U.S. and CANADA LITERATU

NAME: ______

COMPANY: ______

ADDRESS: ______

CITY: ______ STATE: ______ ZIP: ______

COUNTRY: ______

PHONE NO.: ( )

ORDER NO.	TITLE	QTY.		PRICE		TOTAL
			×		=	
			×		=	
			×		=	
			×		=	
			×		=	
			×		=	
			×		=	
			×		=	
			×		=	
			×		=	

Subtotal ______

Must Add Your Local Sales Tax ______

Include postage:
Must add 15% of Subtotal to cover U.S. and Canada postage. (20% all other.) → Postage ______

Total ______

Pay by check, money order, or include company purchase order with this form ($200 minimum). We also accept VISA, MasterCard or American Express. Make payment to Intel Literature Sales. Allow 2-4 weeks for delivery.

☐ VISA ☐ MasterCard ☐ American Express Expiration Date ______

Account No. ______

Signature ______

Mail To: Intel Literature Sales
P.O. Box 7641
Mt. Prospect, IL 60056-7641

International Customers outside the U.S. and Canada should use the International order form on the next page or contact their local Sales Office or Distributor.

For phone orders in the U.S. and Canada
Call Toll Free: (800) 548-4725

Prices good until 12/31/92.
Source HB

INTERNATIONAL LITERATURE ORDER FORM

NAME: ______________________________

COMPANY: ______________________________

ADDRESS: ______________________________

CITY: ______________ STATE: ________ ZIP: ________

COUNTRY: ______________________________

PHONE NO.: (   ) ______________________________

ORDER NO.	TITLE	QTY.		PRICE		TOTAL
			×		=	
			×		=	
			×		=	
			×		=	
			×		=	
			×		=	
			×		=	
			×		=	
			×		=	
			×		=	

Subtotal ________

Must Add Your Local Sales Tax ________

Total ________

PAYMENT

Cheques should be made payable to your ***local*** Intel Sales Office (see inside back cover).

Other forms of payment may be available in your country. Please contact the Literature Coordinator at your ***local*** Intel Sales Office for details.

The completed form should be marked to the attention of the LITERATURE COORDINATOR and returned to your ***local*** Intel Sales Office.

Intel Corporation is a leading supplier of microcomputer components, modules and systems. When Intel first introduced the microprocessor in 1971, it created the era of the microcomputer. Today, Intel architectures are considered world standards. Intel products are used in a wide variety of applications including, embedded systems such as automobiles, avionics systems and telecommunications equipment, and as the CPU in personal computers, network servers and supercomputers. Others bring enhanced capabilities to systems and networks. Intel's mission is to deliver quality products through leading-edge technology.

MICROPROCESSORS

VOLUME II

1992

Intel Corporation makes no warranty for the use of its products and assumes no responsibility for any errors which may appear in this document nor does it make a commitment to update the information contained herein.

Intel retains the right to make changes to these specifications at any time, without notice.

Contact your local sales office to obtain the latest specifications before placing your order.

The following are trademarks of Intel Corporation and may only be used to identify Intel products:

376, Above, ActionMedia, BITBUS, Code Builder, DeskWare, Digital Studio, DVI, EtherExpress, ETOX, FaxBACK, Grand Challenge, i, i287, i386, i387, i486, i487, i750, i860, i960, ICE, iLBX, Inboard, Intel, Intel287, Intel386, Intel387, Intel486, Intel487, intel inside., Intellec, iPSC, iRMX, iSBC, iSBX, iWARP, LANPrint, LANSelect, LANShell, LANSight, LANSpace, LANSpool, MAPNET, Matched, MCS, Media Mail, NetPort, NetSentry, OpenNET, PRO750, ProSolver, READY-LAN, Reference Point, RMX/80, SatisFAXtion, SnapIn 386, Storage Broker, SugarCube, The Computer Inside., TokenExpress, Visual Edge, and WYPIWYF.

MDS is an ordering code only and is not used as a product name or trademark. MDS is a registered trademark of Mohawk Data Sciences Corporation.

CHMOS and HMOS are patented processes of Intel Corp.

Intel Corporation and Intel's FASTPATH are not affiliated with Kinetics, a division of Excelan, Inc. or its FASTPATH trademark or products.

Additional copies of this manual or other Intel literature may be obtained from:

Intel Corporation
Literature Sales
P.O. Box 7641
Mt. Prospect, IL 60056-7641

INTEL SERVICE

INTEL'S COMPLETE SUPPORT SOLUTION WORLDWIDE

Intel Service is a complete support program that provides Intel customers with hardware support, software support, customer training, and consulting services. For detailed information contact your local sales offices.

Service and support are major factors in determining the success of a product or program. For Intel this support includes an international service organization and a breadth of service programs to meet a variety of customer needs. As you might expect, Intel service is extensive. It can start with On-Site Installation and Maintenance for Intel and non-Intel systems and peripherals, Repair Services for Intel OEM Modules and Platforms, Network Operating System support for Novell NetWare and Banyan VINES software, Custom Integration Services for Intel Platforms, Customer Training, and System Engineering Consulting Services. Intel maintains service locations worldwide. So wherever you're using Intel technology, our professional staff is within close reach.

ON-SITE INSTALLATION AND MAINTENANCE

Intel's installation and maintenance services are designed to get Intel and Intel-based systems and the networks they use up and running—fast. Intel's service centers are staffed by trained and certified Customer Engineers throughout the world. Once installed, Intel is dedicated to keeping them running at maximum efficiency, while controlling costs.

REPAIR SERVICES FOR INTEL OEM MODULES AND PLATFORMS

Intel offers customers of its OEM Modules and Platforms a comprehensive set of repair services that reduce the costs of system warranty, maintenance, and ownership. Repair services include module or system testing and repair, module exchange, and spare part sales.

NETWORK OPERATING SYSTEM SUPPORT

An Intel software support contract for Novell NetWare or Banyan VINES software means unlimited access to troubleshooting expertise any time during contract hours—up to seven days per week, twenty-four hours per day. To keep networks current and compatible with the latest software versions, support services include access to minor releases and "patches" as made available by Novell and Banyan.

CUSTOM SYSTEM INTEGRATION SERVICES

Intel Custom System Integration Services enable resellers to order completely integrated systems assembled from a list of Intel386™ and Intel486™ microcomputers and validated hardware and software options. These services are designed to complement the reseller's own integration capabilities. Resellers can increase business opportunities, while controlling overhead and support costs.

CUSTOMER TRAINING

Intel offers a wide range of instructional programs covering various aspects of system design and implementation. In just three to five days a limited number of individuals learn more in a single workshop than in weeks of self-study. Covering a wide variety of topics, Intel's major course categories include: architecture and assembly language, programming and operating systems, BITBUS™, and LAN applications.

SYSTEM ENGINEERING CONSULTING

Intel provides field system engineering consulting services for any phase of your development or application effort. You can use our system engineers in a variety of ways ranging from assistance in using a new product, developing an application, personalizing training and customizing an Intel product to providing technical and management consulting. Working together, we can help you get a successful product to market in the least possible time.

DATA SHEET DESIGNATIONS

Intel uses various data sheet markings to designate each phase of the document as it relates to the product. The marking appears in the upper, right-hand corner of the data sheet. The following is the definition of these markings:

Data Sheet Marking	Description
Product Preview	Contains information on products in the design phase of development. Do not finalize a design with this information. Revised information will be published when the product becomes available.
Advanced Information	Contains information on products being sampled or in the initial production phase of development.*
Preliminary	Contains preliminary information on new products in production.*
No Marking	Contains information on products in full production.*

*Specifications within these data sheets are subject to change without notice. Verify with your local Intel sales office that you have the latest data sheet before finalizing a design.

intel®

Table of Contents

Table of Contents (Continued)

Alphanumeric Index

Alphanumeric Index (Continued)

Intel386™ Microprocessor 4

4

Intel386™ DX MICROPROCESSOR
HIGH PERFORMANCE 32-BIT CHMOS MICROPROCESSOR WITH INTEGRATED MEMORY MANAGEMENT

- **Flexible 32-Bit Microprocessor**
  - **8, 16, 32-Bit Data Types**
  - **8 General Purpose 32-Bit Registers**
- **Very Large Address Space**
  - **4 Gigabyte Physical**
  - **64 Terabyte Virtual**
  - **4 Gigabyte Maximum Segment Size**
- **Integrated Memory Management Unit**
  - **Virtual Memory Support**
  - **Optional On-Chip Paging**
  - **4 Levels of Protection**
  - **Fully Compatible with 80286**
- **Object Code Compatible with All 8086 Family Microprocessors**
- **Virtual 8086 Mode Allows Running of 8086 Software in a Protected and Paged System**
- **Hardware Debugging Support**
- **Optimized for System Performance**
  - **Pipelined Instruction Execution**
  - **On-Chip Address Translation Caches**
  - **20, 25 and 33 MHz Clock**
  - **40, 50 and 66 Megabytes/Sec Bus Bandwidth**
- **High Speed Numerics Support via Intel387™ DX Coprocessor**
- **Complete System Development Support**
  - **Software: C, PL/M, Assembler System Generation Tools**
  - **Debuggers: PSCOPE, ICE™-386**
- **High Speed CHMOS III and CHMOS IV Technology**
- **132 Pin Grid Array Package**
  (See Packaging Specification, Order #231369)

The Intel386 DX Microprocessor is an advanced 32-bit microprocessor designed for applications needing very high performance and optimized for multitasking operating systems. The 32-bit registers and data paths support 32-bit addresses and data types. The processor addresses up to four gigabytes of physical memory and 64 terabytes (2**46) of virtual memory. The integrated memory management and protection architecture includes address translation registers, advanced multitasking hardware and a protection mechanism to support operating systems. In addition, the Intel386 DX allows the simultaneous running of multiple operating systems. Instruction pipelining, on-chip address translation, and high bus bandwidth ensure short average instruction execution times and high system throughput.

The Intel386 DX offers new testability and debugging features. Testability features include a self-test and direct access to the page translation cache. Four new breakpoint registers provide breakpoint traps on code execution or data accesses, for powerful debugging of even ROM-based systems.

Object-code compatibility with all 8086 family members (8086, 8088, 80186, 80188, 80286) means the Intel386 DX offers immediate access to the world's largest microprocessor software base.

4

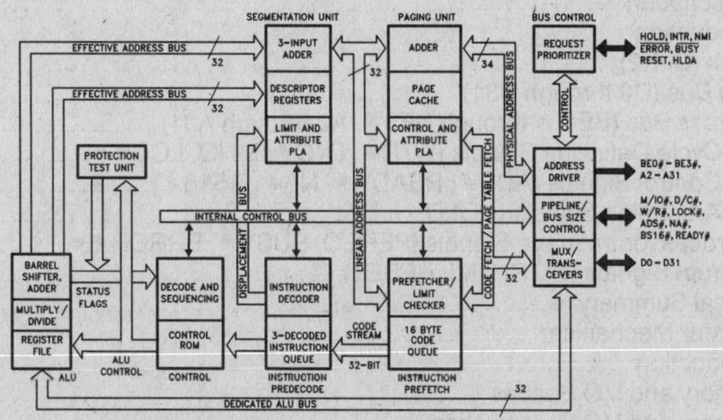

Intel386™ DX Pipelined 32-Bit Microarchitecture

October 1991
Order Number: 231630-009

TABLE OF CONTENTS

CONTENTS

PAGE

CONTENTS

1. PIN ASSIGNMENT

The Intel386 DX pinout as viewed from the top side of the component is shown by Figure 1-1. Its pinout as viewed from the Pin side of the component is Figure 1-2.

V_{CC} and GND connections must be made to multiple V_{CC} and V_{SS} (GND) pins. Each V_{CC} and V_{SS} must be connected to the appropriate voltage level. The circuit board should include V_{CC} and GND planes for power distribution and all V_{CC} and V_{SS} pins must be connected to the appropriate plane.

NOTE:
Pins identified as "N.C." should remain completely unconnected.

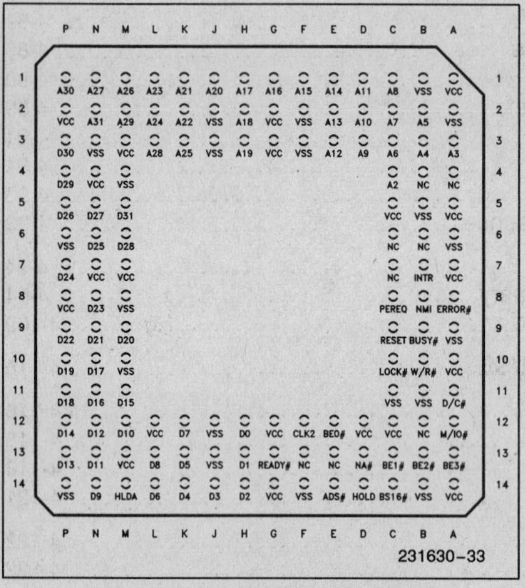

Figure 1-1. Intel386™ DX PGA Pinout—View from Top Side

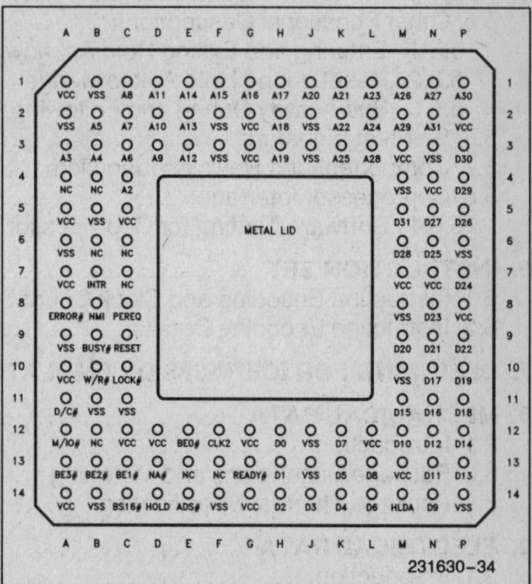

Figure 1-2. Intel386™ DX PGA Pinout—View from Pin Side

Table 1-1. Intel386™ DX PGA Pinout—Functional Grouping

Signal/Pin		Signal/Pin		Signal/Pin		Signal/Pin		Signal/Pin		Signal/Pin	
A2	C4	A24	L2	D6	L14	D28	M6	V_{CC}	C12	V_{SS}	F2
A3	A3	A25	K3	D7	K12	D29	P4		D12		F3
A4	B3	A26	M1	D8	L13	D30	P3		G2		F14
A5	B2	A27	N1	D9	N14	D31	M5		G3		J2
A6	C3	A28	L3	D10	M12	D/C#	A11		G12		J3
A7	C2	A29	M2	D11	N13	ERROR#	A8		G14		J12
A8	C1	A30	P1	D12	N12	HLDA	M14		L12		J13
A9	D3	A31	N2	D13	P13	HOLD	D14		M3		M4
A10	D2	ADS#	E14	D14	P12	INTR	B7		M7		M8
A11	D1	BE0#	E12	D15	M11	LOCK#	C10		M13		M10
A12	E3	BE1#	C13	D16	N11	M/IO#	A12		N4		N3
A13	E2	BE2#	B13	D17	N10	NA#	D13		N7		P6
A14	E1	BE3#	A13	D18	P11	NMI	B8		P2		P14
A15	F1	BS16#	C14	D19	P10	PEREQ	C8		P8	W/R#	B10
A16	G1	BUSY#	B9	D20	M9	READY#	G13	V_{SS}	A2	N.C.	A4
A17	H1	CLK2	F12	D21	N9	RESET	C9		A6		B4
A18	H2	D0	H12	D22	P9	V_{CC}	A1		A9		B6
A19	H3	D1	H13	D23	N8		A5		B1		B12
A20	J1	D2	H14	D24	P7		A7		B5		C6
A21	K1	D3	J14	D25	N6		A10		B11		C7
A22	K2	D4	K14	D26	P5		A14		B14		E13
A23	L1	D5	K13	D27	N5		C5		C11		F13

1.1 PIN DESCRIPTION TABLE

The following table lists a brief description of each pin on the Intel386 DX. The following definitions are used in these descriptions:

#	The named signal is active LOW.
I	Input signal.
O	Output signal.
I/O	Input and Output signal.
—	No electrical connection.

For a more complete description refer to Section 5.2 Signal Description.

Symbol	Type	Name and Function
CLK2	I	**CLK2** provides the fundamental timing for the Intel386 DX.
D_{31}–D_0	I/O	**DATA BUS** inputs data during memory, I/O and interrupt acknowledge read cycles and outputs data during memory and I/O write cycles.
A_{31}–A_2	O	**ADDRESS BUS** outputs physical memory or port I/O addresses.
BE0#–BE3#	O	**BYTE ENABLES** indicate which data bytes of the data bus take part in a bus cycle.
W/R#	O	**WRITE/READ** is a bus cycle definition pin that distinguishes write cycles from read cycles.
D/C#	O	**DATA/CONTROL** is a bus cycle definition pin that distinguishes data cycles, either memory or I/O, from control cycles which are: interrupt acknowledge, halt, and instruction fetching.
M/IO#	O	**MEMORY I/O** is a bus cycle definition pin that distinguishes memory cycles from input/output cycles.
LOCK#	O	**BUS LOCK** is a bus cycle definition pin that indicates that other system bus masters are denied access to the system bus while it is active.
ADS#	O	**ADDRESS STATUS** indicates that a valid bus cycle definition and address (W/R#, D/C#, M/IO#, BE0#, BE1#, BE2#, BE3# and A_{31}–A_2) are being driven at the Intel386 DX pins.
NA#	I	**NEXT ADDRESS** is used to request address pipelining.
READY#	I	**BUS READY** terminates the bus cycle.
BS16#	I	**BUS SIZE 16** input allows direct connection of 32-bit and 16-bit data buses.
HOLD	I	**BUS HOLD REQUEST** input allows another bus master to request control of the local bus.

4

1.1 PIN DESCRIPTION TABLE (Continued)

Symbol	Type	Name and Function
HLDA	O	**BUS HOLD ACKNOWLEDGE** output indicates that the Intel386 DX has surrendered control of its local bus to another bus master.
BUSY#	I	**BUSY** signals a busy condition from a processor extension.
ERROR#	I	**ERROR** signals an error condition from a processor extension.
PEREQ	I	**PROCESSOR EXTENSION REQUEST** indicates that the processor extension has data to be transferred by the Intel386 DX.
INTR	I	**INTERRUPT REQUEST** is a maskable input that signals the Intel386 DX to suspend execution of the current program and execute an interrupt acknowledge function.
NMI	I	**NON-MASKABLE INTERRUPT REQUEST** is a non-maskable input that signals the Intel386 DX to suspend execution of the current program and execute an interrupt acknowledge function.
RESET	I	**RESET** suspends any operation in progress and places the Intel386 DX in a known reset state. See **Interrupt Signals** for additional information.
N/C	—	**NO CONNECT** should always remain unconnected. Connection of a N/C pin may cause the processor to malfunction or be incompatible with future steppings of the Intel386 DX.
V_{CC}	I	**SYSTEM POWER** provides the +5V nominal D.C. supply input.
V_{SS}	I	**SYSTEM GROUND** provides 0V connection from which all inputs and outputs are measured.

2. BASE ARCHITECTURE

2.1 INTRODUCTION

The Intel386 DX consists of a central processing unit, a memory management unit and a bus interface.

The central processing unit consists of the execution unit and instruction unit. The execution unit contains the eight 32-bit general purpose registers which are used for both address calculation, data operations and a 64-bit barrel shifter used to speed shift, rotate, multiply, and divide operations. The multiply and divide logic uses a 1-bit per cycle algorithm. The multiply algorithm stops the iteration when the most significant bits of the multiplier are all zero. This allows typical 32-bit multiplies to be executed in under one microsecond. The instruction unit decodes the instruction opcodes and stores them in the decoded instruction queue for immediate use by the execution unit.

The memory management unit (MMU) consists of a segmentation unit and a paging unit. Segmentation allows the managing of the logical address space by providing an extra addressing component, one that allows easy code and data relocatability, and efficient sharing. The paging mechanism operates beneath and is transparent to the segmentation process, to allow management of the physical address space. Each segment is divided into one or more 4K byte pages. To implement a virtual memory system, the Intel386 DX supports full restartability for all page and segment faults.

Memory is organized into one or more variable length segments, each up to four gigabytes in size. A given region of the linear address space, a segment, can have attributes associated with it. These attributes include its location, size, type (i.e. stack, code or data), and protection characteristics. Each task on an Intel386 DX can have a maximum of 16,381 segments of up to four gigabytes each, thus providing 64 terabytes (trillion bytes) of virtual memory to each task.

The segmentation unit provides four-levels of protection for isolating and protecting applications and the operating system from each other. The hardware enforced protection allows the design of systems with a high degree of integrity.

The Intel386 DX has two modes of operation: Real Address Mode (Real Mode), and Protected Virtual Address Mode (Protected Mode). In Real Mode the Intel386 DX operates as a very fast 8086, but with 32-bit extensions if desired. Real Mode is required primarily to setup the processor for Protected Mode operation. Protected Mode provides access to the sophisticated memory management, paging and privilege capabilities of the processor.

Within Protected Mode, software can perform a task switch to enter into tasks designated as Virtual 8086 Mode tasks. Each such task behaves with 8086 semantics, thus allowing 8086 software (an application program, or an entire operating system) to execute. The Virtual 8086 tasks can be isolated and protected from one another and the host Intel386 DX operating system, by the use of paging, and the I/O Permission Bitmap.

Finally, to facilitate high performance system hardware designs, the Intel386 DX bus interface offers address pipelining, dynamic data bus sizing, and direct Byte Enable signals for each byte of the data bus. These hardware features are described fully beginning in Section 5.

2.2 REGISTER OVERVIEW

The Intel386 DX has 32 register resources in the following categories:

- General Purpose Registers
- Segment Registers
- Instruction Pointer and Flags
- Control Registers
- System Address Registers
- Debug Registers
- Test Registers.

The registers are a superset of the 8086, 80186 and 80286 registers, so all 16-bit 8086, 80186 and 80286 registers are contained within the 32-bit Intel386 DX.

Figure 2-1 shows all of Intel386 DX base architecture registers, which include the general address and data registers, the instruction pointer, and the flags register. The contents of these registers are task-specific, so these registers are automatically loaded with a new context upon a task switch operation.

The base architecture also includes six directly accessible segments, each up to 4 Gbytes in size. The segments are indicated by the selector values placed in Intel386 DX segment registers of Figure 2-1. Various selector values can be loaded as a program executes, if desired.

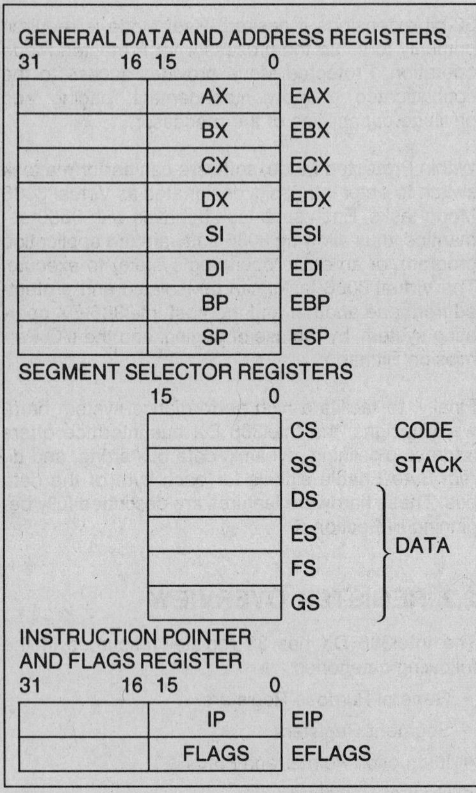

Figure 2-1. Intel386™ DX Base Architecture Registers

The selectors are also task-specific, so the segment registers are automatically loaded with new context upon a task switch operation.

The other types of registers, Control, System Address, Debug, and Test, are primarily used by system software.

2.3 REGISTER DESCRIPTIONS

2.3.1 General Purpose Registers

General Purpose Registers: The eight general purpose registers of 32 bits hold data or address quantities. The general registers, Figure 2-2, support data operands of 1, 8, 16, 32 and 64 bits, and bit fields of 1 to 32 bits. They support address operands of 16 and 32 bits. The 32-bit registers are named EAX, EBX, ECX, EDX, ESI, EDI, EBP, and ESP.

The least significant 16 bits of the registers can be accessed separately. This is done by using the 16-bit names of the registers AX, BX, CX, DX, SI, DI, BP, and SP. When accessed as a 16-bit operand, the upper 16 bits of the register are neither used nor changed.

Finally 8-bit operations can individually access the lowest byte (bits 0–7) and the higher byte (bits 8–15) of general purpose registers AX, BX, CX and DX. The lowest bytes are named AL, BL, CL and DL, respectively. The higher bytes are named AH, BH, CH and DH, respectively. The individual byte accessibility offers additional flexibility for data operations, but is not used for effective address calculation.

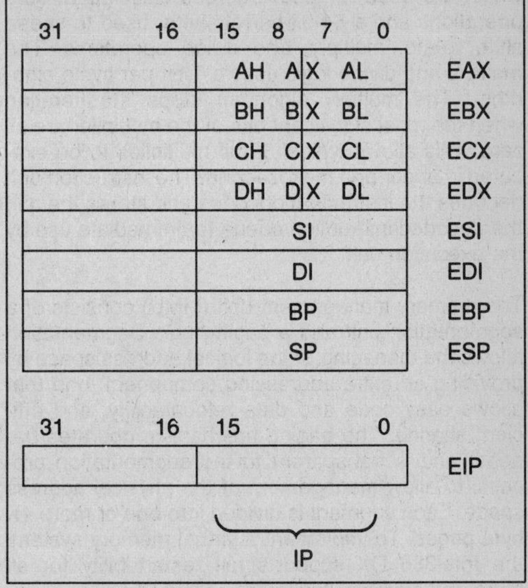

Figure 2-2. General Registers and Instruction Pointer

2.3.2 Instruction Pointer

The instruction pointer, Figure 2-2, is a 32-bit register named EIP. EIP holds the offset of the next instruction to be executed. The offset is always relative to the base of the code segment (CS). The lower 16 bits (bits 0–15) of EIP contain the 16-bit instruction pointer named IP, which is used by 16-bit addressing.

2.3.3 Flags Register

The Flags Register is a 32-bit register named EFLAGS. The defined bits and bit fields within EFLAGS, shown in Figure 2-3, control certain operations and indicate status of the Intel386 DX. The lower 16 bits (bit 0–15) of EFLAGS contain the 16-bit flag register named FLAGS, which is most useful when executing 8086 and 80286 code.

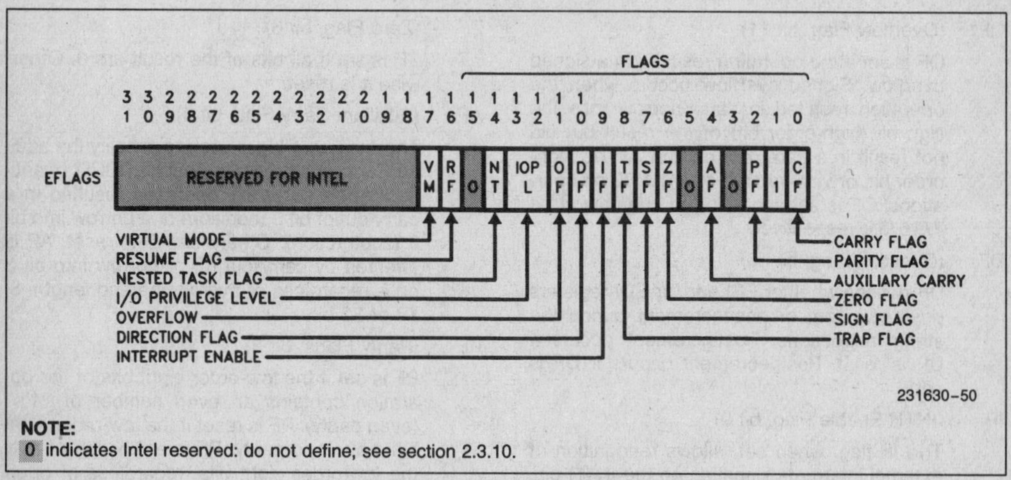

NOTE:
0 indicates Intel reserved: do not define; see section 2.3.10.

Figure 2-3. Flags Register

VM (Virtual 8086 Mode, bit 17)

The VM bit provides Virtual 8086 Mode within Protected Mode. If set while the Intel386 DX is in Protected Mode, the Intel386 DX will switch to Virtual 8086 operation, handling segment loads as the 8086 does, but generating exception 13 faults on privileged opcodes. The VM bit can be set only in Protected Mode, by the IRET instruction (if current privilege level = 0) and by task switches at any privilege level. The VM bit is unaffected by POPF. PUSHF always pushes a 0 in this bit, even if executing in virtual 8086 Mode. The EFLAGS image pushed during interrupt processing or saved during task switches will contain a 1 in this bit if the interrupted code was executing as a Virtual 8086 Task.

RF (Resume Flag, bit 16)

The RF flag is used in conjunction with the debug register breakpoints. It is checked at instruction boundaries before breakpoint processing. When RF is set, it causes any debug fault to be ignored on the next instruction. RF is then automatically reset at the successful completion of every instruction (no faults are signalled) except the IRET instruction, the POPF instruction, (and JMP, CALL, and INT instructions causing a task switch). These instructions set RF to the value specified by the memory image. For example, at the end of the breakpoint service routine, the IRET instruction can pop an EFLAG image having the RF bit set and resume the program's execution at the breakpoint address without generating another breakpoint fault on the same location.

NT (Nested Task, bit 14)

This flag applies to Protected Mode. NT is set to indicate that the execution of this task is nested within another task. If set, it indicates that the current nested task's Task State Segment (TSS) has a valid back link to the previous task's TSS. This bit is set or reset by control transfers to other tasks. The value of NT in EFLAGS is tested by the IRET instruction to determine whether to do an inter-task return or an intra-task return. A POPF or an IRET instruction **will** affect the setting of this bit according to the image popped, at any privilege level.

IOPL (Input/Output Privilege Level, bits 12-13)

This two-bit field applies to Protected Mode. IOPL indicates the numerically maximum CPL (current privilege level) value permitted to execute I/O instructions without generating an exception 13 fault or consulting the I/O Permission Bitmap. It also indicates the maximum CPL value allowing alteration of the IF (INTR Enable Flag) bit when new values are popped into the EFLAG register. POPF and IRET instruction can alter the IOPL field when executed at CPL = 0. Task switches can always alter the IOPL field, when the new flag image is loaded from the incoming task's TSS.

4

OF (Overflow Flag, bit 11)

OF is set if the operation resulted in a signed overflow. Signed overflow occurs when the operation resulted in carry/borrow **into** the sign bit (high-order bit) of the result but did not result in a carry/borrow **out of** the high-order bit, or vice-versa. For 8/16/32 bit operations, OF is set according to overflow at bit 7/15/31, respectively.

DF (Direction Flag, bit 10)

DF defines whether ESI and/or EDI registers postdecrement or postincrement during the string instructions. Postincrement occurs if DF is reset. Postdecrement occurs if DF is set.

IF (INTR Enable Flag, bit 9)

The IF flag, when set, allows recognition of external interrupts signalled on the INTR pin. When IF is reset, external interrupts signalled on the INTR are not recognized. IOPL indicates the maximum CPL value allowing alteration of the IF bit when new values are popped into EFLAGS or FLAGS.

TF (Trap Enable Flag, bit 8)

TF controls the generation of exception 1 trap when single-stepping through code. When TF is set, the Intel386 DX generates an exception 1 trap after the next instruction is executed. When TF is reset, exception 1 traps occur only as a function of the breakpoint addresses loaded into debug registers DR0–DR3.

SF (Sign Flag, bit 7)

SF is set if the high-order bit of the result is set, it is reset otherwise. For 8-, 16-, 32-bit operations, SF reflects the state of bit 7, 15, 31 respectively.

ZF (Zero Flag, bit 6)

ZF is set if all bits of the result are 0. Otherwise it is reset.

AF (Auxiliary Carry Flag, bit 4)

The Auxiliary Flag is used to simplify the addition and subtraction of packed BCD quantities. AF is set if the operation resulted in a carry out of bit 3 (addition) or a borrow into bit 3 (subtraction). Otherwise AF is reset. AF is affected by carry out of, or borrow into bit 3 only, regardless of overall operand length: 8, 16 or 32 bits.

PF (Parity Flags, bit 2)

PF is set if the low-order eight bits of the operation contains an even number of "1's" (even parity). PF is reset if the low-order eight bits have odd parity. PF is a function of only the low-order eight bits, regardless of operand size.

CF (Carry Flag, bit 0)

CF is set if the operation resulted in a carry out of (addition), or a borrow into (subtraction) the high-order bit. Otherwise CF is reset. For 8-, 16- or 32-bit operations, CF is set according to carry/borrow at bit 7, 15 or 31, respectively.

Note in these descriptions, "set" means "set to 1," and "reset" means "reset to 0."

2.3.4 Segment Registers

Six 16-bit segment registers hold segment selector values identifying the currently addressable memory segments. Segment registers are shown in Figure 2-4. In Protected Mode, each segment may range in size from one byte up to the entire linear and physi-

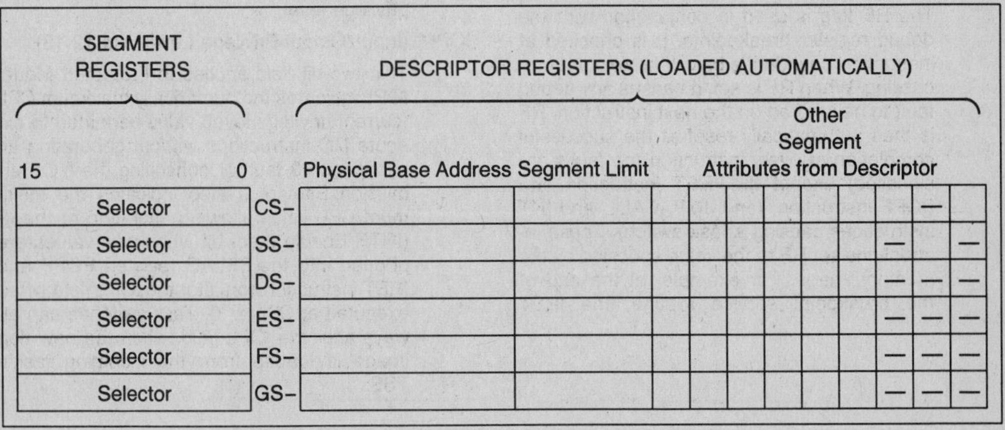

SEGMENT REGISTERS 15 ... 0		DESCRIPTOR REGISTERS (LOADED AUTOMATICALLY) Physical Base Address	Segment Limit	Other Segment Attributes from Descriptor								
Selector	CS–										—	
Selector	SS–									—		—
Selector	DS–									—	—	—
Selector	ES–									—	—	—
Selector	FS–									—	—	—
Selector	GS–									—	—	—

Figure 2-4. Intel386™ DX Segment Registers, and Associated Descriptor Registers

cal space of the machine, 4 Gbytes (2^{32} bytes). If a maximum sized segment is used (limit = FFFFFFFFH) it should be Dword aligned (i.e., the least two significant bits of the segment base should be zero). This will avoid a segment limit violation (exception 13) caused by the wrap around. In Real Address Mode, the maximum segment size is fixed at 64 Kbytes (2^{16} bytes).

The six segments addressable at any given moment are defined by the segment registers CS, SS, DS, ES, FS and GS. The selector in CS indicates the current code segment; the selector in SS indicates the current stack segment; the selectors in DS, ES, FS and GS indicate the current data segments.

2.3.5 Segment Descriptor Registers

The segment descriptor registers are not programmer visible, yet it is very useful to understand their content. Inside the Intel386 DX, a descriptor register (programmer invisible) is associated with each programmer-visible segment register, as shown by Figure 2-4. Each descriptor register holds a 32-bit segment base address, a 32-bit segment limit, and the other necessary segment attributes.

When a selector value is loaded into a segment register, the associated descriptor register is automatically updated with the correct information. In Real Address Mode, only the base address is updated directly (by shifting the selector value four bits to the left), since the segment maximum limit and attributes are fixed in Real Mode. In Protected Mode, the base address, the limit, and the attributes are all updated per the contents of the segment descriptor indexed by the selector.

Whenever a memory reference occurs, the segment descriptor register associated with the segment being used is automatically involved with the memory reference. The 32-bit segment base address becomes a component of the linear address calculation, the 32-bit limit is used for the limit-check operation, and the attributes are checked against the type of memory reference requested.

2.3.6 Control Registers

The Intel386 DX has three control registers of 32 bits, CR0, CR2 and CR3, to hold machine state of a global nature (not specific to an individual task). These registers, along with System Address Registers described in the next section, hold machine state that affects all tasks in the system. To access the Control Registers, load and store instructions are defined.

CR0: Machine Control Register (includes 80286 Machine Status Word)

CR0, shown in Figure 2-5, contains 6 defined bits for control and status purposes. The low-order 16 bits of CR0 are also known as the Machine Status Word, MSW, for compatibility with 80286 Protected Mode. LMSW and SMSW instructions are taken as special aliases of the load and store CR0 operations, where only the low-order 16 bits of CR0 are involved. For compatibility with 80286 operating systems the Intel386 DX LMSW instructions work in an identical fashion to the LMSW instruction on the 80286. (i.e. It only operates on the low-order 16-bits of CR0 and it ignores the new bits in CR0.) New Intel386 DX operating systems should use the MOV CR0, Reg instruction.

The defined CR0 bits are described below.

PG (Paging Enable, bit 31)

the PG bit is set to enable the on-chip paging unit. It is reset to disable the on-chip paging unit.

R (reserved, bit 4)

This bit is reserved by Intel. When loading CR0 care should be taken to not alter the value of this bit.

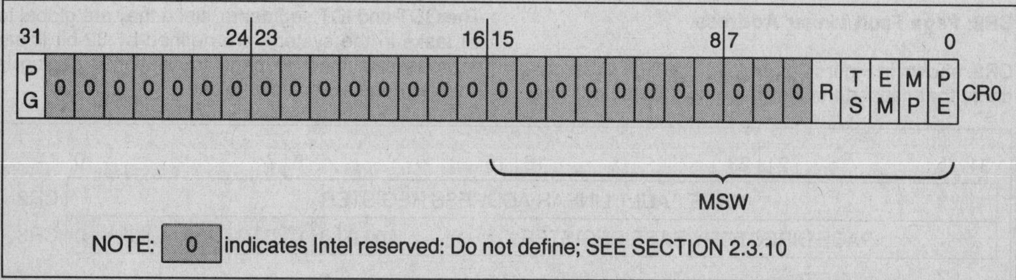

Figure 2-5. Control Register 0

TS (Task Switched, bit 3)

TS is automatically set whenever a task switch operation is performed. If TS is set, a coprocessor ESCape opcode will cause a Coprocessor Not Available trap (exception 7). The trap handler typically saves the Intel387 DX coprocessor context belonging to a previous task, loads the Intel387 DX coprocessor state belonging to the current task, and clears the TS bit before returning to the faulting coprocessor opcode.

EM (Emulate Coprocessor, bit 2)

The EMulate coprocessor bit is set to cause all coprocessor opcodes to generate a Coprocessor Not Available fault (exception 7). It is reset to allow coprocessor opcodes to be executed on an actual Intel387 DX coprocessor (this is the default case after reset). Note that the WAIT opcode is not affected by the EM bit setting.

MP (Monitor Coprocessor, bit 1)

The MP bit is used in conjunction with the TS bit to determine if the WAIT opcode will generate a Coprocessor Not Available fault (exception 7) when TS = 1. When both MP = 1 and TS = 1, the WAIT opcode generates a trap. Otherwise, the WAIT opcode does not generate a trap. Note that TS is automatically set whenever a task switch operation is performed.

PE (Protection Enable, bit 0)

The PE bit is set to enable the Protected Mode. If PE is reset, the processor operates again in Real Mode. PE may be set by loading MSW or CR0. PE can be reset only by a load into CR0. Resetting the PE bit is typically part of a longer instruction sequence needed for proper transition from Protected Mode to Real Mode. Note that for strict 80286 compatibility, PE cannot be reset by the LMSW instruction.

CR1: reserved

CR1 is reserved for use in future Intel processors.

CR2: Page Fault Linear Address

CR2, shown in Figure 2-6, holds the 32-bit linear address that caused the last page fault detected. The error code pushed onto the page fault handler's stack when it is invoked provides additional status information on this page fault.

CR3: Page Directory Base Address

CR3, shown in Figure 2-6, contains the physical base address of the page directory table. The Intel386 DX page directory table is always page-aligned (4 Kbyte-aligned). Therefore the lowest twelve bits of CR3 are ignored when written and they store as undefined.

A task switch through a TSS which **changes** the value in CR3, or an explicit load into CR3 with any value, will invalidate all cached page table entries in the paging unit cache. Note that if the value in CR3 does not change during the task switch, the cached page table entries are not flushed.

2.3.7 System Address Registers

Four special registers are defined to reference the tables or segments supported by the 80286 CPU and Intel386 DX protection model. These tables or segments are:

GDT (Global Descriptor Table),

IDT (Interrupt Descriptor Table),

LDT (Local Descriptor Table),

TSS (Task State Segment).

The addresses of these tables and segments are stored in special registers, the System Address and System Segment Registers illustrated in Figure 2-7. These registers are named GDTR, IDTR, LDTR and TR, respectively. Section 4 **Protected Mode Architecture** describes the use of these registers.

GDTR and IDTR

These registers hold the 32-bit linear base address and 16-bit limit of the GDT and IDT, respectively.

The GDT and IDT segments, since they are global to all tasks in the system, are defined by 32-bit linear addresses (subject to page translation if paging is enabled) and 16-bit limit values.

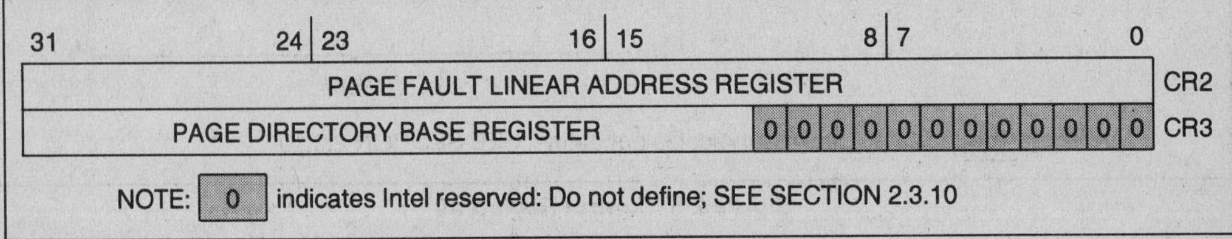

Figure 2-6. Control Registers 2 and 3

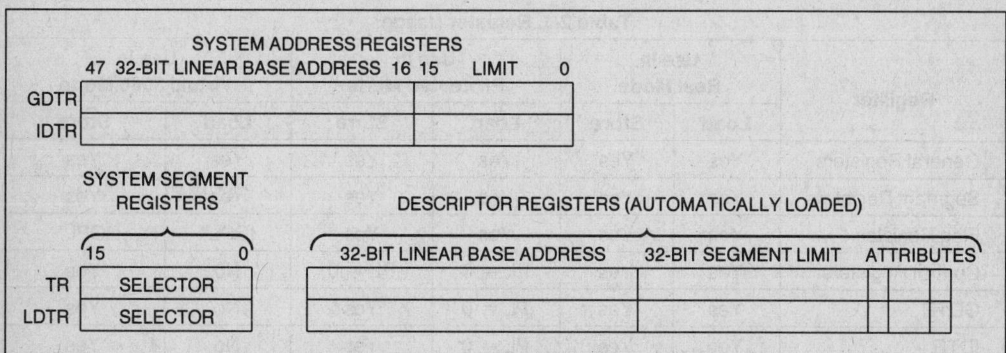

Figure 2-7. System Address and System Segment Registers

LDTR and TR

These registers hold the 16-bit selector for the LDT descriptor and the TSS descriptor, respectively.

The LDT and TSS segments, since they are task-specific segments, are defined by selector values stored in the system segment registers. Note that a segment descriptor register (programmer-invisible) is associated with each system segment register.

2.3.8 Debug and Test Registers

Debug Registers: The six programmer accessible debug registers provide on-chip support for debugging. Debug Registers DR0–3 specify the four linear breakpoints. The Debug Control Register DR7 is used to set the breakpoints and the Debug Status Register DR6, displays the current state of the breakpoints. The use of the debug registers is described in section 2.12 **Debugging support.**

DEBUG REGISTERS

31 … 0	
LINEAR BREAKPOINT ADDRESS 0	DR0
LINEAR BREAKPOINT ADDRESS 1	DR1
LINEAR BREAKPOINT ADDRESS 2	DR2
LINEAR BREAKPOINT ADDRESS 3	DR3
Intel reserved. Do not define.	DR4
Intel reserved. Do not define.	DR5
BREAKPOINT STATUS	DR6
BREAKPOINT CONTROL	DR7

TEST REGISTERS (FOR PAGE CACHE)

31 … 0	
TEST CONTROL	TR6
TEST STATUS	TR7

Figure 2-8. Debug and Test Registers

Test Registers: Two registers are used to control the testing of the RAM/CAM (Content Addressable Memories) in the Translation Lookaside Buffer portion of the Intel386 DX. TR6 is the command test register, and TR7 is the data register which contains the data of the Translation Lookaside buffer test. Their use is discussed in section 2.11 **Testability.**

Figure 2-8 shows the Debug and Test registers.

2.3.9 Register Accessibility

There are a few differences regarding the accessibility of the registers in Real and Protected Mode. Table 2-1 summarizes these differences. See Section 4 **Protected Mode Architecture** for further details.

2.3.10 Compatibility

VERY IMPORTANT NOTE:
COMPATIBILITY WITH FUTURE PROCESSORS

In the preceding register descriptions, note certain Intel386 DX register bits are Intel reserved. When reserved bits are called out, treat them as fully undefined. This is essential for your software compatibility with future processors! Follow the guidelines below:

1) **Do not depend on the states of any undefined bits when testing the values of defined register bits. Mask them out when testing.**
2) **Do not depend on the states of any undefined bits when storing them to memory or another register.**
3) **Do not depend on the ability to retain information written into any undefined bits.**
4) **When loading registers always load the undefined bits as zeros.**

Table 2-1. Register Usage

Register	Use in Real Mode		Use in Protected Mode		Use in Virtual 8086 Mode	
	Load	Store	Load	Store	Load	Store
General Registers	Yes	Yes	Yes	Yes	Yes	Yes
Segment Registers	Yes	Yes	Yes	Yes	Yes	Yes
Flag Register	Yes	Yes	Yes	Yes	IOPL*	IOPL*
Control Registers	Yes	Yes	PL = 0	PL = 0	No	Yes
GDTR	Yes	Yes	PL = 0	Yes	No	Yes
IDTR	Yes	Yes	PL = 0	Yes	No	Yes
LDTR	No	No	PL = 0	Yes	No	No
TR	No	No	PL = 0	Yes	No	No
Debug Control	Yes	Yes	PL = 0	PL = 0	No	No
Test Registers	Yes	Yes	PL = 0	PL = 0	No	No

NOTES:
PL = 0: The registers can be accessed only when the current privilege level is zero.
*IOPL: The PUSHF and POPF instructions are made I/O Privilege Level sensitive in Virtual 8086 Mode.

5) However, registers which have been previously stored may be reloaded without masking.

Depending upon the values of undefined register bits will make your software dependent upon the unspecified Intel386 DX handling of these bits. Depending on undefined values risks making your software incompatible with future processors that define usages for the Intel386 DX-undefined bits. AVOID ANY SOFTWARE DEPENDENCE UPON THE STATE OF UNDEFINED Intel386 DX REGISTER BITS.

2.4 INSTRUCTION SET

2.4.1 Instruction Set Overview

The instruction set is divided into nine categories of operations:

Data Transfer
Arithmetic
Shift/Rotate
String Manipulation
Bit Manipulation
Control Transfer
High Level Language Support
Operating System Support
Processor Control

These Intel386 DX instructions are listed in Table 2-2.

All Intel386 DX instructions operate on either 0, 1, 2, or 3 operands; where an operand resides in a register, in the instruction itself, or in memory. Most zero operand instructions (e.g. CLI, STI) take only one byte. One operand instructions generally are two bytes long. The average instruction is 3.2 bytes long. Since the Intel386 DX has a 16-byte instruction queue, an average of 5 instructions will be prefetched. The use of two operands permits the following types of common instructions:

Register to Register
Memory to Register
Immediate to Register
Register to Memory
Immediate to Memory.

The operands can be either 8, 16, or 32 bits long. As a general rule, when executing code written for the Intel386 DX (32-bit code), operands are 8 or 32 bits; when executing existing 80286 or 8086 code (16-bit code), operands are 8 or 16 bits. Prefixes can be added to all instructions which override the default length of the operands, (i.e. use 32-bit operands for 16-bit code, or 16-bit operands for 32-bit code).

For a more elaborate description of the instruction set, refer to the *Intel386 DX Programmer's Reference Manual.*

2.4.2 Intel386™ DX Instructions

Table 2-2a. Data Transfer

GENERAL PURPOSE	
MOV	Move operand
PUSH	Push operand onto stack
POP	Pop operand off stack
PUSHA	Push all registers on stack
POPA	Pop all registers off stack
XCHG	Exchange Operand, Register
XLAT	Translate
CONVERSION	
MOVZX	Move byte or Word, Dword, with zero extension
MOVSX	Move byte or Word, Dword, sign extended
CBW	Convert byte to Word, or Word to Dword
CWD	Convert Word to DWORD
CWDE	Convert Word to DWORD extended
CDQ	Convert DWORD to QWORD
INPUT/OUTPUT	
IN	Input operand from I/O space
OUT	Output operand to I/O space
ADDRESS OBJECT	
LEA	Load effective address
LDS	Load pointer into D segment register
LES	Load pointer into E segment register
LFS	Load pointer into F segment register
LGS	Load pointer into G segment register
LSS	Load pointer into S (Stack) segment register
FLAG MANIPULATION	
LAHF	Load A register from Flags
SAHF	Store A register in Flags
PUSHF	Push flags onto stack
POPF	Pop flags off stack
PUSHFD	Push EFlags onto stack
POPFD	Pop EFlags off stack
CLC	Clear Carry Flag
CLD	Clear Direction Flag
CMC	Complement Carry Flag
STC	Set Carry Flag
STD	Set Direction Flag

Table 2-2b. Arithmetic Instructions

ADDITION	
ADD	Add operands
ADC	Add with carry
INC	Increment operand by 1
AAA	ASCII adjust for addition
DAA	Decimal adjust for addition
SUBTRACTION	
SUB	Subtract operands
SBB	Subtract with borrow
DEC	Decrement operand by 1
NEG	Negate operand
CMP	Compare operands
DAS	Decimal adjust for subtraction
AAS	ASCII Adjust for subtraction
MULTIPLICATION	
MUL	Multiply Double/Single Precision
IMUL	Integer multiply
AAM	ASCII adjust after multiply
DIVISION	
DIV	Divide unsigned
IDIV	Integer Divide
AAD	ASCII adjust before division

Table 2-2c. String Instructions

MOVS	Move byte or Word, Dword string
INS	Input string from I/O space
OUTS	Output string to I/O space
CMPS	Compare byte or Word, Dword string
SCAS	Scan Byte or Word, Dword string
LODS	Load byte or Word, Dword string
STOS	Store byte or Word, Dword string
REP	Repeat
REPE/ REPZ	Repeat while equal/zero
RENE/ REPNZ	Repeat while not equal/not zero

Table 2-2d. Logical Instructions

LOGICALS	
NOT	"NOT" operands
AND	"AND" operands
OR	"Inclusive OR" operands
XOR	"Exclusive OR" operands
TEST	"Test" operands

Table 2-2d. Logical Instructions (Continued)

SHIFTS	
SHL/SHR	Shift logical left or right
SAL/SAR	Shift arithmetic left or right
SHLD/ SHRD	Double shift left or right
ROTATES	
ROL/ROR	Rotate left/right
RCL/RCR	Rotate through carry left/right

Table 2-2e. Bit Manipulation Instructions

SINGLE BIT INSTRUCTIONS	
BT	Bit Test
BTS	Bit Test and Set
BTR	Bit Test and Reset
BTC	Bit Test and Complement
BSF	Bit Scan Forward
BSR	Bit Scan Reverse

Table 2-2f. Program Control Instructions

CONDITIONAL TRANSFERS	
SETCC	Set byte equal to condition code
JA/JNBE	Jump if above/not below nor equal
JAE/JNB	Jump if above or equal/not below
JB/JNAE	Jump if below/not above nor equal
JBE/JNA	Jump if below or equal/not above
JC	Jump if carry
JE/JZ	Jump if equal/zero
JG/JNLE	Jump if greater/not less nor equal
JGE/JNL	Jump if greater or equal/not less
JL/JNGE	Jump if less/not greater nor equal
JLE/JNG	Jump if less or equal/not greater
JNC	Jump if not carry
JNE/JNZ	Jump if not equal/not zero
JNO	Jump if not overflow
JNP/JPO	Jump if not parity/parity odd
JNS	Jump if not sign
JO	Jump if overflow
JP/JPE	Jump if parity/parity even
JS	Jump if Sign

Table 2-2f. Program Control Instructions (Continued)

UNCONDITIONAL TRANSFERS	
CALL	Call procedure/task
RET	Return from procedure
JMP	Jump
ITERATION CONTROLS	
LOOP	Loop
LOOPE/ LOOPZ	Loop if equal/zero
LOOPNE/ LOOPNZ	Loop if not equal/not zero
JCXZ	JUMP if register CX=0
INTERRUPTS	
INT	Interrupt
INTO	Interrupt if overflow
IRET	Return from Interrupt/Task
CLI	Clear interrupt Enable
STI	Set Interrupt Enable

Table 2-2g. High Level Language Instructions

BOUND	Check Array Bounds
ENTER	Setup Parameter Block for Entering Procedure
LEAVE	Leave Procedure

Table 2-2h. Protection Model

SGDT	Store Global Descriptor Table
SIDT	Store Interrupt Descriptor Table
STR	Store Task Register
SLDT	Store Local Descriptor Table
LGDT	Load Global Descriptor Table
LIDT	Load Interrupt Descriptor Table
LTR	Load Task Register
LLDT	Load Local Descriptor Table
ARPL	Adjust Requested Privilege Level
LAR	Load Access Rights
LSL	Load Segment Limit
VERR/ VERW	Verify Segment for Reading or Writing
LMSW	Load Machine Status Word (lower 16 bits of CR0)
SMSW	Store Machine Status Word

Table 2-2i. Processor Control Instructions

HLT	Halt
WAIT	Wait until BUSY# negated
ESC	Escape
LOCK	Lock Bus

2.5 ADDRESSING MODES

2.5.1 Addressing Modes Overview

The Intel386 DX provides a total of 11 addressing modes for instructions to specify operands. The addressing modes are optimized to allow the efficient execution of high level languages such as C and FORTRAN, and they cover the vast majority of data references needed by high-level languages.

2.5.2 Register and Immediate Modes

Two of the addressing modes provide for instructions that operate on register or immediate operands:

Register Operand Mode: The operand is located in one of the 8-, 16- or 32-bit general registers.

Immediate Operand Mode: The operand is included in the instruction as part of the opcode.

2.5.3 32-Bit Memory Addressing Modes

The remaining 9 modes provide a mechanism for specifying the effective address of an operand. The linear address consists of two components: the segment base address and an effective address. The effective address is calculated by using combinations of the following four address elements:

DISPLACEMENT: An 8-, or 32-bit immediate value, following the instruction.

BASE: The contents of any general purpose register. The base registers are generally used by compilers to point to the start of the local variable area.

INDEX: The contents of any general purpose register except for ESP. The index registers are used to access the elements of an array, or a string of characters.

SCALE: The index register's value can be multiplied by a scale factor, either 1, 2, 4 or 8. Scaled index mode is especially useful for accessing arrays or structures.

Combinations of these 4 components make up the 9 additional addressing modes. There is no performance penalty for using any of these addressing combinations, since the effective address calculation is pipelined with the execution of other instructions. The one exception is the simultaneous use of Base and Index components which requires one additional clock.

As shown in Figure 2-9, the effective address (EA) of an operand is calculated according to the following formula.

EA = Base Reg + (Index Reg * Scaling) + Displacement

Direct Mode: The operand's offset is contained as part of the instruction as an 8-, 16- or 32-bit displacement.
EXAMPLE: INC Word PTR [500]

Register Indirect Mode: A BASE register contains the address of the operand.
EXAMPLE: MOV [ECX], EDX

Based Mode: A BASE register's contents is added to a DISPLACEMENT to form the operands offset.
EXAMPLE: MOV ECX, [EAX+24]

Index Mode: An INDEX register's contents is added to a DISPLACEMENT to form the operands offset.
EXAMPLE: ADD EAX, TABLE[ESI]

Scaled Index Mode: An INDEX register's contents is multiplied by a scaling factor which is added to a DISPLACEMENT to form the operands offset.
EXAMPLE: IMUL EBX, TABLE[ESI*4],7

Based Index Mode: The contents of a BASE register is added to the contents of an INDEX register to form the effective address of an operand.
EXAMPLE: MOV EAX, [ESI] [EBX]

Based Scaled Index Mode: The contents of an INDEX register is multiplied by a SCALING factor and the result is added to the contents of a BASE register to obtain the operands offset.
EXAMPLE: MOV ECX, [EDX*8] [EAX]

Based Index Mode with Displacement: The contents of an INDEX Register and a BASE register's contents and a DISPLACEMENT are all summed together to form the operand offset.
EXAMPLE: ADD EDX, [ESI] [EBP+00FFFFF0H]

Based Scaled Index Mode with Displacement: The contents of an INDEX register are multiplied by a SCALING factor, the result is added to the contents of a BASE register and a DISPLACEMENT to form the operand's offset.
EXAMPLE: MOV EAX, LOCALTABLE[EDI*4] [EBP+80]

4

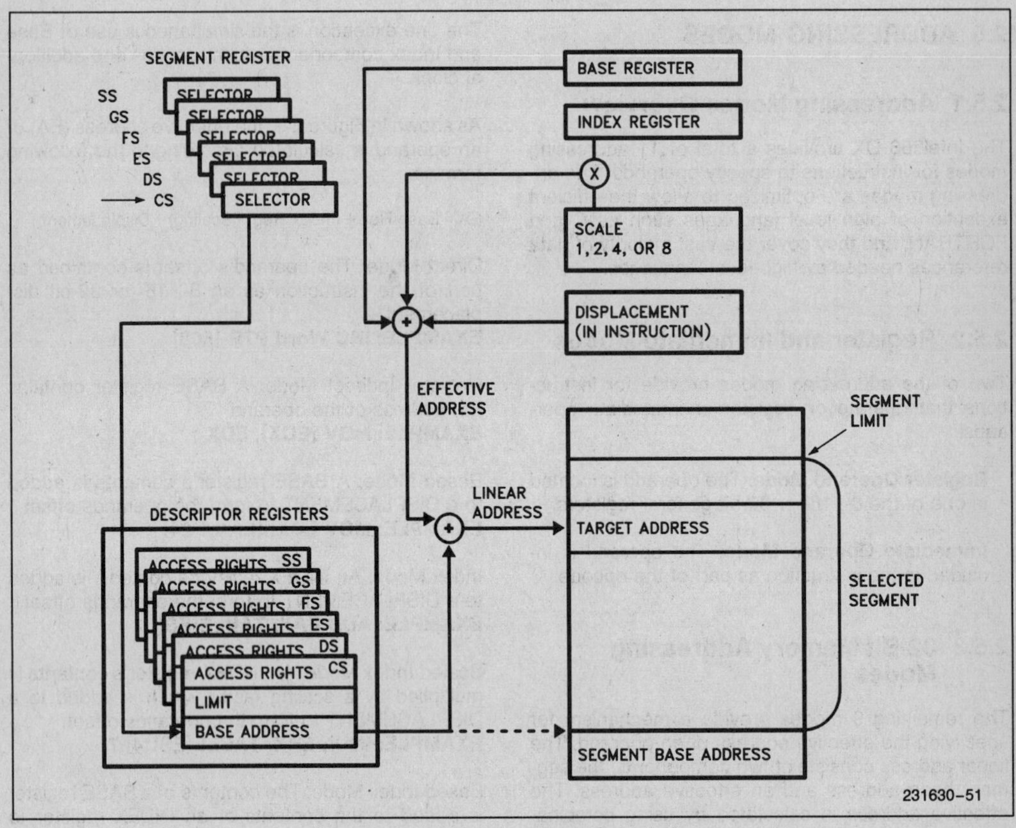

Figure 2-9. Addressing Mode Calculations

2.5.4 Differences Between 16 and 32 Bit Addresses

In order to provide software compatibility with the 80286 and the 8086, the Intel386 DX can execute 16-bit instructions in Real and Protected Modes. The processor determines the size of the instructions it is executing by examining the D bit in the CS segment Descriptor. If the D bit is 0 then all operand lengths and effective addresses are assumed to be 16 bits long. If the D bit is 1 then the default length for operands and addresses is 32 bits. In Real Mode the default size for operands and addresses is 16-bits.

Regardless of the default precision of the operands or addresses, the Intel386 DX is able to execute either 16 or 32-bit instructions. This is specified via the use of override prefixes. Two prefixes, the **Operand Size Prefix** and the **Address Length Prefix**, override the value of the D bit on an individual instruction basis. These prefixes are automatically added by Intel assemblers.

Example: The processor is executing in Real Mode and the programmer needs to access the EAX registers. The assembler code for this might be MOV EAX, 32-bit MEMORYOP, ASM386 Macro Assembler automatically determines that an Operand Size Prefix is needed and generates it.

Example: The D bit is 0, and the programmer wishes to use Scaled Index addressing mode to access an array. The Address Length Prefix allows the use of MOV DX, TABLE[ESI*2]. The assembler uses an Address Length Prefix since, with D=0, the default addressing mode is 16-bits.

Example: The D bit is 1, and the program wants to store a 16-bit quantity. The Operand Length Prefix is used to specify only a 16-bit value; MOV MEM16, DX.

Table 2-3. BASE and INDEX Registers for 16- and 32-Bit Addresses

	16-Bit Addressing	32-Bit Addressing
BASE REGISTER	BX,BP	Any 32-bit GP Register
INDEX REGISTER	SI,DI	Any 32-bit GP Register Except ESP
SCALE FACTOR	none	1, 2, 4, 8
DISPLACEMENT	0, 8, 16 bits	0, 8, 32 bits

The OPERAND LENGTH and Address Length Prefixes can be applied separately or in combination to any instruction. The Address Length Prefix does not allow addresses over 64K bytes to be accessed in Real Mode. A memory address which exceeds FFFFH will result in a General Protection Fault. An Address Length Prefix only allows the use of the additional Intel386 DX addressing modes.

When executing 32-bit code, the Intel386 DX uses either 8-, or 32-bit displacements, and any register can be used as base or index registers. When executing 16-bit code, the displacements are either 8, or 16 bits, and the base and index register conform to the 80286 model. Table 2-3 illustrates the differences.

2.6 DATA TYPES

The Intel386 DX supports all of the data types commonly used in high level languages:

Bit: A single bit quantity.

Bit Field: A group of up to 32 contiguous bits, which spans a maximum of four bytes.

Bit String: A set of contiguous bits, on the Intel386 DX bit strings can be up to 4 gigabits long.

Byte: A signed 8-bit quantity.

Unsigned Byte: An unsigned 8-bit quantity.

Integer (Word): A signed 16-bit quantity.

Long Integer (Double Word): A signed 32-bit quantity. All operations assume a 2's complement representation.

Unsigned Integer (Word): An unsigned 16-bit quantity.

Unsigned Long Integer (Double Word): An unsigned 32-bit quantity.

Signed Quad Word: A signed 64-bit quantity.

Unsigned Quad Word: An unsigned 64-bit quantity.

Offset: A 16- or 32-bit offset only quantity which indirectly references another memory location.

Pointer: A full pointer which consists of a 16-bit segment selector and either a 16- or 32-bit offset.

Char: A byte representation of an ASCII Alphanumeric or control character.

String: A contiguous sequence of bytes, words or dwords. A string may contain between 1 byte and 4 Gbytes.

BCD: A byte (unpacked) representation of decimal digits 0–9.

Packed BCD: A byte (packed) representation of two decimal digits 0–9 storing one digit in each nibble.

When the Intel386 DX is coupled with an Intel387 DX Numerics Coprocessor then the following common Floating Point types are supported.

Floating Point: A signed 32-, 64-, or 80-bit real number representation. Floating point numbers are supported by the Intel387 DX numerics coprocessor.

Figure 2-10 illustrates the data types supported by the Intel386 DX and the Intel387 DX numerics coprocessor.

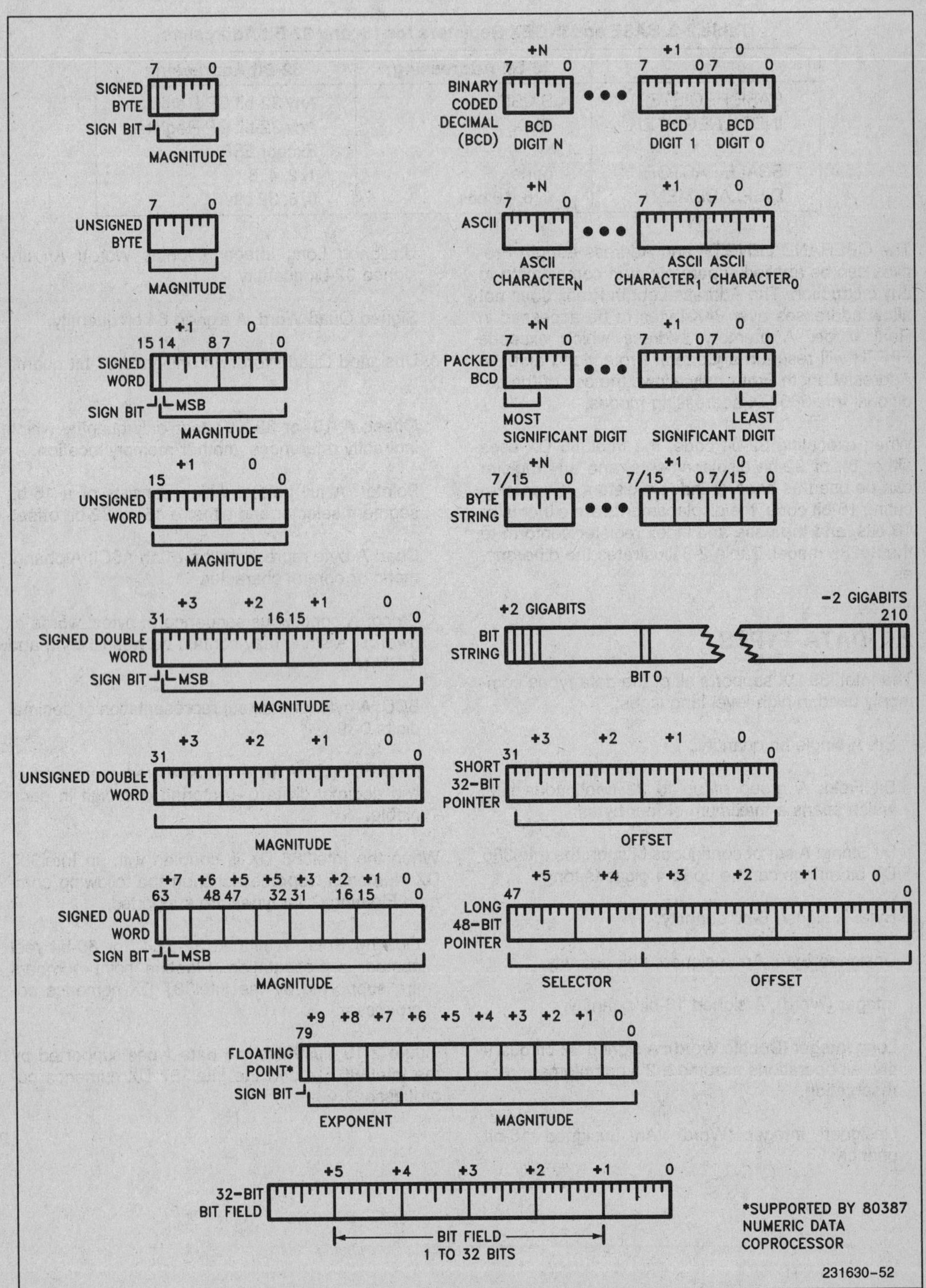

Figure 2-10. Intel386™ DX Supported Data Types

2.7 MEMORY ORGANIZATION

2.7.1 Introduction

Memory on the Intel386 DX is divided up into 8-bit quantities (bytes), 16-bit quantities (words), and 32-bit quantities (dwords). Words are stored in two consecutive bytes in memory with the low-order byte at the lowest address, the high order byte at the high address. Dwords are stored in four consecutive bytes in memory with the low-order byte at the lowest address, the high-order byte at the highest address. The address of a word or dword is the byte address of the low-order byte.

In addition to these basic data types, the Intel386 DX supports two larger units of memory: pages and segments. Memory can be divided up into one or more variable length segments, which can be swapped to disk or shared between programs. Memory can also be organized into one or more 4K byte pages. Finally, both segmentation and paging can be combined, gaining the advantages of both systems. The Intel386 DX supports both pages and segments in order to provide maximum flexibility to the system designer. Segmentation and paging are complementary. Segmentation is useful for organizing memory in logical modules, and as such is a tool for the application programmer, while pages are useful for the system programmer for managing the physical memory of a system.

2.7.2 Address Spaces

The Intel386 DX has three distinct address spaces: **logical, linear,** and **physical**. A **logical** address (also known as a **virtual** address) consists of a selector and an offset. A selector is the contents of a segment register. An offset is formed by summing all of the addressing components (BASE, INDEX, DISPLACEMENT) discussed in section 2.5.3 **Memory Addressing Modes** into an effective address. Since each task on Intel386 DX has a maximum of 16K (2^{14} −1) selectors, and offsets can be 4 gigabytes, (2^{32} bits) this gives a total of 2^{46} bits or 64 terabytes of **logical** address space per task. The programmer sees this virtual address space.

The segmentation unit translates the **logical** address space into a 32-bit **linear** address space. If the paging unit is not enabled then the 32-bit **linear** address corresponds to the **physical** address. The paging unit translates the **linear** address space into the **physical** address space. The **physical address** is what appears on the address pins.

The primary difference between Real Mode and Protected Mode is how the segmentation unit performs the translation of the **logical** address into the **linear** address. In Real Mode, the segmentation unit shifts the selector left four bits and adds the result to the offset to form the **linear** address. While in Protected Mode every selector has a **linear** base address associated with it. The **linear base** address is stored in one of two operating system tables (i.e. the Local Descriptor Table or Global Descriptor Table). The selector's **linear base** address is added to the offset to form the final **linear** address.

Figure 2-11 shows the relationship between the various address spaces.

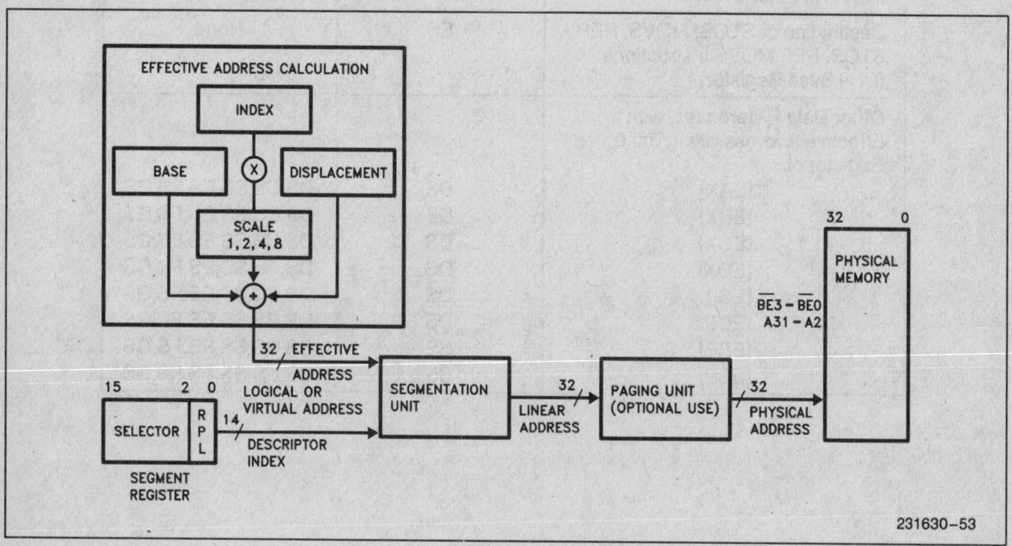

Figure 2-11. Address Translation

2.7.3 Segment Register Usage

The main data structure used to organize memory is the segment. On the Intel386 DX, segments are variable sized blocks of linear addresses which have certain attributes associated with them. There are two main types of segments: code and data, the segments are of variable size and can be as small as 1 byte or as large as 4 gigabytes (2^{32} bytes).

In order to provide compact instruction encoding, and increase processor performance, instructions do not need to explicitly specify which segment register is used. A default segment register is automatically chosen according to the rules of Table 2-4 (Segment Register Selection Rules). In general, data references use the selector contained in the DS register; Stack references use the SS register and Instruction fetches use the CS register. The contents of the Instruction Pointer provides the offset. Special segment override prefixes allow the explicit use of a given segment register, and override the implicit rules listed in Table 2-4. The override prefixes also allow the use of the ES, FS and GS segment registers.

There are no restrictions regarding the overlapping of the base addresses of any segments. Thus, all 6 segments could have the base address set to zero and create a system with a four gigabyte linear address space. This creates a system where the virtual address space is the same as the linear address space. Further details of segmentation are discussed in section 4.1.

2.8 I/O SPACE

The Intel386 DX has two distinct physical address spaces: Memory and I/O. Generally, peripherals are placed in I/O space although the Intel386 DX also supports memory-mapped peripherals. The I/O space consists of 64K bytes, it can be divided into 64K 8-bit ports, 32K 16-bit ports, or 16K 32-bit ports, or any combination of ports which add up to less than 64K bytes. The 64K I/O address space refers to physical memory rather than linear address since I/O instructions do not go through the segmentation or paging hardware. The M/IO# pin acts as an additional address line thus allowing the system designer to easily determine which address space the processor is accessing.

Table 2-4. Segment Register Selection Rules

Type of Memory Reference	Implied (Default) Segment Use	Segment Override Prefixes Possible
Code Fetch	CS	None
Destination of PUSH, PUSHF, INT, CALL, PUSHA Instructions	SS	None
Source of POP, POPA, POPF, IRET, RET instructions	SS	None
Destination of STOS, MOVS, REP STOS, REP MOVS Instructions (DI is Base Register)	ES	None
Other Data References, with Effective Address Using Base Register of:		
[EAX]	DS	DS,CS,SS,ES,FS,GS
[EBX]	DS	DS,CS,SS,ES,FS,GS
[ECX]	DS	DS,CS,SS,ES,FS,GS
[EDX]	DS	DS,CS,SS,ES,FS,GS
[ESI]	DS	DS,CS,SS,ES,FS,GS
[EDI]	DS	DS,CS,SS,ES,FS,GS
[EBP]	SS	DS,CS,SS,ES,FS,GS
[ESP]	SS	DS,CS,SS,ES,FS,GS

The I/O ports are accessed via the IN and OUT I/O instructions, with the port address supplied as an immediate 8-bit constant in the instruction or in the DX register. All 8- and 16-bit port addresses are zero extended on the upper address lines. The I/O instructions cause the M/IO# pin to be driven low.

I/O port addresses 00F8H through 00FFH are reserved for use by Intel.

2.9 INTERRUPTS

2.9.1 Interrupts and Exceptions

Interrupts and exceptions alter the normal program flow, in order to handle external events, to report errors or exceptional conditions. The difference between interrupts and exceptions is that interrupts are used to handle asynchronous external events while exceptions handle instruction faults. Although a program can generate a software interrupt via an INT N instruction, the processor treats software interrupts as exceptions.

Hardware interrupts occur as the result of an external event and are classified into two types: maskable or non-maskable. Interrupts are serviced after the execution of the current instruction. After the interrupt handler is finished servicing the interrupt, execution proceeds with the instruction immediately **after** the interrupted instruction. Sections 2.9.3 and 2.9.4 discuss the differences between Maskable and Non-Maskable interrupts.

Exceptions are classified as faults, traps, or aborts depending on the way they are reported, and whether or not restart of the instruction causing the exception is supported. **Faults** are exceptions that are detected and serviced **before** the execution of the faulting instruction. A fault would occur in a virtual memory system, when the processor referenced a page or a segment which was not present. The operating system would fetch the page or segment from disk, and then the Intel386 DX would restart the instruction. **Traps** are exceptions that are reported immediately **after** the execution of the instruction which caused the problem. User defined interrupts are examples of traps. **Aborts** are exceptions which do not permit the precise location of the instruction causing the exception to be determined. Aborts are used to report severe errors, such as a hardware error, or illegal values in system tables.

Thus, when an interrupt service routine has been completed, execution proceeds from the instruction immediately following the interrupted instruction. On the other hand, the return address from an exception fault routine will always point at the instruction causing the exception and include any leading instruction prefixes. Table 2-5 summarizes the possible interrupts for the Intel386 DX and shows where the return address points.

The Intel386 DX has the ability to handle up to 256 different interrupts/exceptions. In order to service the interrupts, a table with up to 256 interrupt vectors must be defined. The interrupt vectors are simply pointers to the appropriate interrupt service routine. In Real Mode (see section 3.1), the vectors are 4 byte quantities, a Code Segment plus a 16-bit offset; in Protected Mode, the interrupt vectors are 8 byte quantities, which are put in an Interrupt Descriptor Table (see section 4.1). Of the 256 possible interrupts, 32 are reserved for use by Intel, the remaining 224 are free to be used by the system designer.

2.9.2 Interrupt Processing

When an interrupt occurs the following actions happen. First, the current program address and the Flags are saved on the stack to allow resumption of the interrupted program. Next, an 8-bit vector is supplied to the Intel386 DX which identifies the appropriate entry in the interrupt table. The table contains the starting address of the interrupt service routine. Then, the user supplied interrupt service routine is executed. Finally, when an IRET instruction is executed the old processor state is restored and program execution resumes at the appropriate instruction.

The 8-bit interrupt vector is supplied to the Intel386 DX in several different ways: exceptions supply the interrupt vector internally; software INT instructions contain or imply the vector; maskable hardware interrupts supply the 8-bit vector via the interrupt acknowledge bus sequence. Non-Maskable hardware interrupts are assigned to interrupt vector 2.

2.9.3 Maskable Interrupt

Maskable interrupts are the most common way used by the Intel386 DX to respond to asynchronous external hardware events. A hardware interrupt occurs when the INTR is pulled high and the Interrupt Flag bit (IF) is enabled. The processor only responds to interrupts between instructions, (REPeat String instructions, have an "interrupt window", between memory moves, which allows interrupts during long

Table 2-5. Interrupt Vector Assignments

Function	Interrupt Number	Instruction Which Can Cause Exception	Return Address Points to Faulting Instruction	Type
Divide Error	0	DIV, IDIV	YES	FAULT
Debug Exception	1	any instruction	YES	TRAP*
NMI Interrupt	2	INT 2 or NMI	NO	NMI
One Byte Interrupt	3	INT	NO	TRAP
Interrupt on Overflow	4	INTO	NO	TRAP
Array Bounds Check	5	BOUND	YES	FAULT
Invalid OP-Code	6	Any Illegal Instruction	YES	FAULT
Device Not Available	7	ESC, WAIT	YES	FAULT
Double Fault	8	Any Instruction That Can Generate an Exception		ABORT
Coprocessor Segment Overrun	9	ESC	NO	ABORT
Invalid TSS	10	JMP, CALL, IRET, INT	YES	FAULT
Segment Not Present	11	Segment Register Instructions	YES	FAULT
Stack Fault	12	Stack References	YES	FAULT
General Protection Fault	13	Any Memory Reference	YES	FAULT
Intel Reserved	15			
Page Fault	14	Any Memory Access or Code Fetch	YES	FAULT
Coprocessor Error	16	ESC, WAIT	YES	FAULT
Intel Reserved	17–31			
Two Byte Interrupt	0–255	INT n	NO	TRAP

* Some debug exceptions may report both traps on the previous instruction, and faults on the next instruction.

string moves). When an interrupt occurs the processor reads an 8-bit vector supplied by the hardware which identifies the source of the interrupt, (one of 224 user defined interrupts). The exact nature of the interrupt sequence is discussed in section 5.

The IF bit in the EFLAG registers is reset when an interrupt is being serviced. This effectively disables servicing additional interrupts during an interrupt service routine. However, the IF may be set explicitly by the interrupt handler, to allow the nesting of interrupts. When an IRET instruction is executed the original state of the IF is restored.

2.9.4 Non-Maskable Interrupt

Non-maskable interrupts provide a method of servicing very high priority interrupts. A common example of the use of a non-maskable interrupt (NMI) would be to activate a power failure routine. When the NMI input is pulled high it causes an interrupt with an internally supplied vector value of 2. Unlike a normal hardware interrupt, no interrupt acknowledgment sequence is performed for an NMI.

While executing the NMI servicing procedure, the Intel386 DX will not service further NMI requests, until an interrupt return (IRET) instruction is executed or the processor is reset. If NMI occurs while currently servicing an NMI, its presence will be saved for servicing after executing the first IRET instruction. The IF bit is cleared at the beginning of an NMI interrupt to inhibit further INTR interrupts.

2.9.5 Software Interrupts

A third type of interrupt/exception for the Intel386 DX is the software interrupt. An INT n instruction causes the processor to execute the interrupt service routine pointed to by the nth vector in the interrupt table.

A special case of the two byte software interrupt INT n is the one byte INT 3, or breakpoint interrupt. By inserting this one byte instruction in a program, the user can set breakpoints in his program as a debugging tool.

A final type of software interrupt, is the single step interrupt. It is discussed in section 2.12.

2.9.6 Interrupt and Exception Priorities

Interrupts are externally-generated events. Maskable Interrupts (on the INTR input) and Non-Maskable Interrupts (on the NMI input) are recognized at instruction boundaries. When NMI and maskable INTR are **both** recognized at the **same** instruction boundary, the Intel386 DX invokes the NMI service routine first. If, after the NMI service routine has been invoked, maskable interrupts are still enabled, then the Intel386 DX will invoke the appropriate interrupt service routine.

Table 2-6a. Intel386™ DX Priority for Invoking Service Routines in Case of Simultaneous External Interrupts

1. NMI
2. INTR

Exceptions are internally-generated events. Exceptions are detected by the Intel386 DX if, in the course of executing an instruction, the Intel386 DX detects a problematic condition. The Intel386 DX then immediately invokes the appropriate exception service routine. The state of the Intel386 DX is such that the instruction causing the exception can be restarted. If the exception service routine has taken care of the problematic condition, the instruction will execute without causing the same exception.

It is possible for a single instruction to generate several exceptions (for example, transferring a single operand could generate two page faults if the operand location spans two "not present" pages). However, only one exception is generated upon each attempt to execute the instruction. Each exception service routine should correct its corresponding exception, and restart the instruction. In this manner, exceptions are serviced until the instruction executes successfully.

As the Intel386 DX executes instructions, it follows a consistent cycle in checking for exceptions, as shown in Table 2-6b. This cycle is repeated as each instruction is executed, and occurs in parallel with instruction decoding and execution.

Table 2-6b. Sequence of Exception Checking

Consider the case of the Intel386 DX having just completed an instruction. It then performs the following checks before reaching the point where the next instruction is completed:

1. Check for Exception 1 Traps from the instruction just completed (single-step via Trap Flag, or Data Breakpoints set in the Debug Registers).
2. Check for Exception 1 Faults in the next instruction (Instruction Execution Breakpoint set in the Debug Registers for the next instruction).
3. Check for external NMI and INTR.
4. Check for Segmentation Faults that prevented fetching the entire next instruction (exceptions 11 or 13).
5. Check for Page Faults that prevented fetching the entire next instruction (exception 14).
6. Check for Faults decoding the next instruction (exception 6 if illegal opcode; exception 6 if in Real Mode or in Virtual 8086 Mode and attempting to execute an instruction for Protected Mode only (see 4.6.4); or exception 13 if instruction is longer than 15 bytes, or privilege violation in Protected Mode (i.e. not at IOPL or at CPL=0).
7. If WAIT opcode, check if TS=1 and MP=1 (exception 7 if both are 1).
8. If ESCAPE opcode for numeric coprocessor, check if EM=1 or TS=1 (exception 7 if either are 1).
9. If WAIT opcode or ESCAPE opcode for numeric coprocessor, check ERROR# input signal (exception 16 if ERROR# input is asserted).
10. Check in the following order for each memory reference required by the instruction:
    a. Check for Segmentation Faults that prevent transferring the entire memory quantity (exceptions 11, 12, 13).
    b. Check for Page Faults that prevent transferring the entire memory quantity (exception 14).

Note that the order stated supports the concept of the paging mechanism being "underneath" the segmentation mechanism. Therefore, for any given code or data reference in memory, segmentation exceptions are generated before paging exceptions are generated.

4

2.9.7 Instruction Restart

The Intel386 DX fully supports restarting all instructions after faults. If an exception is detected in the instruction to be executed (exception categories 4 through 10 in Table 2-6b), the Intel386 DX invokes the appropriate exception service routine. The Intel386 DX is in a state that permits restart of the instruction, for all cases but those in Table 2-6c. Note that all such cases are easily avoided by proper design of the operating system.

Table 2-6c. Conditions Preventing Instruction Restart

A. An instruction causes a task switch to a task whose Task State Segment is **partially** "not present". (An entirely "not present" TSS is restartable.) Partially present TSS's can be avoided either by keeping the TSS's of such tasks present in memory, or by aligning TSS segments to reside entirely within a single 4K page (for TSS segments of 4K bytes or less).

B. A coprocessor operand wraps around the top of a 64K-byte segment or a 4G-byte segment, and spans three pages, and the page holding the middle portion of the operand is "not present." This condition can be avoided by starting **at a page boundary** any segments containing coprocessor operands if the segments are approximately 64K-200 bytes or larger (i.e. large enough for wraparound of the coprocessor operand to possibly occur).

Note that these conditions are avoided by using the operating system designs mentioned in this table.

2.9.8 Double Fault

A Double Fault (exception 8) results when the processor attempts to invoke an exception service routine for the segment exceptions (10, 11, 12 or 13), but in the process of doing so, detects an exception **other than** a Page Fault (exception 14).

A Double Fault (exception 8) will also be generated when the processor attempts to invoke the Page Fault (exception 14) service routine, and detects an exception other than a second Page Fault. In any functional system, the entire Page Fault service routine must remain "present" in memory.

Double page faults however do not raise the double fault exception. If a second page fault occurs while the processor is attempting to enter the service routine for the first time, then the processor will invoke the page fault (exception 14) handler a second time, rather than the double fault (exception 8) handler. A subsequent fault, though, will lead to shutdown.

When a Double Fault occurs, the Intel386 DX invokes the exception service routine for exception 8.

2.10 RESET AND INITIALIZATION

When the processor is initialized or Reset the registers have the values shown in Table 2-7. The Intel386 DX will then start executing instructions near the top of physical memory, at location FFFFFFF0H. When the first InterSegment Jump or Call is executed, address lines A20-31 will drop low for CS-relative memory cycles, and the Intel386 DX will only execute instructions in the lower one megabyte of physical memory. This allows the system designer to use a ROM at the top of physical memory to initialize the system and take care of Resets.

RESET forces the Intel386 DX to terminate all execution and local bus activity. No instruction execution or bus activity will occur as long as Reset is active. Between 350 and 450 CLK2 periods after Reset becomes inactive the Intel386 DX will start executing instructions at the top of physical memory.

Table 2-7. Register Values after Reset

Register	Value	Note
Flag Word	UUUU0002H	Note 1
Machine Status Word (CR0)	UUUUUUU0H	Note 2
Instruction Pointer	0000FFF0H	
Code Segment	F000H	Note 3
Data Segment	0000H	
Stack Segment	0000H	
Extra Segment (ES)	0000H	
Extra Segment (FS)	0000H	
Extra Segment (GS)	0000H	
DX register	component and stepping ID	Note 5
All other registers	undefined	Note 4

NOTES:

1. EFLAG Register. The upper 14 bits of the EFLAGS register are undefined, VM (Bit 17) and RF (BIT) 16 are 0 as are all other defined flag bits.
2. CR0: (Machine Status Word). All of the defined fields in the CR0 are 0 (PG Bit 31, TS Bit 3, EM Bit 2, MP Bit 1, and PE Bit 0).
3. The Code Segment Register (CS) will have its Base Address set to FFFF0000H and Limit set to 0FFFFH.
4. All undefined bits are Intel Reserved and should not be used.
5. DX register always holds component and stepping identifier (see 5.7). EAX register holds self-test signature if self-test was requested (see 5.6).

2.11 TESTABILITY

2.11.1 Self-Test

The Intel386 DX has the capability to perform a self-test. The self-test checks the function of all of the Control ROM and most of the non-random logic of the part. Approximately one-half of the Intel386 DX can be tested during self-test.

Self-Test is initiated on the Intel386 DX when the RESET pin transitions from HIGH to LOW, and the BUSY# pin is low. The self-test takes about 2**19 clocks, or approximately 26 milliseconds with a 20 MHz Intel386 DX. At the completion of self-test the processor performs reset and begins normal operation. The part has successfully passed self-test if the contents of the EAX register are zero (0). If the results of EAX are not zero then the self-test has detected a flaw in the part.

2.11.2 TLB Testing

The Intel386 DX provides a mechanism for testing the Translation Lookaside Buffer (TLB) if desired. This particular mechanism is unique to the Intel386 DX and may not be continued in the same way in future processors. When testing the TLB paging must be turned off (PG = 0 in CR0) to enable the TLB testing hardware and avoid interference with the test data being written to the TLB.

There are two TLB testing operations: 1) write entries into the TLB, and, 2) perform TLB lookups. Two Test Registers, shown in Figure 2-12, are provided for the purpose of testing. TR6 is the "test command register", and TR7 is the "test data register". The fields within these registers are defined below.

C: This is the command bit. For a write into TR6 to cause an immediate write into the TLB entry, write a 0 to this bit. For a write into TR6 to cause an immediate TLB lookup, write a 1 to this bit.

Linear Address: This is the tag field of the TLB. On a TLB write, a TLB entry is allocated to this linear address and the rest of that TLB entry is set per the value of TR7 and the value just written into TR6. On a TLB lookup, the TLB is interrogated per this value and if one and only one TLB entry matches, the rest of the fields of TR6 and TR7 are set from the matching TLB entry.

Physical Address: This is the data field of the TLB. On a write to the TLB, the TLB entry allocated to the linear address in TR6 is set to this value. On a TLB lookup, the data field (physical address) from the TLB is read out to here.

PL: On a TLB write, PL=1 causes the REP field of TR7 to select which of four associative blocks of the TLB is to be written, but PL=0 allows the internal pointer in the paging unit to select which TLB block is written. On a TLB lookup, the PL bit indicates whether the lookup was a hit (PL gets set to 1) or a miss (PL gets reset to 0).

V: The valid bit for this TLB entry. All valid bits can also be cleared by writing to CR3.

D, D#: The dirty bit for/from the TLB entry.

U, U#: The user bit for/from the TLB entry.

W, W#: The writable bit for/from the TLB entry.

For D, U and W, both the attribute and its complement are provided as tag bits, to permit the option of a "don't care" on TLB lookups. The meaning of these pairs of bits is given in the following table:

X	X#	Effect During TLB Lookup	Value of Bit X after TLB Write
0	0	Miss All	Bit X Becomes Undefined
0	1	Match if X = 0	Bit X Becomes 0
1	0	Match if X = 1	Bit X Becomes 1
1	1	Match all	Bit X Becomes Undefined

For writing a TLB entry:

1. Write TR7 for the desired physical address, PL and REP values.
2. Write TR6 with the appropriate linear address, etc. (be sure to write C = 0 for "write" command).

For looking up (reading) a TLB entry:

1. Write TR6 with the appropriate linear address (be sure to write C=1 for "lookup" command).
2. Read TR7 and TR6. If the PL bit in TR7 indicates a hit, then the other values reveal the TLB contents. If PL indicates a miss, then the other values in TR7 and TR6 are indeterminate.

2.12 DEBUGGING SUPPORT

The Intel386 DX provides several features which simplify the debugging process. The three categories of on-chip debugging aids are:

1) the code execution breakpoint opcode (0CCH),

2) the single-step capability provided by the TF bit in the flag register, and

3) the code and data breakpoint capability provided by the Debug Registers DR0-3, DR6, and DR7.

4

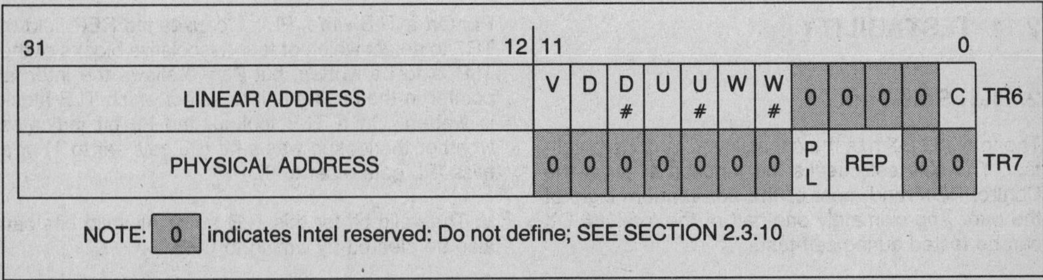

31 ... 12	11											0	
LINEAR ADDRESS	V	D	D#	U	U#	W	W#	0	0	0	0	C	TR6
PHYSICAL ADDRESS	0	0	0	0	0	0	0	PL	REP		0	0	TR7

NOTE: 0 indicates Intel reserved: Do not define; SEE SECTION 2.3.10

Figure 2-12. Test Registers

2.12.1 Breakpoint Instruction

A single-byte-opcode breakpoint instruction is available for use by software debuggers. The breakpoint opcode is 0CCh, and generates an exception 3 trap when executed. In typical use, a debugger program can "plant" the breakpoint instruction at all desired code execution breakpoints. The single-byte breakpoint opcode is an alias for the two-byte general software interrupt instruction, INT n, where n=3. The only difference between INT 3 (0CCh) and INT n is that INT 3 is never IOPL-sensitive but INT n is IOPL-sensitive in Protected Mode and Virtual 8086 Mode.

2.12.2 Single-Step Trap

If the single-step flag (TF, bit 8) in the EFLAG register is found to be set at the end of an instruction, a single-step exception occurs. The single-step exception is auto vectored to exception number 1. Precisely, exception 1 occurs as a trap after the instruction following the instruction which set TF. In typical practice, a debugger sets the TF bit of a flag register image on the debugger's stack. It then typically transfers control to the user program and loads the flag image with a signal instruction, the IRET instruction. The single-step trap occurs after executing one instruction of the user program.

Since the exception 1 occurs as a trap (that is, it occurs after the instruction has already executed), the CS:EIP pushed onto the debugger's stack points to the next unexecuted instruction of the program being debugged. An exception 1 handler, merely by ending with an IRET instruction, can therefore efficiently support single-stepping through a user program.

2.12.3 Debug Registers

The Debug Registers are an advanced debugging feature of the Intel386 DX. They allow data access breakpoints as well as code execution breakpoints. Since the breakpoints are indicated by on-chip registers, an instruction execution breakpoint can be placed in ROM code or in code shared by several tasks, neither of which can be supported by the INT3 breakpoint opcode.

The Intel386 DX contains six Debug Registers, providing the ability to specify up to four distinct breakpoints addresses, breakpoint control options, and read breakpoint status. Initially after reset, breakpoints are in the disabled state. Therefore, no breakpoints will occur unless the debug registers are programmed. Breakpoints set up in the Debug Registers are autovectored to exception number 1.

2.12.3.1 LINEAR ADDRESS BREAKPOINT REGISTERS (DR0–DR3)

Up to four breakpoint addresses can be specified by writing into Debug Registers DR0–DR3, shown in Figure 2-13. The breakpoint addresses specified are 32-bit linear addresses. Intel386 DX hardware continuously compares the linear breakpoint addresses in DR0–DR3 with the linear addresses generated by executing software (a linear address is the result of computing the effective address and adding the 32-bit segment base address). Note that if paging is not enabled the linear address equals the physical address. If paging is enabled, the linear address is translated to a physical 32-bit address by the on-chip paging unit. Regardless of whether paging is enabled or not, however, the breakpoint registers hold linear addresses.

2.12.3.2 DEBUG CONTROL REGISTER (DR7)

A Debug Control Register, DR7 shown in Figure 2-13, allows several debug control functions such as enabling the breakpoints and setting up other control options for the breakpoints. The fields within the Debug Control Register, DR7, are as follows:

LENi (breakpoint length specification bits)

A 2-bit LEN field exists for each of the four breakpoints. LEN specifies the length of the associated breakpoint field. The choices for data breakpoints are: 1 byte, 2 bytes, and 4 bytes. Instruction execu-

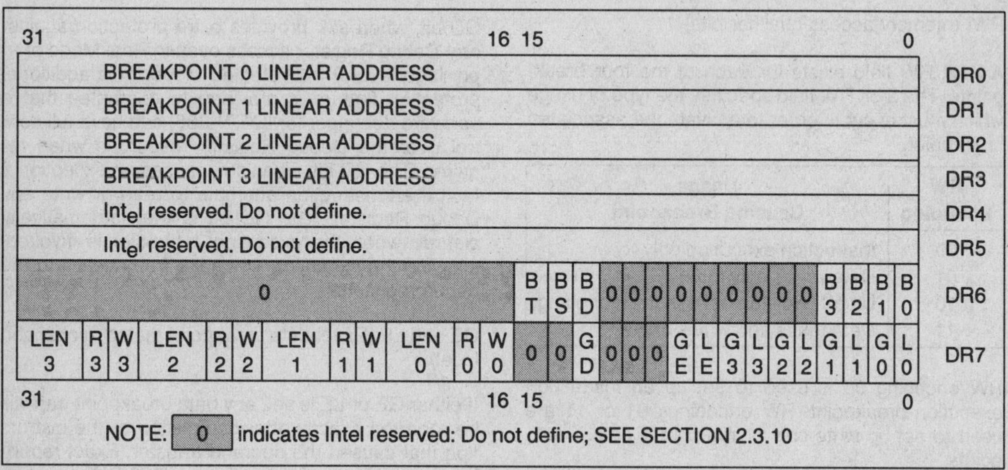

Figure 2-13. Debug Registers

tion breakpoints must have a length of 1 (LENi = 00). Encoding of the LENi field is as follows:

LENi Encoding	Breakpoint Field Width	Usage of Least Significant Bits in Breakpoint Address Register i, (i = 0 − 3)
00	1 byte	All 32-bits used to specify a single-byte breakpoint field.
01	2 bytes	A1–A31 used to specify a two-byte, word-aligned breakpoint field. A0 in Breakpoint Address Register is not used.
10	Undefined—do not use this encoding	
11	4 bytes	A2–A31 used to specify a four-byte, dword-aligned breakpoint field. A0 and A1 in Breakpoint Address Register are not used.

The LENi field controls the size of breakpoint field i by controlling whether all low-order linear address bits in the breakpoint address register are used to detect the breakpoint event. Therefore, all breakpoint fields are aligned; 2-byte breakpoint fields begin on Word boundaries, and 4-byte breakpoint fields begin on Dword boundaries.

The following is an example of various size breakpoint fields. Assume the breakpoint linear address in DR2 is 00000005H. In that situation, the following illustration indicates the region of the breakpoint field for lengths of 1, 2, or 4 bytes.

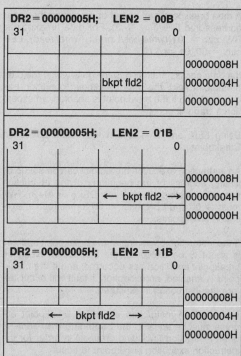

DR2 = 00000005H; LEN2 = 00B

31 0

				00000008H
		bkpt fld2		00000004H
				00000000H

DR2 = 00000005H; LEN2 = 01B

31 0

				00000008H
		← bkpt fld2 →		00000004H
				00000000H

DR2 = 00000005H; LEN2 = 11B

31 0

				00000008H
← bkpt fld2 →				00000004H
				00000000H

RWi (memory access qualifier bits)

A 2-bit RW field exists for each of the four breakpoints. The 2-bit RW field specifies the type of usage which must occur in order to activate the associated breakpoint.

RW Encoding	Usage Causing Breakpoint
00	Instruction execution only
01	Data writes only
10	Undefined—do not use this encoding
11	Data reads and writes only

RW encoding 00 is used to set up an instruction execution breakpoint. RW encodings 01 or 11 are used to set up write-only or read/write data breakpoints.

Note that **instruction execution breakpoints are taken as faults** (i.e. before the instruction executes), but **data breakpoints are taken as traps** (i.e. after the data transfer takes place).

Using LENi and RWi to Set Data Breakpoint i

A data breakpoint can be set up by writing the linear address into DRi (i = 0–3). For data breakpoints, RWi can = 01 (write-only) or 11 (write/read). LEN can = 00, 01, or 11.

If a data access entirely or partly falls within the data breakpoint field, the data breakpoint condition has occurred, and if the breakpoint is enabled, an exception 1 trap will occur.

Using LENi and RWi to Set Instruction Execution Breakpoint i

An instruction execution breakpoint can be set up by writing address of the beginning of the instruction (including prefixes if any) into DRi (i = 0–3). RWi must = 00 and LEN must = 00 for instruction execution breakpoints.

If the instruction beginning at the breakpoint address is about to be executed, the instruction execution breakpoint condition has occurred, and if the breakpoint is enabled, an exception 1 fault will occur before the instruction is executed.

Note that an instruction execution breakpoint address must be equal to the **beginning** byte address of an instruction (including prefixes) in order for the instruction execution breakpoint to occur.

GD (Global Debug Register access detect)

The Debug Registers can only be accessed in Real Mode or at privilege level 0 in Protected Mode. The GD bit, when set, provides extra protection against **any** Debug Register access even in Real Mode or at privilege level 0 in Protected Mode. This additional protection feature is provided to guarantee that a software debugger (or ICE™-386) can have full control over the Debug Register resources when required. The GD bit, when set, causes an exception 1 fault if an instruction attempts to read or write any Debug Register. The GD bit is then automatically cleared when the exception 1 handler is invoked, allowing the exception 1 handler free access to the debug registers.

GE and LE (Exact data breakpoint match, global and local)

If either GE or LE is set, any data breakpoint trap will be reported exactly after completion of the instruction that caused the operand transfer. Exact reporting is provided by forcing the Intel386 DX execution unit to wait for completion of data operand transfers before beginning execution of the next instruction.

If exact data breakpoint match is not selected, data breakpoints may not be reported until several instructions later or may not be reported at all. When enabling a data breakpoint, it is therefore recommended to enable the exact data breakpoint match.

When the Intel386 DX performs a task switch, the LE bit is cleared. Thus, the LE bit supports fast task switching out of tasks, that have enabled the exact data breakpoint match for their task-local breakpoints. The LE bit is cleared by the processor during a task switch, to avoid having exact data breakpoint match enabled in the new task. Note that exact data breakpoint match must be re-enabled under software control.

The Intel386 DX GE bit is unaffected during a task switch. The GE bit supports exact data breakpoint match that is to remain enabled during all tasks executing in the system.

Note that **instruction execution** breakpoints are always reported exactly, whether or not exact data breakpoint match is selected.

Gi and Li (breakpoint enable, global and local)

If either Gi or Li is set then the associated breakpoint (as defined by the linear address in DRi, the length in LENi and the usage criteria in RWi) is enabled. If either Gi or Li is set, and the Intel386 DX detects the ith breakpoint condition, then the exception 1 handler is invoked.

When the Intel386 DX performs a task switch to a new Task State Segment (TSS), all Li bits are cleared. Thus, the Li bits support fast task switching out of tasks that use some task-local breakpoint registers. The Li bits are cleared by the processor during a task switch, to avoid spurious exceptions in the new task. Note that the breakpoints must be re-enabled under software control.

All Intel386 DX Gi bits are unaffected during a task switch. The Gi bits support breakpoints that are active in all tasks executing in the system.

2.12.3.3 DEBUG STATUS REGISTER (DR6)

A Debug Status Register, DR6 shown in Figure 2-13, allows the exception 1 handler to easily determine why it was invoked. Note the exception 1 handler can be invoked as a result of one of several events:

1) DR0 Breakpoint fault/trap.
2) DR1 Breakpoint fault/trap.
3) DR2 Breakpoint fault/trap.
4) DR3 Breakpoint fault/trap.
5) Single-step (TF) trap.
6) Task switch trap.
7) Fault due to attempted debug register access when GD=1.

The Debug Status Register contains single-bit flags for each of the possible events invoking exception 1. Note below that some of these events are faults (exception taken before the instruction is executed), while other events are traps (exception taken after the debug events occurred).

The flags in DR6 are set by the hardware but never cleared by hardware. Exception 1 handler software should clear DR6 before returning to the user program to avoid future confusion in identifying the source of exception 1.

The fields within the Debug Status Register, DR6, are as follows:

Bi (debug fault/trap due to breakpoint 0–3)

Four breakpoint indicator flags, B0–B3, correspond one-to-one with the breakpoint registers in DR0–DR3. A flag Bi is set when the condition described by DRi, LENi, and RWi occurs.

If Gi or Li is set, and if the ith breakpoint is detected, the processor will invoke the exception 1 handler. The exception is handled as a fault if an instruction execution breakpoint occurred, or as a trap if a data breakpoint occurred.

IMPORTANT NOTE: A flag Bi is set whenever the hardware detects a match condition on **enabled** breakpoint i. Whenever a match is detected on at least one **enabled** breakpoint i, the hardware immediately sets all Bi bits corresponding to breakpoint conditions matching at that instant, whether enabled **or not.** Therefore, the exception 1 handler may see that multiple Bi bits are set, but only set Bi bits corresponding to **enabled** breakpoints (Li or Gi set) are **true** indications of why the exception 1 handler was invoked.

BD (debug fault due to attempted register access when GD bit set)

This bit is set if the exception 1 handler was invoked due to an instruction attempting to read or write to the debug registers when GD bit was set. If such an event occurs, then the GD bit is automatically cleared when the exception 1 handler is invoked, allowing handler access to the debug registers.

BS (debug trap due to single-step)

This bit is set if the exception 1 handler was invoked due to the TF bit in the flag register being set (for single-stepping). See section 2.12.2.

BT (debug trap due to task switch)

This bit is set if the exception 1 handler was invoked due to a task switch occurring to a task having an Intel386 DX TSS with the T bit set. (See Figure 4-15a). Note the task switch into the new task occurs normally, but before the first instruction of the task is executed, the exception 1 handler is invoked. With respect to the task switch operation, the operation is considered to be a trap.

2.12.3.4 USE OF RESUME FLAG (RF) IN FLAG REGISTER

The Resume Flag (RF) in the flag word can suppress an instruction execution breakpoint when the exception 1 handler returns to a user program at a user address which is also an instruction execution breakpoint. See section 2.3.3.

3. REAL MODE ARCHITECTURE

3.1 REAL MODE INTRODUCTION

When the processor is reset or powered up it is initialized in Real Mode. Real Mode has the same base architecture as the 8086, but allows access to the 32-bit register set of the Intel386 DX. The addressing mechanism, memory size, interrupt handling, are all identical to the Real Mode on the 80286.

4

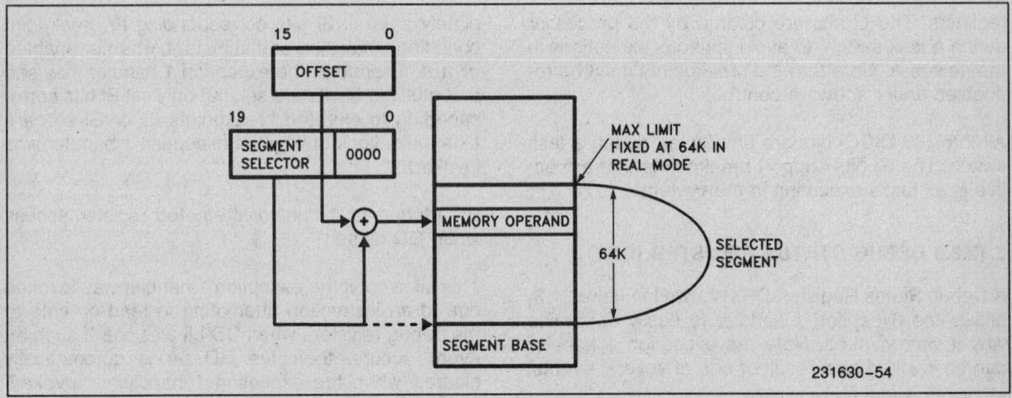

Figure 3-1. Real Address Mode Addressing

All of the Intel386 DX instructions are available in Real Mode (except those instructions listed in 4.6.4). The default operand size in Real Mode is 16-bits, just like the 8086. In order to use the 32-bit registers and addressing modes, override prefixes must be used. In addition, the segment size on the Intel386 DX in Real Mode is 64K bytes so 32-bit effective addresses must have a value less the 0000FFFFH. The primary purpose of Real Mode is to set up the processor for Protected Mode Operation.

The LOCK prefix on the Intel386 DX, even in Real Mode, is more restrictive than on the 80286. This is due to the addition of paging on the Intel386 DX in Protected Mode and Virtual 8086 Mode. Paging makes it impossible to guarantee that repeated string instructions can be LOCKed. The Intel386 DX can't require that all pages holding the string be physically present in memory. Hence, a Page Fault (exception 14) might have to be taken during the repeated string instruction. Therefore the LOCK prefix can't be supported during repeated string instructions.

These are the only instruction forms where the LOCK prefix is legal on the Intel386 DX:

Opcode	Operands (Dest, Source)
BIT Test and SET/RESET/COMPLEMENT	Mem, Reg/immed
XCHG	Reg, Mem
XCHG	Mem, Reg
ADD, OR, ADC, SBB, AND, SUB, XOR	Mem, Reg/immed
NOT, NEG, INC, DEC	Mem

An exception 6 will be generated if a LOCK prefix is placed before any instruction form or opcode not listed above. The LOCK prefix allows indivisible read/modify/write operations on memory operands using the instructions above. For example, even the ADD Reg, Mem is not LOCKable, because the Mem operand is not the destination (and therefore no memory read/modify/operation is being performed).

Since, on the Intel386 DX, repeated string instructions are not LOCKable, it is not possible to LOCK the bus for a long period of time. Therefore, the LOCK prefix is not IOPL-sensitive on the Intel386 DX. The LOCK prefix can be used at any privilege level, but only on the instruction forms listed above.

3.2 MEMORY ADDRESSING

In Real Mode the maximum memory size is limited to 1 megabyte. Thus, only address lines A2–A19 are active. (Exception, the high address lines A20–A31 are high during CS-relative memory cycles until an intersegment jump or call is executed (see section 2.10)).

Since paging is not allowed in Real Mode the linear addresses are the same as physical addresses. Physical addresses are formed in Real Mode by adding the contents of the appropriate segment register which is shifted left by four bits to an effective address. This addition results in a physical address from 00000000H to 0010FFEFH. This is compatible with 80286 Real Mode. Since segment registers are shifted left by 4 bits this implies that Real Mode segments always start on 16 byte boundaries.

All segments in Real Mode are exactly 64K bytes long, and may be read, written, or executed. The Intel386 DX will generate an exception 13 if a data operand or instruction fetch occurs past the end of a segment. (i.e. if an operand has an offset greater than FFFFH, for example a word with a low byte at FFFFH and the high byte at 0000H.)

Segments may be overlapped in Real Mode. Thus, if a particular segment does not use all 64K bytes another segment can be overlayed on top of the unused portion of the previous segment. This allows the programmer to minimize the amount of physical memory needed for a program.

3.3 RESERVED LOCATIONS

There are two fixed areas in memory which are reserved in Real address mode: system initialization area and the interrupt table area. Locations 00000H through 003FFH are reserved for interrupt vectors. Each one of the 256 possible interrupts has a 4-byte jump vector reserved for it. Locations FFFFFFF0H through FFFFFFFFH are reserved for system initialization.

3.4 INTERRUPTS

Many of the exceptions shown in Table 2-5 and discussed in section 2.9 are not applicable to Real Mode operation, in particular exceptions 10, 11, 14, will not happen in Real Mode. Other exceptions have slightly different meanings in Real Mode; Table 3-1 identifies these exceptions.

3.5 SHUTDOWN AND HALT

The HLT instruction stops program execution and prevents the processor from using the local bus until restarted. Either NMI, INTR with interrupts enabled (IF=1), or RESET will force the Intel386 DX out of halt. If interrupted, the saved CS:IP will point to the next instruction after the HLT.

Shutdown will occur when a severe error is detected that prevents further processing. In Real Mode, shutdown can occur under two conditions:

An interrupt or an exception occur (Exceptions 8 or 13) and the interrupt vector is larger than the Interrupt Descriptor Table (i.e. There is not an interrupt handler for the interrupt).

A CALL, INT or PUSH instruction attempts to wrap around the stack segment when SP is not even. (e.g. pushing a value on the stack when SP = 0001 resulting in a stack segment greater than FFFFH)

An NMI input can bring the processor out of shutdown if the Interrupt Descriptor Table limit is large enough to contain the NMI interrupt vector (at least 0017H) and the stack has enough room to contain the vector and flag information (i.e. SP is greater than 0005H). Otherwise shutdown can only be exited via the RESET input.

4. PROTECTED MODE ARCHITECTURE

4.1 INTRODUCTION

The complete capabilities of the Intel386 DX are unlocked when the processor operates in Protected Virtual Address Mode (Protected Mode). Protected Mode vastly increases the linear address space to four gigabytes (2^{32} bytes) and allows the running of virtual memory programs of almost unlimited size (64 terabytes or 2^{46} bytes). In addition Protected Mode allows the Intel386 DX to run all of the existing 8086 and 80286 software, while providing a sophisticated memory management and a hardware-assisted protection mechanism. Protected Mode allows the use of additional instructions especially optimized for supporting multitasking operating systems. The base architecture of the Intel386 DX remains the same, the registers, instructions, and addressing modes described in the previous sections are retained. The main difference between Protected Mode, and Real Mode from a programmer's view is the increased address space, and a different addressing mechanism.

4

Table 3-1

Function	Interrupt Number	Related Instructions	Return Address Location
Interrupt table limit too small	8	INT Vector is not within table limit	Before Instruction
CS, DS, ES, FS, GS Segment overrun exception	13	Word memory reference beyond offset = FFFFH. An attempt to execute past the end of CS segment.	Before Instruction
SS Segment overrun exception	12	Stack Reference beyond offset = FFFFH	Before Instruction

4.2 ADDRESSING MECHANISM

Like Real Mode, Protected Mode uses two components to form the logical address, a 16-bit selector is used to determine the linear base address of a segment, the base address is added to a 32-bit effective address to form a 32-bit linear address. The linear address is then either used as the 32-bit physical address, or if paging is enabled the paging mechanism maps the 32-bit linear address into a 32-bit physical address.

The difference between the two modes lies in calculating the base address. In Protected Mode the selector is used to specify an index into an operating system defined table (see Figure 4-1). The table contains the 32-bit base address of a given segment. The physical address is formed by adding the base address obtained from the table to the offset.

Paging provides an additional memory management mechanism which operates only in Protected Mode. Paging provides a means of managing the very large segments of the Intel386 DX. As such, paging operates beneath segmentation. The paging mechanism translates the protected linear address which comes from the segmentation unit into a physical address. Figure 4-2 shows the complete Intel386 DX addressing mechanism with paging enabled.

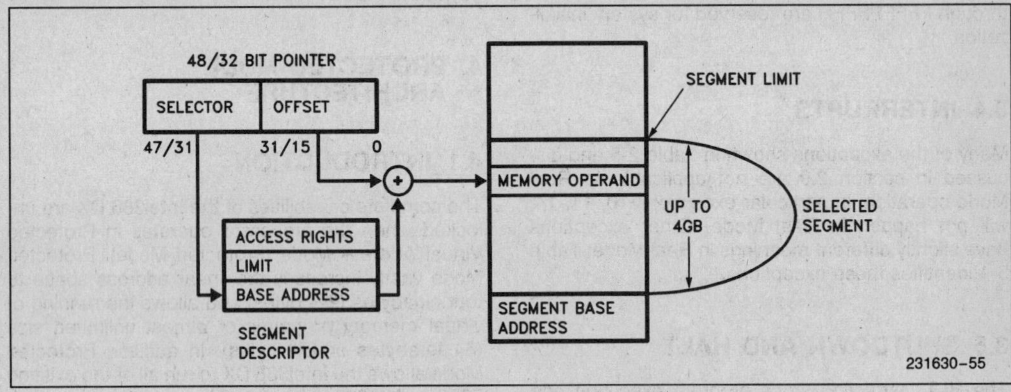

Figure 4-1. Protected Mode Addressing

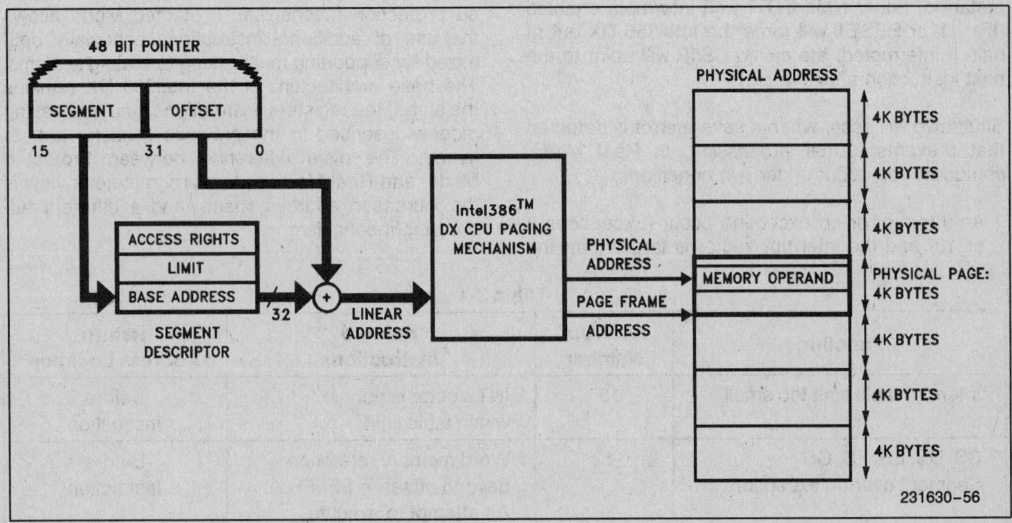

Figure 4-2. Paging and Segmentation

4.3 SEGMENTATION

4.3.1 Segmentation Introduction

Segmentation is one method of memory management. Segmentation provides the basis for protection. Segments are used to encapsulate regions of memory which have common attributes. For example, all of the code of a given program could be contained in a segment, or an operating system table may reside in a segment. All information about a segment is stored in an 8 byte data structure called a descriptor. All of the descriptors in a system are contained in tables recognized by hardware.

4.3.2 Terminology

The following terms are used throughout the discussion of descriptors, privilege levels and protection:

PL: Privilege Level—One of the four hierarchical privilege levels. Level 0 is the most privileged level and level 3 is the least privileged. More privileged levels are numerically smaller than less privileged levels.

RPL: Requestor Privilege Level—The privilege level of the original supplier of the selector. RPL is determined by the **least two** significant bits of a selector.

DPL: Descriptor Privilege Level—This is the least privileged level at which a task may access that descriptor (and the segment associated with that descriptor). Descriptor Privilege Level is determined by bits 6:5 in the Access Right Byte of a descriptor.

CPL: Current Privilege Level—The privilege level at which a task is currently executing, which equals the privilege level of the code segment being executed. CPL can also be determined by examining the lowest 2 bits of the CS register, except for conforming code segments.

EPL: Effective Privilege Level—The effective privilege level is the least privileged of the RPL and DPL. Since smaller privilege level **values** indicate greater privilege, EPL is the numerical maximum of RPL and DPL.

Task: One instance of the execution of a program. Tasks are also referred to as processes.

4.3.3 Descriptor Tables

4.3.3.1 DESCRIPTOR TABLES INTRODUCTION

The descriptor tables define all of the segments which are used in an Intel386 DX system. There are three types of tables on the Intel386 DX which hold descriptors: the Global Descriptor Table, Local Descriptor Table, and the Interrupt Descriptor Table. All of the tables are variable length memory arrays. They can range in size between 8 bytes and 64K bytes. Each table can hold up to 8192 8 byte descriptors. The upper 13 bits of a selector are used as an index into the descriptor table. The tables have registers associated with them which hold the 32-bit linear base address, and the 16-bit limit of each table.

Each of the tables has a register associated with it the GDTR, LDTR, and the IDTR (see Figure 4-3). The LGDT, LLDT, and LIDT instructions, load the base and limit of the Global, Local, and Interrupt Descriptor Tables, respectively, into the appropriate register. The SGDT, SLDT, and SIDT instructions store the base and limit values. These tables are manipulated by the operating system. Therefore, the load descriptor table instructions are privileged instructions.

4.3.3.2 GLOBAL DESCRIPTOR TABLE

The Global Descriptor Table (GDT) contains descriptors which are possibly available to all of the tasks in a system. The GDT can contain any type of segment descriptor except for descriptors which are used for servicing interrupts (i.e. interrupt and trap descriptors). Every Intel386 DX system contains a

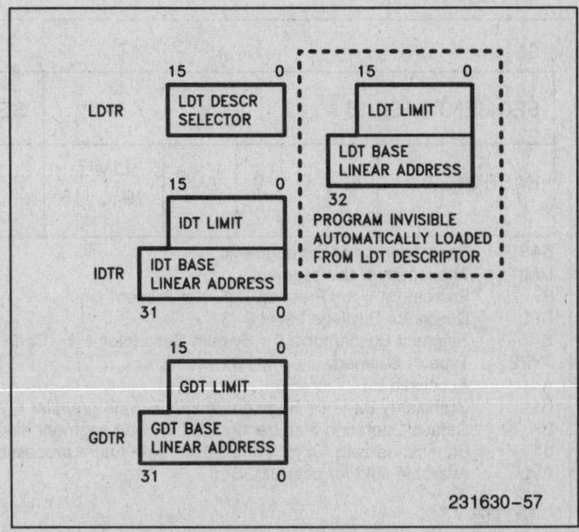

Figure 4-3. Descriptor Table Registers

GDT. Generally the GDT contains code and data segments used by the operating systems and task state segments, and descriptors for the LDTs in a system.

The first slot of the Global Descriptor Table corresponds to the null selector and is not used. The null selector defines a null pointer value.

4.3.3.3 LOCAL DESCRIPTOR TABLE

LDTs contain descriptors which are associated with a given task. Generally, operating systems are designed so that each task has a separate LDT. The LDT may contain only code, data, stack, task gate, and call gate descriptors. LDTs provide a mechanism for isolating a given task's code and data segments from the rest of the operating system, while the GDT contains descriptors for segments which are common to all tasks. A segment cannot be accessed by a task if its segment descriptor does not exist in either the current LDT or the GDT. This provides both isolation and protection for a task's segments, while still allowing global data to be shared among tasks.

Unlike the 6 byte GDT or IDT registers which contain a base address and limit, the visible portion of the LDT register contains only a 16-bit selector. This selector refers to a Local Descriptor Table descriptor in the GDT.

4.3.3.4 INTERRUPT DESCRIPTOR TABLE

The third table needed for Intel386 DX systems is the Interrupt Descriptor Table. (See Figure 4-4.) The IDT contains the descriptors which point to the location of up to 256 interrupt service routines. The IDT may contain only task gates, interrupt gates, and trap gates. The IDT should be at least 256 bytes in size in order to hold the descriptors for the 32 Intel Reserved Interrupts. Every interrupt used by a system must have an entry in the IDT. The IDT entries are referenced via INT instructions, external interrupt vectors, and exceptions. (See 2.9 **Interrupts**).

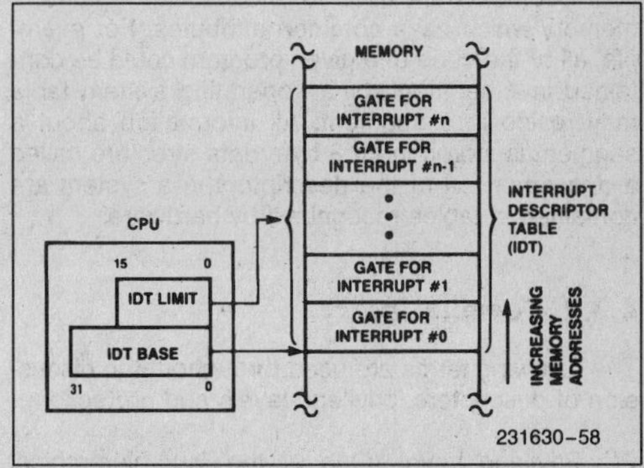

Figure 4-4. Interrupt Descriptor Table Register Use

4.3.4 Descriptors

4.3.4.1 DESCRIPTOR ATTRIBUTE BITS

The object to which the segment selector points to is called a descriptor. Descriptors are eight byte quantities which contain attributes about a given region of linear address space (i.e. a segment). These attributes include the 32-bit base linear address of the segment, the 20-bit length and granularity of the segment, the protection level, read, write or execute privileges, the default size of the operands (16-bit or

31											0	BYTE ADDRESS
SEGMENT BASE 15 . . . 0						SEGMENT LIMIT 15 . . . 0						0
BASE 31 . . . 24	G	D	0	AVL	LIMIT 19 . . . 16	P	DPL	S	TYPE	A	BASE 23 . . . 16	+4

BASE Base Address of the segment
LIMIT The length of the segment
P Present Bit 1 = Present 0 = Not Present
DPL Descriptor Privilege Level 0–3
S Segment Descriptor 0 = System Descriptor 1 = Code or Data Segment Descriptor
TYPE Type of Segment
A Accessed Bit
G Granularity Bit 1 = Segment length is page granular 0 = Segment length is byte granular
D Default Operation Size (recognized in code segment descriptors only) 1 = 32-bit segment 0 = 16-bit segment
0 Bit must be zero (0) for compatibility with future processors
AVL Available field for user or OS

NOTE:
In a maximum-size segment (ie. a segment with G = 1 and segment limit 19...0 = FFFFFH), the lowest 12 bits of the segment base should be zero (ie. segment base 11...000 = 000H).

Figure 4-5. Segment Descriptors

32-bit), and the type of segment. All of the attribute information about a segment is contained in 12 bits in the segment descriptor. Figure 4-5 shows the general format of a descriptor. All segments on the Intel386 DX have three attribute fields in common: the **P** bit, the **DPL** bit, and the **S** bit. The Present **P** bit is 1 if the segment is loaded in physical memory, if P=0 then any attempt to access this segment causes a not present exception (exception 11). The Descriptor Privilege Level **DPL** is a two-bit field which specifies the protection level 0–3 associated with a segment.

The Intel386 DX has two main categories of segments system segments and non-system segments (for code and data). The segment **S** bit in the segment descriptor determines if a given segment is a system segment or a code or data segment. If the S bit is 1 then the segment is either a code or data segment, if it is 0 then the segment is a system segment.

4.3.4.2 Intel386™ DX CODE, DATA DESCRIPTORS (S=1)

Figure 4-6 shows the general format of a code and data descriptor and Table 4-1 illustrates how the bits in the Access Rights Byte are interpreted.

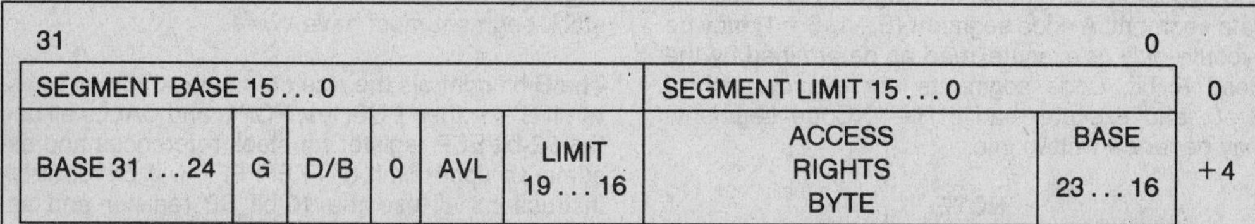

D/B 1=Default Instructions Attributes are 32-Bits
0=Default Instruction Attributes are 16-Bits
AVL Available field for user or OS
G Granularity Bit 1=Segment length is page granular
0=Segment length is byte granular
0 Bit must be zero (0) for compatibility with future processors

NOTE:
In a maximum-size segment (ie. a segment with G=1 and segment limit 19...0=FFFFFH), the lowest 12 bits of the segment base should be zero (ie. segment base 11...000=000H).

Figure 4-6. Segment Descriptors

Table 4-1. Access Rights Byte Definition for Code and Data Descriptions

	Bit Position	Name	Function		
	7	Present (P)	P = 1	Segment is mapped into physical memory.	
			P = 0	No mapping to physical memory exits, base and limit are not used.	
	6–5	Descriptor Privilege Level (DPL)		Segment privilege attribute used in privilege tests.	
	4	Segment Descriptor (S)	S = 1	Code or Data (includes stacks) segment descriptor	
			S = 0	System Segment Descriptor or Gate Descriptor	
Type Field Definition	3	Executable (E)	E = 0	Descriptor type is data segment:	If Data Segment (S = 1, E = 0)
	2	Expansion Direction (ED)	ED 0	Expand up segment, offsets must be ≤ limit.	
			ED = 1	Expand down segment, offsets must be > limit.	
	1	Writeable (W)	W = 0	Data segment may not be written into.	
			W = 1	Data segment may be written into.	
	3	Executable (E)	E = 1	Descriptor type is code segment:	If Code Segment (S = 1, E = 1)
	2	Conforming (C)	C = 1	Code segment may only be executed when CPL ≥ DPL and CPL remains unchanged.	
	1	Readable (R)	R = 0	Code segment may not be read.	
			R = 1	Code segment may be read.	
	0	Accessed (A)	A = 0	Segment has not been accessed.	
			A = 1	Segment selector has been loaded into segment register or used by selector test instructions.	

Code and data segments have several descriptor fields in common. The accessed **A** bit is set whenever the processor accesses a descriptor. The **A** bit is used by operating systems to keep usage statistics on a given segment. The **G** bit, or granularity bit, specifies if a segment length is byte-granular or page-granular. Intel386 DX segments can be one megabyte long with byte granularity (G=0) or four gigabytes with page granularity (G=1), (i.e., 2^{20} pages each page is 4K bytes in length). The granularity is totally unrelated to paging. An Intel386 DX system can consist of segments with byte granularity, and page granularity, whether or not paging is enabled.

The executable **E** bit tells if a segment is a code or data segment. A code segment (E=1, S=1) may be execute-only or execute/read as determined by the Read **R** bit. Code segments are execute only if R=0, and execute/read if R=1. Code segments may never be written into.

NOTE:
Code segments may be modified via aliases. Aliases are writeable data segments which occupy the same range of linear address space as the code segment.

The **D** bit indicates the default length for operands and effective addresses. If D=1 then 32-bit operands and 32-bit addressing modes are assumed. If D=0 then 16-bit operands and 16-bit addressing modes are assumed. Therefore all existing 80286 code segments will execute on the Intel386 DX assuming the D bit is set 0.

Another attribute of code segments is determined by the conforming **C** bit. Conforming segments, C=1, can be executed and shared by programs at different privilege levels. (See section 4.4 **Protection.**)

Segments identified as data segments (E=0, S=1) are used for two types of Intel386 DX segments: stack and data segments. The expansion direction **(ED)** bit specifies if a segment expands downward (stack) or upward (data). If a segment is a stack segment all offsets must be greater than the segment limit. On a data segment all offsets must be less than or equal to the limit. In other words, stack segments start at the base linear address plus the maximum segment limit and grow down to the base linear address plus the limit. On the other hand, data segments start at the base linear address and expand to the base linear address plus limit.

The write **W** bit controls the ability to write into a segment. Data segments are read-only if W=0. The stack segment must have W=1.

The **B** bit controls the size of the stack pointer register. If B=1, then PUSHes, POPs, and CALLs all use the 32-bit ESP register for stack references and assume an upper limit of FFFFFFFFH. If B=0, stack instructions all use the 16-bit SP register and assume an upper limit of FFFFH.

4.3.4.3 SYSTEM DESCRIPTOR FORMATS

System segments describe information about operating system tables, tasks, and gates. Figure 4-7 shows the general format of system segment descriptors, and the various types of system segments. Intel386 DX system descriptors contain a 32-bit base linear address and a 20-bit segment limit. 80286 system descriptors have a 24-bit base address and a 16-bit segment limit. 80286 system descriptors are identified by the upper 16 bits being all zero.

31					16						0	
SEGMENT BASE 15 . . . 0						SEGMENT LIMIT 15 . . . 0						0
BASE 31 . . . 24	G	0	0	0	LIMIT 19 . . . 16	P	DPL	0	TYPE	BASE 23 . . . 16		+4

Type	Defines	Type	Defines
0	Invalid	8	Invalid
1	Available 80286 TSS	9	Available Intel386™ DX TSS
2	LDT	A	Undefined (Intel Reserved)
3	Busy 80286 TSS	B	Busy Intel386™ DX TSS
4	80286 Call Gate	C	Intel386™ DX Call Gate
5	Task Gate (for 80286 or Intel386™ DX Task)	D	Undefined (Intel Reserved)
6	80286 Interrupt Gate	E	Intel386™ DX Interrupt Gate
7	80286 Trap Gate	F	Intel386™ DX Trap Gate

NOTE:
In a maximum-size segment (ie. a segment with G=1 and segment limit 19...0=FFFFFH), the lowest 12 bits of the segment base should be zero (ie. segment base 11...000=000H).

Figure 4-7. System Segments Descriptors

4.3.4.4 LDT DESCRIPTORS (S=0, TYPE=2)

LDT descriptors (S=0 TYPE=2) contain information about Local Descriptor Tables. LDTs contain a table of segment descriptors, unique to a particular task. Since the instruction to load the LDTR is only available at privilege level 0, the DPL field is ignored. LDT descriptors are only allowed in the Global Descriptor Table (GDT).

4.3.4.5 TSS DESCRIPTORS (S=0, TYPE=1, 3, 9, B)

A Task State Segment (TSS) descriptor contains information about the location, size, and privilege level of a Task State Segment (TSS). A TSS in turn is a special fixed format segment which contains all the state information for a task and a linkage field to permit nesting tasks. The TYPE field is used to indicate whether the task is currently BUSY (i.e. on a chain of active tasks) or the TSS is available. The TYPE field also indicates if the segment contains a 80286 or an Intel386 DX TSS. The Task Register (TR) contains the selector which points to the current Task State Segment.

4.3.4.6 GATE DESCRIPTORS (S=0, TYPE=4–7, C, F)

Gates are used to control access to entry points within the target code segment. The various types of gate descriptors are **call** gates, **task** gates, **interrupt** gates, and **trap** gates. Gates provide a level of indirection between the source and destination of the control transfer. This indirection allows the processor to automatically perform protection checks. It also allows system designers to control entry points to the operating system. Call gates are used to change privilege levels (see section 4.4 **Protection**), task gates are used to perform a task switch, and interrupt and trap gates are used to specify interrupt service routines.

Figure 4-8 shows the format of the four types of gate descriptors. Call gates are primarily used to transfer program control to a more privileged level. The call gate descriptor consists of three fields: the access byte, a long pointer (selector and offset) which points to the start of a routine and a word count which specifies how many parameters are to be copied from the caller's stack to the stack of the called routine. The word count field is only used by call gates when there is a change in the privilege level, other types of gates ignore the word count field.

Interrupt and trap gates use the destination selector and destination offset fields of the gate descriptor as a pointer to the start of the interrupt or trap handler routines. The difference between interrupt gates and trap gates is that the interrupt gate disables interrupts (resets the IF bit) while the trap gate does not.

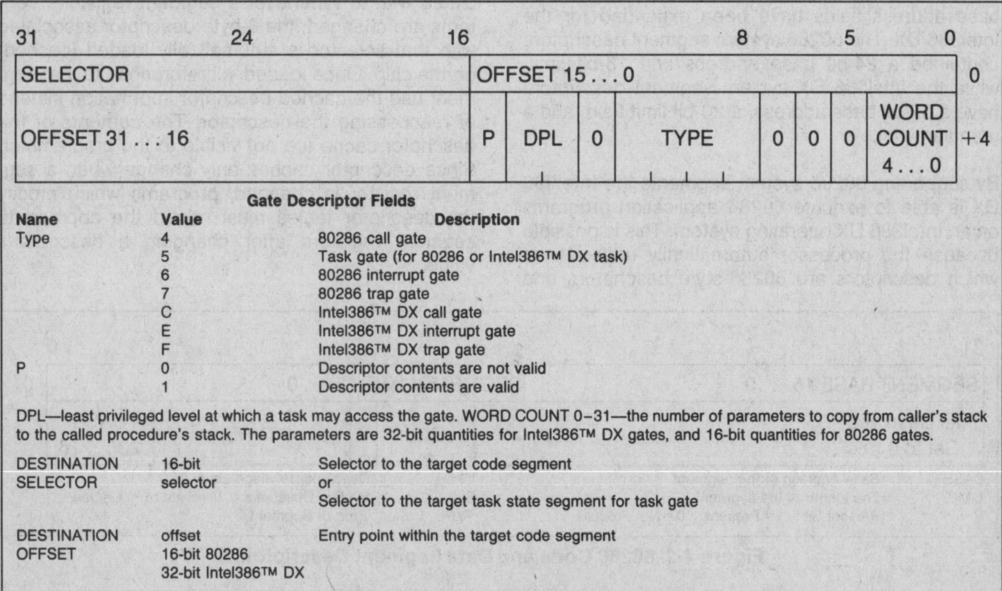

Gate Descriptor Fields

Name	Value	Description
Type	4	80286 call gate
	5	Task gate (for 80286 or Intel386™ DX task)
	6	80286 interrupt gate
	7	80286 trap gate
	C	Intel386™ DX call gate
	E	Intel386™ DX interrupt gate
	F	Intel386™ DX trap gate
P	0	Descriptor contents are not valid
	1	Descriptor contents are valid

DPL—least privileged level at which a task may access the gate. WORD COUNT 0–31—the number of parameters to copy from caller's stack to the called procedure's stack. The parameters are 32-bit quantities for Intel386™ DX gates, and 16-bit quantities for 80286 gates.

DESTINATION SELECTOR	16-bit selector	Selector to the target code segment or Selector to the target task state segment for task gate
DESTINATION OFFSET	offset 16-bit 80286 32-bit Intel386™ DX	Entry point within the target code segment

Figure 4-8. Gate Descriptor Formats

Task gates are used to switch tasks. Task gates may only refer to a task state segment (see section 4.4.6 **Task Switching**) therefore only the destination selector portion of a task gate descriptor is used, and the destination offset is ignored.

Exception 13 is generated when a destination selector does not refer to a correct descriptor type, i.e., a code segment for an interrupt, trap or call gate, a TSS for a task gate.

The access byte format is the same for all gate descriptors. P=1 indicates that the gate contents are valid. P=0 indicates the contents are not valid and causes exception 11 if referenced. DPL is the descriptor privilege level and specifies when this descriptor may be used by a task (see section 4.4 **Protection**). The S field, bit 4 of the access rights byte, must be 0 to indicate a system control descriptor. The type field specifies the descriptor type as indicated in Figure 4-8.

4.3.4.7 DIFFERENCES BETWEEN Intel386™ DX AND 80286 DESCRIPTORS

In order to provide operating system compatibility between the 80286 and Intel386 DX, the Intel386 DX supports all of the 80286 segment descriptors. Figure 4-9 shows the general format of an 80286 system segment descriptor. The only differences between 80286 and Intel386 DX descriptor formats are that the values of the type fields, and the limit and base address fields have been expanded for the Intel386 DX. The 80286 system segment descriptors contained a 24-bit base address and 16-bit limit, while the Intel386 DX system segment descriptors have a 32-bit base address, a 20-bit limit field, and a granularity bit.

By supporting 80286 system segments the Intel386 DX is able to execute 80286 application programs on an Intel386 DX operating system. This is possible because the processor automatically understands which descriptors are 80286-style descriptors and which descriptors are Intel386 DX-style descriptors. In particular, if the upper word of a descriptor is zero, then that descriptor is a 80286-style descriptor.

The only other differences between 80286-style descriptors and Intel386 DX descriptors is the interpretation of the word count field of call gates and the B bit. The word count field specifies the number of 16-bit quantities to copy for 80286 call gates and 32-bit quantities for Intel386 DX call gates. The B bit controls the size of PUSHes when using a call gate; if B=0 PUSHes are 16 bits, if B=1 PUSHes are 32 bits.

4.3.4.8 SELECTOR FIELDS

A selector in Protected Mode has three fields: Local or Global Descriptor Table Indicator (TI), Descriptor Entry Index (Index), and Requestor (the selector's) Privilege Level (RPL) as shown in Figure 4-10. The TI bits select one of two memory-based tables of descriptors (the Global Descriptor Table or the Local Descriptor Table). The Index selects one of 8K descriptors in the appropriate descriptor table. The RPL bits allow high speed testing of the selector's privilege attributes.

4.3.4.9 SEGMENT DESCRIPTOR CACHE

In addition to the selector value, every segment register has a segment descriptor cache register associated with it. Whenever a segment register's contents are changed, the 8-byte descriptor associated with that selector is automatically loaded (cached) on the chip. Once loaded, all references to that segment use the cached descriptor information instead of reaccessing the descriptor. The contents of the descriptor cache are not visible to the programmer. Since descriptor caches only change when a segment register is changed, programs which modify the descriptor tables must reload the appropriate segment registers after changing a descriptor's value.

31					0	
SEGMENT BASE 15 . . . 0	SEGMENT LIMIT 15 . . . 0					0
Intel Reserved Set to 0	P	DPL	S	TYPE	BASE 23 . . . 16	+4

BASE	Base Address of the segment	DPL	Descriptor Privilege Level 0–3
LIMIT	The length of the segment	S	System Descriptor 0=System 1=User
P	Present Bit 1=Present 0=Not Present	TYPE	Type of Segment

Figure 4-9. 80286 Code and Data Segment Descriptors

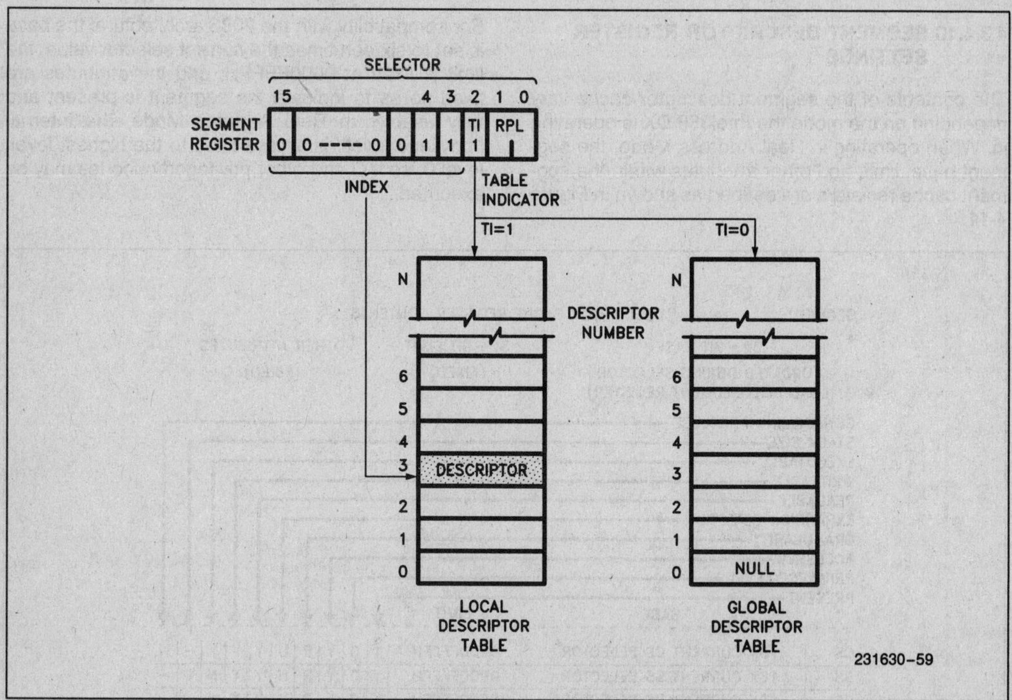

Figure 4-10. Example Descriptor Selection

4

4.3.4.10 SEGMENT DESCRIPTOR REGISTER SETTINGS

The contents of the segment descriptor cache vary depending on the mode the Intel386 DX is operating in. When operating in Real Address Mode, the segment base, limit, and other attributes within the segment cache registers are defined as shown in Figure 4-11.

For compatiblity with the 8086 architecture, the base is set to sixteen times the current selector value, the limit is fixed at 0000FFFFH, and the attributes are fixed so as to indicate the segment is present and fully usable. In Real Address Mode, the internal "privilege level" is always fixed to the highest level, level 0, so I/O and other privileged opcodes may be executed.

SEGMENT — DESCRIPTOR CACHE REGISTER CONTENTS

32-BIT BASE (UPDATED DURING SELECTOR LOAD INTO SEGMENT REGISTER) — 32-BIT LIMIT (FIXED) — OTHER ATTRIBUTES (FIXED)

SEGMENT	BASE	LIMIT	PRESENT	PRIVILEGE LEVEL	ACCESSED	GRANULARITY	EXPANSION DIRECTION	READABLE	WRITEABLE	EXECUTABLE	STACK SIZE	CONFORMING PRIVILEGE
CS	16X CURRENT CS SELECTOR*	0000FFFFH	Y	0	Y	B	U	Y	Y	Y	–	N
SS	16X CURRENT SS SELECTOR	0000FFFFH	Y	0	Y	B	U	Y	Y	N	W	–
DS	16X CURRENT DS SELECTOR	0000FFFFH	Y	0	Y	B	U	Y	Y	N	–	–
ES	16X CURRENT ES SELECTOR	0000FFFFH	Y	0	Y	B	U	Y	Y	N	–	–
FS	16X CURRENT FS SELECTOR	0000FFFFH	Y	0	Y	B	U	Y	Y	N	–	–
GS	16X CURRENT GS SELECTOR	0000FFFFH	Y	0	Y	B	U	Y	Y	N	–	–

231630-60

*Except the 32-bit CS base is initialized to FFFFF000H after reset until first intersegment control transfer (e.g. intersegment CALL, or intersegment JMP, or INT). (See Figure 4-13 Example.)

Key:
- Y = yes
- N = no
- 0 = privilege level 0
- 1 = privilege level 1
- 2 = privilege level 2
- 3 = privilege level 3
- U = expand up
- D = expand down
- B = byte granularity
- P = page granularity
- W = push/pop 16-bit words
- F = push/pop 32-bit dwords
- – = does not apply to that segment cache register

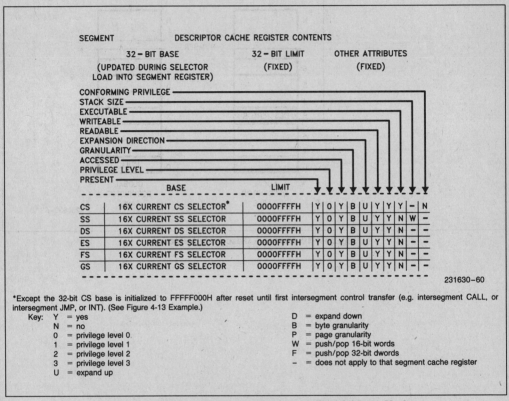

Figure 4-11. Segment Descriptor Caches for Real Address Mode (Segment Limit and Attributes are Fixed)

When operating in Protected Mode, the segment base, limit, and other attributes within the segment cache registers are defined as shown in Figure 4-12. In Protected Mode, each of these fields are defined according to the contents of the segment descriptor indexed by the selector value loaded into the segment register.

SEGMENT — DESCRIPTOR CACHE REGISTER CONTENTS

32-BIT BASE (UPDATED DURING SELECTOR LOAD INTO SEGMENT REGISTER) | 32-BIT LIMIT (UPDATED DURING SELECTOR LOAD INTO SEGMENT REGISTER) | OTHER ATTRIBUTES (UPDATED DURING SELECTOR LOAD INTO SEGMENT REGISTER)

SEGMENT	BASE	LIMIT	PRESENT	PRIVILEGE LEVEL	ACCESSED	GRANULARITY	EXPANSION DIRECTION	READABLE	WRITEABLE	EXECUTABLE	STACK SIZE	CONFORMING PRIVILEGE
CS	BASE PER SEG DESCR	LIMIT PER SEG DESCR	p	d	d	d	d	d	N	Y	–	d
SS	BASE PER SEG DESCR	LIMIT PER SEG DESCR	p	d	d	d	d	r	w	N	d	–
DS	BASE PER SEG DESCR	LIMIT PER SEG DESCR	p	d	d	d	d	d	d	N	–	–
ES	BASE PER SEG DESCR	LIMIT PER SEG DESCR	p	d	d	d	d	d	d	N	–	–
FS	BASE PER SEG DESCR	LIMIT PER SEG DESCR	p	d	d	d	d	d	d	N	–	–
GS	BASE PER SEG DESCR	LIMIT PER SEG DESCR	p	d	d	d	d	d	d	N	–	–

231630-61

Key:
- Y = fixed yes
- N = fixed no
- d = per segment descriptor
- p = per segment descriptor; descriptor must indicate "present" to avoid exception 11 (exception 12 in case of SS)
- r = per segment descriptor, but descriptor must indicate "readable" to avoid exception 13 (special case for SS)
- w = per segment descriptor, but descriptor must indicate "writable" to avoid exception 13 (special case for SS)
- – = does not apply to that segment cache register

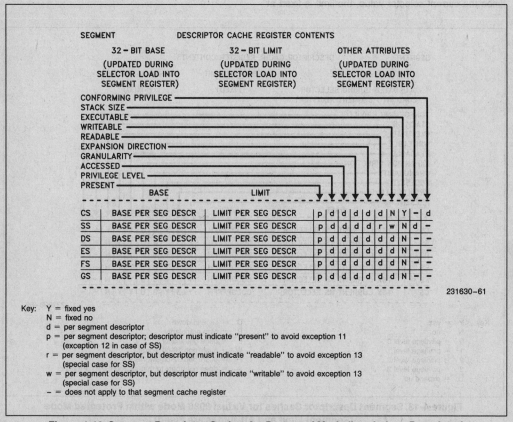

Figure 4-12. Segment Descriptor Caches for Protected Mode (Loaded per Descriptor)

When operating in a Virtual 8086 Mode within the Protected Mode, the segment base, limit, and other attributes within the segment cache registers are defined as shown in Figure 4-13. For compatibility with the 8086 architecture, the base is set to sixteen times the current selector value, the limit is fixed at 0000FFFFH, and the attributes are fixed so as to indicate the segment is present and fully usable. The virtual program executes at lowest privilege level, level 3, to allow trapping of all IOPL-sensitive instructions and level-0-only instructions.

SEGMENT — DESCRIPTOR CACHE REGISTER CONTENTS

32-BIT BASE (UPDATED DURING SELECTOR LOAD INTO SEGMENT REGISTER) — 32-BIT LIMIT (FIXED) — OTHER ATTRIBUTES (FIXED)

SEGMENT	BASE	LIMIT	PRESENT	PRIVILEGE LEVEL	ACCESSED	GRANULARITY	EXPANSION DIRECTION	READABLE	WRITEABLE	EXECUTABLE	STACK SIZE	CONFORMING PRIVILEGE
CS	16X CURRENT CS SELECTOR	0000FFFFH	Y	3	Y	B	U	Y	Y	Y	–	N
SS	16X CURRENT SS SELECTOR	0000FFFFH	Y	3	Y	B	U	Y	Y	N	W	–
DS	16X CURRENT DS SELECTOR	0000FFFFH	Y	3	Y	B	U	Y	Y	N	–	–
ES	16X CURRENT ES SELECTOR	0000FFFFH	Y	3	Y	B	U	Y	Y	N	–	–
FS	16X CURRENT FS SELECTOR	0000FFFFH	Y	3	Y	B	U	Y	Y	N	–	–
GS	16X CURRENT GS SELECTOR	0000FFFFH	Y	3	Y	B	U	Y	Y	N	–	–

231630-62

Key:
- Y = yes
- N = no
- 0 = privilege level 0
- 1 = privilege level 1
- 2 = privilege level 2
- 3 = privilege level 3
- U = expand up
- D = expand down
- B = byte granularity
- P = page granularity
- W = push/pop 16-bit words
- F = push/pop 32-bit dwords
- – = does not apply to that segment cache register

Figure 4-13. Segment Descriptor Caches for Virtual 8086 Mode within Protected Mode (Segment Limit and Attributes are Fixed)

4.4 PROTECTION

4.4.1 Protection Concepts

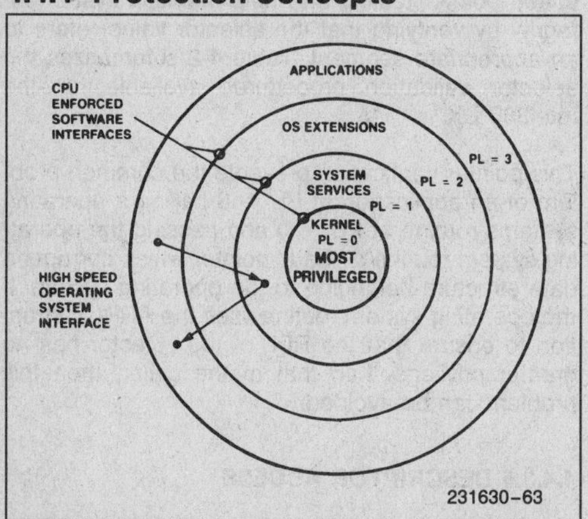

Figure 4-14. Four-Level Hierachical Protection

The Intel386 DX has four levels of protection which are optimized to support the needs of a multi-tasking operating system to isolate and protect user programs from each other and the operating system. The privilege levels control the use of privileged instructions, I/O instructions, and access to segments and segment descriptors. Unlike traditional microprocessor-based systems where this protection is achieved only through the use of complex external hardware and software the Intel386 DX provides the protection as part of its integrated Memory Management Unit. The Intel386 DX offers an additional type of protection on a page basis, when paging is enabled (See section 4.5.3 **Page Level Protection**).

The four-level hierarchical privilege system is illustrated in Figure 4-14. It is an extension of the user/supervisor privilege mode commonly used by minicomputers and, in fact, the user/supervisor mode is fully supported by the Intel386 DX paging mechanism. The privilege levels (PL) are numbered 0 through 3. Level 0 is the most privileged or trusted level.

4.4.2 Rules of Privilege

The Intel386 DX controls access to both data and procedures between levels of a task, according to the following rules.

- Data stored in a segment with privilege level **p** can be accessed only by code executing at a privilege level at least as privileged as **p**.
- A code segment/procedure with privilege level **p** can only be called by a task executing at the same or a lesser privilege level than **p**.

4.4.3 Privilege Levels

4.4.3.1 TASK PRIVILEGE

At any point in time, a task on the Intel386 DX always executes at one of the four privilege levels. The Current Privilege Level (CPL) specifies the task's privilege level. A task's CPL may only be changed by control transfers through gate descriptors to a code segment with a different privilege level. (See section 4.4.4 **Privilege Level Transfers**) Thus, an application program running at PL = 3 may call an operating system routine at PL = 1 (via a gate) which would cause the task's CPL to be set to 1 until the operating system routine was finished.

4.4.3.2 SELECTOR PRIVILEGE (RPL)

The privilege level of a selector is specified by the RPL field. The RPL is the two least significant bits of the selector. The selector's RPL is only used to establish a less trusted privilege level than the current privilege level for the use of a segment. This level is called the task's effective privilege level (EPL). The EPL is defined as being the least privileged (i.e. numerically larger) level of a task's CPL and a selector's RPL. Thus, if selector's RPL = 0 then the CPL always specifies the privilege level for making an access using the selector. On the other hand if RPL = 3 then a selector can only access segments at level 3 regardless of the task's CPL. The RPL is most commonly used to verify that pointers passed to an operating system procedure do not access data that is of higher privilege than the procedure that originated the pointer. Since the originator of a selector can specify any RPL value, the Adjust RPL (ARPL) instruction is provided to force the RPL bits to the originator's CPL.

4.4.3.3 I/O PRIVILEGE AND I/O PERMISSION BITMAP

The I/O privilege level (IOPL, a 2-bit field in the EFLAG register) defines the least privileged level at which I/O instructions can be unconditionally performed. I/O instructions can be unconditionally performed when CPL ≤ IOPL. (The I/O instructions are IN, OUT, INS, OUTS, REP INS, and REP OUTS.) When CPL > IOPL, and the current task is associated with a 286 TSS, attempted I/O instructions cause an exception 13 fault. When CPL > IOPL, and the current task is associated with an Intel386 DX TSS, the I/O Permission Bitmap (part of an Intel386 DX TSS) is consulted on whether I/O to the port is allowed, or an exception 13 fault is to be generated

4

instead. For diagrams of the I/O Permission Bitmap, refer to Figures 4-15a and 4-15b. For further information on how the I/O Permission Bitmap is used in Protected Mode or in Virtual 8086 Mode, refer to section 4.6.4 Protection and I/O Permission Bitmap.

The I/O privilege level (IOPL) also affects whether several other instructions can be executed or cause an exception 13 fault instead. These instructions are called "IOPL-sensitive" instructions and they are CLI and STI. (Note that the LOCK prefix is *not* IOPL-sensitive on the Intel386 DX.)

The IOPL also affects whether the IF (interrupts enable flag) bit can be changed by loading a value into the EFLAGS register. When CPL ≤ IOPL, then the IF bit can be changed by loading a new value into the EFLAGS register. When CPL > IOPL, the IF bit cannot be changed by a new value POP'ed into (or otherwise loaded into) the EFLAGS register; the IF bit merely remains unchanged and no exception is generated.

Table 4-2. Pointer Test Instructions

Instruction	Operands	Function
ARPL	Selector, Register	Adjust Requested Privilege Level: adjusts the RPL of the selector to the numeric maximum of current selector RPL value and the RPL value in the register. Set zero flag if selector RPL was changed.
VERR	Selector	VERify for Read: sets the zero flag if the segment referred to by the selector can be read.
VERW	Selector	VERify for Write: sets the zero flag if the segment referred to by the selector can be written.
LSL	Register, Selector	Load Segment Limit: reads the segment limit into the register if privilege rules and descriptor type allow. Set zero flag if successful.
LAR	Register, Selector	Load Access Rights: reads the descriptor access rights byte into the register if privilege rules allow. Set zero flag if successful.

4.4.3.4 PRIVILEGE VALIDATION

The Intel386 DX provides several instructions to speed pointer testing and help maintain system integrity by verifying that the selector value refers to an appropriate segment. Table 4-2 summarizes the selector validation procedures available for the Intel386 DX.

This pointer verification prevents the common problem of an application at PL = 3 calling a operating systems routine at PL = 0 and passing the operating system routine a "bad" pointer which corrupts a data structure belonging to the operating system. If the operating system routine uses the ARPL instruction to ensure that the RPL of the selector has no greater privilege than that of the caller, then this problem can be avoided.

4.4.3.5 DESCRIPTOR ACCESS

There are basically two types of segment accesses: those involving code segments such as control transfers, and those involving data accesses. Determining the ability of a task to access a segment involves the type of segment to be accessed, the instruction used, the type of descriptor used and CPL, RPL, and DPL as described above.

Any time an instruction loads data segment registers (DS, ES, FS, GS) the Intel386 DX makes protection validation checks. Selectors loaded in the DS, ES, FS, GS registers must refer only to data segments or readable code segments. The data access rules are specified in section 4.2.2 **Rules of Privilege**. The only exception to those rules is readable conforming code segments which can be accessed at any privilege level.

Finally the privilege validation checks are performed. The CPL is compared to the EPL and if the EPL is more privileged than the CPL an exception 13 (general protection fault) is generated.

The rules regarding the stack segment are slightly different than those involving data segments. Instructions that load selectors into SS must refer to data segment descriptors for writeable data segments. The DPL and RPL must equal the CPL. All other descriptor types or a privilege level violation will cause exception 13. A stack not present fault causes exception 12. Note that an exception 11 is used for a not-present code or data segment.

4.4.4 Privilege Level Transfers

Inter-segment control transfers occur when a selector is loaded in the CS register. For a typical system most of these transfers are simply the result of a call

Table 4-3. Descriptor Types Used for Control Transfer

Control Transfer Types	Operation Types	Descriptor Referenced	Descriptor Table
Intersegment within the same privilege level	JMP, CALL, RET, IRET*	Code Segment	GDT/LDT
Intersegment to the same or higher privilege level Interrupt within task may change CPL	CALL	Call Gate	GDT/LDT
	Interrupt Instruction, Exception, External Interrupt	Trap or Interrupt Gate	IDT
Intersegment to a lower privilege level (changes task CPL)	RET, IRET*	Code Segment	GDT/LDT
	CALL, JMP	Task State Segment	GDT
Task Switch	CALL, JMP	Task Gate	GDT/LDT
	IRET** Interrupt Instruction, Exception, External Interrupt	Task Gate	IDT

*NT (Nested Task bit of flag register) = 0
**NT (Nested Task bit of flag register) = 1

or a jump to another routine. There are five types of control transfers which are summarized in Table 4-3. Many of these transfers result in a privilege level transfer. Changing privilege levels is done only via control transfers, by using gates, task switches, and interrupt or trap gates.

Control transfers can only occur if the operation which loaded the selector references the correct descriptor type. Any violation of these descriptor usage rules will cause an exception 13 (e.g. JMP through a call gate, or IRET from a normal subroutine call).

In order to provide further system security, all control transfers are also subject to the privilege rules.

The privilege rules require that:

— Privilege level transitions can only occur via gates.

— JMPs can be made to a non-conforming code segment with the same privilege or to a conforming code segment with greater or equal privilege.

— CALLs can be made to a non-conforming code segment with the same privilege or via a gate to a more privileged level.

— Interrupts handled within the task obey the same privilege rules as CALLs.

— Conforming Code segments are accessible by privilege levels which are the same or less privileged than the conforming-code segment's DPL.

— Both the requested privilege level (RPL) in the selector pointing to the gate and the task's CPL must be of equal or greater privilege than the gate's DPL.

— The code segment selected in the gate must be the same or more privileged than the task's CPL.

— Return instructions that do not switch tasks can only return control to a code segment with same or less privilege.

— Task switches can be performed by a CALL, JMP, or INT which references either a task gate or task state segment who's DPL is less privileged or the same privilege as the old task's CPL.

Any control transfer that changes CPL within a task causes a change of stacks as a result of the privilege level change. The initial values of SS:ESP for privilege levels 0, 1, and 2 are retained in the task state segment (see section 4.4.6 **Task Switching**). During a JMP or CALL control transfer, the new stack pointer is loaded into the SS and ESP registers and the previous stack pointer is pushed onto the new stack.

When RETurning to the original privilege level, use of the lower-privileged stack is restored as part of the RET or IRET instruction operation. For subroutine calls that pass parameters on the stack and cross privilege levels, a fixed number of words (as specified in the gate's word count field) are copied from the previous stack to the current stack. The inter-segment RET instruction with a stack adjustment value will correctly restore the previous stack pointer upon return.

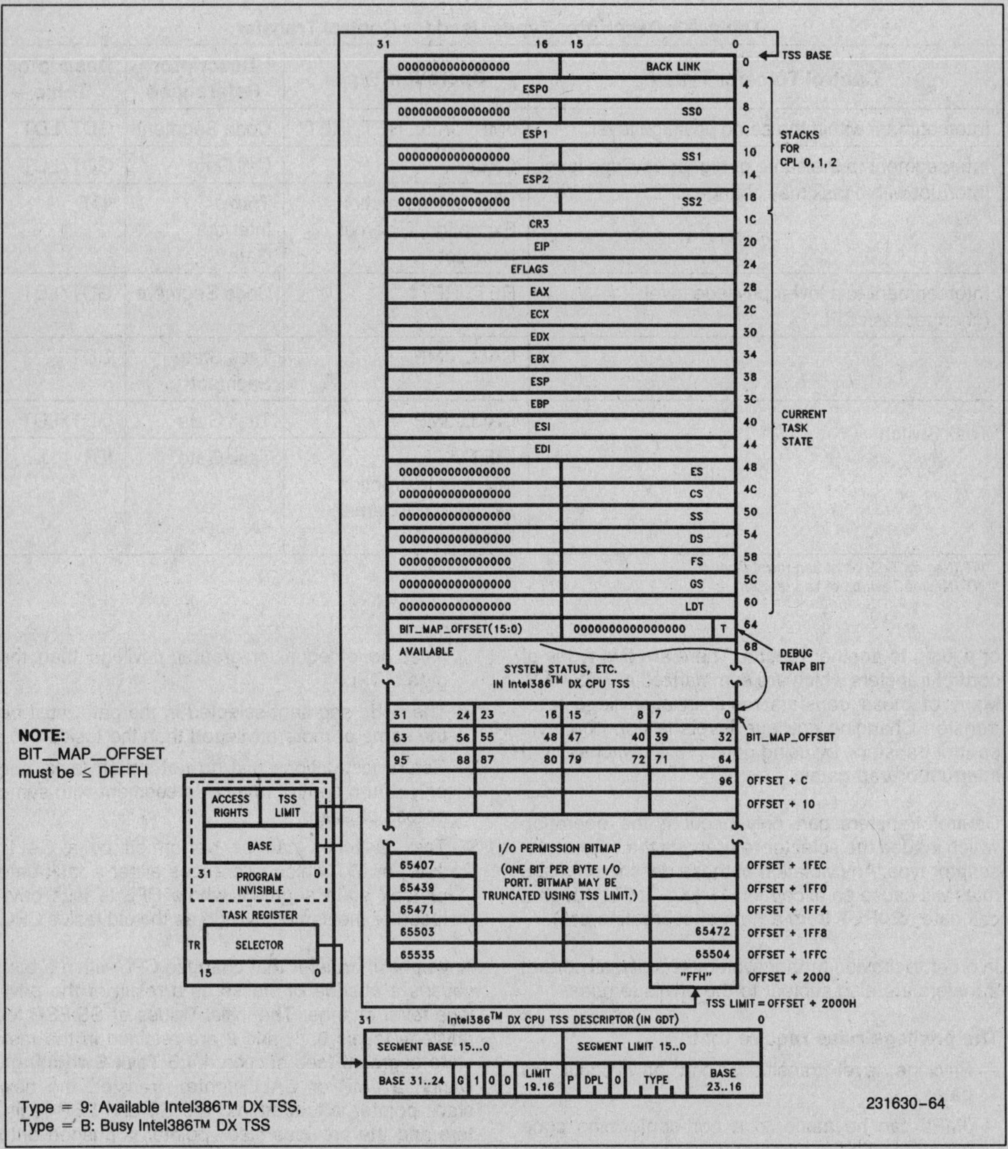

31 ... 16	15 ... 0	Offset	
0000000000000000	BACK LINK	0	← TSS BASE
ESP0		4	STACKS FOR CPL 0, 1, 2
0000000000000000	SS0	8	
ESP1		C	
0000000000000000	SS1	10	
ESP2		14	
0000000000000000	SS2	18	
CR3		1C	CURRENT TASK STATE
EIP		20	
EFLAGS		24	
EAX		28	
ECX		2C	
EDX		30	
EBX		34	
ESP		38	
EBP		3C	
ESI		40	
EDI		44	
0000000000000000	ES	48	
0000000000000000	CS	4C	
0000000000000000	SS	50	
0000000000000000	DS	54	
0000000000000000	FS	58	
0000000000000000	GS	5C	
0000000000000000	LDT	60	
BIT_MAP_OFFSET(15:0)	0000000000000000 T	64	DEBUG TRAP BIT
AVAILABLE		68	

SYSTEM STATUS, ETC. IN Intel386™ DX CPU TSS

31 ... 24	23 ... 16	15 ... 8	7 ... 0	
31 24	23 16	15 8	7 0	BIT_MAP_OFFSET
63 56	55 48	47 40	39 32	
95 88	87 80	79 72	71 64	
			96	OFFSET + C
				OFFSET + 10

I/O PERMISSION BITMAP

(ONE BIT PER BYTE I/O PORT. BITMAP MAY BE TRUNCATED USING TSS LIMIT.)

65407				OFFSET + 1FEC
65439				OFFSET + 1FF0
65471				OFFSET + 1FF4
65503			65472	OFFSET + 1FF8
65535			65504	OFFSET + 1FFC
			"FFH"	OFFSET + 2000

TSS LIMIT = OFFSET + 2000H

NOTE:
BIT_MAP_OFFSET must be ≤ DFFFH

TASK REGISTER: ACCESS RIGHTS, TSS LIMIT, BASE (31 ... 0) — PROGRAM INVISIBLE; TR SELECTOR (15 ... 0)

Intel386™ DX CPU TSS DESCRIPTOR (IN GDT)

31											0
SEGMENT BASE 15...0						SEGMENT LIMIT 15..0					
BASE 31..24	G	1	0	0	LIMIT 19..16	P	DPL	0	TYPE	BASE 23..16	

Type = 9: Available Intel386™ DX TSS,
Type = B: Busy Intel386™ DX TSS

231630-64

Figure 4-15a. Intel386™ DX TSS and TSS Registers

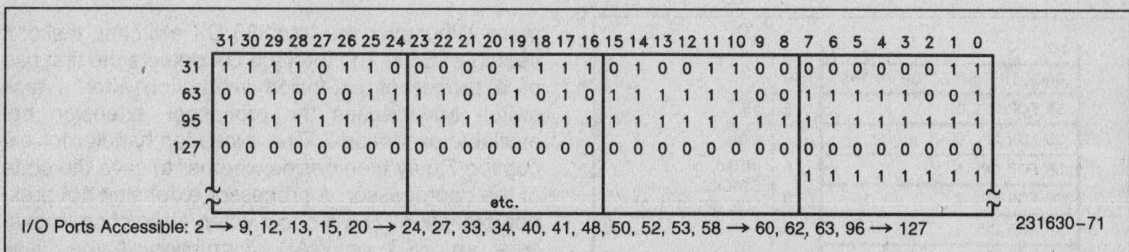

Figure 4-15b. Sample I/O Permission Bit Map

4.4.5 Call Gates

Gates provide protected, indirect CALLs. One of the major uses of gates is to provide a secure method of privilege transfers within a task. Since the operating system defines all of the gates in a system, it can ensure that all gates only allow entry into a few trusted procedures (such as those which allocate memory, or perform I/O).

Gate descriptors follow the data access rules of privilege; that is, gates can be accessed by a task if the EPL, is equal to or more privileged than the gate descriptor's DPL. Gates follow the control transfer rules of privilege and therefore may only transfer control to a more privileged level.

Call Gates are accessed via a CALL instruction and are syntactically identical to calling a normal subroutine. When an inter-level Intel386 DX call gate is activated, the following actions occur.

1. Load CS:EIP from gate check for validity
2. SS is pushed zero-extended to 32 bits
3. ESP is pushed
4. Copy Word Count 32-bit parameters from the old stack to the new stack
5. Push Return address on stack

The procedure is identical for 80286 Call gates, except that 16-bit parameters are copied and 16-bit registers are pushed.

Interrupt Gates and Trap gates work in a similar fashion as the call gates, except there is no copying of parameters. The only difference between Trap and Interrupt gates is that control transfers through an Interrupt gate disable further interrupts (i.e. the IF bit is set to 0), and Trap gates leave the interrupt status unchanged.

4.4.6 Task Switching

A very important attribute of any multi-tasking/multi-user operating systems is its ability to rapidly switch between tasks or processes. The Intel386 DX directly supports this operation by providing a task switch instruction in hardware. The Intel386 DX task switch operation saves the entire state of the machine (all of the registers, address space, and a link to the previous task), loads a new execution state, performs protection checks, and commences execution in the new task, in about 17 microseconds. Like transfer of control via gates, the task switch operation is invoked by executing an inter-segment JMP or CALL instruction which refers to a Task State Segment (TSS), or a task gate descriptor in the GDT or LDT. An INT n instruction, exception, trap, or external interrupt may also invoke the task switch operation if there is a task gate descriptor in the associated IDT descriptor slot.

The TSS descriptor points to a segment (see Figure 4-15) containing the entire Intel386 DX execution state while a task gate descriptor contains a TSS selector. The Intel386 DX supports both 80286 and Intel386 DX style TSSs. Figure 4-16 shows a 80286 TSS. The limit of an Intel386 DX TSS must be greater than 0064H (002BH for a 80286 TSS), and can be as large as 4 Gigabytes. In the additional TSS space, the operating system is free to store additional information such as the reason the task is inactive, time the task has spent running, and open files belong to the task.

Each task must have a TSS associated with it. The current TSS is identified by a special register in the Intel386 DX called the Task State Segment Register (TR). This register contains a selector referring to the task state segment descriptor that defines the current TSS. A hidden base and limit register associated with TR are loaded whenever TR is loaded with a new selector. Returning from a task is accomplished by the IRET instruction. When IRET is executed, control is returned to the task which was interrupted. The current executing task's state is saved in the TSS and the old task state is restored from its TSS.

Several bits in the flag register and machine status word (CR0) give information about the state of a task which are useful to the operating system. The Nested Task (NT) (bit 14 in EFLAGS) controls the function of the IRET instruction. If NT = 0, the IRET instruction performs the regular return; when NT = 1, IRET performs a task switch operation back to the previous task. The NT bit is set or reset in the following fashion:

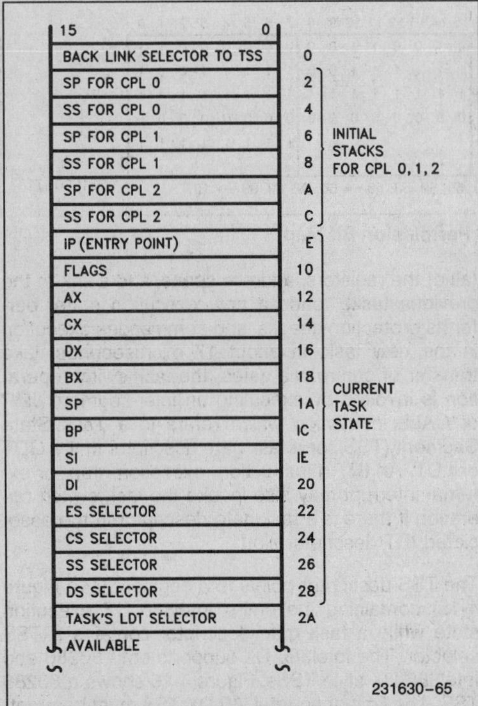

Figure 4-16. 80286 TSS

When a CALL or INT instruction initiates a task switch, the new TSS will be marked busy and the back link field of the new TSS set to the old TSS selector. The NT bit of the new task is set by CALL or INT initiated task switches. An interrupt that does not cause a task switch will clear NT. (The NT bit will be restored after execution of the interrupt handler) NT may also be set or cleared by POPF or IRET instructions.

The Intel386 DX task state segment is marked busy by changing the descriptor type field from TYPE 9H to TYPE BH. An 80286 TSS is marked busy by changing the descriptor type field from TYPE 1 to TYPE 3. Use of a selector that references a busy task state segment causes an exception 13.

The Virtual Mode (VM) bit 17 is used to indicate if a task, is a virtual 8086 task. If VM = 1, then the tasks will use the Real Mode addressing mechanism. The virtual 8086 environment is only entered and exited via a task switch (see section 4.6 **Virtual Mode**).

The coprocessor's state is not automatically saved when a task switch occurs, because the incoming task may not use the coprocessor. The Task Switched (TS) Bit (bit 3 in the CR0) helps deal with the coprocessor's state in a multi-tasking environment. Whenever the Intel386 DX switches tasks, it sets the TS bit. The Intel386 DX detects the first use of a processor extension instruction after a task switch and causes the processor extension not available exception 7. The exception handler for exception 7 may then decide whether to save the state of the coprocessor. A processor extension not present exception (7) will occur when attempting to execute an ESC or WAIT instruction if the Task Switched and Monitor coprocessor extension bits are both set (i.e. TS = 1 and MP = 1).

The **T** bit in the Intel386 DX TSS indicates that the processor should generate a debug exception when switching to a task. If T = 1 then upon entry to a new task a debug exception 1 will be generated.

4.4.7 Initialization and Transition to Protected Mode

Since the Intel386 DX begins executing in Real Mode immediately after RESET it is necessary to initialize the system tables and registers with the appropriate values.

The GDT and IDT registers must refer to a valid GDT and IDT. The IDT should be at least 256 bytes long, and GDT must contain descriptors for the initial code, and data segments. Figure 4-17 shows the tables and Figure 4-18 the descriptors needed for a simple Protected Mode Intel386 DX system. It has a single code and single data/stack segment each four gigabytes long and a single privilege level PL = 0.

The actual method of enabling Protected Mode is to load CR0 with the PE bit set, via the MOV CR0, R/M instruction. This puts the Intel386 DX in Protected Mode.

After enabling Protected Mode, the next instruction should execute an intersegment JMP to load the CS register and flush the instruction decode queue. The final step is to load all of the data segment registers with the initial selector values.

An alternate approach to entering Protected Mode which is especially appropriate for multi-tasking operating systems, is to use the built in task-switch to load all of the registers. In this case the GDT would contain two TSS descriptors in addition to the code and data descriptors needed for the first task. The first JMP instruction in Protected Mode would jump to the TSS causing a task switch and loading all of the registers with the values stored in the TSS. The Task State Segment Register should be initialized to point to a valid TSS descriptor since a task switch saves the state of the current task in a task state segment.

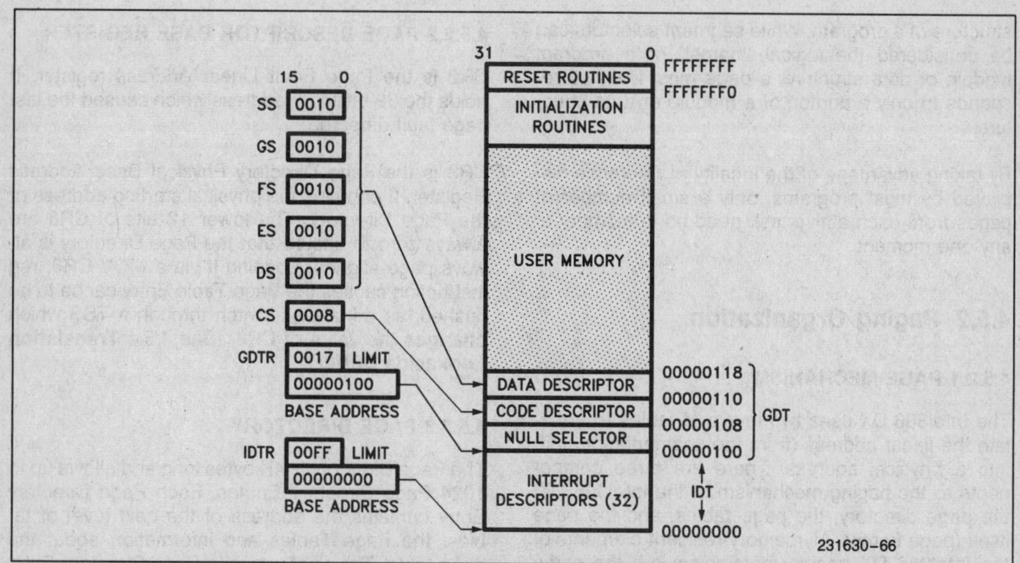

Figure 4-17. Simple Protected System

	31...24						16 / 15							8...0
DATA DESCRIPTOR	SEGMENT BASE 15...0 0118 (H)						SEGMENT LIMIT 15...0 FFFF (H)							
	BASE 31...24 00 (H)	G 1	D 1	0	0	LIMIT 19.16 F (H)	1	0	0	1	0	0	1	0	BASE 23...16 00 (H)
CODE DESCRIPTOR	SEGMENT BASE 15...0 0118 (H)						SEGMENT LIMIT 15...0 FFFF (H)							
	BASE 31...24 00 (H)	G 1	D 1	0	0	LIMIT 19.16 F (H)	1	0	0	1	1	0	1	0	BASE 23...16 00 (H)
	NULL DESCRIPTOR													
	31	24				16	15				8			0

Figure 4-18. GDT Descriptors for Simple System

4.4.8 Tools for Building Protected Systems

In order to simplify the design of a protected multi-tasking system, Intel provides a tool which allows the system designer an easy method of constructing the data structures needed for a Protected Mode Intel386 DX system. This tool is the builder BLD-386™. BLD-386 lets the operating system writer specify all of the segment descriptors discussed in the previous sections (LDTs, IDTs, GDTs, Gates, and TSSs) in a high-level language.

4.5 PAGING

4.5.1 Paging Concepts

Paging is another type of memory management useful for virtual memory multitasking operating systems. Unlike segmentation which modularizes programs and data into variable length segments, paging divides programs into multiple uniform size pages. Pages bear no direct relation to the logical

structure of a program. While segment selectors can be considered the logical "name" of a program module or data structure, a page most likely corresponds to only a portion of a module or data structure.

By taking advantage of the locality of reference displayed by most programs, only a small number of pages from each active task need be in memory at any one moment.

4.5.2 Paging Organization

4.5.2.1 PAGE MECHANISM

The Intel386 DX uses two levels of tables to translate the linear address (from the segmentation unit) into a physical address. There are three components to the paging mechanism of the Intel386 DX: the page directory, the page tables, and the page itself (page frame). All memory-resident elements of the Intel386 DX paging mechanism are the same size, namely, 4K bytes. A uniform size for all of the elements simplifies memory allocation and reallocation schemes, since there is no problem with memory fragmentation. Figure 4-19 shows how the paging mechanism works.

4.5.2.2 PAGE DESCRIPTOR BASE REGISTER

CR2 is the Page Fault Linear Address register. It holds the 32-bit linear address which caused the last page fault detected.

CR3 is the Page Directory Physical Base Address Register. It contains the physical starting address of the Page Directory. The lower 12 bits of CR3 are always zero to ensure that the Page Directory is always page aligned. Loading it via a MOV CR3, reg instruction causes the Page Table Entry cache to be flushed, as will a task switch through a TSS which **changes** the value of CR0. (See 4.5.4 **Translation Lookaside Buffer**).

4.5.2.3 PAGE DIRECTORY

The Page Directory is 4K bytes long and allows up to 1024 Page Directory Entries. Each Page Directory Entry contains the address of the next level of tables, the Page Tables and information about the page table. The contents of a Page Directory Entry are shown in Figure 4-20. The upper 10 bits of the linear address (A22–A31) are used as an index to select the correct Page Directory Entry.

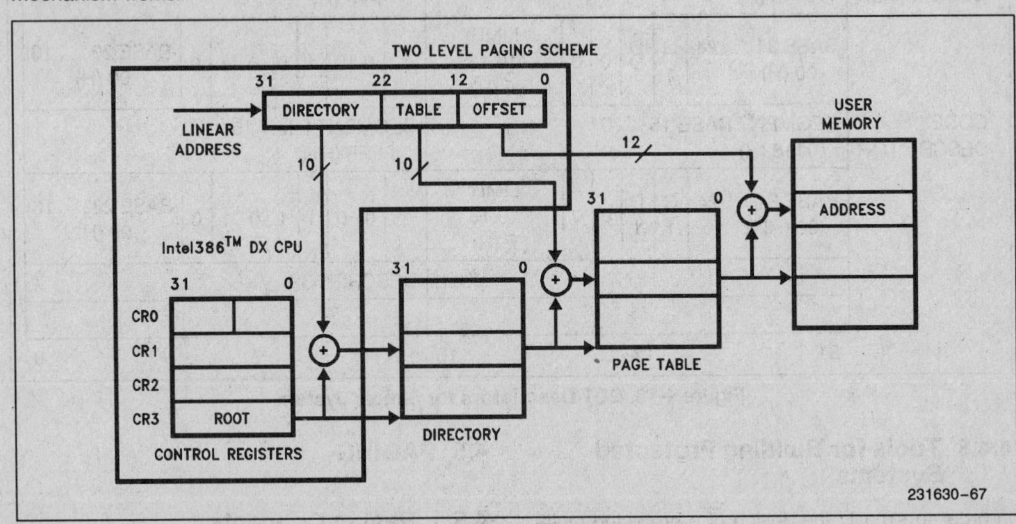

Figure 4-19. Paging Mechanism

31 … 12	11 … 9	8	7	6	5	4	3	2	1	0
PAGE TABLE ADDRESS 31..12	OS RESERVED	0	0	D	A	0	0	U/S	R/W	P

Figure 4-20. Page Directory Entry (Points to Page Table)

31 ... 12	11 10 9	8	7	6	5	4	3	2	1	0
PAGE FRAME ADDRESS 31..12	OS RESERVED	0	0	D	A	0	0	U/S	R/W	P

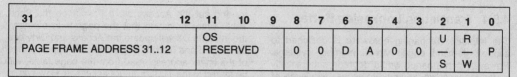

Figure 4-21. Page Table Entry (Points to Page)

4.5.2.4 PAGE TABLES

Each Page Table is 4K bytes and holds up to 1024 Page Table Entries. Page Table Entries contain the starting address of the page frame and statistical information about the page (see Figure 4-21). Address bits A12–A21 are used as an index to select one of the 1024 Page Table Entries. The 20 upper-bit page frame address is concatenated with the lower 12 bits of the linear address to form the physical address. Page tables can be shared between tasks and swapped to disks.

4.5.2.5 PAGE DIRECTORY/TABLE ENTRIES

The lower 12 bits of the Page Table Entries and Page Directory Entries contain statistical information about pages and page tables respectively. The **P** (Present) bit 0 indicates if a Page Directory or Page Table entry can be used in address translation. If P = 1 the entry can be used for address translation; if P = 0 the entry can not be used for translation. Note that the present bit of the page table entry that points to the page where code is currently being executed should always be set. Code that marks its own page not present should not be written. All of the other bits are available for use by the software. For example the remaining 31 bits could be used to indicate where on the disk the page is stored.

The **A** (Accessed) bit 5, is set by the Intel386 DX for both types of entries before a read or write access occurs to an address covered by the entry. The **D** (Dirty) bit 6 is set to 1 before a write to an address covered by that page table entry occurs. The D bit is undefined for Page Directory Entries. When the P, A and D bits are updated by the Intel386 DX, the processor generates a Read-Modify-Write cycle which locks the bus and prevents conflicts with other processors or perpherials. Software which modifies these bits should use the LOCK prefix to ensure the integrity of the page tables in multi-master systems.

The 3 bits marked **OS Reserved** in Figure 4-20 and Figure 4-21 (bits 9–11) are software definable. OSs are free to use these bits for whatever purpose they wish. An example use of the **OS Reserved** bits would be to store information about page aging. By keeping track of how long a page has been in memory since being accessed, an operating system can implement a page replacement algorithm like Least Recently Used.

The (User/Supervisor) U/S bit 2 and the (Read/Write) R/W bit 1 are used to provide protection attributes for individual pages.

4.5.3 Page Level Protection (R/W, U/S Bits)

The Intel386 DX provides a set of protection attributes for paging systems. The paging mechanism distinguishes between two levels of protection: User which corresponds to level 3 of the segmentation based protection, and supervisor which encompasses all of the other protection levels (0, 1, 2). Programs executing at Level 0, 1 or 2 bypass the page protection, although segmentation based protection is still enforced by the hardware.

The U/S and R/W bits are used to provide User/Supervisor and Read/Write protection for individual pages or for all pages covered by a Page Table Directory Entry. The U/S and R/W bits in the first level Page Directory Table apply to all pages described by the page table pointed to by that directory entry. The U/S and R/W bits in the second level Page Table Entry apply only to the page described by that entry. The U/S and R/W bits for a given page are obtained by taking the most restrictive of the U/S and R/W from the Page Directory Table Entries and the Page Table Entries and using these bits to address the page.

Example: If the U/S and R/W bits for the Page Directory entry were 10 and the U/S and R/W bits for the Page Table Entry were 01, the access rights for the page would be 01, the numerically smaller of the two. Table 4-4 shows the affect of the U/S and R/W bits on accessing memory.

Table 4-4. Protection Provided by R/W and U/S

U/S	R/W	Permitted Level 3	Permitted Access Levels 0, 1, or 2
0	0	None	Read/Write
0	1	None	Read/Write
1	0	Read-Only	Read/Write
1	1	Read/Write	Read/Write

However a given segment can be easily made read-only for level 0, 1, or 2 via the use of segmented protection mechanisms. (Section 4.4 **Protection**).

4.5.4 Translation Lookaside Buffer

The Intel386 DX paging hardware is designed to support demand paged virtual memory systems. However, performance would degrade substantially if the processor was required to access two levels of tables for every memory reference. To solve this problem, the Intel386 DX keeps a cache of the most recently accessed pages, this cache is called the Translation Lookaside Buffer (TLB). The TLB is a four-way set associative 32-entry page table cache. It automatically keeps the most commonly used Page Table Entries in the processor. The 32-entry TLB coupled with a 4K page size, results in coverage of 128K bytes of memory addresses. For many common multi-tasking systems, the TLB will have a hit rate of about 98%. This means that the processor will only have to access the two-level page structure on 2% of all memory references. Figure 4-22 illustrates how the TLB complements the Intel386 DX's paging mechanism.

4.5.5 Paging Operation

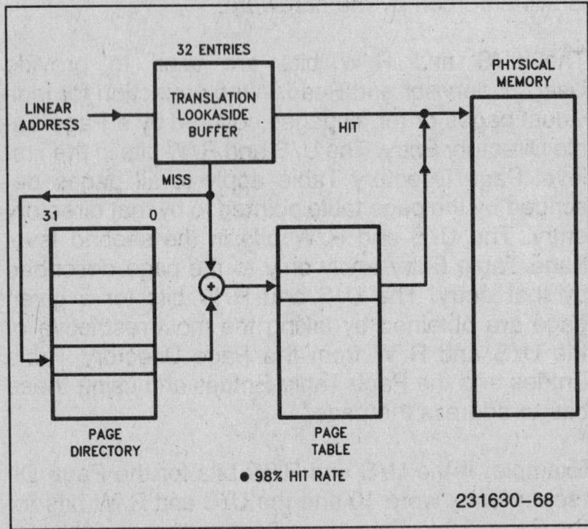

Figure 4-22. Translation Lookaside Buffer

The paging hardware operates in the following fashion. The paging unit hardware receives a 32-bit linear address from the segmentation unit. The upper 20 linear address bits are compared with all 32 entries in the TLB to determine if there is a match. If there is a match (i.e. a TLB hit), then the 32-bit physical address is calculated and will be placed on the address bus.

However, if the page table entry is not in the TLB, the Intel386 DX will read the appropriate Page Directory Entry. If P = 1 on the Page Directory Entry indicating that the page table is in memory, then the Intel386 DX will read the appropriate Page Table Entry and set the Access bit. If P = 1 on the Page Table Entry indicating that the page is in memory, the Intel386 DX will update the Access and Dirty bits as needed and fetch the operand. The upper 20 bits of the linear address, read from the page table, will be stored in the TLB for future accesses. However, if P = 0 for either the Page Directory Entry or the Page Table Entry, then the processor will generate a page fault, an Exception 14.

The processor will also generate an exception 14, page fault, if the memory reference violated the page protection attributes (i.e. U/S or R/W) (e.g. trying to write to a read-only page). CR2 will hold the linear address which caused the page fault. If a second page fault occurs, while the processor is attempting to enter the service routine for the first, then the processor will invoke the page fault (exception 14) handler a second time, rather than the double fault (exception 8) handler. Since Exception 14 is classified as a fault, CS: EIP will point to the instruction causing the page fault. The 16-bit error code pushed as part of the page fault handler will contain status bits which indicate the cause of the page fault.

The 16-bit error code is used by the operating system to determine how to handle the page fault Figure 4-23A shows the format of the page-fault error code and the interpretation of the bits.

NOTE:
Even though the bits in the error code (U/S, W/R, and P) have similar names as the bits in the Page Directory/Table Entries, the interpretation of the error code bits is different. Figure 4-23B indicates what type of access caused the page fault.

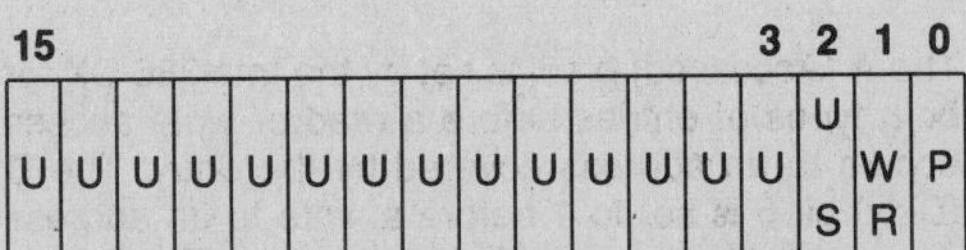

Figure 4-23A. Page Fault Error Code Format

U/S: The U/S bit indicates whether the access causing the fault occurred when the processor was executing in User Mode (U/S = 1) or in Supervisor mode (U/S = 0)

W/R: The W/R bit indicates whether the access causing the fault was a Read (W/R = 0) or a Write (W/R = 1)

P: The P bit indicates whether a page fault was caused by a not-present page (P = 0), or by a page level protection violation (P = 1)

U: UNDEFINED

U/S	W/R	Access Type
0	0	Supervisor* Read
0	1	Supervisor Write
1	0	User Read
1	1	User Write

*Descriptor table access will fault with U/S = 0, even if the program is executing at level 3.

Figure 4-23B. Type of Access Causing Page Fault

4.5.6 Operating System Responsibilities

The Intel386 DX takes care of the page address translation process, relieving the burden from an operating system in a demand-paged system. The operating system is responsible for setting up the initial page tables, and handling any page faults. The operating system also is required to invalidate (i.e. flush) the TLB when any changes are made to any of the page table entries. The operating system must reload CR3 to cause the TLB to be flushed.

Setting up the tables is simply a matter of loading CR3 with the address of the Page Directory, and allocating space for the Page Directory and the Page Tables. The primary responsibility of the operating system is to implement a swapping policy and handle all of the page faults.

A final concern of the operating system is to ensure that the TLB cache matches the information in the paging tables. In particular, any time the operating system sets the P present bit of page table entry to zero, the TLB must be flushed. Operating systems may want to take advantage of the fact that CR3 is stored as part of a TSS, to give every task or group of tasks its own set of page tables.

4.6 VIRTUAL 8086 ENVIRONMENT

4.6.1 Executing 8086 Programs

The Intel386 DX allows the execution of 8086 application programs in both Real Mode and in the Virtual 8086 Mode (Virtual Mode). Of the two methods, Virtual 8086 Mode offers the system designer the most flexibility. The Virtual 8086 Mode allows the execution of 8086 applications, while still allowing the system designer to take full advantage of the Intel386 DX protection mechanism. In particular, the Intel386 DX allows the simultaneous execution of 8086 operating systems and its applications, and an Intel386 DX operating system and both 80286 and Intel386 DX applications. Thus, in a multi-user Intel386 DX computer, one person could be running an MS-DOS spreadsheet, another person using MS-DOS, and a third person could be running multiple Unix utilities and applications. Each person in this scenario would believe that he had the computer completely to himself. Figure 4-24 illustrates this concept.

4.6.2 Virtual 8086 Mode Addressing Mechanism

One of the major differences between Intel386 DX Real and Protected modes is how the segment selectors are interpreted. When the processor is executing in Virtual 8086 Mode the segment registers are used in an identical fashion to Real Mode. The contents of the segment register is shifted left 4 bits and added to the offset to form the segment base linear address.

The Intel386 DX allows the operating system to specify which programs use the 8086 style address mechanism, and which programs use Protected Mode addressing, on a per task basis. Through the use of paging, the one megabyte address space of the Virtual Mode task can be mapped to anywhere in the 4 gigabyte linear address space of the Intel386 DX. Like Real Mode, Virtual Mode effective addresses (i.e., segment offsets) that exceed 64K byte will cause an exception 13. However, these restrictions should not prove to be important, because most tasks running in Virtual 8086 Mode will simply be existing 8086 application programs.

4.6.3 Paging In Virtual Mode

The paging hardware allows the concurrent running of multiple Virtual Mode tasks, and provides protection and operating system isolation. Although it is not strictly necessary to have the paging hardware enabled to run Virtual Mode tasks, it is needed in order to run multiple Virtual Mode tasks or to relocate the address space of a Virtual Mode task to physical address space greater than one megabyte.

The paging hardware allows the 20-bit linear address produced by a Virtual Mode program to be divided into up to 256 pages. Each one of the pages can be located anywhere within the maximum 4 gigabyte physical address space of the Intel386 DX. In addition, since CR3 (the Page Directory Base Register) is loaded by a task switch, each Virtual Mode task can use a different mapping scheme to map pages to different physical locations. Finally, the paging hardware allows the sharing of the 8086 op-

4

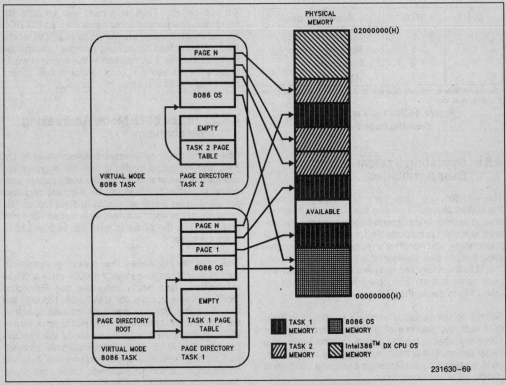

Figure 4-24. Virtual 8086 Environment Memory Management

erating system code between multiple 8086 applications. Figure 4-24 shows how the Intel386 DX paging hardware enables multiple 8086 programs to run under a virtual memory demand paged system.

4.6.4 Protection and I/O Permission Bitmap

All Virtual 8086 Mode programs execute at privilege level 3, the level of least privilege. As such, Virtual 8086 Mode programs are subject to all of the protection checks defined in Protected Mode. (This is different from Real Mode which implicitly is executing at privilege level 0, the level of greatest privilege.) Thus, an attempt to execute a privileged instruction when in Virtual 8086 Mode will cause an exception 13 fault.

The following are privileged instructions, which may be executed only at Privilege Level 0. Therefore, attempting to execute these instructions in Virtual 8086 Mode (or anytime CPL > 0) causes an exception 13 fault:

```
LIDT;    MOV DRn,reg;    MOV reg,DRn;
LGDT;    MOV TRn,reg;    MOV reg,TRn;
LMSW;    MOV CRn,reg;    MOV reg,CRn.
CLTS;
HLT;
```

Several instructions, particularly those applying to the multitasking model and protection model, are available only in Protected Mode. Therefore, attempting to execute the following instructions in Real Mode or in Virtual 8086 Mode generates an exception 6 fault:

```
LTR;     STR;
LLDT;    SLDT;
LAR;     VERR;
LSL;     VERW;
ARPL.
```

The instructions which are IOPL-sensitive in Protected Mode are:

```
IN;      STI;
OUT;     CLI
INS;
OUTS;
REP INS;
REP OUTS;
```

In Virtual 8086 Mode, a slightly different set of instructions are made IOPL-sensitive. The following instructions are IOPL-sensitive in Virtual 8086 Mode:

```
INT n;     STI;
PUSHF;     CLI;
POPF;      IRET
```

The PUSHF, POPF, and IRET instructions are IOPL-sensitive in Virtual 8086 Mode only. This provision allows the IF flag (interrupt enable flag) to be virtualized to the Virtual 8086 Mode program. The INT n software interrupt instruction is also IOPL-sensitive in Virtual 8086 Mode. Note, however, that the INT 3 (opcode 0CCH), INTO, and BOUND instructions are not IOPL-sensitive in Virtual 8086 mode (they aren't IOPL sensitive in Protected Mode either).

Note that the I/O instructions (IN, OUT, INS, OUTS, REP INS, and REP OUTS) are **not** IOPL-sensitive in Virtual 8086 mode. Rather, the I/O instructions become automatically sensitive to the **I/O Permission Bitmap** contained in the **Intel386 DX Task State Segment**. The I/O Permission Bitmap, automatically used by the Intel386 DX in Virtual 8086 Mode, is illustrated by Figures 4.15a and 4-15b.

The I/O Permission Bitmap can be viewed as a 0–64 Kbit bit string, which begins in memory at offset Bit_Map_Offset in the current TSS. Bit_Map_Offset must be ≤ DFFFH so the entire bit map and the byte FFH which follows the bit map are all at offsets ≤ FFFFH from the TSS base. The 16-bit pointer Bit_Map_Offset (15:0) is found in the word beginning at offset 66H (102 decimal) from the TSS base, as shown in Figure 4-15a.

Each bit in the I/O Permission Bitmap corresponds to a single byte-wide I/O port, as illustrated in Figure 4-15a. If a bit is 0, I/O to the corresponding byte-wide port can occur without generating an exception. Otherwise the I/O instruction causes an exception 13 fault. Since every byte-wide I/O port must be protectable, all bits corresponding to a word-wide or dword-wide port must be 0 for the word-wide or dword-wide I/O to be permitted. If all the referenced bits are 0, the I/O will be allowed. If any referenced bits are 1, the attempted I/O will cause an exception 13 fault.

Due to the use of a pointer to the base of the I/O Permission Bitmap, the bitmap may be located anywhere within the TSS, or may be ignored completely by pointing the Bit_Map_Offset (15:0) beyond the limit of the TSS segment. In the same manner, only a small portion of the 64K I/O space need have an associated map bit, by adjusting the TSS limit to truncate the bitmap. This eliminates the commitment of 8K of memory when a complete bitmap is not required, while allowing the fully general case if desired.

EXAMPLE OF BITMAP FOR I/O PORTS 0–255: Setting the TSS limit to {bit_Map_Offset + 31 + 1**} [** see note below] will allow a 32-byte bitmap for the I/O ports #0–255, plus a terminator byte of all 1's [** see note below]. This allows the I/O bitmap to control I/O Permission to I/O port 0–255 while causing an exception 13 fault on attempted I/O to any I/O port 80256 through 65,565.

****IMPORTANT IMPLEMENTATION NOTE:** Beyond the last byte of I/O mapping information in the I/O Permission Bitmap **must** be a byte containing all 1's. The byte of all 1's must be within the limit of the Intel386 DX TSS segment (see Figure 4-15a).

4.6.5 Interrupt Handling

In order to fully support the emulation of an 8086 machine, interrupts in Virtual 8086 Mode are handled in a unique fashion. When running in Virtual Mode all interrupts and exceptions involve a privilege change back to the host Intel386 DX operating system. The Intel386 DX operating system determines if the interrupt comes from a Protected Mode application or from a Virtual Mode program by examining the VM bit in the EFLAGS image stored on the stack.

When a Virtual Mode program is interrupted and execution passes to the interrupt routine at level 0, the VM bit is cleared. However, the VM bit is still set in the EFLAG image on the stack.

The Intel386 DX operating system in turn handles the exception or interrupt and then returns control to the 8086 program. The Intel386 DX operating system may choose to let the 8086 operating system handle the interrupt or it may emulate the function of the interrupt handler. For example, many 8086 operating system calls are accessed by PUSHing parameters on the stack, and then executing an INT n instruction. If the IOPL is set to 0 then all INT n instructions will be intercepted by the Intel386 DX Microprocessor operating system. The Intel386 DX operating system could emulate the 8086 operating system's call. Figure 4-25 shows how the Intel386 DX operating system could intercept an 8086 operating system's call to "Open a File".

An Intel386 DX operating system can provide a Virtual 8086 Environment which is totally transparent to the application software via intercepting and then emulating 8086 operating system's calls, and intercepting IN and OUT instructions.

4.6.6 Entering and Leaving Virtual 8086 Mode

Virtual 8086 mode is entered by executing an IRET instruction (at CPL=0), or Task Switch (at any CPL) to an Intel386 DX task whose Intel386 DX TSS has a FLAGS image containing a 1 in the VM bit position while the processor is executing in Protected Mode. That is, one way to enter Virtual 8086 mode is to switch to a task with an Intel386 DX TSS that has a 1 in the VM bit in the EFLAGS image. The other way is to execute a 32-bit IRET instruction at privilege level 0, where the stack has a 1 in the VM bit in the EFLAGS image. POPF does not affect the VM bit, even if the processor is in Protected Mode or level 0, and so cannot be used to enter Virtual 8086 Mode. PUSHF always pushes a 0 in the VM bit, even if the processor is in Virtual 8086 Mode, so that a program cannot tell if it is executing in REAL mode, or in Virtual 8086 mode.

The VM bit can be set by executing an IRET instruction only at privilege level 0, or by any instruction or Interrupt which causes a task switch in Protected Mode (with VM=1 in the new FLAGS image), and can be cleared only by an interrupt or exception in Virtual 8086 Mode. IRET and POPF instructions executed in REAL mode or Virtual 8086 mode will not change the value in the VM bit.

The transition out of virtual 8086 mode to Intel386 DX protected mode occurs only on receipt of an interrupt or exception (such as due to a sensitive instruction). In Virtual 8086 mode, all interrupts and exceptions vector through the protected mode IDT, and enter an interrupt handler in protected Intel386 DX mode. That is, as part of interrupt processing, the VM bit is cleared.

Because the matching IRET must occur from level 0, if an Interrupt or Trap Gate is used to field an interrupt or exception out of Virtual 8086 mode, the Gate must perform an inter-level interrupt only to level 0. Interrupt or Trap Gates through conforming segments, or through segments with DPL>0, will raise a GP fault with the CS selector as the error code.

4.6.6.1 TASK SWITCHES TO/FROM VIRTUAL 8086 MODE

Tasks which can execute in virtual 8086 mode must be described by a TSS with the new Intel386 DX format (TYPE 9 or 11 descriptor).

A task switch out of virtual 8086 mode will operate exactly the same as any other task switch out of a task with an Intel386 DX TSS. All of the programmer visible state, including the FLAGS register with the VM bit set to 1, is stored in the TSS. The segment registers in the TSS will contain 8086 segment base values rather than selectors.

A task switch into a task described by an Intel386 DX TSS will have an additional check to determine if the incoming task should be resumed in virtual 8086 mode. Tasks described by 80286 format TSSs cannot be resumed in virtual 8086 mode, so no check is required there (the FLAGS image in 80286 format TSS has only the low order 16 FLAGS bits). Before loading the segment register images from an Intel386 DX TSS, the FLAGS image is loaded, so that the segment registers are loaded from the TSS image as 8086 segment base values. The task is now ready to resume in virtual 8086 execution mode.

4.6.6.2 TRANSITIONS THROUGH TRAP AND INTERRUPT GATES, AND IRET

A task switch is one way to enter or exit virtual 8086 mode. The other method is to exit through a Trap or Interrupt gate, as part of handling an interrupt, and to enter as part of executing an IRET instruction. The transition out must use an Intel386 DX Trap Gate (Type 14), or Intel386 DX Interrupt Gate (Type 15), which must point to a non-conforming level 0 segment (DPL=0) in order to permit the trap handler to IRET back to the Virtual 8086 program. The Gate must point to a non-conforming level 0 segment to perform a level switch to level 0 so that the matching IRET can change the VM bit. Intel386 DX gates must be used, since 80286 gates save only the low 16 bits of the FLAGS register, so that the VM bit will not be saved on transitions through the 80286 gates. Also, the 16-bit IRET (presumably) used to terminate the 80286 interrupt handler will pop only the lower 16 bits from FLAGS, and will not affect the VM bit. The action taken for an Intel386 DX Trap or Interrupt gate if an interrupt occurs while the task is executing in virtual 8086 mode is given by the following sequence.

(1) Save the FLAGS register in a temp to push later. Turn off the VM and TF bits, and if the interrupt is serviced by an Interrupt Gate, turn off IF also.

(2) Interrupt and Trap gates must perform a level switch from 3 (where the VM86 program executes) to level 0 (so IRET can return). This process involves a stack switch to the stack given in the TSS for privilege level 0. Save the Virtual 8086 Mode SS and ESP registers to push in a later step. The segment register load of SS will be done as a Protected Mode segment load, since the VM bit was turned off above.

(3) Push the 8086 segment register values onto the new stack, in the order: GS, FS, DS, ES. These are pushed as 32-bit quantities, with undefined values in the upper 16 bits. Then load these 4 registers with null selectors (0).

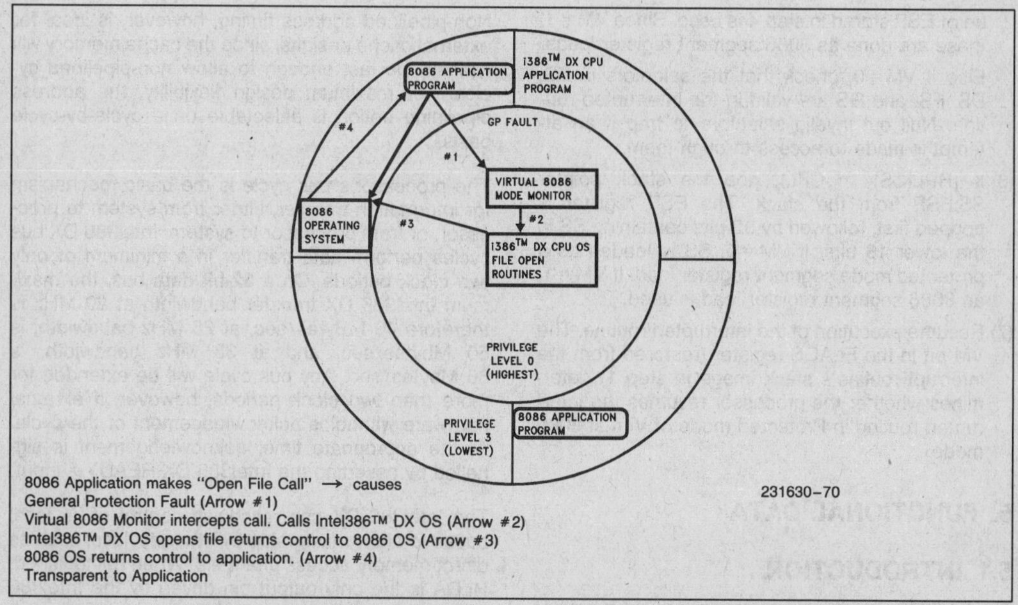

Figure 4-25. Virtual 8086 Environment Interrupt and Call Handling

(4) Push the old 8086 stack pointer onto the new stack by pushing the SS register (as 32-bits, high bits undefined), then pushing the 32-bit ESP register saved above.

(5) Push the 32-bit FLAGS register saved in step 1.

(6) Push the old 8086 instruction pointer onto the new stack by pushing the CS register (as 32-bits, high bits undefined), then pushing the 32-bit EIP register.

(7) Load up the new CS:EIP value from the interrupt gate, and begin execution of the interrupt routine in protected Intel386 DX mode.

The transition out of virtual 8086 mode performs a level change and stack switch, in addition to changing back to protected mode. In addition, all of the 8086 segment register images are stored on the stack (behind the SS:ESP image), and then loaded with null (0) selectors before entering the interrupt handler. This will permit the handler to safely save and restore the DS, ES, FS, and GS registers as 80286 selectors. This is needed so that interrupt handlers which don't care about the mode of the interrupted program can use the same prolog and epilog code for state saving (i.e. push all registers in prolog, pop all in epilog) regardless of whether or not a "native" mode or Virtual 8086 mode program was interrupted. Restoring null selectors to these registers before executing the IRET will not cause a trap in the interrupt handler. Interrupt routines which expect values in the segment registers, or return values in segment registers will have to obtain/return values from the 8086 register images pushed onto the new stack. They will need to know the mode of the interrupted program in order to know where to find/return segment registers, and also to know how to interpret segment register values.

The IRET instruction will perform the inverse of the above sequence. Only the extended Intel386 DXs IRET instruction (operand size = 32) can be used, and must be executed at level 0 to change the VM bit to 1.

(1) If the NT bit in the FLAGs register is on, an inter-task return is performed. The current state is stored in the current TSS, and the link field in the current TSS is used to locate the TSS for the interrupted task which is to be resumed.

Otherwise, continue with the following sequence.

(2) Read the FLAGS image from SS:8[ESP] into the FLAGS register. This will set VM to the value active in the interrupted routine.

(3) Pop off the instruction pointer CS:EIP. EIP is popped first, then a 32-bit word is popped which contains the CS value in the lower 16 bits. If VM = 0, this CS load is done as a protected mode segment load. If VM = 1, this will be done as an 8086 segment load.

(4) Increment the ESP register by 4 to bypass the FLAGS image which was "popped" in step 1.

(5) If VM = 1, load segment registers ES, DS, FS, and GS from memory locations SS:[ESP + 8], SS:[ESP + 12], SS:[ESP + 16], and SS:[ESP + 20], respectively, where the new val-

ue of ESP stored in step 4 is used. Since VM=1, these are done as 8086 segment register loads.

Else if VM=0, check that the selectors in ES, DS, FS, and GS are valid in the interrupted routine. Null out invalid selectors to trap if an attempt is made to access through them.

(6) If (RPL(CS) > CPL), pop the stack pointer SS:ESP from the stack. The ESP register is popped first, followed by 32-bits containing SS in the lower 16 bits. If VM=0, SS is loaded as a protected mode segment register load. If VM=1, an 8086 segment register load is used.

(7) Resume execution of the interrupted routine. The VM bit in the FLAGS register (restored from the interrupt routine's stack image in step 1) determines whether the processor resumes the interrupted routine in Protected mode of Virtual 8086 mode.

5. FUNCTIONAL DATA

5.1 INTRODUCTION

The Intel386 DX features a straightforward functional interface to the external hardware. The Intel386 DX has separate, parallel buses for data and address. The data bus is 32-bits in width, and bidirectional. The address bus outputs 32-bit address values in the most directly usable form for the high-speed local bus: 4 individual byte enable signals, and the 30 upper-order bits as a binary value. The data and address buses are interpreted and controlled with their associated control signals.

A **dynamic data bus sizing** feature allows the processor to handle a mix of 32- and 16-bit external buses on a cycle-by-cycle basis (see **5.3.4 Data Bus Sizing**). If 16-bit bus size is selected, the Intel386 DX automatically makes any adjustment needed, even performing another 16-bit bus cycle to complete the transfer if that is necessary. 8-bit peripheral devices may be connected to 32-bit or 16-bit buses with no loss of performance. A **new address pipelining option** is provided and applies to 32-bit and 16-bit buses for substantially improved memory utilization, especially for the most heavily used memory resources.

The **address pipelining option**, when selected, typically allows a given memory interface to operate with one less wait state than would otherwise be required (see **5.4.2 Address Pipelining**). The pipelined bus is also well suited to interleaved memory designs. When address pipelining is requested by the external hardware, the Intel386 DX will output the address and bus cycle definition of the next bus cycle (if it is internally available) even while waiting for the current cycle to be acknowledged.

Non-pipelined address timing, however, is ideal for external cache designs, since the cache memory will typically be fast enough to allow non-pipelined cycles. For maximum design flexibility, the address pipelining option is selectable on a cycle-by-cycle basis.

The processor's bus cycle is the basic mechanism for information transfer, either from system to processor, or from processor to system. Intel386 DX bus cycles perform data transfer in a minimum of only two clock periods. On a 32-bit data bus, the maximum Intel386 DX transfer bandwidth at 20 MHz is therefore 40 MBytes/sec, at 25 MHz bandwidth, is 50 Mbytes/sec, and at 33 MHz bandwidth, is 66 Mbytes/sec. Any bus cycle will be extended for more than two clock periods, however, if external hardware withholds acknowledgement of the cycle. At the appropriate time, acknowledgement is signalled by asserting the Intel386 DX READY# input.

The Intel386 DX can relinquish control of its local buses to allow mastership by other devices, such as direct memory access channels. When relinquished, HLDA is the only output pin driven by the Intel386 DX providing near-complete isolation of the processor from its system. The near-complete isolation characteristic is ideal when driving the system from test equipment, and in fault-tolerant applications.

Functional data covered in this chapter describes the processor's hardware interface. First, the set of signals available at the processor pins is described (see **5.2 Signal Description**). Following that are the signal waveforms occurring during bus cycles (see **5.3 Bus Transfer Mechanism, 5.4 Bus Functional Description** and **5.5 Other Functional Descriptions**).

5.2 SIGNAL DESCRIPTION

5.2.1 Introduction

Ahead is a brief description of the Intel386 DX input and output signals arranged by functional groups. Note the # symbol at the end of a signal name indicates the active, or asserted, state occurs when the signal is at a low voltage. When no # is present after the signal name, the signal is asserted when at the high voltage level.

Example signal: M/IO# — High voltage indicates Memory selected
— Low voltage indicates I/O selected

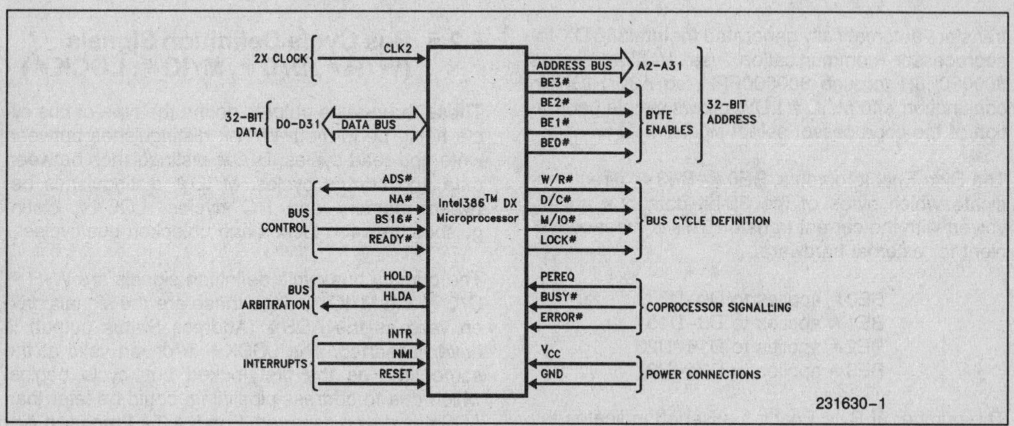

Figure 5-1. Functional Signal Groups

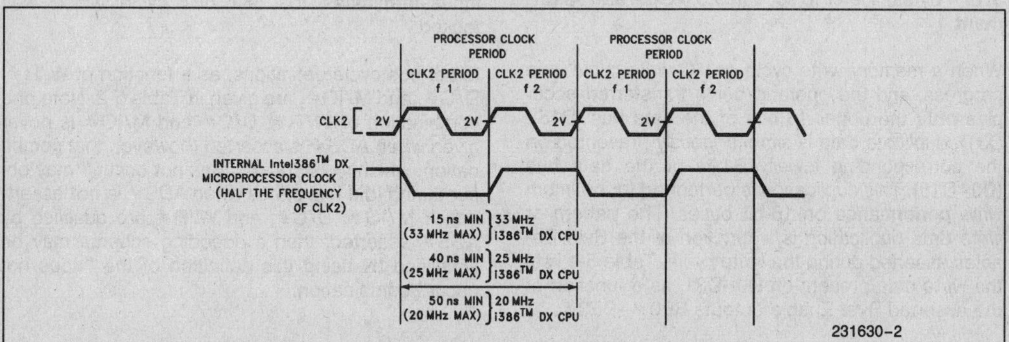

Figure 5-2. CLK2 Signal and Internal Processor Clock

The signal descriptions sometimes refer to AC timing parameters, such as "t_{25} Reset Setup Time" and "t_{26} Reset Hold Time." The values of these parameters can be found in Tables 7-4 and 7-5.

5.2.2 Clock (CLK2)

CLK2 provides the fundamental timing for the Intel386 DX. It is divided by two internally to generate the internal processor clock used for instruction execution. The internal clock is comprised of two phases, "phase one" and "phase two." Each CLK2 period is a phase of the internal clock. Figure 5-2 illustrates the relationship. If desired, the phase of the internal processor clock can be synchronized to a known phase by ensuring the RESET signal falling edge meets its applicable setup and hold times, t_{25} and t_{26}.

5.2.3 Data Bus (D0 through D31)

These three-state bidirectional signals provide the general purpose data path between the Intel386 DX and other devices. Data bus inputs and outputs indicate "1" when HIGH. The data bus can transfer data on 32- and 16-bit buses using a data bus sizing feature controlled by the BS16# input. See section **5.2.6 Bus Contol**. Data bus reads require that read data setup and hold times t_{21} and t_{22} be met for correct operation. In addition, the Intel386 DX requires that all data bus pins be at a valid logic state (high or low) at the end of each read cycle, when READY# is asserted. During any write operation (and during halt cycles and shutdown cycles), the Intel386 DX always drives all 32 signals of the data bus even if the current bus size is 16-bits.

5.2.4 Address Bus (BE0# through BE3#, A2 through A31)

These three-state outputs provide physical memory addresses or I/O port addresses. The address bus is capable of addressing 4 gigabytes of physical memory space (00000000H through FFFFFFFFH), and 64 kilobytes of I/O address space (00000000H through 0000FFFFH) for programmed I/O. I/O transfers automatically generated for Intel386 DX-to-coprocessor communication use I/O addresses 800000F8H through 800000FFH, so A31 HIGH in conjunction with M/IO# LOW allows simple generation of the coprocessor select signal.

The Byte Enable outputs, BE0#–BE3#, directly indicate which bytes of the 32-bit data bus are involved with the current transfer. This is most convenient for external hardware.

BE0# applies to D0–D7
BE1# applies to D8–D15
BE2# applies to D16–D23
BE3# applies to D24–D31

The number of Byte Enables asserted indicates the physical size of the operand being transferred (1, 2, 3, or 4 bytes). Refer to section **5.3.6 Operand Alignment.**

When a memory write cycle or I/O write cycle is in progress, and the operand being transferred occupies **only** the upper 16 bits of the data bus (D16–D31), duplicate data is simultaneously presented on the corresponding lower 16-bits of the data bus (D0–D15). This duplication is performed for optimum write performance on 16-bit buses. The pattern of write data duplication is a function of the Byte Enables asserted during the write cycle. Table 5-1 lists the write data present on D0–D31, as a function of the asserted Byte Enable outputs BE0#–BE3#.

5.2.5 Bus Cycle Definition Signals (W/R#, D/C#, M/IO#, LOCK#)

These three-state outputs define the type of bus cycle being performed. W/R# distinguishes between write and read cycles. D/C# distinguishes between data and control cycles. M/IO# distinguishes between memory and I/O cycles. LOCK# distinguishes between locked and unlocked bus cycles.

The primary bus cycle definition signals are W/R#, D/C# and M/IO#, since these are the signals driven valid as the ADS# (Address Status output) is driven asserted. The LOCK# is driven valid at the same time as the first locked bus cycle begins, which due to address pipelining, could be later than ADS# is driven asserted. See **5.4.3.4 Pipelined Address.** The LOCK# is negated when the READY# input terminates the last bus cycle which was locked.

Exact bus cycle definitions, as a function of W/R#, D/C#, and M/IO#, are given in Table 5-2. Note one combination of W/R#, D/C# and M/IO# is never given when ADS# is asserted (however, that combination, which is listed as "does not occur," may occur during **idle** bus states when ADS# is **not** asserted). If M/IO#, D/C#, and W/R# are qualified by ADS# asserted, then a decoding scheme may be simplified by using this definition of the "does not occur" combination.

Table 5-1. Write Data Duplication as a Function of BE0#–BE3#

Intel386™ DX Byte Enables				Intel386™ DX Write Data				Automatic Duplication?
BE3#	BE2#	BE1#	BE0#	D24–D31	D16–D23	D8–D15	D0–D7	
High	High	High	Low	undef	undef	undef	A	No
High	High	Low	High	undef	undef	B	undef	No
High	Low	High	High	undef	C	undef	C	Yes
Low	High	High	High	D	undef	D	undef	Yes
High	High	Low	Low	undef	undef	B	A	No
High	Low	Low	High	undef	C	B	undef	No
Low	Low	High	High	D	C	D	C	Yes
High	Low	Low	Low	undef	C	B	A	No
Low	Low	Low	High	D	C	B	undef	No
Low	Low	Low	Low	D	C	B	A	No

Key:
D = logical write data d24–d31
C = logical write data d16–d23
B = logical write data d8–d15
A = logical write data d0–d7

Table 5-2. Bus Cycle Definition

M/IO#	D/C#	W/R#	Bus Cycle Type	Locked?
Low	Low	Low	INTERRUPT ACKNOWLEDGE	Yes
Low	Low	High	does not occur	—
Low	High	Low	I/O DATA READ	No
Low	High	High	I/O DATA WRITE	No
High	Low	Low	MEMORY CODE READ	No
High	Low	High	HALT: Address = 2 (BE0# High BE1# High BE2# Low BE3# High A2–A31 Low) SHUTDOWN: Address = 0 (BE0# Low BE1# High BE2# High BE3# High A2–A31 Low)	No
High	High	Low	MEMORY DATA READ	Some Cycles
High	High	High	MEMORY DATA WRITE	Some Cycles

5.2.6 Bus Control Signals (ADS#, READY#, NA#, BS16#)

5.2.6.1 INTRODUCTION

The following signals allow the processor to indicate when a bus cycle has begun, and allow other system hardware to control address pipelining, data bus width and bus cycle termination.

5.2.6.2 ADDRESS STATUS (ADS#)

This three-state output indicates that a valid bus cycle definition, and address (W/R#, D/C#, M/IO#, BE0#–BE3#, and A2–A31) is being driven at the Intel386 DX pins. It is asserted during T1 and T2P bus states (see **5.4.3.2 Non-pipelined Address** and **5.4.3.4 Pipelined Address** for additional information on bus states).

5.2.6.3 TRANSFER ACKNOWLEDGE (READY#)

This input indicates the current bus cycle is complete, and the active bytes indicated by BE0#–BE3# and BS16# are accepted or provided. When READY# is sampled asserted during a read cycle or interrupt acknowledge cycle, the Intel386 DX latches the input data and terminates the cycle. When READY# is sampled asserted during a write cycle, the processor terminates the bus cycle.

READY# is ignored on the first bus state of all bus cycles, and sampled each bus state thereafter until asserted. READY# must eventually be asserted to acknowledge every bus cycle, including Halt Indication and Shutdown Indication bus cycles. When being sampled, READY must always meet setup and hold times t_{19} and t_{20} for correct operation. See all sections of **5.4 Bus Functional Description**.

5.2.6.4 NEXT ADDRESS REQUEST (NA#)

This is used to request address pipelining. This input indicates the system is prepared to accept new values of BE0#–BE3#, A2–A31, W/R#, D/C# and M/IO# from the Intel386 DX even if the end of the current cycle is not being acknowledged on READY#. If this input is asserted when sampled, the next address is driven onto the bus, provided the next bus request is already pending internally. See **5.4.2 Address Pipelining** and **5.4.3 Read and Write Cycles**. NA# must always meet setup and hold times, t_{15} and t_{16}, for correct operation.

5.2.6.5 BUS SIZE 16 (BS16#)

The BS16# feature allows the Intel386 DX to directly connect to 32-bit and 16-bit data buses. Asserting this input constrains the current bus cycle to use only the lower-order half (D0–D15) of the data bus, corresponding to BE0# and BE1#. Asserting BS16# has no additional effect if only BE0# and/or BE1# are asserted in the current cycle. However, during bus cycles asserting BE2# or BE3#, asserting BS16# will automatically cause the Intel386 DX to make adjustments for correct transfer of the upper bytes(s) using only physical data signals D0–D15.

If the operand spans both halves of the data bus and BS16# is asserted, the Intel386 DX will automatically perform another 16-bit bus cycle. BS16# must always meet setup and hold times t_{17} and t_{18} for correct operation.

Intel386 DX I/O cycles are automatically generated for coprocessor communication. Since the Intel386 DX must transfer 32-bit quantities between itself and the Intel387 DX, BS16# *must not* be asserted during Intel387 DX communication cycles.

5.2.7 Bus Arbitration Signals (HOLD, HLDA)

5.2.7.1 INTRODUCTION

This section describes the mechanism by which the processor relinquishes control of its local buses when requested by another bus master device. See **5.5.1 Entering and Exiting Hold Acknowledge** for additional information.

5.2.7.2 BUS HOLD REQUEST (HOLD)

This input indicates some device other than the Intel386 DX requires bus mastership.

HOLD must remain asserted as long as any other device is a local bus master. HOLD is not recognized while RESET is asserted. If RESET is asserted while HOLD is asserted, RESET has priority and places the bus into an idle state, rather than the hold acknowledge (high impedance) state.

HOLD is level-sensitive and is a synchronous input. HOLD signals must always meet setup and hold times t_{23} and t_{24} for correct operation.

5.2.7.3 BUS HOLD ACKNOWLEDGE (HLDA)

Assertion of this output indicates the Intel386 DX has relinquished control of its local bus in response to HOLD asserted, and is in the bus Hold Acknowledge state.

The Hold Acknowledge state offers near-complete signal isolation. In the Hold Acknowledge state, HLDA is the only signal being driven by the Intel386 DX. The other output signals or bidirectional signals (D0–D31, BE0#–BE3#, A2–A31, W/R#, D/C#, M/IO#, LOCK# and ADS#) are in a high-impedance state so the requesting bus master may control them. Pullup resistors may be desired on several signals to avoid spurious activity when no bus master is driving them. See **7.2.3 Resistor Recommendations**. Also, one rising edge occuring on the NMI input during Hold Acknowledge is remembered, for processing after the HOLD input is negated.

In addition to the normal usage of Hold Acknowledge with DMA controllers or master peripherals, the near-complete isolation has particular attractiveness during system test when test equipment drives the system, and in hardware-fault-tolerant applications.

5.2.8 Coprocessor Interface Signals (PEREQ, BUSY#, ERROR#)

5.2.8.1 INTRODUCTION

In the following sections are descriptions of signals dedicated to the numeric coprocessor interface. In addition to the data bus, address bus, and bus cycle definition signals, these following signals control communication between the Intel386 DX and its Intel387 DX processor extension.

5.2.8.2 COPROCESSOR REQUEST (PEREQ)

When asserted, this input signal indicates a coprocessor request for a data operand to be transferred to/from memory by the Intel386 DX. In response, the Intel386 DX transfers information between the coprocessor and memory. Because the Intel386 DX has internally stored the coprocessor opcode being executed, it performs the requested data transfer with the correct direction and memory address.

PEREQ is level-sensitive and is allowed to be asynchronous to the CLK2 signal.

5.2.8.3 COPROCESSOR BUSY (BUSY#)

When asserted, this input indicates the coprocessor is still executing an instruction, and is not yet able to accept another. When the Intel386 DX encounters any coprocessor instruction which operates on the numeric stack (e.g. load, pop, or arithmetic operation), or the WAIT instruction, this input is first automatically sampled until it is seen to be negated. This sampling of the BUSY# input prevents overrunning the execution of a previous coprocessor instruction.

The FNINIT and FNCLEX coprocessor instructions are allowed to execute even if BUSY# is asserted, since these instructions are used for coprocessor initialization and exception-clearing.

BUSY# is level-sensitive and is allowed to be asynchronous to the CLK2 signal.

BUSY# serves an additional function. If BUSY# is sampled LOW at the falling edge of RESET, the Intel386 DX performs an internal self-test (see **5.5.3 Bus Activity During and Following Reset**). If BUSY# is sampled HIGH, no self-test is performed.

5.2.8.4 COPROCESSOR ERROR (ERROR#)

This input signal indicates that the previous coprocessor instruction generated a coprocessor error of a type not masked by the coprocessor's control register. This input is automatically sampled by the Intel386 DX when a coprocessor instruction is encountered, and if asserted, the Intel386 DX generates exception 16 to access the error-handling software.

Several coprocessor instructions, generally those which clear the numeric error flags in the coprocessor or save coprocessor state, do execute without the Intel386 DX generating exception 16 even if ERROR# is asserted. These instructions are FNINIT, FNCLEX, FSTSW, FSTSWAX, FSTCW, FSTENV, FSAVE, FESTENV and FESAVE.

ERROR# is level-sensitive and is allowed to be asynchronous to the CLK2 signal.

5.2.9 Interrupt Signals (INTR, NMI, RESET)

5.2.9.1 INTRODUCTION

The following descriptions cover inputs that can interrupt or suspend execution of the processor's current instruction stream.

5.2.9.2 MASKABLE INTERRUPT REQUEST (INTR)

When asserted, this input indicates a request for interrupt service, which can be masked by the Intel386 DX Flag Register IF bit. When the Intel386 DX responds to the INTR input, it performs two interrupt acknowledge bus cycles, and at the end of the second, latches an 8-bit interrupt vector on D0–D7 to identify the source of the interrupt.

INTR is level-sensitive and is allowed to be asynchronous to the CLK2 signal. To assure recognition of an INTR request, INTR should remain asserted until the first interrupt acknowledge bus cycle begins.

5.2.9.3 NON-MASKABLE INTERRUPT REQUEST (NMI)

This input indicates a request for interrupt service, which cannot be masked by software. The non-maskable interrupt request is always processed according to the pointer or gate in slot 2 of the interrupt table. Because of the fixed NMI slot assignment, no interrupt acknowledge cycles are perfomed when processing NMI.

NMI is rising edge-sensitive and is allowed to be asynchronous to the CLK2 signal. To assure recognition of NMI, it must be negated for at least eight CLK2 periods, and then be asserted for at least eight CLK2 periods.

Once NMI processing has begun, no additional NMI's are processed until after the next IRET instruction, which is typically the end of the NMI service routine. If NMI is re-asserted prior to that time, however, one rising edge on NMI will be remembered for processing after executing the next IRET instruction.

5.2.9.4 RESET (RESET)

This input signal suspends any operation in progress and places the Intel386 DX in a known reset state. The Intel386 DX is reset by asserting RESET for 15 or more CLK2 periods (80 or more CLK2 periods before requesting self test). When RESET is asserted, all other input pins are ignored, and all other bus pins are driven to an idle bus state as shown in Table 5-3. If RESET and HOLD are both asserted at a point in time, RESET takes priority even if the Intel386 DX was in a Hold Acknowledge state prior to RESET asserted.

RESET is level-sensitive and must be synchronous to the CLK2 signal. If desired, the phase of the internal processor clock, and the entire Intel386 DX state can be completely synchronized to external circuitry by ensuring the RESET signal falling edge meets its applicable setup and hold times, t_{25} and t_{26}.

Table 5-3. Pin State (Bus Idle) During Reset

Pin Name	Signal Level During Reset
ADS#	High
D0–D31	High Impedance
BE0#–BE3#	Low
A2–A31	High
W/R#	Low
D/C#	High
M/IO#	Low
LOCK#	High
HLDA	Low

4

5.2.10 Signal Summary

Table 5-4 summarizes the characteristics of all Intel386 DX signals.

Table 5-4. Intel386™ DX Signal Summary

Signal Name	Signal Function	Active State	Input/ Output	Input Synch or Asynch to CLK2	Output High Impedance During HLDA?
CLK2	Clock	—	I	—	—
D0–D31	Data Bus	High	I/O	S	Yes
BE0#–BE3#	Byte Enables	Low	O	—	Yes
A2–A31	Address Bus	High	O	—	Yes
W/R#	Write-Read Indication	High	O	—	Yes
D/C#	Data-Control Indication	High	O	—	Yes
M/IO#	Memory-I/O Indication	High	O	—	Yes
LOCK#	Bus Lock Indication	Low	O	—	Yes
ADS#	Address Status	Low	O	—	Yes
NA#	Next Address Request	Low	I	S	—
BS16#	Bus Size 16	Low	I	S	—
READY#	Transfer Acknowledge	Low	I	S	—
HOLD	Bus Hold Request	High	I	S	—
HLDA	Bus Hold Acknowledge	High	O	—	No
PEREQ	Coprocessor Request	High	I	A	—
BUSY#	Coprocessor Busy	Low	I	A	—
ERROR#	Coprocessor Error	Low	I	A	—
INTR	Maskable Interrupt Request	High	I	A	—
NMI	Non-Maskable Intrpt Request	High	I	A	—
RESET	Reset	High	I	S	—

5.3 BUS TRANSFER MECHANISM

5.3.1 Introduction

All data transfers occur as a result of one or more bus cycles. Logical data operands of byte, word and double-word lengths may be transferred without restrictions on physical address alignment. Any byte boundary may be used, although two or even three physical bus cycles are performed as required for unaligned operand transfers. See **5.3.4 Dynamic Data Bus Sizing** and **5.3.6 Operand Alignment**.

The Intel386 DX address signals are designed to simplify external system hardware. Higher-order address bits are provided by A2–A31. Lower-order address in the form of BE0#–BE3# directly provides linear selects for the four bytes of the 32-bit data bus. Physical operand size information is thereby implicitly provided each bus cycle in the most usable form.

Byte Enable outputs BE0#–BE3# are asserted when their associated data bus bytes are involved with the present bus cycle, as listed in Table 5-5. During a bus cycle, any possible pattern of contiguous, asserted Byte Enable outputs can occur, but never patterns having a negated Byte Enable separating two or three asserted Enables.

Address bits A0 and A1 of the physical operand's base address can be created when necessary (for instance, for MULTIBUS® I or MULTIBUS® II interface), as a function of the lowest-order asserted Byte Enable. This is shown by Table 5-6. Logic to generate A0 and A1 is given by Figure 5-3.

Table 5-5. Byte Enables and Associated Data and Operand Bytes

Byte Enable Signal	Associated Data Bus Signals
BE0#	D0–D7 (byte 0—least significant)
BE1#	D8–D15 (byte 1)
BE2#	D16–D23 (byte 2)
BE3#	D24–D31 (byte 3—most significant)

Table 5-6. Generating A0–A31 from BE0#–BE3# and A2–A31

Intel386™ DX Address Signals						
A31 .... A2			BE3#	BE2#	BE1#	BE0#
Physical Base Address						
A31 .... A2	A1	A0				
A31 .... A2	0	0	X	X	X	Low
A31 .... A2	0	1	X	X	Low	High
A31 .... A2	1	0	X	Low	High	High
A31 .... A2	1	1	Low	High	High	High

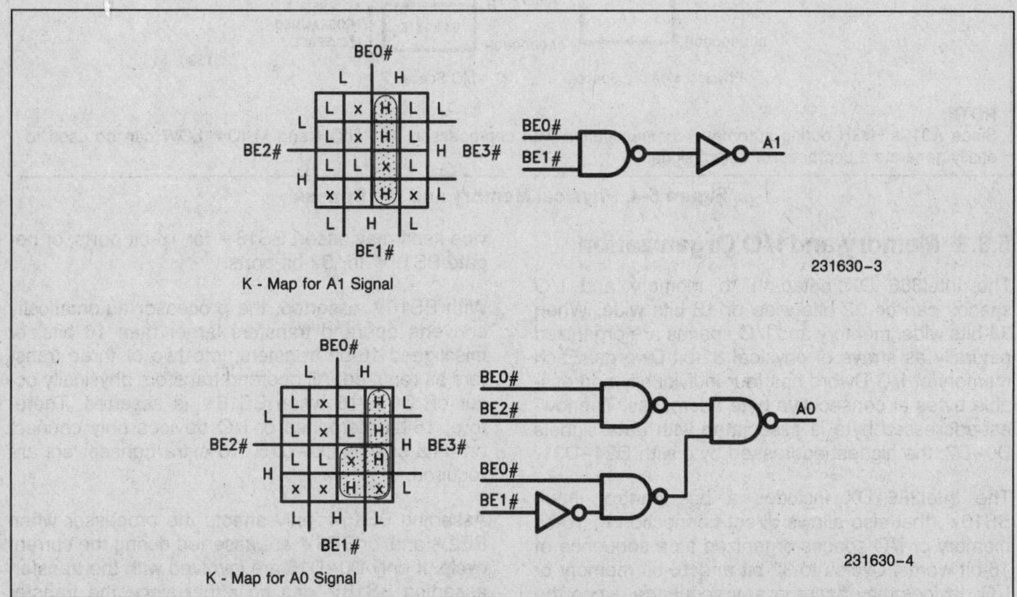

Figure 5-3. Logic to Generate A0, A1 from BE0#–BE3#

Each bus cycle is composed of at least two bus states. Each bus state requires one processor clock period. Additional bus states added to a single bus cycle are called wait states. See **5.4 Bus Functional Description**.

Since a bus cycle requires a minimum of two bus states (equal to two processor clock periods), data can be transferred between external devices and the Intel386 DX at a maximum rate of one 4-byte Dword every two processor clock periods, for a maximum bus bandwidth of 66 megabytes/second (Intel386 DX operating at 33 MHz processor clock rate).

5.3.2 Memory and I/O Spaces

Bus cycles may access physical memory space or I/O space. Peripheral devices in the system may either be memory-mapped, or I/O-mapped, or both. As shown in Figure 5-4, physical memory addresses range from 00000000H to FFFFFFFFH (4 gigabytes) and I/O addresses from 00000000H to 0000FFFFH (64 kilobytes) for programmed I/O. Note the I/O addresses used by the automatic I/O cycles for coprocessor communication are 800000F8H to 800000FFH, beyond the address range of programmed I/O, to allow easy generation of a coprocessor chip select signal using the A31 and M/IO# signals.

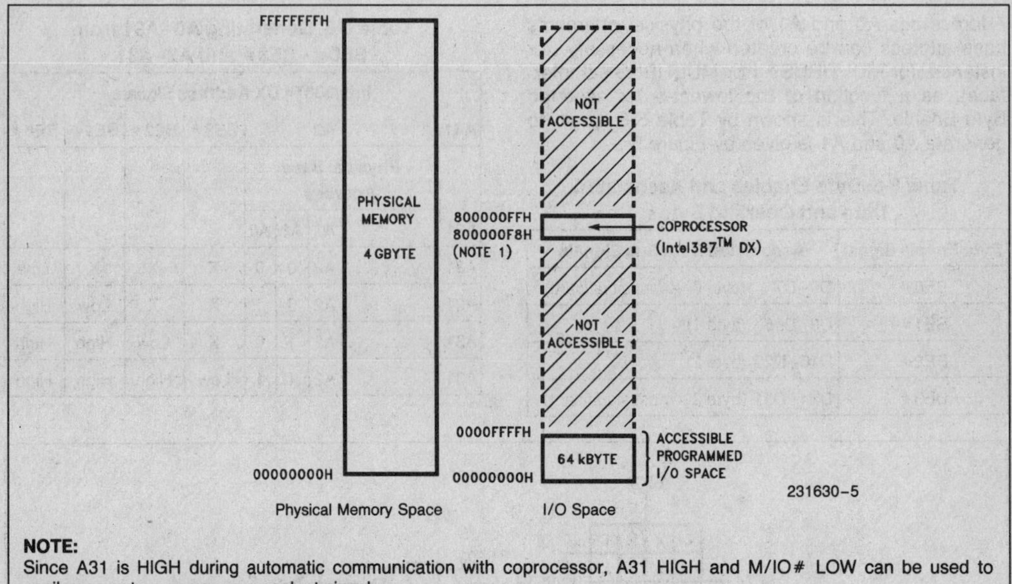

NOTE:
Since A31 is HIGH during automatic communication with coprocessor, A31 HIGH and M/IO# LOW can be used to easily generate a coprocessor select signal.

Figure 5-4. Physical Memory and I/O Spaces

5.3.3 Memory and I/O Organization

The Intel386 DX datapath to memory and I/O spaces can be 32 bits wide or 16 bits wide. When 32-bits wide, memory and I/O spaces are organized naturally as arrays of physical 32-bit Dwords. Each memory or I/O Dword has four individually addressable bytes at consecutive byte addresses. The lowest-addressed byte is associated with data signals D0–D7; the highest-addressed byte with D24–D31.

The Intel386 DX includes a bus control input, BS16#, that also allows direct connection to 16-bit memory or I/O spaces organized as a sequence of 16-bit words. Cycles to 32-bit and 16-bit memory or I/O devices may occur in any sequence, since the BS16# control is sampled during each bus cycle. See **5.3.4 Dynamic Data Bus Sizing**. The Byte Enable signals, BE0#–BE3#, allow byte granularity when addressing any memory or I/O structure, whether 32 or 16 bits wide.

5.3.4 Dynamic Data Bus Sizing

Dynamic data bus sizing is a feature allowing direct processor connection to 32-bit or 16-bit data buses for memory or I/O. A single processor may connect to both size buses. Transfers to or from 32- or 16-bit ports are supported by dynamically determining the bus width during each bus cycle. During each bus cycle an address decoding circuit or the slave device itself may assert BS16# for 16-bit ports, or negate BS16# for 32-bit ports.

With BS16# asserted, the processor automatically converts operand transfers larger than 16 bits, or misaligned 16-bit transfers, into two or three transfers as required. All operand transfers physically occur on D0–D15 when BS16# is asserted. Therefore, 16-bit memories or I/O devices only connect on data signals D0–D15. No extra transceivers are required.

Asserting BS16# only affects the processor when BE2# and/or BE3# are asserted during the current cycle. If only D0–D15 are involved with the transfer, asserting BS16# has no affect since the transfer can proceed normally over a 16-bit bus whether BS16# is asserted or not. In other words, asserting BS16# has no effect when only the lower half of the bus is involved with the current cycle.

There are two types of situations where the processor is affected by asserting BS16#, depending on which Byte Enables are asserted during the current bus cycle:

Upper Half Only:
Only BE2# and/or BE3# asserted.

Upper and Lower Half:
At least BE1#, BE2# asserted (and perhaps also BE0# and/or BE3#).

Effect of asserting BS16# during "upper half only" read cycles:

Asserting BS16# during "upper half only" reads causes the Intel386 DX to read data on the lower 16 bits of the data bus and ignore data on the upper 16 bits of the data bus. Data that would have been read from D16–D31 (as indicated by BE2# and BE3#) will instead be read from D0–D15 respectively.

Effect of asserting BS16# during "upper half only" write cycles:

Asserting BS16# during "upper half only" writes does not affect the Intel386 DX. When only BE2# and/or BE3# are asserted during a write cycle the Intel386 DX always duplicates data signals D16–D31 onto D0–D15 (see Table 5-1). Therefore, no further Intel386 DX action is required to perform these writes on 32-bit or 16-bit buses.

Effect of asserting BS16# during "upper and lower half" read cycles:

Asserting BS16# during "upper and lower half" reads causes the processor to perform two 16-bit read cycles for complete physical operand transfer. Bytes 0 and 1 (as indicated by BE0# and BE1#) are read on the first cycle using D0–D15. Bytes 2 and 3 (as indicated by BE2# and BE3#) are read during the second cycle, again using D0–D15. D16–D31 are ignored during both 16-bit cycles. BE0# and BE1# are always negated during the second 16-bit cycle (See **Figure 5-14, cycles 2 and 2a**).

Effect of asserting BS16# during "upper and lower half" write cycles:

Asserting BS16# during "upper and lower half" writes causes the Intel386 DX to perform two 16-bit write cycles for complete physical operand transfer. All bytes are available the first write cycle allowing external hardware to receive Bytes 0 and 1 (as indicated by BE0# and BE1#) using D0–D15. On the second cycle the Intel386 DX duplicates Bytes 2 and 3 on D0–D15 and Bytes 2 and 3 (as indicated by BE2# and BE3#) are written using D0–D15. BE0# and BE1# are always negated during the second 16-bit cycle. BS16# must be asserted during the second 16-bit cycle. See **Figure 5-14, cycles 1 and 1a.**

5.3.5 Interfacing with 32- and 16-Bit Memories

In 32-bit-wide physical memories such as Figure 5-5, each physical Dword begins at a byte address that is a multiple of 4. A2–A31 are directly used as a Dword select and BE0#–BE3# as byte selects. BS16# is negated for all bus cycles involving the 32-bit array.

When 16-bit-wide physical arrays are included in the system, as in Figure 5-6, each 16-bit physical word begins at a address that is a multiple of 2. Note the address is decoded, to assert BS16# only during bus cycles involving the 16-bit array. (If desiring to

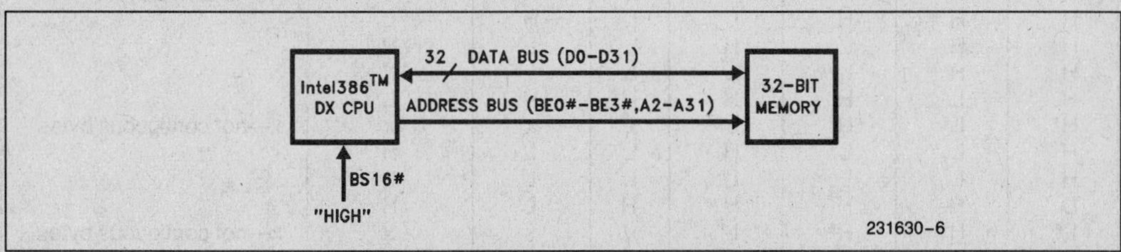

Figure 5-5. Intel386™ DX with 32-Bit Memory

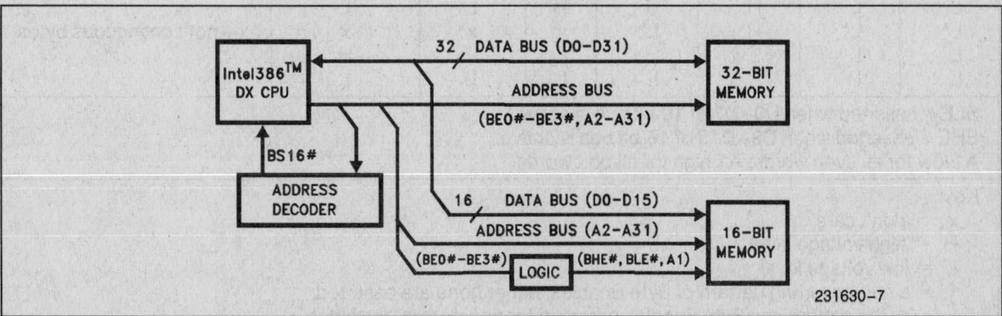

Figure 5-6. Intel386™ DX with 32-Bit and 16-Bit Memory

use pipelined address with 16-bit memories then BE0#-BE3# and W/R# are also decoded to determine when BS16# should be asserted. See **5.4.3.6 Pipelined Address with Dynamic Data Bus Sizing.**)

A2-A31 are directly usable for addressing 32-bit and 16-bit devices. To address 16-bit devices, A1 and two byte enable signals are also needed.

To generate an A1 signal and two Byte Enable signals for 16-bit access, BE0#-BE3# should be decoded as in Table 5-7. Note certain combinations of BE0#-BE3# are never generated by the Intel386 DX, leading to "don't care" conditions in the decoder. Any BE0#-BE3# decoder, such as Figure 5-7, may use the non-occurring BE0#-BE3# combinations to its best advantage.

5.3.6 Operand Alignment

With the flexibility of memory addressing on the Intel386 DX, it is possible to transfer a logical operand that spans more than one physical Dword or word of memory or I/O. Examples are 32-bit Dword operands beginning at addresses not evenly divisible by 4, or a 16-bit word operand split between two physical Dwords of the memory array.

Operand alignment and data bus size dictate when multiple bus cycles are required. Table 5-8 describes the transfer cycles generated for all combinations of logical operand lengths, alignment, and data bus sizing. When multiple bus cycles are required to transfer a multi-byte logical operand, the highest-order bytes are transferred first (but if BS16# asserted requires two 16-bit cycles be performed, that part of the transfer is low-order first).

5.4 BUS FUNCTIONAL DESCRIPTION

5.4.1 Introduction

The Intel386 DX has separate, parallel buses for data and address. The data bus is 32-bits in width, and bidirectional. The address bus provides a 32-bit value using 30 signals for the 30 upper-order address bits and 4 Byte Enable signals to directly indicate the active bytes. These buses are interpreted and controlled via several associated definition or control signals.

Table 5-7. Generating A1, BHE# and BLE# for Addressing 16-Bit Devices

Intel386™ DX Signals				16-Bit Bus Signals			Comments
BE3#	BE2#	BE1#	BE0#	A1	BHE#	BLE# (A0)	
H*	H*	H*	H*	x	x	x	x—no active bytes
H	H	H	L	L	H	L	
H	H	L	H	L	L	H	
H	H	L	L	L	L	L	
H	L	H	H	H	H	L	
H*	L*	H*	L*	x	x	x	x—not contiguous bytes
H	L	L	H	L	L	H	
H	L	L	L	L	L	L	
L	H	H	H	H	L	H	
L*	H*	H*	L*	x	x	x	x—not contiguous bytes
L*	H*	L*	H*	x	x	x	x—not contiguous bytes
L*	H*	L*	L*	x	x	x	x—not contiguous bytes
L	L	H	H	H	L	L	
L*	L*	H*	L*	x	x	x	x—not continguous bytes
L	L	L	H	L	L	H	
L	L	L	L	L	L	L	

BLE# asserted when D0-D7 of 16-bit bus is active.
BHE# asserted when D8-D15 of 16-bit bus is active.
A1 low for all even words; A1 high for all odd words.

Key:
x = don't care
H = high voltage level
L = low voltage level
* = a non-occurring pattern of Byte Enables; either none are asserted, or the pattern has Byte Enables asserted for non-contiguous bytes

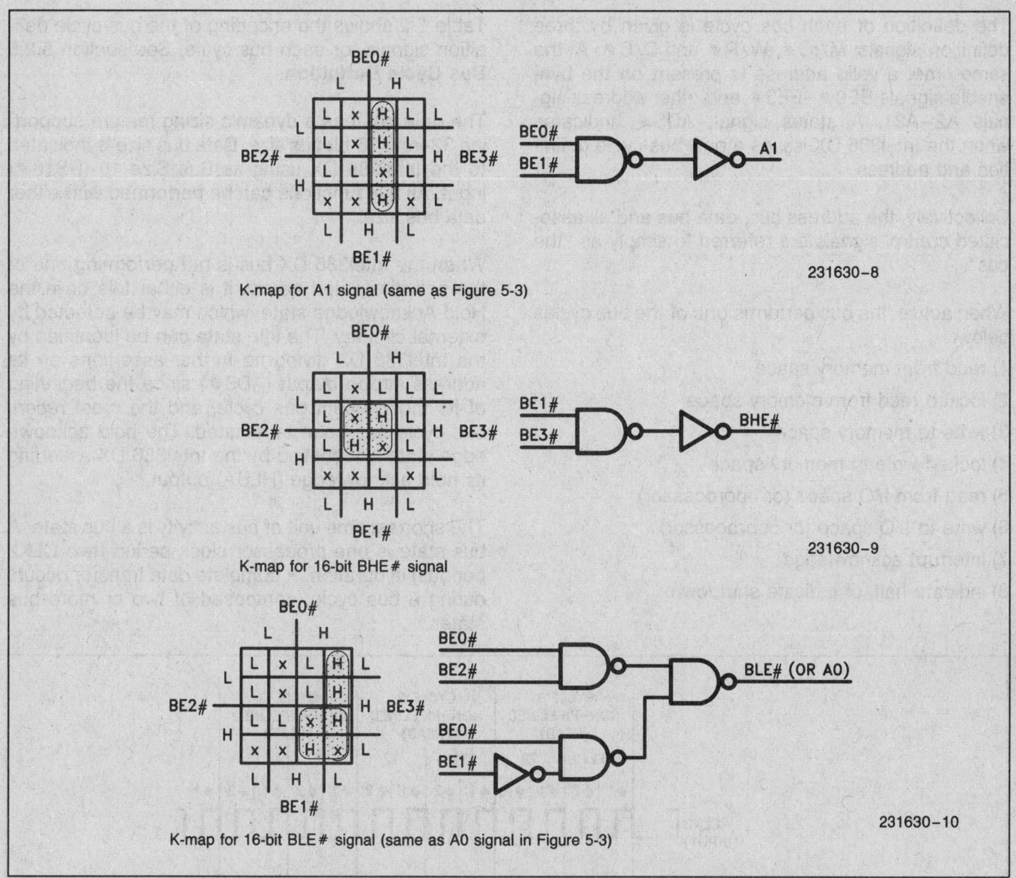

Figure 5-7. Logic to Generate A1, BHE# and BLE# for 16-Bit Buses

Table 5-8. Transfer Bus Cycles for Bytes, Words and Dwords

	Byte-Length of Logical Operand								
	1	2				4			
Physical Byte Address in Memory (low-order bits)	xx	00	01	10	11	00	01	10	11
Transfer Cycles over 32-Bit Data Bus	b	w	w	w	hb,* lb	d	hb l3	hw, lw	h3, lb
Transfer Cycles over 16-Bit Data Bus	b	w	lb, hb	w	hb, lb	lw, hw	hb, lb, mw	hw, lw	mw, hb, lb

Key: b = byte transfer
w = word transfer
l = low-order portion
m = mid-order portion
x = don't care
(shaded) = BS16# asserted causes second bus cycle

3 = 3-byte transfer
d = Dword transfer
h = high-order portion

*For this case, 8086, 8088, 80186, 80188, 80286 transfer lb first, then hb.

The definition of each bus cycle is given by three definition signals: M/IO#, W/R# and D/C#. At the same time, a valid address is present on the byte enable signals BE0#–BE3# and other address signals A2–A31. A status signal, ADS#, indicates when the Intel386 DX issues a new bus cycle definition and address.

Collectively, the address bus, data bus and all associated control signals are referred to simply as "the bus".

When active, the bus performs one of the bus cycles below:

1) read from memory space
2) locked read from memory space
3) write to memory space
4) locked write to memory space
5) read from I/O space (or coprocessor)
6) write to I/O space (or coprocessor)
7) interrupt acknowledge
8) indicate halt, or indicate shutdown

Table 5-2 shows the encoding of the bus cycle definition signals for each bus cycle. See section **5.2.5 Bus Cycle Definition**.

The data bus has a dynamic sizing feature supporting 32- and 16-bit bus size. Data bus size is indicated to the Intel386 DX using its Bus Size 16 (BS16#) input. All bus functions can be performed with either data bus size.

When the Intel386 DX bus is not performing one of the activities listed above, it is either Idle or in the Hold Acknowledge state, which may be detected by external circuitry. The idle state can be identified by the Intel386 DX giving no further assertions on its address strobe output (ADS#) since the beginning of its most recent bus cycle, and the most recent bus cycle has been terminated. The hold acknowledge state is identified by the Intel386 DX asserting its hold acknowledge (HLDA) output.

The shortest time unit of bus activity is a bus state. A bus state is one processor clock period (two CLK2 periods) in duration. A complete data transfer occurs during a bus cycle, composed of two or more bus states.

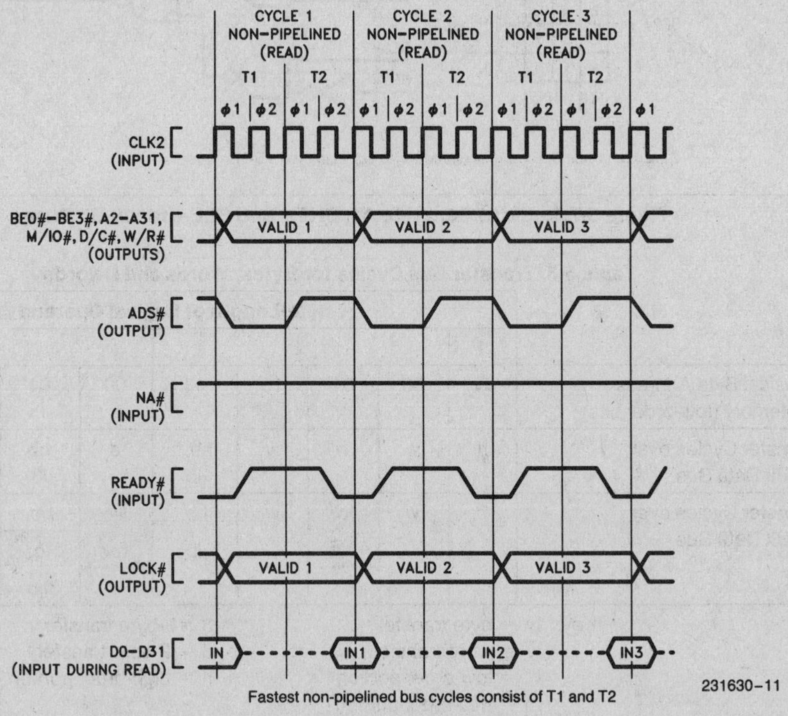

CYCLE 1 NON-PIPELINED (READ) | CYCLE 2 NON-PIPELINED (READ) | CYCLE 3 NON-PIPELINED (READ)

T1 T2 T1 T2 T1 T2

φ1 φ2 φ1 φ2 φ1 φ2 φ1 φ2 φ1 φ2 φ1 φ2 φ1

CLK2 (INPUT)

BE0#–BE3#, A2–A31, M/IO#, D/C#, W/R# (OUTPUTS): VALID 1, VALID 2, VALID 3

ADS# (OUTPUT)

NA# (INPUT)

READY# (INPUT)

LOCK# (OUTPUT): VALID 1, VALID 2, VALID 3

D0–D31 (INPUT DURING READ): IN, IN1, IN2, IN3

Fastest non-pipelined bus cycles consist of T1 and T2

231630–11

Figure 5-8. Fastest Read Cycles with Non-Pipelined Address Timing

The fastest Intel386 DX bus cycle requires only two bus states. For example, three consecutive bus read cycles, each consisting of two bus states, are shown by Figure 5-8. The bus states in each cycle are named **T1** and **T2**. Any memory or I/O address may be accessed by such a two-state bus cycle, if the external hardware is fast enough. The high-bandwidth, two-clock bus cycle realizes the full potential of fast main memory, or cache memory.

Every bus cycle continues until it is acknowledged by the external system hardware, using the Intel386 DX READY# input. Acknowledging the bus cycle at the end of the first T2 results in the shortest bus cycle, requiring only T1 and T2. If READY# is not immediately asserted, however, T2 states are repeated indefinitely until the READY# input is sampled asserted.

5.4.2 Address Pipelining

The address pipelining option provides a choice of bus cycle timings. Pipelined or non-pipelined address timing is selectable on a cycle-by-cycle basis with the Next Address (NA#) input.

When address pipelining is not selected, the current address and bus cycle definition remain stable throughout the bus cycle.

When address pipelining is selected, the address (BE0#–BE3#, A2–A31) and definition (W/R#, D/C# and M/IO#) of the next cycle are available before the end of the current cycle. To signal their availability, the Intel386 DX address status output (ADS#) is also asserted. Figure 5-9 illustrates the fastest read cycles with pipelined address timing.

Note from Figure 5-9 the fastest bus cycles using pipelined address require only two bus states, named **T1P** and **T2P**. Therefore cycles with pipelined address timing allow the same data bandwidth as non-pipelined cycles, but address-to-data access time is increased compared to that of a non-pipelined cycle.

By increasing the address-to-data access time, pipelined address timing reduces wait state requirements. For example, if one wait state is required with non-pipelined address timing, no wait states would be required with pipelined address.

4

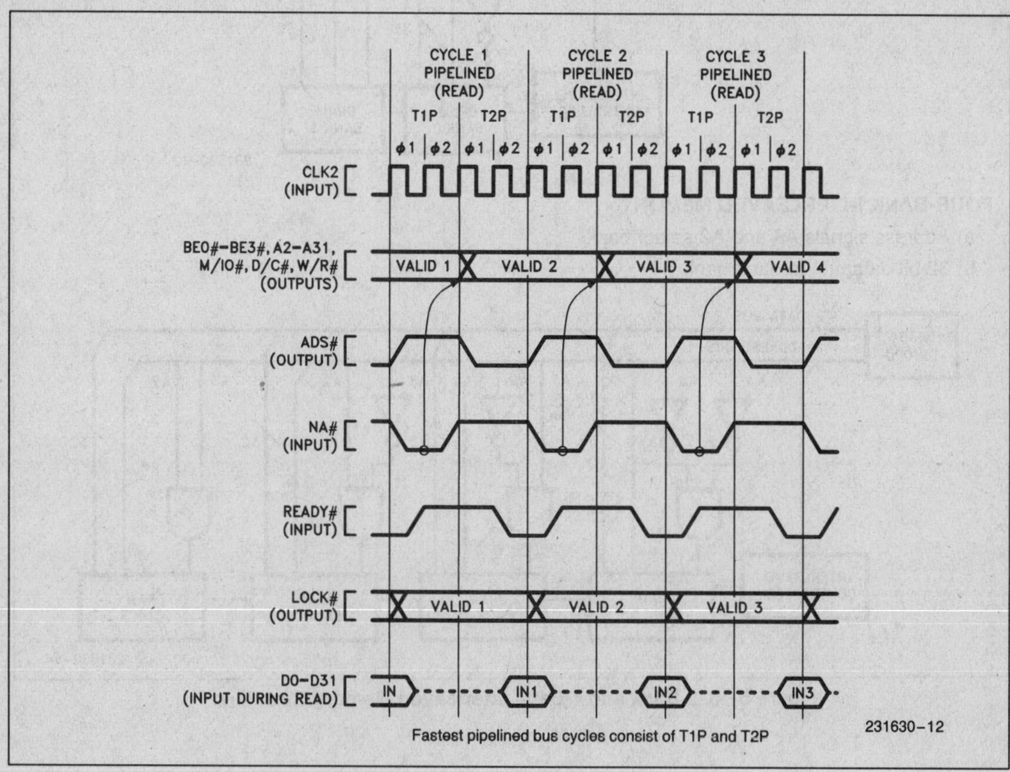

Figure 5-9. Fastest Read Cycles with Pipelined Address Timing

Pipelined address timing is useful in typical systems having address latches. In those systems, once an address has been latched, pipelined availability of the next address allows decoding circuitry to generate chip selects (and other necessary select signals) in advance, so selected devices are accessed immediately when the next cycle begins. In other words, the decode time for the next cycle can be overlapped with the end of the current cycle.

If a system contains a memory structure of two or more interleaved memory banks, pipelined address timing potentially allows even more overlap of activity. This is true when the interleaved memory controller is designed to allow the next memory operation to begin in one memory bank while the current bus cycle is still activating another memory bank. Figure 5-10 shows the general structure of the Intel386 DX with 2-bank and 4-bank interleaved memory. Note each memory bank of the interleaved memory has full data bus width (32-bit data width typically, unless 16-bit bus size is selected).

Further details of pipelined address timing are given in **5.4.3.4 Pipelined Address, 5.4.3.5 Initiating and Maintaining Pipelined Address, 5.4.3.6 Pipelined Address with Dynamic Bus Sizing,** and **5.4.3.7 Maximum Pipelined Address Usage with 16-Bit Bus Size.**

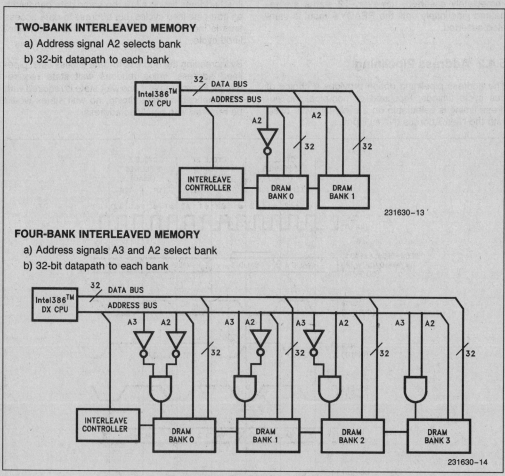

TWO-BANK INTERLEAVED MEMORY

a) Address signal A2 selects bank

b) 32-bit datapath to each bank

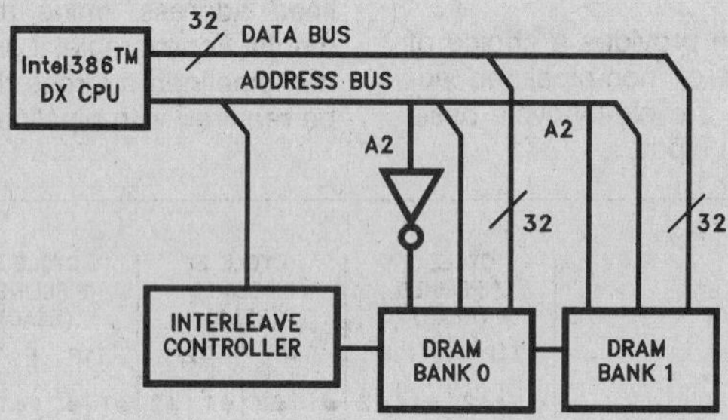

231630–13

FOUR-BANK INTERLEAVED MEMORY

a) Address signals A3 and A2 select bank

b) 32-bit datapath to each bank

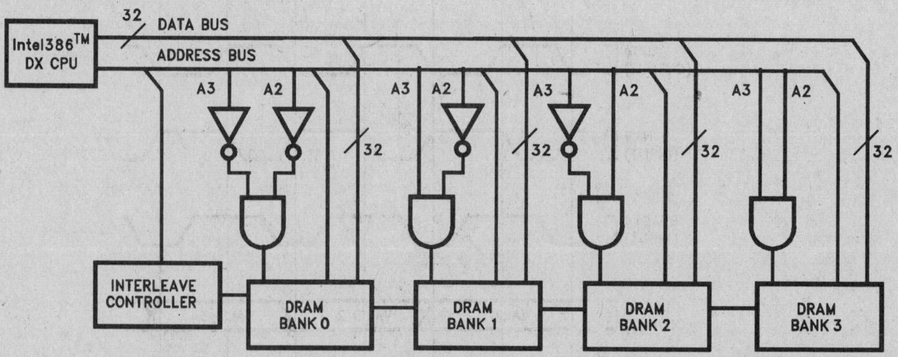

231630–14

Figure 5-10. 2-Bank and 4-Bank Interleaved Memory Structure

5.4.3 Read and Write Cycles

5.4.3.1 INTRODUCTION

Data transfers occur as a result of bus cycles, classified as read or write cycles. During read cycles, data is transferred from an external device to the processor. During write cycles data is transferred in the other direction, from the processor to an external device.

Two choices of address timing are dynamically selectable: non-pipelined, or pipelined. After a bus idle state, the processor always uses non-pipelined address timing. However, the NA# (Next Address) input may be asserted to select pipelined address timing for the next bus cycle. When pipelining is selected and the Intel386 DX has a bus request pending internally, the address and definition of the next cycle is made available even before the current bus cycle is acknowledged by READY#. Generally, the NA# input is sampled each bus cycle to select the desired address timing for the next bus cycle.

Two choices of physical data bus width are dynamically selectable: 32 bits, or 16 bits. Generally, the BS16# (Bus Size 16) input is sampled near the end of the bus cycle to confirm the physical data bus size applicable to the current cycle. Negation of BS16# indicates a 32-bit size, and assertion indicates a 16-bit bus size.

If 16-bit bus size is indicated, the Intel386 DX automatically responds as required to complete the transfer on a 16-bit data bus. Depending on the size and alignment of the operand, another 16-bit bus cycle may be required. Table 5-7 provides all details. When necessary, the Intel386 DX performs an additional 16-bit bus cycle, using D0–D15 in place of D16–D31.

Terminating a read cycle or write cycle, like any bus cycle, requires acknowledging the cycle by asserting the READY# input. Until acknowledged, the processor inserts wait states into the bus cycle, to allow adjustment for the speed of any external device. External hardware, which has decoded the address and bus cycle type asserts the READY# input at the appropriate time.

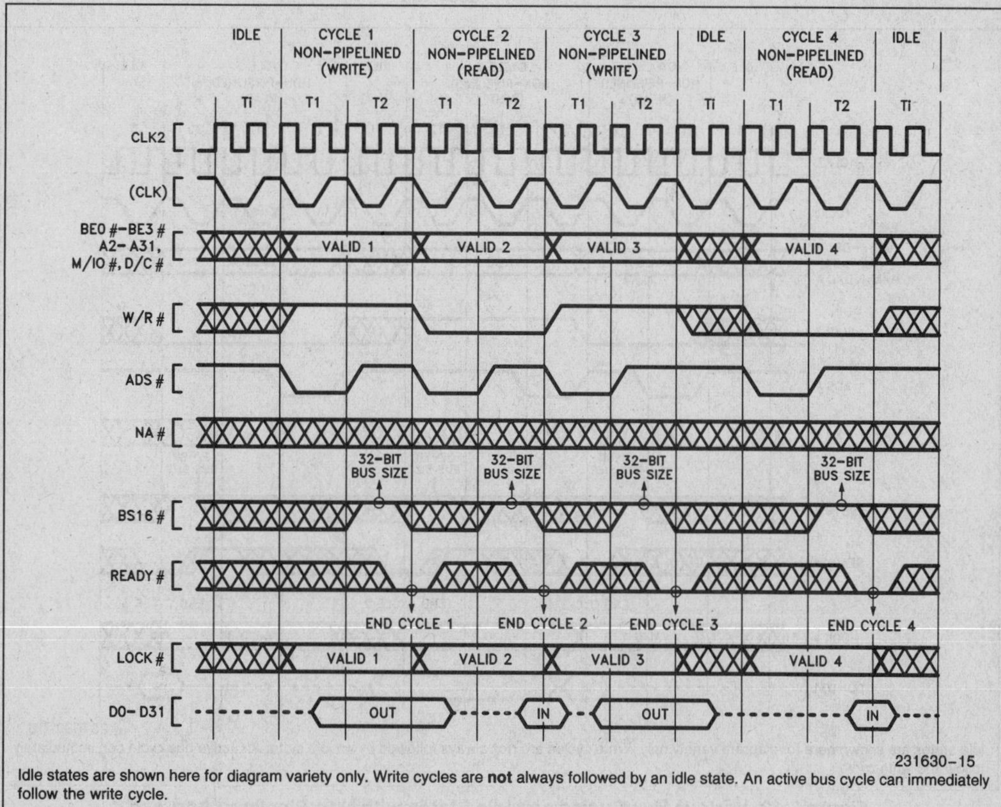

Idle states are shown here for diagram variety only. Write cycles are **not** always followed by an idle state. An active bus cycle can immediately follow the write cycle.

Figure 5-11. Various Bus Cycles and Idle States with Non-Pipelined Address (zero wait states)

At the end of the second bus state within the bus cycle, READY# is sampled. At that time, if external hardware acknowledges the bus cycle by asserting READY#, the bus cycle terminates as shown in Figure 5-11. If READY# is negated as in Figure 5-12, the cycle continues another bus state (a wait state) and READY# is sampled again at the end of that state. This continues indefinitely until the cycle is acknowledged by READY# asserted.

When the current cycle is acknowledged, the Intel386 DX terminates it. When a read cycle is acknowledged, the Intel386 DX latches the information present at its data pins. When a write cycle is acknowledged, the Intel386 DX write data remains valid throughout phase one of the next bus state, to provide write data hold time.

5.4.3.2 NON-PIPELINED ADDRESS

Any bus cycle may be performed with non-pipelined address timing. For example, Figure 5-11 shows a mixture of read and write cycles with non-pipelined address timing. Figure 5-11 shows the fastest possible cycles with non-pipelined address have two bus states per bus cycle. The states are named T1 and T2. In phase one of the T1, the address signals and bus cycle definition signals are driven valid, and to signal their availability, address status (ADS#) is simultaneously asserted.

During read or write cycles, the data bus behaves as follows. If the cycle is a read, the Intel386 DX floats its data signals to allow driving by the external device being addressed. **The Intel386 DX requires that all data bus pins be at a valid logic state (high or low) at the end of each read cycle, when READY# is asserted, even if all byte enables are not asserted. The system MUST be designed to meet this requirement.** If the cycle is a write, data signals are driven by the Intel386 DX beginning in phase two of T1 until phase one of the bus state following cycle acknowledgment.

Figure 5-12 illustrates non-pipelined bus cycles with one wait added to cycles 2 and 3. READY# is sampled negated at the end of the first T2 in cycles 2 and 3. Therefore cycles 2 and 3 have T2 repeated. At the end of the second T2, READY# is sampled asserted.

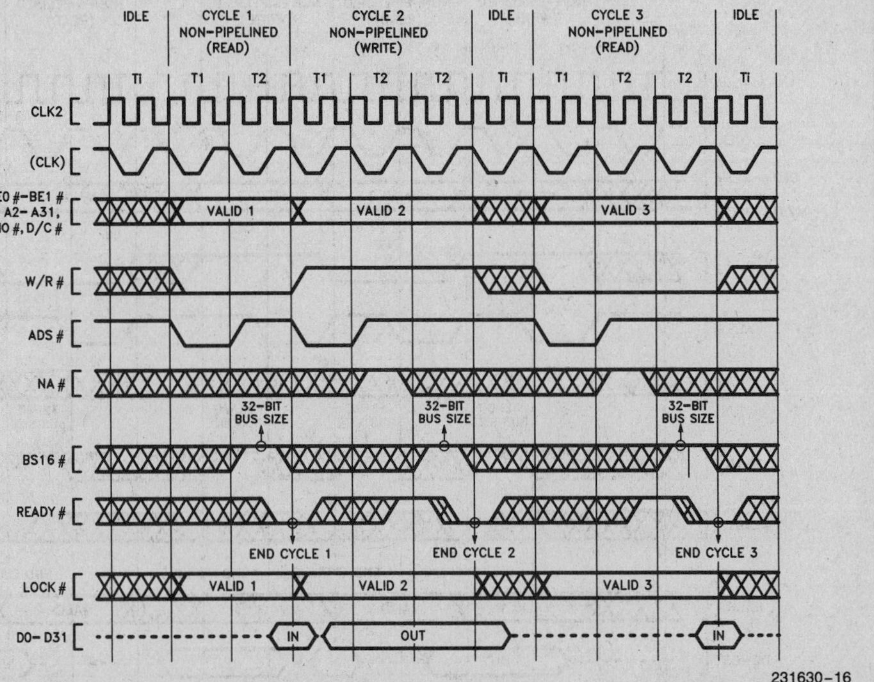

231630–16

Idle states are shown here for diagram variety only. Write cycles are **not** always followed by an idle state. An active bus cycle can immediately follow the write cycle.

Figure 5-12. Various Bus Cycles and Idle States with Non-Pipelined Address (various number of wait states)

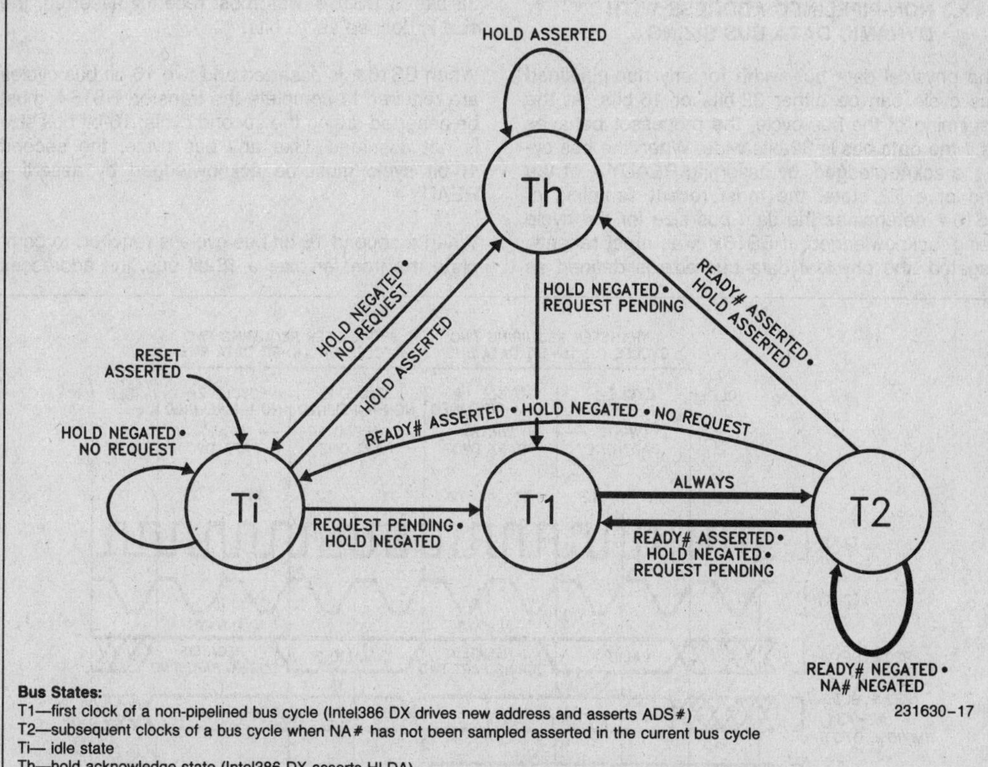

Bus States:
T1—first clock of a non-pipelined bus cycle (Intel386 DX drives new address and asserts ADS#)
T2—subsequent clocks of a bus cycle when NA# has not been sampled asserted in the current bus cycle
Ti— idle state
Th—hold acknowledge state (Intel386 DX asserts HLDA)
The fastest bus cycle consists of two states: T1 and T2.
Four basic bus states describe bus operation when not using pipelined address. These states do include BS16# usage for 32-bit and 16-bit bus size. If asserting BS16# requires a second 16-bit bus cycle to be performed, it is performed before HOLD asserted is acknowledged.

Figure 5-13. Intel386™ DX Bus States (not using pipelined address)

When address pipelining is not used, the address and bus cycle definition remain valid during all wait states. When wait states are added and you desire to maintain non-pipelined address timing, it is necessary to negate NA# during each T2 state except the last one, as shown in Figure 5-12 cycles 2 and 3. If NA# is sampled asserted during a T2 other than the last one, the next state would be T2I (for pipelined address) or T2P (for pipelined address) instead of another T2 (for non-pipelined address).

When address pipelining is not used, the bus states and transitions are completely illustrated by Figure 5-13. The bus transitions between four possible states: T1, T2, Ti, and Th. Bus cycles consist of T1 and T2, with T2 being repeated for wait states. Otherwise, the bus may be idle, in the Ti state, or in hold acknowledge, the Th state.

When address pipelining is not used, the bus state diagram is as shown in Figure 5-13. When the bus is idle it is in state Ti. Bus cycles always begin with T1. T1 always leads to T2. If a bus cycle is not acknowledged during T2 and NA# is negated, T2 is repeated. When a cycle is acknowledged during T2, the following state will be T1 of the next bus cycle if a bus request is pending internally, or Ti if there is no bus request pending, or Th if the HOLD input is being asserted.

The bus state diagram in Figure 5-13 also applies to the use of BS16#. If the Intel386 DX makes internal adjustments for 16-bit bus size, the adjustments do not affect the external bus states. If an additional 16-bit bus cycle is required to complete a transfer on a 16-bit bus, it also follows the state transitions shown in Figure 5-13.

Use of pipelined address allows the Intel386 DX to enter three additional bus states not shown in Figure 5-13. Figure 5-20 in **5.4.3.4 Pipelined Address** is the complete bus state diagram, including pipelined address cycles.

4

5.4.3.3 NON-PIPELINED ADDRESS WITH DYNAMIC DATA BUS SIZING

The physical data bus width for any non-pipelined bus cycle can be either 32-bits or 16-bits. At the beginning of the bus cycle, the processor behaves as if the data bus is 32-bits wide. When the bus cycle is acknowledged, by asserting READY# at the end of a T2 state, the most recent sampling of BS16# determines the data bus size for the cycle being acknowledged. If BS16# was most recently negated, the physical data bus size is defined as 32 bits. If BS16# was most recently asserted, the size is defined as 16 bits.

When BS16# is asserted and two 16-bit bus cycles are required to complete the transfer, BS16# must be asserted during the second cycle; 16-bit bus size is not assumed. Like any bus cycle, the second 16-bit cycle must be acknowledged by asserting READY#.

When a second 16-bit bus cycle is required to complete the transfer over a 16-bit bus, the addresses

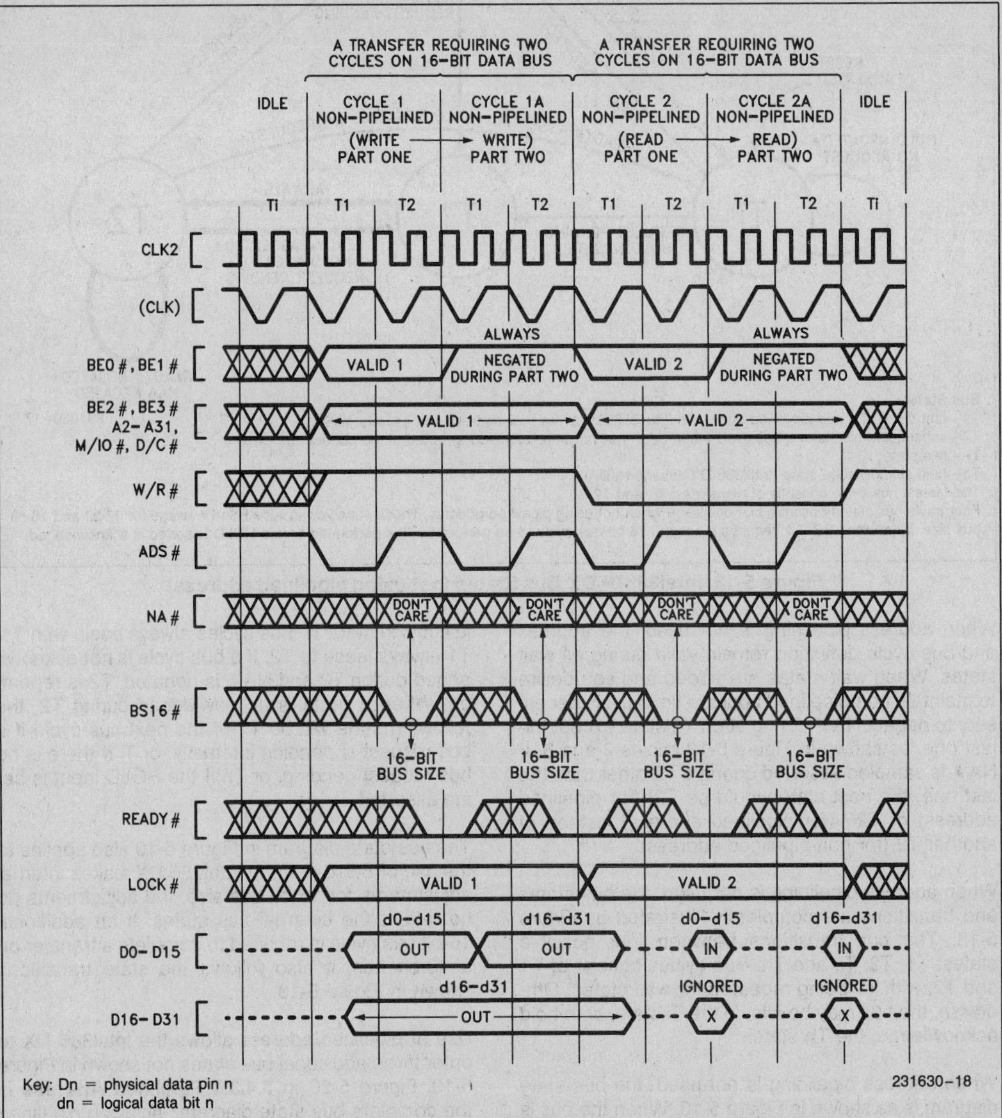

Key: Dn = physical data pin n
dn = logical data bit n

231630–18

Figure 5-14. Asserting BS16# (zero wait states, non-pipelined address)

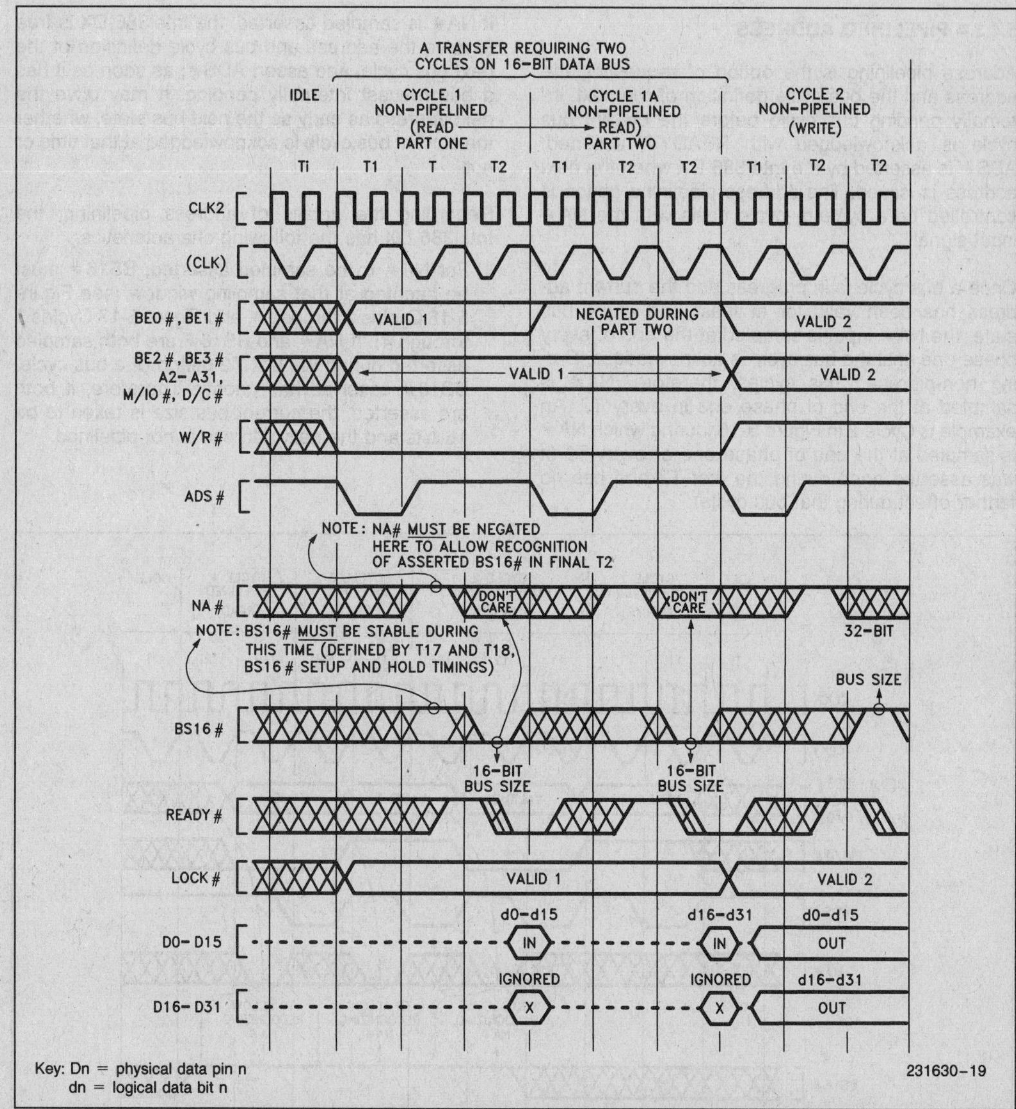

Figure 5-15. Asserting BS16# (one wait state, non-pipelined address)

generated for the two 16-bit bus cycles are closely related to each other. The addresses are the same except BE0# and BE1# are always negated for the second cycle. This is because data on D0–D15 was already transferred during the first 16-bit cycle.

Figures 5-14 and 5-15 show cases where assertion of BS16# requires a second 16-bit cycle for complete operand transfer. Figure 5-14 illustrates cycles without wait states. Figure 5-15 illustrates cycles with one wait state. In Figure 5-15 cycle 1, the bus cycle during which BS16# is asserted, note that NA# must be negated in the T2 state(s) prior to the last T2 state. This is to allow the recognition of BS16# asserted in the final T2 state. Also note that during this state BS16# must be stable (defined by t17 and t18, BS16# setup and hold timings), in order to prevent potential data corruption during split cycle reads. The logic state of BS16# during this time is not important. The relation of NA# and BS16# is given fully in **5.4.3.4 Pipelined Address**, but Figure 5-15 illustrates these precautions you need to know when using BS16# with non-pipelined address.

5.4.3.4 PIPELINED ADDRESS

Address pipelining is the option of requesting the address and the bus cycle definition of the next, internally pending bus cycle before the current bus cycle is acknowledged with READY# asserted. ADS# is asserted by the Intel386 DX when the next address is issued. The address pipelining option is controlled on a cycle-by-cycle basis with the NA# input signal.

Once a bus cycle is in progress and the current address has been valid for at least one entire bus state, the NA# input is sampled at the end of every phase one until the bus cycle is acknowledged. During non-pipelined bus cycles, therefore, NA# is sampled at the end of phase one in every T2. An example is Cycle 2 in Figure 5-16, during which NA# is sampled at the end of phase one of every T2 (it was asserted once during the first T2 and has no further effect during that bus cycle).

If NA# is sampled asserted, the Intel386 DX is free to drive the address and bus cycle definition of the next bus cycle, and assert ADS#, as soon as it has a bus request internally pending. It may drive the next address as early as the next bus state, whether the current bus cycle is acknowledged at that time or not.

Regarding the details of address pipelining, the Intel386 DX has the following characteristics:

1) For NA# to be sampled asserted, BS16# must be negated at that sampling window (see Figure 5-16 Cycles 2 through 4, and Figure 5-17 Cycles 1 through 4). If NA# and BS16# are both sampled asserted during the last T2 period of a bus cycle, BS16# asserted has priority. Therefore, if both are asserted, the current bus size is taken to be 16 bits and the next address is not pipelined.

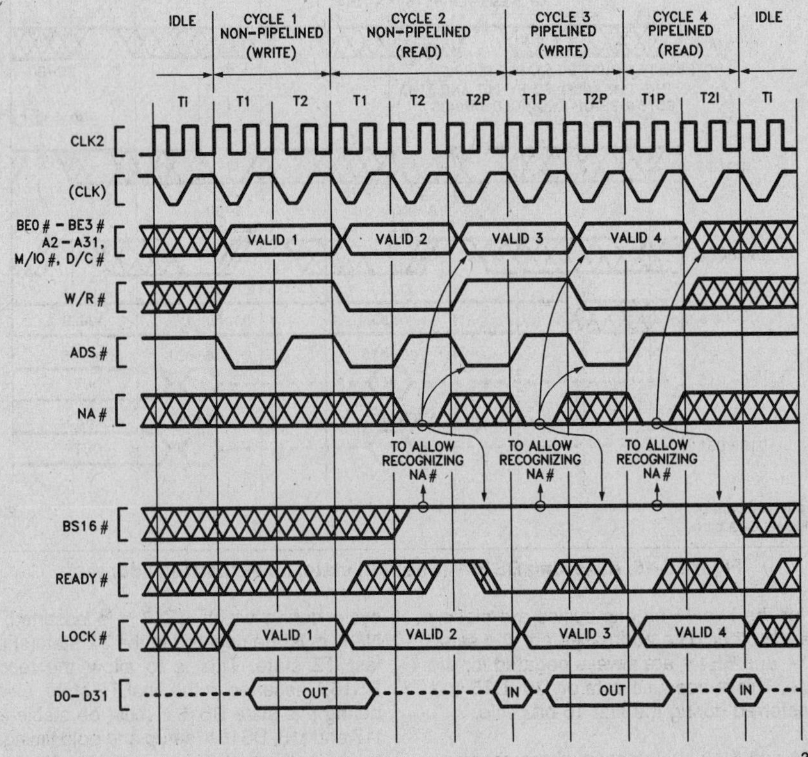

231630-20

Following any idle bus state (Ti), addresses are non-pipelined. Within non-pipelined bus cycles, NA# is only sampled during wait states. Therefore, to begin address pipelining during a group of non-pipelined bus cycles requires a non-pipelined cycle with at least one wait state (Cycle 2 above).

Figure 5-16. Transitioning to Pipelined Address During Burst of Bus Cycles

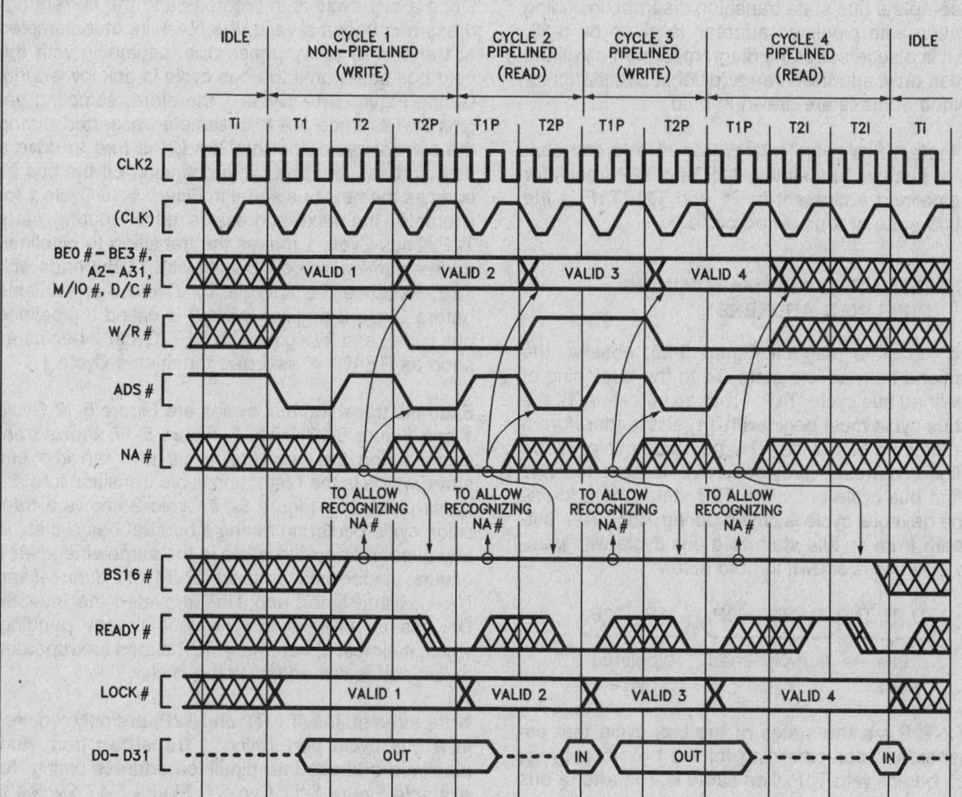

Following any idle bus state (Ti) the address is always non-pipelined and NA# is only sampled during wait states. To start address pipelining after an idle state requires a non-pipelined cycle with at least one wait state (cycle 1 above).
The pipelined cycles (2, 3, 4 above) are shown with various numbers of wait states.

Figure 5-17. Fastest Transition to Pipelined Address Following Idle Bus State

2) The next address may appear as early as the bus state after NA# was sampled asserted (see Figures 5-16 or 5-17). In that case, state T2P is entered immediately. However, when there is not an internal bus request already pending, the next address will not be available immediately after NA# is asserted and T2I is entered instead of T2P (see Figure 5-19 Cycle 3). Provided the current bus cycle isn't yet acknowledged by READY# asserted, T2P will be entered as soon as the Intel386 DX does drive the next address. External hardware should therefore observe the ADS# output as confirmation the next address is actually being driven on the bus.

3) Once NA# is sampled asserted, the Intel386 DX commits itself to the highest priority bus request that is pending internally. It can no longer perform another 16-bit transfer to the same address should BS16# be asserted externally, so thereafter must assume the current bus size is 32 bits. Therefore if NA# is sampled asserted within a bus cycle, BS16# must be negated thereafter in that bus cycle (see Figures 5-16, 5-17, 5-19). Consequently, do not assert NA# during bus cycles which must have BS16# driven asserted. See **5.4.3.6 Dynamic Bus Sizing with Pipelined Address.**

4) Any address which is validated by a pulse on the Intel386 DX ADS# output will remain stable on the address pins for at least two processor clock periods. The Intel386 DX cannot produce a new address more frequently than every two processor clock periods (see Figures 5-16, 5-17, 5-19).

5) Only the address and bus cycle definition of the very next bus cycle is available. The pipelining capability cannot look further than one bus cycle ahead (see Figure 5-19 Cycle 1).

The complete bus state transition diagram, including operation with pipelined address is given by 5-20. Note it is a superset of the diagram for non-pipelined address only, and the three additional bus states for pipelined address are drawn in bold.

The fastest bus cycle with pipelined address consists of just two bus states, T1P and T2P (recall for non-pipelined address it is T1 and T2). T1P is the first bus state of a pipelined cycle.

5.4.3.5 INITIATING AND MAINTAINING PIPELINED ADDRESS

Using the state diagram Figure 5-20, observe the transitions from an idle state, Ti, to the beginning of a pipelined bus cycle, T1P. From an idle state Ti, the first bus cycle must begin with T1, and is therefore a non-pipelined bus cycle. The next bus cycle will be pipelined, however, provided NA# is asserted and the first bus cycle ends in a T2P state (the address for the next bus cycle is driven during T2P). The fastest path from an idle state to a bus cycle with pipelined address is shown in bold below:

Ti, Ti, Ti	T1 - T2 - T2P,	T1P - T2P,
idle states	non-pipelined cycle	pipelined cycle

T1-T2-T2P are the states of the bus cycle that establishes address pipelining for the next bus cycle, which begins with T1P. The same is true after a bus hold state, shown below:

Th, Th, Th,	T1 - T2 - T2P,	T1P - T2P,
hold acknowledge states	non-pipelined cycle	pipelined cycle

The transition to pipelined address is shown functionally by Figure 5-17 Cycle 1. Note that Cycle 1 is used to transition into pipelined address timing for the subsequent Cycles 2, 3 and 4, which are pipelined. The NA# input is asserted at the appropriate time to select address pipelining for Cycles 2, 3 and 4.

Once a bus cycle is in progress and the current address has become valid, the NA# input is sampled at the end of every phase one, beginning with the next bus state, until the bus cycle is acknowledged. During Figure 5-17 Cycle 1 therefore, sampling begins in T2. Once NA# is sampled asserted during the current cycle, the Intel386 DX is free to drive a new address and bus cycle definition on the bus as early as the next bus state. In Figure 5-16 Cycle 1 for example, the next address is driven during state T2P. Thus Cycle 1 makes the transition to pipelined address timing, since it begins with T1 but ends with T2P. Because the address for Cycle 2 is available before Cycle 2 begins, Cycle 2 is called a pipelined bus cycle, and it begins with T1P. Cycle 2 begins as soon as READY# asserted terminates Cycle 1.

Example transition bus cycles are Figure 5-17 Cycle 1 and Figure 5-16 Cycle 2. Figure 5-17 shows transition during the very first cycle after an idle bus state, which is the fastest possible transition into address pipelining. Figure 5-16 Cycle 2 shows a transition cycle occurring during a burst of bus cycles. In any case, a transition cycle is the same whenever it occurs: it consists at least of T1, T2 (you assert NA# at that time), and T2P (provided the Intel386 DX has an internal bus request already pending, which it almost always has). T2P states are repeated if wait states are added to the cycle.

Note three states (T1, T2 and T2P) are only required in a bus cycle performing a **transition** from non-pipelined address into pipelined address timing, for example Figure 5-17 Cycle 1. Figure 5-17 Cycles 2, 3 and 4 show that address pipelining can be maintained with two-state bus cycles consisting only of T1P and T2P.

Once a pipelined bus cycle is in progress, pipelined timing is maintained for the next cycle by asserting NA# and detecting that the Intel386 DX enters T2P during the current bus cycle. The current bus cycle must end in state T2P for pipelining to be maintained in the next cycle. T2P is identified by the assertion of ADS#. Figures 5-16 and 5-17 however, each show pipelining ending after Cycle 4 because Cycle 4 ends in T2I. This indicates the Intel386 DX didn't have an internal bus request prior to the acknowledgement of Cycle 4. If a cycle ends with a T2 or T2I, the next cycle will not be pipelined.

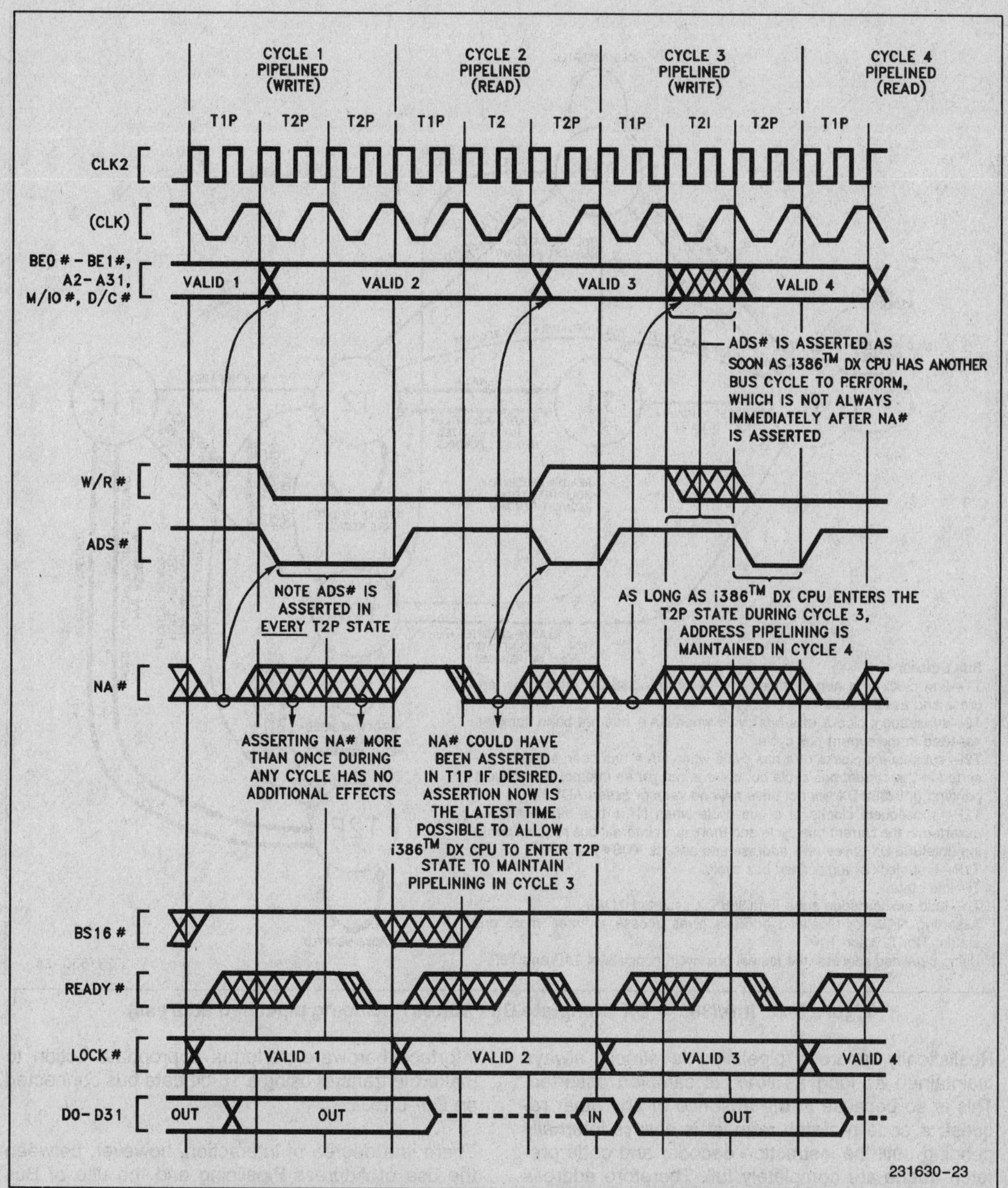

Figure 5-19. Details of Address Pipelining During Cycles with Wait States

4

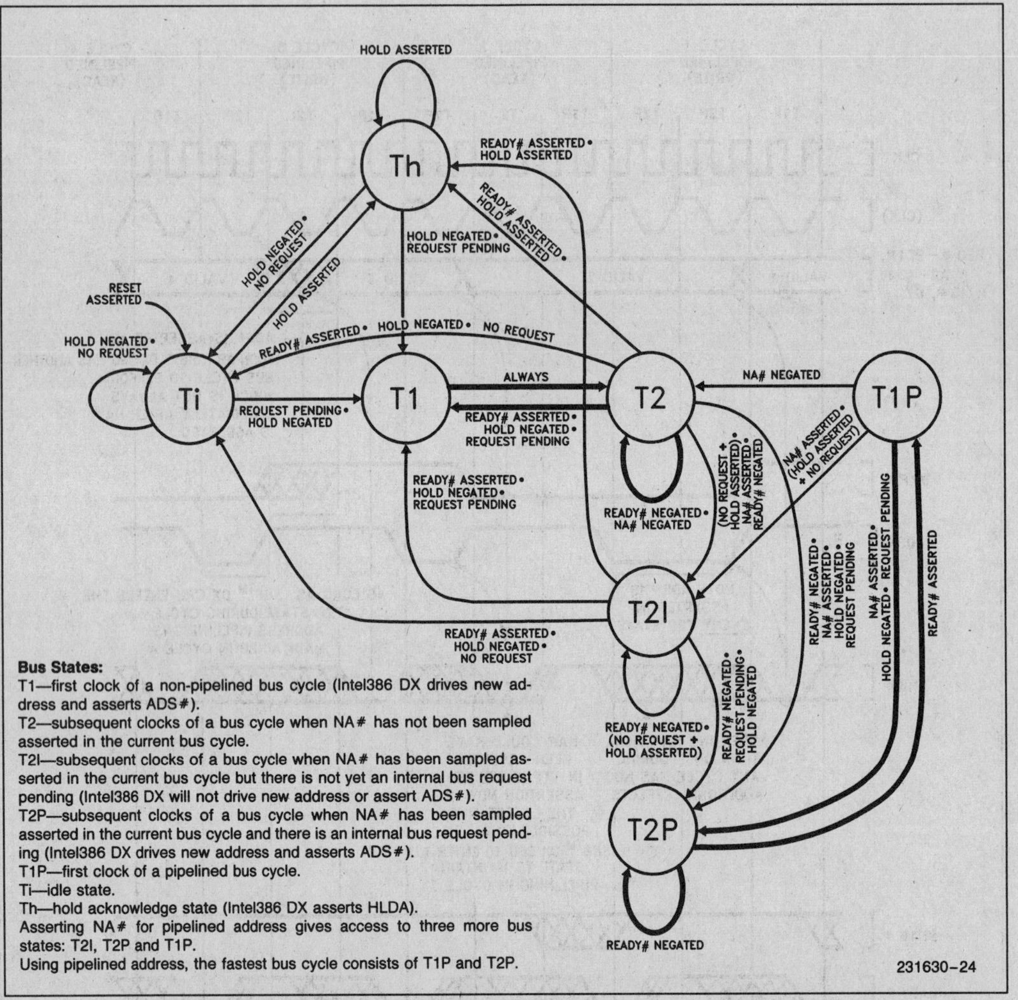

HOLD ASSERTED
Th
READY# ASSERTED • HOLD ASSERTED
READY# ASSERTED • HOLD ASSERTED •
HOLD NEGATED • REQUEST PENDING
HOLD NEGATED • NO REQUEST
HOLD ASSERTED
RESET ASSERTED
HOLD NEGATED • NO REQUEST
READY# ASSERTED • HOLD NEGATED • NO REQUEST
Ti
REQUEST PENDING • HOLD NEGATED
T1
ALWAYS
T2
READY# ASSERTED • HOLD NEGATED • REQUEST PENDING
NA# NEGATED
T1P
READY# ASSERTED • HOLD NEGATED • REQUEST PENDING
READY# NEGATED • NA# NEGATED
(NO REQUEST + HOLD ASSERTED) • NA# ASSERTED • READY# NEGATED
NA# ASSERTED • (HOLD ASSERTED + NO REQUEST)
READY# NEGATED • NA# ASSERTED • HOLD NEGATED • REQUEST PENDING
NA# ASSERTED • HOLD NEGATED • REQUEST PENDING
READY# ASSERTED
T2I
READY# ASSERTED • HOLD NEGATED • NO REQUEST
READY# NEGATED • (NO REQUEST + HOLD ASSERTED)
READY# NEGATED • REQUEST PENDING • HOLD NEGATED
T2P
READY# NEGATED

Bus States:
T1—first clock of a non-pipelined bus cycle (Intel386 DX drives new address and asserts ADS#).
T2—subsequent clocks of a bus cycle when NA# has not been sampled asserted in the current bus cycle.
T2I—subsequent clocks of a bus cycle when NA# has been sampled asserted in the current bus cycle but there is not yet an internal bus request pending (Intel386 DX will not drive new address or assert ADS#).
T2P—subsequent clocks of a bus cycle when NA# has been sampled asserted in the current bus cycle and there is an internal bus request pending (Intel386 DX drives new address and asserts ADS#).
T1P—first clock of a pipelined bus cycle.
Ti—idle state.
Th—hold acknowledge state (Intel386 DX asserts HLDA).
Asserting NA# for pipelined address gives access to three more bus states: T2I, T2P and T1P.
Using pipelined address, the fastest bus cycle consists of T1P and T2P.

231630–24

Figure 5-20. Intel386™ DX Complete Bus States (including pipelined address)

Realistically, address pipelining is almost always maintained as long as NA# is sampled asserted. This is so because in the absence of any other request, a code prefetch request is always internally pending until the instruction decoder and code prefetch queue are completely full. Therefore address pipelining is maintained for long bursts of bus cycles, if the bus is available (i.e., HOLD negated) and NA# is sampled asserted in each of the bus cycles.

5.4.3.6 PIPELINED ADDRESS WITH DYNAMIC DATA BUS SIZING

The BS16# feature allows easy interface to 16-bit data buses. When asserted, the Intel386 DX bus interface hardware performs appropriate action to make the transfer using a 16-bit data bus connected on D0–D15.

There is a degree of interaction, however, between the use of Address Pipelining and the use of Bus Size 16. The interaction results from the multiple bus cycles required when transferring 32-bit operands over a 16-bit bus. If the operand requires both 16-bit halves of the 32-bit bus, the appropriate Intel386 DX action is a second bus cycle to complete the operand's transfer. It is this necessity that conflicts with NA# usage.

When NA# is sampled asserted, the Intel386 DX commits itself to perform the next internally pending bus request, and is allowed to drive the next internally pending address onto the bus. Asserting NA# therefore makes it impossible for the next bus cycle to again access the current address on A2–A31, such as may be required when BS16# is asserted by the external hardware.

To avoid conflict, the Intel386 DX is designed with following two provisions:

1) To avoid conflict, BS16# must be negated in the current bus cycle if NA# has already been sampled asserted in the current cycle. If NA# is sampled asserted, the current data bus size is assumed to be 32 bits.

2) To also avoid conflict, if NA# and BS16# are both asserted during the same sampling window, BS16# asserted has priority and the Intel386 DX acts as if NA# was negated at that time. Internal Intel386 DX circuitry, shown conceptually in Figure 5-18, assures that BS16# is sampled asserted and NA# is sampled negated if both inputs are externally asserted at the same sampling window.

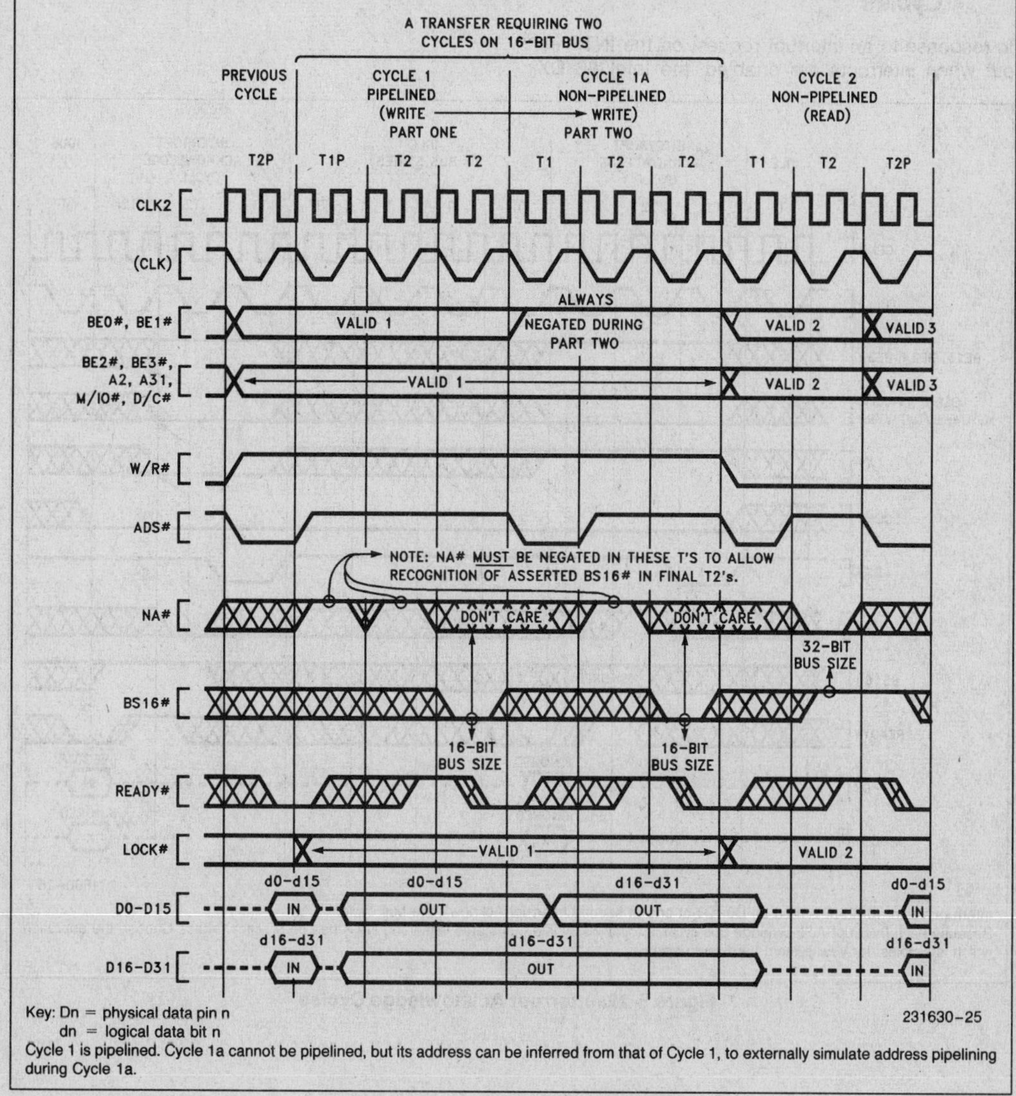

Key: Dn = physical data pin n
dn = logical data bit n

Cycle 1 is pipelined. Cycle 1a cannot be pipelined, but its address can be inferred from that of Cycle 1, to externally simulate address pipelining during Cycle 1a.

Figure 5-21. Using NA# and BS16#

Certain types of 16-bit or 8-bit operands require no adjustment for correct transfer on a 16-bit bus. Those are read or write operands using only the lower half of the data bus, and write operands using only the upper half of the bus since the Intel386 DX simultaneously duplicates the write data on the lower half of the data bus. For these patterns of Byte Enables and the R/W# signals, BS16# need not be asserted at the Intel386 DX allowing NA# to be asserted during the bus cycle if desired.

5.4.4 Interrupt Acknowledge (INTA) Cycles

In response to an interrupt request on the INTR input when interrupts are enabled, the Intel386 DX performs two interrupt acknowledge cycles. These bus cycles are similar to read cycles in that bus definition signals define the type of bus activity taking place, and each cycle continues until acknowledged by READY# sampled asserted.

The state of A2 distinguishes the first and second interrupt acknowledge cycles. The byte address driven during the first interrupt acknowledge cycle is 4 (A31–A3 low, A2 high, BE3#–BE1# high, and BE0# low). The address driven during the second interrupt acknowledge cycle is 0 (A31–A2 low, BE3#–BE1# high, BE0# low).

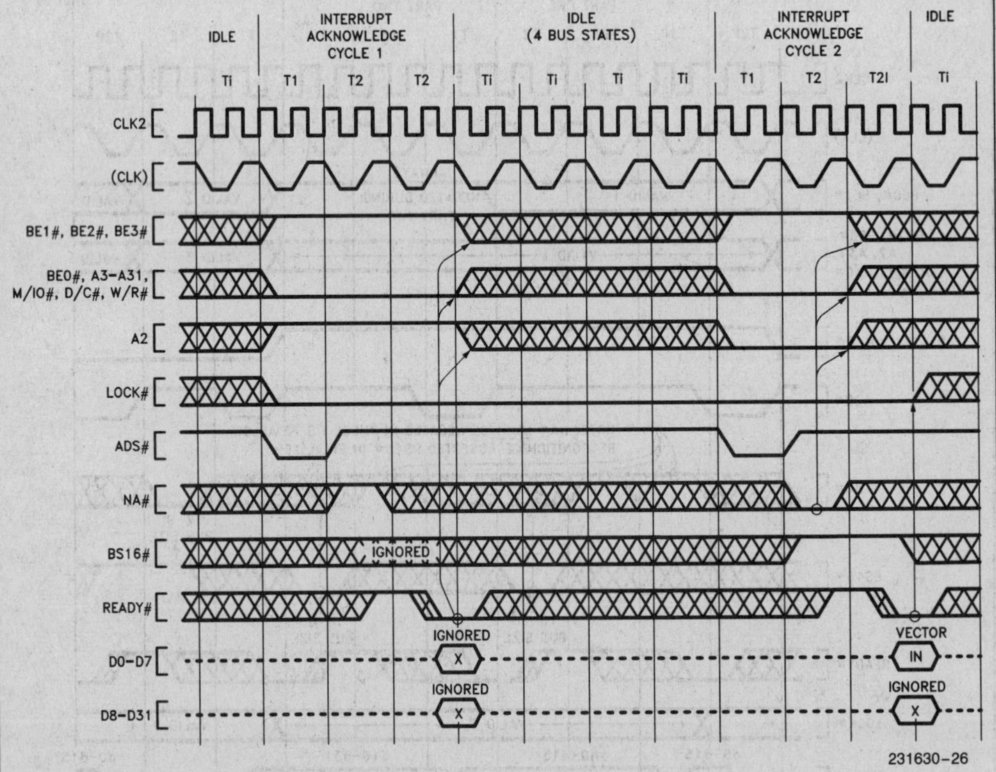

IDLE | INTERRUPT ACKNOWLEDGE CYCLE 1 | IDLE (4 BUS STATES) | INTERRUPT ACKNOWLEDGE CYCLE 2 | IDLE

Ti T1 T2 T2 Ti Ti Ti Ti T1 T2 T2I Ti

CLK2, (CLK), BE1#, BE2#, BE3#, BE0#, A3–A31, M/IO#, D/C#, W/R#, A2, LOCK#, ADS#, NA#, BS16# (IGNORED), READY#, D0–D7 (IGNORED, VECTOR IN), D8–D31 (IGNORED, IGNORED)

231630–26

Interrupt Vector (0–255) is read on D0–D7 at end of second Interrupt Acknowledge bus cycle.
Because each Interrupt Acknowledge bus cycle is followed by idle bus states, asserting NA# has no practical effect. Choose the approach which is simplest for your system hardware design.

Figure 5-22. Interrupt Acknowledge Cycles

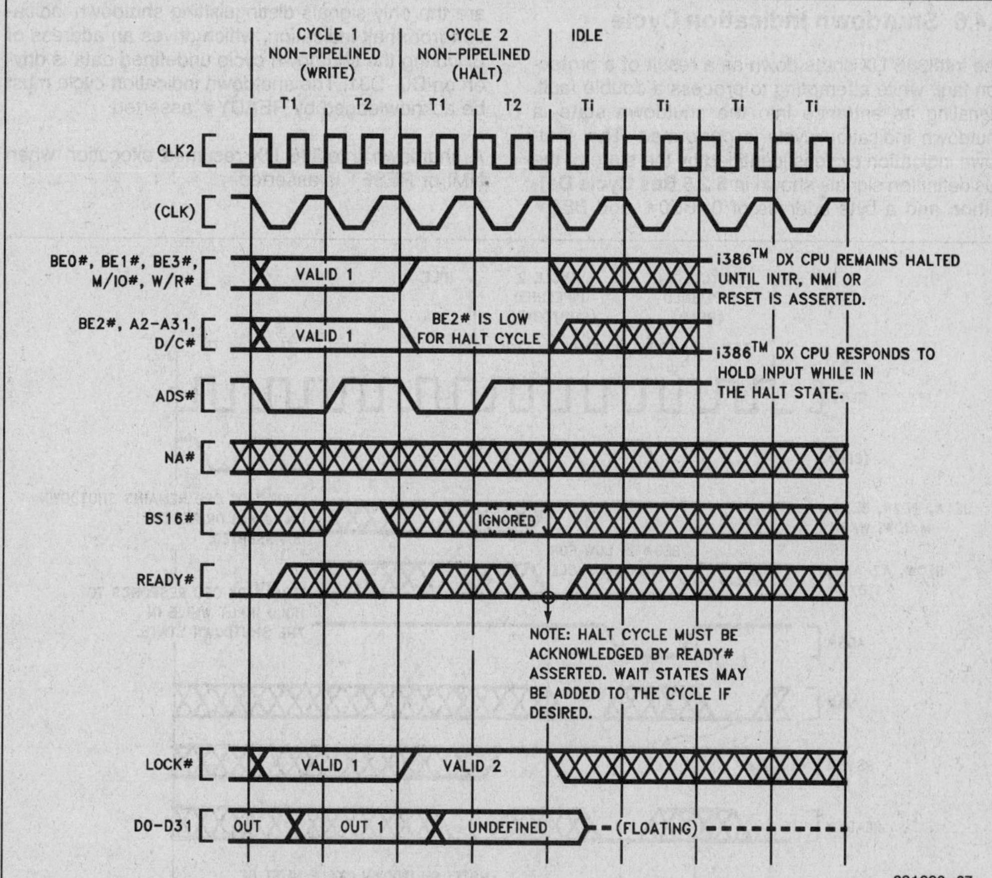

Figure 5-23. Halt Indication Cycle

The LOCK# output is asserted from the beginning of the first interrupt acknowledge cycle until the end of the second interrupt acknowledge cycle. Four idle bus states, Ti, are inserted by the Intel386 DX between the two interrupt acknowledge cycles, allowing for compatibility with spec TRHRL of the 8259A Interrupt Controller.

During both interrupt acknowledge cycles, D0–D31 float. No data is read at the end of the first interrupt acknowledge cycle. At the end of the second interrupt acknowledge cycle, the Intel386 DX will read an external interrupt vector from D0–D7 of the data bus. The vector indicates the specific interrupt number (from 0–255) requiring service.

5.4.5 Halt Indication Cycle

The Intel386 DX halts as a result of executing a HALT instruction. Signaling its entrance into the halt state, a halt indication cycle is performed. The halt indication cycle is identified by the state of the bus definition signals shown in **5.2.5 Bus Cycle Definition** and a byte address of 2. BE0# and BE2# are the only signals distinguishing halt indication from shutdown indication, which drives an address of 0. During the halt cycle undefined data is driven on D0–D31. The halt indication cycle must be acknowledged by READY# asserted.

A halted Intel386 DX resumes execution when INTR (if interrupts are enabled) or NMI or RESET is asserted.

5.4.6 Shutdown Indication Cycle

The Intel386 DX shuts down as a result of a protection fault while attempting to process a double fault. Signaling its entrance into the shutdown state, a shutdown indication cycle is performed. The shutdown indication cycle is identified by the state of the bus definition signals shown in **5.2.5 Bus Cycle Definition** and a byte address of 0. BE0# and BE2# are the only signals distinguishing shutdown indication from halt indication, which drives an address of 2. During the shutdown cycle undefined data is driven on D0–D31. The shutdown indication cycle must be acknowledged by READY# asserted.

A shutdown Intel386 DX resumes execution when NMI or RESET is asserted.

CYCLE 1 PIPELINED (READ)
CYCLE 2 PIPELINED (SHUTDOWN)
IDLE
T1P T2P T1P T2I Ti Ti Ti Ti
CLK2
(CLK)
BE1#, BE2#, BE3#, M/IO#, W/R#
VALID 1
i386™ DX CPU REMAINS SHUTDOWN UNTIL NMI OR RESET IS ASSERTED.
BE0# IS LOW FOR SHUTDOWN CYCLE
BE0#, A2–A31, D/C#
VALID 1
i386™ DX CPU RESPONDS TO HOLD INPUT WHILE IN THE SHUTDOWN STATE.
ADS#
NA#
BS16#
READY#
NOTE: SHUTDOWN CYCLE MUST BE ACKNOWLEDGED BY READY# ASSERTED. WAIT STATES MAY BE ADDED TO THE CYCLE IF DESIRED.
LOCK#
VALID 1
VALID 2
D0–D31
IN
IN 1
UNDEFINED
(FLOATING)
231630–28

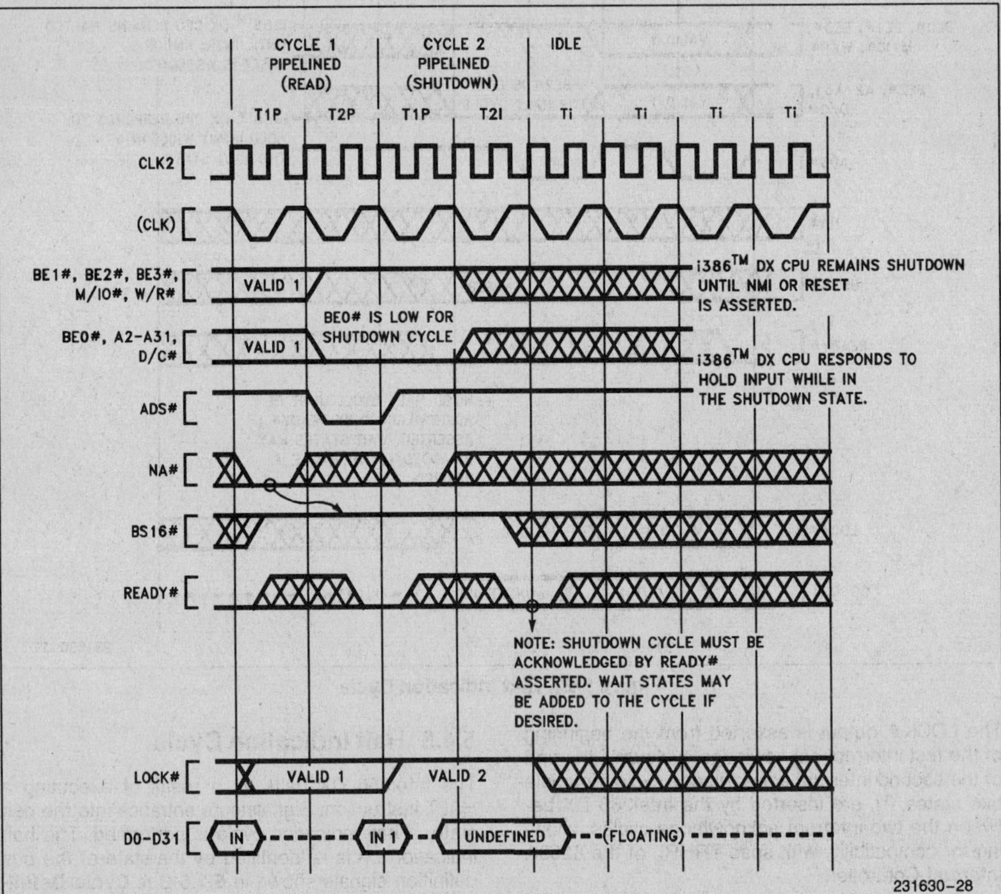

Figure 5-24. Shutdown Indication Cycle

5.5 OTHER FUNCTIONAL DESCRIPTIONS

5.5.1 Entering and Exiting Hold Acknowledge

The bus hold acknowledge state, Th, is entered in response to the HOLD input being asserted. In the bus hold acknowledge state, the Intel386 DX floats all output or bidirectional signals, except for HLDA. HLDA is asserted as long as the Intel386 DX remains in the bus hold acknowledge state. In the bus hold acknowledge state, all inputs except HOLD, RESET, BUSY#, ERROR#, and PEREQ are ignored (also up to one rising edge on NMI is remembered for processing when HOLD is no longer asserted).

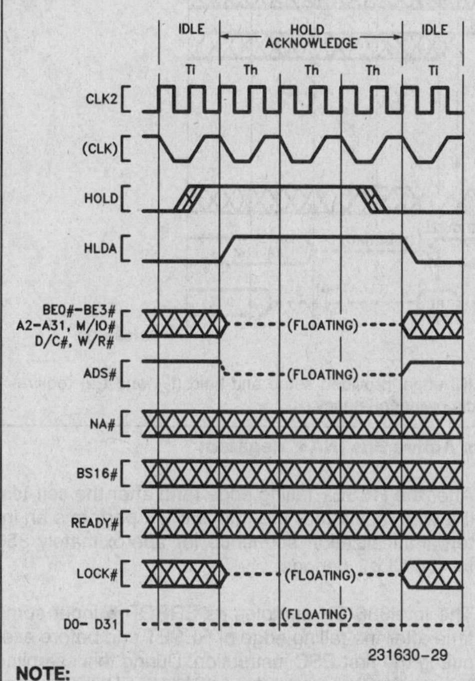

NOTE:
For maximum design flexibility the Intel386 DX has no internal pullup resistors on its outputs. Your design may require an external pullup on ADS# and other Intel386 DX outputs to keep them negated during float periods.

Figure 5-25. Requesting Hold from Idle Bus

Th may be entered from a bus idle state as in Figure 5-25 or after the acknowledgement of the current physical bus cycle if the LOCK# signal is not asserted, as in Figures 5-26 and 5-27. If HOLD is asserted during a locked bus cycle, the Intel386 DX may execute one unlocked bus cycle before acknowledging HOLD. If asserting BS16# requires a second 16-bit bus cycle to complete a physical operand transfer, it is performed before HOLD is acknowledged, although the bus state diagrams in Figures 5-13 and 5-20 do not indicate that detail.

Th is exited in response to the HOLD input being negated. The following state will be Ti as in Figure 5-25 if no bus request is pending. The following bus state will be T1 if a bus request is internally pending, as in Figures 5-26 and 5-27.

Th is also exited in response to RESET being asserted.

If a rising edge occurs on the edge-triggered NMI input while in Th, the event is remembered as a non-maskable interrupt 2 and is serviced when Th is exited, unless of course, the Intel386 DX is reset before Th is exited.

5.5.2 Reset During Hold Acknowledge

RESET being asserted takes priority over HOLD being asserted. Therefore, Th is exited in reponse to the RESET input being asserted. If RESET is asserted while HOLD remains asserted, the Intel386 DX drives its pins to defined states during reset, as in **Table 5-3 Pin State During Reset**, and performs internal reset activity as usual.

If HOLD remains asserted when RESET is negated, the Intel386 DX enters the hold acknowledge state before performing its first bus cycle, provided HOLD is still asserted when the Intel386 DX would otherwise perform its first bus cycle. If HOLD remains asserted when RESET is negated, the BUSY# input is still sampled as usual to determine whether a self test is being requested, and ERROR# is still sampled as usual to determine whether a Intel387 DX coprocessor vs. an 80287 (or none) is present.

5.5.3 Bus Activity During and Following Reset

RESET is the highest priority input signal, capable of interrupting any processor activity when it is asserted. A bus cycle in progress can be aborted at any stage, or idle states or bus hold acknowledge states discontinued so that the reset state is established.

RESET should remain asserted for at least 15 CLK2 periods to ensure it is recognized throughout the Intel386 DX, and at least 80 CLK2 periods if Intel386 DX self-test is going to be requested at the falling edge. RESET asserted pulses less than 15 CLK2 periods may not be recognized. RESET pulses less than 80 CLK2 periods followed by a self-test may

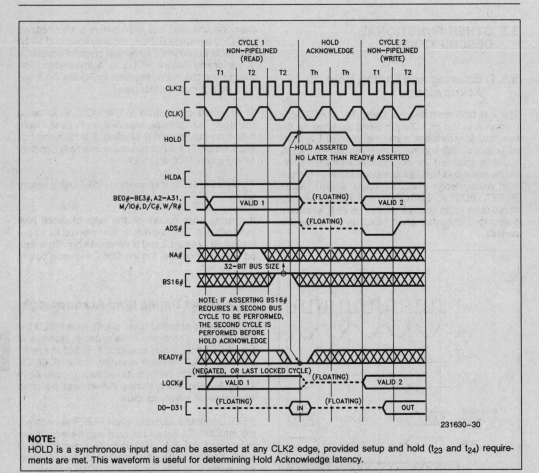

NOTE:
HOLD is a synchronous input and can be asserted at any CLK2 edge, provided setup and hold (t_{23} and t_{24}) requirements are met. This waveform is useful for determining Hold Acknowledge latency.

Figure 5-26. Requesting Hold from Active Bus (NA# negated)

cause the self-test to report a failure when no true failure exists. The additional RESET pulse width is required to clear additional state prior to a valid self-test.

Provided the RESET falling edge meets setup and hold times t_{25} and t_{26}, the internal processor clock phase is defined at that time, as illustrated by Figure 5-28 and Figure 7-7.

A Intel386 DX self-test may be requested at the time RESET is negated by having the BUSY# input at a LOW level, as shown in Figure 5-28. The self-test requires (2^{20}) + approximately 60 CLK2 periods to complete. The self-test duration is not affected by the test results. Even if the self-test indicates a problem, the Intel386 DX attempts to proceed with the reset sequence afterwards.

After the RESET falling edge (and after the self-test if it was requested) the Intel386 DX performs an internal initialization sequence for approximately 350 to 450 CLK2 periods.

The Intel386 DX samples its ERROR# input some time after the falling edge of RESET and before executing the first ESC instruction. During this sampling period BUSY# must be HIGH. If ERROR# was sampled active, the Intel386 DX employs the 32-bit protocol of the Intel387 DX. Even though this protocol was selected, it is still necessary to use a software recognition test to determine the presence or identity of the coprocessor and to assure compatibility with future processors. (See Chapter 11 of the Intel386 DX Programmer's Reference Manual, Order #230985-002).

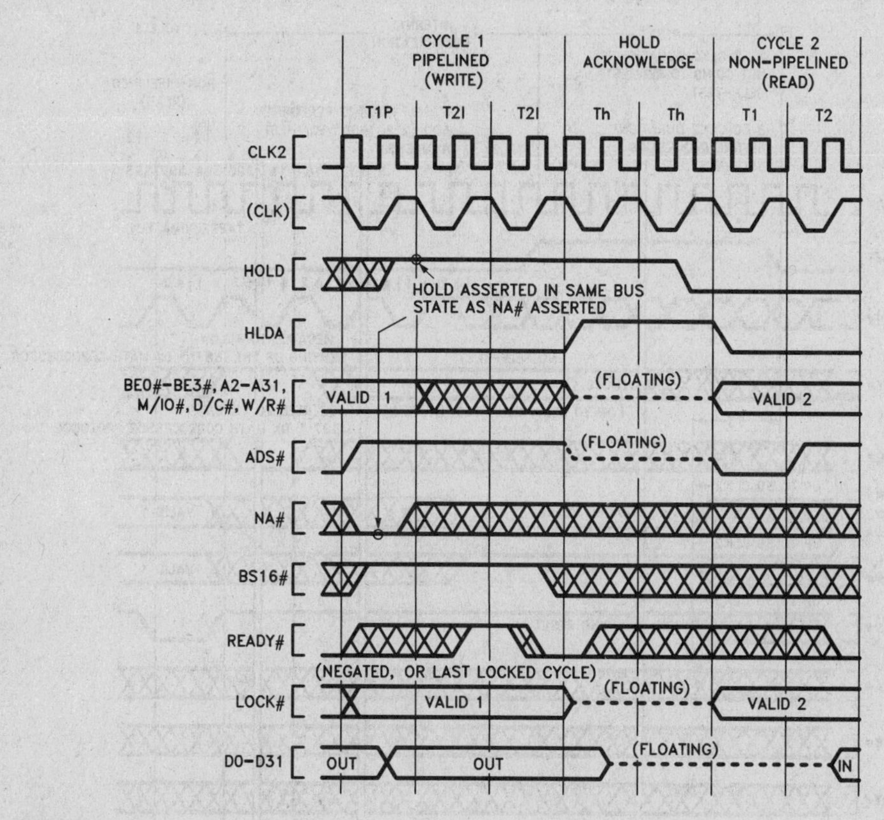

NOTE:
HOLD is a synchronous input and can be asserted at any CLK2 edge, provided setup and hold (t_{23} and t_{24}) requirements are met. This waveform is useful for determining Hold Acknowledge latency.

Figure 5-27. Requesting Hold from Active Bus (NA# asserted)

5.6 SELF-TEST SIGNATURE

Upon completion of self-test, (if self-test was requested by holding BUSY# LOW at least eight CLK2 periods before and after the falling edge of RESET), the EAX register will contain a signature of 00000000h indicating the Intel386 DX passed its self-test of microcode and major PLA contents with no problems detected. The passing signature in EAX, 00000000h, applies to all Intel386 DX revision levels. Any non-zero signature indicates the Intel386 DX unit is faulty.

5.7 COMPONENT AND REVISION IDENTIFIERS

To assist Intel386 DX users, the Intel386 DX after reset holds a component identifier and a revision identifier in its DX register. The upper 8 bits of DX hold 03h as identification of the Intel386 DX component. The lower 8 bits of DX hold an 8-bit unsigned binary number related to the component revision level. The revision identifier begins chronologically with a value zero and is subject to change (typically it will be incremented) with component steppings intended to have certain improvements or distinctions from previous steppings.

These features are intended to assist Intel386 DX users to a practical extent. However, the revision identifier value is not guaranteed to change with every stepping revision, or to follow a completely uniform numerical sequence, depending on the type or intention of revision, or manufacturing materials required to be changed. Intel has sole discretion over these characteristics of the component.

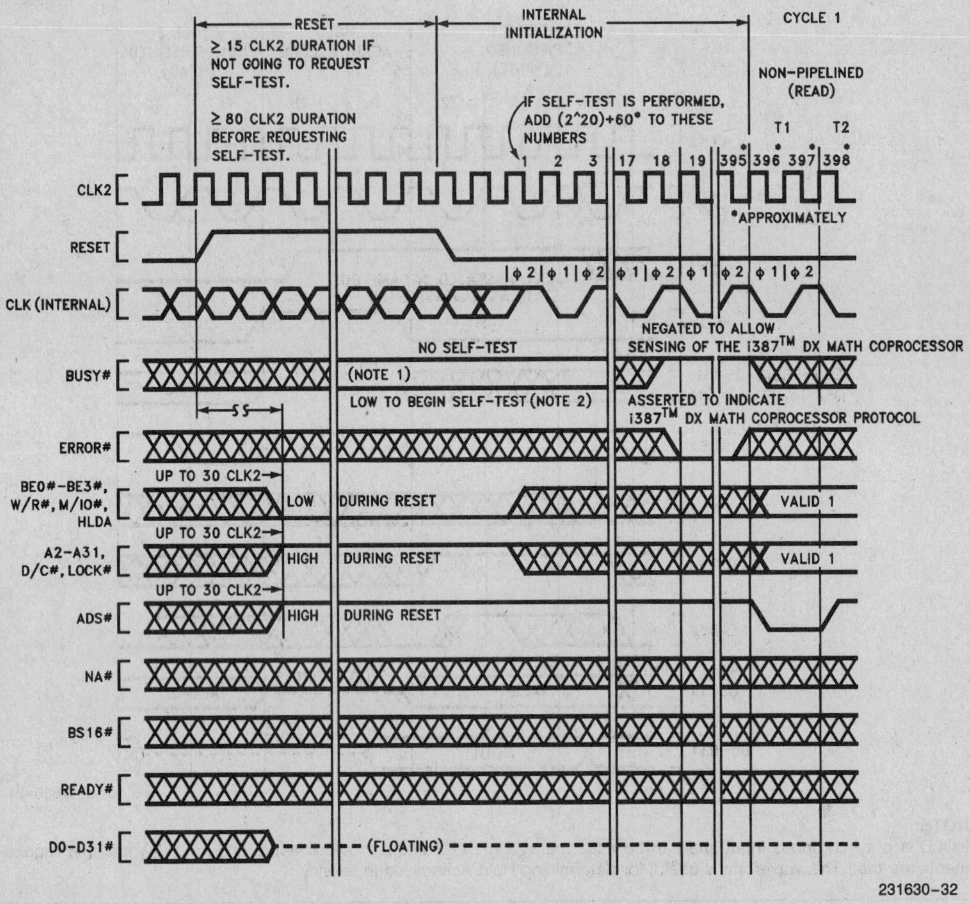

231630-32

NOTES:

1. BUSY# should be held stable for 8 CLK2 periods before and after the CLK2 period in which RESET falling edge occurs.
2. If self-test is requested, the Intel386 DX outputs remain in their reset state as shown here and in Table 5-3.

Figure 5-28. Bus Activity from Reset Until First Code Fetch

Table 5-10. Component and Revision Identifier History

Intel386™ DX Stepping Name	Component Identifier	Revision Identifier	Intel386 DX Stepping Name	Component Identifier	Revision Identifier
B0	03	03	D0	03	05
B1	03	03	D1	03	08

5.8 COPROCESSOR INTERFACING

The Intel386 DX provides an automatic interface for the Intel Intel387 DX numeric floating-point coprocessor. The Intel387 DX coprocessor uses an I/O-mapped interface driven automatically by the Intel386 DX and assisted by three dedicated signals: BUSY#, ERROR#, and PEREQ.

As the Intel386 DX begins supporting a coprocessor instruction, it tests the BUSY# and ERROR# signals to determine if the coprocessor can accept its next instruction. Thus, the BUSY# and ERROR# inputs eliminate the need for any "preamble" bus cycles for communication between processor and coprocessor. The Intel387 DX can be given its command opcode immediately. The dedicated signals provide instruction synchronization, and eliminate the need of using the Intel386 DX WAIT opcode (9Bh) for Intel387 DX coprocessor instruction synchronization (the WAIT opcode was required when 8086 or 8088 was used with the 8087 coprocessor).

Custom coprocessors can be included in Intel386 DX-based systems, via memory-mapped or I/O-mapped interfaces. Such coprocessor interfaces allow a completely custom protocol, and are not limited to a set of coprocessor protocol "primitives". Instead, memory-mapped or I/O-mapped interfaces may use all applicable Intel386 DX instructions for high-speed coprocessor communication. The BUSY# and ERROR# inputs of the Intel386 DX may also be used for the custom coprocessor interface, if such hardware assist is desired. These signals can be tested by the Intel386 DX WAIT opcode (9Bh). The WAIT instruction will wait until the BUSY# input is negated (interruptable by an NMI or enabled INTR input), but generates an exception 16 fault if the ERROR# pin is in the asserted state when the BUSY# goes (or is) negated. If the custom coprocessor interface is memory-mapped, protection of the addresses used for the interface can be provided with the Intel386 DX on-chip paging or segmentation mechanisms. If the custom interface is I/O-mapped, protection of the interface can be provided with the Intel386 DX IOPL (I/O Privilege Level) mechanism.

The Intel387 DX numeric coprocessor interface is I/O mapped as shown in Table 5-11. Note that the Intel387 DX coprocessor interface addresses are beyond the 0h-FFFFh range for programmed I/O. When the Intel386 DX supports the Intel387 DX coprocessor, the Intel386 DX automatically generates bus cycles to the coprocessor interface addresses.

Table 5-11. Numeric Coprocessor Port Addresses

Address in Intel386™ DX I/O Space	Intel387™ DX Coprocessor Register
800000F8h	Opcode Register (32-bit port)
800000FCh	Operand Register (32-bit port)

To correctly map the Intel387 DX coprocessor registers to the appropriate I/O addresses, connect the Intel387 DX coprocessor CMD0# pin directly to the A2 output of the Intel386 DX.

5.8.1 Software Testing for Coprocessor Presence

When software is used to test for coprocessor (Intel387 DX) presence, it should use only the following coprocessor opcodes: FINIT, FNINIT, FSTCW mem, FSTSW mem, FSTSW AX. To use other coprocessor opcodes when a coprocessor is known to be not present, first set EM = 1 in Intel386 DX CR0.

4

6. INSTRUCTION SET

This section describes the Intel386 DX instruction set. A table lists all instructions along with instruction encoding diagrams and clock counts. Further details of the instruction encoding are then provided in the following sections, which completely describe the encoding structure and the definition of all fields occurring within Intel386 DX instructions.

6.1 Intel386™ DX INSTRUCTION ENCODING AND CLOCK COUNT SUMMARY

To calculate elapsed time for an instruction, multiply the instruction clock count, as listed in Table 6-1 below, by the processor clock period (e.g. 50 ns for a 20 MHz Intel386 DX, 40 ns for a 25 MHz Intel386 DX, and 30 ns for a 33 MHz Intel386 DX).

For more detailed information on the encodings of instructions refer to section 6.2 Instruction Encodings. Section 6.2 explains the general structure of instruction encodings, and defines exactly the encodings of all fields contained within the instruction.

Instruction Clock Count Assumptions

1. The instruction has been prefetched, decoded, and is ready for execution.
2. Bus cycles do not require wait states.
3. There are no local bus HOLD requests delaying processor access to the bus.
4. No exceptions are detected during instruction execution.
5. If an effective address is calculated, it does not use two general register components. One register, scaling and displacement can be used within the clock counts shown. However, if the effective address calculation uses two general register components, add 1 clock to the clock count shown.

Instruction Clock Count Notation

1. If two clock counts are given, the smaller refers to a register operand and the larger refers to a memory operand.
2. n = number of times repeated.
3. m = number of components in the next instruction executed, where the entire displacement (if any) counts as one component, the entire immediate data (if any) counts as one component, and each of the **other** bytes of the instruction and prefix(es) each count as one component.

Wait States

Add 1 clock per wait state to instruction execution for each data access.

Table 6-1. Intel386™ DX Instruction Set Clock Count Summary

INSTRUCTION	FORMAT	Clk Count Virtual 8086 Mode	CLOCK COUNT: Real Address Mode or Virtual 8086 Mode	CLOCK COUNT: Protected Virtual Address Mode	NOTES: Real Address Mode or Virtual 8086 Mode	NOTES: Protected Virtual Address Mode
GENERAL DATA TRANSFER						
MOV = Move:						
Register to Register/Memory	1000100w | mod reg r/m		2/2	2/2	b	h
Register/Memory to Register	1000101w | mod reg r/m		2/4	2/4	b	h
Immediate to Register/Memory	1100011w | mod 000 r/m | immediate data		2/2	2/2	b	h
Immediate to Register (short form)	1011 w reg | immediate data		2	2		
Memory to Accumulator (short form)	1010000w | full displacement		4	4	b	h
Accumulator to Memory (short form)	1010001w | full displacement		2	2	b	h
Register Memory to Segment Register	10001110 | mod sreg3 r/m		2/5	18/19	b	h, i, j
Segment Register to Register/Memory	10001100 | mod sreg3 r/m		2/2	2/2	b	h
MOVSX = Move With Sign Extension						
Register From Register/Memory	00001111 | 1011111w | mod reg r/m		3/6	3/6	b	h
MOVZX = Move With Zero Extension						
Register From Register/Memory	00001111 | 1011011w | mod reg r/m		3/6	3/6	b	h
PUSH = Push:						
Register/Memory	11111111 | mod 110 r/m		5	5	b	h
Register (short form)	01010 reg		2	2	b	h
Segment Register (ES, CS, SS or DS)	000 sreg2 110		2	2	b	h
Segment Register (FS or GS)	00001111 | 10 sreg3 000		2	2	b	h
Immediate	011010s0 | immediate data		2	2	b	h
PUSHA = Push All	01100000		18	18	b	h
POP = Pop						
Register/Memory	10001111 | mod 000 r/m		5	5	b	h
Register (short form)	01011 reg		4	4	b	h
Segment Register (ES, SS or DS)	000 sreg 2 111		7	21	b	h, i, j
Segment Register (FS or GS)	00001111 | 10 sreg 3 001		7	21	b	h, i, j
POPA = Pop All	01100001		24	24	b	h
XCHG = Exchange						
Register/Memory With Register	1000011w | mod reg r/m		3/5	3/5	b, f	f, h
Register With Accumulator (short form)	10010 reg		3	3		
IN = Input from:						
Fixed Port	1110010w | port number	†26	12	6*/26**		m
Variable Port	1110110w	†27	13	7*/27**		m
OUT = Output to:						
Fixed Port	1110011w | port number	†24	10	4*/24**		m
Variable Port	1110111w	†25	11	5*/25**		m
LEA = Load EA to Register	10001101 | mod reg r/m		2	2		

* If CPL ≤ IOPL ** If CPL > IOPL

Table 6-1. Intel386™ DX Instruction Set Clock Count Summary (Continued)

INSTRUCTION	FORMAT				Clock Count: Real Address Mode or Virtual 8086 Mode	Clock Count: Protected Virtual Address Mode	Notes: Real Address Mode or Virtual 8086 Mode	Notes: Protected Virtual Address Mode
SEGMENT CONTROL								
LDS = Load Pointer to DS	11000101	mod reg r/m			7	22	b	h, i, j
LES = Load Pointer to ES	11000100	mod reg r/m			7	22	b	h, i, j
LFS = Load Pointer to FS	00001111	10110100	mod reg r/m		7	25	b	h, i, j
LGS = Load Pointer to GS	00001111	10110101	mod reg r/m		7	25	b	h, i, j
LSS = Load Pointer to SS	00001111	10110010	mod reg r/m		7	22	b	h, i, j
FLAG CONTROL								
CLC = Clear Carry Flag	11111000				2	2		
CLD = Clear Direction Flag	11111100				2	2		
CLI = Clear Interrupt Enable Flag	11111010				8	8		m
CLTS = Clear Task Switched Flag	00001111	00000110			6	6	c	l
CMC = Complement Carry Flag	11110101				2	2		
LAHF = Load AH into Flag	10011111				2	2		
POPF = Pop Flags	10011101				5	5	b	h, n
PUSHF = Push Flags	10011100				4	4	b	h
SAHF = Store AH into Flags	10011110				3	3		
STC = Set Carry Flag	11111001				2	2		
STD = Set Direction Flag	11111101				2	2		
STI = Set Interrupt Enable Flag	11111011				8	8		m
ARITHMETIC								
ADD = Add								
Register to Register	000000dw	mod reg r/m			2	2		
Register to Memory	0000000w	mod reg r/m			7	7	b	h
Memory to Register	0000001w	mod reg r/m			6	6	b	h
Immediate to Register/Memory	100000sw	mod 000 r/m	immediate data		2/7	2/7	b	h
Immediate to Accumulator (short form)	0000010w	immediate data			2	2		
ADC = Add With Carry								
Register to Register	000100dw	mod reg r/m			2	2		
Register to Memory	0001000w	mod reg r/m			7	7	b	h
Memory to Register	0001001w	mod reg r/m			6	6	b	h
Immediate to Register/Memory	100000sw	mod 010 r/m	immediate data		2/7	2/7	b	h
Immediate to Accumulator (short form)	0001010w	immediate data			2	2		
INC = Increment								
Register/Memory	1111111w	mod 000 r/m			2/6	2/6	b	h
Register (short form)	01000 reg				2	2		
SUB = Subtract								
Register from Register	001010dw	mod reg r/m			2	2		

Table 6-1. Intel386™ DX Instruction Set Clock Count Summary (Continued)

INSTRUCTION	FORMAT	CLOCK COUNT: Real Address Mode or Virtual 8086 Mode	CLOCK COUNT: Protected Virtual Address Mode	NOTES: Real Address Mode or Virtual 8086 Mode	NOTES: Protected Virtual Address Mode
ARITHMETIC (Continued)					
Register from Memory	0010100w | mod reg r/m	7	7	b	h
Memory from Register	0010101w | mod reg r/m	6	6	b	h
Immediate from Register/Memory	100000sw | mod 101 r/m | immediate data	2/7	2/7	b	h
Immediate from Accumulator (short form)	0010110w | immediate data	2	2		
SBB = Subtract with Borrow					
Register from Register	000110dw | mod reg r/m	2	2		
Register from Memory	0001100w | mod reg r/m	7	7	b	h
Memory from Register	0001101w | mod reg r/m	6	6	b	h
Immediate from Register/Memory	100000sw | mod 011 r/m | immediate data	2/7	2/7	b	h
Immediate from Accumulator (short form)	0001110w | immediate data	2	2		
DEC = Decrement					
Register/Memory	1111111w | reg 001 r/m	2/6	2/6	b	h
Register (short form)	01001 reg	2	2		
CMP = Compare					
Register with Register	001110dw | mod reg r/m	2	2		
Memory with Register	0011100w | mod reg r/m	5	5	b	h
Register with Memory	0011101w | mod reg r/m	6	6	b	h
Immediate with Register/Memory	100000sw | mod 111 r/m | immediate data	2/5	2/5	b	h
Immediate with Accumulator (short form)	0011110w | immediate data	2	2		
NEG = Change Sign	1111011w | mod 011 r/m	2/6	2/6	b	h
AAA = ASCII Adjust for Add	00110111	4	4		
AAS = ASCII Adjust for Subtract	00111111	4	4		
DAA = Decimal Adjust for Add	00100111	4	4		
DAS = Decimal Adjust for Subtract	00101111	4	4		
MUL = Multiply (unsigned)					
Accumulator with Register/Memory	1111011w | mod 100 r/m				
Multiplier-Byte		12–17/15–20	12–17/15–20	b, d	d, h
-Word		12–25/15–28	12–25/15–28	b, d	d, h
-Doubleword		12–41/15–44	12–41/15–44	b, d	d, h
IMUL = Integer Multiply (signed)					
Accumulator with Register/Memory	1111011w | mod 101 r/m				
Multiplier-Byte		12–17/15–20	12–17/15–20	b, d	d, h
-Word		12–25/15–28	12–25/15–28	b, d	d, h
-Doubleword		12–41/15–44	12–41/15–44	b, d	d, h
Register with Register/Memory	00001111 | 10101111 | mod reg r/m				
Multiplier-Byte		12–17/15–20	12–17/15–20	b, d	d, h
-Word		12–25/15–28	12–25/15–28	b, d	d, h
-Doubleword		12–41/15–44	12–41/15–44	b, d	d, h
Register/Memory with Immediate to Register	011010s1 | mod reg r/m | immediate data				
-Word		13–26/14–27	13–26/14–27	b, d	d, h
-Doubleword		13–42/14–43	13–42/14–43	b, d	d, h

Table 6-1. Intel386™ DX Instruction Set Clock Count Summary (Continued)

INSTRUCTION	FORMAT	CLOCK COUNT: Real Address Mode or Virtual 8086 Mode	CLOCK COUNT: Protected Virtual Address Mode	NOTES: Real Address Mode or Virtual 8086 Mode	NOTES: Protected Virtual Address Mode
ARITHMETIC (Continued)					
DIV = Divide (Unsigned)					
Accumulator by Register/Memory	1111011w · mod 110 r/m				
Divisor—Byte		14/17	14/17	b,e	e,h
—Word		22/25	22/25	b,e	e,h
—Doubleword		38/41	38/41	b,e	e,h
IDIV = Integer Divide (Signed)					
Accumulator By Register/Memory	1111011w · mod 111 r/m				
Divisor—Byte		19/22	19/22	b,e	e,h
—Word		27/30	27/30	b,e	e,h
—Doubleword		43/46	43/46	b,e	e,h
AAD = ASCII Adjust for Divide	11010101 · 00001010	19	19		
AAM = ASCII Adjust for Multiply	11010100 · 00001010	17	17		
CBW = Convert Byte to Word	10011000	3	3		
CWD = Convert Word to Double Word	10011001	2	2		
LOGIC					
Shift Rotate Instructions					
Not Through Carry **(ROL, ROR, SAL, SAR, SHL, and SHR)**					
Register/Memory by 1	1101000w · mod TTT r/m	3/7	3/7	b	h
Register/Memory by CL	1101001w · mod TTT r/m	3/7	3/7	b	h
Register/Memory by Immediate Count	1100000w · mod TTT r/m · immed 8-bit data	3/7	3/7	b	h
Through Carry **(RCL and RCR)**					
Register/Memory by 1	1101000w · mod TTT r/m	9/10	9/10	b	h
Register/Memory by CL	1101001w · mod TTT r/m	9/10	9/10	b	h
Register/Memory by Immediate Count	1100000w · mod TTT r/m · immed 8-bit data	9/10	9/10	b	h
	TTT Instruction 000 ROL 001 ROR 010 RCL 011 RCR 100 SHL/SAL 101 SHR 111 SAR				
SHLD = Shift Left Double					
Register/Memory by Immediate	00001111 · 10100100 · mod reg r/m · immed 8-bit data	3/7	3/7		
Register/Memory by CL	00001111 · 10100101 · mod reg r/m	3/7	3/7		
SHRD = Shift Right Double					
Register/Memory by Immediate	00001111 · 10101100 · mod reg r/m · immed 8-bit data	3/7	3/7		
Register/Memory by CL	00001111 · 10101101 · mod reg r/m	3/7	3/7		
AND = And					
Register to Register	001000dw · mod reg r/m	2	2		

Table 6-1. Intel386™ DX Instruction Set Clock Count Summary (Continued)

INSTRUCTION	FORMAT	Clk Count Virtual 8086 Mode	CLOCK COUNT: Real Address Mode or Virtual 8086 Mode	CLOCK COUNT: Protected Virtual Address Mode	NOTES: Real Address Mode or Virtual 8086 Mode	NOTES: Protected Virtual Address Mode
LOGIC (Continued)						
Register to Memory	0010000w mod reg r/m		7	7	b	h
Memory to Register	0010001w mod reg r/m		6	6	b	h
Immediate to Register/Memory	100000sw mod 100 r/m immediate data		2/7	2/7	b	h
Immediate to Accumulator (Short Form)	0010010w immediate data		2	2		
TEST = And Function to Flags, No Result						
Register/Memory and Register	1000010w mod reg r/m		2/5	2/5	b	h
Immediate Data and Register/Memory	1111011w mod 000 r/m immediate data		2/5	2/5	b	h
Immediate Data and Accumulator (Short Form)	1010100w immediate data		2	2		
OR = Or						
Register to Register	000010dw mod reg r/m		2	2		
Register to Memory	0000100w mod reg r/m		7	7	b	h
Memory to Register	0000101w mod reg r/m		6	6	b	h
Immediate to Register/Memory	100000sw mod 001 r/m immediate data		2/7	2/7	b	h
Immediate to Accumulator (Short Form)	0000110w immediate data		2	2		
XOR = Exclusive Or						
Register to Register	001100dw mod reg r/m		2	2		
Register to Memory	0011000w mod reg r/m		7	7	b	h
Memory to Register	0011001w mod reg r/m		6	6	b	h
Immediate to Register/Memory	100000sw mod 110 r/m immediate data		2/7	2/7	b	h
Immediate to Accumulator (Short Form)	0011010w immediate data		2	2		
NOT = Invert Register/Memory	1111011w mod 010 r/m		2/6	2/6	b	h
STRING MANIPULATION						
CMPS = Compare Byte Word	1010011w		10	10	b	h
INS = Input Byte/Word from DX Port	0110110w	†29	15	9*/29**	b	h, m
LODS = Load Byte/Word to AL/AX/EAX	1010110w		5	5	b	h
MOVS = Move Byte Word	1010010w		8	8	b	h
OUTS = Output Byte/Word to DX Port	0110111w	†28	14	8*/28**	b	h, m
SCAS = Scan Byte Word	1010111w		8	8	b	h
STOS = Store Byte/Word from AL/AX/EX	1010101w		5	5	b	h
XLAT = Translate String	11010111		5	5		h
REPEATED STRING MANIPULATION						
Repeated by Count in CX or ECX						
REPE CMPS = Compare String (Find Non-Match)	11110011 1010011w		5+9n	5+9n	b	h

* If CPL ≤ IOPL ** If CPL > IOPL

Table 6-1. Intel386™ DX Instruction Set Clock Count Summary (Continued)

INSTRUCTION	FORMAT					CLOCK COUNT		NOTES	
						Real Address Mode or Virtual 8086 Mode	Protected Virtual Address Mode	Real Address Mode or Virtual 8086 Mode	Protected Virtual Address Mode
REPEATED STRING MANIPULATION (Continued)									
REPNE CMPS = Compare String					Clk Count Virtual 8086 Mode				
(Find Match)	11110010	1010011w				5+9n	5+9n	b	h
REP INS = Input String	11110010	0110110w			†28+6n	14+6n	8+6n*/28+6n**	b	h, m
REP LODS = Load String	11110010	1010110w				5+6n	5+6n	b	h
REP MOVS = Move String	11110010	1010010w				8+4n	8+4n	b	h
REP OUTS = Output String	11110010	0110111w			†26+5n	12+5n	6+5n*/26+5n**	b	h, m
REPE SCAS = Scan String									
(Find Non-AL/AX/EAX)	11110011	1010111w				5+8n	5+8n	b	h
REPNE SCAS = Scan String									
(Find AL/AX/EAX)	11110010	1010111w				5+8n	5+8n	b	h
REP STOS = Store String	11110010	1010101w				5+5n	5+5n	b	h
BIT MANIPULATION									
BSF = Scan Bit Forward	00001111	10111100	mod reg	r/m		11+3n	11+3n	b	h
BSR = Scan Bit Reverse	00001111	10111101	mod reg	r/m		9+3n	9+3n	b	h
BT = Test Bit									
Register/Memory, Immediate	00001111	10111010	mod 100	r/m	immed 8-bit data	3/6	3/6	b	h
Register/Memory, Register	00001111	10100011	mod reg	r/m		3/12	3/12	b	h
BTC = Test Bit and Complement									
Register/Memory, Immediate	00001111	10111010	mod 111	r/m	immed 8-bit data	6/8	6/8	b	h
Register/Memory, Register	00001111	10111011	mod reg	r/m		6/13	6/13	b	h
BTR = Test Bit and Reset									
Register/Memory, Immediate	00001111	10111010	mod 110	r/m	immed 8-bit data	6/8	6/8	b	h
Register/Memory, Register	00001111	10110011	mod reg	r/m		6/13	6/13	b	h
BTS = Test Bit and Set									
Register/Memory, Immediate	00001111	10111010	mod 101	r/m	immed 8-bit data	6/8	6/8	b	h
Register/Memory, Register	00001111	10101011	mod reg	r/m		6/13	6/13	b	h
CONTROL TRANSFER									
CALL = Call									
Direct Within Segment	11101000	full displacement				7+m	7+m	b	r
Register/Memory									
Indirect Within Segment	11111111	mod 010 r/m				7+m/ 10+m	7+m/ 10+m	b	h, r
Direct Intersegment	10011010	unsigned full offset, selector				17+m	34+m	b	j,k,r

NOTES:

† Clock count shown applies if I/O permission allows I/O to the port in virtual 8086 mode. If I/O bit map denies permission exception 13 fault occurs; refer to clock counts for INT 3 instruction.

* If CPL ≤ IOPL   ** If CPL > IOPL

Table 6-1. Intel386™ DX Instruction Set Clock Count Summary (Continued)

INSTRUCTION	FORMAT	CLOCK COUNT: Real Address Mode or Virtual 8086 Mode	CLOCK COUNT: Protected Virtual Address Mode	NOTES: Real Address Mode or Virtual 8086 Mode	NOTES: Protected Virtual Address Mode
CONTROL TRANSFER (Continued)					
Protected Mode Only (Direct Intersegment)					
Via Call Gate to Same Privilege Level			52+m		h,j,k,r
Via Call Gate to Different Privilege Level, (No Parameters)			86+m		h,j,k,r
Via Call Gate to Different Privilege Level, (x Parameters)			94+4x+m		h,j,k,r
From 80286 Task to 80286 TSS			273		h,j,k,r
From 80286 Task to Intel386 DX TSS			298		h,j,k,r
From 80286 Task to Virtual 8086 Task (Intel386 DX TSS)			218		h,j,k,r
From Intel386 DX Task to 80286 TSS			273		h,j,k,r
From Intel386 DX Task to Intel386 DX TSS			300		h,j,k,r
From Intel386 DX Task to Virtual 8086 Task (Intel386 DX TSS)			218		h,j,k,r
Indirect Intersegment	11111111 / mod 011 r/m	22+m	38+m	b	h,j,k,r
Protected Mode Only (Indirect Intersegment)					
Via Call Gate to Same Privilege Level			56+m		h,j,k,r
Via Call Gate to Different Privilege Level, (No Parameters)			90+m		h,j,k,r
Via Call Gate to Different Privilege Level, (x Parameters)			98+4x+m		h,j,k,r
From 80286 Task to 80286 TSS			278		h,j,k,r
From 80286 Task to Intel386 DX TSS			303		h,j,k,r
From 80286 Task to Virtual 8086 Task (Intel386 DX TSS)			222		h,j,k,r
From Intel386 DX Task to 80286 TSS			278		h,j,k,r
From Intel386 DX Task to Intel386 DX TSS			305		h,j,k,r
From Intel386 DX Task to Virtual 8086 Task (Intel386 DX TSS)			222		h,j,k,r
JMP = Unconditional Jump					
Short	11101011 / 8-bit displacement	7+m	7+m		r
Direct within Segment	11101001 / full displacement	7+m	7+m		r
Register/Memory Indirect within Segment	11111111 / mod 100 r/m	7+m/ 10+m	7+m/ 10+m	b	h,r
Direct Intersegment	11101010 / unsigned full offset, selector	12+m	27+m		j,k,r
Protected Mode Only (Direct Intersegment)					
Via Call Gate to Same Privilege Level			45+m		h,j,k,r
From 80286 Task to 80286 TSS			274		h,j,k,r
From 80286 Task to Intel386 DX TSS			301		h,j,k,r
From 80286 Task to Virtual 8086 Task (Intel386 DX TSS)			219		h,j,k,r
From Intel386 DX Task to 80286 TSS			270		h,j,k,r
From Intel386 DX Task to Intel386 DX TSS			303		h,j,k,r
From Intel386 DX Task to Virtual 8086 Task (Intel386 DX TSS)			221		h,j,k,r
Indirect Intersegment	11111111 / mod 101 r/m	17+m	31+m	b	h,j,k,r
Protected Mode Only (Indirect Intersegment)					
Via Call Gate to Same Privilege Level			49+m		h,j,k,r
From 80286 Task to 80286 TSS			279		h,j,k,r
From 80286 Task to Intel386 DX TSS			306		h,j,k,r
From 80286 Task to Virtual 8086 Task (Intel386 DX TSS)			223		h,j,k,r
From Intel386 DX Task to 80286 TSS			275		h,j,k,r
From Intel386 DX Task to Intel386 DX TSS			308		h,j,k,r
From Intel386 DX Task to Virtual 8086 Task (Intel386 DX TSS)			225		h,j,k,r

Table 6-1. Intel386™ DX Instruction Set Clock Count Summary (Continued)

INSTRUCTION	FORMAT			CLOCK COUNT		NOTES	
				Real Address Mode or Virtual 8086 Mode	Protected Virtual Address Mode	Real Address Mode or Virtual 8086 Mode	Protected Virtual Address Mode
CONTROL TRANSFER (Continued)							
RET = Return from CALL:							
Within Segment	11000011			10 + m	10 + m	b	g, h, r
Within Segment Adding Immediate to SP	11000010	16-bit displ		10 + m	10 + m	b	g, h, r
Intersegment	11001011			18 + m	32+m	b	g, h, j, k, r
Intersegment Adding Immediate to SP	11001010	16-bit displ		18 + m	32+m	b	g, h, j, k, r
Protected Mode Only (RET):							
to Different Privilege Level							
Intersegment					69		h, j, k, r
Intersegment Adding Immediate to SP					69		h, j, k, r
CONDITIONAL JUMPS							
NOTE: Times Are Jump "Taken or Not Taken"							
JO = Jump on Overflow							
8-Bit Displacement	01110000	8-bit displ		7 + m or 3	7 + m or 3		r
Full Displacement	00001111	10000000	full displacement	7 + m or 3	7 + m or 3		r
JNO = Jump on Not Overflow							
8-Bit Displacement	01110001	8-bit displ		7 + m or 3	7 + m or 3		r
Full Displacement	00001111	10000001	full displacement	7 + m or 3	7 + m or 3		r
JB/JNAE = Jump on Below/Not Above or Equal							
8-Bit Displacement	01110010	8-bit displ		7 + m or 3	7 + m or 3		r
Full Displacement	00001111	10000010	full displacement	7 + m or 3	7 + m or 3		r
JNB/JAE = Jump on Not Below/Above or Equal							
8-Bit Displacement	01110011	8-bit displ		7 + m or 3	7 + m or 3		r
Full Displacement	00001111	10000011	full displacement	7 + m or 3	7 + m or 3		r
JE/JZ = Jump on Equal/Zero							
8-Bit Displacement	01110100	8-bit displ		7 + m or 3	7 + m or 3		r
Full Displacement	00001111	10000100	full displacement	7 + m or 3	7 + m or 3		r
JNE/JNZ = Jump on Not Equal/Not Zero							
8-Bit Displacement	01110101	8-bit displ		7 + m or 3	7 + m or 3		r
Full Displacement	00001111	10000101	full displacement	7 + m or 3	7 + m or 3		r
JBE/JNA = Jump on Below or Equal/Not Above							
8-Bit Displacement	01110110	8-bit displ		7 + m or 3	7 + m or 3		r
Full Displacement	00001111	10000110	full displacement	7 + m or 3	7 + m or 3		r
JNBE/JA = Jump on Not Below or Equal/Above							
8-Bit Displacement	01110111	8-bit displ		7 + m or 3	7 + m or 3		r
Full Displacement	00001111	10000111	full displacement	7 + m or 3	7 + m or 3		r
JS = Jump on Sign							
8-Bit Displacement	01111000	8-bit displ		7 + m or 3	7 + m or 3		r
Full Displacement	00001111	10001000	full displacement	7 + m or 3	7 + m or 3		r

Table 6-1. Intel386™ DX Instruction Set Clock Count Summary (Continued)

INSTRUCTION	FORMAT				CLOCK COUNT: Real Address Mode or Virtual 8086 Mode	CLOCK COUNT: Protected Virtual Address Mode	NOTES: Real Address Mode or Virtual 8086 Mode	NOTES: Protected Virtual Address Mode
CONDITIONAL JUMPS (Continued)								
JNS = Jump on Not Sign								
8-Bit Displacement	01111001	8-bit displ			7 + m or 3	7 + m or 3		r
Full Displacement	00001111	10001001	full displacement		7 + m or 3	7 + m or 3		r
JP/JPE = Jump on Parity/Parity Even								
8-Bit Displacement	01111010	8-bit displ			7 + m or 3	7 + m or 3		r
Full Displacement	00001111	10001010	full displacement		7 + m or 3	7 + m or 3		r
JNP/JPO = Jump on Not Parity/Parity Odd								
8-Bit Displacement	01111011	8-bit displ			7 + m or 3	7 + m or 3		r
Full Displacement	00001111	10001011	full displacement		7 + m or 3	7 + m or 3		r
JL/JNGE = Jump on Less/Not Greater or Equal								
8-Bit Displacement	01111100	8-bit displ			7 + m or 3	7 + m or 3		r
Full Displacement	00001111	10001100	full displacement		7 + m or 3	7 + m or 3		r
JNL/JGE = Jump on Not Less/Greater or Equal								
8-Bit Displacement	01111101	8-bit displ			7 + m or 3	7 + m or 3		r
Full Displacement	00001111	10001101	full displacement		7 + m or 3	7 + m or 3		r
JLE/JNG = Jump on Less or Equal/Not Greater								
8-Bit Displacement	01111110	8-bit displ			7 + m or 3	7 + m or 3		r
Full Displacement	00001111	10001110	full displacement		7 + m or 3	7 + m or 3		r
JNLE/JG = Jump on Not Less or Equal/Greater								
8-Bit Displacement	01111111	8-bit displ			7 + m or 3	7 + m or 3		r
Full Displacement	00001111	10001111	full displacement		7 + m or 3	7 + m or 3		r
JCXZ = Jump on CX Zero	11100011	8-bit displ			9 + m or 5	9 + m or 5		r
JECXZ = Jump on ECX Zero	11100011	8-bit displ			9 + m or 5	9 + m or 5		r
(Address Size Prefix Differentiates JCXZ from JECXZ)								
LOOP = Loop CX Times	11100010	8-bit displ			11 + m	11 + m		r
LOOPZ/LOOPE = Loop with Zero/Equal	11100001	8-bit displ			11 + m	11 + m		r
LOOPNZ/LOOPNE = Loop While Not Zero	11100000	8-bit displ			11 + m	11 + m		r
CONDITIONAL BYTE SET								
NOTE: Times Are Register/Memory								
SETO = Set Byte on Overflow								
To Register/Memory	00001111	10010000	mod 000	r/m	4/5	4/5		h
SETNO = Set Byte on Not Overflow								
To Register/Memory	00001111	10010001	mod 000	r/m	4/5	4/5		h
SETB/SETNAE = Set Byte on Below/Not Above or Equal								
To Register/Memory	00001111	10010010	mod 000	r/m	4/5	4/5		h

4

Table 6-1. Intel386™ DX Instruction Set Clock Count Summary (Continued)

INSTRUCTION	FORMAT			CLOCK COUNT		NOTES	
				Real Address Mode or Virtual 8086 Mode	Protected Virtual Address Mode	Real Address Mode or Virtual 8086 Mode	Protected Virtual Address Mode
CONDITIONAL BYTE SET (Continued)							
SETNB = Set Byte on Not Below/Above or Equal							
To Register/Memory	00001111	10010011	mod 000 r/m	4/5	4/5		h
SETE/SETZ = Set Byte on Equal/Zero							
To Register/Memory	00001111	10010100	mod 000 r/m	4/5	4/5		h
SETNE/SETNZ = Set Byte on Not Equal/Not Zero							
To Register/Memory	00001111	10010101	mod 000 r/m	4/5	4/5		h
SETBE/SETNA = Set Byte on Below or Equal/Not Above							
To Register/Memory	00001111	10010110	mod 000 r/m	4/5	4/5		h
SETNBE/SETA = Set Byte on Not Below or Equal/Above							
To Register/Memory	00001111	10010111	mod 000 r/m	4/5	4/5		h
SETS = Set Byte on Sign							
To Register/Memory	00001111	10011000	mod 000 r/m	4/5	4/5		h
SETNS = Set Byte on Not Sign							
To Register/Memory	00001111	10011001	mod 000 r/m	4/5	4/5		h
SETP/SETPE = Set Byte on Parity/Parity Even							
To Register/Memory	00001111	10011010	mod 000 r/m	4/5	4/5		h
SETNP/SETPO = Set Byte on Not Parity/Parity Odd							
To Register/Memory	00001111	10011011	mod 000 r/m	4/5	4/5		h
SETL/SETNGE = Set Byte on Less/Not Greater or Equal							
To Register/Memory	00001111	10011100	mod 000 r/m	4/5	4/5		h
SETNL/SETGE = Set Byte on Not Less/Greater or Equal							
To Register/Memory	00001111	01111101	mod 000 r/m	4/5	4/5		h
SETLE/SETNG = Set Byte on Less or Equal/Not Greater							
To Register/Memory	00001111	10011110	mod 000 r/m	4/5	4/5		h
SETNLE/SETG = Set Byte on Not Less or Equal/Greater							
To Register/Memory	00001111	10011111	mod 000 r/m	4/5	4/5		h
ENTER = Enter Procedure	11001000	16-bit displacement, 8-bit level					
L = 0				10	10	b	h
L = 1				12	12	b	h
L > 1				15 + 4(n − 1)	15 + 4(n − 1)	b	h
LEAVE = Leave Procedure	11001001			4	4	b	h

Table 6-1. Intel386™ DX Instruction Set Clock Count Summary (Continued)

INSTRUCTION	FORMAT		CLOCK COUNT		NOTES	
			Real Address Mode or Virtual 8086 Mode	Protected Virtual Address Mode	Real Address Mode or Virtual 8086 Mode	Protected Virtual Address Mode
INTERRUPT INSTRUCTIONS						
INT = Interrupt:						
Type Specified	11001101	type	37		b	
Type 3	11001100		33		b	
INTO = Interrupt 4 if Overflow Flag Set	11001110					
If OF = 1			35		b, e	
If OF = 0			3	3	b, e	
Bound = Interrupt 5 if Detect Value Out of Range	01100010	mod reg r/m				
If Out of Range			44		b, e	e, g, h, j, k, r
If In Range			10	10	b, e	e, g, h, j, k, r
Protected Mode Only (INT)						
INT: Type Specified						
Via Interrupt or Trap Gate to Same Privilege Level				59		g, j, k, r
Via Interrupt or Trap Gate to Different Privilege Level				99		g, j, k, r
From 80286 Task to 80286 TSS via Task Gate				282		g, j, k, r
From 80286 Task to Intel386 DX TSS via Task Gate				309		g, j, k, r
From 80286 Task to virt 8086 md via Task Gate				226		g, j, k, r
From Intel386 DX Task to 80286 TSS via Task Gate				284		g, j, k, r
From Intel386 DX Task to Intel386 DX TSS via Task Gate				311		g, j, k, r
From Intel386 DX Task to virt 8086 md via Task Gate				228		g, j, k, r
From virt 8086 md to 80286 TSS via Task Gate				289		g, j, k, r
From virt 8086 md to Intel386 DX TSS via Task Gate				316		g, j, k, r
From virt 8086 md to priv level 0 via Trap Gate or Interrupt Gate				119		
INT: TYPE 3						
Via Interrupt or Trap Gate to Same Privilege Level				59		g, j, k, r
Via Interrupt or Trap Gate to Different Privilege Level				99		g, j, k, r
From 80286 Task to 80286 TSS via Task Gate				278		g, j, k, r
From 80286 Task to Intel386 DX TSS via Task Gate				305		g, j, k, r
From 80286 Task to Virt 8086 md via Task Gate				222		g, j, k, r
From Intel386 DX Task to 80286 TSS via Task Gate				280		g, j, k, r
From Intel386 DX Task to Intel386 DX TSS via Task Gate				307		g, j, k, r
From Intel386 DX Task to Virt 8086 md via Task Gate				224		g, j, k, r
From virt 8086 md to 80286 TSS via Task Gate				285		g, j, k, r
From virt 8086 md to Intel386 DX TSS via Task Gate				312		g, j, k, r
From virt 8086 md to priv level 0 via Trap Gate or Interrupt Gate				119		
INTO:						
Via Interrupt or Trap Grate to Same Privilege Level				59		g, j, k, r
Via Interrupt or Trap Gate to Different Privilege Level				99		g, j, k, r
From 80286 Task to 80286 TSS via Task Gate				280		g, j, k, r
From 80286 Task to Intel386 DX TSS via Task Gate				307		g, j, k, r
From 80286 Task to virt 8086 md via Task Gate				224		g, j, k, r
From Intel386 DX Task to 80286 TSS via Task Gate				282		g, j, k, r
From Intel386 DX Task to Intel386 DX TSS via Task Gate				309		g, j, k, r
From Intel386 DX Gate				225		g, j, k, r
From virt 8086 md to 80286 TSS via Task Gate				287		g, j, k, r
From virt 8086 md to Intel386 DX TSS via Task Gate				314		g, j, k, r
From virt 8086 md to priv level 0 via Trap Gate or Interrupt Gate				119		

Table 6-1. Intel386™ DX Instruction Set Clock Count Summary (Continued)

INSTRUCTION	FORMAT			CLOCK COUNT: Real Address Mode or Virtual 8086 Mode	CLOCK COUNT: Protected Virtual Address Mode	NOTES: Real Address Mode or Virtual 8086 Mode	NOTES: Protected Virtual Address Mode
INTERRUPT INSTRUCTIONS (Continued)							
BOUND:							
Via Interrupt or Trap Gate to Same Privilege Level					59		g, j, k, r
Via Interrupt or Trap Gate to Different Privilege Level					99		g, j, k, r
From 80286 Task to 80286 TSS via Task Gate					254		g, j, k, r
From 80286 Task to Intel386 DX TSS via Task Gate					284		g, j, k, r
From 80268 Task to virt 8086 Mode via Task Gate					231		g, j, k, r
From Intel386 DX Task to 80286 TSS via Task Gate					264		g, j, k, r
From Intel386 DX Task to Intel386 DX TSS via Task Gate					294		g, j, k, r
From 80368 Task to virt 8086 Mode via Task Gate					243		g, j, k, r,
From virt 8086 Mode to 80286 TSS via Task Gate					264		g, j, k, r
From virt 8086 Mode to Intel386 DX TSS via Task Gate					294		g, j, k, r
From virt 8086 md to priv level 0 via Trap Gate or Interrupt Gate					119		
INTERRUPT RETURN							
IRET = Interrupt Return	11001111			22			g, h, j, k, r
Protected Mode Only (IRET)							
To the Same Privilege Level (within task)					38		g, h, j, k, r
To Different Privilege Level (within task)					82		g, h, j, k, r
From 80286 Task to 80286 TSS					232		h, j, k, r
From 80286 Task to Intel386 DX TSS					265		h, j, k, r
From 80286 Task to Virtual 8086 Task					213		h, j, k, r
From 80286 Task to Virtual 8086 Mode (within task)					60		
From Intel386 DX Task to 80286 TSS					271		h, j, k, r
From Intel386 DX Task to Intel386 DX TSS					275		h, j, k, r
From Intel386 DX Task to Virtual 8086 Task					223		h, j, k, r
From Intel386 DX Task to Virtual 8086 Mode (within task)					60		
PROCESSOR CONTROL							
HLT = HALT	11110100			5	5		l
MOV = Move to and From Control/Debug/Test Registers							
CR0/CR2/CR3 from register	00001111	00100010	1 1 eee reg	11/4/5	11/4/5		l
Register From CR0–3	00001111	00100000	1 1 eee reg	6	6		l
DR0–3 From Register	00001111	00100011	1 1 eee reg	22	22		l
DR6–7 From Register	00001111	00100011	1 1 eee reg	16	16		l
Register from DR6–7	00001111	00100001	1 1 eee reg	14	14		l
Register from DR0–3	00001111	00100001	1 1 eee reg	22	22		l
TR6–7 from Register	00001111	00100110	1 1 eee reg	12	12		l
Register from TR6–7	00001111	00100100	1 1 eee reg	12	12		l
NOP = No Operation	10010000			3	3		
WAIT = Wait until BUSY # pin is negated	10011011			7	7		

Table 6-1. Intel386™ DX Instruction Set Clock Count Summary (Continued)

INSTRUCTION	FORMAT				CLOCK COUNT		NOTES	
					Real Address Mode or Virtual 8086 Mode	Protected Virtual Address Mode	Real Address Mode or Virtual 8086 Mode	Protected Virtual Address Mode
PROCESSOR EXTENSION INSTRUCTIONS								
Processor Extension Escape	11011TTT	mod LLL r/m			See 80287/80Intel387 data sheets for clock counts			h
	TTT and LLL bits are opcode information for coprocessor.							
PREFIX BYTES								
Address Size Prefix	01100111				0	0		
LOCK = Bus Lock Prefix	11110000				0	0		m
Operand Size Prefix	01100110				0	0		
Segment Override Prefix								
CS:	00101110				0	0		
DS:	00111110				0	0		
ES:	00100110				0	0		
FS:	01100100				0	0		
GS:	01100101				0	0		
SS:	00110110				0	0		
PROTECTION CONTROL								
ARPL = Adjust Requested Privilege Level								
From Register/Memory	01100011	mod reg r/m			N/A	20/21	a	h
LAR = Load Access Rights								
From Register/Memory	00001111	00000010	mod reg r/m		N/A	15/16	a	g, h, j, p
LGDT = Load Global Descriptor								
Table Register	00001111	00000001	mod 010 r/m		11	11	b, c	h, l
LIDT = Load Interrupt Descriptor								
Table Register	00001111	00000001	mod 011 r/m		11	11	b, c	h, l
LLDT = Load Local Descriptor								
Table Register to Register/Memory	00001111	00000000	mod 010 r/m		N/A	20/24	a	g, h, j, l
LMSW = Load Machine Status Word								
From Register/Memory	00001111	00000001	mod 110 r/m		11/14	11/14	b, c	h, l
LSL = Load Segment Limit								
From Register/Memory	00001111	00000011	mod reg r/m					
Byte-Granular Limit					N/A	21/22	a	g, h, j, p
Page-Granular Limit					N/A	25/26	a	g, h, j, p
LTR = Load Task Register								
From Register/Memory	00001111	00000000	mod 011 r/m		N/A	23/27	a	g, h, j, l
SGDT = Store Global Descriptor								
Table Register	00001111	00000001	mod 000 r/m		9	9	b, c	h
SIDT = Store Interrupt Descriptor								
Table Register	00001111	00000001	mod 001 r/m		9	9	b, c	h
SLDT = Store Local Descriptor Table Register								
To Register/Memory	00001111	00000000	mod 000 r/m		N/A	2/2	a	h

4

Table 6-1. Intel386™ DX Instruction Set Clock Count Summary (Continued)

INSTRUCTION		FORMAT			CLOCK COUNT		NOTES	
					Real Address Mode or Virtual 8086 Mode	Protected Virtual Address Mode	Real Address Mode or Virtual 8086 Mode	Protected Virtual Address Mode
SMSW	**= Store Machine Status Word**	00001111	00000001	mod 100 r/m	2/2	2/2	b, c	h, l
STR	**= Store Task Register**							
	To Register/Memory	00001111	00000000	mod 001 r/m	N/A	2/2	a	h
VERR	**= Verify Read Accesss**							
	Register/Memory	00001111	00000000	mod 100 r/m	N/A	10/11	a	g, h, j, p
VERW	**= Verify Write Accesss**	00001111	00000000	mod 101 r/m	N/A	15/16	a	g, h, j, p

INSTRUCTION NOTES FOR TABLE 6-1

Notes a through c apply to Intel386 DX Real Address Mode only:

a. This is a Protected Mode instruction. Attempted execution in Real Mode will result in exception 6 (invalid opcode).

b. Exception 13 fault (general protection) will occur in Real Mode if an operand reference is made that partially or fully extends beyond the maximum CS, DS, ES, FS or GS limit, FFFFH. Exception 12 fault (stack segment limit violation or not present) will occur in Real Mode if an operand reference is made that partially or fully extends beyond the maximum SS limit.

c. This instruction may be executed in Real Mode. In Real Mode, its purpose is primarily to initialize the CPU for Protected Mode.

Notes d through g apply to Intel386 DX Real Address Mode and Intel386 DX Protected Virtual Address Mode:

d. The Intel386 DX uses an early-out multiply algorithm. The actual number of clocks depends on the position of the most significant bit in the operand (multiplier).

Clock counts given are minimum to maximum. To calculate actual clocks use the following formula:

Actual Clock = if $m <> 0$ then max ($[\log_2 |m|]$, 3) + b clocks:

if $m = 0$ then $3+b$ clocks

In this formula, m is the multiplier, and

b = 9 for register to register,

b = 12 for memory to register,

b = 10 for register with immediate to register,

b = 11 for memory with immediate to register.

e. An exception may occur, depending on the value of the operand.

f. LOCK# is automatically asserted, regardless of the presence or absence of the LOCK# prefix.

g. LOCK# is asserted during descriptor table accesses.

Notes h through r apply to Intel386 DX Protected Virtual Address Mode only:

h. Exception 13 fault (general protection violation) will occur if the memory operand in CS, DS, ES, FS or GS cannot be used due to either a segment limit violation or access rights violation. If a stack limit is violated, an exception 12 (stack segment limit violation or not present) occurs.

i. For segment load operations, the CPL, RPL, and DPL must agree with the privilege rules to avoid an exception 13 fault (general protection violation). The segment's descriptor must indicate "present" or exception 11 (CS, DS, ES, FS, GS not present). If the SS register is loaded and a stack segment not present is detected, an exception 12 (stack segment limit violation or not present) occurs.

j. All segment descriptor accesses in the GDT or LDT made by this instruction will automatically assert LOCK# to maintain descriptor integrity in multiprocessor systems.

k. JMP, CALL, INT, RET and IRET instructions referring to another code segment will cause an exception 13 (general protection violation) if an applicable privilege rule is violated.

l. An exception 13 fault occurs if CPL is greater than 0 (0 is the most privileged level).

m. An exception 13 fault occurs if CPL is greater than IOPL.

n. The IF bit of the flag register is not updated if CPL is greater than IOPL. The IOPL and VM fields of the flag register are updated only if CPL = 0.

o. The PE bit of the MSW (CR0) cannot be reset by this instruction. Use MOV into CR0 if desiring to reset the PE bit.

p. Any violation of privilege rules as applied to the selector operand does not cause a protection exception; rather, the zero flag is cleared.

q. If the coprocessor's memory operand violates a segment limit or segment access rights, an exception 13 fault (general protection exception) will occur before the ESC instruction is executed. An exception 12 fault (stack segment limit violation or not present) will occur if the stack limit is violated by the operand's starting address.

r. The destination of a JMP, CALL, INT, RET or IRET must be in the defined limit of a code segment or an exception 13 fault (general protection violation) will occur.

6.2 INSTRUCTION ENCODING

6.2.1 Overview

All instruction encodings are subsets of the general instruction format shown in Figure 6-1. Instructions consist of one or two primary opcode bytes, possibly an address specifier consisting of the "mod r/m" byte and "scaled index" byte, a displacement if required, and an immediate data field if required.

Within the primary opcode or opcodes, smaller encoding fields may be defined. These fields vary according to the class of operation. The fields define such information as direction of the operation, size of the displacements, register encoding, or sign extension.

Almost all instructions referring to an operand in memory have an addressing mode byte following the primary opcode byte(s). This byte, the mod r/m byte, specifies the address mode to be used. Certain encodings of the mod r/m byte indicate a second addressing byte, the scale-index-base byte, follows the mod r/m byte to fully specify the addressing mode.

Addressing modes can include a displacement immediately following the mod r/m byte, or scaled index byte. If a displacement is present, the possible sizes are 8, 16 or 32 bits.

If the instruction specifies an immediate operand, the immediate operand follows any displacement bytes. The immediate operand, if specified, is always the last field of the instruction.

Figure 6-1 illustrates several of the fields that can appear in an instruction, such as the mod field and the r/m field, but the Figure does not show all fields. Several smaller fields also appear in certain instructions, sometimes within the opcode bytes themselves. Table 6-2 is a complete list of all fields appearing in the Intel386 DX instruction set. Further ahead, following Table 6-2, are detailed tables for each field.

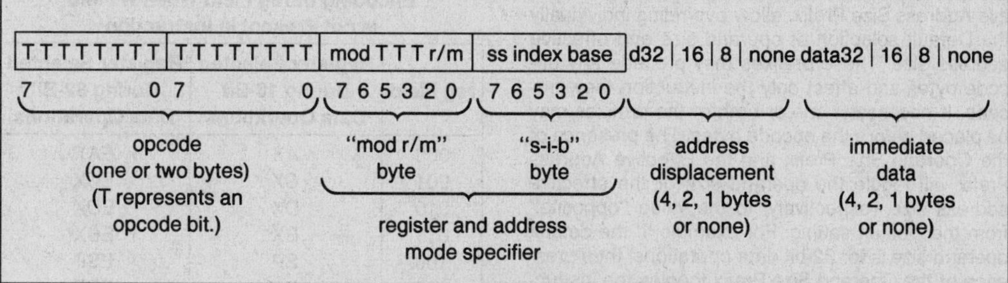

Figure 6-1. General Instruction Format

Table 6-2. Fields within Intel386™ DX Instructions

Field Name	Description	Number of Bits
w	Specifies if Data is Byte or Full Size (Full Size is either 16 or 32 Bits	1
d	Specifies Direction of Data Operation	1
s	Specifies if an Immediate Data Field Must be Sign-Extended	1
reg	General Register Specifier	3
mod r/m	Address Mode Specifier (Effective Address can be a General Register)	2 for mod; 3 for r/m
ss	Scale Factor for Scaled Index Address Mode	2
index	General Register to be used as Index Register	3
base	General Register to be used as Base Register	3
sreg2	Segment Register Specifier for CS, SS, DS, ES	2
sreg3	Segment Register Specifier for CS, SS, DS, ES, FS, GS	3
tttn	For Conditional Instructions, Specifies a Condition Asserted or a Condition Negated	4

Note: Table 6-1 shows encoding of individual instructions.

6.2.2 32-Bit Extensions of the Instruction Set

With the Intel386 DX, the 8086/80186/80286 instruction set is extended in two orthogonal directions: 32-bit forms of all 16-bit instructions are added to support the 32-bit data types, and 32-bit addressing modes are made available for all instructions referencing memory. This orthogonal instruction set extension is accomplished having a Default (D) bit in the code segment descriptor, and by having 2 prefixes to the instruction set.

Whether the instruction defaults to operations of 16 bits or 32 bits depends on the setting of the D bit in the code segment descriptor, which gives the default length (either 32 bits or 16 bits) for both operands and effective addresses when executing that code segment. In the Real Address Mode or Virtual 8086 Mode, no code segment descriptors are used, but a D value of 0 is assumed internally by the Intel386 DX when operating in those modes (for 16-bit default sizes compatible with the 8086/80186/80286).

Two prefixes, the Operand Size Prefix and the Effective Address Size Prefix, allow overriding individually the Default selection of operand size and effective address size. These prefixes may precede any opcode bytes and affect only the instruction they precede. If necessary, one or both of the prefixes may be placed before the opcode bytes. The presence of the Operand Size Prefix and the Effective Address Prefix will toggle the operand size or the effective address size, respectively, to the value "opposite" from the Default setting. For example, if the default operand size is for 32-bit data operations, then presence of the Operand Size Prefix toggles the instruction to 16-bit data operation. As another example, if the default effective address size is 16 bits, presence of the Effective Address Size prefix toggles the instruction to use 32-bit effective address computations.

These 32-bit extensions are available in all Intel386 DX modes, including the Real Address Mode or the Virtual 8086 Mode. In these modes the default is always 16 bits, so prefixes are needed to specify 32-bit operands or addresses. For instructions with more than one prefix, the order of prefixes is unimportant.

Unless specified otherwise, instructions with 8-bit and 16-bit operands do not affect the contents of the high-order bits of the extended registers.

6.2.3 Encoding of Instruction Fields

Within the instruction are several fields indicating register selection, addressing mode and so on. The exact encodings of these fields are defined immediately ahead.

6.2.3.1 ENCODING OF OPERAND LENGTH (w) FIELD

For any given instruction performing a data operation, the instruction is executing as a 32-bit operation or a 16-bit operation. Within the constraints of the operation size, the w field encodes the operand size as either one byte or the full operation size, as shown in the table below.

w Field	Operand Size During 16-Bit Data Operations	Operand Size During 32-Bit Data Operations
0	8 Bits	8 Bits
1	16 Bits	32 Bits

6.2.3.2 ENCODING OF THE GENERAL REGISTER (reg) FIELD

The general register is specified by the reg field, which may appear in the primary opcode bytes, or as the reg field of the "mod r/m" byte, or as the r/m field of the "mod r/m" byte.

Encoding of reg Field When w Field is not Present in Instruction

reg Field	Register Selected During 16-Bit Data Operations	Register Selected During 32-Bit Data Operations
000	AX	EAX
001	CX	ECX
010	DX	EDX
011	BX	EBX
100	SP	ESP
101	BP	EBP
110	SI	ESI
111	DI	EDI

Encoding of reg Field When w Field is Present in Instruction

reg	Register Specified by reg Field During 16-Bit Data Operations: Function of w Field (when w = 0)	(when w = 1)
000	AL	AX
001	CL	CX
010	DL	DX
011	BL	BX
100	AH	SP
101	CH	BP
110	DH	SI
111	BH	DI

reg	Register Specified by reg Field During 32-Bit Data Operations	
	Function of w Field	
	(when w = 0)	(when w = 1)
000	AL	EAX
001	CL	ECX
010	DL	EDX
011	BL	EBX
100	AH	ESP
101	CH	EBP
110	DH	ESI
111	BH	EDI

6.2.3.3 ENCODING OF THE SEGMENT REGISTER (sreg) FIELD

The sreg field in certain instructions is a 2-bit field allowing one of the four 80286 segment registers to be specified. The sreg field in other instructions is a 3-bit field, allowing the Intel386 DX FS and GS segment registers to be specified.

2-Bit sreg2 Field

2-Bit sreg2 Field	Segment Register Selected
00	ES
01	CS
10	SS
11	DS

3-Bit sreg3 Field

3-Bit sreg3 Field	Segment Register Selected
000	ES
001	CS
010	SS
011	DS
100	FS
101	GS
110	do not use
111	do not use

6.2.3.4 ENCODING OF ADDRESS MODE

Except for special instructions, such as PUSH or POP, where the addressing mode is pre-determined, the addressing mode for the current instruction is specified by addressing bytes following the primary opcode. The primary addressing byte is the "mod r/m" byte, and a second byte of addressing information, the "s-i-b" (scale-index-base) byte, can be specified.

The s-i-b byte (scale-index-base byte) is specified when using 32-bit addressing mode and the "mod r/m" byte has r/m = 100 and mod = 00, 01 or 10. When the sib byte is present, the 32-bit addressing mode is a function of the mod, ss, index, and base fields.

The primary addressing byte, the "mod r/m" byte, also contains three bits (shown as TTT in Figure 6-1) sometimes used as an extension of the primary opcode. The three bits, however, may also be used as a register field (reg).

When calculating an effective address, either 16-bit addressing or 32-bit addressing is used. 16-bit addressing uses 16-bit address components to calculate the effective address while 32-bit addressing uses 32-bit address components to calculate the effective address. When 16-bit addressing is used, the "mod r/m" byte is interpreted as a 16-bit addressing mode specifier. When 32-bit addressing is used, the "mod r/m" byte is interpreted as a 32-bit addressing mode specifier.

Tables on the following three pages define all encodings of all 16-bit addressing modes and 32-bit addressing modes.

Encoding of 16-bit Address Mode with "mod r/m" Byte

mod r/m	Effective Address
00 000	DS:[BX+SI]
00 001	DS:[BX+DI]
00 010	SS:[BP+SI]
00 011	SS:[BP+DI]
00 100	DS:[SI]
00 101	DS:[DI]
00 110	DS:d16
00 111	DS:[BX]
01 000	DS:[BX+SI+d8]
01 001	DS:[BX+DI+d8]
01 010	SS:[BP+SI+d8]
01 011	SS:[BP+DI+d8]
01 100	DS:[SI+d8]
01 101	DS:[DI+d8]
01 110	SS:[BP+d8]
01 111	DS:[BX+d8]

mod r/m	Effective Address
10 000	DS:[BX+SI+d16]
10 001	DS:[BX+DI+d16]
10 010	SS:[BP+SI+d16]
10 011	SS:[BP+DI+d16]
10 100	DS:[SI+d16]
10 101	DS:[DI+d16]
10 110	SS:[BP+d16]
10 111	DS:[BX+d16]
11 000	register—see below
11 001	register—see below
11 010	register—see below
11 011	register—see below
11 100	register—see below
11 101	register—see below
11 110	register—see below
11 111	register—see below

Register Specified by r/m During 16-Bit Data Operations

mod r/m	Function of w Field	
	(when w=0)	(when w = 1)
11 000	AL	AX
11 001	CL	CX
11 010	DL	DX
11 011	BL	BX
11 100	AH	SP
11 101	CH	BP
11 110	DH	SI
11 111	BH	DI

Register Specified by r/m During 32-Bit Data Operations

mod r/m	Function of w Field	
	(when w=0)	(when w = 1)
11 000	AL	EAX
11 001	CL	ECX
11 010	DL	EDX
11 011	BL	EBX
11 100	AH	ESP
11 101	CH	EBP
11 110	DH	ESI
11 111	BH	EDI

Encoding of 32-bit Address Mode with "mod r/m" byte (no "s-i-b" byte present):

mod r/m	Effective Address
00 000	DS:[EAX]
00 001	DS:[ECX]
00 010	DS:[EDX]
00 011	DS:[EBX]
00 100	s-i-b is present
00 101	DS:d32
00 110	DS:[ESI]
00 111	DS:[EDI]
01 000	DS:[EAX+d8]
01 001	DS:[ECX+d8]
01 010	DS:[EDX+d8]
01 011	DS:[EBX+d8]
01 100	s-i-b is present
01 101	SS:[EBP+d8]
01 110	DS:[ESI+d8]
01 111	DS:[EDI+d8]

mod r/m	Effective Address
10 000	DS:[EAX+d32]
10 001	DS:[ECX+d32]
10 010	DS:[EDX+d32]
10 011	DS:[EBX+d32]
10 100	s-i-b is present
10 101	SS:[EBP+d32]
10 110	DS:[ESI+d32]
10 111	DS:[EDI+d32]
11 000	register—see below
11 001	register—see below
11 010	register—see below
11 011	register—see below
11 100	register—see below
11 101	register—see below
11 110	register—see below
11 111	register—see below

Register Specified by reg or r/m during 16-Bit Data Operations:

mod r/m	function of w field	
	(when w=0)	(when w=1)
11 000	AL	AX
11 001	CL	CX
11 010	DL	DX
11 011	BL	BX
11 100	AH	SP
11 101	CH	BP
11 110	DH	SI
11 111	BH	DI

Register Specified by reg or r/m during 32-Bit Data Operations:

mod r/m	function of w field	
	(when w=0)	(when w=1)
11 000	AL	EAX
11 001	CL	ECX
11 010	DL	EDX
11 011	BL	EBX
11 100	AH	ESP
11 101	CH	EBP
11 110	DH	ESI
11 111	BH	EDI

4

Encoding of 32-bit Address Mode ("mod r/m" byte and "s-i-b" byte present):

mod base	Effective Address
00 000	DS:[EAX + (scaled index)]
00 001	DS:[ECX + (scaled index)]
00 010	DS:[EDX + (scaled index)]
00 011	DS:[EBX + (scaled index)]
00 100	SS:[ESP + (scaled index)]
00 101	DS:[d32 + (scaled index)]
00 110	DS:[ESI + (scaled index)]
00 111	DS:[EDI + (scaled index)]
01 000	DS:[EAX + (scaled index) + d8]
01 001	DS:[ECX + (scaled index) + d8]
01 010	DS:[EDX + (scaled index) + d8]
01 011	DS:[EBX + (scaled index) + d8]
01 100	SS:[ESP + (scaled index) + d8]
01 101	SS:[EBP + (scaled index) + d8]
01 110	DS:[ESI + (scaled index) + d8]
01 111	DS:[EDI + (scaled index) + d8]
10 000	DS:[EAX + (scaled index) + d32]
10 001	DS:[ECX + (scaled index) + d32]
10 010	DS:[EDX + (scaled index) + d32]
10 011	DS:[EBX + (scaled index) + d32]
10 100	SS:[ESP + (scaled index) + d32]
10 101	SS:[EBP + (scaled index) + d32]
10 110	DS:[ESI + (scaled index) + d32]
10 111	DS:[EDI + (scaled index) + d32]

NOTE:
Mod field in "mod r/m" byte; ss, index, base fields in "s-i-b" byte.

ss	Scale Factor
00	x1
01	x2
10	x4
11	x8

index	Index Register
000	EAX
001	ECX
010	EDX
011	EBX
100	no index reg**
101	EBP
110	ESI
111	EDI

****IMPORTANT NOTE:**
When index field is 100, indicating "no index register," then ss field MUST equal 00. If index is 100 and ss does not equal 00, the effective address is undefined.

6.2.3.5 ENCODING OF OPERATION DIRECTION (d) FIELD

In many two-operand instructions the d field is present to indicate which operand is considered the source and which is the destination.

d	Direction of Operation
0	Register/Memory <- - Register "reg" Field Indicates Source Operand; "mod r/m" or "mod ss index base" Indicates Destination Operand
1	Register <- - Register/Memory "reg" Field Indicates Destination Operand; "mod r/m" or "mod ss index base" Indicates Source Operand

6.2.3.6 ENCODING OF SIGN-EXTEND (s) FIELD

The s field occurs primarily to instructions with immediate data fields. The s field has an effect only if the size of the immediate data is 8 bits and is being placed in a 16-bit or 32-bit destination.

s	Effect on Immediate Data8	Effect on Immediate Data 16|32
0	None	None
1	Sign-Extend Data8 to Fill 16-Bit or 32-Bit Destination	None

6.2.3.7 ENCODING OF CONDITIONAL TEST (tttn) FIELD

For the conditional instructions (conditional jumps and set on condition), tttn is encoded with n indicating to use the condition (n = 0) or its negation (n = 1), and ttt giving the condition to test.

Mnemonic	Condition	tttn
O	Overflow	0000
NO	No Overflow	0001
B/NAE	Below/Not Above or Equal	0010
NB/AE	Not Below/Above or Equal	0011
E/Z	Equal/Zero	0100
NE/NZ	Not Equal/Not Zero	0101
BE/NA	Below or Equal/Not Above	0110
NBE/A	Not Below or Equal/Above	0111
S	Sign	1000
NS	Not Sign	1001
P/PE	Parity/Parity Even	1010
NP/PO	Not Parity/Parity Odd	1011
L/NGE	Less Than/Not Greater or Equal	1100
NL/GE	Not Less Than/Greater or Equal	1101
LE/NG	Less Than or Equal/Greater Than	1110
NLE/G	Not Less or Equal/Greater Than	1111

6.2.3.8 ENCODING OF CONTROL OR DEBUG OR TEST REGISTER (eee) FIELD

For the loading and storing of the Control, Debug and Test registers.

When Interpreted as Control Register Field

eee Code	Reg Name
000	CR0
010	CR2
011	CR3
Do not use any other encoding	

When Interpreted as Debug Register Field

eee Code	Reg Name
000	DR0
001	DR1
010	DR2
011	DR3
110	DR6
111	DR7
Do not use any other encoding	

When Interpreted as Test Register Field

eee Code	Reg Name
110	TR6
111	TR7
Do not use any other encoding	

4

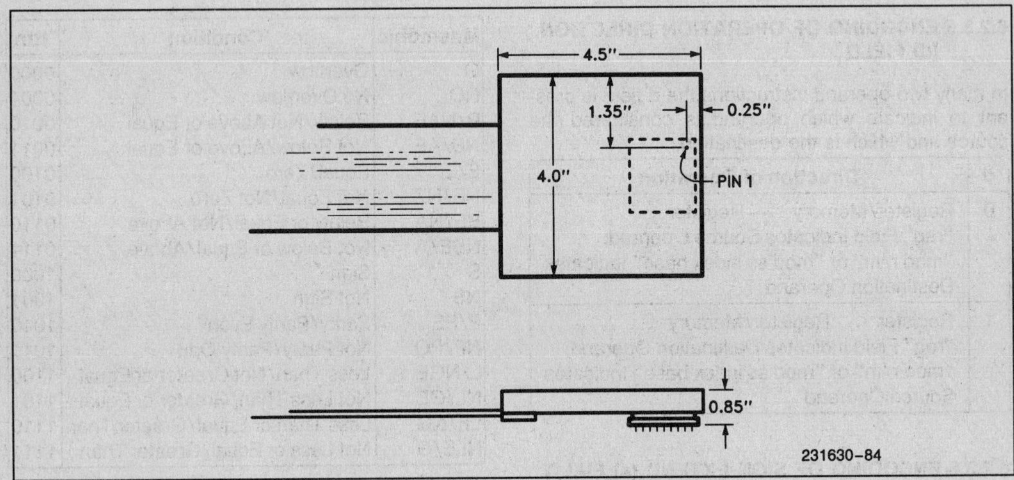

Figure 7-1. Processor Module Dimensions

7. DESIGNING FOR ICE™-Intel386 DX EMULATOR USE

The Intel386 DX in-circuit emulator products are ICE-Intel386 DX 25 MHz or 33 MHz (both referred to as ICE-Intel386 DX emulator). The ICE-Intel386 DX emulator probe module has several electrical and mechanical characteristics that should be taken into consideration when designing the hardware.

Capacitive loading: The ICE-Intel386 DX emulator adds up to 25 pF to each line.

Drive requirement: The ICE-Intel386 DX emulator adds one standard TTL load on the CLK2 line, up to one advanced low-power Schottky TTL load per control signal line, and one advanced low-power Schottky TTL load per address, byte enable, and data line. These loads are within the probe module and are driven by the probe's Intel386 DX component, which has standard drive and loading capability listed in the A.C. and D.C. Specification Tables in Sections 9.4 and 9.5.

Power requirement: For noise immunity the ICE-Intel386 DX emulator probe is powered by the user system. This high-speed probe circuitry draws up to 1.5A plus the maximum I_{CC} from the user Intel386 DX component socket.

Intel386 DX location and orientation: The ICE-Intel386 DX processor module, target-adaptor cable (which does not exist for the ICE-Intel386 DX 33 MHz emulator), and the isolation board used for extra electrical buffering of the emulator initially, require clearance as illustrated in Figures 7-1 and 7-2.

Interface Board and CLK2 speed reduction: When the ICE-Intel386 DX emulator probe is first attached to an unverified user system, the interface board helps the ICE-Intel386 DX emulator function in user systems with bus faults (shorted signals, etc.). After electrical verification it may be removed. Only when the interface board is installed, the user system must have a reduced CLK2 frequency of 25 MHz maximum.

Cache coherence: The ICE-Intel386 DX emulator loads user memory by performing Intel386 DX component write cycles. Note that if the user system is not designed to update or invalidate its cache (if it has a cache) upon processor writes to memory, the cache could contain stale instruction code and/or data. For best use of the ICE-Intel386 DX emulator, the user should consider designing the cache (if any) to update itself automatically when processor writes occur, or find another method of maintaining cache data coherence with main user memory.

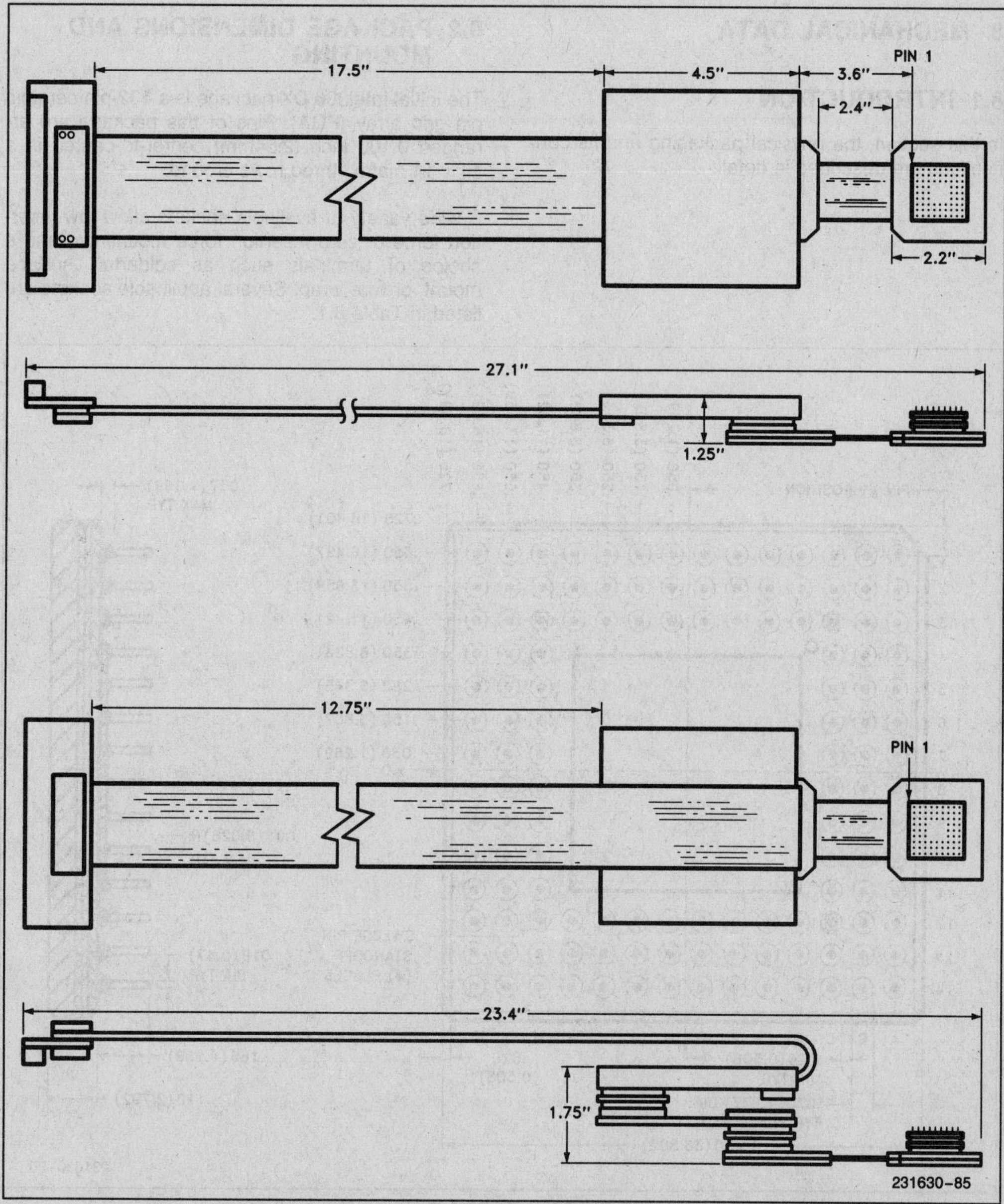

17.5″
4.5″
3.6″
PIN 1
2.4″
2.2″
27.1″
1.25″
12.75″
PIN 1
23.4″
1.75″
231630–85

Figure 7-2. Processor Module, Target-Adapter Cable, and Isolation Board Dimensions

4

8. MECHANICAL DATA

8.1 INTRODUCTION

In this section, the physical packaging and its connections are described in detail.

8.2 PACKAGE DIMENSIONS AND MOUNTING

The initial Intel386 DX package is a 132-pin ceramic pin grid array (PGA). Pins of this package are arranged 0.100 inch (2.54mm) center-to-center, in a 14 x 14 matrix, three rows around.

A wide variety of available sockets allow low insertion force or zero insertion force mountings, and a choice of terminals such as soldertail, surface mount, or wire wrap. Several applicable sockets are listed in Table 8.1.

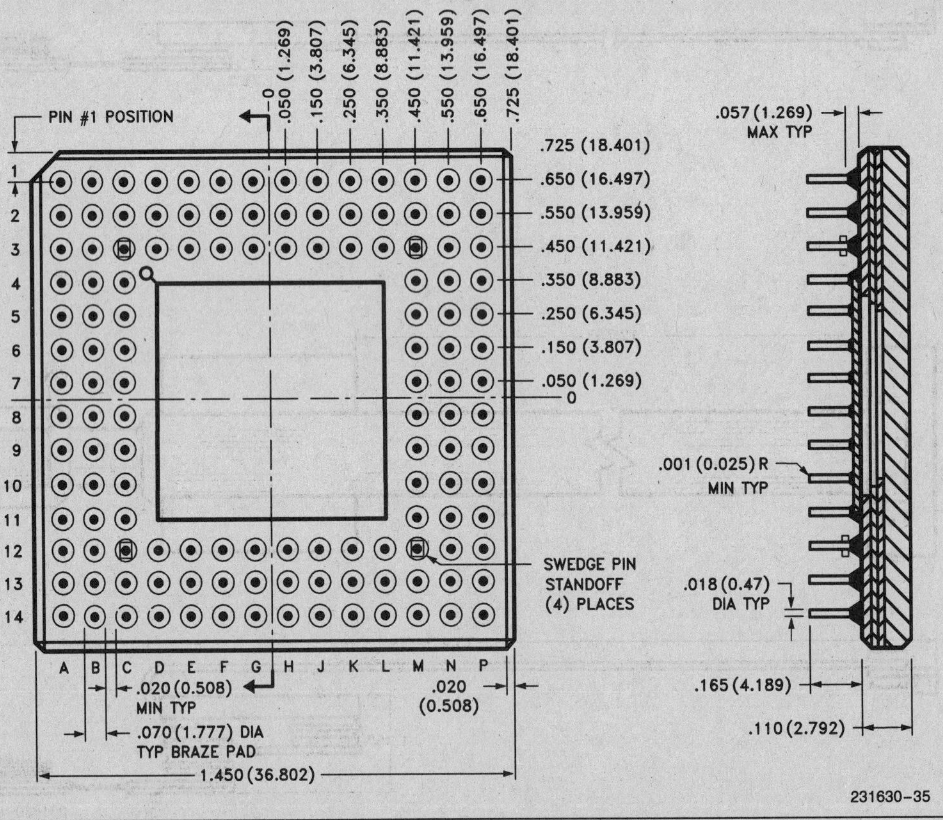

231630-35

Figure 8.1. 132-Pin Ceramic PGA Package Dimensions

Table 8.1. Several Socket Options for 132-Pin PGA

* Low insertion force (LIF) soldertail 55274-1
* Amp tests indicate 50% reduction in insertion force compared to machined sockets

Other socket options
* Zero insertion force (ZIF) soldertail 55583-1
* Zero insertion force (ZIF) Burn-in version 55573-2

Amp Incorporated
(Harrisburg, PA 17105 U.S.A.
Phone 717-564-0100)

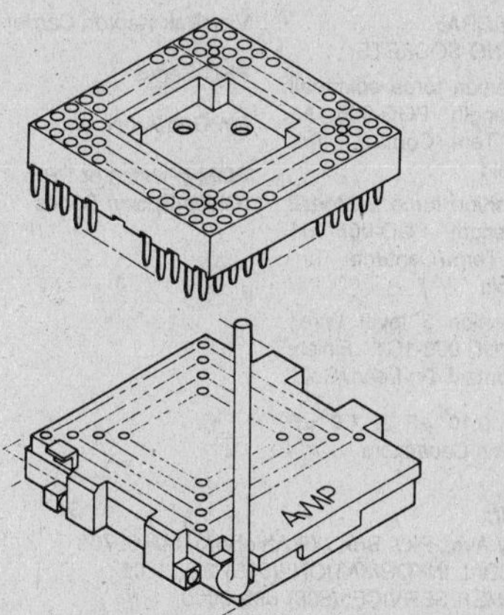

231630-45

Cam handle locks in low profile position when substrate is installed (handle UP for open and DOWN for closed positions)

courtesy Amp Incorporated

Peel-A-Way™ Mylar and Kapton Socket Terminal Carriers
* Low insertion force surface mount CS132-37TG
* Low insertion force soldertail CS132-01TG
* Low insertion force wire-wrap CS132-02TG (two level) CS132-03TG (three-level)
* Low insertion force press-fit CS132-05TG

Advanced Interconnections
(5 Division Street
Warwick, RI 02818 U.S.A.
Phone 401-885-0485)

Peel-A-Way Carrier No. 132:
Kapton Carrier is KS132
Mylar Carrier is MS132

Molded Plastic Body KS132 is shown below:

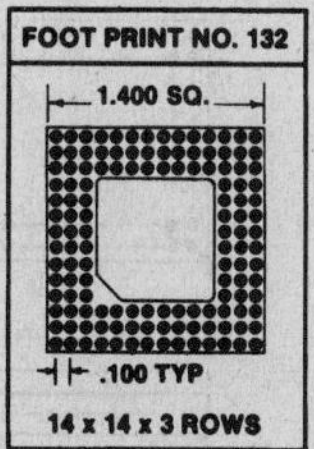

231630-46

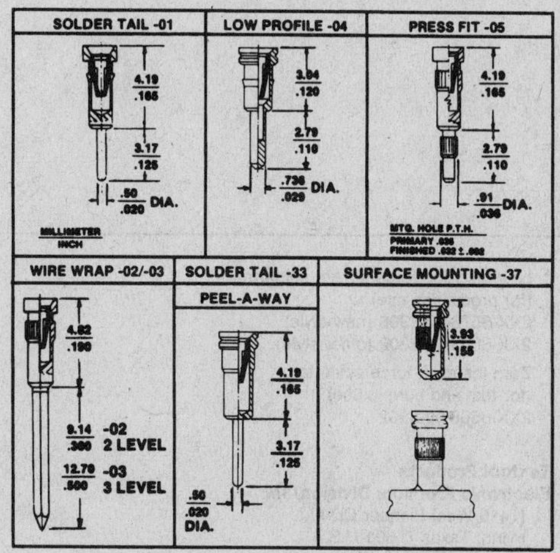

231630-47

courtesy Advanced Interconnections
(Peel-A-Way Terminal Carriers
U.S. Patent No. 4442938)

Table 8.1. Several Socket Options for 132-Pin PGA (Continued)

PIN GRID ARRAY DECOUPLING SOCKETS

* Low insertion force soldertail 0.125 length PGD-005-1A1 Finish: Term/Contact Tin-Lead/Gold
* Low insertion force soldertail 0.180 length PGD-005-1B1 Finish: Term/Contact: Tin-Lead/Gold
* Low insertion 3 level Wire/Wrap PGD-005-1C1 Finish: Term/Contact Tin-Lead/Gold

Includes 0.10 μF & 1.0 μF Decoupling Capacitors

VisinPak Kapton Carrier

PKC Series

Pin Grid Array

PGM (Plastic) or PPS (Glass Epoxy) Series

AUGAT INC.
33 Perry Ave., P.O. Box 779 Attleboro, MA 02703
TECHNICAL INFORMATION: (508) 222-2202
CUSTOMER SERVICE: (508) 699-9800

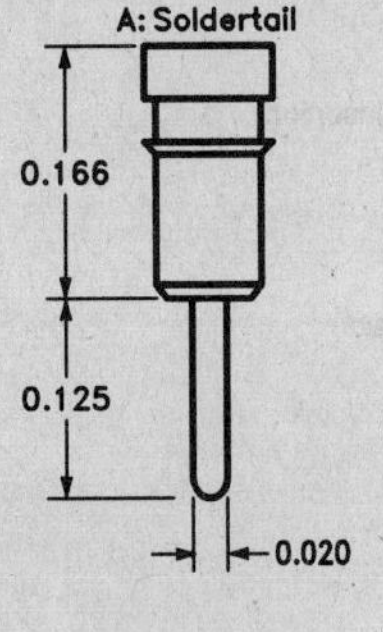

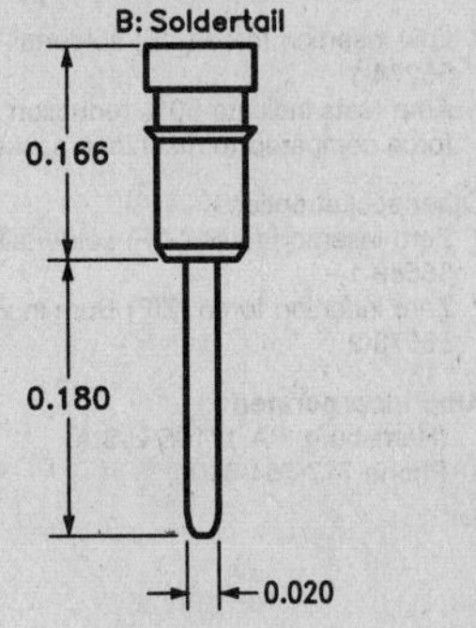

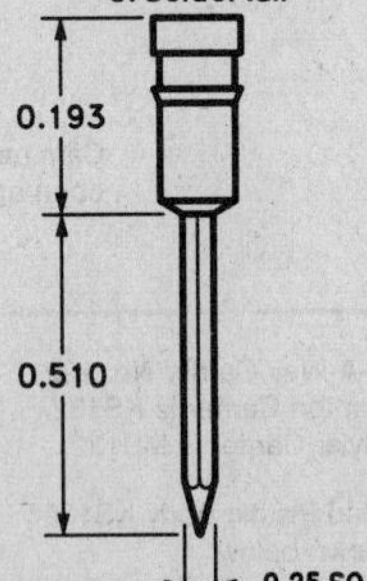

231630-86

* Low insertion force socket soldertail (for production use)
  2XX-6576-00-3308 (new style)
  2XX-6003-00-3302 (older style)
* Zero insertion force soldertail (for test and burn-in use)
  2XX-6568-00-3302

Textool Products
Electronic Products Division/3M
(1410 West Pioneer Drive
Irving, Texas 75601 U.S.A.
Phone 214-259-2676)

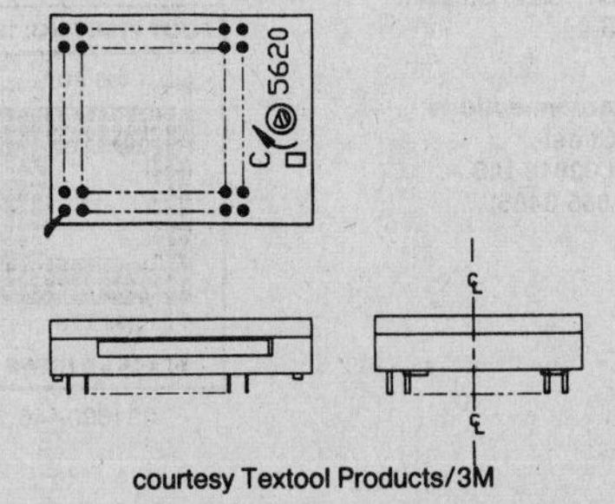

courtesy Textool Products/3M 231630-48

8.3 PACKAGE THERMAL SPECIFICATION

The Intel386 DX is specified for operation when case temperature is within the range of 0°C–85°C. The case temperature may be measured in any environment, to determine whether the Intel386 DX is within specified operating range.

The PGA case temperature should be measured at the center of the top surface opposite the pins, as in Figure 8.2.

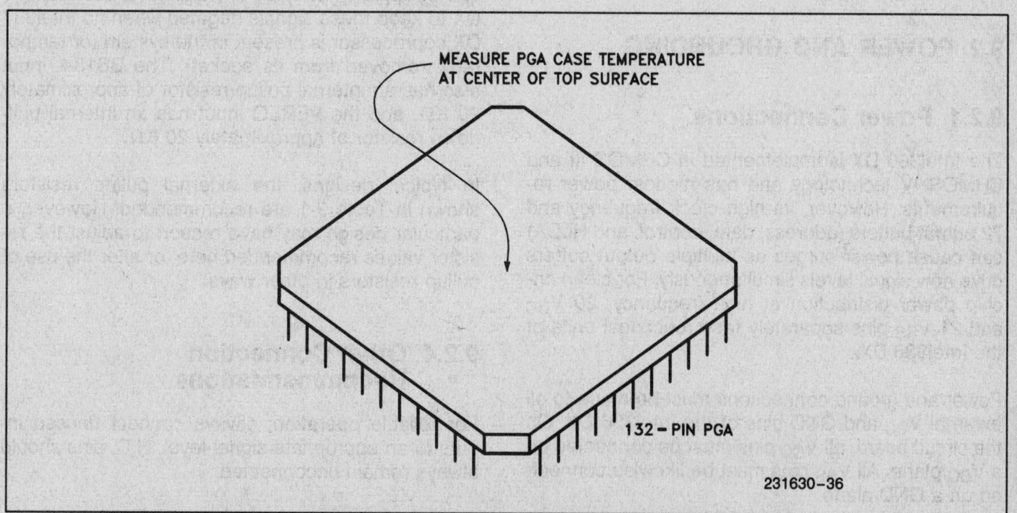

Figure 8.2. Measuring Intel386™ DX PGA Case Temperature

Table 8.2. Intel386™ DX PGA Package Thermal Characteristics

Parameter	Thermal Resistance — °C/Watt						
	Airflow — ft./min (m/sec)						
	0 (0)	50 (0.25)	100 (0.50)	200 (1.01)	400 (2.03)	600 (3.04)	800 (4.06)
θ Junction-to-Case (case measured as Fig. 8-2)	2	2	2	2	2	2	2
θ Case-to-Ambient (no heatsink)	19	18	17	15	12	10	9
θ Case-to-Ambient (with omnidirectional heatsink)	16	15	14	12	9	7	6
θ Case-to-Ambient (with unidirectional heatsink)	15	14	13	11	8	6	5

NOTES:
1. Table 8.2 applies to Intel386™ DX PGA plugged into socket or soldered directly into board.
2. $\theta_{JA} = \theta_{JC} + \theta_{CA}$.
3. $\theta_{J\text{-}CAP}$ = 4°C/w (approx.)
$\theta_{J\text{-}PIN}$ = 4°C/w (inner pins) (approx.)
$\theta_{J\text{-}PIN}$ = 8°C/w (outer pins) (approx.)
4. $T_A = T_C - P * \theta_{CA}$ (ambient temperature)

231630-72

9. ELECTRICAL DATA

9.1 INTRODUCTION

The following sections describe recommended electrical connections for the Intel386 DX, and its electrical specifications.

9.2 POWER AND GROUNDING

9.2.1 Power Connections

The Intel386 DX is implemented in CHMOS III and CHMOS IV technology and has modest power requirements. However, its high clock frequency and 72 output buffers (address, data, control, and HLDA) can cause power surges as multiple output buffers drive new signal levels simultaneously. For clean on-chip power distribution at high frequency, 20 V_{CC} and 21 V_{SS} pins separately feed functional units of the Intel386 DX.

Power and ground connections must be made to all external V_{CC} and GND pins of the Intel386 DX. On the circuit board, all V_{CC} pins must be connected on a V_{CC} plane. All V_{SS} pins must be likewise connected on a GND plane.

9.2.2 Power Decoupling Recommendations

Liberal decoupling capacitance should be placed near the Intel386 DX. The Intel386 DX driving its 32-bit parallel address and data buses at high frequencies can cause transient power surges, particularly when driving large capacitive loads.

Low inductance capacitors and interconnects are recommended for best high frequency electrical performance. Inductance can be reduced by shortening circuit board traces between the Intel386 DX and decoupling capacitors as much as possible. Capacitors specifically for PGA packages are also commercially available, for the lowest possible inductance.

9.2.3 Resistor Recommendations

The ERROR# and BUSY# inputs have resistor pullups of approximately 20 KΩ built-in to the Intel386 DX to keep these signals negated when no Intel387 DX coprocessor is present in the system (or temporarily removed from its socket). The BS16# input also has an internal pullup resistor of approximately 20 KΩ, and the PEREQ input has an internal pulldown resistor of approximately 20 KΩ.

In typical designs, the external pullup resistors shown in Table 9-1 are recommended. However, a particular design may have reason to adjust the resistor values recommended here, or alter the use of pullup resistors in other ways.

9.2.4 Other Connection Recommendations

For reliable operation, always connect unused inputs to an appropriate signal level. N.C. pins should always remain unconnected.

Particularly when not using interrupts or bus hold, (as when first prototyping, perhaps) prevent any chance of spurious activity by connecting these associated inputs to GND:

Pin	Signal
B7	INTR
B8	NMI
D14	HOLD

If not using address pipelining, pullup D13 NA# to V_{CC}.

If not using 16-bit bus size, pullup C14 BS16# to V_{CC}.

Pullups in the range of 20 KΩ are recommended.

Table 9-1. Recommended Resistor Pullups to V_{CC}

Pin and Signal	Pullup Value	Purpose
E14 ADS#	20 KΩ ±10%	Lightly Pull ADS# Negated During Intel386 DX Hold Acknowledge States
C10 LOCK#	20 KΩ ±10%	Lightly Pull LOCK# Negated During Intel386 DX Hold Acknowledge States

9.3 MAXIMUM RATINGS

Table 9-2. Maximum Ratings

Parameter	Intel386™ DX 20, 25, 33 MHz Maximum Rating
Storage Temperature	−65°C to +150°C
Case Temperature Under Bias	−65°C to +110°C
Supply Voltage with Respect to V_{SS}	−0.5V to +6.5V
Voltage on Other Pins	−0.5V to V_{CC} + 0.5V

Table 9-2 is a stress rating only, and functional operation at the maximums is not guaranteed. Functional operating conditions are given in **9.4 D.C. Specifications** and **9.5 A.C. Specifications.**

Extended exposure to the Maximum Ratings may affect device reliability. Furthermore, although the Intel386 DX contains protective circuitry to resist damage from static electric discharge, always take precautions to avoid high static voltages or electric fields.

9.4 D.C. SPECIFICATIONS

Functional Operating Range: V_{CC} = 5V ±5%; T_{CASE} = 0°C to 85°C

Table 9-3. Intel386™ DX D.C. Characteristics

Symbol	Parameter	Intel386™ DX 20 MHz, 25 MHz, 33 MHz		Unit	Test Conditions
		Min	Max		
V_{IL}	Input Low Voltage	−0.3	0.8	V	(Note 1)
V_{IH}	Input High Voltage	2.0	V_{CC} + 0.3	V	
V_{ILC}	CLK2 Input Low Voltage	−0.3	0.8	V	(Note 1)
V_{IHC}	CLK2 Input High Voltage 20 MHz 25 MHz and 33 MHz	 V_{CC} − 0.8 3.7	 V_{CC} + 0.3 V_{CC} + 0.3	 V V	
V_{OL}	Output Low Voltage I_{OL} = 4 mA: A2–A31, D0–D31 I_{OL} = 5 mA: BE0#–BE3#, W/R#, D/C#, M/IO#, LOCK#, ADS#, HLDA		 0.45 0.45	 V V	
V_{OH}	Output High Voltage I_{OH} = 1 mA: A2–A31, D0–D31 I_{OH} = 0.9 mA: BE0#–BE3#, W/R#, D/C#, M/IO#, LOCK#, ADS#, HLDA	 2.4 2.4		 V V	
I_{LI}	Input Leakage Current (For All Pins except BS16#, PEREQ, BUSY#, and ERROR#)		±15	μA	0V ≤ V_{IN} ≤ V_{CC}
I_{IH}	Input Leakage Current (PEREQ Pin)		200	μA	V_{IH} = 2.4V (Note 2)
I_{IL}	Input Leakage Current (BS16#, BUSY#, and ERROR# Pins)		−400	μA	V_{IL} = 0.45 (Note 3)
I_{LO}	Output Leakage Current		±15	μA	0.45V ≤ V_{OUT} ≤ V_{CC}
I_{CC}	Supply Current CLK2 = 40 MHz: with 20 MHz Intel386™ DX CLK2 = 50 MHz: with 25 MHz Intel386™ DX CLK2 = 66 MHz: with 33 MHz Intel386™ DX		 260 320 390	 mA mA mA	(Note 4) I_{CC} Typ. = 200 mA I_{CC} Typ. = 240 mA I_{CC} Typ. = 300 mA
C_{IN}	Input or I/O Capacitance		10	pF	F_C = 1 MHz
C_{OUT}	Output Capacitance		12	pF	F_C = 1 MHz
C_{CLK}	CLK2 Capacitance		20	pF	F_C = 1 MHz

NOTES:
1. The min value, −0.3, is not 100% tested.
2. PEREQ input has an internal pulldown resistor.
3. BS16#, BUSY# and ERROR# inputs each have an internal pullup resistor.
4. CHMOS IV Technology (CHMOS III Max I_{CC} at 20 MHz, 25 MHz = 500 mA, 550 mA).

9.5 A.C. SPECIFICATIONS

9.5.1 A.C. Spec Definitions

The A.C. specifications, given in Tables 9-4, 9-5, and 9-6, consist of output delays, input setup requirements and input hold requirements. All A.C. specifications are relative to the CLK2 rising edge crossing the 2.0V level.

A.C. spec measurement is defined by Figure 9-1. Inputs must be driven to the voltage levels indicated by Figure 9-1 when A.C. specifications are measured. Intel386 DX output delays are specified with minimum and maximum limits, measured as shown. The minimum Intel386 DX delay times are hold times provided to external circuitry. Intel386 DX input setup and hold times are specified as minimums, defining the smallest acceptable sampling window. Within the sampling window, a synchronous input signal must be stable for correct Intel386 DX operation.

Outputs NA#, W/R#, D/C#, M/IO#, LOCK#, BE0#–BE3#, A2–A31 and HLDA only change at the beginning of phase one. D0–D31 (write cycles) only change at the beginning of phase two. The READY#, HOLD, BUSY#, ERROR#, PEREQ and D0–D31 (read cycles) inputs are sampled at the beginning of phase one. The NA#, BS16#, INTR and NMI inputs are sampled at the beginning of phase two.

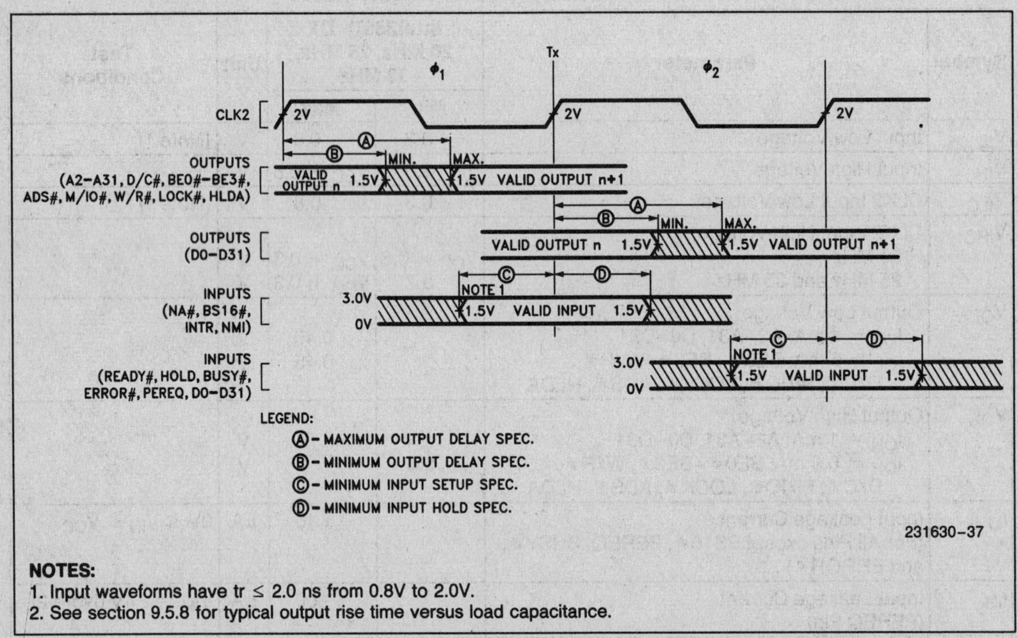

NOTES:
1. Input waveforms have tr ≤ 2.0 ns from 0.8V to 2.0V.
2. See section 9.5.8 for typical output rise time versus load capacitance.

Figure 9-1. Drive Levels and Measurement Points for A.C. Specifications

9.5.2 A.C. Specification Tables

Functional Operating Range: V_{CC} = 5V ±5%; T_{CASE} = 0°C to +85°C

Table 9-4. 33 MHz Intel386™ DX A.C. Characteristics

Symbol	Parameter	33 MHz Intel386™ DX		Unit	Ref. Fig.	Notes
		Min	Max			
	Operating Frequency	8	33.3	MHz		Half of CLK2 Frequency
t1	CLK2 Period	15.0	62.5	ns	9-3	
t2a	CLK2 High Time	6.25		ns	9-3	at 2V
t2b	CLK2 High Time	4.5		ns	9-3	at 3.7V
t3a	CLK2 Low Time	6.25		ns	9-3	at 2V
t3b	CLK2 Low Time	4.5		ns	9-3	at 0.8V
t4	CLK2 Fall Time		4	ns	9-3	3.7V to 0.8V (Note 3)
t5	CLK2 Rise Time		4	ns	9-3	0.8V to 3.7V (Note 3)
t6	A2–A31 Valid Delay	4	15	ns	9-5	C_L = 50 pF
t7	A2–A31 Float Delay	4	20	ns	9-6	(Note 1)
t8	BE0#–BE3#, LOCK# Valid Delay	4	15	ns	9-5	C_L = 50 pF
t9	BE0#–BE3#, LOCK# Float Delay	4	20	ns	9-6	(Note 1)
t10	W/R#, M/IO#, D/C#, Valid Delay	4	15	ns	9-5	C_L = 50 pF
t10a	ADS# Valid Delay	4	14.5	ns	9-5	C_L = 50 pF
t11	W/R#, M/IO#, D/C#, ADS# Float Delay	4	20	ns	9-6	(Note 1)
t12	D0–D31 Write Data Valid Delay	7	24	ns	9-5a	C_L = 50 pF, (Note 4)
t12a	D0–D31 Write Data Hold Time	2			9-5b	C_L = 50 pF
t13	D0–D31 Float Delay	4	17	ns	9-6	(Note 1)
t14	HLDA Valid Delay	4	20	ns	9-6	C_L = 50 pF
t15	NA# Setup Time	5		ns	9-4	
t16	NA# Hold Time	2		ns	9-4	
t17	BS16# Setup Time	5		ns	9-4	
t18	BS16# Hold Time	2		ns	9-4	
t19	READY# Setup Time	7		ns	9-4	
t20	READY# Hold Time	4		ns	9-4	

9.5.2 A.C. Specification Tables (Continued)

Functional Operating Range: V_{CC} = 5V ±5%; T_{CASE} = 0°C to +85°C

Table 9-4. 33 MHz Intel386™ DX A.C. Characteristics (Continued)

Symbol	Parameter	33 MHz Intel386™ DX		Unit	Ref. Fig.	Notes
		Min	Max			
t21	D0–D31 Read Setup Time	5		ns	9-4	
t22	D0–D31 Read Hold Time	3		ns	9-4	
t23	HOLD Setup Time	11		ns	9-4	
t24	HOLD Hold Time	2		ns	9-4	
t25	RESET Setup Time	5		ns	9-7	
t26	RESET Hold Time	2		ns	9-7	
t27	NMI, INTR Setup Time	5		ns	9-4	(Note 2)
t28	NMI, INTR Hold Time	5		ns	9-4	(Note 2)
t29	PEREQ, ERROR#, BUSY# Setup Time	5		ns	9-4	(Note 2)
t30	PEREQ, ERROR#, BUSY# Hold Time	4		ns	9-4	(Note 2)

NOTES:

1. Float condition occurs when maximum output current becomes less than I_{LO} in magnitude. Float delay is not 100% tested.
2. These inputs are allowed to be asynchronous to CLK2. The setup and hold specifications are given for testing purposes, to assure recognition within a specific CLK2 period.
3. Rise and fall times are not tested.
4. Min. time not 100% tested.

9.5.2 A.C. Specification Tables (Continued)

Functional Operating Range: V_{CC} = 5V ±5%; T_{CASE} = 0°C to +85°C

Table 9-5. 25 MHz Intel386™ DX A.C. Characteristics

Symbol	Parameter	25 MHz Intel386™ DX Min	25 MHz Intel386™ DX Max	Unit	Ref. Fig.	Notes
	Operating Frequency	4	25	MHz		Half of CLK2 Frequency
t1	CLK2 Period	20	125	ns	9-3	
t2a	CLK2 High Time	7		ns	9-3	at 2V
t2b	CLK2 High Time	4		ns	9-3	at 3.7V
t3a	CLK2 Low Time	7		ns	9-3	at 2V
t3b	CLK2 Low Time	5		ns	9-3	at 0.8V
t4	CLK2 Fall Time		7	ns	9-3	3.7V to 0.8V
t5	CLK2 Rise Time		7	ns	9-3	0.8V to 3.7V
t6	A2–A31 Valid Delay	4	21	ns	9-5	C_L = 50 pF
t7	A2–A31 Float Delay	4	30	ns	9-6	(Note 1)
t8	BE0#–BE3# Valid Delay	4	24	ns	9-5	C_L = 50 pF
t8a	LOCK# Valid Delay	4	21	ns	9-5	C_L = 50 pF
t9	BE0#–BE3#, LOCK# Float Delay	4	30	ns	9-6	(Note 1)
t10	W/R#, M/IO#, D/C#, ADS# Valid Delay	4	21	ns	9-5	C_L = 50 pF
t11	W/R#, M/IO#, D/C#, ADS# Float Delay	4	30	ns	9-6	(Note 1)
t12	D0–D31 Write Data Valid Delay	7	27	ns	9-5a	C_L = 50 pF
t12a	D0–D31 Write Data Hold Time	2			9-5b	C_L = 50 pF
t13	D0–D31 Float Delay	4	22	ns	9-6	(Note 1)
t14	HLDA Valid Delay	4	22	ns	9-6	C_L = 50 pF
t15	NA# Setup Time	7		ns	9-4	
t16	NA# Hold Time	3		ns	9-4	
t17	BS16# Setup Time	7		ns	9-4	
t18	BS16# Hold Time	3		ns	9-4	
t19	READY# Setup Time	9		ns	9-4	
t20	READY# Hold Time	4		ns	9-4	

4

9.5.2 A.C. Specification Tables (Continued)

Functional Operating Range: V_{CC} = 5V ±5%; T_{CASE} = 0°C to +85°C

Table 9-5. 25 MHz Intel386™ DX A.C. Characteristics (Continued)

Symbol	Parameter	25 MHz Intel386™ DX		Unit	Ref. Fig.	Notes
		Min	Max			
t21	D0–D31 Read Setup Time	7		ns	9-4	
t22	D0–D31 Read Hold Time	5		ns	9-4	
t23	HOLD Setup Time	15		ns	9-4	
t24	HOLD Hold Time	3		ns	9-4	
t25	RESET Setup Time	10		ns	9-7	
t26	RESET Hold Time	3		ns	9-7	
t27	NMI, INTR Setup Time	6		ns	9-4	(Note 2)
t28	NMI, INTR Hold Time	6		ns	9-4	(Note 2)
t29	PEREQ, ERROR#, BUSY# Setup Time	6		ns	9-4	(Note 2)
t30	PEREQ, ERROR#, BUSY# Hold Time	5		ns	9-4	(Notes 2, 3)

NOTES:

1. Float condition occurs when maximum output current becomes less than I_{LO} in magnitude. Float delay is not 100% tested.
2. These inputs are allowed to be asynchronous to CLK2. The setup and hold specifications are given for testing purposes, to assure recognition within a specific CLK2 period.
3.

	Symbol	Parameter	Min
T_C = 0°C	t30	PEREQ, ERROR#, BUSY# Hold Time	4
T_C = +85°C	t30	PEREQ, ERROR#, BUSY# Hold Time	5

9.5.2 A.C. Specification Tables (Continued)

Functional Operating Range: V_{CC} = 5V ±5%; T_{CASE} = 0°C to +85°C

Table 9.6. 20 MHz Intel386™ DX A.C. Characteristics

Symbol	Parameter	20 MHz Intel386™ DX		Unit	Ref. Fig.	Notes
		Min	Max			
	Operating Frequency	4	20	MHz		Half of CLK2 Frequency
t_1	CLK2 Period	25	125	ns	9-3	
t_{2a}	CLK2 High Time	8		ns	9-3	at 2V
t_{2b}	CLK2 High Time	5		ns	9-3	at (V_{CC} − 0.8V)
t_{3a}	CLK2 Low Time	8		ns	9-3	at 2V
t_{3b}	CLK2 Low Time	6		ns	9-3	at 0.8V
t_4	CLK2 Fall Time		8	ns	9-3	(V_{CC} − 0.8V) to 0.8V
t_5	CLK2 Rise Time		8	ns	9-3	0.8V to (V_{CC} − 0.8V)
t_6	A2–A31 Valid Delay	4	30	ns	9-5	C_L = 120 pF
t_7	A2–A31 Float Delay	4	32	ns	9-6	(Note 1)
t_8	BE0#–BE3#, LOCK# Valid Delay	4	30	ns	9-5	C_L = 75 pF
t_9	BE0#–BE3#, LOCK# Float Delay	4	32	ns	9-6	(Note 1)
t_{10}	W/R#, M/IO#, D/C#, ADS# Valid Delay	6	28	ns	9-5	C_L = 75 pF
t_{11}	W/R#, M/IO#, D/C#, ADS# Float Delay	6	30	ns	9-6	(Note 1)
t_{12}	D0–D31 Write Data Valid Delay	4	38	ns	9-5c	C_L = 120 pF
t_{13}	D0–D31 Float Delay	4	27	ns	9-6	(Note 1)
t_{14}	HLDA Valid Delay	6	28	ns	9-6	C_L = 75 pF
t_{15}	NA# Setup Time	9		ns	9-4	
t_{16}	NA# Hold Time	14		ns	9-4	
t_{17}	BS16# Setup Time	13		ns	9-4	
t_{18}	BS16# Hold Time	21		ns	9-4	
t_{19}	READY# Setup Time	12		ns	9-4	
t_{20}	READY# Hold Time	4		ns	9-4	
t_{21}	D0–D31 Read Setup Time	11		ns	9-4	
t_{22}	D0–D31 Read Hold Time	6		ns	9-4	
t_{23}	HOLD Setup Time	17		ns	9-4	
t_{24}	HOLD Hold Time	5		ns	9-4	
t_{25}	RESET Setup Time	12		ns	9-7	

9.5.2 A.C. Specification Tables (Continued)

Functional Operating Range: V_{CC} = 5V ±5%; T_{CASE} = 0°C to +85°C

Table 9-6. 20 MHz Intel386™ DX A.C. Characteristics (Continued)

Symbol	Parameter	20 MHz Intel386™ DX		Unit	Ref. Fig.	Notes
		Min	Max			
t_{26}	RESET Hold Time	4		ns	9-7	
t_{27}	NMI, INTR Setup Time	16		ns	9-4	(Note 2)
t_{28}	NMI, INTR Hold Time	16		ns	9-4	(Note 2)
t_{29}	PEREQ, ERROR#, BUSY# Setup Time	14		ns	9-4	(Note 2)
t_{30}	PEREQ, ERROR#, BUSY# Hold Time	5		ns	9-4	(Note 2)

NOTES:

1. Float condition occurs when maximum output current becomes less than I_{LO} in magnitude. Float delay is not 100% tested.
2. These inputs are allowed to be asynchronous to CLK2. The setup and hold specifications are given for testing purposes, to assure recognition within a specific CLK2 period.

9.5.3 A.C. Test Loads

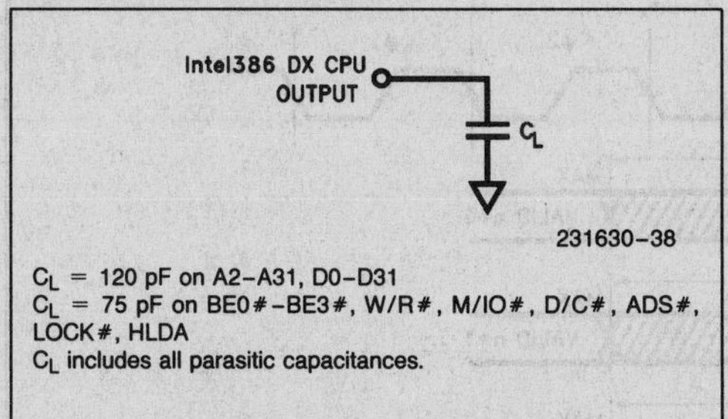

Intel386 DX CPU OUTPUT
C_L
231630-38
C_L = 120 pF on A2–A31, D0–D31
C_L = 75 pF on BE0#–BE3#, W/R#, M/IO#, D/C#, ADS#, LOCK#, HLDA
C_L includes all parasitic capacitances.

Figure 9-2. A.C. Test Load

9.5.4 A.C. Timing Waveforms

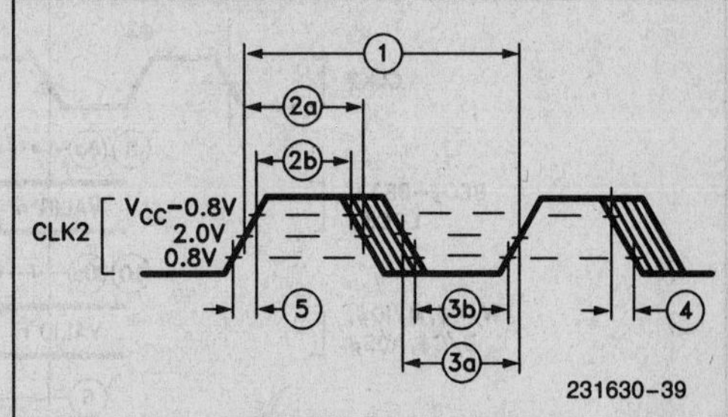

Figure 9-3. CLK2 Timing

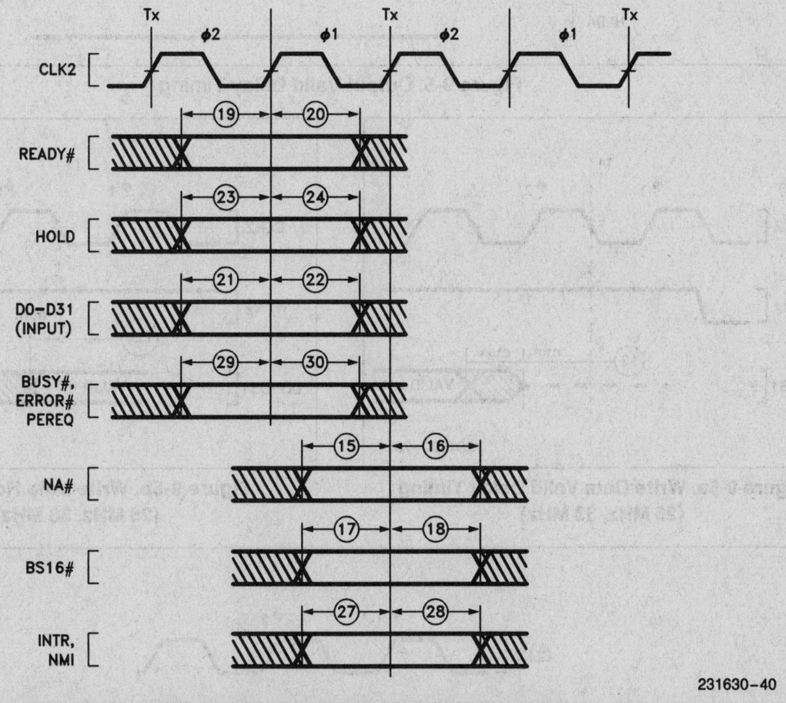

231630-40

Figure 9-4. Input Setup and Hold Timing

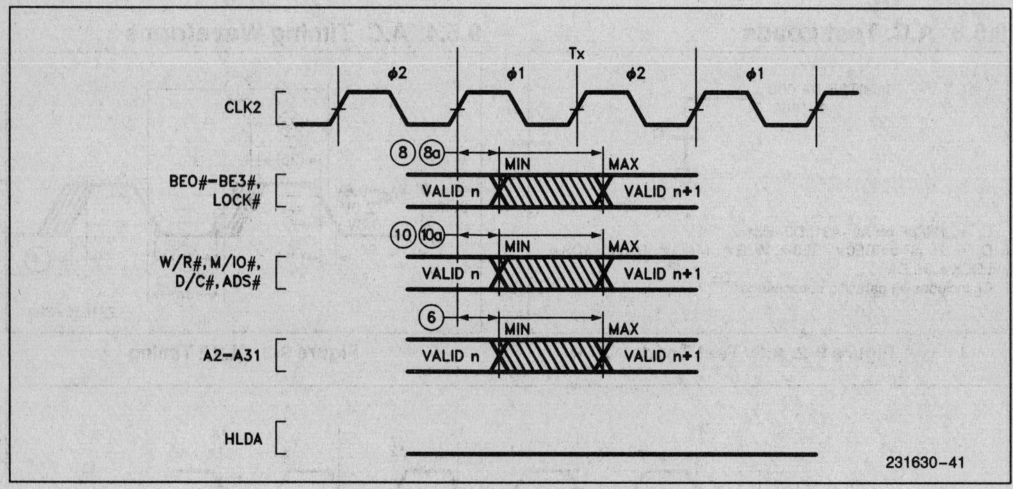

Figure 9-5. Output Valid Delay Timing

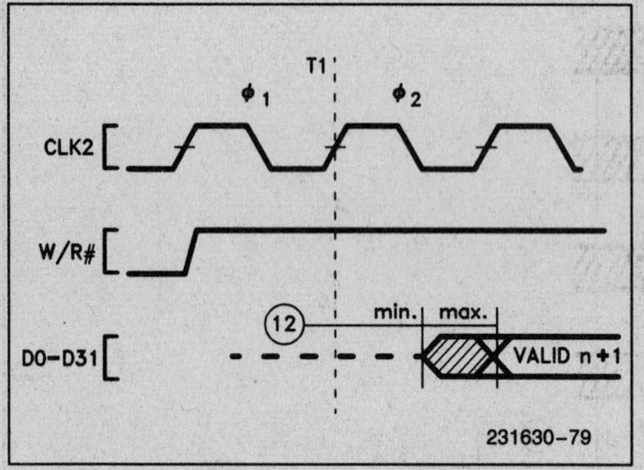

Figure 9-5a. Write Data Valid Delay Timing (25 MHz, 33 MHz)

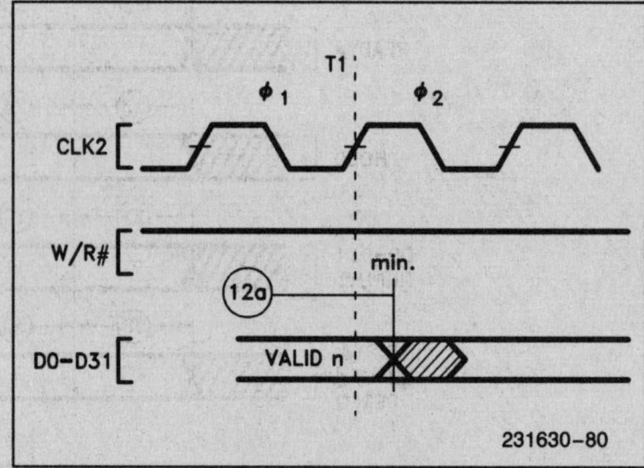

Figure 9-5b. Write Data Hold Timing (25 MHz, 33 MHz)

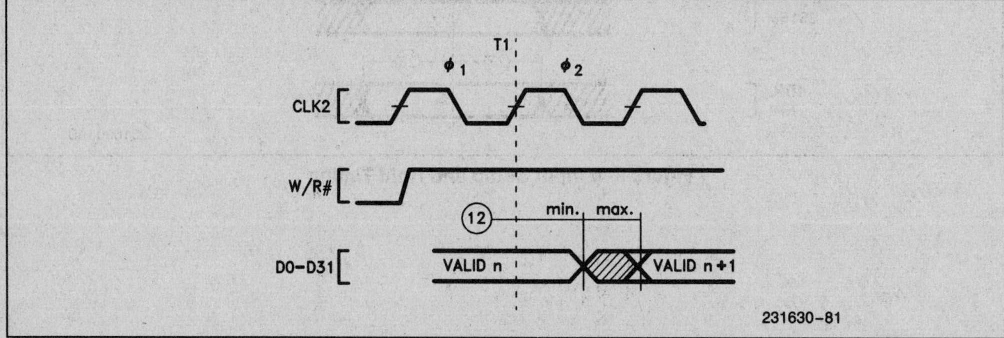

Figure 9-5c. Write Data Valid Delay Timing (20 MHz)

9.5.5 Typical Output Valid Delay Versus Load Capacitance at Maximum Operating Temperature (C_L = 120 pF)

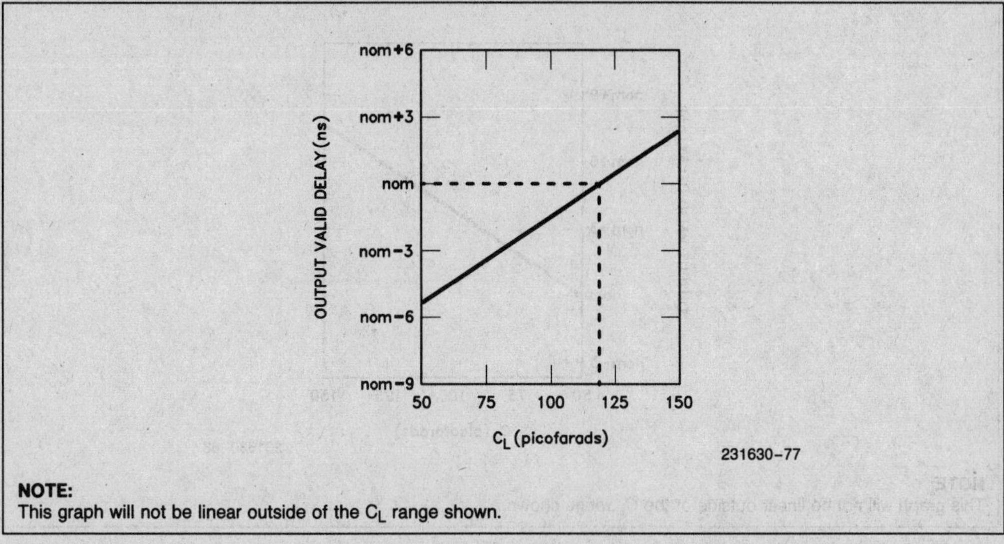

NOTE:
This graph will not be linear outside of the C_L range shown.

9.5.6 Typical Output Valid Delay Versus Load Capacitance at Maximum Operating Temperature (C_L = 75 pF)

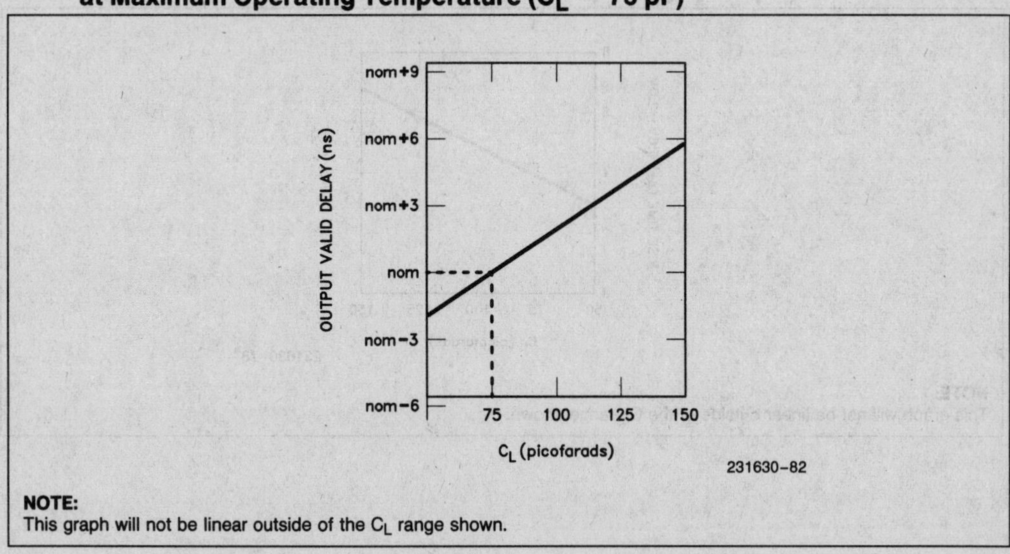

NOTE:
This graph will not be linear outside of the C_L range shown.

4

9.5.7 Typical Output Valid Delay Versus Load Capacitance at Maximum Operating Temperature (C_L = 50 pF)

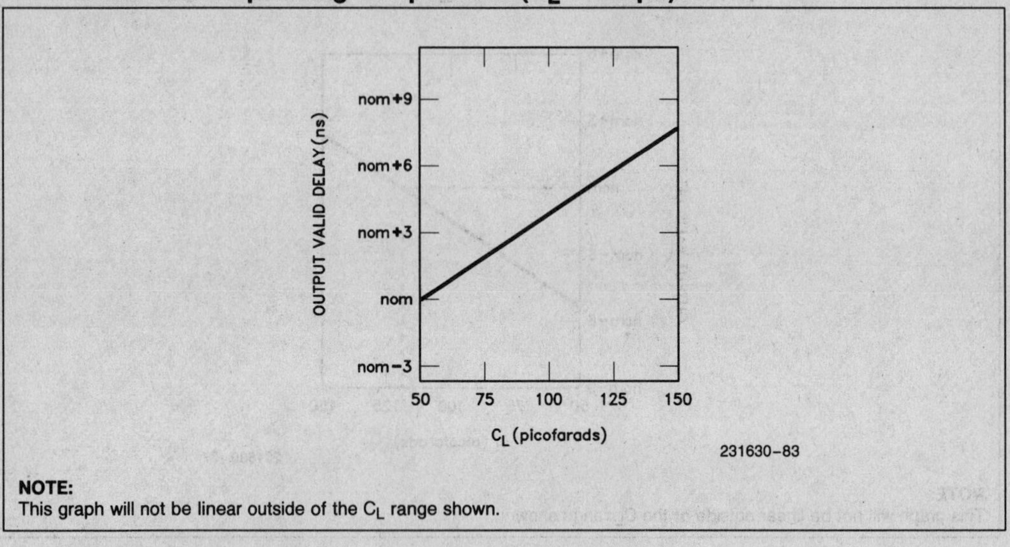

NOTE:
This graph will not be linear outside of the C_L range shown.

9.5.8 Typical Output Rise Time Versus Load Capacitance at Maximum Operating Temperature

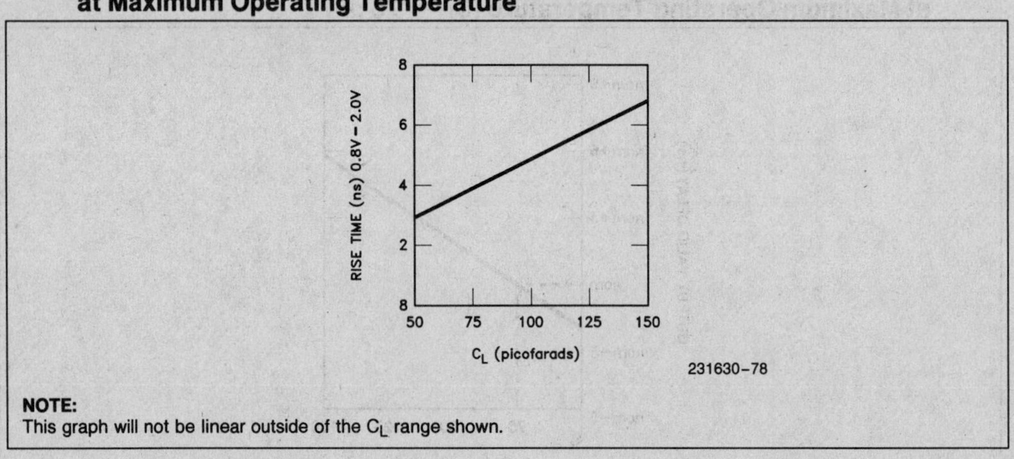

NOTE:
This graph will not be linear outside of the C_L range shown.

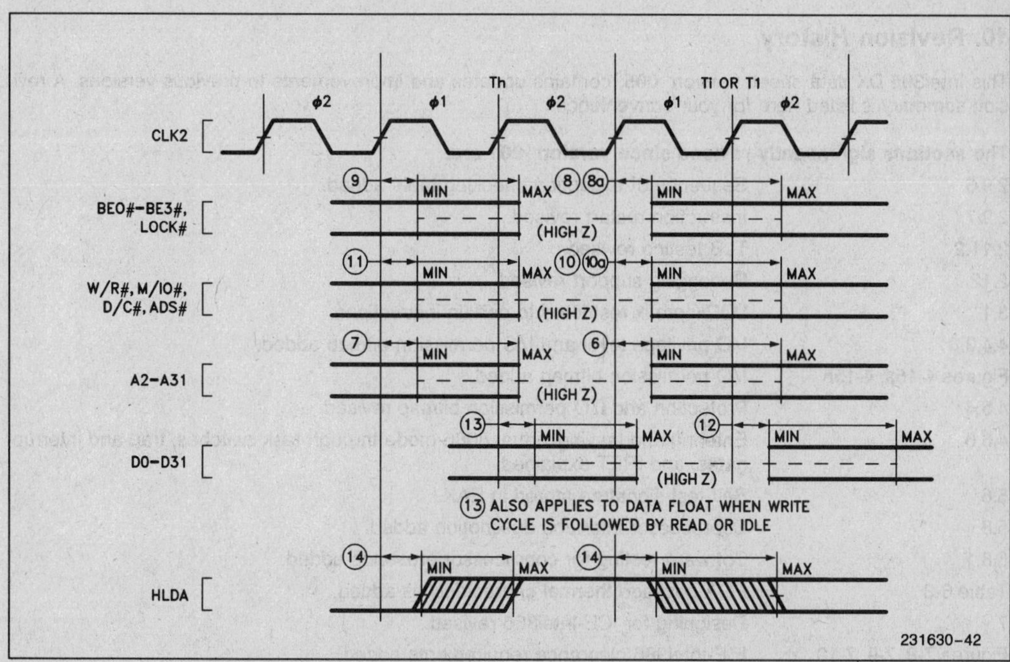

Figure 9-6. Output Float Delay and HLDA Valid Delay Timing

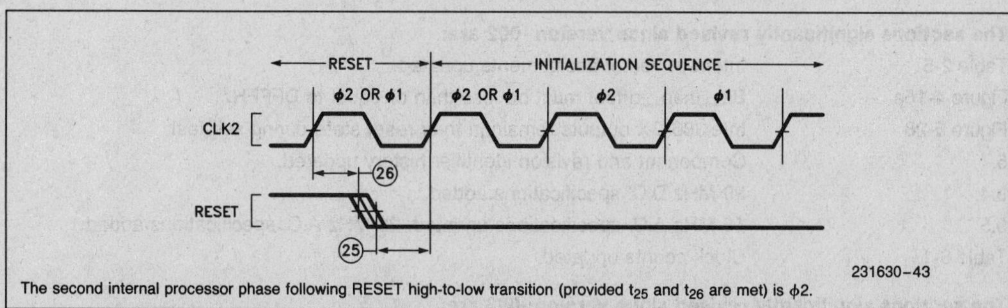

The second internal processor phase following RESET high-to-low transition (provided t_{25} and t_{26} are met) is $\phi 2$.

Figure 9-7. RESET Setup and Hold Timing, and Internal Phase

10. Revision History

This Intel386 DX data sheet, version -005, contains updates and improvements to previous versions. A revision summary is listed here for your convenience.

The sections significantly revised since version -001 are:

2.9.6	Sequence of exception checking table added.
2.9.7	Instruction restart revised.
2.11.2	TLB testing revised.
2.12	Debugging support revised.
3.1	LOCK prefix restricted to certain instructions.
4.4.3.3	I/O privilege level and I/O permission bitmap added.
Figures 4-15a, 4-15b	I/O permission bitmap added.
4.6.4	Protection and I/O permission bitmap revised.
4.6.6	Entering and leaving virtual 8086 mode through task switches, trap and interrupt gates, and IRET explained.
5.6	Self-test signature stored in EAX.
5.8	Coprocessor interface description added.
5.8.1	Software testing for coprocessor presence added.
Table 6-3	PGA package thermal characteristics added.
7.	Designing for ICE-Intel386 revised.
Figures 7-8, 7-9, 7-10	ICE-Intel386 clearance requirements added.
6.2.3.4	Encoding of 32-bit address mode with no "sib" byte corrected.

The sections significantly revised since version -002 are:

Table 2-5	Interrupt vector assignments updated.
Figure 4-15a	Bit_map_offset must be less than or equal to DFFFH.
Figure 5-28	Intel386 DX outputs remain in their reset state during self-test.
5.7	Component and revision identifier history updated.
9.4	20 MHz D.C. specifications added.
9.5	16 MHz A.C. specifications updated. 20 MHz A.C. specifications added.
Table 6-1	Clock counts updated.

The sections significantly revised since version -003 are:

Table 2-6b	Interrupt priorities 2 and 3 interchanged.
2.9.8	Double page faults do not raise double fault exception.
Figure 4-5	Maximum-sized segments must have segments $Base_{11..0} = 0$.
5.4.3.4	BS16# timing corrected.
Figures 5-16, 5-17, 5-19, 5-22	BS16# timing corrected. BS16# must not be asserted once NA# has been sampled asserted in the current bus cycle.
9.5	16 MHz and 20 MHz A.C. specifications revised. All timing parameters are now guaranteed at 1.5V test levels. The timing parameters have been adjusted to remain compatible with previous 0.8V/2.0V specifications.

The sections significantly revised since version -004 are:

Chapter 4	25 MHz Clock data included.
Table 2-4	Segment Register Selection Rules updated.
5.4.4	Interrupt Acknowledge Cycles discussion corrected.
Table 5-10	Additional Stepping Information added.
Table 9-3	I_{CC} values updated.
9.5.2	Table for 25 MHz A.C. Characteristics added. A.C. Characteristics tables reordered.
Figure 9-5	Output Valid Delay Timing Figure reconfigured. Partial data now provided in additional Figures 9-5a and 9-5b.
Table 6-1	Clock counts updated and formats corrected.

The sections significantly revised since version -005 are:

Table of Contents	Simplified.
Chapter 1	Pin Assignment.
2.3.6	Control Register 0.
Table 2-4	Segment override prefixes possible.
Figure 4-6	Note added.
Figure 4-7	Note added.
5.2.3	Data bus state at end of cycle.
5.2.8.4	Coprocessor error.
5.5.3	Bus activity during and following reset.
Figure 5-28	ERROR#.
Chapter 6	Moved forward in datasheet.
Chapter 7	Moved forward in datasheet.
Chapter 8	Upgraded to chapter.
Table 9-3	25 MHz I_{CC} Typ. value corrected.
Table 9-3	33 MHz D.C. Specifications added.
Table 9-4	33 MHz A.C. Specifications added.
Figure 9-5	t8a and t10a added.
Figure 9-5c	Added.
9.5.6	Added derating for $C_L = 75$ pF.
9.5.7	Added derating for $C_L = 50$ pF.
Figure 9.6	t8a and t10a added.

The sections significantly revised since version -006 are:

2.3.4	Alignment of maximum sized segments.
2.9.8	Double page faults do not raise double fault exception.
5.5.3	ERROR# and BUSY# sampling after RESET.
Figure 5-21	BS16# timing altered.
Figure 5-26	READY# timing altered.
Figure 5-28	ERROR# timing corrected.
6.2.3.1	Corrected Encoding of Register Field Chart.
Chapter 7	Updated ICE-Intel386 DX information.
9.5.2	Remove preliminary stamp on 25 MHz A.C. Specifications.
9.5.2	Remove preliminary stamp on 33 MHz A.C. Specifications.

The sections significantly revised since version -007 are:

Table of Contents	Page numbers revised.
Figure 5-15	BS16# timing altered.
Figure 5-22	Previous cycle, T2 changed to Idle cycle, Ti.
6.1	Note about wait states added.
Table 6-1	Opcodes for AND, OR, and XOR instructions corrected.
Table 6-1	Bits 3, 4, and 5 of the "mod r/m" byte corrected for the LTR instruction.
Table 8-2	Reference to Figure 6-4 should be reference Figure 8-2.
Table 8-2	Note #4 added.

The sections significantly revised since version -008 are:

Table 9-3	20, 25, 33 MHz I_{CC} specifications updated.

Intel387™ DX MATH COPROCESSOR

- High Performance 80-Bit Internal Architecture
- Implements ANSI/IEEE Standard 754-1985 for Binary Floating-Point Arithmetic
- Six to Eleven Times 8087/80287 Performance
- Expands Intel386™ DX CPU Data Types to Include 32-, 64-, 80-Bit Floating Point, 32-, 64-Bit Integers and 18-Digit BCD Operands
- Directly Extends Intel386™ DX CPU Instruction Set to Include Trigonometric, Logarithmic, Exponential and Arithmetic Instructions for All Data Types
- Upward Object-Code Compatible from 8087 and 80287
- Full-Range Transcendental Operations for SINE, COSINE, TANGENT, ARCTANGENT and LOGARITHM
- Built-In Exception Handling
- Operates Independently of Real, Protected and Virtual-8086 Modes of the Intel386™ DX Microprocessor
- Eight 80-Bit Numeric Registers, Usable as Individually Addressable General Registers or as a Register Stack
- Available in 68-Pin PGA Package
- One Version Supports 16 MHz–33 MHz Speeds

(See Packaging Spec: Order #231369)

The Intel387™ DX Math CoProcessor (MCP) is an extension of the Intel386™ microprocessor architecture. The combination of the Intel387 DX MCP with the Intel386™ DX Microprocessor dramatically increases the processing speed of computer application software which utilize mathematical operations. This makes an ideal computer workstation platform for applications such as financial modeling and spreadsheets, CAD/CAM, or graphics.

The Intel387 DX Math CoProcessor adds over seventy mnemonics to the Intel386 DX Microprocessor instruction set. Specific Intel387 DX MCP math operations include logarithmic, arithmetic, exponential, and trigonometric functions. The Intel387 DX MCP supports integer, extended integer, floating point and BCD data formats, and fully conforms to the ANSI/IEEE floating point standard.

The Intel387 DX Math CoProcessor is object code compatible with the Intel387 SX MCP, and upward object code compatible from the 80287 and 8087 math coprocessors. Object code for Intel386 DX/Intel387 DX is also compatible with the Intel486™ microprocessor. The Intel387 DX MCP is manufactured on 1 micron, CHMOS IV technology and packaged in a 68-pin PGA package.

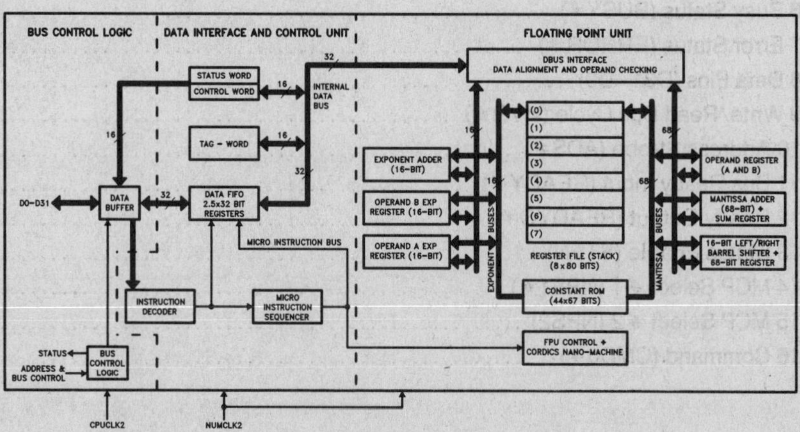

Figure 0.1. Intel387™ DX Math CoProcessor Block Diagram

October 1991
Order Number: 240448-004

Intel387™ DX Math CoProcessor

CONTENTS

CONTENTS

PAGE

FIGURES

CONTENTS

PAGE

FIGURES (Continued)

TABLES

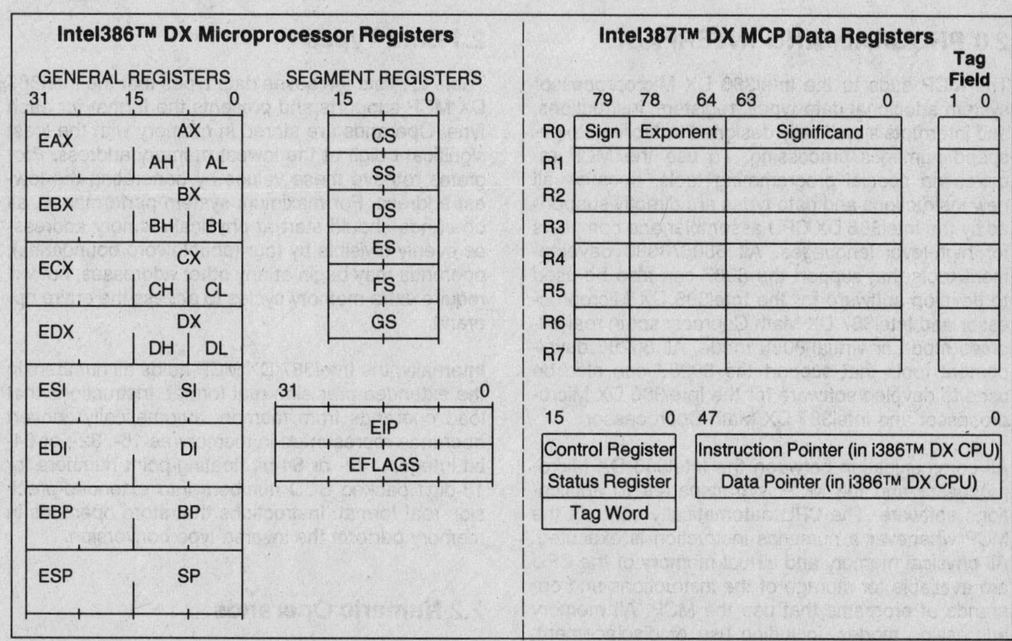

Figure 1.1. Intel386™ DX Microprocessor and Intel387™ DX Math Coprocessor Register Set

1.0 FUNCTIONAL DESCRIPTION

The Intel387™ DX Math Coprocessor provides arithmetic instructions for a variety of numeric data types in Intel386™ DX Microprocessor systems. It also executes numerous built-in transcendental functions (e.g. tangent, sine, cosine, and log functions). The Intel387 DX MCP effectively extends the register and instruction set of a Intel386 DX Microprocessor system for existing data types and adds several new data types as well. Figure 1.1 shows the model of registers visible to programs. Essentially, the Intel387 DX MCP can be treated as an additional resource or an extension to the Intel386 DX Microprocessor. The Intel386 DX Microprocessor together with a Intel387 DX MCP can be used as a single unified system.

The Intel387 DX MCP works the same whether the Intel386 DX Microprocessor is executing in real-address mode, protected mode, or virtual-8086 mode. All memory access is handled by the Intel386 DX Microprocessor; the Intel387 DX MCP merely operates on instructions and values passed to it by the Intel386 DX Microprocessor. Therefore, the Intel387 DX MCP is not sensitive to the processing mode of the Intel386 DX Microprocessor.

In real-address mode and virtual-8086 mode, the Intel386 DX Microprocessor and Intel387 DX MCP are completely upward compatible with software for 8086/8087, 80286/80287 real-address mode, and Intel386 DX Microprocessor and 80287 Coprocessor real-address mode systems.

In protected mode, the Intel386 DX Microprocessor and Intel387 DX MCP are completely upward compatible with software for 80286/80287 protected mode, and Intel386 DX Microprocessor and 80287 Coprocessor protected mode systems.

The only differences of operation that may appear when 8086/8087 programs are ported to a protected-mode Intel386 DX Microprocessor and Intel387 DX MCP system (*not* using virtual-8086 mode), is in the format of operands for the administrative instructions FLDENV, FSTENV, FRSTOR and FSAVE. These instructions are normally used only by exception handlers and operating systems, not by applications programs.

The Intel387 DX MCP contains three functional units that can operate in parallel to increase system performance. The Intel386 DX Microprocessor can be transferring commands and data to the MCP *bus control logic* for the next instruction while the MCP *floating-point unit* is performing the current numeric instruction.

2.0 PROGRAMMING INTERFACE

The MCP adds to the Intel386 DX Microprocessor system additional data types, registers, instructions, and interrupts specifically designed to facilitate high-speed numerics processing. To use the MCP requires no special programming tools, because all new instructions and data types are directly supported by the Intel386 DX CPU assembler and compilers for high-level languages. All 8086/8088 development tools that support the 8087 can also be used to develop software for the Intel386 DX Microprocessor and Intel387 DX Math Coprocessor in real-address mode or virtual-8086 mode. All 80286 development tools that support the 80287 can also be used to develop software for the Intel386 DX Microprocessor and Intel387 DX Math Coprocessor.

All communication between the Intel386 DX Microprocessor and the MCP is transparent to applications software. The CPU automatically controls the MCP whenever a numerics instruction is executed. All physical memory and virtual memory of the CPU are available for storage of the instructions and operands of programs that use the MCP. All memory addressing modes, including use of displacement, base register, index register, and scaling, are available for addressing numerics operands.

Section 6 at the end of this data sheet lists by class the instructions that the MCP adds to the instruction set of the Intel386 DX Microprocessor system.

2.1 Data Types

Table 2.1 lists the seven data types that the Intel387 DX MCP supports and presents the format for each type. Operands are stored in memory with the least significant digit at the lowest memory address. Programs retrieve these values by generating the lowest address. For maximum system performance, all operands should start at physical-memory addresses evenly divisible by four (doubleword boundaries); operands may begin at any other addresses, but will require extra memory cycles to access the entire operand.

Internally, the Intel387 DX MCP holds all numbers in the extended-precision real format. Instructions that load operands from memory automatically convert operands represented in memory as 16-, 32-, or 64-bit integers, 32- or 64-bit floating-point numbers, or 18-digit packed BCD numbers into extended-precision real format. Instructions that store operands in memory perform the inverse type conversion.

2.2 Numeric Operands

A typical MCP instruction accepts one or two operands and produces a single result. In two-operand instructions, one operand is the contents of an MCP register, while the other may be a memory location. The operands of some instructions are predefined; for example FSQRT always takes the square root of the number in the top stack element.

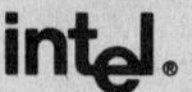

Table 2.1. Intel387™ DX MCP Data Type Representation in Memory

Data Formats	Range	Precision	Most Significant Byte = Highest Addressed Byte (7 0 7 0 7 0 7 0 7 0 7 0 7 0 7 0 7 0 7 0)
Word Integer	$\pm 10^4$	16 Bits	(TWO'S COMPLEMENT) bits 15…0
Short Integer	$\pm 10^9$	32 Bits	(TWO'S COMPLEMENT) bits 31…0
Long Integer	$\pm 10^{18}$	64 Bits	(TWO'S COMPLEMENT) bits 63…0
Packed BCD	$\pm 10^{\pm 18}$	18 Digits	S (79), X (78–72), MAGNITUDE d_{17} d_{16} d_{15} d_{14} d_{13} d_{12} d_{11} d_{10} d_9 d_8 d_7 d_6 d_5 d_4 d_3 d_2 d_1 d_0 … 0
Single Precision	$\pm 10^{\pm 38}$	24 Bits	S (31), BIASED EXPONENT, 23 ▲ I, SIGNIFICAND … 0
Double Precision	$\pm 10^{\pm 308}$	53 Bits	S (63), BIASED EXPONENT, 52 ▲ I, SIGNIFICAND … 0
Extended Precision	$\pm 10^{\pm 4932}$	64 Bits	S (79), BIASED EXPONENT, 64, I (63) ▲, SIGNIFICAND … 0

240448-2

NOTES:

(1) S = Sign bit (0 = positive, 1 = negative)
(2) d_n = Decimal digit (two per byte)
(3) X = Bits have no significance; Intel387™ DX MCP ignores when loading, zeros when storing
(4) ▲ = Position of implicit binary point
(5) I = Integer bit of significand; stored in temporary real, implicit in single and double precision
(6) Exponent Bias (normalized values):
Single: 127 (7FH)
Double: 1023 (3FFH)
Extended Real: 16383 (3FFFH)
(7) Packed BCD: $(-1)^S (D_{17} \ldots D_0)$
(8) Real: $(-1)^S (2^{E-BIAS}) (F_0 F_1 \ldots)$

15							0
TAG (7)	TAG (6)	TAG (5)	TAG (4)	TAG (3)	TAG (2)	TAG (1)	TAG (0)

NOTE:
The index i of tag(i) is **not** top-relative. A program typically uses the "top" field of Status Word to determine which tag(i) field refers to logical top of stack.
TAG VALUES:
00 = Valid
01 = Zero
10 = QNaN, SNaN, Infinity, Denormal and Unsupported Formats
11 = Empty

Figure 2.1. Intel387™ DX MCP Tag Word

2.3 Register Set

Figure 1.1 shows the Intel387 DX MCP register set. When an MCP is present in a system, programmers may use these registers in addition to the registers normally available on the Intel386 DX CPU.

2.3.1 DATA REGISTERS

Intel387 DX MCP computations use the MCP's data registers. These eight 80-bit registers provide the equivalent capacity of twenty 32-bit registers. Each of the eight data registers in the MCP is 80 bits wide and is divided into "fields" corresponding to the MCPs extended-precision real data type.

The Intel387 DX MCP register set can be accessed either as a stack, with instructions operating on the top one or two stack elements, or as a fixed register set, with instructions operating on explicitly designated registers. The TOP field in the status word identifies the current top-of-stack register. A "push" operation decrements TOP by one and loads a value into the new top register. A "pop" operation stores the value from the current top register and then increments TOP by one. Like the Intel386 DX Microprocessor stacks in memory, the MCP register stack grows "down" toward lower-addressed registers.

Instructions may address the data registers either implicitly or explicitly. Many instructions operate on the register at the TOP of the stack. These instructions implicitly address the register at which TOP points. Other instructions allow the programmer to explicitly specify which register to user. This explicit register addressing is also relative to TOP.

2.3.2 TAG WORD

The tag word marks the content of each numeric data register, as Figure 2.1 shows. Each two-bit tag represents one of the eight numerics registers. The principal function of the tag word is to optimize the MCPs performance and stack handling by making it possible to distinguish between empty and nonempty register locations. It also enables exception handlers to check the contents of a stack location without the need to perform complex decoding of the actual data.

MCP BUSY
TOP OF STACK POINTER
CONDITION CODE

15 7 0

B	C3	TOP			C2	C1	C0	ES	SF	PE	UE	OE	ZE	DE	IE

ERROR SUMMARY STATUS
STACK FLAG

EXCEPTION FLAGS:
PRECISION
UNDERFLOW
OVERFLOW
ZERO DIVIDE
DENORMALIZED OPERAND
INVALID OPERATION

240448-3

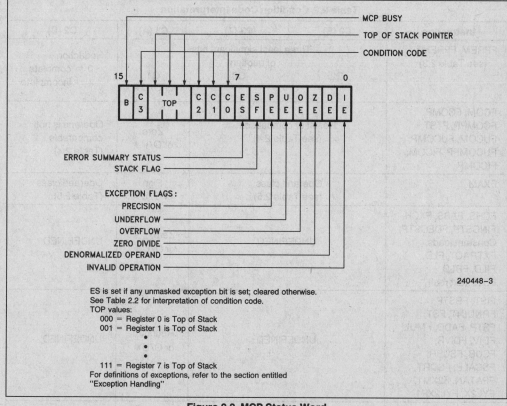

ES is set if any unmasked exception bit is set; cleared otherwise.
See Table 2.2 for interpretation of condition code.
TOP values:
000 = Register 0 is Top of Stack
001 = Register 1 is Top of Stack
•
•
•
111 = Register 7 is Top of Stack
For definitions of exceptions, refer to the section entitled "Exception Handling"

Figure 2.2. MCP Status Word

2.3.3 STATUS WORD

The 16-bit status word (in the status register) shown in Figure 2.2 reflects the overall state of the MCP. It may be read and inspected by CPU code.

Bit 15, the B-bit (busy bit) is included for 8087 compatibility only. It reflects the contents of the ES bit (bit 7 of the status word), not the status of the BUSY# output of the Intel387 DX MCP.

Bits 13–11 (TOP) point to the Intel387 DX MCP register that is the current top-of-stack.

The four numeric condition code bits (C_3–C_0) are similar to the flags in a CPU; instructions that perform arithmetic operations update these bits to reflect the outcome. The effects of these instructions on the condition code are summarized in Tables 2.2 through 2.5.

Bit 7 is the error summary (ES) status bit. This bit is set if any unmasked exception bit is set; it is clear otherwise. If this bit is set, the ERROR# signal is asserted.

Bit 6 is the stack flag (SF). This bit is used to distinguish invalid operations due to stack overflow or underflow from other kinds of invalid operations. When SF is set, bit 9 (C_1) distinguishes between stack overflow ($C_1 = 1$) and underflow ($C_1 = 0$).

Figure 2.2 shows the six exception flags in bits 5–0 of the status word. Bits 5–0 are set to indicate that the MCP has detected an exception while executing an instruction. A later section entitled "Exception Handling" explains how they are set and used.

Note that when a new value is loaded into the status word by the FLDENV or FRSTOR instruction, the value of ES (bit 7) and its reflection in the B-bit (bit 15) are not derived from the values loaded from memory but rather are dependent upon the values of the exception flags (bits 5–0) in the status word and their corresponding masks in the control word. If ES is set in such a case, the ERROR# output of the MCP is activated immediately.

Table 2.2. Condition Code Interpretation

Instruction	C0 (S)	C3 (Z)	C1 (A)	C2 (C)
FPREM, FPREM1 (see Table 2.3)	Three least significant bits of quotient Q2	Q0	Q1 or O/U#	Reduction 0 = complete 1 = incomplete
FCOM, FCOMP, FCOMPP, FTST, FUCOM, FUCOMP, FUCOMPP, FICOM, FICOMP	Result of comparison (see Table 2.4)		Zero or O/U#	Operand is not comparable (Table 2.4)
FXAM	Operand class (see Table 2.5)		Sign or O/U#	Operand class (Table 2.5)
FCHS, FABS, FXCH, FINCSTP, FDECSTP, Constant loads, FXTRACT, FLD, FILD, FBLD, FSTP (ext real)	UNDEFINED		Zero or O/U#	UNDEFINED
FIST, FBSTP, FRNDINT, FST, FSTP, FADD, FMUL, FDIV, FDIVR, FSUB, FSUBR, FSCALE, FSQRT, FPATAN, F2XM1, FYL2X, FYL2XP1	UNDEFINED		Roundup or O/U#	UNDEFINED
FPTAN, FSIN FCOS, FSINCOS	UNDEFINED		Roundup or O/U#, undefined if C2 = 1	Reduction 0 = complete 1 = incomplete
FLDENV, FRSTOR	Each bit loaded from memory			
FLDCW, FSTENV, FSTCW, FSTSW, FCLEX, FINIT, FSAVE	UNDEFINED			

O/U#	When both IE and SF bits of status word are set, indicating a stack exception, this bit distinguishes between stack overflow (C1 = 1) and underflow (C1 = 0).
Reduction	If FPREM or FPREM1 produces a remainder that is less than the modulus, reduction is complete. When reduction is incomplete the value at the top of the stack is a partial remainder, which can be used as input to further reduction. For FPTAN, FSIN, FCOS, and FSINCOS, the reduction bit is set if the operand at the top of the stack is too large. In this case the original operand remains at the top of the stack.
Roundup	When the PE bit of the status word is set, this bit indicates whether the last rounding in the instruction was upward.
UNDEFINED	Do not rely on finding any specific value in these bits.

Table 2.3. Condition Code Interpretation after FPREM and FPREM1 Instructions

Condition Code					Interpretation after FPREM and FPREM1
C2	**C3**	**C1**	**C0**		
1	X	X	X		Incomplete Reduction: further interation required for complete reduction
0	Q1	Q0	Q2	Q MOD8	Complete Reduction: C0, C3, C1 contain three least significant bits of quotient
	0	0	0	0	
	0	1	0	1	
	1	0	0	2	
	1	1	0	3	
	0	0	1	4	
	0	1	1	5	
	1	0	1	6	
	1	1	1	7	

Table 2.4. Condition Code Resulting from Comparison

Order	C3	C2	C0
TOP > Operand	0	0	0
TOP < Operand	0	0	1
TOP = Operand	1	0	0
Unordered	1	1	1

4

Table 2.5. Condition Code Defining Operand Class

C3	C2	C1	C0	Value at TOP
0	0	0	0	+ Unsupported
0	0	0	1	+ NaN
0	0	1	0	− Unsupported
0	0	1	1	− NaN
0	1	0	0	+ Normal
0	1	0	1	+ Infinity
0	1	1	0	− Normal
0	1	1	1	− Infinity
1	0	0	0	+ 0
1	0	0	1	+ Empty
1	0	1	0	− 0
1	0	1	1	− Empty
1	1	0	0	+ Denormal
1	1	1	0	− Denormal

2.3.4 INSTRUCTION AND DATA POINTERS

Because the MCP operates in parallel with the CPU, any errors detected by the MCP may be reported after the CPU has executed the ESC instruction which caused it. To allow identification of the failing numeric instruction, the Intel386 DX Microprocessor and Intel387 DX Math CoProcessor contains two pointer registers that supply the address of the failing numeric instruction and the address of its numeric memory operand (if appropriate).

The instruction and data pointers are provided for user-written error handlers. These registers are actually located in the Intel386 DX CPU, but appear to be located in the MCP because they are accessed by the ESC instructions FLDENV, FSTENV, FSAVE, and FRSTOR. (In the 8086/8087 and 80286/80287, these registers are located in the MCP.) Whenever the Intel386 DX CPU decodes a new ESC instruction, it saves the address of the instruction (including any prefixes that may be present), the address of the operand (if present), and the opcode.

The instruction and data pointers appear in one of four formats depending on the operating mode of the Intel386 DX Microprocessor (protected mode or real-address mode) and depending on the operand-size attribute in effect (32-bit operand or 16-bit operand). When the Intel386 DX Microprocessor is in virtual-8086 mode, the real-address mode formats are used. (See Figures 2.3 through 2.6.) The ESC instructions FLDENV, FSTENV, FSAVE, and FRSTOR are used to transfer these values between the Intel386 DX Microprocessor registers and memory. Note that the value of the data pointer is *undefined* if the prior ESC instruction did not have a memory operand.

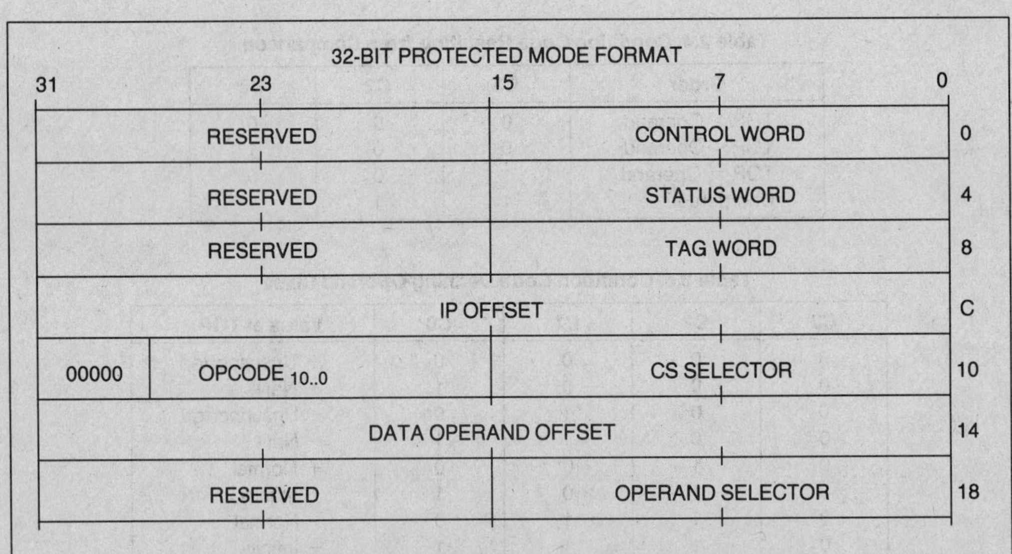

Figure 2.3. Protected Mode Intel387™ DX MCP Instruction and Data Pointer Image in Memory, 32-Bit Format

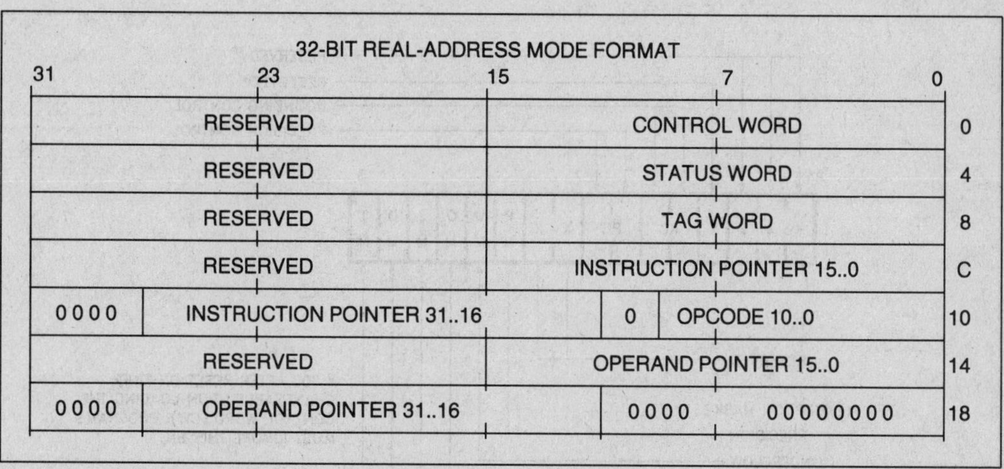

Figure 2.4. Real Mode Intel387™ DX MCP Instruction and Data Pointer Image in Memory, 32-Bit Format

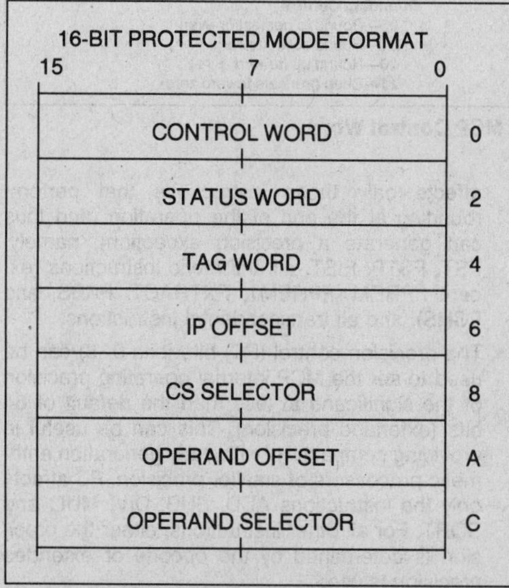

Figure 2.5. Protected Mode Intel387™ DX MCP Instruction and Data Pointer Image in Memory, 16-Bit Format

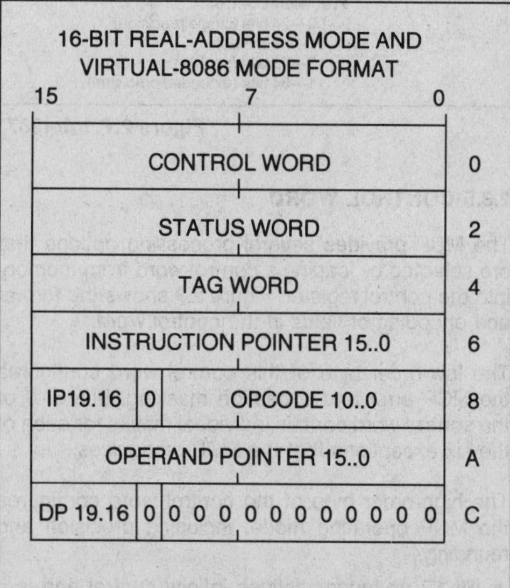

Figure 2.6. Real Mode Intel387™ DX MCP Instruction and Data Pointer Image in Memory, 16-Bit Format

4

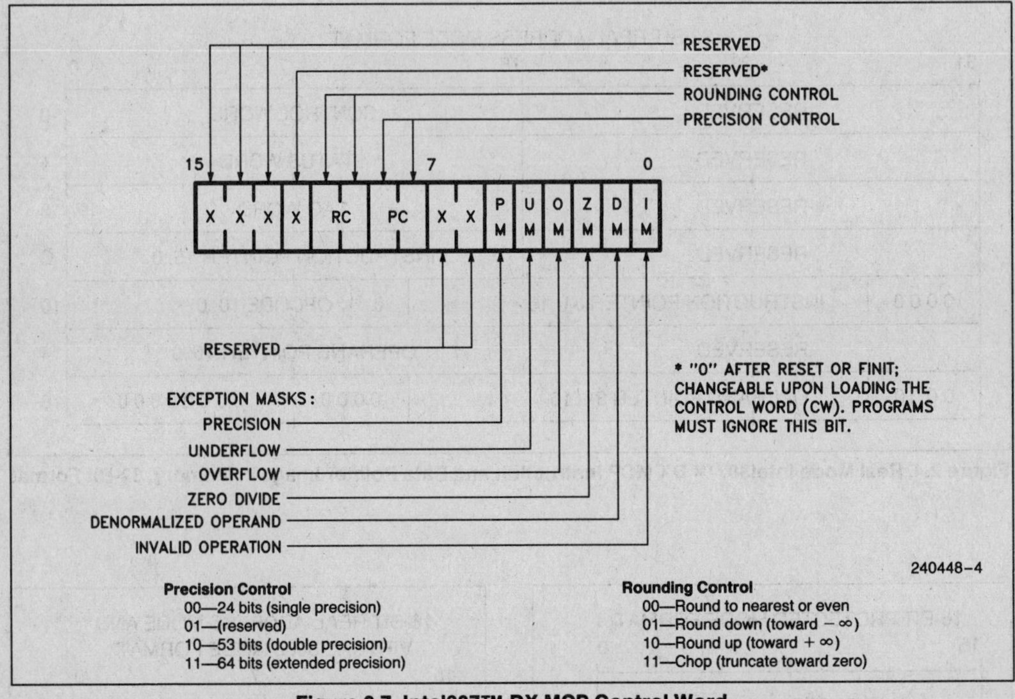

Figure 2.7. Intel387™ DX MCP Control Word

2.3.5 CONTROL WORD

The MCP provides several processing options that are selected by loading a control word from memory into the control register. Figure 2.7 shows the format and encoding of fields in the control word.

The low-order byte of this control word configures the MCP error and exception masking. Bits 5–0 of the control word contain individual masks for each of the six exceptions that the MCP recognizes.

The high-order byte of the control word configures the MCP operating mode, including precision and rounding.

- Bit 12 no longer defines infinity control and is a reserved bit. Only affine closure is supported for infinity arithmetic. The bit is initialized to zero after RESET or FINIT and is changeable upon loading the CW. Programs must ignore this bit.
- The rounding control (RC) bits (bits 11–10) provide for directed rounding and true chop, as well as the unbiased round to nearest even mode specified in the IEEE standard. Rounding control affects only those instructions that perform rounding at the end of the operation (and thus can generate a precision exception); namely, FST, FSTP, FIST, all arithmetic instructions (except FPREM, FPREM1, FXTRACT, FABS, and FCHS), and all transcendental instructions.
- The precision control (PC) bits (bits 9–8) can be used to set the MCP internal operating precision of the significand at less than the default of 64 bits (extended precision). This can be useful in providing compatibility with early generation arithmetic processors of smaller precision. PC affects only the instructions ADD, SUB, DIV, MUL, and SQRT. For all other instructions, either the precision is determined by the opcode or extended precision is used.

2.4 Interrupt Description

Several interrupts of the Intel386 DX CPU are used to report exceptional conditions while executing numeric programs in either real or protected mode. Table 2.6 shows these interrupts and their causes.

Table 2.6. Intel386™ DX Microprocessor Interrupt Vectors Reserved for MCP

Interrupt Number	Cause of Interrupt
7	An ESC instruction was encountered when EM or TS of the Intel386™ DX CPU control register zero (CR0) was set. EM = 1 indicates that software emulation of the instruction is required. When TS is set, either an ESC or WAIT instruction causes interrupt 7. This indicates that the current MCP context may not belong to the current task.
9	An operand of a coprocessor instruction wrapped around an addressing limit (0FFFFH for small segments, 0FFFFFFFFH for big segments, zero for expand-down segments) and spanned inaccessible addresses(1). The failing numerics instruction is not restartable. The address of the failing numerics instruction and data operand may be lost; an FSTENV does not return reliable addresses. As with the 80286/80287, the segment overrun exception should be handled by executing an FNINIT instruction (i.e. an FINIT without a preceding WAIT). The return address on the stack does not necessarily point to the failing instruction nor to the following instruction. The interrupt can be avoided by never allowing numeric data to start within 108 bytes of the end of a segment.
13	The first word or doubleword of a numeric operand is not entirely within the limit of its segment. The return address pushed onto the stack of the exception handler points at the ESC instruction that caused the exception, including any prefixes. The Intel387™ DX MCP has not executed this instruction; the instruction pointer and data pointer register refer to a previous, correctly executed instruction.
16	The previous numerics instruction caused an unmasked exception. The address of the faulty instruction and the address of its operand are stored in the instruction pointer and data pointer registers. Only ESC and WAIT instructions can cause this interrupt. The Intel386™ DX CPU return address pushed onto the stack of the exception handler points to a WAIT or ESC instruction (including prefixes). This instruction can be restarted after clearing the exception condition in the MCP. FNINIT, FNCLEX, FNSTSW, FNSTENV, and FNSAVE cannot cause this interrupt.

1. An operand may wrap around an addressing limit when the segment limit is near an addressing limit and the operand is near the largest valid address in the segment. Because of the wrap-around, the beginning and ending addresses of such an operand will be at opposite ends of the segment. There are two ways that such an operand may also span inaccessible addresses: 1) if the segment limit is not equal to the addressing limit (e.g. addressing limit is FFFFH and segment limit is FFFDH) the operand will span addresses that are not within the segment (e.g. an 8-byte operand that starts at valid offset FFFC will span addresses FFFC–FFFF and 0000-0003; however addresses FFFE and FFFF are not valid, because they exceed the limit); 2) if the operand begins and ends in present and accessible pages but intermediate bytes of the operand fall in a not-present page or a page to which the procedure does not have access rights.

2.5 Exception Handling

The Intel387 DX MCP detects six different exception conditions that can occur during instruction execution. Table 2.7 lists the exception conditions in order of precedence, showing for each the cause and the default action taken by the MCP if the exception is masked by its corresponding mask bit in the control word.

Any exception that is not masked by the control word sets the corresponding exception flag of the status word, sets the ES bit of the status word, and asserts the ERROR# signal. When the CPU attempts to execute another ESC instruction or WAIT, exception 7 occurs. The exception condition must be resolved via an interrupt service routine. The Intel386 DX Microprocessor saves the address of the floating-point instruction that caused the exception and the address of any memory operand required by that instruction.

2.6 Initialization

Intel387 DX MCP initialization software must execute an FNINIT instruction (i.e. an FINIT without a preceding WAIT) to clear ERROR#. After a hardware RESET, the ERROR# output is asserted to indicate that a Intel387 DX MCP is present. To accomplish this, the IE and ES bits of the status word are set, and the IM bit in the control word is reset. After FNINIT, the status word and the control word have the same values as in an 80287 after RESET.

2.7 8087 and 80287 Compatibility

This section summarizes the differences between the Intel387 DX MCP and the 80287. Any migration from the 8087 directly to the Intel387 DX MCP must also take into account the differences between the 8087 and the 80287 as listed in Appendix A.

Many changes have been designed into the Intel387 DX MCP to directly support the IEEE standard in hardware. These changes result in increased performance by eliminating the need for software that supports the standard.

2.7.1 GENERAL DIFFERENCES

The Intel387 DX MCP supports only affine closure for infinity arithmetic, not projective closure. Bit 12 of the Control Word (CW) no longer defines infinity control. It is a reserved bit; but it is initialized to zero after RESET or FINIT and is changeable upon loading the CW. Programs must ignore this bit.

Operands for FSCALE and FPATAN are no longer restricted in range (except for $\pm\infty$); F2XM1 and FPTAN accept a wider range of operands.

The results of transcendental operations may be slightly different from those computed by 80287.

In the case of FPTAN, the Intel387 DX MCP supplies a true tangent result in ST(1), and (always) a floating point 1 in ST.

Rounding control is in effect for FLD *constant*.

Software cannot change entries of the tag word to values (other than empty) that do not reflect the actual register contents.

After reset, FINIT, and incomplete FPREM, the Intel387 DX MCP resets to zero the condition code bits C_3–C_0 of the status word.

In conformance with the IEEE standard, the Intel387 DX MCP does not support the special data formats: pseudozero, pseudo-NaN, pseudoinfinity, and unnormal.

Table 2.7. Exceptions

Exception	Cause	Default Action (if exception is masked)
Invalid Operation	Operation on a signaling NaN, unsupported format, indeterminate form ($0*\infty$, 0/0, $(+\infty)+(-\infty)$, etc.), or stack overflow/underflow (SF is also set).	Result is a quiet NaN, integer indefinite, or BCD indefinite
Denormalized Operand	At least one of the operands is denormalized, i.e. it has the smallest exponent but a nonzero significand.	Normal processing continues
Zero Divisor	The divisor is zero while the dividend is a noninfinite, nonzero number.	Result is ∞
Overflow	The result is too large in magnitude to fit in the specified format.	Result is largest finite value or ∞
Underflow	The true result is nonzero but too small to be represented in the specified format, and, if underflow exception is masked, denormalization causes loss of accuracy.	Result is denormalized or zero
Inexact Result (Precision)	The true result is not exactly representable in the specified format (e.g. 1/3); the result is rounded according to the rounding mode.	Normal processing continues

2.7.2 EXCEPTIONS

A number of differences exist due to changes in the IEEE standard and to functional improvements to the architecture of the Intel387 DX MCP:

1. When the overflow or underflow exception is masked, the Intel387 DX MCP differs from the 80287 in rounding when overflow or underflow occurs. The Intel387 DX MCP produces results that are consistent with the rounding mode.
2. When the underflow exception is masked, the Intel387 DX MCP sets its underflow flag only if there is also a loss of accuracy during denormalization.
3. Fewer invalid-operation exceptions due to denormal operands, because the instructions FSQRT, FDIV, FPREM, and conversions to BCD or to integer normalize denormal operands before proceeding.
4. The FSQRT, FBSTP, and FPREM instructions may cause underflow, because they support denormal operands.
5. The denormal exception can occur during the transcendental instructions and the FXTRACT instruction.
6. The denormal exception no longer takes precedence over all other exceptions.
7. When the denormal exception is masked, the Intel387 DX MCP automatically normalizes denormal operands. The 8087/80287 performs unnormal arithmetic, which might produce an unnormal result.
8. When the operand is zero, the FXTRACT instruction reports a zero-divide exception and leaves $-\infty$ in ST(1).
9. The status word has a new bit (SF) that signals when invalid-operation exceptions are due to stack underflow or overflow.
10. FLD *extended precision* no longer reports denormal exceptions, because the instruction is not numeric.
11. FLD *single/double precision* when the operand is denormal converts the number to extended precision and signals the denormalized operand exception. When loading a signaling NaN, FLD *single/double precision* signals an invalid-operand exception.
12. The Intel387 DX MCP only generates quiet NaNs (as on the 80287); however, the Intel387 DX MCP distinguishes between quiet NaNs and signaling NaNs. Signaling NaNs trigger exceptions when they are used as operands; quiet NaNs do not (except for FCOM, FIST, and FBSTP which also raise IE for quiet NaNs).
13. When stack overflow occurs during FPTAN and overflow is masked, both ST(0) and ST(1) contain quiet NaNs. The 80287/8087 leaves the original operand in ST(1) intact.
14. When the scaling factor is $\pm\infty$, the FSCALE (ST(0), ST(1)) instruction behaves as follows (ST(0) and ST(1) contain the scaled and scaling operands respectively):
    - FSCALE(0, ∞) generates the invalid operation exception.
    - FSCALE(finite, $-\infty$) generates zero with the same sign as the scaled operand.
    - FSCALE(finite, $+\infty$) generates ∞ with the same sign as the scaled operand.

    The 8087/80287 returns zero in the first case and raises the invalid-operation exception in the other cases.
15. The Intel387 DX MCP returns signed infinity/zero as the unmasked response to massive overflow/underflow. The 8087 and 80287 support a limited range for the scaling factor; within this range either massive overflow/underflow do not occur or undefined results are produced.

3.0 HARDWARE INTERFACE

In the following description of hardware interface, the # symbol at the end of a signal name indicates that the active or asserted state occurs when the signal is at a low voltage. When no # is present after the signal name, the signal is asserted when at the high voltage level.

3.1 Signal Description

In the following signal descriptions, the Intel387 DX Math Coprocessor pins are grouped by function as follows:

1. Execution control—CPUCLK2, NUMCLK2, CKM, RESETIN
2. MCP handshake—PEREQ, BUSY#, ERROR#
3. Bus interface pins—D31–D0, W/R#, ADS#, READY#, READYO#
4. Chip/Port Select—STEN, NPS1#, NPS2, CMD0#
5. Power supplies—V_{CC}, V_{SS}

Table 3.1 lists every pin by its identifier, gives a brief description of its function, and lists some of its characteristics. All output signals are tristate; they leave floating state only when STEN is active. The output buffers of the bidirectional data pins D31–D0 are also tristate; they leave floating state only in read cycles when the MCP is selected (i.e. when STEN, NPS1#, and NPS2 are all active).

Figure 3.1 and Table 3.2 together show the location of every pin in the pin grid array.

Table 3.1. Intel387™ DX MCP Pin Summary

Pin Name	Function	Active State	Input/ Output	Referenced To
CPUCLK2	Intel386™ DX CPU CLocK 2		I	
NUMCLK2	Intel387™ DX MCP CLocK 2		I	
CKM	Intel387™ DX MCP CLocKing Mode		I	
RESETIN	System reset	High	I	CPUCLK2
PEREQ	Processor Extension REQuest	High	O	CPUCLK2/STEN
BUSY#	Busy status	Low	O	CPUCLK2/STEN
ERROR#	Error status	Low	O	NUMCLK2/STEN
D31–D0	Data pins	High	I/O	CPUCLK2
W/R#	Write/Read bus cycle	Hi/Lo	I	CPUCLK2
ADS#	ADdress Strobe	Low	I	CPUCLK2
READY#	Bus ready input	Low	I	CPUCLK2
READYO#	Ready output	Low	O	CPUCLK2/STEN
STEN	STatus ENable	High	I	CPUCLK2
NPS1#	MCP select #1	Low	I	CPUCLK2
NPS2	MCP select #2	High	I	CPUCLK2
CMD0#	CoMmanD	Low	I	CPUCLK2
V_{CC}			I	
V_{SS}			I	

NOTE:
STEN is referenced to only when getting the output pins into or out of tristate mode.

Table 3.2. Intel387™ DX MCP Pin Cross-Reference

Pin		Location	Pin		Location	Pin		Location
ADS#	—	K7	D18	—	A8	STEN	—	L4
BUSY#	—	K2	D19	—	B9	W/R#	—	K4
CKM	—	J11	D20	—	B10			
CPUCLK24	—	K10	D21	—	A10	V_{CC}	—	A6, A9, B4,
CMD0#	—	L8	D22	—	B11			E1, F1, F10,
D0	—	H2	D23	—	C10			J2, K5,
D1	—	H1	D24	—	D10			L7
D2	—	G2	D25	—	D11			
D3	—	G1	D26	—	E10	V_{SS}	—	B2, B7, C11,
D4	—	D2	D27	—	E11			E2, F2, F11,
D5	—	D1	D28	—	G10			J1, J10, L5
D6	—	C2	D29	—	G11			
D7	—	C1	D30	—	H10	NO CONNECT	—	K9
D8	—	B1	D31	—	H11	TIE HIGH	—	K3, L9*
D9	—	A2	ERROR#	—	L2			
D10	—	B3	NPS1#	—	L6			
D11	—	A3	NPS2	—	K6			
D12	—	A4	NUMCLK2	—	K11			
D13	—	B5	PEREQ	—	K1			
D14	—	A5	READY#	—	K8			
D15	—	B6	READYO#	—	L3			
D16	—	A7	RESETIN	—	L10			
D17	—	B8						

*Tie high pins may either be tied high with a pullup resistor or connected to V_{CC}.

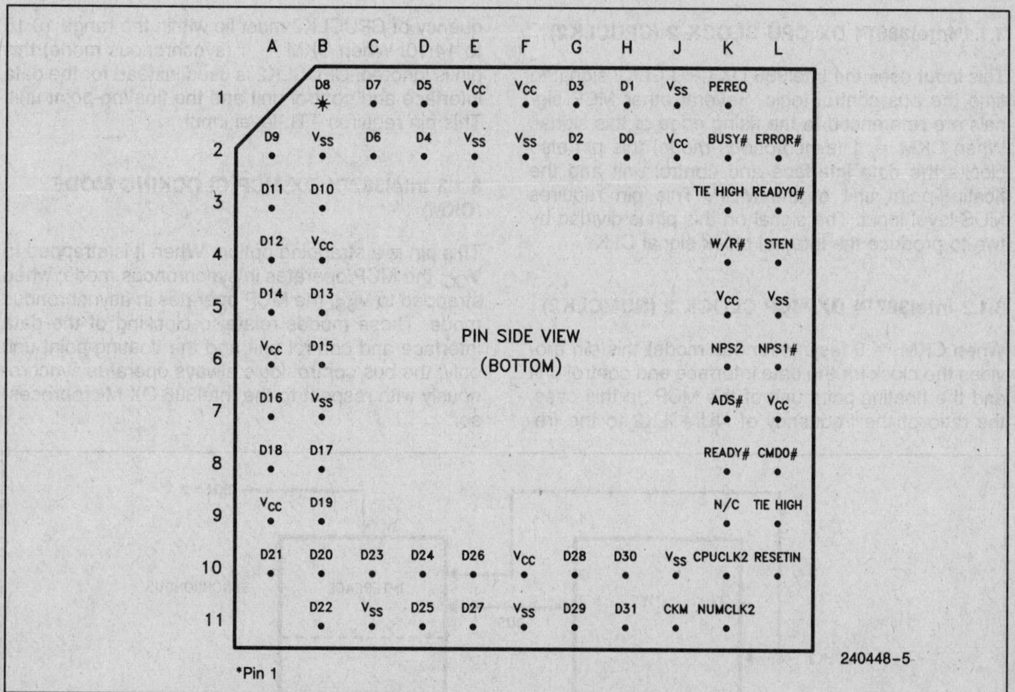

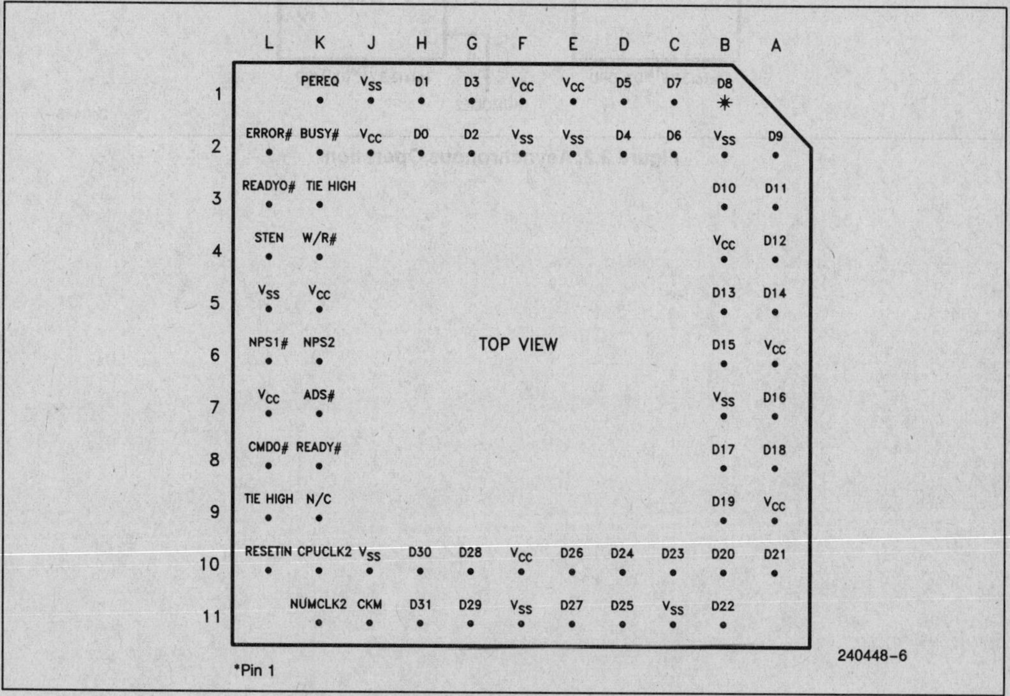

Figure 3.1. Intel387™ DX MCP Pin Configuration

3.1.1 Intel386™ DX CPU CLOCK 2 (CPUCLK2)

This input uses the Intel386 DX CPU CLK2 signal to time the bus control logic. Several other MCP signals are referenced to the rising edge of this signal. When CKM = 1 (synchronous mode) this pin also clocks the data interface and control unit and the floating-point unit of the MCP. This pin requires MOS-level input. The signal on this pin is divided by two to produce the internal clock signal CLK.

3.1.2 Intel387™ DX MCP CLOCK 2 (NUMCLK2)

When CKM = 0 (asynchronous mode) this pin provides the clock for the data interface and control unit and the floating-point unit of the MCP. In this case, the ratio of the frequency of NUMCLK2 to the frequency of CPUCLK2 must lie within the range 10:16 to 14:10. When CKM = 1 (synchronous mode) this pin is ignored; CPUCLK2 is used instead for the data interface and control unit and the floating-point unit. This pin requires TTL-level input.

3.1.3 Intel387™ DX MCP CLOCKING MODE (CKM)

This pin is a strapping option. When it is strapped to V_{CC}, the MCP operates in synchronous mode; when strapped to V_{SS}, the MCP operates in asynchronous mode. These modes relate to clocking of the data interface and control unit and the floating-point unit only; the bus control logic always operates synchronously with respect to the Intel386 DX Microprocessor.

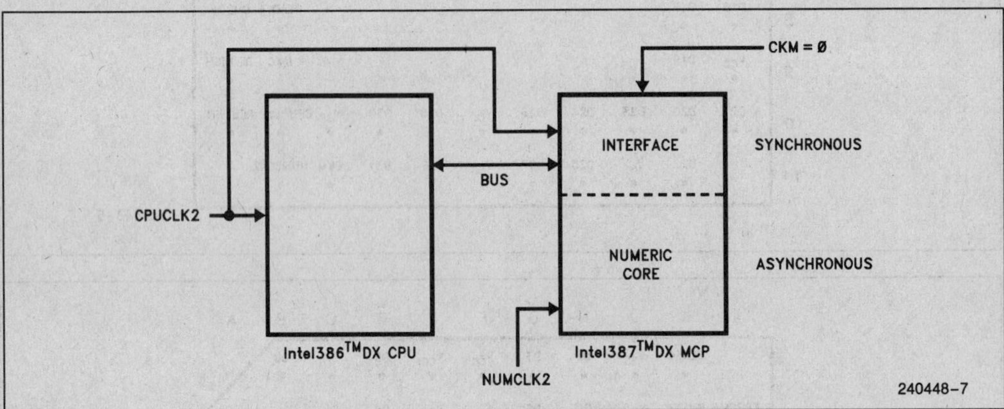

Figure 3.2. Asynchronous Operation

3.1.4 SYSTEM RESET (RESETIN)

A LOW to HIGH transition on this pin causes the MCP to terminate its present activity and to enter a dormant state. RESETIN must remain HIGH for at least 40 NUMCLK2 periods. The HIGH to LOW transitions of RESETIN must be synchronous with CPUCLK2, so that the phase of the internal clock of the bus control logic (which is the CPUCLK2 divided by 2) is the same as the phase of the internal clock of the Intel386 DX CPU. After RESETIN goes LOW, at least 50 NUMCLK2 periods must pass before the first MCP instruction is written into the Intel387 DX MCP. This pin should be connected to the Intel386 DX CPU RESET pin. Table 3.3 shows the status of other pins after a reset.

Table 3.3. Output Pin Status During Reset

Pin Value	Pin Name
HIGH	READYO#, BUSY#
LOW	PEREQ, ERROR#
Tri-State OFF	D31–D0

3.1.5 PROCESSOR EXTENSION REQUEST (PEREQ)

When active, this pin signals to the Intel386 DX CPU that the MCP is ready for data transfer to/from its data FIFO. When all data is written to or read from the data FIFO, PEREQ is deactivated. This signal always goes inactive before BUSY# goes inactive. This signal is referenced to CPUCLK2. It should be connected to the Intel386 DX CPU PEREQ input.

3.1.6 BUSY STATUS (BUSY#)

When active, this pin signals to the Intel386 DX CPU that the MCP is currently executing an instruction. This signal is referenced to CPUCLK2. It should be connected to the Intel386 DX CPU BUSY# pin.

3.1.7 ERROR STATUS (ERROR#)

This pin reflects the ES bits of the status register. When active, it indicates that an unmasked exception has occurred (except that, immediately after a reset, it indicates to the Intel386 DX Microprocessor that a Intel387 DX MCP is present in the system). This signal can be changed to inactive state only by the following instructions (without a preceding WAIT): FNINIT, FNCLEX, FNSTENV, and FNSAVE. This signal is referenced to NUMCLK2. It should be connected to the Intel386 DX CPU ERROR# pin.

3.1.8 DATA PINS (D31–D0)

These bidirectional pins are used to transfer data and opcodes between the Intel386 DX CPU and Intel387 DX MCP. They are normally connected directly to the corresponding Intel386 DX CPU data pins. HIGH state indicates a value of one. D0 is the least significant data bit. Timings are referenced to CPUCLK2.

3.1.9 WRITE/READ BUS CYCLE (W/R#)

This signal indicates to the MCP whether the Intel386 DX CPU bus cycle in progress is a read or a write cycle. This pin should be connected directly to the Intel386 DX CPU W/R# pin. HIGH indicates a write cycle; LOW, a read cycle. This input is ignored if any of the signals STEN, NPS1#, or NPS2 is inactive. Setup and hold times are referenced to CPUCLK2.

3.1.10 ADDRESS STROBE (ADS#)

This input, in conjunction with the READY# input indicates when the MCP bus-control logic may sample W/R# and the chip-select signals. Setup and hold times are referenced to CPUCLK2. This pin should be connected to the Intel386 DX CPU ADS# pin.

4

3.1.11 BUS READY INPUT (READY#)

This input indicates to the MCP when a Intel386 DX CPU bus cycle is to be terminated. It is used by the bus-control logic to trace bus activities. Bus cycles can be extended indefinitely until terminated by READY#. This input should be connected to the same signal that drives the Intel386 DX CPU READY# input. Setup and hold times are referenced to CPUCLK2.

3.1.12 READY OUTPUT (READYO#)

This pin is activated at such a time that write cycles are terminated after two clocks (except FLDENV and FRSTOR) and read cycles after three clocks. In configurations where no extra wait states are required, this pin must directly or indirectly drive the Intel386 DX CPU READY# input. Refer to section 3.4 "Bus Operation" for details. This pin is activated only during bus cycles that select the MCP. This signal is referenced to CPUCLK2.

3.1.13 STATUS ENABLE (STEN)

This pin serves as a chip select for the MCP. When inactive, this pin forces BUSY#, PEREQ, ERROR#, and READYO# outputs into floating state. D31–D0 are normally floating and leave floating state only if STEN is active and additional conditions are met. STEN also causes the chip to recognize its other chip-select inputs. STEN makes it easier to do on-board testing (using the overdrive method) of other chips in systems containing the MCP. STEN should be pulled up with a resistor so that it can be pulled down when testing. In boards that do not use on-board testing, STEN should be connected to V_{CC}. Setup and hold times are relative to CPUCLK2. Note that STEN must maintain the same setup and hold times as NPS1#, NPS2, and CMD0# (i.e. if STEN changes state during a Intel387 DX MCP bus cycle, it should change state during the same CLK period as the NPS1#, NPS2, and CMD0# signals).

3.1.14 MCP Select #1 (NPS1#)

When active (along with STEN and NPS2) in the first period of a Intel386 DX CPU bus cycle, this signal indicates that the purpose of the bus cycle is to communicate with the MCP. This pin should be connected directly to the Intel386 DX CPU M/IO# pin, so that the MCP is selected only when the Intel386 DX CPU performs I/O cycles. Setup and hold times are referenced to CPUCLK2.

3.1.15 MCP SELECT #2 (NPS2)

When active (along with STEN and NPS1#) in the first period of an Intel386 DX CPU bus cycle, this signal indicates that the purpose of the bus cycle is to communicate with the MCP. This pin should be connected directly to the Intel386 DX CPU A31 pin, so that the MCP is selected only when the Intel386 DX CPU uses one of the I/O addresses reserved for the MCP (800000F8 or 800000FC). Setup and hold times are referenced to CPUCLK2.

3.1.16 COMMAND (CMD0#)

During a write cycle, this signal indicates whether an opcode (CMD0# active) or data (CMD0# inactive) is being sent to the MCP. During a read cycle, it indicates whether the control or status register (CMD0# active) or a data register (CMD0# inactive) is being read. CMD0# should be connected directly to the A2 output of the Intel386 DX Microprocessor. Setup and hold times are referenced to CPUCLK2.

3.2 Processor Architecture

As shown by the block diagram on the front page, the MCP is internally divided into three sections: the bus control logic (BCL), the data interface and control unit, and the floating point unit (FPU). The FPU (with the support of the control unit which contains the sequencer and other support units) executes all numerics instructions. The data interface and control unit is responsible for the data flow to and from the FPU and the control registers, for receiving the instructions, decoding them, and sequencing the microinstructions, and for handling some of the administrative instructions. The BCL is responsible for the Intel386 DX CPU bus tracking and interface. The BCL is the only unit in the Intel387 DX MCP that must run synchronously with the Intel386 DX CPU; the rest of the MCP can run asynchronously with respect to the Intel386 DX Microprocessor.

3.2.1 BUS CONTROL LOGIC

The BCL communicates solely with the CPU using I/O bus cycles. The BCL appears to the CPU as a special peripheral device. It is special in two respects: the CPU initiates I/O automatically when it encounters ESC instructions, and the CPU uses reserved I/O addresses to communicate with the BCL. The BCL does not communicate directly with memory. The CPU performs all memory access, transferring input operands from memory to the MCP and transferring outputs from the MCP to memory.

3.2.2 DATA INTERFACE AND CONTROL UNIT

The data interface and control unit latches the data and, subject to BCL control, directs the data to the FIFO or the instruction decoder. The instruction decoder decodes the ESC instructions sent to it by the CPU and generates controls that direct the data flow in the FIFO. It also triggers the microinstruction sequencer that controls execution of each instruction. If the ESC instruction is FINIT, FCLEX, FSTSW, FSTSW AX, or FSTCW, the control executes it independently of the FPU and the sequencer. The data interface and control unit is the one that generates the BUSY#, PEREQ and ERROR# signals that synchronize Intel387 DX MCP activities with the Intel386 DX CPU. It also supports the FPU in all operations that it cannot perform alone (e.g. exceptions handling, transcendental operations, etc.).

3.2.3 FLOATING POINT UNIT

The FPU executes all instructions that involve the register stack, including arithmetic, logical, transcendental, constant, and data transfer instructions. The data path in the FPU is 84 bits wide (68 significant bits, 15 exponent bits, and a sign bit) which allows internal operand transfers to be performed at very high speeds.

3.3 System Configuration

As an extension to the Intel386 DX Microprocessor, the Intel387 DX Math Coprocessor can be connected to the CPU as shown by Figure 3.3. A dedicated

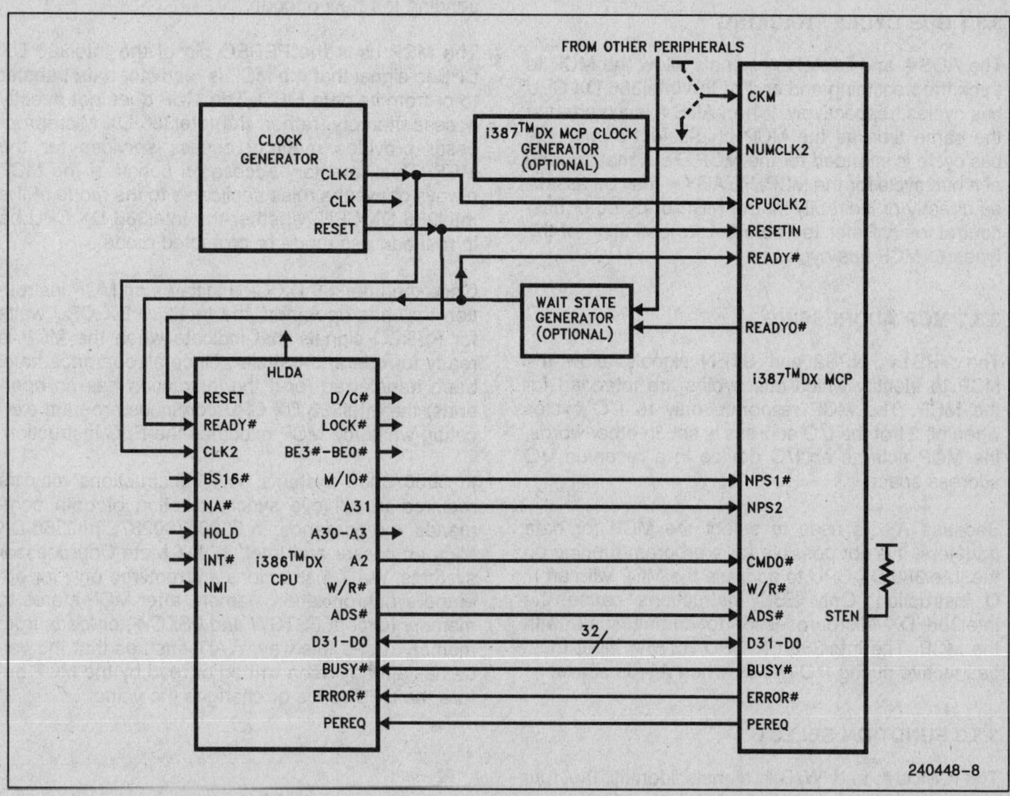

Figure 3.3. Intel386™ DX Microprocessor and Intel387™ DX Math Coprocessor System Configuration

Table 3.4. Bus Cycles Definition

STEN	NPS1#	NPS2	CMD0#	W/R#	Bus Cycle Type
0	x	x	x	x	MCP not selected and all outputs in floating state
1	1	x	x	x	MCP not selected
1	x	0	x	x	MCP not selected
1	0	1	0	0	CW or SW read from MCP
1	0	1	0	1	Opcode write to MCP
1	0	1	1	0	Data read from MCP
1	0	1	1	1	Data write to MCP

communication protocol makes possible high-speed transfer of opcodes and operands between the Intel386 DX CPU and Intel387 DX MCP. The Intel387 DX MCP is designed so that no additional components are required for interface with the Intel386 DX CPU. The Intel387 DX MCP shares the 32-bit wide local bus of the Intel386 DX CPU and most control pins of the Intel387 DX MCP are connected directly to pins of the Intel386 DX Microprocessor.

3.3.1 BUS CYCLE TRACKING

The ADS# and READY# signals allow the MCP to track the beginning and end of the Intel386 DX CPU bus cycles, respectively. When ADS# is asserted at the same time as the MCP chip-select inputs, the bus cycle is intended for the MCP. To signal the end of a bus cycle for the MCP, READY# may be asserted directly or indirectly by the MCP or by other bus-control logic. Refer to Table 3.4 for definition of the types of MCP bus cycles.

3.3.2 MCP ADDRESSING

The NPS1#, NPS2 and STEN signals allow the MCP to identify which bus cycles are intended for the MCP. The MCP responds only to I/O cycles when bit 31 of the I/O address is set. In other words, the MCP acts as an I/O device in a reserved I/O address space.

Because A_{31} is used to select the MCP for data transfers, it is not possible for a program running on the Intel386 DX CPU to address the MCP with an I/O instruction. Only ESC instructions cause the Intel386 DX Microprocessor to communicate with the MCP. The Intel386 DX CPU BS16# input must be inactive during I/O cycles when A_{31} is active.

3.3.3 FUNCTION SELECT

The CMD0# and W/R# signals identify the four kinds of bus cycle: control or status register read, data read, opcode write, data write.

3.3.4 CPU/MCP Synchronization

The pin pairs BUSY#, PEREQ, and ERROR# are used for various aspects of synchronization between the CPU and the MCP.

BUSY# is used to synchronize instruction transfer from the Intel386 DX CPU to the MCP. When the MCP recognizes an ESC instruction, it asserts BUSY#. For most ESC instructions, the Intel386 DX CPU waits for the MCP to deassert BUSY# before sending the new opcode.

The MCP uses the PEREQ pin of the Intel386 DX CPU to signal that the MCP is ready for data transfer to or from its data FIFO. The MCP does not directly access memory; rather, the Intel386 DX Microprocessor provides memory access services for the MCP. Thus, memory access on behalf of the MCP always obeys the rules applicable to the mode of the Intel386 DX CPU, whether the Intel386 DX CPU be in real-address mode or protected mode.

Once the Intel386 DX CPU initiates an MCP instruction that has operands, the Intel386 DX CPU waits for PEREQ signals that indicate when the MCP is ready for operand transfer. Once all operands have been transferred (or if the instruction has no operands) the Intel386 DX CPU continues program execution while the MCP executes the ESC instruction.

In 8086/8087 systems, WAIT instructions may be required to achieve synchronization of both commands and operands. In 80286/80287, Intel386 DX Microprocessor and Intel387 DX Math Coprocessor systems, WAIT instructions are required only for operand synchronization; namely, after MCP stores to memory (except FSTSW and FSTCW) or loads from memory. Used this way, WAIT ensures that the value has already been written or read by the MCP before the CPU reads or changes the value.

Once it has started to execute a numerics instruction and has transferred the operands from the Intel386 DX CPU, the MCP can process the instruction in parallel with and independent of the host CPU. When the MCP detects an exception, it asserts the ERROR# signal, which causes a Intel386 DX CPU interrupt.

3.3.5 SYNCHRONOUS OR ASYNCHRONOUS MODES

The internal logic of the Intel387 DX MCP (the FPU) can either operate directly from the CPU clock (synchronous mode) or from a separate clock (asynchronous mode). The two configurations are distinguished by the CKM pin. In either case, the bus control logic (BCL) of the MCP is synchronized with the CPU clock. Use of asynchronous mode allows the Intel386 DX CPU and the FPU section of the MCP to run at different speeds. In this case, the ratio of the frequency of NUMCLK2 to the frequency of CPUCLK2 must lie within the range 10:16 to 14:10. Use of synchronous mode eliminates one clock generator from the board design.

3.3.6 AUTOMATIC BUS CYCLE TERMINATION

In configurations where no extra wait states are required, READYO# can be used to drive the Intel386 DX CPU READY# input. If this pin is used, it should be connected to the logic that ORs all READY outputs from peripherals on the Intel386 DX CPU bus. READYO# is asserted by the MCP only during I/O cycles that select the MCP. Refer to section 3.4 "Bus Operation" for details.

3.4 Bus Operation

With respect to the bus interface, the Intel387 DX MCP is fully synchronous with the Intel386 DX Microprocessor. Both operate at the same rate, because each generates its internal CLK signal by dividing CPUCLK2 by two.

The Intel386 DX CPU initiates a new bus cycle by activating ADS#. The MCP recognizes a bus cycle, if, during the cycle in which ADS# is activated, STEN, NPS1#, and NPS2 are all activated. Proper operation is achieved if NPS1# is connected to the M/IO# output of the Intel386 DX CPU, and NPS2 to the A31 output. The Intel386 DX CPU's A31 output is guaranteed to be inactive in all bus cycles that do not address the MCP (i.e. I/O cycles to other devices, interrupt acknowledge, and reserved types of bus cycles). System logic must not signal a 16-bit bus cycle via the Intel386 DX CPU BS16# input during I/O cycles when A31 is active.

During the CLK period in which ADS# is activated, the MCP also examines the W/R# input signal to determine whether the cycle is a read or a write cycle and examines the CMD0# input to determine whether an opcode, operand, or control/status register transfer is to occur.

The Intel387 DX MCP supports both pipelined and nonpipelined bus cycles. A nonpipelined cycle is one for which the Intel386 DX CPU asserts ADS# when no other MCP bus cycle is in progress. A pipelined bus cycle is one for which the Intel386 DX CPU asserts ADS# and provides valid next-address and control signals as soon as in the second CLK period after the ADS# assertion for the previous Intel386 DX CPU bus cycle. Pipelining increases the availability of the bus by at least one CLK period. The MCP supports pipelined bus cycles in order to optimize address pipelining by the Intel386 DX CPU for memory cycles.

Bus operation is described in terms of an abstract *state machine*. Figure 3.4 illustrates the states and state transitions for MCP bus cycles:

- T_I is the idle state. This is the state of the bus logic after RESET, the state to which bus logic returns after evey nonpipelined bus cycle, and the state to which bus logic returns after a series of pipelined cycles.
- T_{RS} is the READY# sensitive state. Different types of bus cycle may require a minimum of one or two successive T_{RS} states. The bus logic remains in T_{RS} state until READY# is sensed, at which point the bus cycle terminates. Any number of wait states may be implemented by delaying READY#, thereby causing additional successive T_{RS} states.
- T_P is the first state for every pipelined bus cycle.

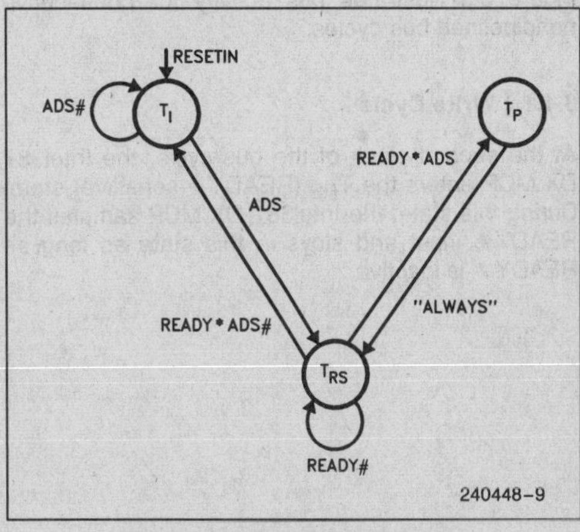

Figure 3.4. Bus State Diagram

4

The READYO# output of the Intel387 DX MCP indicates when a bus cycle for the MCP may be terminated if no extra wait states are required. For all write cycles (except those for the instructions FLDENV and FRSTOR), READYO# is always asserted in the first T_{RS} state, regardless of the number of wait states. For all read cycles and write cycles for FLDENV and FRSTOR, READYO# is always asserted in the second T_{RS} state, regardless of the number of wait states. These rules apply to both pipelined and nonpipelined cycles. Systems designers must use READYO# in one of the following ways:

1. Connect it (directly or through logic that ORs READY signals from other devices) to the READY# inputs of the Intel386 DX CPU and Intel387 DX MCP.
2. Use it as one input to a wait-state generator.

The following sections illustrate different types of MCP bus cycles.

Because different instructions have different amounts of overhead before, between, and after operand transfer cycles, it is not possible to represent in a few diagrams all of the combinations of successive operand transfer cycles. The following bus-cycle diagrams show memory cycles between MCP operand-transfer cycles. Note however that, during the instructions FLDENV, FSTENV, FSAVE, and FRSTOR, some consecutive accesses to the MCP do not have intervening memory accesses. For the timing relationship between operand transfer cycles and opcode write or other overhead activities, see Figure 3.8.

3.4.1 NONPIPELINED BUS CYCLES

Figure 3.5 illustrates bus activity for consecutive nonpipelined bus cycles.

3.4.1.1 Write Cycle

At the second clock of the bus cycle, the Intel387 DX MCP enters the T_{RS} (READY#-sensitive) state. During this state, the Intel387 DX MCP samples the READY# input and stays in this state as long as READY# is inactive.

In write cycles, the MCP drives the READYO# signal for one CLK period beginning with the second CLK of the bus cycle; therefore, the fastest write cycle takes two CLK cycles (see cycle 2 of Figure 3.5). For the instructions FLDENV and FRSTOR, however, the MCP forces a wait state by delaying the activation of READYO# to the second T_{RS} cycle (not shown in Figure 3.5).

When READY# is asserted the MCP returns to the idle state, in which ADS# could be asserted again by the Intel386 DX Microprocessor for the next cycle.

3.4.1.2 Read Cycle

At the second clock of the bus cycle, the MCP enters the T_{RS} state. See Figure 3.5. In this state, the MCP samples the READY# input and stays in this state as long as READY# is inactive.

At the rising edge of CLK in the second clock period of the cycle, the MCP starts to drive the D31–D0 outputs and continues to drive them as long as it stays in T_{RS} state.

In read cycles that address the MCP, at least one wait state must be inserted to insure that the Intel386 DX CPU latches the correct data. Since the MCP starts driving the system data bus only at the rising edge of CLK in the second clock period of the bus cycle, not enough time is left for the data signals to propagate and be latched by the Intel386 DX CPU at the falling edge of the same clock period. The MCP drives the READYO# signal for one CLK period in the third CLK of the bus cycle. Therefore, if the READYO# output is used to drive the Intel386 DX CPU READY# input, one wait state is inserted automatically.

Because one wait state is required for MCP reads, the minimum is three CLK cycles per read, as cycle 3 of Figure 3.5 shows.

When READY# is asserted the MCP returns to the idle state, in which ADS# could be asserted again by the Intel386 DX CPU for the next cycle. The transition from T_{RS} state to idle state causes the MCP to put the tristate D31–D0 outputs into the floating state, allowing another device to drive the system data bus.

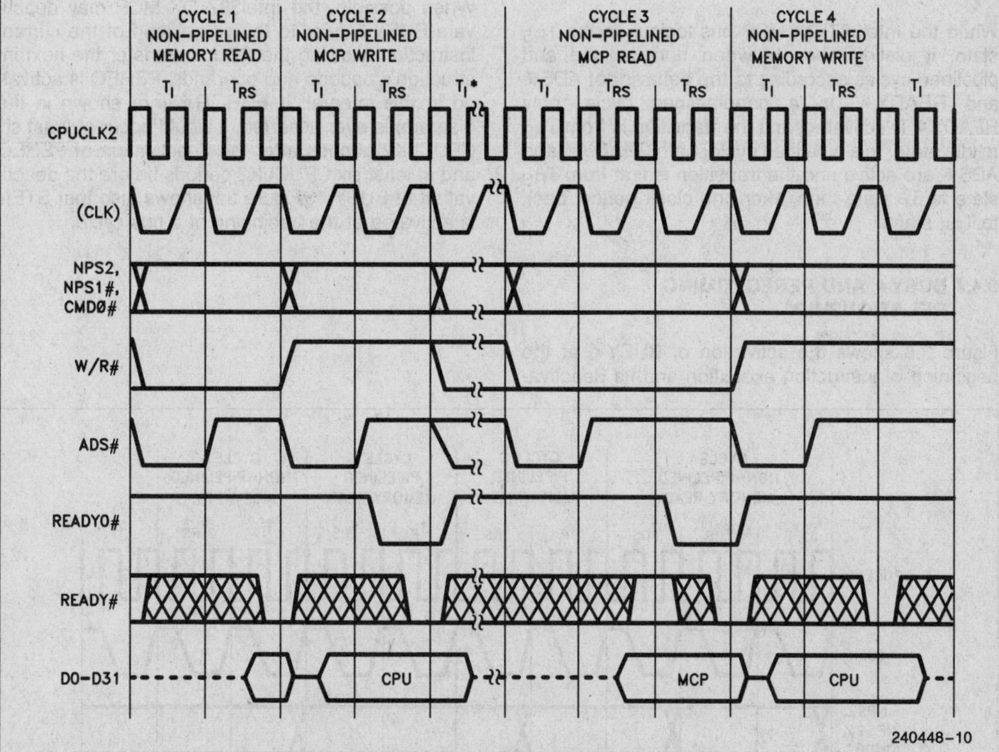

CYCLE 1 NON-PIPELINED MEMORY READ | CYCLE 2 NON-PIPELINED MCP WRITE | CYCLE 3 NON-PIPELINED MCP READ | CYCLE 4 NON-PIPELINED MEMORY WRITE

T_I T_{RS} T_I T_{RS} T_I* T_I T_{RS} T_{RS} T_I T_{RS} T_I

CPUCLK2

(CLK)

NPS2, NPS1#, CMD0#

W/R#

ADS#

READYO#

READY#

D0–D31 CPU MCP CPU

240448–10

Cycles 1 & 2 represent part of the operand transfer cycle for instructions involving either 4-byte or 8-byte operand loads.
Cycles 3 & 4 represent part of the operand transfer cycle for a store operation.
*Cycles 1 & 2 could repeat here or T_I states for various non-operand transfer cycles and overhead.

Figure 3.5. Nonpipelined Read and Write Cycles

3.4.2 PIPELINED BUS CYCLES

Because all the activities of the Intel387 DX MCP bus interface occur either during the T_{RS} state or during the transitions to or from that state, the only difference between a pipelined and a nonpipelined cycle is the manner of changing from one state to another. The exact activities in each state are detailed in the previous section "Nonpipelined Bus Cycles".

When the Intel386 DX CPU asserts ADS# before the end of a bus cycle, both ADS# and READY# are active during a T_{RS} state. This condition causes the MCP to change to a different state named T_P. The MCP activities in the transition from a T_{RS} state to a T_P state are exactly the same as those in the transition from a T_{RS} state to a T_I state in nonpipelined cycles.

T_P state is metastable; therefore, one clock period later the MCP returns to T_{RS} state. In consecutive pipelined cycles, the MCP bus logic uses only T_{RS} and T_P states.

Figure 3.6 shows the fastest transition into and out of the pipelined bus cycles. Cycle 1 in this figure represents a nonpipelined cycle. (Nonpipelined write cycles with only one T_{RS} state (i.e. no wait states) are always followed by another nonpipelined cycle, because READY# is asserted before the earliest possible assertion of ADS# for the next cycle.)

Figure 3.7 shows the pipelined write and read cycles with one additional T_{RS} states beyond the minimum required. To delay the assertion of READY# requires external logic.

3.4.3 BUS CYCLES OF MIXED TYPE

When the Intel387 DX MCP bus logic is in the T_{RS} state, it distinguishes between nonpipelined and pipelined cycles according to the behavior of ADS# and READY#. In a nonpipelined cycle, only READY# is activated, and the transition is from T_{RS} to idle state. In a pipelined cycle, both READY# and ADS# are active and the transition is first from T_{RS} state to T_P state then, after one clock period, back to T_{RS} state.

3.4.4 BUSY# AND PEREQ TIMING RELATIONSHIP

Figure 3.8 shows the activation of BUSY# at the beginning of instruction execution and its deactivation after execution of the instruction is complete. When possible, the Intel387 DX MCP may deactivate BUSY# prior to the completion of the current instruction allowing the CPU to transfer the next instruction's opcode and operands. PEREQ is activated in this interval. If ERROR# (not shown in the diagram) is ever asserted, it would occur at least six CPUCLK2 periods after the deactivation of PEREQ and at least six CPUCLK2 periods before the deactivation of BUSY#. Figure 3.8 shows also that STEN is activated at the beginning of a bus cycle.

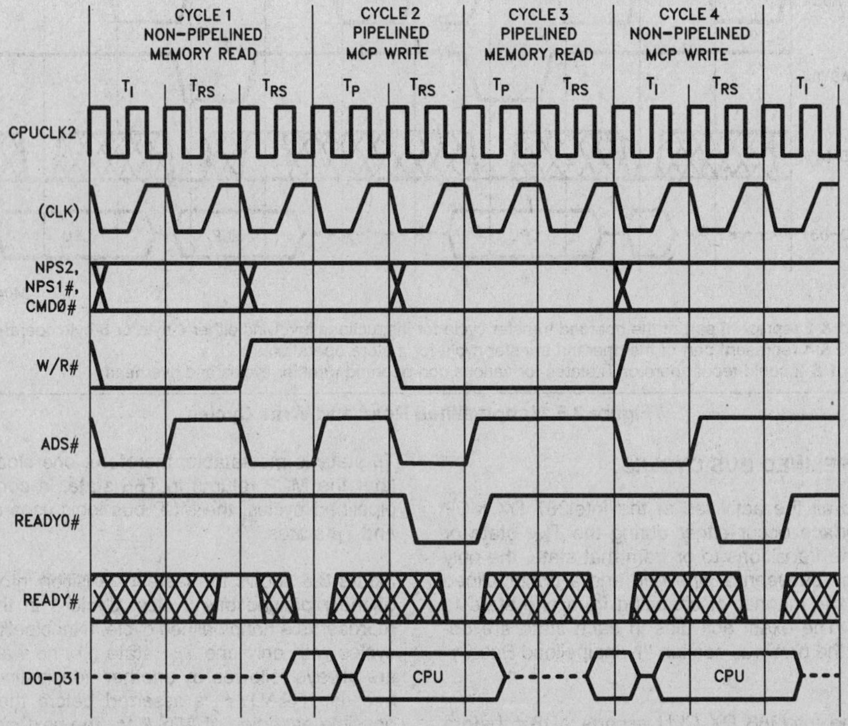

240448–11

Cycle 1–Cycle 4 represent the operand transfer cycle for an instruction involving a transfer of two 32-bit loads in total. The opcode write cycles and other overhead are not shown.
Note that the next cycle will be a pipelined cycle if both READY# and ADS# are sampled active at the end of a T_{RS} state of the current cycle.

Figure 3.6. Fastest Transitions to and from Pipelined Cycles

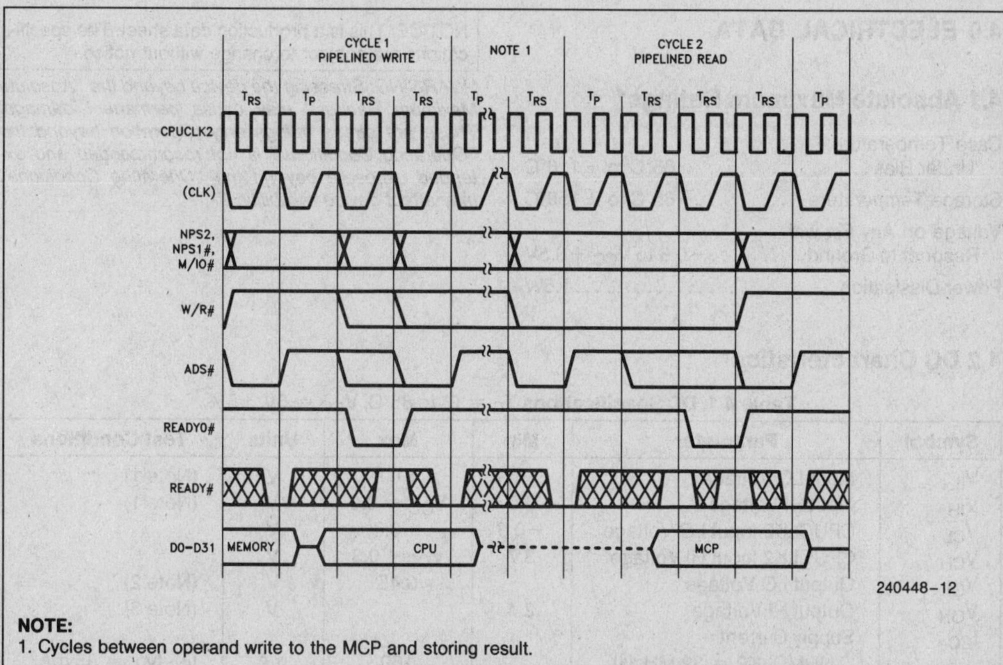

NOTE:
1. Cycles between operand write to the MCP and storing result.

Figure 3.7. Pipelined Cycles with Wait States

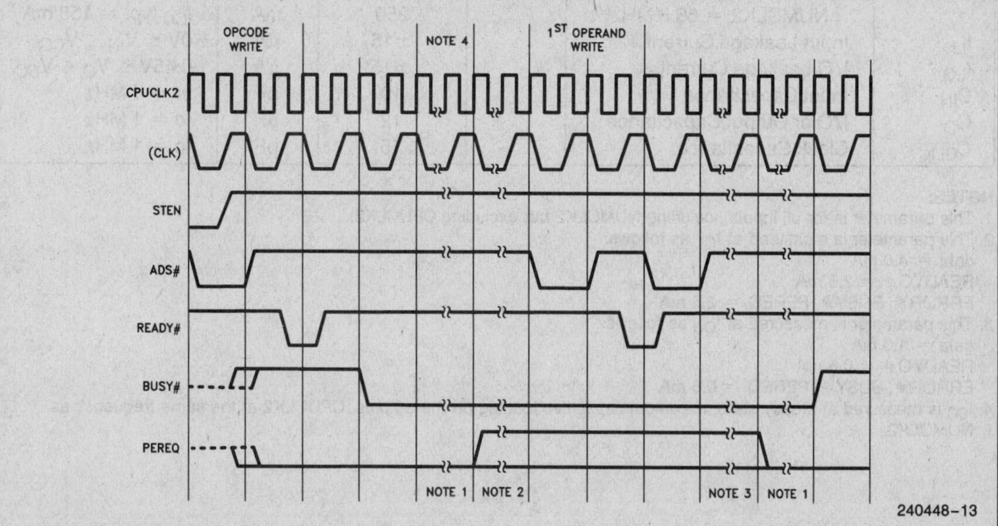

NOTES:
1. Instruction dependent.
2. PEREQ is an asynchronous input to the Intel386™ DX Microprocessor; it may not be asserted (instruction dependent).
3. More operand transfers.
4. Memory read (operand) cycle is not shown.

Figure 3.8. STEN, BUSY# and PEREQ Timing Relationship

4.0 ELECTRICAL DATA

NOTICE: This is a production data sheet. The specifications are subject to change without notice.

4.1 Absolute Maximum Ratings*

Case Temperature T_C
Under Bias .... −65°C to +110°C

Storage Temperature .... −65°C to +150°C

Voltage on Any Pin with
Respect to Ground .... −0.5 to V_{CC} +0.5V

Power Dissipation......................... 1.5W

**WARNING: Stressing the device beyond the "Absolute Maximum Ratings" may cause permanent damage. These are stress ratings only. Operation beyond the "Operating Conditions" is not recommended and extended exposure beyond the "Operating Conditions" may affect device reliability.*

4.2 DC Characteristics

Table 4.1. DC Specifications T_C = 0° to 85°C, V_{CC} = 5V ±5%

Symbol	Parameter	Min	Max	Units	Test Conditions
V_{IL}	Input LO Voltage	−0.3	+0.8	V	(Note 1)
V_{IH}	Input HI Voltage	2.0	V_{CC} + 0.3	V	(Note 1)
V_{CL}	CPUCLK2 Input LO Voltage	−0.3	+0.8	V	
V_{CH}	CPUCLK2 Input HI Voltage	3.7	V_{CC} +0.3	V	
V_{OL}	Output LO Voltage		0.45	V	(Note 2)
V_{OH}	Output HI Voltage	2.4		V	(Note 3)
I_{CC}	Supply Current				
	NUMCLK2 = 32 MHz(4)		160	mA	I_{CC} typ. = 95 mA
	NUMCLK2 = 40 MHz(4)		180	mA	I_{CC} typ. = 105 mA
	NUMCLK2 = 50 MHz(4)		210	mA	I_{CC} typ. = 125 mA
	NUMCLK2 = 66.6 MHz(4)		250	mA	I_{CC} typ. = 150 mA
I_{LI}	Input Leakage Current		±15	μA	$0V \leq V_{IN} \leq V_{CC}$
I_{LO}	I/O Leakage Current		±15	μA	$0.45V \leq V_O \leq V_{CC}$
C_{IN}	Input Capacitance		10	pF	fc = 1 MHz
C_O	I/O or Output Capacitance		12	pF	fc = 1 MHz
C_{CLK}	Clock Capacitance		15	pF	fc = 1 MHz

NOTES:
1. This parameter is for all inputs, including NUMCLK2 but excluding CPUCLK2.
2. This parameter is measured at I_{OL} as follows:
   data = 4.0 mA
   READYO# = 2.5 mA
   ERROR#, BUSY#, PEREQ = 2.5 mA
3. This parameter is measured at I_{OH} as follows:
   data = 1.0 mA
   READYO# = 0.6 mA
   ERROR#, BUSY#, PEREQ = 0.6 mA
4. I_{CC} is measured at steady state, maximum capacitive loading on the outputs, CPUCLK2 at the same frequency as NUMCLK2.

4.3 AC Characteristics

Table 4.2a. Combinations of Bus Interface and Execution Speeds

Functional Block	80387 DX-16	80387 DX-20	80387 DX-25	80387 DX-33
Bus Interface Unit (MHz)	16	20	25	33
Execution Unit (MHz)	16	20	25	33

Table 4.2b. Timing Requirements of the Execution Unit
T_C = 0°C to +85°C, V_{CC} = 5V ±5%

Pin	Symbol	Parameter	16 MHz		20 MHz		25 MHz		33 MHz		Test Conditions	Figure Reference
			Min (ns)	Max (ns)	Min (ns)	Max (ns)	Min (ns)	Max (ns)	Min (ns)	Max (ns)		
NUMCLK2	t1	Period	31.25	125	25	125	20	125	**15**	**125**	2.0V	4.1
NUMCLK2	t2a	High Time	9		8		7		**6.25**		2.0V	
NUMCLK2	t2b	High Time	5		5		4		**4.5**		3.7V	
NUMCLK2	t3a	Low Time	9		8		7		**6.25**		2.0V	
NUMCLK2	t3b	Low Time	7		6		5		**4.5**		0.8V	
NUMCLK2	t4	Fall Time		8		8		7		**6**	3.7V to 0.8V	
NUMCLK2	t5	Rise Time		8		8		7		**6**	0.8V to 3.7V	

Table 4.2c. Timing Requirements of the Bus Interface Unit
T_C = 0°C to +85°C, V_{CC} = 5V ±5%
(All measurements made at 1.5V and C_L = 50 pF unless otherwise specified)

Pin	Symbol	Parameter	16 MHz		20 MHz		25 MHz		33 MHz		Test Conditions	Figure Reference
			Min (ns)	Max (ns)	Min (ns)	Max (ns)	Min (ns)	Max (ns)	Min (ns)	Max (ns)		
CPUCLK2	t1	Period	31.25	125	25	125	20	125	**15**	**125**	2.0V	4.1
CPUCLK2	t2a	High Time	9		8		7		**6.25**		2.0V	
CPUCLK2	t2b	High Time	5		5		4		**4.5**		3.7V	
CPUCLK2	t3a	Low Time	9		8		7		**6.25**		2.0V	
CPUCLK2	t3b	Low Time	7		6		5		**4.5**		0.8V	
CPUCLK2	t4	Fall Time		8		8		7		**4**	3.7V to 0.8V	
CPUCLK2	t5	Rise Time		8		8		7		**4**	0.8V to 3.7V	
NUMCLK2/ CPUCLK2		Ratio	10/16	14/10	10/16	14/10	10/16	14/10	**10/16**	**14/10**		
READYO#	t7	Out Delay	3	34	3	31	3	24	**3**	**17**	C_L = 75 pF†	4.2
READYO# (1)	t7	Out Delay	3	31	3	27	3	21	**3**	**15**	C_L = 25 pF	
PEREQ	t7	Out Delay	5	34	5	34	4	33	**4**	**25**	C_L = 75 pF†	
BUSY#	t7	Out Delay	5	34	5	29	4	29	**4**	**21**	C_L = 75 pF†	
BUSY# (1)	t7	Out Delay	N/A	N/A	N/A	N/A	4	27	**4**	**19**	C_L = 25 pF	
ERROR#	t7	Out Delay	5	34	5	34	4	33	**4**	**25**	C_L = 75 pF†	
D31–D0	t8	Out Delay	1	54	1	54	0	50	**0**	**37**	C_L = 120 pF†	4.3
D31–D0	t10	Setup Time	11		11		11		**8**			
D31–D0	t11	Hold Time	11		11		11		**8**			
D31–D0 (2)	t12*	Float Time	6	33	6	27	5	24	**3**	**19**	C_L = 120 pF†	
PEREQ (2)	t13*	Float Time	1	60	1	50	1	40	**1**	**30**	C_L = 75 pF†	4.5
BUSY# (2)	t13*	Float Time	1	60	1	50	1	40	**1**	**30**	C_L = 75 pF†	
ERROR# (2)	t13*	Float Time	1	60	1	50	1	40	**1**	**30**	C_L = 75 pF†	
READYO# (2)	t13*	Float Time	1	60	1	50	1	40	**1**	**30**	C_L = 75 pF†	

*Float condition occurs when maximum output current becomes less than I_{LO} in magnitude. Float delay is not tested.
†For 25 MHz and 33 MHz, C_L = 50 pF

Table 4.2c. Timing Requirements of the Bus Interface Unit (Continued)
T_C = 0°C to +85°C, V_{CC} = 5V ±5%
(All measurements made at 1.5V and C_L = 50 pF unless otherwise specified)

Pin	Symbol	Parameter	16 MHz		20 MHz		25 MHz		33 MHz		Figure Reference
			Min (ns)	Max (ns)	Min (ns)	Max (ns)	Min (ns)	Max (ns)	Min (ns)	Max (ns)	
ADS#	t14	Setup Time	25		20		15		13		4.3
ADS#	t15	Hold Time	5		5		4		4		
W/R#	t14	Setup Time	25		20		15		13		
W/R#	t15	Hold Time	5		5		4		4		
READY#	t16	Setup Time	20		11		8		7		
READY#	t17	Hold Time	4		4		4		4		
CMD0#	t16	Setup Time	20		18		15		13		
CMD0#	t17	Hold Time	2		2		4		4		
NPS1# NPS2	t16	Setup Time	20		18		15		13		
NPS1# NPS2	t17	Hold Time	2		2		4		4		
STEN	t16	Setup Time	20		20		14		13		
STEN	t17	Hold Time	2		2		2		2		
RESETIN	t18	Setup Time	13		12		10		5		4.4
RESETIN	t19	Hold Time	4		4		3		3		

NOTES:
1. Not tested at 25 pF.
2. Float delay is not tested. Float condition occurs when maximum output current becomes less than I_{LO} in magnitude.

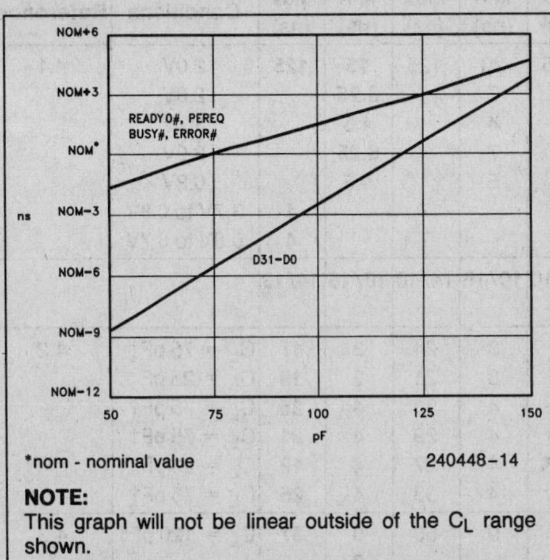

NOTE:
This graph will not be linear outside of the C_L range shown.

Figure 4.0a. Typical Output Valid Delay vs Load Capacitance at Max Operating Temperature

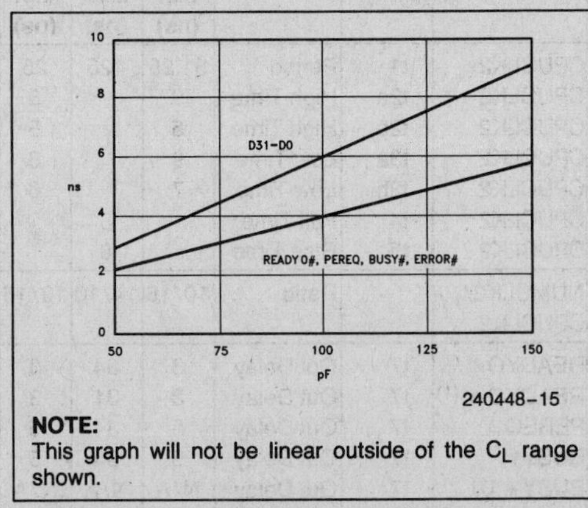

NOTE:
This graph will not be linear outside of the C_L range shown.

Figure 4.0b. Typical Output Rise Time vs Load Capacitance at Max Operating Temperature

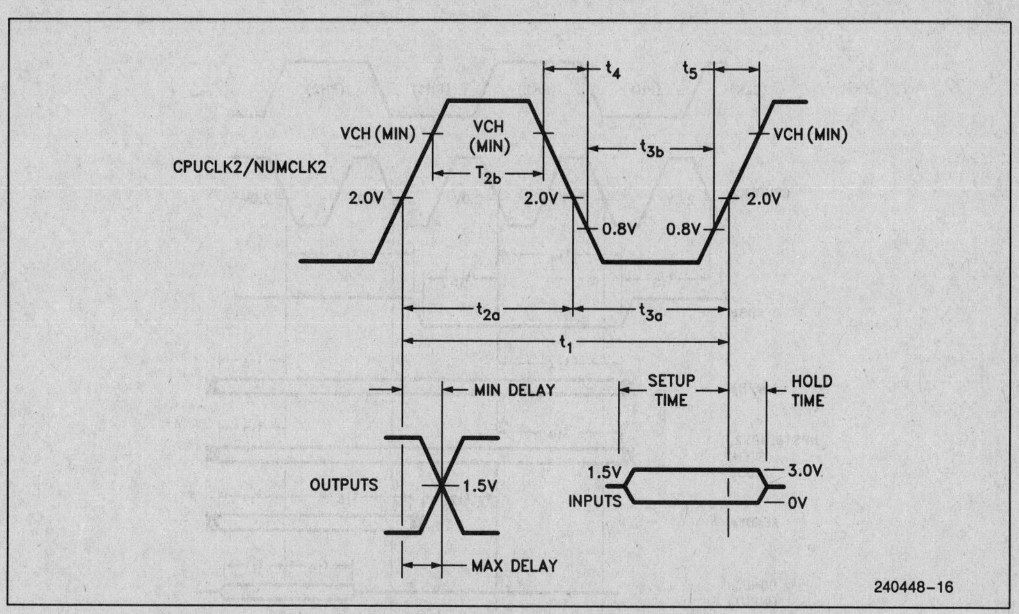

Figure 4.1. CPUCLK2/NUMCLK2 Waveform and Measurement Points for Input/Output A.C. Specifications

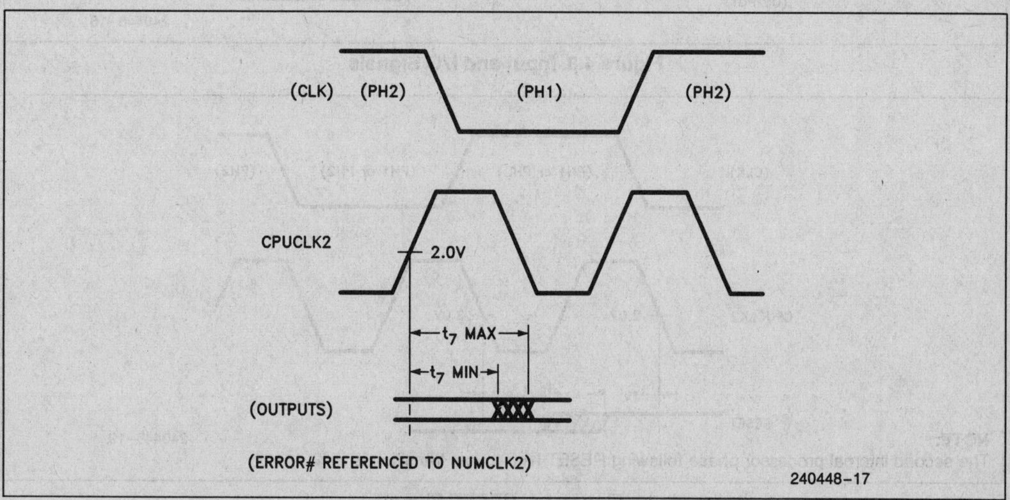

Figure 4.2. Output Signals

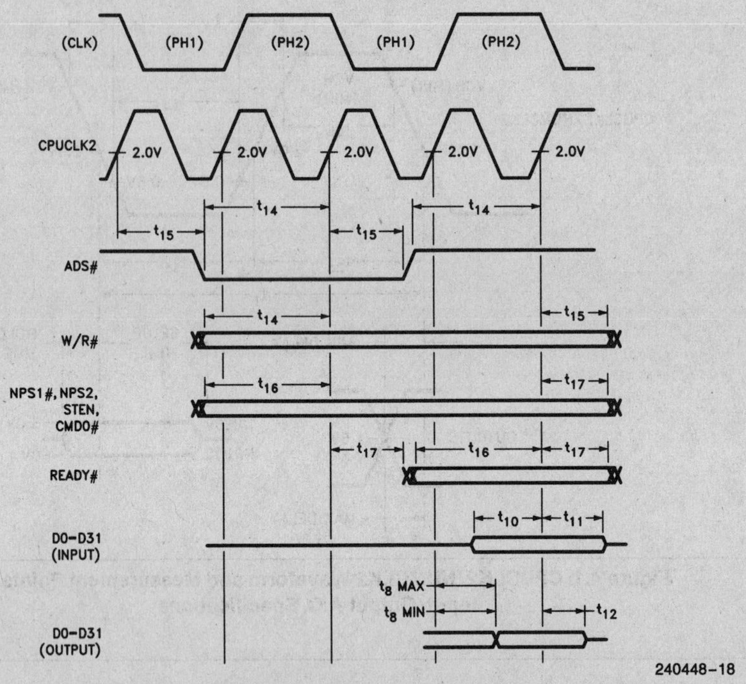

Figure 4.3. Input and I/O Signals

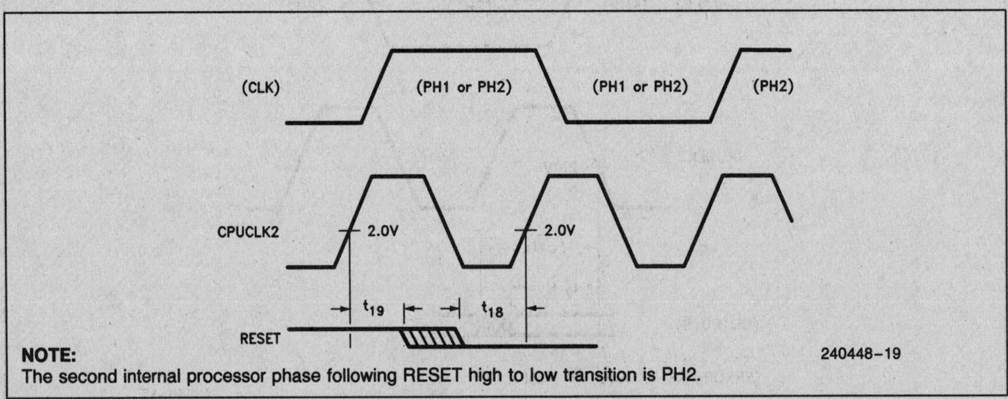

NOTE:
The second internal processor phase following RESET high to low transition is PH2.

Figure 4.4. RESET Signal

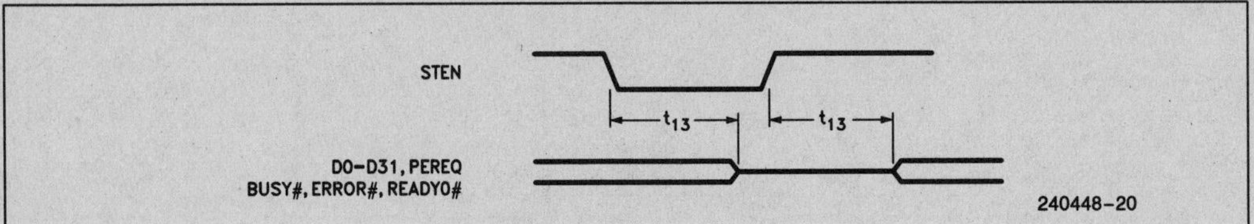

Figure 4.5. Float from STEN

Table 4.3. Other Parameters

Pin	Symbol	Parameter	Min	Max	Units
RESETIN	t30	Duration	40		NUMCLK2
RESETIN	t31	RESETIN Inactive to 1st Opcode Write	50		NUMCLK2
BUSY#	t32	Duration	6		CPUCLK2
BUSY#, ERROR#	t33	ERROR# (In) Active to BUSY# Inactive	6		CPUCLK2
PEREQ, ERROR#	t34	PEREQ Inactive to ERROR# Active	6		CPUCLK2
READY#, BUSY#	t35	READY# Active to BUSY# Active	4	4	CPUCLK2
READY#	t36	Minimum Time from Opcode Write to Opcode/Operand Write	6		CPUCLK2
READY#	t37	Minimum Time from Operand Write to Operand Write	8		CPUCLK2

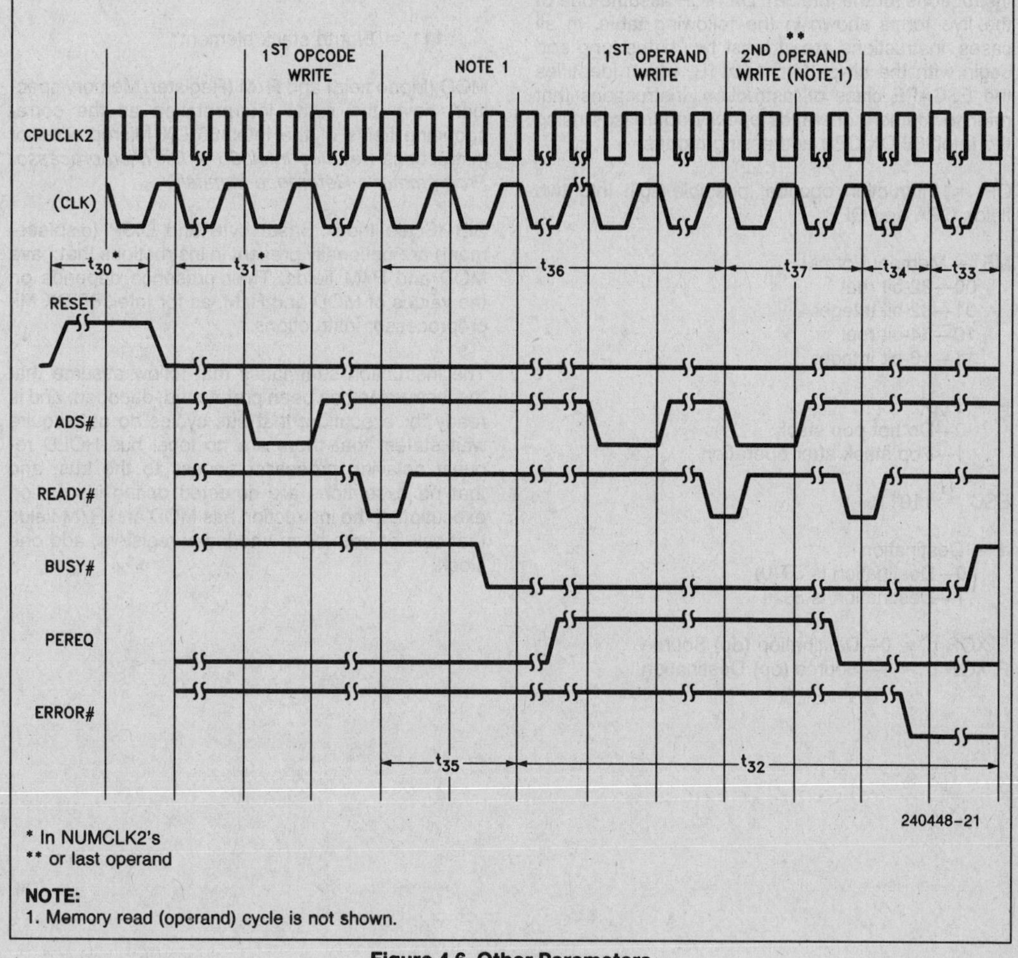

* In NUMCLK2's

** or last operand

NOTE:

1. Memory read (operand) cycle is not shown.

Figure 4.6. Other Parameters

<table>
<tr><th></th><th colspan="9">Instruction</th><th colspan="2" rowspan="2">Optional Fields</th></tr>
<tr><th></th><th colspan="4">First Byte</th><th colspan="5">Second Byte</th></tr>
<tr><td>1</td><td>11011</td><td colspan="2">OPA</td><td>1</td><td colspan="2">MOD</td><td>1</td><td>OPB</td><td>R/M</td><td>SIB</td><td>DISP</td></tr>
<tr><td>2</td><td>11011</td><td colspan="2">MF</td><td>OPA</td><td colspan="2">MOD</td><td colspan="2">OPB</td><td>R/M</td><td>SIB</td><td>DISP</td></tr>
<tr><td>3</td><td>11011</td><td>d</td><td>P</td><td>OPA</td><td>1</td><td>1</td><td colspan="2">OPB</td><td>ST(i)</td><td></td><td></td></tr>
<tr><td>4</td><td>11011</td><td>0</td><td>0</td><td>1</td><td>1</td><td>1</td><td>1</td><td colspan="2">OP</td><td></td><td></td></tr>
<tr><td>5</td><td>11011</td><td>0</td><td>1</td><td>1</td><td>1</td><td>1</td><td>1</td><td colspan="2">OP</td><td></td><td></td></tr>
<tr><td></td><td>15–11</td><td>10</td><td>9</td><td>8</td><td>7</td><td>6</td><td>5</td><td colspan="2">4 3 2 1 0</td><td></td><td></td></tr>
</table>

5.0 Intel387™ DX MCP EXTENSIONS TO THE Intel386™ DX CPU INSTRUCTION SET

Instructions for the Intel387 DX MCP assume one of the five forms shown in the following table. In all cases, instructions are at least two bytes long and begin with the bit pattern 11011B, which identifies the ESCAPE class of instruction. Instructions that refer to memory operands specify addresses using the Intel386 DX CPU addressing modes.

OP = Instruction opcode, possible split into two fields OPA and OPB

MF = Memory Format
- 00—32-bit real
- 01—32-bit integer
- 10—64-bit real
- 11—16-bit integer

P = Pop
- 0—Do not pop stack
- 1—Pop stack after operation

ESC = 11011

d = Destination
- 0—Destination is ST(0)
- 1—Destination is ST(i)

R XOR d = 0—Destination (op) Source
R XOR d = 1—Source (op) Destination

ST(i) = Register stack element *i*
- 000 = Stack top
- 001 = Second stack element
- •
- •
- •
- 111 = Eighth stack element

MOD (Mode field) and R/M (Register/Memory specifier) have the same interpretation as the corresponding fields of the Intel386 DX Microprocessor instructions (refer to *Intel386™ DX Microprocessor Programmer's Reference Manual*).

SIB (Scale Index Base) byte and DISP (displacement) are optionally present in instructions that have MOD and R/M fields. Their presence depends on the values of MOD and R/M, as for Intel386 DX Microprocessor instructions.

The instruction summaries that follow assume that the instruction has been prefetched, decoded, and is ready for execution; that bus cycles do not require wait states; that there are no local bus HOLD request delaying processor access to the bus; and that no exceptions are detected during instruction execution. If the instruction has MOD and R/M fields that call for both base and index registers, add one clock.

Intel387™ DX MCP Extensions to the Intel386™ DX CPU Instruction Set

Instruction	Encoding			Clock Count Range			
	Byte 0	Byte 1	Optional Bytes 2–6	32-Bit Real	32-Bit Integer	64-Bit Real	16-Bit Integer
DATA TRANSFER							
FLD = Load[a]							
Integer/real memory to ST(0)	ESC MF 1	MOD 000 R/M	SIB/DISP	9–18	26–42	16–23	42–53
Long integer memory to ST(0)	ESC 111	MOD 101 R/M	SIB/DISP	26–54			
Extended real memory to ST(0)	ESC 011	MOD 101 R/M	SIB/DISP	12–43			
BCD memory to ST(0)	ESC 111	MOD 100 R/M	SIB/DISP	45–97			
ST(i) to ST(0)	ESC 001	11000 ST(i)		7–12			
FST = Store							
ST(0) to integer/real memory	ESC MF 1	MOD 010 R/M	SIB/DISP	25–43	57–76	32–44	58–76
ST(0) to ST(i)	ESC 101	11010 ST(i)		7–11			
FSTP = Store and Pop							
ST(0) to integer/real memory	ESC MF 1	MOD 011 R/M	SIB/DISP	25–43	57–76	32–44	58–76
ST(0) to long integer memory	ESC 111	MOD 111 R/M	SIB/DISP	60–82			
ST(0) to extended real	ESC 011	MOD 111 R/M	SIB/DISP	46–52			
ST(0) to BCD memory	ESC 111	MOD 110 R/M	SIB/DISP	112–190			
ST(0) to ST(i)	ESC 101	11011 ST (i)		7–11			
FXCH = Exchange							
ST(i) and ST(0)	ESC 001	11001 ST(i)		10–17			
COMPARISON							
FCOM = Compare							
Integer/real memory to ST(0)	ESC MF 0	MOD 010 R/M	SIB/DISP	13–25	34–52	14–27	39–62
ST(i) to ST(0)	ESC 000	11010 ST(i)		13–21			
FCOMP = Compare and pop							
Integer/real memory to ST	ESC MF 0	MOD 011 R/M	SIB/DISP	13–25	34–52	14–27	39–62
ST(i) to ST(0)	ESC 000	11011 ST(i)		13–21			
FCOMPP = Compare and pop twice							
ST(1) to ST(0)	ESC 110	1101 1001		13–21			
FTST = Test ST(0)	ESC 001	1110 0100		17–25			
FUCOM = Unordered compare	ESC 101	11100 ST(i)		13–21			
FUCOMP = Unordered compare and pop	ESC 101	11101 ST(i)		13–21			
FUCOMPP = Unordered compare and pop twice	ESC 010	1110 1001		13–21			
FXAM = Examine ST(0)	ESC 001	11100101		24–37			
CONSTANTS							
FLDZ = Load +0.0 into ST(0)	ESC 001	1110 1110		10–17			
FLD1 = Load +1.0 into ST(0)	ESC 001	1110 1000		15–22			
FLDPI = Load pi into ST(0)	ESC 001	1110 1011		26–36			
FLDL2T = Load $\log_2(10)$ into ST(0)	ESC 001	1110 1001		26–36			

Shaded areas indicate instructions not available in 8087/80287.

NOTE:
a. When loading single- or double-precision zero from memory, add 5 clocks.

Intel387™ DX MCP Extensions to the Intel386™ DX CPU Instruction Set (Continued)

Instruction	Encoding			Clock Count Range			
	Byte 0	Byte 1	Optional Bytes 2–6	32-Bit Real	32-Bit Integer	64-Bit Real	16-Bit Integer
CONSTANTS (Continued)							
FLDL2E = Load $log_2(e)$ into ST(0)	ESC 001	1110 1010		26–36			
FLDLG2 = Load $log_{10}(2)$ into ST(0)	ESC 001	1110 1100		25–35			
FLDLN2 = Load $log_e(2)$ into ST(0)	ESC 001	1110 1101		26–38			
ARITHMETIC							
FADD = Add							
Integer/real memory with ST(0)	ESC MF 0	MOD 000 R/M	SIB/DISP	12–29	34–56	15–34	38–64
ST(i) and ST(0)	ESC d P 0	11000 ST(i)		12–26[b]			
FSUB = Subtract							
Integer/real memory with ST(0)	ESC MF 0	MOD 10 R R/M	SIB/DISP	12–29	34–56	15–34	38–64[c]
ST(i) and ST(0)	ESC d P 0	1110 R R/M		12–26[d]			
FMUL = Multiply							
Integer/real memory with ST(0)	ESC MF 0	MOD 001 R/M	SIB/DISP	19–32	43–71	23–53	46–74
ST(i) and ST(0)	ESC d P 0	1100 1 R/M		17–50[e]			
FDIV = Divide							
Integer/real memory with ST(0)	ESC MF 0	MOD 11 R R/M	SIB/DISP	77-85	101–114[f]	81–91	105–124[g]
ST(i) and ST(0)	ESC d P 0	1111 R R/M		77-80[h]			
FSQRT[i] = Square root	ESC 001	1111 1010		97–111			
FSCALE = Scale ST(0) by ST(1)	ESC 001	1111 1101		44–82			
FPREM = Partial remainder	ESC 001	1111 1000		56–140			
FPREM1 = Partial remainder (IEEE)	ESC 001	1111 0101		81–168			
FRNDINT = Round ST(0) to integer	ESC 001	1111 1100		41–62			
FXTRACT = Extract components of ST(0)	ESC 001	1111 0100		42–63			
FABS = Absolute value of ST(0)	ESC 001	1110 0001		14–21			
FCHS = Change sign of ST(0)	ESC 001	1110 0000		17–24			

Shaded areas indicate instructions not available in 8087/80287.

NOTES:

b. Add 3 clocks to the range when d = 1.
c. Add 1 clock to **each** range when R = 1.
d. Add 3 clocks to the range when d = 0.
e. typical = 52 (When d = 0, 46–54, typical = 49).
f. Add 1 clock to the range when R = 1.
g. 135–141 when R = 1.
h. Add 3 clocks to the range when d = 1.
i. $-0 \leq ST(0) \leq +\infty$.

Intel387™ DX MCP Extensions to the Intel386™ DX CPU Instruction Set (Continued)

Instruction	Encoding Byte 0	Encoding Byte 1	Encoding Optional Bytes 2–6	Clock Count Range
TRANSCENDENTAL				
FCOS[k] = Cosine of ST(0)	ESC 001	1111 1111		122–680
FPTAN[k] = Partial tangent of ST(0)	ESC 001	1111 0010		162–430j
FPATAN = Partial arctangent	ESC 001	1111 0011		250–420
FSIN[k] = Sine of ST(0)	ESC 001	1111 1110		121–680
FSINCOS[k] = Sine and cosine of ST(0)	ESC 001	1111 1011		150–650
F2XM1[l] = $2^{ST(0)} - 1$	ESC 001	1111 0000		167–410
FYL2X[m] = ST(1) * $\log_2$(ST(0))	ESC 001	1111 0001		99–436
FYL2XP1[n] = ST(1) * $\log_2$(ST(0) + 1.0)	ESC 001	1111 1001		210–447
PROCESSOR CONTROL				
FINIT = Initialize MCP	ESC 011	1110 0011		33
FSTSW AX = Store status word	ESC 111	1110 0000		13
FLDCW = Load control word	ESC 001	MOD 101 R/M	SIB/DISP	19
FSTCW = Store control word	ESC 101	MOD 111 R/M	SIB/DISP	15
FSTSW = Store status word	ESC 101	MOD 111 R/M	SIB/DISP	15
FCLEX = Clear exceptions	ESC 011	1110 0010		11
FSTENV = Store environment	ESC 001	MOD 110 R/M	SIB/DISP	103–104
FLDENV = Load environment	ESC 001	MOD 100 R/M	SIB/DISP	71
FSAVE = Save state	ESC 101	MOD 110 R/M	SIB/DISP	375–376
FRSTOR = Restore state	ESC 101	MOD 100 R/M	SIB/DISP	308
FINCSTP = Increment stack pointer	ESC 001	1111 0111		21
FDECSTP = Decrement stack pointer	ESC 001	1111 0110		22
FFREE = Free ST(i)	ESC 101	1100 0 ST(i)		18
FNOP = No operations	ESC 001	1101 0000		12

Shaded areas indicate instructions not available in 8087/80287.

NOTES:

j. These timings hold for operands in the range $|x| < \pi/4$. For operands not in this range, up to 76 additional clocks may be needed to reduce the operand.

k. $0 \leq |\text{ST}(0)| < 2^{63}$.

l. $-1.0 \leq \text{ST}(0) \leq 1.0$.

m. $0 \leq \text{ST}(0) < \infty, -\infty < \text{ST}(1) < +\infty$.

n. $0 \leq |\text{ST}(0)| < (2 - \text{SQRT}(2))/2, -\infty < \text{ST}(1) < +\infty$.

4

APPENDIX A COMPATIBILITY BETWEEN THE 80287 AND THE 8087

The 80286/80287 operating in Real-Address mode will execute 8086/8087 programs without major modification. However, because of differences in the handling of numeric exceptions by the 80287 MCP and the 8087 MCP, exception-handling routines *may* need to be changed.

This appendix summarizes the differences between the 80287 MCP and the 8087 MCP, and provides details showing how 8086/8087 programs can be ported to the 80286/80287.

1. The MCP signals exceptions through a dedicated ERROR# line to the 80286. The MCP error signal does not pass through an interrupt controller (the 8087 INT signal does). Therefore, any interrupt-controller-oriented instructions in numeric exception handlers for the 8086/8087 should be deleted.
2. The 8087 instructions FENI/FNENI and FDISI/FNDISI perform no useful function in the 80287. If the 80287 encounters one of these opcodes in its instruction stream, the instruction will effectively be ignored—none of the 80287 internal states will be updated. While 8086/8087 containing these instructions may be executed on the 80286/80287, it is unlikely that the exception-handling routines containing these instructions will be completely portable to the 80287.
3. Interrupt vector 16 must point to the numeric exception handling routine.
4. The ESC instruction address saved in the 80287 includes any leading prefixes before the ESC opcode. The corresponding address saved in the 8087 does not include leading prefixes.
5. In Protected-Address mode, the format of the 80287's saved instruction and address pointers is different than for the 8087. The instruction opcode is not saved in Protected mode—exception handlers will have to retrieve the opcode from memory if needed.
6. Interrupt 7 will occur in the 80286 when executing ESC instructions with either TS (task switched) or EM (emulation) of the 80286 MSW set (TS = 1 or EM = 1). If TS is set, then a WAIT instruction will also cause interrupt 7. An exception handler should be included in 80286/80287 code to handle these situations.
7. Interrupt 9 will occur if the second or subsequent words of a floating-point operand fall outside a segment's size. Interrupt 13 will occur if the starting address of a numeric operand falls outside a segment's size. An exception handler should be included in 80286/80287 code to report these programming errors.
8. Except for the processor control instructions, all of the 80287 numeric instructions are automatically synchronized by the 80286 CPU—the 80286 automatically tests the BUSY# line from the 80287 to ensure that the 80287 has completed its previous instruction before executing the next ESC instruction. No explicit WAIT instructions are required to assure this synchronization. For the 8087 used with 8086 and 8088 processors, explicit WAITs are required before each numeric instruction to ensure synchronization. Although 8086/8087 programs having explicit WAIT instructions will execute perfectly on the 80286/80287 without reassembly, these WAIT instructions are unnecessary.
9. Since the 80287 does not require WAIT instructions before each numeric instruction, the ASM286 assembler does not automatically generate these WAIT instructions. The ASM86 assembler, however, automatically precedes every ESC instruction with a WAIT instruction. Although numeric routines generated using the ASM86 assembler will generally execute correctly on the 80286/80287, reassembly using ASM286 may result in a more compact code image.

   The processor control instructions for the 80287 may be coded using either a WAIT or No-WAIT form of mnemonic. The WAIT forms of these instructions cause ASM286 to precede the ESC instruction with a CPU WAIT instruction, in the identical manner as does ASM86.

DATA SHEET REVISION REVIEW

The following list represents the key differences between this and the -003 versions of the Intel387™ Math Coprocessor Data Sheet. Please review this summary carefully.

1. Corrected typographical errors.
2. Corrected clock ratio "PIN" name on Table 4.2c to NUMCLK/CPUCLK.

82395DX HIGH PERFORMANCE SMART CACHE

- **Optimized Intel386™ DX Microprocessor Companion**
- **Integrated 16KB Data RAM**
- **4 Way SET Associative with Pseudo LRU Algorithm**
- **Write Buffer Architecture**
- **Integrated 4 Double Word Write Buffer**
- **16 Byte Line Size**
- **Integrated Intel387™ DX Math Coprocessor and Weitek 3167 Floating Point Coprocessor Decode Logic**
- **Concurrent Line Buffer Cacheing**
- **Multiprocessor Support**
- **Expandable - up to 64KB**
- **Supports Intel486™ Microprocessor-like Burst**
- **Dual Bus Architecture**
  - **— Snooping Maintains Cache Coherency**
- **20, 25 and 33MHz Clock**
- **196 lead PQFP package**
  (See Packaging Handbook Order Number 240800-001, Package Type KU)

The 82395DX High Performance 82395DX Smart Cache is a low cost, high integration, 32-Bit peripheral for Intel's i386™ DX Microprocessor. It stores a copy of frequently accessed code or data from main memory to on chip data RAM that can be accessed in zero wait states. The 82395DX enables the 386 DX Microprocessor to run at near its full potential by reducing the average number of wait states seen by the CPU to nearly zero. The dual bus architecture allows another bus master to access the System Bus while the 386 DX Microprocessor can operate out of the 82395DX's cache on the Local Bus. The 82395DX has a snooping mechanism which maintains cache coherency during these cycles.

The 82395DX is completely software transparent, protecting the integrity of system software. High performance, low cost and board space saving are achieved due to the high integration and new write buffer architecture.

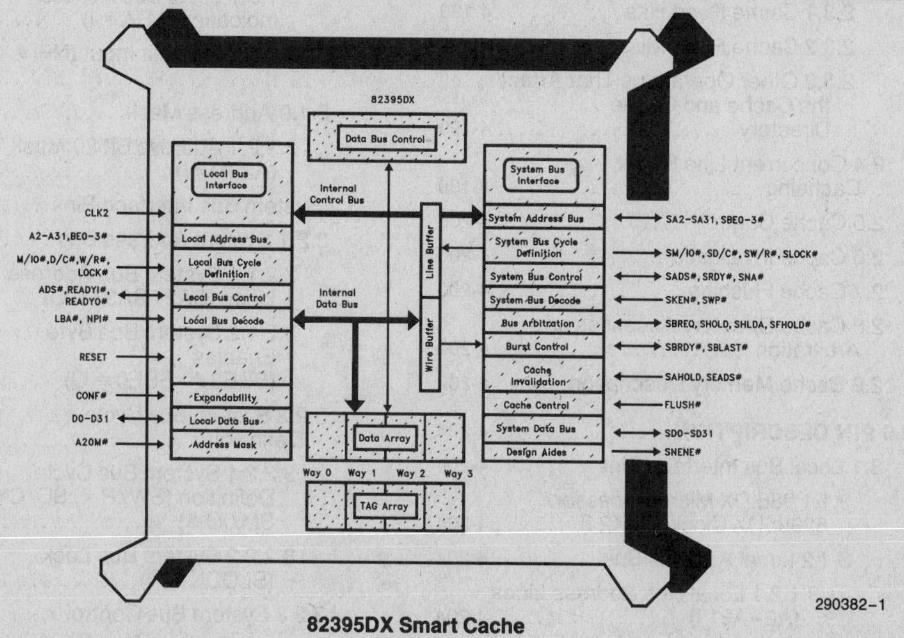

82395DX Smart Cache

Intel387™, Intel386™, and Intel486™ are trademarks of Intel Corporation

October 1991
Order Number: 290382-002

82395DX
HIGH PERFORMANCE SMART CACHE

CONTENTS PAGE

CONTENTS PAGE

CONTENTS

PAGE

CONTENTS

PAGE

4

CONTENTS PAGE

TABLES

CONTENTS PAGE

FIGURES

CONTENTS

CONTENTS

0.0 DESIGNER SUMMARY

0.1 Pin Out

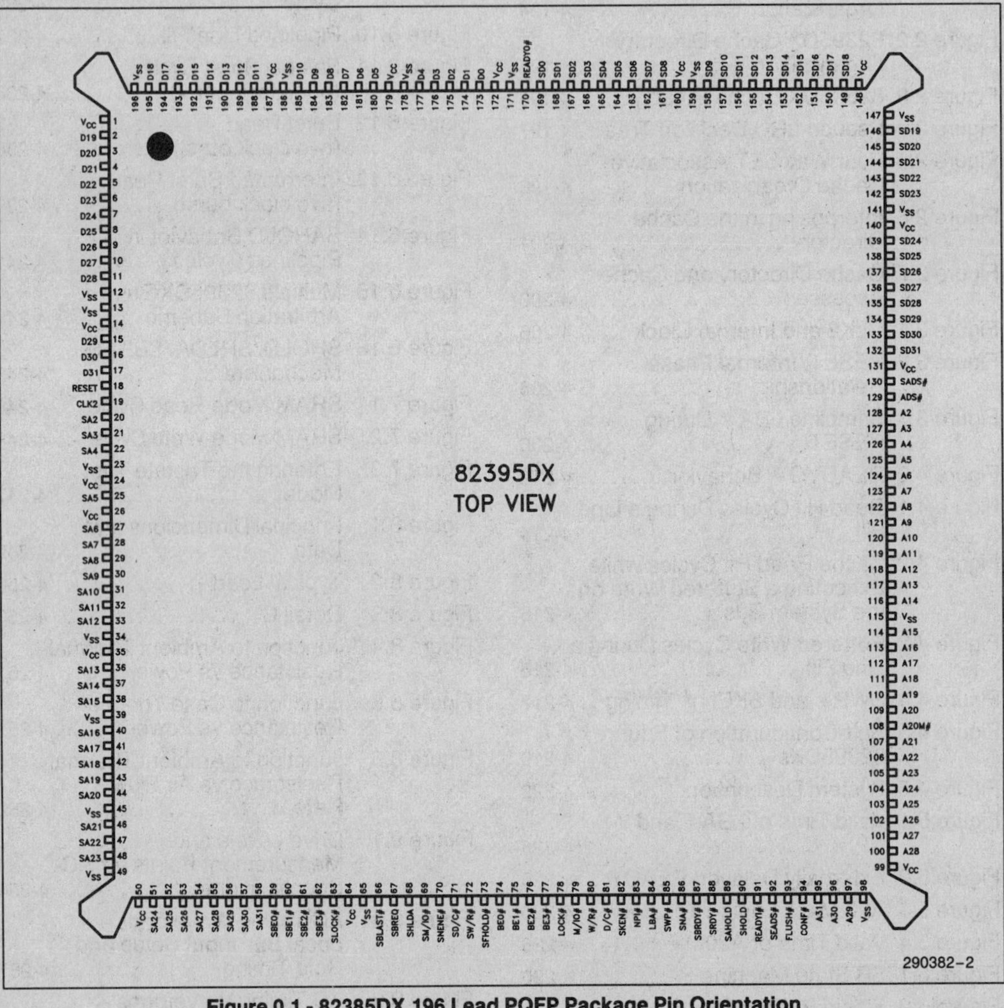

82395DX
TOP VIEW

290382-2

Figure 0.1 - 82385DX 196 Lead PQFP Package Pin Orientation

Pin	Signal	Pin	Signal	Pin	Signal	Pin	Signal
1	VCC	50	VCC	99	VCC	148	VCC
2	D19	51	SA24	100	A28	149	SD18
3	D20	52	SA25	101	A27	150	SD17
4	D21	53	SA26	102	A26	151	SD16
5	D22	54	SA27	103	A25	152	SD15
6	D23	55	SA28	104	A24	153	SD14
7	D24	56	SA29	105	A23	154	SD13
8	D25	57	SA30	106	A22	155	SD12
9	D26	58	SA31	107	A21	156	SD11
10	D27	59	SBE0#	108	A20M#	157	SD10
11	D28	60	SBE1#	109	A20	158	SD9
12	VSS	61	SBE2#	110	A19	159	VSS
13	VSS	62	SBE3#	111	A18	160	VCC
14	VCC	63	SLOCK#	112	A17	161	SD8
15	D29	64	VCC	113	A16	162	SD7
16	D30	65	VSS	114	A15	163	SD6
17	D31	66	SBLAST#	115	VSS	164	SD5
18	RESET	67	SBREQ	116	A14	165	SD4
19	CLK2	68	SHLDA	117	A13	166	SD3
20	SA2	69	SM/IO#	118	A12	167	SD2
21	SA3	70	SNENE#	119	A11	168	SD1
22	SA4	71	SD/C#	120	A10	169	SD0
23	VSS	72	SW/R#	121	A9	170	READY0#
24	VCC	73	SFHOLD#	122	A8	171	VSS
25	SA5	74	BE0#	123	A7	172	VCC
26	VCC	75	BE1#	124	A6	173	D0
27	SA6	76	BE2#	125	A5	174	D1
28	SA7	77	BE3#	126	A4	175	D2
29	SA8	78	LOCK#	127	A3	176	D3
30	SA9	79	M/IO#	128	A2	177	D4
31	SA10	80	W/R#	129	ADS#	178	VSS
32	SA11	81	D/C#	130	SADS#	179	VCC
33	SA12	82	SKEN#	131	VCC	180	D5
34	VSS	83	NPI#	132	SD31	181	D6
35	VCC	84	LBA#	133	SD30	182	D7
36	SA13	85	SWP#	134	SD29	183	D8
37	SA14	86	SNA#	135	SD28	184	D9
38	SA15	87	SBRDY#	136	SD27	185	D10
39	VSS	88	SRDY#	137	SD26	186	VSS
40	SA16	89	SAHOLD	138	SD25	187	VCC
41	SA17	90	SHOLD	139	SD24	188	D11
42	SA18	91	READYI#	140	VCC	189	D12
43	SA19	92	SEADS#	141	VSS	190	D13
44	SA20	93	FLUSH#	142	SD23	191	D14
45	VSS	94	CONF#	143	SD22	192	D15
46	SA21	95	A31	144	SD21	193	D16
47	SA22	96	A30	145	SD20	194	D17
48	SA23	97	A29	146	SD19	195	D18
49	VSS	98	VSS	147	VSS	196	VSS

Table 0.1 - 82395DX 196-Pin PQFP Pin Description

0.2 Quick Pin Reference

What follows is a brief pin description. For more details refer to chapter 3.

Symbol	Type	Function
CLK2	I	This signal provides the fundamental timing for the 82395DX. All external timing parameters are specified with respect to the rising edge of CLK2.
Local Address Bus		
A2–31	I	A2–31 are the Local Bus address lines. These signals along with the byte enable signals, define the physical area of memory or input/output space accessed.
BE0–3#	I	The byte enable signals are used to determine which bytes are accessed in partial cache write cycles. These signals are ignored for Cache Read Hit cycles. For all System Bus memory read cycles (except the last three cycle of a Line Fill), these signals are mirrored by the SBE0–3# signals.
Local Bus Cycle Definition		
W/R# D/C# M/IO#	I I I	The write/read, data/code and memory/input-output signals are the primary bus definition signals directly connected to the 386 DX Microprocessor. They become valid as the ADS# signal is sampled active. The bus definition signals are not driven by the 386 DX Microprocessor during bus hold and follow the timing of the address bus.
LOCK#	I	The Local Bus LOCK# signal indicates that the current bus cycle is LOCK#ed. LOCK#ed cycles are treated as non-cacheable cycles, except that LOCK#ed write hit cycles update the cache.
Local Bus Control		
ADS#	I	The address status pin, an output of the 386 DX Microprocessor, indicates that new and valid information is currently available on the Local Bus. The signals that are valid when ADS# is activated are: A2–31, BE0–3#, W/R#, D/C#, M/IO#, LOCK#, NPI# and LBA#
READYI#	I	This is the READY input signal seen by the Local Bus master. Typically it is a logical OR between the 82395DX generated READYO# and READY# signals generated by other Local Bus masters (optional). It is used by the 82395DX, along with the ADS# signal, to keep track of the 386 DX Microprocessor bus state.
READYO#	I/O	This is the Local Bus READY output that is used to terminate all types of 386 DX Microprocessor bus cycles, except for 386 DX Microprocessor Local Bus cycles which must be terminated by the Local Bus device being accessed. This signal is wired-OR with parallel 82395DX READYO# signals in a multi-82395DX system. The READYO# pin may serve as READY# for the 387 DX Math Coprocessor.
RESET		
RESET	I	The RESET signal forces the 82395DX to begin execution at a known state. The RESET falling edge is used by the 82395DX to set the phase of its internal clock identical to the 386 DX Microprocessors internal clock. RESET falling edge must satisfy the appropriate setup and hold times (T14, T15b) for proper chip operation. RESET must remain active for at least 1ms after the power supply and CLK2 input have reached their proper DC and AC specifications.
Configuration		
CONF#	I	The activity on the CONF# input during and after RESET allows the 82395DX to configure itself to operate in the specified address range. Refer to chapter 4 for 1, 2 or 4 82395DX's operation.

0.2 Quick Pin Reference (Continued)

Symbol	Type	Function
Local Data Bus		
D0–31	I/O	These are the Local Bus data lines of the 82395DX. They must be connected to the D0–31 pins of the 386 DX Microprocessor.
Local Bus Decode Pins		
LBA#	I	This is the Local Bus Access indication. It instructs the 82395DX that the cycle currently in progress is targeted to a Local Bus device. This results in the cycle being ignored by the 82395DX. The 387 DX Math Coprocessor is considered a Local Bus devcie but LBA# need not be generated. If LBA# is asserted at the falling edge of RESET accesses to Weitek 3167 Floating-Point Coprocessor address space are decoded as Local Bus cycles. Note that LBA# cycles have priority over all other cycle types.
NPI#	I	The No Post Input signal instructs the 82395DX that the write cycle currently in progress must not be posted in the write buffer. NPI# is sampled at the falling edge of CLK at the end of T1 (see figure 5.1).
Address Mask		
A20M#	I	Address bit 20 Mask when active, forces the A20 input as seen by the 82395DX to logic "0", regardless of the actual value on the A20 input pin. A20M# emulates the address wraparound at 1 MByte which occurs on the 8086. This pin is asynchronous but must meet setup and hold times (t47 and t48) to guarantee recognition in a specific clock. It must be asserted two clock cycles before ADS# is sampled active (see figure 5.3). It must be stable throughout Local Bus memory cycles.
System Address Bus		
SA2–3 SA4–31	O I/O	These are the System Bus address lines of the 82395DX. When driven by the 82395DX, these signals, along with the System Bus byte enables define the physical area of memory or input/output space being accessed. During bus HOLD or address HOLD, the I/O signals serve as inputs for the cache invalidation cycle.
SB0–3#	O	These are the Byte Enable signals for the System Bus. The 82395DX drives these pins identically to BE0–3# in all System Bus cycles except Line Fills. In Line Fills these signals are driven identically to BE0–3# for the first read cycle of the Line Fill. They are all driven active in the remaining cycles of the Line Fill.
System Bus Cycle Definition		
SW/R# SD/C# SM/IO#	O O O	The System Bus write/read, data/code and memory/input-output signals are the System Bus cycle definition pins. When the 82395DX is the System Bus master, it drives these signals identically to the 386 DX Microprocessor cycle definition encoding.
SLOCK#	O	The System Bus LOCK# signal indicates that the current cycle is LOCK#ed. The 82395DX has exclusive access to the System Bus across bus cycle boundaries until this signal is negated. The 82395DX does not acknowledge a bus HOLD request while this signal is asserted. The 82395DX asserts SLOCK# when the System Bus is available and a LOCK#ed cycle was started on the Local Bus that requires System Bus service. SLOCK# is negated only after completion of all LOCK#ed System Bus cycles and negation of the LOCK# signal.

4

0.2 Quick Pin Reference (Continued)

Symbol	Type	Function
System Bus Control		
SADS#	O	The System Bus ADdress Status signal is used to indicate that new and valid information is currently being driven onto the System Bus. The signals that are valid when SADS# is driven low are: SA2-31, SBE0-3#, SW/R#, SD/C#, SM/IO# and SLOCK#
SRDY#	I	The System Bus ReaDY# signal indicates that the current System Bus cycle is complete. When SRDY# is sampled asserted it indicates one of two things. In response to a read request it indicates that the external system has presented valid data on the system data bus. In response to a write request it indicates that the external system has accepted the 82395DX's data. This signal is ignored when the System Bus is in STi, STH, ST1 or ST1P states. At the first read cycle of a Line Fill SRDY#, SBRDY# and SNA# determine if the Line Fill will proceed as a burst/non-burst, pipelined/non-pipelined Line Fill. Once a burst Line Fill has started, if SRDY# is returned in the 2nd or 3rd DW, the burst Line Fill will be interrupted and the cache will not be updated. The 1st DW will already have been transferred to the CPU. In the 4th DW of a Line Fill both SRDY# and SBRDY# have the same affect. They indicate the end of the Line Fill.
SNA#	I	The System Bus Next Address signal, when active, indicates that a pipelined address cycle will be executed. It is sampled by the 82395DX at the rising edge of CLK in ST2 and ST1P cycles. If this signal is sampled active then burst Line Fills are disabled. This signal is ignored once a burst Line Fill begins.
Bus Arbitration		
SBREQ	O	The System Bus REQuest signal is the internal cycle pending signal. This indicates to the outside world that internally the 82395DX has generated a bus request (due to the CPU's request that requires access to the System Bus). It is generated whether the 82395DX owns the bus or not and can be used to arbitrate among the various masters on the System Bus. If the bus is available and the cycle starts immediately this signal will not be activated for cache read miss cycles.
SHOLD	I	The System Bus HOLD request indicates that another master must have complete control of the entire System Bus. When SHOLD is sampled asserted the 82395DX completes the current System Bus cycle or sequence of LOCK#ed cycles, before driving SHLDA active. In the same clock that SHLDA went active all the System Bus outpus and I/O pins are floated (with the exception of SHLDA and SBREQ). The 82395DX stays in this state until SHOLD is negated. SHOLD is recognized during RESET.
SHLDA	O	The System Bus HOLD Acknowledge signal is driven active by the 82395DX in response to a hold request. It indicates that the 82395DX has given the bus to another System Bus master. It is driven active in the same clock that the 82395DX floats it's System Bus. When leaving a bus HOLD, SHLDA is driven inactive and the 82395DX resumes driving the bus in the same clock. The 82395DX is able to support CPU Local Bus activities during System Bus HOLD.

0.2 Quick Pin Reference (Continued)

Symbol	Type	Function
Bus Arbitration (Continued)		
SFHOLD#	I	The System Bus Fast HOLD Request signal indicates that another master needs immediate access to the System Bus. In response to SFHOLD# being sampled active, the 82395DX stops driving (in the next clock) the System Bus output and I/O pins (except SHLDA and SBREQ). Because the 82395DX always stops driving the System Bus in response to SFHOLD# active, no acknowledge is required. The System Bus output and I/O pins remain in the high impedance state until SFHOLD# is negated. It is the responsibility of the system designer to guarantee that bus cycles that are in progress when SFHOLD# is asserted are terminated correctly. This pin is recognized during RESET.
Burst Control		
SBRDY#	I	The System Bus Burst ReaDY signal performs the same function during a burst cycle that SRDY# does in a non-burst cycle. SBRDY# asserted indicates that the external system has presented valid data on the data pins in response to a burst Line Fill cycle. This signal is ignored when the System Bus is at STi, STH, ST1 or ST1P states. Note that in the fourth bus cycle of a Line Fill, SBRDY# and SRDY# have the same effect on the 82395DX. They indicate the end of the Line Fill. For all cycles other than burst Line Fills, SBRDY# and SRDY# have the same effect on the 82395DX.
SBLAST#	O	The System Bus Burst LAST cycle indicator signal indicates that the next time SBRDY# is returned the burst cycle is complete. It indicates to the external system that the next SBRDY# returned is treated as a normal SRDY# by the 82395DX. Another set of addresses will be driven with SADS# or the System Bus will go idle. SBLAST# is normally active. In a cache read miss cycle, which may proceed as a Line Fill, SBLAST# starts active. After determining whether or not the cycle is cacheable via SKEN#, SBLAST# is driven inactive. If it is a cacheable cycle, and SBRDY# terminates the first DW of the Line Fill, a burst Line Fill, SBLAST# will be driven active when the data is valid for the fourth DW of the Line Fill. If SRDY# terminates the first DW of the Line Fill, a non-burst Line Fill, SBLAST# is driven active in the cycle where SRDY# was sampled active.
Cache Invalidation		
SAHOLD	I	The System Bus Address HOLD request allows another bus master access to the address bus of the 82395DX. This is to indicate the address of an external cycle for performing an internal cache directory lookup and invalidation cycle. In response to this signal the 82395DX stops driving the System Bus address pins in the next cycle. No HOLD Acknowledge is required. Other System Bus signals can remain active during address hold. The 82395DX does not initiate another bus cycle during address hold. This pin is recognized during RESET.
SEADS#	I	The System Bus External ADress Strobe signal indicates that a valid external address has been driven onto the 82395DX System Bus address pins. This address will be used to perform an internal cache invalidation cycle. The maximum invalidation cycle rate is one every two clock cycles.

4

0.2 Quick Pin Reference (Continued)

Symbol	Type	Function
Cache Control		
FLUSH#	I	The FLUSH# pin, when sampled active for four clock cycles or more, causes the 82395DX to invalidate its entire TAG array. In addition, it is used to configure the 82395DX to enter various test modes. For details refer to chapter 7. This signal is asynchronous but must meet setup and hold times to guarantee recognition in any specific clock.
System Data Bus		
SD0–31	I/O	The System Bus Data lines of the 82395DX must be driven with appropriate setup and hold times for proper operation. These signals are driven by the 82395DX only during write cycles.
System Bus Decode Pins		
SKEN#	I	The System Cacheability ENable signal is used to determine if the current cycle running on the System Bus is cacheable or not. When the 82395DX generates a read cycle, SKEN# is sampled one clock before the first SBRDY# or SRDY# or one cycle before the first SNA# is sampled active (see chapter 6). If SKEN# is sampled active the cycle will be transformed into a Line Fill. Otherwise, the cache and cache directory will be unaffected. Note that SKEN# is ignored after the first cycle in a Line Fill. SKEN# is ignored for all System Bus cycles except for cache read miss cycles.
SWP#	I	The System Write Protect indicator signal is used to determine whether the current System Bus Line Fill cycle is write protected or not. In non-pipelined cycles, SWP# is sampled with the first SRDY# or SBRDY# of the Line Fill. In pipelined cycles, SWP# is sampled one clock phase after the first SNA# is sampled active (see figures 6.9-10). The Write Protect bit is sampled together with the TAG of each line in the 82395DX Cache Directory. In every cacheable write cycle the Write Protect bit is read. If active, the cycle will be a write protected cycle which is treated like a cacheable write miss cycle. It is buffered and it does not update the cache even if the addressed location is present in the cache.
Design Aides		
SNENE#	O	The System NExt NEar indicator signal indicates that the current System Bus memory cycle is to the same 2048 byte area as the previous memory cycle. Address lines A11–31 of the current System Bus memory cycle are identical to address lines A11–31 of the previous memory cycle. SNENE# can be used in an external DRAM system to run CAS# only cycles, thereby increasing the throughput of the memory system. SNENE# is valid for all memory cycles, and indicates that the current memory cycle is to the same 2048 byte area, even if there were idle or non-memory bus cycles since the last System Bus memory cycle. For the first cycle after the 82395DX has exited the HOLD state, or after SAHOLD was deactivated, this pin will be inactive.

1.0 82395DX FUNCTIONAL OVERVIEW

1.1 Introduction

The primary function of a cache is to provide local storage for frequently accessed memory locations. The cache intercepts memory references and handles them directly without transferring the request to the System Bus. This results in lower traffic on the System Bus and decreases latency on the local bus. This leads to improved performance for a processor on the Local Bus. By providing fast access to frequently used code and data, the cache is able to reduce the average memory access time of the 386 DX Microprocessor based system.

The 82395DX is a single chip cache subsystem specifically designed for use with the 386 DX Microprocessor. The 82395DX integrates 16KB cache, the Cache Directory and the Cache Control Logic onto one chip.

The 82395DX is expandable such that larger cache sizes are supported by cascading 82395DXs. In a single 82395DX system, the 82395DX can map 4 Giga bytes of main memory into a 16KB cache. In the maximum configuration of a four 82395DX system, the 4 Giga bytes of main memory are mapped into a 64KB cache. The cache is unified for code and data and is transparent to application software. The 82395DX provides a cache consistency mechanism which guarantees that the cache has the most recently updated version of the main memory. Consistency support has no performance impact on the 386 DX Microprocessor. Section 1.2 covers all the 82395DX features.

The 82395DX cache architecture is similar to the i486 Microprocessor's on-chip cache. The cache is four Way set associative with Pseudo LRU replacement algorithm. The line size is 16B and a full line is retrieved from the memory every cache miss. A TAG is associated with every 16B line.

The 82395DX architecture allows for cache read hit cycles to run on the Local Bus even when the System Bus is not available. 82395DX incorporates a new write buffer cache architecture, which allows the 386 DX Microprocessor to continue operation without waiting for write cycles to actually update the main memory.

A detailed description of the cache operation and parameters is included in chapter 2.

The 82395DX has an interface to two electrically isolated busses. The interface to the 386 DX Microprocessor bus is referred to as the Local Bus (LB) interface. The interface to the main memory and other system devices is referred to as the 82395DX System Bus (SB) interface. The SB interface emulates the 386 DX Microprocessor. The SB interface, as does the 386 DX Microprocessor, can be pipelined.

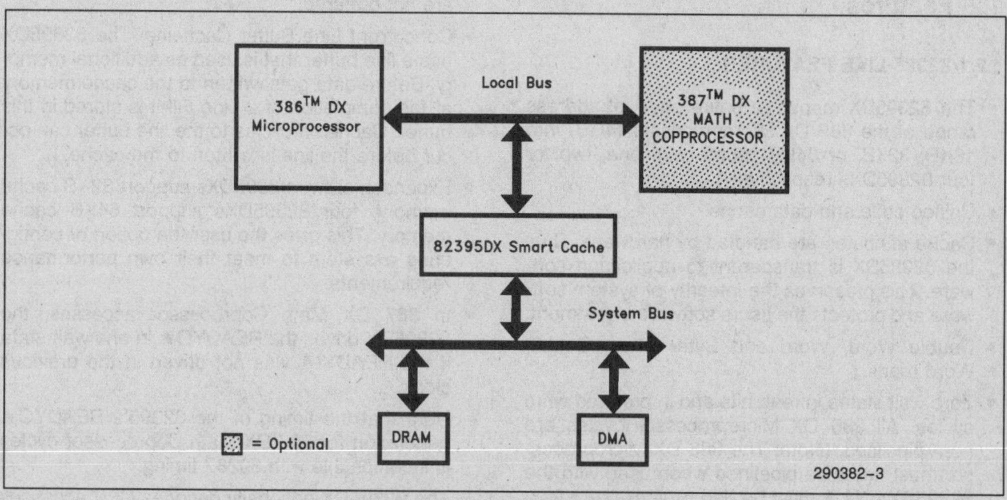

Figure 1.1 - System Block Diagram

4

In addition, it is enhanced by an optional burst mode for Line Fills. The burst mode provides faster line fills by allowing consecutive read cycles to be executed at a rate of up to one DW per clock cycle. Several bus masters (or several 82395DXs) can share the same System Bus and the arbitration is done via the SHOLD/SHLDA/SBREQ mechanism (similar to the i486 Microprocessor) along with SFHOLD#. Using these arbitration mechanisms, the 82395DX is able to support a multiprocessor system (multi 386 DX Microprocessor/82395DX systems sharing the same memory).

Cache consistency is maintained by the SAHOLD/SEADS# snooping mechanism, similar to the i486 microprocessor. The 82395DX is able to run a zero wait state 386 DX Microprocessor non-pipelined read cycle if the data exists in the cache. Memory write cycles can run with zero wait states if the write buffer is not full.

The 82395DX cache organization provides a higher hit rate than other standard configurations. The 82395DX, featuring the new high performance write buffer cache architecture, provides full concurrency between the electrically isolated Local Bus and System Bus. This allows the 82395DX to service read hit cycles on the Local Bus while running line fills or buffered write cycles on the System Bus. Moreover, the user has the option to expand his cache system up to 64KB.

1.2 Features

1.2.1 82385-LIKE FEATURES

- The 82395DX maps the entire physical address range of the 386 DX Microprocessor (4GB) into 16KB, 32KB, or 64KB cache (with one, two, or four 82395DXs respectively).
- Unified code and data cache.
- Cache attributes are handled by hardware. Thus the 82395DX is transparent to application software. This preserves the integrity of system software and protects the users software investment.
- Double Word, Word and Byte writes, Double Word reads.
- Zero wait states in read hits and in buffered write cycles. All 386 DX Microprocessor cycles are non- pipelined. (Note: The 386 DX Microprocessor must never be pipelined when used with the 82395DX - NA# must be tied to Vcc).
- A hardware cache FLUSH# option. The 82395DX will invalidate all the Tag Valid bits in the Cache Directory and clear the System Bus line buffer when FLUSH# is activated for a minimum of four CLK's. The line buffer is also FLUSH#ed.
- The 82395DX supports non-cacheable accesses. The 82395DX internally decodes the 387 DX Math Coprocessor accesses as Local Bus cycles.
- The system bus interface emulates a 386 DX Microprocessor interface.
- The 82395DX supports pipelined and non-pipelined system interface.
- Provides cache consistency (snooping): The 82395DX monitors the System Bus address via SEADS# and invalidates the cache address if the System Bus address matches a cached location.

1.2.2 NEW FEATURES

- 16KB on chip cache arranged in four banks, one bank for each way. In Read hit cycles, one DW is read. In a write hit cycle, any byte within the DW can be written. In cache fill cycle, the whole line (16B) is written. This large line size increases the hit rate over smaller line size caches.
- Cache architecture similar to the i486 Microprocessor cache: Four Way SET associative with Pseudo LRU replacement algorithm. Line size is 16B and a full line is retrieved from memory for every cache miss. Tag, Tag Valid Bit and Write Protect Bit are associated with every Line.
- New write buffer architecture with four DW deep write buffer provides zero wait state memory write cycles. I/O, Halt/Shutdown and LOCK#ed writes are not buffered.
- Concurrent Line Buffer Cacheing: The 82395DX has a line buffer that is used as additional memory. Before data gets written to the cache memory at the completion of a Line Fill it is stored in this buffer. Cache hit cycles to the line buffer can occur before the line is written to the cache.
- Expandable: two 82395DXs support 32KB cache memory, four 82395DXs support 64KB cache memory. This gives the user the option of configuring a system to meet their own performance requirements.
- In 387 DX Math Coprocessor accesses, the 82395DX drives the READYO# in one wait state if the READYI# was not driven in the previous clock.

  Note that the timing of the 82395's READYO# generation for 387 DX Math Coprocessor cycles is incompatible with 80287 timing.
- The 82395DX optionally decodes CPU accesses to Weitek 3167 Floating-Point Coprocessor address space (C0000000H–C1FFFFFFH) as Local Bus cycles. This option is enabled or disabled according to the LBA# pin value at the falling edge of RESET.

- An enhanced System Bus interface:
  a) Burst option is supported in line-fills similar to the i486 Microprocessor. SBRDY# (System Burst READY) is provided in addition to SRDY#. A burst is always a 16 byte cache update which is equivalent to four DW cycles. The i486 Microprocessor burst order is supported.
  b) System cacheability attribute is provided (SKEN#). SKEN# is used to determine whether the current cycle is cacheable. It is used to qualify Line Fill requests.
  c) SHOLD/SHLDA/SBREQ system bus arbitration mechanism is supported, the same as in the i486 Microprocessor. A Multi 386 DX/82395DX cluster can share the same System Bus via this mechanism.
  d) SNENE# output (Next Near) is provided to simplify the interface to DRAM controllers. DRAM page size of 2K is supported.
  e) Fast HOLD function (SFHOLD#) is provided. This function allows for multiprocessor support.
  f) Cache invalidation cycles supported via SEADS#. This is the mechanism used to provide cache coherency.
- Full Local Bus/System Bus concurrency is attained by:
  a) Servicing cache read hit cycles on the Local Bus while completing a Line Fill on the System Bus. The data requested by the 386 DX Microprocessor was provided over the local bus as the first part of the Line Fill.
  b) Servicing cache read hit cycles on the Local Bus while executing buffered write cycles on the system bus.
  c) Servicing cache read hit cycles on the Local Bus while another bus master is running (DMA, other 386 DX Microprocessor, 82395DX, i486 Microprocessor, etc . . .) on the System Bus.
  d) Buffering write cycles on the Local Bus while the system bus is executing other cycles.
- Write protected areas are supported by the SWP# input. This enables caching of ROM space or shadowed ROM space.
- No Post Input (NPI#) provided for disabling of write buffers per cycle. This option supports memory mapped I/O designs.
- A20M# input provided for emulation of 8086 address wrap-around.
- SRAM test mode, in which the TAGRAM and the cache RAM are treated as standard SRAM, is provided. A Tristate Output test mode is also provided for system debugging. In this mode the 82395DX is isolated from the other devices in the board by floating all its outputs.
- Single chip, 196 lead PQFP package, 1 micron CHMOS-IV technology.

2.0 82395DX CACHE SYSTEM DESCRIPTION

2.1 82395DX Cache Organization

The on chip cache memory is a unified code and data cache. The cache organization is 4 Way SET Associative and each Line is 16 bytes wide (see Figure 2.1). The 16K bytes of cache memory are logically organized as 4 4KB banks (4: 1 bank for each Way). Each bank contains 256 16B lines (256: 1 line for each SET).

The Cache Directory is used to determine whether the data in the cache memory is valid for the address being accessed. The Cache Directory contains 256 TAG's (each TAG is 22-bits wide) for each Way, for a total of 1K TAG's (See Figure 2.2). With each 20 bit TAG Address there is a TAG Valid Bit and a Write Protect bit. The Cache Directory also contains the LRU bits. The LRU bits are used to determine which Way to replace whenever the cache needs to be updated with a new line and all four ways contain data.

Table 2.1 lists the 82395DX cache organization.

4

Table 2.1 - 82395DX Cache Organization

Cache Element	82395DX Size/Qty	Comments
TAG	1K	Total number of TAGs
SET	256	Cache Directory Offset
LRU	256	3 bits per SET address
Way	4	4 TAG's per SET address
Line Size	16B	4 DW's
Sector Size	16B	4 DW's, one line per sector
Cache Size	16KB	Expandable to 64KB
Cache Directory	—	TAG address, TAG Valid Bit, and Write Protect Bit for each Way for each SET address (256 SET's × 4 Ways), and LRU bits.
TAG Valid Bit	1K	1 for each TAG in the cache directory, indicates valid data is in the cache memory.
Write Protect Bit	1K	1 for each TAG in the cache directory, indicates that the address is write protected.

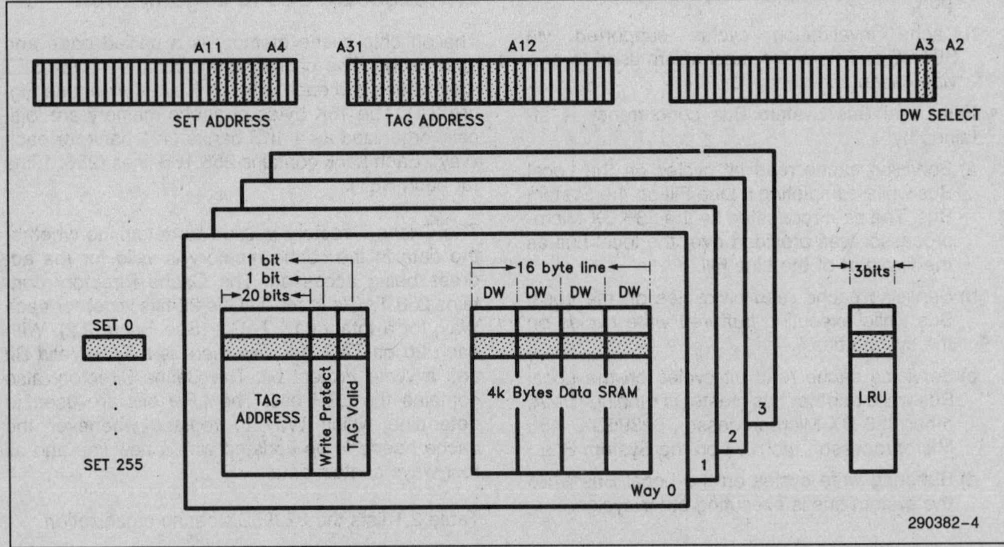

Figure 2.1 - 82395DX Cache Organization

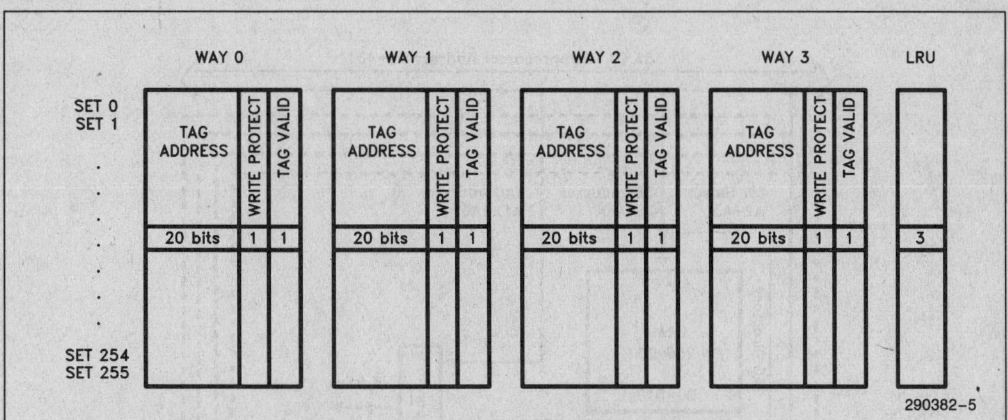

Figure 2.2 - 82395DX Cache Directory Organization

2.1.1 82395DX CACHE STRUCTURE AND TERMINOLOGY

A detailed description of the 82395DX cache parameters are defined here.

A **Line** is the basic unit of data transferred between the cache and main memory. In the 82395DX each Line is 16B. A Line is also known as a transfer block. The decision of a cache "hit or miss" is determined on a per Line basis. A cache hit results when the TAG address of the current address being accessed matches the TAG address in the Cache Directory (see Figure 2.3) and the TAG Valid bit is set. The 82395DX has 1K Lines.

A **TAG** is a storage element of the Cache Directory with which the hit/miss decision is made. The TAG consists of the TAG address (A31–A12), the TAG Valid bit and the Write Protect bit. Since many addresses map to a single line, the TAG is used to determine whether the data associated with the current address is present in the cache memory (a cache hit). This is done through a comparison of the TAG address bits of the current address and the contents of the Cache Directory, along with the TAG Valid bit. Each line in the cache memory has a TAG associated with it.

4

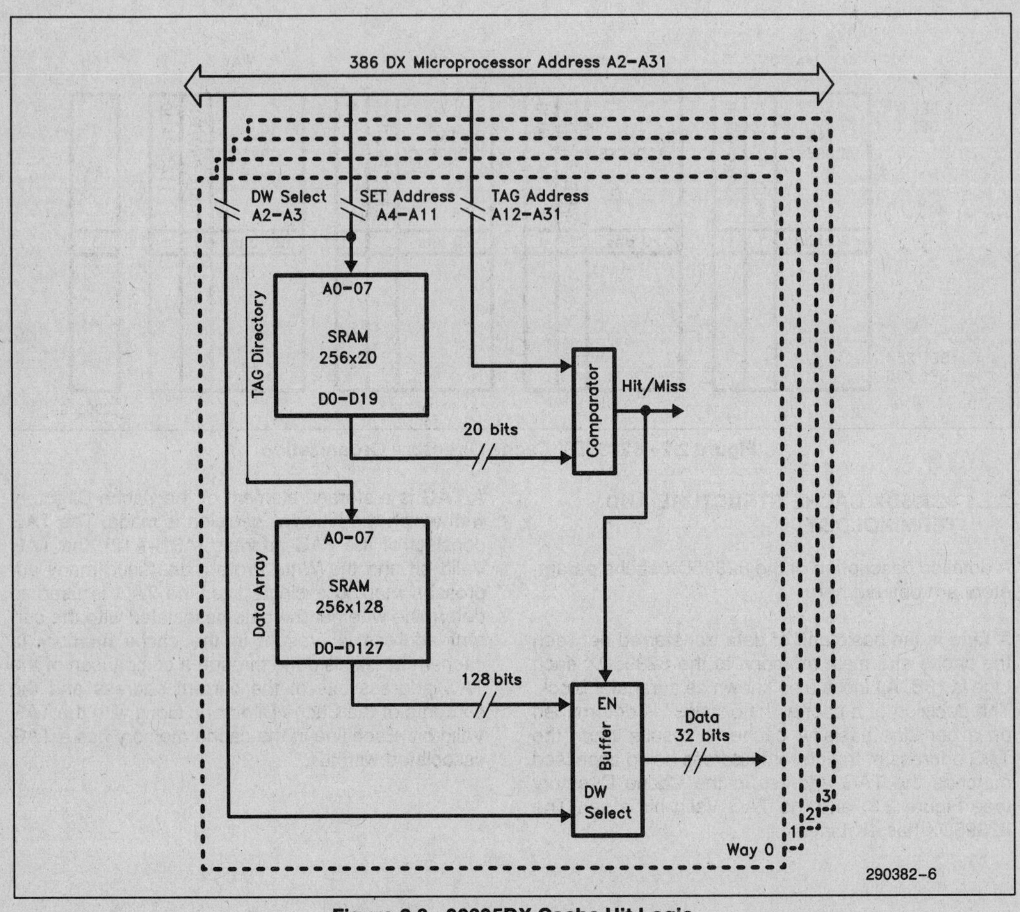

Figure 2.3 - 82395DX Cache Hit Logic

A **TAG Valid Bit** is associated with each TAG address in the Cache Directory. It determines if the data held in the cache memory for the particular TAG address is valid. It is used to determine whether the data in the cache is a match to data in main memory.

A **Write Protect Bit** is also associated with each TAG address in the Cache Directory. This field determines if the cache memory can be written to. It is set by the SWP# pin during Line Fill cycles (see chapter 6).

A **SET** address is a decoded portion of the Local Bus address that maps to 1 TAG address per Way in the Cache Directory. All the TAG's associated with a particular SET are simultaneously compared with the TAG field of the bus address to make the hit/miss decision. The 82395DX provides 256 SET addresses, each SET maps to four lines in the cache memory.

The term **Way** as in 4 Way SET Associative describes the degree of associativity of the cache system. Each Way provides TAG Address, TAG Valid bit, and Write Protect bit storage, 1 entry for each SET address. A simultaneous comparison of one TAG address from each Way with the bus address is done in order to make the hit/miss decision. The 82395DX is 4 Way SET Associative.

Other key 82395DX features include:

Cache Size - The 82395DX contains 16KB of cache memory. This can be expanded by connecting two or four 82395DX's in parallel to get up to 64KB of cache memory. Expanding the cache in this way results in an increased number of Tags with a constant number of lines per Tag. The cache is organized as four banks of 4KB. Each of the four banks corresponds to a particular Way.

Update Policy - The update policy deals with how main memory is updated when a cacheable write cycle is issued on the Local Bus. The 82395DX supports the write buffer policy, similar to the write through policy, which means that main memory is always updated in every write cycle. However, the cache is updated only when the write cycle hits the cache. Also, the 82395DX is able to cache write protected areas, e.g. ROMs, by preventing the cache update if the write cycle hits a write protected line. A write cycle to main memory is buffered as explained in chapter 6.

Replacement - When a new line is needed to update the cache, the Tag Valid bits are checked to see if any of the four ways are available. If they are all valid it is necessary to replace an old line that is already in the cache. In the 82395DX, the Pseudo LRU (least recently used) algorithm is adopted. The Pseudo LRU algorithm targets the least recently used line associated with the SET for replacement. (Pseudo LRU is described in section 2.2.).

Consistency - The 82395DX implements hooks for a consistency mechanism. This is to guarantee that in systems with multiple caches (and/or with multiple bus masters) all processor requests result in returning correct and consistent data. Whenever a system bus master performs memory accesses to data which also exists in the cache, the System Bus master can invalidate that entry in the 82395DX. This invalidation is done by using SEADS# (description in chapter 6).

The invalidation is performed by marking the TAG as invalid (the TAG Valid bit is cleared). Thus, the next time a Local Bus request is made to that location, the 82395DX accesses the main memory to get the most recent copy of the data.

2.2 Pseudo LRU Algorithm

When a line needs to be placed in the internal cache the 82395DX first checks to see if there is a non-valid line in the SET that can be replaced. The validity is checked by looking at the TAG Valid bit. The order that is used for this check is Way 0, Way 1, Way 2, and Way 3. If all four lines associated with the SET are valid, a pseudo Least Recently Used algorithm is used to determine which line will be replaced. If a non-valid line is found, that line is marked for replacement. All the TAG Valid bits are cleared when the 82395DX is RESET or when the cache is FLUSH#ed. Three bits, B0, B1, and B2, are defined for each of the 256 SETs. These bits are called the LRU bits and are stored in the cache directory. The LRU bits are updated for every access to the cache.

If the most recent access to the cache was to Way 0 or Way 1 then B0 is set to 1.

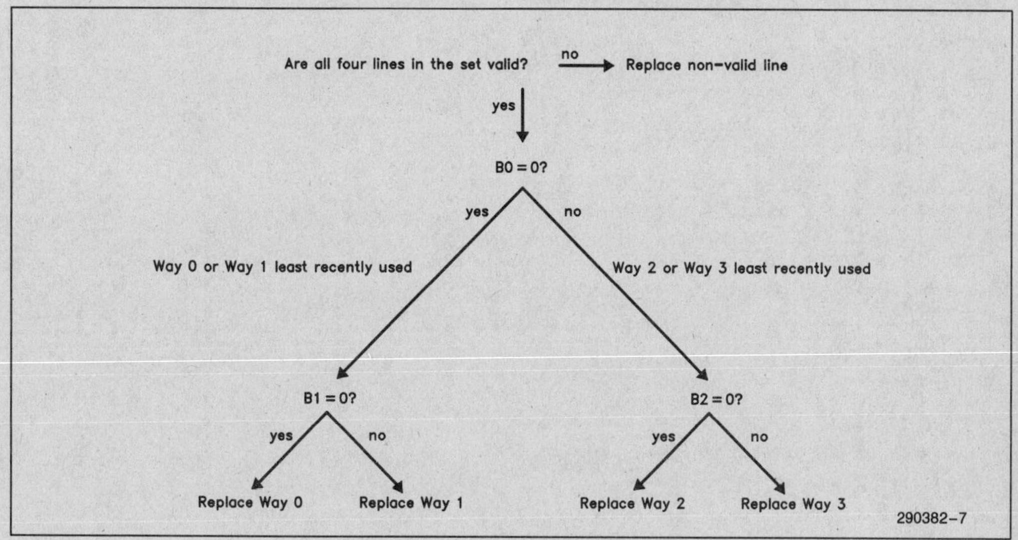

Figure 2.4 - Pseudo LRU Decision Tree

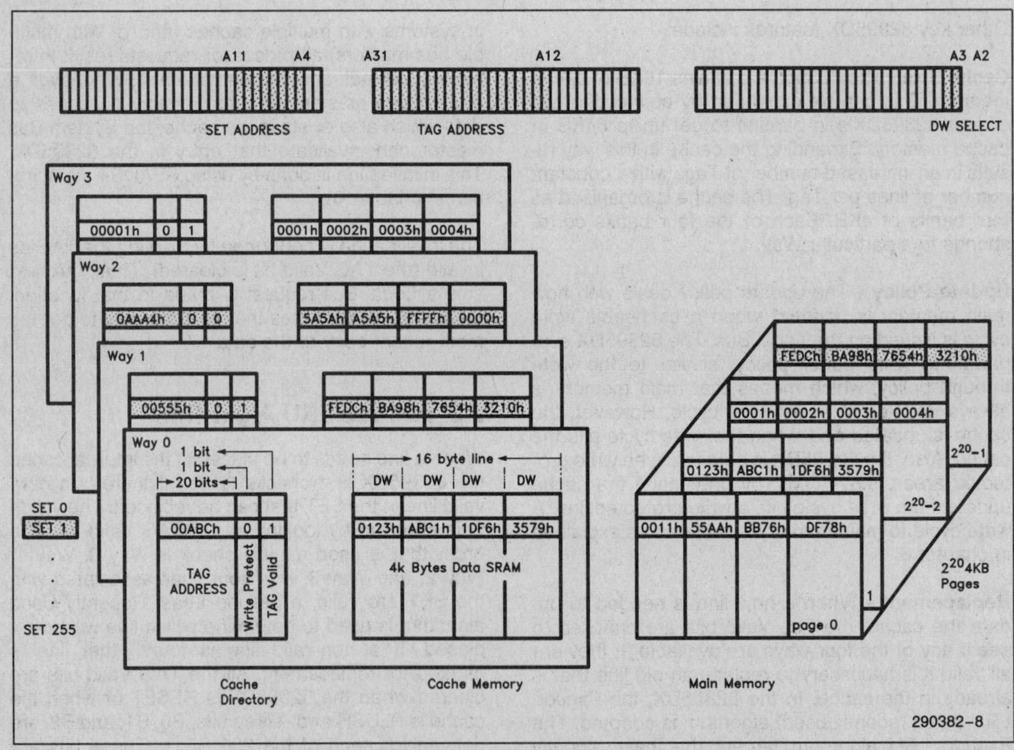

Figure 2.5 - Four Way Set Associative Cache Organization

B0 is set to 0 if the most recent access was to Way 2 or Way 3. If the most recent access to Way 0 or Way 1 was to Way 0, B1 is set to 1. Else B1 is set to 0. If the most recent access to Way 2 or Way 3 was to Way 2, B2 is set to 1. Else B2 is set to 0. See Table 2.2.

The Pseudo LRU algorithm works in the following manner. When a line must be replaced, the cache will first select which of Way 0 and Way 1 or Way 2 and Way 3 was least recently used. Then the cache will select which of the two lines was least recently used and mark it for replacement. The decision tree is shown in Figure 2.4. When the 82395DX is RESET or the cache is FLUSH#ed all the LRU bits are cleared along with the TAG Valid bits.

2.3 Four Way Set Associative Cache Organization

The 82395DX is a four Way SET Associative cache. Figure 2.5 shows the 82395DX's cache organization. For each of the 256 SET's there are four TAG's, one for each Way. The address currently being accessed is decoded into the SET and TAG addresses. If the access was to address 00555004h (SET = 001,TAG = 00555h), the four TAG's in the Cache Directory associated with SET 001 are simultaneously compared with the TAG of the address being accessed. The TAG Valid bits are also checked. If the TAG's match and the TAG Valid bit is set, the access is a hit to the Way where the hit was detected, in this example the hit occurred in Way 1. The data would be retrieved from Way 1 of the cache memory. If the next access was to address 0AAA4007h (SET = 001, TAG = 0AAA4h), the comparison would be done and a TAG match would be found in Way 2. However in this case the TAG Valid bit is cleared so the access is a miss and the data will be retrieved from main memory. The cache memory will also be updated. It is helpful to notice that the main memory is broken into pages by the TAG size. In this case with a 20-bit TAG address there are 2^{20} pages. The smaller the TAG size the fewer pages main memory is broken into. The SET breaks down these memory pages. The larger the SET size the more lines per page.

The following is a description of the interaction between the 386DX Microprocessor, the 82395DXs cache and Cache Directory.

2.3.1 CACHE READ HITS

When the 386 DX Microprocessor initiates a memory read cycle, the 82395DX uses the 8 bit SET address to select 1 of the 256 SET's in the Cache Directory. The four TAG's of this SET are simultaneously compared with address bits A12–A31. The four TAG Valid bits are checked. If any comparison produces a hit the corresponding bank of internal SRAM supplies the 32 bits of data to the 386 DX Microprocessor data bus based on the DW Select bits A2 and A3. The LRU bits are then updated according to the Pseudo LRU algorithm.

2.3.2 CACHE READ MISSES

Like the cache read hit the 82395DX uses the 8 bit SET address to select the 4 TAG's for comparison. If none of these match or if the TAG Valid bit associated with a matching TAG address is cleared the cycle is a miss and the 82395DX retrieves the requested data from main memory. A Line Fill is simultaneously started to read the line of data from system memory and write the line of data into the cache in the Way designated by the LRU bits.

2.3.3 OTHER OPERATIONS THAT AFFECT THE CACHE AND CACHE DIRECTORY

Other operations that affect the cache and Cache Directory include write hits, snoop hits, cache FLUSH#es and 82395DX RESETs. In write hits, the cache is updated along with main memory. The bank that detected the hit is the one that data is written to. The LRU bits are then adjusted according to the Pseudo LRU algorithm. When a cache invalidation cycle occurs (Snoop hit) the tag valid bit is cleared. RESETs and cache FLUSH#es clear all the TAG Valid bits.

2.4 Concurrent Line Buffer Cacheing

This feature of the 82395DX can be broken into two components, Concurrent Line Buffer and Line Buffer Cacheing.

A Concuurent Line Buffer indicates that the DW requested is returned to the 386 DX Microprocessor in the first cycle of a Line Fill. The Local Bus is then free to execute other cycles while the Line Fill is being completed on the System Bus.

Line Buffer Cacheing indicates that the 82395DX serves 386 DX Microprocessor cycles before it updates its Cache Directory. If the 386 DX Microprocessor cycle is to a line which resides in the cache memory, the 82395DX will serve that cycle as a regular cache hit cycle. The cache memory and cache directory are not updated until after the Line Fill is complete (see sections 2.8 and 2.9). The 82395DX keeps the address and data of the retrieved line in an internal buffer, the System Bus line buffer. Any 386 DX Microprocessor read cycle to the same line will be serviced from the line buffer. Until the cache memory and cache directory are updated, any

386 DX Microprocessor read cycle to a Doubleword, which has already been retrieved, will be serviced from the System Bus line buffer. On the other hand, any 386 DX Microprocessor write cycle to the same line will be done to the cache memory after updating the line in the cache. In this case, the write cycle is buffered and the READYO# is activated after updating the line in the cache. However, if the line is Write Protected, the write cycle will be handled as if it is a miss cycle.

A snooping cycle to a line which has not been updated in the cache will invalidate the SB Line Buffer and will prevent the cache update. Also, cache FLUSH will invalidate the buffer. More details about invalidation cycles can be found in chapter 6.

2.5 Cache Control

The cache can be controlled via the SWP# pin. By asserting this pin during the first DW in a Line Fill the 82395DX sets the write protect bit in the Cache Directory making the entry protected from writes.

2.6 Cache Invalidation

Cache invalidation cycles are activated using the SEADS# pin. SAHOLD or SHLDA asserted conditions the 82395DX's system address bus (SA4–SA31) to accept an input. The 82395DX floats its system address bus in the clock immediately after SAHOLD was asserted, or in the clock SHLDA is activated. No address hold acknowledge is required for SAHOLD. SEADS# asserted and the rising edge of CLK2 indicate that the address on the System Bus is valid. SEADS# is not conditioned by SAHOLD or SHLDA being asserted. The 82395DX will read the address and perform an internal cache invalidation cycle to the address indicated. The internal cache invalidation cycle is serviced 1 cycle after SEADS# was sampled active (or 2 cycles after SEADS# was sampled active if there is contention between the Cache Directory Snoop (CDS) cycle and a Cache Directory Lookup (CDL) cycle, see 2.8 and Figure 2.6). To actually invalidate the address the 82395DX clears the tag valid bit.

2.7 Cache Flushing

The user has an option of clearing the cache by activating the FLUSH# input. When sampling the FLUSH# input low for four clocks, the 82395DX resets all the tag valid bits and the LRU bits of the Cache Directory. Thus, all the banks of the cache are invalidated. Also, the SB Line Buffer is invalidated. The FLUSH# input must have at least eight CLK periods in order to be recognized. If FLUSH is activated for longer than four CLKs, the 82395DX will handle all accesses as misses and it will not update the Cache Directory (the Cache Directory will be FLUSH#ed as long as the FLUSH# input is low). The cache is also FLUSH#ed during RESET.

2.8 Cache Directory Accesses and Arbitration

There are five types of accesses to the cache directory. Each access is a one clock cycle:

1) Cache Directory Look-Up
2) Cache Directory Update
3) Cache Directory Snoop
4) Testability Accesses
5) Cache Directory FLUSH#

A description of each of these accesses follows:

1) **Cache Directory Look-up cycle (CDL):** A 386 DX Microprocessor access in which the hit/miss decision is made. The Cache Directory is accessed by the 386 DX Microprocessor address bus directly from the pins. CDL is executed whenever ADS# is activated, in both read and write cycles. The LRU bits are updated in every CDL hit cycle so the accessed "Way" becomes the most recently used. The LRU bits are read in every CDL miss cycle to indicate the "Way" to be updated in the Cache Directory Update cycle. Also, the WP bit is read.

2) **Cache Directory Update cycle (CDU):** A write cycle to the cache directory due to a previous miss. The CDU cycle can be caused by a TAG mismatch (either a Tag Address mismatch or a cleared TAG Valid bit). In both cases, the new TAG is written to the "Way" indicated by the LRU bits read by the previous CDL miss cycle. Also, the TAG Valid bit is turned on and the LRU algorithm is updated so the accessed "Way" becomes the most recently used. The WP bit is written according to the sampled SWP# input. The Cache Directory is accessed by the internally latched 386 DX Microprocessor address bus. Simultaneously with the CDU cycle, the cache memory is updated.

3) **Cache Directory Snooping cycle (CDS):** A Cache Directory look-up cycle initiated by the System Bus, in response to an access to a memory location that is shared with another system master, followed by a conditional invalidation of the TAG Valid bit. If the look-up cycle results in a hit, the corresponding TAG Valid bit in the Way which detected the HIT will be cleared. CDS cycles do not affect the LRU bits. The Cache Directory is accessed by the internally latched System Bus address.

4) **Testability accesses (CDT):** Cache Directory read and write cycles performed in SRAM test mode. During the TEST accesses, 25 bits of each entry (20 for the TAG, one for the TAG Valid BIT, one for the WP bit and 3 for the LRU bits) are read or written. No comparison is done. CDT cycles are used for debugging purposes so CDT cycles do not contend with other cycles.

5) **Cache Directory FLUSH cycle (CDF):** During RESET or as a result of a FLUSH# request generated by activating the FLUSH# input, all the TAG Valid bits and the LRU bits are cleared as well as the Line Buffer. CDF is a one clock cycle if FLUSH# is active for four clocks. If FLUSH# is activated longer, the CDF cycle is N−3 clocks, where N is the number of clocks FLUSH# is activated for. The actual clearing of the valid bits occurs seven clocks after the activation of FLUSH#. Two clocks are for internal synchronization and four for recognizing FLUSH# asserted. It has higher priority than all other cycles. CDF cycle may occur simultaneously with any other cycle but the result is always a FLUSH#ed Cache Directory.

The 82395DX performs the CDL cycle in T1 state. The CDU cycle, in general, is performed in the clock after the last SRDY# or SBRDY# of the Line Fill cycle and the CDS cycle one clock after sampling the SEADS# active (see more details on snooping cycles in chapter 6). Supporting concurrent activities on local and system busses causes CDL cycles to be requested in any clock during the execution with a maximum rate of a CDL cycle every other clock.

The following arbitration mechanism guarantees resolution of any possible contention between CDL, CDU and CDS cycles:

1. The priority order is CDL, CDS and CDU. CDL has the highest priority, CDU has the lowest.
2. In case of simultaneous CDL and CDS cycles, the CDS will be delayed by one clock. So, the maximum latency in executing the invalidation cycle is two clocks after sampling the SEADS# active. Since the maximum rate of each of the CDL and the CDS cycles is one every other clock, the 82395DX is able to interpose the CDL and CDS cycles such that both are serviced. Figure 2.6 clarifies the interposing in the Cache Directory between the 386 DX Microprocessor and the System Bus.
3. CDU cycle is executed in any clock after the last SRDY# or SBRDY# in which neither CDL nor CDS cycles are requested. The worst case is the case where immediately after the read miss, the 386 DX Microprocessor runs consecutive read hits while the System Bus is running invalidation cycles every other clock. In this case, the CDU cycle is postponed until a free clock is inserted, which may occur due to slower look-up rate (in case of read miss, non-cacheable read, etc...), or due to slower SEADS# rate.

Since every CDU cycle is synchronized with the cache update (CU - writing the retrieved line into the cache), a possible contention on the cache can occur between a cache update cycle and a cache write cycle (CW - cache is written due to a write hit cycle). In this case, the CW cycle is executed, and the CDU and CU cycles are delayed.

4

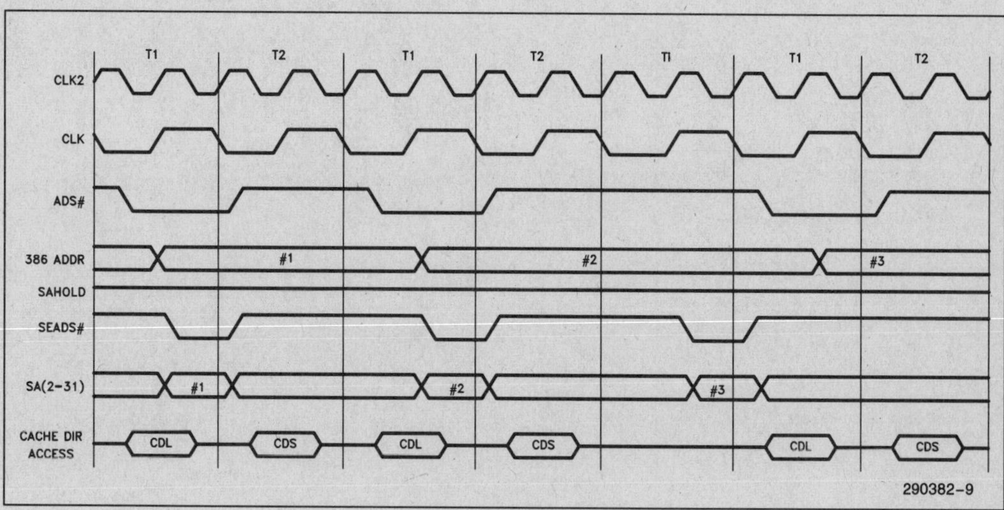

Figure 2.6 - Interposing in the Cache Directory

2.9 Cache Memory Description

The 82395DX cache memory is constructed of four banks, each bank is 1K double words (4KB) and represents a "Way". For example, if the read cycle is to Way 0, bank 0 will be read. The basic cache element is a Line. The cache is able to write a full line or any byte within the line. Reads are done by DW only.

There are four types of accesses to the cache data memory. Each access is a one clock cycle:

1) Cache Read cycle
2) Cache Write cycle
3) Cache Update cycle
4) Testability Access

A description of each type of access follows:

1) **Cache Read cycle (CR):** CR cycle occurs simultaneously with Cache Directory look-up (CDL) cycle if the cycle is a read. In case of a hit, the cache bank in which the hit was detected is read. In CR cycle, the A2–3 address lines select the requested DW within the line.

2) **Cache Write cycle (CW):** CW cycle occurs one clock after the Cache Directory look-up cycle (CDL) if the cycle is a write hit and the WP bit is not set. The cache bank in which the hit was detected is updated. In CW cycle, the A2–3 address lines and the four BE# lines select the required bytes within the line to be written. For all write hit cycles, READYO# is returned simultaneously with the CW cycle unless the write buffer is full. When the write buffer is full the first cycle buffered must be completed on the system bus before READYO# can be asserted.

3) **Cache Update cycle (CU):** CU cycle occurs simultaneously with every Cache Directory update cycle (CDU). The full line is written.

4) **Testability accesses (CT):** cache read and write cycles performed by the 82395DX TEST machine. During the TEST accesses, the cache memory acts as a standard RAM. CT cycles are used for debugging purposes so CT cycles do not contend with other cycles.

The Cache Directory arbitration rules guarantee that contention will not occur in the cache accesses. This is since CR is synchronized with the CDL cycle, CU is synchronized with CDU cycle, CW cannot occur simultaneously with CR cycles (ADS# not activated while READYO# is returned since 386 DX Microprocessor is not pipelined) and finally the possible contention of CW and CU is resolved. See figure 2.7 for an example of Cache Directory and cache memory accesses during a typical cycle execution.

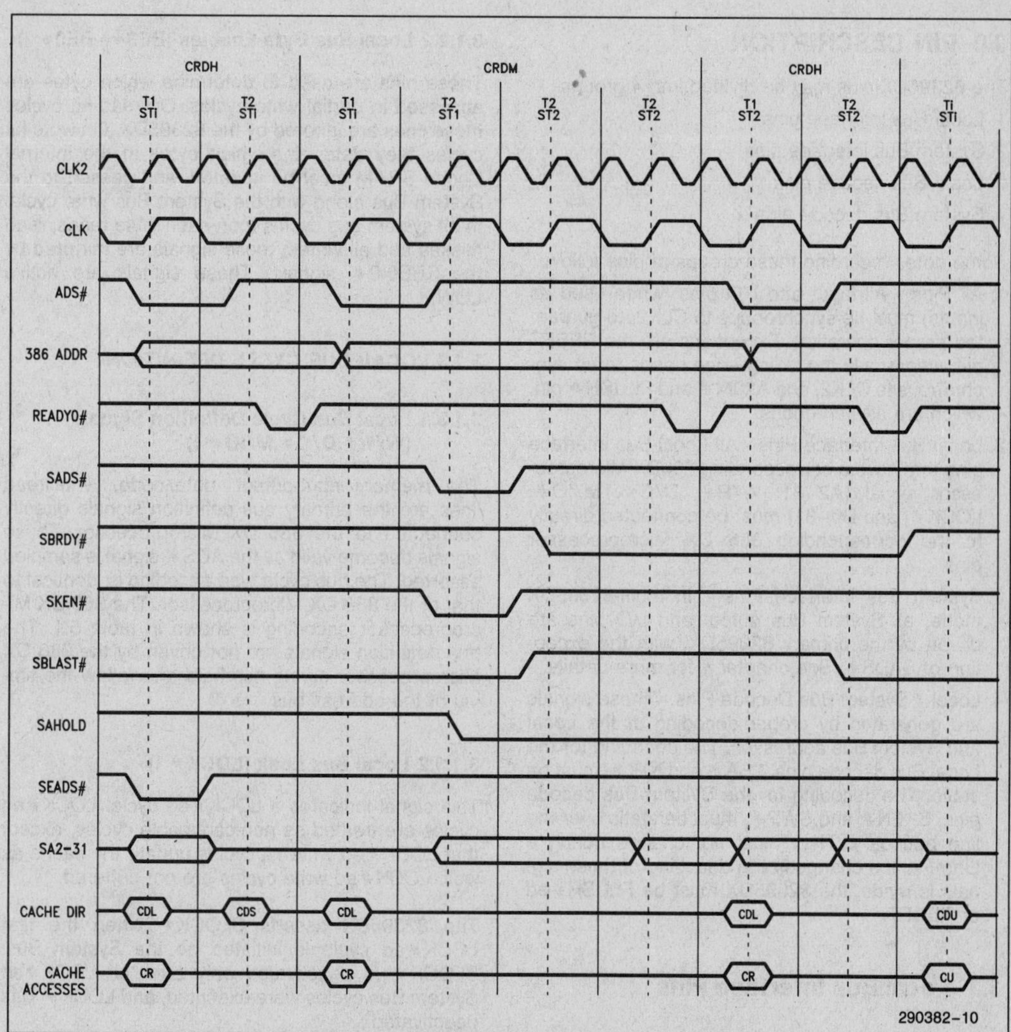

Figure 2.7 - Cache Directory and Cache Accesses

4

3.0 PIN DESCRIPTION

The 82395DX pins may be divided into 4 groups:

1. Local Bus interface pins
2. System Bus interface pins
3. Local Bus decode pins
4. System Bus decode pins

Some notes regarding these groups of pins follow:

1. All Pins - All input and I/O pins (when used as inputs) must be synchronous to CLK2, to guarantee proper operation. Exceptions are the RESET pin, where only the falling edge needs to be synchronous to CLK2, and A20M# and FLUSH# pin, which are asynchronous.
2. Local Bus Interface Pins - All Local Bus interface pins that have a corresponding 386DX Microprocessor signal (A2–31, W/R#, D/C#, M/IO#, LOCK#, and D0–31) must be connected directly to the corresponding 386 DX Microprocessor pins.
3. System Bus Interface Pins - In multi-82395DX mode, all System Bus output and I/O pins are driven by the primary 82395DX, with the exception of SADS#. See chapter 4 for more details.
4. Local / System Bus Decode Pins - These signals are generated by proper decoding of the Local and System Bus addresses. The decoding for the Local Bus decode pins, LBA# and NPI#, must be static. The decoding for the System Bus decode pins, SKEN# and SWP#, must be static over the line boundary. They must not change during a Line Fill. If a change in the decoding of these signals is made, the 82395DX must be FLUSH#ed or RESET.

3.1 Local Bus Interface Pins

3.1.1 386 DX MICROPROCESSOR/82395DX CLOCK (CLK2 I)

This signal provides the fundamental timing for the 82395DX. The 82395DX, like the 386 DX Microprocessor, divides CLK2 by two to generate the internal clock. The phase of the internal 82395DX clock is synchronized to the internal CPU clock phase by the RESET signal. All external timing parameters are specified with respect to CLK2.

3.1.2 LOCAL ADDRESS BUS

3.1.2.1 Local Bus Address Lines (A2–A31 I)

These signals, along with the byte enable signals, define the physical area of memory or I/O accessed.

3.1.2.2 Local Bus Byte Enables (BE3#–BE0# I)

These pins are used to determine which bytes are accessed in partial write cycles. On read-hit cycles these lines are ignored by the 82395DX. On write hit cycles they determine which bytes in the internal Cache SRAM must be updated, and passed to the System Bus along with the System Bus write cycle. In all system bus cycles (non-cacheable reads, read misses and all writes) these signals are mirrored by the SBE0-3# signals. These signals are active LOW.

3.1.3 LOCAL BUS CYCLE DEFINITION

3.1.3.1 Local Bus Cycle Definition Signals (W/R#,D/C#,M/IO# I)

The memory/input-output, data/code, write/read lines are the primary bus definition signals directly connected to the 386 DX Microprocessor. These signals become valid as the ADS# signal is sampled asserted. The bus cycle type encoding is identical to that of the 386 DX Microprocessor. The 386 DX Microprocessor encoding is shown in table 5.1. The bus definition signals are not driven by the 386 DX Microprocessor during bus hold and follow the timing of the address bus.

3.1.3.2 Local Bus Lock (LOCK# I)

This signal indicates a LOCK#ed cycle. LOCK#ed cycles are treated as non-cacheable cycles, except that LOCK#ed write hit cycles update the cache as well. LOCK#ed write cycles are not buffered.

The 82395DX asserts SLOCK# when the first LOCK#ed cycle is initiated on the System Bus. SLOCK# is deactivated only after all LOCK#ed System Bus cycles were executed, and LOCK# was deactivated.

3.1.4 LOCAL BUS CONTROL

3.1.4.1 Address Status (ADS# I)

The address status pin, an output of the 386 DX Microprocessor, indicates that new, valid address and cycle definition information is currently available on the Local Bus. The signals that are valid when ADS# is activated are:

A(2-31), BE(0-3)#, W/R#, D/C#, M/IO#, LOCK#, NPI# and LBA#

3.1.4.2 Local Bus Ready (READYI# I)

This is the ready input signal seen by the local bus master. Typically it is a logical OR between the 82395DX generated READYO# signal and other (optional) READY# signals generated by other Local Bus masters. It is used by the 82395DX, along with the ADS# signal, to keep track of the 386 DX Microprocessor bus state. Do not drive READYI# during T1. Do not delay READYI# from READY0#. (READYI# can be delayed from READY0# as long as the delay does not extend into the next clock cycle.)

3.1.4.3 Local Bus Ready Output (READYO# I/O)

This output is returned to the 386 DX Microprocessor to terminate all types of 386 DX Microprocessor bus cycles, except for Local Bus cycles. This signal is wire-ORed with parallel 82395DX READYO# signals (if more than one 82395DX is used on a 386 DX Microprocessor bus). For more details on READYO# functionality in a multi-82395DX system, refer to Chapter 4.

The READYO# may serve as READY# signal for the 387 DX Math Coprocessor. For details, refer to Chapter 5.

This pin is used during the self configuration sequence, after RESET. For details, refer to Chapter 4.

3.1.5 RESET (RESET I)

This signal forces the 82395DX to begin execution at a known state. RESET falling edge is used by the 82395DX to set the phase of its internal clock identical to the 386 DX Microprocessor internal clock. The RESET falling edge must satisfy the appropriate setup and hold times for proper chip operation. RESET must remain active for at least 1ms after power supply and CLK2 input have reached their proper DC and AC specifications.

The RESET input is used for three purposes: first, it RESETs the 82395DX and brings it to a known state. Second, it is used to synchronize the internal 82395DX clock phase to that of the 386 DX Microprocessor. Third, it initiates a self-configuration sequence in which the 82395DX determines the number of parallel 82395DX devices in the system and it's own configuration (Primary / Secondary and address space).

On power up, RESET must be active for at least 1 millisecond after power has stabilized to a voltage within spec, and after CLK2 input has stabilized to voltage and frequency within spec. This is to allow the internal circuitry to stabilize. Otherwise, RESET must be active for at least 10 clock cycles.

No access to the 82395DX is allowed for 128 clock cycles after the RESET falling edge. During RESET, all other input pins are ignored, except SHOLD, SAHOLD and SFHOLD#. Unlike the 386 DX Microprocessor, the 82395DX can respond to a System Bus HOLD request by floating its bus and asserting SHLDA even while RESET is asserted. Also the 82395DX can respond to a System Bus address HOLD request by floating its address bus. The status of the 82395DX outputs during RESET is shown in Table 3.2.

The 82395DX samples the LBA#pin during RESET and enables the decoding of Weitek 3167 Floating-Point Coprocessor address space if it is sampled low (active).

The user must make sure SAHOLD and FLUSH# are not asserted at the falling edge of RESET. If they are the Tristate Test Mode will be entered. The user must also insure that FLUSH# does not get asserted for one clock cycle while SAHOLD is negated for the same CLK cycle prior to RESET falling. If this condition exists a reserved mode will be entered.

3.1.6 CONFIGURATION (CONF# I)

The activity on this input during and after RESET allows the 82395DX to configure itself to operate in the specified address range.

Refer to Chapter 4 for more details. This pin is active LOW.

3.1.7 LOCAL DATA BUS

3.1.7.1 Local Bus Data Lines (D0–D31 I/O)

These are the Local Bus data lines of the 82395DX and must be connected to the D0–D31 signals of the Local Bus.

3.1.8 LOCAL BUS DECODE PINS

These signals are generated by proper decoding of the local bus address. The decoding of these signals must be static, the decoding must not change during normal operation of the 82395DX. If a change in the decoding of these signals is made, the 82395DX must be FLUSH#ed or RESET. These signals must be stable throughout the local bus cycle (refer to Figure 5.1).

3.1.8.1 Local Bus Access Indication (LBA# I)

This signal instructs the 82395DX that the cycle currently in progress is targeted to a Local Bus device, and must therefore be ignored by the 82395DX. The 387 DX Math Coprocessor is considered a Local Bus Device, but LBA# need not be generated for 387 DX Math Coprocessor accesses. Weitek 3167 Floating-Point Coprocessor address space may also be decoded internally as Local Bus cycles. Note that LBA# has priority over all other types of cycles. This signal is active LOW.

3.1.8.2 No Post Input (NPI# I)

This signal instructs the 82395DX that the write cycle currently in progress must not be posted (buffered) in the write buffer. NPI# is sampled on the falling edge of CLK following the address change, see figure 5.1. NPI# is ignored during read cycles. This signal is active LOW.

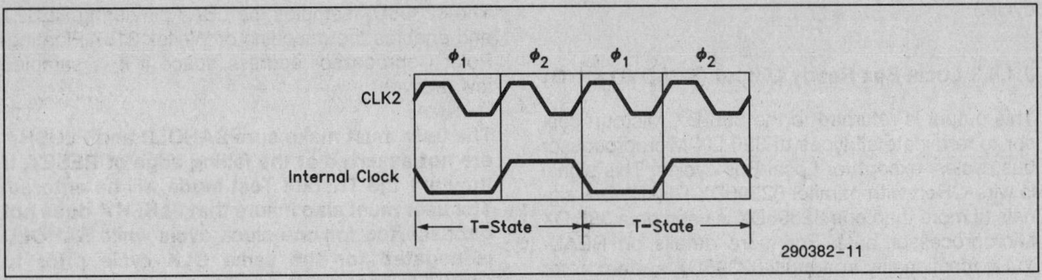

Figure 3.1 - CLK2 and Internal Clock

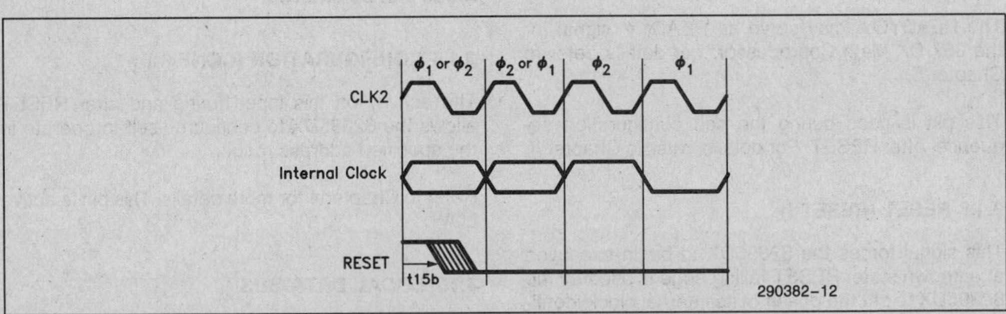

Figure 3.2 - RESET/Internal Phase Relationship

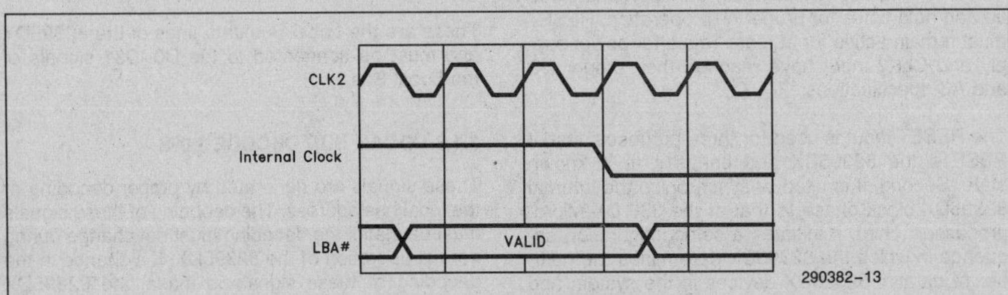

Figure 3.3 - Sampling LBA# During RESET

3.1.9 ADDRESS MASK

3.1.9.1 Address Bit 20 Mask (A20M# I)

This pin, when active (low), forces the A20 input as seen by the 82395DX to logic '0', regardless of the actual value on the A20 input pin. It must be asserted two clock cycles before ADS# for proper operation. A20M# emulates the address wraparound at 1 MByte which occurs on the 8086. This pin is asynchronous but must meet setup and hold times to guarantee recognition in a specific clock. It must be stable throughout Local Bus memory cycles.

3.2 System Bus Interface Pins

3.2.1 SYSTEM ADDRESS BUS

3.2.1.1 System Bus Address Lines (SA2–SA31 I/O *)

* SA2-3 are outputs only.

These are the SYSTEM BUS address lines of the 82395DX. When driven by the 82395DX, these signals, along with the System Bus byte enables define the physical area of memory or I/O accessed.

Activation of SEADS# conditions these signals to serve as inputs for the snooping cycle.

3.2.1.2 System Bus Byte Enables (SBE0#–SBE3# O)

These are the byte enable signals for the System Bus. The 82395DX drives these pins identically to BE0#–BE3# in all System Bus cycles except Line Fills. In Line Fills these signals are driven identically to BE0#–BE3# in the first read cycle of the Line Fill. They are all driven active in the remaining cycles of the Line Fill.

The system memory must ignore these pins during Line Fill, and return all four bytes. These signals are active low.

3.2.2 SYSTEM BUS CYCLE DEFINITION

3.2.2.1 System Bus Cycle Definition (SW/R#,SD/C#,SM/IO# O)

These are the System Bus cycle definition pins. When the 82395DX is the SYSTEM BUS master, it drives these signals identically to the 386 DX Microprocessor encoding.

3.2.2.2 System Bus Lock (SLOCK# O)

The SYSTEM BUS LOCK pin is one of the bus cycle definition pins. It indicates that the current bus cycle is LOCK#ed: that the 82395DX (on behalf of the CPU) must be allowed exclusive access to the System Bus across bus cycle boundaries until this signal is de-asserted. The 82395DX does not acknowledge a bus hold request when this signal is asserted. The 82395DX asserts SLOCK# when the first LOCK#ed cycle is initiated on the System Bus; SLOCK# is deactivated only after all LOCK#ed System Bus cycles were executed, and LOCK# was deactivated. SLOCK# is active LOW.

3.2.3 SYSTEM BUS CONTROL

3.2.3.1 System Bus Address Status (SADS# O)

The address status pin is used to indicate that new, valid address and cycle definition information is currently being driven onto the address, byte enables and cycle definition lines of the System Bus. SADS# can be used as an indication of a new cycle start. SADS# is driven active in the same clock as the addresses are driven. SADS# is not valid until a specified setup time before the CLK falling edge, and must be sampled by CLK falling edge before it is used by the system. This signal is active LOW.

SADS# can float from the active (low) state in pipelined cycles when SFHOLD# is activated in ST2P. SADS# floats from phi2 while being driven from phi1. It is always driven high before it is floated except for when SFHOLD# is asserted in ST2P. Drive SFHOLD# active to the 82395DX only after SADS# has been driven in pipelined cycles or use external latches to drive SADS# after SFHOLD# is deactivated.

3.2.3.2 System Bus Ready (SRDY# I)

The SRDY# signal indicates that the current bus cycle is complete. When SRDY# is sampled asserted it indicates that the external system has presented valid data on the data pins in response to a read cycle or that the external system has accepted the 82395DX data in response to a write request. This signal is ignored when the SYSTEM BUS is at STi, STH, ST1 or ST1P states.

At the first read cycle of a Line Fill, if SBRDY# is returned active and both SRDY# and SNA# are returned inactive, a burst Line Fill will be executed. If SRDY# is returned active and SNA# is returned inactive, a non-burst non-pipelined Line Fill will be executed. If SNA# is returned active and SRDY# is inactive, a non-burst pipelined line fill will be executed.

4

Once a burst Line Fill has started, if SRDY# is returned in the second or third DW of the transfer, the burst Line Fill will be interrupted and the cache will not be updated. The first DW will already have been transferred to the CPU. Note that in the last (fourth) bus cycle in a Line Fill, SBRDY# and SRDY# have the same effect on the 82395DX. They indicate the end of the Line Fill. This signal is active LOW.

3.2.3.3 System Bus Next Address (SNA# I)

This input, when active, indicates that a pipelined address cycle can be executed. It is sampled by the 82395DX in the same timing as the 386 DX Microprocessor samples NA#. If this signal is sampled active, then SBRDY# is treated as SRDY#, i.e. burst Line Fill is disabled. This signal is ignored once a burst Line Fill has started, as well as during the fourth DW of a Line Fill.

3.2.4 BUS ARBITRATION

3.2.4.1 System Bus Request (SBREQ O)

SBREQ is the internal cycle pending signal. This indicates to the outside world that internally the 82395DX has generated a bus request (due to a CPU's request that requires access to the System Bus). It is generated whether the 82395DX owns the bus or not and can be used to arbitrate among the various masters on the system bus. In read misses, if the bus is available and the cycle starts immediately, this signal will not be activated at all. This signal is active HIGH.

3.2.4.2 System Bus Hold Request (SHOLD I)

This signal allows another bus master complete control of the entire System Bus. In response to this pin, the 82395DX floats all its system bus interface output and input/output pins (With the exception of SHLDA and SBREQ) and asserts SHLDA after completing its current bus cycle or sequence of LOCK#ed cycles. The 82395DX maintains its bus in this state until SHOLD is deasserted. SHOLD is active HIGH. SHOLD is recognized during reset.

3.2.4.3 System Bus Hold Acknowledge (SHLDA O)

This signal goes active in response to a hold request presented on the SHOLD pin and indicates that the 82395DX has given the bus to another System Bus master. It is driven active in the same clock that the 82395DX floats its bus. When leaving a bus hold, SHLDA is driven inactive in one clock and the 82395DX resumes driving the bus. Depending on internal requests the 82395DX may, or may not begin a System Bus cycle in the clock where SHLDA is driven inactive. The 82395DX is able to support CPU Local Bus activities during System Bus hold, since the internal cache is able to satisfy the majority of those requests. This signal is active HIGH.

3.2.4.4 System Bus Fast Hold Request (SFHOLD# I)

This input allows another bus master immediate access to the System Bus. In response to this signal, the 82395DX stops driving the System Bus output and input/output pins (with the exception of SHLDA and SBREQ) in the next CLK cycle. Note that the same signals are tristated in response to a SHOLD request. Because the 82395DX always stops driving the System Bus in response to SFHOLD# active, no acknowledge is needed.

The bus remains in the high impedance state until SFHOLD# is negated.

Note that SRDY# is internally inactivated during SFHOLD# cycles. The only affect of SFHOLD# being asserted is forcing the System Bus output and I/O buffers into their high impedance state. It is the responsibility of the system designer to guarantee that bus cycles which are in progress when SFHOLD# is asserted are terminated correctly.

This pin is recognized during RESET and is active low.

3.2.5 BURST CONTROL

3.2.5.1 System Bus Burst Ready (SBRDY# I)

This signal performs the same function during a burst cycle that SRDY# does in a non-burst cycle. SBRDY# asserted indicates that the external system has presented valid data on the data pins in response to a burst Line Fill cycle. This signal is ignored when the SYSTEM BUS is at STi, STH, ST1 or ST1P states.

Note that in the last (fourth) bus cycle in a Line Fill, SBRDY# and SRDY# have the same effect on the 82395DX. They indicate the end of the Line Fill. For all cycles that cannot run in burst, e.g. noncacheable cycles, non Line Fill cycles (or pipelined Line Fill), SBRDY# has the same effect on the 82395DX as the normal SRDY# pin. This signal is active LOW.

3.2.5.2 System Bus Burst Last Cycle Indicator (SBLAST# O)

The system burst last cycle signal indicates that the next time SBRDY# is returned the burst transfer is complete. In other words, it indicates to the external system that the next SBRDY# returned is treated as a normal SRDY# by the 82395DX, i.e., another set of addresses will be driven with SADS# or the System Bus will go idle. SBLAST# is normally active. In a cache read miss cycle, which may proceed as a Line Fill, SBLAST# starts active and later follows SKEN# by one clock. SBLAST# is active during non-burst Line Fill cycles. Refer to Chapter 6 for more details. This signal is active LOW.

3.2.6 CACHE INVALIDATION

3.2.6.1 System Bus Address Hold (SAHOLD I)

This is the Address Hold request. It allows another bus master access to the address bus of the 82395DX in order to indicate the address of an external cycle for performing an internal Cache Directory lookup and invalidation cycle. In response to this signal, the 82395DX immediately (in the next cycle) stops driving the entire system address bus (SA2–SA31). Because the 82395DX always stops driving the address bus, in response to system bus address hold request, no hold acknowledge is required. Only the address bus will be floated during address hold, other signals can remain active. For example, data can be returned for a previously specified bus cycle during address hold. The 82395DX does not initiate another bus cycle during address hold.

This pin is recognized during RESET. However, since the entire cache is invalidated by reset, any invalidation cycles run will be superfluous. This signal is active high.

3.2.6.2 System Bus External Address Strobe (SEADS# I)

This signal indicates that a valid external address has been driven onto the 82395DX pins and that this address must be used to perform an internal cache invalidation cycle. Maximum allowed invalidation cycle rate is one every two clock cycles. This signal is active low.

3.2.7 CACHE CONTROL

3.2.7.1 Flush (FLUSH# I)

This pin, when sampled active for four clock cycles or more, causes the 82395DX to invalidate its entire Tag Array. In addition, it is used to configure the 82395DX to enter various test modes. For details refer to Chapter 7. This pin is asynchronous but must meet setup and hold times to guarantee recognition in any specific clock. This signal is active LOW.

3.2.8 SYSTEM DATA BUS

3.2.8.1 System Bus Data Lines (SD0–SD31 I/O)

These are the System Bus data lines of the 82395DX. The lines must be driven with appropriate setup and hold times for proper operation. These signals are driven by the 82395DX only during write cycles.

3.2.9 SYSTEM BUS DECODE PINS

3.2.9.1 System Cacheability Enable (SKEN# I)

This is the cache enable pin. It is used to determine whether the current cycle running on the System Bus is cacheable or not. When the 82395DX generates a read cycle that may be cached, this pin is sampled 1 CLK before the first SBRDY#, SRDY# or SNA# is sampled active (for detailed timing description, refer to Chapter 6). If sampled active, the cycle will be transformed into a Line Fill. Otherwise, the Cache and Cache Directory will be unaffected. Note that SKEN# is ignored after the first cycle in a Line Fill. SKEN# is ignored during all System Bus cycles except for cacheable read miss cycles. This signal is active LOW.

4

3.2.9.2 System Write Protect Indication (SWP# I)

This is the write protect indicator pin. It is used to determine whether the address of the current system bus Line Fill cycle is write protected or not.

In non-pipelined cycles, the SWP# is sampled with the first SRDY# or SBRDY# of a system Line Fill cycle. In pipelined cycles, SWP# is sampled at the last ST2 stage, or at ST1P; in other words, one clock phase after SNA# is sampled active.

The write protect indicator is sampled together with the TAG address of each line in the 82395DX Cache Directory. In every cacheable write cycle, the write protect indicator is read. If active, the cycle will be a Write Protected cycle which is treated like a cacheable write miss cycle. It is buffered and it does not update the cache even if the addressed location is present in the cache. The signal is active LOW.

3.2.10 DESIGN AIDES

3.2.10.1 System Next Near Indication (SNENE# O)

This signal indicates that the current System Bus memory cycle is to the same 2048 Byte area as the previous memory cycle. Address lines A11–A31 of the current System Bus memory cycle are identical to the address lines A11–A31 of the previous memory cycle.

This signal can be used in an external DRAM system to run CAS# only cycles, therefore increasing the throughput of the memory system. SNENE# is valid for all memory cycles, and indicates that the current memory cycle is to the same 2048 Byte area, even if there were idle or non-memory bus cycles since the last System Bus memory cycle.

For the first memory cycle after the 82395DX has exited the HOLD state, or after SAHOLD was deactivated, this pin will be inactive. This signal is active low.

3.3 Pinout Summary Tables

Table 3.1 - Input Pins

Name	Function	Synchronous/ Asynchronous	Active Level
CLK2	Clock		
RESET	Reset	Asynchronous*	High
BE0–3#	Local Bus Byte Enables	Synchronous	Low
A2–31	Local Bus Address Lines	Synchronous	—
W/R#	Local Bus Write/Read	Synchronous	—
D/C#	Local Bus Data/Control	Synchronous	—
M/IO#	Local Bus Memory/Input-Output	Synchronous	—
LOCK#	Local Bus LOCK	Synchronous	Low
ADS#	Local Bus Address Strobe	Synchronous	Low
READYI#	Local Bus READY	Synchronous	Low
LBA#	Local Bus Access Indication	Synchronous	Low
NPI#	No Post Input	Synchronous	Low
FLUSH#	FLUSH the 82395DX Cache	Asynchronous	Low
A20M#	Address Bit 20 Mask	Asynchronous	Low
CONF#	Configuration	Synchronous	Low
SHOLD	System Bus Hold Request	Synchronous	High
SRDY#	System Bus READY	Synchronous	Low
SNA#	System Bus Next Address Indication	Synchronous	Low
SBRDY#	System Bus Burst Ready	Synchronous	Low
SKEN#	System Cacheability Indication	Synchronous	Low
SWP#	System Write Protect Indication	Synchronous	Low
SAHOLD	System Bus Address HOLD	Synchronous	High
SEADS#	System Bus External Address Strobe	Synchronous	Low
SFHOLD#	System Bus Fast HOLD Request	Synchronous	Low

* The falling edge of RESET needs to be synchronous to CLK2 but the rising edge is asynchronous.

Table 3.2 - Output Pins

Name	Function	When Floated	State at RESET	Active Level
SBE0-3#	System Bus Byte Enables	SHLDA/SFHOLD#	Low	Low
SADS#	System Bus Address Strobe (1)	SHLDA/SFHOLD#	High	Low
SD/C#	System Bus Data/Control	SHLDA/SFHOLD#	High	—
SM/IO#	System Bus Memory/Input-Output	SHLDA/SFHOLD#	Low	—
SW/R#	System Bus Write/Read	SHLDA/SFHOLD#	Low	—
SHLDA	System Bus HOLD Acknowledge	—	Low (2)	High
SBREQ	System Bus Request	—	Low	High
SLOCK#	System Bus LOCK	SHLDA/SFHOLD#	High	Low
SBLAST#	System Bus Burst Last Cycle Indication	SHLDA/SFHOLD#	Low	Low
SA2-3	System Bus Address (2 lowest order bits)	SHLDA/SAHOLD/ SFHOLD#	High	—
SNENE#	System Bus Next Near Indication	SHLDA/SFHOLD#	High	Low

NOTES:
1. SADS# is driven active in ST1/ST2P and inactive for one phase in the first ST2/ST1P following the activation. SADS# is driven high before it is floated.
2. Unless SHOLD is asserted

Table 3.3 - Input-Output Pins

Name	Function	When Floated	State(1) at RESET	Active Level
D0-31	Local Data Bus (2)	Always Except READs	z	—
SD0-31	System Data Bus	Always Except WRITEs	z	—
SA4-31	System Bus Address (except the 2 lowest order bits)	SHLDA/SAHOLD/ SFHOLD#	High	—
READYO#	Local Bus READY	See Sec 4.6	High	Low

(1) Provided SHOLD, SAHOLD, and SFHOLD# are inactive
(2) Local Data is driven only in T2.

4.0 BASIC FUNCTIONAL DESCRIPTION

The 82395DX has an interface to the 386 DX Microprocessor (Local Bus) and to the System Bus. The System Bus interface emulates the 386 DX Microprocessor bus such that the system will view the 82395DX as the front end of a 386 DX Microprocessor. Some optional enhancements, like burst support, are provided to maximize the performance.

When ADS# is sampled active, the 82395DX decodes the 386 DX Microprocessor cycle definition signals (M/IO#, D/C#, W/R# and LOCK#), as well as two Local Bus decode signals (LBA# and NPI#), to determine how to respond. LBA# indicates that the current cycle is addressed to a Local Bus device; NPI# indicates that the current memory write cycle must not be buffered. In addition, the 82395DX internally decodes the 386 DX Microprocessor accesses to the 387 DX Math Coprocessor / Weitek 3167 Floating-Point Coprocessor as Local Bus accesses. The result of the address, cycle definition and cycle qualification decoding is two categories of accesses, the Local Bus accesses (LBA# active or 387 DX Math Coprocessor / Weitek 3167 Floating-Point Coprocessor accesses) and 82395DX accesses. In 387 DX Math Coprocessor accesses, the 82395DX drives the READYO# signal active after one wait state, if the READYI# was not sampled active. Local Bus accesses are ignored by the 82395DX.

Any 82395DX access can be either to a cacheable address or to a non-cacheable address. Non-cacheable addresses are all I/O and system accesses with SKEN# returned inactive. Non-cacheable cycles are all cycles to non-cacheable addresses, LOCK#ed read cycles and Halt/Shutdown cycles. All other cycles are cacheable. For more details about non-cacheable cycles, refer to section 4.2. Non-cacheable cycles pass through the cache. They are always forwarded to the System Bus.

Cacheable read cycles can be either hit or miss. Cacheable read hit cycles are serviced by the internal cache and they don't require System Bus service. A cacheable read miss cycle generates a series of four System Bus read cycles, called a Line Fill. Of the four cycles, the first cycle is for reading the requested data while all four are for filling the cache line. The System Bus has the ability to provide the system cacheability attribute to the 82395DX Line Fill request, via the SKEN# input, and the system write protection indicator, via the SWP# input. Refer to chapter 6 for more information about Line Fill cycles.

Cacheable write cycles, as any write cycles, are forwarded to the system bus. The write buffer algorithm terminates the write cycle on the Local Bus, allowing the 386 DX Microprocessor to continue processing in 0 wait states, while the 82395DX executes the write cycles on the System Bus. All cacheable write hit cycles, except protected writes, update the cache in a byte basis i.e. only the selected bytes are updated. Cacheable write misses do not update the cache (the 82395DX does not allocate on writes). All cacheable write cycles, except LOCK#ed writes, are buffered (unless NPI# pin is sampled active).

Cache consistency is provided by the SAHOLD, SEADS# mechanism. If any bus master performs a memory cycle which disturbs the data consistency, the address of this cycle must be provided to the 82395DX using the SAHOLD, SEADS# mechanism. Then, the 82395DX checks if that memory location resides in the cache. If it does, the 82395DX invalidates that line in the cache by marking it as invalid in the Cache Directory. The 82395DX interposes the Cache Directory between the 386DX Microprocessor and the System Bus such that the 386 DX Microprocessor is not forced to wait due to snooping and none of the snooping cycles are missed due to 386 DX Microprocessor accesses (see figure 2.6). Cacheability is resolved on the system side using the SKEN# input. SKEN# is sampled one clock before the first SRDY#/SBRDY# in nonpipelined Line Fill cycles. In pipelined Line Fill cycles, SKEN# is sampled one clock phase before sampling SNA# active. SKEN# is always sampled at PHI1.

Note that the 82395DX does not support pipelining of the 386DX Microprocessor Local Bus. The NA# input on the 386 DX Microprocessor must be tied to Vcc.

4.1 Cacheable Accesses

In a cacheable access, the 82395DX performs a cache directory look-up cycle. This is to determine if the requested data exists in the cache and to read the write protection bit. In parallel, the 82395DX performs a cache read cycle if the access is a read, or prepares the cache for a write cycle if the access is a write.

4.1.1 CACHEABLE READ HIT ACCESSES

If the Cache Directory look-up for a cacheable read access results in a hit (the requested data exists in the cache), the 82395DX drives the local data bus by the data provided from the internal cache. It also drives the 386DX Microprocessor READY# (by activating the 82395DX READYO#), so that the 386 DX Microprocessor gets the required data directly from the cache without any wait states.

The 82395DX is a four Way SET associative cache, so only one of the four ways (four banks) is selected to supply data to the 386 DX Microprocessor. The Way in which the hit occurred will provide the data. Also, the replacement algorithm (LRU) is updated such that the Way in which the hit occurred is marked as the most recently used.

4.1.2 CACHEABLE READ MISS ACCESSES

READYO# is always activated in the first T2 of cache read miss cycles. In order to meet the timing requirements READYO# must be activated prior to the hit/miss decision. Once the hit/miss decision is made and the cycle is a miss, READYO# is deactivated. This activation only occurs prior to the max valid delay specification (t20 max). After the max valid delay spec, READYO# will always be stable. See Figure 4.0. READYO# must not be sent to any edge triggered logic.

If the Cache Directory look-up results in a miss, the 82395DX transfers the request to the System Bus in order to read the data from the main memory and for

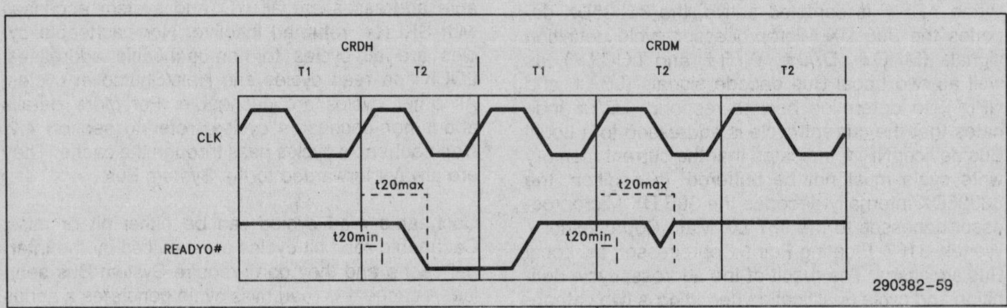

Figure 4.0 READYO# Behavior

updating the cache. A full line is updated in cache update cycle. As a result of a cache miss, the 82395DX performs four System Bus accesses to read four DWs from the DRAM, and write the four DWs to the cache. This is called a Line Fill cycle. The first DW accessed in a Line Fill cycle is for the DW which the 386 DX Microprocessor requested and the 82395DX provides the data and drives the READYO# one clock after it gets the first DW from the SB.

The 82395DX provides the option of supporting burst bus in order to minimize the latency of a line fill. Also, the 82395DX provides the SKEN# input, which, if inactive, converts a Line Fill cycle to a non-cacheable cycle. Write protection is also provided. The write protection indicator is stored together with the TAG Valid bit and the TAG field of every line in the Cache Directory. For more details refer to chapter 6.

The 82395DX features Line Buffer cacheing. In a Line Fill the data for the four DWs is stored in a buffer, the Line Buffer, as it is accumulated. After filling the Line Buffer, the 82395DX performs the Cache Update and the Cache Directory Update. The updated Way is the least recently used Way flagged by the Pseudo LRU algorithm during the Cache Directory Lookup cycle, if all the Ways are valid. If there is a non-valid Way it will be updated.

The SRDY# (System Bus READY#) active indicates the completion of the system bus cycle and SBRDY# (System Bus Burst READY#) active indicates the completion of a burst System Bus cycle. In a 386 DXMicroprocessor-like system, the 82395DX drives the 386 DX Microprocessor READY# one clock after the first SRDY# and, in a burst system, one clock after the first SBRDY#. This frees up the Local Bus, allowing the 386 DX Microprocessor to execute the next instruction, while filling the cache.

So, during Line Fills, there is no advantage in driving the 386 DX Microprocessor into the pipelined mode. **Therefore, the 82395DX does not drive the 386 DX Microprocessor's NA# at all. NA# must be tied to VCC.**

4.1.2.1 Burst Bus

The 82395DX offers an option to minimize the latency in Line Fills. This option is the burst bus and is only applicable to Line Fill cycles. By generation of a burst bus compatible DRAM controller, one which generates SBRDY# and SBLAST# to take advantage of the 82395DX's burst feature, the number of cycles required for a Line Fill to be completed is significantly reduced. Details of burst Line Fills can be found in chapter 6. The burst feature uses the i486 Microprocessor burst order to fill the 16 byte cache line (see Table 6.1).

4.1.3 CACHE WRITE ACCESSES

The 82395DX supports the write buffer policy, which means that main memory is always updated in any write cycle. However, the cache is updated only when the write cycle hits the cache and the accessed address is not write protected. In cache write misses, the cache is not updated (allocation in writes is not supported).

The 82395DX has a write buffer of four DWs. Only the cacheable write cycles, except LOCKed writes, are buffered so, if the write buffer is not full, the 82395DX buffers the cycle. This means that the data, address and cycle definition signals are written in one entry of the write buffer and the 82395DX drives the READYO# in the first T2 so all the buffered write cycles run without wait states. If the write buffer is full, the 82395DX delays the READYO# until the completion of the execution of the first buffered write cycle. The execution of the buffered write cycles depends on the availability of the System Bus. In non-buffered write cycles, e.g. I/O writes, the 386 DX Microprocessor is forced to wait until the execution of all the buffered writes and the non-buffered write (READYO# is driven one clock after the SRDY# of the non-buffered write). More details about the write buffer can be found in chapter 6.

In cacheable non-write protected write hit cycles, only the appropriate bytes within the line are updated. The updated bytes are selected by decoding the A2, A3 and the four BE# lines. The LRU is updated so that the hit Way is the most recently used, as in cache read hit cycles.

All cacheable writes, whether hits or misses, are executed on the system bus. The System Bus write cycle address, data and cycle definition signals are the same as the 386 DX Microprocessor signals. All buffered writes run with zero wait states if the write buffer is not full.

Table 4.1 - 386 DX Microprocessor Bus Cycle Definition with Cacheability

M/IO#	D/C#	W/R#	386 DX Microprocessor Cycle Definition	Cacheable/ Non-cacheable	Writes Posted
0	0	0	Interrupt Acknowledge	Non-cacheable	—
0	0	1	Undefined	—	—
0	1	0	I/O Read	Non-cacheable	—
0	1	1	I/O Write	Non-cacheable	No
1	0	0	Memory Code Read	Cacheable	—
1	0	1	Halt/Shutdown	Non-cacheable	—
1	1	0	Memory Data Read	Cacheable	—
1	1	1	Memory Data Write	Cacheable	Yes

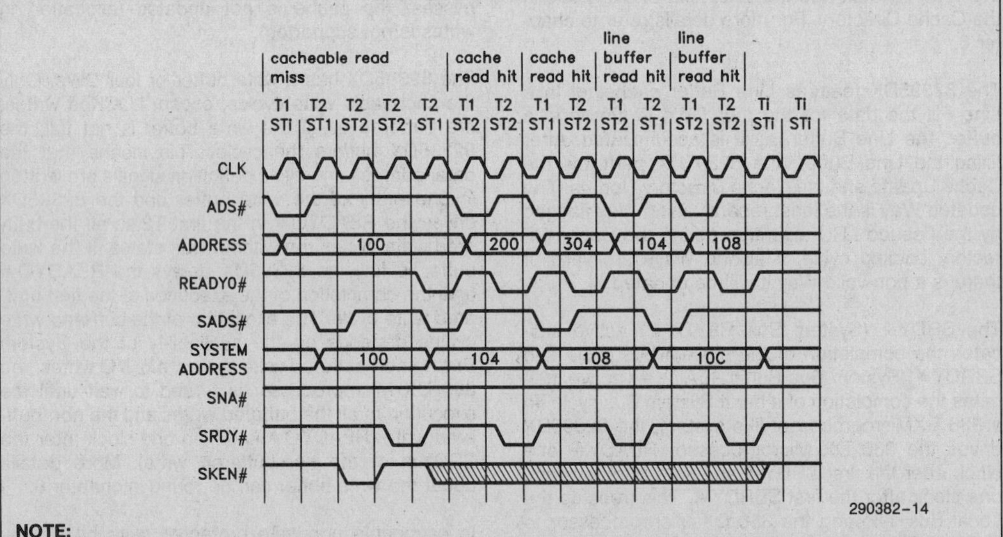

NOTE:
The second and third reads are to a different line and are serviced from the cache while the fourth and fifth reads are to the same line and are serviced from the line buffer.

Figure 4.1 - Read Hit Cycles During a Line Fill

4.2 Noncacheable System Bus Accesses

Non-cacheable cycles are any of the following 82395DX cycles:

1) All I/O cycles.
2) All LOCKed read cycles.
3) Halt/Shutdown cycles.
4) SRAM mode cycles not addressing the internal cache or Tagram.

All the above cycles are defined as non-cacheable by the Local Bus interface controller. In addition, Line Fill cycles in which the SKEN# signal was returned inactive are aborted. They are called Aborted Line Fills (ALF).

Non-cacheable cycles are never serviced from the cache and they don't update the cache. They are always referred to the System Bus. In non-cacheable cycles, the 82395DX transfers to the System Bus the exact 386 DX Microprocessor bus cycle.

Description of LOCKed cycles can be found in chapter 5.

4.3 Local and System Bus Concurrency

Concurrency between local and System Busses is supported in several cases:

1. Read hit cycles can run while executing a Line Fill on the System Bus. Refer to timing diagram 4.1.
2. Read hit cycles can run while executing buffered write cycles on System Bus. Refer to timing diagram 4.2.
3. Write cycles are buffered while the System Bus is running other cycles, including other buffered writes. They are also buffered when another bus master is using the System Bus (e.g. DMA, other CPU). Refer to timing diagram 4.3.
4. Read hit cycles can run while another System Bus master is using the System Bus.

The first case is established by providing the data which the 386 DX Microprocessor requested first and later the 82395DX continues filling its line while it is servicing new cache read hit cycles. The 82395DX updates its cache and cache directory after completing the System Bus Line Fill cycle. Meanwhile, any 386 DX Microprocessor read cycles will be serviced from the cache if they hit the cache. In case the 386 DX Microprocessor read cycles are consecutive such that the 386 DX Microprocessor is requesting a double-word which belongs to the same line currently retrieved by the System Bus Line Fill cycle and the requested DW was already retrieved, the 82395DX provides the requested DW in zero wait states (a Line Buffer hit). If the requested DW wasn't already retrieved, it will be read after completing the Line Fill.

The second and third cases are attained by having the Four DW deep write buffer which is described in chapter 6. The READYO# signal is driven active after latching the write cycle, so all buffered cycles will run without wait states. This releases the 386 DX Microprocessor to issue a new cycle, which can also run without wait states if it does not require system bus service. Two examples are in the case of a cache read hit cycle, or another buffered write cycle, which does not require immediate System Bus service. In the case of a write cycle to the same line currently retrieved, the write cycle will wait until the Line Fill is complete and then the selected bytes within the line are written in the cache. READYO# is returned after the cache is written.

Whenever the System Bus is released to any bus master, the 82395DX activates the snooping function. The maximum rate of snooping cycles is a cycle every other clock. Although the snooping support requires accessing the 82395DX cache directory, the 82395DX is able to interpose the cache directory accesses between the 386 DX Microprocessor cycles and the snooping device such that zero wait state cache read hit cycles are supported. All the snooping cycles are also serviced. This is how the fourth case is provided. For more details, refer to chapter 6.

4

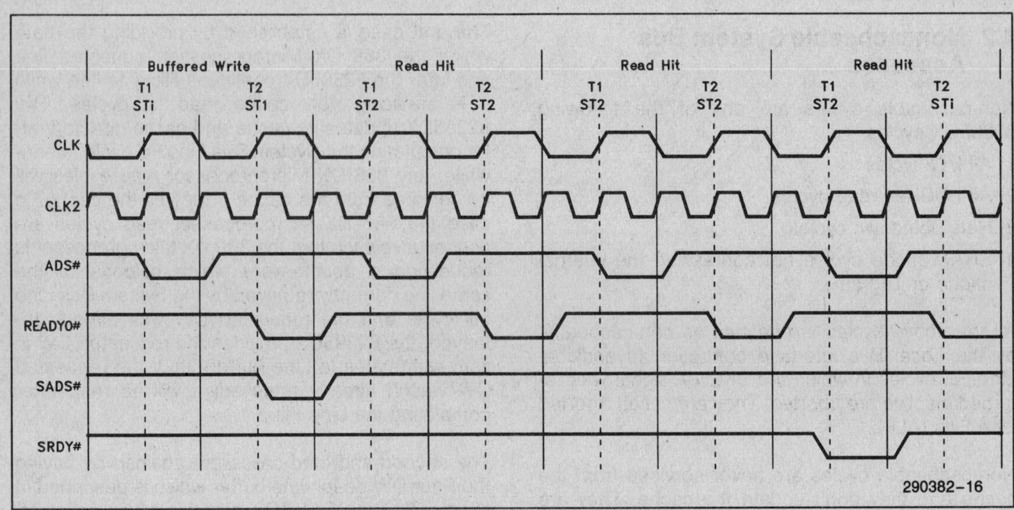

Figure 4.2 - Cache Read Hit Cycles while Executing a Buffered Write on the System Bus

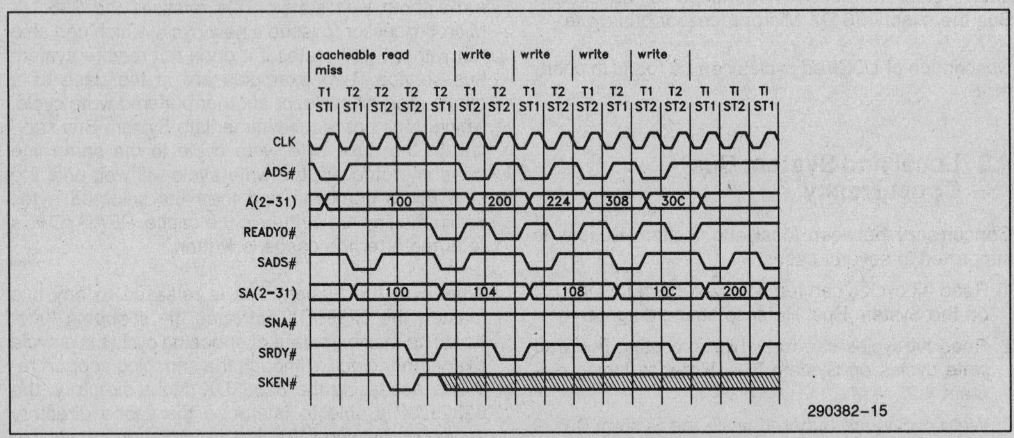

Figure 4.3 - Buffered Write Cycles During a Line Fill

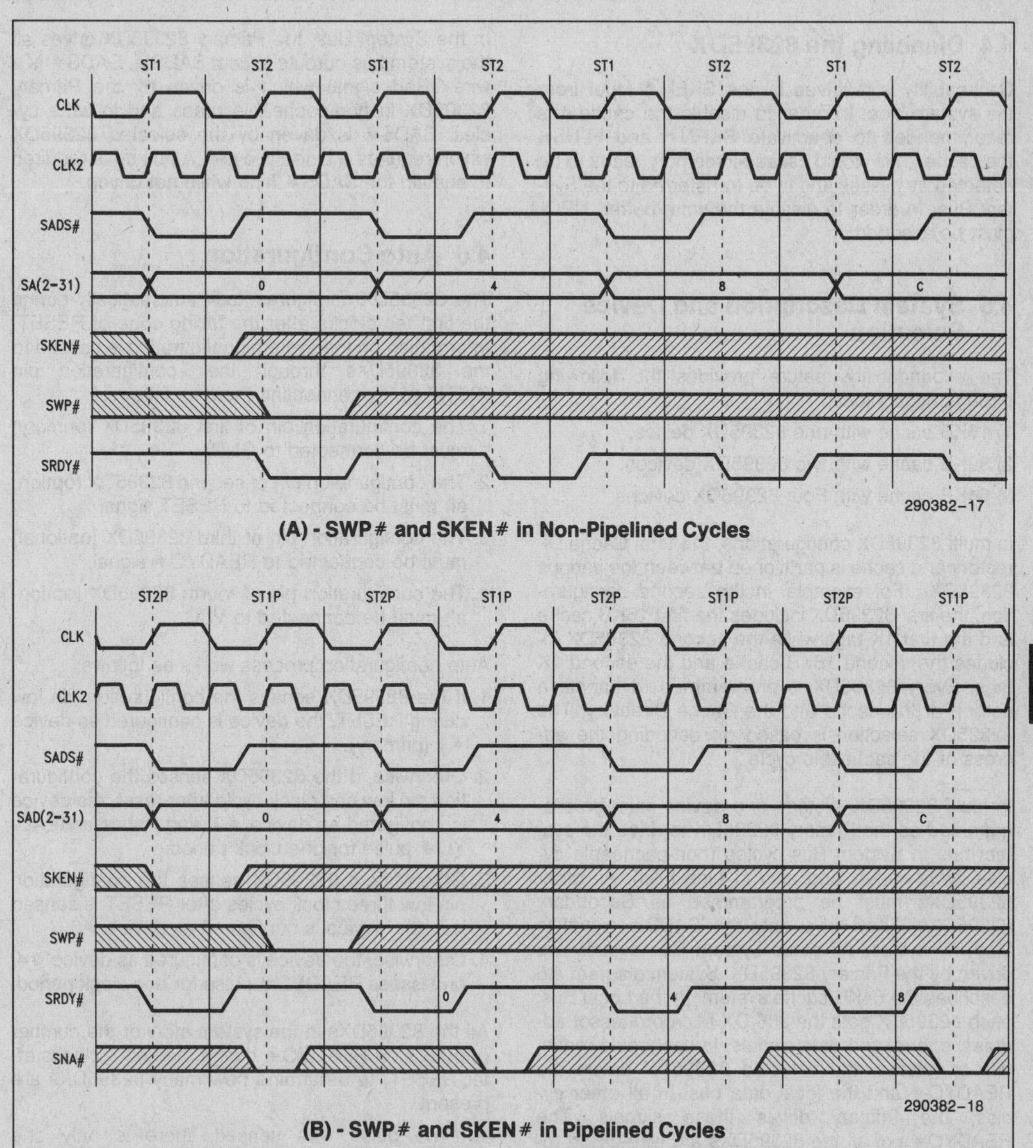

(A) - SWP# and SKEN# in Non-Pipelined Cycles

(B) - SWP# and SKEN# in Pipelined Cycles

Figure 4.4 - SWP# and SKEN# Timing

4.4 Disabling the 82395DX

Cacheability is resolved by the SKEN# input from the system side. In order to disable the cache it is recommended to deactivate SKEN# and FLUSH the cache. This would cause all memory reads to be detected as misses and to be transferred to the System Bus. In order to disable the write buffer, NPI# must be asserted.

4.5 System Description and Device Selection

The expandability feature provides the following three configurations:

1) 16KB cache with one 82395DX device.

2) 32KB cache with two 82395DX devices.

3) 64KB cache with Four 82395DX devices.

In multi 82395DX configurations, the total Cache Directory and cache is partitioned between the various 82395DXs. For example, in the second configuration, the first 82395DX includes the first 16KB cache and the first 1K tags while the second 82395DX includes the second 16KB cache and the second 1K tags. Every 82395DX is programmed to handle a portion of the cache and the Cache Directory. The 82395DX selection is based on decoding the address of the cacheable cycle.

In multi 82395DX system, one device must be programmed as the Primary 82395DX to drive the system bus in System Bus cycles (non-cacheable cycles, write cycles and also in Line Fills). All other 82395DXs must be programmed as Secondary 82395DXs. They drive only the SADS# signal in Line Fill cycles. All other System Bus signals are driven by the Primary 82395DX. System diagram 4.6 describes the 64KB cache system. In the Local Bus, each 82395DX gets the 386 DX Microprocessor address, control and data signals. In cacheable reads, hits or misses, the selected 82395DX drives the READYO# and the local data bus. In all other cycles, the Primary drives these signals. The READYO#s of all the 82395DXs are wire-ORed together and they can be logically ORed with the READYO#s of local bus devices. An External pull-up must exist on the 82395DX READYO# to sustain it high. The selected 82395DX drives the READYO# low and keeps it low while the READYI# is not sampled active. Immediately with sampling the READYI# active, the selected 82395DX drives the READYO# high for one phase and floats it in the next phase. Therefore, zero wait state cycles are supported.

In the System Bus, the Primary 82395DX drives all the system bus outputs except SADS#. SADS# is a wire-ORed signal which is driven by the Primary 82395DX in non-cacheable reads and in write cycles. SADS# is driven by the selected 82395DX which requires a Line Fill cycle. A pull-up is required to sustain the SADS# high while not driven.

4.6 Auto Configuration

The 82395DX configures itself automatically during the first ten clocks after the falling edge of RESET. Information on the system configuration is passed to the 82395DXs through their configuration pin (CONF#), by connecting them as follows:

1. The configuration pin of first 82395DX (primary) must be connected to GND.
2. The configuration pin of second 82395DX (optional) must be connected to RESET signal.
3. The configuration pin of third 82395DX (optional) must be connected to READYO# signal.
4. The configuration pin of fourth 82395DX (optional) must be connected to VCC.

Auto configuration process works as follows:

1. If the 82395DX senses the configuration pin low during RESET, the device is configured as device #1 (primary).
2. Otherwise, if the 82395DX senses the configuration pin low one clock cycle after reset, the device is configured as device #2, and issues a READYO# pulse for one clock period.
3. Otherwise, if 82395DX senses the configuration pin low three clock cycles after RESET is sensed low, the device is configured as device #3.
4. Otherwise, the device is configured as device #4, and issues READYO# pulse for one clock period.

All the 82395DXs in the system monitor the number of pulses on READYO# during the first 4 clocks after RESET, to determine how many 82395DXs are present.

1. If no pulse was sensed, there is only one 82395DX.
2. If one pulse is sensed, there are two 82395DXs in the system.
3. If two pulses were sensed, there are 4 82395DXs in the system.

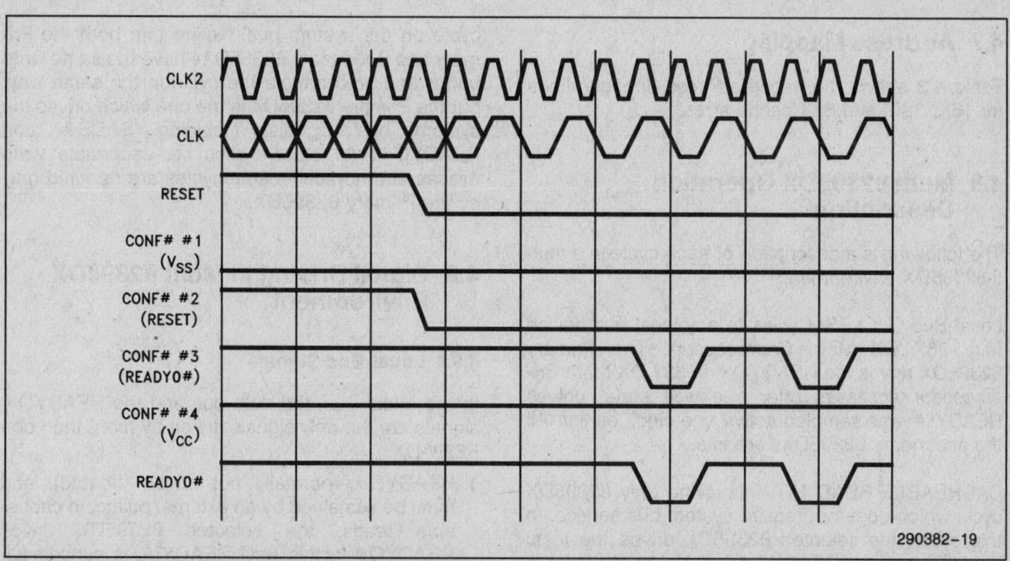

Figure 4.5 - Self Configuration of Four 82395DXs

4

4.7 Address Mapping

Table 4.2 shows the cache address configurations for 16K, 32K, and 64K cache sizes.

4.8 Multi 82395DX Operation Description

The following is a description of each cycle in a multi-82395DX environment:

Local Bus CYCLES: Cycles to any local bus device (e.g. 387 DX Math Coprocessor). The Primary 82395DX drives the READYO# in 387 DX Math Coprocessor accesses after one wait state, unless READYI# was sampled active one clock earlier. All the secondary 82395DXs are idle.

CACHEABLE READ HIT: this is the only 82395DX cycle which does not require system bus service. In this cycle, the selected 82395DX drives the local data bus and the READYO# in T2. Also, it updates its LRU bits.

CACHEABLE READ MISS: As soon as the system bus is available, the selected 82395DX, which detected the miss, drives the SADS#. In parallel, the Primary 82395DX drives the system bus address and control signals. After receiving the first SRDY# or SBRDY# and after sampling the SKEN# active, the selected 82395DX samples the system data and one clock later it provides it to the 386 DX Microprocessor and drives the READYO# active. Then, it continues in filling the line and, after collecting the four DWs, it updates its cache and Cache Directory.

CACHEABLE WRITE HITS: the selected 82395DX updates its cache, except for write protected cycles. The Primary 82395DX, however, executes the write cycle on the system bus. Notice that both the Primary and Secondary 82395DXs have the same write buffer and both handle the cycle in the same way, but the Primary 82395DX is the one which drives the system bus signals, including SADS# and READYO#. All other cycles i.e. cacheable write misses and non-cacheable cycles are handled only by the Primary 82395DX.

4.9 Signal Driving in Multi 82395DX Environment

4.9.1 Local Bus Signals

In the Local Bus, the data bus and the READYO# signals are the only signals driven by more than one 82395DX.

1. READYO#: normally not driven (floated), and must be sustained by an external pullup. In cacheable reads, the selected 82395DX drives READYO# active until READYI# is sensed active, than it drives READYO# inactive for one clock phase and then floats it. In other cycles, the primary 82395DX drives READYO# in the same manner.
2. Data Bus: The selected (or primary) 82395DX drives the data bus in the T2 state of read cycles, which ensures no contention with the 386 DX Microprocessor when a write cycle follows a read cycle.

4.9.2 SYSTEM BUS SIGNALS

In the System Bus, the Primary 82395DX drives all the System Bus signals except SADS#. So, the jeopardy of contention exists on the SADS# signal

Table 4.2 - Address Mapping for 1-4 82395DX Systems

Device No.	Total Devices in System	Address Decoding	Primary/ Secondary	Cache Data Mapping	Cache Directory SETs
1	1	—	P	0KB-16KB	0-255
1	2	A12#	P	0KB-16KB	0-255
2	2	A12	S	16KB-32KB	256-511
1	4	A13#*A12#	P	0KB-16KB	0-255
2	4	A13#*A12	S	16KB-32KB	256-511
3	4	A13 *A12#	S	32KB-48KB	512-767
4	4	A13 *A12	S	48KB-64KB	768-1023

only. SADS# is normally not driven (floated), and must be sustained by an external pullup. Every 82395DX, Primary or Secondary, after driving the SADS# active in ST1 or ST2P, will drive it inactive for one clock phase in ST2 or ST1P, and float it afterwards.

In Line Fills, the SADS# is driven by the selected 82395DX which detected the miss. In all other cycles e.g. write cycles, the SADS# is driven by the Primary 82395DX.

4.10 SHOLD/SHLDA/SBREQ Arbitration Mechanism

The Primary 82395DX is responsible for handling the SHOLD/SHLDA/SBREQ mechanism. Assuming that the SHOLD is acknowledged, the Primary 82395DX floats all its outputs immediately after completing the system bus cycle in which SHOLD was activated and it drives SHLDA active. This enables the bus master to get control of the bus. When the bus master completes its cycles, it drives the SHOLD signal inactive. Then the Primary 82395DX gets the bus back by driving the SHLDA inactive.

The Secondary 82395DXs get the SHOLD input in order to monitor the bus activity but they don't drive the SHLDA. Secondary 82395DXs do not drive the SADS# in Hold states. The Primary 82395DX drives the SBREQ signal in all System Bus cycles. In Line Fill cycles, the SBREQ signal is driven active one clock later than in other cycles. Of course, this is applicable for the case the System Bus is not available. If the System Bus is available, the SBREQ will not be driven in Line fill cycles. For more details about system arbitration, refer to Chapter 6.

4.11 System Description

A 386 DX Microprocessor/ 82395DX-based system includes the processor, optional Local bus devices (e.g. 387 DX Math Coprocessor), cache system (one 82395DX or more) and System Bus devices (memory, I/O devices and other non-cacheable devices). The 82395DX is the interface between the Local Bus and the System Bus.

A Local Bus address decoder must be used to generate LBA# and NPI# signals, and a System Bus address decoder must be used to generate SKEN# and SWP# signals.

The 82395DX READYO# may be logically ORed with READYO#s of other Local Bus devices. However, this is not required unless a Local Bus device,

Table 4.3 - Local Bus Signal Connections in Multi-82395DX Systems

Primary 82395DX Only		Each 82395DX in the System	
Signal	Type	Signal	Type
		CLK2	I
		D0-D31	I/O
		A2-A31	I
		RESET	I
		BE0-3#	I
		W/R#	I
		D/C#	I
		M/IO#	I
		LOCK#	I
		ADS#	I
		READYI#	I
		LBA#	I
		NPI#	I
		FLUSH#	I
		A20M#	I
		CONF#	I
		READYO#	I/O

other than 387 DX Math Coprocessor, exists on the local bus (82395DX generates a READY signal for the 387 DX Math Coprocessor). The 386 DX Microprocessor READY# input signal must also be driven to the 82395DX READYI# pin, so that the 82395DX will be able to track the Local Bus cycles correctly.

To allow for expanding the cache system beyond 16KB, up to four 82395DX devices may be connected in parallel. Two 82395DX outputs are Wire-ORed between the parallel 82395DXs: READYO# and SADS#. Each of the 82395DXs' CONF# input must be tied to a different signal, to program each one of them to a distinct address decoding.

Figure 4.6 describes a maximum 386 DX Microprocessor/82395DX system, with 387 DX Math Coprocessor, four 82395DX devices, READY# generation logic and Local Bus/System Bus address decoders.

Note that optional elements in Figure 4.6 are drawn with dotted line. The Local Bus includes CLK2, RESET, BE3#-BE0#, A2-A31, D0-D31, W/R#, D/C#, M/IO#, LOCK# and ADS#. The System Bus can be broken into two groups. Those pins connected only to the primary 82395DX (82395DX #1) and those connected to each 82395DX in the system (82395DX #1-#4). See Table 4.4.

4

Table 4.4 - System Bus Signal Connections in Multi-82395DX Systems

Primary 82395DX Only		Each 82395DX in the System	
Signal	**Type**	**Signal**	**Type**
SA2–3	O	SD0–31	I/O
SW/R#	O	SA4–31*	I/O
SD/C#	O	SADS#	O
SM/IO#	O	SRDY#	I
SLOCK#	O	SBRDY#	I
SBREQ	O	SNA#	I
SHLDA	O	SHOLD	I
SBLAST#	O	SAHOLD	I
SNENE#	O	SEADS#	I
		SFHOLD#	I
		SKEN#	I
		SWP#	I

*SA4–31 are connected to each 82395DX in the system for snooping purposes but are driven only by the primary 82395DX.

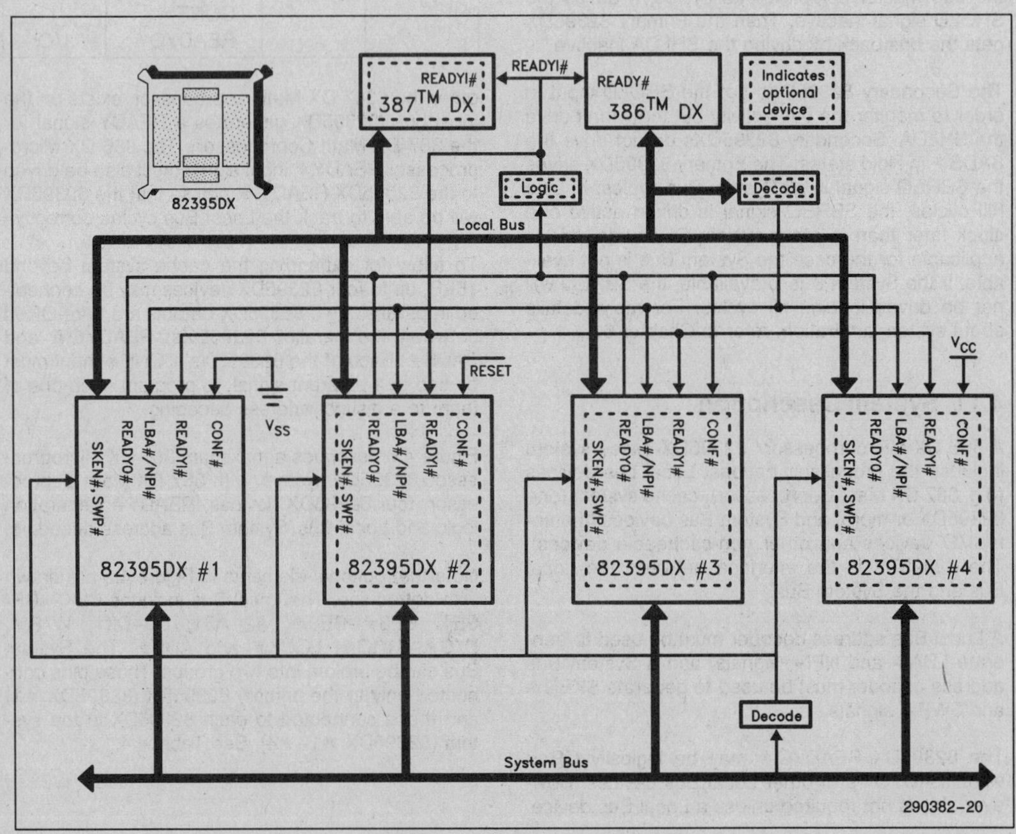

Figure 4.6 - System Description

5.0 PROCESSOR INTERFACE

The 82395DX runs synchronously with the 386 DX Microprocessor. It is a slave on the Local Bus, and it buffers between the Local Bus and the System Bus. Most of the 82395DX cycles are serviced from the internal cache, and some (82395DX cache misses, non cacheable accesses, etc.) require an access to the System Bus to complete the transaction.

To achieve maximum performance, the 82395DX serves cache hits and buffered write cycles in zero wait- state, non-pipelined cycles. The 82395DX requires that the CPU is never driven to pipelined cycles, i.e. the 386 DX Microprocessor NA# input must be strapped to inactive (high) state.

The 82395DX is directly connected to all local bus address and data lines, byte enable lines, and bus cycle definition signals. The 82395DX returns READYO# to the 386 DX Microprocessor, and keeps track of the 386 DX Microprocessor cycle status by receiving READYI# (which is the 386 DX Microprocessor READY#).

A multi 82395DX system description was presented in chapter 4.

5.1 Hardware Interface

The 82395DX requires minimal hardware on the Local Bus. Other than the 386 DX Microprocessor and other Local Bus resources (i.e. 387 DX Math Coprocessor) and the 82395DX(s) (1-4 depending on the system). Ready logic and a Local Bus decoder are optional since the user can wire OR the READYO#s and tie LBA# and NPI# high if no addresses are to be local or non-buffered. The SRAM and buffers have been integrated on chip to simplify the design. Refer to Figure 4.6.

5.2 Nonpipelined Local Bus

The 82395DX does not pipeline the Local Bus. READYO# gets returned to the 386 DX Microprocessor one cycle after SRDY# or SBRDY# are driven into the 82395DX after the first DW of a Line Fill. This allows the Local Bus to be free to execute 386 DX Microprocessor cycles while the System Bus fills the cache line (see chapter 6).This takes away the advantage gained by pipelining the Local Bus.

5.3 Local Bus Response Hit Cycles

The 82395DX's Local Bus response to hit cycles are described here:

1) Cache Read Hit (CRDH) Cycle — READYO# gets returned in T2. The Data is valid to the 386 DX Microprocessor on the rising edge of CLK2.

2) Cache Write Hit (CWTH), Buffered — Like in CRDH cycles the 82395DX returns READYO# in T2 so that the cycle runs with zero wait states on the Local Bus. The write cycle is placed in the write buffer and will be performed when the System Bus is available. If the System Bus is on HOLD up to four write cycles can be buffered before introducing any wait states on the Local Bus.

3) CWTH, Non-Buffered — In the case of a non-buffered write hit cycle the write buffers can not be used so the 386 DX Microprocessor must wait until the System Bus is free to do the write. READYO# is returned to the cycle after SRDY# is driven to the 82395DX.

5.4 Local Bus Response to Miss Cycles

In a Cache Read Miss (CRDM) cycle a Line Fill is performed on the System Bus. READYO# is returned to the 386 DX Microprocessor one cycle after SRDY# or SBRDY# for the first DW of the Line Fill is driven into the 82395DX.

5.5 Local Bus Control Signals — ADS#, READYI#

ADS# and READYI# are the two bus control inputs used by the 82395DX to determine the status of the Local Bus cycle. ADS# denotes the beginning of a 386 DX Microprocessor cycle and READYI# is the 386 DX Microprocessor cycle terminator.

ADS# active and M/IO# = 1 invokes a look-up request to the 82395DX's cache directory; the look-up is performed in T1 state. The Cache Directory access is simultaneous with all other cycle qualification activities, this Way the hit/miss decision becomes the last in the cycle qualification process. This parallelism enhances performance, and enables the 82395DX to respond to ADS# within one clock period. If the cycle is to a Local Bus device (LBA# asserted) or is non-cacheable, the hit/miss decision is ignored.

5.6 82395's Response to the 386 DX Microprocessor Cycles

Tables 5.2 - 5.4 show the 82395DX's response to the various 386 DX Microprocessor cycles. They depict the activity in the internal cache, cache directory, the System Bus and write buffers in response to various cycle definition signals. Special cycles such as: LOCK, HALT/SHUTDOWN, WP, LBA, NPI are discussed separately below.

5.6.1 LOCKED CYCLES

The 386 DX Microprocessor LOCK#ed cycles are all those cycles in which LOCK# is active. The 82395DX forces all LOCK#ed cycles to run on the System Bus. The 82395DX starts the LOCK#ed cycle after it has emptied its write buffers.

If the LOCK#ed cycle is cacheable the 82395DX will respond as follows (see table 5.2):

Cache Read Miss (CRDM) — handled similar to a non cacheable cycle.

Cache Read Hit (CRDH) — handled similar to a non cacheable cycle (LRU bits are not updated).

Cache Write Miss (CWTM) — the cache is not updated, the write is not buffered.

Cache Write Hit (CWTH) — the cache is updated if the line is not write protected. The write is not buffered. Note that this write is not buffered even though it is cacheable. The LRU mechanism is updated.

If the LOCK#ed cycle is non-cacheable (e.g. IO cycle, INTA cycle) then it will be performed as a common non-cacheable cycle with the addition of asserting SLOCK# on the System Bus.

Conceptually, a LOCK# cycle on the Local Bus is reflected into an SLOCK# cycle on the System Bus. Detailed timing considerations were presented in chapter 3. SLOCK# becomes inactive only after LOCK# has become inactive. If there are idle clocks in between the LOCK#ed cycles but LOCK# is still active - SLOCK# will remain active as well. **A consequence of this is that SLOCK# is negated one clock after LOCK# is negated.**

During LOCK#ed cycles on System Bus (i.e. when SLOCK# signal is active), the 82395DX does not acknowledge hold requests so the whole sequence of LOCK#ed cycles will run without interruption by another master.

Note that when a LOCK#ed LBA# cycle runs on the Local Bus, and the System Bus is idle and not at HLDA state, SLOCK# will be asserted even though the LBA# cycle will not be transferred to the system bus.

5.6.2 I/O, HALT/SHUTDOWN

I/O and HALT/SHUTDOWN cycles are handled as non-cacheable cycles. They are neither cached nor kept in the write buffer. The 386 DX Microprocessor HALT/SHUTDOWN cycles are memory write cycles to code area (i.e. M/IO# = 1, D/C# = 0). The 82395DX completes I/O and HALT/ SHUTDOWN cycles by returning READYO#, after receiving the SRDY#.

5.6.3 LBA# CYCLES

LBA# cycles are all the 386 DX Microprocessor cycles in which LBA# is active, or all cycles in which the 387 DX Math Coprocessor or Weitek 3167 Floating-Point Coprocessor is addressed. A CPU access to I/O space with A31 = 1 is decoded as a 387 DX Math Coprocessor access. A CPU access to memory space C0000000H through C1FFFFFFH is decoded as a Weitek 3167 Floating-Point Coprocessor access, provided that the Weitek decoding is enabled.

When an LBA# cycle is detected all other attributes are ignored. If a 387 DX Math Coprocessor access is decoded, READYO# is activated as described in section 5.6. No other activity takes place.

5.6.4 NPI# CYCLES

NPI# cycles are all the 386 DX Microprocessor memory write cycles in which NPI# is active. In response to a cycle with NPI# active, the 82395DX first executes all pending write cycles in the write buffer (if any), and then executes the current write cycle on the System Bus. READYO# is returned to the CPU only after SRDY# for the current write cycle is returned to the 82395DX.

All NPI# cycles must have at least one wait state on the System Bus or be done to non-cacheable memory.

NPI# is ignored for read cycles, as well as all write cycles that cannot be buffered.

5.6.5 LBA#/NPI# TIMING

These inputs must be valid throughout the 386 DX Microprocessor bus cycle, namely in T1 and all T2 states (See Figure 5.1).

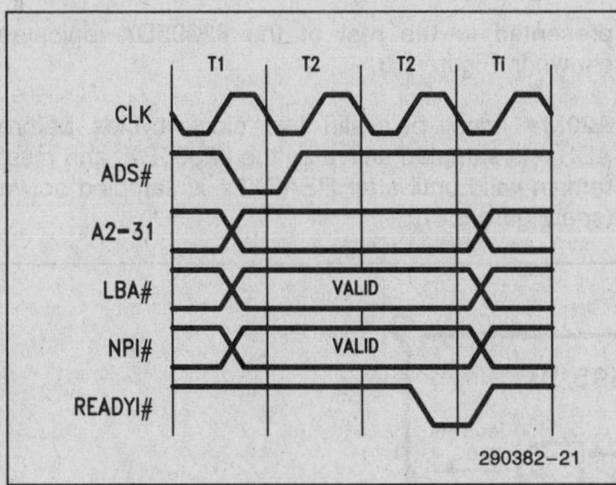

Figure 5.1 - Valid Time of LBA# and NPI#

5.7 82395DX READYO# Generation

The 82395DX READYO# generation rules are listed below:

CRDH cycles (non-LOCK#ed), READYO# is activated during the first T2 state, so the cycle runs with zero wait states.

CRDM cycles - READYO# is returned one clock after the first SRDY# or SBRDY#.

Non cacheable reads - READYO# is returned one clock after SRDY# or SBRDY#.

All cacheable writes (with the exception of LOCK#ed writes) are buffered. These cycles may be divided into two categories:

(a) The first four write cycles — while the write buffer is not fully exploited. READYO# is returned in zero wait states. The address and the data are registered in the write buffer.

(b) When the write buffer is full — READYO# is delayed until one clock after the SRDY# or SBRDY# of the first write cycle in the buffer. In other words the fifth write waits until there is one vacant entry in the write buffer.

Non cacheable writes (plus LOCK#ed writes) — these writes are not buffered. READYO# is returned one clock after SRDY# or SBRDY# of the same cycle.

READYO# activation during SRAM mode is described in Chapter 7. READYO# activation during self configuration is listed in Chapter 4.

In all 387 DX Math Coprocessor accesses, the 82395DX monitors the READYI#. If it wasn't activated immediately after ADS#, READYO# will be activated in the next clock i.e. a one wait state cycle. So, the 82395DX READYO# can be used to terminate any 387 DX Math Coprocessor access.

Note that the timing of the 82395's READYO# generation for 387 DX Math Coprocessor cycles is incompatible with 80287 timing. When activated, READYO# remains active until READYI# is sampled active. This procedure enables adding control logic to control the 386 DX Microprocessor READYI# generation (see Figure 5.2).

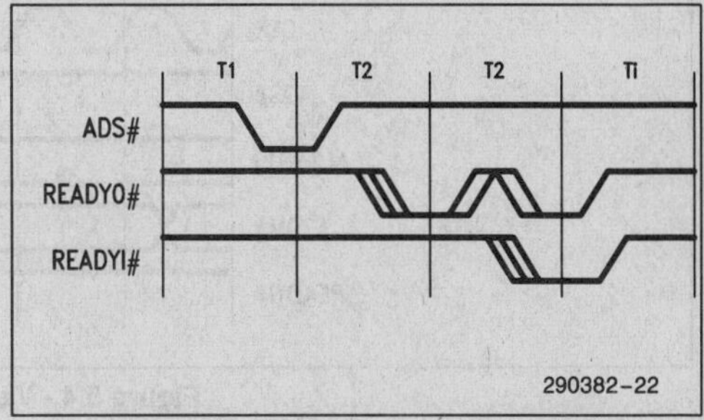

Figure 5.2 - Externally Delayed READY

In a multi-82395DX system, each device on the Local Bus must be able to return READYO#. Therefore, READYO# is wired OR on the Local Bus. READYO# is normally floated, and it is connected to the positive power supply by a pull-up resistor. An external OR gate ORs the 82395DXs' READYO#s with the READYO# of all other Local Bus devices.

5.8 A20 Mask Signal

The A20M# signal is provided to allow for emulation of the address wraparound at 1 MByte which occurs on the 8086. A20M# pin is synchronized internally by the 82395DX, then ANDed with the A20 input pin. The product of synchronized A20M# and A20 is presented to the rest of the 82395DX logic, as shown in Figure 5.3.

A20M# must be valid two clock cycles before ADS# is sampled active by the 82395DX, and must remain valid until after READYI# is sampled active (see Figure 5.4).

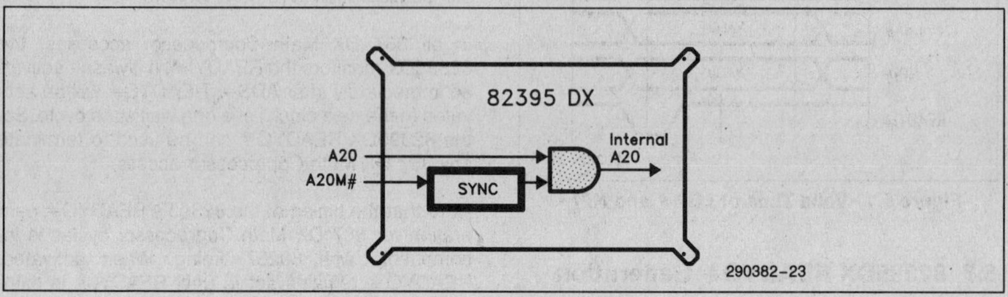

Figure 5.3 - A20 Mask Logic

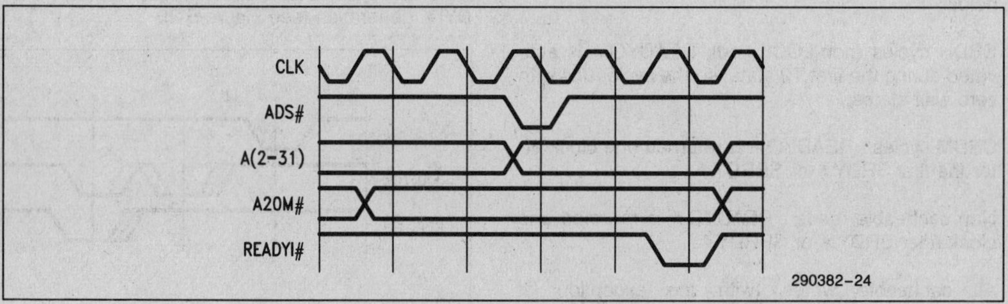

Figure 5.4 - Valid Time of A20M#

5.9 82395DX Cycle Overview

Table 5.1 - 386 DX Microprocessor Bus Cycle Definition

M/IO#	D/C#	W/R#	386 DX Microprocessor Cycle Definition
0	0	0	Interrupt Acknowledge
0	0	1	Undefined
0	1	0	I/O Read
0	1	1	I/O Write
1	0	0	Memory Code Read
1	0	1	Halt/Shutdown
1	1	0	Memory Data Read
1	1	1	Memory Data Write

Table 5.2 describes the activity in the cache, in the Tagram, on the System Bus and in the write buffers. The cycles are defined in table 5.1. Table 5.2 is sorted in a descending order. The more dominant the attribute the higher it is located. For example, if the cycle is both LBA# and I/O it is considered an LBA# cycle. Table 5.2 is for non test modes.

Table 5.2 - Activity by Functional Groupings

Cycle Type	WP	Cache	TAGRAM		System Bus	Posted Write	Comm.
			LRU	TAG			
1. LBA & 387/Weitek Cycles	N/A	—	—	—	—	N/A	
2. I/O Write, I/O Read, Halt/Shutdown, INTA, LOCK#ed Read	N/A	—	—	—	Non Cacheable Cycle	No	2
3. LOCK#ed Write Hit	Yes		Update	—	Memory Write	No	2
4. LOCK#ed Write Hit	No	Cache Write	Update	—	Memory Write	No	2
5. LOCK#ed Write Miss	N/A	—	—	—	Memory Write	No	2
6. Other Read Hit	N/A	Cache Read	Update	—	—	N/A	1
7. Other Read Miss SKEN# Active	N/A	Cache Write	Update	Update	Line Fill	N/A	2
8. Other Read Miss SKEN# Inactive	N/A	—	—	—	Noncacheable Read No Line Fill	N/A	2
9. Other Write Hit NPI# Inactive	Yes	—	Update	—	Memory Write	Yes	1
10. Other Write Hit NPI# Active	Yes	—	Update	—	Memory Write	No	2
11. Other Write Hit NPI# Inactive	No	Cache Write	Update	—	Memory Write	Yes	1
12. Other Write Hit NPI# Active	No	Cache Write	Update	—	Memory Write	No	2
13. Other Write Miss NPI# Inactive	N/A	—	—	—	Memory Write	Yes	1
14. Other Write Miss NPI# Active	N/A	—	—	—	Memory Write	No	2

4

Table 5.3 describes line buffer hit cycles. Hit/miss here means to the specific DW in the line buffer.

Table 5.3. Activity in Line Buffer Hit Cycles

Cycle Type	WP	Cache	TAGRAM		System Bus	Posted Write	Comm.
			LRU	TAG			
15. LOCK#ed Write	Yes	—	—	—	Memory Write	No	2
16. LOCK#ed Write	No	Cache Write	—	—	Memory Write	No	4
17. Read Hit	N/A	LB Read	—	—	—	N/A	1
18. Read Miss	N/A	LB Read	—	—	—	N/A	3
19. Other Write NPI# Inactive	Yes	—	—	—	Memory Write	Yes	6
20. Other Write NPI# Active	Yes	—	—	—	Memory Write	No	2
21. Other Write NPI# Inactive	No	Cache Write	—	—	Memory Write	Yes	5
22. Other Write NPI# Inactive	No	Cache Write	—	—	Memory Write	No	4

Table 5.4 describes the line buffer hit cycles, when the Line Fill is interrupted (by: FLUSH#, snoop hit to the line buffer or interrupted burst, even if the Line Fill continues on the System Bus in the first two cases). The table includes only the cycles which wait to the end of the Line Fill or to the CPU cache update. Hit/Miss here means to the right DW in the line buffer.

Table 5.4. Activity in the Line Buffer During ALF Cycles

Cycle Type	WP	Cache	TAGRAM		System Bus	Posted Write	Comm.
			LRU	TAG			
23. LOCK#ed Write	N/A	—	—	—	Memory Write	No	2
24. Read Miss (Restart)	N/A	Cache Write	Update	Replace	Line Fill	N/A	2
25. Other Write NPI# Inactive	N/A	—	—	—	Memory Write	Yes	5
26. Other Write NPI# Active	N/A	—	—	—	Memory Write	No	2

Table 5.5 depicts the 82395DX Test Cycles.

Table 5.5. Activity in Test Cycles

Cycle Type	WP	A16	Cache	TAGRAM		System Bus	Posted Write	Comm.
				LRU	TAG			
27. High Impedance	N/A	N/A	—	—	—	—	N/A	
28. SRAM Mode Read Add 256K-512K	N/A	0	—	LRU RD	TAG RD	—	N/A	
29. SRAM Mode Read Add 256K-512K	N/A	1	Cache	—	—	—	N/A	
30. SRAM Mode Write Add 256K-512K	N/A	0	—	LRU WR	TAG WR	—	N/A	
31. SRAM Mode Write Add 256K-512K	N/A	1	Cache Write	—	—	—	N/A	
32. SRAM Mode Read Add <>256K-512K	N/A	N/A	—	—	—	Noncacheable Cycle	No	2
33. SRAM Mode Write Add <>256K-512K	N/A	N/A	—	—	—	Noncacheable Cycle	N/A	

Remarks for Tables 5-2 through 5-5:

1. READYO# is active in the first T2. (In read cycles, in write it depends if the write buffer is full).
2. READYO# is active one clock cycle after SRDY#/SBRDY# of this cycle is asserted. In case of Line Fill, READYO# is active one clock cycle after first SRDY#/SBRDY# of this cycle is asserted.
3. READYO# is active immediately after the current line fill is finished.
4. READYO# is active after the previous line fill and the write cycle are terminated by SRDY# or SBRDY#, and the cache is updated.
5. READYO# is active after the cache is updated for the previous Line Fill, or after the Line Fill is aborted.
6. READYO# is active on the third T2 (2 wait states) if the write buffer is not full.
7. "OTHER" means the cycle does not fall within the first five categories.

6.0 SYSTEM BUS INTERFACE

The System Bus (SB) interface is similar to the 386 DX Microprocessor interface. It runs synchronously to the 386 DX Microprocessor clock. In general, the interface is similar to the 82385 in terms of: System Bus pipelining, snooping support and write cycle buffering. In addition, the following enhancements are provided:

1) Line Fill buffer.

2) Optional burst Line Fill.

3) System cacheability attribute, SKEN#.

4) System Write Protection attribute, SWP#.

5) The SBREQ/SHOLD/SHLDA arbitration mechanism to support multi master systems.

6) The SEADS# snooping mechanism to support concurrency on the System Bus and on the general purpose bus.

7) SFHOLD# mechanism to resolve deadlocks in multiprocessing systems.

8) Four Double-Word write buffer (16 bytes).

9) SNENE# (System NExt NEar) function to simplify the design of page mode DRAM system, and save wait states.

The 82395DX System Bus interface has identical bus signals to the 386 DX Microprocessor bus. It has the bus control signals (SADS#, SRDY# and SNA#), the cycle definition signals (SLOCK#, SW/R#, SD/C# and SM/IO#), the address and byte enable signals (SA2–SA31 and SBE0#–SBE3#) and the data signals (SD0–SD31). In addition, the 82395DX has the SBRDY# signal for burst support. The SKEN# signal for the system cacheability attribute. The SWP# signal for the system Write Protection attribute. The SAHOLD and SEADS# signals for snooping support. The SBREQ, SHOLD and SHLDA signals for system arbitration. And SNENE# for DRAM hook-up. Also, the 82395DX provides a signal, SBLAST#, which when asserted, indicates that the current cycle is the last cycle in a burst transfer.

4

The 82395DX System Bus interface can support any device, non cacheable, I/O or cacheable memory with any number of wait states. However, zero wait state non-posted writes are not allowed. The 82395DX is able to support one clock burst cycles. The 82395's System Bus state machine is similar to the 386 DX Microprocessor bus state machine (refer to the "386 DX Microprocessor data sheet"). Note that during burst Line Fill, the 82395DX remains is ST2 state until SRDY# or SBRDY# is asserted for the fourth cycle of the burst transfer. Figure 6.1 describes the 82395's System Bus state machine.

RDY = SRDY# + SBRDY#

Request Pending = A cycle pending execution on the System Bus and SAHOLD inactive

290382-25

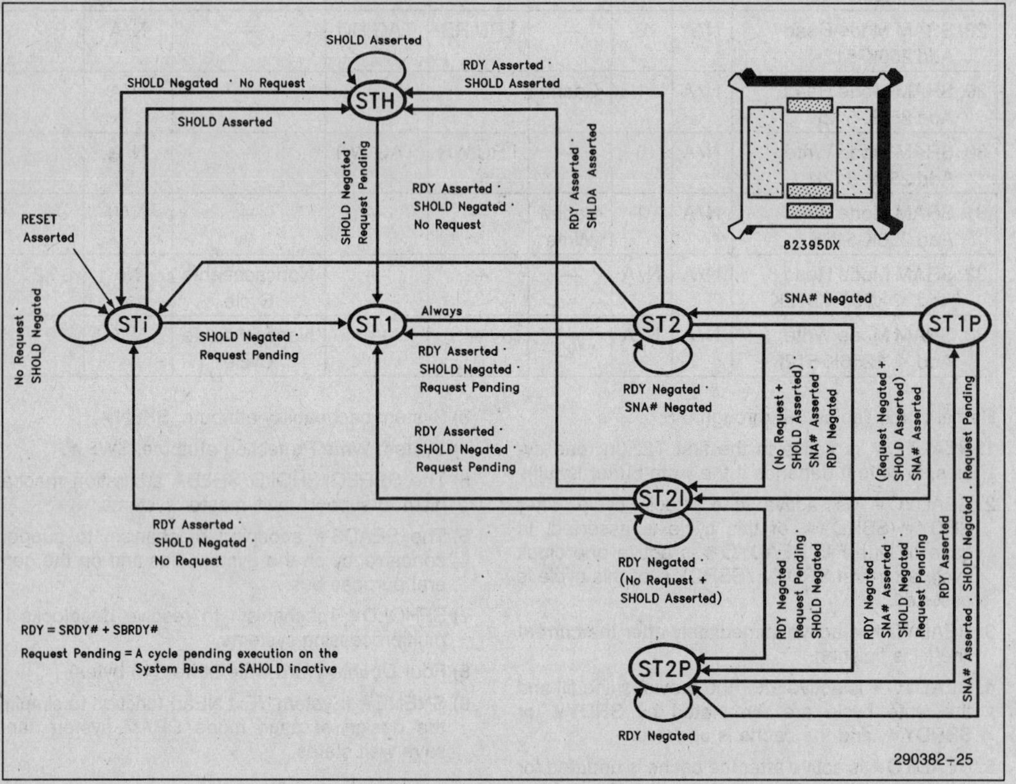

Figure 6.1 - SB State Machine

6.1 System Bus Cycle Types

Following five types of SB cycles are supported:

1) Buffered write cycle
2) Non buffered write cycle
3) Buffered/non-buffered write protected cycles.
4) Non cacheable read cycle
5) Cacheable read cycle

6.1.1 BUFFERED WRITE CYCLE

All the cacheable write cycles, except LOCK#ed write cycles or non-buffered write cycles (as indicated by NPI# pin sampled active), are buffered. These cycles are terminated on the Local Bus before they are terminated on the System Bus.

The following Figures (6.2 - 6.3) include waveforms of several cases of buffered write cycles:

The 82395DX has a four DW deep write buffer but five writes cycles can be buffered if one of the buffered writes is being executed.

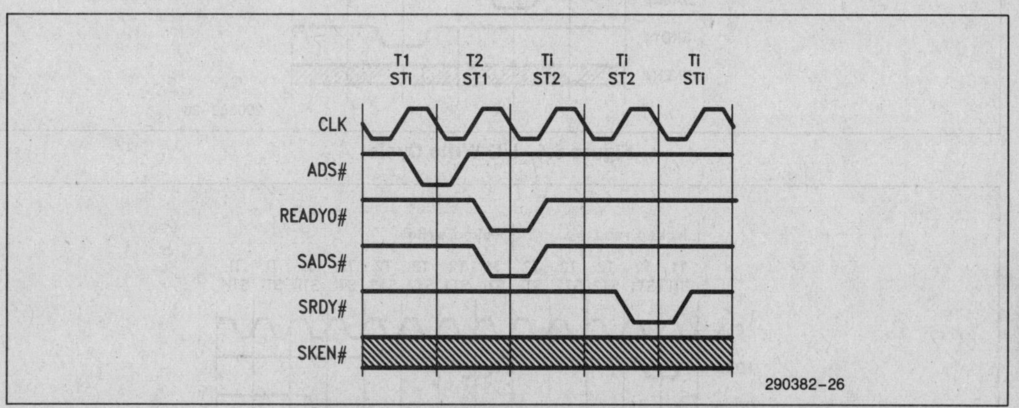

Figure 6.2 - Single Buffered Write Cycle

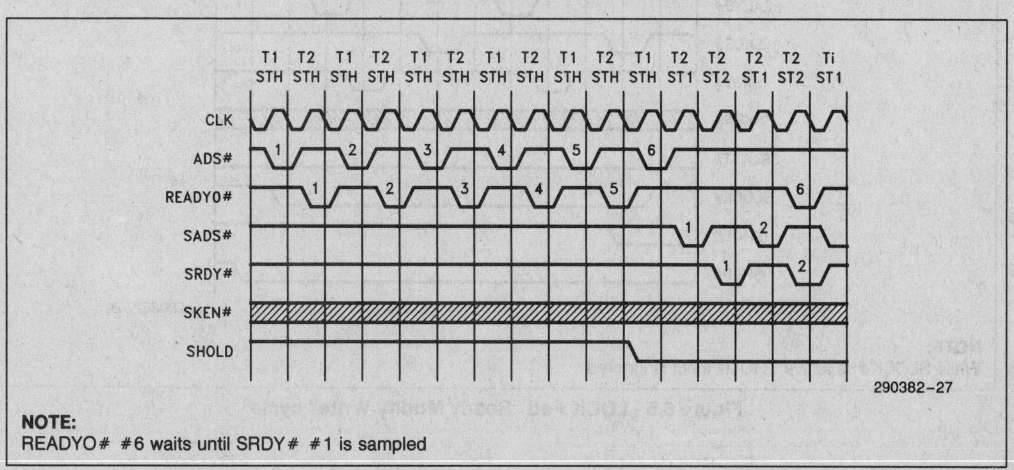

NOTE:
READYO# #6 waits until SRDY# #1 is sampled

Figure 6.3 - Multiple Buffered Write Cycles During System Bus HOLD

4

6.1.2 NON-BUFFERED WRITE CYCLE

These cycles are terminated on the System Bus one clock before they are terminated on the Local Bus.

The following Figures (6.4 - 6.5) include waveforms of several cases of non buffered write cycles.

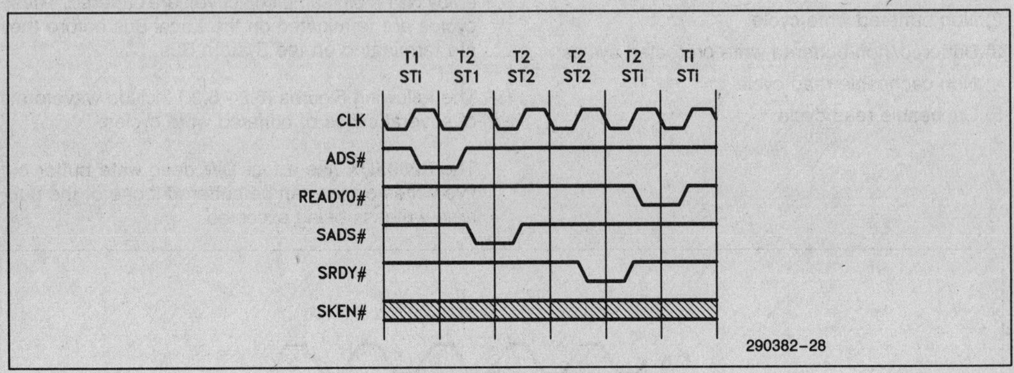

Figure 6.4 - I/O Write Cycle

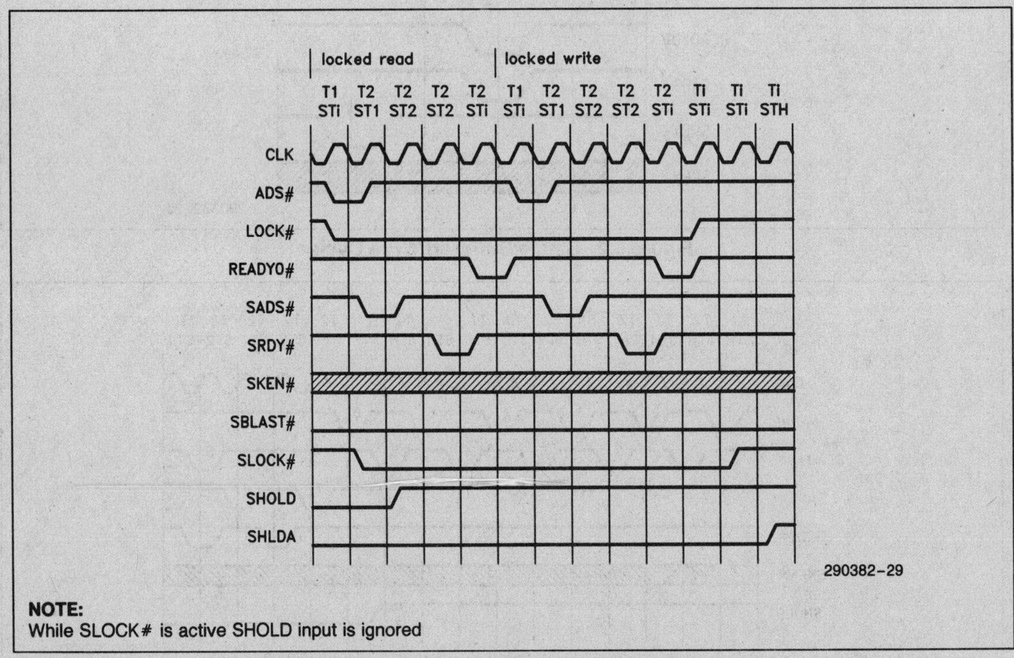

NOTE:
While SLOCK# is active SHOLD input is ignored

Figure 6.5 - LOCK#ed "Ready Modify Write" cycle

6.1.3 WRITE PROTECTED CYCLES

The Write Protection attribute is provided by the system bus SWP# input. The SWP# is sampled with the first SRDY# or SBRDY# in every Line Fill cycle. The write protection indicator is registered in the Cache Directory together with the TAG address and TAG Valid bit of every line. In every cacheable write cycle, the write protection indicator is read simultaneously with the Hit/Miss decision. If the write cycle is a hit and the write protection indicator is set, the cache will not be updated. In all other cases, the write protection indicator is ignored.

6.1.4 NON-CACHEABLE READ CYCLE

Non cacheable read cycles are terminated on the System Bus one clock before they are terminated on the Local Bus.

The following Figures (6.6 - 6.7) include waveforms of several cases of non cacheable read cycles.

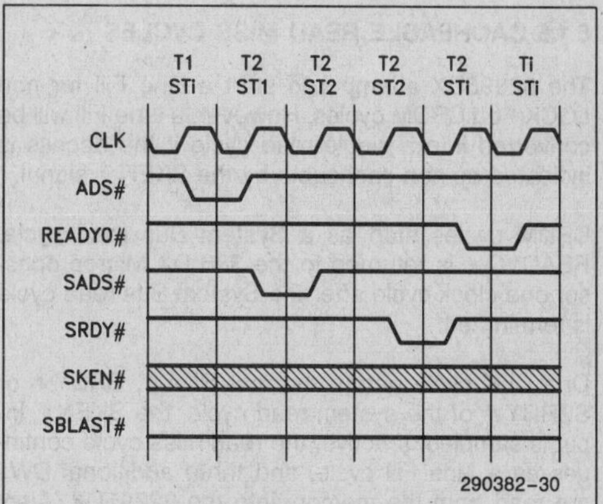

Figure 6.6 - I/O Read Cycle

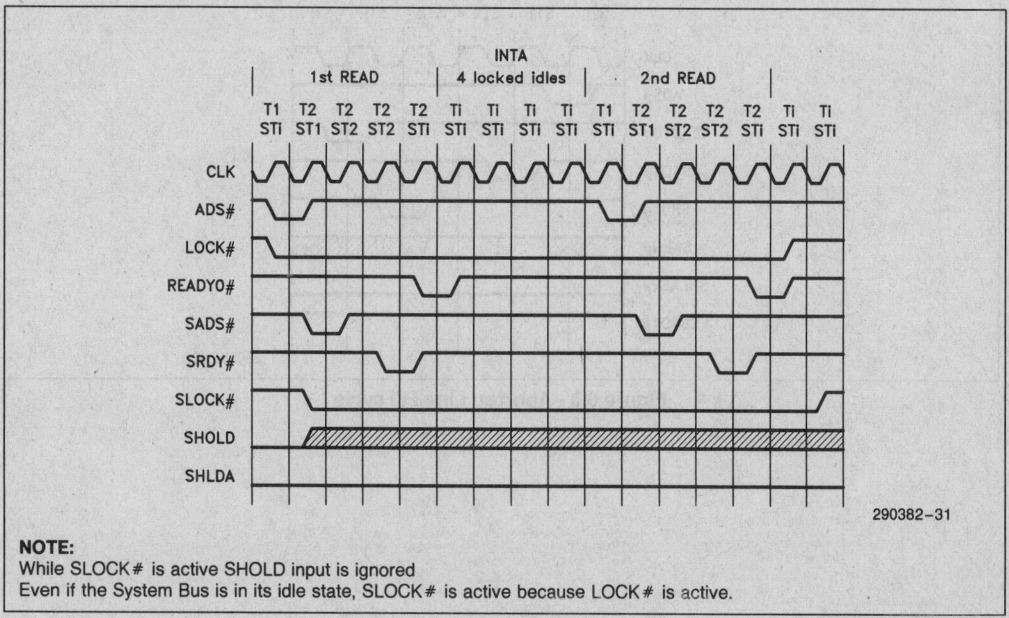

NOTE:
While SLOCK# is active SHOLD input is ignored
Even if the System Bus is in its idle state, SLOCK# is active because LOCK# is active.

Figure 6.7 - INTA LOCK#ed Cycle

6.1.5 CACHEABLE READ MISS CYCLES

The 82395DX attempts to start a Line Fill for non LOCK#ed CRDM cycles. However, a Line Fill will be converted into a single read cycle if the access is indicated as non-cacheable by the SKEN# signal.

CRDM cycles start as a System Bus read cycle. READYO# is returned to the 386 DX Microprocessor one clock cycle after the System Bus read cycle is terminated.

One CLK cycle before the first SNA#, SRDY# or SBRDY# of the system read cycle, the SKEN# input is sampled. If active, the read miss cycle continues as a Line Fill cycle, and three additional DWs are read from the memory into the 82395DX. Also, the SWP# input will be sampled with the first SNA#, SRDY# or SBRDY# so the WP flag of the line will be updated in the Cache Directory.

6.1.5.1 Aborted Line Fill (ALF) Cycles

The System Bus can respond that the area of memory included in a particular request is non-cacheable, by returning SKEN# inactive. As soon as the 82395DX samples SKEN# inactive, it converts the cycle from a cache Line Fill, which requires additional read cycles to be completed, to a single cycle.

In this case SBLAST# will stay active. Also, the 82395DX will not generate another system cycle for the same Line Fill, because the cycle has already been finished by the first SBRDY# or SRDY# after SKEN# was sampled inactive.

The following Figure 6.8 includes waveforms of an ALF cycle.

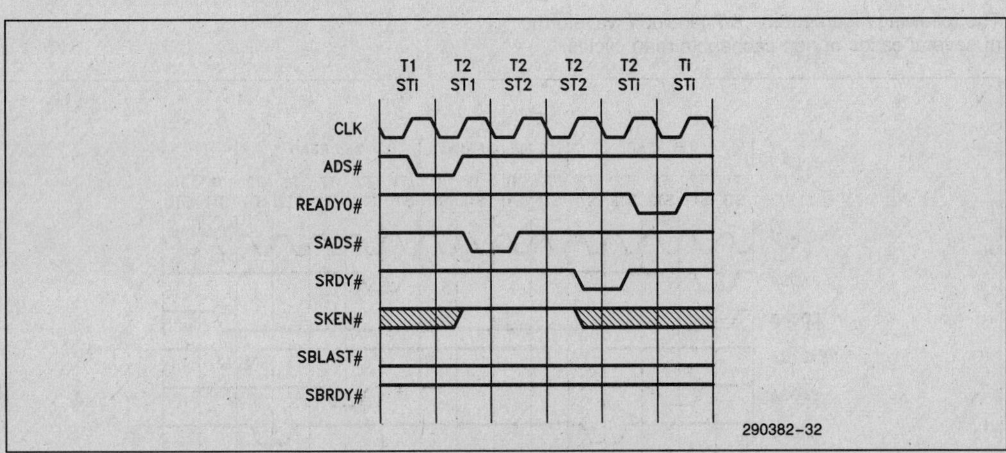

Figure 6.8 - Aborted Line Fill cycle

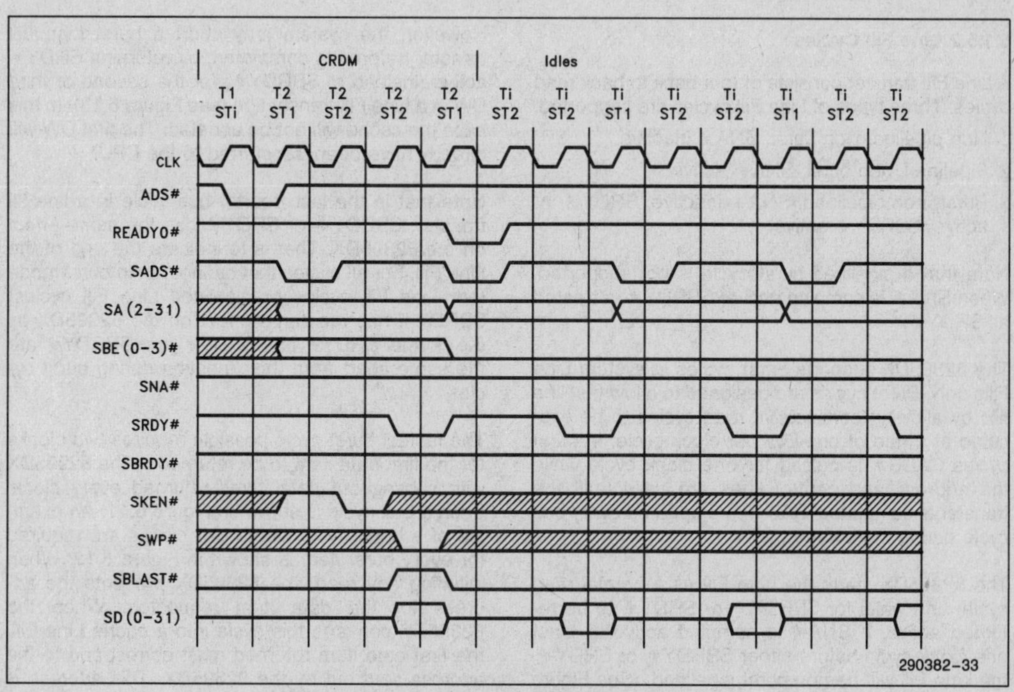

Figure 6.9 - Line Fill Without Burst or Pipeline

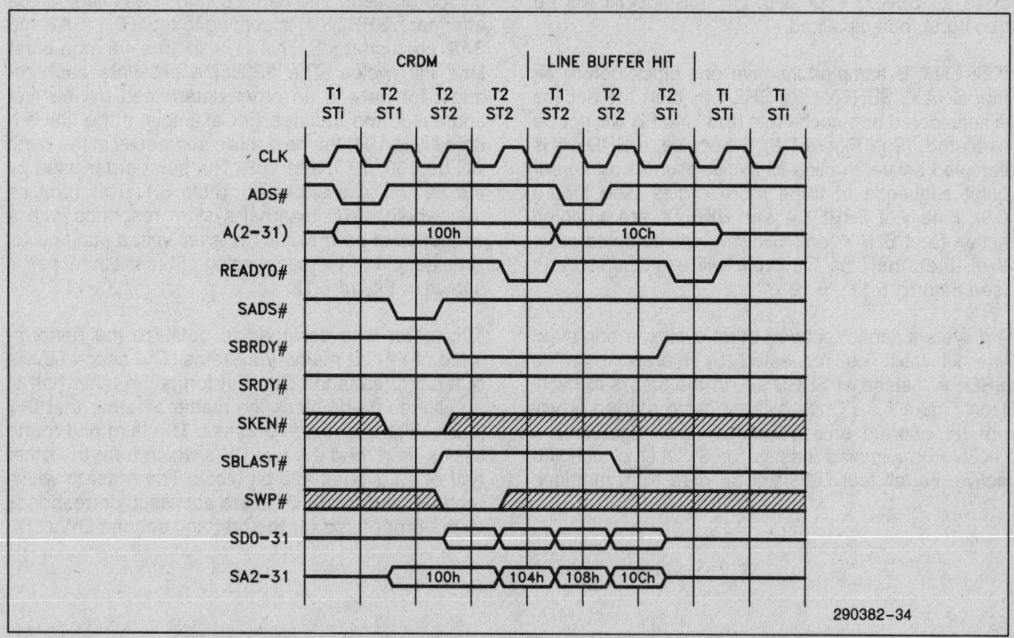

Figure 6.9A - Burst Mode Line Fill followed by a Line Buffer Hit Cycle

4

6.1.5.2 Line Fill Cycles

A Line Fill transfer consists of four back to back read cycles. Three types of Line Fill cycles are supported:

1. Non pipeline, Non burst, SNA# inactive.
2. Pipelined, non burst, SNA# active.
3. Burst, non pipelined, SNA# inactive, SRDY# inactive, SBRDY# active.

Note that a pipelined burst cycle is not supported. When SNA# is sampled active, SBRDY# is treated as SRDY#.

The 82395DX supports burst cycles in system Line Fills only. Burst cycles are designed to allow fast line fills by allowing consecutive read cycles to be executed at a rate of one DW per clock cycle. In burst cycles SADS# is pulsed for one clock cycle while the address and control lines are valid until the transfer is completed. SA2–3 are updated every bus cycle during the burst transfer.

The 82395DX starts the Line Fill as a normal read cycle, and waits for SBRDY# or SRDY# to be returned active. If SNA# is sampled active at least one clock cycle before either SBRDY# or SRDY#, the Line Fill will be non burst pipelined. (See Figure 6.10). If SNA# is sampled active at the same clock cycle as SBRDY# or SRDY#, the line fill will be non-burst, non-pipelined.

If SKEN# is sampled inactive one clock before either SNA#, SBRDY# or SRDY#, then the access is considered non-cacheable and Line Fill will not be executed. (See Figure 6.8) Otherwise, if SRDY# is sampled active, the line fill cycle resumes as a non-burst sequence of three more cycles (see Figure 6.9). Finally, if SBRDY# and SKEN# are sampled active (and SNA# and SRDY# are sampled inactive), then the Line Fill cycle will be a burst cycle (see Figures 6.11 - 6.12).

If a system cannot support burst cycles, a non burst line fill must be requested by merely returning SRDY# instead of SBRDY#, in the first read cycle (see Figure 6.9). Once a burst cycle started, it will not be aborted until it's completed, regardless if SKEN# is sampled inactive or SHOLD is sampled active, i.e. all four DWs will be read from memory. However, the system may abort a burst Line Fill transfer before it's completed, by returning SRDY# active (instead of SBRDY#) for the second or third DW in a Line Fill transaction (see Figure 6.13). In this case the cache will not be updated. The first DW will already have been transferred to the CPU.

Note that in the last (fourth) bus cycle in a line fill transfer, SBRDY# or SRDY# has the same effect on the 82395DX. That is to indicate the end of the Line Fill. For all cycles that cannot run in burst mode (non-Line Fill cycles or pipelined Line Fill cycles) SBRDY# has the same effect on the 82395DX as the normal SRDY# pin. SRDY# and SBRDY# are the same apart from their function during burst cycles.

The fastest burst cycle possible requires two clocks for the first data item to be returned to the 82395DX with subsequent data items returned every clock. Such a bus cycle is shown in Figure 6.11. An example of a burst cycle where two clocks are required for every burst item is shown in Figure 6.12. When initiating any read, the 82395DX presents the address for the data item requested. When the 82395DX converts this cycle into a cache Line Fill, the first data item returned must correspond to the address sent out by the 82395DX. This address is the original address that is requested by the 386 DX Microprocessor. The 82395DX updates this address after each SBRDY# according to table 6.1 (SA2 and SA3 are updated). This is also true for non-burst Line Fill cycles. The 82395DX presents each request for data in an order determined by the first address in the transfer. For example, if the first address was 104, the next three addresses in the burst will be 100, 10C, and 108. The burst order used by the 82395DX is shown in Table 6.1. This remains true whether the external system responds with a sequence of normal bus cycles or with a burst cycle. An example of the sequencing of burst addresses is shown in Figure 6.12.

This order was designed to optimize the performance of 64- bit memory systems. The second cycle of a burst reads the DW that forms the other half of an aligned 64-bit block, no matter whether that DW is at a higher or lower address. The third and fourth cycles then read the two DWs which form the other half of an aligned 128-bit block. The order in which the third and fourth DWs are accessed corresponds to the order used for the first and second DWs.

Table 6.1 - Line Fill Address Order

First Address	Second Address	Third Address	Fourth Address
0	4	8	C
4	0	C	8
8	C	0	4
C	8	4	0

In the following cases, a Line Fill cycle will not update the cache:

1. Aborted burst: burst cycle will be aborted if SRDY# is returned active in the second or third bus cycle. The Line Fill will not resume, and the cache will not be updated.
2. Snoop hit to line buffer: If, during a Line Fill transfer, a snoop cycle is initiated after the first SRDY# or SBRDY#, and the address matches the address of the line being retrieved, the Line Fill cycle will continue as usual but the cache will not be updated.
3. FLUSH during Line Fill cycle: the Line Fill cycle will continue as usual, but the cache will not be updated.

Figures (6.9 - 6.13) include waveforms of several cases of Line Fill cycles.

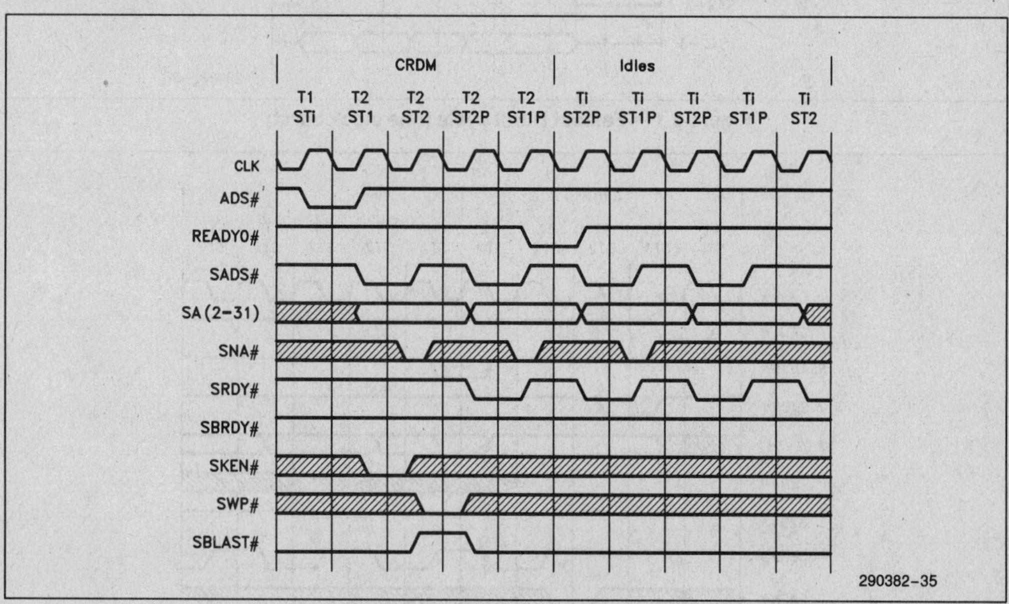

Figure 6.10 - Pipelined Line Fill

4

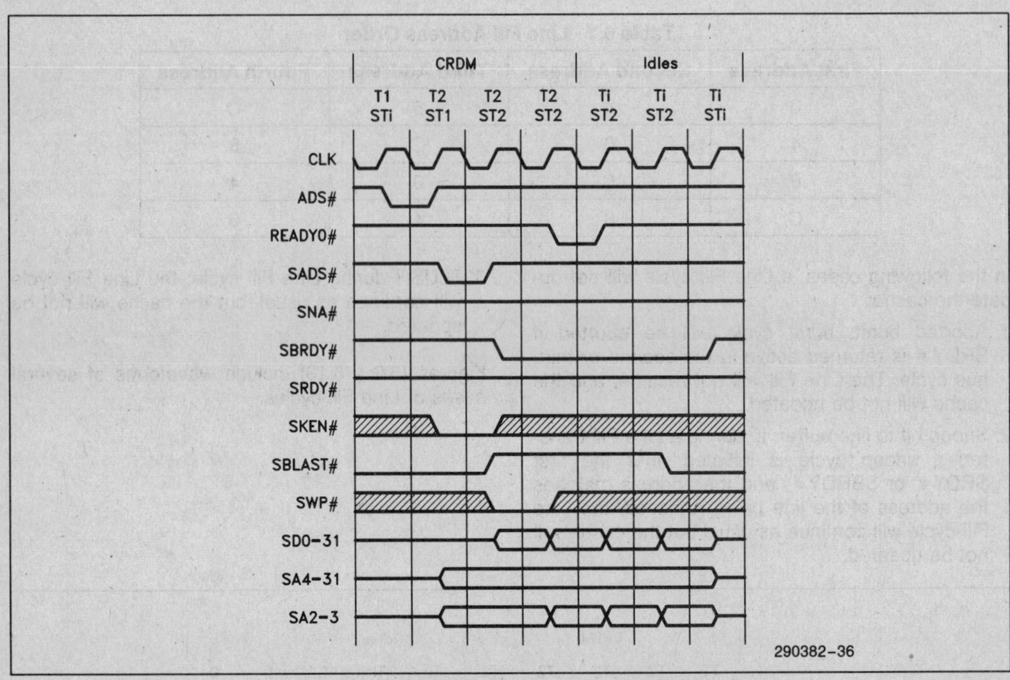

Figure 6.11 - Fastest Burst cycle (one clock burst)

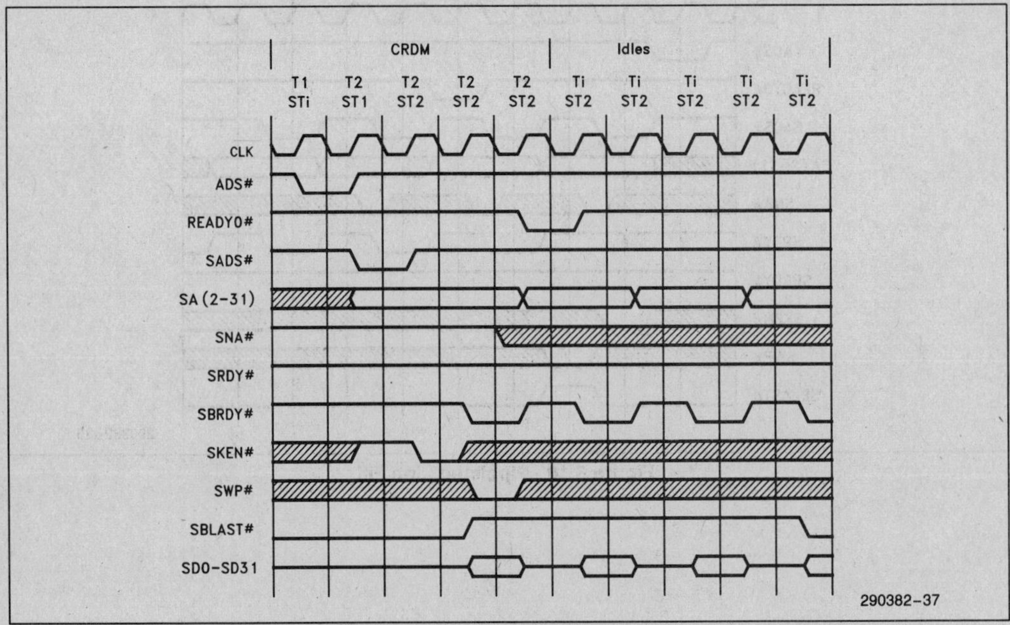

Figure 6.12 - Burst Read (2 clock burst)

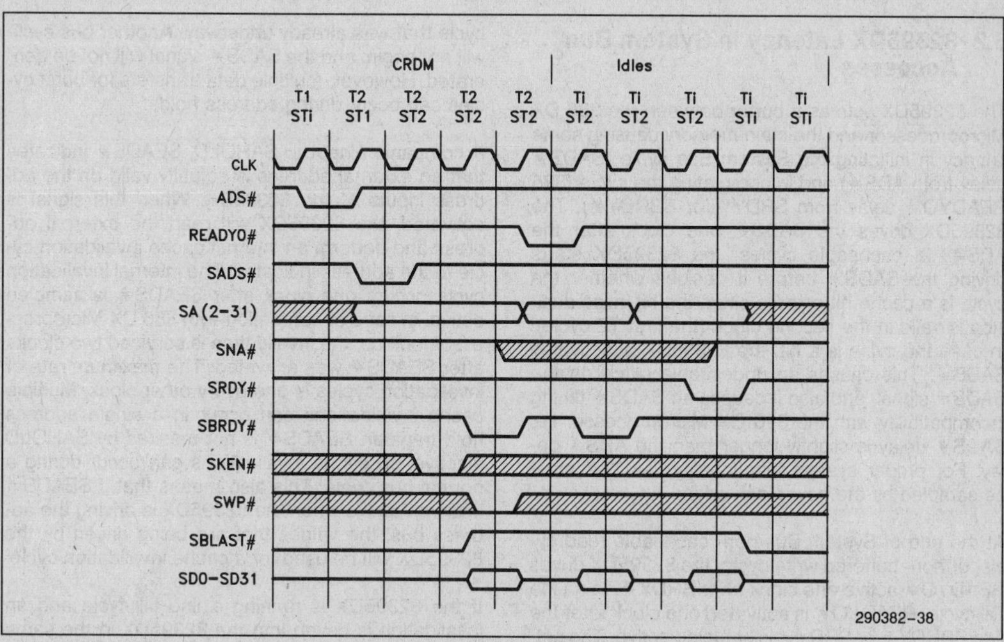

Figure 6.13 - Interrupted Burst Read (2 clock burst)

4

6.2 82395DX Latency in System Bus Accesses

The 82395DX acts as a buffer between the 386 DX Microprocessor and the main memory causing some latency in initiating the System Bus cycle (SADS# delay from ADS#) and in completing the cycle (386 READYO# delay from SRDY# or SBRDY#). The 82395DX drives the SADS# one clock after the ADS#. In cacheable cycles, the 82395DX starts driving the SADS# before it decides whether the cycle is a cache hit or miss since the hit/miss decision is valid in the second clock (the first T2 cycle). In case the cycle is a hit, the 82395DX deactivates SADS#. This causes an undesirable glitch on the SADS# signal, and also it causes an SADS# timing incompatibility with the 386 DX Microprocessor i.e. SADS# delay is slightly longer than the ADS# delay. For proper system functionality, SADS# must be sampled by the next clock edge.

At the end of System Bus non- cacheable read cycle, or non- buffered write cycle, the 82395DX drives READYO# active one clock after SRDY#. In a Line Fill cycle, READYO# is activated one clock after the first SBRDY# or SRDY# is sampled active. The setup timing requirements of SRDY# and system data force one wait state at the end of the cycle.

6.3 SHLDA Latency

For non-LOCK#ed cycles the worst case delay between SHOLD and SHLDA would be when SHOLD is activated during ST2P state, followed by a Line Fill. In this case, the HOLD request will be acknowledged only after the Line Fill is completed. In LOCKed cycles SHLDA will not be asserted until after SLOCK# is negated. The latency would be:

Latency = (Number of ST2Pcycles) + (Number of Line Fill cycles) OR (Number of LOCK#ed cycles)

6.4 Cache Consistency Support

The 82395DX supports snooping using the SEADS# mechanism. Besides insuring the consistency, this mechanism provides multi processing support by having the 82395DX System Bus and the Local Bus running concurrently.

The 82395DX will always float its address bus in the clock immediately following the one in which SAHOLD is received. Thus, no address hold acknowledge is required. When the address bus is floated, the rest of the 82395DX's System Bus will remain active, so that data can be received from a bus cycle that was already underway. Another bus cycle will not begin, and the SADS# signal will not be generated. However, multiple data transfers for burst cycles can occur during address holds.

A companion input to SAHOLD, SEADS# indicates that an external address is actually valid on the address inputs of the 82395DX. When this signal is activated, the 82395DX will read the external address and perform an internal cache invalidation cycle to the address indicated. The internal invalidation cycle occurs one clock after SEADS# is sampled active. In case of contention with 386 DX Microprocessor look up, the invalidation is serviced two clocks after SEADS# was activated. The maximum rate of invalidation cycles is one every other clock. Multiple cache invalidations can occur in a single address hold transfer. SEADS# is not masked by SAHOLD inactive, so cache invalidations can occur during a normal bus cycle. This also means that if SEADS# is driven active when the 82395DX is driving the address bus, the values that are being driven by the 82395DX will be used for a cache invalidation cycle.

If the 82395DX is running a line fill cycle and an invalidation is driven into the 82395DX in the same clock the first data is returned, or in any subsequent clock, the 82395DX will invalidate that line even if it is the same cache line that the 82395DX is currently filling.

SAHOLD in pipelined cycles: The activation of SAHOLD only causes the system address to be floated in the next clock without changing the behavior of pipelined cycles. If SAHOLD is activated before entering the ST2P state, the 82395DX will move into non-pipeline and drive the SADS# only after the deactivation of SAHOLD. However, if SAHOLD is asserted in the ST2P state and the Nth cycle has already started, the system address is floated but SADS# is kept active until SRDY# (for the N-1 th cycle) is returned. It is the system designers' responsibility to latch the address bus. Note that the address driven on the System Bus after SAHOLD is deasserted (in pipelined cycles) depends on whether SNA# has been sampled active during the SAHOLD state and another cycle is pending. As seen from Figure 6.14, the (N+1)th address will be driven by the 82395DX once SAHOLD was deactivated and SNA# was sampled active, provided there is a cycle pending in the 82395DX. The following figures describe the 82395DX behavior in two cases. First, when SNA# is sampled active and second, in the case of SNA# sampled inactive.

Note that the maximum rate of snooping cycles is every other clock. The first clock edge in which SEADS# is sampled active causes the 82395DX to

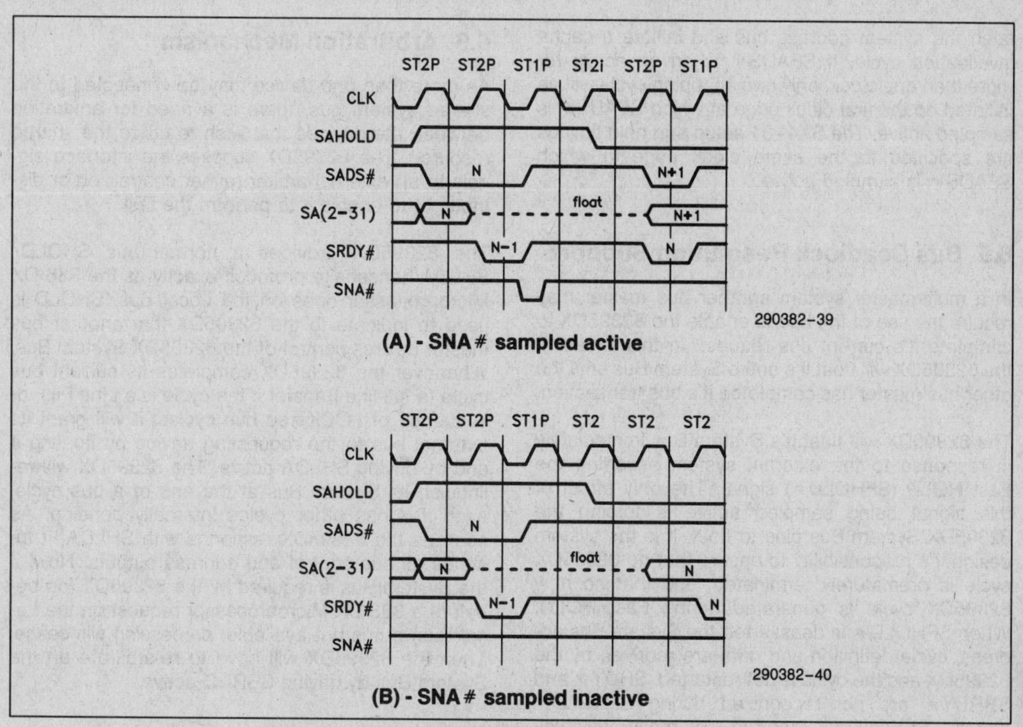

Figure 6.14 - SAHOLD Behavior in Pipelined Cycles

latch the system address bus and initiate a cache invalidation cycle. If SEADS# is driven active for more than one clock, only one snooping cycle will be initiated on the first clock edge at which SEADS# is sampled active. The SA4–31 setup and hold timings are specified to the same clock edge in which SEADS# is sampled active.

6.5 Bus Deadlock Resolution Support

In a multi-master system another bus master may require the use of the bus to enable the 82395DX to complete it's current bus request. In this situation, the 82395DX will float it's entire System Bus until the other bus master has completed it's bus transaction.

The 82395DX will float it's System Bus immediately in response to the external system asserting the Fast HOLD (SFHOLD#) signal. The only effect of this signal being sampled active is forcing the 82395DX System Bus pins to float. It is the system designer's responsibility to ensure that no 82395DX cycle is prematurely terminated, and that no new 82395DX cycle is generated during Fast HOLD. When SFHOLD# is deasserted the System Bus address, cycle definition and data are redriven by the 82395DX and the cycle is not restarted. SRDY# and SBRDY# are not recognized during SFHOLD# states. SFHOLD# asserted internally disables SRDY# and SBRDY#.

6.6 Arbitration Mechanism

As more than one device may be connected to the shared system bus, there is a need for arbitration between the devices that wish to utilize the shared resource. The 82395DX supplies the interface signals to an external arbiter (either centralized or distributed) to enable it to perform the task.

The 82395DX provides a normal bus SHOLD/SHLDA handshake protocol, exactly as the 386 DX Microprocessor does on the Local Bus. SHOLD is used to indicate to the 82395DX that another bus master desires control of the 82395DX System Bus. Whenever the 82395DX completes its current bus cycle (a full line transfer if the cycle is a Line Fill), or sequence of LOCK#ed bus cycles, it will grant its external bus to the requesting device by floating it and by driving SHLDA active. The 82395DX will relinquish its System Bus at the end of a bus cycle, even if it has other cycles internally pending. As soon as the 82395DX responds with SHLDA, it tri-states all bus control and address outputs. Now, if the System Bus is required by the 82395DX (on behalf of a 386 DX Microprocessor request on the Local Bus) but is not available, processing will cease. Then the 82395DX will have to re-arbitrate on the System Bus by driving SBREQ active.

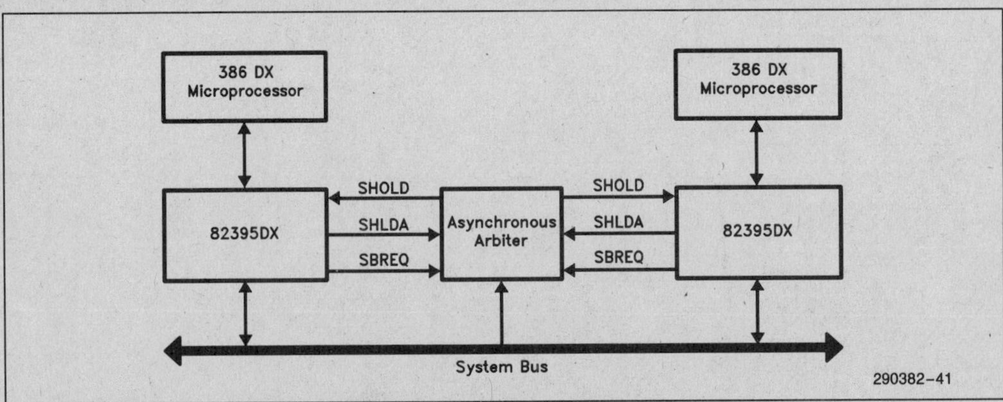

Figure 6.15 - Multiple 82395DX Bus Arbitration Scheme

The SBREQ output is activated whenever the 82395DX has internally generated a bus cycle request. It is inactivated immediately after the 82395DX asserts SADS# of the cycle. By examining this signal, external logic can determine when the 82395DX requires the use of the System Bus and intelligently arbitrate the System Bus among multiple processors. This pin is always driven, regardless of the state of bus hold (See Figure 6.16).

The SHOLD input has higher priority than the pending request. In the case of LOCK#ed System Bus cycles, SHOLD requests will not be acknowledged. Another case is a non-burst Line Fill, where SHOLD is acknowledged after reading the fourth DW, even though SHOLD was activated before.

6.7 Next Near Cycles

For all System Bus cycles, the 82395DX generates a signal, SNENE#, to indicate that the current cycle is in the same 2048 Byte area as the previous memory cycle. Namely, it indicates that address lines A11–A31 of the current System Bus memory cycle are identical to address lines A11–A31 of the previous memory cycle. This signal can be used by an external DRAM system to run CAS# only cycles, therefore increasing the throughput of the memory system. SNENE# timing is identical to system address timing, namely it is valid from SADS# active until SRDY# or SBRDY# is sampled active (non-pipelined cycles) or until SNA# is sampled active (pipelined cycles). SNENE# is valid for all memory cycles, and must be ignored in I/O and idle cycles.

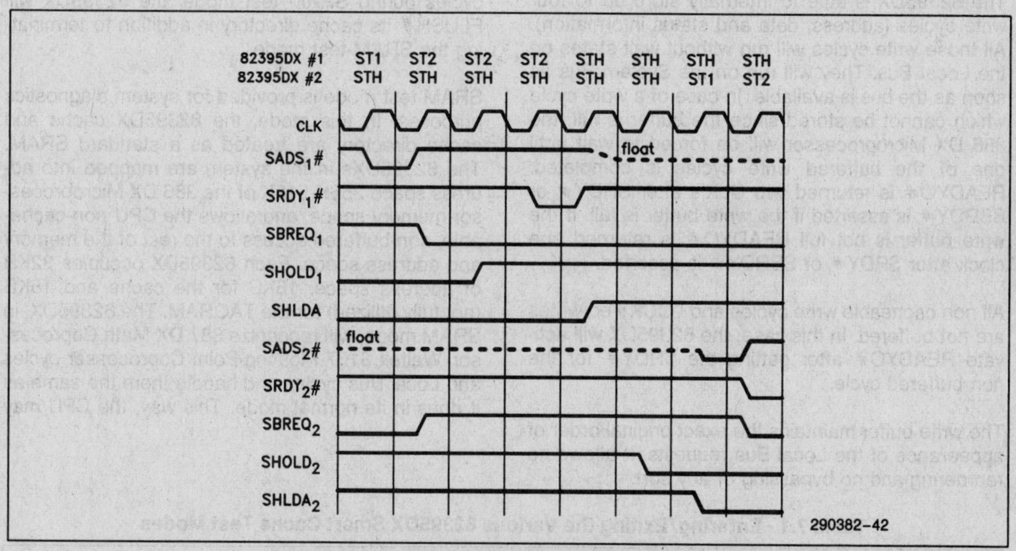

Figure 6.16 - SHOLD/SHLDA/SBREQ Mechanism

After the 82395DX exits the SHOLD state, SNENE# is always inactive. SNENE# is always inactive in the first memory cycle after a Halt/Shutdown cycle.

If SAHOLD is sampled active while the System Bus is idle, the next 82395DX cycle will have SNENE# inactive. If SAHOLD is sampled active while the 82395DX is running a System Bus cycle, SNENE# will not change until the next SADS# is issued. During SHLDA, SNENE# is floated and the first cycle after SHLDA is deactivated will have SNENE# inactive. SNENE# can run in the pipeline, the same as the system address.

6.8 Write Buffer

The 82395DX is able to internally store up to four write cycles (address, data and status information). All those write cycles will run without wait states on the Local Bus. They will run on the System Bus as soon as the bus is available. In case of a write cycle which cannot be stored since the buffer is full, the 386 DX Microprocessor will be forced to wait until one of the buffered write cycles is completed. READYO# is returned two CLK's after SRDY# or SBRDY# is asserted if the write buffer is full. If the write buffer is not full READYO# is returned one clock after SRDY# or SBRDY# is asserted.

All non cacheable write cycles and LOCK#ed writes are not buffered. In this case, the 82395DX will activate READYO# after getting the SRDY# for the non buffered cycle.

The write buffer maintains the exact original order of appearance of the Local Bus requests. It allows no reordering and no bypassing of any sort.

7.0 TESTABILITY FEATURES

This chapter discusses the requirements for properly testing an 82395DX based system after power up and during normal system operation.

7.1 SRAM Test Mode

This mode is invoked by driving the FLUSH# pin active for less than four clocks during normal operation. SRAM test mode may only be invoked when the 82395DX is in idle state, namely there is no cycle in progress, and no cycle is pending in the 82395DX. The 82395DX exits this mode with subsequent activation of the FLUSH# pin for minimum of 1 clock cycle. If FLUSH# is activated for at least four clock cycles during SRAM test mode, the 82395DX will FLUSH# its cache directory in addition to terminating the SRAM test mode.

SRAM test mode is provided for system diagnostics purposes. In this mode, the 82395DX cache and cache directory are treated as a standard SRAM. The 82395DXs in the system are mapped into address space 256K-512K of the 386 DX Microprocessor memory space, and allows the CPU non-cacheable, non-buffered access to the rest of the memory and address space. Each 82395DX occupies 32KB of address space: 16KB for the cache and 16KB (not fully utilized) for the TAGRAM. The 82395DX, in SRAM mode, will recognize 387 DX Math Coprocessor/Weitek 3167 Floating-Point Coprocessor cycles and Local Bus cycles and handle them the same as it does in its normal mode. This way, the CPU may

Table 7.1 - Entering/Exiting the Various 82395DX Smart Cache Test Modes

Operating Mode	FLUSH#	SAHOLD	Comments
Tristate Test Mode	0	1	Sampled 1 CLK prior to RESET falling. Exit by next activation of RESET with FLUSH# and SAHOLD deactivated.
SRAM Test Mode	0	X	FLUSH# activation for less than four CLKs during normal mode. Exit with activation of FLUSH# for a minimum of one CLK.
Reserved Mode	0	0	Sampled 1 CLK prior to RESET falling.
Normal Mode	1	X	

execute code that tests the 82395DX as a regular memory component, with the only limitation that no code or data may reside in the memory space 256K-512K during this mode. During SRAM test mode, all accesses to memory space other than 256K-512K are handled exactly as in normal mode with the following exceptions:

1. All read cycles are non-cacheable - read hits are not serviced from the cache and read misses don't cause Line Fills.
2. All write cycles are not buffered.
3. All write cycles do not update the cache.
4. Snooping is disabled.

The local address pins indicate the 82395DX internal addresses. The partitioning is as follows:

- A16=0 selects the cache directory. A16=1 select the cache.
- A15–14 select the "way".
- A12 and A13 select one 82395DX in a multi 82395DX system.
- A11–A4 are the set address.
- A3–2 select a DW in the line. Applicable in cache accesses (A16=1).

The user can write to any byte in any line in case of a cache write cycle and write to all the Tagram fields (25 bits) in one Way in one Tagram write cycle. The memory mapping of the SRAM mode is the described in Table 7.2.

As can be seen from Table 7.2, the address space allocated for either Tagram or Cache is 4096 (4K) addresses per way, per 82395DX. The address allocation within each 4K segment is shown in Tables 7.3 and 7.4.

The data presented on the 82395DX local data pins is the SRAM data input. The SRAM data output is also driven on the local data pins. The BE(0–3)# pins indicate the bytes which must be written. During SRAM test mode, all the AC specifications are met. Figures 7.1 and 7.2 depict the SRAM mode read and write cycles respectively. Note that two wait states are inserted during SRAM test mode read cycles and one wait state is inserted in write cycles. The system may extend the number of wait states by gating READYO# for any number of clock cycles (1 clock cycle in Figure 7.1, 0 clock cycles in Figure 7.2).

The user can write to any byte in any line in case of a cache write cycle and write to all the Tagram fields (25 bits) in one way in one Tagram write cycle. The memory mapping of the SRAM test mode described in Table 7.2.

Table 7.2 - SRAM Memory Map

Cache/Tagram	Way	82395DX	Start Address
Cache	3	4	0005F000 h
Cache	3	3	0005E000 h
Cache	3	2	0005D000 h
Cache	3	1	0005C000 h
Cache	2	4	0005B000 h
Cache	2	3	0005A000 h
Cache	2	2	00059000 h
Cache	2	1	00058000 h
Cache	1	4	00057000 h
Cache	1	3	00056000 h
Cache	1	2	00055000 h
Cache	1	1	00054000 h
Cache	0	4	00053000 h
Cache	0	3	00052000 h
Cache	0	2	00051000 h
Cache	0	1	00050000 h
Tagram	3	4	0004F000 h
Tagram	3	3	0004E000 h
Tagram	3	2	0004D000 h
Tagram	3	1	0004C000 h
Tagram	2	4	0004B000 h
Tagram	2	3	0004A000 h
Tagram	2	2	00049000 h
Tagram	2	1	00048000 h
Tagram	1	4	00047000 h
Tagram	1	3	00046000 h
Tagram	1	2	00045000 h
Tagram	1	1	00044000 h
Tagram	0	4	00043000 h
Tagram	0	3	00042000 h
Tagram	0	2	00041000 h
Tagram	0	1	00040000 h

As can be seen from Tables 7.3 and 7.4, the address space allocated for either Tagram or Cache is 4096 (4K) addresses per way, per 82395DX. The address allocation within each 4K segment is shown in Table 7.3 for the Cache and Table 7.4 for the Tagram.

Table 7.3 - Cache Address Allocation

SET	DW	Start Address
255	3	FFC h
255	2	FF8 h
255	1	FF4 h
255	0	FF0 h
.	.	.
	.	.
	.	.
.	.	.
1	3	01C h
1	2	018 h
1	1	014 h
1	0	010 h
0	3	00C h
0	2	008 h
0	1	004 h
0	0	000 h

Table 7.4 - TAGRAM Address Allocation

SET	Start Address
255	FFC h
255	FF8 h
255	FF4 h
255	FF0 h
.	.
	.
	.
.	.
1	01C h
1	018 h
1	014 h
1	010 h
0	00C h
0	008 h
0	004 h
0	000 h

Double Word format in Tagram read/write:

31–25	24–22	21	20–1	0
0 0 0 0 0 0 0	LRU	V	TAG	WP

V = TAG Valid bit
WP = Write Protect bit
"0" = Indicates don't care bits. Writing to these bits will have no effect. When reading the Tagram these bits will have a value of 0.

NOTE:
In Tagram accesses, BE0#-BE3# are ignored in both read and write cycles.

The data presented on the 82395DX D0–D31 pins is the SRAM data input for write cycles and is also the SRAM data output for read cycles during the SRAM test mode. The BE3#–BE0# pins indicate the bytes which will be written to. During SRAM test mode all the AC specifications are met. Figures 7.1 and 7.2 depict the SRAM test mode read and write cycles respectively. The system may extend the number of wait states by gating READYO# for any number of clock cycles (one clock cycle in Figure 7.1, zero in Figure 7.2).

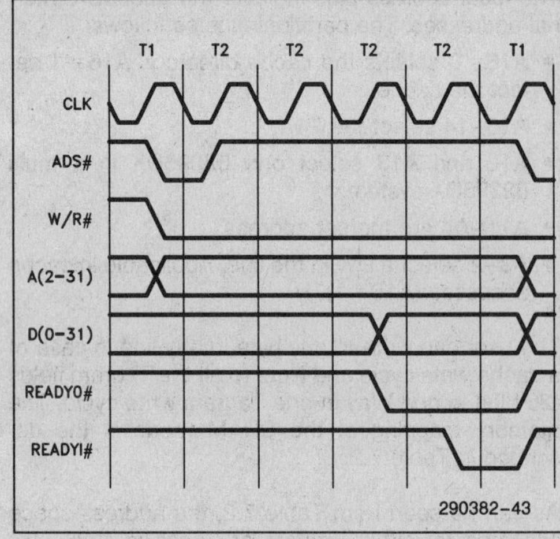

Figure 7.1 - SRAM Mode Read Cycle

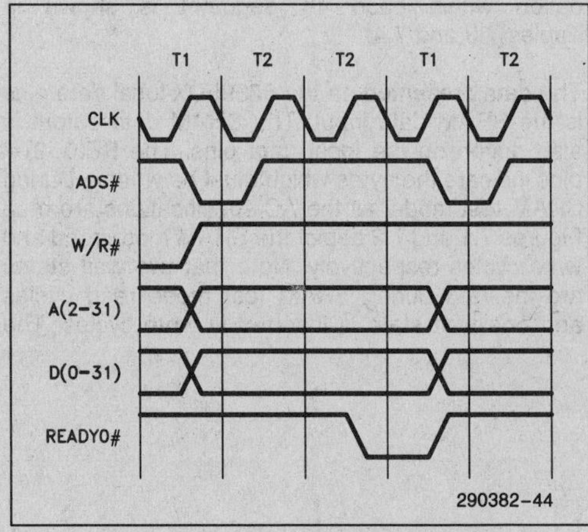

Figure 7.2 - SRAM Mode Write Cycle

7.2 Tristate Output Test Mode

The 82395DX provides the option of isolating itself from other devices on the board for system debugging, by floating all it's outputs. Output tristate mode is invoked by driving the SAHOLD and FLUSH# pins active during RESET. The 82395DX will remain in this mode after RESET is deactivated, if SAHOLD and FLUSH# pins are sampled active in the CLK2 prior to RESET going low (See Figure 7.3). The 82395DX exits this mode with the next activation of RESET with SAHOLD or FLUSH# driven inactive.

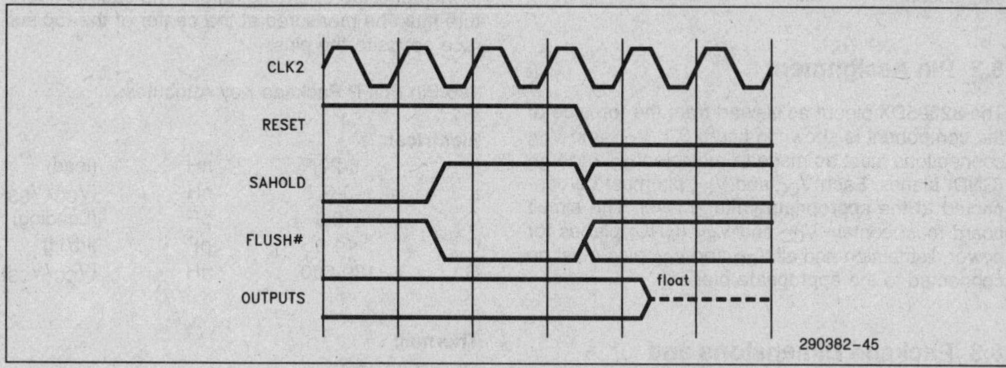

Figure 7.3 - Entering the Tristate Test Mode

4

8.0 MECHANICAL DATA

8.1 Introduction

This chapter discusses the physical package and its connections.

8.2 Pin Assignment

The 82395DX pinout as viewed from the top side of the component is shown in figure 0.1. V_{CC} and V_{SS} connections must be made to multiple V_{CC} and V_{SS} (GND) planes. Each V_{CC} and V_{SS} pin must be connected to the appropriate voltage level. The circuit board must contain V_{CC} and V_{SS} (GND) planes for power distribution and all V_{CC} and V_{SS} pins must be connected to the appropriate planes.

8.3 Package Dimensions and Mounting

The 82395DX package is a 196 lead plastic quad flat pack (PQFP). For information on dimensions refer to Table 8.1 and Figures 8.1–8.3.

8.4 Package Thermal Specification

The 82395DX is specified for operation when the case temperature is within the range of 0–85 °C. The case temperature may be measured in any environment, to determine whether the 82395DX is within the specified operating range. The case temperature must be measured at the center of the top surface opposite the pins.

196 Pin PQFP Package Key Attributes:

Electrical:

L	6-20	nH	(lead)
L	3-6	nH	(V_{CC}/V_{SS})
C	<2.3	pF	(Loading)
C	<1.6	pF	(ld/ld)
C	130-200	nH	(V_{CC}/V_{SS})

Thermal:

"See Table 8.1".

Lead Stiffness:

In-Plane	17	gm/mil
Transverse	18	gm/mil

Thermal characterization of the 196 lead PQFP package yielded the information contained in Figures 8.4–8.6.

Table 8.1 - 196 Lead PQFP Package Typical Thermal Characteristics

Parameter	Thermal Resistance—°C/Watt							
	Airflow LFM							
	0	50	100	200	400	600	800	1000
θ_{JC}	5	5	5	5	5	5	5	5
θ_{JA}	24	22	21	19	17	15	14	13

NOTES:
1. Table 8.1 applies to the 82395DX Smart Cache PQFP plugged into the socket or soldered directly onto the board.
2. $\theta_{CA} = \theta_{JA} - \theta_{JC}$, where θ_{CA} is the case to ambient thermal resistance, θ_{JA} is the junction to ambient thermal resistance and θ_{JC} is the junction to case thermal resistance.

The ambient temperature must be controlled to prevent T_{CASE} from being violated. The ambient temperature can be calculated from the thermal resistance values with the following equations:

$$T_J = T_{CASE} + P * \theta_{JC}$$

$$T_{amb} = T_J - P * \theta_{JA}$$

$$T_{CASE} = T_{amb} + P * [\theta_{JA} - \theta_{JC}]$$

Values for θ_{JA} and θ_{JC} are given in Table 8.1 for the 196 lead PQFP package at various airflow rates. Table 8.2 shows the maximum T_{amb} allowable (without exceding T_{CASE}) at various airflows. Note that T_{amb} can be improved further by attaching "fins" or a "heat sink" to the package.

Table 8.2 - Ambient Temperature Requirements

Using I_{CC2}	Ambient Temperature Not to Exceed T_{CASE} = 85°C							
	Airflow LFM							
	0	50	100	200	400	600	800	1000
T_{amb} @ 33 MHz (°C)	40.4	45.1	47.4	52.1	56.8	61.5	63.9	66.2
T_{amb} @ 25 MHz (°C)	45.1	49.3	51.4	55.6	59.8	64.0	66.1	68.7
T_{amb} @ 20 MHz (°C)	48.0	51.9	53.8	57.7	61.6	65.5	67.5	69.4

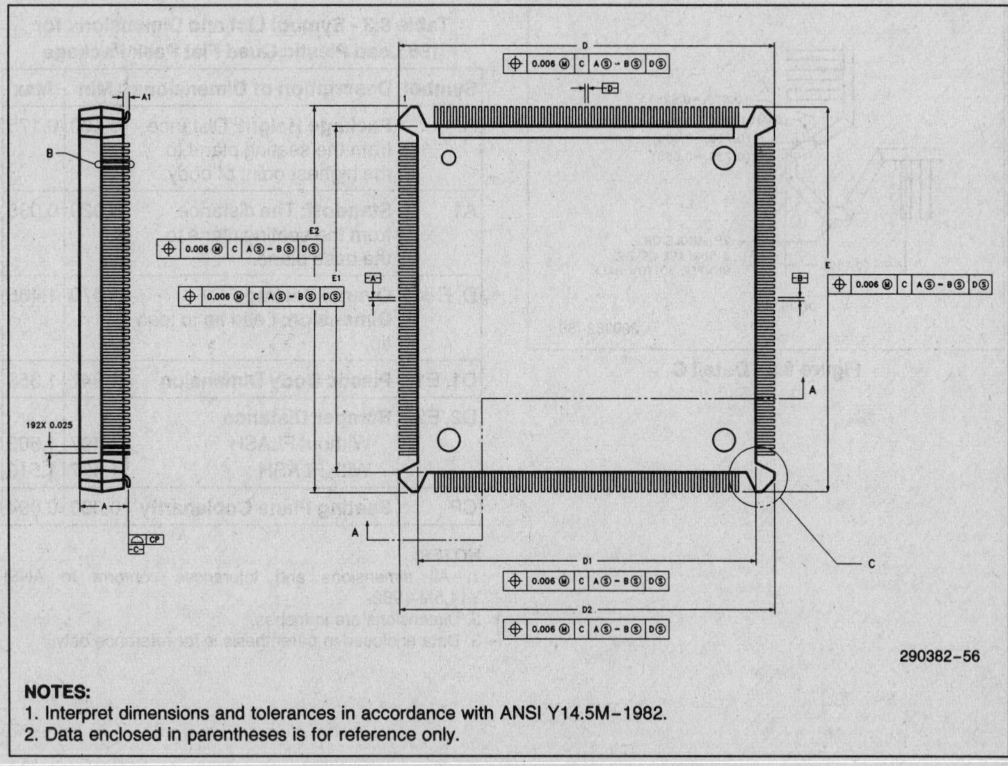

NOTES:
1. Interpret dimensions and tolerances in accordance with ANSI Y14.5M–1982.
2. Data enclosed in parentheses is for reference only.

Figure 8.1 - Principal Dimensions and Data

4

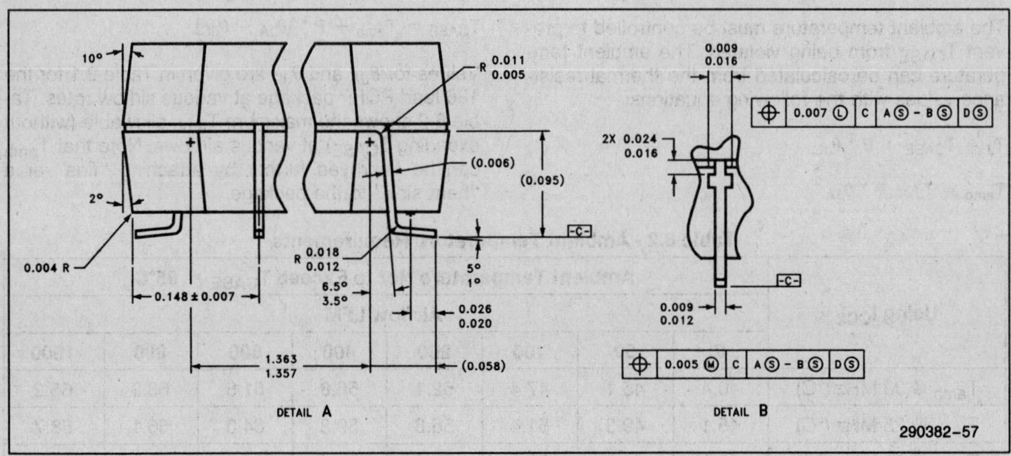

Figure 8.2 - Typical Lead

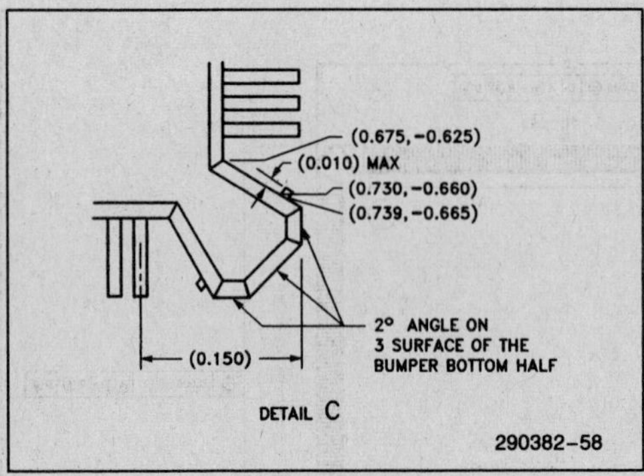

Figure 8.3 - Detail C

Table 8.3 - Symbol List and Dimensions for 196 Lead Plastic Quad Flat Pack Package

Symbol	Description of Dimensions	Min	Max
A	**Package Height:** Distance from the seating plane to the highest point of body.	0.160	0.175
A1	**Standoff:** The distance from the seating plane to the base plane.	0.020	0.035
D, E	**Overall Package Dimension:** Lead tip to lead tip.	1.470	1.485
D1, E1	**Plastic Body Dimension**	1.347	1.353
D2, E2	**Bumper Distance**		
	Without FLASH	1.497	1.503
	With FLASH	1.497	1.510
CP	**Seating Plane Coplanarity**	0.000	0.004

NOTES:
1. All dimensions and tolerances conform to ANSI Y14.5M-1982.
2. Dimensions are in inches.
3. Data enclosed in parenthesis is for reference only.

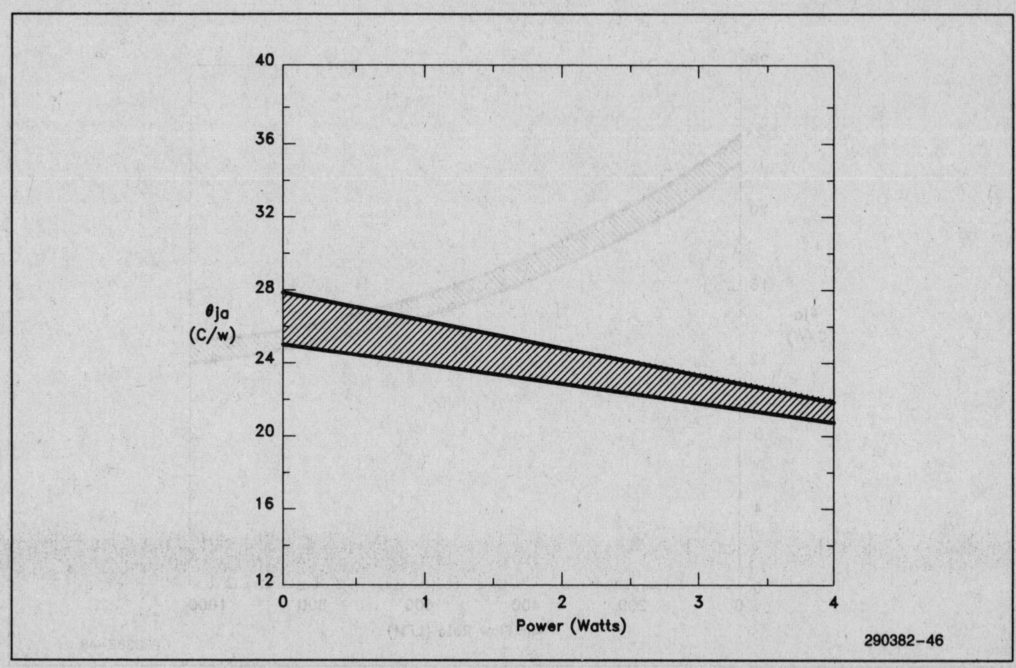

Figure 8.4 - Junction to Ambient Thermal Resistance vs Power

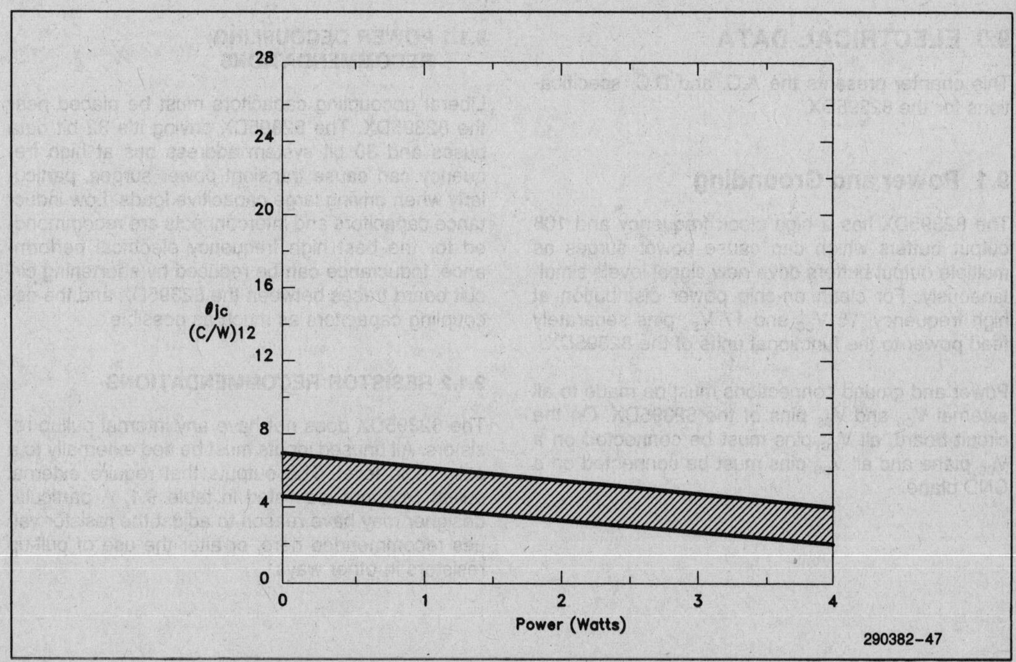

Figure 8.5 - Junction to Case Thermal Resistance vs Power

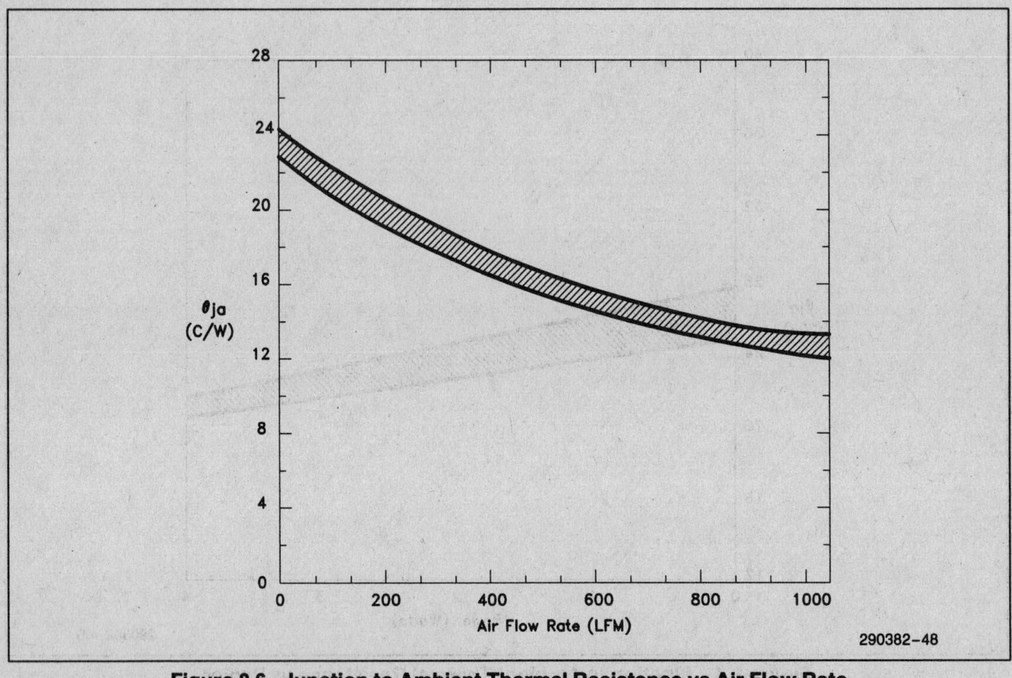

Figure 8.6 - Junction to Ambient Thermal Resistance vs Air Flow Rate

9.0 ELECTRICAL DATA

This chapter presents the A.C. and D.C. specifications for the 82395DX.

9.1 Power and Grounding

The 82395DX has a high clock frequency and 108 output buffers which can cause power surges as multiple output buffers drive new signal levels simultaneously. For clean on-chip power distribution at high frequency, 15 V_{CC} and 17 V_{SS} pins separately feed power to the functional units of the 82395DX.

Power and ground connections must be made to all external V_{CC} and V_{SS} pins of the 82395DX. On the circuit board, all V_{CC} pins must be connected on a V_{CC} plane and all V_{SS} pins must be connected on a GND plane.

9.1.1 POWER DECOUPLING RECOMMENDATIONS

Liberal decoupling capacitors must be placed near the 82395DX. The 82395DX driving it's 32 bit data buses and 30 bit system address bus at high frequency can cause transient power surges, particularly when driving large capacitive loads. Low inductance capacitors and interconnects are recommended for the best high frequency electrical performance. Inductance can be reduced by shortening circuit board traces between the 82395DX and the decoupling capacitors as much as possible.

9.1.2 RESISTOR RECOMMENDATIONS

The 82395DX does not have any internal pullup resistors. All unused inputs must be tied externally to a solid logic level. The outputs that require external pullup resistors are listed in table 9.1. A particular designer may have reason to adjust the resistor values recommended here, or alter the use of pull-up resistors in other ways.

9.2 Absolute Maximum Ratings

Storage Temperature .... −65 °C to 150 °C

Case Temperature under Bias .... −65 °C to 110 °C

Supply voltage with Respect to V_{SS} .... −0.5V to 6.5V

Voltage on Other Pins .... −0.5V to V_{CC} +0.5V

NOTICE: This data sheet contains information on products in the sampling and initial production phases of development. The specifications are subject to change without notice. Verify with your local Intel Sales office that you have the latest data sheet before finalizing a design.

**WARNING: Stressing the device beyond the "Absolute Maximum Ratings" may cause permanent damage. These are stress ratings only. Operation beyond the "Operating Conditions" is not recommended and extended exposure beyond the "Operating Conditions" may affect device reliability.*

Table 9.1 - Pullup Resistor Recommendations

Signal	Pullup Value	Purpose
READYO#	20K Ohms ±10%	Lightly pull READYO# inactive when the 82345DX is not driving it. Allows the selected 82395DX to drive READYO# while it is inactive for the others.
SADS#	20K Ohms ±10%	Lightly pull SADS# inactive when the 82345DX is not driving it. Allows the selected 82395DX to drive SADS# while it is inactive for the others.
SLOCK#	20K Ohms ±10%	Lightly pull SLOCK# inactive for 82395DX SHOLD states.

9.3 DC SPECIFICATIONS Tcase = 0°C to +85°C, Vcc = 5V ±5%

Table 9.2 - DC Specifications

Symbol	Parameter	Limits		Units	Test Conditions
		Min	Max		
VIL	Input Low Voltage	−0.3	0.8	V	
VIH	Input High Voltage	2.0	Vcc+0.3	V	
VCIL	CMOS Input Low	−0-.3	0.8	V	See Note 6
VCIH	CMOS Input High	Vcc−0.8	Vcc+0.3	V	See Note 6
VOL	Output Low Voltage		0.45	V	See Note 1
VOH	Output High Voltage	2.4		V	See Note 2
VCOL	CMOS Output Low Voltage		0.45	V	See Notes 1,7
VCOH	CMOS Output High Voltage	Vcc−0.45		V	See Notes 2,7
ILI	Input Leakage		±15	uA	OV<Vin<Vcc
ILO	Output Leakage		±15	uA	0.45V<Vout<Vcc
Cin	Cap. Input		10	pF	See Note 4
I_{CC}	Power Supply Current 33 MHz @ T_{CASE} = 0°C		650	mA	See Note 3
	Power Supply Current 25 MHz @ T_{CASE} = 0°C		600	mA	See Note 3
	Power Supply Current 20 MHz @ T_{CASE} = 0°C		550	mA	See Note 3

4

9.3 DC SPECIFICATIONS Tcase = 0°C to +85°C, Vcc = 5V ±5% (Continued)

Table 9.2 - DC Specifications (Continued)

Symbol	Parameter	Limits		Units	Test Conditions
		Min	Max		
I_{CC2}	Power Supply Current 33 MHz @ T_{CASE} = 85°C		470	mA	See Note 8
	Power Supply Current 25 MHz @ T_{CASE} = 85°C		420	mA	See Note 8
	Power Supply Current 20 MHz @ T_{CASE} = 85°C		390	mA	See Note 8

NOTES:
1. This parameter is measured at IOL=4mA for all the outputs.
2. This parameter is measured at IOH=1mA for all the outputs.
3. Measured with inputs driven to CMOS levels, V_{CC} = 5.25V, T_{CASE} = 0°C, using a test pattern consisting of 33% read, 33% write and 33% idle cycles. Refer to Table 8.2 for the ambient temperature requirements.
4. CLK2 input capacitance is 20pF.
5. No activity on the Local/System Bus.
6. Applies to CLK2, READYO# inputs.
7. Applies to READYO# output.
8. I_{CC2} was measured using V_{CC} of 5.0V at T_{CASE} = 85°C. This I_{CC} measurement is representative of the worst case I_{CC} at T_{CASE} = 85°C with the outputs unloaded. This is not 100% tested.

9.4 AC Characteristics

Some of the 82395DX AC parameters are clock-frequency dependent. Thus, while the part functions properly at the entire frequency range specified by the t1 spec, the AC parameters are guaranteed at three distinct frequencies only: 20MHz, 25MHz and 33MHz. Note that, for example, when a 33MHz part operates at 25Mhz CLK frequency, the AC parameters under "25MHz" column must be used.

- Functional operating range: VCC = 5V ±5%, Tcase = 0°C to +85°C.
- All AC parameters are measured relative to 1.5V for falling and rising, CLK2 is at 2V.
- All outputs tested at a 50pF load. In case of overloaded signals, the derating factor is 1ns for every extra 25pF load.
- All parameters are referred to PHI1 unless otherwise noted.
- The reference Figure of CLK2 parameters and AC measurements level is Figure 9.1 and RESET and internal phase is Figure 3.2.
- Dynamic frequency changes are not allowed.

9.4.1 TIMING CONSIDERATIONS FOR CACHE EXTENSIONS

The values listed in Tables 9.3 and 9.4 for the AC parameters are valid for a design using one 82395DX with its 16KB cache or two 82395DXs to extend the cache size to 32KB. For a design using four 82395DXs to extend the cache size to 64KB, some timing adjustments must be made due to the increased capacitive load on the signal traces. The capacitive derating curve (see Figure 9.6) must be used to accurately determine the impact on AC timings.

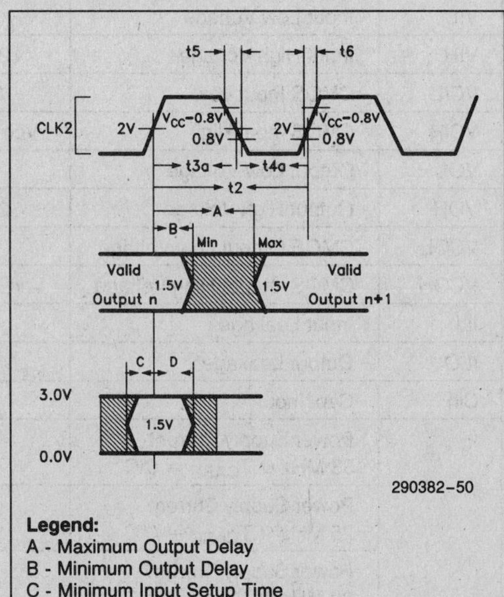

Figure 9.1 - Drive Levels and Measurement Points for AC Specifications

9.4.2 AC CHARACTERISTICS TABLES Tcase = 0°C to 85°C, Vcc = 5V ±5%

Table 9.3 - Local Bus Signal AC Parameters

Symbol	Parameter	20 MHz		25 MHz		33 MHz		Units	Notes
		Min	Max	Min	Max	Min	Max		
t1	Operating Frequency	15.4	20	15.4	25	15.4	33	MHz	Internal CLK
t2	CLK2 Period	25	32.5	20	32.5	15	32.5	ns	
t3a	CLK2 High Time	8		7		6.25		ns	Measured at 2V
t3b	CLK2 High Time	5		5		4.5		ns	Measured at 3.7V
t4a	CLK2 Low Time	8		7		6.25		ns	Measured at 2V
t4b	CLK2 Low Time	6		5		4.5		ns	Measured at 0.8V
t5	CLK2 Fall Time		7		7		4	ns	Note 1
t6	CLK2 Rise Time		7		7		4	ns	Note 2
t7a	A2–A31 Setup Time	24		17		13		ns	
t7b	LOCK# Setup Time	12		11		9		ns	
t7c	BE0–3# Setup Time	18		14		13		ns	
t8	A2–A31, BE0–3#, LOCK# Hold Time	3		3		3		ns	
t9a	M/IO#, D/C#, W/R# Setup Time	20		17		13		ns	
t9b	ADS# Setup Time	23		17		13.5		ns	
t10	M/IO#, D/C#, W/R#, ADS# Hold Time	3		3		3		ns	
t11	READYI# Setup Time	12		9		7		ns	
t12	READYI# Hold Time	4		4		4		ns	
t13	LBA#, NPI# Setup Time	10		9		5.5		ns	Note 7
t14	RESET Setup Time	12		10		5		ns	
t15a	LBA#, NPI# Hold Time	3		3		3		ns	
t15b	RESET Hold Time	4		3		2		ns	
t16	D0–31 Setup Time	10		11		4		ns	Note 3
t17	D0–31 Hold Time	2		2		2		ns	Note 3
t18	D0–31 Valid Delay	3	38	3	32	3	24	ns	
t19	D0–31 Float Delay		25		20		17	ns	Note 5
t20	READYO# Valid Delay	4	32	4	25	4	17.5	ns	
t21	READYO# Float Delay		25		20		15	ns	Notes 4,5
t22	READYO# Setup Time	16		13		11		ns	
t23	READYO# Hold Time	4		4		4		ns	
t24a	CONF# Setup Time	12		10		5		ns	Note 8
t24b	CONF# Setup Time	16		13		11		ns	Note 9
t25a	CONF# Hold Time	4		3		2		ns	Note 8
t25b	CONF# Hold Time	4		4		4		ns	Note 9

4

Table 9.4 - System Bus Signal AC Parameters

Symbol	Parameter	20 MHz		25 MHz		33 MHz		Units	Notes
		Min	Max	Min	Max	Min	Max		
t31	SA2-31, SBE0-3#, SLOCK#, SD/C#, SW/R#, SM/IO# Valid Delay	3	28	3	21	3	15	ns	
t32	SA2-31, SBE0-3#, SLOCK#, SD/C#, SW/R#, SM/IO# Float Delay	3	30	3	30	3	20	ns	Note 5
t33	SBLAST#, SHLDA, SBREQ, SNENE# Valid Delay	3	28	3	22	3	20	ns	
t34	SBLAST#, SNENE# Float Delay	3	30	3	25	3	20	ns	Note 5
t35	SD0-31 Write Data Valid Delay	3	38	3	27	3	24	ns	Note 4
t36	SD0-31 Float Delay		27		22	3	17	ns	Notes 4,5
t37	SA4-31 Setup Time	10		9		7		ns	
t38	SA4-31 Hold Time	3		3		3		ns	
t39	SD0-31 Read Setup Time	11		7		5		ns	
t40	SD0-31 Read Hold Time	3		3		3		ns	
t41	SNA# Setup Time	18		13		7		ns	Note 3
t42	SNA# Hold Time	3		3		3		ns	Note 3
t43a	SKEN# Setup Time	17		12		6.5		ns	
t43b	SHOLD, SAHOLD, SFHOLD# Setup Time	18		15		12		ns	
t43c	SWP# Setup Time	17		12		10		ns	
t44	SHOLD, SKEN#, SWP#, SFHOLD#, SAHOLD Hold Time	3		3		3		ns	
t45a	SEADS# Setup Time	14		11		7		ns	
t45b	SRDY#, SBRDY# Setup Time	14		11		9		ns	
t46	SEADS#, SRDY#, SBRDY# Hold Time	4		4		4		ns	
t47	FLUSH#, A20M# Setup Time	18		13		8		ns	Note 6
t48	FLUSH#, A20M# Hold Time	3		3		3		ns	Note 6
t49	SADS# Valid Delay	3	28	3	22	3	16	ns	
t50	SADS# Float Delay		25		20		15	ns	Notes 4,5

NOTES:
1. Tf is Measured at 3.7V to 0.8V. Tf is not 100% tested.
2. Tr is Measured at 0.8V to 3.7V. Tr is not 100% tested.
3. The specification is relative to PHI2 i.e. signal sampled by PHI2.
4. The specification is relative to PHI2 i.e. signal driven by PHI2.
5. Float condition occurs when maximum output current becomes less than ILO in magnitude. Float delay is not 100% tested.
6. The signal is allowed to be asynchronous to CLK2. The setup and hold specifications are given for testing purposes, to assure recognition within a specific CLK2 period.
7. The signal is not sampled. It must be valid through the entire cycle (as the Address lines).
8. When tested as the second 82395DX.
9. When tested as the third 82395DX.

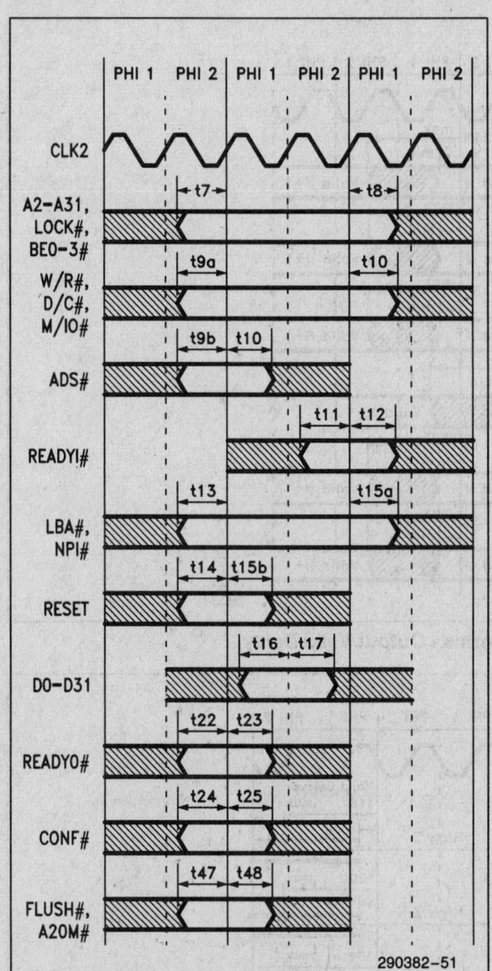

Figure 9.2 - AC Timing Waveforms - Local Bus Input Setup and Hold Timing

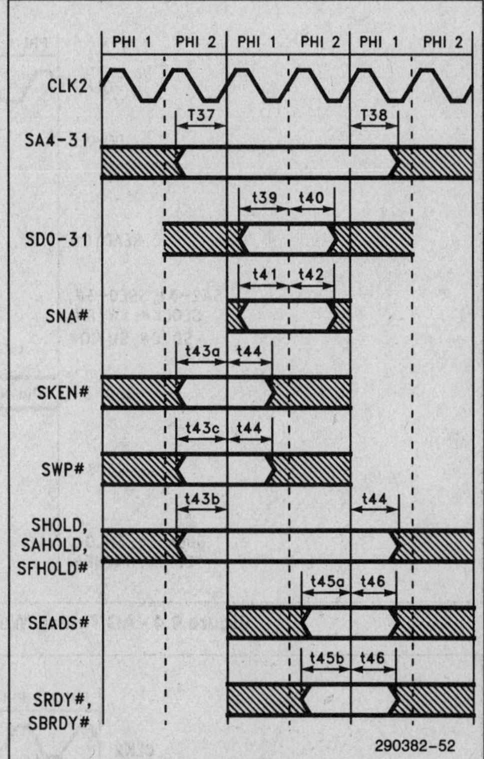

Figure 9.3 - AC Timing Waveforms - System Bus Input Setup and Hold Timing

4

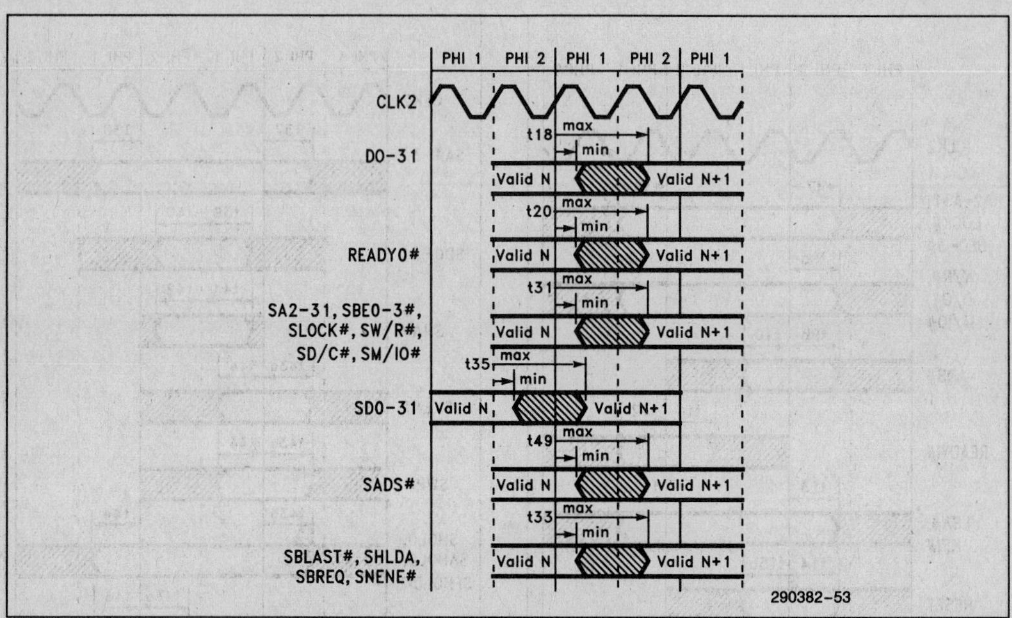

Figure 9.4 - AC Timing Waveforms - Output Valid Delay

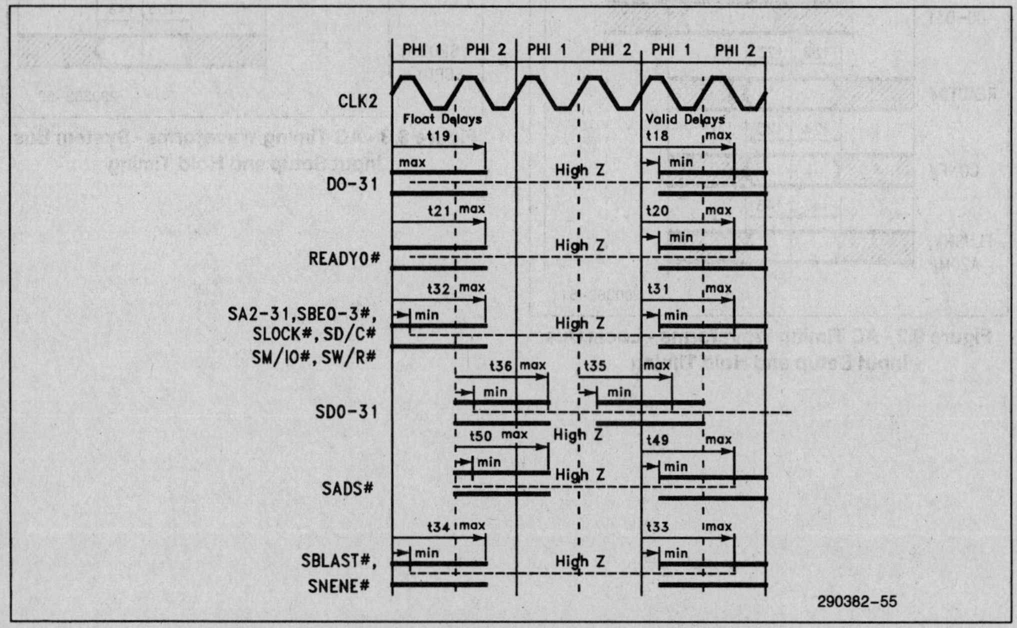

Figure 9.5 - AC Timing Waveforms - Output Float Delays

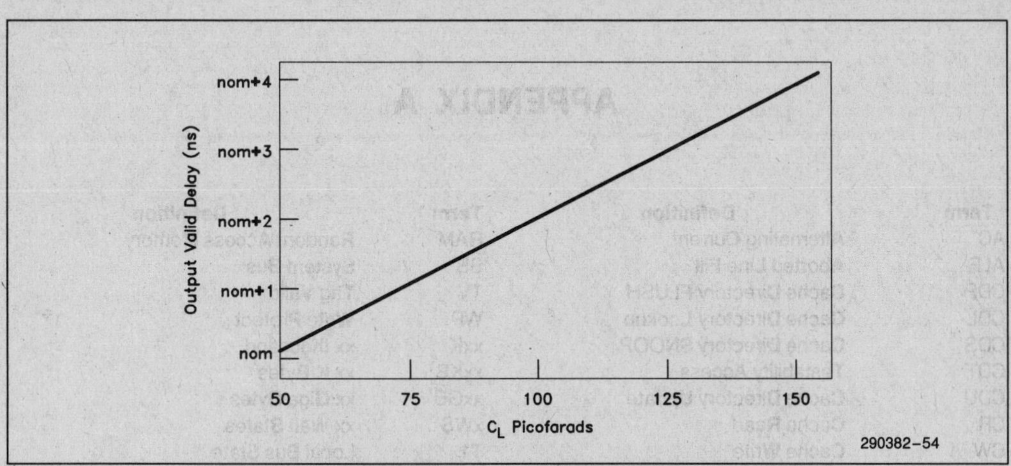

Figure 9.6 - Typical Output Valid Delay vs Load Capacitance at Maximum Operating Temperature (C_L = 50pF)

APPENDIX A

Term	Definition	Term	Definition
AC	Alternating Current	RAM	Random Access Memory
ALF	Aborted Line Fill	SB	System Bus
CDF	Cache Directory FLUSH	TV	Tag Valid
CDL	Cache Directory Lookup	WP	Write Protect
CDS	Cache Directory SNOOP	xxK	xx thousand
CDT	Testability Access	xxKB	xx K Bytes
CDU	Cache Directory Update	xxGB	xx Giga Bytes
CR	Cache Read	xWS	xx Wait States
CW	Cache Write	T1	Local Bus State
CU	Cache Update	T2	Local Bus State
CT	Testability Access	TI	Local Bus State
CPU	Central Processing Unit	TH	Local Bus State
CHMOS	Complimentary High Performance	ST1	System Bus State
	Metal Oxide Semiconductor	ST1P	System Bus State
CRDH	Cache Read Hit	ST2	System Bus State
CRDM	Cache Read Miss	ST2P	System Bus State
CWTH	Cache Write Hit	STI	System Bus State
DC	Direct Current	STH	System Bus State
DRAM	Dynamic Random Access Memory	PHI1	1st CLK2 cycle in a 2 CLK2 CLK cycle
DMA	Direct Memory Access	PHI2	2nd CLK2 cycle in a 2 CLK2 CLK cycle
DW	Double Word	C	Celsius
GND	Ground	V	Volts
I/O	Input/Output	μA	10^{-6} Amps
LB	Local Bus	mA	10^{-3} Amps
LBA	Local Bus Access	pF	10^{-12} Farads
LRU	Least Recently Used	MHz	10^{6} Hertz
PQFP	Plastic Quad Flat Pack	ns	10^{-9} seconds

82385 HIGH PERFORMANCE 32-BIT CACHE CONTROLLER

- **Improves 386™ DX System Performance**
  - **—Reduces Average CPU Wait States to Nearly Zero**
  - **—Zero Wait State Read Hit**
  - **—Zero Wait State Posted Memory Writes**
  - **—Allows Other Masters to Access the System Bus More Readily**
- **Hit Rates up to 99%**
- **Optimized as 386 DX Companion**
  - **—Simple 386 DX Interface**
  - **—Part of 386 DX-Based Compute Engine Including 387™ DX Math Coprocessor and 82380 Integrated System Peripheral**
  - **—20 MHz, 25 MHz, and 33 MHz Operation**
- **Software Transparent**
- **Synchronous Dual Bus Architecture**
  - **—Bus Watching Maintains Cache Coherency**
- **Maps Full 386 DX Address Space (4 Gigabytes)**
- **Flexible Cache Mapping Policies**
  - **—Direct Mapped or 2-Way Set Associative Cache Organization**
  - **—Supports Non-Cacheable Memory Space**
  - **—Unified Cache for Code and Data**
- **Integrates Cache Directory and Cache Management Logic**
- **High Speed CHMOS* IV Technology**
- **132-Pin PGA Package**
- **132-Lead Plastic Quad Flat Pack (PQFP)**

4

The 82385 Cache Controller is a high performance 32-bit peripheral for the Intel386 Microprocessor. It stores a copy of frequently accessed code and data from main memory in a zero wait state local cache memory. The 82385 enables the 386 DX to run at its full potential by reducing the average number of CPU wait states to nearly zero. The dual bus architecture of the 82385 allows other masters to access system resources while the 386 DX operates locally out of its cache. In this situation, the 82385's "bus watching" mechanism preserves cache coherency by monitoring the system bus address lines at no cost to system or local throughput.

The 82385 is completely software transparent, protecting the integrity of system software. High performance and board savings are achieved because the 82385 integrates a cache directory and all cache management logic on one chip.

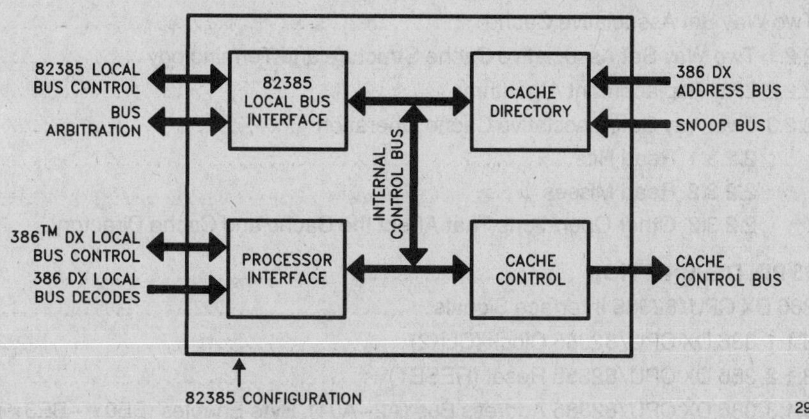

82385 Internal Block Diagram

*CHMOS is a patented process of Intel Corporation.
Intel386™, 386™ DX, 387™ DX are trademarks of Intel Corporation.

December 1990
Order Number: 290143-006

CONTENTS

CONTENTS

PAGE

4

CONTENTS

PAGE

CONTENTS

1.0 82385 FUNCTIONAL OVERVIEW

The 82385 Cache Controller is a high performance 32-bit peripheral for the Intel386 microprocessor. This chapter provides an overview of the 82385, and of the basic architecture and operation of an 386 DX CPU/82385 system.

1.1 82385 OVERVIEW

The main function of a cache memory system is to provide fast local storage for frequently accessed code and data. The cache system intercepts 386 DX memory references to see if the required data resides in the cache. If the data resides in the cache (a hit), it is returned to the 386 DX without incurring wait states. If the data is not cached (a miss), the reference is forwarded to the system and the data retrieved from main memory. An efficient cache will yield a high "hit rate" (the ratio of cache hits to total 386 DX accesses), such that the majority of accesses are serviced with zero wait states. The net effect is that the wait states incurred in a relatively infrequent miss are averaged over a large number of accesses, resulting in an average of nearly zero wait states per access. Since cache hits are serviced locally, a processor operating out of its local cache has a much lower "bus utilization" which reduces system bus bandwidth requirements, making more bandwidth available to other bus masters.

The 82385 Cache Controller integrates a cache directory and all cache management logic required to support an external 32 Kbyte cache. The cache directory structure is such that the entire physical address range of the 386 DX (4 Gigabytes) is mapped into the cache. Provision is made to allow areas of memory to be set aside as non-cacheable. The user has two cache organization options: direct mapped and 2-way set associative. Both provide the high hit rates necessary to make a large, relatively slow main memory array look like a fast, zero wait state memory to the 386 DX.

1.2 SYSTEM OVERVIEW I: BUS STRUCTURE

A good grasp of the bus structure of a 386 DX CPU/82385 system is essential in understanding both the 82385 and its role in an 386 DX system. The following is a description of this structure.

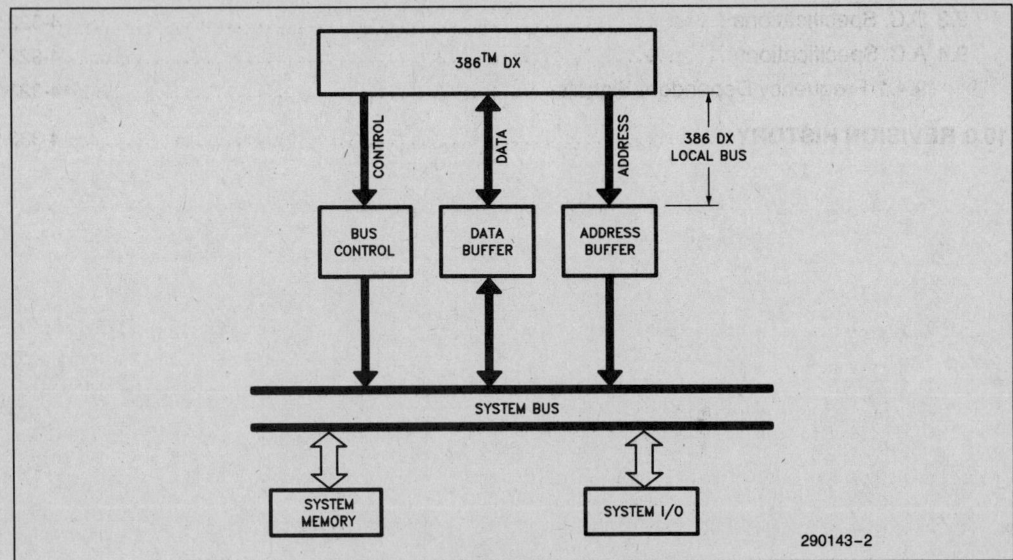

Figure 1-1. 386 DX System Bus Structure

1.2.1 386 DX Local Bus/82385 Local Bus/System Bus

Figure 1-1 depicts the bus structure of a typical 386 DX system. The "386 DX Local Bus" consists of the physical 386 DX address, data, and control busses. The local address and data busses are buffered and/or latched to become the "system" address and data busses. The local control bus is decoded by bus control logic to generate the various system bus read and write commands.

The addition of an 82385 Cache Controller causes a separation of the 386 DX bus into two distinct busses: the actual 386 DX local bus and the "82385 Local Bus" (Figure 1-2). The 82385 local bus is designed to look like the front end of an 386 DX by providing 82385 local bus equivalents to all appropriate 386 DX signals. The system ties to this "386 DX-like" front end just as it would to an actual 386 DX. The 386 DX simply sees a fast system bus, and the system sees a 386 DX front end with low bus bandwidth requirements. The cache subsystem is transparent to both. Note that the 82385 local bus is not simply a buffered version of the 386 DX bus, but rather is distinct from, and able to operate in parallel with the 386 DX bus. Other masters residing on either the 82385 local bus or system bus are free to manage system resources while the 386 DX operates out of its cache.

1.2.2 Bus Arbitration

The 82385 presents the "386 DX-like" interface which is called the 82385 local bus. Whereas the 386 DX provides a Hold Request/Hold Acknowledge bus arbitration mechanism via its HOLD and HLDA pins, the 82385 provides an equivalent mechanism via its BHOLD and BHLDA pins. (These signals are described in Section 3.7.) When another master requests the 82385 local bus, it issues the request to the 82385 via BHOLD. Typically, at the end of the current 82385 local bus cycle, the 82385 will release the 82385 local bus and acknowledge the request via BHLDA. The 386 DX is of course free to continue operating on the 386 DX local bus while another master owns the 82385 local bus.

1.2.3 Master/Slave Operation

The above 82385 local bus arbitration discussion is true when the 82385 is programmed for "Master" mode operation. The user can, however, configure the 82385 for "Slave" mode operation. (Programming is done via a hardware strap option.) The roles of BHOLD and BHLDA are reversed for an 82385 in slave mode; BHOLD is now an output indicating a request to control the bus, and BHLDA is an input indicating that a request has been granted. An 82385 programmed in slave mode drives the 82385 local bus only when it has requested and subsequently been granted bus control. This allows multiple 386 DX CPU/82385 subsystems to reside on the same 82385 local bus (Figure 1-3).

4

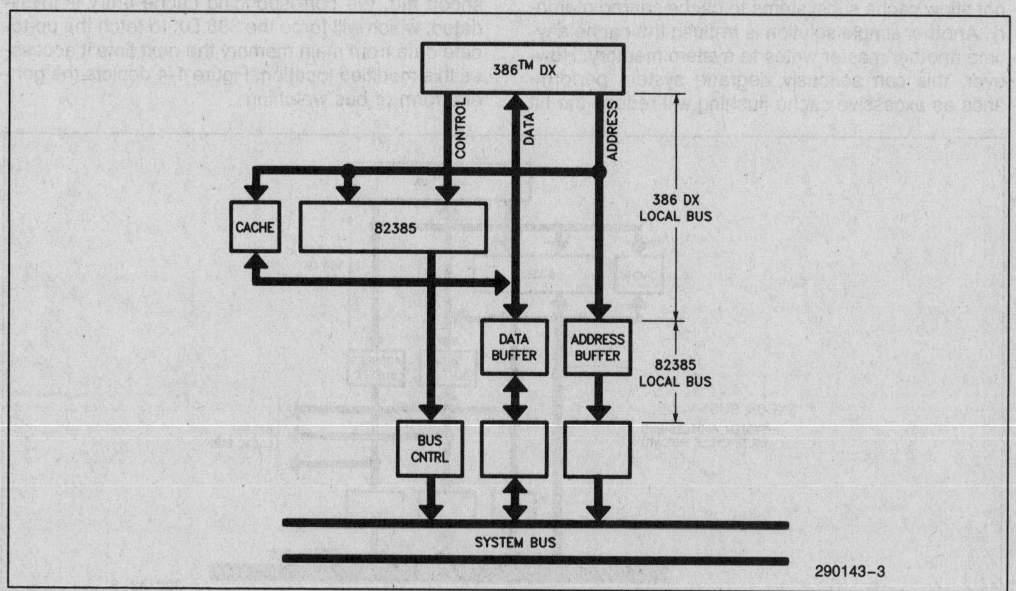

Figure 1-2. 386™ DX CPU/82385 System Bus Structure

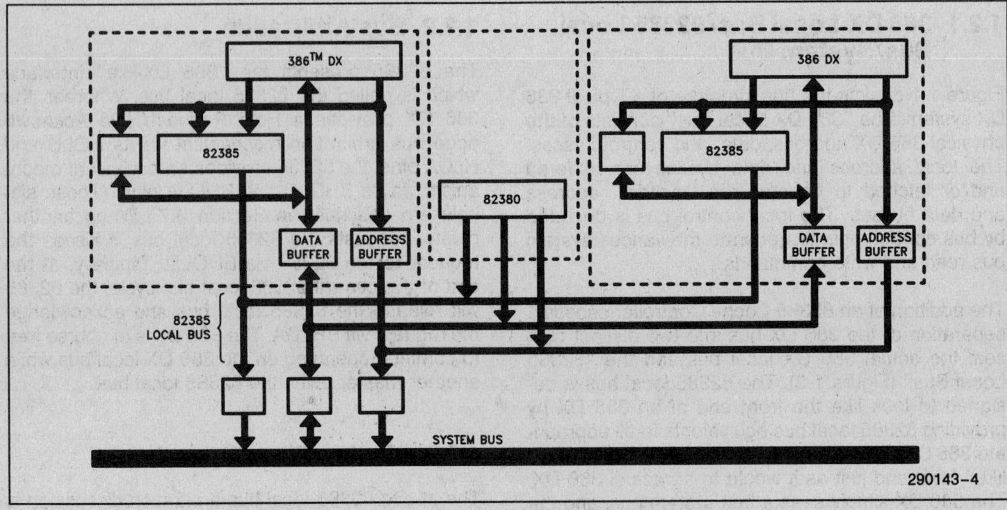

Figure 1-3. Multi-Master/Multi-Cache Environment

1.2.4 Cache Coherency

Ideally, a cache contains a copy of the most heavily used portions of main memory. To maintain cache "coherency" is to make sure that this local copy is identical to main memory. In a system where multiple masters can access the same memory, there is always a risk that one master will alter the contents of a memory location that is duplicated in the local cache of another master. (The cache is said to contain "stale" data.) One rather restrictive solution is to not allow cache subsystems to cache shared memory. Another simple solution is to flush the cache anytime another master writes to system memory. However, this can seriously degrade system performance as excessive cache flushing will reduce the hit rate of what may otherwise be a highly efficient cache.

The 82385 preserves cache coherency via "bus watching" (also called snooping), a technique that neither impacts performance nor restricts memory mapping. An 82385 that is not currently bus master monitors system bus cycles, and when a write cycle by another master is detected (a snoop), the system address is sampled and used to see if the referenced location is duplicated in the cache. If so (a snoop hit), the corresponding cache entry is invalidated, which will force the 386 DX to fetch the up-to-date data from main memory the next time it accesses this modified location. Figure 1-4 depicts the general form of bus watching.

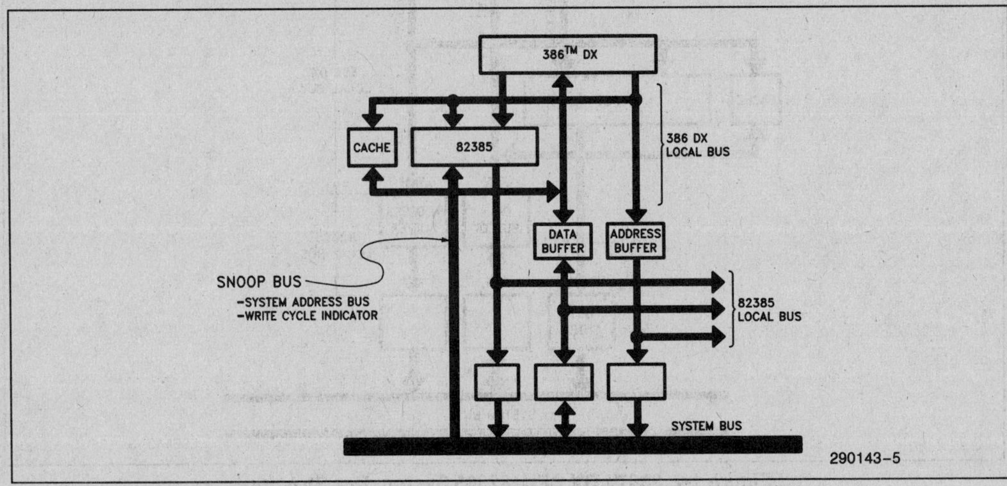

Figure 1-4. 82385 Bus Watching—Monitor System Bus Write Cycles

1.3 SYSTEM OVERVIEW II: BASIC OPERATION

This discussion is an overview of the basic operation of an 386 DX CPU/82385 system. Items discussed include the 82385's response to all 386 DX cycles, including interrupt acknowledges, halts, and shutdowns. Also discussed are non-cacheable and local accesses.

1.3.1 386 DX Memory Code and Data Read Cycles

1.3.1.1 READ HITS

When the 386 DX initiates a memory code or data read cycle, the 82385 compares the high order bits of the 386 DX address bus with the appropriate addresses (tags) stored in its on-chip directory. (The directory structure is described in Chapter 2.) If the 82385 determines that the requested data is in the cache, it issues the appropriate control signals that direct the cache to drive the requested data onto the 386 DX data bus, where it is read by the 386 DX. The 82385 terminates the 386 DX cycle without inserting any wait states.

1.3.1.2 READ MISSES

If the 82385 determines that the requested data is not in the cache, the request is forwarded to the 82385 local bus and the data retrieved from main memory. As the data returns from main memory, it is directed to the 386 DX and also written into the cache. Concurrently, the 82385 updates the cache directory such that the next time this particular piece of information is requested by the 386 DX, the 82385 will find it in the cache and return it with zero wait states.

The basic unit of transfer between main memory and cache memory in a cache subsystem is called the line size. In an 82385 system, the line size is one 32-bit aligned doubleword. During a read miss, all four 82385 local bus byte enables are active. This ensures that a full 32-bit entry is written into the cache. (The 386 DX simply ignores what it did not request.) In any other type of 386 DX cycle that is forwarded to the 82385 local bus, the logic levels of the 386 DX byte enables are duplicated on the 82385 local bus.

The 82385 does not actively fetch main memory data independently of the 386 DX. The 82385 is essentially a passive device which only monitors the address bus and activates control signals. The read miss is the only mechanism by which main memory data is copied into the cache and validated in the cache directory.

In an isolated read miss, the number of wait states seen by the 386 DX is that required by the system memory to respond with data plus the cache comparison cycle (hit/miss decision). The cache system must determine that the cycle is a miss before it can begin the system memory access. However, since misses most often occur consecutively, the 82385 will begin 386 DX address pipelined cycles to effectively "hide" the comparison cycle beyond the first miss (refer to Section 4.1.3).

The 82385 can execute a main memory access on the 82385 local bus only if it currently owns the bus. If not, an 82385 in master mode will run the cycle after the current master releases the bus. An 82385 in slave mode will issue a hold request, and will run the cycle as soon as the request is acknowledged. (This is true for any read or write cycle that needs to run on the 82385 local bus.)

1.3.2 386 DX Memory Write Cycles

The 82385's "posted write" capability allows the majority of 386 DX memory write cycles to run with zero wait states. The primary memory update policy implemented in a posted write is the traditional cache "write through" technique, which implies that main memory is always updated in any memory write cycle. If the referenced location also happens to reside in the cache (a write hit), the cache is updated as well.

Beyond this, a posted write latches the 386 DX address, data, and cycle definition signals, and the 386 DX local bus cycle is terminated without any wait states, even though the corresponding 82385 local bus cycle is not yet completed, or perhaps not even started. A posted write is possible because the 82385's bus state machine, which is almost identical to the 386 DX bus state machine, is able to run 82385 local bus cycles independently of the 386 DX. The only time the 386 DX sees write cycle wait states is when a previously latched (posted) write has not yet been completed on the 82385 local bus or during an I/O write (which is not posted). A 386 DX write can be posted even if the 82385 does not currently own the 82385 local bus. In this case, an 82385 in master mode will run the cycle as soon as the current master releases the bus, and an 82385 in slave mode will request the bus and run the cycle when the request is acknowledged. The 386 DX is free to continue operating out of its cache (on the 386 DX local bus) during this time.

1.3.3 Non-Cacheable Cycles

Non-cacheable cycles fall into one of two categories: cycles decoded as non-cacheable, and cycles that are by default non-cacheable according to the 82385's design. All non-cacheable cycles are forwarded to the 82385 local bus. Non-cacheable cycles have no effect on the cache or cache directory.

The 82385 allows the system designer to define areas of main memory as non-cacheable. The 386 DX address bus is decoded and the decode output is connected to the 82385's non-cacheable access (NCA#) input. This decoding is done in the first 386 DX bus state in which the non-cacheable cycle address becomes available. Non-cacheable read cycles resemble cacheable read miss cycles, except that the cache and cache directory are unaffected. NCA defined non-cacheable writes, like most writes, are posted.

The 82385 defines certain cycles as non-cacheable without using its non-cacheable access input. These include I/O cycles, interrupt acknowledge cycles, and halt/shutdown cycles. I/O reads and interrupt acknowledge cycles execute as any other non-cacheable read. I/O write cycles are not posted. The 386 DX is not allowed to continue until a ready signal is returned from the system. Halt/Shutdown cycles are posted. During a halt/shutdown condition, the 82385 local bus duplicates the behavior of the 386 DX, including the ability to recognize and respond to a BHOLD request. (The 82385's bus watching mechanism is functional in this condition.)

1.3.3.1 16-BIT MEMORY SPACE

The 82385 does not cache 16-bit memory space (as decoded by the 386 DX BS16# input), but does make provisions to handle 16-bit space as non-cacheable. (There is no 82385 equivalent to the 386 DX BS16# input.) In a system without an 82385, the 386 DX BS16# input need not be asserted until the last state of a 16-bit cycle for the 386 DX to recognize it as such (unless NA# is sampled active earlier in the cycle.) The 82385, however, needs this information earlier, specifically at the end of the first 386 DX bus state in which the address of the 16-bit cycle becomes available. The result is that in a system without an 82385, 16-bit devices can inform the 386 DX that they are 16-bit devices "on the fly," while in a system with an 82385, devices decoded as 16-bit (using the 386 DX BS16#) must be located in address space set aside for 16-bit devices. If 16-bit space is decoded according to 82385 guidelines (as described later in the data sheet), then the 82385 will handle 16-bit cycles just like the 386 DX does, including effectively locking the two halves of a non-aligned 16-bit transfer from interruption by another master.

1.3.4 386 DX Local Bus Cycles

386 DX Local Bus Cycles are accesses to resources on the 386 DX local bus other than to the 82385 itself. The 82385 simply ignores these accesses: they are neither forwarded to the system nor do they affect the cache. The designer sets aside memory and/or I/O space for local resources by decoding the 386 DX address bus and feeding the decode to the 82385's local bus access (LBA#) input. The designer can also decode the 386 DX cycle definition signals to keep specific 386 DX cycles from being forwarded to the system. For example, a multi-processor design may wish to capture and remedy a 386 DX shutdown locally without having it detected by the rest of the system. Note that in such a design, the local shutdown cycle must be terminated by local bus control logic. The 387 Math Coprocessor is considered a 386 DX local bus resource, but it need not be decoded as such by the user since the 82385 is able to internally recognize 387 accesses via the M/IO# and A31 pins.

1.3.5 Summary of 82385 Response to All 386 DX Cycles

Table 1-1 summarizes the 82385 response to all 386 DX bus cycles, as conditioned by whether or not the cycle is decoded as local or non-cacheable. The table describes the impact of each cycle on the cache and on the cache directory, and whether or not the cycle is forwarded to the 82385 local bus. Whenever the 82385 local bus is marked "IDLE", it implies that this bus is available to other masters.

Table 1-1. 82385 Response to 386 DX Cycles

386 DX Bus Cycle Definition					82385 Response when Decoded as Cacheable			82385 Response when Decoded as Non-Cacheable			82385 Response when Decoded as an 386 DX Local Bus Access		
M/IO#	D/C#	W/R#	386 DX Cycle		Cache	Cache Directory	82385 Local Bus	Cache	Cache Directory	82385 Local Bus	Cache	Cache Directory	82385 Local Bus
0	0	0	INT ACK	N/A	—	—	INT ACK	—	—	INT ACK	—	—	IDLE
0	0	1	UNDEFINED	N/A			UNDEFINED			UNDEFINED			IDLE
0	1	0	I/O READ	N/A	—	—	I/O READ	—	—	I/O READ	—	—	IDLE
0	1	1	I/O WRITE	N/A	—	—	I/O WRITE	—	—	I/O WRITE	—	—	IDLE
1	0	0	MEM CODE READ	HIT	CACHE READ	—	IDLE	—	—	MEM CODE READ	—	—	IDLE
				MISS	CACHE WRITE	DATA VALIDATION	MEM CODE READ						
1	0	1	HALT/ SHUTDOWN	N/A	—	—	HALT/ SHUTDOWN	—	—	HALT/ SHUTDOWN	—	—	IDLE
1	1	0	MEM DATA READ	HIT	CACHE READ	—	IDLE	—	—	MEM DATA READ	—	—	IDLE
				MISS	CACHE WRITE	DATA VALIDATION	MEM DATA READ						
1	1	1	MEM DATA WRITE	HIT	CACHE WRITE	—	MEM DATA WRITE	—	—	MEM DATA WRITE	—	—	IDLE
				MISS	—	—	MEM DATA WRITE						

NOTES:

- A dash (—) indicates that the cache and cache directory are unaffected. This table does not reflect how an access affects the LRU bit.
- An "IDLE" 82385 Local Bus implies that this bus is available to other masters.
- The 82385's response to 80387 accesses is the same as when decoded as an 386 DX Local Bus access.
- The only other operations that affect the cache directory are:
  1. RESET or Cache Flush—all tag valid bits cleared.
  2. Snoop Hit—corresponding line valid bit cleared.

4

1.3.6 Bus Watching

As previously discussed, the 82385 "qualifies" an 386 DX bus cycle in the first bus state in which the address and cycle definition signals of the cycle become available. The cycle is qualified as read or write, cacheable or non-cacheable, etc. Cacheable cycles are further classified as hit or miss according to the results of the cache comparison, which accesses the 82385 directory and compares the appropriate directory location (tag) to the current 386 DX address. If the cycle turns out to be non-cacheable or a 386 DX local bus access, the hit/miss decision is ignored. The cycle qualification requires one 386 DX state. Since the fastest 386 DX access is two states, the second state can be used for bus watching.

When the 82385 does not own the system bus, it monitors system bus cycles. If another master writes into main memory, the 82385 latches the system address and executes a cache look-up to see if the altered main memory location resides in the cache. If so (a snoop hit), the cache entry is marked invalid in the cache directory. Since the directory is at most only being used every other state to qualify 386 DX accesses, snoop look-ups are interleaved between 386 DX local bus look-ups. The cache directory is time multiplexed between the 386 DX address and the latched system address. The result is that all snoops are caught and serviced without slowing down the 386 DX, even when running zero wait state hits on the 386 DX local bus.

1.3.7 Cache Flush

The 82385 offers a cache flush input. When activated, this signal causes the 82385 to invalidate all data which had previously been cached. Specifically, all tag valid bits are cleared. (Refer to the 82385 directory structure in Chapter 2.) Therefore, the cache is empty and subsequent cycles are misses until the 386 DX begins repeating the new accesses (hits). The primary use of the FLUSH input is for diagnostics and multi-processor support.

NOTE:
The use of this pin as a coherency mechanism may impact software transparency.

2.0 82385 CACHE ORGANIZATION

The 82385 supports two cache organizations: a simple direct mapped organization and a slightly more complex, higher performance two way set associative organization. The choice is made by strapping an 82385 input (2W/D#) either high or low. This chapter describes the structure and operation of both organizations.

2.1 DIRECT MAPPED CACHE

2.1.1 Direct Mapped Cache Structure and Terminology

Figure 2-1 depicts the relationship between the 82385's internal cache directory, the external cache memory, and the 386 DX's 4 Gigabyte physical address space. The 4 Gigabytes can conceptually be thought of as cache "pages" each being 8K doublewords (32 Kbytes) deep. The page size matches the cache size. The cache can be further divided into 1024 (0 thru 1023) sets of eight doublewords (8 x 32 bits). Each 32-bit doubleword is called a "line." The unit of transfer between the main memory and cache is one line.

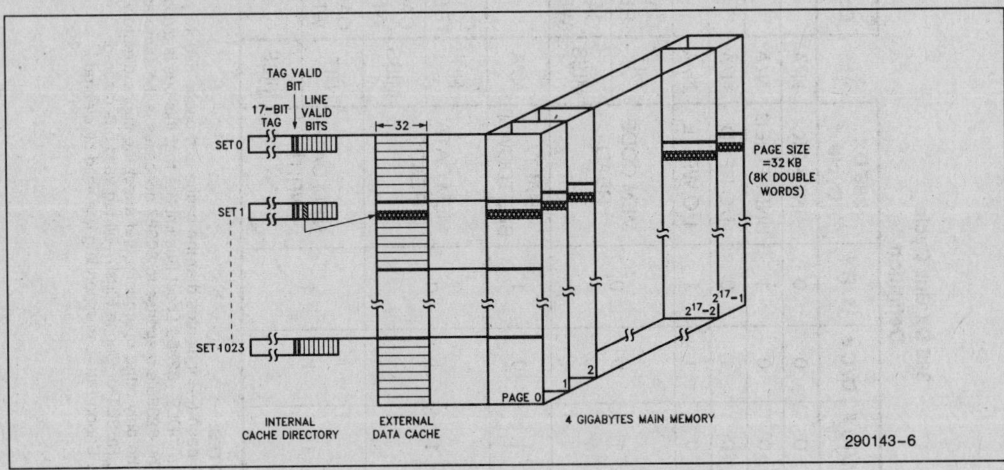

Figure 2-1. Direct Mapped Cache Organization

Each block in the external cache has an associated 26-bit entry in the 82385's internal cache directory. This entry has three components: a 17-bit "tag," a "tag valid" bit, and eight "line valid" bits. The tag acts as a main memory page number (17 tag bits support 2^{17} pages). For example, if line 9 of page 2 currently resides in the cache, then a binary 2 is stored in the Set 1 tag field. (For any 82385 direct mapped cache page in main memory, Set 0 consists of lines 0–7, Set 1 consists of lines 8–15, etc. Line 9 is shaded in Figure 2-1.) An important characteristic of a direct mapped cache is that line 9 of any page can only reside in line 9 of the cache. All identical page offsets map to a single cache location.

The data in a cache set is considered valid or invalid depending on the status of its tag valid bit. If clear, the entire set is considered invalid. If true, an individual line within the set is considered valid or invalid depending on the status of its line valid bit.

The 82385 sees the 386 DX address bus (A2–A31) as partitioned into three fields: a 17-bit "tag" field (A15–A31), a 10-bit "set-address" field (A5–A14), and a 3-bit "line select" field (A2–A4). (See Figure 2-2.) The lower 13 address bits (A2–A14) also serve as the "cache address" which directly selects one of 8K doublewords in the external cache.

2.1.2 Direct Mapped Cache Operation

The following is a description of the interaction between the 386 DX, cache, and cache directory.

2.1.2.1 READ HITS

When the 386 DX initiates a memory read cycle, the 82385 uses the 10-bit set address to select one of 1024 directory entries, and the 3-bit line select field to select one of eight line valid bits within the entry. The 13-bit cache address selects the corresponding doubleword in the cache. The 82385 compares the 17-bit tag field (A15–A31 of the 386 DX access) with the tag stored in the selected directory entry. If the tag and upper address bits match, and if both the tag and appropriate line valid bits are set, the result is a hit, and the 82385 directs the cache to drive the selected doubleword onto the 386 DX data bus. A read hit does not alter the contents of the cache or directory.

2.1.2.2 READ MISSES

A read miss can occur in two ways. The first is known as a "line" miss, and occurs when the tag and upper address bits match and the tag valid bit is set, but the line valid bit is clear. The second is called a "tag" miss, and occurs when either the tag and upper address bits do not match, or the tag valid bit is clear. (The line valid bit is a "don't care" in a tag miss.) In both cases, the 82385 forwards the 386 DX reference to the system, and as the returning data is fed to the 386 DX, it is written into the cache and validated in the cache directory.

In a line miss, the incoming data is validated simply by setting the previously clear line valid bit. In a tag miss, the upper address bits overwrite the previously stored tag, the tag valid bit is set, the appropriate line valid bit is set, and the other seven line valid bits are cleared. Subsequent tag hits with line misses will only set the appropriate line valid bit. (Any data associated with the previous tag is no longer considered resident in the cache.)

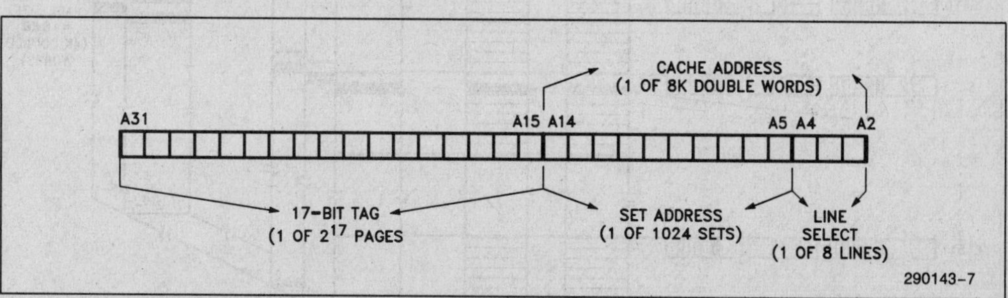

Figure 2-2. 386 DX Address Bus Bit Fields—Direct Mapped Organization

2.1.2.3 OTHER OPERATIONS THAT AFFECT THE CACHE AND CACHE DIRECTORY

The other operations that affect the cache and/or directory are write hits, snoop hits, cache flushes, and 82385 resets. In a write hit, the cache is updated along with main memory, but the directory is unaffected. In a snoop hit, the cache is unaffected, but the affected line is invalidated by clearing its line valid bit in the directory. Both an 82385 reset and cache flush clear all tag valid bits.

When an 386 DX CPU/82385 system "wakes up" upon reset, all tag valid bits are clear. At this point, a read miss is the only mechanism by which main memory data is copied into the cache and validated in the cache directory. Assume an early 386 DX code access seeks (for the first time) line 9 of page 2. Since the tag valid bit is clear, the access is a tag miss, and the data is fetched from main memory. Upon return, the data is fed to the 386 DX and simultaneously written into line 9 of the cache. The set directory entry is updated to show this line as valid. Specifically, the tag and appropriate line valid bits are set, the remaining seven line valid bits cleared, and a binary 2 written into the tag. Since code is sequential in nature, the 386 DX will likely next want line 10 of page 2, then line 11, and so on. If the 386 DX sequentially fetches the next six lines, these fetches will be line misses, and as each is fetched from main memory and written into the cache, its corresponding line valid bit is set. This is the basic flow of events that fills the cache with valid data. Only after a piece of data has been copied into the cache and validated can it be accessed in a zero wait state read hit. Also, a cache entry must have been validated before it can be subsequently altered by a write hit, or invalidated by a snoop hit.

An extreme example of "thrashing" is if line 9 of page two is an instruction to jump to line 9 of page one, which is an instruction to jump back to line 9 of page two. Thrashing results from the direct mapped cache characteristic that all identical page offsets map to a single cache location. In this example, the page one access overwrites the cached page two data, and the page two access overwrites the cached page one data. As long as the code jumps back and forth the hit rate is zero. This is of course an extreme case. The effect of thrashing is that a direct mapped cache exhibits a slightly reduced overall hit rate as compared to a set associative cache of the same size.

2.2 TWO WAY SET ASSOCIATIVE CACHE

2.2.1 Two Way Set Associative Cache Structure and Terminology

Figure 2-3 illustrates the relationship between the directory, cache, and 4 Gigabyte address space.

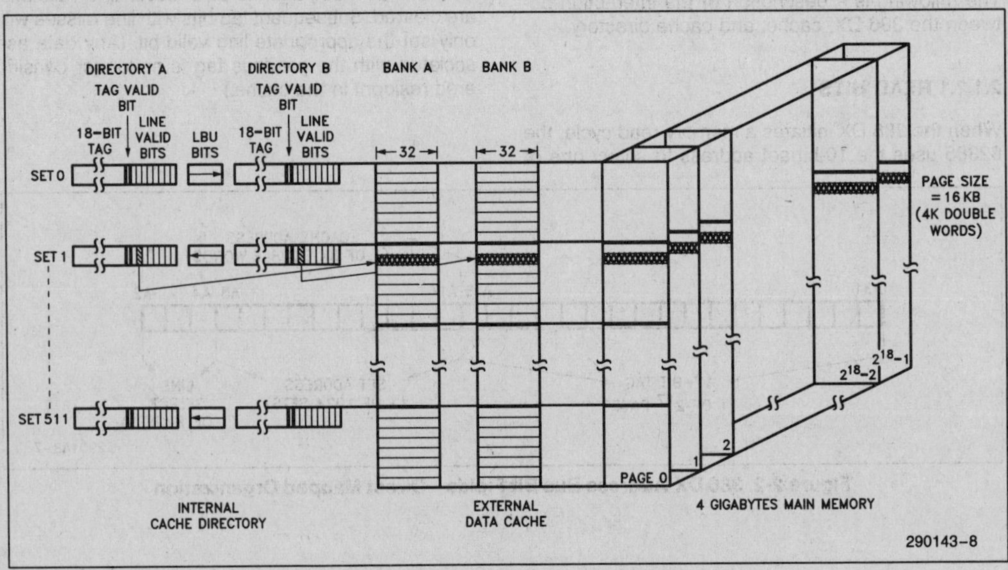

Figure 2-3. Two-Way Set Associative Cache Organization

Whereas the direct mapped cache is organized as one bank of 8K doublewords, the two way set associative cache is organized as two banks (A and B) of 4K doublewords each. The page size is halved, and the number of pages doubled. (Note the extra tag bit.) The cache now has 512 sets in each bank. (Two banks times 512 sets gives a total of 1024. The structure can be thought of as two half-sized direct mapped caches in parallel.) The performance advantage over a direct mapped cache is that all identical page offsets map to two cache locations instead of one, reducing the potential for thrashing. The 82385's partitioning of the 386 DX address bus is depicted in Figure 2-4.

2.2.2 LRU Replacement Algorithm

The two way set associative directory has an additional feature: the "least recently used" or LRU bit. In the event of a read miss, either bank A or bank B will be updated with new data. The LRU bit flags the candidate for replacement. Statistically, of two blocks of data, the block most recently used is the block most likely to be needed again in the near future. By flagging the least recently used block, the 82385 ensures that the cache block replaced is the least likely to have data needed by the CPU.

2.2.3 Two Way Set Associative Cache Operation

2.2.3.1 READ HITS

When the 386 DX initiates a memory read cycle, the 82385 uses the 9-bit set address to select one of 512 sets. The two tags of this set are simultaneously compared with A14–A31, both tag valid bits checked, and both appropriate line valid bits checked. If either comparison produces a hit, the corresponding cache bank is directed to drive the selected doubleword onto the 386 DX data bus. (Note that both banks will never concurrently cache the same main memory location.) If the requested data resides in bank A, the LRU bit is pointed toward B. If B produces the hit, the LRU bit is pointed toward A.

2.2.3.2 READ MISSES

As in direct mapped operation, a read miss can be either a line or tag miss. Let's start with a tag miss example. Assume the 386 DX seeks line 9 of page 2, and that neither the A or B directory produces a tag match. Assume also, as indicated in Figure 2-3, that the LRU bit points to A. As the data returns from main memory, it is loaded into offset 9 of bank A. Concurrently, this data is validated by updating the set 1 directory entry for bank A. Specifically, the upper address bits overwrite the previous tag, the tag valid bit is set, the appropriate line valid bit is set, and the other seven line valid bits cleared. Since this data is the most recently used, the LRU bit is turned toward B. No change to bank B occurs.

If the next 386 DX request is line 10 of page two, the result will be a line miss. As the data returns from main memory, it will be written into offset 10 of bank A (tag hit/line miss in bank A), and the appropriate line valid bit will be set. A line miss in one bank will cause the LRU bit to point to the other bank. In this example, however, the LRU bit has already been turned toward B.

2.2.3.3 OTHER OPERATIONS THAT AFFECT THE CACHE AND CACHE DIRECTORY

Other operations that affect the cache and cache directory are write hits, snoop hits, cache flushes, and 82385 resets. A write hit updates the cache along with main memory. If directory A detects the hit, bank A is updated. If directory B detects the hit, bank B is updated. If one bank is updated, the LRU bit is pointed toward the other.

If a snoop hit invalidates an entry, for example, in cache bank A, the corresponding LRU bit is pointed toward A. This ensures that invalid data is the prime candidate for replacement in a read miss. Finally, resets and flushes behave just as they do in a direct mapped cache, clearing all tag valid bits.

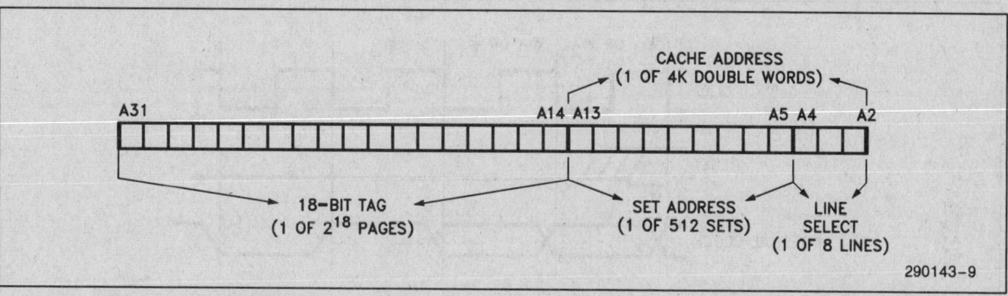

Figure 2-4. 386 DX Address Bus Bit Fields—Two-Way Set Associative Organization

3.0 82385 PIN DESCRIPTION

The 82385 creates the 82385 local bus, which is a functional 386 DX interface. To facilitate understanding, 82385 local bus signals go by the same name as their 386 DX equivalents, except that they are preceded by the letter "B". The 82385 local bus equivalent to ADS# is BADS#, the equivalent to NA# is BNA#, etc. This convention applies to bus states as well. For example, BT1P is the 82385 local bus state equivalent to the 386 DX T1P state.

3.1 386 DX CPU/82385 INTERFACE SIGNALS

These signals form the direct interface between the 386 DX and 82385.

3.1.1 386 DX CPU/82385 Clock (CLK2)

CLK2 provides the fundamental timing for an 386 DX CPU/82385 system, and is driven by the same source that drives the 386 DX CLK2 input. The 82385, like the 386 DX, divides CLK2 by two to generate an internal "phase indication" clock. (See Figure 3-1.) The CLK2 period whose rising edge drives the internal clock low is called PHI1, and the CLK2 period that drives the internal clock high is called PHI2. A PHI1-PHI2 combination (in that order) is known as a "T" state, and is the basis for 386 DX bus cycles.

3.1.2 386 DX CPU/82385 Reset (RESET)

This input resets the 82385, bringing it to an initial known state, and is driven by the same source that drives the 386 DX RESET input. A reset effectively flushes the cache by clearing all cache directory tag valid bits. The falling edge of RESET is synchronized to CLK2, and used by the 82385 to properly establish the phase of its internal clock. (See Figure 3-2.) Specifically, the second internal phase following the falling edge of RESET is PHI2.

3.1.3 386 DX CPU/82385 Address Bus (A2–A31), Byte Enables (BE0#–BE3#), and Cycle Definition Signals (M/IO#, D/C#, W/R#, LOCK#)

The 82385 directly connects to these 386 DX outputs. The 386 DX address bus is used in the cache directory comparison to see if data referenced by 386 DX resides in the cache, and the byte enables inform the 82385 as to which portions of the data bus are involved in an 386 DX cycle. The cycle definition signals are decoded by the 82385 to determine the type of cycle the 386 DX is executing.

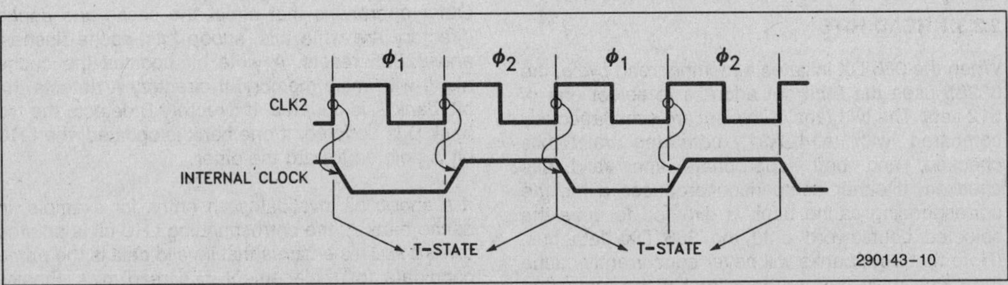

Figure 3-1. CLK2 and Internal Clock

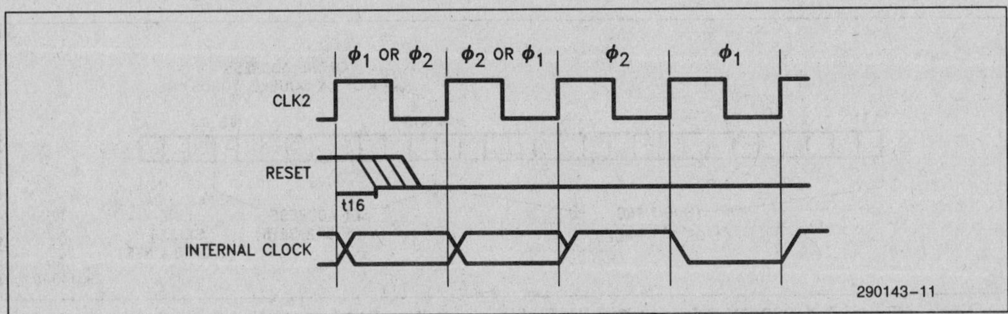

Figure 3-2. Reset/Internal Phase Relationship

3.1.4 386 DX CPU/82385 Address Status (ADS#) and Ready Input (READYI#)

ADS#, a 386 DX output, tells the 82385 that new address and cycle definition information is available. READYI#, an input to both the 386 DX (via the 386 DX READY# input pin) and 82385, indicates the completion of an 386 DX bus cycle. ADS# and READYI# are used to keep track of the 386 DX bus state.

3.1.5 386 DX Next Address Request (NA#)

This 82385 output controls 386 DX pipelining. It can be tied directly to the 386 DX NA# input, or it can be logically "AND"ed with other 386 DX local bus next address requests.

3.1.6 Ready Output (READYO#) and Bus Ready Enable (BRDYEN#)

The 82385 directly terminates all but two types of 386 DX bus cycles with its READYO# output. 386 DX local bus cycles must be terminated by the local device being accessed. This includes devices decoded using the 82385 LBA# signal and 80387 accesses. The other cycles not directly terminated by the 82385 are 82385 local bus reads, specifically cache read misses and non-cacheable reads. (Recall that the 82385 forwards and runs such cycles on the 82385 bus.) In these cycles the signal that terminates the 82385 local bus access is BREADY#, which is gated through to the 386 DX local bus such that the 386 DX and 82385 local bus cycles are concurrently terminated. BRDYEN# is used to gate the BREADY# signal to the 386 DX.

3.2 CACHE CONTROL SIGNALS

These 82385 outputs control the external 32 KB cache data memory.

3.2.1 Cache Address Latch Enable (CALEN)

This signal controls the latch (typically an F or AS series 74373) that resides between the low order 386 DX address bits and the cache SRAM address inputs. (The outputs of this latch are the "cache address" described in the previous chapter.) When CALEN is high the latch is transparent. The falling edge of CALEN latches the current inputs which remain applied to the cache data memory until CALEN returns to an active high state.

3.2.2 Cache Transmit/Receive (CT/R#)

This signal defines the direction of an optional data transceiver (typically an F or AS series 74245) between the cache and 386 DX data bus. When high, the transceiver is pointed towards the 386 DX local data bus (the SRAMs are output enabled). When low, the transceiver points towards the cache data memory. A transceiver is required if the cache is designed with SRAMs that lack an output enable control. A transceiver may also be desirable in a system that has a heavily loaded 386 DX local data bus. These devices are not necessary when using SRAMs which incorporate an output enable.

3.2.3 Cache Chip Selects (CS0#–CS3#)

These active low signals tie to the cache SRAM chip selects, and individually enable the four bytes of the 32-bit wide cache. CS0# enables D0–D7, CS1# enables D8–D15, CS2# enables D16–D23, and CS3# enables D24–D31. During read hits, all four bytes are enabled regardless of whether or not all four 386 DX byte enables are active. (The 386 DX ignores what it did not request.) Also, all four cache bytes are enabled in a read miss so as to update the cache with a complete line (double word). In a write hit, only those cache bytes that correspond to active byte enables are selected. This prevents cache data from being corrupted in a partial doubleword write.

3.2.4 Cache Output Enables (COEA#, COEB#) and Write Enables (CWEA#, CWEB#)

COEA# and COEB# are active low signals which tie to the cache SRAM or Transceiver output enables and respectively enable cache bank A or B. The state of DEFOE# (define cache output enable), an 82385 configuration input, determines the functional definition of COEA# and COEB#.

If DEFOE# = V_{IL}, in a two-way set associative cache, either COEA# or COEB# is active during read hit cycles only, depending on which bank is selected. In a direct mapped cache, both are activated during read hits, so the designer is free to use either one. This COEx# definition best suites cache SRAMs with output enables.

If DEFOE# = V_{IH}, COEx# is active during read hit, read miss (cache update) and write hit cycles only. This COEx# definition suites cache SRAMs without output enables. In such systems, transceivers are needed and their output enables must be active for writing, as well as reading, the cache SRAMs.

4

CWEA# and CWEB# are active low signals which tie to the cache SRAM write enables, and respectively enable cache bank A or B to receive data from the 386 DX data bus (386 DX write hit or read miss update). In a two-way set associative cache, one or the other is enabled in a read miss or write hit. In a direct mapped cache, both are activated, so the designer is free to use either one.

The various cache configurations supported by the 82385 are described in Chapter 4.

3.3 386 DX LOCAL BUS DECODE INPUTS

These 82385 inputs are generated by decoding the 386 DX address and cycle definition lines. These active low inputs are sampled at the end of the first state in which the address of a new 386 DX cycle becomes available (T1 or first T2P).

3.3.1 386 DX Local Bus Access (LBA#)

This input identifies an 386 DX access as directed to a resource (other than the cache) on the 386 DX local bus. (The 387 Numerics Coprocessor is considered a 386 DX local bus resource, but LBA# need not be generated as the 82385 internally decodes 387 accesses.) The 82385 simply ignores these cycles. They are neither forwarded to the system nor do they affect the cache or cache directory. Note that LBA# has priority over all other types of cycles. If LBA# is asserted, the cycle is interpreted as an 386 DX local bus access, regardless of the cycle type or status of NCA# or X16#. This allows any 386 DX cycle (memory, I/O, interrupt acknowledge, etc.) to be kept on the 386 local bus if desired.

3.3.2 Non-Cacheable Access (NCA#)

This active low input identifies a 386 DX cycle as non-cacheable. The 82385 forwards non-cacheable cycles to the 82385 local bus and runs them. The cache and cache directory are unaffected.

NCA# allows a designer to set aside a portion of main memory as non-cacheable. Potential applications include memory-mapped I/O and systems where multiple masters access dual ported memory via different busses. Another possibility makes use of the 386 DX D/C# output. The 82385 by default implements a unified code and data cache, but driving NCA# directly by D/C# creates a data only cache. If D/C# is inverted first, the result is a code only cache.

3.3.3 16-Bit Access (X16#)

X16# is an active low input which identifies 16-bit memory and/or I/O space, and the decoded signal that drives X16# should also drive the 386 DX BS16# input. 16-bit accesses are treated like non-cacheable accesses: they are forwarded to and executed on the 82385 local bus with no impact on the cache or cache directory. In addition, the 82385 locks the two halves of a non-aligned 16-bit transfer from interruption by another master, as does the 386 DX.

3.4 82385 LOCAL BUS INTERFACE SIGNALS

The 82385 presents a "386 DX-like" front end to the system, and the signals discussed in this section are 82385 local bus equivalents to actual 386 DX signals. These signals are named with respect to their 386 DX counterparts, but with the letter "B" appended to the front.

Note that the 82385 itself does not have equivalent output signals to the 386 DX data bus (D0–D31), address bus (A2–A31), and cycle definition signals (M/IO#, D/C#, W/R#). The 82385 data bus (BD0–BD31) is actually the system side of a latching transceiver, and the 82385 address bus and cycle definition signals (BA2–BA31, BM/IO#, BD/C#, BW/R#) are the outputs of an edge-triggered latch. The signals that control this data transceiver and address latch are discussed in Section 3.5.

3.4.1 82385 Bus Byte Enables (BBE0#–BBE3#)

BBE0#–BBE3# are the 82385 local bus equivalents to the 386 DX byte enables. In a cache read miss, the 82385 drives all four signals low, regardless of whether or not all four 386 DX byte enables are active. This ensures that a complete line (doubleword) is fetched from main memory for the cache update. In all other 82385 local bus cycles, the 82385 duplicates the logic levels of the 386 DX byte enables. The 82385 tri-states these outputs when it is not the current bus master.

3.4.2 82385 Bus Lock (BLOCK#)

BLOCK# is the 82385 local bus equivalent to the 386 DX LOCK# output, and distinguishes between locked and unlocked cycles. When the 386 DX runs a locked sequence of cycles (and LBA# is negated), the 82385 forwards and runs the sequence on the 82385 local bus, regardless of whether any locations referenced in the sequence reside in the cache. A read hit will be run as if it is a read miss, but a write hit will update the cache as well as being completed to system memory. In keeping with 386 DX behavior, the 82385 does not allow another master to interrupt the sequence. BLOCK# is tri-stated when the 82385 is not the current bus master.

3.4.3 82385 Bus Address Status (BADS#)

BADS# is the 82385 local bus equivalent of ADS#, and indicates that a valid address (BA2–BA31, BBE0#–BBE3#) and cycle definition (BM/IO#, BW/R#, BD/C#) is available. It is asserted in BT1 and BT2P states, and is tri-stated when the 82385 does not own the bus.

3.4.4 82385 Bus Ready Input (BREADY#)

82385 local bus cycles are terminated by BREADY#, just as 386 DX cycles are terminated by the 386 DX READY# input. In 82385 local bus read cycles, BREADY# is gated by BRDYEN# onto the 386 DX local bus, such that it terminates both the 386 DX and 82385 local bus cycles.

3.4.5 82385 Bus Next Address Request (BNA#)

BNA# is the 82385 local bus equivalent to the 386 DX NA# input, and indicates that the system is prepared to accept a pipelined address and cycle definition. If BNA# is asserted and the new cycle information is available, the 82385 begins a pipelined cycle on the 82385 local bus.

3.5 82385 BUS DATA TRANSCEIVER AND ADDRESS LATCH CONTROL SIGNALS

The 82385 data bus is the system side of a latching transceiver (typically an F or AS series 74646), and the 82385 address bus and cycle definition signals are the outputs of an edge-triggered latch (F or AS series 74374). The following is a discussion of the 82385 outputs that control these devices. An important characteristic of these signals and the devices they control is that they ensure that BD0–BD31, BA2–BA31, BM/IO#, BD/C#, and BW/R# reproduce the functionality and timing behavior of their 386 DX equivalents.

3.5.1 Local Data Strobe (LDSTB), Data Output Enable (DOE#), and Bus Transmit/Receive (BT/R#)

These signals control the latching data transceiver. BT/R# defines the transceiver direction. When high, the transceiver drives the 82385 data bus in write cycles. When low, the transceiver drives the 386 DX data bus in 82385 local bus read cycles. DOE# enables the transceiver outputs.

The rising edge of LDSTB latches the 386 DX data bus in all write cycles. The interaction of this signal and the latching transceiver is used to perform the 82385's posted write capability.

3.5.2 Bus Address Clock Pulse (BACP) and Bus Address Output Enable (BAOE#)

These signals control the latch that drives BA2–BA31, BM/IO#, BW/R#, and BD/C#. In any 386 DX cycle that is forwarded to the 82385 local bus, the rising edge of BACP latches the 386 DX address and cycle definition signals. BAOE# enables the latch outputs when the 82385 is the current bus master and disables them otherwise.

4

3.6 STATUS AND CONTROL SIGNALS

3.6.1 Cache Miss Indication (MISS#)

This output accompanies cacheable read and write miss cycles. This signal transitions to its active low state when the 82385 determines that a cacheable 386 DX access is a miss. Its timing behavior follows that of the 82385 local bus cycle definition signals (BM/IO#, BD/C#, BW/R#) so that it becomes available with BADS# in BT1 or the first BT2P. MISS# is floated when the 82385 does not own the bus, such that multiple 82385's can share the same node in multi-cache systems. (As discussed in Chapter 7, this signal also serves a reserved function in testing the 82385.)

3.6.2 Write Buffer Status (WBS)

The latching data transceiver is also known as the "posted write buffer." WBS indicates that this buffer contains data that has not yet been written to the system even though the 386 DX may have begun its next cycle. It is activated when 386 DX data is latched, and deactivated when the corresponding

82385 local bus write cycle is completed (BREADY#). (As discussed in Chapter 7, this signal also serves a reserved function in testing the 82385.)

WBS can serve several functions. In multi-processor applications, it can act as a coherency mechanism by informing a bus arbiter that it should let a write cycle run on the system bus so that main memory has the latest data. If any other 82385 cache subsystems are on the bus, they will monitor the cycle via their bus watching mechanisms. Any 82385 that detects a snoop hit will invalidate the corresponding entry in its local cache.

3.6.3 Cache Flush (FLUSH)

When activated, this signal causes the 82385 to clear all of its directory tag valid bits, effectively flushing the cache. (As discussed in Chapter 7, this signal also serves a reserved function in testing the 82385.) The primary use of the FLUSH input is for diagnostics and multi-processor support. The use of this pin as a coherency mechanism may impact software transparency.

The FLUSH input must be held active for at least 4 CLK (8 CLK2) cycles to complete the flush sequence. If FLUSH is still active after 4 CLK cycles, any accesses to the cache will be misses and the cache will not be updated (since FLUSH is active).

3.7 BUS ARBITRATION SIGNALS (BHOLD AND BHLDA)

In master mode, BHOLD is an input that indicates a request by a slave device for bus ownership. The 82385 acknowledges this request via its BHLDA output. (These signals function identically to the 386 DX HOLD and HLDA signals.)

The roles of BHOLD and BHLDA are reversed for an 82385 in slave mode. BHOLD is now an output indicating a request for bus ownership, and BHLDA an input indicating that the request has been granted.

3.8 COHERENCY (BUS WATCHING) SUPPORT SIGNALS (SA2–SA31, SSTB#, SEN)

These signals form the 82385's bus watching interface. The Snoop Address Bus (SA2–SA31) connects to the system address lines if masters reside at both the system and 82385 local bus levels, or the 82385 local bus address lines if masters reside only at the 82385 local bus level. Snoop Strobe (SSTB#) indicates that a valid address is on the snoop address inputs. Snoop Enable (SEN) indicates that the cycle is a write. In a system with masters only at the 82385 local bus level, SA2–SA31, SSTB#, and SEN can be driven respectively by BA2–BA31, BADS#, and BW/R# without any support circuitry.

3.9 CONFIGURATION INPUTS (2W/D#, M/S#, DEFOE#)

These signals select the configurations supported by the 82385. They are hardware strap options and must not be changed dynamically. 2W/D# (2-Way/Direct Mapped Select) selects a two-way set associative cache when tied high, or a direct mapped cache when tied low. M/S# (Master/Slave Select) chooses between master mode (M/S# high) and slave mode (M/S# low). DEFOE# defines the functionality of the 82385 cache output enables (COEA# and COEB#). DEFOE# allows the 82385 to interface to SRAMs with output enables (DEFOE# low) or to SRAMs requiring transceivers (DEFOE# high).

4.0 386 DX LOCAL BUS INTERFACE

The following is a detailed description of how the 82385 interfaces to the 386 DX and to 386 DX local bus resources. Items specifically addressed are the interfaces to the 386 DX, the cache SRAMs, and the 387 Numerics Coprocessor.

The many timing diagrams in this and the next chapter provide insight into the dual pipelined bus structure of a 386 DX CPU/82385 system. It's important to realize, however, that one need not know every possible cycle combination to use the 82385. The interface is simple, and the dual bus operation invisible to the 386 DX and system. To facilitate discussion of the timing diagrams, several conventions have been adopted. Refer to Figure 4-2A, and note that 386 DX bus cycles, 386 DX bus states, and 82385 bus states are identified along the top. All states can be identified by the "frame numbers" along the bottom. The cycles in Figure 4-2A include a cache read hit (CRDH), a cache read miss (CRDM), and a write (WT). WT represents any write, cacheable or not. When necessary to distinguish cacheable writes, a write hit goes by CWTH and a write miss by CWTM. Non-cacheable system reads go by SBRD. Also, it is assumed that system bus pipelining occurs even though the BNA# signal is not shown. When the system pipeline begins is a function of the system bus controller.

386 DX bus cycles can be tracked by ADS# and READYI#, and 82385 cycles by BADS# and BREADY#. These four signals are thus a natural

choice to help track parallel bus activity. Note in the timing diagrams that 386 DX cycles are numbered using ADS# and READYI#, and 82385 cycles using BADS# and BREADY#. For example, when the address of the first 386 DX cycle becomes available, the corresponding assertion of ADS# is marked "1", and the READYI# pulse that terminates the cycle is marked "1" as well. Whenever a 386 DX cycle is forwarded to the system, its number is forwarded as well so that the corresponding 82385 bus cycle can be tracked by BADS# and BREADY#.

The "N" value in the timing diagrams is the assumed number of main memory wait states inserted in a non-pipelined 82385 bus cycle. For example, a non-pipelined access to N=2 memory requires a total of four bus states, while a pipelined access requires three. (The pipeline advantage effectively hides one main memory wait state.)

4.1 PROCESSOR INTERFACE

This section presents the 386 DX CPU /82385 hardware interface and discusses the interaction and timing of this interface. Also addressed is how to decode the 386 DX address bus to generate the 82385 inputs LBA#, NCA#, and X16#. (Recall that LBA# allows memory and/or I/O space to be set aside for 386 DX local bus resources; NCA# allows system memory to be set aside as non-cacheable; and X16# allows system memory and/or I/O space to be reserved for 16-bit resources.) Finally, the 82385's handling of 16-bit space is discussed.

4.1.1 Hardware Interface

Figure 4-1 is a diagram of an 386 DX CPU/82385 system, which can be thought of as three distinct interfaces. The first is the 386 DX CPU/82385 interface (including the Ready Logic). The second is the cache interface, as depicted by the cache control bus in the upper left corner of Figure 4-1. The third is the 82385 bus interface, which includes both direct connects and signals that control the 74374 address/cycle definition latch and 74646 latching data transceiver. (The 82385 bus interface is the subject of the next chapter.)

As seen in Figure 4-1, the 386 DX CPU/82385 interface is a straightforward connection. The only necessary support logic is that required to sum all ready sources.

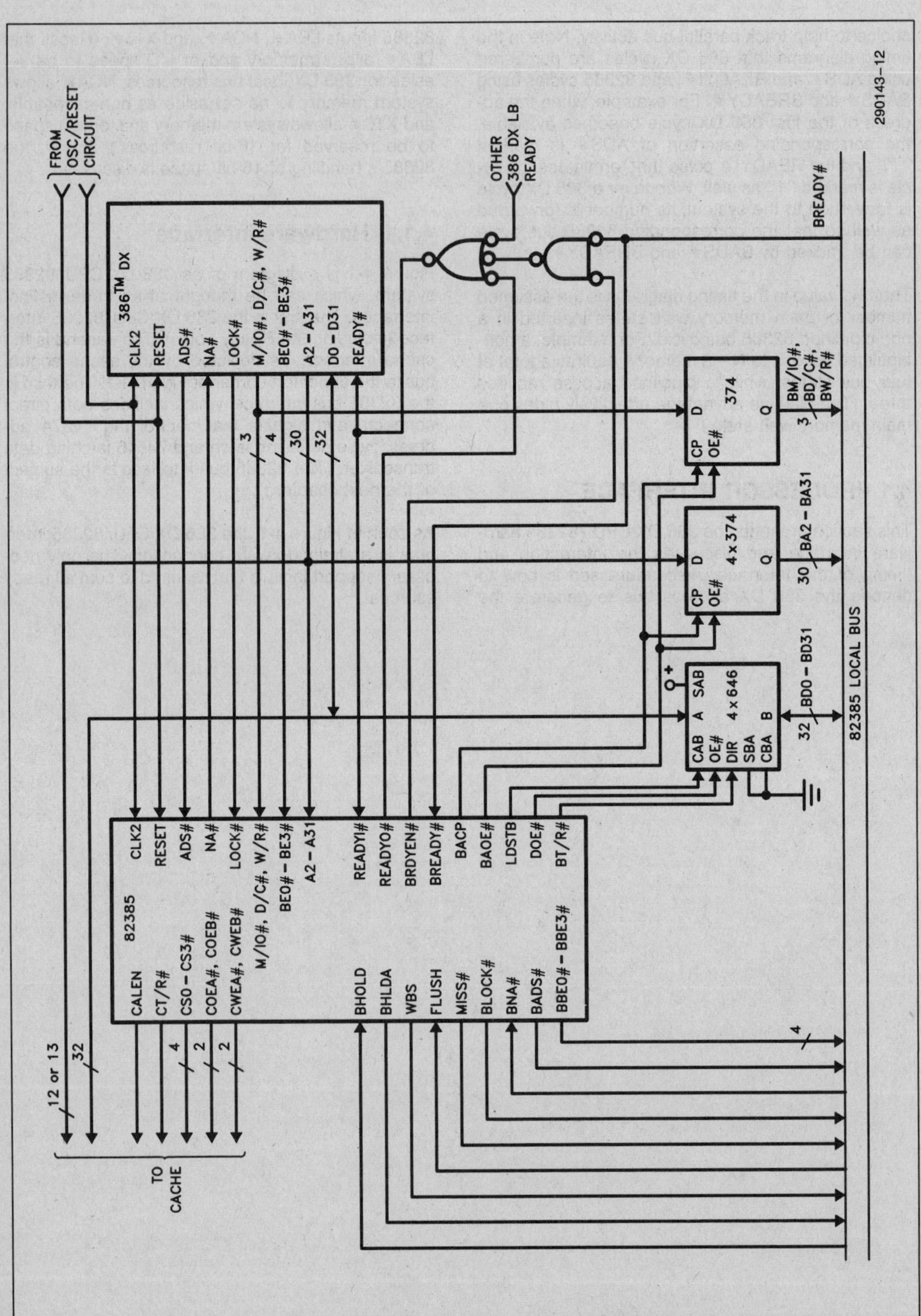

Figure 4-1. 386 DX CPU/82385 Interface

4.1.2 Ready Generation

Note in Figure 4-1 that the ready logic consists of two gates. The upper three-input AND gate (shown as a negative logic OR) sums all 386 DX local bus ready sources. One such source is the 82385 READYO# output, which terminates read hits and posted writes. The output of this gate drives the 386 DX READY# input and is monitored by the 82385 (via READYI#) to track the 386 DX bus state.

When the 82385 forwards a 386 DX read cycle to the 82385 bus (cache read miss or non-cacheable read), it does not directly terminate the cycle via READYO#. Instead, the 386 DX and 82385 bus cycles are concurrently terminated by a system ready source. This is the purpose of the additional two-input OR gate (negative logic AND) in Figure 4-1. When the 82385 forwards a read to the 82385 bus, it asserts BRDYEN# which enables the system ready signal (BREADY#) to directly terminate the 386 DX bus cycle.

Figures 4-2A and 4-2B illustrate the behavior of the signals involved in ready generation. Note in cycle 1 of Figure 4-2A that the 82385 READYO# directly terminates the hit cycle. In cycle 2, READYO# is not activated. Instead the 82385 BRDYEN# is activated in BT2, BT2P, or BT2I states such that BREADY# can concurrently terminate the 386 DX and 82385 bus cycles (frame 6). Cycle 3 is a posted write. The write data becomes available in T1P (frame 7), and

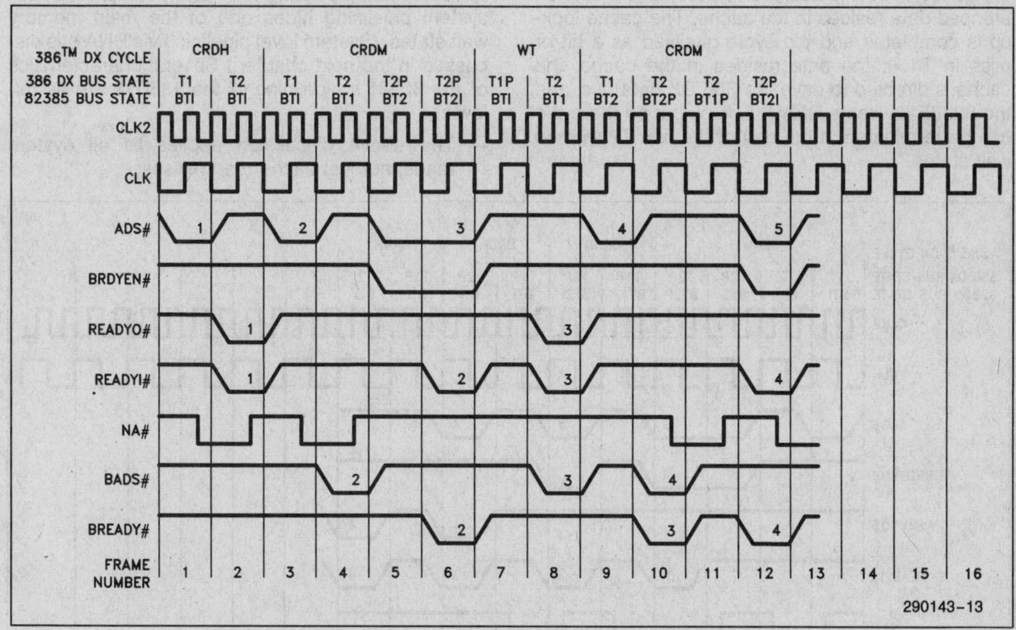

Figure 4-2A. READYO#, BRDYEN#, and NA# (N=1)

the address, data, and cycle definition of the write are latched in T2 (frame 8). The 386 DX cycle is terminated by READYO# in frame 8 with no wait states. The 82385, however, sees the write cycle through to completion on the 82385 bus where it is terminated in frame 10 by BREADY#. In this case, the BREADY# signal is not gated through to the 386 DX . Refer to Figures 4-2A and 4-2B for clarification.

4.1.3. NA# and 386 DX Local Bus Pipelining

Cycle 1 of Figure 4-2A is a typical cache read hit. The 386 DX address becomes available in T1, and the 82385 uses this address to determine if the referenced data resides in the cache. The cache look-up is completed and the cycle qualified as a hit or miss in T1. If the data resides in the cache, the cache is directed to drive the 386 DX data bus, and the 82385 drives its READYO# output so the cycle can be terminated at the end of the first T2 with no wait states.

Although cycle 2 starts out like cycle 1, at the end of T1 (frame 3), it is qualified as a miss and forwarded to the 82385 bus. The 82385 bus cycle begins one state after the 386 DX bus cycle, implying a one wait state overhead associated with cycle 2 due to the look-up. When the 82385 encounters the miss, it immediately asserts NA#, which puts the 386 DX into pipelined mode. Once in pipelined mode, the 82385 is able to qualify an 386 DX cycle using the 386 DX pipelined address and control signals. The result is that the cache look-up state is hidden in all but the first of a contiguous sequence of read misses. This is shown in the first two cycles, both read misses, of Figure 4-2B. The CPU sees the look-up state in the first cycle, but not in the second. In fact, the second miss requires a total of only two states, as not only does 386 DX pipelining hide the look-up state, but system pipelining hides one of the main memory wait states. (System level pipelining via BNA# is discussed in the next chapter.) Several characteristics of the 82385's pipelining of the 386 DX are as follows:

— The above discussion applies to all system reads, not just cache read misses.

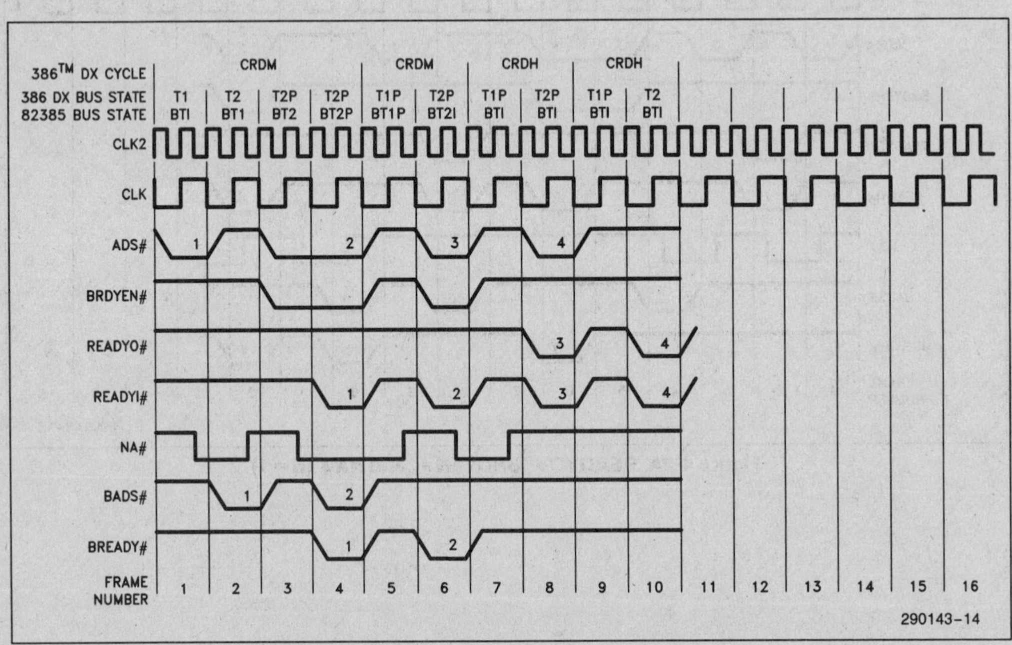

Figure 4-2B. READYO#, BRDYEN#, and NA# (N = 1)

— The 82385 provides the fastest possible switch to pipelining, T1-T2-T2P. The exception to this is when a system read follows a posted write. In this case, the sequence is T1-T2-T2-T2P. (Refer to cycle 4 of Figure 4-2A.) The number of T2 states is dependent on the number of main memory wait states.

— Refer to the read hit in Figure 4-2A (cycle 1), and note that NA# is actually asserted before the end of T1, before the hit/miss decision is made. This is of no consequence since even though NA# is sampled active in T2, the activation of READYO# in the same T2 renders NA# a "don't care". NA# is asserted in this manner to meet 386 DX timing requirements and to ensure the fastest possible switch to pipelined mode.

— All read hits and the majority of writes can be serviced by the 82385 with zero wait states in non-pipelined mode, and the 82385 accordingly attempts to run all such cycles in non-pipelined mode. An exception is seen in the hit cycles (cycles 3 and 4) of Figure 4-2B. The 82385 does not know soon enough that cycle 3 is a hit, and thus sustains the pipeline. The result is that three sequential hits are required before the 386 DX is totally out of pipelined mode. (The three hits look like T1P-T2P, T1P-T2, T1-T2.) Note that this does not occur if the number of main memory wait states is equal to or greater than two.

As far as the design is concerned, NA# is generally tied directly to the 386 DX NA# input. However, other local NA# sources may be logically "AND"ed with the 82385 NA# output if desired. It is essential, however, that no device other than the 82385 drive the 386 DX NA# input unless that device resides on the 386 DX local bus in space decoded via LBA#. If desired, the 82385 NA# output can be ignored and the 386 DX NA# input tied high. The 386 DX NA# input should never be tied low, which would always keep it active.

4.1.4 LBA#, NCA#, and X16# Generation

The 82385 input signals LBA#, NCA# and X16# are generated by decoding the 386 DX address (A2–A31) and cycle definition (W/R#, D/C#, M/IO#) lines. The 82385 samples them at the end of the first state in which they become available, which is either T1 or the first T2P cycle. The decode configuration and timings are illustrated respectively in Figures 4-3A and 4-3B.

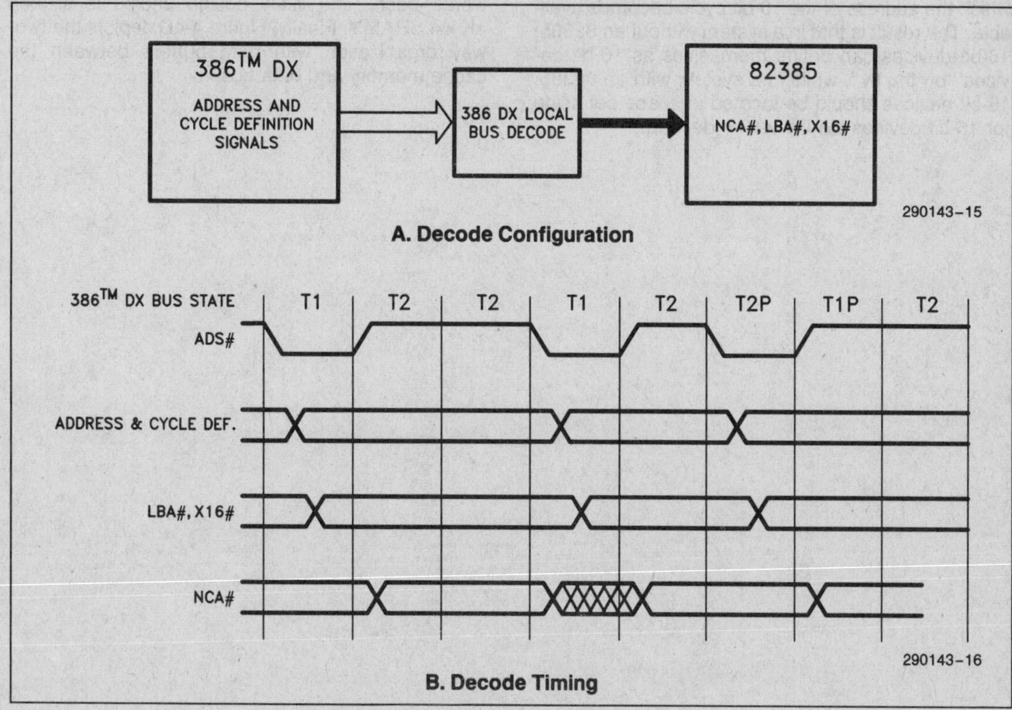

A. Decode Configuration

B. Decode Timing

Figure 4-3. NCA#, LBA#, X16# Generation

4.1.5 82385 Handling of 16-Bit Space

As discussed previously, the 82385 does not cache devices decoded as 16-bit. Instead it makes provision to accommodate 16-bit space as non-cacheable via the X16# input. X16# is generated when the user decodes the 386 DX address and cycle definition lines for the BS16# input of the 386 DX (Figure 4-3). The decode output now drives both the 386 DX BS16# input and the 82385 X16# input. Cycles decoded this way are treated as non-cacheable. They are forwarded to and executed on the 82385 bus, but have no impact on the cache or cache directory. The 82385 also monitors the 386 DX byte enables in a 16-bit cycle to see if an additional cycle is required to complete the transfer. Specifically, a second cycle is required if (BE0# OR BE1#) AND (BE2# OR BE3#) is asserted in the current cycle. The 82385, like the 386 DX , will not allow the two halves of a 16-bit transfer to be interrupted by another master. There is an important distinction between the handling of 16-bit space in a 386 DX system with an 82385 as compared to a system without an 82385. The 386 DX BS16# input need not be asserted until the last state of a 16-bit cycle for the 386 DX to recognize it as such. The 82385, however, needs the information earlier, specifically at the end of the first 386 DX bus state (T1 or first T2P) in which the address of the 16-bit cycle becomes available. The result is that in a system without an 82385, 16-bit devices can define themselves as 16-bit devices "on the fly", while in a system with an 82385, 16-bit devices should be located in space set aside for 16-bit devices via the X16# decode.

4.2 CACHE INTERFACE

The following is a description of the external data cache and 82385 cache interface.

4.2.1 Cache Configurations

The 82385 controls the cache memory via the control signals shown in Figure 4-1. These signals drive one of four possible cache configurations, as depicted in Figures 4-4A through 4-4D. Figure 4-4A shows a direct mapped cache organized as 8K doublewords. The likely design choice is four 8K x 8 SRAMs. Figure 4-4B depicts the same cache memory but with a data transceiver between the cache and 386 DX data bus. In this configuration, CT/R# controls the transceiver direction, COEA# drives the transceiver output enable. (COEB# could also be used, and DEFOE# is strapped high.) A data buffer is required if the chosen SRAM does not have a separate output enable. Additionally, buffers may be used to ease SRAM timing requirements or in a system with a heavily loaded data bus. (Guidelines for SRAM selection are included in Chapter 6.)

Figure 4-4C depicts a two-way set associative cache organized as two banks (A and B) of 4K doublewords each. The likely design choice is sixteen 4K x 4 SRAM's. Finally, Figure 4-4D depicts the two-way organization with data buffers between the cache memory and data bus.

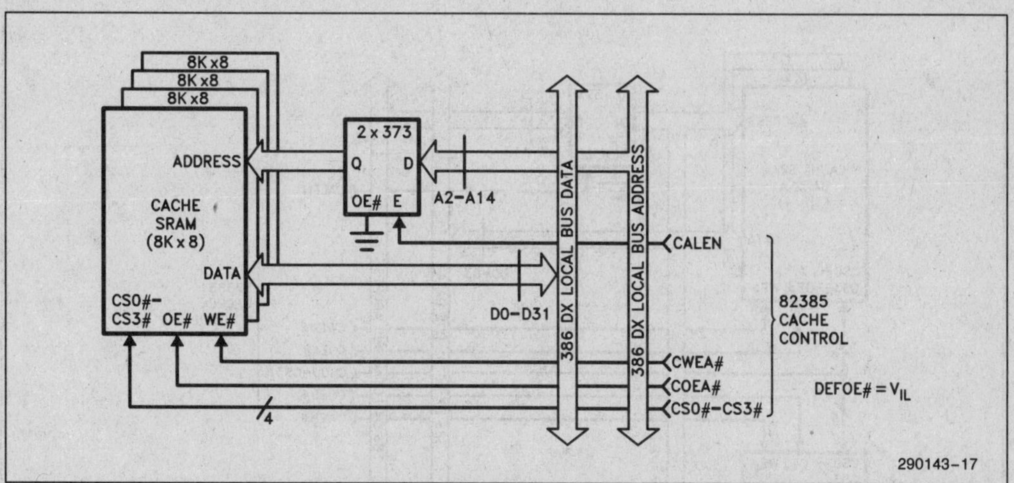

Figure 4-4A. Direct Mapped Cache without Data Buffers

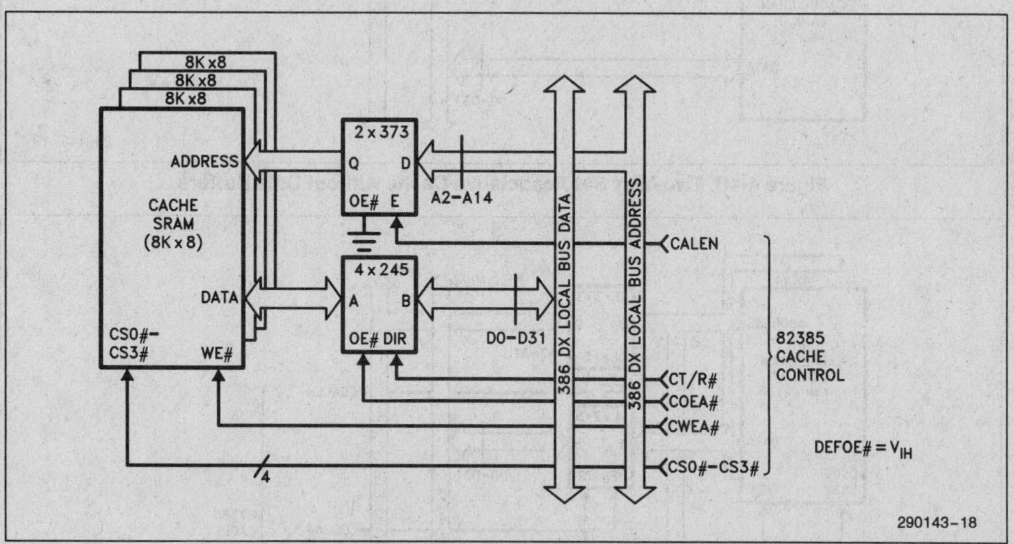

Figure 4-4B. Direct Mapped Cache with Data Buffers

4

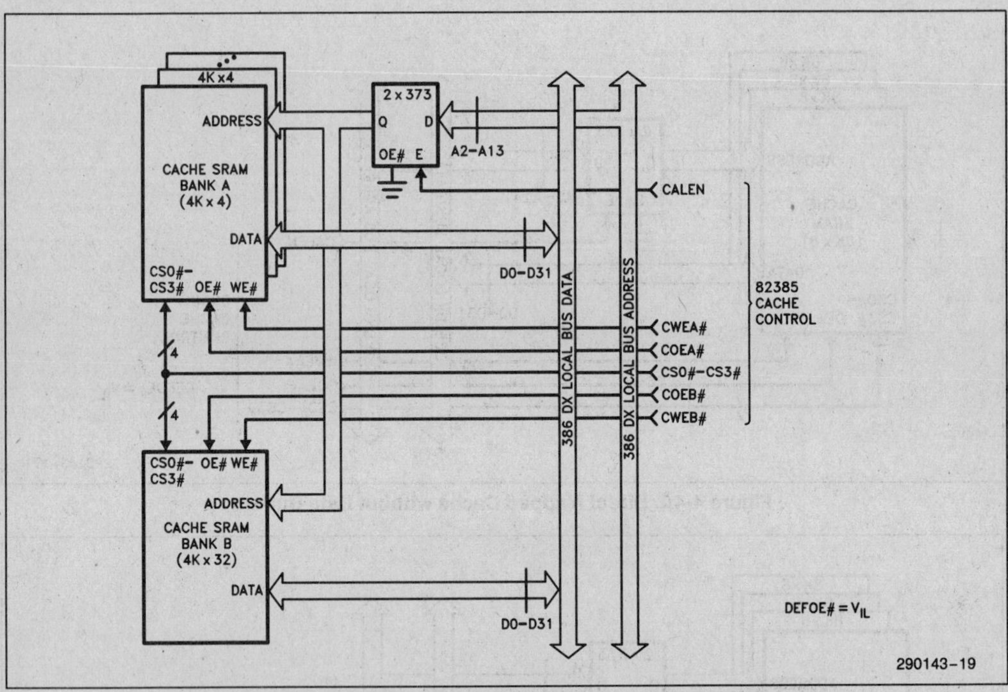

Figure 4-4C. Two-Way Set Associative Cache without Data Buffers

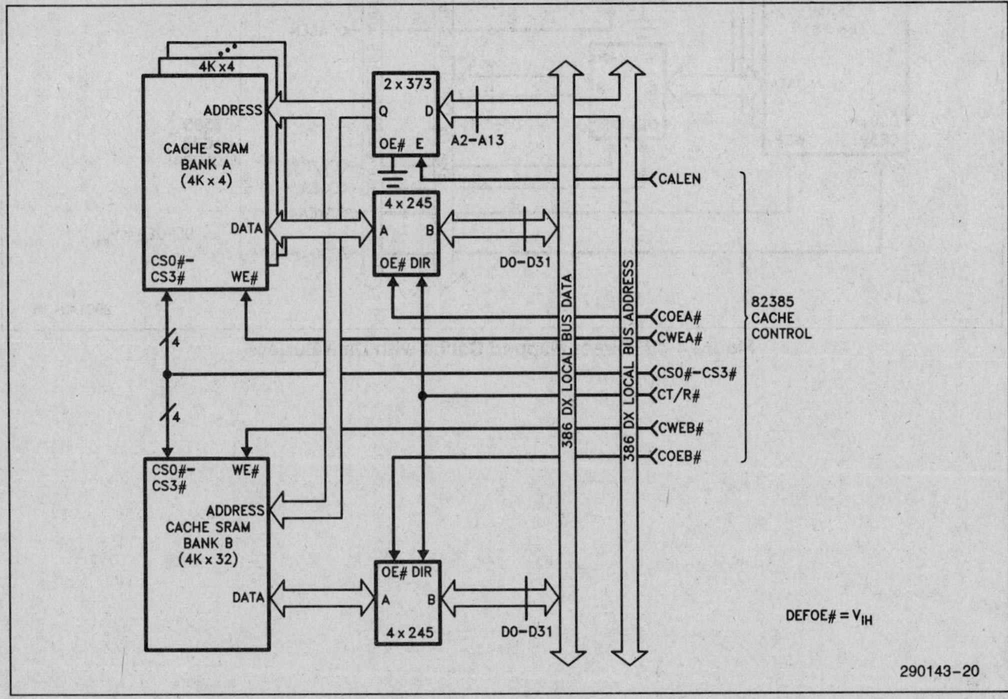

Figure 4-4D. Two-Way Set Associative Cache with Data Buffers

4.2.2 Cache Control—Direct Mapped

Figure 4-5A illustrates the timing of cache read and write hits, while Figure 4-5B illustrates cache updates. In a read hit, the cache output enables are driven from the beginning of T2 (cycle 1 of Figure 4-5A). If at the end of T1 the cycle is qualified as a cacheable read, the output enables are asserted on the assumption that the cycle will be a hit. (Driving the output enables before the actual hit/miss decision is made eases SRAM timing requirements.)

Cycle 1 of Figure 4-5B illustrates what happens when the assumption of a hit turns out to be wrong. Note that the output enables are asserted at the beginning of T2, but then disabled at the end of T2. Once the output enables are inactive, the 82385 turns the transceiver around (via CT/R#) and drives the write enables to begin the cache update cycle. Note in Figure 4-5B that once the 386 DX is in pipelined mode, the output enables need not be driven prior to a hit/miss decision, since the decision is made earlier via the pipelined address information.

One consequence of driving the output enables low in a miss before the hit/miss decision is made is that since the cache starts driving the 386 DX data bus,

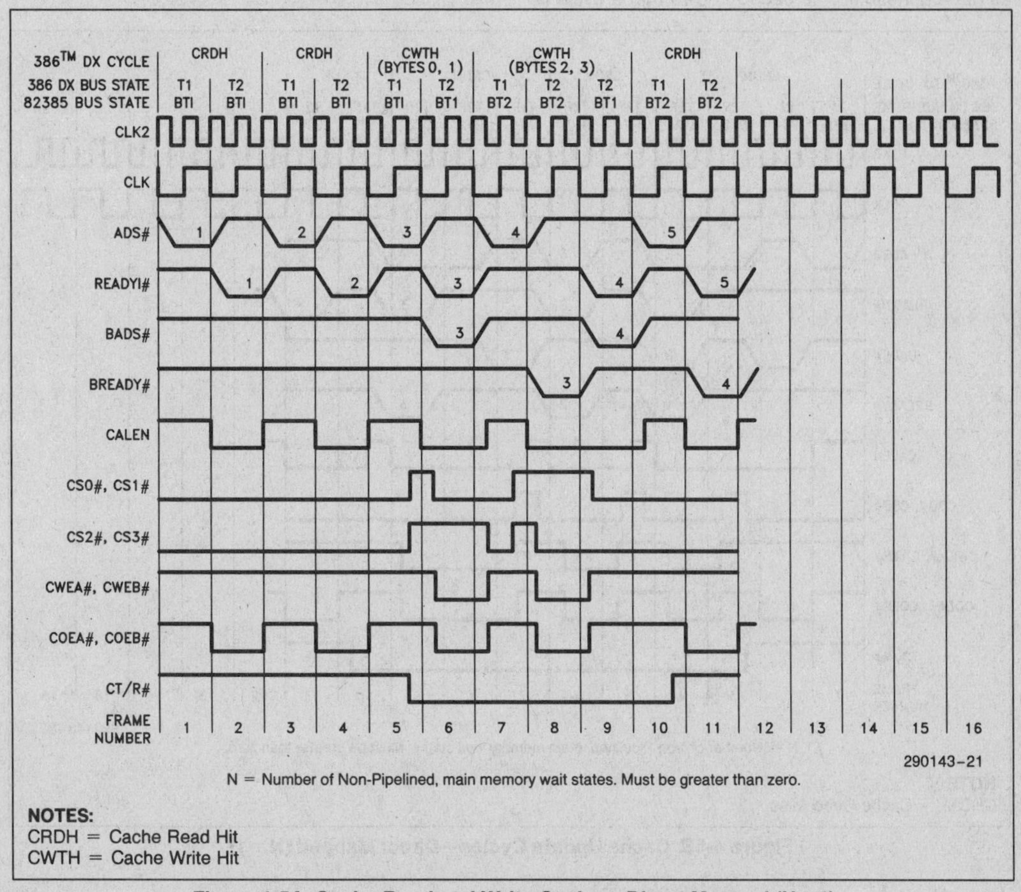

Figure 4-5A. Cache Read and Write Cycles—Direct Mapped (N = 1)

the 82385 cannot enable the 74646 transceiver (Figure 4-1) until after the cache outputs are disabled. (The timing of the 74646 control signals is described in the next chapter.) The result is that the 74646 cannot be enabled soon enough to support N=0 main memory ("N" was defined in section 4.0 as the number of non-pipelined main memory wait states). This means that memory which can run with zero wait states in a non-pipelined cycle should not be mapped into cacheable memory. This should not present a problem, however, as a main memory system built with N=0 memory has no need of a cache. (The main memory is as fast as the cache.) Zero wait state memory can be supported if it is decoded as non-cacheable. The 82385 knows that a cycle is non-cacheable in time not to drive the cache output enables, and can thus enable the 74646 sooner.

In a write hit, the 82385 only updates the cache bytes that are meant to be updated as directed by the 386 DX byte enables. This prevents corrupting cache data in partial doubleword writes. Note in Figure 4-5A that the appropriate bytes are selected via the cache byte select lines CS0#-CS3#. In a read hit, all four select lines are driven as the 386 DX will simply ignore data it does not need. Also, in a cache update (read miss), all four selects are active in order to update the cache with a complete line (doubleword).

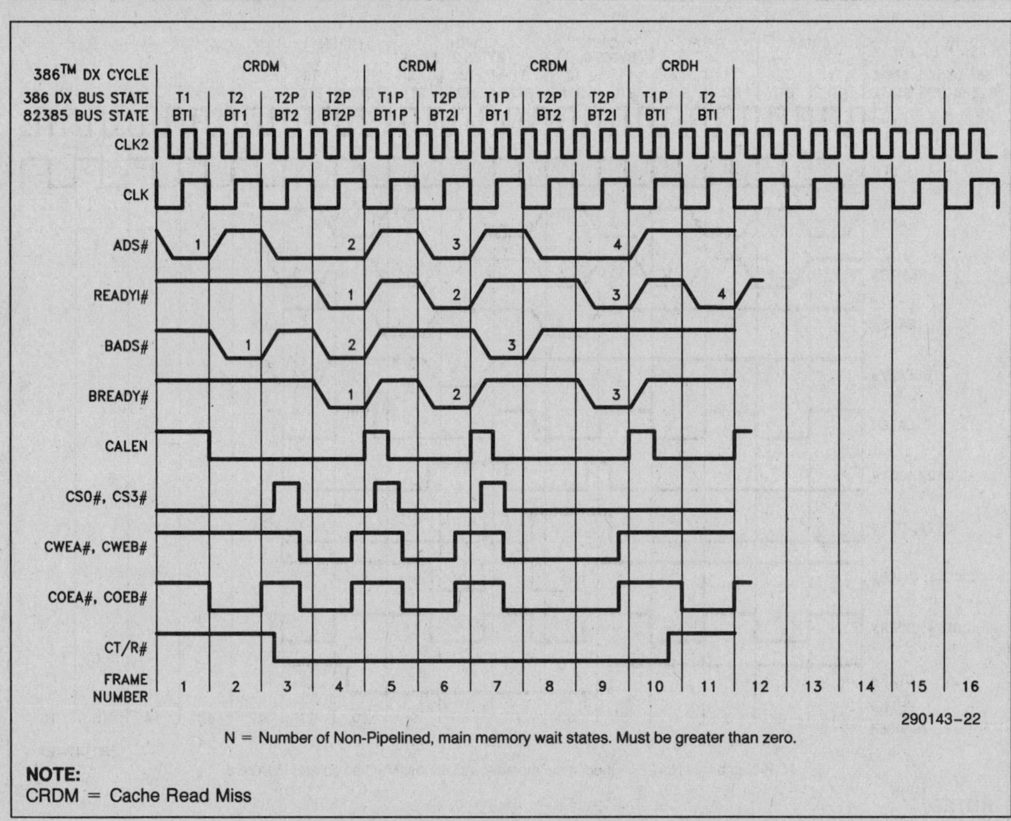

Figure 4-5B. Cache Update Cycles—Direct Mapped (N = 1)

4.2.3 Cache Control—Two-Way Set Associative

Figures 4-6A and 4-6B illustrate the timing of cache read hits, write hits, and updates for a two-way set associative cache. (Note that the cycle sequences are the same as those in Figures 4-5A and 4-5B.) In a cache read hit, only one bank on the other is enabled to drive the 386 DX data bus, so unlike the control of a direct mapped cache, the appropriate cache output enable cannot be driven until the outcome of the hit/miss decision is known. (This implies stricter SRAM timing requirements for a two-way set associative cache.) In write hits and read misses, only one bank or the other is updated.

4.3 387™ DX INTERFACE

The 387 DX Math Coprocessor interfaces to the 386 DX just as it would in a system without an 82385. The 387 DX READYO# output is logically "AND"ed along with all other 386 DX local bus ready sources (Figure 4-1), and the output is fed to the 387 DX READY#, 82385 READYI#, and 386 DX READY# inputs.

The 386 DX uniquely addresses the 387 DX by driving M/IO# low and A31 high. The 82385 decodes this internally and treats 387 DX accesses in the same way it treats 386 DX cycles in which LBA# is asserted, it ignores them.

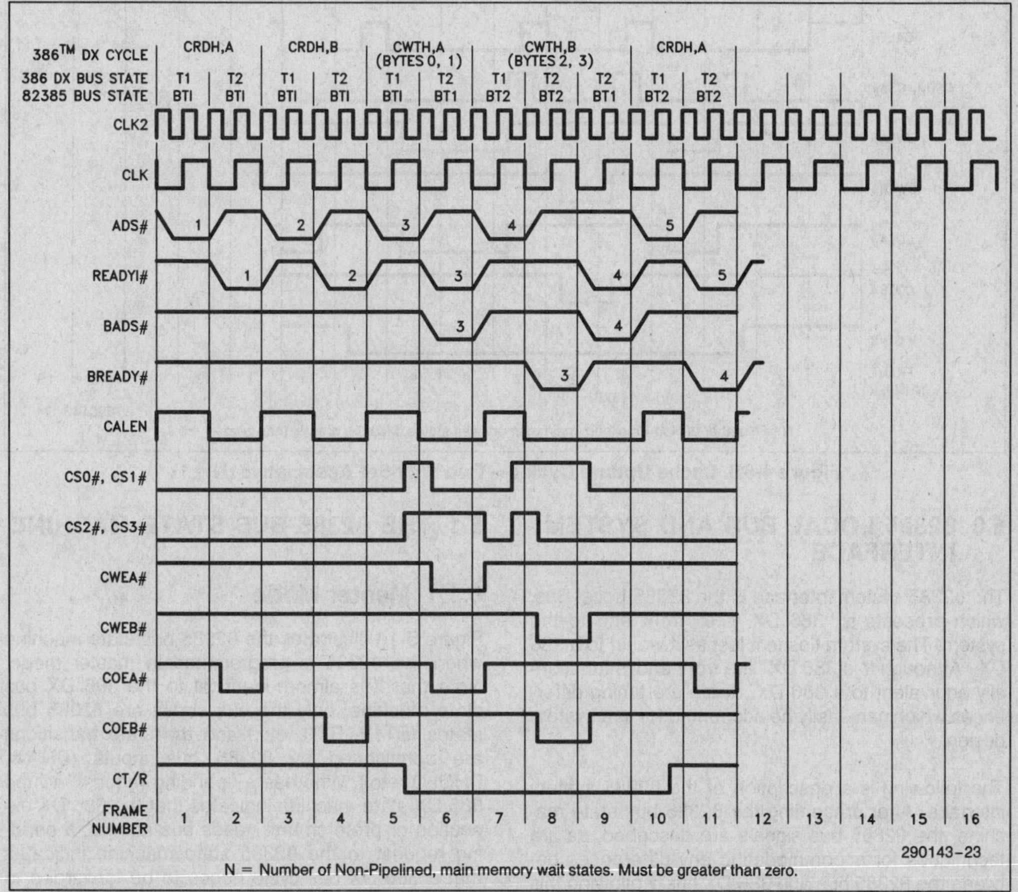

Figure 4-6A. Cache Read and Write Cycles—Two Way Set Associative (N = 1)

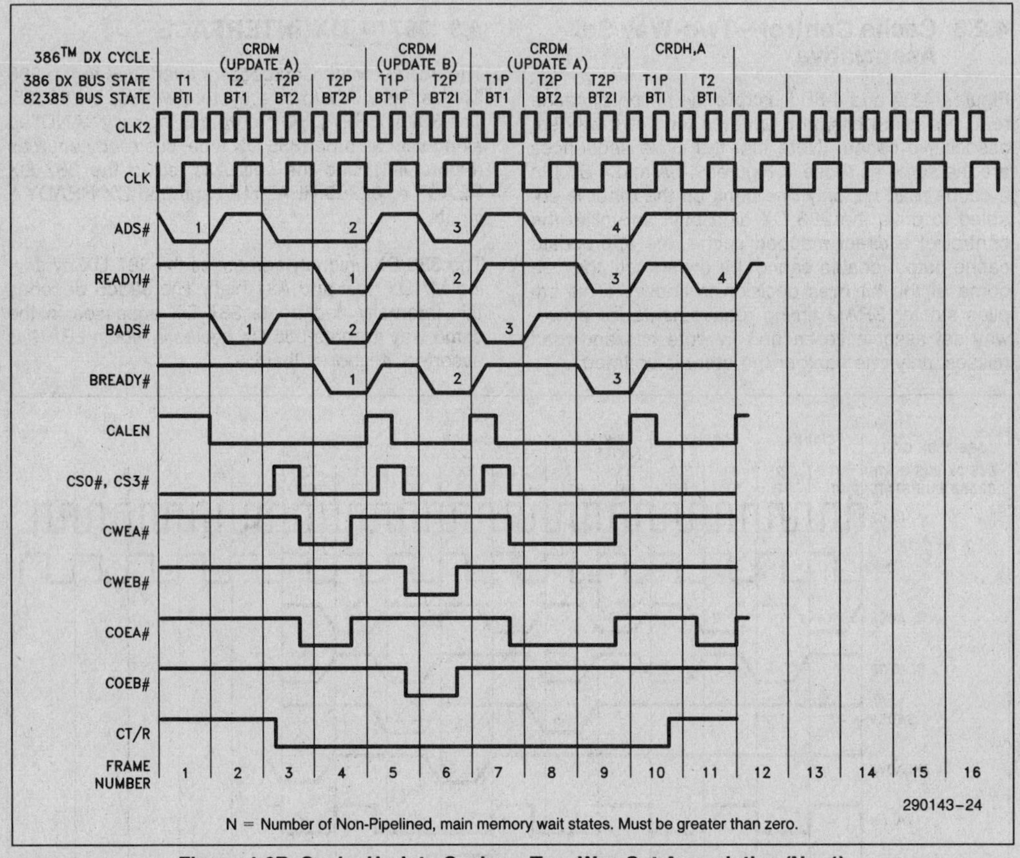

Figure 4-6B. Cache Update Cycles—Two Way Set Associative (N = 1)

5.0 82385 LOCAL BUS AND SYSTEM INTERFACE

The 82385 system interface is the 82385 Local Bus, which presents a "386 DX -like" front end to the system. The system ties to it just as it would to a 386 DX . Although this 386 DX -like front end is functionally equivalent to a 386 DX , there are timing differences which can easily be accounted for in a system design.

The following is a description of the 82385 system interface. After presenting the 82385 bus state machine, the 82385 bus signals are described, as are techniques for accommodating any differences between the 82385 bus and 386 DX bus. Following this is a discussion of the 82385's condition upon reset.

5.1 THE 82385 BUS STATE MACHINE

5.1.1 Master Mode

Figure 5-1A illustrates the 82385 bus state machine when the 82385 is programmed in master mode. Note that it is almost identical to the 386 DX bus state machine, only the bus states are 82385 bus states (BT1P, BTH, etc.) and the state transitions are conditioned by 82385 bus inputs (BNA#, BHOLD, etc.). Whereas a "pending request" to the 386 DX state machine indicates that the 386 DX execution or prefetch unit needs bus access, a pending request to the 82385 state machine indicates that a 386 DX bus cycle needs to be forwarded to the system (read miss, non-cacheable read, write,

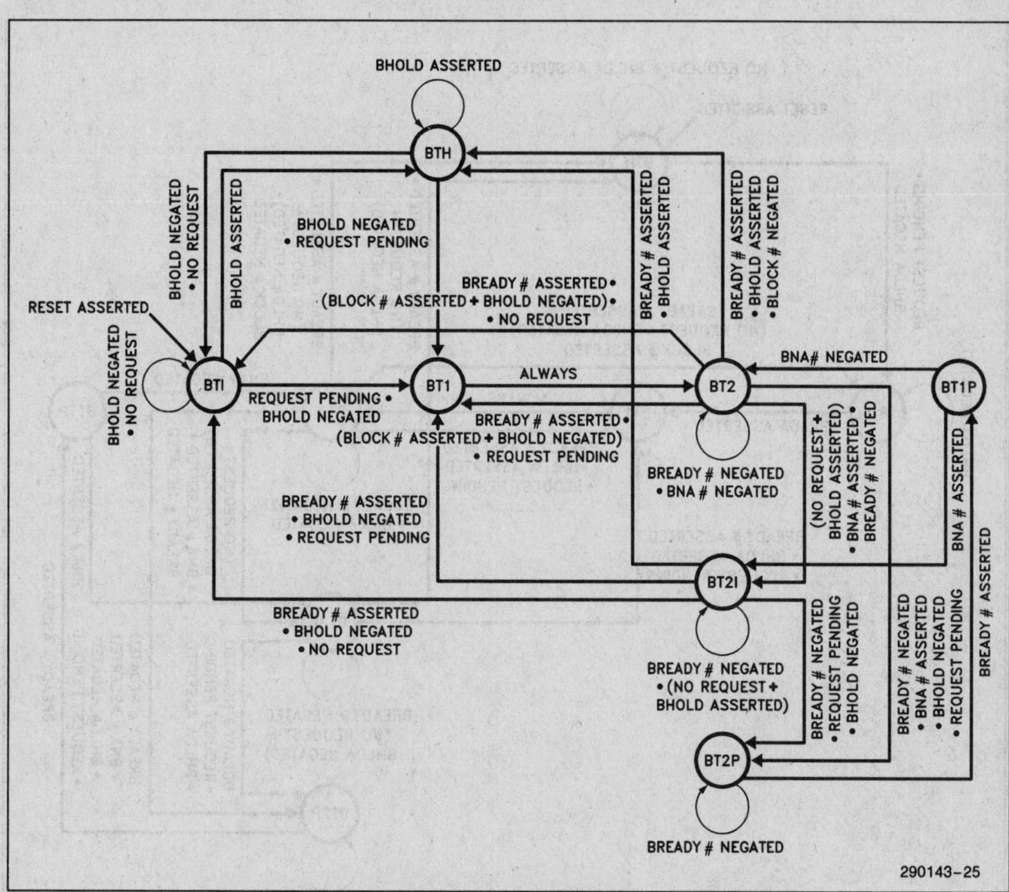

Figure 5-1A. 82385 Local Bus State Machine—Master Mode

4

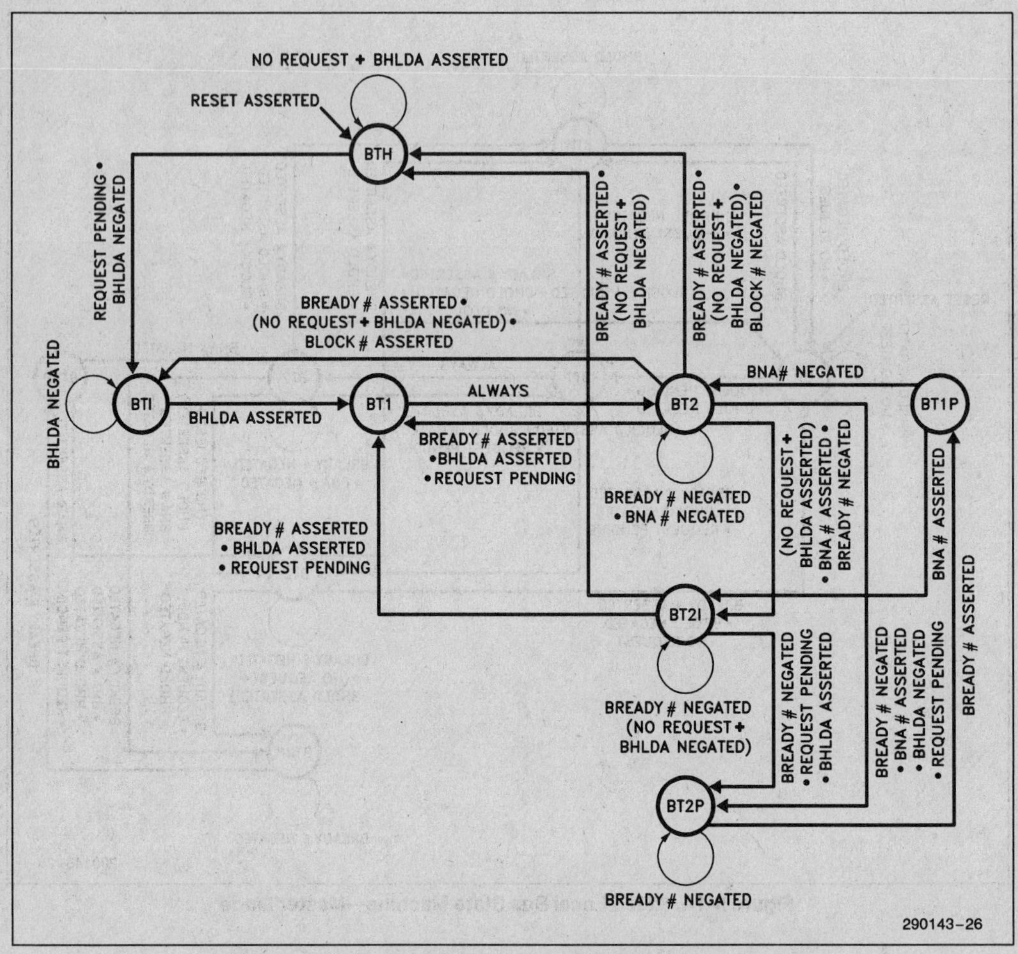

Figure 5-1B. 82385 Local Bus State Machine—Slave Mode

etc.). The only difference between the state machines is that the 82385 does not implement a direct BT1P–BT2P transition. If BNA# is asserted in BT1P, the resulting state sequence is BT1P-BT2I-BT2P. The 82385's ability to sustain a pipeline is not affected by the lack of this state transition.

5.1.2 Slave Mode

The 82385's slave mode state machine (Figure 5-1B) is similar to the master mode machine except that now transitions are conditioned by BHLDA rather than BHOLD. (Recall that in slave mode, the roles of BHOLD and BHLDA are reversed from their master mode roles.) Figure 5-2 clarifies slave mode state machine operation. Upon reset, a slave mode 82385 enters the BTH state. When the 386 DX of the slave 82385 subsystem has a cycle that needs to be forwarded to the system, the 82385 moves to BTI and issues a hold request via BHOLD. It is important to note that a slave mode 82385 does not drive the bus in a BTI state. When the master or bus arbiter returns BHLDA, the slave 82385 enters BT1 and runs the cycle. When the cycle is completed, and if no additional requests are pending, the 82385 moves back to BTH and disables BHOLD.

If, while a slave 82385 is running a cycle, the master or arbiter drops BHLDA (Figure 5-2B), the 82385 will complete the current cycle, move to BTH and remove the BHOLD request. If the 82385 still had cycles to run when it was kicked off the bus, it will immediately assert a new BHOLD and move to BTI to await bus acknowledgement. Note, however, that it will only move to BTI if BHLDA is negated, ensuring that the handshake sequence is completed.

There are several cases in which a slave 82385 will not immediately release the bus if BHLDA is dropped. For example, if BHLDA is dropped during a BT2P state, the 82385 has already committed to the next system bus pipelined cycle and will execute it before releasing the bus. Also, the 82385 will complete the second half of a two-cycle 16-bit transfer, or will complete a sequence of locked cycles before releasing the bus. This should not present any problems, as a properly designed arbiter will not assume that the 82385 has released the bus until it sees BHOLD become inactive.

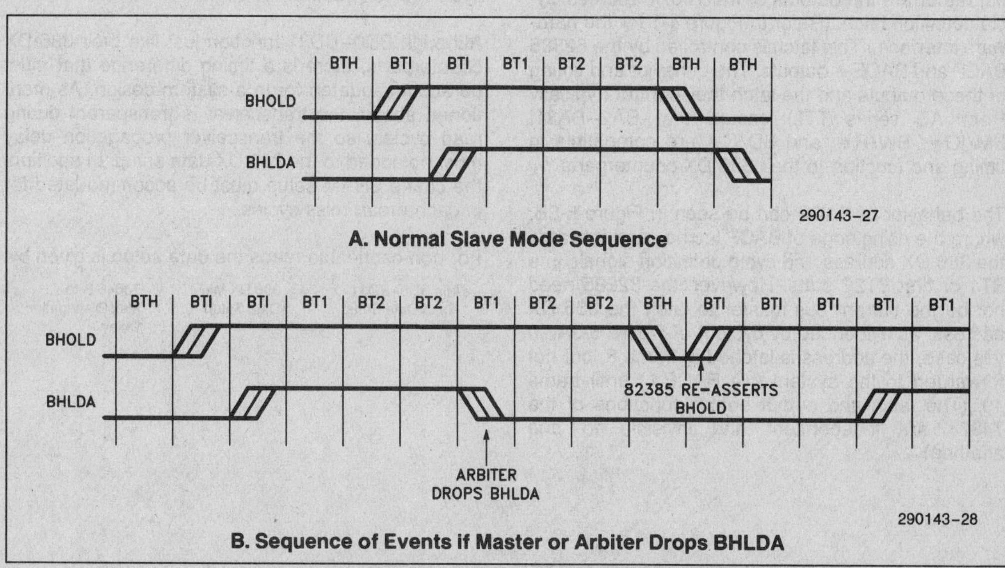

A. Normal Slave Mode Sequence

B. Sequence of Events if Master or Arbiter Drops BHLDA

Figure 5-2. BHOLD/BHLDA—Slave Mode

5.2 The 82385 Local Bus

The 82385 bus can be broken up into two groups of signals: those which have direct 386 DX counterparts, and additional status and control signals provided by the 82385. The operation and interaction of all 82385 bus signals are depicted in Figures 5-3A through 5-3L for a wide variety of cycle sequences. These diagrams serve as a reference for the 82385 bus discussion and provide insight into the dual bus operation of the 82385.

5.2.1 82385 Bus Counterparts to 386 DX Signals

The following sections discuss the signals presented on the 82385 local bus which are functional equivalents to the signals present at the 386 DX local bus.

5.2.1.1 ADDRESS BUS (BA2–BA31) AND CYCLE DEFINITION SIGNALS (BM/IO#, BD/C#, BW/R#)

These signals are not driven directly by the 82385, but rather are the outputs of the 74374 address/cycle definition latch. (Refer to Figure 4-1 for the hardware interface.) This latch is controlled by the 82385 BACP and BAOE# outputs. The behavior and timing of these outputs and the latch they control (typically F or AS series TTL) ensure that BA2–BA31, BM/IO#, BW/R#, and BD/C# are compatible in timing and function to their 386 DX counterparts.

The behavior of BACP can be seen in Figure 5-3B, where the rising edge of BACP latches and forwards the 386 DX address and cycle definition signals in a BT1 or first BT2P state. However, the 82385 need not be the current bus master to latch the 386 DX address, as evidenced by cycle 4 of Figure 5-3A. In this case, the address is latched in frame 8, but not forwarded to the system (via BAOE#) until frame 10. (The latch and output enable functions of the 74374 are independent and invisible to one another.)

Note that in frames 2 and 6 the BACP pulses are marked "False." The reason is that BACP is issued and the address latched before the hit/miss determination is made. This ensures that should the cycle be a miss, the 82385 bus can move directly into BT1 without delay. In the case of a hit, the latched address is simply never qualified by the assertion of BADS#. The 82385 bus stays in BTI if there is no access pending (new cycle is a hit) and no bus activity. It will move to and stay in BT2I if the system has requested a pipelined cycle and the 82385 does not have a pending bus access (new cycle is a hit).

5.2.1.2 DATA BUS (BD0–BD31)

The 82385 data bus is the system side of the 74646 latching transceiver. (See Figure 4-1.) This device is controlled by the 82385 outputs LDSTB, DOE#, and BT/R#. LDSTB latches data in write cycles, DOE# enables the transceiver outputs, and BT/R# controls the transceiver direction. The interaction of these signals and the transceiver is such that BD0–BD31 behave just like their 386 DX counterparts. The transceiver is configured such that data flow in write cycles (A to B) is latched, and data flow in read cycles (B to A) is flow-through.

Although BD0–BD31 function just like their 386 DX counterparts, there is a timing difference that must be accommodated for in a system design. As mentioned above, the transceiver is transparent during read cycles, so the transceiver propagation delay must be added to the 386 DX data setup. In addition, the cache SRAM setup must be accommodated for in cache read miss cycles.

For non-cacheable reads the data setup is given by:

Min BD0–BD31 Read Data Setup = 386 DX Min Data Setup + 74646 B-to-A Max Propagation Delay

The required BD0–BD31 setup in a cache read miss is given by:

Min BD0–BD31 Read Data Setup	=	74646 B-to-A Max Propagation Delay	+	Cache SRAM Min Write Setup
	+	One CLK2 Period	−	82385 CWEA# or CWEB# Min Delay

If a data buffer is located between the 386 DX data bus and the cache SRAMs, then its maximum propagation delay must be added to the above formula as well. A design analysis should be completed for every new design to determine actual margins.

A design can accommodate the increased data setup by choosing appropriately fast main memory DRAMs and data buffers. Alternatively, a designer may deal with the longer setup by inserting an extra wait state into cache read miss cycles. If an additional state is to be inserted, the system bus controller should sample the 82385 MISS# output to distinguish read misses from cycles that do not require the longer setup. Tips on using the 82385 MISS# signal are presented later in this chapter.

The behavior of LDSTB, DOE#, and BT/R# can be understood via Figures 5-3A through 5-3L. Note that in cycle 1 of Figure 5-3A (a non-cacheable system read), DOE# is activated midway through BT1, but in cycle 1 of Figure 5-3B (a cache read miss), DOE# is not activated until midway through BT2. The reason is that in a cacheable read cycle, the cache SRAMs are enabled to drive the 386 DX data bus before the outcome of the hit/miss decision (in anticipation of a hit). In cycle 1 of Figure 5-3B, the assertion of DOE# must be delayed until after the 82385 has disabled the cache output buffers. The result is that N=0 main memory should not be mapped into the cache.

5.2.1.3 BYTE ENABLES (BBE0#–BBE3#)

These outputs are driven directly by the 82385, and are completely compatible in timing and function with their 386 DX counterparts. When a 386 DX cycle is forwarded to the 82385 bus, the 386 DX byte enables are duplicated on BBE0#–BBE3#. The one exception is a cache read miss, during which BBE0#–BBE3# are all active regardless of the status of the 386 DX byte enables. This ensures that the cache is updated with a valid 32-bit entry.

5.2.1.4 ADDRESS STATUS (BADS#)

BADS# is identical in function and timing to its 386 DX counterpart. It is asserted in BT1 and BT2P states, and indicates that valid address and cycle definition (BA2–BA31, BBE0#–BBE3#, BM/IO#, BW/R#, BD/C#) information is available on the 82385 bus.

5.2.1.5 READY (BREADY#)

The 82385 BREADY# input terminates 82385 bus cycles just as the 386 DX READY# input terminates 386 DX bus cycles. The behavior of BREADY# is the same as that of READY#, but note in the A.C. timing specifications that a cache read miss requires a longer BREADY# setup than do other cycles. This must be accommodated for in ready logic design.

5.2.1.6 NEXT ADDRESS (BNA#)

BNA# is identical in function and timing to its 386 DX counterpart. Note that in Figures 5-3A through 5-3L, BNA# is assumed asserted in every BT1P or first BT2 state. Along with the 82385's pipelining of the 386 DX , this ensures that the timing diagrams accurately reflect the full pipelined nature of the dual bus structure.

5.2.1.7 BUS LOCK (BLOCK#)

The 386 DX flags a locked sequence of cycles by asserting LOCK#. During a locked sequence, the 386 DX does not acknowledge hold requests, so the sequence executes without interruption by another master. The 82385 forces all locked 386 DX cycles to run on the 82385 bus (unless LBA# is active), regardless of whether or not the referenced location resides in the cache. In addition, a locked sequence of 386 DX cycles is run as a locked sequence on the 82385 bus; BLOCK# is asserted and the 82385 does not allow the sequence to be interrupted. Locked writes (hit or miss) and locked read misses affect the cache and cache directory just as their unlocked counterparts do. A locked read hit, however, is handled differently. The read is necessarily

4

forced to run on the 82385 local bus, and as the data returns from main memory, it is "re-copied" into the cache. (See Figure 5-3L.) The directory is not changed as it already indicates that this location exists in the cache. This activity is invisible to the system and ensures that semaphores are properly handled.

BLOCK# is asserted during locked 82385 bus cycles just as LOCK# is asserted during locked 386 DX cycles. The BLOCK# maximum valid delay, however, differs from that of LOCK#, and this must be accounted for in any circuitry that makes use of BLOCK#. The difference is due to the fact that LOCK#, unlike the other 386 DX cycle definition signals, is not pipelined. The situation is clarified in Figure 5-3K. In cycle 2 the state of LOCK# is not known before the corresponding system read starts (Frames 4 and 5). In this case, LOCK# is asserted at the beginning of T1P, and the delay for BLOCK# to become active is the delay of LOCK# from the 386 DX plus the propagation delay through the 82385. This occurs because T1P and the corresponding BT1P are concurrent (Frame 5). The result is that BLOCK# should not be sampled at the end of BT1P. The first appropriate sampling point is midway through the next state, as shown in Frame 6. In Figure 5-3L, the maximum delay for BLOCK# to become valid in Frame 4 is the same as the maximum delay for LOCK# to become valid from the 386 DX. This is true since the pipelining issue discussed above does not occur.

The 82385 should negate BLOCK# after BREADY# of the last 82385 Locked Cycle was asserted and Lock turns inactive. This means that in a sequence of cycles which begins with a 82385 Locked Cycle and goes on with all the possible Locked Cycles (other 82385 cycles, idles, and local cycles), while LOCK# is continuously active, the 82385 will maintain BLOCK# active continuously. Another implication is that in a Locked Posted Write Cycle followed by non-locked sequence, BLOCK# is negated one CLK after BREADY# of the write cycle. In other 82385 Locked Cycles, followed by non-locked sequences, BLOCK# is negated one CLK after LOCK# is negated, which occurs two CLKs after BREADY# is asserted. In the last case BLOCK# active moves by one CLK to the non-locked sequence.

The arbitration rules of Locked Cycles are:

MASTER MODE:

BHOLD input signal is ignored when BLOCK# or internal lock (16-bit non-aligned cycle) are active. BHLDA output signal remains inactive, and BAOE# output signal remains active at that time interval.

SLAVE MODE:

The 82385 does not relinquish the system bus if BLOCK# or internal lock are active. The BHOLD output signal remains active when BLOCK# or internal lock is active plus one CLK. The BHLDA input signal is ignored when BLOCK# or the internal lock is active plus one CLK. This means the 82385 slave does not respond to BHLDA inactivation. The BAOE# output signal remains active during the same time interval.

5.2.2 Additional 82385 Bus Signals

The 82385 bus provides two status outputs and one control input that are unique to cache operation and thus have no 386 DX counterparts. The outputs are MISS#, and WBS, and the input is FLUSH.

5.2.2.1 CACHE READ/WRITE MISS INDICATION (MISS#)

MISS# can be thought of as an extra 82385 bus cycle definition signal similar to BM/IO#, BW/R#, and BD/C#, that distinguishes cacheable read and write misses from other cycles. MISS#, like the other definition signals, becomes valid with BADS# (BT1 or first BT2P). The behavior of MISS# is illustrated in Figures 5-3B, 5-3C, and 5-3J. The 82385 floats MISS# when another master owns the bus, allowing multiple 82385s to share the same node in multi-cache systems. MISS# should thus be lightly pulled up (~20 KΩ) to keep it negated during hold (BTH) states.

MISS# can serve several purposes. As discussed previously, the BD0–BD31 and BREADY# setup times in a cache read miss are longer than in other cycles. A bus controller can distinguish these cycles by gating MISS# with BW/R#. MISS# may also prove useful in gathering 82385 system performance data.

5.2.2.2 WRITE BUFFER STATUS (WBS)

WBS is activated when 386 DX write cycle data is latched into the 74646 latching transceiver (via LDSTB). It is deactivated upon completion of the write cycle on the 82385 bus when the 82385 sees the BREADY# signal. WBS behavior is illustrated in Figures 5-3F through 5-3J, and potential applications are discussed in Chapter 3.

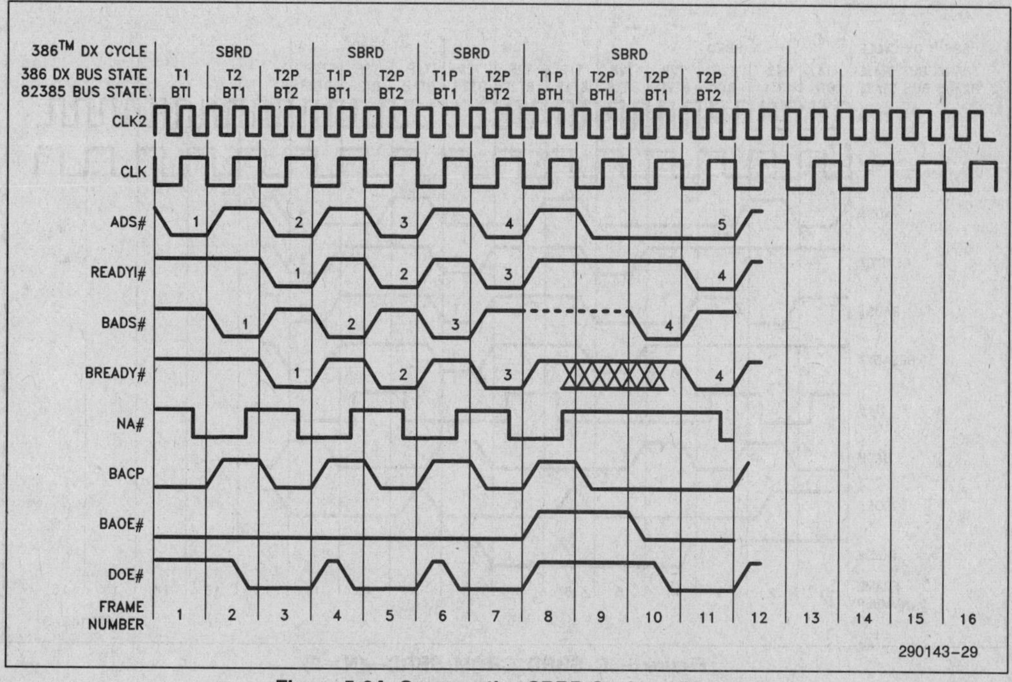

Figure 5-3A. Consecutive SBRD Cycles—(N = 0)

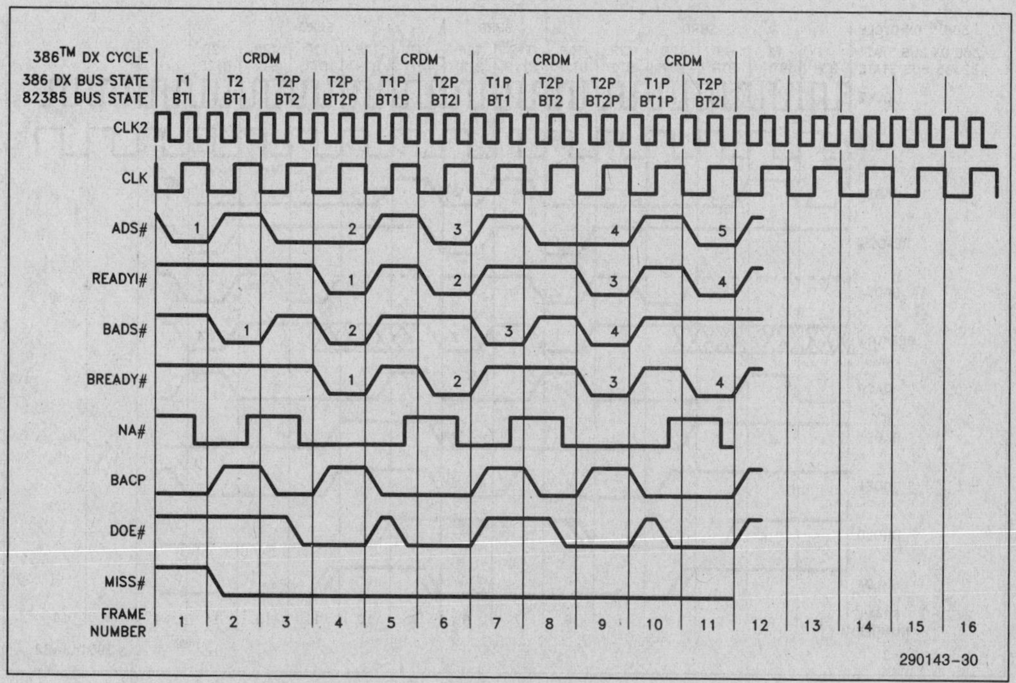

Figure 5-3B. Consecutive CRDM Cycles—(N = 1)

4

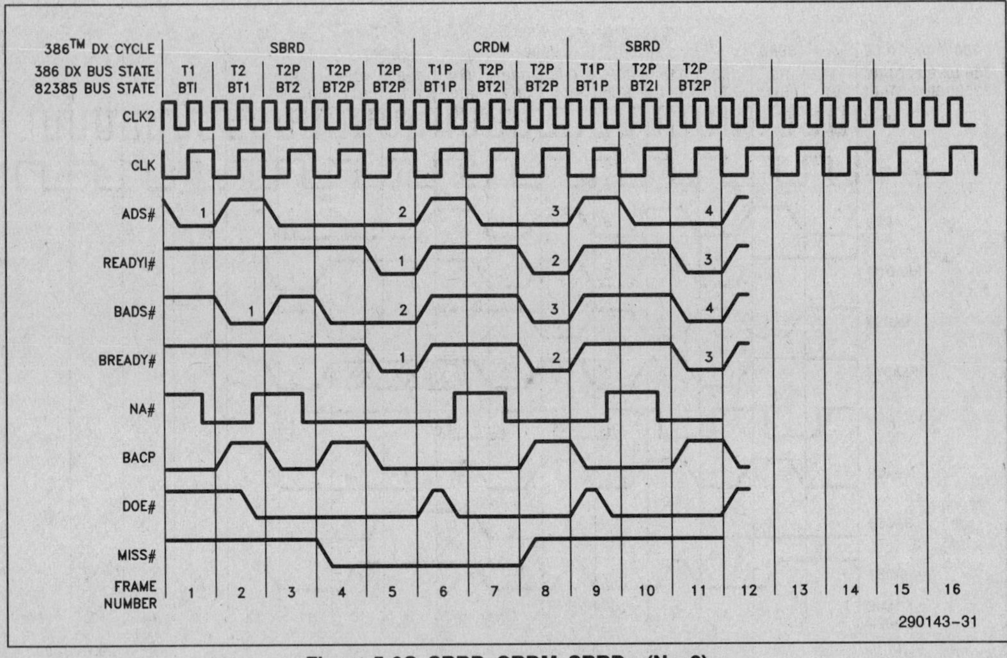

Figure 5-3C. SBRD, CRDM, SBRD—(N = 2)

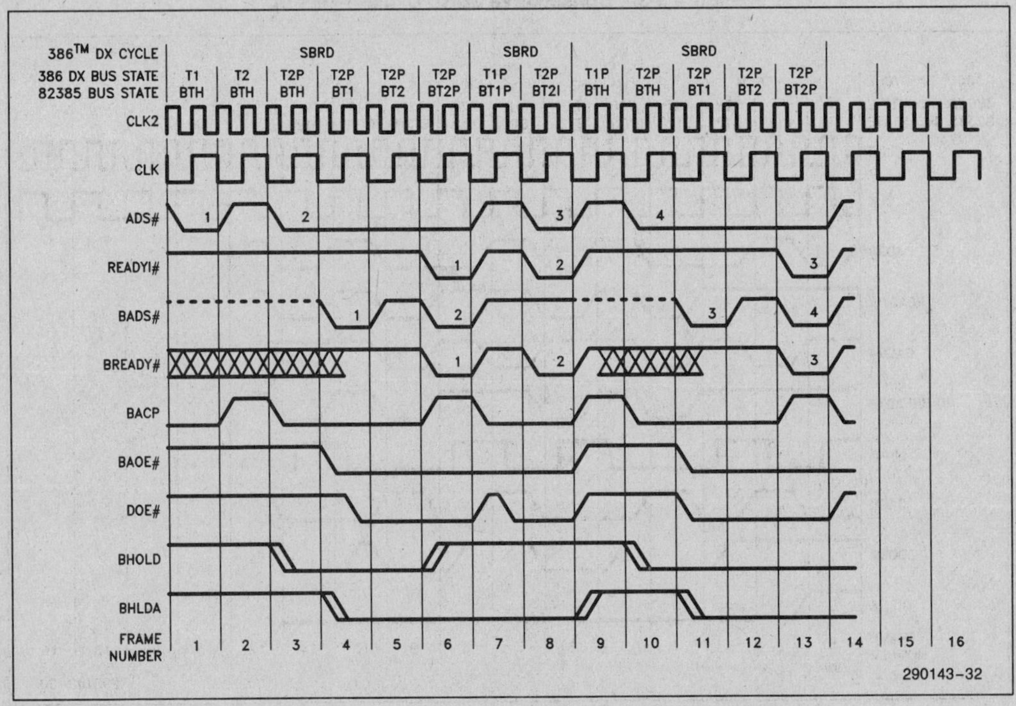

Figure 5-3D. SBRD Cycles Interleaved with BTH States—(N = 1)

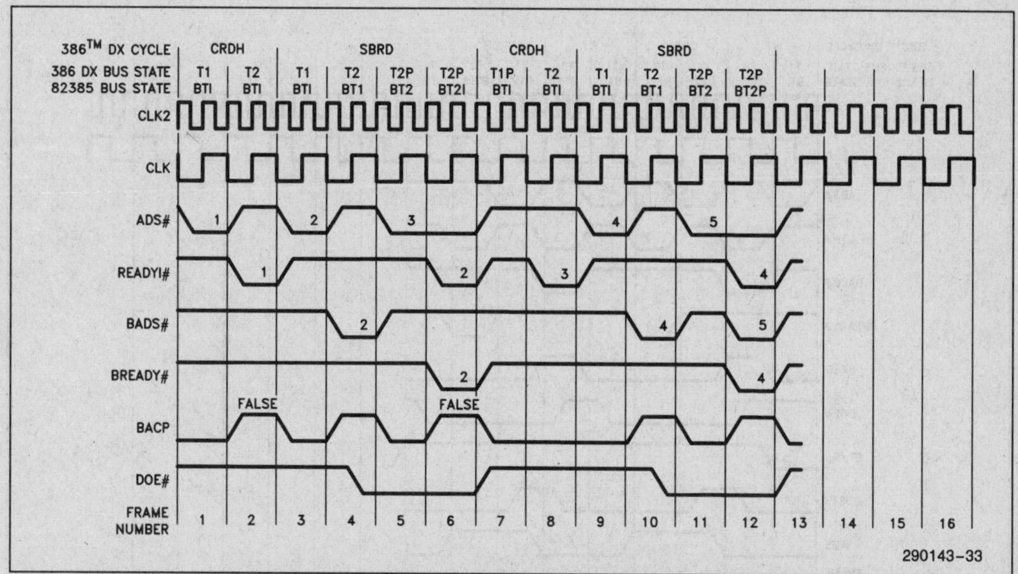

Figure 5-3E. Interleaved SBRD/CRDH Cycles—(N = 1)

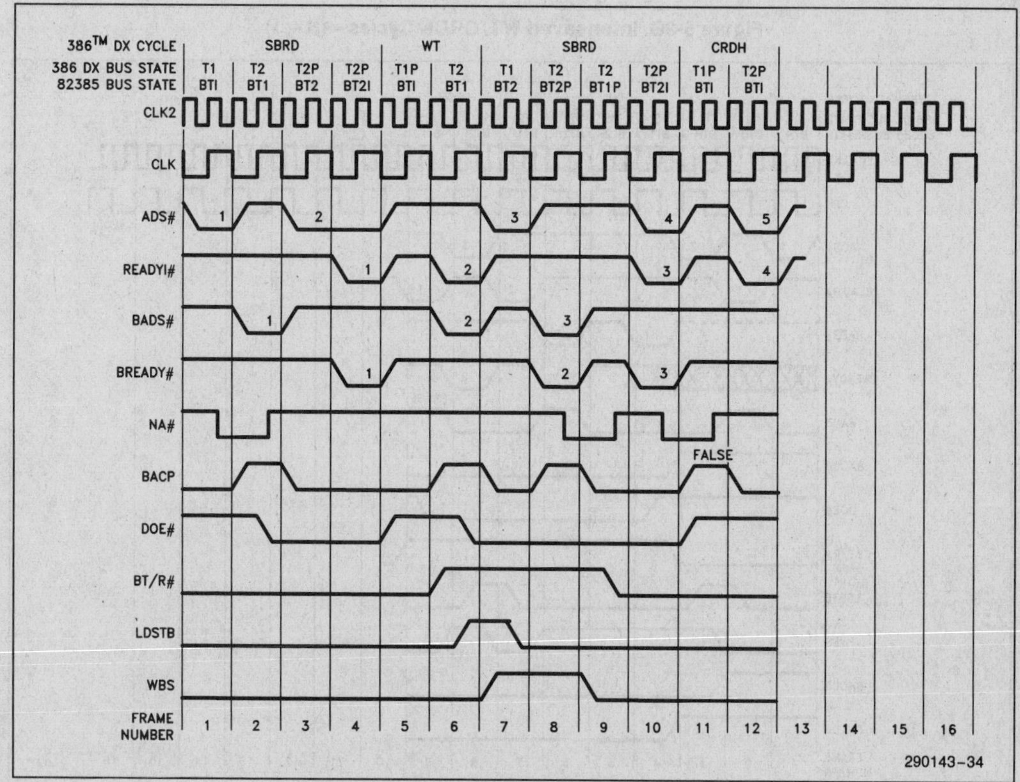

386™ DX CYCLE
SBRD
WT
SBRD
CRDH
386 DX BUS STATE
82385 BUS STATE
T1 BTI
T2 BT1
T2P BT2
T2P BT2I
T1P BTI
T2 BT1
T1 BT2
T2 BT2P
T2 BT1P
T2P BT2I
T1P BTI
T2P BTI
CLK2
CLK
ADS#
READYI#
BADS#
BREADY#
NA#
FALSE
BACP
DOE#
BT/R#
LDSTB
WBS
FRAME NUMBER
1 2 3 4 5 6 7 8 9 10 11 12 13 14 15 16
290143-34

Figure 5-3F. SBRD, WT, SBRD, CRDH—(N = 1)

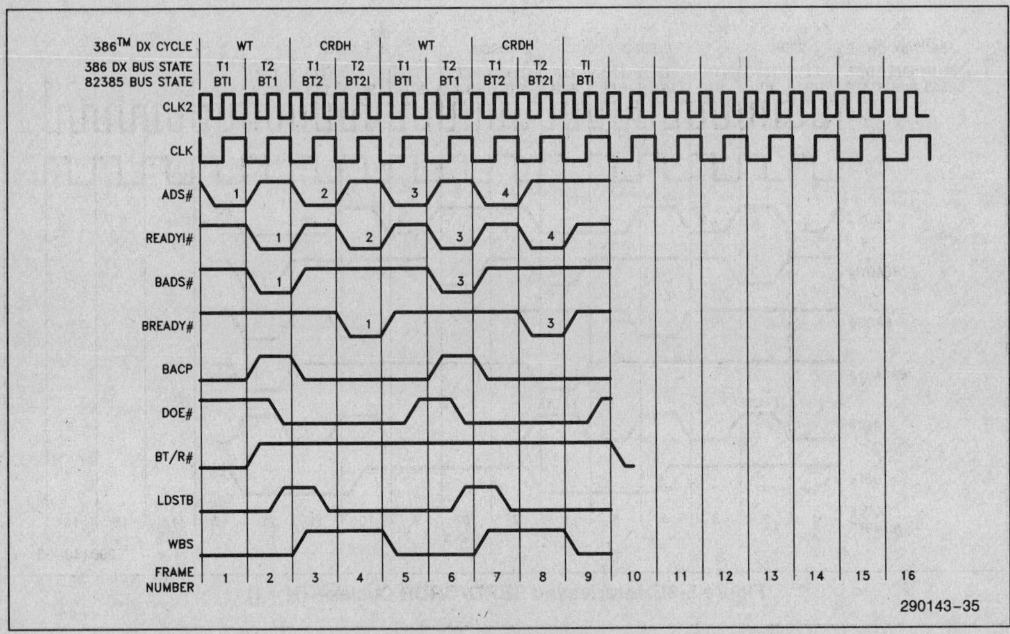

Figure 5-3G. Interleaved WT/CRDH Cycles—(N = 1)

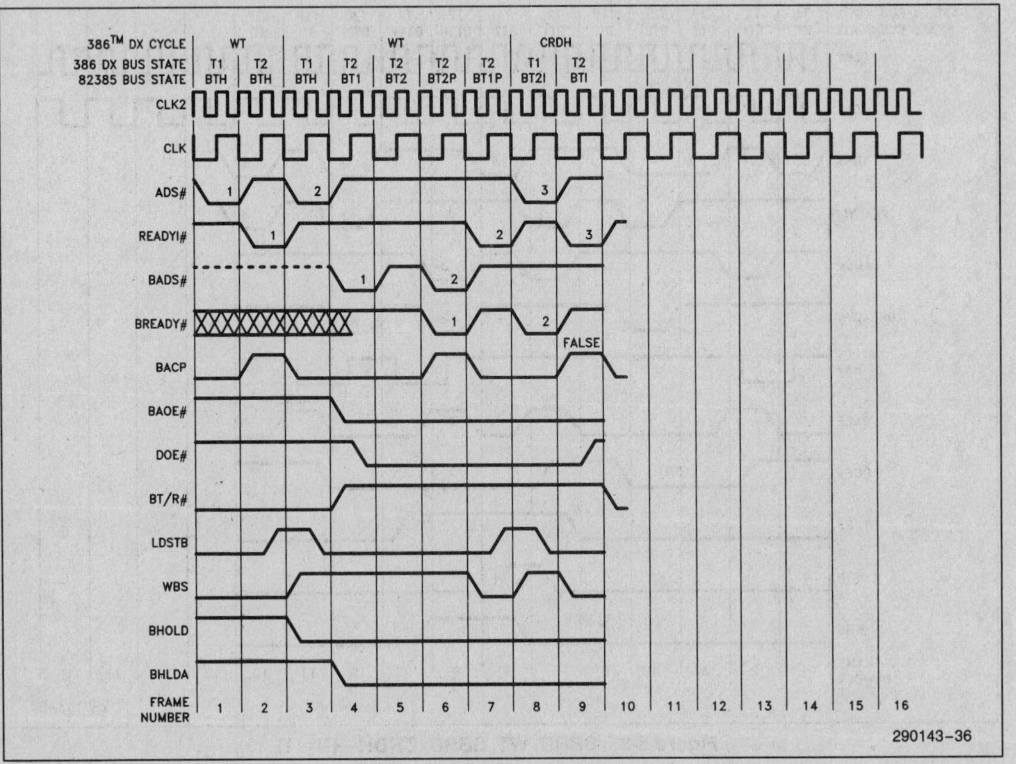

386™ DX CYCLE: WT, WT, CRDH

386 DX BUS STATE: T1 T2 T1 T2 T2 T2 T2 T1 T2

82385 BUS STATE: BTH BTH BTH BT1 BT2 BT2P BT1P BT2I BTI

CLK2

CLK

ADS#

READYI#

BADS#

BREADY#

FALSE

BACP

BAOE#

DOE#

BT/R#

LDSTB

WBS

BHOLD

BHLDA

FRAME NUMBER: 1 2 3 4 5 6 7 8 9 10 11 12 13 14 15 16

290143-36

Figure 5-3H. WT, WT, CRDH—(N = 1)

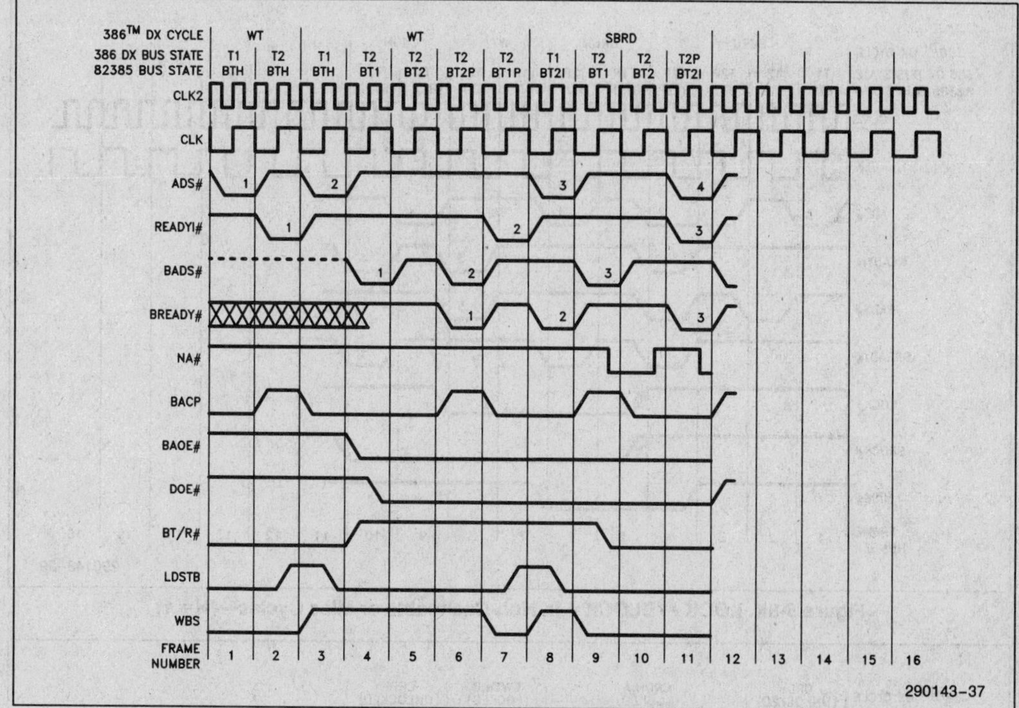

386™ DX CYCLE: WT, WT, SBRD
386 DX BUS STATE: T1, T2, T1, T2, T2, T2, T2, T1, T2, T2, T2P
82385 BUS STATE: BTH, BTH, BTH, BT1, BT2, BT2P, BT1P, BT2I, BT1, BT2, BT2I
CLK2, CLK, ADS#, READYI#, BADS#, BREADY#, NA#, BACP, BAOE#, DOE#, BT/R#, LDSTB, WBS
FRAME NUMBER: 1 2 3 4 5 6 7 8 9 10 11 12 13 14 15 16

290143-37

Figure 5-3I. WT, WT, SBRD—(N = 1)

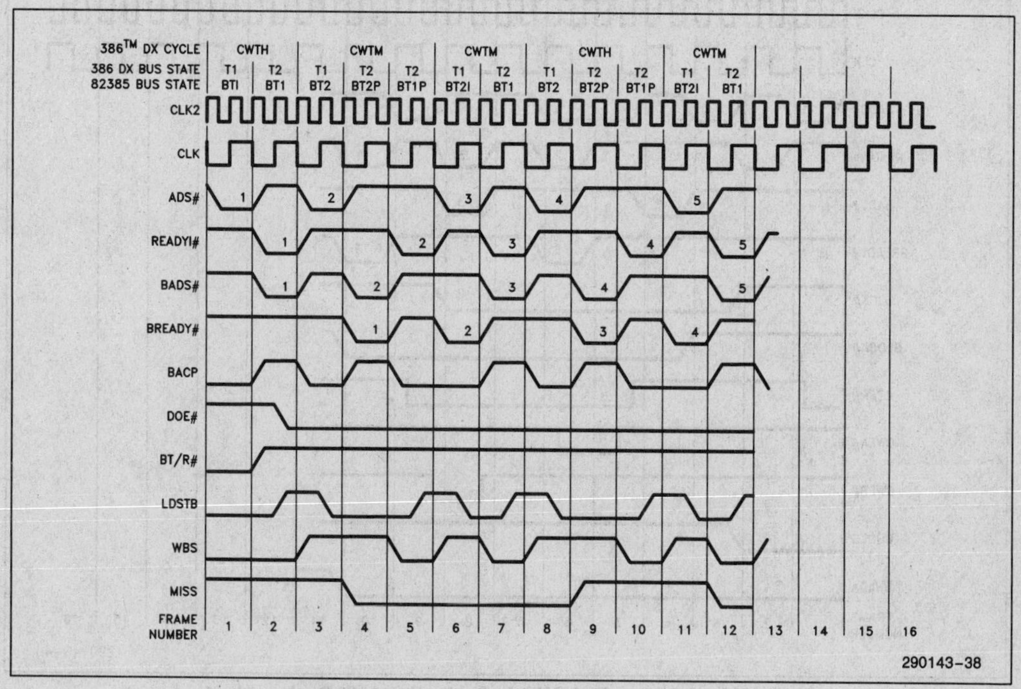

Figure 5-3J. Consecutive Write Cycles—(N = 1)

4

386™ DX CYCLE
SBRD
CRDM
WT
CRDH
386 DX BUS STATE
82385 BUS STATE
T1 BTI
T2 BT1
T2P BT2
T2P BT2P
T1P BT1P
T2P BT2I
T1P BTI
T2 BT1
T1 BT2
T2 BT2I
CLK2
CLK
ADS#
READYI#
BADS#
BREADY#
LOCK#
BLOCK#
MISS#
FRAME NUMBER
1 2 3 4 5 6 7 8 9 10 11 12 13 14 15 16
290143-39

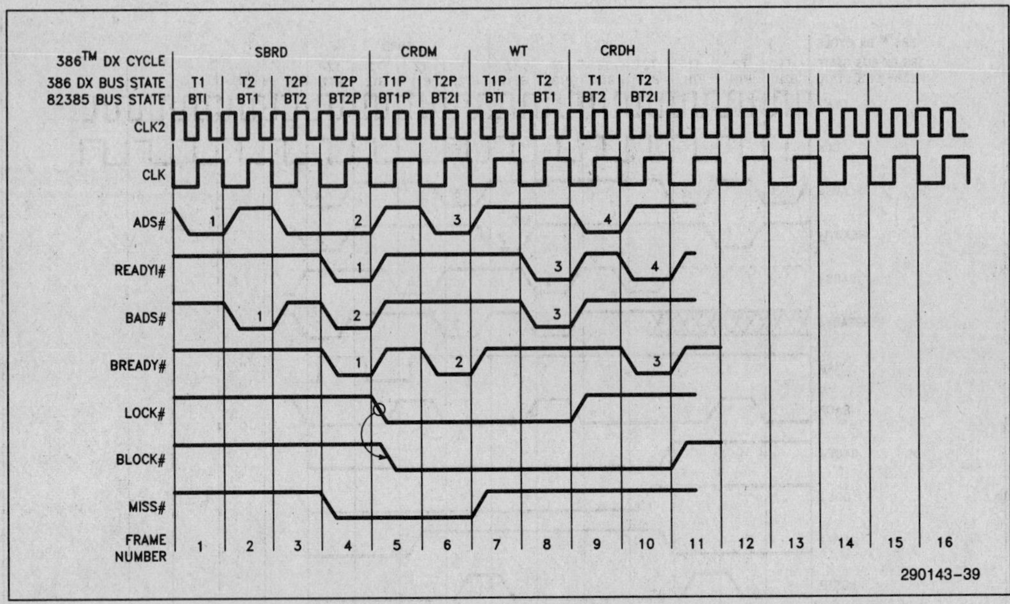

Figure 5-3K. LOCK#/BLOCK# in Non-Cacheable or Miss Cycles—(N = 1)

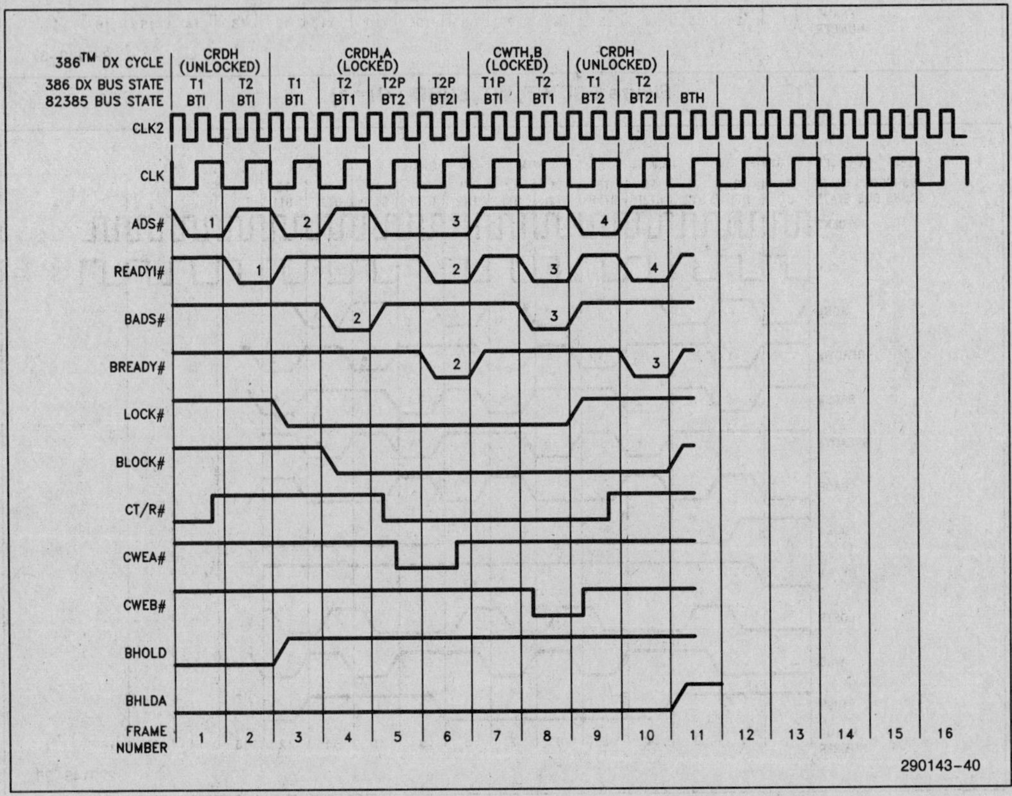

386™ DX CYCLE
CRDH (UNLOCKED)
CRDH,A (LOCKED)
CWTH,B (LOCKED)
CRDH (UNLOCKED)
386 DX BUS STATE
82385 BUS STATE
T1 BTI
T2 BTI
T1 BTI
T2 BT1
T2P BT2
T2P BT2I
T1P BTI
T2 BT1
T1 BT2
T2 BT2I
BTH
CLK2
CLK
ADS#
READYI#
BADS#
BREADY#
LOCK#
BLOCK#
CT/R#
CWEA#
CWEB#
BHOLD
BHLDA
FRAME NUMBER
1 2 3 4 5 6 7 8 9 10 11 12 13 14 15 16
290143-40

Figure 5-3L. LOCK#/BLOCK# in Cache Read Hit Cycle—(N = 1)

5.2.2.3 CACHE FLUSH (FLUSH)

FLUSH is an 82385 input which is used to reset all tag valid bits within the cache directory. The FLUSH input must be kept active for at least 4 CLK (8 CLK2) periods to complete the directory flush. Flush is generally used in diagnostics but can also be used in applications where snooping cannot guarantee coherency.

5.3 BUS WATCHING (SNOOP) INTERFACE

The 82385's bus watching interface consists of the snoop address (SA2–SA31), snoop strobe (SSTB#), and snoop enable (SEN) inputs. If masters reside at the system bus level, then the SA2–SA31 inputs are connected to the system address lines and SEN the system bus memory write command. SSTB# indicates that a valid address is present on the system bus. Note that the snoop bus inputs are synchronous, so care must be taken to ensure that they are stable during their sample windows. If no master resides beyond the 82385 bus level, then the 82385 inputs SA2–SA31, SEN, and SSTB# can respectively tie directly to BA2–BA31, BW/R#, and BADS# of the other system bus master (see Figure 5.5). However, it is recommended that SEN be driven by the logical "AND" of BW/R# and BM/IO# so as to prevent I/O writes from unnecessarily invalidating cache data.

When the 82385 detects a system write by another master and the conditions in Figure 5.4 are met: CLK2 PHI1 rising (CLK falling), BHLDA asserted, SEN asserted, SSTB# asserted, it internally latches SA2–SA31 and runs a cache look-up to see if the altered main memory location is duplicated in the cache. If yes (a snoop hit), the line valid bit associated with that cache entry is cleared. An important feature of the 82385 is that even if the 386 DX is running zero wait state hits out of the cache, all snoops are serviced. This is accomplished by time multiplexing the cache directory between the 386 DX address and the latched system address. If the SSTB# signal occurs during an 82385 comparison cycle (for the 386 DX), the 386 DX cycle has the highest priority in accessing the cache directory. This takes the first of the two 386 DX states. The other state is then used for the snoop comparison. This worst case example, depicted in Figure 5-4, shows the 386 DX running zero wait state hits on the 386 DX local bus, and another master running zero wait state writes on the 82385 bus. No snoops are missed, and no performance penalty incurred.

5.4 RESET DEFINITION

Table 5-1 summarizes the states of all 82385 outputs during reset and initialization. A slave mode 82385 tri-states its "386 DX-like" front end. A master mode 82385 emits a pulse stream on its BACP output. As the 386 DX address and cycle definition lines reach their reset values, this stream will latch the reset values through to the 82385 bus.

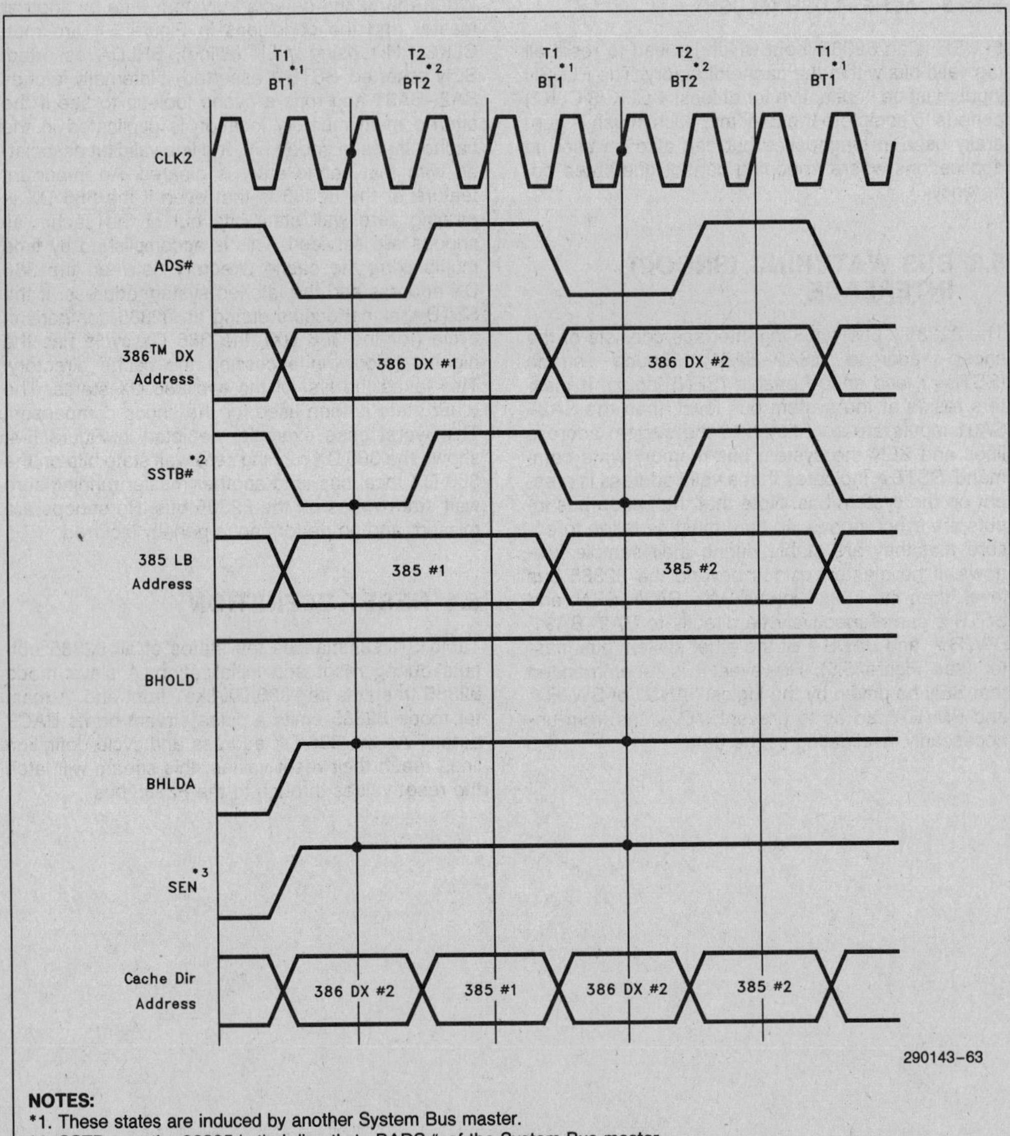

NOTES:
*1. These states are induced by another System Bus master.
*2. SSTB# on the 82385 is tied directly to BADS# of the System Bus master.
*3. SEN on the 82385 is tied directly to BW/R# of the System Bus master.

Figure 5.4. Interleaved Snoop and 386 DX Accesses to the Cache Directory

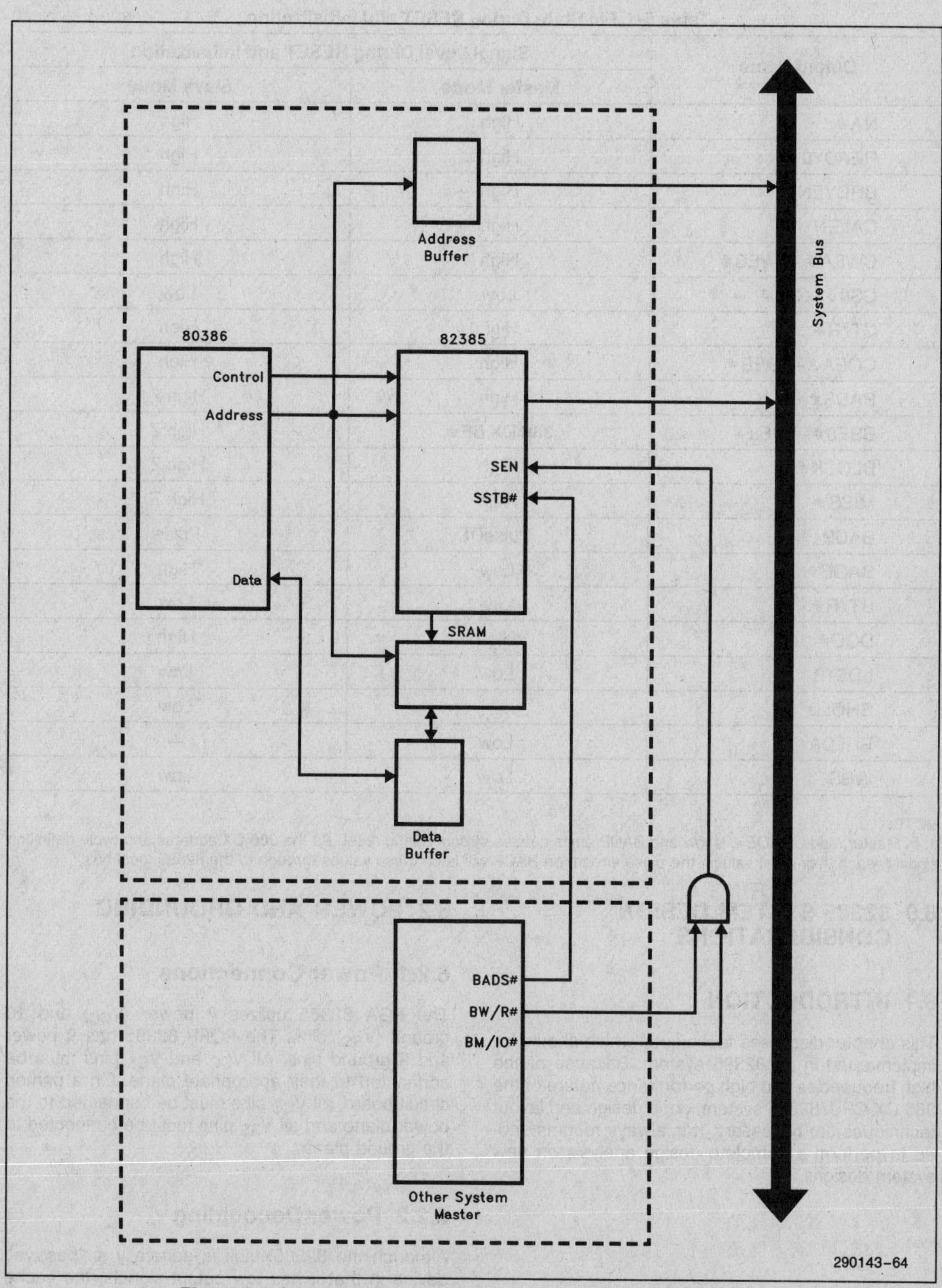

Figure 5.5. Snooping Connections in a Multi Master Environment

Table 5-1. Pin State During RESET and Initialization

Output Name	Signal Level During RESET and Initialization	
	Master Mode	Slave Mode
NA#	High	High
READY0#	High	High
BRDYEN#	High	High
CALEN	High	High
CWEA#-CWEB#	High	High
CS0#-CS3#	Low	Low
CT/R#	High	High
COEA#-COEB#	High	High
BADS#	High	High Z
BBE0#-BBE3#	386 DX BE#	High Z
BLOCK#	High	High Z
MISS#	High	High Z
BACP	Pulse(1)	Pulse
BAOE#	Low	High
BT/R#	Low	Low
DOE#	High	High
LDSTB	Low	Low
BHOLD	—	Low
BHLDA	Low	—
WBS	Low	Low

NOTE:
1. In Master Mode, BAOE# is low and BACP emits a pulse stream during reset. As the 386 DX address and cycle definition signals reach their reset values, the pulse stream on BACP will latch these values through to the 82385 local bus.

6.0 82385 SYSTEM DESIGN CONSIDERATIONS

6.1 INTRODUCTION

This chapter discusses techniques which should be implemented in an 82385 system. Because of the high frequencies and high performance nature of the 386 DX CPU/82385 system, good design and layout techniques are necessary. It is always recommended to perform a complete design analysis on new system designs.

6.2 POWER AND GROUNDING

6.2.1 Power Connections

The PGA 82385 utilizes 8 power (V_{CC}) and 10 ground (V_{SS}) pins. The PQFP 82385 has 9 power and 9 ground pins. All V_{CC} and V_{SS} pins must be connected to their appropriate plane. On a printed circuit board, all V_{CC} pins must be connected to the power plane and all V_{SS} pins must be connected to the ground plane.

6.2.2 Power Decoupling

Although the 82385 itself is generally a "passive" device in that it has few output signals, the cache subsystem as a whole is quite active. Therefore, many decoupling capacitors should be placed around the 82385 cache subsystem.

Low inductance capacitors and interconnects are recommended for best high frequency electrical performance. Inductance can be reduced by shortening circuit board traces between the decoupling capacitors and their respective devices as much as possible. Capacitors specifically for PGA packages are also commercially available, for the lowest possible inductance.

6.2.3 Resistor Recommendations

Because of the dual bus structure of the 82385 subsystem (386 DX Local Bus and 82385 Local Bus), any signals which are recommended to be pulled up will be respective to one of the busses. The following sections will discuss signals for both busses.

6.2.3.1 386 DX LOCAL BUS

For typical designs, the pullup resistors shown in Table 6-1 are recommended. This table correlates to Chapter 7 of the 386 DX Data Sheet. However, particular designs may have a need to differ from the listed values. Design analysis is recommended to determine specific requirements.

6.2.3.2 82385 LOCAL BUS

Pullup resistor recommendations for the 82385 Local Bus signals are shown in Table 6-2. Design analysis is necessary to determine if deviations to the typical values given is needed.

Table 6-1. Recommended Resistor Pullups to V_{CC} (386 DX Local Bus)

Pin and Signal	Pullup Value	Purpose
ADS# PGA E13 PQFP 123	20 KΩ ±10%	Lightly Pull ADS# Negated for 386 DX Hold States
LOCK# PGA F13 PQFP 118	20 KΩ ±10%	Lightly Pull LOCK# Negated for 386 DX Hold States

Table 6-2. Recommended Resistor Pullups to V_{CC} (82385 Local Bus)

Signal and Pin	Pullup Value	Purpose
BADS# PGA N9 PQFP 89	20 KΩ ±10%	Lightly Pull BADS# Negated for 82385 Hold States
BLOCK# PGA P9 PQFP 86	20 KΩ ±10%	Lightly Pull BLOCK# Negated for 82385 Hold States
MISS# PGA N8 PQFP 85	20 KΩ ±10%	Lightly Pull MISS# Negated for 82385 Hold States

6.3 82385 SIGNAL CONNECTIONS

6.3.1 Configuration Inputs

The 82385 configuration signals (M/S#, 2W/D#, DEFOE#) must be connected (pulled up) to the appropriate logic level for the system design. There is also a reserved 82385 input which must be tied to the appropriate level. Refer to Table 6-3 for the signals and their required logic level.

Table 6-3. 82385 Configuration Inputs Logic Levels

Pin and Signal	Logic Level	Purpose
M/S# PGA B13 PQFP 129	High	Master Mode Operation
	Low	Slave Mode Operation
2W/D# PGA D12 PQFP 127	High	2-Way Set Associative
	Low	Direct Mapped
Resrved PGA L14 PQFP 102	High	Must be tied to V_{CC} via a pull-up for proper functionality
DEFOE# PGA A14 PQFP 128	N/A	Define Cache Output Enables. Allows use of any SRAM.

NOTE:
The listed 82385 pins which need to be tied high should use a pull-up resistor in the range of 5 KΩ to 20 KΩ.

4

6.3.2 CLK2 and RESET

The 82385 has two inputs to which the 386 DX CLK2 signal must be connected. One is labeled CLK2 (82385 PGA pin C13, PQFP lead 126) and the other is labeled BCLK2 (82385 PGA pin L13, PQFP lead 103). These two inputs must be tied together on the printed circuit board.

The 82385 also has two reset inputs. RESET (82385 PGA pin D13, PQFP lead 125) and BRESET (82385 PGA pin K12, PQFP lead 104) must be connected on the printed circuit board.

6.4 UNUSED PIN REQUIREMENTS

For reliable operation, ALWAYS connect unused inputs to a valid logic level. As is the case with most other CMOS processes, a floating input will increase the current consumption of the component and give an indeterminate state to the component.

6.5 CACHE SRAM REQUIREMENTS

The 82385 offers the option of using SRAMs with or without an output enable pin. This is possible by inserting a transceiver between the SRAMs and the 386 DX local data bus and strapping DEFOE# to the appropriate logic level for a given system configuration. This transceiver may also be desirable in a system which has a very heavily loaded 386 DX local data bus. The following sections discuss the SRAM requirements for all cache configurations.

6.5.1 Cache Memory without Transceivers

As discussed in Section 3.2, the 82385 presents all of the control signals necessary to access the cache memory. The SRAM chip selects, write enables, and output enables are driven directly by the 82385. Table 6-4 lists the required SRAM specifications. These specifications allow for zero margins. They should be used as guides for the actual system design.

6.5.2 Cache Memory With Transceivers

To implement an 82385 subsystem using cache memory transceivers, COEA# or COEB# must be used as output enable signals for the transceivers and DEFOE# must be appropriately strapped for proper COEx# functionality (since the cache SRAM transceivers must be enabled for writes as well as reads). DEFOE# must be tied high when using cache SRAM transceivers. In a 2-way set associative organization, COEA# enables the transceiver for bank A and COEB# enables the bank B transceiver. A direct mapped cache may use either COEA# or COEB# to enable the transceiver. Table 6-5 lists the required SRAM specifications. These specifications allow for zero margin. They should be used as guides for the actual system design.

Table 6-4. SRAM Specs for Non-Buffered Cache Memory

SRAM Spec Requirements	Direct Mapped			2-Way Set Associative		
	20	25	33	20	25	33
Read Cycle Requirements						
Address Access (MAX)	44	36	27	42	34	27
Chip Select Access (MAX)	56	44	35	56	41	35
OE# to Data Valid (MAX)	19	13	10	14	13	10
OE# to Data Float (MAX)	20	15	10	20	15	10
Write Cycle Requirements						
Chip Select to End of Write (MIN)	30	25	20	30	25	20
Address Valid to End of Write (MIN)	42	37	29	40	37	29
Write Pulse Width (MIN)	30	25	20	30	25	20
Data Setup (MAX)	—	—	—	—	—	—
Data Hold (MIN)	4	4	2	4	4	2

Table 6-5. SRAM Specs for Buffered Cache Memory

SRAM Spec Requirements	Direct Mapped			2-Way Set Associative		
	20	25	33	20	25	33
Read Cycle Requirements						
Address Access (MAX)	37	29	20	35	29	20
Chip Select Access (MAX)	48	36	27	48	36	27
OE# to Data Valid (MAX)	N/A	N/A	N/A	N/A	N/A	N/A
OE# to Data Float (MAX)	N/A	N/A	N/A	N/A	N/A	N/A
Write Cycle Requirements						
Chip Select to End of Write (MIN)	30	25	20	30	23	20
Address Valid to End of Write (MIN)	42	37	29	40	36	27
Write Pulse Width (MIN)	30	25	20	30	25	20
Data Setup (MAX)	15	10	10	15	10	10
Data Hold (MIN)	3	3	3	3	3	3

7.0 SYSTEM TEST CONSIDERATIONS

7.1 INTRODUCTION

Power On Self Testing (POST) is performed by most systems after a reset. This chapter discusses the requirements for properly testing an 82385 based system after power up.

7.2 MAIN MEMORY (DRAM) TESTING

Most systems perform a memory test by writing a data pattern and then reading and comparing the data. This test may also be used to determine the total available memory within the system. Without properly taking into account the 82385 cache memory, the memory test can give erroneous results. This will occur if the cache responds with read hits during the memory test routine.

7.2.1 Memory Testing Routine

In order to properly test main memory, the test routine must not read from the same block consecutively. For instance, if the test routine writes a data pattern to the first 32 kbytes of memory (0000–7FFFH), reads from the same block, writes a new pattern to the same locations (0000–7FFFH), and reads the new pattern, the second pattern tested would have had data returned from the 82385 cache memory. Therefore, it is recommended that the test routine work with a memory block of at least 64 kbytes. This will guarantee that no 32 kbyte block will be read twice consecutively.

7.3 82385 CACHE MEMORY TESTING

With the addition of SRAMs for the cache memory, it may be desirable for the system to be able to test the cache SRAMs during system diagnostics. This requires the test routine to access only the cache memory. The requirements for this routine are based on where it resides within the memory map. This can be broken into two areas: the routine residing in cacheable memory space or the routine residing in either non-cacheable memory or on the 386 DX local bus (using the LBA# input).

7.3.1 Test Routine in the NCA# or LBA# Memory Map

In this configuration, the test routine will never be cached. The recommended method is code which will access a single 32 kbyte block during the test. Initially, a 32 kbyte read (assume 0000–7FFFH) must be executed. This will fill the cache directory with the address information which will be used in the diagnostic procedure. Then, a 32 kbyte write to the same address locations (0000–7FFFH) will load the cache with the desired test pattern (due to write hits). The comparison can be made by completing another 32 kbyte read (same locations, 0000–7FFFH), which will be cache read hits. Subsequent writes and reads to the same addresses will enable various patterns to be tested.

7.3.2 Test Routine in Cacheable Memory

In this case, it must be understood that the diagnostic routine must reside in the cache memory before the actual data testing can begin. Otherwise, when the 386 DX performs a code fetch, a location within the cache memory which is to be tested will be altered due to the read miss (code fetch) update.

The first task is to load the diagnostic routine into the top of the cache memory. It must be known how much memory is required for the code as the rest of the cache memory will be tested as in the earlier method. Once the diagnostics have been cached (via read updates), the code will perform the same type of read/write/read/compare as in the routine explained in the above section. The difference is that now the amount of cache memory to be tested is 32 kbytes minus the length of the test routine.

7.4 82385 CACHE DIRECTORY TESTING

Since the 82385 does not directly access the data bus, it is not possible to easily complete a comparison of the cache directory. (The 82385 can serially transmit its directory contents. See Section 7.5.) However, the cache memory tests described in Section 7.3 will indicate if the directory is working properly. Otherwise, the data comparison within the diagnostics will show locations which fail.

There is a slight possibility that the cache memory comparison could pass even if locations within the directory gave false hit/miss results. This could cause the comparison to always be performed to main memory instead of the cache and give a proper comparison to the 386 DX . The solution here is to use the MISS# output of the 82385 as an indicator to a diagnostic port which can be read by the 386 DX . It could also be used to flag an interrupt if a failure occurs.

The implementation of these techniques in the diagnostics will assure proper functionality of the 82385 subsystem.

7.5 SPECIAL FUNCTION PINS

As mentioned in Chapter 3, there are three 82385 pins which have reserved functions in addition to their normal operational functions. These pins are MISS#, WBS, and FLUSH.

As discussed previously, the 82385 performs a directory flush when the FLUSH input is held active for at least 4 CLK (8 CLK2) cycles. However, the FLUSH pin also serves as a diagnostic input to the 82385. The 82385 will enter a reserved mode if the FLUSH pin is high at the falling edge of RESET.

If, during normal operation, the FLUSH input is active for only one CLK (2 CLK2) cycle/s, the 82385 will enter another reserved mode. Therefore it must be guaranteed that FLUSH is active for at least the 4 CLK (8 CLK2) cycle specification.

WBS and MISS# serve as outputs in the 82385 reserved modes.

8.0 MECHANICAL DATA

8.1 INTRODUCTION

This chapter discusses the physical package and its connections in detail.

8.2 PIN ASSIGNMENT

The 82385 pinout as viewed from the top side of the component is shown by Figure 8-1. Its pinout as viewed from the Pin side of the component is shown in Figure 8-2.

V_{CC} and V_{SS} connections must be made to multiple V_{CC} and V_{SS} (GND) pins. Each V_{CC} and V_{SS} must be connected to the appropriate voltage level. The circuit board should include V_{CC} and GND planes for power distribution and all V_{CC} and V_{SS} pins must be connected to the appropriate plane.

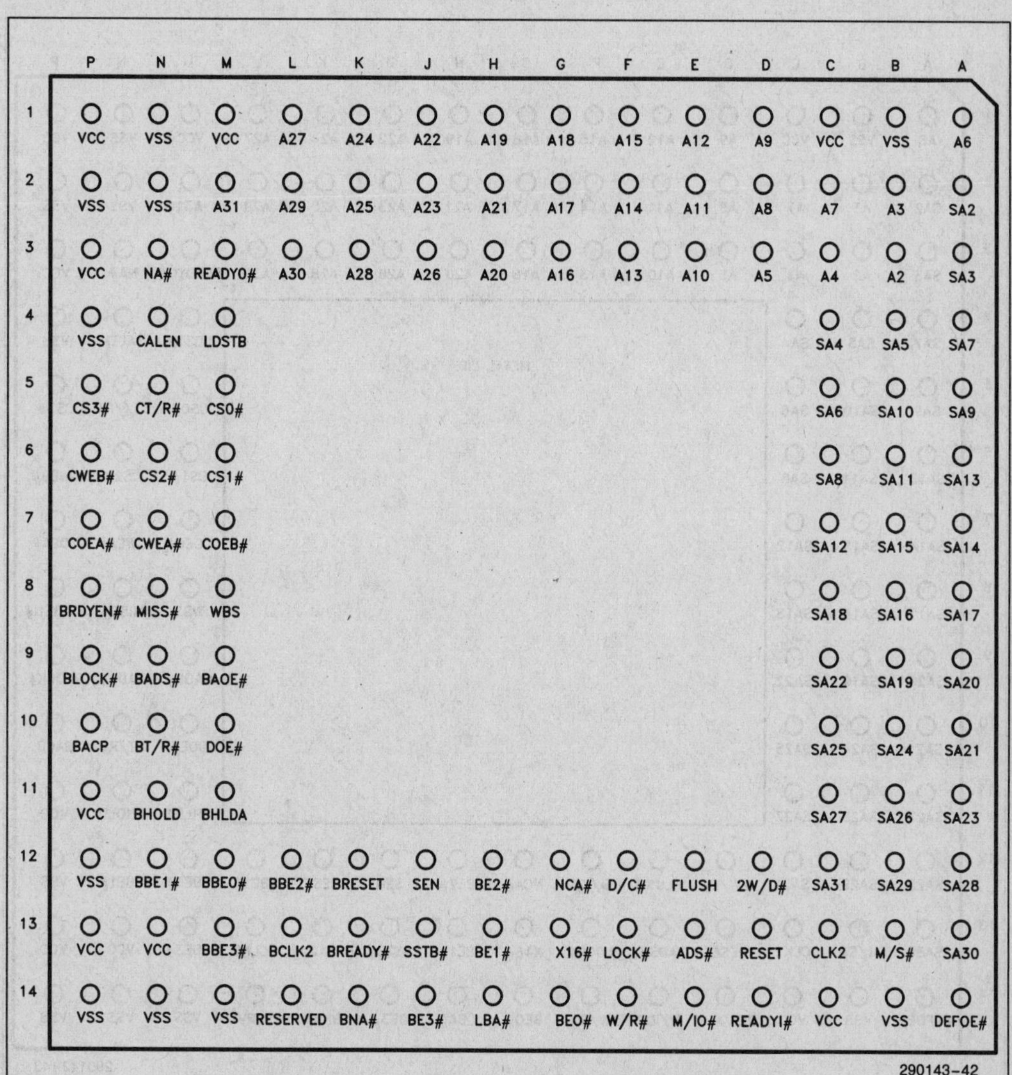

Figure 8-1. 82385 PGA Pinout—View from TOP Side

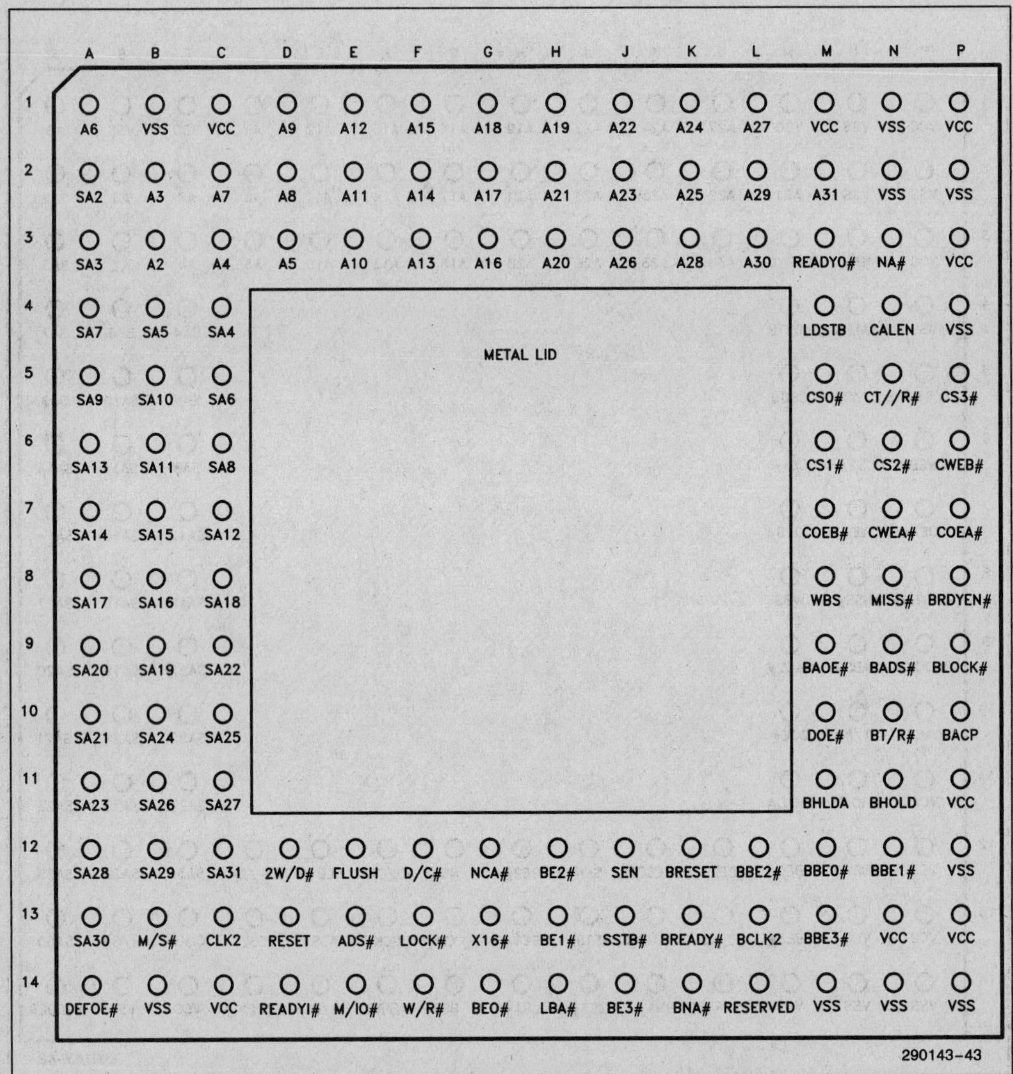

Figure 8-2. 82385 PGA Pinout—View from PIN Side

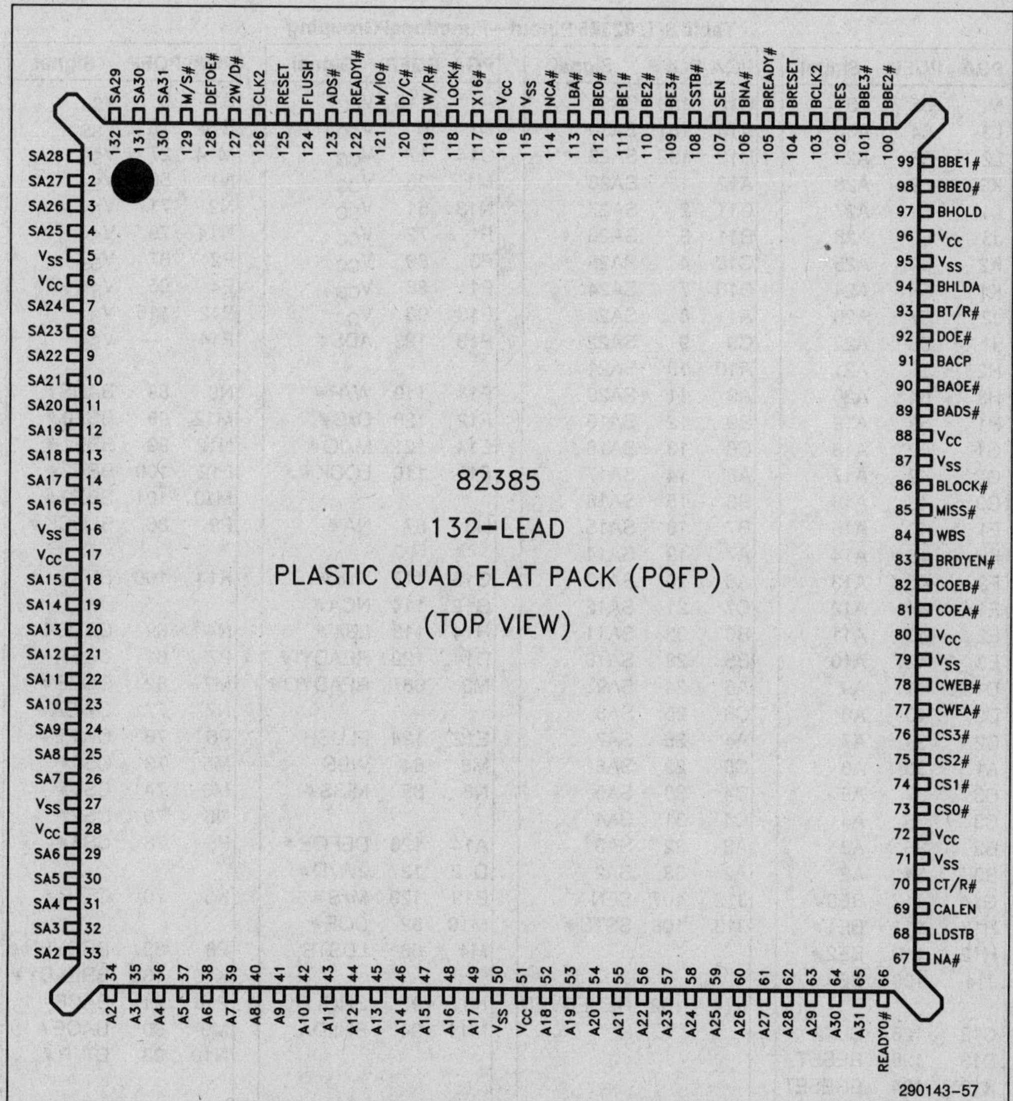

Figure 8-3. 82385 PQFP Pinout—View from TOP Side

4

Table 8-1. 82385 Pinout—Functional Grouping

PGA	PQFP	Signal
M2	65	A31
L3	64	A30
L2	63	A29
K3	62	A28
L1	61	A27
J3	60	A26
K2	59	A25
K1	58	A24
J2	57	A23
J1	56	A22
H2	55	A21
H3	54	A20
H1	53	A19
G1	52	A18
G2	49	A17
G3	48	A16
F1	47	A15
F2	46	A14
F3	45	A13
E1	44	A12
E2	43	A11
E3	42	A10
D1	41	A9
D2	40	A8
C2	39	A7
A1	38	A6
D3	37	A5
C3	36	A4
B2	35	A3
B3	34	A2
G14	112	BE0#
H13	111	BE1#
H12	110	BE2#
J14	109	BE3#
C13	126	CLK2
D13	125	RESET
K12	104	BRESET
L13	103	BCLK2

PGA	PQFP	Signal
C12	130	SA31
A13	131	SA30
B12	132	SA29
A12	1	SA28
C11	2	SA27
B11	3	SA26
C10	4	SA25
B10	7	SA24
A11	8	SA23
C9	9	SA22
A10	10	SA21
A9	11	SA20
B9	12	SA19
C8	13	SA18
A8	14	SA17
B8	15	SA16
B7	18	SA15
A7	19	SA14
A6	20	SA13
C7	21	SA12
B6	22	SA11
B5	23	SA10
A5	24	SA9
C6	25	SA8
A4	26	SA7
C5	29	SA6
B4	30	SA5
C4	31	SA4
A3	32	SA3
A2	33	SA2
J12	107	SEN
J13	108	SSTB#
L14	102	RESERVED

PGA	PQFP	Signal
—	116	V_{CC}
C1	6	V_{CC}
C14	17	V_{CC}
M1	28	V_{CC}
N13	51	V_{CC}
P1	72	V_{CC}
P3	80	V_{CC}
P11	88	V_{CC}
P13	96	V_{CC}
E13	123	ADS#
F14	119	W/R#
F12	120	D/C#
E14	121	M/IO#
F13	118	LOCK#
N3	67	NA#
G13	117	X16#
G12	114	NCA#
H14	113	LBA#
D14	122	READYI#
M3	66	READYO#
E12	124	FLUSH
M8	84	WBS
N8	85	MISS#
A14	128	DEFOE#
D12	127	2W/D#
B13	129	M/S#
M10	92	DOE#
M4	68	LDSTB
N11	97	BHOLD
M11	94	BHLDA

PGA	PQFP	Signal
B1	5	V_{SS}
B14	16	V_{SS}
M14	27	V_{SS}
N1	50	V_{SS}
N2	71	V_{SS}
N14	79	V_{SS}
P2	87	V_{SS}
P4	95	V_{SS}
P12	115	V_{SS}
P14	—	V_{SS}
N9	89	BADS#
M12	98	BBE0#
N12	99	BBE1#
L12	100	BBE2#
M13	101	BBE3#
P9	86	BLOCK#
K14	106	BNA#
N4	69	CALEN
P7	81	COEA#
M7	82	COEB#
N7	77	CWEA#
P6	78	CWEB#
M5	73	CS0#
M6	74	CS1#
N6	75	CS2#
P5	76	CS3#
N5	70	CT/R#
P8	83	BRDYEN#
K13	105	BREADY#
P10	91	BACP
M9	90	BAOE#
N10	93	BT/R#

8.3 PACKAGE DIMENSIONS AND MOUNTING

The 82385 package is a 132-pin ceramic Pin Grid Array (PGA). The pins are arranged 0.100 inch (2.5 mm) center-to-center, in a 14 x 14 matrix, three rows around (Figure 8-3).

A wide variety of available sockets allow low insertion force or zero insertion force mounting. These come in a choice of terminals such as soldertail, surface mount, or wire wrap.

8.4 PACKAGE THERMAL SPECIFICATION

The PGA case temperature should be measured at the center of the top surface opposite the pins, as in Figure 8-4. The case temperature may be measured in any environment to determine whether or not the 82385 is within the specified operating range.

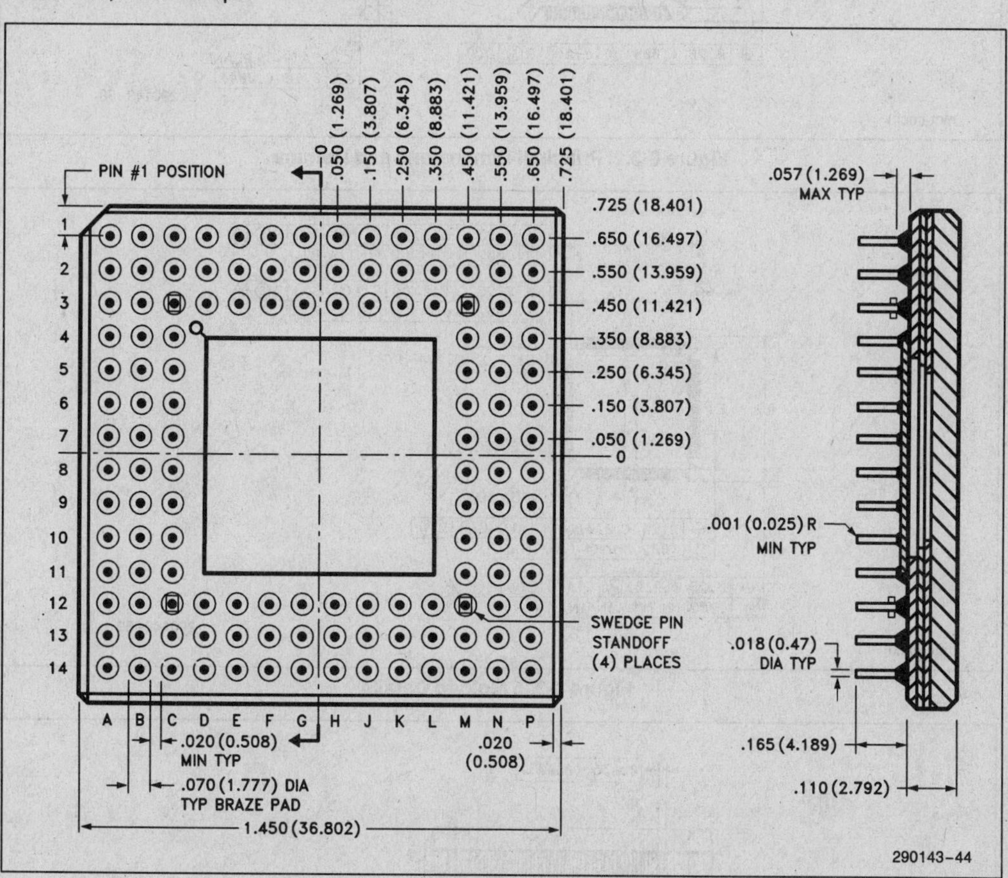

Figure 8-3.1. 132-Pin PGA Package Dimensions

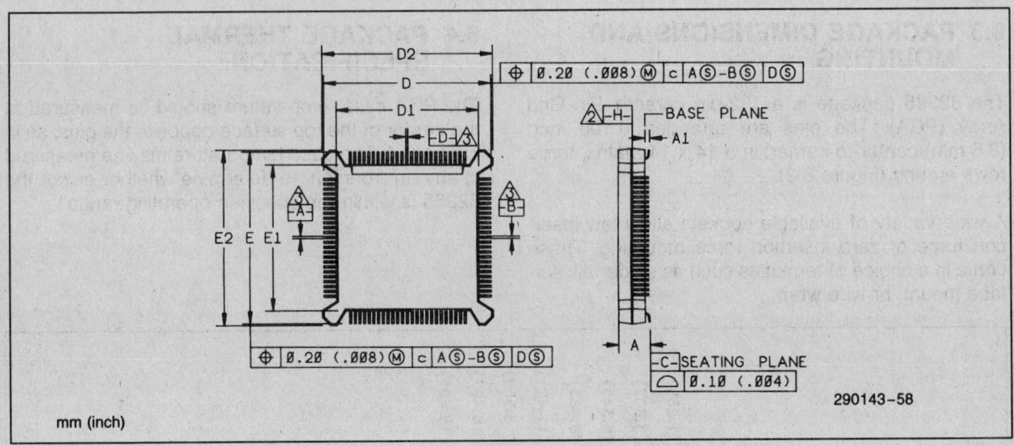

Figure 8-3.2. Principal Dimensions and Datums

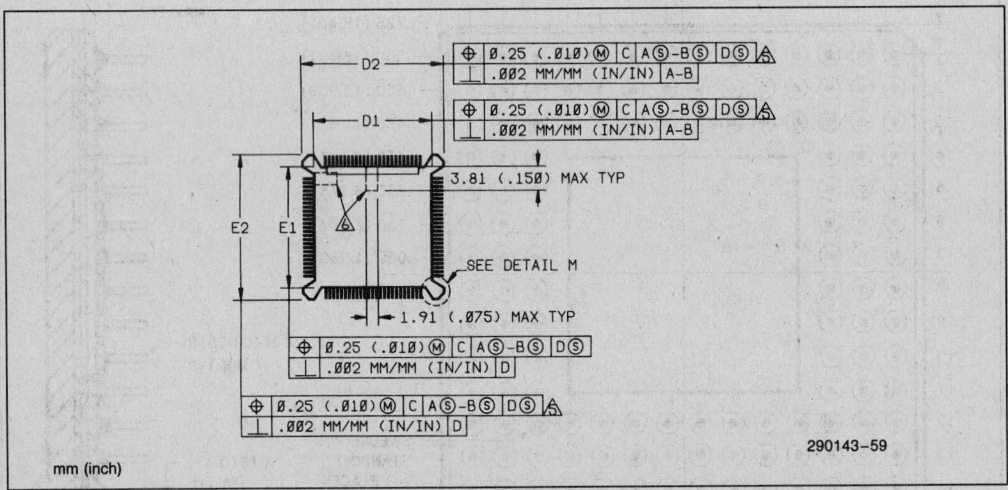

Figure 8-3.3. Molded Details

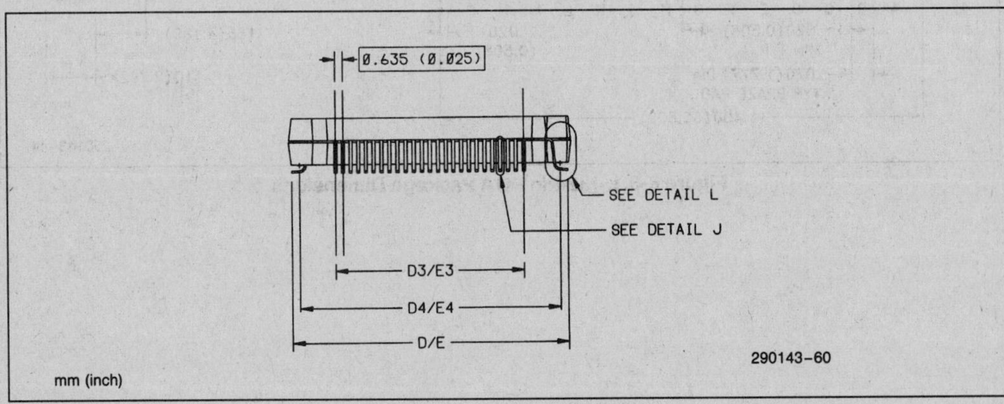

Figure 8-3.4. Terminal Details

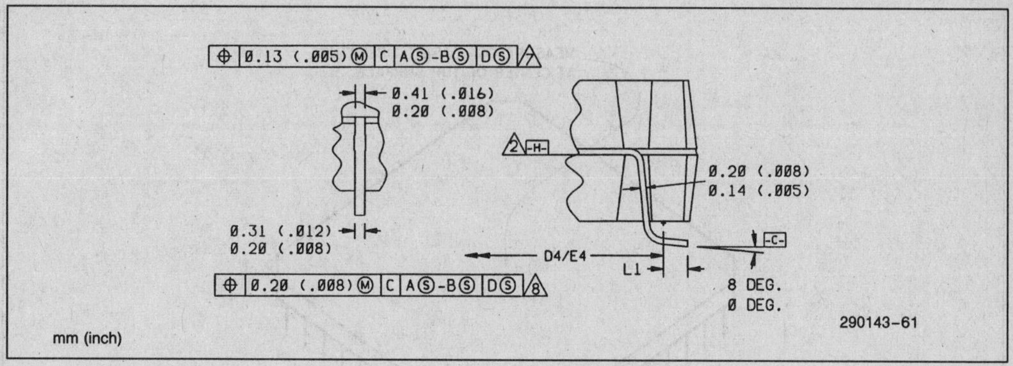

Figure 8-3.5. Typical Lead

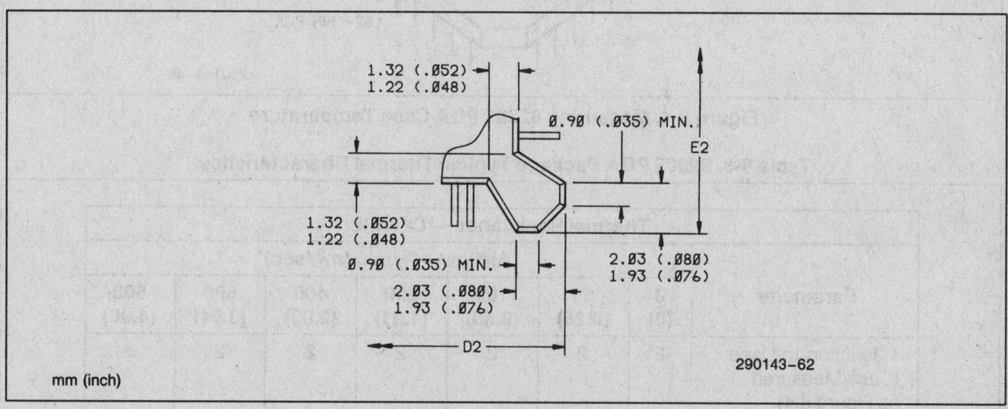

Figure 8-3.6. Detail M

PLASTIC QUAD FLAT PACK

Table 8-2. Symbol List for Plastic Quad Flat Pack

Letter or Symbol	Description of Dimensions
A	Package height: distance from seating plane to highest point of body
A1	Standoff: Distance from seating plane to base plane
D/E	Overall package dimension: lead tip to lead tip
D1/E1	Plastic body dimension
D2/E2	Bumper Distance
D3/E3	Footprint
L1	Foot length
N	Total number of leads

NOTES:

1. All dimensions and tolerances conform to ANSI Y14.5M-1982.
2. Datum plane -H- located at the mold parting line and coincident with the bottom of the lead where lead exits plastic body.
3. Datums A–B and -D- to be determined where center leads exit plastic body at datum plane -H-.
4. Controlling Dimension, Inch.
5. Dimensions D1, D2, E1 and E2 are measured at the mold parting line and do not include mode protrusion. Allowable mold protrusion of 0.18mm (0.007 in.) per side.
6. Pin 1 identifier is located within one of the two zones indicated.
7. Measured at datum plane -H-.
8. Measured at seating plane datum -C-.

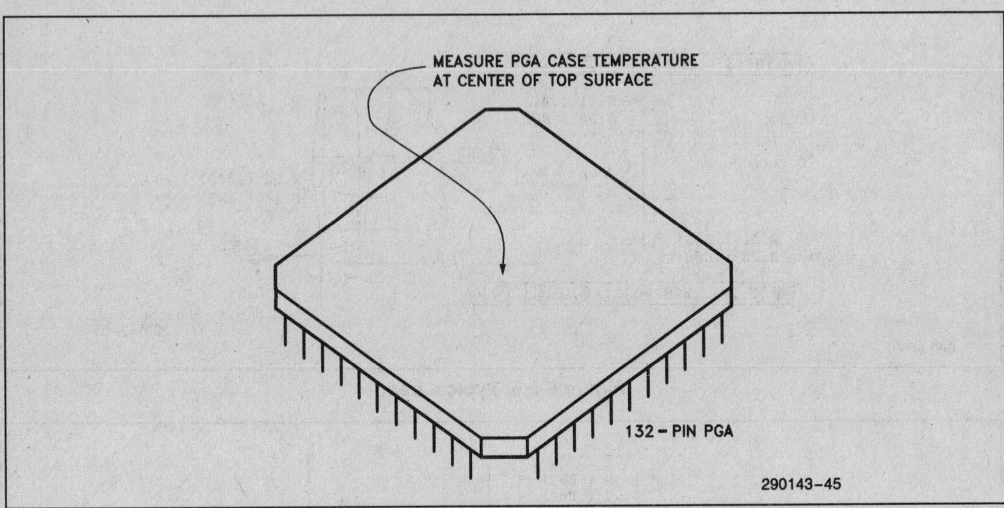

Figure 8-4. Measuring 82385 PGA Case Temperature

Table 8-3. 82385 PGA Package Typical Thermal Characteristics.

Thermal Resistance—°C/Watt							
Parameter	**Airflow—f³/min (m³/sec)**						
	0 (0)	**50 (0.25)**	**100 (0.50)**	**200 (1.01)**	**400 (2.03)**	**600 (3.04)**	**800 (4.06)**
θ Junction-to-Case (Case Measured as Figure 8.4)	2	2	2	2	2	2	2
θ Case-to-Ambient (No Heatsink)	19	18	17	15	12	10	9
θ Case-to-Ambient (with Omnidirectional Heatsink)	16	15	14	12	9	7	6
θ Case-to-Ambient (with Unidirectional Heatsink)	15	14	13	11	8	6	5

NOTES:
1. Table 8-3 applies to 82385 PGA plugged into socket or soldered directly onto board.
2. $\theta_{JA} = \theta_{JC} + \theta_{CA}$.
3. $\theta_{J\text{-}CAP}$ = 4°C/W (approx.)
   $\theta_{J\text{-}PIN}$ = 4°C/W (inner pins) (approx.)
   $\theta_{J\text{-}PIN}$ = 8°C/W (outer pins) (approx.)

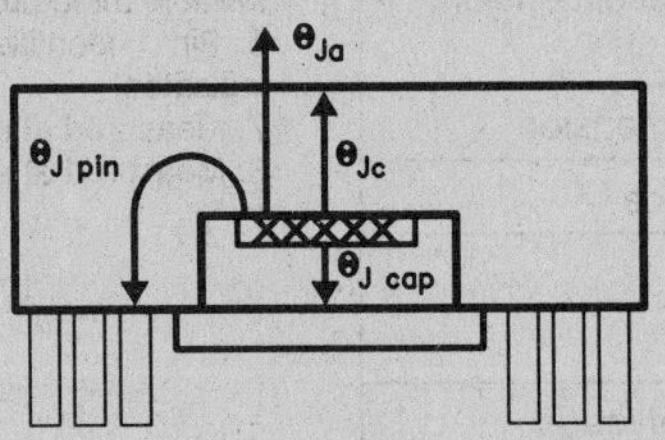

Table 8-4. 82385 132-Lead PQFP Package Typical Thermal Characteristics

Parameter	Thermal Resistance—°C/Watt						
	Airflow—lfm						
	0	50	100	200	400	600	800
θ Junction-to-Case (Case Measured as Figure 8.4)	5	5	5	5	5	5	5
θ Case-to-Ambient (No Heatsink)	23.5	22.0	20.5	17.5	14.0	11.5	9.5
θ Case-to-Ambient (with Omnidirectional Heatsink)	TO BE DEFINED						
θ Case-to-Ambient (with Unidirectional Heatsink)	TO BE DEFINED						

NOTES:
1. Table 8-4 applies to 82385 PQFP plugged into socket or soldered directly onto board.
2. $\theta_{JA} = \theta_{JC} + \theta_{CA}$.
3. $\theta_{J\text{-}CAP}$ = 4°C/W (approx.)
   $\theta_{J\text{-}PIN}$ = 4°C/W (inner pins) (approx.)
   $\theta_{J\text{-}PIN}$ = 8°C/W (outer pins) (approx.)

4

9.0 ELECTRICAL DATA

9.1 INTRODUCTION

This chapter presents the A.C. and D.C. specifications for the 82385.

9.2 MAXIMUM RATINGS

Storage Temperature .... −65°C to +150°C

Case Temperature under Bias ... −65°C to +110°C

Supply Voltage with Respect to V_{SS} .... −0.5V to +6.5V

Voltage on Any Other Pin .... −0.5V to V_{CC} + 0.5V

NOTE:
Stress above those listed may cause permanent damage to the device. This is a stress rating only and functional operation at these or any other conditions above those listed in the operational sections of this specification is not implied.

Exposure to absolute maximum rating conditions for extended periods may affect device reliability. Although the 82385 contains protective circuitry to resist damage from static electrical discharges, always take precautions against high static voltages or electric fields.

9.3 D.C. SPECIFICATIONS V_{CC} = 5V ±5%; V_{SS} = 0V

Table 9-1. D.C. Specifications

Symbol	Parameter	Min	Max	Unit	Test Condition
V_{IL}	Input Low Voltage	−0.3	0.8	V	(Note 1)
V_{IH}	Input High Voltage	2.0	V_{CC} + 0.3	V	
V_{CL}	CLK2, BCLK2 Input Low	−0.3	0.8	V	(Note 1)
V_{CH}	CLK2, BCLK2 Input High	3.7	V_{CC} + 0.3	V	
V_{OL}	Output Low Voltage		0.45	V	I_{OL} = 4 mA
V_{OH}	Output High Voltage	2.4		V	I_{OH} = −1 mA
I_{CC}	Supply Current		300	mA	(Note 2) (Note 4)
I_{LI}	Input Leakage Current		±15	μA	$0V < V_{IN} \leq V_{CC}$
I_{LO}	Output Leakage Current		±15	μA	$0.45 < V_{OUT} < V_{CC}$
C_{IN}	Input Capacitance		10	pF	(Note 3)
C_{OUT}	Output Capacitance		10	pF	(Note 3)
C_{CLK}	CLK2 Input Capacitance		15	pF	(Note 3)

NOTES:
1. Minimum value is not 100% tested.
2. I_{CC} is specified with inputs driven to CMOS levels. I_{CC} may be higher if driven to TTL levels.
3. Not 100% tested. Test conditions f_C = 1 MHz, Inputs = 0V, T_{CASE} = Room.
4. 300 mA is the maximum I_{CC} at 33 MHz.
   275 mA is the maximum I_{CC} at 25 MHz.
   250 mA is the maximum I_{CC} at 20 MHz.

9.4 A.C. SPECIFICATIONS

The A.C. specifications given in the following tables consist of output delays and input setup requirements. The A.C. diagram's purpose is to illustrate the clock edges from which the timing parameters are measured. The reader should not infer any other timing relationships from them. For specific information on timing relationships between signals, refer to the appropriate functional section.

A.C. spec measurement is defined in Figure 9-1. Inputs must be driven to the levels shown when A.C. specifications are measured. 82385 output delays are specified with minimum and maximum limits, which are measured as shown. 82385 input setup and hold times are specified as minimums and define the smallest acceptable sampling window. Within the sampling window, a synchronous input signal must be stable for correct 82385 operation.

9.4.1 Frequency Dependent Signals

The 82385 has signals whose output valid delays are dependent on the clock frequency. These signals are marked in the A.C. Specification Tables with a Note 1.

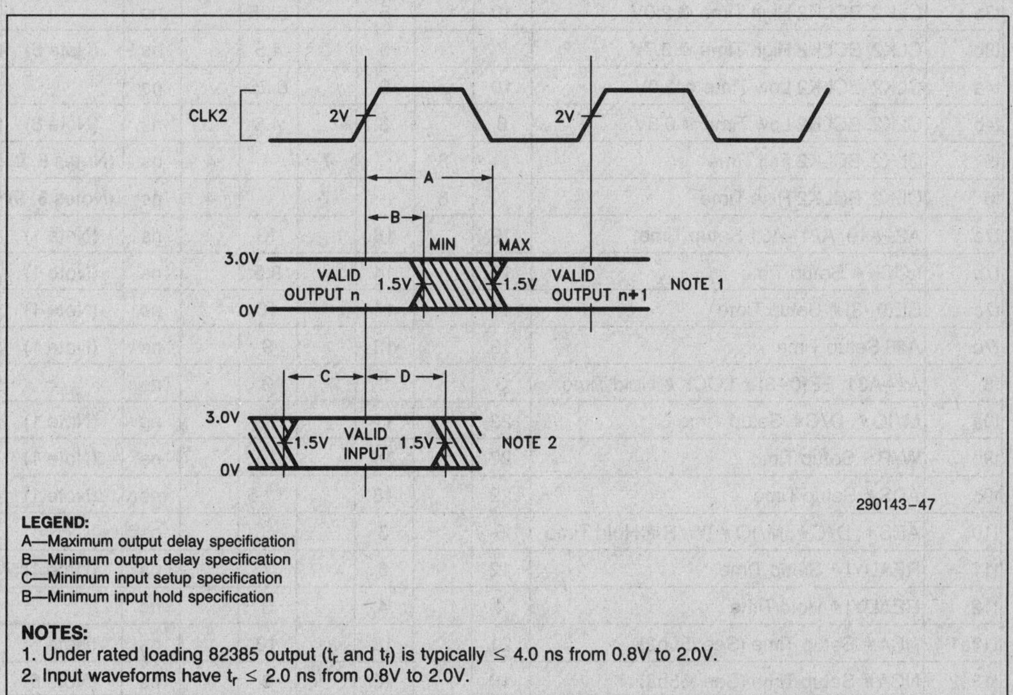

Figure 9-1. Drive Levels and Measurement Points for A.C. Specification

4

A.C. SPECIFICATION TABLES

Many of the A.C. Timing parameters are frequency dependent. The frequency dependent A.C. Timing parameters are guaranteed only at the maximum specified operating frequency.

Table 9-2. 82385 A.C. Timing Specifications

$V_{CC} = 5.0 \pm 5\%$

Symbol	Parameter	20 MHz		25 MHz		33 MHz		Units	Notes
		Min	Max	Min	Max	Min	Max		
T_{CASE}	Case Temperature	0	85	0	75	0	75	°C	
t1	Operating Frequency	15.40	20.00	15.40	25.00	15.40	33.33	MHz	
t2	CLK2, BCLK2 Clock Period	25.00	32.50	20.00	32.50	15.00	32.50	ns	
t3a	CLK2, BCLK2 High Time @ 2.0V	10		8		6.25		ns	
t3b	CLK2, BCLK2 High Time @ 3.7V	7		5		4.5		ns	(Note 8)
t4a	CLK2, BCLK2 Low Time @ 2.0V	10		8		6.25		ns	
t4b	CLK2, BCLK2 Low Time @ 0.8V	8		6		4.5		ns	(Note 8)
t5	CLK2, BCLK2 Fall Time		8		7		4	ns	(Notes 8, 9)
t6	CLK2, BCLK2 Rise Time		8		7		4	ns	(Notes 8, 9)
t7a	A2–A19, A21–A31 Setup Time	19		18		13		ns	(Note 1)
t7b	LOCK# Setup Time	16		14		9.5		ns	(Note 1)
t7c	BE(0–3)# Setup Time	19		14		10		ns	(Note 1)
t7d	A20 Setup Time	13		13		9		ns	(Note 1)
t8	A2–A31, BE(0–3)# LOCK# Hold Time	3		3		3		ns	
t9a	M/IO#, D/C# Setup Time	22		17		13		ns	(Note 1)
t9b	W/R# Setup Time	22		18		13		ns	(Note 1)
t9c	ADS# Setup Time	22		18		13.5		ns	(Note 1)
t10	ADS#, D/C#, M/IO#, W/R# Hold Time	5		3		3		ns	
t11	READYI# Setup Time	12		8		7		ns	(Note 1)
t12	READYI# Hold Time	4		4		3		ns	
t13a1	NCA# Setup Time (See t55b2)	21		18		13		ns	(Note 6)
t13a2	NCA# Setup Time (See t55b3)	16		13		9		ns	(Note 6)
t13b	LBA# Setup Time	10		8		5.75		ns	
t13c	X16# Setup Time	10		7		5.5		ns	
t14a	NCA# Hold Time	4		3		3		ns	
t14b	LBA#, X16# Hold Time	4		3		3		ns	
t15	RESET, BRESET Setup Time	12		10		8		ns	
t16	RESET, BRESET Hold Time	4		3		2		ns	
t17	NA# Valid Delay	15	34	4	27	4	19.2	ns	(25 pF Load) (Note 1)
t18	READYO# Valid Delay	4	28	4	22	3	15	ns	(25 pF Load) (Note 1)
t19	BRDYEN# Valid Delay	4	28	4	21	3	13	ns	

Table 9-2. 82385 A.C. Timing Specifications (Continued)
$V_{CC} = 5.0 \pm 5\%$

Symbol	Parameter	20 MHz		25 MHz		33 MHz		Units	Notes
		Min	Max	Min	Max	Min	Max		
t21a1	CALEN Rising, PHI1	3	24	4	21	3	15	ns	
t21a2	CALEN Falling, PHI1	3	24	4	21	3	15	ns	
t21a3	CALEN Falling in T1P, PHI2	3	24	4	21	3	15	ns	
t21b	CALEN Rising Following CWTH Cycle	3	34	4	27	3	20	ns	(Note 1)
t21c	CALEN Pulse Width	10		10		10		ns	
t21d	CALEN Rising to CS# Falling	13		13		13		ns	
t22a1	CWEx# Falling, PHI1 (CWTH)	4	25	4	23	3	18	ns	(Note 1)
t22a2	CWEx# Falling, PHI2 (CRDM)	4	25	4	23	3	18	ns	(Note 1)
t22b	CWEx# Pulse Width	30		25		20		ns	(Notes 1, 2)
t22c1	CWEx# Rising, PHI1 (CWTH)	4	25	4	21	3	16	ns	(Note 1)
t22c2	CWEx# Rising, PHI2 (CRDM)	12	25	8	21	6	16	ns	(Note 1)
t23a	CS(0–3)# Rising	12	37	9	29	3	25	ns	(Note 1)
t23b	COEx# Falling to CS(0–3)# Falling	0		0		0		ns	(Note 1)
t24	CT/R# Valid Delay	12	38	9	30	3	22	ns	(Note 1)
t25a	COEx# Falling (Direct)	1	22	4	19.5	3	15	ns	(25 pF Load)
t25b	COEx# Falling (2-Way)	1	24.5	4	19.5	3	15	ns	(25 pF Load) (Note 1)
t25c1	COEx# Rising Delay @ T_{CASE} = Min	5	17	4	17.5	3	12	ns	(25 pF Load)
t25c2	COEx# Rising Delay @ T_{CASE} = Max	5	19	4	19.5	3	12	ns	(25 pF Load)
t25d	CWEx# Falling to COEx# Falling or CWEx# Rising to COEX# Rising when DEFOE# = V_{CC}	0	5	0	5	0	5	ns	(25 pF Load)
t26	CS(0–3)# Falling to CWEx# Rising	30		25		20		ns	(Notes 1, 2)
t27	CWEx# Falling to CS(0–3)# Falling	0		0		0		ns	
t28a	CWEx# Rising to CALEN Rising	0		0		2		ns	
t28b	CWEx# Rising to CS(0–3)# Falling	0		0		2		ns	
t31	SA(2–31) Setup Time	19		10		8		ns	
t32	SA(2–31) Hold Time	3		3		3		ns	
t33	BADS# Valid Delay	6	28	4	21	3	16	ns	(Note 1)
t34	BADS# Float Delay	6	30	4	30	4	25	ns	(Note 3)
t35	BNA# Setup Time	9		7		7		ns	
t36	BNA# Hold Time	15		4		2		ns	
t37	BREADY# Setup Time	26		18		13		ns	(Note 1)
t38	BREADY# Hold Time	4		3		2		ns	
t40a	BACP Rising Delay	4	20	4	16	2	12	ns	
t40b	BACP Falling Delay	4	22	4	20	2	18	ns	

4

Table 9-2. 82385 A.C. Timing Specifications (Continued)
$V_{CC} = 5.0 \pm 5\%$

Symbol	Parameter	20 MHz		25 MHz		33 MHz		Units	Notes
		Min	Max	Min	Max	Min	Max		
t41	BAOE# Valid Delay	4	18	4	15	2	12	ns	
t43a	BT/R# Valid Delay	2	19	4	16	2	14	ns	
t43b1	DOE# Falling Delay	2	23	4	20	2	16	ns	
t43b2	DOE# Rising Delay @ T_{CASE} = Min	4	17	4	17	2	12	ns	
t43b3	DOE# Rising Delay @ T_{CASE} = Max	4	19	4	19	2	14	ns	
t43c	LDSTB Valid Delay	2	26	2	21	2	16	ns	
t44a	SEN Setup Time	11		9		7		ns	
t44b	SSTB# Setup Time	11		5		5		ns	
t45	SEN, SSTB# Hold Time	5		5		2		ns	
M/S# = V_{CC} (Master Mode)									
t_{46}	BHOLD Setup Time	17		15		11		ns	
t47	BHOLD Hold Time	5		3		2		ns	
t48	BHLDA Valid Delay	5	28	4	23	3	16	ns	
M/S# = V_{SS} (Slave Mode)									
t49	BHLDA Setup Time	17		15		11		ns	
t50	BHLDA Hold Delay	5		3		2		ns	
t51	BHOLD Valid Delay	5	28	4	23	3	18	ns	
t55a	BLOCK# Valid Delay	4	30	4	26	3	20	ns	(Notes 1,5)
t55b1	BBE(0–3)# Valid Delay	4	30	4	26	3	20	ns	(Notes 1, 7)
t55b2	BBE(0–3#) Valid Delay	4	30	4	26	3	20	ns	(Notes 1, 7)
t55b3	BBE(0–3)# Valid Delay	4	36	4	32	3	23	ns	(Notes 1, 7)
t55c	LOCK# Valid to BLOCK# Valid	0	30	0	26	0	20	ns	(Notes 1, 5)
t56	MISS# Valid Delay	4	35	4	30	3	22	ns	(Note 1)
t57	MISS#, BBE(0–3)#, BLOCK# Float Delay	4	32	4	30	4	25	ns	(Note 3)
t58	WBS Valid Delay	4	37	4	25	3	16	ns	(Note 1)
t59	FLUSH Setup Time	16		12		10		ns	
t60	FLUSH Hold Time	5		5		3		ns	
t61	FLUSH Setup to RESET Falling	26		21		16		ns	(Note 4)
t62	FLUSH Hold to RESET Falling	26		21		16		ns	(Note 4)

NOTES:
1. Frequency dependent specification.
2. Used for cache data memory (SRAM) specifications.
3. Float times not 100% tested.
4. This feature is tested only at 16 MHz.
5. BLOCK# delay is either from BPHI1 or from 386 LOCK#. Refer to Figure 5-3K and 5-3L in the 82385 data sheet.
6. NCA# setup time is now specified to the rising edge of PHI2 in the state after 386 DX addresses become valid (either the first T2 or the state after the first T2P).
7. BBE# Valid delay is a function of NCA# setup.
8. Not 100% tested.
9. t5 is measured from 0.8V to 3.7V.
   t6 is measured from 3.7V to 0.8V
   This parameter is not 100% tested and is guaranteed by Intel's test methodology.

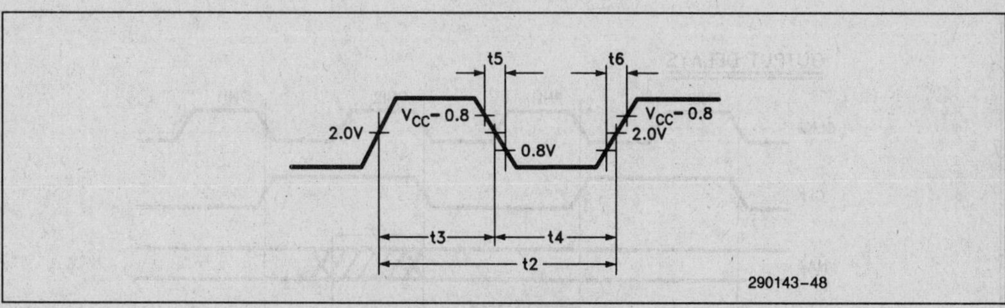

Figure 9-2. CLK2, BCLK2 Timing

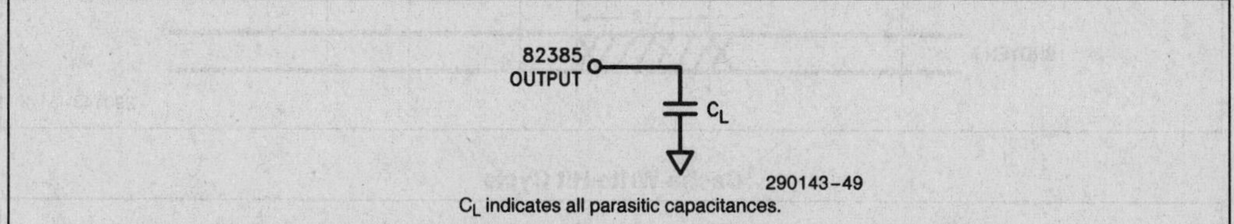

Figure 9-3. A.C. Test Load

386 DX Interface Parameters

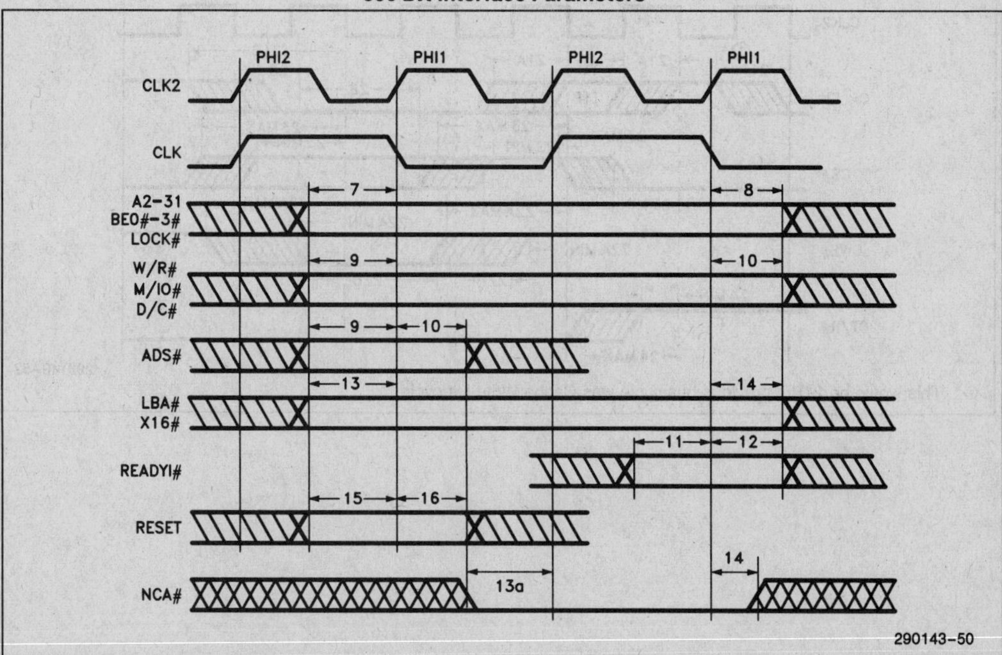

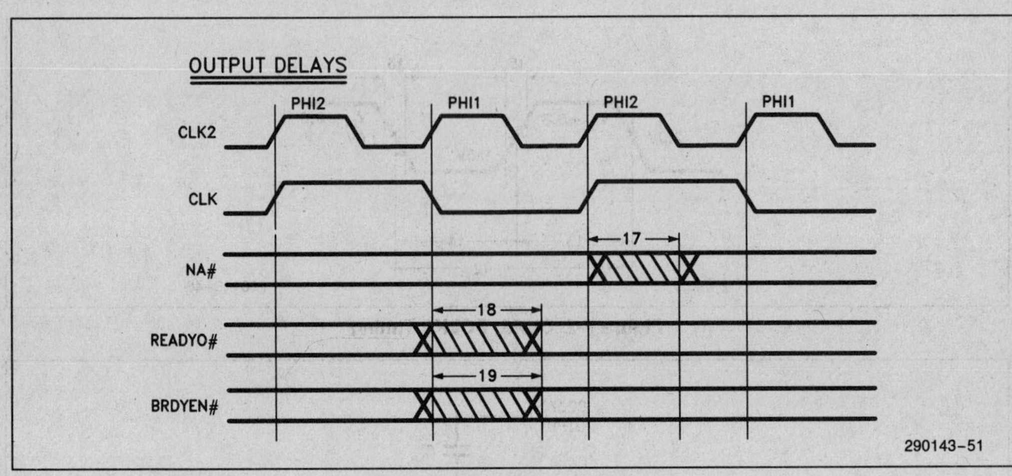

Cache Write Hit Cycle

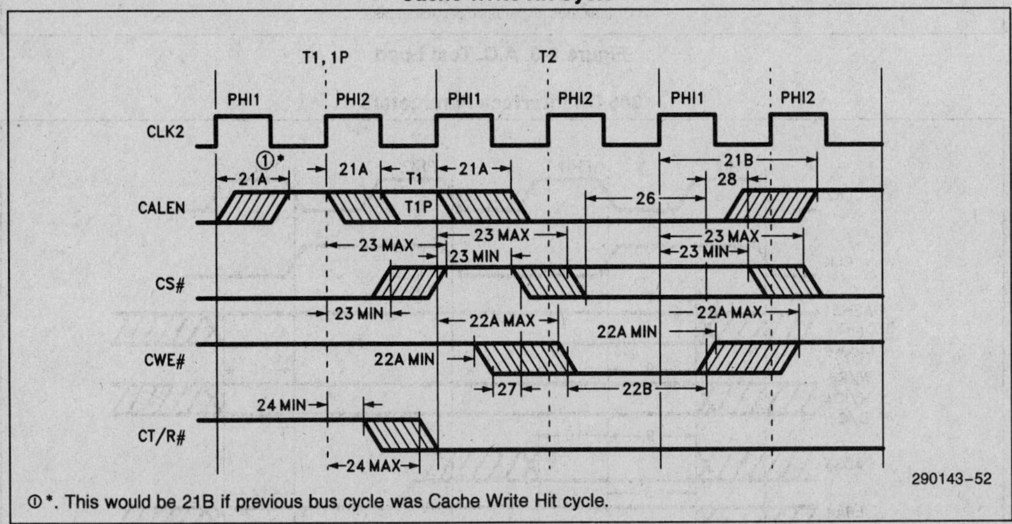

①*. This would be 21B if previous bus cycle was Cache Write Hit cycle.

Cache Read Miss (Cache Update Cycle)

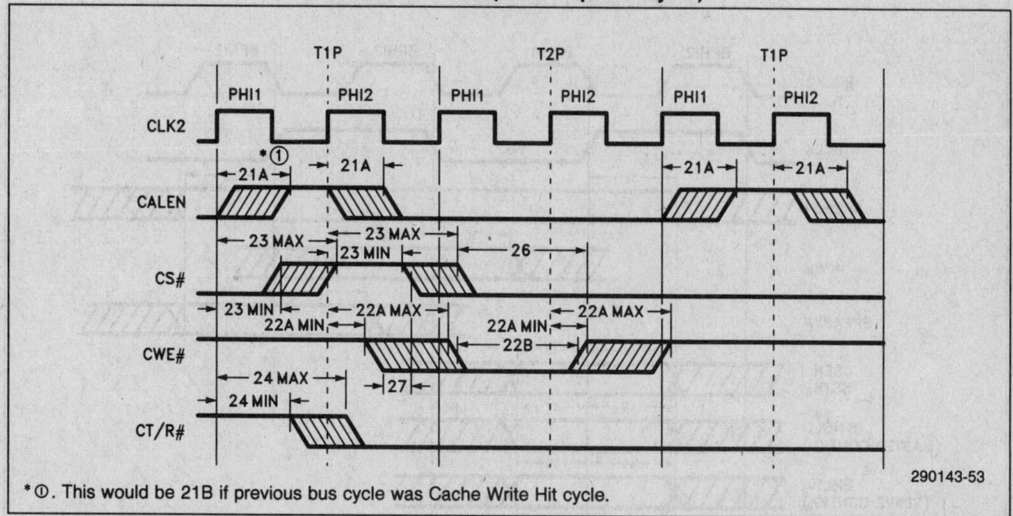

*①. This would be 21B if previous bus cycle was Cache Write Hit cycle.

Cache Read Cycle

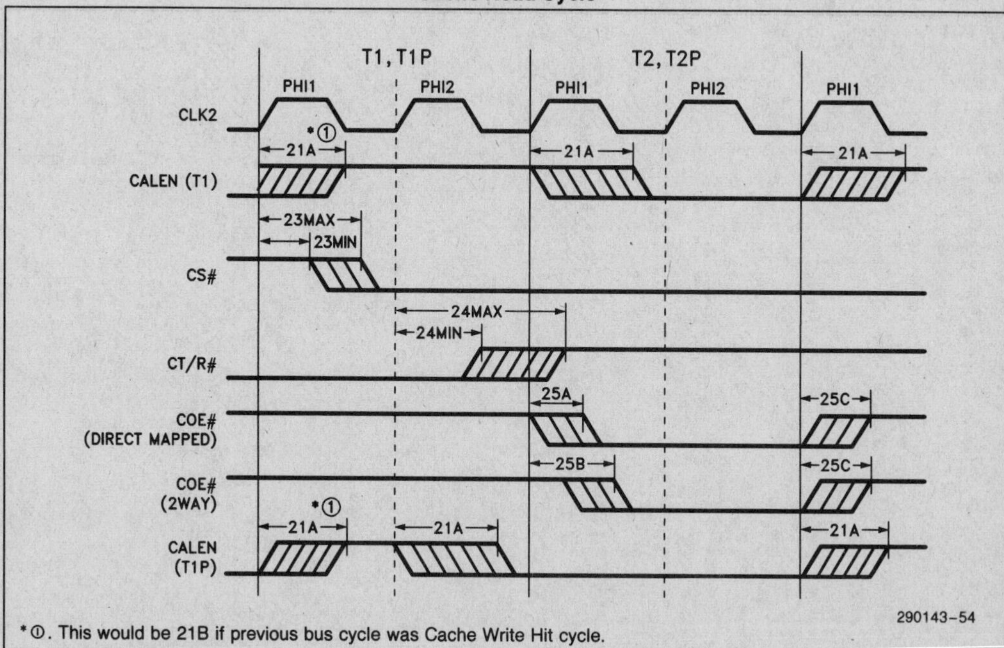

*①. This would be 21B if previous bus cycle was Cache Write Hit cycle.

System Bus Interface Parameters

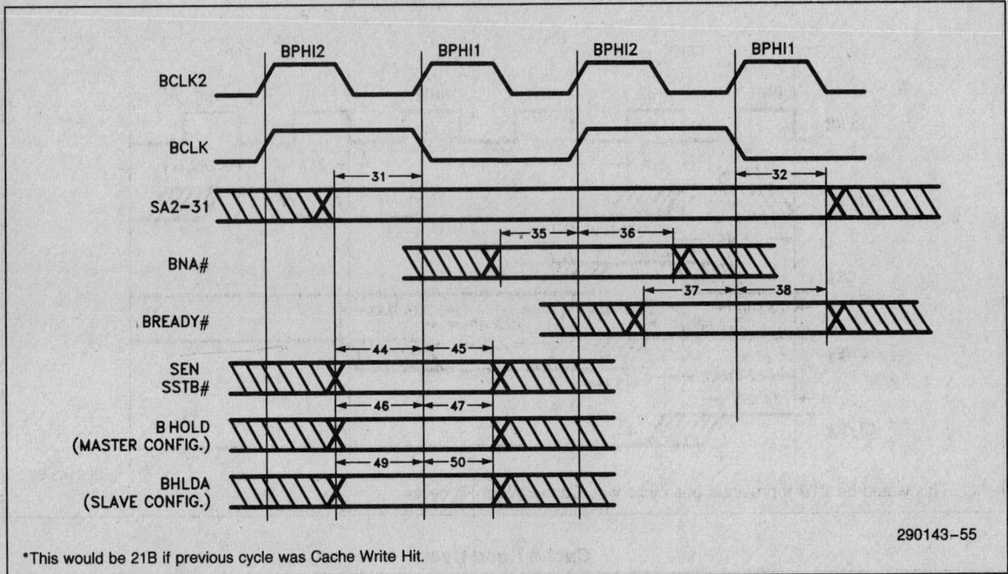

*This would be 21B if previous cycle was Cache Write Hit.

System Bus Interface Parameters (Continued)

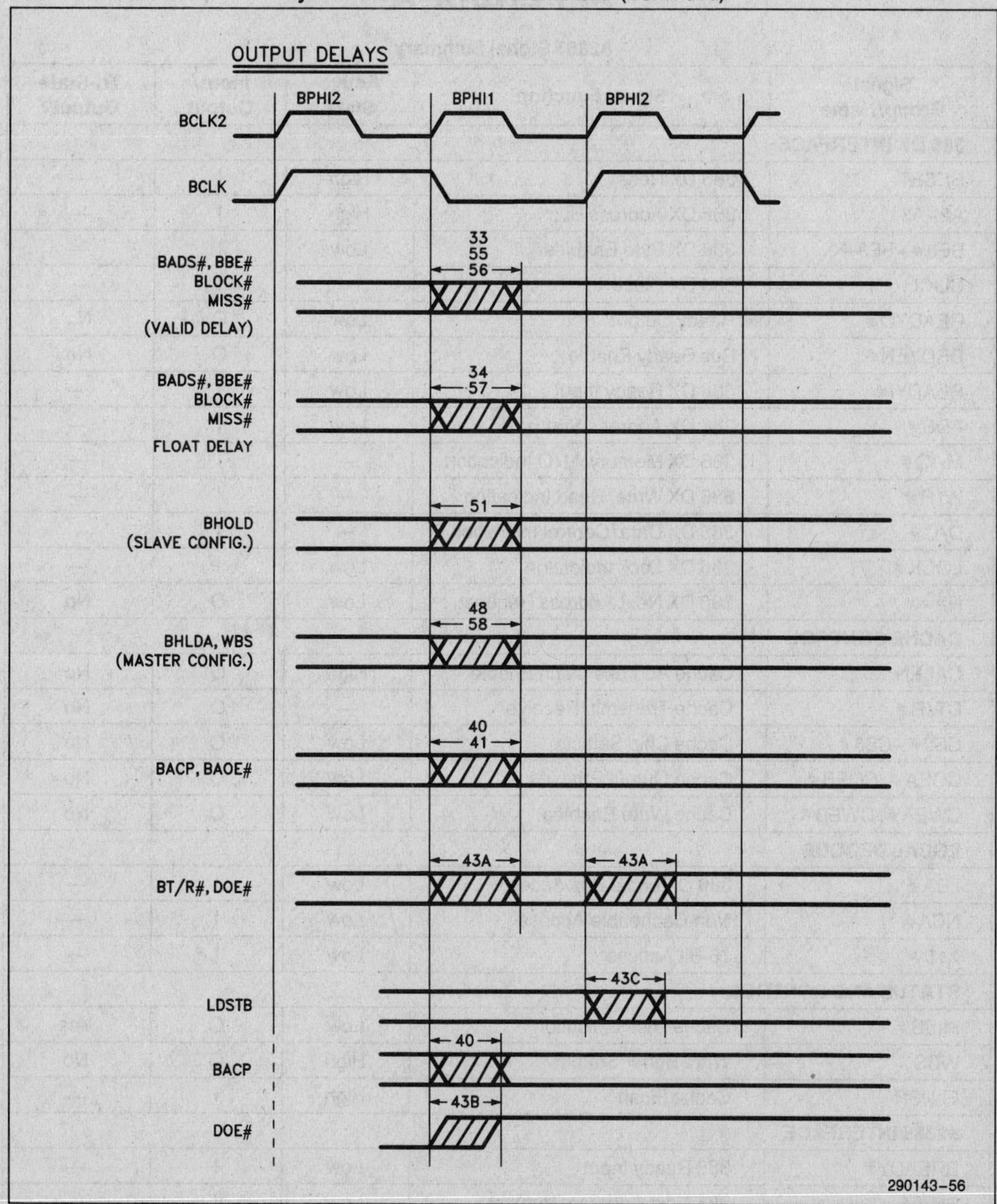

290143-56

APPENDIX A

82385 Signal Summary

Signal Group/Name	Signal Function	Active State	Input/ Output	Tri-State Output?
386 DX INTERFACE				
RESET	386 DX Reset	High	I	—
A2–A31	386 DX Address Bus	High	I	—
BE0#–BE3#	386 DX Byte Enables	Low	I	—
CLK2	386 DX Clock	—	I	—
READYO#	Ready Output	Low	O	No
BRDYEN#	Bus Ready Enable	Low	O	No
READYI#	386 DX Ready Input	Low	I	—
ADS#	386 DX Address Status	Low	I	—
M/IO#	386 DX Memory / I/O Indication	—	I	—
W/R#	386 DX Write/Read Indication	—	I	—
D/C#	386 DX Data/Control Indication	—	I	—
LOCK#	386 DX Lock Indication	Low	I	—
NA#	386 DX Next Address Request	Low	O	No
CACHE CONTROL				
CALEN	Cache Address Latch Enable	High	O	No
CT/R#	Cache Transmit/Receive	—	O	No
CS0#–CS3#	Cache Chip Selects	Low	O	No
COEA#, COEB#	Cache Output Enables	Low	O	No
CWEA#, CWEB#	Cache Write Enables	Low	O	No
LOCAL DECODE				
LBA#	386 DX Local Bus Access	Low	I	—
NCA#	Non-Cacheable Access	Low	I	—
X16#	16-Bit Access	Low	I	—
STATUS AND CONTROL				
MISS#	Cache Miss Indication	Low	O	Yes
WBS	Write Buffer Status	High	O	No
FLUSH	Cache Flush	High	I	—
82385 INTERFACE				
BREADY#	385 Ready Input	Low	I	—
BNA#	385 Next Address Request	Low	I	—
BLOCK#	385 Lock Indication	Low	O	Yes
BADS#	385 Address Status	Low	O	Yes
BBE0#–BBE3#	385 Byte Enables	Low	O	Yes

82385 Signal Summary (Continued)

Signal Group/Name	Signal Function	Active State	Input/ Output	Tri-State Output?
DATA/ADDR CONTROL				
LDSTB	Local Data Strobe	Pos. Edge	O	No
DOE#	Data Output Enable	Low	O	No
BT/R#	Bus Transmit/Receive	—	O	No
BACP	Bus Address Clock Pulse	Pos. Edge	O	No
BAOE#	Bus Address Output Enable	Low	O	No
CONFIGURATION				
2W/D#	2-Way/Direct Map Select	—	I	—
M/S#	Master/Slave Select	—	I	—
DEFOE#	Define Cache Output Enable	—	1	—
COHERENCY				
SA2–SA31	Snoop Address Bus	High	I	—
SSTB#	Snoop Strobe	Low	I	—
SEN	Snoop Enable	High	I	—
ARBITRATION				
BHOLD	Hold	High	I/O	No
BHLDA	Hold Acknowledge	High	I/O	No

10.0 REVISION HISTORY

DOCUMENT: ADVANCE INFORMATION DATA SHEET
PRIOR REV: 290143-003 September 1988
NEW REV: 290143-004 September 1989

Change #	Page #	Para. #	Change
1.	Throughout	Fig. 8-3	PQFP Package added
2.	Throughout	Tables 8-2, 8-3	PQFP Info
3.	Throughout	Table 8-4	PQFP Thermal Resistance
4.	Throughout		A.C. Specifications Unified (20 MHz, 25 MHz, 33 MHz)
5.	Throughout		DEFOE# Specifications added to device

intel®

APPLICATION NOTE

AP-442

June 1990

33 MHz 386™ System Design Considerations

SHAHZAD BAQAI

KIYOSHI NISHIDE

Order Number: 240725-001

33 MHz 386™ SYSTEM DESIGN CONSIDERATIONS

CONTENTS

CONTENTS

4

RELATED DOCUMENTATION

This Application Note should be used in conjunction with the 386™ DX microprocessor Data Sheet (Order Number 231630-007) and the 386™ DX Hardware Reference Manual (Order Number 231732-004). A list of related references is provided in the appendix for getting more information on high speed design issues.

INTRODUCTION

The 386™ DX Microprocessor is an advanced 32-bit microprocessor designed using Intel's CHMOS IV process for applications which require very high performance. It is optimized for multitasking operating systems. The 32-bit register and data paths support 32-bit address and data types allowing up to four gigabytes of physical memory and 64 terabytes of virtual memory to be addressed. The integrated memory management and protection architecture includes address translation registers, advanced multitasking hardware and a protection mechanism to support operating systems. In addition, the 386 DX microprocessor allows the simultaneous running of DOS with other operating systems.

Instruction pipelining, on chip address translation and high bus bandwidth ensure short average instruction execution times and high system throughput. To facilitate high performance system hardware designs, the 386 DX microprocessor bus interface offers address pipelining, dynamic data bus sizing and direct byte enable signals for each byte of the data bus.

This Application Note is intended to show how to complete a successful design of a 'Core' system using the 386 DX-33, the 33 MHz clock version. A Core system is a minimum system configuration, in this case comprising the CPU, the 82385 32-bit Cache controller, Dynamic and Static RAM and an I/O mechanism with which to communicate with the CPU.

The Application Note examines the design techniques necessary when executing a design at this frequency. Many of the methods used at lower frequencies, such as 16 MHz and 20 MHz, are no longer valid at this higher frequency. Phenomena, whose effects are negligible at the lower frequencies, must be taken into account in the design. The physical positioning of components relative to each other plays a significant part in the success of the design, since transmission line effects (reflection, radiation) are no longer negligible.

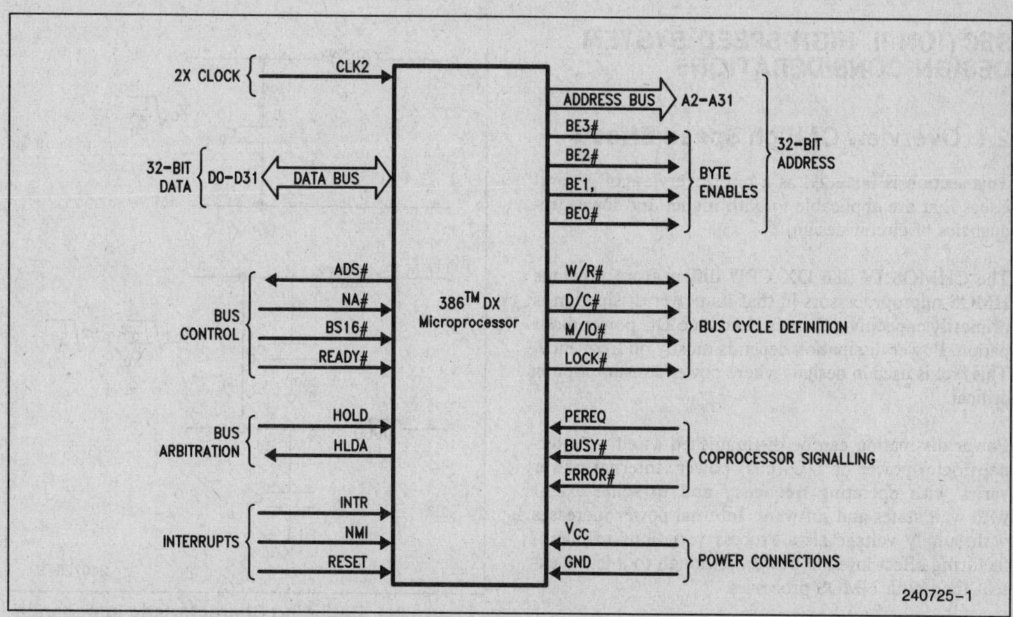

Figure 1-1. Functional Signal Groups

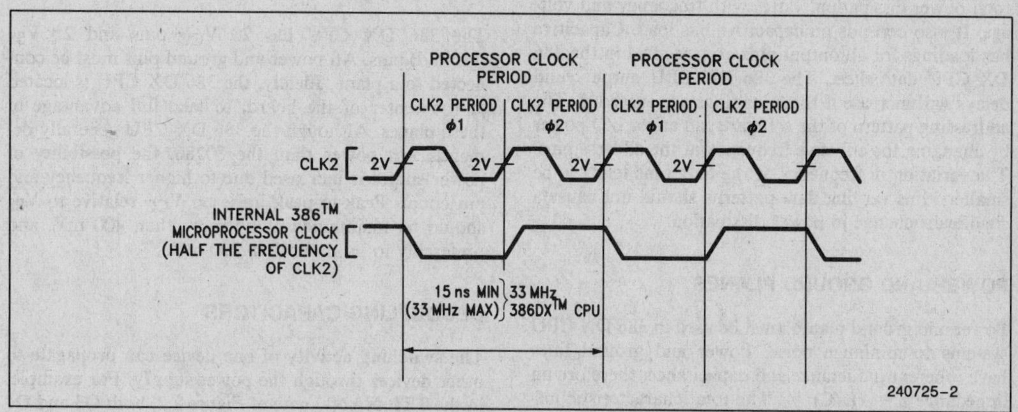

Figure 1-2. CLK2 Signal and Internal Processor Clock

4

SECTION II. HIGH SPEED SYSTEM DESIGN CONSIDERATIONS

2.1 Overview Of High Speed Effects

This section is included as a brief overview of general issues that are applicable to both higher and lower frequencies of circuit design.

The CHMOS IV 386 DX CPU differs from previous HMOS microprocessors in that its power dissipation is primarily capacitive; there is almost no DC power dissipation. Power dissipation depends mostly on frequency. This fact is used in designs where power consumption is critical.

Power dissipation can be distinguished as either internal (logic) power or I/O (bus) power. Internal power varies with operating frequency and to some extent with wait states and software. Internal power increases with supply voltage also. Process variations in manufacturing affect internal power, although to a lesser extent than with NMOS processes.

I/O power, which accounts for roughly one-fifth of the total power dissipation, varies with frequency and voltage. It also depends on capacitive bus load. Capacitive bus loadings for all output pins are specified in the 386 DX CPU data sheet. The 386 DX CPU output valid delays will increase if these loadings are exceeded. The addressing pattern of the software can affect I/O power by changing the effective frequency at the address pins. The variation in frequency at the data pins tends to be smaller; thus varying data patterns should not cause a significant change in power dissipation.

POWER AND GROUND PLANES

Power and ground planes must be used in 386 DX CPU systems to minimize noise. Power and ground lines have inherent inductance and capacitance, therefore an impedance $z = (L/C)^{*1/2}$. The total characteristic impedance for the power supply can be reduced by adding more lines. This effect is illustrated in 2.1 which shows that two lines in parallel have half the impedance of one. To reduce the impedance even further, the user should add more lines. In the limit, an infinite number of parallel lines, or a plane, results in the lowest impedance. Planes also provide the best distribution of power and ground.

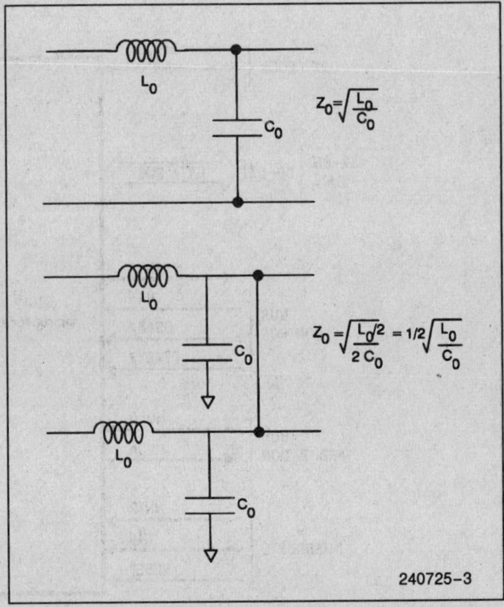

Figure 2-1. Reducing Characteristic Impedance

The 386 DX CPU has 20 V_{CC} pins and 21 V_{SS} (ground) pins. All power and ground pins must be connected to a plane. Ideally, the 386 DX CPU is located at the center of the board, to take full advantage of these planes. Although the 386 DX CPU generally demands less power than the 80286, the possibility of power surges is increased due to higher frequency and pin count. Peak-to-peak noise on V_{CC} relative to V_{SS} should be maintained at no more than 400 mV, and preferably to no more than 200 mV.

DECOUPLING CAPACITORS

The switching activity of one device can propagate to other devices through the power supply. For example, in the TTL NAND gate of Figure 2.2, both Q3 and Q4 transistors are on for a short time when the output is switching. This increased load causes a negative spike on V_{CC} and a positive spike on ground.

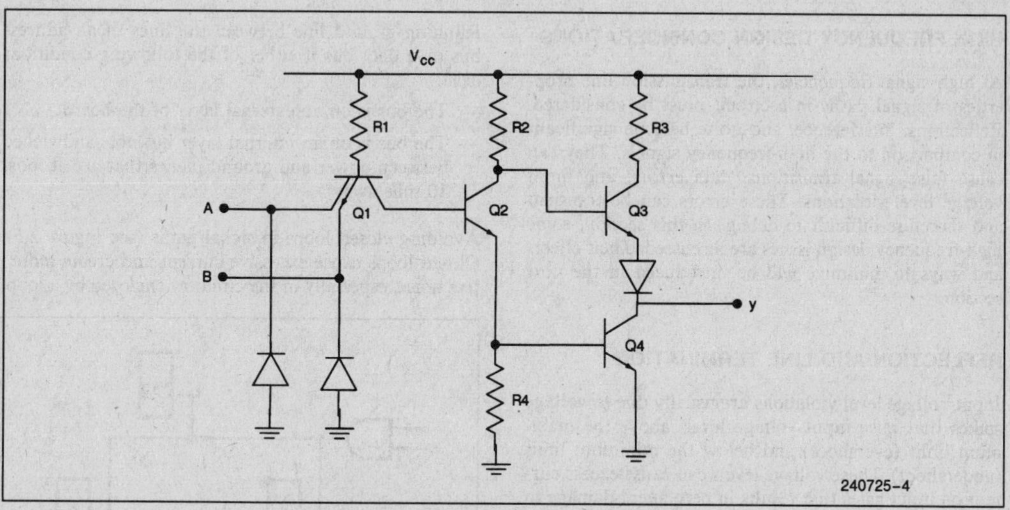

Figure 2-2. Circuit without Decoupling

In synchronous systems in which many gates switch simultaneously, the result is signifcant noise on the power and ground lines.

Decoupling capacitors placed across the device between Vcc and ground reduce Voltage spikes by supplying the extra current needed during switching. These capacitors should be placed close to their devices because the inductance or connection lines negates their effect.

When selecting decoupling capacitors, the user should provide 0.01 microfarads for each device and 0. 1 microfarads for every 20 gates. Radio-frequency capacitors must be used; they should be distributed evenly over the board to be most effective. In addition, the board should be decoupled from the external supply line with a 2.2 microfarad capacitor.

Chip capacitors (surface-mount) are preferable because they exhibit lower inductance and require less total board space. They should be connected as in Figure 2.3. Leaded capacitors can also be used if the leads are kept as short as possible. Six leaded capacitors are required to match the effectiveness of one chip capacitor, but because only a limited number can fit around the 386 DX, the configuration in Figure 2.4 results.

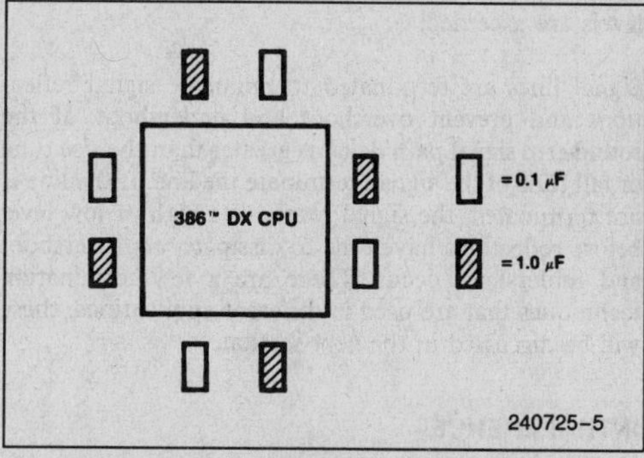

Figure 2-3. Decoupling Chip Capacitors

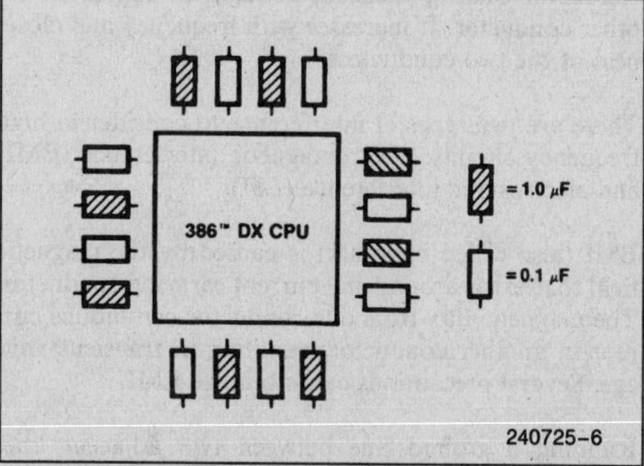

Figure 2-4. Decoupling Leaded Capacitors

HIGH FREQUENCY DESIGN CONSIDERATIONS

At high signal frequencies, the transmission line properties of signal paths in a circuit must be considered. Reflections, interference, and noise become significant in comparison to the high-frequency signals. They can cause false signal transitions, data errors, and input voltage level violations. These errors can be transient and therefore difficult to debug. In this section, some high-frequency design issues are discussed. Their effects and ways to minimize will be introduced in the next section.

REFLECTION AND LINE TERMINATION

Input voltage level violations are usually due to voltage spikes that raise input voltage levels above the maximum limit (overshoot) and below the minimum limit (undershoot). These voltage levels can cause excess current on input gates that results in permanent damage to the device. Even if no damage occurs, most devices are not guaranteed to function as specified if input voltage levels are exceeded.

Signal lines are terminated to minimize signal reflections and prevent overshoot and undershoot. If the round-trip signal path delay is greater than the rise time or fall time of the signal, terminate the line. If the line is not terminated, the signal reaches its high or low level before reflections have time to dissipate, and overshoot and undershoot occur. There are a few termination techniques that are used in different applications, these will be discussed in the next section.

INTERFERENCE

Interference is the result of electrical activity in one conductor causing transient voltages to appear in another conductor. It increases with frequency and closeness of the two conductors.

There are two types of interference to consider in high frequency circuits: electromagnetic interference (EMI) and electrostatic interference (ESI).

EMI (also called crosstalk) is caused by the magnetic field that exists around any current carrying conductor. The magnetic flux from one conductor can induce current in another conductor, resulting in transient voltage. Several precautions can minimize EMI.

Running a ground line between two adjacent lines wherever they traverse a long section of the circuit board. The ground line should be grounded at both ends.

Running ground line between the lines of an address bus or a data bus if either of the following conditions exist.

— The bus is on an external layer of the board.

— The bus is on an internal layer but not sandwiched between power and ground planes that are at most 10 mils away.

Avoiding closed loops in signal paths (see Figure 2.5). Closed loops cause excessive current and create inductive noise, especially in the circuitry enclosed by a loop.

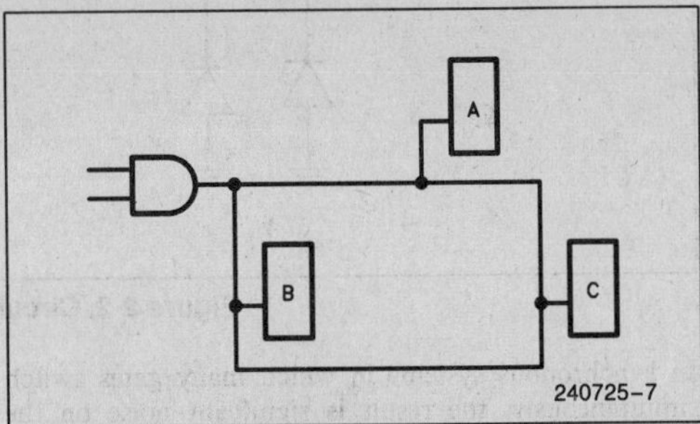

Figure 2-5. Avoid Closed-Loop Signal Paths

ESI is caused by the capacitive coupling of two adjacent conductors. The conductors act as the plates of a capacitor; a charge built up on one induces the opposite charge on the other.

The following steps reduce ESI:

Separating signal lines so that capacitive coupling becomes negligible.

Running a ground line between two lines to cancel the electrostatic fields.

LATCHUP

Latchup is a condition in a CMOS circuit in which V_{CC} becomes shorted to Vss. Intel's CHMOS IV process is immune to latchup under normal operating conditions. Latchup can be triggered when the voltage limits on I/O pins are exceeded, causing internal PN junctions to become forward biased. The following guidelines help prevent latchup:

Observing the maximum rating for input voltage on I/O pins.

Never applying power to an 386 DX CPU pin or a device connected to an 386 DX CPU pin before applying power to the 386 DX CPU itself.

Preventing overshoot and undershoot on I/O pins by adding line termination and by designing to reduce noise and reflection on signal lines.

THERMAL CHARACTERISTICS

The thermal specification for the 386 DX CPU defines the maximum case temperature. This section describes how to ensure that an 386 DX CPU system meets this specification.

Thermal specifications for the 386 DX CPU are designed to guarantee a tolerable temperature at the surface of the 386 DX CPU chip. This temperature (called the junction temperature) can be determined from external measurements using the known thermal charactcristics of the package. Two equations for calculating junction temperature are as follows:

$T_j = T_a + (@j_a * PD)$ and

$T_j = T_c + (@j_c * PD)$

where:

T_j = Junction Temperature

$@j_a$ = Junction to ambient temperature coeff.

T_c = Case Temperature

T_a = Ambient Temperature

$@j_c$ = Junction to Case

PD = Power Dissapation temperature coeff.

Case temperature calculations offer several advantages over ambient temperature calculations.

Case temperature is easier to measure accurately than ambient temperature because the measurement is localized to a single point (top center of the package).

The worst-case junction temperature (T_j) is lower when calculated with case temperature for the following reasons:

— The junction-to-case thermal coefficient ($@j_c$) is lower than the junction-to-ambient thermal coefficient ($@j_a$); therefore, calculated junction temperature varies less with power dissipation (PD).

— $@j_c$ is not affected by airflow in the system; $@j_a$ varies with air flow.

With the case-temperature specification, the designer can either set the ambient temperature or use fans to control case temperature. Finned heat sinks or conductive cooling may also be used in environments where the use of fans is precluded. To approximate the case temperature for various environments, the two equations above should be combined by setting the junction temperature equal for both, resulting in this equation:

$$T_a = T_c - ((@j_a - @j_c) * PD)$$

The current data sheet should be consulted to determine the values of @ja (for the system's air flow) and ambient temperature that will yield the desired case temperature. Whatever the conditions are, the case temperature is easy to verify.

2.2 Transmission Line Effects

As a general rule, any interconnection is considered a transmission line when the time required for the signal to travel the length of the interconnection is greater than one-eighth of the signal rise time. (True K. M., "Reflection: Computations and Waveforms, The Interface Handbook", Fairchild Corp, Mountain View, CA, 1975, Ch. 3). As frequencies increase, designers must account for the negative effects associated with transmission lines. The section that follows will attempt to describe these effects and provide some suggestions for minimizing their negative effect on the system.

Before describing each effect, it is important to know how to characterize a trace on different types of transmision lines. This includes knowing the characteristic impedance of a trace, Z_o, and the propagation delay for a given trace, t_{pd}. These parameters will be used in determining what effects must be accounted for and to select component values used in minimizing the effects.

TRANSMISSION LINES TYPES

Although many types of transmission lines (conductors) exist, those most commonly used on the printed circuit boards are microstrip lines, strip lines, printed circuit traces, side-by-side conductors and flat conductors.

MICRO STRIP LINES

The micro strip trace consists of a signal plane that is seperated from a ground plane by a dielectric as shown in Figure 2.6. G-10 fiber-glass epoxy, which is most common, has an $e_r = 5$ where e_r is the dielctric constant of the insulation. Let:

w = the width of the signal line (inches)

t = the thickness of copper

h = the height of dielectric for controlled impedance (inches)

The characteristic impedance Z_O, is a function of dielectric constant and the geometry of the board. This is given by:

$$Z_O = (87/(e_r + 1.41))^{1/2} \ln (5.98/0.8\,w + t)\ \Omega$$

where e_r is the relative dielectric constant of the board material.

The propagation delay (t_{pd}) associated with the trace is a function of the dielectric only.

$$t_{pd} = 1.017\,(0.475e_r + 0.67)^{1/2}\ \text{ns/ft}$$

STRIP LINES

A strip line is a strip conductor centered in a dielectric medium between two voltage planes. The characteristic impedance is given by:

$$Z_O = 60/(e_r)^{1/2} \ln (5.98b/(0.8W + t))\ \Omega$$

where b = distance between the planes for the controlled impedance as shown in Figure 2.10

The propagation delay is given by:

$$t_{pd} = 1.017\,(e_r)^{1/2}\ \text{ns/ft}$$

Typical values of the characteristic impedance and propagation delay of these types of lines are:

$$Z_O = 50\Omega$$

$$t_{pd} = 2\ \text{ns/ft (or 6 in/ns)}$$

2.3 Reflection

The first effect is reflection. As the name indicates it is the reflection of a signal as it propagates down the trace. The reflection results from a mismatch in impedance. The impedance of a transmission line is a function of the geometry of the line, its distance from the ground plane, and the loads long the line. Any discontinuity in the impedance will cause reflections.

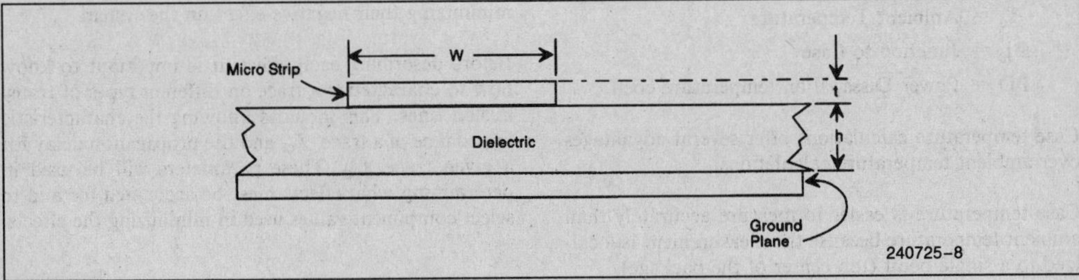

Figure 2-6. Micro Strip Lines

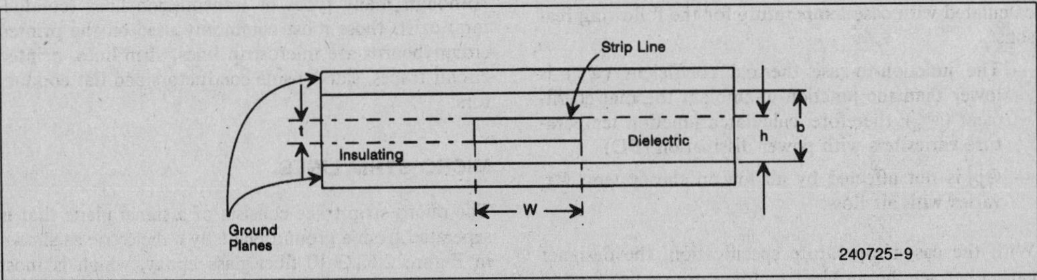

Figure 2-7. Strip Lines

Impedance mismatch occurs between the transmission line characteristic impedance and the input or output impedance of the devices that are connected to the line. The result is that the signals are reflected back and forth on the line. These reflections can attentuate or reinforce the signal depending upon the phase relationships. The results of these reflections include overshoot, undershoot, ringing and other undesirable effects.

At lower edge rates, the effects of these reflections are not severe. However at higher rates, the rise time of the signal is short with respect to the propagation delay. Thus it can cause problems as shown in Figure 2-8.

Overshoot occurs when the voltage level exceeds the maximum (upper) limit of the output voltage, while undershoot occurs when the level passes below the minimum (lower) limit. These conditions can cause excess current on the input gates which results in permanent damage to the device.

The amount of reflection voltage can be easily calculated. Figure 2-9 shows a system exhibiting reflections.

The magnitude of a reflection is usually represented in terms of a reflection coefficient. This is illustrated in the following equations:

$$T = v_r/v_i = \text{Reflected voltage/Incident voltage}$$

$$T_{load} = (Z_{load} - Z_O)/(Z_{load} + Z_O)$$

$$T_{source} = (Z_{source} - Z_O)/(Z_{source} + Z_O)$$

Reflections voltage V_r is given by V_i, the voltage incident at the point of the reflections, and the reflection coefficient.

The model transmission line can now be completed. In Figure 2-9, the voltage seen at point A is given by the following equation:

$$V_a = V_s * Z_O/(Z_O + Z_s)$$

This voltage V_a enters the transmission line at "A" and appears at "B" delayed by t_{pd}.

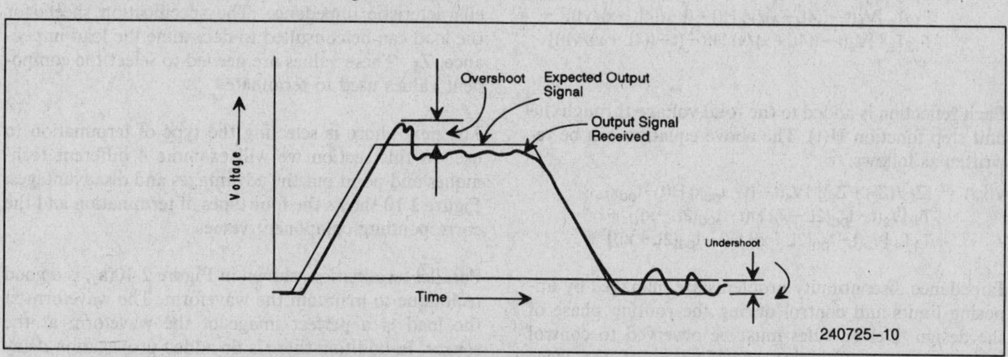

Figure 2-8. Overshoot and Undershoot Effects

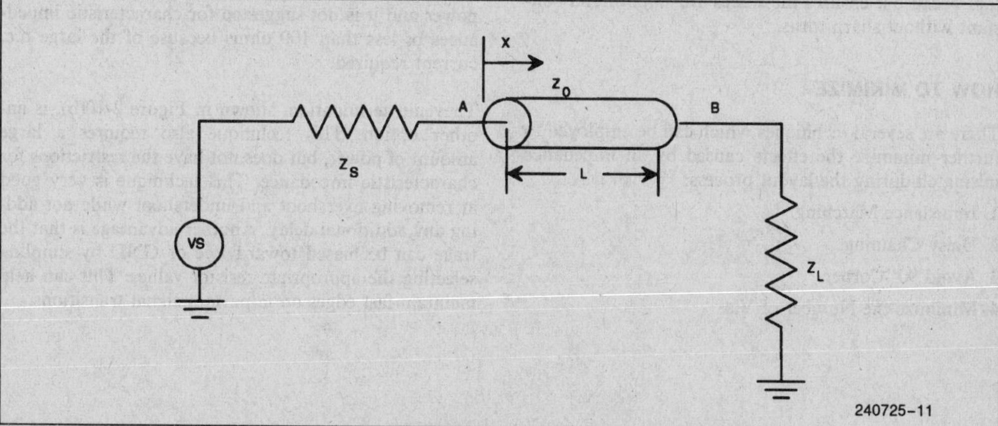

Figure 2-9. Loaded Transmission Line

$$V_b(t - x/t)\ H(t - x/v)$$

where x = distance along the transmission line from point "A" and H(t) is the unit step function. The waveform encounters the loads ZL, and this may cause reflection. The reflected wave enters the transmission line at "B" and appears at point "A" after time delay (t_{pd}):

$$V_{r1} = T_{load} * V_b$$

This phenomenon continues infinitely, but it is negligible after 3 or 4 reflections. Hence:

$$V_{r2} = T_{source} * V_{r1}$$

Each reflected waveform is treated as a seperate source that is independent of the reflection coefficient at that point and the incident waveform. Thus the waveform from any point and on the transmission line and at any given time is as follows:

$$\begin{aligned} V(x,t) = {} & (Z_O/(Z_O+Z_s))\ \{V_s(t-(x/v))\ H(t-(x/v)) + \\ & T_1\ [V_s(t-((2L-x)/v)\ H(t-(t-((2L-x)/v)))] + \\ & T_1T_s\ [V_s(t-((2L+x)/v)\ H(t-(t-((2L+x)/v)))] + \\ & T_{12}T_s\ [V_s(t-((4L-x)/v)\ H(t-(t-((4L-x)/v)))] + \\ & T_{12}T_s^2\ [V_s(t-((4L+x)/v)\ H(t-(t-((4L+x)/v)))] \\ & + \ldots \} \end{aligned}$$

Each reflection is added to the total voltage through the unit step function H(t). The above equation can be rewritten as follows:

$$\begin{aligned} V(x,t) = {} & (Z_O/(Z_O+Z_s))\ \{V_s(t-(t-t_{pd}x)\ H(t-t_{pd}x) + \\ & T_1\ [V_s(t-t_{pd}(2L-x))\ H(t-t_{pd}(2L-x))] + \\ & T_1T_s\ [V_s(t-t_{pd}(2L+x))\ H(t-t_{pd}(2L+x))] + \ldots \} \end{aligned}$$

Impedance discontinuity problems are managed by imposing limits and control during the routing phase of the design. Design rules must be observed to control trace geometry, including specification of the trace width and spacing for each layer. This is very important because it ensures the traces are smooth and constant without sharp turns.

HOW TO MINIMIZE

There are several techniques which can be employed to further minimize the effects caused by an impedance mismatch during the layout process:

1. Impedance Matching
2. Daisy Chaining
3. Avoid 90° Corners
4. Minimize the Number of Vias

IMPEDANCE MATCHING

Impedance matching is the process of matching the impedance of the the source or load to the impedance of the trace. This matching is accomplished using a technique called termination. Termination makes the effective source or load impedance, seen by the trace, to be approximately equal to the characteristic impedance of the trace. Before terminating a line one must determine if termination is required. This is done by a simple calculation. If the propagation delay down a trace from source to destination is greater than or equal to one-third the signals rise time, termination is needed. (i. e. $T_{pd} \geq \frac{1}{3} t_r$). The rise time is the 0%-100% rise time specified for the source. If this value is specified for 10%-90% or 20%-80%, it must be scaled by multiplying the specified value by 1.25 or 1.67, respectively. The propagation delay is caculated by multiplying the trace propagation delay, t_{pd}, descibed earlier by the trace length.

Once it is determined that termination is needed, use the equation described earlier to calculate the trace's characteristic impedance. The specification sheets for the load can be consulted to determine the load impedance, Z_L. These values are needed to select the component values used to terminate.

The next chore is selecting the type of termination to use. In this section we will examine 4 different techniques and point out the advantages and disadvantages. Figure 2.10 shows the four types of termination and the corresponding component values.

Parallel termination, shown in Figure 2-10(a), is a good technique to maintain the waveform. The waveform at the load is a perfect image of the waveform at the source. In addition there is no added propagation delay associated with this technique. The disadvantage of this technique is that it requires a fair amount of additional power and it is not suggested for characteristic impedances of less than 100 ohms because of the large d.c. current required.

Thevenin termination, shown in Figure 2-10(b), is another option. This technique also requires a large amount of power, but does not have the restrictions for characteristic impedance. This technique is very good at removing overshoot and undershoot while not adding any additional delay. Another advantage is that the trace can be biased toward Vcc or GND by simpling selecting the appropriate resistor values. This can help maintain fast edges on important signal transitions.

Name	Circuitry	Advantages	Disadvantages
Parallel	R $R = Z_O$	Waveform at receiver is almost perfect image of input Bipolar/Advanced CMOS No added T_{PD}	High power dissipation $Z_O \geq 100\Omega$, else D.C. current limit
Thevenin	V_{CC} R R $R = 2 Z_O$	Good overshoot and undershoot suppression Bipolar or Bipolar/CMOS systems No added T_{PD}	High power dissipation

Figure 2-10(a). Termination Techniques

Name	Circuitry	Advantages	Disadvantages
Series	R $R = Z_O - Z_{OUT}$	Low power consumption CMOS—CMOS Systems Easy to adjust signal amplitude to match switching threshold	Added T_{PD}
A.C.	R C $R = Z_O$, C = 200 pF–500 pF	Low—medium power dissipation (capacitor blocks D.C. coupling of signal) No added delays High-speed CMOS families	Two added components

Figure 2-10(b). Termination Techniques

Series termination, shown in Figure 2-10(b), is a very easy technique of matching impedance. It only requires on resistor and very little additional power is required. In addition the resistor value can be selected to provide constructive or destructive reflections and thus alter the signal amplitude to match the switching threshold. The major disadvantage of this technique is the added delay it introduces.

The fourth technique is A.C. termination, shown in Figure 2-10(b). It requires a small amount of additional power, this is decreased over parallel termination by the introduction of the capacitor, and adds no extra delay to the path. The major disadvantage is that it requires two extra components.

After examing the systems needs and selecting a termination technique, the impedance values determined earlier, Z_O and Z_L, can be used to determine the component values to implement the termination. These values should be seen as a starting point and may be altered to remove a specific problem experienced on a signal or to bias signals in an appropriate fashion.

DAISY CHAINING

Another technique of minimizing reflections is to daisy-chain signals, shown in Figure 2-11. This means to run a single trace from a source and to distribute the loads along this trace. The alternative is to run multiple traces from the source to each load. Each trace will have reflections of its own and these will be transmitted down the other traces once they have returned to the source. To manage such a system separate termination would be required for each branch. To eliminate these multiple terminators from T-connections, high frequency designs are routed as daisy chains.

Because each gate provides its own impedance load along the chain, it is necessary to distribute these loads evenly along the length of the chain. Hence, the impedance along the chain will change in a series of steps and is easier to match. The overall speed of this line is faster and predictable. Also all loads should be placed at equal distances (regular intervals).

90 DEGREE ANGLES

Eliminating 90° angles also minimizes reflections. It is much more desirable to use 45° or 135° angles as shown in Figure 2-12.

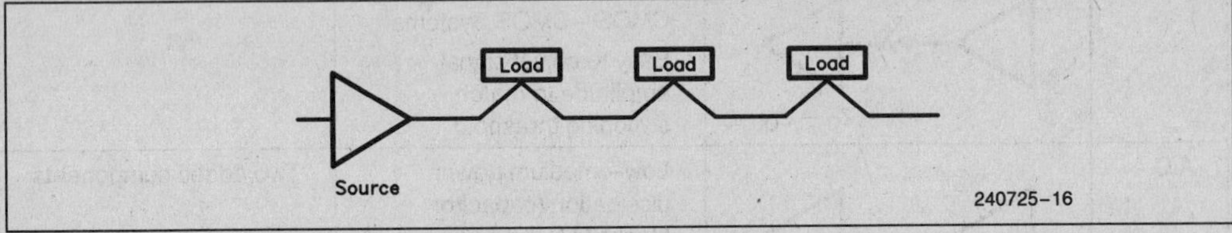

Figure 2-11. Daisy Chaining

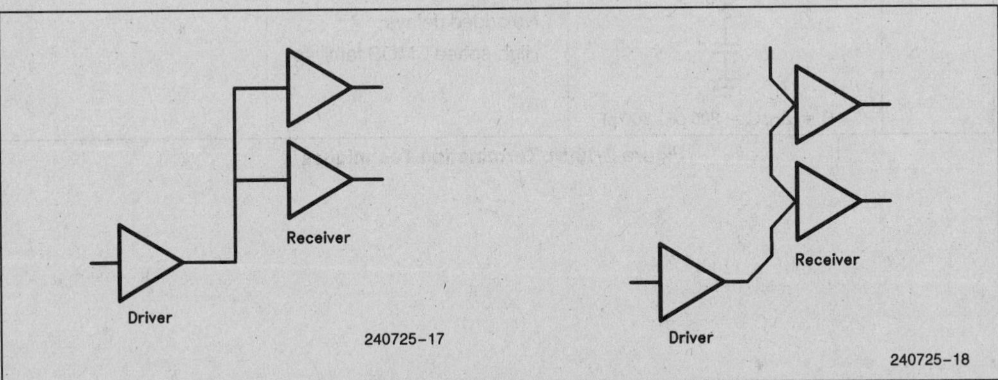

Figure 2-12. Avoiding 90 Degree Angles

VIAS (FEED THROUGH CONNECTIONS)

Another impedance source that degrades high frequency circuit performance is the via. Expert layout techniques can reduce vias to avoid reflection sites on PCBs.

Following these guidelines will not guarantee elimination of all reflections, but they will minimize the number and size.

2.4 Cross Talk

Cross talk is another negative effect of transmission lines. It is a problem at high frequencies because, as operating frequency increase, the signal wavelength become comparable to the length of the interconnections on the PC board. In general, interference such as cross talk, occurs when electrical activity in one conductor causes a transient voltage to appear in another conductor. Main factors that increase interference in any circuit are:

1. Variation of current and voltage in the lines causes frequency interference. This interence increases with increase in frequency.
2. Coupling occurs when conductors are in close proximity.

Cross talk is the phenomenom of a signal in one trace producing a similar signal in an adjacent trace. It may not be a carbon copy of the original signal. It may only be occasional noise that corrupts the integrity of the second signal. The easiest way to minimize crosstalk is to eliminate or at least minimize the number of parallel traces. Parallel traces can be on a single layer or on adjacent signal layers.

There are three ways that parallel traces can couple and thereby produce a signal or at least influence the signal on a second trace. These methods of coupling are inductive, radiative, and capacitive. Inductive coupling is where the two traces act as inductors. The field produced by a signal in one trace induces a current in the second trace. Radiative coupling occurs when the two parallel traces act as a dipole, an antenna. One radiates a signal and the other receives it, thus corupting the signal already present on the trace. The final method is capacitive coupling. Two parallel traces separated by a dielectric act as a capacitor. If both traces are in a high state and one transitions to a low. The capacitor will try to maintain the high and thus cause a slow transition time on the second trace. These effects can be minimized by reducing the number of parallel traces.

HOW TO MINIMIZE

When laying out a board for an high speed 386 DX based system, several guidelines should be followed to minimize crosstalk. Some of them are as follows:

1. To reduce crosstalk, it is necesary to minimize the common impedance paths.
2. Run a ground line between two adjacent lines. The lines should be grounded at both ends.
3. Seperate the address and data busses by a ground line. This technique may however be expensive due to large number of address and data lines.
4. Remove closed loop signal paths which create inductive noise.
5. Capacitive coupling can be reduced by reducing the number of parellel traces. Parallel traces can be minimized by insuring that signals on adjacent signal layers run orthogonal, perpendicular. Ground planes or traces can be inserted to provide shielding. A ground plane between signal layers eliminates any coupling that could occur. On a single trace, a ground trace can be run between traces to prevent coupling.

In some instances it is necessary to run traces parallel to each other. In these cases try to make the distance as short as possible and choose signals in which the transition time is not as critical so that the coupling effects do not produce problems. In addition the coupling can be minimized by increasing the spacing between parallel traces.

2.5 Skew

Skew is another effect of transmission lines. This is very important in a synchronous system. Long traces add propagation delay. A longer trace or a load placed further down a trace will experience more delay than a short trace or loads very close to the source. This must be taken into account when doing the worst case timing analysis. In a system where events must occur synchronous to a clock signal, it is important to make sure the signal is available to all input a sufficient amount of time prior to the corresponding clock edge. When performing the component placement this is one of the considerations that must be accounted for.

These guidelines have always been recommended for board design; however, they are much more important at higher frequencies. At the slower frequencies designers could ignore these practices occassionally and not experience difficulties. This is not the case at higher frequencies.

2.6 DC Loading

To maintain proper logic levels, all digital signal outputs have a maximum load, they are capable of driving. DC loading is the constant current required by an input in either the high or the low state. It limits the ability of a device driving the bus to maintain proper logic levels. For a 386 DX based system, a careful analysis must be performed to ensure that in a worst case situation no loading limits are exceeded. Even if a bus is loaded slightly beyond its worst case limit, it might cause problems if a batch of parts whose input loading is close to maximum is encountered. Proper logic level will then fail to be maintained and unreliable operation may result. Marginal loading problems are particularly insidious, since the effect is often erratic operation and non repetitive errors that are extremely difficult to track down. For both the high and low logic levels, the sum of the currents required by all the inputs and the leakage currents of all outputs (drivers) on the bus must be added together. This sum must be less than the output capability of the weakest driver. Since the 386 DX is a CHMOS device having negligible dc loading, the main contributors to dc loading will be the TTL devices.

2.7 AC Loading

The AC or capacitive loading is caused by the input capacitance of each device and limits the speed at which a device driving a bus signal can change the state from high to low or low to high. Designers of microprocessor systems have traditionally calculated load capacitance of their systems by determining the number of devices and their individual capacitance loading attached to a signal plus the amount of trace capacitance. Typically, the trace capacitance was a set "lumped" number of pf (i.e. 2 pf to 3 pf per inch) when it is thought of at all. This lumped method is a general rule-of-thumb which generates a good first pass approximation. For low frequency designs, the lumped method works since system and component margins are large enough to cover any minor differences due to the approximation.

For high frequency designs, the component and system margins are no longer available to the designer. With less than 1 ns of margin, even the amount of trace capacitance can make a circuit path critical.

A more accurate calculation of capacitive loading can be derived by modeling the device loads and system traces as a series of Transmission Lines Theory. Transmission Line Theory provides a more accurate picture of system loading in high frequency systems. In addition, it allows new factors such as inductance and the effect of reflections upon the quality of the signal waveform to be factored into consideration.

2.8 Derating Curve and Its Effects:

A derating curve is a graph that plots the output buffer against the capacitive load. The curve is used to analyze a signal delay without necessitating a simulation every time the processor's loading changes. This graph assumes the lumped capacitance model to calculate the total capacitance. The delay in the graph should be added to the specified AC timing value for the device that is driving the load. The derating curve is different for different devices because each device has different output buffers.

A derating curve is generated by tying the chip's output buffers to a range of capacitors. The voltage and resistance values chosen for the output buffers are at the highest specified temperature and are rising (worst case) values. The value of the capacitors centres around the AC timing values for the chip. For 33 MHz and above, this is 50 pF. Since the AC timing specifications are measured for a signal reaching 1.5 V. A curve is then drawn from kthe range of time and capacitance values, with 50 pF representing the average and with nominal or zero derating. These curves are valid only for 50 pF–150 pF load range. Beyond this range the output buffers are not characterized. The the derating curve for the 386 DX are shown in 2-13. These curves use the lumped capacitance model for circuit capacitance measurements and must be modified slightly when doing worst-case calculations that involve transmission line effects.

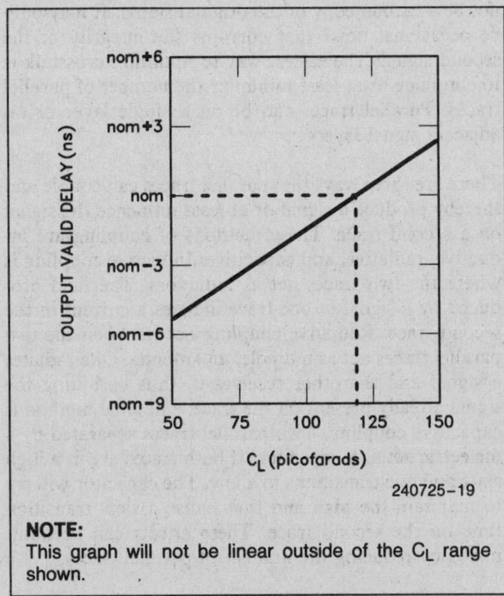

Figure 2-13. Typical Output Valid Delay Versus Load Capacitance at Maximum Operating Temperature (C_L = 120 pF)

2.9 High Speed Clock Circuits

For performance at high frequencies, the clock signal (CLK2) for the 386 DX CPU must be free of noise and within the specifcations listed in the 386 DX CPU data sheet. Achieving the proper clock routing around a 33 MHz printed circuit board is delicate because a myriad of problems, some of them subtle, can arise design guidelines are not followed. For example, fast clock edges cause reflections from high impedance terminations. These reflections can cause significant signal degradation in systems operating at 33 MHz clock rates. This section covers some design guidelines which should be observed to properly lay out the clock lines for efficient 386 DX operation.

- Since the rise/fall time of the clock signal is typically in the range of 2-4 ns, the reflections at this speed could result in undesirable noise and unacceptable signal degradation. The degree of reflections depends on the impedance of the traces of the clock connections. These reflections can be optimized by terminating the CLK2 output with proper terminations and by keeping length of the traces as short as possible. The preferred method is to connect all of the loads via a single trace as shown in Figure 2-14, thus avoiding the extra stubs associated with each load. The loads should be as close to one another as possible. Multiple clock sources should be for distributed loads.
- A less desirable method is the star connection layout in which the clock traces branch to the load as closely as posssible (Figure 2-15). In this layout, the stubs should be kept as short as possible. The maximum allowable length of the traces depends upon the frequency and the total fanout, but the length of all the traces in the star connection should be equal. Lengths of less than one inch are recommended. In this method the CLK2 signal is terminated by a series resistor. The resistor value is calculated by measuring the total capacitive load on the CLK2 signal and referring to Figure 2-16. If the total capacitive load is less than 80 pF, the user should add capacitors to make up the diference. Because of the high frequency of CLK2, the terminating resistor must have low inductance; carbon resistors are recommended.
- Use an oscilloscope to compare the CLK2 waveform with those in Figure 2-17.

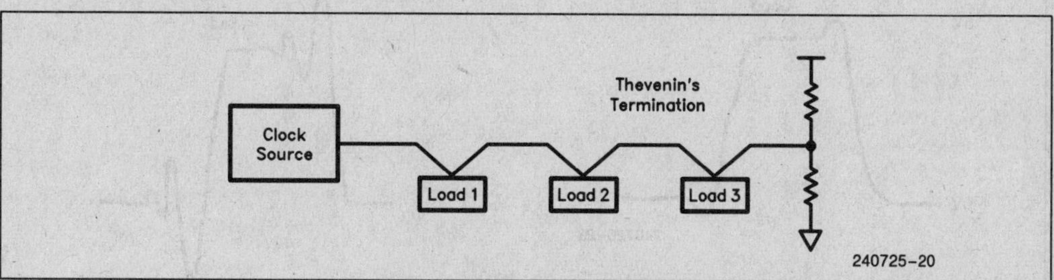

Figure 2-14. Clock Routing

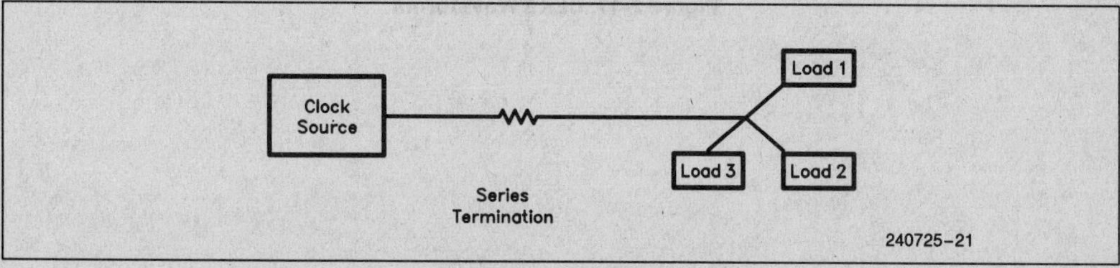

Figure 2-15. Star Connection

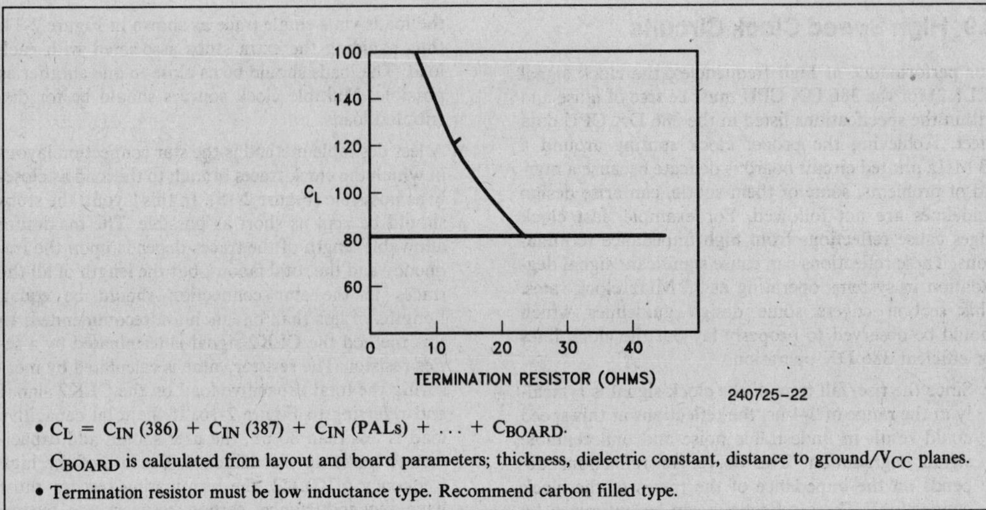
100
140
120
C_L 100
80
60
0
10
20
30
40
TERMINATION RESISTOR (OHMS)
240725-22
• $C_L = C_{IN}$ (386) + C_{IN} (387) + C_{IN} (PALs) + ... + C_{BOARD}.
C_{BOARD} is calculated from layout and board parameters; thickness, dielectric constant, distance to ground/V_{CC} planes.
• Termination resistor must be low inductance type. Recommend carbon filled type.

Figure 2-16. CLK2 Series Termination

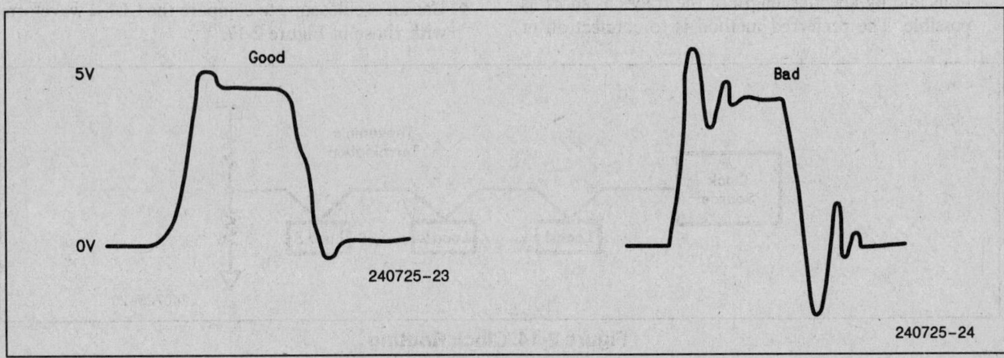
5V
Good
0V
240725-23
Bad
240725-24

Figure 2-17. CLK2 Waveforms

SECTION III. DESIGN EXAMPLE

At higher processor speeds the window of time available to perform specific tasks become very small. This window can be equated to multiples of the CLK2 period. Within this time signals must be supplied from a source and reach a destination in time to meet any setup requirements. At 16 MHz the CLK2 period is 31 ns. At 33 MHz it shrinks to half this value, 15 ns. The longer time allowed the use of slower logic families and the delays associated with longer traces. As the window decreases system designers have to practice more care in the selection of logic families and in the choices made for component placement and signal routing on PCBs. This section attempts to list the signal paths whose worst case timing analysis results in very small margins and therefore require closer attention from designers to guarantee that all a. c. timing specifications are met.

This section also includes a sample design based on 33 MHz version of the 386 DX. It should not be taken as a recommended design. The circuit is used only to highlight the design considerations for high speed systems.

3.1 System Architecture

Figure 3.1 shows the system block diagram. It has four major subsystems.

1) CPU subsystem

2) DRAM subsystem

3) Cache subsystem

4) ROM and I/O subsystem

The system has 1 megabytes of Page-Mode DRAMS (60 ns RAS access time), 128 kilobytes of EPROMS (200 ns access time), an 8259A-2, and an 82510. The cache subsystem is optional. Schematics and PAL codes are given in appendix A and B respectively.

3.2 CPU Subsystem

The CPU subsystem consists of the 386 DX microprocessor, a clock and reset circuitry, and bus control logic. Clean and proper clock is very important in the designs at high frequencies.

RESET STATE MACHINE

This state machine is used to generate three control signals, namely RESET, REFREQ and CLK. The CLK signal is half of the CPU clock, CLK2 and is used mainly in I/O and EPROM subsystem.

RESET is generated through the input from RESET triggering circuitry (as shown in the CPU schematic). The min RESET Setup and Hold time for operation at 33 MHz are 5 ns and 2 ns respectively.

A 61.44 KHz clock is used to produce a synchronous refresh request (REFREQ) signal for the DRAM controller, which employ a transparent, distributed, DRAM refresh technique that allows the processor and cache to run while the refresh cycle is in progress.

3.3 DRAM Subsystem

An non-interleaved DRAM system is used in the sample board, which simplifies the design. Since the board provide caching, the performance of DRAM subsystem is outweighed by the simplicity and economy of the design. It employs a transparent, distributed, DRAM refresh technique which allows the processor and cache to run while the refresh cycle is in progress. It uses the 3-state capability of the 16R8-7 and the 74ACT258 to multiplex the refresh address. A further consideration is the choice of DRAM devices. If one uses a memory device such as the AAA2801 (which supports a CAS# before RAS# refresh and provides an internal refresh counter) further simplifications can be made in both the circuitry and the control logic.

DRAM CONTROL STATE MACHINE

The state machine is implemented with three 16R8-type E-speed PALs (see page 4 of the schematics). E-speed PALs must be used since the CLK2 frequency, 66.67 MHz, is higher than the maximum clock frequency of the D-speed PALs.

In order to generate DRAM control signals with smallest delay from the CLK2 edges, all state machines are implemented as Moore machines. The state machines flip-flops generate most of the DRAM control signals directly. This is an expensive design approach in terms of hardware but allows signal timings and skews to be fine tuned.

DRAM CYCLES—NO CACHE CONFIGURATION

Pages C-1 through C-4 show examples of DRAM cycles. In order to hide the DRAM page hit-or-miss decision time, the DRAM controller always tries to put the 386 DX in pipelined mode. The first read cycle requires only two wait states since RAS# has been precharged (see page C-1). The second cycle takes only two clock cycles. The second cycle is a pipelined, page-hit read cycle, which is the best case. The third cycle is a pipelined, page-hit write cycle. This cycle requires one wait state. DRAMs capture data at the falling edge of CAS# during Early Write cycles. The 386 DX drives

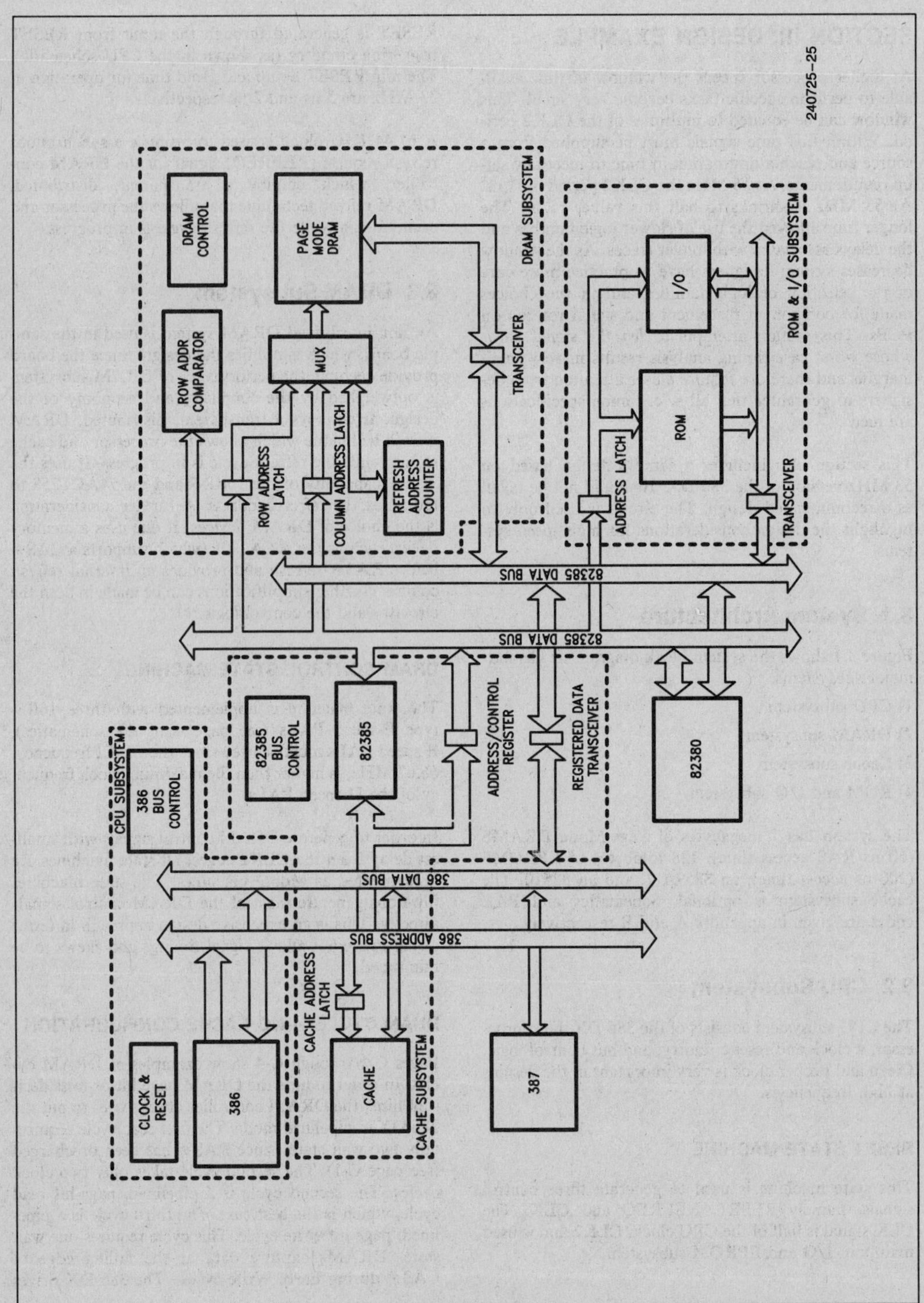

Figure 3-1. Block Diagram

valid write data at the rising edge in the middle of Tip (edge C) with a max prop delay of 24 ns (T12 max). This means that the CAS# is generated after the rising edge in the middle of the second T2p (edge A). CAS# is, therefore, generated at the end of RAS# hold time with respect to CAS# (if the next cycle is a page miss, RAS# will go inactive at the end of the current write cycle), and so on.

The fifth cycle is a page miss, which is actually detected at the end of the fourth cycle (page C-2). Since the DRAM controller must wait for minimum RAS# precharge time, the fifth cycle requires three wait states. The sixth cycle is also a page miss. This cycle, however, requires only two wait states because the miss was detected early enough in the previous cycle to have RAS# precharged by the end of the T1p. If the seventh cycle is another page miss, it will require three wait states.

The eighth cycle is ended with T2i. Consequently, the ninth cycle must wait for minimum RAS# precharge time and requires three wait states.

A DRAM refresh cycle is shown on page C-4. The DRAM address multiplexer output is disabled, and the refresh address counter output is enabled. The cycle does a RAS# only refresh cycle where only RAS# is asserted with a proper refresh address. After the refresh cycle is completed, a read cycle which has been suspended due to the refresh is resumed.

STATE DIAGRAMS

Pages B-1 through B-11 show state diagrams of the DRAM controller. The precharge state machine on page B-2 measures the required RAS# precharge time and CAS#-to-RAS# precharge time. The CAS#-READY# state machine on page B-2 implements a pin strap option of having or not having the 82385. For no cache configuration, the Cache variable must be forced low.

TIMING CALCULATIONS

Timing equations are described on pages D-1 and D-2. Their corresponding results are given on pages D-3 through D-7.

Capacitive load on the 386 DX address bus was assumed to be less than 85 pF. Capacitive load on the DRAM address bus was calculated to be less than 22 pF.

3.4 CACHE Subsystem

At 33 MHz DRAM speeds are not fast enough to design zero wait state memory systems. A cache can be used to take advantage of the higher performance available from the higher speed 386 DX microprocessors. The cache takes advantage of the faster SRAM while keeping system costs down by using the cheaper but slower DRAMs.

Details of the cache subsystem are shown on Figure 3.2 and 3.3. The 82385 address and data busses are interfaced to the 386 DX address and data busses via 74AS574s and 74AS646s. Static RAMs (20 ns access time) are used for the cache memory.

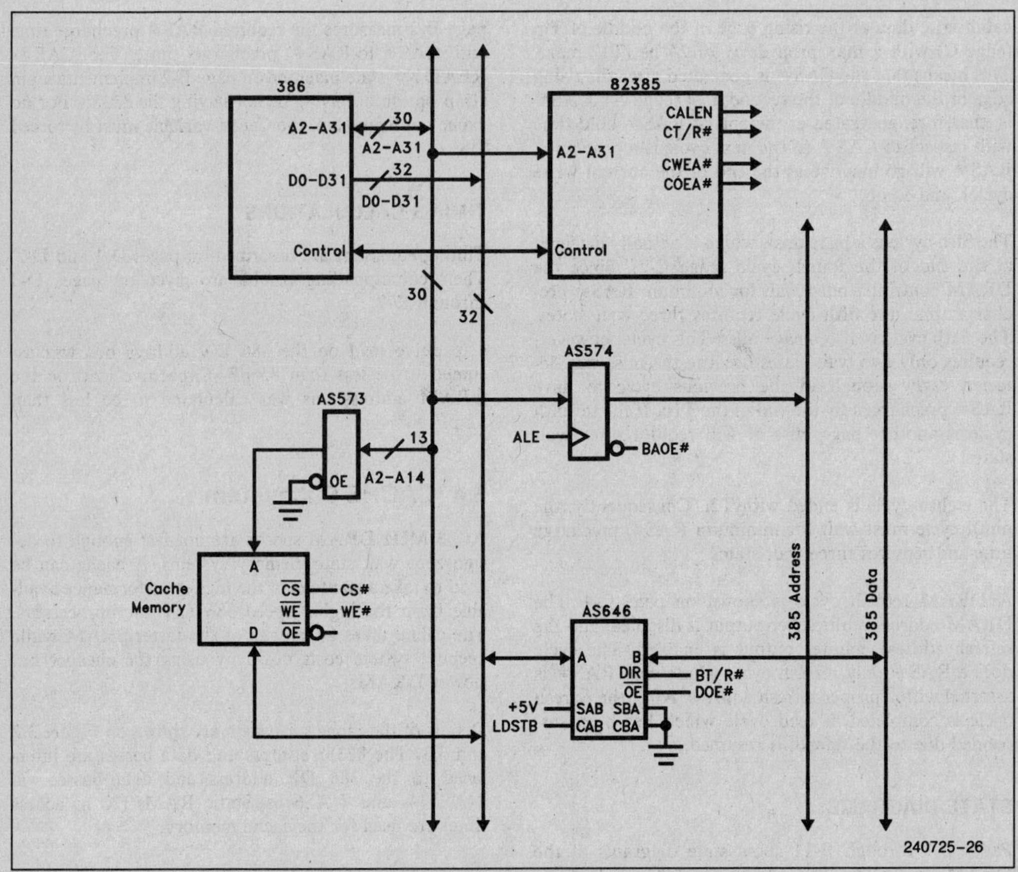

Figure 3-2. Block Diagram of Cache Subsystem

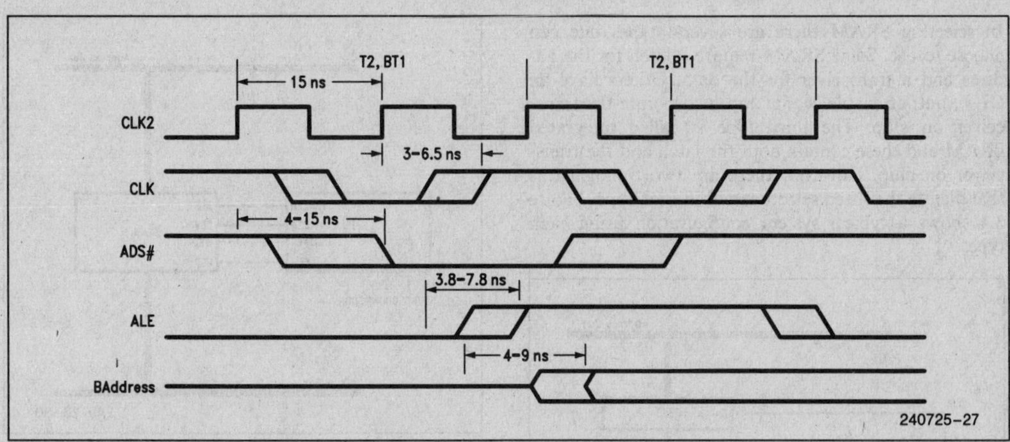

Figure 3-3. Address Valid Delay for Cache Subsystem

4

In selecting SRAM there are several types one can choose to use. Some SRAM require a latch for the address and a transceiver for the data. Others have an OE#, output enable, signal and incorporate the transceiver on chip. The third type is called integrated SRAM and these contain both the latch and the transceiver on chip. However, there are two timing paths that dictate the speed selection within each type. Figure 3.4 shows a typical system configuration using each type.

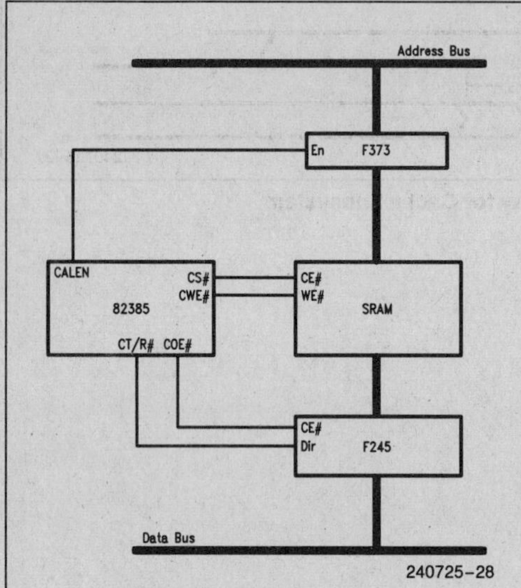

Figure 3.4(a) SRAM w/o OE#

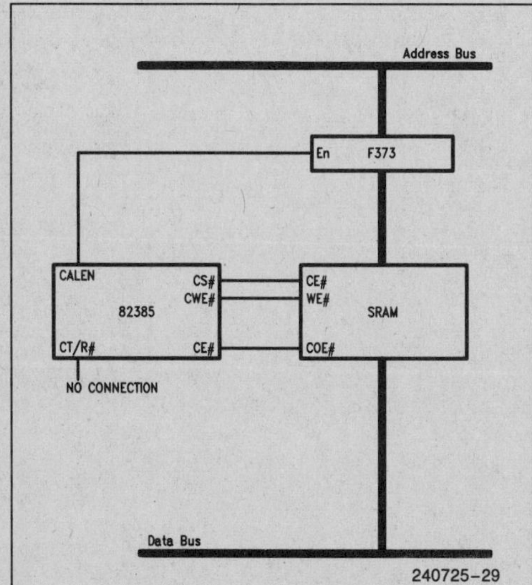

Figure 3.4(b) SRAM with OE# Control

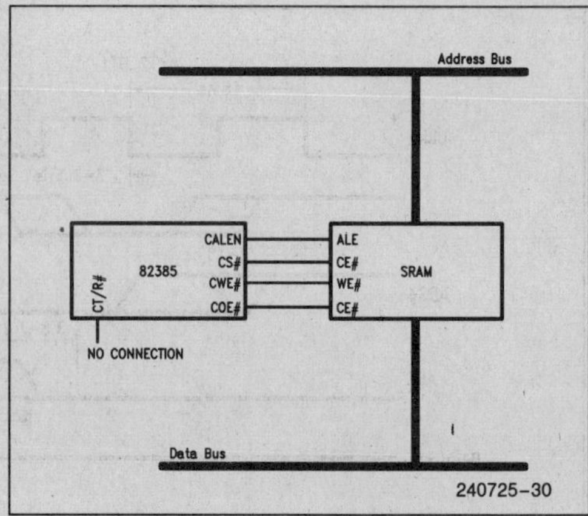

Figure 3-4. (c) Integrated SRAM

The critical times for the SRAM are the SRAM OE# to data delay and the SRAM address to data delay. The following analysis applies to SRAMs with an OE# signal as shown in Figure 3.4b. First examine the path of OE# to data. This path must be completed within 2 CLK periods. The COE# signal from the 385 Cache Controller must be valid and the SRAM must drive data onto the data bus so that the data setup time of the 386 DX CPU is met.

2 X CLK2 period - t_{25b} 82385 COE# valid delay (max) - SRAM access time (OE# to data) - t_{21} 386 DX data setup ≥ 0

Using the specified values from the data sheets reveals that the SRAM must have an OE# to data delay of 10ns or less. The other path is for the address to become available and data to reach the 386 DX CPU. This path has 4 CLK2 periods. The 385 Cache Controller must supply the CALEN signal to pass the address to the SRAM and then the SRAM must drive the data on the data bus so that the data setup time is met on the 386 DX CPU.

4 X CLK2 period - t_{21b} 82385 CALEN valid delay (max) - t_{pd} (x373 latch) - SRAM access time (address to data) - t_{21} 386 DX data setup ≥ 0

Once again using the data sheet the access time can be determined. Depending on the type of transparent latch the SRAM needs an address to data access time of 20ns or 25ns. If an F series 373 is used the faster 20ns SRAM must be used, but if an FCT373a or PCT373a is used the 25ns SRAM is sufficient.

The A_{20} path is another path with a small margin. The reason is the AND gate that many designers insert to provide 1MB wraparound of address in real mode. Figure 3.5 shows the circuit block diagram. A_{20} must leave the 386 DX and reach the 385 Cache Controller within 2 CLK2 periods.

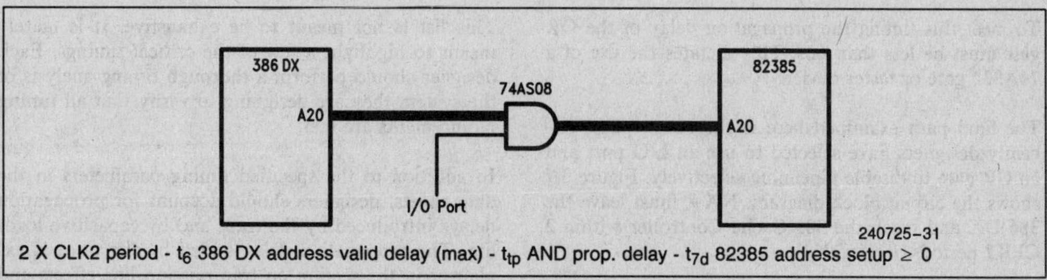

2 X CLK2 period - t_6 386 DX address valid delay (max) - t_{tp} AND prop. delay - t_{7d} 82385 address setup ≥ 0

Figure 3-5. Critical Timing A20

To meet this timing the propagation delay of the AND gate must be less than 6ns. This dictates the use of a 74AS08 gate or faster device.

Analysis of the LOCK# path also shows a small margin. The reason is the OR gate that many designers insert to disable the LOCK# signal to the 385 Cache Controller. This allows locked accesses to be cached. Figure 3.6 shows the circuit block diagram. LOCK# must leave the 386 DX and reach the 385 Cache Controller within 2 CLK2 periods.

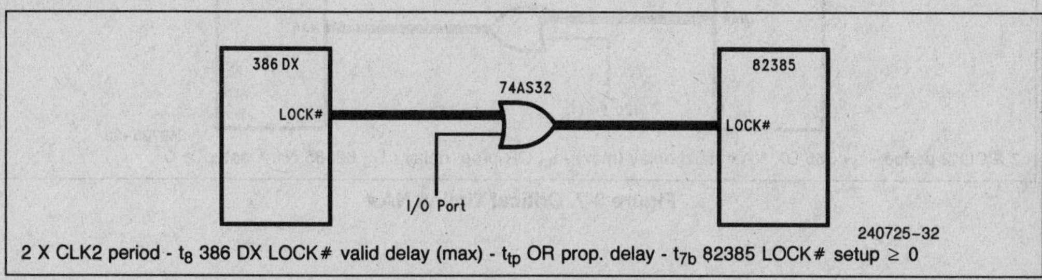

2 X CLK2 period - t_8 386 DX LOCK# valid delay (max) - t_{tp} OR prop. delay - t_{7b} 82385 LOCK# setup ≥ 0

Figure 3-6. Critical Timing Lock#

4

To meet this timing the propagation delay of the OR gate must be less than 6ns. This dictates the use of a 74AS32 gate or faster device.

The final path examined here is the NA# path. Recently designers have selected to use an I/O port and an OR gate to disable pipelining selectively. Figure 3.7 shows the circuit block diagram. NA# must leave the 386 DX and reach the 385 Cache Controller within 2 CLK2 periods.

Using the specified values in the appropriate data sheets results in the need for the propagation delay of the OR gate must be no greater than 5.8ns. This dictates the use of a 74AS32 gate or faster device.

This list is not meant to be exhaustive. It is merely meant to highlight a few of the critical timings. Each designer should perform a thorough timing analysis of the system they are designing to verify that all timing requirements are met.

In addition to the specified timing parameters in the data sheets, designers should account for propagation delays introduced by the trace and by capacitive loading. The propagation delay added by the trace is explained in the section on transmission line effects and supplies an equation to determine the amount of delay.

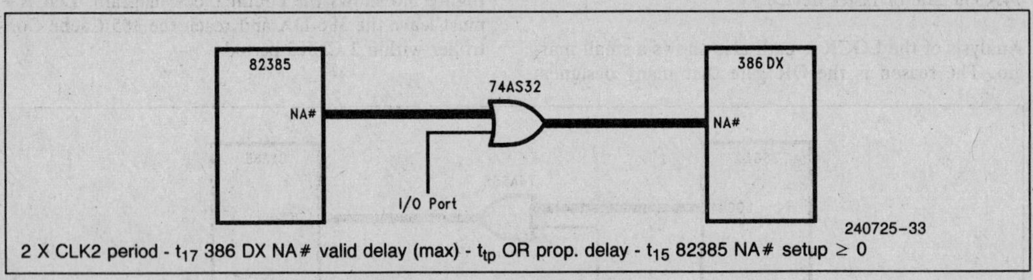

2 X CLK2 period - t_{17} 386 DX NA# valid delay (max) - t_{tp} OR prop. delay - t_{15} 82385 NA# setup ≥ 0

Figure 3-7. Critical Timing NA#

Another factor that becomes more important at higher frequencies is loading. DC loading and especially capacitive loading must be considered during the design stage. If the board is to be assembled and tested in stages, then the DC loads should be considered for all configurations of the board. Most termination techniques require additional current. If a board has a marginal loading situation, one is limited in one's choices of termination techniques. If a capacitive loading problem exists, the timing situations can become extremely difficult at higher frequencies. If timing is critical, do not overload the capacitance at which a device was tested. If a device is overloaded, derating must be taken into consideration.

Capacitive loading also introduces a delay on signals. Many components including the 386 DX include a capacitive derating curve in the data sheet. To use the curve in the 386 DX data sheet, the capacitive load must be calculated. This is done by summing the input capacitances of all devices driven by a given output from the 386 Microprocessor. Find this value on the X-axis of the derating curve in the data sheet and move up till the derating curve is intersected. Then move at a right angle to the left until intersecting the Y-axis. A value of nom+ or nom− something is found. This is the nominal value plus or minus some amount. The nominal value is the value found in the data sheet. Add the offset from the curve to this nominal value to get the resulting delay corresponding to the capacitive loading in the system. Note: The trace capacitance was not included in this calculation. It is accounted for in the trace propagation delay mentioned earlier.

DRAM CYCLES WITH 82385 ENABLED

When the 82385 is enabled (the CACHE variable of the state machine on page B-2 is forced High), the DRAM controller inserts one extra wait state in all read cycles. This extra time is needed to allow a cache update cycle to occur after each cache read miss cycle. During a cache update cycle, the read data from DRAMs must propagate through the 74AS646 and the 74F245 (optional) and must be ready for a SRAM write cycle with enough setup time.

Timing diagrams on pages C-5 through C-9 show cache and DRAM cycles.

TIMING CALCULATIONS

Timing equations are found on pages D-8 and D-9. Only tCAS, tRAC, tCAC, tAA, tPC, and tCAP are different in this configuration. Actual values for DRAM timings are found on page D-10.

3.5 I/O - EPROM Subsystem

A block diagram of the I/O-EPROM subsystem is shown on Figure 3.8. This subsystem has separate address and data busses. The address bus is 14 bits wide, and the data bus is 16 bits wide.

The bus controller is designed with B-speed PALs which are clocked by the CLK# signal (Figure 3.8). There are a few unique design issues in this scheme.

As shown on Figure 3.10, ADS# is now an asynchronous signal for the state machine. It is impossible for the state machine to capture valid ADS# without re-synchronization of the signal. To guarantee recognition of valid ADS#, two D flip-flop is clocked by CLK# and provides a synchronous ADS# (or Latched ADS#) which is in phase with the state machine.

The second issue is its asynchronous nature of the state machine output signal. With the state machine running almost asynchronously to CLK2 (B PALs also have a long clock-to-output propagation delay), signals generated by the state machine must be re-synchronized before they are returned to the 386 DX. Signals that go to I/O devices and EPROMs need no re-synchronization since these devices are asynchronous. Signals which require re-synchronization are BS16# and DEN#. Each rising edge of DEN# is synchronized to CLK2 by a J-K flip-flop as shown on Figure 3.9. This is important to avoid bus contention after an I/O or EPROM read-cycle. BS16# is synchronized to CLK2 by D flip-flops.

EPROM and I/O cycle timings are shown on pages C-10 through C-13. The worst case is a write cycle to the 82510 and may require as many as 14 wait states.

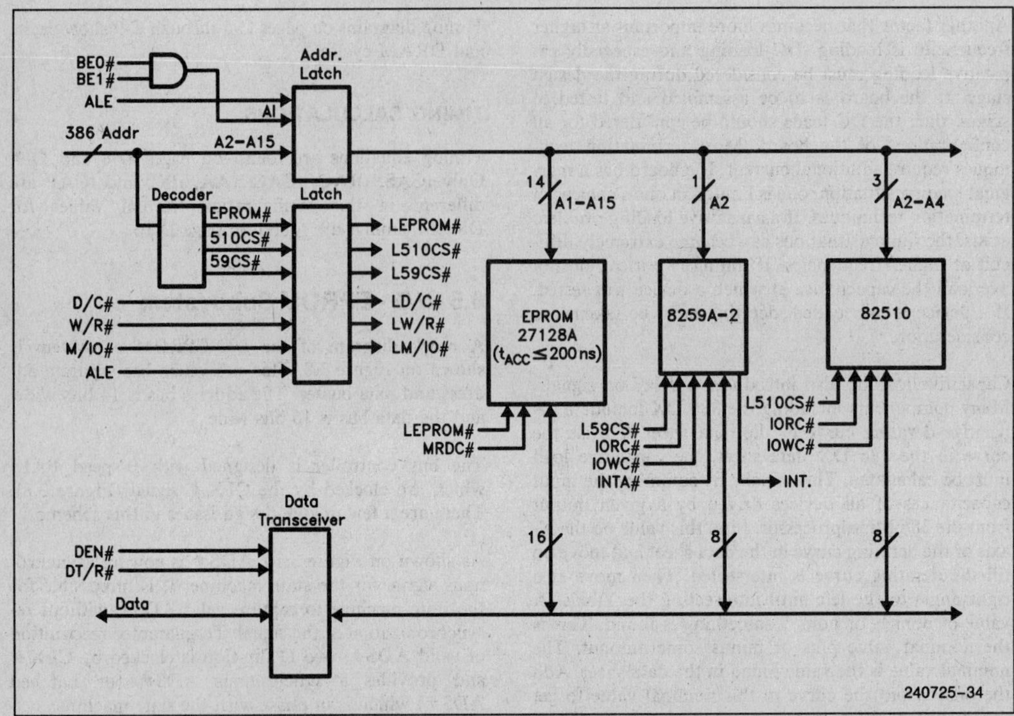

Figure 3-8. Block Diagram of I/O, EPROM Subsystem

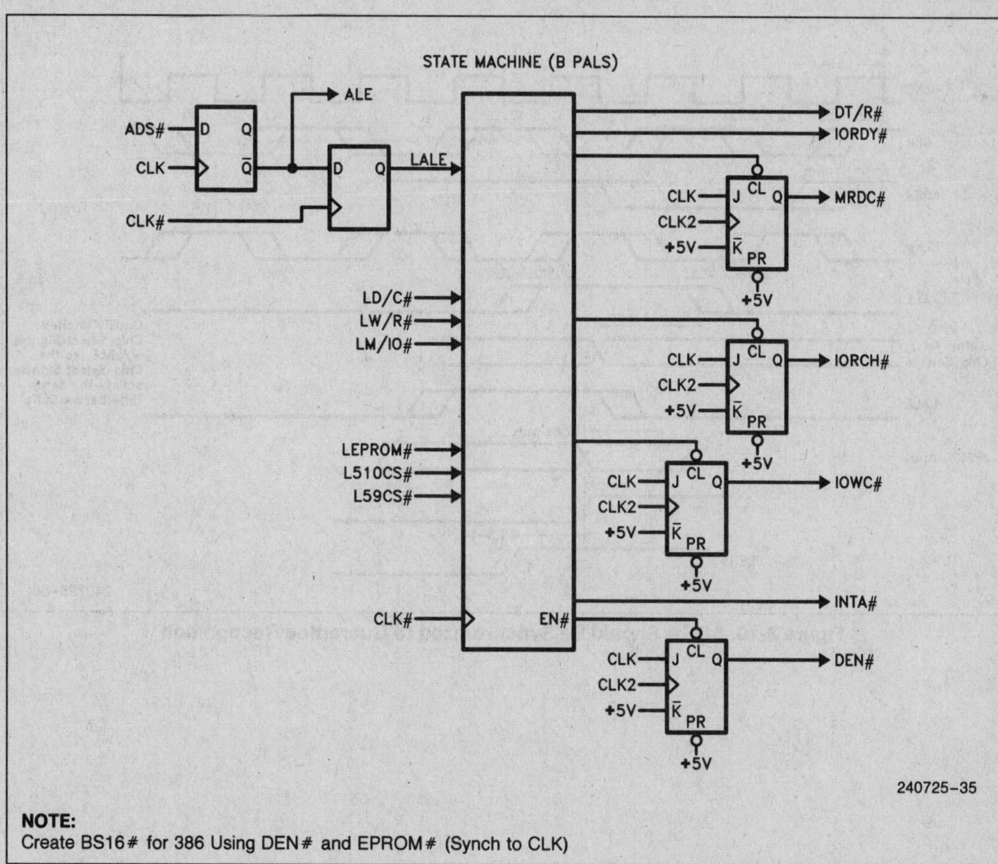

NOTE:
Create BS16# for 386 Using DEN# and EPROM# (Synch to CLK)

Figure 3-9. Control Logic for I/O, EPROM Subsystem

4

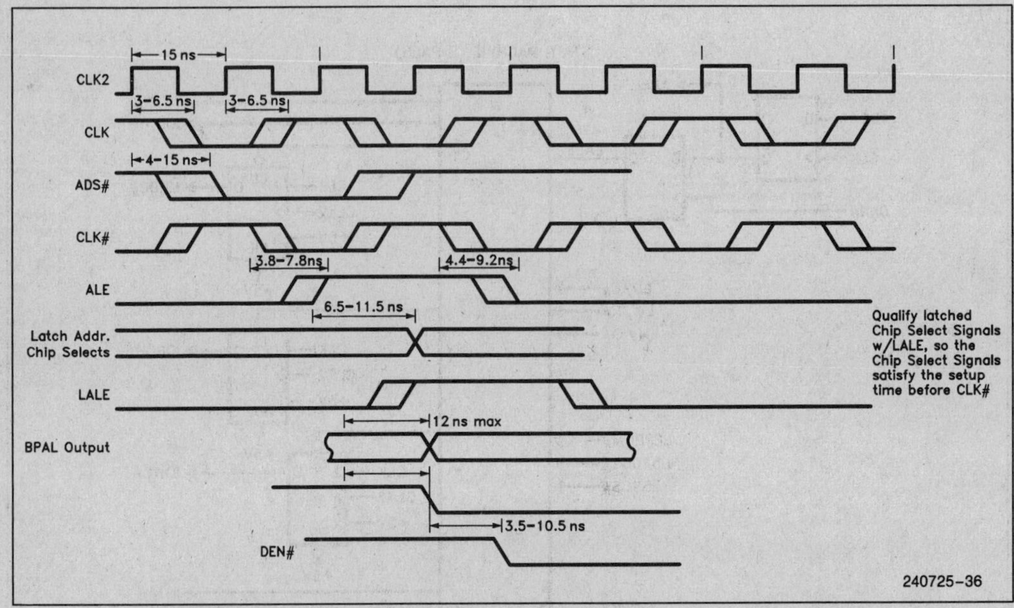

Figure 3-10. ADS# Should Be Synchronized to Guarantee Recognition

APPENDIX A
SCHEMATICS

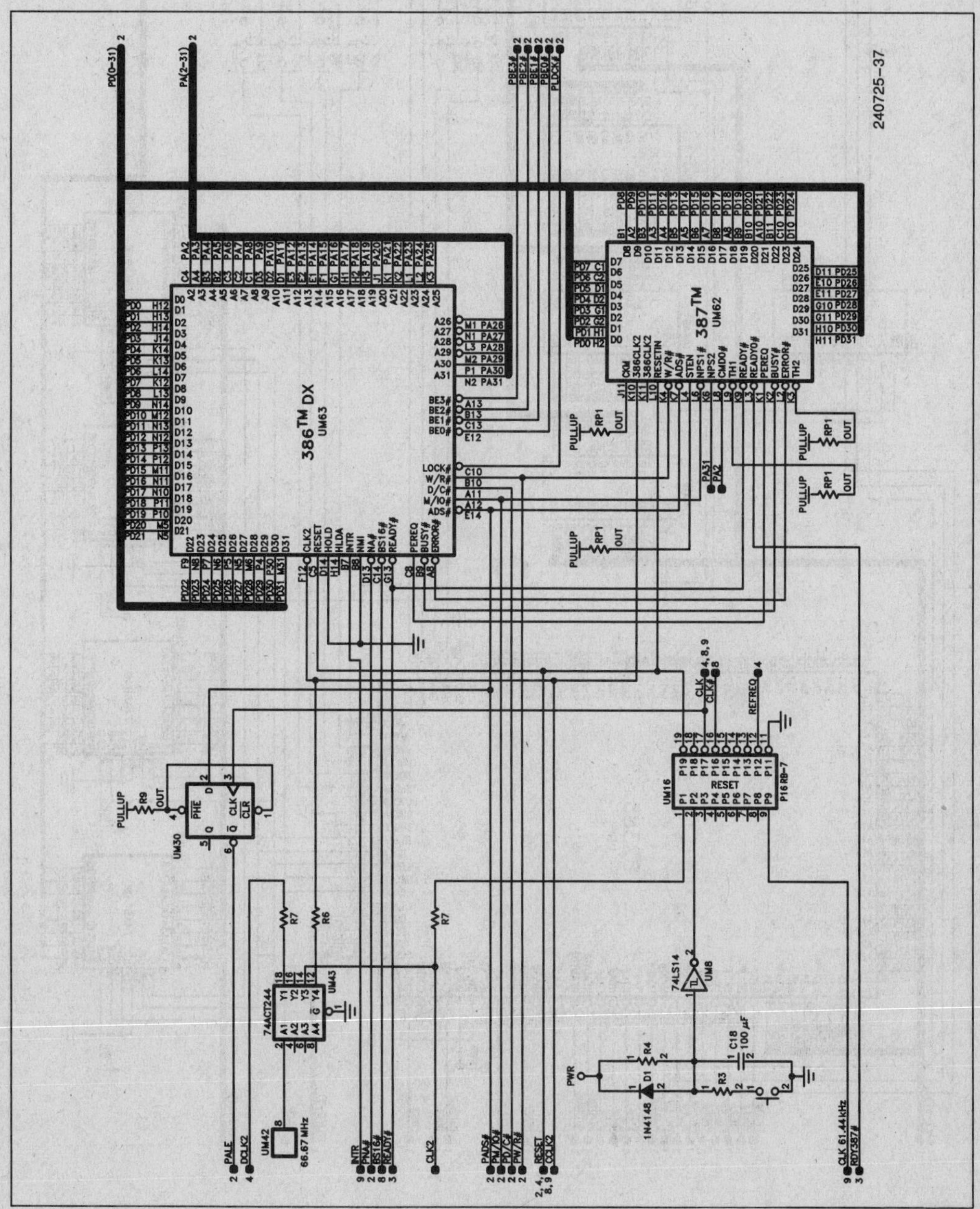

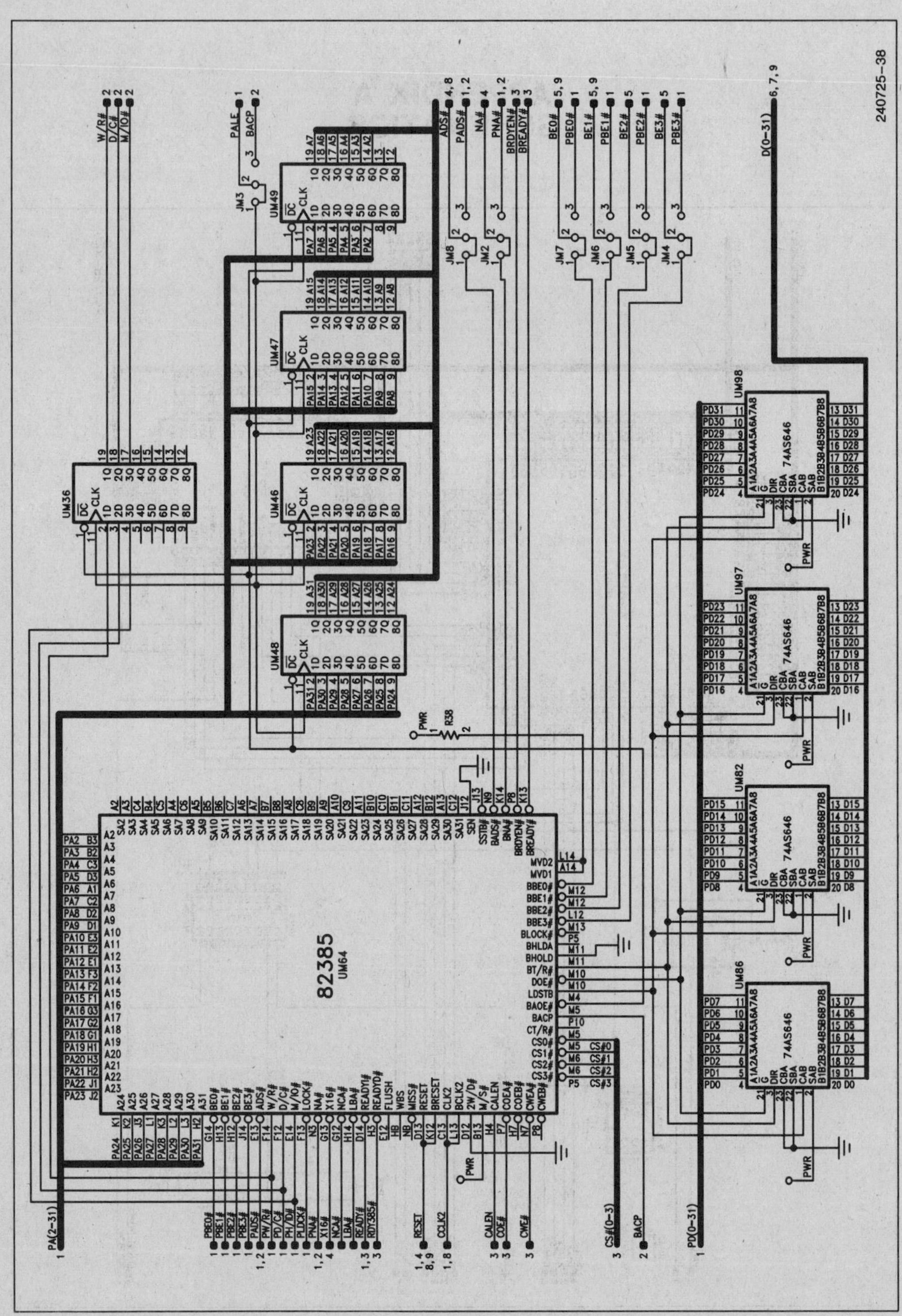

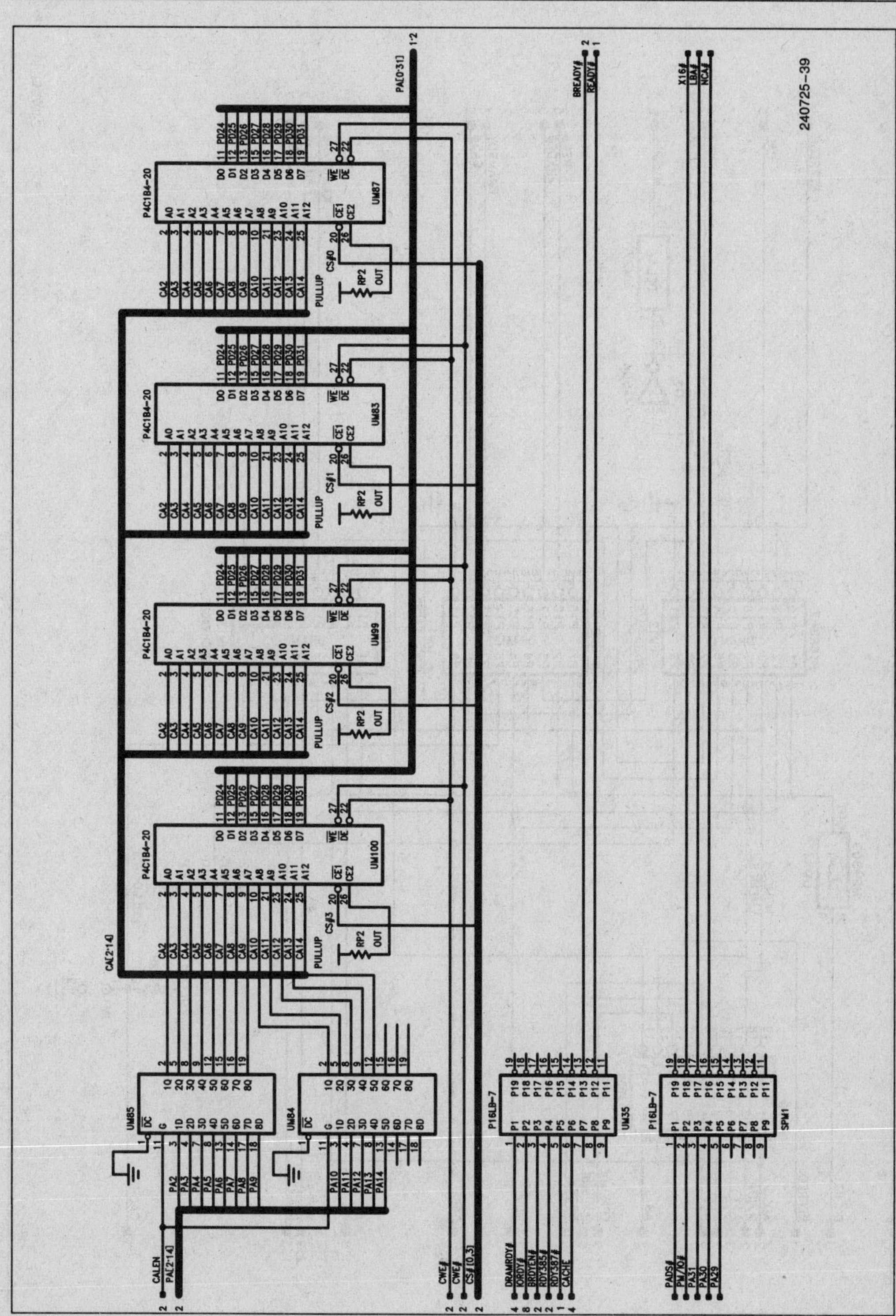
P4C1B4-20
UM87
UM83
UM99
UM100
UM85
UM84
P16L8-7
UM35
SPM1
PULLUP
RP2
OUT
CS#0
CS#1
CS#2
CS#3
PA[0-31]
CA[2-14]
CALEN
PA[2-14]
CWE#
CS#[0,3]
DRAMRDY#
IORDY#
BRDYEN#
RDY385#
RDY387#
CACHE
BREADY#
READY#
PADS#
PM/IO#
PA31
PA30
PA29
X16#
LBA#
NCA#

240725-39

4

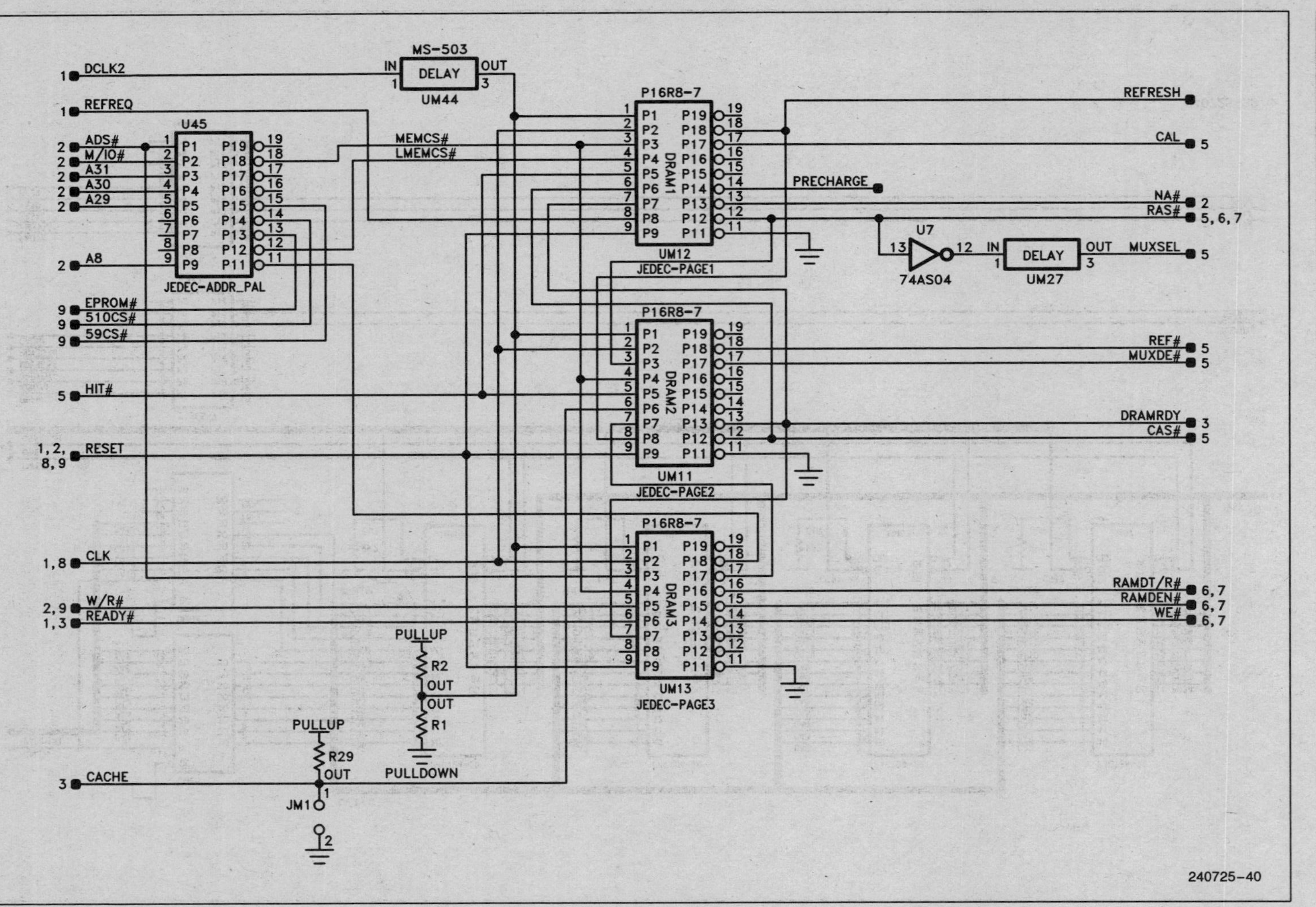

MS-503
DELAY
UM44
IN 1
OUT 3
DCLK2 1
REFREQ 1
U45
JEDEC-ADDR_PAL
ADS# 2
M/IO# 2
A31 2
A30 2
A29 2
A8 2
EPROM# 9
510CS# 9
59CS# 9
HIT# 5
RESET 1, 2, 8, 9
CLK 1, 8
W/R# 2, 9
READY# 1, 3
CACHE 3
MEMCS#
LMEMCS#
P16R8-7
DRAM1
UM12
JEDEC-PAGE1
DRAM2
UM11
JEDEC-PAGE2
DRAM3
UM13
JEDEC-PAGE3
REFRESH
CAL 5
PRECHARGE
NA# 2
RAS# 5, 6, 7
U7
74AS04
DELAY
UM27
MUXSEL 5
REF# 5
MUXDE# 5
DRAMRDY 3
CAS# 5
RAMDT/R# 6, 7
RAMDEN# 6, 7
WE# 6, 7
PULLUP
R2
R1
PULLDOWN
R29
JM1
240725-40

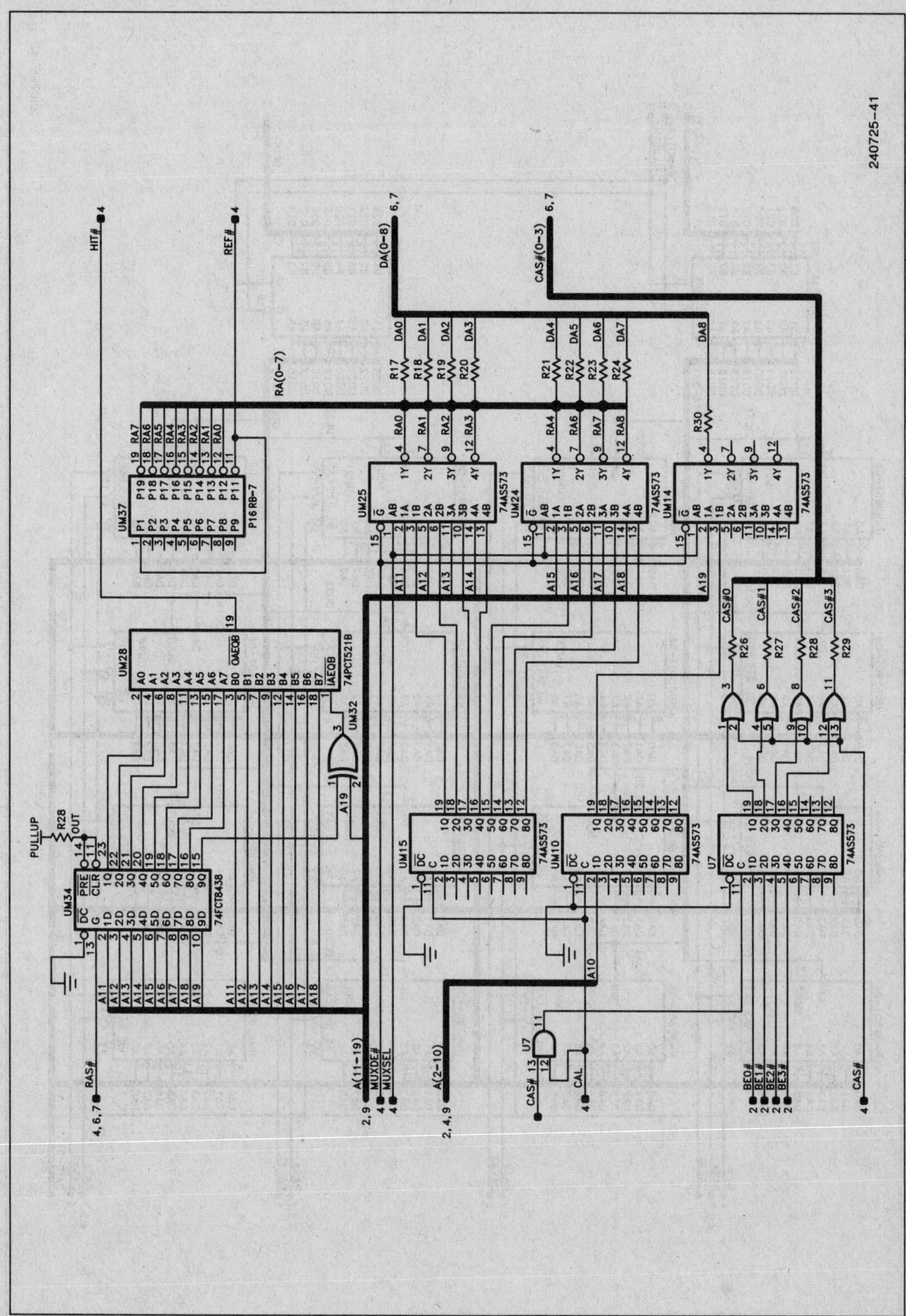
240725-41
HIT#
REF#
DA(0-8)
CAS#(0-3)
RA(0-7)
UM37
P16R8-7
UM28
74PCT521B
UM32
UM34
74FCT8438
PULLUP
R28
OUT
UM25
UM24
UM14
74AS573
UM15
UM10
U7
74AS573
R17
R18
R19
R20
R21
R22
R23
R24
R30
R26
R27
R28
R29
CAS#0
CAS#1
CAS#2
CAS#3
RAS#
A(11-19)
MUXDE#
MUXSEL
A(2-10)
CAS#
CAL
BE0#
BE1#
BE2#
BE3#
A10
A19

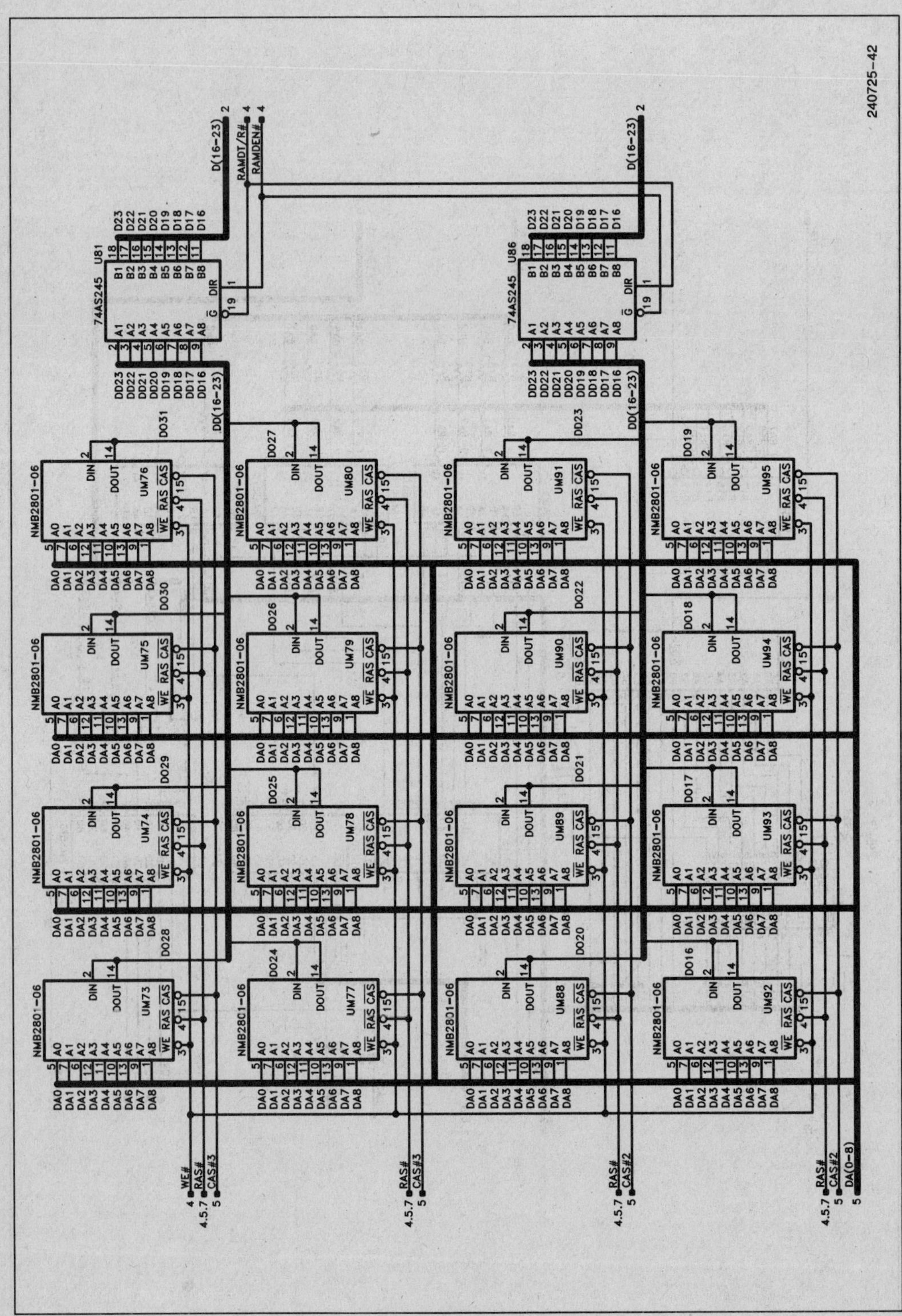

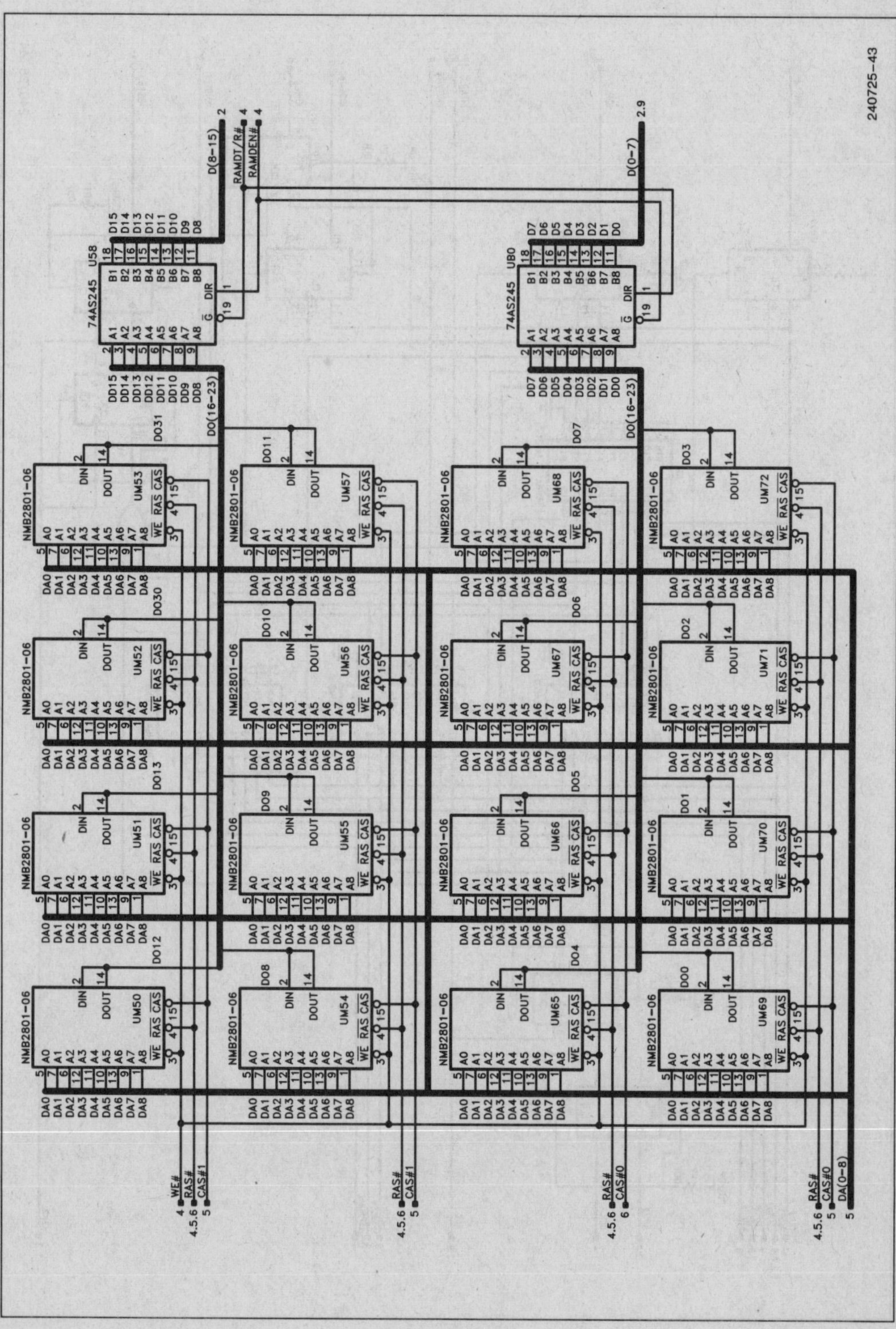

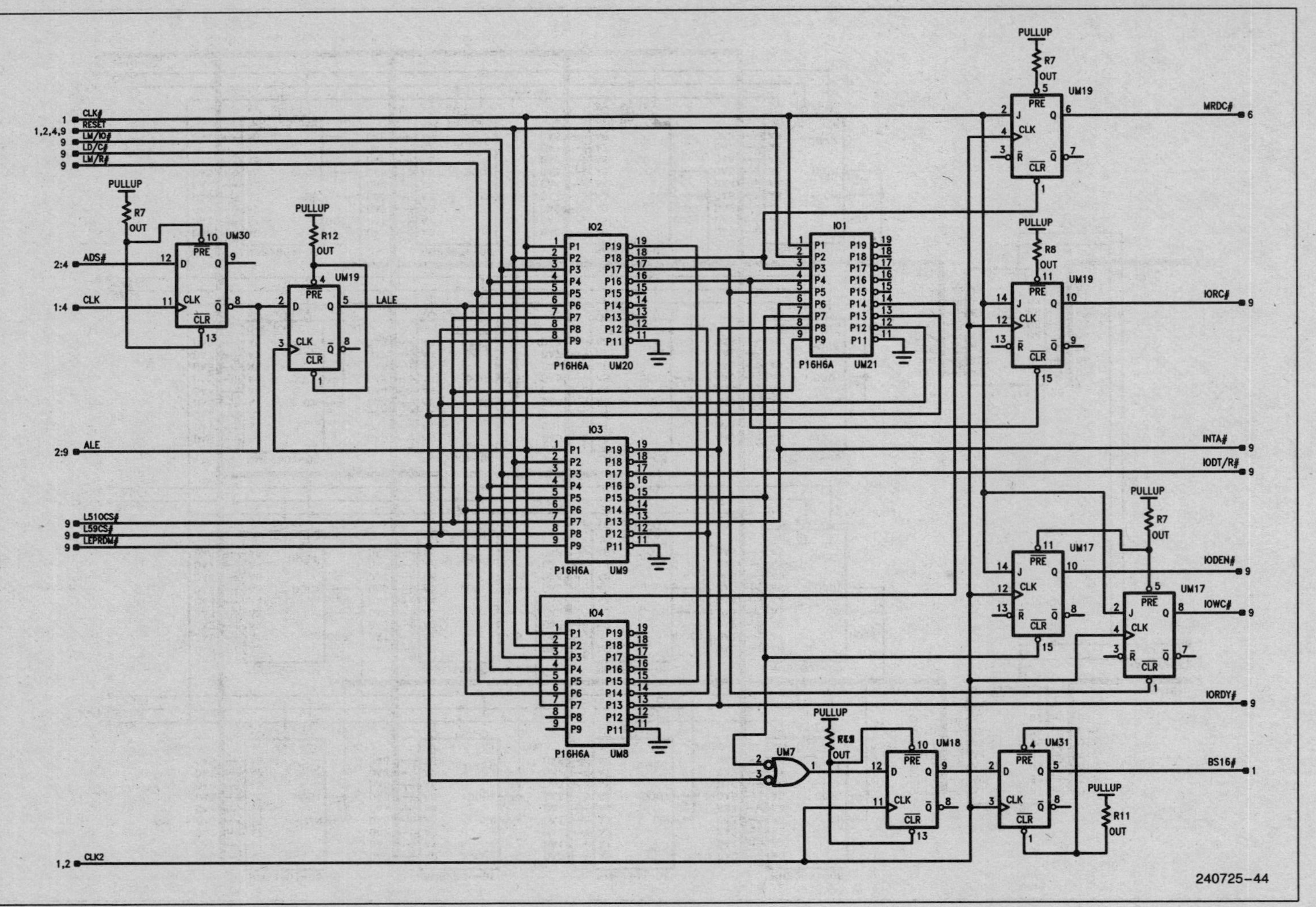
MRDC#
IORC#
INTA#
IODT/R#
IODEN#
IOWC#
IORDY#
BS16#
PULLUP
UM19
UM17
UM31
UM18
UM7
UM30
UM21
UM20
UM9
UM8
IO1
IO2
IO3
IO4
P16H6A
LALE
CLK#
RESET
LM/IO#
LD/C#
LM/R#
ADS#
CLK
ALE
L510CS#
L59CS#
LEPROM#
CLK2

240725-44

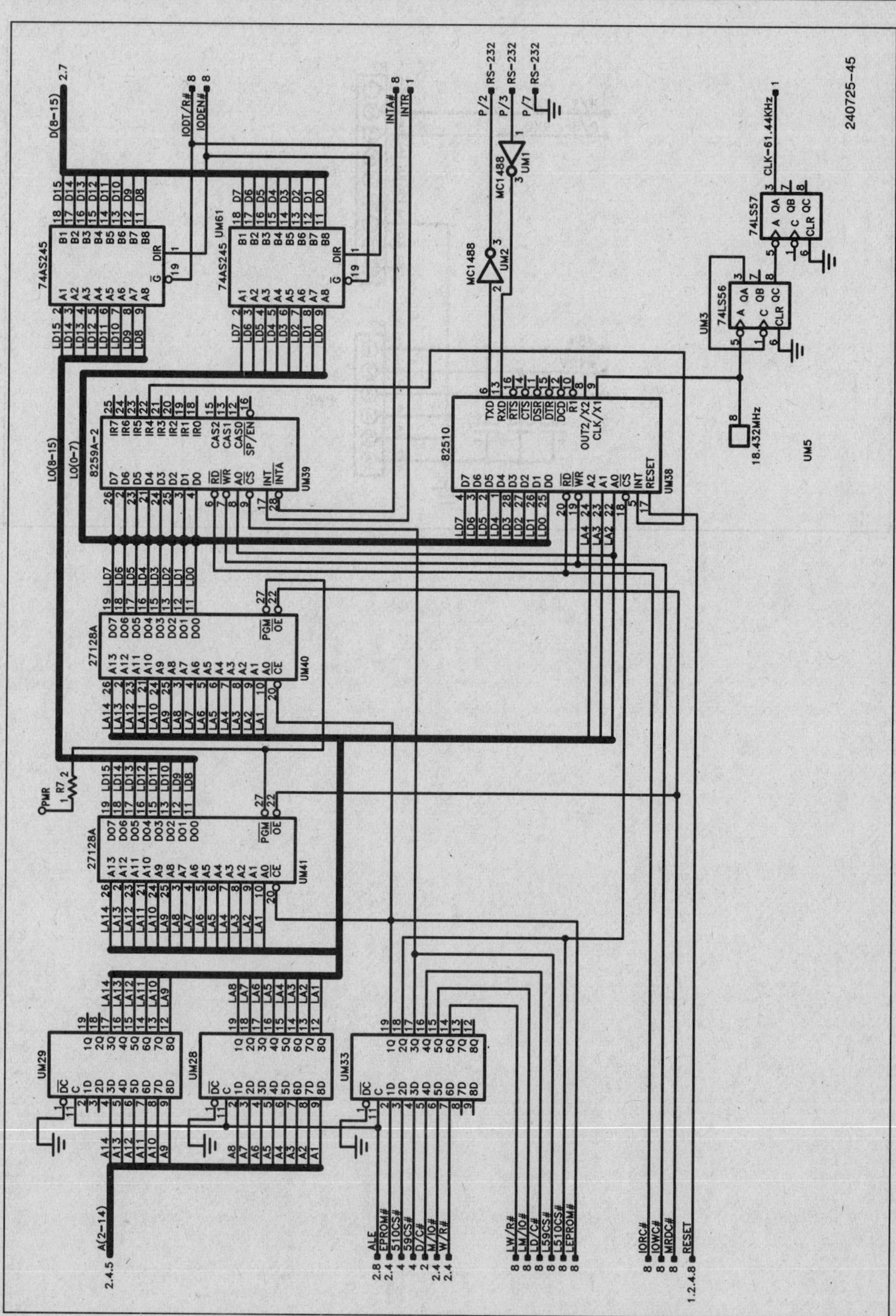
240725-45

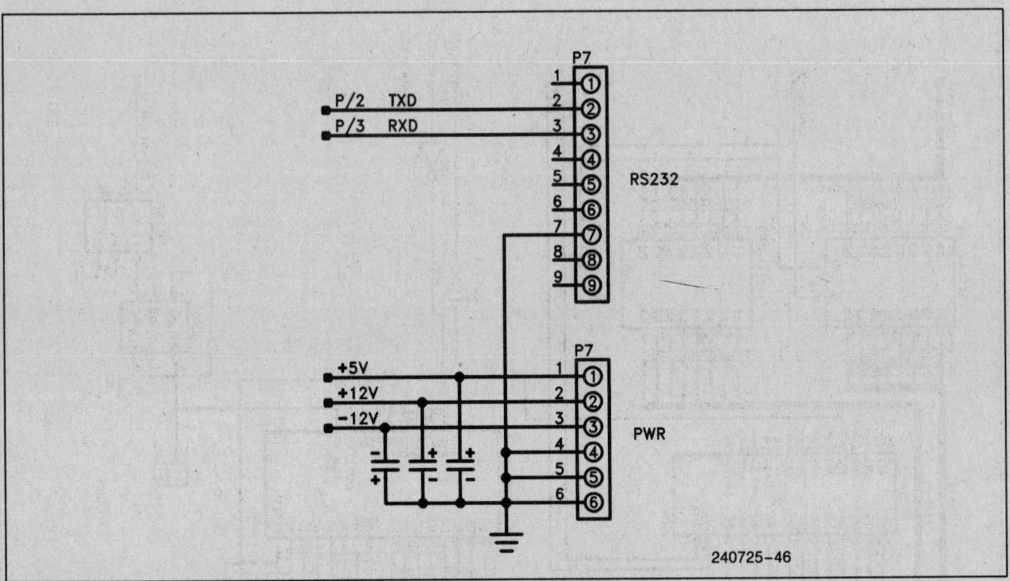
P7
P/2 TXD
P/3 RXD
RS232
P7
+5V
+12V
-12V
PWR
240725-46

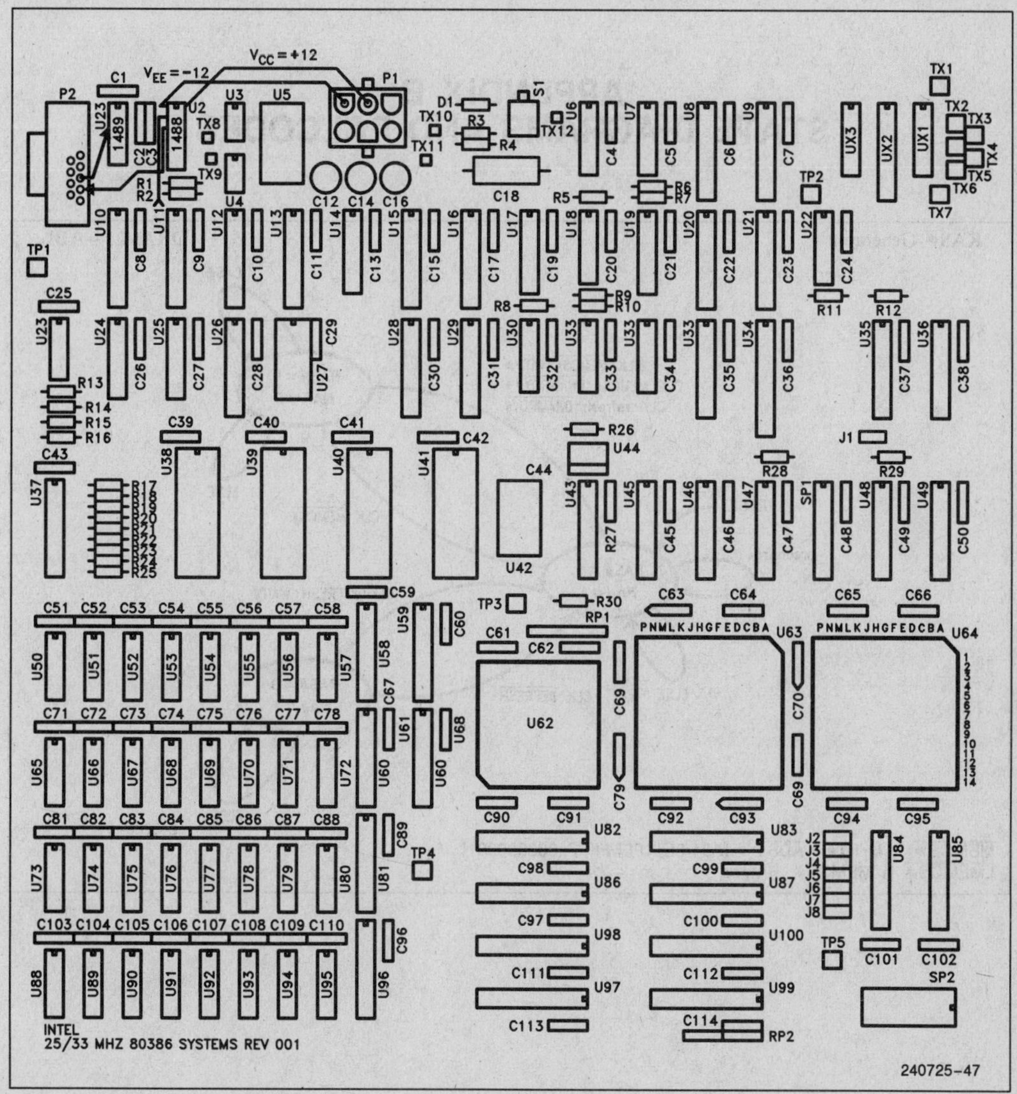
V_{CC} = +12
V_{EE} = −12
INTEL
25/33 MHZ 80386 SYSTEMS REV 001
240725-47

APPENDIX B
STATE DIAGRAMS AND PALCODES

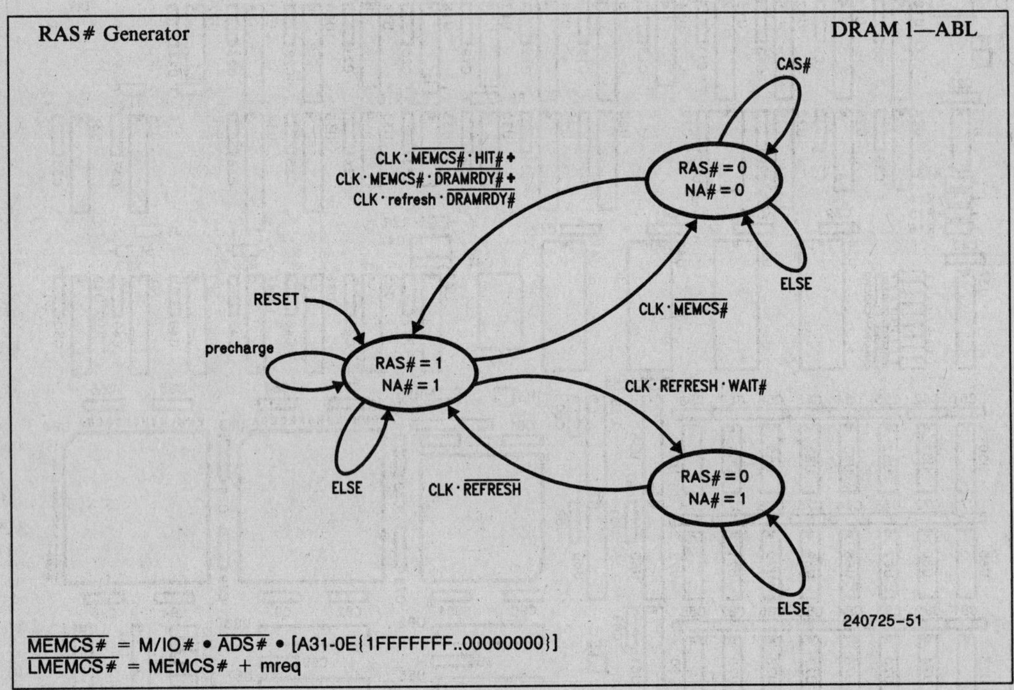

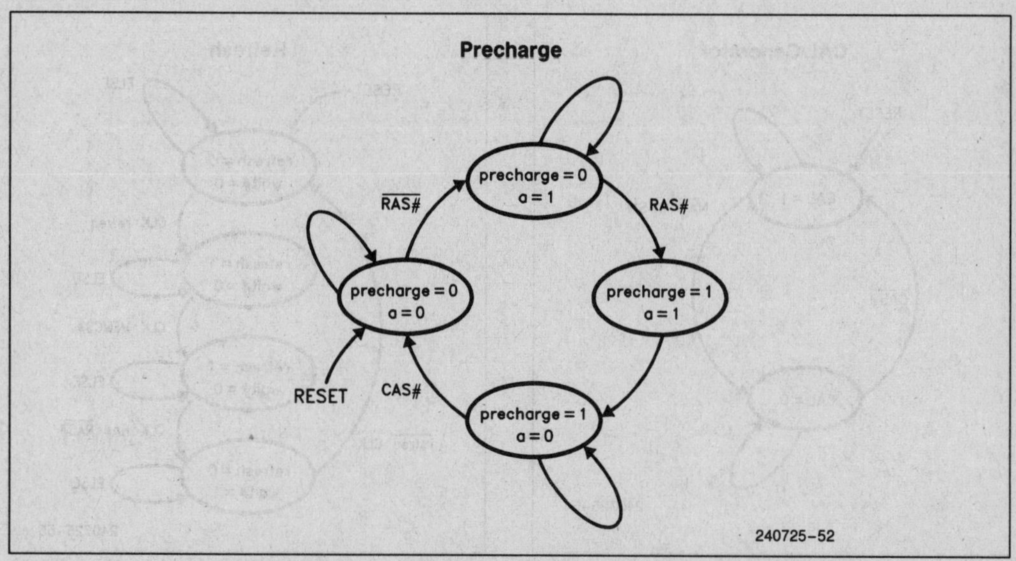

240725-52

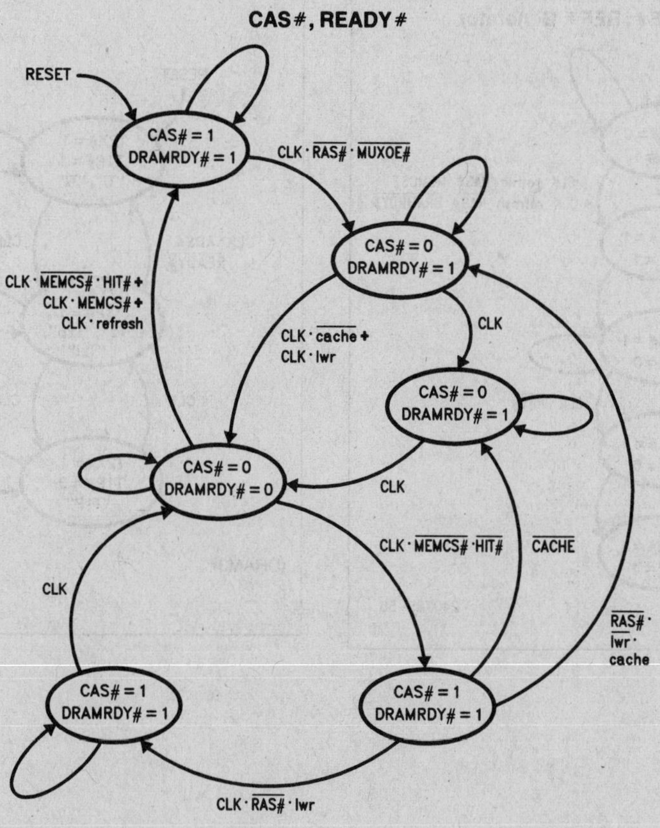

CAS#, READY#

RESET
CAS# = 1
DRAMRDY# = 1
CLK · $\overline{\text{RAS\#}}$ · $\overline{\text{MUXOE\#}}$
CAS# = 0
DRAMRDY# = 1
CLK · $\overline{\text{MEMCS\#}}$ · HIT# +
CLK · MEMCS# +
CLK · refresh
CLK · $\overline{\text{cache}}$ +
CLK · lwr
CLK
CAS# = 0
DRAMRDY# = 1
CAS# = 0
DRAMRDY# = 0
CLK
CLK · $\overline{\text{MEMCS\#}}$ · $\overline{\text{HIT\#}}$
$\overline{\text{CACHE}}$
CLK
$\overline{\text{RAS\#}}$ ·
$\overline{\text{lwr}}$ ·
cache
CAS# = 1
DRAMRDY# = 1
CAS# = 1
DRAMRDY# = 1
CLK · $\overline{\text{RAS\#}}$ · lwr

240725-53

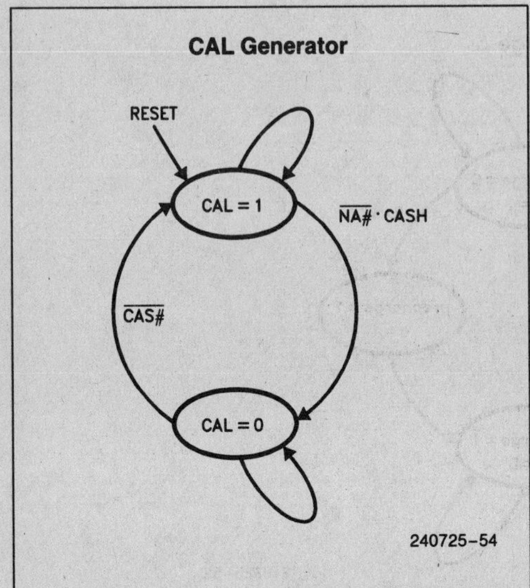
CAL Generator
RESET
CAL = 1
NA# · CASH
CAS#
CAL = 0
240725-54

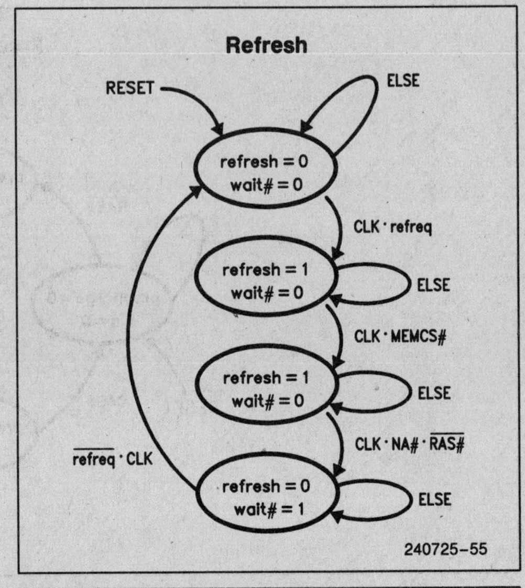
Refresh
RESET
ELSE
refresh = 0
wait# = 0
CLK · refreq
refresh = 1
wait# = 0
ELSE
CLK · MEMCS#
refresh = 1
wait# = 0
ELSE
CLK · NA# · RAS#
refreq · CLK
refresh = 0
wait# = 1
ELSE
240725-55

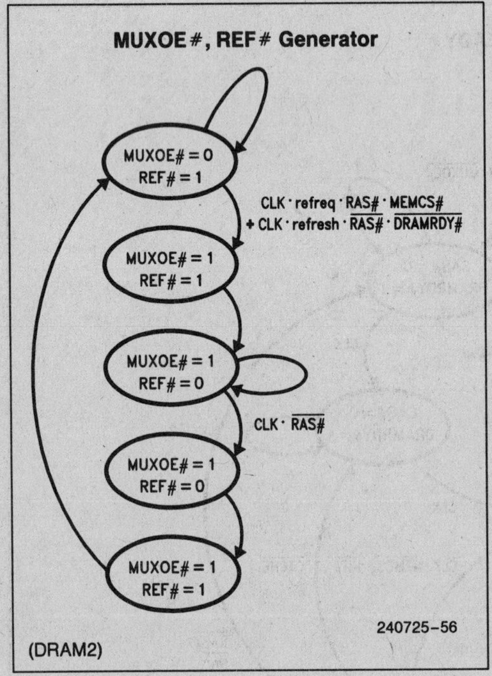
MUXOE#, REF# Generator
MUXOE# = 0
REF# = 1
CLK · refreq · RAS# · MEMCS#
+ CLK · refresh · RAS# · DRAMRDY#
MUXOE# = 1
REF# = 1
MUXOE# = 1
REF# = 0
CLK · RAS#
MUXOE# = 1
REF# = 0
MUXOE# = 1
REF# = 1
240725-56
(DRAM2)

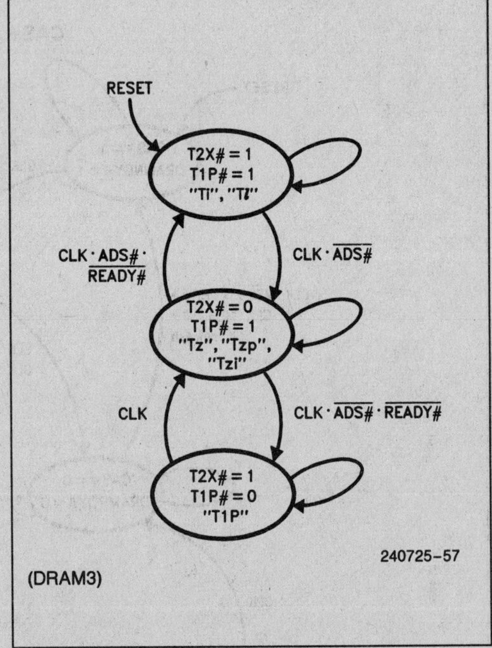
RESET
T2X# = 1
T1P# = 1
"Ti", "T2"
CLK · ADS# · READY#
CLK · ADS#
T2X# = 0
T1P# = 1
"Tz", "Tzp", "Tzi"
CLK
CLK · ADS# · READY#
T2X# = 1
T1P# = 0
"T1P"
240725-57
(DRAM3)

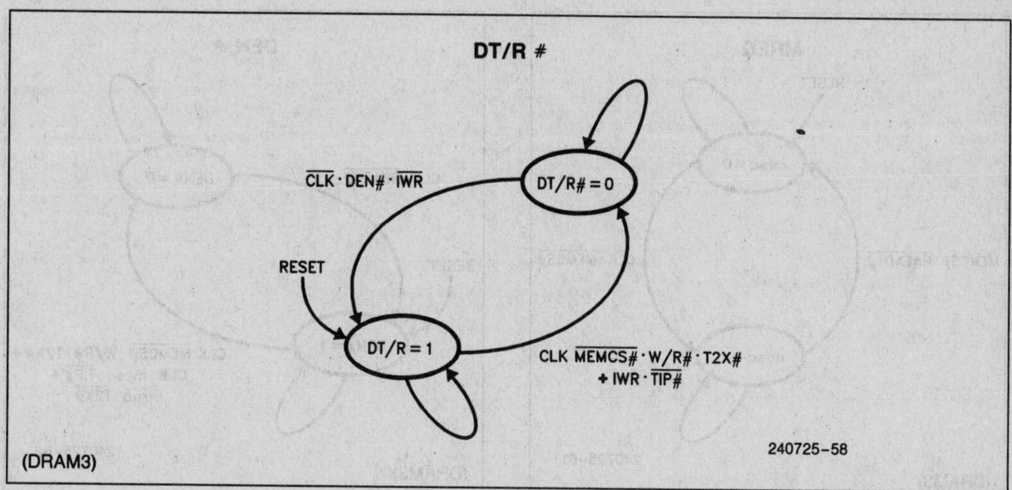

(DRAM3) 240725-58

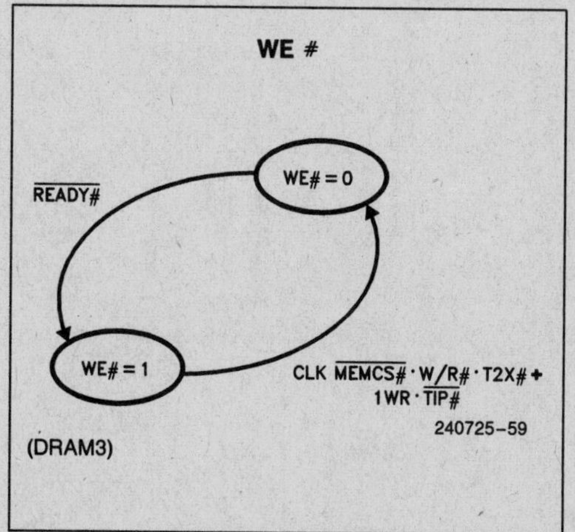

(DRAM3) 240725-59

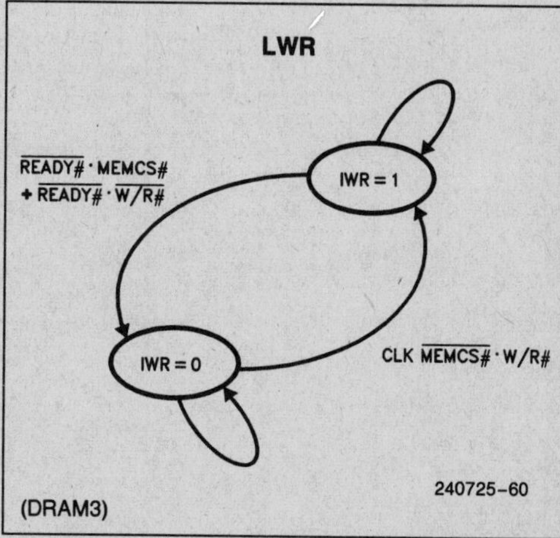

(DRAM3) 240725-60

4

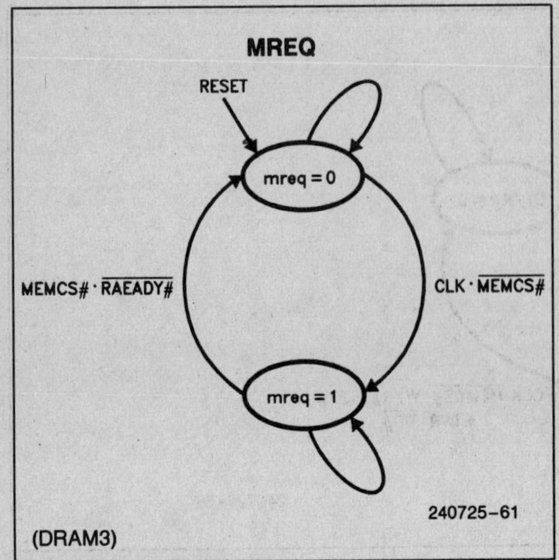

240725-61

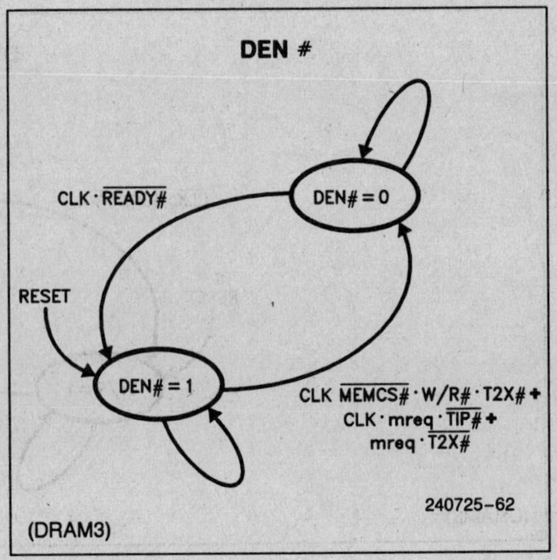

240725-62

```
module        RESET_GEN flag '-r3'

title   'RESET_GENERATION_LOGIC - INTEL CORPORATION'

    RESET_PAL     device       'P16R8';

    x = .X.;            "ABEL don't care symbol
    c = .C.;            "ABEL clocking input sybol

" Inputs

    CLK2    pin   1;   "CLK2
    RESTRIG pin   2;   "signal from reset circuitry
    CLK_61  pin   9;   "61.44KHz clock

" Outputs

    REFREQ  pin  12;   "REFREQ, sync 61.44KHz clock
    RFQTMP  pin  13;   "temporary stage in sync of 61.44MHz clk
    CLK-    pin  16;   "CLK#
    CLK     pin  17;   "CLK = CLK2 / 2
    RESTMP  pin  18;   "temporary stage in generating RESET
    RESET   pin  19;   "RESET

equations

    CLK := (!CLK # (!RESTMP & RESET));
    CLK- := CLK;
    RESTMP := RESTRIG;
    RESET := RESTMP;
    RFQTMP := CLK_61;
    REFREQ := RFQTMP;

 test_vectors

    ([CLK2, CLK_61, RESTRIG, CLK, CLK-, RESTMP, RESET, RFQTMP, REFREQ] ->
     [CLK, CLK-, RESTMP, RESET, RFQTMP, REFREQ])

"    C  C  R  C  C  R  R  R  R      C  C  R  R  R  R
"    L  L  E  L  L  E  E  F  E      L  L  E  E  F  E
"    K  K  S  K  K  S  S  Q  F      K  K  S  S  Q  F
"    2  _  T     -  T  E  T  R         -  T  E  T  R
"       6  R        M  T  M  E            M  T  M  E
"       1  I        P     P  Q            P     P  Q
"          G

    [c, x, 1, x, x, x, x, x, x] -> [x, x, 1, x, x, x];
    [c, x, 1, x, x, 1, x, x, x] -> [x, x, 1, 1, x, x];
    [c, x, 0, x, x, 1, x, x, x] -> [x, x, 0, 1, x, x];

    [c, x, x, x, x, 0, 1, x, x] -> [1, x, x, x, x, x];  " clk generation
    [c, x, x, 1, x, x, 0, x, x] -> [0, 1, x, x, x, x];
    [c, x, x, 0, x, x, x, x, x] -> [1, 0, x, x, x, x];
```

240725-48

PAL Codes: RESET

4

```
    [c, x, x, 1, x, 1, x, x, x] -> [0, 1, x, x, x, x];

    [c, x, 0, x, x, x, x, x, x] -> [x, x, 0, x, x, x];  " restmp gen
    [c, x, x, x, x, 0, x, x, x] -> [x, x, x, 0, x, x];  " reset gen
    [c, x, 1, x, x, x, x, x, x] -> [x, x, 1, x, x, x];

    [c, x, x, x, x, 1, x, x, x] -> [x, x, x, 1, x, x];

    [c, 0, x, x, x, x, x, x, x] -> [x, x, x, x, 0, x];  " 61.44KHz clk
    [c, x, x, x, x, x, x, 0, x] -> [x, x, x, x, x, 0];
    [c, 1, x, x, x, x, x, x, x] -> [x, x, x, x, 1, x];
    [c, x, x, x, x, x, x, 1, x] -> [x, x, x, x, x, 1];

end RESET_GEN;
```

240725-49

```
ABEL(tm) 3.10  -  Document Generator            14-Feb-90 09:53 AM
RESET_GENERATION_LOGIC - INTEL CORPORATION
Equations for Module RESET_GEN

Device RESET_PAL

- Reduced Equations:

    !CLK := (CLK & !RESET # CLK & RESTMP);

    !CLK~ := (!CLK);

    !RESTMP := (!RESTRIG);

    !RESET := (!RESTMP);

    !RFQTMP := (!CLK_61);

    !REFREQ := (!RFQTMP);
```

240725-D4

PAL Codes: RESET (Continued)

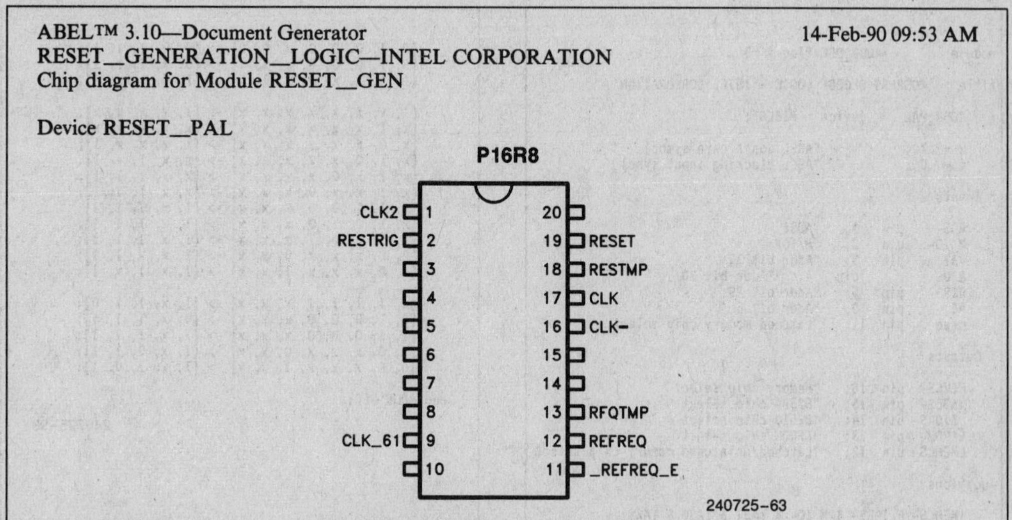

ABEL™ 3.10—Document Generator
14-Feb-90 09:53 AM
RESET_GENERATION_LOGIC—INTEL CORPORATION
Chip diagram for Module RESET_GEN
Device RESET_PAL
P16R8
CLK2 1
RESTRIG 2
3
4
5
6
7
8
CLK_61 9
10
20
19 RESET
18 RESTMP
17 CLK
16 CLK-
15
14
13 RFQTMP
12 REFREQ
11 _REFREQ_E
240725-63

PAL Codes: RESET (Continued)

```
module         ADDR_DEC flag '-r3'

title   'ADDRESS_DECODE_LOGIC - INTEL CORPORATION'

    ADDR_PAL      device   'P16L8';

    x = .X.;             "ABEL don't care symbol
    c = .C.;             "ABEL clocking input sybol

" Inputs

    ADS~     pin   1;    "ADS#
    M_IO~    pin   2;    "M/IO#
    A31      pin   3;    "Addr bit 31
    A30            pin   4;   "Addr bit 30
    A29      pin   5;    "Addr bit 29
    A6       pin   9;    "Addr bit 6
    mreq     pin  11;    "Latched memory chip select

" Outputs

    MEMCS~  pin  18;     "Memory chip select
    _59CS~  pin  15;     "8259A chip select
    _510CS~ pin  14;     "82510 chip select
    EPRDM~  pin  13;     "EPROM chip select
    LMEMCS~ pin  12;     "Latched/unlatched memory chip select

equations

    !MEMCS~ = !ADS~ & M_IO~ & !A31 & !A30 & !A29;
    !LMEMCS~ = (!ADS~ & M_IO~ & !A31 & !A30 & !A29) # mreq;
    !_59CS~ = !M_IO~ & !A6;
    !_510CS~ = !M_IO~ & A6;
    !EPRDM~ =  M_IO~ & A31 & A30 & A29;


 test_vectors

    ([ADS~, M_IO~, A31, A30, A29, A6, mreq, MEMCS~] ->
     [MEMCS~, LMEMCS~, _59CS~, _510CS~, EPRDM~])

"    A  M  A  A  A  A  m  M      M  L  5  5  E
"    D  _  3  3  2  6  r  E      E  M  9  1  P
"    S  I  1  0  9     e  M      M  E  C  0  R
"    ~  O              q  C      C  M  S  C  D
"       ~                 S      S  C  ~  S  M
"                         ~      ~  S     ~  ~
"                                   ~
"

    [1, x, x, x, x, x, 0, 1] -> [1, 1, x, x, x];

    [1, x, x, x, x, x, 1, 1] -> [1, 0, x, x, x];  "LMEMCS~
    [0, 1, 0, 0, 0, x, x, x] -> [0, x, 1, 1, 1];
```

240725-92

```
    [0, 1, 0, 0, 0, x, 0, 0] -> [0, 0, 1, 1, 1];
    [0, 1, 0, 0, 0, x, x, x] -> [0, x, 1, 1, 1];
    [1, x, x, x, x, x, 1, 0] -> [1, 0, x, x, x];

    [1, x, x, x, x, x, x, x] -> [1, x, x, x, x];  "---CS~
    [x, 1, x, x, x, x, x, x] -> [x, x, 1, 1, x];
    [x, 0, x, x, x, x, x, x] -> [1, x, x, x, 1];
    [x, 1, 0, x, x, x, x, x] -> [x, x, 1, 1, 1];
    [x, 1, x, 0, x, x, x, x] -> [x, x, 1, 1, 1];
    [x, 1, x, x, 0, x, x, x] -> [x, x, 1, 1, 1];
    [x, 1, 1, 0, 0, x, x, x] -> [1, x, 1, 1, 1];
    [x, 1, 0, 1, 0, x, x, x] -> [1, x, 1, 1, 1];
    [x, 1, 0, 0, 1, x, x, x] -> [1, x, 1, 1, 1];
    [x, 0, x, x, x, 0, x, x] -> [1, x, x, 1, 1];
    [x, 0, x, x, x, 1, x, x] -> [1, x, 1, x, 1];

    [x, 1, 1, 1, 1, x, x, x] -> [1, x, 1, 1, 0];
    [0, 1, 0, 0, 0, x, x, x] -> [0, x, 1, 1, 1];
    [1, 1, 0, 0, 0, x, x, x] -> [1, x, 1, 1, 1];
    [0, 0, x, x, x, 0, x, x] -> [1, x, 0, 1, 1];
    [0, 0, x, x, x, 1, x, x] -> [1, x, 1, 0, 1];

end ADDR_DEC;
```

240725-93

PAL Codes: Address Decoder

```
ABEL(tm) 3.10  -  Document Generator                14-Feb-90 09:50 AM
ADDRESS_DECODE_LOGIC - INTEL CORPORATION
Equations for Module ADDR_DEC

Device ADDR_PAL

- Reduced Equations:

    !MEMCS~ = (!A29 & !A30 & !A31 & !ADS~ & M_IO~);

    !LMEMCS~ = (mreq # !A29 & !A30 & !A31 & !ADS~ & M_IO~);

    !_59CS~ = (!A6 & !M_IO~);

    !_510CS~ = (A6 & !M_IO~);

    !EPRDM~ = (A29 & A30 & A31 & M_IO~);
```

240725-D5

PAL Codes: Address Decoder (Continued)

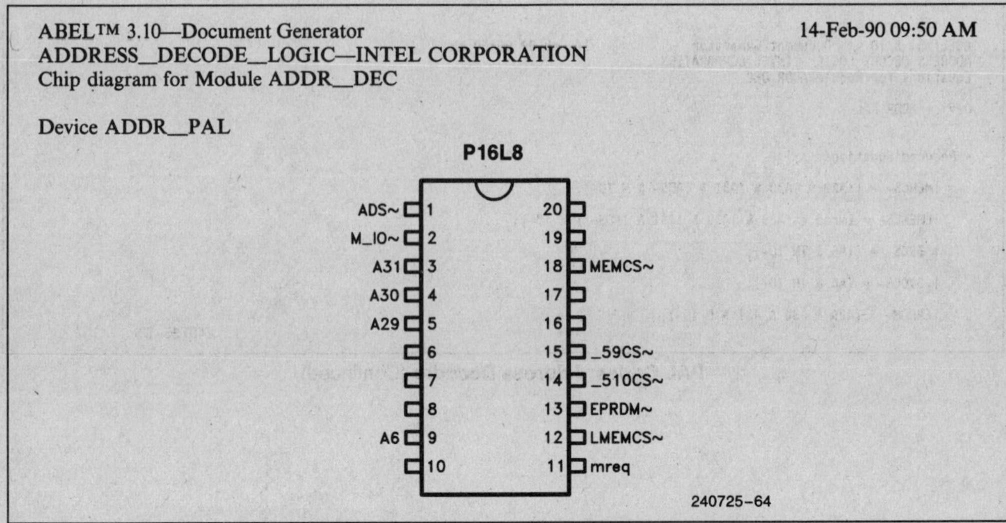

PAL Codes: Address Decoder (Continued)

```
module        PAGE_MODE_DRAM_CTRL_1  flag '-r3'

title   'PAGE MODE DRAM CONTROLLER - PAL 1, INTEL CORPORATION'

    PAGE1    device      'P16R8';

    x        =     .X.;         " ABEL 'don't care' symbol
    c        =     .C.;         " ABEL 'clocking input' symbol

" Inputs

    CLK2     pin   1;    "80386 CLK2
    CLK      pin   2;    "Processor Clock
    MEMCS~   pin   3;    "Memory Chip Select
    LMEMCS~  pin   4;    "Latched/Unlatched Memory Chip Select
    HIT~     pin   5;    "DRAM Page Hit Signal
    CAS~     pin   6;    "Column Address Strobe
    DRAMRDY~       pin   7;   "DRAM Ready Signal
    refreq   pin   8;    "Refresh Request Signal
    RESET    pin   9;    "System Reset

" Outputs

    RAS~     pin   12;    "Row Address Strobe
    NA~      pin   13;    "Next Address Signal
    precharge      pin  14;    "RAS Precharge Signal
    a        pin   15;
    wait~    pin   16;    "delays RAS~ until refresh adress is valid
    CAL      pin   17;    "Column Address Latch
    refresh  pin   18;    "Refresh Signal (active once refresh is acknowledged.)

    unused   pin   19;    "

state_diagram [RAS~, NA~]

    state [1, 1]:    if precharge then [1, 1] else
                  if (CLK & refresh & wait~) then [0, 1] else
                  if (CLK & !LMEMCS~& !refresh) then [0, 0] else [1, 1];
    state [0, 0]:    if RESET then [1, 1] else
                  if CAS~ then [0, 0] else
                  if (CLK & !MEMCS~ & HIT~ #
                    CLK & MEMCS~ & !DRAMRDY~ #
                    CLK & refresh & !DRAMRDY~) then [1, 1] else [0, 0];
    state [0, 1]:    if RESET then [1, 1] else
                  if (CLK & !refresh) then [1, 1] else [0, 1];
    state [1, 0]:    goto [1, 1];

state_diagram [precharge, a]

    state [0, 0]:    if (!RAS~) then [0, 1] else [0, 0];
    state [0, 1]:    if (RESET) then [0, 0] else
                  if (RAS~) then [1, 1] else [0, 1];
    state [1, 1]:    goto [1, 0];
    state [1, 0]:    if (CAS~) then [0, 0] else [1, 0];
```

240725-94

PAL Codes: DRAM 1

```
state_diagram [CAL]

    state [1]:      if (!NA~ & CAS~) then [0] else [1];
    state [0]:      if (RESET) then [1] else
              if (!CAS~) then [1] else [0];

state_diagram [refresh, wait~]

    state[0, 0]:    if (CLK & refreq) then [1, 0] else [0, 0];
    state[1, 0]:    if (RESET) then [0,0] else
                        if (CLK & MEMCS~) then [1, 1] else [1, 0];
    state[1, 1]:    if (RESET) then [0,0] else
                        if (CLK & NA~ & !RAS~) then [0, 1] else [1, 1];
    state[0, 1]:    if (RESET) then [0,0] else
                        if (CLK & !refreq) then [0, 0] else [0, 1];

test_vectors

    ([CLK2,CLK,MEMCS~,LMEMCS~,HIT~,CAS~,DRAMRDY~,refreq,RESET] ->
     [RAS~,NA~,precharge,CAL,refresh])

"    C  C  M  L  H  C  D  r  R     R  N  p  C  r
"    L  L  E  M  I  A  R  e  E     A  A  r  A  e
"    K  K  M  E  T  S  A  f  S     S  ~  e  L  f
"    2     C  M  ~  ~  M  r  E     ~     c     r
"          S  C        R  e  T           h     e
"          ~  S        D  q              a     s
"             ~        Y                 r     h
"                      ~                 g
"                                        e

    [c, x, x, x, x, x, 1, x, 1] -> [1, 1, x, 1, 0];
    [c, x, x, x, x, x, 1, x, 1] -> [1, 1, x, 1, 0];
    [c, 1, 1, 1, x, 1, 1, 0, 0] -> [1, 1, x, 1, 0]; "Ti, phase 1
    [c, 0, 1, 1, x, 1, 1, 0, 0] -> [1, 1, x, 1, 0]; "    phase 2
    [c, 1, 1, 1, x, 1, 1, 0, 0] -> [1, 1, x, 1, 0]; "T1, Read, Non-Pipelined
    [c, 0, 0, 0, x, 1, 1, 0, 0] -> [1, 1, 0, 1, 0];
    [c, 1, 0, 0, x, 1, 1, 0, 0] -> [0, 0, 0, 1, 0]; "T2
    [c, 0, 1, 0, x, 1, 1, 0, 0] -> [0, 0, 0, 0, 0];
    [c, 1, 1, 0, x, 1, 1, 0, 0] -> [0, 0, 0, 0, 0]; "T2P
    [c, 0, 0, 0, x, 0, 1, 0, 0] -> [0, 0, 0, 1, 0]; "      Page Hit
    [c, 1, 0, 0, 0, 0, 1, 0, 0] -> [0, 0, 0, 1, 0]; "T2P
    [c, 0, 0, 0, 0, 0, 0, 0, 0] -> [0, 0, 0, 1, 0];
    [c, 1, 0, 0, 0, 0, 0, 0, 0] -> [0, 0, 0, 1, 0]; "T1P, Read, Pipelined
    [c, 0, 1, 0, 0, 1, 1, 0, 0] -> [0, 0, 0, 0, 0];
    [c, 1, 1, 0, 0, 0, 1, 0, 0] -> [0, 0, 0, 1, 0]; "T2P
    [c, 0, 0, 0, 0, 0, 0, 0, 0] -> [0, 0, 0, 1, 0];
    [c, 1, 0, 0, 0, 0, 0, 0, 0] -> [0, 0, 0, 1, 0]; "T1P, Write
    [c, 0, 1, 0, 0, 1, 1, 0, 0] -> [0, 0, 0, 0, 0];
    [c, 1, 1, 0, 0, 1, 1, 0, 0] -> [0, 0, 0, 0, 0]; "T2P
    [c, 0, 0, 0, 0, 1, 1, 0, 0] -> [0, 0, 0, 0, 0];
    [c, 1, 0, 0, 0, 1, 1, 0, 0] -> [0, 0, 0, 0, 0]; "T2P
    [c, 0, 0, 0, 0, 0, 0, 0, 0] -> [0, 0, 0, 1, 0];
```

240725–95

PAL Codes: DRAM 1 (Continued)

```
[c, 1, 0, 0, 0, 0, 0, 0, 0] -> [0, 0, 0, 1, 0]; "T1P
[c, 0, 1, 0, 0, 1, 1, 0, 0] -> [0, 0, 0, 0, 0];
[c, 1, 1, 0, 0, 0, 1, 0, 0] -> [0, 0, 0, 1, 0]; "T2P
[c, 0, 0, 0, 0, 0, 0, 0, 0] -> [0, 0, 0, 1, 0]; "    Page Miss
[c, 1, 0, 0, 1, 0, 0, 0, 0] -> [1, 1, 0, 1, 0]; "T1P
[c, 0, 1, 0, 1, 1, 1, 0, 0] -> [1, 1, 1, 1, 0];
[c, 1, 1, 0, 1, 1, 1, 0, 0] -> [1, 1, 1, 1, 0]; "T2
[c, 0, 1, 0, 1, 1, 1, 0, 0] -> [1, 1, 0, 1, 0];
[c, 1, 1, 0, 1, 1, 1, 0, 0] -> [0, 0, 0, 1, 0]; "T2
[c, 0, 1, 0, 1, 1, 1, 0, 0] -> [0, 0, 0, 0, 0];
[c, 1, 1, 0, 1, 1, 1, 0, 0] -> [0, 0, 0, 0, 0]; "T2P
[c, 0, 0, 0, x, 0, 1, 0, 0] -> [0, 0, 0, 1, 0];
[c, 1, 0, 0, 1, 0, 1, 0, 0] -> [1, 1, 0, 1, 0]; "T2P
[c, 0, 0, 0, 1, 0, 0, 0, 0] -> [1, 1, 1, 1, 0];
[c, 1, 0, 0, 1, 0, 0, 0, 0] -> [1, 1, 1, 1, 0]; "T1P
[c, 0, 1, 0, 1, 1, 1, 0, 0] -> [1, 1, 0, 1, 0];
[c, 1, 1, 0, 1, 1, 1, 0, 0] -> [0, 0, 0, 1, 0]; "T2
[c, 0, 1, 0, 1, 1, 1, 0, 0] -> [0, 0, 0, 0, 0];
[c, 1, 1, 0, 1, 1, 1, 0, 0] -> [0, 0, 0, 0, 0]; "T2P
[c, 0, 0, 0, 1, 0, 1, 0, 0] -> [0, 0, 0, 1, 0];
[c, 1, 0, 0, 0, 0, 1, 0, 0] -> [0, 0, 0, 1, 0]; "T2P
[c, 0, 0, 0, 0, 0, 0, 0, 0] -> [0, 0, 0, 1, 0];
[c, 1, 0, 0, 0, 0, 0, 0, 0] -> [0, 0, 0, 1, 0]; "T1P
[c, 0, 1, 0, 0, 1, 1, 0, 0] -> [0, 0, 0, 0, 0];
[c, 1, 1, 0, 0, 0, 1, 0, 0] -> [0, 0, 0, 1, 0]; "T2P
[c, 0, 0, 0, 0, 0, 0, 0, 0] -> [0, 0, 0, 1, 0];
[c, 1, 0, 0, 0, 0, 0, 0, 0] -> [0, 0, 0, 1, 0]; "T1P
[c, 0, 1, 0, 0, 1, 1, 0, 0] -> [0, 0, 0, 0, 0];
[c, 1, 1, 0, 0, 0, 1, 0, 0] -> [0, 0, 0, 1, 0]; "T2i
[c, 0, 1, 0, 0, 0, 0, 0, 0] -> [0, 0, 0, 1, 0];
[c, 1, 1, 1, 0, 0, 0, 0, 0] -> [1, 1, 0, 1, 0]; "T1
[c, 0, 0, 0, x, 1, 1, 0, 0] -> [1, 1, 1, 1, 0];
[c, 1, 0, 0, x, 1, 1, 0, 0] -> [1, 1, 1, 1, 0]; "T2
[c, 0, 1, 0, x, 1, 1, 0, 0] -> [1, 1, 0, 1, 0];
[c, 1, 1, 0, x, 1, 1, 0, 0] -> [0, 0, 0, 1, 0]; "T2
[c, 0, 1, 0, x, 1, 1, 0, 0] -> [0, 0, 0, 0, 0];
[c, 1, 1, 0, x, 1, 1, 0, 0] -> [0, 0, 0, 0, 0]; "T2P
[c, 0, 0, 0, x, 0, 1, 0, 0] -> [0, 0, 0, 1, 0];
[c, 1, 0, 0, 0, 0, 1, 0, 0] -> [0, 0, 0, 1, 0]; "T2P
[c, 0, 0, 0, 0, 0, 0, 0, 0] -> [0, 0, 0, 1, 0];
[c, 1, 0, 0, 0, 0, 0, 0, 0] -> [0, 0, 0, 1, 0]; "T1P
[c, 0, 1, 0, 0, 1, 1, 0, 0] -> [0, 0, 0, 0, 0];
[c, 1, 1, 0, 0, 0, 1, 0, 0] -> [0, 0, 0, 1, 0]; "T2P
[c, 0, 0, 0, 0, 0, 0, 0, 0] -> [0, 0, 0, 1, 0];
[c, 1, 0, 0, 0, 0, 0, 0, 0] -> [0, 0, 0, 1, 0]; "T1P
[c, 0, 1, 0, 0, 1, 1, 1, 0] -> [0, 0, 0, 0, 0];
[c, 1, 1, 0, 0, 0, 1, 1, 0] -> [0, 0, 0, 1, 1]; "T2P
[c, 0, 0, 0, 0, 0, 0, 1, 0] -> [0, 0, 0, 1, 1];
[c, 1, 0, 0, 0, 0, 0, 1, 0] -> [1, 1, 0, 1, 1]; "T1P, Refresh
[c, 0, 1, 0, 0, 1, 1, 1, 0] -> [1, 1, 1, 1, 1];
[c, 1, 1, 0, 0, 1, 1, 1, 0] -> [1, 1, 1, 1, 1]; "T2
[c, 0, 1, 0, 0, 1, 1, 1, 0] -> [1, 1, 0, 1, 1];
[c, 1, 1, 0, 0, 1, 1, 1, 0] -> [0, 1, 0, 1, 1]; "T2
[c, 0, 1, 0, 0, 1, 1, 0, 0] -> [0, 1, 0, 1, 1];
```

240725-96

```
    [c, 1, 1, 0, 0, 1, 1, 0, 0] -> [0, 1, 0, 1, 0]; "T2
    [c, 0, 1, 0, 0, 1, 1, 0, 0] -> [0, 1, 0, 1, 0];
    [c, 1, 1, 0, 0, 1, 1, 0, 0] -> [1, 1, 0, 1, 0]; "T2, Pending Read
    [c, 0, 1, 0, 0, 1, 1, 0, 0] -> [1, 1, 1, 1, 0];
    [c, 1, 1, 0, 0, 1, 1, 0, 0] -> [1, 1, 1, 1, 0]; "T2
    [c, 0, 1, 0, 0, 1, 1, 0, 0] -> [1, 1, 0, 1, 0];
    [c, 1, 1, 0, 0, 1, 1, 0, 0] -> [0, 0, 0, 1, 0]; "T2
    [c, 0, 1, 0, 0, 1, 1, 0, 0] -> [0, 0, 0, 0, 0];
    [c, 1, 1, 0, 0, 1, 1, 0, 0] -> [0, 0, 0, 0, 0]; "T2P
    [c, 0, 0, 0, 0, 0, 1, 0, 0] -> [0, 0, 0, 1, 0];
    [c, 1, 0, 0, 0, 0, 1, 0, 0] -> [0, 0, 0, 1, 0]; "T2P
    [c, 0, 0, 0, 0, 0, 0, 0, 0] -> [0, 0, 0, 1, 0];
    [c, 1, 0, 0, 0, 0, 0, 0, 0] -> [0, 0, 0, 1, 0]; "T1P

end PAGE_MODE_DRAM_CTRL_1;
```

240725-97

PAL Codes: DRAM 1 (Continued)

```
ABEL(tm) 3.10  -  Document Generator              15-Feb-90 05:47 PM
PAGE MODE DRAM CONTROLLER - PAL 1, INTEL CORPORATION
Equations for Module PAGE_MODE_DRAM_CTRL_1

Device PAGE1


- Reduced Equations:

    !RAS~ := (NA~ & !RAS~ & !RESET & refresh
              # DRAMRDY~ & !HIT~ & !NA~ & !RAS~ & !RESET
              # DRAMRDY~ & MEMCS~ & !NA~ & !RAS~ & !RESET
              # !HIT~ & !MEMCS~ & !NA~ & !RAS~ & !RESET & !refresh
              # !CLK & !RAS~ & !RESET
              # CAS~ & !NA~ & !RAS~ & !RESET
              # CLK & !LMEMCS~ & NA~ & RAS~ & !precharge & !refresh
              # CLK & NA~ & RAS~ & !precharge & refresh & wait~);


    !NA~ := (DRAMRDY~ & !HIT~ & !NA~ & !RAS~ & !RESET
             # DRAMRDY~ & MEMCS~ & !NA~ & !RAS~ & !RESET
             # !HIT~ & !MEMCS~ & !NA~ & !RAS~ & !RESET & !refresh
             # !CLK & !NA~ & !RAS~ & !RESET
             # CAS~ & !NA~ & !RAS~ & !RESET
             # CLK & !LMEMCS~ & NA~ & RAS~ & !precharge & !refresh);


    !precharge := (CAS~ & !a
                   # !RAS~ & !precharge
                   # RESET & !precharge
                   # !a & !precharge);


    !a := (precharge # RESET & a # RAS~ & !a);

    !CAL := (!CAL & CAS~ & !RESET # CAL & CAS~ & !NA~);

    !refresh := (!refresh & wait~
                 # CLK & NA~ & !RAS~ & wait~
                 # RESET & refresh
                 # !refreq & !refresh
                 # !CLK & !refresh);


    !wait~ := (CLK & !refreq & !refresh
               # !MEMCS~ & !wait~
               # !CLK & !wait~
               # RESET
               # !refresh & !wait~);
```

240725-50

PAL Codes: DRAM 1 (Continued)

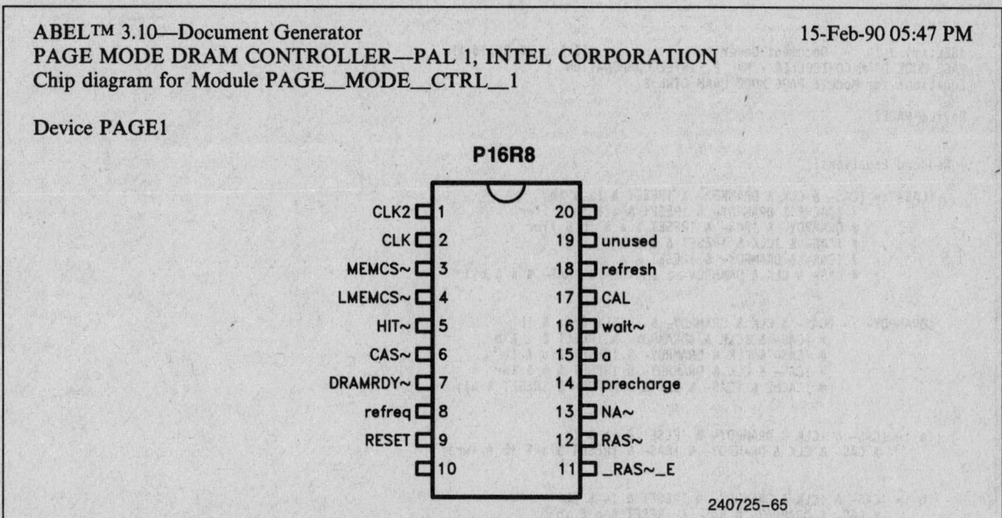
ABEL™ 3.10—Document Generator
15-Feb-90 05:47 PM
PAGE MODE DRAM CONTROLLER—PAL 1, INTEL CORPORATION
Chip diagram for Module PAGE__MODE__CTRL__1
Device PAGE1
P16R8
CLK2 1
CLK 2
MEMCS~ 3
LMEMCS~ 4
HIT~ 5
CAS~ 6
DRAMRDY~ 7
refreq 8
RESET 9
10
20
19 unused
18 refresh
17 CAL
16 wait~
15 a
14 precharge
13 NA~
12 RAS~
11 _RAS~_E
240725-65

PAL Codes: DRAM 1 (Continued)

```
ABEL(tm) 3.10  -  Document Generator                15-Feb-90 06:16 PM
PAGE MODE DRAM CONTROLLER - PAL 2, INTEL CORPORATION
Equations for Module PAGE_MODE_DRAM_CTRL_2

Device PAGE2


- Reduced Equations:

    !CAS~ := (CAS~ & CLK & DRAMRDY~ & !RESET & !a & !b
           # !CACHE & DRAMRDY~ & !RESET & a & !b & !lwr
           # DRAMRDY~ & !RAS~ & !RESET & a & !b & !lwr
           # !CAS~ & !CLK & !RESET & a & b
           # !CAS~ & DRAMRDY~ & !RESET & a
           # CAS~ & CLK & DRAMRDY~ & !MUXOE~ & !RAS~ & a & b);

    !DRAMRDY~ := (CAS~ & CLK & DRAMRDY~ & !RESET & !a & !b
               # !CAS~ & !CLK & !DRAMRDY~ & !RESET & a & b
               # !CAS~ & CLK & DRAMRDY~ & !RESET & a & !b
               # !CAS~ & CLK & DRAMRDY~ & !RESET & a & lwr
               # !CACHE & !CAS~ & CLK & DRAMRDY~ & !RESET & a);

    !a := (CAS~ & !CLK & DRAMRDY~ & !RESET & !a & !b
        # CAS~ & CLK & DRAMRDY~ & !RAS~ & !RESET & a & !b & lwr);

    !b := (CAS~ & !CLK & DRAMRDY~ & !RESET & !a & !b
        # CAS~ & DRAMRDY~ & RAS~ & !RESET & a & !b
        # !CACHE & CAS~ & DRAMRDY~ & !RESET & a & !b
        # CAS~ & DRAMRDY~ & !RESET & a & !b & lwr
        # !CAS~ & CLK & !DRAMRDY~ & !MEMCS~ & !RAS~ & !RESET & a & b &
      !refresh
        # !CAS~ & !CLK & DRAMRDY~ & !RESET & a & !b
        # CACHE & !CAS~ & CLK & DRAMRDY~ & !RESET & a & b & !lwr);

    !MUXOE~ := (!MUXOE~ & !REF~
             # REF~ & !r
             # MUXOE~ & RESET
             # DRAMRDY~ & !MUXOE~ & !RAS~
             # !MEMCS~ & !MUXOE~ & RAS~
             # !MUXOE~ & !refresh
             # !CLK & !MUXOE~);

    !REF~ := (MUXOE~ & !RESET & r);

    !r := (MUXOE~ & !REF~ & !RESET & !r
        # CLK & MUXOE~ & !RAS~ & !REF~ & !RESET);
```

240725–98

PAL Codes: DRAM 2

ABEL™ 3.10—Document Generator 15-Feb-90 06:16 PM
PAGE MODE DRAM CONTROLLER—PAL 2, INTEL CORPORATION
Chip diagram for Module PAGE_MODE_DRAM_CTRL_2

Device PAGE2

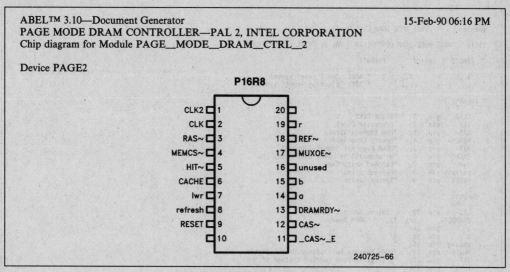

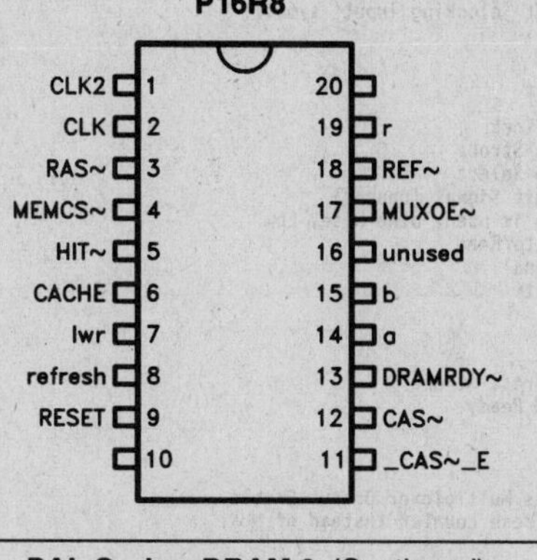

PAL Codes: DRAM 2 (Continued)

```
module        PAGE_MODE_DRAM_CTRL_2  flag '-r3'

title   'PAGE MODE DRAM CONTROLLER - PAL 2, INTEL CORPORATION'

    PAGE2    device      'P16R8';

    x        =     .X.;         " ABEL 'don't care' symbol
    c        =     .C.;         " ABEL 'clocking input' symbol

" Inputs

    CLK2    pin   1;   "80386 CLK2
    CLK     pin   2;   "Processor Clock
    RAS~    pin   3;   "Row Address Strobe
    MEMCS~  pin   4;   "Memory Chip Select
    HIT~    pin   5;   "DRAM Page Hit Signal (unused)
    CACHE   pin   6;   "Hi when 385 is used; otherwise, Low
    lwr     pin   7;   "Latched Write/Read
    refresh pin   8;   "Refresh Signal
    RESET   pin   9;   "System Reset

" Outputs

    CAS~    pin  12;    "Column Address Strobe
    DRAMRDY~     pin  13;    "DRAM Ready
    a       pin  14;    "
    b       pin  15;    "
    unused  pin  16;    "
    MUXOE~  pin  17;    "DRAM Address Multiplexer Output Enable
    REF~    pin  18;    "Enables refresh counter instead of MUX
    r       pin  19;

    cstate  =  [CAS~, DRAMRDY~,a, b];
    idle    =  [ 1 ,  1     ,1, 1];  "Idle
    start   =  [ 0 ,  1     ,1, 1];  "CAS~ Active
    wait    =  [ 0,   1     ,1, 0];  "CAS~ Active, Wait State
    active  =  [ 0 ,  0     ,1, 1];  "CAS~ and DRAMRDY~ Active
    inactive_1    = [ 1 ,  1     ,1,  0];    "Page Hit,  CAS~  and  DRAMRDY-
Inactive
    inactive_2    = [ 1 ,  1     ,0,  0];    "Page Hit,  CAS~  and  DRAMRDY-
Inactive
    illegal_a    =  [0,0,0,0];
    illegal_b    =  [0,0,0,1];
    illegal_c    =  [0,0,1,0];
    illegal_d    =  [0,1,0,0];
    illegal_e    =  [0,1,0,1];
    illegal_f    =  [1,0,0,1];
    illegal_g    =  [1,0,1,0];
    illegal_h    =  [1,0,1,1];
    illegal_i    =  [1,1,0,1];
    illegal_j    =  [1,0,0,0];

    muxstate      =  [MUXOE~, REF~, r];
    enabled =  [  0    ,  1    , 1];  "Multiplexer Outputs Enabled
```

240725-99

PAL Codes: DRAM 2 (Continued)

```
    disabled_1     = [  1   ,  1    , 1];  "Multiplexer Outputs Disabled
    disabled_2     = [  1   ,  0    , 1];  "Refresh Address Enabled
    disabled_3     = [  1   ,  0    , 0];  "Wait for RAS#
    disabled_4     = [  1   ,  1    , 0];  "Refresh Address Disabled
    illegal_z      = [0,0,0];
    illegal_y      = [0,0,1];
    illegal_x      = [0,1,0];

state_diagram cstate

    state idle:       if (CLK & !RAS~ & !MUXOE~) then start else idle;
    state start:      if RESET then idle else
                  if (CLK & !CACHE # CLK & lwr) then active else
                  if CLK then wait else start;
    state wait:       if RESET then idle else
                  if CLK then active else wait;
    state active:     if RESET then idle else
                  if (CLK & !MEMCS~ & RAS~ #
                    CLK & MEMCS~ #
                    CLK & refresh) then idle else
                  if (CLK & !MEMCS~ & !RAS~) then inactive_1
                  else active;
    state inactive_1: if RESET then idle else
                  if (CLK & !RAS~ & lwr) then inactive_2 else
                  if (!RAS~ & !lwr & CACHE) then start else
                  if (!lwr & !CACHE) then wait else
                  inactive_1;
    state inactive_2: if RESET then idle else
                  if CLK then active else inactive_2;
    state illegal_a:  goto idle;
    state illegal_b:  goto idle;
    state illegal_c:  goto idle;
    state illegal_d:  goto idle;
    state illegal_e:  goto idle;
    state illegal_f:  goto idle;
    state illegal_g:  goto idle;
    state illegal_h:  goto idle;
    state illegal_i:  goto idle;
    state illegal_j:  goto idle;

state_diagram muxstate

    state enabled:    if (CLK & refresh & RAS~ & MEMCS~ #
                   CLK & refresh & !RAS~ & !DRAMRDY~) then
                   disabled_1 else enabled;
    state disabled_1: if (RESET) then enabled else disabled_2;
    state disabled_2: if (RESET) then enabled else
                  if (CLK & !RAS~) then disabled_3 else disabled_2;
    state disabled_3: if (RESET) then enabled else disabled_4;
    state disabled_4: goto enabled;
    state illegal_z:  goto enabled;
    state illegal_y:  goto enabled;
    state illegal_x:  goto enabled;
```

240725-A0

PAL Codes: DRAM 2 (Continued)

4

```
test_vectors

    ([CLK2,CLK,MEMCS~,lwr,HIT~,RAS~,refresh,RESET,CACHE] ->
     [CAS~,DRAMRDY~,MUXOE~,REF~])

"   C  C  M  l  H  R  r  R  C      C  D  M  R
"   L  L  E  w  I  A  e  E  A      A  R  U  E
"   K  K  M  r  T  S  f  S  C      S  A  X  F
"   2     C     ~  ~  r  E  H      ~  M  O  ~
"         S           e  T  E         R  E
"         ~           s               D  ~
"                     h               Y
"                        ~

    [c, x, x, 0, x, x, x, 1, 0] -> [1, 1, 0, 1]; "Cache disabled
    [c, x, x, 0, x, x, x, 1, 0] -> [1, 1, 0, 1];
    [c, 0, 1, 0, x, 1, 0, 0, 0] -> [1, 1, 0, 1]; "Ti
    [c, 1, 1, 0, x, 1, 0, 0, 0] -> [1, 1, 0, 1];
    [c, 0, 0, 0, x, 1, 0, 0, 0] -> [1, 1, 0, 1]; "T1
    [c, 1, 0, 0, x, 1, 0, 0, 0] -> [1, 1, 0, 1];
    [c, 0, 1, 0, x, 0, 0, 0, 0] -> [1, 1, 0, 1]; "T2
    [c, 1, 1, 0, x, 0, 0, 0, 0] -> [0, 1, 0, 1];
    [c, 0, 0, 0, x, 0, 0, 0, 0] -> [0, 1, 0, 1]; "T2P
    [c, 1, 0, 0, 0, 0, 0, 0, 0] -> [0, 0, 0, 1];
    [c, 0, 0, 0, 0, 0, 0, 0, 0] -> [0, 0, 0, 1]; "T2P
    [c, 1, 0, 0, 0, 0, 0, 0, 0] -> [1, 1, 0, 1];
    [c, 0, 1, 0, 0, 0, 0, 0, 0] -> [0, 1, 0, 1]; "T1P
    [c, 1, 1, 0, 0, 0, 0, 0, 0] -> [0, 0, 0, 1];
    [c, 0, 0, 0, 0, 0, 0, 0, 0] -> [0, 0, 0, 1]; "T2P
    [c, 1, 0, 0, 0, 0, 0, 0, 0] -> [1, 1, 0, 1];
    [c, 0, 1, 1, 0, 0, 0, 0, 0] -> [1, 1, 0, 1]; "T1P
    [c, 1, 1, 1, 0, 0, 0, 0, 0] -> [1, 1, 0, 1];
    [c, 0, 0, 1, 0, 0, 0, 0, 0] -> [1, 1, 0, 1]; "T2P
    [c, 1, 0, 1, 0, 0, 0, 0, 0] -> [0, 0, 0, 1];
    [c, 0, 0, 1, 0, 0, 0, 0, 0] -> [0, 0, 0, 1]; "T2p
    [c, 1, 0, 0, 0, 0, 0, 0, 0] -> [1, 1, 0, 1];
    [c, 0, 1, 0, 0, 0, 0, 0, 0] -> [0, 1, 0, 1]; "T1P
    [c, 1, 1, 0, 0, 0, 0, 0, 0] -> [0, 0, 0, 1];
    [c, 0, 0, 0, 0, 0, 0, 0, 0] -> [0, 0, 0, 1]; "T2P
    [c, 1, 0, 0, 1, 1, 0, 0, 0] -> [1, 1, 0, 1];
    [c, 0, 1, 0, 1, 1, 0, 0, 0] -> [1, 1, 0, 1]; "T1P
    [c, 1, 1, 0, 1, 1, 0, 0, 0] -> [1, 1, 0, 1];
    [c, 0, 1, 0, 1, 1, 0, 0, 0] -> [1, 1, 0, 1]; "T2
    [c, 1, 1, 0, 1, 1, 0, 0, 0] -> [1, 1, 0, 1];
    [c, 0, 1, 0, 1, 0, 0, 0, 0] -> [1, 1, 0, 1]; "T2
    [c, 1, 1, 0, 1, 0, 0, 0, 0] -> [0, 1, 0, 1];
    [c, 0, 0, 0, x, 0, 0, 0, 0] -> [0, 1, 0, 1]; "T2P
    [c, 1, 0, 0, 1, 0, 0, 0, 0] -> [0, 0, 0, 1];
    [c, 0, 0, 1, 1, 1, 0, 0, 0] -> [0, 0, 0, 1]; "T2P
    [c, 1, 0, 0, 1, 1, 0, 0, 0] -> [1, 1, 0, 1];
    [c, 0, 1, 1, 1, 1, 0, 0, 0] -> [1, 1, 0, 1]; "T1P
    [c, 1, 1, 1, 1, 1, 0, 0, 0] -> [1, 1, 0, 1];
```

240725–A1

PAL Codes: DRAM 2 (Continued)

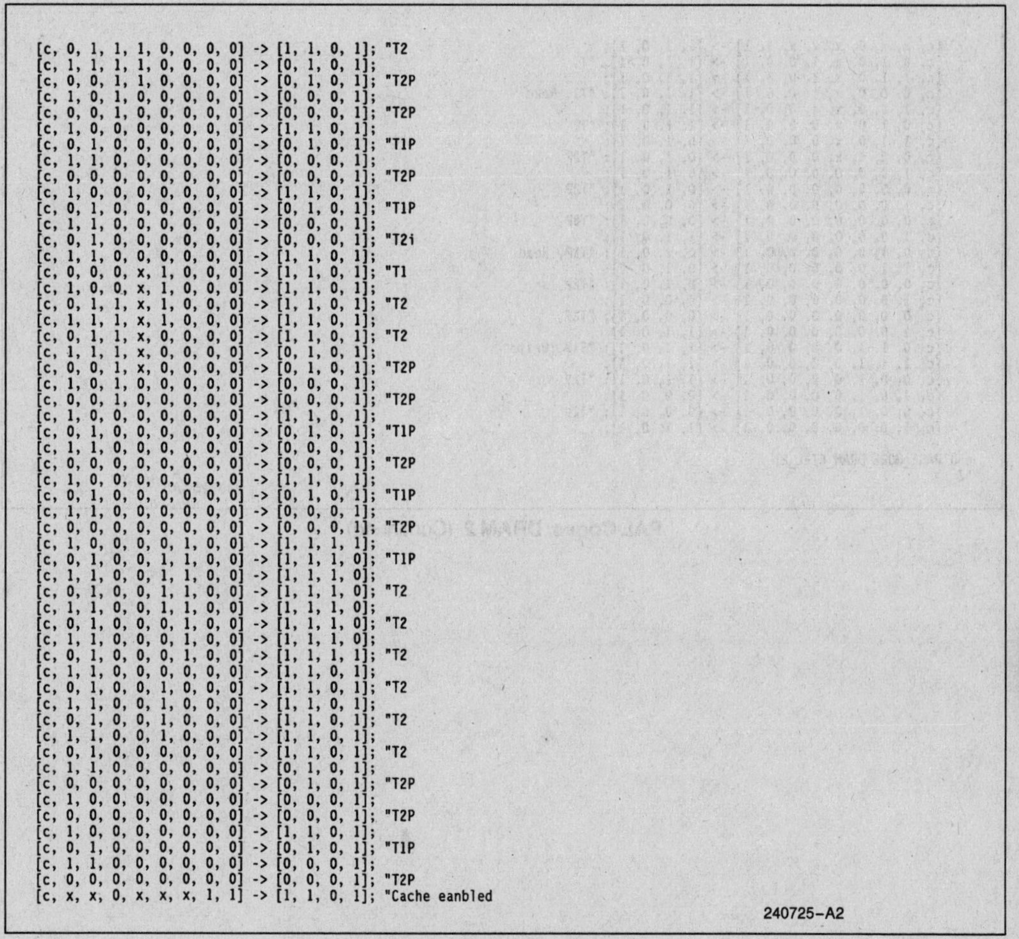

```
[c, 0, 1, 1, 1, 0, 0, 0, 0] -> [1, 1, 0, 1]; "T2
[c, 1, 1, 1, 1, 0, 0, 0, 0] -> [0, 1, 0, 1];
[c, 0, 0, 1, 1, 0, 0, 0, 0] -> [0, 1, 0, 1]; "T2P
[c, 1, 0, 1, 0, 0, 0, 0, 0] -> [0, 0, 0, 1];
[c, 0, 0, 1, 0, 0, 0, 0, 0] -> [0, 0, 0, 1]; "T2P
[c, 1, 0, 0, 0, 0, 0, 0, 0] -> [1, 1, 0, 1];
[c, 0, 1, 0, 0, 0, 0, 0, 0] -> [0, 1, 0, 1]; "T1P
[c, 1, 1, 0, 0, 0, 0, 0, 0] -> [0, 0, 0, 1];
[c, 0, 0, 0, 0, 0, 0, 0, 0] -> [0, 0, 0, 1]; "T2P
[c, 1, 0, 0, 0, 0, 0, 0, 0] -> [1, 1, 0, 1];
[c, 0, 1, 0, 0, 0, 0, 0, 0] -> [0, 1, 0, 1]; "T1P
[c, 1, 1, 0, 0, 0, 0, 0, 0] -> [0, 0, 0, 1];
[c, 0, 1, 0, 0, 0, 0, 0, 0] -> [0, 0, 0, 1]; "T2i
[c, 1, 1, 0, 0, 0, 0, 0, 0] -> [1, 1, 0, 1];
[c, 0, 0, 0, x, 1, 0, 0, 0] -> [1, 1, 0, 1]; "T1
[c, 1, 0, 0, x, 1, 0, 0, 0] -> [1, 1, 0, 1];
[c, 0, 1, 1, x, 1, 0, 0, 0] -> [1, 1, 0, 1]; "T2
[c, 1, 1, 1, x, 1, 0, 0, 0] -> [1, 1, 0, 1];
[c, 0, 1, 1, x, 0, 0, 0, 0] -> [1, 1, 0, 1]; "T2
[c, 1, 1, 1, x, 0, 0, 0, 0] -> [0, 1, 0, 1];
[c, 0, 0, 1, x, 0, 0, 0, 0] -> [0, 1, 0, 1]; "T2P
[c, 1, 0, 1, 0, 0, 0, 0, 0] -> [0, 0, 0, 1];
[c, 0, 0, 1, 0, 0, 0, 0, 0] -> [0, 0, 0, 1]; "T2P
[c, 1, 0, 0, 0, 0, 0, 0, 0] -> [1, 1, 0, 1];
[c, 0, 1, 0, 0, 0, 0, 0, 0] -> [0, 1, 0, 1]; "T1P
[c, 1, 1, 0, 0, 0, 0, 0, 0] -> [0, 0, 0, 1];
[c, 0, 0, 0, 0, 0, 0, 0, 0] -> [0, 0, 0, 1]; "T2P
[c, 1, 0, 0, 0, 0, 0, 0, 0] -> [1, 1, 0, 1];
[c, 0, 1, 0, 0, 0, 0, 0, 0] -> [0, 1, 0, 1]; "T1P
[c, 1, 1, 0, 0, 0, 0, 0, 0] -> [0, 0, 0, 1];
[c, 0, 0, 0, 0, 0, 0, 0, 0] -> [0, 0, 0, 1]; "T2P
[c, 1, 0, 0, 0, 0, 1, 0, 0] -> [1, 1, 1, 1];
[c, 0, 1, 0, 0, 1, 1, 0, 0] -> [1, 1, 1, 0]; "T1P
[c, 1, 1, 0, 0, 1, 1, 0, 0] -> [1, 1, 1, 0];
[c, 0, 1, 0, 0, 1, 1, 0, 0] -> [1, 1, 1, 0]; "T2
[c, 1, 1, 0, 0, 1, 1, 0, 0] -> [1, 1, 1, 0];
[c, 0, 1, 0, 0, 0, 1, 0, 0] -> [1, 1, 1, 0]; "T2
[c, 1, 1, 0, 0, 0, 1, 0, 0] -> [1, 1, 1, 0];
[c, 0, 1, 0, 0, 0, 1, 0, 0] -> [1, 1, 1, 1]; "T2
[c, 1, 1, 0, 0, 0, 0, 0, 0] -> [1, 1, 0, 1];
[c, 0, 1, 0, 0, 1, 0, 0, 0] -> [1, 1, 0, 1]; "T2
[c, 1, 1, 0, 0, 1, 0, 0, 0] -> [1, 1, 0, 1];
[c, 0, 1, 0, 0, 1, 0, 0, 0] -> [1, 1, 0, 1]; "T2
[c, 1, 1, 0, 0, 1, 0, 0, 0] -> [1, 1, 0, 1];
[c, 0, 1, 0, 0, 0, 0, 0, 0] -> [1, 1, 0, 1]; "T2
[c, 1, 1, 0, 0, 0, 0, 0, 0] -> [0, 1, 0, 1];
[c, 0, 0, 0, 0, 0, 0, 0, 0] -> [0, 1, 0, 1]; "T2P
[c, 1, 0, 0, 0, 0, 0, 0, 0] -> [0, 0, 0, 1];
[c, 0, 0, 0, 0, 0, 0, 0, 0] -> [0, 0, 0, 1]; "T2P
[c, 1, 0, 0, 0, 0, 0, 0, 0] -> [1, 1, 0, 1];
[c, 0, 1, 0, 0, 0, 0, 0, 0] -> [0, 1, 0, 1]; "T1P
[c, 1, 1, 0, 0, 0, 0, 0, 0] -> [0, 0, 0, 1];
[c, 0, 0, 0, 0, 0, 0, 0, 0] -> [0, 0, 0, 1]; "T2P
[c, x, x, 0, x, x, x, 1, 1] -> [1, 1, 0, 1]; "Cache eanbled
```

240725-A2

PAL Codes: DRAM 2 (Continued)

4

```
[c, x, x, 0, x, x, x, 1, 1] -> [1, 1, 0, 1];
[c, 0, 1, 0, x, 1, 0, 0, 1] -> [1, 1, 0, 1]; "Ti
[c, 1, 1, 0, x, 1, 0, 0, 1] -> [1, 1, 0, 1];
[c, 0, 0, 0, x, 1, 0, 0, 1] -> [1, 1, 0, 1]; "T1, Read
[c, 1, 0, 0, x, 1, 0, 0, 1] -> [1, 1, 0, 1];
[c, 0, 1, 0, x, 0, 0, 0, 1] -> [1, 1, 0, 1]; "T2
[c, 1, 1, 0, x, 0, 0, 0, 1] -> [0, 1, 0, 1];
[c, 0, 0, 0, x, 0, 0, 0, 1] -> [0, 1, 0, 1]; "T2P
[c, 1, 0, 0, 0, 0, 0, 0, 1] -> [0, 1, 0, 1];
[c, 0, 0, 0, 0, 0, 0, 0, 1] -> [0, 1, 0, 1]; "T2P
[c, 1, 0, 0, 0, 0, 0, 0, 1] -> [0, 0, 0, 1];
[c, 0, 0, 0, 0, 0, 0, 0, 1] -> [0, 0, 0, 1]; "T2P
[c, 1, 0, 0, 0, 0, 0, 0, 1] -> [1, 1, 0, 1];
[c, 0, 1, 0, 0, 0, 0, 0, 1] -> [0, 1, 0, 1]; "T1P, Read
[c, 1, 1, 0, 0, 0, 0, 0, 1] -> [0, 1, 0, 1];
[c, 0, 0, 0, 0, 0, 0, 0, 1] -> [0, 1, 0, 1]; "T2P
[c, 1, 0, 0, 0, 0, 0, 0, 1] -> [0, 0, 0, 1];
[c, 0, 0, 0, 0, 0, 0, 0, 1] -> [0, 0, 0, 1]; "T2P
[c, 1, 0, 0, 0, 0, 0, 0, 1] -> [1, 1, 0, 1];
[c, 0, 1, 1, 0, 0, 0, 0, 1] -> [1, 1, 0, 1]; "T1P, Write
[c, 1, 1, 1, 0, 0, 0, 0, 1] -> [1, 1, 0, 1];
[c, 0, 0, 1, 0, 0, 0, 0, 1] -> [1, 1, 0, 1]; "T2P
[c, 1, 0, 1, 0, 0, 0, 0, 1] -> [0, 0, 0, 1];
[c, 0, 0, 1, 0, 0, 0, 0, 1] -> [0, 0, 0, 1]; "T2p
[c, 1, 0, 0, 0, 0, 0, 0, 1] -> [1, 1, 0, 1];

end PAGE_MODE_DRAM_CTRL_2;
^Z
```

240725-A3

PAL Codes: DRAM 2 (Continued)

```
module        PAGE_MODE_DRAM_CTRL_3  flag '-r3'

title   'PAGE MODE DRAM CONTROLLER - PAL 3, INTEL CORPORATION'

    PAGE3    device       'P16R8';

    x        =     .X.;         " ABEL 'don't care' symbol
    c        =     .C.;         " ABEL 'clocking input' symbol

" Inputs

    CLK2     pin   1;   "80386 CLK2
    CLK      pin   2;   "Processor Clock
    ADS~     pin   3;   "Address Strobe
    MEMCS~   pin   4;   "Memory Chip Select
    WR             pin   5;   "Write/Read
    READY~   pin   6;   "System Ready
    DRMRDY~  pin   7;   "DRAM Ready
    unused1  pin   8;
    RESET    pin   9;   "System Reset

" Outputs

    T2X~     pin   12;    "active during T2, T2p, and T2i
    T1P~     pin   13;    "active during T1p
    WE~      pin   14;    "DRAM Write Enable
    DEN~     pin   15;    "DRAM Data Bus Transceiver Enable
    DTR      pin   16;    "DRAM Data Bus Transceiver R/W# Direction signal
    lwr      pin   17;    "Latched Write/Read
    mreq     pin   18;    "Latched Memory Chip Select
    unused2  pin   19;    "

state_diagram [T2X~, T1P~]

    state [1, 1]:    if (CLK & !ADS~) then [0, 1] else [1, 1];
    state [0, 1]:    if RESET then [1, 1] else
                  if (CLK & !ADS~ & !READY~) then [1, 0] else
                  if (CLK & ADS~ & !READY~) then [1, 1] else [0, 1];
    state [1, 0]:    if RESET then [1, 1] else
                  if (CLK) then [0, 1] else [1, 0];
    state [0, 0]:    goto [1, 1];

state_diagram [WE~]

    state [1]:       if (CLK & !MEMCS~ & WR & T2X~ #
                 lwr & !T1P~) then [0] else [1];
    state [0]:       if (RESET) then [1] else
              if (CLK & !READY~) then [1] else [0];

state_diagram [DEN~]

    state [1]:       if (CLK & !MEMCS~ & !WR & T2X~ #
                 mreq & !T2X~ #
                 CLK & mreq & !T1P~) then [0] else [1];
```

240725-A4

PAL Codes: DRAM 3

```
    state [0]:      if RESET then [1] else
              if (CLK & !READY~) then [1] else [0];

state_diagram [DTR]

    state [1]:      if (CLK & !MEMCS~ & WR & T2X~ #
                lwr & !T1P~) then [0] else [1];
    state [0]:      if (RESET) then [1] else
              if (!CLK & DEN~ & !lwr) then [1] else [0];

state_diagram [lwr]

    state [0]:      if (CLK & !MEMCS~ & WR) then [1] else [0];
    state [1]:      if (RESET) then [0] else
              if (!READY~ & MEMCS~ #
                 !READY~ & !WR) then [0] else [1];

state_diagram [mreq]

    state [0]:      if (CLK & !MEMCS~) then [1] else [0];
    state [1]:      if RESET then [0] else
              if (!READY~ & MEMCS~) then [0] else [1];

test_vectors

    ([CLK2,CLK,ADS~,WR,MEMCS~,READY~,RESET] ->
     [T2X~,T1P~,DEN~,lwr,WE~,DTR, mreq])

"     C  C  A  W  M  R  R      T  T  D  l  W  D  m
"     L  L  D  R  E  E  E      2  1  E  w  E  T  r
"     K  K  S     M  A  S      X  P  N  r  ~  R  e
"     2     ~     C  D  E      ~  ~  ~           q
"                 S  Y  T
"                 ~  ~

    [c, x, x, x, x, x, 1] -> [1, 1, 1, 0, 1, 1, x];
    [c, x, x, x, x, x, 1] -> [1, 1, 1, 0, 1, 1, 0];
    [c, 1, 1, x, 1, 1, 0] -> [1, 1, 1, 0, 1, 1, 0];
    [c, 0, 1, x, 1, 1, 0] -> [1, 1, 1, 0, 1, 1, 0]; "Ti
    [c, 1, 1, x, 1, 1, 0] -> [1, 1, 1, 0, 1, 1, 0];
    [c, 0, 0, 0, 0, 1, 0] -> [1, 1, 1, 0, 1, 1, 0]; "T1
    [c, 1, 0, 0, 0, 1, 0] -> [0, 1, 0, 0, 1, 1, 1];
    [c, 0, 1, 0, 1, 1, 0] -> [0, 1, 0, 0, 1, 1, 1]; "T2
    [c, 1, 1, 0, 1, 1, 0] -> [0, 1, 0, 0, 1, 1, 1];
    [c, 0, 0, 0, 0, 1, 0] -> [0, 1, 0, 0, 1, 1, 1]; "T2
    [c, 1, 0, 0, 0, 1, 0] -> [0, 1, 0, 0, 1, 1, 1];
    [c, 0, 0, 0, 0, 0, 0] -> [0, 1, 0, 0, 1, 1, 1]; "T2P
    [c, 1, 0, 0, 0, 0, 0] -> [1, 0, 1, 0, 1, 1, 1];
    [c, 0, 1, 0, 1, 1, 0] -> [1, 0, 1, 0, 1, 1, 1]; "T1P
    [c, 1, 1, 0, 1, 1, 0] -> [0, 1, 0, 0, 1, 1, 1];
    [c, 0, 0, 1, 0, 0, 0] -> [0, 1, 0, 0, 1, 1, 1]; "T2P
    [c, 1, 0, 1, 0, 0, 0] -> [1, 0, 1, 1, 1, 1, 1];
    [c, 0, 1, 1, 1, 1, 0] -> [1, 0, 1, 1, 0, 0, 1]; "T1P
    [c, 1, 1, 1, 1, 1, 0] -> [0, 1, 0, 1, 0, 0, 1];
```

240725-A5

PAL Codes: DRAM 3 (Continued)

```
[c, 0, 0, 0, 0, 1, 0] -> [0, 1, 0, 1, 0, 0, 1]; "T2P
[c, 1, 0, 0, 0, 1, 0] -> [0, 1, 0, 1, 0, 0, 1];
[c, 0, 0, 0, 0, 0, 0] -> [0, 1, 0, 0, 0, 0, 1]; "T2P
[c, 1, 0, 0, 0, 0, 0] -> [1, 0, 1, 0, 1, 0, 1];
[c, 0, 1, 0, 1, 1, 0] -> [1, 0, 1, 0, 1, 1, 1]; "T1P
[c, 1, 1, 0, 1, 1, 0] -> [0, 1, 0, 0, 1, 1, 1];
[c, 0, 0, 0, 0, 0, 0] -> [0, 1, 0, 0, 1, 1, 1]; "T2P
[c, 1, 0, 0, 0, 0, 0] -> [1, 0, 1, 0, 1, 1, 1];
[c, 0, 1, 0, 1, 1, 0] -> [1, 0, 1, 0, 1, 1, 1]; "T1p
[c, 1, 1, 0, 1, 1, 0] -> [0, 1, 0, 0, 1, 1, 1];
[c, 0, 1, 0, 1, 1, 0] -> [0, 1, 0, 0, 1, 1, 1]; "T2
[c, 1, 1, 0, 1, 1, 0] -> [0, 1, 0, 0, 1, 1, 1];
[c, 0, 1, 0, 1, 1, 0] -> [0, 1, 0, 0, 1, 1, 1]; "T2
[c, 1, 1, 0, 1, 1, 0] -> [0, 1, 0, 0, 1, 1, 1];
[c, 0, 0, 1, 0, 1, 0] -> [0, 1, 0, 0, 1, 1, 1]; "T2P
[c, 1, 0, 1, 0, 1, 0] -> [0, 1, 0, 1, 1, 1, 1];
[c, 0, 0, 1, 0, 0, 0] -> [0, 1, 0, 1, 1, 1, 1]; "T2p
[c, 1, 0, 1, 0, 0, 0] -> [1, 0, 1, 1, 1, 1, 1];
[c, 0, 1, 1, 1, 1, 0] -> [1, 0, 1, 1, 0, 0, 1]; "T1P
[c, 1, 1, 1, 1, 1, 0] -> [0, 1, 0, 1, 0, 0, 1];
[c, 0, 1, 1, 1, 1, 0] -> [0, 1, 0, 1, 0, 0, 1]; "T2
[c, 1, 1, 1, 1, 1, 0] -> [0, 1, 0, 1, 0, 0, 1];
[c, 0, 0, 0, 0, 1, 0] -> [0, 1, 0, 1, 0, 0, 1]; "T2P
[c, 1, 0, 0, 0, 1, 0] -> [0, 1, 0, 1, 0, 0, 1];
[c, 0, 0, 0, 0, 0, 0] -> [0, 1, 0, 0, 0, 0, 1]; "T2P
[c, 1, 0, 0, 0, 0, 0] -> [1, 0, 1, 0, 1, 0, 1];
[c, 0, 1, 0, 1, 1, 0] -> [1, 0, 1, 0, 1, 1, 1]; "T1P
[c, 1, 1, 0, 1, 1, 0] -> [0, 1, 0, 0, 1, 1, 1];
[c, 0, 0, 0, 0, 0, 0] -> [0, 1, 0, 0, 1, 1, 1]; "T2P
[c, 1, 0, 0, 0, 0, 0] -> [1, 0, 1, 0, 1, 1, 1];
[c, 0, 1, 0, 1, 1, 0] -> [1, 0, 1, 0, 1, 1, 1]; "T1P
[c, 1, 1, 0, 1, 1, 0] -> [0, 1, 0, 0, 1, 1, 1];
[c, 0, 1, 0, 1, 0, 0] -> [0, 1, 0, 0, 1, 1, 0]; "T2i
[c, 1, 1, 0, 1, 0, 0] -> [1, 1, 1, 0, 1, 1, 0];
[c, 0, 0, 1, 0, 1, 0] -> [1, 1, 1, 0, 1, 1, 0]; "T1
[c, 1, 0, 1, 0, 1, 0] -> [0, 1, 1, 1, 0, 0, 1];
[c, 0, 1, 1, 1, 1, 0] -> [0, 1, 0, 1, 0, 0, 1]; "T2
[c, 1, 1, 1, 1, 1, 0] -> [0, 1, 0, 1, 0, 0, 1];
[c, 0, 1, 1, 1, 1, 0] -> [0, 1, 0, 1, 0, 0, 1]; "T2
[c, 1, 1, 1, 1, 1, 0] -> [0, 1, 0, 1, 0, 0, 1];
[c, 0, 0, 0, 0, 1, 0] -> [0, 1, 0, 1, 0, 0, 1]; "T2P
[c, 1, 0, 0, 0, 1, 0] -> [0, 1, 0, 1, 0, 0, 1];
[c, 0, 0, 0, 0, 0, 0] -> [0, 1, 0, 0, 0, 0, 1]; "T2P
[c, 1, 0, 0, 0, 0, 0] -> [1, 0, 1, 0, 1, 0, 1];
[c, 0, 1, 0, 1, 1, 0] -> [1, 0, 1, 0, 1, 1, 1]; "T1P
[c, 1, 1, 0, 1, 1, 0] -> [0, 1, 0, 0, 1, 1, 1];
[c, 0, 0, 0, 0, 0, 0] -> [0, 1, 0, 0, 1, 1, 1]; "T2P
[c, 1, 0, 0, 0, 0, 0] -> [1, 0, 1, 0, 1, 1, 1];
[c, 0, 1, 0, 1, 1, 0] -> [1, 0, 1, 0, 1, 1, 1]; "T1P
[c, 1, 1, 0, 1, 1, 0] -> [0, 1, 0, 0, 1, 1, 1];
[c, 0, 0, 0, 0, 0, 0] -> [0, 1, 0, 0, 1, 1, 1]; "T2P
[c, 1, 0, 0, 0, 0, 0] -> [1, 0, 1, 0, 1, 1, 1];
[c, 0, 1, 0, 1, 1, 0] -> [1, 0, 1, 0, 1, 1, 1]; "T1P
[c, 1, 1, 0, 1, 1, 0] -> [0, 1, 0, 0, 1, 1, 1];
```

240725-A6

```
    [c, 0, 1, 0, 1, 1, 0] -> [0, 1, 0, 0, 1, 1, 1]; "T2
    [c, 1, 1, 0, 1, 1, 0] -> [0, 1, 0, 0, 1, 1, 1];
    [c, 0, 1, 0, 1, 1, 0] -> [0, 1, 0, 0, 1, 1, 1]; "T2
    [c, 1, 1, 0, 1, 1, 0] -> [0, 1, 0, 0, 1, 1, 1];
    [c, 0, 1, 0, 1, 1, 0] -> [0, 1, 0, 0, 1, 1, 1]; "T2
    [c, 1, 1, 0, 1, 1, 0] -> [0, 1, 0, 0, 1, 1, 1];
    [c, 0, 1, 0, 1, 1, 0] -> [0, 1, 0, 0, 1, 1, 1]; "T2
    [c, 1, 1, 0, 1, 1, 0] -> [0, 1, 0, 0, 1, 1, 1];
    [c, 0, 1, 0, 1, 1, 0] -> [0, 1, 0, 0, 1, 1, 1]; "T2
    [c, 1, 1, 0, 1, 1, 0] -> [0, 1, 0, 0, 1, 1, 1];
    [c, 0, 1, 0, 1, 1, 0] -> [0, 1, 0, 0, 1, 1, 1]; "T2
    [c, 1, 1, 0, 1, 1, 0] -> [0, 1, 0, 0, 1, 1, 1];
    [c, 0, 0, 0, 0, 1, 0] -> [0, 1, 0, 0, 1, 1, 1]; "T2P
    [c, 1, 0, 0, 0, 1, 0] -> [0, 1, 0, 0, 1, 1, 1];
    [c, 0, 0, 0, 0, 0, 0] -> [0, 1, 0, 0, 1, 1, 1]; "T2P
    [c, 1, 0, 0, 0, 0, 0] -> [1, 0, 1, 0, 1, 1, 1];
    [c, 0, 1, 0, 1, 1, 0] -> [1, 0, 1, 0, 1, 1, 1]; "T1P
    [c, 1, 1, 0, 1, 1, 0] -> [0, 1, 0, 0, 1, 1, 1];
    [c, 0, 0, 0, 0, 0, 0] -> [0, 1, 0, 0, 1, 1, 1]; "T2P

end PAGE_MODE_DRAM_CTRL_3;
```

240725-A7

PAL Codes: DRAM 3 (Continued)

4

```
ABEL(tm) 3.10  -  Document Generator           14-Feb-90 09:54 AM
PAGE MODE DRAM CONTROLLER - PAL 3, INTEL CORPORATION
Equations for Module PAGE_MODE_DRAM_CTRL_3

Device PAGE3


- Reduced Equations:

    !T2X~ := (CLK & !RESET & !T1P~ & T2X~
            # READY~ & !RESET & T1P~ & !T2X~
            # !CLK & !RESET & T1P~ & !T2X~
            # !ADS~ & CLK & T1P~ & T2X~);


    !T1P~ := (!CLK & !RESET & !T1P~ & T2X~
            # !ADS~ & CLK & !READY~ & !RESET & T1P~ & !T2X~);


    !WE~ := (READY~ & !RESET & !WE~
           # !CLK & !RESET & !WE~
           # !T1P~ & WE~ & lwr
           # CLK & !MEMCS~ & T2X~ & WE~ & WR);


    !DEN~ := (!DEN~ & READY~ & !RESET
            # !CLK & !DEN~ & !RESET
            # CLK & DEN~ & !T1P~ & mreq
            # DEN~ & !T2X~ & mreq
            # CLK & DEN~ & !MEMCS~ & T2X~ & !WR);


    !DTR := (!DTR & !RESET & lwr
           # !DEN~ & !DTR & !RESET
           # CLK & !DTR & !RESET
           # DTR & !T1P~ & lwr
           # CLK & DTR & !MEMCS~ & T2X~ & WR);


    !lwr := (!READY~ & !WR
           # MEMCS~ & !READY~
           # RESET & lwr
           # !WR & !lwr
           # MEMCS~ & !lwr
           # !CLK & !lwr);


    !mreq := (MEMCS~ & !READY~
            # RESET & mreq
            # MEMCS~ & !mreq
            # !CLK & !mreq);
```

240725-A8

PAL Codes: DRAM 3 (Continued)

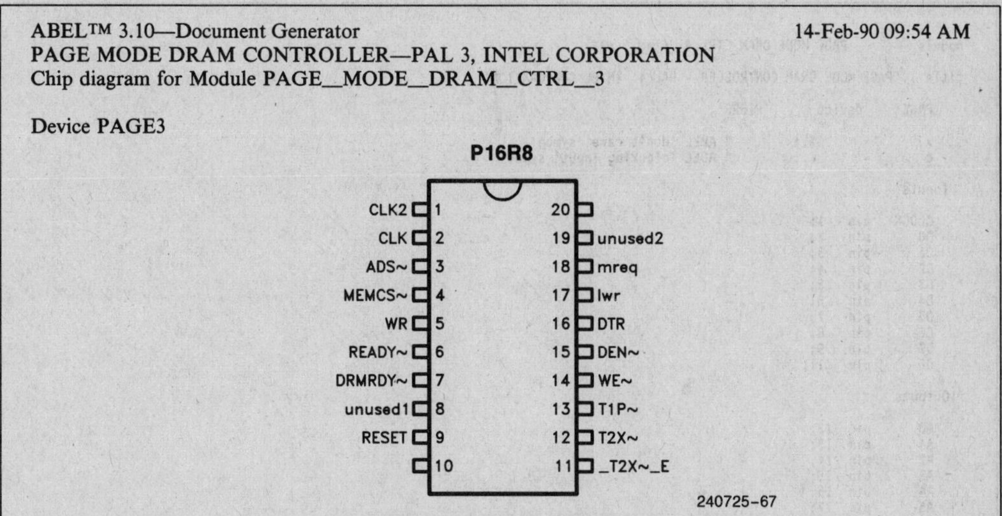
ABEL™ 3.10—Document Generator
14-Feb-90 09:54 AM
PAGE MODE DRAM CONTROLLER—PAL 3, INTEL CORPORATION
Chip diagram for Module PAGE__MODE__DRAM__CTRL__3
Device PAGE3
P16R8
CLK2 1
CLK 2
ADS~ 3
MEMCS~ 4
WR 5
READY~ 6
DRMRDY~ 7
unused1 8
RESET 9
10
20
19 unused2
18 mreq
17 lwr
16 DTR
15 DEN~
14 WE~
13 T1P~
12 T2X~
11 _T2X~_E
240725-67

PAL Codes: DRAM 3 (Continued)

```
module        PAGE_MODE_DRAM_CTRL_4  flag '-r3'

title   'PAGE MODE DRAM CONTROLLER - PAL 4, INTEL CORPORATION'

    PAGE4    device      'P16R8';

    x        =     .X.;          " ABEL 'don't care' symbol
    c        =     .C.;          " ABEL 'clocking input' symbol

" Inputs

    CLOCK   pin   1;
    D0      pin   2;
    D1      pin   3;
    D2      pin   4;
    D3      pin   5;
    D4      pin   6;
    D5      pin   7;
    D6      pin   8;
    D7      pin   9;
    OE      pin   11;

" Outputs

    A0      pin  12;
    A1      pin  13;
    A2      pin  14;
    A3      pin  15;
    A4      pin  16;
    A5      pin  17;
    A6      pin  18;
    A7      pin  19;

addr = [A7..A0];

equations

    addr := addr + 1;

end PAGE_MODE_DRAM_CTRL_4;
```

240725-A9

PAL Codes: DRAM 4

```
ABEL(tm) 3.10  -  Document Generator            14-Feb-90 09:54 AM
PAGE MODE DRAM CONTROLLER - PAL 4, INTEL CORPORATION
Equations for Module PAGE_MODE_DRAM_CTRL_4

Device PAGE4

- Reduced Equations:

    !A7 := (A0 & A1 & A2 & A3 & A4 & A5 & A6 & A7
            # !A0 & !A7
            # !A1 & !A7
            # !A2 & !A7
            # !A3 & !A7
            # !A4 & !A7
            # !A5 & !A7
            # !A6 & !A7);

    !A6 := (A0 & A1 & A2 & A3 & A4 & A5 & A6
            # !A0 & !A6
            # !A1 & !A6
            # !A2 & !A6
            # !A3 & !A6
            # !A4 & !A6
            # !A5 & !A6);

    !A5 := (A0 & A1 & A2 & A3 & A4 & A5
            # !A0 & !A5
            # !A1 & !A5
            # !A2 & !A5
            # !A3 & !A5
            # !A4 & !A5);

    !A4 := (A0 & A1 & A2 & A3 & A4
            # !A0 & !A4
            # !A1 & !A4
            # !A2 & !A4
            # !A3 & !A4);

    !A3 := (A0 & A1 & A2 & A3 # !A0 & !A3 # !A1 & !A3 # !A2 & !A3);

    !A2 := (A0 & A1 & A2 # !A0 & !A2 # !A1 & !A2);

    !A1 := (A0 & A1 # !A0 & !A1);

    !A0 := (A0);
```

240725-B0

PAL Codes: DRAM 4 (Continued)

4

ABEL™ 3.10—Document Generator 14-Feb-90 09:54 AM
PAGE MODE DRAM CONTROLLER—PAL 4, INTEL CORPORATION
Chip diagram for Module PAGE_MODE_DRAM_CTRL_4

Device PAGE4

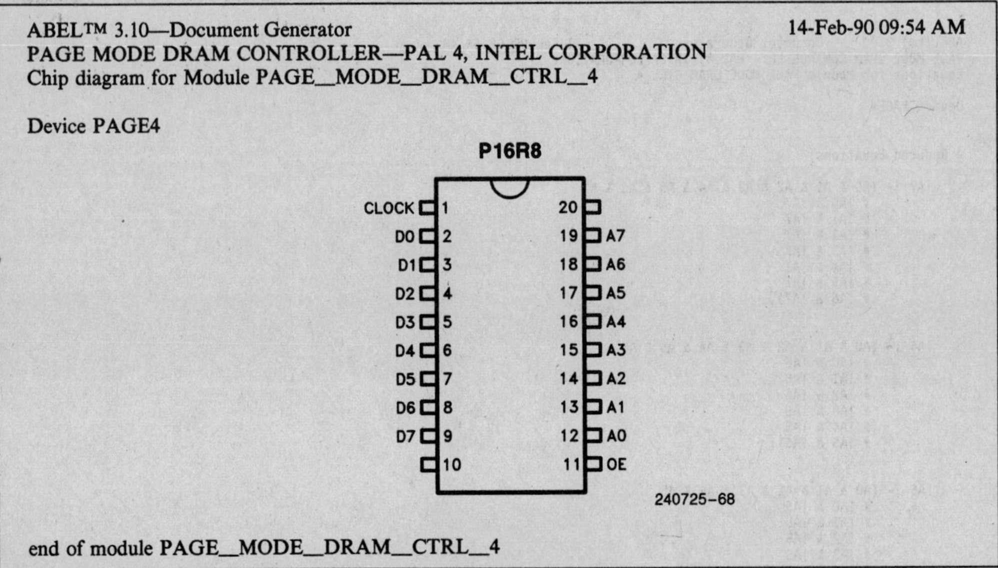

end of module PAGE_MODE_DRAM_CTRL_4

PAL Codes: DRAM 4 (Continued)

```
module     IO_CTRL_1  flag '-r3'

title      'IO BUS CONTROLLER - PAL 1, INTEL CORPORATION'

    IO1    device      'P16R4';

    x           =     .X.;              " ABEL 'don't care' symbol
    c           =     .C.;              " ABEL 'clocking input' symbol

" Inputs

    CLK         pin   1;    "Processor Clock
    RESET       pin   2;    "System Reset
    MRDC~       pin   3;    "Memory (EPROM) Read Command
    IORC~       pin   4;    "I/O Read Command
    IOWC~       pin   5;    "I/O Write Command
    INTA~       pin   6;    "Interrupt Acknowledge
    DEN~        pin   7;    "I/O Bus Data Transceiver Enable
    IORDY~      pin   8;    "I/O-EPROM Ready
    L510CS~     pin   9;    "82510 Chip Select
    OEN~        pin   11;   "PAL output Enable
    L59CS~      pin   12;   "8259A-2 Chip Select
    LEPROM~     pin   13;   "EPROM Chip Select
    unused_0    pin   18;   "
    unused_1    pin   19;   "

" Outputs

    delay       pin   14;   "
    s2          pin   15;   "
    s1          pin   16;   "
    s0          pin   17;   "

    dstate      =   [delay, s2, s1, s0];
    idle        =   [  1  , 1 , 1 , 1 ];
    start       =   [  1  , 1 , 1 , 0 ];
    wait_14     =   [  1  , 0 , 1 , 0 ];
    wait_13     =   [  1  , 0 , 1 , 1 ];
    wait_12     =   [  1  , 0 , 0 , 0 ];
    wait_11     =   [  1  , 1 , 0 , 0 ];
    wait_10     =   [  1  , 1 , 0 , 1 ];
    active      =   [  0  , 1 , 1 , 1 ];

state_diagram dstate

    state idle:     if (!DEN~ & !MRDC~ # !DEN~ & !IORC~ #
                        !DEN~ & !IOWC~ # !DEN~ & !INTA~) then start
                    else idle;
    state start:    if (!L510CS~ & !IOWC~) then wait_14 else
                    if (!L510CS~ & !IORC~) then wait_13 else
                    if (!L59CS~ & !IOWC~) then wait_11 else
                    if (!LEPROM~ # !L59CS~ & !IORC~ # !INTA~) then wait_10;
    state wait_14: goto wait_13;
```

240725-B1

```
    state wait_13: goto wait_12;
    state wait_12: goto wait_11;
    state wait_11: goto wait_10;
    state wait_10: goto active;
    state active:  if !IORDY~ then idle else active;

end IO_CTRL_1;
^Z
```

240725-B2

PAL Codes: IO-1

```
ABEL(tm) 3.10  -  Document Generator              15-Feb-90 06:40 PM
IO BUS CONTROLLER - PAL 1, INTEL CORPORATION
Equations for Module IO_CTRL_1

Device IO1

- Reduced Equations:

    !delay := (IORDY~ & !delay & s0 & s1 & s2 # delay & s0 & !s1 & s2);

    !s2 := (delay & s1 & !s2
           # !IORC~ & !L510CS~ & delay & !s0 & s1
           # !IOWC~ & !L510CS~ & delay & !s0 & s1);

    !s1 := (delay & !s0 & !s1
           # delay & s0 & s1 & !s2
           # !INTA~ & IORC~ & IOWC~ & delay & !s0 & s2
           # IORC~ & IOWC~ & !LEPROM~ & delay & !s0 & s2
           # !IORC~ & L510CS~ & !L59CS~ & delay & !s0 & s2
           # !INTA~ & L510CS~ & delay & !s0 & s2
           # L510CS~ & !LEPROM~ & delay & !s0 & s2
           # !IOWC~ & L510CS~ & !L59CS~ & delay & !s0 & s2);

    !s0 := (delay & !s0 & !s1 & !s2
           # delay & s0 & s1 & !s2
           # !IOWC~ & !L59CS~ & delay & !s0 & s1 & s2
           # !IOWC~ & !L510CS~ & delay & !s0 & s1 & s2
           # !DEN~ & !INTA~ & delay & s0 & s1
           # !DEN~ & !IOWC~ & delay & s0 & s1
           # !DEN~ & !IORC~ & delay & s0 & s1
           # !DEN~ & !MRDC~ & delay & s0 & s1);
```

240725-B3

PAL Codes: IO-1 (Continued)

ABEL™ 3.10—Document Generator 15-Feb-90 06:40 PM
IO BUS CONTROLLER—PAL 1, INTEL CORPORATION
Chip diagram for Module IO__CTRL__1

Device IO1

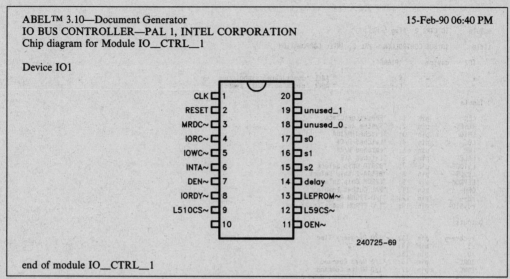

Signal	Pin	Pin	Signal
CLK	1	20	
RESET	2	19	unused_1
MRDC~	3	18	unused_0
IORC~	4	17	s0
IOWC~	5	16	s1
INTA~	6	15	s2
DEN~	7	14	delay
IORDY~	8	13	LEPROM~
L510CS~	9	12	L59CS~
	10	11	OEN~

240725-69

end of module IO__CTRL__1

PAL Codes: IO-1 (Continued)

```
module     IO_CTRL_2  flag '-r3'

title     'IO BUS CONTROLLER - PAL 2, INTEL CORPORATION'

    IO2    device     'P16R6';

    x          =     .X.;               " ABEL 'don't care' symbol
    c          =     .C.;               " ABEL 'clocking input' symbol

" Inputs

    CLK        pin   1;   "Processor Clock
    RESET      pin   2;   "System Reset
    LMIO       pin   3;   "Latched M/IO#
    LDC        pin   4;   "Latched D/C#
    LWR        pin   5;   "Latched W/R#
    LALE       pin   6;   "Latched ALE
    L510CS-    pin   7;   "82510 Chip Select
    L59CS-     pin   8;   "8259A-2 Chip Select
    LEPROM-    pin   9;   "EPROM Chip Select
    OEN-       pin  11;   "PAL Output Enable
    rdy-       pin  12;   "I/O-EPROM Ready (n-1)
    rdy510-    pin  19;   "I/O-EPROM Ready (n-2)

" Outputs

    recovery   pin  13;   "I/O Recovery Time
    s1         pin  14;   "
    s0         pin  15;   "
    IORC-      pin  16;   "I/O Read Command
    IOWC-      pin  17;   "I/O Write Command
    MRDC-      pin  18;   "Memory (EPROM) Read Command

    rstate     = [recovery, s1, s0];
    idle       = [  0      , 1 , 0 ];
    active     = [  0      , 1 , 1 ];
    inactive_0 = [  1      , 1 , 1 ];
    inactive_1 = [  1      , 0 , 1 ];
    inactive_2 = [  1      , 0 , 0 ];
    inactive_3 = [  1      , 1 , 0 ];
    illegal_a  = [  0      , 0 , 0 ];
    illegal_b  = [  0      , 0 , 1 ];


state_diagram rstate

    state idle:         if (!IORC- # !IOWC-) then active else idle;
    state active:       if (IORC- # IOWC-) then inactive_0 else active;
    state inactive_0:   goto inactive_1;
    state inactive_1:   goto inactive_2;
    state inactive_2:   goto inactive_3;
    state inactive_3:   goto idle;
    state illegal_a:    goto idle;
    state illegal_b:    goto idle;
```

240725–B4

```
state_diagram [IOWC-]

    state [1]: if (!recovery & !LMIO & LDC & LWR & (!L510CS- # !L59CS-))
               then [0] else [1];
    state [0]: if RESET then [1] else
               if (!L510CS- & !rdy510- # !rdy-) then [1] else [0];

state_diagram [IORC-]

    state [1]: if (!recovery & !LMIO & LDC & !LWR & (!L510CS- # !L59CS-))
               then [0] else [1];
    state [0]: if RESET then [1] else
               if !rdy- then [1] else [0];

state_diagram [MRDC-]

    state [1]: if (LALE & LMIO & !LWR & !LEPROM-) then [0] else [1];
    state [0]: if RESET then [1] else
               if !rdy- then [1] else [0];

end IO_CTRL_2;

^Z
```

240725–B5

PAL Codes: IO-2

```
ABEL(tm) 3.10  -  Document Generator            14-Feb-90 09:34 AM
IO BUS CONTROLLER - PAL 2, INTEL CORPORATION
Equations for Module IO_CTRL_2

Device IO2

- Reduced Equations:

    !recovery := (!recovery & !s1 # !IORC~ & !IOWC~ & !recovery # !s0 & s1);

    !s1 := (recovery & s0);

    !s0 := (recovery & !s0 # !s1 # IORC~ & IOWC~ & !s0);

    !IOWC~ := (!IOWC~ & !RESET & rdy510~ & rdy~
              # !IOWC~ & L510CS~ & !RESET & rdy~
              # IOWC~ & !L59CS~ & LDC & !LMIO & LWR & !recovery
              # IOWC~ & !L510CS~ & LDC & !LMIO & LWR & !recovery);


    !IORC~ := (!IORC~ & !RESET & rdy~
              # IORC~ & !L59CS~ & LDC & !LMIO & !LWR & !recovery
              # IORC~ & !L510CS~ & LDC & !LMIO & !LWR & !recovery);


    !MRDC~ := (!MRDC~ & !RESET & rdy~
              # LALE & !LEPROM~ & LMIO & !LWR & MRDC~);
```

240725-B6

PAL Codes: IO-2 (Continued)

4

ABEL™ 3.10—Document Generator 14-Feb-90 09:34 AM
IO BUS CONTROLLER—PAL 2, INTEL CORPORATION
Chip diagram for Module IO__CTRL__2

Device IO2

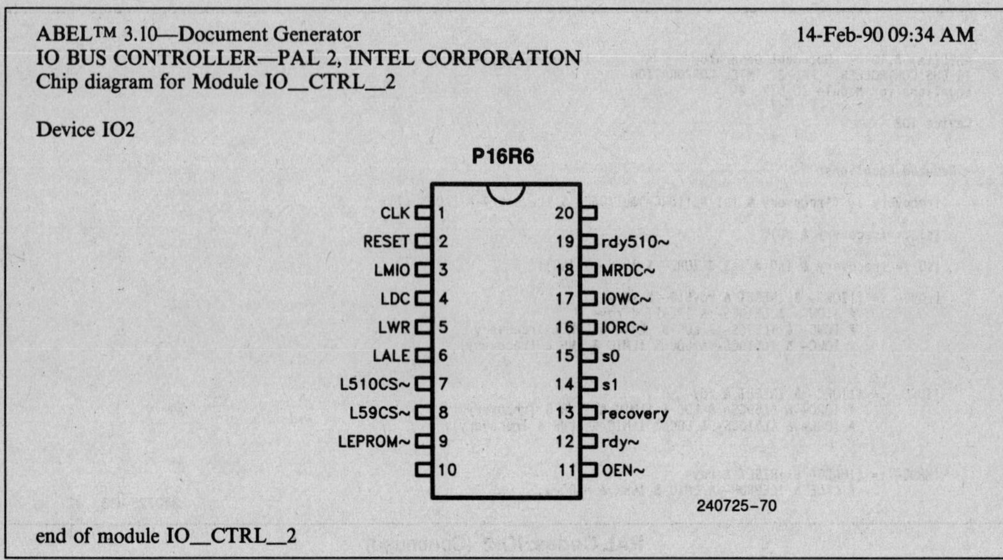

end of module IO__CTRL__2

PAL Codes: IO-2 (Continued)

```
module      IO_CTRL_3  flag '-r3'

title       'IO BUS CONTROLLER - PAL 2, INTEL CORPORATION'

    IO3     device       'P16R6';

    x           =      .X.;              " ABEL 'don't care' symbol
    c           =      .C.;              " ABEL 'clocking input' symbol

" Inputs

    CLK         pin   1;    "Processor Clock
    RESET       pin   2;    "System Reset
    LMIO        pin   3;    "Latched M/IO#
    LDC         pin   4;    "Latched D/C#
    LWR         pin   5;    "Latched W/R#
    LALE        pin   6;    "Latched ALE
    L510CS~     pin   7;    "82510 Chip Select
    L59CS~      pin   8;    "8259A-2 Chip Select
    LEPROM~     pin   9;    "EPROM Chip Select
    OEN~        pin  11;    "PAL Output Enable
    rdy~        pin  12;    "I/O-EPROM Ready (n-1)
    IORDY~      pin  19;    "I/O-EPROM Ready

" Outputs

    INTA~       pin  13;    "Interrupt Acknowledge
    st0         pin  14;    "
    DEN~        pin  15;    "I/O Bus Transceiver Enable
    st1         pin  16;    "
    DTR         pin  17;    "I/O Bus Transceiver Direction
    st2         pin  18;    "

state_diagram [INTA~, st0]

    state [1, 1]:  if (!LMIO & !LDC & !LWR & LALE) then [1, 0] else [1, 1];
    state [1, 0]:  if RESET then [1, 1] else
                   if !LALE then [0, 0] else [1, 0];
    state [0, 0]:  if RESET then [1, 1] else
                   if !rdy~ then [1, 1] else [0, 0];
    state [0, 1]:  goto [1, 1];

state_diagram [DEN~, st1]

    state [1, 1]:  if LALE & (!LEPROM~ # !L510CS~ # !L59CS~) then [1, 0] else

                   if !INTA~ then [0, 0] else [1, 1];
    state [1, 0]:  if RESET then [1, 1] else
                   if !LALE then [0, 0] else [1, 0];
    state [0, 0]:  if RESET then [1, 1] else
                   if !rdy~ then [1, 1] else [0, 0];
    state [0, 1]:  goto [1, 1];

state_diagram [DTR, st2]
```

240725-B7

```
    state [1, 1]:  if LALE & (!LEPROM~ # !L510CS~ # !L59CS~) & LWR then [0, 1]

                   else [1, 1];
    state [0, 1]:  if RESET then [1, 1] else
                   if !IORDY~ then [0, 0] else [0, 1];
    state [0, 0]:  goto [1, 1];
    state [1, 0]:  goto [1, 1];

end IO_CTRL_3;
^Z
```

240725-B8

PAL Codes: IO-3

```
ABEL(tm) 3.10  -  Document Generator            15-Feb-90 06:45 PM
IO BUS CONTROLLER - PAL 2, INTEL CORPORATION
Equations for Module IO_CTRL_3

Device IO3

- Reduced Equations:

    !INTA~ := (!INTA~ & !RESET & rdy~ & !st0
             # INTA~ & !LALE & !RESET & !st0);


    !st0 := (!RESET & rdy~ & !st0
           # INTA~ & !RESET & !st0
           # INTA~ & LALE & !LDC & !LMIO & !LWR & st0);


    !DEN~ := (!DEN~ & !RESET & rdy~ & !st1
            # DEN~ & !LALE & !RESET & !st1
            # DEN~ & !INTA~ & L510CS~ & L59CS~ & LEPROM~ & st1
            # DEN~ & !INTA~ & !LALE & st1);


    !st1 := (!RESET & rdy~ & !st1
           # DEN~ & !RESET & !st1
           # DEN~ & !INTA~ & st1
           # DEN~ & !L59CS~ & LALE & st1
           # DEN~ & !L510CS~ & LALE & st1
           # DEN~ & LALE & !LEPROM~ & st1);


    !DTR := (!DTR & !RESET & st2
           # DTR & !L59CS~ & LALE & LWR & st2
           # DTR & !L510CS~ & LALE & LWR & st2
           # DTR & LALE & !LEPROM~ & LWR & st2);


    !st2 := (!DTR & !IORDY~ & !RESET & st2);
```

240725-B9

PAL Codes: IO-3 (Continued)

ABEL™ 3.10—Document Generator 15-Feb-90 06:45 PM
IO BUS CONTROLLER—PAL 2, INTEL CORPORATION
Chip diagram for Module IO__CTRL__3

Device IO3

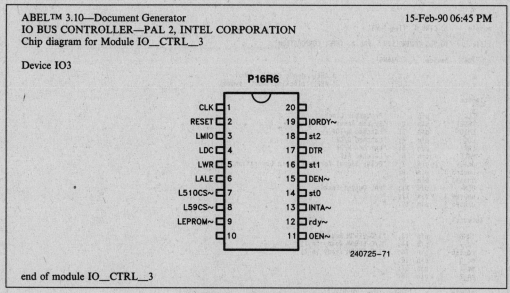

P16R6

Signal	Pin	Pin	Signal
CLK	1	20	
RESET	2	19	IORDY~
LMIO	3	18	st2
LDC	4	17	DTR
LWR	5	16	st1
LALE	6	15	DEN~
L510CS~	7	14	st0
L59CS~	8	13	INTA~
LEPROM~	9	12	rdy~
	10	11	OEN~

240725-71

end of module IO__CTRL__3

PAL Codes: IO-3 (Continued)

4

```
module    IO_CTRL_4  flag '-r3'

title     'IO BUS CONTROLLER - PAL 2, INTEL CORPORATION'

    IO4    device       'P16R6';

    x            =      .X.;                  " ABEL 'don't care' symbol
    c            =      .C.;                  " ABEL 'clocking input' symbol

" Inputs

    CLK          pin   1;    "Processor Clock
    RESET        pin   2;    "System Reset
    LMIO         pin   3;    "Latched M/IO#
    LDC          pin   4;    "Latched D/C#
    LWR          pin   5;    "Latched W/R#
    LALE         pin   6;    "Latched ALE
    delay        pin   7;    "Delay Signal for Wait State Generation
    unused_0     pin   8;    "
    unused_1     pin   9;    "
    OEN~         pin  11;    "PAL Output Enable
    unused_3     pin  12;    "
    unused_4     pin  19;    "

" Outputs

    IORDY~       pin  13;    "I/O-EPROM Ready
    rdy~         pin  14;    "I/O-EPROM Ready (n-1)
    rdy510~      pin  15;    "I/O-EPROM Ready (n-2)
    nc_0         pin  16;    "
    nc_1         pin  17;    "
    nc_2         pin  18;    "

    rstate     =  [IORDY~, rdy~, rdy510~];
    idle       =  [   1  ,  1  ,    1   ];
    rdy2       =  [   1  ,  1  ,    0   ];
    rdy1       =  [   1  ,  0  ,    1   ];
    rdy0       =  [   0  ,  1  ,    1   ];
    illegal_a  =  [   1  ,  0  ,    0   ];
    illegal_b  =  [   0  ,  0  ,    0   ];
    illegal_c  =  [   0  ,  0  ,    1   ];
    illegal_d  =  [   0  ,  1  ,    0   ];

state_diagram rstate

    state idle:         if (LMIO & !LDC & LWR & LALE) then rdy1 else
                        if !delay then rdy2 else idle;
    state rdy2:         if RESET then idle else rdy1;
    state rdy1:         if RESET then idle else
                        if !LALE then rdy0 else rdy1;
    state rdy0:         goto idle;
    state illegal_a:    goto idle;
    state illegal_b:    goto idle;
    state illegal_c:    goto idle;
```

240725-C0

PAL Codes: IO-4

```
    state illegal_d:    goto idle;

end IO_CTRL_4;
^Z
```

240725–C1

```
ABEL(tm) 3.10  -  Document Generator                15-Feb-90 06:55 PM
IO BUS CONTROLLER - PAL 2, INTEL CORPORATION
Equations for Module IO_CTRL_4

Device IO4


- Reduced Equations:

    !IORDY~ := (IORDY~ & !LALE & !RESET & rdy510~ & !rdy~);

    !rdy~ := (IORDY~ & LALE & !RESET & rdy510~ & !rdy~
            # IORDY~ & !RESET & !rdy510~ & rdy~
            # IORDY~ & LALE & !LDC & LMIO & LWR & rdy510~ & rdy~);


    !rdy510~ := (IORDY~ & !LALE & !delay & rdy510~ & rdy~
               # IORDY~ & !LWR & !delay & rdy510~ & rdy~
               # IORDY~ & LDC & !delay & rdy510~ & rdy~
               # IORDY~ & !LMIO & !delay & rdy510~ & rdy~);
```

240725–C2

PAL Codes: IO-4 (Continued)

4

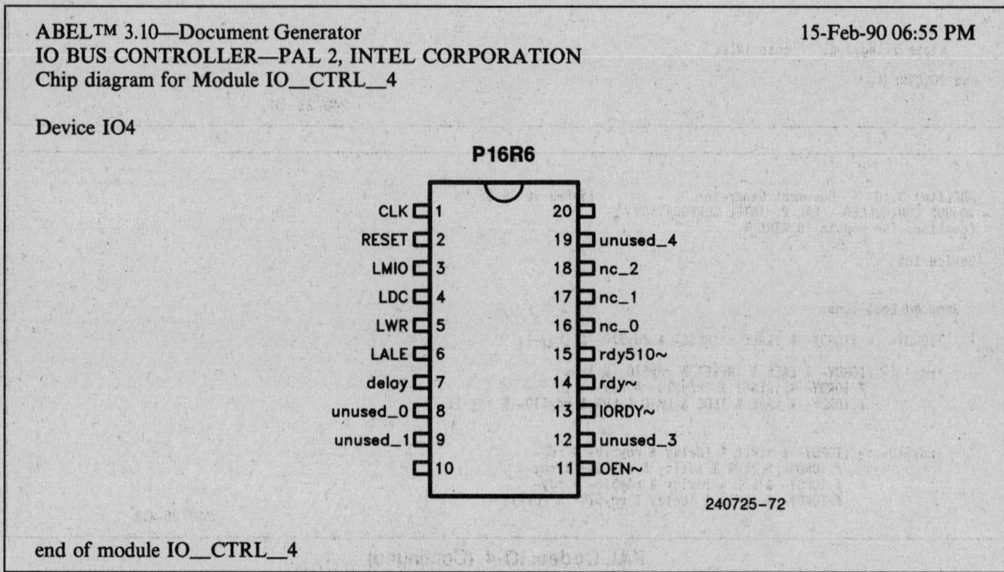
ABEL™ 3.10—Document Generator
15-Feb-90 06:55 PM
IO BUS CONTROLLER—PAL 2, INTEL CORPORATION
Chip diagram for Module IO__CTRL__4
Device IO4
P16R6
CLK 1
RESET 2
LMIO 3
LDC 4
LWR 5
LALE 6
delay 7
unused_0 8
unused_1 9
10
20
19 unused_4
18 nc_2
17 nc_1
16 nc_0
15 rdy510~
14 rdy~
13 IORDY~
12 unused_3
11 OEN~
240725-72
end of module IO__CTRL__4

PAL Codes: IO-4 (Continued)

```
module         LADDR_DEC flag '-r3'

title   'LOCAL_DECODE_LOGIC - INTEL CORPORATION'

    LADDR_PAL     device       'P16L8';

    x = .X.;              "ABEL don't care symbol
    c = .C.;              "ABEL clocking input symbol
    h = 1;                "logic 1
    l = 0;                "logic 0

" Inputs

    ADS~    pin   1;   "ADS#
    M_IO~   pin   2;   "M/IO#
    A31     pin   3;   "Addr bit 31
    A30           pin   4;   "Addr bit 30
    A29     pin   5;   "Addr bit 29

" Outputs

    X16~    pin  18;   "indicates a 16-bit access
    LBA~    pin  17;   "local bus access
    NCA~    pin  16;   "non-cache access

equations

    !X16~ =  !ADS~ & M_IO~ & A31 & A30 & A29;
    LBA~  =  h;
    NCA~  =  h;

end LADDR_DEC;
```

240725-C3

```
ABEL(tm) 3.10  -  Document Generator           14-Feb-90 09:51 AM
LOCAL_DECODE_LOGIC - INTEL CORPORATION
Equations for Module LADDR_DEC

Device LADDR_PAL


- Reduced Equations:

    !X16~ = (A29 & A30 & A31 & !ADS~ & M_IO~);

    !LBA~ = (0);

    !NCA~ = (0);
```

240725-C4

PAL Codes: Local Decoder

4

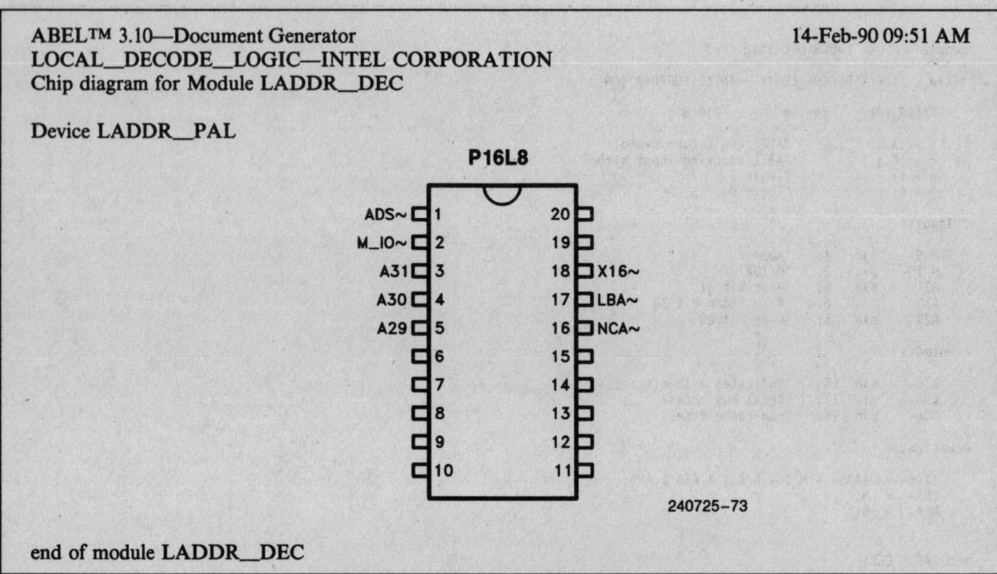

PAL Codes: Local Decoder (Continued)

```
module          READY flag '-r3'

title   'READY_LOGIC - INTEL CORPORATION'

    RDY     device       'P16L8';

" Inputs

    DRAMRDY-        pin   1;   "DRAM READY#
    IORDY-   pin   2;   "IO/EPROM READY#
    RDYEN-   pin   3;   "RDYEN# of 82385
    RDY385-  pin   4;   "READYO# OF 82385
    RDY387-  pin   5;   "READYO# OF 82387
    CACHE    pin   6;   "High if cache exits; otherwise, Low

" Outputs

    READY~  pin  12;   "READY# for 80386
    BREADY~ pin  13;   "BREADY# for 82385

equations

    !BREADY~ = !DRAMRDY~ # !IORDY~;
    !READY~ = (CACHE & !RDY385~) # !RDY387~ #
              (CACHE & !RDYEN~ & (!DRAMRDY~ # !IORDY~) #
              !CACHE & (!DRAMRDY~ # !IORDY~));

end READY;
```

240725-C5

```
ABEL(tm) 3.10  -  Document Generator        15-Feb-90 07:02 PM
READY_LOGIC - INTEL CORPORATION
Equations for Module READY

Device RDY


- Reduced Equations:

    !BREADY~ = (!IORDY~ # !DRAMRDY~);

    !READY~ = (!CACHE & !IORDY~
              # !CACHE & !DRAMRDY~
              # !IORDY~ & !RDYEN~
              # !DRAMRDY~ & !RDYEN~
              # !RDY387~
              # CACHE & !RDY385~);
```

240725-C6

PAL Codes: Ready

4

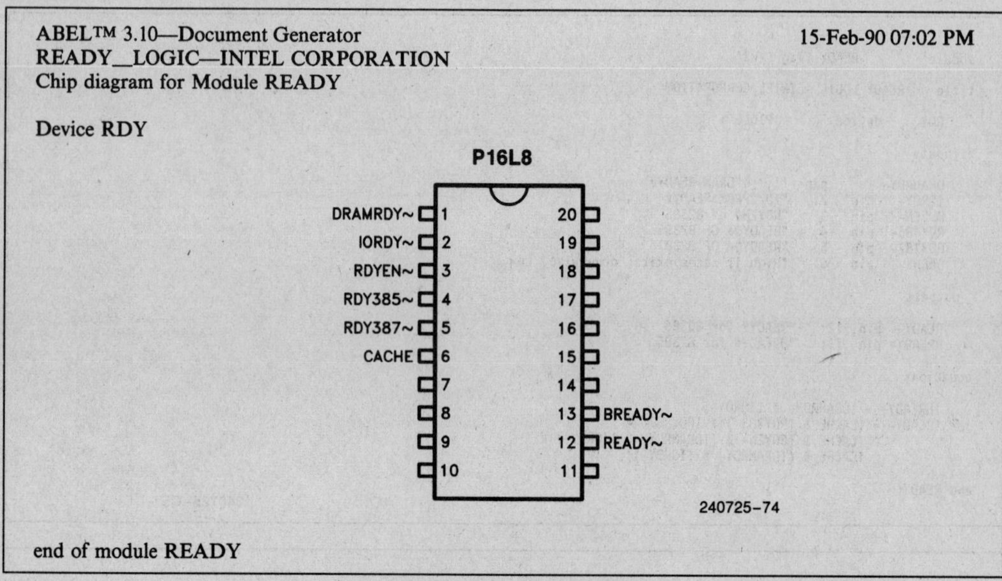
ABEL™ 3.10—Document Generator
15-Feb-90 07:02 PM
READY_LOGIC—INTEL CORPORATION
Chip diagram for Module READY
Device RDY
P16L8
DRAMRDY~ 1
IORDY~ 2
RDYEN~ 3
RDY385~ 4
RDY387~ 5
CACHE 6
7
8
9
10
20
19
18
17
16
15
14
13 BREADY~
12 READY~
11
240725-74
end of module READY

PAL Codes: Ready (Continued)

APPENDIX C
TIMING EQUATIONS

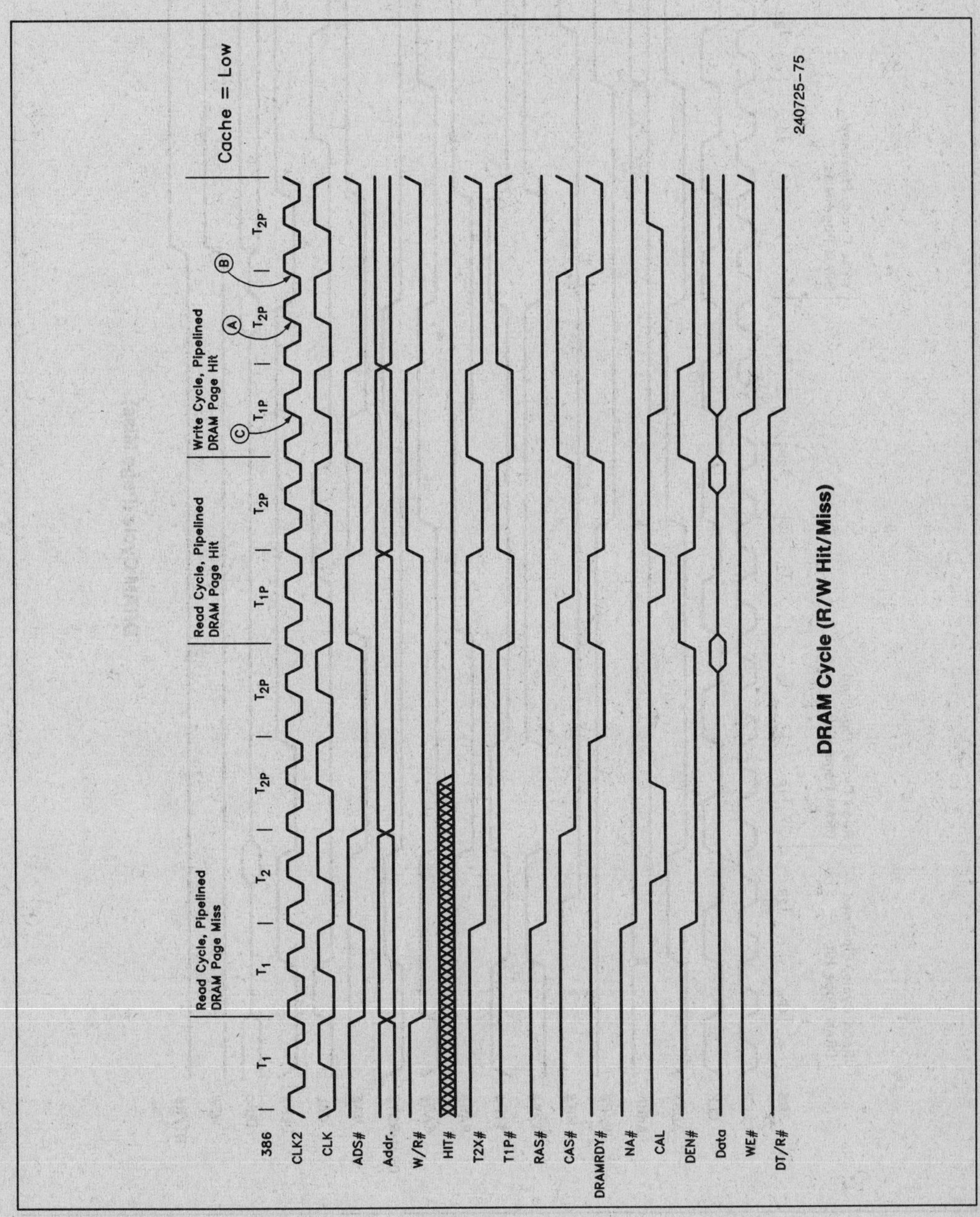

DRAM Cycle (R/W Hit/Miss)

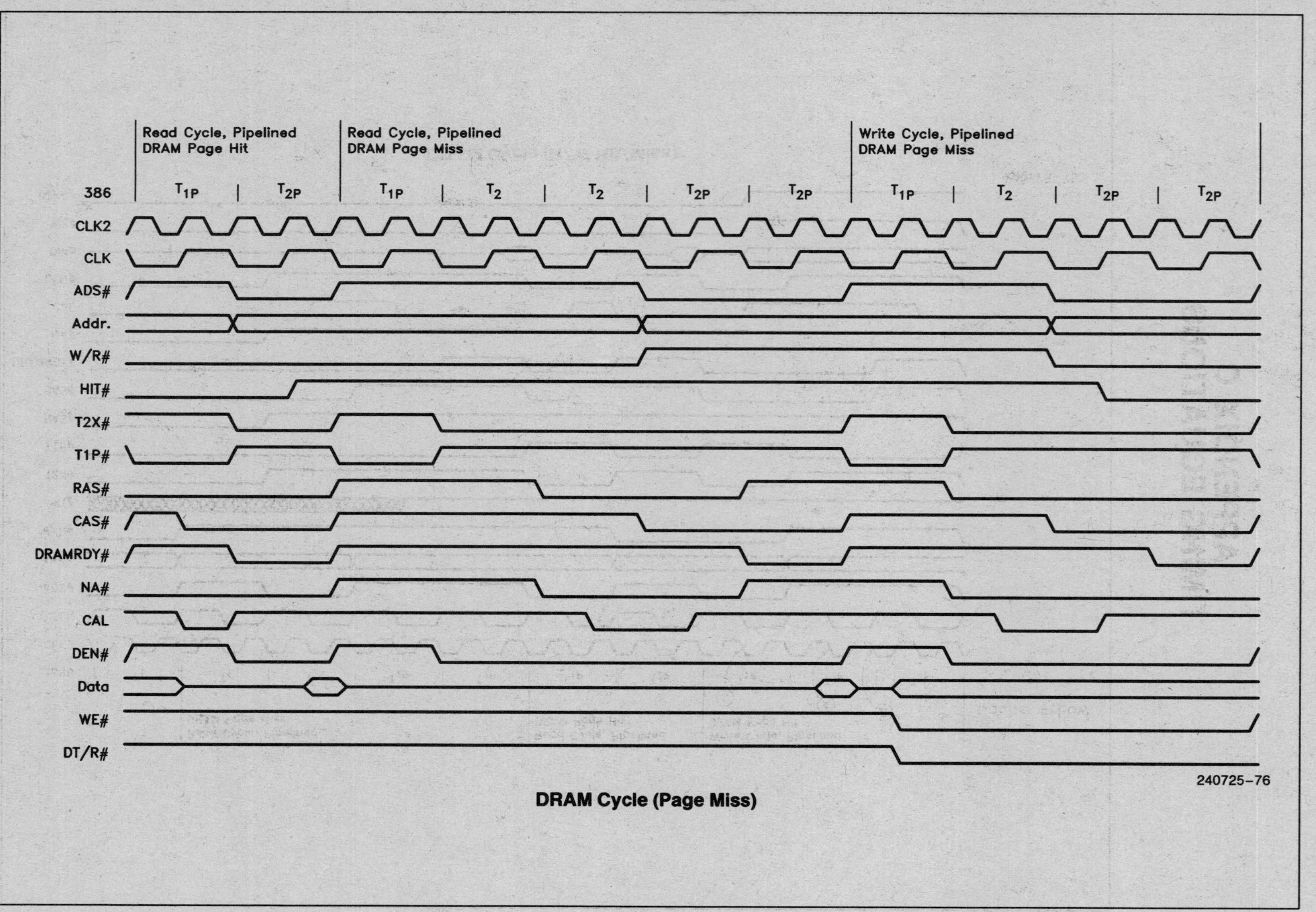

DRAM Cycle (Page Miss)

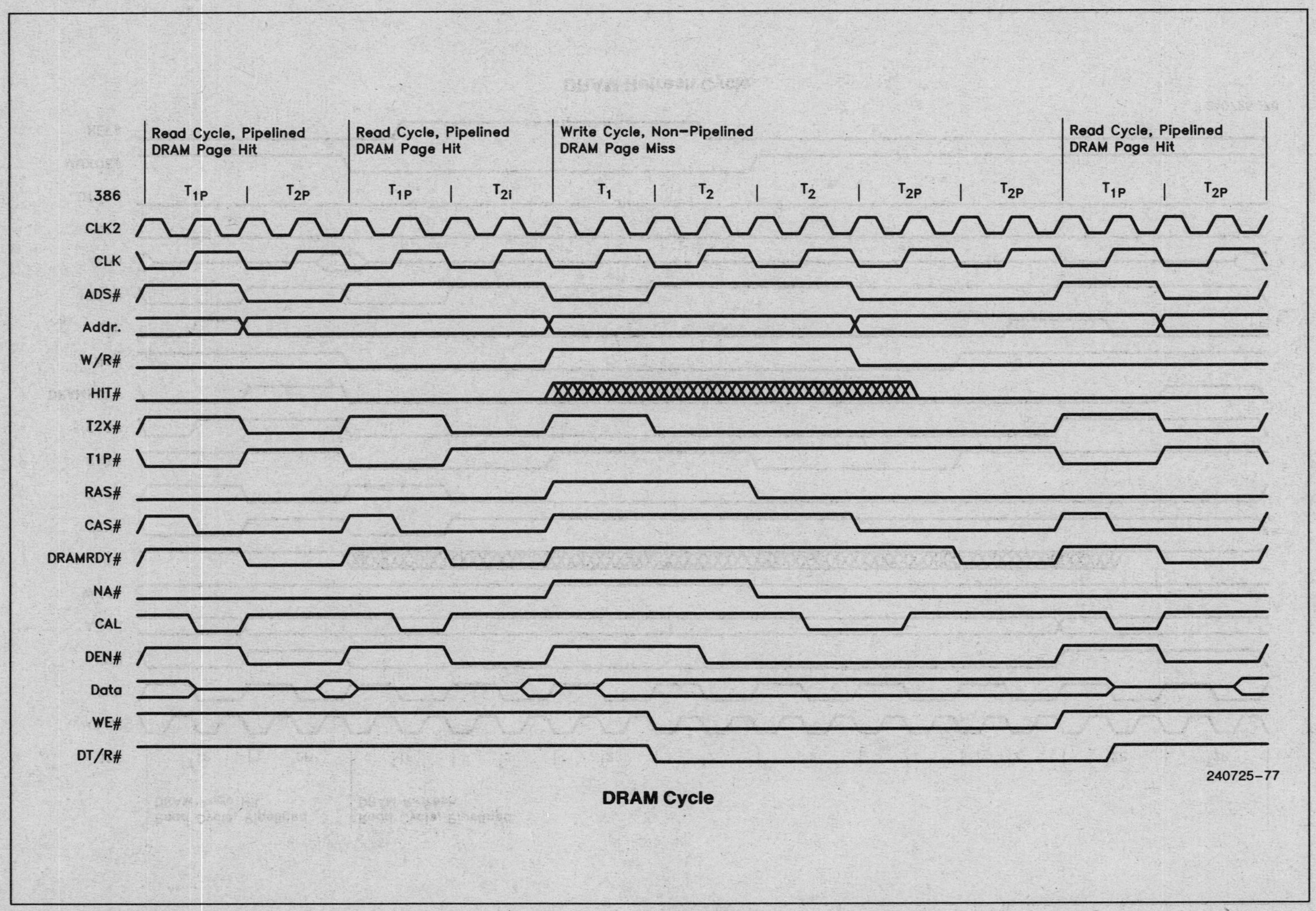
Read Cycle, Pipelined DRAM Page Hit
Read Cycle, Pipelined DRAM Page Hit
Write Cycle, Non-Pipelined DRAM Page Miss
Read Cycle, Pipelined DRAM Page Hit
386
T1P | T2P | T1P | T2I | T1 | T2 | T2 | T2P | T2P | T1P | T2P
CLK2
CLK
ADS#
Addr.
W/R#
HIT#
T2X#
T1P#
RAS#
CAS#
DRAMRDY#
NA#
CAL
DEN#
Data
WE#
DT/R#
240725-77

DRAM Cycle

4

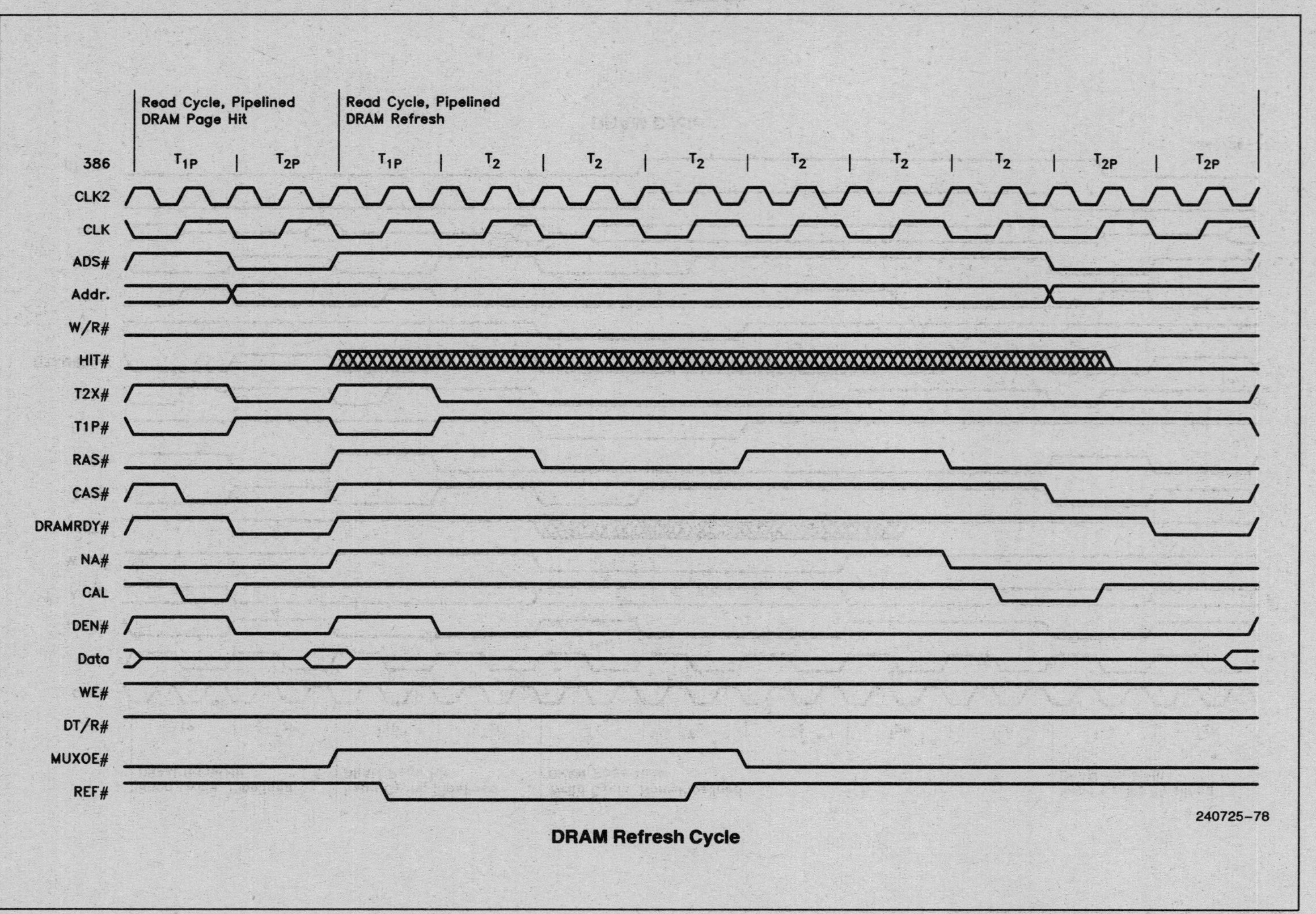

DRAM Refresh Cycle

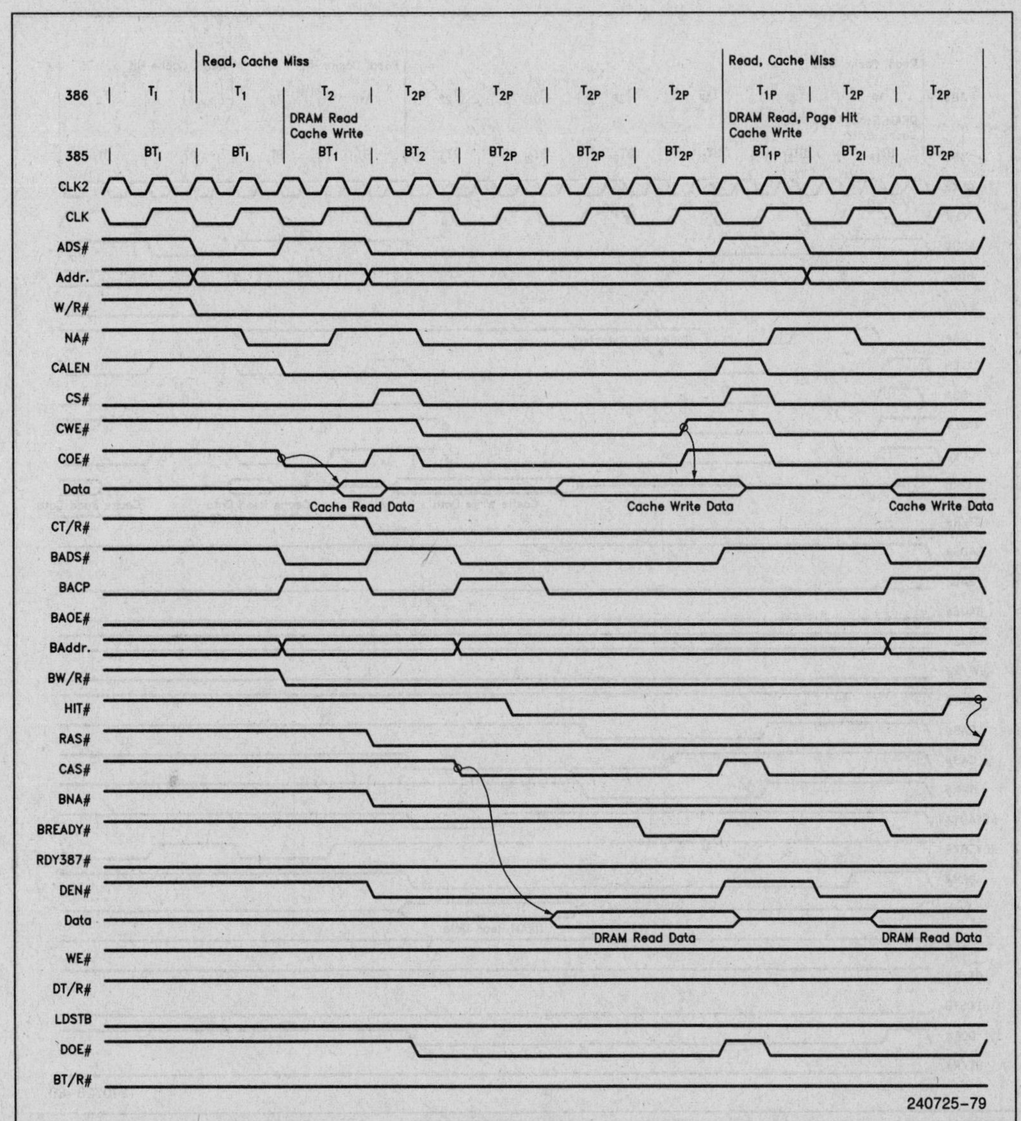
Read, Cache Miss
Read, Cache Miss
386
T1
T1
T2
T2P
T2P
T2P
T2P
T1P
T2P
T2P
DRAM Read
Cache Write
DRAM Read, Page Hit
Cache Write
385
BT1
BT1
BT1
BT2
BT2P
BT2P
BT2P
BT1P
BT2I
BT2P
CLK2
CLK
ADS#
Addr.
W/R#
NA#
CALEN
CS#
CWE#
COE#
Data
Cache Read Data
Cache Write Data
Cache Write Data
CT/R#
BADS#
BACP
BAOE#
BAddr.
BW/R#
HIT#
RAS#
CAS#
BNA#
BREADY#
RDY387#
DEN#
Data
DRAM Read Data
DRAM Read Data
WE#
DT/R#
LDSTB
DOE#
BT/R#
240725-79

Cache Cycle

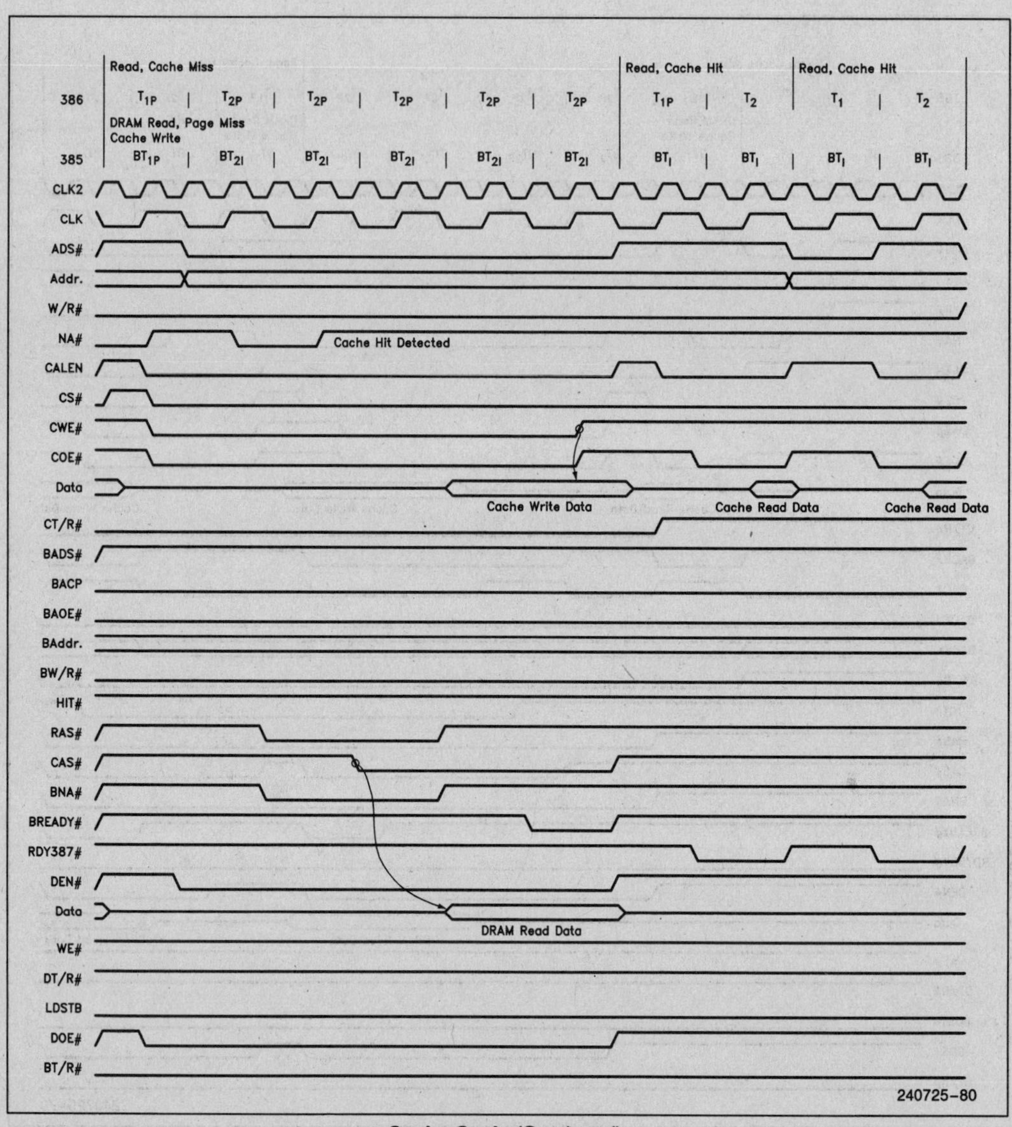

Cache Cycle (Continued)

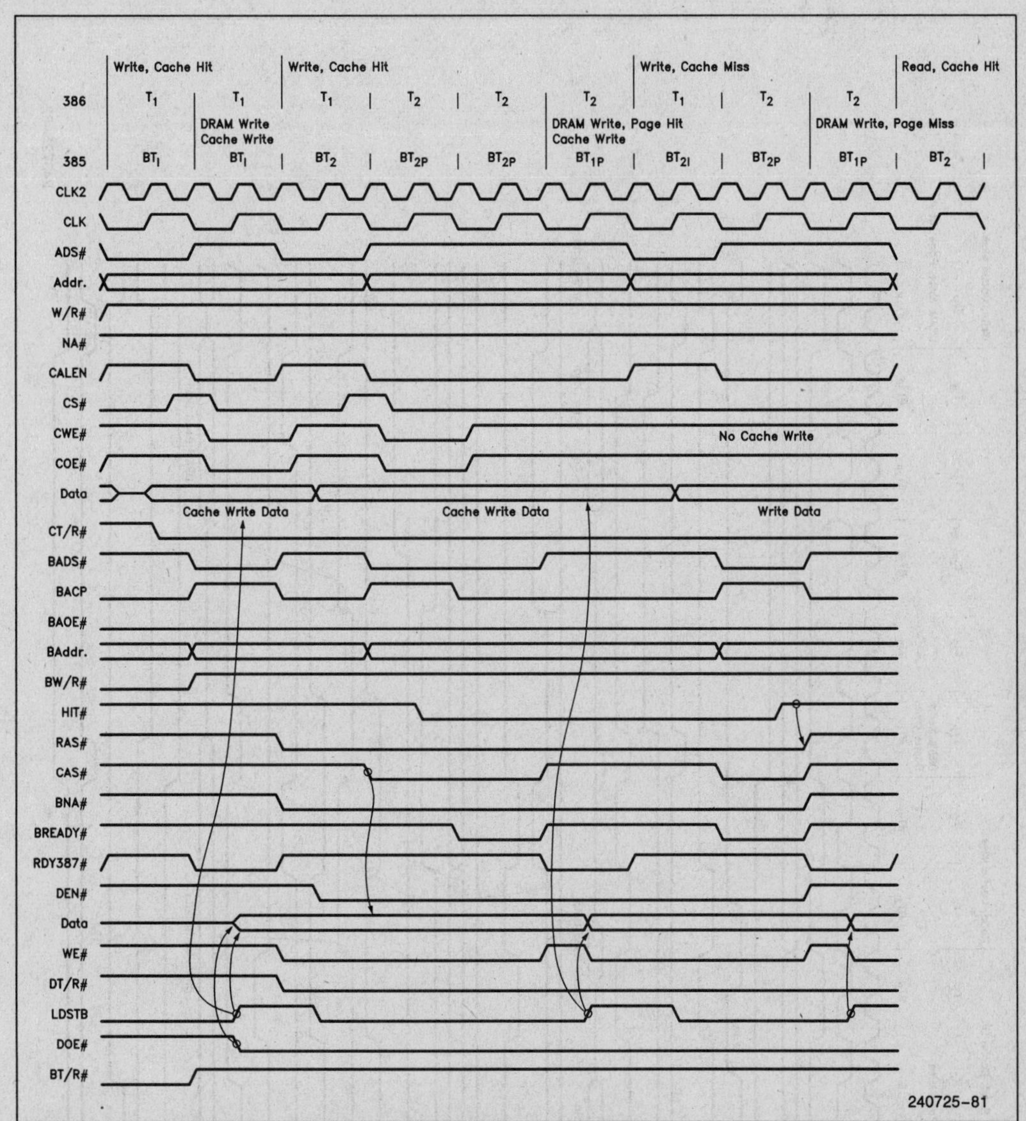

Cache Cycle (Continued)

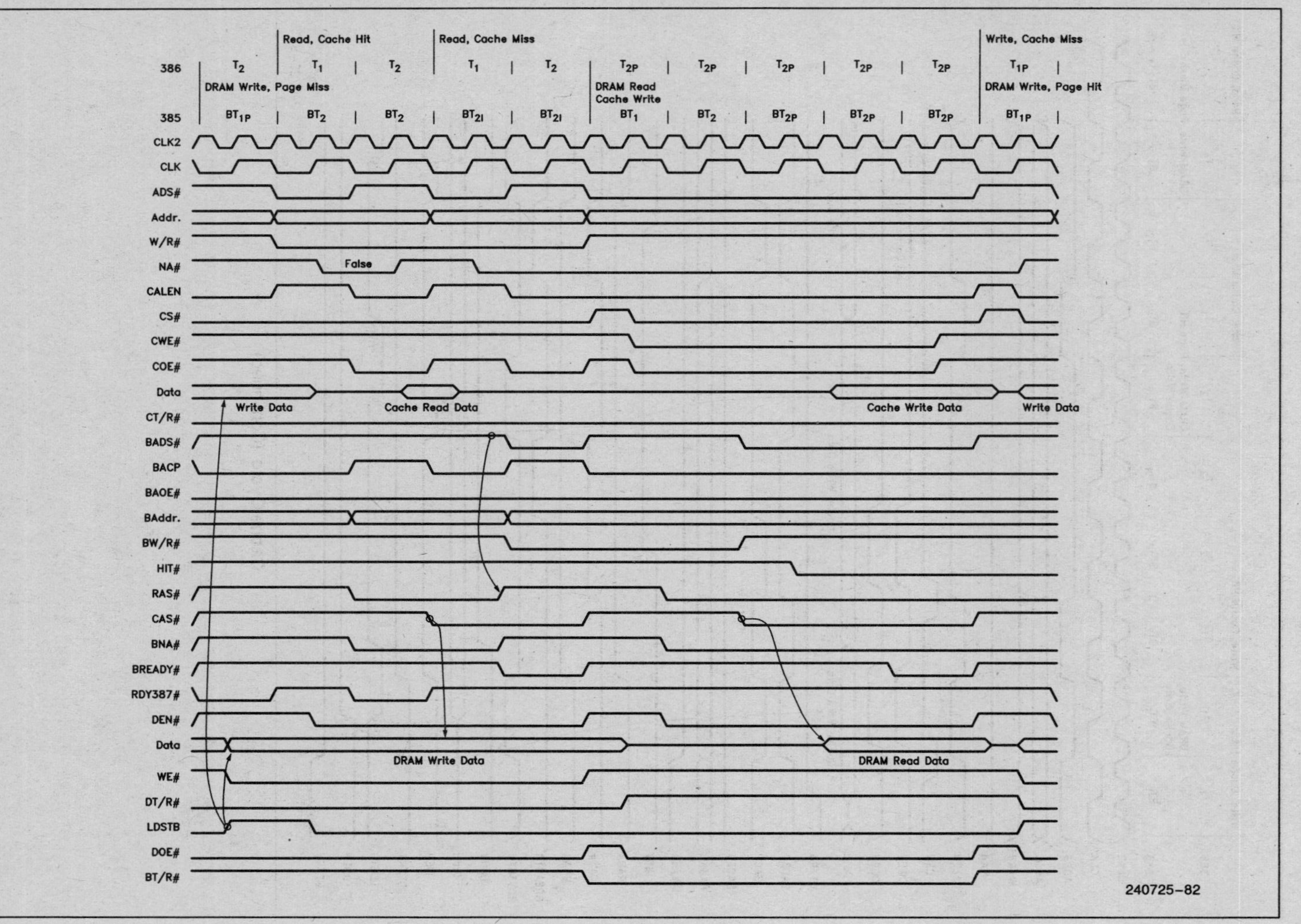

Cache Cycle (Continued)

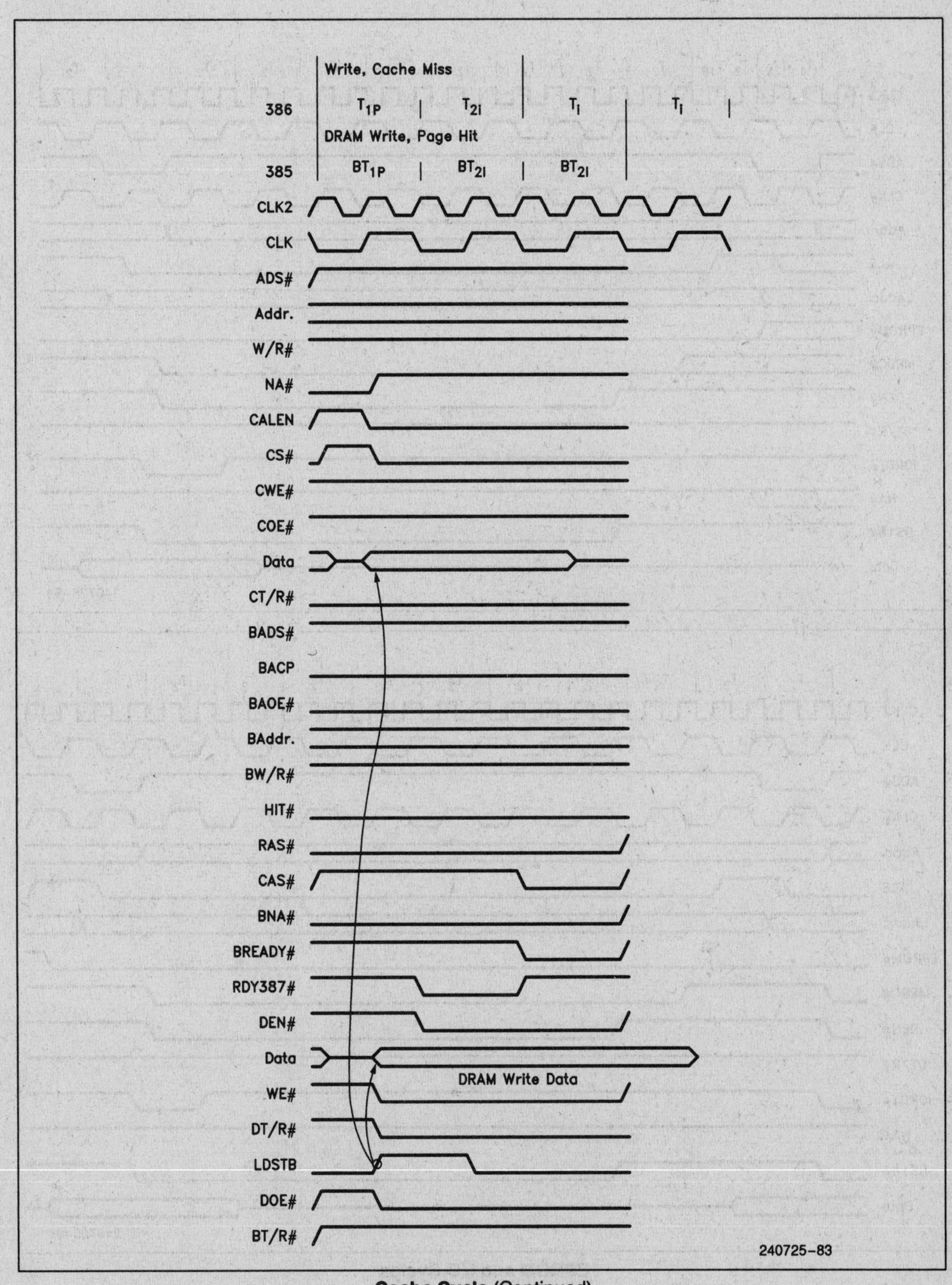

Cache Cycle (Continued)

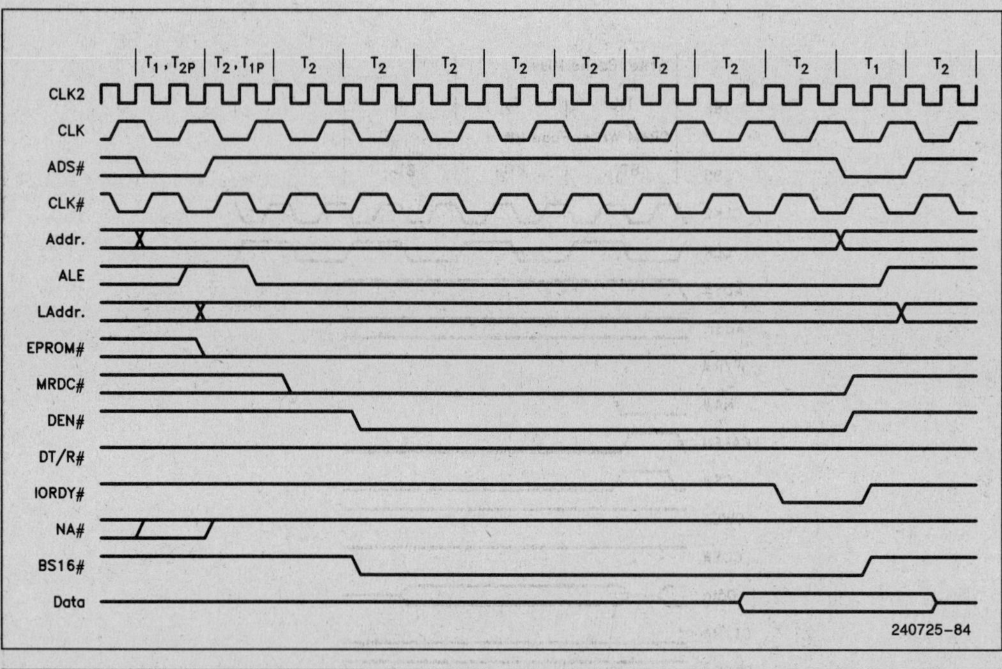

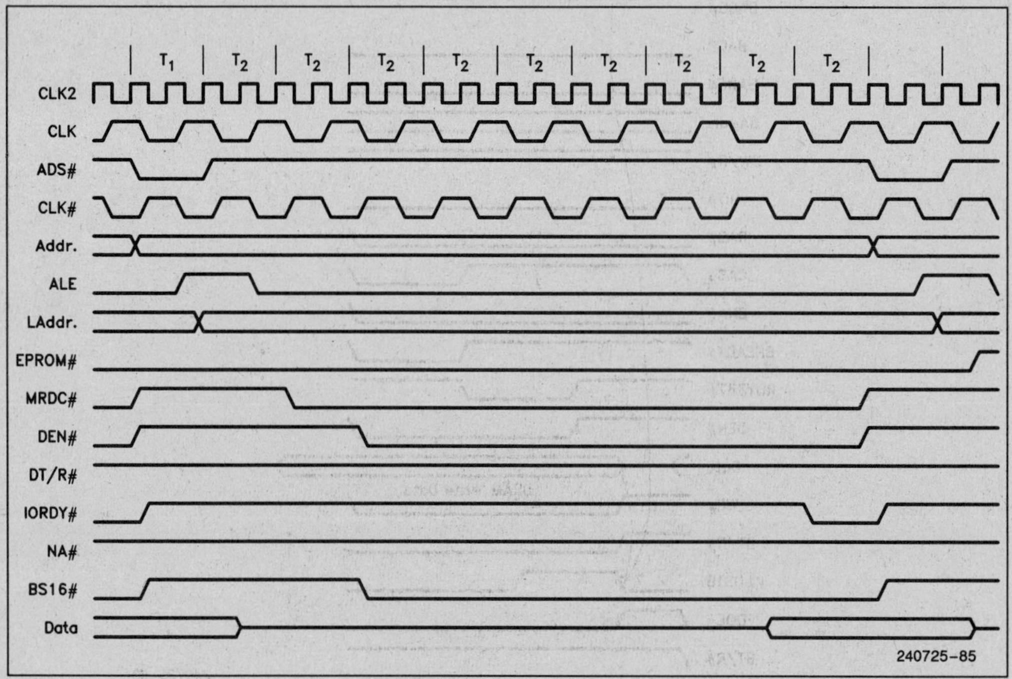

EPROM and I/O Cycles

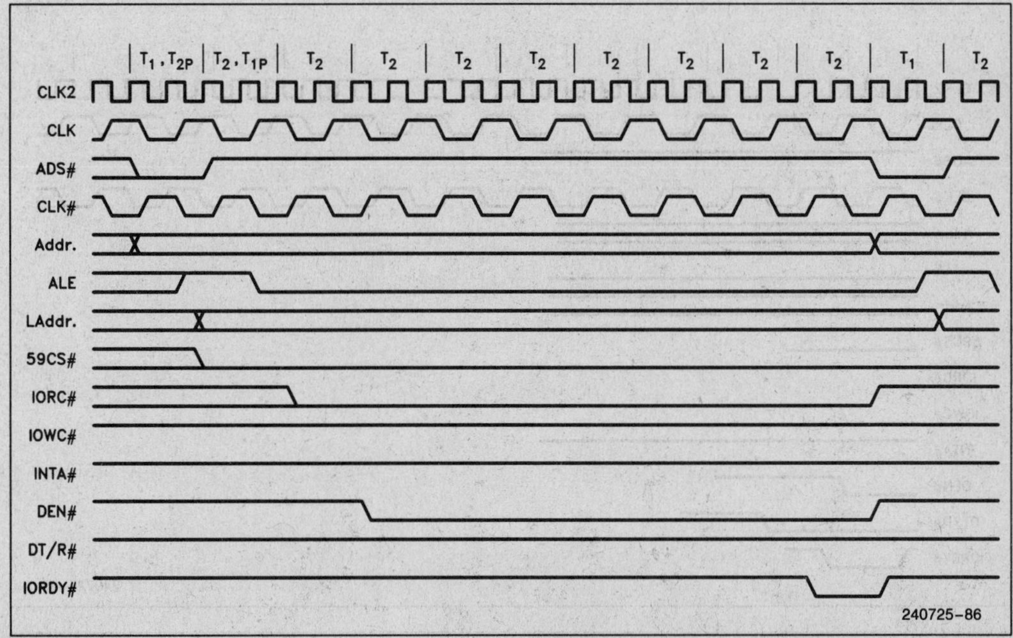

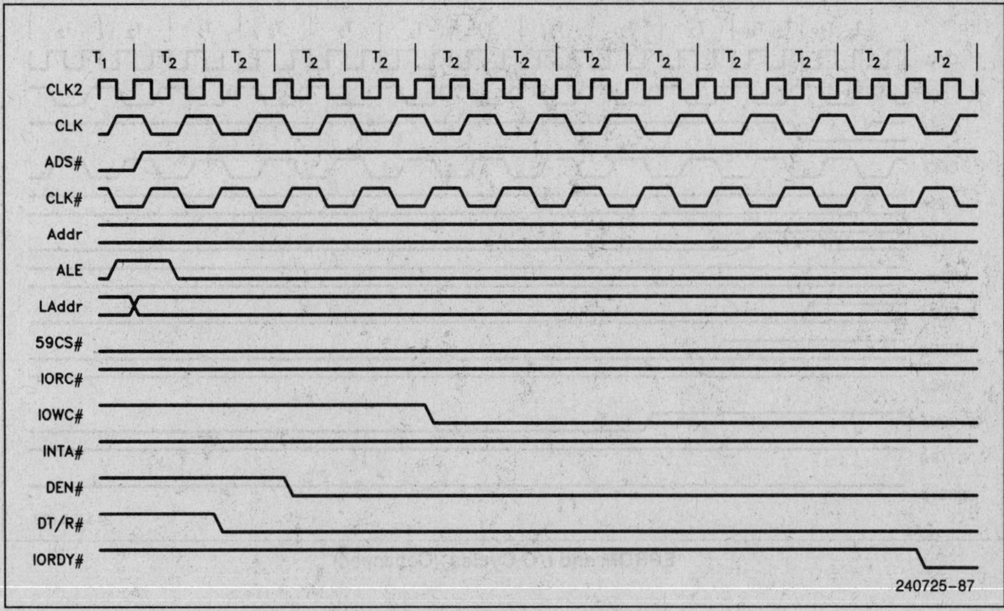

EPROM and I/O Cycles (Continued)

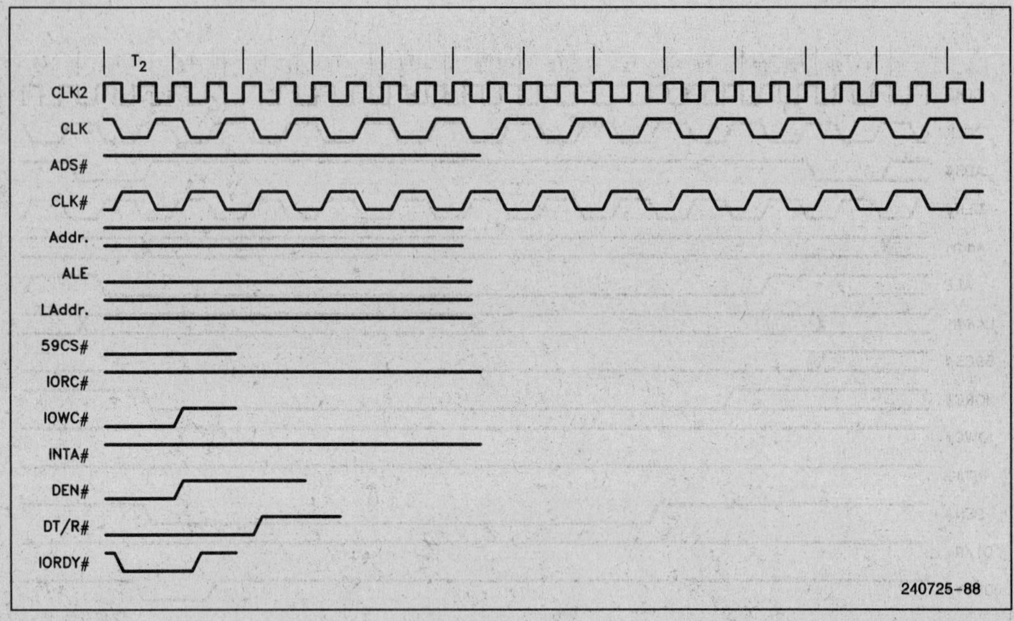

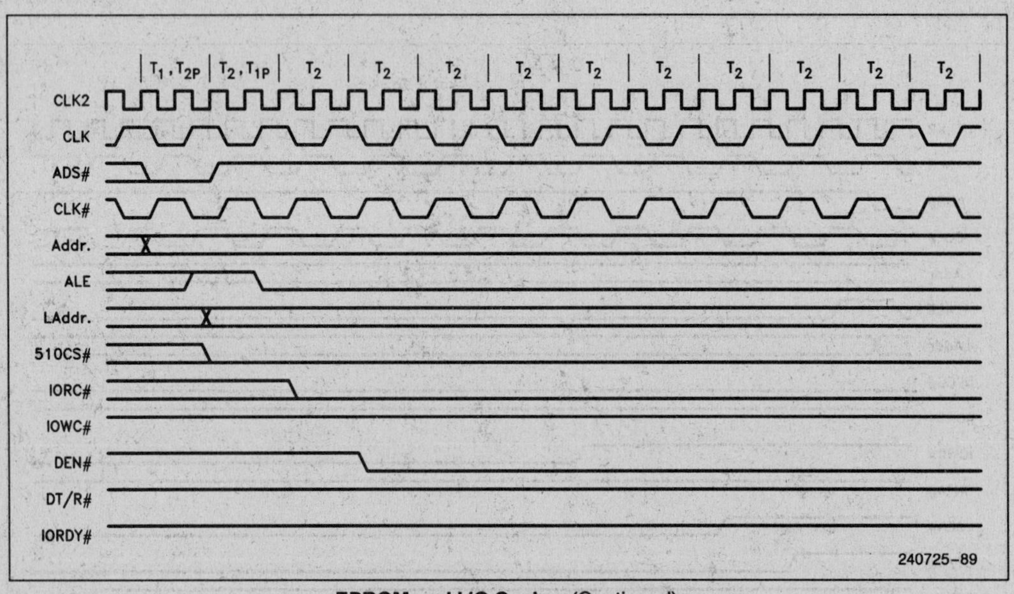

EPROM and I/O Cycles (Continued)

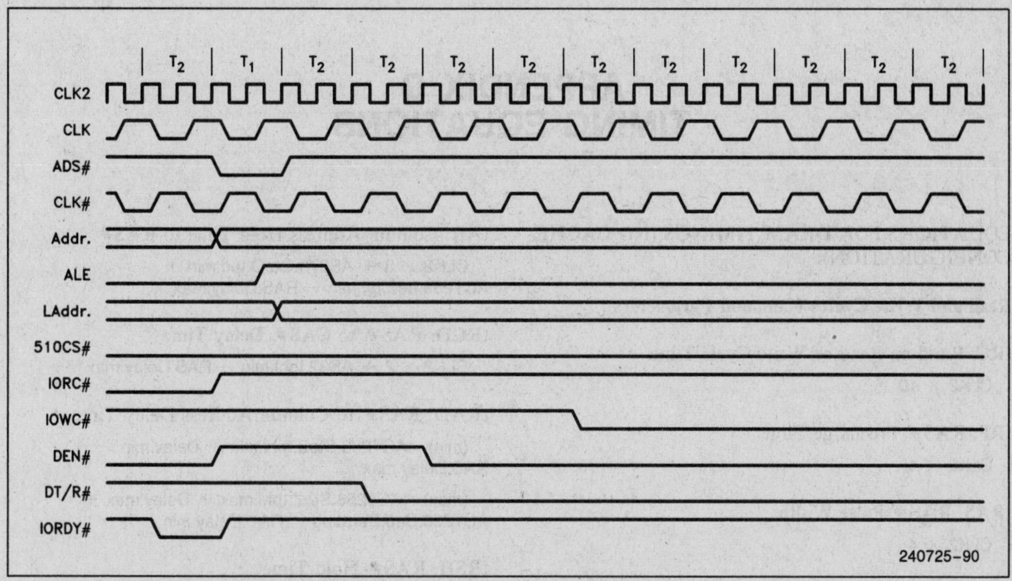

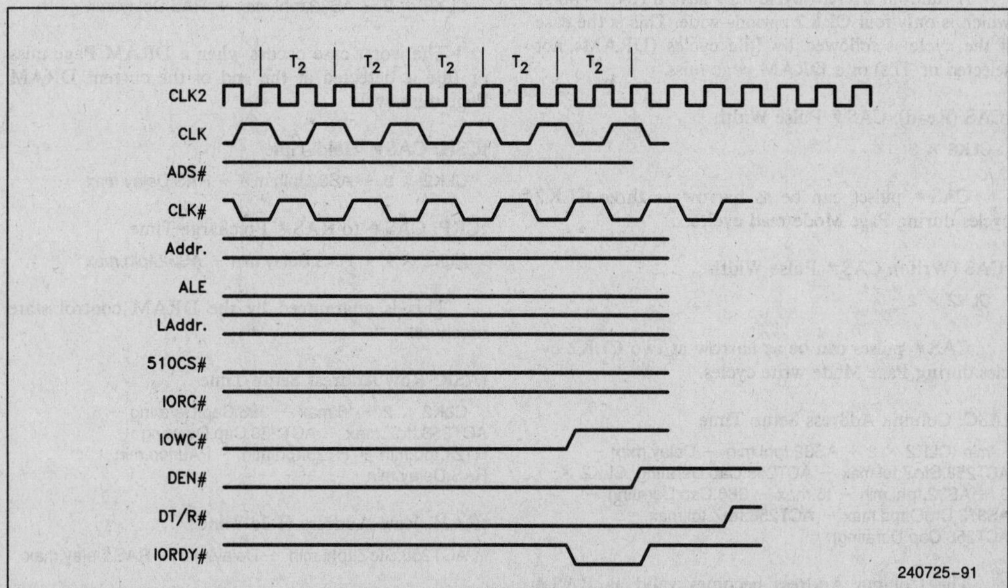

EPROM and I/O Cycles (Continued)

4

APPENDIX D
TIMING EQUATIONS

EQUATIONS FOR DRAM TIMINGS (NO CACHE CONFIGURATION):

Read and Write Cycles (Common Parameters):

tRC: Random Read or Write Cycle Time

CLK2 × 10

tRP: RAS# Precharge Time

CLK2 × 4

tRAS: RAS# Pulse Width

CLK2 × 4

A random DRAM cycle may have a RAS# pulse which is only four CLK2 periods wide. This is the case if the cycle is followed by Idle cycles (DRAMs not selected or Ti's) or a DRAM page miss.

tCAS (Read): CAS# Pulse Width

CLK2 × 3

CAS# pulses can be as narrow as three CLK2 cycles during Page Mode read cycles.

tCAS (Write): CAS# Pulse Width

CLK2 × 2

CAS# pulses can be as narrow as two CLK2 cycles during Page Mode write cycles.

tASC: Column Address Setup Time

min (CLK2 × 2 + AS32.tphl.min − Delay.max − ACT258.StoZ.tpl.max − ACT258.Cap.Derating, CLK2 × 3 + AS32.tphl.min − t6.max − 386.Cap.Derating − AS373.DtoO.tpd.max − ACT258.ItoZ.tpl.max − ACT258.Cap.Derating)

The Column Address becomes valid as RAS# switches from High to Low or as the 386 address becomes valid while RAS# is already Low (i.e., Page Mode, Pipelined cycles)

tCAH: Column Address Hold Time

CLK2 + AS373.GtoO.tpd.min + ACT258.ItoZ.tpl.min − AS32.tphl.max

The CAL (Column Address Latch) signal is activated one CLK2 period after the active-going edge of CAS#.

tAR: Column Address Hold Time to RAS#

CLK2 × 3 + AS373.GtoO.tpd.min + ACT258.ItoZ.tpl.min − RAS.Delay.max

tRCD: RAS# to CAS# Delay Time

CLK2 × 2 + AS32.tphl.min − RAS.Delay.max

tRAD: RAS# to Column Address Delay Time

(min) ACT258.StoZ.tphl.min + Delay.min − RAS.Delay.max

(max) ACT258.StoZ.tphl.max + Delay.max + ACT258.Cap.Derating − RAS.Delay.min

tRSH: RAS# Hold Time

CLK2 × 2 − AS32.tphl.max + RAS.Delay.min

The worst case occurs when a DRAM Page miss or Idle is detected at the end of the current DRAM Page miss cycle.

tCSH: CAS# Hold Time

CLK2 × 6 + AS32.tplh.min − RAS.Delay.max

tCRP: CAS# to RAS# Precharge Time

CLK2 × 2 + RAS.Delay.min − AS32.tplh.max

This is guaranteed by the DRAM control state machine.

tASR: Row Address Setup Time

CLK2 × 2 − t6.max − 386.Cap.Derating − ACT258.ItoZ.max − ACT258.Cap.Derating + H124.tpd.min + H125.tpd.min + PAL.tco.min + RAS.Delay.min

tRAH: Row Address Hold Time

ACT258.StoZ.tphl.min + Delay.min − RAS.Delay.max

tT: Transition Time (Rise and Fall)

tREF: Refresh Period

tREF2: Refresh Period

Read Cycles:

tRAC: Access Time

CLK2 × 6 − H124.tpd.max − H125.tpd.max − PAL.tco.max − t21.min − F245.max − RAS.Delay.max

tCAC: Access Time from CAS#

CLK2 × 3 − H124.tpd.max − H125.tpd.max − PAL.tco.max − AS32.tphl.max − t21.min − F245.max

tAA: Access Time from Address

CLK2 × 6 − t6.max − 386.Cap.Derating − AS373.DtoO.max − ACT258.ItoZ.tp.max − ACT258.Cap.Derating − t21.min − F245.max

tRCS: Read Command Setup Time

CLK2 + AS32.tphl.min

tRCH: Read Command Hold Time to CAS#

CLK2 − AS32.tplh.max

tRRH: Read Command Hold Time to RAS#

CLK2 − RAS.Delay.max

tOFF: Output Buffer Turn-off Time

CLK2 × 2 + F245.tzh.min

Write Cycles:

tWCS: Write Command Setup Time

CLK2 × 3 + AS32.tphl.min

tWCH: Write Command Hold Time

CLK2 × 2 − AS32.tplh.max

tWCR: Write Command Hold Time to RAS#

CLK2 × 6 − RAS.Delay.max

tWP: Write Command Pulse Width

CLK2 × 5

tRWL: Write Command to RAS# Lead Time

CLK2 × 5 + RAS.Delay.min

tCWL: Write Command to CAS# Lead Time

CLK2 × 5

tDS: Data-in Setup Time

CLK2 × 3 + H124.tp.min + H125.tp.min + AS32.tphl.min − T12.max − F245.tp.max

tDH: Data-in Hold Time

CLK2 × 2 + F245.tpz.min − AS32.tphl.max

tDHR: Data-in Hold Time to RAS#

CLK2 × 6 + F245.tpz.max + RAS.Delay.min

Page Mode Cycles:

tPC: Page Mode Cycle Time

CLK2 × 4

tRAPC: Page Mode RAS# Pulse Width

CLK2 × 4

tRSW: RAS# to Second WE# Delay Time

CLK2 × 7 − RAS.Delay.max

tCP: CAS# Precharge Time

CLK2

tWI: Write Invalid Time

CLK2

tCAP: Access Time from Column Precharge Time

CLK2 × 4 − H124.tp.max − H125.tp.max − PAL.tco.max − t21.min − F245.max

80386 A.C. SPECIFICATIONS

Symbol	Parameter	80386-33 Minimum	80386-33 Maximum
	Operating Frequency	8.00	33.33
t1	CLK2 Period	15.00	62.50
t2a	CLK2 High Time	6.25	
t2b	CLK2 High Time	4.50	
t3a	CLK2 Low Time	6.25	
t3b	CLK2 Low Time	4.50	
t4	CLK2 Fall Time		4.00
t5	CLK2 Rise Time		4.00
t6	A2-A31 Valid Delay	4.00	15.00
t7	A2-A31 Float Delay	4.00	20.00
t8	BE0#-BE3#, LOCK# Valid Delay	4.00	15.00
t9	BE0#-BE3#, LOCK# Float Delay	4.00	20.00
t10	W/R#, M/IO#, D/C#, ADS# Valid Delay	4.00	15.00
t11	W/R#, M/IO#, D/C#, ADS# Float Delay	4.00	25.00
t12	D0-D31 Write Data Valid Delay	5.00	24.00
t13	D0-D31 Float Delay	4.00	17.00
t14	HLDA Valid Delay	4.00	20.00
t15	NA# Setup Time	5.00	
t16	NA# Hold Time	3.00	
t17	BS16# Setup Time	5.00	
t18	BS16# Hold Time	3.00	
t19	Ready# Setup Time	7.00	
t20	Ready# Hold Time	4.00	
t21	D0-D31 Read Setup Time	5.00	
t22	D0-D31 Read Hold Time	3.00	
t23	HOLD Setup Time	11.00	
t24	HOLD Hold Time	3.00	
t25	RESET Setup Time	8.00	
t26	RESET Hold Time	3.00	
t27	NMI, INTR Setup Time	5.00	
t28	NMI, INTR Hold Time	5.00	
t29	PEREQ, ERROR#, BUSY# Setup Time	5.00	
t30	PEREQ, ERROR#, BUSY# Hold Time	4.00	

PAL SPECIFICATIONS

Symbol	Parameter	Minimum	Maximum
ts	Input or Feedback Setup Time	7.00	
tco	Clock to Output	3.00	6.50

ROW ADDRESS LATCH SPECIFICATIONS
74FCT843B (IDT)

Symbol	Parameter	50 pF Minimum	Maximum
tplh	Dn to On Propagation Delay	3.00	6.50
tphl		3.00	6.50
tplh	G to On Propagation Delay	6.00	8.00
tphl		4.00	8.00
ts	Setup Time	2.00	
th	Hold Time	3.00	

240725-C7

Timings for No Cache Configuration

ROW ADDRESS COMPARATOR SPECIFICATIONS
74PCT521B (Performance)

Symbol	Parameter	Minimum	Maximum
tplh	An or Bn to Q Propagation Delay	1.50	5.50
tphl		1.50	5.50
tplh	I to Q Propagation Delay	1.50	4.60
tphl		1.50	4.60

DRAM ADDRESS MULTIPLEXER SPECIFICATIONS
74ACT258

Symbol	Parameter	Minimum	Maximum
tplh	S to Zn Propagation Delay	1.00	11.50
tphl		1.00	11.00
tplh	E# to Zn Propagation Delay	1.00	9.50
tphl		1.00	9.50
tplh	In to Zn Propagation Delay	1.00	9.50
tphl		1.00	8.00

DATA TRANSCEIVER SPECIFICATIONS
74F245

Symbol	Parameter	Minimum	Maximum
tplh	An to Bn or Bn to An Propagation Delay	2.50	7.00
tphl		2.50	7.00
tzh	Output Enable Time	3.00	8.00
tzl		3.50	9.00
tphz	Output Disable Time	3.00	7.50
tplz		2.00	7.50

COLUMN ADDRESS LATCH SPECIFICATIONS
74AS573

Symbol	Parameter	Minimum	Maximum
tplh	Dn to On Propagation Delay	3.00	6.00
tphl		3.00	6.00
tplh	G to On Propagation Delay	6.00	11.50
tphl		4.00	7.50
ts	Setup Time	2.00	
th	Hold Time	3.00	

RAS# DELAY

Symbol	Parameter	Minimum	Maximum
tp	Propagation Delay	0.00	0.00

240725-C8

Timings for No Cache Configuration (Continued)

4

OR SPECIFICATIONS
74AS32

Symbol	Parameter	Minimum	Maximum
tplh	Propagation Delay	1.00	5.80
tphl		1.00	5.80

DRAM TIMING REQUIREMENTS

Symbol	Parameter	For 80386-33 Minimum	For 80386-33 Maximum	Timing Margin (NMB 2801-06) Minimum	Timing Margin (NMB 2801-06) Maximum
Read and Write Cycles (Common Parameters):					
tRC	Random Read or Write Cycle Time	150.00		29.00	
tRP	RAS# Precharge Time	60.00		5.00	
tRAS	RAS# Pulse Width	60.00		0.00	
tCAS	CAS# Pulse Width (Read)	45.00		34.00	
tCAS	CAS# Pulse Width (Write)	30.00		25.00	
tASC	Column Address Setup Time	9.70		9.70	
tCAH	Column Address Hold Time	14.20		8.20	
tAR	Column Address Hold Time to RAS#	50.00		10.00	
tRCD	RAS# to CAS# Delay Time	31.00		25.00	14.00
tRAD	RAS# to Column Address Delay Time	5.00	21.30	1.00	6.70
tRSH	RAS# Hold Time	24.20		9.20	
tCSH	CAS# Hold Time	91.00		51.00	
tCRP	CAS# to RAS# Precharge Time	24.20		21.20	
tASR	Row Address Setup Time	5.45		3.45	
tRAH	Row Address Hold Time	5.00		3.00	
tT	Transition Time (Rise and Fall)				
tREF	Refresh Period				
tREF2	Refresh Period				
Read Cycles:					
tRAC	Access Time	68.25		8.25	
tCAC	Access Time from CAS#	17.45		6.45	
tAA	Access Time from Address	41.20		9.20	
tRCS	Read Command Setup Time	16.00		16.00	
tRCH	Read Command Hold Time to CAS#	9.20		9.20	
tRRH	Read Command Hold Time to RAS#	15.00		15.00	
tOFF	Output Buffer Turn-off Time		33.00		16.00
Write Cycles:					
tWCS	Write Command Setup Time	46.00		46.00	
tWCH	Write Command Hold Time	24.20		19.20	
tWCR	Write Command Hold Time to RAS#	90.00		50.00	
tWP	Write Command Pulse Width	75.00		70.00	
tRWL	Write Command to RAS# Lead Time	75.00		62.00	
tCWL	Write Command to CAS# Lead Time	75.00		70.00	
tDS	Data-in Setup Time	17.75		17.75	
tDH	Data-in Hold Time	26.20		21.20	
tDHR	Data-in Hold Time to RAS#	97.50		57.50	
Page Mode Cycles:					
tPC	Page Mode Cycle Time	60.00		23.00	
tRAPC	Page Mode RAS# Pulse Width	60.00			
tRSW	RAS# to Second WE# Delay Time	105.00			
tCP	CAS# Precharge Time	15.00		10.00	
tWI	Write Invalid Time	15.00			
tCAP	Access Time from Column Precharge Time		38.25		4.25

240725-C9

Timings for No Cache Configuration (Continued)

ADDRESS DECODER REQUIREMENTS

Symbol	Parameter	For 80386-33 Minimum	Maximum
tpd	Available Propagation Delay		8.75

ROW ADDRESS COMPARATOR REQUIREMENTS

Symbol	Parameter	For 80386-33 Minimum	Maximum
tpd	Available Propagation Delay		8.75

NA# SETUP TIME

Symbol	Parameter	Minimum	Maximum
tNA#	Available NA# Setup Time	5.25	

QUAD TTL TO 10KH-ECL TRANSLATOR
MC10H124

Symbol	Parameter	Minimum	Maximum
tpd	Propagation Delay	2.75	3.25

QUAD 10KH-ECL to TTL TRANSLATOR
MC10H125

Symbol	Parameter	Minimum	Maximum
tpd	Propagation Delay	0.00	0.00

DELAY ELEMENT

Symbol	Parameter	Minimum	Maximum
tpd	Propagation Delay	4.00	6.00

240725-D0

Timings for No Cache Configuration (Continued)

DRAM SPECIFICATIONS

Symbol	NMB 2801-06 Minimum	NMB 2801-06 Maximum	VITELIC V53C256 (70 ns) Minimum	VITELIC V53C256 (70 ns) Maximum
tRC	121.00		130.00	
tRP	55.00		50.00	
tRAS	60.00	100000	70.00	75000.00
tCAS	11.00		15, 20	75000.00
tCAS	5.00			
tASC	0.00		0.00	
tCAH	6.00		15.00	
tAR	40.00		55.00	
tRCD	6.00	45.00	25.00	55.00
tRAD	4.00	28.00	20.00	35.00
tRSH	15.00		15, 25	
tCSH	40.00		70.00	
tCRP	3.00		15.00	
tASR	2.00		0.00	
tRAH	2.00		15.00	
tT			3.00	25.00
tREF				
tREF2				
tRAC		60.00		70.00
tCAC		11.00		15.00
tAA		32.00		35.00
tRCS	0.00		0.00	
tRCH	0.00		5.00	
tRRH	0.00		5.00	
tOFF		17.00	0.00	15.00
tWCS	0.00		0.00	
tWCH	5.00		15.00	
tWCR	40.00		55.00	
tWP	5.00		15.00	
tRWL	13.00		20.00	
tCWL	5.00		20.00	
tDS	0.00		0.00	
tDH	5.00		15.00	
tDHR	40.00		55.00	
tPC	37.00		50.00	
tRAPC				
tRSW				
tCP	5.00		15.00	
tWI				
tCAP		34.00		45.00

240725-D1

CAPACITIVE LOAD TIMING DERATING FOR 74ACT258

Load Capacitance (pF)	Additional Propagation Delay (ns)
60.00	0.26 (p = 0.02625q - 1.3125)
80.00	0.79
100.00	0.89 (p = 0.022q - 1.3125)
120.00	1.33
140.00	1.77
160.00	2.21
180.00	2.65
200.00	3.09
220.00	3.83 (p = 0.01666q + 0.1666)
240.00	4.17
260.00	4.50
280.00	4.83
300.00	5.17

DRAM ADDRESS BUS TIMING DERATING

Reason	Capacitive Load (pF)	Additional Propagation Delay (ns)
DRAM Address Inputs	160.00	
F258 Output		
Microstrip/Strip Lines	60.00	
TOTAL	220.00 ===>	3.80

240725-D2

Timings for No Cache Configuration (Continued)

EQUATIONS FOR DRAM TIMINGS (82385 Active):

Read and Write Cycles (Common Parameters):

tRC: Random Read or Write Cycle Time

CLK2 × 10

tRP: RAS# Precharge Time

CLK2 × 4

tRAS: RAS# Pulse Width

CLK2 × 4

A random DRAM cycle may have a RAS# pulse which is only four CLK2 periods wide. This is the case if the cycle is followed by Idle cycles (DRAMs not selected or Ti's) or a DRAM page miss.

tCAS (Read): CAS# Pulse Width

CLK2 × 5

CAS# pulses can be as narrow as five CLK2 cycles during Page Mode read cycles.

tCAS (Write): CAS# Pulse Width

CLK2 × 2

CAS# pulses can be as narrow as two CLK2 cycles during Page Mode write cycles.

tASC: Column Address Setup Time

min (CLK2 × 2 + AS32.tphl.min − Delay.max − ACT258.StoZ.tpl.max − ACT258.Cap.Derating, CLK2 × 3 + AS32.tphl.min − t6.max − 386.Cap.Derating − AS373.DtoO.tpd.max − ACT258.ItoZ.tpl.max − ACT258.Cap.Derating)

The Column Address becomes valid as RAS# switches from High to Low or as the 386 address becomes valid while RAS# is already Low (i.e., Page Mode, Pipelined cycles)

tCAH: Column Address Hold Time

CLK2 + AS373.GtoO.tpd.min + ACT258.ItoZ.tpl.min − AS32.tphl.max

The CAL (Column Address Latch) signal is activated one CLK2 period after the active-going edge of CAS#.

tAR: Column Address Hold Time to RAS#

CLK2 × 3 + AS373.GtoO.tpd.min + ACT258.ItoZ.tpl.min − RAS.Delay.max

tRCD: RAS# to CAS# Delay Time

CLK2 × 2 + AS32.tphl.min − RAS.Delay.max

tRAD: RAS# to Column Address Delay Time

(min) ACT258.StoZ.tphl.min + Delay.min − RAS.Delay.max

(max) ACT258.StoZ.tphl.max + Delay.max + ACT258.Cap.Derating − RAS.Delay.min

tRSH: RAS# Hold Time

CLK2 × 2 − AS32.tphl.max + RAS.Delay.min

The worst case occurs when a DRAM Page miss or Idle is detected at the end of the current DRAM Page miss cycle.

tCSH: CAS# Hold Time

CLK2 × 6 + AS32.tphl.min − RAS.Delay.max

tCRP: CAS# to RAS# Precharge Time

CLK2 × 2 + RAS.Delay.min − AS32.tplh.max

This is guaranteed by the DRAM control state machine.

tASR: Row Address Setup Time

CLK2 × 2 − t6.max − 386.Cap.Derating − ACT258.ItoZ.max − ACT258.Cap.Derating + H124.tpd.min + H125.tpd.min + PAL.tco.min + RAS.Delay.min

tRAH: Row Address Hold Time

ACT258.StoZ.tphl.min + Delay.min − RAS.Delay.max

tT: Transition Time (Rise and Fall)

tREF: Refresh Period

tREF2: Refresh Period

4

Read Cycles:

tRAC: Access Time

CLK2 × 8 − H124.tpd.max − H125.tpd.max − PAL.tco.max − − F245.max − AS646.tpd.max − F245.max − RAS.Delay.max − SRAM.tDW − CLK2 + 385.t22a.min

tCAC: Access Time from CAS#

CLK2 × 5 − H124.tpd.max − H125.tpd.max − PAL.tco.max − AS32.tphl.max − F245.max − AS646.tpd.max − F245.max − SRAM.tDW − CLK2 + 385.t22a.min

tAA: Access Time from Address

CLK2 × 8 − t6.max − 386.Cap.Derating − AS373.DtoO.max − ACT258.ItoZ.tp.max − ACT258.Cap.Derating − F245.max − AS646.tpd.max − F245.max − SRAM.tDW − CLK2 + 385.t22a.min

tRCS: Read Command Setup Time

CLK2 + AS32.tphl.min

tRCH: Read Command Hold Time to CAS#

CLK2 − AS32.tplh.max

tRRH: Read Command Hold Time to RAS#

CLK2 − RAS.Delay.max

tOFF: Output Buffer Turn-off Time

CLK2 × 2 + F245.tzh.min

Write Cycles:

tWCS: Write Command Setup Time

CLK2 × 3 + AS32.tphl.min

tWCH: Write Command Hold Time

CLK2 × 2 − AS32.tplh.max

tWCR: Write Command Hold Time to RAS#

CLK2 × 6 − RAS.Delay.max

tWP: Write Command Pulse Width

CLK2 × 5

tRWL: Write Command to RAS# Lead Time

CLK2 × 5 + RAS.Delay.min

tCWL: Write Command to CAS# Lead Time

CLK2 × 5

tDS: Data-in Setup Time

CLK2 × 3 + H124.tp.min + H125.tp.min + AS32.tphl.min − − 385.t43c.max − AS646.GotO.tp.max − F245.tp.max

tDH: Data-in Hold Time

CLK2 × 2 + F245.tpz.min − AS32.tphl.max

tDHR: Data-in Hold Time to RAS#

CLK2 × 6 + F245.tpz.max + RAS.Delay.min

Page Mode Cycles:

tPC: Page Mode Cycle Time

CLK2 × 6

tRAPC: Page Mode RAS# Pulse Width

CLK2 × 4

tRSW: RAS# to Second WE# Delay Time

CLK2 × 7 − RAS.Delay.max

tCP: CAS# Precharge Time

CLK2

tWI: Write Invalid Time

CLK2

tCAP: Access Time from Column Precharge Time

CLK2 × 6 − H124.tp.max − H125.tp.max − PAL.tco.max − − F245.max − AS646.tpd.max − F245.max − SRAM.tDW − CLK2 + 385.t22a.min

DRAM TIMING REQUIREMENTS

Symbol	Parameter	For 80386-33 Minimum	For 80386-33 Maximum	Timing Margin (NMB 2801-06) Minimum	Timing Margin (NMB 2801-06) Maximum
Read and Write Cycles (Common Parameters):					
tRC	Random Read or Write Cycle Time	150.00		29.00	
tRP	RAS# Precharge Time	60.00		5.00	
tRAS	RAS# Pulse Width	60.00		0.00	
tCAS	CAS# Pulse Width (Read)	75.00		64.00	
tCAS	CAS# Pulse Width (Write)	30.00		25.00	
tASC	Column Address Setup Time	9.70		9.70	
tCAH	Column Address Hold Time	14.20		8.20	
tAR	Column Address Hold Time to RAS#	50.00		10.00	
tRCD	RAS# to CAS# Delay Time	31.00		25.00	14.00
tRAD	RAS# to Column Address Delay Time	5.00	21.30	1.00	6.70
tRSH	RAS# Hold Time	24.20		9.20	
tCSH	CAS# Hold Time	91.00		51.00	
tCRP	CAS# to RAS# Precharge Time	24.20		21.20	
tASR	Row Address Setup Time	6.20		4.20	
tRAH	Row Address Hold Time	5.00		3.00	
tT	Transition Time (Rise and Fall)				
tREF	Refresh Period				
tREF2	Refresh Period				
Read Cycles:					
tRAC	Access Time	67.50		7.50	
tCAC	Access Time from CAS#	16.70		5.70	
tAA	Access Time from Address	37.70		5.70	
tRCS	Read Command Setup Time	20.80		20.80	
tRCH	Read Command Hold Time to CAS#	9.20		9.20	
tRRH	Read Command Hold Time to RAS#	15.00		15.00	
tOFF	Output Buffer Turn-off Time		33.00		16.00
Write Cycles:					
tWCS	Write Command Setup Time	46.00		46.00	
tWCH	Write Command Hold Time	24.20		19.20	
tWCR	Write Command Hold Time to RAS#	90.00		50.00	
tWP	Write Command Pulse Width	75.00		70.00	
tRWL	Write Command to RAS# Lead Time	75.00		62.00	
tCWL	Write Command to CAS# Lead Time	75.00		70.00	
tDS	Data-in Setup Time	9.00		9.00	
tDH	Data-in Hold Time	31.70		26.70	
tDHR	Data-in Hold Time to RAS#	97.50		57.50	
Page Mode Cycles:					
tPC	Page Mode Cycle Time	90.00		53.00	
tRAPC	Page Mode RAS# Pulse Width	60.00			
tRSW	RAS# to Second WE# Delay Time	105.00			
tCP	CAS# Precharge Time	15.00		10.00	
tWI	Write Invalid Time	15.00			
tCAP	Access Time from Column Precharge Time		37.50		3.50

240725-D3

Timings with Cache Active

APPENDIX E
REFERENCES

REFERENCES

Advanced CMOS Logic Designer's Handbook, Texas Instruments Inc., 1988.

Blood W., *MECL System Design Handbook*, Motorola Corp., 1983.

Keeler R., "High Speed Digital Printed Circuit Boards," *Electronic Packaging & Production*, pp. 140-145, Jan. 1986.

Tomlinson J., "Avoid The Pitfalls of High Speed Logic Design," *Electronic Design*, pp. 75-84, Nov. 9, 1989.

Pace C., "Terminate Bus Lines to Avoid Overshoot and Ringing," *EDN*, pp. 227-234, Sept. 17, 1987.

Royle D., "Rules Tell Whether Interconnections Act Like Transmission Lines," *EDN*, pp. 131-136, June 23, 1988.

Royle D., "Correct Signal Faults by Implementing Line-Analysis Theory," *EDN*, pp. 143-148, June 23, 1988.

Winchester E., "Guidelines Help You Design High-Speed PC Boards," *EDN*, pp. 221-226, Nov. 28, 1985.

Yeargan J. R., Day R. L., and Nguyen T., "Effects of Printed Circuit Board Transmission Lines an Loading on Gate Performance," *IEEE Transactions on Industrial Electronics*, Vol. IE-34, no. 3, pp. 399-405, Aug. 1987.

intel®

ADVANCE INFORMATION

Intel386™ SL MICROPROCESSOR SuperSet
Highly-Integrated Static Intel386™ Microprocessor
Complete ISA Peripheral Subsystem
System-Wide Power Management

- Static Intel386™ CPU Core
  - Runs MS-DOS*, WINDOWS*, OS/2* and UNIX*
  - Object Code Compatible with Intel 8086, 80286 and Intel386 Microprocessors
- Architecture Extension for Power Management Transparent to Operating Systems and Applications
- Complete ISA System, with Extended Support
  - Full ISA Bus Control, Status and Address and Data Interface Logic, with Full 24 mA Drive
  - Compatible ISA Bus Peripherals
  - System I/O Decoding, Programmable Chip Selects and Support Interfaces
  - High-Speed Peripheral Interface Bus (PI-Bus Support)
  - New ideaPort Interface for Hardware Expansion
- Integrated Cache Controller and Tag RAM(1)
  - No-Glue Cache SRAM Interface
  - 16k, 32k, or 64 kByte Cache Size
  - Direct, 2-Way or 4-Way Set Associative Organization
- Programmable Memory Control
  - No-Glue, Page-Mode DRAM Interface
  - SRAM Support for Lowest Power
  - 512k to 32 MBytes
  - Full Hardware LIM EMS 4.0

NOTE:
1. The Cache Controller is not integrated into the 16 MHz speed variant of the Intel386™ SL microprocessor.

4

The Intel386™ SL Microprocessor SuperSet combines an ISA bus compatible personal computer's microprocessor, memory controller, cache controller and peripheral subsystems into just two Very Large Scale Integration (VLSI) devices. The product's high-integration and power conservation features reduce the size and power consumption typically associated with fully Industry Standard Architecture (ISA) bus compatible systems. In addition, new expandability and flexibility features offer the capability for continued innovation in battery-operated, space-constrained systems. The SL SuperSet brings 100% ISA-Bus compatibility to system designs ranging from the smallest palm-top and notebook PCs to expandable lap-top systems.

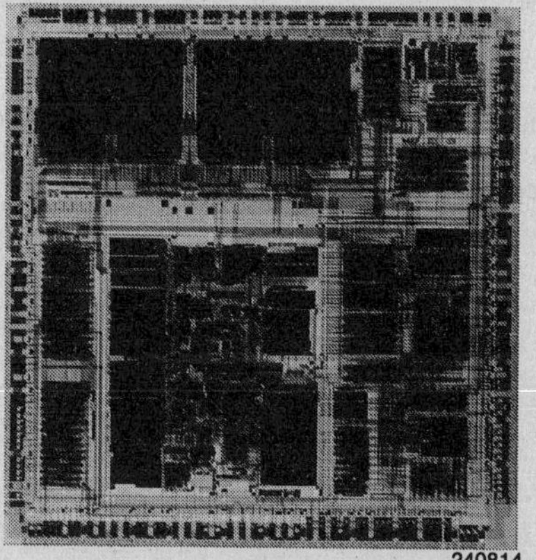

240814-1

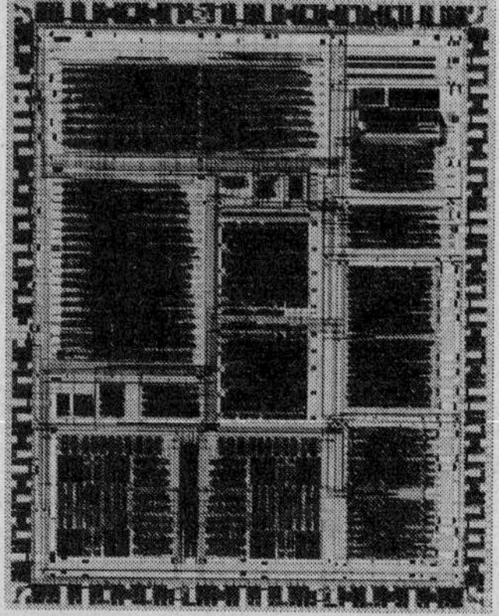

240814-2

Figure 1-1. Die Photograph of the Intel386™ SL Microprocessor (left) and 82360SL ISA Peripheral I/O (right)

September 1991
Order Number: 240814-003

Intel386™ SL MICROPROCESSOR
Intel386™ Microprocessor Core, with Integrated Memory and Cache Controllers and System Power Management
Fully-Static CHMOS IV Technology

- **Static Intel386™ CPU Core**
  - Optimized and Compatible with Standard Operating System Software such as: MS-DOS*, WINDOWS*, OS/2* and UNIX*
  - Object Code Compatible with Intel 8086, 80286 and Intel386 Microprocessors
  - Runs All Desk-Top Applications, 16- or 32-Bit
  - D.C. to 25 MHz Operation
  - 20 Megabytes Physical Memory/ 64 Terabytes Virtual Memory
  - 4 Gigabyte Maximum Segment Size
  - High Integration, Low Power Intel CHMOS IV Process Technology
- **Transparent Power-Management System Architecture**
  - System Management Mode Architecture Extension for Truly Compatible Systems
  - Power Management Transparent to Operating Systems and Application Programs
  - Programmable Hardware Supports Custom Power-Control Methods
- **Direct Drive Bus Interfaces**
  - Full ISA Bus Interface, with 24 mA Drive
  - High Speed Peripheral Interface Bus
- **Integrated Cache Controller and Tag RAM(1)**
  - No-Glue Cache SRAM Interface
  - 16k, 32k, or 64 kByte Cache Size
  - Direct, 2-Way or 4-Way Set Associative Organization
  - Write Posting—Posted Memory Writes
  - 16-Bit Line Size—Reduces Bus Utilization for Cache Line Fills
  - Write-Thru, with SmartHit Algorithm for Reduced Main Memory Power Consumption
- **Programmable Memory Control**
  - No-Glue, Page-Mode DRAM Interface
  - SRAM Support for Lowest Power
  - 1, 2, or 4 Banks Interleaved, with Programmable Wait States
  - 512k to 20 MBytes
  - Advanced, Flexible Address-Map Configuration
  - Full Hardware LIM EMS 4.0 Address Translation to 32 Megabytes without Waitstate Penalty

NOTE:

1. The Cache Controller is not integrated into the 16 MHz speed variant of the Intel386™ SL microprocessor.

82360SL I/O Subsystem
Complete ISA Peripheral Subsystem
Integrated System Power Management
Fully-Static CHMOS IV Technology

- **Complete ISA System, with Extended Support**
  - — Full ISA Bus Control, Status and Address and Data Interface Logic, with Full 24 mA Drive
  - — Compatible ISA Bus Peripherals:
    - •Two 8237 Direct Memory Access Controllers
    - •Two 8254 Programmable Timer Counters (6 Timer/Counter Channels)
    - •Two 8259A Programmable Interrupt Controllers (15 Channels)
    - •Enhanced LS612 Page Memory Mapper
    - •One 146818 Compatible Real Time Clock w/256-byte CMOS RAM
    - •Two 16450 Compatible Serial Port Controllers
    - •One 8-Bit Parallel I/O Port with High Speed Protocol (Centronics or Bi-Directional)
  - — Additional System I/O Decoding, Programmable Chip Selects and Support Interfaces:
    - •Full Integrated Drive Electronics (I.D.E.) Hard Disk Interface
    - •Floppy Disk Controller
    - •Keyboard Controller Chip Selects and Support Logic
  - — External Real Time Clock Support
  - — PS/2 and EISA Control/Status Ports
  - — Local Memory and ISA-Bus Memory Refresh Control
  - — New ideaPort Interface for Hardware Expansion
- **Transparent Power-Management System Architecture**
  - — Architecture Extension for Truely Compatible Systems
  - — Transparent to Operating Systems and Applications Programs
  - — Programmable Hardware Supports Custom Power-Control Methods
  - — Integrated Power Management Unit Manages Power-Events Safely

4

Intel386™ SL Microprocessor SuperSet Intel386™ SL CPU and 82360SL I/O

1.0 INTRODUCTION

This document provides the pinouts, signal descriptions, and D.C./A.C. electrical characteristics of the Intel386™ SL CPU and 82360SL ISA I/O Peripheral device. Consult Intel for the most recent design-in information. For a thorough description of any functional topic, other than the parametric specifications, please consult the latest Intel386 SL Microprocessor SuperSet System Design Guide (Order No. 240816), and the Intel386 SL Microprocessor SuperSet Programmer's Guide (Order No. 240815).

Overview

The Intel386 SL Microprocessor SuperSet is an extremely flexible pair of components marking a new milestone in microcomputer technology. Included in the pair are a Intel386 Architecture Central Processing Unit (CPU), a memory subsystem controller capable of controlling either DRAM or SRAM, address translation and remapping logic, a cache memory controller in the 20 MHz and 25 MHz speed variants, and an extensive collection of ISA bus compatible peripheral functions.

The SL SuperSet allows the personal computer designer to take advantage of the highest level of system integration, while preserving complete freedom in selecting system features, power/performance trade-offs, and value-added enhancements.

Essentially, all of the components needed to build an ISA bus compatible personal computer have been combined within just two components: the Intel386 SL microprocessor and memory control system, and the 82360SL ISA peripheral I/O and power management subsystem. The only other components needed for a complete personal computer are the main DRAM or optional static memory subsystem, optional cache SRAM and a graphics controller. A minimal amount of commodity Small Scale Integration (SSI) logic or Medium Scale Integration (MSI) logic buffers may be required for design-specific interface to peripheral devices on the ISA bus.

Systems based on the SL SuperSet typically include the functional blocks shown in Figure 1-2.

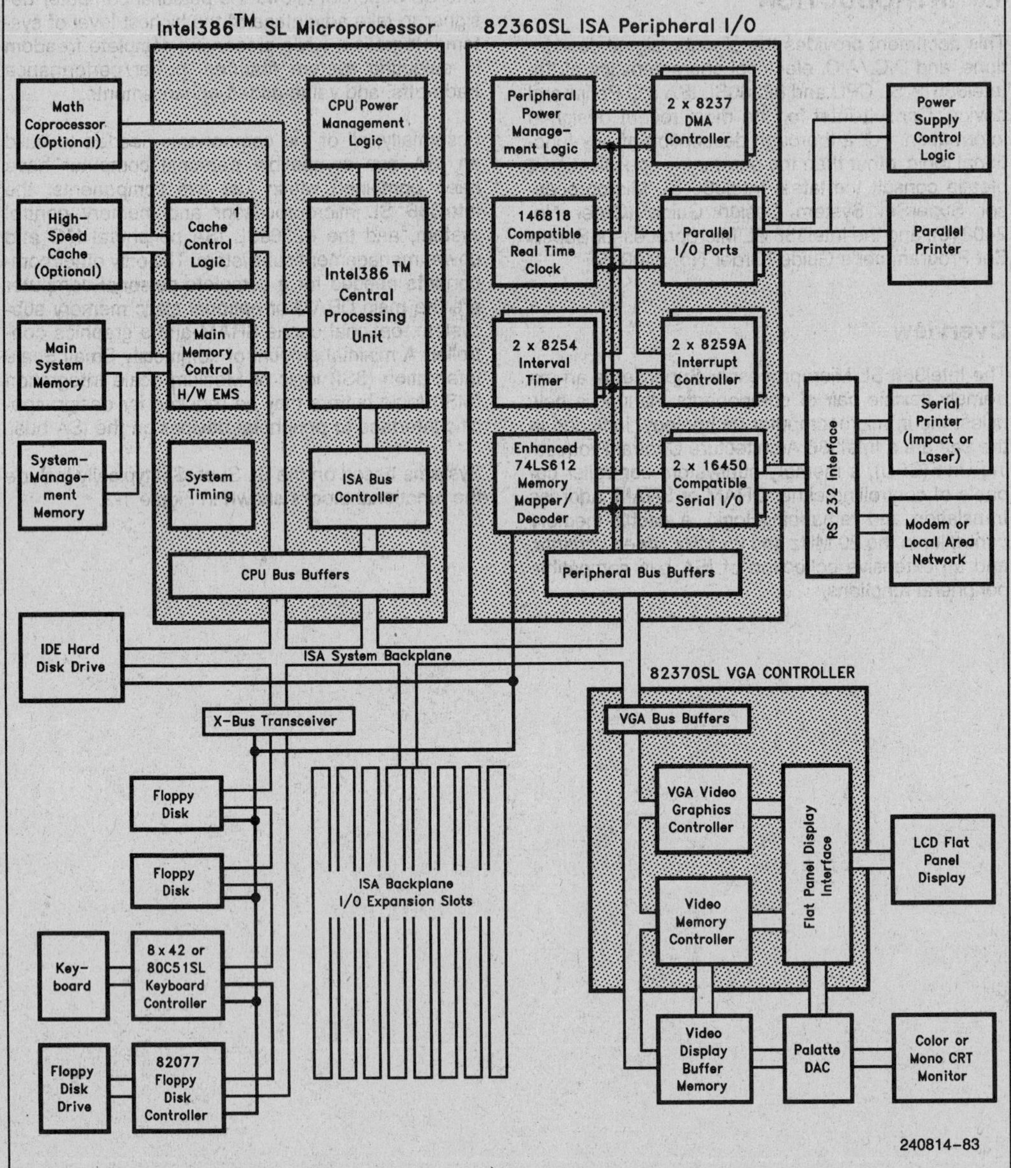

NOTE:
1. Only available in 20 MHz and 25 MHz speed variants.

Figure 1-2. Intel386™ SL Microprocessor-Based System Functional Block Diagram

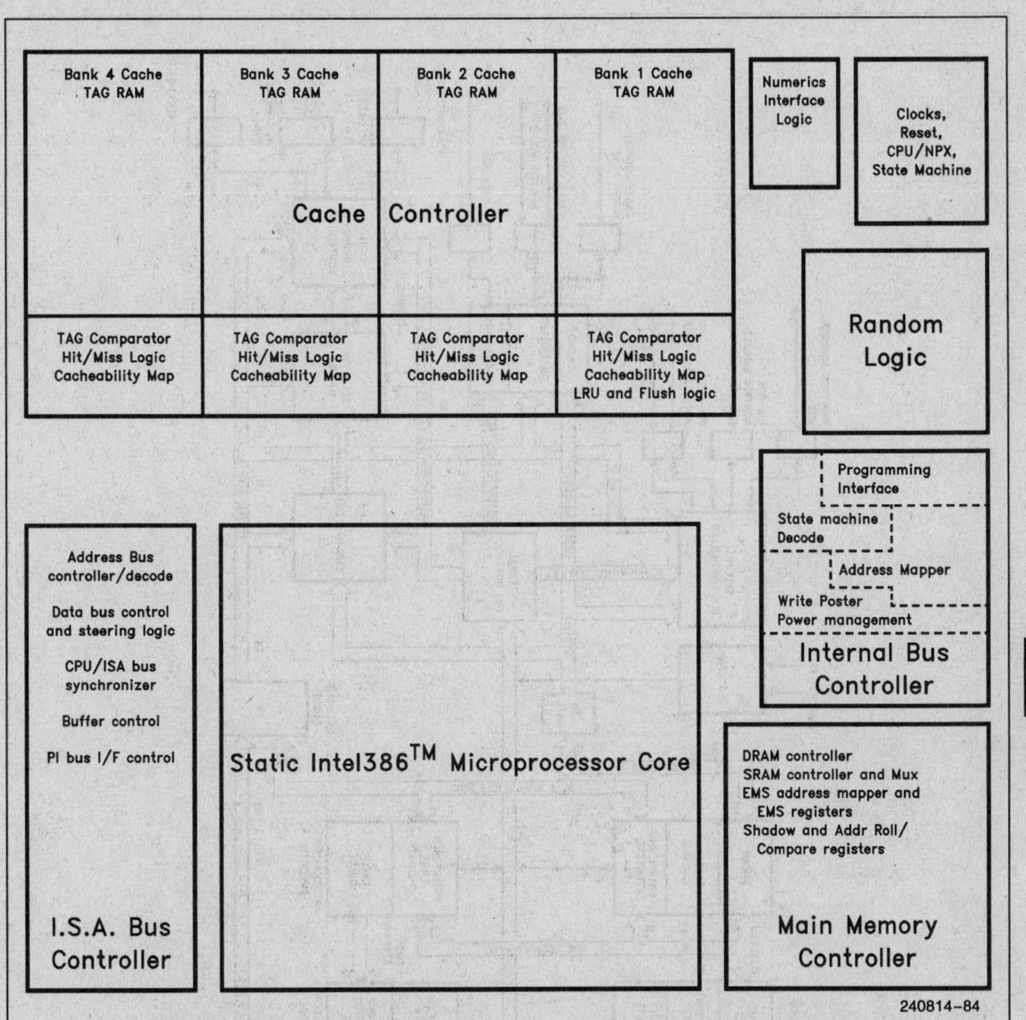

Figure 1-3a. Intel386™ SL Microprocessor Internal Functional Modules

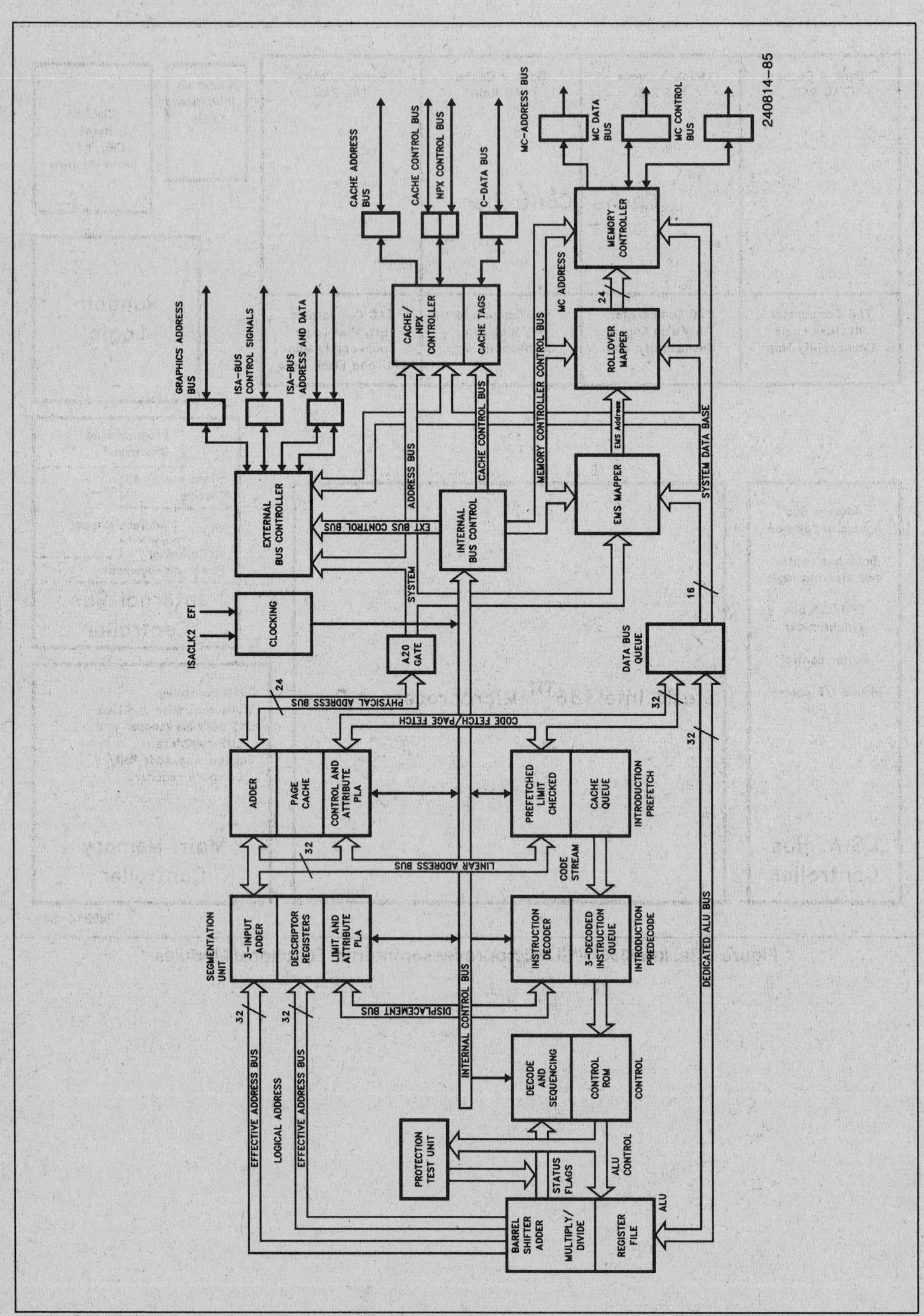

Figure 1-3b. Intel386™ SL Microprocessor Micro-Architecture

Intel386™ SL Microprocessor: Central Processing Unit (CPU) and Memory Controller Subsystem

The Intel386 SL microprocessor is a highly-integrated, complete microprocessor and memory controller subsystem. At the heart of the Intel386 SL microprocessor is a CHMOS static Intel386 CPU core. The Intel386 CPU core has been fully optimized to reduce run-time power requirements, and includes a key architectural extension required by battery-operated systems.

The Intel386 SL processor is the first member of the Intel386 microprocessor product line to implement a CPU with the System Management Mode extension. The System Management Mode is a new CPU operating-mode which allows system vendors to rid their systems of the backwards-compatibility problems that plague battery-operated PCs. This Intel386 architecture extension eliminates portable-system conflicts by providing a safe, new operating level for the battery management firmware developed by system designers. With the Intel386 SL CPU, firmware will execute transparently to every application, operating system and CPU mode, thus avoiding the compatibility conflicts which were once unavoidable.

The Intel386 SL microprocessor retains the paged-memory-management system, and all other key features which are common to the Intel386™ architecture. In addition, on-chip hardware implements the Expanded Memory Specification (E.M.S.) address translation compatible with the current Lotus/Intel/Microsoft (L.I.M.) E.M.S. 4.0 standard. Additional address-mapping and control logic integrated in the Intel386 SL CPU allows BIOS ROMs to be "shadowed" by faster memory devices, and supports a variety of common memory roll-over and back-fill schemes. The Intel386 SL CPU contains all of the control and interface logic needed to directly drive large main memory and an optional cache memory subsystem.

The Intel386 SL CPU contains bus drivers and control circuitry for two expansion interfaces. A Peripheral Interface Bus (PI-Bus) provides high-speed communication with fast devices such as VGA and FLASH™ Disk. The Industry Standard Architecture (ISA) bus provides a common interface for the wealth of third party ISA bus compatible I/O peripheral and expansion memory add-in boards. On-chip data-byte steering logic, address decoding and mapping logic automatically routes each memory or I/O operation to the appropriate local memory, cache, PI-Bus or ISA expansion bus.

All system configuration logic in the Intel386 SL processor subsystem is initialized under software control.

The system designer only has to program the processor in order to support multiple system hardware designs where many devices of less flexibility were once required. System characteristics such as memory type, size, speed, organization, and mapping; cache size, organization and mapping; and peripheral selection, configuration and mapping are configured under software control. Thereafter, all memory and I/O transfer requests are automatically sent to the appropriate memory space or expansion bus, fully-transparent to existing operating system software and application programs.

Figure 1-3a shows the functional blocks and Figure 1.3b shows the microarchitecture of the Intel386 SL processor.

82360SL I/O: Integrated ISA Peripheral and Power Management Device

The 82360SL Peripheral I/O contains dedicated logic to perform a number of CPU, memory, and peripheral support functions. The 82360SL device also contains an extensive set of programmable power management facilities which allow minimized system energy requirements for battery-powered portable computers.

The 82360SL includes a complete set of on-chip peripheral device functions including two 16450 compatible serial ports, one 8-bit Centronics interface or bi-directional parallel port, two 8254 compatible timer counters, two 8259 compatible interrupt controllers, two 8237 compatible DMA controllers, one 74LS612 compatible DMA page register, one 146818 compatible Real-time clock/calendar with an additional 128 bytes of battery backed CMOS RAM and an integrated drive electronics (IDE) hard disk drive interface. The Intel 82360SL also contains highly programmable chip selects and complete peripheral interface logic for direct keyboard and floppy disk controller support. The peripheral registers and functions behave exactly as the discrete components commonly found in industry standard personal computers. The peripheral logic is enhanced for static operation by supporting write only registers as read/write.

The processor and memory support functions contained in the 82360SL device eliminate most of the external random-logic "glue" that might otherwise be required. The 82360SL device provides internal programmable-frequency clock generators for the ISA bus backplane, and video subsystems. A programmable, low-power DRAM refresh timer is also provided to maintain system memory integrity during the power saving suspend state.

The 82360SL also contains a flexible set of hardware functions to support the growing sophistication in power management schemes required by portable systems. Numerous hardware timers, event monitors and I/O interfaces can programmably monitor and control system activity. Firmware developed by the system designer allocates and directs the hardware to fulfill the unique power management needs of a given system configuration.

All of the standard peripheral registers, clock-generation logic, and power-management facilities have been designed to ensure complete compatibility with existing operating systems and applications software.

Figure 1-4 shows the functional blocks and micro-architecture of the 82360SL I/O subsystem.

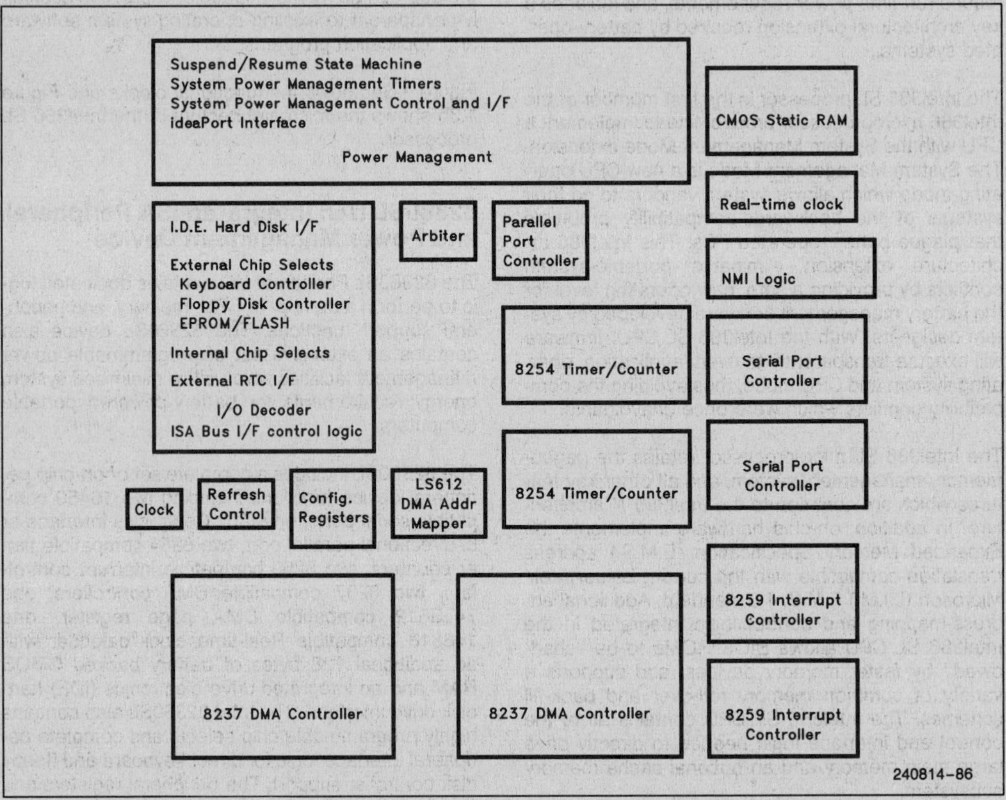

Figure 1-4a. 82360SL ISA Peripheral I/O Internal Functional Modules

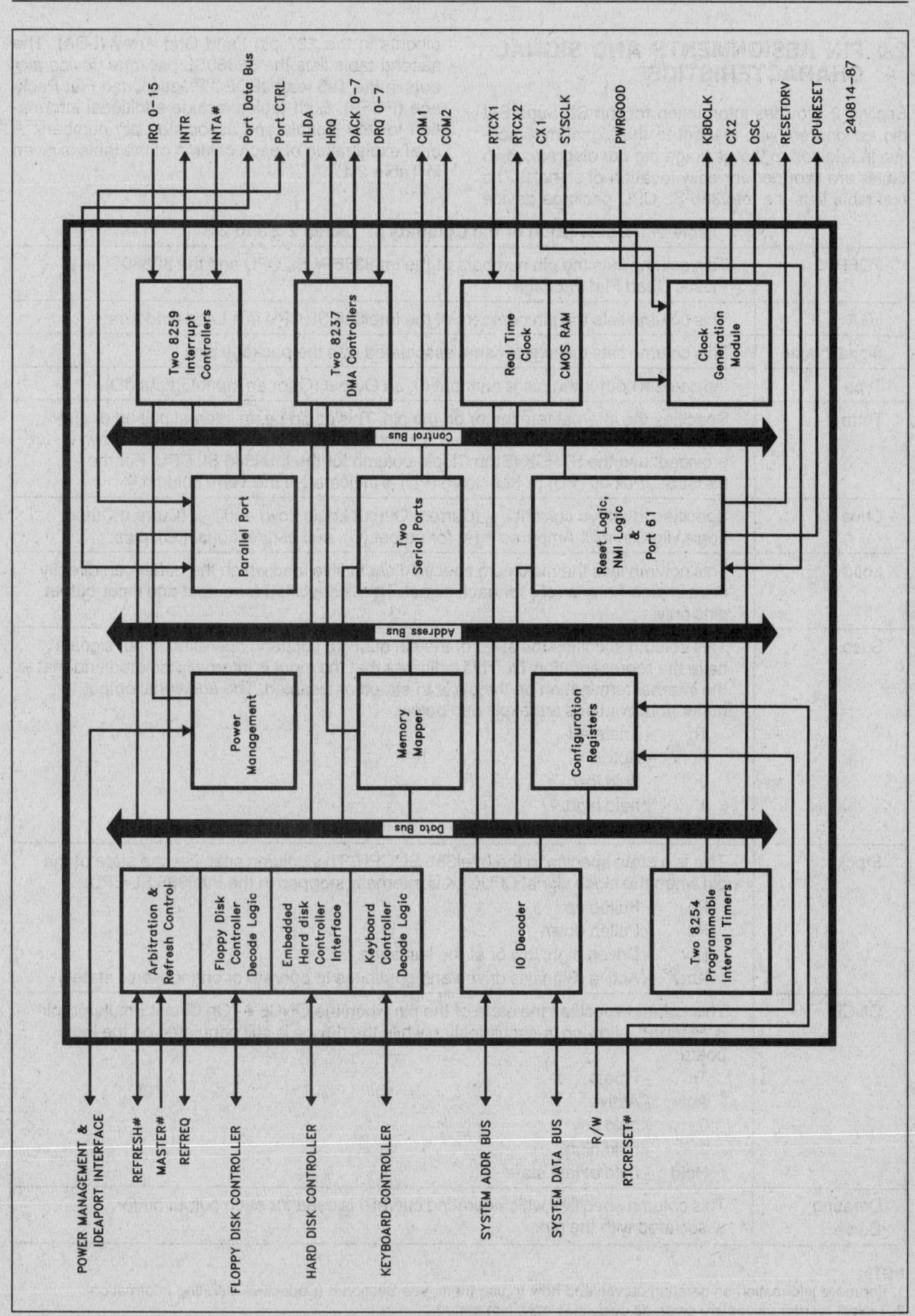

Figure 1-4b. 82360SL Functional Block Diagram

4

2.0 PIN ASSIGNMENTS AND SIGNAL CHARACTERISTICS

Section 2 provides information for the SL SuperSet pin assignment with respect to the signal mnemonics. In addition to the package pin out diagrams, two tables are provided for easy location of signals. The first table lists the Intel386 SL CPU package device pinouts in the 227 pin Land Grid Array (LGA). The second table lists the 82360SL package device pinouts in the 196 lead JEDEC Plastic Quad Flat Package (PQFP). Both tables include additional information for the signals and associated pin numbers. A brief explanation of each column of the table is given in Table 2-1.

Table 2-1. Description of the Columns of Tables 2-2 and 2-3

PQFP	This column lists the pin numbers of the Intel386™ SL CPU and the 82360SL in a Plastic Quad Flat Package.
LGA	This column lists the pin numbers of the Intel386 SL CPU in a Land Grid Array.
Signal Name	This column lists the signal name associated with the package pins.
Type	Indicates whether the pin is an Input (I), an Output (O) or an Input-Output (IO).
Term	Specifies the internal terminator on the pin. This could be an internal pull-up or pull-down resistor value or a hold circuit. To find out whether a pull-up or a pull-down is provided, use the STPCK (Stop Clock) column for the Intel386 SL CPU. For the 82360SL, Pull-up (PU) or Pull-down (PD) is indicated in the Term column.[2]
Drive	Specifies the drive current I_{OL} (Current Output Logic Low) and I_{OH} (Current Output Logic High) in milli-Amperes (mA) for output (O), and bi-directional (IO), pins.
Load	This column lists the maximum specified capacitive load which the buffer can directly drive in pico-Farads (pF) for each signal. This is specified for output and input-output pins only.
Susp.	This column specifies the state of the pin during a suspend operation. Input signals have the representation Tri. This indicates that the input is internally isolated and that the internal termination on the pin is tri-stated or disabled. The additional output buffer abbreviations are explained below. Tri - Tristated Actv - Active 0 - held low 1 - held high Hold - held at last state
Stpck.	This is a state specific to the Intel386 SL CPU. This column specifies the state of the pin when the clock signal CPUCLK is internally stopped in the Intel386 SL CPU. Pu - Pulled up Pd - Pulled down Drv - Driven high, low or at the last state Actv - Active (Signal is driven and continues to operate or change logic states)
ONCE	This column specifies the state of the pin when the ONCE# (On Circuit Emulator) pin is asserted, allowing in-circuit testing while the device is still populated on the logic board. Tri - Floats Actv - Active 0 - held low 1 - held high Hold - held at last state
Derating Curve	This column specifies which derating curve[1] is used for each output buffer associated with the pin.

NOTE:
1. For more information on derating curves and how to use them, see Section 8 (Capacitive Derating Information).
2. Typical resistor values are given as guidelines only. Not tested.

THE INTEL386™ SL CPU PINOUT DIAGRAM

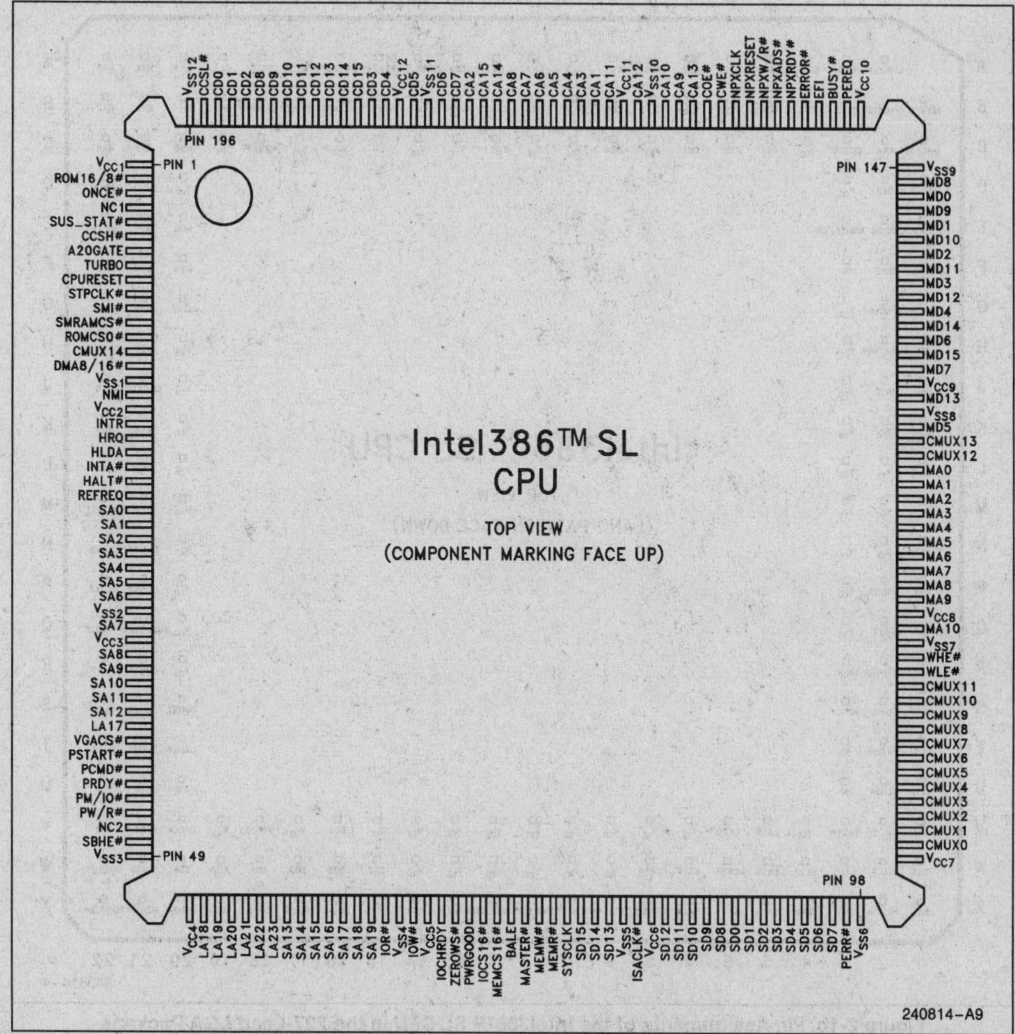

Figure 2-1a. Top View of the Pinout of the Intel386™ SL CPU in a PQFP Package

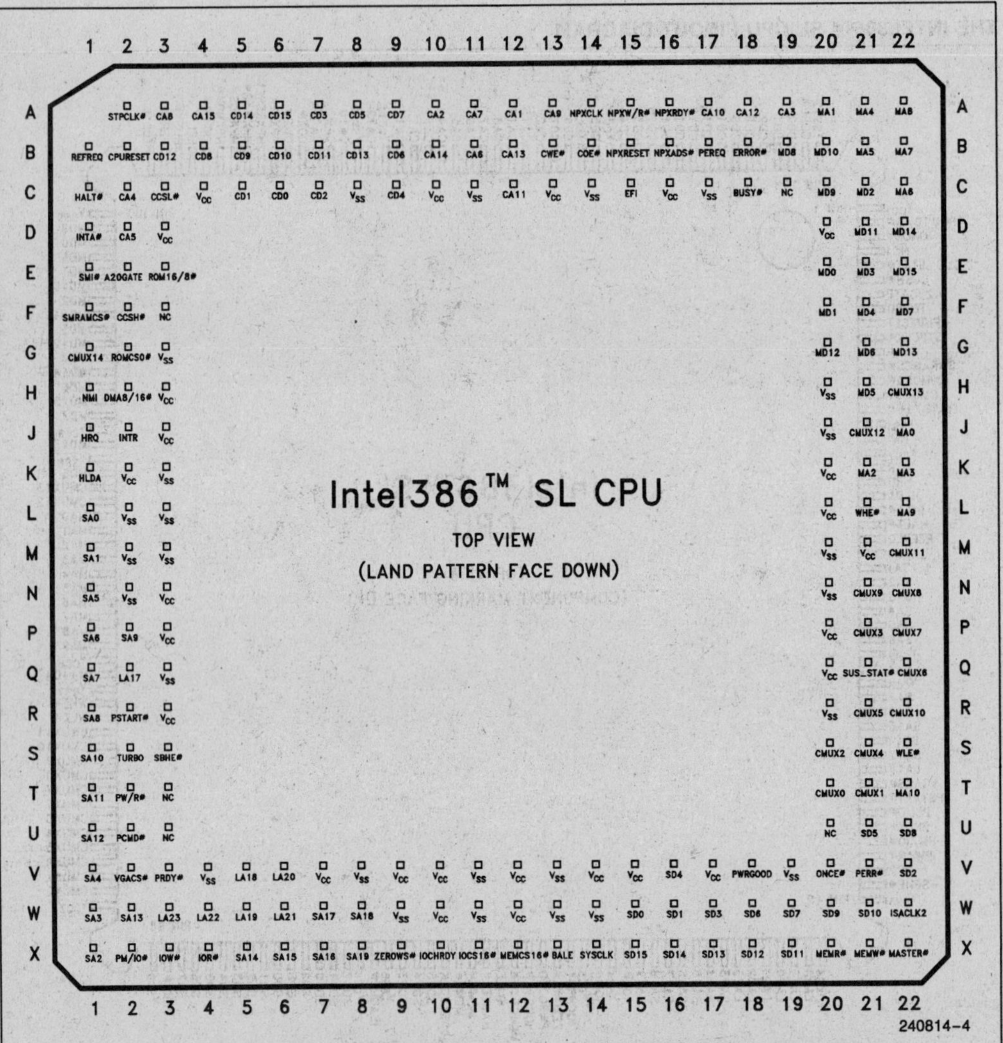

Intel386™ SL CPU

TOP VIEW

(LAND PATTERN FACE DOWN)

	1	2	3	4	5	6	7	8	9	10	11	12	13	14	15	16	17	18	19	20	21	22
A		STPCLK#	CA8	CA15	CD14	CD15	CD3	CD5	CD7	CA2	CA7	CA1	CA9	NPXCLK	NPXW/R#	NPXRDY#	CA10	CA12	CA3	MA1	MA4	MA8
B	REFREQ	CPURESET	CD12	CD8	CD9	CD10	CD11	CD13	CD6	CA14	CA6	CA13	CWE#	COE#	NPXRESET	NPXADS#	PEREQ	ERROR#	MD8	MD10	MA5	MA7
C	HALT#	CA4	CCSL#	V_{CC}	CD1	CD0	CD2	V_{SS}	CD4	V_{CC}	V_{SS}	CA11	V_{CC}	V_{SS}	EFI	V_{CC}	V_{SS}	BUSY#	NC	MD9	MD2	MA6
D	INTA#	CA5	V_{CC}																	V_{CC}	MD11	MD14
E	SMI#	A20GATE	ROM16/8#																	MD0	MD3	MD15
F	SMRAMCS#	CCSH#	NC																	MD1	MD4	MD7
G	CMUX14	ROMCS0#	V_{SS}																	MD12	MD6	MD13
H	NMI	DMA8/16#	V_{CC}																	V_{SS}	MD5	CMUX13
J	HRQ	INTR	V_{CC}																	V_{SS}	CMUX12	MA0
K	HLDA	V_{CC}	V_{SS}																	V_{CC}	MA2	MA3
L	SA0	V_{SS}	V_{SS}																	V_{CC}	WHE#	MA9
M	SA1	V_{SS}	V_{SS}																	V_{SS}	V_{CC}	CMUX11
N	SA5	V_{SS}	V_{CC}																	V_{SS}	CMUX9	CMUX8
P	SA6	SA9	V_{CC}																	V_{CC}	CMUX3	CMUX7
Q	SA7	LA17	V_{SS}																	V_{CC}	SUS_STAT#	CMUX6
R	SA8	PSTART#	V_{CC}																	V_{SS}	CMUX5	CMUX10
S	SA10	TURBO	SBHE#																	CMUX2	CMUX4	WLE#
T	SA11	PW/R#	NC																	CMUX0	CMUX1	MA10
U	SA12	PCMD#	NC																	NC	SD5	SD8
V	SA4	VGACS#	PRDY#	V_{SS}	LA18	LA20	V_{CC}	V_{SS}	V_{CC}	V_{CC}	V_{SS}	V_{CC}	V_{SS}	V_{CC}	V_{CC}	SD4	V_{CC}	PWRGOOD	V_{SS}	ONCE#	PERR#	SD2
W	SA3	SA13	LA23	LA22	LA19	LA21	SA17	SA18	V_{SS}	V_{CC}	V_{SS}	V_{CC}	V_{SS}	V_{SS}	SD0	SD1	SD3	SD6	SD7	SD9	SD10	ISACLK2
X	SA2	PM/IO#	IOW#	IOR#	SA14	SA15	SA16	SA19	ZEROWS#	IOCHRDY	IOCS16#	MEMCS16#	BALE	SYSCLK	SD15	SD14	SD13	SD12	SD11	MEMR#	MEMW#	MASTER#

240814-4

Figure 2-1b. Pin Assignments of the Intel386™ SL CPU in the 227-Lead LGA Package (Top View—Land Pattern Facing Down, Component Marking Facing Up)

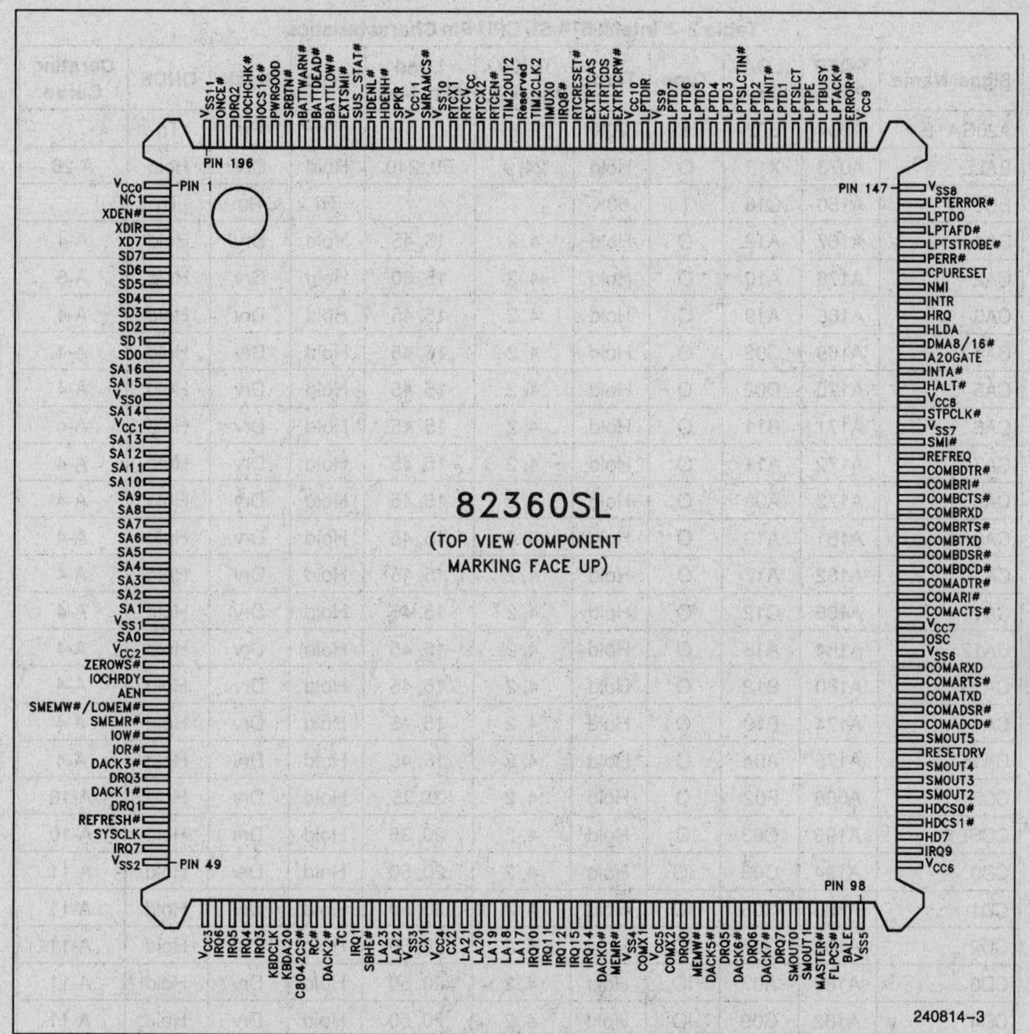

Figure 2-2. Pin Assignments for the 82360SL in a 196-Lead Plastic Quad Flat Package

4

Table 2-2. Intel386™ SL CPU Pin Characteristics

Signal Name	PQFP Pin #	LGA Pin #	Type	Term	Drive I_{OL}, I_{OH}	Load Min, Max	Susp	Stpck	ONCE	Derating Curve
A20GATE	A007	E02	I	20K			Tri	Pu	Tri	
BALE	A073	X13	O	Hold	24, 4	50, 240	Hold	Drv	Hold	A-26
BUSY#	A150	C18	I	60K			Tri	Pu	Tri	
CA1	A167	A12	O	Hold	4, 2	15, 45	Hold	Drv	Hold	A-4
CA2	A176	A10	O	Hold	4, 2	15, 60	Hold	Drv	Hold	A-5
CA3	A168	A19	O	Hold	4, 2	15, 45	Hold	Drv	Hold	A-4
CA4	A169	C02	O	Hold	4, 2	15, 45	Hold	Drv	Hold	A-4
CA5	A170	D02	O	Hold	4, 2	15, 45	Hold	Drv	Hold	A-4
CA6	A171	B11	O	Hold	4, 2	15, 45	Hold	Drv	Hold	A-4
CA7	A172	A11	O	Hold	4, 2	15, 45	Hold	Drv	Hold	A-4
CA8	A173	A03	O	Hold	4, 2	15, 45	Hold	Drv	Hold	A-4
CA9	A161	A13	O	Hold	4, 2	15, 45	Hold	Drv	Hold	A-4
CA10	A162	A17	O	Hold	4, 2	15, 45	Hold	Drv	Hold	A-4
CA11	A166	C12	O	Hold	4, 2	15, 45	Hold	Drv	Hold	A-4
CA12	A164	A18	O	Hold	4, 2	15, 45	Hold	Drv	Hold	A-4
CA13	A160	B12	O	Hold	4, 2	15, 45	Hold	Drv	Hold	A-4
CA14	A174	B10	O	Hold	4, 2	15, 45	Hold	Drv	Hold	A-4
CA15	A175	A04	O	Hold	4, 2	15, 45	Hold	Drv	Hold	A-4
CCSH#	A006	F02	O	Hold	4, 2	20,35	Hold	Drv	Hold	A-10
CCSL#	A195	C03	O	Hold	4, 2	20, 35	Hold	Drv	Hold	A-10
CD0	A194	C06	IO	Hold	4, 2	20, 50	Hold	Drv	Hold	A-11
CD1	A193	C05	IO	Hold	4, 2	20, 50	Hold	Drv	Hold	A-11
CD2	A192	C07	IO	Hold	4, 2	20, 50	Hold	Drv	Hold	A-11
CD3	A183	A07	IO	Hold	4, 2	20, 50	Hold	Drv	Hold	A-11
CD4	A182	C09	IO	Hold	4, 2	20, 50	Hold	Drv	Hold	A-11
CD5	A180	A08	IO	Hold	4, 2	20, 50	Hold	Drv	Hold	A-11
CD6	A178	B09	IO	Hold	4, 2	20, 50	Hold	Drv	Hold	A-11
CD7	A177	A09	IO	Hold	4, 2	20, 50	Hold	Drv	Hold	A-11
CD8	A191	B04	IO	Hold	4, 2	20, 50	Hold	Drv	Hold	A-11
CD9	A190	B05	IO	Hold	4, 2	20, 50	Hold	Drv	Hold	A-11
CD10	A189	B06	IO	Hold	4, 2	20, 50	Hold	Drv	Hold	A-11
CD11	A188	B07	IO	Hold	4, 2	20, 50	Hold	Drv	Hold	A-11
CD12	A187	B03	IO	Hold	4, 2	20, 50	Hold	Drv	Hold	A-11
CD13	A186	B08	IO	Hold	4, 2	20, 50	Hold	Drv	Hold	A-11

Table 2-2. Intel386™ SL CPU Pin Characteristics (Continued)

Signal Name	PQFP Pin #	LGA Pin #	Type	Term	Drive I_{OL}, I_{OH}	Load Min, Max	Susp	Stpck	ONCE	Derating Curve
CD14	A185	A05	IO	Hold	4, 2	20, 50	Hold	Drv	Hold	A-11
CD15	A184	A06	IO	Hold	4, 2	20, 50	Hold	Drv	Hold	A-11
CMUX0	A100	T20	O	Hold	4, 2	15, 72	Hold(1)	Drv	Hold	A-6
CMUX1	A101	T21	O	Hold	4, 2	15, 72	Hold(1)	Drv	Hold	A-6
CMUX2	A102	S20	O	Hold	4, 2	15, 72	Hold(1)	Drv	Hold	A-6
CMUX3	A103	P21	O	Hold	4, 2	15, 72	Hold(1)	Drv	Hold	A-6
CMUX4	A104	S21	O	Hold	4, 2	15, 72	Hold(1)	Drv	Hold	A-6
CMUX5	A105	R21	O	Hold	4, 2	15, 72	Hold(1)	Drv	Hold	A-6
CMUX6	A106	Q22	O	Hold	4, 2	15, 72	Hold(1)	Drv	Hold	A-6
CMUX7	A107	P22	O	Hold	4, 2	15, 72	Hold(1)	Drv	Hold	A-6
CMUX8	A108	N22	O	Hold	4, 2	32, 136	Hold(1)	Drv	Hold	A-21
CMUX9	A109	N21	O	Hold	4, 2	32, 136	Hold(1)	Drv	Hold	A-21
CMUX10	A110	R22	O	Hold	4, 2	32, 136	Hold(1)	Drv	Hold	A-21
CMUX11	A111	M22	O	Hold	4, 2	32, 136	Hold(1)	Drv	Hold	A-21
CMUX12	A127	J21	IO	Hold	4, 2	8, 32	Hold	Drv	Hold	A-2
CMUX13	A128	H22	IO	Hold	4, 2	8, 32	Hold	Drv	Hold	A-2
CMUX14	A014	G01	O	Hold	4, 2	20, 65	Hold	Drv	Hold	A-16
COE#	A159	B14	O	Hold	4, 2	15, 45	Hold	Drv	Hold	A-7
CPURESET	A009	B02	I	20K			Actv	Pd	Tri	
CWE#	A158	B13	O	Hold	4, 2	15, 45	Hold	Drv	Hold	A-8
DMA8/16#	A015	H02	I	60K			Tri	Pu	Tri	
EFI	A151	C15	I				Actv		Tri	
ERROR#	A152	B18	I	60K			Tri	Pu	Tri	
HALT#	A023	C01	O	Hold	4, 2	20, 65	Hold	Drv	Hold	A-16
HLDA	A021	K01	O	Hold	4, 2	20, 65	Hold	Drv	Hold	A-16
HRQ	A020	J01	I	20K			Tri	Pd	Tri	
INTA#	A022	D01	O	Hold	4, 2	20, 65	Hold	Drv	Hold	A-16
INTR	A019	J02	I	20K			Tri	Pd	Tri	
IOCHRDY	A068	X10	IO	1K	24, 4	50, 240	Tri	Pu	Tri	A-22
IOCS16#	A071	X11	IO	1K	24, 4	50, 240	Tri	Pu	Tri	A-23
IOR#	A064	X04	IO	60K	24, 4	50, 240	Tri	Pu	Tri	A-24
IOW#	A065	X03	IO	60K	24, 4	50, 240	Tri	Pu	Tri	A-24
ISACLK2	A082	W22	I				Actv		Tri	
LA17	A040	Q02	IO	Hold	24, 4	50, 240	Hold	Drv	Hold	A-25
LA18	A051	V05	IO	Hold	24, 4	50, 240	Hold	Drv	Hold	A-25
LA19	A052	W05	IO	Hold	24, 4	50, 240	Hold	Drv	Hold	A-25

NOTE:
1. These pins are driven during the suspend state if suspend refresh is enabled.

4

Table 2-2. Intel386™ SL CPU Pin Characteristics (Continued)

Signal Name	PQFP Pin #	LGA Pin #	Type	Term	Drive I_{OL}, I_{OH}	Load Min, Max	Susp	Stpck	ONCE	Derating Curve
LA20	A053	V06	IO	Hold	24, 4	50, 240	Hold	Drv	Hold	A-25
LA21	A054	W06	IO	Hold	24, 4	50, 240	Hold	Drv	Hold	A-25
LA22	A055	W04	IO	Hold	24, 4	50, 240	Hold	Drv	Hold	A-25
LA23	A056	W03	IO	Hold	24, 4	50, 240	Hold	Drv	Hold	A-25
MA0	A126	J22	O	Hold	4, 2	32, 240	Hold(1)	Drv	Hold	A-20
MA1	A125	A20	O	Hold	4, 2	32, 240	Hold(1)	Drv	Hold	A-20
MA2	A124	K21	O	Hold	4, 2	32, 240	Hold(1)	Drv	Hold	A-20
MA3	A123	K22	O	Hold	4, 2	32, 240	Hold(1)	Drv	Hold	A-20
MA4	A122	A21	O	Hold	4, 2	32, 240	Hold(1)	Drv	Hold	A-20
MA5	A121	B21	O	Hold	4, 2	32, 240	Hold(1)	Drv	Hold	A-20
MA6	A120	C22	O	Hold	4, 2	32, 240	Hold(1)	Drv	Hold	A-20
MA7	A119	B22	O	Hold	4, 2	32, 240	Hold(1)	Drv	Hold	A-20
MA8	A118	A22	O	Hold	4, 2	32, 240	Hold(1)	Drv	Hold	A-20
MA9	A117	L22	O	Hold	4, 2	32, 240	Hold(1)	Drv	Hold	A-20
MA10	A115	T22	O	Hold	4, 2	32, 240	Hold(1)	Drv	Hold	A-20
MASTER#	A074	X22	I	1K			Tri	Pu	Tri	
MD0	A145	E20	IO	Hold	4, 2	8, 32	Hold	Drv	Hold	A-1
MD1	A143	F20	IO	Hold	4, 2	8, 32	Hold	Drv	Hold	A-1
MD2	A141	C21	IO	Hold	4, 2	8, 32	Hold	Drv	Hold	A-1
MD3	A139	E21	IO	Hold	4, 2	8, 32	Hold	Drv	Hold	A-1
MD4	A137	F21	IO	Hold	4, 2	8, 32	Hold	Drv	Hold	A-1
MD5	A129	H21	IO	Hold	4, 2	8, 32	Hold	Drv	Hold	A-1
MD6	A135	G21	IO	Hold	4, 2	8, 32	Hold	Drv	Hold	A-1
MD7	A133	F22	IO	Hold	4, 2	8, 32	Hold	Drv	Hold	A-1
MD8	A146	B19	IO	Hold	4, 2	8, 32	Hold	Drv	Hold	A-1
MD9	A144	C20	IO	Hold	4, 2	8, 32	Hold	Drv	Hold	A-1
MD10	A142	B20	IO	Hold	4, 2	8, 32	Hold	Drv	Hold	A-1
MD11	A140	D21	IO	Hold	4, 2	8, 32	Hold	Drv	Hold	A-1
MD12	A138	G20	IO	Hold	4, 2	8, 32	Hold	Drv	Hold	A-1
MD13	A131	G22	IO	Hold	4, 2	8, 32	Hold	Drv	Hold	A-1
MD14	A136	D22	IO	Hold	4, 2	8, 32	Hold	Drv	Hold	A-1
MD15	A134	E22	IO	Hold	4, 2	8, 32	Hold	Drv	Hold	A-1
MEMCS16#	A072	X12	IO	1K	24, 4	50, 240	Tri	Pu	Tri	A-23
MEMR#	A076	X20	IO	60K	24, 4	20, 240	Tri	Pu	Tri	A-12
MEMW#	A075	X21	IO	60K	24, 4	20, 240	Tri	Pu	Tri	A-12
NMI	A017	H01	I	20K			Tri	Pd	Tri	

NOTE:
1. These pins are driven in the suspend state if suspend refresh is enabled.

Table 2-2. Intel386™ SL CPU Pin Characteristics (Continued)

Signal Name	PQFP Pin #	LGA Pin #	Type	Term	Drive I_{OL}, I_{OH}	Load Min, Max	Susp	Stpck	ONCE	Derating Curve
NPXADS#	A154	B16	O	Hold	4, 2	20, 32	Hold	Drv	Hold	A-13
NPXCLK	A157	A14	O	Hold	4, 2	20, 40	Hold	Drv	Tri	A-14
NPXRDY#	A153	A16	I	20K			Tri	Pd	Tri	
NPXRESET	A156	B15	O	Hold	4, 2	20, 32	Hold	Drv	Hold	A-15
NPXW/R#	A155	A15	O	Hold	4, 2	20, 32	Hold	Drv	Tri	A-13
ONCE#	A003	V20	I	60K			Actv	Pu	Actv	
PCMD#	A043	U02	O	Hold	4, 2	20, 65	Hold	Drv	Hold	A-16
PEREQ	A149	B17	I	20K			Tri	Pd	Tri	
PERR#	A097	V21	O	Hold	4, 2	8, 32	Hold	Drv	Hold	A-3
PM/IO#	A045	X02	O	Hold	4, 2	20, 65	Hold	Drv	Hold	A-16
PRDY#	A044	V03	I	60K			Tri	Pu	Tri	
PSTART#	A042	R02	O	Hold	4, 2	20, 65	Hold	Drv	Tri	A-16
PW/R#	A046	T02	O	Hold	4, 2	20, 65	Hold	Drv	Hold	A-16
PWRGOOD	A070	V18	I				Actv	Actv	Tri	
REFREQ	A024	B01	I	Hold			Actv	Actv	Tri	
ROM16/8#	A002	E03	I	60K			Tri	Pu	Tri	
ROMCS0#	A013	G02	O	Hold	4, 2	20, 65	Hold	Drv	Hold	A-16
SA0	A025	L01	IO	Hold	24, 4	50, 240	Hold	Drv	Hold	A-25
SA1	A026	M01	IO	Hold	24, 4	50, 240	Hold	Drv	Hold	A-25
SA2	A027	X01	IO	Hold	24, 4	50, 240	Hold	Drv	Hold	A-25
SA3	A028	W01	IO	Hold	24, 4	50, 240	Hold	Drv	Hold	A-25
SA4	A029	V01	IO	Hold	24, 4	50, 240	Hold	Drv	Hold	A-25
SA5	A030	N01	IO	Hold	24, 4	50, 240	Hold	Drv	Hold	A-25
SA6	A031	P01	IO	Hold	24, 4	50, 240	Hold	Drv	Hold	A-25
SA7	A033	Q01	IO	Hold	24, 4	50, 240	Hold	Drv	Hold	A-25
SA8	A035	R01	IO	Hold	24, 4	50, 240	Hold	Drv	Hold	A-25
SA9	A036	P02	IO	Hold	24, 4	50, 240	Hold	Drv	Hold	A-25
SA10	A037	S01	IO	Hold	24, 4	50, 240	Hold	Drv	Hold	A-25
SA11	A038	T01	IO	Hold	24, 4	50, 240	Hold	Drv	Hold	A-25
SA12	A039	U01	IO	Hold	24, 4	50, 240	Hold	Drv	Hold	A-25
SA13	A057	W02	IO	Hold	24, 4	50, 240	Hold	Drv	Hold	A-25
SA14	A058	X05	IO	Hold	24, 4	50, 240	Hold	Drv	Hold	A-25
SA15	A059	X06	IO	Hold	24, 4	50, 240	Hold	Drv	Hold	A-25
SA16	A060	X07	IO	Hold	24, 4	50, 240	Hold	Drv	Hold	A-25

Table 2-2. Intel386™ SL CPU Pin Characteristics (Continued)

Signal Name	PQFP Pin #	LGA Pin #	Type	Term	Drive I_{OL}, I_{OH}	Load Min, Max	Susp	Stpck	ONCE	Derating Curve
SA17	A061	W07	O	Hold	24, 4	50, 240	Hold	Drv	Hold	A-25
SA18	A062	W08	O	Hold	24, 4	50, 240	Hold	Drv	Hold	A-25
SA19	A063	X08	O	Hold	24, 4	50, 240	Hold	Drv	Hold	A-25
SBHE#	A048	S03	IO	Hold	24, 4	20, 240	Hold	Drv	Hold	A-17
SD0	A089	W15	IO	60K	24, 4	50, 240	Tri	Pu	Tri	A-26
SD1	A090	W16	IO	60K	24, 4	50, 240	Tri	Pu	Tri	A-26
SD2	A091	V22	IO	60K	24, 4	50, 240	Tri	Pu	Tri	A-26
SD3	A092	W17	IO	60K	24, 4	50, 240	Tri	Pu	Tri	A-26
SD4	A093	V16	IO	60K	24, 4	50, 240	Tri	Pu	Tri	A-26
SD5	A094	U21	IO	60K	24, 4	50, 240	Tri	Pu	Tri	A-26
SD6	A095	W18	IO	60K	24, 4	50, 240	Tri	Pu	Tri	A-26
SD7	A096	W19	IO	60K	24, 4	50, 240	Tri	Pu	Tri	A-26
SD8	A088	U22	IO	60K	24, 4	50, 240	Tri	Pu	Tri	A-26
SD9	A087	W20	IO	60K	24, 4	50, 240	Tri	Pu	Tri	A-26
SD10	A086	W21	IO	60K	24, 4	50, 240	Tri	Pu	Tri	A-26
SD11	A085	X19	IO	60K	24, 4	50, 240	Tri	Pu	Tri	A-26
SD12	A084	X18	IO	60K	24, 4	50, 240	Tri	Pu	Tri	A-26
SD13	A080	X17	IO	60K	24, 4	50, 240	Tri	Pu	Tri	A-26
SD14	A079	X16	IO	60K	24, 4	50, 240	Tri	Pu	Tri	A-26
SD15	A078	X15	IO	60K	24, 4	50, 240	Tri	Pu	Tri	A-26
SMI#	A011	E01	I	60K			Tri	Pu	Tri	
SMRAMCS#	A012	F01	O	Hold	4, 2	20, 65	Drv	Drv	Hold	A-18
STPCLK#	A010	A02	I	60K			Tri	Pu	Tri	
SUS_STAT#	A005	Q21	I	60K			Actv	Actv	Tri	
SYSCLK	A077	X14	O	Hold	4, 2	20, 120	Hold	Drv	Hold	A-19
TURBO	A008	S02	I	60K			Tri	Pu	Tri	
VGACS#	A041	V02	O	Hold	4, 2	20, 65	Hold	Drv	Hold	A-16
WHE#	A113	L21	O	Hold	4, 2	15, 136	Hold(1)	Drv	Hold	A-9
WLE#	A112	S22	O	Hold	4, 2	15, 136	Hold(1)	Drv	Hold	A-9
ZEROWS#	A069	X09	I	700			Tri	Pu	Tri	

Power Pins

V_{CC} PQFP: A001, A018, A034, A050, A067, A083, A099, A116, A132, A148, A165, A181
LGA: C04, C10, C13, C16, D03, D20, H03, J03, K02, K20, L20, M21, N03 , P03, P20, Q20, R03, V07, V17, V15, V14, V12, V10, V09, W10, W12

V_{SS} PQFP: A016, A032, A049, A065, A081, A098, A114, A130, A147, A163, A179, A196
LGA: C08, C11, C14, C17, G03, H20, J20, K03, L02, L03, M02, M03, M20, N02, N20, Q03, R20, V04, V08, V19, V13, V11, W09, W11, W13, W14

No Connects
PQFP: A004, A047
LGA: C19, F03, T03, U03, U20

NOTE:
1. These pins are driven inactive in the suspend state if suspend refresh is enabled.

Table 2-3. 82360SL Pin Characteristics

Signal Name	PQFP Pin #	Type	Term	Drive I_{OL}, I_{OH}	Load Min, Max	Susp	ONCE	Derating Curve
A20GATE	B135	O		12, 2	20, 50	Tri	Tri	B-7
AEN	B37	O		24, 4	50, 240	Tri	Tri	B-4
BALE	B97	I				Tri	Tri	
BATTDEAD#	B188	I				Actv	Tri	
BATTLOW#	B187	I				Actv	Tri	
BATTWARN#	B189	I	60K PU			Tri	Tri	
C8042CS#	B57	O		12, 2	20, 50	Tri	Tri	B-7
COMACTS#	B117	I	60K PU			Tri	Tri	
COMADCD#	B109	I	60K PU			Tri	Tri	
COMADSR#	B110	I	60K PU			Tri	Tri	
COMADTR#	B119	O		12, 2	20, 50	Tri	Tri	B-7
COMARI#	B118	I	60K PU			Actv	Tri	
COMARTS#	B112	O		12, 2	20, 50	Tri	Tri	B-7
COMARXD	B113	I	20K PD			Tri	Tri	
COMATXD	B111	O		12, 2	20, 50	Tri	Tri	B-7
COMBCTS#	B125	I	60K PU			Tri	Tri	
COMBDCD#	B120	I	60K PU			Tri	Tri	
COMBDSR#	B121	I	60K PU			Tri	Tri	
COMBDTR#	B127	O		12, 2	20, 50	Tri	Tri	B-7
COMBRI#	B126	I	60K PU			Actv	Tri	
COMBRTS#	B123	O		12, 2	20, 50	Tri	Tri	B-7
COMBRXD	B124	I	20K PD			Tri	Tri	
COMBTXD	B122	O		12, 2	20, 50	Tri	Tri	B-7
COMX1	B82	I				Tri	Tri	
COMX2	B84	O				1	1	B-7
CPURESET	B141	O		12, 2	20, 50	Actv	Tri	B-7
CX1	B66	I				Tri	Tri	
CX2	B68	O				1	1	B-7
DACK0#	B79	O		12, 2	20, 50	Tri	Tri	B-7
DACK1#	B44	O		12, 2	20, 50	Tri	Tri	B-7
DACK2#	B59	O		12, 2	20, 50	Tri	Tri	B-7
DACK3#	B42	O		12, 2	20, 50	Tri	Tri	B-7
DACK5#	B87	O		12, 2	20, 50	Tri	Tri	B-7
DACK6#	B89	O		12, 2	20, 50	Tri	Tri	B-7
DACK7#	B91	O		12, 2	20, 50	Tri	Tri	B-7

4

Table 2-3. 82360SL Pin Characteristics (Continued)

Signal Name	PQFP Pin #	Type	Term	Drive I_{OL}, I_{OH}	Load Min, Max	Susp	ONCE	Derating Curve
DMA8/16#	B136	O		12, 2	20, 50	Tri	Tri	B-7
DRQ0	B85	I	20K PD			Tri	Tri	
DRQ1	B45	I	20K PD			Tri	Tri	
DRQ2	B194	I	20K PD			Tri	Tri	
DRQ3	B43	I	20K PD			Tri	Tri	
DRQ5	B88	I	20K PD			Tri	Tri	
DRQ6	B90	I	20K PD			Tri	Tri	
DRQ7	B92	I	20K PD			Tri	Tri	
ERROR#	B149	I	60K PU			Tri	Tri	
EXTRTCRW#	B166	O	60K PU	12, 2	20, 50	1	Tri	B-7
EXTRTCAS	B168	O	20K PD	12, 2	20, 50	0	Tri	B-7
EXTRTCDS	B167	O	60K PU	12, 2	20, 50	1	Tri	B-7
EXTSMI#	B186	I	60K PU			Tri	Tri	
FLPCS#	B96	O		12, 2	20, 50	Tri	Tri	B-7
HALT#	B133	I	60K PU			Tri	Tri	
HD7	B101	IO	60K PU	24, 4	20, 100	Tri	Tri	B-3
HDCS0#	B103	O		12, 2	20, 50	Tri	Tri	B-7
HDCS1#	B102	O		12, 2	20, 50	Tri	Tri	B-7
HDENH#	B183	O		12, 2	20, 50	Tri	Tri	B-7
HDENL#	B184	O		12, 2	20, 50	Tri	Tri	B-7
HLDA	B137	I	20K PD			Tri	Tri	
HRQ	B138	O		12, 2	20, 50	Tri	Tri	B-7
IMUX0	B171	I	20K PD			Tri	Tri	
INTA#	B134	I	60K PU			Tri	Tri	
INTR	B139	O		12, 2	20, 50	Tri	Tri	B-7
IOCHCK#	B193	I	4.7K PU			Tri	Tri	
IOCHRDY	B36	IO OD		24, 4	20, 240	Tri	Tri	B-8
IOCS16#	B192	I				Tri		
IOR#	B41	IO		24, 4	50, 240	Tri	Tri	B-2
IOW#	B40	IO		24, 4	50, 240	Tri	Tri	B-2
IRQ1	B61	I	10K PU			Tri	Tri	
IRQ3	B54	I	10K PU			Tri	Tri	
IRQ4	B53	I	10K PU			Tri	Tri	
IRQ5	B52	I	10K PU			Tri	Tri	
IRQ6	B51	I	10K PU			Tri	Tri	
IRQ7	B48	I	10K PU			Tri	Tri	

Table 2-3. 82360SL Pin Characteristics (Continued)

Signal Name	PQFP Pin #	Type	Term	Drive I_{OL}, I_{OH}	Load Min, Max	Susp	ONCE	Derating Curve
IRQ8#	B170	I	20K PD			Actv	Tri	
IRQ9	B100	I	10K PU			Tri	Tri	
IRQ10	B74	I	10K PU			Tri	Tri	
IRQ11	B75	I	10K PU			Tri	Tri	
IRQ12	B76	I	10K PU			Tri	Tri	
IRQ14	B78	I	10K PU			Tri	Tri	
IRQ15	B77	I	10K PU			Tri	Tri	
KBDA20	B56	I	60K PU			Tri	Tri	
KBDCLK	B55	O		12, 2	20, 50	Tri	Tri	B-7
LA17	B73	IO		24, 4	50, 240	Tri	Tri	B-1
LA18	B72	IO		24, 4	50, 240	Tri	Tri	B-1
LA19	B71	IO		24, 4	50, 240	Tri	Tri	B-1
LA20	B70	IO		24, 4	50, 240	Tri	Tri	B-1
LA21	B69	IO		24, 4	50, 240	Tri	Tri	B-1
LA22	B64	IO		24, 4	50, 240	Tri	Tri	B-1
LA23	B63	IO		24, 4	50, 240	Tri	Tri	B-1
LPTACK#	B150	I	60K PU			Tri	Tri	
LPTAFD#	B144	O OD(1)	4.7K PU	12	20, 100	Tri	Tri	B-6
LPTBUSY	B151	I	20K PU			Tri	Tri	
LPTD0	B145	IO	20K PD	8, 2	20, 100	Tri	Tri	B-5
LPTD1	B154	IO	20K PD	8, 2	20, 100	Tri	Tri	B-5
LPTD2	B156	IO	20K PD	8, 2	20, 100	Tri	Tri	B-5
LPTD3	B158	IO	20K PD	8, 2	20, 100	Tri	Tri	B-5
LPTD4	B159	IO	20K PD	8, 2	20, 100	Tri	Tri	B-5
LPTD5	B160	IO	20K PD	8, 2	20, 100	Tri	Tri	B-5
LPTD6	B161	IO	20K PD	8, 2	20, 100	Tri	Tri	B-5
LPTD7	B162	IO	20K PD	8, 2	20, 100	Tri	Tri	B-5
LPTDIR	B164	O OD(1)	4.7K PU	12	20, 100	Tri	Tri	B-6
LPTERROR#	B146	I	60K PU			Tri	Tri	
LPTINIT#	B155	O OD(1)	4.7K PU	12	20, 100	Tri	Tri	B-6
LPTPE	B152	I	20K PD			Tri	Tri	
LPTSLCT	B153	I	20K PD			Tri	Tri	
LPTSLCTIN#	B157	O OD(1)	4.7K PU	12	20, 100	Tri	Tri	B-6
LPTSTROBE#	B143	O OD(1)	4.7K PU	12	20, 100	Tri	Tri	B-6

NOTE:
1. These outputs become CMOS drivers when bit 7 of the FPP_CNTL register is set.

4

Table 2-3. 82360SL Pin Characteristics (Continued)

Signal Name	PQFP Pin #	Type	Term	Drive I_{OL}, I_{OH}	Load Min, Max	Susp	ONCE	Derating Curve
MASTER#	B95	I				Tri	Tri	
MEMR#	B80	IO		24, 4	20, 240	Tri	Tri	B-2
MEMW#	B86	IO		24, 4	20, 240	Tri	Tri	B-2
NC	B2							
NMI	B140	O		12, 2	20, 50	Tri	Tri	B-7
ONCE#	B195	I	60K PU			Tri	Actv	
OSC	B115	O		24	50, 240	Tri	Tri	B-4
PERR#	B142	I	60K PU			Tri	Tri	
PWRGOOD	B191	I				Actv	Tri	
RC#	B58	I	60K PU			Tri	Tri	
REFREQ	B128	O		12, 2	20, 50	Actv	Tri	B-7
REFRESH#	B46	IO OD	300 PU	8	50, 240	Tri	Tri	B-4
RESETDRV	B107	O		24	50, 240	Tri	Tri	B-4
RTCEN#	B175	I				Actv	Tri	
RTCRESET#	B169	I				Actv	Tri	
RTCVCC	B177							
RTCX1	B178	I				Actv	Tri	
RTCX2	B176	O				Actv	1	B-7
Reserved	B173							
SA0	B33	IO		24, 4	50, 240	Tri	Tri	B-1
SA1	B31	IO		24, 4	50, 240	Tri	Tri	B-1
SA2	B30	IO		24, 4	50, 240	Tri	Tri	B-1
SA3	B29	IO		24, 4	50, 240	Tri	Tri	B-1
SA4	B28	IO		24, 4	50, 240	Tri	Tri	B-1
SA5	B27	IO		24, 4	50, 240	Tri	Tri	B-1
SA6	B26	IO		24, 4	50, 240	Tri	Tri	B-1
SA7	B25	IO		24, 4	50, 240	Tri	Tri	B-1
SA8	B24	IO		24, 4	50, 240	Tri	Tri	B-1
SA9	B23	IO		24, 4	50, 240	Tri	Tri	B-1
SA10	B22	IO		24, 4	50, 240	Tri	Tri	B-1
SA11	B21	IO		24, 4	50, 240	Tri	Tri	B-1
SA12	B20	IO		24, 4	50, 240	Tri	Tri	B-1
SA13	B19	IO		24, 4	50, 240	Tri	Tri	B-1

Table 2-3. 82360SL Pin Characteristics (Continued)

Signal Name	PQFP Pin #	Type	Term	Drive I_{OL}, I_{OH}	Load Min, Max	Susp	ONCE	Derating Curve
SA14	B17	IO		24, 4	50, 240	Tri	Tri	B-1
SA15	B15	IO		24, 4	50, 240	Tri	Tri	B-1
SA16	B14	IO		24, 4	50, 240	Tri	Tri	B-1
SBHE#	B62	O		24, 4	50, 240	Tri	Tri	B-4
SD0	B13	IO		24, 4	50, 240	Tri	Tri	B-2
SD1	B12	IO		24, 4	50, 240	Tri	Tri	B-2
SD2	B11	IO		24, 4	50, 240	Tri	Tri	B-2
SD3	B10	IO		24, 4	50, 240	Tri	Tri	B-2
SD4	B9	IO		24, 4	50, 240	Tri	Tri	B-2
SD5	B8	IO		24, 4	50, 240	Tri	Tri	B-2
SD6	B7	IO		24, 4	50, 240	Tri	Tri	B-2
SD7	B6	IO		24, 4	50, 240	Tri	Tri	B-2
SMEMR#/LOMEM#	B39	O	60K PU	24, 4	50, 240	Tri	Tri	B-4
SMEMW#	B38	O	60K PU	24, 4	50, 240	Tri	Tri	B-4
SMI#	B129	O		12, 2	20, 50	Tri	Tri	B-7
SMOUT0	B93	O		12, 2	20, 50	Tri	Tri	B-7
SMOUT1	B94	O		12, 2	20, 50	Tri	Tri	B-7
SMOUT2	B104	O		12, 2	20, 50	Tri	Tri	B-7
SMOUT3	B105	O		12, 2	20, 50	Tri	Tri	B-7
SMOUT4	B106	O		12, 2	20, 50	Tri	Tri	B-7
SMOUT5	B108	O		12, 2	20, 50	Tri	Tri	B-7
SMRAMCS#	B180	I	60K PU			Tri	Tri	
SPKR	B182	O		12, 2	20, 50	Tri	Tri	B-7
SRBTN#	B190	I				Actv	Tri	
STPCLK#	B131	O		12, 2	20, 50	Tri	Tri	B-7
SUS_STAT#	B185	O		12, 2	20, 50	Actv	Tri	B-7
SYSCLK	B47	I				Tri	Tri	
TC	B60	O		24, 4	50, 240	Tri	Tri	B-4
TIM2CLK2	B172	I	20K PD			Tri	Tri	
TIM2OUT2	B174	O		12, 2	20, 50	Tri	Tri	B-7

Table 2-3. 82360SL Pin Characteristics (Continued)

Signal Name	PQFP Pin #	Type	Term	Drive I_{OL}, I_{OH}	Load Min, Max	Susp	ONCE	Derating Curve
XD7	B5	IO	60K PU	24, 4	20, 100	Tri	Tri	B-3
XDEN#	B3	O		12, 2	20, 50	Tri	Tri	B-7
XDIR	B4	O		12, 2	20, 50	Tri	Tri	B-7
ZEROWS#	B35	O OD		24, 4	50, 240	Tri	Tri	B-4

Power Pins

V_{CC} : B001, B018, B034, B050, B067, B083, B099, B116, B132, B148, B165, B181

V_{SS} : B016, B032, B049, B065, B081, B098, B114, B130, B147, B163, B179, B196

3.0 SIGNAL DESCRIPTIONS

Intel386™ SL Microprocessor

The following table provides a brief description of the signals of the Intel386 SL CPU. Signal names which end with the character "#" indicate that the corresponding signal is low when active.

<table>
<tr><th>Symbol</th><th>Name and Function</th></tr>
<tr><td>A20GATE</td><td>A20 Gate: This active HIGH input signal controls the Intel386 SL CPU A20 address line. When LOW this signal forces the Intel386 SL CPU to mask off (force LOW) the internal physical address signal A20. When this signal is HIGH, A20 is available on the System Address (SA) bus. When A20 gate is LOW this allows emulation of the 8086 1 Mbyte address "wrap-around".</td></tr>
<tr><td>BALE</td><td>Bus Address Latch Enable (ISA bus signal): This active HIGH output signal is used for two purposes. BALE is used to latch the address lines on the LA bus (LA17–LA23) on the falling edge of BALE. BALE is also used to qualify ISA bus cycles for signals on the Peripherial Interface (PI) bus (PM/IO# and PW/R#). On the falling edge of BALE, PM/IO# and PW/R# can be sampled to determine the type of ISA bus cycle that is going to occur. BALE may be used to qualify and generate buffered control and status signals to the ISA expansion bus. The PI bus signal decoding is as follows:
<table>
<tr><th>Type of Bus Cycle</th><th>PM/IO#</th><th>PW/R#</th></tr>
<tr><td>Memory Read</td><td>1</td><td>0</td></tr>
<tr><td>Memory Write</td><td>1</td><td>1</td></tr>
<tr><td>I/O Read</td><td>0</td><td>0</td></tr>
<tr><td>I/O Write</td><td>0</td><td>1</td></tr>
<tr><td>Interrupt Acknowledge</td><td>0</td><td>1</td></tr>
<tr><td>HALT (address = 2)*</td><td>1</td><td>1</td></tr>
<tr><td>Shutdown (address = 0)*</td><td>1</td><td>1</td></tr>
</table>
*Note that BALE is not generated for these cycles, however the PM/IO# and PW/R# will reflect these states during HALT and Shutdown bus cycles where BALE is driven in typical ISA bus systems. Memory read/write, IO read/write and interrupt/interrupt acknowledge cycles correspond to the standard ISA bus cycle.</td></tr>
<tr><td>BUSY#</td><td>BUSY: This active LOW input signal indicates a busy condition from a math co-processor (MCP).</td></tr>
<tr><td>CA[15:1]</td><td>Cache Address Bus: This is the address bus output used to select the memory cell in the cache memory. The CA2 signal is also connected to the CMD0# input of the MCP indicating Opcode (when high) or Data (when low) during a write cycle and control/status register (high) or data register (low) during a read. CA2 is used to address the upper or lower DWORD port of the MCP.</td></tr>
<tr><td>CCSH#</td><td>Cache Chip Select High Byte: This active LOW output is used to enable the upper byte of the cache SRAMs. This signal should be connected to the upper byte cache SRAM chip-select input.</td></tr>
<tr><td>CCSL#</td><td>Cache Chip Select Low Byte: This active LOW output is used to enable the lower byte of the cache SRAMs. This signal should be connected to the lower byte cache SRAM chip-select input.</td></tr>
<tr><td>CD[15:0]</td><td>Cache Data Bus: This is the bi-directional data bus used to transfer data between the cache SRAMs and the Intel386 SL CPU. The Cache Data bus is also used to transfer data between the MCP and the Intel386 SL CPU.</td></tr>
</table>

4

Intel386™ SL Microprocessor Signal Descriptions (Continued)

Symbol	Name and Function
CMUX0 (CASL3#/ DIR)	**CPU Multiplexed Pin Zero:** This output signal has two functions. When the Intel386 SL CPU Memory Controller Unit is configured as a DRAM controller then this pin becomes "CASL3#" and should be connected to the lower byte of DRAM bank 3 CAS# input. When the Intel386 SL CPU Memory Controller Unit is configured as an SRAM controller this signal becomes the direction control (DIR) and should be connected to the direction control input of the SRAM data transceiver.
CMUX1 (CASH3#/ LE)	**CPU Multiplexed Pin One:** This output signal has two functions. When the Intel386 SL CPU Memory Controller Unit is configured as a DRAM controller then this pin becomes "CASH3#" and should be connected to the upper byte of DRAM bank 3 CAS# input. When the Intel386 SL CPU Memory Controller Unit is configured as a SRAM controller this signal becomes "LE" and should be connected to the latch enable input of the SRAM address latch. This pin is disabled when SUS_STAT# is active (LOW) and the system is not performing a suspend refresh operation. When the pin is disabled the output is sustained at the previous state by internal "keepers".
CMUX2 (CASL2#/ DEN3#)	**CPU Multiplexed Pin Two:** This output signal has two functions. When the Intel386 SL CPU Memory Controller Unit is configured as a DRAM controller this pin becomes "CASL2#" and should be connected to the lower byte of DRAM bank 2 CAS# input. When the Intel386 SL CPU Memory Controller Unit is configured as a SRAM controller this pin becomes "DEN3#" and should be connected to the data transceiver enable input for bank 3 of the SRAM memory subsystem. This pin is disabled when SUS_STAT# is active (LOW) and the system is not performing a suspend refresh operation. When the pin is disabled the output is sustained at the previous state by internal "keepers".
CMUX3 (CASH2#/ DEN2#)	**CPU Multiplexed Pin Three:** This output signal has two functions. When the Intel386 SL CPU Memory Controller Unit is configured as a DRAM controller this pin becomes "CASH2#" and should be connected to the upper byte of DRAM bank 2 CAS# input. When the Intel386 SL CPU Memory Controller Unit is configured as a SRAM controller this pin becomes "DEN2#" and should be connected to the data transceiver enable input for bank 2 of the SRAM memory subsystem. This pin is disabled when SUS_STAT# is active (LOW) and the system is not performing a suspend refresh operation. When the pin is disabled the output is sustained at the previous state by internal "keepers".
CMUX4 (CASL1#/ DEN1#	**CPU Multiplexed Pin Four:** This output signal has two functions. When the Intel386 SL CPU Memory Controller Unit is configured as a DRAM controller this pin becomes "CASL1#" and should be connected to the lower byte of DRAM bank 1 CAS# input. When the Intel386 SL CPU Memory Controller Unit is configured as a SRAM controller this pin becomes "DEN1#" and should be connected to the data transceiver enable input for bank 1 of the SRAM memory subsystem. This pin is disabled when SUS_STAT# is active (LOW) and the system is not performing a suspend refresh operation. When the pin is disabled the output is sustained at the previous state by internal "keepers".

NOTE:
Pins CMUX4 and CMUX5 both carry the signal DEN1# in the SRAM mode. This is done to provide increased drive capacity on the DEN1# signal.

Intel386™ SL Microprocessor Signal Descriptions (Continued)

Symbol	Name and Function
CMUX5 (CASH1#/ DEN1#)	**CPU Multiplexed Pin Five:** This output signal has two functions. When the Intel386 SL CPU Memory Controller Unit is configured as a DRAM controller this pin becomes "CASH1#" and should be connected to the upper byte of DRAM bank 1 CAS# input. When the Intel386 SL CPU Memory Controller Unit is configured as a SRAM controller this pin becomes "DEN1#" and should be connected to the data transceiver enable input for bank 1 of the SRAM memory subsystem. This pin is disabled when SUS_STAT# is active (LOW) and the system is not performing a suspend refresh operation. When the pin is disabled the output is sustained at the previous state by internal "keepers".
CMUX6 (CASL0#/ DEN0#)	**CPU Multiplexed Pin Six:** This output signal has two functions. When the Intel386 SL CPU Memory Controller Unit is configured as a DRAM controller this pin becomes "CASL0#" and should be connected to the lower byte of DRAM bank 0 CAS# input. When the Intel386 SL CPU Memory Controller Unit is configured as a SRAM controller this pin becomes "DEN0#" and should be connected to the data transceiver enable input for bank 0 of the SRAM memory subsystem. This pin is disabled when SUS_STAT# is active (LOW) and the system is not performing a suspend refresh operation. When the pin is disabled the output is sustained at the previous state by internal "keepers".
CMUX7 (CASH0#/ DEN0#)	**CPU Multiplexed Pin Seven:** This output signal has two functions. When the Intel386 SL CPU Memory Controller Unit is configured as a DRAM controller this pin becomes "CASH0#" and should be connected to the upper byte of DRAM bank 0 CAS# input. When the Intel386 SL CPU Memory Controller Unit is configured as a SRAM controller this pin becomes "DEN0#" and should be connected to the data transceiver enable input for bank 0 of the SRAM memory subsystem. This pin is disabled when SUS_STAT# is active (LOW) and the system is not performing a suspend refresh operation. When the pin is disabled the output is sustained at the previous state by internal "keepers".
CMUX8 (RAS3#/ CE3#)	**CPU Multiplexed Pin Eight:** This output signal has two functions. When the Intel386 SL CPU Memory Controller Unit is configured as a DRAM controller this pin becomes "RAS3#" and should be connected to the upper and lower byte of DRAM bank 3 RAS# inputs. When the Intel386 SL CPU Memory Controller Unit is configured as a SRAM controller then this pin becomes "CE3#" and should be connected to the upper and lower byte of the SRAM chip-select, or to the chip-select decode logic for bank 3 of the SRAM memory subsystem. This pin is disabled when SUS_STAT# is active (LOW) and the system is not performing a suspend refresh operation. When the pin is disabled the output is sustained at the previous state by internal "keepers".
CMUX9 (RAS2#/ CE2#)	**CPU Multiplexed Pin Nine:** This output signal has two functions. When the Intel386 SL CPU Memory Controller Unit is configured as a DRAM controller this pin becomes "RAS2#" and should be connected to the upper and lower byte of DRAM bank 2 RAS# inputs. When the Intel386 SL CPU Memory Controller Unit is configured as a SRAM controller this pin becomes "CE2#" and should be connected to the upper and lower byte of the SRAM chip-select, or to the chip-select decode logic for bank 2 of the SRAM memory subsystem. This pin is disabled when SUS_STAT# is active (LOW) and the system is not performing a suspend refresh operation. When the pin is disabled the output is sustained at the previous state by internal "keepers".

NOTES:

Pins CMUX4 and CMUX5 both carry the signal DEN1# in the SRAM mode. This is done to provide increased drive capacity on the DEN1# signal.

Pins CMUX6 and CMUX7 both carry the signal DEN0# in the SRAM mode. This is done to provide increased drive capacity on the DEN0# signal.

Intel386™ SL Microprocessor Signal Descriptions (Continued)

Symbol	Name and Function
CMUX10 (RAS1#/ CE1#)	**CPU Multiplexed Pin Ten:** This output signal has two functions. When the Intel386 SL CPU Memory Controller Unit is configured as a DRAM controller this pin becomes "RAS1#" and should be connected to the upper and lower byte of DRAM bank 1 RAS# inputs. When the Intel386 SL CPU Memory Controller Unit is configured as a SRAM controller this pin becomes "CE1#" and should be connected to the upper and lower byte of the SRAM chip-select, or to the chip-select decode logic for bank 1 of the SRAM memory subsystem. This pin is disabled when SUS_STAT# is active (LOW) and the system is not performing a suspend refresh operation. When the pin is disabled the output is sustained at the previous state by internal "keepers".
CMUX11 (RAS0#/ CE0#)	**CPU Multiplexed Pin Eleven:** This output signal has two functions. When the Intel386 SL CPU Memory Controller Unit is configured as a DRAM controller this pin becomes "RAS0#" and should be connected to the upper and lower byte of DRAM bank 0 RAS# inputs. When the Intel386 SL CPU Memory Controller Unit is configured as a SRAM controller this pin becomes "CE0#" and should be connected to the upper and lower byte of the SRAM chip-select, or to the chip-select decode logic for bank 0 of the SRAM memory subsystem. This pin is disabled when SUS_STAT# is active (LOW) and the system is not performing a suspend refresh operation. When the pin is disabled the output is sustained at the previous state by internal "keepers".
CMUX12 (PARL/ OLE#)	**CPU Multiplexed Pin Twelve:** This output signal has two functions. When the Intel386 SL CPU Memory Controller Unit is configured as a DRAM controller this pin becomes "PARL" and should be connected to the lower byte of DRAM bank 0 data parity bit. When the Intel386 SL CPU Memory Controller Unit is configured as a SRAM controller this pin becomes "OLE#" and should be connected to the lower byte of the SRAM output enable input of the SRAM memory subsystem. This pin is disabled when SUS_STAT# is active (LOW) and the system is not performing a suspend refresh operation. When the pin is disabled the output is sustained at the previous state by internal "keepers".
CMUX13 (PARH/ OHE#)	**CPU Multiplexed Pin Thirteen:** This output signal has two functions. When the Intel386 SL CPU Memory Controller Unit is configured as a DRAM controller this pin becomes "PARH" and should be connected to the upper byte of DRAM bank 0 data parity bit. When the Intel386 SL CPU Memory Controller Unit is configured as a SRAM controller this pin becomes "OHE#" and should be connected to the upper byte of the SRAM output enable input of the SRAM memory subsystem. This pin is disabled when SUS_STAT# is active (LOW) and the system is not performing a suspend refresh operation. When the pin is disabled the output is sustained at the previous state by internal "keepers".
CMUX14 (ROMCS1#/ FLSHDCS#)	**CPU Multiplexed Pin 14:** This output signal has two functions. The Intel386 SL CPU can be configured to use this pin as either a BIOS ROM chip-select (ROMCS1#), or a FLASH disk chip-select signal (FLSHDCS#). In either case, the signal is driven LOW when an access to the selected interface occurs.
COE#	**Cache Output Enable:** This active LOW output signal is used to indicate a read access to the CACHE SRAMs, and is used to enable the cache SRAMs' output buffers. This signal should be connected to the output enable signals of the upper and lower byte cache SRAMs.
CPURESET	**CPU Reset:** This active HIGH input forces the Intel386 SL CPU to execute a reset to the internal CPU core and state machines. The configuration registers are not reset.

Intel386™ SL Microprocessor Signal Descriptions (Continued)

Symbol	Name and Function
CWE#	**Cache Write Enable:** This active LOW output is used to indicate a write (LOW) access to the cache SRAMs. This signal should be connected to the write enable signal of the upper and lower cache SRAMs.
DMA8/16#	**DMA 8-bit or 16-bit Cycle:** This input, in conjunction with HRQ, indicates to 386 SL CPU if an 8-bit or 16-bit DMA access is occurring. If an 8-bit DMA access is occurring, the Intel386 SL CPU will swap the upper byte of data to the lower data byte for upper byte accesses.
EFI	**External Frequency Input.** This is an oscillator input. This clock controls all CPU core and memory controller timings and is equal to twice the desired processor frequency (CPUCLK).
ERROR#	**Numerics ERROR:** This active LOW input to the Intel386 SL CPU is generated from a math co-processor (MCP). It also indicates to the 82360SL that an unmasked exception has occurred in the MCP. ERROR# is provided to allow numerics error handling compatible with the ISA bus compatible Personal Computer.
HALT#	**HALT:** This active LOW output indicates to external devices that the Intel386 SL CPU has executed a HALT instruction (address = 2) or a shutdown condition (address = 0). This can be used as an indicator for devices to assert the STPCLK# signal.
HLDA	**HoLD Acknowledge:** This active HIGH output indicates to external devices that the Intel386 SL CPU has relinquished control of the ISA bus. At this time the Intel386 SL CPU has floated the address and control signals of the ISA bus.
HRQ	**Hold ReQuest:** This active HIGH input indicates to the Intel386 SL CPU that an external device wishes to take control of the ISA bus.
INTA#	**INTerrupt Acknowledge:** This active LOW output indicates that the Intel386 SL CPU is executing an interrupt acknowledge bus cycle. During this process an external interrupt device will pass an interrupt vector to the Intel386 SL CPU.
INTR	**Interrupt Request:** This active HIGH input indicates to the Intel386 SL CPU that an external device is requesting the execution of an interrupt service routine.
IOCHRDY	**I/O CHannel ReaDY:** This active HIGH input indicates that the I/O Channel, (ISA expansion bus), is ready to terminate the bus cycle. The ISA expansion bus is a normally ready bus and IOCHRDY is active HIGH. When an ISA bus peripheral needs to extend the standard 3 SYSCLK, 16-bit ISA bus cycle the peripheral device asserts IOCHRDY LOW.
IOCS16#	**I/O Chip Select 16:** This active LOW input indicates that an ISA bus peripheral wishes to execute a 16-bit I/O cycle. This signal has an active pull-up, when not driven the default I/O bus cycle is 8 bits.
IOR#	**I/O Read:** This active LOW signal indicates that the ISA bus is executing an I/O read cycle.
IOW#	**I/O Write:** This active LOW signal indicates that the ISA bus is executing an I/O write cycle.
ISACLK2	**ISA Clock Two:** This is an oscillator input. This clock controls all of the ISA bus timings and is equal to twice the SYSCLK frequency. Normally the ISA bus SYSCLK is 8 MHz, and the ISACLK2 oscillator is 16 MHz.

4

Intel386™ SL Microprocessor Signal Descriptions (Continued)

Symbol	Name and Function
LA[23:17]	**Latchable local Address bus:** This is the unlatched local address of the ISA bus for access to memory above 1 megabyte. The LA bus is also used by the Peripherial Interface (PI) Bus.
MA[10:0]	**Memory controller Multiplexed Address bus:** This is the address bus output for the Memory Controller Unit. The 22-bit address is output in a row/column fashion for both DRAM and SRAM memory subsystems. The Memory Controller Unit places the ROW address out first and qualifies it by the RASx# signal going active in DRAM mode or the LE signal going active in the SRAM mode. The column address is then placed on the Memory Address bus and is qualified by the CASXx# signals going active for the DRAM mode. This pin is disabled when SUS_STAT# is active (LOW). When the pin is disabled the output is sustained at the previous state by internal "keepers".
MASTER#	**Master:** This active LOW input indicates that an ISA bus peripheral is controlling the bus. The peripheral device asserts this signal in conjunction with a DMA request (DRQ) line or the HRQ (hold request) to gain control of the bus. When the MASTER# signal is asserted LOW along with HRQ being asserted HIGH or a DRQ line being asserted HIGH, the Intel386 SL CPU will float all address, data and control signals on the ISA bus.
MD[15:0]	**Memory controller local Memory Data bus:** This is the bi-directional data bus of the Memory Controller Unit. All accesses by the Memory Controller Unit that transfer data between the Intel386 SL CPU and SRAM or DRAM use the Memory Data Bus. This pin is disabled when SUS_STAT# is active (low) and the system is not performing a suspend refresh operation. When the pin is disabled the output is sustained at the previous state by internal "keepers".
MEMCS16#	**MEMory Chip Select 16:** This active LOW input indicates that an ISA bus peripheral wishes to execute a 16-bit memory cycle. This signal has an active pull-up, when not driven the default memory bus cycle is 8 bits.
MEMR#	**MEMory Read:** This bi-directional active LOW signal indicates when a memory read access is taking place on the ISA bus. When the Intel386 SL CPU is performing a memory read to the ISA bus it is an output, when the DMA or Bus Master is accessing memory on the ISA bus, the DMA device or Master drives MEMR#.
MEMW#	**MEMory Write:** This bi-directional active LOW signal indicates when a memory write access is taking place on the ISA bus. When the Intel386 SL CPU is performing a memory write to the ISA bus it is an output, when the DMA or Bus Master is accessing memory on the ISA bus, the DMA controller or Bus Master drives MEMW#.
N/C	**No connection:** These pins must not be connected to any voltage, but must be left floating in order to guarantee proper operation of the Intel386 SL CPU and to maintain compatibility with future Intel Processors.
NMI	**Non-Maskable Interrupt:** This rising edge sensitive input will latch a request to the Intel386 SL CPU for a non-maskable interrupt on a LOW-to-HIGH transition.
NPXADS#	**Numerics ADdress Strobe:** This active LOW output signal indicates the start of a math co-process (MCP) data transfer cycle.
NPXCLK	**Numerics Clock:** This output signal is used to drive the MCP clock input.
NPXRDY#	**Numerics Ready:** This active LOW input is used to terminate a MCP bus cycle. This signal is low for I/O and data operand MCP cycles.

Intel386™ SL Microprocessor Signal Descriptions (Continued)

Symbol	Name and Function
NPXRESET	**Numerics Reset:** This active HIGH output signal is used to reset the MCP.
NPXW/R#	**Numerics Write or Read:** This output signal indicates the type of data transfer that is being performed between the Intel386 SL CPU and the MCP. When high this signal indicates a MCP write, when low this signal indicates a MCP read.
ONCE#	**ON-board Circuit Emulation:** This active LOW input signal floats the neccessary outputs from the Intel386 SL CPU allowing an in-circuit emulation (ICE™-Intel386™ SL) module to drive the Intel386 SL CPU signals. This allows an emulator to be used for system testing and developement while the Intel386 SL CPU and the 82360SL are still physically populated on the system motherboard. The state of all Intel386 SL CPU and 82360SL signals when ONCE# is asserted low is summarized in section 2, (Intel386 SL CPU and 82360SL signal characteristics). Note that the ONCE# pin of the Intel386 SL CPU should not be connected to the ONCE# pin of the 82360 SL I/O.
PCMD#	**PI-BUS Command:** This active LOW output indicates that valid write data is on the System data bus (SD[15:0]) signals, or that the Intel386 SL CPU is ready to sample valid read data from the PI bus for Peripherial Interface bus cycles.
PEREQ	**Processor Extension Request:** This active HIGH input signal indicates that the MCP has data to transfer to or from the Intel386 SL CPU.
PERR#	**Parity ERRor:** This active LOW output indicates to an external device that the Intel386 SL CPU Memory Controller Unit has detected a memory parity error. The PERROR# signal is used by the 82360SL to generate NMI back to the Intel386 SL CPU.
PM/IO#	**PI-BUS Memory or I/O:** This output indicates the type of bus cycle the Intel386 SL CPU is executing on the Peripherial Interface Bus (PI-bus): Either a Memory (HIGH) or I/O (LOW) cycle.
PRDY#	**PI-BUS Ready:** This active LOW input is used to terminate Peripherial Interface bus cycles. The Peripheral Interface Bus is a normally not-ready bus, and will continue the bus cycle until the PRDY# is activated or a Peripherial Interface Time-out occurs.
PSTART#	**PI-BUS START:** This active LOW output indicates that the address (SA[19:0], LA[23:17] and SBHE#), command signals (PM/IO# and PW/R#) and chip-selects (VGACS# or FLSHDCS#) are valid for a Peripheral Interface Bus cycle.
PW/R#	**PI-BUS Write or Read:** This output indicates the type of bus cycle the Intel386 SL CPU is executing on the Peripheral Interface Bus: Either a Write (HIGH) or Read (LOW) cycle.
PWRGOOD	**Power Good:** This active HIGH input indicates that power to the system is good. This signal is generated by the power supply circuitry, and a LOW level on this signal causes the Intel386 SL to totally reset: The CPU core is reset, internal state machines are reset, all configuration registers are reset. Power Good should be low for a specified minimum number of CPU clocks for valid recognition in order to perform a global Intel386 SL CPU reset.
REFREQ	**REFresh REQuest:** This active HIGH input indicates that the Intel386 SL CPU should execute an internal DRAM refresh cycle to the on-board local memory.
ROM16/8#	**ROM 16-bits or 8-bits:** This input configuration signal pin selects if the BIOS interface is a 16-bit (when high) or 8-bit interface (when low). This pin has an internal pull-up resistor defaulting to a 16-bit wide BIOS EPROM.
ROMCS0#	**ROM Chip Select 0:** This LOW true output provides the chip select for the System BIOS EPROM.
SA[19:0]	**System Address Bus:** This is the bi-directional system address of the ISA bus, as well as the Peripheral Interface Bus. SA[16:0] are inputs during DMA and Master operation. SA[19:17] are outputs only since a 8237 compatible DMA controller accesses up to 64 kBytes at a time. The 74LS612 module in the 82360SL is used to furnish the DMA upper addresses for DMA access to 16 Megabyte.

4

Intel386™ SL Microprocessor Signal Descriptions (Continued)

Symbol	Name and Function
SBHE#	**System Byte High Enable:** When this output signal is LOW, it indicates that data is being transferred on the upper byte of the 16-bit data bus (SD[15:8]).
SD[15:0]	**System Data Bus:** This 16-bit bi-directional data bus is used to transfer data between the Intel386 SL CPU and the ISA bus. The system data bus is also used to transfer data between the Intel386 SL CPU and the Peripherial Interface (PI-BUS).
SMI#	**System power Management Interrupt:** This falling edge sensitive input latches a Power Management interrupt request with a High-to-Low edge. The SMI# is the highest priority interrupt in the Intel386 SL processor.
SMRAMCS#	**System power Management RAM Chip Select:** This active LOW output is used to select an external system power management SM-RAM, and to indicate to the 82360SL device when accesses to the system power management SM-RAM are occurring.
STPCLK#	**Stop Clock:** This active LOW input stops the clock to the internal Intel386 CPU core. (This signal is functionally tested by the execution of HALT or I/O read instructions.)
SYSCLK	**System Clock:** This is a clock output equal to one half of the ISACLK2 input frequency.
SUS_STAT#	**SUSpend STATus:** This active LOW input indicates to the Intel386 SL CPU that system power is being turned off. The Intel386 SL CPU will respond by electrically isolating selected pins as indicated in Section 2, (Intel386 SL CPU signal characteristics).
TURBO	**Turbo:** This active HIGH input signal indicates to Intel386 SL CPU when to enter "Turbo Mode". Turbo Mode is defined as the CPU executing at full speed, the default speed for the system. When this signal is forced inactive LOW, the Intel386 SL CPU executes from a divide by two or a divide by four clock as defined by the De-turbo bit in the CPUPWRMODE register. When this signal is HIGH, the CPU executes from a clock as defined by the Fast CPU clock field in the CPUPWRMODE register.
V_{CC}	**System Power:** Provides the +5V nominal D.C. supply inputs.
VGACS#	**VGA Chip-select:** This active LOW output is asserted anytime an access occurs to the user defined VGA address space.
V_{SS}	**System Ground:** Provides the 0V connection from which all inputs and outputs are referenced.
WHE#	**Write High Enable:** This active LOW output indicates that a write access to the upper byte of the Intel386 SL CPU memory bus is occurring when the Memory Controller Unit is configured for SRAM mode. When in DRAM mode, the signal is active anytime a write access occurs. This output should be connected to the write enable of the upper byte for either DRAM or SRAM memory subsystems. This pin is driven inactive during a suspend operation.
WLE#	**Write Low Enable:** This active LOW output indicates that a write access to the lower byte of the Intel386 SL CPU memory bus is occurring when the Memory Controller Unit is configured for SRAM mode. When in DRAM mode, the signal is active anytime a write access occurs. This output should be connected to the write enable of the lower byte for either DRAM or SRAM memory subsystems. This pin is driven inactive during a suspend operation.
ZEROWS#	**ZERO Wait State (ISA bus signal):** This active LOW input indicates that an ISA bus peripheral wishes to execute a zero wait state bus cycle (the normal default 16-bit ISA bus memory or I/O cycle is 3 SYSCLKs or one PC/AT equivalent wait state). When ZEROWS# is driven low, a 16-bit bus cycle will occur in two SYSCLKs. When ZEROWS# is driven low for an 8-bit memory cycle the default 6 SYSCLK bus cycle is shortened to 3 SYSCLKs.

3.0 SIGNAL DESCRIPTIONS (Continued)

82360SL ISA Peripheral I/O

The following table provides a brief description of the signals of the 82360SL I/O. Signal names which end with the character "#" indicate that the corresponding signal is low true when active.

Symbol	Name and Function
A20GATE	**A20 Gate (direct to CPU):** This active HIGH output signal allows the Intel386 SL CPU to pass A20 on the system address bus. When this signal is LOW, A20 is masked to allow emulation of an 8086.
AEN	**Address ENabled (ISA-bus signal):** This active HIGH output indicates a DMA access or refresh. The 82360SL drives this signal high to signify a valid DMA address. It is used by bus slaves to decode I/O ports. All ports must be decoded for AEN low. There are no DMA cycles to addressed I/O ports.
BALE	**Buffered Address Latch Enable (ISA-bus signal):** This active HIGH input to the 82360SL is driven by the Intel386 SL CPU during standard ISA bus cycles. During ISA bus memory and I/O cycles BALE is used to indicate valid addresses at the start of a bus cycle. SA[19:0] are valid on the falling edge and LA[23:17] are valid while BALE is high. BALE is is also driven high by the Intel386 SL CPU and remains high during DMA, REFRESH and Master cycles.
BATTDEAD#	**BATTery DEAD:** This signal acts as a reset to the state machines connected to RTCVCC. This signal must be connected to an RC combination which will allow it to meet the AC specification Ct 250.
BATTLOW#	**BATTery LOW:** This active LOW input indicates that the battery power is low. BATTLOW# is typically driven by a D.C. to D.C. power converter associated with the battery power supply. A thermal power monitor indicates that the main battery power is dropping below the adequate charge level to sustain operation. If this signal is asserted LOW a SMI request will be generated. The feature is enabled via S/W control. The signal will also prevent a resume operation if asserted LOW.
BATTWARN#	**BATTery WARNing:** This active LOW input indicates the battery has minimal charge left (eg. one half an hour of full power use remaining). It is used to generate a battery low warning tone.
C8042CS#	**Keyboard controller Chip Select:** This active LOW output is driven when there is an I/O read or write to the Keyboard Controller Ports 60 or 64 hex.
COM(A,B)CTS#	**Clear To Send:** This active LOW input indicates to the Serial Port Controller for COMA or COMB that a serial device is clear to accept data. This signal is typically used for a modem control function. A change in the state of this signal generates a modem status interrupt. The modem or data set asserts this signal when it is ready to accept data for transmission.
COM(A,B)DCD#	**Data Carrier Detect:** This active LOW input indicates that the Serial Port Controller COMA or COMB has detected a data carrier from the data set of a serial device. Typically this signal is from a modem.
COM(A,B)DSR#	**Data Set Ready:** This active LOW input signal is used by the modem or data set to indicate that the modem or data set is ready to establish the communication link and transfer data with the Serial Port Controller.
COM(A,B)DTR#	**Data Terminal Ready:** This active LOW output signal informs the modem or data set that the Serial Port Controller is ready to communicate.
COM(A,B)RXD	**Serial data Receive:** This input signal is used to receive serial data. Each character can consist of from five to eight bits of data with one start bit and one, one and a half or two stop bits. The least significant bit is received first.

4

82360SL ISA Peripheral I/O Signal Descriptions (Continued)

Symbol	Name and Function
COM(A,B)RI#	**Ring Indicator:** This active LOW input signal is used for a modem control function. A change in the state (either from high to low or from low to high) of this signal generates a modem status interrupt. The modem or data set asserts this signal to indicate that it has detected a telephone ring. This will cause the 82360SL to wake the Intel386 SL CPU from a suspended state if modem ring is enabled as a wake-up event.
COM(A,B)RTS#	**Request To Send:** This active LOW output signal informs the modem or data set that the Serial Port Controller is ready to send data.
COM(A,B)TXD	**Serial data transmission:** This output signal is used to transmit data serially between the Serial Port Controller and serial device. Each character can consist of five to eight bits of data with one start bit and either one, one and a half, or two stop bits. The least significant bit is transmitted first. The control of the format of a character is defined under S/W control via the Line Control Register. Please consult the Intel386 SL Microprocessor SuperSet Programmer's Reference Manual for additional information. Information regarding the functional timing specifications of transmitted and recieved serial data may be found in sections 6 and 7 (A.C. timing specifications and timing diagrams).
COMX1,COMX2	**Crystal oscillator input and output pins:** The crystal attached to these signals should be tuned to 1.8432 Mhz. The on-chip oscillator uses an external crystal and tank circuit to generate an internal clock. This clock is used to generate the various baud rates for the serial ports. Optionally an external oscillator may be connected to the COMX1 input.
CPURESET	**CPU RESET:** This active HIGH output is connected directly to the Intel386 SL CPU to provide a reset of the Intel386 CPU core. CPURESET always occurs during a PWRGOOD reset. CPURESET may also be generated by RC# from a keyboard controller, Fast Reset from I/O Port 92 or other programmable Reset, or a resume from suspend.
CX1,CX2	**Crystal oscillator input and output pins:** The crystal should be tuned to 14.31818 Mhz. It is used for the ISA bus signal OSC signal and is internally divided by 12 to clock the timer counters. The oscillator input may be directly driven from an external source.
DACK[7:5], [3:0]#	**DMA ACKnowledge channel n (ISA bus signal):** The 82360SL DMA controller drives the respective DMA acknowledge signal low after a device has requested DMA service. The corresponding output signal indicates that the DMA channel transfer may begin.
DMA8/16#	**DMA 8-bit or 16-bit cycle:** This output signal is directly connected to the Intel386 SL CPU. When the signal is HIGH it indicates that the current DMA cycle is 8-bit. When this signal is low it indicates that the DMA cycle is using a 16-bit channel.
DRQ[7:5], [3:0]	**DMA ReQuest channel n (ISA bus signal):** These input signals are used to request DMA service from devices residing on the ISA bus. An ISA bus device drives this signal to request service from the appropriate DMA channel by asserting this signal high.
ERROR#	**MCP ERROR:** This signal is an active LOW input to the 82360SL. The math coprocessor error signal generates a IRQ13 through the 82360SL.
EXTSMI#	**EXTernal System Management Interrupt request:** This active low input will generate a SMI request if the function is enabled.
EXTRTCAS	**EXTernal RTC Address Strobe:** This output signal is active HIGH when there is a write access to the RTC I/O address port and when an external RTC is selected.
EXTRTCDS	**EXTernal RTC read Data Strobe:** This output signal is active LOW when there is a read access to an external RTC I/O data port and when an external RTC is selected.
EXTRTCRW#	**EXTernal RTC (Real Time Clock) Read/Write:** This output signal is active LOW when there is a write access to an external RTC I/O data port and when an external RTC is selected.

82360SL ISA Peripheral I/O Signal Descriptions (Continued)

Symbol	Name and Function
FLPCS#	**FLoPpy Chip Select:** This LOW true output signal is the chip select for the floppy disk controller I/O ports 03F0–03F5 and 3F7 hex.
HALT#	**HALT:** This LOW true input signal is driven by the Intel386 SL CPU and indicates when the CPU has executed a HLT instruction (address = 2) or is in a shutdown condition (address = 0).
HD7	**HD-bus Data bit HD7:** The bi-directional System Data Bit 7 is controlled separately for the Integrated Drive Electronics (I.D.E.) hard disk drive and floppy disk drive. This is provided to accommodate the I/O address 3F7 hex which is split between the floppy disk drive controller and I.D.E. hard disk. Data transfer between storage peripherals connected to the I.D.E. Hard Disk and Floppy Disk and the 82360SL are on separate busses. Data bit 7 has to be separated from data bits [6:0]. The 82360SL controls and buffers data bit 7 seperately.
HDCS[1:0]#	**Hard Disk Chip Select:** These LOW true output signals are the I.D.E. hard disk drive chip selects decoded from the I/O address ports 01F0–01F7h (HDCS0#) and 03F6–03F7h (HDCS1#).
HDEN(H,L)#	**Hard Disk buffer ENable:** These LOW true output signals control the I.D.E. hard disk data buffers, high and low bytes.
HLDA	**HoLD Acknowledge (direct to CPU):** This HIGH true input signal indicates that the Intel386 SL CPU has released the ISA bus for refresh, DMA or master cycles.
HRQ	**Hold ReQuest (direct to CPU):** This active HIGH output signal indicates a request to the Intel386 SL CPU to release the ISA bus when the 82360SL requests the bus for ISA bus style refresh, DMA or master mode cycles.
IMUX0	This pin is multiplexed. It can be used as Timer 2 gate 2 input or an external audio input.
INTA#	**INTerrupt Acknowledge (direct to CPU):** This active LOW input to the 82360SL indicates that the Intel386 SL CPU has recognized an interrupt and will initiate an interrupt acknowledge bus cycle. The INTA bus cycle is comprised of two eight-bit I/O cycles in which the interrupt vector transferred on the second eight-bit I/O write of the INTA cycle.
INTR	**INTerrupt Request (direct to CPU):** This active HIGH output requests a standard maskable interrupt to the Intel386 SL CPU.
IOCHCK#	**IO CHannel ChecK (ISA bus signal):** This maskable active LOW input is driven by a device on the ISA bus typically used to indicate a parity error on the ISA bus. This signal is one of the possible sources which may generate an NMI. NMI generation via IO Channel Check may be enabled or disabled using PORT 61 (IOCKEN). NMI may be masked using the ISA bus compatible NMI control port at I/O 70 hex bit 7.
IOCHRDY	**I/O CHannel ReaDY (ISA bus signal):** This active HIGH I/O signal is used by the 82360SL DMA controller to extend ISA bus cycles. IOCHRDY is also used to extend bus cycles for I/O device trapping. Additional wait states extend the bus cycle, allowing for start up during Resume mode. The ISA bus is a normally ready bus, an external device can extend a DMA cycle or ISA bus cycle by deasserting this signal (driven low). This signal is normally high on the ISA bus.
IOCS16#	**16-bit I/O Chip Select (ISA bus signal):** This active LOW input signal to the 82360SL is used to indicate a 16-bit I/O bus cycle. The I.D.E. hard disk high byte buffer enable is generated when IOCS16# is driven low during an I.D.E. 16-bit I/O access. IOCS16# is also an input to the Intel386 SL CPU driven by devices residing on the ISA bus to indicate a 16-bit I/O bus cycle.

4

82360SL ISA Peripheral I/O Signal Descriptions (Continued)

Symbol	Name and Function
IOR#	**I/O Read (ISA bus signal):** This bi-directional active LOW signal is an input during normal accesses to I/O ports. When low this signal indicates an I/O read. This signal is an output from the 82360SL during DMA bus cycles for I/O to memory transfers.
IOW#	**I/O Write (ISA bus signal):** This bi-directional active LOW signal is an input during normal accesses to I/O ports. When low this signal indicates and I/O write. This signal is an output from the 82360SL during DMA bus cycles for memory to I/O transfers.
IRQ[15, 14, 12–9, 7–3, 1]	**Interrupt ReQuest n (ISA bus signal):** These active HIGH input signals are used to request interrupt service. The interrupt request lines are driven by devices on the ISA bus which have a corresponding interrupt service routine associated with the interrupt vector and interrupt request.
IRQ8#	**Interrupt ReQuest 8:** This active LOW signal is used by the external Real Time Clock to request interrupt service.
KBDA20	**KeyBoarD A20 gate:** This active HIGH input is "ORed" with internal bits to produce A20GATE which goes to the Intel386 SL CPU. The bit is connected to port 2, bit 1 of an 8042 in a standard ISA bus compatible system.
KBDCLK	**KeyBoarD CLocK:** This output signal is used to drive the clock input to the keyboard controller. It is derived from the 8 MHz SYSCLK and can be divided by 1, 2, 4 or stopped.
LA[23:17]	**Local Address bus (ISA bus signal):** These are input signals to the 82360SL during memory transfers (decoding for X-bus buffer controls) and output signals during DMA accesses and refresh. The latchable address lines allow access to physical memory on the ISA bus to 16 megabytes.
LPTACK#	**Line PrinTer ACKnowledge:** Active LOW input signal which is part of the parallel port data handshake. The line printer asserts this signal to show that data transfer was complete and that it is ready for the next transfer. If the interrupt enable bit is set in the LPT control register, this signal can be used to generate an interrupt.
LPTAFD#	**Line Printer Auto line FeeD:** This signal is an active LOW output from 82360SL to a printer. When asserted, it instructs the printing device to insert a line feed at the end of every line. In the Fast parallel port mode, this signal is used as a data strobe. It can be used to latch data during write cycles and to enable buffers during read cycles.
LPTBUSY	**Line PrinTer BUSY:** This signal is an active HIGH input to 82360SL. The printer asserts this signal when it is not ready to accept further data from 82360SL. In the Fast parallel port mode this signal is active LOW.
LPTD[7:0]	**Line printer Data bus:** These signals are the 8-bit bi-directional data bus for the parallel port. In PC/AT mode these signals are output only. The 82360SL also supports a bidirectional mode for the PS/2 style parallel port.
LPTDIR	**Line PrinTer DIRection:** This active HIGH output signal is only valid in bidirectional mode for data transfer using the parallel port. This signal is LOW in ISA compatible and Fast parallel port modes. In the PS-2 expanded mode, this signal is LOW for writes and HIGH for reads.
LPTERROR#	**Line PrinTer ERROR:** This active LOW input signal is driven by a peripheral device to flag an error condition.
LPTINIT#	**Line PrinTer InITialize:** This active LOW output from 82360SL instructs the peripheral to initialize itself.
LPTPE	**Line PrinTer Paper End:** This active HIGH input to 82360SL signals that the printer has run out of paper when asserted.
LPTSLCT	**Line PrinTer SeLeCTed:** This active HIGH input signal is asserted by the printer to confirm that it has been selected.

82360SL ISA Peripheral I/O Signal Descriptions (Continued)

Symbol	Name and Function
LPTSLCTIN#	**Line PrinTer SeLeCT IN:** This active LOW output signal is asserted to select the printer interfaced to the parallel port. In the Fast parallel port mode, this signal is used as an address strobe. It indicates that an access is being made to the port X7Bh.
LPTSTROBE#	**Line PrinTer STROBE:** This active LOW output signal is used to strobe data into the peripheral device. The parallel port controls are read and written through I/O registers. In the Fast parallel port mode, this signal is used to indicate a write cycle.
MASTER#	**ISA bus MASTER (ISA bus signal):** This active LOW input signal is used by the 82360 SL to determine when to go into an external master refresh arbitration mode. In this mode, the master controls the REFRESH signal but the 82360SL generates the address, the REFREQ# signal, the AEN and command signals.
MEMR#	**MEMory cycle Read (ISA bus signal):** This bi-directional active LOW signal indicates a read cycle anywhere in the 16 Mbyte memory address space. During memory read cycles to memory on the ISA bus, this signal is an input into the 82360SL. MEMR# is driven by the 82360SL during DMA cycles.
MEMW#	**MEMory cycle Write (ISA bus signal):** This bi-directional active LOW signal indicates a write cycle anywhere in the 16 Mbyte memory address space. During memory write cycles to memory on the ISA bus, this signal is an input. MEMW# is an output from the 82360SL during DMA cycles.
N/C	**No Connection:** These signals must not be connected to any voltage. The No Connection signals must be left floating in order to guarantee proper operation of the 82360SL and compatibility with future Intel processors.
NMI	**Non Maskable Interrupt (direct to CPU):** This active HIGH output is directly connected to the Intel386 SL CPU. The 82360SL asserts NMI to request the Intel386 SL CPU to service a high priority non-maskable interrupt. The low to high transition of this signal is recognized by the Intel386 SL CPU.
ONCE#	**ON-board Circuit Emulation:** This active LOW input pin floats the appropriate outputs of the 82360SL as indicated in Section 2 pin assignments. This allows the system to be tested with external logic while the 82360SL is still physically populated on the motherboard. Note that the ONCE# pin on the 82360SL I/O should not be connected to the ONCE# pin on the Intel386 SL CPU.
OSC	**OSCillator (ISA bus signal):** This is the 14.31818 Mhz output signal with a 50% duty cycle and is asynchronous to SYSCLK.
PERR#	**Parity ERRor (direct from CPU):** This active LOW input signal is connected to the output of the Intel386 SL CPU. When the Intel386 SL CPU detects a parity error from the local DRAM subsystem it drives this signal to the 82360SL. The system memory parity error will generate a NMI via the 82360SL when NMI is enabled via I/O port 70h bit 7 and PERR# is enabled via port 61h.
PWRGOOD	**PoWeR GOOD:** This active HIGH input is typically supplied by the power supply. When Power good is activated high this indicates that the supply voltage is stable. Power Good low is also used to generate System Reset, RESETDRV, and CPURESET.
RC#	**Reset CPU:** This active low input is typically driven by the keyboard controller. RC# is "ORed" with internal bits to produce a programmable pulse width CPURESET signal. It is connected to port 2, bit 0 of an 8042 in a standard ISA bus compatible system.
REFREQ	**REFresh REQuest (direct to CPU):** This active HIGH output signal is directly connected to the Intel386 SL CPU. When Refresh Request is asserted it indicates that the Intel386 SL CPU should refresh the local DRAM subsystem.
REFRESH#	**System REFRESH (ISA bus signal):** This active LOW input signal indicates a refresh cycle. It is driven for the duration of the cycle. It is an input during master generated refresh bus cycles.

4

82360SL ISA Peripheral I/O Signal Descriptions (Continued)

Symbol	Name and Function
RESETDRV	**RESET DRiVe (ISA bus signal):** This active HIGH output is the main system cold reset, generated from the power supply "power good" signal and by system resume.
RTCEN#	**RTC ENable:** This active LOW input signal should be strapped to GND or RTCVCC depending on whether an internal or external RTC is used in the system. The 82360SL on-chip real time clock and CMOS RAM are enabled by this signal when LOW.
RTCRESET#	**Internal RTC RESET input:** This active LOW input signal is used to reset the internal RTC status and flag registers, (typically when the RTC battery has been changed).
RTCVCC	This is a separate power supply input for the internal RTC. It should be connected to a 3V battery when the system is fully off and 5V during active operation.
RTCX1,RTCX2	**RTC Crystal oscillator input and output pins:** The crystal should be tuned to 32.768 Khz. It is used for the RTC and system power management state machines. The oscillator may be driven directly from the input signal.
SA[16:0]	**System Address bus (ISA bus signal):** The bi-directional system address bus is an input for decoding internal I/O registers and an output during DMA and refresh cycles.
SBHE#	**System Byte High Enable (ISA bus signal):** The active LOW output signal indicates when there is valid data on the upper data byte of the system data bus.
SD[7:0]	**System Data bus (ISA bus signal):** This is the bidirectional system data bus. The 82360SL directly drives the ISA bus system data bits [7:0] without external transceivers or buffers. 8-bit data is transferred to and from the 82360SL with these signals.
SMEMR#/ LOMEM#	**System MEMory Read (ISA bus signal):** This multiplexed signal has two functions. When configured as SMEMR#, this signal is driven by the 82360SL to signify a memory read cycle to the bottom 1 Mbyte address range. It is used by ISA bus compatible slaves which decode SA[19:0] during memory cycles. When configured as LOMEM#, this signal indicates that the lower 1 Mbyte is being addressed.
SMEMW#	**System MEMory Write (ISA bus signal):** This signal is driven by the 82360SL to signify memory write cycle to the bottom 1 Mbyte address range. It is used by ISA bus compatible slaves which decode SA[19:0] during memory cycles.
SMI#	**System Management Interrupt (direct to CPU):** This active LOW output is directly connected to the Intel386 SL CPU. When the falling edge of SMI# is detected by the Intel386 SL CPU it generates the highest priority interrupt when enabled. The typical use of SMI# is for power management.
SMOUT[5:0]	**System Management OUTput control:** These six outputs can be connected to control the power circuits for various devices in the system. These output pins are directly controlled by the SMOUT__CNTRL register.
SMRAMCS#	**System Management RAM Chip Select:** This active LOW input is driven by the Intel386SL CPU whenever the Intel386 SL CPU is accessing the System Management SM-RAM. It is active even when SM-RAM is part of the Intel386 SL CPU system memory RAM. The 82360SL uses the SMRAMCS# to determine when the SMI code is being executed on the ISA bus, and enables the X-bus control signals.
SPKR	**SPeaKeR output:** This is the output of the 8254 megacell, timer/counter #1, channel 2, or directly driven through IMUX0, or from the 8254 megacell, timer/counter #2, channel 1 depending on the programming. This output signal is typically connected to an external speaker. There is additional circuitry to ensure that the signal is low when not being used.
SRBTN#	**Suspend/Resume BuTtoN:** This active LOW input generates a SMI requesting a system suspend or resume. Activation of this input can be used as a wake up event for the STPCLK# signal.

82360SL ISA Peripheral I/O Signal Descriptions (Continued)

Symbol	Name and Function
STPCLK#	**SToP CLocK:** This active LOW output signal stops the clock to the Intel386 CPU core of the Intel386 SL Microprocessor. Stop clock is directly connected to the Intel386 SL CPU from the 82360SL. The 82360SL activates this signal upon detection of a halt bus cycle or when an I/O read to the stop clock register in the 82360SL occurs.
SYSCLK	**SYStem CLocK (ISA bus signal):** This signal is an output from the Intel386 SL CPU and an input to the 82360SL. The SYSCLK signal is used to clock the ISA bus state machines and is also used to derive the internal DMA clock signal and to generate the KBDCLK output in the 82360SL. The SYSCLK is the 8 MHz typical clock which is one half of the frequency of ISACLK2.
SUS_STAT#	**SUSpend STATus:** The 82360SL power management controls this active low output signal to switch the power off to all non-critical devices during a suspend.
TC	**Terminal Count (ISA bus signal):** This active HIGH output signal is used to indicate the termination of a DMA transfer.
TIM2CLK2	**TIMer 2 CLK:** This is the input clock for timer/counter #2, channel 2 when it is programmed to be used in the General Purpose (GP) mode.
TIM2OUT2	**TIMer 2 OUTput:** This signal is the frequency output from timer/counter #2 and can be used as a general purpose timer/counter output when programmed for GP mode.
V_{CC}	**System Power:** Provides the +5V nominal D.C. supply inputs for the 82360SL.
V_{SS}	**System Ground:** Provides the 0V connection from which all inputs and outputs are referenced.
XD7	**X-bus Data bit XD7:** I/O port 3F7h is split between the floppy and hard disk and the storage peripherals which transfer data reside on separate busses. Data bit XD7 is separated from bits XD[6:0]. The 82360SL separately controls and buffers bit XD7 to isolate data bit 7 from the floppy disk and I.D.E. hard disk.
XDEN#	**X-bus Data ENable:** This active LOW output signal is used to control the X-bus data transceiver. It is only activated by the 82360SL on valid accesses to X-bus peripherals.
XDIR	**X-bus data DIRection:** This active HIGH output signal controls the direction of the X-bus and HD-bus data transceivers. XDIR is high for read cycles.
ZEROWS#	**ZERO Wait State (ISA-bus signal):** This active LOW output signal is driven by the 82360SL when it can accept a zero wait state write cycle.

4

4.0 PACKAGE THERMAL SPECIFICATIONS

The SL SuperSet is specified for functional operation with a temperature range from 0 to 90 degrees Celcius for the Intel386 SL CPU and the 82360SL. The case temperature should be measured in the operating environment to determine whether the SL SuperSet is within the specified operating temperature range. The case temperature should be measured at the center of the top surface of the package. When the SL SuperSet devices have a supply voltage applied the operating temperature range is applicable rather than the storage temperature.

The following definitions and assumptions are used to determine the recommended maximum case temperature for the Intel386 SL CPU and 82360SL:

T_A = Ambient Temperature in degrees Celcius

T_C = Case temperature in degrees Celcius

θ_{JC} = Package thermal resistance between junction and case

θ_{JA} = Package thermal resistance between junction and ambient

T_J = Junction Temperature

P = Power Consumption in Watts

The ambient temperature can be evaluated by using the values of thermal resistance between junction and case, θ_{JC} and the thermal resistance between junction and ambient θ_{JA} in the following equations:

$$T_J = T_C + P^*\theta_{JC}$$

$$T_A = T_J - P^*\theta_{JA}$$

$$T_C = T_A + P^*[\theta_{JA} - \theta_{JC}]$$

Values for θ_{JA} and θ_{JC} are given in Table 4-1 for the 196-lead PQFP Intel386 SL CPU, the 82360SL I/O and the 227-lead LGA Intel386 SL CPU.

Table 4-1. Thermal Resistances (°C/W) θ_{JC} and θ_{JA}

Package	θ_{JC} °C/W	θ_{JA} (°C/W) versus Airflow—ft/min (m/sec)			
		0 (0)	**200 (1.01)**	**400 (2.03)**	**600 (3.04)**
196L PQFP	6	23	19	16	13.5
227L LGA(1)	5	15	12	10.5	9.5

NOTE:
1. These values reflect use of a typical LGA socket.

ABSOLUTE MAXIMUM RATINGS

Table 4-2 provides environmental stress ratings for the packaged SL SuperSet devices. Functional operation at the storage maximum and minimum ratings is not implied or guaranteed.

Extended exposure to maximum ratings may affect device reliability. Further, precautions should be taken to avoid high static voltages and electric fields to prevent static electric discharge.

Other system components such as the memory subsystem (DRAM/SRAM), storage peripherals (hard disk/floppy disk), I/O and display subsystem may reduce the absolute maximum storage temperature conditions due to the inherent physical characteristics of the other components.

Table 4-2. Maximum Ratings

Parameter	Maximum Rating
1. Storage Temperature	−65°C to +150°C
2. Case Temperature under Bias	0°C to +90°C (Note 1)
3. Supply Voltage with Respect to V_{SS}	−0.5V to +6.5V
4. Voltage on Other Pins	−0.5V to (V_{CC} + 0.5V)

NOTE:
1. Case temperature under Bias maximum rating also includes the case where the Intel386 SL CPU and 82360SL are in suspend or standby mode. In standby mode and in specific cases in suspend mode, power is applied to the SL SuperSet for operation of the Real-Time Clock and DRAM refresh.

4

5.0 D.C. SPECIFICATIONS

Intel386™ SL CPU D.C. Specifications

Functional operating range: V_{CC} = 5V ± 10%; T_{CASE} = 0°C to 90°C

Table 5-1. D.C. Voltage Specifications

Symbol	Parameter	Min	Max	Unit	Notes
V_{IL}	Input Low Voltage	−0.3	0.8	V	Tested at 4 MHz. Min value for system design reference only.
V_{IH}	Input High Voltage	2.0	V_{CC} + 0.3	V	Tested at 4 MHz. Min value for system design reference only.
V_{ILC}	EFI/ISACLK2 Input Low Voltage	−0.3	0.8	V	Tested at 4 MHz, CMOS Logic Levels. Min value for system design reference only.
V_{IHC}	EFI/ISACLK2 Input High Voltage	V_{CC} − 0.8	V_{CC} − 0.3	V	At 4 MHz, CMOS Logic Levels. Min value for system design reference only.
V_{OL}	Output Low Voltage				
	I_{OL} = 4 mA		0.5	V	At 4 MHz (Note 1)
	I_{OL} = 24 mA		0.5	V	At 4 MHz (Note 2)
V_{OH}	Output High Voltage				
	I_{OH} = −2 mA	2.4		V	At 4 MHz (Note 1)
	I_{OH} = −0.2 mA	V_{CC} − 0.5		V	At 4 MHz (Note 2)
	I_{OH} = −4 mA	2.4		V	At 4 MHz (Note 2)
	I_{OH} = −0.18 mA	V_{CC} − 0.5		V	At 4 MHz (Note 1)

Table 5-2. Leakage Current and Sustaining Current Specifications

Symbol	Parameter	Min	Max	Unit	Notes
I_{IL}	Input Leakage Current Condition 1: When SUS_STAT# and/or ONCE# not active.				
	Pins with internal 60k PU		−120	μA	$V_{IL} = 0.45V$
	Pins with internal 20k PD		300	μA	$V_{IH} = 2.4V$
	Pins with internal 1K PU		−15	mA	$V_{IL} = 0.45V$
	Other Input Pins		±15	μA	$0V < V_{IN} < V_{CC}$
	Condition 2: When SUS_STAT# and/or ONCE# active.		±15	μA	$0V < V_{IN} < V_{CC}$
I_{LO}	Output Leakage Current Condition 1: When SUS_STAT# and/or ONCE# not active				
	Pins with internal 60k PU		−150	μA	$V_{OUT} = 0.45V$
	Pins with internal 1K PU		−24	mA	$V_{OUT} = 0.45V$
	Other Output Pins		±15	μA	$0.45V < V_{OUT} < V_{CC}$
	Condition 2: When SUS_STAT# and/or ONCE# active		±15	μA	$0.45V < V_{OUT} < V_{CC}$
I_{BHL}	Input Sustaining Current (Bus Hold Low)		38	μA	$V_{IN} = 0.8V$ (Note 3)
I_{BHH}	Input Sustaining Current (Bus Hold High)		−60	μA	$V_{IN} = 3.0V$ (Note 4)
I_{BHLO}	Bus Hold Low Overdrive	300		μA	(Note 5)
I_{BHHO}	Bus Hold High Overdrive	−550		μA	(Note 6)

Table 5-3. Capacitance D.C. Specifications

Symbol	Parameter	Min	Max	Unit	Notes
C_{IN}	Input Capacitance		10	pF	EFI = 1 MHz (Note 7)
C_{OUT}	Output or I/O Capacitance		20	pF	EFI = 1 MHz (Note 7)
C_{CLK}	EFI Capacitance		15	pF	EFI = 1 MHz (Note 7)

NOTES:

1. List of pins which have 24 mA/4 mA I_{OL}/I_{OH} specification, (reference section 2).
2. Other output pins which do not belong to list in Note 1, (reference Section 2).
3. This is the maximum current the bus hold circuit can sink without raising the node above 0.8V. I_{BHL} should be measured after lowering V_{IN} to Ground (0V) and then raising to 0.8V.
4. This is the maximum current the bus hold circuit can source without lowering the node voltage below 3.0V. I_{BHH} should be measured after raising V_{IN} to V_{CC} and then lowering to 3.0V.
5. An external driver must source at least I_{BHLO} to switch this node from low to high.
6. An external driver must sink at least I_{BHHO} to switch this node from high to low.
7. Guaranteed by design characterization.

FUNCTIONAL OPERATING RANGE: V_{CC} = 5V ±10%; T_{CASE} = 0°C to 90°C.

Table 5-4. Intel386™ SL CPU I_{CC} Specifications

Symbol	Parameter	Typ	Max	Unit	Notes
I_{CC} (16 MHz)	Supply Current		450	mA	(Note 1a)
	Notebook Configuration	350		mA	(Note 2)
	Desktop Configuration	450		mA	(Note 3)
I_{CC} (20 MHz)	Supply Current		525	mA	(Note 1b)
	Notebook Configuration	400		mA	(Note 2)
	Desktop Configuration	500		mA	(Note 3)
I_{CC} (25 MHz)	Supply Current		600	mA	(Note 1c)
	Notebook Configuration	500		mA	(Note 2)
	Desktop Configuration	570		mA	(Note 3)
I_{CCS1}	Supply Current with the STPCLK Signal Asserted	50		mA	(Note 4)
I_{CCS2}	Supply Current in Suspend Mode with Oscillators OFF and Suspend Refresh ON	0.3		mA	(Note 5)
I_{CCS3}	Supply Current in Suspend Mode with Oscillators OFF and Suspend Refresh OFF	0.2	2	mA	(Note 6)

NOTES:

1a. Tested with V_{CC} = 5.5V, EFI = 32 MHz, ISACLK2 = 16 MHz, 50 pF capacitive loads and no resistive load on the outputs.

1b. Tested with V_{CC} = 5.5V, EFI = 40 MHz, ISACLK2 = 16 MHz, 50 pF capacitive loads and no resistive load on the outputs.

1c. Tested with V_{CC} = 5.5V, EFI = 50 MHz, ISACLK2 = 16 MHz, 50 pF capacitive loads and no resistive load on the outputs.

2. Notebook system configuration consists of 1 bank of 1 MB × 4 DRAMs with 1 MB × 1 DRAMs for parity (2 MB total memory with Cache enabled (Cache is disabled in the 16 MHz part with no cache SRAM). 25 pF capacitive loading on PI-bus control/status signals, 100 pF capacitive loading on the ISA bus signals and SYSCLK.
3. Desktop system configuration consists of 4 banks of DRAM in the configuration ((1 MB × 4) × 2 + 1 MB × 1) for banks 0 and 1 and (1 MB × 9) for banks 3 and 4 (20 MB total memory). Cache is enabled with 2 × (16K × 16) SRAMs and 240 pF on the ISA bus signals including SYSCLK from 8 ISA slots.
4. STPCLK signal asserted, all external oscillators free running, no cycles on cache, memory or ISA bus. Typically with V_{CC} = 5V, EFI = 40 MHz, ISACLK2 = 16 MHz, 50 pF capacitive loads and no resistive loads on the outputs.
5. Suspend mode and all external oscillators turned OFF (in a fixed logic state), no cycles on cache, memory or ISA bus. The REFREQ signal is active causing memory refreshes to the on-board DRAM memory during suspend. Typically with V_{CC} = 5V, 50 pF capacitive loads and no resistive loads on the outputs.
6. Tested with V_{CC} = 5.5V, 50 pF capacitive loads and no resistive load on the outputs. The 386 SL CPU is in suspend mode and all external oscillators turned OFF (in a fixed logic state), no cycles on cache, memory or ISA bus. The REFREQ signal is turned OFF (Refresh is not required if the on-board memory consists of battery backed SRAMs).

Intel386™ SL CPU I_{CC} Specifications: Special Topics

DETERMINING I_{CC} WITH SLOW CLOCK CONTROL

The Intel386 SL CPU supports CPU clock division which reduces power consumption of the CPU core logic. The EFI clock input is similar to the CLK2 input found on the Intel386 CPU. However, the internal CPUCLK signal in the Intel386 SL CPU is not always one half of the frequency of the EFI input. An internal clock divider and synchronizer allows the CPU core clock to be slowed down and even stopped. However, additional internal logic such as the memory controller and cache controller continue to use half the EFI frequency. Therefore, when calculating the theoretical power consumption with CPU clock division it is important to recognize that a fixed constant (K) value of power is required by the Intel386 SL CPU.

The value K is constant only if the ISA bus loading is constant. Figure 5-1 shows the value of K for different values of ISA bus capacitance.

I_{CC}(divided clock) = [{(I_{CC}*(normal clock) - K}*n] + K

I_{CC}(normal clock) = The I_{CC} value calculated from the following section.

n = The fractional value that the clock is divided (e.g., divide by 2 = 0.5)

K = Is a constant in MilliAmps which determined by reading the value in Figure 5-1.

To determine the maximum current for the Intel386 SL CPU with EFI divider perform the following steps:

1. Sum the total capacitive load of all active ISA bus output signals from the Intel386 SL CPU to all devices.
2. From Figure 5-1 draw a line from the horizontal axis (capacitance) where it intersects the diagonal line.
3. From Figure 5-1 draw a perpendicular line to the vertical axis to determine K.
4. Solve the equation for I_{CC} (divided clock).

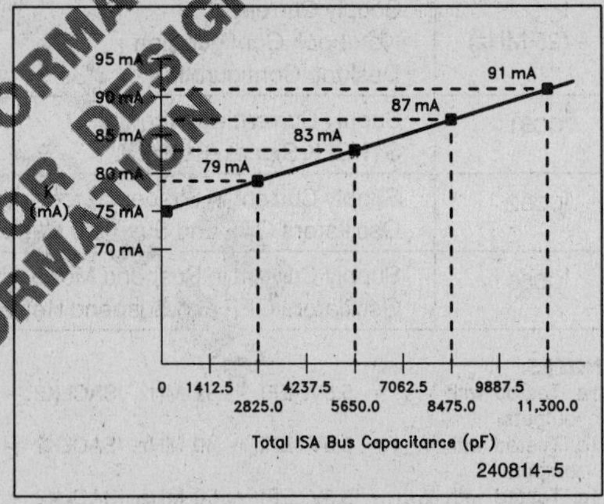

Figure 5-1. Variation of the constant current (K) with respect to the total ISA bus capacitance

POWER VARIATIONS WITH CAPACITIVE LOADS AT VARIOUS VOLTAGES

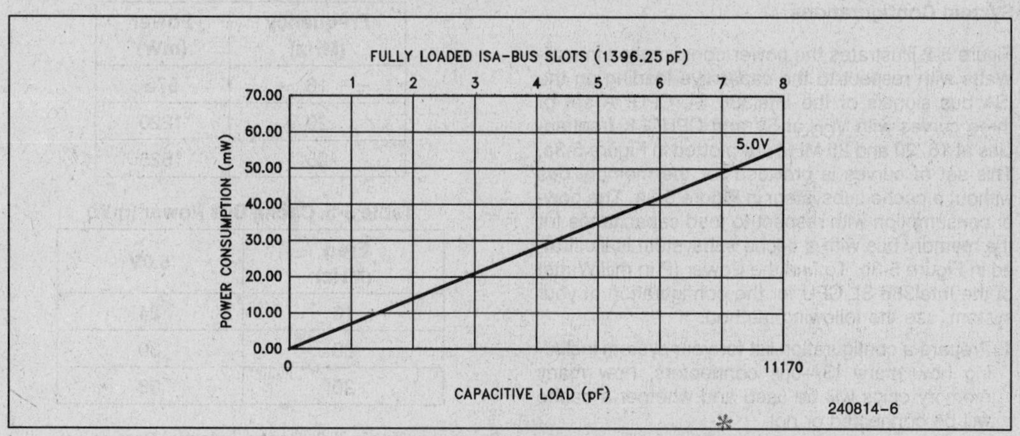

Figure 5-2. ISA Bus

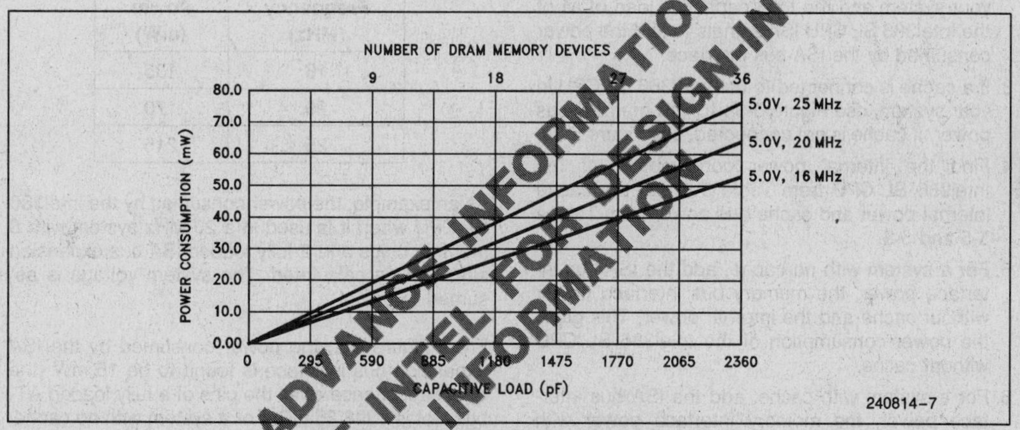

Figure 5-3a. Memory Bus without Cache

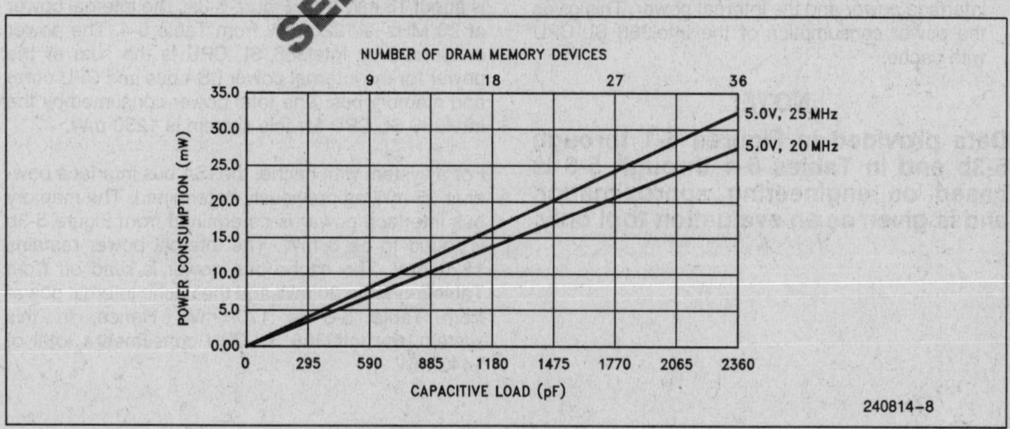

Figure 5-3b. Memory Bus with Cache

Calculation of I_{CC} for Various SL SuperSet System Configurations

Figure 5-2 illustrates the power consumption in milliWatts with respect to the capacitive loading on the ISA bus signals of the Intel386 SL CPU. A set of three curves with V_{CC} at 5V and CPUCLK frequencies at 16, 20 and 25 MHZ are plotted in Figure 5-3a. This set of curves is provided for the memory bus without a cache subsystem in Figure 5-3a. The power consumption with respect to load capacitance for the memory bus with a cache subsystem is illustrated in Figure 5-3b. To find the Power (P in milliWatts) of the Intel386 SL CPU for the configuration of your system, use the following method.

1. Prepare a configuration list for your system including how many ISA-bus connectors, how many memory chips will be used and whether a cache will be connected or not.
2. From the curves in Figure 5-2, use the voltage of your system and the total capactive load of all of the Intel386 SL CPU ISA signals to find the power consumed by the ISA-bus interface.
3. If a cache is connected to the Intel386 SL CPU in your system, use Figure 5-3b to find memory bus power. If cache is not connected, use Figure 5-3a.
4. Find the internal power consumption of the Intel386 SL CPU from Table 5-4 and the cache internal power and cache bus power from Tables 5-5 and 5-6.
5. For a system with no cache, add the ISA-bus interface power, the memory bus interface power without cache and the internal power. This gives the power consumption of the Intel386 SL CPU without cache.
6. For a system with cache, add the ISA bus interface power, the memory interface power with cache, the cache internal power, the cache bus interface power and the internal power. This gives the power consumption of the Intel386 SL CPU with cache.

NOTE:

Data provided in Figures 5-1 through 5-3b and in Tables 5-4 through 5-6 is based on engineering approximation and is given as an evaluation tool only.

Table 5-4. Internal Power

Frequency (MHz)	Power (mW)
16	975
20	1220
25	1525

Table 5-5. Cache Bus Power (mW)

Freq. (MHz)	5.0V
16	24
20	30
25	38

Table 5-6. Cache Internal Power

Frequency (MHz)	Power (mW)
16	135
20	170
25	215

As an example, the power consumed by the Intel386 SL CPU when it is used in a 20 MHz system with 8 memory chips and 2 fully loaded ISA bus expansion slots will be calculated. The system voltage is assumed to be 5V.

From Figure 5-2, the power consumed by the ISA expansion bus interface is found to be 15 mW (the total capacitance of all the pins of a fully loaded AT-bus slot is 1396.25 pF). For a system with no cache, the power consumed by the memory bus for 8 chips is about 15 mW from Figure 5-3a. The internal power at 20 MHz is 1220 mW from Table 5-4. The power consumed by Intel386 SL CPU is the sum of the power for the internal power (ISA bus and CPU core) and memory bus. The total power consumed by the Intel386 SL CPU for this system is 1250 mW.

For a system with cache, the ISA bus interface power is 15 mW as previously determined. The memory bus interface power is determined from Figure 5-3b is found to be 8 mW. The internal power remains 1220 mW. The cache bus power is read off from Table 5-5 to be 30 mW and the cache internal power from Table 5-6 is 170 mW. Hence, in this system, the Intel386 SL CPU consumes a total of 1443 mW.

82360SL D.C. Specifications

Functional operating range: V_{CC} = 5.0V ±10%, T_{CASE} = 0°C to 90°C.

Table 5-7. 82360SL D.C. Specifications

Symbol	Parameter	Min	Typ	Max	Unit	Notes
V_{IL}	Input Low Voltage	−0.3		0.8 0.8 0.8 0.8	V V V V	(Note 16) (Note 12) (Note 13) (Note 14)
V_{IH}	Input High Voltage	2.0 V_{CC} − 0.3 2.0 3.4 1.5		V_{CC} + 0.3	V V V V V	(Note 17) (Note 2) (Note 12) (Note 13) (Note 14)
I_{LI}	Input Leakage Current			±15	μA	(Note 1)
I_{LO}	Output Leakage Current			±15	μA	
C_{IN}	Input Capacitance			15	pF	(Note 15)
C_{OUT}	Output or I/O Capacitance			15	pF	(Note 15)
I_{CCS1}	Suspend with Slow Refresh		200	400	μA	(Note 9)
I_{CCS2}	Suspend without Slow Refresh		150	350	μA	(Note 9)
I_{CC}	Power Supply Current		50	100	mA	(Note 10)
D.C. Specifications for Standard ISA Bus Signals						
V_{OL}	Output Low Voltage			0.5	V	I_{OL} = 24 mA (Note 4)
V_{OH}	Output High Voltage	2.4			V	I_{OH} = −4.0 mA (Note 4)
D.C. Specifications for Parallel Port						
V_{OL}	Output Low Voltage			0.5	V	I_{OL} = 8 mA (Note 3)
V_{OH}	Output High Voltage	2.4			V	I_{OH} = −2 mA (Note 3)
D.C. Specifications for Open Drain Outputs						
V_{OL}	Output Low Voltage			0.5	V	I_{OL} = 24 mA (Note 5) I_{OL} = 12 mA (Note 6) I_{OL} = 8 mA (Note 11)
D.C. Specifications for All Other Outputs						
V_{OL}	Output Low Voltage			0.5	V	I_{OL} = 12 mA (Note 7)
V_{OH}	Output High Voltage	2.4			V	I_{OH} = −2 mA (Note 7)
D.C. Specifications for Power-Down Mode						
V_{BATT}	Battery Supply Voltage	2.5			V	
I_{BATT}	Battery Supply Current		20 10	75 35	μA μA	V_{BATT} = 5V V_{BATT} = 2.5V (Note 8)
V_{OL}	Output Low Voltage			0.4 0.5	V V	I_{OL} = 4 mA I_{OL} = 8 mA
V_{OH}	Output High Voltage	2.0			V	I_{OH} = −2 mA

NOTES:

1. No pullup or pulldown.
2. For inputs—COMX1, CX1, RTCX1
3. For outputs—LPTD7:0
4. For outputs—OSC, AEN, SA16:0, LA23:17, MEMR#, MEMW#, IOR#, IOW#, SMEMW#, SMEMR#, SBHE#, TC, SD7:0, XD7, HD7, RESETDRV.
5. ZEROWS#, IOCHRDY.
6. LPTSTROBE#, LPTAFD, LPTINIT#, LPTSLCTIN#, LPTDIR.
7. For all other outputs of the module.
8. Measured at V_{CC} = 0V, V_{BATT} = 3.0V, 32 kHz RTC clock with input rise time and fall time, $t_r = t_f < 50$ ns.
9. RTC clock at 32 kHz; Timer Clock, Serial clock and SYSCLK stopped; V_{CC} = 5.5V and RTCVCC = 5.5V, C_L = 50 pF with outputs unloaded.

NOTES (Continued):
10. I_{CC} tests at maximum frequency with no resisitive loads on the outputs.
11. REFRESH#
12. For RTC oscillator at 3V V_{CC}.
13. For all oscillators at 5V V_{CC}.
14. For all input buffers at 3V V_{CC}.
15. Characterized by design.
16. Min for system design reference only.
17. Max for system design reference only.

6.0 SL SuperSet TIMING SPECIFICATIONS

A.C. Specification Definitions

The A.C. specifications given in Tables 6.0 and 6.1 consist of output delays, input setup requirements and input hold requirements. A.C. specifications may be relative to a clock edge or another signal edge.

All Intel386 SL CPU clock related specifications reference EFI except ISA bus timing which reference ISACLK2. All 82360SL clock related timings reference SYSCLK edges.

A.C. specifications are defined in Figure 6.1. All clock related specifications are tested at the voltage levels shown. Output to output specifications are derived from tested clock related timings.

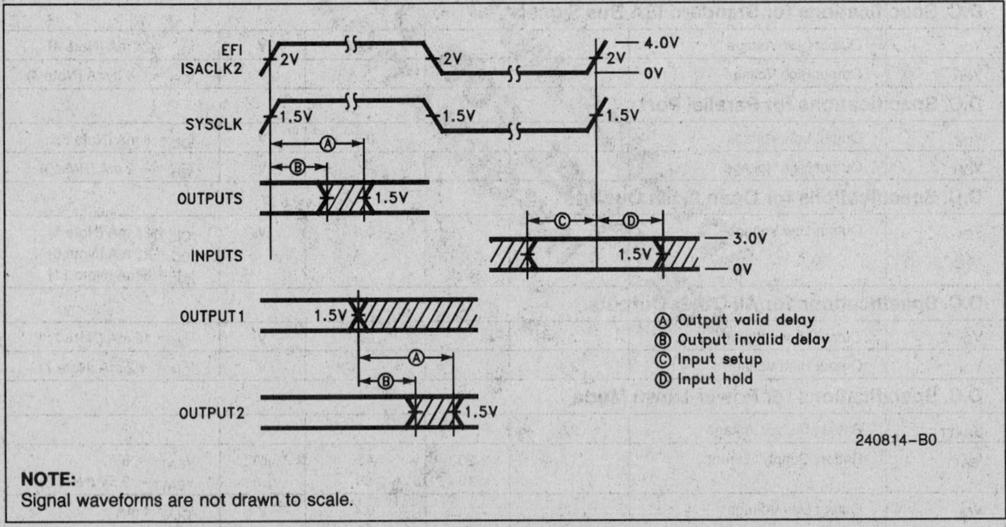

Figure 6-1. Drive Levels and Measurement Points for A.C. Specifications

6.0 SL SuperSet TIMING SPECIFICATIONS (Continued)

Table 6.0. Intel386 SL CPU A.C. Specifications

Symbol	Parameter	Min	Max	Unit	Derating	Figure	Notes
ISA-Bus Clock Timings							
Ct 201	ISACLK2 Period	62.5		ns		7.1.2	(Note 1)
Ct 202	ISACLK2 High Time at 2V	28	32.5	ns		7.1.2	(Note 1)
Ct 203	ISACLK2 Low Time at 2V	28	32.5	ns		7.1.2	(Note 1)
Ct 204	ISACLK2 Fall Time from (V_{CC} − 0.8V) to 0.8V		8	ns		7.1.2	(Note 1)
Ct 205	ISACLK2 Rise Time from 0.8V to (V_{CC} − 0.8V)		8	ns		7.1.2	(Note 1)
Ct 206	ISACLK2 to SYSCLK Delay, Falling to Rising Edge	2	32	ns	FR; SR	7.1.2	
Ct 207	ISACLK2 to SYSCLK Delay, Falling to Falling Edge	2	32	ns	FF; SF	7.12	
Ct 211	SYSCLK Period	125		ns		7.1.2	(Note 2)
Ct 212	SYSCLK High Time at 1.5V	55		ns		7.1.2	(Note 2)
Ct 213	SYSCLK Low Time at 1.5V	57		ns		7.1.2	(Note 2)
Ct 214	SYSCLK Fall Time from (V_{CC} − 0.8V) to 0.8V		10	ns		7.1.2	(Note 2)
Ct 215	SYSCLK Rise Time from 0.8V to (V_{CC} − 0.8V)		10	ns		7.1.2	(Note 2)
Ct 272a	A20GATE Setup to EFI (PH1)	11		ns			(Note 3)
Ct 272b	A20GATE Hold Time	16		ns			(Note 3)

NOTES:

1. ISACLK2 minimum period, high and low times are specified with ISACLK2 input = 16 MHz and SYSCLK output = 8 MHz. The ISACLK2 input specifications are provided to ensure that the SYSCLK output, period, minimum high and low time, rise and fall time and ISACLK2 to SYSCLK skew are met.
2. SYSCLK period, low and high time are tested at 1.5V thresholds. All other parameters are guaranteed by design characterization.
3. A20GATE is an asynchronous input to the Intel386 SL CPU. Setup and hold times with respect to EFI are provided for test purposes only.

4

6.0 SL SuperSet TIMING SPECIFICATIONS (Continued)

Table 6.0. Intel386 SL CPU A.C. Specifications (Continued)

Symbol	Parameter	Min	Max	Unit	Derating	Figure	Notes
ISA-Bus Timings							
Ct 221	BALE Active Delay from T_S phi 2 Low		52	ns	SR	7.1.12	Nt1
Ct 222	BALE Inactive Delay from T_C phi 1 Low	5	52	ns	FF; SF	7.1.12	
Ct 223	LA17–23 Valid Delay from T_C or T_C phi 2 Low		52	ns	S	7.1.12	
Ct 224	LA17–23 Invalid Delay from T_C phi 2 Low	0		ns	F	7.1.12	
Ct 225	SA1–19 Valid Delay from T_S phi 2 Low		38	ns	S	7.1.12	
Ct 226	SA0–19, SBHE#, LA17–23 Valid Setup to phi 1 Low (External Master)	18		ns		7.1.12	
Ct 227	SA1–19 Invalid Delay from T_S or Ti phi 2 Low	0		ns	F	7.1.12	
Ct 228	SA0, SBHE# Valid Delay from T_S phi 2 Low		52	ns	SF	7.1.12	
Ct 229	SA0, SBHE# Invalid Delay from T_S or Ti phi 2 Low	0	45	ns	FR; SR	7.1.12	
Ct 230	MEMR#, MEMW# Active from T_C phi 1 Low (16-bit MEMR#/MEMW#, HALT# Cycles)	7	45	ns	FF; SF	7.1.18	
Ct 231	Command Active Setup to phi 1 Low (External Master)	18		ns		7.1.27	
Ct 232	HALT# Valid Delay from phi 1 Low		34	ns	SF		NT8
Ct 233	Command Inactive to Float Delay from TI phi 1 Low (External Master)		45	ns	S	7.1.27	
Ct 234	Command Active Delay from T_C phi 2 Low (IOR#/IOW# 8-, 16-Bit; MEMR#/MEMW# 8-Bit)	7	45	ns	FF; SF	7.1.27	
Ct 235	Command Inactive Delay from Teoc phi 1 Low (MEMR#/MEMW#, IOR#/IOW# and HALT#)	7	45	ns	FR; SR		NT2
Ct 238	MEMCS16# Setup to T_C phi 1 Low	0		ns		7.1.13	NT6, NT12
Ct 239	MEMCS16# Hold from T_C phi 1 Low	25		ns		7.1.13	NT6, NT12
Ct 240	IOCS16# Setup to T_C phi 1 Low	45		ns		7.1.15	NT7
Ct 241	IOCS16# Hold from Teoc phi 1 Low	0		ns		7.1.16	NT7
Ct 242	ZEROWS# Setup to T_C phi 2 Low	0		ns		7.1.15	NT7, NT9
Ct 244	ZEROWS# Hold from T_C phi 2 Low	10		ns		7.1.15	NT7, NT9
Ct 245	MEMCS16# Active Delay from Valid Address (External Master Cycles)		64	ns	SF	7.1.28b	
Ct 246	SD0–15 Valid Setup to IOR#/MEMR#, INTA# Inactive	63		ns		7.1.13	Ext. Master
Ct 247	SD0–15 Hold from IOR#/MEMR#, INTA# Inactive	0				7.1.12	Read Cycle,
Ct 248	SD0–7 Valid Delay from T_S phi 2 Low	30	65	ns	F; S	7.1.12	Write Cycle
Ct 249	SD8–15 Valid Delay from T_S phi 2 Low	37	65	ns	F; S		Write Cycle
Ct 250	SD0–15 Invalid Delay from Teoc phi 2 Low	12		ns		7.1.12	Write Cycle

6.0 SL SuperSet TIMING SPECIFICATIONS (Continued)

Table 6.0. Intel386 SL CPU A.C. Specifications (Continued)

Symbol	Parameter	Min	Max	Unit	Derating	Figure	Notes
ISA-Bus Timings (Continued)							
Ct 251	IOCHRDY Setup to T_C phi 2 Low	6		ns		7.1.14	
Ct 251a	IOCHRDY Inactive Setup to T_C phi 1 Low	45		ns			
Ct 252	IOCHRDY Hold from T_C phi 2 Low	8		ns		7.1.14	NT11
Ct 259	INTA Active Delay from T_C phi 2 Low		45	ns			NT16
Ct 260	INTA Inactive Delay from Teoc phi 1 Low		60	ns			NT17
Ct 261	HRQ Setup to T_C or Ti phi 2 Low	15		ns		7.1.24	
Ct 262	HRQ Hold from Th phi 2 Low	5		ns		7.1.24	
Ct 263	HLDA Active Delay from Th phi 1 Low	0	38	ns	FR; SR	7.1.24	NT3
Ct 264	HLDA Inactive Delay from Th phi 1 Low	7	38	ns	FF; SF	7.1.24	
Ct 265	DMA8/16# Setup to Th phi 2 Low	15		ns		7.1.24	NT13, NT14, NT15
Ct 266	MASTER# Setup to Th phi 2 Low	15		ns		7.1.26	NT15
Ct 267	REFREQ Setup to Ti or T_C phi 2 Low	16		ns		7.1.25	
Ct 268	VGACS# Active Delay from LA[23:17]		35	ns	SF	7.1.10	
Ct 269	VGACS# Inactive Delay from LA[23:17]		41	ns	SR	7.1.10	
Ct 269a	VGACS# Active Delay from T_S phi 2 Low		41	ns	SF		
Ct 269b	VGACS# Inactive Delay from T_S phi 2 Low		41	ns	SR		
Ct 270	ROMCSO#/CMUX14# Active Delay from T_S phi 2 Low		41	ns	SF	7.1.11	NT18
Ct 271	ROMCSO#/CMUX14# Inactive Delay from T_S phi 2 Low	25		ns	FR	7.1.11	NT18
Ct 272	ROMCSO#/CMUX14# Active Delay from Address		41	ns	SF	7.1.9	NT19
Ct 273	ROMCSO#/CMUX14# Inactive Delay from Address		41	ns	SR	7.1.9	NT19
Ct 274	SMRAMCS# Active Delay from T_S phi 2 Low	5	49	ns	FF; SF	7.1.11	NT18
Ct 275	SMRAMCS# Inactive Delay from T_S or Ti phi 2 Low	10	49	ns	FR; SR	7.1.11	NT18
Ct 275a	TURBO Setup	16		ns			Asynch

4

6.0 SL SuperSet TIMING SPECIFICATIONS (Continued)

Table 6.0. Intel386 SL CPU A.C. Specifications (Continued)

Symbol	Parameter	Min	Max	Unit	Derating	Figure	Notes
ISA-Bus Timings (Continued)							
Ct 276	SD15–0 Valid Delay from IOCHRDY Asserted (External Master)		48	ns	SR, S	7.1.28b	
Ct 277	SD15–0 Data Invalid Delay from MEMR# Inactive (External Master)	7		ns	F	7.1.28b	
Ct 278	SD15–0 Data Invalid Delay from IOR# Inactive (External Master)	7		ns	F	7.1.28a	
Ct 279	SD15–0 Data Setup to MEMW# Active (External Master)	-45		ns		7.1.28b	
Ct 280	SD15–0 Data Hold from MEMW# Inactive (External Master)	0		ns		7.1.28b	
Ct 281	SD15–0 Setup to IOW# Active (External Master)	0		ns		7.1.28a	
Ct 282	BALE Active Delay from Th phi 1 Low (External Master)		45	ns	SR	7.1.26	
Ct 283	BALE Inactive from Th phi 1 Low (External Master)		45	ns	SF	7.1.26	
Ct 284	LA23–17, SA19–0, SBHE# Float to Invalid Delay from Th phi 2 (External Master)		54	ns	S	7.1.26	
Ct 285	LA23–17, SA19–0, SBHE# Invalid to Float Delay from Th phi 1 (External Master)		54	ns	S	7.1.26	
Ct 286	SA19–17 Delay from LA19–17 (DMA Cycle)	10	45	ns	F, F; S, S	7.1.24	
Ct 287	Command Float to Inactive from Th phi 2 Low (External Master)		45	ns	S	7.1.24	
Ct 288	Address Setup to Command Active (External Master)	28		ns		7.1.28a	
Ct 289	SA15–0 Hold after IOR# or IOW# Inactive (External Master)	15		ns		7.1.28a	
Ct 290	IOCS16# Active Delay from Valid Address (External Master)		64	ns	SF	7.1.28a	
Ct 291	SD15–0 Delay from IOR# Active (External Master Read from CPU I/O Ports)		65	ns	S	7.1.28a	
Ct 292	SD15–0 Valid Delay from phi 2 Low (External Master Read from On Board Memory)		95	ns	S		
Ct 293	SD15–0 Hold from IOW# Inactive (External Master)	15		ns		7.1.28a	
Ct 294	Byte Swap Delay (External Master)	10	72	ns	F; S	7.1.26	NT5

6.0 SL SuperSet TIMING SPECIFICATIONS (Continued)

Table 6.0. Intel386 SL CPU A.C. Specifications (Continued)

Symbol	Parameter	Min	Max	Unit	Derating	Figure	Notes
ISA-Bus Timings (Continued)							
Ct 295	IOCHRDY Invalid from Command Active (External Master)		44	ns	SF	7.1.28b	
Ct 296	IOCHRDY Active Delay from phi 2 Low (External Master)		85	ns	SR	7.1.28b	
Ct 298	IOCS16# Inactive Delay from Address (External Master)		110	ns	SR	7.1.28a	NT20
Ct 299	IOCS16#/MEMCS16#/MASTER# Float to High Delay		78	ns			NT20

NOTES:

NT1. The ISA bus timings are specified in a synchronous manner with respect to the ISACLK2 input. ISACLK2 input is 16 MHz, which is twice the frequency of the SYSCLK output. Each SYSCLK period represents one T-state and each T-state corresponds to either the beginning of a bus cycle (T_S—Send Status), middle of a bus cycle (T_C—execute command), end of cycle (T_{eoc}), hold (T_h) or idle (T_i). T-States, (T_S, T_C, T_{eoc} and T_i) are comprised of two ISACLK2 periods (Phi 1 and Phi 2). The ISACLK2 Periods or Phases, (Phi 1 and Phi 2), falling or rising edge are used to reference the synchronous ISA parameters. ISACLK2 Phi 1 falling edge leads SYSCLK rising edge, ISACLK2 Phi 2 falling edge leads SYSCLK falling edge.

NT2. T_{eoc} represents the End of Cycle. The falling edge of ISACLK2 Phi 2 during T_C indicates T_{eoc}.

NT3. After HLDA (Hold Acknowledge) is de-asserted, the Intel386 SL CPU drives the address bus with the previous address that was latched prior to the beginning of the HLDA cycle. The term "invalid" refers to this latched address. The latched address may or may not be valid for the next CPU bus cycle. At the start of the next CPU bus cycle on an external bus a valid address will be placed on the address bus.

NT4. INTR, NMI, SMI#, and TURBO are asynchronous inputs with respect to ISACLK2 and SYSCLK. These are input signals to the Intel386 SL CPU. Setup and hold times with respect to the ISACLK2 input are provided for reference. The minimum setup and hold times are specified for valid recognition at a specific clock edge in other timing diagrams with the EFI clock input.

NT5. The setup time is required to ensure that byte swapping is not delayed when an external master reads from an 8-bit device on an odd byte address boundary.

NT6. MEMCS16# is sampled on the falling edge of ISACLK2 Phi 2.

NT7. IOCS16# and ZEROWS# are sampled on the falling edge of ISACLK2 Phi 1.

NT8. HALT timing is identical to a 16-bit ISA bus default memory bus cycle except that no BALE or Status Signal is asserted.

NT9. ZEROWS# and IOCHRDY should not both be driven LOW during the same bus cycle.

NT11. IOCHRDY de-asserted (LOW) is sampled on the falling edge of ISACLK2 Phi 2 when Command is active (LOW). De-asserting IOCHRDY# adds incremental wait states (1 SYSCLK long). IOCHRDY should not be held LOW longer than 17 SYSCLKs (2.1 μs.)

NT12. ROM read bus cycles are similar to 8/16 bit ISA bus memory read bus cycles except that MEMCS# is ignored. The strapping pin ROM16/8# is sampled to determine if the ROM read is an 8-bit or 16-bit memory read. Additionally ROMCS0# and/or ROMCS1# are asserted during a ROM read.

NT13. DMA bus cycles are not supported to On-board I/O ports. AEN is HIGH during MASTER, DMA and access to the configuration registers.

NT14. Byte swap timing for 8-bit DMA bus cycles is identical to that of an external master.

NT15. During DMA cycles the Intel386 SL CPU drives SA17–19 with the value of LA17–19 while HLDA is active. During other Slave cycles (i.e., Refresh and External Master) the Intel386 SL CPU does not drive SA17–19.

NT16. During the INTA# cycle, SD8–15 should not change state. During the first INTA# pulse SD0–15 are ignored. The second INTA# pulse in an INTA# bus cycle indicates a bus cycle that is similar to an 8-bit I/O read in which the interrupt vector is read from SD0–7.

NT17. The 8259 INTA# minimum pulse width is 160 ns.

NT18. ROMCS0#, ROMCS1# and SMRAMCS# are specified with respect to ISACLK2 when the CPU is the bus master.

NT19. ROMCS0#, ROMCS1# and SMRAMCS# are specified with respect to valid address when an external master controls the bus.

NT20. The low to high or float to high delays on these signals are guaranteed for four ISA slots with a total of 160 pF capacitive load. The 386 SL CPU will pull these signals high at a slew rate of (160/C)*0.021 V/ns where C is the total capacitive load on the signal pin. To use 8 slots, these signals must be pulled up with 300Ω resistors.

6.0 SL SuperSet TIMING SPECIFICATIONS (Continued)

Table 6.0. Intel386 SL CPU A.C. Specifications 16 MHz

Symbol	Parameter	Min	Max	Unit	Derating	Figure	Notes
General: 16 MHz							
Ct 101	EFI Period	31.25	500	ns		7.1.1	(Note 1)
Ct 102a	EFI High Time at 2V	9		ns		7.1.1	
Ct 102b	EFI High Time at 3.7V	6		ns		7.1.1	
Ct 103a	EFI Low Time at 2V	9		ns		7.1.1	
Ct 103b	EFI Low Time at 0.8V	7		ns		7.1.1	
Ct 104	EFI Fall Time from (V_{CC} − 0.8V) to 0.8V		8	ns		7.1.1	
Ct 105	EFI Rise Time 0.8V to (V_{CC} − 0.8V)		8	ns		7.1.1	
Ct 111	PWRGOOD Minimum Pulse Width	1		EFI			
Ct 111a	PWRGOOD Setup to EFI	12		ns			(Note 2)
Ct 111b	PWRGOOD Hold Time	4		ns			
Ct 112	CPURESET Minimum Pulse Width	1		EFI			
Ct 112a	CPURESET—Setup to EFI	12		ns			(Note 2)
Ct 112b	CPURESET Hold Time	4		ns			
Ct 113a	STPCLK# Setup to EFI	15		ns			(Note 2)
Ct 113b	STPCLK# Hold Time	20		ns			
Ct 114a	SUS_STAT# Setup to EFI	20		ns			(Note 2)
Ct 114b	SUS_STAT# Hold Time	15		ns			
Ct 115	ONCE# Minimum Pulse Width	35		ns			
Ct 115a	ONCE# Setup to EFI	20		ns			(Note 2)
Ct 115b	ONCE# Hold Time	15		ns			
Ct 116a	SMI# Setup to EFI	15		ns			(Note 2)
Ct 116b	SMI# Hold Time	21		ns			
Ct 117a	INTR Setup to EFI	15		ns			(Note 2)
Ct 117b	INTR Hold Time	45		ns			
Ct 118a	NMI Setup to EFI	11		ns			(Note 2)
Ct 118b	NMI Hold Time	16		ns			

NOTES:

1. EFI maximum period is specified only for the case where a MCP (Math co-processor) is present in the system. NPXCLK period, high and low time are tested at 2V. All other parameters are guaranteed by design characterization.
2. A20GATE, CPURESET, INTR, NMI, ONCE#, PWRGOOD, SMI#, STPCLK# and SUS_STAT# are asynchronous inputs to the Intel386 SL CPU. Setup and hold times with respect to the EFI input are provided for test purposes only. The minimum setup and hold times are specified for valid recognition at a specific clock edge. The minimum valid pulse width can be extrapolated from the setup and hold times with respect to EFI.

6.0 SL SuperSet TIMING SPECIFICATIONS (Continued)

Table 6.0. Intel386 SL CPU A.C. Specifications 16 MHz (Continued)

Symbol	Parameter	Min	Max	Unit	Derating	Figure	Notes
PI-Bus Timings: 16 MHz							
Ct 301	Min. Chip Select and Command Setup to PSTART# Active	42.5		ns	SF, SF	7.1.7	C_R = Min, C_T = Max
Ct 302	Min. Chip Select and Command Hold from PSTART# Active	80		ns	FF, FR	7.1.7	C_R = Max, C_T = Min
Ct 304	Min. Read Data Setup Time to PCMD# Inactive	21		ns		7.1.7	
Ct 305	Min. Read Data Hold Time from PCMD# Inactive	12		ns		7.1.7	
Ct 307	Maximum Write Data Valid Delay from PSTART# Active		64	ns	SF, S	7.1.7	C_R = Min, C_T = Max
Ct 308	Min. Write Data Invalid Delay from PCMD# Inactive	31		ns	FF, F	7.1.7	C_R = Max, C_T = Min
Ct 309	Min Address Setup Time to PSTART# Active	32.5		ns	SF, S	7.1.7	C_R = Min, C_T = Max
Ct 310	Min Address Hold Time from PSTART# Active	62		ns	FF, F	7.1.7	C_R = Max, C_T = Min
Ct 311	PSTART# Pulse Width	55		ns		7.1.7	
Ct 312	Min Delay from PSTART# Active to PCMD# Active	50		ns	SF, SF	7.1.7	C_R = Max, C_T = Min
Ct 313	Min Delay from PRDY# Active to PCMD# Inactive	37.5		ns	FR	7.1.7	
Ct 314	Min Delay from PCMD# Inactive to PSTART# Active	0		ns	FR, FF	7.1.7	C_R = Max, C_T = Max
External Master Timings: SYSCLK at 8 MHz (Slave CPU)							
Ct 321	PW/R# Valid Delay		35	ns	SF	7.1.8	ATCLK2 Sync.
Ct 321	PM/IO# Valid Delay		35	ns	SF	7.1.8	ATCLK2 Sync.
Ct 321	VGACS# Valid Delay		35	ns	SF	7.1.8	ATCLK2 Sync.
Ct 325	PSTART# Valid Delay		34	ns	SF	7.1.8	ATCLK2 Sync.
Ct 326	PCMD# Valid Delay		34	ns	SF	7.1.8	ATCLK2 Sync.
Ct 327a	PRDY# Set-up	5		ns		7.1.8	ATCLK2 Sync.
Ct 327b	PRDY# Hold	25		ns		7.1.8	ATCLK2 Sync.

NOTES:
1. VGACS#, FLSHDCS#, PW/R#, PM/IO# and Addresses change for each subsequent read or write.
2. PSTART# indicates a new cycle in which address, status and chip selects are valid before PSTART# is asserted LOW. PRDY# terminates each bus cycle and a new PSTART# is driven if a new address and status signals are available.
3. C_R is the capacitive load on the reference signal.
4. C_T is the capacitive load on the target signal.

4

6.0 SL SuperSet TIMING SPECIFICATIONS (Continued)

Table 6.0. Intel386 SL CPU A.C. Specifications 16 MHz (Continued)

Symbol	Parameter	Min	Max	Unit	Derating	Figure	Notes
Math Coprocessor Timings: 16 MHz							
Ct 421	CA2 Valid Delay (NPX Cyc)	3	25	ns	FR, F; SR, S	7.1.3	
Ct 422	NPXADS# Valid Delay	5	27	ns	FR, FF; SR, SF	7.1.3	
Ct 423	NPXW/R# Valid Delay	5	27	ns	FR, FF; SR, SF	7.1.3	
Ct 424	CD Valid Delay (NPX Cycle)	2	35	ns	FR, F; SR, S	7.1.4	
Ct 425a	NPXRDY# Setup	16		ns		7.1.5	
Ct 425b	NPXRDY# Hold	3		ns		7.1.5	
Ct 426a	BUSY#, PEREQ, ERROR# Setup to NPXCLK phi1 high	23		ns		7.1.5	
Ct 426b	BUSY#, PEREQ, ERROR# Hold from NPXCLK phi1 high	5		ns		7.1.5	
Ct 427a	CD Setup (NPX Cycle)	12		ns		7.1.3	
Ct 427b	CD Hold (NPX Cycle)	6		ns		7.1.3	
Ct 441	NPXCLK Period	31.25	500	ns		7.1.1	(Note 1)
Ct 442a	NPXCLK High Time 2V	8		ns		7.1.1	(Note 1)
Ct 442b	NPXCLK High Time 3.7V	5		ns		7.1.1	
Ct 443a	NPXCLK Low Time 2V	8		ns		7.1.1	(Note 1)
Ct 443b	NPXCLK Low Time 0.8V	6		ns		7.1.1	
Ct 444	NPXCLK Fall Time (V_{CC} − 0.8V) to 0.8V		8	ns		7.1.1	
Ct 445	NPXCLK Rise Time 0.8V to (V_{CC} − 0.8V)		8	ns		7.1.1	
Ct 446	NPXCLK to NPXRESET inactive delay	3	18	ns	FR, FF; SR, SF		
SRAM Mode: 16 MHz Timings							
Ct 501	Access Time from OE#	50		ns	SF, S	7.1.30	2 Wait State
Ct 502	Access Time from OE#	60		ns	SF, S		3 Wait State
Ct 503	CE# Setup to OE# Active	50		ns	SF, SF		2 Wait State
Ct 504	CE# Setup to OE# Active	50		ns	SF, SF		3 Wait State
Ct 505	Addr Setup to OE# Active	50		ns	SF, S		2 Wait State
Ct 506	Addr Setup to OE# Active	50		ns	SF, S		3 Wait State
Ct 507	CE# Setup to WE# Active	0		ns	SF, SF		2 Wait State
Ct 508	CE# Setup to WE# Active	0		ns	SF, SF		3 Wait State
Ct 509	Addr Setup to WE# Active	0		ns	SF, S		2 Wait State
Ct 510	Addr Setup to WE# Active	0		ns	SF, S		3 Wait State
Ct 511	WE# Active Pulse Width	90		ns	S		2 Wait State
Ct 512	WE# Active Pulse Width	100		ns	S		3 Wait State

NOTE:
1. NPXCLK maximum period is specified only for the case where a MCP (Math Co-processor) is present in the system. NPXCLK period, high and low time are tested at 2V. All other parameters are guaranteed by design characterization.

6.0 SL SuperSet TIMING SPECIFICATIONS (Continued)

Table 6.0. Intel386 SL CPU A.C. Specifications 16 MHz (Continued)

Symbol	Parameter	Min	Max	Unit	Derating	Figure	Notes
SRAM Mode: 16 MHz Timings (Continued)							
Ct 513	WE# Recovery Time	10		ns	SR, S		2 Wait State
Ct 514	WE# Recovery Time	10		ns	SR, S		3 Wait State
Ct 515	Write Data Setup to WE# Inactive	40		ns	SR, S		2 Wait State
Ct 516	Write Data Setup to WE# Inactive	50		ns	SR, S		3 Wait State
Ct 517	Write Data Hold from WE# Inactive	0		ns	FR, F	*	2 Wait State
Ct 518	Write Data Hold from WE# Inactive	0		ns	FR, F		3 Wait State
Ct 519	DIR Setup to OE# Active	0		ns	SF, S		2 Wait State
Ct 520	DIR Setup to OE# Active	0		ns	SF, S		3 Wait State
Ct 523	OE# Inactive Setup to DEN# Active	40		ns	SF, SR		2 Wait State
Ct 524	OE# Inactive Setup to DEN# Active	50		ns	SF, SR		3 Wait State
Ct 525	DIR Inactive Setup to WE# Active	0		ns	SF, S		2 Wait State
Ct 526	DIR Inactive Setup to WE# Active	0		ns	SF, S		3 Wait State
Ct 527	DEN# Hold from WE# Inactive	0		ns	FR, FR		2 Wait State
Ct 528	DEN# Hold from WE# Inactive	0		ns	FR, FR		3 Wait State
Ct 529	DIR Inactive Setup to DEN# Active	0		ns	SF, S		2 Wait State
Ct 530	DIR Inactive Setup to DEN# Active	0		ns	SF, S	7.1.30	3 Wait State
Ct 531	DIR Hold from DEN# Inactive	0		ns	FR, F		2 Wait State
Ct 532	DIR Hold from DEN# Inactive	0		ns	FR, F		3 Wait State
Ct 533	DIR Setup to DEN# Active	0	73	ns	FF, F; SF, S		2 Wait State
Ct 534	DIR Setup to DEN# Active	0	73	ns	FF, F; SF, S		3 Wait State
Ct 535	Upper Addr Setup to LE Inactive	8		ns	SF, S		2 Wait State
Ct 536	Upper Addr Setup to LE Inactive	8		ns	SF, S		3 Wait State
Ct 537	Upper Addr Hold from LE Inactive	4		ns	SF, S		2 Wait State
Ct 538	Upper Addr Hold from LE Inactive	4		ns	SF, S		3 Wait State
Ct 539	LE Active Pulse Width	8		ns	F		2 Wait State
Ct 540	LE Active Pulse Width	8		ns	F		3 Wait State
Ct 541	Addr Valid Delay from LE Inactive		60	ns	SF, S		2 Wait State
Ct 542	Addr Valid Delay from LE Inactive		80	ns	SF, S		3 Wait State
Ct 543	Read Data Hold from OE# Inactive	0		ns			2 Wait State
Ct 544	Read Data Hold from OE# Inactive	0		ns			3 Wait State

6.0 SL SuperSet TIMING SPECIFICATIONS (Continued)

Table 6.0. Intel386 SL CPU A.C. Specifications 16 MHz (Continued)

Symbol	Alt Symbol	Parameter	Min	Max	Unit	Derating	Figure	Notes	
DRAM Mode: 16 MHz Timings									
Ct 601	t_{ASR}	Row Addr Setup to RAS# Active	0		ns		7.1.29	F1 Mode	C_R = Max, C_T = Max
Ct 602		Row Addr Setup to RAS# Active	7		ns	SF, S		F2 Mode	
Ct 603		Row Addr Setup to RAS# Active	7		ns			P1 Mode	
Ct 605	tRAH	Row Addr Hold from RAS# Active	25		ns	SF, S		F1 Mode	C_R = Max, C_T = Max
Ct 606		Row Addr Hold from RAS# Active	25		ns			F2 Mode	
Ct 607		Row Addr Hold from RAS# Active	25		ns			P1 Mode	
Ct 609	tASC	Col Addr Setup to CAS# Active	0		ns	SF, S		F1 Mode	C_R = Max, C_T = Max
Ct 610		Col Addr Setup to CAS# Active	0		ns			F2 Mode	
Ct 611		Col Addr Setup to CAS# Active	0		ns			P1 Mode	
Ct 613	tCAH	Col Addr Hold from CAS# Active	20		ns	SF, S		F1 Mode	C_R = Max, C_T = Max
Ct 614		Col Addr Hold from CAS# Active	20		ns			F2 Mode	
Ct 615		Col Addr Hold from CAS# Active	25		ns			P1 Mode	
Ct 617	tRCD	RAS# to CAS# Delay	25		ns	SF, SF		F1 Mode	C_R = Max, C_T = Max
Ct 618		RAS# to CAS# Delay	25		ns			F2 Mode	
Ct 619		RAS# to CAS# Delay	25		ns			P1 Mode	
Ct 621	tCSH	CAS# Hold Time from RAS# Active	100		ns	SF, SR		F1 Mode	C_R = Max, C_T = Max
Ct 622		CAS# Hold Time from RAS# Active	100		ns			F2 Mode	
Ct 623		CAS# Hold Time from RAS# Active	100		ns			P1 Mode	
Ct 625	tRSH	RAS# Hold Time from CAS# Active	30		ns	SF, SR		F1 Mode	C_R = Max, C_T = Max
Ct 626		RAS# Hold Time from CAS# Active	45		ns			F2 Mode	
Ct 627		RAS# Hold Time from CAS# Active	45		ns			P1 Mode	
Ct 629	tWCS	WE# Setup to CAS# Active (Write)	0		ns	SF, SF		F1 Mode	C_R = Max, C_T = Max
Ct 630		WE# Setup to CAS# Active (Write)	0		ns			F2 Mode	
Ct 631		WE# Setup to CAS# Active (Write)	0		ns			P1 Mode	
Ct 633	tWCH	WE# Hold from CAS# Active (Write)	25		ns	SF, SR		F1 Mode	C_R = Max, C_T = Max
Ct 634		WE# Hold from CAS# Active (Write)	25		ns			F2 Mode	
Ct 635		WE# Hold from CAS# Active (Write)	25		ns			P1 Mode	
Ct 637	tRCS	WE# Inactive Setup to CAS# Active (Read)	0		ns	SF, SR		F1 Mode	C_R = Max, C_T = Max
Ct 638		WE# Inactive Setup to CAS# Active (Read)	0		ns			F2 Mode	
Ct 639		WE# Inactive Setup to CAS# Active (Read)	0		ns			P1 Mode	
Ct 641	tRCH	WE# Inactive Hold from CAS# Inactive (Read)	0		ns	SR, SF		F1 Mode	C_R = Max, C_T = Max
Ct 642		WE# Inactive Hold from CAS# Inactive (Read)	0		ns			F2 Mode	
Ct 643		WE# Inactive Hold from CAS# Inactive (Read)	0		ns			P1 Mode	

6.0 SL SuperSet TIMING SPECIFICATIONS (Continued)

Table 6.0. Intel386 SL CPU A.C. Specifications 16 MHz (Continued)

Symbol	Alt Symbol	Parameter	Min	Max	Unit	Derating	Figure	Notes	
DRAM Mode: 16 MHz Timings (Continued)									
Ct 645		Write Data Setup to CAS# Active	0		ns			F1 Mode	
Ct 646	tWDS	Write Data Setup to CAS# Active	0		ns	SF, S		F2 Mode	C_R = Max, C_T = Max
Ct 647		Write Data Setup to CAS# Active	0		ns			P1 Mode	
Ct 649		Write Data Hold from CAS# Active	20		ns			F1 Mode	
Ct 650	tWDH	Write Data Hold from CAS# Active	20		ns	SF, S		F2 Mode	C_R = Max, C_T = Max
Ct 651		Write Data Hold from CAS# Active	20		ns			P1 Mode	
Ct 653		Access Time from RAS# Active	100		ns			F1 Mode	
Ct 654	tRAC	Access Time from RAS# Active	100		ns			F2 Mode	
Ct 655		Access Time from RAS# Active	100		ns			P1 Mode	
Ct 657		Access Time from CAS# Active	30		ns			F1 Mode	
Ct 658	tCAC	Access Time from CAS# Active	30		ns			F2 Mode	
Ct 659		Access Time from CAS# Active	50		ns			P1 Mode	
Ct 661		Read Data Hold from CAS# Inactive	0		ns			F1 Mode	
Ct 662	tRDH	Read Data Hold from CAS# Inactive	0		ns			F2 Mode	
Ct 663		Read Data Hold from CAS# Inactive	0		ns			P1 Mode	
Ct 665		RAS# Active Pulse Width	100		ns			F1 Mode	
Ct 666	tRAS	RAS# Active Pulse Width	100		ns		7.1.29	F2 Mode	
Ct 667		RAS# Active Pulse Width	100		ns			P1 Mode	
Ct 669		CAS# Active Pulse Width	30		ns			F1 Mode	
Ct 670	tCAS	CAS# Active Pulse Width	30		ns			F2 Mode	
Ct 671		CAS# Active Pulse Width	45		ns			P1 Mode	
Ct 673		RAS# Precharge Pulse Width	90		ns			F1 Mode	
Ct 674	tRP	RAS# Precharge Pulse Width	90		ns			F2 Mode	
Ct 675		RAS# Precharge Pulse Width	90		ns			P1 Mode	
Ct 677		CAS# Precharge Pulse Width	20		ns			F1 Mode	
Ct 678	tCP	CAS# Precharge Pulse Width	20		ns			F2 Mode	
Ct 679		CAS# Precharge Pulse Width	25		ns			P1 Mode	
Ct 681		PARx# Setup to CAS# Active (Write)	0		ns			F1 Mode	
Ct 682	tPSW	PARx# Setup to CAS# Active (Write)	0		ns	SF, SF		F2 Mode	C_R = Max, C_T = Max
Ct 683		PARx# Setup to CAS# Active (Write)	0		ns			P1 Mode	
Ct 685		PARx# Hold from CAS# Active (Write)	20		ns			F1 Mode	
Ct 686	tPHW	PARx# Hold from CAS# Active (Write)	20		ns	SF, SR		F2 Mode	C_R = Max, C_T = Max
Ct 687		PARx# Hold from CAS# Active (Write)	20		ns			P1 Mode	

4

6.0 SL SuperSet TIMING SPECIFICATIONS (Continued)

Table 6.0. Intel386 SL CPU A.C. Specifications 16 MHz (Continued)

Symbol	Alt Symbol	Parameter	Min	Max	Unit	Derating	Figure	Notes
DRAM Mode: 16 MHz Timings (Continued)								
Ct 689	tPVR	PARx# Valid from CAS# Active (Read)	30		ns		7.1.29	F1 Mode
Ct 690		PARx# Valid from CAS# Active (Read)	30		ns			F2 Mode
Ct 691		PARx# Valid from CAS# Active (Read)	50		ns			P1 Mode
Ct 693	tPHR	PARx# Hold from CAS# Inactive (Read)	0		ns			F1 Mode
Ct 694		PARx# Hold from CAS# Inactive (Read)	0		ns			F2 Mode
Ct 695		PARx# Hold from CAS# Inactive (Read)	0		ns			P1 Mode
Other DRAM Timings								
Ct 701	tPED	PERR# Delay from SYSCLK		38	ns	SF	7.1.34	
Ct 702	tCSR	CAS# Setup to RAS# Active (DRAM Refresh)	10		ns	SF, SF	7.1.31	C_R = Max C_T = Max
Ct 703	tCHR	CAS# Hold from RAS# Active (DRAM Refresh)	30		ns	FF, FR	7.1.31	C_R = Min C_T = Min
Ct 704	tWSR	WE# Setup to RAS# Active (DRAM Refresh)	15		ns	SF, SF	7.1.31	C_R = Min, C_T = Max
Ct 705	tWHR	WE# Hold from RAS# Active (DRAM Refresh)	15		ns	FF, FR	7.1.31	C_R = Min C_T = Min
Ct 706	tRDS	RAS# Active Delay from SYSCLK (DRAM DMA/Master)		55	ns	SF	7.1.33	
Ct 707	tADS	Address Valid Delay from SYSCLK (DRAM DMA/Master)		65	ns	S	7.1.32	
Ct 710	tRSF	RAS# Pulse Width in Suspend Refresh Mode	160		ns			

6.0 SL SuperSet TIMING SPECIFICATIONS (Continued)

Table 6.0. Intel386 SL CPU A.C. Specifications 20 MHz

Symbol	Parameter	Min	Max	Unit	Derating	Figure	Notes
General: 20 MHz							
Ct 101	EFI Period	25	500	ns		7.1.1	(Note 1)
Ct 102a	EFI High Time at 2V	8		ns		7.1.1	
Ct 102b	EFI High Time at 3.7V	5		ns	*	7.1.1	
Ct 103a	EFI Low Time at 2V	8		ns		7.1.1	
Ct 103b	EFI Low Time at 0.8V	6		ns		7.1.1	
Ct 104	EFI Fall Time from (V_{CC} − 0.8V) to 0.8V		8	ns		7.1.1	
Ct 105	EFI Rise Time 0.8V to (V_{CC} − 0.8V)		8	ns		7.1.1	
Ct 111	PWRGOOD Minimum Pulse Width	1		EFI			
Ct 111a	PWRGOOD Setup to EFI	12		ns			(Note 2)
Ct 111b	PWRGOOD Hold Time	4		ns			
Ct 112	CPURESET Minimum Pulse Width	1		EFI			
Ct 112a	CPURESET—Setup to EFI	12		ns			(Note 2)
Ct 112b	CPURESET Hold Time	4		ns			
Ct 113a	STPCLK# Setup to EFI	15		ns			(Note 2)
Ct 113b	STPCLK# Hold Time	20		ns			
Ct 114a	SUS_STAT# Setup to EFI	20		ns			(Note 2)
Ct 114b	SUS_STAT# Hold Time	15		ns			
Ct 115	ONCE# Minimum Pulse Width	35		ns			
Ct 115a	ONCE# Setup to EFI	20		ns			(Note 2)
Ct 115b	ONCE# Hold Time	15		ns			
Ct 116a	SMI# Setup to EFI	15		ns			(Note 2)
Ct 116b	SMI# Hold Time	21		ns			
Ct 117a	INTR Setup to EFI	15		ns			(Note 2)
Ct 117b	INTR Hold Time	45		ns			
Ct 118a	NMI Setup to EFI	11		ns			(Note 2)
Ct 118b	NMI Hold Time	16		ns			

NOTES:
1. EFI maximum period is specified only for the case where a MCP (Math co-processor) is present in the system. NPXCLK period, high and low time are tested at 2V. All other parameters are guaranteed by design characterization.
2. A20GATE, CPURESET, INTR, NMI, ONCE#, PWRGOOD, SMI#, STPCLK# and SUS_STAT# are asynchronous inputs to the Intel386 SL CPU. Setup and hold times with respect to the EFI input are provided for test purposes only. The minimum setup and hold times are specified for valid recognition at a specific clock edge. The minimum valid pulse width can be extrapolated from the setup and hold times with respect to EFI.

4

6.0 SL SuperSet TIMING SPECIFICATIONS (Continued)

Table 6.0. Intel386 SL CPU A.C. Specifications 20 MHz (Continued)

Symbol	Parameter	Min	Max	Unit	Derating	Figure	Notes
PI-Bus Timings: 20 MHz							
Ct 301	Min. Chip Select and Command Setup to PSTART# Active	30		ns	SF, SF	7.1.7	C_R = Min, C_T = Max
Ct 302	Min. Chip Select and Command Hold from PSTART# Active	48		ns	FF, FR	7.1.7	C_R = Max, C_T = Min
Ct 304	Min. Read Data Setup Time to PCMD# Inactive	30		ns		7.1.7	
Ct 305	Min. Read Data Hold Time from PCMD# Inactive	9		ns		7.1.7	
Ct 307	Maximum Write Data Valid Delay from PSTART# Active		57	ns	SF, S	7.1.7	C_R = Min, C_T = Max
Ct 308	Min. Write Data Invalid Delay from PCMD# Inactive	25		ns	FF, F	7.1.7	C_R = Max, C_T = Min
Ct 309	Min Address Setup Time to PSTART# Active	20		ns	SF, S	7.1.7	C_R = Min, C_T = Max
Ct 310	Min Address Hold Time from PSTART# Active	50		ns	FF, F	7.1.7	C_R = Max, C_T = Min
Ct 311	PSTART# Pulse Width	45		ns		7.1.7	
Ct 312	Min Delay from PSTART# Active to PCMD# Active	40		ns	SF, SF	7.1.7	C_R = Max, C_T = Min
Ct 313	Min Delay from PRDY# Active to PCMD# Inactive	32		ns	FR	7.1.7	
Ct 314	Min Delay from PCMD# Inactive to PSTART# Active	0		ns	FR, FF	7.1.7	C_R = Max, C_T = Max
External Master Timings: SYSCLK at 8 MHz (Slave CPU)							
Ct 321	PW/R# Valid Delay		35	ns		7.1.8	ATCLK2 Sync.
Ct 321	PM/IO# Valid Delay		35	ns		7.1.8	ATCLK2 Sync.
Ct 321	VGACS# Valid Delay		35	ns		7.1.8	ATCLK2 Sync.
Ct 325	PSTART# Valid Delay		24	ns		7.1.8	ATCLK2 Sync.
Ct 326	PCMD# Valid Delay		24	ns		7.1.8	ATCLK2 Sync.
Ct 327a	PRDY# Set-up	5		ns		7.1.8	ATCLK2 Sync.
Ct 327b	PRDY# Hold	25		ns		7.1.8	ATCLK2 Sync.

NOTES:

1. VGACS#, FLSHDCS#, PW/R#, PM/IO# and Addresses change for each subsequent read or write.
2. PSTART# indicates a new cycle in which address, status and chip selects are valid before PSTART# is asserted LOW. PRDY# terminates each bus cycle and a new PSTART# is driven if a new address and status signals are available.
3. C_R is the capacitive load on the reference signal.
4. C_T is the capacitive load on the target signal.

6.0 SL SuperSet TIMING SPECIFICATIONS (Continued)

Table 6.0. Intel386 SL CPU A.C. Specifications 20 MHz (Continued)

Symbol	Parameter	Min	Max	Unit	Derating	Figure	Notes
Cache Bus Timing: 20 MHz							
Ct 401	CABUS Valid to CD Bus Valid		36	ns		7.1.6	
Ct 402	COE# Pulse Width	60		ns	SF, SR	7.1.6	
Ct 403	CCSH#, CCSL# Active to CD Bus Valid		36	ns		7.1.6	
Ct 404a	COE# Active to CD Bus Valid		25	ns		7.1.6	
Ct 404b	CDBUS Hold from COE# Inactive	0		ns		7.1.6	
Ct 405	CABUS Valid to CWE# Inactive	36		ns	SR, S	7.1.6	C_R = Min, C_T = Max
Ct 406	CWE# Active Width	35		ns	SF, SR	7.1.6	
Ct 407	CDBUS Setup to CWE# Inactive	25		ns	SR, S	7.1.6	C_R = Min, C_T = Max
Ct 408	CDBUS Hold to CWE# Inactive	0		ns	SR, S	7.1.6	C_R = Max, C_T = Max
Ct 409	CABUS Hold to CWE# Inactive	0		ns	SR, S	7.1.6	C_R = Max, C_T = Min
Math Coprocessor Timings: 20 MHz							
Ct 421	CA2 Valid Delay (NPX Cyc)	3	25	ns	FR, F; SR, S	7.1.3	
Ct 422	NPXADS# Valid Delay	6	27	ns	FR, FF; SR, SF	7.1.3	
Ct 423	NPXW/R# Valid Delay	5	27	ns	FR, FF; SR, SF	7.1.3	
Ct 424	CD Valid Delay (NPX Cycle)	2	35	ns	FR, F; SR, S	7.1.4	
Ct 425a	NPXRDY# Setup	16		ns		7.1.5	
Ct 425b	NPXRDY# Hold	3		ns		7.1.5	
Ct 426a	BUSY#, PEREQ, ERROR# Setup to NPXCLK phi1 high	19		ns		7.1.5	
Ct 426b	BUSY#, PEREQ, ERROR# Hold from NPXCLK phi1 high	5		ns		7.1.5	
Ct 427a	CD Setup (NPX Cycle)	12		ns		7.1.3	
Ct 427b	CD Hold (NPX Cycle)	6		ns		7.1.3	

6.0 SL SuperSet TIMING SPECIFICATIONS (Continued)

Table 6.0. Intel386 SL CPU A.C. Specifications 20 MHz (Continued)

Symbol	Parameter	Min	Max	Unit	Derating	Figure	Notes
Math Coprocessor Timings: 20 MHz (Continued)							
Ct 441	NPXCLK Period	25	500	ns		7.1.1	(Note 1)
Ct 442a	NPXCLK High Time 2V	7		ns		7.1.1	(Note 1)
Ct 442b	NPXCLK High Time 3.7V	4		ns		7.1.1	
Ct 443a	NPXCLK Low Time 2V	7		ns		7.1.1	(Note 1)
Ct 443b	NPXCLK Low Time 0.8V	5		ns		7.1.1	
Ct 444	NPXCLK Fall Time (V_{CC} − 0.8V) to 0.8V		8	ns		7.1.1	
Ct 445	NPXCLK Rise Time 0.8V to (V_{CC} − 0.8V)		8	ns		7.1.1	
Ct 446	NPXCLK to NPXRESET inactive delay	3	14	ns	FR, FF, SR, SF		
SRAM Mode: 20 MHz Timings							
Ct 501	Access Time from OE#	40		ns	SF, S		2 Wait State
Ct 502	Access Time from OE#	50		ns	SF, S		3 Wait State
Ct 503	CE# Setup to OE# Active	40		ns	SF, SF		2 Wait State
Ct 504	CE# Setup to OE# Active	40		ns	SF, SF		3 Wait State
Ct 505	Addr Setup to OE# Active	40		ns	SF, S		2 Wait State
Ct 506	Addr Setup to OE# Active	40		ns	SF, S		3 Wait State
Ct 507	CE# Setup to WE# Active	0		ns	SF, SF		2 Wait State
Ct 508	CE# Setup to WE# Active	0		ns	SF, SF		3 Wait State
Ct 509	Addr Setup to WE# Active	0		ns	SF, S	7.1.30	2 Wait State
Ct 510	Addr Setup to WE# Active	0		ns	SF, S		3 Wait State
Ct 511	WE# Active Pulse Width	70		ns	S		2 Wait State
Ct 512	WE# Active Pulse Width	90		ns	S		3 Wait State
Ct 513	WE# Recovery Time	10		ns	SR, S		2 Wait State
Ct 514	WE# Recovery Time	10		ns	SR, S		3 Wait State
Ct 515	Write Data Setup to WE# Inactive	39		ns	SR, S		2 Wait State
Ct 516	Write Data Setup to WE# Inactive	44		ns	SR, S		3 Wait State
Ct 517	Write Data Hold from WE# Inactive	0		ns	FR, F		2 Wait State
Ct 518	Write Data Hold from WE# Inactive	0		ns	FR, F		3 Wait State

NOTE:
1. NPXCLK maximum period is specified only for the case where a MCP (Math Co-processor) is present in the system. NPXCLK period, high and low time are tested at 2V. All other parameters are guaranteed by design characterization.

6.0 SL SuperSet TIMING SPECIFICATIONS (Continued)

Table 6.0. Intel386 SL CPU A.C. Specifications 20 MHz (Continued)

Symbol	Parameter	Min	Max	Unit	Derating	Figure	Notes
SRAM Mode: 20 MHz Timings (Continued)							
Ct 519	DIR Setup to OE# Active	0		ns	SF, S	*	2 Wait State
Ct 520	DIR Setup to OE# Active	0		ns	SF, S		3 Wait State
Ct 523	OE# Inactive Setup to DEN# Active	30		ns	SF, SR		2 Wait State
Ct 524	OE# Inactive Setup to DEN# Active	40		ns	SF, SR		3 Wait State
Ct 525	DIR Inactive Setup to WE# Active	0		ns	SF, S		2 Wait State
Ct 526	DIR Inactive Setup to WE# Active	0		ns	SF, S		3 Wait State
Ct 527	DEN# Hold from WE# Inactive	0		ns	FR, FR		2 Wait State
Ct 528	DEN# Hold from WE# Inactive	0		ns	FR, FR		3 Wait State
Ct 529	DIR Inactive Setup to DEN# Active	0		ns	SF, S		2 Wait State
Ct 530	DIR Inactive Setup to DEN# Active	0		ns	SF, S		3 Wait State
Ct 531	DIR Hold from DEN# Inactive	0		ns	FR, F		2 Wait State
Ct 532	DIR Hold from DEN# Inactive	0		ns	FR, F		3 Wait State
Ct 533	DIR Setup to DEN# Active	0	60	ns	FF, F; SF, S	7.1.30	2 Wait State
Ct 534	DIR Setup to DEN# Active	0	60	ns	FF, F; SF, S		3 Wait State
Ct 535	Upper Addr Setup to LE Inactive	8		ns	SF, S		2 Wait State
Ct 536	Upper Addr Setup to LE Inactive	8		ns	SF, S		3 Wait State
Ct 537	Upper Addr Hold from LE Inactive	4		ns	SF, S		2 Wait State
Ct 538	Upper Addr Hold from LE Inactive	4		ns	SF, S		3 Wait State
Ct 539	LE Active Pulse Width	8		ns	F		2 Wait State
Ct 540	LE Active Pulse Width	8		ns	F		3 Wait State
Ct 541	Addr Valid Delay from LE Inactive		50	ns	SF, S		2 Wait State
Ct 542	Addr Valid Delay from LE Inactive		70	ns	SF, S		3 Wait State
Ct 543	Read Data Hold from OE# Inactive	0		ns			2 Wait State
Ct 544	Read Data Hold from OE# Inactive	0		ns			3 Wait State

4

6.0 SL SuperSet TIMING SPECIFICATIONS (Continued)

Table 6.0. Intel386 SL CPU A.C. Specifications 20 MHz (Continued)

Symbol	Alt Symbol	Parameter	Min	Max	Unit	Derating	Figure	Notes	
DRAM Mode: 20 MHz Timings									
Ct 601	t_{ASR}	Row Addr Setup to RAS# Active	0		ns		7.1.29	F1 Mode	C_R = Max, C_T = Max
Ct 602		Row Addr Setup to RAS# Active	7		ns	SF, S		F2 Mode	
Ct 603		Row Addr Setup to RAS# Active	7		ns			P1 Mode	
Ct 605	tRAH	Row Addr Hold from RAS# Active	20		ns	SF, S		F1 Mode	C_R = Max, C_T = Max
Ct 606		Row Addr Hold from RAS# Active	20		ns			F2 Mode	
Ct 607		Row Addr Hold from RAS# Active	20		ns			P1 Mode	
Ct 609	tASC	Col Addr Setup to CAS# Active	0		ns	SF, S		F1 Mode	C_R = Max, C_T = Max
Ct 610		Col Addr Setup to CAS# Active	0		ns			F2 Mode	
Ct 611		Col Addr Setup to CAS# Active	0		ns			P1 Mode	
Ct 613	tCAH	Col Addr Hold from CAS# Active	15		ns	SF, S		F1 Mode	C_R = Max, C_T = Max
Ct 614		Col Addr Hold from CAS# Active	15		ns			F2 Mode	
Ct 615		Col Addr Hold from CAS# Active	25		ns			P1 Mode	
Ct 617	tRCD	RAS# to CAS# Delay	25		ns	SF, SF		F1 Mode	C_R = Max, C_T = Max
Ct 618		RAS# to CAS# Delay	25		ns			F2 Mode	
Ct 619		RAS# to CAS# Delay	25		ns			P1 Mode	
Ct 621	tCSH	CAS# Hold Time from RAS# Active	80		ns	SF, SR		F1 Mode	C_R = Max, C_T = Max
Ct 622		CAS# Hold Time from RAS# Active	100		ns			F2 Mode	
Ct 623		CAS# Hold Time from RAS# Active	100		ns			P1 Mode	
Ct 625	tRSH	RAS# Hold Time from CAS# Active	25		ns	SF, SR		F1 Mode	C_R = Max, C_T = Max
Ct 626		RAS# Hold Time from CAS# Active	30		ns			F2 Mode	
Ct 627		RAS# Hold Time from CAS# Active	45		ns			P1 Mode	
Ct 629	tWCS	WE# Setup to CAS# Active (Write)	0		ns	SF, SF		F1 Mode	C_R = Max, C_T = Max
Ct 630		WE# Setup to CAS# Active (Write)	0		ns			F2 Mode	
Ct 631		WE# Setup to CAS# Active (Write)	0		ns			P1 Mode	
Ct 633	tWCH	WE# Hold from CAS# Active (Write)	20		ns	SF, SR		F1 Mode	C_R = Max, C_T = Max
Ct 634		WE# Hold from CAS# Active (Write)	20		ns			F2 Mode	
Ct 635		WE# Hold from CAS# Active (Write)	20		ns			P1 Mode	
Ct 637	tRCS	WE# Inactive Setup to CAS# Active (Read)	0		ns	SF, SR		F1 Mode	C_R = Max, C_T = Max
Ct 638		WE# Inactive Setup to CAS# Active (Read)	0		ns			F2 Mode	
Ct 639		WE# Inactive Setup to CAS# Active (Read)	0		ns			P1 Mode	
Ct 641	tRCH	WE# Inactive Hold from CAS# Inactive (Read)	0		ns	SR, SF		F1 Mode	C_R = Max, C_T = Max
Ct 642		WE# Inactive Hold from CAS# Inactive (Read)	0		ns			F2 Mode	
Ct 643		WE# Inactive Hold from CAS# Inactive (Read)	0		ns			P1 Mode	

6.0 SL SuperSet TIMING SPECIFICATIONS (Continued)

Table 6.0. Intel386 SL CPU A.C. Specifications 20 MHz (Continued)

Symbol	Alt Symbol	Parameter	Min	Max	Unit	Derating	Figure		Notes
DRAM Mode: 20 MHz Timings (Continued)									
Ct 645		Write Data Setup to CAS# Active	0		ns			F1 Mode	
Ct 646	tWDS	Write Data Setup to CAS# Active	0		ns	SF, S		F2 Mode	C_R = Max, C_T = Max
Ct 647		Write Data Setup to CAS# Active	0		ns			P1 Mode	
Ct 649		Write Data Hold from CAS# Active	20		ns			F1 Mode	
Ct 650	tWDH	Write Data Hold from CAS# Active	20		ns	SF, S		F2 Mode	C_R = Max, C_T = Max
Ct 651		Write Data Hold from CAS# Active	20		ns			P1 Mode	
Ct 653		Access Time from RAS# Active	80		ns	*		F1 Mode	
Ct 654	tRAC	Access Time from RAS# Active	100		ns			F2 Mode	
Ct 655		Access Time from RAS# Active	100		ns			P1 Mode	
Ct 657		Access Time from CAS# Active	25		ns			F1 Mode	
Ct 658	tCAC	Access Time from CAS# Active	30		ns			F2 Mode	
Ct 659		Access Time from CAS# Active	40		ns			P1 Mode	
Ct 661		Read Data Hold from CAS# Inactive	0		ns			F1 Mode	
Ct 662	tRDH	Read Data Hold from CAS# Inactive	0		ns			F2 Mode	
Ct 663		Read Data Hold from CAS# Inactive	0		ns			P1 Mode	
Ct 665		RAS# Active Pulse Width	80		ns			F1 Mode	
Ct 666	tRAS	RAS# Active Pulse Width	100		ns		7.1.29	F2 Mode	
Ct 667		RAS# Active Pulse Width	100		ns			P1 Mode	
Ct 669		CAS# Active Pulse Width	25		ns			F1 Mode	
Ct 670	tCAS	CAS# Active Pulse Width	30		ns			F2 Mode	
Ct 671		CAS# Active Pulse Width	45		ns			P1 Mode	
Ct 673		RAS# Precharge Pulse Width	70		ns			F1 Mode	
Ct 674	tRP	RAS# Precharge Pulse Width	90		ns			F2 Mode	
Ct 675		RAS# Precharge Pulse Width	90		ns			P1 Mode	
Ct 677		CAS# Precharge Pulse Width	15		ns			F1 Mode	
Ct 678	tCP	CAS# Precharge Pulse Width	15		ns			F2 Mode	
Ct 679		CAS# Precharge Pulse Width	25		ns			P1 Mode	
Ct 681		PARx# Setup to CAS# Active (Write)	0		ns			F1 Mode	
Ct 682	tPSW	PARx# Setup to CAS# Active (Write)	0		ns	SF, SF		F2 Mode	C_R = Max, C_T = Max
Ct 683		PARx# Setup to CAS# Active (Write)	0		ns			P1 Mode	
Ct 685		PARx# Hold from CAS# Active (Write)	20		ns			F1 Mode	
Ct 686	tPHW	PARx# Hold from CAS# Active (Write)	20		ns	SF, SR		F2 Mode	C_R = Max, C_T = Max
Ct 687		PARx# Hold from CAS# Active (Write)	20		ns			P1 Mode	

4

6.0 SL SuperSet TIMING SPECIFICATIONS (Continued)

Table 6.0. Intel386 SL CPU A.C. Specifications 20 MHz (Continued)

Symbol	Alt Symbol	Parameter	Min	Max	Unit	Derating	Figure	Notes
DRAM Mode: 20 MHz Timings (Continued)								
Ct 689	tPVR	PARx# Valid from CAS# Active (Read)	25		ns		7.1.29	F1 Mode
Ct 690		PARx# Valid from CAS# Active (Read)	30		ns			F2 Mode
Ct 691		PARx# Valid from CAS# Active (Read)	42		ns			P1 Mode
Ct 693	tPHR	PARx# Hold from CAS# Inactive (Read)	0		ns			F1 Mode
Ct 694		PARx# Hold from CAS# Inactive (Read)	0		ns			F2 Mode
Ct 695		PARx# Hold from CAS# Inactive (Read)	0		ns			P1 Mode
Other DRAM Timings								
Ct 701	tPED	PERR# Delay from SYSCLK		38	ns	SF	7.1.34	
Ct 702	tCSR	CAS# Setup to RAS# Active (DRAM Refresh)	10		ns	SF, SF	7.1.31	C_R = Max, C_T = Max
Ct 703	tCHR	CAS# Hold from RAS# Active (DRAM Refresh)	30		ns	FF, FR	7.1.31	C_R = Min, C_T = Min
Ct 704	tWSR	WE# Setup to RAS# Active (DRAM Refresh)	15		ns	SF, SF	7.1.31	C_R = Min, C_T = Max
Ct 705	tWHR	WE# Hold from RAS# Active (DRAM Refresh)	15		ns	FF, FR	7.1.31	C_R = Min, C_T = Min
Ct 706	tRDS	RAS# Active Delay from SYSCLK (DRAM DMA/Master)		55	ns	SF	7.1.33	
Ct 707	tADS	Address Valid Delay from SYSCLK (DRAM DMA/Master)		65	ns	S	7.1.32	
Ct 710	tRSF	RAS# Pulse Width in Suspend Refresh Mode	160		ns			

6.0 SL SuperSet TIMING SPECIFICATIONS (Continued)

Table 6.0. Intel386 SL CPU A.C. Specifications 25 MHz

Symbol	Parameter	Min	Max	Unit	Derating	Figure	Notes
General: 25 MHz							
Ct 101	EFI Period	20	500	ns		7.1.1	(Note 1)
Ct 102a	EFI High Time at 2V	7		ns		7.1.1	
Ct 102b	EFI High Time at 3.7V	4		ns		7.1.1	
Ct 103a	EFI Low Time at 2V	7		ns		7.1.1	
Ct 103b	EFI Low Time at 0.8V	5		ns		7.1.1	
Ct 104	EFI Fall Time from (V_{CC} − 0.8V) to 0.8V		7	ns		7.1.1	
Ct 105	EFI Rise Time 0.8V to (V_{CC} − 0.8V)		7	ns		7.1.1	
Ct 111	PWRGOOD Minimum Pulse Width	2		EFI			
Ct 111a	PWRGOOD Setup to EFI	10		ns			(Note 2)
Ct 111b	PWRGOOD Hold Time	3		ns			
Ct 112	CPURESET Minimum Pulse Width	1		EFI			
Ct 112a	CPURESET—Setup to EFI	10		ns			(Note 2)
Ct 112b	CPURESET Hold Time	3		ns			
Ct 113a	STPCLK# Setup to EFI	10		ns			(Note 2)
Ct 113b	STPCLK# Hold Time	3		ns			
Ct 114a	SUS_STAT# Setup to EFI	10		ns			(Note 2)
Ct 114b	SUS_STAT# Hold Time	3		ns			
Ct 115	ONCE# Minimum Pulse Width	35		ns			
Ct 115a	ONCE# Setup to EFI	10		ns			(Note 2)
Ct 115b	ONCE# Hold Time	3		ns			
Ct 116a	SMI# Setup to EFI	11		ns			(Note 2)
Ct 116b	SMI# Hold Time	15		ns			
Ct 117a	INTR Setup to EFI	11		ns			(Note 2)
Ct 117b	INTR Hold Time	16		ns			
Ct 118a	NMI Setup to EFI	11		ns			(Note 2)
Ct 118b	NMI Hold Time	16		ns			

NOTES:

1. EFI maximum period is specified only for the case where a MCP (Math co-processor) is present in the system. NPXCLK period, high and low time are tested at 2V. All other parameters are guaranteed by design characterization.
2. A20GATE, CPURESET, INTR, NMI, ONCE#, PWRGOOD, SMI#, STPCLK# and SUS_STAT# are asynchronous inputs to the Intel386 SL CPU. Setup and hold times with respect to the EFI input are provided for test purposes only. The minimum setup and hold times are specified for valid recognition at a specific clock edge. The minimum valid pulse width can be extrapolated from the setup and hold times with respect to EFI.

6.0 SL SuperSet TIMING SPECIFICATIONS (Continued)

Table 6.0. Intel386 SL CPU A.C. Specifications 25 MHz (Continued)

Symbol	Parameter	Min	Max	Unit	Derating	Figure	Notes
PI-Bus Timings: 25 MHz							
Ct 301	Min. Chip Select and Command Setup to PSTART# Active	20		ns	SF, SF	7.1.7	C_R = Min, C_T = Max
Ct 302	Min. Chip Select and Command Hold from PSTART# Active	38		ns	FF, FR	7.1.7	C_R = Max, C_T = Min
Ct 304	Min. Read Data Setup Time to PCMD# Inactive	48		ns		7.1.7	
Ct 305	Min. Read Data Hold Time from PCMD# Inactive	12		ns		7.1.7	
Ct 307	Maximum Write Data Valid Delay from PSTART# Active		52	ns	SF, S	7.1.7	C_R = Min, C_T = Max
Ct 308	Min. Write Data Invalid Delay from PCMD# Inactive	20		ns	FF, F	7.1.7	C_R = Max, C_T = Min
Ct 309	Min Address Setup Time to PSTART# Active	10		ns	SF, S	7.1.7	C_R = Min, C_T = Max
Ct 310	Min Address Hold Time from PSTART# Active	40		ns	FF, F	7.1.7	C_R = Max, C_T = Min
Ct 311	PSTART# Pulse Width	35		ns		7.1.7	
Ct 312	Min Delay from PSTART# Active to PCMD# Active	30		ns	SF, SF	7.1.7	C_R = Max, C_T = Min
Ct 313	Min Delay from PRDY# Active to PCMD# Inactive	26		ns	FR	7.1.7	
Ct 314	Min Delay from PCMD# Inactive to PSTART# Active	0		ns	FR, FF	7.1.7	C_R = Max, C_T = Max
External Master Timings: SYSCLK at 8 MHz (Slave CPU)							
Ct 321	PW/R# Valid Delay		35	ns	SF	7.1.8	ATCLK2 Sync.
Ct 321	PM/IO# Valid Delay		35	ns	SF	7.1.8	ATCLK2 Sync.
Ct 321	VGACS# Valid Delay		35	ns	SF	7.1.8	ATCLK2 Sync.
Ct 325	PSTART# Valid Delay		24	ns	SF	7.1.8	ATCLK2 Sync.
Ct 326	PCMD# Valid Delay		24	ns	SF	7.1.8	ATCLK2 Sync.
Ct 327a	PRDY# Set-up	5		ns		7.1.8	ATCLK2 Sync.
Ct 327b	PRDY# Hold	25		ns		7.1.8	ATCLK2 Sync.

NOTES:
1. VGACS#, FLSHDCS#, PW/R#, PM/IO# and Addresses change for each subsequent read or write.
2. PSTART# indicates a new cycle in which address, status and chip selects are valid before PSTART# is asserted LOW. PRDY# terminates each bus cycle and a new PSTART# is driven if a new address and status signals are available.
3. C_R is the capacitive load on the reference signal.
4. C_T is the capacitive load on the target signal.

6.0 SL SuperSet TIMING SPECIFICATIONS (Continued)

Table 6.0. Intel386 SL CPU A.C. Specifications 25 MHz (Continued)

Symbol	Parameter	Min	Max	Unit	Derating	Figure	Notes
Cache Bus Timing: 25 MHz							
Ct 401	CABUS Valid to CD Bus Valid		25	ns		7.1.6	
Ct 402	COE# Pulse Width	45		ns	SF, SR	7.1.6	
Ct 403	CCSH#, CCSL# Active to CD Bus Valid		25	ns		7.1.6	
Ct 404a	COE# Active to CD Bus Valid		15	ns		7.1.6	
Ct 404b	CDBUS Hold from COE# Inactive	0		ns		7.1.6	
Ct 405	CABUS Valid to CWE# Inactive	26		ns	SR, S	7.1.6	C_R = Min, C_T = Max
Ct 406	CWE# Active Width	25		ns	SF, SR	7.1.6	
Ct 407	CDBUS Setup to CWE# Inactive	15		ns	SR, S	7.1.6	C_R = Min, C_T = Max
Ct 408	CDBUS Hold to CWE# Inactive	0		ns	SR, S	7.1.6	C_R = Max, C_T = Max
Ct 409	CABUS Hold to CWE# Inactive	0		ns	SR, S	7.1.6	C_R = Max, C_T = Min
Math Coprocessor Timings: 25 MHz							
Ct 421	CA2 Valid Delay (NPX Cyc)	2	20	ns	FR, F; SR, S	7.1.3	
Ct 422	NPXADS# Valid Delay	4	23	ns	FR, FF; SR, SF	7.1.3	
Ct 423	NPXW/R# Valid Delay	4	23	ns	FR, FF; SR, SF	7.1.3	
Ct 424	CD Valid Delay (NPX Cycle)	0	35	ns	FR, F; SR, S	7.1.4	
Ct 425a	NPXRDY# Setup	14		ns		7.1.5	
Ct 425b	NPXRDY# Hold	3		ns		7.1.5	
Ct 426a	BUSY#, PEREQ, ERROR# Setup to NPXCLK phi1 high	19		ns		7.1.5	
Ct 426b	BUSY#, PEREQ, ERROR# Hold from NPXCLK phi1 high	4		ns		7.1.5	
Ct 427a	CD Setup (NPX Cycle)	9		ns		7.1.3	
Ct 427b	CD Hold (NPX Cycle)	5		ns		7.1.3	

4

6.0 SL SuperSet TIMING SPECIFICATIONS (Continued)

Table 6.0. Intel386 SL CPU A.C. Specifications 25 MHz (Continued)

Symbol	Parameter	Min	Max	Unit	Derating	Figure	Notes
Math Coprocessor Timings: 25 MHz (Continued)							
Ct 441	NPXCLK Period	20	500	ns		7.1.1	(Note 1)
Ct 442a	NPXCLK High Time 2V	6		ns		7.1.1	(Note 1)
Ct 442b	NPXCLK High Time 3.7V	3		ns		7.1.1	
Ct 443a	NPXCLK Low Time 2V	6		ns		7.1.1	(Note 1)
Ct 443b	NPXCLK Low Time 0.8V	4		ns	*	7.1.1	
Ct 444	NPXCLK Fall Time (V_{CC} − 0.8V) to 0.8V		7	ns		7.1.1	
Ct 445	NPXCLK Rise Time 0.8V to (V_{CC} − 0.8V)		7	ns		7.1.1	
Ct 446	NPXCLK to NPXRESET inactive delay	3	12	ns	FR, FP, SR, SF		
SRAM Mode: 25 MHz Timings							
Ct 501	Access Time from OE#	30		ns	SF, S	7.1.30	2 Wait State
Ct 502	Access Time from OE#	40		ns	SF, S		3 Wait State
Ct 503	CE# Setup to OE# Active	30		ns	SF, SF		2 Wait State
Ct 504	CE# Setup to OE# Active	30		ns	SF, SF		3 Wait State
Ct 505	Addr Setup to OE# Active	30		ns	SF, S		2 Wait State
Ct 506	Addr Setup to OE# Active	30		ns	SF, S		3 Wait State
Ct 507	CE# Setup to WE# Active	0		ns	SF, SF		2 Wait State
Ct 508	CE# Setup to WE# Active	0		ns	SF, SF		3 Wait State
Ct 509	Addr Setup to WE# Active	0		ns	SF, S		2 Wait State
Ct 510	Addr Setup to WE# Active	0		ns	SF, S		3 Wait State
Ct 511	WE# Active Pulse Width	55		ns	S		2 Wait State
Ct 512	WE# Active Pulse Width	70		ns	S		3 Wait State
Ct 513	WE# Recovery Time	5		ns	SR, S		2 Wait State
Ct 514	WE# Recovery Time	10		ns	SR, S		3 Wait State
Ct 515	Write Data Setup to WE# Inactive	35		ns	SR, S		2 Wait State
Ct 516	Write Data Setup to WE# Inactive	40		ns	SR, S		3 Wait State
Ct 517	Write Data Hold from WE# Inactive	0		ns	FR, F		2 Wait State
Ct 518	Write Data Hold from WE# Inactive	0		ns	FR, F		3 Wait State

NOTE:
1. NPXCLK maximum period is specified only for the case where a MCP (Math Co-processor) is present in the system. NPXCLK period, high and low time are tested at 2V. All other parameters are guaranteed by design characterization.

6.0 SL SuperSet TIMING SPECIFICATIONS (Continued)

Table 6.0. Intel386 SL CPU A.C. Specifications 25 MHz (Continued)

Symbol	Parameter	Min	Max	Unit	Derating	Figure	Notes
SRAM Mode: 25 MHz Timings (Continued)							
Ct 519	DIR Setup to OE# Active	0		ns	SF, S		2 Wait State
Ct 520	DIR Setup to OE# Active	0		ns	SF, S		3 Wait State
Ct 523	OE# Inactive Setup to DEN# Active	25		ns	SF, SR		2 Wait State
Ct 524	OE# Inactive Setup to DEN# Active	30		ns	SF, SR		3 Wait State
Ct 525	DIR Inactive Setup to WE# Active	0		ns	SF, S		2 Wait State
Ct 526	DIR Inactive Setup to WE# Active	0		ns	SF, S		3 Wait State
Ct 527	DEN# Hold from WE# Inactive	0		ns	FR, FR		2 Wait State
Ct 528	DEN# Hold from WE# Inactive	0		ns	FR, FR		3 Wait State
Ct 529	DIR Inactive Setup to DEN# Active	0		ns	SF, S		2 Wait State
Ct 530	DIR Inactive Setup to DEN# Active	0		ns	SF, S		3 Wait State
Ct 531	DIR Hold from DEN# Inactive	0		ns	FR, F		2 Wait State
Ct 532	DIR Hold from DEN# Inactive	0		ns	FR, F		3 Wait State
Ct 533	DIR Setup to DEN# Active	0	50	ns	FF, F; SF, S	7.1.30	2 Wait State
Ct 534	DIR Setup to DEN# Active	0	50	ns	FF, F; SF, S		3 Wait State
Ct 535	Upper Addr Setup to LE Inactive	8		ns	SF, S		2 Wait State
Ct 536	Upper Addr Setup to LE Inactive	8		ns	SF, S		3 Wait State
Ct 537	Upper Addr Hold from LE Inactive	4		ns	SF, S		2 Wait State
Ct 538	Upper Addr Hold from LE Inactive	4		ns	SF, S		3 Wait State
Ct 539	LE Active Pulse Width	8		ns	F		2 Wait State
Ct 540	LE Active Pulse Width	8		ns	F		3 Wait State
Ct 541	Addr Valid Delay from LE Inactive		40	ns	SF, S		2 Wait State
Ct 542	Addr Valid Delay from LE Inactive		60	ns	SF, S		3 Wait State
Ct 543	Read Data Hold from OE# Inactive	0		ns			2 Wait State
Ct 544	Read Data Hold from OE# Inactive	0		ns			3 Wait State

6.0 SL SuperSet TIMING SPECIFICATIONS (Continued)

Table 6.0. Intel386 SL CPU A.C. Specifications 25 MHz (Continued)

Symbol	Alt Symbol	Parameter	Min	Max	Unit	Derating	Figure	Notes	
DRAM Mode: 25 MHz Timings									
Ct 601		Row Addr Setup to RAS# Active	*		ns			F1 Mode	
Ct 602	tASR	Row Addr Setup to RAS# Active	7		ns	SF, S		F2 Mode	C_R = Max, C_T = Max
Ct 603		Row Addr Setup to RAS# Active	7		ns			P1 Mode	
Ct 605		Row Addr Hold from RAS# Active	*		ns			F1 Mode	
Ct 606	tRAH	Row Addr Hold from RAS# Active	15		ns	SF, S		F2 Mode	C_R = Max, C_T = Max
Ct 607		Row Addr Hold from RAS# Active	15		ns			P1 Mode	
Ct 609		Col Addr Setup to CAS# Active	*		ns			F1 Mode	
Ct 610	tASC	Col Addr Setup to CAS# Active	0		ns	SF, S		F2 Mode	C_R = Max, C_T = Max
Ct 611		Col Addr Setup to CAS# Active	0		ns			P1 Mode	
Ct 613		Col Addr Hold from CAS# Active	*		ns			F1 Mode	
Ct 614	tCAH	Col Addr Hold from CAS# Active	15		ns	SF, S		F2 Mode	C_R = Max, C_T = Max
Ct 615		Col Addr Hold from CAS# Active	20		ns			P1 Mode	
Ct 617		RAS# to CAS# Delay	*		ns			F1 Mode	
Ct 618	tRCD	RAS# to CAS# Del,ay	20		ns	SF, SF		F2 Mode	C_R = Max, C_T = Max
Ct 619		RAS# to CAS# Delay	20		ns			P1 Mode	
Ct 621		CAS# Hold Time from RAS# Active	*		ns			F1 Mode	
Ct 622	tCSH	CAS# Hold Time from RAS# Active	80		ns	SF, SR	7.1.29	F2 Mode	C_R = Max, C_T = Max
Ct 623		CAS# Hold Time from RAS# Active	80		ns			P1 Mode	
Ct 625		RAS# Hold Time from CAS# Active	*		ns			F1 Mode	
Ct 626	tRSH	RAS# Hold Time from CAS# Active	30		ns	SF, SR		F2 Mode	C_R = Max, C_T = Max
Ct 627		RAS# Hold Time from CAS# Active	45		ns			P1 Mode	
Ct 629		WE# Setup to CAS# Active (Write)	*		ns			F1 Mode	
Ct 630	tWCS	WE# Setup to CAS# Active (Write)	0		ns	SF, SF		F2 Mode	C_R = Max, C_T = Max
Ct 631		WE# Setup to CAS# Active (Write)	0		ns			P1 Mode	
Ct 633		WE# Hold from CAS# Active (Write)	*		ns			F1 Mode	
Ct 634	tWCH	WE# Hold from CAS# Active (Write)	20		ns	SF, SR		F2 Mode	C_R = Max, C_T = Max
Ct 635		WE# Hold from CAS# Active (Write)	20		ns			P1 Mode	
Ct 637		WE# Inactive Setup to CAS# Active (Read)	*		ns			F1 Mode	
Ct 638	tRCS	WE# Inactive Setup to CAS# Active (Read)	0		ns	SF, SR		F2 Mode	C_R = Max, C_T = Max
Ct 639		WE# Inactive Setup to CAS# Active (Read)	0		ns			P1 Mode	
Ct 641		WE# Inactrive Hold from CAS# Inactive (Read)	*		ns			F1 Mode	
Ct 642	tRCH	WE# Inactive Hold from CAS# Inactive (Read)	0		ns	SR, SF		F2 Mode	C_R = Max, C_T = Max
Ct 643		WE# Inactive Hold from CAS# Inactive (Read)	0		ns			P1 Mode	

6.0 SL SuperSet TIMING SPECIFICATIONS (Continued)

Table 6.0. Intel386 SL CPU A.C. Specifications 25 MHz (Continued)

Symbol	Alt Symbol	Parameter	Min	Max	Unit	Derating	Figure	Notes	
DRAM Mode: 25 MHz Timings (Continued)									
Ct 645		Write Data Setup to CAS# Active	*		ns			F1 Mode	
Ct 646	tWDS	Write Data Setup to CAS# Active	0		ns	SF, S		F2 Mode	C_R = Max, C_T = Max
Ct 647		Write Data Setup to CAS# Active	0		ns			P1 Mode	
Ct 649		Write Data Hold from CAS# Active	*		ns			F1 Mode	
Ct 650	tWDH	Write Data Hold from CAS# Active	15		ns	SF, S		F2 Mode	C_R = Max, C_T = Max
Ct 651		Write Data Hold from CAS# Active	20		ns			P1 Mode	
Ct 653		Access Time from RAS# Active	*		ns			F1 Mode	
Ct 654	tRAC	Access Time from RAS# Active	80		ns			F2 Mode	
Ct 655		Access Time from RAS# Active	80		ns			P1 Mode	
Ct 657		Access Time from CAS# Active	*		ns			F1 Mode	
Ct 658	tCAC	Access Time from CAS# Active	23		ns			F2 Mode	
Ct 659		Access Time from CAS# Active	40		ns			P1 Mode	
Ct 661		Read Data Hold from CAS# Inactive	*		ns			F1 Mode	
Ct 662	tRDH	Read Data Hold from CAS# Inactive			ns			F2 Mode	
Ct 663		Read Data Hold from CAS# Inactive	0		ns			P1 Mode	
Ct 665		RAS# Active Pulse Width	*		ns			F1 Mode	
Ct 666	tRAS	RAS# Active Pulse Width	80		ns		7.1.29	F2 Mode	
Ct 667		RAS# Active Pulse Width	80		ns			P1 Mode	
Ct 669		CAS# Active Pulse Width	*		ns			F1 Mode	
Ct 670	tCAS	CAS# Active Pulse Width	27		ns			F2 Mode	
Ct 671		CAS# Active Pulse Width	40		ns			P1 Mode	
Ct 673		RAS# Precharge Pulse Width	*		ns			F1 Mode	
Ct 674	tRP	RAS# Precharge Pulse Width	70		ns			F2 Mode	
Ct 675		RAS# Precharge Pulse Width	70		ns			P1 Mode	
Ct 677		CAS# Precharge Pulse Width	*		ns			F1 Mode	
Ct 678	tCP	CAS# Precharge Pulse Width	15		ns			F2 Mode	
Ct 679		CAS# Precharge Pulse Width	25		ns			P1 Mode	
Ct 681		PARx# Setup to CAS# Active (Write)	*		ns			F1 Mode	
Ct 682	tPSW	PARx# Setup to CAS# Active (Write)	0		ns	SF, SF		F2 Mode	C_R = Max, C_T = Max
Ct 683		PARx# Setup to CAS# Active (Write)	0		ns			P1 Mode	
Ct 685		PARx# Hold from CAS# Active (Write)	*		ns			F1 Mode	
Ct 686	tPHW	PARx# Hold from CAS# Active (Write)	20		ns	SF, SR		F2 Mode	C_R = Max, C_T = Max
Ct 687		PARx# Hold from CAS# Active (Write)	20		ns			P1 Mode	

NOTE:
*F1 mode will not be available at 25 MHz.

4

6.0 SL SuperSet TIMING SPECIFICATIONS (Continued)

Table 6.0. Intel386 SL CPU A.C. Specifications 25 MHz (Continued)

Symbol	Alt Symbol	Parameter	Min	Max	Unit	Derating	Figure	Notes
DRAM Mode: 25 MHz Timings (Continued)								
Ct 689	tPVR	PARx# Valid from CAS# Active (Read)			ns		7.1.29	F1 Mode
Ct 690		PARx# Valid from CAS# Active (Read)	23		ns			F2 Mode
Ct 691		PARx# Valid from CAS# Active (Read)	40		ns			P1 Mode
Ct 693	tPHR	PARx# Hold from CAS# Inactive (Read)			ns			F1 Mode
Ct 694		PARx# Hold from CAS# Inactive (Read)	0		ns			F2 Mode
Ct 695		PARx# Hold from CAS# Inactive (Read)	0		ns			P1 Mode
Other DRAM Timings								
Ct 701	tPED	PERR# Delay from SYSCLK		38	ns	SF	7.1.34	
Ct 702	tCSR	CAS# Setup to RAS# Active (DRAM Refresh)	10		ns	SF, SF	7.1.31	C_R = Max, C_T = Max
Ct 703	tCHR	CAS# Hold from RAS# Active (DRAM Refresh)	30		ns	FF, FR	7.1.31	C_R = Min, C_T = Min
Ct 704	tWSR	WE# Setup to RAS# Active (DRAM Refresh)	15		ns	SF, SF	7.1.31	C_R = Min, C_T = Max
Ct 705	tWHR	WE# Hold from RAS# Active (DRAM Refresh)	15		ns	FF, FR	7.1.31	C_R = Min, C_T = Min
Ct 706	tRDS	RAS# Active Delay from SYSCLK (DRAM DMA/Master)		55	ns	SF	7.1.33	
Ct 707	tADS	Address Valid Delay from SYSCLK (DRAM DMA/Master)		65	ns	S	7.1.32	
Ct 710	tRSF	RAS# Pulse Width in Suspend Refresh Mode	160		ns			

6.0 SL SuperSet TIMING SPECIFICATIONS (Continued)

Table 6.1. 82360SL I/O Timing Specifications(1)

Symbol	Parameter	Min	Max	Unit	Derating	Figure	Notes
It1	SYSCLK Period	125		ns		7.2.1	
It2	SYSCLK Low Time @V_{IL} = 1.5V	55		ns		7.2.1	
It3	SYSCLK High Time @V_{IL} = 1.5V	50		ns		7.2.1	
It4	SYSCLK Rise Time and Fall time		10	ns		7.2.2	
It5a	RESETDRV from SYSCLK		125		S		
It6a	A20GATE Active (HIGH) Delay from KBDA20 Active (HIGH)		30	ns	SR	7.2.1	
It6b	A20GATE Active (HIGH) Delay from SYSCLK		45	ns	SR	7.2.1	
It7	SYSCLK to KBDCLK Delay		30	ns		7.2.1	(Note 3)
It8a	RC#/PERR#/IOCHCK# Pulse Width	250		ns		7.2.2	
It8b	RC#/PERR#/IOCHCK# Setup to SYSCLK Falling Edge	12		ns		7.2.1	(Note 3)
It9a	Programmable CPURESET Active (HIGH) from SYSCLK	5	50	ns	FR, SR	7.2.1	
It10a	NMI Active (HIGH) from SYSCLK		125	ns	SR	7.2.1	(Note 3)
It10b	NMI Inactive from IOW# Active (LOW)	0			FF	7.2.1	
It11	RTCRESET# Pulse Width	5		μs		7.2.1	
It14	BALE hold from SYSCLK	2	45	ns		7.2.3	
It15	IOR#/IOW#/INTA# Input Active (LOW) Delay from SYSCLK Low		20	ns		7.2.1	
It15a	IOR#/IOW#/MEMW# Output Active (LOW) Delay from SYSCLK		90	ns	SF	7.2.8	
It16	IOR#/IOW#/INTA#/MEMW#/MEMR# Input Inactive from SYSCLK		35	ns		7.2.3	
It16a	IOR#/IOW# Output Inactive from SYSCLK		120	ns	SR	7.2.8	
It17	ZEROWS# Output Active from SYSCLK		65	ns	SF	7.2.4	
It18	ZEROWS# Output Inactive from SYSCLK	0		ns	SR	7.2.4	
It19	BALE Setup to SYSCLK (DMA Cycle)	18		ns		7.2.7	
It20	IOCHRDY Input Active Setup to SYSCLK	15		ns		7.2.7	
It20a	IOCHRDY Input Inactive Setup to SYSCLK	15		ns		7.2.7	
It21	DMA8/16# Active Delay from SYSCLK		65	ns	SF	7.2.7	
It22	DMA8/16# Inactive Delay from SYSCLK (4 MHz DMACLK)		65	ns	SR	7.2.7	
It22a	DMA8/16# Inactive Delay from SYSCLK Low (8 MHz DMACLK)		65	ns	SR	7.2.23	
It23	AEN Active from HLDA Active		35	ns	SR	7.2.7	

NOTE:
1. The A.C. specifications given in Table 6.1 are made with the assumption that the input signals IOR#, IOW#, BALE, SYSCLK and SA[16:0] do not vary independently (i.e., they all have either max delays or min delays and one signal cannot have a max delay while another has a min delay). This condition is guaranteed when these signals are driven by the Intel386 SL CPU. If used in a system where this condition does not hold true, Intel does not guarantee the timings of the output signals of the 82360 SL I/O.

4

6.0 SL SuperSet TIMING SPECIFICATIONS (Continued)

Table 6.1. 82360SL I/O Timing Specifications (Continued)

Symbol	Parameter	Min	Max	Unit	Derating	Figure	Notes
It24	AEN Inactive Delay from HLDA Inactive		35	ns	SF	7.2.7	
It25	SA15:0, SBHE# Valid Delay from SYSCLK	10	120	ns	F, S	7.2.7	
It26	SA16 (Only if DMA8/16# = 0) SA15:0, SHBE# Valid Output Hold from SYSCLK	6		ns		7.2.10	
It26a	SA16 (Only if DMA 8/16# = 1), LA17:23 Valid Output Hold from IOR#/IOW#/MEMR#/MEMW# Output	10		ns		7.2.24	
It26f	SA16:0, LA17:23, SBHE# Float Delay from SYSCLK		90	ns	S	7.2.10	
It27	DACKx# Active Delay from SYSCLK (4 MHz DMACLK)		75	ns	SF	7.2.7	
It27a	DACKx# Active Delay from SYSCLK Low (8 MHz DMACLK)		75	ns	SF	7.2.8	
It28	DACKx# Inactive Delay from SYSCLK (4 MHz DMACLK)		75	ns	SR	7.2.7	
It28a	DACKx# Inactive Delay from SYSCLK Low (8 MHz DMACLK)		75	ns	SR	7.2.8	
It29	IOR#/IOW#/MEMW# Float-to-Drive-Inactive from SYSCLK		75	ns		7.2.23	
It30	IOR#/IOW#/MEMW# Float Delay from SYSCLK		75	ns		7.2.23	
It30a	SMRAMCS# Setup to MEMR#/MEMW# Active	10		ns	FF	7.2.11	
It31	MEMR#/MEMW# Input Active Delay from SYSCLK		70	ns		7.2.11	
It31a	MEMR#/MEMW# Output Active Delay from SYSCLK		70	ns	SF	7.2.8	
It32a	MEMR#/MEMW# Output Inactive Delay from SYSCLK		75	ns	SR	7.2.7	
It33	T/C Active Delay from SYSCLK		85	ns	SR	7.2.7	
It34	T/C Inactive Delay from SYSCLK		85	ns	SF	7.2.7	
It35	TIM2CLK2 Period	125		ns		7.2.2	
It36	TIM2CLK2 Low Time	55		ns		7.2.2	
It37	TIM2CLK2 High Time	55		ns		7.2.2	
It38	TIM2CLK2 Rise Time		25	ns		7.2.2	
It39	TIM2CLK2 Fall Time		25	ns		7.2.2	
It40	TIM2GAT2 High Pulse Width	45		ns		7.2.22	
It41	TIM2GAT2 Low Pulse Width	45		ns		7.2.22	
It42	TIM2GAT2 Setup to TIM2CLK2	45		ns		7.2.22	

6.0 SL SuperSet TIMING SPECIFICATIONS (Continued)

Table 6.1. 82360SL I/O Timing Specifications (Continued)

Symbol	Parameter	Min	Max	Unit	Derating	Figure	Notes
It43	TIM2GAT2 Hold from TIM2CLK2	45		ns		7.2.22	
It44	TIM2OUT2 from TIM2CLK2 High to Low		110	ns	SR	7.2.22	
It45	TIM2OUT2 from TIM2GAT2 High to Low		110	ns	SR	7.2.22	
It46	SPKR Active Delay from TIM2GAT2 (When EXTAUD is Set)		120	ns	SR	7.2.22	
It50	REFRESH# Active to MEMR# Output Active	150		ns	FF	7.2.10	
It52	Address Valid to MEMR# Active	40		ns	S, SF	7.2.10	
It53	MEMR# Output Inactive from IOCHRDY Input Low to High (During a Master Refresh)	125		ns	FR	7.2.10	
It55	IOCHRDY Pulse Width		750	ns	*	7.2.10	
It56	MEMR# Output Pulse Width for Refresh	2		SYSCLK		7.2.10	
It59	FLPCS#/C8042CS# Active Setup to Command Active	10		ns	FF	7.2.13	
It59a	HDCS0#/HDCS1# Active Setup to Command Active	45		ns	FF	7.2.13	
It60	FLPCS#/C8042CS#/HDCS0#/HDCS1# Output Hold from Command Inactive	10		ns	FR	7.2.13	
It60a	SMRAMCS# Hold from MEMR#/MEMW#	10		ns		7.2.11	
It69	DRQx Setup to SYSCLK High to Low	0		ns		7.2.5	
It78	EXTSMI# Input Pulse Width	1		SYSCLK		7.2.26	
It79	EXTRTCAS Pulse Width	3	4	SYSCLK		7.2.14	
It80	IOCS16# Setup to Command	10		ns		7.2.18	
It81	IOCS16# Hold from Command	10		ns		7.2.18	
It82	STPCLK# Delay from SYSCLK		100	ns	SF	7.2.25	
It82a	STPCLK# Output Pulse Width	2		SYSCLK		7.2.25	
It83	SMI# from SYSCLK		100	ns	SF	7.2.25	
It84	SMOUTx from SYSCLK		110	ns	S	7.2.25	
It85	SUS_STAT# from SYSCLK		100	ns	SF	7.2.25	(Note 3)
It86	IOCHRDY Output High to Low from Command		24	ns	SF	7.2.23	
It94	Delay from IOW# to Modem Output (RTS#, DTR#)		200	ns	SF	7.2.20	
It109	KBDCLK Period (8 MHz)	125		ns		7.2.2	
	KBDCLK Period (4 MHz)	250		ns		7.2.2	
	KBDCLK Period (2 MHz)	500		ns		7.2.2	
It110	KBDCLK High Time (8 MHz)	40		ns		7.2.2	
	KBDCLK High Time (4 MHz)	95		ns		7.2.2	
	KBDCLK High Time (2 MHz)	200		ns		7.2.2	

6.0 SL SuperSet TIMING SPECIFICATIONS (Continued)

Table 6.1. 82360SL I/O Timing Specifications (Continued)

Symbol	Parameter	Min	Max	Unit	Derating	Figure	Notes
It111	KBDCLK Low Time (8 MHz)	40		ns		7.2.2	
	KBDCLK Low Time (4 MHz)	95		ns		7.2.2	
	KBDCLK Low Time (2 MHz)	200		ns		7.2.2	
It117	HRQ Inactive to HLDA Inactive	185		ns	FF	7.2.5	
It118	HLDA Inactive to HRQ Active (Back to Back Hold Acknowledge Cycles)	0		ns	FR		(Note 3)
It120	IRQ1, 6, 10: 12, 14, 15, ERROR#, IRQ8# Pulse Width	100		ns		7.2.21	
It121	INTR Output Delay from IRQ1, 6, 10: 12, 14, 15, ERROR#, IRQ8#		100	ns	SR	7.2.21	
It122	Data Output Valid from INTA# Active		120	ns	S	7.2.21	
It123	Data Output Hold from INTA# Inactive	0		ns	F	7.2.21	
It123f	Data Float from INTA# Inactive		35	ns		7.2.21	
It124a	SD7 Read Data Output Hold from MEMR# Inactive	0		ns		7.2.11	
It124f	SD7 Float from MEMR# Inactive		35	ns		7.2.11	
It125	Write Data Input Setup to MEMW# Active	40		ns		7.2.12	
It125a	XD7 Output Valid from MEMW# Active		60	ns	S	7.2.12	
It126	Write Data Input Hold from MEMW#	15		ns		7.2.12	
It126a	XD7 Output Hold from MEMW# Inactive	5		ns	F	7.2.12	
It126f	XD7 Float from MEMW# Inactive		45	ns		7.2.12	
It129	SMEMR#/SMEMW# Active from MEMR#/MEMW#		30	ns	SF	7.2.11	
It129a	SMEMR#/SMEMW# Inactive from MEMR#/MEMW# Inactive	3	30	ns	FR, SR	7.2.11	
It130	LOMEM# Output Active Setup to MEMR#/MEMW# Input Active	3		ns	FF	7.2.11	
It130a	LOMEM# Output Inactive Setup to MEMR#/MEMW# Input Active	5		ns	FR	7.2.11	
It140	LPTSTROBE#/LPTSLCTIN#/LPTAFD# Output Delay from Command		45	ns	SF	7.2.27	(Note 1)
It141	LPTD Output from LPTSTROBE#/LPTSLCTIN#/LPTAFD# Active		15	ns	SF, S	7.2.27	(Note 1)
It142	LPTD Output Hold from LPTSLCTIN#/LPTAFD# Inactive	50		ns	SR, S	7.2.27	(Note 1)
It143	LPTD Input Setup to LPTSLCTIN#/LPTAFD# Inactive during Read	210		ns		7.2.27	(Note 1)
It144	LPTD Input hold from LPTSLCTIN#/LPTAFD# Inactive during Read	0		ns		7.2.27	(Note 1)
It145	IOCHRDY Output Low from LPTBUSY Low		40	ns	SF	7.2.27	(Note 1)
It200	BALE Active from SYSCLK Low	2	35	ns		7.2.3	
It201	Write Data Input Setup to IOW# Active	40		ns		7.2.3	

6.0 SL SuperSet TIMING SPECIFICATIONS (Continued)

Table 6.1. 82360SL I/O Timing Specifications (Continued)

Symbol	Parameter	Min	Max	Unit	Derating	Figure	Notes
It202	Write Data Input Hold from IOW# Inactive	25		ns		7.2.3	
It203	Read Data Output Setup to IOR# Inactive	62		ns	F	7.2.3	
It204	Read Data Output Hold from IOR# Inactive	0		ns	F	7.2.3	
It204f	Data Bus Float from IOR#/MEMR#		35	ns		7.2.3	
It205	BALE Active Pulse Width	50		ns		7.2.3	
It206	SA Address Input Valid Setup to BALE Inactive	40		ns		7.2.3	
It208a	LA Address Input Valid Setup to BALE Active	40		ns		7.2.11	
It208b	LA Address Input Valid Hold from BALE Inactive	55		ns		7.2.11	
It209	IOW# to EXTRTCAS		130	ns	SR	7.2.15	
It210	XD7 Output Valid from IOW# Active		60	ns	S	7.2.14	
It211	XD7 Output Hold from IOW# Inactive	5		ns	F	7.2.14	
It211f	XD7 Output Float from IOW# Inactive		45	ns		7.2.14	
It212	EXTRTCRW#/EXTRTCDS Active from Command Active		50	ns	SF; SR	7.2.16	
It213	EXTRTCRW#/ EXTRTCDS Hold from Command Inactive		35	ns	SR; SF	7.2.16	
It214	XDEN# Output Delay from IOR#/IOW#, MEMR#/MEMW# Inputs	10	75	ns	FF, SF	7.2.11	
It214a	XDEN# Output Delay from IOR#/IOW# Output	5	75	ns	FF, FF SF, SF	7.2.24	
It215a	XDEN# Output Active from XDIR Output Active	0		ns	FR, FF	7.2.11	
It215b	XDIR Output Inactive from XDEN# Output Inactive	5		ns	FR, FF	7.2.11	
It216a	SD7 Read Data Output Delay from XD7 Input		35	ns	S	7.2.11	
It216b	SD7 Read Data Output Delay from HD7 Input		50	ns	S	7.2.18	
It217	SD7 Read Data Output Hold from IOR# Inactive	0		ns	F	7.2.13	
It217f	SD7 Float from IOR# Inactive		35	ns		7.2.13	
It218	Address Input Hold from Command Inactive	40		ns		7.2.3	
It219	HDENL#/HDENH# Output Active Delay from Command		35	ns	SF	7.2.18	
It219a	HDENL#/HDENH# Output Inactive Delay from Command Inactive	5		ns	FR	7.2.18	
It220	HD7 Output Valid from IOW# Active		45	ns	S	7.2.19	
It221	HD7 Output Hold from IOW# Inactive	10		ns	F	7.2.19	
It221f	HD7 Output Float from IOW# Inactive		35	ns		7.2.19	

4

6.0 SL SuperSet TIMING SPECIFICATIONS (Continued)

Table 6.1. 82360SL I/O Timing Specifications (Continued)

Symbol	Parameter	Min	Max	Unit	Derating	Figure	Notes
It223	HALT# Input Valid from SYSCLK Low		20			7.2.1	
It224	XD7/HD7 Input Setup to IOR#/MEMR#	60		ns		7.2.13	
It225	XD7/HD7 Input Hold from IOR#/MEMR#	0		ns		7.2.13	
It230	XD7 Output Valid from EXTRTCRW# Active		35	ns	S	7.2.17	
It231	XD7 Output Hold from EXTRTCRW# Inactive	0		ns	F	7.2.17	
It231f	XD7 Output Float from EXTRTCRW#		35	ns		7.2.17	
It250	BATTDEAD# Inactive from Stable RTCVCC	2		ms		7.2.26	(Note 2)
It251	EXTSMI# active to SMI# Active (for Minimum Programmed Count)	1	2.1	ms		7.2.26	(Note 2)
It252	SMI# Active from SRBTN#/BATT Low# Active (for Minimum Programmed Count)	128	256	ms		7.2.26	(Note 2)
It253	Advanced Power Management (APM) SMI# Active from IOW# Active	2	3	SYSCLK	FF, SF	7.7.26	(Note 2)
It254	COMARI#/COMBRI#/SRBTN# Pulse Width	1		RTCCLK		7.2.26	(Note 2)
It305	SA16, LA23:17 Valid Delay from SYSCLK	10	165	ns	F, S	7.2.7	
It311	HRQ Output Active from SYSCLK		45	ns	SR	7.2.6	
It312	HLDA Setup to SYSCLK	18		ns		7.2.6	
It314	HRQ Inactive from SYSCLK	5		ns	FF	7.2.6	
It317	REFREQ Active from SYSCLK		45	ns	SR	7.2.6	
It319	REFREQ Inactive from SYSCLK		45	ns	SF	7.2.6	
It320	Normal REFREQ to Slow REFREQ Delay (when Going to Suspend)	0.5	2	RTCCLK		7.2.24	
It321	Slow REFREQ Active Delay to SUS_STAT# Active	2	2	RTCCLK		7.2.24	
It322	MASTER# Active to REFRESH# Input Active Delay	25		ns		7.2.9	
It324	REFRESH# Output Active from HLDA		35	ns	SF	7.2.6	
It325	REFRESH# Output Inactive from SYSCLK	5		ns	FR	7.2.6	
It326	REFRESH# Input Active to REFREQ Active		30	ns	SR	7.2.9	
It327	REFRESH# Input Inactive to REFREQ Inactive	0		ns	FF	7.2.9	
It328	REFRESH# Pulse Width	4	5	SYSCLK		7.2.6	
It329	REFREQ Pulse Width during Master# Cycle	4	5	SYSCLK		7.2.9	
It330	DACKx# to MASTER# Delay	0		ns	SF, SF	7.2.9	
It331	AEN Delay from MASTER#	0	49	ns	FR, FF SR, SF	7.2.9	
It332	Alternate Master Drives Address and Data		125	ns		7.2.9	
It333	MASTER# Delay from DRQx Inactive		100	ns	SF	7.2.9	
It334	Alternate Master Tri-States Bus Signal	0		ns		7.2.9	

NOTES:
1. Fast parallel port specifications are applicable for I/O accesses to ports 37B–37F and 27B–27F.
2. These specifications are for power management.
3. These specifications are for test purposes only.

7.0 SL SuperSet TIMING DIAGRAMS

7.1 Intel386™ SL CPU Timing Diagrams

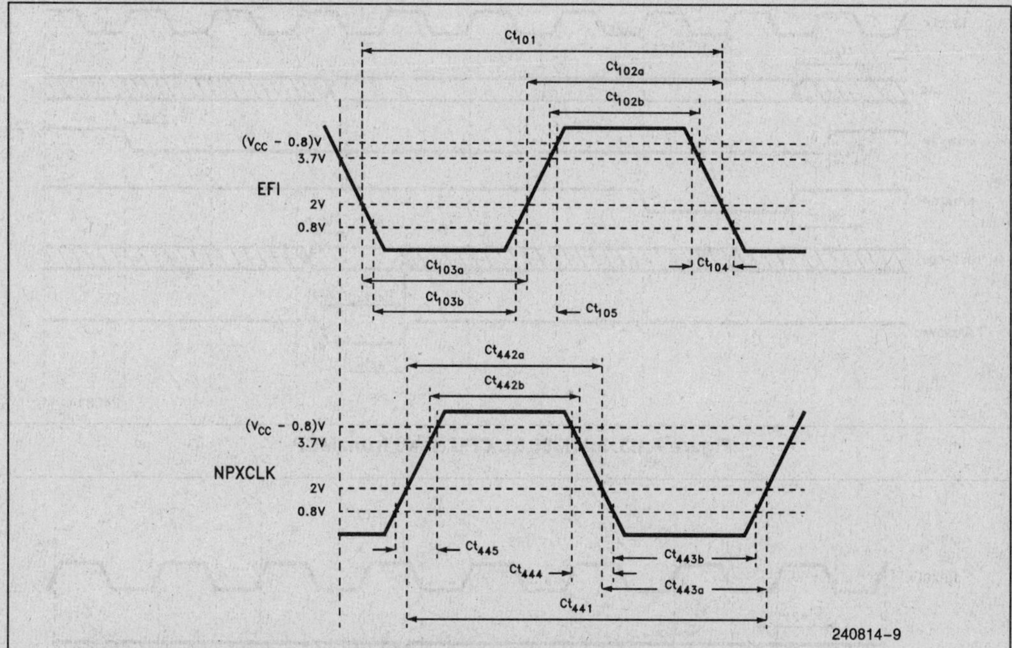

Figure 7.1.1. Clocks

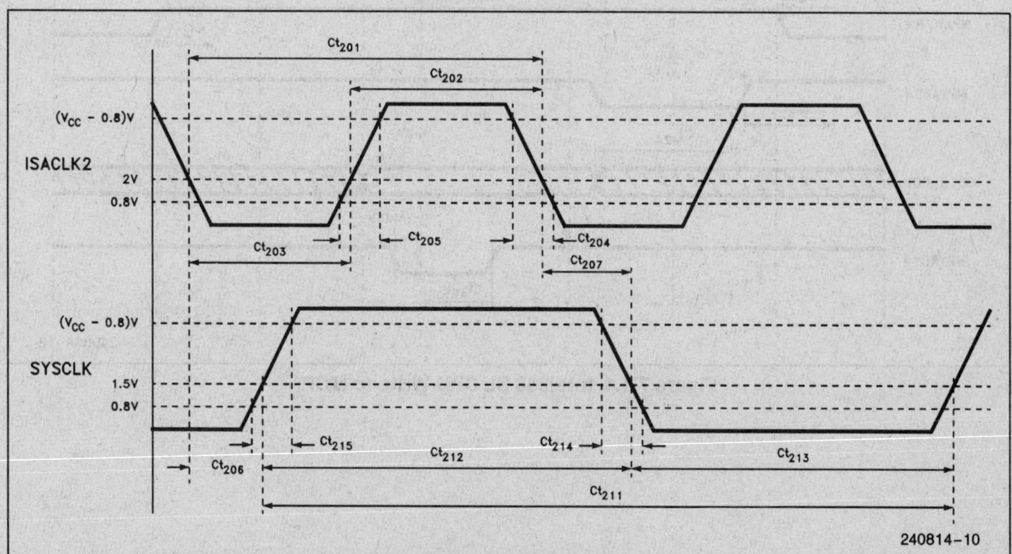

Figure 7.1.2. Clocks

7.1 Intel386™ SL CPU Timing Diagrams (Continued)

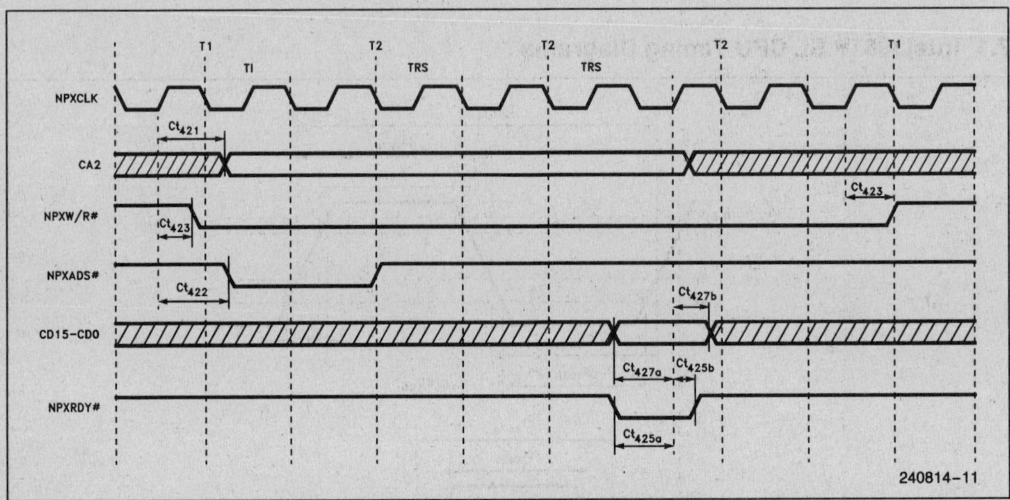

Figure 7.1.3. Intel386 SL CPU Read from MCP

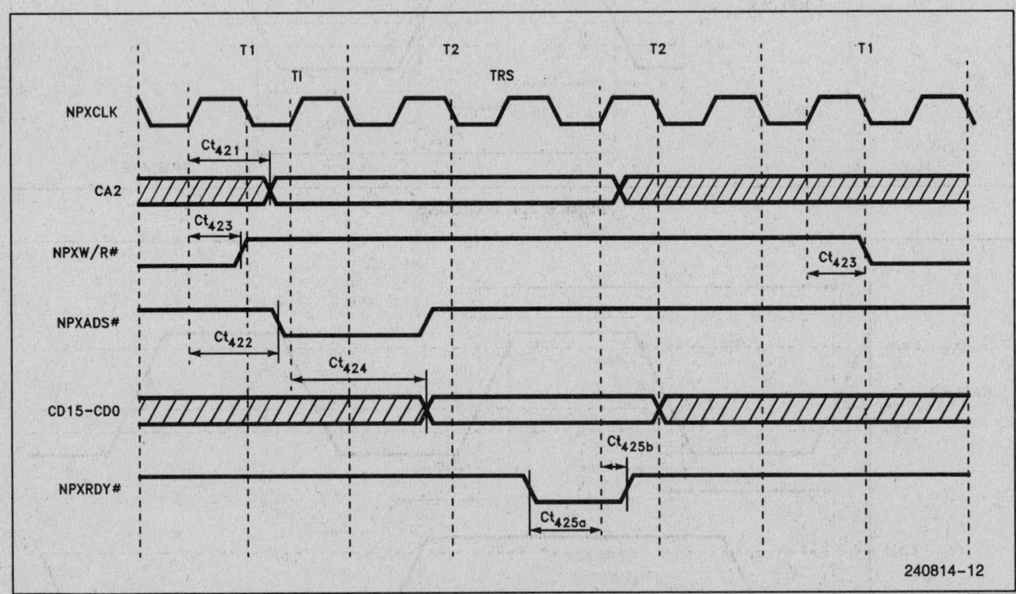

Figure 7.1.4. Intel386 SL CPU Write to MCP

7.1 Intel386™ SL CPU Timing Diagrams (Continued)

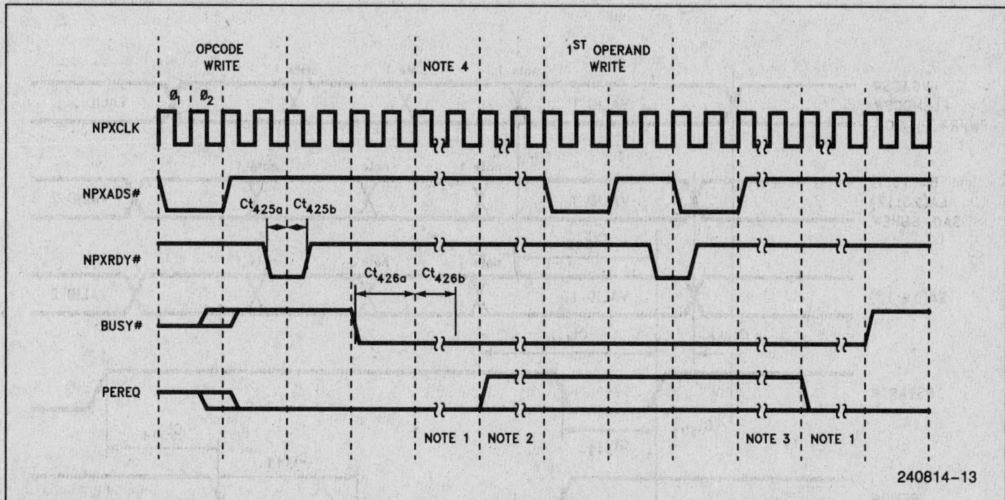

NOTES:
1. Instruction dependent.
2. PEREQ is an asynchronous input to the Intel386 SL CPU. Instruction dependent as to when it is asserted.
3. Additional operand transfers.
4. Memory read (operand) cycles not shown.

Figure 7.1.5. MCP BUSY# and PEREQ Timings

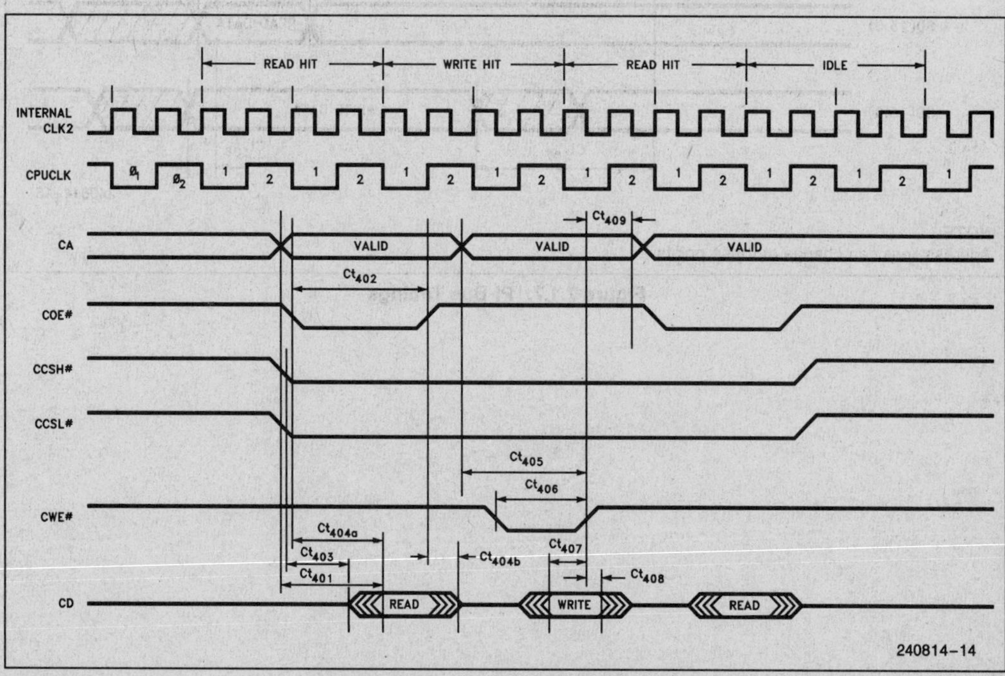

Figure 7.1.6. Cache Read/Write Hit Cycles

7.1 Intel386™ SL CPU Timing Diagrams (Continued)

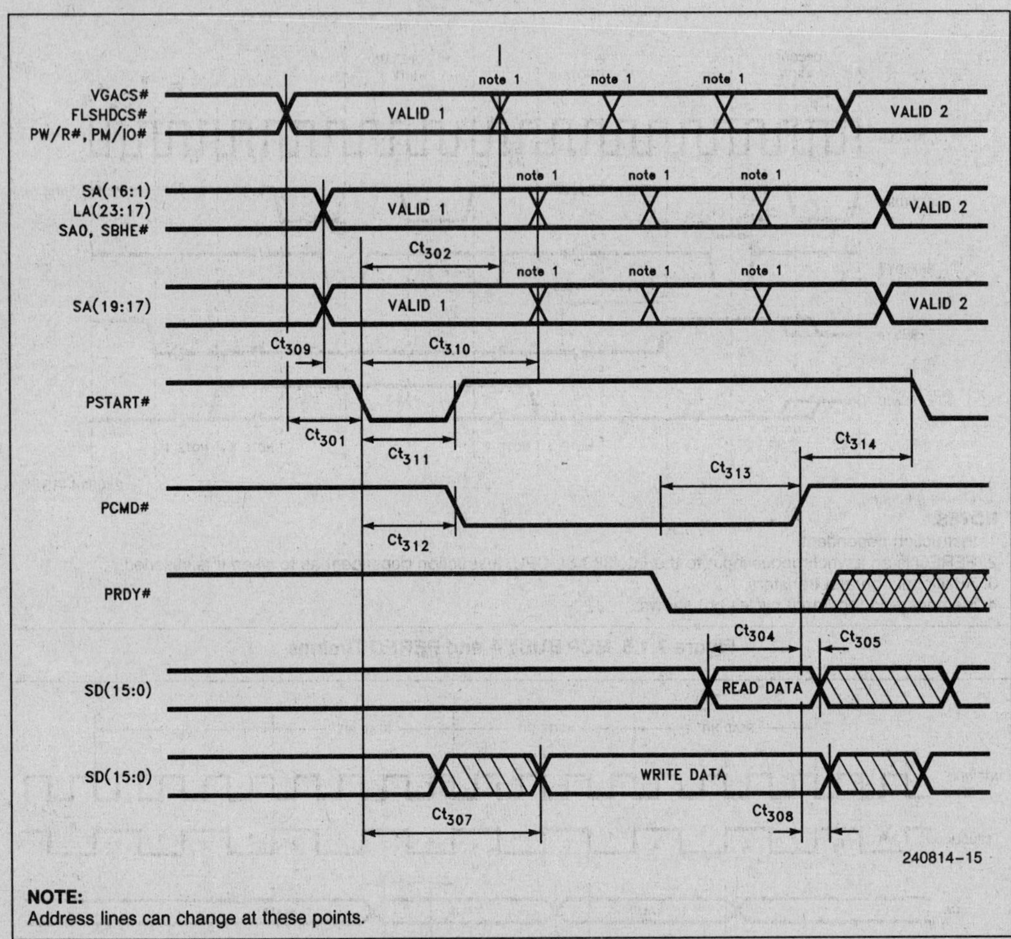

NOTE:
Address lines can change at these points.

Figure 7.1.7. PI-Bus Timings

7.1 Intel386™ SL CPU Timing Diagrams (Continued)

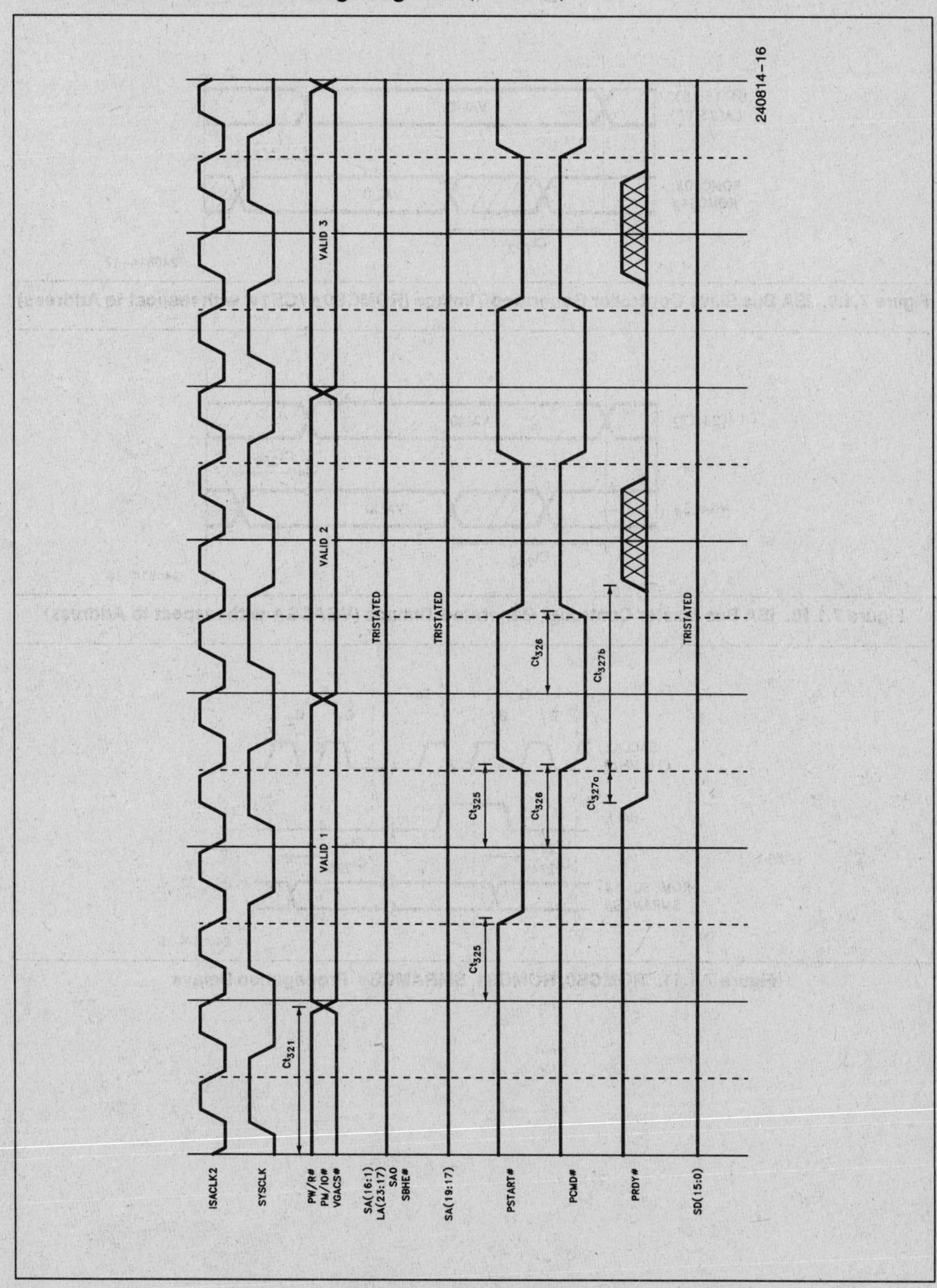

Figure 7.1.8. PI-Bus Slave Controller Generated Timings

7.1 Intel386™ SL CPU Timing Diagrams (Continued)

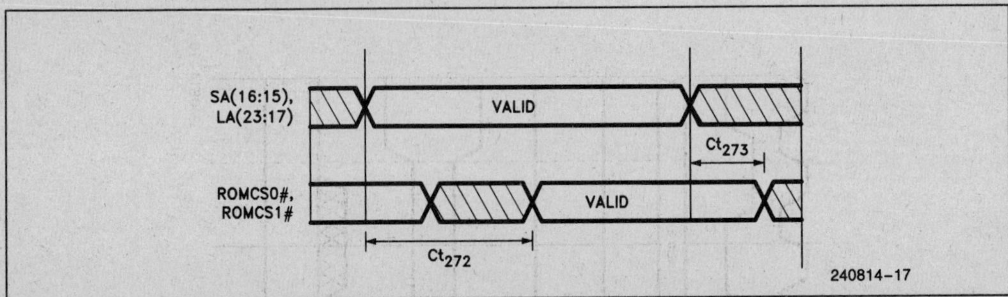

Figure 7.1.9. ISA Bus Slave Controller Generated Timings (ROMCS0#/CS1# with respect to Address)

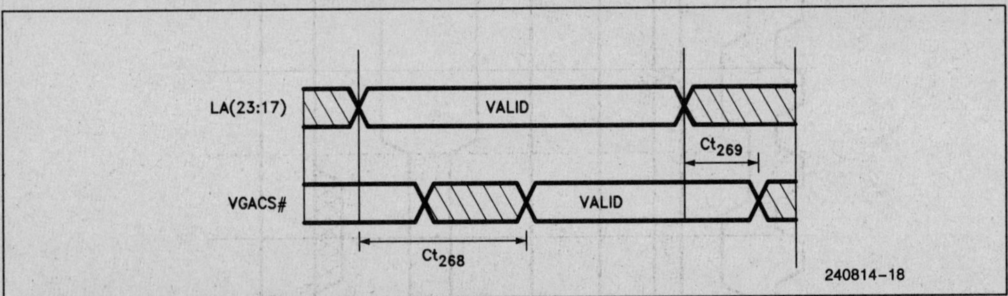

Figure 7.1.10. ISA Bus Master Controller Generated Timings (VGACS# with respect to Address)

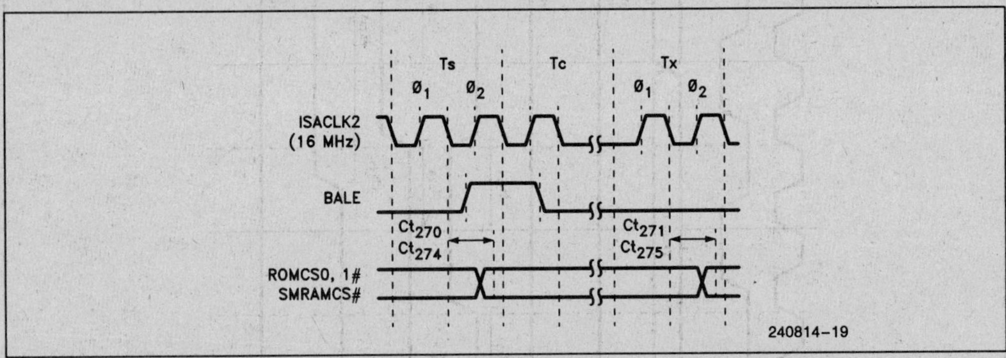

Figure 7.1.11. ROMCS0, ROMCS1, SMRAMCS# Propagation Delays

7.1 Intel386™ SL CPU Timing Diagrams (Continued)

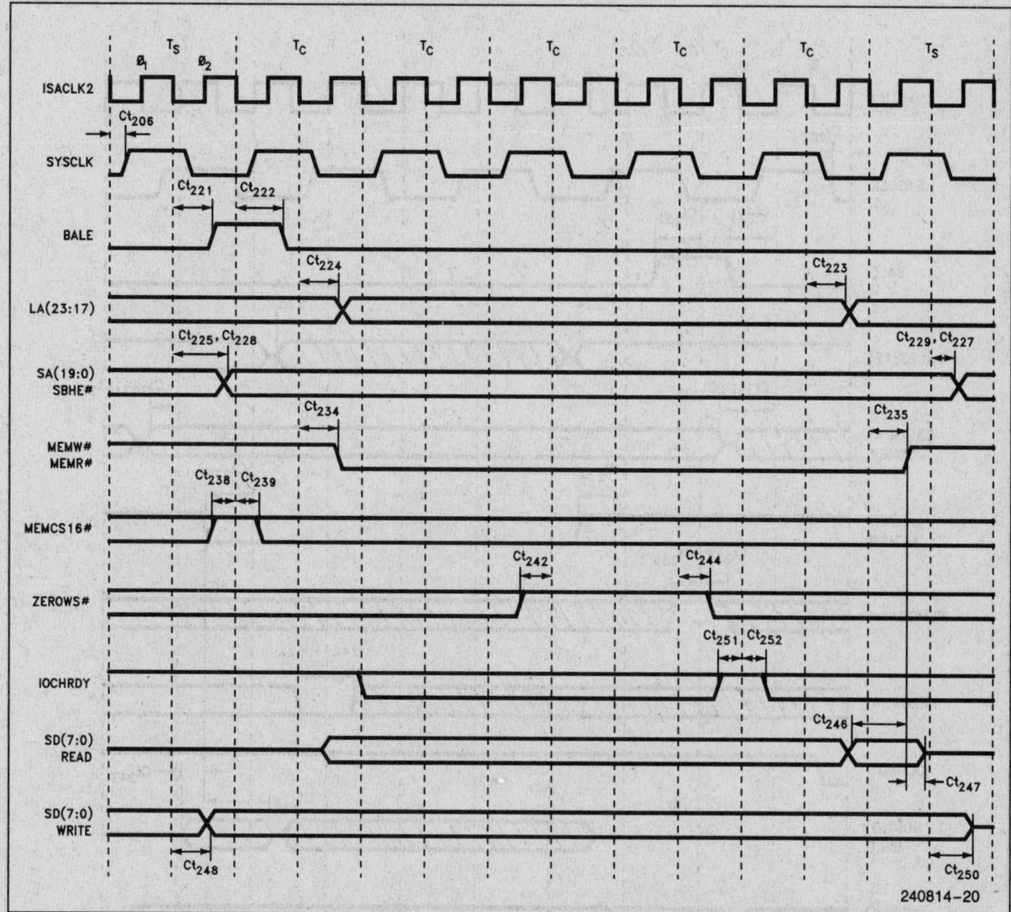

Figure 7.1.12. ISA Bus 8-Bit Memory Read/Write Standard ISA BUS Cycle (6 SYSCLKs)

4

7.1 Intel386™ SL CPU Timing Diagrams (Continued)

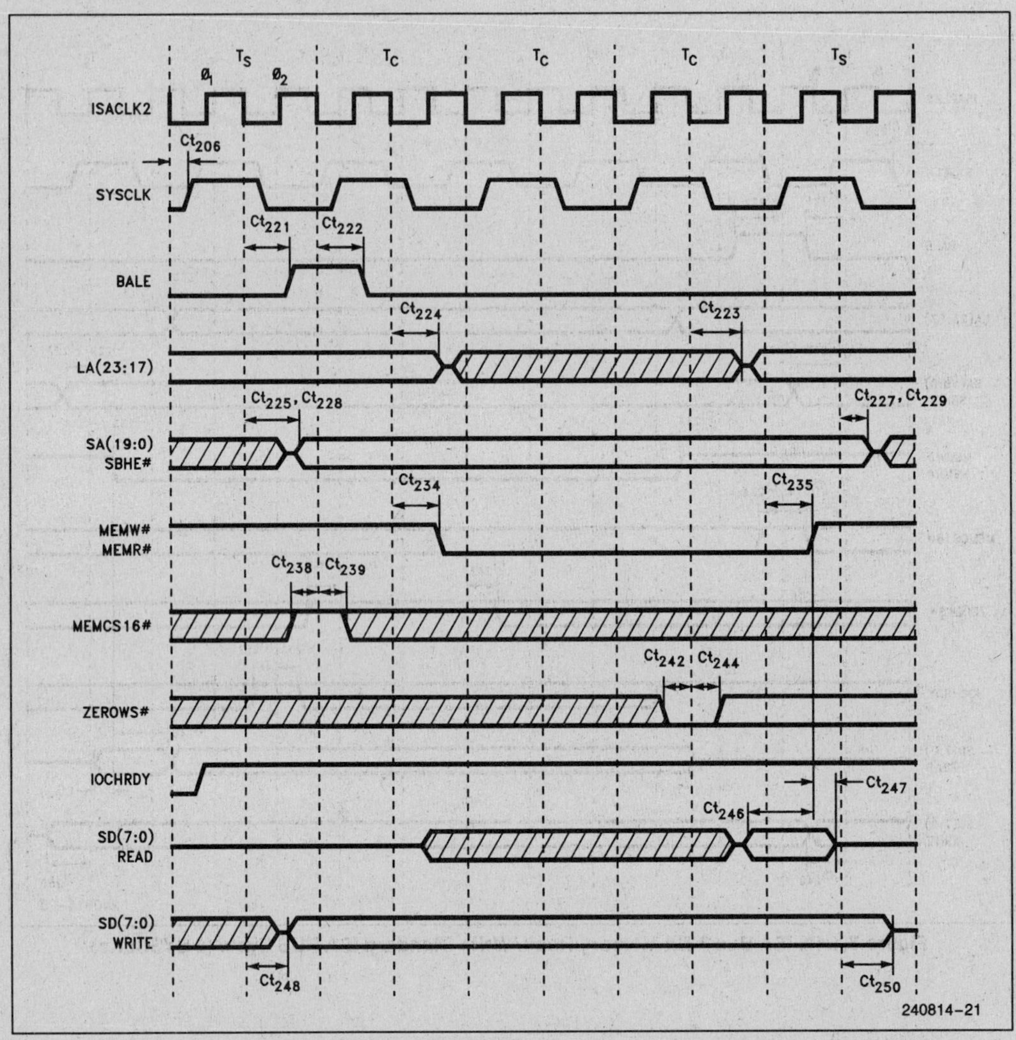

Figure 7.1.13. ISA Bus 8-Bit Memory Read/Write with ZEROWS# Asserted (3 SYSCLKs)

7.1 Intel386™ SL CPU Timing Diagrams (Continued)

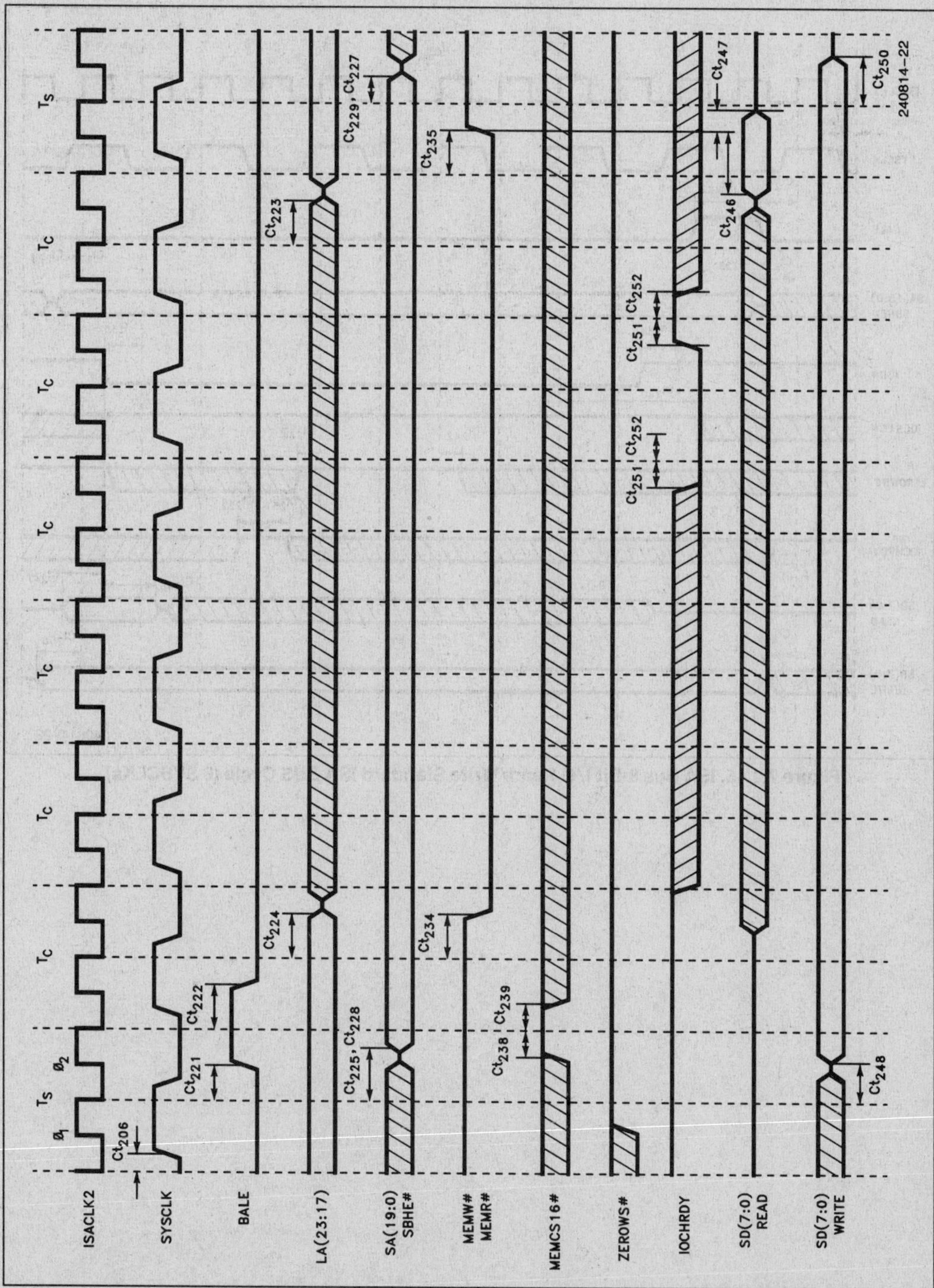

Figure 7.1.14. ISA Bus 8-Bit Memory Read/Write with IOCHRDY De-Asserted (Added Wait States)

7.1 Intel386™ SL CPU Timing Diagrams (Continued)

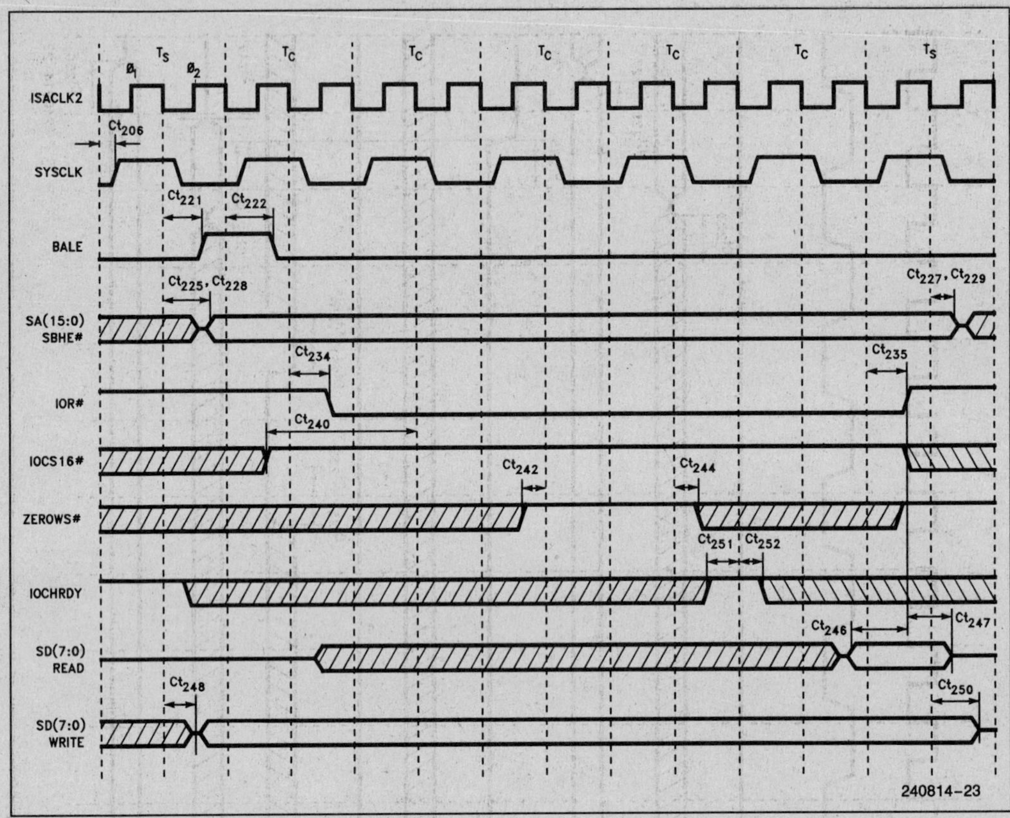

Figure 7.1.15. ISA Bus 8-Bit I/O Read/Write Standard ISA BUS Cycle (6 SYSCLKs)

7.1 Intel386™ SL CPU Timing Diagrams (Continued)

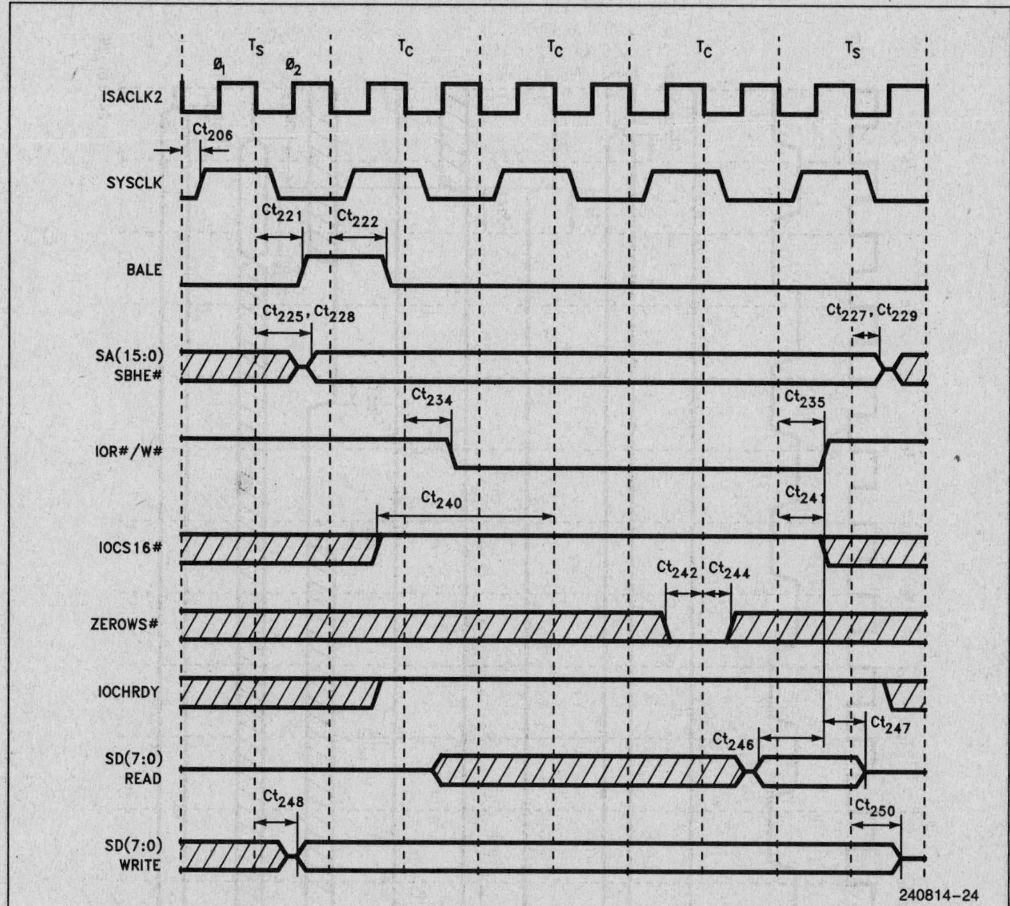

Figure 7.1.16. ISA Bus 8-Bit I/O Read/Write with ZEROWS# Asserted (3 SYSCLKs)

7.1 Intel386™ SL CPU Timing Diagrams (Continued)

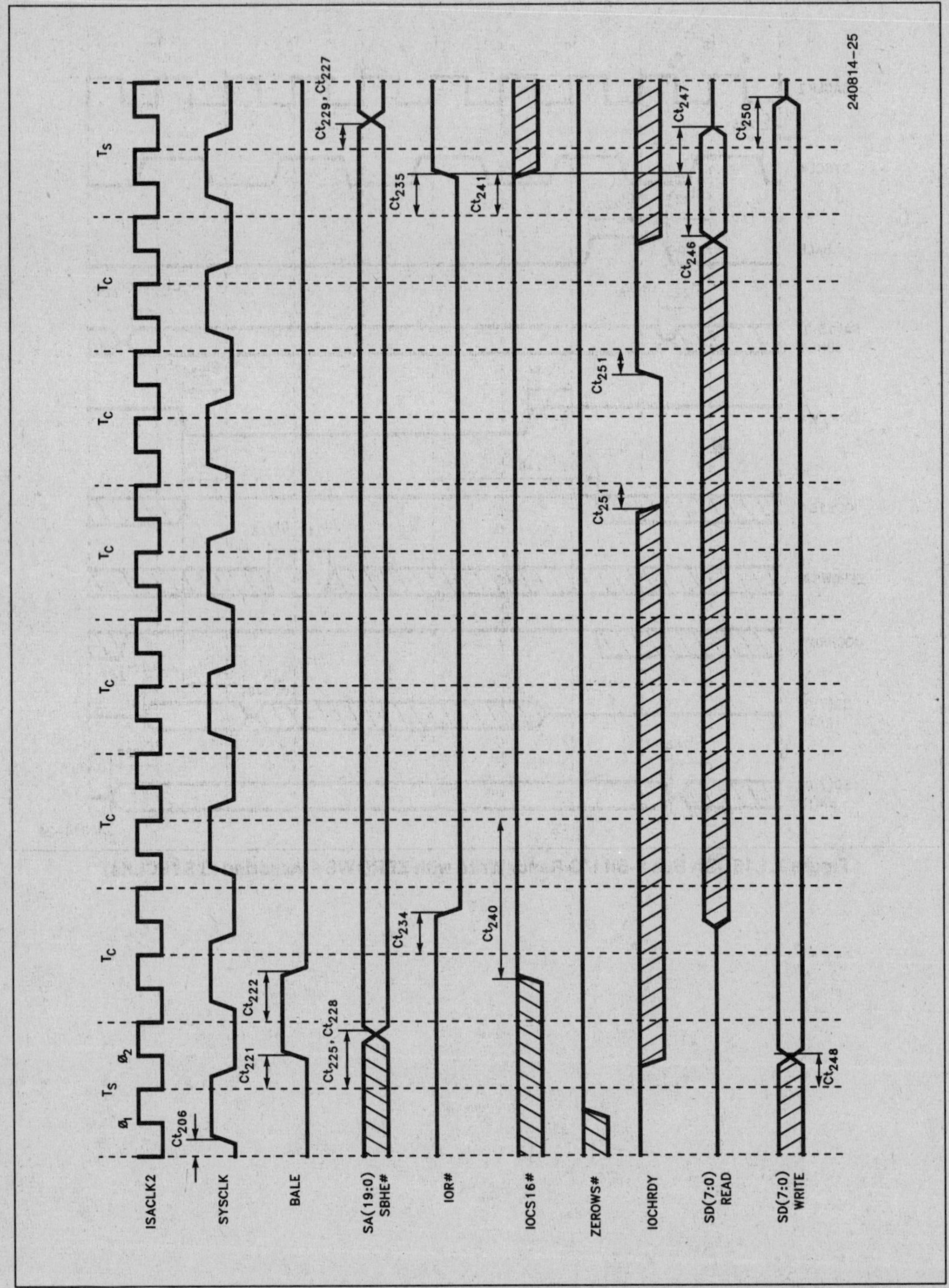

Figure 7.1.17. ISA Bus 8-Bit I/O Read/Write with IOCHRDY De-Asserted (Added Wait States)

7.1 Intel386™ SL CPU Timing Diagrams (Continued)

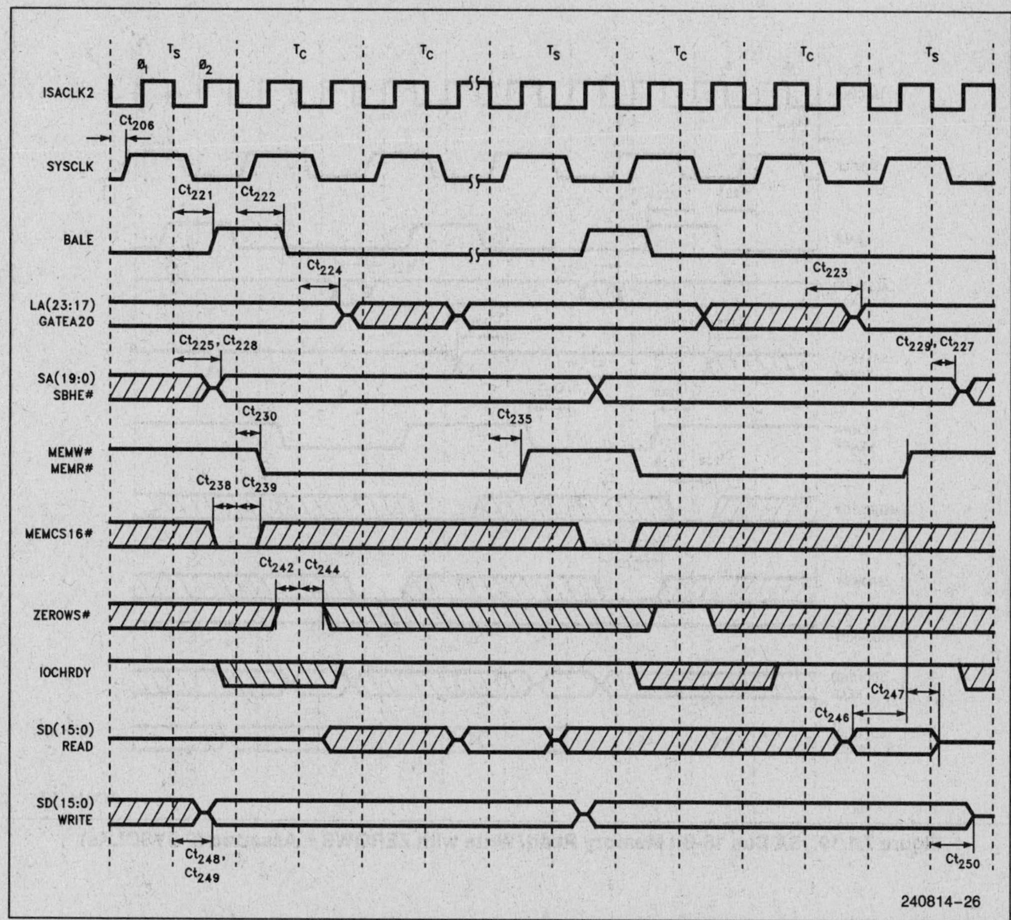

Figure 7.1.18. ISA Bus 16-Bit Memory Read/Write Standard ISA BUS Cycle (3 SYSCLKs)

7.1 Intel386™ SL CPU Timing Diagrams (Continued)

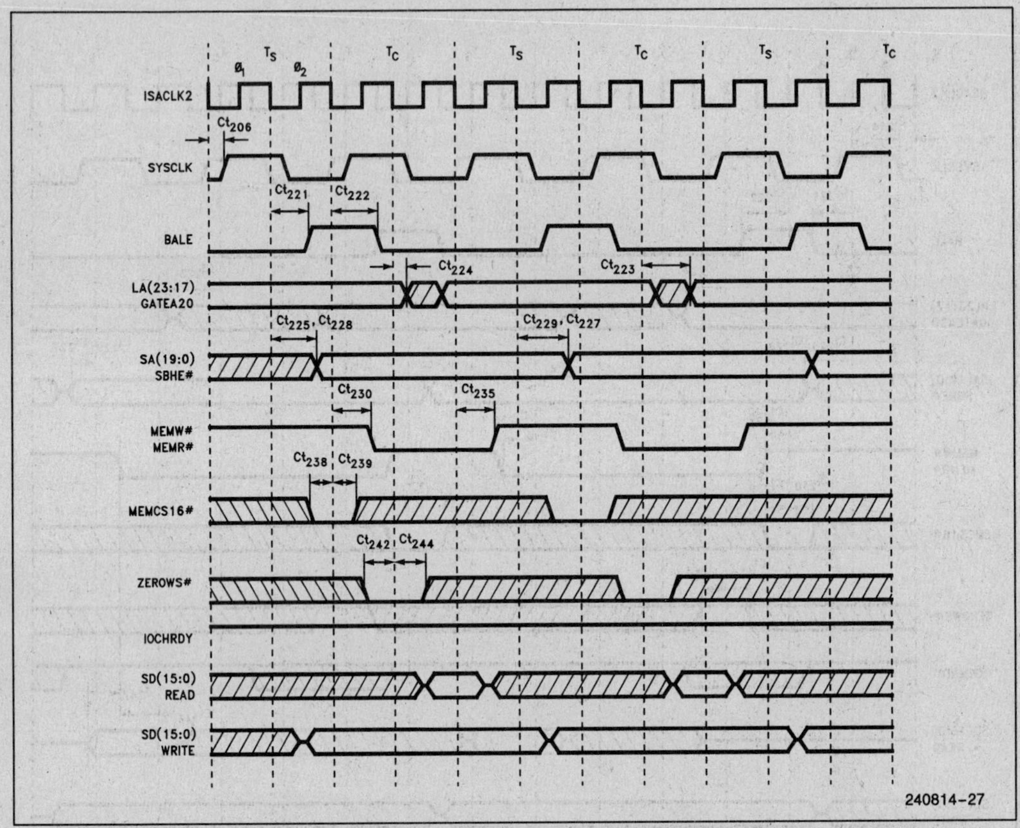

Figure 7.1.19. ISA Bus 16-Bit Memory Read/Write with ZEROWS# Asserted (2 SYSCLKs)

7.1 Intel386™ SL CPU Timing Diagrams (Continued)

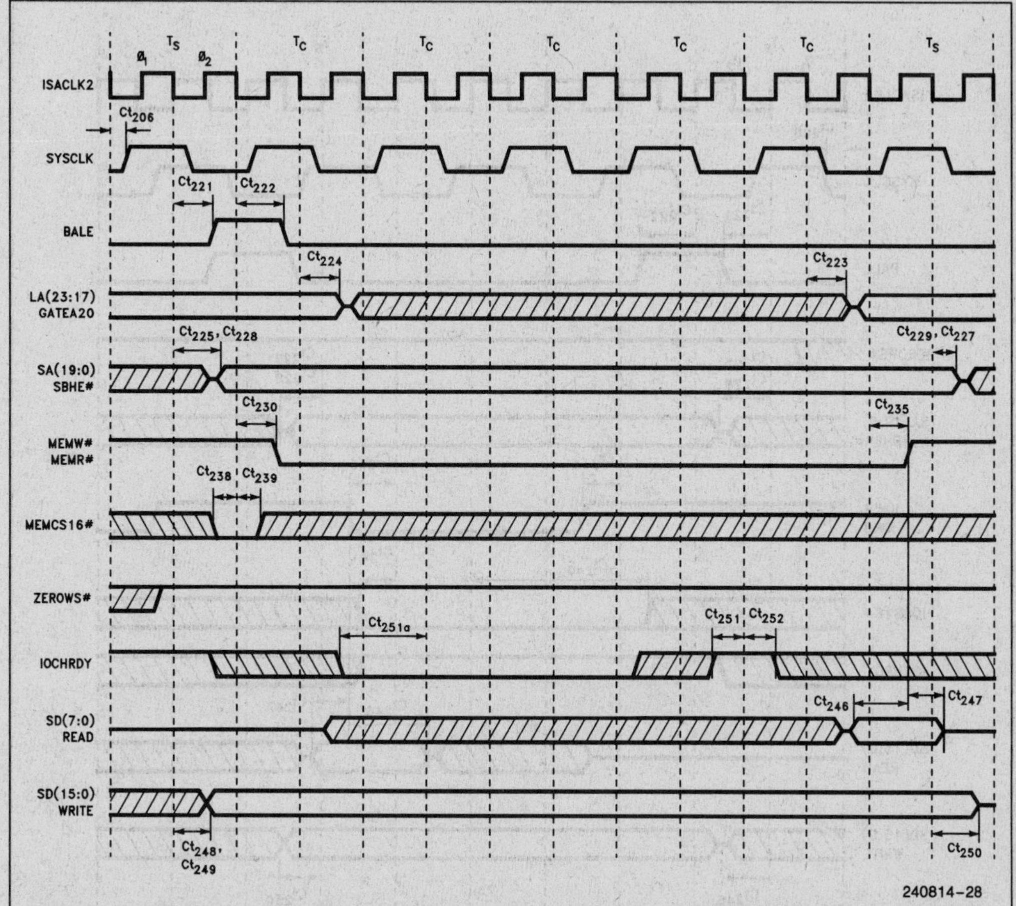

Figure 7.1.20. ISA Bus 16-Bit Memory Read/Write with IOCHRDY De-Asserted (Added Wait States)

4

7.1 Intel386™ SL CPU Timing Diagrams (Continued)

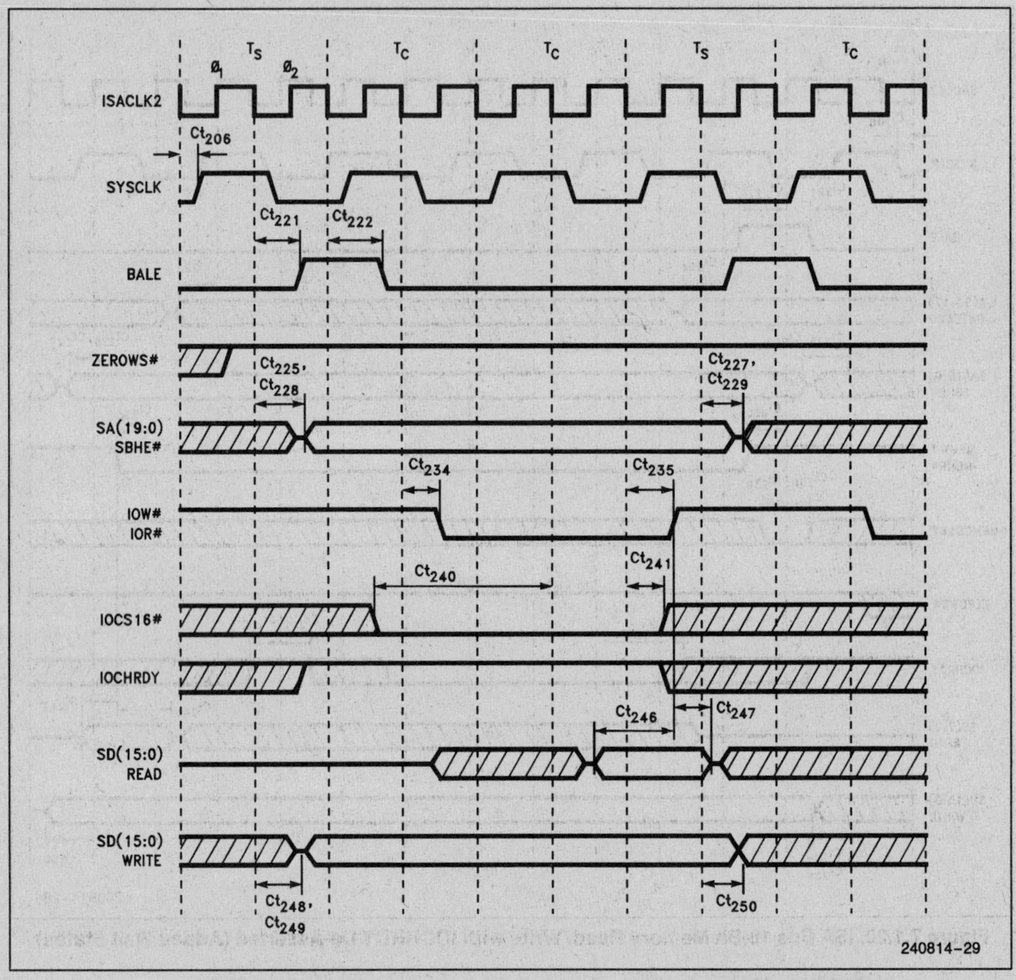

Figure 7.1.21. ISA Bus 16-Bit I/O Read/Write Standard ISA BUS Cycle (3 SYSCLKs)

7.1 Intel386™ SL CPU Timing Diagrams (Continued)

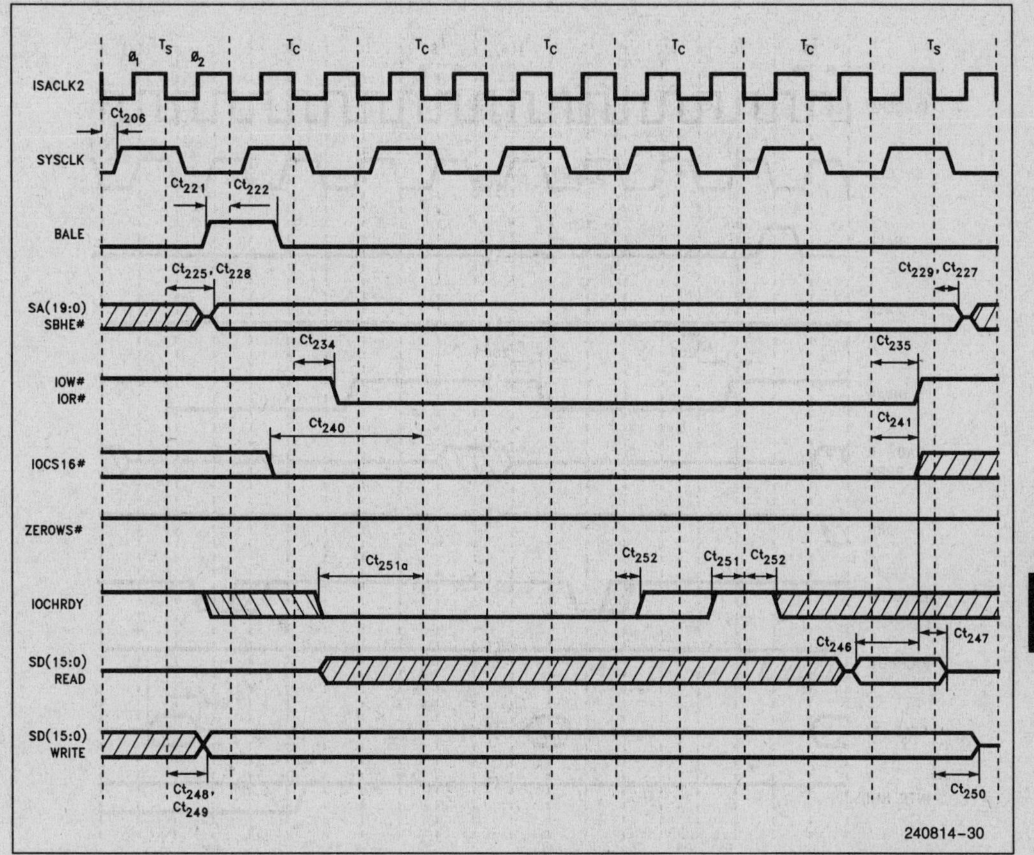

Figure 7.1.22. ISA Bus 16-Bit I/O Read/Write with IOCHRDY De-Asserted (Added Wait States)

7.1 Intel386™ SL CPU Timing Diagrams (Continued)

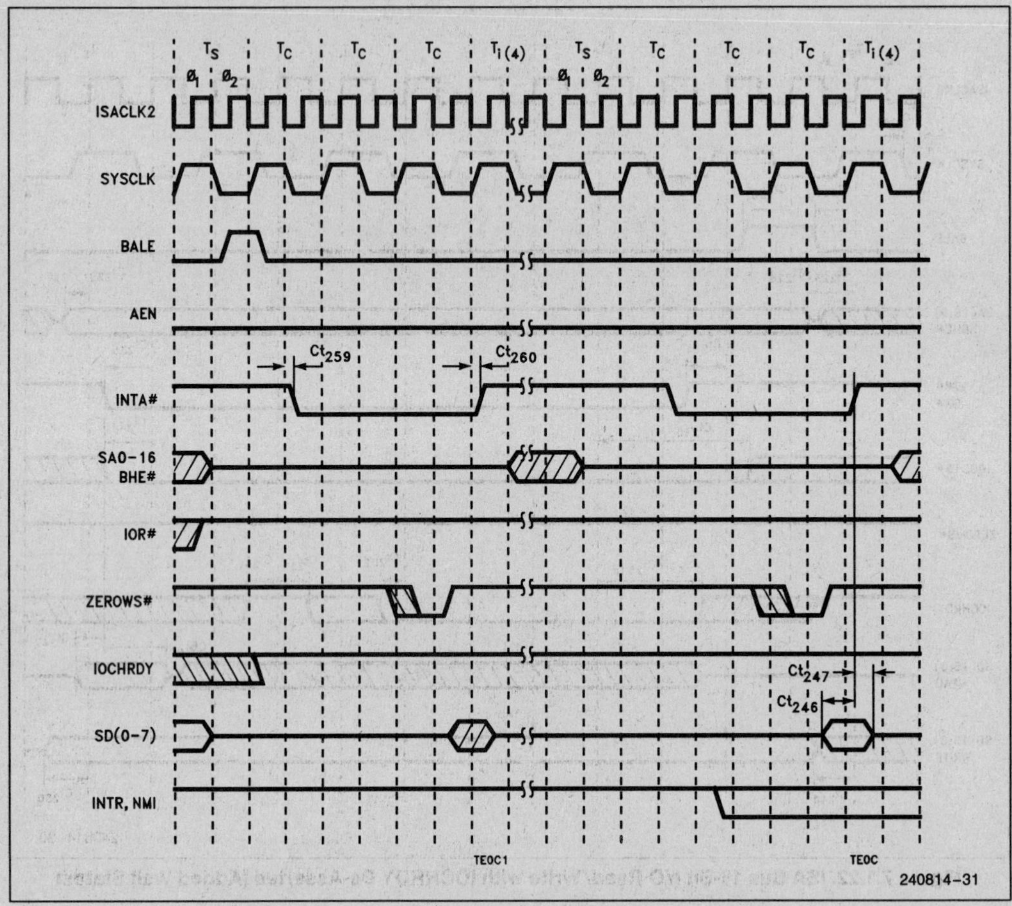

Figure 7.1.23. ISA Bus Interrupt Acknowledge Bus Cycle

7.1 Intel386™ SL CPU Timing Diagrams (Continued)

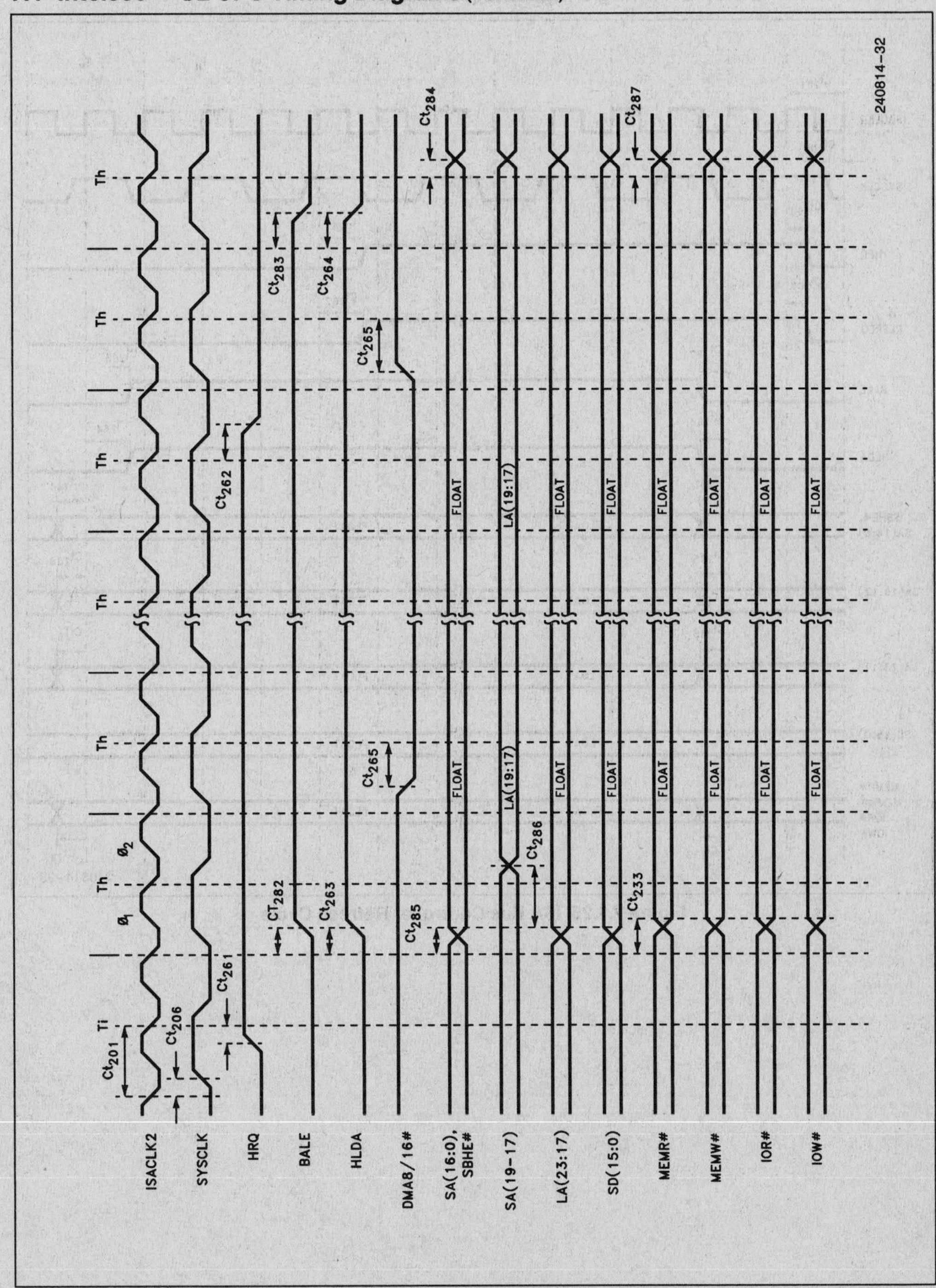

Figure 7.1.24. ISA Bus Controller DMA Cycle

7.1 Intel386™ SL CPU Timing Diagrams (Continued)

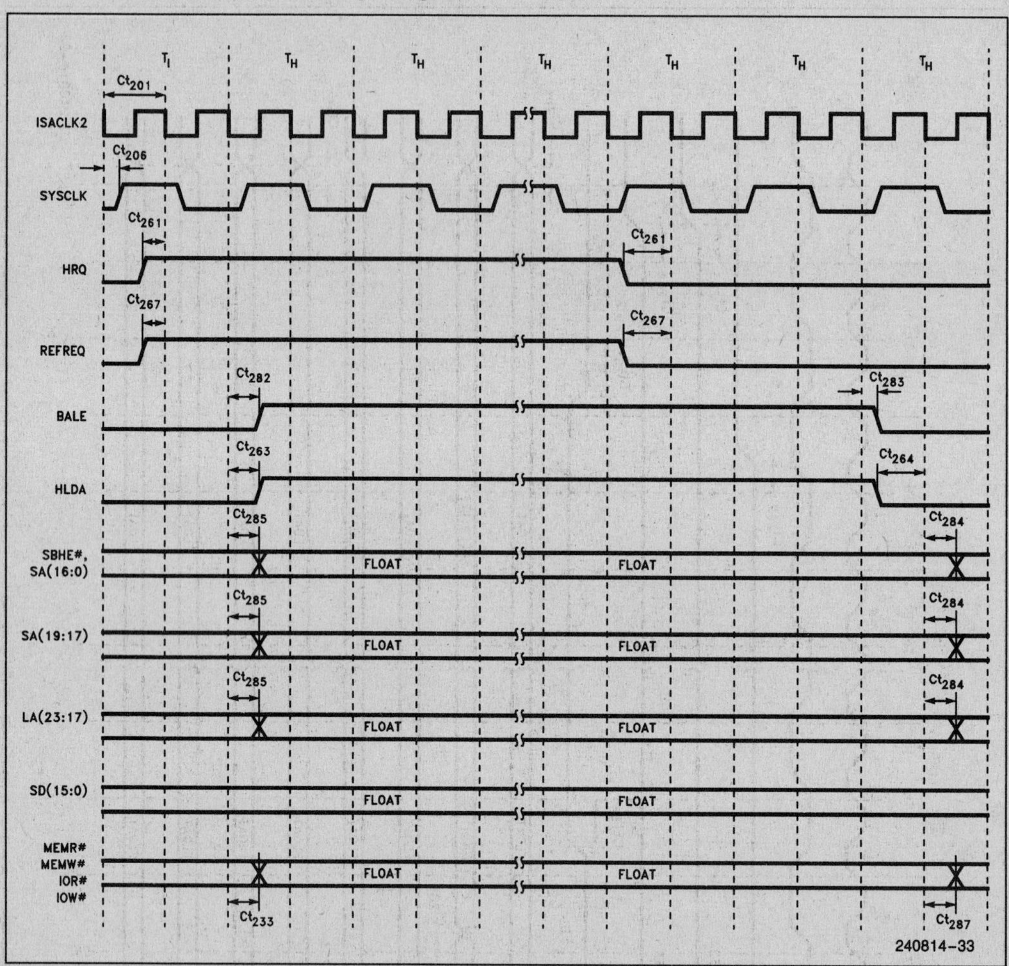

Figure 7.1.25. ISA Bus Controller Refresh Cycle

7.1 Intel386™ SL CPU Timing Diagrams (Continued)

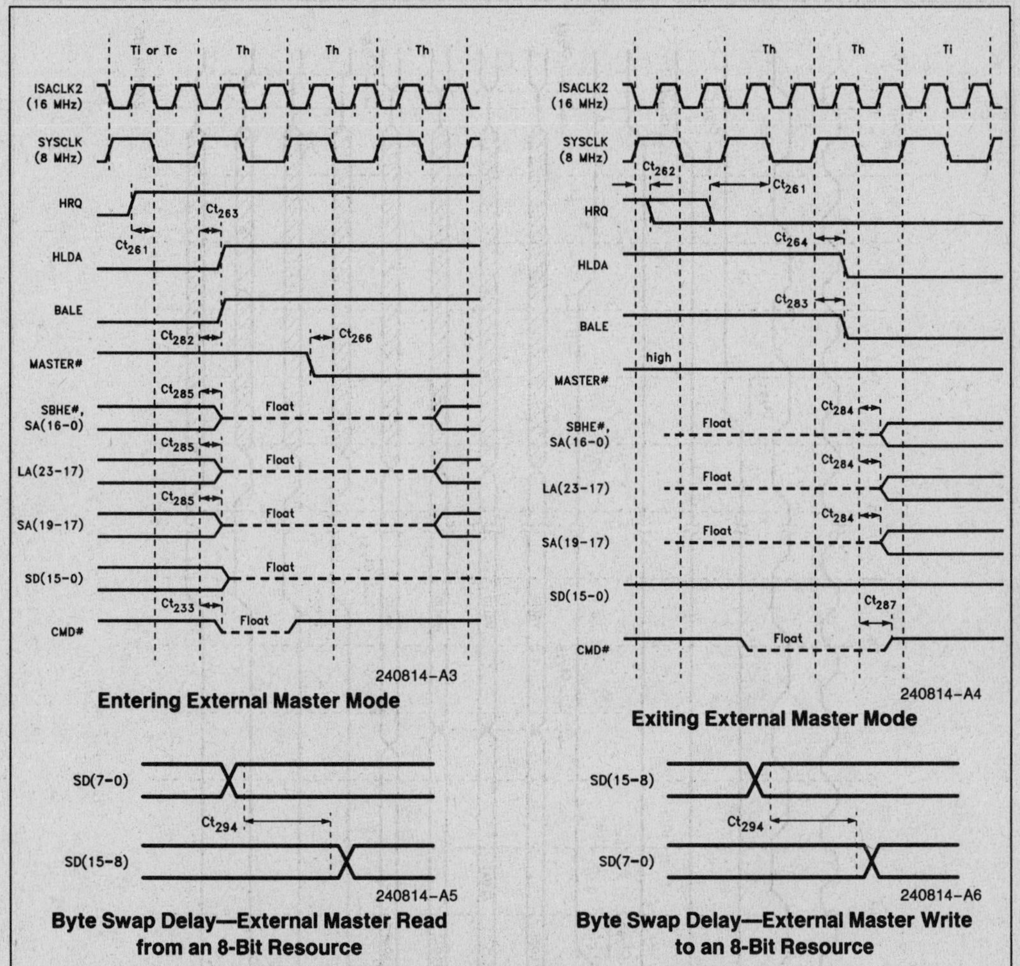

Figure 7.1.26. ISA Bus External Bus Master

4

7.1 Intel386™ SL CPU Timing Diagrams (Continued)

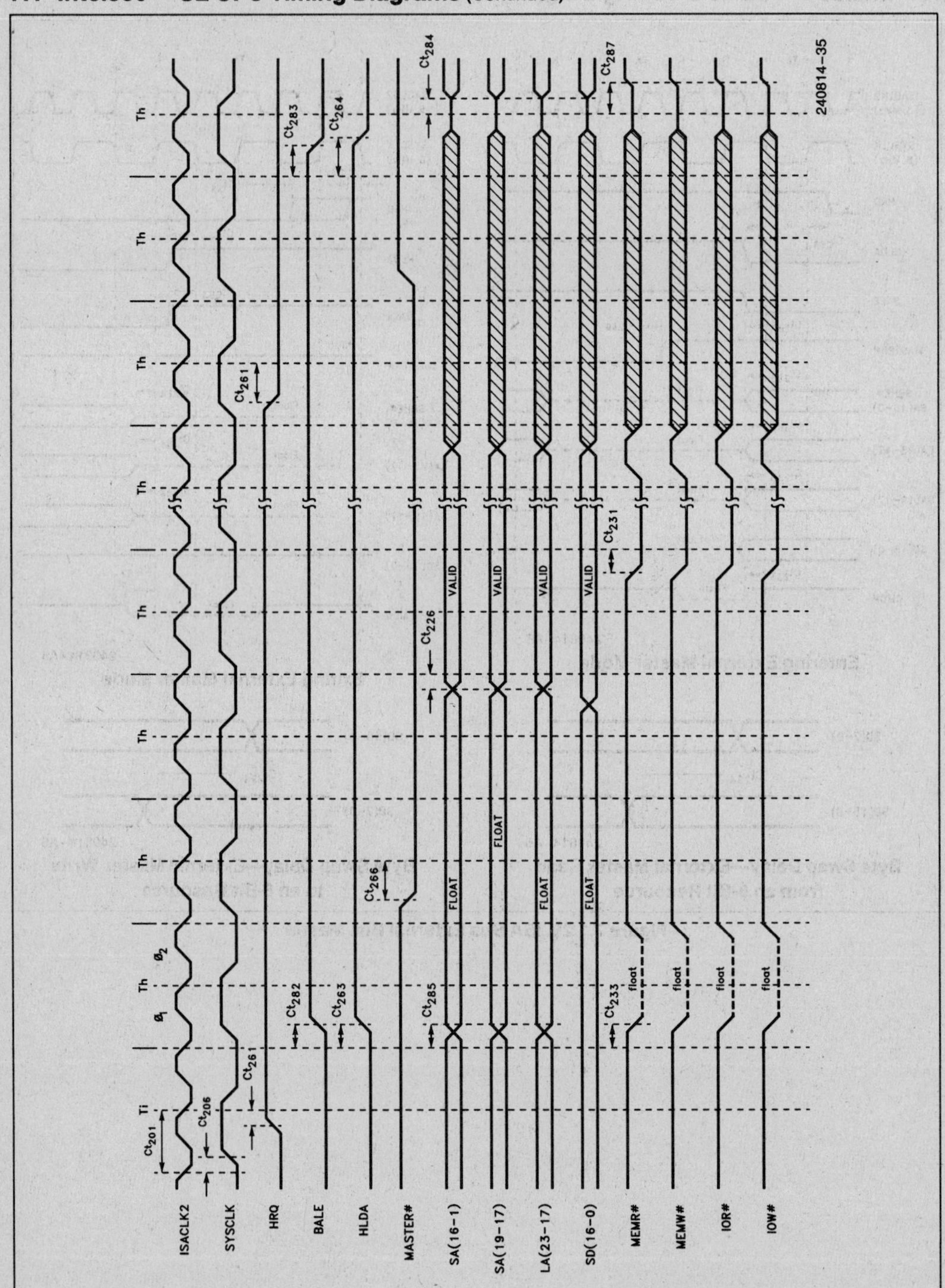

Figure 7.1.27. ISA Bus External Bus Master to Off-Board I/O Ports (No Byte-Swapping)

7.1 Intel386™ SL CPU Timing Diagrams (Continued)

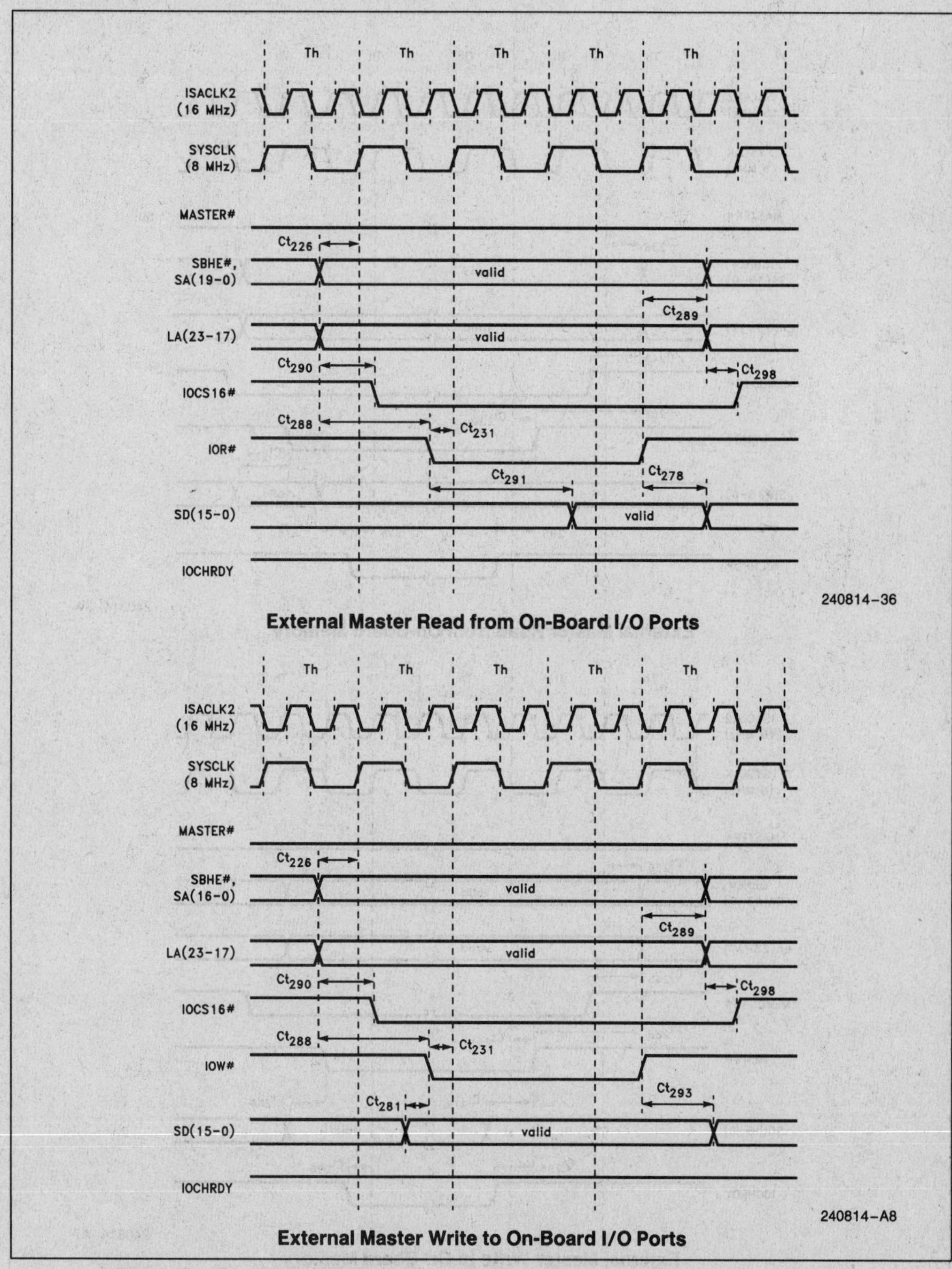

Figure 7.1.28a. ISA Bus External Bus Master to On-Board I/O Ports (Read/Write)

4

7.1 Intel386™ SL CPU Timing Diagrams (Continued)

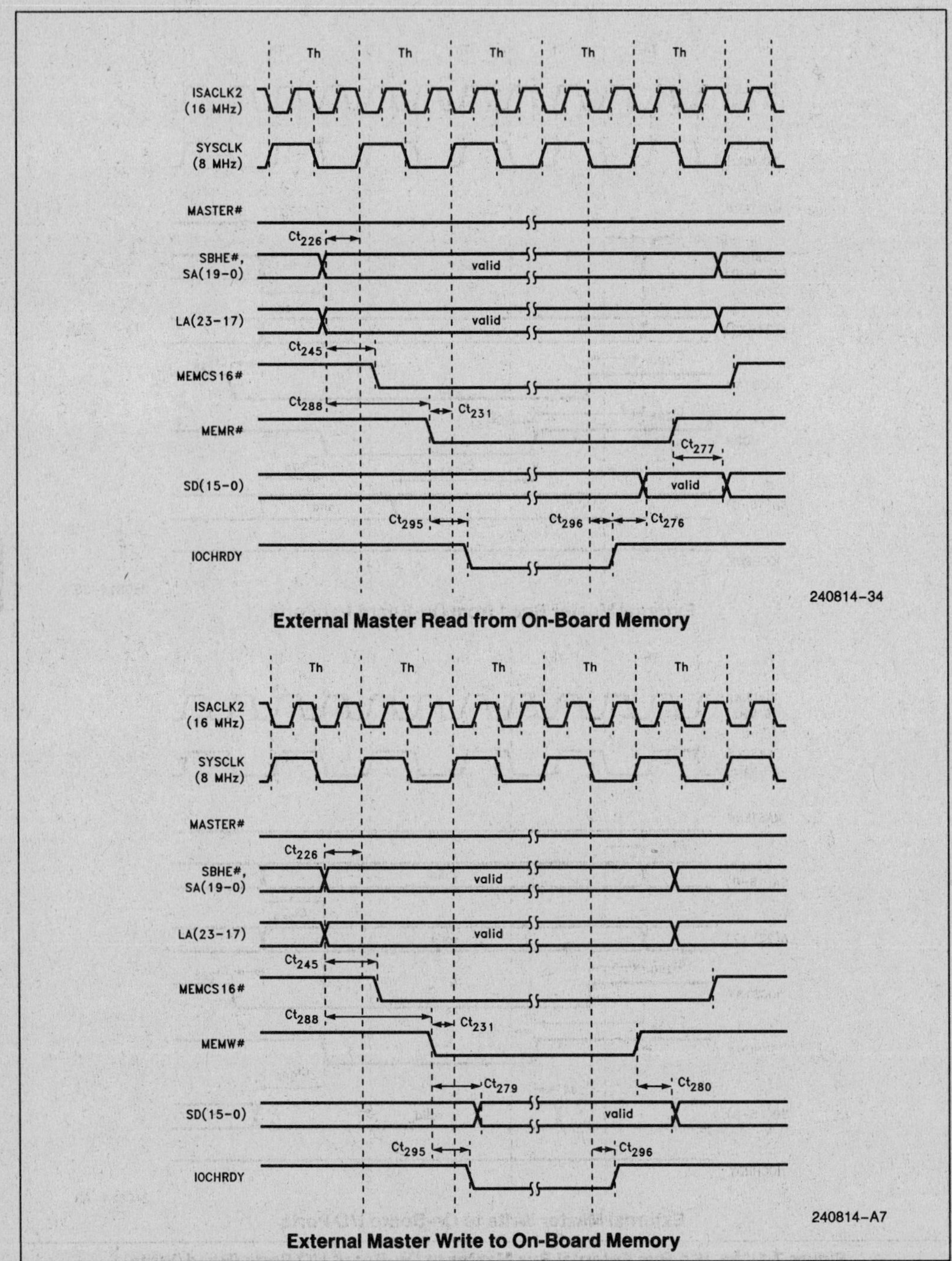

External Master Read from On-Board Memory

External Master Write to On-Board Memory

Figure 7.1.28b. ISA Bus External Bus Master Accesses to On-Board Memory

7.1 Intel386™ SL CPU Timing Diagrams (Continued)

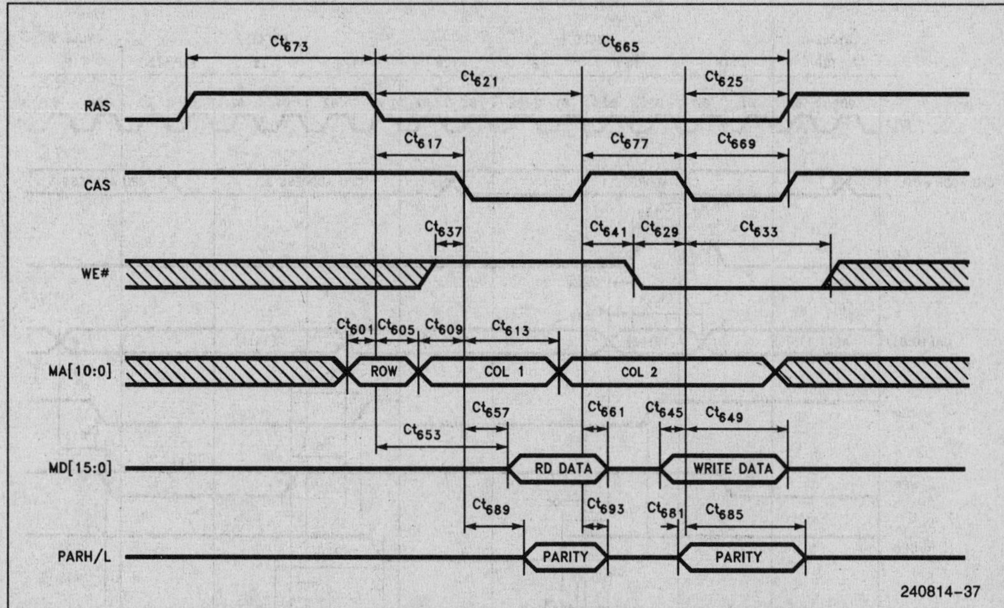

Figure 7.1.29. Intel386™ SL CPU Memory Controller Timings (DRAM Timing Parameters)

7.1 Intel386™ SL CPU Timing Diagrams (Continued)

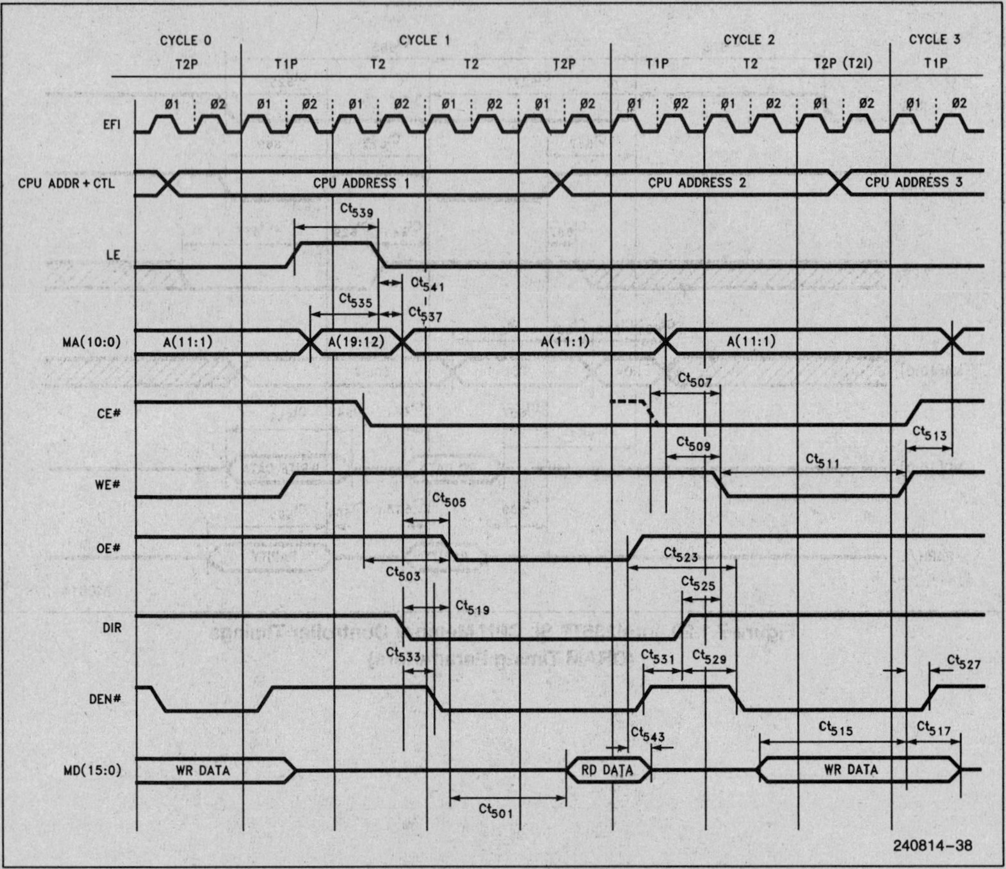

240814-38

Figure 7.1.30. Intel386™ SL CPU Memory Controller Timings (SRAM Mode Timing Parameters; 2 Wait States)

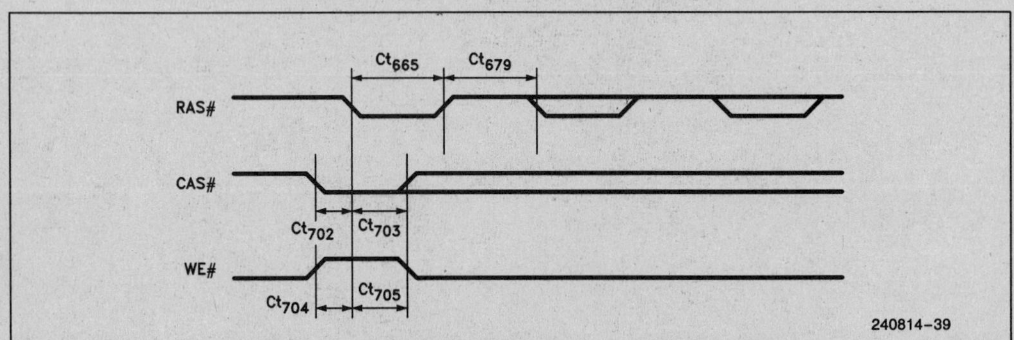

Figure 7.1.31. Intel386™ SL CPU Memory Controller Timings (CAS# before RAS# Refresh Timings)

7.1 Intel386™ SL CPU Timing Diagrams (Continued)

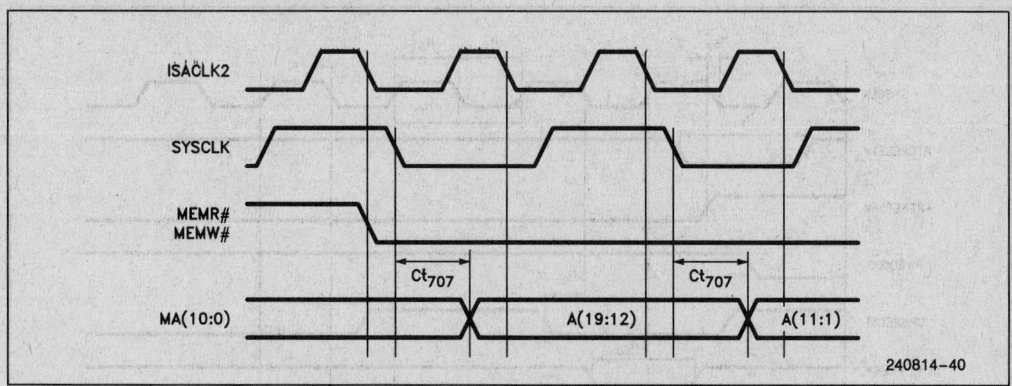

Figure 7.1.32. REFRESH, DMA/MASTER Timing Diagrams (Address Active Delay from SYSCLK)

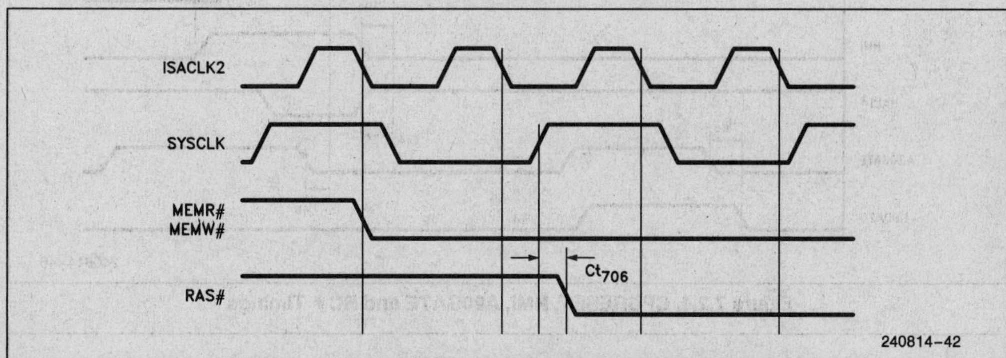

Figure 7.1.33. REFRESH, DMA/MASTER Timing Diagrams (RAS# Active Delay from SYSCLK)

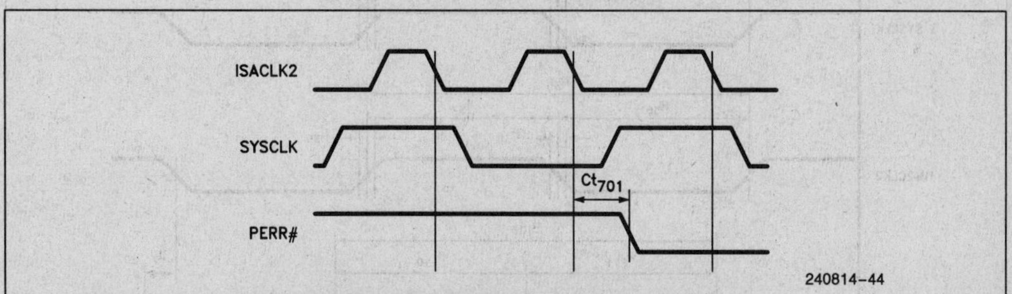

Figure 7.1.34. PERROR Timing Diagram (PERR# Active Delay from SYSCLK)

7.2 82360SL Timing Diagrams

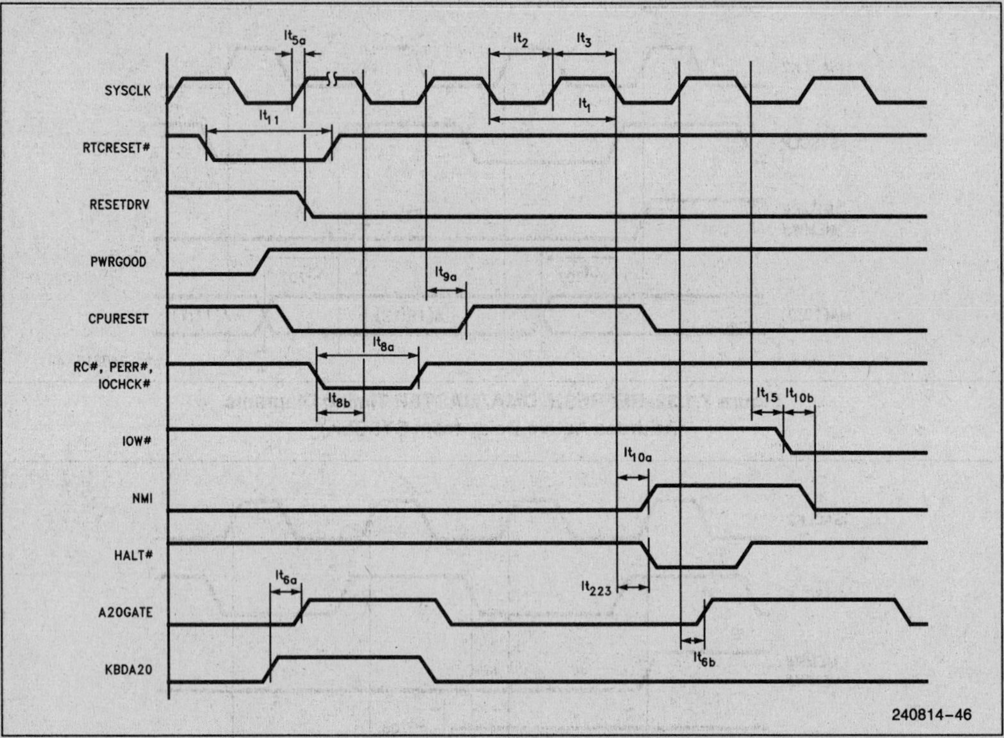

240814-46

Figure 7.2.1. CPURESET, NMI, A20GATE and RC# Timings

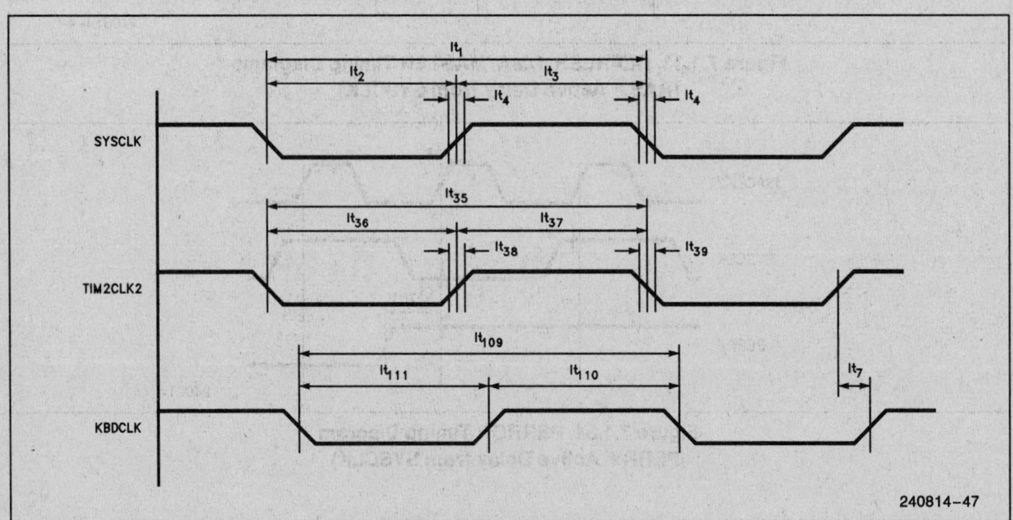

Figure 7.2.2. Clock Timings

7.2 82360SL Timing Diagrams (Continued)

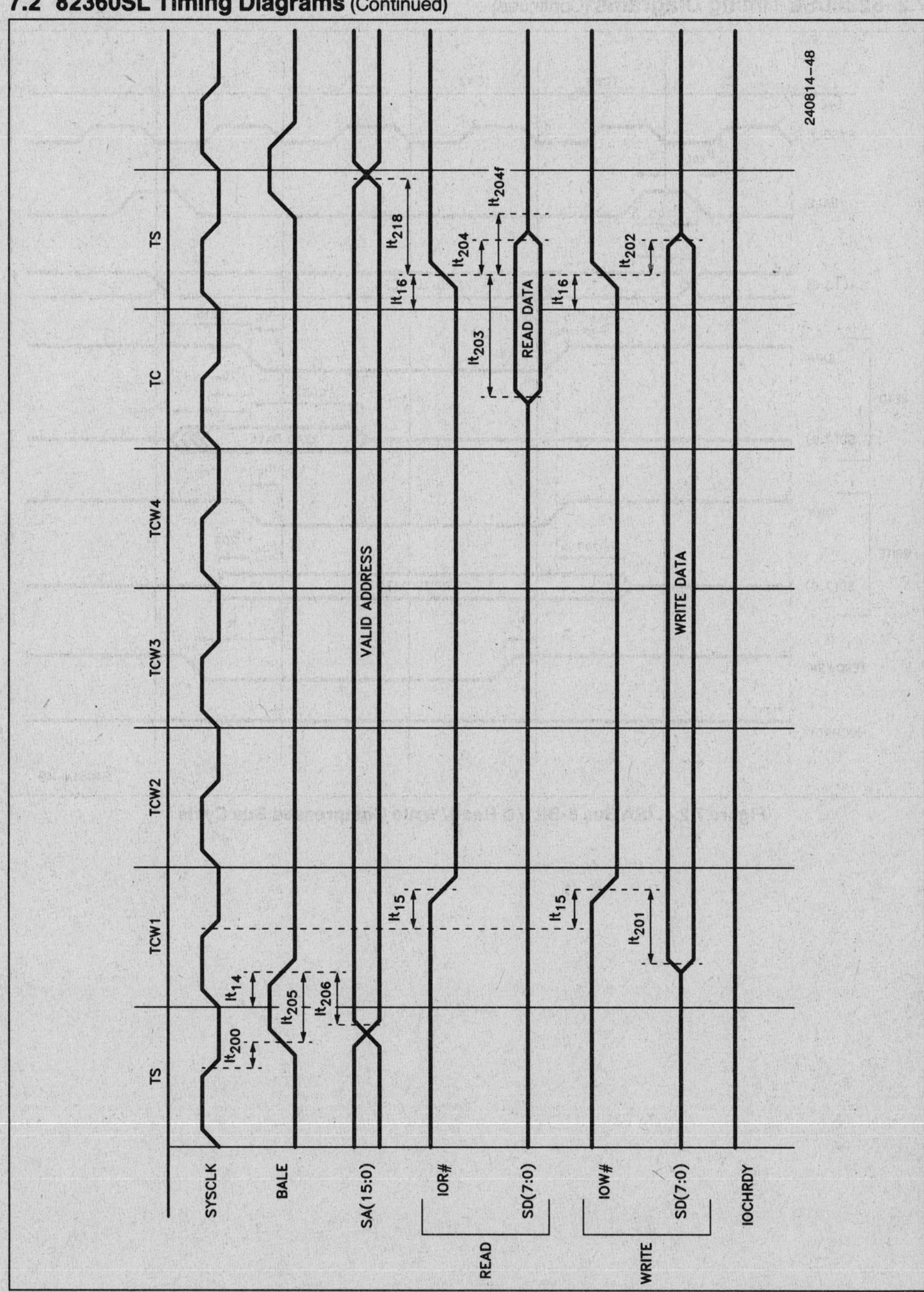

Figure 7.2.3. ISA Bus 8-Bit I/O Read/Write Default Bus Cycle (6 SYSCLKs)

7.2 82360SL Timing Diagrams (Continued)

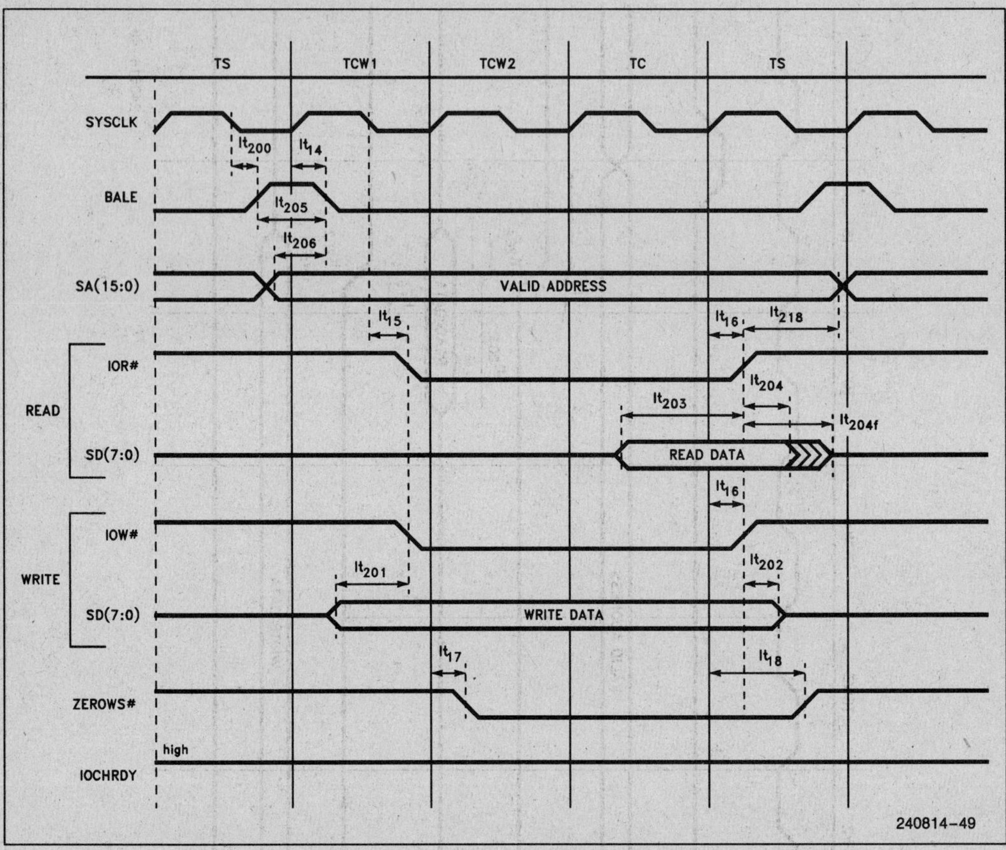

Figure 7.2.4. ISA Bus 8-Bit I/O Read/Write Compressed Bus Cycle

7.2 82360SL Timing Diagrams (Continued)

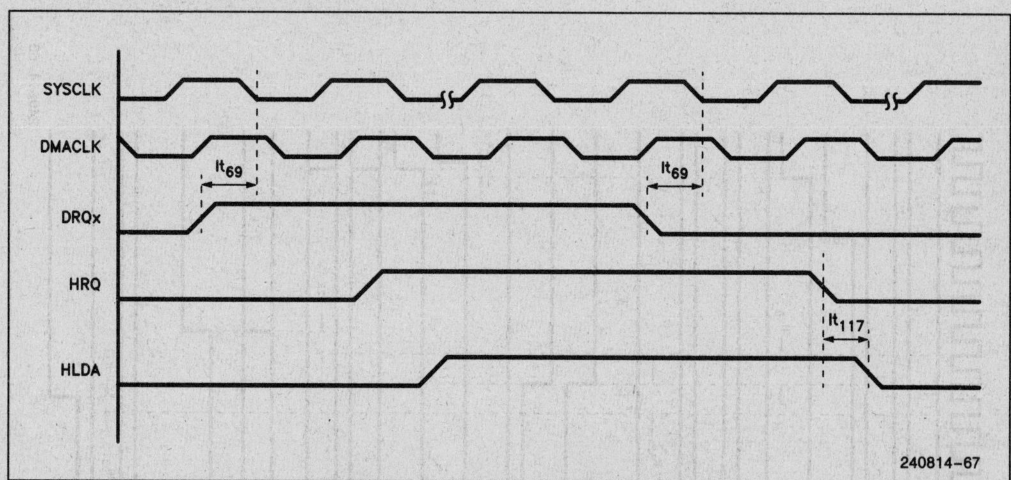

Figure 7.2.5. DMA Controller Timings

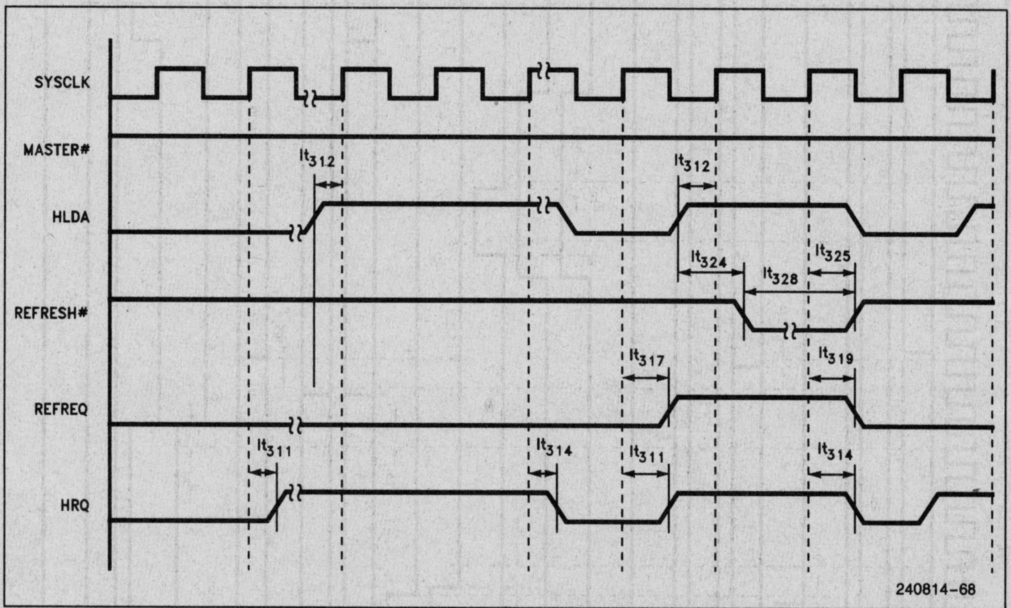

Figure 7.2.6. Refresh Arbitration Timings

4

7.2 82360SL Timing Diagrams (Continued)

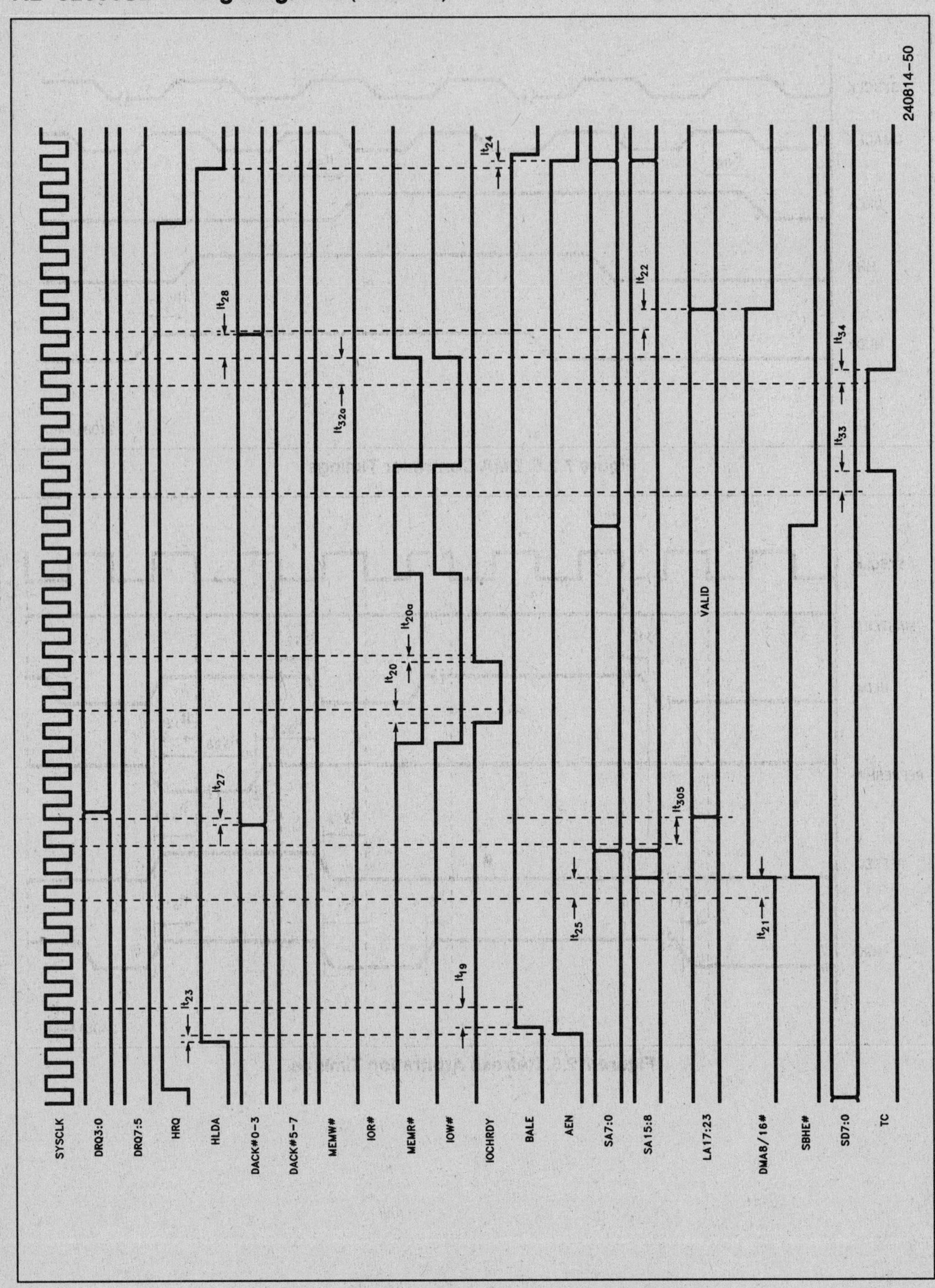

Figure 7.2.7. DMA Memory Read Timings (4 MHz)

7.2 82360SL Timing Diagrams (Continued)

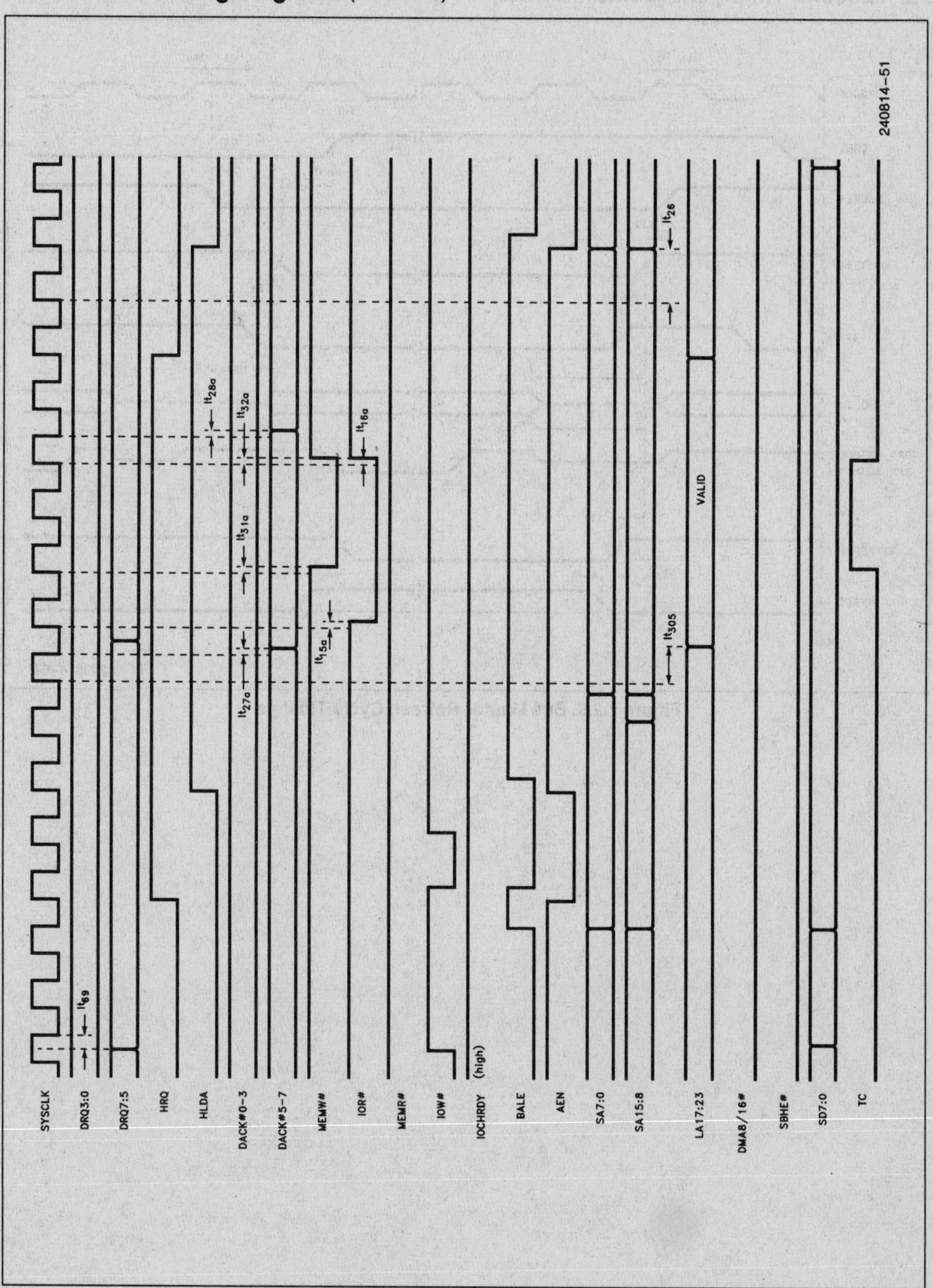

Figure 7.2.8. DMA Memory Write Timings (8 MHz)

7.2 82360SL Timing Diagrams (Continued)

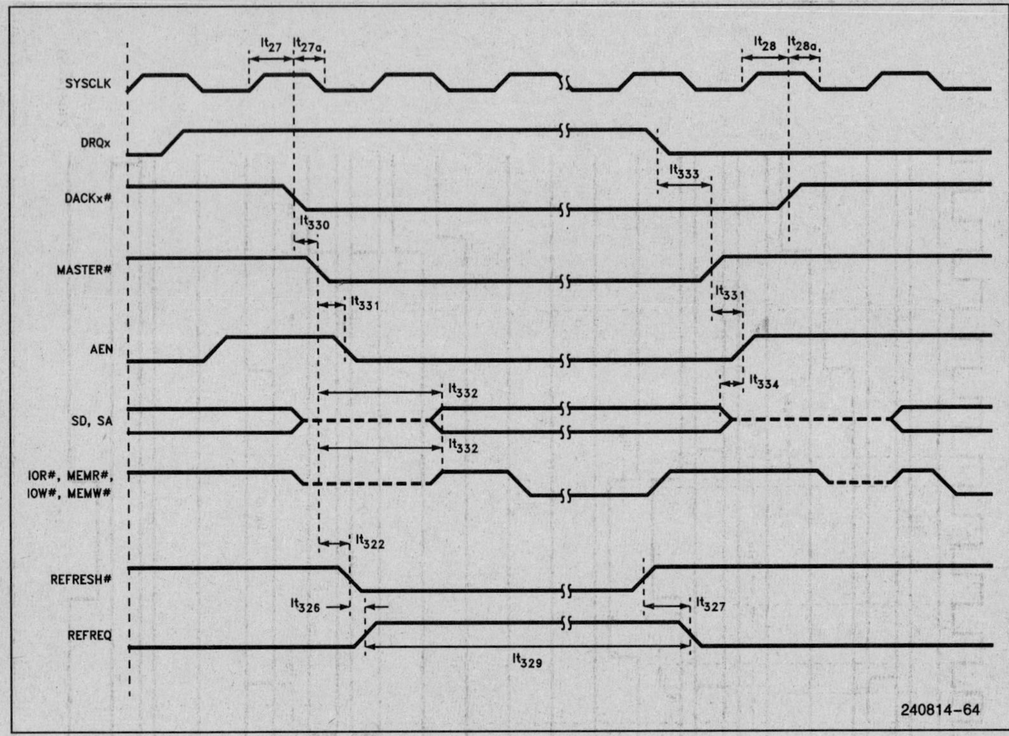

Figure 7.2.9. Bus Master Refresh Cycle Timings

7.2 82360SL Timing Diagrams (Continued)

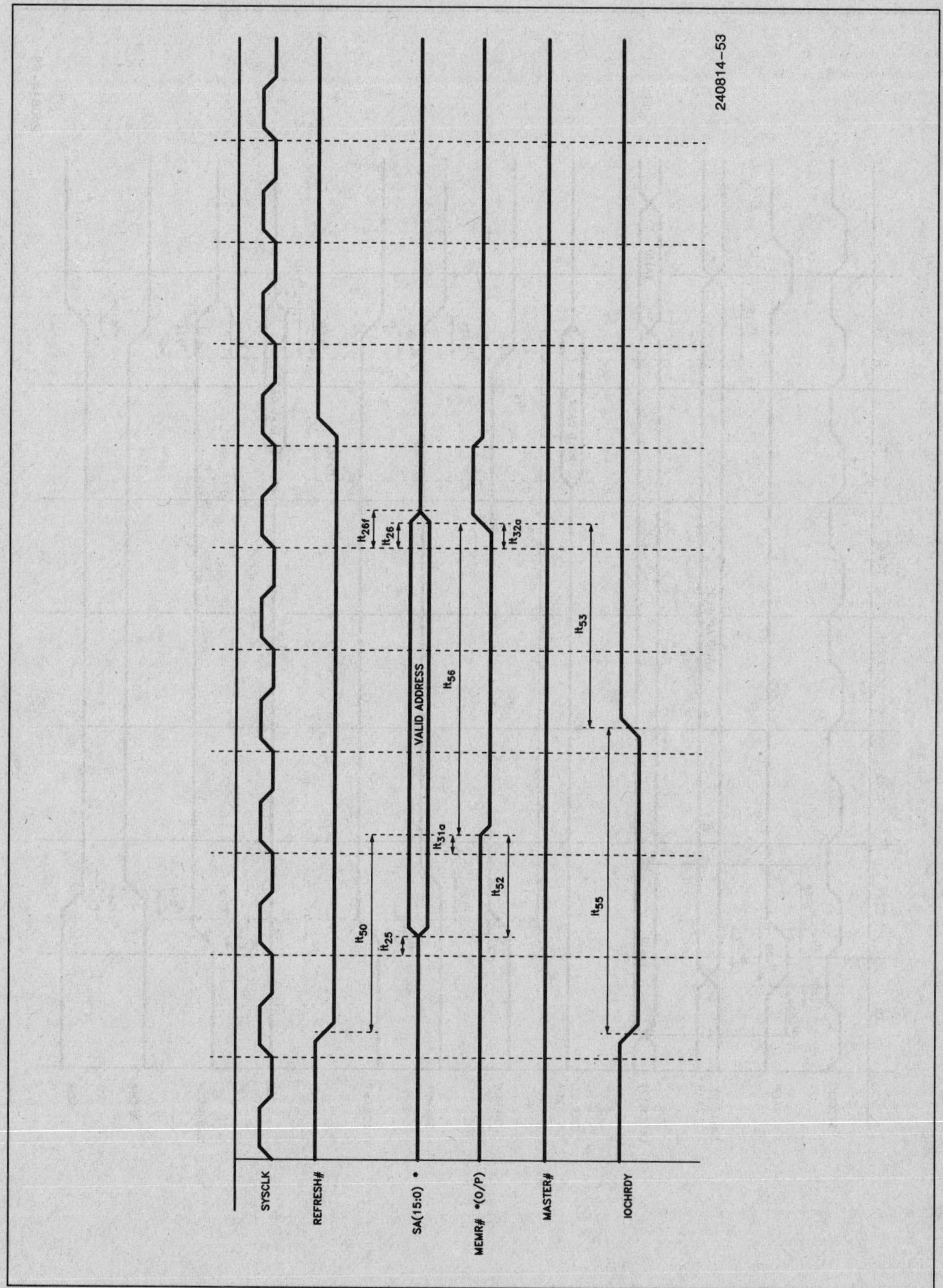

Figure 7.2.10. ISA Bus Master Refresh Cycle with IOCHRDY Timings

7.2 82360SL Timing Diagrams (Continued)

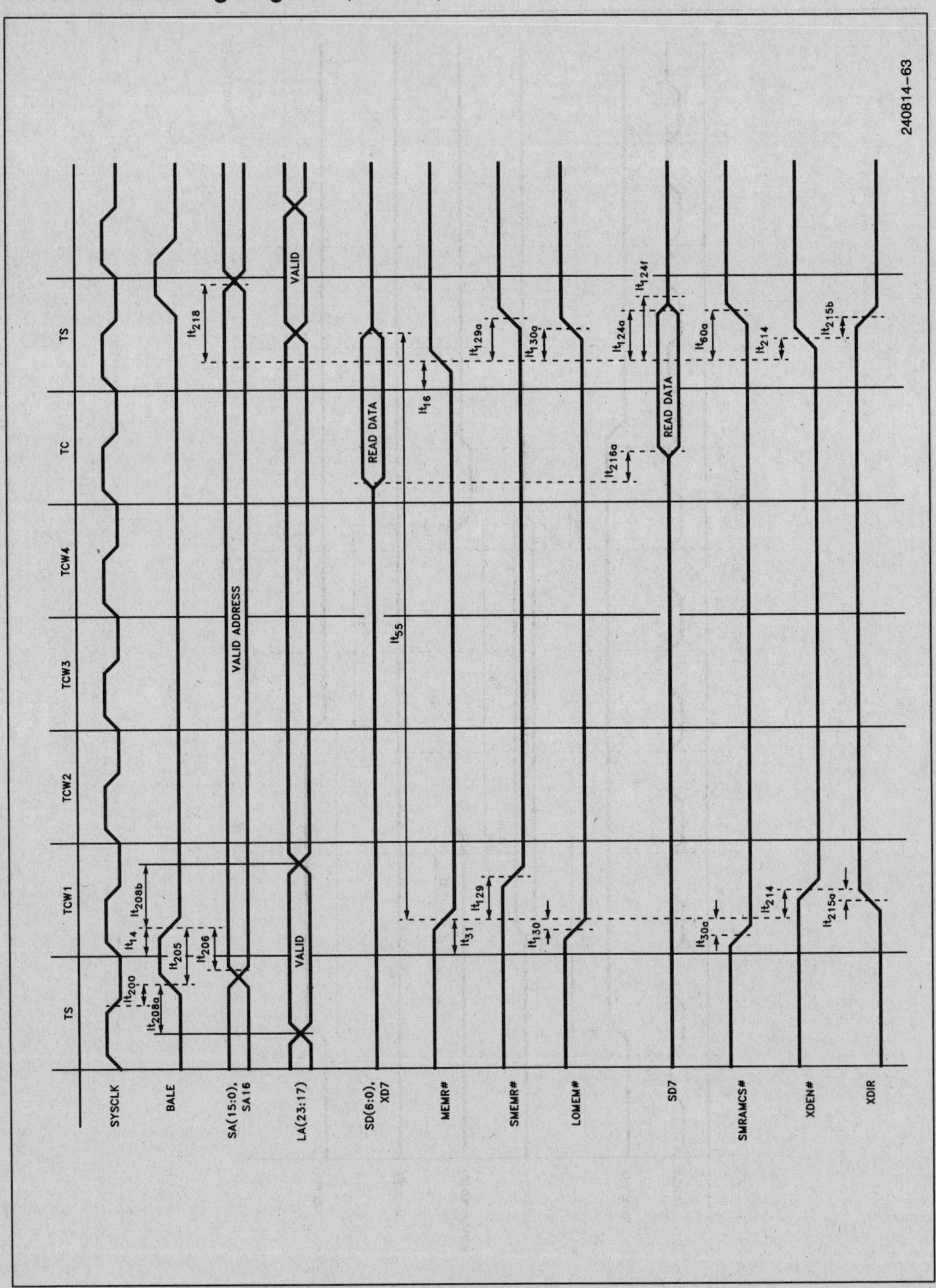

Figure 7.2.11. X-Bus Control Signals—Memory Read Timings

7.2 82360SL Timing Diagrams (Continued)

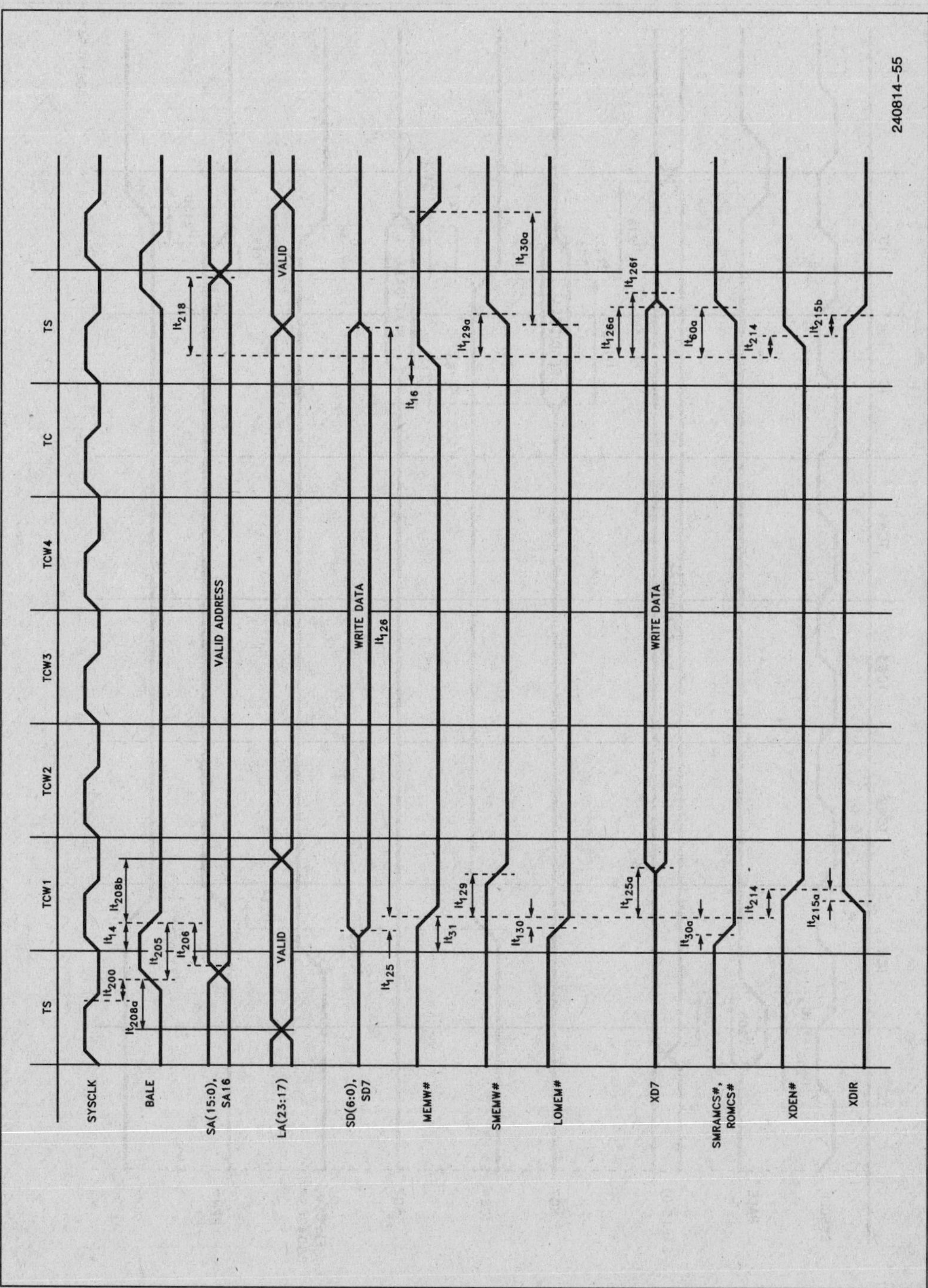

Figure 7.2.12. X-Bus Control Signals—Memory Write Timings

7.2 82360SL Timing Diagrams (Continued)

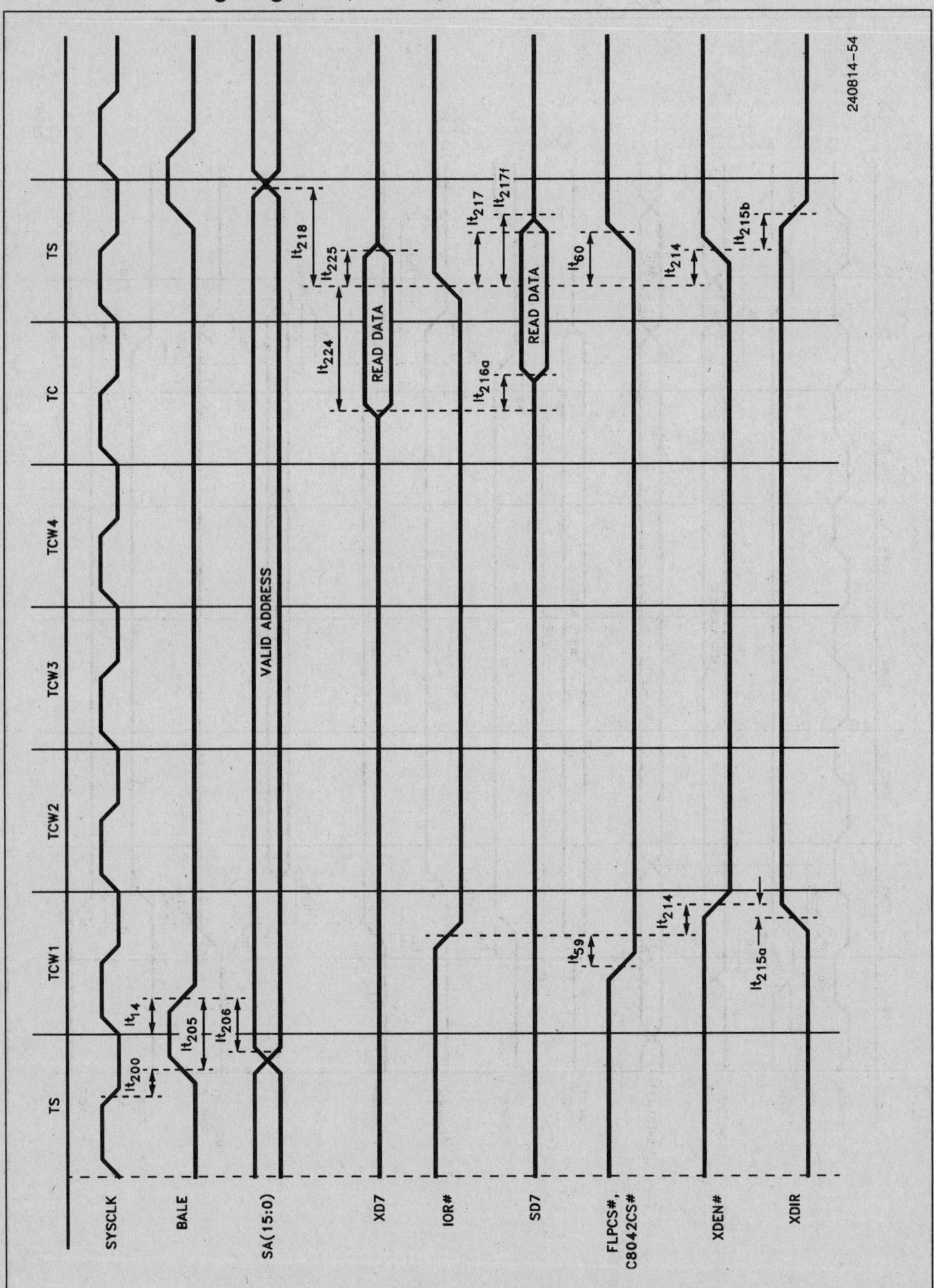

Figure 7.2.13. X-Bus Control Signals—I/O Read Timings

7.2 82360SL Timing Diagrams (Continued)

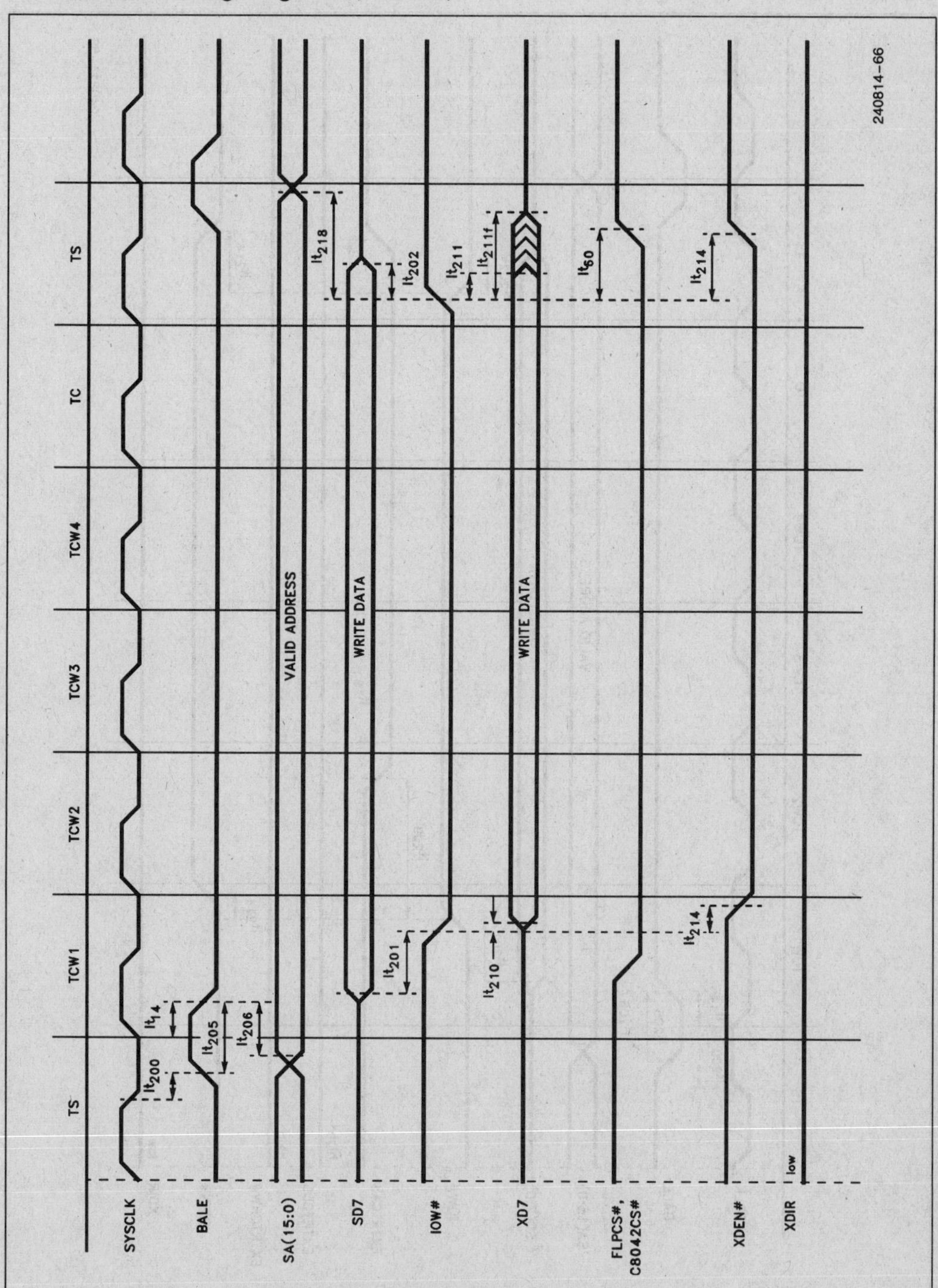

Figure 7.2.14. X-Bus Control Signals—I/O Write Timings

7.2 82360SL Timing Diagrams (Continued)

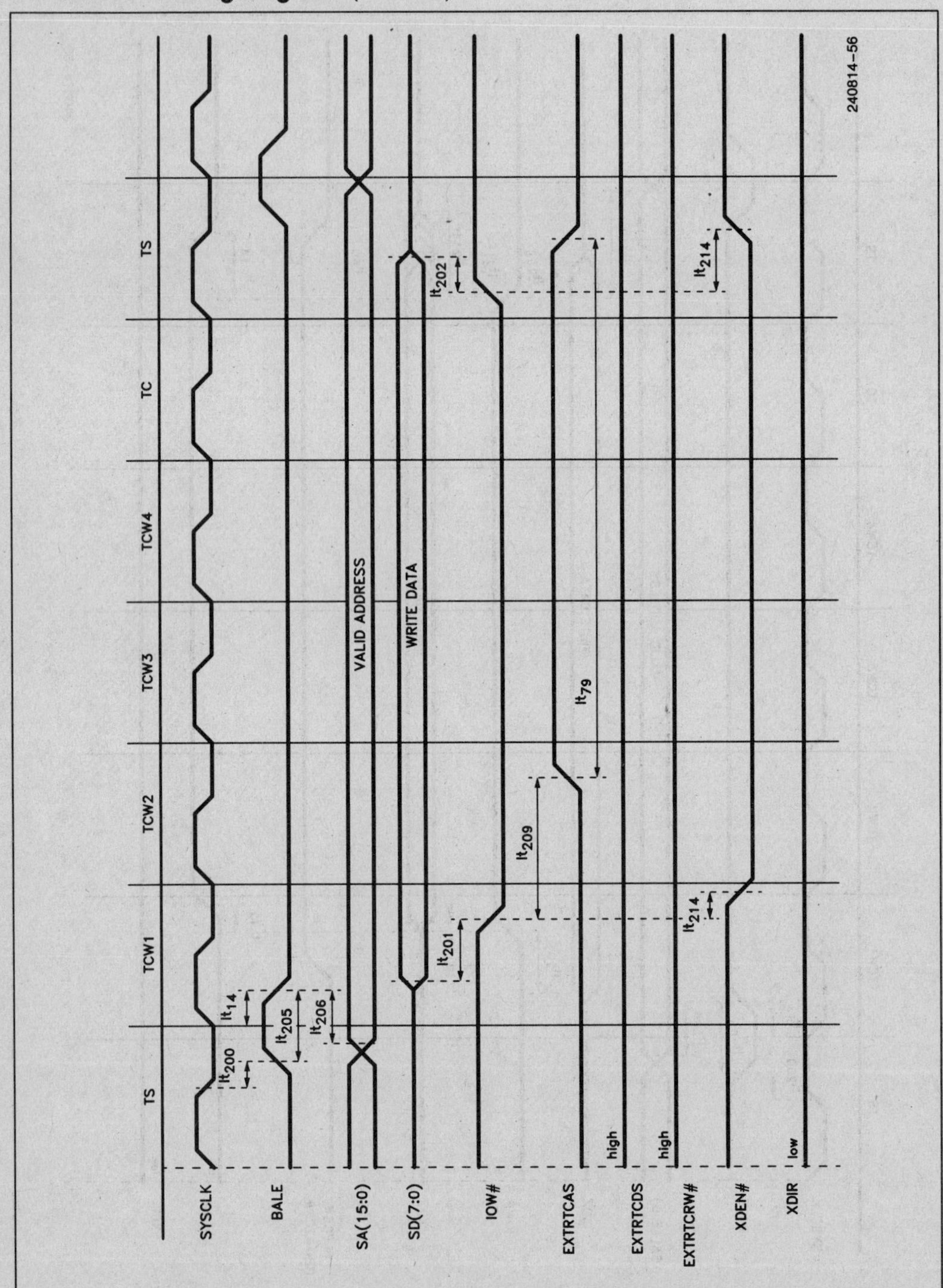

Figure 7.2.15. I/O Port 70 Hex Write—External RTC Timings

7.2 82360SL Timing Diagrams (Continued)

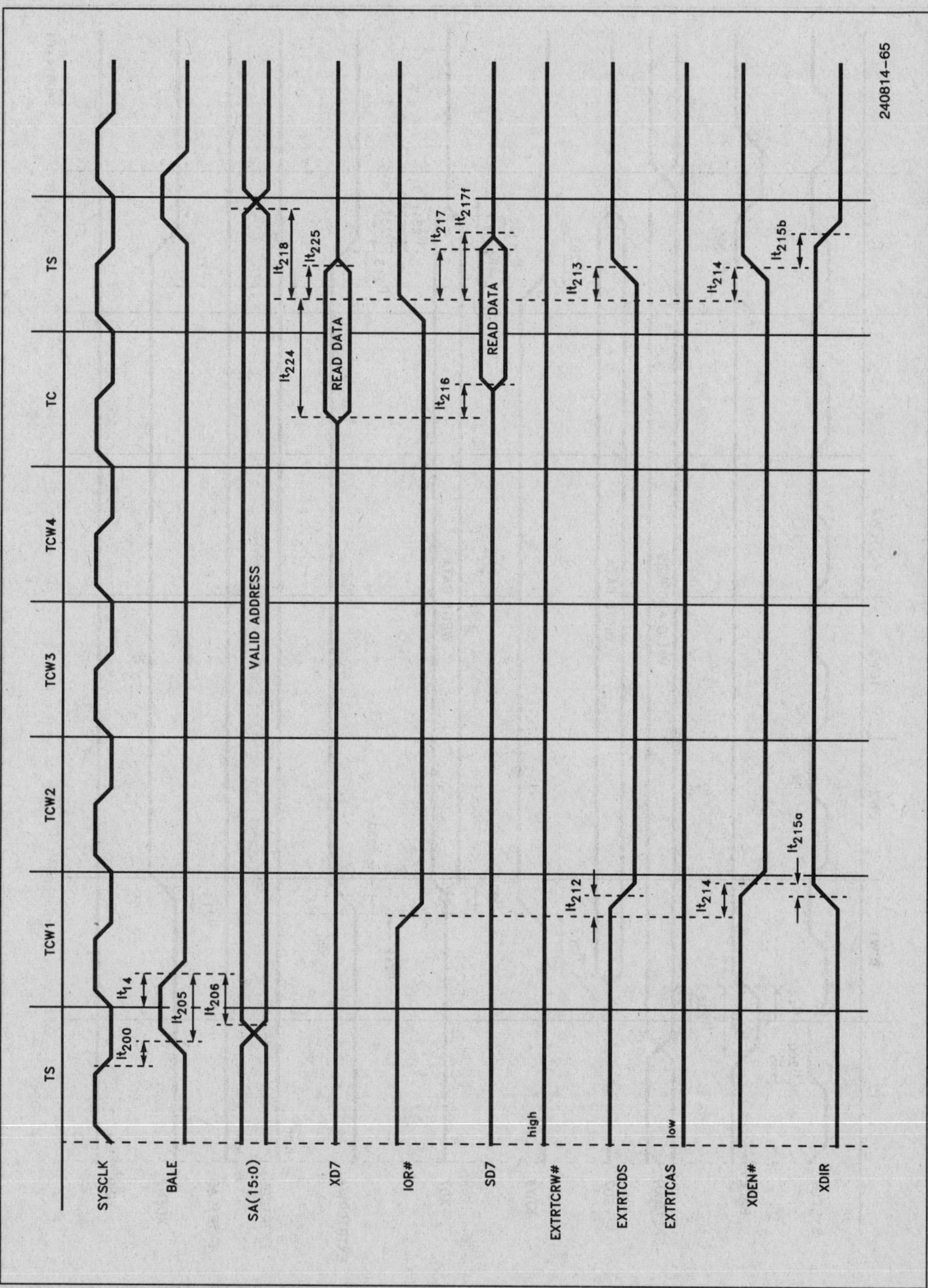

Figure 7.2.16. I/O Port 71 Hex Read—External RTC Timings

7.2 82360SL Timing Diagrams (Continued)

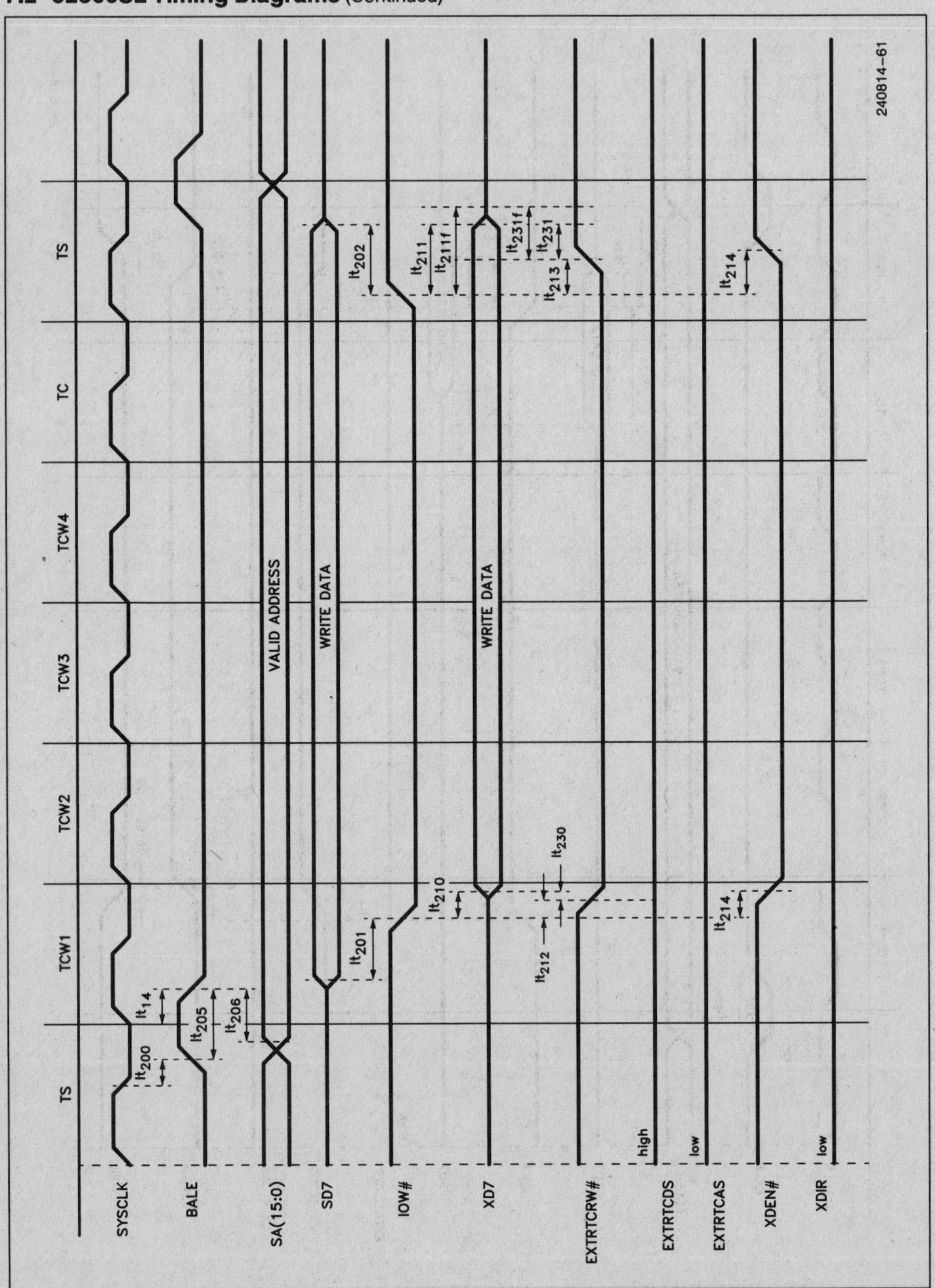

Figure 7.2.17. I/O Port 71 Hex Write—External RTC Timings

7.2 82360SL Timing Diagrams (Continued)

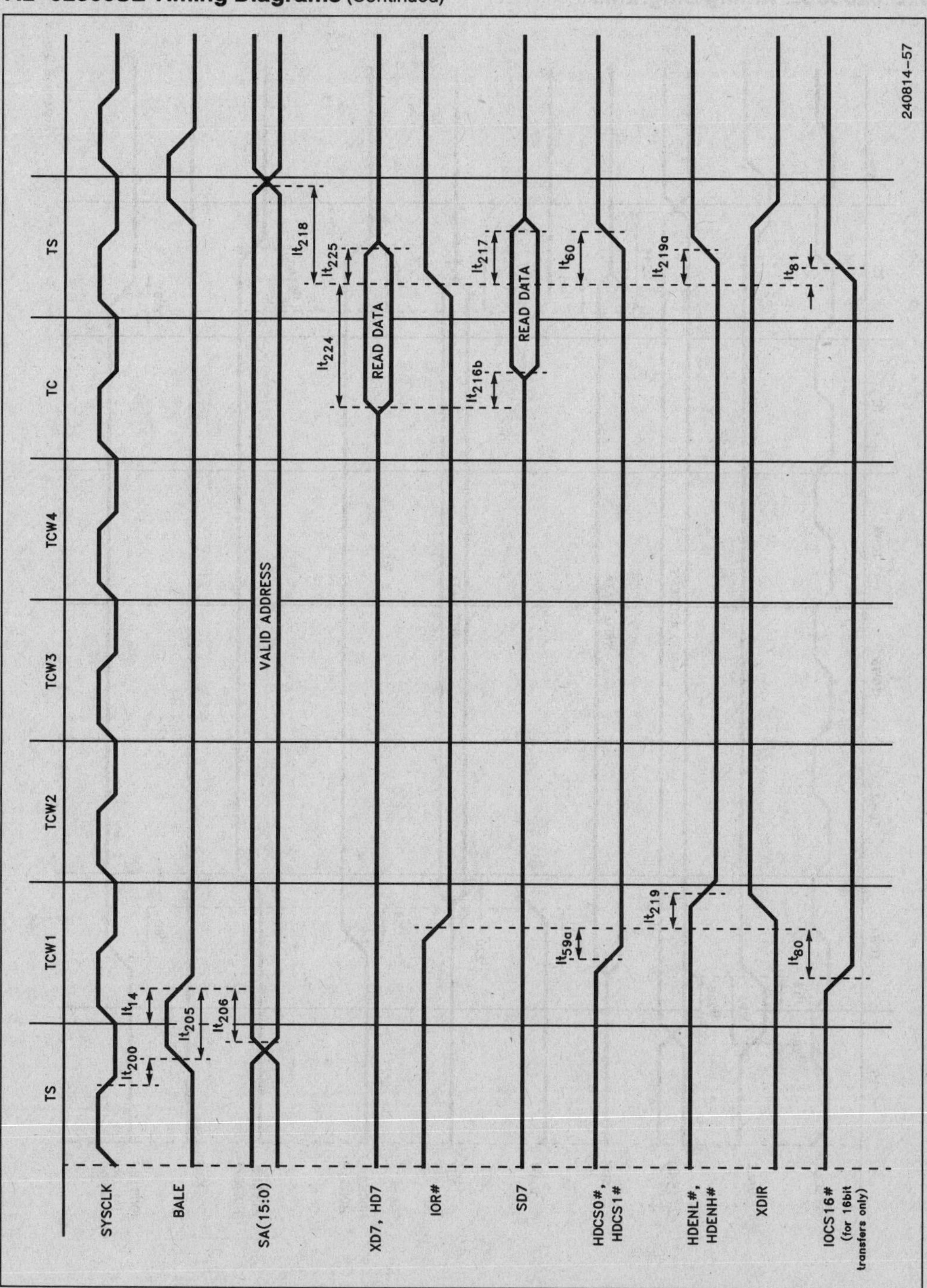

Figure 7.2.18. I.D.E. Hard Disk Control Signals—I/O Read Timings

7.2 82360SL Timing Diagrams (Continued)

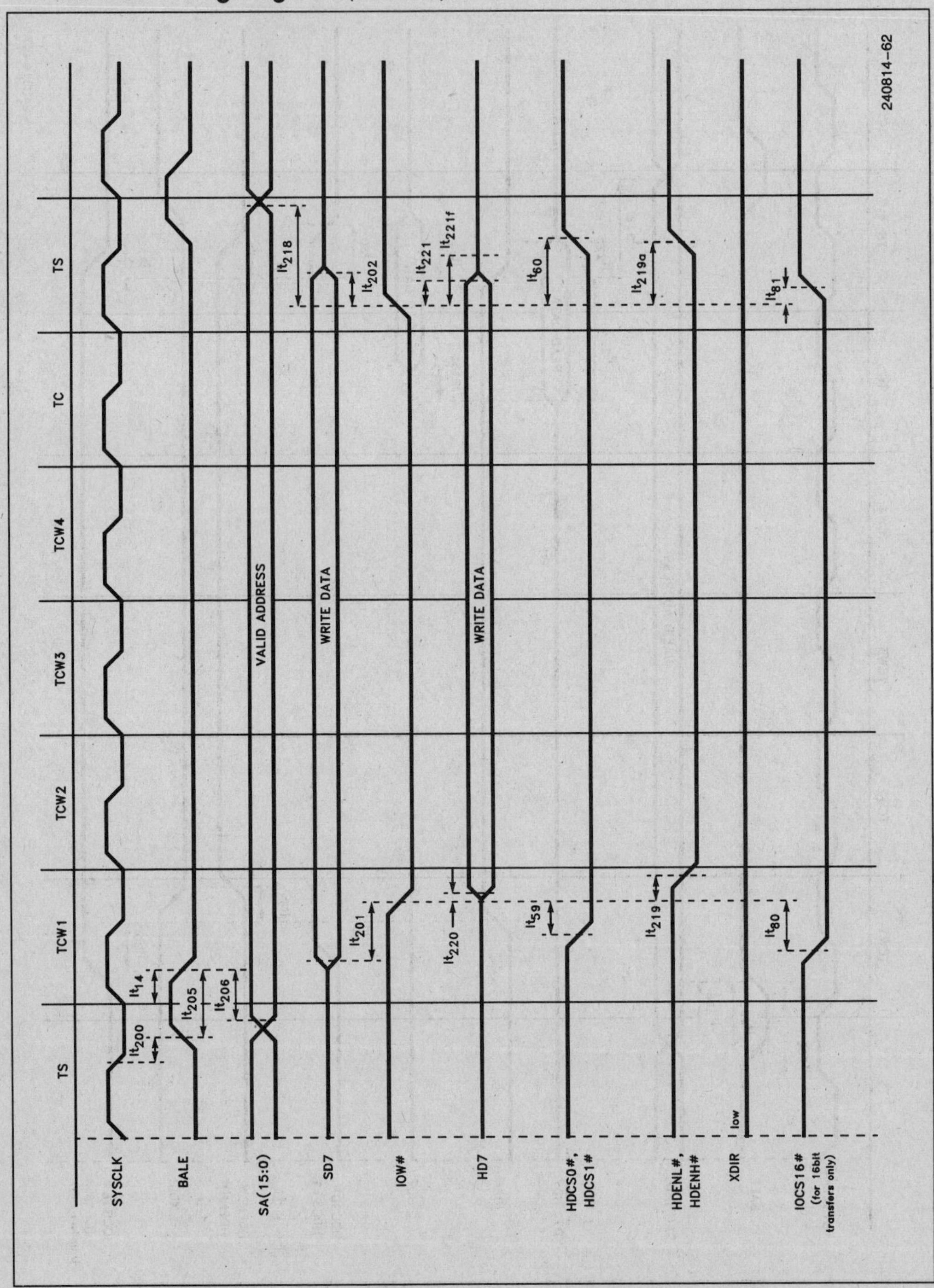

Figure 7.2.19. I.D.E. Hard Disk Control Signals—I/O Write Timings

7.2 82360SL Timing Diagrams (Continued)

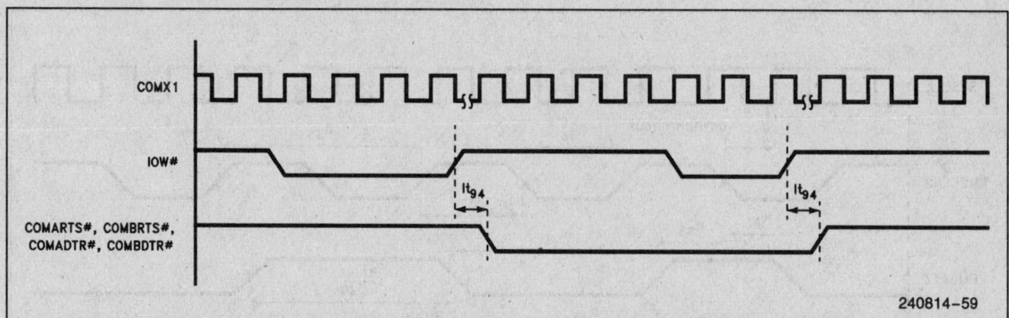

Figure 7.2.20. Serial Port Controller—Modem Control Signal Timings

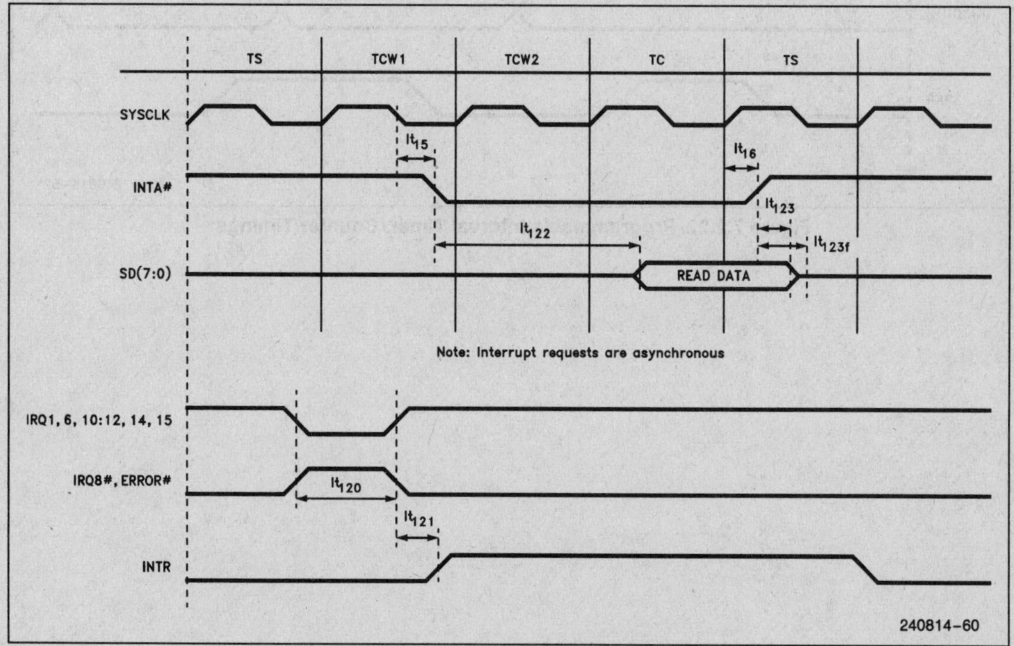

Figure 7.2.21. Interrupt Controller Timings

4

7.2 82360SL Timing Diagrams (Continued)

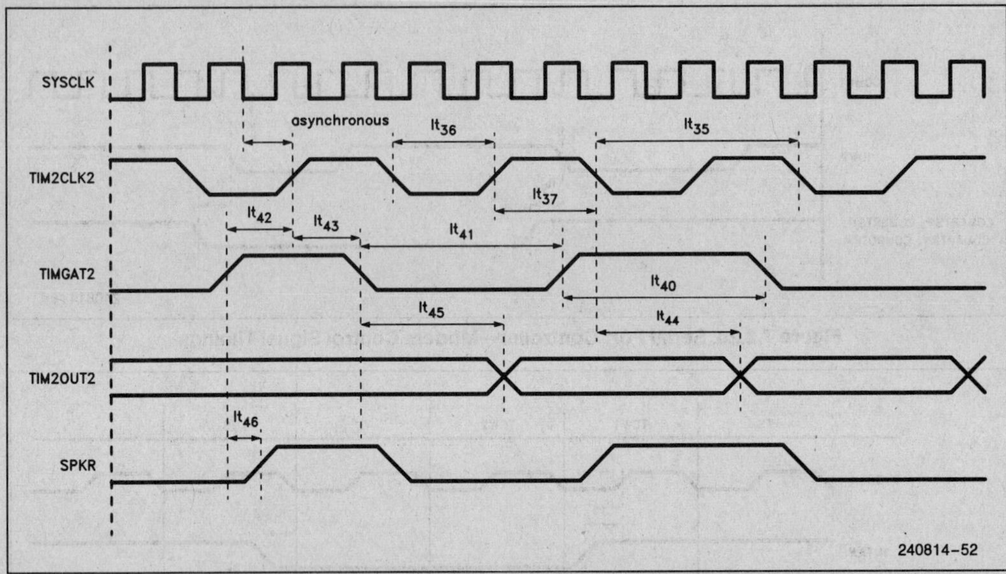

Figure 7.2.22. Programmable Interval Timer/Counter Timings

7.2 82360SL Timing Diagrams (Continued)

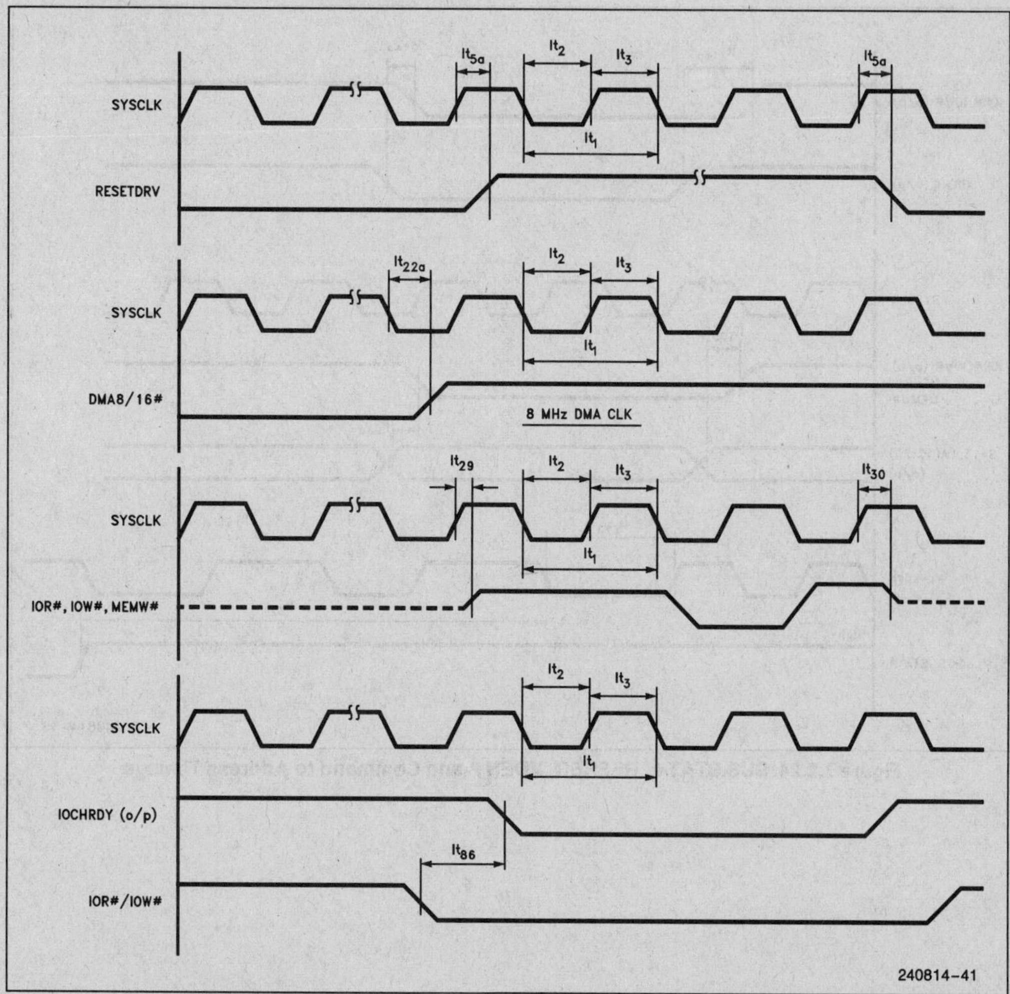

Figure 7.2.23. RESETDRV, DMA8/16#, Command Signals and IOCHRDY with Respect to SYSCLK

4

7.2 82360SL Timing Diagrams (Continued)

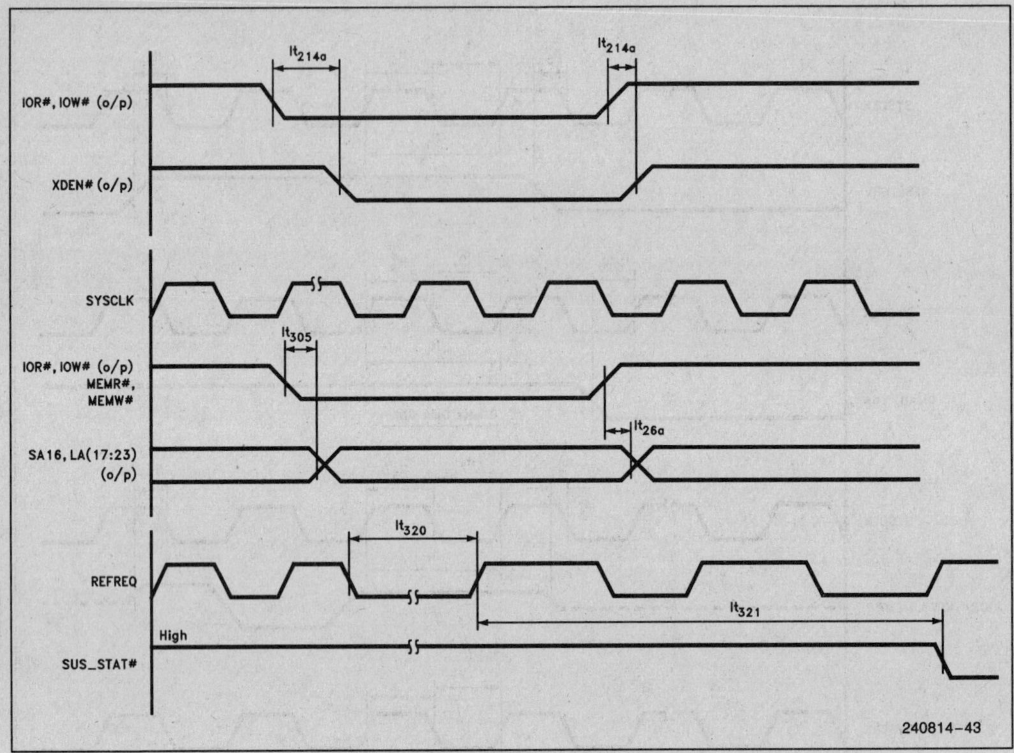

Figure 7.2.24. SUS.STAT#, REFREQ, XDEN# and Command to Address Timings

7.2 82360SL Timing Diagrams (Continued)

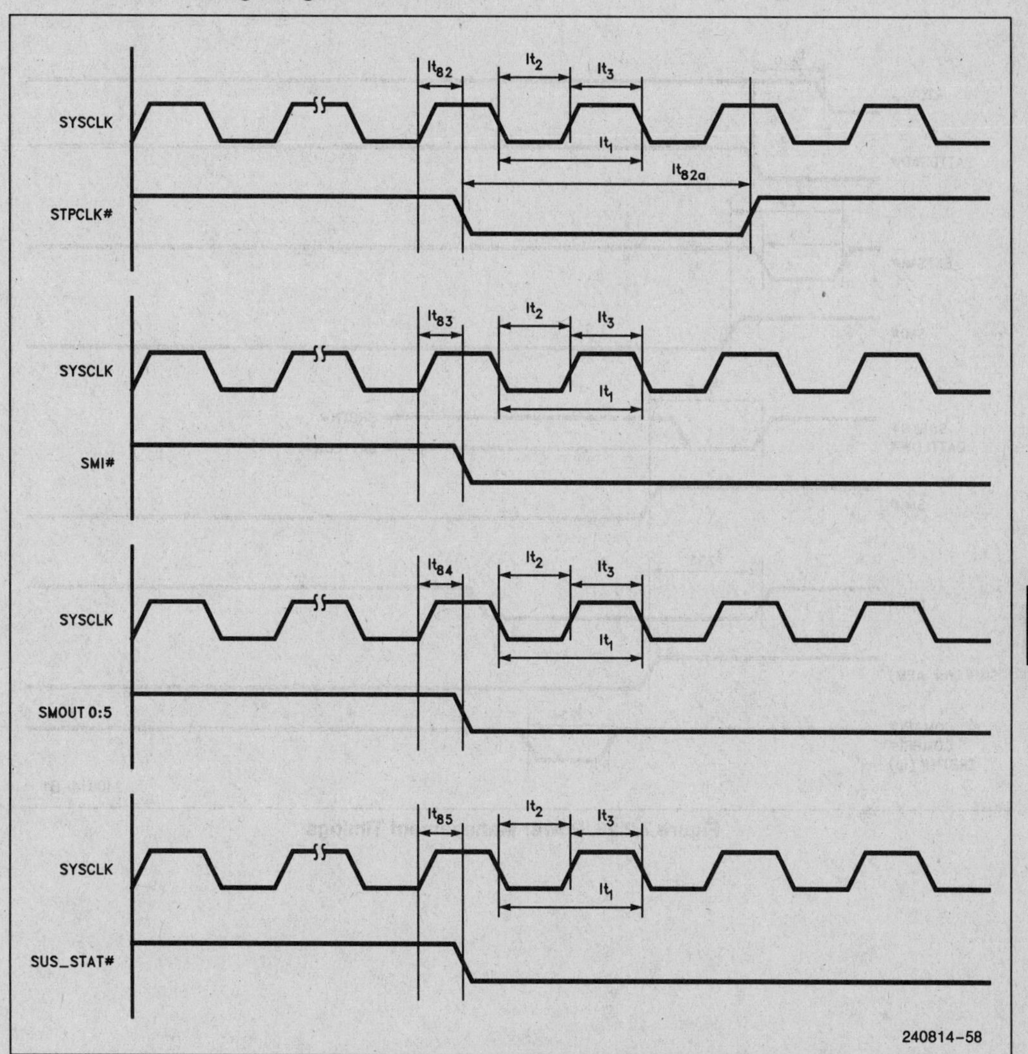

Figure 7.2.25. System Power Management Control Signal Timings

7.2 82360SL Timing Diagrams (Continued)

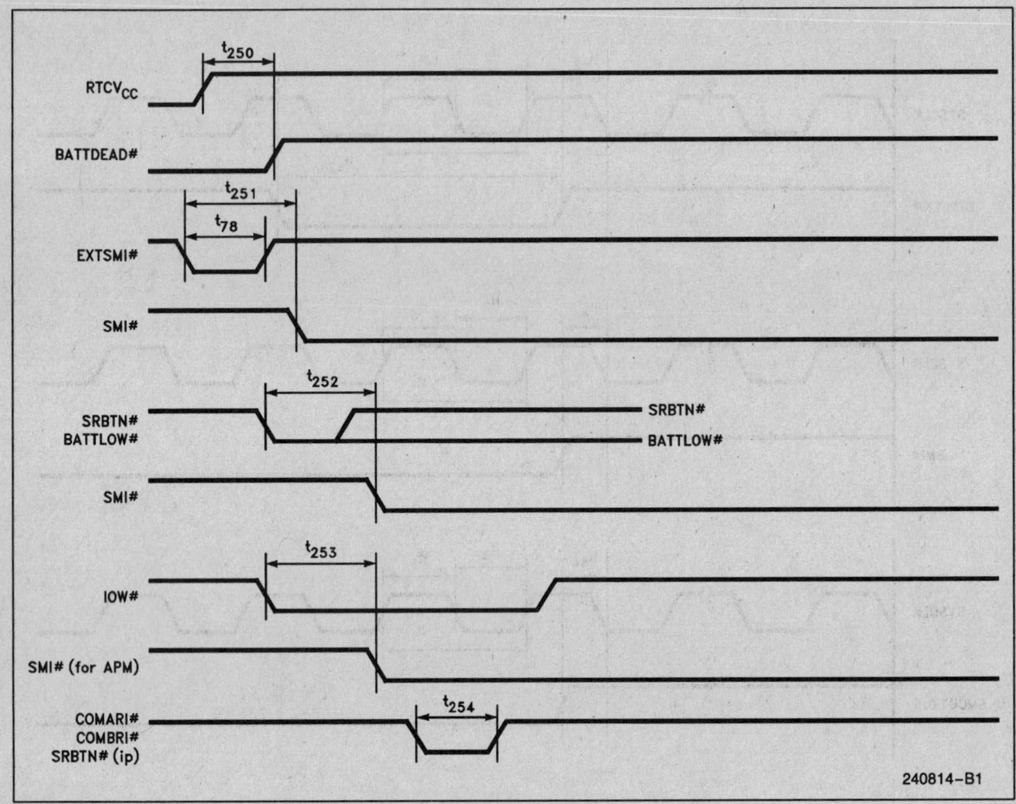

Figure 7.2.26. Power Management Timings

7.2 82360SL Timing Diagrams (Continued)

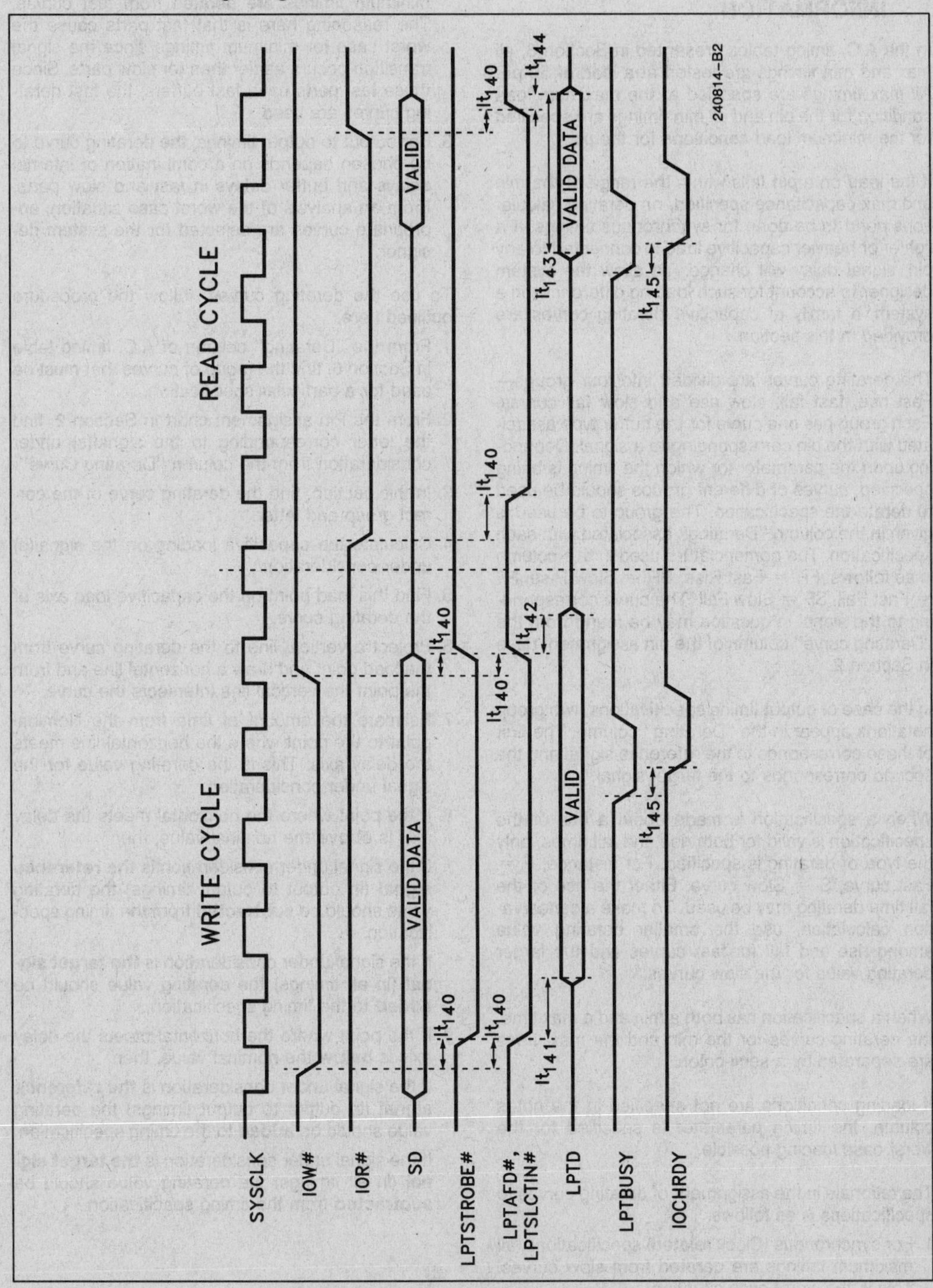

Figure 7.2.27. Fast Parallel Port Timing

8.0 CAPACITIVE DERATING INFORMATION

In the A.C. timing tables presented in Section 6, all max and min timings are tested at a load of 50 pF. All max timings are specified at the maximum load condition for the pin and all min timings are specified for the minimum load conditions for the pin.

If the load on a pin falls within the range of the min and max capacitance specified, no derating calculations need to be done for synchronous timings. If a lighter or heavier capacitive load is connected to any pin, signal delay will change. To allow the system designer to account for such loading differences in a system, a family of capacitive derating curves are provided in this section.

The derating curves are divided into four groups—Fast rise, fast fall, slow rise and slow fall curves. Each group has one curve for the buffer type associated with the pin corresponding to a signal. Depending upon the parameter for which the timing is being specified, curves of different groups should be used to derate the specification. The group to be used is given in the column "Derating" associated with each specification. The nomenclature used in this column is as follows: FR = Fast Rise, SR = Slow Rise, FF = Fast Fall, SF = Slow Fall. The curve corresponding to the signal in question may be found from the "Derating curve" column of the pin assignment table in Section 2.

In the case of output timing specifications, two group notations appear in the "Derating" column. The first of these corresponds to the reference signal and the second corresponds to the target signal.

When a specification is made about a bus or the specification is valid for both rise and fall times, only the type of derating is specified. For instance, F = Fast curve, S = Slow curve. Either the rise or the fall time derating may be used. To make a conservation calculation, use the smaller derating value among rise and fall for fast curves and the larger derating value for the slow curves.

When a specification has both a min and a max time, the derating curves for the min and the max times are separated by a semi-colon.

If loading conditions are not specified in the notes column, the timing parameter is specified for the worst case loading possible.

The rationale in the assignment of derating curves to specifications is as follows.

1. For synchronous (Clock related) specifications, all maximum timings are derated from slow curves. This is the worst case situation.
2. For synchronous (Clock related) specifications, all minimum timings are derated from fast curves. The reasoning here is that fast parts cause the worst case for minimum timings since the signal transition occurs earlier than for slow parts. Since these fast parts have fast buffers, the fast derating curves are used.
3. For output to output timings, the derating curve to be chosen depends on a combination of internal delays and buffer delays in fast and slow parts. From an analysis of the worst case situation, appropriate curves are selected for the system designer.

To use the derating curves, follow the procedure outlined here.

1. From the "Derating" column of A.C. timing table in Section 6, find the group of curves that must be used for a particular specification.
2. From the Pin assignment chart in Section 2, find the letter corresponding to the signal(s) under consideration from the column "Derating Curve".
3. In this section, find the derating curve of the correct group and letter.
4. Calculate the capacitive loading on the signal(s) under consideration.
5. Find this load point on the capacitive load axis of the derating curve.
6. Project a vertical line to the derating curve from the load point and draw a horizontal line and from the point the vertical line intersects the curve.
7. Estimate the amount of time from the Nominal point to the point where the horizontal line meets the delay axis. This is the derating value for the signal under consideration.
8. If the point where the horizontal meets the delay axis is **above** the nominal value, then

   If the signal under consideration is **the reference signal** (in output to output timings) the derating value should be **subtracted** from the timing specification.

   If the signal under consideration is **the target signal** (in all timings) the derating value should be **added** to the timing specification.
9. If the point where the horizontal meets the delay axis is **below** the nominal value, then

   If the signal under consideration is **the reference signal** (in output to output timings) the derating value should be **added** to the timing specification.

   If the signal under consideration is **the target signal** (in all timings) the derating value should be **subtracted** from the timing specification.

In some output to output specifications, the loads are not at the nominal points for the curves specified. The loads at which the specifications are made are indicated in the notes column. The same procedure as above may be used for derating except that a nominal point corresponding to the load specified must first be found on the curve specified.

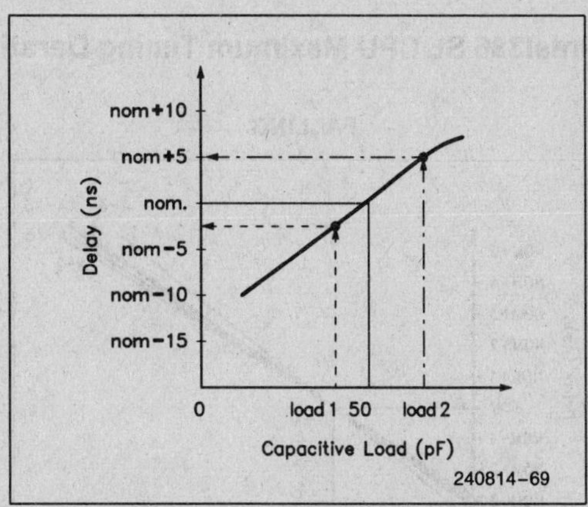

Using The Capacitive Derating Curves

Intel386 SL CPU Maximum Timing Derating Curves

FALLING

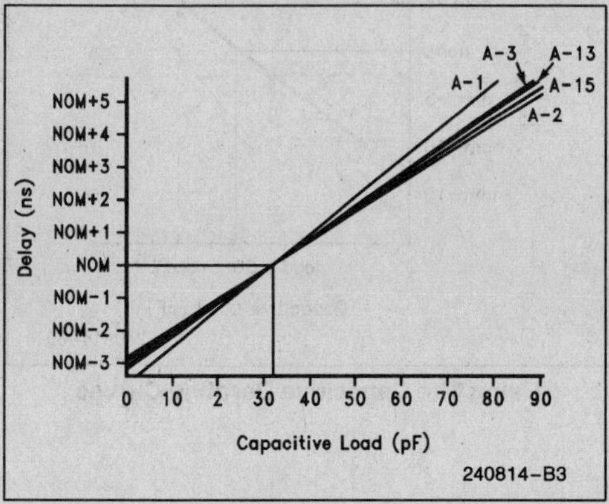

Figure 8.1a

RISING

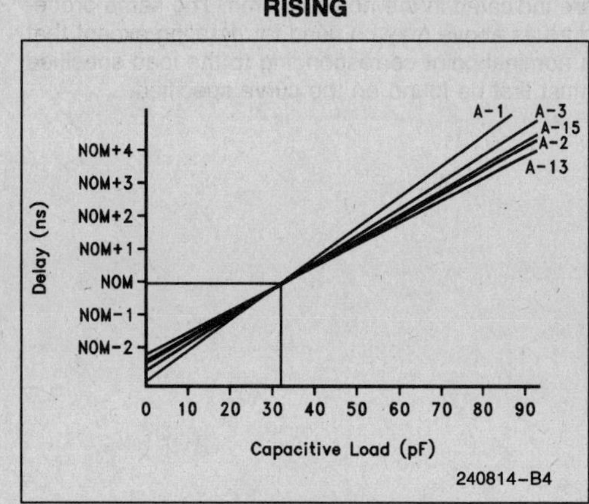

Figure 8.1b

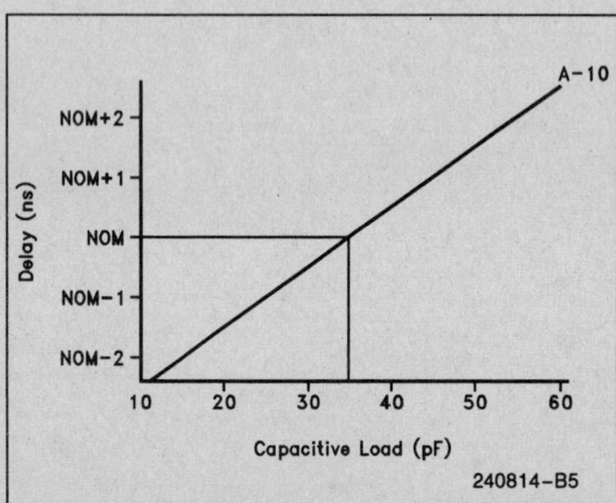

Figure 8.2a

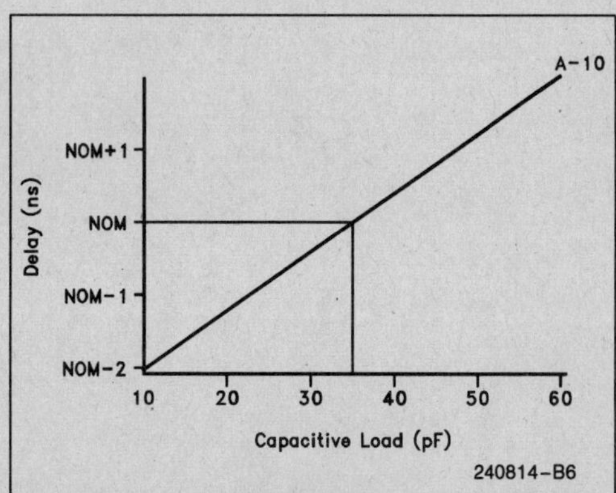

Figure 8.2b

Intel386 SL CPU Maximum Timing Derating Curves (Continued)

FALLING **RISING**

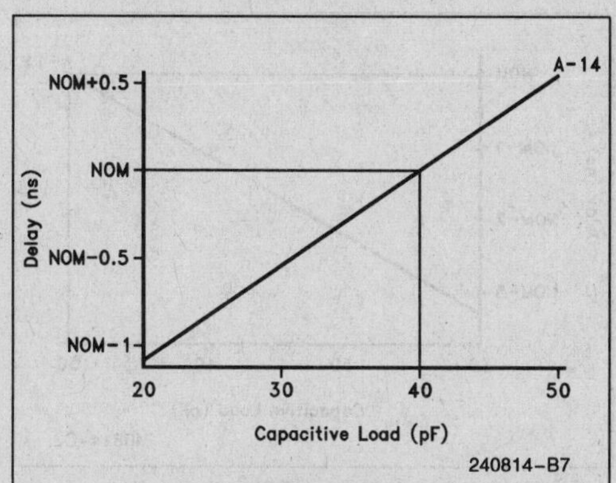

Figure 8.3a

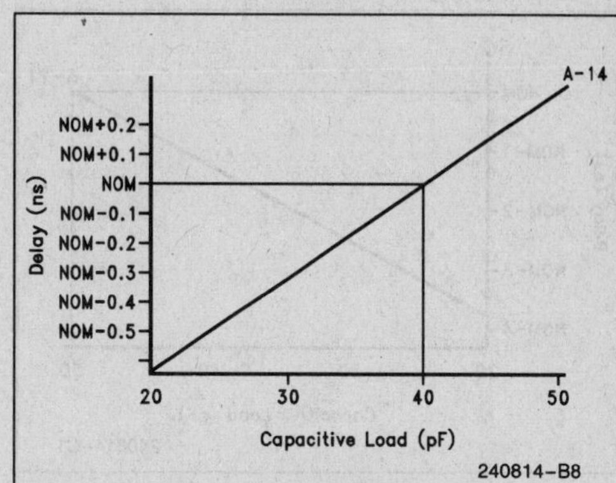

Figure 8.3b

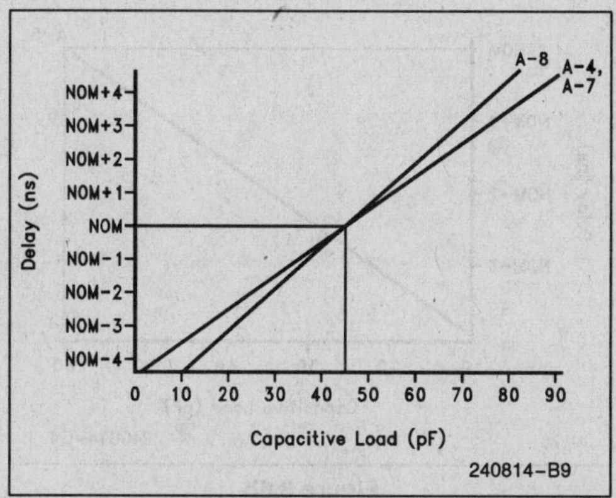

Figure 8.4a

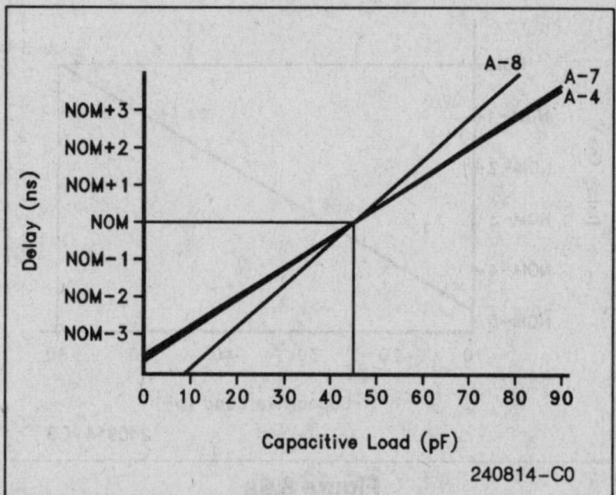

Figure 8.4b

4

Intel386 SL CPU Maximum Timing Derating Curves (Continued)

FALLING **RISING**

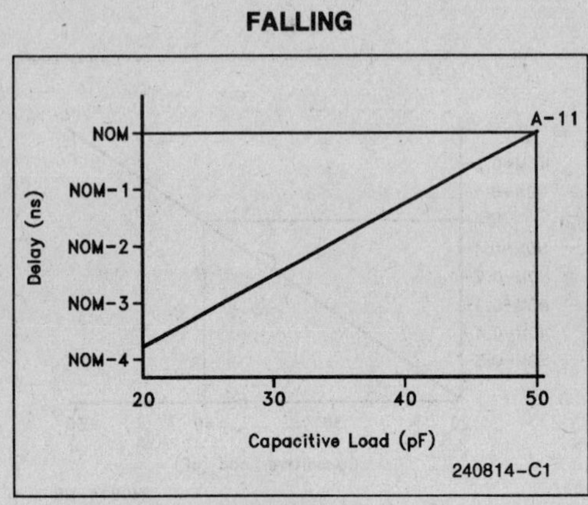

Figure 8.5a

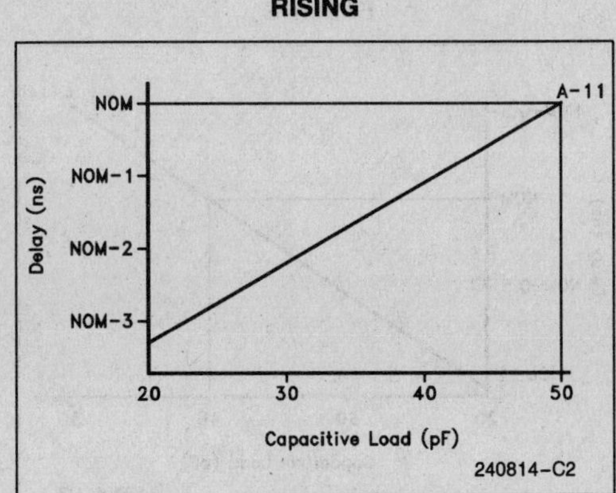

Figure 8.5b

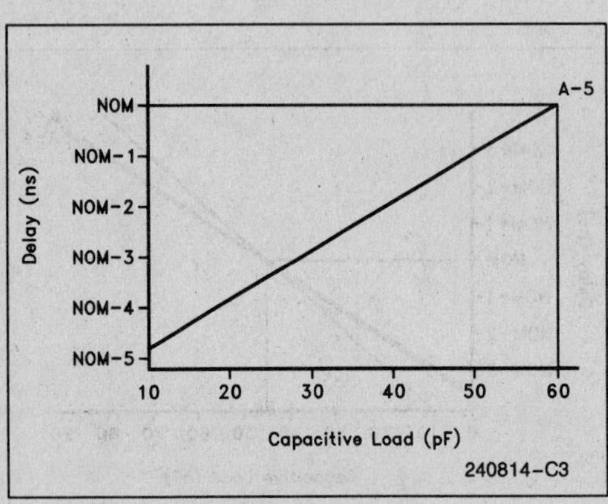

Figure 8.6a

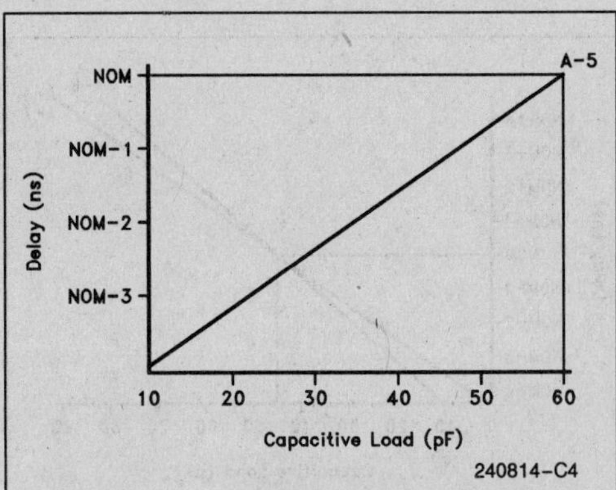

Figure 8.6b

Intel386 SL CPU Maximum Timing Derating Curves (Continued)

FALLING

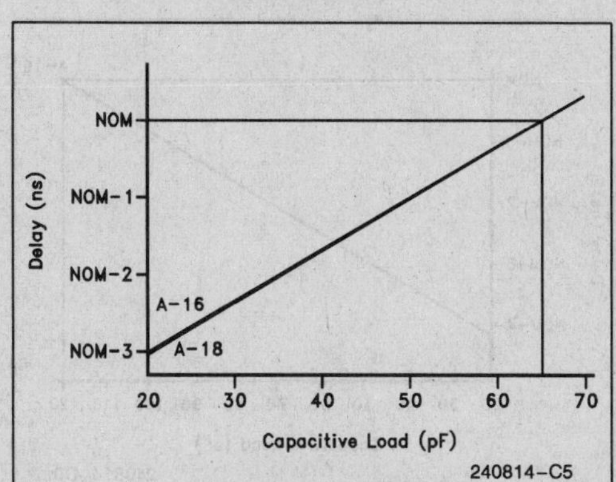

Figure 8.7a

RISING

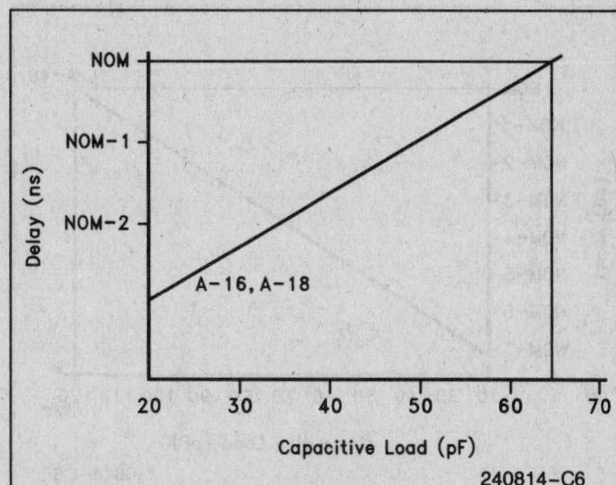

Figure 8.7b

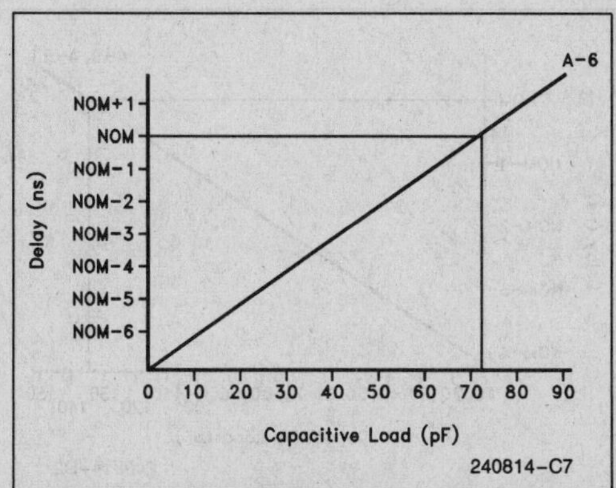

Figure 8.8a

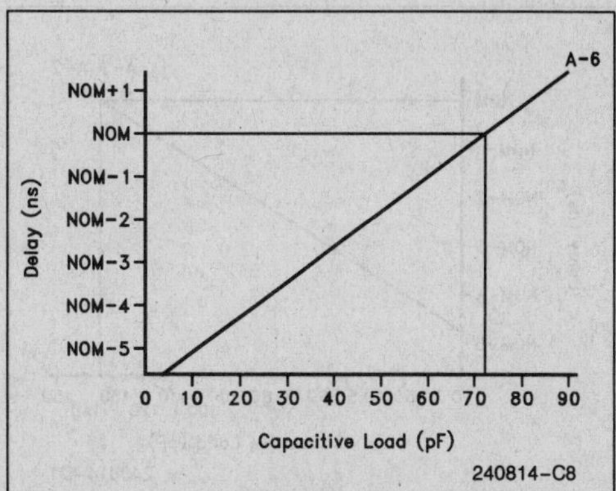

Figure 8.8b

4

Intel386 SL CPU Maximum Timing Derating Curves (Continued)

FALLING | **RISING**

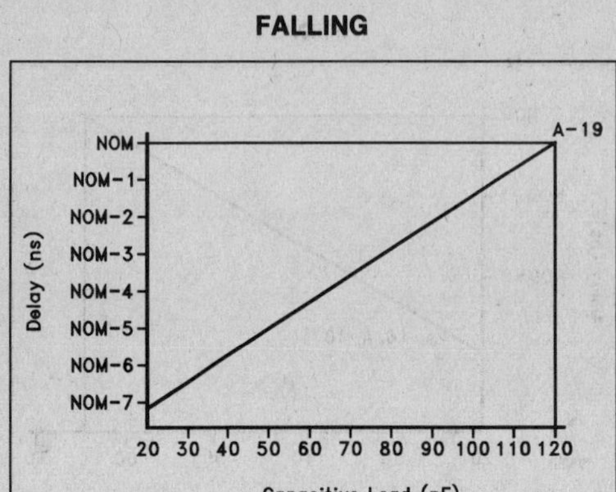

Figure 8.9a

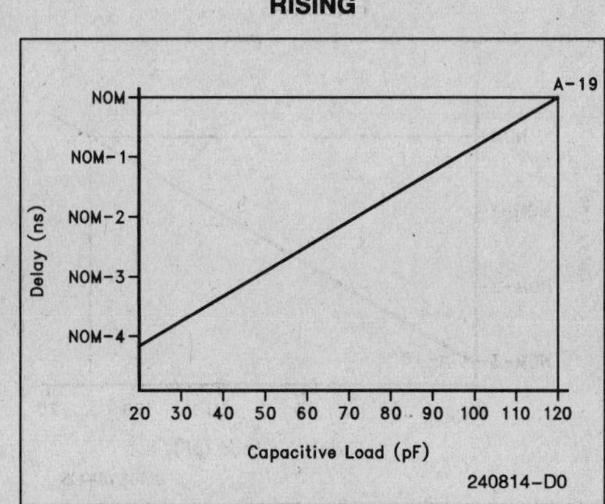

Figure 8.9b

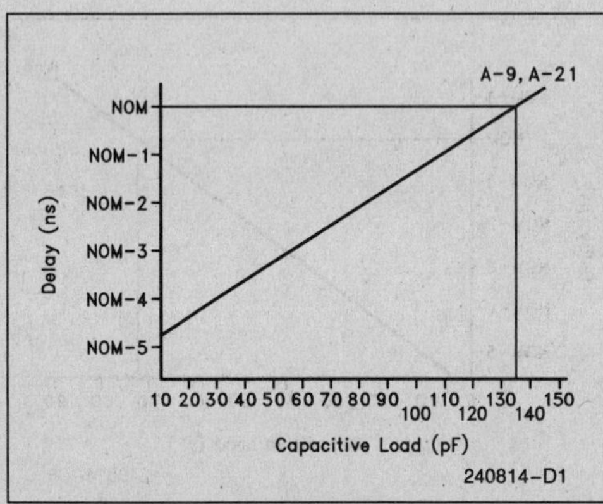

Figure 8.10a

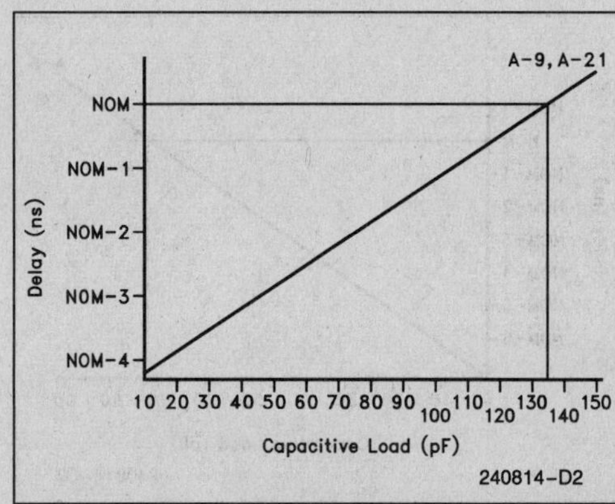

Figure 8.10b

Intel386 SL CPU Maximum Timing Derating Curves (Continued)

FALLING **RISING**

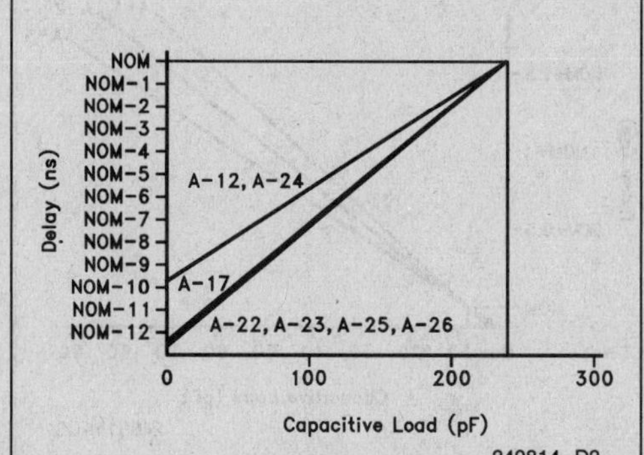

Figure 8.11a

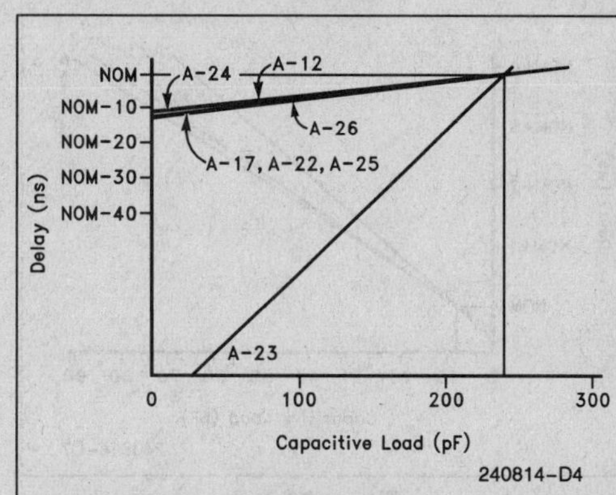

Figure 8.11b

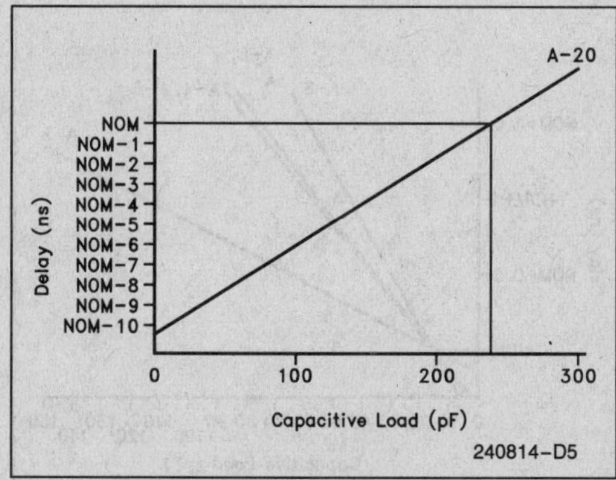

Figure 8.12a

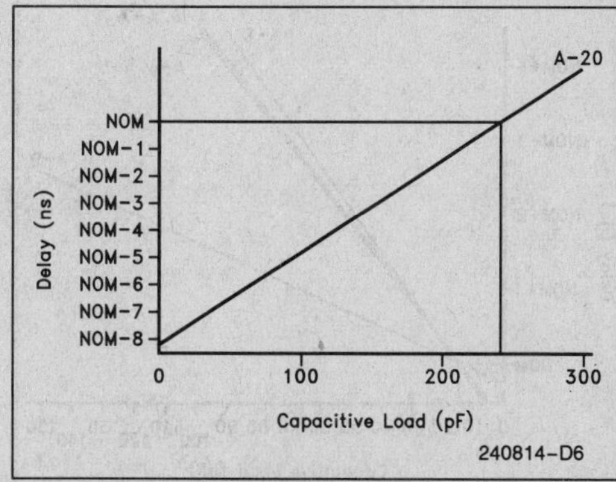

Figure 8.12b

4

Intel386 SL CPU Minimum Timing Derating Curves

FALLING

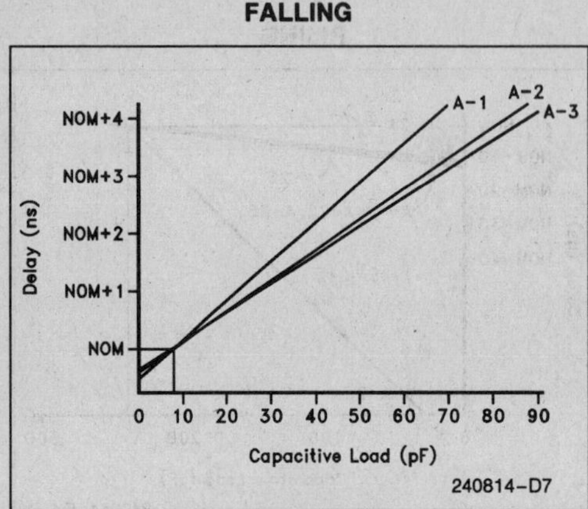

Figure 8.13a

RISING

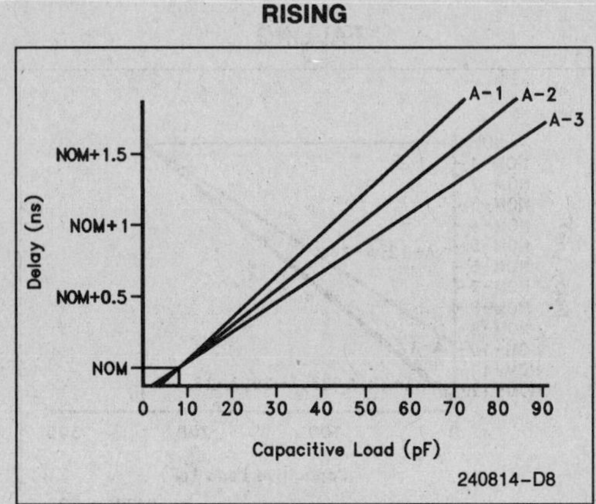

Figure 8.13b

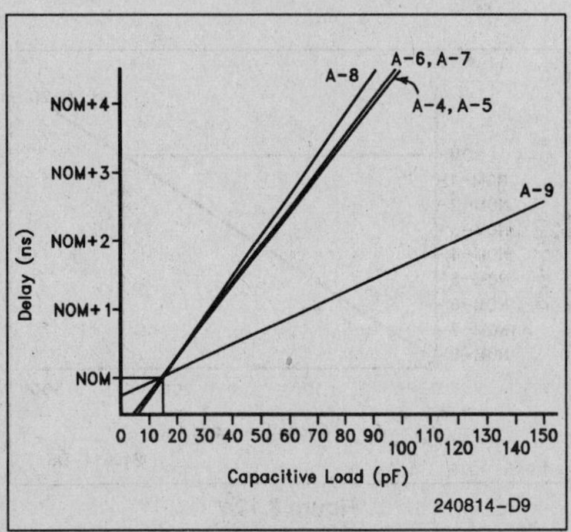

Figure 8.14a

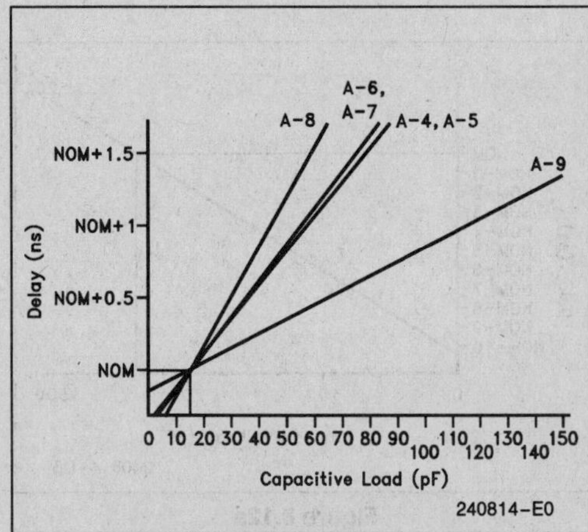

Figure 8.14b

Intel386 SL CPU Minimum Timing Derating Curves (Continued)

FALLING

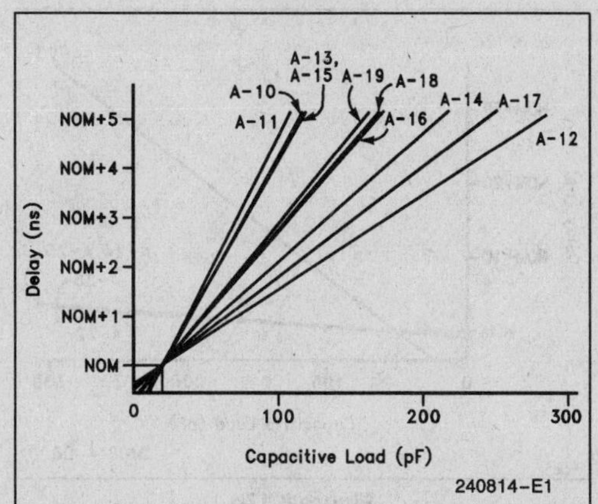

Figure 8.15a

RISING

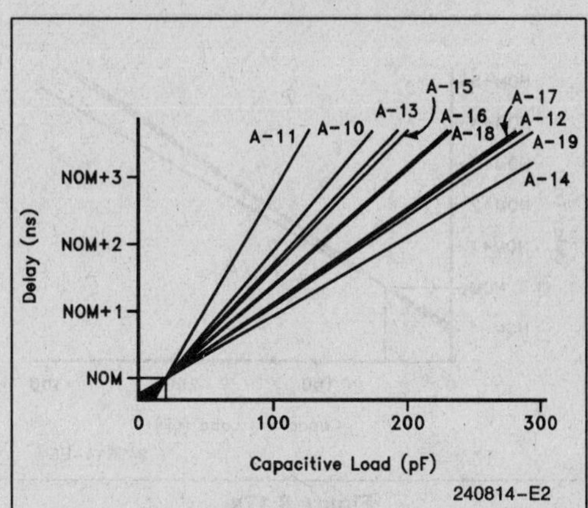

Figure 8.15b

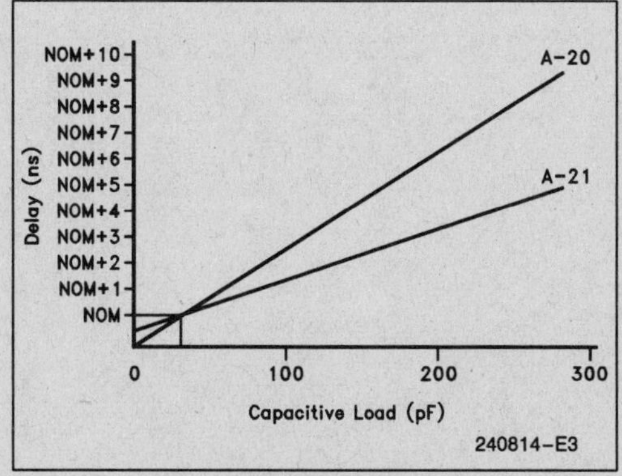

Figure 8.16a

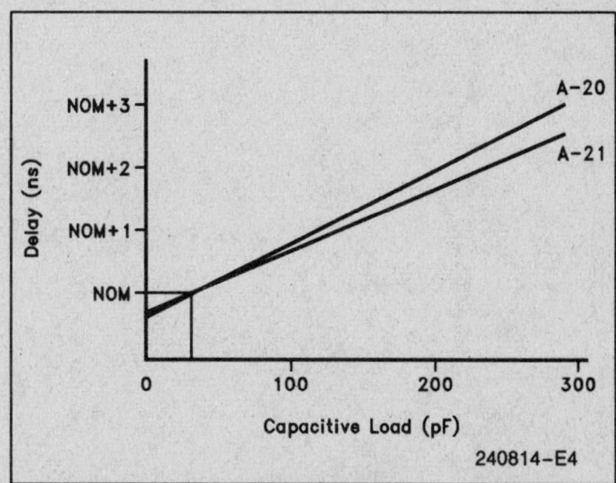

Figure 8.16b

4

Intel386 SL CPU Minimum Timing Derating Curves (Continued)

FALLING

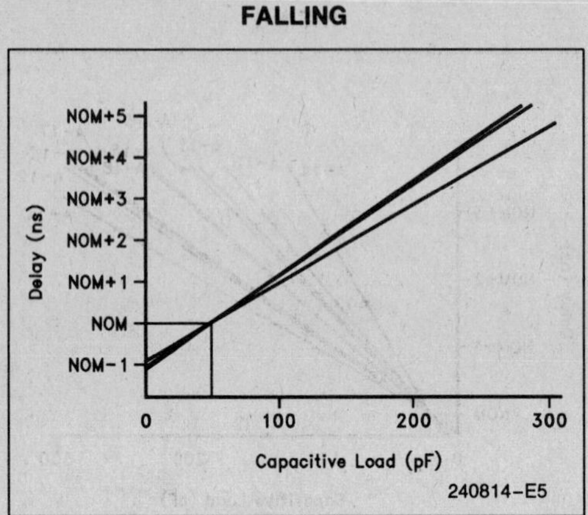

Figure 8.17a

RISING

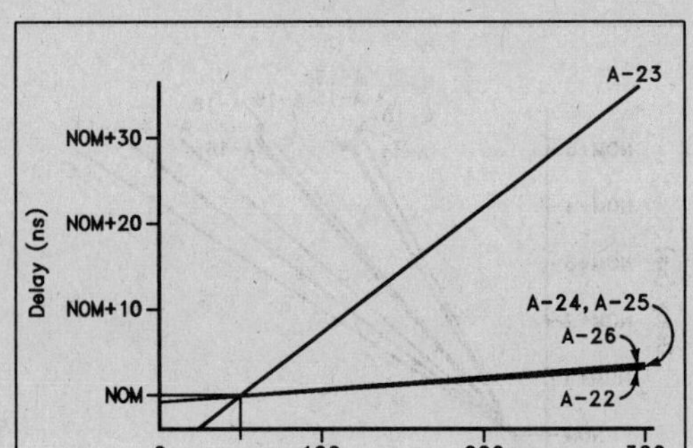

Figure 8.17b

82360SL I/O Maximum Timing Derating Curves

FALLING

RISING

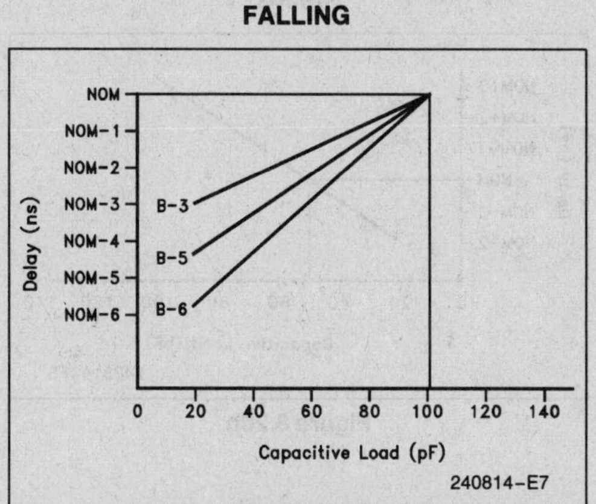

Figure 8.18a

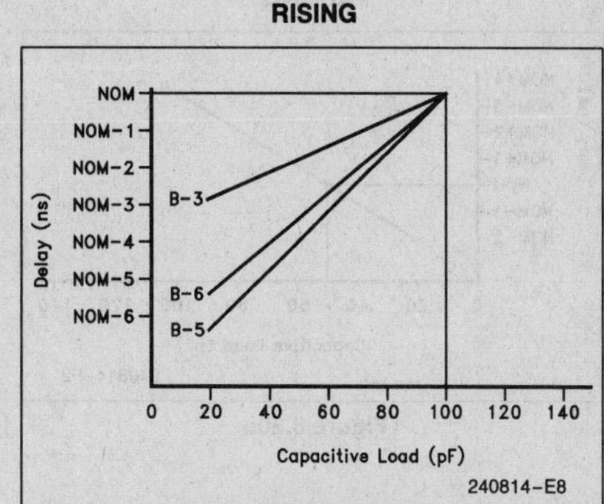

Figure 8.18b

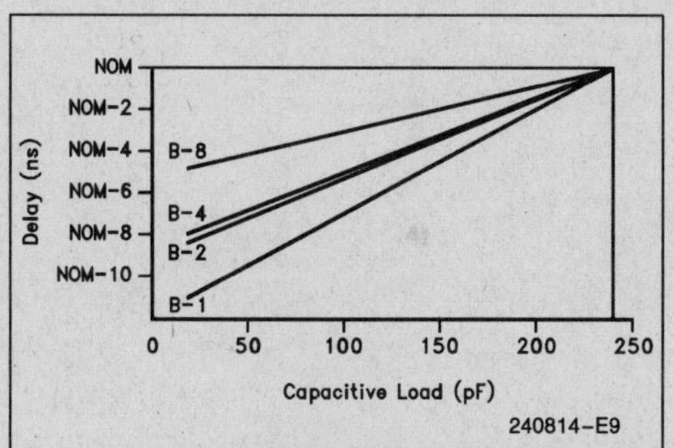

Figure 8.19a

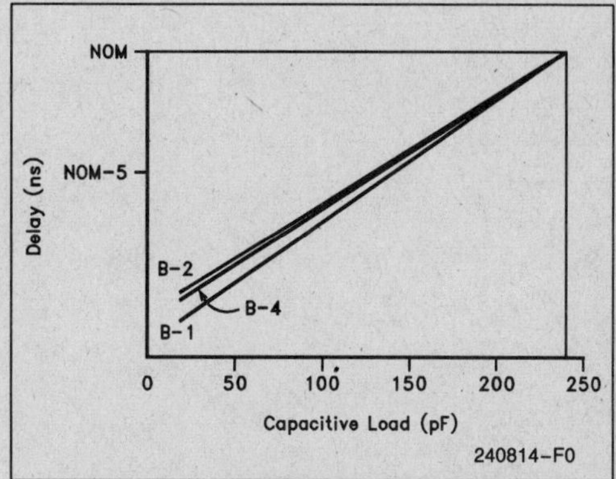

Figure 8.19b

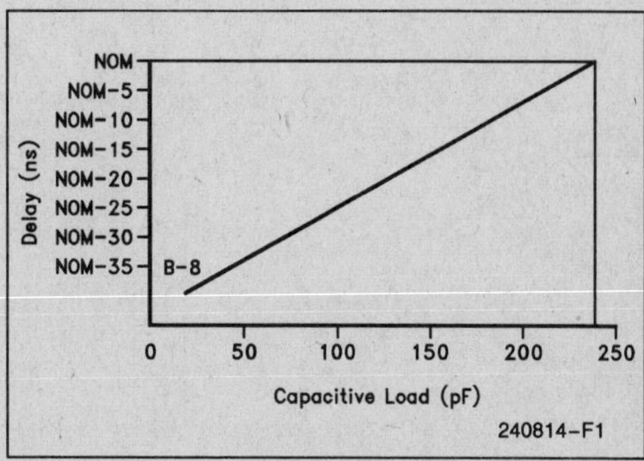

Figure 8.19c

82360SL I/O Maximum Timing Derating Curves (Continued)

FALLING

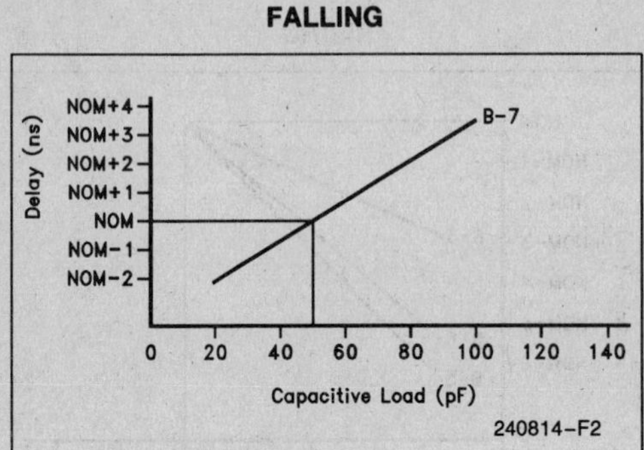

Figure 8.20a

RISING

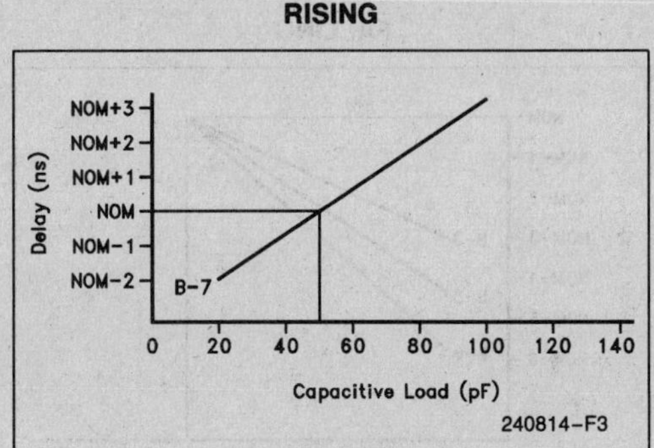

Figure 8.20b

82360SL I/O Minimum Timing Derating Curves (Continued)

FALLING

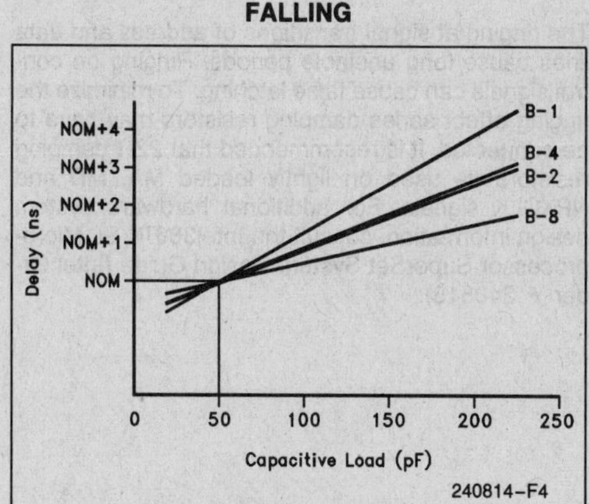

Figure 8.21a

RISING

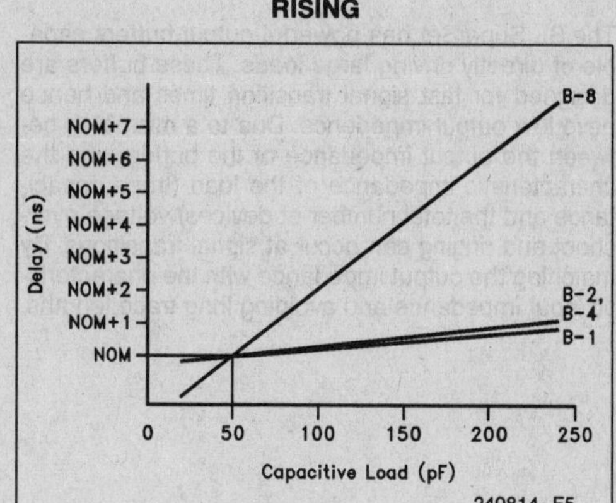

Figure 8.21b

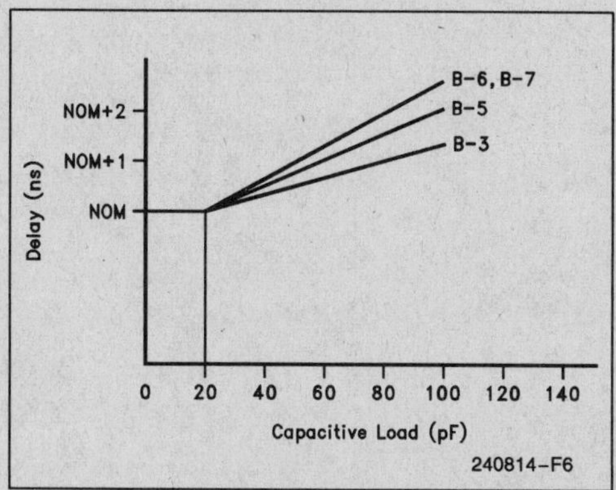

Figure 8.22a

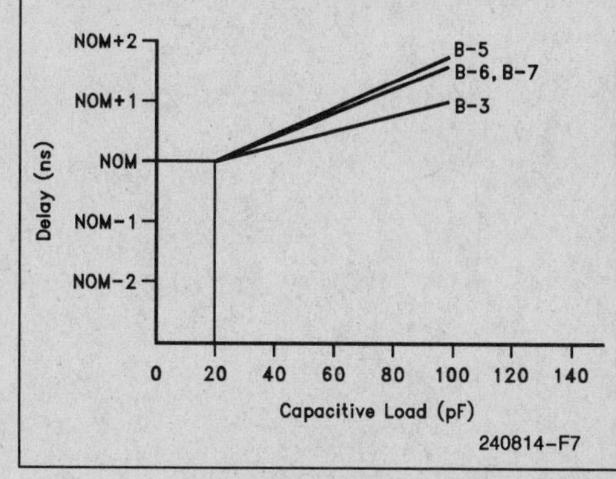

Figure 8.22b

4

9.0 DAMPING RESISTOR REQUIREMENTS

The SL SuperSet has powerful output buffers capable of directly driving large loads. These buffers are designed for fast signal transition times and hence have low output impedence. Due to a mismatch between the output impedance of the buffers and the characteristic impedance of the load (trace capacitance and the total number of devices) voltage overshoot and ringing can occur at signal transitions. By matching the output impedance with the characteristic input impedance and avoiding long trace lengths, the system designer can minimize the transmission line reflections and ringing.

The ringing at signal transitions of address and data lines cause long unstable periods. Ringing on control signals can cause false latching. To minimize the ringing effect series damping resistors may have to be connected. It is recommended that 22Ω damping resistors be used on lightly loaded MA, MD and NPXCLK signals. For additional hardware system design information, consult the Intel386™ SL Microprocessor SuperSet System Design Guide (Intel Order # 240816).

10.0 MECHANICAL DETAILS OF LGA AND PQFP PACKAGES

This section contains mechanical details of the two types of packages used in the SL SuperSet to help design the parts in. For more detailed information on packages and package types, please refer to *"Surface Mount Technology Guide"* (Order #240585)

227L CERAMIC LAND GRID ARRAY (CAVITY UP)

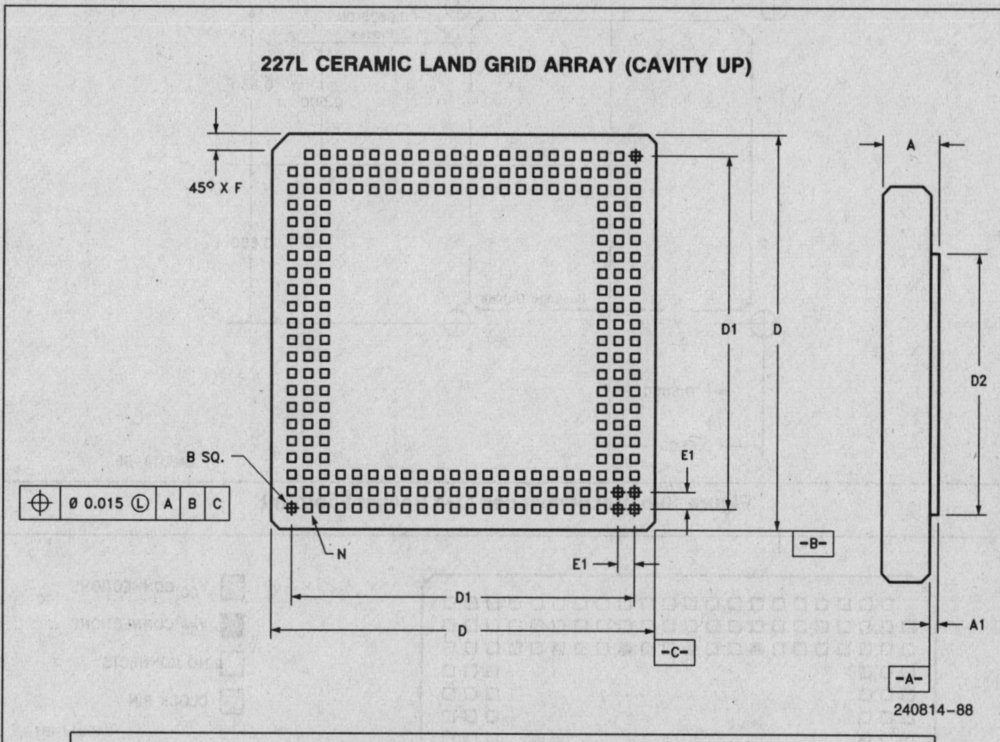

Symbol	Millimeters			Inches		
	Min	Max	Notes	Min	Max	Notes
1	3.56	4.06		0.097	0.120	
A1	0.33	0.43		0.009	0.017	
B	0.69	0.84		0.027	0.033	
D	28.96	29.46		1.140	1.160	
D1	26.67		Basic	1.050		Basic
D2		24.13			0.950	
e1	1.27		Basic	0.050		Basic
F	1.65	2.16		0.065	0.085	
N	227			227		
Issue	4/17/90					

Family: Ceramic Land Grid Array Package

Figure 10-1a. Principal Dimensions of the Intel386™ SL CPU in a 227-Lead LGA Package

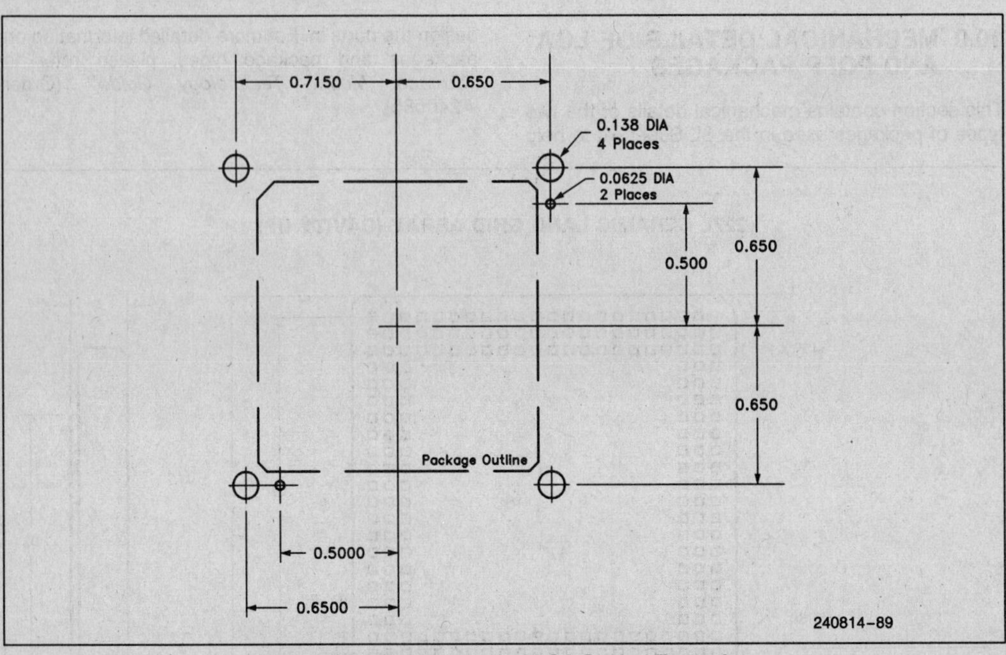

Figure 10-b. Recommended LGA Socket Footprint

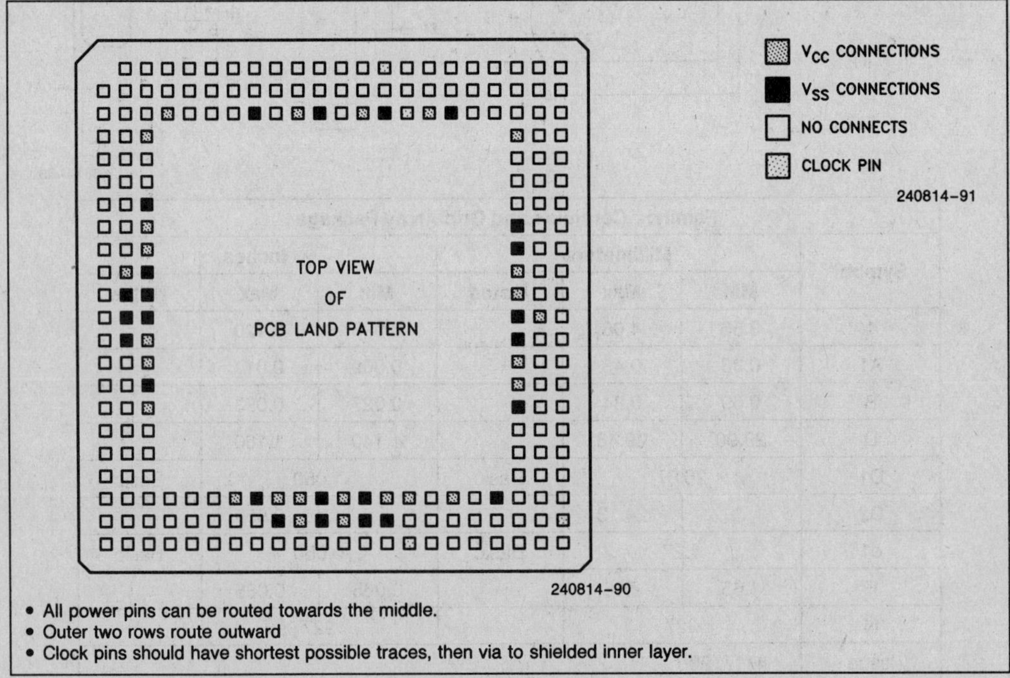

- All power pins can be routed towards the middle.
- Outer two rows route outward
- Clock pins should have shortest possible traces, then via to shielded inner layer.

Figure 10-1c. Recommended Signal Routing for LGA Package

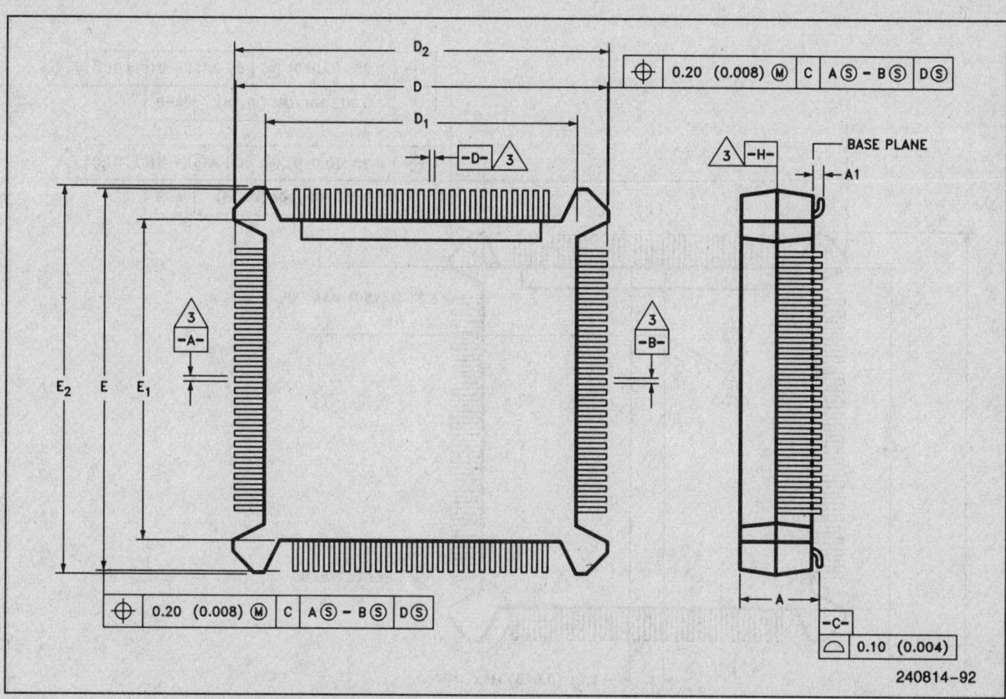

Figure 10-2a. Principle Dimensions of the 82360SL I/O in the 196-Lead PQFP Package

Family: 196-Lead Plastic Quad Flat Package (PQFP) 0.025 Inch (0.635mm) Pitch

Symbol	Millimeters		Inches	
	Min	Max	Min	Max
A = Package Height: Distance from seating plane to highest point of the body	4.06	4.32	0.160	0.170
A1 = Standoff: Distance from Seating Plane to Base Plane	0.51	0.76	0.020	0.030
D/E = Overall Package Dimension: Lead Tip to Lead Tip	37.47	37.72	1.475	1.485
D1/E1 = Plastic Body Dimension	34.21	34.37	1.347	1.353
D2/E2 = Bumper Distance	38.02	38.18	1.497	1.503
D3/E3 = Lead Dimension	30.48 Ref		1.200 Ref	
D4/E4 = Foot Radius Location	36.14	36.49	1.423	1.437
L1 = Foot Length	0.51	0.76	0.020	0.030

NOTES:
1. All PQFP case outlines are being presented as standards to the JEDEC.
2. Typical board footprint area for the 196-lead PQFP is 1.500 inches x 1.5000 inches.
3. All dimensions and tolerance conform to ANSI Y14.5M-1982.
4. Datum Plane -H- located at the molding parting line and coincident with the bottom of the lead where the lead exits the plastic body.
5. Datums A-B and -D- to be determined where the center lead exits the plastic body at datum plane -H-.
6. Controlling dimension in inches.
7. Dimensions D1, D2, E1, and E2 are measured at the molding parting line and do not include mold protrusions.
8. Pin 1 identifier is located within one of the two zones indicated.
9. Measured at datum plane -H-.
10. Measured at seating plane datum -C-.

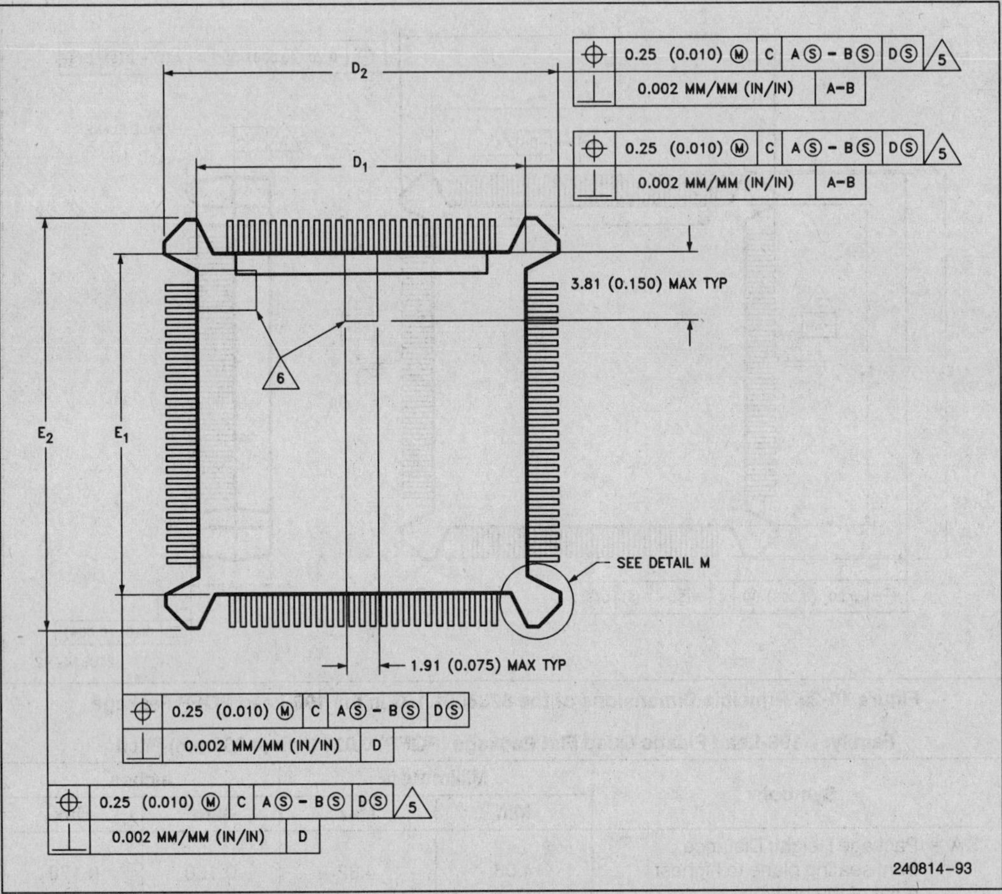

D2
D1
E2
E1
⌖ 0.25 (0.010) Ⓜ | C | AⓈ − BⓈ | DⓈ | 5
⊥ 0.002 MM/MM (IN/IN) | A−B
3.81 (0.150) MAX TYP
6
SEE DETAIL M
1.91 (0.075) MAX TYP
⌖ 0.25 (0.010) Ⓜ | C | AⓈ − BⓈ | DⓈ
⊥ 0.002 MM/MM (IN/IN) | D
⌖ 0.25 (0.010) Ⓜ | C | AⓈ − BⓈ | DⓈ | 5
⊥ 0.002 MM/MM (IN/IN) | D
240814–93

Figure 10-2b. Detailed Dimensions of the 82360SL I/O in the 196-Lead PQFP—Molded Details

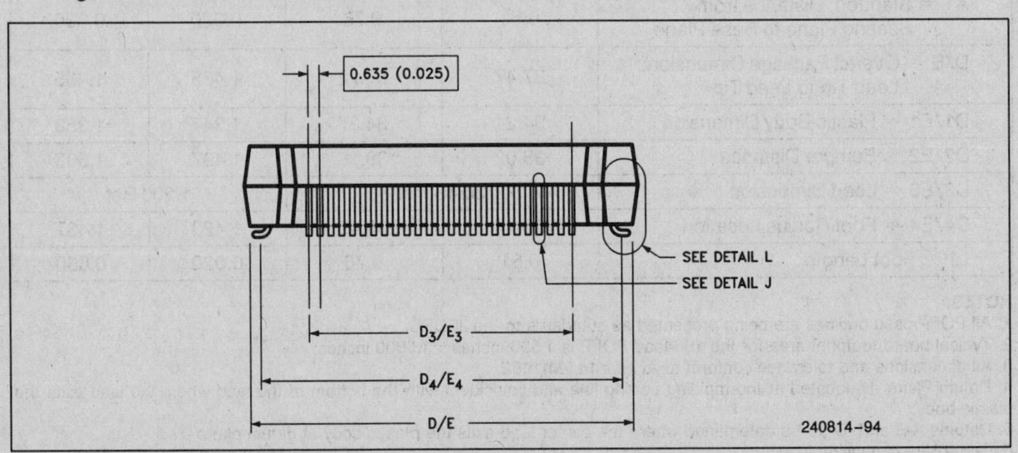

Figure 10-2c. Detailed Dimensions of the 82360SL I/O in the 196-Lead—Terminal Details

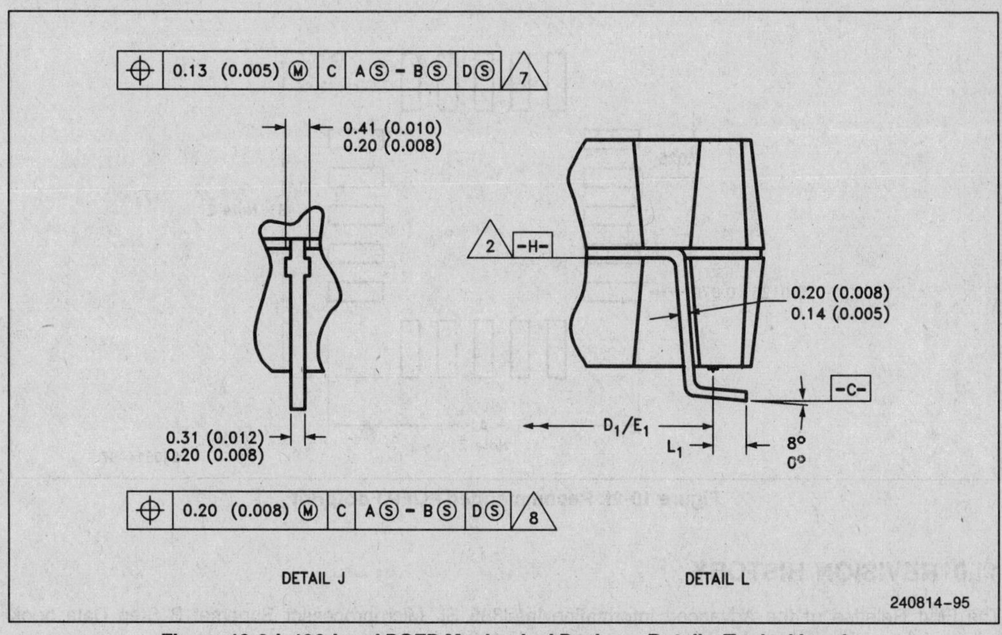

Figure 10-2d. 196-Lead PQFP Mechanical Package Detail—Typical Lead

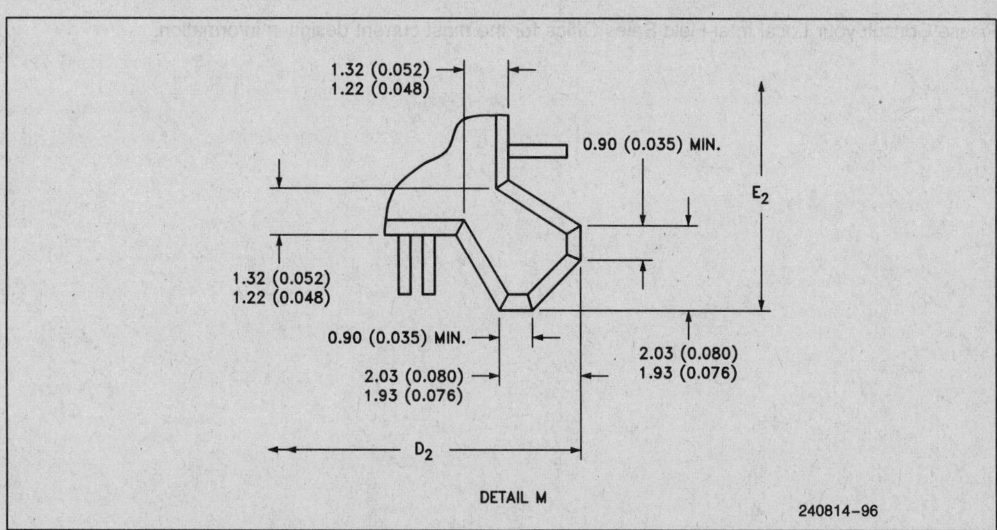

Figure 10-2e. 196-Lead PQFP Mechanical Package Detail—Protective Bumper

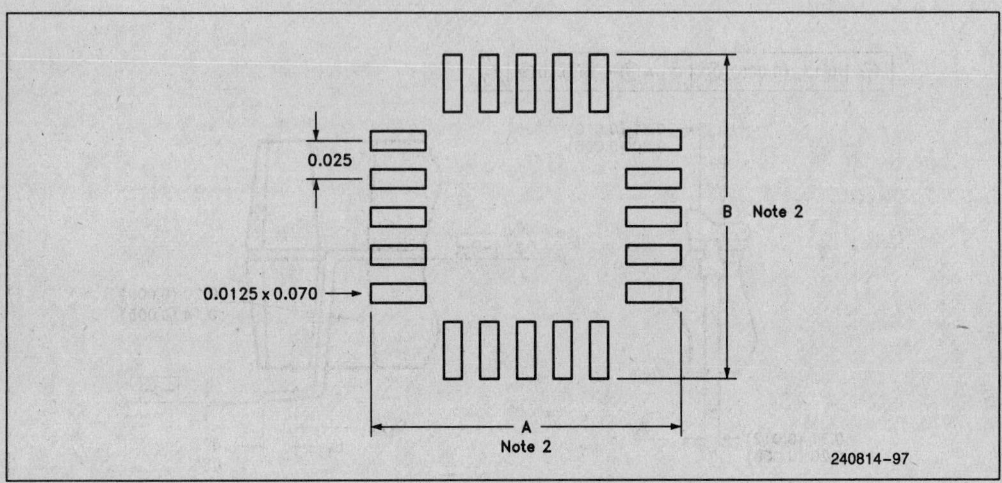

Figure 10-2f. Recommended PQFP Footprint

11.0 REVISION HISTORY

The First Release of the Advanced Information Intel386 SL Microprocessor Superset B Step Data book reflects information believed to be accurate as of July 1991.

Please Consult your Local Intel Field Sales Office for the most current design-in information.

Intel386™ SX MICROPROCESSOR

- **Full 32-Bit Internal Architecture**
  - **— 8-, 16-, 32-Bit Data Types**
  - **— 8 General Purpose 32-Bit Registers**
- **Runs Intel386™ Software in a Cost Effective 16-Bit Hardware Environment**
  - **— Runs Same Applications and O.S.'s as the Intel386™ DX Processor**
  - **— Object Code Compatible with 8086, 80186, 80286, and Intel386 Processors**
  - **— Runs MS-DOS*, OS/2* and UNIX****
- **Very High Performance 16-Bit Data Bus**
  - **— 16 MHz and 20 MHz Clock**
  - **— Two-Clock Bus Cycles**
  - **— 20 Megabytes/Sec Bus Bandwidth**
  - **— Address Pipelining Allows Use of Slower/Cheaper Memories**
- **Integrated Memory Management Unit**
  - **— Virtual Memory Support**
  - **— Optional On-Chip Paging**
  - **— 4 Levels of Hardware Enforced Protection**
  - **— MMU Fully Compatible with Those of the 80286 and Intel386 DX CPUs**
- **Virtual 8086 Mode Allows Execution of 8086 Software in a Protected and Paged System**
- **Large Uniform Address Space**
  - **— 16 Megabyte Physical**
  - **— 64 Terabyte Virtual**
  - **— 4 Gigabyte Maximum Segment Size**
- **High Speed Numerics Support with the Intel387™ SX Coprocessor**
- **On-Chip Debugging Support Including Breakpoint Registers**
- **Complete System Development Support**
  - **— Software: C, PL/M, Assembler**
  - **— Debuggers: PMON-Intel386 DX, ICE™-386 SX**
  - **— Extensive Third-Party Support: C, Pascal, FORTRAN, BASIC, Ada*** on VAX®†, UNIX**, MS-DOS*, and Other Hosts**
- **High Speed CHMOS IV Technology**
- **Operating Frequency:**
  - **— Standard (Intel386 SX -20, -16) Min/Max Frequency (4/20, 4/16) MHz**
  - **— Low Power (Intel386 SX -20, -16, -12) Min/Max Frequency (2/20, 2/16, 2/12) MHz**
- **100-Pin Plastic Quad Flatpack Package**
  (See Packaging Outlines and Dimensions #231369)

4

The Intel386™ SX Microprocessor is a 32-bit CPU with a 16-bit external data bus and a 24-bit external address bus. The Intel386 SX CPU brings the high-performance software of the Intel386™ Architecture to midrange systems. It provides the performance benefits of a 32-bit programming architecture with the cost savings associated with 16-bit hardware systems.

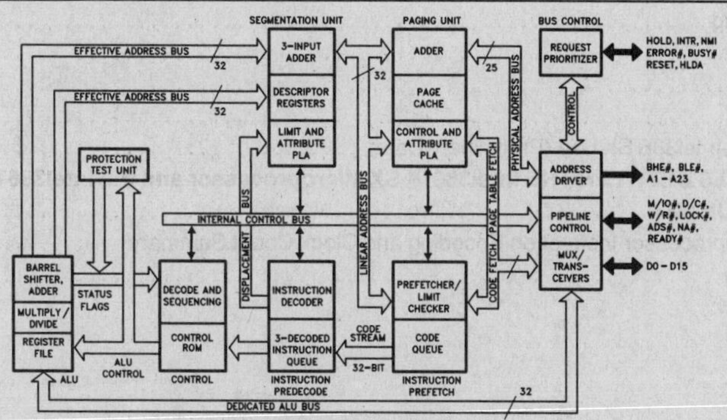

240187-47

Intel386™ SX Pipelined 32-Bit Microarchitecture

†VAX® is a registered trademark of the Digital Equipment Corporation.
*MS-DOS and OS/2 are trademarks of Microsoft Corporation.
**UNIX is a trademark of AT&T.
***Ada is a trademark of the Department of Defense.
i386™, i387™, Intel386™, Intel387™ are trademarks of Intel Corporation.

October 1991
Order Number: 240187-007

1.0 PIN DESCRIPTION

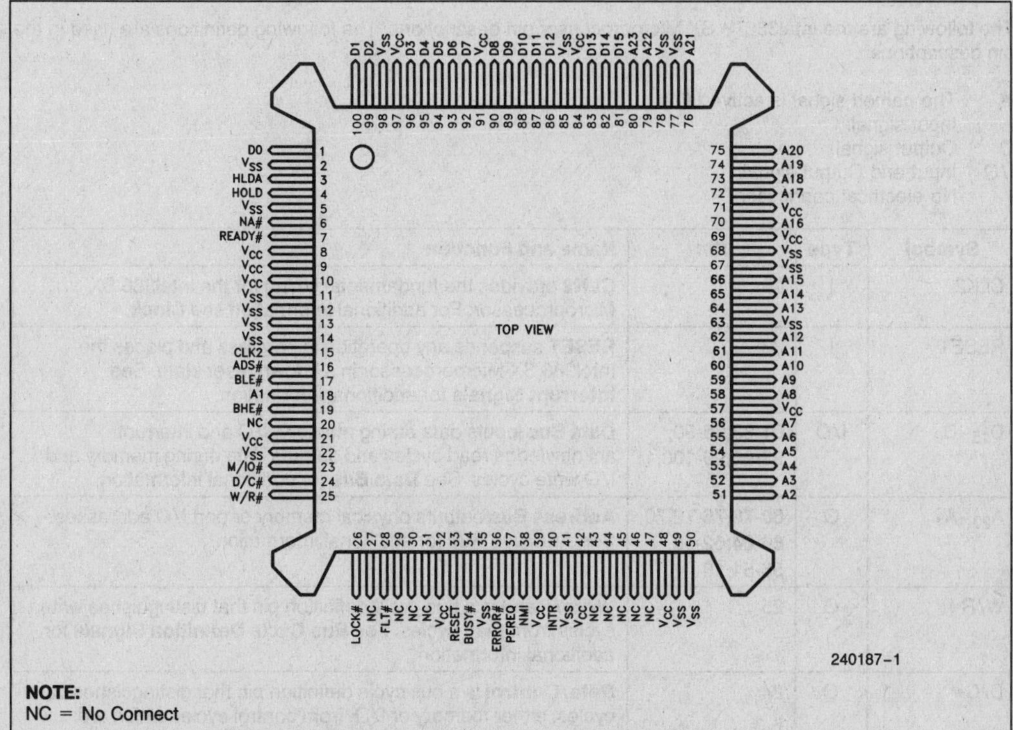

NOTE:
NC = No Connect

Figure 1.1. Intel386™ SX Microprocessor Pin out Top View

Table 1.1. Alphabetical Pin Assignments

Address		Data		Control		N/C	V_{CC}	V_{SS}
A_1	18	D_0	1	ADS#	16	20	8	2
A_2	51	D_1	100	BHE#	19	27	9	5
A_3	52	D_2	99	BLE#	17	29	10	11
A_4	53	D_3	96	BUSY#	34	30	21	12
A_5	54	D_4	95	CLK2	15	31	32	13
A_6	55	D_5	94	D/C#	24	43	39	14
A_7	56	D_6	93	ERROR#	36	44	42	22
A_8	58	D_7	92	FLT#	28	45	48	35
A_9	59	D_8	90	HLDA	3	46	57	41
A_{10}	60	D_9	89	HOLD	4	47	69	49
A_{11}	61	D_{10}	88	INTR	40		71	50
A_{12}	62	D_{11}	87	LOCK#	26		84	63
A_{13}	64	D_{12}	86	M/IO#	23		91	67
A_{14}	65	D_{13}	83	NA#	6		97	68
A_{15}	66	D_{14}	82	NMI	38			77
A_{16}	70	D_{15}	81	PEREQ	37			78
A_{17}	72			READY#	7			85
A_{18}	73			RESET	33			98
A_{19}	74			W/R#	25			
A_{20}	75							
A_{21}	76							
A_{22}	79							
A_{23}	80							

1.0 PIN DESCRIPTION (Continued)

The following are the Intel386™ SX Microprocessor pin descriptions. The following definitions are used in the pin descriptions:

#	The named signal is active LOW.
I	Input signal.
O	Output signal.
I/O	Input and Output signal.
-	No electrical connection.

Symbol	Type	Pin	Name and Function
CLK2	I	15	**CLK2** provides the fundamental timing for the Intel386 SX Microprocessor. For additional information see **Clock.**
RESET	I	33	**RESET** suspends any operation in progress and places the Intel386 SX Microprocessor in a known reset state. See **Interrupt Signals** for additional information.
D_{15}–D_0	I/O	81-83,86-90, 92-96,99-100,1	**Data Bus** inputs data during memory, I/O and interrupt acknowledge read cycles and outputs data during memory and I/O write cycles. See **Data Bus** for additional information.
A_{23}–A_1	O	80-79,76-72,70, 66-64,62-58, 56-51,18	**Address Bus** outputs physical memory or port I/O addresses. See **Address Bus** for additional information.
W/R#	O	25	**Write/Read** is a bus cycle definition pin that distinguishes write cycles from read cycles. See **Bus Cycle Definition Signals** for additional information.
D/C#	O	24	**Data/Control** is a bus cycle definition pin that distinguishes data cycles, either memory or I/O, from control cycles which are: interrupt acknowledge, halt, and code fetch. See **Bus Cycle Definition Signals** for additional information.
M/IO#	O	23	**Memory/IO** is a bus cycle definition pin that distinguishes memory cycles from input/output cycles. See **Bus Cycle Definition Signals** for additional information.
LOCK#	O	26	**Bus Lock** is a bus cycle definition pin that indicates that other system bus masters are not to gain control of the system bus while it is active. See **Bus Cycle Definition Signals** for additional information.
ADS#	O	16	**Address Status** indicates that a valid bus cycle definition and address (W/R#, D/C#, M/IO#, BHE#, BLE# and A_{23}–A_1 are being driven at the Intel386 SX Microprocessor pins. See **Bus Control Signals** for additional information.
NA#	I	6	**Next Address** is used to request address pipelining. See **Bus Control Signals** for additional information.
READY#	I	7	**Bus Ready** terminates the bus cycle. See **Bus Control Signals** for additional information.
BHE#, BLE#	O	19,17	**Byte Enables** indicate which data bytes of the data bus take part in a bus cycle. See **Address Bus** for additional information.

1.0 PIN DESCRIPTION (Continued)

Symbol	Type	Pin	Name and Function
HOLD	I	4	**Bus Hold Request** input allows another bus master to request control of the local bus. See **Bus Arbitration Signals** for additional information.
HLDA	O	3	**Bus Hold Acknowledge** output indicates that the Intel386 SX Microprocessor has surrendered control of its local bus to another bus master. See **Bus Arbitration Signals** for additional information.
INTR	I	40	**Interrupt Request** is a maskable input that signals the Intel386 SX Microprocessor to suspend execution of the current program and execute an interrupt acknowledge function. See **Interrupt Signals** for additional information.
NMI	I	38	**Non-Maskable Interrupt Request** is a non-maskable input that signals the Intel386 SX Microprocessor to suspend execution of the current program and execute an interrupt acknowledge function. See **Interrupt Signals** for additional information.
BUSY#	I	34	**Busy** signals a busy condition from a processor extension. See **Coprocessor Interface Signals** for additional information.
ERROR#	I	36	**Error** signals an error condition from a processor extension. See **Coprocessor Interface Signals** for additional information.
PEREQ	I	37	**Processor Extension Request** indicates that the processor has data to be transferred by the Intel386 SX Microprocessor. See **Coprocessor Interface Signals** for additional information.
FLT#	I	28	**Float** is an input which forces all bidirectional and output signals, including HLDA, to the tri-state condition. This allows the electrically isolated Intel386SX PQFP to use ONCE (On-Circuit Emulation) method without removing it from the PCB. See **Float** for additional information.
N/C	-	20, 27, 29-31, 43-47	**No Connects** should always be left unconnected. Connection of a N/C pin may cause the processor to malfunction or be incompatible with future steppings of the Intel386 SX Microprocessor.
V_{CC}	I	8-10,21,32,39 42,48,57,69, 71,84,91,97	**System Power** provides the +5V nominal DC supply input.
V_{SS}	I	2,5,11-14,22 35,41,49-50, 63,67-68, 77-78,85,98	**System Ground** provides the 0V connection from which all inputs and outputs are measured.

4

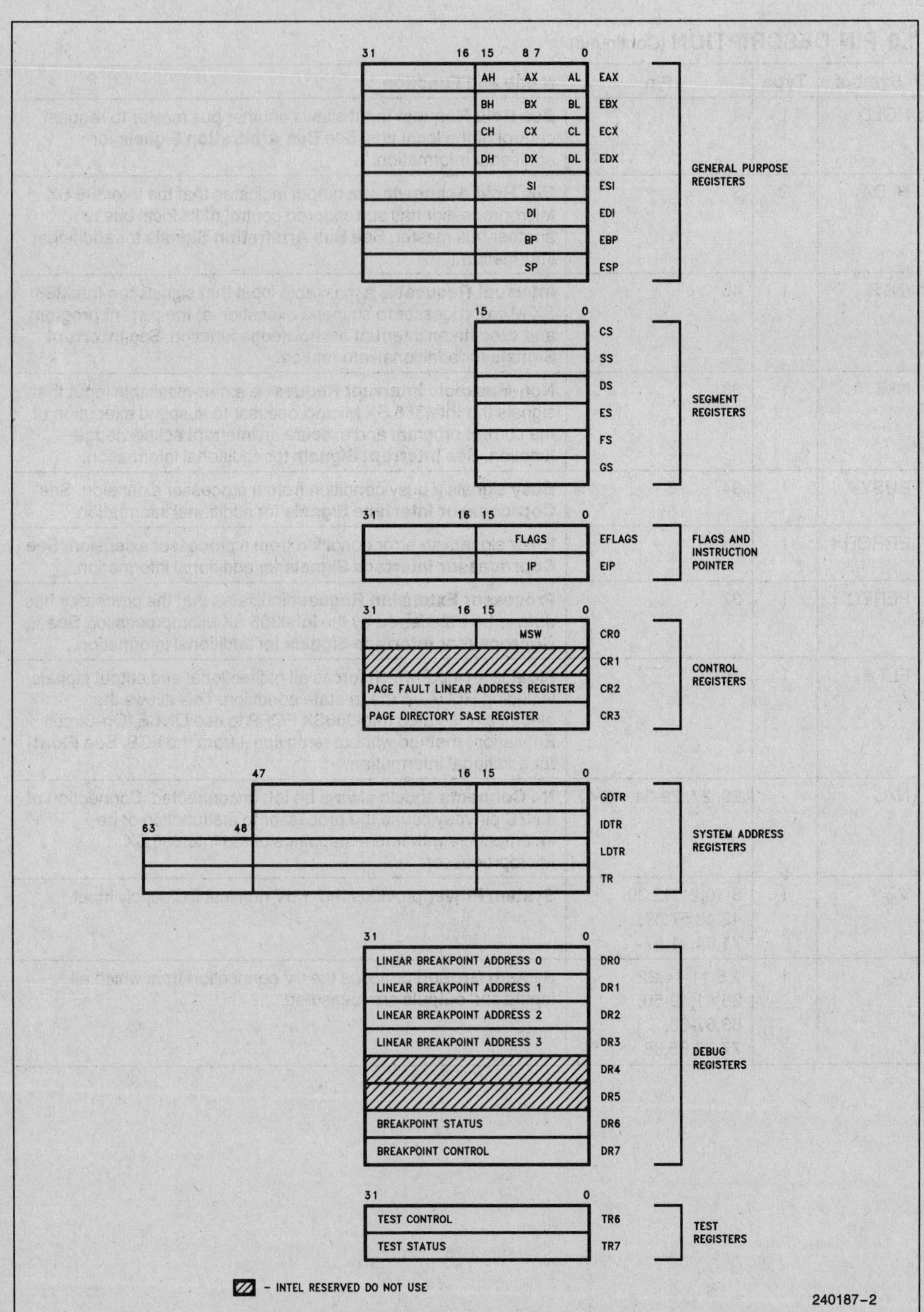

Figure 2.1. Intel386™ SX Microprocessor Registers

INTRODUCTION

The Intel386 SX Microprocessor is 100% object code compatible with the Intel386 DX, 286 and 8086 microprocessors. System manufacturers can provide Intel386 DX CPU based systems optimized for performance and Intel386 SX CPU based systems optimized for cost, both sharing the same operating systems and application software. Systems based on the Intel386 SX CPU can access the world's largest existing microcomputer software base, including the growing 32-bit software base. Only the Intel386 architecture can run UNIX, OS/2 and MS-DOS.

Instruction pipelining, high bus bandwidth, and a very high performance ALU ensure short average instruction execution times and high system throughput. The Intel386 SX CPU is capable of execution at sustained rates of 2.5–3.0 million instructions per second.

The integrated memory management unit (MMU) includes an address translation cache, advanced multi-tasking hardware, and a four-level hardware-enforced protection mechanism to support operating systems. The virtual machine capability of the Intel386 SX CPU allows simultaneous execution of applications from multiple operating systems such as MS-DOS and UNIX.

The Intel386 SX CPU offers on-chip testability and debugging features. Four breakpoint registers allow conditional or unconditional breakpoint traps on code execution or data accesses for powerful debugging of even ROM-based systems. Other testability features include self-test, tri-state of output buffers, and direct access to the page translation cache.

The new Low Power Intel386 SX CPU brings the benefits of Intel's Intel386 Microprocessor 32-bit architecture to the mainstream Laptop and Notebook personal computer applications. With its power saving 2 MHz sleep-mode and extended functional temperature range of 0°C to 100°C T_{CASE}, the Lower Power Intel386 SX CPU specifically satisfies the power consumption and heat dissipation requirements of today's small form factor computers.

2.0 BASE ARCHITECTURE

The Intel386 SX Microprocessor consists of a central processing unit, a memory management unit and a bus interface.

The central processing unit consists of the execution unit and the instruction unit. The execution unit contains the eight 32-bit general purpose registers which are used for both address calculation and data operations and a 64-bit barrel shifter used to speed shift, rotate, multiply, and divide operations. The instruction unit decodes the instruction opcodes and stores them in the decoded instruction queue for immediate use by the execution unit.

The memory management unit (MMU) consists of a segmentation unit and a paging unit. Segmentation allows the managing of the logical address space by providing an extra addressing component, one that allows easy code and data relocatability, and efficient sharing. The paging mechanism operates beneath and is transparent to the segmentation process, to allow management of the physical address space.

The segmentation unit provides four levels of protection for isolating and protecting applications and the operating system from each other. The hardware enforced protection allows the design of systems with a high degree of integrity.

The Intel386 SX Microprocessor has two modes of operation: Real Address Mode (Real Mode), and Protected Virtual Address Mode (Protected Mode). In Real Mode the Intel386 SX Microprocessor operates as a very fast 8086, but with 32-bit extensions if desired. Real Mode is required primarily to set up the processor for Protected Mode operation.

Within Protected Mode, software can perform a task switch to enter into tasks designated as Virtual 8086 Mode tasks. Each such task behaves with 8086 semantics, thus allowing 8086 software (an application program or an entire operating system) to execute. The Virtual 8086 tasks can be isolated and protected from one another and the host Intel386 SX Microprocessor operating system by use of paging.

Finally, to facilitate high performance system hardware designs, the Intel386 SX Microprocessor bus interface offers address pipelining and direct Byte Enable signals for each byte of the data bus.

2.1 Register Set

The Intel386 SX Microprocessor has thirty-four registers as shown in Figure 2-1. These registers are grouped into the following seven categories:

General Purpose Registers: The eight 32-bit general purpose registers are used to contain arithmetic and logical operands. Four of these (EAX, EBX, ECX, and EDX) can be used either in their entirety as 32-bit registers, as 16-bit registers, or split into pairs of separate 8-bit registers.

Segment Registers: Six 16-bit special purpose registers select, at any given time, the segments of memory that are immediately addressable for code, stack, and data.

Flags and Instruction Pointer Registers: The two 32-bit special purpose registers in figure 2.1 record or control certain aspects of the Intel386 SX Microprocessor state. The EFLAGS register includes status and control bits that are used to reflect the outcome of many instructions and modify the semantics of some instructions. The Instruction Pointer, called EIP, is 32 bits wide. The Instruction Pointer controls instruction fetching and the processor automatically increments it after executing an instruction.

Control Registers: The four 32-bit control register are used to control the global nature of the Intel386 SX Microprocessor. The CR0 register contains bits that set the different processor modes (Protected, Real, Paging and Coprocessor Emulation). CR2 and CR3 registers are used in the paging operation.

System Address Registers: These four special registers reference the tables or segments supported by the 80286/Intel386 SX/Intel386 DX CPU's protection model. These tables or segments are:

GDTR (Global Descriptor Table Register),
IDTR (Interrupt Descriptor Table Register),
LDTR (Local Descriptor Table Register),
TR (Task State Segment Register).

Debug Registers: The six programmer accessible debug registers provide on-chip support for debugging. The use of the debug registers is described in Section 2.10 **Debugging Support**.

Test Registers: Two registers are used to control the testing of the RAM/CAM (Content Addressable Memories) in the Translation Lookaside Buffer portion of the Intel386 SX Microprocessor. Their use is discussed in **Testability**.

EFLAGS REGISTER

The flag register is a 32-bit register named EFLAGS. The defined bits and bit fields within EFLAGS, shown in Figure 2.2, control certain operations and indicate the status of the Intel386 SX Microprocessor. The lower 16 bits (bits 0–15) of EFLAGS contain the 16-bit flag register named FLAGS. This is the default flag register used when executing 8086, 80286, or real mode code. The functions of the flag bits are given in Table 2.1.

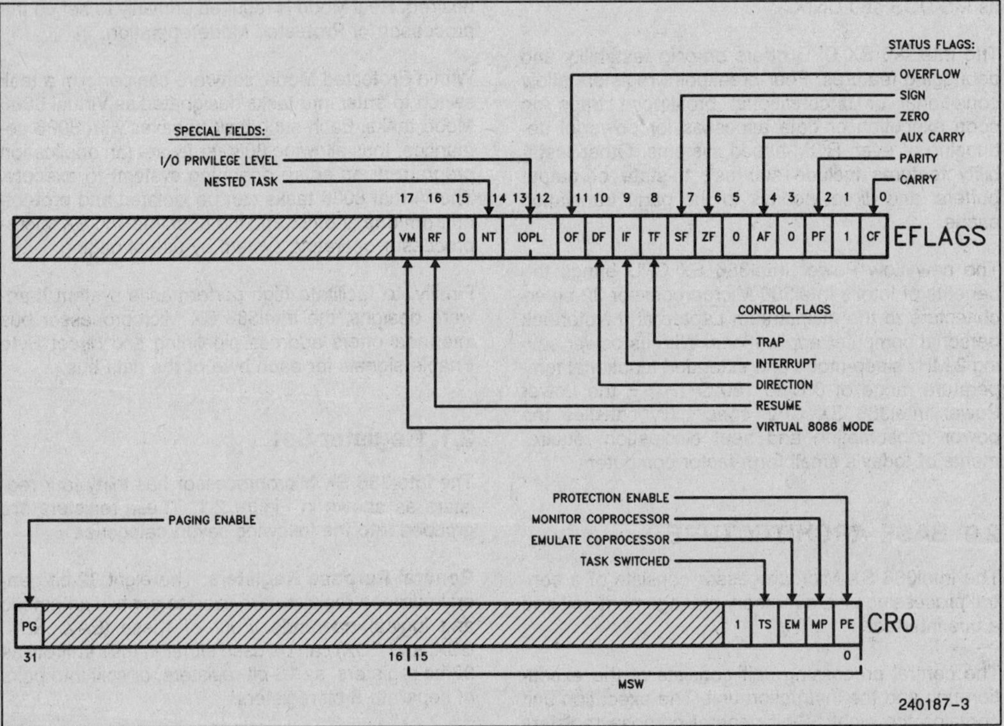

240187–3

Figure 2.2. Status and Control Register Bit Functions

Table 2.1. Flag Definitions

Bit Position	Name	Function
0	CF	Carry Flag—Set on high-order bit carry or borrow; cleared otherwise.
2	PF	Parity Flag—Set if low-order 8 bits of result contain an even number of 1-bits; cleared otherwise.
4	AF	Auxiliary Carry Flag—Set on carry from or borrow to the low order four bits of AL; cleared otherwise.
6	ZF	Zero Flag—Set if result is zero; cleared otherwise.
7	SF	Sign Flag—Set equal to high-order bit of result (0 if positive, 1 if negative).
8	TF	Single Step Flag—Once set, a single step interrupt occurs after the next instruction executes. TF is cleared by the single step interrupt.
9	IF	Interrupt-Enable Flag—When set, maskable interrupts will cause the CPU to transfer control to an interrupt vector specified location.
10	DF	Direction Flag—Causes string instructions to auto-increment (default) the appropriate index registers when cleared. Setting DF causes auto-decrement.
11	OF	Overflow Flag—Set if the operation resulted in a carry/borrow into the sign bit (high-order bit) of the result but did not result in a carry/borrow out of the high-order bit or vice-versa.
12,13	IOPL	I/O Privilege Level—Indicates the maximum Current Privilege Level (CPL) permitted to execute I/O instructions without generating an exception 13 fault or consulting the I/O permission bit map while executing in protected mode. For virtual 86 mode it indicates the maximum CPL allowing alteration of the IF bit. See Section 4.2 for a further discussion and definitions on various privilege levels.
14	NT	Nested Task—Set if the execution of the current task is nested within another task. Cleared otherwise.
16	RF	Resume Flag—Used in conjunction with debug register breakpoints. It is checked at instruction boundaries before breakpoint processing. If set, any debug fault is ignored on the next instruction.
17	VM	Virtual 8086 Mode—If set while in protected mode, the Intel386 SX Microprocessor will switch to virtual 8086 operation, handling segment loads as the 8086 does, but generating exception 13 faults on privileged opcodes.

4

CONTROL REGISTERS

The Intel386 SX Microprocessor has three control registers of 32 bits, CR0, CR2 and CR3, to hold the machine state of a global nature. These registers are shown in Figures 2.1 and 2.2. The defined CR0 bits are described in Table 2.2.

Table 2.2. CR0 Definitions

Bit Position	Name	Function
0	PE	Protection mode enable—places the Intel386 SX Microprocessor into protected mode. If PE is reset, the processor operates again in Real Mode. PE may be set by loading MSW or CR0. PE can be reset only by loading CR0, it cannot be reset by the LMSW instruction.
1	MP	Monitor coprocessor extension—allows WAIT instructions to cause a processor extension not present exception (number 7).
2	EM	Emulate processor extension—causes a processor extension not present exception (number 7) on ESC instructions to allow emulating a processor extension.
3	TS	Task switched—indicates the next instruction using a processor extension will cause exception 7, allowing software to test whether the current processor extension context belongs to the current task.
31	PG	Paging enable bit—is set to enable the on-chip paging unit. It is reset to disable the on-chip paging unit.

2.2 Instruction Set

The instruction set is divided into nine categories of operations:

Data Transfer
Arithmetic
Shift/Rotate
String Manipulation
Bit Manipulation
Control Transfer
High Level Language Support
Operating System Support
Processor Control

These instructions are listed in Table 9.1 **Instruction Set Clock Count Summary**.

All Intel386 SX Microprocessor instructions operate on either 0, 1, 2 or 3 operands; an operand resides in a register, in the instruction itself, or in memory. Most zero operand instructions (e.g CLI, STI) take only one byte. One operand instructions generally are two bytes long. The average instruction is 3.2 bytes long. Since the Intel386 SX Microprocessor has a 16 byte prefetch instruction queue, an average of 5 instructions will be prefetched. The use of two operands permits the following types of common instructions:

Register to Register
Memory to Register
Immediate to Register
Memory to Memory
Register to Memory
Immediate to Memory.

The operands can be either 8, 16, or 32 bits long. As a general rule, when executing code written for the Intel386 SX Microprocessor (32-bit code), operands are 8 or 32 bits; when executing existing 8086 or 80286 code (16-bit code), operands are 8 or 16 bits. Prefixes can be added to all instructions which override the default length of the operands (i.e. use 32-bit operands for 16-bit code, or 16-bit operands for 32-bit code).

2.3 Memory Organization

Memory on the Intel386 SX Microprocessor is divided into 8-bit quantities (bytes), 16-bit quantities (words), and 32-bit quantities (dwords). Words are stored in two consecutive bytes in memory with the low-order byte at the lowest address. Dwords are stored in four consecutive bytes in memory with the low-order byte at the lowest address. The address of a word or dword is the byte address of the low-order byte.

In addition to these basic data types, the Intel386 SX Microprocessor supports two larger units of memory: pages and segments. Memory can be divided up into one or more variable length segments, which can be swapped to disk or shared between programs. Memory can also be organized into one or more 4K byte pages. Finally, both segmentation and paging can be combined, gaining the advantages of both systems. The Intel386 SX Microprocessor supports both pages and segmentation in order to provide maximum flexibility to the system designer. Segmentation and paging are complementary. Segmentation is useful for organizing memory in logical modules, and as such is a tool for the application programmer, while pages are useful to the system programmer for managing the physical memory of a system.

ADDRESS SPACES

The Intel386 SX Microprocessor has three types of address spaces: **logical**, **linear**, and **physical**. A **logical** address (also known as a **virtual** address) consists of a selector and an offset. A selector is the contents of a segment register. An offset is formed by summing all of the addressing components (BASE, INDEX, DISPLACEMENT), discussed in section 2.4 **Addressing Modes**, into an effective address. This effective address along with the selector is known as the logical address. Since each task on the Intel386 SX Microprocessor has a maximum of 16K ($2^{14}-1$) selectors, and offsets can be 4 gigabytes (with paging enabled) this gives a total of 2^{46} bits, or 64 terabytes, of **logical** address space per task. The programmer sees the logical address space.

The segmentation unit translates the **logical** address space into a 32-bit **linear** address space. If the paging unit is not enabled then the 32-bit **linear** address is truncated into a 24-bit **physical** address. The **physical address** is what appears on the address pins.

The primary differences between Real Mode and Protected Mode are how the segmentation unit performs the translation of the **logical** address into the **linear** address, size of the address space, and paging capability. In Real Mode, the segmentation unit shifts the selector left four bits and adds the result to the effective address to form the **linear** address. This **linear** address is limited to 1 megabyte. In addition, real mode has no paging capability.

Protected Mode will see one of two different address spaces, depending on whether or not paging is enabled. Every selector has a **logical base** address associated with it that can be up to 32 bits in length. This 32-bit **logical base** address is added to the effective address to form a final 32-bit **linear**

4

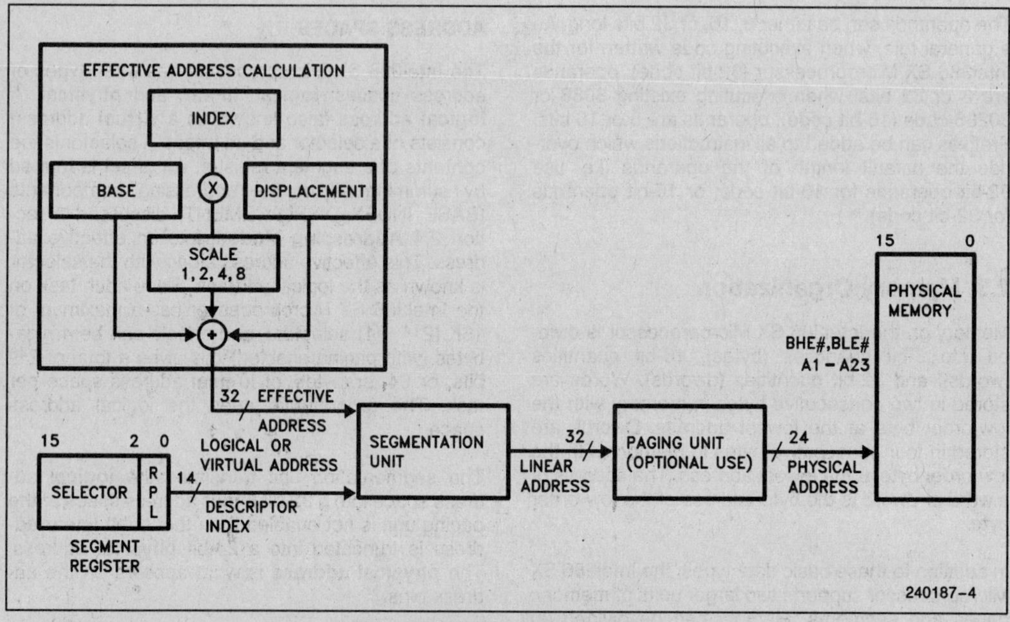

Figure 2.3. Address Translation

address. If paging is disabled this final **linear** address reflects physical memory and is truncated so that only the lower 24 bits of this address are used to address the 16 megabyte memory address space. If paging is enabled this final **linear** address reflects a 32-bit address that is translated through the paging unit to form a 16-megabyte physical address. The **logical base** address is stored in one of two operating system tables (i.e. the Local Descriptor Table or Global Descriptor Table).

Figure 2.3 shows the relationship between the various address spaces.

SEGMENT REGISTER USAGE

The main data structure used to organize memory is the segment. On the Intel386 SX Microprocessor, segments are variable sized blocks of linear addresses which have certain attributes associated with them. There are two main types of segments, code and data. The segments are of variable size and can be as small as 1 byte or as large as 4 gigabytes (2^{32} bits).

In order to provide compact instruction encoding and increase processor performance, instructions do not need to explicitly specify which segment register is used. The segment register is automatically chosen according to the rules of Table 2.3 (Segment Register Selection Rules). In general, data references use the selector contained in the DS register, stack references use the SS register and instruction fetches use the CS register. The contents of the Instruction Pointer provide the offset. Special segment override prefixes allow the explicit use of a given segment register, and override the implicit rules listed in Table 2.3. The override prefixes also allow the use of the ES, FS and GS segment registers.

There are no restrictions regarding the overlapping of the base addresses of any segments. Thus, all 6 segments could have the base address set to zero and create a system with a four gigabyte linear address space. This creates a system where the virtual address space is the same as the linear address space. Further details of segmentation are discussed in chapter 4 **PROTECTED MODE ARCHITECTURE.**

2.4 Addressing Modes

The Intel386 SX Microprocessor provides a total of 8 addressing modes for instructions to specify operands. The addressing modes are optimized to allow the efficient execution of high level languages such as C and FORTRAN, and they cover the vast majority of data references needed by high-level languages.

REGISTER AND IMMEDIATE MODES

Two of the addressing modes provide for instructions that operate on register or immediate operands:

Table 2.3. Segment Register Selection Rules

Type of Memory Reference	Implied (Default) Segment Use	Segment Override Prefixes Possible
Code Fetch	CS	None
Destination of PUSH, PUSHF, INT, CALL, PUSHA Instructons	SS	None
Source of POP, POPA, POPF, IRET, RET Instructions	SS	None
Destination of STOS, MOVE, REP STOS, and REP MOVS instructions	ES	None
Other data references, with effective address using base register of:		
[EAX]	DS	CS,SS,ES,FS,GS
[EBX]	DS	CS,SS,ES,FS,GS
[ECX]	DS	CS,SS,ES,FS,GS
[EDX]	DS	CS,SS,ES,FS,GS
[ESI]	DS	CS,SS,ES,FS,GS
[EDI]	DS	CS,SS,ES,FS,GS
[EBP]	SS	CS,DS,ES,FS,GS
[ESP]	SS	CS,DS,ES,FS,GS

Register Operand Mode: The operand is located in one of the 8, 16 or 32-bit general registers.

Immediate Operand Mode: The operand is included in the instruction as part of the opcode.

32-BIT MEMORY ADDRESSING MODES

The remaining 6 modes provide a mechanism for specifying the effective address of an operand. The linear address consists of two components: the segment base address and an effective address. The effective address is calculated by summing any combination of the following three address elements (see figure 2.3):

DISPLACEMENT: an 8, 16 or 32-bit immediate value, following the instruction.

BASE: The contents of any general purpose register. The base registers are generally used by compilers to point to the start of the local variable area.

INDEX: The contents of any general purpose register except for ESP. The index registers are used to access the elements of an array, or a string of characters. The index register's value can be multiplied by a scale factor, either 1, 2, 4 or 8. The scaled index is especially useful for accessing arrays or structures.

Combinations of these 3 components make up the 6 additional addressing modes. There is no performance penalty for using any of these addressing combinations, since the effective address calculation is pipelined with the execution of other instructions. The one exception is the simultaneous use of Base and Index components which requires one additional clock.

As shown in Figure 2.4, the effective address (EA) of an operand is calculated according to the following formula:

$$EA = Base_{Register} + (Index_{Register} * scaling) + Displacement$$

1. **Direct Mode:** The operand's offset is contained as part of the instruction as an 8, 16 or 32-bit displacement.
2. **Register Indirect Mode:** A BASE register contains the address of the operand.
3. **Based Mode:** A BASE register's contents are added to a DISPLACEMENT to form the operand's offset.
4. **Scaled Index Mode:** An INDEX register's contents are multiplied by a SCALING factor, and the result is added to a DISPLACEMENT to form the operand's offset.

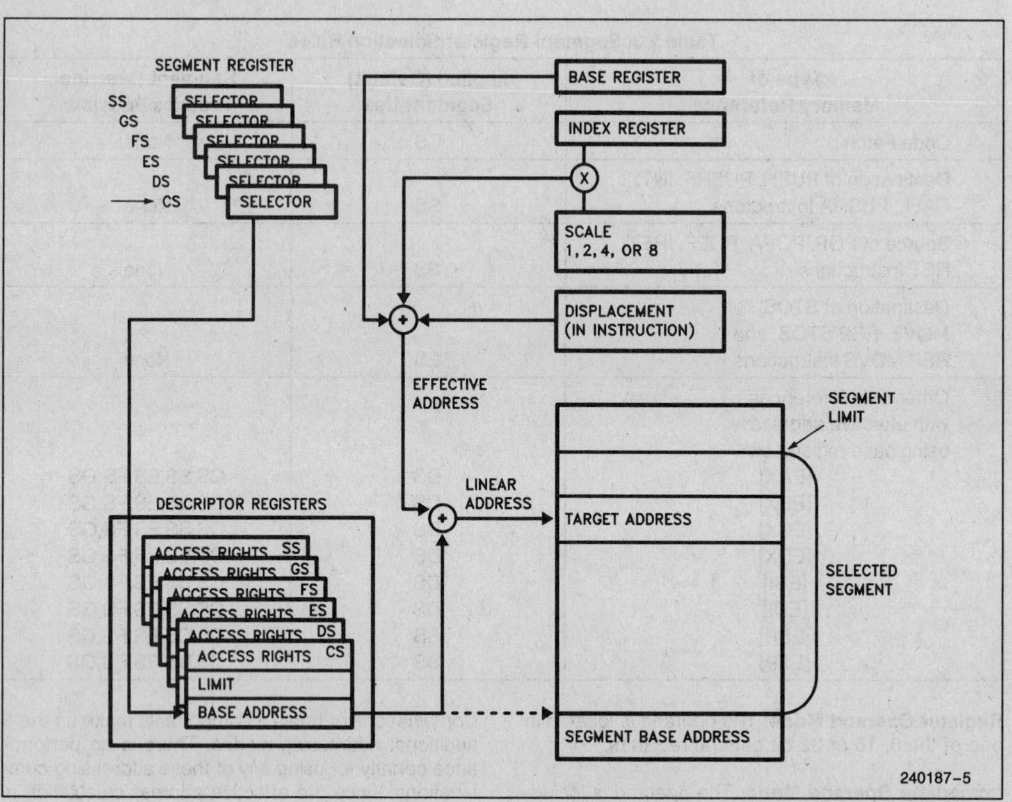

Figure 2.4. Addressing Mode Calculations

5. **Based Scaled Index Mode:** The contents of an INDEX register are multiplied by a SCALING factor, and the result is added to the contents of a BASE register to obtain the operand's offset.
6. **Based Scaled Index Mode with Displacement:** The contents of an INDEX register are multiplied by a SCALING factor, and the result is added to the contents of a BASE register and a DISPLACEMENT to form the operand's offset.

DIFFERENCES BETWEEN 16 AND 32 BIT ADDRESSES

In order to provide software compatibility with the 8086 and the 80286, the Intel386 SX Microprocessor can execute 16-bit instructions in Real and Protected Modes. The processor determines the size of the instructions it is executing by examining the D bit in a Segment Descriptor. If the D bit is 0 then all operand lengths and effective addresses are assumed to be 16 bits long. If the D bit is 1 then the default length for operands and addresses is 32 bits. In Real Mode the default size for operands and addresses is 16 bits.

Regardless of the default precision of the operands or addresses, the Intel386 SX Microprocessor is able to execute either 16 or 32-bit instructions. This is specified through the use of override prefixes. Two prefixes, the **Operand Length Prefix** and the **Address Length Prefix**, override the value of the D bit on an individual instruction basis. These prefixes are automatically added by assemblers.

The Operand Length and Address Length Prefixes can be applied separately or in combination to any instruction. The Address Length Prefix does not allow addresses over 64K bytes to be accessed in Real Mode. A memory address which exceeds 0FFFFH will result in a General Protection Fault. An Address Length Prefix only allows the use of the additional Intel386 SX Microprocessor addressing modes.

When executing 32-bit code, the Intel386 SX Microprocessor uses either 8 or 32-bit displacements, and any register can be used as base or index registers. When executing 16-bit code, the displacements are either 8 or 16-bits, and the base and index register conform to the 80286 model. Table 2.4 illustrates the differences.

Table 2.4. BASE and INDEX Registers for 16- and 32-Bit Addresses

	16-Bit Addressing	32-Bit Addressing
BASE REGISTER	BX,BP	Any 32-bit GP Register
INDEX REGISTER	SI,DI	Any 32-bit GP Register Except ESP
SCALE FACTOR	None	1, 2, 4, 8
DISPLACEMENT	0, 8, 16-bits	0, 8, 32-bits

2.5 Data Types

The Intel386 SX Microprocessor supports all of the data types commonly used in high level languages:

Bit: A single bit quantity.

Bit Field: A group of up to 32 contiguous bits, which spans a maximum of four bytes.

Bit String: A set of contiguous bits; on the Intel386 SX Microprocessor, bit strings can be up to 4 gigabits long.

Byte: A signed 8-bit quantity.

Unsigned Byte: An unsigned 8-bit quantity.

Integer (Word): A signed 16-bit quantity.

Long Integer (Double Word): A signed 32-bit quantity. All operations assume a 2's complement representation.

Unsigned Integer (Word): An unsigned 16-bit quantity.

Unsigned Long Integer (Double Word): An unsigned 32-bit quantity.

Signed Quad Word: A signed 64-bit quantity.

Unsigned Quad Word: An unsigned 64-bit quantity.

Pointer: A 16 or 32-bit offset-only quantity which indirectly references another memory location.

Long Pointer: A full pointer which consists of a 16-bit segment selector and either a 16 or 32-bit offset.

Char: A byte representation of an ASCII Alphanumeric or control character.

String: A contiguous sequence of bytes, words or dwords. A string may contain between 1 byte and 4 gigabytes

BCD: A byte (unpacked) representation of decimal digits 0–9.

Packed BCD: A byte (packed) representation of two decimal digits 0–9 storing one digit in each nibble.

When the Intel386 SX Microprocessor is coupled with its numerics coprocessor, the Intel387 SX, then the following common floating point types are supported:

Floating Point: A signed 32, 64, or 80-bit real number representation. Floating point numbers are supported by the Intel387 SX numerics coprocessor.

Figure 2.5 illustrates the data types supported by the Intel386 SX Microprocessor and the Intel387 SX.

2.6 I/O Space

The Intel386 SX Microprocessor has two distinct physical address spaces: physical memory and I/O. Generally, peripherals are placed in I/O space although the Intel386 SX Microprocessor also supports memory-mapped peripherals. The I/O space consists of 64K bytes which can be divided into 64K 8-bit ports or 32K 16-bit ports, or any combination of ports which add up to no more than 64K bytes. The 64K I/O address space refers to physical addresses rather than linear addresses since I/O instructions do not go through the segmentation or paging hardware. The M/IO# pin acts as an additional address line, thus allowing the system designer to easily determine which address space the processor is accessing.

The I/O ports are accessed by the IN and OUT instructions, with the port address supplied as an immediate 8-bit constant in the instruction or in the DX register. All 8-bit and 16-bit port addresses are zero extended on the upper address lines. The I/O instructions cause the M/IO# pin to be driven LOW. I/O port addresses 00F8H through 00FFH are reserved for use by Intel.

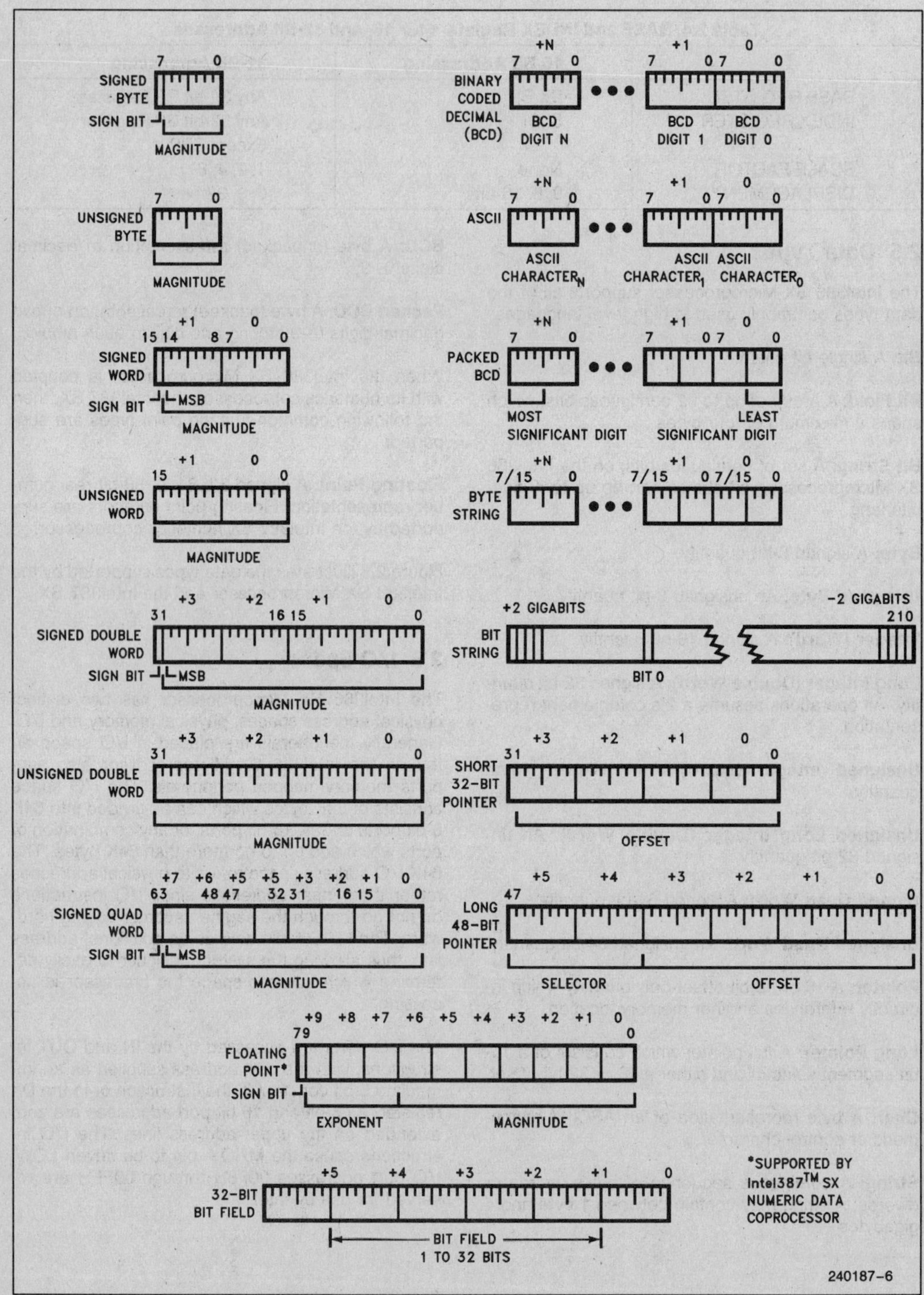

Figure 2.5. Intel386™ SX Microprocessor Supported Data Types

Table 2.5. Interrupt Vector Assignments

Function	Interrupt Number	Instruction Which Can Cause Exception	Return Address Points to Faulting Instruction	Type
Divide Error	0	DIV, IDIV	YES	FAULT
Debug Exception	1	any instruction	YES	TRAP*
NMI Interrupt	2	INT 2 or NMI	NO	NMI
One Byte Interrupt	3	INT	NO	TRAP
Interrupt on Overflow	4	INTO	NO	TRAP
Array Bounds Check	5	BOUND	YES	FAULT
Invalid OP-Code	6	Any illegal instruction	YES	FAULT
Device Not Available	7	ESC, WAIT	YES	FAULT
Double Fault	8	Any instruction that can generate an exception		ABORT
Coprocessor Segment Overrun	9	ESC	NO	ABORT
Invalid TSS	10	JMP, CALL, IRET, INT	YES	FAULT
Segment Not Present	11	Segment Register Instructions	YES	FAULT
Stack Fault	12	Stack References	YES	FAULT
General Protection Fault	13	Any Memory Reference	YES	FAULT
Page Fault	14	Any Memory Access or Code Fetch	YES	FAULT
Coprocessor Error	16	ESC, WAIT	YES	FAULT
Intel Reserved	17–32			
Two Byte Interrupt	0–255	INT n	NO	TRAP

*Some debug exceptions may report both traps on the previous instruction and faults on the next instruction.

2.7 Interrupts and Exceptions

Interrupts and exceptions alter the normal program flow in order to handle external events, report errors or exceptional conditions. The difference between interrupts and exceptions is that interrupts are used to handle asynchronous external events while exceptions handle instruction faults. Although a program can generate a software interrupt via an INT N instruction, the processor treats software interrupts as exceptions.

Hardware interrupts occur as the result of an external event and are classified into two types: maskable or non-maskable. Interrupts are serviced after the execution of the current instruction. After the interrupt handler is finished servicing the interrupt, execution proceeds with the instruction immediately **after** the interrupted instruction.

Exceptions are classified as faults, traps, or aborts, depending on the way they are reported and whether or not restart of the instruction causing the exception is supported. **Faults** are exceptions that are detected and serviced **before** the execution of the faulting instruction. **Traps** are exceptions that are reported immediately **after** the execution of the instruction which caused the problem. **Aborts** are exceptions which do not permit the precise location of the instruction causing the exception to be determined.

Thus, when an interrupt service routine has been completed, execution proceeds from the instruction immediately following the interrupted instruction. On the other hand, the return address from an exception fault routine will always point to the instruction causing the exception and will include any leading instruction prefixes. Table 2.5 summarizes the possible interrupts for the Intel386 SX Microprocessor and shows where the return address points to.

The Intel386 SX Microprocessor has the ability to handle up to 256 different interrupts/exceptions. In order to service the interrupts, a table with up to 256 interrupt vectors must be defined. The interrupt vectors are simply pointers to the appropriate interrupt service routine. In Real Mode, the vectors are 4-byte quantities, a Code Segment plus a 16-bit offset; in Protected Mode, the interrupt vectors are 8 byte quantities, which are put in an Interrupt Descriptor Table. Of the 256 possible interrupts, 32 are reserved for use by Intel and the remaining 224 are free to be used by the system designer.

INTERRUPT PROCESSING

When an interrupt occurs, the following actions happen. First, the current program address and Flags are saved on the stack to allow resumption of the interrupted program. Next, an 8-bit vector is supplied to the Intel386 SX Microprocessor which identifies the appropriate entry in the interrupt table. The table contains the starting address of the interrupt service routine. Then, the user supplied interrupt service routine is executed. Finally, when an IRET instruction is executed the old processor state is restored and program execution resumes at the appropriate instruction.

The 8-bit interrupt vector is supplied to the Intel386 SX Microprocessor in several different ways: exceptions supply the interrupt vector internally; software INT instructions contain or imply the vector; maskable hardware interrupts supply the 8-bit vector via the interrupt acknowledge bus sequence. Non-Maskable hardware interrupts are assigned to interrupt vector 2.

Maskable Interrupt

Maskable interrupts are the most common way to respond to asynchronous external hardware events. A hardware interrupt occurs when the INTR is pulled HIGH and the Interrupt Flag bit (IF) is enabled. The processor only responds to interrupts between instructions (string instructions have an 'interrupt window' between memory moves which allows interrupts during long string moves). When an interrupt occurs the processor reads an 8-bit vector supplied by the hardware which identifies the source of the interrupt (one of 224 user defined interrupts).

Interrupts through interrupt gates automatically reset IF, disabling INTR requests. Interrupts through Trap Gates leave the state of the IF bit unchanged. Interrupts through a Task Gate change the IF bit according to the image of the EFLAGs register in the task's Task State Segment (TSS). When an IRET instruction is executed, the original state of the IF bit is restored.

Non-Maskable Interrupt

Non-maskable interrupts provide a method of servicing very high priority interrupts. When the NMI input is pulled HIGH it causes an interrupt with an internally supplied vector value of 2. Unlike a normal hardware interrupt, no interrupt acknowledgment sequence is performed for an NMI.

While executing the NMI servicing procedure, the Intel386 SX Microprocessor will not service any further NMI request or INT requests until an interrupt return (IRET) instruction is executed or the processor is reset. If NMI occurs while currently servicing an NMI, its presence will be saved for servicing after executing the first IRET instruction. The IF bit is cleared at the beginning of an NMI interrupt to inhibit further INTR interrupts.

Software Interrupts

A third type of interrupt/exception for the Intel386 SX Microprocessor is the software interrupt. An INT n instruction causes the processor to execute the interrupt service routine pointed to by the nth vector in the interrupt table.

A special case of the two byte software interrupt INT n is the one byte INT 3, or breakpoint interrupt. By inserting this one byte instruction in a program, the user can set breakpoints in his program as a debugging tool.

A final type of software interrupt is the single step interrupt. It is discussed in **Single Step Trap.**

INTERRUPT AND EXCEPTION PRIORITIES

Interrupts are externally generated events. Maskable Interrupts (on the INTR input) and Non-Maskable Interrupts (on the NMI input) are recognized at instruction boundaries. When NMI and maskable INTR are **both** recognized at the **same** instruction boundary, the Intel386 SX Microprocessor invokes the NMI service routine first. If maskable interrupts are still enabled after the NMI service routine has been invoked, then the Intel386 SX Microprocessor will invoke the appropriate interrupt service routine.

As the Intel386 SX Microprocessor executes instructions, it follows a consistent cycle in checking for exceptions, as shown in Table 2.6. This cycle is repeated as each instruction is executed, and occurs in parallel with instruction decoding and execution.

INSTRUCTION RESTART

The Intel386 SX Microprocessor fully supports restarting all instructions after Faults. If an exception is detected in the instruction to be executed (exception categories 4 through 10 in Table 2.6), the Intel386 SX Microprocessor invokes the appropriate exception service routine. The Intel386 SX Microprocessor is in a state that permits restart of the instruction, for all cases but those given in Table 2.7. Note that all such cases will be avoided by a properly designed operating system.

Table 2.6. Sequence of Exception Checking

Consider the case of the Intel386 SX Microprocessor having just completed an instruction. It then performs the following checks before reaching the point where the next instruction is completed:

1. Check for Exception 1 Traps from the instruction just completed (single-step via Trap Flag, or Data Breakpoints set in the Debug Registers).
2. Check for external NMI and INTR.
3. Check for Exception 1 Faults in the next instruction (Instruction Execution Breakpoint set in the Debug Registers for the next instruction).
4. Check for Segmentation Faults that prevented fetching the entire next instruction (exceptions 11 or 13).
5. Check for Page Faults that prevented fetching the entire next instruction (exception 14).
6. Check for Faults decoding the next instruction (exception 6 if illegal opcode; exception 6 if in Real Mode or in Virtual 8086 Mode and attempting to execute an instruction for Protected Mode only; or exception 13 if instruction is longer than 15 bytes, or privilege violation in Protected Mode (i.e. not at IOPL or at CPL=0).
7. If WAIT opcode, check if TS=1 and MP=1 (exception 7 if both are 1).
8. If ESCape opcode for numeric coprocessor, check if EM=1 or TS=1 (exception 7 if either are 1).
9. If WAIT opcode or ESCape opcode for numeric coprocessor, check ERROR# input signal (exception 16 if ERROR# input is asserted).
10. Check in the following order for each memory reference required by the instruction:
    a. Check for Segmentation Faults that prevent transferring the entire memory quantity (exceptions 11, 12, 13).
    b. Check for Page Faults that prevent transferring the entire memory quantity (exception 14).

NOTE:
Segmentation exceptions are generated before paging exceptions.

Table 2.7. Conditions Preventing Instruction Restart

1. An instruction causes a task switch to a task whose Task State Segment is **partially** 'not present' (An entirely 'not present' TSS is restartable). Partially present TSS's can be avoided either by keeping the TSS's of such tasks present in memory, or by aligning TSS segments to reside entirely within a single 4K page (for TSS segments of 4K bytes or less).
2. A coprocessor operand wraps around the top of a 64K-byte segment or a 4G-byte segment, and spans three pages, and the page holding the middle portion of the operand is 'not present'. This condition can be avoided by starting **at a page boundary** any segments containing coprocessor operands if the segments are approximately 64K-200 bytes or larger (i.e. large enough for wraparound of the coprocessor operand to possibly occur).

Note that these conditions are avoided by using the operating system designs mentioned in this table.

Table 2.8. Register Values after Reset

Register	Value	Note
Flag Word (EFLAGS)	uuuu0002H	Note 1
Machine Status Word (CR0)	uuuuuu10H	
Instruction Pointer (EIP)	0000FFF0H	
Code Segment (CS)	F000H	Note 2
Data Segment (DS)	0000H	Note 3
Stack Segment (SS)	0000H	
Extra Segment (ES)	0000H	Note 3
Extra Segment (FS)	0000H	
Extra Segment (GS)	0000H	
EAX register	0000H	Note 4
EDX register	component and stepping ID	Note 5
All other registers	undefined	Note 6

NOTES:
1. EFLAG Register. The upper 14 bits of the EFLAGS register are undefined, all defined flag bits are zero.
2. The Code Segment Register (CS) will have its Base Address set to 0FFFF0000H and Limit set to 0FFFFH.
3. The Data and Extra Segment Registers (DS, ES) will have their Base Address set to 000000000H and Limit set to 0FFFFH.
4. If self-test is selected, the EAX register should contain a 0 value. If a value of 0 is not found then the self-test has detected a flaw in the part.
5. EDX register always holds component and stepping identifier.
6. All undefined bits are Intel Reserved and should not be used.

DOUBLE FAULT

A Double Fault (exception 8) results when the processor attempts to invoke an exception service routine for the segment exceptions (10, 11, 12 or 13), but in the process of doing so detects an exception **other than** a Page Fault (exception 14).

One other cause of generating a Double Fault is the Intel386 SX Microprocessor detecting any other exception when it is attempting to invoke the Page Fault (exception 14) service routine (for example, if a Page Fault is detected when the Intel386 SX Microprocessor attempts to invoke the Page Fault service routine). Of course, in any functional system, not only in Intel386 SX Microprocessor-based systems, the entire page fault service routine must remain 'present' in memory.

2.8 Reset and Initialization

When the processor is initialized or Reset the registers have the values shown in Table 2.8. The Intel386 SX Microprocessor will then start executing instructions near the top of physical memory, at location 0FFFFF0H. When the first Intersegment Jump or Call is executed, address lines $A_{20}-A_{23}$ will drop LOW for CS-relative memory cycles, and the Intel386 SX Microprocessor will only execute instructions in the lower one megabyte of physical memory. This allows the system designer to use a shadow ROM at the top of physical memory to initialize the system and take care of Resets.

RESET forces the Intel386 SX Microprocessor to terminate all execution and local bus activity. No instruction execution or bus activity will occur as long as Reset is active. Between 350 and 450 CLK2 periods after Reset becomes inactive, the Intel386 SX Microprocessor will start executing instructions at the top of physical memory.

2.9 Testability

The Intel386 SX Microprocessor, like the Intel386 Microprocessor, offers testability features which include a self-test and direct access to the page translation cache.

SELF-TEST

The Intel386 SX Microprocessor has the capability to perform a self-test. The self-test checks the function of all of the Control ROM and most of the non-random logic of the part. Approximately one-half of the Intel386 SX Microprocessor can be tested during self-test.

Self-Test is initiated on the Intel386 SX Microprocessor when the RESET pin transitions from HIGH to LOW, and the BUSY# pin is LOW. The self-test takes about 2^{20} clocks, or approximately 33 milliseconds with a 16 MHz Intel386 SX CPU. At the completion of self-test the processor performs reset and begins normal operation. The part has successfully passed self-test if the contents of the EAX are zero. If the results of the EAX are not zero then the self-test has detected a flaw in the part.

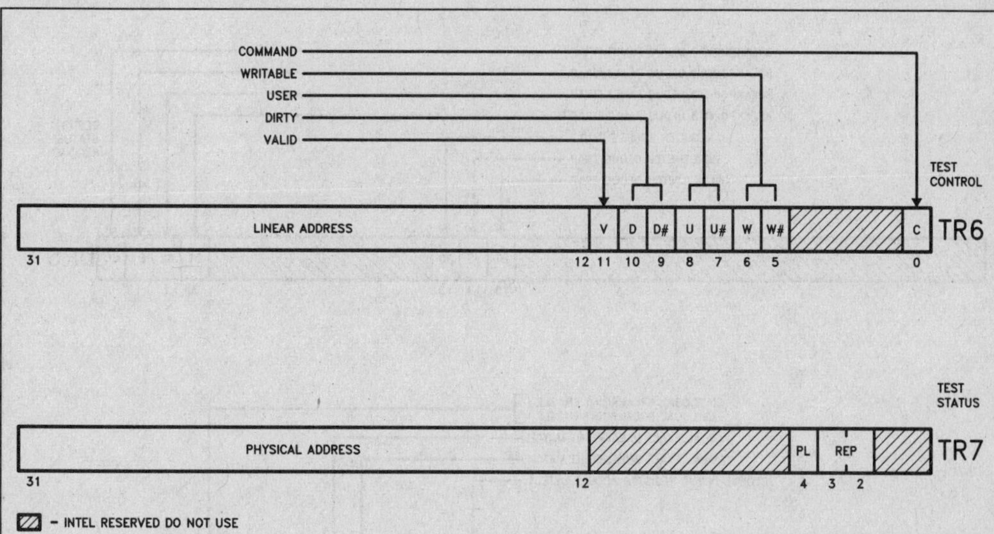

Figure 2.6. Test Registers

TLB TESTING

The Intel386 SX Microprocessor also provides a mechanism for testing the Translation Lookaside Buffer (TLB) if desired. This particular mechanism may not be continued in the same way in future processors.

There are two TLB testing operations: 1) writing entries into the TLB, and, 2) performing TLB lookups. Two Test Registers, shown in Figure 2.6, are provided for the purpose of testing. TR6 is the "test command register", and TR7 is the "test data register". For a more detailed explanation of testing the TLB, see the Intel386™ SX Microprocessor Programmer's Reference Manual.

2.10 Debugging Support

The Intel386 SX Microprocessor provides several features which simplify the debugging process. The three categories of on-chip debugging aids are:

1. The code execution breakpoint opcode (0CCH).
2. The single-step capability provided by the TF bit in the flag register.
3. The code and data breakpoint capability provided by the Debug Registers DR0–3, DR6, and DR7.

BREAKPOINT INSTRUCTION

A single-byte software interrupt (Int 3) breakpoint instruction is available for use by software debuggers. The breakpoint opcode is 0CCh, and generates an exception 3 trap when executed.

SINGLE-STEP TRAP

If the single-step flag (TF, bit 8) in the EFLAG register is found to be set at the end of an instruction, a single-step exception occurs. The single-step exception is auto vectored to exception number 1.

DEBUG REGISTERS

The Debug Registers are an advanced debugging feature of the Intel386 SX Microprocessor. They allow data access breakpoints as well as code execution breakpoints. Since the breakpoints are indicated by on-chip registers, an instruction execution breakpoint can be placed in ROM code or in code shared by several tasks, neither of which can be supported by the INT 3 breakpoint opcode.

The Intel386 SX Microprocessor contains six Debug Registers, consisting of four breakpoint address registers and two breakpoint control registers. Initially after reset, breakpoints are in the disabled state; therefore, no breakpoints will occur unless the debug registers are programmed. Breakpoints set up in the Debug Registers are auto-vectored to exception 1. Figure 2.7 shows the breakpoint status and control registers.

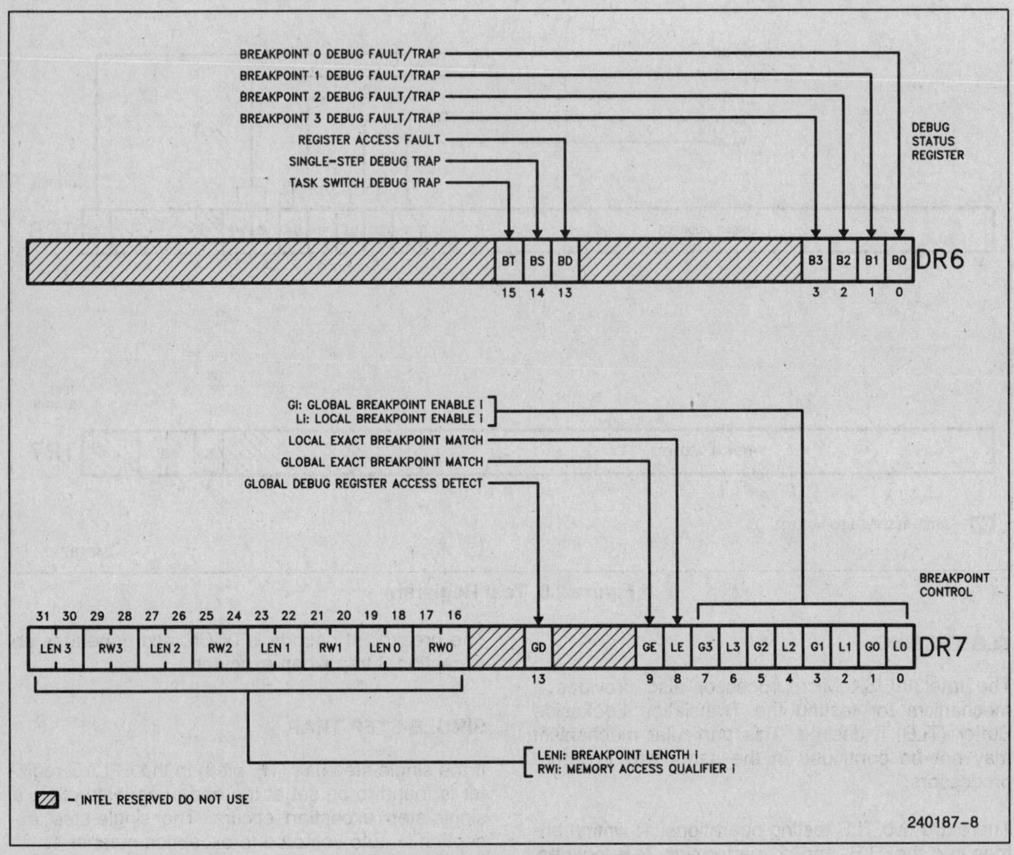

Figure 2.7. Debug Registers

3.0 REAL MODE ARCHITECTURE

When the processor is reset or powered up it is initialized in Real Mode. Real Mode has the same base architecture as the 8086, but allows access to the 32-bit register set of the Intel386 SX Microprocessor. The addressing mechanism, memory size, and interrupt handling are all identical to the Real Mode on the 80286.

The default operand size in Real Mode is 16 bits, as in the 8086. In order to use the 32-bit registers and addressing modes, override prefixes must be used. In addition, the segment size on the Intel386 SX Microprocessor in Real Mode is 64K bytes so 32-bit addresses must have a value less then 0000FFFFH. The primary purpose of Real Mode is to set up the processor for Protected Mode operation.

3.1 Memory Addressing

In Real Mode the linear addresses are the same as physical addresses (paging is not allowed). Physical addresses are formed in Real Mode by adding the contents of the appropriate segment register which is shifted left by four bits to an effective address. This addition results in a 20-bit physical address or a 1 megabyte address space. Since segment registers are shifted left by 4 bits, Real Mode segments always start on 16-byte boundaries.

All segments in Real Mode are exactly 64K bytes long, and may be read, written, or executed. The Intel386 SX Microprocessor will generate an exception 13 if a data operand or instruction fetch occurs past the end of a segment.

Table 3.1. Exceptions in Real Mode

Function	Interrupt Number	Related Instructions	Return Address Location
Interrupt table limit too small	8	INT vector is not within table limit	Before Instruction
CS, DS, ES, FS, GS Segment overrun exception	13	Word memory reference with offset = 0FFFFH. an attempt to execute past the end of CS segment.	Before Instruction
SS Segment overrun exception	12	Stack Reference beyond offset = 0FFFFH	Before Instruction

3.2 Reserved Locations

There are two fixed areas in memory which are reserved in Real address mode: the system initialization area and the interrupt table area. Locations 00000H through 003FFH are reserved for interrupt vectors. Each one of the 256 possible interrupts has a 4-byte jump vector reserved for it. Locations 0FFFFF0H through 0FFFFFFH are reserved for system initialization.

3.3 Interrupts

Many of the exceptions discussed in section 2.7 are not applicable to Real Mode operation; in particular, exceptions 10, 11 and 14 do not occur in Real Mode. Other exceptions have slightly different meanings in Real Mode; Table 3.1 identifies these exceptions.

3.4 Shutdown and Halt

The HLT instruction stops program execution and prevents the processor from using the local bus until restarted. Either NMI, FLT#, INTR with interrupts enabled (IF=1), or RESET will force the Intel386 SX Microprocessor out of halt. If interrupted, the saved CS:IP will point to the next instruction after the HLT.

Shutdown will occur when a severe error is detected that prevents further processing. In Real Mode, shutdown can occur under two conditions:

1. An interrupt or an exception occurs (Exceptions 8 or 13) and the interrupt vector is larger than the Interrupt Descriptor Table.
2. A CALL, INT or PUSH instruction attempts to wrap around the stack segment when SP is not even.

An NMI input can bring the processor out of shutdown if the Interrupt Descriptor Table limit is large enough to contain the NMI interrupt vector (at least 000FH) and the stack has enough room to contain the vector and flag information (i.e. SP is greater that 0005H). Otherwise, shutdown can only be exited by a processor reset.

3.5 LOCK operation

The LOCK prefix on the Intel386 SX Microprocessor, even in Real Mode, is more restrictive than on the 80286. This is due to the addition of paging on the Intel386 SX Microprocessor in Protected Mode and Virtual 8086 Mode. The LOCK prefix is not supported during repeat string instructions.

The only instruction forms where the LOCK prefix is legal on the Intel386 SX Microprocessor are shown in Table 3.2.

Table 3.2. Legal Instructions for the LOCK Prefix

Opcode	Operands (Dest, Source)
BIT Test and SET/RESET /COMPLEMENT	Mem, Reg/Immediate
XCHG	Reg, Mem
XCHG	Mem, Reg
ADD, OR, ADC, SBB, AND, SUB, XOR	Mem, Reg/Immediate
NOT, NEG, INC, DEC	Mem

An exception 6 will be generated if a LOCK prefix is placed before any instruction form or opcode not listed above. The LOCK prefix allows indivisible read/modify/write operations on memory operands using the instructions above.

The LOCK prefix is not IOPL-sensitive on the Intel386 SX Microprocessor. The LOCK prefix can be used at any privilege level, but only on the instruction forms listed in Table 3.2.

4

4.0 PROTECTED MODE ARCHITECTURE

The complete capabilities of the Intel386 SX Microprocessor are unlocked when the processor operates in Protected Virtual Address Mode (Protected Mode). Protected Mode vastly increases the linear address space to four gigabytes (2^{32} bytes) and allows the running of virtual memory programs of almost unlimited size (64 terabytes (2^{46} bytes)). In addition, Protected Mode allows the Intel386 SX Microprocessor to run all of the existing Intel386 DX CPU (using only 16 megabytes of physical memory), 80286 and 8086 CPU's software, while providing a sophisticated memory management and a hardware-assisted protection mechanism. Protected Mode allows the use of additional instructions specially optimized for supporting multitasking operating systems. The base architecture of the Intel386 SX Microprocessor remains the same; the registers, instructions, and addressing modes described in the previous sections are retained. The main difference between Protected Mode and Real Mode from a programmer's viewpoint is the increased address space and a different addressing mechanism.

4.1 Addressing Mechanism

Like Real Mode, Protected Mode uses two components to form the logical address; a 16-bit selector is used to determine the linear base address of a segment, the base address is added to a 32-bit effective address to form a 32-bit linear address. The linear address is then either used as a 24-bit physical address, or if paging is enabled the paging mechanism maps the 32-bit linear address into a 24-bit physical address.

The difference between the two modes lies in calculating the base address. In Protected Mode, the selector is used to specify an index into an operating system defined table (see Figure 4.1). The table contains the 32-bit base address of a given segment. The physical address is formed by adding the base address obtained from the table to the offset.

Paging provides an additional memory management mechanism which operates only in Protected Mode. Paging provides a means of managing the very large segments of the Intel386 SX Microprocessor, as paging operates beneath segmentation. The page mechanism translates the protected linear address which comes from the segmentation unit into a physical address. Figure 4.2 shows the complete Intel386 SX Microprocessor addressing mechanism with paging enabled.

4.2 Segmentation

Segmentation is one method of memory management. Segmentation provides the basis for protection. Segments are used to encapsulate regions of memory which have common attributes. For example, all of the code of a given program could be contained in a segment, or an operating system table may reside in a segment. All information about each segment is stored in an 8 byte data structure called a descriptor. All of the descriptors in a system are contained in descriptor tables which are recognized by hardware.

TERMINOLOGY

The following terms are used throughout the discussion of descriptors, privilege levels and protection:

PL: Privilege Level—One of the four hierarchical privilege levels. Level 0 is the most privileged level and level 3 is the least privileged.

RPL: Requestor Privilege Level—The privilege level of the original supplier of the selector. RPL is determined by the least two significant bits of a selector.

DPL: Descriptor Privilege Level—This is the least privileged level at which a task may access that descriptor (and the segment associated with that descriptor). Descriptor Privilege Level is determined by bits 6:5 in the Access Right Byte of a descriptor.

CPL: Current Privilege Level—The privilege level at which a task is currently executing, which equals the privilege level of the code segment being executed. CPL can also be determined by examining the lowest 2 bits of the CS register, except for conforming code segments.

EPL: Effective Privilege Level—The effective privilege level is the least privileged of the RPL and the DPL. EPL is the numerical maximum of RPL and DPL.

Task: One instance of the execution of a program. Tasks are also referred to as processes.

DESCRIPTOR TABLES

The descriptor tables define all of the segments which are used in a Intel386 SX Microprocessor system. There are three types of tables which hold descriptors: the Global Descriptor Table, Local Descriptor Table, and the Interrupt Descriptor Table. All of the tables are variable length memory arrays and can vary in size from 8 bytes to 64K bytes. Each table can hold up to 8192 8-byte descriptors. The upper 13 bits of a selector are used as an index into the descriptor table. The tables have registers associated with them which hold the 32-bit linear base address and the 16-bit limit of each table.

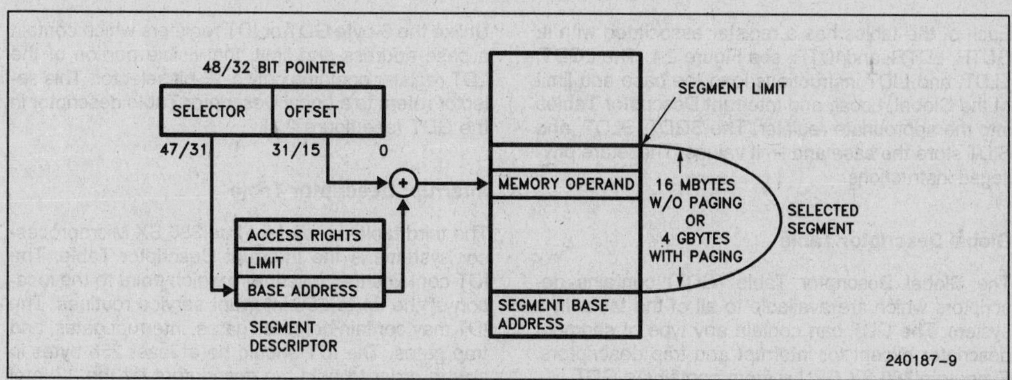

Figure 4.1. Protected Mode Addressing

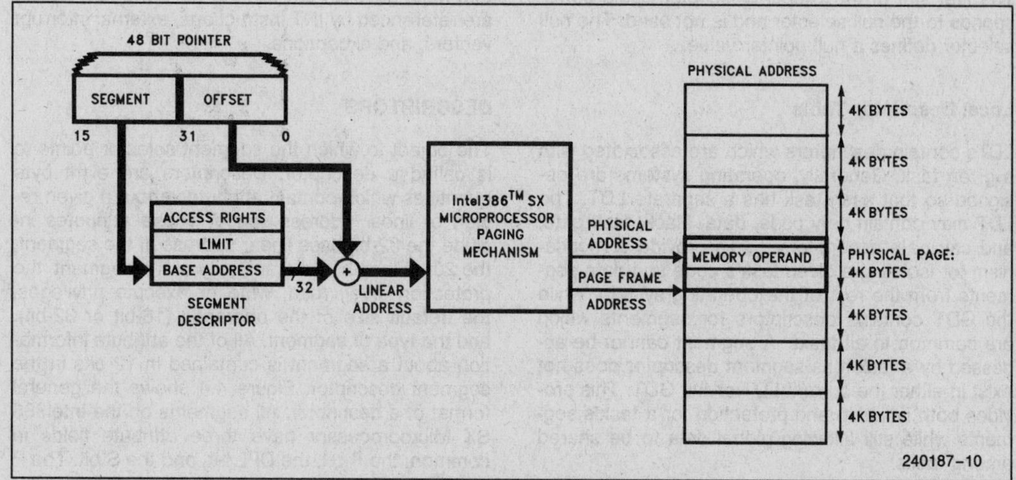

Figure 4.2. Paging and Segmentation

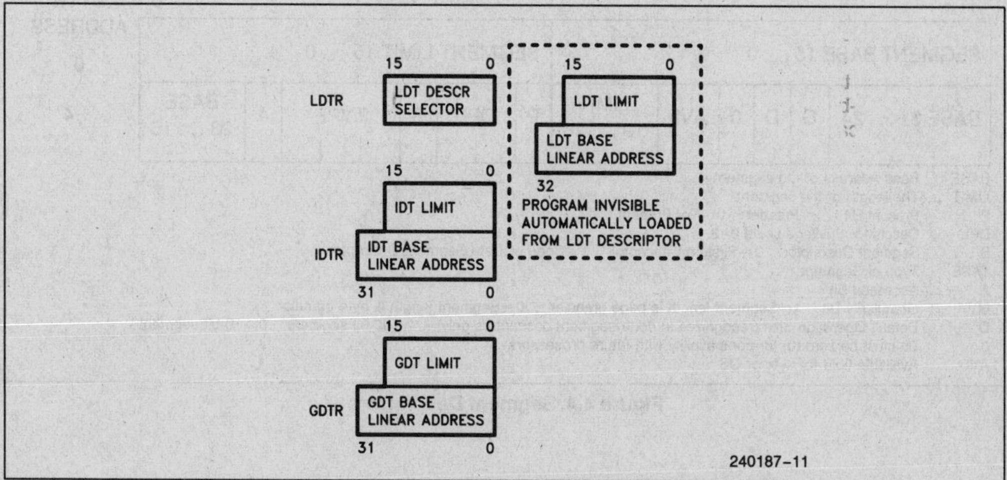

Figure 4.3. Descriptor Table Registers

Each of the tables has a register associated with it: GDTR, LDTR, and IDTR; see Figure 2.1. The LGDT, LLDT, and LIDT instructions load the base and limit of the Global, Local, and Interrupt Descriptor Tables into the appropriate register. The SGDT, SLDT, and SIDT store the base and limit values. These are privileged instructions.

Global Descriptor Table

The Global Descriptor Table (GDT) contains descriptors which are available to all of the tasks in a system. The GDT can contain any type of segment descriptor except for interrupt and trap descriptors. Every Intel386 SX CPU system contains a GDT.

The first slot of the Global Descriptor Table corresponds to the null selector and is not used. The null selector defines a null pointer value.

Local Descriptor Table

LDTs contain descriptors which are associated with a given task. Generally, operating systems are designed so that each task has a separate LDT. The LDT may contain only code, data, stack, task gate, and call gate descriptors. LDTs provide a mechanism for isolating a given task's code and data segments from the rest of the operating system, while the GDT contains descriptors for segments which are common to all tasks. A segment cannot be accessed by a task if its segment descriptor does not exist in either the current LDT or the GDT. This provides both isolation and protection for a task's segments while still allowing global data to be shared among tasks.

Unlike the 6-byte GDT or IDT registers which contain a base address and limit, the visible portion of the LDT register contains only a 16-bit selector. This selector refers to a Local Descriptor Table descriptor in the GDT (see figure 2.1).

Interrupt Descriptor Table

The third table needed for Intel386 SX Microprocessor systems is the Interrupt Descriptor Table. The IDT contains the descriptors which point to the location of the up to 256 interrupt service routines. The IDT may contain only task gates, interrupt gates, and trap gates. The IDT should be at least 256 bytes in size in order to hold the descriptors for the 32 Intel Reserved Interrupts. Every interrupt used by a system must have an entry in the IDT. The IDT entries are referenced by INT instructions, external interrupt vectors, and exceptions.

DESCRIPTORS

The object to which the segment selector points to is called a descriptor. Descriptors are eight byte quantities which contain attributes about a given region of linear address space. These attributes include the 32-bit base linear address of the segment, the 20-bit length and granularity of the segment, the protection level, read, write or execute privileges, the default size of the operands (16-bit or 32-bit), and the type of segment. All of the attribute information about a segment is contained in 12 bits in the segment descriptor. Figure 4.4 shows the general format of a descriptor. All segments on the Intel386 SX Microprocessor have three attribute fields in common: the P bit, the DPL bit, and the S bit. The P

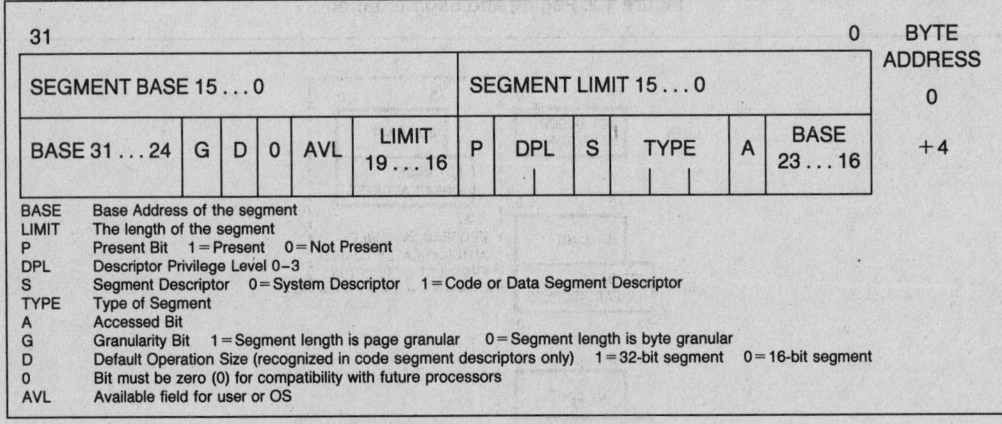

Figure 4.4. Segment Descriptors

(Present) Bit is 1 if the segment is loaded in physical memory. If P=0 then any attempt to access this segment causes a not present exception (exception 11). The Descriptor Privilege Level, DPL, is a two bit field which specifies the protection level, 0–3, associated with a segment.

The Intel386 SX Microprocessor has two main categories of segments: system segments and non-system segments (for code and data). The segment bit, S, determines if a given segment is a system segment or a code or data segment. If the S bit is 1 then the segment is either a code or data segment; if it is 0 then the segment is a system segment.

Code and Data Descriptors (S=1)

Figure 4.5 shows the general format of a code and data descriptor and Table 4.1 illustrates how the bits in the Access Right Byte are interpreted.

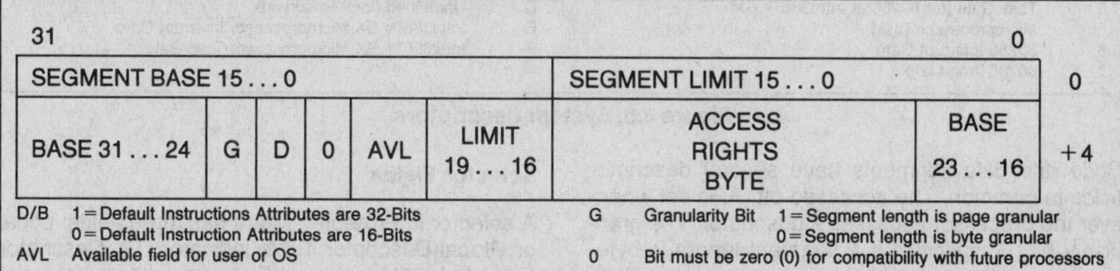

Figure 4.5. Code and Data Descriptors

Table 4.1. Access Rights Byte Definition for Code and Data Descriptors

Bit Position	Name	Function	
7	Present (P)	P = 1 Segment is mapped into physical memory. P = 0 No mapping to physical memory exists, base and limt are not used.	
6–5	Descriptor Privilege Level (DPL)	Segment privilege attribute used in privilege tests.	
4	Segment Descriptor (S)	S = 1 Code or Data (includes stacks) segment descriptor S = 0 System Segment Descriptor or Gate Descriptor	
3 2 1	Executable (E) Expansion Direction (ED) Writeable (W)	E = 0 Descriptor type is data segment: ED = 0 Expand up segment, offsets must be ≤ limit. ED = 1 Expand down segment, offsets must be > limit. W = 0 Data segment may not be written into. W = 1 Data segment may be written into.	If Data Segment (S = 1, E = 0)
3 2 1	Executable (E) Conforming (C) Readable (R)	E = 1 Descriptor type is code segment: C = 1 Code segment may only be executed when CPL ≥ DPL and CPL remains unchanged. R = 0 Code segment may not be read. R = 1 Code segment may be read.	If Code Segment (S = 1, E = 1)
0	Accessed (A)	A = 0 Segment has not been accessed. A = 1 Segment selector has been loaded into segment register or used by selector test instructions.	

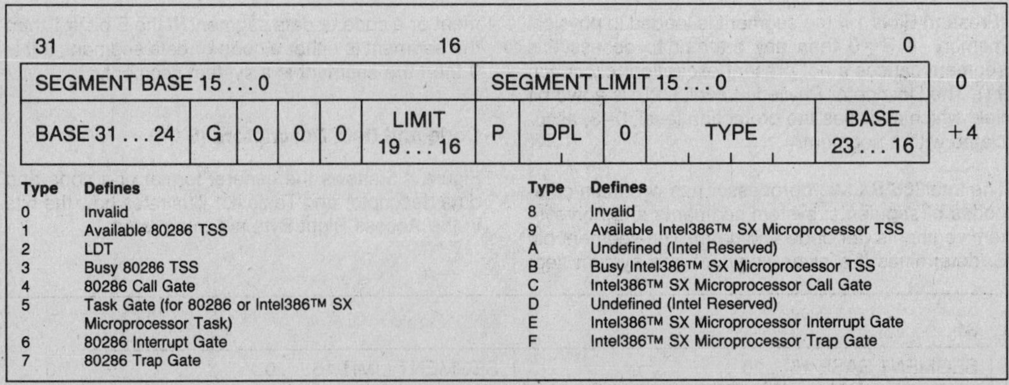

Type	Defines	Type	Defines
0	Invalid	8	Invalid
1	Available 80286 TSS	9	Available Intel386™ SX Microprocessor TSS
2	LDT	A	Undefined (Intel Reserved)
3	Busy 80286 TSS	B	Busy Intel386™ SX Microprocessor TSS
4	80286 Call Gate	C	Intel386™ SX Microprocessor Call Gate
5	Task Gate (for 80286 or Intel386™ SX Microprocessor Task)	D	Undefined (Intel Reserved)
		E	Intel386™ SX Microprocessor Interrupt Gate
6	80286 Interrupt Gate	F	Intel386™ SX Microprocessor Trap Gate
7	80286 Trap Gate		

Figure 4.6. System Descriptors

Code and data segments have several descriptor fields in common. The accessed bit, A, is set whenever the processor accesses a descriptor. The granularity bit, G, specifies if a segment length is byte-granular or page-granular.

System Descriptor Formats (S=0)

System segments describe information about operating system tables, tasks, and gates. Figure 4.6 shows the general format of system segment descriptors, and the various types of system segments. Intel386 SX system descriptors (which are the same as Intel386 DX CPU system descriptors) contain a 32-bit base linear address and a 20-bit segment limit. 80286 system descriptors have a 24-bit base address and a 16-bit segment limit. 80286 system descriptors are identified by the upper 16 bits being all zero.

Differences Between Intel386™ SX Microprocessor and 80286 Descriptors

In order to provide operating system compatibility with the 80286 the Intel386 SX CPU supports all of the 80286 segment descriptors. The 80286 system segment descriptors contain a 24-bit base address and 16-bit limit, while the Intel386 SX CPU system segment descriptors have a 32-bit base address, a 20-bit limit field, and a granularity bit. The word count field specifies the number of 16-bit quantities to copy for 80286 call gates and 32-bit quantities for Intel386 SX CPU call gates.

Selector Fields

A selector in Protected Mode has three fields: Local or Global Descriptor Table indicator (TI), Descriptor Entry Index (Index), and Requestor (the selector's) Privilege Level (RPL) as shown in Figure 4.7. The TI bit selects either the Global Descriptor Table or the Local Descriptor Table. The Index selects one of 8k descriptors in the appropriate descriptor table. The RPL bits allow high speed testing of the selector's privilege attributes.

Segment Descriptor Cache

In addition to the selector value, every segment register has a segment descriptor cache register associated with it. Whenever a segment register's contents are changed, the 8-byte descriptor associated with that selector is automatically loaded (cached) on the chip. Once loaded, all references to that segment use the cached descriptor information instead of reaccessing the descriptor. The contents of the descriptor cache are not visible to the programmer. Since descriptor caches only change when a segment register is changed, programs which modify the descriptor tables must reload the appropriate segment registers after changing a descriptor's value.

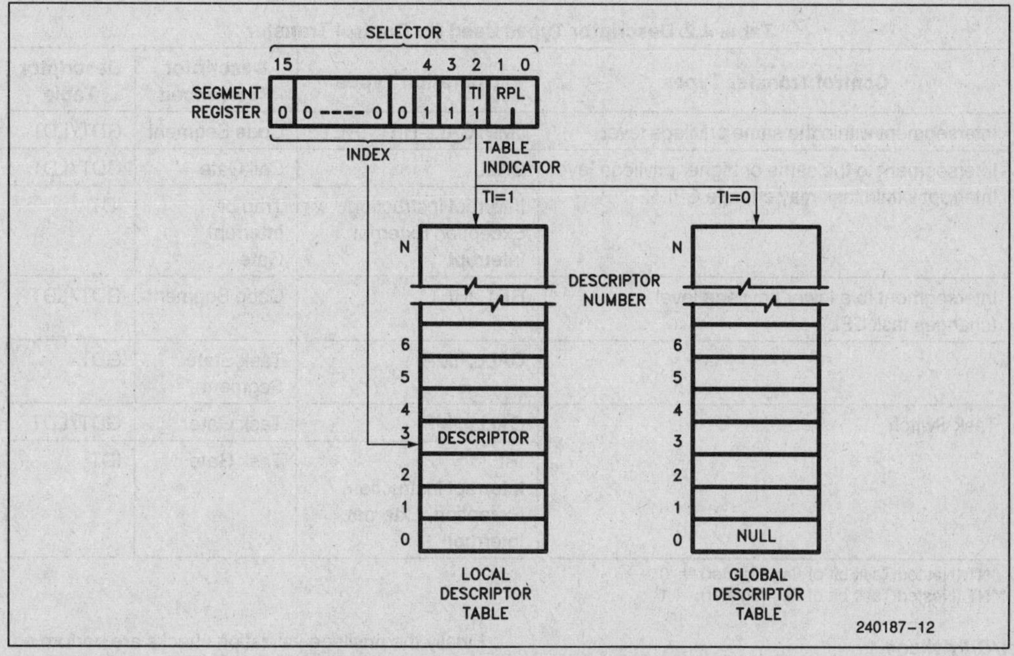

Figure 4.7. Example Descriptor Selection

4.3 Protection

The Intel386 SX Microprocessor has four levels of protection which are optimized to support a multi-tasking operating system and to isolate and protect user programs from each other and the operating system. The privilege levels control the use of privileged instructions, I/O instructions, and access to segments and segment descriptors. The Intel386 SX Microprocessor also offers an additional type of protection on a page basis when paging is enabled.

The four-level hierarchical privilege system is an extension of the user/supervisor privilege mode commonly used by minicomputers. The user/supervisor mode is fully supported by the Intel386 SX Microprocessor paging mechanism. The privilege levels (PL) are numbered 0 through 3. Level 0 is the most privileged level.

RULES OF PRIVILEGE

The Intel386 SX Microprocessor controls access to both data and procedures between levels of a task, according to the following rules.

— Data stored in a segment with privilege level **p** can be accessed only by code executing at a privilege level at least as privileged as **p**.

— A code segment/procedure with privilege level **p** can only be called by a task executing at the same or a lesser privilege level than **p**.

PRIVILEGE LEVELS

At any point in time, a task on the Intel386 SX Microprocessor always executes at one of the four privilege levels. The Current Privilege Level (CPL) specifies what the task's privilege level is. A task's CPL may only be changed by control transfers through gate descriptors to a code segment with a different privilege level. Thus, an application program running at PL = 3 may call an operating system routine at PL = 1 (via a gate) which would cause the task's CPL to be set to 1 until the operating system routine was finished.

Selector Privilege (RPL)

The privilege level of a selector is specified by the RPL field. The selector's RPL is only used to establish a less trusted privilege level than the current privilege level of the task for the use of a segment. This level is called the task's effective privilege level (EPL). The EPL is defined as being the least privileged (numerically larger) level of a task's CPL and a selector's RPL. The RPL is most commonly used to verify that pointers passed to an operating system procedure do not access data that is of higher privilege than the procedure that originated the pointer. Since the originator of a selector can specify any RPL value, the Adjust RPL (ARPL) instruction is provided to force the RPL bits to the originator's CPL.

Table 4.2. Descriptor Types Used for Control Transfer

Control Transfer Types	Operation Types	Descriptor Referenced	Descriptor Table
Intersegment within the same privilege level	JMP, CALL RET, IRET*	Code Segment	GDT/LDT
Intersegment to the same or higher privilege level Interrupt within task may change CPL	CALL	Call Gate	GDT/LDT
	Interrupt instruction Exception External Interrupt	Trap or Interrupt Gate	IDT
Intersegment to a lower privilege level (changes task CPL)	RET, IRET*	Code Segment	GDT/LDT
	CALL, JMP	Task State Segment	GDT
Task Switch	CALL, JMP	Task Gate	GDT/LDT
	IRET** Interrupt instruction, Exception, External Interrupt	Task Gate	IDT

*NT (Nested Task bit of flag register) = 0
**NT (Nested Task bit of flag register) = 1

I/O Privilege

The I/O privilege level (IOPL) lets the operating system code executing at CPL=0 define the least privileged level at which I/O instructions can be used. An exception 13 (General Protection Violation) is generated if an I/O instruction is attempted when the CPL of the task is less privileged then the IOPL. The IOPL is stored in bits 13 and 14 of the EFLAGS register. The following instructions cause an exception 13 if the CPL is greater than IOPL: IN, INS, OUT, OUTS, STI, CLI, LOCK prefix.

Descriptor Access

There are basically two types of segment accesses: those involving code segments such as control transfers, and those involving data accesses. Determining the ability of a task to access a segment involves the type of segment to be accessed, the instruction used, the type of descriptor used and CPL, RPL, and DPL as described above.

Any time an instruction loads a data segment register (DS, ES, FS, GS) the Intel386 SX Microprocessor makes protection validation checks. Selectors loaded in the DS, ES, FS, GS registers must refer only to data segment or readable code segments.

Finally the privilege validation checks are performed. The CPL is compared to the EPL and if the EPL is more privileged than the CPL, an exception 13 (general protection fault) is generated.

The rules regarding the stack segment are slightly different than those involving data segments. Instructions that load selectors into SS must refer to data segment descriptors for writeable data segments. The DPL and RPL must equal the CPL of all other descriptor types or a privilege level violation will cause an exception 13. A stack not present fault causes an exception 12.

PRIVILEGE LEVEL TRANSFERS

Inter-segment control transfers occur when a selector is loaded in the CS register. For a typical system most of these transfers are simply the result of a call or a jump to another routine. There are five types of control transfers which are summarized in Table 4.2. Many of these transfers result in a privilege level transfer. Changing privilege levels is done only by control transfers, using gates, task switches, and interrupt or trap gates.

Control transfers can only occur if the operation which loaded the selector references the correct descriptor type. Any violation of these descriptor usage rules will cause an exception 13.

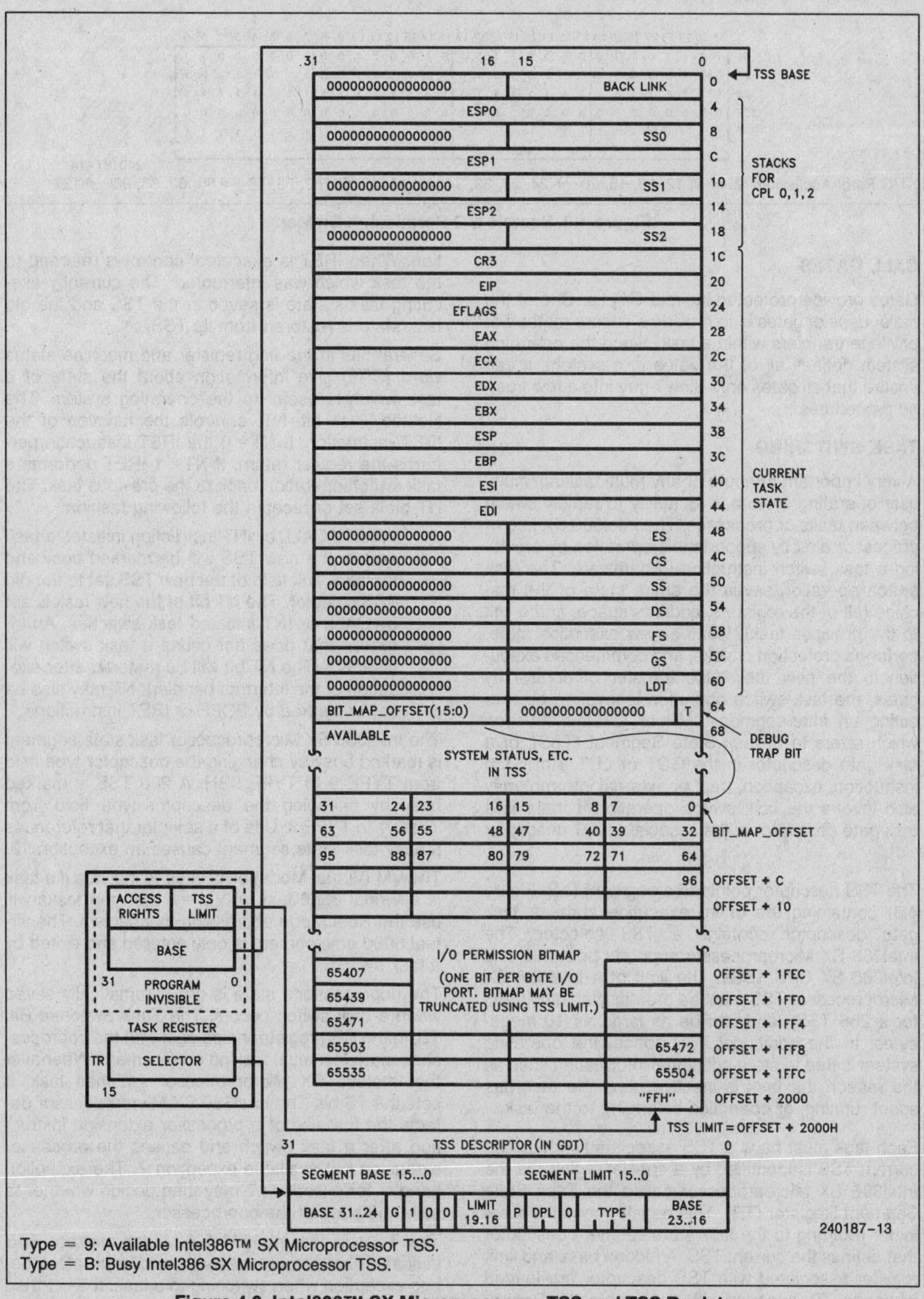

Type = 9: Available Intel386™ SX Microprocessor TSS.
Type = B: Busy Intel386 SX Microprocessor TSS.

Figure 4.8. Intel386™ SX Microprocessor TSS and TSS Registers

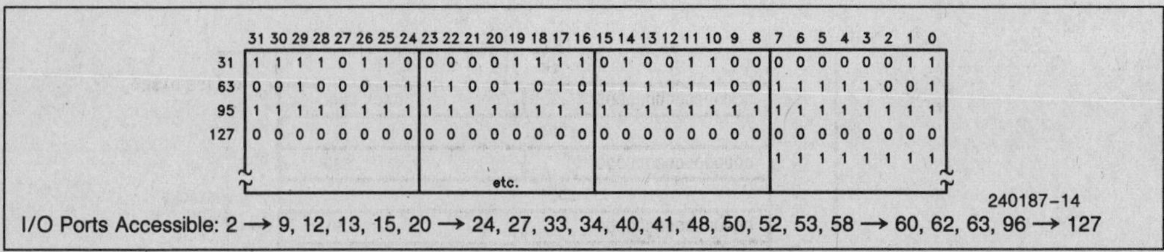

Figure 4.9. Sample I/O Permission Bit Map

CALL GATES

Gates provide protected indirect CALLs. One of the major uses of gates is to provide a secure method of privilege transfers within a task. Since the operating system defines all of the gates in a system, it can ensure that all gates only allow entry into a few trusted procedures.

TASK SWITCHING

A very important attribute of any multi-tasking/multi-user operating system is its ability to rapidly switch between tasks or processes. The Intel386 SX Microprocessor directly supports this operation by providing a task switch instruction in hardware. The task switch operation saves the entire state of the machine (all of the registers, address space, and a link to the previous task), loads a new execution state, performs protection checks, and commences execution in the new task. Like transfer of control by gates, the task switch operation is invoked by executing an inter-segment JMP or CALL instruction which refers to a Task State Segment (TSS), or a task gate descriptor in the GDT or LDT. An INT n instruction, exception, trap, or external interrupt may also invoke the task switch operation if there is a task gate descriptor in the associated IDT descriptor slot.

The TSS descriptor points to a segment (see Figure 4.8) containing the entire execution state. A task gate descriptor contains a TSS selector. The Intel386 SX Microprocessor supports both 286 and Intel386 SX CPU TSSs. The limit of a Intel386 SX Microprocessor TSS must be greater than 64H (2BH for a 286 TSS), and can be as large as 16 megabytes. In the additional TSS space, the operating system is free to store additional information such as the reason the task is inactive, time the task has spent running, or open files belonging to the task.

Each task must have a TSS associated with it. The current TSS is identified by a special register in the Intel386 SX Microprocessor called the Task State Segment Register (TR). This register contains a selector referring to the task state segment descriptor that defines the current TSS. A hidden base and limit register associated with TSS descriptor are loaded whenever TR is loaded with a new selector. Returning from a task is accomplished by the IRET instruction. When IRET is executed, control is returned to the task which was interrupted. The currently executing task's state is saved in the TSS and the old task state is restored from its TSS.

Several bits in the flag register and machine status word (CR0) give information about the state of a task which is useful to the operating system. The Nested Task bit, NT, controls the function of the IRET instruction. If NT = 0 the IRET instruction performs the regular return. If NT = 1 IRET performs a task switch operation back to the previous task. The NT bit is set or reset in the following fashion:

> When a CALL or INT instruction initiates a task switch, the new TSS will be marked busy and the back link field of the new TSS set to the old TSS selector. The NT bit of the new task is set by CALL or INT initiated task switches. An interrupt that does not cause a task switch will clear NT (The NT bit will be restored after execution of the interrupt handler). NT may also be set or cleared by POPF or IRET instructions.

The Intel386 SX Microprocessor task state segment is marked busy by changing the descriptor type field from TYPE 9 to TYPE 0BH. A 286 TSS is marked busy by changing the descriptor type field from TYPE 1 to TYPE 3. Use of a selector that references a busy task state segment causes an exception 13.

The VM (Virtual Mode) bit is used to indicate if a task is a Virtual 8086 task. If VM = 1 then the tasks will use the Real Mode addressing mechanism. The virtual 8086 environment is only entered and exited by a task switch.

The coprocessor's state is not automatically saved when a task switch occurs. The Task Switched Bit, TS, in the CR0 register helps deal with the coprocessor's state in a multi-tasking environment. Whenever the Intel386 SX Microprocessor switches task, it sets the TS bit. The Intel386 SX Microprocessor detects the first use of a processor extension instruction after a task switch and causes the processor extension not available exception 7. The exception handler for exception 7 may then decide whether to save the state of the coprocessor.

The T bit in the Intel386 SX Microprocessor TSS indicates that the processor should generate a debug exception when switching to a task. If T = 1 then upon entry to a new task a debug exception 1 will be generated.

INITIALIZATION AND TRANSITION TO PROTECTED MODE

Since the Intel386 SX Microprocessor begins executing in Real Mode immediately after RESET it is necessary to initialize the system tables and registers with the appropriate values. The GDT and IDT registers must refer to a valid GDT and IDT. The IDT should be at least 256 bytes long, and the GDT must contain descriptors for the initial code and data segments.

Protected Mode is enabled by loading CR0 with PE bit set. This can be accomplished by using the **MOV CR0, R/M** instruction. After enabling Protected Mode, the next instruction should execute an intersegment JMP to load the CS register and flush the instruction decode queue. The final step is to load all of the data segment registers with the initial selector values.

An alternate approach to entering Protected Mode is to use the built in task-switch to load all of the registers. In this case the GDT would contain two TSS descriptors in addition to the code and data descriptors needed for the first task. The first JMP instruction in Protected Mode would jump to the TSS causing a task switch and loading all of the registers with the values stored in the TSS. The Task State Segment Register should be initialized to point to a valid TSS descriptor.

4.4 Paging

Paging is another type of memory management useful for virtual memory multi-tasking operating systems. Unlike segmentation, which modularizes programs and data into variable length segments, paging divides programs into multiple uniform size pages. Pages bear no direct relation to the logical structure of a program. While segment selectors can be considered the logical 'name' of a program module or data structure, a page most likely corresponds to only a portion of a module or data structure.

PAGE ORGANIZATION

The Intel386 SX Microprocessor uses two levels of tables to translate the linear address (from the segmentation unit) into a physical address. There are three components to the paging mechanism of the Intel386 SX Microprocessor: the page directory, the page tables, and the page itself (page frame). All memory-resident elements of the Intel386 SX Microprocessor paging mechanism are the same size, namely 4K bytes. A uniform size for all of the elements simplifies memory allocation and reallocation schemes, since there is no problem with memory fragmentation. Figure 4.10 shows how the paging mechanism works.

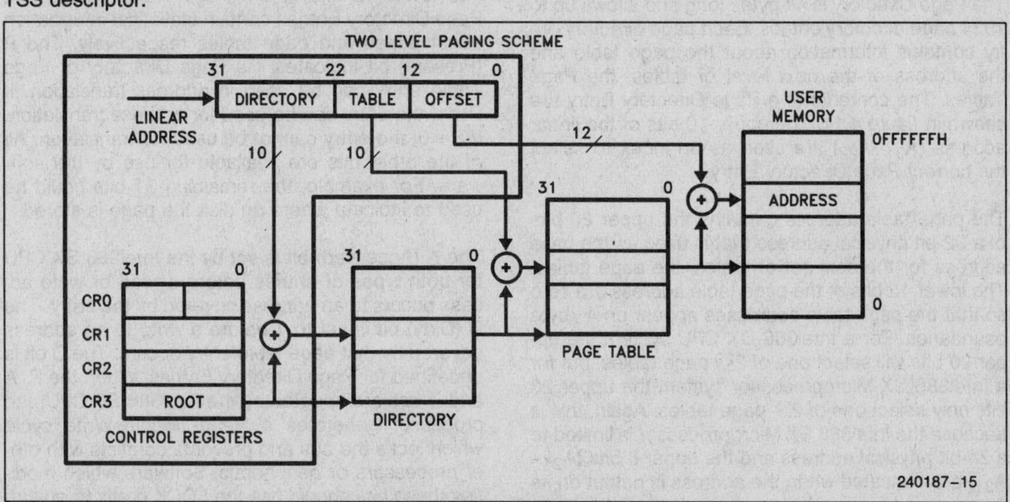

Figure 4.10. Paging Mechanism

31 — 12	11 — 9	8	7	6	5	4	3	2	1	0
PAGE TABLE ADDRESS 31..12	System Software Defineable	0	0	D	A	0	0	U/S	R/W	P

Figure 4.11. Page Directory Entry (Points to Page Table)

31 ... 12	11 10 9	8	7	6	5	4	3	2	1	0
PAGE FRAME ADDRESS 31..12	System Software Defineable	0	0	D	A	0	0	U/S	R/W	P

Figure 4.12. Page Table Entry (Points to Page)

Page Fault Register

CR2 is the Page Fault Linear Address register. It holds the 32-bit linear address which caused the last Page Fault detected.

Page Descriptor Base Register

CR3 is the Page Directory Physical Base Address Register. It contains the physical starting address of the Page Directory (this value is truncated to a 24-bit value associated with the Intel386 SX CPU's 16 megabyte physical memory limitation). The lower 12 bits of CR3 are always zero to ensure that the Page Directory is always page aligned. Loading it with a **MOV CR3, reg** instruction causes the page table entry cache to be flushed, as will a task switch through a TSS which changes the value of CR0.

Page Directory

The Page Directory is 4k bytes long and allows up to 1024 page directory entries. Each page directory entry contains information about the page table and the address of the next level of tables, the Page Tables. The contents of a Page Directory Entry are shown in figure 4.11. The upper 10 bits of the linear address ($A_{31}-A_{22}$) are used as an index to select the correct Page Directory Entry.

The page table address contains the upper 20 bits of a 32-bit physical address that is used as the base address for the next set of tables, the page tables. The lower 12 bits of the page table address are zero so that the page table addresses appear on 4 kbyte boundaries. For a Intel386 DX CPU system the upper 20 bits will select one of 2^{20} page tables, but for a Intel386 SX Microprocessor system the upper 20 bits only select one of 2^{12} page tables. Again, this is because the Intel386 SX Microprocessor is limited to a 24-bit physical address and the upper 8 bits ($A_{24}-A_{31}$) are truncated when the address is output on its 24 address pins.

Page Tables

Each Page Table is 4K bytes long and allows up to 1024 Page table Entries. Each page table entry contains information about the Page Frame and its address. The contents of a Page Table Entry are shown in figure 4.12. The middle 10 bits of the linear address ($A_{21}-A_{12}$) are used as an index to select the correct Page Table Entry.

The Page Frame Address contains the upper 20 bits of a 32-bit physical address that is used as the base address for the Page Frame. The lower 12 bits of the Page Frame Address are zero so that the Page Frame addresses appear on 4 kbyte boundaries. For an Intel386 DX CPU system the upper 20 bits will select one of 2^{20} Page Frames, but for an Intel386 SX Microprocessor system the upper 20 bits only select one of 2^{12} Page Frames. Again, this is because the Intel386 SX Microprocessor is limited to a 24-bit physical address space and the upper 8 bits ($A_{24}-A_{31}$) are truncated when the address is output on its 24 address pins.

Page Directory/Table Entries

The lower 12 bits of the Page Table Entries and Page Directory Entries contain statistical information about pages and page tables respectively. The P (Present) bit indicates if a Page Directory or Page Table entry can be used in address translation. If P=1, the entry can be used for address translation. If P=0, the entry cannot be used for translation. All of the other bits are available for use by the software. For example, the remaining 31 bits could be used to indicate where on disk the page is stored.

The A (Accessed) bit is set by the Intel386 SX CPU for both types of entries before a read or write access occurs to an address covered by the entry. The D (Dirty) bit is set to 1 before a write to an address covered by that page table entry occurs. The D bit is undefined for Page Directory Entries. When the P, A and D bits are updated by the Intel386 SX CPU, the processor generates a Read- Modify-Write cycle which locks the bus and prevents conflicts with other processors or peripherals. Software which modifies these bits should use the LOCK prefix to ensure the integrity of the page tables in multi-master systems.

The 3 bits marked system software definable in Figures 4.11 and Figure 4.12 are software definable. System software writers are free to use these bits for whatever purpose they wish.

PAGE LEVEL PROTECTION (R/W, U/S BITS)

The Intel386 SX Microprocessor provides a set of protection attributes for paging systems. The paging mechanism distinguishes between two levels of protection: User, which corresponds to level 3 of the segmentation based protection, and supervisor which encompasses all of the other protection levels (0, 1, 2). Programs executing at Level 0, 1 or 2 bypass the page protection, although segmentation-based protection is still enforced by the hardware.

The U/S and R/W bits are used to provide User/Supervisor and Read/Write protection for individual pages or for all pages covered by a Page Table Directory Entry. The U/S and R/W bits in the second level Page Table Entry apply only to the page described by that entry. While the U/S and R/W bits in the first level Page Directory Table apply to all pages described by the page table pointed to by that directory entry. The U/S and R/W bits for a given page are obtained by taking the most restrictive of the U/S and R/W from the Page Directory Table Entries and using these bits to address the page.

TRANSLATION LOOKASIDE BUFFER

The Intel386 SX Microprocessor paging hardware is designed to support demand paged virtual memory systems. However, performance would degrade substantially if the processor was required to access two levels of tables for every memory reference. To solve this problem, the Intel386 SX Microprocessor keeps a cache of the most recently accessed pages, this cache is called the Translation Lookaside Buffer (TLB). The TLB is a four-way set associative 32-entry page table cache. It automatically keeps the most commonly used page table entries in the processor. The 32-entry TLB coupled with a 4K page size results in coverage of 128K bytes of memory addresses. For many common multi-tasking systems, the TLB will have a hit rate of greater than 98%. This means that the processor will only have to access the two-level page structure for less than 2% of all memory references.

PAGING OPERATION

The paging hardware operates in the following fashion. The paging unit hardware receives a 32-bit linear address from the segmentation unit. The upper 20 linear address bits are compared with all 32 entries in the TLB to determine if there is a match. If there is a match (i.e. a TLB hit), then the 24-bit physical address is calculated and is placed on the address bus.

If the page table entry is not in the TLB, the Intel386 SX Microprocessor will read the appropriate Page Directory Entry. If P=1 on the Page Directory Entry, indicating that the page table is in memory, then the Intel386 SX Microprocessor will read the appropriate Page Table Entry and set the Access bit. If P=1 on the Page Table Entry, indicating that the page is in memory, the Intel386 SX Microprocessor will update the Access and Dirty bits as needed and fetch the operand. The upper 20 bits of the linear address, read from the page table, will be stored in the TLB for future accesses. If P=0 for either the Page Directory Entry or the Page Table Entry, then the processor will generate a page fault Exception 14.

The processor will also generate a Page Fault (Exception 14) if the memory reference violated the page protection attributes. CR2 will hold the linear address which caused the page fault. Since Exception 14 is classified as a fault, CS:EIP will point to the instruction causing the page-fault. The 16-bit error code pushed as part of the page fault handler will contain status bits which indicate the cause of the page fault.

The 16-bit error code is used by the operating system to determine how to handle the Page Fault. Figure 4.13 shows the format of the Page Fault error code and the interpretation of the bits. Even though the bits in the error code (U/S, W/R, and P) have similar names as the bits in the Page Directory/Table Entries, the interpretation of the error code bits is different. Figure 4.14 indicates what type of access caused the page fault.

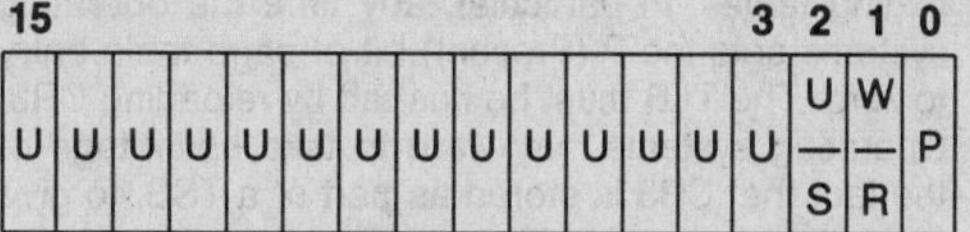

Figure 4.13. Page Fault Error Code Format

U/S: The U/S bit indicates whether the access causing the fault occurred when the processor was executing in User Mode (U/S = 1) or in Supervisor mode (U/S = 0)

W/R: The W/R bit indicates whether the access causing the fault was a Read (W/R = 0) or a Write (W/R = 1)

P: The P bit indicates whether a page fault was caused by a not-present page (P = 0), or by a page level protection violation (P = 1)

U = Undefined

U/S	W/R	Access Type
0	0	Supervisor* Read
0	1	Supervisor Write
1	0	User Read
1	1	User Write

*Descriptor table access will fault with U/S = 0, even if the program is executing at level 3.

Figure 4.14. Type of Access Causing Page Fault

OPERATING SYSTEM RESPONSIBILITIES

When the operating system enters or exits paging mode (by setting or resetting bit 31 in the CR0 register) a short JMP must be executed to flush the Intel386 SX Microprocessor's prefetch queue. This ensures that all instructions executed after the address mode change will generate correct addresses.

The Intel386 SX Microprocessor takes care of the page address translation process, relieving the burden from an operating system in a demand-paged system. The operating system is responsible for setting up the initial page tables and handling any page faults. The operating system also is required to invalidate (i.e. flush) the TLB when any changes are made to any of the page table entries. The operating system must reload CR3 to cause the TLB to be flushed.

Setting up the tables is simply a matter of loading CR3 with the address of the Page Directory, and allocating space for the Page Directory and the Page Tables. The primary responsibility of the operating system is to implement a swapping policy and handle all of the page faults.

A final concern of the operating system is to ensure that the TLB cache matches the information in the paging tables. In particular, any time the operating systems sets the P (Present) bit of page table entry to zero. The TLB must be flushed by reloading CR3. Operating systems may want to take advantage of the fact that CR3 is stored as part of a TSS, to give every task or group of tasks its own set of page tables.

4.5 Virtual 8086 Environment

The Intel386 SX Microprocessor allows the execution of 8086 application programs in both Real Mode and in the Virtual 8086 Mode. The Virtual 8086 Mode allows the execution of 8086 applications, while still allowing the system designer to take full advantage of the Intel386 SX CPU's protection mechanism.

VIRTUAL 8086 ADDRESSING MECHANISM

One of the major differences between Intel386 SX CPU Real and Protected modes is how the segment selectors are interpreted. When the processor is executing in Virtual 8086 Mode, the segment registers are used in a fashion identical to Real Mode. The contents of the segment register are shifted left 4 bits and added to the offset to form the segment base linear address.

The Intel386 SX Microprocessor allows the operating system to specify which programs use the 8086 address mechanism and which programs use Protected Mode addressing on a per task basis. Through the use of paging, the one megabyte address space of the Virtual Mode task can be mapped to anywhere in the 4 gigabyte linear address space of the Intel386 SX Microprocessor. Like Real Mode, Virtual Mode addresses that exceed one megabyte will cause an exception 13. However, these restrictions should not prove to be important, because most tasks running in Virtual 8086 Mode will simply be existing 8086 application programs.

PAGING IN VIRTUAL MODE

The paging hardware allows the concurrent running of multiple Virtual Mode tasks, and provides protection and operating system isolation. Although it is not strictly necessary to have the paging hardware enabled to run Virtual Mode tasks, it is needed in order to run multiple Virtual Mode tasks or to relocate the address space of a Virtual Mode task to physical address space greater than one megabyte.

The paging hardware allows the 20-bit linear address produced by a Virtual Mode program to be divided into as many as 256 pages. Each one of the pages can be located anywhere within the maximum 16 megabyte physical address space of the Intel386 SX Microprocessor. In addition, since CR3 (the Page Directory Base Register) is loaded by a task switch, each Virtual Mode task can use a different mapping scheme to map pages to different physical locations. Finally, the paging hardware allows the sharing of the 8086 operating system code between multiple 8086 applications.

PROTECTION AND I/O PERMISSION BIT MAP

All Virtual Mode programs execute at privilege level 3. As such, Virtual Mode programs are subject to all of the protection checks defined in Protected Mode. This is different than Real Mode, which implicitly is executing at privilege level 0. Thus, an attempt to execute a privileged instruction in Virtual Mode will cause an exception 13 fault.

The following are privileged instructions, which may be executed only at Privilege Level 0. Attempting to execute these instructions in Virtual 8086 Mode (or anytime CPL ≥ 0) causes an exception 13 fault:

```
LIDT;   MOV DRn,REG;   MOV reg,DRn;
LGDT;   MOV TRn,reg;   MOV reg,TRn;
LMSW;   MOV CRn,reg;   MOV reg,CRn;

CLTS;
HLT;
```

Several instructions, particularly those applying to the multitasking and the protection model, are available only in Protected Mode. Therefore, attempting to execute the following instructions in Real Mode or in Virtual 8086 Mode generates an exception 6 fault:

LTR;	STR;
LLDT;	SLDT;
LAR;	VERR;
LSL;	VERW;
ARPL;	

The instructions which are IOPL sensitive in Protected Mode are:

IN;	STI;
OUT;	CLI
INS;	
OUTS;	
REP INS;	
REP OUTS;	

In Virtual 8086 Mode the following instructions are IOPL-sensitive:

INT n;	STI;
PUSHF;	CLI;
POPF;	IRET;

The PUSHF, POPF, and IRET instructions are IOPL-sensitive in Virtual 8086 Mode only. This provision allows the IF flag to be virtualized to the virtual 8086 Mode program. The INT n software interrupt instruction is also IOPL-sensitive in Virtual 8086 mode. Note that the INT 3, INTO, and BOUND instructions are not IOPL-sensitive in Virtual 8086 Mode.

The I/O instructions that directly refer to addresses in the processor's I/O space are IN, INS, OUT, and OUTS. The Intel386 SX Microprocessor has the ability to selectively trap references to specific I/O addresses. The structure that enables selective trapping is the *I/O Permission Bit Map* in the TSS segment (see Figures 4.8 and 4.9). The I/O permission map is a bit vector. The size of the map and its location in the TSS segment are variable. The processor locates the I/O permission map by means of the **I/O map base** field in the fixed portion of the TSS. The **I/O map base** field is 16 bits wide and contains the offset of the beginning of the I/O permission map.

In protected mode when an I/O instruction (IN, INS, OUT or OUTS) is encountered, the processor first checks whether CPL≤IOPL. If this condition is true, the I/O operation may proceed. If not true, the processor checks the I/O permission map (in Virtual 8086 Mode, the processor consults the map without regard for the IOPL).

Each bit in the map corresponds to an I/O port byte address; for example, the bit for port 41 is found at **I/O map base** +5, bit offset 1. The processor tests all the bits that correspond to the I/O addresses spanned by an I/O operation; for example, a double word operation tests four bits corresponding to four adjacent byte addresses. If any tested bit is set, the processor signals a general protection exception. If all the tested bits are zero, the I/O operations may proceed.

It is not necessary for the I/O permission map to represent all the I/O addresses. I/O addresses not spanned by the map are treated as if they had one-bits in the map. The **I/O map base** should be at least one byte less than the TSS limit, the last byte beyond the I/O mapping information must contain all 1's.

Because the I/O permission map is in the TSS segment, different tasks can have different maps. Thus, the operating system can allocate ports to a task by changing the I/O permission map in the task's TSS.

IMPORTANT IMPLEMENTATION NOTE: Beyond the last byte of I/O mapping information in the I/O permission bit map **must** be a byte containing all 1's. The byte of all 1's must be within the limit of the Intel386 SX CPU TSS segment (see Figure 4.8).

Interrupt Handling

In order to fully support the emulation of an 8086 machine, interrupts in Virtual 8086 Mode are handled in a unique fashion. When running in Virtual Mode all interrupts and exceptions involve a privilege change back to the host Intel386 SX Microprocessor operating system. The Intel386 SX Microprocessor operating system determines if the interrupt comes from a Protected Mode application or from a Virtual Mode program by examining the VM bit in the EFLAGS image stored on the stack.

When a Virtual Mode program is interrupted and execution passes to the interrupt routine at level 0, the VM bit is cleared. However, the VM bit is still set in the EFLAG image on the stack.

The Intel386 SX Microprocessor operating system in turn handles the exception or interrupt and then returns control to the 8086 program. The Intel386 SX Microprocessor operating system may choose to let the 8086 operating system handle the interrupt or it may emulate the function of the interrupt handler. For example, many 8086 operating system calls are accessed by PUSHing parameters on the stack, and then executing an INT n instruction. If the IOPL is set to 0 then all INT n instructions will be intercepted by the Intel386 SX Microprocessor operating system.

An Intel386 SX Microprocessor operating system can provide a Virtual 8086 Environment which is totally transparent to the application software by intercepting and then emulating 8086 operating system's calls, and intercepting IN and OUT instructions.

Entering and Leaving Virtual 8086 Mode

Virtual 8086 mode is entered by executing a 32-bit IRET instruction at CPL=0 where the stack has a 1 in the VM bit of its EFLAGS image, or a Task Switch (at any CPL) to a Intel386 SX Microprocessor task whose Intel386 SX CPU TSS has a EFLAGS image containing a 1 in the VM bit position while the processor is executing in the Protected Mode. POPF does not affect the VM bit but a PUSHF always pushes a 0 in the VM bit.

The transition out of Virtual 8086 mode to protected mode occurs only on receipt of an interrupt or exception. In Virtual 8086 mode, all interrupts and exceptions vector through the protected mode IDT, and enter an interrupt handler in protected mode. As part of the interrupt processing the VM bit is cleared.

Because the matching IRET must occur from level 0, Interrupt or Trap Gates used to field an interrupt or exception out of Virtual 8086 mode must perform an inter-level interrupt only to level 0. Interrupt or Trap Gates through conforming segments, or through segments with DPL>0, will raise a GP fault with the CS selector as the error code.

Task Switches To/From Virtual 8086 Mode

Tasks which can execute in Virtual 8086 mode must be described by a TSS with the Intel386 SX CPU format (type 9 or 11 descriptor). A task switch out of virtual 8086 mode will operate exactly the same as any other task switch out of a task with a Intel386 SX CPU TSS. All of the programmer visible state, including the EFLAGS register with the VM bit set to 1, is stored in the TSS. The segment registers in the TSS will contain 8086 segment base values rather than selectors.

A task switch into a task described by a Intel386 SX CPU TSS will have an additional check to determine if the incoming task should be resumed in Virtual 8086 mode. Tasks described by 286 format TSSs cannot be resumed in Virtual 8086 mode, so no check is required there (the FLAGS image in 286 format TSS has only the low order 16 FLAGS bits). Before loading the segment register images from a Intel386 SX CPU TSS, the FLAGS image is loaded, so that the segment registers are loaded from the TSS image as 8086 segment base values. The task is now ready to resume in Virtual 8086 mode.

Transitions Through Trap and Interrupt Gates, and IRET

A task switch is one way to enter or exit Virtual 8086 mode. The other method is to exit through a Trap or Interrupt gate, as part of handling an interrupt, and to enter as part of executing an IRET instruction. The transition out must use a Intel386 SX CPU Trap Gate (Type 14), or Intel386 SX CPU Interrupt Gate (Type 15), which must point to a non-conforming level 0 segment (DPL=0) in order to permit the trap handler to IRET back to the Virtual 8086 program. The Gate must point to a non-conforming level 0 segment to perform a level switch to level 0 so that the matching IRET can change the VM bit. Intel386 SX CPU gates must be used since 286 gates save only the low 16 bits of the EFLAGS register (the VM bit will not be saved). Also, the 16-bit IRET used to terminate the 286 interrupt handler will pop only the lower 16 bits from FLAGS, and will not affect the VM bit. The action taken for a Intel386 SX CPU Trap or Interrupt gate if an interrupt occurs while the task is executing in virtual 8086 mode is given by the following sequence:

1. Save the FLAGS register in a temp to push later. Turn off the VM, TF, and IF bits.
2. Interrupt and Trap gates must perform a level switch from 3 (where the Virtual 8086 Mode program executes) to level 0 (so IRET can return).
3. Push the 8086 segment register values onto the new stack, in this order: GS, FS, DS, ES. These are pushed as 32-bit quantities. Then load these 4 registers with null selectors (0).
4. Push the old 8086 stack pointer onto the new stack by pushing the SS register (as 32-bits), then pushing the 32-bit ESP register saved above.
5. Push the 32-bit EFLAGS register saved in step 1.
6. Push the old 8086 instruction onto the new stack by pushing the CS register (as 32-bits), then pushing the 32-bit EIP register.
7. Load up the new CS:EIP value from the interrupt gate, and begin execution of the interrupt routine in protected mode.

The transition out of V86 mode performs a level change and stack switch, in addition to changing back to protected mode. Also all of the 8086 segment register images are stored on the stack (behind the SS:ESP image), and then loaded with null (0) selectors before entering the interrupt handler. This will permit the handler to safely save and restore the DS, ES, FS, and GS registers as 286 selectors. This is needed so that interrupt handlers which don't care about the mode of the interrupted program can use the same prologue and epilogue code for state saving regardless of whether or not a 'native' mode or Virtual 8086 Mode program was interrupted. Restoring null selectors to these registers before executing the IRET will cause a trap in the interrupt handler. Interrupt routines which expect or return values in the segment registers will have to obtain/return values from the 8086 register images pushed onto the new stack. They will need to know the mode of the interrupted program in order to know where to find/return segment registers, and also to know how to interpret segment register values.

The IRET instruction will perform the inverse of the above sequence. Only the extended IRET instruction (operand size=32) can be used and must be executed at level 0 to change the VM bit to 1.

1. If the NT bit in the FLAGS register is on, an intertask return is performed. The current state is stored in the current TSS, and the link field in the current TSS is used to locate the TSS for the interrupted task which is to be resumed. Otherwise, continue with the following sequence:
2. Read the FLAGS image from SS:8[ESP] into the FLAGS register. This will set VM to the value active in the interrupted routine.
3. Pop off the instruction pointer CS:EIP. EIP is popped first, then a 32-bit word is popped which contains the CS value in the lower 16 bits. If VM=0, this CS load is done as a protected mode segment load. If VM=1, this will be done as an 8086 segment load.
4. Increment the ESP register by 4 to bypass the FLAGS image which was 'popped' in step 1.
5. If VM=1, load segment registers ES, DS, FS, and GS from memory locations SS:[ESP+8], SS:[ESP+12], SS:[ESP+16], and SS:[ESP=20], respectively, where the new value of ESP stored in step 4 is used. Since VM=1, these are done as 8086 segment register loads.

   Else if VM=0, check that the selectors in ES, DS, FS, and GS are valid in the interrupted routine. Null out invalid selectors to trap if an attempt is made to access through them.
6. If RPL(CS)>CPL, pop the stack pointer SS:ESP from the stack. The ESP register is popped first, followed by 32-bits containing SS in the lower 16 bits. If VM=0, SS is loaded as a protected mode segment register load. If VM=1, an 8086 segment register load is used.
7. Resume execution of the interrupted routine. The VM bit in the FLAGS register (restored from the interrupt routine's stack image in step 1) determines whether the processor resumes the interrupted routine in Protected mode or Virtual 8086 Mode.

5.0 FUNCTIONAL DATA

The Intel386 SX Microprocessor features a straightforward functional interface to the external hardware. The Intel386 SX Microprocessor has separate parallel buses for data and address. The data bus is 16-bits in width, and bi-directional. The address bus outputs 24-bit address values using 23 address lines and two byte enable signals.

The Intel386 SX Microprocessor has two selectable address bus cycles: address pipelined and non-address pipelined. The address pipelining option allows as much time as possible for data access by starting the pending bus cycle before the present bus cycle is finished. A non-pipelined bus cycle gives the highest bus performance by executing every bus cycle in two processor CLK cycles. For maximum design flexibility, the address pipelining option is selectable on a cycle-by-cycle basis.

The processor's bus cycle is the basic mechanism for information transfer, either from system to processor, or from processor to system. Intel386 SX Microprocessor bus cycles perform data transfer in a minimum of only two clock periods. The maximum transfer bandwidth at 16 MHz is therefore 16 Mbytes/sec. However, any bus cycle will be extended for more than two clock periods if external hardware withholds acknowledgement of the cycle.

4

The Intel386 SX Microprocessor can relinquish control of its local buses to allow mastership by other devices, such as direct memory access (DMA) channels. When relinquished, HLDA is the only output pin driven by the Intel386 SX Microprocessor, providing near-complete isolation of the processor from its system (all other output pins are in a float condition).

5.1 Signal Description Overview

Ahead is a brief description of the Intel386 SX Microprocessor input and output signals arranged by functional groups. Note the # symbol at the end of a signal name indicates the active, or asserted, state occurs when the signal is at a LOW voltage. When no # is present after the signal name, the signal is asserted when at the HIGH voltage level.

Example signal: M/IO# — HIGH voltage indicates Memory selected
— LOW voltage indicates I/O selected

The signal descriptions sometimes refer to AC timing parameters, such as 't_{25} Reset Setup Time' and 't_{26} Reset Hold Time.' The values of these parameters can be found in Table 7.4.

CLOCK (CLK2)

CLK2 provides the fundamental timing for the Intel386 SX Microprocessor. It is divided by two internally to generate the internal processor clock used for instruction execution. The internal clock is comprised of two phases, 'phase one' and 'phase two'. Each CLK2 period is a phase of the internal clock. Figure 5.2 illustrates the relationship. If desired, the phase of the internal processor clock can be synchronized to a known phase by ensuring the falling edge of the RESET signal meets the applicable setup and hold times t_{25} and t_{26}.

DATA BUS (D_{15}–D_0)

These three-state bidirectional signals provide the general purpose data path between the Intel386 SX Microprocessor and other devices. The data bus outputs are active HIGH and will float during bus hold acknowledge. Data bus reads require that read-data setup and hold times t_{21} and t_{22} be met relative to CLK2 for correct operation.

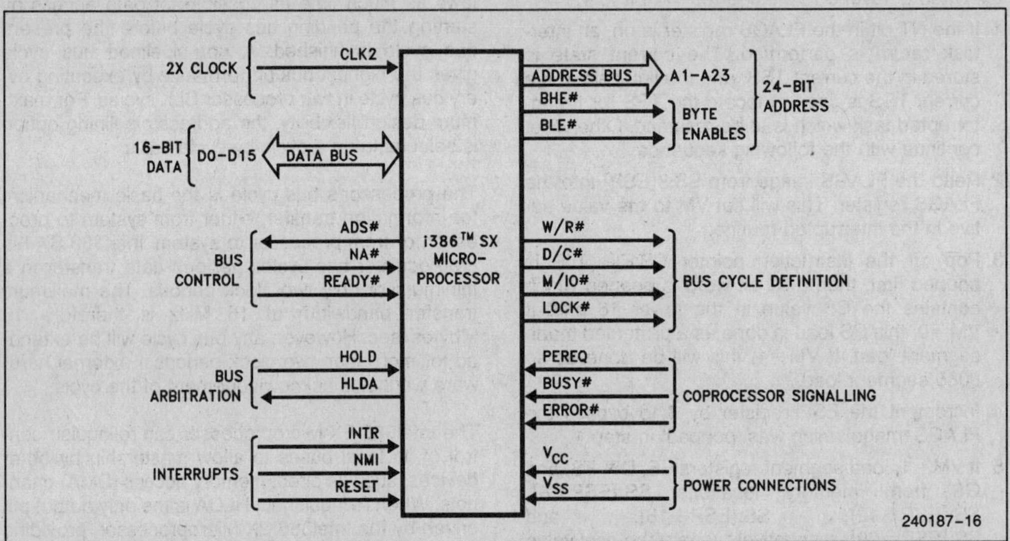

Figure 5.1. Functional Signal Groups

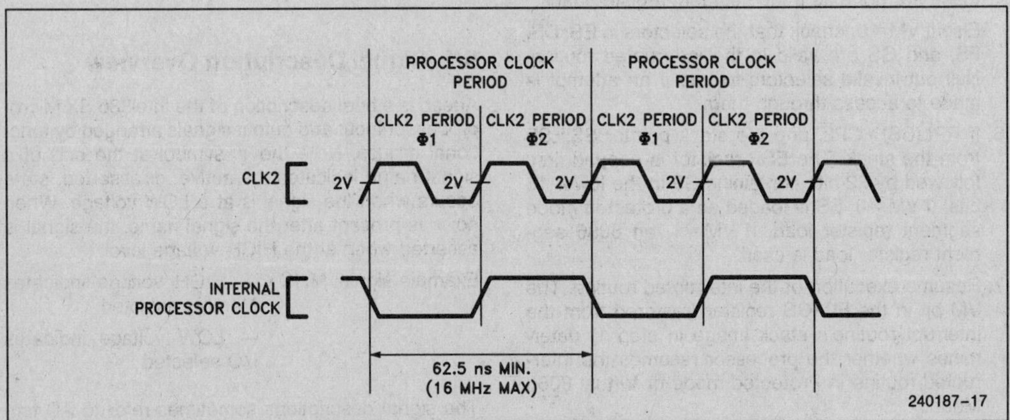

Figure 5.2. CLK2 Signal and Internal Processor Clock

ADDRESS BUS (A_{23}–A_1, BHE#, BLE#)

These three-state outputs provide physical memory addresses or I/O port addresses. A_{23}–A_{16} are LOW during I/O transfers except for I/O transfers automatically generated by coprocessor instructions. During coprocessor I/O transfers, A_{22}–A_{16} are driven LOW, and A_{23} is driven HIGH so that this address line can be used by external logic to generate the coprocessor select signal. Thus, the I/O address driven by the Intel386 SX Microprocessor for coprocessor commands is 8000F8H, the I/O addresses driven by the Intel386 SX Microprocessor for coprocessor data are 8000FCH or 8000FEH for cycles to the Intel387™ SX.

The address bus is capable of addressing 16 megabytes of physical memory space (000000H through FFFFFFH), and 64 kilobytes of I/O address space (000000H through 00FFFFH) for programmed I/O. The address bus is active HIGH and will float during bus hold acknowledge.

The Byte Enable outputs, BHE# and BLE#, directly indicate which bytes of the 16-bit data bus are involved with the current transfer. BHE# applies to D_{15}–D_8 and BLE# applies to D_7–D_0. If both BHE# and BLE# are asserted, then 16 bits of data are being transferred. See Table 5.1 for a complete decoding of these signals. The byte enables are active LOW and will float during bus hold acknowledge.

BUS CYCLE DEFINITION SIGNALS (W/R#, D/C#, M/IO#, LOCK#)

These three-state outputs define the type of bus cycle being performed: W/R# distinguishes between write and read cycles, D/C# distinguishes between data and control cycles, M/IO# distinguishes between memory and I/O cycles, and LOCK# distinguishes between locked and unlocked bus cycles. All of these signals are active LOW and will float during bus acknowledge.

The primary bus cycle definition signals are W/R#, D/C# and M/IO#, since these are the signals driven valid as ADS# (Address Status output) becomes active. The LOCK# is driven valid at the same time the bus cycle begins, which due to address pipelining, could be after ADS# becomes active. Exact bus cycle definitions, as a function of W/R#, D/C#, and M/IO# are given in Table 5.2.

LOCK# indicates that other system bus masters are not to gain control of the system bus while it is active. LOCK# is activated on the CLK2 edge that begins the first locked bus cycle (i.e., it is not active at the same time as the other bus cycle definition pins) and is deactivated when ready is returned at the end of the last bus cycle which is to be locked. The beginning of a bus cycle is determined when READY# is returned in a previous bus cycle and another is pending (ADS# is active) or by the clock edge in which ADS# is driven active if the bus was idle. This means that it follows more closely with the write data rules when it is valid, but may cause the bus to be locked longer than desired. The LOCK# signal may be explicitly activated by the LOCK prefix on certain instructions. LOCK# is always asserted when executing the XCHG instruction, during descriptor updates, and during the interrupt acknowledge sequence.

Table 5.1. Byte Enable Definitions

BHE#	BLE#	Function
0	0	Word Transfer
0	1	Byte transfer on upper byte of the data bus, D_{15}–D_8
1	0	Byte transfer on lower byte of the data bus, D_7–D_0
1	1	Never occurs

Table 5.2. Bus Cycle Definition

M/IO#	D/C#	W/R#	Bus Cycle Type	Locked?
0	0	0	Interrupt Acknowledge	Yes
0	0	1	does not occur	—
0	1	0	I/O Data Read	No
0	1	1	I/O Data Write	No
1	0	0	Memory Code Read	No
1	0	1	Halt: Address = 2, BHE# = 1, BLE# = 0 / Shutdown: Address = 0, BHE# = 1, BLE# = 0	No
1	1	0	Memory Data Read	Some Cycles
1	1	1	Memory Data Write	Some Cycles

4

BUS CONTROL SIGNALS (ADS#, READY#, NA#)

The following signals allow the processor to indicate when a bus cycle has begun, and allow other system hardware to control address pipelining and bus cycle termination.

Address Status (ADS#)

This three-state output indicates that a valid bus cycle definition and address (W/R#, D/C#, M/IO#, BHE#, BLE# and A_{23}–A_1) are being driven at the Intel386 SX Microprocessor pins. ADS# is an active LOW output. Once ADS# is driven active, valid address, byte enables, and definition signals will not change. In addition, ADS# will remain active until its associated bus cycle begins (when READY# is returned for the previous bus cycle when running pipelined bus cycles). When address pipelining is utilized, maximum throughput is achieved by initiating bus cycles when ADS# and READY# are active in the same clock cycle. ADS# will float during bus hold acknowledge. See sections **Non-Pipelined Address** and **Pipelined Address** for additional information on how ADS# is asserted for different bus states.

Transfer Acknowledge (READY#)

This input indicates the current bus cycle is complete, and the active bytes indicated by BHE# and BLE# are accepted or provided. When READY# is sampled active during a read cycle or interrupt acknowledge cycle, the Intel386 SX Microprocessor latches the input data and terminates the cycle. When READY# is sampled active during a write cycle, the processor terminates the bus cycle.

READY# is ignored on the first bus state of all bus cycles, and sampled each bus state thereafter until asserted. READY# must eventually be asserted to acknowledge every bus cycle, including Halt Indication and Shutdown Indication bus cycles. When being sampled, READY# must always meet setup and hold times t_{19} and t_{20} for correct operation.

Next Address Request (NA#)

This is used to request address pipelining. This input indicates the system is prepared to accept new values of BHE#, BLE#, A_{23}–A_1, W/R#, D/C# and M/IO# from the Intel386 SX Microprocessor even if the end of the current cycle is not being acknowledged on READY#. If this input is active when sampled, the next address is driven onto the bus, provided the next bus request is already pending internally. NA# is ignored in CLK cycles in which ADS# or READY# is activated. This signal is active LOW and must satisfy setup and hold times t_{15} and t_{16} for correct operation. See **Pipelined Address** and **Read and Write Cycles** for additional information.

BUS ARBITRATION SIGNALS (HOLD, HLDA)

This section describes the mechanism by which the processor relinquishes control of its local buses when requested by another bus master device. See **Entering and Exiting Hold Acknowledge** for additional information.

Bus Hold Request (HOLD)

This input indicates some device other than the Intel386 SX Microprocessor requires bus mastership. When control is granted, the Intel386 SX Microprocessor floats A_{23}–A_1, BHE#, BLE#, D_{15}–D_0, LOCK#, M/IO#, D/C#, W/R# and ADS#, and then activates HLDA, thus entering the bus hold acknowledge state. The local bus will remain granted to the requesting master until HOLD becomes inactive. When HOLD becomes inactive, the Intel386 SX Microprocessor will deactivate HLDA and drive the local bus (at the same time), thus terminating the hold acknowledge condition.

HOLD must remain asserted as long as any other device is a local bus master. External pull-up resistors may be required when in the hold acknowledge state since none of the Intel386 SX Microprocessor floated outputs have internal pull-up resistors. See **Resistor Recommendations** for additional information. HOLD is not recognized while RESET is active. If RESET is asserted while HOLD is asserted, RESET has priority and places the bus into an idle state, rather than the hold acknowledge (high-impedance) state.

HOLD is a level-sensitive, active HIGH, synchronous input. HOLD signals must always meet setup and hold times t_{23} and t_{24} for correct operation.

Bus Hold Acknowledge (HLDA)

When active (HIGH), this output indicates the Intel386 SX Microprocessor has relinquished control of its local bus in response to an asserted HOLD signal, and is in the bus Hold Acknowledge state.

The Bus Hold Acknowledge state offers near-complete signal isolation. In the Hold Acknowledge state, HLDA is the only signal being driven by the Intel386 SX Microprocessor. The other output signals or bidirectional signals (D_{15}–D_0, BHE#, BLE#, A_{23}–A_1, W/R#, D/C#, M/IO#, LOCK# and ADS#) are in a high-impedance state so the requesting bus master may control them. These pins remain OFF throughout the time that HLDA remains active (see Table 5.3)). Pull-up resistors may be desired on several signals to avoid spurious activity when no bus master is driving them. See **Resistor Recommendations** for additional information.

When the HOLD signal is made inactive, the Intel386 SX Microprocessor will deactivate HLDA and drive the bus. One rising edge on the NMI input is remembered for processing after the HOLD input is negated.

Table 5.3. Output pin State During HOLD

Pin Value	Pin Names
1	HLDA
Float	LOCK#, M/IO#, D/C#, W/R#, ADS#, A_{23}–A_1, BHE#, BLE#, D_{15}–D_0

In addition to the normal usage of Hold Acknowledge with DMA controllers or master peripherals, the near-complete isolation has particular attractiveness during system test when test equipment drives the system, and in hardware fault-tolerant applications.

HOLD Latencies

The maximum possible HOLD latency depends on the software being executed. The actual HOLD latency at any time depends on the current bus activity, the state of the LOCK# signal (internal to the CPU) activated by the LOCK# prefix, and interrupts. The Intel386 SX Microprocessor will not honor a HOLD request until the current bus operation is complete.

The Intel386 SX Microprocessor breaks 32-bit data or I/O accesses into 2 internally locked 16-bit bus cycles; the LOCK# signal is not asserted. The Intel386 SX Microprocessor breaks unaligned 16-bit or 32-bit data or I/O accesses into 2 or 3 internally locked 16-bit bus cycles. Again, the LOCK# signal is not asserted but a HOLD request will not be recognized until the end of the entire transfer.

Wait states affect HOLD latency. The Intel386 SX Microprocessor will not honor a HOLD request until the end of the current bus operation, no matter how many wait states are required. Systems with DMA where data transfer is critical must insure that READY# returns sufficiently soon.

COPROCESSOR INTERFACE SIGNALS (PEREQ, BUSY#, ERROR#)

In the following sections are descriptions of signals dedicated to the numeric coprocessor interface. In addition to the data bus, address bus, and bus cycle definition signals, these following signals control communication between the Intel386 SX Microprocessor and its Intel387™ SX processor extension.

Coprocessor Request (PEREQ)

When asserted (HIGH), this input signal indicates a coprocessor request for a data operand to be transferred to/from memory by the Intel386 SX Microprocessor. In response, the Intel386 SX Microprocessor transfers information between the coprocessor and memory. Because the Intel386 SX Microprocessor has internally stored the coprocessor opcode being executed, it performs the requested data transfer with the correct direction and memory address.

PEREQ is a level-sensitive active HIGH asynchronous signal. Setup and hold times, t_{29} and t_{30}, relative to the CLK2 signal must be met to guarantee recognition at a particular clock edge. This signal is provided with a weak internal pull-down resistor of around 20 K-ohms to ground so that it will not float active when left unconnected.

Coprocessor Busy (BUSY#)

When asserted (LOW), this input indicates the coprocessor is still executing an instruction, and is not yet able to accept another. When the Intel386 SX Microprocessor encounters any coprocessor instruction which operates on the numerics stack (e.g. load, pop, or arithmetic operation), or the WAIT instruction, this input is first automatically sampled until it is seen to be inactive. This sampling of the BUSY# input prevents overrunning the execution of a previous coprocessor instruction.

The FNINIT, FNSTENV, FNSAVE, FNSTSW, FNSTCW and FNCLEX coprocessor instructions are allowed to execute even if BUSY# is active, since these instructions are used for coprocessor initialization and exception-clearing.

BUSY# is an active LOW, level-sensitive asynchronous signal. Setup and hold times, t_{29} and t_{30}, rela-

4

tive to the CLK2 signal must be met to guarantee recognition at a particular clock edge. This pin is provided with a weak internal pull-up resistor of around 20 K-ohms to Vcc so that it will not float active when left unconnected.

BUSY# serves an additional function. If BUSY# is sampled LOW at the falling edge of RESET, the Intel386 SX Microprocessor performs an internal self-test (see **Bus Activity During and Following Reset**. If BUSY# is sampled HIGH, no self-test is performed.

Coprocessor Error (ERROR#)

When asserted (LOW), this input signal indicates that the previous coprocessor instruction generated a coprocessor error of a type not masked by the coprocessor's control register. This input is automatically sampled by the Intel386 SX Microprocessor when a coprocessor instruction is encountered, and if active, the Intel386 SX Microprocessor generates exception 16 to access the error-handling software.

Several coprocessor instructions, generally those which clear the numeric error flags in the coprocessor or save coprocessor state, do execute without the Intel386 SX Microprocessor generating exception 16 even if ERROR# is active. These instructions are FNINIT, FNCLEX, FNSTSW, FNSTSWAX, FNSTCW, FNSTENV and FNSAVE.

ERROR# is an active LOW, level-sensitive asynchronous signal. Setup and hold times, t_{29} and t_{30}, relative to the CLK2 signal must be met to guarantee recognition at a particular clock edge. This pin is provided with a weak internal pull-up resistor of around 20 K-ohms to Vcc so that it will not float active when left unconnected.

INTERRUPT SIGNALS (INTR, NMI, RESET)

The following descriptions cover inputs that can interrupt or suspend execution of the processor's current instruction stream.

Maskable Interrupt Request (INTR)

When asserted, this input indicates a request for interrupt service, which can be masked by the Intel386 SX CPU Flag Register IF bit. When the Intel386 SX Microprocessor responds to the INTR input, it performs two interrupt acknowledge bus cycles and, at the end of the second, latches an 8-bit interrupt vector on D_7–D_0 to identify the source of the interrupt.

INTR is an active HIGH, level-sensitive asynchronous signal. Setup and hold times, t_{27} and t_{28}, relative to the CLK2 signal must be met to guarantee recognition at a particular clock edge. To assure recognition of an INTR request, INTR should remain active until the first interrupt acknowledge bus cycle begins. INTR is sampled at the beginning of every instruction in the Intel386 SX Microprocessor's Execution Unit. In order to be recognized at a particular instruction boundary, INTR must be active at least eight CLK2 clock periods before the beginning of the instruction. If recognized, the Intel386 SX Microprocessor will begin execution of the interrupt.

Non-Maskable Interrupt Request (NMI))

This input indicates a request for interrupt service which cannot be masked by software. The non-maskable interrupt request is always processed according to the pointer or gate in slot 2 of the interrupt table. Because of the fixed NMI slot assignment, no interrupt acknowledge cycles are performed when processing NMI.

NMI is an active HIGH, rising edge-sensitive asynchronous signal. Setup and hold times, t_{27} and t_{28}, relative to the CLK2 signal must be met to guarantee recognition at a particular clock edge. To assure recognition of NMI, it must be inactive for at least eight CLK2 periods, and then be active for at least eight CLK2 periods before the beginning of the instruction boundary in the Intel386 SX Microprocessor's Execution Unit.

Once NMI processing has begun, no additional NMI's are processed until after the next IRET instruction, which is typically the end of the NMI service routine. If NMI is re-asserted prior to that time, however, one rising edge on NMI will be remembered for processing after executing the next IRET instruction.

Interrupt Latency

The time that elapses before an interrupt request is serviced (interrupt latency) varies according to several factors. This delay must be taken into account by the interrupt source. Any of the following factors can affect interrupt latency:

1. If interrupts are masked, an INTR request will not be recognized until interrupts are reenabled.
2. If an NMI is currently being serviced, an incoming NMI request will not be recognized until the Intel386 SX Microprocessor encounters the IRET instruction.
3. An interrupt request is recognized only on an instruction boundary of the Intel386 SX Microprocessor's Execution Unit except for the following cases:
   - Repeat string instructions can be interrupted after each iteration.

— If the instruction loads the Stack Segment register, an interrupt is not processed until after the following instruction, which should be an ESP. This allows the entire stack pointer to be loaded without interruption.

— If an instruction sets the interrupt flag (enabling interrupts), an interrupt is not processed until after the next instruction.

The longest latency occurs when the interrupt request arrives while the Intel386 SX Microprocessor is executing a long instruction such as multiplication, division, or a task-switch in the protected mode.

4. Saving the Flags register and CS:EIP registers.
5. If interrupt service routine requires a task switch, time must be allowed for the task switch.
6. If the interrupt service routine saves registers that are not automatically saved by the Intel386 SX Microprocessor.

RESET

This input signal suspends any operation in progress and places the Intel386 SX Microprocessor in a known reset state. The Intel386 SX Microprocessor is reset by asserting RESET for 15 or more CLK2 periods (80 or more CLK2 periods before requesting self-test). When RESET is active, all other input pins, except FLT#, are ignored, and all other bus pins are driven to an idle bus state as shown in Table 5.5. If RESET and HOLD are both active at a point in time, RESET takes priority even if the Intel386 SX Microprocessor was in a Hold Acknowledge state prior to RESET active.

RESET is an active HIGH, level-sensitive synchronous signal. Setup and hold times, t_{25} and t_{26}, must be met in order to assure proper operation of the Intel386 SX Microprocessor.

Table 5.5. Pin State (Bus Idle) During Reset

Pin Name	Signal Level During Reset
ADS#	1
D_{15}–D_0	Float
BHE#, BLE#	0
A_{23}–A_1	1
W/R#	0
D/C#	1
M/IO#	0
LOCK#	1
HLDA	0

5.2 Bus Transfer Mechanism

All data transfers occur as a result of one or more bus cycles. Logical data operands of byte and word lengths may be transferred without restrictions on physical address alignment. Any byte boundary may be used, although two physical bus cycles are performed as required for unaligned operand transfers.

The Intel386 SX Microprocessor address signals are designed to simplify external system hardware. Higher-order address bits are provided by A_{23}–A_1. BHE# and BLE# provide linear selects for the two bytes of the 16-bit data bus.

Byte Enable outputs BHE# and BLE# are asserted when their associated data bus bytes are involved with the present bus cycle, as listed in Table 5.6.

Table 5.6. Byte Enables and Associated Data and Operand Bytes

Byte Enable Signal	Associated Data Bus Signals	
BLE#	D_7–D_0	(byte 0 — least significant)
BHE#	D_{15}–D_8	(byte 1 — most significant)

Each bus cycle is composed of at least two bus states. Each bus state requires one processor clock period. Additional bus states added to a single bus cycle are called wait states. See section **5.4 Bus Functional Description**.

5.3 Memory and I/O Spaces

Bus cycles may access physical memory space or I/O space. Peripheral devices in the system may either be memory-mapped, or I/O-mapped, or both. As shown in Figure 5.3, physical memory addresses range from 000000H to 0FFFFFFH (16 megabytes) and I/O addresses from 000000H to 00FFFFH (64 kilobytes). Note the I/O addresses used by the automatic I/O cycles for coprocessor communication are 8000F8H to 8000FFH, beyond the address range of programmed I/O, to allow easy generation of a coprocessor chip select signal using the A_{23} and M/IO# signals.

5.4 Bus Functional Description

The Intel386 SX Microprocessor has separate, parallel buses for data and address. The data bus is 16-bits in width, and bidirectional. The address bus provides a 24-bit value using 23 signals for the 23 upper-order address bits and 2 Byte Enable signals to directly indicate the active bytes. These buses are interpreted and controlled by several definition signals.

The definition of each bus cycle is given by three signals: M/IO#, W/R# and D/C#. At the same time, a valid address is present on the byte enable signals, BHE# and BLE#, and the other address signals A_{23}–A_1. A status signal, ADS#, indicates

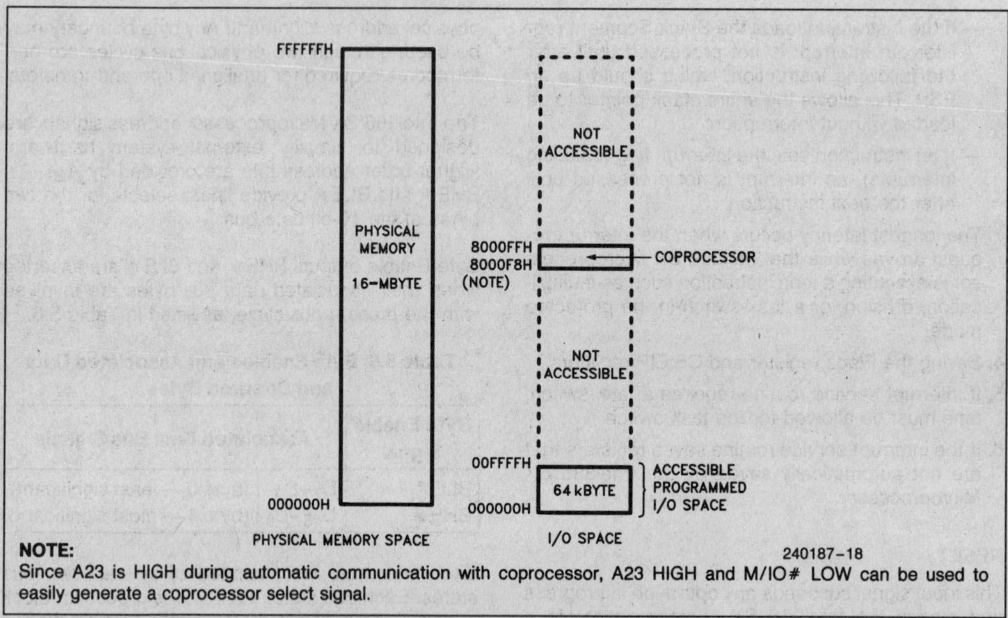

NOTE:
Since A23 is HIGH during automatic communication with coprocessor, A23 HIGH and M/IO# LOW can be used to easily generate a coprocessor select signal.

Figure 5.3. Physical Memory and I/O Spaces

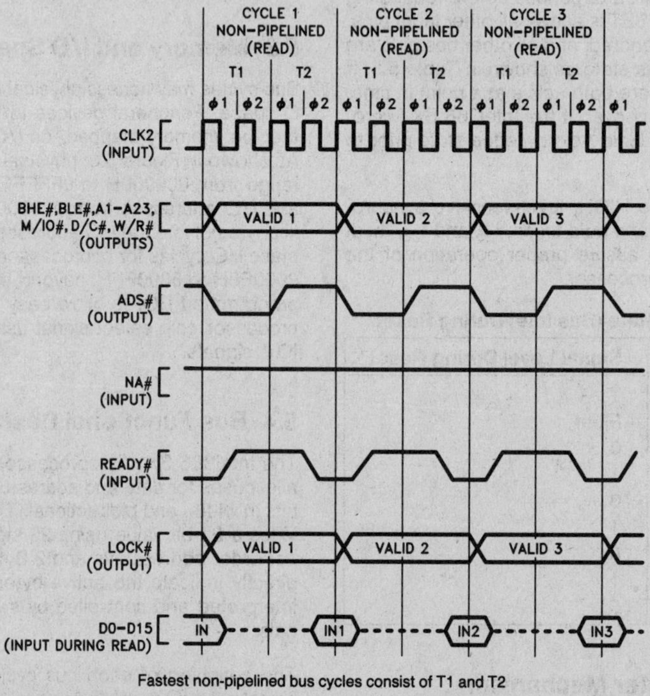

CYCLE 1 NON-PIPELINED (READ) | CYCLE 2 NON-PIPELINED (READ) | CYCLE 3 NON-PIPELINED (READ)

T1 T2 T1 T2 T1 T2

φ1 φ2 φ1 φ2 φ1 φ2 φ1 φ2 φ1 φ2 φ1 φ2 φ1

CLK2 (INPUT)

BHE#, BLE#, A1–A23, M/IO#, D/C#, W/R# (OUTPUTS) — VALID 1, VALID 2, VALID 3

ADS# (OUTPUT)

NA# (INPUT)

READY# (INPUT)

LOCK# (OUTPUT) — VALID 1, VALID 2, VALID 3

D0–D15 (INPUT DURING READ) — IN, IN1, IN2, IN3

240187–19

Fastest non-pipelined bus cycles consist of T1 and T2

Figure 5.4. Fastest Read Cycles with Non-pipelined Address Timing

when the Intel386 SX Microprocessor issues a new bus cycle definition and address.

Collectively, the address bus, data bus and all associated control signals are referred to simply as 'the bus'. When active, the bus performs one of the bus cycles below:

1. Read from memory space
2. Locked read from memory space
3. Write to memory space
4. Locked write to memory space
5. Read from I/O space (or coprocessor)
6. Write to I/O space (or coprocessor)
7. Interrupt acknowledge (always locked)
8. Indicate halt, or indicate shutdown

Table 5.2 shows the encoding of the bus cycle definition signals for each bus cycle. See **Bus Cycle Definition Signals** for additional information.

When the Intel386 SX Microprocessor bus is not performing one of the activities listed above, it is either Idle or in the Hold Acknowledge state, which may be detected externally. The idle state can be identified by the Intel386 SX Microprocessor giving no further assertions on its address strobe output (ADS#) since the beginning of its most recent bus cycle, and the most recent bus cycle having been terminated. The hold acknowledge state is identified by the Intel386 SX Microprocessor asserting its hold acknowledge (HLDA) output.

The shortest time unit of bus activity is a bus state. A bus state is one processor clock period (two CLK2 periods) in duration. A complete data transfer occurs during a bus cycle, composed of two or more bus states.

The fastest Intel386 SX Microprocessor bus cycle requires only two bus states. For example, three consecutive bus read cycles, each consisting of two bus states, are shown by Figure 5.4. The bus states in each cycle are named T1 and T2. Any memory or I/O address may be accessed by such a two-state bus cycle, if the external hardware is fast enough.

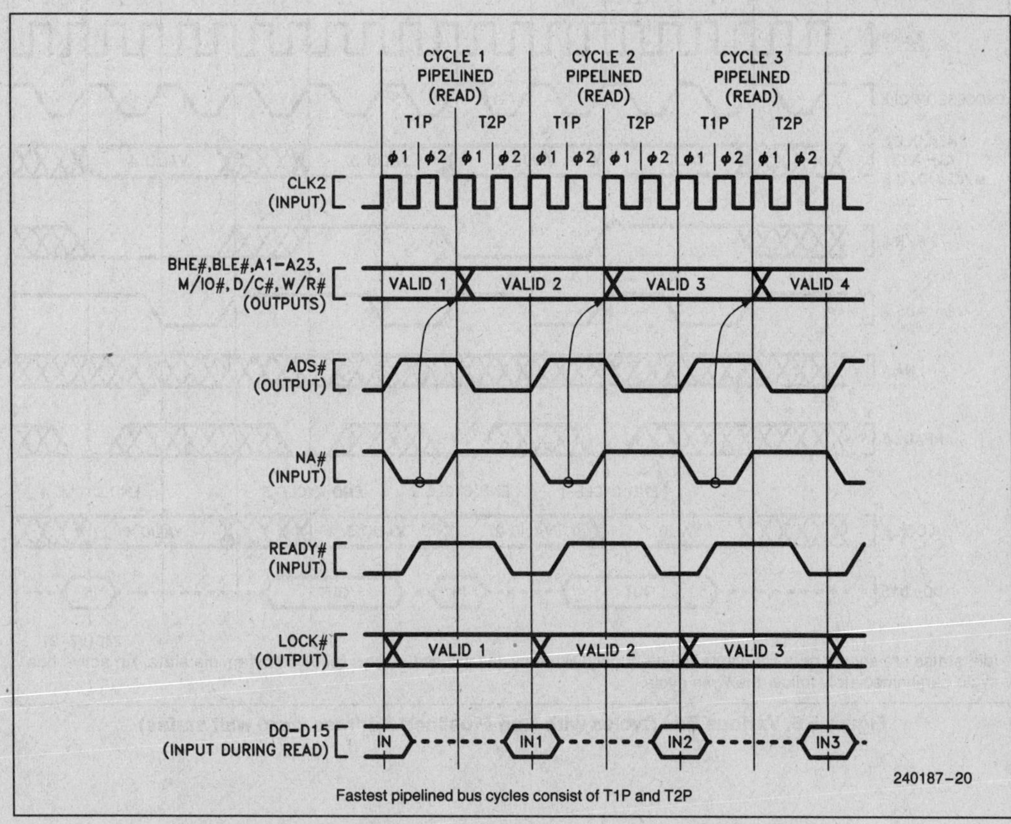

Figure 5.5. Fastest Read Cycles with Pipelined Address Timing

Every bus cycle continues until it is acknowledged by the external system hardware, using the Intel386 SX Microprocessor READY# input. Acknowledging the bus cycle at the end of the first T2 results in the shortest bus cycle, requiring only T1 and T2. If READY# is not immediately asserted however, T2 states are repeated indefinitely until the READY# input is sampled active.

The address pipelining option provides a choice of bus cycle timings. Pipelined or non-pipelined address timing is selectable on a cycle-by-cycle basis with the Next Address (NA#) input.

When address pipelining is selected the address (BHE#, BLE# and A_{23}–A_1) and definition (W/R#, D/C#, M/IO# and LOCK#) of the next cycle are available before the end of the current cycle. To signal their availability, the Intel386 SX Microprocessor address status output (ADS#) is asserted. Figure 5.5 illustrates the fastest read cycles with pipelined address timing.

Note from Figure 5.5 the fastest bus cycles using pipelined address require only two bus states, named **T1P** and **T2P**. Therefore cycles with pipelined address timing allow the same data bandwidth as non-pipelined cycles, but address-to-data access time is increased by one T-state time compared to that of a non-pipelined cycle.

READ AND WRITE CYCLES

Data transfers occur as a result of bus cycles, classified as read or write cycles. During read cycles, data is transferred from an external device to the processor. During write cycles, data is transferred from the processor to an external device.

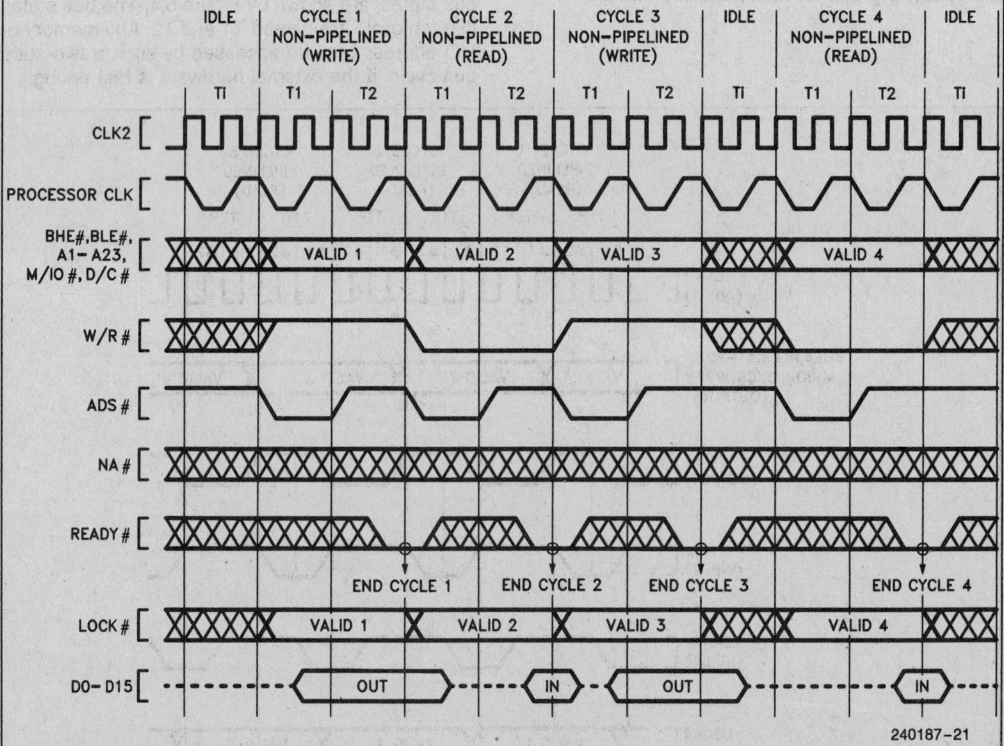

240187–21

Idle states are shown here for diagram variety only. Write cycles are **not** always followed by an idle state. An active bus cycle can immediately follow the write cycle.

Figure 5.6. Various Bus Cycles with Non-Pipelined Address (zero wait states)

Two choices of address timing are dynamically selectable: non-pipelined or pipelined. After an idle bus state, the processor always uses non-pipelined address timing. However the NA# (Next Address) input may be asserted to select pipelined address timing for the next bus cycle. When pipelining is selected and the Intel386 SX Microprocessor has a bus request pending internally, the address and definition of the next cycle is made available even before the current bus cycle is acknowledged by READY#.

Terminating a read or write cycle, like any bus cycle, requires acknowledging the cycle by asserting the READY# input. Until acknowledged, the processor inserts wait states into the bus cycle, to allow adjustment for the speed of any external device. External hardware, which has decoded the address and bus cycle type, asserts the READY# input at the appropriate time.

At the end of the second bus state within the bus cycle, READY# is sampled. At that time, if external hardware acknowledges the bus cycle by asserting READY#, the bus cycle terminates as shown in Figure 5.6. If READY# is negated as in Figure 5.7, the Intel386 SX Microprocessor executes another bus state (a wait state) and READY# is sampled again at the end of that state. This continues indefinitely until the cycle is acknowledged by READY# asserted.

When the current cycle is acknowledged, the Intel386 SX Microprocessor terminates it. When a read cycle is acknowledged, the Intel386 SX Microprocessor latches the information present at its data pins. When a write cycle is acknowledged, the Intel386 SX CPU's write data remains valid throughout phase one of the next bus state, to provide write data hold time.

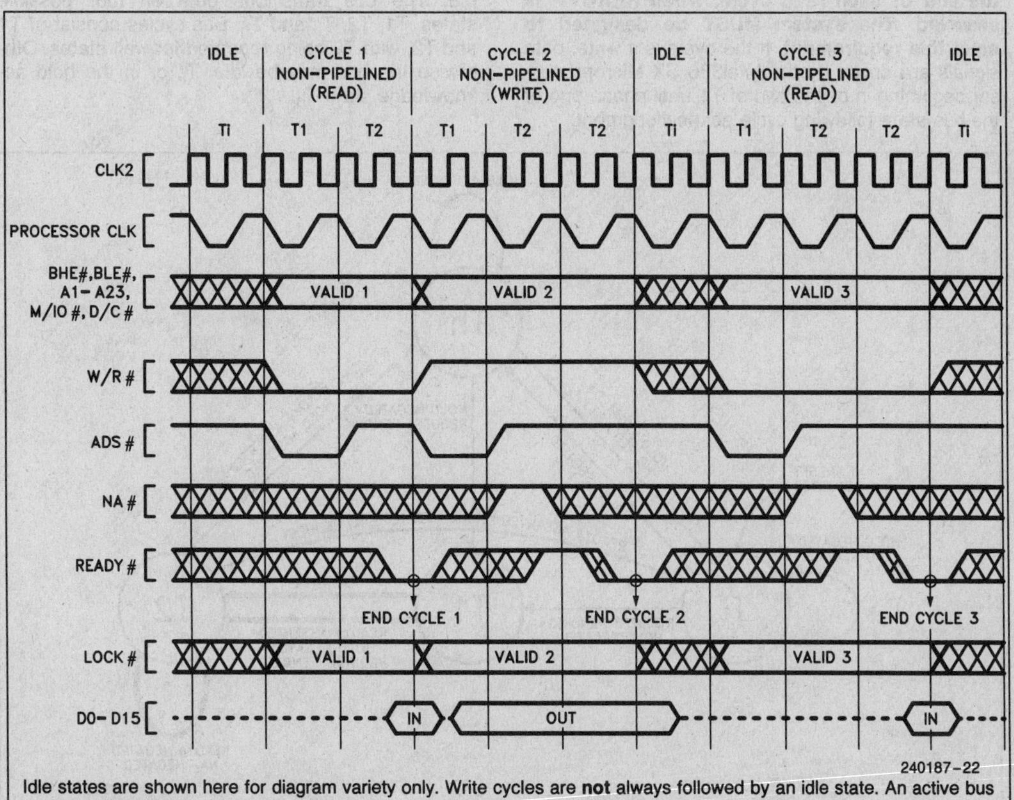

Idle states are shown here for diagram variety only. Write cycles are **not** always followed by an idle state. An active bus cycle can immediately follow the write cycle.

Figure 5.7. Various Bus Cycles with Non-Pipelined Address (various number of wait states)

Non-Pipelined Address

Any bus cycle may be performed with non-pipelined address timing. For example, Figure 5.6 shows a mixture of read and write cycles with non-pipelined address timing. Figure 5.6 shows that the fastest possible cycles with non-pipelined address have two bus states per bus cycle. The states are named T1 and T2. In phase one of T1, the address signals and bus cycle definition signals are driven valid and, to signal their availability, address strobe (ADS#) is simultaneously asserted.

During read or write cycles, the data bus behaves as follows. If the cycle is a read, the Intel386 SX Microprocessor floats its data signals to allow driving by the external device being addressed. **The Intel386 SX Microprocessor requires that all data bus pins be at a valid logic state (HIGH or LOW) at the end of each read cycle, when READY# is asserted. The system MUST be designed to meet this requirement.** If the cycle is a write, data signals are driven by the Intel386 SX Microprocessor beginning in phase two of T1 until phase one of the bus state following cycle acknowledgment.

Figure 5.7 illustrates non-pipelined bus cycles with one wait state added to Cycles 2 and 3. READY# is sampled inactive at the end of the first T2 in Cycles 2 and 3. Therefore Cycles 2 and 3 have T2 repeated again. At the end of the second T2, READY# is sampled active.

When address pipelining is not used, the address and bus cycle definition remain valid during all wait states. When wait states are added and it is desirable to maintain non-pipelined address timing, it is necessary to negate NA# during each T2 state except the last one, as shown in Figure 5.7 Cycles 2 and 3. If NA# is sampled active during a T2 other than the last one, the next state would be T2I or T2P instead of another T2.

When address pipelining is not used, the bus states and transitions are completely illustrated by Figure 5.8. The bus transitions between four possible states, T1, T2, T_i, and T_h. Bus cycles consist of T1 and T2, with T2 being repeated for wait states. Otherwise the bus may be idle, T_i, or in the hold acknowledge state T_h.

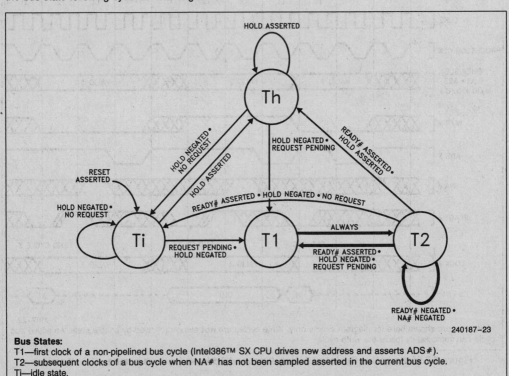

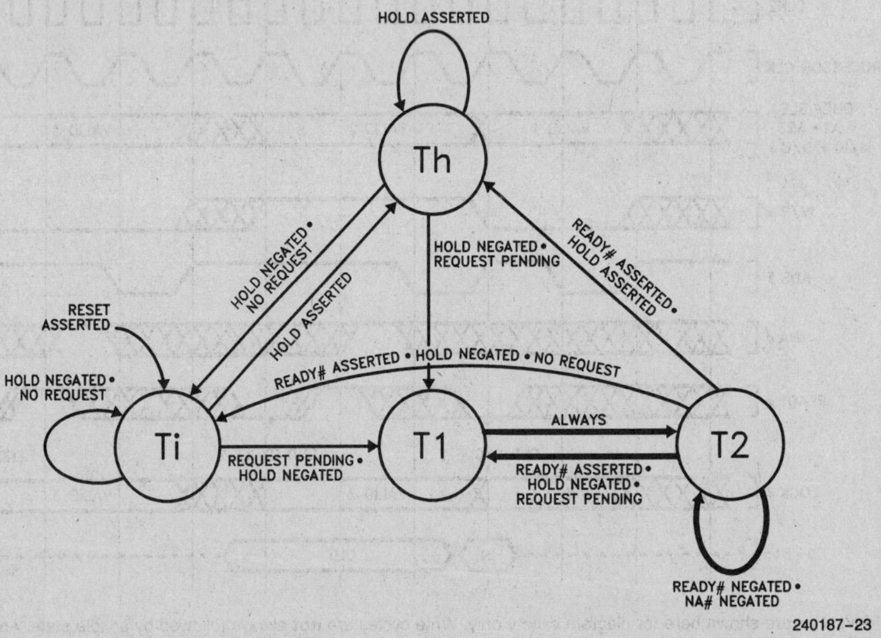

Bus States:
T1—first clock of a non-pipelined bus cycle (Intel386™ SX CPU drives new address and asserts ADS#).
T2—subsequent clocks of a bus cycle when NA# has not been sampled asserted in the current bus cycle.
Ti—idle state.
Th—hold acknowledge state (Intel386 SX CPU asserts HLDA).
The fastest bus cycle consists of two states T1 and T2.
Four basic bus states describe bus operation when not using pipelined address.

Figure 5.8. Bus States (not using pipelined address)

Bus cycles always begin with T1. T1 always leads to T2. If a bus cycle is not acknowledged during T2 and NA# is inactive, T2 is repeated. When a cycle is acknowledged during T2, the following state will be T1 of the next bus cycle if a bus request is pending internally, or T_i if there is no bus request pending, or T_h if the HOLD input is being asserted.

Use of pipelined address allows the Intel386 SX Microprocessor to enter three additional bus states not shown in Figure 5.8. Figure 5.12 is the complete bus state diagram, including pipelined address cycles.

Pipelined Address

Address pipelining is the option of requesting the address and the bus cycle definition of the next internally pending bus cycle before the current bus cycle is acknowledged with READY# asserted. ADS# is asserted by the Intel386 SX Microprocessor when the next address is issued. The address pipelining option is controlled on a cycle-by-cycle basis with the NA# input signal.

Once a bus cycle is in progress and the current address has been valid for at least one entire bus state, the NA# input is sampled at the end of every phase one until the bus cycle is acknowledged. During non-pipelined bus cycles NA# is sampled at the end of phase one in every T2. An example is Cycle 2 in Figure 5.9, during which NA# is sampled at the end of phase one of every T2 (it was asserted once during the first T2 and has no further effect during that bus cycle).

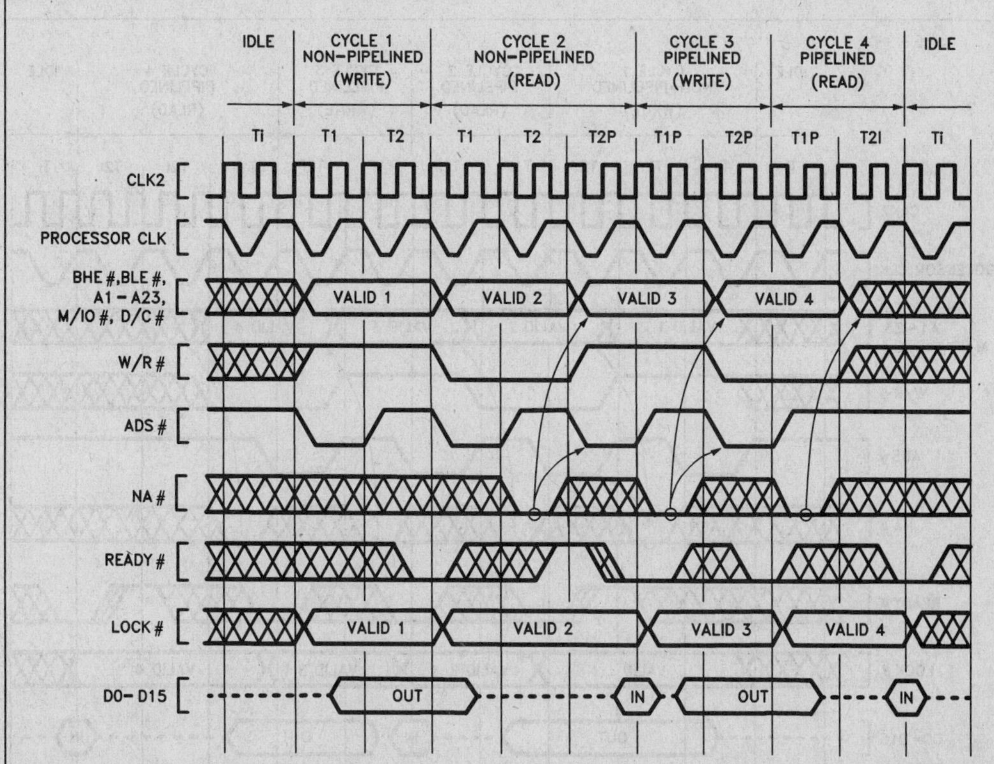

Following any idle bus state (Ti), addresses are non-pipelined. Within non-pipelined bus cycles, NA# is only sampled during wait states. Therefore, to begin address pipelining during a group of non-pipelined bus cycles requires a non-pipelined cycle with at least one wait state (Cycle 2 above).

Figure 5.9. Transitioning to Pipelined Address During Burst of Bus Cycles

If NA# is sampled active, the Intel386 SX Microprocessor is free to drive the address and bus cycle definition of the next bus cycle, and assert ADS#, as soon as it has a bus request internally pending. It may drive the next address as early as the next bus state, whether the current bus cycle is acknowledged at that time or not.

Regarding the details of address pipelining, the Intel386 SX Microprocessor has the following characteristics:

1. The next address may appear as early as the bus state after NA# was sampled active (see Figures 5.9 or 5.10). In that case, state T2P is entered immediately. However, when there is not an internal bus request already pending, the next address will not be available immediately after NA# is asserted and T2I is entered instead of T2P (see Figure 5.11 Cycle 3). Provided the current bus cycle isn't yet acknowledged by READY# asserted, T2P will be entered as soon as the Intel386 SX Microprocessor does drive the next address. External hardware should therefore observe the ADS# output as confirmation the next address is actually being driven on the bus.
2. Any address which is validated by a pulse on the ADS# output will remain stable on the address pins for at least two processor clock periods. The Intel386 SX Microprocessor cannot produce a new address more frequently than every two processor clock periods (see Figures 5.9, 5.10, and 5.11).
3. Only the address and bus cycle definition of the very next bus cycle is available. The pipelining capability cannot look further than one bus cycle ahead (see Figure 5.11 Cycle 1).

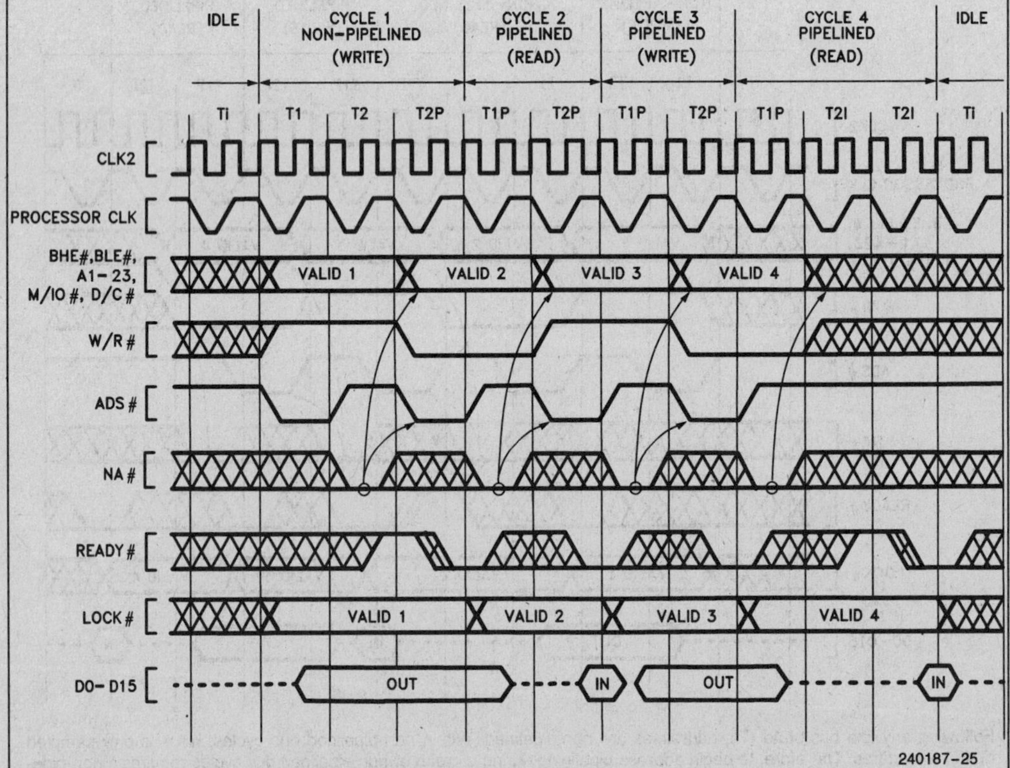

IDLE | CYCLE 1 NON-PIPELINED (WRITE) | CYCLE 2 PIPELINED (READ) | CYCLE 3 PIPELINED (WRITE) | CYCLE 4 PIPELINED (READ) | IDLE

Ti T1 T2 T2P T1P T2P T1P T2P T1P T2I T2I Ti

CLK2

PROCESSOR CLK

BHE#, BLE#, A1-23, M/IO#, D/C# — VALID 1, VALID 2, VALID 3, VALID 4

W/R#

ADS#

NA#

READY#

LOCK# — VALID 1, VALID 2, VALID 3, VALID 4

D0-D15 — OUT, IN, OUT, IN

240187-25

Following any bus state (Ti) the address is always non-pipelined and NA# is only sampled during wait states. To start address pipelining after an idle state requires a non-pipelined cycle with at least one wait state (cycle 1 above)
The pipelined cycles (2, 3, 4 above) are shown with various numbers of wait states.

Figure 5.10. Fastest Transition to Pipelined Address Following Idle Bus State

The complete bus state transition diagram, including operation with pipelined address is given by Figure 5.12. Note it is a superset of the diagram for non-pipelined address only, and the three additional bus states for pipelined address are drawn in bold.

The fastest bus cycle with pipelined address consists of just two bus states, T1P and T2P (recall for non-pipelined address it is T1 and T2). T1P is the first bus state of a pipelined cycle.

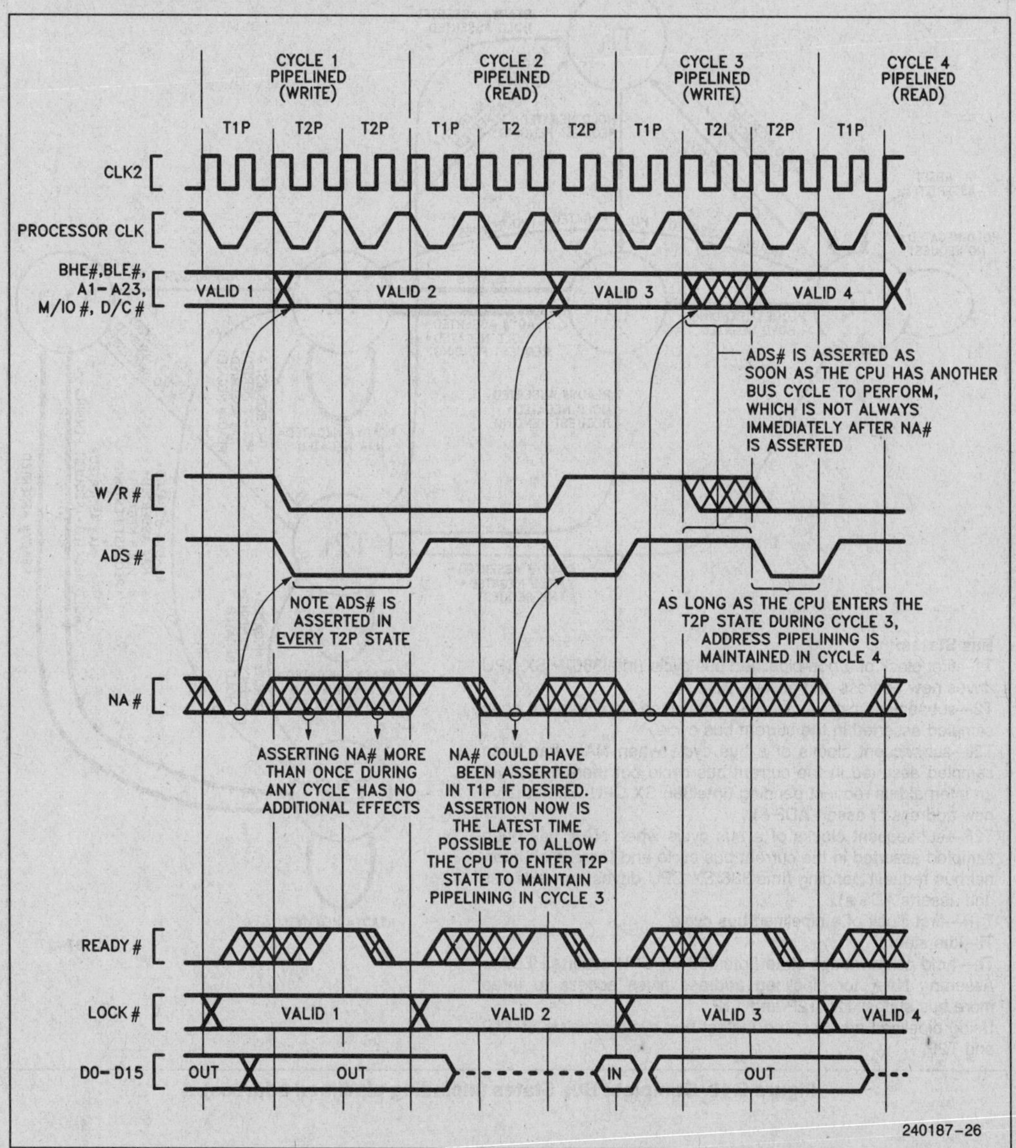

Figure 5.11. Details of Address Pipelining During Cycles with Wait States

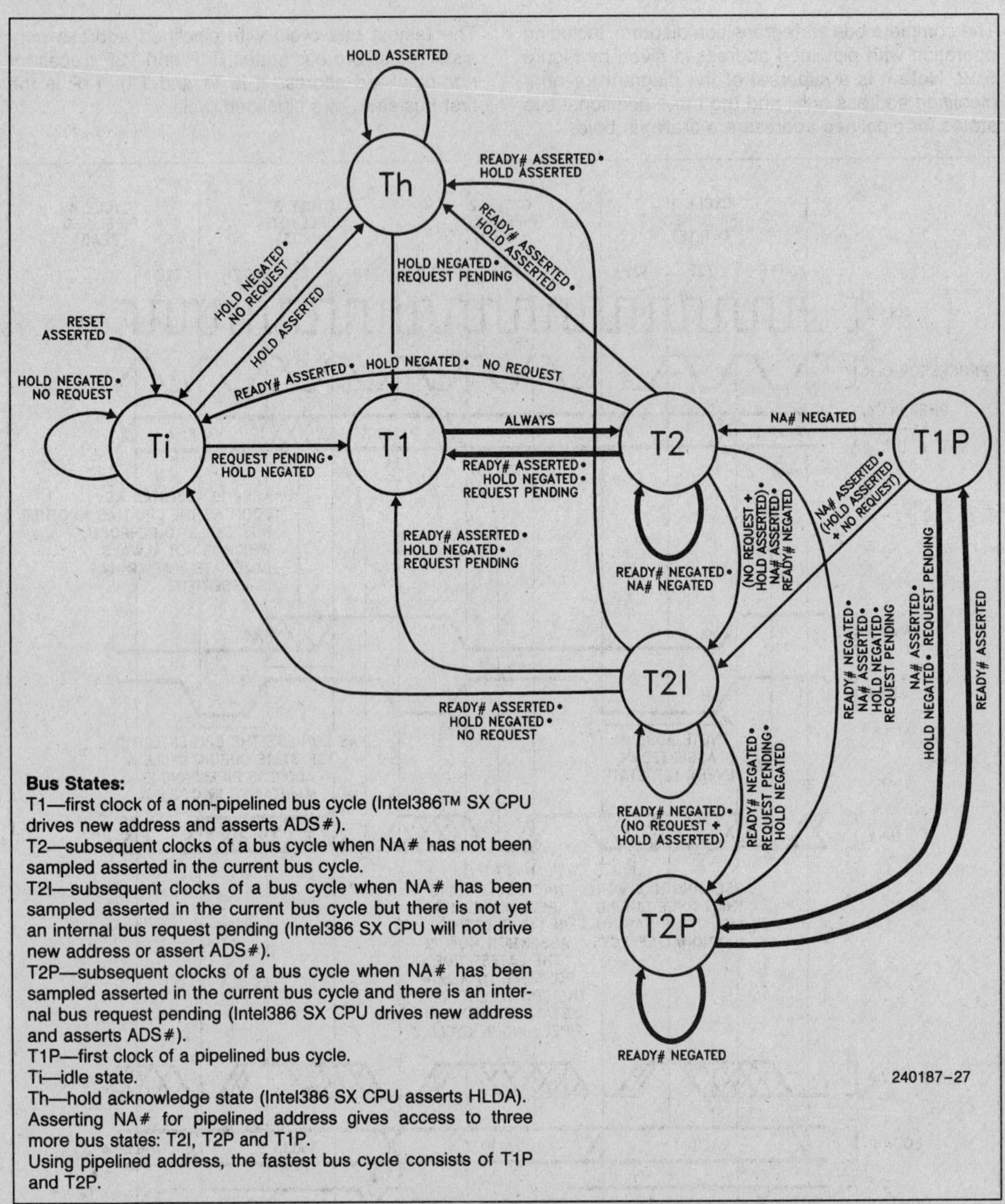

Figure 5.12. Complete Bus States (including pipelined address)

Initiating and Maintaining Pipelined Address

Using the state diagram Figure 5.12, observe the transitions from an idle state, T_i, to the beginning of a pipelined bus cycle T1P. From an idle state, T_i, the first bus cycle must begin with T1, and is therefore a non-pipelined bus cycle. The next bus cycle will be pipelined, however, provided NA# is asserted and the first bus cycle ends in a T2P state (the address for the next bus cycle is driven during T2P). The fastest path from an idle state to a bus cycle with pipelined address is shown in bold below:

T_i, T_i, T_i,	**T1 - T2 - T2P,**	**T1P - T2P,**
idle states	non-pipelined cycle	pipelined cycle

T1-T2-T2P are the states of the bus cycle that establish address pipelining for the next bus cycle, which begins with T1P. The same is true after a bus hold state, shown below:

T_h, T_h, T_h,	**T1 - T2 - T2P,**	**T1P - T2P,**
hold acknowledge states	non-pipelined cycle	pipelined cycle

The transition to pipelined address is shown functionally by Figure 5.10 Cycle 1. Note that Cycle 1 is used to transition into pipelined address timing for the subsequent Cycles 2, 3 and 4, which are pipelined. The NA# input is asserted at the appropriate time to select address pipelining for Cycles 2, 3 and 4.

Once a bus cycle is in progress and the current address has been valid for one entire bus state, the NA# input is sampled at the end of every phase one until the bus cycle is acknowledged. Sampling begins in T2 during Cycle 1 in Figure 5.10. Once NA# is sampled active during the current cycle, the Intel386 SX Microprocessor is free to drive a new address and bus cycle definition on the bus as early as the next bus state. In Figure 5.10 Cycle 1 for example, the next address is driven during state T2P. Thus Cycle 1 makes the transition to pipelined address timing, since it begins with T1 but ends with T2P. Because the address for Cycle 2 is available before Cycle 2 begins, Cycle 2 is called a pipelined bus cycle, and it begins with T1P. Cycle 2 begins as soon as READY# asserted terminates Cycle 1.

Examples of transition bus cycles are Figure 5.10 Cycle 1 and Figure 5.9 Cycle 2. Figure 5.10 shows transition during the very first cycle after an idle bus state, which is the fastest possible transition into address pipelining. Figure 5.9 Cycle 2 shows a transition cycle occurring during a burst of bus cycles. In any case, a transition cycle is the same whenever it occurs: it consists at least of T1, T2 (NA# is asserted at that time), and T2P (provided the Intel386 SX Microprocessor has an internal bus request already pending, which it almost always has). T2P states are repeated if wait states are added to the cycle.

Note that only three states (T1, T2 and T2P) are required in a bus cycle performing a **transition** from non-pipelined address into pipelined address timing, for example Figure 5.10 Cycle 1. Figure 5.10 Cycles 2, 3 and 4 show that address pipelining can be maintained with two-state bus cycles consisting only of T1P and T2P.

Once a pipelined bus cycle is in progress, pipelined timing is maintained for the next cycle by asserting NA# and detecting that the Intel386 SX Microprocessor enters T2P during the current bus cycle. The current bus cycle must end in state T2P for pipelining to be maintained in the next cycle. T2P is identified by the assertion of ADS#. Figures 5.9 and 5.10 however, each show pipelining ending after Cycle 4 because Cycle 4 ends in T2I. This indicates the Intel386 SX Microprocessor didn't have an internal bus request prior to the acknowledgement of Cycle 4. If a cycle ends with a T2 or T2I, the next cycle will not be pipelined.

Realistically, address pipelining is almost always maintained as long as NA# is sampled asserted. This is so because in the absence of any other request, a code prefetch request is always internally pending until the instruction decoder and code prefetch queue are completely full. Therefore, address pipelining is maintained for long bursts of bus cycles, if the bus is available (i.e., HOLD inactive) and NA# is sampled active in each of the bus cycles.

INTERRUPT ACKNOWLEDGE (INTA) CYCLES

In response to an interrupt request on the INTR input when interrupts are enabled, the Intel386 SX Microprocessor performs two interrupt acknowledge cycles. These bus cycles are similar to read cycles in that bus definition signals define the type of bus activity taking place, and each cycle continues until acknowledged by READY# sampled active.

The state of A_2 distinguishes the first and second interrupt acknowledge cycles. The byte address driven during the first interrupt acknowledge cycle is 4 (A_{23}–A_3, A_1, BLE# LOW, A_2 and BHE# HIGH). The byte address driven during the second interrupt acknowledge cycle is 0 (A_{23}–A_1, BLE# LOW, and BHE# HIGH).

The LOCK# output is asserted from the beginning of the first interrupt acknowledge cycle until the end of the second interrupt acknowledge cycle. Four idle bus states, T_i, are inserted by the Intel386 SX Microprocessor between the two interrupt acknowledge cycles for compatibility with spec TRHRL of the 8259A Interrupt Controller.

During both interrupt acknowledge cycles, D_{15}–D_0 float. No data is read at the end of the first interrupt acknowledge cycle. At the end of the second interrupt acknowledge cycle, the Intel386 SX Microprocessor will read an external interrupt vector from D_7–D_0 of the data bus. The vector indicates the specific interrupt number (from 0–255) requiring service.

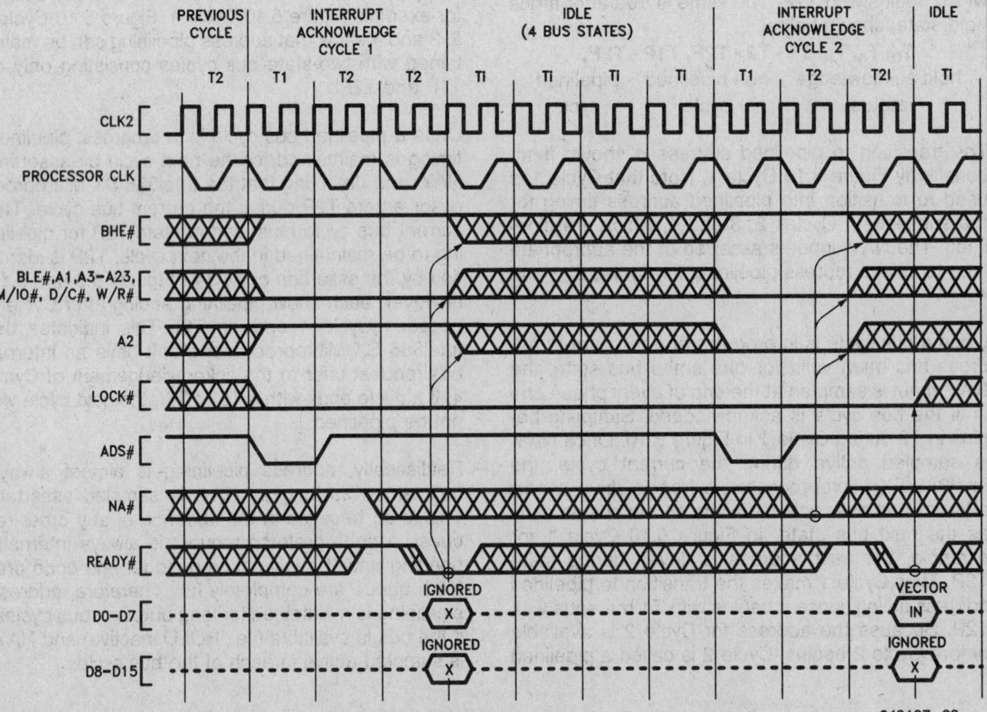

PREVIOUS CYCLE | INTERRUPT ACKNOWLEDGE CYCLE 1 | IDLE (4 BUS STATES) | INTERRUPT ACKNOWLEDGE CYCLE 2 | IDLE

T2 T1 T2 T2 Ti Ti Ti Ti T1 T2 T2I Ti

CLK2
PROCESSOR CLK
BHE#
BLE#,A1,A3-A23, M/IO#, D/C#, W/R#
A2
LOCK#
ADS#
NA#
READY#
D0-D7 — IGNORED X — VECTOR IN
D8-D15 — IGNORED X — IGNORED X

240187-28

Interrupt Vector (0–255) is read on D0–D7 at end of second interrupt Acknowledge bus cycle.
Because each Interrupt Acknowledge bus cycle is followed by idle bus states. asserting NA# has no practical effect.
Choose the approach which is simplest for your system hardware design.

Figure 5.13. Interrupt Acknowledge Cycles

HALT INDICATION CYCLE

The execution unit halts as a result of executing a HLT instruction. Signaling its entrance into the halt state, a halt indication cycle is performed. The halt indication cycle is identified by the state of the bus definition signals shown on page 40, **Bus Cycle Definition Signals**, and an address of 2. The halt indication cycle must be acknowledged by READY# asserted. A halted Intel386 SX Microprocessor resumes execution when INTR (if interrupts are enabled), NMI or RESET is asserted.

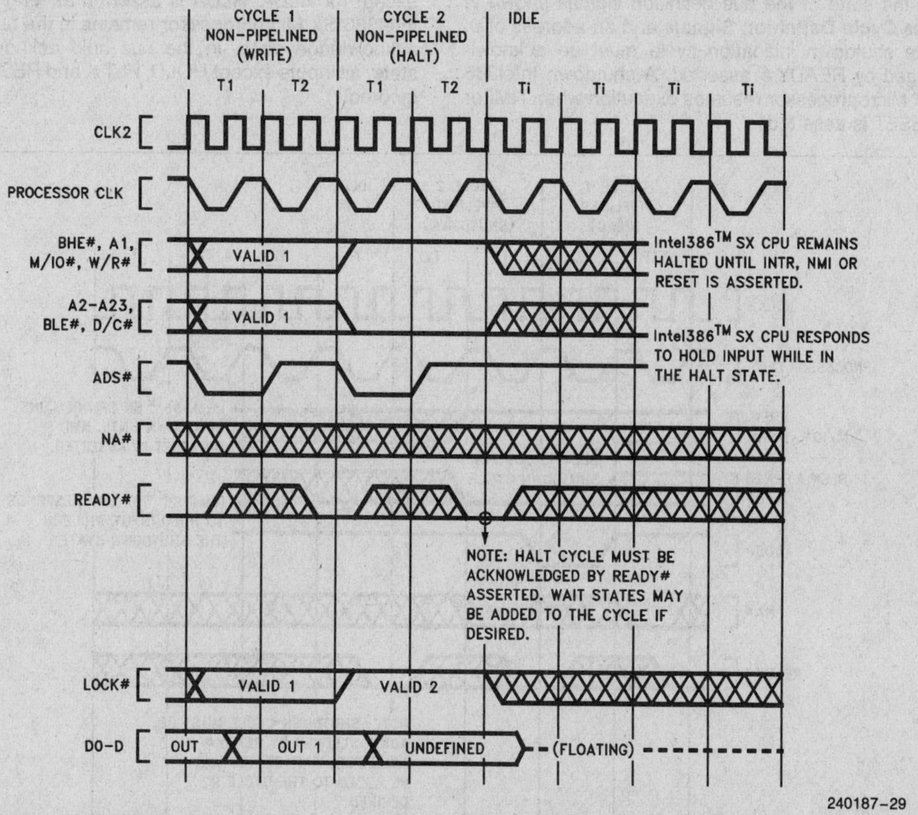

240187–29

Figure 5.14. Example Halt Indication Cycle from Non-Pipelined Cycle

SHUTDOWN INDICATION CYCLE

The Intel386 SX Microprocessor shuts down as a result of a protection fault while attempting to process a double fault. Signaling its entrance into the shutdown state, a shutdown indication cycle is performed. The shutdown indication cycle is identified by the state of the bus definition signals shown in **Bus Cycle Definition Signals** and an address of 0. The shutdown indication cycle must be acknowledged by READY# asserted. A shutdown Intel386 SX Microprocessor resumes execution when NMI or RESET is asserted.

ENTERING AND EXITING HOLD ACKNOWLEDGE

The bus hold acknowledge state, T_h, is entered in response to the HOLD input being asserted. In the bus hold acknowledge state, the Intel386 SX Microprocessor floats all outputs or bidirectional signals, except for HLDA. HLDA is asserted as long as the Intel386 SX Microprocessor remains in the bus hold acknowledge state. In the bus hold acknowledge state, all inputs except HOLD, FLT# and RESET are ignored.

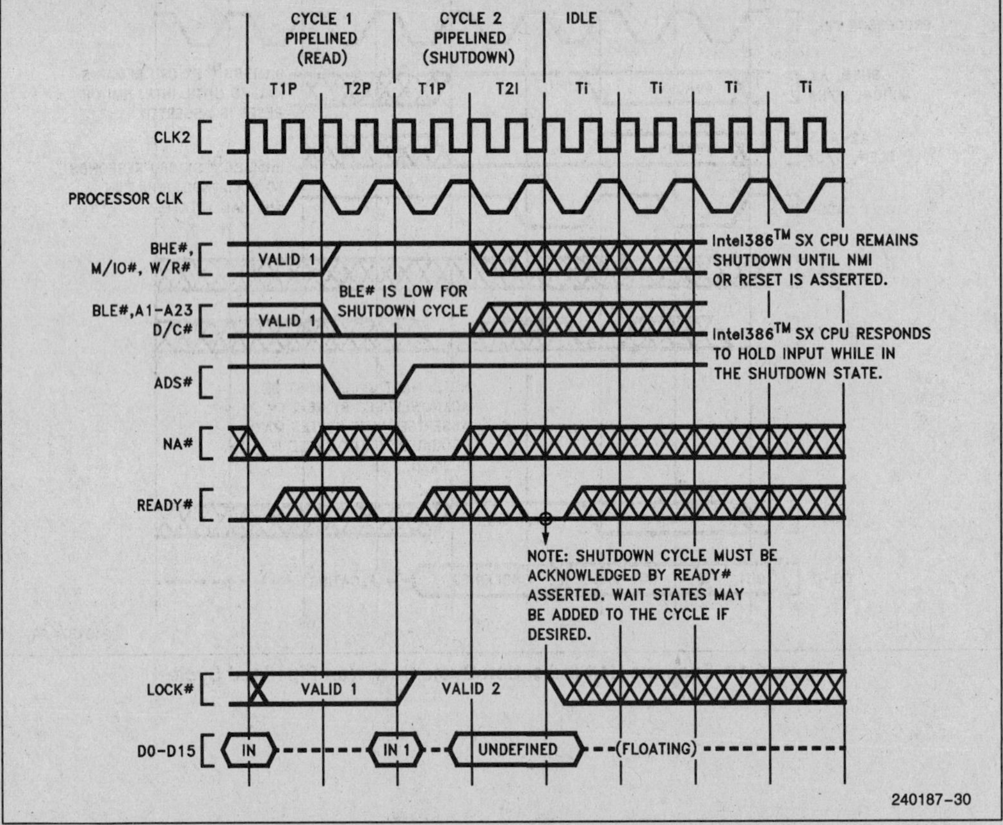

Figure 5.15. Example Shutdown Indication Cycle from Non-Pipelined Cycle

T_h may be entered from a bus idle state as in Figure 5.16 or after the acknowledgement of the current physical bus cycle if the LOCK# signal is not asserted, as in Figures 5.17 and 5.18.

T_h is exited in response to the HOLD input being negated. The following state will be T_i as in Figure 5.16 if no bus request is pending. The following bus state will be T1 if a bus request is internally pending, as in Figures 5.17 and 5.18. T_h is exited in response to RESET being asserted.

If a rising edge occurs on the edge-triggered NMI input while in T_h, the event is remembered as a non-maskable interrupt 2 and is serviced when T_h is exited unless the Intel386 SX Microprocessor is reset before T_h is exited.

RESET DURING HOLD ACKNOWLEDGE

RESET being asserted takes priority over HOLD being asserted. If RESET is asserted while HOLD remains asserted, the Intel386 SX Microprocessor drives its pins to defined states during reset, as in **Table 5.5 Pin State During Reset**, and performs internal reset activity as usual.

If HOLD remains asserted when RESET is inactive, the Intel386 SX Microprocessor enters the hold acknowledge state before performing its first bus cycle, provided HOLD is still asserted when the Intel386 SX Microprocessor would otherwise perform its first bus cycle.

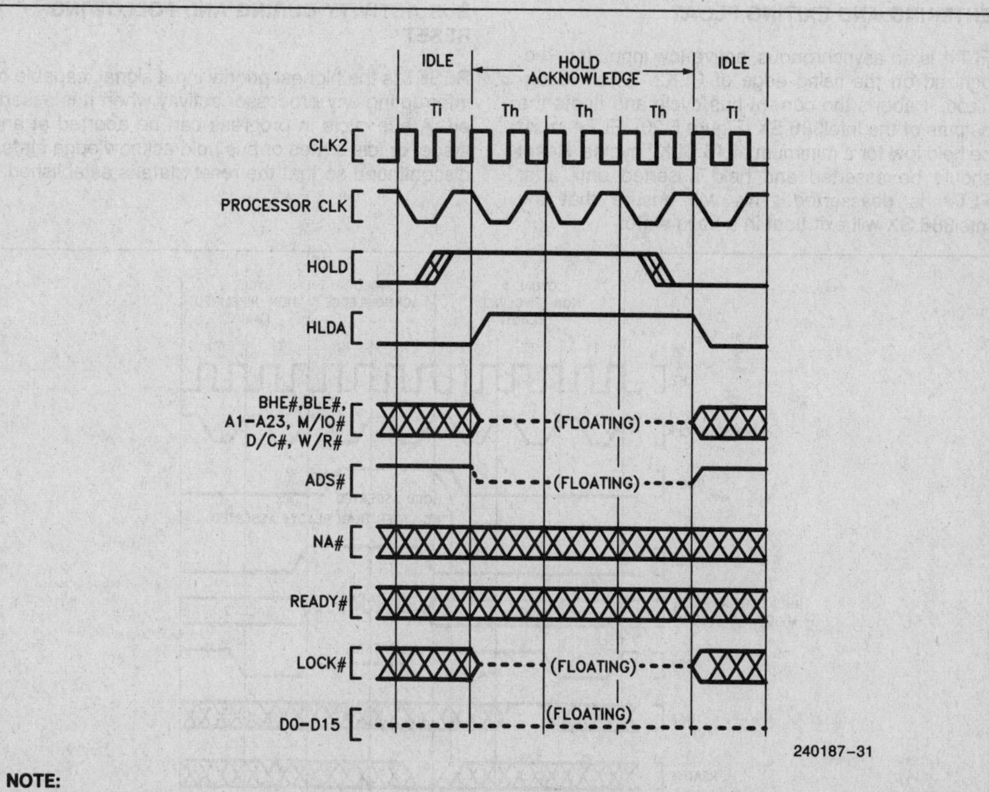

NOTE:
For maximum design flexibility the Intel386™ SX CPU has no internal pullup resistors on its outputs. Your design may require an external pullup on ADS# and other outputs to keep them negated during float periods.

Figure 5.16. Requesting Hold from Idle Bus

FLOAT

Activating the FLT# input floats all Intel386 SX bidirectional and output signals, including HLDA. Asserting FLT# isolates the Intel386 SX from the surrounding circuitry.

As the Intel386 SX is packaged in a surface mount PQFP, it cannot be removed from the motherboard when In-Circuit Emulation (ICE) is needed. The FLT# input allows the Intel386 SX to be electrically isolated from the surrounding circuitry. This allows connection of an emulator to the Intel386 SX PQFP without removing it from the PCB. This method of emulation is referred to as ON-Circuit Emulation (ONCE).

ENTERING AND EXITING FLOAT

FLT# is an asynchronous, active-low input. It is recognized on the rising edge of CLK2. When recognized, it aborts the current bus cycle and floats the outputs of the Intel386 SX (Figure 5.20). FLT# must be held low for a minimum of 16 CLK2 cycles. Reset should be asserted and held asserted until after FLT# is deasserted. This will ensure that the Intel386 SX will exit float in a valid state.

Asserting the FLT# input unconditionally aborts the current bus cycle and forces the Intel386 SX into the FLOAT mode. Since activating FLT# unconditionally forces the Intel386 SX into FLOAT mode, the Intel386 SX is not guaranteed to enter FLOAT in a valid state. After deactivating FLT#, the Intel386 SX is not guaranteed to exit FLOAT mode in a valid state. This is not a problem as the FLT# pin is meant to be used only during ONCE. After exiting FLOAT, the Intel386 SX must be reset to return it to a valid state. Reset should be asserted before FLT# is deasserted. This will ensure that the Intel386 SX will exit float in a valid state.

FLT# has an internal pull-up resistor, and if it is not used it should be unconnected.

BUS ACTIVITY DURING AND FOLLOWING RESET

RESET is the highest priority input signal, capable of interrupting any processor activity when it is asserted. A bus cycle in progress can be aborted at any stage, or idle states or bus hold acknowledge states discontinued so that the reset state is established.

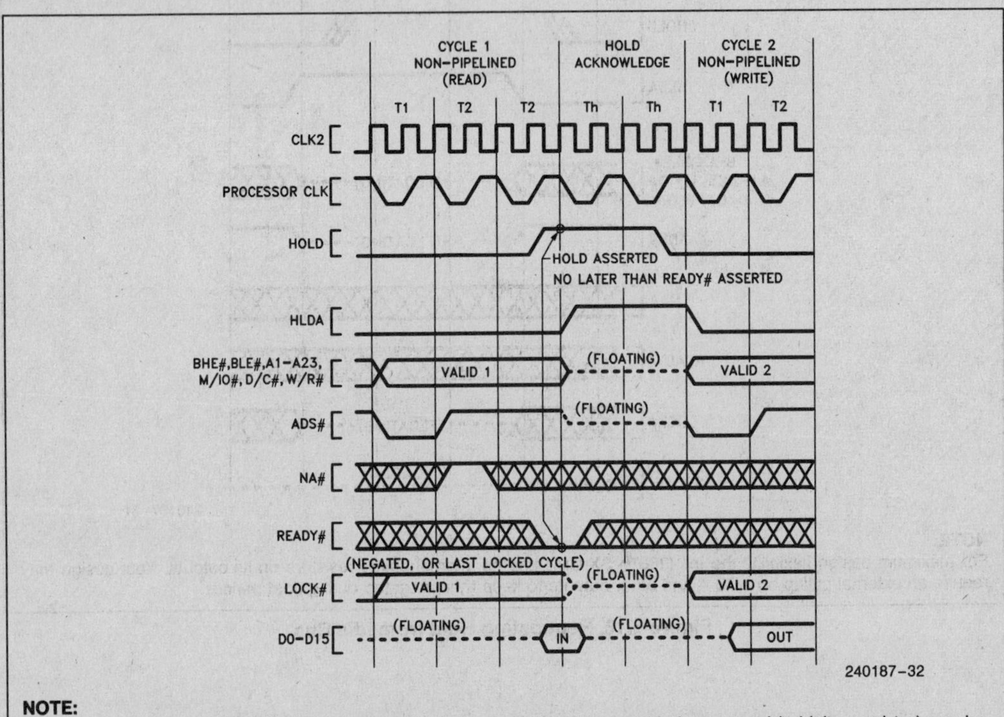

NOTE:
HOLD is a synchronous input and can be asserted at any CLK2 edge, provided setup and hold (t_{23} and t_{24}) requirements are met. This waveform is useful for determining Hold Acknowledge latency.

Figure 5.17. Requesting Hold from Active Bus (NA# inactive)

RESET should remain asserted for at least 15 CLK2 periods to ensure it is recognized throughout the Intel386 SX Microprocessor, and at least 80 CLK2 periods if self-test is going to be requested at the falling edge. RESET asserted pulses less than 15 CLK2 periods may not be recognized. RESET pulses less than 80 CLK2 periods followed by a self-test may cause the self-test to report a failure when no true failure exists.

Provided the RESET falling edge meets setup and hold times t_{25} and t_{26}, the internal processor clock phase is defined at that time as illustrated by Figure 5.19 and Figure 7.7.

A self-test may be requested at the time RESET goes inactive by having the BUSY# input at a LOW level as shown in Figure 5.19. The self-test requires approximately $(2^{20} + 60)$ CLK2 periods to complete. The self-test duration is not affected by the test results. Even if the self-test indicates a problem, the Intel386 SX Microprocessor attempts to proceed with the reset sequence afterwards.

After the RESET falling edge (and after the self-test if it was requested) the Intel386 SX Microprocessor performs an internal initialization sequence for approximately 350 to 450 CLK2 periods.

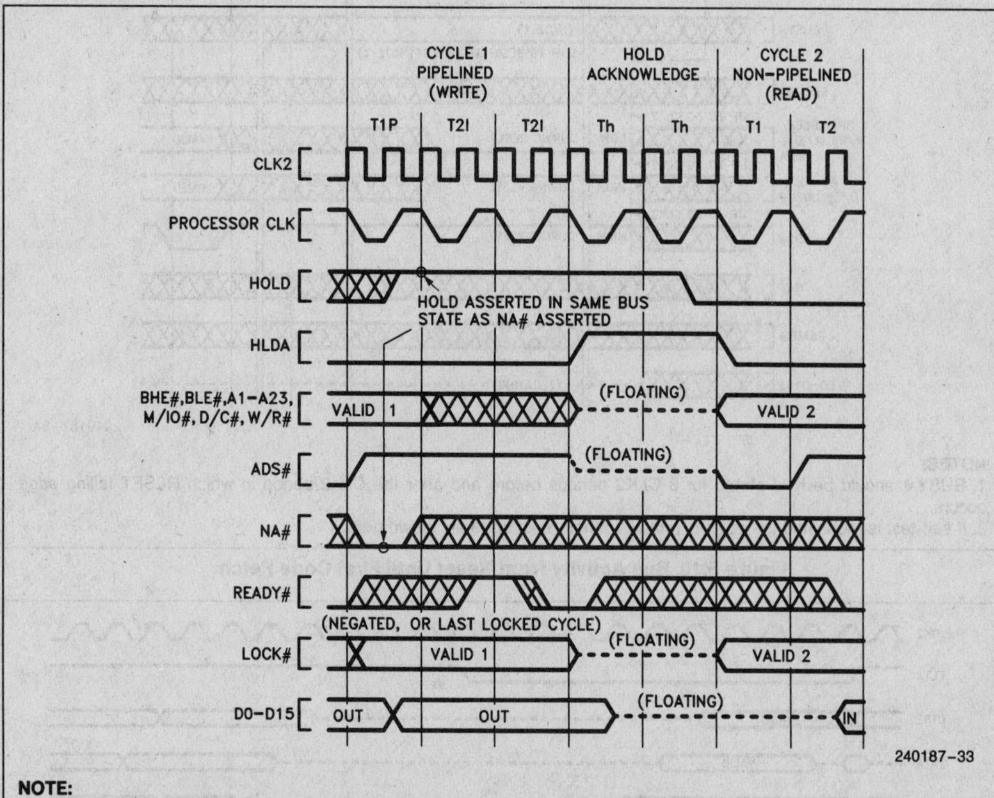

NOTE:
HOLD is a synchronous input and can be asserted at any CLK2 edge, provided setup and hold (t23 and t24) requirements are met. This waveform is useful for determining Hold Acknowledge latency.

Figure 5.18. Requesting Hold from Idle Bus (NA# active)

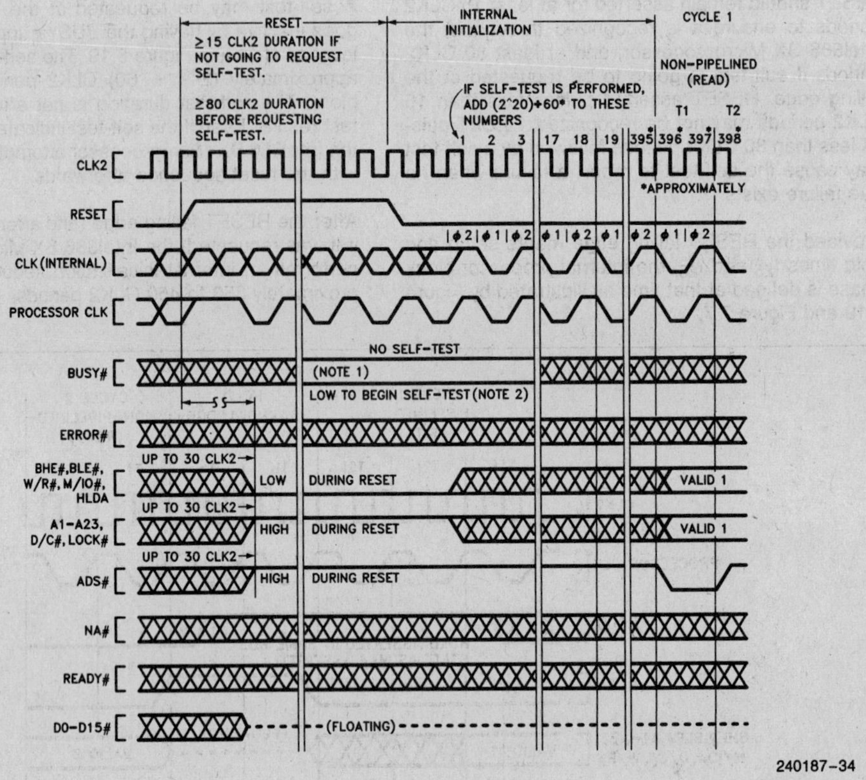

RESET

≥15 CLK2 DURATION IF NOT GOING TO REQUEST SELF-TEST.

≥80 CLK2 DURATION BEFORE REQUESTING SELF-TEST.

INTERNAL INITIALIZATION

IF SELF-TEST IS PERFORMED, ADD (2^20)+60* TO THESE NUMBERS

CYCLE 1

NON-PIPELINED (READ)

T1 T2

1 2 3 17 18 19 395 396 397 398

*APPROXIMATELY

CLK2

RESET

CLK (INTERNAL)

PROCESSOR CLK

BUSY#

NO SELF-TEST

(NOTE 1)

LOW TO BEGIN SELF-TEST (NOTE 2)

ERROR#

UP TO 30 CLK2

BHE#, BLE#, W/R#, M/IO#, HLDA — LOW DURING RESET — VALID 1

A1–A23, D/C#, LOCK# — HIGH DURING RESET — VALID 1

ADS# — HIGH DURING RESET

NA#

READY#

D0–D15# — (FLOATING)

240187-34

NOTES:

1. BUSY# should be held stable for 8 CLK2 periods before and after the CLK2 period in which RESET falling edge occurs.
2. If self-test is requested the outputs remain in their reset state as shown here.

Figure 5.19. Bus Activity from Reset Until First Code Fetch

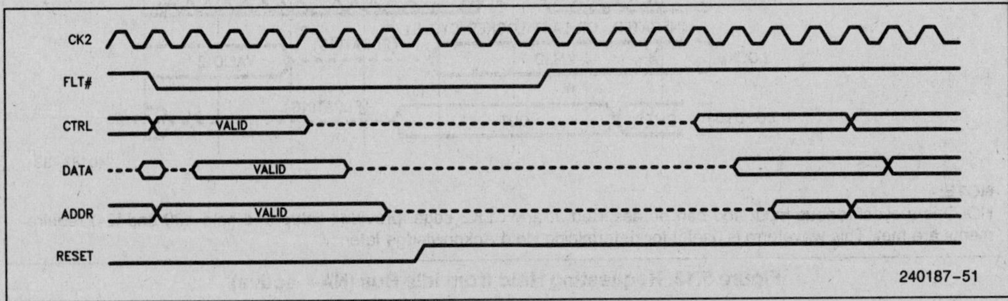

Figure 5.20. Entering and Exiting, FLT#

5.5 Self-test Signature

Upon completion of self-test (if self-test was requested by driving BUSY# LOW at the falling edge of RESET) the EAX register will contain a signature of 00000000H indicating the Intel386 SX Microprocessor passed its self-test of microcode and major PLA contents with no problems detected. The passing signature in EAX, 00000000H, applies to all revision levels. Any non-zero signature indicates the unit is faulty.

5.6 Component and Revision Identifiers

To assist users, the Intel386 SX Microprocessor after reset holds a component identifier and revision identifier in its DX register. The upper 8 bits of DX hold 23H as identification of the Intel386 SX Microprocessor (the lower nibble, 03H, refers to the Intel386 DX Architecture. The upper nibble, 02H, refers to the second member of the IntelIntel386 DX Family). The lower 8 bits of DX hold an 8-bit unsigned binary number related to the component revision level. The revision identifier will, in general, chronologically track those component steppings which are intended to have certain improvements or distinction from previous steppings. The Intel386 SX Microprocessor revision identifier will track that of the Intel386 DX CPU where possible.

The revision identifier is intended to assist users to a practical extent. However, the revision identifier value is not guaranteed to change with every stepping revision, or to follow a completely uniform numerical sequence, depending on the type or intention of revision, or manufacturing materials required to be changed. Intel has sole discretion over these characteristics of the component.

Table 5.7. Component and Revision Identifier History

Stepping	Revision Identifier
A0	04H
B	05H
C	08H
D	08H

5.7 Coprocessor Interfacing

The Intel386 SX Microprocessor provides an automatic interface for the Intel Intel387 SX numeric floating-point coprocessor. The Intel387 SX coprocessor uses an I/O mapped interface driven automatically by the Intel386 SX Microprocessor and assisted by three dedicated signals: BUSY#, ERROR# and PEREQ.

As the Intel386 SX Microprocessor begins supporting a coprocessor instruction, it tests the BUSY# and ERROR# signals to determine if the coprocessor can accept its next instruction. Thus, the BUSY# and ERROR# inputs eliminate the need for any 'preamble' bus cycles for communication between processor and coprocessor. The Intel387™ SX can be given its command opcode immediately. The dedicated signals provide instruction synchronization, and eliminate the need of using the WAIT opcode (9BH) for Intel387™ SX instruction synchronization (the WAIT opcode was required when the 8086 or 8088 was used with the 8087 coprocessor).

Custom coprocessors can be included in Intel386 SX Microprocessor based systems by memory-mapped or I/O-mapped interfaces. Such coprocessor interfaces allow a completely custom protocol, and are not limited to a set of coprocessor protocol 'primitives'. Instead, memory-mapped or I/O-mapped interfaces may use all applicable instructions for high-speed coprocessor communication. The BUSY# and ERROR# inputs of the Intel386 SX Microprocessor may also be used for the custom coprocessor interface, if such hardware assist is desired. These signals can be tested by the WAIT opcode (9BH). The WAIT instruction will wait until the BUSY# input is inactive (interruptable by an NMI or enabled INTR input), but generates an exception 16 fault if the ERROR# pin is active when the BUSY# goes (or is) inactive. If the custom coprocessor interface is memory-mapped, protection of the addresses used for the interface can be provided with the Intel386 SX CPU's on-chip paging or segmentation mechanisms. If the custom interface is I/O-mapped, protection of the interface can be provided with the IOPL (I/O Privilege Level) mechanism.

The Intel387™ SX numeric coprocessor interface is I/O mapped as shown in Table 5.8. Note that the Intel387™ SX coprocessor interface addresses are beyond the 0H-0FFFFH range for programmed I/O. When the Intel386 SX Microprocessor supports the Intel387™ SX coprocessor, the Intel386 SX Microprocessor automatically generates bus cycles to the coprocessor interface addresses.

Table 5.8. Numeric Coprocessor Port Addresses

Address in Intel386™ SX CPU I/O Space	Intel387™ SX Coprocessor Register
8000F8H	Opcode Register
8000FCH/8000FEH*	Operand Register

*Generated as 2nd bus cycle during Dword transfer.

To correctly map the Intel387™ SX registers to the appropriate I/O addresses, connect the CMD0 and CMD1 lines of the Intel387™ SX as listed in Table 5.9.

Table 5.9. Connections for CMD0 and CMD1 Inputs for the Intel387™ SX

Signal	Connection
CMD0	Connect directly to Intel386™ SX CPU A2 signal
CMD1	Connect to ground.

Software Testing for Coprocessor Presence

When software is used to test for coprocessor (Intel387 SX) presence, it should use only the following coprocessor opcodes: FINIT, FNINIT, FSTCW mem, FSTSW mem and FSTSW AX. To use other coprocessor opcodes when a coprocessor is known to be not present, first set EM = 1 in the Intel386 SX CPU's CR0 register.

6.0 PACKAGE THERMAL SPECIFICATIONS

The Intel386 SX Microprocessor is specified for operation when case temperature is within the range of 0°C–100°C. The case temperature may be measured in any environment, to determine whether the Intel386 SX Microprocessor is within specified operating range. The case temperature should be measured at the center of the top surface opposite the pins.

The ambient temperature is guaranteed as long as T_c is not violated. The ambient temperature can be calculated from the θ_{jc} and θ_{ja} from the following equations:

$$T_j = T_c + P^*\theta_{jc}$$

$$T_a = T_j - P^*\theta_{ja}$$

$$T_c = T_a + P^*[\theta_{ja} - \theta_{jc}]$$

Values for θ_{ja} and θ_{jc} are given in table 6.1 for the 100 lead fine pitch. θ_{ja} is given at various airflows. Table 6.2 shows the maximum T_a allowable (without exceeding T_c) at various airflows. Note that T_a can be improved further by attaching 'fins' or a 'heat sink' to the package.

7.0 ELECTRICAL SPECIFICATIONS

The following sections describe recommended electrical connections for the Intel386 SX Microprocessor, and its electrical specifications.

7.1 Power and Grounding

The Intel386 SX Microprocessor is implemented in CHMOS IV technology and has modest power requirements. However, its high clock frequency and 47 output buffers (address, data, control, and HLDA) can cause power surges as multiple output buffers drive new signal levels simultaneously. For clean on-chip power distribution at high frequency, 14 Vcc and 18 Vss pins separately feed functional units of the Intel386 SX Microprocessor.

Power and ground connections must be made to all external Vcc and V_{SS} pins of the Intel386 SX Microprocessor. On the circuit board, all Vcc pins should be connected on a Vcc plane and all Vss pins should be connected on a GND plane.

POWER DECOUPLING RECOMMENDATIONS

Liberal decoupling capacitors should be placed near the Intel386 SX Microprocessor. The Intel386 SX Microprocessor driving its 24-bit address bus and 16-bit data bus at high frequencies can cause transient power surges, particularly when driving large capacitive loads. Low inductance capacitors and interconnects are recommended for best high frequency electrical performance. Inductance can be reduced by shortening circuit board traces between the Intel386 SX Microprocessor and decoupling capacitors as much as possible.

Table 6.1. Thermal Resistances (°C/Watt) θ_{jc} and θ_{ja}.

Package	θjc	θ_{ja} versus Airflow - ft/min (m/sec)					
		0 (0)	200 (1.01)	400 (2.03)	600 (3.04)	800 (4.06)	1000 (5.07)
100 Lead Fine Pitch	7.5	34.5	29.5	25.5	22.5	21.5	21

Table 6.2. Maximum T_a at various airflows.

Package	Frequency	T_A(°C) versus Airflow - ft/min (m/sec)					
		0 (0)	200 (1.01)	400 (2.03)	600 (3.04)	800 (4.06)	1000 (5.07)
100L PQFP Fine Pitch	16 MHz	74	80	83	86	89	90
	20 MHz	70	77	80	84	87	88

NOTE:
The numbers in Table 6.2 were calculated using an I_{CC} of 200 mA at 16 MHz and 230 mA at 20 MHz, which is representative of the worst case I_{CC} at T_C = 100°C with the outputs unloaded.

Table 7.1. Recommended Resistor Pull-ups to Vcc

Pin	Signal	Pull-up Value	Purpose
16	ADS#	20 K-Ohm ± 10%	Lightly pull ADS# inactive during Intel386™ SX CPU hold acknowledge states
26	LOCK#	20 K-Ohm ± 10%	Lightly pull LOCK# inactive during Intel386™ SX CPU hold acknowledge states

RESISTOR RECOMMENDATIONS

The ERROR#, FLT# and BUSY# inputs have internal pull-up resistors of approximately 20 K-Ohms and the PEREQ input has an internal pull-down resistor of approximately 20 K-Ohms built into the Intel386 SX Microprocessor to keep these signals inactive when the Intel387 SX is not present in the system (or temporarily removed from its socket).

In typical designs, the external pull-up resistors shown in Table 7.1 are recommended. However, a particular design may have reason to adjust the resistor values recommended here, or alter the use of pull-up resistors in other ways.

OTHER CONNECTION RECOMMENDATIONS

For reliable operation, always connect unused inputs to an appropriate signal level. N/C pins should always remain **unconnected. Connection of N/C pins to Vcc or Vss will result in component malfunction or incompatibility with future steppings of the Intel386 SX Microprocessor.**

Particularly when not using interrupts or bus hold (as when first prototyping), prevent any chance of spurious activity by connecting these associated inputs to GND:

Pin	Signal
40	INTR
38	NMI
4	HOLD

If not using address pipelining, connect pin 6, NA#, through a pull-up in the range of 20 K-Ohms to Vcc.

7.2 Maximum Ratings

Table 7.2. Maximum Ratings

Parameter	Maximum Rating
Storage temperature	−65 °C to 150 °C
Case temperature under bias	−65 °C to 110 °C
Supply voltage with respect to Vss	−.5V to 6.5V
Voltage on other pins	−.5V to (Vcc + .5)V

Table 7.2 gives stress ratings only, and functional operation at the maximums is not guaranteed. Functional operating conditions are given in section **7.3, D.C. Specifications**, and section **7.4, A.C. Specifications**.

Extended exposure to the Maximum Ratings may affect device reliability. Furthermore, although the Intel386 SX Microprocessor contains protective circuitry to resist damage from static electric discharge, always take precautions to avoid high static voltages or electric fields.

4

7.3 D.C. Specifications

Functional operating range: Vcc = 5V ± 10%; T_{CASE} = 0°C to 100°C

Table 7.3. Intel386™ SX D.C. Characteristics

Symbol	Parameter	Intel386™SX 20 MHz, 16 MHz, 12 MHz (LP Only) Min	Max	Unit	Test Condition
V_{IL}	Input LOW Voltage	−0.3	+0.8	V	
V_{IH}	Input HIGH Voltage	2.0	Vcc+0.3	V	
V_{ILC}	CLK2 Input LOW Voltage	−0.3	+0.8	V	
V_{IHC}	CLK2 Input HIGH Voltage	Vcc−0.8	Vcc+0.3	V	
V_{OL}	Output LOW Voltage I_{OL}=4mA: A_{23}–A_1,D_{15}–D_0 I_{OL}=5mA: BHE#,BLE#,W/R#, D/C#,M/IO#,LOCK#, ADS#,HLDA		 0.45 0.45	 V V	
V_{OH}	Output high voltage I_{OH}= −1mA: A_{23}–A_1,D_{15}–D_0 I_{OH}= −0.2 mA: A_{23}–A_1,D_{15}–D_0 I_{OH}= −0.9mA: BHE#,BLE#,W/R#, D/C#,M/IO#,LOCK#, ADS#,HLDA I_{OH}= −0.18 mA: BHE#,BLE#,W/R#, D/C#,M/IO#,LOCK#, ADS#,HLDA	 2.4 Vcc−0.5 2.4 Vcc−0.5		 V V V	
I_{LI}	Input leakage current (for all pins except PEREQ, BUSY#, FLT# and ERROR#)		±15	μA	0V≤V_{IN}≤Vcc
I_{IH}	Input Leakage Current (PEREQ pin)		200	μA	V_{IH}=2.4V, Note 1
I_{IL}	Input Leakage Current (BUSY#, ERROR# and FLT# Pins)		−400	μA	V_{IL}=0.45V, Note 2
I_{LO}	Output leakage current		±15	μA	0.45V≤V_{OUT}≤Vcc
I_{CC}	Supply Current CLK2 = 4 MHz: with 20, 16, or 12 MHz Intel386 SX (LP) CLK2 = 24 MHz: with 12 MHz Intel386 SX CLK2 = 32 MHz: with 16 MHz Intel386 SX CLK2 = 40 MHz: with 20 MHz Intel386 SX		 140 245 275 305	 mA mA mA mA	 I_{CC} typ = 70 mA, Note 3 I_{CC} typ = 140 mA, Note 3 I_{CC} typ = 175 mA, Note 3 I_{CC} Typ = 200 mA, Note 3
C_{IN}	Input capacitance		10	pF	Fc=1 MHz, Note 4
C_{OUT}	Output or I/O capacitance		12	pF	Fc=1 MHz, Note 4
C_{CLK}	CLK2 Capacitance		20	pF	Fc=1 MHz, Note 4

Tested at the minimum operating frequency of the part.

NOTES:
1. PEREQ input has an internal pull-down resistor.
2. BUSY#, FLT# and ERROR# inputs each have an internal pull-up resistor.
3. Icc max measurement at worst case load, frequency, Vcc and temperature.
4. Not 100% tested.

7.4 A.C. Specifications

The A.C. specifications given in Table 7.4 consist of output delays, input setup requirements and input hold requirements. All A.C. specifications are relative to the CLK2 rising edge crossing the 2.0V level.

A.C. spec measurement is defined by Figure 7.1. Inputs must be driven to the voltage levels indicated by Figure 7.1 when A.C. specifications are measured. Output delays are specified with minimum and maximum limits measured as shown. The minimum delay times are hold times provided to external circuitry. Input setup and hold times are specified as minimums, defining the smallest acceptable sampling window. Within the sampling window, a synchronous input signal must be stable for correct operation.

Outputs NA#, W/R#, D/C#, M/IO#, LOCK#, BHE#, BLE#, A_{23}–A_1 and HLDA only change at the beginning of phase one. D_{15}–D_0 (write cycles) only change at the beginning of phase two. The READY#, HOLD, BUSY#, ERROR#, PEREQ, FLT# and D_{15}–D_0 (read cycles) inputs are sampled at the beginning of phase one. The NA#, INTR and NMI inputs are sampled at the beginning of phase two.

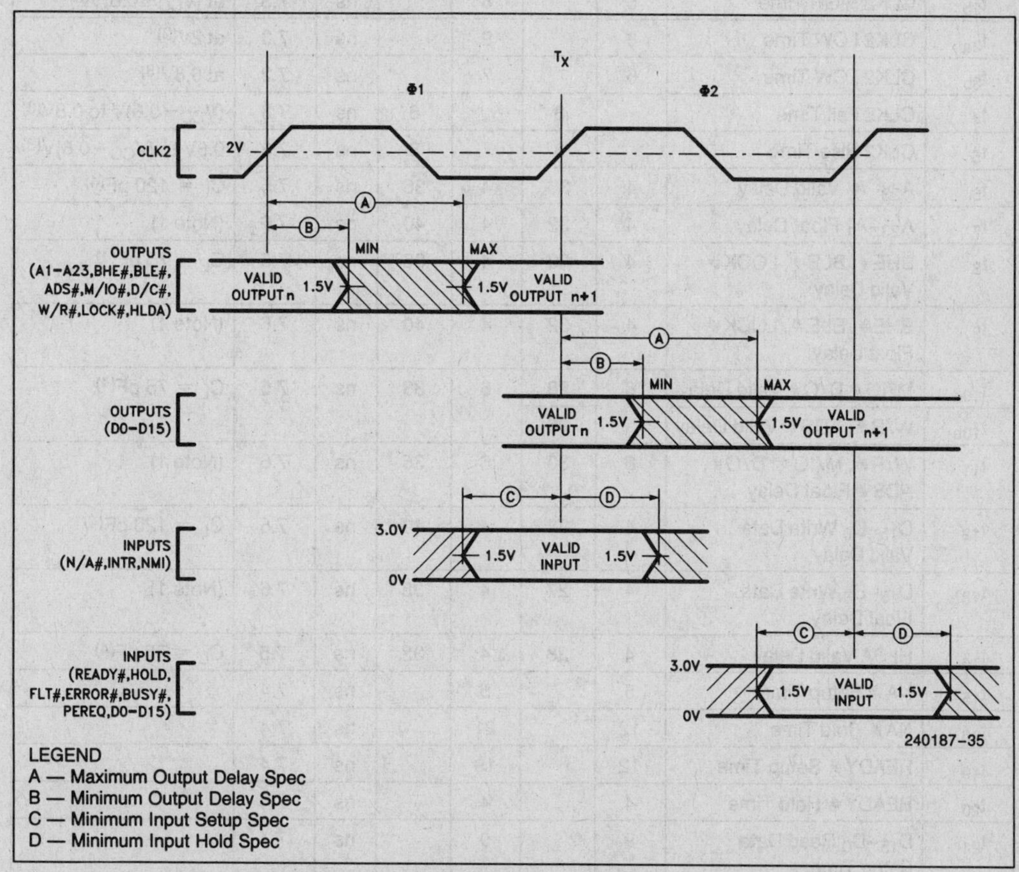

Figure 7.1. Drive Levels and Measurement Points for A.C. Specifications

A.C. SPECIFICATIONS TABLES

Functional operating range: V_{CC} = 5V ±10%; T_{CASE} = 0°C to 100°C

Table 7.4. Intel386™ SX A.C. Characteristics

Symbol	Parameter	20 MHz Intel386 SX		16 MHz Intel386 SX		Unit	Figure	Notes
		Min	Max	Min	Max			
	Operating Frequency	4	20	4	16	MHz		Half CLK2 Frequency
t_1	CLK2 Period	25	125	31	125	ns	7.3	
t_{2a}	CLK2 HIGH Time	8		9		ns	7.3	at 2V(3)
t_{2b}	CLK2 HIGH Time	5		5		ns	7.3	at (V_{CC} − 0.8)V(3)
t_{3a}	CLK2 LOW Time	8		9		ns	7.3	at 2V(3)
t_{3b}	CLK2 LOW Time	6		7		ns	7.3	at 0.8V(3)
t_4	CLK2 Fall Time		8		8	ns	7.3	(V_{CC} − 0.8)V to 0.8V(3)
t_5	CLK2 Rise Time		8		8	ns	7.3	0.8V to (V_{CC} − 0.8)V(3)
t_6	A_{23}–A_1 Valid Delay	4	30	4	36	ns	7.5	C_L = 120 pF(4)
t_7	A_{23}–A_1 Float Delay	4	32	4	40	ns	7.6	(Note 1)
t_8	BHE#, BLE#, LOCK# Valid Delay	4	30	4	36	ns	7.5	C_L = 75 pF(4)
t_9	BHE#, BLE#, LOCK# Float Delay	4	32	4	40	ns	7.6	(Note 1)
t_{10a}	M/IO# D/C# Valid Delay	6	28	6	33	ns	7.5	C_L = 75 pF(4)
t_{10b}	W/R#, ADS# Valid Delay		26					
t_{11}	W/R#, M/IO#, D/C#, ADS# Float Delay	6	30	6	35	ns	7.6	(Note 1)
t_{12}	D_{15}–D_0 Write Data Valid Delay	4	38	4	40	ns	7.5	C_L = 120 pF(4)
t_{13}	D_{15}–D_0 Write Data Float Delay	4	27	4	35	ns	7.6	(Note 1)
t_{14}	HLDA Valid Delay	4	28	4	33	ns	7.5	C_L = 75 pF(4)
t_{15}	NA# Setup Time	5		5		ns	7.4	
t_{16}	NA# Hold Time	12		21		ns	7.4	
t_{19}	READY# Setup Time	12		19		ns	7.4	
t_{20}	READY# Hold Time	4		4		ns	7.4	
t_{21}	D_{15}–D_0 Read Data Setup Time	9		9		ns	7.4	
t_{22}	D_{15}–D_0 Read Data Hold Time	6		6		ns	7.4	
t_{23}	HOLD Setup Time	17		26		ns	7.4	
t_{24}	HOLD Hold Time	5		5		ns	7.4	
t_{25}	RESET Setup Time	12		13		ns	7.7	
t_{26}	RESET Hold Time	4		4		ns	7.7	

Functional operating range: V_{CC} = 5V ±10%; T_{CASE} = 0°C to 100°C

Table 7.4. Intel386™ SX A.C. Characteristics (Continued)

Symbol	Parameter	20 MHz Intel386 SX		16 MHz Intel386 SX		Unit	Figure	Notes
		Min	Max	Min	Max			
t_{27}	NMI, INTR Setup Time	16		16		ns	7.4	(Note 2)
t_{28}	NMI, INTR Hold Time	16		16		ns	7.4	(Note 2)
t_{29}	PEREQ, ERROR#, BUSY#, FLT# Setup Time	14		16		ns	7.4	(Note 2)
t_{30}	PEREQ, ERROR#, BUSY#, FLT# Hold Time	5		5		ns	7.4	(Note 2)

Table 7.5. Low Power (LP) Intel386™ SX A.C. Characteristics

Symbol	Parameter	20 MHz Intel386 SX		16 MHz Intel386 SX		12 MHz Intel386 SX		Unit	Figure	Notes
		Min	Max	Min	Max	Min	Max			
	Operating Frequency	2	20	2	16	2	12.5	MHz		Half CLK2 Frequency
t_1	CLK2 Period	25	250	31	250	40	250	ns	7.3	
t_{2a}	CLK2 HIGH Time	8		9		11		ns	7.3	at 2V (Note 3)
t_{2b}	CLK2 HIGH Time	5		5		7		ns	7.3	at (V_{CC} − 0.8V)(3)
t_{3a}	CLK2 LOW Time	8		9		11		ns	7.3	at 2V(3)
t_{3b}	CLK2 LOW Time	6		7		9		ns	7.3	at 0.8V(3)
t_4	CLK2 Fall Time		8		8		8	ns	7.3	(V_{CC} − 0.8V) to 0.8V(3)
t_5	CLK2 Rise Time		8		8		8	ns	7.3	0.8V to (V_{CC} − 0.8V)(3)
t_6	A_{23}–A_1 Valid Delay	4	30	4	36	4	42	ns	7.5	C_L = 120 pF(4)
t_7	A_{23}–A_1 Float Delay	4	32	4	40	4	45	ns	7.6	(Note 1)
t_8	BHE#, BLE#, LOCK# Valid Delay	4	30	4	36	4	36	ns	7.5	C_L = 75 pF
t_9	BHE#, BLE#, LOCK# Float Delay	4	32	4	40	4	40	ns	7.6	(Note 1)
t_{10}	M/IO#, D/C#, W/R#, ADS# Valid Delay	6	28	6	33	4	33	ns	7.5	C_L = 75 pF
t_{11}	M/IO#, D/C#, W/R#, ADS# Float Delay	6	30	6	35	4	35	ns	7.6	(Note 1)
t_{12}	D15–D0 Write Data Valid Delay	4	38	4	40	4	50	ns	7.5	C_L = 120 pF(4)
t_{13}	D15–D0 Write Data Float Delay	4	27	4	35	4	40	ns	7.6	(Note 1)
t_{14}	HLDA Valid Delay	4	28	6	33	4	33	ns	7.5	C_L = 75 pF(4)
t_{15}	NA# Setup Time	5		5		7		ns	7.4	
t_{16}	NA# Hold Time	12		21		21		ns	7.4	

Functional operating range: V_{CC} = 5V ± 10%; T_{CASE} = 0°C to 100°C

Table 7.5. Low Power (LP) Intel386™ SX A.C. Characteristics (Continued)

Symbol	Parameter	20 MHz Intel386 SX		16 MHz Intel386 SX		12 MHz Intel386 SX		Unit	Figure	Notes
		Min	Max	Min	Max	Min	Max			
t_{19}	READY# Setup Time	12		19		19		ns	7.4	
t_{20}	READY# Hold Time	4		4		4		ns	7.4	
t_{21}	D15–D0 Read Data Setup Time	9		9		9		ns	7.4	
t_{22}	D15–D0 Read Data Hold Time	6		6		6		ns	7.4	
t_{23}	HOLD Setup Time	17		26		26		ns	7.4	
t_{24}	HOLD Hold Time	5		5		7		ns	7.4	
t_{25}	RESET Setup Time	12		13		15		ns	7.7	
t_{26}	RESET Hold Time	4		4		6		ns	7.7	
t_{27}	NMI, INTR Setup Time	16		16		16		ns	7.4	(Note 2)
t_{28}	NMI, INTR Hold Time	16		16		16		ns	7.4	(Note 2)
t_{29}	PEREQ, ERROR#, BUSY#, FLT# Setup Time	14		16		16		ns	7.4	(Note 2)
t_{30}	PEREQ, ERROR#, BUSY#, FLT# Hold Time	5		5		5		ns	7.4	(Note 2)

NOTES:
1. Float condition occurs when maximum output current becomes less than I_{LO} in magnitude. Float delay is not 100% tested.
2: These inputs are allowed to be asynchronous to CLK2. The setup and hold specifications are given for testing purposes, to assure recognition within a specific CLK2 period.
3: These are not tested. They are guaranteed by design characterization.
4: Tested with C_L set at 50 pf and derated to support the indicated distributed capacitive load. See Figures 7.8 though 7.10 for the capacitive derating curve.

A.C. TEST LOADS

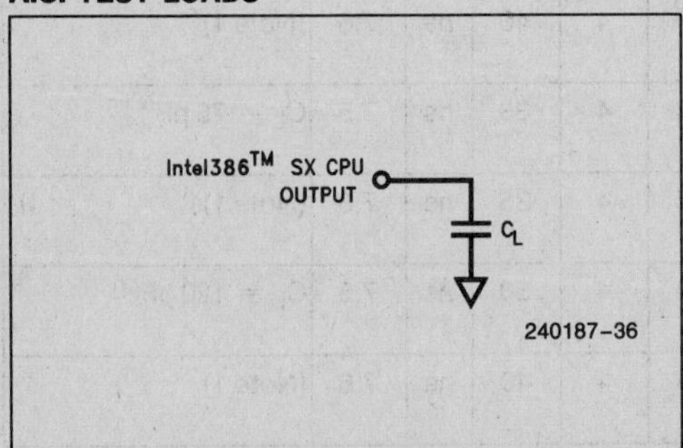

Figure 7.2. A.C. Test Loads

A.C. TIMING WAVEFORMS

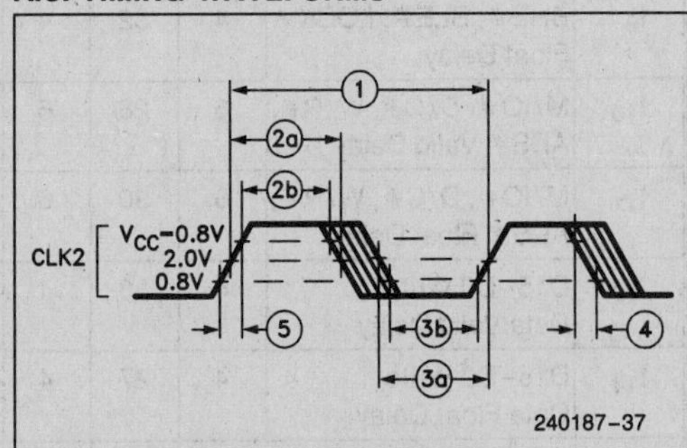

Figure 7.3. CLK2 Waveform

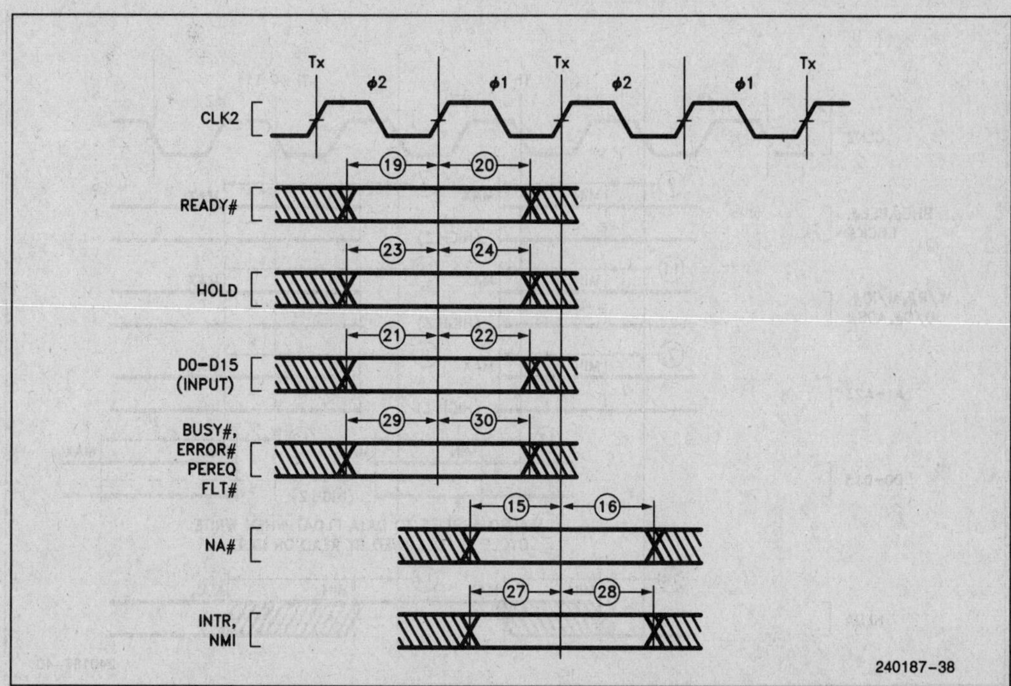

Figure 7.4. A.C. Timing Waveforms—Input Setup and Hold Timing

4

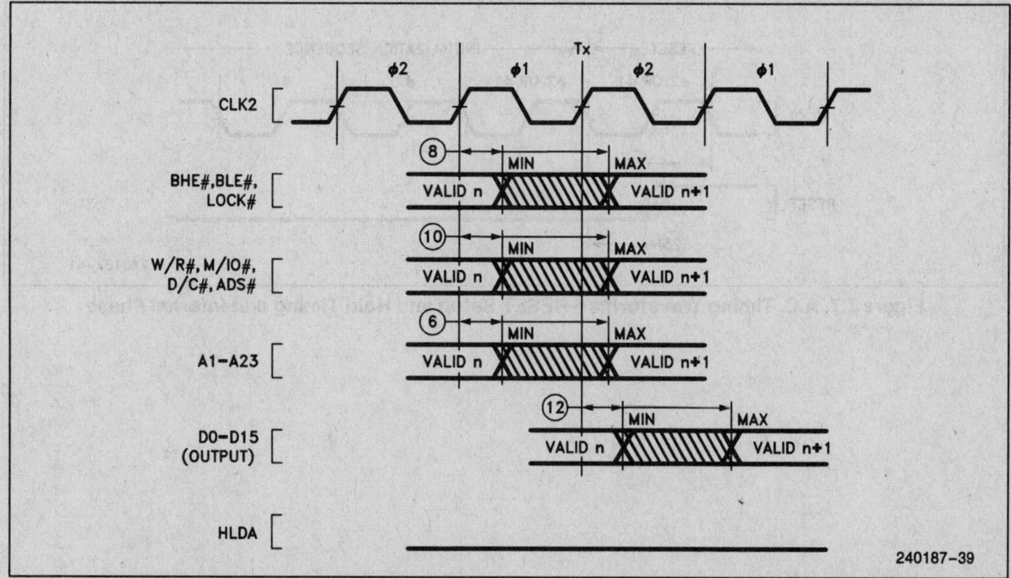

Figure 7.5. A.C. Timing Waveforms—Output Valid Delay Timing

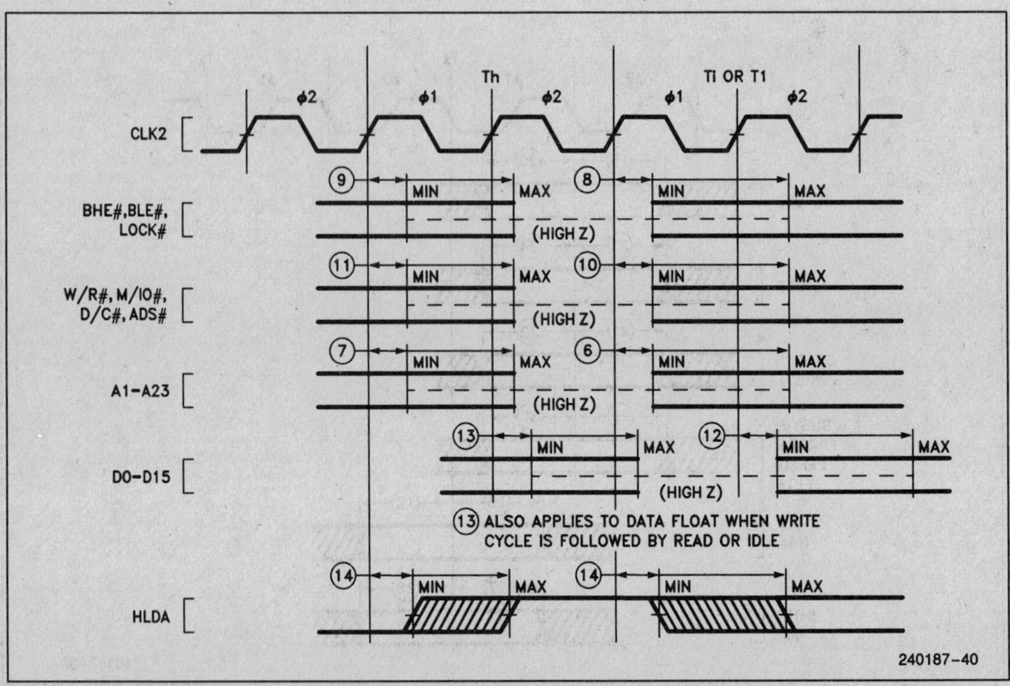

Figure 7.6. A.C. Timing Waveforms—Output Float Delay and HLDA Valid Delay Timing

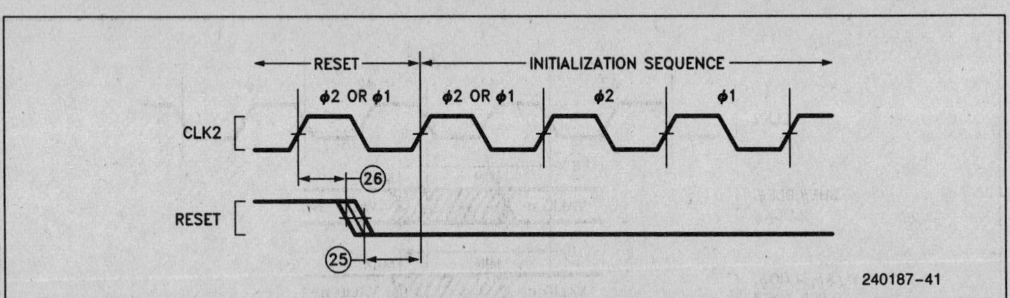

Figure 7.7. A.C. Timing Waveforms—RESET Setup and Hold Timing and Internal Phase

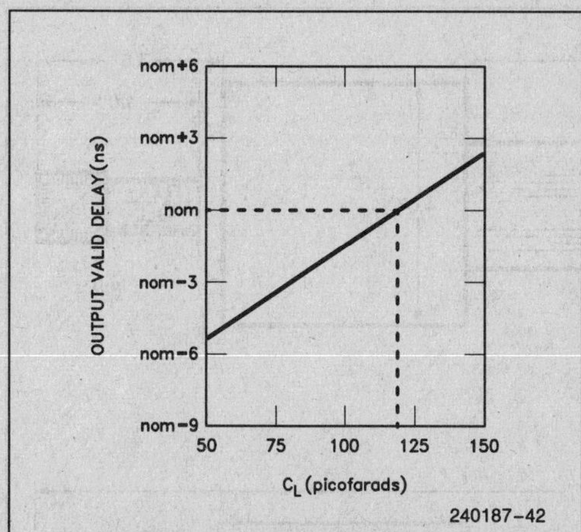

Figure 7.8. Typical Output Valid Delay versus Load Capacitance at Maximum Operating Temperature (C_L = 120 pF)

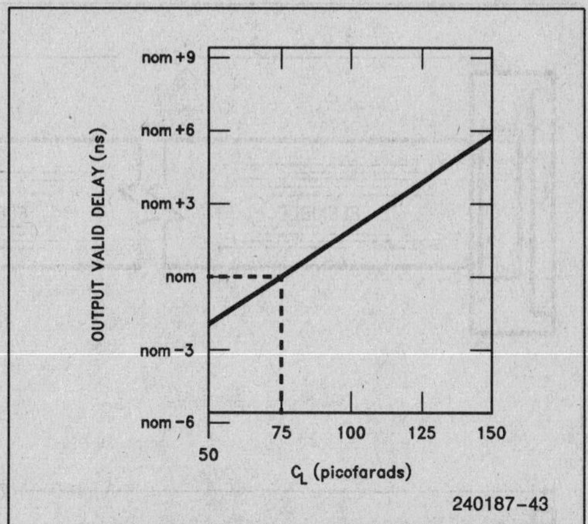

Figure 7.9. Typical Output Valid Delay versus Load Capacitance at Maximum Operating Temperature (C_L = 75 pF)

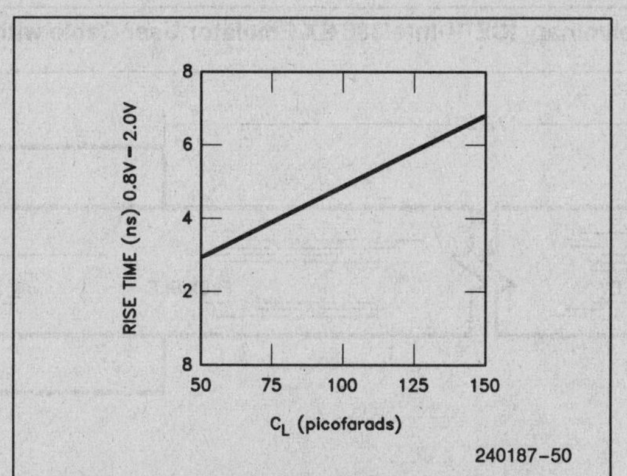

Figure 7.10. Typical Output Rise Time versus Load Capacitance at Maximum Operating Temperature

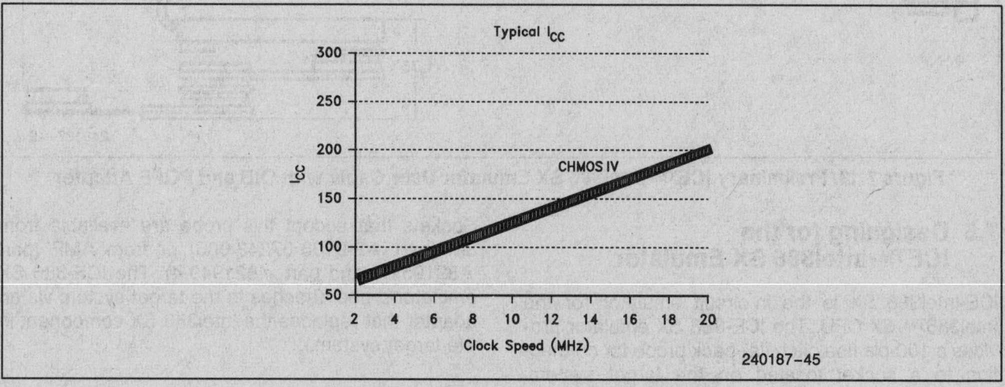

Figure 7.11. Typical I_{CC} vs Frequency

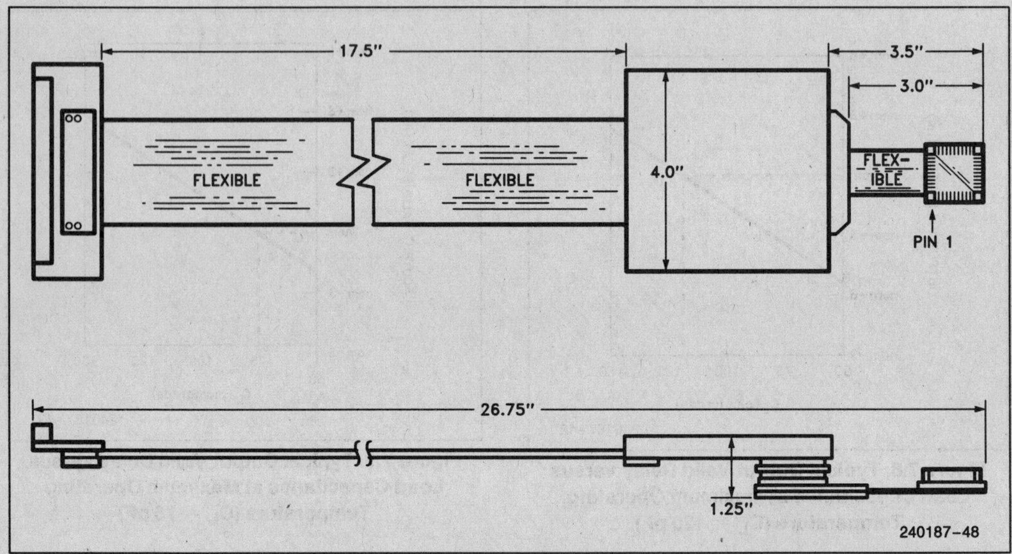

Figure 7.12. Preliminary ICE™-Intel386 SX Emulator User Cable with PQFP Adapter

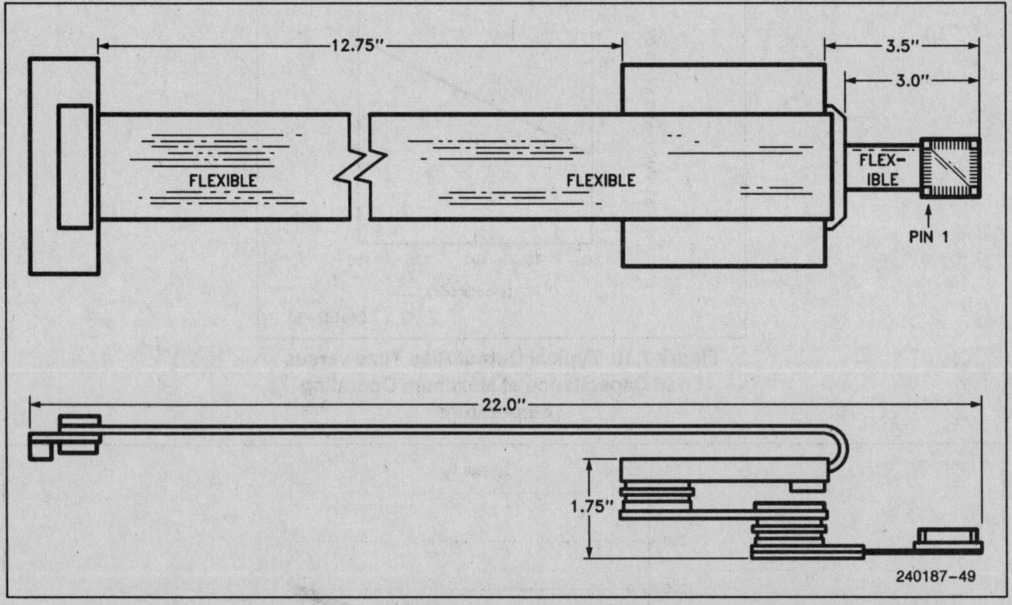

Figure 7.13. Preliminary ICE™-Intel386 SX Emulator User Cable with OIB and PQFP Adapter

7.5 Designing for the ICE™-Intel386 SX Emulator

ICE-Intel386 SX is the in-circuit emulator for the Intel386™ SX CPU. The ICE-386 SX emulator provides a 100-pin fine pitch flat-pack probe for connection to a socket located on the target system. Sockets that accept this probe are available from 3M (part #2-0100-07243-000) or from AMP (part #821959-1 and part #821949-4). The ICE-386 SX emulator probe attaches to the target system via an adapter that replaces the Intel386 SX component in the target system.

Due to the high operating frequency of Intel386 SX CPU based systems, there is no buffering between the Intel386 SX emulation processor (on the emulator probe) and the target system. A direct result of the non-buffered interconnect is that the ICE-Intel386 SX emulator shares the address and data busses with the target system.

In order to avoid problems with the shared bus and maintain signal integrity, the system designer must adhere to the following guidelines:

1. The bus controller must only enable data transceivers onto the data bus during valid read cycles (initiated by assertion of ADS#) of the Intel386 SX CPU, other local devices or other bus masters.
2. Before another bus master drives the local processor address bus, the other master must gain control of the address bus by asserting HOLD and receiving the HLDA response.
3. The emulation processor receives the RESET signal 2 or 4 CLK2 cycles later than an Intel386 SX CPU would, and responds to RESET later. Correct phase of the response is guaranteed.

In order to avoid problems that might arise due to the shared busses, an Optional use Isolation Board (OIB) is included with the emulator hardware. The OIB may be used to provide buffering between the emulation processor and the target system, but inserts a delay of approximately 10 ns in signal path.

In addition to the above considerations, the ICE-386 SX emulator processor module has several electrical and mechanical characteristics that should be taken into consideration when designing the Intel386 SX CPU system.

Capacitive Loading: ICE-Intel386 SX adds up to 27 pF to each Intel386 SX CPU signal.

Drive Requirements: ICE-Intel386 SX adds one FAST TTL load on the CLK2, control, address, and data lines. These loads are within the processor module and are driven by the Intel386 SX CPU emulation processor, which has standard drive and loading capability listed in Tables 7.3 and 7.4.

Power Requirements: For noise immunity and CMOS latch-up protection the ICE-Intel386 SX emulator processor module is powered by the user system.

The circuitry on the processor module draws up to 1.4A including the maximum Intel386 SX CPU I_{CC} from the user Intel386 SX CPU socket.

Intel386 SX CPU Location and Orientation: The ICE-Intel386 SX emulator processor module may require lateral clearance. Figure 7.12 shows the clearance requirements of the iMP adapter. The optional isolation board (OIB), which provides extra electrical buffering and has the same lateral clearance requirements as Figure 7.12, adds an additional 0.5 inches to the vertical clearance requirement. This is illustrated in Figure 7.13.

Optional Isolation Board (OIB) and the CLK2 speed reduction: Due to the unbuffered probe design, the ICE-Intel386 SX emulator is susceptible to errors on the user's bus. The OIB allows the ICE-Intel386 SX emulator to function in user systems with faults (shorted signals, etc.). After electrical verification the OIB may be removed. When the OIB is installed, the user system must have a maximum CLK2 frequency of 20 MHz.

8.0 DIFFERENCES BETWEEN THE Intel386 SX CPU AND THE Intel386 DX CPU

The following are the major differences between the Intel386 SX CPU and the Intel386 DX CPU:

1. The Intel386 SX CPU generates byte selects on BHE# and BLE# (like the 8086 and 80286) to distinguish the upper and lower bytes on its 16-bit data bus. The Intel386 DX CPU uses four byte selects, BE0#-BE3#, to distinguish between the different bytes on its 32-bit bus.
2. The Intel386 SX CPU has no bus sizing option. The Intel386 DX CPU can select between either a 32-bit bus or a 16-bit bus by use of the BS16# input. The Intel386 SX CPU has a 16-bit bus size.
3. The NA# pin operation in the Intel386 SX CPU is identical to that of the NA# pin on the Intel386 DX CPU with one exception: the Intel386 DX CPU NA# pin cannot be activated on 16-bit bus cycles (where BS16# is LOW in the Intel386 DX CPU case), whereas NA# can be activated on any Intel386 SX CPU bus cycle.
4. The contents of all Intel386 SX CPU registers at reset are identical to the contents of the Intel386 DX CPU registers at reset, except the DX register. The DX register contains a component-stepping identifier at reset, i.e.

   in Intel386 DX CPU, DH = 3 indicates Intel386 DX CPU after reset
   DL = revision number;
   in Intel386 SX CPU, DH = 23H indicates Intel386 SX CPU after reset
   DL = revision number.

5. The Intel386 DX CPU uses A_{31} and M/IO# as selects for the numerics coprocessor. The Intel386 SX CPU uses A_{23} and M/IO# as selects.
6. The Intel386 DX CPU prefetch unit fetches code in four-byte units. The Intel386 SX CPU prefetch unit reads two bytes as one unit (like the 80286). In BS16 mode, the Intel386 DX CPU takes two consecutive bus cycles to complete a prefetch request. If there is a data read or write request after the prefetch starts, the Intel386 DX CPU will fetch all four bytes before addressing the new request.
7. Both Intel386 DX CPU and Intel386 SX CPU have the same logical address space. The only difference is that the Intel386 DX CPU has a 32-bit physical address space and the Intel386 SX CPU has a 24-bit physical address space. The Intel386 SX CPU has a physical memory address space of up to 16 megabytes instead of the 4 gigabytes available to the Intel386 DX CPU. Therefore, in Intel386 SX CPU systems, the operating system must be aware of this physical memory limit and should allocate memory for applications programs within this limit. If a Intel386 DX CPU system uses only the lower 16 megabytes of physical address, then there will be no extra effort required to migrate Intel386 DX CPU software to the Intel386 SX CPU. Any application which uses more than 16 megabytes of memory can run on the Intel386 SX CPU if the operating system utilizes the Intel386 SX CPU's paging mechanism. In spite of this difference in physical address space, the Intel386 SX CPU and Intel386 DX CPU can run the same operating systems and applications within their respective physical memory constraints.
8. The Intel386 SX has an input called FLT# which tri-states all bidirectional and output pins, including HLDA#, when asserted. It is used with ON Circuit Emulation (ONCE).

9.0 INSTRUCTION SET

This section describes the instruction set. Table 9.1 lists all instructions along with instruction encoding diagrams and clock counts. Further details of the instruction encoding are then provided in the following sections, which completely describe the encoding structure and the definition of all fields occurring within instructions.

9.1 Intel386 SX CPU Instruction Encoding and Clock Count Summary

To calculate elapsed time for an instruction, multiply the instruction clock count, as listed in Table 9.1 below, by the processor clock period (e.g. 62.5 ns for an Intel386 SX Microprocessor operating at 16 MHz). The actual clock count of an Intel386 SX Microprocessor program will average 5% more than the calculated clock count due to instruction sequences which execute faster than they can be fetched from memory.

Instruction Clock Count Assumptions

1. The instruction has been prefetched, decoded, and is ready for execution.
2. Bus cycles do not require wait states.
3. There are no local bus HOLD requests delaying processor access to the bus.
4. No exceptions are detected during instruction execution.
5. If an effective address is calculated, it does not use two general register components. One register, scaling and displacement can be used within the clock counts shown. However, if the effective address calculation uses two general register components, add 1 clock to the clock count shown.

Instruction Clock Count Notation

1. If two clock counts are given, the smaller refers to a register operand and the larger refers to a memory operand.
2. n = number of times repeated.
3. m = number of components in the next instruction executed, where the entire displacement (if any) counts as one component, the entire immediate data (if any) counts as one component, and all other bytes of the instruction and prefix(es) each count as one component.

Misaligned or 32-Bit Operand Accesses

— If instructions accesses a misaligned 16-bit operand or 32-bit operand on even address add:
  2* clocks for read or write
  4** clocks for read and write

— If instructions accesses a 32-bit operand on odd address add:
  4* clocks for read or write
  8** clocks for read and write

Wait States

Wait states add 1 clock per wait state to instruction execution for each data access.

Table 9-1. Instruction Set Clock Count Summary

INSTRUCTION	FORMAT		CLOCK COUNT		NOTES	
		Clk Count Virtual 8086 Mode	Real Address Mode or Virtual 8086 Mode	Protected Virtual Address Mode	Real Address Mode or Virtual 8086 Mode	Protected Virtual Address Mode
GENERAL DATA TRANSFER						
MOV = Move:						
Register to Register/Memory	1000100w · mod reg r/m		2/2	2/2*	b	h
Register/Memory to Register	1000101w · mod reg r/m		2/4	2/4*	b	h
Immediate to Register/Memory	1100011w · mod 000 r/m · immediate data		2/2	2/2*	b	h
Immediate to Register (short form)	1011 w reg · immediate data		2	2		
Memory to Accumulator (short form)	1010000w · full displacement		4*	4*	b	h
Accumulator to Memory (short form)	1010001w · full displacement		2*	2*	b	h
Register Memory to Segment Register	10001110 · mod sreg3 r/m		2/5	22/23	b	h, i, j
Segment Register to Register/Memory	10001100 · mod sreg3 r/m		2/2	2/2	b	h
MOVSX = Move With Sign Extension						
Register From Register/Memory	00001111 · 1011111w · mod reg r/m		3/6*	3/6*	b	h
MOVZX = Move With Zero Extension						
Register From Register/Memory	00001111 · 1011011w · mod reg r/m		3/6*	3/6*	b	h
PUSH = Push:						
Register/Memory	11111111 · mod 110 r/m		5/7*	7/9*	b	h
Register (short form)	01010 reg		2	4	b	h
Segment Register (ES, CS, SS or DS) (short form)	000 sreg2 110		2	4	b	h
Segment Register (ES, CS, SS, DS, FS or GS)	00001111 · 10 sreg3 000		2	4	b	h
Immediate	011010s0 · immediate data		2	4	b	h
PUSHA = Push All	01100000		18	34	b	h
POP = Pop						
Register/Memory	10001111 · mod 000 r/m		5/7	7/9	b	h
Register (short form)	01011 reg		6	6	b	h
Segment Register (ES, CS, SS or DS) (short form)	000 sreg 2 111		7	25	b	h, i, j
Segment Register (ES, CS, SS or DS), FS or GS	00001111 · 10 sreg 3 001		7	25	b	h, i, j
POPA = Pop All	01100001		24	40	b	h
XCHG = Exchange						
Register/Memory With Register	1000011w · mod reg r/m		3/5**	3/5**	b, f	f, h
Register With Accumulator (short form)	10010 reg		3	3		
IN = Input from:						
Fixed Port	1110010w · port number	†26	12*	6*/26*		s/t,m
Variable Port	1110110w	†27	13*	7*/27*		s/t,m
OUT = Output to:						
Fixed Port	1110011w · port number	†24	10*	4*/24*		s/t,m
Variable Port	1110111w	†25	11*	5*/25*		s/t,m
LEA = Load EA to Register	10001101 · mod reg r/m		2	2		

Table 9-1. Instruction Set Clock Count Summary (Continued)

INSTRUCTION	FORMAT	CLOCK COUNT: Real Address Mode or Virtual 8086 Mode	CLOCK COUNT: Protected Virtual Address Mode	NOTES: Real Address Mode or Virtual 8086 Mode	NOTES: Protected Virtual Address Mode
SEGMENT CONTROL					
LDS = Load Pointer to DS	11000101 | mod reg r/m	7*	26*/28*	b	h, i, j
LES = Load Pointer to ES	11000100 | mod reg r/m	7*	26*/28*	b	h, i, j
LFS = Load Pointer to FS	00001111 | 10110100 | mod reg r/m	7*	29*/31*	b	h, i, j
LGS = Load Pointer to GS	00001111 | 10110101 | mod reg r/m	7*	26*/28*	b	h, i, j
LSS = Load Pointer to SS	00001111 | 10110010 | mod reg r/m	7*	26*/28*	b	h, i, j
FLAG CONTROL					
CLC = Clear Carry Flag	11111000	2	2		
CLD = Clear Direction Flag	11111100	2	2		
CLI = Clear Interrupt Enable Flag	11111010	8	8		m
CLTS = Clear Task Switched Flag	00001111 | 00000110	5	5	c	l
CMC = Complement Carry Flag	11110101	2	2		
LAHF = Load AH into Flag	10011111	2	2		
POPF = Pop Flags	10011101	5	5	b	h, n
PUSHF = Push Flags	10011100	4	4	b	h
SAHF = Store AH into Flags	10011110	3	3		
STC = Set Carry Flag	11111001	2	2		
STD = Set Direction Flag	11111101	2	2		
STI = Set Interrupt Enable Flag	11111011	8	8		m
ARITHMETIC					
ADD = Add					
Register to Register	000000dw | mod reg r/m	2	2		
Register to Memory	0000000w | mod reg r/m	7**	7**	b	h
Memory to Register	0000001w | mod reg r/m	6*	6*	b	h
Immediate to Register/Memory	100000sw | mod 000 r/m | immediate data	2/7**	2/7**	b	h
Immediate to Accumulator (short form)	0000010w | immediate data	2	2		
ADC = Add With Carry					
Register to Register	000100dw | mod reg r/m	2	2		
Register to Memory	0001000w | mod reg r/m	7**	7**	b	h
Memory to Register	0001001w | mod reg r/m	6*	6*	b	h
Immediate to Register/Memory	100000sw | mod 010 r/m | immediate data	2/7**	2/7**	b	h
Immediate to Accumulator (short form)	0001010w | immediate data	2	2		
INC = Increment					
Register/Memory	1111111w | mod 000 r/m	2/6**	2/6**	b	h
Register (short form)	01000 reg	2	2		
SUB = Subtract					
Register from Register	001010dw | mod reg r/m	2	2		

Table 9-1. Instruction Set Clock Count Summary (Continued)

INSTRUCTION	FORMAT				CLOCK COUNT Real Address Mode or Virtual 8086 Mode	CLOCK COUNT Protected Virtual Address Mode	NOTES Real Address Mode or Virtual 8086 Mode	NOTES Protected Virtual Address Mode
ARITHMETIC (Continued)								
Register from Memory	0010100w	mod reg r/m			7**	7**	b	h
Memory from Register	0010101w	mod reg r/m			6*	6*	b	h
Immediate from Register/Memory	100000sw	mod 101 r/m	immediate data		2/7**	2/7**	b	h
Immediate from Accumulator (short form)	0010110w	immediate data			2	2		
SBB = Subtract with Borrow								
Register from Register	000110dw	mod reg r/m			2	2		
Register from Memory	0001100w	mod reg r/m			7**	7**	b	h
Memory from Register	0001101w	mod reg r/m			6*	6*	b	h
Immediate from Register/Memory	100000sw	mod 011 r/m	immediate data		2/7**	2/7**	b	h
Immediate from Accumulator (short form)	0001110w	immediate data			2	2		
DEC = Decrement								
Register/Memory	1111111w	reg 001 r/m			2/6	2/6	b	h
Register (short form)	01001 reg				2	2		
CMP = Compare								
Register with Register	001110dw	mod reg r/m			2	2		
Memory with Register	0011100w	mod reg r/m			5*	5*	b	h
Register with Memory	0011101w	mod reg r/m			6*	6*.	b	h
Immediate with Register/Memory	100000sw	mod 111 r/m	immediate data		2/5*	2/5*	b	h
Immediate with Accumulator (short form)	0011110w	immediate data			2	2		
NEG = Change Sign	1111011w	mod 011 r/m			2/6*	2/6*	b	h
AAA = ASCII Adjust for Add	00110111				4	4		
AAS = ASCII Adjust for Subtract	00111111				4	4		
DAA = Decimal Adjust for Add	00100111				4	4		
DAS = Decimal Adjust for Subtract	00101111				4	4		
MUL = Multiply (unsigned)								
Accumulator with Register/Memory	1111011w	mod 100 r/m						
Multiplier-Byte					12-17/15-20*	12-17/15-20*	b, d	d, h
-Word					12-25/15-28*	12-25/15-28*	b, d	d, h
-Doubleword					12-41/17-46*	12-41/17-46*	b, d	d, h
IMUL = Integer Multiply (signed)								
Accumulator with Register/Memory	1111011w	mod 101 r/m						
Multiplier-Byte					12-17/15-20*	12-17/15-20*	b, d	d, h
-Word					12-25/15-28*	12-25/15-28*	b, d	d, h
-Doubleword					12-41/17-46*	12-41/17-46*	b, d	d, h
Register with Register/Memory	00001111	10101111	mod reg r/m					
Multiplier-Byte					12-17/15-20*	12-17/15-20*	b, d	d, h
-Word					12-25/15-28*	12-25/15-28*	b, d	d, h
-Doubleword					12-41/17-46*	12-41/17-46*	b, d	d, h
Register/Memory with Immediate to Register	011010s1	mod reg r/m	immediate data					
-Word					13-26	13-26/14-27	b, d	d, h
-Doubleword					13-42	13-42/16-45	b, d	d, h

4

Table 9-1. Instruction Set Clock Count Summary (Continued)

INSTRUCTION	FORMAT	Clock Count: Real Address Mode or Virtual 8086 Mode	Clock Count: Protected Virtual Address Mode	Notes: Real Address Mode or Virtual 8086 Mode	Notes: Protected Virtual Address Mode
ARITHMETIC (Continued)					
DIV = Divide (Unsigned)					
Accumulator by Register/Memory	1111011w | mod 110 r/m				
Divisor—Byte		14/17	14/17	b,e	e,h
—Word		22/25	22/25	b,e	e,h
—Doubleword		38/43	38/43	b,e	e,h
IDIV = Integer Divide (Signed)					
Accumulator By Register/Memory	1111011w | mod 111 r/m				
Divisor—Byte		19/22	19/22	b,e	e,h
—Word		27/30	27/30	b,e	e,h
—Doubleword		43/48	43/48	b,e	e,h
AAD = ASCII Adjust for Divide	11010101 | 00001010	19	19		
AAM = ASCII Adjust for Multiply	11010100 | 00001010	17	17		
CBW = Convert Byte to Word	10011000	3	3		
CWD = Convert Word to Double Word	10011001	2	2		
LOGIC					
Shift Rotate Instructions					
Not Through Carry **(ROL, ROR, SAL, SAR, SHL, and SHR)**					
Register/Memory by 1	1101000w | mod TTT r/m	3/7**	3/7**	b	h
Register/Memory by CL	1101001w | mod TTT r/m	3/7*	3/7*	b	h
Register/Memory by Immediate Count	1100000w | mod TTT r/m | immed 8-bit data	3/7*	3/7*	b	h
Through Carry **(RCL and RCR)**					
Register/Memory by 1	1101000w | mod TTT r/m	9/10*	9/10*	b	h
Register/Memory by CL	1101001w | mod TTT r/m	9/10*	9/10*	b	h
Register/Memory by Immediate Count	1100000w | mod TTT r/m | immed 8-bit data	9/10*	9/10*	b	h
	TTT Instruction 000 ROL 001 ROR 010 RCL 011 RCR 100 SHL/SAL 101 SHR 111 SAR				
SHLD = Shift Left Double					
Register/Memory by Immediate	00001111 | 10100100 | mod reg r/m | immed 8-bit data	3/7**	3/7**		
Register/Memory by CL	00001111 | 10100101 | mod reg r/m	3/7**	3/7**		
SHRD = Shift Right Double					
Register/Memory by Immediate	00001111 | 10101100 | mod reg r/m | immed 8-bit data	3/7**	3/7**		
Register/Memory by CL	00001111 | 10101101 | mod reg r/m	3/7**	3/7**		
AND = And					
Register to Register	001000dw | mod reg r/m	2	2		

Table 9-1. Instruction Set Clock Count Summary (Continued)

INSTRUCTION	FORMAT			Clk Count Virtual 8086 Mode	CLOCK COUNT: Real Address Mode or Virtual 8086 Mode	CLOCK COUNT: Protected Virtual Address Mode	NOTES: Real Address Mode or Virtual 8086 Mode	NOTES: Protected Virtual Address Mode
LOGIC (Continued)								
Register to Memory	0010000w	mod reg r/m			7**	7**	b	h
Memory to Register	0010001w	mod reg r/m			6*	6*	b	h
Immediate to Register/Memory	1000000w	mod 100 r/m	immediate data		2/7*	2/7**	b	h
Immediate to Accumulator (Short Form)	0010010w	immediate data			2	2		
TEST = And Function to Flags, No Result								
Register/Memory and Register	1000010w	mod reg r/m			2/5*	2/5*	b	h
Immediate Data and Register/Memory	1111011w	mod 000 r/m	immediate data		2/5*	2/5*	b	h
Immediate Data and Accumulator (Short Form)	1010100w	immediate data			2	2		
OR = Or								
Register to Register	000010dw	mod reg r/m			2	2		
Register to Memory	0000100w	mod reg r/m			7**	7**	b	h
Memory to Register	0000101w	mod reg r/m			6*	6*	b	h
Immediate to Register/Memory	1000000w	mod 001 r/m	immediate data		2/7**	2/7**	b	h
Immediate to Accumulator (Short Form)	0000110w	immediate data			2	2		
XOR = Exclusive Or								
Register to Register	001100dw	mod reg r/m			2	2		
Register to Memory	0011000w	mod reg r/m			7**	7**	b	h
Memory to Register	0011001w	mod reg r/m			6*	6*	b	h
Immediate to Register/Memory	1000000w	mod 110 r/m	immediate data		2/7**	2/7**	b	h
Immediate to Accumulator (Short Form)	0011010w	immediate data			2	2		
NOT = Invert Register/Memory	1111011w	mod 010 r/m			2/6**	2/6**	b	h
STRING MANIPULATION								
CMPS = Compare Byte Word	1010011w				10*	10*	b	h
INS = Input Byte/Word from DX Port	0110110w			†29	15	9*/29**	b	s/t, h, m
LODS = Load Byte/Word to AL/AX/EAX	1010110w				5	5*	b	h
MOVS = Move Byte Word	1010010w				7	7**	b	h
OUTS = Output Byte/Word to DX Port	0110111w			†28	14	8*/28*	b	s/t, h, m
SCAS = Scan Byte Word	1010111w				7*	7*	b	h
STOS = Store Byte/Word from AL/AX/EX	1010101w				4*	4*	b	h
XLAT = Translate String	11010111				5*	5*		h
REPEATED STRING MANIPULATION								
Repeated by Count in CX or ECX								
REPE CMPS = Compare String								
(Find Non-Match)	11110011	1010011w			5 + 9n**	5 + 9n**	b	h

Table 9-1. Instruction Set Clock Count Summary (Continued)

INSTRUCTION	FORMAT	Clk Count Virtual 8086 Mode	CLOCK COUNT: Real Address Mode or Virtual 8086 Mode	CLOCK COUNT: Protected Virtual Address Mode	NOTES: Real Address Mode or Virtual 8086 Mode	NOTES: Protected Virtual Address Mode
REPEATED STRING MANIPULATION (Continued)						
REPNE CMPS = Compare String						
(Find Match)	11110010 | 1010011w		5+9n**	5+9n**	b	h
REP INS = Input String	11110010 | 0110110w	†	13+6n*	7+6n*/27+6n*	b	s/t, h, m
REP LODS = Load String	11110010 | 1010110w		5+6n*	5+6n*	b	h
REP MOVS = Move String	11110010 | 1010010w		7+4n*	7+4n**	b	h
REP OUTS = Output String	11110010 | 0110111w	†	12+5n*	6+5n*/26+5n*	b	s/t, h, m
REPE SCAS = Scan String						
(Find Non-AL/AX/EAX)	11110011 | 1010111w		5+8n*	5+8n*	b	h
REPNE SCAS = Scan String						
(Find AL/AX/EAX)	11110010 | 1010111w		5+8n*	5+8n*	b	h
REP STOS = Store String	11110010 | 1010101w		5+5n*	5+5n*	b	h
BIT MANIPULATION						
BSF = Scan Bit Forward	00001111 | 10111100 | mod reg r/m		10+3n*	10+3n**	b	h
BSR = Scan Bit Reverse	00001111 | 10111101 | mod reg r/m		10+3n*	10+3n**	b	h
BT = Test Bit						
Register/Memory, Immediate	00001111 | 10111010 | mod 100 r/m | immed 8-bit data		3/6*	3/6*	b	h
Register/Memory, Register	00001111 | 10100011 | mod reg r/m		3/12*	3/12*	b	h
BTC = Test Bit and Complement						
Register/Memory, Immediate	00001111 | 10111010 | mod 111 r/m | immed 8-bit data		6/8*	6/8*	b	h
Register/Memory, Register	00001111 | 10111011 | mod reg r/m		6/13*	6/13*	b	h
BTR = Test Bit and Reset						
Register/Memory, Immediate	00001111 | 10111010 | mod 110 r/m | immed 8-bit data		6/8*	6/8*	b	h
Register/Memory, Register	00001111 | 10110011 | mod reg r/m		6/13*	6/13*	b	h
BTS = Test Bit and Set						
Register/Memory, Immediate	00001111 | 10111010 | mod 101 r/m | immed 8-bit data		6/8*	6/8*	b	h
Register/Memory, Register	00001111 | 10101011 | mod reg r/m		6/13*	6/13*	b	h
CONTROL TRANSFER						
CALL = Call						
Direct Within Segment	11101000 | full displacement		7+m*	9+m*	b	r
Register/Memory						
Indirect Within Segment	11111111 | mod 010 r/m		7+m*/10+m*	9+m/12+m*	b	h, r
Direct Intersegment	10011010 | unsigned full offset, selector		17+m*	42+m*	b	j,k,r

NOTE:
† Clock count shown applies if I/O permission allows I/O to the port in virtual 8086 mode. If I/O bit map denies permission exception 13 fault occurs; refer to clock counts for INT 3 instruction.

Table 9-1. Instruction Set Clock Count Summary (Continued)

INSTRUCTION	FORMAT	CLOCK COUNT: Real Address Mode or Virtual 8086 Mode	CLOCK COUNT: Protected Virtual Address Mode	NOTES: Real Address Mode or Virtual 8086 Mode	NOTES: Protected Virtual Address Mode
CONTROL TRANSFER (Continued)					
Protected Mode Only (Direct Intersegment)					
Via Call Gate to Same Privilege Level			64+m		h,j,k,r
Via Call Gate to Different Privilege Level, (No Parameters)			98+m		h,j,k,r
Via Call Gate to Different Privilege Level, (x Parameters)			106+8x+m		h,j,k,r
From 286 Task to 286 TSS			285		h,j,k,r
From 286 Task to Intel386™ SX CPU TSS			310		h,j,k,r
From 286 Task to Virtual 8086 Task (Intel386 SX CPU TSS)			229		h,j,k,r
From Intel386 SX CPU Task to 286 TSS			285		h,j,k,r
From Intel386 SX CPU Task to Intel386 SX CPU TSS			392		h,j,k,r
From Intel386 SX CPU Task to Virtual 8086 Task (Intel386 SX CPU TSS)			309		h,j,k,r
Indirect Intersegment	11111111 | mod 011 r/m	30+m	46+m	b	h,j,k,r
Protected Mode Only (Indirect Intersegment)					
Via Call Gate to Same Privilege Level			68+m		h,j,k,r
Via Call Gate to Different Privilege Level, (No Parameters)			102+m		h,j,k,r
Via Call Gate to Different Privilege Level, (x Parameters)			110+8x+m		h,j,k,r
From 286 Task to 286 TSS					h,j,k,r
From 286 Task to Intel386 SX CPU TSS					h,j,k,r
From 286 Task to Virtual 8086 Task (Intel386 SX CPU TSS)					h,j,k,r
From Intel386 SX CPU Task to 286 TSS					h,j,k,r
From Intel386 SX CPU Task to Intel386 SX CPU TSS			399		h,j,k,r
From Intel386 SX CPU Task to Virtual 8086 Task (Intel386 SX CPU TSS)					h,j,k,r
JMP = Unconditional Jump					
Short	11101011 | 8-bit displacement	7+m	7+m		r
Direct within Segment	11101001 | full displacement	7+m	7+m		r
Register/Memory Indirect within Segment	11111111 | mod 100 r/m	9+m/14+m	9+m/14+m	b	h,r
Direct Intersegment	11101010 | unsigned full offset, selector	16+m	31+m		j,k,r
Protected Mode Only (Direct Intersegment)					
Via Call Gate to Same Privilege Level			53+m		h,j,k,r
From 286 Task to 286 TSS					h,j,k,r
From 286 Task to Intel386 SX CPU TSS					h,j,k,r
From 286 Task to Virtual 8086 Task (Intel386 SX CPU TSS)					h,j,k,r
From Intel386 SX CPU Task to 286 TSS					h,j,k,r
From Intel386 SX CPU Task to Intel386 SX CPU TSS					h,j,k,r
From Intel386 SX CPU Task to Virtual 8086 Task (Intel386 SX CPU TSS)			395		h,j,k,r
Indirect Intersegment	11111111 | mod 101 r/m	17+m	31+m	b	h,j,k,r
Protected Mode Only (Indirect Intersegment)					
Via Call Gate to Same Privilege Level			49+m		h,j,k,r
From 286 Task to 286 TSS					h,j,k,r
From 286 Task to Intel386 SX CPU TSS					h,j,k,r
From 286 Task to Virtual 8086 Task (Intel386 SX CPU TSS)					h,j,k,r
From Intel386 SX CPU Task to 286 TSS					h,j,k,r
From Intel386 SX CPU Task to Intel386 SX CPU TSS			328		h,j,k,r
From Intel386 SX CPU Task to Virtual 8086 Task (Intel386 SX CPU TSS)					h,j,k,r

4

Table 9-1. Instruction Set Clock Count Summary (Continued)

INSTRUCTION	FORMAT			CLOCK COUNT: Real Address Mode or Virtual 8086 Mode	CLOCK COUNT: Protected Virtual Address Mode	NOTES: Real Address Mode or Virtual 8086 Mode	NOTES: Protected Virtual Address Mode
CONTROL TRANSFER (Continued)							
RET = Return from CALL:							
Within Segment	11000011				12+m	b	g, h, r
Within Segment Adding Immediate to SP	11000010	16-bit displ			12+m	b	g, h, r
Intersegment	11001011				36+m	b	g, h, j, k, r
Intersegment Adding Immediate to SP	11001010	16-bit displ			36+m	b	g, h, j, k, r
Protected Mode Only (RET):							
to Different Privilege Level							
Intersegment					72		h, j, k, r
Intersegment Adding Immediate to SP					72		h, j, k, r
CONDITIONAL JUMPS							
NOTE: Times Are Jump "Taken or Not Taken"							
JO = Jump on Overflow							
8-Bit Displacement	01110000	8-bit displ		7+m or 3	7+m or 3		r
Full Displacement	00001111	10000000	full displacement	7+m or 3	7+m or 3		r
JNO = Jump on Not Overflow							
8-Bit Displacement	01110001	8-bit displ		7+m or 3	7+m or 3		r
Full Displacement	00001111	10000001	full displacement	7+m or 3	7+m or 3		r
JB/JNAE = Jump on Below/Not Above or Equal							
8-Bit Displacement	01110010	8-bit displ		7+m or 3	7+m or 3		r
Full Displacement	00001111	10000010	full displacement	7+m or 3	7+m or 3		r
JNB/JAE = Jump on Not Below/Above or Equal							
8-Bit Displacement	01110011	8-bit displ		7+m or 3	7+m or 3		r
Full Displacement	00001111	10000011	full displacement	7+m or 3	7+m or 3		r
JE/JZ = Jump on Equal/Zero							
8-Bit Displacement	01110100	8-bit displ		7+m or 3	7+m or 3		r
Full Displacement	00001111	10000100	full displacement	7+m or 3	7+m or 3		r
JNE/JNZ = Jump on Not Equal/Not Zero							
8-Bit Displacement	01110101	8-bit displ		7+m or 3	7+m or 3		r
Full Displacement	00001111	10000101	full displacement	7+m or 3	7+m or 3		r
JBE/JNA = Jump on Below or Equal/Not Above							
8-Bit Displacement	01110110	8-bit displ		7+m or 3	7+m or 3		r
Full Displacement	00001111	10000110	full displacement	7+m or 3	7+m or 3		r
JNBE/JA = Jump on Not Below or Equal/Above							
8-Bit Displacement	01110111	8-bit displ		7+m or 3	7+m or 3		r
Full Displacement	00001111	10000111	full displacement	7+m or 3	7+m or 3		r
JS = Jump on Sign							
8-Bit Displacement	01111000	8-bit displ		7+m or 3	7+m or 3		r
Full Displacement	00001111	10001000	full displacement	7+m or 3	7+m or 3		r

Table 9-1. Instruction Set Clock Count Summary (Continued)

INSTRUCTION	FORMAT				CLOCK COUNT		NOTES	
					Real Address Mode or Virtual 8086 Mode	Protected Virtual Address Mode	Real Address Mode or Virtual 8086 Mode	Protected Virtual Address Mode
CONDITIONAL JUMPS (Continued)								
JNS = Jump on Not Sign								
8-Bit Displacement	01111001	8-bit displ			7+m or 3	7+m or 3		r
Full Displacement	00001111	10001001	full displacement		7+m or 3	7+m or 3		r
JP/JPE = Jump on Parity/Parity Even								
8-Bit Displacement	01111010	8-bit displ			7+m or 3	7+m or 3		r
Full Displacement	00001111	10001010	full displacement		7+m or 3	7+m or 3		r
JNP/JPO = Jump on Not Parity/Parity Odd								
8-Bit Displacement	01111011	8-bit displ			7+m or 3	7+m or 3		r
Full Displacement	00001111	10001011	full displacement		7+m or 3	7+m or 3		r
JL/JNGE = Jump on Less/Not Greater or Equal								
8-Bit Displacement	01111100	8-bit displ			7+m or 3	7+m or 3		r
Full Displacement	00001111	10001100	full displacement		7+m or 3	7+m or 3		r
JNL/JGE = Jump on Not Less/Greater or Equal								
8-Bit Displacement	01111101	8-bit displ			7+m or 3	7+m or 3		r
Full Displacement	00001111	10001101	full displacement		7+m or 3	7+m or 3		r
JLE/JNG = Jump on Less or Equal/Not Greater								
8-Bit Displacement	01111110	8-bit displ			7+m or 3	7+m or 3		r
Full Displacement	00001111	10001110	full displacement		7+m or 3	7+m or 3		r
JNLE/JG = Jump on Not Less or Equal/Greater								
8-Bit Displacement	01111111	8-bit displ			7+m or 3	7+m or 3		r
Full Displacement	00001111	10001111	full displacement		7+m or 3	7+m or 3		r
JCXZ = Jump on CX Zero	11100011	8-bit displ			9+m or 5	9+m or 5		r
JECXZ = Jump on ECX Zero	11100011	8-bit displ			9+m or 5	9+m or 5		r
(Address Size Prefix Differentiates JCXZ from JECXZ)								
LOOP = Loop CX Times	11100010	8-bit displ			11+m	11+m		r
LOOPZ/LOOPE = Loop with Zero/Equal	11100001	8-bit displ			11+m	11+m		r
LOOPNZ/LOOPNE = Loop While Not Zero	11100000	8-bit displ			11+m	11+m		r
CONDITIONAL BYTE SET								
NOTE: Times Are Register/Memory								
SETO = Set Byte on Overflow								
To Register/Memory	00001111	10010000	mod 000	r/m	4/5*	4/5*		h
SETNO = Set Byte on Not Overflow								
To Register/Memory	00001111	10010001	mod 000	r/m	4/5*	4/5*		h
SETB/SETNAE = Set Byte on Below/Not Above or Equal								
To Register/Memory	00001111	10010010	mod 000	r/m	4/5*	4/5*		h

4

Table 9-1. Instruction Set Clock Count Summary (Continued)

INSTRUCTION	FORMAT			CLOCK COUNT		NOTES	
				Real Address Mode or Virtual 8086 Mode	Protected Virtual Address Mode	Real Address Mode or Virtual 8086 Mode	Protected Virtual Address Mode
CONDITIONAL BYTE SET (Continued)							
SETNB = Set Byte on Not Below/Above or Equal							
To Register/Memory	00001111	10010011	mod 000 r/m	4/5*	4/5*		h
SETE/SETZ = Set Byte on Equal/Zero							
To Register/Memory	00001111	10010100	mod 000 r/m	4/5*	4/5*		h
SETNE/SETNZ = Set Byte on Not Equal/Not Zero							
To Register/Memory	00001111	10010101	mod 000 r/m	4/5*	4/5*		h
SETBE/SETNA = Set Byte on Below or Equal/Not Above							
To Register/Memory	00001111	10010110	mod 000 r/m	4/5*	4/5*		h
SETNBE/SETA = Set Byte on Not Below or Equal/Above							
To Register/Memory	00001111	10010111	mod 000 r/m	4/5*	4/5*		h
SETS = Set Byte on Sign							
To Register/Memory	00001111	10011000	mod 000 r/m	4/5*	4/5*		h
SETNS = Set Byte on Not Sign							
To Register/Memory	00001111	10011001	mod 000 r/m	4/5*	4/5*		h
SETP/SETPE = Set Byte on Parity/Parity Even							
To Register/Memory	00001111	10011010	mod 000 r/m	4/5*	4/5*		h
SETNP/SETPO = Set Byte on Not Parity/Parity Odd							
To Register/Memory	00001111	10011011	mod 000 r/m	4/5*	4/5*		h
SETL/SETNGE = Set Byte on Less/Not Greater or Equal							
To Register/Memory	00001111	10011100	mod 000 r/m	4/5*	4/5*		h
SETNL/SETGE = Set Byte on Not Less/Greater or Equal							
To Register/Memory	00001111	01111101	mod 000 r/m	4/5*	4/5*		h
SETLE/SETNG = Set Byte on Less or Equal/Not Greater							
To Register/Memory	00001111	10011110	mod 000 r/m	4/5*	4/5*		h
SETNLE/SETG = Set Byte on Not Less or Equal/Greater							
To Register/Memory	00001111	10011111	mod 000 r/m	4/5*	4/5*		h
ENTER = Enter Procedure	11001000	16-bit displacement, 8-bit level					
L = 0				10	10	b	h
L = 1				14	14	b	h
L > 1				17 + 8(n − 1)	17 + 8(n − 1)	b	h
LEAVE = Leave Procedure	11001001			4	4	b	h

Table 9-1. Instruction Set Clock Count Summary (Continued)

INSTRUCTION	FORMAT	CLOCK COUNT: Real Address Mode or Virtual 8086 Mode	CLOCK COUNT: Protected Virtual Address Mode	NOTES: Real Address Mode or Virtual 8086 Mode	NOTES: Protected Virtual Address Mode
INTERRUPT INSTRUCTIONS					
INT = Interrupt:					
Type Specified	11001101 | type	37		b	
Type 3	11001100	33		b	
INTO = Interrupt 4 if Overflow Flag Set	11001110				
If OF = 1		35		b, e	
If OF = 0		3	3	b, e	
Bound = Interrupt 5 if Detect Value Out of Range	01100010 | mod reg r/m				
If Out of Range		44		b, e	e, g, h, j, k, r
If In Range		10	10	b, e	e, g, h, j, k, r
Protected Mode Only (INT)					
INT: Type Specified					
Via Interrupt or Trap Gate					
Via Interrupt or Trap Gate to Same Privilege Level			71		g, j, k, r
to Different Privilege Level			111		g, j, k, r
From 286 Task to 286 TSS via Task Gate			438		g, j, k, r
From 286 Task to Intel386™ SX CPU TSS via Task Gate			465		g, j, k, r
From 286 Task to virt 8086 md via Task Gate			382		g, j, k, r
From Intel386™ SX CPU Task to 286 TSS via Task Gate			440		g, j, k, r
From Intel386™ SX CPU Task to Intel386™ SX CPU TSS via Task Gate			467		g, j, k, r
From Intel386™ SX CPU Task to virt 8086 md via Task Gate			384		g, j, k, r
From virt 8086 md to 286 TSS via Task Gate			445		g, j, k, r
From virt 8086 md to Intel386™ SX CPU TSS via Task Gate			472		g, j, k, r
From virt 8086 md to priv level 0 via Trap Gate or Interrupt Gate			275		
INT: TYPE 3					
Via Interrupt or Trap Gate to Same Privilege Level			71		g, j, k, r
Via Interrupt or Trap Gate to Different Privilege Level			111		g, j, k, r
From 286 Task to 286 TSS via Task Gate			382		g, j, k, r
From 286 Task to Intel386™ SX CPU TSS via Task Gate			409		g, j, k, r
From 286 Task to Virt 8086 md via Task Gate			326		g, j, k, r
From Intel386™ SX CPU Task to 286 TSS via Task Gate			384		g, j, k, r
From Intel386™ SX CPU Task to Intel386™ SX CPU TSS via Task Gate			411		g, j, k, r
From Intel386™ SX CPU Task to Virt 8086 md via Task Gate			328		g, j, k, r
From virt 8086 md to 286 TSS via Task Gate			389		g, j, k, r
From virt 8086 md to Intel386™ SX CPU TSS via Task Gate			416		g, j, k, r
From virt 8086 md to priv level 0 via Trap Gate or Interrupt Gate			223		
INTO:					
Via Interrupt or Trap Grate to Same Privilege Level			71		g, j, k, r
Via Interrupt or Trap Gate to Different Privilege Level			111		g, j, k, r
From 286 Task to 286 TSS via Task Gate			384		g, j, k, r
From 286 Task to Intel386™ SX CPU TSS via Task Gate			411		g, j, k, r
From 286 Task to virt 8086 md via Task Gate			328		g, j, k, r
From Intel386™ SX CPU Task to 286 TSS via Task Gate			Intel386 DX		g, j, k, r
From Intel386™ SX CPU Task to Intel386™ SX CPU TSS via Task Gate			413		g, j, k, r
From Intel386™ SX CPU Task to virt 8086 md via Task Gate			329		g, j, k, r
From virt 8086 md to 286 TSS via Task Gate			391		g, j, k, r
From virt 8086 md to Intel386™ SX CPU TSS via Task Gate			418		g, j, k, r
From virt 8086 md to priv level 0 via Trap Gate or Interrupt Gate			223		

Table 9-1. Instruction Set Clock Count Summary (Continued)

INSTRUCTION	FORMAT			CLOCK COUNT: Real Address Mode or Virtual 8086 Mode	CLOCK COUNT: Protected Virtual Address Mode	NOTES: Real Address Mode or Virtual 8086 Mode	NOTES: Protected Virtual Address Mode
INTERRUPT INSTRUCTIONS (Continued)							
BOUND:							
Via Interrupt or Trap Gate to Same Privilege Level					71		g, j, k, r
Via Interrupt or Trap Gate to Different Privilege Level					111		g, j, k, r
From 286 Task to 286 TSS via Task Gate					358		g, j, k, r
From 286 Task to Intel386™ SX CPU TSS via Task Gate					388		g, j, k, r
From 268 Task to virt 8086 Mode via Task Gate					335		g, j, k, r
From Intel386 SX CPU Task to 286 TSS via Task Gate					368		g, j, k, r
From Intel386 SX CPU Task to Intel386 SX CPU TSS via Task Gate					398		g, j, k, r
From Intel386 SX CPU Task to virt 8086 Mode via Task Gate					347		g, j, k, r,
From virt 8086 Mode to 286 TSS via Task Gate					368		g, j, k, r
From virt 8086 Mode to Intel386 SX CPU TSS via Task Gate					398		g, j, k, r
From virt 8086 md to priv level 0 via Trap Gate or Interrupt Gate					223		
INTERRUPT RETURN							
IRET = Interrupt Return	11001111			24			g, h, j, k, r
Protected Mode Only (IRET)							
To the Same Privilege Level (within task)					42		g, h, j, k, r
To Different Privilege Level (within task)					86		g, h, j, k, r
From 286 Task to 286 TSS					285		h, j, k, r
From 286 Task to Intel386 SX CPU TSS					318		h, j, k, r
From 286 Task to Virtual 8086 Task					267		h, j, k, r
From 286 Task to Virtual 8086 Mode (within task)					113		
From Intel386 SX CPU Task to 286 TSS					324		h, j, k, r
From Intel386 SX CPU Task to Intel386 SX CPU TSS					328		h, j, k, r
From Intel386 SX CPU Task to Virtual 8086 Task					377		h, j, k, r
From Intel386 SX CPU Task to Virtual 8086 Mode (within task)					113		
PROCESSOR CONTROL							
HLT = HALT	11110100			5	5		l
MOV = Move to and From Control/Debug/Test Registers							
CR0/CR2/CR3 from register	00001111	00100010	1 1 eee reg	10/4/5	10/4/5		l
Register From CR0–3	00001111	00100000	1 1 eee reg	6	6		l
DR0–3 From Register	00001111	00100011	1 1 eee reg	22	22		l
DR6–7 From Register	00001111	00100011	1 1 eee reg	16	16		l
Register from DR6–7	00001111	00100001	1 1 eee reg	14	14		l
Register from DR0–3	00001111	00100001	1 1 eee reg	22	22		l
TR6–7 from Register	00001111	00100110	1 1 eee reg	12	12		l
Register from TR6–7	00001111	00100100	1 1 eee reg	12	12		l
NOP = No Operation	10010000			3	3		
WAIT = Wait until BUSY# pin is negated	10011011			6	6		

Table 9-1. Instruction Set Clock Count Summary (Continued)

INSTRUCTION	FORMAT			CLOCK COUNT: Real Address Mode or Virtual 8086 Mode	CLOCK COUNT: Protected Virtual Address Mode	NOTES: Real Address Mode or Virtual 8086 Mode	NOTES: Protected Virtual Address Mode
PROCESSOR EXTENSION INSTRUCTIONS							
Processor Extension Escape	11011TTT	mod LLL r/m		See Intel387SX data sheet for clock counts			h
	TTT and LLL bits are opcode information for coprocessor.						
PREFIX BYTES							
Address Size Prefix	01100111			0	0		
LOCK = Bus Lock Prefix	11110000			0	0		m
Operand Size Prefix	01100110			0	0		
Segment Override Prefix							
CS:	00101110			0	0		
DS:	00111110			0	0		
ES:	00100110			0	0		
FS:	01100100			0	0		
GS:	01100101			0	0		
SS:	00110110			0	0		
PROTECTION CONTROL							
ARPL = Adjust Requested Privilege Level							
From Register/Memory	01100011	mod reg r/m		N/A	20/21**	a	h
LAR = Load Access Rights							
From Register/Memory	00001111	00000010	mod reg r/m	N/A	15/16*	a	g, h, j, p
LGDT = Load Global Descriptor							
Table Register	00001111	00000001	mod 010 r/m	11*	11*	b, c	h, l
LIDT = Load Interrupt Descriptor							
Table Register	00001111	00000001	mod 011 r/m	11*	11*	b, c	h, l
LLDT = Load Local Descriptor							
Table Register to Register/Memory	00001111	00000000	mod 010 r/m	N/A	20/24*	a	g, h, j, l
LMSW = Load Machine Status Word							
From Register/Memory	00001111	00000001	mod 110 r/m	10/13	10/13*	b, c	h, l
LSL = Load Segment Limit							
From Register/Memory	00001111	00000011	mod reg r/m				
Byte-Granular Limit				N/A	20/21*	a	g, h, j, p
Page-Granular Limit				N/A	25/26*	a	g, h, j, p
LTR = Load Task Register							
From Register/Memory	00001111	00000000	mod 001 r/m	N/A	23/27*	a	g, h, j, l
SGDT = Store Global Descriptor							
Table Register	00001111	00000001	mod 000 r/m	9*	9*	b, c	h
SIDT = Store Interrupt Descriptor							
Table Register	00001111	00000001	mod 001 r/m	9*	9*	b, c	h
SLDT = Store Local Descriptor Table Register							
To Register/Memory	00001111	00000000	mod 000 r/m	N/A	2/2*	a	h

4

Table 9-1. Instruction Set Clock Count Summary (Continued)

INSTRUCTION		FORMAT			CLOCK COUNT		NOTES	
					Real Address Mode or Virtual 8086 Mode	Protected Virtual Address Mode	Real Address Mode or Virtual 8086 Mode	Protected Virtual Address Mode
PROTECTION CONTROL (Continued)								
SMSW	**= Store Machine Status Word**	00001111	00000001	mod 100 r/m	2/2*	2/2*	b, c	h, l
STR	**= Store Task Register**							
	To Register/Memory	00001111	00000000	mod 001 r/m	N/A	2/2*	a	h
VERR	**= Verify Read Access**							
	Register/Memory	00001111	00000000	mod 100 r/m	N/A	10/11*	a	g, h, j, p
VERW	**= Verify Write Access**	00001111	00000000	mod 101 r/m	N/A	15/16*	a	g, h, j, p

INSTRUCTION NOTES FOR TABLE 9-1

Notes a through c apply to Real Address Mode only:

a. This is a Protected Mode instruction. Attempted execution in Real Mode will result in exception 6 (invalid opcode).

b. Exception 13 fault (general protection) will occur in Real Mode if an operand reference is made that partially or fully extends beyond the maximum CS, DS, ES, FS or GS limit, FFFFH. Exception 12 fault (stack segment limit violation or not present) will occur in Real Mode if an operand reference is made that partially or fully extends beyond the maximum SS limit.

c. This instruction may be executed in Real Mode. In Real Mode, its purpose is primarily to initialize the CPU for Protected Mode.

Notes d through g apply to Real Address Mode and Protected Virtual Address Mode:

d. The Intel386 SX CPU uses an early-out multiply algorithm. The actual number of clocks depends on the position of the most significant bit in the operand (multiplier).

Clock counts given are minimum to maximum. To calculate actual clocks use the following formula:

Actual Clock = if $m <> 0$ then max ($[\log_2 |m|]$, 3) + b clocks:

if $m = 0$ then $3 + b$ clocks

In this formula, m is the multiplier, and

$b = 9$ for register to register,

$b = 12$ for memory to register,

$b = 10$ for register with immediate to register,

$b = 11$ for memory with immediate to register.

e. An exception may occur, depending on the value of the operand.

f. LOCK# is automatically asserted, regardless of the presence or absence of the LOCK# prefix.

g. LOCK# is asserted during descriptor table accesses.

Notes h through r apply to Protected Virtual Address Mode only:

h. Exception 13 fault (general protection violation) will occur if the memory operand in CS, DS, ES, FS or GS cannot be used due to either a segment limit violation or access rights violation. If a stack limit is violated, an exception 12 (stack segment limit violation or not present) occurs.

i. For segment load operations, the CPL, RPL, and DPL must agree with the privilege rules to avoid an exception 13 fault (general protection violation). The segment's descriptor must indicate "present" or exception 11 (CS, DS, ES, FS, GS not present). If the SS register is loaded and a stack segment not present is detected, an exception 12 (stack segment limit violation or not present) occurs.

j. All segment descriptor accesses in the GDT or LDT made by this instruction will automatically assert LOCK# to maintain descriptor integrity in multiprocessor systems.

k. JMP, CALL, INT, RET and IRET instructions referring to another code segment will cause an exception 13 (general protection violation) if an applicable privilege rule is violated.

l. An exception 13 fault occurs if CPL is greater than 0 (0 is the most privileged level).

m. An exception 13 fault occurs if CPL is greater than IOPL.

n. The IF bit of the flag register is not updated if CPL is greater than IOPL. The IOPL and VM fields of the flag register are updated only if CPL = 0.

o. The PE bit of the MSW (CR0) cannot be reset by this instruction. Use MOV into CR0 if desiring to reset the PE bit.

p. Any violation of privilege rules as applied to the selector operand does not cause a protection exception; rather, the zero flag is cleared.

q. If the coprocessor's memory operand violates a segment limit or segment access rights, an exception 13 fault (general protection exception) will occur before the ESC instruction is executed. An exception 12 fault (stack segment limit violation or not present) will occur if the stack limit is violated by the operand's starting address.

r. The destination of a JMP, CALL, INT, RET or IRET must be in the defined limit of a code segment or an exception 13 fault (general protection violation) will occur.

s/t. The instruction will execute in s clocks if CPL ≤ IOPL. If CPL > IOPL, the instruction will take t clocks.

9.2 INSTRUCTION ENCODING

9.2.1 Overview

All instruction encodings are subsets of the general instruction format shown in Figure 8-1. Instructions consist of one or two primary opcode bytes, possibly an address specifier consisting of the "mod r/m" byte and "scaled index" byte, a displacement if required, and an immediate data field if required.

Within the primary opcode or opcodes, smaller encoding fields may be defined. These fields vary according to the class of operation. The fields define such information as direction of the operation, size of the displacements, register encoding, or sign extension.

Almost all instructions referring to an operand in memory have an addressing mode byte following the primary opcode byte(s). This byte, the mod r/m byte, specifies the address mode to be used. Certain encodings of the mod r/m byte indicate a second addressing byte, the scale-index-base byte, follows the mod r/m byte to fully specify the addressing mode.

Addressing modes can include a displacement immediately following the mod r/m byte, or scaled index byte. If a displacement is present, the possible sizes are 8, 16 or 32 bits.

If the instruction specifies an immediate operand, the immediate operand follows any displacement bytes. The immediate operand, if specified, is always the last field of the instruction.

Figure 9-1 illustrates several of the fields that can appear in an instruction, such as the mod field and the r/m field, but the Figure does not show all fields. Several smaller fields also appear in certain instructions, sometimes within the opcode bytes themselves. Table 9-2 is a complete list of all fields appearing in the instruction set. Further ahead, following Table 9-2, are detailed tables for each field.

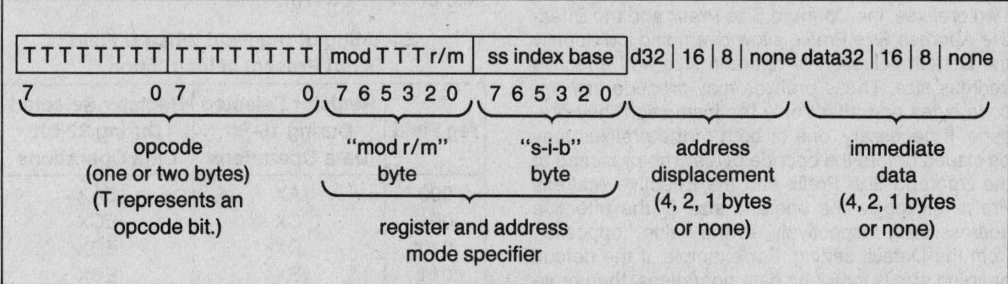

Figure 9-1. General Instruction Format

Table 9-2. Fields within Instructions

Field Name	Description	Number of Bits
w	Specifies if Data is Byte or Full Size (Full Size is either 16 or 32 Bits	1
d	Specifies Direction of Data Operation	1
s	Specifies if an Immediate Data Field Must be Sign-Extended	1
reg	General Register Specifier	3
mod r/m	Address Mode Specifier (Effective Address can be a General Register)	2 for mod; 3 for r/m
ss	Scale Factor for Scaled Index Address Mode	2
index	General Register to be used as Index Register	3
base	General Register to be used as Base Register	3
sreg2	Segment Register Specifier for CS, SS, DS, ES	2
sreg3	Segment Register Specifier for CS, SS, DS, ES, FS, GS	3
tttn	For Conditional Instructions, Specifies a Condition Asserted or a Condition Negated	4

Note: Table 9-1 shows encoding of individual instructions.

9.2.2 32-Bit Extensions of the Instruction Set

With the Intel386 SX CPU, the 8086/80186/80286 instruction set is extended in two orthogonal directions: 32-bit forms of all 16-bit instructions are added to support the 32-bit data types, and 32-bit addressing modes are made available for all instructions referencing memory. This orthogonal instruction set extension is accomplished having a Default (D) bit in the code segment descriptor, and by having 2 prefixes to the instruction set.

Whether the instruction defaults to operations of 16 bits or 32 bits depends on the setting of the D bit in the code segment descriptor, which gives the default length (either 32 bits or 16 bits) for both operands and effective addresses when executing that code segment. In the Real Address Mode or Virtual 8086 Mode, no code segment descriptors are used, but a D value of 0 is assumed internally by the Intel386 SX CPU when operating in those modes (for 16-bit default sizes compatible with the 8086/80186/80286).

Two prefixes, the Operand Size Prefix and the Effective Address Size Prefix, allow overriding individually the Default selection of operand size and effective address size. These prefixes may precede any opcode bytes and affect only the instruction they precede. If necessary, one or both of the prefixes may be placed before the opcode bytes. The presence of the Operand Size Prefix and the Effective Address Prefix will toggle the operand size or the effective address size, respectively, to the value "opposite" from the Default setting. For example, if the default operand size is for 32-bit data operations, then presence of the Operand Size Prefix toggles the instruction to 16-bit data operation. As another example, if the default effective address size is 16 bits, presence of the Effective Address Size prefix toggles the instruction to use 32-bit effective address computations.

These 32-bit extensions are available in all modes, including the Real Address Mode or the Virtual 8086 Mode. In these modes the default is always 16 bits, so prefixes are needed to specify 32-bit operands or addresses. For instructions with more than one prefix, the order of prefixes is unimportant.

Unless specified otherwise, instructions with 8-bit and 16-bit operands do not affect the contents of the high-order bits of the extended registers.

9.2.3 Encoding of Instruction Fields

Within the instruction are several fields indicating register selection, addressing mode and so on. The exact encodings of these fields are defined immediately ahead.

9.2.3.1 ENCODING OF OPERAND LENGTH (w) FIELD

For any given instruction performing a data operation, the instruction is executing as a 32-bit operation or a 16-bit operation. Within the constraints of the operation size, the w field encodes the operand size as either one byte or the full operation size, as shown in the table below.

w Field	Operand Size During 16-Bit Data Operations	Operand Size During 32-Bit Data Operations
0	8 Bits	8 Bits
1	16 Bits	32 Bits

9.2.3.2 ENCODING OF THE GENERAL REGISTER (reg) FIELD

The general register is specified by the reg field, which may appear in the primary opcode bytes, or as the reg field of the "mod r/m" byte, or as the r/m field of the "mod r/m" byte.

Encoding of reg Field When w Field is not Present in Instruction

reg Field	Register Selected During 16-Bit Data Operations	Register Selected During 32-Bit Data Operations
000	AX	EAX
001	CX	ECX
010	DX	EDX
011	BX	EBX
100	SP	ESP
101	BP	EBP
101	SI	ESI
101	DI	EDI

Encoding of reg Field When w Field is Present in Instruction

Register Specified by reg Field During 16-Bit Data Operations:		
reg	Function of w Field	
	(when w = 0)	(when w = 1)
000	AL	AX
001	CL	CX
010	DL	DX
011	BL	BX
100	AH	SP
101	CH	BP
110	DH	SI
111	BH	DI

Register Specified by reg Field During 32-Bit Data Operations		
reg	Function of w Field	
	(when w = 0)	(when w = 1)
000	AL	EAX
001	CL	ECX
010	DL	EDX
011	BL	EBX
100	AH	ESP
101	CH	EBP
110	DH	ESI
111	BH	EDI

9.2.3.3 ENCODING OF THE SEGMENT REGISTER (sreg) FIELD

The sreg field in certain instructions is a 2-bit field allowing one of the four 80286 segment registers to be specified. The sreg field in other instructions is a 3-bit field, allowing the Intel386 SX CPU FS and GS segment registers to be specified.

2-Bit sreg2 Field

2-Bit sreg2 Field	Segment Register Selected
00	ES
01	CS
10	SS
11	DS

3-Bit sreg3 Field

3-Bit sreg3 Field	Segment Register Selected
000	ES
001	CS
010	SS
011	DS
100	FS
101	GS
110	do not use
111	do not use

9.2.3.4 ENCODING OF ADDRESS MODE

Except for special instructions, such as PUSH or POP, where the addressing mode is pre-determined, the addressing mode for the current instruction is specified by addressing bytes following the primary opcode. The primary addressing byte is the "mod r/m" byte, and a second byte of addressing information, the "s-i-b" (scale-index-base) byte, can be specified.

The s-i-b byte (scale-index-base byte) is specified when using 32-bit addressing mode and the "mod r/m" byte has r/m = 100 and mod = 00, 01 or 10. When the sib byte is present, the 32-bit addressing mode is a function of the mod, ss, index, and base fields.

The primary addressing byte, the "mod r/m" byte, also contains three bits (shown as TTT in Figure 8-1) sometimes used as an extension of the primary opcode. The three bits, however, may also be used as a register field (reg).

When calculating an effective address, either 16-bit addressing or 32-bit addressing is used. 16-bit addressing uses 16-bit address components to calculate the effective address while 32-bit addressing uses 32-bit address components to calculate the effective address. When 16-bit addressing is used, the "mod r/m" byte is interpreted as a 16-bit addressing mode specifier. When 32-bit addressing is used, the "mod r/m" byte is interpreted as a 32-bit addressing mode specifier.

Tables on the following three pages define all encodings of all 16-bit addressing modes and 32-bit addressing modes.

Encoding of 16-bit Address Mode with "mod r/m" Byte

mod r/m	Effective Address
00 000	DS:[BX+SI]
00 001	DS:[BX+DI]
00 010	SS:[BP+SI]
00 011	SS:[BP+DI]
00 100	DS:[SI]
00 101	DS:[DI]
00 110	DS:d16
00 111	DS:[BX]
01 000	DS:[BX+SI+d8]
01 001	DS:[BX+DI+d8]
01 010	SS:[BP+SI+d8]
01 011	SS:[BP+DI+d8]
01 100	DS:[SI+d8]
01 101	DS:[DI+d8]
01 110	SS:[BP+d8]
01 111	DS:[BX+d8]

mod r/m	Effective Address
10 000	DS:[BX+SI+d16]
10 001	DS:[BX+DI+d16]
10 010	SS:[BP+SI+d16]
10 011	SS:[BP+DI+d16]
10 100	DS:[SI+d16]
10 101	DS:[DI+d16]
10 110	SS:[BP+d16]
10 111	DS:[BX+d16]
11 000	register—see below
11 001	register—see below
11 010	register—see below
11 011	register—see below
11 100	register—see below
11 101	register—see below
11 110	register—see below
11 111	register—see below

Register Specified by r/m During 16-Bit Data Operations

mod r/m	Function of w Field	
	(when w=0)	(when w=1)
11 000	AL	AX
11 001	CL	CX
11 010	DL	DX
11 011	BL	BX
11 100	AH	SP
11 101	CH	BP
11 110	DH	SI
11 111	BH	DI

Register Specified by r/m During 32-Bit Data Operations

mod r/m	Function of w Field	
	(when w=0)	(when w=1)
11 000	AL	EAX
11 001	CL	ECX
11 010	DL	EDX
11 011	BL	EBX
11 100	AH	ESP
11 101	CH	EBP
11 110	DH	ESI
11 111	BH	EDI

Encoding of 32-bit Address Mode with "mod r/m" byte (no "s-i-b" byte present):

mod r/m	Effective Address
00 000	DS:[EAX]
00 001	DS:[ECX]
00 010	DS:[EDX]
00 011	DS:[EBX]
00 100	s-i-b is present
00 101	DS:d32
00 110	DS:[ESI]
00 111	DS:[EDI]
01 000	DS:[EAX+d8]
01 001	DS:[ECX+d8]
01 010	DS:[EDX+d8]
01 011	DS:[EBX+d8]
01 100	s-i-b is present
01 101	SS:[EBP+d8]
01 110	DS:[ESI+d8]
01 111	DS:[EDI+d8]

mod r/m	Effective Address
10 000	DS:[EAX+d32]
10 001	DS:[ECX+d32]
10 010	DS:[EDX+d32]
10 011	DS:[EBX+d32]
10 100	s-i-b is present
10 101	SS:[EBP+d32]
10 110	DS:[ESI+d32]
10 111	DS:[EDI+d32]
11 000	register—see below
11 001	register—see below
11 010	register—see below
11 011	register—see below
11 100	register—see below
11 101	register—see below
11 110	register—see below
11 111	register—see below

Register Specified by reg or r/m during 16-Bit Data Operations:

mod r/m	function of w field	
	(when w=0)	(when w=1)
11 000	AL	AX
11 001	CL	CX
11 010	DL	DX
11 011	BL	BX
11 100	AH	SP
11 101	CH	BP
11 110	DH	SI
11 111	BH	DI

Register Specified by reg or r/m during 32-Bit Data Operations:

mod r/m	function of w field	
	(when w=0)	(when w=1)
11 000	AL	EAX
11 001	CL	ECX
11 010	DL	EDX
11 011	BL	EBX
11 100	AH	ESP
11 101	CH	EBP
11 110	DH	ESI
11 111	BH	EDI

4

Encoding of 32-bit Address Mode ("mod r/m" byte and "s-i-b" byte present):

mod base	Effective Address
00 000	DS:[EAX + (scaled index)]
00 001	DS:[ECX + (scaled index)]
00 010	DS:[EDX + (scaled index)]
00 011	DS:[EBX + (scaled index)]
00 100	SS:[ESP + (scaled index)]
00 101	DS:[d32 + (scaled index)]
00 110	DS:[ESI + (scaled index)]
00 111	DS:[EDI + (scaled index)]
01 000	DS:[EAX + (scaled index) + d8]
01 001	DS:[ECX + (scaled index) + d8]
01 010	DS:[EDX + (scaled index) + d8]
01 011	DS:[EBX + (scaled index) + d8]
01 100	SS:[ESP + (scaled index) + d8]
01 101	SS:[EBP + (scaled index) + d8]
01 110	DS:[ESI + (scaled index) + d8]
01 111	DS:[EDI + (scaled index) + d8]
10 000	DS:[EAX + (scaled index) + d32]
10 001	DS:[ECX + (scaled index) + d32]
10 010	DS:[EDX + (scaled index) + d32]
10 011	DS:[EBX + (scaled index) + d32]
10 100	SS:[ESP + (scaled index) + d32]
10 101	SS:[EBP + (scaled index) + d32]
10 110	DS:[ESI + (scaled index) + d32]
10 111	DS:[EDI + (scaled index) + d32]

NOTE:
Mod field in "mod r/m" byte; ss, index, base fields in "s-i-b" byte.

ss	Scale Factor
00	x1
01	x2
10	x4
11	x8

index	Index Register
000	EAX
001	ECX
010	EDX
011	EBX
100	no index reg**
101	EBP
110	ESI
111	EDI

****IMPORTANT NOTE:**
When index field is 100, indicating "no index register," then ss field MUST equal 00. If index is 100 and ss does not equal 00, the effective address is undefined.

9.2.3.5 ENCODING OF OPERATION DIRECTION (d) FIELD

In many two-operand instructions the d field is present to indicate which operand is considered the source and which is the destination.

d	Direction of Operation
0	Register/Memory <-- Register "reg" Field Indicates Source Operand; "mod r/m" or "mod ss index base" Indicates Destination Operand
1	Register <-- Register/Memory "reg" Field Indicates Destination Operand; "mod r/m" or "mod ss index base" Indicates Source Operand

9.2.3.6 ENCODING OF SIGN-EXTEND (s) FIELD

The s field occurs primarily to instructions with immediate data fields. The s field has an effect only if the size of the immediate data is 8 bits and is being placed in a 16-bit or 32-bit destination.

s	Effect on Immediate Data8	Effect on Immediate Data 16|32
0	None	None
1	Sign-Extend Data8 to Fill 16-Bit or 32-Bit Destination	None

9.2.3.7 ENCODING OF CONDITIONAL TEST (tttn) FIELD

For the conditional instructions (conditional jumps and set on condition), tttn is encoded with n indicating to use the condition (n = 0) or its negation (n = 1), and ttt giving the condition to test.

Mnemonic	Condition	tttn
O	Overflow	0000
NO	No Overflow	0001
B/NAE	Below/Not Above or Equal	0010
NB/AE	Not Below/Above or Equal	0011
E/Z	Equal/Zero	0100
NE/NZ	Not Equal/Not Zero	0101
BE/NA	Below or Equal/Not Above	0110
NBE/A	Not Below or Equal/Above	0111
S	Sign	1000
NS	Not Sign	1001
P/PE	Parity/Parity Even	1010
NP/PO	Not Parity/Parity Odd	1011
L/NGE	Less Than/Not Greater or Equal	1100
NL/GE	Not Less Than/Greater or Equal	1101
LE/NG	Less Than or Equal/Greater Than	1110
NLE/G	Not Less or Equal/Greater Than	1111

9.2.3.8 ENCODING OF CONTROL OR DEBUG OR TEST REGISTER (eee) FIELD

For the loading and storing of the Control, Debug and Test registers.

When Interpreted as Control Register Field

eee Code	Reg Name
000	CR0
010	CR2
011	CR3
Do not use any other encoding	

When Interpreted as Debug Register Field

eee Code	Reg Name
000	DR0
001	DR1
010	DR2
011	DR3
110	DR6
111	DR7
Do not use any other encoding	

When Interpreted as Test Register Field

eee Code	Reg Name
110	TR6
111	TR7
Do not use any other encoding	

DATA SHEET REVISION REVIEW

The following list represents key differences between this and the -002 version of the Intel386™ SX microprocessor data sheet. Please review the summary carefully.

1. Removed CHMOS III in the features summary regarding High Speed CHMOS technology.
2. Table 5.7, D-Step revision identifier is added.
3. Table 7.3, I_{CC} supply current for CLK2 = 40 MHz with 20 MHz Intel386 SX has a typical I_{CC} of 200 mA.
4. Table 7.5, t_4 CLK2 fall time and t_5 CLK2 rise time have no minimum time for all speeds but maximum time for all speeds is 8 ns.
5. Figure 7.11, CHMOS III characteristics for typical I_{CC} has been taken out.

intel®

Intel387™ SX MATH COPROCESSOR

- Interfaces with Intel386™ SX and Intel386 SL Microprocessors
- Expands Intel386 SX CPU Data Types to Include 32-, 64-, 80-Bit Floating Point, 32-, 64-Bit Integers and 18-Digit BCD Operands
- High Performance 80-Bit Internal Architecture
- Two to Three Times 8087/80287 Performance at Equivalent Clock Speed
- Implements ANSI/IEEE Standard 754-1985 for Binary Floating-Point Arithmetic
- Fully compatible with the Intel387™ Math CoProcessor. Implements all Intel387 MCP architectural enhancements over 8087 and 80287
- Upward Object-Code Compatible from 8087 and 80287
- Directly Extends Intel386 SX CPU Instruction Set to Trigonometric, Logarithmic, Exponential, and Arithmetic Instructions for All Data Types
- Full-Range Transcendental Operations for SINE, COSINE, TANGENT, ARCTANGENT, and LOGARITHM
- Operates Independently of Real, Protected, and Virtual-8086 Modes of the Intel386 SX Microprocessor
- Eight 80-Bit Numeric Registers, Usable as Individually Addressable General Registers or as a Register Stack
- Available in a 68-pin PLCC Package (see Packaging Specs: Order #231369)

The Intel387 SX Math CoProcessor is an extension to the Intel386 microprocessor architecture. The combination of the Intel387 SX with the Intel386 SX or the Intel386 SL microprocessor dramatically increases the processing speed of computer application software which utilizes mathematical operations. This makes an ideal computer workstation platform for applications such as financial modeling and spreadsheets, CAD/CAM, or graphics.

The Intel387 SX Math CoProcessor adds over seventy mnemonics to the Intel386 SX microprocessor instruction set. Specific Intel387 SX math operations include logarithmic, arithmetic, exponential, and trigonometric functions. The Intel387 SX supports integer, extended integer, floating point and BCD data formats, and fully conforms to the ANSI/IEEE floating point standard.

The Intel387 SX Math CoProcessor is object code compatible with the Intel387 DX and upward object code compatible from the 80287 and 8087 Math CoProcessors. The Intel387 SX is manufactured with Intel's CHMOS III technology and packaged in a 68-pin PLCC package. A low power consumption option allows use in laptop or notebook applications with the Intel386 SL microprocessor.

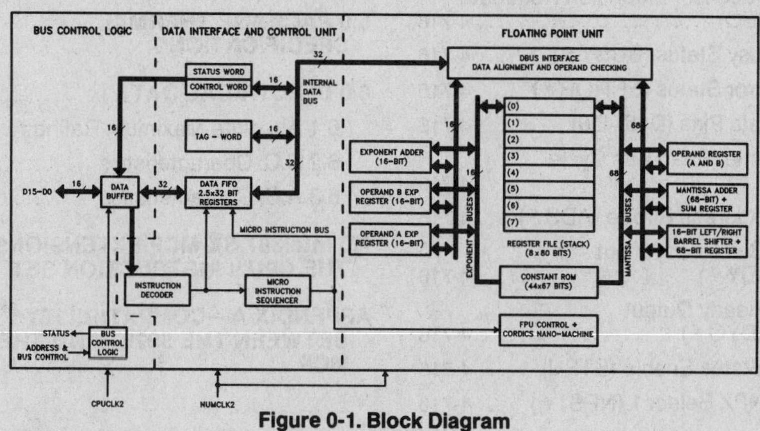

Figure 0-1. Block Diagram

October 1991
Order Number: 240225-008

Intel387™ SX Math CoProcessor

CONTENTS PAGE

CONTENTS PAGE

CONTENTS PAGE

FIGURES

CONTENTS PAGE

TABLES

4

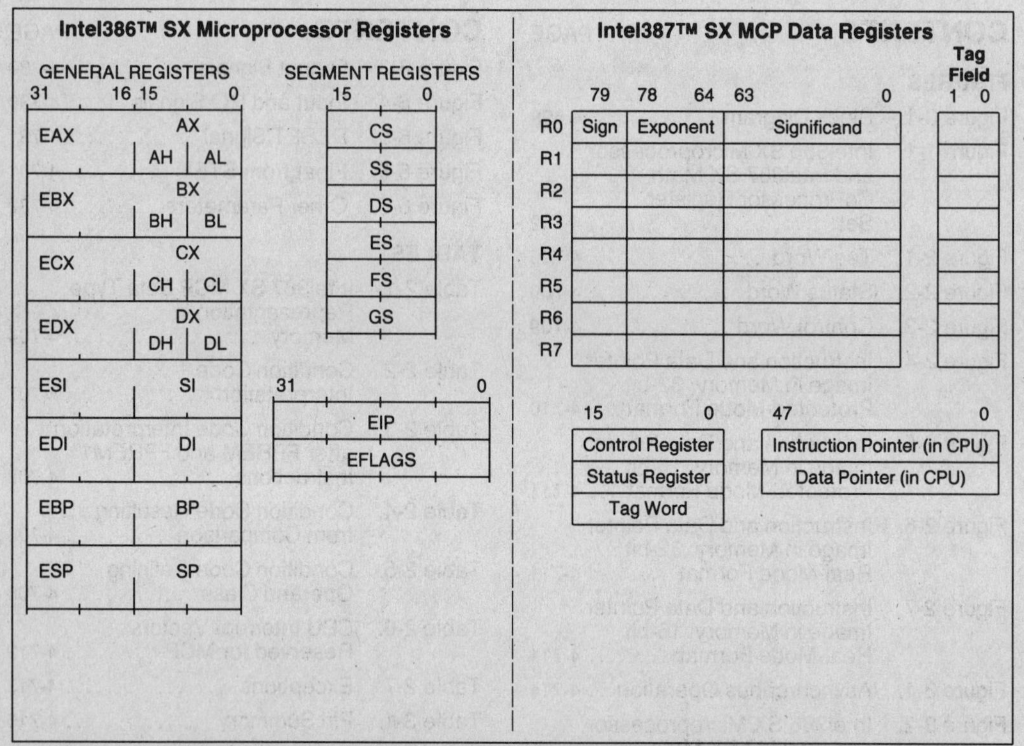

Intel386™ SX Microprocessor Registers

GENERAL REGISTERS (bits 31, 16 15, 0)

EAX — AX — AH | AL
EBX — BX — BH | BL
ECX — CX — CH | CL
EDX — DX — DH | DL
ESI — SI
EDI — DI
EBP — BP
ESP — SP

SEGMENT REGISTERS (bits 15, 0)

CS
SS
DS
ES
FS
GS

(bits 31, 0)

EIP
EFLAGS

Intel387™ SX MCP Data Registers

	Sign (79)	Exponent (78–64)	Significand (63–0)	Tag Field (1 0)
R0				
R1				
R2				
R3				
R4				
R5				
R6				
R7				

(bits 15, 0)

Control Register
Status Register
Tag Word

(bits 47, 0)

Instruction Pointer (in CPU)
Data Pointer (in CPU)

Figure 1-1. Intel386™ SX Microprocessor and Intel387™ SX Math CoProcessor Register Set

1.0 FUNCTIONAL DESCRIPTION

The Intel387 SX Math CoProcessor (MCP) provides arithmetic instructions for a variety of numeric data types. It also executes numerous built-in transcendental functions (e.g. tangent, sine, cosine, and log functions). The Intel387 SX MCP effectively extends the register and instruction set of its CPU for existing data types and adds several new data types as well. Figure 1-1 shows the model of registers visible to Intel386 SX Microprocessor and Intel387 SX Math CoProcessor applications programs. Essentially, the Intel387 SX Math CoProcessor can be treated as an additional resource or an extension to the Intel386 SX Microprocessor. The Intel386 SX Microprocessor together with a Intel387 SX MCP can be used as a single unified system, the Intel386 SX Microprocessor and Intel387 SX Math CoProcessor.

The Intel387 SX Math CoProcessor works the same whether the CPU is executing in real-address mode, protected mode, or virtual-8086 mode. All references to memory for numerics data or status information are performed by the CPU, and therefore obey the memory-management and protection rules of the CPU mode currently in effect. The Intel387 SX Math CoProcessor merely operates on instructions and values passed to it by the CPU and therefore is not sensitive to the processing mode of the CPU.

In real-address mode and virtual-8086 mode, the Intel386 SX Microprocessor and Intel387 SX Math CoProcessor are completely upward compatible with software for the 8086/8087 and 80286/80287 real-address mode systems.

In protected mode, the Intel386 SX Microprocessor and Intel387 SX Math CoProcessor are completely upward compatible with software for the 80286/80287 protected mode system.

In all modes, the Intel386 SX Microprocessor and Intel387 SX Math CoProcessor are completely compatible with software for the Intel386 Microprocessor/Intel387 Math CoProcessor system.

The only differences of operation that may appear when 8086/8087 programs are ported to the protected-mode Intel386 SX Microprocessor and Intel387 SX Math CoProcessor system (*not* using virtual-8086 mode) is in the format of operands for the administrative instructions FLDENV, FSTENV, FRSTOR, and FSAVE. These instructions are normally used only by exception handlers and operating systems, not by applications programs.

2.0 PROGRAMMING INTERFACE

The Intel387 SX MCP adds to an Intel386 SX Microprocessor system additional data types, registers, instructions, and interrupts specifically designed to facilitate high-speed numerics processing. To use the Intel387 SX MCP requires no special programming tools, because all new instructions and data types are directly supported by the assembler and compilers for high-level languages. All Intel386 Microprocessor development tools that support Intel387 MCP programs can also be used to develop software for the Intel386 SX Microprocessor and the Intel387 SX Math CoProcessor. All 8086/8088 development tools that support the 8087 can also be used to develop software for the Intel386 SX Microprocessor and the Intel387 SX Math CoProcessor in real-address mode or virtual-8086 mode. All 80286 development tools that support the 80287 can also be used to develop software for the Intel386 SX Microprocessor and the Intel387 SX Math CoProcessor.

The Intel387 SX MCP supports all Intel387 MCP instructions. The Intel386 SX Microprocessor and Intel387 SX Math CoProcessor support all the same programs and give the same results as an Intel386 Microprocessor and an Intel387 Math CoProcessor.

All communication between the CPU and the MCP is transparent to applications software. The CPU automatically controls the MCP whenever a numerics instruction is executed. All physical memory and virtual memory of the CPU are available for storage of the instructions and operands of programs that use the MCP. All memory addressing modes, including use of displacement, base register, index register, and scaling, are available for addressing numerics operands.

Section 7 at the end of this data sheet lists by class the instructions that the Intel387 SX MCP adds to the instruction set of an Intel386 SX Microprocessor system.

2.1 Data Types

Table 2-1 lists the seven data types that the MCP supports and presents the format for each type. Operands are stored in memory with the least significant digit at the lowest memory address. Programs retrieve these values by generating the lowest address. For maximum system performance, all operands should start at physical-memory addresses that correspond to the word size of the CPU; operands may begin at any other addresses, but will require extra memory cycles to access the entire operand.

Internally, the MCP holds all numbers in the extended-precision real format. Instructions that load operands from memory automatically convert operands represented in memory as 16-, 32-, or 64-bit integers, 32- or 64-bit floating-point numbers, or 18-digit packed BCD numbers into extended-precision real format. Instructions that store operands in memory perform the inverse type conversion.

2.2 Numeric Operands

A typical MCP instruction accepts one or two operands and produces one (or sometimes two) results. In two-operand instructions, one operand is the contents of a MCP register, while the other may be a memory location. The operands of some instructions are predefined; for example, FSQRT always takes the square root of the number in the top stack element.

Table 2-1. Intel387™ SX MCP Data Type Representation in Memory

Data Formats	Range	Precision	Most Significant Byte = HIGHEST ADDRESSED BYTE (7 0 7 0 7 0 7 0 7 0 7 0 7 0 7 0 7 0 7 0)
Word Integer	$\pm 10^4$	16 Bits	(TWO'S COMPLEMENT) bits 15–0
Short Integer	$\pm 10^9$	32 Bits	(TWO'S COMPLEMENT) bits 31–0
Long Integer	$\pm 10^{18}$	64 Bits	(TWO'S COMPLEMENT) bits 63–0
Packed BCD	$\pm 10^{18}$	18 Digits	S (79), X (78–72), MAGNITUDE: d_{17} d_{16} d_{15} d_{14} d_{13} d_{12} d_{11} d_{10} d_9 d_8 d_7 d_6 d_5 d_4 d_3 d_2 d_1 d_0 (to 0)
Single Precision	$\pm 10^{\pm 38}$	24 Bits	S (31), BIASED EXPONENT, SIGNIFICAND (23–0); I▲ at 23
Double Precision	$\pm 10^{\pm 308}$	53 Bits	S (63), BIASED EXPONENT, SIGNIFICAND (52–0); I▲ at 52
Extended Precision	$\pm 10^{\pm 4932}$	64 Bits	S (79), BIASED EXPONENT (to 64), I (63)▲, SIGNIFICAND (to 0)

240225–2

NOTES:

(1) S = Sign bit (0 = positive, 1 = negative)
(2) d_n = Decimal digit (two per byte)
(3) X = Bits have no significance; MCP ignores when loading, zeros when storing
(4) ▲ = Position of implicit binary point
(5) I = Integer bit of significand; stored in temporary real, implicit in single and double precision
(6) Exponent Bias (normalized values):
Single: 127 (7FH)
Double: 1023 (3FFH)
Extended REal: 16383 (3FFFH)
(7) Packed BCD: $(-1)^S (D_{17}..D_0)$
(8) Real: $(-1)^S (2^{E-BIAS}) (F_0\ F_1...)$

2.3 Register Set

Figure 1-1 shows the Intel387 SX MCP register set. When an MCP is present in a system, programmers may use these registers in addition to the registers normally available on the CPU.

2.3.1 DATA REGISTERS

Intel387 SX MCP computations use the MCP's data registers. These eight 80-bit registers provide the equivalent capacity of 20 32-bit registers. Each of the eight data registers in the MCP is 80 bits wide and is divided into "fields" corresponding to the MCP's extended-precision real data type.

The MCP register set can be accessed either as a stack, with instructions operating on the top one or two stack elements, or as individually addressable registers. The TOP field in the status word identifies the current top-of-stack register. A "push" operation decrements TOP by one and loads a value into the new top register. A "pop" operation stores the value from the current top register and then increments TOP by one. The MCP register stack grows "down" toward lower-addressed registers.

Instructions may address the data registers either implicitly or explicitly. Many instructions operate on the register at the TOP of the stack. These instructions implicitly address the register at which TOP points. Other instructions allow the programmer to explicitly specify which register to use. This explicit register addressing is also relative to TOP.

2.3.2 TAG WORD

The tag word marks the content of each numeric data register, as Figure 2-1 shows. Each two-bit tag represents one of the eight data registers. The principal function of the tag word is to optimize the MCP's performance and stack handling by making it possible to distinguish between empty and nonempty register locations. It also enables exception handlers to identify special values (e.g. NaNs or denormals) in the contents of a stack location without the need to perform complex decoding of the actual data.

2.3.3 STATUS WORD

The 16-bit status word (in the status register) shown in Figure 2-2 reflects the overall state of the MCP. It may be read and inspected by programs.

Bit 15, the B-bit (busy bit) is included for 8087 compatibility only. It always has the same value as the ES bit (bit 7 of the status word); it does **not** indicate the status of the BUSY# output of the MCP.

Bits 13–11 (TOP) point to the MCP register that is the current top-of-stack.

The four numeric condition code bits (C_3–C_0) are similar to the flags in a CPU; instructions that perform arithmetic operations update these bits to reflect the outcome. The effects of these instructions on the condition code are summarized in Tables 2-2 through 2-5.

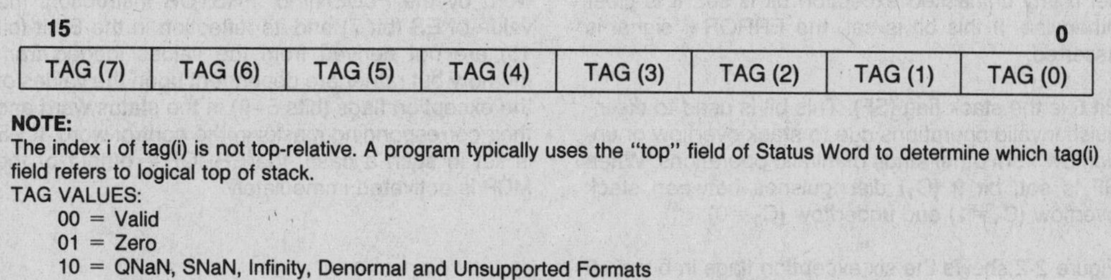

Figure 2-1. Tag Word

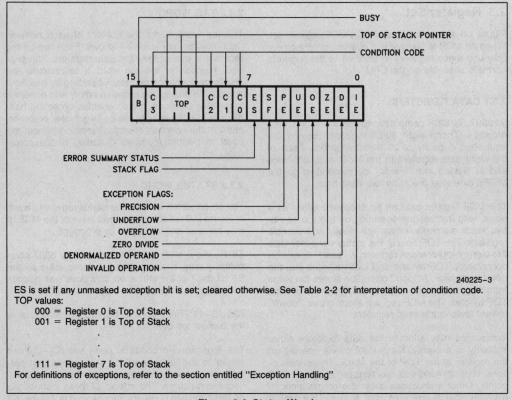

ES is set if any unmasked exception bit is set; cleared otherwise. See Table 2-2 for interpretation of condition code.

TOP values:

000 = Register 0 is Top of Stack
001 = Register 1 is Top of Stack
.
.
.
111 = Register 7 is Top of Stack

For definitions of exceptions, refer to the section entitled "Exception Handling"

Figure 2-2. Status Word

Bit 7 is the error summary (ES) status bit. This bit is set if any unmasked exception bit is set; it is clear otherwise. If this bit is set, the ERROR# signal is asserted.

Bit 6 is the stack flag (SF). This bit is used to distinguish invalid operations due to stack overflow or underflow from other kinds of invalid operations. When SF is set, bit 9 (C_1) distinguishes between stack overflow ($C_1 = 1$) and underflow ($C_1 = 0$).

Figure 2-2 shows the six exception flags in bits 5–0 of the status word. Bits 5–0 are set to indicate that the MCP has detected an exception while executing an instruction. A later section entitled "Exception Handling" explains how they are set and used.

Note that when a new value is loaded into the status word by the FLDENV or FRSTOR instruction, the value of ES (bit 7) and its reflection in the B-bit (bit 15) are not derived from the values loaded from memory but rather are dependent upon the values of the exception flags (bits 5–0) in the status word and their corresponding masks in the control word. If ES is set in such a case, the ERROR# output of the MCP is activated immediately.

Table 2-2. Condition Code Interpretation

Instruction	C0 (S)	C3 (Z)	C1 (A)	C2 (C)
FPREM, FPREM1 (see Table 2.3)	Three least significant bits of quotient Q2	Q0	Q1 or O/U#	Reduction 0 = complete 1 = incomplete
FCOM, FCOMP, FCOMPP, FTST, FUCOM, FUCOMP, FUCOMPP, FICOM, FICOMP	Result of comparison (see Table 2.4)		Zero or O/U#	Operand is not comparable (Table 2.4)
FXAM	Operand class (see Table 2.5)		Sign or O/U#	Operand class (Table 2.5)
FCHS, FABS, FXCH, FINCSTP, FDECSTP, Constant loads, FXTRACT, FLD, FILD, FBLD, FSTP (ext real)	UNDEFINED		Zero or O/U#	UNDEFINED
FIST, FBSTP, FRNDINT, FST, FSTP, FADD, FMUL, FDIV, FDIVR, FSUB, FSUBR, FSCALE, FSQRT, FPATAN, F2XM1, FYL2X, FYL2XP1	UNDEFINED		Roundup or O/U#	UNDEFINED
FPTAN, FSIN FCOS, FSINCOS	UNDEFINED		Roundup or O/U#, undefined if C2 = 1	Reduction 0 = complete 1 = incomplete
FLDENV, FRSTOR	Each bit loaded from memory			
FLDCW, FSTENV, FSTCW, FSTSW, FCLEX, FINIT, FSAVE	UNDEFINED			

O/U# When both IE and SF bits of status word are set, indicating a stack exception, this bit distinguishes between stack overflow (C1 = 1) and underflow (C1 = 0).

Reduction If FPREM or FPREM1 produces a remainder that is less than the modulus, reduction is complete. When reduction is incomplete the value at the top of the stack is a partial remainder, which can be used as input to further reduction. For FPTAN, FSIN, FCOS,and FSINCOS, the reudction bit is set if the oeprand at the top of the stack is too large. In this case the original operand remains at the top of the stack.

Roundup When the PE bit of the status word is set, this bit indicates whether the last rounding in the instruction was upward.

UNDEFINED Do not rely on finding any specific value in these bits.

4

Table 2-3. Condition Code Interpretation after FPREM and FPREM1 Instructions

Condition Code				Interpretation after FPREM and FPREM1	
C2	C3	C1	C0		
1	X	X	X	Incomplete Reduction: further interation required for complete reduction	
	Q1	Q0	Q2	Q MOD8	
0	0	0	0	0	Complete Reduction: C0, C3, C1 contain three least significant bits of quotient
	0	1	0	1	
	1	0	0	2	
	1	1	0	3	
	0	0	1	4	
	0	1	1	5	
	1	0	1	6	
	1	1	1	7	

Table 2-4. Condition Code Resulting from Comparison

Order	C3	C2	C0
TOP > Operand	0	0	0
TOP < Operand	0	0	1
TOP = Operand	1	0	0
Unordered	1	1	1

Table 2-5. Condition Code Defining Operand Class

C3	C2	C1	C0	Value at TOP
0	0	0	0	+ Unsupported
0	0	0	1	+ NaN
0	0	1	0	− Unsupported
0	0	1	1	− NaN
0	1	0	0	+ Normal
0	1	0	1	+ Infinity
0	1	1	0	− Normal
0	1	1	1	− Infinity
1	0	0	0	+ 0
1	0	0	1	+ Empty
1	0	1	0	− 0
1	0	1	1	− Empty
1	1	0	0	+ Denormal
1	1	1	0	− Denormal

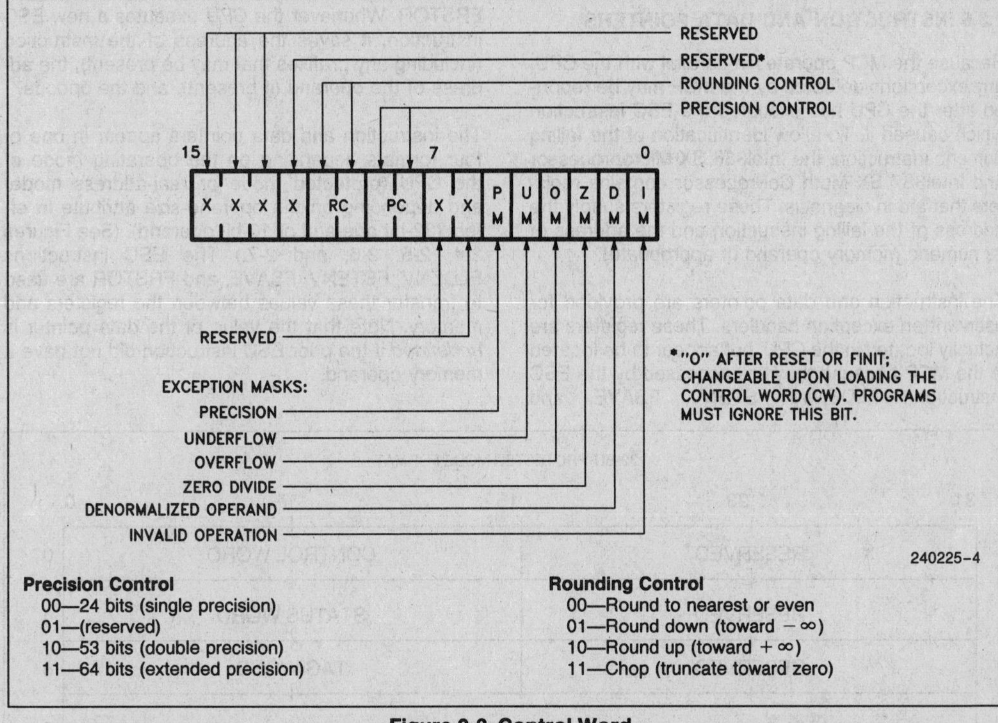

Figure 2-3. Control Word

2.3.4 CONTROL WORD

The MCP provides several processing options that are selected by loading a control word from memory into the control register. Figure 2-3 shows the format and encoding of fields in the control word.

The low-order byte of this control word configures exception masking. Bits 5–0 of the control word contain individual masks for each of the six exceptions that the MCP recognizes.

The high-order byte of the control word configures the MCP operating mode, including precision, rounding, and infinity control.

- The "infinity control bit" (bit 12) is not meaningful to the Intel387 SX MCP, and programs must ignore its value. To maintain compatibility with the 8087 and 80287, this bit can be programmed; however, regardless of its value, the Intel387 SX MCP always treats infinity in the affine sense ($-\infty < +\infty$). This bit is initialized to zero both after a hardware reset and after the FINIT instruction.
- The rounding control (RC) bits (bits 11–10) provide for directed rounding and true chop, as well as the unbiased round to the nearest even mode specified in the IEEE standard. Rounding control affects only those instructions that perform rounding at the end of the operation (and thus can generate a precision exception); namely, FST, FSTP, FIST, all arithmetic instructions (except FPREM, FPREM1, FXTRACT, FABS, and FCHS), and all transcendental instructions.
- The precision control (PC) bits (bits 9–8) can be used to set the MCP internal operating precision of the significand at less than the default of 64 bits (extended precision). This can be useful in providing compatibility with early generation arithmetic processors of smaller precision. PC affects only the instructions ADD, SUB, DIV, MUL, and SQRT. For all other instructions, either the precision is determined by the opcode or extended precision is used.

2.3.5 INSTRUCTION AND DATA POINTERS

Because the MCP operates in parallel with the CPU, any exceptions detected by the MCP may be reported after the CPU has executed the ESC instruction which caused it. To allow identification of the failing numeric instruction, the Intel386 SX Microprocessor and Intel387 SX Math CoProcessor contains registers that aid in diagnosis. These registers supply the address of the failing instruction and the address of its numeric memory operand (if appropriate).

The instruction and data pointers are provided for user-written exception handlers. These registers are actually located in the CPU, but appear to be located in the MCP because they are accessed by the ESC instructions FLDENV, FSTENV, FSAVE, and FRSTOR. Whenever the CPU executes a new ESC instruction, it saves the address of the instruction (including any prefixes that may be present), the address of the operand (if present), and the opcode.

The instruction and data pointers appear in one of four formats depending on the operating mode of the CPU (protected mode or real-address mode) and depending on the operand-size attribute in effect (32-bit operand or 16-bit operand). (See Figures 2-4, 2-5, 2-6, and 2-7.) The ESC instructions FLDENV, FSTENV, FSAVE, and FRSTOR are used to transfer these values between the registers and memory. Note that the value of the data pointer is *undefined* if the prior ESC instruction did not have a memory operand.

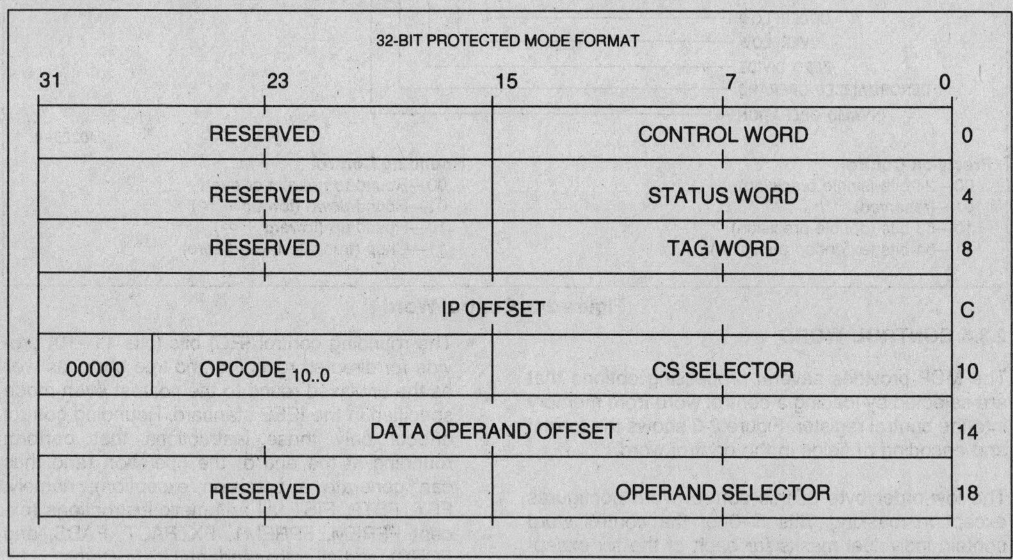

Figure 2-4.Instruction and Data Pointer Image in Memory, 32-bit Protected-Mode Format

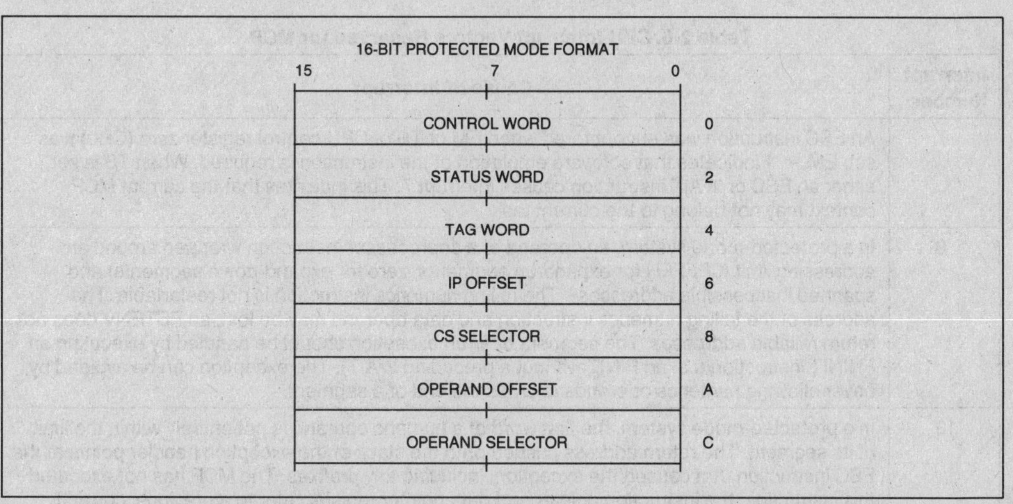

Figure 2-5. Instruction and Data Pointer Image in Memory, 16-bit Protected-Mode Format

32-BIT REAL-ADDRESS MODE FORMAT

31 … 16		15 … 0		Offset
RESERVED		CONTROL WORD		0
RESERVED		STATUS WORD		4
RESERVED		TAG WORD		8
RESERVED		INSTRUCTION POINTER 15..0		C
0000	INSTRUCTION POINTER 31..16	0	OPCODE 10..0	10
RESERVED		OPERAND POINTER 15..0		14
0000	OPERAND POINTER 31..16	0000	00000000	18

Figure 2-6. Instruction and Data Pointer Image in Memory, 32-bit Real-Mode Format

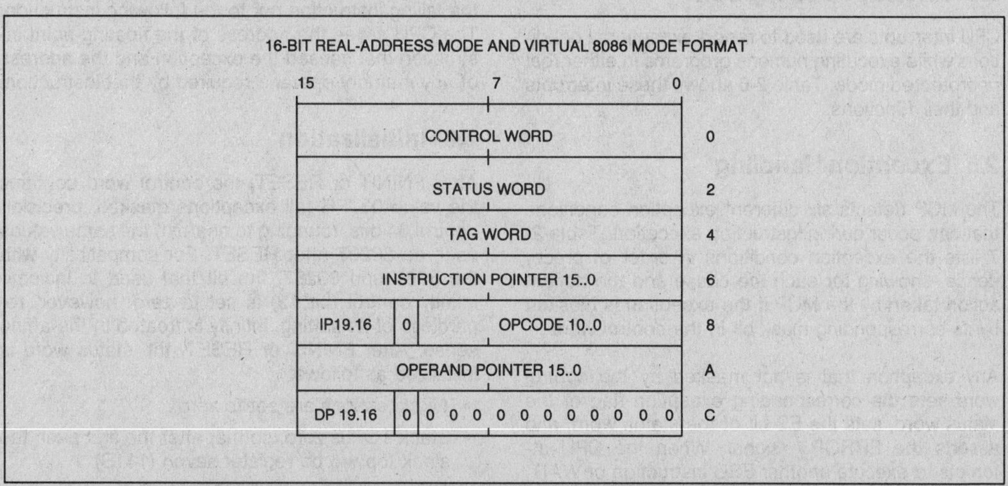

Figure 2-7. Instruction and Data Pointer Image in Memory, 16-bit Real-Mode Format

Table 2-6. CPU Interrupt Vectors Reserved for MCP

Interrupt Number	Cause of Interrupt
7	An ESC instruction was encountered when EM or TS of CPU control register zero (CR0) was set. EM = 1 indicates that software emulation of the instruction is required. When TS is set, either an ESC or WAIT instruction causes interrupt 7. This indicates that the current MCP context may not belong to the current task.
9	In a protected-mode system, an operand of a coprocessor instruction wrapped around an addressing limit (0FFFFH for expand-up segments, zero for expand-down segments) and spanned inaccessible addresses[a]. The failing numerics instruction is not restartable. The address of the failing numerics instruction and data operand may be lost; an FSTENV does not return reliable addresses. The segment overrun exception should be handled by executing an FNINIT instruction (i.e. an FINIT without a preceding WAIT). The exception can be avoided by never allowing numerics operands to cross the end of a segment.
13	In a protected-mode system, the first word of a numeric operand is not entirely within the limit of its segment. The return address pushed onto the stack of the exception handler points at the ESC instruction that caused the exception, including any prefixes. The MCP has not executed this instruction; the instruction pointer and data pointer register refer to a previous, correctly executed instruction.
16	The previous numerics instruction caused an unmasked exception. The address of the faulty instruction and the address of its operand are stored in the instruction pointer and data pointer registers. Only ESC and WAIT instructions can cause this interrupt. The CPU return address pushed onto the stack of the exception handler points to a WAIT or ESC instruction (including prefixes). This instruction can be restarted after clearing the exception condition in the MCP. FNINIT, FNCLEX, FNSTSW, FNSTENV, and FNSAVE cannot cause this interrupt.

a. An operand may wrap around an addressing limit when the segment limit is near an addressing limit and the operand is near the largest valid address in the segment. Because of the wrap-around, the beginning and ending addresses of such an operand will be at opposite ends of the segment. There are two ways that such an operand may also span inaccessible addresses: 1) if the segment limit is not equal to the addressing limit (e.g. addressing limit is FFFFH and segment limit is FFFDH) the operand will span addresses that are not within the segment (e.g. an 8-byte operand that starts at valid offset FFFCH will span addresses FFFC–FFFFH and 0000-0003H; however addresses FFFEH and FFFFH are not valid, because they exceed the limit); 2) if the operand begins and ends in present and accessible segments but intermediate bytes of the operand fall in a not-present page or in a segment or page to which the procedure does not have access rights.

2.4 Interrupt Description

CPU interrupts are used to report exceptional conditions while executing numeric programs in either real or protected mode. Table 2-6 shows these interrupts and their functions.

2.5 Exception Handling

The MCP detects six different exception conditions that can occur during instruction execution. Table 2-7 lists the exception conditions in order of precedence, showing for each the cause and the default action taken by the MCP if the exception is masked by its corresponding mask bit in the control word.

Any exception that is not masked by the control word sets the corresponding exception flag of the status word, sets the ES bit of the status word, and asserts the ERROR# signal. When the CPU attempts to execute another ESC instruction or WAIT, exception 16 occurs. The exception condition must be resolved via an interrupt service routine. The return address pushed onto the CPU stack upon entry to the service routine does not necessarily point to the failing instruction nor to the following instruction. The CPU saves the address of the floating-point instruction that caused the exception and the address of any memory operand required by that instruction.

2.6 Initialization

After FNINIT or RESET, the control word contains the value 037FH (all exceptions masked, precision control 64 bits, rounding to nearest) the same values as in an 80287 after RESET. For compatibility with the 8087 and 80287, the bit that used to indicate infinity control (bit 12) is set to zero; however, regardless of its setting, infinity is treated in the affine sense. After FNINIT or RESET, the status word is initialized as follows:

- All exceptions are set to zero.
- Stack TOP is zero, so that after the first push the stack top will be register seven (111B).
- The condition code C_3–C_0 is undefined.
- The B-bit is zero.

Table 2-7. Exceptions

Exception	Cause	Default Action (if exception is masked)
Invalid Operation	Operation on a signalling NaN, unsupported format, indeterminate for (0-∞, 0/0, (+∞) + (−∞), etc.), or stack overflow/underflow (SF is also set)	Result is a quiet NaN, integer indefinite, or BCD indefinte
Denormalized Operand	At least one of the operands is denormalized, i.e., it has the smallest exponent but a nonzero significand.	Normal processing continues
Zero Divisor	The divisor is zero while the dividend is a noninfinite, nonzero number	Result is ∞
Overflow	The result is too large in magnitude to fit in the specified format	Result is largest finite value or ∞
Underflow	The true result is nonzero but too small to be represented in the specified format, and, if underflow exception is masked, denormalization causes the loss of accuracy.	Result is denormalized or zero
Inexact Result (Precision	The true result is not exactly representable in the specified format (e.g. 1/3); the result is rounded according to the rounding mode.	Normal processing continues

The tag word contains FFFFH (all stack locations are empty).

The Intel386 SX Microprocessor and Intel387 SX Math CoProcessor initialization software must execute an FNINIT instruction (i.e an FINIT without a preceding WAIT) after RESET. The FNINIT is not strictly required for the 80287 software, but Intel recommends its use to help ensure upward compatibility with other processors. After a hardware RESET, the ERROR# output is asserted to indicate that a Intel387 SX MCP is present. To accomplish this, the IE and ES bits of the status word are set, and the IM bit in the control word is cleared. After FNINIT, the status word and the control word have the same values as in an 80287 after RESET.

2.7 8087 and 80287 Compatibility

This section summarizes the differences between the Intel387 SX MCP and the 80287. Any migration from the 8087 directly to the Intel387 SX MCP must also take into account the differences between the 8087 and the 80287 as listed in Appendix A.

Many changes have been designed into the Intel387 SX MCP to directly support the IEEE standard in hardware. These changes result in increased performance by eliminating the need for software that supports the standard.

2.7.1 GENERAL DIFFERENCES

The Intel387 SX MCP supports only affine closure for infinity arithmetic, not projective closure.

Operands for FSCALE and FPATAN are no longer restricted in range (except for ±∞); F2XM1 and FPTAN accept a wider range of operands.

Rounding control is in effect for FLD *constant*.

Software cannot change entries of the tag word to values (other than empty) that differ from actual register contents.

After reset, FINIT, and incomplete FPREM, the Intel387 SX MCP resets to zero the condition code bits C_3-C_0 of the status word.

In conformance with the IEEE standard, the Intel387 SX MCP does not support the special data formats pseudozero, pseudo-NaN, pseudoinfinity, and unnormal.

The denormal exception has a different purpose on the Intel387 SX MCP. A system that uses the denormal-exception handler solely to normalize the denormal operands, would better mask the denormal exception on the Intel387 SX MCP. The Intel387 SX MCP automatically normalizes denormal operands when the denormal exception is masked.

4

2.7.2 EXCEPTIONS

A number of differences exist due to changes in the IEEE standard and to functional improvements to the architecture of the Intel387 SX MCP:

1. When the overflow or underflow exception is masked, the Intel387 SX MCP differs from the 80287 in rounding when overflow or underflow occurs. The Intel387 SX MCP produces results that are consistent with the rounding mode.
2. When the underflow exception is masked, the Intel387 SX MCP sets its underflow flag only if there is also a loss of accuracy during denormalization.
3. Fewer invalid-operation exceptions due to denormal operands, because the instructions FSQRT, FDIV, FPREM, and conversions to BCD or to integer normalize denormal operands before proceeding.
4. The FSQRT, FBSTP, and FPREM instructions may cause underflow, because they support denormal operands.
5. The denormal exception can occur during the transcendental instructions and the FXTRACT instruction.
6. The denormal exception no longer takes precedence over all other exceptions.
7. When the denormal exception is masked, the Intel387 SX MCP automatically normalizes denormal operands. The 8087/80287 performs unnormal arithmetic, which might produce an unnormal result.
8. When the operand is zero, the FXTRACT instruction reports a zero-divide exception and leaves $-\infty$ in ST(1).
9. The status word has a new bit (SF) that signals when invalid-operation exceptions are due to stack underflow or overflow.
10. FLD *extended precision* no longer reports denormal exceptions, because the instruction is not numeric.
11. FLD *single/double precision* when the operand is denormal converts the number to extended precision and signals the denormalized operand exception. When loading a signalling NaN, FLD *single/double precision* signals an invalid-operand exception.
12. The Intel387 SX MCP only generates quiet NaNs (as on the 80287); however, the Intel387 SX MCP distinguishes between quiet NaNs and signaling NaNs. Signaling NaNs trigger exceptions when they are used as operands; quiet NaNs do not (except for FCOM, FIST, and FBSTP which also raise IE for quiet NaNs).
13. When stack overflow occurs during FPTAN and overflow is masked, both ST(0) and ST(1) contain quiet NaNs. The 80287/8087 leaves the original operand in ST(1) intact.
14. When the scaling factor is $\pm\infty$, the FSCALE (ST(0), ST(1)) instruction behaves as follows (ST(0) and ST(1) contain the scaled and scaling operands respectively):
    - FSCALE(0, ∞) generates the invalid operation exception.
    - FSCALE(finite, $-\infty$) generates zero with the same sign as the scaled operand.
    - FSCALE(finite, $+\infty$) generates ∞ with the same sign as the scaled operand.

    The 8087/80287 returns zero in the first case and raises the invalid-operation exception in the other cases.
15. The Intel387 SX MCP returns signed infinity/zero as the unmasked response to massive overflow/underflow. The 8087 and 80287 support a limited range for the scaling factor; within this range either massive overflow/underflow do not occur or undefined results are produced.

3.0 HARDWARE INTERFACE

In the following description of hardware interface, the # symbol at the end of a signal name indicates that the active or asserted state occurs when the signal is at a low voltage. When no # is present after the signal name, the signal is asserted when at the high voltage level.

3.1 Signal Description

In the following signal descriptions, the Intel387 SX MCP pins are grouped by function as shown by Table 3-1. Table 3-1 lists every pin by its identifier, gives a brief description of its function, and lists some of its characteristics (Refer to Figure 5-1 and Table 5-1 for pin configuration).

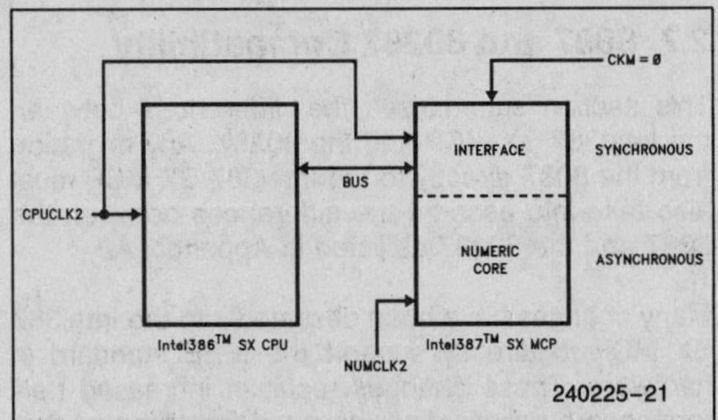

Figure 3-1. Asynchronous Operation

Table 3-1. Pin Summary

Pin Name	Function	Active State	Input/ Output	Referenced To...
Execution Control				
CPUCLK2	Intel386™ SX Microprocessor CLocK 2		I	
NUMCLK2	MCP CLocK 2		I	
CKM	MCP ClocKing Mode		I	
RESETIN	System reset	High	I	CPUCLK2
MCP Handshake				
PEREQ	Processor Extension REQuest	High	O	STEN/CPUCLK2
BUSY#	Busy status	Low	O	STEN/CPUCLK2
ERROR#	Error status	Low	O	STEN/NUMCLK2
Bus Interface				
D15–D0	Data pins	High	I/O	CPUCLK2
W/R#	Write/Read bus cycle	Hi/Lo	I	CPUCLK2
ADS#	ADdress Strobe	Low	I	CPUCLK2
READY#	Bus ready input	Low	I	CPUCLK2
READYO#	Ready output	Low	O	STEN/CPUCLK2
Chip/Port Select				
STEN	STatus ENable	High	I	CPUCLK2
NPS1#	NPX select #1	Low	I	CPUCLK2
NPS2	NPX select #2	High	I	CPUCLK2
CMD0#	CoMmanD	Low	I	CPUCLK2
Power and Ground				
V_{CC}	System power			
V_{SS}	System ground			

All output signals are tristate; they leave floating state only when STEN is active. The output buffers of the bidirectional data pins D15–D0 are also tristate; they leave the floating state only during cycles when the MCP is selected (i.e. when STEN, NPS1#, and NPS2 are all active).

3.1.1 Intel386 SX CPU CLOCK 2 (CPUCLK2)

This input uses the CLK2 signal of the CPU to time the bus control logic. Several other MCP signals are referenced to the rising edge of this signal. When CKM = 1 (synchronous mode) this pin also clocks the data interface and control unit and the floating-point unit of the MCP. This pin requires MOS-level input. The signal on this pin is divided by two to produce the internal clock signal CLK.

3.1.2 Intel387 SX MCP CLOCK 2 (NUMCLK2)

When CKM = 0 (asynchronous mode) this pin provides the clock for the data interface and control unit and the floating-point unit of the MCP. In this case, the ratio of the frequency of NUMCLK2 to the frequency of CPUCLK2 must lie within the range 10:16 to 14:10. When CKM = 1 (synchronous mode) signals on this pin are ignored; CPUCLK2 is used instead for the data interface and control unit and the floating-point unit. This pin requires MOS-level input and should be tied low if not used.

3.1.3 CLOCKING MODE (CKM)

This pin is a strapping option. When it is strapped to V_{CC} (HIGH), the MCP operates in synchronous mode; when strapped to V_{SS} (LOW), the MCP operates in asynchronous mode. These modes relate to clocking of the data interface and control unit and the floating-point unit only; the bus control logic always operates synchronously with respect to the CPU.

3.1.4 SYSTEM RESET (RESETIN)

A LOW to HIGH transition on this pin causes the MCP to terminate its present activity and to enter a dormant state. RESETIN must remain active (HIGH) for at least 40 NUMCLK2 periods.

The HIGH to LOW transitions of RESETIN must be synchronous with CPUCLK2, so that the phase of the internal clock of the bus control logic (which is the CPUCLK2 divided by two) is the same as the phase of the internal clock of the CPU. After RESETIN goes LOW, at least 50 NUMCLK2 periods must pass before the first MCP instruction is written into the MCP. This pin should be connected to the CPU RESET pin. Table 3-1 shows the status of the output pins during the reset sequence. After a reset, all output pins return to their inactive states.

Table 3-2. Output Pin Status during Reset

Pin Value	Pin Name
HIGH	READYO#, BUSY#
LOW	PEREQ, ERROR#
Tri-State OFF	D15–D0

3.1.5 PROCESSOR EXTENSION REQUEST (PEREQ)

When active, this pin signals to the CPU that the MCP is ready for data transfer to/from its data FIFO. When all data is written to or read from the data FIFO, PEREQ is deactivated. This signal always goes inactive before BUSY# goes inactive. This signal is referenced to CPUCLK2. It should be connected to the CPU PEREQ input.

3.1.6 BUSY STATUS (BUSY#)

When active, this pin signals to the CPU that the MCP is currently executing an instruction. This signal is referenced to CPUCLK2. It should be connected to the CPU BUSY# pin.

3.1.7 ERROR STATUS (ERROR#)

This pin reflects the ES bit of the status register. When active, it indicates that an unmasked exception has occurred. This signal can be changed to inactive state only by the following instructions (without a preceding WAIT): FNINIT, FNCLEX, FNSTENV, FNSAVE, FLDCW, FLDENV, and FRSTOR. This pin is referenced to NUMCLK2. It should be connected to the ERROR# pin of the CPU.

3.1.8 DATA PINS (D15–D0)

These bidirectional pins are used to transfer data and opcodes between the CPU and MCP. They are normally connected directly to the corresponding CPU data pins. HIGH state indicates a value of one. D0 is the least significant data bit. Timings are referenced to CPUCLK2.

3.1.9 WRITE/READ BUS CYCLE (W/R#)

This signal indicates to the MCP whether the CPU bus cycle in progress is a read or a write cycle. This pin should be connected directly to the CPU's W/R# pin. HIGH indicates a write cycle; LOW a read cycle. This input is ignored if any of the signals STEN, NPS1#, or NPS2 are inactive. Setup and hold times are referenced to CPUCLK2.

3.1.10 ADDRESS STROBE (ADS#)

This input, in conjunction with the READY# input, indicates when the MCP bus-control logic may sample W/R# and the chip-select signals. Setup and hold times are referenced to CPUCLK2. This pin should be connected to the ADS# pin of the CPU.

3.1.11 BUS READY INPUT (READY#)

This input indicates to the MCP when a CPU bus cycle is to be terminated. It is used by the bus-control logic to trace bus activities. Bus cycles can be extended indefinitely until terminated by READY#. This input should be connected to the same signal that drives the CPU's READY# input. Setup and hold times are referenced to CPUCLK2.

3.1.12 READY OUTPUT (READYO#)

This pin is activated at such a time that write cycles are terminated after two clocks (except FLDENV and FRSTOR) and read cycles after three clocks. In configurations where no extra wait states are required, this pin must directly or indirectly drive the READY# input of the CPU. Refer to the section entitled "Bus Operation" for details. This pin is activated only during bus cycles that select the MCP. This signal is referenced to CPUCLK2.

3.1.13 STATUS ENABLE (STEN)

This pin serves as a chip select for the MCP. When inactive, this pin forces, BUSY#, PEREQ#, ERROR#, and READYO# outputs into floating state. D15–D0 are normally floating; they leave floating state only if STEN is active and additional conditions are met. STEN also causes the chip to recognize its other chip-select inputs. STEN makes it easier to do on-board testing (using the overdrive method) of other chips in systems containing the MCP. STEN should be pulled up with a resistor so that it can be pulled down when testing. In boards that do not use on-board testing STEN should be connected to V_{CC}. Setup and hold times are relative to CPUCLK2. Note that STEN must maintain the same setup and hold times as NPS1#, NPS2, and CMD0# (i.e. if STEN changes state during an MCP bus cycle, it must change state during the same CLK period as the NPS1#, NPS2, and CMD0# signals).

3.1.14 NPX SELECT 1 (NPS1#)

When active (along with STEN and NPS2) in the first period of a CPU bus cycle, this signal indicates that the purpose of the bus cycle is to communicate with the MCP. This pin should be connected directly to the M/IO# pin of the CPU, so that the MCP is selected only when the CPU performs I/O cycles. Setup and hold times are referenced to CPUCLK2.

3.1.15 NPX SELECT 2 (NPS2)

When active (along with STEN and NPS1#) in the first period of a CPU bus cycle, this signal indicates that the purpose of the bus cycle is to communicate with the MCP. This pin should be connected directly to the A23 pin of the CPU, so that the MCP is selected only when the CPU issues one of the I/O addresses reserved for the MCP (8000F8H, 8000FCH or 8000FEH which is treated as 8000FCH by the MCP). Setup and hold times are referenced to CPUCLK2.

3.1.16 COMMAND (CMD0#)

During a write cycle, this signal indicates whether an opcode (CMD0# active) or data (CMD0# inactive) is being sent to the MCP. During a read cycle, it indicates whether the control or status register (CMD0# active) or a data register (CMD0# inactive) is being read. CMD0# should be connected directly to the A2 output of the CPU. Setup and hold times are referenced to CPUCLK2.

3.1.17 SYSTEM POWER (V_{CC})

System power provides the +5V DC supply input. All V_{CC} pins should be tied together on the circuit board and local decoupling capacitors should be used between V_{CC} and V_{SS}.

3.1.18 SYSTEM GROUND (V_{SS})

All V_{SS} pins should be tied together on the circuit board and local decoupling capacitors should be used between V_{CC} and V_{SS}.

3.2 System Configuration

The Intel387 SX Math CoProcessor is designed to interface with the Intel386 SX Microprocessor as shown by Figure 3-1. A dedicated communication protocol makes possible high-speed transfer of opcodes and operands between the CPU and MCP. The Intel387 SX MCP is designed so that no additional components are required for interface with the CPU. Most control pins of the MCP are connected directly to pins of the CPU.

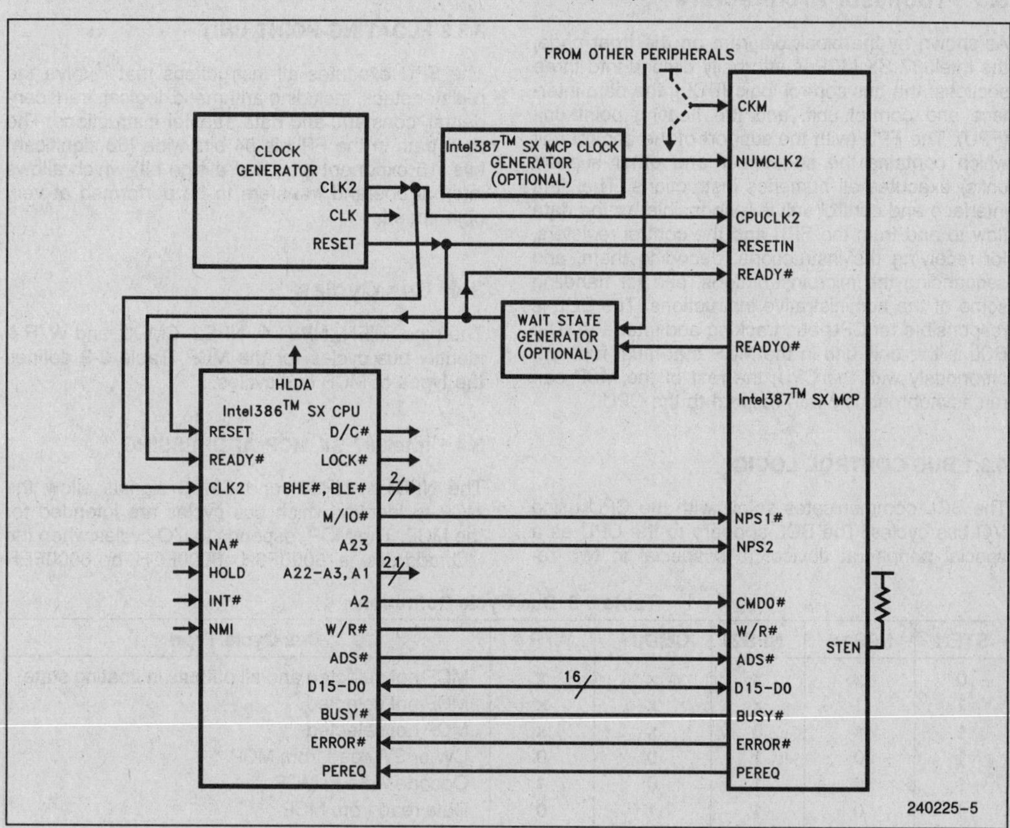

Figure 3-2. Intel386™ SX CPU and Intel387™ SX MCP System Configuration

4

The interface between the MCP and the CPU has these characteristics:

- The MCP shares the local bus of the Intel386 SX Microprocessor.
- The CPU and MCP share the same reset signals. They may also share the same clock input; however, for greatest performance, an external oscillator may be needed.
- The corresponding BUSY#, ERROR#, and PEREQ pins are connected together.
- The MCP NPS1# and NPS2 inputs are connected to the latched CPU M/IO# and A23 outputs respectively. For MCP cycles, M/IO# is always LOW and A23 always HIGH.
- The MCP input CMD0 is connected to the latched A_2 output. The Intel386 SX Microprocessor generates address 8000F8H when writing a command and address 8000FCH or 8000FEH (treated as 8000FCH by the Intel387 SX MCP) when writing or reading data. It does not generate any other addresses during MCP bus cycles.

3.3 Processor Architecture

As shown by the block diagram on the front page, the Intel387 SX MCP is internally divided into three sections: the bus control logic (BCL), the data interface and control unit, and the floating point unit (FPU). The FPU (with the support of the control unit which contains the sequencer and other support units) executes all numerics instructions. The data interface and control unit is responsible for the data flow to and from the FPU and the control registers, for receiving the instructions, decoding them, and sequencing the microinstructions, and for handling some of the administrative instructions. The BCL is responsible for CPU bus tracking and interface. The BCL is the only unit in the MCP that must run synchronously with the CPU; the rest of the MCP can run asynchronously with respect to the CPU.

3.3.1 BUS CONTROL LOGIC

The BCL communicates solely with the CPU using I/O bus cycles. The BCL appears to the CPU as a special peripheral device. It is special in two respects: the CPU initiates I/O automatically when it encounters ESC instructions, and the CPU uses reserved I/O addresses to communicate with the BCL. The BCL does not communicate directly with memory. The CPU performs all memory access, transferring input operands from memory to the MCP and transferring outputs from the MCP to memory.

3.3.2 DATA INTERFACE AND CONTROL UNIT

The data interface and control unit latches the data and, subject to BCL control, directs the data to the FIFO or the instruction decoder. The instruction decoder decodes the ESC instructions sent to it by the CPU and generates controls that direct the data flow in the FIFO. It also triggers the microinstruction sequencer that controls execution of each instruction. If the ESC instruction is FINIT, FCLEX, FSTSW, FSTSW AX, FSTCW, FSETPM, or FRSTPM, the control executes it independently of the FPU and the sequencer. The data interface and control unit is the one that generates the BUSY#, PEREQ, and ERROR# signals that synchronize MCP activities with the CPU.

3.3.3 FLOATING-POINT UNIT

The FPU executes all instructions that involve the register stack, including arithmetic, logical, transcendental, constant, and data transfer instructions. The data path in the FPU is 84 bits wide (68 significant bits, 15 exponent bits, and a sign bit) which allows internal operand transfers to be performed at very high speeds.

3.4 Bus Cycles

The pins STEN, NPS1#, NPS2, CMD0, and W/R# identify bus cycles for the MCP. Table 3-3 defines the types of MCP bus cycles.

3.4.1 Intel387 SX MCP ADDRESSING

The NPS1#, NPS2, and CMD0 signals allow the MCP to identify which bus cycles are intended for the MCP. The MCP responds to I/O cycles when the I/O address is 8000F8H, 8000FCH or 8000FEH

Table 3-3. Bus Cycle Definition

STEN	NPS1#	NPS2	CMD0#	W/R#	Bus Cycle Type
0	x	x	x	x	MCP not selected and all outputs in floating state
1	1	x	x	x	MCP not selected
1	x	0	x	x	MCP not selected
1	0	1	0	0	CW or SW read from MCP
1	0	1	0	1	Opcode write to MCP
1	0	1	1	0	Data read from MCP
1	0	1	1	1	Data write to MCP

(treated as 8000FCH by the Intel387 SX MCP). The MCP responds to I/O cycles when bit 23 of the I/O address is set. In other words, the MCP acts as an I/O device in a reserved I/O address space.

Because A23 is used to select the Intel387 SX Math CoProcessor for data transfers, it is not possible for a program running on the CPU to address the MCP with an I/O instruction. Only ESC instructions cause the CPU to communicate with the MCP.

3.4.2 CPU/MCP SYNCHRONIZATION

The pins BUSY#, PEREQ, and ERROR# are used for various aspects of synchronization between the CPU and the MCP.

BUSY# is used to synchronize instruction transfer from the CPU to the MCP. When the MCP recognizes an ESC instruction, it asserts BUSY#. For most ESC instructions, the CPU waits for the MCP to deassert BUSY# before sending the new opcode.

The MCP uses the PEREQ pin of the CPU to signal that the MCP is ready for data transfer to or from its data FIFO. The MCP does not directly access memory; rather, the CPU provides memory access services for the MCP. (For this reason, memory access on behalf of the MCP always obeys the protection rules applicable to the current CPU mode.) Once the CPU initiates a MCP instruction that has operands, the CPU waits for PEREQ signals that indicate when the MCP is ready for operand transfer. Once all operands have been transferred (or if the instruction has no operands) the CPU continues program execution while the MCP executes the ESC instruction.

In 8086/8087 systems, WAIT instructions may be required to achieve synchronization of both commands and operands. In the Intel386 SX Microprocessor and Intel387 SX Math CoProcessor systems, however, WAIT instructions are required only for operand synchronization; namely, after MCP stores to memory (except FSTSW and FSTCW) or loads from memory. (In 80286/80287 systems, WAIT is required before FLDENV and FRSTOR; with the Intel386 SX Microprocessor and Intel387 SX Math CoProcessor, WAIT is not required in these cases.) Used this way, WAIT ensures that the value has already been written or read by the MCP before the CPU reads or changes the value.

Once it has started to execute a numerics instruction and has transferred the operands from the CPU, the MCP can process the instruction in parallel with and independent of the host CPU. When the MCP detects an exception, it asserts the ERROR# signal, which causes a CPU interrupt.

3.4.3 SYNCHRONOUS OR ASYNCHRONOUS MODES

The internal logic of the MCP (the FPU) can operate either directly from the CPU clock (synchronous mode) or from a separate clock (asynchronous mode). The two configurations are distinguished by the CKM pin. In either case, the bus control logic (BCL) of the MCP is synchronized with the CPU clock. Use of asynchronous mode allows the CPU and the FPU section of the MCP to run at different speeds. In this case, the ratio of the frequency of NUMCLK2 to the frequency of CPUCLK2 must lie within the range 10:16 to 14:10. Use of synchronous mode eliminates one clock generator from the board design.

3.4.4 AUTOMATIC BUS CYCLE TERMINATION

In configurations where no extra wait states are required, READYO# can drive the CPU's READY# input. If this pin is used, it should be connected to the logic that ORs all READY outputs from peripherals on the CPU bus. READYO# is asserted by the MCP only during I/O cycles that select the MCP. Refer to Section 4.0 "Bus Operation" for details.

4.0 BUS OPERATION

With respect to bus interface, the Intel387 SX MCP is fully synchronous with the CPU. Both operate at the same rate, because each generates its internal CLK signal by dividing CPUCLK2 by two. Furthermore, both internal CLK signals are in phase, because they are synchronized by the same RESETIN signal.

A bus cycle for the MCP starts when the CPU activates ADS# and drives new values on the address and cycle-definition lines. The MCP examines the address and cycle-definition lines in the same CLK period during which ADS# is activated. This CLK period is considered the first CLK of the bus cycle. During this first CLK period, the MCP also examines the R/W# input signal to determine whether the cycle is a read or a write cycle and examines the CMD0 input to determine whether an opcode, operand, or control/status register transfer is to occur.

The Intel387 SX MCP supports both pipelined (i.e. overlapped) and nonpipelined bus cycles. A nonpipelined cycle is one for which the CPU asserts ADS# when no other MCP bus cycle is in progress. A pipelined bus cycle is one for which the CPU asserts ADS# and provides valid next-address and control signals before the prior MCP cycle terminates. The CPU may do this as early as the second CLK period after asserting ADS# for the prior cycle. Pipelining increases the availability of the bus by at least one CLK period. The Intel387 SX MCP supports pipelined bus cycles in order to optimize address pipelining by the CPU for memory cycles.

Bus operation is described in terms of an abstract state machine. Figure 4-1 illustrates the states and state transitions for MCP bus cycles:

- T_I is the idle state. This is the state of the bus logic after RESET, the state to which bus logic returns after every nonpipelined bus cycle, and the state to which bus logic returns after a series of pipelined cycles.
- T_{RS} is the READY#-sensitive state. Different types of bus cycles may require a minimum of one or two successive T_{RS} states. The bus logic remains in T_{RS} state until READY#is sensed, at which point the bus cycle terminates. Any number of wait states may be implemented by delaying READY#, thereby causing additional successive T_{RS} states.
- T_P is the first state for every pipelined bus cycle. This state is not used by nonpipelined cycles.

Note that the bus logic tracks the bus state regardless of the values on the chip/port select pins.

The READYO# output of the MCP indicates when an MCP bus cycle may be terminated if no extra wait states are required. For all write cycles (except those for the instructions FLDENV and FRSTOR), READYO# is always asserted during the first T_{RS} state, regardless of the number of wait states. For all read cycles and write cycles for FLDENV and FRSTOR, READYO# is always asserted in the second T_{RS} state, regardless of the number of wait states. These rules apply to both pipelined and nonpipelined cycles. Systems designers may use READYO# in one of the following ways:

1. Connect it (directly or through logic that ORs READY# signals from other devices) to the READY# inputs of the CPU and MCP.
2. Use it as one input to a wait-state generator.

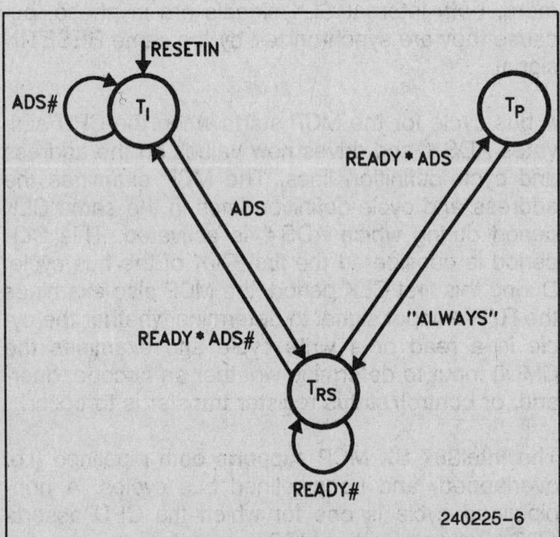

Figure 4-1. Bus State Diagram

The following sections illustrate different types of Intel387 SX MCP bus cycles. Because different instructions have different amounts of overhead before, between, and after operand transfer cycles, it is not possible to represent in a few diagrams all of the combinations of successive operand transfer cycles. The following bus-cycle diagrams show memory cycles between MCP operand-transfer cycles. Note, that during FRSTOR some consecutive accesses to the MCP do not have intervening memory accesses. For the timing relationship between operand transfer cycles and opcode write or other overhead activities, see the figure "Other Parameters" in section 6.

4.1 Nonpipelined Bus Cycles

Figure 4-2 illustrates bus activity for consecutive nonpipelined bus cycles.

At the second clock of the bus cycle, the MCP enters the T_{RS} state. During this state, it samples the READY# input and stays in this state as long as READY# is inactive.

4.1.1 WRITE CYCLE

In write cycles, the MCP drives the READYO# signal for one CLK period during the second CLK period of the cycle (i.e. the first T_{RS} state); therefore, the fastest write cycle takes two CLK periods (see cycle 2 of Figure 4-2). For the instructions FLDENV and FRSTOR, however, the MCP forces a wait state by delaying the activation of READYO# to the second T_{RS} state (not shown in Figure 4-2).

The MCP samples the D15–D0 inputs into data latches at the falling edge of CLK as long as it stays in T_{RS} state.

When READY# is asserted, the MCP returns to the idle state. Simultaneously with the MCP's entering the idle state, the CPU may assert ADS# again, signaling the beginning of yet another cycle.

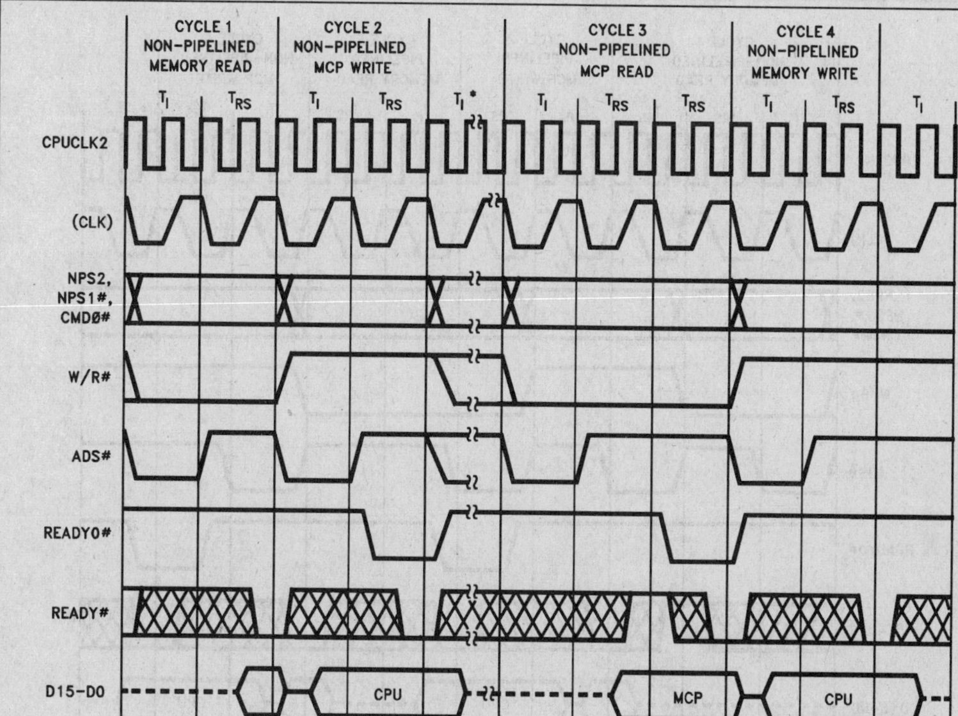

Cycles 1 & 2 represent part of the operand transfer cycle for instructions involving either 4-byte or 8-byte operand loads.
Cycles 3 & 4 represent part of the operand transfer cycle for a store operation.
*Cycles 1 & 2 could repeat here or T_I states for various non-operand transfer cycles and overhead.

Figure 4-2. Nonpipelined Read and Write Cycles

4.1.2 READ CYCLE

At the rising edge of CLK in the second CLK period of the cycle (i.e. the first T_{RS} state), the MCP starts to drive the D15–D0 outputs and continues to drive them as long as it stays in T_{RS} state.

At least one wait state must be inserted to ensure that the CPU latches the correct data. Because the MCP starts driving the data bus only at the rising edge of CLK in the second clock period of the bus cycle, not enough time is left for the data signals to propagate and be latched by the CPU before the next falling edge of CLK. Therefore, the MCP does not drive the READYO# signal until the third CLK period of the cycle. Thus, if the READYO# output drives the CPU's READY# input, one wait state is automatically inserted.

Because one wait state is required for MCP reads, the minimum length of a MCP read cycle is three CLK periods, as cycle 3 of Figure 4-2 shows.

When READY# is asserted, the MCP returns to the idle state. Simultaneously with the MCP's entering the idle state, the CPU may assert ADS# again, signaling the beginning of yet another cycle. The transition from T_{RS} state to idle state causes the MCP to put the tristate D15–D0 outputs into the floating state, allowing another device to drive the data bus.

4.2 Pipelined Bus Cycles

Because all the activities of the MCP bus interface occur either during the T_{RS} state or during the transitions to or from that state, the only difference between a pipelined and a nonpipelined cycle is the manner of changing from one state to another. The exact activities during each state are detailed in the previous section "Nonpipelined Bus Cycles".

When the CPU asserts ADS# before the end of a bus cycle, both ADS# and READY# are active dur-

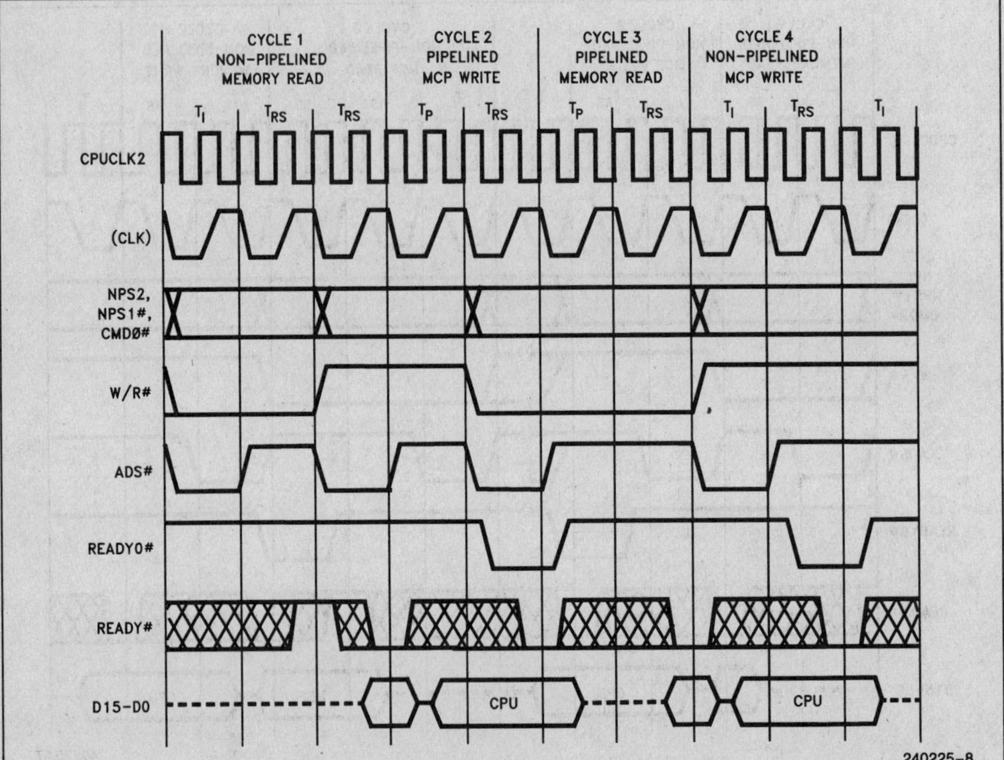

Cycle 1–Cycle 4 represent the operand transfer cycle for an instruction involving a transfer of two 32-bit loads in total. The opcode write cycles and other overhead are not shown.
Note that the next cycle will be a pipelined cycle if both READY# and ADS# are sampled active at the end of a T_{RS} state of the current cycle.

Figure 4-3. Fastest Transitions to and from Pipelined Cycles

ing a T_{RS} state. This condition causes the MCP to change to a different state named T_P. One clock period after a T_P state, the MCP always returns to T_{RS} state. In consecutive pipelined cycles, the MCP bus logic uses only the T_{RS} and T_P states.

Figure 4-3 shows the fastest transitions into and out of the pipelined bus cycles. Cycle 1 in the figure represents a nonpipelined cycle. (Nonpipelined write cycles with only one T_{RS} state (i.e. no wait states) are always followed by another nonpipelined cycle, because READY# is asserted before the earliest possible assertion of ADS# for the next cycle.)

Figure 4-4 shows pipelined write and read cycles with one additional T_{RS} state beyond the minimum required. To delay the assertion of READY# requires external logic.

4.3 Bus Cycles of Mixed Type

When the MCP bus logic is in the T_{RS} state, it distinguishes between nonpipelined and pipelined cycles according to the behavior of ADS# and READY#. In a nonpipelined cycle, only READY# is activated, and the transition is from T_{RS} state to idle state. In a

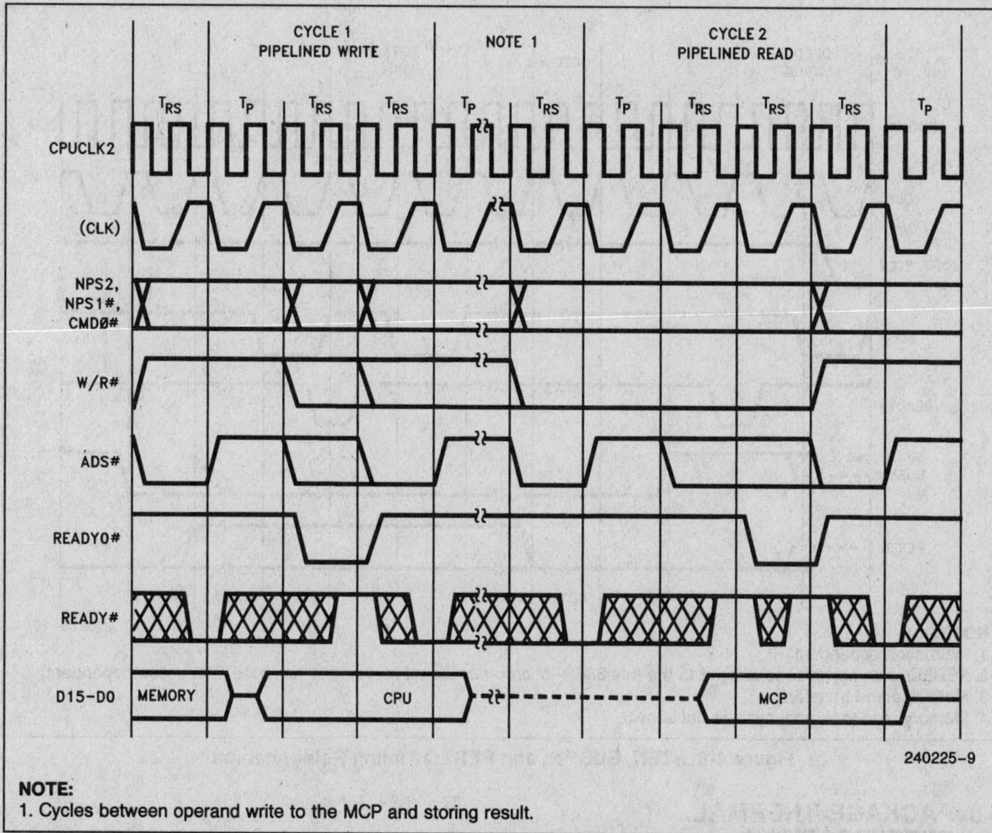

NOTE:
1. Cycles between operand write to the MCP and storing result.

Figure 4-4. Pipelined Cycles with Wait States

pipelined cycle, both READY# and ADS# are active, and the transition is first from T_{RS} state to T_P state, then, after one clock period, back to T_{RS} state.

4.4 BUSY# and PEREQ Timing Relationship

Figure 4-5 shows the activation of BUSY# at the beginning of instruction execution and its deactivation upon completion of the instruction. PEREQ is activated within this interval. If ERROR# (not shown in the figure) is ever asserted, it would be asserted at least six CPUCLK2 periods after the deactivation of PEREQ and would be deasserted at least six CPUCLK2 periods before the deactivation of BUSY#. Figure 4-5 also shows that STEN is activated at the beginning of a MCP bus cycle.

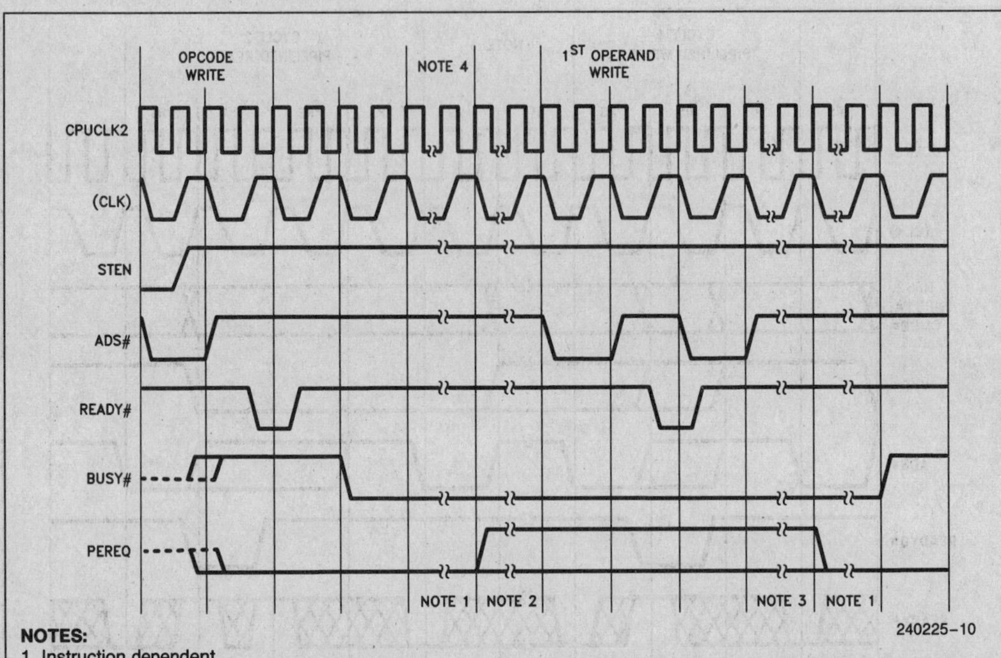

NOTES:
1. Instruction dependent.
2. PEREQ is an asynchronous input to the Intel386™ Microprocessor; it may not be asserted (instruction dependent).
3. More operand transfers.
4. Memory read (operand) cycle is not shown.

Figure 4-5. STEN, BUSY#, and PEREQ Timing Relationships

5.0 PACKAGE THERMAL SPECIFICATIONS

The Intel387 SX Math CoProcessor is specified for operation when case temperature is within the range of 0°C–100°C. The case temperature may be measured in any environment, to determine whether the Intel387 SX Math CoProcessor is within specified operating range. The case temperature should be measured at the center of the top surface opposite the pins.

The ambient temperature is guaranteed as long as T_c is not violated. The ambient temperature can be calculated from the θ_{jc} and θ_{ja} from the following equations:

$$T_j = T_c + P * \theta_{jc}$$

$$T_a = T_j - P * \theta_{ja}$$

$$T_c = T_a + P * [\theta_{ja} - \theta_{jc}]$$

Values for θ_{ja} and θ_{jc} are given in Table 5-1 for the 68-pin PLCC. θ_{ja} is given at various airflows. Table 5-2 shows the maximum T_a allowable (without exceeding T_c) at various airflows. Note that T_a can be improved further by attaching 'fins' or a 'heat sink' to the package. P is calculated by using the maximum hot I_{CC}.

Table 5-1. Thermal Resistances (°C/Watt) θ_{jc} and θ_{ja}

Package	θ_{jc}	θ_{ja} versus Airflow - ft/min (m/sec)					
		0 (0)	200 (1.01)	400 (2.03)	600 (3.04)	800 (4.06)	1000 (5.07)
68-Pin PLCC	8	30	25	20	15.5	13	12

Table 5-2. Maximum T_A at Various Airflows

Package	T_A(°C) versus Airflow - ft/min (m/sec)					
	0 (0)	200 (1.01)	400 (2.03)	600 (3.04)	800 (4.06)	1000 (5.07)
68-Pin PLCC	54.7	61.6	68.5	74.6	78.1	79.5

Max. T_A calculated at Max V_{CC} and Max I_{CC}.

Figure 5-1 shows the locations of pins on the chip package. Table 5-3 helps to locate pin identifiers in Figure 5-1.

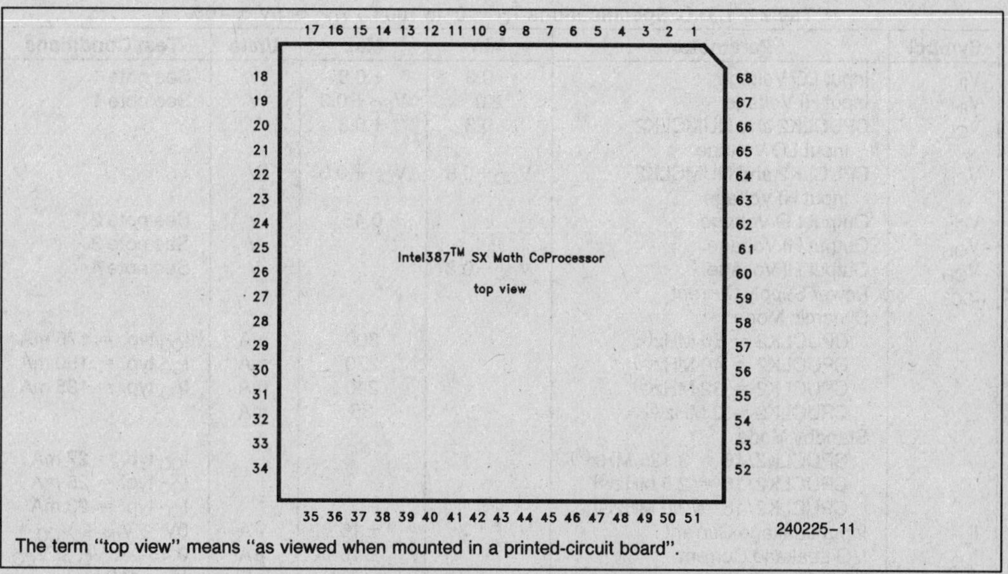

The term "top view" means "as viewed when mounted in a printed-circuit board".

Figure 5-1. PLCC Pin Configuration

Table 5-3. Pin Cross-Reference

1 — n.c.	18 — n.c.	35 — ERROR#	52 — n.c.
2 — D07	19 — D00	36 — BUSY#	53 — NUMCLK2
3 — D06	20 — D01	37 — V_{CC}	54 — CPUCLK2
4 — V_{CC}	21 — V_{SS}	38 — V_{SS}	55 — V_{SS}
5 — V_{SS}	22 — V_{CC}	39 — V_{CC}	56 — PEREQ
6 — D05	23 — D02	40 — STEN	57 — READYO#
7 — D04	24 — D08	41 — W/R#	58 — V_{CC}
8 — D03	25 — V_{SS}	42 — V_{SS}	59 — CKM
9 — V_{CC}	26 — V_{CC}	43 — V_{CC}	60 — V_{SS}
10 — n.c.	27 — V_{SS}	44 — NPS1#	61 — V_{SS}
11 — D15	28 — D09	45 — NPS2	62 — V_{CC}
12 — D14	29 — D10	46 — V_{CC}	63 — V_{SS}
13 — V_{CC}	30 — D11	47 — ADS#	64 — V_{CC}
14 — V_{SS}	31 — V_{CC}	48 — CMD0#	65 — n.c.
15 — D13	32 — V_{SS}	49 — READY#	66 — V_{SS}
16 — D12	33 — V_{CC}	50 — V_{CC}	67 — n.c.
17 — n.c.	34 — V_{SS}	51 — RESETIN	68 — n.c.

n.c.—The corresponding pins of the Intel387™ SX MCP are left unconnected.

6.0 ELECTRICAL DATA

6.1 Absolute Maximum Ratings

NOTE:
Stresses above those listed may cause permanent damage to the device. This is a stress rating only and functional operation of the device at these or any other conditions above those indicated in the operational sections of this specification is not implied. Exposure to absolute maximum rating conditions for extended periods may affect device reliability.

Case temperature T_C under bias ......0°C to 100°C
Storage temperature .... −65°C to +150°C
Voltage on any pin with respect to ground −0.5 to V_{CC}+0.5V
Power dissipation ....1.5 Watt

6.2 D.C. Characteristics

Table 6-1. D.C. Specifications T_C = 0° to 100°C, V_{CC} = 5V ± 10%

Symbol	Parameter	Min	Max	Units	Test Conditions
V_{IL}	Input LO Voltage	−0.3	+0.8	V	See note 1
V_{IH}	Input HI Voltage	2.0	V_{CC}+0.3	V	See note 1
V_{CL}	CPUCLK2 and NUMCLK2 Input LO Voltage	−0.3	+0.8	V	
V_{CH}	CPUCLK2 and NUMCLK2 Input HI Voltage	V_{CC}−0.8	V_{CC}+0.3	V	
V_{OL}	Output LO Voltage		0.45	V	See note 2
V_{OH}	Output HI Voltage	2.4		V	See note 3
V_{OH}	Output HI Voltage	V_{CC}−0.8		V	See note 4
I_{CC}	Power Supply Current				
	Dynamic Mode				
	CPUCLK2 = 50 MHz(5)		300	mA	I_{CC} typ. = 175 mA
	CPUCLK2 = 40 MHz(5)		270	mA	I_{CC} typ. = 160 mA
	CPUCLK2 = 32 MHz(5)		240	mA	I_{CC} typ. = 135 mA
	CPUCLK2 = 2 MHz(5)		85	mA	
	Standby Mode				
	CPUCLK2/16 = 3.125 MHz(6)				I_{CC} typ. = 27 mA
	CPUCLK2/16 = 2.5 MHz(6)				I_{CC} typ. = 25 mA
	CPUCLK2/16 = 2.0 MHz(6)				I_{CC} typ. = 23 mA
I_{LI}	Input Leakage Current		±15	μA	$0V \le V_{IN} \le V_{CC}$
I_{LO}	I/O Leakage Current		±15	μA	$0.45V \le V_O \le V_{CC}$
C_{IN}	Input Capacitance		10	pF	fc = 1MHz
C_O	I/O or Output Capacitance		12	pF	fc = 1MHz
C_{CLK}	Clock Capacitance		20	pF	fc = 1MHz

NOTES:
1. This parameter is for all inputs, excluding the clock inputs.
2. This parameter is measured at I_{OL} as follows:
   data = 4.0mA
   READY0#, ERROR#, BUSY#, PEREQ = 2.5mA
3. This parameter is measured at I_{OH} as follows:
   data = 1.0mA
   READY0#, ERROR#, BUSY#, PEREQ = 0.6mA
4. This parameter is measured at I_{OH} as follows:
   data = 0.2mA
   READY0#, ERROR#, BUSY#, PEREQ = 0.12mA
5. Synchronous Clock Mode (CKM = 1). I_{CC} is measured at steady state, maximum capacitive loading on the outputs, and worst-case D.C. level at the inputs.
6. Supports the Intel386™SL Power Management Feature.
   Synchronous clock mode, all control inputs are inactive, and the MCP is not executing an instruction. I_{CC} is measured at maximum capacitive loading on the outputs and worst case D.C. level at the inputs.

6.3 A.C. Characteristics

Table 6-2a. Combinations of Bus Interface and Execution Speeds

Functional Block	80387SX-16	80387SX-20	80387SX-25
Bus Interface Unit (MHz)	16	20	25
Execution Unit (MHz)	16	20	25

Table 6-2b. Timing Requirements of Execution Unit T_C = 0° to 100° C, V_{CC} = 5V ± 10%

Pin	Symbol	Parameter	16 MHz		20 MHz		25 MHz		Test Conditions	Refer to Figure
			Min (ns)	Max (ns)	Min (ns)	Max (ns)	Min (ns)	Max (ns)		
NUMCLK2	t1	Period	31.25	500	25	500	20	500	2.0V	6.2
NUMCLK2	t2a	High Time	8		7		6		2.0V	
NUMCLK2	t2b	High Time	5		4		3		V_{CC}−0.8V	
NUMCLK2	t3a	Low Time	8		7		6		2.0V	
NUMCLK2	t3b	Low Time	6		5		4		0.8V	
NUMCLK2	t4	Fall Time		8		8		7	From V_{CC}−0.8 to 0.8V	(Note 1)
NUMCLK2	t5	Rise Time		8		8		7	From 0.8 to V_{CC}−0.8V	

NOTE:
1. If not used (CKM = 1), tie LOW.

Table 6-2c. Timing Requirements of Bus Interface Unit T_C = 0° to 100° C, V_{CC} = 5V ± 10%
(All measurements made at 1.5V unless otherwise specified.)

Pin	Symbol	Parameter	16 MHz		20 MHz		25 MHz		Test Conditions	Refer to Figure
			Min (ns)	Max (ns)	Min (ns)	Max (ns)	Min (ns)	Max (ns)		
CPUCLK2	t1	Period	31.25	500	25	500	20	500	2.0V	6.2
CPUCLK2	t2a	High Time	8		7		6		2.0V	
CPUCLK2	t2b	High Time	5		4		3		V_{CC}−0.8V	
CPUCLK2	t3a	Low Time	8		7		6		2.0V	
CPUCLK2	t3b	Low Time	6		5		4		0.8V	
CPUCLK2	t4	Fall Time		8		8		7	From V_{CC}−0.8 to 0.8V	
CPUCLK2	t5	Rise Time		8		8		7	From 0.8 to V_{CC}−0.8V	
NUMCLK2/ CPUCLK2		Ratio	10/16	14/10	10/16	14/10	10/16	14/10		
READYO#	t7	Out Delay	4	34	4	31	4	26	C_L = 75pf	6.3
READYO#	t7	Out Delay	4	31	4	27	4	21	C_L = 25pf**	
PEREQ	t7	Out Delay	5	34	5	34	4	23	C_L = 75pf	
BUSY#	t7	Out Delay	5	34	5	29	4	23	C_L = 75pf	
ERROR#	t7	Out Delay	5	34	5	34	4	23	C_L = 75pf	
D15–D0	t8	Out Delay	1	54	1	54	0	50	C_L = 120pf	6.4
D15–D0	t10	Setup Time	11		11		11			
D15–D0	t11	Hold Time	11		11		11			
D15–D0	t12*	Float Time	6	33	6	27	5	24	C_L = 120pf	
PEREQ	t13*	Float Time	1	60	1	50	1	40	C_L = 75pf	6.6
BUSY#	t13*	Float Time	1	60	1	50	1	40	C_L = 75pf	
ERROR#	t13*	Float Time	1	60	1	50	1	40	C_L = 75pf	
READYO#	t13*	Float Time	1	60	1	50	1	40	C_L = 75pf	
ADS#	t14	Setup Time	26		21		16			6.4
ADS#	t15	Hold Time	4		4		4			
W/R#	t14	Setup Time	26		21		16			
W/R#	t15	Hold Time	4		4		4			
READY#	t16	Setup Time	19		12		10			6.4
READY#	t17	Hold Time	4		4		3			
CMD0#	t16	Setup Time	21		19		16			
CMD0#	t17	Hold Time	2		2		2			
NPS1#, NPS2	t16	Setup Time	21		19		16			
NPS1#, NPS2	t17	Hold Time	2		2		2			
STEN	t16	Setup Time	21		21		15			
STEN	t17	Hold Time	2		2		2			

Table 6-2c. Timing Requirements of Bus Interface Unit $T_C = 0° \text{ to } 100° C, V_{CC} = 5V \pm 10\%$ (Continued)

Pin	Symbol	Parameter	16 MHz (1.5V)		20 MHz (1.5V)		25 MHz		Test Conditions	Refer to Figure
			Min (ns)	Max (ns)	Min (ns)	Max (ns)	Min (ns)	Max (ns)		
RESETIN	t18	Setup Time	13		11		8			6.5
RESETIN	t19	Hold Time	3		3		3			

NOTES:
*Float condition occurs when maximum output current becomes less than I_{LO} in magnitude. Float delay is not tested.
**Not tested at 25 pf.

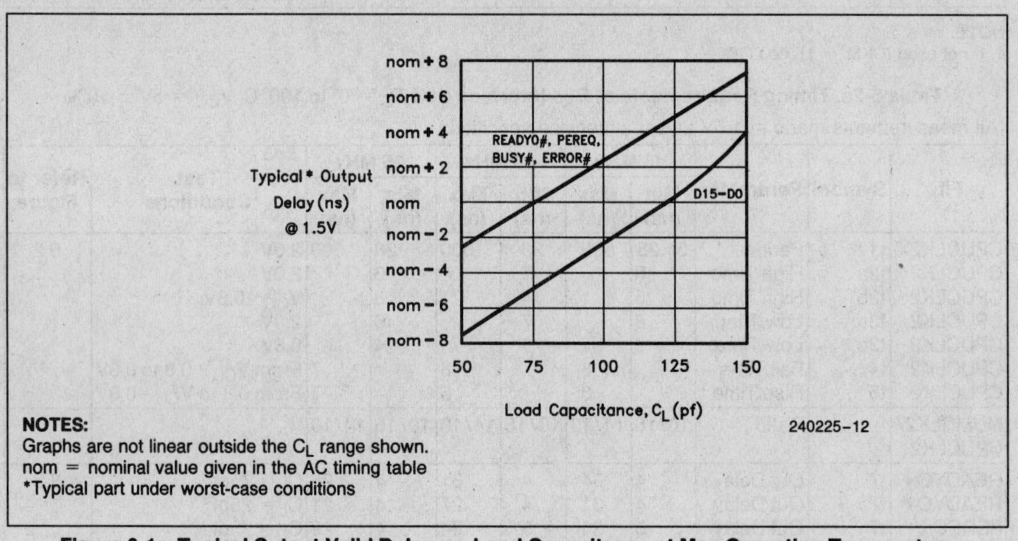

NOTES:
Graphs are not linear outside the C_L range shown.
nom = nominal value given in the AC timing table
*Typical part under worst-case conditions

Figure 6-1a. Typical Output Valid Delay vs. Load Capacitance at Max Operating Temperature

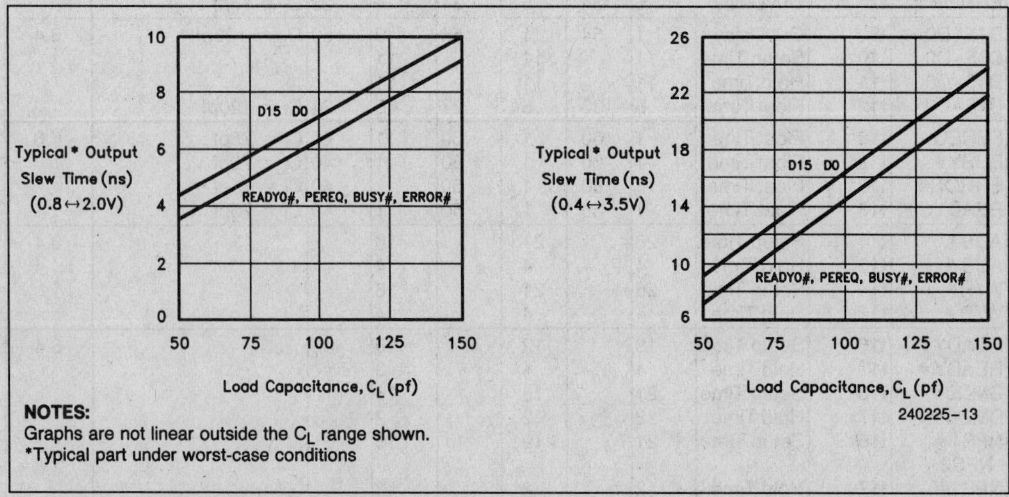

NOTES:
Graphs are not linear outside the C_L range shown.
*Typical part under worst-case conditions

Figure 6-1b. Typical Output Slew Time vs. Load Capacitance at Max Operating Temperature

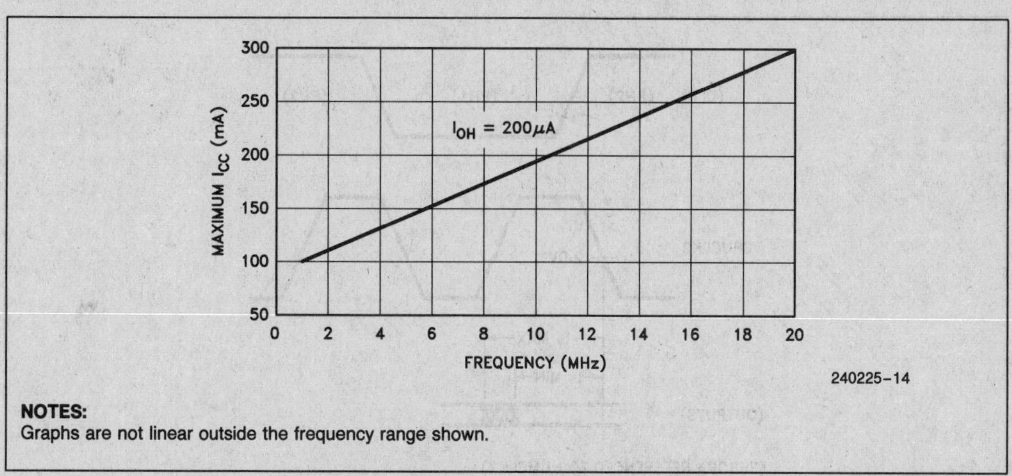

NOTES:
Graphs are not linear outside the frequency range shown.

Figure 6-1c. Maximum I_{CC} vs. Frequency

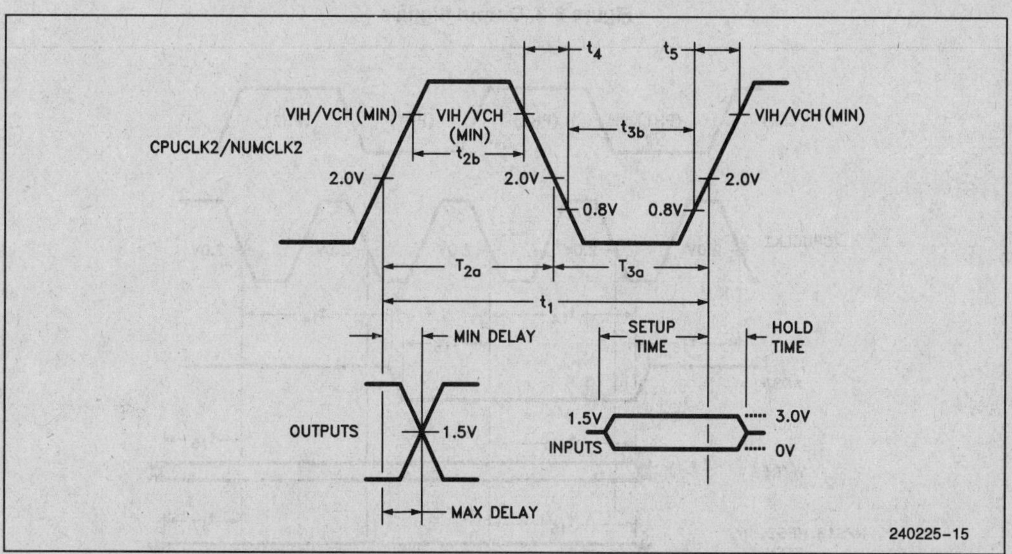

Figure 6-2. CPUCLK2/NUMCLK2 Waveform and Measurement Points for Input/Output

4

(CLK)
(PH2)
(PH1)
(PH2)
CPUCLK2
2.0V
t7 MAX
t7 MIN
(OUTPUTS)
(ERROR# REFERENCED TO NUMCLK2)
240225-16

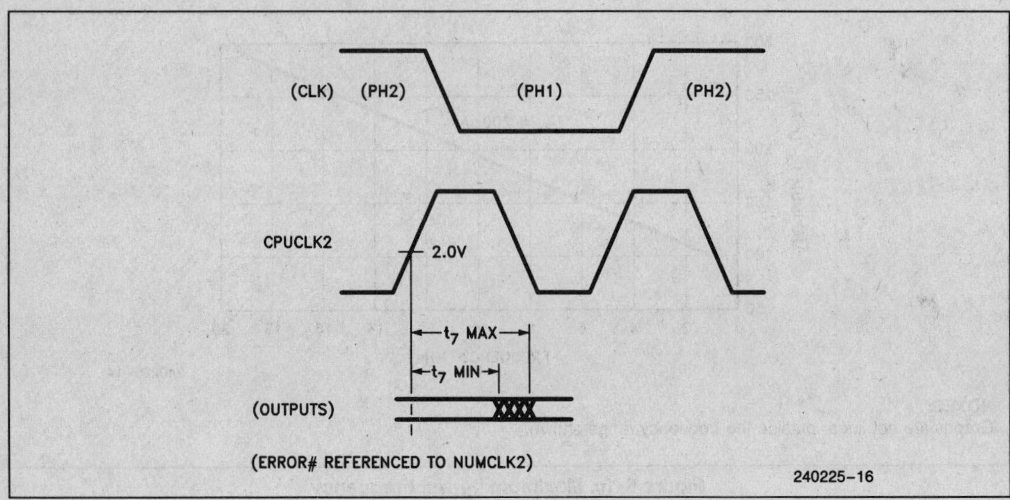

Figure 6-3. Output Signals

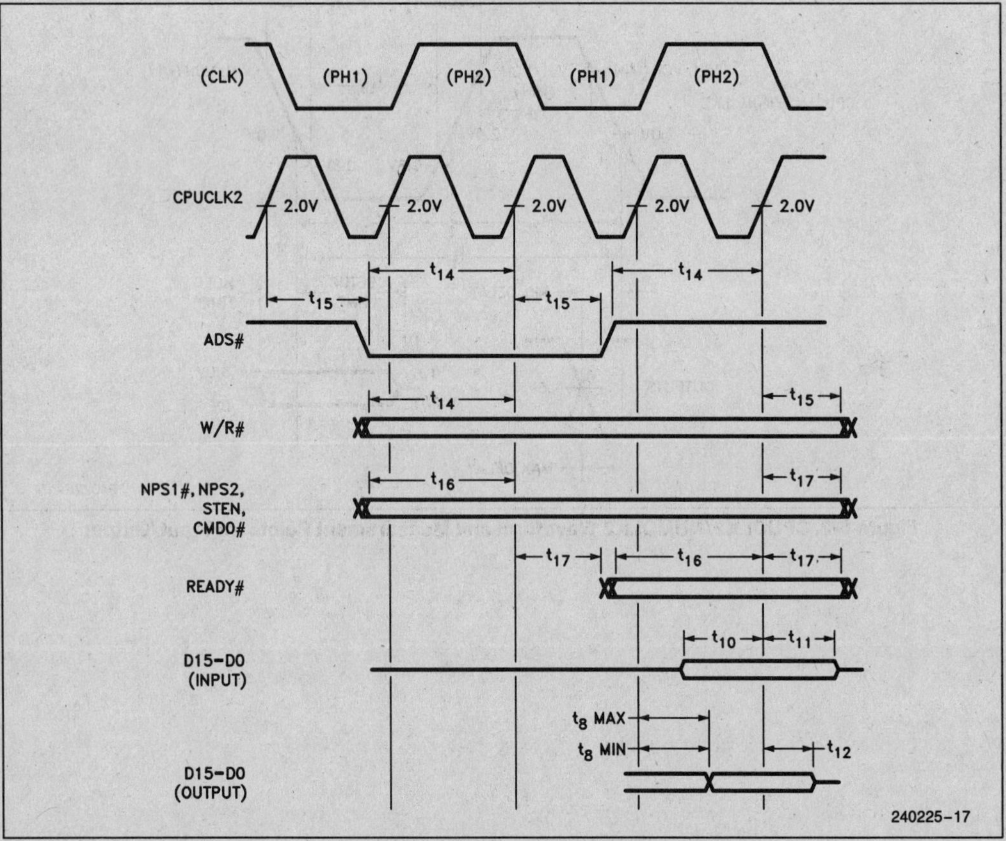

(CLK)
(PH1)
(PH2)
(PH1)
(PH2)
CPUCLK2
2.0V
2.0V
2.0V
2.0V
2.0V
t14
t14
t15
t15
ADS#
t14
t15
W/R#
t16
t17
NPS1#, NPS2, STEN, CMD0#
t17
t16
t17
READY#
t10
t11
D15-D0 (INPUT)
t8 MAX
t8 MIN
t12
D15-D0 (OUTPUT)
240225-17

Figure 6-4. Input and I/O Signals

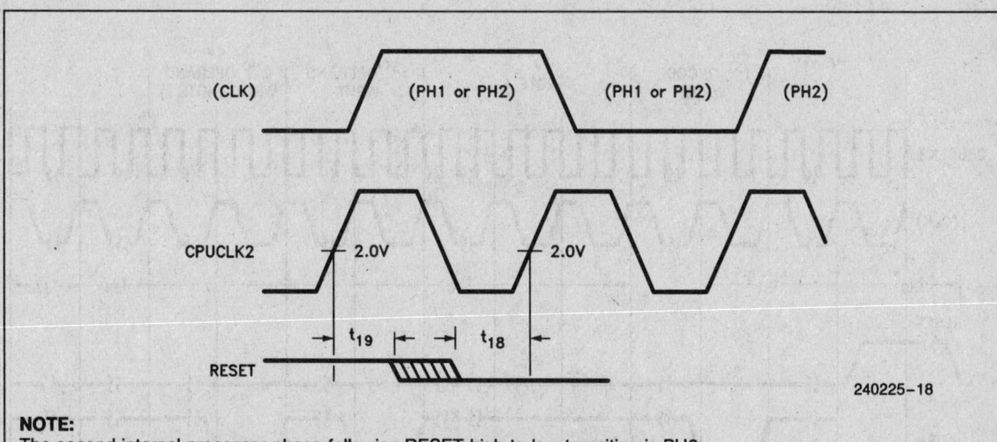

Figure 6-5. RESET Signal

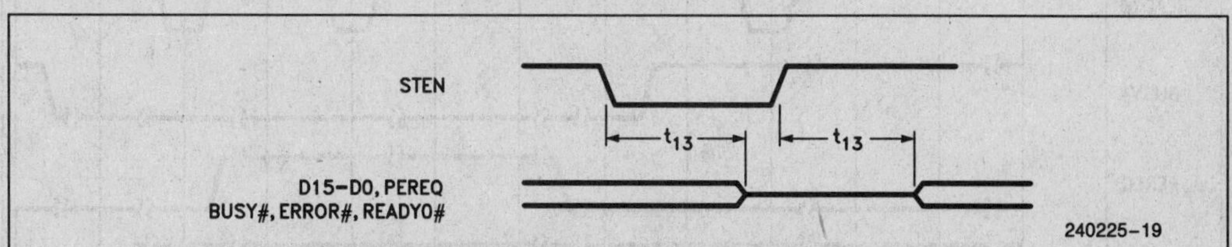

Figure 6-6. Float from STEN

Table 6-3. Other Parameters

Pin	Symbol	Parameter	Min	Max	Units
RESETIN	t30	Duration	40		NUMCLK2
RESETIN	t31	RESETIN inactive to 1st opcode write	50		NUMCLK2
BUSY#	t32	Duration	6		CPUCLK2
BUSY#, ERROR#	t33	ERROR# (in)active to BUSY# inactive	6		CPUCLK2
PEREQ, ERROR#	t34	PEREQ inactive to ERROR# active	6		CPUCLK2
READY#, BUSY#	t35	READY# active to BUSY# active	4	4	CPUCLK2
READY#	t36	Minimum time from opcode write to opcode/operand write	4		CPUCLK2
READY#	t37	Minimum time from operand write to operand write	4		CPUCLK2

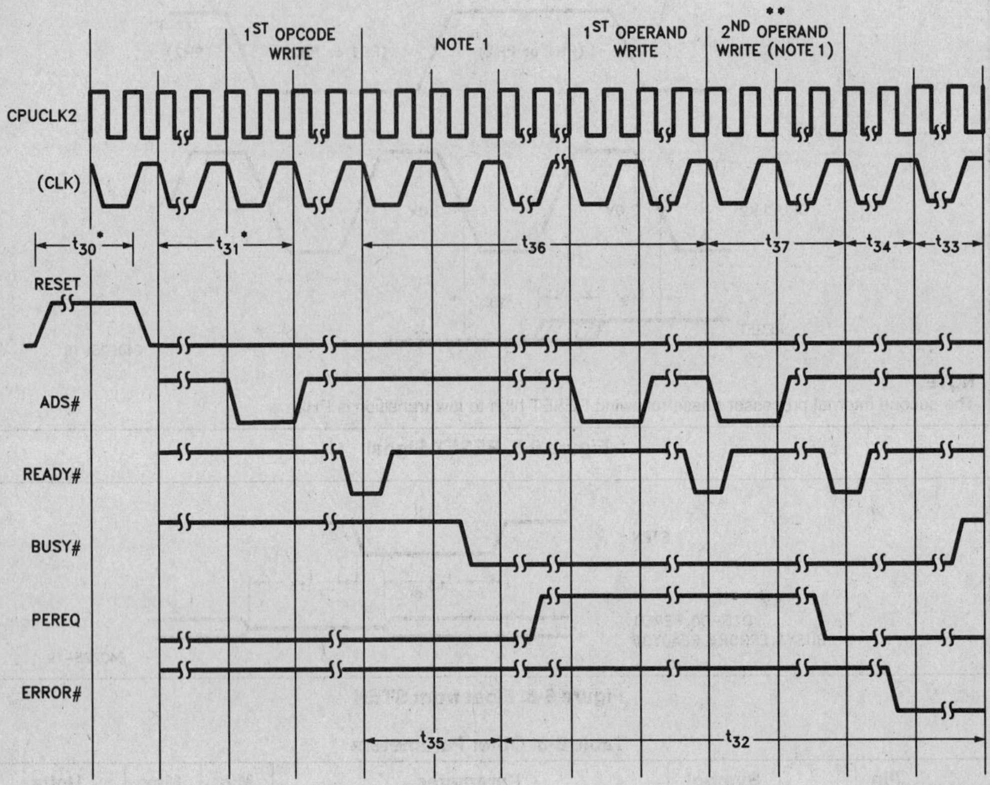

240225-20

* In NUMCLK2's

** or last operand

NOTE:

1. Memory read (operand) cycle is not shown.

Figure 6-7. Other Parameters

7.0 Intel387 SX MCP EXTENSIONS TO THE CPU'S INSTRUCTION SET

Instructions for the Intel387 SX MCP assume one of the five forms shown in Table 7-1. In all cases, instructions are at least two bytes long and begin with the bit pattern 11011B, which identifies the ESCAPE class of instruction. Instructions that refer to memory operands specify addresses using the CPU's addressing modes.

MOD (Mode field) and R/M (Register/Memory specifier) have the same interpretation as the corresponding fields of CPU instructions (refer to Programmer's Reference Manual for the CPU). SIB (Scale Index Base) byte and DISP (displacement) are optionally present in instructions that have MOD and R/M fields. Their presence depends on the values of MOD and R/M, as for instructions of the CPU.

The instruction summaries that follow assume that the instruction has been prefetched, decoded, and is ready for execution; that bus cycles do not require wait states; that there are no local bus HOLD requests delaying processor access to the bus; and that no exceptions are detected during instruction execution. If the instruction has MOD and R/M fields that call for both base and index registers, add one clock.

Table 7-1. Instruction Formats

	Instruction									Optional Fields	
	First Byte				Second Byte						
1	11011	OPA		1	MOD		1	OPB	R/M	SIB	DISP
2	11011	MF		OPA	MOD		OPB*		R/M	SIB	DISP
3	11011	d	P	OPA	1	1	OPB*		ST(i)		
4	11011	0	0	1	1	1	1	OP			
5	11011	0	1	1	1	1	1	OP			
	15–11	10	9	8	7	6	5	4 3	2 1 0		

OP = Instruction opcode, possibly split into two fields OPA and OPB
MF = Memory Format
  00—32-bit real
  01—32-bit integer
  10—64-bit real
  11—16-bit integer
d = Destination
  0—Destination is ST(0)
  1—Destination is ST(i)
R XOR d = 0—Destination (op) Source
R XOR d = 1—Source (op) Destination
*In FSUB and FDIV, the low-order bit of OPB is the R (reversed) bit
P = POP
  0—Do not pop stack
  1—Pop stack after operation
ESC = 11011
ST(i) = Register stack element i
  000 = Stack top
  001 = Second stack element
  .
  .
  .
  111 = Eighth stack element

Intel387™ SX MCP Extension to the Intel386™ SX Microprocessor Instruction Set

Instruction	Encoding			Clock Count Range			
	Byte 0	Byte 1	Optional Bytes 2–6	32-Bit Real	32-Bit Integer	64-Bit Real	16-Bit Integer
DATA TRANSFER							
FLD = Load[a]							
Integer/real memory to ST(0)	ESC MF 1	MOD 000 R/M	SIB/DISP	24	49–56	33	61–65
Long integer memory to ST(0)	ESC 111	MOD 101 R/M	SIB/DISP	64–75			
Extended real memory to ST(0)	ESC 011	MOD 101 R/M	SIB/DISP	52			
BCD memory to ST(0)	ESC 111	MOD 100 R/M	SIB/DISP	274–283			
ST(i) to ST(0)	ESC 001	11000 ST(i)		14			
FST = Store							
ST(0) to integer/real memory	ESC MF 1	MOD 010 R/M	SIB/DISP	49	84–98	55	82–95
ST(0) to ST(i)	ESC 101	11010 ST(i)		11			
FSTP = Store and Pop							
ST(0) to integer/real memory	ESC MF 1	MOD 011 R/M	SIB/DISP	49	84–98	55	82–95
ST(0) to long integer memory	ESC 111	MOD 111 R/M	SIB/DISP	90–107			
ST(0) to extended real	ESC 011	MOD 111 R/M	SIB/DISP	63			
ST(0) to BCD memory	ESC 111	MOD 110 R/M	SIB/DISP	522–544			
ST(0) to ST(i)	ESC 101	11011 ST (i)		12			
FXCH = Exchange							
ST(i) and ST(0)	ESC 001	11001 ST(i)		18			
COMPARISON							
FCOM = Compare							
Integer/real memory to ST(0)	ESC MF 0	MOD 010 R/M	SIB/DISP	30	60–67	39	71–75
ST(i) to ST(0)	ESC 000	11010 ST(i)		24			
FCOMP = Compare and pop							
Integer/real memory to ST	ESC MF 0	MOD 011 R/M	SIB/DISP	30	60–67	39	71–75
ST(i) to ST(0)	ESC 000	11011 ST(i)		26			
FCOMPP = Compare and pop twice							
ST(1) to ST(0)	ESC 110	1101 1001		26			
FTST = Test ST(0)	ESC 001	1110 0100		28			
FUCOM = Unordered compare	ESC 101	11100 ST(i)		24			
FUCOMP = Unordered compare and pop	ESC 101	11101 ST(i)		26			
FUCOMPP = Unordered compare and pop twice	ESC 010	1110 1001		26			
FXAM = Examine ST(0)	ESC 001	11100101		30-38			
CONSTANTS							
FLDZ = Load +0.0 into ST(0)	ESC 001	1110 1110		20			
FLD1 = Load +1.0 into ST(0)	ESC 001	1110 1000		24			
FLDPI = Load pi into ST(0)	ESC 001	1110 1011		40			
FLDL2T = Load $\log_2(10)$ into ST(0)	ESC 001	1110 1001		40			

Shaded areas indicate instructions not available in 8087/80287.

NOTE:
a. When loading single- or double-precision zero from memory, add 5 clocks.

Intel387™ SX MCP Extension to the Intel386™ SX Microprocessor Instruction Set (Continued)

Instruction	Encoding			Clock Count Range			
	Byte 0	Byte 1	Optional Bytes 2–6	32-Bit Real	32-Bit Integer	64-Bit Real	16-Bit Integer
CONSTANTS (Continued)							
FLDL2E = Load $log_2(e)$ into ST(0)	ESC 001	1110 1010		40			
FLDLG2 = Load $log_{10}(2)$ into ST(0)	ESC 001	1110 1100		41			
FLDLN2 = Load $log_e(2)$ into ST(0)	ESC 001	1110 1101		41			
ARITHMETIC							
FADD = Add							
Integer/real memory with ST(0)	ESC MF 0	MOD 000 R/M	SIB/DISP	28–36	61–76	37–45	71–85
ST(i) and ST(0)	ESC d P 0	11000 ST(i)		23–31[b]			
FSUB = Subtract							
Integer/real memory with ST(0)	ESC MF 0	MOD 10 R R/M	SIB/DISP	28–36	61–76	36–44	71–83[c]
ST(i) and ST(0)	ESC d P 0	1110 R R/M		26–34[d]			
FMUL = Multiply							
Integer/real memory with ST(0)	ESC MF 0	MOD 001 R/M	SIB/DISP	31–39	65–86	40–65	76–87
ST(i) and ST(0)	ESC d P 0	1100 1 R/M		29–57[e]			
FDIV = Divide							
Integer/real memory with ST(0)	ESC MF 0	MOD 11 R R/M	SIB/DISP	93	124–131[f]	102	136–140[g]
ST(i) and ST(0)	ESC d P 0	1111 R R/M		88[h]			
FSQRT[i] = Square root	ESC 001	1111 1010		122–129			
FSCALE = Scale ST(0) by ST(1)	ESC 001	1111 1101		67–86			
FPREM = Partial remainder	ESC 001	1111 1000		74–155			
FPREM1 = Partial remainder (IEEE)	ESC 001	1111 0101		95–185			
FRNDINT = Round ST(0) to integer	ESC 001	1111 1100		66–80			
FXTRACT = Extract components of ST(0)	ESC 001	1111 0100		70–76			
FABS = Absolute value of ST(0)	ESC 001	1110 0001		22			
FCHS = Change sign of ST(0)	ESC 001	1110 0000		24–25			

Shaded areas indicate instructions not available in 8087/80287.

NOTES:
b. Add 3 clocks to the range when d = 1.
c. Add 1 clock to **each** range when R = 1.
d. Add 3 clocks to the range when d = 0.
e. typical = 52 (When d = 0, 46–54, typical = 49).
f. Add 1 clock to the range when R = 1.
g. 135–141 when R = 1.
h. Add 3 clocks to the range when d = 1.
i. $-0 \leq ST(0) \leq +\infty$.

4

Intel387™ SX MCP Extension to the Intel386™ SX Microprocessor Instruction Set (Continued)

Instruction	Encoding Byte 0	Encoding Byte 1	Encoding Optional Bytes 2–6	Clock Count Range
TRANSCENDENTAL				
FCOS[k] = Cosine of ST(0)	ESC 001	1111 1111		123–772[j]
FPTAN[k] = Partial tangent of ST(0)	ESC 001	1111 0010		191–497[j]
FPATAN = Partial arctangent	ESC 001	1111 0011		314–487
FSIN[k] = Sine of ST(0)	ESC 001	1111 1110		122–771[j]
FSINCOS[k] = Sine and cosine of ST(0)	ESC 001	1111 1011		194–809[j]
F2XM1[l] = $2^{ST(0)} - 1$	ESC 001	1111 0000		211–476
FYL2X[m] = ST(1) * $\log_2$(ST(0))	ESC 001	1111 0001		120–538
FYL2XP1[n] = ST(1) * $\log_2$(ST(0) + 1.0)	ESC 001	1111 1001		257–547
PROCESSOR CONTROL				
FINIT = Initialize MCP	ESC 011	1110 0011		33
FSTSW AX = Store status word	ESC 111	1110 0000		13
FLDCW = Load control word	ESC 001	MOD 101 R/M	SIB/DISP	19
FSTCW = Store control word	ESC 101	MOD 111 R/M	SIB/DISP	15
FSTSW = Store status word	ESC 101	MOD 111 R/M	SIB/DISP	15
FCLEX = Clear exceptions	ESC 011	1110 0010		11
FSTENV = Store environment	ESC 001	MOD 110 R/M	SIB/DISP	103–104
FLDENV = Load environment	ESC 001	MOD 100 R/M	SIB/DISP	71
FSAVE = Save state	ESC 101	MOD 110 R/M	SIB/DISP	475–476
FRSTOR = Restore state	ESC 101	MOD 100 R/M	SIB/DISP	388
FINCSTP = Increment stack pointer	ESC 001	1111 0111		21
FDECSTP = Decrement stack pointer	ESC 001	1111 0110		22
FFREE = Free ST(i)	ESC 101	1100 0 ST(i)		18
FNOP = No operations	ESC 001	1101 0000		12

Shaded areas indicate instructions not available in 8087/80287.

NOTES:

j. These timings hold for operands in the range $|x| < \pi/4$. For operands not in this range, up to 76 additional clocks may be needed to reduce the operand.

k. $0 \le |ST(0)| < 2^{63}$.

l. $-1.0 \le ST(0) \le 1.0$.

m. $0 \le ST(0) < \infty, -\infty < ST(1) < +\infty$.

n. $0 \le |ST(0)| < (2 - SQRT(2))/2, -\infty < ST(1) < +\infty$.

APPENDIX A
COMPATIBILITY BETWEEN THE 80287 AND THE 8087

The 80286/80287 operating in Real-Address mode will execute 8086/8087 programs without major modification. However, because of differences in the handling of numeric exceptions by the 80287 MCP and the 8087 MCP, exception-handling routines *may* need to be changed.

This appendix summarizes the differences between the 80287 MCP and the 8087 MCP, and provides details showing how 8086/8087 programs can be ported to the 80286/80287.

1. The MCP signals exceptions through a dedicated ERROR# line to the 80286. The MCP error signal does not pass through an interrupt controller (the 8087 INT signal does). Therefore, any interrupt-controller-oriented instructions in numeric exception handlers for the 8086/8087 should be deleted.
2. The 8087 instructions FENI/FNENI and FDISI/FNDISI perform no useful function in the 80287. If the 80287 encounters one of these opcodes in its instruction stream, the instruction will effectively be ignored—none of the 80287 internal states will be updated. While 8086/8087 containing these instructions may be executed on the 80286/80287, it is unlikely that the exception-handling routines containing these instructions will be completely portable to the 80287.
3. Interrupt vector 16 must point to the numeric exception handling routine.
4. The ESC instruction address saved in the 80287 includes any leading prefixes before the ESC opcode. The corresponding address saved in the 8087 does not include leading prefixes.
5. In Protected-Address mode, the format of the 80287's saved instruction and address pointers is different than for the 8087. The instruction opcode is not saved in Protected mode—exception handlers will have to retrieve the opcode from memory if needed.
6. Interrupt 7 will occur in the 80286 when executing ESC instructions with either TS (task switched) or EM (emulation) of the 80286 MSW set (TS = 1 or EM = 1). If TS is set, then a WAIT instruction will also cause interrupt 7. An exception handler should be included in 80286/80287 code to handle these situations.
7. Interrupt 9 will occur if the second or subsequent words of a floating-point operand fall outside a segment's size. Interrupt 13 will occur if the starting address of a numeric operand falls outside a segment's size. An exception handler should be included in 80286/80287 code to report these programming errors.
8. Except for the processor control instructions, all of the 80287 numeric instructions are automatically synchronized by the 80286 CPU—the 80286 automatically tests the BUSY# line from the 80287 to ensure that the 80287 has completed its previous instruction before executing the next ESC instruction. No explicit WAIT instructions are required to assure this synchronization. For the 8087 used with 8086 and 8088 processors, explicit WAITs are required before each numeric instruction to ensure synchronization. Although 8086/8087 programs having explicit WAIT instructions will execute perfectly on the 80286/80287 without reassembly, these WAIT instructions are unnecessary.
9. Since the 80287 does not require WAIT instructions before each numeric instruction, the ASM286 assembler does not automatically generate these WAIT instructions. The ASM86 assembler, however, automatically precedes every ESC instruction with a WAIT instruction. Although numeric routines generated using the ASM86 assembler will generally execute correctly on the 80286/80287, reassembly using ASM286 may result in a more compact code image.

   The processor control instructions for the 80287 may be coded using either a WAIT or No-WAIT form of mnemonic. The WAIT forms of these instructions cause ASM286 to precede the ESC instruction with a CPU WAIT instruction, in the identical manner as does ASM86.

4

DATA SHEET REVISION REVIEW

The following list represents the key differences between this and the -007 version of the Intel387 SX Math CoProcessor Data Sheet. Please review this summary carefully.

1. Intel387 SX MCP 25 MHz A.C. and D.C. specifications added.

82396SX SMART CACHE

- **Optimized Intel386™ SX Microprocessor Companion**
- **4 Way SET Associative with Pseudo LRU Algorithm**
- **Write Buffer Architecture**
- **Integrated 4 Word Write Buffer**
- **Integrated Intel387™ SX Math Coprocessor Decode Logic**
- **132 Lead PQFP Package**
- **Intel486™ SX Microprocessor like Burst**
- **Integrated 16 KB Data RAM**
- **16-Byte Line Size**
- **Dual Bus Architecture — Snooping Maintains Cache Coherency**
- **20 MHz Clock**
- **Concurrent Line Buffer Cacheing**
- **1K of TAG RAM**
- **Non-Sectored Architecture**

The 82396SX Smart Cache (part number 82396SX) is a low cost, single chip, 16-bit peripheral for Intel's i386™ SX Microprocessor. By storing frequently accessed code or data from main memory the 82396SX Smart Cache enables the i386™ SX Microprocessor to run at near zero wait states. The dual bus architecture allows another bus master to access the System Bus while the i386™ SX Microprocessor operates out of the 82396SX Smart Cache on the Local Bus. The 82396SX Smart Cache has a snooping mechanism which maintains cache coherency with main memory during these cycles.

The 82396SX Smart Cache is completely software transparent, protecting the integrity of system software. The advanced architectural features of the 82596SX Smart Cache offer high performance with a cache data RAM size that can be integrated on a single chip, offering the board space and cost savings needed in an i386™ SX Microprocessor based system.

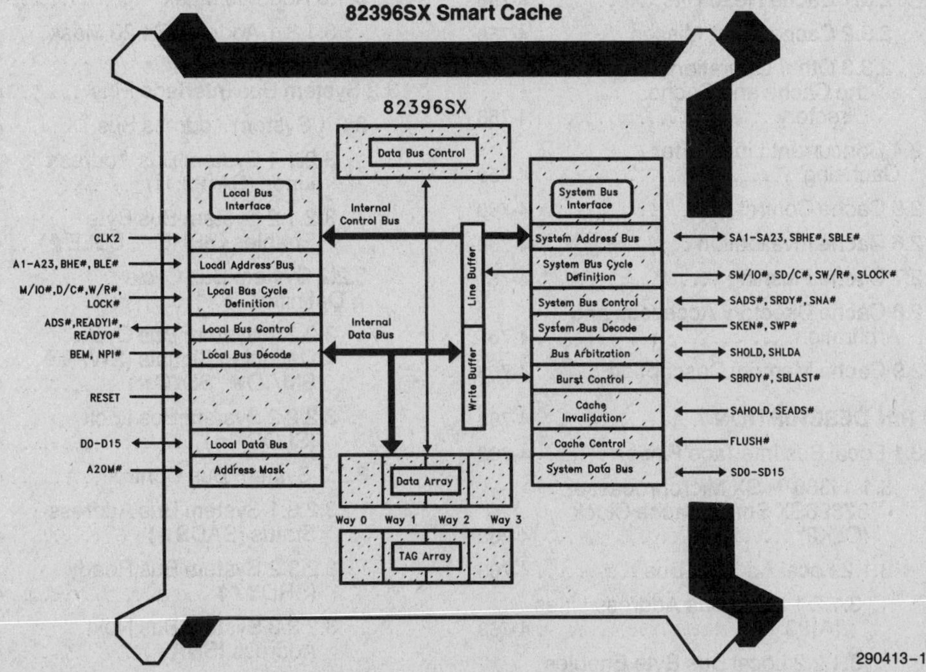

September 1991
Order Number: 290413-001

82396SX Smart Cache

CONTENTS PAGE

CONTENTS PAGE

CONTENTS PAGE

CONTENTS PAGE

4

CONTENTS PAGE

CONTENTS PAGE

CONTENTS PAGE

FIGURES

CONTENTS PAGE

CONTENTS PAGE

TABLES

CONTENTS PAGE

0.0 DESIGNER SUMMARY

0.1 Pin Out

Figure 0.1 82396SX Smart Cache 132 Lead PQFP Package Pin Orientation

4

Table 0.1 82396SX Smart Cache 132 Pin PQFP Pin Description

Pin	Signal	Pin	Signal	Pin	Signal	Pin	Signal
1	V_{CC}	34	V_{SS}	67	V_{CC}	100	V_{SS}
2	D11	35	SA23	68	A22	101	SD10
3	D12	36	SBLE#	69	A21	102	SD9
4	D13	37	SBHE#	70	A20	103	SD8
5	V_{SS}	38	SLOCK#	71	A20M#	104	V_{CC}
6	D14	39	SBLAST#	72	A19	105	V_{SS}
7	D15	40	SHLDA	73	A18	106	SD7
8	V_{CC}	41	SM/IO#	74	A17	107	SD6
9	V_{SS}	42	SD/C#	75	A16	108	SD5
10	RESET	43	SW/R#	76	A15	109	SD4
11	CLK2	44	BLE#	77	A14	110	SD3
12	SA1	45	V_{CC}	78	A13	111	SD2
13	SA2	46	BHE#	79	A12	112	SD1
14	SA3	47	LOCK#	80	A11	113	SD0
15	SA4	48	M/IO#	81	A10	114	V_{CC}
16	SA5	49	W/R#	82	A9	115	V_{SS}
17	SA6	50	D/C#	83	A8	116	READYO#
18	SA7	51	V_{SS}	84	A7	117	V_{SS}
19	SA8	52	V_{CC}	85	V_{SS}	118	V_{CC}
20	SA9	53	SKEN#	86	A6	119	D0
21	SA10	54	NPI#	87	A5	120	D1
22	SA11	55	SWP#	88	A4	121	D2
23	SA12	56	SNA#	89	A3	122	D3
24	SA13	57	SBRDY#	90	A2	123	D4
25	SA14	58	SRDY#	91	A1	124	D5
26	SA15	59	SAHOLD	92	ADS#	125	D6
27	SA16	60	SHOLD	93	SADS#	126	D7
28	SA17	61	READYI#	94	SD15	127	V_{SS}
29	SA18	62	SEADS#	95	SD14	128	V_{CC}
30	SA19	63	FLUSH#	96	SD13	129	D8
31	SA20	64	BEM	97	SD12	130	D9
32	SA21	65	A23	98	SD11	131	D10
33	SA22	66	V_{SS}	99	V_{CC}	132	V_{SS}

0.2 Quick Pin Reference

What follows is a brief pin description. For more details refer to Chapter 3.

Symbol	Type	Function
CLK2	I	This signal provides the fundamental timing for the 82396SX Smart Cache. All external timing parameters are specified with respect to the rising edge of CLK2.
Local Address Bus		
A[23:1]	I	A[23:1] are the Local Bus address lines. These signals along with the byte enable signals, define the physical area of memory or input/output space accessed.
BHE#, BLE#	I	The byte enable signals are used to determine which bytes are accessed in partial cache write cycles. These signals are ignored for Cache Read Hit cycles. For all System Bus memory read cycles (except the last seven cycles of a Line Fill), these signals are mirrored by the SBHE#, SBLE# signals. (See also SBHE#, SBLE# and BEM.)
Local Bus Cycle Definition		
W/R# D/C# M/IO#	I I I	The write/read, data/code and memory/input-output signals are the primary bus definition signals directly connected to the i386™ SX Microprocessor. They become valid as the ADS# signal is sampled active. The bus definition signals are not driven by the i386™ SX Microprocessor during bus hold and follow the timing of the address bus.
LOCK#	I	The Local Bus LOCK# signal indicates that the current bus cycle is LOCK#ed. LOCK#ed cycles are treated as non-cacheable cycles, except that LOCK#ed write hit cycles update the cache.
Local Bus Control		
ADS#	I	The address status pin, an output of the i386™ SX Microprocessor, indicates that new and valid information is currently available on the Local Bus. The signals that are valid when ADS# is activated are: A[23:1], BHE#, BLE#, W/R#, D/C#, M/IO#, LOCK#, NPI#, BEM
READYI#	I	This is the READY input signal seen by the Local Bus master. Typically it is a logical OR between the READYO# generated by the 82396SX Smart Cache and the READY# signal generated by the i387™ SX Math Coprocessor. It is used by the 82396SX Smart Cache, along with the ADS# signal, to keep track of the i386™ SX Microprocessor bus state.
READYO#	O	This is the Local Bus READY output that is used to terminate all types of i386™ SX Microprocessor bus cycles, except for i387™ SX Math Coprocessor cycles. Assertion of READYO# indicates the completion of the cycle on the Local Bus. The cycle can be concurrently running on the System Bus allowing the dual bus nature of the 82396SX Smart Cache to be utilized. The READYO# pin may serve as READY# for the i387™ SX Math Coprocessor.
Reset		
RESET	I	The RESET signal forces the 82396SX Smart Cache to begin execution at a known state. The RESET falling edge is used by the 82396SX Smart Cache to set the phase of its internal clock identical to the i386™ SX Microprocessors internal clock. RESET falling edge must satisfy the appropriate setup and hold times (T14, T15b) for proper chip operation. RESET must remain active for at least 1ms after the power supply and CLK2 input have reached their proper DC and AC specifications.
Local Data Bus		
D[15:0]	I/O	These are the Local Bus data lines of the 82396SX Smart Cache. They must be connected to the D[15:0] pins of the i386™ SX Microprocessor.
Local Bus Decode Pins		
NPI#	I	The No Post Input signal instructs the 82396SX Smart Cache that the write cycle currently in progress must not be posted in the write buffer. NPI# is sampled at the falling edge of CLK at the end of T1 (see Figure 5.1).

0.2 Quick Pin Reference (Continued)

Symbol	Type	Function
Local Bus Decode Pins (Continued)		
BEM	I	The Byte Enable Mask signal, when asserted, causes the local bus byte enable signals to be masked so that both system bus byte enables are asserted on memory read cycles. If BEM is asserted during cacheble read cycles and that cycle requires a Line Fill (cache read miss), then both bytes will be accessed during the first cycle of the Line Fill. If BEM is not used (tied low), the system must return valid data for both bytes on the first access of a Line Fill, because SBHE# and SBLE# will be the same as BHE# and BLE# during the first access of a Line Fill and are not always active.
Address Mask		
A20M#	I	Address bit 20 Mask when active, forces the A20 input as seen by the 82396SX Smart Cache to logic '0', regardless of the actual value on the A20 input pin. A20M# emulates the address wraparound at 1 MByte which occurs on the 8086. This pin is asynchronous but must meet setup and hold times (t47 and t48) to guarantee recognition in a specific clock. It must be asserted two clock cycles before ADS# is sampled active (see figure 5.3). It must be stable throughout Local Bus memory cycles.
System Address Bus		
SA[3:1] SA[23:4]	O I/O	These are the System Bus address lines of the 82396SX Smart Cache. When driven by the 82396SX Smart Cache, these signals, along with the System Bus byte enables define the physical area of memory or input/output space being accessed. During bus HOLD or address HOLD, the 20 MSB serve as inputs for the cache invalidation cycle.
SBHE#, SBLE#	O	These are the Byte Enable signals for the System Bus. When BEM is inactive, the 82396SX Smart Cache drives these pins identically to BHE# and BLE# in all System Bus cycles except Line Fills. In Line Fills these signals are driven identically to BHE# and BLE# for the first read cycle of the Line Fill. They are both driven active in the remaining cycles of the Line Fill. When BEM is active, the 82396SX Smart Cache will assert SBHE# and SBLE# for all non-locked memory read cycles.
System Bus Cycle Definition		
SW/R# SD/C# SM/IO#	O O O	The System Bus write/read, data/code and memory/input- output signals are the System Bus cycle definition pins. When the 82396SX Smart Cache is the System Bus master, it drives these signals identically to the i386™ SX Microprocessor cycle definition encoding.
SLOCK#	O	The System Bus LOCK signal indicates that the current cycle is LOCK#ed. The 82396SX Smart Cache has exclusive access to the System Bus across bus cycle boundries until this signal is negated. The 82396SX Smart Cache does not acknowledge a bus HOLD request while this signal is asserted. The 82396SX Smart Cache asserts SLOCK# when the System Bus is available and a LOCK#ed cycle was started on the Local Bus that requires System Bus service. SLOCK# is negated only after completion of all LOCK#ed System Bus cycles and negation of the LOCK# signal.
System Bus Control		
SADS#	O	The System Bus Address Status signal is used to indicate that new and valid information is currently being driven onto the System Bus. The signals that are valid when SADS# is driven low are: SA[23:1], SBHE#, SBLE#, SW/R#, SD/C#, SM/IO# and SLOCK#

0.2 Quick Pin Reference (Continued)

Symbol	Type	Function
System Bus Control (Continued)		
SRDY#	I	The System Bus ReaDY# signal indicates that the current System Bus cycle is complete. When SRDY# is sampled asserted it indicates one of two things. In response to a read request it indicates that the external system has presented valid data on the system data bus. In response to a write request it indicates that the external system has accepted the 82396SX Smart Cache's data. This signal is ignored when the System Bus is in STi, STH, ST1 or ST1P states. At the first read cycle of a Line Fill SRDY#, SBRDY# and SNA# determine if the Line Fill will proceed as a burst/non-burst, pipelined/non-pipelined Line Fill. Once a burst Line Fill has started, if SRDY# is returned in the 2nd through the 7th word, the burst Line Fill will be interrupted and the cache will not be updated. The 1st word will already have been transferred to the CPU. In the 8th word of a Line Fill both SRDY# and SBRDY# have the same effect. They indicate the end of the Line Fill.
SNA#	I	The System Bus Next Address signal, when active, indicates that a pipelined address cycle will be executed. It is sampled by the 82396SX Smart Cache at the rising edge of CLK in ST2 and ST1P cycles. SNA# is ignored during the eighth word of the Line Fill. If this signal is sampled active for the first word of the Line Fill then burst Line Fills are disabled.
Bus Arbitration		
SHOLD	I	The System Bus HOLD request indicates that another master must have complete control of the entire System Bus. When SHOLD is sampled asserted the 82396SX Smart Cache completes the current System Bus cycle or sequence of LOCK#ed cycles, before driving SHLDA active. In the same clock that SHLDA went active all the System Bus outputs and I/O pins are floated (with the exception of SHLDA). The 82396SX Smart Cache stays in this state until SHOLD is negated. SHOLD is recognized during RESET.
SHLDA	O	The System Bus HOLD Acknowledge signal is driven active by the 82396SX Smart Cache in response to a hold request. It indicates that the 82396SX Smart Cache has given the bus to another System Bus master. It is driven active in the same clock that the 82396SX Smart Cache floats it's System Bus. When leaving a bus HOLD, SHLDA is driven inactive and the 82396SX Smart Cache resumes driving the bus in the same clock. The 82396SX Smart Cache is able to support CPU Local Bus activities during System Bus HOLD.
Burst Control		
SBRDY#	I	The System Bus Burst ReaDY signal performs the same function during a burst cycle that SRDY# does in a non-burst cycle. SBRDY# asserted indicates that the external system has presented valid data on the data pins in response to a burst Line Fill cycle. This signal is ignored when the System Bus is at STi, STH, ST1 or ST1P states. Note that in the eighth bus cycle of a Line Fill, SBRDY# and SRDY# have the same effect on the 82396SX Smart Cache. They indicate the end of the Line Fill. For all cycles other than burst Line Fills, SBRDY# and SRDY# have the same effect on the 82396SX Smart Cache.

0.2 Quick Pin Reference (Continued)

Symbol	Type	Function
Burst Control (Continued)		
SBLAST#	O	The System Bus Burst LAST cycle indicator signal indicates that the next time SBRDY# is returned the burst cycle is complete. It indicates to the external system that the next SBRDY# returned is treated as a normal SRDY# by the 82396SX Smart Cache. Another set of addresses will be driven with SADS# or the System Bus will go idle. SBLAST# is normally active. In a cache read miss cycle, which may proceed as a Line Fill, SBLAST# starts active. After determining whether or not the cycle is cacheable via SKEN#, SBLAST# is driven inactive. If it is a cacheable cycle, and SBRDY# terminates the first word of the Line Fill, a burst Line Fill, SBLAST# will be driven active when the data is valid for the eighth word of the Line Fill. If SRDY# terminates the first word of the Line Fill, a non-burst Line Fill, SBLAST# is driven active in the cycle where SRDY# was sampled active.
Cache Invalidation		
SAHOLD	I	The System Bus Address HOLD request allows another bus master access to the address bus of the 82396SX Smart Cache. This is to indicate the address of an external cycle for performing an internal cache directory lookup and invalidation cycle. In response to this signal the 82396SX Smart Cache stops driving the System Bus address pins in the next cycle. No HOLD Acknowledge is required. Other System Bus signals can remain active during address hold. The 82396SX Smart Cache does not initiate another bus cycle during address hold. This pin is recognized during RESET.
SEADS#	I	The System Bus External Address Strobe signal indicates that a valid external address has been driven onto the 82396SX Smart Cache System Bus address pins. This address will be used to perform an internal cache invalidation cycle. The maximum invalidation cycle rate is one every two clock cycles.
Cache Control		
FLUSH#	I	The FLUSH# pin, when sampled active for four clock cycles or more, causes the 82396SX Smart Cache to invalidate its entire TAG array. In addition, it is used to configure the 82396SX Smart Cache to enter various test modes. For details refer to chapter 7. This signal is asynchronous but must meet setup and hold times to guarantee recognition in any specific clock.
System Data Bus		
SD[15:0]	I/O	The System Bus Data lines of the 82396SX Smart Cache must be driven with appropriate setup and hold times for proper operation. These signals are driven by the 82396SX Smart Cache only during write cycles.
System Bus Decode Pins		
SKEN#	I	The System Cacheability Enable signal is used to determine if the current cycle running on the System Bus is cacheable or not. When the 82396SX Smart Cache generates a read cycle, SKEN# is sampled one clock before the first SBRDY# or SRDY# or one cycle before the first SNA# is sampled active (see chapter 6). If SKEN# is sampled active the cycle will be transformed into a Line Fill. Otherwise, the cache and cache directory will be unaffected. Note that SKEN# is ignored after the first cycle in a Line Fill. SKEN# is ignored for all System Bus cycles except for cache read miss cycles.
SWP#	I	The System Write Protect indicator signal is used to determine whether the current System Bus Line Fill cycle is write protected or not. In non-pipelined cycles, SWP# is sampled with the first SRDY# or SBRDY# of the Line Fill. In pipelined cycles, SWP# is sampled one clock phase after the first SNA# is sampled active (see figures 6.9-10). The Write Protect bit is sampled together with the TAG of each line in the 82396SX Smart Cache Cache Directory. In every cacheable write cycle the Write Protect bit is read. If active, the cycle will be a write protected cycle which is treated like a cacheable write miss cycle. It is buffered and it does not update the cache even if the addressed location is present in the cache.

1.0 82396SX SMART CACHE FUNCTIONAL OVERVIEW

1.1 Introduction

The primary function of a cache is to provide local storage for frequently accessed memory locations. The cache intercepts memory references and handles them directly without transferring the request to the System Bus. This results in lower traffic on the System Bus and decreases latency on the Local Bus. This leads to improved performance for a processor on the Local Bus. It also increases potential system performance by reducing each processor's demand for System Bus bandwidth, thus allowing more processors or system masters in the system. By providing fast access to frequently used code and data the cache is able to reduce the average memory access time of the i386™ SX Microprocessor based system.

The 82396SX Smart Cache is a single chip cache subsystem specifically designed for use with the i386™ SX Microprocessor. The 82396SX Smart Cache integrates 16KB cache, the Cache Directory and the cache control logic onto one chip. The cache is unified for code and data and is transparent to application software. The 82396SX Smart Cache provides a cache consistency mechanism which guarantees that the cache has the most recently updated version of the main memory. Consistency support has no performance impact on the i386™ SX Microprocessor. Section 1.2 covers all the 82396SX Smart Cache features.

The 82396SX Smart Cache architecture is similar to the i486™ SX Microprocessor's on-chip cache. The cache is four Way SET associative with Pseudo LRU (Least Recently Used) replacement algorithm. The

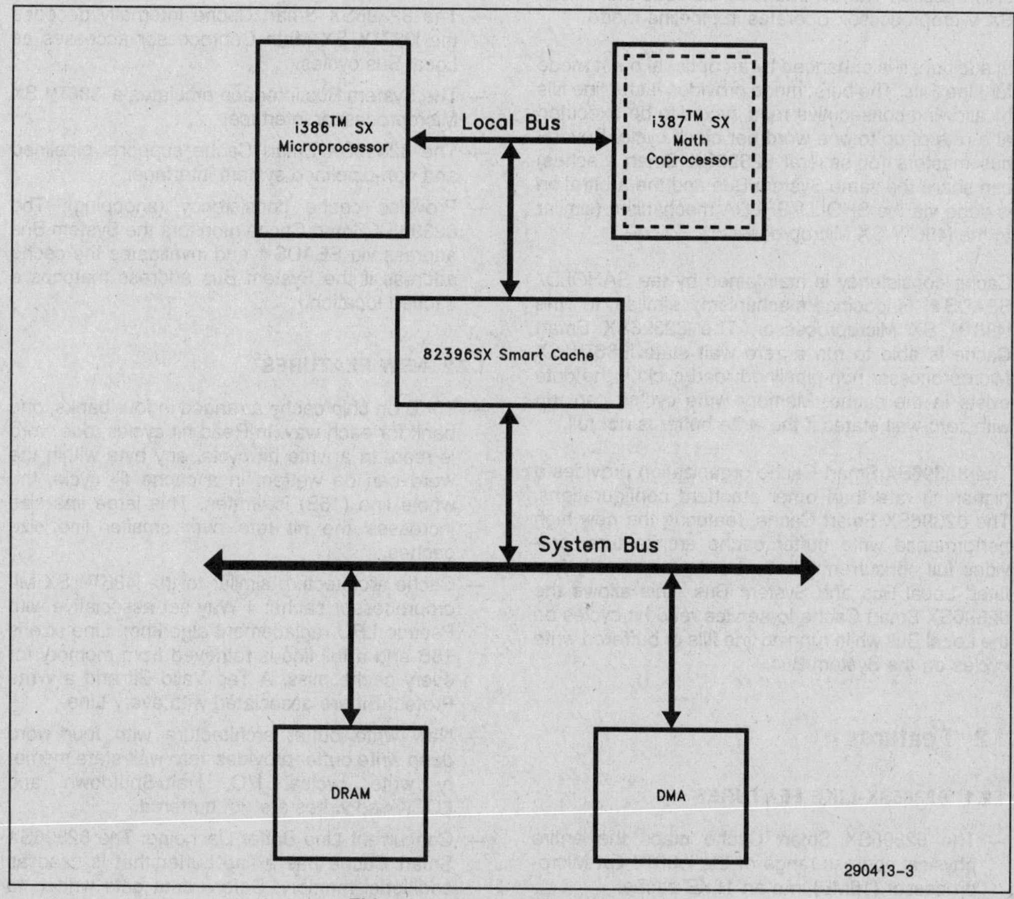

Figure 1.1 System Block Diagram

4

line size is 16B and a full line is retrieved from the memory for every cache miss. A TAG is associated with every 16B line. The 82396SX Smart Cache architecture allows for cache read hit cycles to run on the Local Bus even when the System Bus is not available. 82396SX Smart Cache incorporates a new write buffer cache architecture, which allows the i386™ SX Microprocessor to continue operation without waiting for write cycles to actually update the main memory.

A detailed description of the cache operation and parameters is included in Chapter 2.

The 82396SX Smart Cache has an interface to two electrically isolated busses. The interface to the i386™ SX Microprocessor bus is referred to as the Local Bus (LB) interface. The interface to the main memory and other system devices is referred to as the 82396SX Smart Cache System Bus (SB) interface. The SB interface emulates the i386™ SX Microprocessor. The SB interface, as does the i386™ SX Microprocessor, operates in pipeline mode.

In addition, it is enhanced by an optional burst mode for Line Fills. The burst mode provides faster line fills by allowing consecutive read cycles to be executed at a rate of up to one word per clock cycle. Several bus masters (or several 82396SX Smart Caches) can share the same System Bus and the arbitration is done via the SHOLD/SHLDA mechanism (similar to the i486™ SX Microprocessor).

Cache consistency is maintained by the SAHOLD/SEADS# snooping mechanism, similar to the i486™ SX Microprocessor. The 82396SX Smart Cache is able to run a zero wait state i386™ SX Microprocessor non-pipelined read cycle if the data exists in the cache. Memory write cycles can run with zero wait states if the write buffer is not full.

The 82396SX Smart Cache organization provides a higher hit rate than other standard configurations. The 82396SX Smart Cache, featuring the new high performance write buffer cache architecture, provides full concurrency between the electrically isolated Local Bus and System Bus. This allows the 82396SX Smart Cache to service read hit cycles on the Local Bus while running line fills or buffered write cycles on the System Bus.

1.2 Features

1.2.1 82385SX-LIKE FEATURES

- The 82396SX Smart Cache maps the entire physical address range of the i386™ SX Microprocessor (16MB) into an 16KB cache.
- Unified code and data cache.
- Cache attributes are handled by hardware. Thus the 82396SX Smart Cache is transparent to application software. This preserves the integrity of system software and protects the users software investment.
- Word and Byte writes, Word reads.
- Zero wait states in read hits and in buffered write cycles. All i386™ SX Microprocessor cycles are non-pipelined (Note: The i386™ SX Microprocessor must never be pipelined when used with the 82396SX Smart Cache - NA# must be tied to Vcc).
- A hardware cache FLUSH# option. The 82396SX Smart Cache will invalidate all the Tag Valid bits in the Cache Directory and clear the System Bus line buffer when FLUSH# is activated for a minimum of four CLK's.
- The 82396SX Smart Cache supports non-cacheable accesses.
- The 82396SX Smart Cache internally decodes the i387™ SX Math Coprocessor accesses as Local Bus cycles.
- The System Bus interface emulates a i386™ SX Microprocessor interface.
- The 82396SX Smart Cache supports pipelined and non-pipelined system interface.
- Provides cache consistency (snooping): The 82396SX Smart Cache monitors the System Bus address via SEADS# and invalidates the cache address if the System Bus address matches a cached location.

1.2.2 NEW FEATURES

- 16KB on chip cache arranged in four banks, one bank for each way. In Read hit cycles, one word is read. In a write hit cycle, any byte within the word can be written. In a cache fill cycle, the whole line (16B) is written. This large line size increases the hit rate over smaller line size caches.
- Cache architecture similar to the i486™ SX Microprocessor cache: 4 Way set associative with Pseudo LRU replacement algorithm. Line size is 16B and a full line is retrieved from memory for every cache miss. A Tag Valid Bit and a Write Protect Bit are associated with every Line.
- New write buffer architecture with four word deep write buffer provides zero wait state memory write cycles. I/O, Halt/Shutdown and LOCK#ed writes are not buffered.
- Concurrent Line Buffer Cacheing: The 82396SX Smart Cache has a line buffer that is used as additional memory. Before data gets written to

the cache memory at the completion of a Line Fill it is stored in this buffer. Cache hit cycles to the line buffer can occur before the line is written to the cache.

— In i387™ SX Math Coprocessor accesses, the 82396SX Smart Cache drives the READYO# in one wait state if the READYI# was not driven in the previous clock.

  Note that the timing of the 82396SX Smart Cache's READYO# generation for i387™ SX Math Coprocessor cycles is incompatible with 80287 timing.

— An enhanced System Bus interface:

  a) Burst option is supported in line-fills similar to the i486™ SX Microprocessor. SBRDY# (System Burst READY) is provided in addition to SRDY#. A burst is always a 16 byte line fill (cache update) which is equivalent to eight word cycles.

  b) System cacheability attribute is provided (SKEN#). SKEN# is used to determine whether the current cycle is cacheable. It is used to qualify Line Fill requests.

  c) SHOLD/SHLDA system bus arbitration mechanism is supported. A Multi i386™ SX / 82396SX Smart Cache cluster can share the same System Bus via this mechanism.

  f) Cache invalidation cycles supported via SEADS#. This is used to provide cache coherency.

— Full Local Bus/System Bus concurrency is attained by:

  a) Servicing cache read hit cycles on the Local Bus while completing a Line Fill on the System Bus. The data requested by the i386™ SX Microprocessor is provided over the local bus as the first word of the Line Fill.

  b) Servicing cache read hit cycles on the Local Bus while executing buffered write cycles on the system bus.

  c) Servicing cache read hit cycles on the Local Bus while another bus master is running (DMA, other i386™ SX Microprocessor, 82396SX Smart Cache, i486™ SX Microprocessor, etc . . .) on the System Bus.

  d) Buffering write cycles on the Local Bus while the system bus is executing other cycles.

— Write protected areas are supported by the SWP# input. This enables caching of ROM space or shadowed ROM space.

— No Post Input (NPI#) provided for disabling of write buffers per cycle. This option supports memory mapped I/O designs.

— Byte Enable Mask (BEM) is provided to mask the processor byte enables during a memory read cycle.

— A20M# input provided for emulation of 8086 address wrap-around.

— SRAM test mode, in which the TAGRAM and the cache RAM are treated as standard SRAM, is provided. A Tristate Output test mode is also provided for system debugging. In this mode the 82396SX Smart Cache is isolated from the other devices in the board by floating all its outputs.

— Single chip, 132 lead PQFP package, 1 micron CHMOS-IV technology.

2.0 82396SX SMART CACHE SYSTEM DESCRIPTION

2.1 82396SX Smart Cache Organization

The on chip cache memory is a unified code and data cache. The cache organization is 4 Way SET Associative and each Line is 16 bytes wide (see Figure 2.1). The 16K bytes of cache memory are logically organized as 4 4KB banks (4: 1 bank for each Way). Each bank contains 256 16B lines (256: 1 line for each SET).

The Cache Directory is used to determine whether the data in the cache memory is valid for the address being accessed. The Cache Directory contains 256 TAG's (each TAG is 14-bits wide) for each Way, for a total of 1K TAG's (See Figure 2.2). With each 12 bit TAG Address there is a TAG Valid bit and a Write Protect bit. The Cache Directory also contains the LRU bits. The LRU bits are used to determine which Way to replace whenever the cache needs to be updated with a new line and all four ways contain valid data.

Table 2.1 lists the 82396SX Smart Cache organization.

4

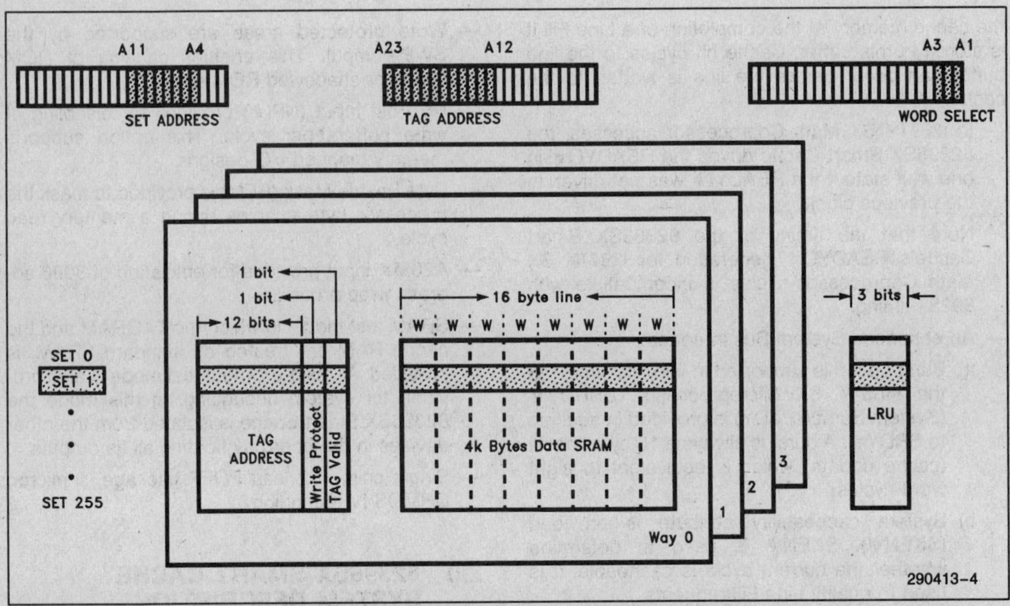

Figure 2.1. 82396SX Smart Cache Organization

Table 2.1 82396SX Smart Cache Organization

Cache Element	82396SX Size/Qty	Comments
TAG	1K	Total number of TAGs
SET	256	Cache Directory Offset
LRU	256x3	3 bits per SET address
Way	4	4 TAG's per SET address
Line Size	16B	8 Words
Sector Size	16B	8 words, one line per sector
Cache Size	16KB	
Cache Directory	—	TAG address, TAG Valid Bit, and Write Protect Bit for each Way for each SET address (256 SET's x 4 Ways), and LRU bits.
TAG Valid Bit	1K	1 for each TAG in the cache directory, indicates valid data is in the cache memory.
Write Protect Bit	1K	1 for each TAG in the cache directory, indicates that the address is write protected.

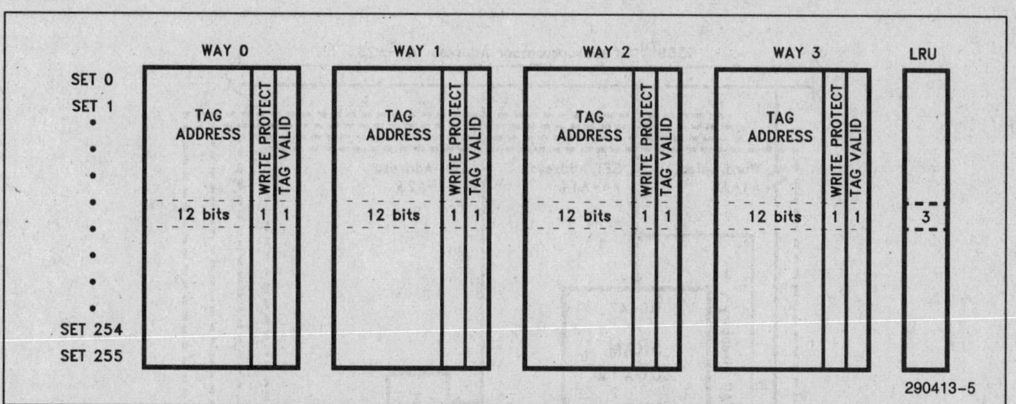

Figure 2.2. 82396SX Smart Cache Directory Organization

2.1.1 82396SX SMART CACHE STRUCTURE AND TERMINOLOGY

A detailed description of the 82396SX Smart Cache parameters are defined here.

A **Line** is the basic unit of data transferred between the cache and main memory. In the 82396SX Smart Cache each Line is 16B. A Line is also known as a transfer block. The decision of a cache "hit or miss" is determined on a per Line basis. A cache hit results when the TAG address of the current address being accessed matches the TAG address in the Cache Directory (see Figure 2.3) and the TAG Valid bit is set. The 82396SX Smart Cache has 1K Lines.

A **TAG** is a storage element of the Cache Directory with which the hit/miss decision is made. The TAG consists of the TAG address (A[23:12]), the TAG Valid bit and the Write Protect bit. Since many addresses map to a single line, the TAG is used to determine whether the data associated with the current address is present in the cache memory (a cache hit). This is done through a comparison of the TAG address bits of the current address with the four TAG address fields associated with the current address's SET. The four TAG Valid bits are also checked. Each line in the cache memory has a TAG associated with it.

A **TAG Valid Bit** is associated with each TAG address in the Cache Directory. It determines if the data held in the cache memory for the particular TAG address is valid. It is used to determine whether the data in the cache is a match to data in main memory.

A **Write Protect Bit** is also associated with each TAG address in the Cache Directory. This field determines if the cache memory can be written to. It is set by the SWP# pin during Line Fill cycles (see Chapter 6).

A **SET** address is a decoded portion of the Local Bus address that maps to 1 TAG address per Way in the Cache Directory. All the TAG's associated with a particular SET are simultaneously compared with the TAG field of the bus address to make the hit/miss decision. The 82396SX Smart Cache provides 256 SET addresses, each SET maps to four lines in the cache memory.

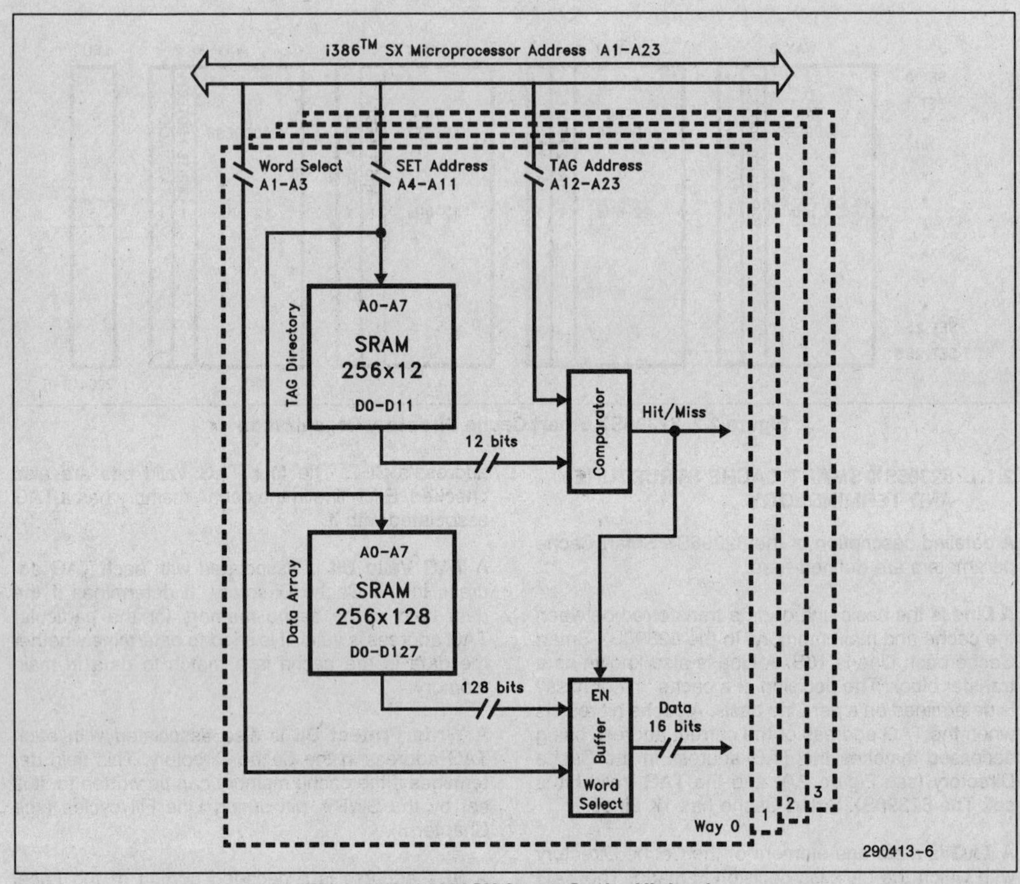

Figure 2.3. 82396SX Smart Cache Hit Logic

The term **Way** as in 4 Way SET Associative describes the degree of associativity of the cache system. Each Way provides TAG Address, TAG Valid bit, and Write Protect bit storage, 1 entry for each SET address. A simultaneous comparison of one TAG address from each Way with the bus address is done in order to make the hit/miss decision. The 82396SX Smart Cache is 4 Way SET Associative.

Other key 82396SX Smart Cache features include:

Cache Size - The 82396SX Smart Cache contains 16KB of cache memory. The cache is organized as four banks of 4KB. Each of the four banks corresponds to a particular Way.

Update Policy - The update policy deals with how main memory is updated when a cacheable write cycle is issued on the Local Bus. The 82396SX Smart Cache supports the write buffer policy, similar to the write through policy, which means that main memory is always updated in every write cycle. However, the cache is updated only when the write cycle hits the cache. Also, the 82396SX Smart Cache is able to cache write protected areas, e.g. ROMs, by preventing the cache update if the write cycle hits a write protected line. A write cycle to main memory is buffered as explained in Chapter 6.

Replacement - When a new line is needed to update the cache, the Tag Valid bits are checked to see if any of the four ways are available. If they are all valid it is necessary to replace an old line that is already in the cache. In the 82396SX Smart Cache, the Pseudo LRU (least recently used) algorithm is adopted. The Pseudo LRU algorithm targets the least recently used line associated with the SET for replacement. (See Section 2.2 for Pseudo LRU description.)

Consistency - The 82396SX Smart Cache contains hooks for a consistency mechanism. This is to guarantee that in systems with multiple caches (and/or with multiple bus masters) all processor requests result in returning correct and consistent data. Whenever a system bus master performs memory accesses to data which also exists in the cache, the System Bus master can invalidate that entry in the 82396SX Smart Cache. This invalidation is done by using SEADS# (description in Chapter 6).

The invalidation is performed by marking the TAG as invalid (the TAG Valid bit is cleared). Thus, the next time a Local Bus request is made to that location, the 82396SX Smart Cache accesses the main memory to get the most recent copy of the data.

2.2 Pseudo LRU Algorithm

When a line needs to be placed in the internal cache the 82396SX Smart Cache first checks to see if there is a non-valid line in the SET that can be replaced. The validity of a line is determined by the TAG Valid bit which is associated with this line. The order that is used for this check is Way 0, Way 1, Way 2, and Way 3. If all four lines associated with the SET are valid, a pseudo Least Recently Used algorithm is used to determine which line will be replaced. If a non-valid line is found, that line is marked for replacement. All the TAG Valid bits are cleared when the 82396SX Smart Cache is RESET or when the cache is FLUSHed. Three bits, B0, B1, and B2, are defined for each of the 256 SETs. These bits are called the LRU bits and are stored in the cache directory. The LRU bits are updated for every access to the cache.

If the most recent access to the cache was to Way 0 or Way 1 then B0 is set to 1. B0 is set to 0 if the most recent access was to Way 2 or Way 3. If the most recent access to Way 0 or Way 1 was to Way 0, B1 is set to 1. Else B1 is set to 0. If the most recent access to Way 2 or Way 3 was to Way 2, B2 is set to 1. Else B2 is set to 0.

The Pseudo LRU algorithm works in the following manner. When a line must be replaced, the cache will first select which of Way 0 and Way 1 or Way 2 and Way 3 was least recently used. Then the cache will select which of the two lines was least recently used and mark it for replacement. The decision tree is shown in Figure 2.4. When the 82396SX Smart Cache is RESET or the cache is FLUSHed all the LRU bits are cleared along with the TAG Valid bits.

4

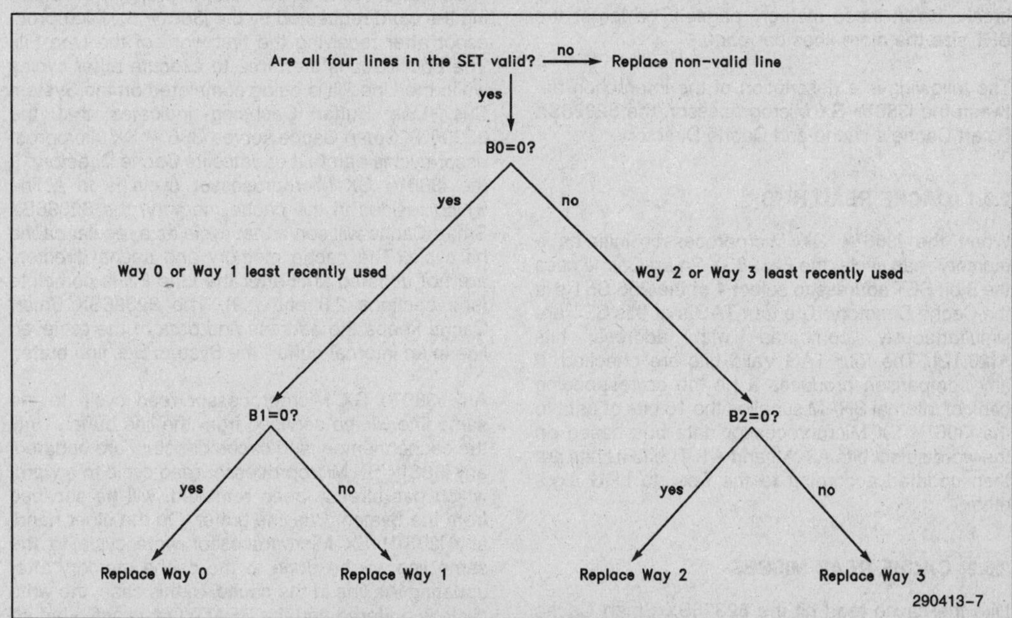

Figure 2.4 Pseudo LRU Decision Tree

2.3 Four Way Set Associative Cache Organization

The 82396SX Smart Cache is a four Way SET Associative cache. Figure 2.5 shows the 82396SX Smart Cache's cache organization. For each of the 256 SET's there are four TAG's, one for each Way. The address currently being accessed is decoded into the SET and TAG addresses. If the access was to address 001014h (SET=01, TAG=001h), the four TAG's in the Cache Directory associated with SET 01 are simultaneously compared with the TAG of the address being accessed. The TAG Valid bits are also checked. If the TAG's match and the TAG Valid bit is set, the access is a hit to the Way where the hit was detected, in this example the hit occurred in Way 1. The data would be retrieved from Way 1 of the cache memory. If the next access was to address 54801Eh (SET=01, TAG=548h), the comparison would be done and a TAG match would be found in Way 2. However in this case the TAG Valid bit is cleared so the access is a miss and the data will be retrieved from main memory. The cache memory will also be updated. It is helpful to notice that the main memory is broken into pages by the TAG size. In this case with a 12 bit TAG address there are 2^{12} pages. The smaller the TAG size the fewer pages main memory is broken into. The SET breaks down these memory pages. The larger the SET size the more lines per page.

The following is a description of the interaction between the i386™ SX Microprocessor, the 82396SX Smart Cache's cache and Cache Directory.

2.3.1 CACHE READ HITS

When the i386™ SX Microprocessor initiates a memory read cycle, the 82396SX Smart Cache uses the 8 bit SET address to select 1 of the 256 SET's in the Cache Directory. The four TAG's of this SET are simultaneously compared with address bits A[23:12]. The four TAG Valid bits are checked. If any comparison produces a hit the corresponding bank of internal SRAM supplies the 16 bits of data to the i386™ SX Microprocessor data bus based on the word select bits A3, A2 and A1. The LRU bits are then updated according to the Pseudo LRU algorithm.

2.3.2 CACHE READ MISSES

Like the cache read hit the 82396SX Smart Cache uses the 8 bit SET address to select the 4 TAG's for comparison. If none of these match or if the TAG Valid bit associated with a matching TAG address is cleared the cycle is a miss and the 82396SX Smart Cache retrieves the requested data from main memory. A Line Fill is simultaneously started to read the line of data from system memory and write the line of data into the cache in the Way designated by the LRU bits.

2.3.3 OTHER OPERATIONS THAT AFFECT THE CACHE AND CACHE DIRECTORY

Other operations that affect the cache and Cache Directory include write hits, snoop hits, cache FLUSHes and 82396SX Smart Cache RESETs. In write hits, the cache is updated along with main memory. The bank that detected the hit is the one that data is written to. The LRU bits are then adjusted according to the Pseudo LRU algorithm. When a cache invalidation cycle occurs (Snoop HIT) the tag valid bit is cleared. RESETs and cache FLUSHes clear all the TAG Valid bits.

2.4 Concurrent Line Buffer Cacheing

This feature of the 82396SX Smart Cache can be broken into two components, Concurrent Line Buffer and Line Buffer Cacheing.

A Concurrent Line Buffer has the property of returning the word requested by the i386™ SX Microprocessor after receiving the first word of the Line Fill. The Local Bus is then free to execute other cycles while the Line Fill is being completed on the System Bus. Line Buffer Cacheing indicates that the 82396SX Smart Cache serves i386™ SX Microprocessor cycles before it updates its Cache Directory. If the i386™ SX Microprocessor cycle is to a line which resides in the cache memory, the 82396SX Smart Cache will serve that cycle as a regular cache hit cycle. The cache memory and cache directory are not updated until after the Line Fill is complete (see sections 2.8 and 2.9). The 82396SX Smart Cache keeps the address and data of the retrieved line in an internal buffer, the System Bus line buffer.

Any i386™ SX Microprocessor read cycle to the same line will be serviced from the line buffer. Until the cache memory and cache directory are updated, any i386™ SX Microprocessor read cycle to a word, which has already been retrieved, will be serviced from the System Bus line buffer. On the other hand, any i386™ SX Microprocessor write cycle to the same line will be done to the cache memory after updating the line in the cache. In this case, the write cycle is buffered and the READYO# is activated after updating the line in the cache. However, if the line is Write Protected, the write cycle will be handled as if it is a miss cycle.

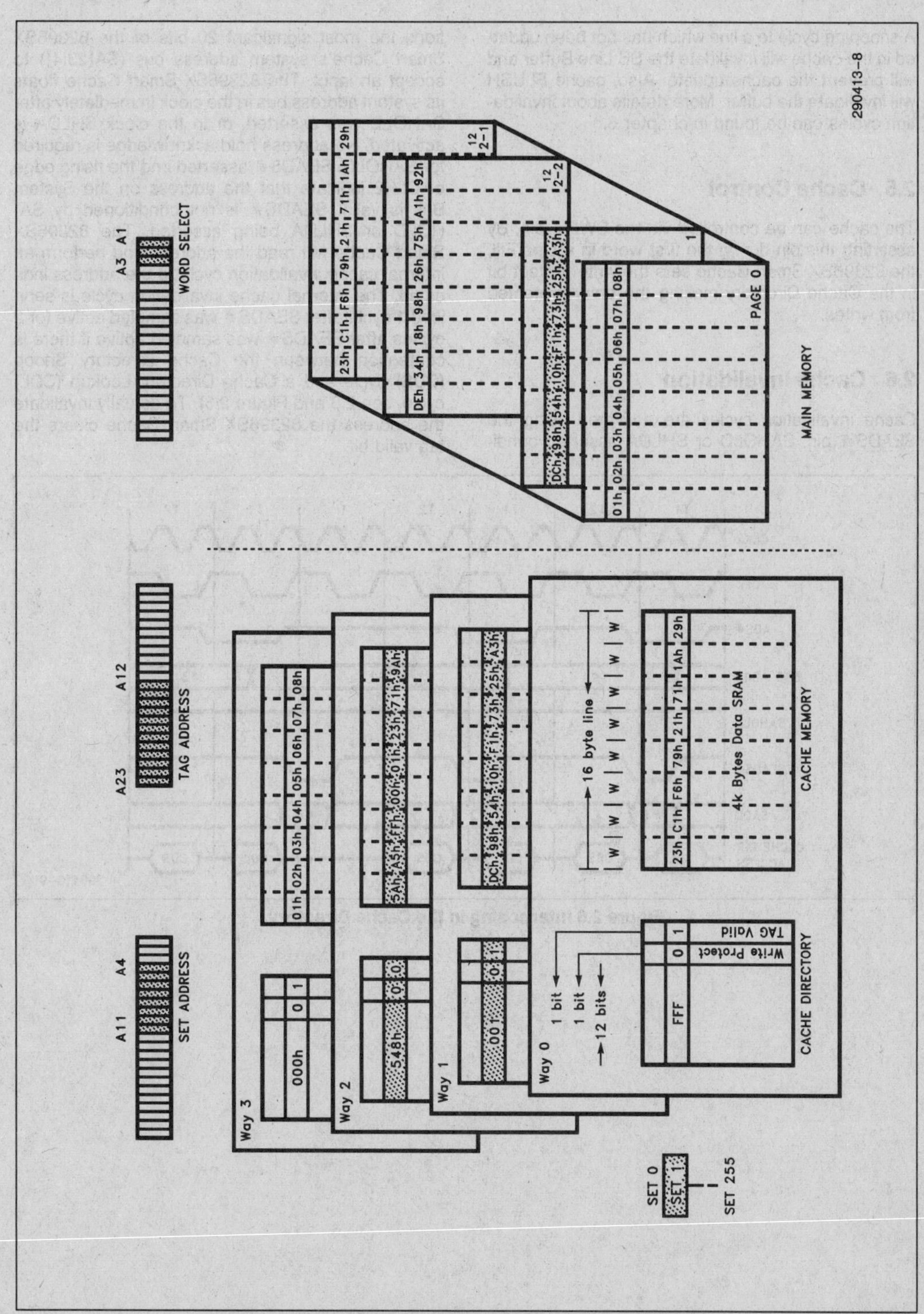

Figure 2.5 Four Way Set Associative Cache Organization

A snooping cycle to a line which has not been updated in the cache will invalidate the SB Line Buffer and will prevent the cache update. Also, cache FLUSH will invalidate the buffer. More details about invalidation cycles can be found in chapter 6.

2.5 Cache Control

The cache can be controlled via the SWP# pin. By asserting this pin during the first word in a Line Fill, the 82396SX Smart Cache sets the write protect bit in the Cache Directory making the entry protected from writes.

2.6 Cache Invalidation

Cache invalidation cycles are activated using the SEADS# pin. SAHOLD or SHLDA asserted conditions the most significant 20 bits of the 82396SX Smart Cache's system address bus (SA[23:4]) to accept an input. The 82396SX Smart Cache floats its system address bus in the clock immediately after SAHOLD was asserted, or in the clock SHLDA is activated. No address hold acknowledge is required for SAHOLD. SEADS# asserted and the rising edge of CLK2 indicate that the address on the System Bus is valid. SEADS# is not conditioned by SAHOLD or SHLDA being asserted. The 82396SX Smart Cache will read the address and perform an internal cache invalidation cycle to the address indicated. The internal cache invalidation cycle is serviced 1 cycle after SEADS# was sampled active (or 2 cycles after SEADS# was sampled active if there is contention between the Cache Directory Snoop (CDS) cycle and a Cache Directory Lookup (CDL) cycle, see 2.8 and Figure 2.6). To actually invalidate the address the 82396SX Smart Cache clears the tag valid bit.

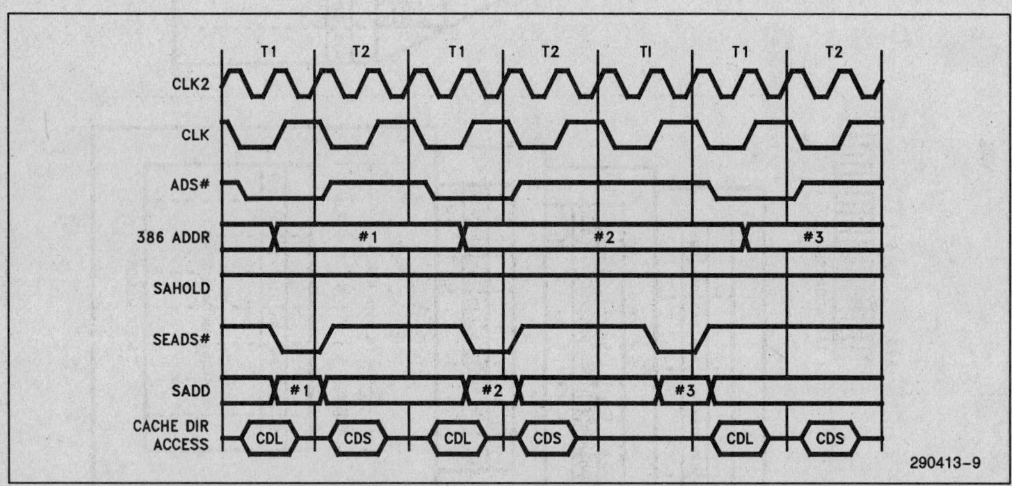

Figure 2.6 Interposing in the Cache Directory

2.7 Cache Flushing

The user has an option of clearing the cache by activating the FLUSH# input. When sampling the FLUSH# input low for at least four clocks, the 82396SX Smart Cache resets all the tag valid bits and the LRU bits of the Cache Directory. Thus, all the banks of the cache are invalidated. Also, the SB Line Buffer is invalidated. The FLUSH# input must have at least four CLK periods in order to be recognized. If FLUSH# is activated for longer than four CLKs, the 82396SX Smart Cache will handle all accesses as misses and it will not update the Cache Directory (the Cache Directory will be FLUSHed as long as the FLUSH# input is low). The cache is also FLUSHed during RESET. See Section 3.2.7.1.

2.8 Cache Directory Accesses and Arbitration

There are five types of accesses to the cache directory. Each access is a one clock cycle:

1) **Cache Directory Look-Up**
2) **Cache Directory Update**
3) **Cache Directory Snoop**
4) **Testability Accesses**
5) **Cache Directory FLUSH**

A description of each of these accesses follows:

1) **Cache Directory Look-up cycle (CDL):** A i386™ SX Microprocessor access in which the hit/miss decision is made. The Cache Directory is accessed by the i386™ SX Microprocessor address bus directly from the pins. CDL is executed whenever ADS# is activated, in both read and write cycles. The LRU bits are updated in every CDL hit cycle so the accessed "Way" becomes the most recently used. The LRU bits are read in every CDL miss cycle to indicate the "Way" to be updated in the Cache Directory Update cycle. Also, the WP bit is read.

2) **Cache Directory Update cycle (CDU):** A write cycle to the cache directory due to a previous miss. The CDU cycle can be caused by a TAG mismatch (either a Tag Address mismatch or a cleared TAG Valid bit). In both cases, the new TAG is written to the "Way" indicated by the LRU bits read by the previous CDL miss cycle. Also, the TAG Valid bit is turned on and the LRU algorithm is updated so the accessed "Way" becomes the most recently used. The WP bit is written according to the sampled SWP# input. The Cache Directory is accessed by the internally latched i386™ SX Microprocessor address bus. Simultaneously with the CDU cycle, the cache memory is updated.

3) **Cache Directory Snooping cycle (CDS):** A Cache Directory look-up cycle initiated by the System Bus, in response to an access to a memory location that is shared with another system master, followed by a conditional invalidation of the TAG Valid bit. If the look-up cycle results in a hit, the corresponding TAG Valid bit in the Way which detected the HIT will be cleared. CDS cycles do not affect the LRU bits. The Cache Directory is accessed by the internally latched System Bus address.

4) **Testability accesses (CDT):** Cache Directory read and write cycles performed in SRAM test mode. During the TEST accesses, the Cache Directory is read or written. No comparison is done. CDT cycles are used for debugging purposes so CDT cycles do not contend with other cycles. (See Section 7.1.)

5) **Cache Directory FLUSH cycle (CDF):** During RESET or as a result of a FLUSH# request generated by activating the FLUSH# input, all the TAG Valid bits and the LRU bits are cleared as well as the Line Buffer. CDF is one clock cycle wide if FLUSH# is active for four CLKs. If FLUSH# is activated longer the CDF cycle is N-3 CLKs, where N is the number of CLKs FLUSH# is activated for. The actual clearing of the valid bits occurs 7 CLKs after the activation of FLUSH#. Two clocks are for internal synchronization and four for recognizing FLUSH# asserted. It has higher priority than all other cycles. A CDF cycle may occur simultaneously with any other cycle but the result is always a FLUSH#ed Cache Directory.

The 82396SX Smart Cache performs the CDL cycle in T1 state. The CDU cycle, in general, is performed in the clock after the last SRDY# or SBRDY# of the Line Fill cycle. The CDS cycle is performed one clock after sampling the SEADS# active (see more details on snooping cycles in chapter 6). Supporting concurrent activities on local and system busses causes CDL cycles to be requested in any clock during the execution with a maximum rate of a CDL cycle every other clock.

4

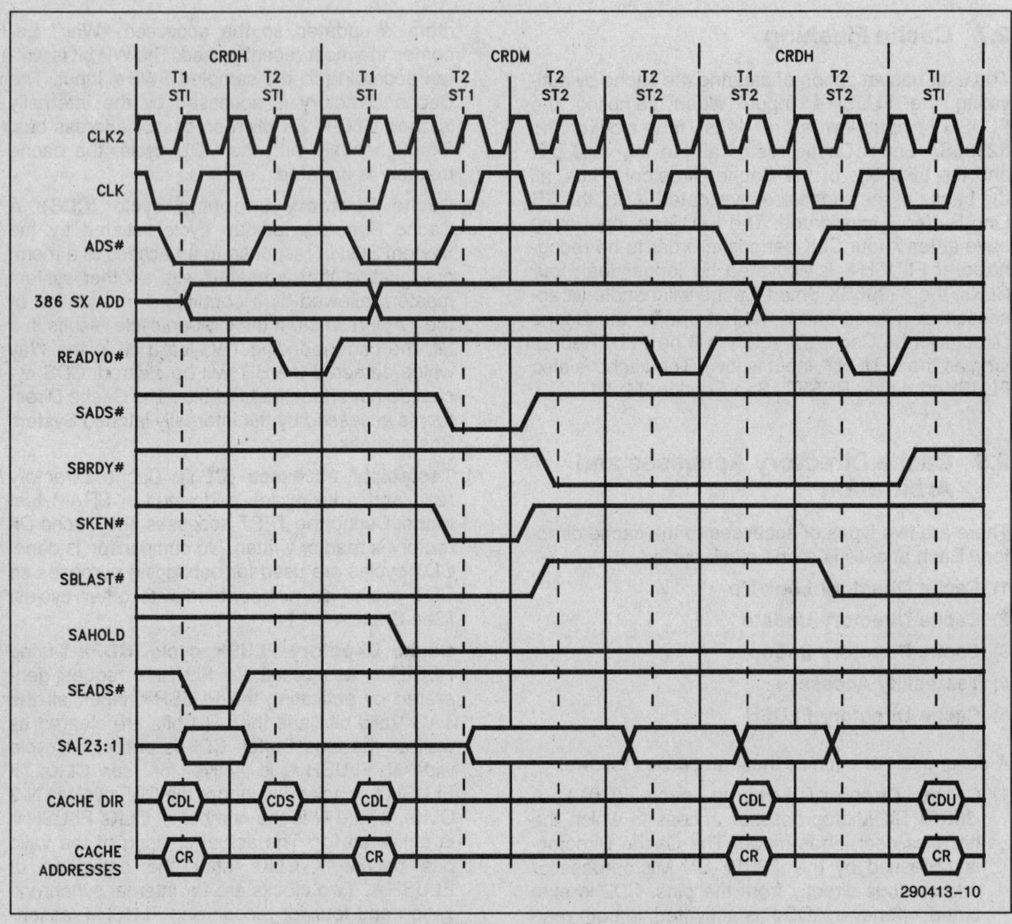

Figure 2.7 Cache Directory and Cache Accesses

The following arbitration mechanism guarantees resolution of any possible contention between CDL, CDU and CDS cycles:

1. The priority order is CDL, CDS and CDU. CDL has the highest priority, CDU has the lowest.
2. In case of simultaneous CDL and CDS cycles, the CDS will be delayed by one clock. So, the maximum latency in executing the invalidation cycle is two clocks after sampling the SEADS# active. Since the maximum rate of each of the CDL and the CDS cycles is one every other clock, the 82396SX Smart Cache is able to interpose the CDL and CDS cycles such that both are serviced. Figure 2.6 clarifies the interposing in the Cache Directory between the i386™ SX Microprocessor and the System Bus.
3. CDU cycle is executed in any clock after the last SRDY# or SBRDY# in which neither CDL nor CDS cycles are requested. The worst case is the case where immediately after the read miss, the i386™ SX Microprocessor runs consecutive read hits while the System Bus is running invalidation cycles every other clock. In this case, the CDU cycle is postponed until a free clock is inserted, which may occur due to slower look-up rate (in case of read miss, non-cacheable read,etc . . .), or due to a slower SEADS# rate.

Since every CDU cycle is synchronized with the cache update (CU - writing the retrieved line into the cache), a possible contention on the cache can occur between a cache update cycle and a cache write cycle (CW - cache is written due to a write hit cycle). In this case, the CW cycle is executed, and the CDU and CU cycles are delayed.

2.9 Cache Memory Description

The 82396SX Smart Cache memory is constructed of four banks,each bank is 2K words (4KB) and represents a "Way". For example, if the read cycle is to Way 0, bank 0 will be read. The basic cache element is a Line. The cache is able to write a full line or any byte within the line. Reads are done by word only.

There are four types of accesses to the cache data memory. Each access is a one clock cycle:

1) **Cache Read cycle**
2) **Cache Write cycle**
3) **Cache Update cycle**
4) **Testability Access**

A description of each type of access follows:

1) **Cache Read cycle (CR):** CR cycle occurs simultaneously with Cache Directory look-up cycle (CDL) if the cycle is a read. In case of a hit, the cache bank in which the hit was detected is read. In CR cycle, the A1-3 address lines select the requested word within the line.
2) **Cache Write cycle (CW):** CW cycle occurs one clock after the Cache Directory look-up cycle (CDL) if the cycle is a write hit and the WP bit is not set. The cache bank in which the hit was detected is updated. In CW cycle, the A1-3 address lines and BHE#, BLE# lines select the required bytes within the line to be written. For all write hit cycles, READYO# is returned simultaneously with the CW cycle unless the write buffer is full. When the write buffer is full the first cycle buffered must be completed on the system bus before READYO# can be asserted.
3) **Cache Update cycle (CU):** CU cycle occurs simultaneously with every Cache Directory update cycle (CDU). The full line is written.
4) **Testability accesses (CT):** cache read and write cycles performed by the 82396SX Smart Cache TEST machine. During the TEST accesses, the cache memory acts as a standard RAM. CT cycles are used for debugging purposes so CT cycles do not contend with other cycles.

The Cache Directory arbitration rules guarantee that contention will not occur in the cache accesses. This is since CR is synchronized with CDL cycle, CU is synchronized with CDU cycle, CW cannot occur simultaneously with CR cycles (ADS# not activated while READYO# is returned since i386™ SX Microprocessor is not pipelined) and finally the possible contention of CW and CU is resolved. See figure 2.7 for an example of Cache Directory and cache memory accesses during a typical cycle execution.

3.0 PIN DESCRIPTION

The 82396SX Smart Cache pins may be divided into 4 groups:

1. Local Bus interface pins
2. System Bus interface pins
3. Local Bus decode pins
4. System Bus decode pins

Some notes regarding these groups of pins follow:

1. All Pins - All input and I/O pins (when used as inputs) must be synchronous to CLK2, to guarantee proper operation. Exceptions are the RESET pin, where only the falling edge needs to be synchronous to CLK2, and A20M# and FLUSH# pins, which are asynchronous.
2. Local Bus Interface Pins - All Local Bus interface pins that have a corresponding i386™ SX Microprocessor signal (A1–23, W/R#, D/C#, M/IO#, LOCK#, and D0-15) must be connected directly to the corresponding i386™ SX Microprocessor pins.
3. Local / System Bus Decode Pins - These signals are generated by proper decoding of the Local and System Bus addresses. The decoding for the Local Bus decode pins, NPI# and BEM, must be static. The decoding for the System Bus Decode pins, SKEN# and SWP#, must be static over the line boundary. They must not change during a Line Fill. If a change in the decoding of any of these signals is made, the 82396SX Smart Cache must be FLUSH#ed or RESET.

4

3.1 Local Bus Interface Pins

3.1.1 i386™ SX MICROPROCESSOR/82396SX SMART CACHE CLOCK (CLK2 I)

This signal provides the fundamental timing for the 82396SX Smart Cache. The 82396SX Smart Cache, like the i386™ SX Microprocessor, divides CLK2 by two to generate the internal clock. The phase of the internal 82396SX Smart Cache clock is synchronized to the internal CPU clock phase by the RESET signal. All external timing parameters are specified with respect to the rising edge of CLK2. Dynamic frequency changes are not allowed.

3.1.2 LOCAL ADDRESS BUS

3.1.2.1 Local Bus Address Lines (A[23:1] I)

These signals, along with the byte enable signals, define the physical area of memory or I/O accessed.

3.1.2.2 Local Bus Byte Enables (BHE#,BLE# I)

These pins are used to determine which bytes are accessed in partial write cycles. On read-hit cycles those lines are ignored by the 82396SX Smart Cache. On write hit cycles they determine which bytes in the internal Cache SRAM must be updated, and passed to the System Bus along with the System Bus write cycle. If BEM is inactive, these signals are mirrored by SBHE# and SBLE# for all writes, non-cacheable reads and the first access of a Line Fill. These signals are active LOW.

3.1.3 LOCAL BUS CYCLE DEFINITION

3.1.3.1 Local Bus Cycle Definition Signals (W/R#,D/C#,M/IO# I)

The memory/input-output, data/code, write/read lines are the primary bus definition signals directly connected to the i386™ SX Microprocessor. These signals become valid as the ADS# signal is sampled asserted. The bus cycle type encoding is identical to that of the i386™ SX Microprocessor. The i386™ SX Microprocessor encoding is shown in table 5.1. The bus definition signals are not driven by the i386™ SX Microprocessor during bus hold and follow the timing of the address bus.

3.1.3.2 Local Bus Lock (LOCK# I)

This signal indicates a LOCK#ed cycle. LOCK#ed cycles are treated as non-cacheable cycles, except that LOCK#ed write hit cycles update the cache as well. LOCK#ed write cycles are not buffered.

The 82396SX Smart Cache asserts SLOCK# when the first LOCK#ed cycle is initiated on the System Bus. SLOCK# is deactivated only after all LOCK#ed System Bus cycles were executed, and LOCK# was deactivated.

3.1.4 LOCAL BUS CONTROL

3.1.4.1 Address Status (ADS# I)

The address status pin, an output of the i386™ SX Microprocessor, indicates that new, valid address and cycle definition information is currently available on the Local Bus. The signals that are valid when ADS# is activated are:

A(1–23), BHE#, BLE#, W/R#, D/C#, M/IO#, LOCK#, NPI# and BEM

3.1.4.2 Local Bus Ready (READYI# I)

This is the ready input signal seen by the Local Bus master. Typically it is a logical OR between the 82396SX Smart Cache generated READYO# signal and the i387™ SX Math Coprocessor READY# signal. It is used by the 82396SX Smart Cache, along with the ADS# signal, to keep track of the i386™ SX Microprocessor bus state. READYI# should not be driven active during T1 and should not be delayed from READYO# by one or more clocks.

3.1.4.3 Local Bus Ready Output (READYO# O)

This output is returned to the i386™ SX Microprocessor to terminate all types of i386™ SX Microprocessor bus cycles, except for Local Bus cycles.

The READYO# may serve as READY# signal for the i387™ SX Math Coprocessor. For details, refer to Chapter 5.

3.1.5 RESET (RESET I)

This signal forces the 82396SX Smart Cache to begin execution at a known state. The RESET falling edge is used by the 82396SX Smart Cache to set the phase of its internal clock identical to the i386™ SX Microprocessor internal clock. The RESET falling edge must satisfy the appropriate setup and hold times for proper chip operation. RESET must remain active for at least 1ms after power supply and CLK2 input have reached their proper DC and AC specifications.

The RESET input is used for two purposes: first, it RESETs the 82396SX Smart Cache and brings it to a known state. Second, it is used to synchronize the internal 82396SX Smart Cache clock phase to that of the i386™ SX Microprocessor.

On power up, RESET must be active for at least 1 millisecond after power has stabilized to a voltage within spec, and after CLK2 input has stabilized to voltage and frequency within spec. This is to allow the internal circuitry to stabilize. Otherwise, RESET must be active for at least 10 clock cycles.

No access to the 82396SX Smart Cache is allowed for 128 clock cycles after the RESET falling edge. During RESET, all other input pins are ignored, except SHOLD, and SAHOLD. Unlike the i386™ SX Microprocessor, the 82396SX Smart Cache can respond to a System Bus HOLD request by floating its bus and asserting SHLDA even while RESET is asserted. Also the 82396SX Smart Cache can respond to a System Bus address HOLD request by floating its address bus. The status of the 82396SX Smart Cache outputs during RESET is shown in Table 3.2.

The user must not drive SAHOLD and FLUSH# active during the two CLK2s prior to driving RESET inactive. If they do the Tristate Test Mode will be entered. The user must also insure that FLUSH# does not get activated for one CLK cycle while SAHOLD is deactivated for the same CLK cycle prior to RESET falling. If this condition exists a reserved mode will be entered (See Chapter 7).

3.1.6 LOCAL DATA BUS

3.1.6.1 Local Bus Data Lines (D[15:0] I/O)

These are the Local Bus data lines of the 82396SX Smart Cache and must be connected to the D[15:0] signals of the Local Bus.

3.1.7 LOCAL BUS DECODE PIN

3.1.7.1 No Post Input (NPI# I)

This signal instructs the 82396SX Smart Cache that the write cycle currently in progress must not be posted (buffered) in the write buffer. NPI# is sampled on the falling edge of CLK following the address change, see figure 5.1. NPI# is ignored during read cycles. This signal is active LOW.

3.1.7.2 Byte Enable Mask (BEM I)

The Byte Enable Mask signal, when asserted, causes the local bus byte enable signals to be masked so that both system bus byte enables are asserted on non-locked memory read cycles. If BEM is asserted during cacheable read cycles and that cycle requires a Line Fill (cache read miss), then both bytes will be accessed during the first cycle of the Line Fill. If BEM is not used (tied low), the system must return valid data for both bytes on the first access of a Line Fill to ensure that the cache stores valid data for both bytes in case the processor requested one. This signal is active HIGH.

4

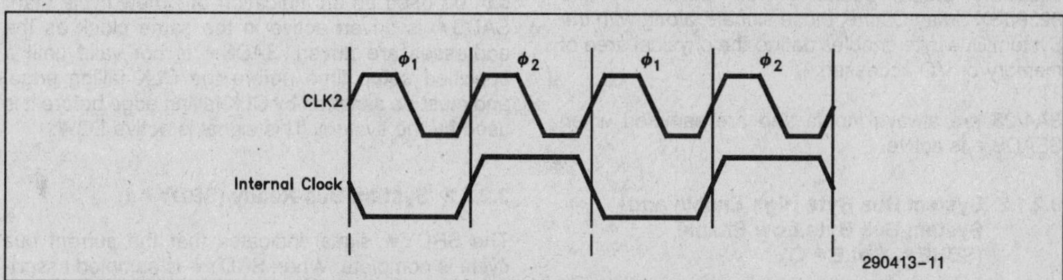

Figure 3.1 CLK2 and Internal Clock

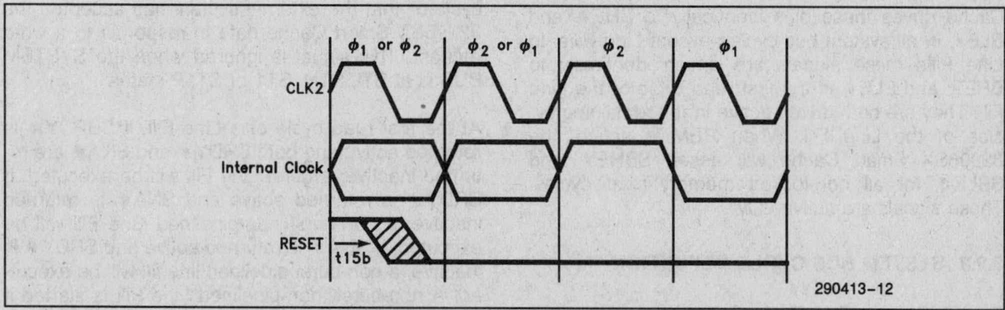

Figure 3.2 RESET/Internal Phase Relationship

3.1.8 ADDRESS MASK

3.1.8.1 Address Bit 20 Mask (A20M# I)

This pin, when active (low), forces the A20 input as seen by the 82396SX Smart Cache to logic '0', regardless of the actual value on the A20 input pin. It must be asserted two clock cycles before ADS# for proper operation. A20M# emulates the address wraparound at 1 Mbyte which occurs on the 8086. This pin is asynchronous but must meet setup and hold times to guarantee recognition in a specific clock. It must be stable throughout Local Bus memory cycles.

3.2 System Bus Interface Pins

3.2.1 SYSTEM ADDRESS BUS

3.2.1.1 System Bus Address Lines (SA[23:1] I/O *)

* SA1–3 are outputs only.

These are the SYSTEM BUS address lines of the 82396SX Smart Cache. When driven by the 82396SX Smart Cache, these signals, along with the System Bus byte enables define the physical area of memory or I/O accessed.

SA4-23 are always inputs and are sampled when SEADS# is active.

3.2.1.2 System Bus Byte High Enable and System Bus Byte Low Enable (SBHE#, SBLE# O)

These are the Byte Enable signals for the System Bus. When BEM is inactive the 82396SX Smart Cache drives these pins identically to BHE# and BLE# in all system bus cycles except Line Fills. In Line Fills these signals are driven identically to BHE# and BLE# in the first read cycle of the Line Fill. They are both driven active in the remaining cycles of the Line Fill. When BEM is active, the 82396SX Smart Cache will assert SBHE# and SBLE# for all non-locked memory read cycles. These signals are active LOW.

3.2.2 SYSTEM BUS CYCLE DEFINITION

3.2.2.1 System Bus Cycle Definition (SW/R#, SD/C#, SM/IO# O)

These are the System Bus cycle definition pins. When the 82396SX Smart Cache is the System Bus master, it drives these signals identically to the i386™ SX Microprocessor encoding.

3.2.2.2 System Bus Lock (SLOCK# O)

The System Bus LOCK pin is one of the bus cycle definition pins. It indicates that the current bus cycle is LOCK#ed: that the 82396SX Smart Cache (on behalf of the CPU) must be allowed exclusive access to the System Bus across bus cycle boundaries until this signal is de-asserted. The 82396SX Smart Cache does not acknowledge a bus hold request when this signal is asserted.

The 82396SX Smart Cache asserts SLOCK# when the first LOCK#ed cycle is initiated on the System Bus. SLOCK# is deactivated only after all LOCK#ed System Bus cycles were executed, and LOCK# was deactivated. SLOCK# is active LOW.

3.2.3 SYSTEM BUS CONTROL

3.2.3.1 System Bus Address Status (SADS# O)

The address status pin is used to indicate that new, valid address and cycle definition information is currently being driven onto the address, byte enable and cycle definition lines of the System Bus. SADS# can be used as an indication of a new cycle start. SADS# is driven active in the same clock as the addresses are driven. SADS# is not valid until a specified setup time before the CLK falling edge, and must be sampled by CLK falling edge before it is used by the system. This signal is active LOW.

3.2.3.2 System Bus Ready (SRDY# I)

The SRDY# signal indicates that the current bus cycle is complete. When SRDY# is sampled asserted it indicates that the external system has presented valid data on the data pins in response to a read cycle or that the external system has accepted the 82396SX Smart Cache data in response to a write request. This signal is ignored when the SYSTEM BUS is at STi, STH, ST1 or ST1P states.

At the first read cycle of a Line Fill, if SBRDY# is returned active and both SRDY# and SNA# are returned inactive, a burst Line Fill will be executed. If SRDY# is returned active and SNA# is returned inactive, a non-burst non-pipelined Line Fill will be executed. If SNA# is returned active and SRDY# is inactive, a non-burst pipelined line fill will be executed. A non-burst, non-pipelined Line Fill is started if SRDY# or SBRDY# is active during ST2 together with SNA# active.

Once a burst Line Fill has started, if SRDY# is returned in the second through the seventh word of the transfer, the burst Line Fill will be interrupted and the cache will not be updated. The first word will already have been transferred to the CPU. Note that in the last (eighth) bus cycle in a Line Fill, SBRDY# and SRDY# have the same effect on the 82396SX Smart Cache. They indicate the end of the Line Fill. This signal is active LOW.

3.2.3.3 System Bus Next Address (SNA# I)

This input, when active, indicates that a pipelined address cycle can be executed. It is sampled by the 82396SX Smart Cache in the same timing as the i386™ SX Microprocessor samples NA#. If this signal is sampled active, then SBRDY# is treated as SRDY#, i.e. burst Line Fills are disabled. This signal is ignored once a burst Line Fill has started as well as during the eighth word of a Line Fill.

3.2.4 BUS ARBITRATION

3.2.4.1 System Bus Hold Request (SHOLD I)

This signal allows another bus master complete control of the entire System Bus. In response to this pin, the 82396SX Smart Cache floats all its system bus interface output and input/output pins (With the Exception of SHLDA) and asserts SHLDA after completing its current bus cycle or sequence of LOCK#ed cycles. The 82396SX Smart Cache maintains its bus in this state until SHOLD is deasserted. SHOLD is active HIGH. SHOLD is recognized during reset.

3.2.4.2 System Bus Hold Acknowledge (SHLDA O)

This signal goes active in response to a hold request presented on the SHOLD pin and indicates that the 82396SX Smart Cache has given the bus to another System Bus master. It is driven active in the same clock that the 82396SX Smart Cache floats its bus. When leaving a bus hold, SHLDA is driven inactive in one clock and the 82396SX Smart Cache resumes driving the bus. Depending on internal requests the 82396SX Smart Cache may, or may not begin a System Bus cycle in the clock where SHLDA is driven inactive. The 82396SX Smart Cache is able to support CPU Local Bus activities during System Bus hold, since the internal cache is able to satisfy the majority of those requests. This signal is active HIGH.

3.2.5 BURST CONTROL

3.2.5.1 System Bus Burst Ready (SBRDY# I)

This signal performs the same function during a burst cycle that SRDY# does in a non-burst cycle. SBRDY# asserted indicates that the external system has presented valid data on the data pins in response to a burst Line Fill cycle. This signal is ignored when the SYSTEM BUS is at STi, STH, ST1 or ST1P states.

Note that in the last (eighth) bus cycle in a Line Fill, SBRDY# and SRDY# have the same effect on the 82396SX Smart Cache. They indicate the end of Line Fill. For all cycles that cannot run in burst, e.g. noncacheable cycles, non Line Fill cycles (or pipelined Line Fill), SBRDY# has the same effect on the 82396SX Smart Cache as the normal SRDY# pin. This signal is active LOW.

3.2.5.2 System Bus Burst Last Cycle Indicator (SBLAST# O)

The system burst last cycle signal indicates that the next time SBRDY# is returned the burst transfer is complete. In other words, it indicates to the external system that the next SBRDY# returned is treated as a normal SRDY# by the 82396SX Smart Cache, i.e., another set of addresses will be driven with SADS# or the SYSTEM BUS will go idle. SBLAST# is normally active. In a cache read miss cycle, which may proceed as a Line Fill, SBLAST# starts active and later follows SKEN# by one clock. SBLAST# is active during non-burst Line Fill cycles. Refer to Chapter 6 for more details. This signal is active LOW.

3.2.6 CACHE INVALIDATION

3.2.6.1 System Bus Address Hold (SAHOLD I)

This is the Address Hold request. It allows another bus master access to the address bus of the 82396SX Smart Cache in order to indicate the address of an external cycle for performing an internal Cache Directory lookup and invalidation cycle. In response to this signal, the 82396SX Smart Cache immediately (in the next cycle) stops driving the entire system address bus (SA[23:1]). Because the 82396SX Smart Cache always stops driving the address bus, in response to system bus address hold request, no hold acknowledge is required. Only the address bus will be floated during address hold, Other signals can remain active. For example, data can be returned for a previously specified bus cycle during address hold. The 82396SX Smart Cache does not initiate another bus cycle during address hold.

This pin is recognized during RESET. However, since the entire cache is invalidated by reset, any invalidation cycles run will be superfluous. This signal is active high.

4

3.2.6.2 System Bus External Address Strobe (SEADS# I)

This signal indicates that a valid external address has been driven onto the 82396SX Smart Cache pins and that this address must be used to perform an internal cache invalidation cycle. Maximum allowed invalidation cycle rate is one every two clock cycles. This signal is active LOW.

3.2.7 CACHE CONTROL

3.2.7.1 Flush (FLUSH# I)

This pin, when sampled active for four clock cycles or more, causes the 82396SX Smart Cache to invalidate its entire Tag Array. In addition, it is used to configure the 82396SX Smart Cache to enter various test modes. For details refer to Chapter 7. This pin is asynchronous but must meet setup and hold times to guarantee recognition in any specific clock. This signal is active LOW.

Activation of FLUSH# does not prevent Line Fills. Although the TAG Valid bit will be cleared, the Line Fill can still occur on the System Bus. To prevent a Line Fill from occurring, the SKEN# signal must be deactivated.

3.2.8 SYSTEM DATA BUS

3.2.8.1 System Bus Data Lines (SD[15:0] I/O)

These are the SYSTEM BUS data lines of the 82396SX Smart Cache. The lines must be driven with appropriate setup and hold times for proper operation. These signals are driven by the 82396SX Smart Cache only during write cycles.

3.2.9 SYSTEM BUS DECODE PINS

3.2.9.1 System Cacheability Enable (SKEN# I)

This is the cache enable pin. It is used to determine whether the current cycle running on the System Bus is cacheable or not. When the 82396SX Smart Cache generates a read cycle that may be cached, this pin is sampled 1 CLK before the first SBRDY#, SRDY# or SNA# is sampled active (for detailed timing description, refer to Chapter 6). If sampled active, the cycle will be transformed into a Line Fill. Otherwise, the Cache and Cache Directory will be unaffected. Note that SKEN# is ignored after the first cycle in a Line Fill. SKEN# is ignored during all System Bus cycles except for cacheable read miss cycles. This signal is active LOW.

3.2.9.2 System Write Protect Indication (SWP# I)

This is the write protect indicator pin. It is used to determine whether the address of the current system bus Line Fill cycle is write protected or not.

In non-pipelined cycles, the SWP# is sampled with the first SRDY# or SBRDY# of a system Line Fill cycle. In pipelined cycles, SWP# is sampled at the last ST2 stage, or at ST1P; in other words, one clock phase after SNA# is sampled active.

The write protect indicator is sampled together with the TAG address of each line in the 82396SX Smart Cache Directory. In every cacheable write cycle, the write protect indicator is read. If active, the cycle will be a Write Protected cycle which is treated like cacheable write miss cycle. It is buffered and it does not update the cache even if the addressed location is present in the cache. The signal is active LOW.

3.3 Pinout Summary Tables

Table 3.1 Input Pins

Name	Function	Synchronous/ Asynchronous	Active Level
CLK2	Clock		
RESET	Reset	Asynchronous*	High
BHE#	Local Bus Byte High Enable	Synchronous	Low
BLE#	Local Bus Byte Low Enable	Synchronous	Low
A1–23	Local Bus Address Lines	Synchronous	—
W/R#	Local Bus Write/Read	Synchronous	—
D/C#	Local Bus Data/Code	Synchronous	—
M/IO#	Local Bus Memory/Input-Output	Synchronous	—
LOCK#	Local Bus LOCK	Synchronous	Low
ADS#	Local Bus Address Strobe	Synchronous	Low
READYI#	Local Bus READY	Synchronous	Low
NPI#	No Post Input	Synchronous	Low
BEM	Byte Enable Mask	Synchronous	High
FLUSH#	FLUSH# the 82396SX Smart Cache	Asynchronous	Low
A20M#	Address Bit 20 Mask	Asynchronous	Low
SHOLD	SYSTEM BUS Hold Request	Synchronous	High
SRDY#	SYSTEM BUS READY	Synchronous	Low
SNA#	SYSTEM BUS Next Address Indication	Synchronous	Low
SBRDY#	SYSTEM BUS Burst Ready	Synchronous	Low
SKEN#	System Cacheability Indication	Synchronous	Low
SWP#	System Write Protect Indication	Synchronous	Low
SAHOLD	SYSTEM BUS Address HOLD	Synchronous	High
SEADS#	SYSTEM BUS External Address Strobe	Synchronous	Low

* The falling edge of RESET needs to be synchronous to CLK2 but the rising edge is asynchronous.

Table 3.2 Output Pins

Name	Function	When Floated	State(3) at RESET	Active Level
SBHE#	SYSTEM BUS Byte High Enable	SHLDA	Low	Low
SBLE#	SYSTEM BUS Byte Low Enable	SHLDA	Low	Low
SADS#	SYSTEM BUS Address Strobe	SHLDA(1)	High	Low
SD/C#	SYSTEM BUS Data/Code	SHLDA	High	—
SM/IO#	SYSTEM BUS Memory/Input-Output	SHLDA	Low	—
SW/R#	SYSTEM BUS Write/Read	SHLDA	Low	—
SHLDA	SYSTEM BUS HOLD Acknowledge	—	Low(2)	High
SLOCK#	SYSTEM BUS LOCK	SHLDA	High	Low
SBLAST#	SYSTEM BUS Burst Last Cycle Indication	SHLDA	Low	Low
SA1–3	SYSTEM BUS Address (3 lowest order bits)	SHLDA/SAHOLD	High	—

(1) SADS# is driven high before it is floated in each first ST2/ST1P
(2) Unless SHOLD is asserted
(3) Provided SHOLD and SAHOLD are inactive

Table 3.3 Input-Output Pins

Name	Function	When Floated	State(1) at RESET	Active Level
D0–15	Local Data Bus(2)	Always Except READs	Z	—
SD0–15	System Data Bus(3)	Always Except WRITEs	Z	—
SA4–23	SYSTEM BUS Address (except the 3 lowest order bits)	SHLDA/SAHOLD	High	—
READYO#	Local Bus READY(2)		High	Low

(1) Provided SHOLD and SAHOLD are inactive
(2) This signal is driven only in T2
(3) This signal is driven only in ST2

4.0 BASIC FUNCTIONAL DESCRIPTION

The 82396SX Smart Cache has an interface to the i386™ SX Microprocessor (Local Bus) and to the System Bus. The System Bus interface emulates the i386™ SX Microprocessor bus such that the system will view the 82396SX Smart Cache as the front end of a i386™ SX Microprocessor. Some optional enhancements, like burst support, are provided to maximize the performance.

When ADS# is sampled active, the 82396SX Smart Cache decodes the i386™ SX Microprocessor cycle definition signals (M/IO#, D/C#, W/R# and LOCK#), as well as the Local Bus decode signal (NPI# and BEM), to determine how to respond. NPI# indicates that the current memory write cycle must not be buffered. In addition, the 82396SX Smart Cache internally decodes the i386™ SX Microprocessor accesses to the i387™ SX Math Coprocessor as Local Bus accesses. The result of the address, cycle definition and cycle qualification decoding is two categories of accesses, i387™ SX Math Coprocessor and 82396SX Smart Cache accesses. In i387™ SX Math Coprocessor accesses, the 82396SX Smart Cache drives the READYO# signal active after one wait state, if the READYI# was not sampled active.

Any 82396SX Smart Cache access can be either to a cacheable address or to a non-cacheable address. Non-cacheable addresses are all I/O and system accesses with SKEN# returned inactive. Non-cacheable cycles are all cycles to non-cacheable addresses, LOCK#ed read cycles and Halt/Shutdown cycles. All other cycles are cacheable. For more details about non-cacheable cycles, refer to Section 4.2. Non-cacheable cycles pass through the cache. They are always forwarded to the System Bus.

Cacheable read cycles can be either hit or miss. Cacheable read hit cycles are serviced by the internal cache and they don't require System Bus service. A cacheable read miss cycle generates a series of eight System Bus read cycles, called a Line Fill. Of the eight cycles, the first cycle is for reading the requested data while all eight are for filling the cache line. The System Bus has the ability to provide the system cacheability attribute to the 82396SX Smart Cache Line Fill request, via the SKEN# input, and the system write protection indicator, via the SWP# input. Refer to chapter 6 for more information about Line Fill cycles.

Cacheable write cycles, as any write cycles, are forwarded to the System Bus. The write buffer algorithm terminates the write cycle on the Local Bus, allowing the i386™ SX Microprocessor to continue processing in zero wait states, while the 82396SX Smart Cache executes the write cycles on the System Bus. All cacheable write hit cycles, except protected writes, update the cache on a byte basis i.e. only the selected bytes are updated. Cacheable write misses do not update the cache (the 82396SX Smart Cache does not allocate on writes). All cacheable write cycles, except LOCK#ed writes, are buffered (unless the NPI# pin is sampled active).

Cache consistency is provided by SEADS#. If any bus master performs a memory cycle which disturbs the data consistency, the address can be provided to the 82396SX Smart Cache by the other bus master using SAHOLD or SHOLD/SHLDA. Then, the 82396SX Smart Cache checks if that memory location resides in the cache. If it does, the 82396SX Smart Cache invalidates that line in the cache by marking it as invalid in the Cache Directory. The 82396SX Smart Cache interposes the Cache Directory between the i386™ SX Microprocessor and the System Bus such that the i386™ SX Microprocessor is not forced to wait due to snooping and none of the snooping cycles are missed due to i386™ SX Microprocessor accesses (see Figure 2.6).

Cacheability is resolved on the system side using the SKEN# input. SKEN# is sampled one clock before the first SRDY#/SBRDY# in non pipelined Line Fill cycles. In pipelined Line Fill cycles, SKEN# is sampled one clock phase before sampling SNA# active. SKEN# is always sampled at PHI1.

Note that the 82396SX Smart Cache does not support pipelining of the i386™ SX Microprocessor Local Bus. The NA# input on the i386™ SX Microprocessor must be tied to Vcc.

4.1 Cacheable Accesses

In a cacheable access, the 82396SX Smart Cache performs a cache directory look-up cycle. This is to determine if the requested data exists in the cache and to read the write protection bit. In parallel, the 82396SX Smart Cache performs a cache read cycle if the access is a read, or prepares the cache for a write cycle if the access is a write.

4.1.1 CACHEABLE READ HIT ACCESSES

If the Cache Directory look-up for a cacheable read access results in a hit (the requested data exists in the cache), the 82396SX Smart Cache drives the local data bus by the data provided from the internal cache. It also drives the i386™ SX Microprocessor READY# (by activating the 82396SX Smart Cache READYO#), so that the i386™ SX Microprocessor gets the required data directly from the cache without any wait states.

The 82396SX Smart Cache is a four Way set associative cache, so only one of the four ways (four banks) is selected to supply data to the i386™ SX Microprocessor. The Way in which the hit occurred will provide the data. Also, the replacement algorithm (LRU) is updated such that the Way in which the hit occurred is marked as the most recently used.

4.1.2 CACHEABLE READ MISS ACCESSES

READYO# is always activated in the first T2 of cache read miss cycles. In order to meet the timing requirements READYO# must be activated prior to the hit/miss decision. Once the hit/miss decision is made and the cycle is a miss, READYO# is deactivated. This activation only occurs prior to the max valid delay specification (t20 max). After the max valid delay spec, READYO# will always be stable. See Figure 4.0.

If the Cache Directory look-up results in a miss, the 82396SX Smart Cache transfers the request to the System Bus in order to read the data from the main memory and for updating the cache. A full line is updated in a cache update cycle. As a result of a cache miss, the 82396SX Smart Cache performs eight System Bus accesses to read eight words from the DRAM, and write the eight words to the cache. This is called a Line Fill cycle. The first word accessed in a Line Fill cycle is for the word which the i386™ SX Microprocessor requested and the 82396SX Smart Cache provides the data and drives the READYO# one clock after it gets the first word from the System Bus.

The 82396SX Smart Cache provides the option of supporting burst bus in order to minimize the latency of a line fill. Also, the 82396SX Smart Cache provides the SKEN# input, which, if inactive, converts a Line Fill cycle to a non-cacheable cycle. Write protection is also provided. The write protection indicator is stored together with the TAG Valid bit and the TAG field of every line in the Cache Directory. For more details refer to Chapter 6.

The 82396SX Smart Cache features Line Buffer cacheing. In a Line Fill the data for the eight words is stored in a buffer, the Line Buffer, as it is accumulated. After filling the Line Buffer, the 82396SX Smart Cache performs the Cache Update and the Cache Directory Update. If the access is a hit to the line buffer it can be serviced in zero wait states. The updated Way is the least recently used Way flagged by the Pseudo LRU algorithm during the Cache Directory Lookup cycle if all Ways are valid. If there is a non-valid Way it will be updated.

The SRDY# (System Bus READY#) active indicates the completion of the System Bus cycle and

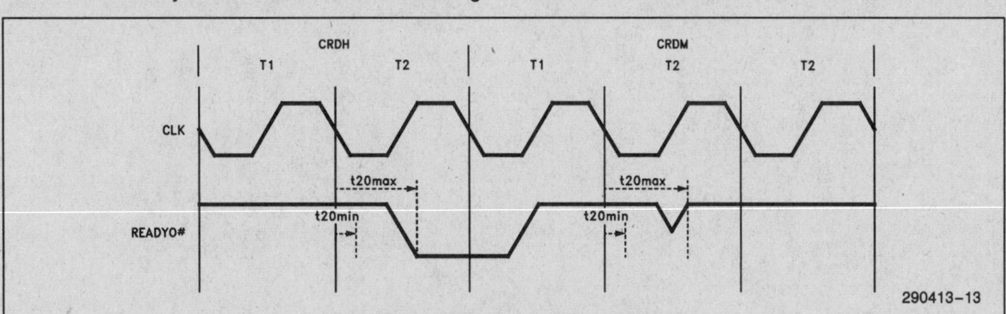

Figure 4.0 READYO# Behavior

SBRDY# (System Bus Burst READY#) active indicates the completion of a burst System Bus cycle. In a i386™ SX Microprocessor-like system, the 82396SX Smart Cache drives the i386™ SX Microprocessor READY# one clock after the first SRDY# and, in a burst system, one clock after the first SBRDY#. This frees up the Local Bus, allowing the i386™ SX Microprocessor to execute the next instruction, while filling the cache. So, during Line Fills, there is no advantage in driving the i386™ SX Microprocessor into the pipelined mode. **Therefore, the 82396SX Smart Cache does not drive the i386™ SX Microprocessor's NA# at all. NA# must be tied to VCC.**

4.1.2.1 Burst Bus

The 82396SX Smart Cache offers an option to minimize the latency in Line Fills. This option is the burst bus and is only applicable to Line Fill cycles. By generation of a burst bus compatible DRAM controller, one which generates SBRDY# and SBLAST# to take advantage of the 82396SX Smart Cache's burst feature, the number of cycles required for a Line Fill to be completed is significantly reduced. Details of burst Line Fills can be found in Chapter 6.

4.1.3 CACHE WRITE ACCESSES

The 82396SX Smart Cache supports the write buffer policy, which means that main memory is always updated in any write cycle. However, the cache is updated only when the write cycle hits the cache and the accessed address is not write protected. In cache write misses, the cache is not updated (allocation in writes is not supported).

The 82396SX Smart Cache has a write buffer of four words. Only the cacheable write cycles, except LOCK#ed writes, are buffered so, if the write buffer is not full, the 82396SX Smart Cache buffers the cycle. This means that the data, address and cycle definition signals are written in one entry of the write buffer and the 82396SX Smart Cache drives the READYO# in the first T2 so all the buffered write cycles run without wait states. If the write buffer is full, the 82396SX Smart Cache delays the READYO# until the completion of the execution of the first buffered write cycle. The execution of the buffered write cycles depends on the availability of the System Bus. In a non-buffered write cycle, e.g. I/O writes, the i386™ SX Microprocessor is forced to wait until the execution of all the buffered writes and the non-buffered write. READYO# is driven one clock after the SRDY# of the non-buffered write. More details about the write buffer can be found in Chapter 6.

In cacheable non-write protected write hit cycles, only the appropriate bytes within the line are updated. The updated bytes are selected by decoding A1–A3 and the BHE# and BLE# lines. The LRU is updated so that the hit Way is the most recently used, as in cache read hit cycles.

All cacheable writes, whether hits or misses, are executed on the System Bus. The System Bus write cycle address, data and cycle definition signals are the same as the i386™ SX Microprocessor signals. All buffered writes run with zero wait states if the write buffer is not full.

4.2 Noncacheable System Bus Accesses

Non-cacheable cycles are any of the following 82396SX Smart Cache cycles:

1) All I/O cycles.
2) All LOCK#ed read cycles.
3) Halt/Shutdown cycles.
4) SRAM mode cycles not addressing the internal cache or Tagram.

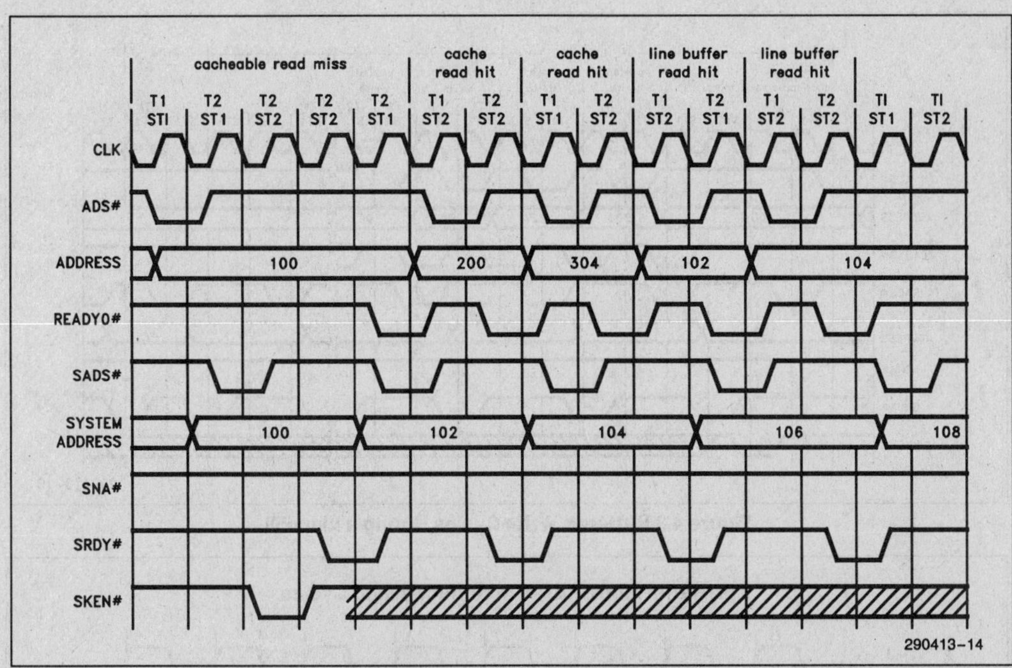

Figure 4.1 Read Hit Cycles During Line Fill

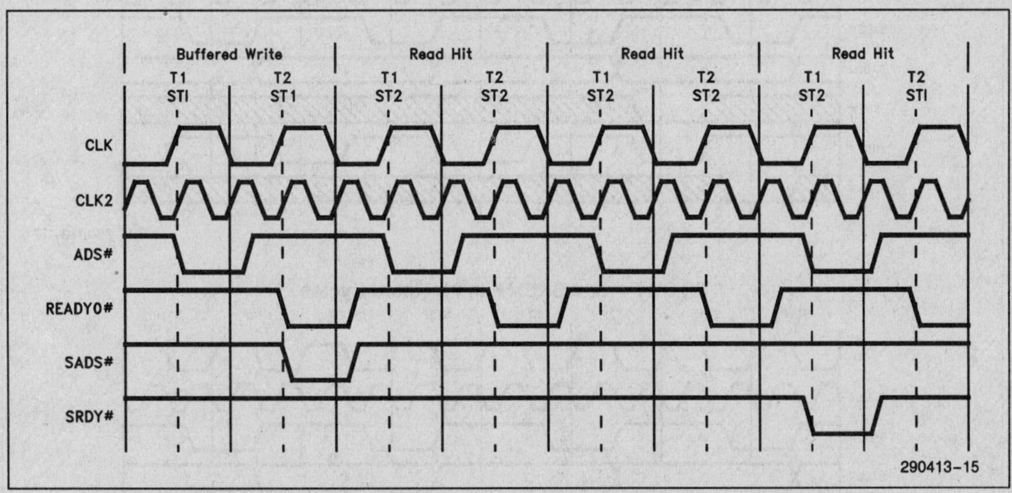

Figure 4.2 Cache Read Hit Cycles While Executing a Buffered Write on the System Bus.

4

LINE FILL
write
cacheable read miss
posted write
posted write
posted write
posted write
T1 STI
T2 ST1
T2 ST2
T2 ST2
T2 ST1
T1 ST2
T2 ST2
T1 ST1
T2 ST2
T1 ST2
T2 ST1
T1 ST2
T2 ST2
TI ST1
TI ST2
TI ST2
TI ST1
TI ST2
TI ST1
CLK
ADS#
ADDRESS
100
200
224
308
30C
READYO#
SADS#
SYSTEM ADDRESS
100
102
104
106
10E
200
SNA#
SRDY#
SKEN#
290413-16

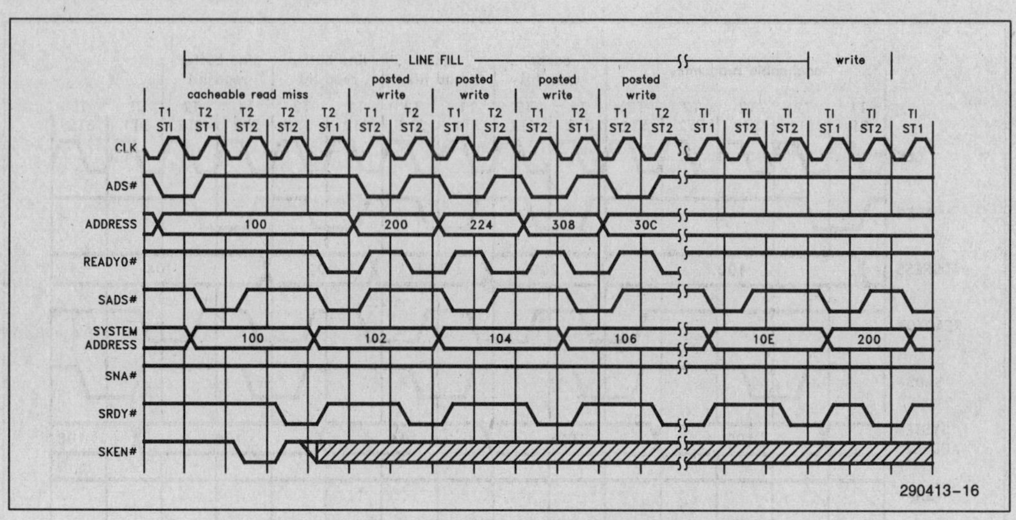

Figure 4.3 Buffered Write Cycles During a Line Fill

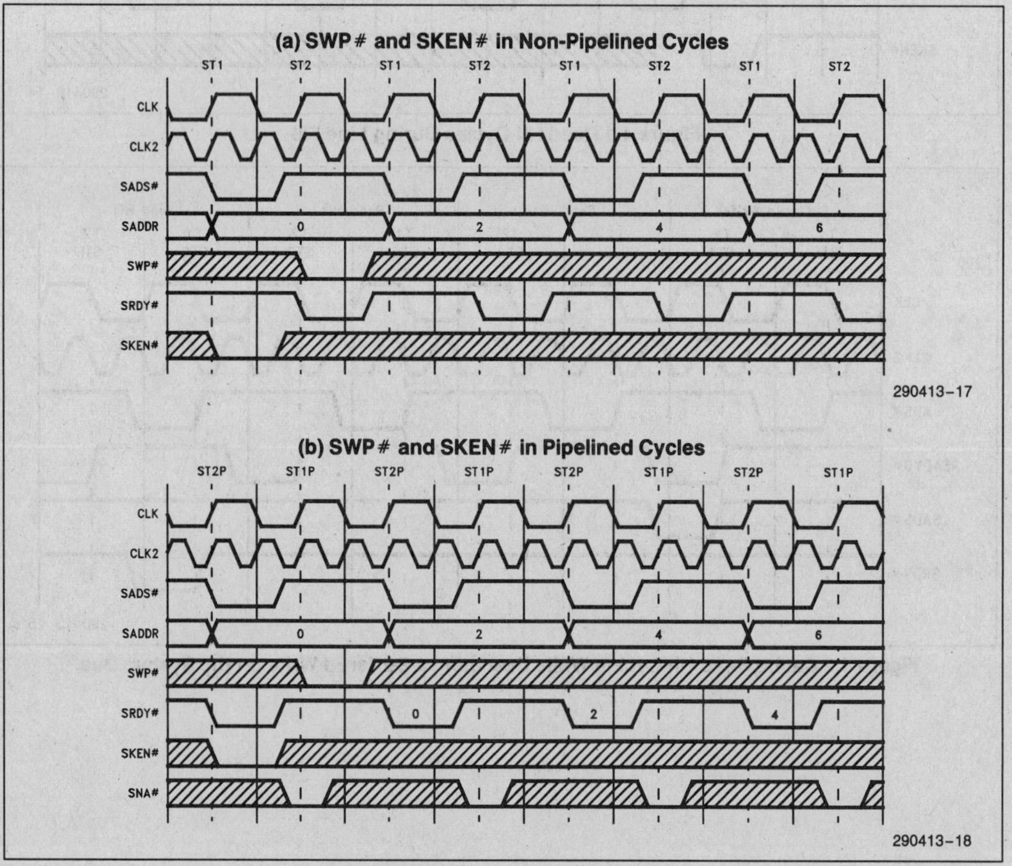

(a) SWP# and SKEN# in Non-Pipelined Cycles
ST1
ST2
ST1
ST2
ST1
ST2
ST1
ST2
CLK
CLK2
SADS#
SADDR
0
2
4
6
SWP#
SRDY#
SKEN#
290413-17
(b) SWP# and SKEN# in Pipelined Cycles
ST2P
ST1P
ST2P
ST1P
ST2P
ST1P
ST2P
ST1P
CLK
CLK2
SADS#
SADDR
0
2
4
6
SWP#
SRDY#
0
2
4
SKEN#
SNA#
290413-18

Figure 4.4 SWP# and SKEN# Timing

Table 4.1 i386™ SX Microprocessor Bus Cycle Definition with Cacheability

M/IO#	D/C#	W/R#	i386™ SX Microprocessor Cycle Definition	Cacheable/ Non-Cacheable	Writes Posted
0	0	0	Interrupt Acknowledge	Non-cacheable	—
0	0	1	Undefined	—	—
0	1	0	I/O Read	Non-cacheable	—
0	1	1	I/O Write	Non-cacheable	No
1	0	0	Memory Code Read	Cacheable(1)	—
1	0	1	Halt/Shutdown	Non-cacheable	No
1	1	0	Memory Data Read	Cacheable(1)	—
1	1	1	Memory Data Write	Cacheable(1)	Yes(2)

NOTES:
1. Cacheability is controlled by SKEN# and SWP#.
2. Writes are not posted if NPI# is asserted.

All the above cycles are defined as non-cacheable by the Local Bus interface controller. In addition, Line Fill cycles in which the SKEN# was returned inactive are aborted. They are called Aborted Line Fills (ALF).

Non-cacheable cycles are never serviced from the cache and they don't update the cache. They are always referred to the System Bus. In non-cacheable cycles, the 82396SX Smart Cache transfers to the System Bus the exact i386™ SX Microprocessor bus cycle.

A description of LOCK#ed cycles can be found in Chapter 5.

4.3 Local and System Bus Concurrency

Concurrency between local and System Busses is supported in several cases:

1. Read hit cycles can run while executing a Line Fill on the System Bus. Refer to timing diagram 4.1.
2. Read hit cycles can run while executing buffered write cycles on System Bus. Refer to timing diagram 4.2.
3. Write cycles are buffered while the System Bus is running other cycles, including other buffered writes. They are also buffered when another bus master is using the System Bus (e.g. DMA, other CPU). Refer to timing diagrams 4.3 and 6.3.
4. Read hit cycles can run while another System Bus master is using the System Bus.

The first case is established by providing the data which the i386™ SX Microprocessor requested first and later the 82396SX Smart Cache continues filling its line while it is servicing new read hit cycles. The 82396SX Smart Cache updates its cache and cache directory after completing the System Bus Line Fill cycle. Meanwhile, any i386™ SX Microprocessor read cycles will be serviced from the cache if they hit the cache. In case the i386™ SX Microprocessor read cycles are consecutive such that the i386™ SX Microprocessor is requesting a word which belongs to the same line currently retrieved by the System Bus Line Fill cycle and the requested word was already retrieved, the 82396SX Smart Cache provides the requested word in zero wait states (a Line Buffer hit). If the requested word wasn't already retrieved, it will be read after completing the Line Fill.

The second and third cases are attained by having the 4 word deep write buffer which is described in chapter 6. The READYO# is driven active after latching the write cycle, so all buffered cycles will run without wait states on the Local Bus. This releases the i386™ SX Microprocessor to issue a new cycle, which can also run without wait states if it does not require system bus service. Two examples are in the case of a read hit cycle, or another buffered write cycle, which does not require immediate System Bus service. In the case of a write cycle to the same line currently retrieved, the write cycle will wait until the Line Fill is complete and then the selected bytes within the line are written in the cache. READYO# is returned after the cache is written.

4

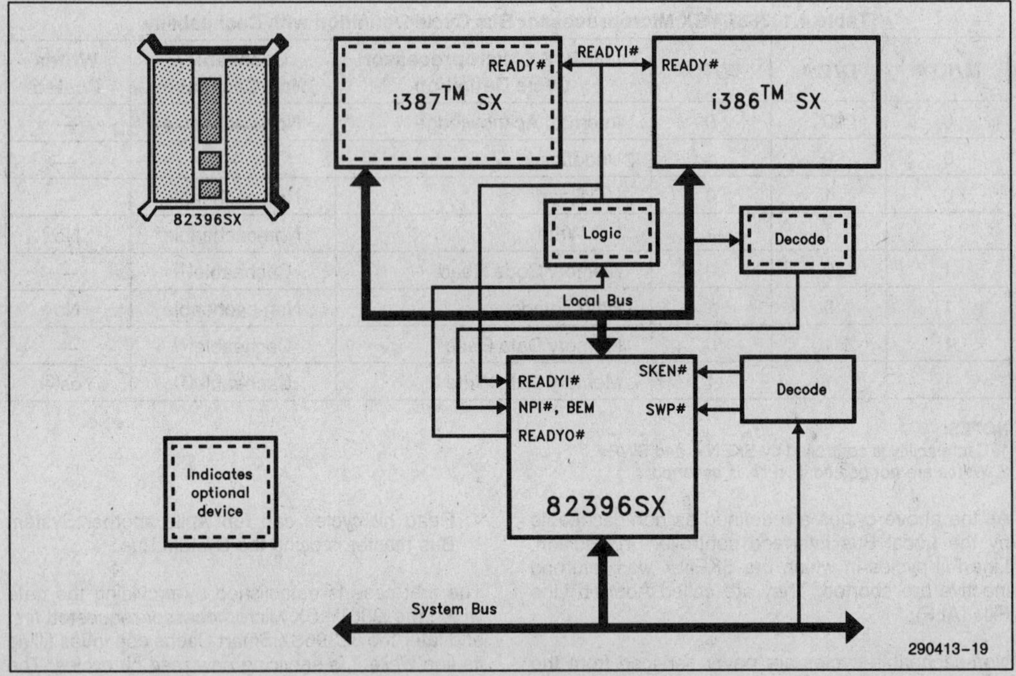

Figure 4.5 System Description

Whenever the System Bus is released to any bus master, the 82396SX Smart Cache activates the snooping function. The maximum rate of snooping cycles is a cycle every other clock. Although the snooping support requires accessing the 82396SX Smart Cache Directory, the 82396SX Smart Cache is able to interpose the cache directory accesses between the i386™ SX Microprocessor cycles and the snooping device such that zero wait state read hit cycles are supported. All the snooping cycles are also serviced. This is how the fourth case is provided. For more details, refer to Chapter 6.

4.4 Disabling the 82396SX Smart Cache

Cacheability is resolved by the SKEN# input from the system side. In order to disable the cache it is recommended to deactivate SKEN#, and assert FLUSH# (See Section 3.2.7.1). This would cause all memory reads to be detected as misses and to be transferred to the System Bus. In order to disable the write buffer, NPI# must be asserted.

5.0 PROCESSOR INTERFACE

The 82396SX Smart Cache runs synchronously with the i386™ SX Microprocessor. It is a slave on the Local Bus, and it buffers between the Local Bus and the System Bus. Most of the 82396SX Smart Cache cycles are serviced from the internal cache, and some (82396SX Smart Cache misses, non cacheable accesses, etc.) require an access to the System Bus to complete the transaction.

To achieve maximum performance, the 82396SX Smart Cache serves cache hits and buffered write cycles in zero wait-state, non- pipelined cycles. The 82396SX Smart Cache requires that the CPU is never driven to pipelined cycles, i.e. **the i386™ SX Microprocessor NA# input must be strapped to the inactive (high) state.**

The 82396SX Smart Cache is directly connected to all local bus address and data lines, byte enable lines, and bus cycle definition signals. The 82396SX Smart Cache returns READYO# to the i386™ SX Microprocessor, and keeps track of the i386™ SX Microprocessor cycle status by receiving READYI# (which is the i386™ SX Microprocessor READY#).

5.1 Hardware Interface

The 82396SX Smart Cache requires minimal hardware on the Local Bus. All that is needed is the i386™ SX Microprocessor and other Local Bus resources (i.e. i387™ SX Math Coprocessor) and the 82396SX Smart Cache. A decoder for generating NPI# (Non-Posted Input) and BEM (Byte Enable Mask) is optional. The SRAM and buffers have been integrated on chip to simplify the design. Refer to Figure 4.5.

5.2 Nonpipelined Local Bus

The 82396SX Smart Cache does not pipeline the Local Bus. READYO# gets returned to the i386™ SX Microprocessor one cycle after SRDY# or SBRDY# is driven into the 82396SX Smart Cache after the first word of a Line Fill. This allows the Local Bus to be free to execute i386™ SX Microprocessor cycles while the System Bus fills the cache line (see Chapter 6).This takes away the advantage gained by pipelining the Local Bus.

5.3 Local Bus Response to Hit Cycles

The 82396SX Smart Cache's Local Bus response to hit cycles are described here:

1) Cache Read Hit (CRDH) Cycle - READYO# gets returned in T2. The data is valid to the i386™ SX Microprocessor on the rising edge of CLK2.
2) Cache Write Hit (CWTH), Buffered - Like in CRDH cycles the 82396SX Smart Cache returns READYO# in T2 so that the cycle runs with zero wait states on the Local Bus. The write cycle is placed in the write buffer and will be performed when the System Bus is available. If the System Bus is on HOLD up to four write cycles can be buffered before introducing any wait states on the Local Bus.
3) CWTH, Non-Buffered - In the case of a non-buffered write hit cycle the write buffers can not be used so the i386™ SX Microprocessor must wait until the System Bus is free to do the write. READYO# is returned the cycle after SRDY# is driven to the 82396SX Smart Cache.

5.4 Local Bus Response to Miss Cycles

In a Cache Read Miss (CRDM) cycle a Line Fill is performed on the System Bus. READYO# is returned to the i386™ SX Microprocessor one cycle after SRDY# or SBRDY# for the first word of the Line Fill is driven into the 82396SX Smart Cache.

A Cache Write Miss (CWTM) cycle is forwarded to the System Bus consistent with the write buffer policy. The cache is not updated.

5.5 Local Bus Control Signals - ADS#, READYI#

ADS# and READYI# are the two bus control inputs used by the 82396SX Smart Cache to determine the status of the Local Bus cycle. ADS# denotes the beginning of a i386™ SX Microprocessor cycle and READYI# is the i386™ SX Microprocessor cycle terminator.

ADS# active and M/IO# = 1 invokes a look-up request to the 82396SX Smart Cache's cache directory; the look-up is performed in T1 state. The Cache Directory access is simultaneous with all other cycle qualification activities, this Way the hit/miss decision becomes the last in the cycle qualification process. This parallelism enhances performance, and enables the 82396SX Smart Cache to respond to ADS# within one clock period. If the cycle is noncacheable, the hit/miss decision is ignored.

READYI# should not be driven active during T1 and should not be delayed from READYO# by one or more clocks.

5.6 82396SX Smart Cache's Response to the i386™ SX Microprocessor Cycles

Tables 5.2 - 5.4 show the 82396SX Smart Cache's response to the various i386™ SX Microprocessor cycles. They depict the activity in the internal cache, cache directory, the System Bus and write buffers in response to various cycle definition signals. Special cycles such as: LOCK, HALT/SHUTDOWN, WP, NPI are discussed separately below.

5.6.1 LOCKED CYCLES

The i386™ SX Microprocessor LOCK#ed cycles are all those cycles in which LOCK# is active. The 82396SX Smart Cache forces all LOCK#ed cycles to run on the System Bus. The 82396SX Smart Cache starts the LOCK#ed cycle after it has emptied its write buffers.

4

If the LOCK#ed cycle is cacheable the 82396SX Smart Cache will respond as follows (see Table 5.2):

Cache Read Miss (CRDM) - handled similar to a non cacheable cycle.

Cache Read Hit (CRDH) - handled similar to a non cacheable cycle (LRU bits are not updated).

Cache Write Miss (CWTM) - the cache is not updated, the write is not buffered.

Cache Write Hit (CWTH) - the cache is updated if the line is not write protected. The write is not buffered. Note that this write is not buffered even though it is cacheable. The LRU mechanism is updated.

If the LOCK#ed cycle is non-cacheable (e.g. IO cycle, INTA cycle) then it will be performed as a common non-cacheable cycle with the addition of asserting SLOCK# on the System Bus.

Conceptually, a LOCK# cycle on the Local Bus is reflected into an SLOCK# cycle on the System Bus. SLOCK# becomes inactive only after LOCK# has become inactive. If there are idle clocks in between the LOCK#ed cycles but LOCK# is still active - SLOCK# will remain active as well. **A consequence of this is that SLOCK# is negated one clock after LOCK# is negated.**

During LOCK#ed cycles on System Bus (i.e. when SLOCK# signal is active), the 82396SX Smart Cache does not acknowledge hold requests, so the whole sequence of LOCK#ed cycles will run without interruption by another master.

5.6.2 I/O, HALT/SHUTDOWN

I/O and HALT/SHUTDOWN cycles are handled as non-cacheable cycles. They are neither cached nor kept in the write buffer. The i386™ SX Microprocessor HALT/SHUTDOWN cycles are memory write cycles to code area (i.e. M/IO# = 1, D/C# = 0). The 82396SX Smart Cache completes I/O and HALT/SHUTDOWN cycles by returning READYO#, after receiving the SBRDY# or SRDY#.

5.6.3 NPI# CYCLES

NPI# cycles are all the i386™ SX Microprocessor memory write cycles in which NPI# is active. In response to a write cycle with NPI# active, the 82396SX Smart Cache first executes all pending write cycles in the write buffer (if any), and than executes the current write cycle on the System Bus. READYO# is returned to the CPU only after SRDY# for the current write cycle is returned to the 82396SX Smart Cache.

All NPI# cycles must have at least one wait state on the System Bus or be done to non-cacheable memory. NPI# is ignored for read cycles, as well as all write cycles that cannot be buffered.

5.6.4 NPI#/BEM TIMING

These inputs must be valid throughout the i386™ SX Microprocessor bus cycle, namely in T1 and all T2 states (See Figure 5.1).

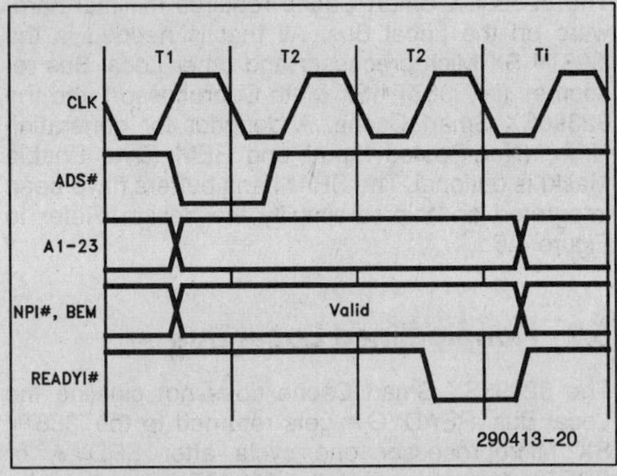

Figure 5.1 Valid Time of NPI# and BEM

5.7 82396SX Smart Cache READYO# Generation

The 82396SX Smart Cache READYO# generation rules are listed below:

CRDH cycles (non-LOCK#ed), READYO# is activated during the first T2 state, so the cycle runs with zero wait states.

CRDM cycles - READYO# is returned one clock after the first SRDY# or SBRDY# associated with this read cycle is returned.

Non cacheable reads - READYO# is returned one clock after SRDY# or SBRDY#.

All cacheable writes (with the exception of LOCK#ed writes) are buffered. These cycles may be divided into two categories:

(a) The first four write cycles - while the write buffer is not fully exploited. READYO# is returned with zero wait states. The address and the data are registered in the write buffer.

(b) When the write buffer is full - READYO# is delayed until one clock after the SRDY# or SBRDY# of the first write cycle in the buffer. In other words the fifth write waits until there is one vacant entry in the write buffer.

Non cacheable writes (plus LOCK#ed writes) - these writes are not buffered. READYO# is returned one clock after SRDY# or SBRDY# of the same cycle.

READYO# activation during SRAM test mode are listed in Chapter 7.

In all i387™ SX Math Coprocessor accesses, the 82396SX Smart Cache monitors the READYI#. If it wasn't activated immediately after ADS#, READYO# will be activated in the next clock i.e. a one wait state cycle. So, the 82396SX Smart Cache READYO# can be used to terminate any i387™ SX Math Coprocessor access.

Note that the timing of the 82396SX Smart Cache's READYO# generation for i387™ SX Math Coprocessor cycles is incompatible with 80287 timing. When activated, READYO# remains active until READYI# is sampled active. This procedure enables adding control logic to control the i386™ SX Microprocessor READYI# generation (see figure 5.2).

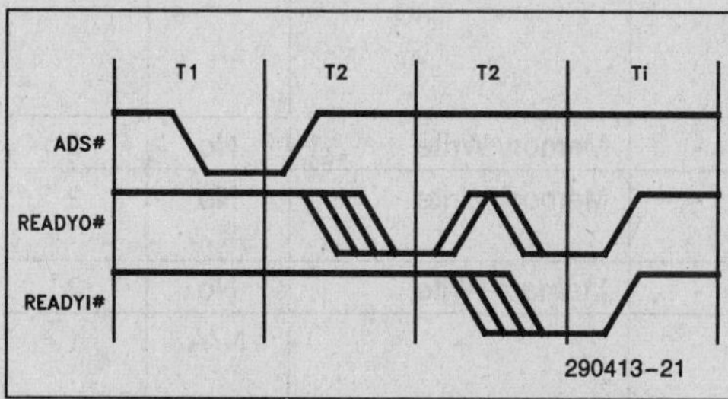

Figure 5.2 Externally Delayed READY

5.8 A20 Mask Signal

The A20M# signal is provided to allow for emulation of the address wraparound at 1 Mbyte which occurs on the 8086. A20M# pin is synchronized internally by the 82396SX Smart Cache, then ANDed with the A20 input pin. The product of synchronized A20M# and A20 is presented to the rest of the 82396SX Smart Cache logic, as shown in Figure 5.3. A20M# must be valid two clock cycles before ADS# is sampled active by the 82396SX Smart Cache, and must remain valid until after READYI# is sampled active (see Figure 5.4).

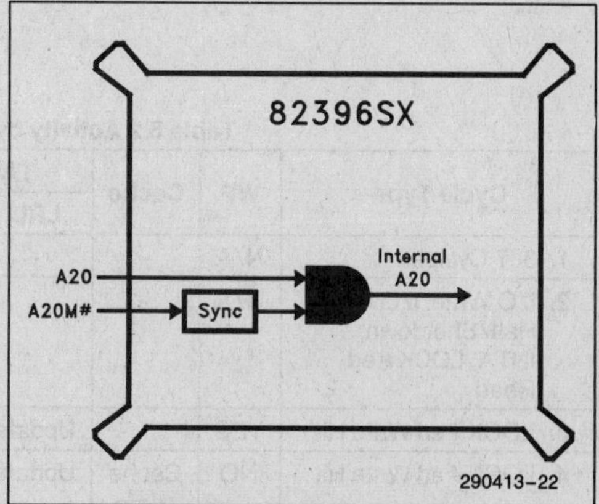

Figure 5.3 A20 Mask Logic

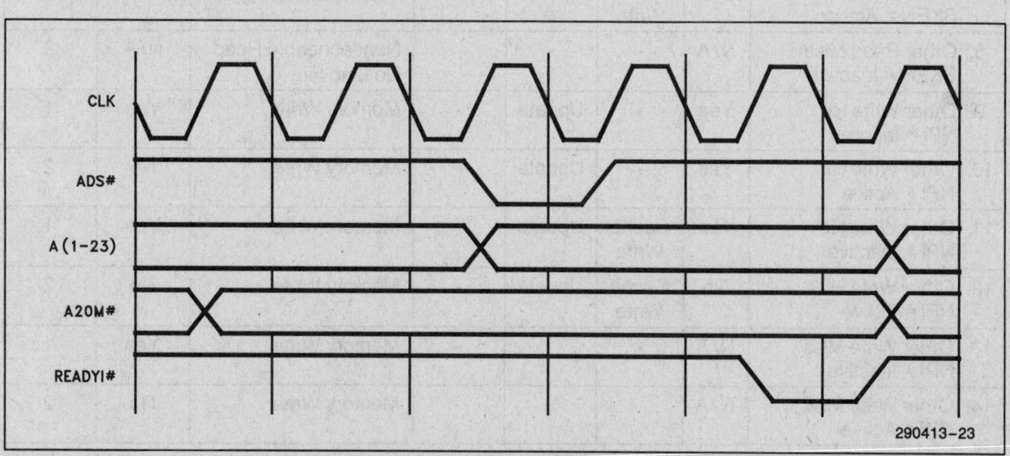

Figure 5.4 Valid Time of A20M#

5.9 82396SX Smart Cache Cycle Overview

Table 5.2 describes the activity in the cache, in the Tagram, on the System Bus and in the write buffers. The cycles are defined in table 5.1. Table 5.2 is sorted in a descending order. The more dominant the attribute the higher it is located. Table 5.2 is for non test modes.

Table 5.1 i386™ SX Microprocessor Bus Cycle Definition

M/IO#	D/C#	W/R#	i386™ SX Microprocessor Cycle Definition
0	0	0	Interrupt Acknowledge
0	0	1	Undefined
0	1	0	I/O Read
0	1	1	I/O Write
1	0	0	Memory Code Read
1	0	1	Halt/Shutdown
1	1	0	Memory Data Read
1	1	1	Memory Data Write

Table 5.2 Activity by Functional Groupings

Cycle Type	WP	Cache	TAGRAM		System Bus	Posted Write	Comm.
			LRU	TAG			
1. 387 Cycles	N/A	-	-	-	-	N/A	
2. I/O Write, I/O Read, Halt/Shutdown, INTA, LOCK#ed Read	N/A	-	-	-	Non Cacheable Cycle	No	2
3. LOCK#ed Write Hit	YES		Update	-	Memory Write	No	2
4. LOCK#ed Write Hit	NO	Cache Write	Update	-	Memory Write	No	2
5. LOCK#ed Write Miss	N/A	-	-	-	Memory Write	No	2
6. Other Read Hit	N/A	Cache Read	Update	-	-	N/A	1
7. Other Read Miss SKEN# Active	N/A	Cache Write	Update	Update	Line Fill	N/A	2
8. Other Read Miss SKEN# Inactive	N/A	-	-	-	Noncacheable Read No Line Fill	N/A	2
9. Other Write Hit NPI# Inactive	Yes	-	Update	-	Memory Write	Yes	1
10. Other Write Hit NPI# Active	Yes	-	Update	-	Memory Write	No	2
11. Other Write Hit NPI# Inactive	No	Cache Write	Update	-	Memory Write	Yes	1
12. Other Write Hit NPI# Active	No	Cache Write	Update	-	Memory Write	No	2
13. Other Write Miss NPI# Inactive	N/A	-	-	-	Memory Write	Yes	1
14. Other Write Miss NPI# Active	N/A	-	-	-	Memory Write	No	2

Table 5.3 describes line buffer hit cycles. Hit/miss here means to the specific word in the line buffer.

Table 5.3

Cycle Type	WP	Cache	TAGRAM		System Bus	Posted Write	Comm.
			LRU	TAG			
15. LOCK#ed Write	Yes	-	-	-	Memory Write	No	2
16. LOCK#ed Write	No	Cache Write	-	-	Memory Write	No	4
17. Read Hit	N/A	LB Read	-	-	-	N/A	1
18. Read Miss	N/A	LB Read	-	-	-	N/A	3
19. Other Write NPI# Inactive	Yes	-	-	-	Memory Write	Yes	6
20. Other Write NPI# Active	Yes	-	-	-	Memory Write	No	2
21. Other Write NPI# Inactive	No	Cache Write	-	-	Memory Write	Yes	5
22. Other Write NPI# Active	No	Cache	-	-	Memory Write	No	4

Table 5.4 describes the line buffer hit cycles, when the Line Fill is interrupted (by: FLUSH#, snoop hit to the line buffer or interrupted burst, even if the Line Fill continues on the System Bus in the first two cases). The table includes only the cycles which wait to the end of the Line Fill or to the CPU cache update. Hit/miss here means to the specific word in the line buffer.

Table 5.4

Cycle Type	WP	Cache	TAGRAM		System Bus	Posted Write	Comm.
			LRU	TAG			
23. LOCK#ed Write	N/A	-	-	-	Memory Write	No	2
24. Read Miss (Restart)	N/A	Cache Write	Update	Replace	Line Fill	N/A	2
25. Other Write NPI# Inactive	N/A	-	-	-	Memory Write	Yes	5
26. Other Write NPI# Active	N/A	-	-	-	Memory Write	No	2

4

Table 5.5 depicts the 82396SX Smart Cache Test Cycles.

Table 5.5

Cycle Type	WP	A16	Cache	TAGRAM		System Bus	Posted Write	Comm.
				LRU	TAG			
27. High Impedance	N/A	N/A	-	-	-	-	N/A	
28. SRAM Mode Read Add 256K–512K	N/A	0	-	LRU RD	TAG RD	-	N/A	
29. SRAM Mode Read Add 256K–512K	N/A	1	Cache Read	-	-	-	N/A	
30. SRAM Mode Write Add 256K–512K	N/A	0	-	LRU WR	TAG WR	-	N/A	
31. SRAM Mode Write Add 256K–512K	N/A	1	Cache Write	-	-	-	N/A	
32. SRAM Mode Read Add <> 256K–512K	N/A	N/A	-	-	-	Noncacheable Cycle	No	2
33. SRAM Mode Write Add <> 256K–512K	N/A	N/A	-	-	-	Noncacheable Cycle	N/A	

Remarks for Tables 5-2 through 5-5:

1. READYO# is active in the first T2. (In read cycles, in write it depends if the write buffer is full).
2. READYO# is active one clock cycle after SRDY#/SBRDY# of this cycle is asserted. In case of Line Fill, READYO# is active one clock cycle after first SRDY#/SBRDY# of this cycle is asserted.
3. READYO# is active immediately after the current line fill is finished.
4. READYO# is active after the previous line fill and the write cycle are terminated by SRDY# or SBRDY#, and the cache is updated.
5. READYO# is active after the cache is updated for the previous Line Fill, or after the Line Fill is aborted.
6. READYO# is active on the third T2 (2 wait states) if the write buffer is not full.
7. "OTHER" means the cycle does not fall within the first five categories.

6.0 SYSTEM BUS INTERFACE

The System Bus (SB) interface is similar to the i386™ SX Microprocessor interface. It runs synchronously to the i386™ SX Microprocessor clock. In general, the interface is similar to the 82385SX in terms of: System Bus pipelining, snooping support, multi master arbitration support and write cycle buffering. In addition, the following enhancements are provided:

1) Line Fill buffer.
2) Optional burst Line Fill.
3) System cacheability attribute, SKEN#.
4) System Write Protection attribute, SWP#.
5) The SEADS# snooping mechanism to support concurrency on the System Bus and on the general purpose bus.
6) Four word write buffer (8 bytes).

The 82396SX Smart Cache System Bus interface has identical bus signals to the i386™ SX Microprocessor bus. It has the bus control signals (SADS#, SRDY# and SNA#), the cycle definition signals (SLOCK#, SW/R#, SD/C# and SM/IO#), the address and byte enable signals (SA[23:1], SBHE# and SBLE#) and the data signals (SD[15:0]). In addition, the 82396SX Smart Cache has the SBRDY# signal for burst support. The SKEN# signal is used for identifying system cacheability. The SWP# signal is used for identifying system write protection. The SEADS# signal is used for snooping support. The SHOLD and SHLDA signals are used for system arbitration. Also, the 82396SX Smart Cache provides a signal, SBLAST#, which when asserted, indicates that the current cycle is the last cycle in a burst transfer.

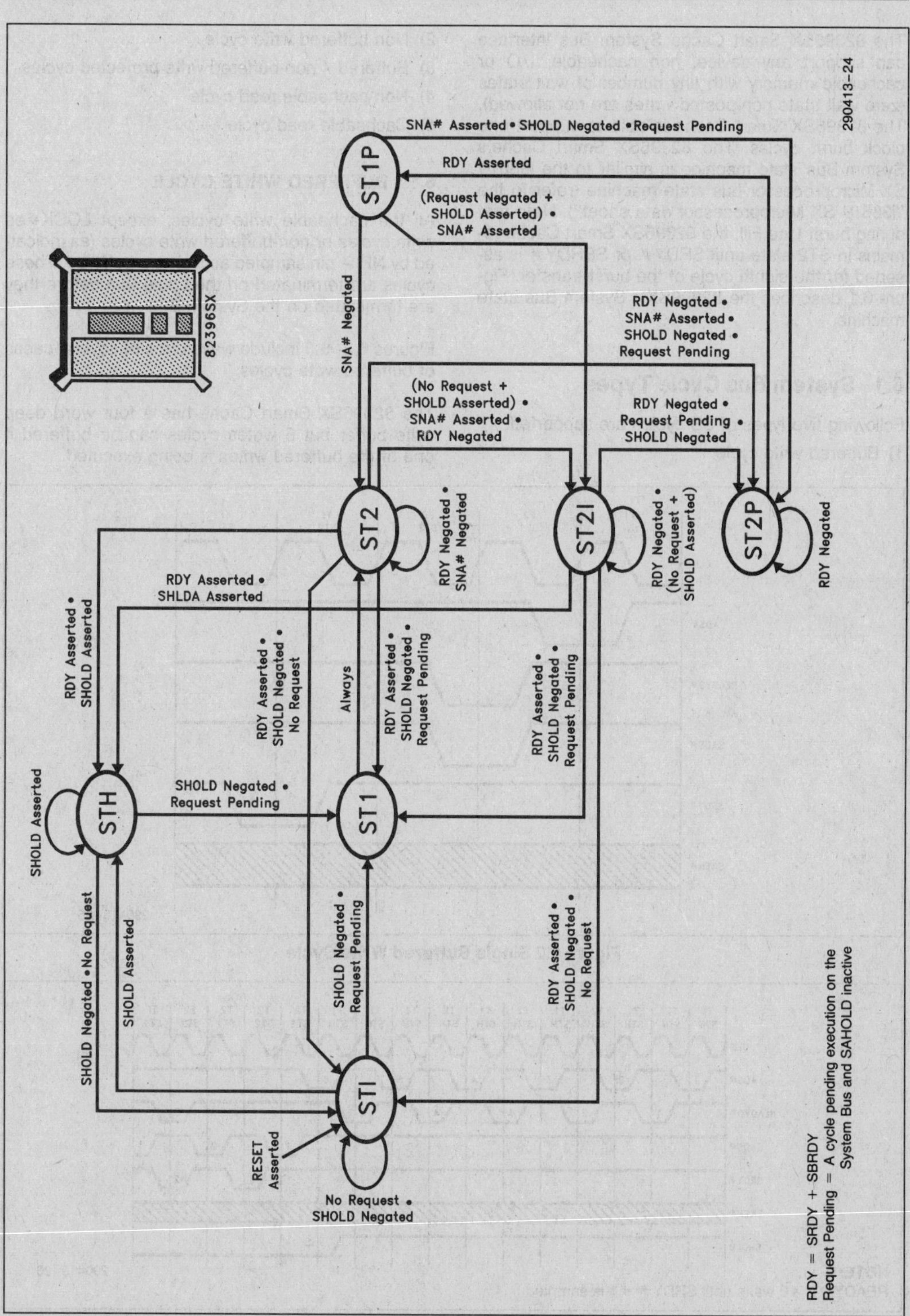

Figure 6.1 SB State Machine

The 82396SX Smart Cache System Bus interface can support any device, non cacheable, I/O or cacheable memory with any number of wait states (zero wait state non-posted writes are not allowed). The 82396SX Smart Cache is able to support one clock burst cycles. The 82396SX Smart Cache's System Bus state machine is similar to the i386™ SX Microprocessor bus state machine (refer to the "i386™ SX Microprocessor data sheet"). Note that during burst Line Fill, the 82396SX Smart Cache remains in ST2 state until SRDY# or SBRDY# is asserted for the eighth cycle of the burst transfer. Figure 6.1 describes the 82396SX's System Bus state machine.

6.1 System Bus Cycle Types

Following five types of SB cycles are supported:

1) Buffered write cycle
2) Non buffered write cycle
3) Buffered / non-buffered write protected cycles.
4) Non cacheable read cycle
5) Cacheable read cycle

6.1.1 BUFFERED WRITE CYCLE

All the cacheable write cycles, except LOCK#ed write cycles or non-buffered write cycles (as indicated by NPI# pin sampled active), are buffered. These cycles are terminated on the Local Bus before they are terminated on the System Bus.

Figures 6.2–6.3 include waveforms of several cases of buffered write cycles:

The 82396SX Smart Cache has a four word deep write buffer but 5 writes cycles can be buffered if one of the buffered writes is being executed.

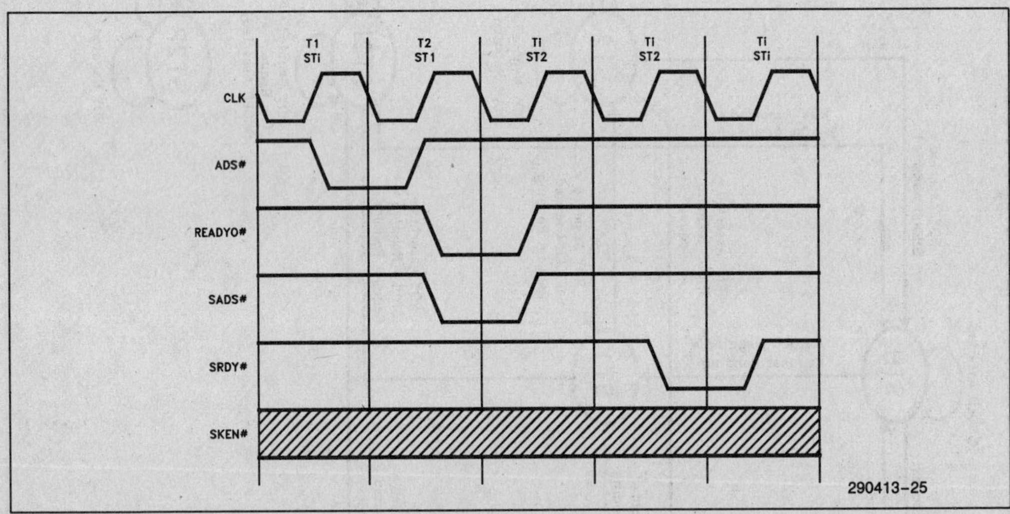

Figure 6.2 Single Buffered Write Cycle

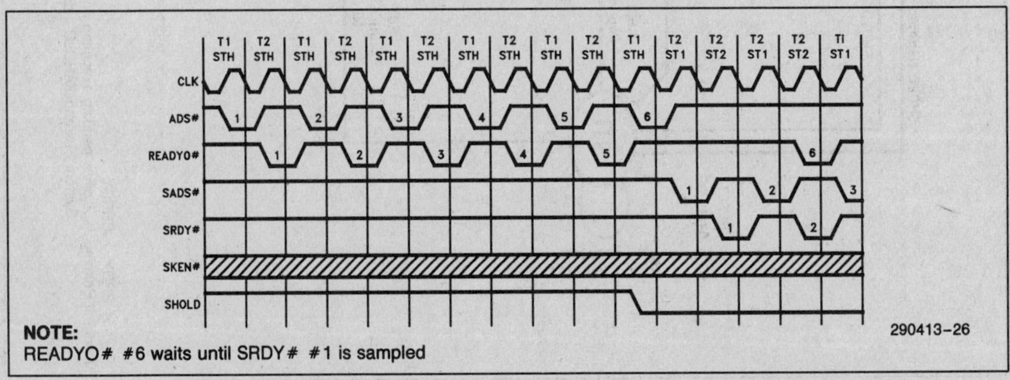

NOTE:
READYO# #6 waits until SRDY# #1 is sampled

Figure 6.3 Multiple Buffered Write Cycles During System Bus HOLD

6.1.2 NON-BUFFERED WRITE CYCLE

These cycles are terminated on the System Bus one clock before they are terminated on the Local Bus. The following Figures (6.4 - 6.5) include waveforms of several cases of non buffered write cycles.

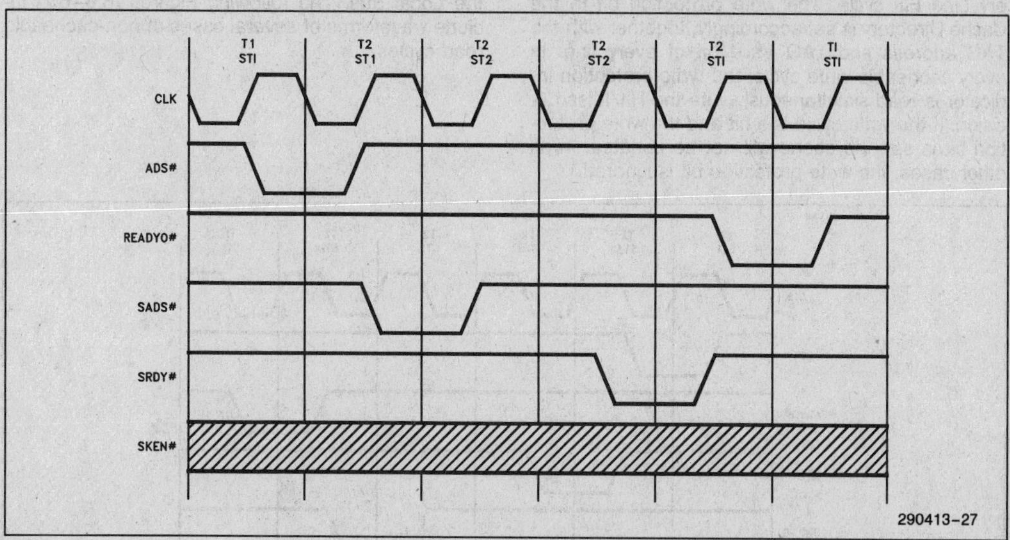

Figure 6.4 I/O Write Cycle

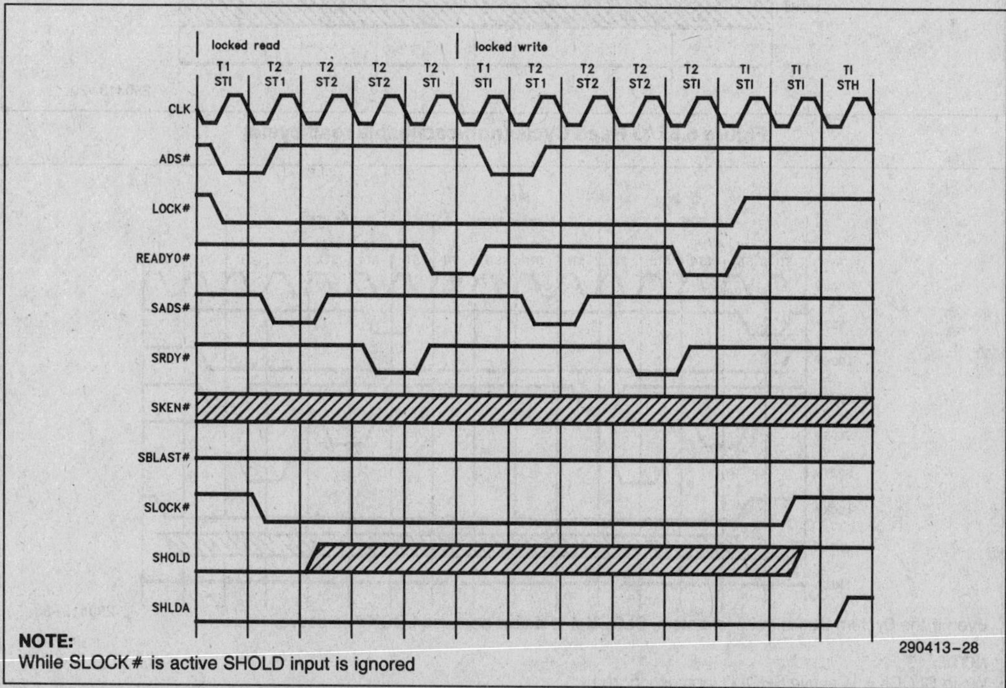

Figure 6.5 LOCKed "Read Modify Write" Cycle

6.1.3 WRITE PROTECTED CYCLES

The Write Protection attribute is provided by the System Bus SWP# input. The SWP# is sampled in every Line Fill cycle. The write protection bit in the Cache Directory is set accordingly, together with the TAG address and TAG Valid bit of every line. In every cacheable write cycle, the write protection indicator is read simultaneously with the Hit/Miss decision. If the write cycle is a hit and the write protection bit is set, the cache will not be updated. In all other cases, the write protection bit is ignored.

6.1.4 NON-CACHEABLE READ CYCLE

Non cacheable read cycles are terminated on the System Bus one clock before they are terminated on the Local Bus. The following Figures (6.6–6.7) include waveforms of several cases of non-cacheable read cycles.

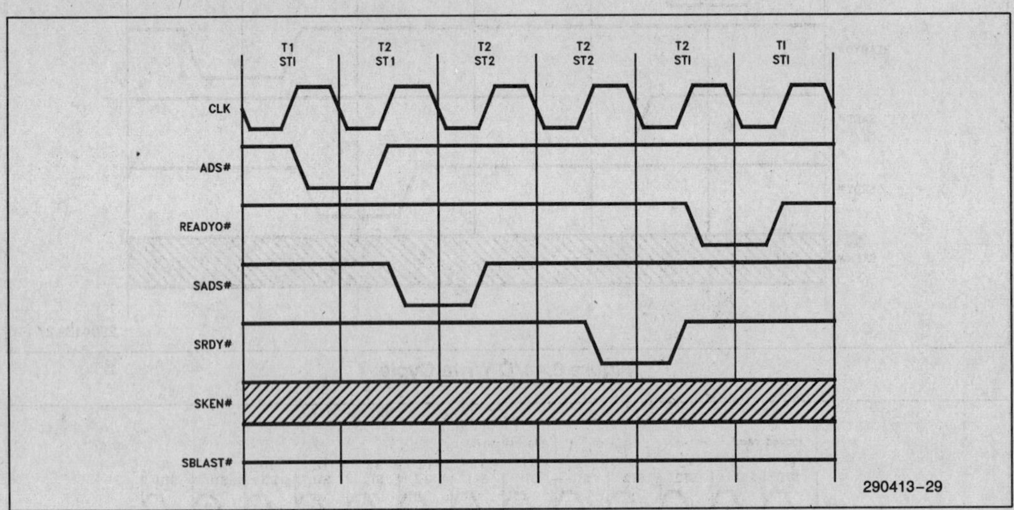

Figure 6.6 I/O Read Cycle (non-cacheable read cycle)

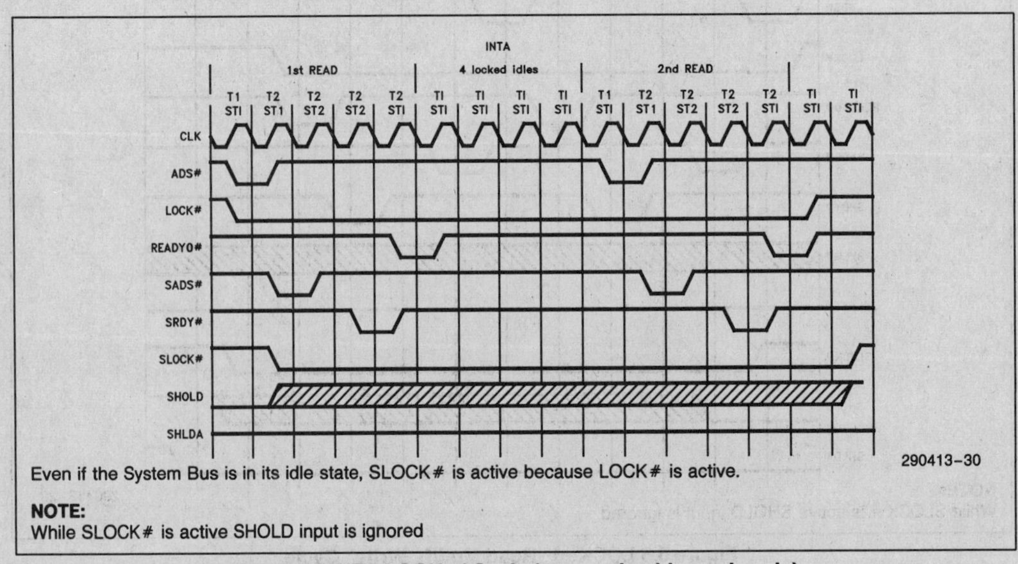

Even if the System Bus is in its idle state, SLOCK# is active because LOCK# is active.

NOTE:
While SLOCK# is active SHOLD input is ignored

Figure 6.7 INTA LOCKed Cycle (non-cacheable read cycle)

6.1.5 CACHEABLE READ MISS CYCLES

The 82396SX Smart Cache attempts to start a Line Fill for non LOCK#ed CRDM cycles. However, a Line Fill will be converted into a single read cycle if the access is indicated as non-cacheable by the SKEN# signal.

CRDM cycles start as a System Bus read cycle. READYO# is returned to the i386™ SX Microprocessor one clock cycle after System Bus read cycle is terminated.

One CLK cycle before the first SNA#, SRDY# or SBRDY# of the system read cycle the SKEN# input is sampled. If active, the read miss cycle continues as a Line Fill cycle, and seven additional words are read from the memory into the 82396SX Smart Cache. Also, the SWP# input will be sampled with the first SNA#, SRDY# or SBRDY# so the WP flag of the line will be updated in the Cache Directory.

6.1.5.1 Aborted Line Fill (ALF) Cycles

The System Bus can respond that the area of memory included in a particular request is non-cacheable, by returning SKEN# inactive. As soon as the 82396SX Smart Cache samples SKEN# inactive, it converts the cycle from a cache Line Fill, which requires seven additional read cycles to be completed, to a single cycle.

In this case SBLAST# will stay active. Also, the 82396SX Smart Cache will not generate another system cycle for the same Line Fill, because the cycle has already been finished by the first SBRDY# or SRDY# after SKEN# was sampled inactive.

Figure 6.8 includes waveforms of an ALF cycle.

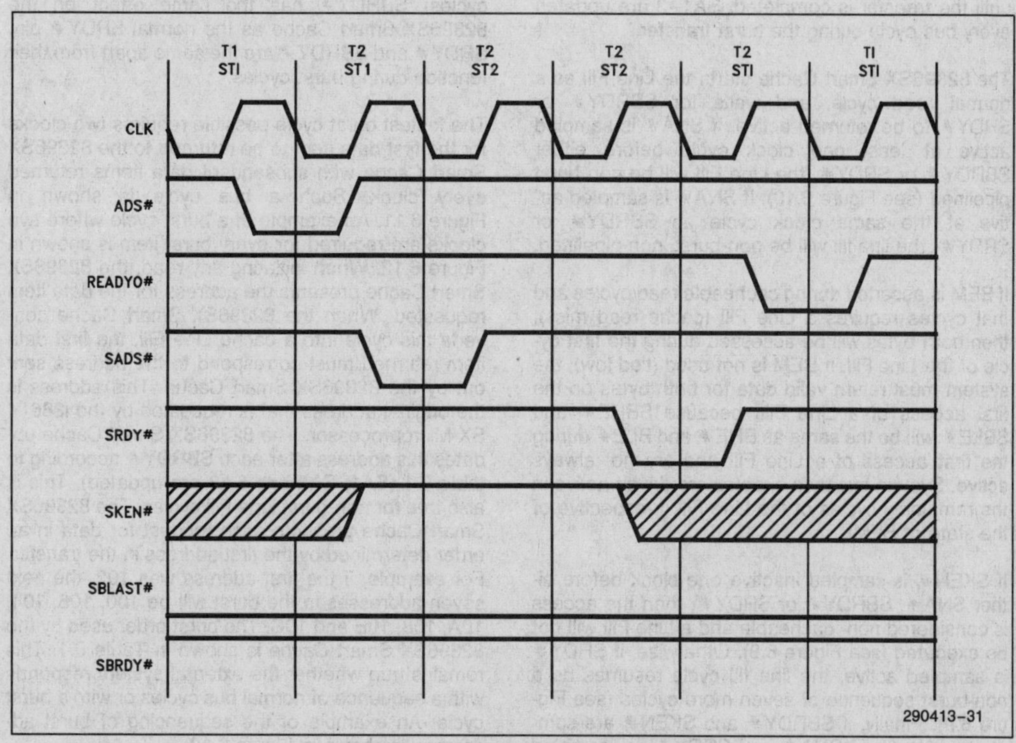

Figure 6.8 Aborted Line Fill Cycle

6.1.5.2 Line Fill Cycles

A Line Fill transfer consists of eight back to back read cycles. Three types of Line Fill cycles are supported:

1. Non pipeline, Non burst, SNA# inactive.
2. Pipelined, non burst, SNA# active.
3. Burst, non pipelined, SNA# inactive, SRDY# inactive, SBRDY# active.

Note that a pipelined burst cycle is not supported. When SNA# is sampled active, SBRDY# is treated as SRDY#.

The 82396SX Smart Cache supports burst cycles in system Line Fills only. Burst cycles are designed to allow fast line fills by allowing consecutive read cycles to be executed at a rate of one word per clock cycle. In burst cycles SADS# is pulsed for one clock cycle while the address and control lines are valid until the transfer is completed. SA1–3 are updated every bus cycle during the burst transfer.

The 82396SX Smart Cache starts the Line Fill as a normal read cycle, and waits for SBRDY# or SRDY# to be returned active. If SNA# is sampled active at least one clock cycle before either SBRDY# or SRDY#, the Line Fill will be non burst pipelined (see Figure 6.10). If SNA# is sampled active at the same clock cycle as SBRDY# or SRDY#, the line fill will be non-burst, non-pipelined.

If BEM is asserted during cacheable read cycles and that cycles requires a Line Fill (cache read miss), then both bytes will be accessed during the first cycle of the Line Fill. If BEM is not used (tied low), the system must return valid data for both bytes on the first access of a Line Fill, because SBHE# and SBLE# will be the same as BHE# and BLE# during the first access of a Line Fill and are not always active. System bus byte enables are driven active in the remaining cycles of the Line Fill (irrespective of the state of BEM).

If SKEN# is sampled inactive one clock before either SNA#, SBRDY# or SRDY#, then the access is considered non- cacheable and a Line Fill will not be executed (see Figure 6.8). Otherwise, if SRDY# is sampled active, the line fill cycle resumes as a non-burst sequence of seven more cycles (see Figure 6.9). Finally, if SBRDY# and SKEN# are sampled active (and SNA# and SRDY# are sampled inactive), then the Line Fill cycle will be a burst cycle (see Figures 6.11 - 6.12). If a system cannot support burst cycles, a non burst line fill must be requested by merely returning SRDY# instead of SBRDY#, in the first read cycle (see Figure 6.9). Once a burst cycle has started, it will not be aborted until it's completed, regardless if SKEN# is sampled inactive or SHOLD is sampled active, i.e. all eight words will be read from memory. However, the system may abort a burst Line Fill transfer before it's completed, by returning SRDY# active (instead of SBRDY#) for the second through the seventh word in a Line Fill transaction (see Figure 6.13). In this case the cache will not be updated. The first word will already have been transferred to the CPU.

Note that in the last (eighth) bus cycle in a Line Fill transfer, SBRDY# or SRDY# has the same effect on the 82396SX Smart Cache. That is to indicate the end of the Line Fill. For all cycles that cannot run in burst mode (non-Line Fill cycles or pipelined Line Fill cycles) SBRDY# has the same effect on the 82396SX Smart Cache as the normal SRDY# pin. SRDY# and SBRDY# are the same apart from their function during burst cycles.

The fastest burst cycle possible requires two clocks for the first data item to be returned to the 82396SX Smart Cache with subsequent data items returned every clock. Such a bus cycle is shown in Figure 6.11. An example of a burst cycle where two clocks are required for every burst item is shown in Figure 6.12. When initiating any read, the 82396SX Smart Cache presents the address for the data item requested. When the 82396SX Smart Cache converts this cycle into a cache Line Fill, the first data item returned must correspond to the address sent out by the 82396SX Smart Cache. This address is the original address that is requested by the i386™ SX Microprocessor. The 82396SX Smart Cache updates this address after each SBRDY# according to table 6.1 (SA1, SA2 and SA3 are updated). This is also true for non-burst Line Fill cycles. The 82396SX Smart Cache presents each request for data in an order determined by the first address in the transfer. For example, if the first address was 102, the next seven addresses in the burst will be 100, 106, 104, 10A, 108, 10E and 10C. The burst order used by the 82396SX Smart Cache is shown in Table 6.1. This remains true whether the external system responds with a sequence of normal bus cycles or with a burst cycle. An example of the sequencing of burst addresses is shown in Figure 6.12.

In the following cases, a Line Fill cycle will not update the cache:

1. Aborted burst: A burst cycle will be aborted if SRDY# is returned active in the second through the seventh bus cycle. The Line Fill will not resume, and the cache will not be updated.
2. Snoop hit to line buffer:

   If, during a Line Fill transfer, a snoop cycle is initiated after the first SRDY# or SBRDY#, and the address matches the address of the line being retrieved, the Line Fill cycle will continue as usual but the cache will not be updated.
3. FLUSH during Line Fill cycle: the Line Fill cycle will continue as usual, but the cache will not be updated.

Figures 6.9 - 6.13 include waveforms of several cases of Line Fill cycles.

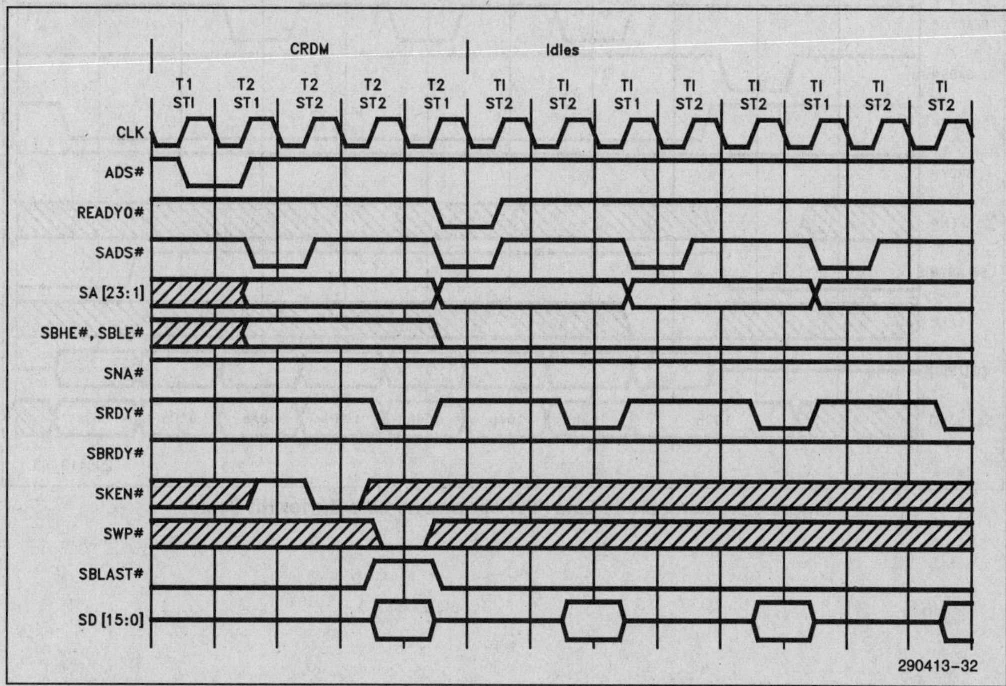

Figure 6.9 Line Fill without Burst or Pipeline (One Wait State—First Four Cycles Shown)

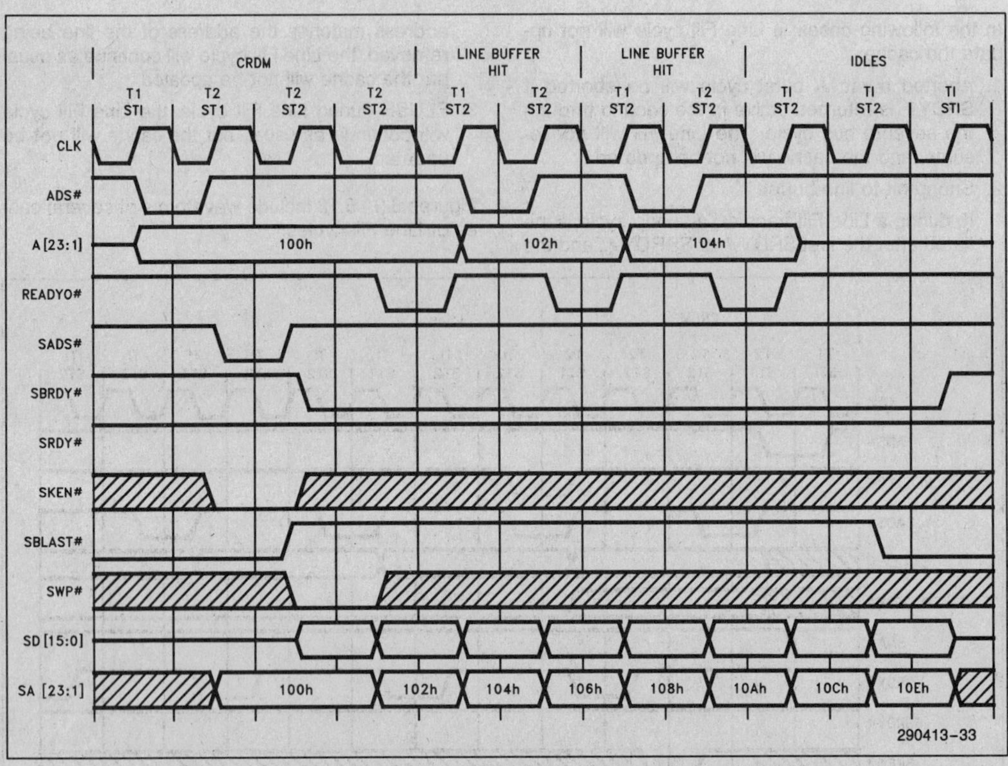

Figure 6.9A Burst Mode Line Fill Followed by Line Buffer Hit Cycles

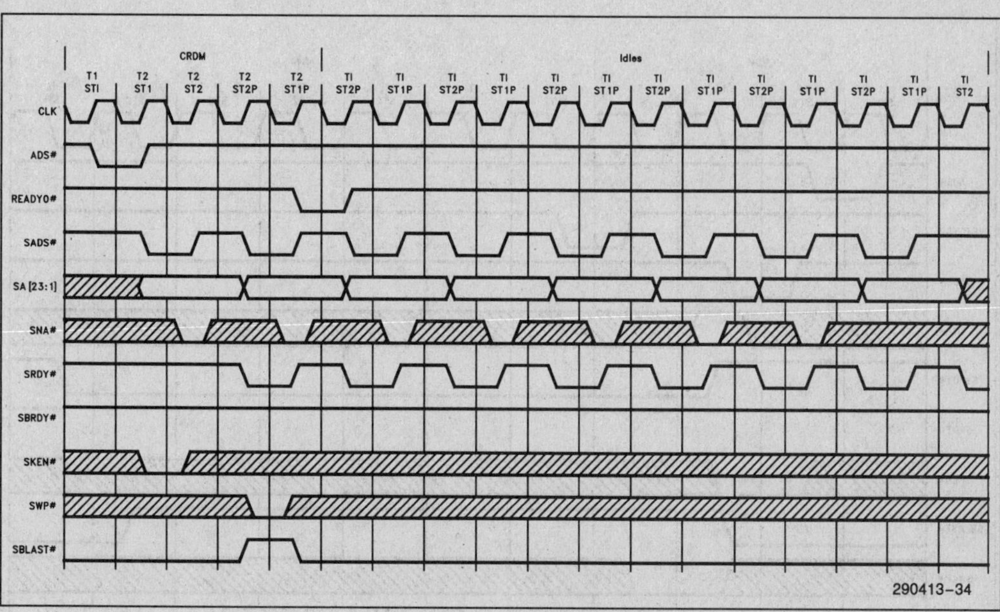

Figure 6.10 Pipelined Line Fill

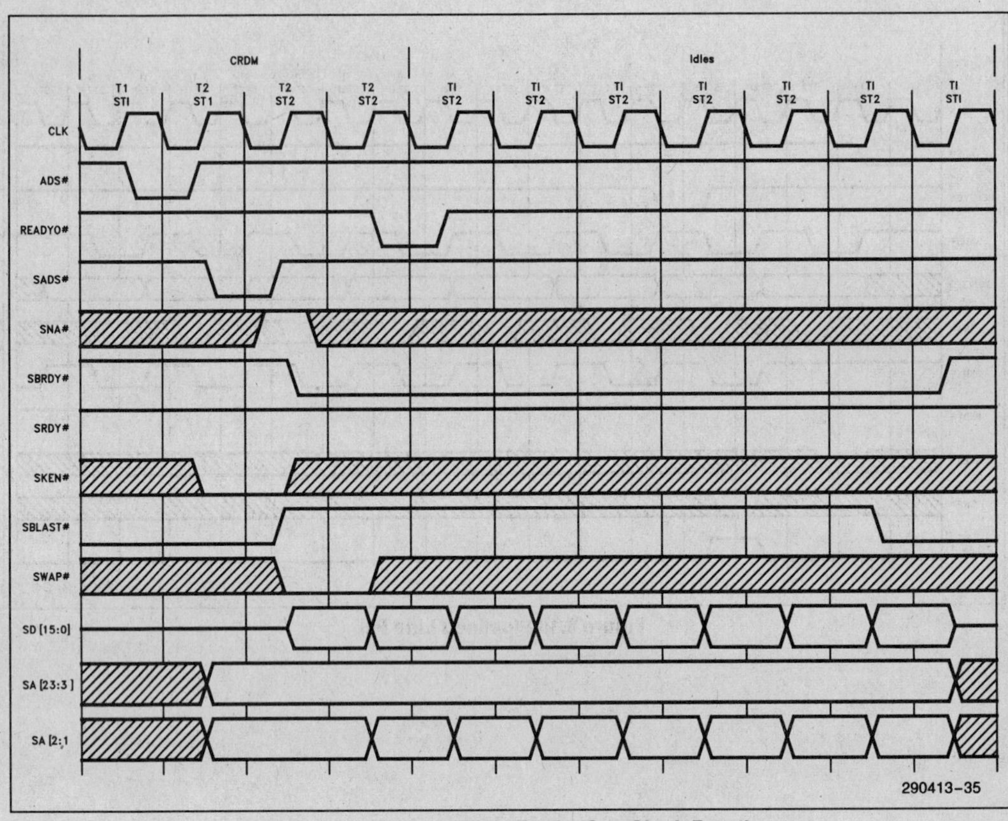

Figure 6.11 Fastest Burst Cycle (One Clock Burst)

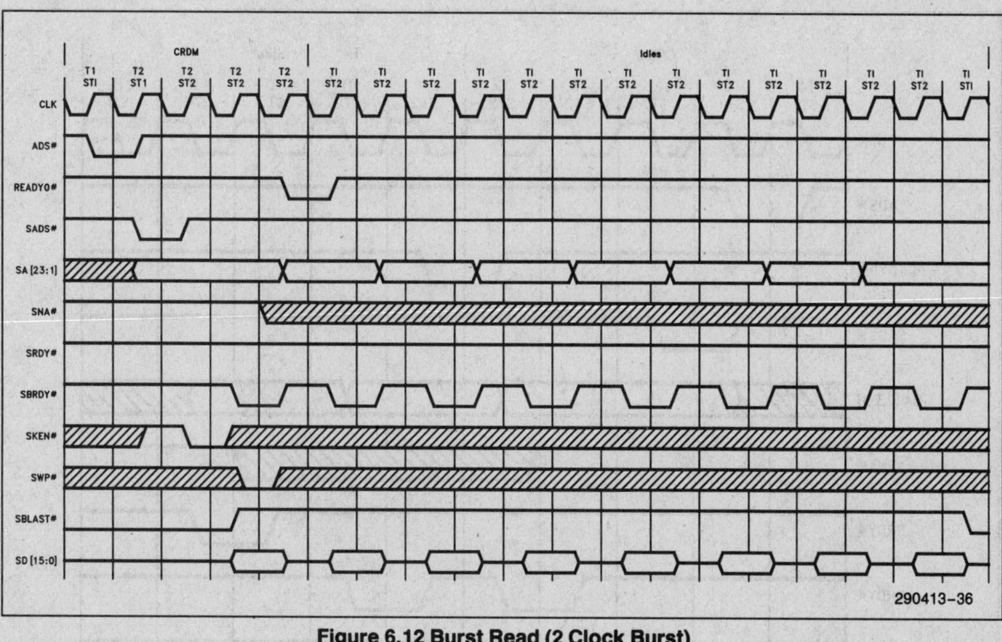

Figure 6.12 Burst Read (2 Clock Burst)

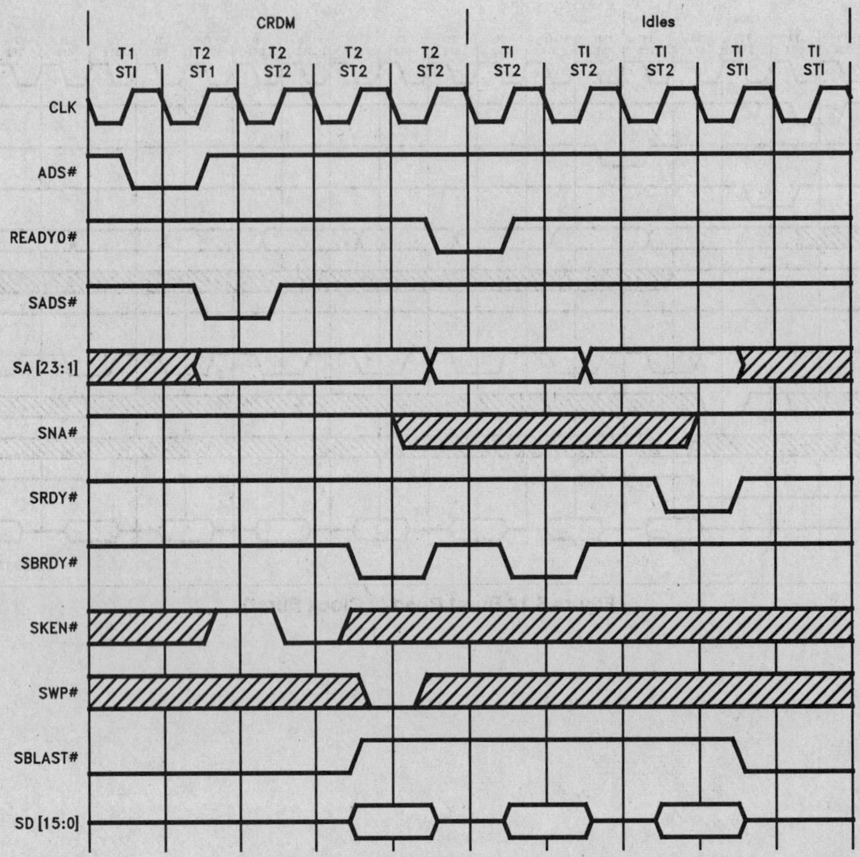

Figure 6.13 Interrupted Burst Read (2 Clock Burst)

Table 6.1 Line Fill Address Order

82396SX Smart Cache Line Fill Order (SA[3:1])							
Word within Line Fill							
1st	**2nd**	**3rd**	**4th**	**5th**	**6th**	**7th**	**8th**
0	2	4	6	8	A	C	E
2	0	6	4	A	8	E	C
4	6	0	2	C	E	8	A
6	4	2	0	E	C	A	8
8	A	C	E	0	2	4	6
A	8	E	C	2	0	6	4
C	E	8	A	4	6	0	2
E	C	A	8	6	4	2	0

6.2 82396SX Smart Cache Latency In System Bus Accesses

The 82396SX Smart Cache acts as a buffer between the i386™ SX Microprocessor and the main memory causing some latency in initiating the System Bus cycle (SADS# delay from ADS#) and in completing the cycle (386 READYO# delay from SRDY# or SBRDY#). The 82396SX Smart Cache drives the SADS# one clock after the ADS#. In cacheable cycles, the 82396SX Smart Cache starts driving the SADS# before it decides whether the cycle is a cache hit or miss since the hit/miss decision is valid in the second clock (the first T2 cycle). In case the cycle is a hit, the 82396SX Smart Cache deactivates SADS#. This causes a glitch on the SADS# signal. For proper system functionality, SADS# must be sampled by the next clock edge. This signal will be stable by its maximum specification in all cycles.

At the end of a System Bus non-cacheable read cycle, or non- buffered write cycle, the 82396SX Smart Cache drives READYO# active one clock after SRDY# or SBRDY#. In a Line Fill cycle, READYO# is activated one clock after the first SBRDY# or SRDY# is sampled active. The setup timing requirements of SRDY# and system data force one wait state at the end of the cycle.

6.3 SHLDA Latency

For non-LOCK#ed cycles the worst case delay between SHOLD and SHLDA would be when SHOLD is activated during ST2P state, followed by a Line Fill. In this case, the HOLD request will be acknowledged only after the Line Fill is completed. In LOCKed cycles SHLDA will not be asserted until after SLOCK# is negated. The latency would be:

Latency = (Number of ST2P cycles) + (Number of Line Fill cycles) OR (Number of LOCK#ed cycles)

6.4 Cache Consistency Support

The 82396SX Smart Cache supports snooping using the SEADS# mechanism. Besides insuring the consistency, this mechanism provides multi processing support by having the 82396SX Smart Cache System Bus and the Local Bus running concurrently. SEADS# must be synchronized to CLK2 for proper operation.

The 82396SX Smart Cache will always float its address bus in the clock immediately following the one in which SAHOLD is received. Thus, no address hold acknowledge is required. When the address bus is floated, the rest of the 82396SX Smart Cache's System Bus will remain active, so that data can be received from a bus cycle that was already underway. Another bus cycle will not begin, and the SADS# signal will not be generated. However, multiple data transfers for burst cycles can occur during address holds.

SEADS# indicates that an external address is actually valid on the address inputs of the 82396SX Smart Cache. When this signal is activated, the 82396SX Smart Cache will read the external address and perform an internal cache invalidation cycle to the address indicated. The internal invalidation cycle occurs one clock after SEADS# is sampled active. In case of contention with i386™ SX Microprocessor look up, the invalidation is serviced two clocks after SEADS# was activated. The maximum rate of invalidation cycles is one every other clock. Multiple cache invalidations can occur in a single address hold transfer. SEADS# is not masked by SAHOLD inactive, so cache invalidations can occur during a normal bus cycle. Activate SEADS# only when SAHOLD or SHLDA are active.

If the 82396SX Smart Cache is running a line fill cycle and an invalidation is driven into the 82396SX Smart Cache in the same clock the first data is returned, or in any subsequent clock, the 82396SX Smart Cache will invalidate that line even if it is the same cache line that the 82396SX Smart Cache is currently filling.

SAHOLD in pipelined cycles: The activation of SAHOLD only causes the system address to be floated in the next clock without changing the behavior of pipelined cycles. If SAHOLD is activated before entering the ST2P state, the 82396SX Smart Cache will move into non-pipeline and drive the SADS# only after the deactivation of SAHOLD. However, if SAHOLD is asserted in the ST2P state and the Nth cycle has already started, the system address is floated but SADS# is kept active until SRDY# (for the N-1 th cycle) is returned. It is the system responsibility to latch the address bus. Note that the address driven on the System Bus after SAHOLD is deasserted (in pipelined cycles) depends on whether SNA# has been sampled active during the SAHOLD state and another cycle is pending. As seen from Figure 6.14, the (N+1)th address will be driven by the 82396SX Smart Cache once SAHOLD was deactivated and SNA# was sampled active, provided there is a cycle pending in the 82396SX Smart Cache. The following figures describe the 82396SX Smart Cache behavior in two cases. First, when SNA# is sampled active and second, in the case of SNA# sampled inactive.

Note that the maximum rate of snooping cycles is every other clock. The first clock edge in which SEADS# is sampled active causes the 82396SX Smart Cache to latch the system address bus and initiate a cache invalidation cycle. If SEADS# is driven active for more than one clock, only one snooping cycle will be initiated on the first clock edge at which SEADS# is sampled active. The SA[23:1] setup and hold timings are specified to the same clock edge in which SEADS# is sampled active.

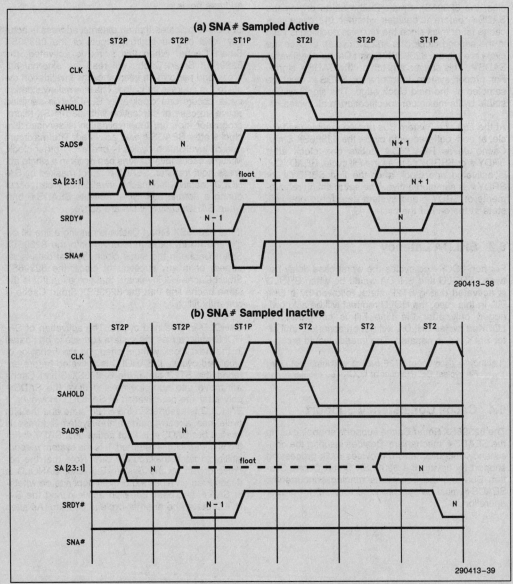

Figure 6.14 SAHOLD Behavior in Pipelined Cycles

6.5 Write Buffer

The 82396SX Smart Cache is able to internally store up to four write cycles (address, data and status information). All those write cycles will run without wait states on the Local Bus. They will run on the System Bus as soon as the bus is available. In case of a write cycle which cannot be stored since the buffer is full, the i386™ SX Microprocessor will be forced to wait until one of the buffered write cycles is completed. READYO# is returned two clocks after SRDY# or SBRDY# is asserted if the write buffer is full. If the write buffer is not full READYO# is returned one clock after SRDY# or SBRDY# is asserted.

All non cacheable write cycles and LOCK#ed writes are not buffered. In this case, the 82396SX Smart Cache will activate READYO# after getting the SRDY# for the non buffered cycle.

The write buffer maintains the exact original order of appearance of the Local Bus requests. It allows no reordering and no bypassing of any sort.

7.0 TESTABILITY FEATURES

This chapter discusses the requirements for properly testing an 82396SX Smart Cache based system after power up and during normal system operation.

Table 7.1 describes how to enter and exit the various 82396SX Smart Cache test modes.

7.1 SRAM Test Mode

This mode is invoked by driving the FLUSH# pin active for less than four clocks during normal operation. SRAM test mode may only be invoked when the 82396SX Smart Cache is in idle state, namely there is no cycle in progress, and no cycle is pending in the 82396SX Smart Cache. The 82396SX Smart Cache exits this mode with subsequent activation of the FLUSH# pin for minimum of one clock cycle. If FLUSH# is activated for at least four clock cycles during SRAM test mode, the 82396SX Smart Cache will FLUSH# its cache directory in addition to terminating the SRAM test mode.

SRAM test mode is provided for system diagnostics purposes. In this mode, the 82396SX Smart Cache cache and cache directory are treated as a standard SRAM. The 82396SX Smart Cache in the system is mapped into address space 256K-512K of the i386™ SX Microprocessor memory space, and allows the CPU non-cacheable, non- buffered access to the rest of the memory and address space. The 82396SX Smart Cache occupies 32KB of address space: 16KB for the cache and 16KB for the TAGRAM (not fully utilized). The 82396SX Smart Cache, in SRAM mode, will recognize i387™ SX Math Coprocessor cycles handle them the same as it does in its normal mode. This way, the CPU may

Table 7-1. Entering/Exiting the Various 82396SX Smart Cache Test Modes

Operating Mode	FLUSH#	SAHOLD	Comments
Tristate Test Mode	0	1	Sampled 1 CLK prior to RESET falling. Exit by next activation of RESET with FLUSH# and SAHOLD deactivated.
SRAM Test Mode	0	X	FLUSH# activation for less than four CLKs during normal mode. Exit with activation of FLUSH# for a minimum of one CLK.
Reserved Mode	0	0	Sampled 1 CLK prior to RESET falling.
Normal Mode	1	X	

4

execute code that tests the 82396SX Smart Cache as a regular memory component, with the only limitation that no code or data may reside in the memory space 256K-512K during this mode. During SRAM test mode, all accesses to memory space other than 256K-512K are handled exactly as in normal mode with the following exceptions:

1. All read cycles are non-cacheable - read hits are not serviced from the cache and read misses don't cause Line Fills.
2. All write cycles are not buffered.
3. All write cycles do not update the cache.
4. Snooping is disabled.

The local address pins indicate the 82396SX Smart Cache internal addresses. The partitioning is as follows:

- A17 = 1 is reserve in this space.
- A16 = 0 selects the cache directory. A16 = 1 select the cache.
- A15–14 select the "way".
- A11–A4 are the set address.
- A3–1 select a word in the line. Applicable in cache accesses (A16 = 1).

The user can write to any byte in any line in case of a cache write cycle and write to the Tagram fields in one Way in one Tagram write cycle. The memory mapping of the SRAM mode is the described in Table 7.2.

The address space allocated for either Tagram or Cache is 4096 (4K) addresses per way, as can be seen from Table 7.2. The address allocation within each 4K segment is shown in Tables 7.3 and 7.4.

The data presented on the 82396SX Smart Cache local data pins is the SRAM data input. The SRAM data output is also driven on the local data pins. The BHE#, BLE# pins indicate the bytes which must be written. During SRAM test mode, all the AC specifications are met. Figures 7.1 and 7.2 depict the SRAM mode read and write cycles respectively. Note that two wait states are inserted during SRAM test mode read cycles and one wait state is inserted in write cycles. The system may extend the number of wait states by gating READYO# for any number of clock cycles (1 clock cycle in Figure 7.1, 0 clock cycles in Figure 7.2).

The user can write to any byte in any line in case of a cache write cycle and write to specific Tagram fields in one way in one Tagram write cycle. The fields that can be written to are described in Table 7.5. The memory mapping of the SRAM test mode described in Table 7.2.

Table 7.2 SRAM Memory Map

Cache/Tagram	Way	Start Address
Cache	3	05C000h
Cache	2	058000h
Cache	1	054000h
Cache	0	050000h
Tagram	3	04C000h
Tagram	2	048000h
Tagram	1	044000h
Tagram	0	040000h

As can be seen from the above table, the address space allocated for either Tagram or Cache is 4096 (4K) addresses per way. The address allocation within each 4K segment is shown in Table 7.3 for the Cache and Table 7.4 for the Tagram.

Table 7.3 Cache Address Allocation

SET	Word	Start Address
255	7	FFE h
255	6	FFC h
255	5	FFA h
255	4	FF8 h
255	3	FF6 h
255	2	FF4 h
255	1	FF2 h
255	0	FF0 h
.	.	.
.	.	.
2	7	02E h
2	6	02C h
2	5	02A h
2	4	028 h
2	3	026 h
2	2	024 h
2	1	022 h
2	0	020 h
1	7	01E h
1	6	01C h
1	5	01A h
1	4	018 h
1	3	016 h
1	2	014 h
1	1	012 h
1	0	010 h
0	7	00E h
0	6	00C h
0	5	00A h
0	4	008 h
0	3	006 h
0	2	004 h
0	1	002 h
0	0	000 h

Table 7.4 Tagram Address Allocation

SET	Start Address	SET	Start Address	SET	Start Address
255	FFE h	2	02A h	1	014 h
255	FFC h	2	028 h	1	012 h
255	FFA h	2	026 h	1	010 h
255	FF8 h	2	024 h	0	00E h
255	FF6 h	2	022 h	0	00C h
255	FF4 h	2	020 h	0	00A h
255	FF2 h	1	01E h	0	008 h
255	FF0 h	1	01C h	0	006 h
.	.	1	01A h	0	004 h
.	.	1	018 h	0	002 h
2	02E h	1	016 h	0	000 h
2	02C h				

Table 7.5 SRAM Test Mode Cache Directory Bit Map Format in Tagram Read/Writes:

Word Format in Tagram Write:

Local Data Bus

15	14	13	12	11	10	9	8	7	6	5	4	3	2	1	0
LRU B2	LRU B1	LRU B0 & V	A23	A22	A21	A20	A19	A18	A17	A16	A15	A14	A13	A12	WP

(Data written to D13 writes to LRU bit B0 and to the Valid bit)

Word Format in Tagram Read:

Way 0

Local Data Bus

15	14	13	12	11	10	9	8	7	6	5	4	3	2	1	0
0	LRU B0	V	A23	A22	A21	A20	A19	A18	A17	A16	A15	A14	A13	A12	WP

Way 1

Local Data Bus

15	14	13	12	11	10	9	8	7	6	5	4	3	2	1	0
0	LRU B1	V	A23	A22	A21	A20	A19	A18	A17	A16	A15	A14	A13	A12	WP

Way 2

Local Data Bus

15	14	13	12	11	10	9	8	7	6	5	4	3	2	1	0
0	LRU B2	V	A23	A22	A21	A20	A19	A18	A17	A16	A15	A14	A13	A12	WP

Way 3

Local Data Bus

15	14	13	12	11	10	9	8	7	6	5	4	3	2	1	0
0	0	V	A23	A22	A21	A20	A19	A18	A17	A16	A15	A14	A13	A12	WP

V = TAG Valid bit
WP = Write Protect bit
"0" - Indicates don't care bits. Writing to these bits will have no effect. When reading the Tagram these bits will have a value of 0.

NOTE:
In Tagram accesses, BHE# and BLE# are ignored in both read and write cycles.

The data presented on the 82396SX Smart Cache D[15:0] pins is the SRAM data input for write cycles and is also the SRAM data output for read cycles during the SRAM test mode. The BHE# and BLE# pins indicate the bytes which will be written to. During SRAM test mode all the AC specifications are met. Figures 7.1 and 7.2 depict the SRAM test mode read and write cycles respectively. The system may extend the number of wait states by gating READYO# for any number of clock cycles (one clock cycle in Figure 7.1, zero in Figure 7.2).

7.2 Tristate Output Test Mode

The 82396SX Smart Cache provides the option of isolating itself from other devices on the board for system debugging, by floating all it's outputs.

Output tristate mode is invoked by driving the SAHOLD and FLUSH# pins active during RESET. The 82396SX Smart Cache will remain in this mode after RESET is deactivated, if SAHOLD and FLUSH# pins are sampled active during the two CLK2s preceding the deactivation of RESET. The 82396SX Smart Cache exits this mode with the next activation of RESET with SAHOLD or FLUSH# driven inactive.

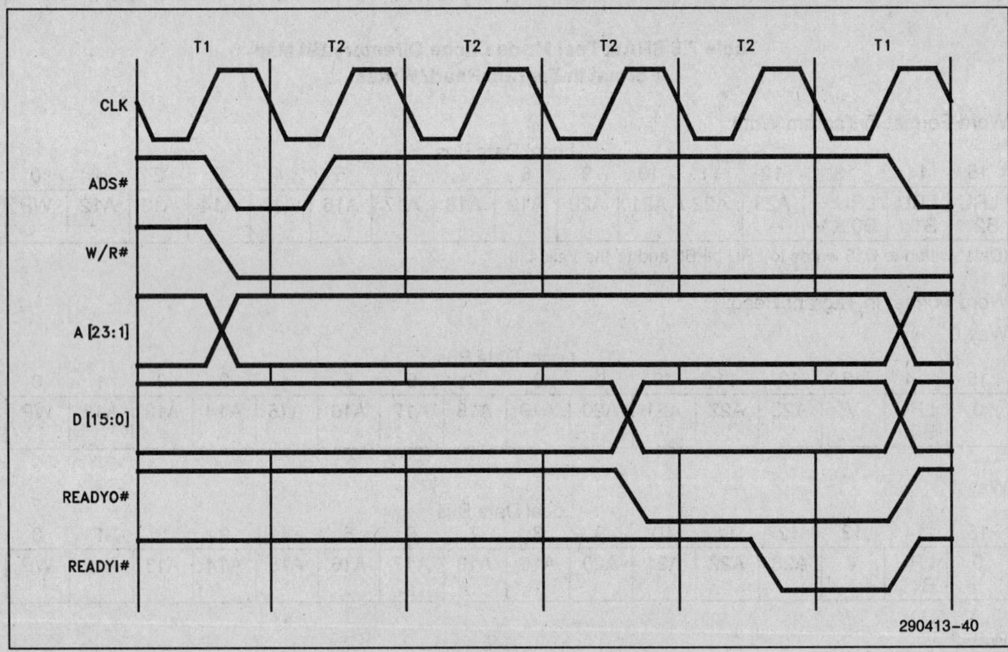

Figure 7.1 SRAM Mode Read Cycle

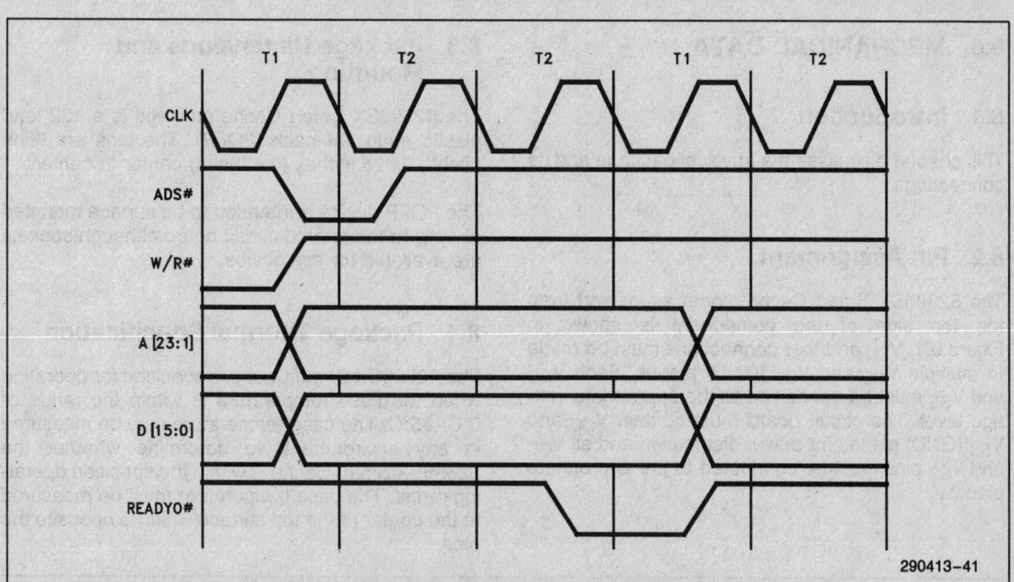

Figure 7.2 SRAM Mode Write Cycle

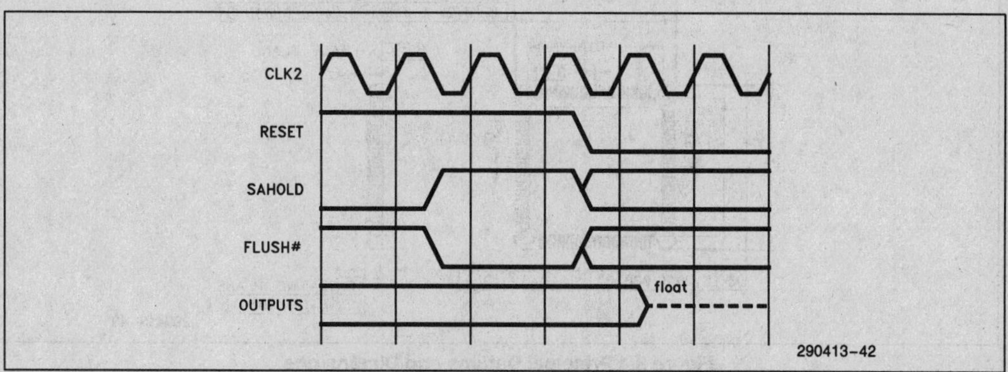

Figure 7.3 Entering the Tristate Test Mode

4

8.0 MECHANICAL DATA

8.1 Introduction

This chapter discusses the physical package and its connections.

8.2 Pin Assignment

The 82396SX Smart Cache pinout as viewed from the top side of the component is shown in Figure 0.1. V_{CC} and V_{SS} connections must be made to multiple V_{CC} and V_{SS} (GND) planes. Each V_{CC} and V_{SS} must be connected to the appropriate voltage level. The circuit board must contain V_{CC} and V_{SS} (GND) planes for power distribution and all V_{CC} and V_{SS} pins must be connected to the appropriate planes.

8.3 Package Dimensions and Mounting

The 82396SX Smart Cache package is a 132 lead plastic quad flat pack (PQFP). The pins are "fine pitch", 0.025 inches (0.635mm) center to center.

The PQFP device is intended to be surface mounted directly to the printed circuit board although sockets are available for this device.

8.4 Package Thermal Specification

The 82396SX Smart Cache is specified for operation when the case temperature is within the range of 0°C–85°C. The case temperature may be measured in any environment, to determine whether the 82396SX Smart Cache is within the specified operating range. The case temperature must be measured at the center of the top surface which is opposite the pins.

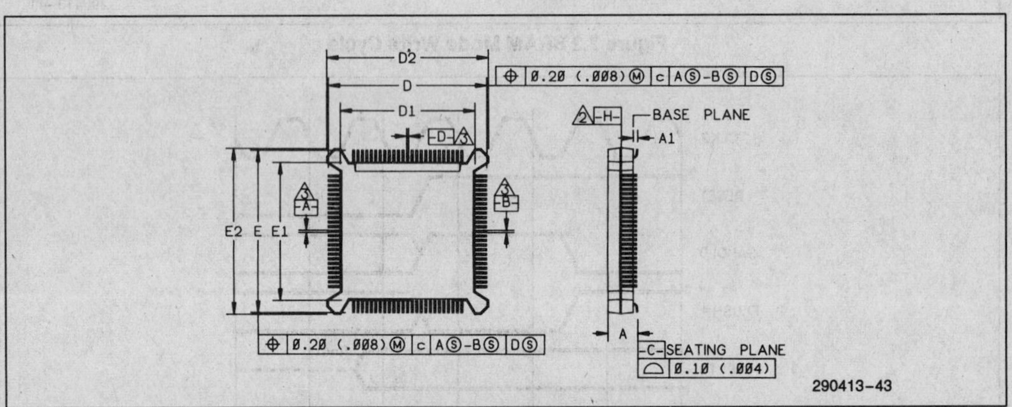

Figure 8.1 Principal Datums and Dimensions

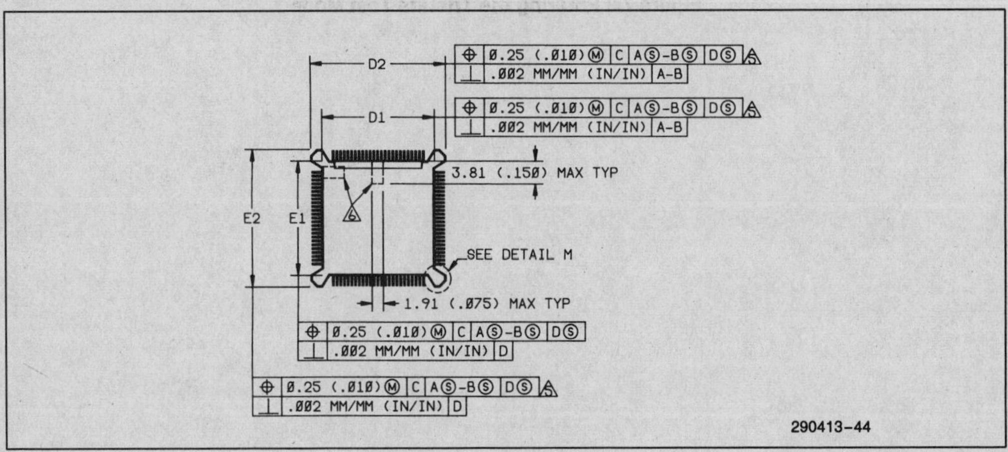

Figure 8.2 Molded Details

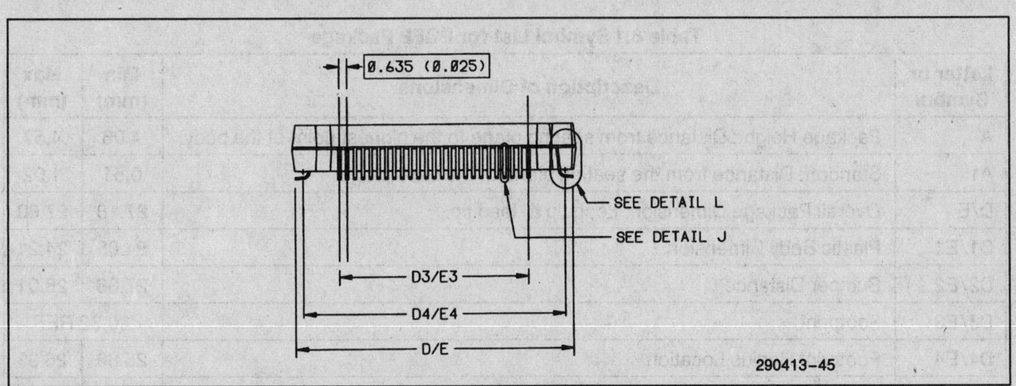

Figure 8.3 Terminal Details

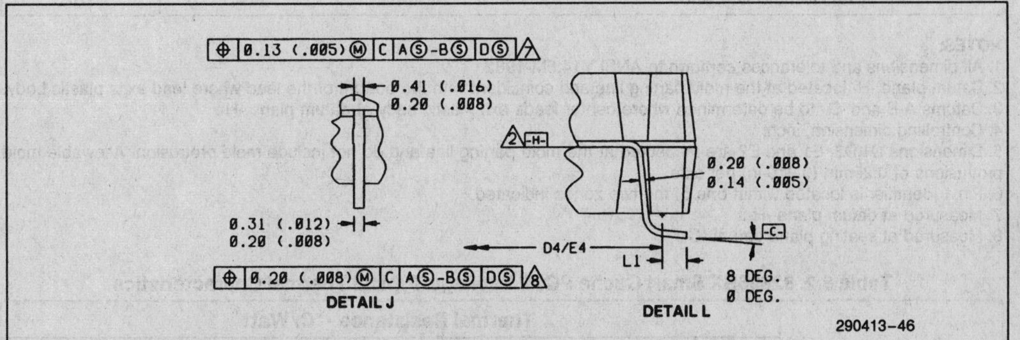

Figure 8.4 Typical Lead

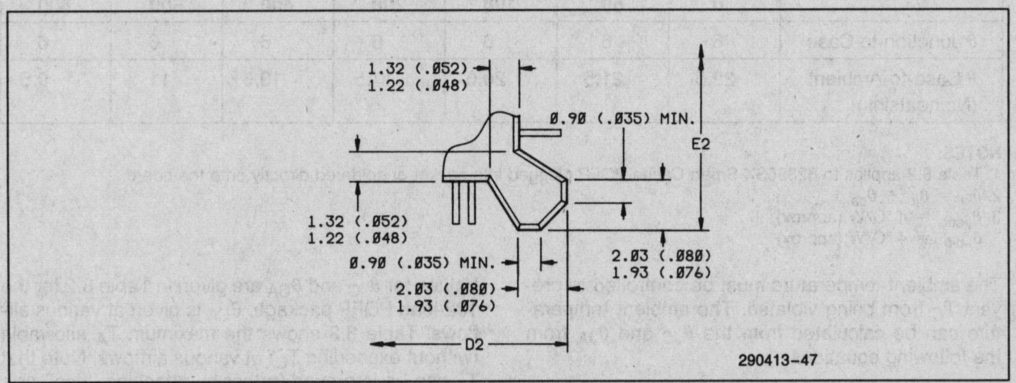

Figure 8.5 Detail M

Table 8.1 Symbol List for PQFP Package

Letter or Symbol	Description of Dimensions	Min (mm)	Max (mm)
A	Package Height: Distance from seating plane to the highest point of the body.	4.06	4.57
A1	Standoff: Distance from the seating plane to the base plane.	0.51	1.02
D/E	Overall Package Dimension: Lead tip to lead tip.	27.18	27.69
D1/E1	Plastic Body Dimension	24.05	24.21
D2/E2	Bumper Distance	27.86	28.01
D3/E3	Footprint	20.32 REF	
D4/E4	Footprint Radius Location	25.89	26.33
L1	Foot Length	0.51	0.76
N	Total Number of Leads	132	

NOTES:
1. All dimensions and tolerances conform to ANSI Y14.5M-1982.
2. Datum plane -H- located at the mold parting line and coincident with the bottom of the lead where lead exits plastic body.
3. Datums A-B and -D- to be determined where center leads exit plastic body at datum plane -H-.
4. Controlling dimension, inch.
5. Dimensions D1,D2, E1 and E2 are measured at the mold parting line and do not include mold protrusion. Allowable mold protrusions of 0.25mm (0.010 in) per side.
6. Pin 1 identifier is located within one of the two zones indicated.
7. Measured at datum plane -H-.
8. Measured at seating plane datum -C-.

Table 8.2. 82396SX Smart Cache PQFP Package Typical Thermal Characteristics

Parameter	Thermal Resistance - °C/Watt						
	Airflow - LFM						
	0	50	100	200	400	600	800
θ Junction-to-Case	6	6	6	6	6	6	6
θ Case-to-Ambient (No heatsink)	22.5	21.5	20.0	17.5	13.5	11	9.5

NOTES:
1. Table 8.2 applies to 82396SX Smart Cache PQFP plugged into socket or soldered directly onto the board.
2. $\theta_{ja} = \theta_{jc} + \theta_{ca}$
3. $\theta_{j\text{-cap}} = 4$ °C/W (approx)
   $\theta_{j\text{-pin}} = 4$ °C/W (approx)

The ambient temperature must be controlled to prevent T_C from being violated. The ambient temperature can be calculated from the θ_{JC} and θ_{JA} from the following equations:

$$T_{DIE} = T_C + P * \theta_{JC}$$

$$T_A = T_{DIE} - P * \theta_{JA}$$

$$T_C = T_A + P * [\theta_{JA} - \theta_{JC}]$$

Values for θ_{JC} and θ_{CA} are given in Table 8.2 for the 132-lead PQFP package. θ_{CA} is given at various airflows. Table 8.3 shows the maximum T_A allowable (without exceeding T_C) at various airflows. Note that T_A can be improved further by attaching "fins" or a "heat sink" to the package.

Table 8-3. Ambient Temperature vs. Airflow

Symbol	Airflow—LFM						
	0	50	100	200	400	600	800
θ_{JA}	28.5	27.5(1)	26.0(1)	23.5	19.5	17.0(1)	15.5(1)
T_A (°C)	49.0	50.6	53.0	57.0	63.4	67.4	69.8

NOTE:
The numbers in Table 8.3 were calculated using V_{CC} of 5.0V and an I_{CC} of 320 mA. This I_{CC} measurement is representative of the worst case I_{CC} at T_C = 85°C with the outputs unloaded.
1. These values have been either interpolated or extrapolated.

9.0 ELECTRICAL DATA

This chapter presents the A.C. and D.C. specifications for the 82396SX Smart Cache.

9.1 Power and Grounding

The 82396SX Smart Cache has a high clock frequency and 66 output buffers which can cause power surges as multiple output buffers drive new signal levels simultaneously. For clean on-chip power distribution at high frequency, 10 Vcc and 12 Vss pins separately feed power to the functional units of the 82396SX Smart Cache.

Power and ground connections must be made to all external Vcc and Vss pins of the 82396SX Smart Cache. On the circuit board, all Vcc pins must be connected on a Vcc plane and all Vss pins must be connected on a GND plane.

9.1.1 POWER DECOUPLING RECOMMENDATIONS

A liberal amount of decoupling capacitors must be placed near the 82396SX Smart Cache. The 82396SX Smart Cache driving its 16 bit local and system data buses and 23 bit system address bus at high frequency can cause transient power surges, particularly when driving large capacitive loads. Low inductance capacitors and interconnects are recommended for the best high frequency electrical performance. Inductance can be reduced by shortening circuit board traces between the 82396SX Smart Cache and the decoupling capacitors as much as possible.

9.1.2 RESISTOR RECOMMENDATIONS

The 82396SX Smart Cache does not have any internal pullup resistors. All unused inputs must be pulled up to a solid logic level through a 20 kΩ resistor. The outputs that require external pullup resistors are listed in Table 9.1. A particular designer may have reason to adjust the resistor values recommended here, or alter the use of pull-up resistors in other ways.

9.2 Absolute Maximum Ratings

Storage Temperature .... −65°C to +150°C
Case Temperature under Bias ... −65°C to +110°C
Supply Voltage with
Respect to V_{SS} .... −0.5V to +6.5V
Voltage on Other Pins ...... −0.5V to V_{CC} + 0.5V.

Table 9.1 Pullup Resistor Recommendations

Signal	Pullup Value	Purpose
SADS#	20KΩ ±10%	Lightly pull SADS# inactive while 82396SX Smart Cache is not driving it.
READYO#	20KΩ ±10%	Lightly pull READYO# inactive while 82396SX Smart Cache is not driving it.
SLOCK#	20KΩ ±10%	Lightly pull SLOCK# inactive for 82396SX Smart Cache SHOLD states.

4

9.3 D.C. Specifications T_{CASE} = 0°C to +85°C, V_{CC} = 5V ±5%

Table 9.2 DC Specifications

Symbol	Parameter	Limits		Units	Test Conditions
		Min	Max		
V_{IL}	Input Low Voltage	−0.3	0.8	V	
V_{IH}	Input High Volt.	2.0	V_{CC} + 0.3	V	
V_{CIL}	CMOS Input Low	−0.3	0.8	V	See Note 6
V_{CIH}	CMOS Input High	V_{CC} − 0.8	V_{CC} + 0.3	V	See Note 6
V_{OL}	Output Low Volt.		0.45	V	See Note 1
V_{OH}	Output High Volt.	2.4		V	See Note 2
V_{COL}	CMOS Output Low Volt.		0.45	V	See Notes 1,7
V_{COH}	CMOS Output High Volt.	V_{CC} − 0.45		V	See Notes 2,7
I_{LI}	Input Leakage		± 15	μA	$0V < V_{IN} < V_{CC}$
I_{LO}	Output Leakage		±15	Ua	$0.45V < V_{OUT} < V_{CC}$
C_{IN}	Cap. Input		10	pF	See Note 4
I_{CC}	Power Supply Current @ 0°C		525	mA	See Note 3
I_{CC2}	Power Supply Current @ +85°C		320	mA	See Note 8

NOTES:
1) This parameter is measured at IOL=4mA for all the outputs.
2) This parameter is measured at IOH=1mA for all the outputs.
3) Measured with inputs driven to CMOS levels, V_{CC} = 5.25V, 0°C, using a test pattern consisting of 40% read, 40% write, and 20% idle cycles. Due to the self-heating of the part after power is applied, this I_{CC} value will be reduced in actual applications. Refer to Table 8.3 for the ambient temperature requirements.
4) CLK2 input capacitance is 20pF.
5) No activity on the Local/System Bus.
6) Applies to CLK2, READYO# inputs.
7) Applies to READYO# output.
8) I_{CC2} was calculated using V_{CC} of 5.0V at T_C = 85°C. This I_{CC} measurement is representative of the worst case I_{CC} at T_C = 85°C with the outputs unloaded. This is not 100% tested.

9.4 A.C. Characteristics

Some of the 82396SX Smart Cache AC parameters are clock- frequency dependent. Thus, while the part functions properly at the entire frequency range specified by the T1 spec, the AC parameters are guaranteed at one distinct frequency only: 20MHz.

- Functional operating range: V_{CC} = 5V ±5%, T_{CASE} = 0°C to 85°C.
- All AC parameters are measured relative to 1.5V for falling and rising, CLK2 is at 2V.
- All outputs tested at a 50 pF load. In case of overloaded signals, the derating factor is 1 ns for every extra 25 pF load.
- All parameters are referred to PHI1 unless otherwise noted.
- The reference figure of CLK2 parameters and AC measurements level is Figure 9.1 and RESET and internal phase is Figure 3.2.

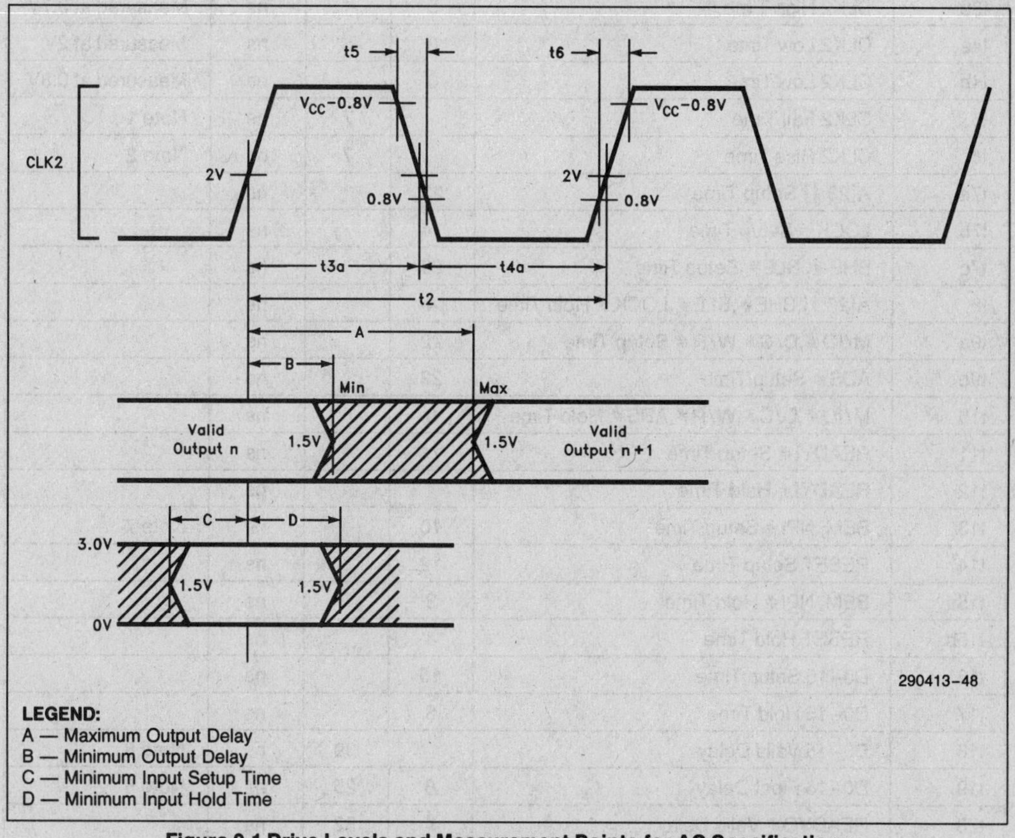

Figure 9.1 Drive Levels and Measurement Points for AC Specifications

9.4.1 A.C. CHARACTERISTICS TABLES T_{CASE} = 0°C to +85°C, V_{CC} = 5V ±5%

Table 9.3 Local Bus Singal AC Parameters

Symbol	Parameter	20 MHz		Units	Notes
		Min	Max		
t1	Operating Frequency	15.4	20	MHz	Internal CLK
t2	CLK2 Period	25	32.5	ns	
t3a	CLK2 High Time	8		ns	Measured at 2V
t3b	CLK2 High Time	5		ns	Measured at 3.7V
t4a	CLK2 Low Time	8		ns	Measured at 2V
t4b	CLK2 Low Time	6		ns	Measured at 0.8V
t5	CLK2 Fall Time		7	ns	Note 1
t6	CLK2 Rise Time		7	ns	Note 2
t7a	A[23:1] Setup Time	23		ns	
t7b	LOCK# Setup Time	14		ns	
t7c	BHE#, BLE# Setup Time	20		ns	
t8	A[23:1],BHE#,BLE#,LOCK# Hold Time	4		ns	
t9a	M/IO#,D/C#,W/R# Setup Time	22		ns	
t9b	ADS# Setup Time	23		ns	
t10	M/IO#,D/C#,W/R#,ADS# Hold Time	5		ns	
t11	READYI# Setup Time	11		ns	
t12	READYI# Hold Time	4		ns	
t13	BEM, NPI# Setup Time	10		ns	Note 7
t14	RESET Setup Time	12		ns	
t15a	BEM, NPI# Hold Time	3		ns	
t15b	RESET Hold Time	4		ns	
t16	D0–15 Setup Time	15		ns	
t17	D0–15 Hold Time	3		ns	
t18	D0–15 Valid Delay		39	ns	Note 8
t19	D0–15 Float Delay	6	25	ns	Note 5
t20	READYO# Valid Delay	4	32	ns	
t21	READYO# Float Delay		25	ns	Notes 4,5

Table 9.4 System Bus Singal AC Parameters

Symbol	Parameter	20 MHz		Units	Notes
		Min	Max		
t31	SA1–23, SBLE#, SBHE#, SLOCK# SD/C#, SW/R#, SM/IO# Valid Delay	4	18	ns	
t31a	SADS# Valid Delay	4	18	ns	
t32	SA1–23, SBHE#, SBLE#, SLOCK#, SD/C#, SW/R#, SM/IO# Float Delay	4	30	ns	Note 5
t32a	SADS# Float Delay	4	30	ns	Notes 4,5
t33	SBLAST#,SHLDA Valid Delay	4	26	ns	
t34	SBLAST# Float Delay	4	30	ns	Note 5
t35	SD[15:0] Write Data Valid Del.	4	33	ns	Note 4
t36	SD[15:0] Float Delay	4	27	ns	Notes 4,5
t37	SA[23:4] Setup Time	10		ns	
t38	SA[23:4] Hold Time	4		ns	
t39	SD[15:0] Read Setup Time	9		ns	
t40	SD[15:0] Read Hold Time	5		ns	
t41	SNA# Setup Time	5		ns	Note 3
t42	SNA# Hold Time	12		ns	Note 3
t43a	SKEN# Setup Time	9		ns	
t43b	SHOLD,SAHOLD Setup Time	17		ns	
t43c	SWP# Setup Time	17		ns	
t44a	SHOLD, SWP# Hold Time	3		ns	
t44b	SKEN# Hold Time	4		ns	
t44c	SAHOLD Hold Time	4		ns	
t45a	SEADS# Setup Time	12		ns	
t45b	SRDY#,SBRDY# Setup Time	12		ns	
t46	SEADS#,SRDY#,SBRDY# Hold Time	4		ns	
t47	FLUSH,A20M# Setup Time	18		ns	Note 6
t48	FLUSH,A20M# Hold Time	3		ns	Note 6

NOTES:
1. Tf is Measured at 3.7V to 0.8V. Tf is not 100% tested.
2. Tr is Measured at 0.8V to 3.7V. Tr is not 100% tested.
3. The specification is relative to PHI2 i.e. signal sampled by PHI2.
4. The specification is relative to PHI2 i.e. signal driven by PHI2.
5. Float condition occurs when maximum output current becomes less than ILO in magnitude. Float delay is not 100% tested.
6. The signal is allowed to be asynchronous to CLK2. The setup and hold specifications are given for testing purposes, to assure recognition within a specific CLK2 period.
7. The signal is not sampled. It must be valid through the entire cycle (as the Address lines).
8. For Data min Valid Delay see min float times (local data lines are floated in the next cycle after being driven active).

4

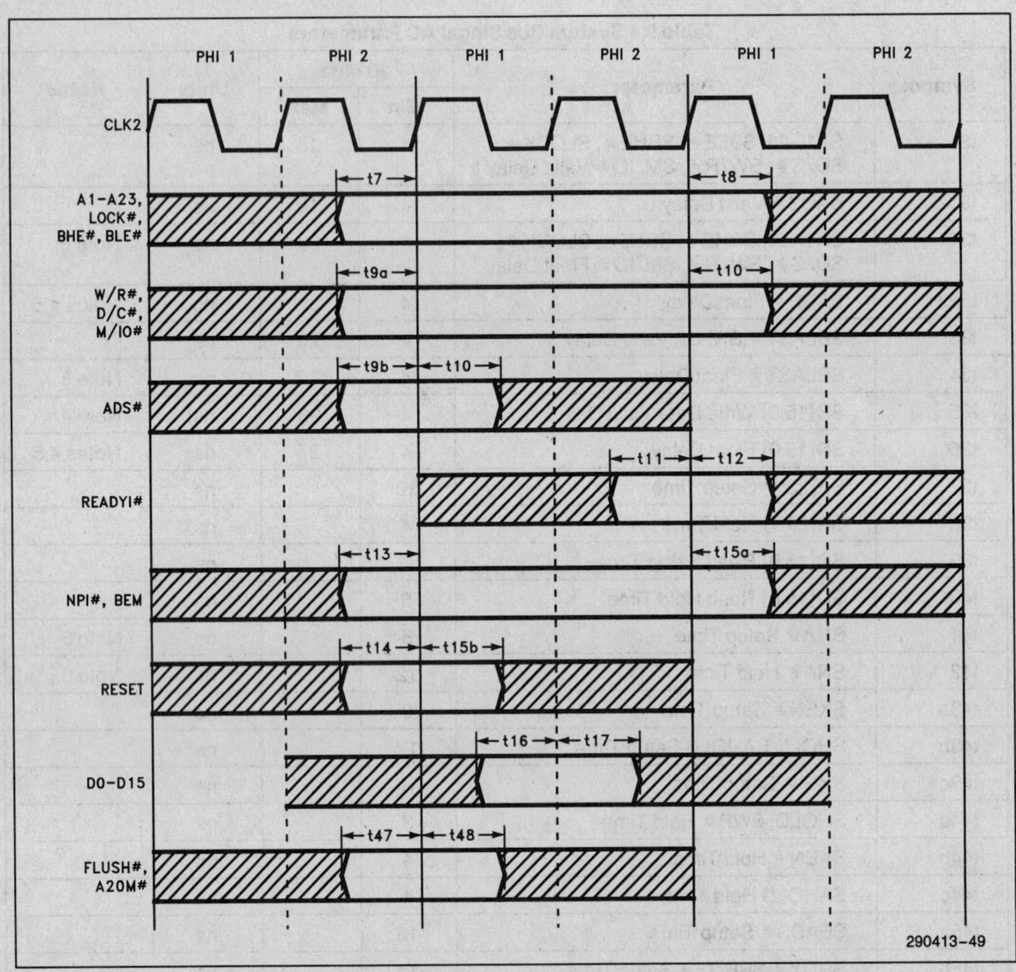

Figure 9.2 AC Timing Waveforms - Local Bus Input Setup and Hold Timing

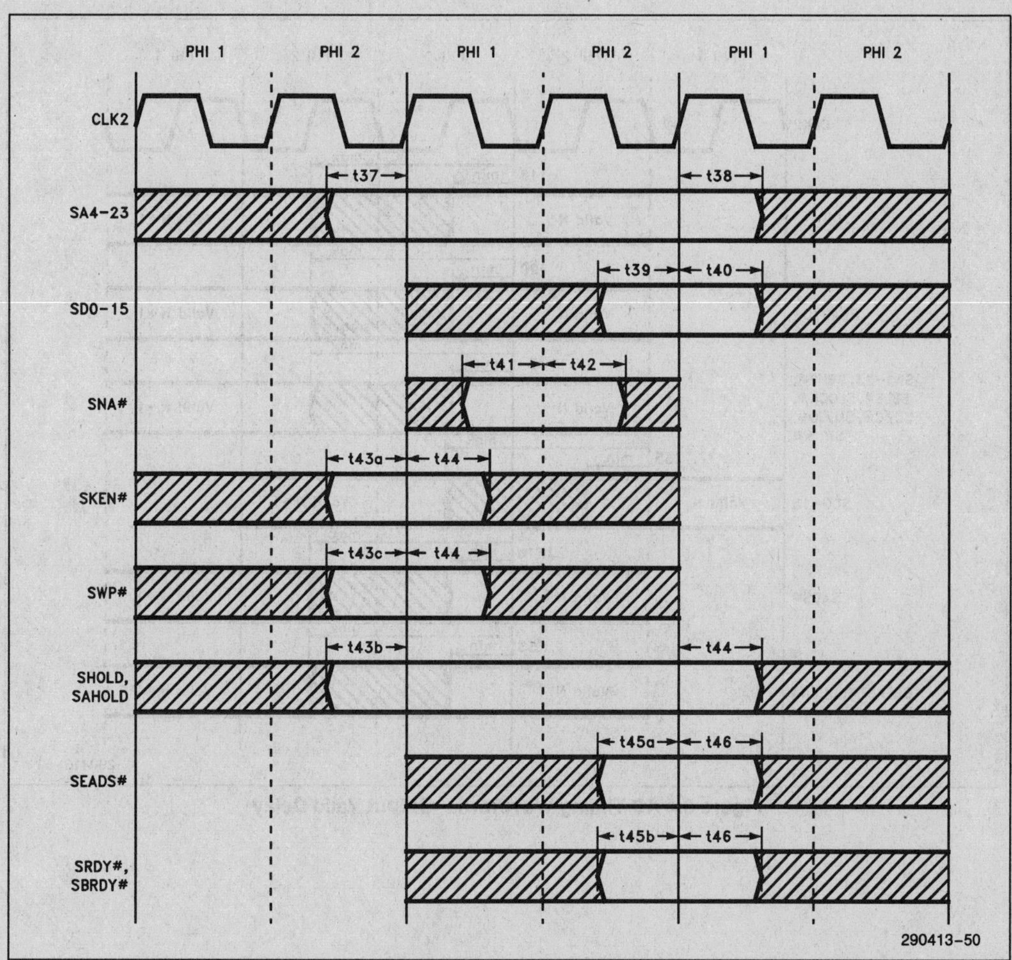

Figure 9.3 AC Timing Waveforms - System Bus Input Setup and Hold Timing

4

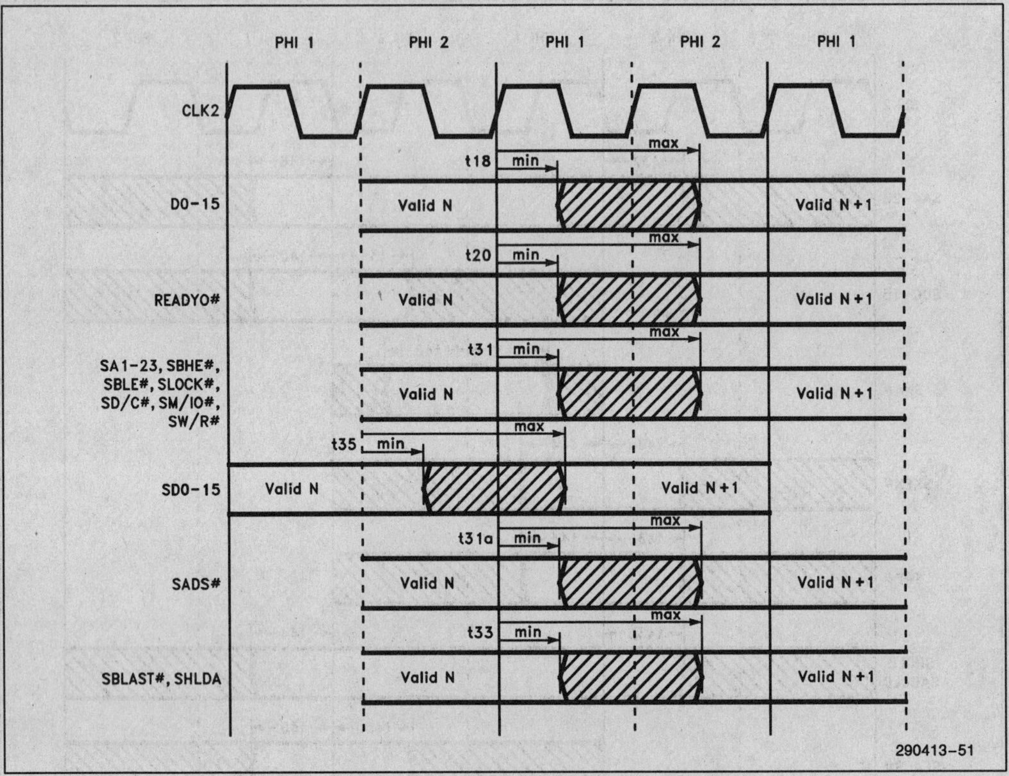

PHI 1 PHI 2 PHI 1 PHI 2 PHI 1

CLK2

t18 min max
D0-15 Valid N Valid N+1

t20 min max
READYO# Valid N Valid N+1

t31 min max
SA1-23, SBHE#, SBLE#, SLOCK#, SD/C#, SM/IO#, SW/R# Valid N Valid N+1

t35 min max
SD0-15 Valid N Valid N+1

t31a min max
SADS# Valid N Valid N+1

t33 min max
SBLAST#, SHLDA Valid N Valid N+1

290413-51

Figure 9.4 AC Timing Waveform - Output Valid Delay

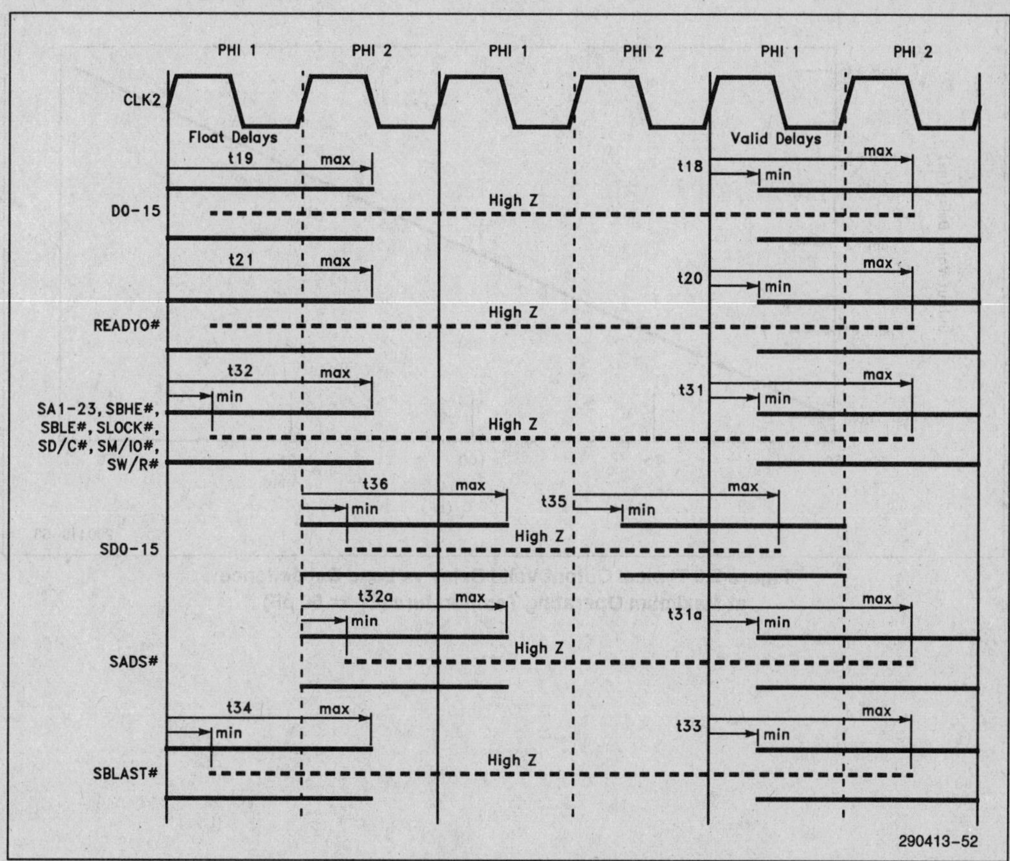

Figure 9.5 AC Timing Waveform - Output Float Delays

4

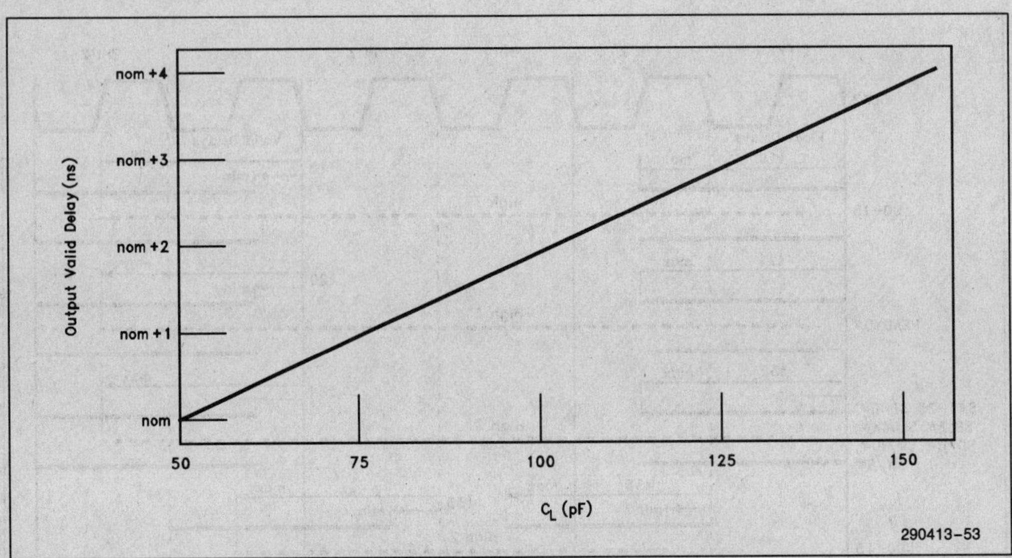

Figure 9.6 Typical Output Valid Delay vs Load Capacitance at Maximum Operating Temperature (C_L = 50 pF)

APPENDIX A

Term	Definition
AC	Alternating Current
ALF	Aborted Line Fill
B	Byte
CDF	Cache Directory FLUSH
CDL	Cache Directory Lookup
CDS	Cache Directory SNOOP
CDT	Testability Access
CDU	Cache Directory Update
CR	Cache Read
CW	Cache Write
CU	Cache Update
CT	Testability Access
CPU	Central Processing Unit
CHMOS	Complimentary High Performance Metal Oxide Semiconductor
CRDH	Cache Read Hit
CRDM	Cache Read Miss
CWTH	Cache Write Hit
DC	Direct Current
MSB	Most Significant Bit(s)
DRAM	Dynamic Random Access Memory
DMA	Direct Memory Access
DW	Double Word
GND	Ground
I/O	Input/Output
LB	Local Bus
LRU	Least Recently Used
PQFP	Plastic Quad Flat Pack

Term	Definition
RAM	Random Access Memory
SB	System Bus
TV	Tag Valid
WP	Write Protect
W	Word
xxK	xx thousand
xxKB	xx K Bytes
xxGB	xx Giga Bytes
xWS	xx Wait States
T1	Local Bus State
T2	Local Bus State
TI	Local Bus State
TH	Local Bus State
ST1	System Bus State
ST1P	System Bus State
ST2	System Bus State
ST2P	System Bus State
STI	System Bus State
STH	System Bus State
PHI1	1st CLK2 cycle in a 2 CLK2 CLK cycle
PHI2	2nd CLK2 cycle in a 2 CLK2 CLK cycle
C	Celsius
V	Volts
μA	10^{-6} Amps
mA	10^{-3} Amps
pF	10^{-12} Farads
MHz	10^{6} Hertz
ns	10^{-9} seconds

4

APPENDIX B

386 SMART CACHE TO 82396SX SMART CACHE DESIGN DIFFERENCES

The 82396SX Smart Cache has the same functional features as the 386 Smart Cache (82395DX) except as noted below.

Cache Architecture

Table B-1. 82395DX/82396SX Architectural Comparison

Feature	82395DX	82396SX
Cache Size	16K	16K
Associativity	4 Way	4 Way
Line Size	16B	16B
Lines/Sector	1	1
Write Buffer	4 DW	4 W
Expandability	to 32K or 64K	none
Line Fill	4DW serial burst or pipelined	8 W serial burst or pipelined
Address Bus's	A[31:2], SA[31:2]	A[23:1], SA[23:1]
Data Bus's	D[31:0], SD[31:0]	D[15:0], SD[15:0]
Bus Width	BE[3:0]#, SBE[3:0]#	BHE#, BLE#, SBHE#, SBLE#

82396SX Smart Cache Pin Definitions

The 82396SX Smart Cache will have the same pins as the 386 Smart Cache (82395DX) except as noted below.

SNENE# The 82396SX Smart Cache does not have an SNENE# pin. Page hit/miss decisions will be made by the DRAM controller.

LBA# Local Bus resources are not supported (the 82396SX Smart Cache will decode i387™ SX cycles and provide READYO# to the processor).

SBREQ SBREQ is not provided on the 82396SX Smart Cache.

SFHOLD# SFHOLD# is not provided on the 82396SX Smart Cache.

BE[3:0]# Replaced by BHE# and BLE#.

SBE[3:0]# Replaced by SBHE# and SBLE#.

BEM The 386 Smart Cache does not have BEM pin.

A[31:2] Modified to A[23:1] for the 16M address range of the 82396SX Smart Cache.

SA[31:2] Modified to SA[23:1] for the 16M address range of the 82396SX Smart Cache.

D[31:0] Modified to D[15:0] for the 16 bit data bus width of the 82396SX Smart Cache.

SD[31:0] Modified to SD[15:0] for the 16 bit system data bus width of the 82396SX Smart Cache.

82396SX Smart Cache Address Differences

Table B-2. 82396SX Smart Cache Address Differences

Device	TAG	SET	DW/W	Byte
82395DX	A[31:12]	A[11:4]	A[3:2]	BE[3:0]#
82396SX	A[23:12]	A[11:4]	A[3:1]	BHE#, BLE#

82396SX Smart Cache Line Fill Order

The Line Fill order for burst and non-burst Line Fill cycles is shown in Table B-3.

Table B-3. 82396SX Smart Cache Line Fill Order

82396SX Smart Cache Line Fill Order (SA[3:1])							
Word within Line Fill							
1st	2nd	3rd	4th	5th	6th	7th	8th
0	2	4	6	8	A	C	E
2	0	6	4	A	8	E	C
4	6	0	2	C	E	8	A
6	4	2	0	E	C	A	8
8	A	C	E	0	2	4	6
A	8	E	C	2	0	6	4
C	E	8	A	4	6	0	2
E	C	A	8	6	4	2	0

82396SX Smart Cache SRAM Test Mode

The following cache directory bits are accessed via the 16-bit data bus when the cache directory is selected during SRAM Test Mode.

Table B-4. SRAM Test Mode Cache Directory Bit Map

Word Format in Tagram Write:

Local Data Bus

15	14	13	12	11	10	9	8	7	6	5	4	3	2	1	0
LRU B2	LRU B1	LRU B0 & V	A23	A22	A21	A20	A19	A18	A17	A16	A15	A14	A13	A12	WP

(Data written to D13 writes to LRU bit B0 and to the Valid bit)

Word Format in Tagram Read:

Way 0

Local Data Bus

15	14	13	12	11	10	9	8	7	6	5	4	3	2	1	0
0	LRU B0	V	A23	A22	A21	A20	A19	A18	A17	A16	A15	A14	A13	A12	WP

Way 1

Local Data Bus

15	14	13	12	11	10	9	8	7	6	5	4	3	2	1	0
0	LRU B1	V	A23	A22	A21	A20	A19	A18	A17	A16	A15	A14	A13	A12	WP

Way 2

Local Data Bus

15	14	13	12	11	10	9	8	7	6	5	4	3	2	1	0
0	LRU B2	V	A23	A22	A21	A20	A19	A18	A17	A16	A15	A14	A13	A12	WP

Way 3

Local Data Bus

15	14	13	12	11	10	9	8	7	6	5	4	3	2	1	0
0	0	V	A23	A22	A21	A20	A19	A18	A17	A16	A15	A14	A13	A12	WP

V = TAG Valid bit
WP = Write Protect bit
"0" - Indicates don't care bits. Writing to these bits will have no effect. When reading the Tagram these bits will have a value of 0.

NOTE:
In Tagram accesses, BHE# and BLE# are ignored in both read and write cycles.

82396SX SMART CACHE SRAM TEST MODE—ADDRESS MAPPING

The following tables show the address mapping for the SRAM test mode.

Table B-5. SRAM Test Mode Address Decoding Signals

Address Decoding - Local Address Pins

Signal	Pins
Cache/Tagram#	[A16]
Way	[A15:A14]
Set	[A11:A4]
Addr Space 256K-512K	[A23:A17]
Word	[A3:A1]
Byte	BHE#,BLE#
Unused	A[13:12] = 00

NOTE:
No code or data should reside between 256K-512K.

Table B-6. SRAM Test Mode Start Address Memory Map

Cache/Tagram	Way	Start Address
Cache	3	05C000h
Cache	2	058000h
Cache	1	054000h
Cache	0	050000h
Tagram	3	04C000h
Tagram	2	048000h
Tagram	1	044000h
Tagram	0	040000h

Table B-7. SRAM Test Mode Cache Address Allocation

SET	Word	Start Address
255	7	FFE h
255	6	FFC h
255	5	FFA h
255	4	FF8 h
255	3	FF6 h
255	2	FF4 h
255	1	FF2 h
255	0	FF0 h
.	.	.
.	.	.
2	7	02E h
2	6	02C h
2	5	02A h
2	4	028 h
2	3	026 h
2	2	024 h
2	1	022 h
2	0	020 h
1	7	01E h
1	6	01C h
1	5	01A h
1	4	018 h
1	3	016 h
1	2	014 h
1	1	012 h
1	0	010 h
0	7	00E h
0	6	00C h
0	5	00A h
0	4	008 h
0	3	006 h
0	2	004 h
0	1	002 h
0	0	000 h

Table B-8. SRAM Test Mode Tagram Address Allocation

SET	Start Address
255	FFE h
255	FFC h
255	FFA h
255	FF8 h
255	FF6 h
255	FF4 h
255	FF2 h
255	FF0 h
.	.
.	.
2	02E h
2	02C h
2	02A h
2	028 h
2	026 h
2	024 h
2	022 h
2	020 h
1	01E h
1	01C h
1	01A h
1	018 h
1	016 h
1	014 h
1	012 h
1	010 h
0	00E h
0	00C h
0	00A h
0	008 h
0	006 h
0	004 h
0	002 h
0	000 h

82385SX
HIGH PERFORMANCE CACHE CONTROLLER

- **Improves 386™ SX System Performance**
  - **—Reduces Average CPU Wait States to Nearly Zero**
  - **—Zero Wait State Read Hit**
  - **—Zero Wait State Posted Memory Writes**
  - **—Allows Other Masters to Access the System Bus More Readily**
- **Hit Rates up to 99%**
- **Optimized as 386 SX Companion**
  - **—Simple 386 SX Interface**
  - **—Part of Intel386™-Based Compute Engine Including 387™ SX Math Coprocessor and 82370 Integrated System Peripheral**
  - **—16 MHz and 20 MHz Operation**
- **Software Transparent**
- **Synchronous Dual Bus Architecture**
  - **—Bus Watching Maintains Cache Coherency**
- **Maps Full 386 SX Address Space**
- **Flexible Cache Mapping Policies**
  - **—Direct Mapped or 2-Way Set Associative Cache Organization**
  - **—Supports Non-Cacheable Memory Space**
  - **—Unified Cache for Code and Data**
- **Integrates Cache Directory and Cache Management Logic**
- **High Speed CHMOS Technology**
  - **—132-Pin PGA and 132-Lead PQFP**

The 82385SX Cache Controller is a high performance peripheral for Intel's 386™ SX Microprocessor. It stores a copy of frequently accessed code and data from main memory in a zero wait state local cache memory. The 82385SX allows the 386 SX Microprocessor to run near its full potential by reducing the average number of CPU wait states to nearly zero. The dual bus architecture of the 82385SX allows other masters to access system resources while the 386 SX CPU operates locally out of its cache. In this situation, the 82385SX's "bus watching" mechanism preserves cache coherency by monitoring the system bus address lines at no cost to system or local throughput.

The 82385SX is completely software transparent, protecting the integrity of system software. High performance and board space savings are achieved because the 82385SX integrates a cache directory and all cache management logic on one chip.

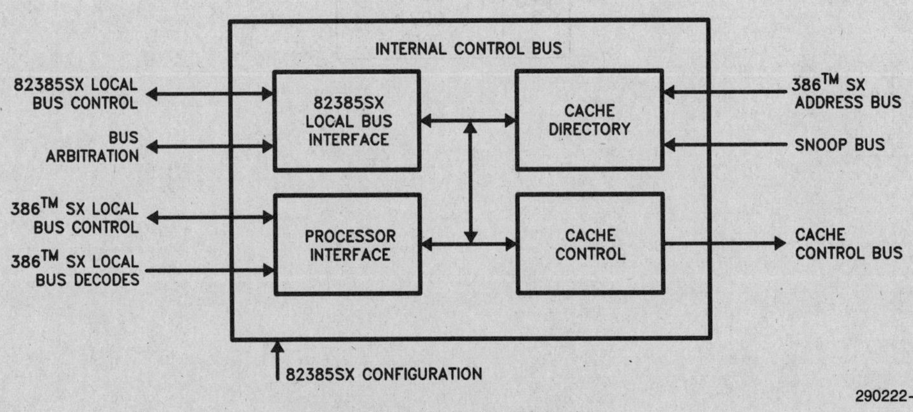

82385SX Internal Block Diagram

October 1990
Order Number: 290222-003

CONTENTS

PAGE

CONTENTS

PAGE

CONTENTS

CONTENTS

1.0 82385SX FUNCTIONAL OVERVIEW

The 82385SX Cache Controller is a high performance peripheral for Intel's 386™ SX microprocessor. This chapter provides an overview of the 82385SX, and of the basic architecture and operation of a 386 SX CPU/82385SX system.

1.1 82385SX Overview

The main function of a cache memory system is to provide fast local storage for frequently accessed code and data. The cache system intercepts 386 SX memory references to see if the required data resides in the cache. If the data resides in the cache (a hit), it is returned to the 386 SX without incurring wait states. If the data is not cached (a miss), the reference is forwarded to the system and the data retrieved from main memory. An efficient cache will yield a high "hit rate" (the ratio of cache hits to total 386 SX accesses), such that the majority of accesses are serviced with zero wait states. The net effect is that the wait states incurred in a relatively infrequent miss are averaged over a large number of accesses, resulting in an average of nearly zero wait states per access. Since cache hits are serviced locally, a processor operating out of its local cache has a much lower "bus utilization" which reduces system bus bandwidth requirements, making more bandwidth available to other bus masters.

The 82385SX Cache Controller integrates a cache directory and all cache management logic required to support an external 16 kbyte cache. The cache directory structure is such that the entire physical address range of the 386 SX is mapped into the cache. Provision is made to allow areas of memory to be set aside as non-cacheable. The user has two cache organization options: direct mapped and 2-way set associative. Both provide the high hit rates necessary to make a large, relatively slow main memory array look like fast, zero wait state memory to the 386 SX.

A good hit rate is an essential ingredient of a successful cache implementation. Hit rate is the measure of how efficient a cache is in maintaining a copy of the most frequently requested code and data. However, efficiency is not the only factor for performance consideration. Just as essential are sound cache management policies. These policies refer to the handling of 386 SX writes, preservation of cache coherency, and ease of system design. The 82385SX's "posted write" capability allows the majority of 386 SX writes, including most non-cacheable cycles, to run with zero wait states, and the 82385SX's "bus watching" mechanism preserves cache coherency with no impact on system performance. Physically, the 82385SX ties directly to the 386 SX with virtually no external logic.

1.2 System Overview I: Bus Structure

A good grasp of bus structure of a 386 SX CPU/82385SX system is essential in understanding both the 82385SX and its role in a 386 SX system. The following is a description of this structure.

1.2.1 386™ SX LOCAL BUS/82385SX LOCAL BUS/SYSTEM BUS

Figure 1-1 depicts the bus structure of a typical 386 SX system. The "386 SX Local Bus" consists of the physical 386 SX address, data, and control busses. The local address and data busses are buffered and/or latched to become the "system" address and data busses. The local control bus is decoded by bus control logic to generate the various system bus read and write commands.

The addition of an 82385SX Cache Controller causes a separation of the 386 SX bus into two distinct busses: the actual 386 SX local bus and the "82385SX Local Bus" (Figure 1-2). The 82385SX local bus is designed to look like the front end of a 386 SX by providing 82385SX local bus equivalents to all appropriate 386 SX signals. The system ties to this "386 SX-like" front end just as it would to an actual 386 SX. The 386 SX simply sees a fast system bus, and the system sees a 386 SX front end with low bus bandwidth requirements. The cache subsystem is transparent to both. Note that the 82385SX local bus is not simply a buffered version of the 386 SX bus, but rather is distinct from, and able to operate in parallel with the 386 SX bus. Other masters residing on either the 82385SX local bus or system bus are free to manage system resources while the 386 SX operates out of its cache.

1.2.2 BUS ARBITRATION

The 82385SX presents the "386 SX-like" interface which is called the 82385SX local bus. Whereas the 386 SX provides a Hold Request/ Hold Acknowledge bus arbitration mechanism via its HOLD and HLDA pins, the 82385SX provides an equivalent mechanism via its BHOLD and BHLDA pins. (These signals are described in Section 3.7.) When another master requests the 82385SX local bus, it issues the request to the 82385SX via BHOLD. Typically, at the end of the current 82385SX local bus cycle, the 82385SX will release the 82385SX local bus and acknowledge the request via BHLDA. The 386 SX is of course free to continue operating on the 386 SX local bus while another master owns the 82385SX local bus.

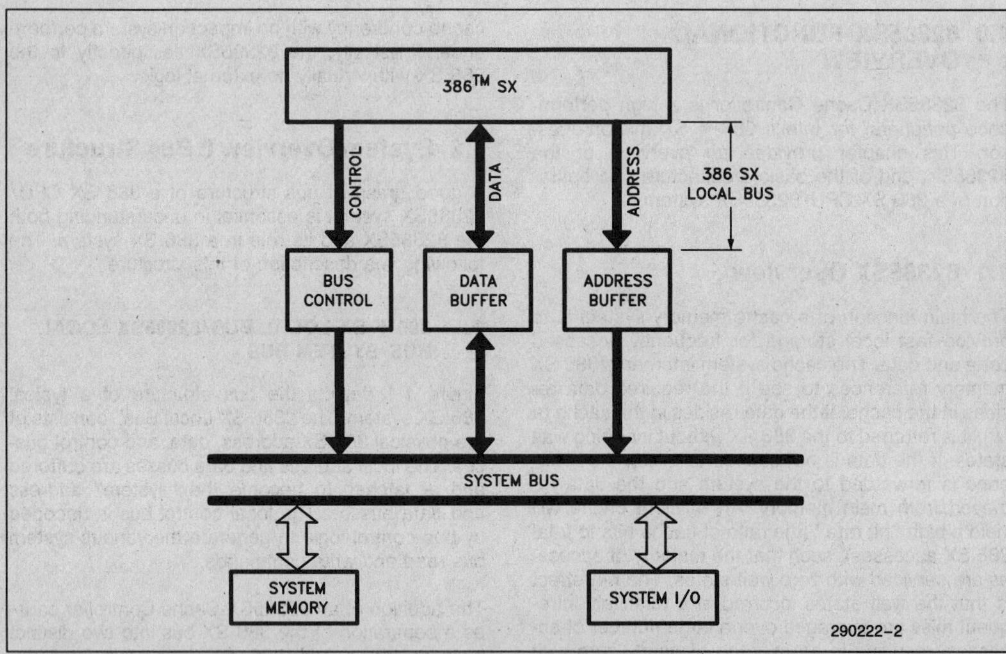

Figure 1-1. 386™ SX System Bus Structure

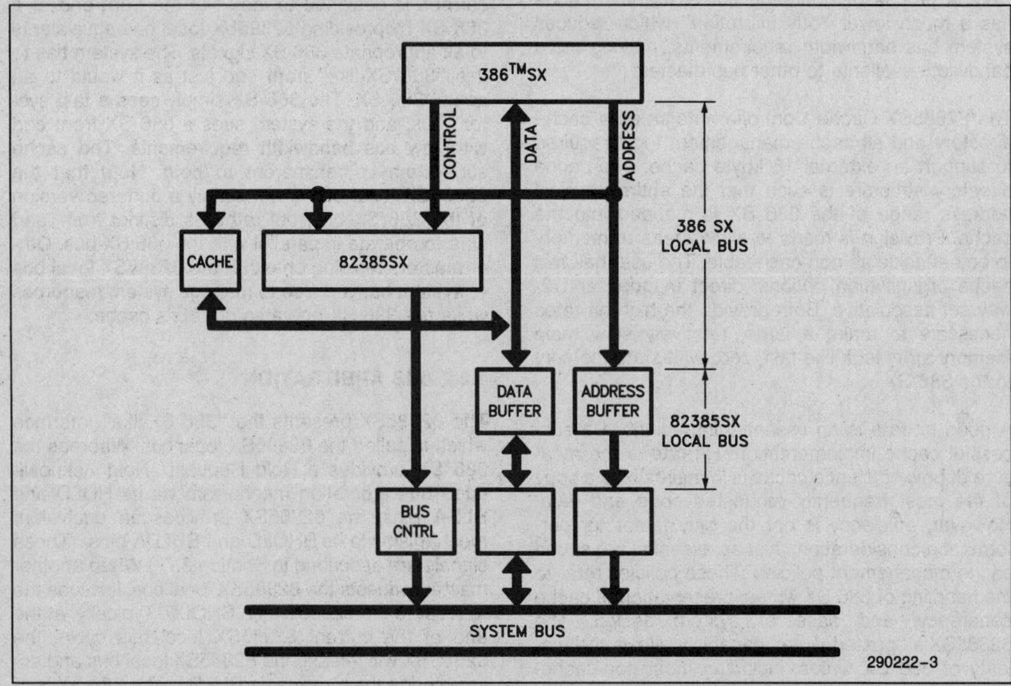

Figure 1-2. 386™ SX and 82385SX System Bus Structure

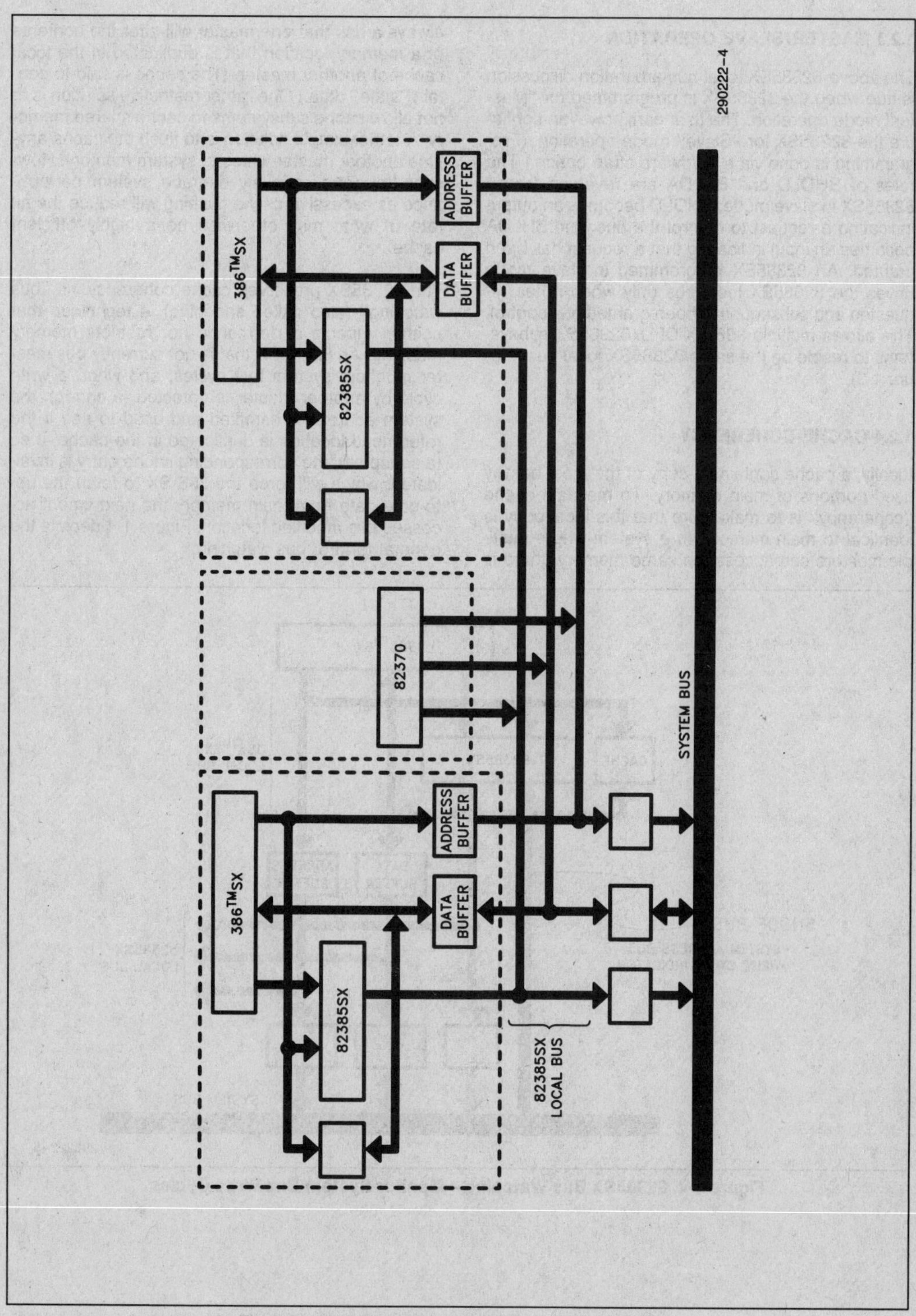

Figure 1-3. Multi-Master/Multi-Cache Environment

4

1.2.3 MASTER/SLAVE OPERATION

The above 82385SX local bus arbitration discussion is true when the 82385SX is programmed for "Master" mode operation. The user can, however, configure the 82385SX for "Slave" mode operation. (Programming is done via a hardware strap option.) The roles of BHOLD and BHLDA are reversed for an 82385SX in slave mode; BHOLD becomes an output indicating a request to control the bus, and BHLDA becomes an input indicating that a request has been granted. An 82385SX programmed in slave mode drives the 82385SX local bus only when it has requested and subsequently been granted bus control. This allows multiple 386 SX CPU/82385SX subsystems to reside on the same 82385SX local bus (Figure 1-3).

1.2.4 CACHE COHERENCY

Ideally, a cache contains a copy of the most heavily used portions of main memory. To maintain cache "coherency" is to make sure that this local copy is identical to main memory. In a system where multiple masters can access the same memory, there is always a risk that one master will alter the contents of a memory location that is duplicated in the local cache of another master. (The cache is said to contain "stale" data.) One rather restrictive solution is to not allow cache subsystems to cache shared memory. Another simple solution is to flush the cache anytime another master writes to system memory. However, this can seriously degrade system performance as excessive cache flushing will reduce the hit rate of what may otherwise be a highly efficient cache.

The 82385SX preserves cache coherency via "bus watching" (also called snooping), a technique that neither impacts performance nor restricts memory mapping. An 82385SX that is not currently bus master monitors system bus cycles, and when a write cycle by another master is detected (a snoop), the system address is sampled and used to see if the referenced location is duplicated in the cache. If so (a snoop hit), the corresponding cache entry is invalidated, which will force the 386 SX to fetch the up-to-date data from main memory the next time it accesses this modified location. Figure 1-4 depicts the general form of bus watching.

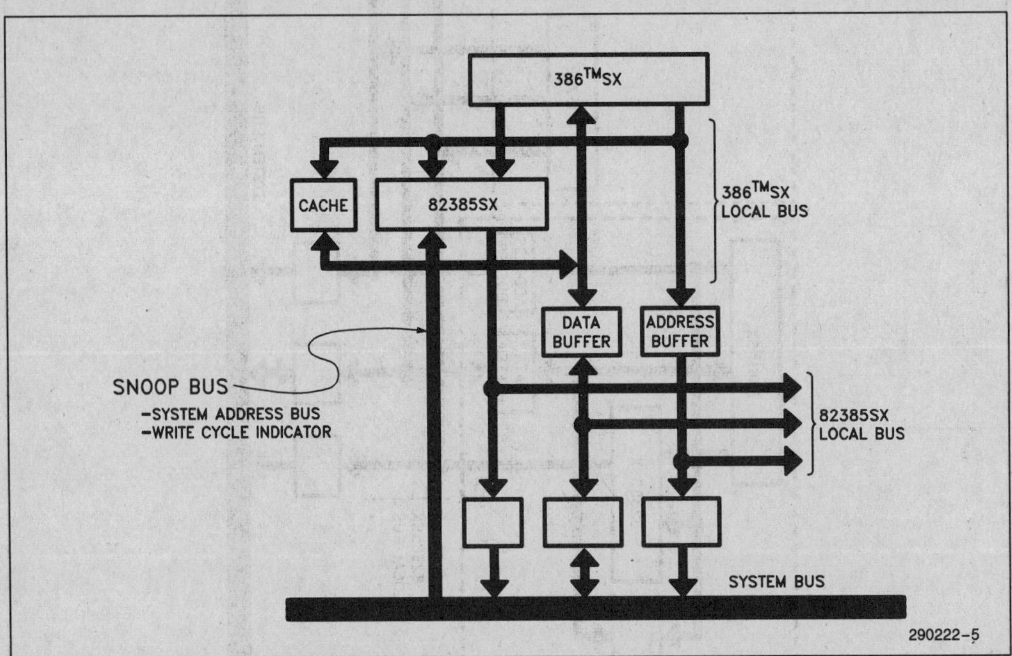

Figure 1-4. 82385SX Bus Watching—Monitor System Bus Write Cycles

1.3 System Overview II: Basic Operation

This discussion is an overview of the basic operation of a 386 SX CPU/82385SX system. Items discussed include the 82385SX's response to all 386 SX cycles, including interrupt acknowledges, halts, and shutdowns. Also discussed are non-cacheable and local accesses.

1.3.1 386™ SX MEMORY CODE AND DATA READ CYCLES

1.3.1.1 Read Hits

When the 386 SX initiates a memory code or data read cycle, the 82385SX compares the high order bits of the 386 SX address bus with the appropriate addresses (tags) stored in its on-chip directory. (The directory structure is described in Section 2.1.1) If the 82385SX determines that the requested data is in the cache, it issues the appropriate control signals that direct the cache to drive the requested data onto the 386 SX data bus, where it is read by the 386 SX. The 82385SX terminates the 386 SX cycle without inserting any wait states.

1.3.1.2 Read Misses

If the 82385SX determines that the requested data is not in the cache, the request is forwarded to the 82385SX local bus and the data retrieved from main memory. As the data returns from main memory, it is directed to the 386 SX and also written into the cache. Concurrently, the 82385SX updates the cache directory such that the next time this particular piece of information is requested by the 386 SX, the 82385SX will find it in the cache and return it with zero wait states.

The basic unit of transfer between main memory and cache memory in a cache subsystem is called the line size. In an 82385SX system, the line size is one 16-bit word. During a read miss, both 82385SX local bus byte enables are active. This insures that the 16-bit entry is written into the cache. (The 386 SX simply ignores what it did not request.) In any other type of 386 SX cycle that is forwarded to the 82385SX local bus, the logic levels of the 386 SX byte enables are duplicated on the 82385SX local bus.

The 82385SX does not actively fetch main memory data independently of the 386 SX. The 82385SX is essentially a passive device which only monitors the address bus and activates control signals. The read miss is the only mechanism by which main memory data is copied into the cache and validated in the cache directory.

In an isolated read miss, the number of wait states seen by the 386 SX is that required by the system memory to respond with data plus the cache comparison cycle (hit/miss decision). The cache system must determine that the cycle is a miss before it can begin the system memory access. However, since misses most often occur consecutively, the 82385SX will begin 386 SX address pipelined cycles to effectively "hide" the comparison cycle beyond the first miss (refer to Section 4.1.3).

The 82385SX can execute a memory access on the 82385SX local bus only if it currently owns the bus. If not, an 82385SX in master mode will run the cycle after the current master releases the bus. An 82385SX in slave mode will issue a hold request, and will run the cycle as soon as the request is acknowledged. (This is true for any read or write cycle that needs to run on the 82385SX local bus.)

1.3.2 386™ SX MEMORY WRITE CYCLES

The 82385SX's "posted write" capability allows the majority of 386 SX memory write cycles to run with zero wait states. The primary memory update policy implemented in a posted write is the traditional cache "write through" technique, which implies that main memory is always updated in any memory write cycle. If the referenced location also happens to reside in the cache (a write hit), the cache is updated as well.

Beyond this, a posted write latches the 386 SX address, data, and cycle definition signals, and the 386 SX local bus is terminated without any wait states, even though the corresponding 82385SX local bus cycle is not yet completed, or perhaps not even started. A posted write is possible because the 82385SX's bus state machine, which is almost identical to the 386 SX bus state machine, is able to run 82385SX local bus cycles independently of the 386 SX. The only time the 386 SX sees write cycle wait states is when a previously latched (posted) write has not yet been completed on the 82385SX local bus or during an I/O write (which is not posted). An 386 SX write can be posted even if the 82385SX does not currently own the 82385SX local bus. In this case, an 82385SX in master mode will run the cycle as soon as the current master releases the bus, and an 82385SX in slave mode will request the bus and run the cycle when the request is acknowledged. The 386 SX is free to continue operating out of its cache (on the 386 SX local bus) during this time.

1.3.3 NON-CACHEABLE CYCLES

Non-cacheable cycles fall into one of two categories: cycles decoded as non-cacheable, and cycles

4

that are by default non-cacheable according to the 82385SX's design. All non-cacheable cycles are forwarded to the 82385SX local bus. Non-cacheable cycles have no effect on the cache or cache directory.

The 82385SX allows the system designer to define areas of main memory as non-cacheable. The 386 SX address bus is decoded and the decode output is connected to the 82385SX's non-cacheable access (NCA#) input. This decoding is done in the first 386 SX bus state in which the non-cacheable cycle address becomes available. Non-cacheable read cycles resemble cacheable read miss cycles, except that the cache and cache directory are unaffected. NCA# defined non-cacheable writes, like most writes, are posted.

The 82385SX defines certain cycles as non-cacheable without using its non-cacheable access input. These include I/O cycles, interrupt acknowledge cycles, and halt/shutdown cycles. I/O reads and interrupt acknowledge cycles execute as any other non-cacheable read. I/O write cycles are not posted. The 386 SX is not allowed to continue until a ready signal is returned from the system. Halt/Shutdown cycles are posted. During a halt/shutdown condition, the 82385SX local bus duplicates the behavior of the 386 SX, including the ability to recognize and respond to a BHOLD request. (The 82385SX's bus watching mechanism is functional in this condition.)

1.3.4 386™ SX LOCAL BUS CYCLES

386 SX Local Bus Cycles are accesses to resources on the 386 SX local bus other than to the 82385SX itself. The 82385SX simply ignores these accesses: they are neither forwarded to the system nor do they affect the cache. The designer sets aside memory and/or I/O space for local resources by decoding the 386 SX address bus and feeding the decode to the 82385SX's local bus access (LBA#) input. The designer can also decode the 386 SX cycle definition signals to keep specific 386 SX cycles from being forwarded to the system. For example, a multiprocessor design may wish to capture and remedy a 386 SX shutdown locally without having it detected by the rest of the system. Note that in such a design, the local shutdown cycle must be terminated by local bus control logic. The 387 SX Math Coprocessor is considered a 386 SX local bus resource, but it need not be decoded as such by the user since the 82385SX is able to internally recognize 387 SX accesses via the M/IO# and A23 pins.

1.3.5 SUMMARY OF 82385SX RESPONSE TO ALL 386™ SX CYCLES

Table 1-1 summarizes the 82385SX response to all 386 SX bus cycles, as conditioned by whether or not the cycle is decoded as local or non-cacheable. The table describes the impact of each cycle on the cache and on the cache directory, and whether or not the cycle is forwarded to the 82385SX local bus. Whenever the 82385SX local bus is marked "IDLE", it implies that this bus is available to other masters.

1.3.6 BUS WATCHING

As previously discussed, the 82385SX "qualifies" a 386 SX bus cycle in the first bus state in which the address and cycle definition signals of the cycle become available. The cycle is qualified as read or write, cacheable or non-cacheable, etc. Cacheable cycles are further classified as hit or miss according to the results of the cache comparison, which accesses the 82385SX directory and compares the appropriate directory location (tag) to the current 386 SX address. If the cycle turns out to be non-cacheable or a 386 SX local bus access, the hit/miss decision is ignored. The cycle qualification requires one 386 SX state. Since the fastest 386 SX access is two states, the second state can be used for bus watching.

When the 82385SX does not own the system bus, it monitors system bus cycles. If another master writes into main memory, the 82385SX latches the system address and executes a cache look-up to see if the altered main memory location resides in the cache. If so (a snoop hit), the cache entry is marked invalid in the cache directory. Since the directory is at most only being used every other state to qualify 386 SX accesses, snoop look-ups are interleaved between 386 SX local bus look-ups. The cache directory is time multiplexed between the 386 SX address and the latched system address. The result is that all snoops are caught and serviced without slowing down the 386 SX, even when running zero wait state hits on the 386 SX local bus.

1.3.7 CACHE FLUSH

The 82385SX offers a cache flush input. When activated, this signal causes the 82385SX to invalidate all data which had previously been cached. Specifically, all tag valid bits are cleared. (Refer to the 82385SX directory structure in Section 2.1.1.) There-

Table 1-1. 82385SX Response to 386™ SX Cycles

386 SX Bus Cycle Definition					82385SX Response when Decoded as Cacheable			82385SX Response when Decoded as Non-Cacheable			82385SX Response when Decoded as a 386SX Local Bus Access		
M/IO#	D/C#	W/R#	386 SX Cycle		Cache	Cache Directory	82385SX Local Bus	Cache	Cache Directory	82385SX Local Bus	Cache	Cache Directory	82385SX Local Bus
0	0	0	INT ACK	N/A	—	—	INT ACK	—	—	INT ACK	—	—	IDLE
0	0	1	UNDEFINED	N/A			UNDEFINED			UNDEFINED			IDLE
0	1	0	I/O READ	N/A	—	—	I/O READ	—	—	I/O READ	—	—	IDLE
0	1	1	I/O WRITE	N/A	—	—	I/O WRITE	—	—	I/O WRITE	—	—	IDLE
1	0	0	MEM CODE READ	HIT	CACHE READ	—	IDLE	—	—	MEM CODE READ	—	—	IDLE
				MISS	CACHE WRITE	DATA VALIDATION	MEM CODE READ						
1	0	1	HALT/ SHUTDOWN	N/A	—	—	HALT/ SHUTDOWN	—	—	HALT/ SHUTDOWN	—	—	IDLE
1	1	0	MEM DATA READ	HIT	CACHE READ	—	IDLE	—	—	MEM DATA READ	—	—	IDLE
				MISS	CACHE WRITE	DATA VALIDATION	MEM DATA READ						
1	1	1	MEM DATA WRITE	HIT	CACHE WRITE	—	MEM DATA WRITE	—	—	MEM DATA WRITE	—	—	IDLE
				MISS	—	—	MEM DATA WRITE						

NOTES:

- A dash (—) indicates that the cache and cache directory are unaffected. This table does not reflect how an access affects the LRU bit.
- An "IDLE" 82385SX Local Bus implies that this bus is available to other masters.
- The 82385SX's response to 387™ SX accesses is the same as when decoded as a 386 SX Local Bus Access.
- The only other operations that affect the cache directory are:

1. RESET or Cache Flush—all tag valid bits cleared.
2. Snoop Hit—corresponding line valid bit cleared.

fore, the cache is empty and subsequent cycles are misses until the 386 SX begins repeating the new accesses (hits). The primary use of the FLUSH input is for diagnostics and multi-processor support.

NOTE:
The use of this pin as a coherency mechanism may impact software transparency.

2.0 82385SX CACHE ORGANIZATION

The 82385SX supports two cache organizations: a simple direct mapped organization and a slightly more complex, higher performance two way set associative organization. The choice is made by strapping an 82385SX input (2W/D#) either high or low. This chapter describes the structure and operation of both organizations.

2.1 Direct Mapped Cache

2.1.1 DIRECT MAPPED CACHE STRUCTURE AND TERMINOLOGY

Figure 2-1 depicts the relationship between the 82385SX's internal cache directory, the external cache memory, and the 386 SX's physical address space. The 386 SX address space can conceptually be thought of as cache "pages" each being 8K words (16 Kbytes) deep. The page size matches the cache size. The cache can be further divided into 1024 (0 thru 1023) sets of eight words (8 x 16 bits). Each 16-bit word is called a "line". The unit of transfer between the main memory and cache is one line.

Each block in the external cache has an associated 19-bit entry in the 82385SX's internal cache directory. This entry has three components: a 10-bit "tag", a "tag valid" bit, and eight "line valid" bits. The tag acts as a main memory page number (10 tag bits support 2^{10} pages). For example, if line 9 of page 2 currently resides in the cache, then a binary 2 is stored in the Set 1 tag field. (For any 82385SX direct mapped cache page in main memory, Set 0 consists of lines 0–7, Set 1 consists of lines 8–15, etc. Line 9 is shaded in Figure 2-1.) An important characteristic of a direct mapped cache is that line 9 of any page can only reside in line 9 of the cache. All identical page offsets map to a single cache location.

The data in a cache set is considered valid or invalid depending on the status of its tag valid bit. If clear, the entire set is considered invalid. If true, an individual line within the set is considered valid or invalid depending on the status of its line valid bit.

The 82385SX sees the 386 SX address bus (A1–A23) as partitioned into three fields: a 10-bit "tag"

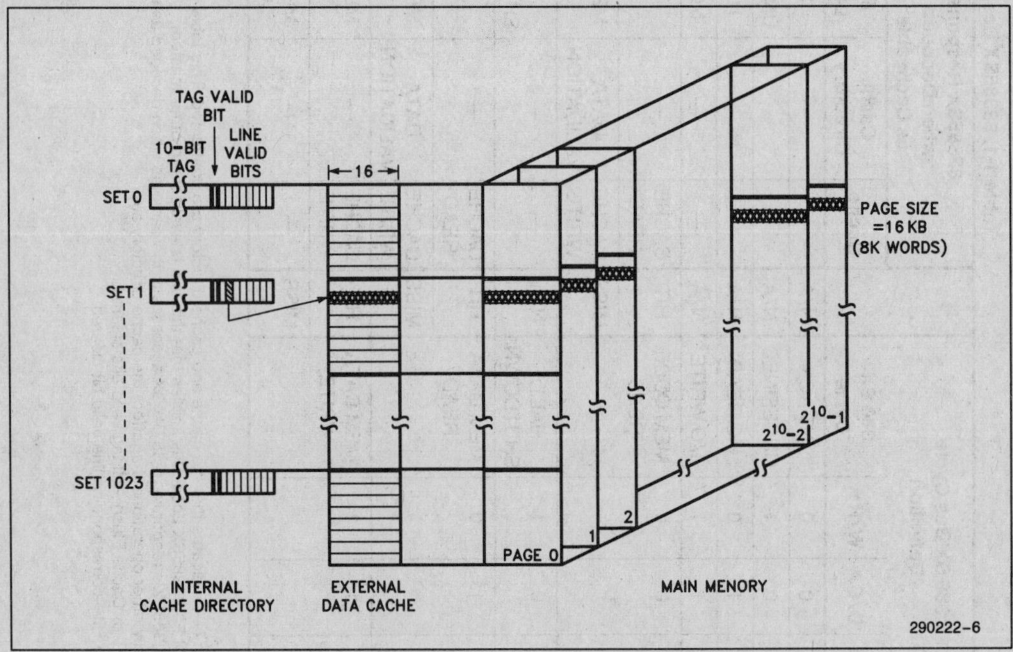

Figure 2-1. Direct Mapped Cache Organiztion

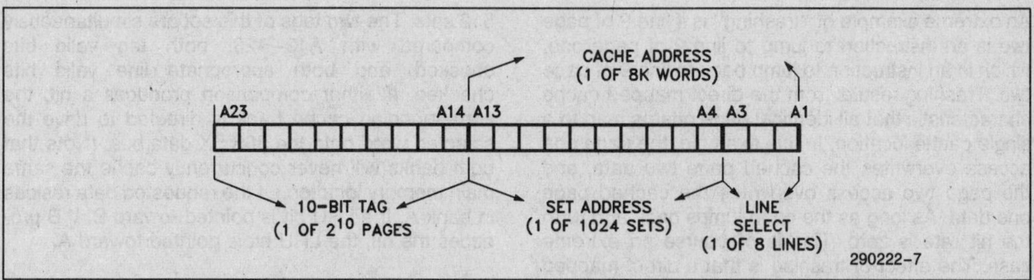

Figure 2-2. 386™ SX Address Bus Bit Fields—Direct Mapped Organization

field (A14–A23), a 10-bit "set address" field (A4–A13), and a 3-bit "line select" field (A1–A3). (See Figure 2-2.) The lower 13 address bits (A1–A13) also serve as the "cache address" which directly selects one of 8K words in the external cache.

2.1.2 DIRECT MAPPED CACHE OPERATION

The following is a description of the interaction between the 386 SX, cache, and cache directory.

2.1.2.1 Read Hits

When the 386 SX initiates a memory read cycle, the 82385SX uses the 10-bit set address to select one of 1024 directory entries, and the 3-bit line select field to select one of eight line valid bits within the entry. The 13-bit cache address selects the corresponding word in the cache. The 82385SX compares the 10-bit tag field (A14–A23 of the 386 SX access) with the tag stored in the selected directory entry. If the tag and upper address bits match, and if both the tag and appropriate line valid bits are set, the result is a hit, and the 82385SX directs the cache to drive the selected word onto the 386 SX data bus. A read hit does not alter the contents of the cache or directory.

2.1.2.2 Read Misses

A read miss can occur in two ways. The first is known as a "line" miss, and occurs when the tag and upper address bits match and the tag valid bit is set, but the line valid bit is clear. The second is called a "tag" miss, and occurs when either the tag and upper address bits do not match, or the tag valid bit is clear. (The line valid bit is a "don't care" in a tag miss.) In both cases, the 82385SX forwards the 386 SX reference to the system, and as the returning data is fed to the 386 SX, it is written into the cache and validated in the cache directory.

In a line miss, the incoming data is validated simply by setting the previously clear line valid bit. In a tag miss, the upper address bits overwrite the previously stored tag, the tag valid bit is set, the appropriate line valid bit is set, and the other seven line valid bits are cleared. Subsequent tag hits with line misses will only set the appropriate line valid bit. (Any data associated with the previous tag is no longer considered resident in the cache.)

2.1.2.3 Other Operations That Affect the Cache and Cache Directory

The other operations that affect the cache and/or directory are write hits, snoop hits, cache flushes, and 82385SX resets. In a write hit, the cache is updated along with main memory, but the directory is unaffected. In a snoop hit, the cache is unaffected, but the affected line is invalidated by clearing its line valid bit in the directory. Both an 82385SX reset and cache flush clear all tag valid bits.

When a 386 SX CPU/82385SX system "wakes up" upon reset, all tag valid bits are clear. At this point, a read miss is the only mechanism by which main memory data is copied into the cache and validated in the cache directory. Assume an early 386 SX code access seeks (for the first time) line 9 of page 2. Since the tag valid bit is clear, the access is a tag miss, and the data is fetched from main memory. Upon return, the data is fed to the 386 SX and simultaneously written into line 9 of the cache. The set directory entry is updated to show this line as valid. Specifically, the tag and appropriate line valid bits are set, the remaining seven line valid bits cleared, and binary 2 written into the tag. Since code is sequential in nature, the 386 SX will likely next want line 10 of page 2, then line 11, and so on. If the 386 SX sequentially fetches the next six lines, these fetches will be line misses, and as each is fetched from main memory and written into the cache, its corresponding line valid bit is set. This is the basic flow of events that fills the cache with valid data. Only after a piece of data has been copied into the cache and validated can it be accessed in a zero wait state read hit. Also, a cache entry must have been validated before it can be subsequently altered by a write hit, or invalidated by a snoop hit.

An extreme example of "trashing" is if line 9 of page two is an instruction to jump to line 9 of page one, which is an instruction to jump back to line 9 of page two. Trashing results from the direct mapped cache characteristic that all identical page offsets map to a single cache location. In this example, the page one access overwrites the cached page two data, and the page two access overwrites the cached page one data. As long as the code jumps back and forth the hit rate is zero. This is of course an extreme case. The effect of trashing is that a direct mapped cache exhibits a slightly reduced overall hit rate as compared to a set associative cache of the same size.

2.2 Two Way Set Associative Cache

2.2.1 TWO WAY SET ASSOCIATIVE CACHE STRUCTURE AND TERMINOLOGY

Figure 2-3 illustrates the relationship between the directory, cache, and 386 SX address space. Whereas the direct mapped cache is organized as one bank of 8K words, the two way set associative cache is organized as two banks (A and B) of 4K words each. The page size is halved, and the number of pages doubled. (Note the extra tag bit.) The cache now has 512 sets in each bank. (Two banks times 512 sets gives a total of 1024. The structure can be thought of as two half-sized direct mapped caches in parallel.) The performance advantage over a direct mapped cache is that all identical page offsets map to two cache locations instead of one, reducing the potential for thrashing. The 82385SX's partitioning of the 386 SX address bus is depicted in Figure 2-4.

2.2.2 LRU REPLACEMENT ALGORITHM

The two way set associative directory has an additional feature: the "least recently used" or LRU bit. In the event of a read miss, either bank A or bank B will be updated with new data. The LRU bit flags the candidate for replacement. Statistically, of two blocks of data, the block most recently used is the block most likely to be needed again in the near future. By flagging the least recently used block, the 82385SX ensures that the cache block replaced is the least likely to have data needed by the CPU.

2.2.3 TWO WAY SET ASSOCIATIVE CACHE OPERATION

2.2.3.1 Read Hits

When the 386 SX initiates a memory read cycle, the 82385SX uses the 9-bit set address to select one of 512 sets. The two tags of this set are simultaneously compared with A13–A23, both tag valid bits checked, and both appropriate line valid bits checked. If either comparison produces a hit, the corresponding cache bank is directed to drive the selected word onto the 386 SX data bus. (Note that both banks will never concurrently cache the same main memory location.) If the requested data resides in bank A, the LRU bit is pointed toward B. If B produces the hit, the LRU bit is pointed toward A.

2.2.3.2 Read Misses

As in direct mapped operation, a read miss can be either a line or tag miss. Let's start with a tag miss example. Assume the 386 SX seeks line 9 of page 2, and that neither the A or B directory produces a tag match. Assume also, as indicated in Figure 2-3, that the LRU bit points to A. As the data returns from main memory, it is loaded into offset 9 of bank A. Concurrently, this data is validated by updating the set 1 directory entry for bank A. Specifically, the upper address bits overwite the previous tag, the tag valid bit is set, the appropriate line valid bit is set, and the other seven line valid bits cleared. Since this data is the most recently used, the LRU bit is turned toward B. No change to bank B occurs.

If the next 386 SX request is line 10 of page two, the result will be a line miss. As the data returns from main memory, it will be written into offset 10 of bank A (tag hit/line miss in bank A), and the appropriate line valid bit will be set. A line miss in one bank will cause the LRU bit to point to the other bank. In this example, however, the LRU bit has already been turned toward B.

2.2.3.3 Other Operations That Affect the Cache and Cache Directory

Other operations that affect the cache and cache directory are write hits, snoop hits, cache flushes, and 82385SX resets. A write hit updates the cache along with main memory. If directory A detects the hit, bank A is updated. If directory B detects the hit, bank B is updated. If one bank is updated, the LRU bit is pointed towards the other.

If a snoop hit invalidates an entry, for example, in cache bank A, the corresponding LRU bit is pointed toward A. This insures that invalid data is the prime candidate for replacement in a read miss. Finally, resets and flushes behave just as they do in a direct mapped cache, clearing all tag valid bits.

3.0 82385SX PIN DESCRIPTION

The 82385SX creates the 82385SX local bus, which is a functional 386 SX interface. To facilitate under-

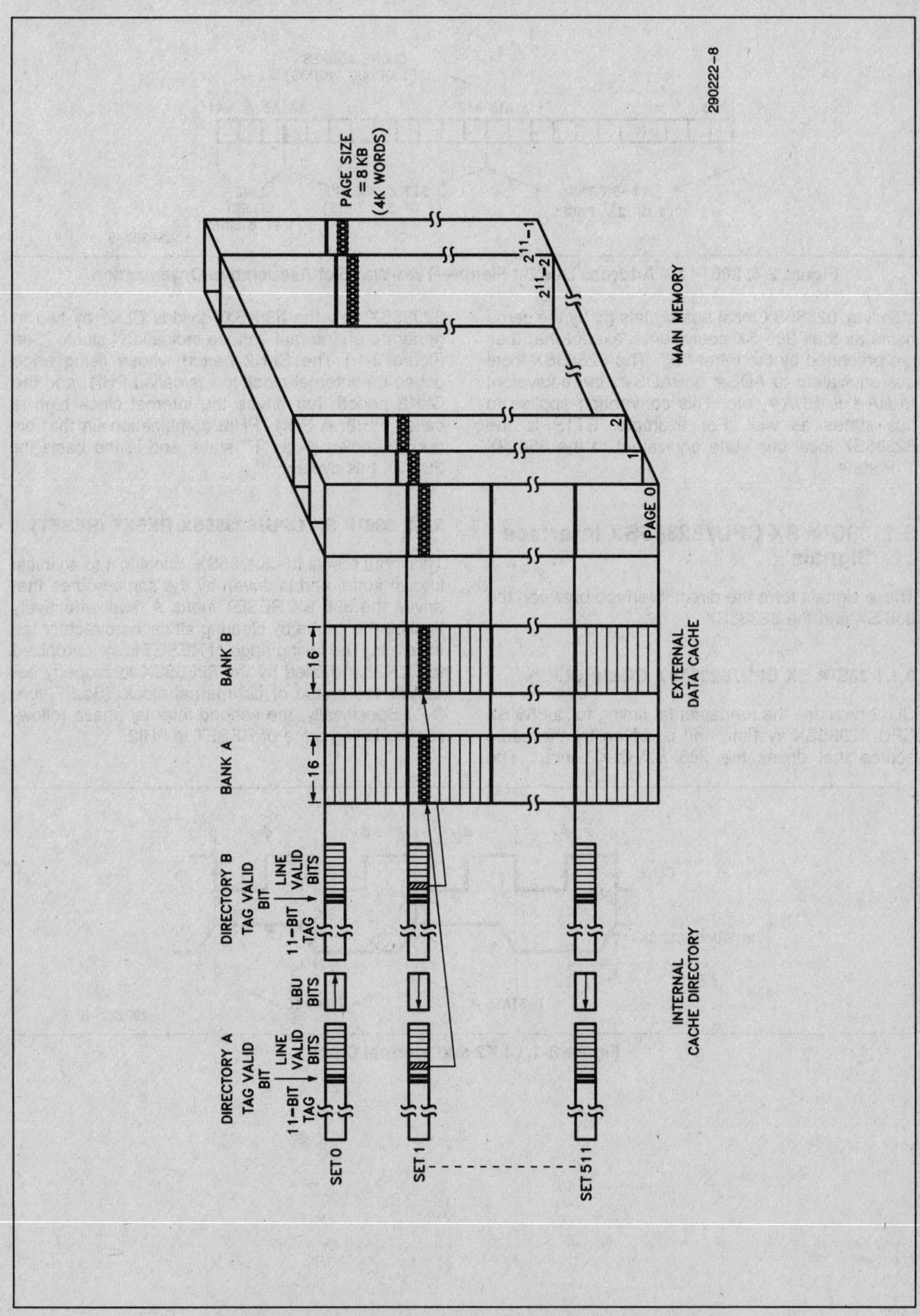

Figure 2-3. Two-Way Set Associative Cache Organization

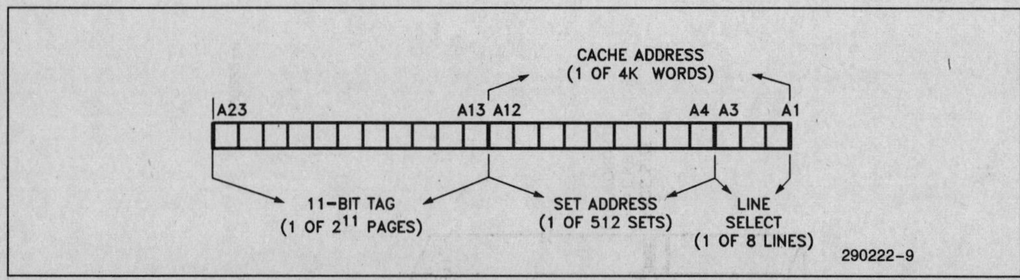

Figure 2-4. 386™ SX Address Bus Bit Fields—Two-Way Set Associative Organization

standing, 82385SX local bus signals go by the same name as their 386 SX equivalents, except that they are preceded by the letter "B". The 82385SX local bus equivalent to ADS# is BADS#, the equivalent to NA# is BNA#, etc. This convention applies to bus states as well. For example, BT1P is the 82385SX local bus state equivalent to the 386 SX T1P state.

3.1 386™ SX CPU/82385SX Interface Signals

These signals form the direct interface between the 386 SX and the 82385SX.

3.1.1 386™ SX CPU/82385SX Clock (CLK2)

CLK2 provides the fundamental timing for a 386 SX CPU/82385SX system, and is driven by the same source that drives the 386 SX CLK2 input. The 82385SX, like the 386 SX, divides CLK2 by two to generate an internal "phase indication" clock. (See Figure 3-1.) The CLK2 period whose rising edge drives the internal clock low is called PHI1, and the CLK2 period that drives the internal clock high is called PHI2. A PHI1-PHI2 combination (in that order) is known as a "T" state, and is the basis for 386 SX bus cycles.

3.1.2 386™ SX CPU/82385SX RESET (RESET)

This input resets the 82385SX, bringing it to an initial known state, and is driven by the same source that drives the 386 SX RESET input. A reset effectively flushes the cache by clearing all cache directory tag valid bits. The falling edge of RESET is synchronized to CLK2, and used by the 82385SX to properly establish the phase of its internal clock. (See Figure 3-2.) Specifically, the second internal phase following the falling edge of RESET is PHI2.

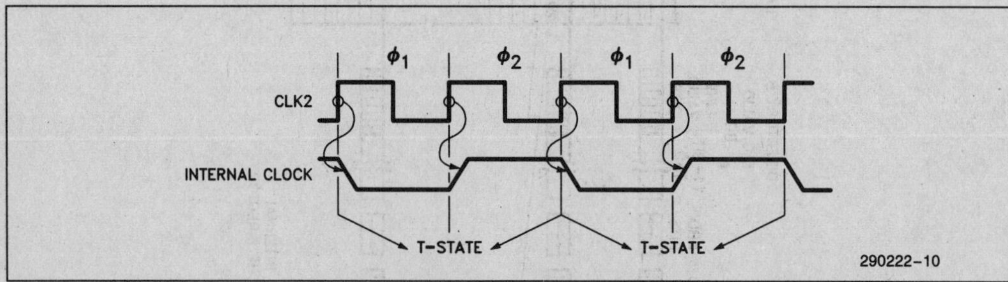

Figure 3-1. CLK2 and Internal Clock

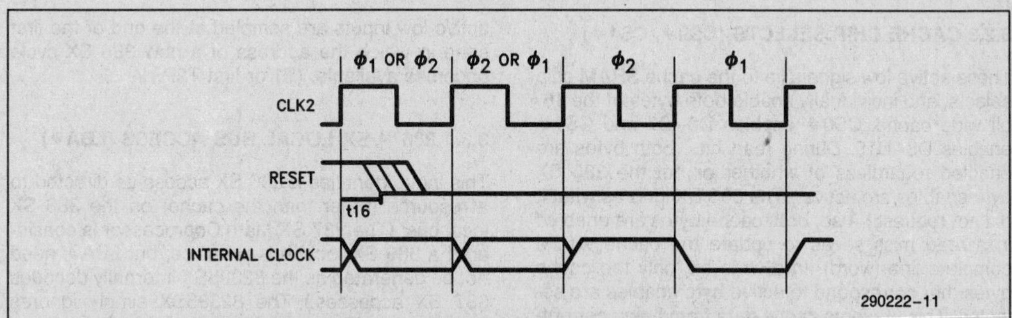

Figure 3-2. Reset/Internal Phase Relationship

3.1.3 386™ SX CPU/82385SX ADDRESS BUS (A1–A23), BYTE ENABLES (BHE#, BLE#), AND CYCLE DEFINITION SIGNALS (M/IO#, D/C#, W/R#, LOCK#)

The 82385SX directly connects to these 386 SX outputs. The 386 SX address bus is used in the cache directory comparison to see if data referenced by 386 SX resides in the cache, and the byte enables inform the 82385SX as to which portions of the data bus are involved in a 386 SX cycle. The cycle definition signals are decoded by the 82385SX to determine the type of cycle the 386 SX is executing.

3.1.4 386™ SX CPU/82385SX ADDRESS STATUS (ADS#) AND READY INPUT (READYI#)

ADS#, a 386 SX output, tells the 82385SX that new address and cycle definition information is available. READYI#, an input to both the 386 SX (via the 386 SX READY# input pin) and 82385SX, indicates the completion of a 386 SX bus cycle. ADS# and READYI# are used to track the 386 SX bus state.

3.1.5 386™ SX NEXT ADDRESS REQUEST (NA#)

This 82385SX output controls 386 SX pipelining. It can be tied directly to the 386 SX NA# input, or it can be logically "AND"ed with other 386 SX local bus next address requests.

3.1.6 READY OUTPUT (READYO#) AND BUS READY ENABLE (BRDYEN#)

The 82385SX directly terminates all but two types of 386 SX bus cycles with its READYO# output. 386 SX local bus cycles must be terminated by the local device being accessed. This includes devices decoded using the 82385SX LBA# signal and 387 accesses. The other cycles not directly terminated by the 82385SX are 82385SX local bus reads, specifically cache read misses and non-cacheable reads. (Recall that the 82385SX forwards and runs such cycles on the 82385SX bus.) In these cycles the signal that terminates the 82385SX local bus access is BREADY# which is gated through to the 386 SX local bus such that the 386 SX and 82385SX local bus cycles are concurrently terminated. BRDYEN# is used to gate the BREADY# signal to the 386 SX.

3.2 Cache Control Signals

These 82385SX outputs control the external 16 KB cache data memory.

3.2.1 CACHE ADDRESS LATCH ENABLE (CALEN)

This signal controls the latch (typically an F or AS series 74373) that resides between the low order 386 SX address bits and the cache SRAM address inputs. (The outputs of this latch are the "cache address" described in the previous chapter.) When CALEN is high the latch is transparent. The falling edge of CALEN latches the current inputs which remain applied to the cache data memory until CALEN returns to an active high state.

3.2.2 CACHE TRANSMIT/RECEIVE (CT/R#)

This signal defines the direction of an optional data transceiver (typically an F or AS series 74245) between the cache and 386 SX data bus. When high, the transceiver is pointed towards the 386 SX local data bus (the SRAMs are output enabled). When low, the transceiver points towards the cache data memory. A transceiver is required if the cache is designed with SRAMs that lack an output enable control. A transceiver may also be desirable in a system that has a heavily loaded 386 SX local data bus. These devices are not necessary when using SRAMs which incorporate an output enable.

3.2.3 CACHE CHIP SELECTS (CS0#, CS1#)

These active low signals tie to the cache SRAM chip selects, and individually enable both bytes of the 16-bit wide cache. CS0# enables D0–D7 and CS1# enables D8–D15. During read hits, both bytes are enabled regardless of whether or not the 386 SX byte enables are active. (The 386 SX ignores what it did not request.) Also, both cache bytes are enabled in a read miss so as to update the cache with a complete line (word). In a write hit, only the cache bytes that correspond to active byte enables are selected. This prevents cache data from being corrupted in a partial word write.

3.2.4 CACHE OUTPUT ENABLES (COEA#, COEB#) AND WRITE ENABLES (CWEA#, CWEB#)

COEA# and COEB# are active low signals which tie to the cache SRAM or Transceiver output enables and respectively enable cache bank A or B. The state of DEFOE# (define cache output enable), an 82385SX configuration input, determines the functional definition of COEA# and COEB#.

If DEFOE# = V_{IL}, in a two-way set associative cache, either COEA# or COEB# is active during read hit cycles only, depending on which bank is selected. In a direct mapped cache, both are activated during read hits, so the designer is free to use either one. This COEx# definition best suits cache SRAMs with output enables.

If DEFOE# = V_{IH}, COEx# is active during a read hit, read miss (cache update) and write hit cycles only. This COEx# definition best suits cache SRAMs without output enables. In such systems, transceivers are needed and their output enables must be active for writing, as well as reading, the cache SRAMs.

CWEA# and CWEB# are active low signals which tie to the cache SRAM write enables, and respectively enable cache bank A or B to receive data from the 386 SX data bus (386 SX write hit or read miss update). In a two-way set associative cache, one or the other is enabled in a read miss or write hit. In a direct mapped cache, both are activated, so the designer is free to use either one.

The various cache configurations supported by the 82385SX are described in Section 4.2.1.

3.3 386™ SX Local Bus Decode Inputs

These 82385SX inputs are generated by decoding the 386 SX address and cycle definition lines. These active low inputs are sampled at the end of the first state in which the address of a new 386 SX cycle becomes available. (T1 or first T2P.)

3.3.1 386™ SX LOCAL BUS ACCESS (LBA#)

This input identifies a 386 SX access as directed to a resource (other than the cache) on the 386 SX local bus. (The 387 SX Math Coprocessor is considered a 386 SX local bus resource, but LBA# need not be generated as the 82385SX internally decodes 387 SX accesses.) The 82385SX simply ignores these cycles. They are neither forwarded to the system nor do they affect the cache or cache directory. Note that LBA# has priority over all other types of cycles. If LBA# is asserted, the cycle is interpreted as a 386 SX local bus access, regardless of the cycle type or status of NCA#. This allows any 386 SX cycle (memory, I/O, interrupt acknowledge, etc.) to be kept on the 386 SX local bus if desired.

3.3.2 NON-CACHEABLE ACCESS (NCA#)

This active low input identifies a 386 SX cycle as non-cacheable. The 82385SX forwards non-cacheable cycles to the 82385SX local bus and runs them. The cache and cache directory are unaffected.

NCA# allows a designer to set aside a portion of main memory as non-cacheable. Potential applications include memory-mapped I/O and systems where multiple masters access dual ported memory via different busses. Another possibility makes use of the 386 SX D/C# output. The 82385SX by default implements a unified code and data cache, but driving NCA# directly by D/C# creates a data only cache. If D/C# is inverted first, the result is a code only cache.

3.4 82385SX Local Bus Interface Signals

The 82385SX presents an "386 SX-like" front end to the system, and the signals discussed in this section are 82385SX local bus equivalents to actual 386 SX signals. These signals are named with respect to their 386 SX counterparts, but with the letter "B" appended to the front.

Note that the 82385SX itself does not have equivalent output signals to the 386 SX data bus (D0–D15) address bus (A1–A23), and cycle definition signals (M/IO#, D/C#, W/R#). The 82385SX data bus (BD0–BD15) is actually the system side of a latching transceiver, and the 82385SX address bus and cycle definition signals (BA1–BA23, BM/IO#, BD/C#,

BW/R#) are the outputs of an edge-triggered latch. The signals that control this data transceiver and address latch are discussed in Section 3.5.

3.4.1 82385SX BUS BYTE ENABLES (BBHE#, BBLE#)

BBHE# and BBLE# are the 82385SX local bus equivalents to the 386 SX byte enables. In a cache read miss, the 82385SX drives both signals low, regardless of whether or not the 386 SX byte enables are active. This insures that a complete line (word) is fetched from main memory for the cache update. In all other 82385SX local bus cycles, the 82385SX duplicates the logic levels of the 386 SX byte enables. The 82385SX tri-states these outputs when it is not the current bus master.

3.4.2 82385SX BUS LOCK (BLOCK#)

BLOCK# is the 82385SX local bus equivalent to the 386 SX LOCK# output, and distinguishes between locked and unlocked cycles. When the 386 SX runs a locked sequence of cycles (and LBA# is negated), the 82385SX forwards and runs the sequence on the 82385SX local bus, regardless of whether any locations referenced in the sequence reside in the cache. A read hit will be run as if it is a read miss, but a write hit will update the cache as well as being completed to system memory. In keeping with 386 SX behavior, the 82385SX does not allow another master to interrupt the sequence. BLOCK# is tri-stated when the 82385SX is not the current bus master.

3.4.3 82385SX BUS ADDRESS STATUS (BADS#)

BADS# is the 82385SSX local bus equivalent of ADS#, and indicates that a valid address (BA1–BA23, BBHE#, BBLE#) and cycle definition (BM/IO#, BW/R#, BD/C#) are available. It is asserted in BT1 and BT2P states, and is tri-stated when the 82385SX does not own the bus.

3.4.4 82385SX BUS READY INPUT (BREADY#)

82385SX local bus cycles are terminated by BREADY#, just as 386 SX cycles are terminated by the 386 SX READY# input. In 82385SX local bus read cycles, BREADY# is gated by BRDYEN# onto the 386 SX local bus, such that it terminates both the 386 SX and 82385SX local bus cycles.

3.4.5 82385SX BUS NEXT ADDRESS REQUEST (BNA#)

BNA# is the 82385SX local bus equivalent to the 386 SX NA# input, and indicates that the system is prepared to accept a pipelined address and cycle definition. If BNA# is asserted and the new cycle information is available, the 82385SX begins a pipelined cycle on the 82385SX local bus.

3.5 82385SX Bus Data Transceiver and Address Latch Control Signals

The 82385SX data bus is the system side of a latching transceiver (typically for F or AS series 74646), and the 82385SX address bus and cycle definition signals are the outputs of an edge-triggered latch (F or AS series 74374). The following is a discussion of the 82385SX outputs that control these devices. An important characteristic of these signals and the devices they control is that they ensure that BD0–BD15, BA1–BA23, BM/IO#, BD/C# and BW/R# reproduce the functionality and timing behavior of their 386 SX equivalents.

3.5.1 LOCAL DATA STROBE (LDSTB), DATA OUTPUT ENABLE (DOE#), AND BUS TRANSMIT/RECEIVE (BT/R#)

These signals control the latching data transceiver. BT/R# defines the transceiver direction. When high, the transceiver drives the 82385SX data bus in write cycles. When low, the transceiver drives the 386 SX data bus in 82385SX local bus read cycles. DOE# enables the transceiver outputs.

The rising edge of LDSTB latches the 386 SX data bus in all write cycles. The interaction of this signal and the latching transceiver is used to perform the 82385SX's posted write capability.

3.5.2 BUS ADDRESS CLOCK PULSE (BACP) AND BUS ADDRESS OUTPUT ENABLE (BAOE#)

These signals control the latch that drives BA1–BA23, BM/IO#, BW/R#, and BD/C#. In any 386 SX cycle that is forwarded to the 82385SX local bus, the rising edge of BACP latches the 386 SX address and cycle definition signals. BAOE# enables the latch outputs when the 82385SX is the current bus master and disables them otherwise.

3.6 Status and Control Signals

3.6.1 CACHE MISS INDICATION (MISS#)

This output accompanies cacheable read and write miss cycles. This signal transitions to its active low state when the 82385SX determines that a cacheable 386 SX access is a miss. Its timing behavior

4

follows that of the 82385SX local bus cycle definition signals (BM/IO#, BD/C#, BW/R#) so that it becomes available with BADS# in BT1 or the first BT2P. MISS# is floated when the 82385SX does not own the bus, such that multiple 82385SX's can share the same node in multi-cache systems. (As discussed in Chapter 7, this signal also serves a reserved function in testing the 82385SX.)

3.6.2 WRITE BUFFER STATUS (WBS)

The latching data transceiver is also known as the "posted write buffer". WBS indicates that this buffer contains data that has not yet been written to the system even though the 386 SX may have begun its next cycle. It is activated when 386 SX data is latched, and deactivated when the corresponding 82385SX local bus write cycle is completed (BREADY#). (As discussed in Chapter 7, this signal also serves a reserved function in testing the 82385SX.)

WBS can serve several functions. In multi-processor applications, it can act as a coherency mechanism by informing a bus arbiter that it should let a write cycle run on the system bus so that main memory has the latest data. If any other 82385SX cache subsystems are on the bus, they will monitor the cycle via their bus watching mechanisms. Any 82385SX that detects a snoop hit will invalidate the corresponding entry in its local cache.

3.6.3 CACHE FLUSH (FLUSH)

When activated, this signal causes the 82385SX to clear all of its directory tag valid bits, effectively flushing the cache. (As discussed in Chapter 7, this signal also serves a reserved function in testing the 82385SX.) The primary use of the FLUSH input is for diagnostics and multi-processor support. The use of this pin as a coherency mechanism may impact software transparency.

The FLUSH input must be held active for at least 4 CLK (8 CLK2) cycles to complete the flush sequence. If FLUSH is still active after 4 CLK cycles, any accesses to the cache will be misses and the cache will not be updated (since FLUSH is active).

3.7 Bus Arbitration Signals (BHOLD and BHLDA)

In master mode, BHOLD is an input that indicates a request by a slave device for bus ownership. The 82385SX acknowledges this request via its BHLDA output. (These signals function identically to the 386 SX HOLD and HLDA signals.)

The roles of BHOLD and BHLDA are reversed for an 82385SX in slave mode. BHOLD is now an output indicating a request for bus ownership, and BHLDA an input indicating that the request has been granted.

3.8 Coherency (Bus Watching) Support Signals (SA1–SA23, SSTB#, SEN)

These signals form the 82385SX's bus watching interface. The Snoop Address Bus (SA1–SA23) connects to the system address lines if masters reside at both the system and 82385SX local bus levels, or the 82385SX local bus address lines if masters reside only at the 82385SX local bus level. Snoop Strobe (SSTB#) indicates that a valid address is on the snoop address inputs. Snoop Enable (SEN) indicates that the cycle is a write. In a system with masters only at the 82385SX local bus level, SA1–SA23, SSTB#, and SEN can be driven respectively by BA1–BA23, BADS#, and BW/R# without any support circuitry.

3.9 Configuration Inputs (2W/D#, M/S#, DEFOE#)

These signals select the configurations supported by the 82385SX. They are hardware strap options and must not be changed dynamically. 2W/D# (2-Way/Direct Mapped Select) selects a two-way set associative cache when tied high, or a direct mapped cache when tied low. M/S# (Master/Slave Select) chooses between master mode (M/S# high) and slave mode (M/S# low). DEFOE# defines the functionality of the 82385SX cache output enables (COEA# and COEB#). DEFOE# allows the 82385SX to interface to SRAMs with output enables (DEFOE# low) or to SRAMs requiring transceivers (DEFOE# high).

3.10 Reserved Pins (RES)

Some pins on the 82385SX are reserved for internal testing and future cache features. To assure compatibility and functionality, these reserved pins must be configured as shown in Table 3.10.1.

Table 3.10.1. Reserved Pin Connections

PGA Pin Location	PQFP Pin Location	Logic Level
A12	1	High
A13	131	High
B10	7	High
B11	3	High
B12	132	High
C10	4	High
C11	2	High
G13	117	High
H12	110	High
J3	60	High
J14	109	High
K1	58	High
K2	59	High
K3	62	High
L1	61	High
L2	63	High
L3	64	High
L12	100	No Connect
L14	102	High
M13	101	No Connect
N6	75	No Connect
P5	76	No Connect

4.0 386 SX LOCAL BUS INTERFACE

The following is a detailed description of how the 82385SX interfaces to the 386 SX and to 386 SX local bus resources. Items specifically addressed are the interfaces to the 386 SX, the cache SRAMs, and the 387 SX Math Coprocessor.

The many timing diagrams in this and the next chapter provide insight into the dual pipelined bus structure of a 386 SX CPU/82385SX system. It's important to realize, however, that one need not know every possible cycle combination to use the 82385SX. The interface is simple, and the dual bus operation invisible to the 386 SX and system. To facilitate discussion of the timing diagrams, several conventions have been adopted. Refer to Figure 4-2A, and note that 386 SX bus cycles, 386 SX bus states, and 82385SX bus states are identified along the top. All states can be identified by the "frame numbers" along the bottom. The cycles in Figure 4-2A include a cache read hit (CRDH), a cache read miss (CRDM), and a write (WT). WT represents any write, cacheable or not. When necessary to distinguish cacheable writes, a write hit goes by CWTH and a write miss by CWTM. Non-cacheable system reads go by SBRD. Also, it is assumed that system bus pipelining occurs even though the BNA# signal is not shown. When the system pipeline begins is a function of the system bus controller.

386 SX bus cycles can be tracked by ADS# and READYI#, and 82385SX cycles by BADS# and BREADY#. These four signals are thus a natural choice to help track parallel bus activity. Note in the timing diagrams that 386 SX cycles are numbered using ADS# and READYI#, and 82385SX cycles using BADS# and BREADY#. For example, when the address of the first 386 SX cycle becomes available, the corresponding assertion of ADS# is marked "1", and the READYI# pulse that terminates the cycle is marked "1" as well. Whenever a 386 SX cycle is forwarded to the system, its number is forwarded as well so that the corresponding 82385SX bus cycle can be tracked by BADS# and BREADY#.

The "N" value in the timing diagrams is the assumed number of main memory wait states inserted in a non-pipelined 82385SX bus cycle. For example, a non-pipelined access to N=2 memory requires a total of four bus states, while a pipelined access requires three. (The pipeline advantage effectively hides one main memory wait state.)

4.1 Processor Interface

4

This section presents the 386 SX CPU/82385SX hardware interface and discusses the interaction and timing of this interface. Also addressed is how to decode the 386 SX address bus to generate the 82385SX inputs LBA# and NCA#. (Recall that LBA# allows memory and/or I/O space to be set aside for 386 SX local bus resources; and NCA# allows system memory to be set aside as non-cacheable.)

4.1.1 HARDWARE INTERFACE

Figure 4-1 is a diagram of a 386 SX CPU/82385SX system, which can be thought of as three distinct interfaces. The first is the 386 SX CPU/82385SX interface (including the Ready Logic). The second is the cache interface, as depicted by the cache control bus in the upper left corner of Figure 4-1. The third is the 82385SX bus interface, which includes both direct connects and signals that control the 74374 address/cycle definition latch and 74646 latching data transceiver. (The 82385SX bus interface is the subject of the next chapter.)

As seen in Figure 4-1, the 386 SX CPU/82385SX interface is a straightforward connection. The only necessary support logic is that required to sum all ready sources.

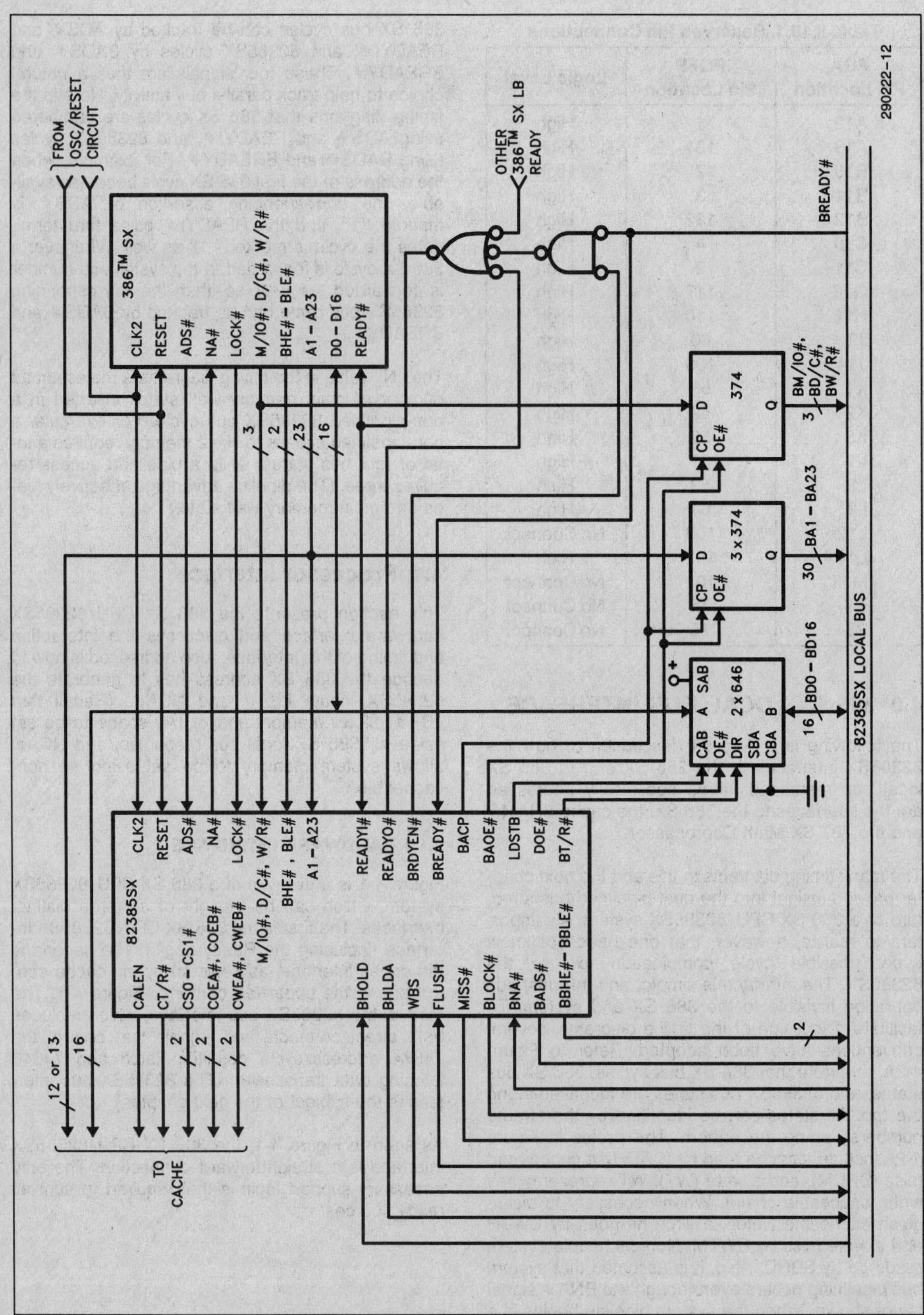

Figure 4-1. 386™ SX CPU/82385SX Interface

4.1.2 READY GENERATION

Note in Figure 4-1 that the ready logic consists of two gates. The upper three-input AND gate (shown as a negative logic OR) sums all 386 SX local bus ready sources. One such source is the 82385SX READYO# output, which terminates read hits and posted writes. The output of this gate drives the 386 SX READY# input and is monitored by the 82385SX (via READYI#) to track the 386 SX bus state.

When the 82385SX forwards a 386 SX read cycle to the 82385SX bus (cache read miss or non-cacheable read), it does not directly terminate the cycle via READYO#. Instead, the 386 SX and 82385SX bus cycles are concurrently terminated by a system ready source. This is the purpose of the additional two-input OR gate (negative logic AND) in Figure 4-1. When the 82385SX forwards a read to the 82385SX bus, it asserts BRDYEN# which enables the system ready signal (BREADY#) to directly terminate the 386 SX bus cycle.

Figure 4-2A and 4-2B illustrate the behavior of the signals involved in ready generation. Note in cycle 1 of Figure 4-2A that the 82385SX READYO# directly terminates the hit cycle. In cycle 2, READYO# is not activated. Instead the 82385SX BRDYEN# is activated in BT2, BT2P, or BT2I states such that BREADY# can concurrently terminate the 386 SX and 82385SX bus cycles (frame 6). Cycle 3 is a posted write. The write data becomes available in T1P (frame 7), and the address, data, and cycle definition of the write are latched in T2 (frame 8). The 386 SX cycle is terminated by READYO# in frame 8 with no wait states. The 82385SX, however, sees the write cycle through to completion on the 82385SX bus where it is terminated in frame 10 by BREADY#. In this case, the BREADY# signal is not gated through to the 386 SX. Refer to Figures 4-2A and 4-2B for clarification.

4.1.3 NA# AND 386 SX LOCAL BUS PIPELINING

Cycle 1 of Figure 4-2A is a typical cache read hit. The 386 SX address becomes available in T1, and the 82385SX uses this address to determine if the referenced data resides in the cache. The cache look-up is completed and the cycle qualified as a hit or miss in T1. If the data resides in the cache, the cache is directed to drive the 386 SX data bus, and the 82385SX drives its READYO# output so the cycle can be terminated at the end of the first T2 with no wait states.

Although cycle 2 starts out like cycle 1, at the end of T1 (frame 3), it is qualified as a miss and forwarded to the 82385SX bus. The 82385SX bus cycle begins one state after the 386 SX bus cycle, implying a one wait state overhead associated with cycle 2 due to the look-up. When the 82385SX encounters the miss, it immediately asserts NA#, which puts the 386 SX into pipelined mode. Once in pipelined mode, the 82385SX is able to qualify a 386 SX cycle using the 386 SX pipelined address and control signals. The result is that the cache look-up state is hidden in all but the first of a contiguous sequence of read misses. This is shown in the first two cycles, both read misses, of Figure 4-2B. The CPU sees the look-up state in the first cycle, but not in the second. In fact, the second miss requires a total of only two states, as not only does 386 SX pipelining hide the look-up state, but system pipelining hides one of the main memory wait states. (System level pipelining via BNA# is discussed in the next chapter.) Several characteristics of the 82385SX's pipelining of the 386 SX are as follows:

- The above discussion applies to all system reads, not just cache read misses.
- The 82385SX provides the fastest possible switch to pipelining, T1-T2-T2P. The exception to this is when a system read follows a posted write. In this case, the sequence is T1-T2-T2-T2P. (Refer to cycle 4 of Figure 4-2A.) The number of T2 states is dependent on the number of main memory wait states.
- Refer to the read hit in Figure 4-2A (cycle 1), and note that NA# is actually asserted before the end of T1, before the hit/miss decision is made. This is of no consequence since even though NA# is sampled active in T2, the activation of READYO# in the same T2 renders NA# a "don't care". NA# is asserted in this manner to meet 386 SX timing requirements and to insure the fastest possible switch to pipelined mode.
- All read hits and the majority of writes can be serviced by the 82385SX with zero wait states in non-pipelined mode, and the 82385SX accordingly attempts to run all such cycles in non-pipelined mode. An exception is seen in the hit cycles (cycles 3 and 4) of Figure 4-2B. The 82385SX does not know soon enough that cycle 3 is a hit, and thus sustains the pipeline. The result is that three sequential hits are required before the 386 SX is totally out of pipelined mode. (The three hits look like T1P-T2P, T1P-T2, T1-T2.) Note that this does not occur if the number of main memory wait states is equal to or greater than two.

As far as the design is concerned, NA# is generally tied directly to the 386 SX NA# input. However, other local NA# sources may be logically "AND"ed with the 82385SX NA# output if desired. It is essential, however, that no device other than the 82385SX drive the 386 SX NA# input unless that device re-

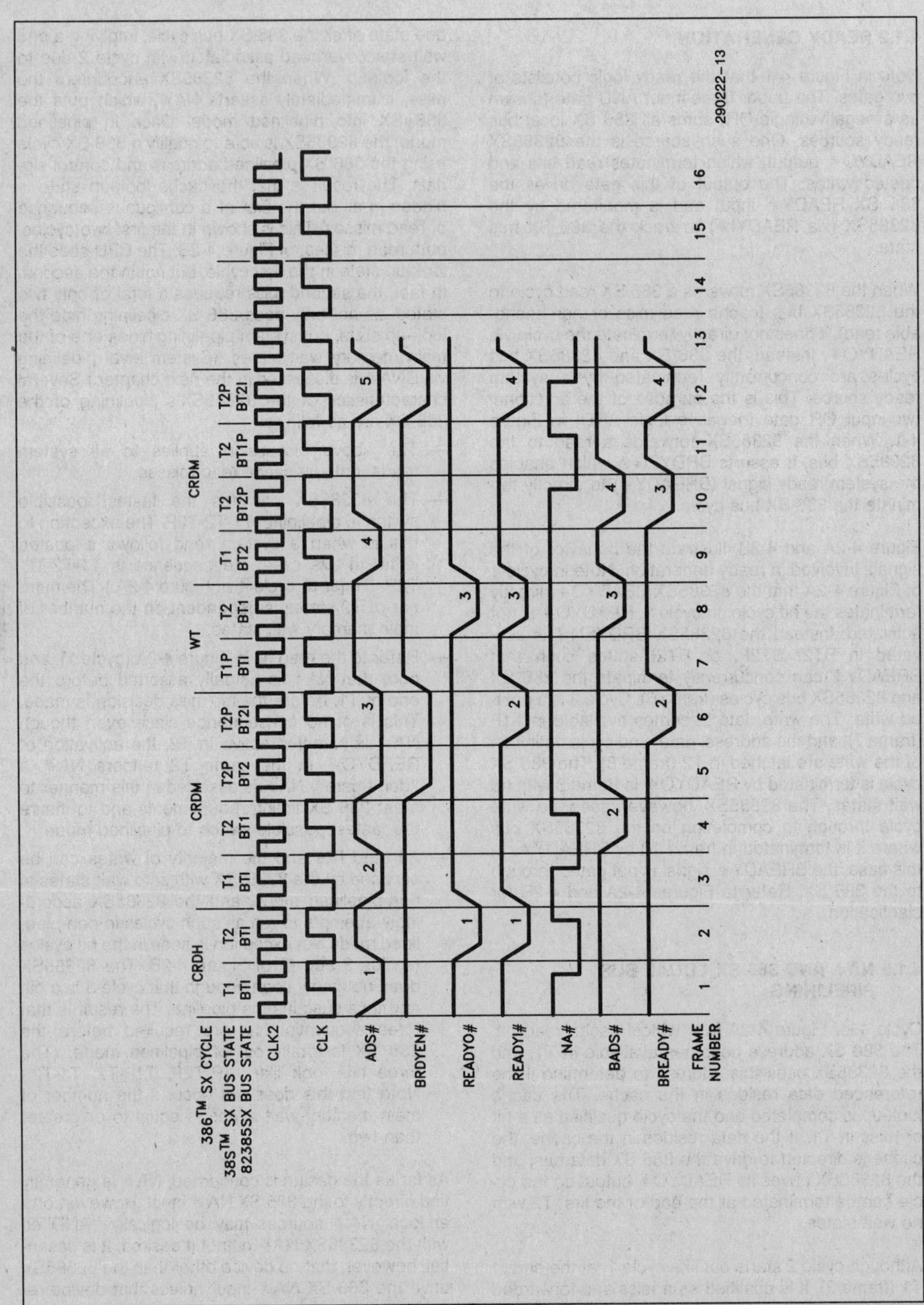

Figure 4-2A. READYO#, BRDYEN#, and NA# (N = 1)

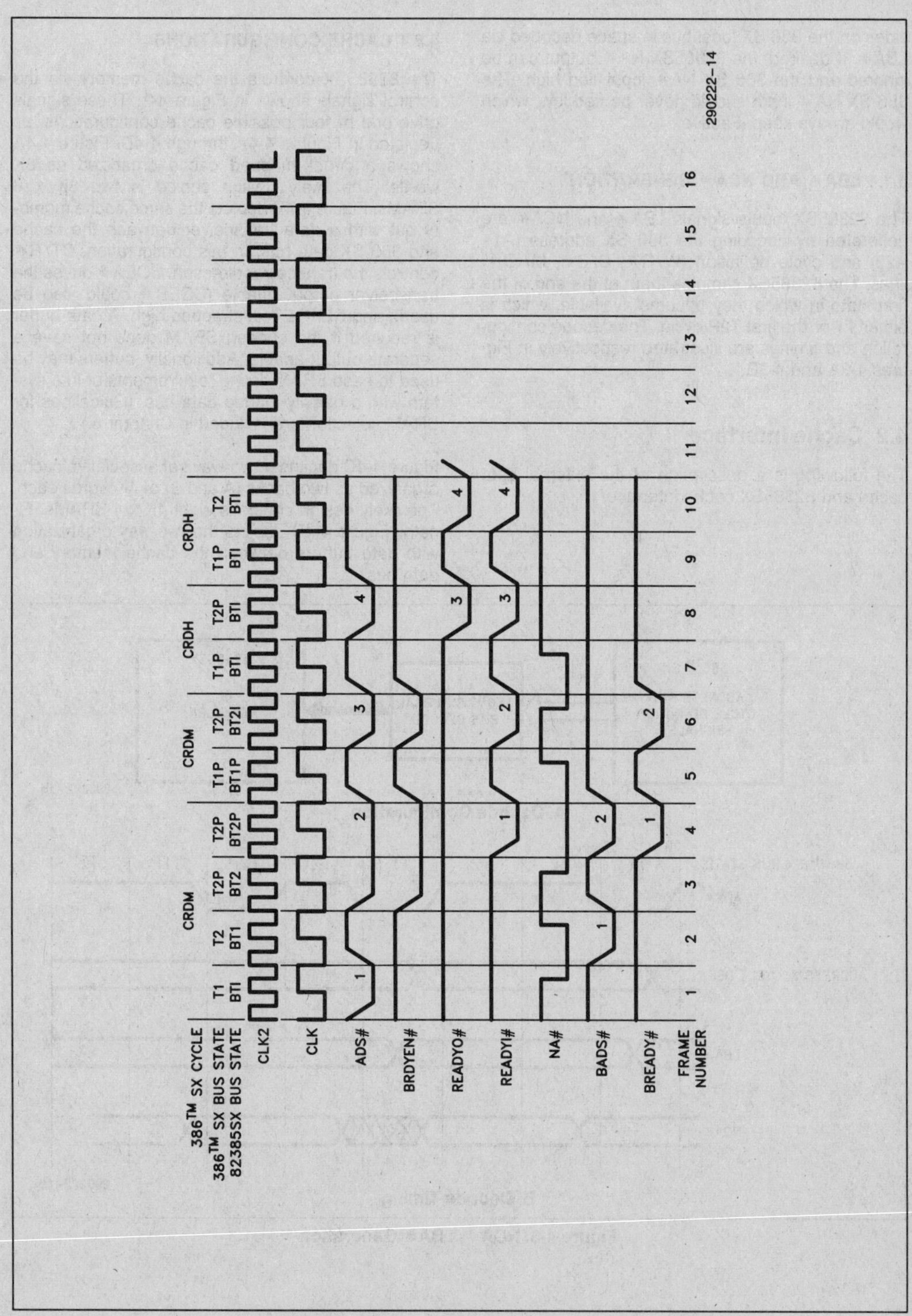

Figure 4-2B. READYO#, BRDYEN#, and NA# (N = 1)

4

sides on the 386 SX local bus in space decoded via LBA#. If desired, the 82385SX NA# output can be ignored and the 386 SX NA# input tied high. The 386 SX NA# input should never be tied low, which would always keep it active.

4.1.4 LBA# AND NCA# GENERATION

The 82385SX inputs signals LBA# and NCA# are generated by decoding the 386 SX address (A1–A23) and cycle definition (W/R#, D/C#, M/IO#) lines. The 82385SX samples them at the end of the first state in which they become available, which is either T1 or the first T2P cycle. The decode configuration and timings are illustrated respectively in Figures 4-3A and 4-3B.

4.2 Cache Interface

The following is a description of the external data cache and 82385SX cache interface.

4.2.1 CACHE CONFIGURATIONS

The 82385SX controls the cache memory via the control signals shown in Figure 4-1. These signals drive one of four possible cache configurations, as depicted in Figures 4-4A through 4-4D. Figure 4-4A shows a direct mapped cache organized as 8K words. The likely design choice is two 8K x 8 SRAMs. Figure 4-4B depicts the same cache memory but with a data transceiver between the cache and 386 SX data bus. In this configuration, CT/R# controls the transceiver direction, COEA# drives the transceiver output enable (COEB# could also be used), and DEFOE# is strapped high. A data buffer is required if the chosen SRAM does not have a separate output enable. Additionally, buffers may be used to ease SRAM timing requirements or in a system with a heavily loaded data bus. (Guidelines for SRAM selection are included in Chapter 6.)

Figure 4-4C depicts a two-way set associative cache organized as two banks (A and B) of 4K words each. The likely design choice is eight 4K x 4 SRAMs. Finally, Figure 4-4D depicts the two-way organization with data buffers between the cache memory and data bus.

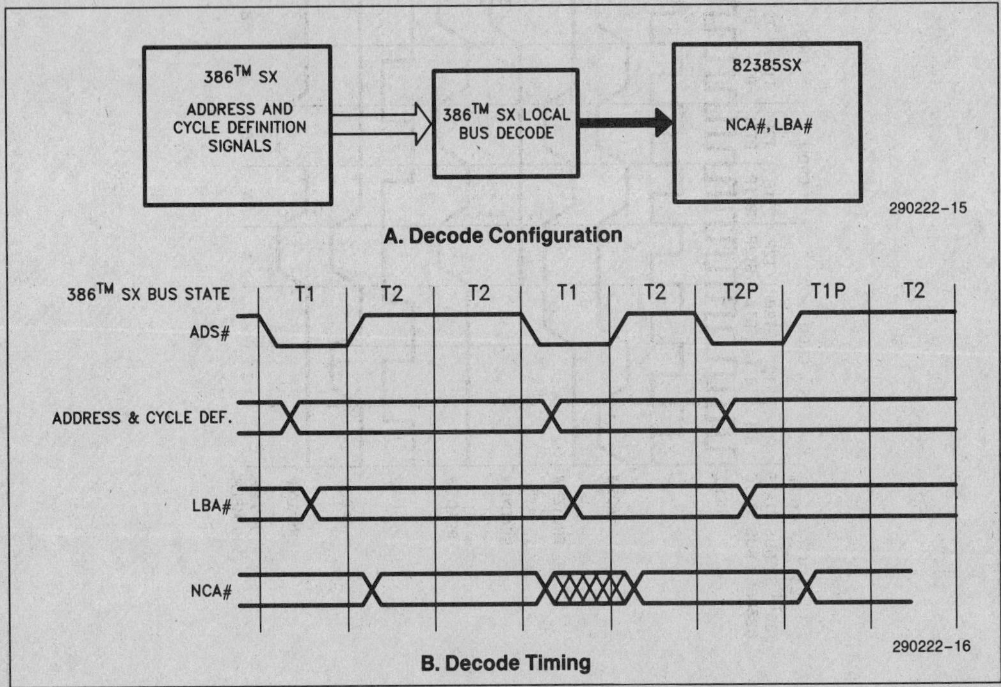

Figure 4-3. NCA#, LBA# Generation

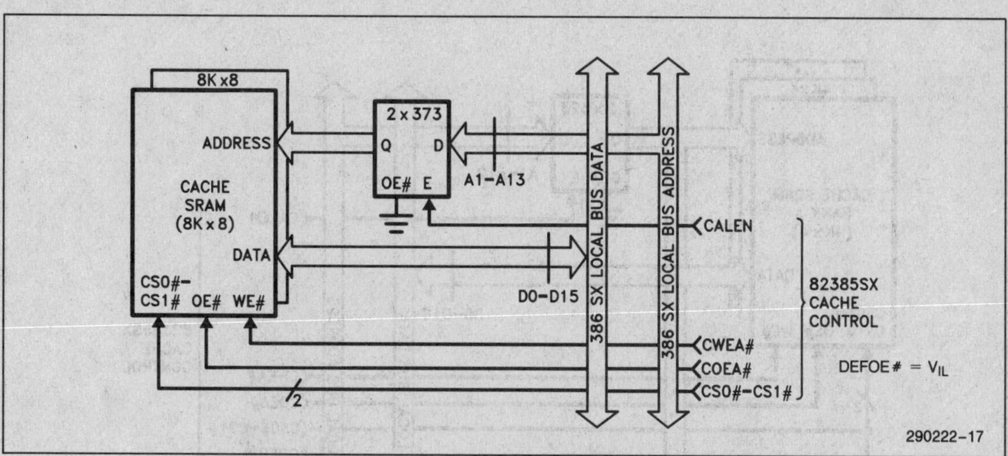

Figure 4-4A. Direct Mapped Cache without Data Buffers

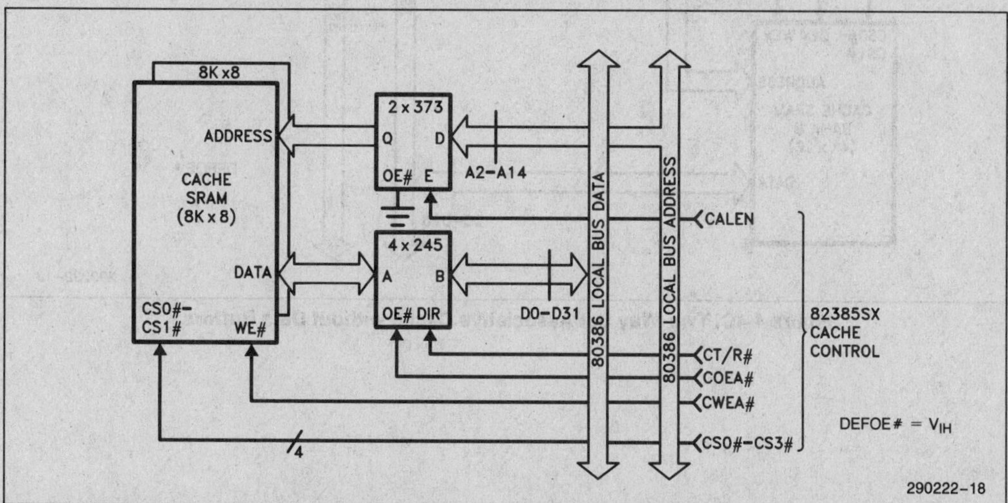

Figure 4-4B. Direct Mapped Cache with Data Buffers

4

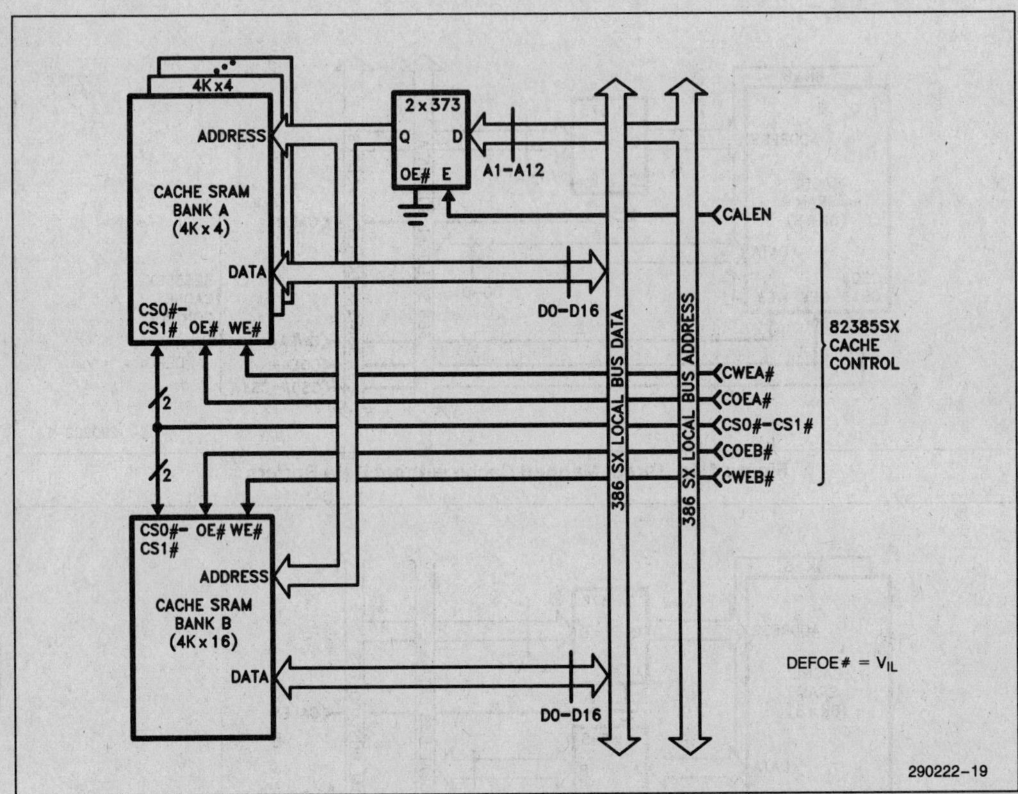

Figure 4-4C. Two-Way Set Associative Cache without Data Buffers

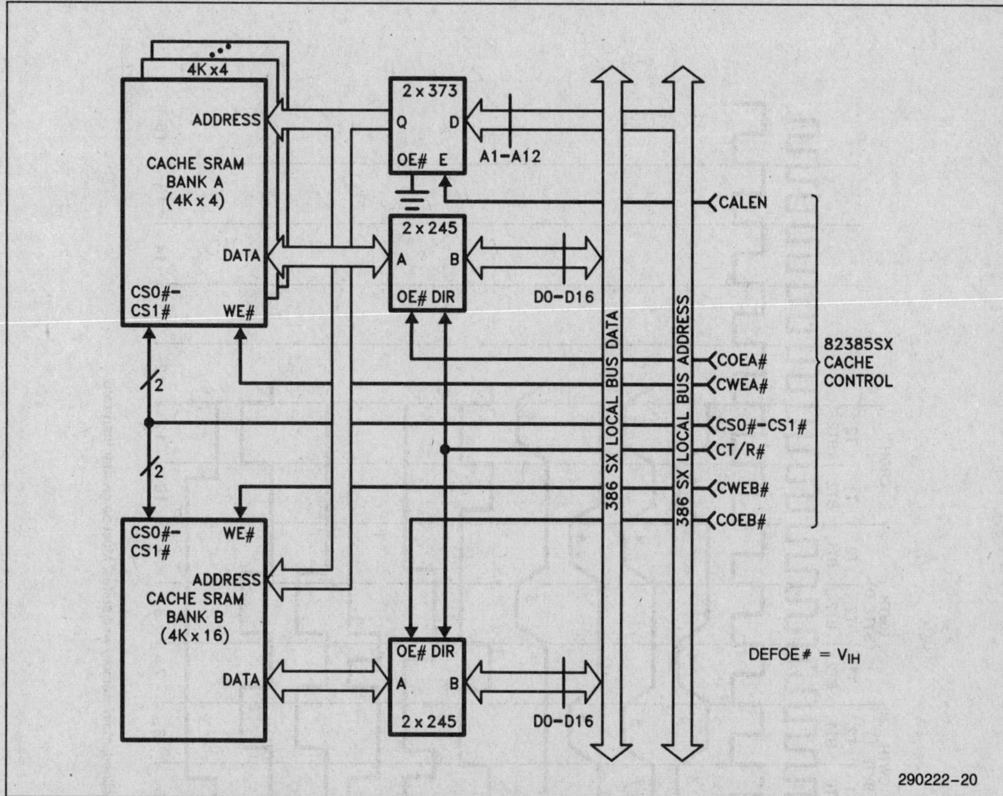

Figure 4-4D. Two-Way Set Associative Cache with Data Buffers

4.2.2 CACHE CONTROL . . . DIRECT MAPPED

Figure 4-5A illustrates the timing of cache read and write hits, while Figure 4-5B illustrates cache updates. In a read hit, the cache output enables are driven from the beginning of T2 (cycle 1 of Figure 4-5A). If at the end of T1 the cycle is qualified as a cacheable read, the output enables are asserted on the assumption that the cycle will be a hit. (Driving the output enables before the actual hit/miss decision is made eases SRAM timing requirements.)

Cycle 1 of Figure 4-5B illustrates what happens when the assumption of a hit turns out to be wrong. Note that the output enables are asserted at the beginning of of T2, but then disabled at the end of T2. Once the output enables are inactive, the 82385SX turns the transceiver around (via CT/R#) and drives the write enables to begin the cache update cycle. Note in Figure 4-5B that once the 386 SX is in pipelined mode, the output enables need not be driven prior to a hit/miss decision, since the decision is made earlier via the pipelined address information.

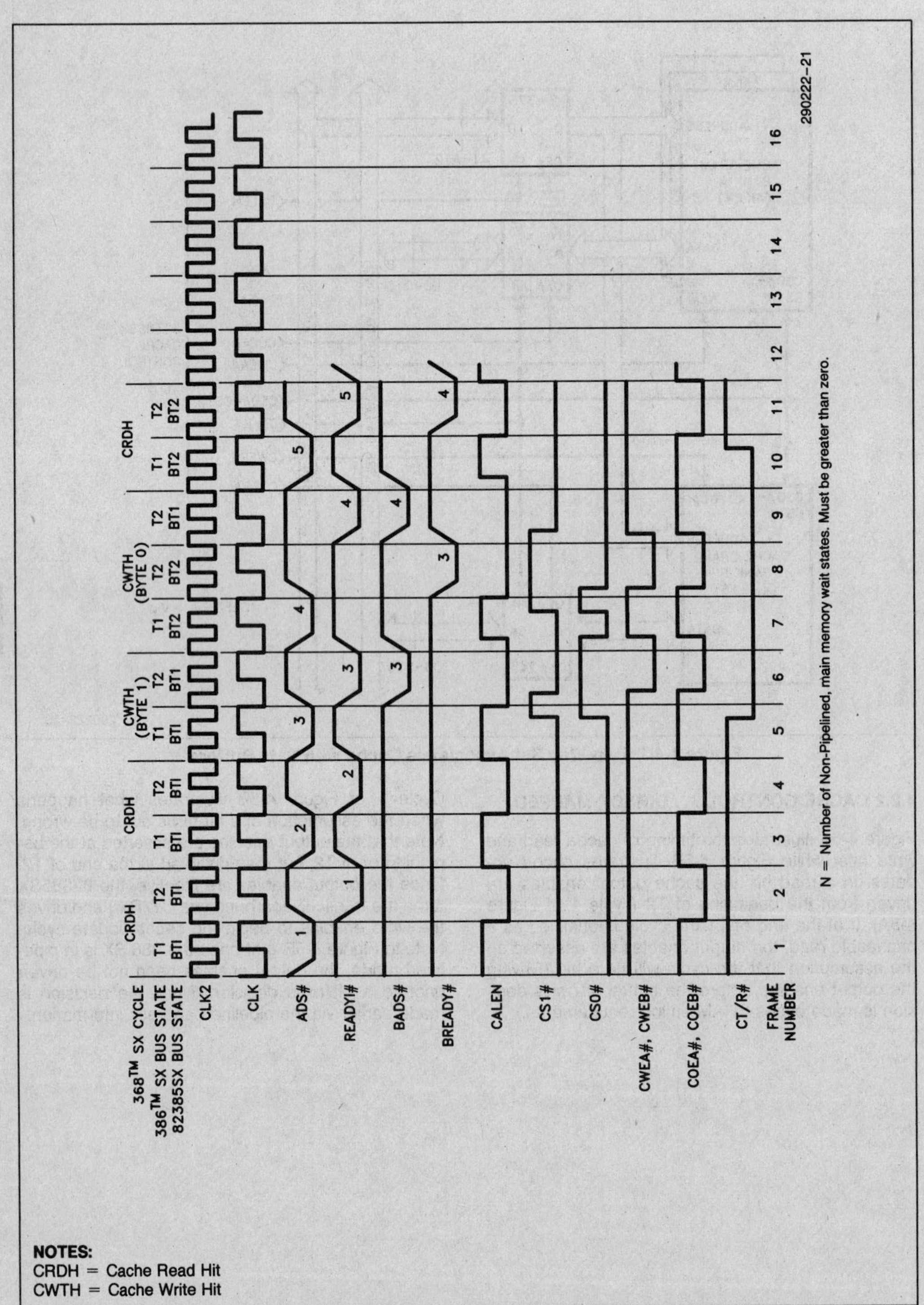

NOTES:
CRDH = Cache Read Hit
CWTH = Cache Write Hit

Figure 4-5A. Cache Read and Write Cycles—Direct Mapped (N = 1)

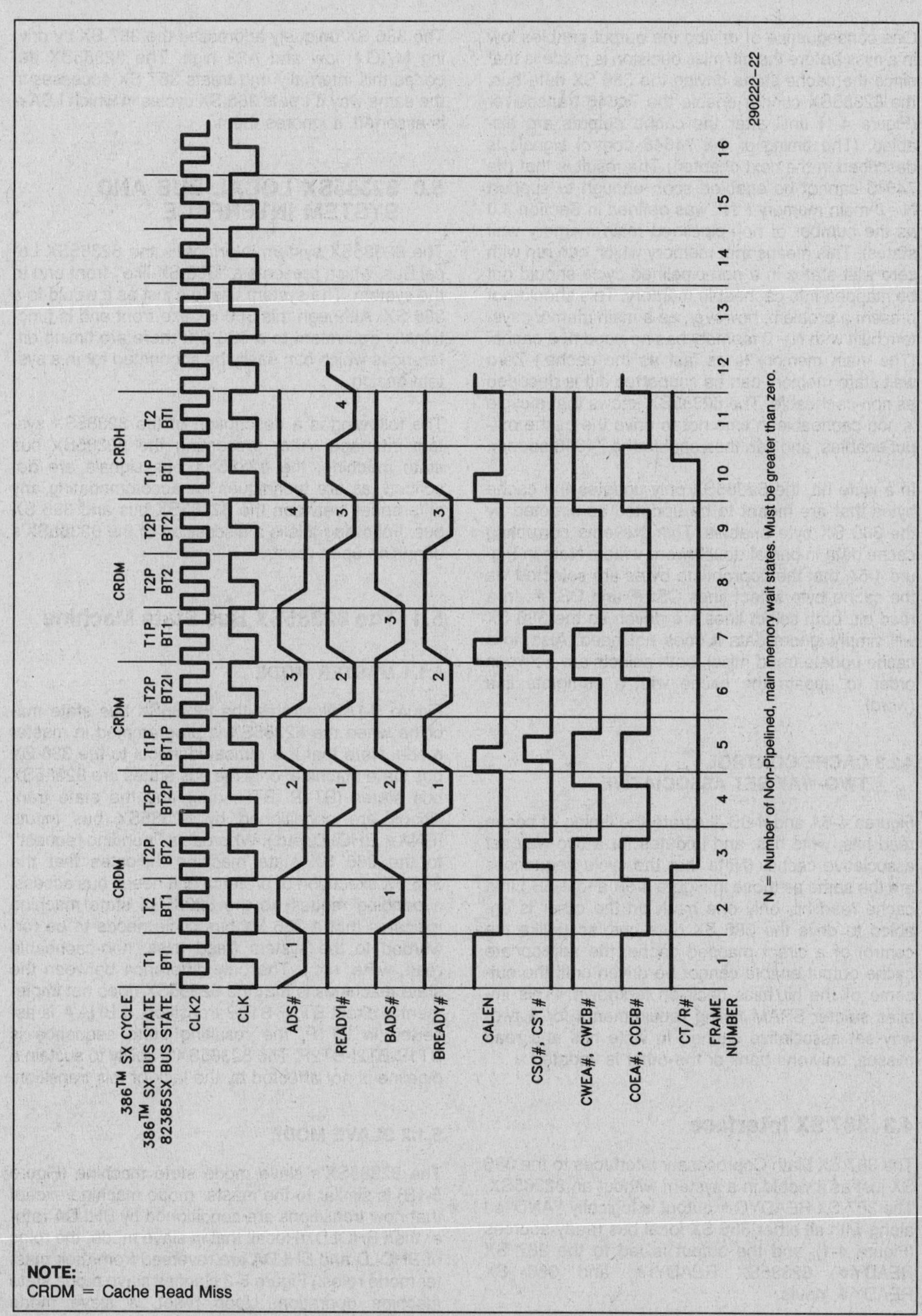

NOTE:
CRDM = Cache Read Miss

Figure 4-5B. Cache Update Cycles—Direct Mapped (N = 1)

One consequence of driving the output enables low in a miss before the hit/miss decision is made is that since the cache starts driving the 386 SX data bus, the 82385SX cannot enable the 74646 transceiver (Figure 4-1) until after the cache outputs are disabled. (The timing of the 74646 control signals is described in the next chapter.) The result is that the 74646 cannot be enabled soon enough to support N=0 main memory ("N" was defined in Section 4.0 as the number of non-pipelined main memory wait states). This means that memory which can run with zero wait states in a non-pipelined cycle should not be mapped into cacheable memory. This should not present a problem, however, as a main memory system built with N=0 memory has no need of a cache. (The main memory is as fast as the cache.) Zero wait state memory can be supported if it is decoded as non-cacheable. The 82385SX knows that a cycle is non-cacheable in time not to drive the cache output enables, and can thus enable the 74646 sooner.

In a write hit, the 82385SX only updates the cache bytes that are meant to be updated as directed by the 386 SX byte enables. This prevents corrupting cache data in partial doubleword writes. Note in Figure 4-5A that the appropriate bytes are selected via the cache byte select lines CS0# and CS1#. In a read hit, both select lines are driven as the 386 SX will simply ignore data it does not need. Also, in a cache update (read miss), both selects are active in order to update the cache with a complete line (word).

4.2.3 CACHE CONTROL ... TWO-WAY SET ASSOCIATIVE

Figures 4-6A and 4-6B illustrate the timing of cache read hits, write hits, and updates for a two-way set associative cache. (Note that the cycle sequences are the same as those in Figure 4-5A and 4-5B.) In a cache read hit, only one bank on the other is enabled to drive the 386 SX data bus, so unlike the control of a direct mapped cache, the appropriate cache output enable cannot be driven until the outcome of the hit/miss decision is known. (This implies stricter SRAM timing requirements for a two-way set associative cache.) In write hits and read misses, only one bank or the other is updated.

4.3 387 SX Interface

The 387 SX Math Coprocessor interfaces to the 386 SX just as it would in a system without an 82385SX. The 387 SX READYO# output is logically "AND"ed along with all other 386 SX local bus ready sources (Figure 4-1), and the output is fed to the 387 SX READY#, 82385SX READYI#, and 386 SX READY# inputs.

The 386 SX uniquely addresses the 387 SX by driving M/IO# low and A23 high. The 82385SX decodes this internally and treats 387 SX accesses in the same way it treats 386 SX cycles in which LBA# is asserted, it ignores them.

5.0 82385SX LOCAL BUS AND SYSTEM INTERFACE

The 82385SX system interface is the 82385SX Local Bus, which presents a "386 SX-like" front end to the system. The system ties to it just as it would to a 386 SX. Although this 386 SX-like front end is functionally equivalent to a 386 SX, there are timing differences which can easily be accounted for in a system design.

The following is a description of the 82385SX system interface. After presenting the 82385SX bus state machine, the 82385SX bus signals are described, as are techniques for accommodating any differences between the 82385SX bus and 386 SX bus. Following this is a discussion of the 82385SX's condition upon reset.

5.1 The 82385SX Bus State Machine

5.1.1 MASTER MODE

Figure 5-1A illustrates the 82385SX bus state machine when the 82385SX is programmed in master mode. Note that it is almost identical to the 386 SX bus state machine, only the bus states are 82385SX bus states (BT1P, BTH, etc.) and the state transitions are conditioned by 82385SX bus inputs (BNA# BHOLD, etc.). Whereas a "pending request" to the 386 SX state machine indicates that the 386 SX execution or prefetch unit needs bus access, a pending request to the 82385SX state machine indicates that a 386 SX bus cycle needs to be forwarded to the system (read miss, non-cacheable read, write, etc.). The only difference between the state machines is that the 82385SX does not implement a direct BT1P-BT2P transition. If BNA# is asserted in BT1P, the resulting state sequence is BT1P-BT2I-BT2P. The 82385SX's ability to sustain a pipeline is not affected by the lack of this transition.

5.1.2 SLAVE MODE

The 82385SX's slave mode state machine (Figure 5-1B) is similar to the master mode machine except that now transitions are conditioned by BHLDA rather than BHOLD. (Recall that in slave mode, the roles of BHOLD and BHLDA are reversed from their master mode roles.) Figure 5-2 clarifies slave mode state machine operation. Upon reset, a slave mode

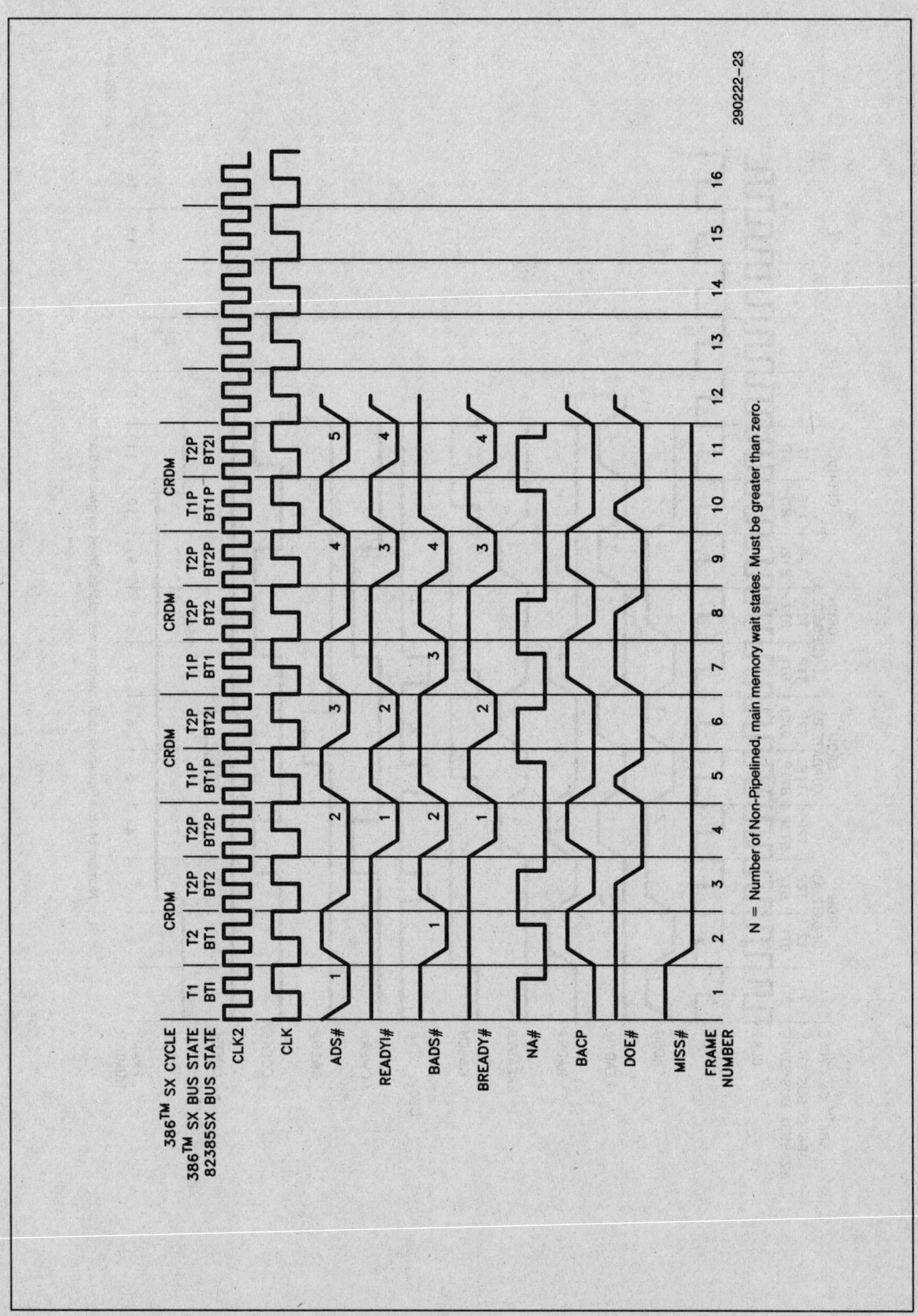

Figure 4-6A. Cache Read and Write Cycles—Two Way Associative (N = 1)

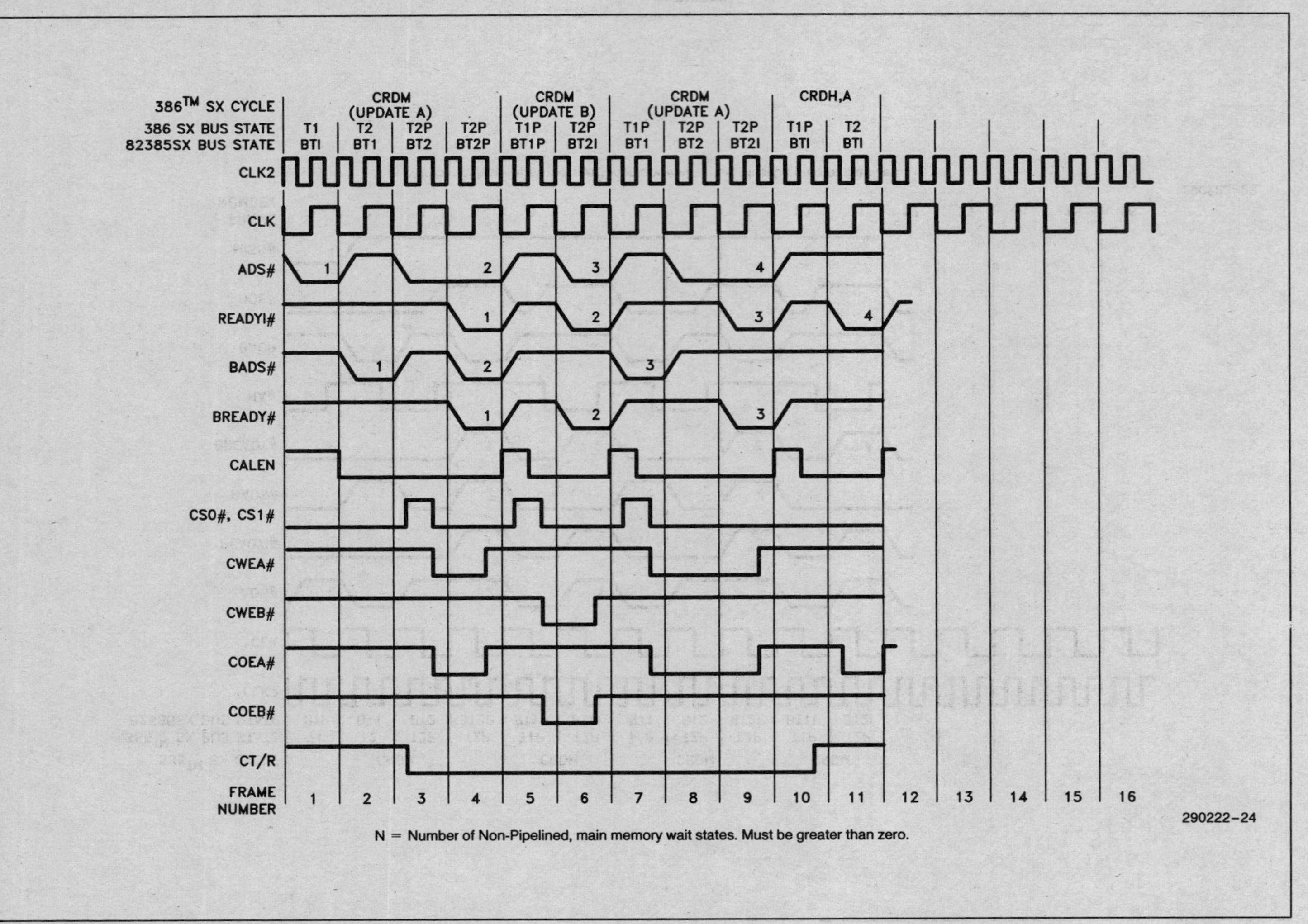

Figure 4-6B. Cache Update Cycles—Two Way Set Associative (N = 1)

82385SX enters the BTH state. When the 386 SX of the slave 82385SX subsystem has a cycle that needs to be forwarded to the system, the 82385SX moves to BTI and issues a hold request via BHOLD. It is important to note that a slave mode 82385SX does not drive the bus in a BTI state. When the master or bus arbiter returns BHLDA, the slave 82385SX enters BT1 and runs the cycle. When the cycle is completed, and if no additional requests are pending, the 82385SX moves back to BTH and disables BHOLD.

If, while a slave 82385SX is running a cycle, the master or arbiter drops BHLDA (Figure 5-2B), the 82385SX will complete the current cycle, move to BTH and remove the BHOLD request. If the 82385SX still had cycles to run when it was kicked off the bus, it will immediately assert a new BHOLD and move to BTI to await bus acknowledgement. Note, however, that it will only move to BTI if BHLDA is negated, insuring that the handshake sequence is completed.

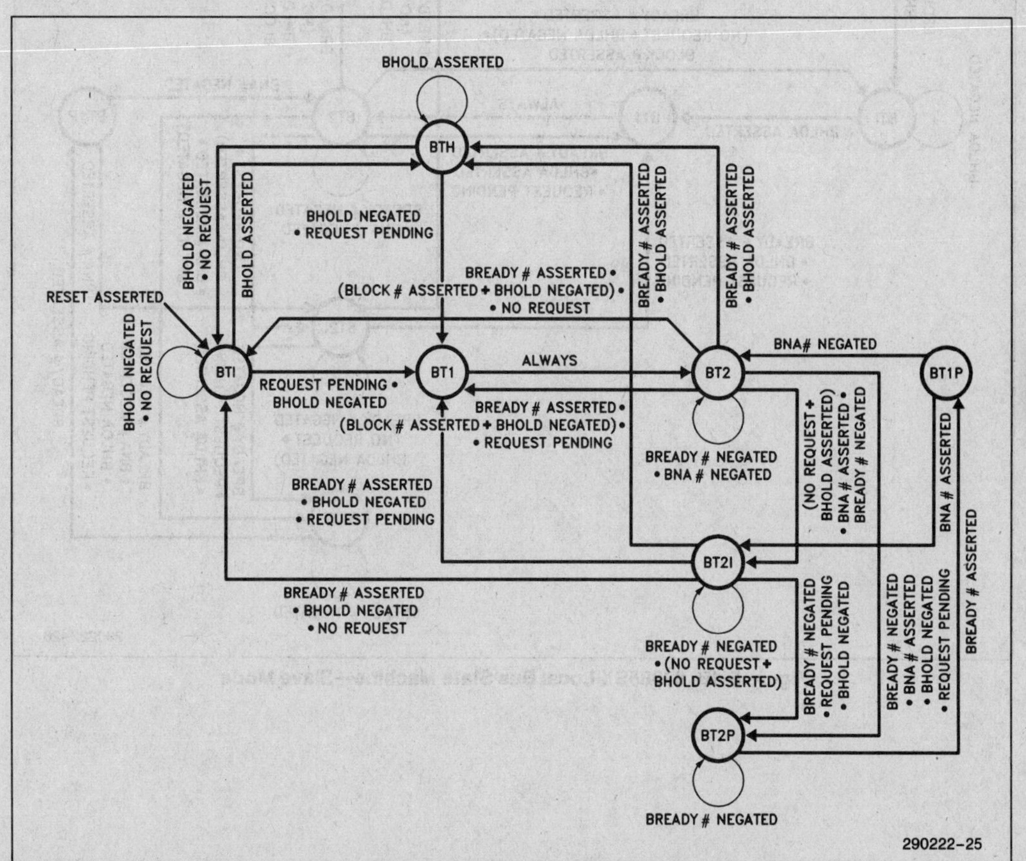

Figure 5-1A. 82385SX Local Bus State Machine—Master Mode

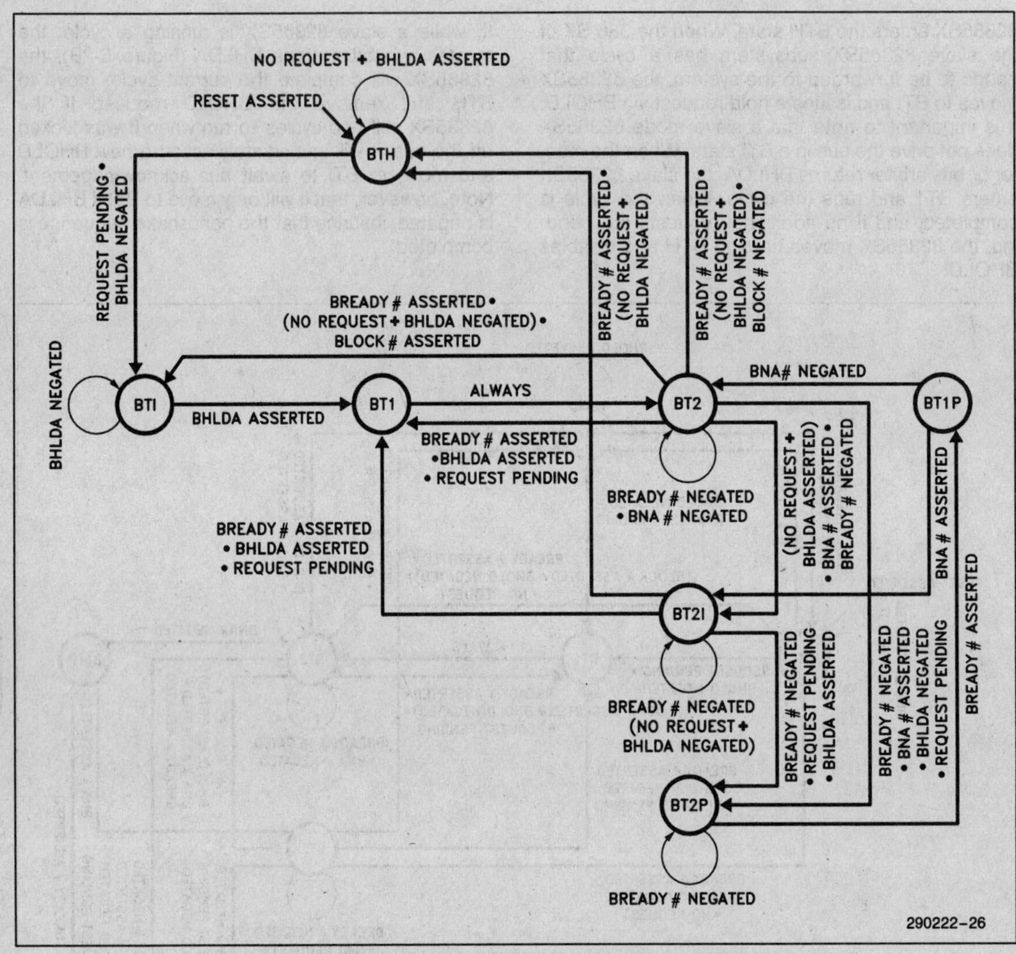

Figure 5-1B. 82385SX Local Bus State Machine—Slave Mode

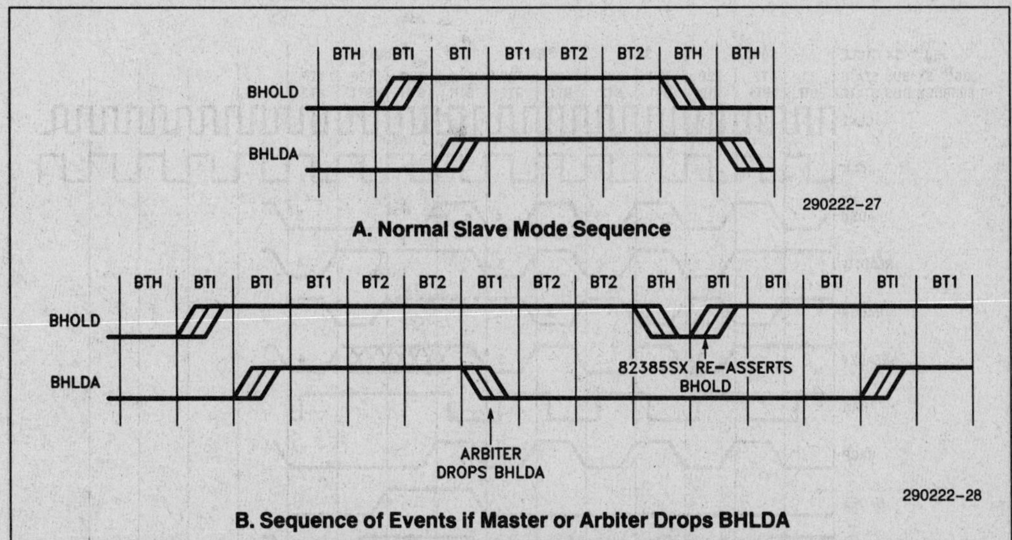

A. Normal Slave Mode Sequence

B. Sequence of Events if Master or Arbiter Drops BHLDA

Figure 5-2. BHOLD/BHLDA—Slave Mode

There are several cases in which a slave 82385SX will not immediately release the bus if BHLDA is dropped. For example, if BHLDA is dropped during a BT2P state, the 82385SX has already committed to the next system bus pipelined cycle and will execute it before releasing the bus. Also, the 82385SX will complete a sequence of locked cycles before releasing the bus. This should not present any problems, as a properly designed arbiter will not assume that the 82385SX has released the bus until it sees BHOLD become inactive.

5.2 The 82385SX Local Bus

The 82385SX bus can be broken up into two groups of signals: those which have direct 386 SX counterparts, and additional status and control signals provided by the 82385SX. The operation and interaction of all 82385SX bus signals are depicted in Figures 5-3A through 5-3L for a wide variety of cycle sequences. These diagrams serve as a reference for the 82385SX bus discussion and provide insight into the dual bus operation of the 82385SX.

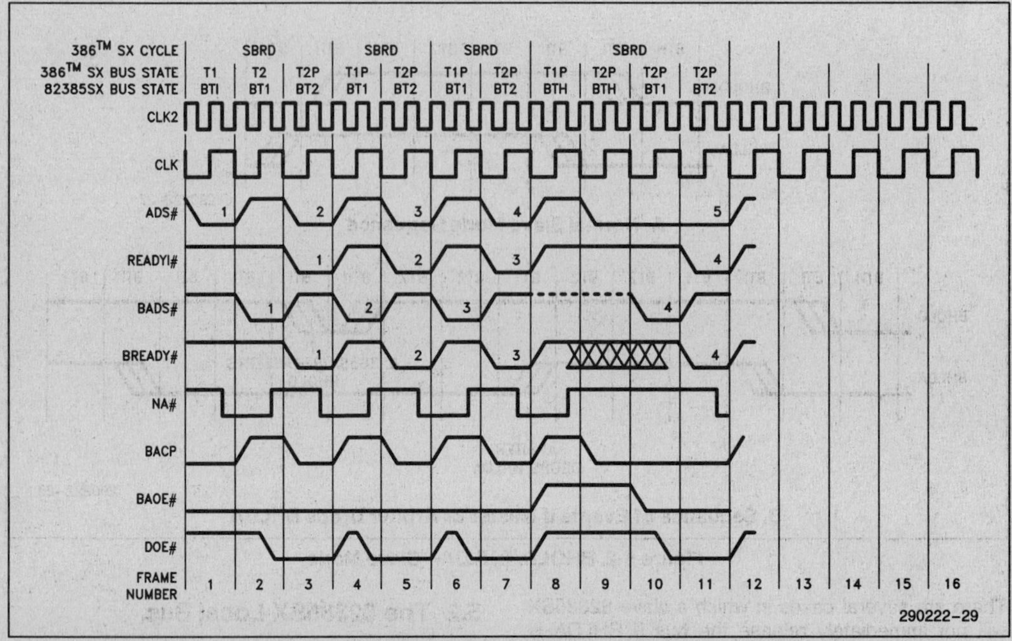

Figure 5-3A. Consecutive SBRD Cycles—(N = 0)

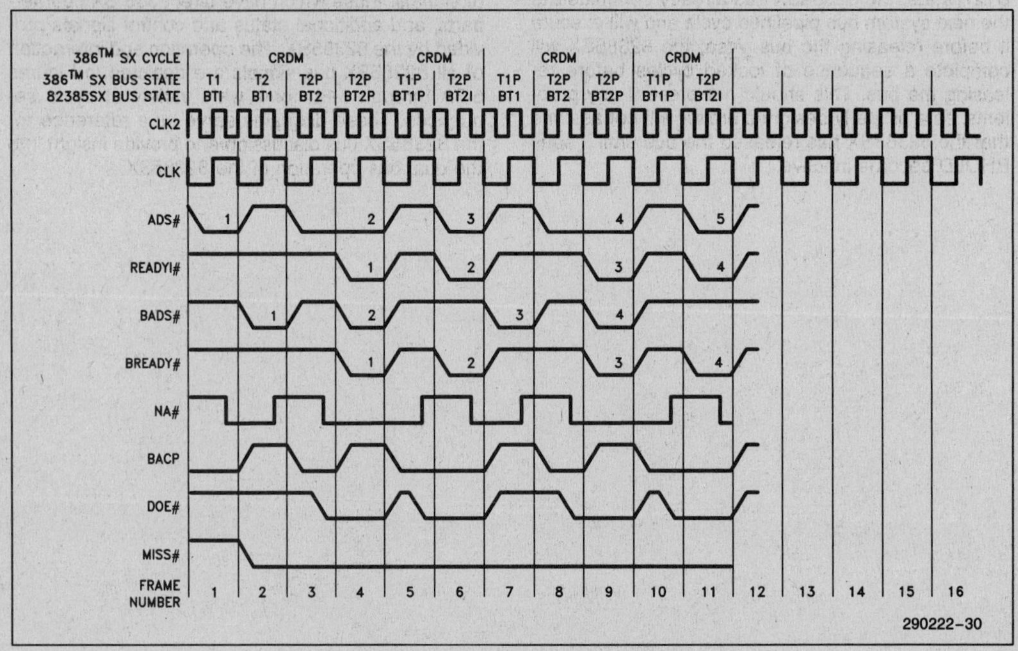

Figure 5-3B. Consecutive CRDM Cycles—(N = 1)

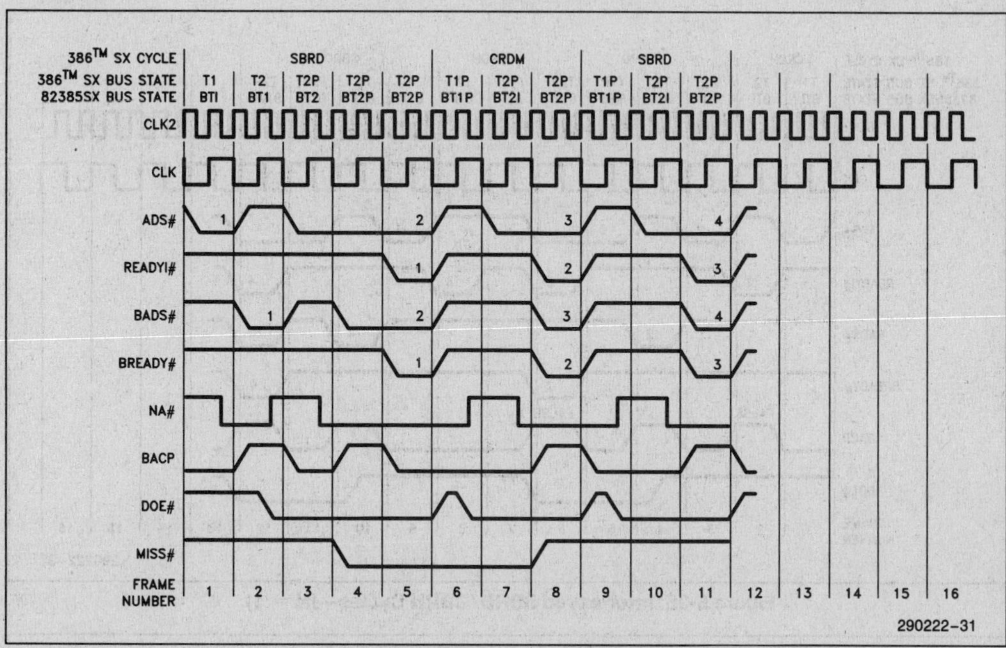

Figure 5-3C. SBRD, CRDM, SBRD—(N = 2)

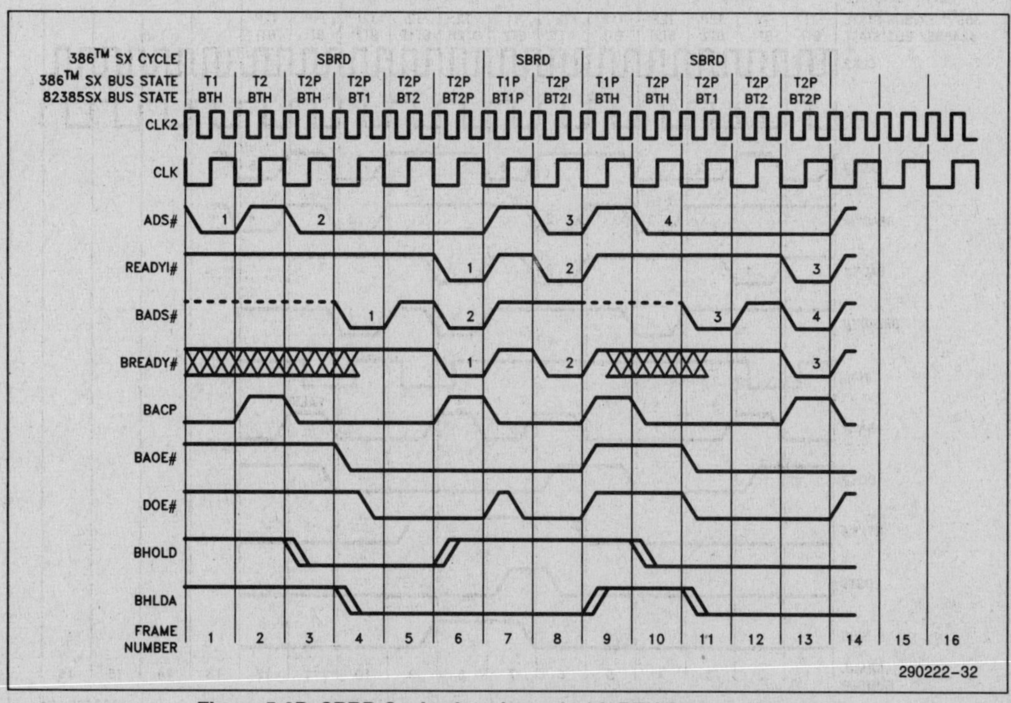

Figure 5-3D. SBRD Cycles Interleaved with BTH States—(N = 1)

386™ SX CYCLE
CRDH
SBRD
CRDH
SBRD
386™ SX BUS STATE
T1 T2 T1 T2 T2P T2P T1P T2 T1 T2 T2P T2P
82385SX BUS STATE
BTI BTI BTI BT1 BT2 BT2I BTI BTI BTI BT1 BT2 BT2P
CLK2
CLK
ADS#
READYI#
BADS#
BREADY#
BACP
FALSE
FALSE
DOE#
FRAME NUMBER
1 2 3 4 5 6 7 8 9 10 11 12 13 14 15 16
290222-33

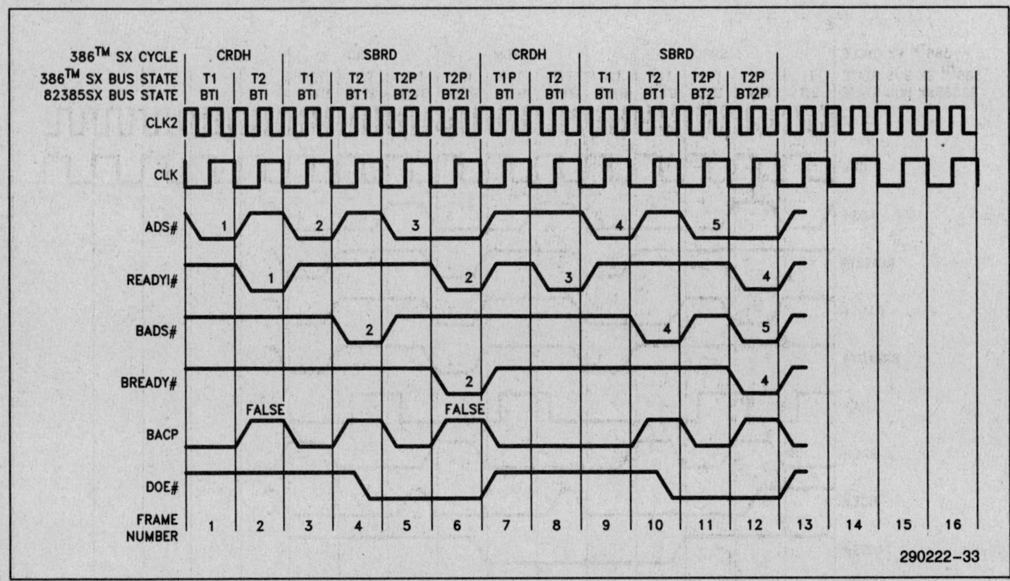

Figure 5-3E. Interleaved SBRD/CDRH Cycles—(N = 1)

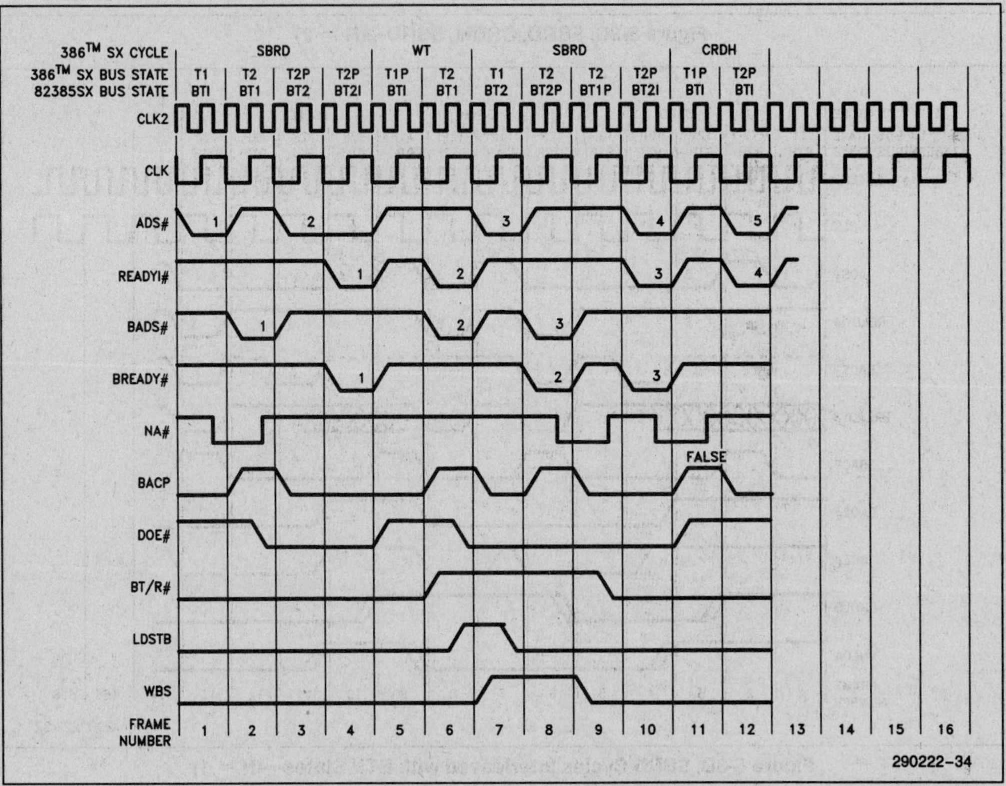

386™ SX CYCLE
SBRD
WT
SBRD
CRDH
386™ SX BUS STATE
T1 T2 T2P T2P T1P T2 T1 T2 T2 T2P T1P T2P
82385SX BUS STATE
BTI BT1 BT2 BT2I BTI BT1 BT2 BT2P BT1P BT2I BTI BTI
CLK2
CLK
ADS#
READYI#
BADS#
BREADY#
NA#
BACP
FALSE
DOE#
BT/R#
LDSTB
WBS
FRAME NUMBER
1 2 3 4 5 6 7 8 9 10 11 12 13 14 15 16
290222-34

Figure 5-3F. SBRD, WT, SBRD, CRDH—(N = 1)

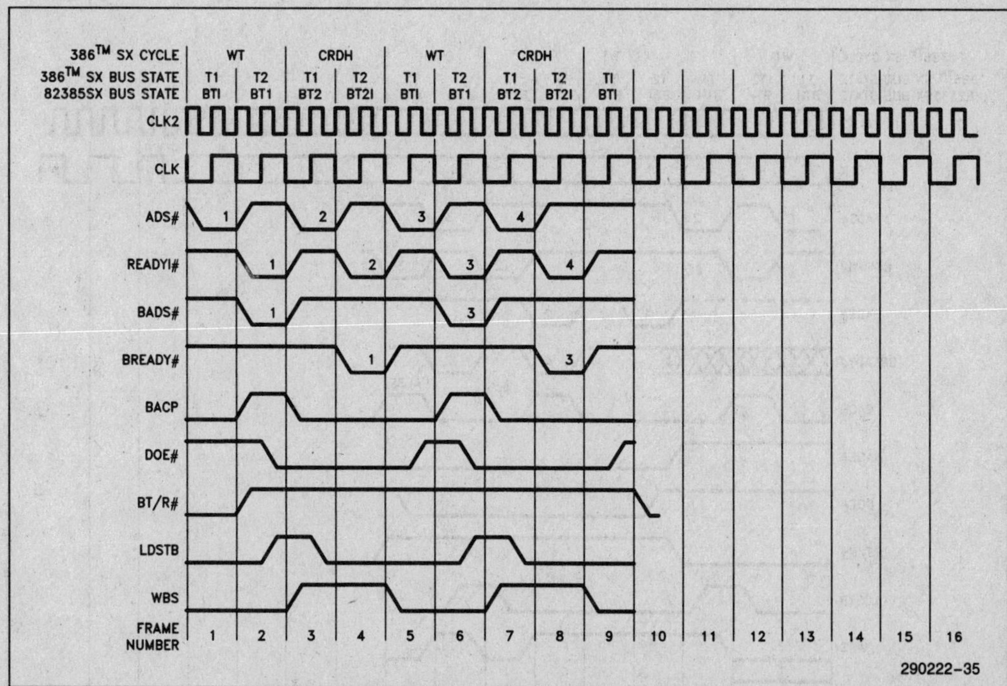

Figure 5-3G. Interleaved WT/CRDH Cycles—(N = 1)

4

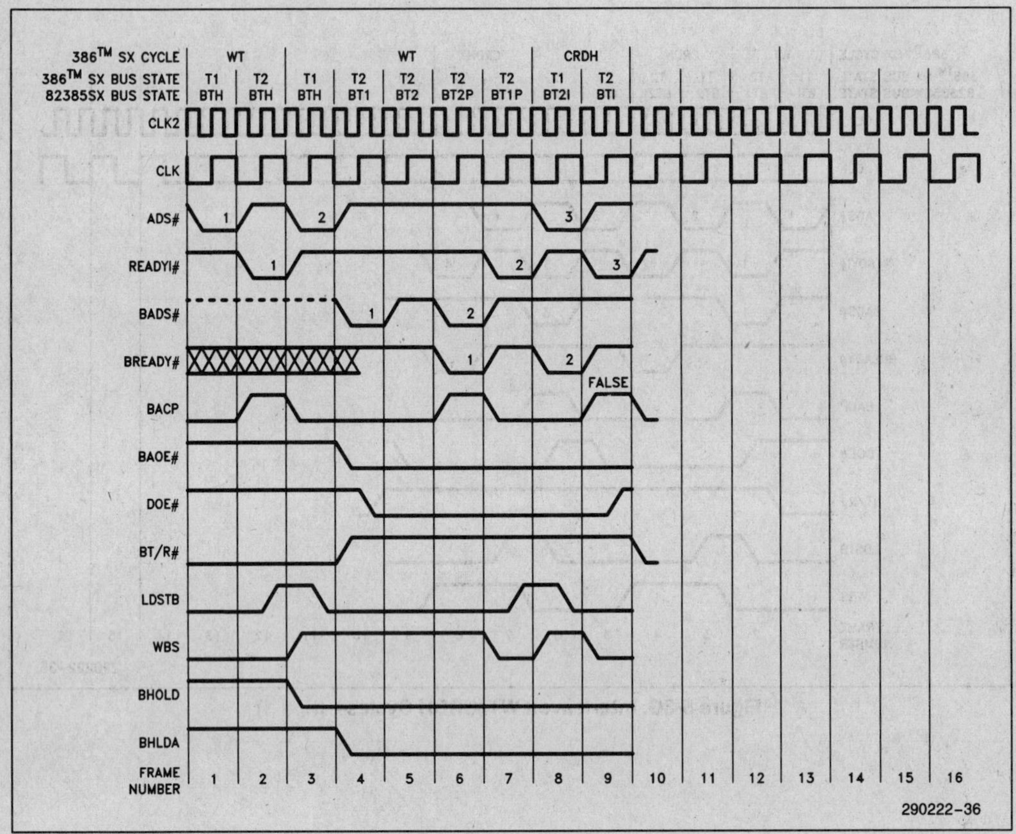

Figure 5-3H. WT, WT, CRDH—(N = 1)

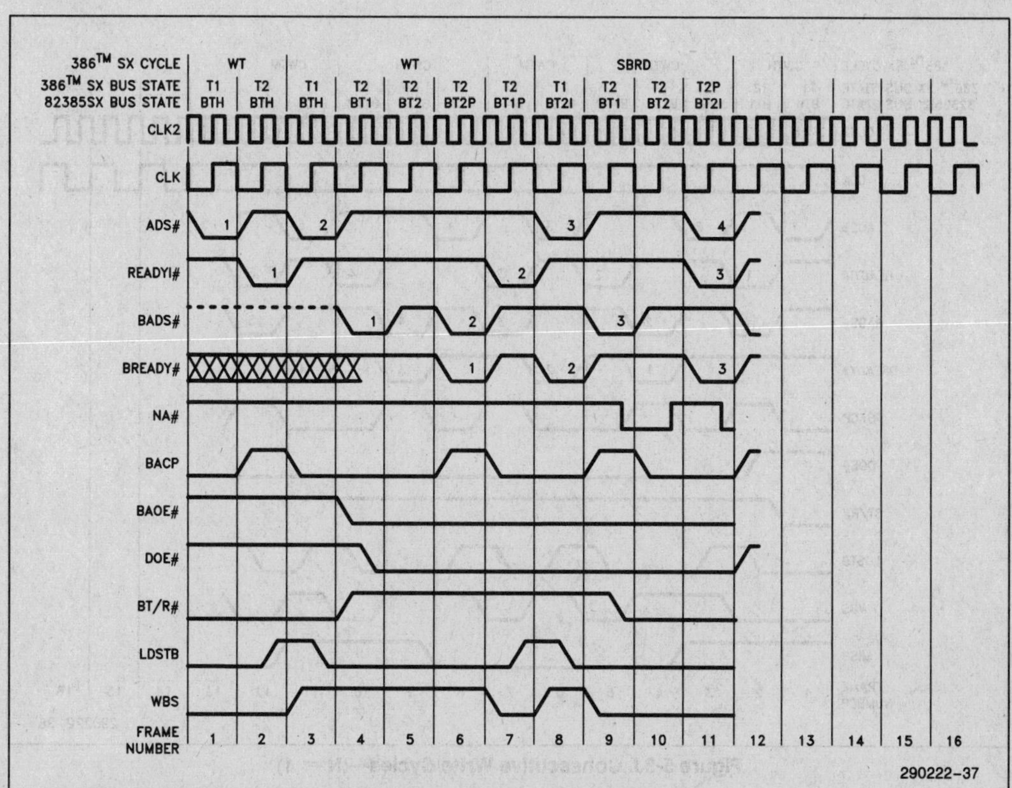

Figure 5-3l. WT, WT, SBRD—(N = 1)

4

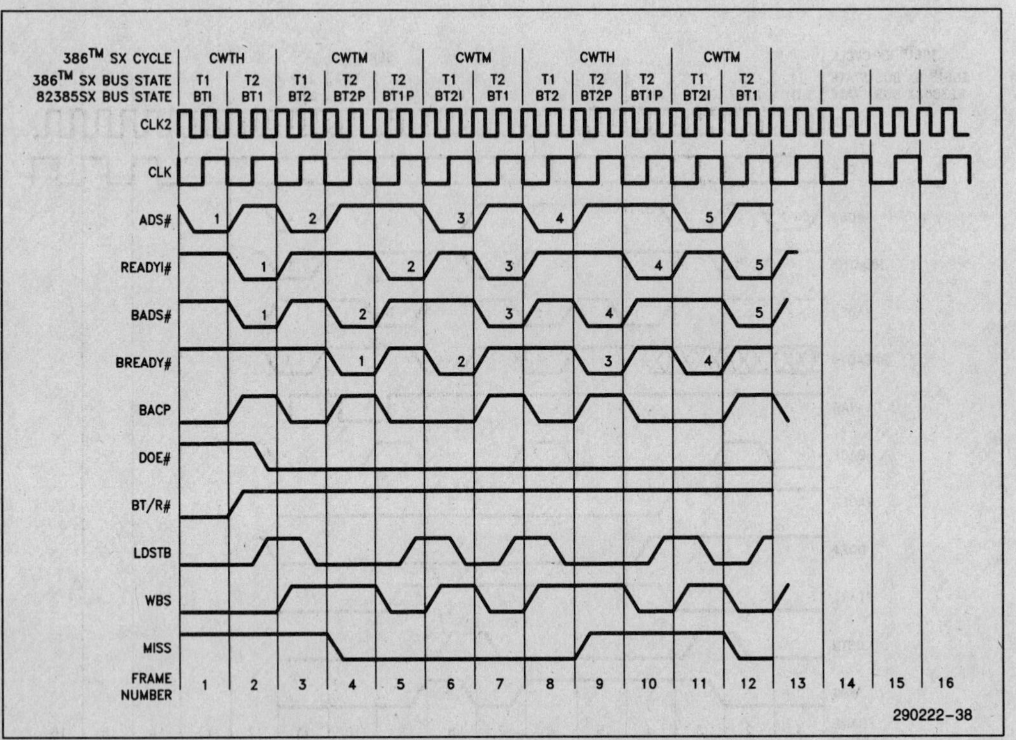

386™ SX CYCLE
CWTH
CWTM
CWTM
CWTH
CWTM
386™ SX BUS STATE
T1 T2 T1 T2 T2 T1 T2 T1 T2 T2 T1 T2
82385SX BUS STATE
BTI BT1 BT2 BT2P BT1P BT2I BT1 BT2 BT2P BT1P BT2I BT1
CLK2
CLK
ADS#
READYI#
BADS#
BREADY#
BACP
DOE#
BT/R#
LDSTB
WBS
MISS
FRAME NUMBER
1 2 3 4 5 6 7 8 9 10 11 12 13 14 15 16
290222-38

Figure 5-3J. Consecutive Write Cycles—(N = 1)

386™ SX CYCLE
SBRD
CRDM
WT
CRDH
386™ SX BUS STATE
T1 T2 T2P T2P T1P T2P T1P T2 T1 T2
82385SX BUS STATE
BTI BT1 BT2 BT2P BT1P BT2I BTI BT1 BT2 BT2I
CLK2
CLK
ADS#
READYI#
BADS#
BREADY#
LOCK#
BLOCK#
MISS#
FRAME NUMBER
1 2 3 4 5 6 7 8 9 10 11 12 13 14 15 16
290222-39

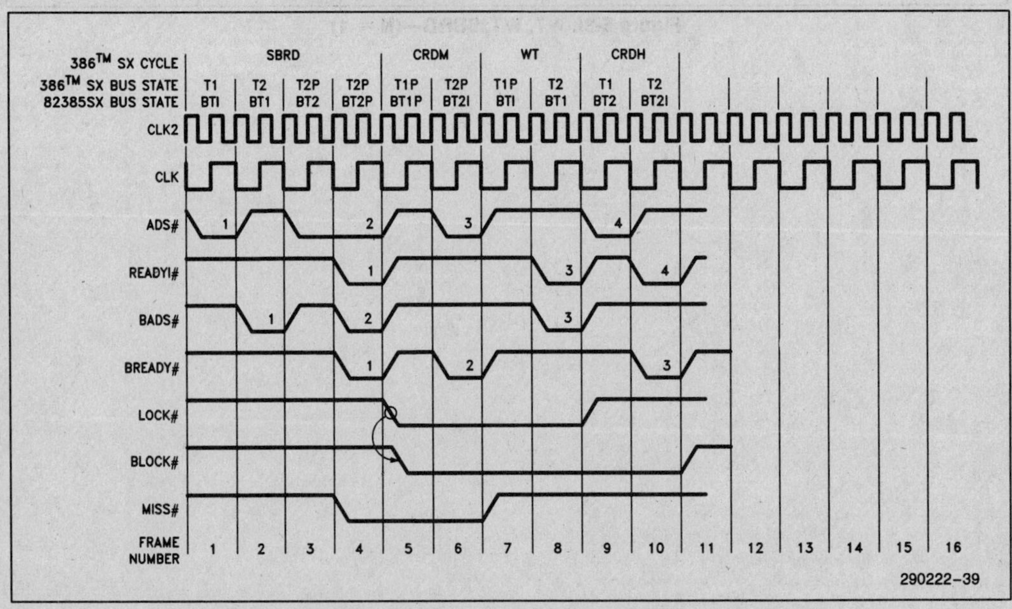

Figure 5-3K. LOCK#/BLOCK# in Non-Cacheable or Miss Cycles—(N = 1)

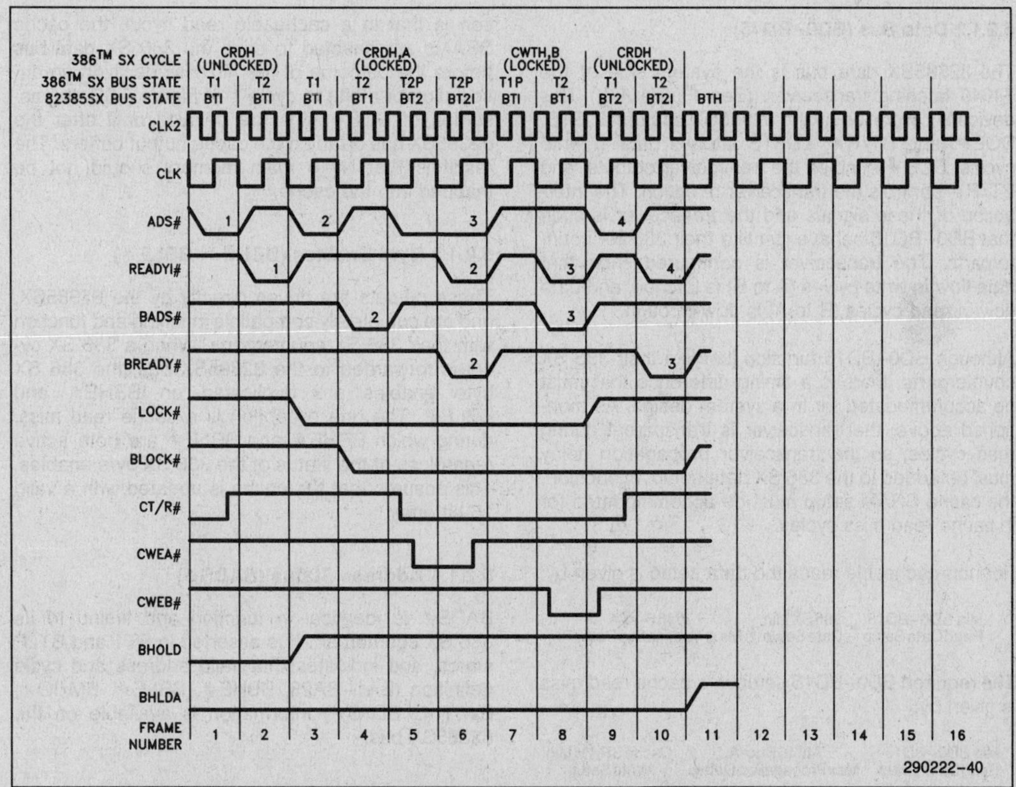

Figure 5-3L. LOCK#/BLOCK# in Cache Read Hit Cycle—(N = 1)

5.2.1 82385SX BUS COUNTERPARTS TO 386™ SX SIGNALS

The following sections discuss the signals presented on the 82385SX local bus which are functional equivalents to the signals present at the 386 SX local bus.

5.2.1.1 Address Bus (BA1–BA23) and Cycle Definition Signals (BM/IO#, BD/C#, BW/R#)

These signals are not driven directly by the 82385SX, but rather are the outputs of the 74374 address/cycle definition latch. (Refer to Figure 4-1 for the hardware interface.) This latch is controlled by the 82385SX BACP and BAOE# outputs. The behavior and timing of these outputs and the latch they control (typically F or AS series TTL) ensure that BA1–BA23, BM/IO#, BW/R#, and BD/C# are compatible in timing and function to their 386 SX counterparts.

The behavior of BACP can be seen in Figure 5-3B, where the rising edge of BACP latches and forwards the 386 SX address and cycle definition signals in a BT1 or first BT2P state. However, the 82385SX need not be the current bus master to latch the 386 SX address, as evidenced by cycle 4 of Figure 5-3A. In this case, the address is latched in frame 8, but not forwarded to the system (via BAOE#) until frame 10. (The latch and output enable functions of the 74374 are independent and invisible to one another.)

Note that in frames 2 and 6 the BACP pulses are marked "False". The reason is that BACP is issued and the address latched before the hit/miss determination is made. This ensures that should the cycle be a miss, the 82385SX bus can move directly into BT1 without delay. In the case of a hit, the latched address is simply never qualified by the assertion of BADS#. The 82385SX bus stays in BTI if there is no access pending (new cycle is a hit) and no bus activity. It will move to and stay in BT2I if the system has requested a pipelined cycle and the 82385SX does not have a pending bus access (new cycle is a hit).

5.2.1.2 Data Bus (BD0–BD15)

The 82385SX data bus is the system side of the 74646 latching transceiver. (See Figure 4-1.) This device is controlled by the 82385SX outputs LDSTB, DOE#, and BT/R#. LDSTB latches data in write cycles, DOE# enables the transceiver outputs, and BT/R# controls the transceiver direction. The interaction of these signals and the transceiver is such that BD0–BD15 behave just like their 386 SX counterparts. The transceiver is configured such that data flow in write cycles (A to B) is latched, and data flow in read cycles (B to A) is flow-through.

Although BD0–BD15 function just like their 386 SX counterparts, there is a timing difference that must be accommodated for in a system design. As mentioned above, the transceiver is transparent during read cycles, so the transceiver propagation delay must be added to the 386 SX data setup. In addition, the cache SRAM setup must be accommodated for in cache read miss cycles.

For non-cacheable reads the data setup is given by:

$$\begin{array}{c}\text{Min BD0–BD15}\\ \text{Read Data Setup}\end{array} = \begin{array}{c}\text{386SX Min}\\ \text{Data Setup}\end{array} + \begin{array}{c}\text{74646 B-to-A}\\ \text{Max Propagation Delay}\end{array}$$

The required BD0–BD15 setup in a cache read miss is given by:

$$\begin{array}{c}\text{Min BD0–BD15}\\ \text{Read Data Setup}\end{array} = \begin{array}{c}\text{74646 B-to-A}\\ \text{Max Propagation Delay}\end{array} + \begin{array}{c}\text{Cache SRAM Min}\\ \text{Write Setup}\end{array} + \begin{array}{c}\text{One CLK2}\\ \text{Period}\end{array} - \begin{array}{c}\text{82385SX CWEA\# or}\\ \text{CWEB\# Min Delay}\end{array}$$

If a data buffer is located between the 386 SX data bus and the cache SRAMs, then its maximum propagation delay must be added to the above formula as well. A design analysis should be completed for every new design to determine actual margins.

A design can accommodate the increased data setup by choosing appropriately fast main memory DRAMs and data buffers. Alternatively, a designer may deal with the longer setup by inserting an extra wait state into cache read miss cycles. If an additional state is to be inserted, the system bus controller should sample the 82385SX MISS# output to distinquish read misses from cycles that do not require the longer setup. Tips on using the 82385SX MISS# signal are presented later in this chapter.

The behavior of LDSTB, DOE#, and BT/R# can be understood via Figures 5-3A through 5-3L. Note that in cycle 1 of Figure 5-3A (A non-cacheable system read), DOE# is activated midway through BT1, but in cycle 1 of Figure 5-3B (a cache read miss), DOE# is not activated until midway through BT2. The reason is that in a cacheable read cycle, the cache SRAMs are enabled to drive the 386 SX data bus before the outcome of the hit/miss decision (in anticipation of a hit.) In cycle 1 of Figure 5-3B, the assertion of DOE# must be delayed until after the 82385SX has disabled the cache output buffers. The result is that N=0 main memory should not be mapped into the cache.

5.2.1.3 Byte Enables (BBHE#, BBLE#)

These outputs are driven directly by the 82385SX, and are completely compatible in timing and function with their 386 SX counterparts. When a 386 SX cycle is forwarded to the 82385SX bus, the 386 SX byte enables are duplicated on BBHE# and BBLE#. The one exception is a cache read miss, during which BBHE# and BBLE# are both active regardless of the status of the 386 SX byte enables. This ensures that the cache is updated with a valid 16-bit entry.

5.2.1.4 Address Status (BADS#)

BADS# is identical in function and timing to its 386 SX counterpart. It is asserted in BT1 and BT2P states, and indicates that valid address and cycle definition (BA1–BA23, BBHE#, BBLE#, BM/IO#, BW/R#, BD/C#) information is available on the 82385SX bus.

5.2.1.5 Ready (BREADY#)

The 82385SX BREADY# input terminates 82385SX bus cycles just as the 386 SX READY# input terminates 386 SX bus cycles. The behavior of BREADY# is the same as that of READY#, but note in the A.C timing specifications that a cache read miss requires a longer BREADY# setup than do other cycles. This must be accommodated for in ready logic design.

5.2.1.6 Next Address (BNA#)

BNA# is identical in function and timing to its 386 SX counterpart. Note that in Figures 5-3A through 5-3L, BNA# is assumed asserted in every BT1P or first BT2 state. Along with the 82385SX's pipelining of the 386 SX, this ensures that the timing diagrams accurately reflect the full pipelined nature of the dual bus structure.

5.2.1.7 Bus Lock (BLOCK#)

The 386 SX flags a locked sequence of cycles by asserting LOCK#. During a locked sequence, the 386 SX does not acknowledge hold requests, so the sequence executes without interruption by another master. The 82385SX forces all locked 386 SX cycles to run on the 82385SX bus (unless LBA# is active), regardless of whether or not the referenced location resides in the cache. In addition, a locked sequence of 386 SX cycles is run as a locked sequence on the 82385SX bus; BLOCK# is asserted and the 82385SX does not allow the sequence to be interrupted. Locked writes (hit or miss) and locked read misses affect the cache and cache directory just as their unlocked counterparts do. A locked read hit, however, is handled differently. The read is necessarily forced to run on the 82385SX local bus, and as the data returns from main memory, it is "re-copied" into the cache. (See Figure 5-3L.) The directory is not changed as it already indicates that this location exists in the cache. This activity is invisible to the system and ensures that semaphores are properly handled.

BLOCK# is asserted during locked 82385SX bus cycles just as LOCK# is asserted during locked 386 SX cycles. The BLOCK# maximum valid delay, however, differs from that of LOCK#, and this must be accounted for in any circuitry that makes use of BLOCK#. The difference is due to the fact that LOCK#, unlike the other 386 SX cycle definition signals, is not pipelined. The situation is clarified in Figure 5-3K. In cycle 2 the state of LOCK# is not known before the corresponding system read starts (Frame 4 and 5). In this case, LOCK# is asserted at the beginning of T1P, and the delay for BLOCK# to become active is the delay of LOCK# from the 386 SX plus the propagation delay through the 82385SX. This occurs because T1P and the corresponding BT1P are concurrent (Frame 5). The result is that BLOCK# should not be sampled at the end of BT1P. The first appropriate sampling point is midway through the next state, as shown in Frame 6. In Figure 5-3L, the maximum delay for BLOCK# to become valid in Frame 4 is the same as the maximum delay for LOCK# to become valid from the 386 SX. This is true since the pipelining issue discussed above does not occur.

The 82385 should negate BLOCK# after: BREADY# of the last 82385 Locked Cycle was asserted AND LOCK# turns inactive.

This means that in a sequence of cycles which begins with a 82385 Locked Cycle and goes on with all the possible Locked Cycles (other 82385 cycles, idles, and local cycles), while LOCK# is continuously active, the 82385 will maintain BLOCK# active continuously. Another implication is that in a Locked Posted Write Cycle followed by non-locked sequence, BLOCK# is negated one CLK after BREADY# of the write cycle. In other 82385 Locked Cycles, followed by non-locked sequences, BLOCK# is negated one CLK after LOCK# is negated, which occurs two CLKs after BREADY# is asserted. In the last case BLOCK# active moves by one CLK to the non-locked sequence.

The arbitration rules of Locked Cycles are:

MASTER MODE:

BHOLD input signal is ignored when BLOCK# or internal lock (16-bit non-aligned cycle) are active. BHLDA output signal remains inactive, and BAOE# output signal remains active at that time interval.

SLAVE MODE:

The 82385 does not relinquish the system bus if BLOCK# or internal lock are active. The BHOLD output signal remains active when BLOCK# or internal lock is active plus one CLK. The BHLDA input signal is ignored when BLOCK# or the internal lock is active plus one CLK. This means the 82385 slave does not respond to BHLDA inactivation. The BAOE# output signal remains active during the same time interval.

5.2.2 ADDITIONAL 82385SX BUS SIGNALS

The 82385SX bus provides two status outputs and one control input that are unique to cache operation and thus have no 386 SX counterparts. The outputs are MISS# and WBS, and the input is FLUSH.

5.2.2.1 Cache Read/Write Miss Indication (MISS#)

MISS# can be thought of as an extra 82385SX bus cycle definition signal similar to BM/IO#, BW/R#, and BD/C#, that distinguishes cacheable read and write misses from other cycles. MISS#, like the other definition signals, becomes valid with BADS# (BT1 or first BT2P). The behavior of MISS# is illustrated in Figures 5-3B, 5-3C, and 5-3J. The 82385SX floats MISS# when another master owns the bus, allowing multiple 82385SXs to share the same node in multi-cache systems. MISS# should thus be lightly pulled up (~20K) to keep it negated during hold (BTH) states.

MISS# can serve several purposes. As discussed previously, the BD0–BD15 and BREADY# setup times in a cache read miss are longer than in other cycles. A bus controller can distinguish these cycles by gating MISS# with BW/R#. MISS# may also prove useful in gathering 82385SX system performance data.

5.2.2.2 WRITE BUFFER STATUS (WBS)

WBS is activated when 386 SX write cycle data is latched into the 74676 latching transceiver (via LDSTB). It is deactivated upon completion of the write cycle on the 82385SX bus when the 82385SX sees the BREADY# signal. WBS behavior is illustrated in Figures 5-3F through 5-3J, and potential applications are discussed in Chapter 3.

5.2.2.3 Cache Flush (FLUSH)

FLUSH is an 82385SX input which is used to reset all tag valid bits within the cache directory. The FLUSH input must be kept active for at least 4 CLK (8 CLK2) periods to complete the directory flush. Flush is generally used in diagnostics but can also be used in applications where snooping cannot guarantee coherency.

5.3 Bus Watching (Snoop) Interface

The 82385SX's bus watching interface consists of the snoop address (SA1–SA23), snoop strobe (SSTB#), and snoop enable (SEN) inputs. If masters reside at the system bus level, then the SA1–SA23 inputs are connected to the system address lines and SEN the system bus memory write command. SSTB# indicates that a valid address is present on the system bus. Note that the snoop bus inputs are synchronous, so care must be taken to ensure that they are stable during their sample windows. If no master resides beyond the 82385 bus level, then the 82385 inputs SA1–SA23, SEN, and SSTB# can respectively tie directly to BA1–BA23, BW/R#, and BADS# of the other system bus master (see Figure 5.5). However, it is recommended that SEN be driven by the logical "AND" of BW/R# and BM/IO# so as to prevent I/O writes from unnecessarily invalidating cache data.

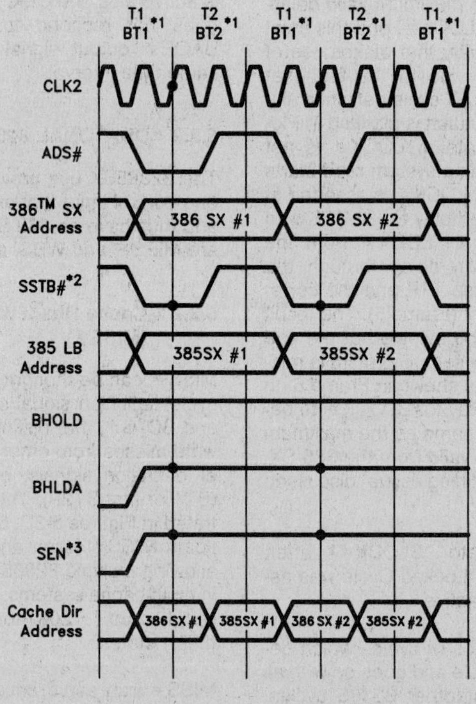

T1 BT1 *1 | T2 BT2 *1 | T1 BT1 *1 | T2 BT2 *1 | T1 BT1 *1

CLK2

ADS#

386™ SX Address: 386 SX #1, 386 SX #2

SSTB# *2

385 LB Address: 385SX #1, 385SX #2

BHOLD

BHLDA

SEN *3

Cache Dir Address: 386 SX #1, 385SX #1, 386 SX #2, 385SX #2

290222–41

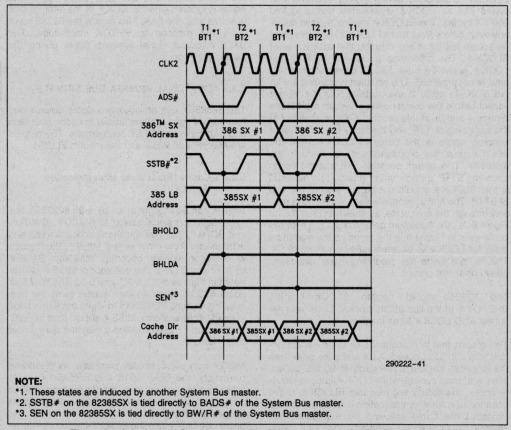

NOTE:
*1. These states are induced by another System Bus master.
*2. SSTB# on the 82385SX is tied directly to BADS# of the System Bus master.
*3. SEN on the 82385SX is tied directly to BW/R# of the System Bus master.

Figure 5.4. Interleaved Snoop and 386™ SX Accesses to the Cache Directory

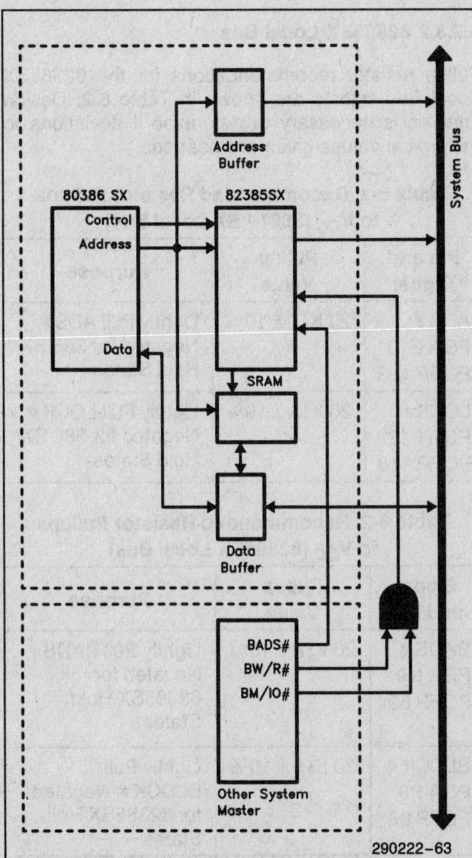

Figure 5.5. Snooping Connections in a Multi Master Environment

When the 82385SX detects a system write by another master and the conditions in Figure 5.4 are met: CLK2 PHI1 rising (CLK falling), BHLDA asserted, SEN asserted, SSTB# asserted, it internally latches SA1–SA23 and runs a cache look-up to see if the altered main memory location is duplicated in the cache. If yes (a snoop hit), the line valid bit associated with that cache entry is cleared. An important feature of the 82385SX is that even the 386 SX is running zero wait state hits out of the cache, all snoops are serviced. This is accomplished by time multiplexing the cache directory between the 386 SX address and the latched system address. If the SSTB# signal occurs during an 82385SX comparison cycle (for the 386 SX), the 386 SX cycle has the highest priority in accessing the cache directory. This takes the first of the two 386 SX states. The other state is then used for the snoop comparison. This worst case example, depicted in Figure 5.4, shows the 386 SX running zero wait state hits on the 386 SX local bus, and another master running zero wait state writes on the 82385SX bus. No snoops are missed, and no performance penalty incurred.

5.4 Reset Definition

Table 5-1 summarizes the states of all 82385SX outputs during reset and initialization. A slave mode 82385SX tri-states its "386 SX-like" front end. A master mode 82385SX emits a pulse stream on its BACP output. As the 386 SX address and cycle definition lines reach their reset values, this stream will latch the reset values through to the 82385SX bus.

Table 5-1. Pin State during RESET and Initialization

Output Name	Signal Level during RESET and Initialization	
	Master Mode	Slave Mode
NA#	High	High
READY0#	High	High
BRDYEN#	High	High
CALEN	High	High
CWEA#–CWEB#	High	High
CS0#, CS1#	Low	Low
CT/R#	High	High
COEA#–COEB#	High	High
BADS#	High	High Z
BBHE#, BBLE#	386 BE#	High Z
BLOCK#	High	High Z
MISS#	High	High Z
BACP	Pulse(1)	Pulse
BAOE#	Low	High
BT/R#	Low	Low
DOE#	High	High
LDSTB	Low	Low
BHOLD	—	Low
BHLDA	Low	—
WBS	Low	Low

NOTE:
1. In Master Mode, BAOE# is low and BACP emits a pulse stream during reset. As the 386 SX address and cycle definition signals reach their reset values, the pulse stream on BACP will latch these values through to the 82385SX local bus.

4

6.0 82385SX SYSTEM DESIGN CONSIDERATIONS

6.1 Introduction

This chapter discusses techniques which should be implemented in an 82385SX system. Because of the high frequencies and high performance nature of the 386 SX CPU/82385SX system, good design and layout techniques are necessary. It is always recommended to perform a complete design analysis of new system designs.

6.2 Power and Grounding

6.2.1 POWER CONNECTIONS

The 82385SX utilizes 8 power (V_{CC}) and 10 ground (V_{SS}) pins. All V_{CC} and V_{SS} pins must be connected to their appropriate plane. On a printed circuit board, all V_{CC} pins must be connected to the power plane and all V_{SS} pins must be connected to the ground plane.

6.2.2 POWER DECOUPLING

Although the 82385SX itself is generally a "passive" device in that it has a few output signals, the cache subsystem as a whole is quite active. Therefore, many decoupling capacitors should be placed around the 82385SX cache subsystem.

Low inductance capacitors and interconnects are recommended for best high frequency electrical performance. Inductance can be reduced by shortening circuit board traces between the decoupling capacitors and their respective devices as much as possible. Capacitors specifically for PGA packages are also commercially available, for the lowest possible inductance.

6.2.3 RESISTOR RECOMMENDATIONS

Because of the dual structure of the 82385SX subsystem (386 SX Local Bus and 82385SX Local Bus), any signals which are recommended to be pulled up will be respective to one of the busses. The following sections will discuss signals for both busses.

6.2.3.1 386 SX LOCAL BUS

For typical designs, the pullup resistors shown in Table 6-1 are recommended. This table correlates to Chapter 7 of the 386 SX Data Sheet. However, particular designs may have a need to differ from the listed values. Design analysis is recommended to determine specific requirements.

6.2.3.2 82835SX Local Bus

Pullup resistor recommendations for the 82385SX Local Bus signals are shown in Table 6-2. Design analysis is necessary to determine if deviations to the typical values given are needed.

Table 6-1. Recommended Resistor Pullups to V_{CC} (386™ SX Local Bus)

Pin and Signal	Pullup Value	Purpose
ADS# PGA E13 PQFP 123	20 KΩ ±10%	Lightly Pull ADS# Negated for 386 SX Hold States
LOCK# PGA F13 PQFP 118	20 KΩ ±10%	Lightly Pull LOCK# Negated for 386 SX Hold States

Table 6-2. Recommended Resistor Pullups to V_{CC} (82385SX Local Bus)

Signal and Pin	Pullup Value	Purpose
BADS# PGA N9 PQFP 89	20 KΩ ±10%	Lightly Pull BADS# Negated for 82385SX Hold States
BLOCK# PGA P9 PQFP 86	20 KΩ ±10%	Lightly Pull BLOCK# Negated for 82385SX Hold States
MISS# PGA N8 PQFP 85	20 KΩ ±10%	Lightly Pull MISS# Negated for 82385SX Hold States

6.3 82385SX Signal Connections

6.3.1 CONFIGURATION INPUTS

The 82835 configuration signals (M/S#, 2W/D#, DEFOE#) must be connected (pulled up) to the appropriate logic level for the system design. There is also a reserved 82385SX input which must be tied to the appropriate level. Refer to Table 6-3 for the signals and their required logic level.

Table 6-3. 82385SX Configuration Inputs Logic Levels

Pin and Signal	Logic Level	Purpose
M/S# PGA B13 PQFP 124	High	Master Mode Operation
	Low	Slave Mode Operation
2W/D# PGA D12 PQFP 127	High	2-Way Set Associative
	Low	Direct Mapped
Reserved PGA L14 PQFP 102	High	Must be tied to V_{CC} via a pull-up for proper functionality
DEFOE# PGA A14 PQFP 128	N/A	Define Cache Output Enable. Allows use of any SRAM.

NOTE:
The listed 82385SX pins which need to be tied high should use a pull-up resistor in the range of 5 KΩ to 20 KΩ.

6.3.2 CLK2 and RESET

The 82385SX has two inupts to which the 386 SX CLK2 signal must be connected. One is labeled CLK2 (82385SX pin C13) and the other is labeled BCLK2 (82385SX pin L13). These two inputs must be tied together on the printed circuit board.

The 82385SX also has two reset inputs. RESET (82385SX pin D13) and BRESET (82385SX pin K12) must be connected on the printed circuit board.

6.4 Unused Pin Requirements

For reliable operation, ALWAYS connect unused inputs to a valid logic level. As is the case with most other CMOS processes, a floating input will increase the current consumption of the component and give an indeterminate state to the component.

6.5 Cache SRAM Requirements

The 82385SX offers the option of using SRAMs with or without an output enable pin. This is possible by inserting a transceiver between the SRAMs and the 386 SX local data bus and strapping DEFOE# to the appropriate logic level for a given system configuration. This transceiver may also be desirable in a system which has a very heavily loaded 386 SX local data bus. The following sections discuss the SRAM requirements for all cache configurations.

6.5.1 CACHE MEMORY WITHOUT TRANSCEIVERS

As discussed in Section 3.2, the 82385SX presents all of the control signals necessary to access the cache memory. The SRAM chip selects, write enables, and output enables are driven directly by the 82385SX. Table 6-4 lists the required SRAM specifications. These specifications allow for zero margins. They should be used as guides for the actual system design.

Table 6-4. SRAM Specs for Non-Buffered Cache Memory

SRAM Spec Requirements	Direct Mapped 16 MHz	Direct Mapped 20 MHz	2-Way Set Associative 16 MHz	2-Way Set Associative 20 MHz
Read Cycle Requirements				
Address Access (MAX)	64 ns	44 ns	62 ns	42 ns
Chip Select Access (MAX)	76	56	76	56
OE# to Data Valid (MAX)	25	19	19	14
OE# to Data Float (MAX)	20	20	20	20
Write Cycle Requirements				
Chip Select to End of Write (MIN)	40	30	40	30
Address Valid to End of Write (MIN)	58	42	56	40
Write Pulse Width (MIN)	40	30	40	30
Data Setup (MAX)	—	—	—	—
Data Hold (MIN)	4	4	4	4

6.5.2 CACHE MEMORY WITH TRANSCEIVERS

To implement an 82385SX subsystem using cache memory transceivers, COEA# or COEB# must be used as output enable signals for the transceivers and DEFOE# must be appropriately strapped for proper COEx# functionality (since the cache SRAM transceivers must be enabled for writes as well as reads). DEFOE# must be tied high when using cache SRAM transceivers. In a 2-way set associative organization, COEA# enables the transceiver for bank A and COEB# enables the bank B transceiver. A direct mapped cache may use either COEA# or COEB# to enable the transceiver. Table 6-5 lists the required SRAM specifications. These specifications allow for zero margin. They should be used as guides for the actual system design.

7.0 SYSTEM TEST CONSIDERATIONS

7.1 Introduction

Power On Self Testing (POST) is performed by most systems after a reset. This chapter discusses the requirements for properly testing an 82385SX based system after power up.

7.2 Main Memory (DRAM) Testing

Most systems perform a memory test by writing a data pattern and then reading and comparing the data. This test may also be used to determine the total available memory within the system. Without properly taking into account the 82385SX cache memory, the memory test can give erroneous results. This will occur if the cache responds with read hits during the memory test routine.

7.2.1 MEMORY TESTING ROUTINE

In order to properly test main memory, the test routine must not read from the same block consecutively. For instance, if the test routine writes a data pattern to the first 16 Kbytes of memory (0000–3FFFH), reads from the same block, writes a new pattern to the same locations (0000–3FFFH), and read the new pattern, the second pattern tested would have had data returned from the 82385SX cache memory. Therefore, it is recommended that the test routine work with a memory block of at least 32 Kbytes. This will guarantee that no 16 Kbyte block will be read twice consecutively.

7.3 82385SX Cache Memory Testing

With the addition of SRAMs for the cache memory, it may be desirable for the system to be able to test the cache SRAMs during system diagnostics. This requires the test routine to access only the cache memory. The requirements for this routine are based on where it resides within the memory map. This can

Table 6-5. SRAM Specs for Buffered Cache Memory

SRAM Spec Requirements	Direct Mapped 16 MHz	Direct Mapped 20 MHz	2-Way Set Associative 16 MHz	2-Way Set Associative 20 MHz
Read Cycle Requirements				
Address Access (MAX)	57 ns	37 ns	55 ns	35 ns
Chip Select Access (MAX)	68	48	68	48
OE# to Data Valid (MAX)	N/A	N/A	N/A	N/A
OE# to Data Float (MAX)	N/A	N/A	N/A	N/A
Write Cycle Requirements				
Chip Select to End of Write (MIN)	40	30	40	30
Address Valid to End of Write (MIN)	58	42	56	40
Write Pulse Width (MIN)	40	30	40	30
Data Setup (MAX)	25	15	25	15
Data Hold (MIN)	3	3	3	3

be broken into two areas: the routine residing in cacheable memory space or the routine residing in either non-cacheable memory or on the 386 SX local bus (using the LBA# input).

7.3.1 TEST ROUTINE IN THE NCA# OR LBA# MEMORY MAP

In this configuration, the test routine will never be cached. The recommended method is code which will access a single 16 Kbyte block during the test. Initially, a 16 Kbyte read (assume 0000–3FFFH) must be executed. This will fill the cache directory with the address information which will be used in the diagnostic procedure. Then, a 16 Kbyte write to the same address locations (0000–3FFFH) will load the cache with the desired test pattern (due to write hits). The comparison can be made by completing another 16 Kbyte read (same locations, 0000–3FFFH), which will be cache read hits. Subsequent writes and reads to the same addresses will enable various patterns to be tested.

7.3.2 TEST ROUTINE IN CACHEABLE MEMORY

In this case, it must be understood that the diagnostic routine must reside in the cache memory before the actual data testing can begin. Otherwise, when the 386 SX performs a code fetch, a location within the cache memory which is to be tested will be altered due to the read miss (code fetch) update.

The first task is to load the diagnostic routine into the top of the cache memory. It must be known how much memory is required for the code as the rest of the cache memory will be tested as in the earlier method. Once the diagnostics have been cached (via read updates), the code will perform the same type of read/write/read/compare as in the routine explained in the above section. The difference is that now the amount of cache memory to be tested is 16 Kbytes minus the length of the test routine.

7.4 82385SX Cache Directory Testing

Since the 82385SX does not directly access the data bus, it is not possible to easily complete a comparison of the cache directory. (The 82385SX can serially transmit its directory contents. See Section 7.5.) However, the cache memory tests described in Section 7.3 will indicate if the directory is working properly. Otherwise, the data comparison within the diagnostics will show locations which fail.

There is a slight possibility that the cache memory comparison could pass even if locations within the directory gave false hit/miss results. This could cause the comparison to always be performed to main memory instead of the cache and give a proper comparison to the 386 SX. The solution here is to use the MISS# output of the 82385SX as an indicator to a diagnostic port which can be read by the 386 SX. It could also be used to flag an interrupt if a failure occurs.

The implementation of these techniques in the diagnostics will assure proper functionality of the 82385SX subsystem.

7.5 Special Function Pins

As mentioned in Chapter 3, there are three 82385SX pins which have reserved functions in addition to their normal operational functions. These pins are MISS#, WBS, and FLUSH.

As discussed previously, the 82385SX performs a directory flush when the FLUSH input is held active for at least 4 CLK (8 CLK2) cycles. However, the FLUSH pin also serves as a diagnostic input to the 82385SX. The 82385SX will enter a reserved mode if the FLUSH pin is high at the falling edge of RESET.

If, during normal operation, the FLUSH input is active for only one CLK (2 CLK2) cycle/s, the 82385SX will enter another reserved mode. Therefore it must be guaranteed that FLUSH is active for at least the 4 CLK (8 CLK2) cycle specification.

WBS and MISS# serve as outputs in the 82385SX reserved modes.

8.0 MECHANICAL DATA

8.1 Introduction

This chapter discusses the physical package and its connections in detail.

8.2 Pin Assignment

The 82385SX PGA pinout as viewed from the top side of the component is shown by Figure 8-1. Its pinout as viewed from the Pin side of the component is shown in Figure 8-2.

The 82385SX Plastic Quad Flat Pack (PQFP) pinout from the top side of the component is shown by Figure 8-3.

V_{CC} and V_{SS} connections must be made to multiple V_{CC} and V_{SS} (GND) pins. Each V_{CC} and V_{SS} must be connected to the appropriate voltage level. The circuit board should include V_{CC} and GND planes for power distribution and all V_{CC} and V_{SS} pins must be connected to the appropriate plane.

	P	N	M	L	K	J	H	G	F	E	D	C	B	A
1	V_{CC}	V_{SS}	V_{CC}	RES	RES	A21	A18	A17	A14	A11	A8	V_{CC}	V_{SS}	A5
2	V_{SS}	V_{SS}	A23	RES	RES	A22	A20	A16	A13	A10	A7	A6	A2	SA1
3	V_{CC}	NA#	READYO#	RES	RES	RES	A19	A15	A12	A9	A4	A3	A1	SA2
4	V_{SS}	CALEN	LDSTB									SA3	SA4	SA6
5	RES	CT/R#	CS0#									SA5	SA9	SA8
6	CWEB#	RES	CS1#									SA7	SA10	SA12
7	COEA#	CWEA#	COEB#									SA11	SA14	SA13
8	BRDYEN#	MISS#	WBS									SA17	SA15	SA16
9	BLOCK#	BADS#	BAOE#									SA21	SA18	SA19
10	BACP	BT/R#	DOE#									RES	RES	SA20
11	V_{CC}	BHOLD	BHLDA									RES	RES	SA22
12	V_{SS}	BBHE#	BBLE#	RES	BRESET	SEN	RES	NCA#	D/C#	FLUSH	2W/D#	SA23	RES	RES
13	V_{CC}	V_{CC}	RES	BCLK2	BREADY#	SSTB#	BHE#	RES	LOCK#	ADS#	RESET	CLK2	M/S#	RES
14	V_{SS}	V_{SS}	V_{SS}	RES	BNA#	RES	LBA#	BLE#	W/R#	M/IO#	READYI#	V_{CC}	V_{SS}	DEFOE#

290222-42

Figure 8-1. 82385SX PGA Pinout—View from TOP Side

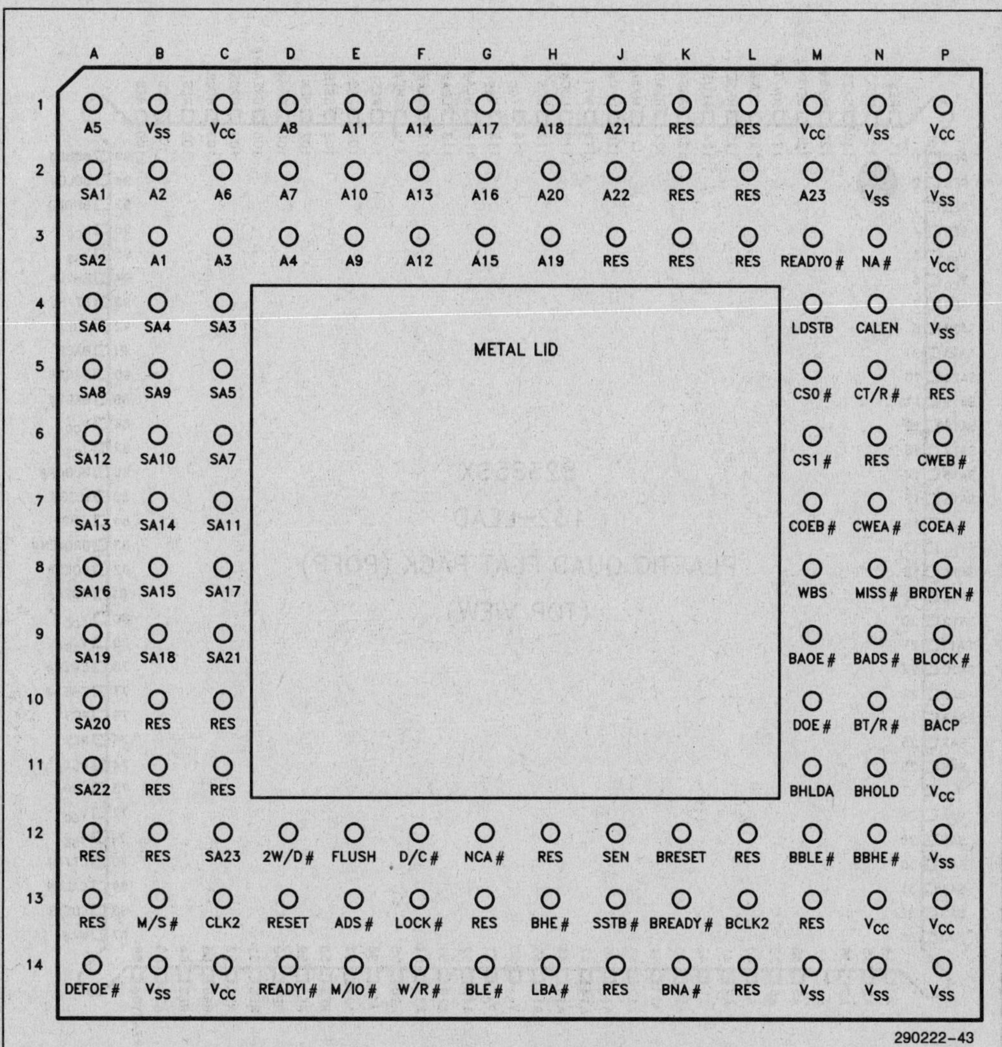

Figure 8-2. 82385SX PGA Pinout—View from PIN Side

4

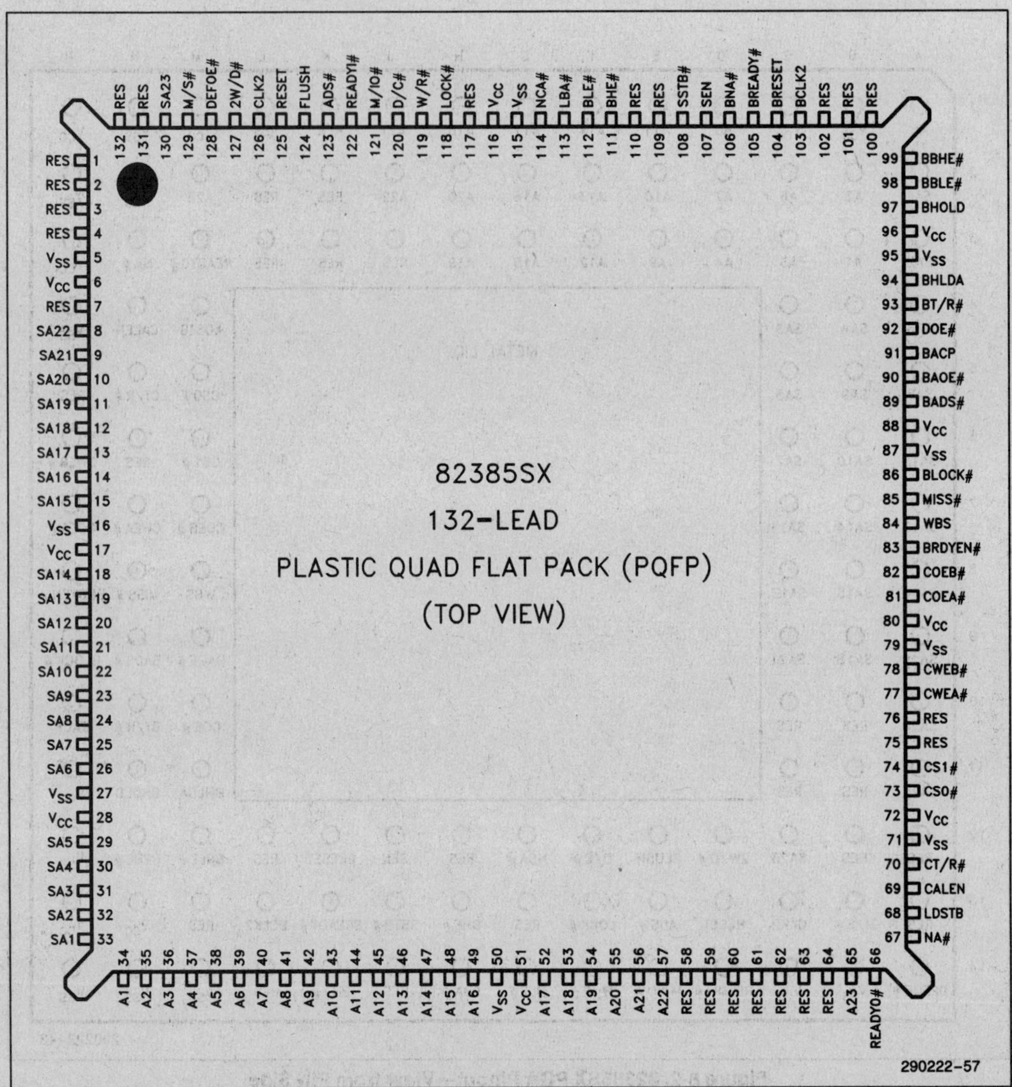

Figure 8-3. 82385SX PQFP Pinout—View from TOP Side

Table 8-1. 82385SX Pinout—Functional Grouping

PGA	PQFP	Signal
M2	65	A23
J2	57	A22
J1	56	A21
H2	55	A20
H3	54	A19
H1	53	A18
G1	52	A17
G2	49	A16
G3	48	A15
F1	47	A14
F2	46	A13
F3	45	A12
E1	44	A11
E2	43	A10
E3	42	A9
D1	41	A8
D2	40	A7
C2	39	A6
A1	38	A5
D3	37	A4
C3	36	A3
B2	35	A2
B3	34	A1
G14	112	BLE#
H13	111	BHE#
C13	126	CLK2
D13	125	RESET
K12	104	BRESET
L13	103	BCLK2
F14	119	W/R#
F12	120	D/C#
E14	121	M/IO#
F13	118	LOCK#
E13	123	ADS#
G12	114	NCA#
H14	113	LBA#
D14	122	READYI#
M3	66	READYO#
C12	130	SA23
A11	8	SA22
C9	9	SA21
A10	10	SA20
A9	11	SA19
B9	12	SA18
C8	13	SA17
A8	14	SA16
B8	15	SA15
B7	18	SA14
A7	19	SA13
A6	20	SA12
C7	21	SA11
B6	22	SA10
B5	23	SA9
A5	24	SA8
C6	25	SA7
A4	26	SA6
C5	29	SA5
B4	30	SA4
C4	31	SA3
A3	32	SA2
A2	33	SA1
J12	107	SEN#
J13	108	SSTB#
C1	6	V_{CC}
C14	17	V_{CC}
M1	28	V_{CC}
N13	51	V_{CC}
P1	72	V_{CC}
P3	80	V_{CC}
P11	88	V_{CC}
P13	96	V_{CC}
—	116	V_{CC}
N3	67	NA#
E12	124	FLUSH
M8	84	WBS
N8	85	MISS#
A14	128	DEFOE#
B13	129	M/S#
D12	127	2W/D#
M10	92	DOE#
M4	68	LDSTB
N11	97	BHOLD
M11	94	BHLDA
B1	5	V_{SS}
B14	16	V_{SS}
M14	27	V_{SS}
N1	50	V_{SS}
N2	71	V_{SS}
N14	79	V_{SS}
P2	87	V_{SS}
P4	95	V_{SS}
P12	115	V_{SS}
P14	—	V_{SS}
N9	89	BADS#
M12	98	BBLE#
N12	99	BBHE#
P9	86	BLOCK#
K14	106	BNA#
N4	69	CALEN
P7	81	COEA#
M7	82	COEB#
N7	77	CWEA#
P6	78	CWEB#
M5	73	CS0#
M6	74	CS1#
N5	70	CT/R#
P8	83	BRDYEN#
K13	105	BREADY#
P10	91	BACP
M9	90	BAOE#
N10	93	BT/R#
A12	1	V_{CC} (*)
A13	131	V_{CC} (*)
B10	7	V_{CC} (*)
B11	3	V_{CC} (*)
B12	132	V_{CC} (*)
C10	4	V_{CC} (*)
C11	2	V_{CC} (*)
G13	117	V_{CC} (*)
H12	110	V_{CC} (*)
J3	60	V_{CC} (*)
J14	109	V_{CC} (*)
K1	58	V_{CC} (*)
K2	59	V_{CC} (*)
K3	62	V_{CC} (*)
L1	61	V_{CC} (*)
L2	63	V_{CC} (*)
L3	64	V_{CC} (*)
L12	100	N.C. (*)
L14	102	V_{CC} (*)
M13	101	N.C. (*)
N6	75	N.C. (*)
P5	76	N.C. (*)

*Reserved pins, N.C. indicates a no connect.

4

8.3 Package Dimensions and Mounting

The 82385SX PGA package is a 132-pin ceramic Pin Grid Array. The pins are arranged 0.100 inch (2.54 mm) center-to-center, in a 14 × 14 matrix, three rows around.

A wide variety of available PGA sockets allow low insertion force or zero insertion force mounting. These come in a choice of terminals such as solder-tail, surface mount, or wire wrap.

The 82385SX PQFP is a 132-lead Plastic Quad Flat Pack. The pins are "fine pitch", 0.025 inches (0.635 mm) center to center.

The PQFP device is intended to be surface mounted directly to the printed board although sockets are available for this device.

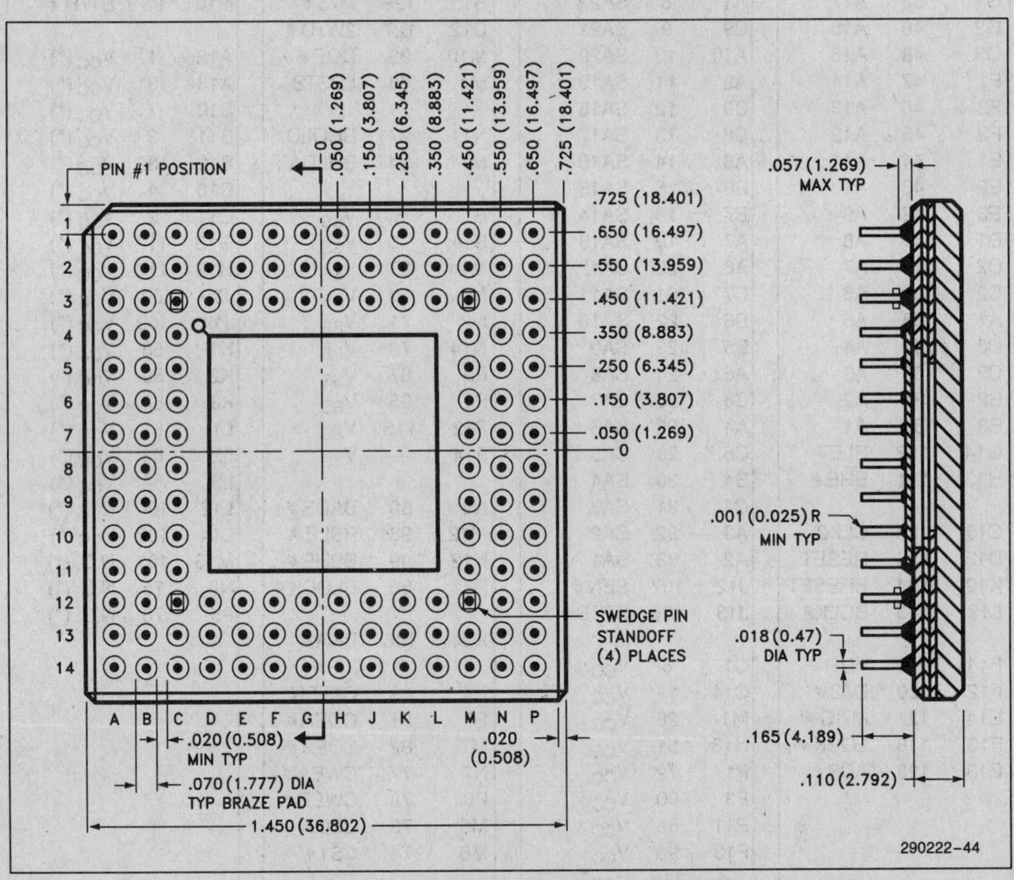

Figure 8-3.1. 132-Pin PGA Package Dimensions

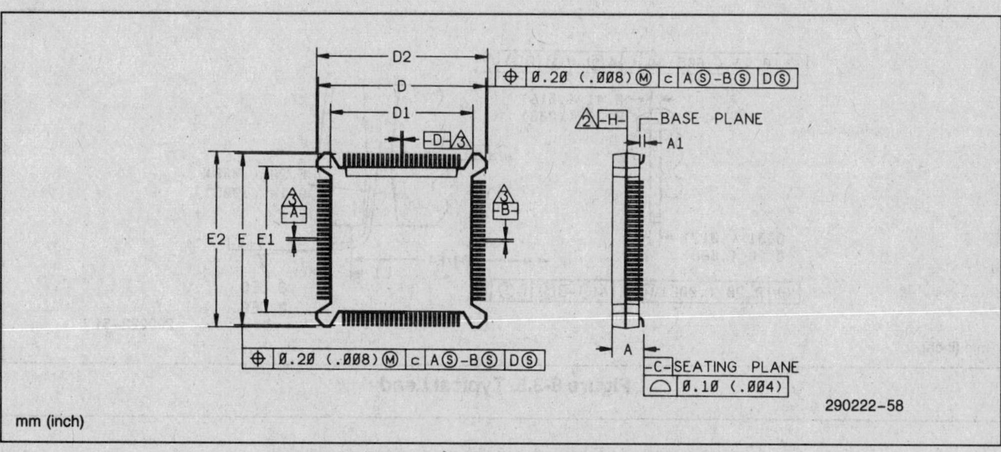

Figure 8-3.2. Principal Dimensions and Datums

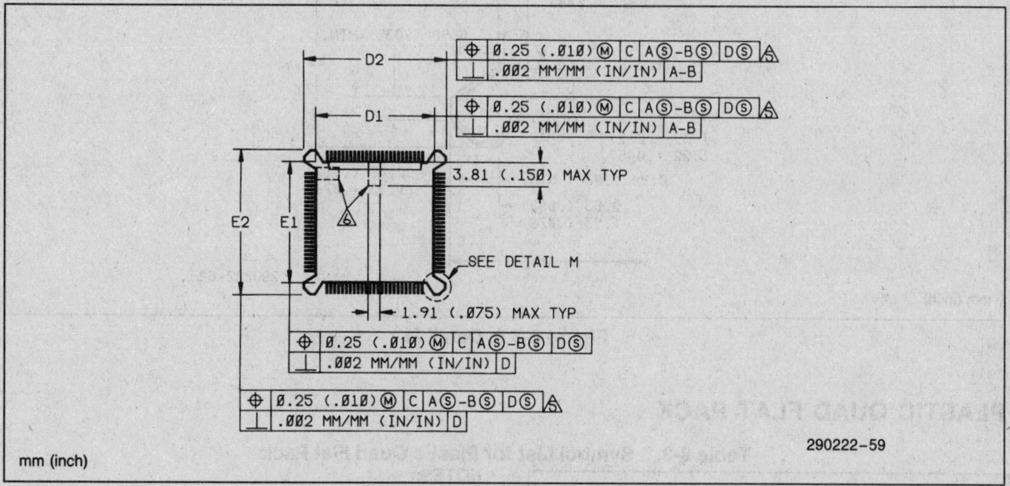

Figure 8-3.3. Molded Details

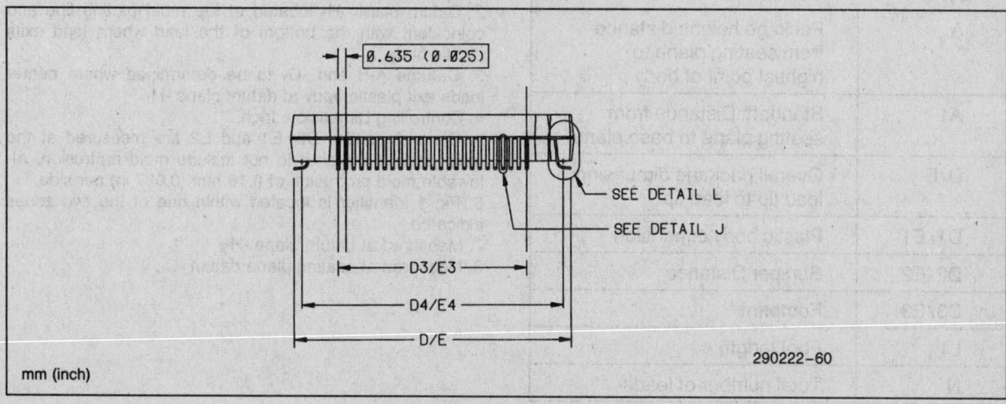

Figure 8-3.4. Terminal Details

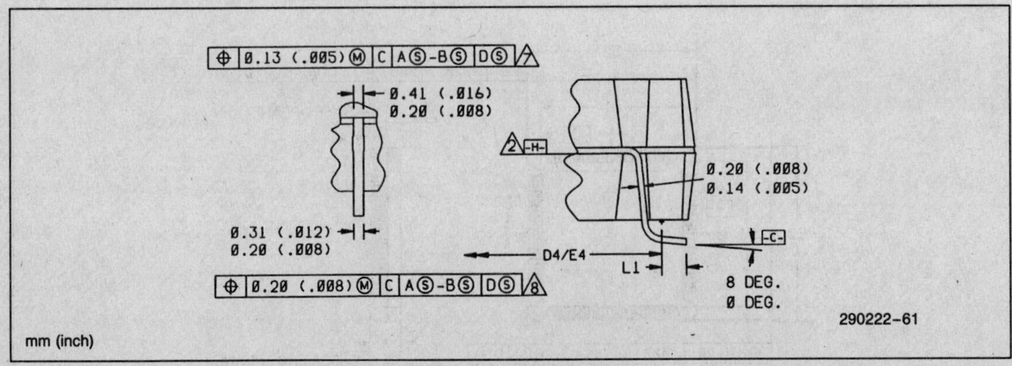

Figure 8-3.5. Typical Lead

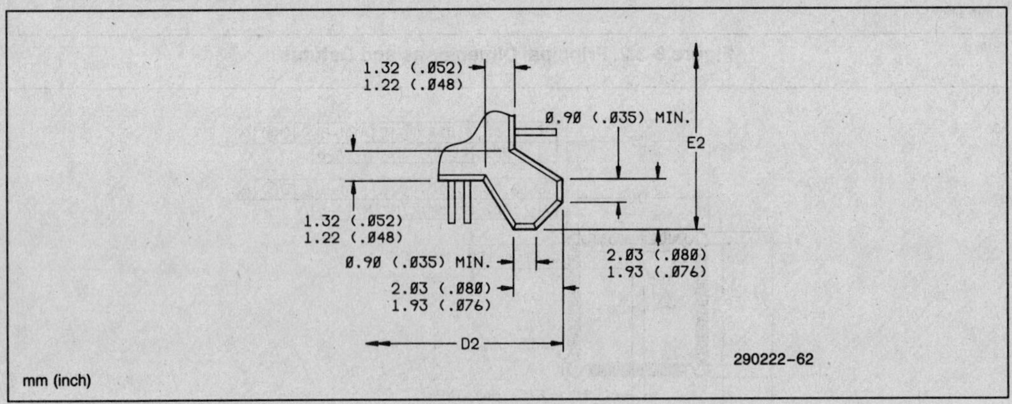

Figure 8-3.6. Detail M

PLASTIC QUAD FLAT PACK

Table 8-3.1. Symbol List for Plastic Quad Flat Pack

Letter or Symbol	Description of Dimensions
A	Package height: distance from seating plane to highest point of body
A1	Standoff: Distance from seating plane to base plane
D/E	Overall package dimension: lead tip to lead tip
D1/E1	Plastic body dimension
D2/E2	Bumper Distance
D3/E3	Footprint
L1	Foot length
N	Total number of leads

NOTES:

1. All dimensions and tolerances conform to ANSI Y14.5M-1982.
2. Datum plane -H- located at the mold parting line and coincident with the bottom of the lead where lead exits plastic body.
3. Datums A-B and -D- to be determined where center leads exit plastic body at datum plane -H-.
4. Controlling Dimension, Inch.
5. Dimensions D1, D2, E1 and E2 are measured at the mold parting line and do not include mold protrusion. Allowable mold protrusion of 0.18 mm (0.007 in) per side.
6. Pin 1 identifier is located within one of the two zones indicated.
7. Measured at datum plane -H-.
8. Measured at seating plane datum -C-.

Table 8-3.2. PQFP Dimensions and Tolerances

Intel Case Outline Drawings
Plastic Quad Flat Pack
0.025 Inch Pitch

Symbol	Description	Min	Max
N	Leadcount	132	
A	Package Height	0.160	0.170
A1	Standoff	0.020	0.030
D, E	Terminal Dimension	1.075	1.085
D1, E1	Package Body	0.947	0.953
D2, E2	Bumper Distance	1.097	1.103
D3, E3	Lead Dimension	0.800 REF	
L1	Foot Length	0.020	0.030
Issue	IWS Preliminary 1/15/87		

Intel Case Outline Drawings
Plastic Quad Flat Pack
0.64 mm Pitch

Symbol	Description	Min	Max
N	Leadcount	132	
A	Package Height	4.06	4.32
A1	Standoff	0.51	0.76
D, E	Terminal Dimension	27.31	27.56
D1, E1	Package Body	24.05	24.21
D2, E2	Bumper Distance	27.86	28.02
D3, E3	Lead Dimension	20.32 REF	
L1	Foot Length	0.51	0.76
Issue	IWS Preliminary 1/15/87		

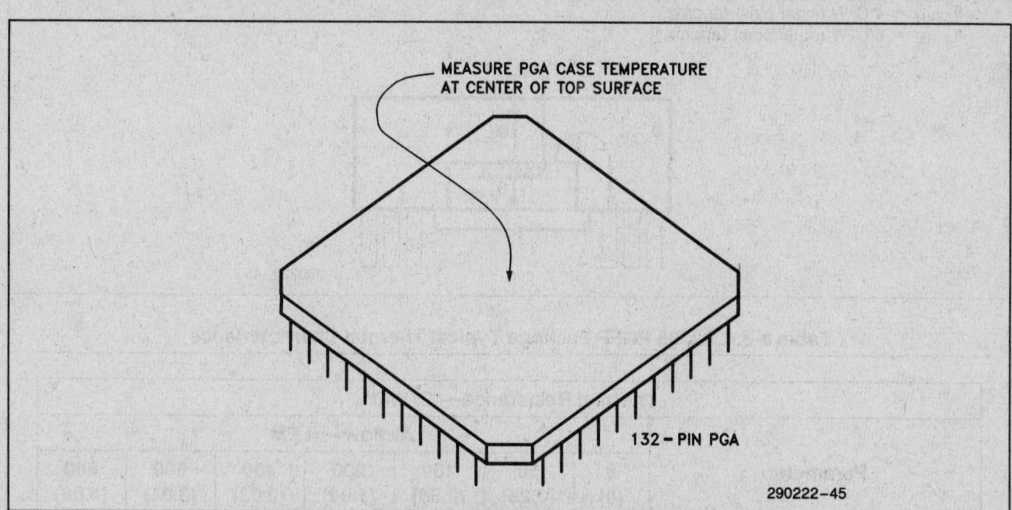

Figure 8-3.7. Measuring 82385SX PGA Case Temperature

Table 8-3.3. 82385SX PGA Package Typical Thermal Characteristics

Thermal Resistance—°C/Watt							
Parameter	Airflow—f^3/min (m^3/sec)						
	0 (0)	50 (0.25)	100 (0.50)	200 (1.01)	400 (2.03)	600 (3.04)	800 (4.06)
θ Junction-to-Case (Case Measured as Figure 8-3.7)	2	2	2	2	2	2	2
θ Case-to-Ambient (No Heatsink)	19	18	17	15	12	10	9
θ Case-to-Ambient (with Omnidirectional Heatsink)	16	15	14	12	9	7	6
θ Case-to-Ambient (with Unidirectional Heatsink)	15	14	13	11	8	6	5

NOTES:
1. Table 8-3.3 applies to 82385SX PGA plugged into socket or soldered directly onto board.
2. $\theta_{JA} = \theta_{JC} + \theta_{CA}$.
3. $\theta_{J\text{-}CAP}$ = 4°C/W (approx.)
   $\theta_{J\text{-}PIN}$ = 4°C/W (inner pins) (approx.)
   $\theta_{J\text{-}PIN}$ = 8°C/W (outer pins) (approx.)

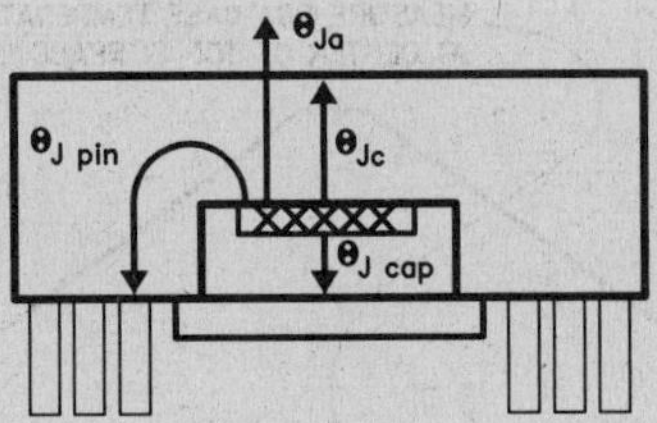

290222–46

Table 8-3.4. 82385 PQFP Package Typical Thermal Characteristics

Thermal Resistance—°C/Watt							
Parameter	Airflow—/LFM						
	0 (0)	50 (0.25)	100 (0.50)	200 (1.01)	400 (2.03)	600 (3.04)	800 (4.06)
θ Junction-to-Case (Case Measured as Figure 8-3.7)	5	5	5	5	5	5	5
θ Case-to-Ambient (No Heatsink)	23.5	22.0	20.5	17.5	14.0	11.5	9.5
θ Case-to-Ambient (with Omnidirectional Heatsink)	TO BE DEFINED						
θ Case-to-Ambient (with Unidirectional Heatsink)	TO BE DEFINED						

NOTES:
1. Table 8-3.4 applies to 82385SX PQFP plugged into socket or soldered directly onto board.
2. $\theta_{JA} = \theta_{JC} + \theta_{CA}$.
3. $\theta_{J\text{-}CAP}$ = 4°C/W (approx.)
   $\theta_{J\text{-}PIN}$ = 4°C/W (inner pins) (approx.)
   $\theta_{J\text{-}PIN}$ = 8°C/W (outer pins) (approx.)

8.4 Package Thermal Specification

The case temperature should be measured at the center of the top surface as in Figure 8-3.7 for PGA or Table 8-3.3 for PQFP. The case temperature may be measured in any environment to determine whether or not the 82385SX is within the specified operating range.

9.0 ELECTRICAL DATA

9.1 Introduction

This chapter presents the A.C. and D.C specifications for the 82385SX.

9.2 Maximum Ratings

Storage Temperature .... −65°C to +150°C

Case Temperature under Bias ... −65°C to +110°C

Supply Voltage with Respect to V_{SS} .... −0.5V to +6.5V

Voltage on Any Other Pin .... −0.5V to V_{CC} + 0.5V

NOTE:

Stress above those listed may cause permanent damage to the device. This is a stress rating only and functional operation at these or any other conditions above those listed in the operational sections of this specification is not implied.

Exposure to absolute maximum rating conditions for extended periods may affect device reliability. Although the 82385SX contains protective circuitry to resist damage from static electric discharges, always take precautions against high static voltages or electric fields.

9.3 D.C. Specifications T_{CASE} = 0°C to +85°C; V_{CC} = 5V ±5%; V_{SS} = 0V

Table 9-1. D.C. Specifications (16 MHz and 20 MHz)

Symbol	Parameter	Min	Max	Unit	Test Condition
V_{IL}	Input Low Voltage	−0.3	0.8	V	(Noe 1)
V_{IH}	Input High Voltage	2.0	V_{CC} + 0.3	V	
V_{CL}	CLK2, BCLK2 Input Low	−0.3	0.8	V	(Note 1)
V_{CH}	CLK2, BCLK2 Input High	V_{CC} − 0.8	V_{CC} + 0.3	V	
V_{OL}	Output Low Voltage		0.45	V	I_{OL} = 4 mA
V_{OH}	Output High Voltage	2.4		V	I_{OH} = −1 mA
I_{CC}	Power Supply Current		275	mA	(Note 2)
I_{LI}	Input Leakage Current		±15	μA	0V < V_{IN} < V_{CC}
I_{LO}	Output Leakage Current		±15	μA	0.45V < V_{OUT} < V_{CC}
C_{IN}	Input Capacitance		10	pF	(Note 3)
C_{CLK}	CLK2 Input Capacitance		20	pF	(Note 3)

NOTES:
1. Minimum value is not 100% tested.
2. I_{CC} is specified with inputs driven to CMOS levels. I_{CC} may be higher if driven to TTL levels.
3. Sampled only.

9.4 A.C. Specifications

The A.C. specifications given in the following tables consist of output delays and input setup requirements. The A.C. diagram's purpose is to illustrate the clock edges from which the timing parameters are measured. The reader should not infer any other timing relationships from them. For specific information on timing relationships between signals, refer to the appropriate functional section.

A.C. spec measurement is defined in Figure 9-1. Inputs must be driven to the levels shown when A.C. specifications are measured. 82385SX output delays are specified with minimum and maximum limits, which are measured as shown. 82385SX input setup and hold times are specified as minimums and define the smallest acceptable sampling window. Within the sampling window, a synchronous input signal must be stable for correct 82385SX operation.

9.4.1 FREQUENCY DEPENDENT SIGNALS

The 82385SX has signals whose output valid delays are dependent on the clock frequency. These signals are marked in the A.C. Specification Tables with a Note 1.

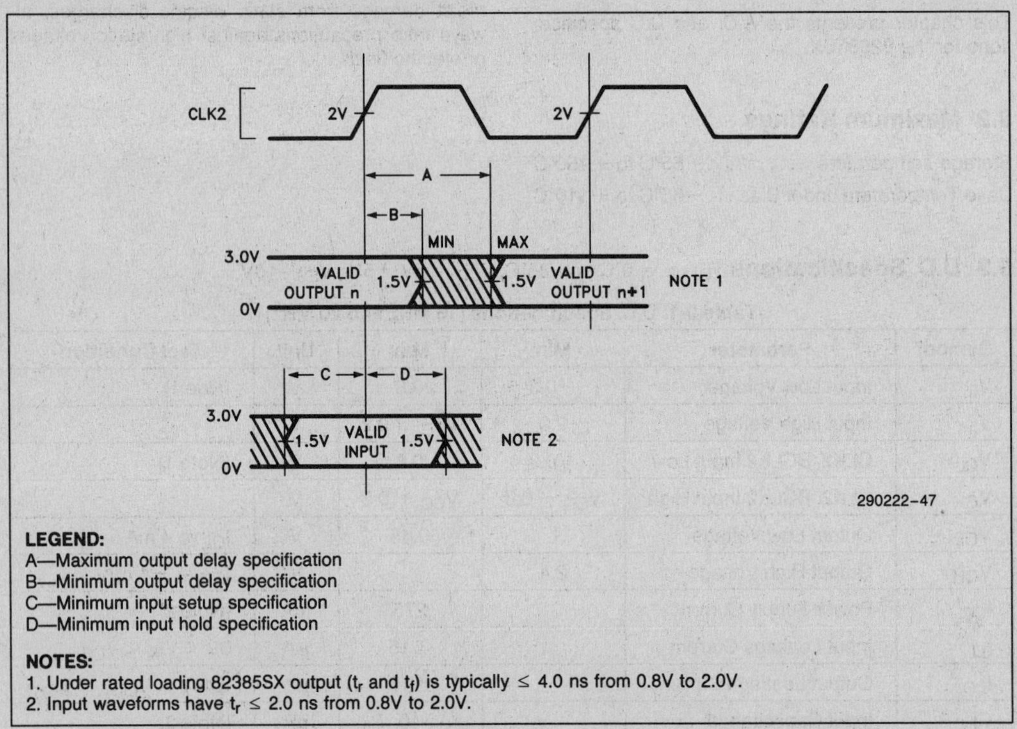

LEGEND:
A—Maximum output delay specification
B—Minimum output delay specification
C—Minimum input setup specification
D—Minimum input hold specification

NOTES:
1. Under rated loading 82385SX output (t_r and t_f) is typically ≤ 4.0 ns from 0.8V to 2.0V.
2. Input waveforms have t_r ≤ 2.0 ns from 0.8V to 2.0V.

Figure 9-1. Drive Levels and Measurement Points for A.C. Specification

A.C. SPECIFICATION TABLES

Functional operating range: V_{CC} = 5V ±5%; T_{CASE} = 0°C to +85°C

A.C. Specifications at 16 MHz

Symbol	Parameter	Min	Max	Units	Notes
t1	Operating Frequency	15.4	16	MHz	
t2	CLK2, BCLK2 Period	31.25	32.5	ns	
t3a	CLK2, BCLK2 High Time @ 2V	10		ns	
t3b	CLK2, BCLK2 High Time @ 3.7V	7		ns	3
t4a	CLK2, BCLK2 Low Time @ 2V	10		ns	
t4b	CLK2, BCLK2 Low Time @ 0.8V	7		ns	3
t5	CLK2, BCLK2 Fall Time		8	ns	3, 9
t6	CLK2, BCLK2 Rise Time		8	ns	3, 9
t7a	A4–A12 Setup Time	30		ns	1
t7b	LOCK# Setup Time	19		ns	1
t7c	BLE#, BHE# Setup Time	21		ns	1
t7d	A1–A3, A13–A23 Setup Time	23		ns	1
t8	A1–A23, BLE#, BHE#, LOCK# Hold	3		ns	
t9a	M/IO#, D/C# Setup Time	30		ns	1
t9b	W/R# Setup Time	30		ns	1
t9c	ADS# Setup Time	30		ns	1
t10	M/IO#, D/C#, W/R#, ADS# Hold Time	5		ns	
t11	READYI# Setup Time	19		ns	1
t12	READYI# Hold Time	4		ns	
t13a1	NCA# Setup Time (See t55b2)	27		ns	6
t13a2	NCA# Setup Time (See t55b3)	20		ns	6
t13b	LBA# Setup Time	16		ns	
t14a	NCA# Hold Time	4		ns	
t14b	LBA# Hold Time	4		ns	
t15	RESET, BRESET Setup Time	13		ns	
t16	RESET, BRESET Hold Time	4		ns	
t17	NA# Valid Delay	12	42	ns	1 (25 pF Load)
t18	READYO# Valid Delay	3	31	ns	1 (25 pF Load)
t19	BRDYEN# Valid Delay	3	31	ns	
t21a1	CALEN Rising, PHI1	3	30	ns	
t21a2	CALEN Falling, PHI1	3	30	ns	
t21a3	CALEN Falling in T1P, PHI2	3	30	ns	
t21b	CALEN Rising Following CWTH	3	39	ns	1
t21c	CALEN Pulse Width	10		ns	
t21d	CALEN Rising to CS# Falling	13		ns	

A.C. SPECIFICATION TABLES (Continued)

Functional operating range: V_{CC} = 5V ±5%; T_{CASE} = 0°C to +85°C

A.C. Specifications at 16 MHz (Continued)

Symbol	Parameter	Min	Max	Units	Notes
t22a1	CWEx# Falling, PHI1 (CWTH)	4	31	ns	1
t22a2	CWEx# Falling, PHI2 (CRDM)	4	31	ns	1
t22b	CWEx# Pulse Width	40		ns	1, 2
t22c1	CWEx# Rising, PHI1 (CWTH)	4	31	ns	1
t22c2	CWEx# Rising, PHI2 (CRDM)	4	31	ns	1
t23a1	CS1#, CS2# Rising, PHI1 (CRDM)	6	41	ns	1
t23a2	CS1#, CS2# Rising, PHI2 (CWTH)	6	41	ns	1
t23a3	CS1#, CS2# Falling, PHI1 (CWTH)	6	41	ns	1
t23a4	CS1#, CS2# Falling, PHI2 (CRDM)	6	41	ns	1
t24a1	CT/R# Rising, PHI2 (CRDH)	6	43	ns	1
t24a2	CT/R# Falling, PHI1 (CRDH)	6	43	ns	1
t24a3	CT/R# Falling, PHI2 (CRDH)	6	43	ns	1
t25a	COEA#, COEB# Falling (Direct)	4	33	ns	(25 pF Load)
t25b	COEA#, COEB# Falling (2-Way)	4	34	ns	1 (25 pF Load)
t25c1	COEx# Rising Delay @ T_{CASE} = 0C	4	20	ns	(25 pF Load)
t25c2	COEx# Rising Delay @ T_{CASE} = T_{MAX}	4	20	ns	(25 pF Load)
t23b	COEx# Falling to CSx# Rising	0		ns	
t25d	CWEx# Falling to COEx# Falling or CWEx# Rising to COEx# Rising	0	10	ns	(25 pF Load)
t26	CS0#, CS1# Falling to CWEx# Rising	40		ns	1, 2
t27	CWEx# Falling to CS0#, CS1# Falling	0		ns	
t28a	CWEx# Rising to CALEN Rising	0		ns	
t28b	CWEx# Rising to CS0#, CS1# Falling	0		ns	
t31	SA(1-23) Setup Time	25		ns	
t32	SA(1-23) Hold Time	3		ns	
t33	BADS# Valid Delay	4	33	ns	1
t34	BADS# Float Delay	4	33	ns	3
t35	BNA# Setup Time	11		ns	
t36	BNA# Hold Time	15		ns	
t37	BREADY# Setup Time	31		ns	1
t38	BREADY# Hold Time	4		ns	
t40a	BACP Rising Delay	0	26	ns	
t40b	BACP Falling Delay	0	28	ns	
t41	BAOE# Valid Delay	3	23	ns	

A.C. SPECIFICATION TABLES (Continued)

Functional operating range: V_{CC} = 5V ±5%; T_{CASE} = 0°C to +85°C

A.C. Specifications at 16 MHz (Continued)

Symbol	Parameter	Min	Max	Units	Notes
t43a	BT/R# Valid Delay	2	27	ns	
t43b1	DOE# Falling Delay	2	30	ns	
t43b2	DOE# Rising Delay @ T_{CASE} = 0C	3	23	ns	
t43b3	DOE# Rising Delay @ T_{CASE} = T_{MAX}	3	26	ns	
t43c	LDSTB Valid Delay	2	33	ns	
t44a	SEN Setup Time	15		ns	
t44b	SSTB# Setup Time	15		ns	
t45	SEN, SSTB# Hold Time	5		ns	
t46	BHOLD Setup Time	26		ns	
t47	BHOLD Hold Time	5		ns	
t48	BHLDA Valid Delay	3	33	ns	
t55a	BLOCK# Valid Delay	3	36	ns	1, 5
t55b1	BBxE# Valid Delay	3	36	ns	1, 7
t55b2	BBxE# Valid Delay	3	36	ns	1, 7
t55b3	BBxE# Valid Delay	3	43	ns	1, 7
t55c	LOCK# Falling to BLOCK# Falling	0	36	ns	1, 5
t56	MISS# Valid Delay	3	43	ns	1
t57	MISS#, BBxE#, BLOCK# Float Delay	4	40	ns	3
t58	WBS Valid Delay	3	39	ns	1
t59	FLUSH Setup Time	21		ns	
t60	FLUSH Hold Time	5		ns	
t61	FLUSH Setup to RESET Low	31		ns	
t62	FLUSH Hold from RESET Low	31		ns	

4

A.C. SPECIFICATION TABLES

Functional operating range: V_{CC} = 5V ±5%; T_{CASE} = 0°C to +85°C

A.C. Specifications at 20 MHz

Symbol	Parameter	Min	Max	Units	Notes
t1	Operating Frequency	15.4	20	MHz	
t2	CLK2, BCLK2 Period	25	32.5	ns	
t3a	CLK2, BCLK2 High Time @ 2V	10		ns	
t3b	CLK2, BCLK2 High Time @ 3.7V	7		ns	3
t4a	CLK2, BCLK2 Low Time @ 2V	10		ns	
t4b	CLK2, BCLK2 Low Time @ 0.8V	7		ns	3
t5	CLK2, BCLK2 Fall Time		8	ns	3, 9
t6	CLK2, BCLK2 Rise Time		8	ns	3, 9
t7a1	A4–A12 Setup Time	20		ns	1
t7a2	A1–A3, A13–A19, A21–A23 Setup Time	18		ns	1
t7a3	A20 Setup Time	16		ns	1
t7b	LOCK# Setup Time	16		ns	1
t7c	BLE#, BHE# Setup Time	18		ns	1
t8	A1–A23, BLE#, BHE#, LOCK# Hold	3		ns	
t9a	M/IO#, D/C# Setup Time	20		ns	1
t9b	W/R# Setup Time	20		ns	1
t9c	ADS# Setup Time	22		ns	1
t10	M/IO#, D/C#, W/R#, ADS# Hold Time	5		ns	
t11	READYI# Setup Time	12		ns	1
t12	READYI# Hold Time	4		ns	
t13a1	NCA# Setup Time (See t55b2)	21		ns	6
t13a2	NCA# Setup Time (See t55b3)	16		ns	6
t13b	LBA# Setup Time	10		ns	
t14a	NCA# Hold Time	4		ns	
t14b	LBA# Hold Time	4		ns	
t15	RESET, BRESET Setup Time	12		ns	
t16	RESET, BRESET Hold Time	4		ns	
t17	NA# Valid Delay	12	34	ns	1 (25 pF Load)
t18	READYO# Valid Delay	3	26	ns	1 (25 pF Load)
t19	BRDYEN# Valid Delay	3	26	ns	
t21a1	CALEN Rising, PHI1	3	24	ns	
t21a2	CALEN Falling, PHI1	3	24	ns	
t21a3	CALEN Falling in T1P, PHI2	3	24	ns	
t21b	CALEN Rising Following CWTH	3	34	ns	1
t21c	CALEN Pulse Width	10		ns	

A.C. SPECIFICATION TABLES (Continued)

Functional operating range: V_{CC} = 5V ±5%; T_{CASE} = 0°C to +85°C

A.C. Specifications at 20 MHz (Continued)

Symbol	Parameter	Min	Max	Units	Notes
t21d	CALEN Rising to CS# Falling	13		ns	
t22a1	CWEx# Falling, PHI1 (CWTH)	4	27	ns	1
t22a2	CWEx# Falling, PHI2 (CRDM)	4	27	ns	1
t22b	CWEx# Pulse Width	30		ns	1, 2
t22c1	CWEx# Rising, PHI1 (CWTH)	4	27	ns	1
t22c2	CWEx# Rising, PHI2 (CRDM)	4	27	ns	1
t23a1	CS1#, CS2# Rising, PHI1 (CRDM)	6	37	ns	1
t23a2	CS1#, CS2# Rising, PHI2 (CWTH)	6	37	ns	1
t23a3	CS1#, CS2# Falling, PHI1 (CWTH)	6	37	ns	1
t23a4	CS1#, CS2# Falling, PHI2 (CRDM)	6	37	ns	1
t24a1	CT/R# Rising, PHI2 (CRDH)	6	38	ns	1
t24a2	CT/R# Falling, PHI1 (CRDH)	6	38	ns	1
t24a3	CT/R# Falling, PHI2 (CRDH)	6	38	ns	1
t25a	COEA#, COEB# Falling (Direct)	4	22	ns	(25 pF Load)
t25b	COEA#, COEB# Falling (2-Way)	4	24.5	ns	1 (25 pF Load)
t25c	COEx# Rising Delay	5	17	ns	(25 pF Load)
CACHE SRAM WRITE CYCLES					
t23b	COEx# Falling to CSx# Rising	0		ns	8
t25d	CWEx# Falling to COEx# Falling or CWEx# Rising to COEx# Rising	0	10	ns	8 (25 pF Load)
t26	CS0#, CS1# Falling to CWEx# Rising	30		ns	1, 2
t27	CWEx# Falling to CS0#, CS1# Falling	0		ns	
t28a	CWEx# Rising to CALEN Rising	0		ns	
t28b	CWEx# Rising to CS0#, CS1# Falling	0		ns	
t31	SA(1–23) Setup Time	19		ns	
t32	SA(1–23) Hold Time	3		ns	
t33	BADS# Valid Delay	4	28	ns	1
t34	BADS# Float Delay	4	30	ns	3
t35	BNA# Setup Time	9		ns	
t36	BNA# Hold time	15		ns	
t37	BREADY# Setup Time	26		ns	1
t38	BREADY# Hold Time	4		ns	
t40a	BACP Rising Delay	0	20	ns	
t40b	BACP Falling Delay	0	22	ns	

A.C. SPECIFICATION TABLES (Continued)

Functional operating range: V_{CC} = 5V ±5%; T_{CASE} = 0°C to +85°C

A.C. Specifications at 20 MHz (Continued)

Symbol	Parameter	Min	Max	Units	Notes
t41	BAOE# Valid Delay	3	18	ns	
t43a	BT/R# Valid Delay	2	19	ns	
t43b1	DOE# Falling Delay	2	23	ns	
t43b2	DOE# Rising Delay @ T_{CASE} = 0C	4	17	ns	
t43b3	DOE# Rising Delay @ T_{CASE} = T_{MAX}	4	19	ns	
t43c	LDSTB Valid Delay	2	26	ns	
t44a	SEN Setup Time	11		ns	
t44b	SSTB# Setup Time	11		ns	
t45	SEN, SSTB# Hold Time	5		ns	
t46	BHOLD Setup Time	17		ns	
t47	BHOLD Hold Time	5		ns	
t48	BHLDA Valid Delay	3	28	ns	
t55a	BLOCK# Valid Delay	3	30	ns	1, 5
t55b1	BBxE# Valid Delay	3	30	ns	1, 7
t55b2	BBxE# Valid Delay	3	30	ns	1, 7
t55b3	BBxE# Valid Delay	3	36	ns	1, 7
t55c	LOCK# Falling to BLOCK# Falling	0	30	ns	1, 5
t56	MISS# Valid Delay	3	35	ns	1
t57	MISS#, BBxE#, BLOCK# Float Delay	4	32	ns	3
t58	WBS Valid Delay	3	37	ns	1
t59	FLUSH Setup Time	16		ns	
t60	FLUSH Hold Time	5		ns	
t61	FLUSH Setup to RESET Low	26		ns	
t62	FLUSH Hold from RESET Low	26		ns	

82385SX A.C. Specification Notes:

1. Frequency dependent specifications.
2. Used for cache data memory (SRAM) specifications.
3. This parameter is sampled, not 100% tested. Guaranteed by design.
5. BLOCK# delay is either from BPHI1 or from 386 LOCK#. Refer to Figures 5-3K and 5-3L in the 82385SX data sheet.
6. NCA# setup time is now specified to the rising edge of BPHI2 in the state after 386 SX addresses become valid (either the state after the first T2 or after the first T2P).
7. BBxE# Valid Delay is a function of NCA# setup.
   BBxE# valid delay:
   t55b1 For cacheable system bus accesses
   t55b2 For NCA# setup < t13a1
   t55b3 For t13a2 < NCA# setup < t13a1
8. t23b and t25d are only valid specifications when DEFOE# = V_{CC}. Otherwise, if DEFOE# = V_{SS}, COEx# is never asserted during cache SRAM write cycles. If DEFOE# = V_{SS}, t23b and t25d are Not Applicable.
9. t5 is measured from 0.8V to 3.7V. t6 is measured from 3.7V to 0.8V.

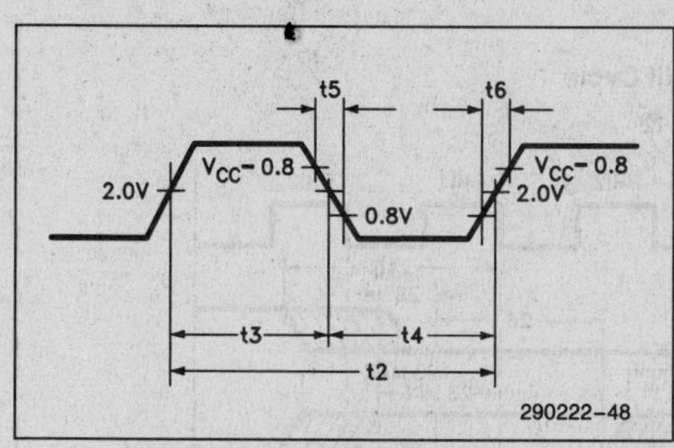

Figure 9-2. CLK2, BCLK2 Timing

82385SX OUTPUT

C_L

290222-49

Figure 9-3. A.C. Test Load

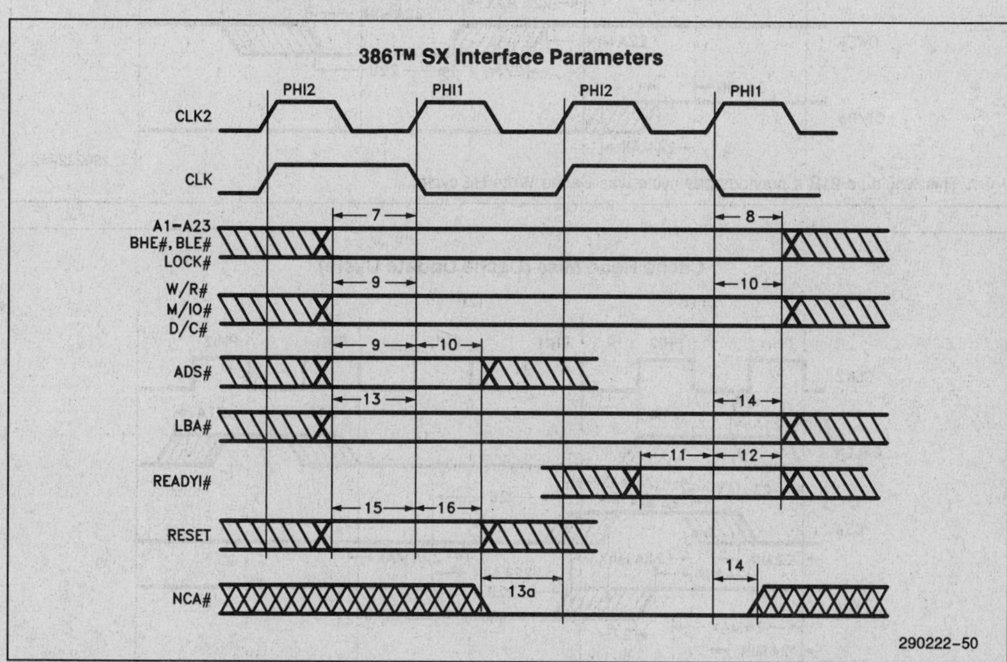

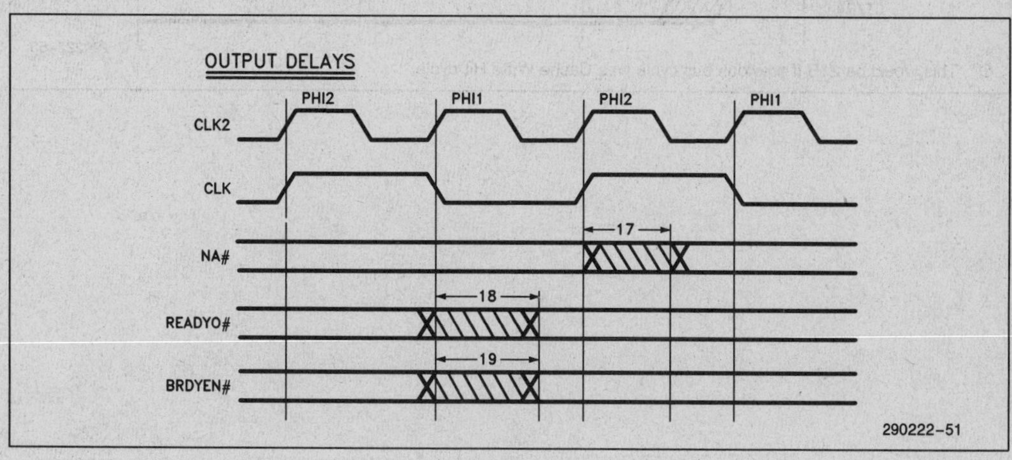

4

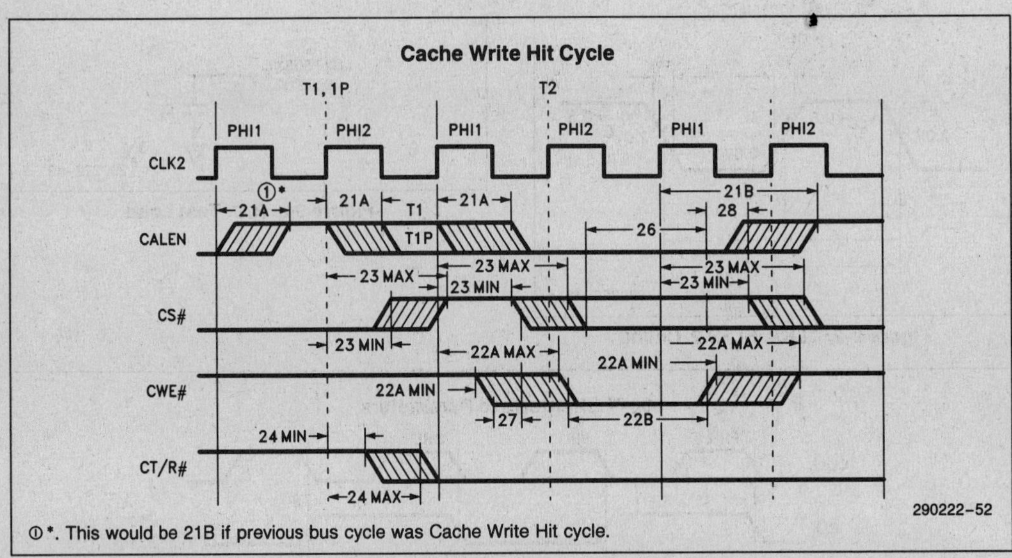

①*. This would be 21B if previous bus cycle was Cache Write Hit cycle.

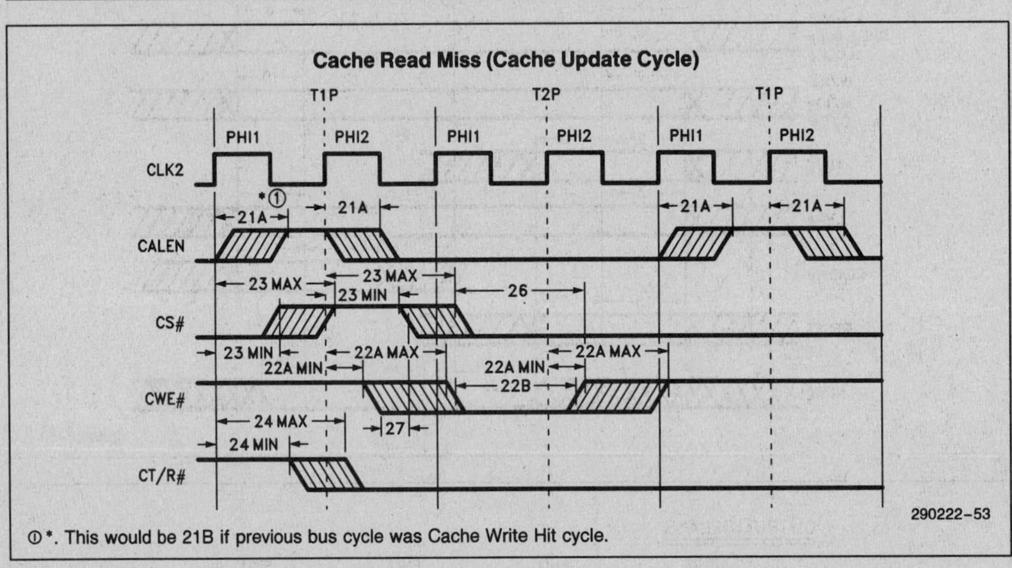

①*. This would be 21B if previous bus cycle was Cache Write Hit cycle.

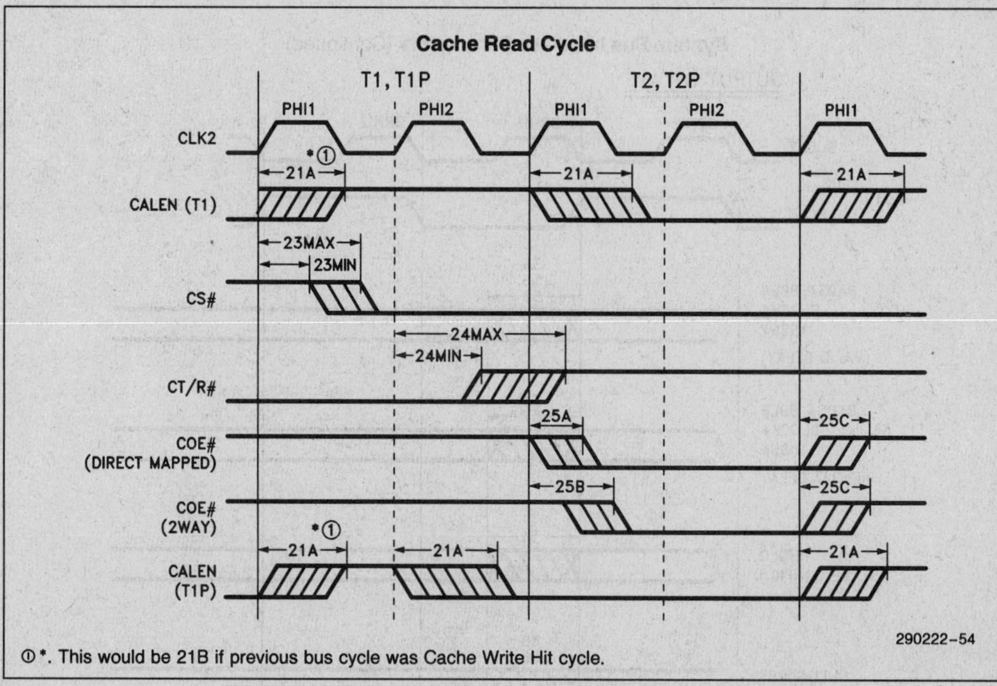

① *. This would be 21B if previous bus cycle was Cache Write Hit cycle.

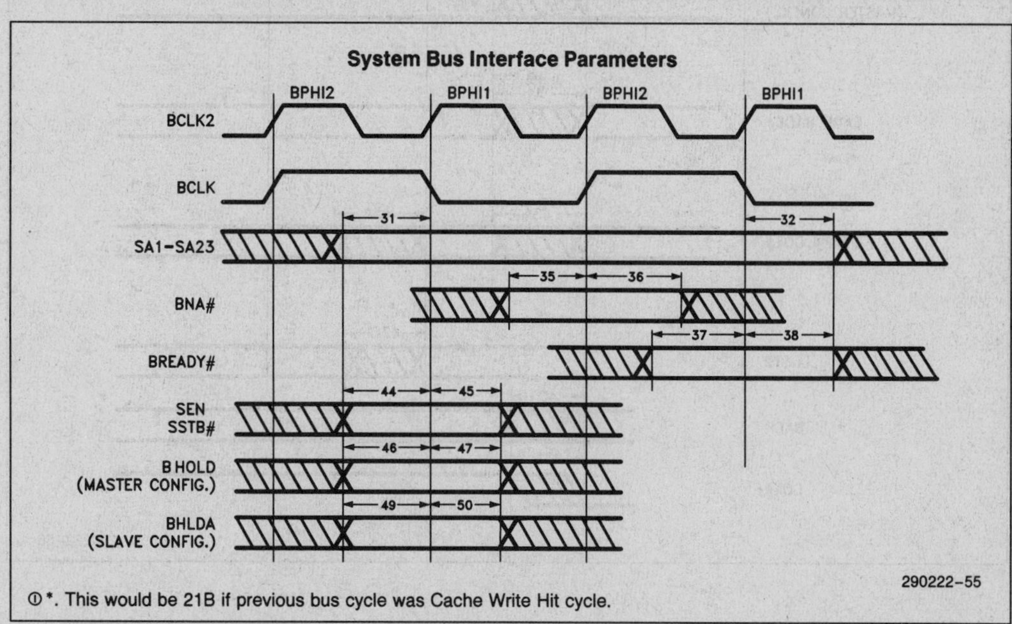

① *. This would be 21B if previous bus cycle was Cache Write Hit cycle.

4

System Bus Interface Parameters (Continued)

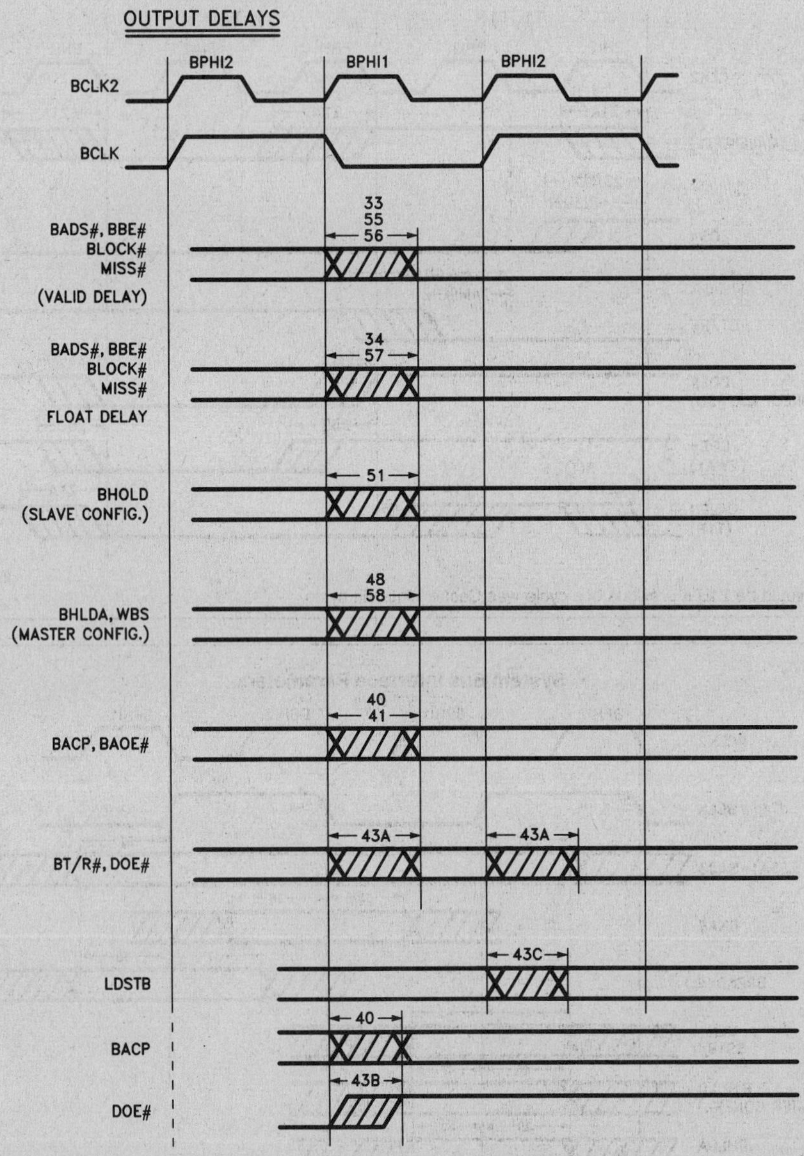

OUTPUT DELAYS

APPENDIX A

82385SX Signal Summary

Signal Group/Name	Signal Function	Active State	Input/ Output	Tri-State Output?
386 SX INTERFACE				
RESET	386 SX Reset	High	I	—
A1–A23	386 SX Address Bus	High	I	—
BHE#, BLE#	386 SX Byte Enables	Low	I	—
CLK2	386 SX Clock	—	I	—
READYO#	Ready Output	Low	O	No
BRDYEN#	Bus Ready Enable	Low	O	No
READYI#	386 SX Ready Input	Low	I	—
ADS#	386 SX Address Status	Low	I	—
M/IO#	386 SX Memory / I/O Indication	—	I	—
W/R#	386 SX Write/Read Indication	—	I	—
D/C#	386 SX Data/Control Indication	—	I	—
LOCK#	386 SX Lock Indication	Low	I	—
NA#	386 SX Next Address Request	Low	O	No
CACHE CONTROL				
CALEN	Cache Address Latch Enable	High	O	No
CT/R#	Cache Transmit/Receive	—	O	No
CS0#, CS1#	Cache Chip Selects	Low	O	No
COEA#, COEB#	Cache Output Enables	Low	O	No
CWEA#, CWEB#	Cache Write Enables	Low	O	No
LOCAL DECODE				
LBA#	386 SX Local Bus Access	Low	I	—
NCA#	Non-Cacheable Access	Low	I	—
STATUS AND CONTROL				
MISS#	Cache Miss Indication	Low	O	Yes
WBS	Write Buffer Status	High	O	No
FLUSH	Cache Flush	High	I	—

82385SX Signal Summary (Continued)

Signal Group/Name	Signal Function	Active State	Input/ Output	Tri-State Output?
82385SX INTERFACE				
BREADY#	82385SX Ready Input	Low	I	—
BNA#	82385SX Next Address Request	Low	I	—
BLOCK#	82385SX Lock Indication	Low	O	Yes
BADS#	82385SX Address Status	Low	O	Yes
BBHE#, BBLE#	82385SX Byte Enables	Low	O	yes
DATA/ADDR CONTROL				
LDSTB	Local Data Strobe	Pos. Edge	O	No
DOE#	Data Output Enable	Low	O	No
BT/R#	Bus Transmit/Receive	—	O	No
BACP	Bus Address Clock Pulse	Pos. Edge	O	No
BAOE#	Bus Address Output Enable	Low	O	No
CONFIGURATION				
2W/D#	2-Way/Direct Map Select	—	I	—
M/S#	Master/Slave Select	—	I	—
DEFOE#	Define Cache Output Enable	—	I	—
COHERENCY				
SA1–SA23	Snoop Address Bus	High	I	—
SSTB#	Snoop Strobe	Low	I	—
SEN	Snoop Enable	High	I	—
ARBITRATION				
BHOLD	Hold	High	I/O	No
BHLDA	Hold Acknowledge	High	I/O	No

82380 HIGH PERFORMANCE 32-BIT DMA CONTROLLER WITH INTEGRATED SYSTEM SUPPORT PERIPHERALS

- **High Performance 32-Bit DMA Controller**
  - **—50 MBytes/sec Maximum Data Transfer Rate at 25 MHz**
  - **—8 Independently Programmable Channels**
- **20-Source Interrupt Controller**
  - **—Individually Programmable Interrupt Vectors**
  - **—15 External, 5 Internal Interrupts**
  - **—82C59A Superset**
- **Four 16-Bit Programmable Interval Timers**
  - **—82C54 Compatible**
- **Programmable Wait State Generator**
  - **—0 to 15 Wait States Pipelined**
  - **—1 to 16 Wait States Non-Pipelined**
- **DRAM Refresh Controller**
- **80386 Shutdown Detect and Reset Control**
  - **—Software/Hardware Reset**
- **High Speed CHMOS III Technology**
- **132-Pin PGA Package**
  (See Packaging Handbook Order 240800-001, Package Type A)
- **Optimized for use with the 80386 Microprocessor**
  - **—Resides on Local Bus for Maximum Bus Bandwidth**
  - **—16, 20, and 25 MHz Clock**

The 82380 is a multi-function support peripheral that integrates system functions necessary in an 80386 environment. It has eight channels of high performance 32-bit DMA with the most efficient transfer rates possible on the 80386 bus. System support peripherals integrated into the 82380 provide Interrupt Control, Timers, Wait State generation, DRAM Refresh Control, and System Reset logic.

4

The 82380's DMA Controller can transfer data between devices of different data path widths using a single channel. Each DMA channel operates independently in any of several modes. Each channel has a temporary data storage register for handling non-aligned data without the need for external alignment logic.

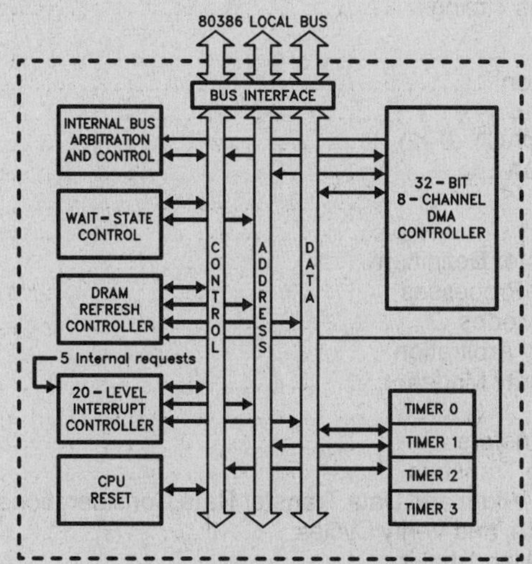

290128-1

82380 Internal Block Diagram

September 1991
Order Number: 290128-006

TABLE OF CONTENTS

CONTENTS PAGE

CONTENTS

PAGE

CONTENTS

CONTENTS

PAGE

1.0 FUNCTIONAL OVERVIEW

The 82380 contains several independent functional modules. The following is a brief discussion of the components and features of the 82380. Each module has a corresponding detailed section later in this data sheet. Those sections should be referred to for design and programming information.

1.1 82380 Architecture

The 82380 is comprised of several computer system functions that are normally found in separate LSI and VLSI components. These include: a high-performance, eight-channel, 32-bit Direct Memory Access Controller; a 20-level Programmable Interrupt Controller which is a superset of the 82C59A; four 16-bit Programmable Interval Timers which are functionally equivalent to the 82C54 timers; a DRAM Refresh Controller; a Programmable Wait State Generator; and system reset logic. The interface to the 82380 is optimized for high-performance operation with the 80386 microprocessor.

The 82380 operates directly on the 80386 bus. In the Slave mode, it monitors the state of the processor at all times and acts or idles according to the commands of the host. It monitors the address pipeline status and generates the programmed number of wait states for the device being accessed. The 82380 also has logic to reset the 80386 via hardware or software reset requests and processor shutdown status.

After a system reset, the 82380 is in the Slave mode. It appears to the system as an I/O device. It becomes a bus master when it is performing DMA transfers.

To maintain compatibility with existing software, the registers within the 82380 are accessed as bytes. If the internal logic of the 82380 requires a delay before another access by the processor, wait states are automatically inserted into the access cycle. This allows the programmer to write initialization routines, etc. without regard to hardware recovery times.

Figure 1-1 shows the basic architectural components of the 82380. The following sections briefly discuss the architecture and function of each of the distinct sections of the 82380.

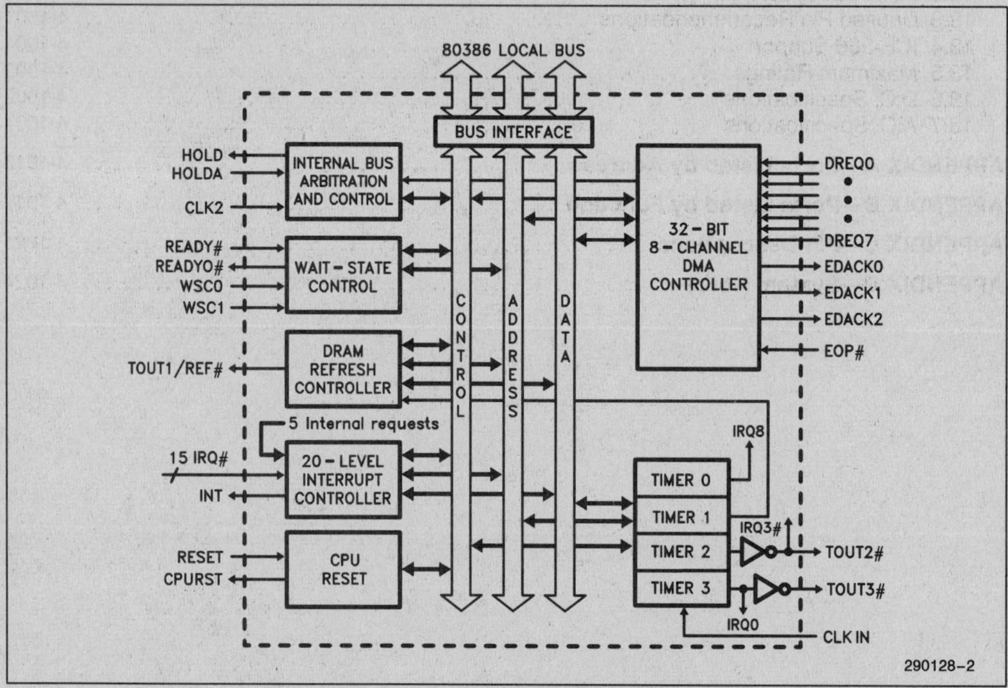

Figure 1-1. Architecture of the 82380

1.1.1 DMA CONTROLLER

The 82380 contains a high-performance, 8-channel, 32-bit DMA controller. It is capable of transferring any combination of bytes, words, and double words. The addresses of both source and distination can be independently incremented, decremented or held constant, and cover the entire 32-bit physical address space of the 80386. It can disassemble and assemble misaligned data via a 32-bit internal temporary data storage register. Data transferred between devices of different data path widths can also be assembled and disassembled using the internal temporary data storage register. The DMA Controller can also transfer aligned data between I/O and memory on the fly, allowing data transfer rates up to 32 megabytes per second for an 82380 operating at 16 MHz. Figure 1-2 illustrates the functional components of the DMA Controller.

There are twenty-four general status and command registers in the 82380 DMA Controller. Through these registers any of the channels may be programmed into any of the possible modes. The operating modes of any one channel are independent of the operation of the other channels.

Each channel has three programmable registers which determine the location and amount of data to be transferred:

Byte Count Register—Number of bytes to transfer. (24-bits)

Requester Register—Address of memory or peripheral which is requesting DMA service. (32-bits)

Target Register—Address of peripheral or memory which will be accessed. (32-bits)

There are also port addresses which, when accessed, cause the 82380 to perform specific functions. The actual data written does not matter, the act of writing to the specific address causes the command to be executed. The commands which operate in this mode are: Master Clear, Clear Terminal Count Interrupt Request, Clear Mask Register, and Clear Byte Pointer Flip-Flop.

DMA transfers can be done between all combinations of memory and I/O; memory-to-memory, memory-to-I/O, I/O-to-memory, and I/O-to-I/O. DMA service can be requested through software and/or hardware. Hardware DMA acknowledge signals are available for all channels (except channel 4) through an encoded 3-bit DMA acknowledge bus (EDACK0–2).

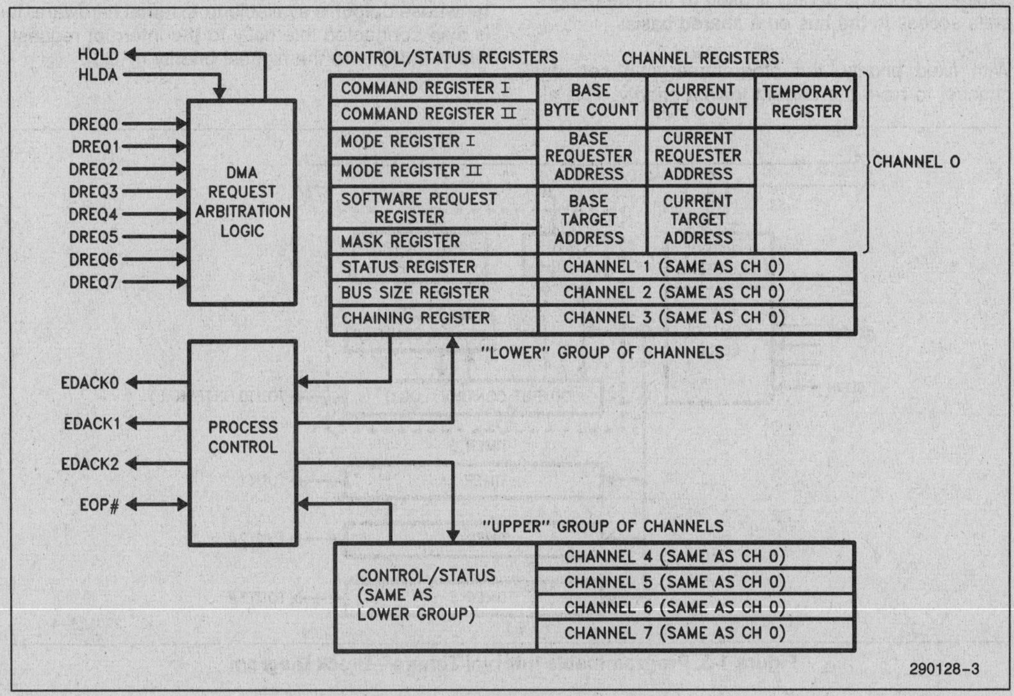

Figure 1-2. 82380 DMA Controller

The 82380 DMA controller transfers blocks of data (buffers) in three modes: Single Buffer, Buffer Auto-Initialize, and Buffer Chaining. In the Single Buffer Process, the 82380 DMA Controller is programmed to transfer one particular block of data. Successive transfers then require reprogramming of the DMA channel. Single Buffer transfers are useful in systems where it is known at the time the transfer begins what quantity of data is to be transferred, and there is a contiguous block of data area available.

The Buffer Auto-Initialize Process allows the same data area to be used for successive DMA transfers without having to reprogram the channel.

The Buffer Chaining Process allows a program to specify a list of buffer transfers to be executed. The 82380 DMA Controller, through interrupt routines, is reprogrammed from the list. The channel is reprogrammed for a new buffer before the current buffer transfer is complete. This pipelining of the channel programming process allows the system to allocate non-contiguous blocks of data storage space, and transfer all of the data with one DMA process. The buffers that make up the chain do not have to be in contiguous locations.

Channel priority can be fixed or rotating. Fixed priority allows the programmer to define the priority of DMA channels based on hardware or other fixed parameters. Rotating priority is used to provide peripherals access to the bus on a shared basis.

With fixed priority, the programmer can set any channel to have the current lowest priority. This allows the user to reset or manually rotate the priority schedule without reprogramming the command registers.

1.1.2 PROGRAMMABLE INTERVAL TIMERS

Four 16-bit programmable interval timers reside within the 82380. These timers are identical in function to the timers in the 82C54 Programmable Interval Timer. All four of the timers share a common clock input which can be independent of the system clock. The timers are capable of operating in six different modes. In all of the modes, the current count can be latched and read by the 80386 at any time, making these very versatile event timers. Figure 1-3 shows the functional components of the Programmable Interval Timers.

The outputs of the timers are directed to key system functions, making system design simpler. Timer 0 is routed directly to an interrupt input and is not available externally. This timer would typically be used to generate time-keeping interrupts.

Timers 1 and 2 have outputs which are available for general timer/counter purposes as well as special functions. Timer 1 is routed to the refresh control logic to provide refresh timing. Timer 2 is connected to an interrupt request input to provide other timer functions. Timer 3 is a general purpose timer/counter whose output is available to external hardware. It is also connected internally to the interrupt request which defaults to the highest priority (IRQ0).

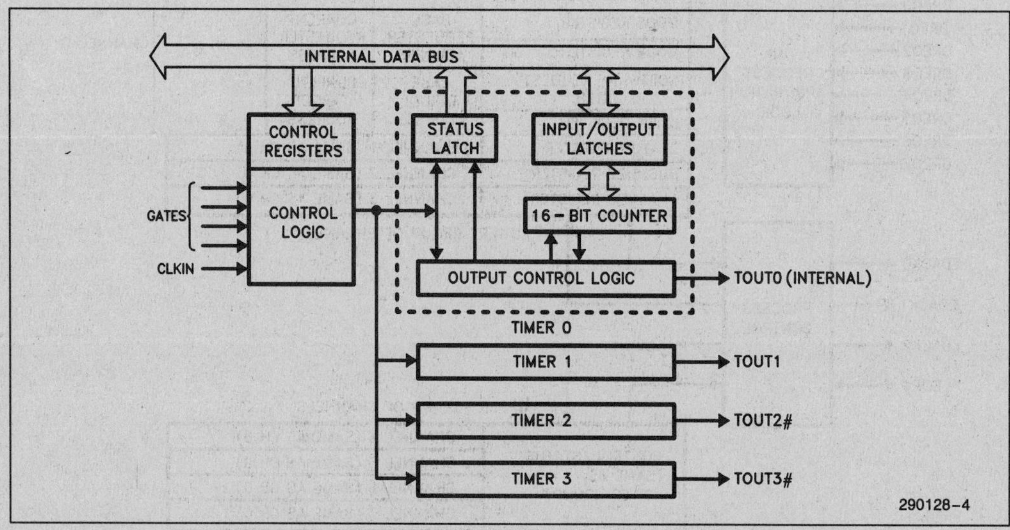

Figure 1-3. Programmable Interval Timers—Block Diagram

1.1.3 INTERRUPT CONTROLLER

The 82380 has the equivalent of three enhanced 82C59A Programmable Interrupt Controllers. These controllers can all be operated in the Master mode, but the priority is always as if they were cascaded. There are 15 interrupt request inputs provided for the user, all of which can be inputs from external slave interrupt controllers. Cascading 82C59As to these request inputs allows a possible total of 120 external interrupt requests. Figure 1-4 is a block diagram of the 82380 Interrupt Controller.

Each of the interrupt request inputs can be individually programmed with its own interrupt vector, allowing more flexibility in interrupt vector mapping than was available with the 82C59A. An interrupt is provided to alert the system that an attempt is being made to program the vectors in the method of the 82C59A. This provides compatibility of existing software that used the 82C59A or 8259A with new designs using the 82380.

In the event of an unrequested or otherwise erroneous interrupt acknowledge cycle, the 82380 Interrupt Controller issues a default vector. This vector, programmed by the system software, will alert the system of unsolicited interrupts of the 80386.

The functions of the 82380 Interrupt Controller are identical to the 82C59A, except in regards to programming the interrupt vectors as mentioned above. Interrupt request inputs are programmable as either edge or level triggered and are software maskable. Priority can be either fixed or rotating and interrupt requests can be nested.

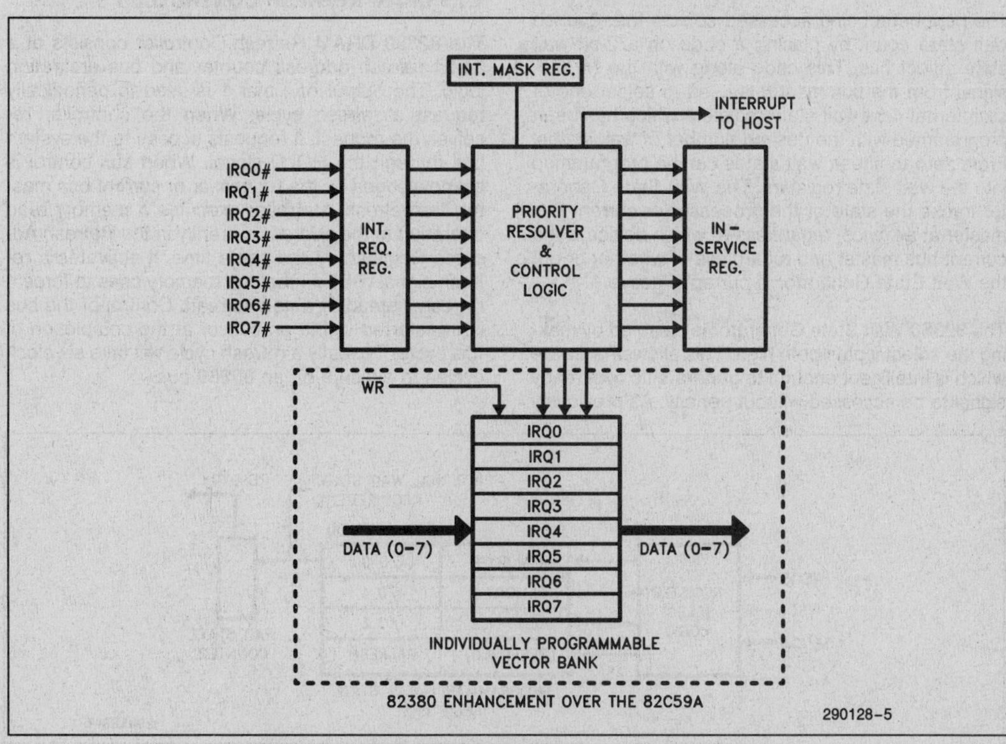

Figure 1-4. 82380 Interrupt Controller—Block Diagram

Enhancements are added to the 82380 for cascading external interrupt controllers. Master to Slave handshaking takes place on the data bus, instead of dedicated cascade lines.

1.1.4 WAIT STATE GENERATOR

The Wait State Generator is a programmable READY generation circuit for the 80386 bus. A peripheral requiring wait states can request the Wait State Generator to hold the processor's READY input inactive for a predetermined number of bus states. Six different wait state counts can be programmed into the Wait State Generator by software; three for memory accesses and three for I/O accesses. A block diagram of the 82380 Wait State Generator is shown in Figure 1-5.

The peripheral being accessed selects the required wait state count by placing a code on a 2-bit wait state select bus. This code along with the M/IO# signal from the bus master is used to select one of six internal 4-bit wait state registers which has been programmed with the desired number of wait states. From zero to fifteen wait states can be programmed into the wait state registers. The Wait State Generator tracks the state of the processor or current bus master at all times, regardless of which device is the current bus master and regardless of whether or not the Wait State Generator is currently active.

The 82380 Wait State Generator is disabled by making the select inputs both high. This allows hardware which is intelligent enough to generate its own ready signal to be accessed without penalty. As previously mentioned, deselecting the Wait State Generator does not disable its ability to determine the proper number of wait states due to pipeline status in subsequent bus cycles.

The number of wait states inserted into a pipelined bus cycle is the value in the selected wait state register. If the bus master is operating in the non-pipelined mode, the Wait State Generator will increase the number of wait states inserted into the bus cycle by one.

On reset, the Wait State Generator's registers are loaded with the value FFH, giving the maximum number of wait states for any access in which the wait state select inputs are active.

1.1.5 DRAM REFRESH CONTROLLER

The 82380 DRAM Refresh Controller consists of a 24-bit refresh address counter and bus arbitration logic. The output of Timer 1 is used to periodically request a refresh cycle. When the controller receives the request, it requests access to the system bus through the HOLD signal. When bus control is acknowledged by the processor or current bus master, the refresh controller executes a memory read operation at the address currently in the Refresh Address Register. At the same time, it activates a refresh signal (REF#) that the memory uses to force a refresh instead of a normal read. Control of the bus is transferred to the processor at the completion of this cycle. Typically a refresh cycle will take six clock cycles to execute on an 80386 bus.

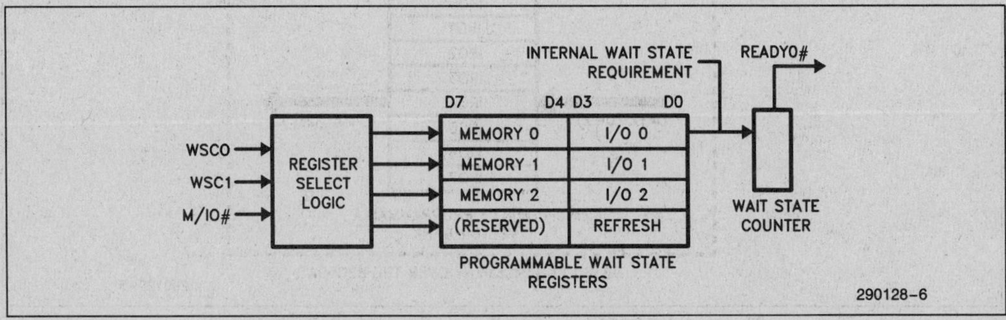

Figure 1-5. 82380 Wait State Generator—Block Diagram

The 82380 DRAM Refresh Controller has the highest priority when requesting bus access and will interrupt any active DMA process. This allows large blocks of data to be moved by the DMA controller without affecting the refresh function. Also the DMA controller is not required to completely relinquish the bus, the refresh controller simply steals a bus cycle between DMA accesses.

The amount by which the refresh address is incremented is programmable to allow for different bus widths and memory bank arrangements.

1.1.6 CPU RESET FUNCTION

The 82380 contains a special reset function which can respond to hardware reset signals from the 82384, as well as a software reset command. The circuit will hold the 80386's RESET line active while an external hardware reset signal is present at its RESET input. It can also reset the 80386 processor as the result of a software command. The software reset command causes the 82380 to hold the processor's RESET line active for a minimum of 62 CLK2 cycles; enough time to allow an 80386 to re-initialize.

The 82380 can be programmed to sense the shutdown detect code on the status lines from the 80386. If the Shutdown Detect function is enabled, the 82380 will automatically reset the processor. A diagnostic register is available which can be used to determine the cause of reset.

1.1.7 REGISTER MAP RELOCATION

After a hardware reset, the internal registers of the 82380 are located in I/O space beginning at port address 0000H. The map of the 82380's registers is relocatable via a software command. The default mapping places the 82380 between I/O addresses 0000H and 00DBH. The relocation register allows this map to be moved to any even 256-byte boundary in the processor's 16-bit I/O address space or any even 16-Mbyte boundary in the 32-bit memory address space.

1.2 Host Interface

The 82380 is designed to operate efficiently on the local bus of an 80386 microprocessor. The control signals of the 82380 are identical in function to those of the 80386. As a slave, the 82380 operates with all of the features available on the 80386 bus. When the 82380 is in the Master mode, it looks identical to the 80386 to the connected devices.

The 82380 monitors the bus at all times, and determines whether the current bus cycle is a pipelined or non-pipelined access. All of the status signals of the processor are monitored.

The control, status, and data registers within the 82380 are located at fixed addresses relative to each other, but the group can be relocated to either memory or I/O space and to different locations within those spaces.

As a Slave device, the 82380 monitors the control/status lines of the CPU. The 82380 will generate all of the wait states it needs whenever it is accessed. This allows the programmer the freedom of accessing 82380 registers without having to insert NOPs in the program to wait for slower 82380 internal registers.

The 82380 can determine if a current bus cycle is a pipelined or a non-pipelined cycle. It does this by monitoring the ADS# and READY# signals and thereby keeping track of the current state of the 80386.

As a bus master, the 82380 looks like an 80386 to the rest of the system. This enables the designer greater flexibility in systems which include the 82380. The designer does not have to alter the interfaces of any peripherals designed to operate with the 80386 to accommodate the 82380. The 82380 will access any peripherals on the bus in the same manner as the 80386, including recognizing pipelined bus cycles.

The 82380 is accessed as an 8-bit peripheral. This is done to maintain compatibility with existing system architectures and software. The 80386 places the data of all 8-bit accesses either on D (0–7) or D (8–15). The 82380 will only accept data on these lines when in the Slave mode. When in the Master mode, the 82380 is a full 32-bit machine, sending and receiving data in the same manner as the 80386.

1.3 IBM PC* System Compatibility

The 82380 is an 80386 companion device designed to provide an enhancement of the system functions common to most small computer systems. It is modeled after and is a superset of the Intel peripheral products found in the IBM PC, PC-AT, and other popular small computers.

2.0 80386 HOST INTERFACE

The 82380 contains a set of interface signals to operate efficiently with the 80386 host processor. These signals were designed so that minimal hardware is needed to connect the 82380 to the 80386.

Figure 2-1 depicts a typical system configuration with the 80386 processor. As shown in the diagram, the 82380 is designed to interface directly with the 80386 bus.

*IBM PC and IBM PC-AT are registered trademarks of International Business Machines Inc.

Since the 82380 is residing on the opposite side of the data bus transceiver (with respect to the rest of the peripherals in the system), it is important to note that the transceiver should be controlled so that contention between the data bus transceiver and the 82380 will not occur. In order to do this, port address decoding logic should be included in the direction and enable control logic of the transceiver. When any of the 82380 internal registers is read, the data bus transceiver should be disabled so that only the 82380 will drive the local bus.

This section describes the basic bus functions of the 82380 to show how this device interacts with the 80386 processor. Other signals which are not directly related to the host interface will be discussed in their associated functional block description.

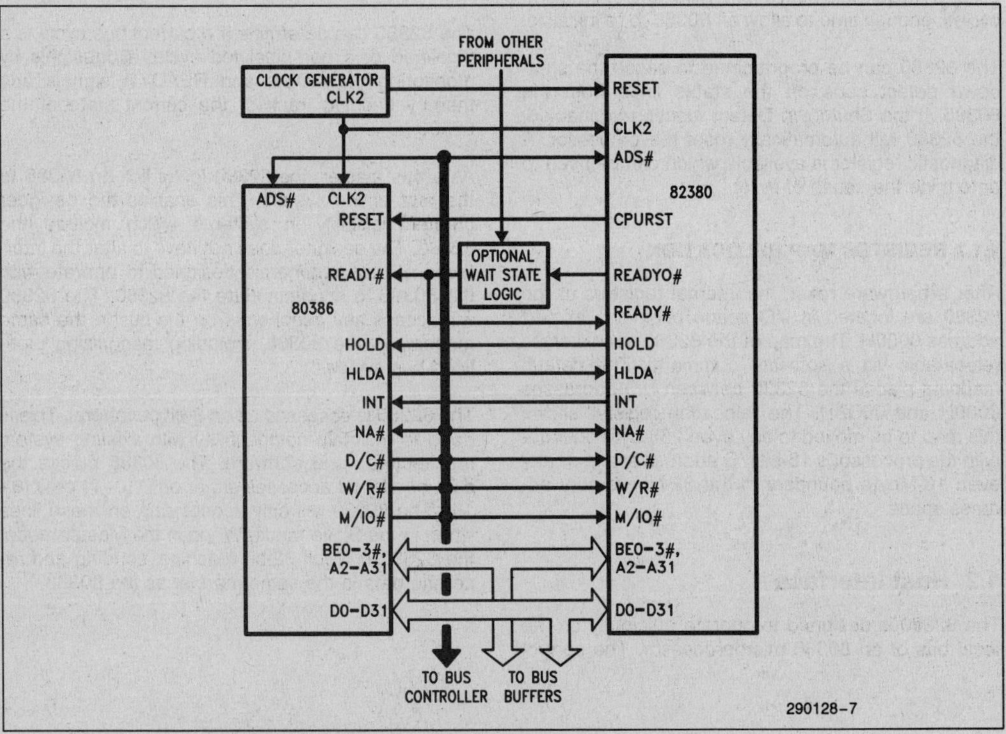

Figure 2-1. 80386/82380 System Configuration

2.1 Master and Slave Modes

At any time, the 82380 acts as either a Slave device or a Master device in the system. Upon reset, the 82380 will be in the Slave Mode. In this mode, the 80386 processor can read/write into the 82380 internal registers. Initialization information may be programmed into the 82380 during Slave Mode.

When DMA service (including DRAM Refresh Cycles generated by the 82380) is requested, the 82380 will request and subsequently get control of the 80386 local bus. This is done through the HOLD and HLDA (Hold Acknowledge) signals. When the 80386 processor responds by asserting the HLDA signal, the 82380 will switch into Master Mode and perform DMA transfers. In this mode, the 82380 is the bus master of the system. It can read/write data from/to memory and peripheral devices. The 82380 will return to the Slave Mode upon completion of DMA transfers, or when HLDA is negated.

2.2 80386 Interface Signals

As mentioned in the Architecture section, the Bus Interface module of the 82380 (see Figure 1-1) contains signals that are directly connected to the 80386 host processor. This module has separate 32-bit Data and Address busses. Also, it has additional control signals to support different bus operations on the system. By residing on the 80386 local bus, the 82380 shares the same address, data and control lines with the processor. The following subsections discuss the signals which interface to the 80386 host processor.

2.2.1 CLOCK (CLK2)

The CLK2 input provides fundamental timing for the 82380. It is divided by two internally to generate the 82380 internal clock. Therefore, CLK2 should be driven with twice the 80386's frequency. In order to maintain synchronization with the 80386 host processor, the 82380 and the 80386 should share a common clock source.

The internal clock consists of two phases: PHI1 and PHI2. Each CLK2 period is a phase of the internal clock. PHI2 is usually used to sample input and set up internal signals and PHI1 is for latching internal data. Figure 2-2 illustrates the relationship of CLK2 and the 82380 internal clock signals. The CPURST signal generated by the 82380 guarantees that the 80386 will wake up in phase with PHI1.

2.2.2 DATA BUS (D0–D31)

This 32-bit three-state bidirectional bus provides a general purpose data path between the 82380 and the system. These pins are tied directly to the corresponding Data Bus pins of the 80386 local bus. The Data Bus is also used for interrupt vectors generated by the 82380 in the Interrupt Acknowledge cycle.

During Slave I/O operations, the 82380 expects a single byte to be written or read. When the 80386 host processor writes into the 82380, either D0–D7 or D8–D15 will be latched into the 82380, depending upon how the Byte Enable (BE0#–BE#3) signals are driven. The 82380 does not need to look at D16–D31 since the 80386 duplicates the single byte

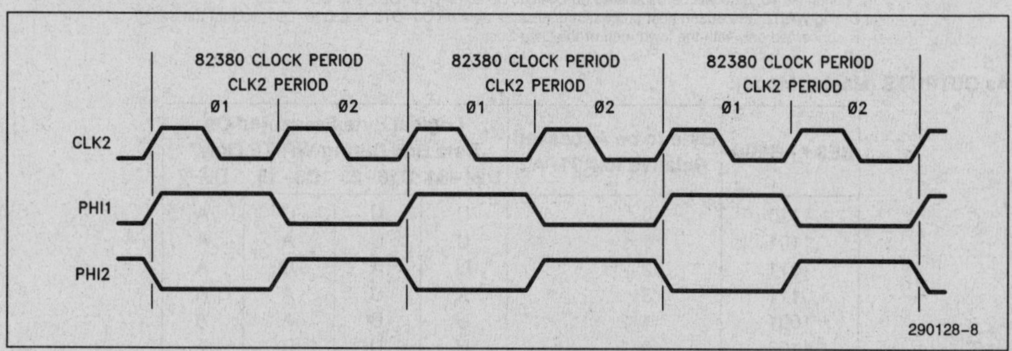

Figure 2-2. CLK2 and 82380 Internal Clock

4

data on both halves of the bus. When the 80386 host processor reads from the 82380, the single byte data will be duplicated four times on the Data Bus; i.e., on D0–D7, D8–D15, D16–D23 and D24–D31.

During Master Mode, the 82380 can transfer 32-, 16-, and 8-bit data between memory (or I/O devices) and I/O devices (or memory) via the Data Bus.

2.2.3 ADDRESS BUS (A31–A2)

These three-state bidirectional signals are connected directly to the 80386 Address Bus. In the Slave Mode, they are used as input signals so that the processor can address the 82380 internal ports/registers. In the Master Mode, they are used as output signals by the 82380 to address memory and peripheral devices. The Address Bus is capable of addressing 4 G-bytes of physical memory space (00000000H to FFFFFFFFH), and 64 K-bytes of I/O addresses (00000000H to 0000FFFFH).

2.2.4 BYTE ENABLE (BE3#–BE0#)

These bidirectional pins select specific byte(s) in the double word addressed by A31–A2. Similar to the Address Bus function, these signals are used as inputs to address internal 82380 registers during Slave Mode operation. During Master Mode operation, they are used as outputs by the 82380 to address memory and I/O locations.

NOTE:

In addition to the above function, BE3# is used to enable a production test mode and must be LOW during reset. The 80386 processor will automatically hold BE3# LOW during RESET.

The definitions of the Byte Enable signals depend upon whether the 82380 is in the Master or Slave Mode. These definitions are depicted in Table 2-1.

Table 2-1. Byte Enable Signals

As INPUTS (Slave Mode):

BE3#–BE0#	Implied A1, A0	Data Bits Written to 82380*
XXX0	00	D0–D7
XX01	01	D8–D15
X011	10	D0–D7
X111	11	D8–D15

X-DON'T CARE
*During READ, data will be duplicated on D0–D7, D8–D15, D16–D23, and D24–D31.
During WRITE, the 80386 host processor duplicates data on D0–D15, and D16–D31, so that the 82380 is concerned only with the lower half of the Data Bus.

As OUTPUTS (Master Mode):

BE3#–BE0#	Byte to be Accessed Relative to A31–A2	Logical Byte Presented On Data Bus During WRITE Only*			
		D24–31	D16–23	D8–15	D0–7
1110	0	U	U	U	A
1101	1	U	U	A	A
1011	2	U	A	U	A
0111	3	A	U	A	A
1001	1, 2	U	B	A	A
1100	0, 1	U	U	B	A
0011	2, 3	B	A	B	A
1000	0, 1, 2	U	C	B	A
0001	1, 2, 3	C	B	A	A
0000	0, 1, 2, 3	D	C	B	A

U = Undefined
A = Logical D0–D7
B = Logical D8–D15
C = Logical D16–D23
D = Logical D24–D31
*Actual number of bytes accessed depends upon the programmed data path width.

2.2.5 BUS CYCLE DEFINITION SIGNALS (D/C#, W/R#, M/IO#)

These three-state bidirectional signals define the type of bus cycle being performed. W/R# distinguishes between write and read cycles. D/C# distinguishes between processor data and control cycles. M/IO# distinguishes between memory and I/O cycles.

During Slave Mode, these signals are driven by the 80386 host processor; during Master Mode, they are driven by the 82380. In either mode, these signals will be valid when the Address Status (ADS#) is driven LOW. Exact bus cycle definitions are given in Table 2-2. Note that some combinations are recognized as inputs, but not generated as outputs. In the Master Mode, D/C# is always HIGH.

2.2.6 ADDRESS STATUS (ADS#)

This bidirectional signal indicates that a valid address (A2–A31, BE0#–BE3#) and bus cycle definition (W/R#, D/C#, M/IO#) is being driven on the bus. In the Master Mode, it is driven by the 82380 as an output. In the Slave Mode, this signal is monitored as an input by the 82380. By the current and past status of ADS# and the READY# input, the 82380 is able to determine, during Slave Mode, if the next bus cycle is a pipelined address cycle. ADS# is asserted during T1 and T2P bus states (see Bus State Definition).

Note that during the idle states at the beginning and the end of a DMA process, neither the 80386 nor the 82380 is driving the ADS# signal; i.e., the signal is left floated. Therefore, it is important to use a pull-up resistor (approximately 10 KΩ) on the ADS# signal.

2.2.7 TRANSFER ACKNOWLEDGE (READY#)

This input indicates that the current bus cycle is complete. In the Master Mode, assertion of this signal indicates the end of a DMA bus cycle. In the Slave Mode, the 82380 monitors this input and ADS# to detect a pipelined address cycles. This signal should be tied directly to the READY# input of the 80386 host processor.

2.2.8 NEXT ADDRESS REQUEST (NA#)

This input is used to indicate to the 82380 in the Master Mode that the system is requesting address pipelining. When driven LOW by either memory or peripheral devices during Master Mode, it indicates that the system is prepared to accept a new address and bus cycle definition signals from the 82380 before the end of the current bus cycle. If this input is active when sampled by the 82380, the next address is driven onto the bus, provided a bus request is already pending internally.

This input pin is monitored only in the Master Mode. In the Slave Mode, the 82380 uses the ADS# and READY# signals to determine address pipelining cycles, and NA# will be ignored.

2.2.9 RESET (RESET, CPURST)

RESET

This synchronous input suspends any operation in progress and places the 82380 in a known initial state. Upon reset, the 82380 will be in the Slave Mode waiting to be initialized by the 80386 host processor. The 82380 is reset by asserting RESET for 15 or more CLK2 periods. When RESET is asserted, all other input pins are ignored, and all other bus pins are driven to an idle bus state as shown in Table 2-3. The 82380 will determine the phase of its internal clock following RESET going inactive.

Table 2-2. Bus Cycle Definition

M/IO#	D/C#	W/R#	As INPUTS	As OUTPUTS
0	0	0	Interrupt Acknowledge	NOT GENERATED
0	0	1	UNDEFINED	NOT GENERATED
0	1	0	I/O Read	I/O Read
0	1	1	I/O Write	I/O Write
1	0	0	UNDEFINED	NOT GENERATED
1	0	1	HALT if BE(3–0)# = X011 SHUTDOWN if BE (3–0)# = XXX0	NOT GENERATED
1	1	0	Memory Read	Memory Read
1	1	1	Memory Write	Memory Write

Table 2-3. Output Signals Following RESET

Signal	Level
A2–A31, D0–D31, BE0#–BE3#	Float
D/C#, W/R#, M/IO#, ADS#	Float
READYO#	'1'
EOP#	'1' (Weak Pull-UP)
EDACK2–EDACK0	'100'
HOLD	'0'
INT	UNDEFINED*
TOUT1/REF#, TOUT2#/IRQ3#, TOUT3#	UNDEFINED*
CPURST	'0'

*The Interrupt Controller and Programmable Interval Timer are initialized by software commands.

RESET is level-sensitive and must be synchronous to the CLK2 signal. Therefore, this RESET input should be tied to the RESET output of the Clock Generator. The RESET setup and hold time requirements are shown in Figure 2.3.

CPURST

This output signal is used to reset the 80386 host processor. It will go active (HIGH) whenever one of the following events occurs: a) 82380's RESET input is active; b) a software RESET command is issued to the 82380; or c) when the 82380 detects a processor Shutdown cycle and when this detection feature is enabled (see CPU Reset and Shutdown Detect). When activated, CPURST will be held active for 62 CLK2 periods. The timing of CPURST is such that the 80386 processor will be in synchronization with the 82380. This timing is shown in Figure 2-4.

2.2.10 INTERRUPT OUT (INT)

This output pin is used to signal the 80386 host processor that one or more interrupt requests (either internal or external) are pending. The processor is expected to respond with an Interrupt Acknowledge cycle. This signal should be connected directly to the Maskable Interrupt Request (INTR) input of the 80386 host processor.

2.3 82380 Bus Timing

The 82380 internally divides the CLK2 signal by two to generate its internal clock. Figure 2-2 shows the relationship of CLK2 and the internal clock. The internal clock consists of two phases: PHI1 and PHI2. Each CLK2 period is a phase of the internal clock. In Figure 2-2, both PHI1 and PHI2 of the 82380 internal clock are shown.

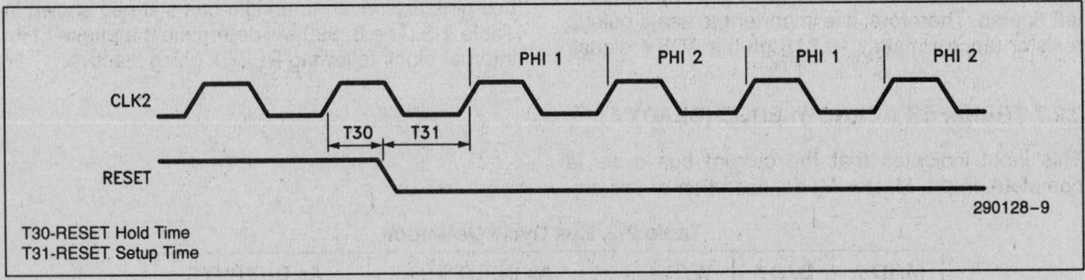

Figure 2-3. RESET Timing

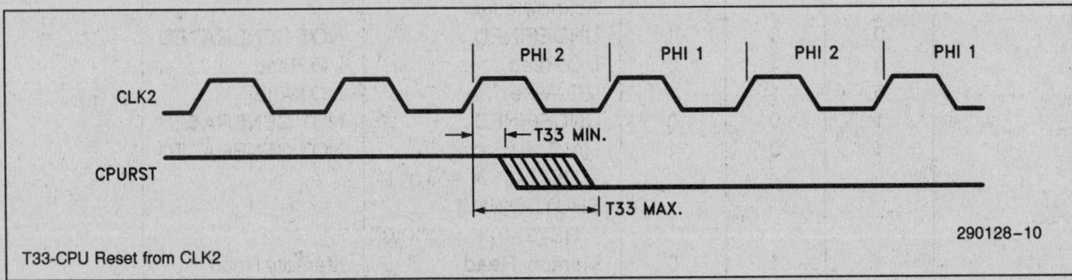

Figure 2-4. CPURST Timing

In the 82380, whether it is in the Master or Slave Mode, the shortest time unit of bus activity is a bus state. A bus state, which is also referred as a 'T-state', is defined as one 82380 PHI2 clock period (i.e., two CLK2 periods). Recall in Table 2-2, there are six different types of bus cycles in the 82380 as defined by the M/IO#, D/C# and W/R# signals. Each of these bus cycles is composed of two or more bus states. The length of a bus cycle depends on when the READY# input is asserted (i.e., driven LOW).

2.3.1 ADDRESS PIPELINING

The 82380 supports Address Pipelining as an option in both the Master and Slave Mode. This feature typically allows a memory or peripheral device to operate with one less wait state than would otherwise be required. This is possible because during a pipelined cycle, the address and bus cycle definition of the next cycle will be generated by the bus master while waiting for the end of the current cycle to be acknowledged. The pipelined bus is especially well suited for interleaved memory environment. For 16 MHz interleaved memory designs with 100 ns access time DRAMs, zero wait state memory accesses can be achieved when pipelined addressing is selected.

In the Master Mode, the 82380 is capable of initiating, on a cycle-by-cycle basis, either a pipelined or non-pipelined access depending upon the state of the NA# input. If a pipelined cycle is requested (indicated by NA# being driven LOW), the 82380 will drive the address and bus cycle definition of the next cycle as soon as there is an internal bus request pending.

In the Slave Mode, the 82380 is constantly monitoring the ADS# and READY# signals on the processor local bus to determine if the current bus cycle is a pipelined cycle. If a pipelined cycle is detected, the 82380 will request one less wait state from the processor if the Wait State Generator feature is selected. On the other hand, during an 82380 internal register access in a pipelined cycle, it will make use of the advance address and bus cycle information. In all cases, Address Pipelining will result in a savings of one wait state.

2.3.2 MASTER MODE BUS TIMING

When the 82380 is in the Master Mode, it will be in one of six bus states. Figure 2-5 shows the complete bus state diagram of the Master Mode, including pipelined address states. As seen in the figure, the 82380 state diagram is very similar to that of the 80386. The major difference is that in the 82380, there is no Hold state. Also, in the 82380, the conditions for some state transitions depend upon whether it is the end of a DMA process*.

NOTE:
*The term 'end of a DMA process' is loosely defined here. It depends on the DMA modes of operation as well as the state of the EOP# and DREQ inputs. This is explained in detail in section 3—DMA Controller.

The 82380 will enter the idle state, Ti, upon RESET and whenever the internal address is not available at the end of a DMA cycle or at the end of a DMA process. When address pipelining is not used (NA# is not asserted), a new bus cycle always begins with state T1. During T1, address and bus cycle definition signals will be driven on the bus. T1 is always followed by T2.

If a bus cycle is not acknowledged (with READY#) during T2 and NA# is negated, T2 will be repeated. When the end of the bus cycle is acknowledged during T2, the following state will be T1 of the next bus cycle (if the internal address latch is loaded and if this is not the end of the DMA process). Otherwise, the Ti state will be entered. Therefore, if the memory or peripheral accessed is fast enough to respond within the first T2, the fastest non-pipelined cycle will take one T1 and one T2 state.

Use of the address pipelining feature allows the 82380 to enter three additional bus states: T1P, T2P, and T2i. T1P is the first bus state of a pipelined bus cycle. T2P follows T1P (or T2) if NA# is asserted when sampled. The 82380 will drive the bus with the address and bus cycle definition signals of the next cycle during T2P. From the state diagram, it can be seen that after an idle state Ti, the first bus cycle must begin with T1, and is therefore a non-pipelined bus cycle. The next bus cycle can be pipelined if NA# is asserted and the previous bus cycle ended in a T2P state. Once the 82380 is in a pipelined cycle and provided that NA# is asserted in subsequent cycles, the 82380 will be switching between T1P and T2P states. If the end of the current bus cycle is not acknowledged by the READY# input, the 82380 will extend the cycle by adding T2P states. The fastest pipelined cycle will consist of one T1P and one T2P state.

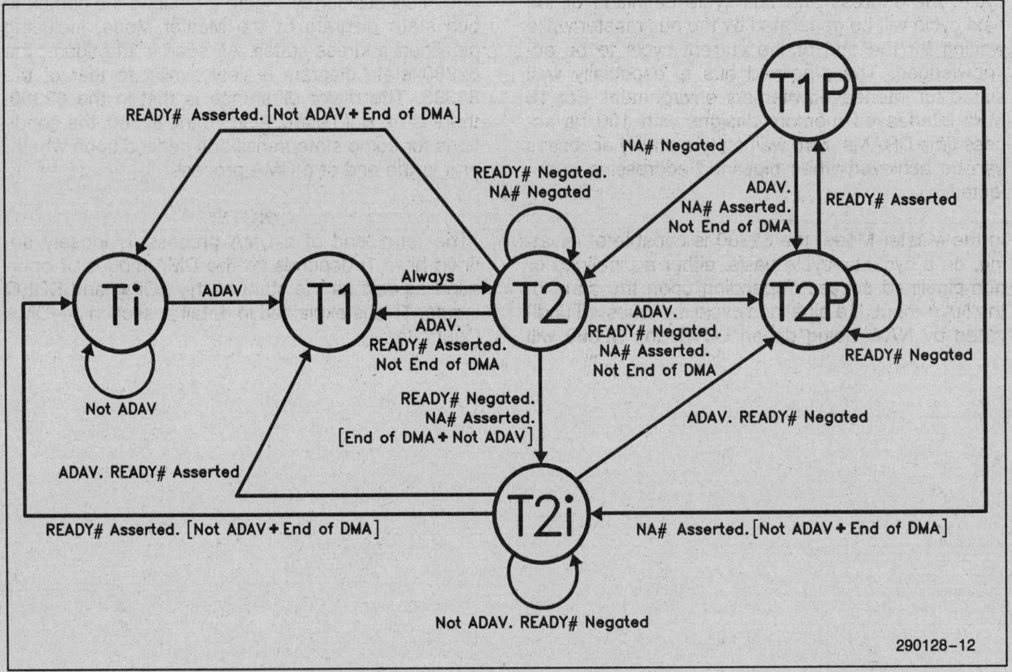

NOTE:
ADAV—Internal Address Available

Figure 2-5. Master Mode State Diagram

The 82380 will enter state T2i when NA# is asserted and when one of the following two conditions occurs. The first condition is when the 82380 is in state T2. T2i will be entered if READY# is not asserted and there is no next address available. This situation is similar to a wait state. The 82380 will stay in T2i for as long as this condition exists. The second condition which will cause the 82380 enter T2i is when the 82380 is in state T1P. Before going to state T2P, the 82380 needs to wait in state T2i until the next address is available. Also, in both cases, if the DMA process is complete, the 82380 will enter the T2i state in order to finish the current DMA cycle.

Figure 2-6 is a timing diagram showing non-pipelined bus accesses in the Master Mode. Figure 2-7 shows the timing of pipelined accesses in the Master Mode.

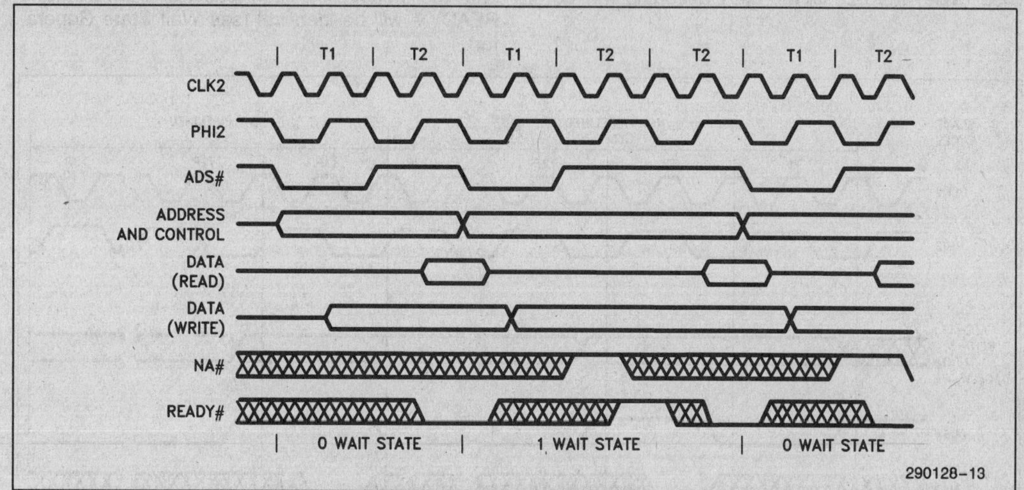

Figure 2-6. Non-Pipelined Bus Cycles

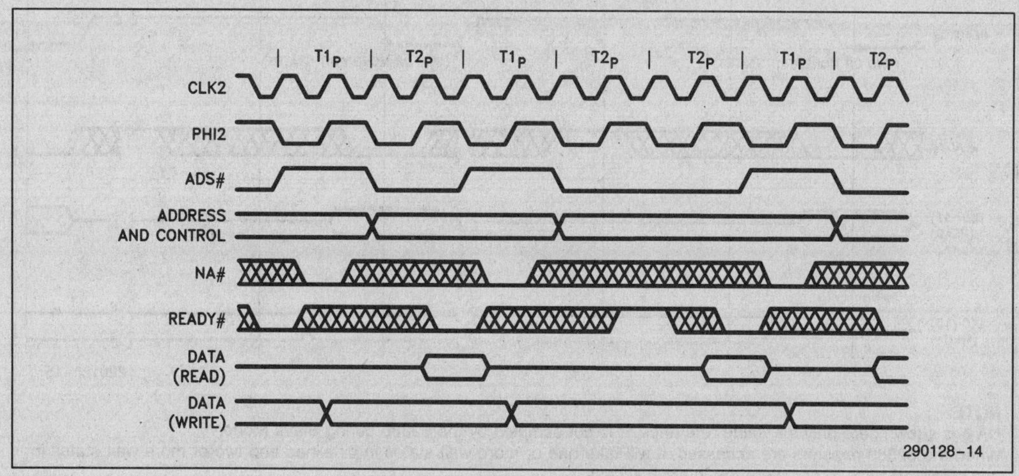

Figure 2-7. Pipelined Bus Cycles

2.3.3 SLAVE MODE BUS TIMING

Figure 2-8 shows the Slave Mode bus timing in both pipelined and non-pipelined cycles when the 82380 is being accessed. Recall that during Slave Mode, the 82380 will constantly monitor the ADS# and READY# signals to determine if the next cycle is pipelined. In Figure 2-8, the first cycle is non-pipelined and the second cycle is pipelined. In the pipelined cycle, the 82380 will start decoding the address and bus cycle signals one bus state earlier than in a non-pipelined cycle.

The READY# input signal is sampled by the 80386 host processor to determine the completion of a bus cycle. This occurs during the end of every T2 and T2P state. Normally, the output of the 82380 Wait State Generator, READYO#, is directly connected to the READY# input of the 80386 host processor and the 82380. In such case, READYO# and READY# will be identical (see Wait State Generator).

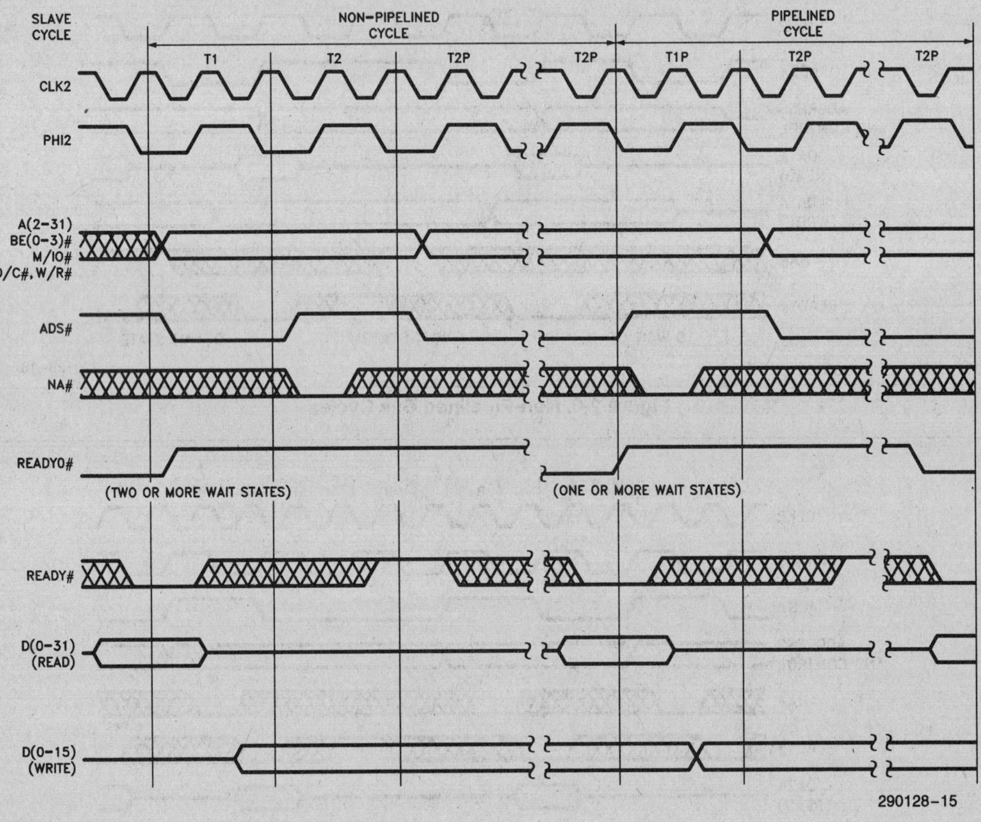

SLAVE CYCLE
NON-PIPELINED CYCLE
PIPELINED CYCLE
T1 T2 T2P T2P T1P T2P T2P
CLK2
PHI2
A(2–31) BE(0–3)# M/IO# D/C#, W/R#
ADS#
NA#
READYO#
(TWO OR MORE WAIT STATES)
(ONE OR MORE WAIT STATES)
READY#
D(0–31) (READ)
D(0–15) (WRITE)

290128–15

NOTE:
NA# is shown here only for timing reference. It is not sampled by the 82380 during Slave Mode.
When the 82380 registers are accessed, it will take one or more wait states in pipelined and two or more wait states in non-pipelined cycle to complete the internal access.

Figure 2-8. Slave Read/Write Timing

3.0 DMA Controller

The 82380 DMA Controller is capable of transferring data between any combination of memory and/or I/O, with any combination (8-, 16-, or 32-bits) of data path widths. Bus bandwidth is optimized through the use of an internal temporary register which can disassemble or assemble data to or from either an aligned or a non-aligned destination or source. Figure 3-1 is a block diagram of the 82380 DMA Controller.

The 82380 has eight channels of DMA. Each channel operates independently of the others. Within the operation of the individual channels, there are many different modes of data transfer available. Many of the operating modes can be intermixed to provide a very versatile DMA controller.

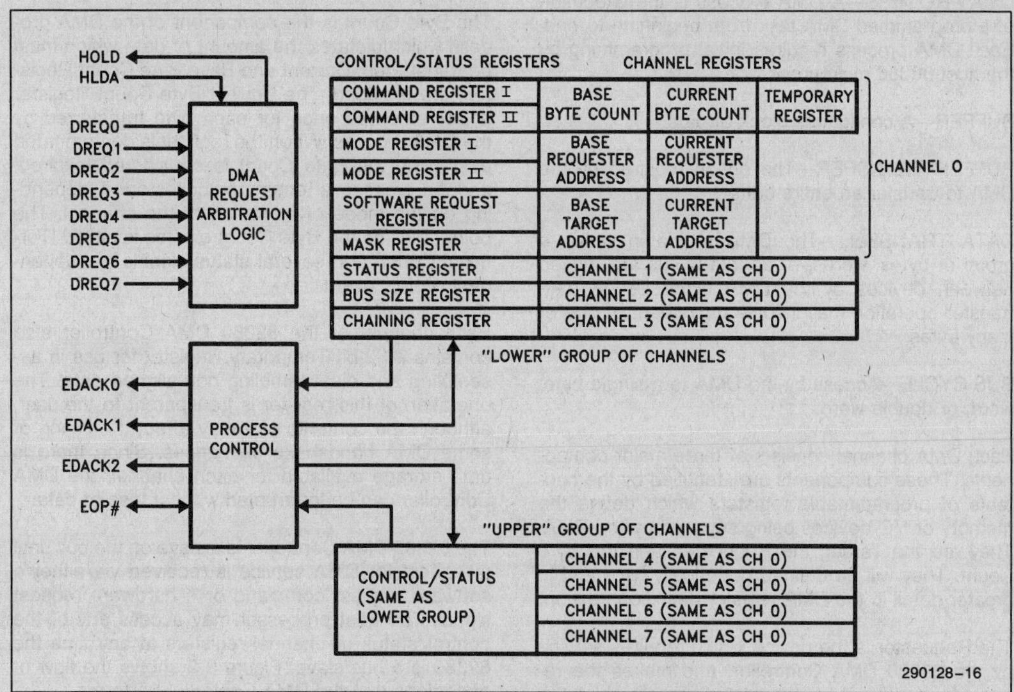

Figure 3-1. 82380 DMA Controller Block Diagram

3.1 Functional Description

In describing the operation of the 82380's DMA Controller, close attention to terminology is required. Before entering the discussion of the function of the 82380 DMA Controller, the following explanations of some of the terminology used herein may be of benefit. First, a few terms for clarification:

DMA PROCESS—A DMA process is the execution of a programmed DMA task from beginning to end. Each DMA process requires initial programming by the host 80386 microprocessor.

BUFFER—A contiguous block of data.

BUFFER TRANSFER—The action required by the DMA to transfer an entire buffer.

DATA TRANSFER—The DMA action in which a group of bytes, words, or double words are moved between devices by the DMA Controller. A data transfer operation may involve movement of one or many bytes.

BUS CYCLE—Access by the DMA to a single byte, word, or double word.

Each DMA channel consists of three major components. These components are identified by the contents of programmable registers which define the memory or I/O devices being serviced by the DMA. They are the Target, the Requester, and the Byte Count. They will be defined generically here and in greater detail in the DMA register definition section.

The Requester is the device which requires service by the 82380 DMA Controller, and makes the request for service. All of the control signals which the DMA monitors or generates for specific channels are logically related to the Requester. Only the Requester is considered capable of initiating or terminating a DMA process.

The Target is the device with which the Requester wishes to communicate. As far as the DMA process is concerned, the Target is a slave which is incapable of control over the process.

The direction of data transfer can be either from Requester to Target or from Target to Requester; i.e., each can be either a source or a destination.

The Requester and Target may each be either I/O or memory. Each has an address associated with it that can be incremented, decremented, or held constant. The addresses are stored in the Requester Address Registers and Target Address Registers, respectively. These registers have two parts: one which contains the current address being used in the DMA process (Current Address Register), and one which holds the programmed base address (Base Address Register). The contents of the Base Registers are never changed by the 82380 DMA Controller. The Current Registers are incremented or decremented according to the progress of the DMA process.

The Byte Count is the component of the DMA process which dictates the amount of data which must be transferred. Current and Base Byte Count Registers are provided. The Current Byte Count Register is decremented once for each byte transferred by the DMA process. When the register is decremented past zero, the Byte Count is considered 'expired' and the process is terminated or restarted, depending on the mode of operation of the channel. The point at which the Byte Count expires is called 'Terminal Count' and several status signals are dependent on this event.

Each channel of the 82380 DMA Controller also contains a 32-bit Temporary Register for use in assembling and disassembling non-aligned data. The operation of this register is transparent to the user, although the contents of it may affect the timing of some DMA handshake sequences. Since there is data storage available for each channel, the DMA Controller can be interrupted without loss of data.

The 82380 DMA Controller is a slave on the bus until a request for DMA service is received via either a software request command or a hardware request signal. The host processor may access any of the control/status or channel registers at any time the 82380 is a bus slave. Figure 3-2 shows the flow of operations that the DMA Controller performs.

At the time a DMA service request is received, the DMA Controller issues a bus hold request to the host processor. The 82380 becomes the bus master when the host relinquishes the bus by asserting a hold acknowledge signal. The channel to be serviced will be the one with the highest priority at the time the DMA Controller becomes the bus master. The DMA Controller will remain in control of the bus until the hold acknowledge signal is removed, or until the current DMA transfer is complete.

While the 82380 DMA Controller has control of the bus, it will perform the required data transfer(s). The type of transfer, source and destination addresses, and amount of data to transfer are programmed in the control registers of the DMA channel which received the request for service.

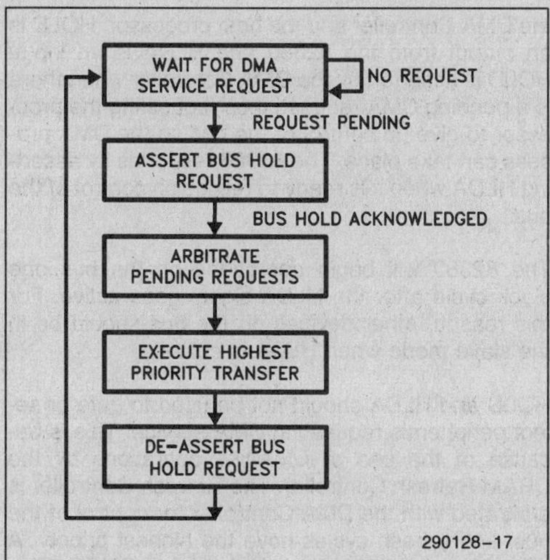

Figure 3-2. Flow of DMA Controller Operation

At completion of the DMA process, the 82380 will remove the bus hold request. At this time the 82380 becomes a slave again, and the host returns to being a master. If there are other DMA channels with requests pending, the controller will again assert the hold request signal and restart the bus arbitration and switching process.

3.2 Interface Signals

There are fourteen control signals dedicated to the DMA process. They include eight DMA Channel Requests (DREQn), three Encoded DMA Acknowledge signals (EDACKn), Processor Hold and Hold Acknowledge (HOLD, HLDA), and End-Of-Process (EOP#). The DREQn inputs and EDACK(0–2) outputs are handshake signals to the devices requiring DMA service. The HOLD output and HLDA input are handshake signals to the host processor. Figure 3-3 shows these signals and how they interconnect between the 82380 DMA Controller, and the Requester and Target devices.

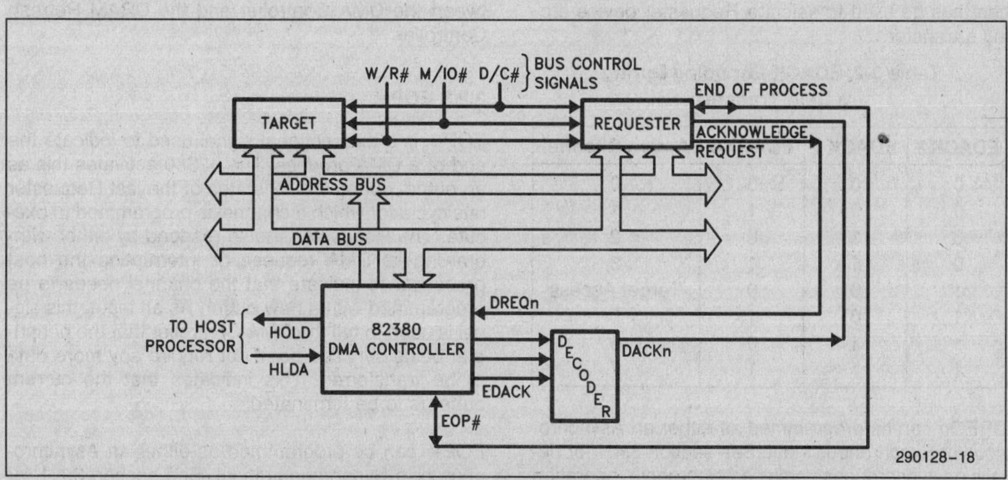

Figure 3-3. Requester, Target, and DMA Controller Interconnection (2-Cycle Configuration)

3.2.1 DREQn and EDACK(0-2)

These signals are the handshake signals between the peripheral and the 82380. When the peripheral requires DMA service, it asserts the DREQn signal of the channel which is programmed to perform the service. The 82380 arbitrates the DREQn against other pending requests and begins the DMA process after finishing other higher priority processes.

When the DMA service for the requested channel is in progress, the EDACK(0-2) signals represent the DMA channel which is accessing the Requester. The 3-bit code on the EDACK(0-2) lines indicates the number of the channel presently being serviced. Table 3-2 shows the encoding of these signals. Note that Channel 4 does not have a corresponding hardware acknowledge.

The DMA acknowledge (EDACK) signals indicate the active channel only during DMA accesses to the Requester. During accesses to the Target, EDACK(0-2) has the idle code (100). EDACK(0-2) can thus be used to select a Requester device during a transfer.

Table 3-2. EDACK Encoding During a DMA Transfer

EDACK2	EDACK1	EDACK0	Active Channel
0	0	0	0
0	0	1	1
0	1	0	2
0	1	1	3
1	0	0	Target Access
1	0	1	5
1	1	0	6
1	1	1	7

DREQn can be programmed as either an Asynchronous or Synchronous input. See section 3.4.1 for details on synchronous versus asynchronous operation of this pin.

The EDACKn signals are always active. They either indicate 'no acknowledge' or they indicate a bus access to the requester. The acknowledge code is either 100, for an idle DMA or during a DMA access to the Target, or 'n' during a Requester access, where n is the binary value representing the channel. A simple 3-line to 8-line decoder can be used to provide discrete acknowledge signals for the peripherals.

3.2.2 HOLD and HLDA

The Hold Request (HOLD) and Hold Acknowledge (HLDA) signals are the handshake signals between the DMA Controller and the host processor. HOLD is an output from the 82380 and HLDA is an input. HOLD is asserted by the DMA Controller when there is a pending DMA request, thus requesting the processor to give up control of the bus so the DMA process can take place. The 80386 responds by asserting HLDA when it is ready to relinquish control of the bus.

The 82380 will begin operations on the bus one clock cycle after the HLDA signal goes active. For this reason, other devices on the bus should be in the slave mode when HLDA is active.

HOLD and HLDA should not be used to gate or select peripherals requesting DMA service. This is because of the use of DMA-like operations by the DRAM Refresh Controller. The Refresh Controller is arbitrated with the DMA Controller for control of the bus, and refresh cycles have the highest priority. A refresh cycle will take place between DMA cycles without relinquishing bus control. See section 3.4.3 for a more detailed discussion of the interaction between the DMA Controller and the DRAM Refresh Controller.

3.2.3 EOP#

EOP# is a bi-directional signal used to indicate the end of a DMA process. The 82380 activates this as an output during the T2 states of the last Requester bus cycle for which a channel is programmed to execute. The Requester should respond by either withdrawing its DMA request, or interrupting the host processor to indicate that the channel needs to be programmed with a new buffer. As an input, this signal is used to tell the DMA Controller that the peripheral being serviced does not require any more data to be transferred. This indicates that the current buffer is to be terminated.

EOP# can be programmed as either an Asynchronous or a Synchronous input. See section 3.4.1 for details on synchronous versus asynchronous operation of this pin.

3.3 Modes of Operation

The 82380 DMA Controller has many independent operating functions. When designing peripheral interfaces for the 82380 DMA Controller, all of the functions or modes must be considered. All of the channels are independent of each other (except in priority of operation) and can operate in any of the modes. Many of the operating modes, though independently programmable, affect the operation of other modes. Because of the large number of combinations possible, each programmable mode is discussed here with its affects on the operation of other modes. The entire list of possible combinations will not be presented.

Table 3-1 shows the categories of DMA features available in the 82380. Each of the five major categories is independent of the others. The sub-categories are the available modes within the major function or mode category. The following sections explain each mode or function and its relation to other features.

Table 3-1. DMA Operating Modes

I. **Target/Requester Definition**
  a. Data Transfer Direction
  b. Device Type
  c. Increment/Decrement/Hold

II. **Buffer Processes**
  a. Single Buffer Process
  b. Buffer Auto-Initialize Process
  c. Buffer Chaining Process

III. **Data Transfer/Handshake Modes**
  a. Single Transfer Mode
  b. Demand Transfer Mode
  c. Block Transfer Mode
  d. Cascade Mode

IV. **Priority Arbitration**
  a. Fixed
  b. Rotating
  c. Programmable Fixed

V. **Bus Operation**
  a. Fly-By (Single-Cycle)/Two-Cycle
  b. Data Path Width
  c. Read, Write, or Verify Cycles

3.3.1 TARGET/REQUESTER DEFINITION

All DMA transfers involve three devices: the DMA Controller, the Requester, and the Target. Since the devices to be accessed by the DMA Controller vary widely, the operating characteristics of the DMA Controller must be tailored to the Requester and Target devices.

The Requester can be defined as either the source or the destination of the data to be transferred. This is done by specifying a Write or a Read transfer, respectively. In a Read transfer, the Target is the data source and the Requester is the destination for the data. In a Write transfer, the Requester is the source and the Target in the destination.

The Requester and Target addresses can each be independently programmed to be incremented, decremented, or held constant. As an example, the 82380 is capable of reversing a string or data by having a Requester address increment and the Target address decrement in a memory-to-memory transfer.

3.3.2 BUFFER TRANSFER PROCESSES

The 82380 DMA Controller allows three programmable Buffer Transfer Processes. These processes define the logical way in which a buffer of data is accessed by the DMA.

The three Buffer Transfer Processes include the Single Buffer Process, the Buffer Auto-Initialize Process, and the Buffer Chaining Process. These processes require special programming considerations. See the DMA Programming section for more details on setting up the Buffer Transfer Processes.

Single Buffer Process

The Single Buffer Process allows the DMA channel to transfer only one buffer of data. When the buffer has been completely transferred (Current Byte Count decremented past zero or EOP# input active), the DMA process ends and the channel becomes idle. In order for that channel to be used again, it must be reprogrammed.

The single Buffer Process is usually used when the amount of data to be transferred is known exactly, and it is also known that there is not likely to be any data to follow before the operating system can reprogram the channel.

Buffer Auto-Initialize Process

The Buffer Auto-Initialize Process allows multiple groups of data to be transferred to or from a single buffer. This process does not require reprogramming. The Current Registers are automatically reprogrammed from the Base Registers when the current process is terminated, either by an expired Byte Count or by an external EOP# signal. The data transferred will always be between the same Target and Requester.

The auto-initialization/process-execution cycle is repeated, with a HOLD/HLDA re-arbitration, until the channel is either disabled or re-programmed.

Buffer Chaining Process

The Buffer Chaining Process is useful for transferring large quantities of data into non-contiguous buffer areas. In this process, a single channel is used to process data from several buffers, while having to program the channel only once. Each new buffer is programmed in a pipelined operation that provides the new buffer information while the old buffer is being processed. The chain is created by loading new buffer information while the 82380 DMA Controller is processing the Current Buffer. When the Current Buffer expires, the 82380 DMA Controller automatically restarts the channel using the new buffer information.

Loading the new buffer information is done by an interrupt routine which is requested by the 82380. Interrupt Request 1 (IRQ1) is tied internally to the 82380 DMA Controller for this purpose. IRQ1 is generated by the 82380 when the new buffer information is loaded into the channel's Current Registers, leaving the Base Registers 'empty'. The interrupt service routine loads new buffer information into the Base Registers. The host processor is required to load the information for another buffer before the current Byte Count expires. The process repeats until the host programs the channel back to single buffer operation, or until the channel runs out of buffers.

The channel runs out of buffers when the Current Buffer expires and the Base Registers have not yet been loaded with new buffer information. When this occurs, the channel must be reprogrammed.

If an external EOP# is encountered while executing a Buffer Chaining Process, the current buffer is considered expired and the new buffer information is loaded into the Current Registers. If the Base Registers are 'empty', the chain is terminated.

The channel uses the Base Target Address Register as an indicator of whether or not the Base Registers are full. When the most significant byte of the Base Target Register is loaded, the channel considers all of the Base Registers loaded, and removes the interrupt request. This requires that the other Base Registers (Base Requester Address, Last Byte Count) must be loaded before the Base Target Address Register. The reason for implementing the reloading process this way is that, for most applications, the Byte Count and the Requester will not change from one buffer to the next, and therefore do not need to be reprogrammed. The details of programming the channel for the Buffer Chaining Process can be found in the section of DMA programming.

3.3.3 DATA TRANSFER MODES

Three Data Transfer modes are available in the 82380 DMA Controller. They are the Single Transfer, Block Transfer, and Demand Transfer Modes. These transfer modes can be used in conjunction with any one of three Buffer Transfer modes: Single Buffer, Auto-Initialized Buffer, and Buffer Chaining. Any Data Transfer Modes can be used under any of the Buffer Transfer Modes. These modes are independently available for all DMA channels.

Different devices being serviced by the DMA Controller require different handshaking sequences for data transfers to take place. Three handshaking modes are available on the 82380, giving the designer the opportunity to use the DMA Controller as efficiently as possible. The speed at which data can be presented or read by a device can affect the way a DMA controller uses the host's bus, thereby affecting not only data throughput during the DMA process, but also affecting the host's performance by limiting its access to the bus.

Single Transfer Mode

In the Single Transfer Mode, one data transfer to or from the Requester is performed by the DMA Controller at a time. The DREQn input is arbitrated and the HOLD/HLDA sequence is executed for each transfer. Transfers continue in this manner until the Byte Count expires, or until EOP# is sampled active. If the DREQn input is held active continuously, the entire DREQ-HOLD-HLDA-DACK sequence is repeated over and over until the programmed number of bytes has been transferred. Bus control is released to the host between each transfer. Figure 3-4 shows the logical flow of events which make up a buffer transfer using the Single Transfer Mode. Refer to section 3.4 for an explanation of the bus control arbitration procedure.

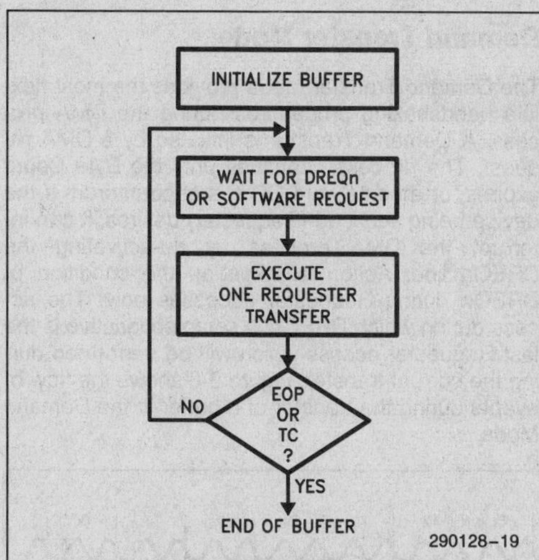

Figure 3-4. Buffer Transfer in Single Transfer Mode

The Single Transfer Mode is used for devices which require complete handshake cycles with each data access. Data is transferred to or from the Requester only when the Requester is ready to perform the transfer. Each transfer requires the entire DREQ-HOLD-HLDA-DACK handshake cycle. Figure 3-5 shows the timing of the Single Transfer Mode cycles.

Block Transfer Mode

In the Block Transfer Mode, the DMA process is initiated by a DMA request and continues until the Byte count expires, or until EOP# is activated by the Requester. The DREQn signal need only be held active until the first Requester access. Only a refresh cycle will interrupt the block transfer process.

Figure 3-6 illustrates the operation of the DMA during the Block Transfer Mode. Figure 3-7 shows the timing of the handshake signals during Block Mode Transfers.

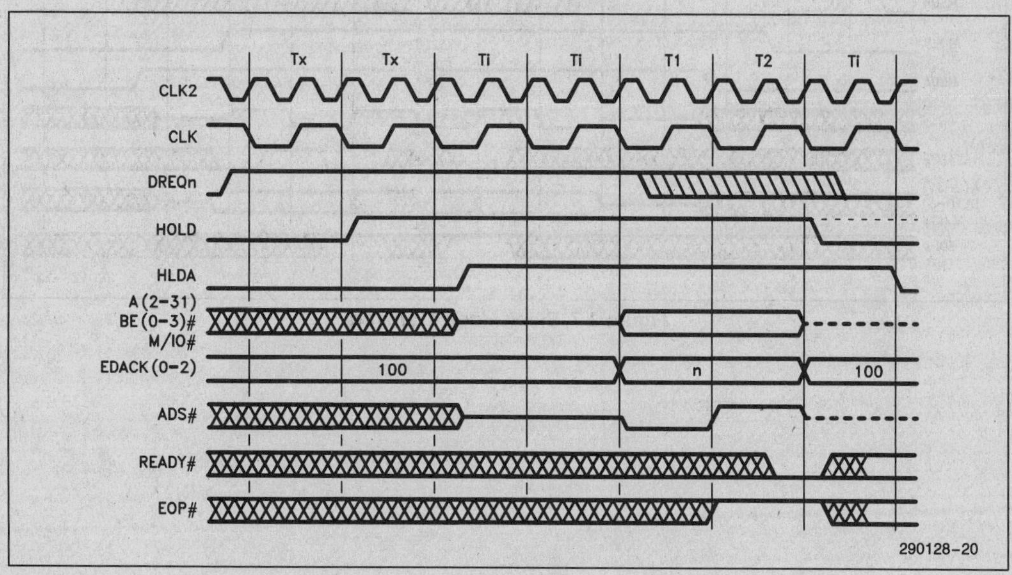

Figure 3-5. DMA Single Transfer Mode

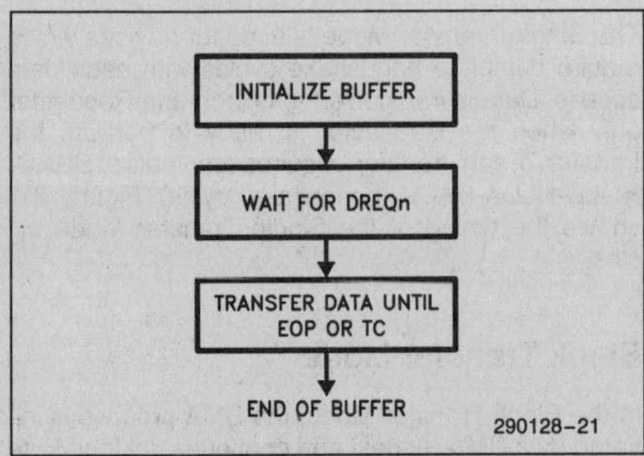

Figure 3-6. Buffer Transfer in Block Transfer Mode

Demand Transfer Mode

The Demand Transfer Mode provides the most flexible handshaking procedures during the DMA process. A Demand Transfer is initiated by a DMA request. The process continues until the Byte Count expires, or an external EOP# is encountered. If the device being serviced (Requester) desires, it can interrupt the DMA process by de-activating the DREQn line. Action is taken on the condition of DREQn during Requester accesses only. The access during which DREQn is sampled inactive is the last Requester access which will be performed during the current transfer. Figure 3-8 shows the flow of events during the transfer of a buffer in the Demand Mode.

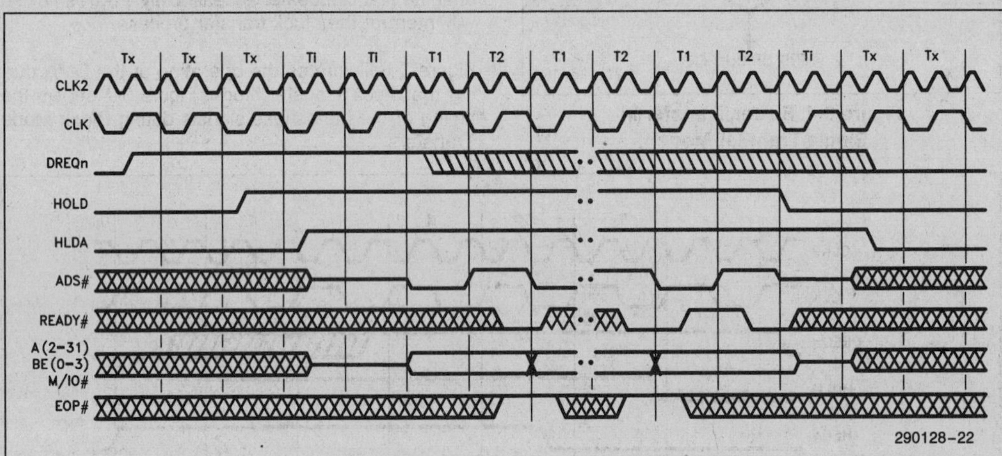

Figure 3-7. Block Mode Transfers

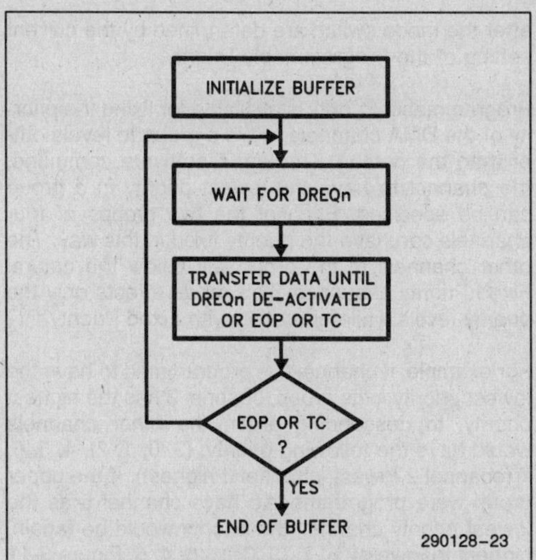

Figure 3-8. Buffer Transfer in Demand Transfer Mode

When the DREQn line goes inactive, the DMA controller will complete the current transfer, including any necessary accesses to the Target, and relinquish control of the bus to the host. The current process information is saved (byte count, Requester and Target addresses, and Temporary Register).

The Requester can restart the transfer process by reasserting DREQn. The 82380 will arbitrate the request with other pending requests and begin the process where it left off. Figure 3-9 shows the timing of handshake signals during Demand Transfer Mode operation.

Using the Demand Transfer Mode allows peripherals to access memory in small, irregular bursts without wasting bus control time. The 82380 is designed to give the best possible bus control latency in the Demand Transfer Mode. Bus control latency is defined here as the time from the last active bus cycle of the previous bus master to the first active bus cycle of the new bus master. The 82380 DMA Controller will perform its first bus access cycle two bus states after HLDA goes active. In the typical configuration, bus control is returned to the host one bus state after the DREQn goes inactive.

There are two cases where there may be more than one bus state of bus control latency at the end of a transfer. The first is at the end of an Auto-Initialize process, and the second is at the end of a process where the source is the Requester and Two-Cycle transfers are used.

When a Buffer Auto-Initialize Process is complete, the 82380 requires seven bus states to reload the

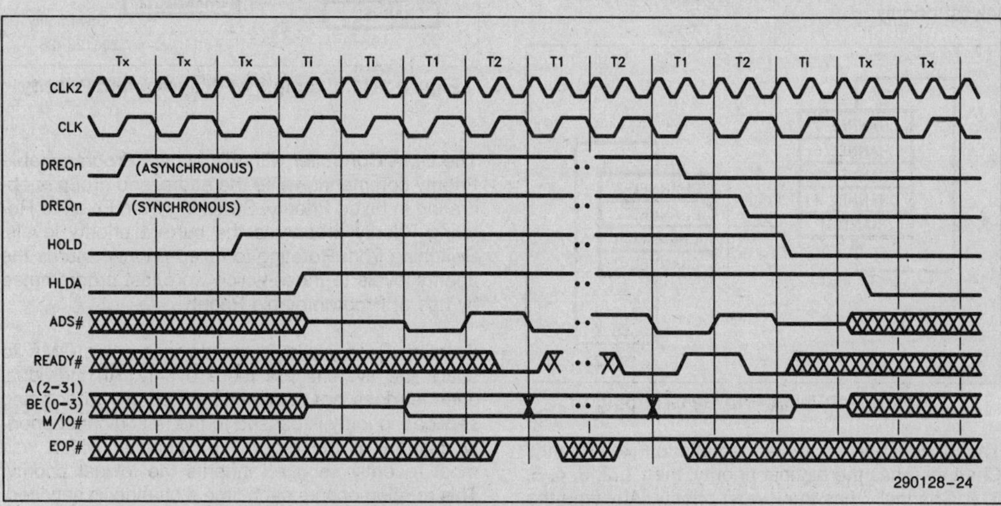

Figure 3-9. Demand Mode Transfers

Current Registers from the Base Registers of the Auto-Initialized channel. The reloading is done while the 82380 is still the bus master so that it is prepared to service the channel immediately after relinquishing the bus, if necessary.

In the case where the Requester is the source, and Two-Cycle transfers are being used, there are two extra idle states at the end of the transfer process. This occurs due to housekeeping in the DMA's internal pipeline. These two idle states are present only after the very last Requester access, before the DMA Controller de-activates the HOLD signal.

3.3.4 CHANNEL PRIORITY ARBITRATION

DMA channel priority can be programmed into one of two arbitration methods: Fixed or Rotating. The four lower DMA channels and the four upper DMA channels operate as if they were two separate DMA controllers operating in cascade. The lower group of four channels (0–3) is always prioritized between channels 7 and 4 of the upper group of channels (4–7). Figure 3-10 shows a pictorial representation of the priority grouping.

The priority can thus be set up as rotating for one group of channels and fixed for the other, or any other combination. While in Fixed Priority, the programmer can also specify which channel has the lowest priority.

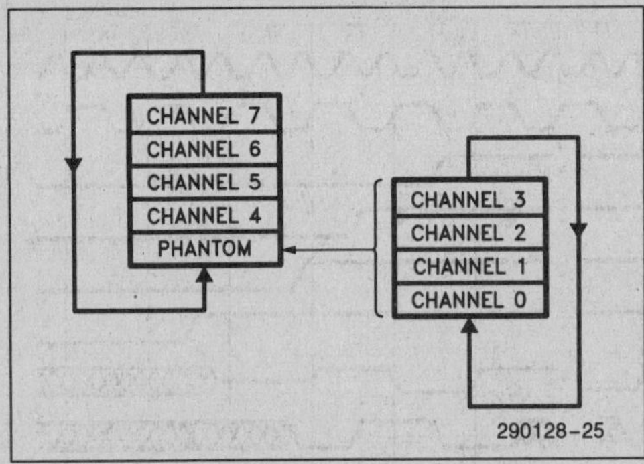

Figure 3-10. DMA Priority Grouping

The 82380 DMA Controller defaults to Fixed Priority. Channel 0 has the highest priority, then 1, 2, 3, 4, 5, 6, 7. Channel 7 has the lowest priority. Any time the DMA Controller arbitrates DMA requests, the requesting channel with the highest priority will be serviced next.

Fixed Priority can be entered into at any time by a software command. The priority levels in effect after the mode switch are determined by the current setting of the Programmable Priority.

Programmable Priority is available for fixing the priority of the DMA channels within a group to levels other than the default. Through a software command, the channel to have the lowest priority in a group can be specified. Each of the two groups of four channels can have the priority fixed in this way. The other channels in the group will follow the natural Fixed Priority sequence. This mode affects only the priority levels while operating with Fixed Priority.

For example, if channel 2 is programmed to have the lowest priority in its group, channel 3 has the highest priority. In descending order, the other channels would have the following priority: (3, 0, 1, 2), 4, 5, 6, 7 (channel 2 lowest, channel 3 highest). If the upper group were programmed to have channel 5 as the lowest priority channel, the priority would be (again, highest to lowest): 6, 7, (3, 0, 1, 2), 4, 5. Figure 3-11 shows this example pictorially. The lower group is always prioritized as a fifth channel of the upper group (between channels 4 and 7).

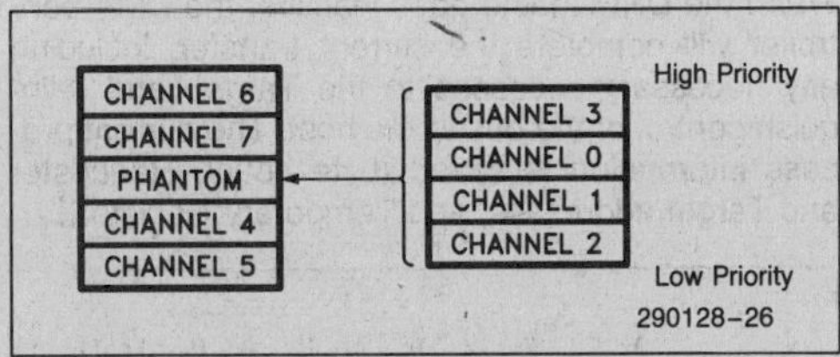

Figure 3-11. Example of Programmed Priority

The DMA Controller will only accept Programmable Priority commands while the addressed group is operating in Fixed Priority. Switching from Fixed to Rotating Priority preserves the current priority levels. Switching from Rotating to Fixed Priority returns the priority levels to those which were last programmed by use of Programmable Priority.

Rotating Priority allows the devices using DMA to share the system bus more evenly. An individual channel does not retain highest priority after being serviced, priority is passed to the next highest priority channel in the group. The channel which was most recently serviced inherits the lowest priority. This rotation occurs each time a channel is serviced. Figure 3-12 shows the sequence of events as priority is passed between channels. Note that the lower group rotates within the upper group, and that servicing a channel within the lower group causes rotation within the group as well as rotation of the upper group.

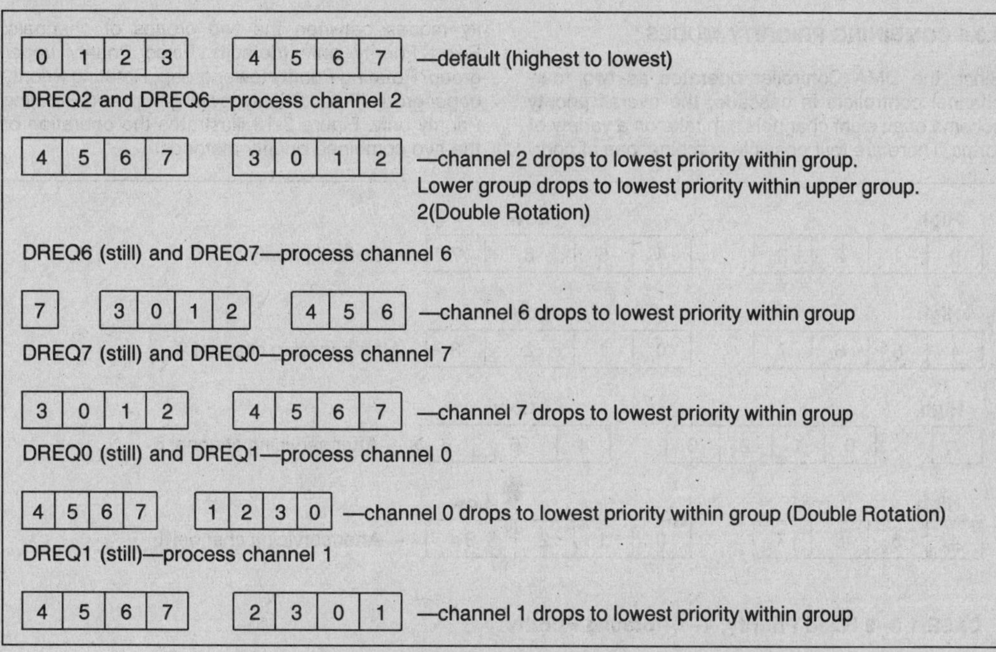

Figure 3-12. Rotating Channel Priority. Lower and Upper groups are programmed for the Rotating Priority Mode.

4

3.3.5 COMBINING PRIORITY MODES

Since the DMA Controller operates as two four-channel controllers in cascade, the overall priority scheme of all eight channels can take on a variety of forms. There are four possible combinations of priority modes between the two groups of channels: Fixed Priority only (default), Fixed Priority upper group/Rotating Priority lower group, Rotating Priority upper group/Fixed Priority lower group, and Rotating Priority only. Figure 3-13 illustrates the operation of the two combined priority methods.

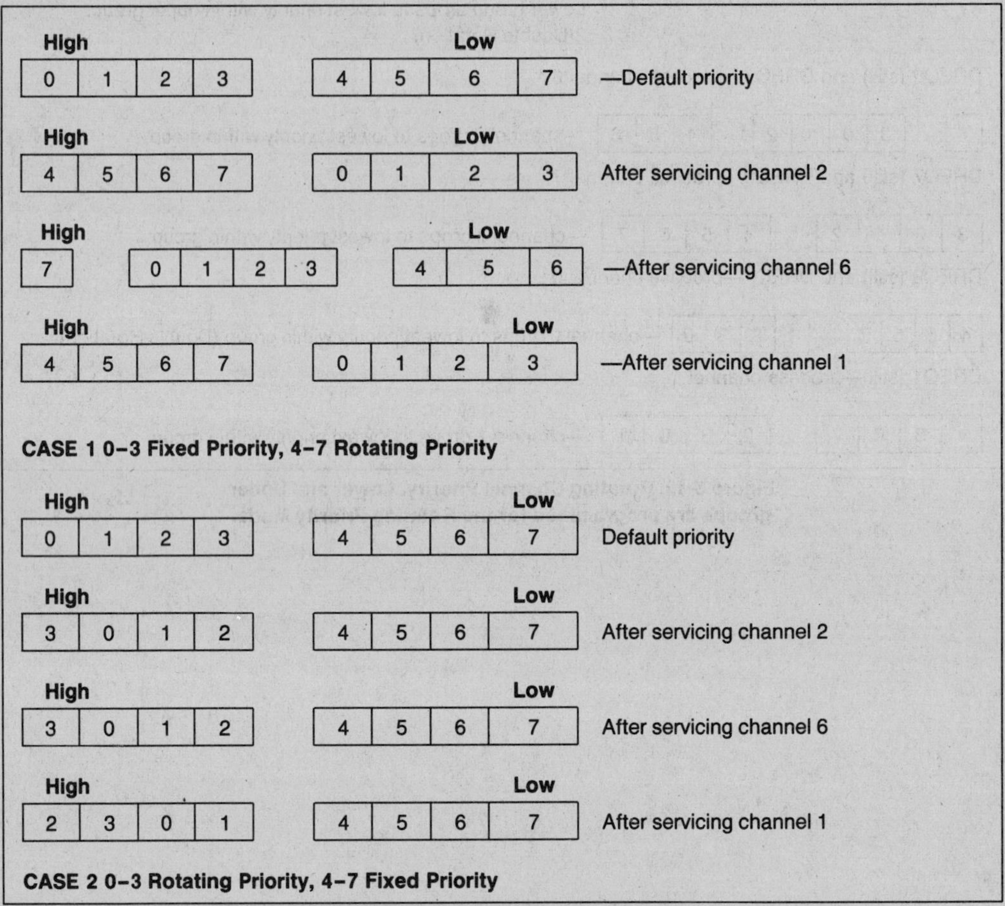

Figure 3-13. Combining Priority Modes

3.3.6 BUS OPERATION

Data may be transferred by the DMA Controller using two different bus cycle operations: Fly-By (one-cycle) and Two-Cycle. These bus handshake methods are selectable independently for each channel through a command register. Device data path widths are independently programmable for both Target and Requester. Also selectable through software is the direction of data transfer. All of these parameters affect the operation of the 82380 on a bus-cycle by bus-cycle basis.

3.3.6.1 Fly-By Transfers

The Fly-By Transfer Mode is the fastest and most efficient way to use the 82380 DMA Controller to transfer data. In this method of transfer, the data is written to the destination device at the same time it is read from the source. Only one bus cycle is used to accomplish the transfer.

In the Fly-By Mode, the DMA acknowledge signal is used to select the Requester. The DMA Controller simultaneously places the address of the Target on the address bus. The state of M/IO# and W/R# during the Fly-By transfer cycle indicate the type of Target and whether the target is being written to or read from. The Target's Bus Size is used as an incrementer for the Byte Count. The Requester address registers are ignored during Fly-By transfers.

Note that memory-to-memory transfers cannot be done using the Fly-By Mode. Only one memory or I/O address is generated by the DMA Controller at a time during Fly-By transfers. Only one of the devices being accessed can be selected by an address. Also, the Fly-By method of data transfer limits the hardware to accesses of devices with the same data bus width. The Temporary Registers are not affected in the Fly-By Mode.

Fly-By transfers also require that the data paths of the Target and Requester be directly connected. This requires that successive Fly-By accesses be to doubleword boundaries, or that the Requester be capable of switching its connections to the data bus.

3.3.6.2 Two-Cycle Transfers

Two-Cycle transfers can also be performed by the 82380 DMA Controller. These transfers require at least two bus cycles to execute. The data being transferred is read into the DMA Controller's Temporary Register during the first bus cycle(s). The second bus cycle is used to write the data from the Temporary Register to the destination.

If the addresses of the data being transferred are not word or doubleword aligned, the 82380 will recognize the situation and read and write the data in groups of bytes, placing them always at the proper destination. This process of collecting the desired bytes and putting them together is called 'byte assembly'. The reverse process (reading from aligned locations and writing to non-aligned locations) is called 'byte disassembly'.

The assembly/disassembly process takes place transparent to the software, but can only be done while using the Two-Cycle transfer method. The 82380 will always perform the assembly/disassembly process as necessary for the current data transfer. Any data path widths for either the Requester or Target can be used in the Two-Cycle Mode. This is very convenient for interfacing existing 8- and 16-bit peripherals to the 80386's 32-bit bus.

The 82380 DMA Controller always attempts to fill the Temporary Register from the source before writing any data to the destination. If the process is terminated before the Temporary Register is filled (TC or EOP#), the 82380 will write the partial data to the destination. If a process is temporarily suspended (such as when DREQn is de-activated during a demand transfer), the contents of a partially filled Temporary Register will be stored within the 82380 until the process is restarted.

For example, if the source is specified as an 8-bit device and the destination as a 32-bit device, there will be four reads as necessary from the 8-bit source to fill the Temporary Register. Then the 82380 will write the 32-bit contents to the destination. This cycle will repeat until the process is terminated or suspended.

Note that for a Single-Cycle transfer mode of operation (see section 3.3.3), the internal circuitry of the DMA Controller actually executes single transfers by removing the DREQ from the internal arbitration. Thus single transfers from an 8-bit requester to a 32-bit target will consist of four complete and independent 8-bit requester cycles, between which bus control is released and re-requested. Finally, the 32-bit data will be transferred to the target device from the temporary register before the fifth requester cycle.

With Two-Cycle transfers, the devices that the 82380 accesses can reside at any address within I/O or memory space. The device must be able to decode the byte-enables (BEn#). Also, if the device cannot accept data in byte quantities, the programmer must take care not to allow the DMA Controller to access the device on any address other than the device boundary.

3.3.6.3 Data Path Width and Data Transfer Rate Considerations

The number of bus cycles used to transfer a single 'word' of data is affected by whether the Two-Cycle or the Fly-By (Single-Cycle) transfer method is used.

The number of bus cycles used to transfer data directly affects the data transfer rate. Inefficient use of bus cycles will decrease the effective data transfer rate that can be obtained. Generally, the data transfer rate is halved by using Two-Cycle transfers instead of Fly-By transfers.

The choice of data path widths of both Target and Requester affects the data transfer rate also. During each bus cycle, the largest pieces of data possible should be transferred.

The data path width of the devices to be accessed must be programmed into the DMA controller. The 82380 defaults after reset to 8-bit-to-8-bit data transfers, but the Target and Requester can have different data path widths, independent of each other and independent of the other channels. Since this is a software programmable function, more discussion of the uses of this feature are found in the section on programming.

3.3.6.4 Read, Write, and Verify Cycles

Three different bus cycle types may be used in a data transfer. They are the Read, Write, and Verify cycles. These cycle types dictate the way in which the 82380 operates on the data to be transferred.

A Read Cycle transfers data from the Target to the Requester. A Write Cycle transfers data from the Requester to the target. In a Fly-By transfer, the address and bus status signals indicate the access (read or write) to the Target; the access to the Requester is assumed to be the opposite.

The Verify Cycle is used to perform a data read only. No write access is indicated or assumed in a Verify Cycle. The Verify Cycle is useful for validating block fill operations. An external comparator must be provided to do any comparisons on the data read.

3.4 Bus Arbitration and Handshaking

Figure 3-14 shows the flow of events in the DMA request arbitration process. The arbitration sequence starts when the Requester asserts a DREQn (or DMA service is requested by software). Figure 3-15 shows the timing of the sequence of events following a DMA request. This sequence is executed for each channel that is activated. The DREQn signal can be replaced by a software DMA channel request with no change in the sequence.

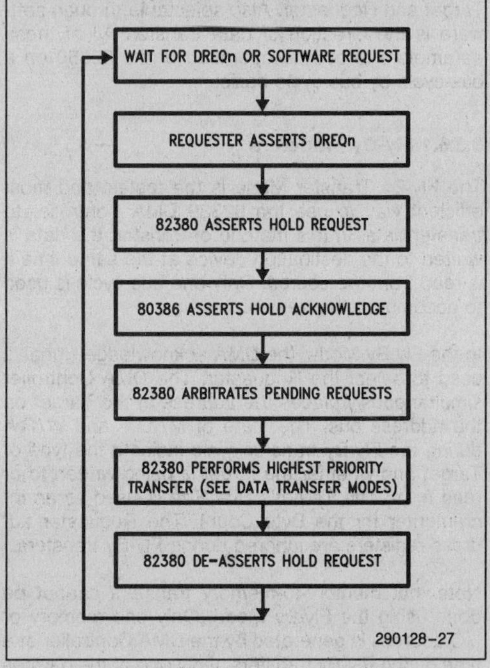

Figure 3-14. Bus Arbitration and DMA Sequence

After the Requester asserts the service request, the 82380 will request control of the bus via the HOLD signal. The 82380 will always assert the HOLD signal one bus state after the service request is asserted. The 80386 responds by asserting the HLDA signal, thus releasing control of the bus to the 82380 DMA Controller.

Priority of pending DMA service requests is arbitrated during the first state after HLDA is asserted by the 80386. The next state will be the beginning of the first transfer access of the highest priority process.

When the 82380 DMA Controller is finished with its current bus activity, it returns control of the bus to the host processor. This is done by driving the HOLD signal inactive. The 82380 does not drive any address or data bus signals after HOLD goes low. It enters the Slave Mode until another DMA process is requested. The processor acknowledges that it has regained control of the bus by forcing the HLDA signal inactive. Note that the 82380's DMA Controller will not re-request control of the bus until the entire HOLD/HLDA handshake sequence is complete.

The 82380 DMA Controller will terminate a current DMA process for one of three reasons: expired byte count, end-of-process command (EOP# activated) from a peripheral, or de-activated DMA request signal. In each case, the controller will de-assert HOLD immediately after completing the data transfer in progress. These three methods of process termination are illustrated in Figures 3-16, 3-19, and 3-18, respectively.

An expired byte count indicates that the current process is complete as programmed and the channel has no further transfers to process. The channel must be restarted according to the currently programmed Buffer Transfer Mode, or reprogrammed completely, including a new Buffer Transfer Mode.

If the peripheral activates the EOP# signal, it is indicating that it will not accept or deliver any more data for the current buffer. The 82380 DMA Controller considers this as a completion of the channel's current process and interprets the condition the same way as if the byte count expired.

The action taken by the 82380 DMA Controller in response to a de-activated DREQn signal depends on the Data Transfer Mode of the channel. In the Demand Mode, data transfers will take place as long as the DREQn is active and the byte count has not expired. In the Block Mode, the controller will complete the entire block transfer without relinquishing

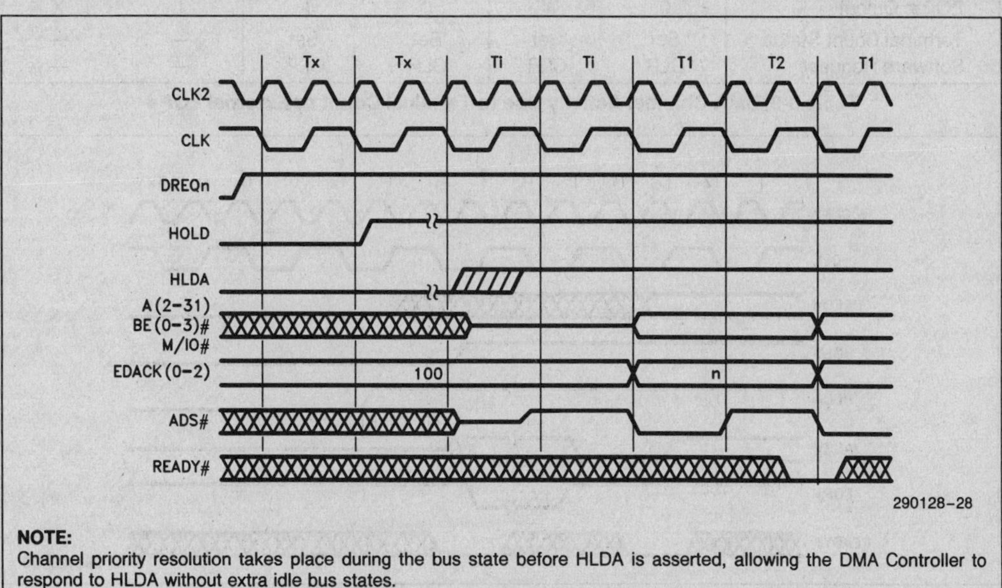

NOTE:
Channel priority resolution takes place during the bus state before HLDA is asserted, allowing the DMA Controller to respond to HLDA without extra idle bus states.

Figure 3-15. Beginning of a DMA process

the bus, even if DREQn goes inactive before the transfer is complete. In the Single Mode, the controller will execute single data transfers, relinquishing the bus between each transfer, as long as DREQn is active.

Normal termination of a DMA process due to expiration of the byte count (Terminal Count-TC) is shown in Figure 3-16. The condition of DREQn is ignored until after the process is terminated. If the channel is programmed to auto-initialize, HOLD will be held active for an additional seven clock cycles while the auto-initialization takes place.

Table 3-3 shows the DMA channel activity due to EOP# or Byte Count expiring (Terminal Count).

Buffer Process:	Single or Chaining-Base Empty		Auto-Initialize		Chaining-Base Loaded	
Event						
Terminal Count	True	X	True	X	True	X
EOP# Input	X	0	X	0	X	0
Results						
Current Registers	—	—	Load	Load	Load	Load
Channel Mask	Set	Set	—	—	—	—
EOP# Output	0	X	0	X	1	X
Terminal Count Status	Set	Set	Set	Set	—	—
Software Request	CLR	CLR	CLR	CLR	—	—

Table 3-3. DMA Channel Activity Due to Terminal Count or External EOP#

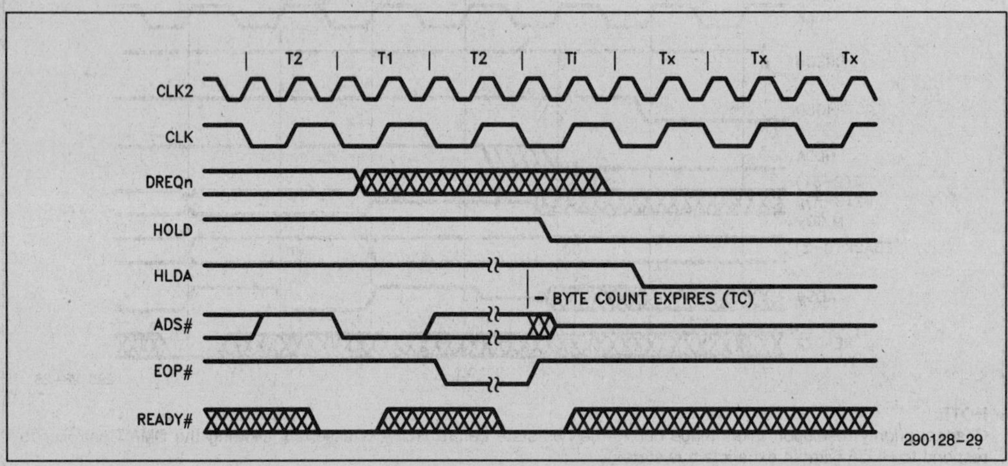

Figure 3-16. Termination of a DMA Process Due to Expiration of Current Byte Count

The 82380 always relinquishes control of the bus between channel services. This allows the hardware designer the flexibility to externally arbitrate bus hold requests, if desired. If another DMA request is pending when a higher priority channel service is completed, the 82380 will relinquish the bus until the hold acknowledge is inactive. One bus state after the HLDA signal goes inactive, the 82380 will assert HOLD again. This is illustrated in Figure 3-17.

3.4.1 SYNCHRONOUS AND ASYNCHRONOUS SAMPLING OF DREQn AND EOP#

As an indicator that a DMA service is to be started, DREQn is always sampled asynchronously. It is sampled at the beginning of a bus state and acted upon at the end of the state. Figure 3-15 illustrates the start of a DMA process due to a DREQn input.

The DREQn and EOP# inputs can be programmed to be sampled either synchronously or asynchronously to signal the end of a transfer.

The synchronous mode affords the Requester one bus state of extra time to react to an access. This means the Requester can terminate a process on the current access, without losing any data. The asynchronous mode requires that the input signal be presented prior to the beginning of the last state of the Requester access.

The timing relationships of the DREQn and EOP# signals to the termination of a DMA transfer are shown in Figures 3-18 and 3-19. Figure 3-18 shows the termination of a DMA transfer due to inactive DREQn. Figure 3-19 shows the termination of a DMA process due to an active EOP# input.

In the Synchronous Mode, DREQn and EOP# are sampled at the end of the last state of every Requester data transfer cycle. If EOP# is active or DREQn is inactive at this time, the 82380 recognizes this access to the Requester as the last transfer. At this point, the 82380 completes the transfer in progress, if necessary, and returns bus control to the host.

In the asynchronous mode, the inputs are sampled at the beginning of every state of a Requester access. The 82380 waits until the end of the state to act on the input.

DREQn and EOP# are sampled at the latest possible time when the 82380 can determine if another transfer is required. In the Synchronous Mode, DREQn and EOP# are sampled on the trailing edge of the last bus state before another data access cycle begins. The Asynchronous Mode requires that the signals be valid one clock cycle earlier.

4

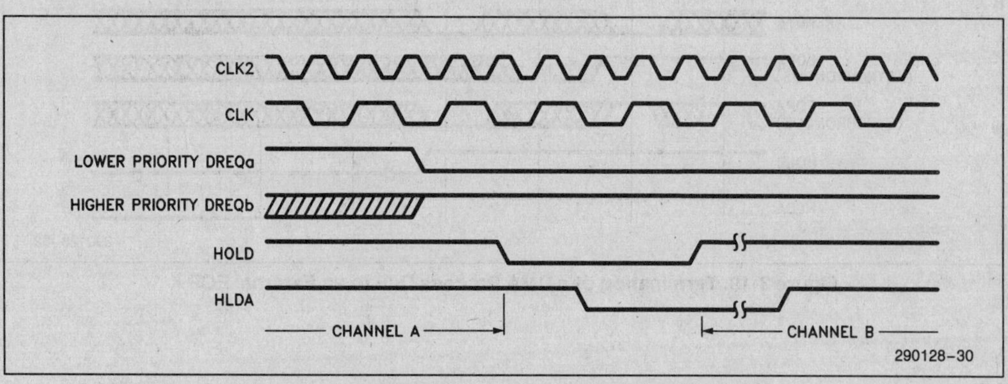

Figure 3-17. Switching between Active DMA Channels

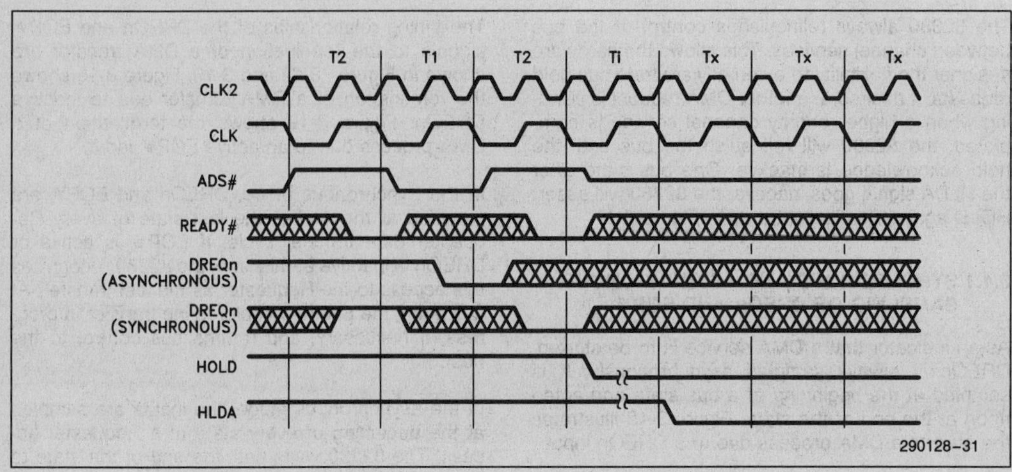

Figure 3-18. Termination of a DMA Process Due to De-Asserting DREQn

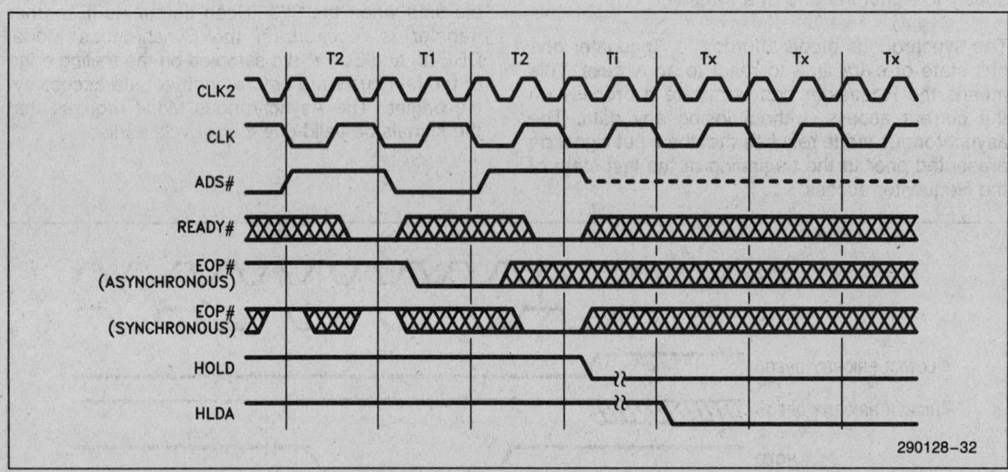

Figure 3-19. Termination of a DMA Process Due to an External EOP#

While in the Pipeline Mode, if the NA# signal is sampled active during a transfer, the end of the state where NA# was sampled active is when the 82380 decides whether to commit to another transfer. The device must de-assert DREQn or assert EOP# before NA# is asserted, otherwise the 82380 will commit to another, possibly undesired, transfer.

Synchronous DREQn and EOP# sampling allows the peripheral to prevent the next transfer from occurring by de-activating DREQn or asserting EOP# during the current Requester access, before the 82380 DMA Controller commits itself to another transfer. The DMA Controller will not perform the next transfer if it has not already begun the bus cycle. Asynchronous sampling allows less stringent timing requirements than the Synchronous Mode, but requires that the DREQn signal be valid at the beginning of the next to last bus state of the current Requester access.

Using the Asynchronous Mode with zero wait states can be very difficult. Since the addresses and control signals are driven by the 82380 near half-way through the first bus state of a transfer, and the Asynchronous Mode requires that DREQn be active before the end of the state, the peripheral being accessed is required to present DREQn only a few nanoseconds after the control information is available. This means that the peripheral's control logic must be extremely fast (practically non-causal). An alternative is the Synchronous Mode.

3.4.2 ARBITRATION OF CASCADED MASTER REQUESTS

The Cascade Mode allows another DMA-type device to share the bus by arbitrating its bus accesses with the 82380's. Seven of the eight DMA channels (0–3 and 5–7) can be connected to a cascaded device. The cascaded device requests bus control through the DREQn line of the channel which is programmed to operate in Cascade Mode. Bus hold acknowledge is signaled to the cascaded device through the EDACK lines. When the EDACK lines are active with the code for the requested cascade channel, the bus is available to the cascaded master device.

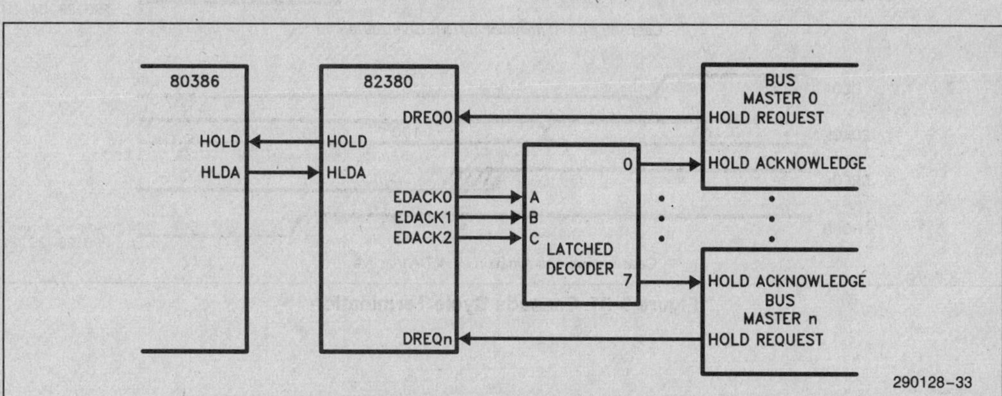

Figure 3-20. Cascaded Bus Master

A Cascade cycle begins the same way a regular DMA cycle begins. The requesting bus master asserts the DREQn line on the 82380. This bus control request arbitrated as any other DMA request would be. If any channel receives a DMA request, the 82380 requests control of the bus. When the host acknowledges that it has released bus control, the 82380 acknowledges to the requesting master that it may access the bus. The 82380 enters an idle state until the new master relinquishes control.

A cascade cycle will be terminated by one of two events: DREQn going inactive, or HLDA going inactive. The normal way to terminate the cascade cycle is for the cascaded master to drop the DREQn signal. Figure 3-21 shows the two cascade cycle termination sequences.

The Refresh Controller may interrupt the cascaded master to perform a refresh cycle. If this occurs, the 82380 DMA Controller will de-assert the EDACK signal (hold acknowledge to cascaded master) and wait for the cascaded master to remove its hold request. When the 82380 regains bus control, it will perform the refresh cycle in its normal fashion. After the refresh cycle has been completed, and if the cascaded device has re-asserted its request, the 82380 will return control to the cascaded master which was interrupted.

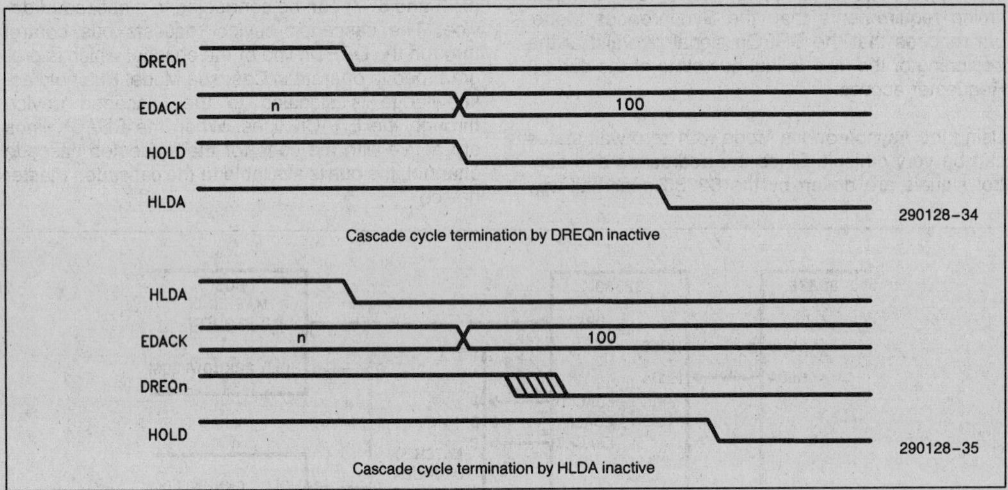

Figure 3-21. Cascade Cycle Termination

The 82380 assumes that it is the only device monitoring the HLDA signal. If the system designer wishes to place other devices on the bus as bus masters, the HLDA from the processor must be intercepted before presenting it to the 82380. Using the Cascade capability of the 82380 DMA Controller offers a much better solution.

3.4.3 ARBITRATION OF REFRESH REQUESTS

The arbitration of refresh requests by the DRAM Refresh Controller is slightly different from normal DMA channel request arbitration. The 82380 DRAM Refresh Controller always has the highest priority of any DMA process. It also can interrupt a process in progress. Two types of processes in progress may be encountered: normal DMA, and bus master cascade.

In the event of a refresh request during a normal DMA process, the DMA Controller will complete the data transfer in progress and then execute the refresh cycle before continuing with the current DMA process. The priority of the interrupted process is not lost. If the data transfer cycle interrupted by the Refresh Controller is the last of a DMA process, the refresh cycle will always be executed before control of the bus is transferred back to the host.

When the Refresh Controller request occurs during a cascade cycle, the Refresh Controller must be assured that the cascaded master device has relinquished control of the bus before it can execute the refresh cycle. To do this, the DMA Controller drops the EDACK signal to the cascaded master and waits for the corresponding DREQn input to go inactive. By dropping the DREQn signal, the cascaded master relinquishes the bus. The Refresh Controller then performs the refresh cycle. Control of the bus is returned to the cascaded master if DREQn returns to an active state before the end of the refresh cycle, otherwise control is passed to the processor and the cascaded master loses its priority.

3.5 DMA Controller Register Overview

The 82380 DMA Controller contains 44 registers which are accessable to the host processor. Twenty-four of these registers contain the device addresses and data counts for the individual DMA channels (three per channel). The remaining registers are control and status registers for initiating and monitoring the operation of the 82380 DMA Controller. Table 3-4 lists the DMA Controller's registers and their accessability.

Register Name	Access
Control/Status Register—One Each Per Group	
Command Register I	Write Only
Command Register II	Write Only
Mode Register I	Write Only
Mode Register II	Write Only
Software Request Register	Read/Write
Mask Set-Reset Register	Write Only
Mask Read-Write Register	Read/Write
Status Register	Read Only
Bus Size Register	Write Only
Chaining Register	Read/Write
Channel Registers—One Each Per Channel	
Base Target Address	Write Only
Current Target Address	Read Only
Base Requester Address	Write Only
Current Requester Address	Read Only
Base Byte Count	Write Only
Current Byte Count	Read Only

Table 3-4. DMA Controller Registers

3.5.1 CONTROL/STATUS REGISTERS

The following registers are available to the host processor for programming the 82380 DMA Controller into its various modes and for checking the operating status of the DMA processes. Each set of four DMA channels has one of each of these registers associated with it.

Command Register I

Enables or disables the DMA channels as a group. Sets the Priority Mode (Fixed or Rotating) of the group. This write-only register is cleared by a hardware reset, defaulting to all channels enabled and Fixed Priority Mode.

Command Register II

Sets the sampling mode of the DREQn and EOP# inputs. Also sets the lowest priority channel for the group in the Fixed Priority Mode. The functions programmed through Command Register II default after a hardware reset to: asynchronous DREQn and EOP#, and channels 3 and 7 lowest priority.

Mode Register I

Mode Register I is identical in function to the Mode register of the 8237A. It programs the following functions for an individually selected channel:

Type of Transfer—read, write, verify
Auto—Initialize—enable or disable
Target Address Count—increment or decrement
Data Transfer Mode—demand, single, block, cascade

Mode Register I functions default to the following after reset: verify transfer, Auto-Initialize disabled, Increment Target address, Demand Mode.

Mode Register II

Programs the following functions for an individually selected channel:

Target Address Hold—enable or disable
Requester Address Count—increment or decrement
Requester Address Hold—enable or disable
Target Device Type—I/O or Memory
Requester Device Type—I/O or Memory
Transfer Cycles—Two-Cycle or Fly-By

Mode Register II functions are defined as follows after a hardware reset: Disable Target Address Hold, Increment Requester Address, Target (and Requester) in memory, Fly-By Transfer Cycles. Note: Requester Device Type ignored in Fly-By Transfers.

Software Request Register

The DMA Controller can respond to service requests which are initiated by software. Each channel has an internal request status bit associated with it. The host processor can write to this register to set or reset the request bit of a selected channel.

The status of the group's software DMA service requests can be read from this register as well. Each request bit is cleared upon Terminal Count or external EOP#.

The software DMA requests are non-maskable and subject to priority arbitration with all other software and hardware requests. The entire register is cleared by a hardware reset.

Mask Registers

Each channel has associated with it a mask bit which can be set/reset to disable/enable that channel. Two methods are available for setting and clearing the mask bits. The Mask Set/Reset Register is a write-only register which allows the host to select an individual channel and either set or reset the mask bit for that channel only. The Mask Read/Write Register is available for reading the mask bit status and for writing mask bits in groups of four.

The mask bits of a group may be cleared in one step by executing the Clear Mask Command. See the DMA Programming section for details. A hardware reset sets all of the channel mask bits, disabling all channels.

Status Register

The Status register is a read-only register which contains the Terminal Count (TC) and Service Request status for a group. Four bits indicate the TC status and four bits indicate the hardware request status for the four channels in the group. The TC bits are set when the Byte Count expires, or when an external EOP# is asserted. These bits are cleared by reading from the Status Register. The Service Request bit for a channel indicates when there is a hardware DMA request (DREQn) asserted for that channel. When the request has been removed, the bit is cleared.

Bus Size Register

This write-only register is used to define the bus size of the Target and Requester of a selected channel. The bus sizes programmed will be used to dictate the sizes of the data paths accessed when the DMA channel is active. The values programmed into this register affect the operation of the Temporary Register. Any byte-assembly required to make the transfers using the specified data path widths will be done in the Temporary Register. The Bus Size register of the Target is used as an increment/decrement value for the Byte Counter and Target Address when in the Fly-By Mode. Upon reset, all channels default to 8-bit Targets and 8-bit Requesters.

Chaining Register

As a command or write register, the Chaining register is used to enable or disable the Chaining Mode for a selected channel. Chaining can either be disabled or enabled for an individual channel, independently of the Chaining Mode status of other channels. After a hardware reset, all channels default to Chaining disabled.

When read by the host, the Chaining Register provides the status of the Chaining Interrupt of each of the channels. These interrupt status bits are cleared when the new buffer information has been loaded.

3.5.2 CHANNEL REGISTERS

Each channel has three individually programmable registers necessary for the DMA process; they are the Base Byte Count, Base Target Address, and Base Requester Address registers. The 24-bit Base

Byte Count register contains the number of bytes to be transferred by the channel. The 32-bit Base Target Address Register contains the beginning address (memory or I/O) of the Target device. The 32-bit Base Requester Address register contains the base address (memory or I/O) of the device which is to request DMA service.

Three more registers for each DMA channel exist within the DMA Controller which are directly related to the registers mentioned above. These registers contain the current status of the DMA process. They are the Current Byte Count register, the Current Target Address, and the Current Requester Address. It is these registers which are manipulated (incremented, decremented, or held constant) by the 82380 DMA Controller during the DMA process. The Current registers are loaded from the Base registers.

The Base registers are loaded when the host processor writes to the respective channel register addresses. Depending on the mode in which the channel is operating, the Current registers are typically loaded in the same operation. Reading from the channel register addresses yields the contents of the corresponding Current register.

To maintain compatibility with software which accesses an 8237A, a Byte Pointer Flip-Flop is used to control access to the upper and lower bytes of some words of the Channel Registers. These words are accessed as byte pairs at single port addresses. The Byte Pointer Flip-Flop acts as a one-bit pointer which is toggled each time a qualifying Channel Register byte is accessed. It always points to the next logical byte to be accessed of a pair of bytes.

The Channel registers are arranged as pairs of words, each pair with its own port address. Addressing the port with the Byte Pointer Flip-Flop reset accesses the least significant byte of the pair. The most significant byte is accessed when the Byte Pointer is set.

For compatibility with existing 8237A designs, there is one exception to the above statements about the Byte Pointer Flip-Flop. The third byte (bits 16–23) of the Target Address is accessed through its own port address. The Byte Pointer Flip-Flop is not affected by any accesses to this byte.

The upper eight bits of the Byte Count Register are cleared when the least significant byte of the register is loaded. This provides compatibility with software which accesses an 8237A. The 8237A has 16-bit Byte Count Registers.

3.5.3 TEMPORARY REGISTERS

Each channel has a 32-bit Temporary Register used for temporary data storage during two-cycle DMA transfers. It is this register in which any necessary byte assembly and disassembly of non-aligned data is performed. Figure 3-22 shows how a block of data will be moved between memory locations with different boundaries. Note that the order of the data does not change.

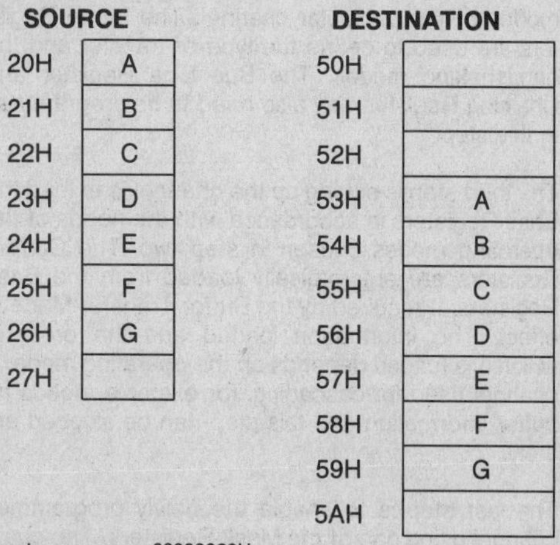

SOURCE		DESTINATION	
20H	A	50H	
21H	B	51H	
22H	C	52H	
23H	D	53H	A
24H	E	54H	B
25H	F	55H	C
26H	G	56H	D
27H		57H	E
		58H	F
		59H	G
		5AH	

Target = source = 00000020H
Requester = destination = 00000053H
Byte Count = 000006H

Figure 3-22. Transfer of Data between Memory Locations with Different Boundaries. This will be the result, independent of data path width.

If the destination is the Requester and an early process termination has been indicated by the EOP# signal or DREQn inactive in the Demand Mode, the Temporary Register is not affected. If data remains in the Temporary Register due to differences in data path widths of the Target and Requester, it will not be transferred or otherwise lost, but will be stored for later transfer.

If the destination is the Target and the EOP# signal is sensed active during the Requester access of a transfer, the DMA Controller will complete the transfer by sending to the Target whatever information is in the Temporary Register at the time of process termination. This implies that the Target could be accessed with partial data. For this reason it is advisable to have an I/O device designated as a Requester, unless it is capable of handling partial data transfers.

3.6 DMA Controller Programming

Programming a DMA Channel to perform a needed DMA function is in general a four step process. First the global attributes of the DMA Controller are programmed via the two Command Registers. These global attributes include: priority levels, channel group enables, priority mode, and DREQn/EOP# input sampling.

The second step involves setting the operating modes of the particular channel. The Mode Registers are used to define the type of transfer and the handshaking modes. The Bus Size Register and Chaining Register may also need to be programmed in this step.

The third step is setting up the channel is to load the Base Registers in accordance with the needs of the operating modes chosen in step two. The Current Registers are automatically loaded from the Base Registers, if required by the Buffer Transfer Mode in effect. The information loaded and the order in which it is loaded depends on the operating mode. A channel used for cascading, for example, needs no buffer information and this step can be skipped entirely.

The last step is to enable the newly programmed channel using one of the Mask Registers. The channel is then available to perform the desired data transfer. The status of the channel can be observed at any time through the Status Register, Mask Register, Chaining Register, and Software Request register.

Once the channel is programmed and enabled, the DMA process may be initiated in one of two ways, either by a hardware DMA request (DREQn) or a software request (Software Request Register).

Once programmed to a particular Process/Mode configuration, the channel will operate in that configuration until programmed otherwise. For this reason, restarting a channel after the current buffer expires does not require complete reprogramming of the channel. Only those parameters which have changed need to be reprogrammed. The Byte Count Register is always changed and must be reprogrammed. A Target or Requester Address Register which is incremented or decremented should be reprogrammed also.

3.6.1 BUFFER PROCESSES

The Buffer Process is determined by the Auto-Initialize bit of Mode Register I and the Chainlng Register. If Auto-Initialize is enabled, Chaining should not be used.

3.6.1.1 Single Buffer Process

The Single Buffer Process is programmed by disabling Chaining via the Chaining Register and programming Mode Register I for non-Auto-Initialize.

3.6.1.2 Buffer Auto-Initialize Process

Setting the Auto-Initialize bit in Mode Register I is all that is necessary to place the channel in this mode. Buffer Auto-Initialize must not be enabled simultaneous to enabling the Buffer Chaining Mode as this will have unpredictable results.

Once the Base Registers are loaded, the channel is ready to be enabled. The channel will reload its Current Registers from the Base Registers each time the Current Buffer expires, either by an expired Byte Count or an external EOP#.

3.6.1.3 Buffer Chaining Process

The Buffer Chaining Process is entered into from the Single Buffer Process. The Mode Registers should be programmed first, with all of the Transfer Modes defined as if the channel were to operate in the Single Buffer Process. The channel's Base and Current Registers are then loaded. When the channel has been set up in this way, and the chaining interrupt service routine is in place, the Chaining Process can be entered by programming the Chaining Register. Figure 3.23 illustrates the Buffer Chaining Process.

An interrupt (IRQ1) will be generated immediately after the Chaining Process is entered, as the channel then perceives the Base Registers as empty and in need of reloading. It is important to have the interrupt service routine in place at the time the Chaining Process is entered into. The interrupt request is removed when the most significant byte of the Base Target Address is loaded.

The interrupt will occur again when the first buffer expires and the Current Registers are loaded from the Base Registers. The cycle continues until the Chaining Process is disabled, or the host fails to respond to IRQ1 before the Current Buffer expires.

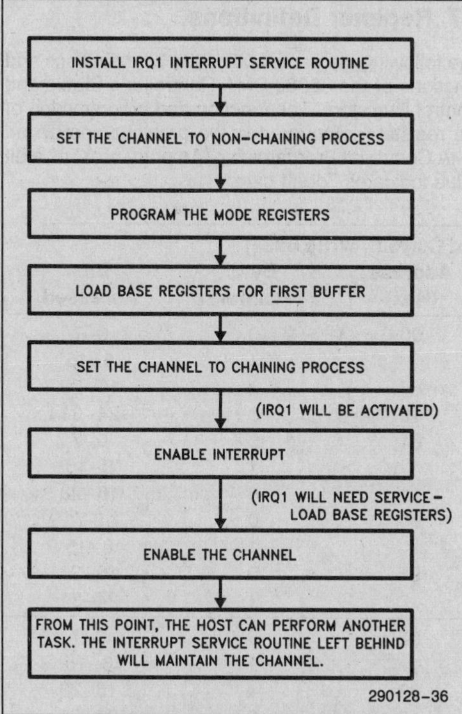

Figure 3-23. Flow of Events in the Buffer Chaining Process

Exiting the Chaining Process can be done by resetting the Chaining Mode Register. If an interrupt is pending for the channel when the Chaining Register is reset, the interrupt request will be removed. The Chaining Process can be temporarily disabled by setting the channel's Mask bit in the Mask Register.

The interrupt service routine for IRQ1 has the responsibility of reloading the Base Register as necessary. It should check the status of the channel to determine the cause of channel expiration, etc. It should also have access to operating system information regarding the channel, if any exists. The IRQ1 service routine should be capable of determining whether the chain should be continued or terminated and act on that information.

3.6.2 DATA TRANSFER MODES

The Data Transfer Modes are selected via Mode Register I. The Demand, Single, and Block Modes are selected by bits D6 and D7. The individual transfer type (Fly-By vs Two-Cycle, Read-Write-Verify, and I/O vs Memory) is programmed through both of the Mode registers.

3.6.3 CASCADED BUS MASTERS

The Cascade Mode is set by writing ones to D7 and D6 of Mode Register I. When a channel is programmed to operate in the Cascade Mode, all of the other modes associated with Mode Registers I and II are ignored. The priority and DREQn/EOP# definitions of the Command Registers will have the same effect on the channel's operation as any other mode.

3.6.4 SOFTWARE COMMANDS

There are five port addresses which, when written to, command certain operations to be performed by the 82380 DMA Controller. The data written to these locations is not of consequence, writing to the location is all that is necessary to command the 82380 to perform the indicated function. Following are descriptions of the command function.

Clear Byte Pointer Flip-Flop—location 000CH

Resets the Byte Pointer Flip-Flop. This command should be performed at the beginning of any access to the channel registers in order to be assured of beginning at a predictable place in the register programming sequence.

Master Clear—location 000DH

All DMA functions are set to their default states. This command is the equivalent of a hardware reset to the DMA Controller. Functions other than those in the DMA Controller section of the 82380 are not affected by this command.

Clear Mask Register —Channels 0-3—location 000EH
Channels 4-7—location 00CEH

This command simultaneously clears the Mask Bits of all channels in the addressed group, enabling all of the channels in the group.

Clear TC Interrupt Request—location 001EH

This command resets the Terminal Count Interrupt Request Flip-Flop. It is provided to allow the program which made a software DMA request to acknowledge that it has responded to the expiration of the requested channel(s).

3.7 Register Definitions

The following diagrams outline the bit definitions and functions of the 82380 DMA Controller's Status and Control Registers. The function and programming of the registers is covered in the previous section on DMA Controller Programming. An entry of 'X' as a bit value indicates "don't care."

Channel Registers Channel	Register Name	(Read Current, Write Base) Address (Hex)	Byte Pointer	Bits Accessed
Channel 0	Target Address	00	0	0-7
			1	8-15
		87	x	16-23
		10	0	24-31
	Byte Count	01	0	0-7
			1	8-15
		11	0	16-23
	Requester Address	90	0	0-7
			1	8-15
		91	0	16-23
			1	24-31
Channel 1	Target Address	02	0	0-7
			1	8-15
		83	x	16-23
		12	0	24-31
	Byte Count	03	0	0-7
			1	8-15
		13	0	16-23
	Requester Address	92	0	0-7
			1	8-15
		93	0	16-23
			1	24-31

Channel Registers Channel	Register Name	(Read Current, Write Base) Address (Hex)	Byte Pointer	Bits Accessed
Channel 2	Target Address	04	0	0–7
			1	8–15
		81	x	16–23
		14	0	24–31
	Byte Count	05	0	0–7
			1	8–15
		15	0	16–23
	Requester Address	94	0	0-7
			1	8–15
		95	0	16–23
			1	24–31
Channel 3	Target Address	06	0	0–7
			1	8–15
		82	x	16–23
		16	0	24–31
	Byte Count	07	0	0–7
			1	8–15
		17	0	16–23
	Requester Address	96	0	0-7
			1	8–15
		97	0	16–23
			1	24–31
Channel 4	Target Address	C0	0	0–7
			1	8–15
		8F	x	16–23
		D0	0	24–31
	Byte Count	C1	0	0–7
			1	8–15
		D1	0	16–23
	Requester Address	98	0	0-7
			1	8–15
		99	0	16–23
			1	24–31
Channel 5	Target Address	C2	0	0–7
			1	8–15
		8B	x	16–23
		D2	0	24–31
	Byte Count	C3	0	0–7
			1	8–15
		D3	0	16–23
	Requester Address	9A	0	0-7
			1	8–15
		9B	0	16–23
			1	24–31

Channel Registers Channel	Register Name	(Read Current, Write Base) Address (Hex)	Byte Pointer	Bits Accessed
Channel 6	Target Address	C4	0	0–7
			1	8–15
		89	x	16–23
		D4	0	24–31
	Byte Count	C5	0	0–7
			1	8–15
		D5	0	16–23
	Requester Address	9C	0	0-7
			1	8–15
		9D	0	16–23
			1	24–31
Channel 7	Target Address	C6	0	0–7
			1	8–15
		8A	x	16–23
		D6	0	24–31
	Byte Count	C7	0	0–7
			1	8–15
		D7	0	16–23
	Requester Address	9E	0	0-7
			1	8–15
		9F	0	16–23
			1	24–31

Command Register I (Write Only)

Port Address—Channels 0-3—0008H
Channels 4-7—00C8H

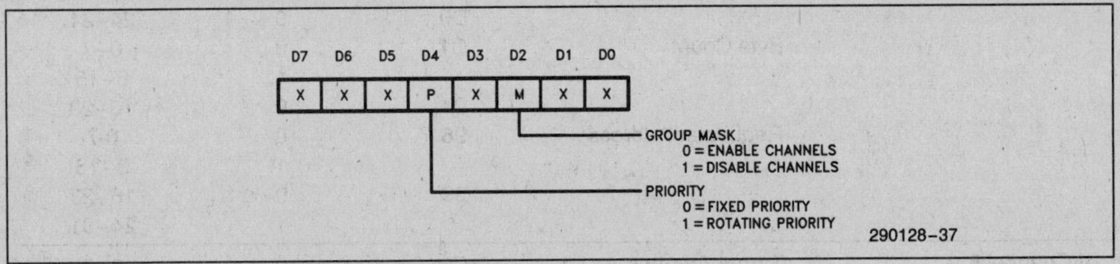

Command Register II (Write Only)

Port Addresses—Channels 0-3—001AH
Channels 4-7—00DAH

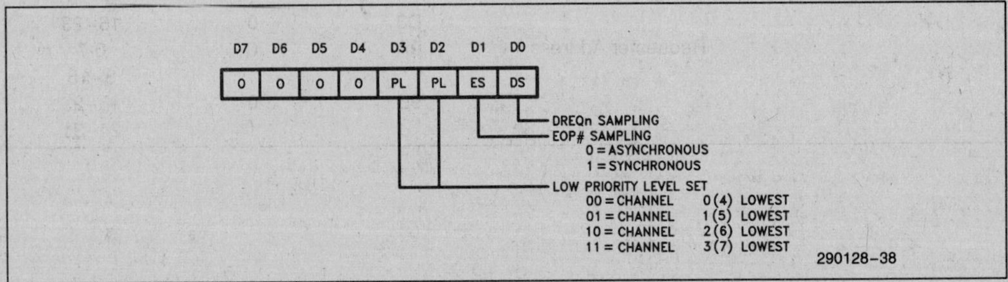

Mode Register I (Write Only)

Port Addresses—Channels 0-3—000BH
Channels 4-7—00CBH

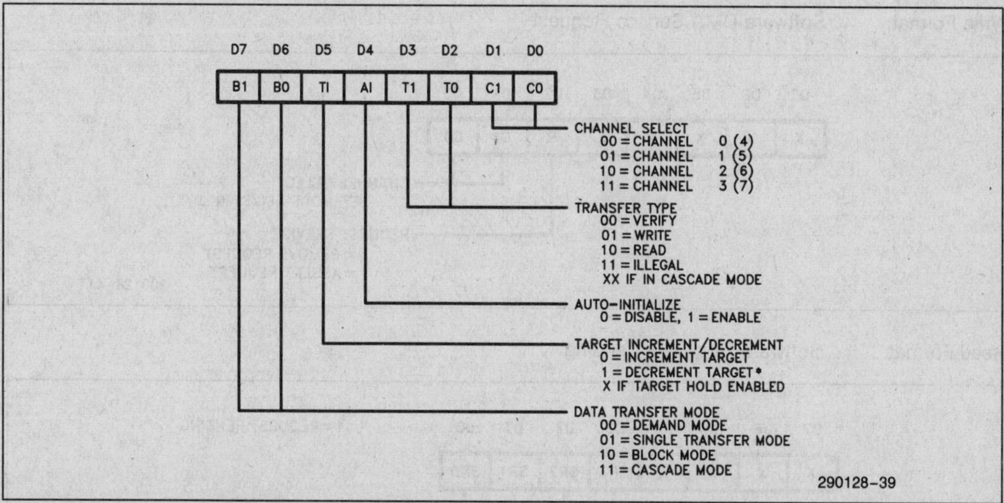

* Target and Requester DECREMENT is allowed only for byte transfers.

Mode Register II (Write Only)

Port Addresses—Channels 0-3—001BH
Channels 4-7—00DBH

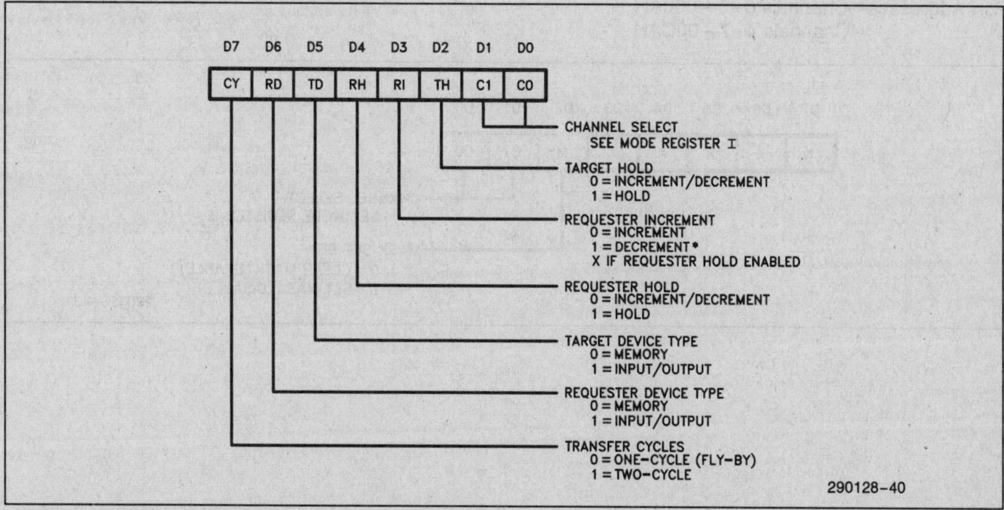

* Target and Requester DECREMENT is allowed only for byte transfers.

Software Request Register (Read/Write)

Port Addresses—Channels 0-3—0009H
Channels 4-7—00C9H

Write Format: Software DMA Service Request

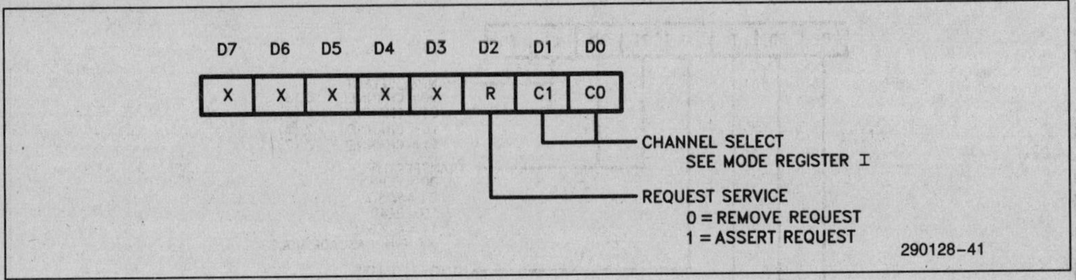

Read Format: Software Requests Pending

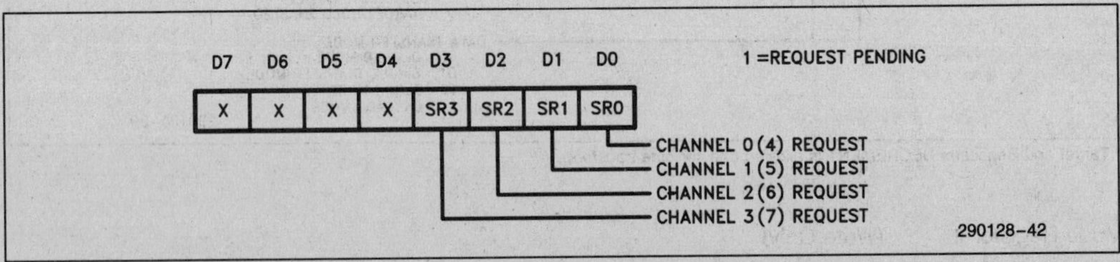

Mask Set/Reset Register Individual Channel Mask (Write Only)

Port Addresses—Channels 0-3—000AH
Channels 4-7—00CAH

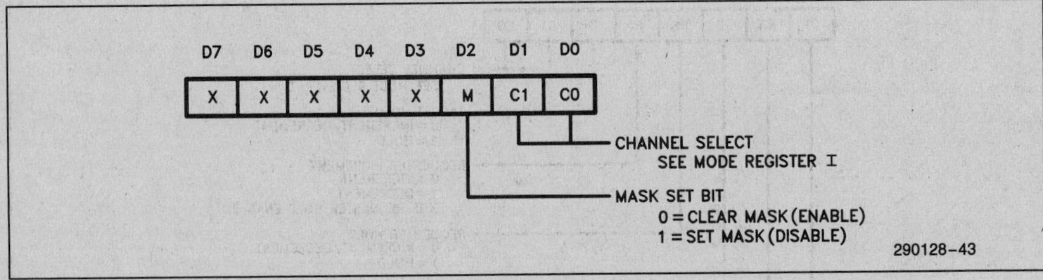

Mask Read/Write Register Group Channel Mask (Read/Write)

Port Addresses—Channels 0-3—000FH
Channels 4-7—00CFH

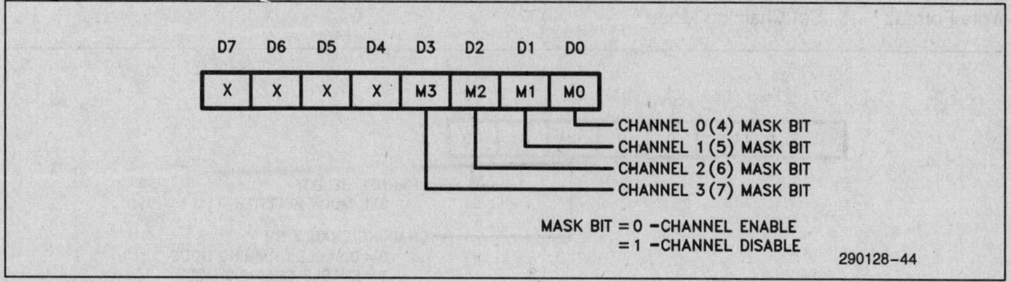

Status Register Channel Process Status (Read Only)

Port Addresses—Channels 0-3—0008H
Channels 4-7—00C8H

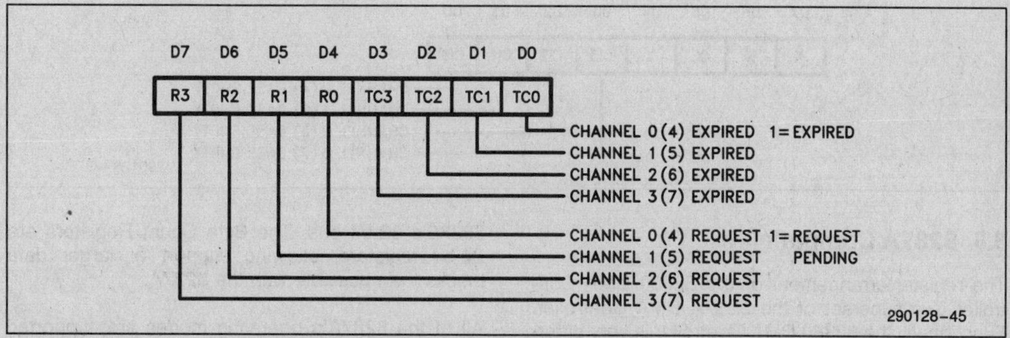

Bus Size Register Set Data Path Width (Write Only)

Port Addresses—Channels 0-3—0018H
Channels 4-7—00D8H

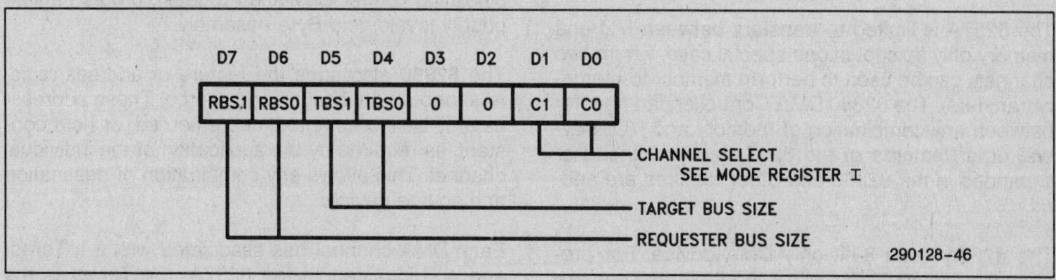

Bus Size Encoding:
00 = Reserved by Intel
01 = 32-bit Bus
10 = 16-bit Bus
11 = 8-bit Bus

Chaining Register (Read/Write)

Port Addresses—Channels 0-3—0019H
Channels 4-7—00D9H

Write Format: Set Chaining Mode

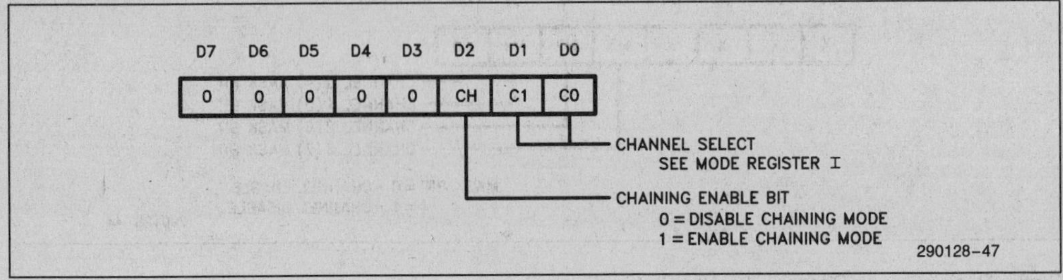

Read Format: Channel Interrupt Status

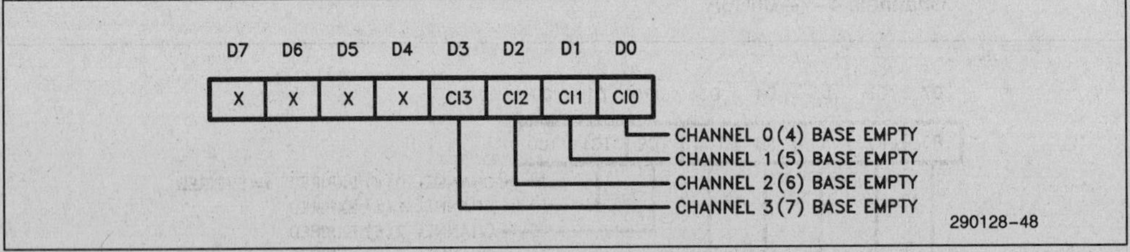

3.8 8237A Compatibility

The register arrangement of the 82380 DMA Controller is a superset of the 8237A DMA Controller. Functionally the 82380 DMA Controller is very different from the 8237A. Most of the functions of the 8237A are performed also by the 82380. The following discussion points out the differences between the 8237A and the 82380.

The 8237A is limited to transfers between I/O and memory only (except in one special case, where two channels can be used to perform memory-to-memory transfers). The 82380 DMA Controller can transfer between any combination of memory and I/O. Several other features of the 8237A are enhanced or expanded in the 82380 and other features are added.

The 8237A is an 8-bit only DMA device. For programming compatibility, all of the 8-bit registers are preserved in the 82380. The 82380 is programmed via 8-bit registers. The address registers in the 82380 are 32-bit registers in order to support the 80386's 32-bit bus. The Byte Count Registers are 24-bit registers, allowing support of larger data blocks than possible with the 8237A.

All of the 8237A's operating modes are supported by the 82380 (except the cumbersome two-channel memory-to-memory transfer). The 82380 performs memory-to-memory transfers using only one channel. The 82380 has the added features of buffer pipelining (Buffer Chaining Process), programmable priority levels, and Byte Assembly.

The 82380 also adds the feature of address registers for both destination and source. These addresses may be incremented, decremented, or held constant, as required by the application of the individual channel. This allows any combination of destination and source device.

Each DMA channel has associated with it a Target and a Requester. In the 8237A, the Target is the device which can be accessed by the address register, the Requester is the device which is accessed by the DMA Acknowledge signals and must be an I/O device.

4.0 Programmable Interrupt Controller (PIC)

4.1 Functional Description

The 82380 Programmable Interrupt Controller (PIC) consists of three enhanced 82C59A Interrupt Contollers. These three controllers together provide 15 external and 5 internal interrupt request inputs. Each external request input can be cascaded with an additional 82C59A slave collector. This scheme allows the 82380 to support a maximum of 120 (15 x 8) external interrupt request inputs.

Following one or more interrupt requests, the 82380 PIC issues an interrupt signal to the 80386. When the 80386 host processor responds with an interrupt acknowledge signal, the PIC will arbitrate between the pending interrupt requests and place the interrupt vector associated with the highest priority pending request on the data bus.

The major enhancement in the 82380 PIC over the 82C59A is that each of the interrupt request inputs can be individually programmed with its own interrupt vector, allowing more flexibility in interrupt vector mapping.

4.1.1 INTERNAL BLOCK DIAGRAM

The block diagram of the 82380 Programmable Interrupt Controller is shown in Figure 4-1. Internally, the PIC consists of three 82C59A banks: A, B and C. The three banks are cascaded to one another: C is cascaded to B, B is cascaded to A. The INT output of Bank A is used externally to interrupt the 80386.

Bank A has nine interrupt request inputs (two are unused), and Banks B and C have eight interrupt request inputs. Of the fifteen external interrupt request inputs, two are shared by other functions. Specifically, the Interrupt Request 3 input (IRQ3#) can be used as the Timer 2 output (TOUT2#). This pin can be used in three different ways: IRQ3# input only, TOUT2# output only, or using TOUT2# to generate an IRQ3# interrupt request. Also, the Interrupt Request 9 input (IRQ 9#) can be used as DMA Request 4 input (DREQ4). Typically, only IRQ9# or DREQ4 can be used at a time.

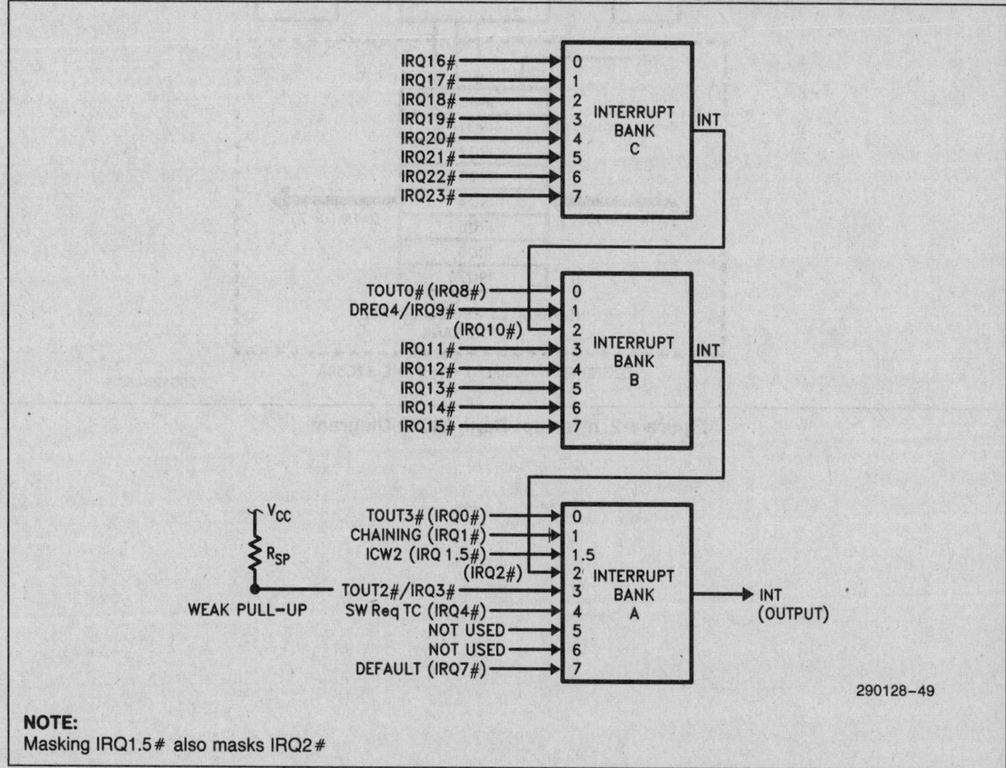

NOTE:
Masking IRQ1.5# also masks IRQ2#

Figure 4-1. Interrupt Controller Block Diagram

4

4.1.2 INTERRUPT CONTROLLER BANKS

All three banks are identical, with the exception of the IRQ1.5 on Bank A. Therefore, only one bank will be discussed. In the 82380 PIC, all external requests can be cascaded into and each interrupt controller bank behaves like a master. As compared to the 82C59A, the enhancements in the banks are:

— All interrupt vectors are individually programmable. (In the 82C59A, the vectors must be programmed in eight consecutive interrupt vector locations.)

— The cascade address is provided on the Data Bus (D0–D7). (In the 82C59A, three dedicated control signals (CAS0, CAS1, CAS2) are used for master/slave cascading.)

The block diagram of a bank is shown in Figure 4-2. As can be seen from this figure, the bank consists of six major blocks: the Interrupt Request Register (IRR), the In-Service Register (ISR), the Interrupt Mask Register (IMR), the Priority Resolver (PR), the Vector Register (VR), and the Control Logic. The functional description of each block follows.

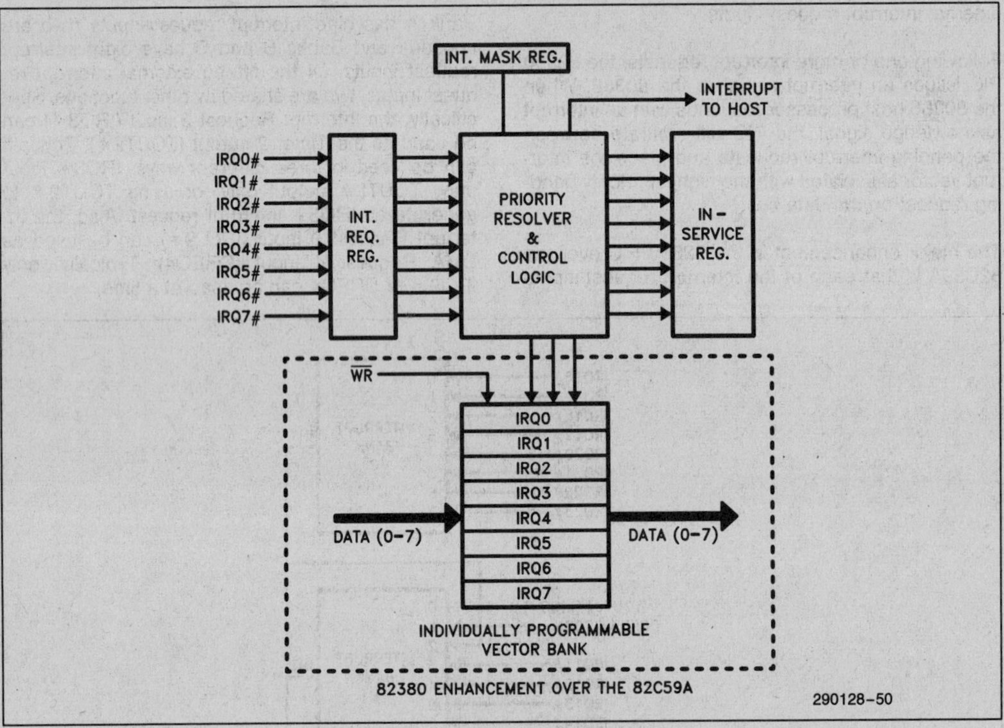

INT. MASK REG.
INTERRUPT TO HOST
IRQ0#
IRQ1#
IRQ2#
IRQ3#
IRQ4#
IRQ5#
IRQ6#
IRQ7#
INT. REQ. REG.
PRIORITY RESOLVER & CONTROL LOGIC
IN-SERVICE REG.
WR
IRQ0
IRQ1
IRQ2
IRQ3
IRQ4
IRQ5
IRQ6
IRQ7
DATA (0–7)
DATA (0–7)
INDIVIDUALLY PROGRAMMABLE VECTOR BANK
82380 ENHANCEMENT OVER THE 82C59A
290128–50

Figure 4-2. Interrupt Bank Block Diagram

INTERRUPT REQUEST (IRR) AND IN-SERVICE REGISTER (ISR)

The interrupts at the Interrupt Request (IRQ) input lines are handled by two registers in cascade, the Interrupt Request Register (IRR) and the In-Service Register (ISR). The IRR is used to store all interrupt levels which are requesting service; and the ISR is used to store all interrupt levels which are being serviced.

PRIORITY RESOLVER (PR)

This logic block determines the priorities of the bits set in the IRR. The highest priority is selected and strobed into the corresponding bit of the ISR during an Interrupt Acknowledge cycle.

INTERRUPT MASK REGISTER (IMR)

The IMR stores the bits which mask the interrupt lines to be masked (disabled). The IMR operates on the IRR. Masking of a higher priority input will not affect the interrupt request lines of lower priority.

VECTOR REGISTERS (VR)

This block contains a set of Vector Registers, one for each interrupt request line, to store the pre-programmed interrupt vector number. The corresponding vector number will be driven onto the Data Bus of the 82380 during the Interrupt Acknowledge cycle.

CONTROL LOGIC

The Control Logic coordinates the overall operations of the other internal blocks within the same bank. This logic will drive the Interrupt Output signal (INT) HIGH when one or more unmasked interrupt inputs are active (LOW). The INT output signal goes directly to the 80386 (in Bank A) or to another bank to which this bank is cascaded (see Figure 4-1). Also, this logic will recognize an Interrupt Acknowledge cycle (via M/IO#, D/C# and W/R# signals). During this bus cycle, the Control Logic will enable the corresponding Vector Register to drive the interrupt vector onto the Data Bus.

In Bank A, the Control Logic is also responsible for handling the special ICW2 interrupt request input (IRQ1.5#).

4.2 Interface Signals

4.2.1 INTERRUPT INPUTS

There are 15 external Interrupt Request inputs and 5 internal Interrupt Requests. The external request inputs are: IRQ3#, IRQ9#, IRQ11# to IRQ23#. They are shown in bold arrows in Figure 4-1. All IRQ inputs are active LOW and they can be programmed (via a control bit in the Initialization Command Word 1 (ICW1)) to be either edge-triggered or level-triggered. In order to be recognized as a valid interrupt request, the interrupt input must be active (LOW) until the first INTA# cycle (see Bus Functional Description).

Note that all 15 external Interrupt Request inputs have weak internal pull-up resistors.

As mentioned earlier, an 82C59A can be cascaded to each external interrupt input to expand the interrupt capacity to a maximum of 120 levels. Also, two of the interrupt inputs are dual functions: IRQ3# can be used as Timer 2 output (TOUT2#) and IRQ9# can be used as DREQ4 input. IRQ3# is a bidirectional dual function pin. This interrupt request input is wired-OR with the output of Timer 2 (TOUT2#). If only IRQ3# function is to be used, Timer 2 should be programmed so that OUT2 is LOW. Note that TOUT2# can also be used to generate an interrupt request to IRQ3# input.

The five internal interrupt requests serve special system functions. They are shown in Table 4-1. The following paragraphs describe these interrupts.

Table 4-1. 82380 Internal Interrupt Requests

Interrupt Request	Interrupt Source
IRQ0#	Timer 3 Output (TOUT3#)
IRQ8#	Timer 0 Output (TOUT0#)
IRQ1#	DMA Chaining Request
IRQ4#	DMA Terminal Count
IRQ1.5#	ICW2 Written

TIMER 0 AND TIMER 3 INTERRUPT REQUESTS [IRQ0#]

IRQ8# and IRQ0# interrupt requests are initiated by the output of Timers 0 and 3, respectively. Each of these requests is generated by an edge-detector flip-flop. The flip-flops are activated by the following conditions:

Set— Rising edge of timer output (TOUT);

Clear— Interrupt acknowledge for this request; OR Request is masked (disabled); OR Hardware Reset.

4

CHAINING AND TERMINAL COUNT INTERRUPTS [IRQ1#]

These interrupt requests are generated by the 82380 DMA Controller. The chaining request (IRQ1#) indicates that the DMA Base Register is not loaded. The Terminal Count request (IRQ4#) indicates that a software DMA request was cleared.

ICW2 INTERRUPT REQUEST [IRQ1.5#]

Whenever an Initialization Control Word 2 (ICW2) is written to a Bank, a special ICW2 interrupt request is generated. The interrupt will be cleared when the newly programmed ICW2 Register is read. This interrupt request is in Bank A at level 1.5. This interrupt request is internally ORed with the Cascaded Request from Bank B and is always assigned a higher priority than the Cascaded Request.

This special interrupt is provided to support compatibility with the original 82C59A. A detailed description of this interrupt is discussed in the Programming section.

DEFAULT INTERRUPT [IRQ7#]

During an Interrupt Acknowledge cycle, if there is no active pending request, the PIC will automatically generate a default vector. This vector corresponds to the IRQ7# vector in Bank A.

4.2.2 INTERRUPT OUTPUT (INT)

The INT output pin is taken directly from bank A. This signal should be tied to the Maskable Interrupt Request (INTR) of the 80386. When this signal is active (HIGH), it indicates that one or more internal/external interrupt requests are pending. The 80386 is expected to respond with an interrupt acknowledge cycle.

4.3 Bus Functional Description

The INT output of bank A will be activated as a result of any unmasked interrupt request. This may be a non-cascaded or cascaded request. After the PIC has driven the INT signal HIGH, 80386 will respond by performing two interrupt acknowledge cycles. The timing diagram in Figure 4-3 shows a typical interrupt acknowledge process between the 82380 and the 80386 CPU.

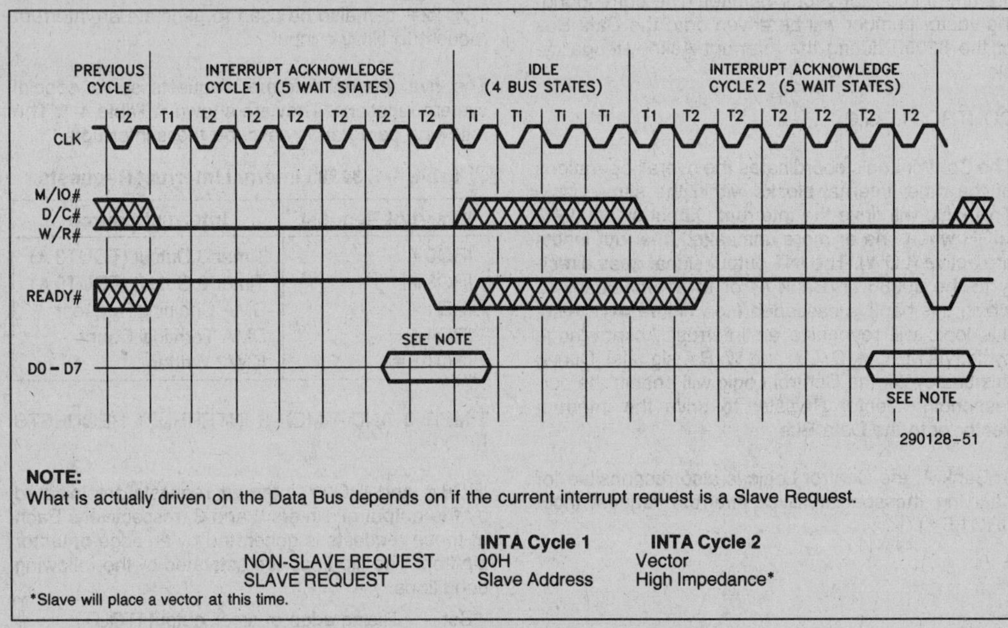

NOTE:
What is actually driven on the Data Bus depends on if the current interrupt request is a Slave Request.

	INTA Cycle 1	INTA Cycle 2
NON-SLAVE REQUEST	00H	Vector
SLAVE REQUEST	Slave Address	High Impedance*

*Slave will place a vector at this time.

Figure 4-3. Interrupt Acknowledge Cycle

After activating the INT signal, the 82380 monitors the status lines (M/IO#, D/C#, W/R#) and waits for the 80386 to initiate the first interrupt acknowledge cycle. In the 80386 environment, two successive interrupt acknowledge cycles (INTA) marked by M/IO# = LOW, D/C# = LOW, and W/R# = LOW are performed. During the first INTA cycle, the PIC will determine the highest priority request. Assuming this interrupt input has no external Slave Controller cascaded to it, the 82380 will drive the Data Bus with 00H in the first INTA cycle. During the second INTA cycle, the 82380 PIC will drive the Data Bus with the corresponding preprogrammed interrupt vector.

If the PIC determines (from the ICW3) that this interrupt input has an external Slave Controller cascaded to it, it will drive the Data Bus with the specific Slave Cascade Address (instead of 00H) during the first INTA cycle. This Slave Cascade Address is the preprogrammed content in the corresponding Vector Register. This means that no Slave Address should be chosen to be 00H. Note that the Slave Address and Interrupt Vector are different interpretations of the same thing. They are both the contents of the programmable Vector Register. During the second INTA cycle, the Data Bus will be floated so that the external Slave Controller can drive its interrupt vector on the bus. Since the Slave Interrupt Controller resides on the system bus, bus transceiver enable and direction control logic must take this into consideration.

In order to have a successful interrupt service, the interrupt request input must be held active (LOW) until the beginning of the first interrupt acknowledge cycle. If there is no pending interrupt request when the first INTA cycle is generated, the PIC will generate a default vector, which is the IRQ7 vector (bank A level 7).

According to the Bus Cycle definition of the 80386, there will be four Bus Idle States between the two interrupt acknowledge cycles. These idle bus cycles will be initiated by the 80386. Also, during each interrupt acknowledge cycle, the internal Wait State Generator of the 82380 will automatically generate the required number of wait states for internal delays.

4.4 Mode of Operation

A variety of modes and commands are available for controlling the 82380 PIC. All of them are programmable; that is, they may be changed dynamically under software control. In fact, each bank can be programmed individually to operate in different modes. With these modes and commands, many possible configurations are conceivable, giving the user enough versatility for almost any interrupt controlled application.

This section is not intended to show how the 82380 PIC can be programmed. Rather, it describes the operation in different modes.

4.4.1 END-OF-INTERRUPT

Upon completion of an interrupt service routine, the interrupted bank needs to be notified so its ISR can be updated. This allows the PIC to keep track of which interrupt levels are in the process of being serviced and their relative priorities. Three different End-Of-Interrupt (EOI) formats are available. They are: Non-Specific EOI Command, Specific EOI Command, and Automatic EOI Mode. Selection of which EOI to use is dependent upon the interrupt operations the user wishes to perform.

If the 82380 is NOT programmed in the Automatic EOI Mode, an EOI command must be issued by the 80386 to the specific 82380 PIC Controller Bank. Also, if this controller bank is cascaded to another internal bank, an EOI command must also be sent to the bank to which this bank is cascaded. For example, if an interrupt request of Bank C in the 82380 PIC is serviced, an EOI should be written into Bank C, Bank B and Bank A. If the request comes from an external interrupt controller cascaded to Bank C, then an EOI should be written into the external controller as well.

NON-SPECIFIC EOI COMMAND

A Non-Specific EOI command sent from the 80386 lets the 82380 PIC bank know when a service routine has been completed, without specification of its exact interrupt level. The respective interrupt bank automatically determines the interrupt level and resets the correct bit in the ISR.

To take advantage of the Non-Specific EOI, the interrupt bank must be in a mode of operation in which it can predetermine its in-service routine levels. For this reason, the Non-Specific EOI command should only be used when the most recent level acknowledged and serviced is always the highest priority level (i.e., in the Fully Nested Mode structure to be described below). When the interrupt bank receives a Non-Specific EOI command, it simply resets the highest priority ISR bit to indicate that the highest priority routine in service is finished.

Special consideration should be taken when deciding to use the Non-Specific EOI command. Here are two operating conditions in which it is best NOT used since the Fully Nested Mode structure will be destroyed:

— Using the Set Priority command within an interrupt service routine.

— Using a Special Mask Mode.

These conditions are covered in more detail in their own sections, but are listed here for reference.

SPECIFIC EOI COMMAND

Unlike a Non-Specific EOI command which automatically resets the highest priority ISR bit, a Specific EOI command specifies an exact ISR bit to be reset. Any one of the IRQ levels of an interrupt bank can be specified in the command.

The Specific EOI command is needed to reset the ISR bit of a completed service routine whenever the interrupt bank is not able to automatically determine it. The Specific EOI command can be used in all conditions of operation, including those that prohibit Non-Specific EOI command usage mentioned above.

AUTOMATIC EOI MODE

When programmed in the Automatic EOI Mode, the 80386 no longer needs to issue a command to notify the interrupt bank it has completed an interrupt routine. The interrupt bank accomplishes this by performing a Non-Specific EOI automatically at the end of the second INTA cycle.

Special consideration should be taken when deciding to use the Automatic EOI Mode because it may disturb the Fully Nested Mode structure. In the Automatic EOI Mode, the ISR bit of a routine in service is reset right after it is acknowledged, thus leaving no designation in the ISR that a service routine is being executed. If any interrupt request within the same bank occurs during this time and interrupts are enabled, it will get serviced regardless of its priority. Therefore, when using this mode, the 80386 should keep its interrupt request input disabled during execution of a service routine. By doing this, higher priority interrupt levels will be serviced only after the completion of a routine in service. This guideline restores the Fully Nested Mode structure. However, in this scheme, a routine in service cannot be interrupted since the host's interrupt request input is disabled.

4.4.2 INTERRUPT PRIORITIES

The 82380 PIC provides various methods for arranging the interrupt priorities of the interrupt request inputs to suit different applications. The following subsections explain these methods in detail.

4.4.2.1 Fully Nested Mode

The Fully Nested Mode of operation is a general purpose priority mode. This mode supports a multi-level interrupt structure in which all of the Interrupt Request (IRQ) inputs within one bank are arranged from highest to lowest.

Unless otherwise programmed, the Fully Nested Mode is entered by default upon initialization. At this time, IRQ0# is assigned the highest priority (priority = 0) and IRQ7# the lowest (priority = 7). This default priority can be changed, as will be explained later in the Rotating Priority Mode.

When an interrupt is acknowledged, the highest priority request is determined from the Interrupt Request Register (IRR) and its vector is placed on the bus. In addition, the corresponding bit in the In-Service Register (ISR) is set to designate the routine in service. This ISR bit will remain set until the 80386 issues an End Of Interrupt (EOI) command immediately before returning from the service routine; or alternately, if the Automatic End Of Interrupt (AEOI) bit is set, the ISR bit will be reset at the end of the second INTA cycle.

While the ISR bit is set, all further interrupts of the same or lower priority are inhibited. Higher level interrupts can still generate an interrupt, which will be acknowledged only if the 80386 internal interrupt enable flip-flop has been re-enabled (through software inside the current service routine).

4.4.2.2 Automatic Rotation—Equal Priority Devices

Automatic rotation of priorities serves in applications where the interrupting devices are of equal priority within an interrupt bank. In this kind of environment, once a device is serviced, all other equal priority peripherals should be given a chance to be serviced before the original device is serviced again. This is accomplished by automatically assigning a device the lowest priority after being serviced. Thus, in the worst case, the device would have to wait until all other peripherals connected to the same bank are serviced before it is serviced again.

There are two methods of accomplishing automatic rotation. One is used in conjunction with the Non-Specific EOI command and the other is used with the Automatic EOI mode. These two methods are discussed below.

ROTATE ON NON-SPECIFIC EOI COMMAND

When the Rotate On Non-Specific EOI command is issued, the highest ISR bit is reset as in a normal Non-Specific EOI command. However, after it is reset, the corresponding Interrupt Request (IRQ) level is assigned the lowest priority. Other IRQ priorities rotate to conform to the Fully Nested Mode based on the newly assigned low priority.

Figure 4-4 shows how the Rotate On Non-Specific EOI command affects the interrupt priorities. Assume the IRQ priorities were assigned with IRQ0 the highest and IRQ7 the lowest. IRQ6 and IRQ4 are already in service but neither is completed. Being the higher priority routine, IRQ4 is necessarily the routine being executed. During the IRQ4 routine, a rotate on Non-Specific EOI command is executed. When this happens, Bit 4 in the ISR is reset. IRQ4 then becomes the lowest priority and IRQ5 becomes the highest.

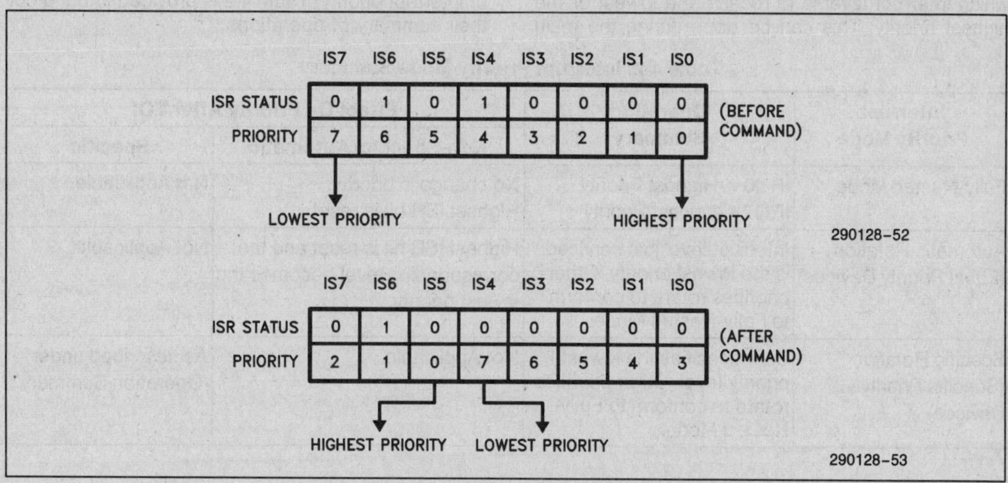

Figure 4-4. Rotate On Non-Specific EOI Command

ROTATE ON AUTOMATIC EOI MODE

The Rotate On Automatic EOI Mode works much like the Rotate On Non-Specific EOI Command. The main difference is that priority rotation is done automatically after the second INTA cycle of an interrupt request. To enter or exit this mode, a Rotate-On-Automatic-EOI Set Command and Rotate-On-Automatic-EOI Clear Command is provided. After this mode is entered, no other commands are needed as in the normal Automatic EOI Mode. However, it must be noted again that when using any form of the Automatic EOI Mode, special consideration should be taken. The guideline presented in the Automatic EOI Mode also applies here.

4.4.2.3 Specific Rotation—Specific Priority

Specific rotation gives the user versatile capabilities in interrupt controlled operations. It serves in those applications in which a specific device's interrupt priority must be altered. As opposed to Automatic Rotation which will automatically set priorities after each interrupt request is serviced, specific rotation is completely user controlled. That is, the user selects which interrupt level is to receive the lowest or the highest priority. This can be done during the main program or within interrupt routines. Two specific rotation commands are available to the user: Set Priority Command and Rotate On Specific EOI Command.

SET PRIORITY COMMAND

The Set Priority Command allows the programmer to assign an IRQ level the lowest priority. All other interrupt levels will conform to the Fully Nested Mode based on the newly assigned low priority.

ROTATE ON SPECIFIC EOI COMMAND

The Rotate On Specific EOI Command is literally a combination of the Set Priority Command and the Specific EOI Command. Like the Set Priority Command, a specified IRQ level is assigned lowest priority. Like the Specific EOI Command, a specified level will be reset in the ISR. Thus, this command accomplishes both tasks in one single command.

4.4.2.4 Interrupt Priority Mode Summary

In order to simplify understanding the many modes of interrupt priority, Table 4-2 is provided to bring out their summary of operations.

Table 4-2. Interrupt Priority Mode Summary

Interrupt Priority Mode	Operation Summary	Effect On Priority After EOI	
		Non-Specific/Automatic	Specific
Fully-Nested Mode	IRQ0#-Highest Priority IRQ7#-Lowest Priority	No change in priority. Highest ISR bit is reset.	Not Applicable.
Automatic Rotation (Equal Priority Devices)	Interrupt level just serviced is the lowest priority. Other priorities rotate to conform to Fully-Nested Mode.	Highest ISR bit is reset and the corresponding level becomes the lowest priority.	Not Applicable.
Specific Rotation (Specific Priority Devices)	User specifies the lowest priority level. Other priorities rotate to conform to Fully-Nested Mode.	Not Applicable.	As described under 'Operation Summary'.

4.4.3 INTERRUPT MASKING

VIA INTERRUPT MASK REGISTER

Each bank in the 82380 PIC has an Interrupt Mask Register (IMR) which enhances interrupt control capabilities. This IMR allows individual IRQ masking. When an IRQ is masked, its interrupt request is disabled until it is unmasked. Each bit in the 8-bit IMR disables one interrupt channel if it is set (HIGH). Bit 0 masks IRQ0, Bit 1 masks IRQ1 and so forth. Masking an IRQ channel will only disable the corresponding channel and does not affect the others operations.

The IMR acts only on the output of the IRR. That is, if an interrupt occurs while its IMR bit is set, this request is not 'forgotten'. Even with an IRQ input masked, it is still possible to set the IRR. Therefore, when the IMR bit is reset, an interrupt request to the 80386 will then be generated, providing that the IRQ request remains active. If the IRQ request is removed before the IMR is reset, the Default Interrupt Vector (Bank A, level 7) will be generated during the interrupt acknowledge cycle.

SPECIAL MASK MODE

In the Fully Nested Mode, all IRQ levels of lower priority than the routine in service are inhibited. However, in some applications, it may be desirable to let a lower priority interrupt request to interrupt the routine in service. One method to achieve this is by using the Special Mask Mode. Working in conjunction with the IMR, the Special Mask Mode enables interrupts from all levels except the level in service. This is usually done inside an interrupt service routine by masking the level that is in service and then issuing the Special Mask Mode Command. Once the Special Mask Mode is enabled, it remains in effect until it is disabled.

4.4.4 EDGE OR LEVEL INTERRUPT TRIGGERING

Each bank in the 82380 PIC can be programmed independently for either edge or level sensing for the interrupt request signals. Recall that all IRQ inputs are active LOW. Therefore, in the edge triggered mode, an active edge is defined as an input transition from an inactive (HIGH) to active (LOW) state. The interrupt input may remain active without generating another interrupt. During level triggered mode, an interrupt request will be recognized by an active (LOW) input, and there is no need for edge detection. However, the interrupt request must be removed before the EOI Command is issued, or the 80386 must be disabled to prevent a second false interrupt from occurring.

In either modes, the interrupt request input must be active (LOW) during the first INTA cycle in order to be recognized. Otherwise, the Default Interrupt Vector will be generated at level 7 of Bank A.

4.4.5 INTERRUPT CASCADING

As mentioned previously, the 82380 allows for external Slave interrupt controllers to be cascaded to any of its external interrupt request pins. The 82380 PIC indicates that a external Slave Controller is to be serviced by putting the contents of the Vector Register associated with the particular request on the 80386 Data Bus during the first INTA cycle (instead of 00H during a non-slave service). The external logic should latch the vector on the Data Bus using the INTA status signals and use it to select the external Slave Controller to be serviced (see Figure 4-5). The selected Slave will then respond to the second INTA cycle and place its vector on the Data Bus. This method requires that if external Slave Controllers

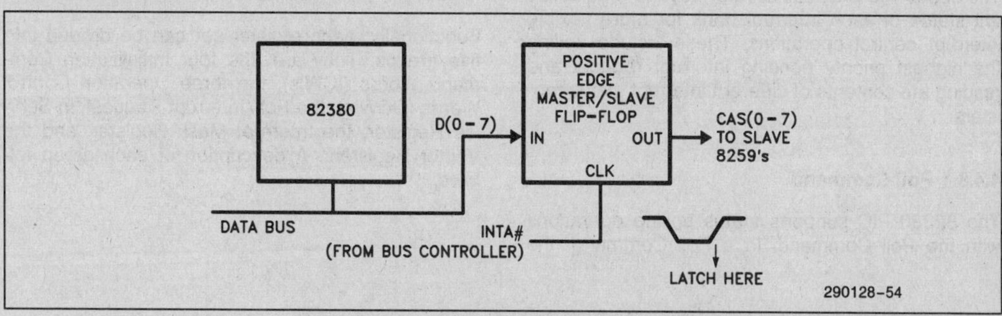

Figure 4-5. Slave Cascade Address Capturing

are used in the system, no vector should be programmed to 00H.

Since the external Slave Cascade Address is provided on the Data Bus during INTA cycle 1, an external latch is required to capture this address for the Slave Controller. A simple scheme is depicted in Figure 4-5.

4.4.5.1 Special Fully Nested Mode

This mode will be used where cascading is employed and the priority is to be conserved within each Slave Controller. The Special Fully Nested Mode is similar to the 'regular' Fully Nested Mode with the following exceptions:

— When an interrupt request from a Slave Controller is in service, this Slave Controller is not locked out from the Master's priority logic. Further interrupt requests from the higher priority logic within the Slave Controller will be recognized by the 82380 PIC and will initiate interrupts to the 80386. In comparing to the 'regular' Fully Nested Mode, the Slave Controller is masked out when its request is in service and no higher requests from the same Slave Controller can be serviced.

— Before exiting the interrupt service routine, the software has to check whether the interrupt serviced was the only request from the Slave Controller. This is done by sending a Non-Specific EOI Command to the Slave Controller and then reading its In Service Register. If there are no requests in the Slave Controller, a Non-Specific EOI can be sent to the corresponding 82380 PIC bank also. Otherwise, no EOI should be sent.

4.4.6 READING INTERRUPT STATUS

The 82380 PIC provides several ways to read different status of each interrupt bank for more flexible interrupt control operations. These include polling the highest priority pending interrupt request and reading the contents of different interrupt status registers.

4.4.6.1 Poll Command

The 82380 PIC supports status polling operations with the Poll Command. In a Poll Command, the pending interrupt request with the highest priority can be determined. To use this command, the INT output is not used, or the 80386 interrupt is disabled. Service to devices is achieved by software using the Poll Command.

This mode is useful if there is a routine command common to several levels so that the INTA sequence is not needed. Another application is to use the Poll Command to expand the number of priority levels.

Notice that the ICW2 mechanism is not supported for the Poll Command. However, if the Poll Command is used, the programmable Vector Registers are of no concern since no INTA cycle will be generated.

4.4.6.2 Reading Interrupt Registers

The contents of each interrupt register (IRR, ISR, and IMR) can be read to update the user's program on the present status of the 82380 PIC. This can be a versatile tool in the decision making process of a service routine, giving the user more control over interrupt operations.

The reading of the IRR and ISR contents can be performed via the Operation Control Word 3 by using a Read Status Register Command and the content of IMR can be read via a simple read operation of the register itself.

4.5 Register Set Overview

Each bank of the 82380 PIC consists of a set of 8-bit registers to control its operations. The address map of all the registers is shown in Table 4-3. Since all three register sets are identical in functions, only one set will be described.

Functionally, each register set can be divided into five groups. They are: the four Initialization Command Words (ICW's), the three Operation Control Words (OCW's), the Poll/Interrupt Request/In-Service Register, the Interrupt Mask Register, and the Vector Registers. A description of each group follows.

Table 4-3. Interrupt Controller Register Address Map

Port Address	Access	Register Description
20H	Write	Bank B ICW1, OCW2, or OCW3
	Read	Bank B Poll, Request or In-Service Status Register
21H	Write	Bank B ICW2, ICW3, ICW4, OCW1
	Read	Bank B Mask Register
22H	Read	Bank B ICW2
28H	Read/Write	IRQ8 Vector Register
29H	Read/Write	IRQ9 Vector Register
2AH	Read/Write	Reserved
2BH	Read/Write	IRQ11 Vector Register
2CH	Read/Write	IRQ12 Vector Register
2DH	Read/Write	IRQ13 Vector Register
2EH	Read/Write	IRQ14 Vector Register
2FH	Read/Write	IRQ15 Vector Register
A0H	Write	Bank C ICW1, OCW2, or OCW3
	Read	Bank C Poll, Request or In-Service Status Register
A1H	Write	Bank C ICW2, ICW3, ICW4, OCW1
	Read	Bank C Mask Register
A2H	Read	Bank C ICW2
A8H	Read/Write	IRQ16 Vector Register
A9H	Read/Write	IRQ17 Vector Register
AAH	Read/Write	IRQ18 Vector Register
ABH	Read/Write	IRQ19 Vector Register
ACH	Read/Write	IRQ20 Vector Register
ADH	Read/Write	IRQ21 Vector Register
AEH	Read/Write	IRQ22 Vector Register
AFH	Read/Write	IRQ23 Vector Register
30H	Write	Bank A ICW1, OCW2, or OCW3
	Read	Bank A Poll, Request or In-Service Status Register
31H	Write	Bank A ICW2, ICW3, ICW4, OCW1
	Read	Bank A Mask Register
32H	Read	Bank ICW2
38H	Read/Write	IRQ0 Vector Register
39H	Read/Write	IRQ1 Vector Register
3AH	Read/Write	IRQ1.5 Vector Register
3BH	Read/Write	IRQ3 Vector Register
3CH	Read/Write	IRQ4 Vector Register
3DH	Read/Write	Reserved
3EH	Read/Write	Reserved
3FH	Read/Write	IRQ7 Vector Register

4

4.5.1 INITIALIZATION COMMAND WORDS (ICW)

Before normal operation can begin, the 82380 PIC must be brought to a known state. There are four 8-bit Initialization Command Words in each interrupt bank to setup the necessary conditions and modes for proper operation. Except for the second common word (ICW2) which is a read/write register, the other three are write-only registers. Without going into detail of the bit definitions of the command words, the following subsections give a brief description of what functions each command word controls.

ICW1

The ICW1 has three major functions. They are:

- To select between the two IRQ input triggering modes (edge-or level-triggered);
- To designate whether or not the interrupt bank is to be used alone or in the cascade mode. If the cascade mode is desired, the interrupt bank will accept ICW3 for further cascade mode programming. Otherwise, no ICW3 will be accepted;
- To determine whether or not ICW4 will be issued; that is, if any of the ICW4 operations are to be used.

ICW2

ICW2 is provided for compatibility with the 82C59A only. Its contents do not affect the operation of the interrupt bank in any way. Whenever the ICW2 of any of the three banks is written into, an interrupt is generated from Bank A at level 1.5. The interrupt request will be cleared after the ICW2 register has been read by the 80386. The user is expected to program the corresponding vector register or to use it as an indicator that an attempt was made to alter the contents. Note that each ICW2 register has different addresses for read and write operations.

ICW3

The interrupt bank will only accept an ICW3 if programmed in the external cascade mode (as indicated in ICW1). ICW3 is used for specific programming within the cascade mode. The bits in ICW3 indicate which interrupt request inputs have a Slave cascaded to them. This will subsequently affect the interrupt vector generation during the interrupt acknowledge cycles as described previously.

ICW4

The ICW4 is accepted only if it was selected in ICW1. This command word register serves two functions:

- To select either the Automatic EOI mode or software EOI mode;
- To select if the Special Nested mode is to be used in conjunction with the cascade mode.

4.5.2 OPERATION CONTROL WORDS (OCW)

Once initialized by the ICW's, the interrupt banks will be operating in the Fully Nested Mode by default and they are ready to accept interrupt requests. However, the operations of each interrupt bank can be further controlled or modified by the use of OCW's. Three OCW's are available for programming various modes and commands. Note that all OCW's are 8-bit write-only registers.

The modes and operations controlled by the OCW's are:

- Fully Nested Mode;
- Rotating Priority Mode;
- Special Mask Mode;
- Poll Mode;
- EOI Commands;
- Read Status Commands.

OCW1

OCW1 is used solely for masking operations. It provides a direct link to the Interrupt Mask Register (IMR). The 80386 can write to this OCW register to enable or disable the interrupt inputs. Reading the pre-programmed mask can be done via the Interrupt Mask Register which will be discussed shortly.

OCW2

OCW2 is used to select End-Of-Interrupt, Automatic Priority Rotation, and Specific Priority Rotation operations. Associated commands and modes of these operations are selected using the different combinations of bits in OCW2.

Specifically, the OCW2 is used to:

- Designate an interrupt level (0–7) to be used to reset a specific ISR bit or to set a specific priority. This function can be enabled or disabled;
- Select which software EOI command (if any) is to be executed (i.e., Non-Specific or Specific EOI);
- Enable one of the priority rotation operations (i.e., Rotate On Non-Specific EOI, Rotate On Automatic EOI, or Rotate on Specific EOI).

OCW3

There are three main categories of operation that OCW3 controls. That are summarized as follows:

— To select and execute the Read Status Register Commands, either reading the Interrupt Request Register (IRR) or the In-Service Register (ISR);

— To issue the Poll Command. The Poll Command will override a Read Register Command if both functions are enabled simultaneously;

— To set or reset the Special Mask Mode.

4.5.3 POLL/INTERRUPT REQUEST/IN-SERVICE STATUS REGISTER

As the name implies, this 8-bit read-only register has multiple functions. Depending on the command issued in the OCW3, the content of this register reflects the result of the command executed. For a Poll Command, the register read contains the binary code of the highest priority level requesting service (if any). For a Read IRR Command, the register content will show the current pending interrupt request(s). Finally, for a Read ISR Command, this register will specify all interrupt levels which are being serviced.

4.5.4 INTERRUPT MASK REGISTER (IMR)

This is a read-only 8-bit register which, when read, will specify all interrupt levels within the same bank that are masked.

4.5.5 VECTOR REGISTER (VR)

Each interrupt request input has an 8-bit read/write programmable vector register associated with it. The registers should be programmed to contain the interrupt vector for the corresponding request. The contents of the Vector Register will be placed on the Data Bus during the INTA cycles as described previously.

4.6 Programming

Programming the 82380 PIC is accomplished by using two types of command words: ICW's and OCW's. All modes and commands explained in the previous sections are programmable using the ICW's and OCW's. The ICW's are issued from the 80386 in a sequential format and are used to setup the banks in the 82380 PIC in an initial state of operation. The OCW's are issued as needed to vary and control the 82380 PIC's operations.

Both ICW's and OCW's are sent by the 80386 to the interrupt banks via the Data Bus. Each bank distinguishes between the different ICW's and OCW's by the I/O address map, the sequence they are issued (ICW's only), and by some dedicated bits among the ICW's and OCW's.

All three interrupt banks are programmed in a similar way. Therefore, only a single bank will be described.

4.6.1 INITIALIZATION (ICW)

Before normal operation can begin, each bank must be initialized by programming a sequence of two to four bytes written into the ICW's.

Figure 4-6 shows the initialization flow for an interrupt bank. Both ICW1 and ICW2 must be issued for any form of operation. However, ICW3 and ICW4 are used only if designated in ICW1. Once initialized, if any programming changes within the ICW's are to be made, the entire ICW sequence must be reprogrammed, not just an individual ICW.

Note that although the ICW2's in the 82380 PIC do not affect the Bank's operation, they still must be programmed in order to preserve the compatibility with the 82C59A. The contents programmed are not relevant to the overall operations of the interrupt banks. Also, whenever one of the three ICW2's is programmed, an interrupt level 1.5 in Bank A will be generated. This interrupt request will be cleared upon reading of the ICW2 registers. Since the three ICW2's share the same interrupt level and the system may not know the origin of the interrupt, all three ICW2's must be read.

However, it is not necessary to provide an interrupt service routine for the ICW2 interrupt. One way to avoid this is as follows. At the beginning of the initialization of the interrupt banks, the 80386 interrupt should be disabled. After each ICW2 register write operation is performed during the initialization, the corresponding ICW2 register is read. This read operation will clear the interrupt request of the 82380. At the end of the initialization, the 80386 interrupt is re-enabled. With this method, the 80386 will not detect the ICW2 interrupt request, thus eliminating the need of an interrupt service routine.

Certain internal setup conditions occur automatically within the interrupt bank after the first ICW (ICW1) has been issued. They are:

— The edge sensitive circuit is reset, which means that following initialization, an interrupt request input must make a HIGH-to-LOW transition to generate an interrupt;

— The Interrupt Mask Register (IMR) is cleared; that is, all interrupt inputs are enabled;

— IRQ7 input of each bank is assigned priority 7 (lowest);

— Special Mask Mode is cleared and Status Read is set to IRR;

— If no ICW4 is needed, then no Automatic-EOI is selected.

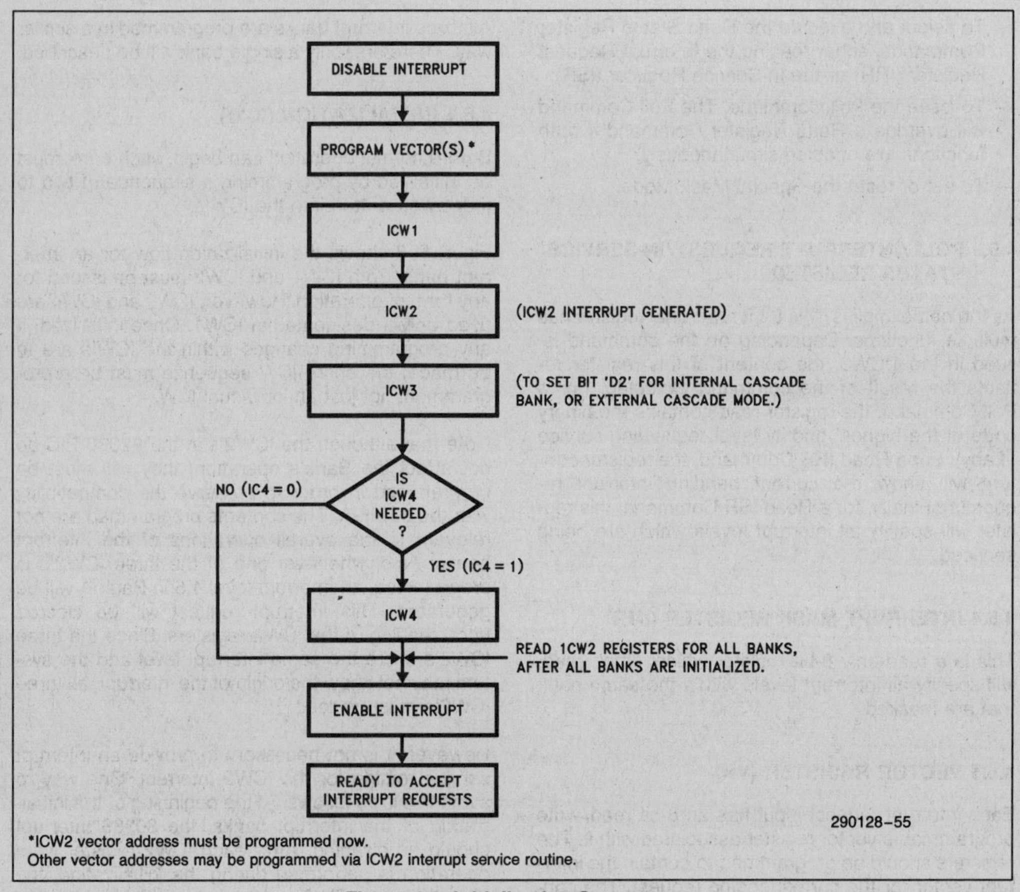

Figure 4-6. Initialization Sequence

4.6.2 VECTOR REGISTERS (VR)

Each interrupt request input has a separate Vector Register. These Vector Registers are used to store the pre-programmed vector number corresponding to their interrupt sources. In order to guarantee proper interrupt handling, all Vector Registers must be programmed with the predefined vector numbers. Since an interrupt request will be generated whenever an ICW2 is written during the initialization sequence, it is important that the Vector Register of IRQ1.5 in Bank A should be initialized and the interrupt service routine of this vector is set up before the ICW's are written.

4.6.3 OPERATION CONTROL WORDS (OCW)

After the ICW's are programmed, the operations of each interrupt controller bank can be changed by writing into the OCW's as explained before. There is no special programming sequence required for the OCW's. Any OCW may be written at any time in order to change the mode of or to perform certain operations on the interrupt banks.

4.6.3.1 Read Status and Poll Commands (OCW3)

Since the reading of IRR and ISR status as well as the result of a Poll Command are available on the same read-only Status Register, a special Read Status/Poll Command must be issued before the Poll/Interrupt Request/In-Service Status Register is read. This command can be specified by writing the required control word into OCW3. As mentioned earlier, if both the Poll Command and the Status Read Command are enabled simultaneously, the Poll Command will override the Status Read. That is, after the command execution, the Status Register will contain the result of the Poll Command.

Note that for reading IRR and ISR, there is no need to issue a Read Status Command to the OCW3 every time the IRR or ISR is to be read. Once a Read Status Command is received by the interrupt bank, it 'remembers' which register is selected. However, this is not true when the Poll Command is used.

In the Poll Command, after the OCW3 is written, the 82380 PIC treats the next read to the Status Register as an interrupt acknowledge. This will set the appropriate IS bit if there is a request and read the priority level. Interrupt Request input status remains unchanged from the Poll Command to the Status Read.

In addition to the above read commands, the Interrupt Mask Register (IMR) can also be read. When read, this register reflects the contents of the preprogrammed OCW1 which contains information on which interrupt request(s) is(are) currently disabled.

4.7 Register Bit Definition

INITIALIZATION COMMAND WORD 1 (ICW1)

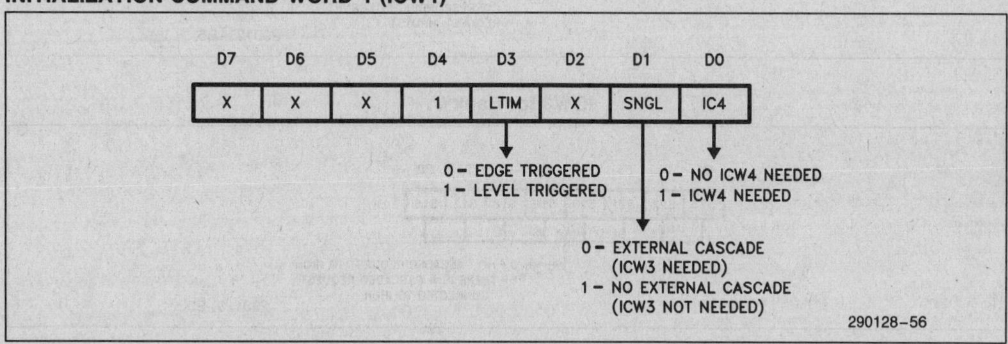

INITIALIZATION COMMAND WORD 2 (ICW2)

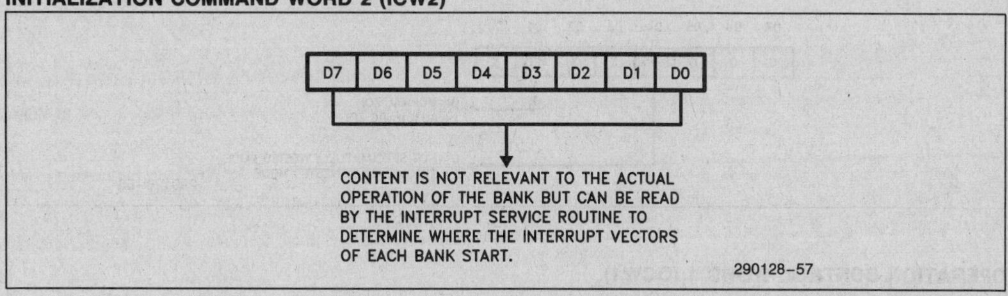

INITIALIZATION COMMAND WORD 3 (ICW3)

ICW3 for Bank A:

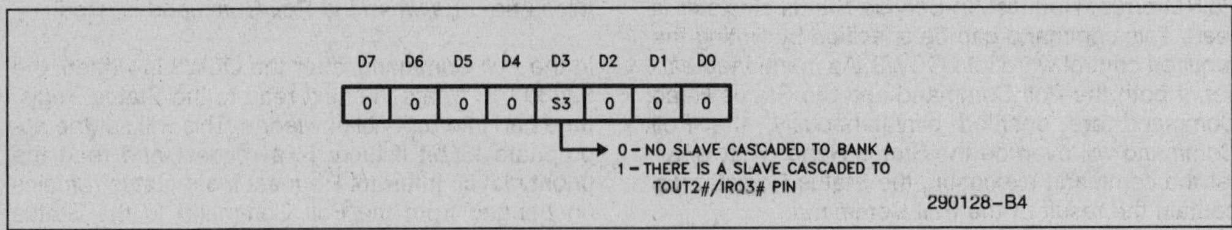

290128-B4

ICW3 for Bank B:

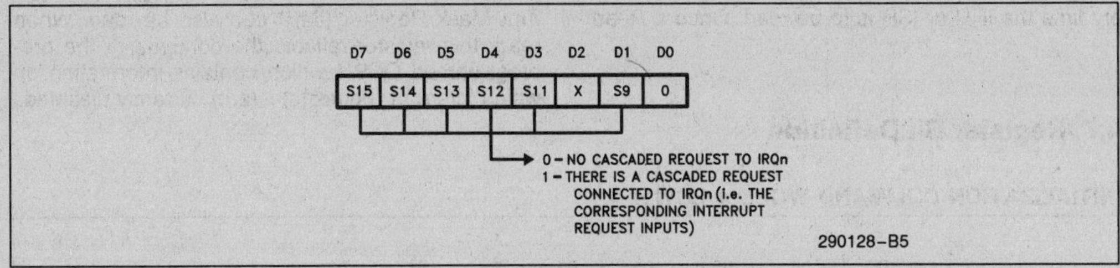

290128-B5

ICW3 for Bank C:

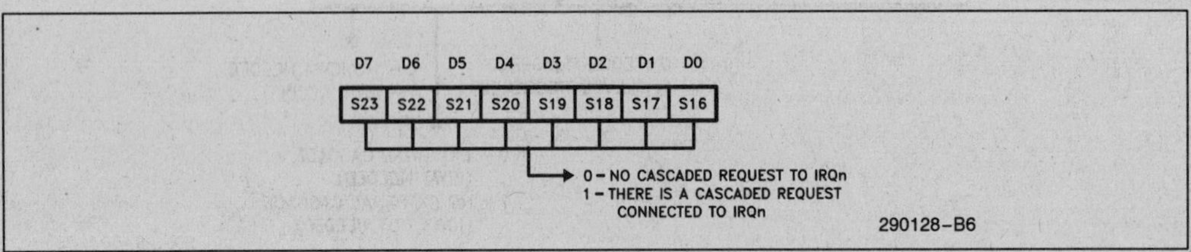

290128-B6

INITIALIZATION COMMAND WORD 4 (ICW4)

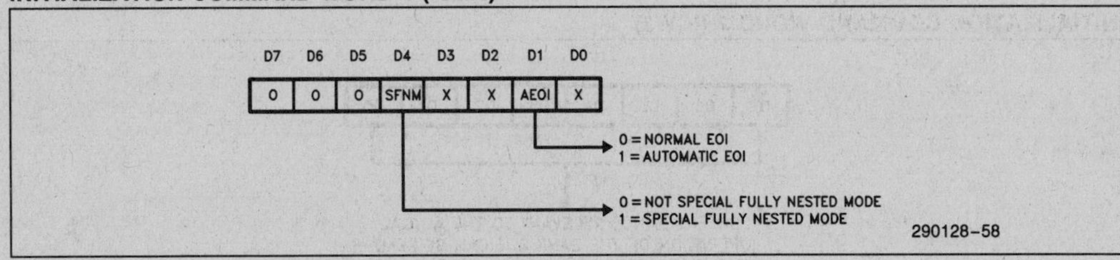

290128-58

OPERATION CONTROL WORD 1 (OCW1)

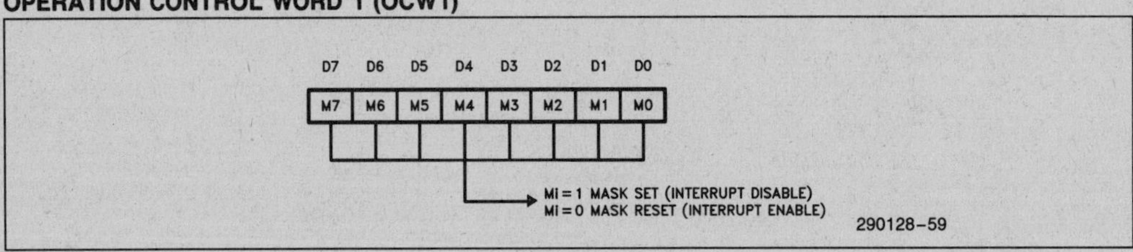

290128-59

OPERATION CONTROL WORD 2 (OCW2)

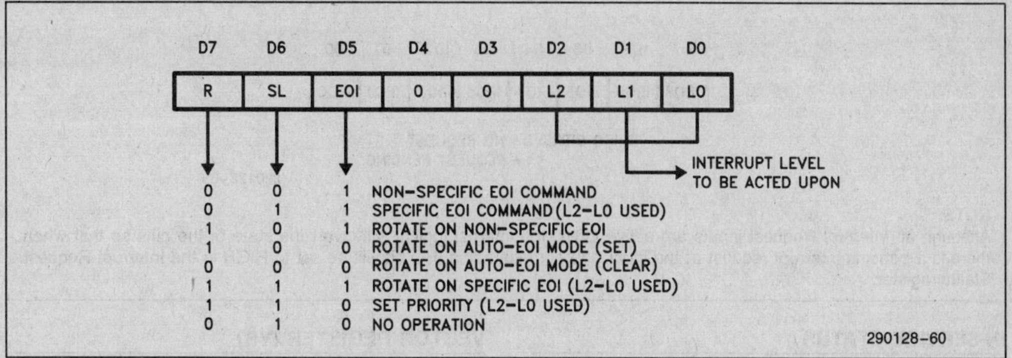

290128-60

OPERATION CONTROL WORD 3 (OCW3)

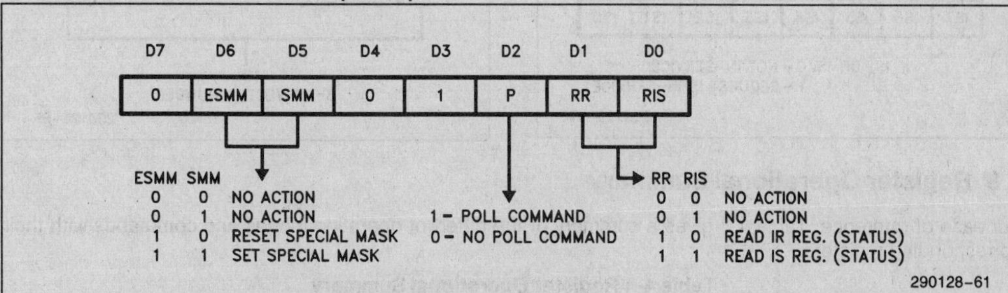

290128-61

ESMM—Enable Special Mask Mode. When this bit is set to 1, it enables the SMM bit to set or reset the Special Mask Mode. When this bit is set to 0, SMM bit becomes don't care.

SMM—Special Mask Mode. If ESMM = 1 and SMM = 1, the interrupt controller bank will enter Special Mask Mode. If ESMM = 1 and SMM = 0, the bank will revert to normal mask mode. When ESMM = 0, SMM has no effect.

Poll/Interrupt Request/In-Service Status Register

POLL COMMAND STATUS

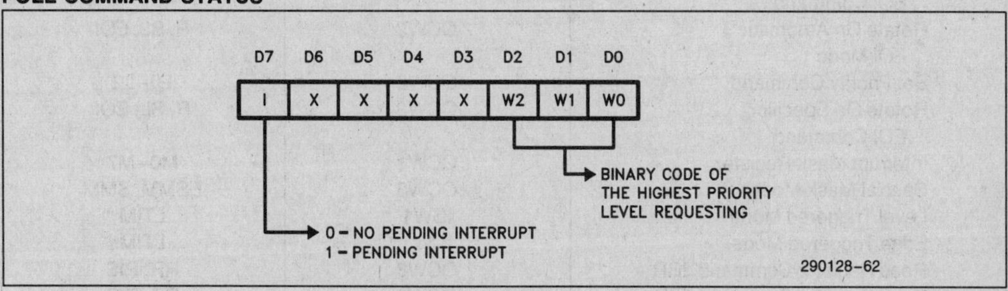

290128-62

INTERRUPT REQUEST STATUS

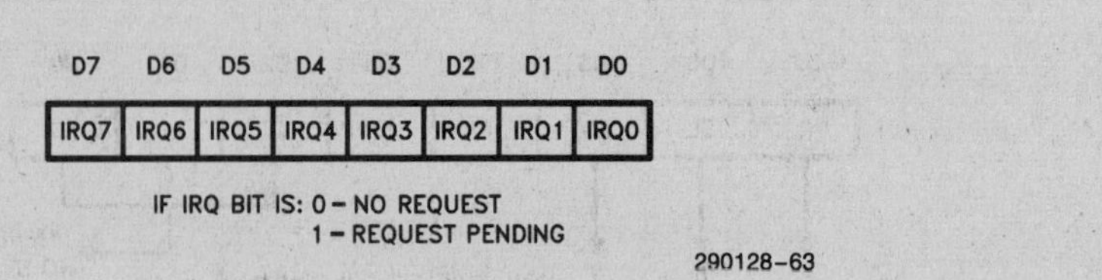

NOTE:
Although all Interrupt Request inputs are active LOW, the internal logical will invert the state of the pins so that when there is a pending interrupt request at the input, the corresponding IRQ bit will be set to HIGH in the Interrupt Request Status register.

IN-SERVICE STATUS

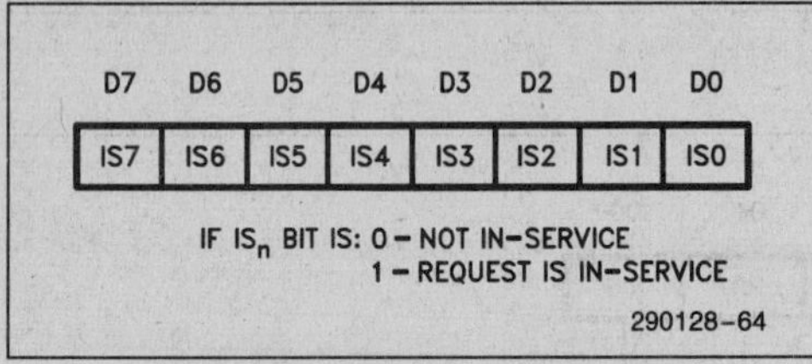

VECTOR REGISTER (VR)

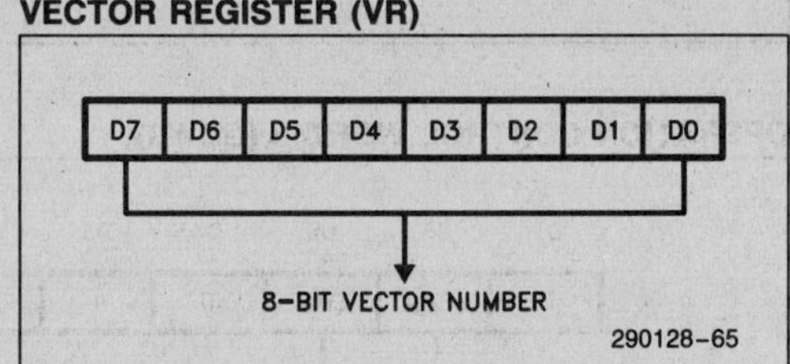

4.8 Register Operational Summary

For ease of reference, Table 4-4 gives a summary of the different operating modes and commands with their corresponding registers.

Table 4-4 Register Operational Summary

Operational Description	Command Words	Bits
Fully Nested Mode	OCW-Default	—
Non-specific EOI Command	OCW2	EOI
Specific EOI Command	OCW2	SL, EOI, LO–L2
Automatic EOI Mode	ICW1, ICW4	IC4, AEOI
Rotate On Non-Specific EOI Command	OCW2	EOI
Rotate On Automatic EOI Mode	OCW2	R, SL, EOI
Set Priority Command	OCW2	L0–L2
Rotate On Specific EOI Command	OCW2	R, SL, EOI
Interrupt Mask Register	OCW1	M0–M7
Special Mask Mode	OCW3	ESMM, SMM
Level Triggered Mode	ICW1	LTIM
Edge Triggered Mode	ICW1	LTIM
Read Register Command, IRR	OCW3	RR, RIS
Read Register Command, ISR	OCW3	RR, RIS
Red IMR	IMR	M0–M7
Poll Command	OCW3	P
Special Fully Nested Mode	ICW2, ICW4	IC4, SFNM

5.0 PROGRAMMABLE INTERVAL TIMER

5.1 Functional Description

The 82380 contains four independently Programmable Interval Timers: Timer 0–3. All four timers are functionally compatible to the Intel 82C54. The first three timers (Timer 0–2) have specific functions. The fourth timer, Timer 3, is a general purpose timer. Table 5-1 depicts the functions of each timer. A brief description of each timer's function follows.

Table 5-1. Programmable Interval Timer Functions

Timer	Output	Function
0	IRQ8	Event Based IRQ8 Generator
1	TOUT1/REF#	Gen. Purpose/DRAM Refresh Req.
2	TOUT2#/IRQ3#	Gen. Purpose/Speaker Out/IRQ3#
3	TOUT3#	Gen. Purpose/IRQ0 Generator

TIMER 0— Event Based IRQ8 Generator

Timer 0 is intended to be used as an Event Counter. The output of this timer will generate an Interrupt Request 8 (IRQ8) upon a rising edge of the timer output (TOUT0). Typically, this timer is used to implement a time-of-day clock or system tick. The Timer 0 output is not available as an external signal.

TIMER 1— General Purpose/DRAM Refresh Request

The output of Timer 1, TOUT1, can be used as a general purpose timer or as a DRAM Refresh Request signal. The rising edge of this output creates a DRAM refresh request to the 82380 DRAM Refresh Controller. Upon reset, the Refresh Request function is disabled, and the output pin is the Timer 1 output.

TIMER 2—General Purpose/Speaker Out/IRQ3#

The Timer 2 output, TOUT2#, could be used to support tone generation to an external speaker. This pin is a bidirectional signal. When used as an input, a logic LOW asserted at this pin will generate an Interrupt Register 3 (IRQ3#) (see Programmable Interrupt Controller).

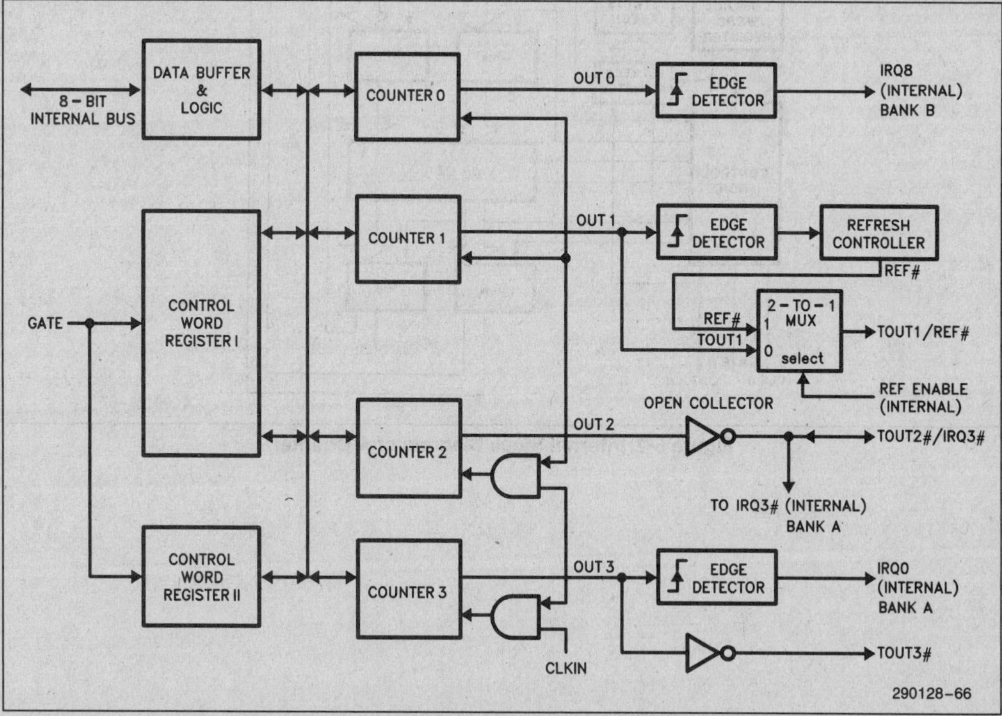

Figure 5-1. Block Diagram of Programmable Interval Timer

TIMER 3—General Purpose/Interrupt Request 0 Generator

The output of Timer 3 is fed to an edge detector and generates an Interrupt Request 0 (IRQ0) in the 82380. The inverted output of this timer (TOUT3#) is also available as an external signal for general purpose use.

5.1.1 INTERNAL ARCHITECTURE

The functional block diagram of the Programmable Interval Timer section is shown in Figure 5-1. Following is a description of each block.

DATA BUFFER & READ/WRITE LOGIC

This part of the Programmable Interval Timer is used to interface the four timers to the 82380 internal bus. The Data Buffer is for transferring commands and data between the 8-bit internal bus and the timers. The Read/Write Logic accepts inputs from the internal bus and generates signals to control other functional blocks within the timer section.

CONTROL WORD REGISTERS I & II

The Control Word Registers are write-only registers. They are used to control the operating modes of the timers. Control Word Register I controls Timers 0, 1 and 2, and Control Word Register II controls Timer 3. Detailed description of the Control Word Registers will be included in the Register Set Overview section.

COUNTER 0, COUNTER 1,
COUNTER 2, COUNTER 3

Counters 0, 1, 2, and 3 are the major parts of Timers 0, 1, 2, and 3, respectively. These four functional blocks are identical in operation, so only a single counter will be described. The internal block diagram of one counter is shown in Figure 5-2.

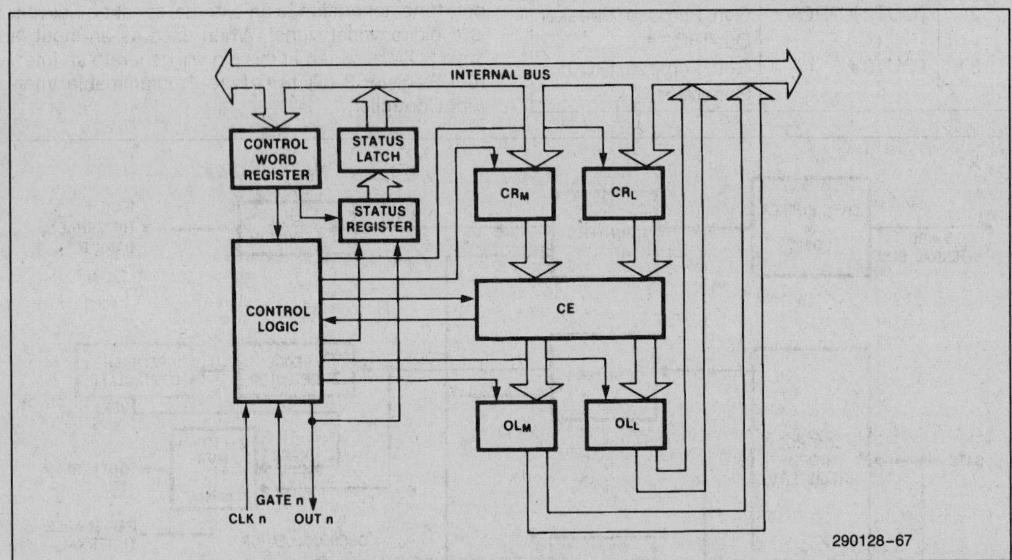

Figure 5-2. Internal Block Diagram of A Counter

The four counters share a common clock input (CLKIN), but otherwise are fully independent. Each counter is programmable to operate in a different Mode.

Although the Control Word Register is shown in the Figure 5-2, it is not part of the counter itself. Its programmed contents are used to control the operations of the counters.

The Status Register, when latched, contains the current contents of the Control Word Register and status of the output and Null Count Flag (see Read Back Command).

The Counting Element (CE) is the actual counter. It is a 16-bit presettable synchronous down counter.

The Output Latches (OL) contain two 8-bit latches (OLM and OLL). Normally, these latches 'follow' the content of the CE. OLM contains the most significant byte of the counter and OLL contains the least significant byte. If the Counter Latch Command is sent to the counter, OL will latch the present count until read by the 80386 and then return to follow the CE. One latch at a time is enabled by the timer's Control Logic to drive the internal bus. This is how the 16-bit Counter communicates over the 8-bit internal bus. Note that CE cannot be read. Whenever the count is read, it is one of the OL's that is being read.

When a new count is written into the counter, the value will be stored in the Count Registers (CR), and transferred to CE. The transferring of the contents from CR's to CE is defined as 'loading' of the counter. The Count Register contains two 8-bit registers: CRM (which contains the most significant byte) and CRL (which contains the least significant byte). Similar to the OL's, the Control Logic allows one register at a time to be loaded from the 8-bit internal bus. However, both bytes are transferred from the CR's to the CE simultaneously. Both CR's are cleared when the Counter is programmed. This way, if the Counter has been programmed for one byte count (either the most significant or the least significant byte only), the other byte will be zero. Note that CE cannot be written into directly. Whenever a count is written, it is the CR that is being written.

As shown in the diagram, the Control Logic consists of three signals: CLKIN, GATE, and OUT. CLKIN and GATE will be discussed in detail in the section that follows. OUT is the internal output of the counter. The external outputs of some timers (TOUT) are the inverted version of OUT (see TOUT1, TOUT2#, TOUT3#). The state of OUT depends on the mode of operation of the timer.

5.2 Interface Signals

5.2.1 CLKIN

CLKIN is an input signal used by all four timers for internal timing reference. This signal can be independent of the 82380 system clock, CLK2. In the following discussion, each 'CLK Pulse' is defined as the time period between a rising edge and a falling edge, in that order, of CLKIN.

During the rising edge of CLKIN, the state of GATE is sampled. All new counts are loaded and counters are decremented on the falling edge of CLKIN.

Please note that there are restrictions on the CLKIN signal during WRITE cycles to the 82380 timer unit. Refer to the appendix of this data manual for details on this issue.

5.2.2 TOUT1, TOUT2#, TOUT3#

TOUT1, TOUT2# and TOUT3# are the external output signals of Timer 1, Timer 2 and Timer 3, respectively. TOUT2# and TOUT3# are the inverted signals of their respective counter outputs, OUT. There is no external output for Timer 0.

If Timer 2 is to be used as a tone generator of a speaker, external buffering must be used to provide sufficient drive capability.

The Outputs of Timer 2 and 3 are dual function pins. The output pin of Timer 2 (TOUT2#/IRQ3#), which is a bidirectional open-collector signal, can also be used as interrupt request input. When the interrupt function is enabled (through the Programmable Interrupt Controller), a LOW on this input will generate an Interrupt Request 3# to the 82380 Programmable Interrupt Controller. This pin has a weak internal pull-up resistor. To use the IRQ3# function, Timer 2 should be programmed so that OUT2 is LOW. Additionally, OUT3 of Timer 3 is connected to an edge detector which will generate an Interrupt Request 0 (IRQ0) to the 82380 after the rising edge of OUT3 (see Figure 5-1).

5.2.3 GATE

GATE is not an externally controllable signal. Rather, it can be software controlled with the Internal Control Port. The state of GATE is always sampled on the rising edge of CLKIN. Depending on the mode of operation, GATE is used to enable/disable counting or trigger the start of an operation.

For Timer 0 and 1, GATE is always enabled (HIGH). For Timer 2 and 3, GATE is connected to Bit 0 and

6, respectively, of an Internal Control Port (at address 61H) of the 82380. After a hardware reset, the state of GATE of Timer 2 and 3 is disabled (LOW).

5.3 Modes of Operation

Each timer can be independently programmed to operate in one of six different modes. Timers are programmed by writing a Control Word into the control Word Register followed by an Initial Count (see Programming).

The following are defined for use in describing the different modes of operation.

CLK Pulse—A rising edge, then a falling edge, in that order of CLKIN.
Trigger—A rising edge of a timer's GATE input.
Timer/Counter Loading—The transfer of a count from Count Register (CR) to Count Element (CE).

Note that figures 5-3 through 5-8 show the logical outputs of the timer units, OUT_X. This signal polarity does not reflect that of the $TOUT_X$ signals. See the first paragraph of Section 5.2.2.

5.3.1 MODE 0—INTERRUPT ON TERMINAL COUNT

Mode 0 is typically used for event counting. After the Control Word is written, OUT is initially LOW, and will remain LOW until the counter reaches zero. OUT then goes HIGH and remains HIGH until a new count or a new Mode 0 Control Word is written into the counter.

In this mode, GATE = HIGH enables counting; GATE = LOW disables counting. However, GATE has no effect on OUT.

After the Control Word and initial count are written to a timer, the initial count will be loaded on the next CLK pulse. This CLK pulse does not decrement the count, so for an initial count of N, OUT does not go HIGH until N + 1 CLK pulses after the initial count is written.

If a new count is written to the timer, it will be loaded on the next CLK pulse and counting will continue from the new count. If a two-byte count is written, the following happens:

1. Writing the first byte disables counting, OUT is set LOW immediately (i.e., no CLK pulse required).
2. Writing the second byte allows the new count to be loaded on the next CLK pulse.

This allows the counting sequence to be synchronized by software. Again, OUT does not go HIGH until N + 1 CLK pulses after the new count of N is written.

If an initial count is written while GATE is LOW, the counter will be loaded on the next CLK pulse. When GATE goes HIGH, OUT will go HIGH N CLK pulses later; no CLK pulse is needed to load the counter as this has already been done.

5.3.2 MODE 1—GATE RETRIGGERABLE ONE-SHOT

In this mode, OUT will be initially HIGH. OUT will go LOW on the CLK pulse following a trigger to start the one-shot operation. The OUT signal will then remain LOW until the timer reaches zero. At this point, OUT will stay HIGH until the next trigger comes in. Since the state of GATE signals of Timer 0 and 1 are internally set to HIGH.

After writing the Control Word and initial count, the timer is considered 'armed'. A trigger results in loading the timer and setting OUT LOW on the next CLK pulse. Therefore, an initial count of N will result in a one-shot pulse width of N CLK cycles. Note that this one-shot operation is retriggerable; i.e., OUT will remain LOW for N CLK pulses after every trigger. The one-shot operation can be repeated without rewriting the same count into the timer.

If a new count is written to the timer during a one-shot operation, the current one-shot pulse width will not be affected until the timer is retriggered. This is because loading of the new count to CE will occur only when the one-shot is triggered.

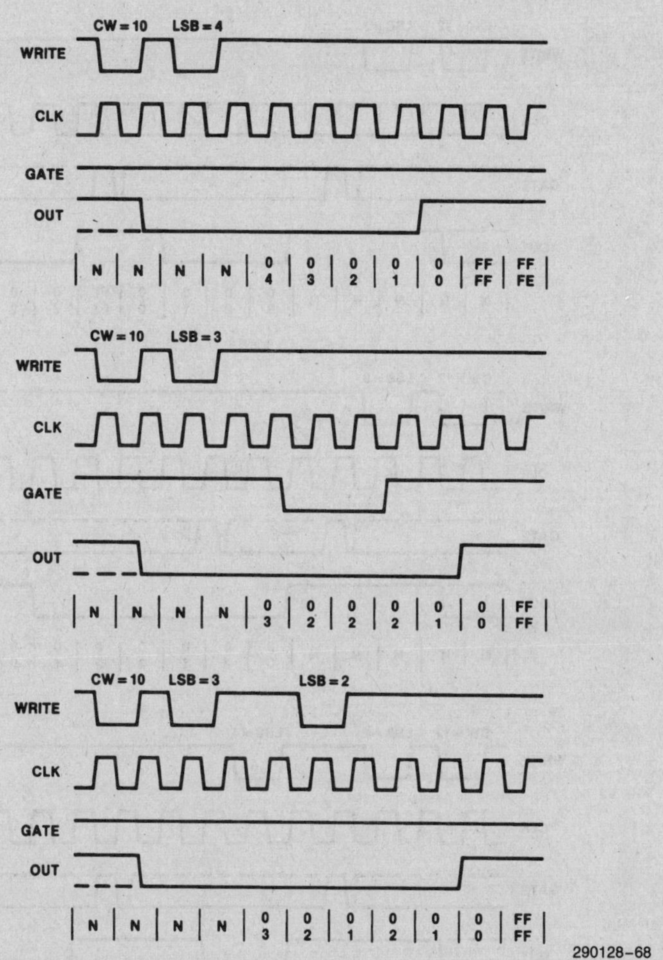

NOTES:

The following conventions apply to all mode timing diagrams.

1. Counters are programmed for binary (not BCD) counting and for reading/writing least significant byte (LSB) only.
2. The counter is always selected ($\overline{CS}$ always low).
3. CW stands for "Control Word"; CW = 10 means a control word of 10, Hex is written to the counter.
4. LSB stands for "least significant byte" of count.
5. Numbers below diagrams are count values.
   The lower number is the least significant byte.
   The upper number is the most significant byte. Since the counter is programmed to read/write LSB only, the most significant byte cannot be read.
   N stands for an undefined count.
   Vertical lines show transitions between count values.

Figure 5-3. Mode 0

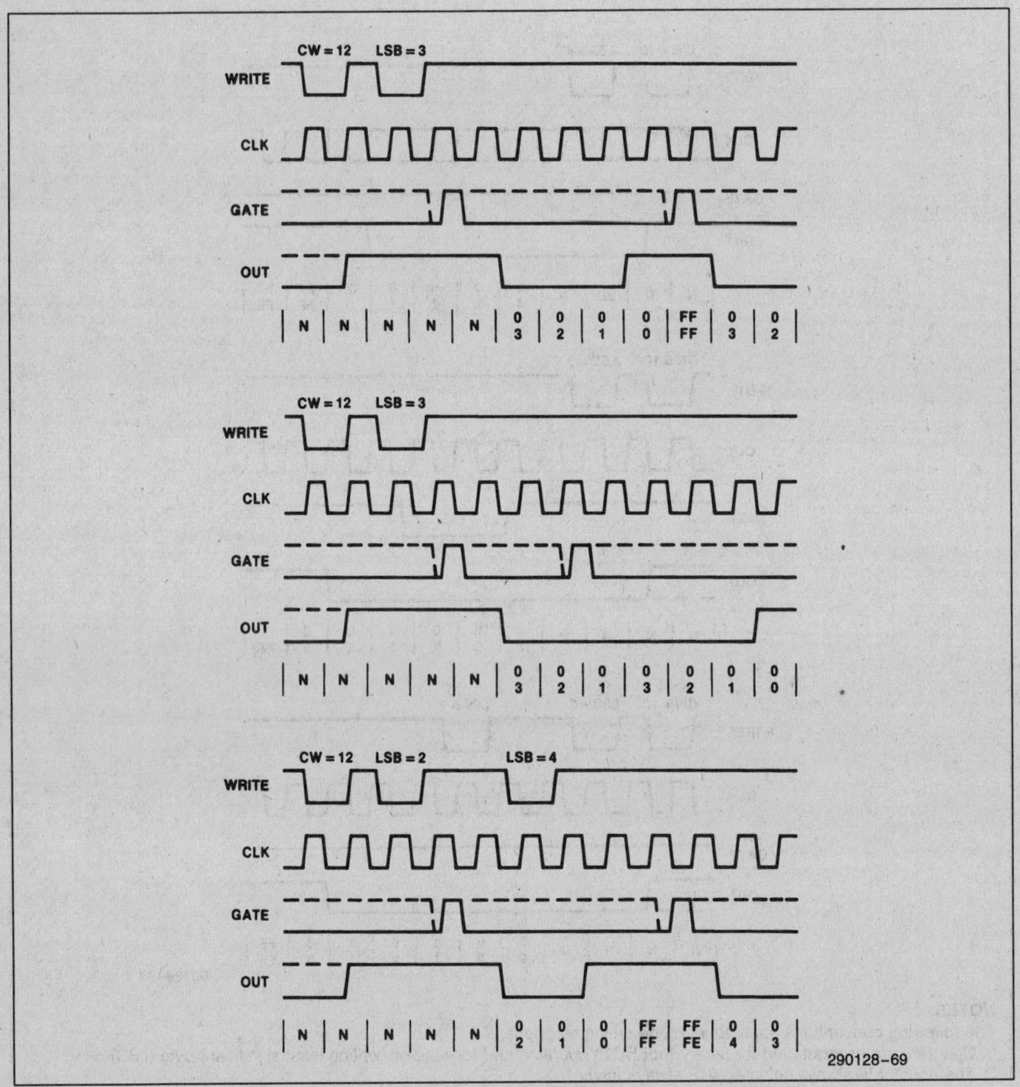

Figure 5-4. Mode 1

5.3.3 MODE 2—RATE GENERATOR

This mode is a divide-by-N counter. It is typically used to generate a Real Time Clock interrupt. OUT will initially be HIGH. When the initial count has decremented to 1, OUT goes LOW for one CLK pulse, then OUT goes HIGH again. Then the timer reloads the initial count and the process is repeated. In other words, this mode is periodic since the same sequence is repeated itself indefinitely. For an initial count of N, the sequence repeats every N CLK cycles.

Similar to Mode 0, GATE = HIGH enables counting, where GATE = LOW disables counting. If GATE goes LOW during an output pulse (LOW), OUT is set HIGH immediately. A trigger (rising edge on GATE) will reload the timer with the initial count on the next CLK pulse. Then, OUT will go LOW (for one CLK pulse) N CLK pulses after the new trigger. Thus, GATE can be used to synchronize the timer.

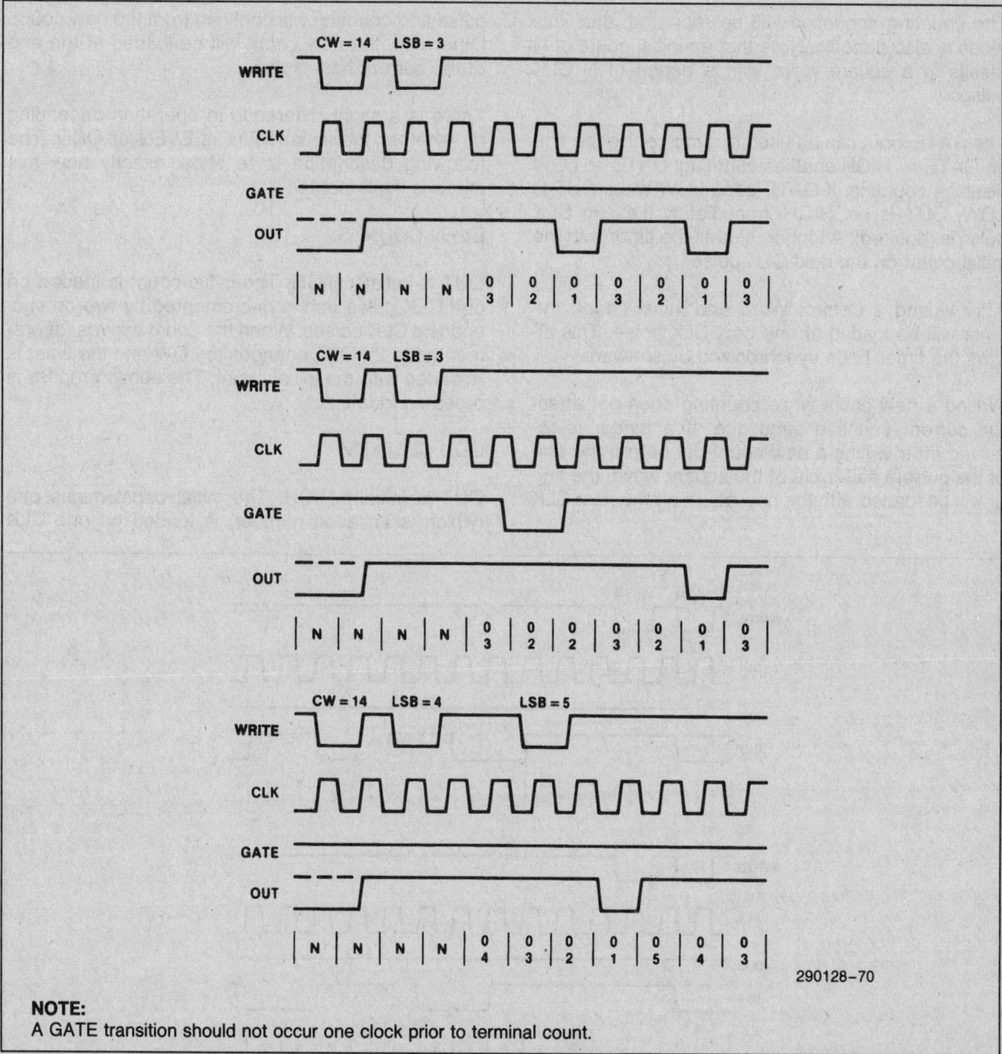

NOTE:
A GATE transition should not occur one clock prior to terminal count.

Figure 5-5. Mode 2

After writing a Control Word and initial count, the timer will be loaded on the next CLK pulse. OUT goes LOW (for the CLK pulse) N CLK pulses after the initial count is written. This is another way the timer may be synchronized by software.

Writing a new count while counting does not affect the current counting sequence because the new count will not be loaded until the end of the current counting cycle. If a trigger is received after writing a new count but before the end of the current period, the timer will be loaded with the new count on the next CLK pulse after the trigger, and counting will continue with the new count.

5.3.4 MODE 3—SQUARE WAVE GENERATOR

Mode 3 is typically used for Baud Rate generation. Functionally, this mode is similar to Mode 2 except for the duty cycle of OUT. In this mode, OUT will be initially HIGH. When half of the initial count has expired, OUT goes low for the remainder of the count.

The counting sequence will be repeated, thus this mode is also periodic. Note that an initial count of N results in a square wave with a period of N CLK pulses.

The GATE input can be used to synchronize the timer. GATE = HIGH enables counting; GATE = LOW disables counting. If GATE goes LOW while OUT is LOW, OUT is set HIGH immediately (i.e., no CLK pulse is required). A trigger reloads the timer with the initial count on the next CLK pulse.

After writing a Control Word and initial count, the timer will be loaded on the next CLK pulse. This allows the timer to be synchronized by software.

Writing a new count while counting does not affect the current counting sequence. If a trigger is received after writing a new count but before the end of the current half-cycle of the square wave, the timer will be loaded with the new count on the next CLK pulse and counting will continue from the new count. Otherwise, the new count will be loaded at the end of the current half-cycle.

There is a slight difference in operation depending on whether the initial count is EVEN or ODD. The following description is to show exactly how this mode is implemented.

EVEN COUNTS:

OUT is initially HIGH. The initial count is loaded on one CLK pulse and is decremented by two on succeeding CLK pulses. When the count expires (decremented to 2), OUT changes to LOW and the timer is reloaded with the initial count. The above process is repeated indefinitely.

ODD COUNTS:

OUT is initially HIGH. The initial count minus one (which is an even number) is loaded on one CLK

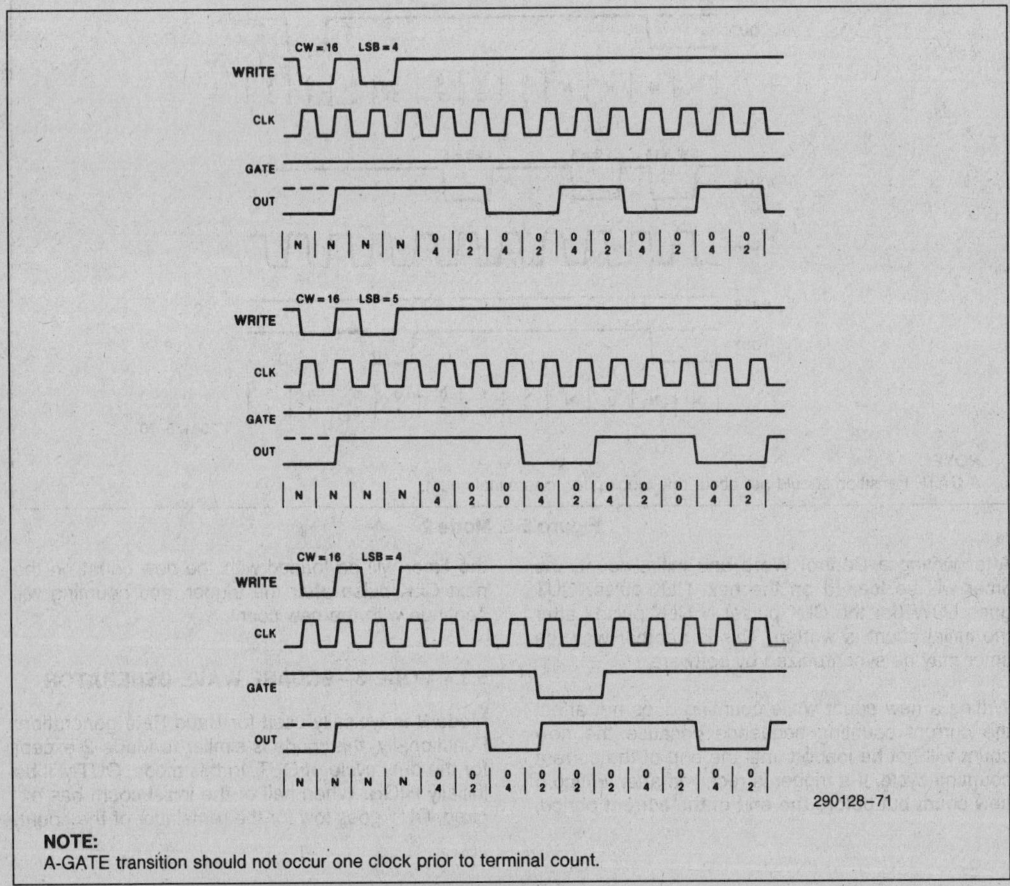

NOTE:
A-GATE transition should not occur one clock prior to terminal count.

Figure 5-6. Mode 3

pulse and is decremented by two on succeeding CLK pulses. One CLK pulse after the count expires (decremented to 2), OUT goes LOW and the timer is loaded with the initial count minus one again. Succeeding CLK pulses decrement the count by two. When the count expires, OUT goes HIGH immediately and the timer is reloaded with the initial count minus one. The above process is repeated indefinitely. So for ODD counts, OUT will be HIGH for (N + 1)/2 counts and LOW for (N − 1)/2 counts.

5.3.5 MODE 4—INITIAL COUNT TRIGGERED STROBE

This mode allows a strobe pulse to be generated by writing an initial count to the timer. Initially, OUT will be HIGH. When a new initial count is written into the timer, the counting sequence will begin. When the initial count expires (decremented to 1), OUT will go LOW for one CLK pulse and then go HIGH again.

Again, GATE = HIGH enables counting while GATE = LOW disables counting. GATE has no effect on OUT.

After writing the Control Word and initial count, the timer will be loaded on the next CLK pulse. This CLK pulse does not decrement the count, so for an initial count of N, OUT does not strobe LOW until N + 1 CLK pulses after initial count is written.

If a new count is written during counting, it will be loaded in the next CLK pulse and counting will continue from the new count.

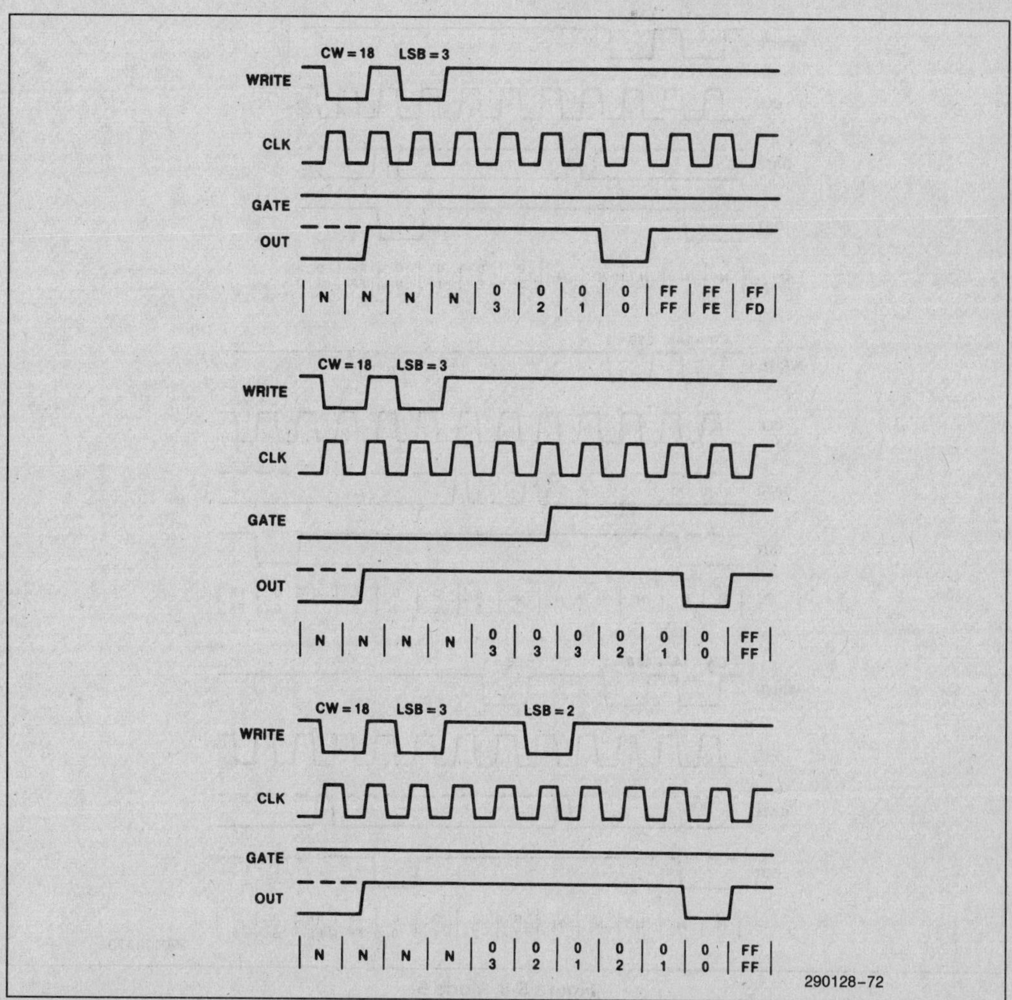

Figure 5-7. Mode 4

If a two-byte count is written, the following will occur:

1. Writing the first byte has no effect on counting.
2. Writing the second byte allows the new count to be loaded on the next CLK pulse.

OUT will strobe LOW N + 1 CLK pulses after the new count of N is written. Therefore, when the strobe pulse will occur after a trigger depends on the value of the initial count loaded.

5.3.6 MODE 5—GATE RETRIGGERABLE STROBE

Mode 5 is very similar to Mode 4 except the count sequence is triggered by the GATE signal instead of by writing an initial count. Initially, OUT will be HIGH. Counting is triggered by a rising edge of GATE. When the initial count has expired (decremented to 1), OUT will go LOW for one CLK pulse and then go HIGH again.

After loading the Control Word and initial count, the Count Element will not be loaded until the CLK pulse after a trigger. This CLK pulse does not decrement the count. Therefore, for an initial count of N, OUT does not strobe LOW until N + 1 CLK pulses after a trigger.

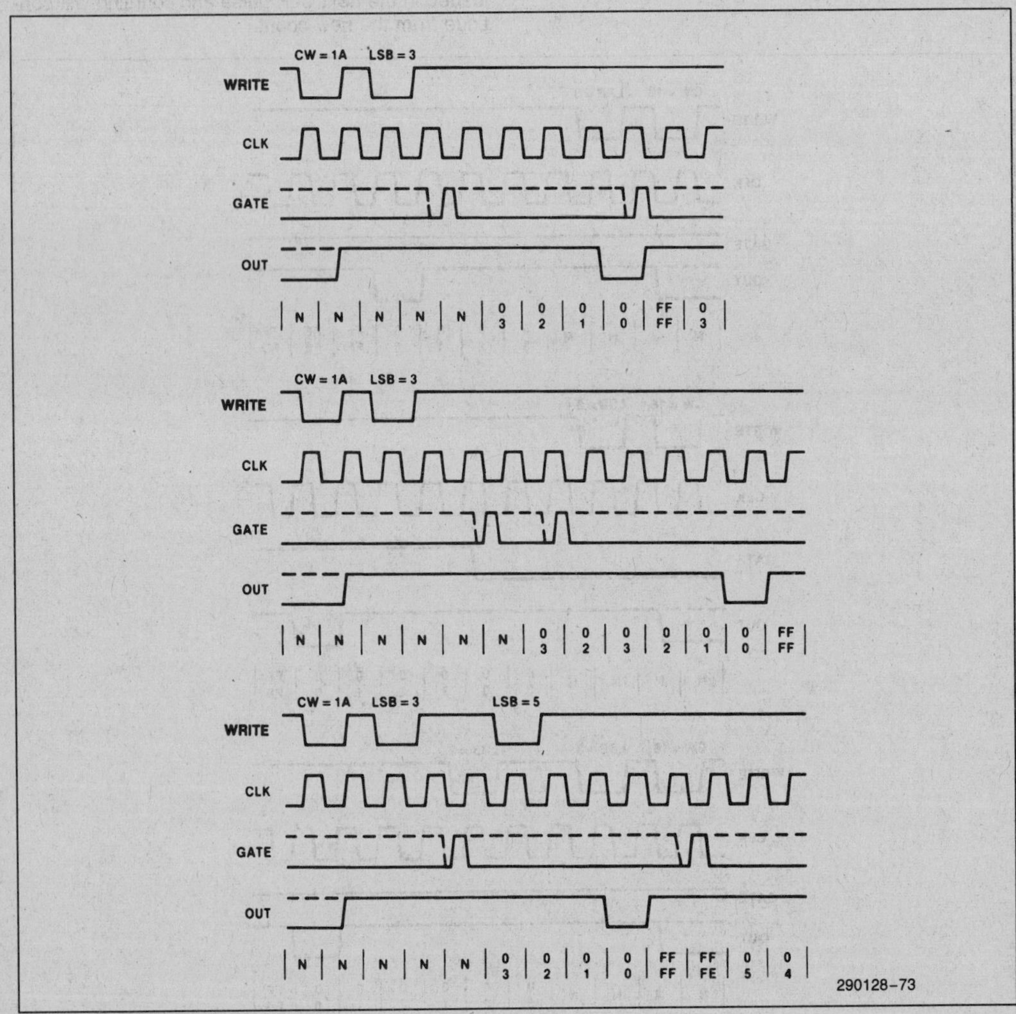

Figure 5-8. Mode 5

SUMMARY OF GATE OPERATIONS

Mode	GATE LOW or Going LOW	GATE Rising	GATE HIGH
0	Disable Count	No Effect	Enable Count
1	No Effect	1. Initiate Count 2. Reset Output After Next Clock	No Effect
2	1. Disable Count 2. Sets Output HIGH Immediately	Initiate Count	Enable Count
3	1. Disable Count 2. Sets Output HIGH Immediately	Initiate Count	Enable Count
4	Disable Count	No Effect	Enable Count
5	No Effect	Initiate Count	No Effect

The counting sequence is retriggerable. Every trigger will result in the timer being loaded with the initial count on the next CLK pulse.

If the new count is written during counting, the current counting sequence will not be affected. If a trigger occurs after the new count is written but before the current count expires, the timer will be loaded with the new count on the next CLK pulse and a new count sequence will start from there.

5.3.7 OPERATION COMMON TO ALL MODES

5.3.7.1 GATE

The GATE input is always sampled on the rising edge of CLKIN. In Modes 0, 2, 3 and 4, the GATE input is level sensitive. The logic level is sampled on the rising edge of CLKIN. In Modes 1, 2, 3 and 5, the GATE input is rising edge sensitive. In these modes, a rising edge of GATE (trigger) sets an edge sensitive flip-flop in the timer. The flip-flop is reset immediately after it is sampled. This way, a trigger will be detected no matter when it occurs; i.e., a HIGH logic level does not have to be maintained until the next rising edge of CLKIN. Note that in Modes 2 and 3, the GATE input is both edge and level sensitive.

5.3.7.2 Counter

New counts are loaded and counters are decremented on the falling edge of CLKIN. The largest possible initial count is 0. This is equivalent to 2**16 for binary counting and 10**4 for BCD counting.

Note that the counter does not stop when it reaches zero. In Modes 0, 1, 4, and 5, the counter 'wraps around' to the highest count: either FFFF Hex for binary counting or 9999 for BCD counting, and continues counting. Modes 2 and 3 are periodic. The counter reloads itself with the initial count and continues counting from there.

The minimum and maximum initial count in each counter depends on the mode of operation. They are summarized below.

Mode	Min	Max
0	1	0
1	1	0
2	2	0
3	2	0
4	1	0
5	1	0

5.4 Register Set Overview

The Programmable Interval Timer module of the 82380 contains a set of six registers. The port address map of these registers is shown in Table 5-2.

Table 5-2. Timer Register Port Address Map

Port Address	Description
40H	Counter 0 Register (read/write)
41H	Counter 1 Register (read/write)
42H	Counter 2 Register (read/write)
43H	Control Word Register I (Counter 0, 1 & 2) (write-only)
44H	Counter 3 Register (read/write)
45H	Reserved
46H	Reserved
47H	Control Word Register II (Counter 3) (write-only)

4

5.4.1 COUNTER 0, 1, 2, 3 REGISTERS

These four 8-bit registers are functionally identical. They are used to write the initial count value into the respective timer. Also, they can be used to read the latched count value of a timer. Since they are 8-bit registers, reading and writing of the 16-bit initial count must follow the count format specified in the Control Word Registers; i.e., least significant byte only, most significant byte only, or least significant byte then most significant byte (see Programming).

5.4.2 CONTROL WORD REGISTER I & II

There are two Control Word Registers associated with the Timer section. One of the two registers (Control Word Register I) is used to control the operations of Counters 0, 1, and 2 and the other (Control Word Register II) is for Counter 3. The major functions of both Control Word Registers are listed below:

— Select the timer to be programmed.

— Define which mode the selected timer is to operate in.

— Define the count sequence; i.e., if the selected timer is to count as a Binary Counter or a Binary Coded Decimal (BCD) Counter.

— Select the byte access sequence during timer read/write operations; i.e., least significant byte only, most significant byte only, or least significant byte first, then most significant byte.

Also, the Control Word Registers can be programmed to perform a Counter Latch Command or a Read Back Command which will be described later.

5.5 Programming

5.5.1 INITIALIZATION

Upon power-up or reset, the state of all timers is undefined. The mode, count value, and output of all timers are random. From this point on, how each timer operates is determined solely by how it is programmed. Each timer must be programmed before it can be used. Since the outputs of some timers can generate interrupt signals to the 82380, all timers should be initialized to a known state.

Timers are programmed by writing a Control Word into their respective Control Word Registers. Then, an Initial Count can be written into the corresponding Count Register. In general, the programming procedure is very flexible. Only two conventions need to be remembered:

1. For each timer, the Control Word must be written before the initial count is written.
2. The 16-bit initial count must follow the count format specified in the Control Word (least significant byte only, most significant byte only, or least significant byte first, followed by most significant byte).

Since the two Control Word Registers and the four Counter Registers have separate addresses, and each timer can be individually selected by the appropriate Control Word Register, no special instruction sequence is required. Any programming sequence that follows the conventions above is acceptable.

A new initial count may be written to a timer at any time without affecting the timer's programmed mode in any way. Count sequence will be affected as described in the Modes of Operation section. Note that the new count must follow the programmed count format.

If a timer is previously programmed to read/write two-byte counts, the following precaution applies. A program must not transfer control between writing the first and second byte to another routine which also writes into the same timer. Otherwise, the read/write will result in incorrect count.

Whenever a Control Word is written to a timer, all control logic for that timer(s) is immediately reset (i.e., no CLK pulse is required). Also, the corresponding output pin, TOUT(#), goes to a known initial state.

5.5.2 READ OPERATION

Three methods are available to read the current count as well as the status of each timer. They are: Read Counter Registers, Counter Latch Command and Read Back Command. Following is a description of these methods.

READ COUNTER REGISTERS

The current count of a timer can be read by performing a read operation on the corresponding Counter Register. The only restriction of this read operation is that the CLKIN of the timers must be inhibited by using external logic. Otherwise, the count may be in the process of changing when it is read, giving an undefined result. Note that since all four timers are sharing the same CLKIN signal, inhibiting CLKIN to read a timer will unavoidably disable the other timers also. This may prove to be impractical. Therefore, it is suggested that either the Counter Latch Command or the Read Back Command be used to read the current count of a timer.

Another alternative is to temporarily disable a timer before reading its Counter Register by using the GATE input. Depending on the mode of operation, GATE = LOW will disable the counting operation. However, this option is available on Timer 2 and 3 only, since the GATE signals of the other two timers are internally enabled all the time.

COUNTER LATCH COMMAND

A Counter Latch Command will be executed whenever a special Control Word is written into a Control Word Register. Two bits written into the Control Word Register distinguish this command from a 'regular' Control Word (see Register Bit Definition). Also, two other bits in the Control Word will select which counter is to be latched.

Upon execution of this command, the selected counter's Output Latch (OL) latches the count at the time the Counter Latch Command is received. This count is held in the latch until it is read by the 80386, or until the timer is reprogrammed. The count is then unlatched automatically and the OL returns to 'following' the Counting Element (CE). This allows reading the contents of the counters 'on the fly' without affecting counting in progress. Multiple Counter Latch Commands may be used to latch more than one counter. Each latched count is held until it is read. Counter Latch Commands do not affect the programmed mode of the timer in any way.

If a counter is latched, and at some time later, it is latched again before the prior latched count is read, the second Counter Latch Command is ignored. The count read will then be the count at the time the first command was issued.

In any event, the latched count must be read according to the programmed format. Specifically, if the timer is programmed for two-byte counts, two bytes must be read. However, the two bytes do not have to be read right after the other. Read/write or programming operations of other timers may be performed between them.

Another feature of this Counter Latch Command is that read and write operations of the same timer may be interleaved. For example, if the timer is programmed for two-byte counts, the following sequence is valid.

1. Read least significant byte.
2. Write new least significant byte.
3. Read most significant byte.
4. Write new most significant byte.

If a timer is programmed to read/write two-byte counts, the following precaution applies. A program must not transfer control between reading the first and second byte to another routine which also reads from that same timer. Otherwise, an incorrect count will be read.

READ BACK COMMAND

The Read Back Command is another special Command Word operation which allows the user to read the current count value and/or the status of the selected timer(s). Like the Counter Latch Command, two bits in the Command Word identify this as a Read Back Command (see Register Bit Definition).

The Read Back Command may be used to latch multiple counter Output Latches (OL's) by selecting more than one timer within a Command Word. This single command is functionally equivalent to several Counter Latch Commands, one for each counter to be latched. Each counter's latched count will be held until it is read by the 80386 or until the timer is reprogrammed. The counter is automatically unlatched when read, but other counters remain latched until they are read. If multiple Read Back commands are issued to the same timer without reading the count, all but the first are ignored; i.e., the count read will correspond to the very first Read Back Command issued.

As mentioned previously, the Read Back Command may also be used to latch status information of the selected timer(s). When this function is enabled, the status of a timer can be read from the Counter Register after the Read Back Command is issued. The status information of a timer includes the following:

1. Mode of timer:

   This allows the user to check the mode of operation of the timer last programmed.

2. State of TOUT pin of the timer:

   This allows the user to monitor the counter's output pin via software, possibly eliminating some hardware from a system.

3. Null Count/Count available:

   The Null Count Bit in the status byte indicates if the last count written to the Count Register (CR) has been loaded into the Counting Element (CE). The exact time this happens depends on the mode of the timer and is described in the Programming section. Until the count is loaded into the Counting Element (CE), it cannot be read from the timer. If the count is latched or read before this occurs, the count value will not reflect the new count just written.

If multiple status latch operations of the timer(s) are performed without reading the status, all but the first command are ignored; i.e., the status read in will correspond to the first Read Back Command issued.

Both the current count and status of the selected timer(s) may be latched simultaneously by enabling both functions in a single Read Back Command. This is functionally the same as issuing two separate Read Back Commands at once. Once again, if multiple read commands are issued to latch both the count and status of a timer, all but the first command will be ignored.

If both count and status of a timer are latched, the first read operation of that timer will return the latched status, regardless of which was latched first. The next one or two (if two count bytes are to be read) read operations return the latched count. Note that subsequent read operations on the Counter Register will return the unlatched count (like the first read method discussed).

5.6 Register Bit Definitions

COUNTER 0, 1, 2, 3 REGISTER (READ/WRITE)

Port Address	Description
40H	Counter 0 Register (read/write)
41H	Counter 1 Register (read/write)
42H	Counter 2 Register (read/write)
44H	Counter 3 Register (read/write)
45H	Reserved
46H	Reserved

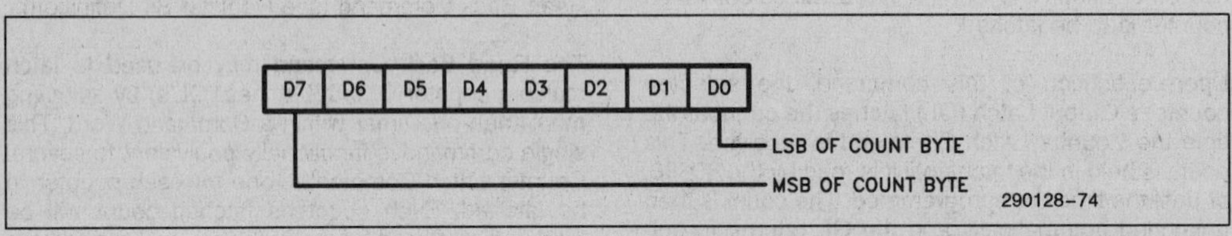

Note that these 8-bit registers are for writing and reading of one byte of the 16-bit count value, either the most significant or the least significant byte.

CONTROL WORD REGISTER I & II (WRITE-ONLY)

Port Address	Description
43H	Control Word Register I (Counter 0, 1, 2) (write-only)
47H	Control Word Register II (Counter 3) (write-only)

CONTROL WORD REGISTER I

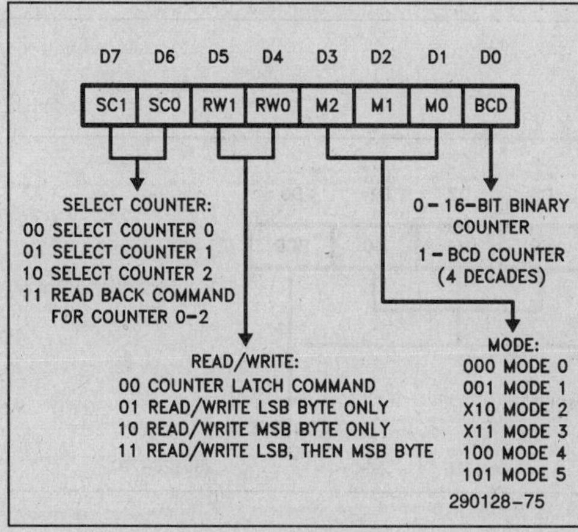

290128–75

CONTROL WORD REGISTER II

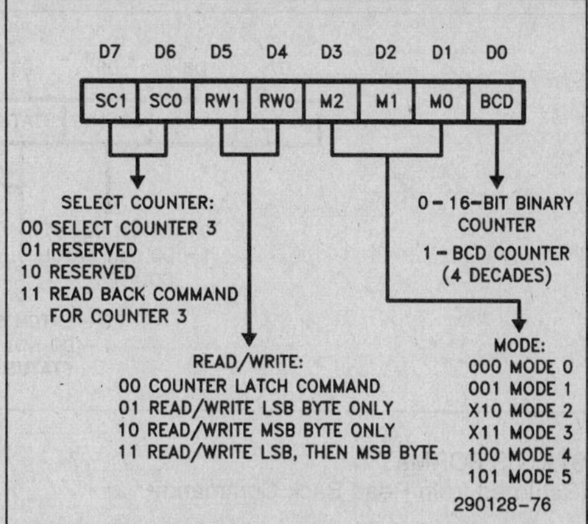

290128–76

COUNTER LATCH COMMAND FORMAT
(Write to Control Word Register)

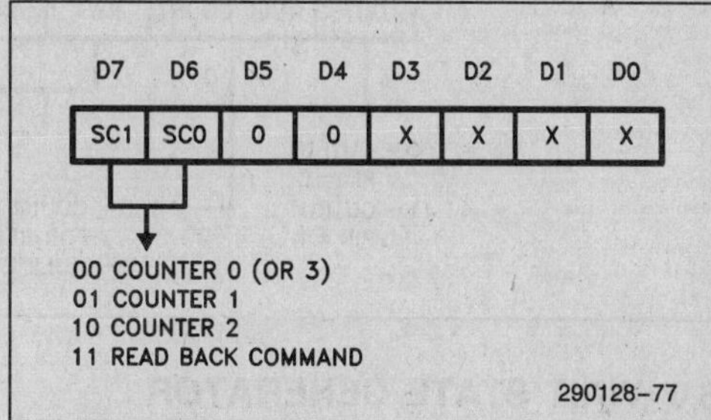

290128–77

Mode	Timer 0	Timer 1	Timer 2	Timer 3	Gate Trigger Edge	Gate Trigger Level	
0						X	Interrupt on Terminal Count
1	NA	NA	①	①	X		Gate Retriggerable One Shot
2					X	X	Rate Generator
3					X	X	Square Wave Generator
4						X	Initial Count Triggered Strobe
5	NA	NA	①	①	X		Gate Retriggerable Strobe

① = Must use Port 61 to generate ⁄ edge.
NA = Not Applicable

READ BACK COMMAND FORMAT
(Write to Control Word Register)

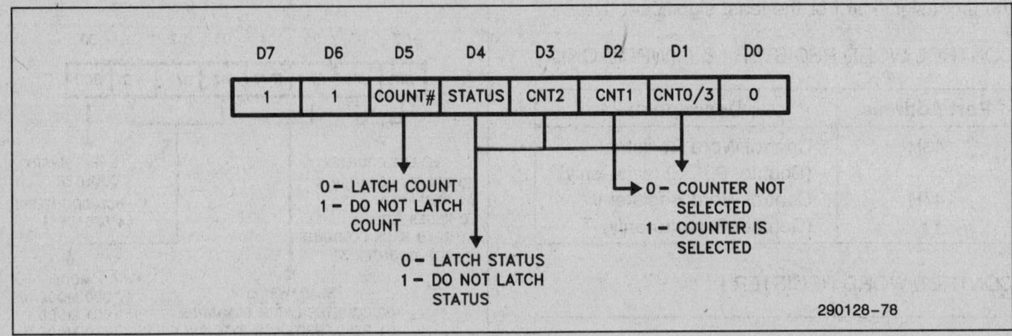

STATUS FORMAT
(Returned from Read Back Command)

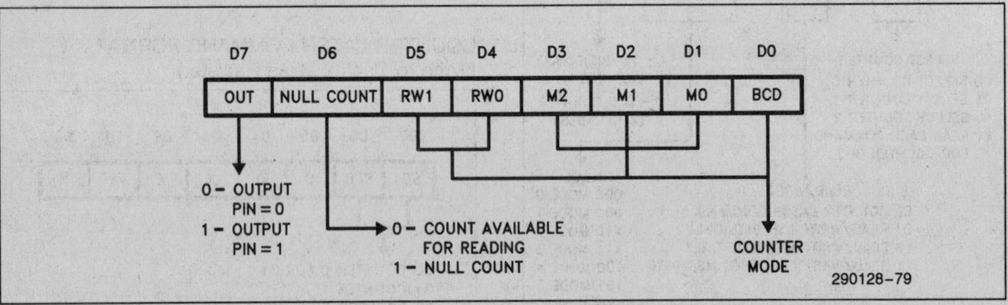

6.0 WAIT STATE GENERATOR

6.1 Functional Description

The 82380 contains a programmable Wait State Generator which can generate a pre-programmed number of wait states during both CPU and DMA initiated bus cycles. This Wait State Generator is capable of generating 1 to 16 wait states in non-pipelined mode, and 0 to 15 wait states in pipelined mode. Depending on the bus cycle type and the two Wait State Control inputs (WSC 0–1), a pre-programmed number of wait states in the selected Wait State Register will be generated.

The Wait State Generator can also be disabled to allow the use of devices capable of generating their own READY# signals. Figure 6-1 is a block diagram of the Wait State Generator.

6.2 Interface Signals

The following describes the interface signals which affect the operation of the Wait State Generator. The READY#, WSC0 and WSC1 signals are inputs. READYO# is the ready output signal to the host processor.

6.2.1 READY#

READY# is an active LOW input signal which indicates to the 82380 the completion of a bus cycle. In the Master mode (e.g., 82380 initiated DMA transfer), this signal is monitored to determine whether a peripheral or memory needs wait states inserted in the current bus cycle. In the Slave mode, it is used (together with the ADS# signal) to trace CPU bus cycles to determine if the current cycle is pipelined.

6.2.2 READYO#

READYO# (Ready Out#) is an active LOW output signal and is the output of the Wait State Generator. The number of wait states generated depends on the WSC(0–1) inputs. Note that special cases are handled for access to the 82380 internal registers and for the Refresh cycles. For 82380 internal register access, READYO# will be delayed to take into account the command recovery time of the register. One or more wait states will be generated in a pipelined cycle. During refresh, the number of wait states will be determined by the preprogrammed value in the Refresh Wait State Register.

In the simplest configuration, READYO# can be connected to the READY# input of the 82380 and the 80386 CPU. This is, however, not always the case. If external circuitry is to control the READY# inputs as well, additional logic will be required (see Application Issues).

6.2.3 WSC(0–1)

These two Wait State Control inputs select one of the three pre-programmed 8-bit Wait State Registers which determines the number of wait states to be generated. The most significant half of the three Wait State Registers corresponds to memory accesses, the least significant half to I/O accesses. The combination WSC(0–1) = 11 disables the Wait State Generator.

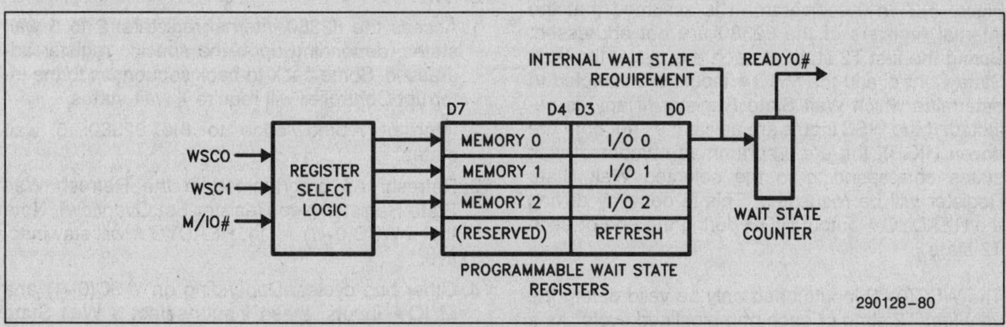

Figure 6-1. Wait State Generator Block Diagram

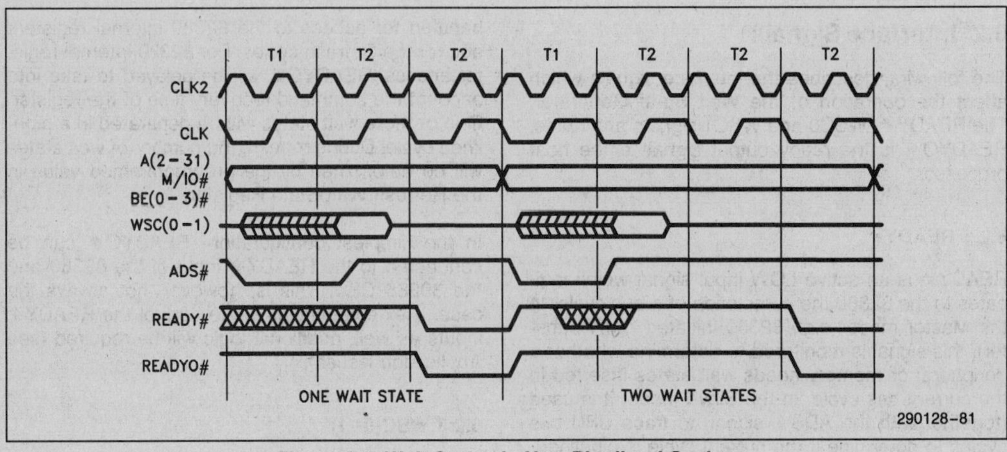

Figure 6-2. Wait States in Non-Pipelined Cycles

6.3 Bus Function

6.3.1 WAIT STATES IN NON-PIPELINED CYCLE

The timing diagram of two typical non-pipelined cycles with 82380 generated wait states is shown in Figure 6-2. In this diagram, it is assumed that the internal registers of the 82380 are not addressed. During the first T2 state of each bus cycle, the Wait State Control and the M/IO# inputs are sampled to determine which Wait State Register (if any) is selected. If the WSC inputs are active (i.e., not both are driven HIGH), the pre-programmed number of wait states corresponding to the selected Wait State Register will be requested. This is done by driving the READYO# output HIGH during the end of each T2 state.

The WSC(0–1) inputs need only be valid during the very first T2 state of each non-pipelined cycle. As a general rule, the WSC inputs are sampled on the rising edge of the next clock (82384 CLK) after the last state when ADS# (Address Status) is asserted.

The number of wait states generated depends on the type of bus cycle, and the number of wait states requested. The various combinations are discussed below.

1. Access the 82380 internal registers: 2 to 5 wait states, depending upon the specific register addressed. Some back-to-back sequences to the Interrupt Controller will require 7 wait states.
2. Interrupt Acknowledge to the 82380: 5 wait states.
3. Refresh: As programmed in the Refresh Wait State Register (see Register Set Overview). Note that if WSC(0–1) = 11, READYO# will stay inactive.
4. Other bus cycles: Depending on WSC(0–1) and M/IO# inputs, these inputs select a Wait State Register in which the number of wait states will be equal to the pre-programmed wait state count in the register plus 1. The Wait State Register selection is defined as follows (Table 6-1).

Table 6-1. Wait State Register Selection

M/IO#	WSC(1–0)	Register Selected
0	00	WAIT REG 0 (I/O half)
0	01	WAIT REG 1 (I/O half)
0	10	WAIT REG 2 (I/O half)
1	00	WAIT REG 0 (MEM half)
1	01	WAIT REG 1 (MEM half)
1	10	WAIT REG 2 (MEM half)
X	11	Wait State Gen. Disabled

The Wait State Control signals, WSC(0–1), can be generated with the address decode and the Read/Write control signals as shown in Figure 6-3.

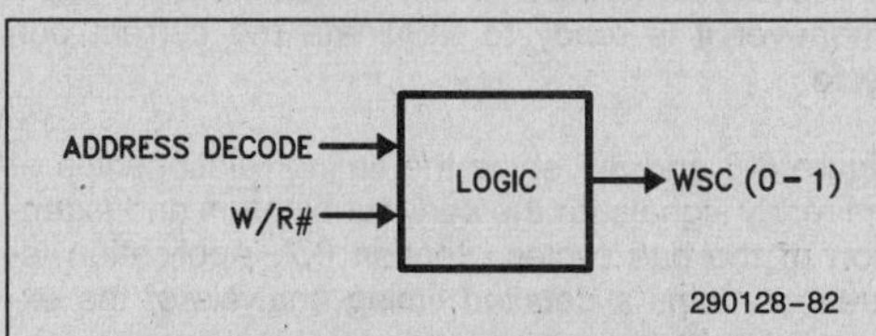

Figure 6-3. WSC(0–1) Generation

Note that during HALT and SHUTDOWN, the number of wait states will depend on the WSC(0–1) inputs, which will select the memory half of one of the Wait State Registers (see CPU Reset and Shutdown Detect).

6.3.2 WAIT STATES IN PIPELINED CYCLE

The timing diagram of two typical pipelined cycles with 82380 generated wait states is shown in Figure 6-4. Again, in this diagram, it is assumed that the 82380 internal registers are not addressed. As defined in the timing of the 80386 processor, the Address (A 2–31), Byte Enable (BE 0–3), and other control signals (M/IO#, ADS#) are asserted one T state earlier than in a non-pipelined cycle; i.e., they are asserted at T2P. Similar to the non-pipelined case, the Wait State Control (WSC) inputs are sampled in the middle of the state after the last state when the ADS# signal is asserted. Therefore, the WSC inputs should be asserted during the T1P state of each pipelined cycle (which is one T state earlier than in the non-pipelined cycle).

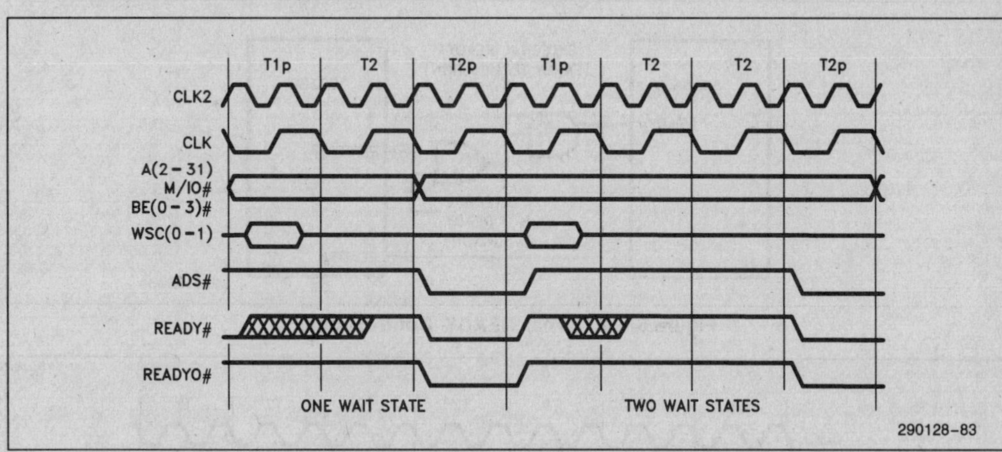

Figure 6-4. Wait State in Pipelined Cycles

The number of wait states generated in a pipelined cycle is selected in a similar manner as in the non-pipelined case discussed in the previous section. The only difference here is that the actual number of wait states generated will be one less than that of the non-pipelined cycle. This is done automatically by the Wait State Generator.

6.3.3 EXTENDING AND EARLY TERMINATING BUS CYCLE

The 82380 allows external logic to either add wait states or cause early termination of a bus cycle by controlling the READY# input to the 82380 and the host processor. A possible configuration is shown in Figure 6-5.

The EXT. RDY# (External Ready) signal of Figure 6-5 allows external devices to cause early termination of a bus cycle. When this signal is asserted LOW, the output of the circuit will also go LOW (even though the READYO# of the 82380 may still be HIGH). This output is fed to the READY# input of the 80386 and the 82380 to indicate the completion of the current bus cycle.

Similarly, the EXT. NOT READY (External Not Ready) signal is used to delay the READY# input of the processor and the 82380. As long as this signal is driven HIGH, the output of the circuit will drive the READY# Input HIGH. This will effectively extend the duration of a bus cycle. However, it is important to note that if the two-level logic is not fast enough to satisfy the READY# setup time, the OR gate should be eliminated. Instead, the 82380 Wait State Generator can be disabled by driving both WSC(0–1) HIGH. In this case, the addressed memory or I/O device should activate the external READY# input whenever it is ready to terminate the current bus cycle.

Figure 6-6 and 6-7 show the timing relationships of the ready signals for the early termination and extension of the bus cycles. Section 6.7, Application Issues, contains a detailed timing analysis of the external circuit.

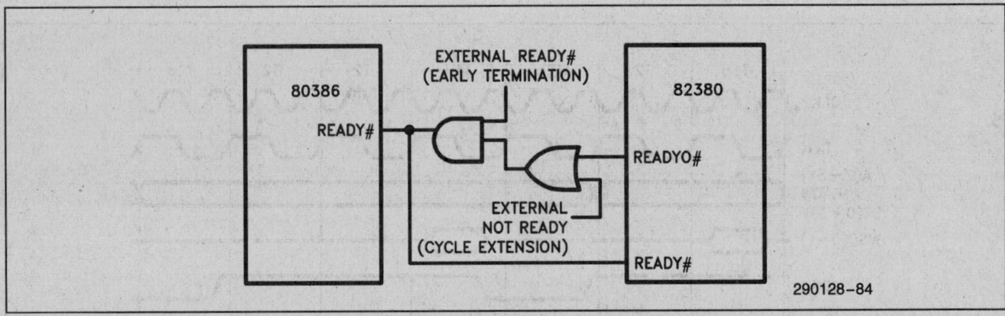

Figure 6-5. External 'READY' Control Logic

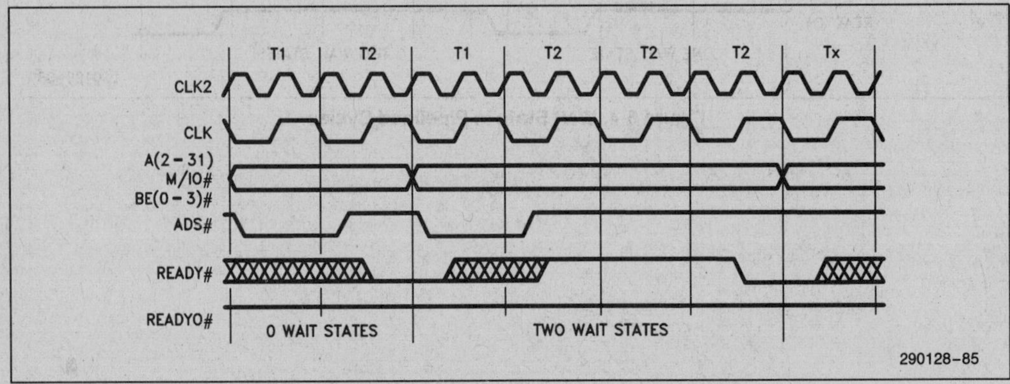

Figure 6-6. Early Termination of Bus Cycle By 'READY#'

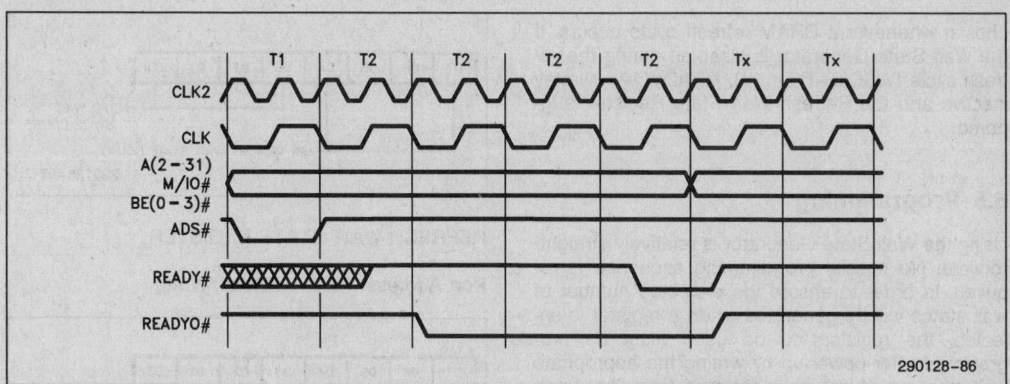

Figure 6-7. Extending Bus Cycle by 'READY#'

Due to the following implications, it should be noted that early termination of bus cycles in which 82380 internal registers are accessed is not recommended.

1. Erroneous data may be read from or written into the addressed register.
2. The 82380 must be allowed to recover either before HLDA (Hold Acknowledge) is asserted or before another bus cycle into an 82380 internal register is initiated.

   The recovery time, in bus periods, equals the remaining wait states that were avoided plus 4.

6.4 Register Set Overview

Altogether, there are four 8-bit internal registers associated with the Wait State Generator. The port address map of these registers is shown below in Table 6-2. A detailed description of each follows.

Table 6-2. Register Address Map

Port Address	Description
72H	Wait State Reg 0 (read/write)
73H	Wait State Reg 1 (read/write)
74H	Wait State Reg 2 (read/write)
75H	Ref. Wait State Reg (read/write)

WAIT STATE REGISTER 0, 1, 2

These three 8-bit read/write registers are functionally identical. They are used to store the pre-programmed wait state count. One half of each register contains the wait state count for I/O accesses while the other half contains the count for memory accesses. The total number of wait states generated will depend on the type of bus cycle. For a non-pipelined cycle, the actual number of wait states requested is equal to the wait state count plus 1. For a pipelined cycle, the number of wait states will be equal to the wait state count in the selected register. Therefore, the Wait State Generator is capable of generating 1 to 16 wait states in non-pipelined mode, and 0 to 15 wait states in pipelined mode.

Note that the minimum wait state count in each register is 0. This is equivalent to 0 wait states for a pipelined cycle and 1 wait state for a non-pipelined cycle.

REFRESH WAIT STATE REGISTER

Similar to the Wait State Registers discussed above, this 4-bit register is used to store the number of wait states to be generated during the DRAM refresh cycle. Note that the Refresh Wait State Register is not selected by the WSC inputs. It will automatically be chosen whenever a DRAM refresh cycle occurs. If the Wait State Generator is disabled during the refresh cycle (WSC(0–1) = 11), READYO# will stay inactive and the Refresh Wait State Register is ignored.

6.5 Programming

Using the Wait State Generator is relatively straightforward. No special programming sequence is required. In order to ensure the expected number of wait states will be generated when a register is selected, the registers to be used must be programmed after power-up by writing the appropriate wait state count into each register. Note that upon hardware reset, all Wait State Registers are initialized with the value FFH, giving the maximum number of wait states possible. Also, each register can be read to check the wait state count previously stored in the register.

6.6 Register Bit Definition

WAIT STATE REGISTER 0, 1, 2

Port Address	Description
72H	Wait State Register 0 (read/write)
73H	Wait State Register 1 (read/write)
74H	Wait State Register 2 (read/write)

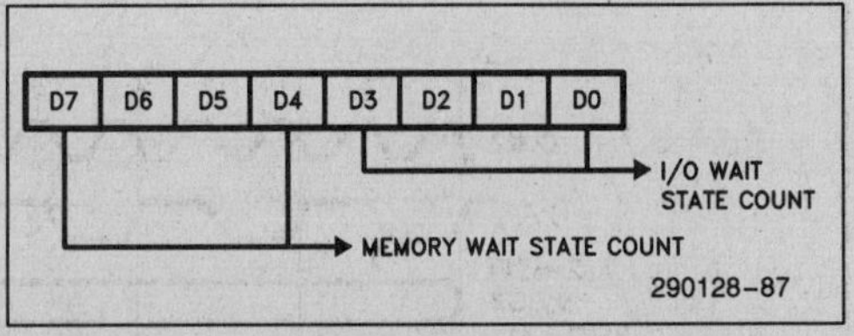

290128–87

REFRESH WAIT STATE REGISTER

Port Address: 75H (Read/Write)

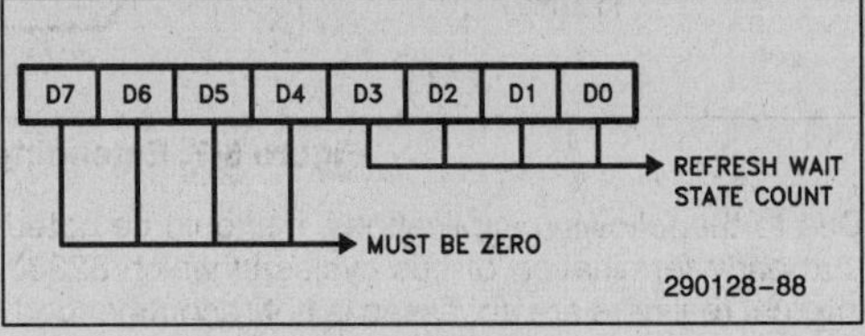

290128–88

6.7 Application Issues

6.7.1 EXTERNAL 'READY' CONTROL LOGIC

As mentioned in section 6.3.3, wait state cycles generated by the 82380 can be terminated early or extended longer by means of additional external logic (see Figure 6-5). In order to ensure that the READY# input timing requirement of the 80386 and the 82380 is satisfied, special care must be taken when designing this external control logic. This section addresses the design requirements.

A simplified block diagram of the external logic along with the READY# tiiming diagram is shown in Figure 6-8. The purpose is to determine the maximum delay time allowed in the external control logic in order to satisfy the READY# setup time.

First, it will be assumed that the 80386 is running at 16 MHz (i.e., CLK2 and 32 MHz). Therefore, one bus state (two CLK2 periods) will be equivalent to 62.5 nsec. According to the AC specifications of the 82380, the maximum delay time for valid READYO# signal is 31 ns after the rising edge of CLK2 in the beginning of T2 (for non-pipelined cycle) or T2P (for pipelined cycle). Also, the minimum READY# setup time of the 80386 and the 82380 should be 20 ns before the rising edge of CLK2 at the beginning of the next bus state. This limits the total delay time for the external READY# control logic to be 11 ns (62.5-31-21) in order to meet the READY# setup timing requirement.

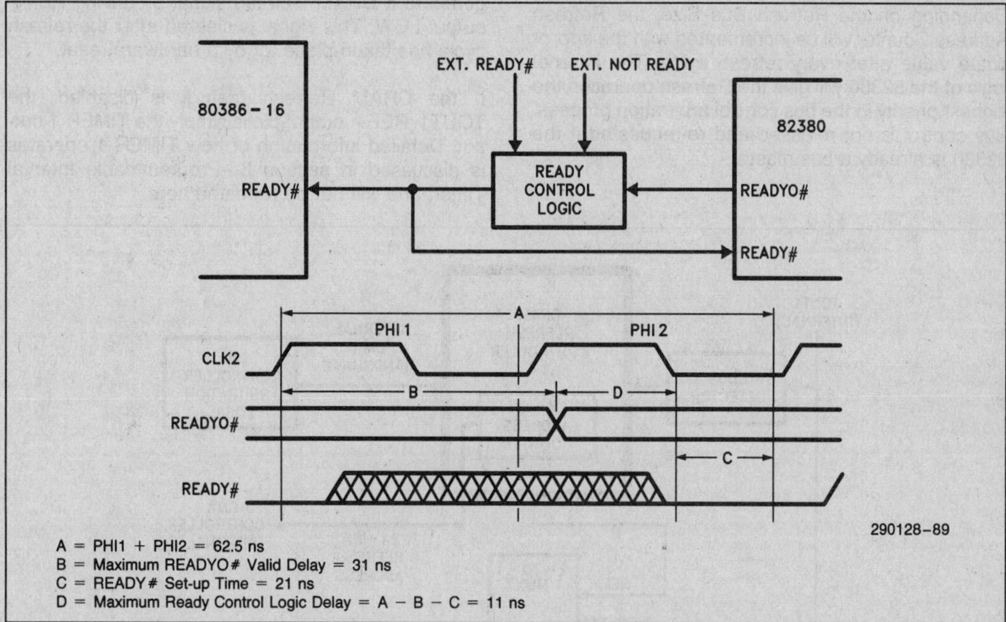

Figure 6-8. 'READY' Timing Consideration

7.0 DRAM REFRESH CONTROLLER

7.1 Functional Description

The 82380 DRAM Refresh Controller consists of a 24-bit Refresh Address Counter and Refresh Request logic for DRAM refresh operations (see Figure 7-1). TIMER 1 can be used as a trigger signal to the DRAM Refresh Request logic. The Refresh Bus Size can be programmed to be 8-, 16-, or 32-bit wide. Depending on the Refresh Bus Size, the Refresh Address Counter will be incremented with the appropriate value after every refresh cycle. The internal logic of the 82380 will give the Refresh operation the highest priority in the bus control arbitration process. Bus control is not released and re-requested if the 82380 is already a bus master.

7.2 Interface Signals

7.2.1 TOUT1/REF#

The dual function output pin of TIMER 1 (TOUT1/REF#) can be programmed to generate DRAM Refresh signal. If this feature is enabled, the rising edge of TIMER 1 output (TOUT1) will trigger the DRAM Refresh Request logic. After some delay for gaining access of the bus, the 82380 DRAM Controller will generate a DRAM Refresh signal by driving REF# output LOW. This signal is cleared after the refresh cycle has taken place, or by a hardware reset.

If the DRAM Refresh feature is disabled, the TOUT1/REF# output pin is simply the TIMER 1 output. Detailed information of how TIMER 1 operates is discussed in section 6—Programmable Interval Timer, and will not be repeated here.

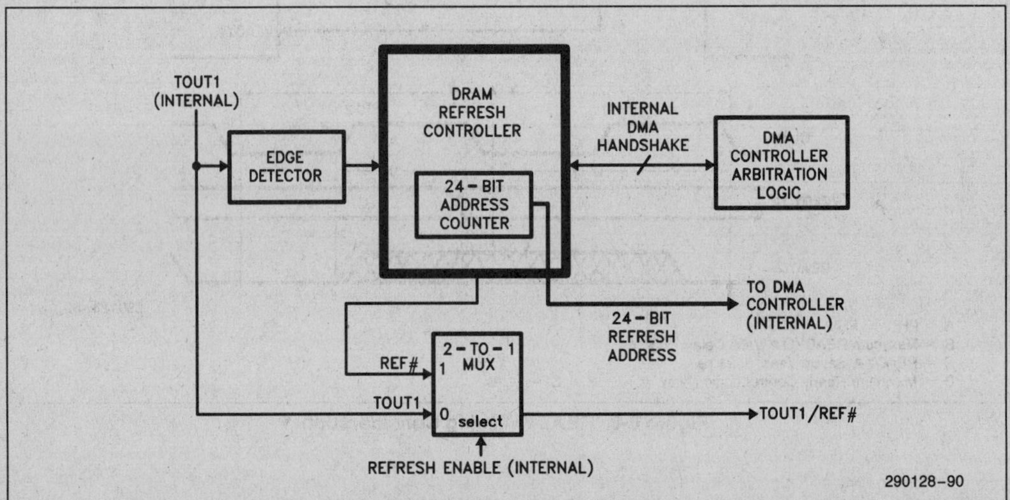

Figure 7-1. DRAM Refresh Controller

7.3 Bus Function

7.3.1 ARBITRATION

In order to ensure data integrity of the DRAMs, the 82380 gives the DRAM Refresh signal the highest priority in the arbitration logic. It allows DRAM Refresh to interrupt a DMA in progress in order to perform the DRAM Refresh cycle. The DMA service will be resumed after the refresh is done.

In case of a DRAM Refresh during a DMA process, the cascaded device will be requested to get off the bus. This is done by deasserting the EDACK signal. Once DREQn goes inactive, the 82380 will perform the refresh operation. Note that the DMA controller does not completely relinquish the system bus during refresh. The Refresh Generator simply 'steals' a bus cycle between DMA accesses.

Figure 7-2 shows the timing diagram of a Refresh Cycle. Upon expiration of TIMER 1, the 82380 will try to take control of the system bus by asserting HOLD. As soon as the 82380 see HLDA go active, the DRAM Refresh Cycle will be carried out by activating the REF# signal as well as the refresh address and control signals on the system bus (Note that REF# will not be active until two CLK periods after HLDA is asserted). The address bus will contain the 24-bit address currently in the Refresh Address Counter. The control signals are driven the same way as in a Memory Read cycle. This 'read' operation is complete when the READY# signal is driven LOW. Then, the 82380 will relinquish the bus by de-asserting HOLD. Typically, a Refresh Cycle without wait states will take five bus states to execute. If 'n' wait states are added, the Refresh Cycle will last for five plus 'n' bus states.

How often the Refresh Generation will initiate a refresh cycle depends on the frequency of CLKIN as well as TIMER1's programmed mode of operation. For this specific application, TIMER1 should be programmed to operate in Mode 2 or 3 to generate a constant clock rate. See section 6—Programmable Interval Timer for more information on programming the timer. One DRAM Refresh Cycle will be generated each time TIMER 1 expires (when TOUT1 changes to LOW to HIGH).

The Wait State Generator can be used to insert wait states during a refresh cycle. The 82380 will automatically insert the desired number of wait states as programmed in the Refresh Wait State Register (see Wait State Generator).

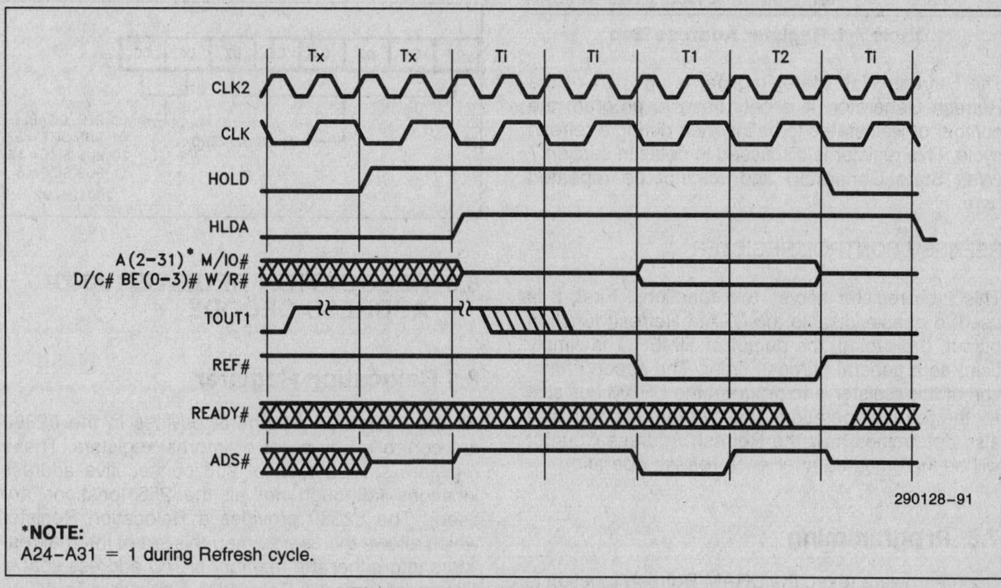

Figure 7-2. 82380 Refresh Cycle

7.4 Modes of Operation

7.4.1 WORD SIZE AND REFRESH ADDRESS COUNTER

The 82380 supports 8-, 16- and 32-bit refresh cycle. The bus width during a refresh cycle is programmable (see Programming). The bus size can be programmed via the Refresh Control Register (see Register Overview). If the DRAM bus size is 8-, 16-, or 32-bits, the Refresh Address Counter will be incremented by 1, 2, or 4, respectively.

The Refresh Address Counter is cleared by a hardware reset.

7.5 Register Set Overview

The Refresh Generator has two internal registers to control its operation. They are the Refresh Control Register and the Refresh Wait State Register. Their port address map is shown in Table 7-1 below.

Port Address	Description
1CH	Refresh Control Reg. (read/write)
75H	Ref. Wait State Reg. (read/write)

Table 7-1. Register Address Map

The Refresh Wait State Register is not part of the Refresh Generator. It is only used to program the number of wait states to be inserted during a refresh cycle. This register is discussed in detail in section 7 (Wait State Generator) and will not be repeated here.

REFRESH CONTROL REGISTER

This 2-bit register serves two functions. First, it is used to enable/disable the DRAM Refresh function output. If disabled, the output of TIMER 1 is simply used as a general purpose timer. The second function of this register is to program the DRAM bus size for the refresh operation. The programmed bus size also determines how the Refresh Address Counter will be incremented after each refresh operation.

7.6 Programming

Upon hardware reset, the DRAM Refresh function is disabled (the Refresh Control Register is cleared). The following programming steps are needed before the Refresh Generator can be used. Since the rate of refresh cycles depends on how TIMER 1 is programmed, this timer must be initialized with the desired mode of operation as well as the correct refresh interval (see Programming Interval Timer). Whether or not wait states are to be generated during a refresh cycle, the Refresh Wait State Register must also be programmed with the appropriate value. Then, the DRAM Refresh feature must be enabled and the DRAM bus width should be defined. These can be done in one step by writing the appropriate control word into the Refresh Control Register (see Register Bit Definition). After these steps are done, the refresh operation will automatically be invoked by the Refresh Generator upon expiration of Timer 1.

In addition to the above programming steps, it should be noted that after reset, although the TOUT1/REF# becomes the Timer 1 output, the state of this pin is undefined. This is because the Timer module has not been initialized yet. Therefore, if this output is used as a DRAM Refresh signal, this pin should be disqualified by external logic until the Refresh function is enabled. One simple solution is to logically AND this output with HLDA, since HLDA should not be active after reset.

7.7 Register Bit Definition

REFRESH CONTROL REGISTER
Port Address: 1CH (Read/Write)

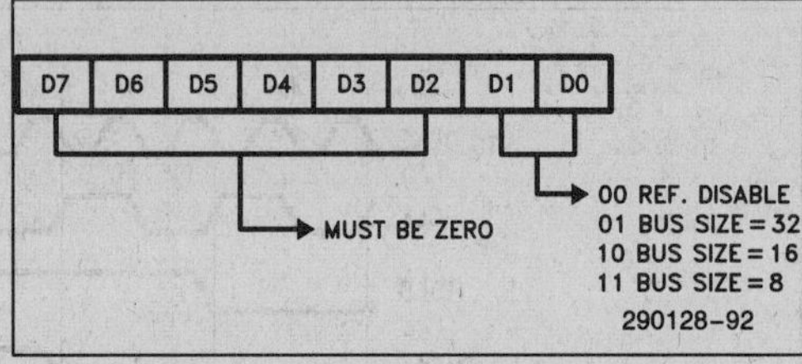

8.0 RELOCATION REGISTER AND ADDRESS DECODE

8.1 Relocation Register

All the integrated peripheral devices in the 82380 are controlled by a set of internal registers. These registers span a total of 256 consecutive address locations (although not all the 256 locations are used). The 82380 provides a Relocation Register which allows the user to map this set of internal registers into either the memory or I/O address space. The function of the Relocation Register is to define the base address of the internal register set of the 82380 as well as if the registers are to be memory- or I/O-mapped. The format of the Relocation Register is depicted in Figure 8-1.

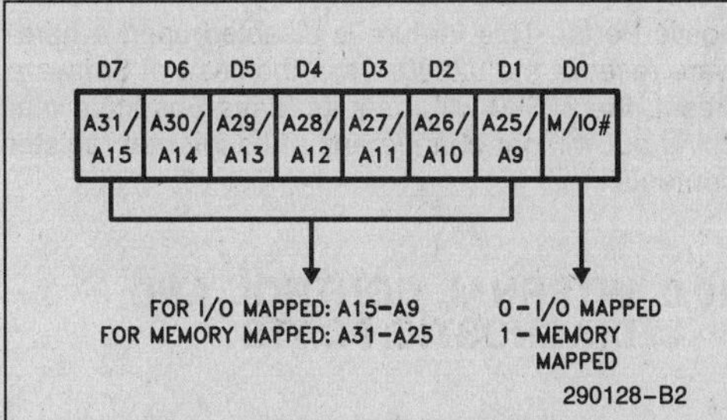

Figure 8-1. Relocation Register

Note that the Relocation Register is part of the internal register set of the 82380. It has a port address of 7FH. Therefore, any time the content of the Relocation Register is changed, the physical location of this register will also be moved. Upon reset of the 82380, the content of the Relocation Register will be cleared. This implies that the 82380 will respond to its I/O addresses in the range of 0000H to 00FFH.

8.1.1 I/O-MAPPED 82380

As shown in the figure, Bit 0 of the Relocation Register determines whether the 82380 registers are to be memory-mapped or I/O-mapped. When Bit 0 is set to '0', the 82380 will respond to I/O Addresses. Address signals BE0#–BE3#, A2–A7 will be used to select one of the internal registers to be accessed. Bit 1 to Bit 7 of the Relocation Register will correspond to A9 to A15 of the Address bus, respectively. Together with A8 implied to be '0', A15 to A8 will be fully decoded by the 82380. The following shows how the 82380 is mapped into the I/O address space.

Example

Relocation Register = 11001110 (0CEH)

82380 will respond to I/O address range from 0CE00H to 0CEFFH.

Therefore, this I/O mapping mechanism allows the 82380 internal registers to be located on any even, contiguous, 256 byte boundary of the system I/O space.

Port Address: 7FH (Read/Write)

8.1.2 MEMORY-MAPPED 82380

When Bit 0 of the Relocation Register is set to '1', the 82380 will respond to memory addresses. Again, Address signals BE0#–BE3#, A2–A7 will be used to select one of the internal registers to be accessed. Bit 1 to Bit 7 of the Relocation Register will correspond to A25–A31, respectively. A24 is assumed to be '0', and A8–A23 are ignored. Consider the following example.

Example

Relocation Register = 10100111 (0A7H)

The 82380 will respond to memory addresses in the range of 0A6XXXX00H to 0A6XXXXFFH (where 'X' is don't care).

This scheme implies that the internal register can be located in any even, contiguous, 2**24 byte page of the memory space.

8.2 Address Decoding

As mentioned previously, the 82380 internal registers do not occupy the entire contiguous 256 address locations. Some of the locations are 'unoccupied'. The 82380 always decodes the lower 8 address bits (A0–A7) to determine if any one of its registers is being accessed. If the address does not correspond to any of its registers, the 82380 will not respond. This allows external devices to be located within the 'holes' in the 82380 address space. Note that there are several unused addresses reserved for future Intel peripheral devices.

9.0 CPU RESET AND SHUTDOWN DETECT

4

The 82380 will activate the CPURST signal to reset the host processor when one of the following conditions occurs:

— 82380 RESET is active;

— 82380 detects a 80386 Shutdown cycle (this feature can be disabled);

— CPURST software command is issued to 80386.

Whenever the CPURST signal is activated, the 82380 will reset its own internal Slave-Bus state machine.

9.1 Hardware Reset

Following a hardware reset, the 82380 will assert its CPURST output to reset the host processor. This output will stay active for as long as the RESET input is active. During a hardware reset, the 82380 internal registers will be initialized as defined in the corresponding functional descriptions.

9.2 Software Reset

CPURST can be generated by writing the following bit pattern into 82380 register location 64H.

D7							D0
1	1	1	1	X	X	X	0

X = Don't Care

The Write operation into this port is considered as an 82380 access and the internal Wait State Generator will automatically determine the required number of wait states. The CPURST will be active following the completion of the Write cycle to this port. This signal will last for 80 CLK2 periods. The 82380 should not be accessed until the CPURST is deactivated.

This internal port is Write-Only and the 82380 will not respond to a Read operation to this location. Also, during a CPU software reset command, the 82380 will reset its Slave-Bus state machine. However, its internal registers remain unchanged. This allows the operating system to distinguish a 'warm' reset by reading any 82380 internal register previously programmed for a non-default value. The Diagnostic registers can be used or this purpose (see Internal Control and Diagnostic Ports).

9.3 Shutdown Detect

The 82380 is constantly monitoring the Bus Cycle Definition signals (M/IO#, D/C#, R/W#) and is able to detect when the 80386 executes a Shutdown bus cycle. Upon detection of a processor shutdown, the 82380 will activate the CPURST output for 62 CLK2 periods to reset the host processor. This signal is generated after the Shutdown cycle is terminated by the READY# signal.

Although the 82380 Wait State Generator will not automatically respond to a Shutdown (or Halt) cycle, the Wait State Control inputs (WSC0, WSC1) can be used to determine the number of wait states in the same manner as other non-82380 bus cycle.

This Shutdown Detect feature can be enabled or disabled by writing a control bit in the Internal Control Port at address 61H (see Internal Control and Diagnostic Ports). This feature is disabled upon a hardware reset of the 82380. As in the case of Software Reset, the 82380 will reset its Slave-Bus state machine but will not change any of its internal register contents.

10.0 INTERNAL CONTROL AND DIAGNOSTIC PORTS

10.1 Internal Control Port

The format of the Internal Control Port of the 82380 is shown in Figure 10.1. This Control Port is used to enable/disable the Processor Shutdown Detect mechanism as well as controlling the Gate inputs of the Timer 2 and 3. Note that this is a Write-Only port. Therefore, the 82380 will not respond to a read operation to this port. Upon hardware reset, this port will be cleared; i.e., the Shutdown Detect feature and the Gate inputs of Timer 2 and 3 are disabled.

10.2 Diagnostic Ports

Two 8-bit read/write Diagnostic Ports are provided in the 82380. These are two storage registers and have no effect on the operation of the 82380. They can be used to store checkpoint data or error codes in the power-on sequence and in the diagnostic service routines. As mentioned in CPU RESET AND SHUTDOWN DETECT section, these Diagnostic Ports can be used to distinguish between 'cold' and 'warm' reset. Upon hardware reset, both Diagnostic Ports are cleared. The address map of these Diagnostic Ports is shown in Figure 10-2.

Port	Address
Diagnostic Port 1 (Read/Write)	80H
Diagnostic Port 2 (Read/Write)	88H

Figure 10-2. Address Map of Diagnostic Ports

Port Address: 61H (Write Only)

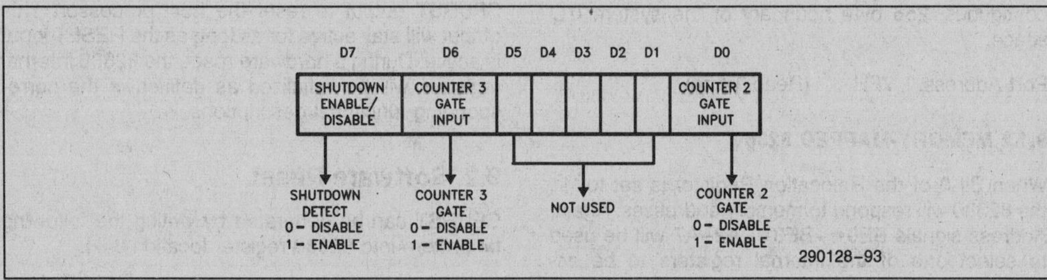

Figure 10-1. Internal Control Port

11.0 INTEL RESERVED I/O PORTS

There are eleven I/O ports in the 82380 address space which are reserved for Intel future peripheral device use only. Their address locations are: 2AH, 3DH, 3EH, 45H, 46H, 76H, 77H, 7DH, 7EH, CCH and CDH. These addresses should not be used in the system since the 82380 may respond to read/write operations to these locations and bus contention may occur if any peripheral is assigned to the same address location.

12.0 MECHANICAL DATA

12.1 Introduction

In this section, the physical package and its connections are described in detail.

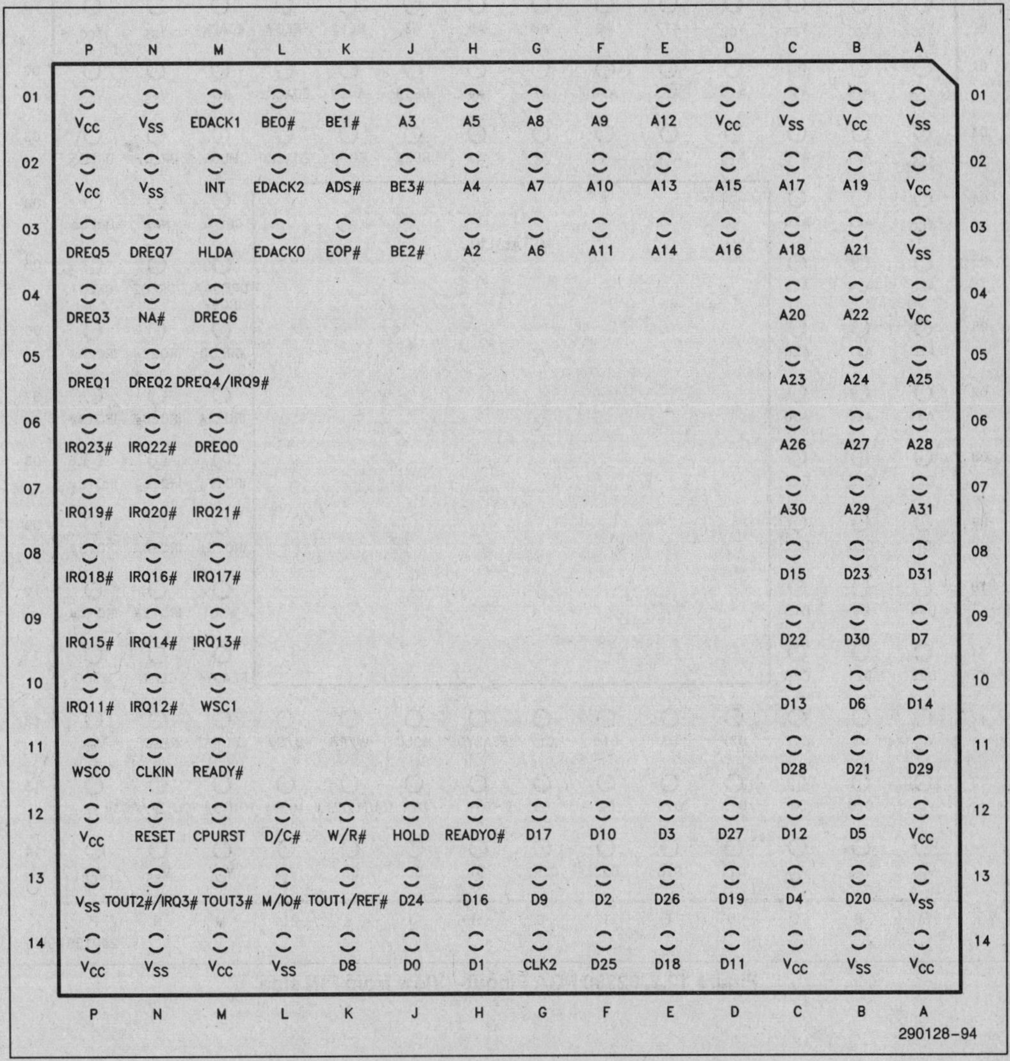

	P	N	M	L	K	J	H	G	F	E	D	C	B	A
01	V_{CC}	V_{SS}	EDACK1	BE0#	BE1#	A3	A5	A8	A9	A12	V_{CC}	V_{SS}	V_{CC}	V_{SS}
02	V_{CC}	V_{SS}	INT	EDACK2	ADS#	BE3#	A4	A7	A10	A13	A15	A17	A19	V_{CC}
03	DREQ5	DREQ7	HLDA	EDACK0	EOP#	BE2#	A2	A6	A11	A14	A16	A18	A21	V_{SS}
04	DREQ3	NA#	DREQ6									A20	A22	V_{CC}
05	DREQ1	DREQ2	DREQ4/IRQ9#									A23	A24	A25
06	IRQ23#	IRQ22#	DREQ0									A26	A27	A28
07	IRQ19#	IRQ20#	IRQ21#									A30	A29	A31
08	IRQ18#	IRQ16#	IRQ17#									D15	D23	D31
09	IRQ15#	IRQ14#	IRQ13#									D22	D30	D7
10	IRQ11#	IRQ12#	WSC1									D13	D6	D14
11	WSC0	CLKIN	READY#									D28	D21	D29
12	V_{CC}	RESET	CPURST	D/C#	W/R#	HOLD	READYO#	D17	D10	D3	D27	D12	D5	V_{CC}
13	V_{SS}	TOUT2#/IRQ3#	TOUT3#	M/IO#	TOUT1/REF#	D24	D16	D9	D2	D26	D19	D4	D20	V_{SS}
14	V_{CC}	V_{SS}	V_{CC}	V_{SS}	D8	D0	D1	CLK2	D25	D18	D11	V_{CC}	V_{SS}	V_{CC}

290128-94

Figure 12.1. 82380 PGA Pinout—View from TOP side

12.2 Pin Assignment

The 82380 pinout as viewed from the top side of the component is shown in Figure 12.1. Its pinout as viewed from the pin side of the component is shown in Figure 12.2.

V_{CC} and GND connections must be made to multiple V_{CC} and V_{SS} (GND) pins. Each V_{CC} and V_{SS} MUST be connected to the appropriate voltage level. The circuit board should include V_{CC} and GND planes for power distribution and all V_{CC} pins must be connected to the appropriate plane.

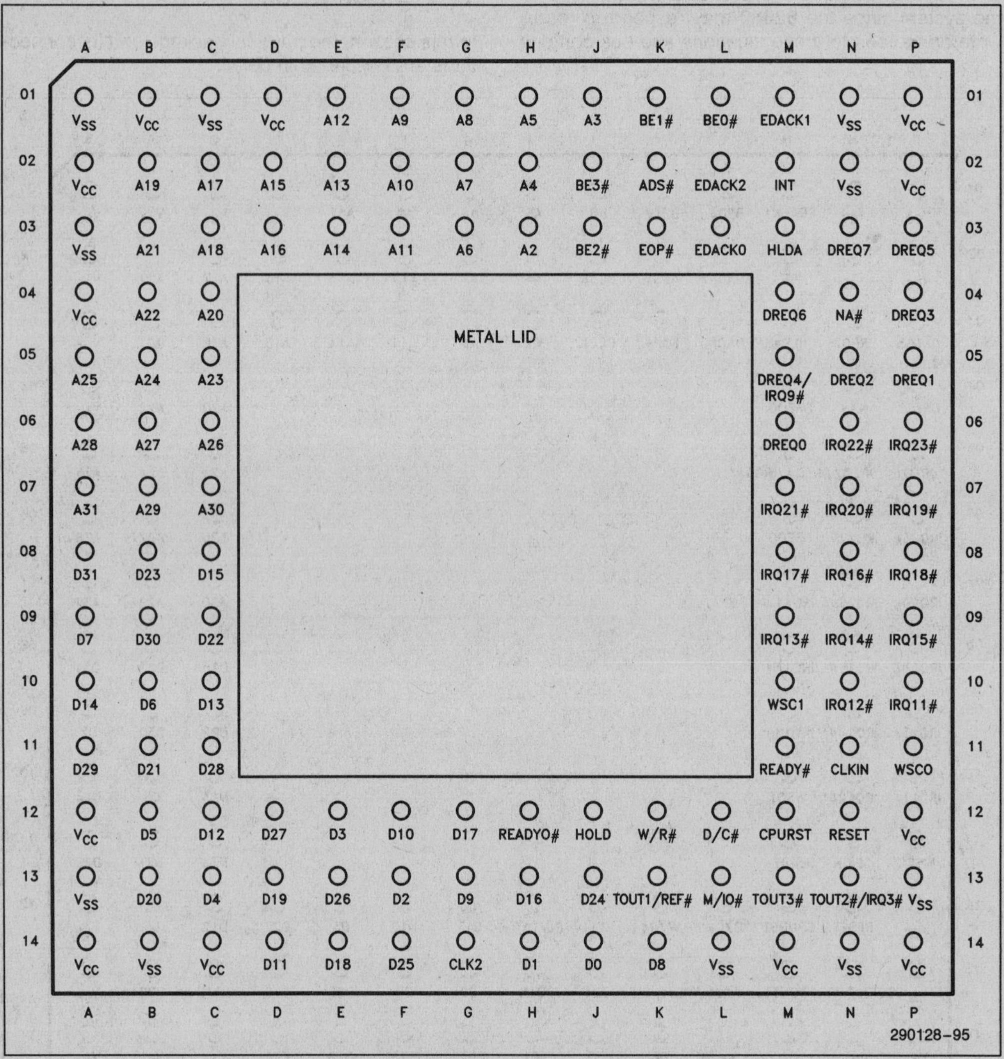

	A	B	C	D	E	F	G	H	J	K	L	M	N	P	
01	V_{SS}	V_{CC}	V_{SS}	V_{CC}	A12	A9	A8	A5	A3	BE1#	BE0#	EDACK1	V_{SS}	V_{CC}	01
02	V_{CC}	A19	A17	A15	A13	A10	A7	A4	BE3#	ADS#	EDACK2	INT	V_{SS}	V_{CC}	02
03	V_{SS}	A21	A18	A16	A14	A11	A6	A2	BE2#	EOP#	EDACK0	HLDA	DREQ7	DREQ5	03
04	V_{CC}	A22	A20									DREQ6	NA#	DREQ3	04
05	A25	A24	A23				METAL LID					DREQ4/ IRQ9#	DREQ2	DREQ1	05
06	A28	A27	A26									DREQ0	IRQ22#	IRQ23#	06
07	A31	A29	A30									IRQ21#	IRQ20#	IRQ19#	07
08	D31	D23	D15									IRQ17#	IRQ16#	IRQ18#	08
09	D7	D30	D22									IRQ13#	IRQ14#	IRQ15#	09
10	D14	D6	D13									WSC1	IRQ12#	IRQ11#	10
11	D29	D21	D28									READY#	CLKIN	WSC0	11
12	V_{CC}	D5	D12	D27	D3	D10	D17	READYO#	HOLD	W/R#	D/C#	CPURST	RESET	V_{CC}	12
13	V_{SS}	D20	D4	D19	D26	D2	D9	D16	D24	TOUT1/REF#	M/IO#	TOUT3#	TOUT2#/IRQ3#	V_{SS}	13
14	V_{CC}	V_{SS}	V_{CC}	D11	D18	D25	CLK2	D1	D0	D8	V_{SS}	V_{CC}	V_{SS}	V_{CC}	14
	A	B	C	D	E	F	G	H	J	K	L	M	N	P	

290128-95

Figure 12.2. 82380 PGA Pinout—View from PIN side

Table 12-1. 82380 PGA Pinout—Functional Grouping

Pin/Signal		Pin/Signal		Pin/Signal		Pin/Signal	
A7	A31	A8	D31	P12	V_{CC}	L14	V_{SS}
C7	A30	B9	D30	M14	V_{CC}	A1	V_{SS}
B7	A29	A11	D29	P1	V_{CC}	P13	V_{SS}
A6	A28	C11	D28	P2	V_{CC}	N1	V_{SS}
B6	A27	D12	D27	P14	V_{CC}	N2	V_{SS}
C6	A26	E13	D26	D1	V_{CC}	C1	V_{SS}
A5	A25	F14	D25	C14	V_{CC}	A3	V_{SS}
B5	A24	J13	D24	B1	V_{CC}	B14	V_{SS}
C5	A23	B8	D23	A2	V_{CC}	A13	V_{SS}
B4	A22	C9	D22	A4	V_{CC}	N14	V_{SS}
B3	A21	B11	D21	A12	V_{CC}		
C4	A20	B13	D20	A14	V_{CC}	P6	IRQ23#
B2	A19	D13	D19			N6	IRQ22#
C3	A18	E14	D18	G14	CLK2	M7	IRQ21#
C2	A17	G12	D17	L12	D/C#	N7	IRQ20#
D3	A16	H13	D16	K12	W/R#	P7	IRQ19#
D2	A15	C8	D15	L13	M/IO#	P8	IRQ18#
E3	A14	A10	D14	K2	ADS#	M8	IRQ17#
E2	A13	C10	D13	N4	NA#	N8	IRQ16#
E1	A12	C12	D12	J12	HOLD	P9	IRQ15#
F3	A11	D14	D11	M3	HLDA	N9	IRQ14#
F2	A10	F12	D10	M6	DREQ0	M9	IRQ13#
F1	A9	G13	D9	P5	DREQ1	N10	IRQ12#
G1	A8	K14	D8	N5	DREQ2	P10	IRQ11#
G2	A7	A9	D7	P4	DREQ3	M2	INT
G3	A6	B10	D6	M5	DREQ4/IRQ9#		
H1	A5	B12	D5	P3	DREQ5	N11	CLKIN
H2	A4	C13	D4	M4	DREQ6	K13	TOUT1/REF#
J1	A3	E12	D3	N3	DREQ7	N13	TOUT2#/IRQ3#
H3	A2	F13	D2			M13	TOUT3#
J2	BE3#	H14	D1	K3	EOP#	M11	READY#
J3	BE2#	J14	D0	L3	EDACK0	H12	READYO#
K1	BE1#			M1	EDACK1	P11	WSC0
L1	BE0#	N12	RESET	L2	EDACK2	M10	WSC1
		M12	CPURST				

12.3 Package Dimensions and Mounting

The 82380 package is a 132-pin ceramic Pin Grid Array (PGA). The pins are arranged 0.100 inch (2.54 mm) center-to-center, in a 14 x 14 matrix, three rows around.

A wide variety of available sockets allow low insertion force or zero insertion force mountings, and a choice of terminals such as soldertail, surface mount, or wire wrap. Several applicable sockets are listed in Figure 12-4.

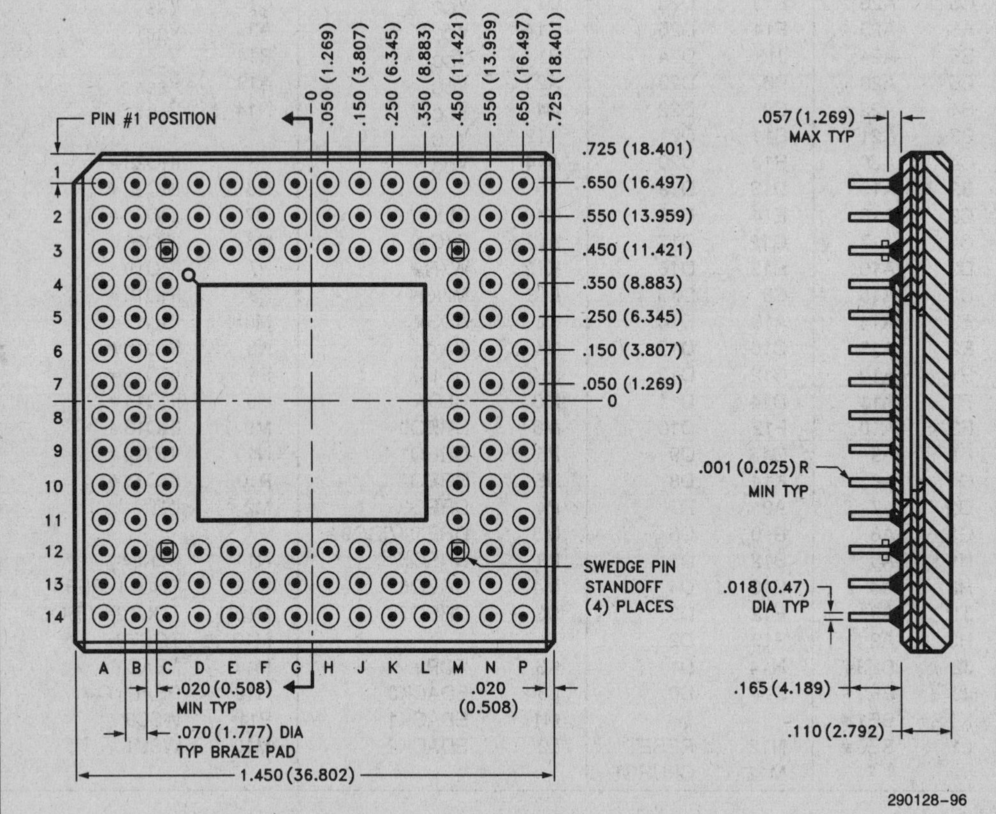

Figure 12.3. 132-Pin Ceramic PGA Package Dimensions

- Low insertion force (LIF) soldertail 55274-1
  - Amp tests indicate 50% reduction in insertion force compared to machined sockets

Other socket options
- Zero insertion force (ZIF) soldertail 55583-1
- Zero insertion force (ZIF) Burn-in version 55573-2

Amp Incorporated
(Harrisburg, PA 17105 U.S.A.
Phone 717-564-0100)

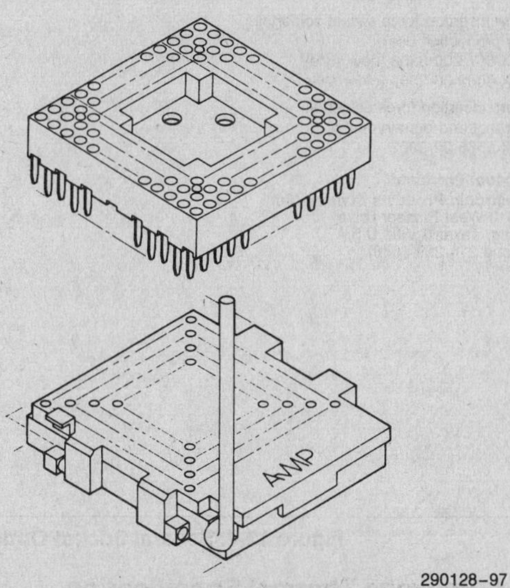

290128–97

Cam handle locks in low profile position when substrate is installed (handle UP for open and DOWN for closed positions)

courtesy Amp Incorporated

Peel-A-Way™ Mylar and Kapton Socket Terminal Carriers
- Low insertion force surface mount CS132-37TG
- Low insertion force soldertail CS132-01TG
- Low insertion force wire-wrap CS132-02TG (two level) CS132-03TG (three-level)
- Low insertion force press-fit CS132-05TG

Advanced Interconnections
(5 Division Street
Warwick, RI 02818 U.S.A.
Phone 401-885-0485)

Peel-A-Way Carrier No. 132;
Kapton Carrier is KS132
Mylar Carrier is MS132

Molded Plastic Body KS132 is shown below:

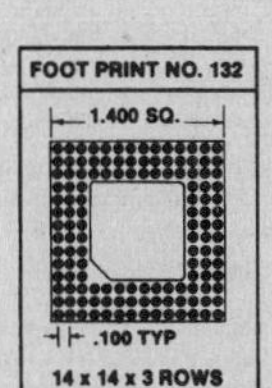

290128–98

SOLDER TAIL -01
4.19 / .165
3.17 / .125
.50 / .020 DIA.
MILLIMETER / INCH
LOW PROFILE -04
3.04 / .120
2.79 / .110
.736 / .029 DIA.
PRESS FIT -05
4.19 / .165
2.79 / .110
.91 / .036 DIA.
MTG. HOLE P.T.H.
WIRE WRAP -02/-03
4.82 / .190
9.14 / .360 -02 2 LEVEL
12.70 / .500 -03 3 LEVEL
SOLDER TAIL -33
PEEL-A-WAY
4.19 / .165
3.17 / .125
.50 / .020 DIA.
SURFACE MOUNTING -37
3.93 / .155

290128–99

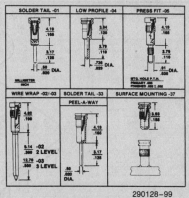

courtesy Advanced Interconnections
(Peel-A-Way Terminal Carriers
U.S. Patent No. 4442938)

Figure 12-4. Several Socket Options for 132-pin PGA

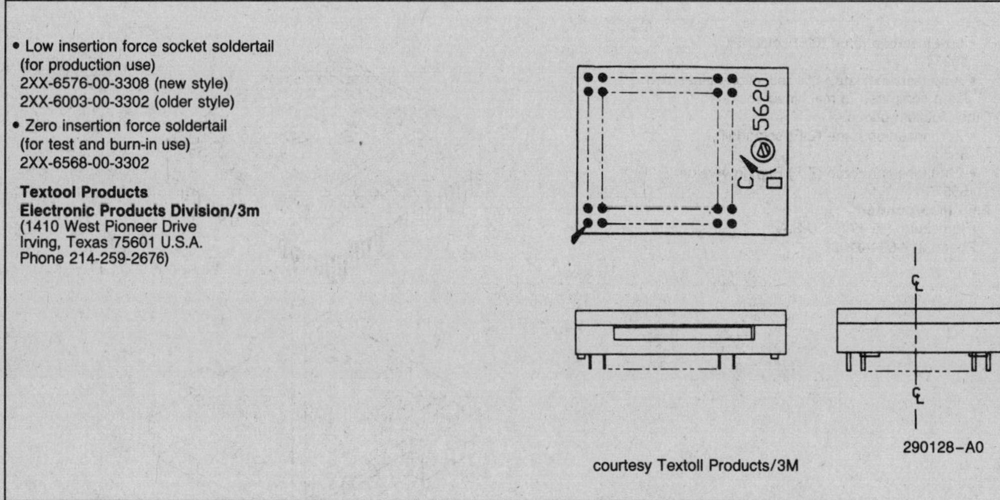

• Low insertion force socket soldertail
(for production use)
2XX-6576-00-3308 (new style)
2XX-6003-00-3302 (older style)
• Zero insertion force soldertail
(for test and burn-in use)
2XX-6568-00-3302
Textool Products
Electronic Products Division/3m
(1410 West Pioneer Drive
Irving, Texas 75601 U.S.A.
Phone 214-259-2676)
5620
courtesy Textoll Products/3M
290128–A0

Figure 12-4. Several Socket Options for 132-pin PGA (Continued)

12.4 Package Thermal Specification

The 82380 is specified for operation when case temperature is within the range of 0°C −85°C. The case temperature may be measured in any environment, to determine whether the 82380 is within the specified operating range.

The PGA case temperature should be measured at the center of the top surface opposite the pins, as in Figure 12.5.

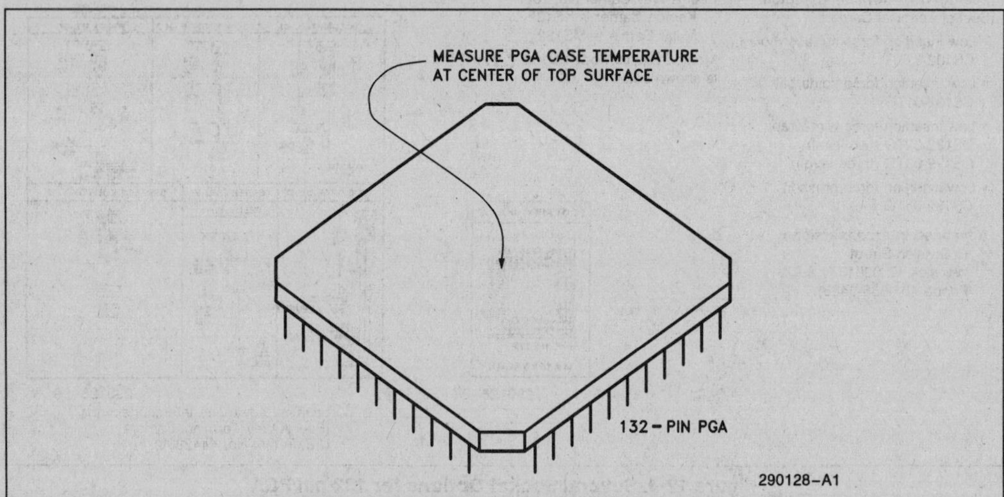

Figure 12.5. Measuring 82380 PGA Case Temperature

Thermal Resistance—°C/Watt							
	Airflow—f³/min (m³/sec)						
Parameter	0 (0)	50 (0.25)	100 (0.50)	200 (1.01)	400 (2.03)	600 (3.04)	800 (4.06)
θ Junction-to-Case (case measured as Fig. 6.4)	2	2	2	2	2	2	2
θ Case-to-Ambient (no heatsink)	19	18	17	15	12	10	9
θ Case-to-Ambient (with omnidirectional heatsink)	16	15	14	12	9	7	6
θ Case-to-Ambient (with unidirectional heatsink)	15	14	13	11	8	6	5

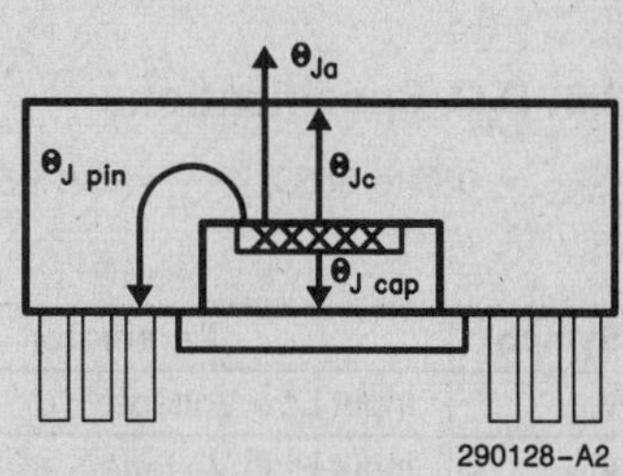

NOTES:
1. Table 12-6 applies to 82380 PGA plugged into socket or soldered directly into board.
2. $\theta_{JA} = \theta_{JC} + \theta_{CA}$.
3. $\theta_{J\text{-}CAP}$ = 4°C/W (approx.)
   $\theta_{J\text{-}PIN}$ = 4°C/W (inner pins) (approx.)
   $\theta_{J\text{-}PIN}$ = 8°C/W (outer pins) (approx.)

Figure 12-6. 82380 PGA Package Typical Thermal Characteristics

4

13.0 ELECTRICAL DATA

13.1 Power and Grounding

The large number of output buffers (address, data and control) can cause power surges as multiple output buffers drive new signal levels simultaneously. The 22 V_{CC} and V_{SS} pins of the 82380 each feed separate functional units to minimize switching induced noise effects. All V_{CC} pins of the 82380 must be connected on the circuit board.

13.2 Power Decoupling

Liberal decoupling capacitance should be placed close to the 82380. The 82380 driving its 32-bit parallel address and data buses at high frequencies can cause transient power surges when driving large capacitive loads. Low inductance capacitors and interconnects are recommended for the best reliability at high frequencies. Low inductance capacitors are available specifically for Pin Grid Array packages.

13.3 Unused Pin Recommendations

For reliable operation, ALWAYS connect unused inputs to a valid logic level. As is the case with most other CMOS processes, a floating input will increase the current consumption of the component and give an indeterminate state to the component.

13.4 ICE-386 Support

The 82380 specifications provide sufficient drive capability to support the ICE386. On the pins that are generally shared between the 80386 and the 82380, the additional loading represented by the ICE386 was allowed for in the design of the 82380.

13.5 Maximum Ratings

Storage Temperature .... −65°C to +150°C
Case temperature Under Bias ... −65°C to +110°C
Supply Voltage with Respect to V_{SS} .... −0.5V to +6.5V
Voltage on any other Pin ..... −0.5V to V_{CC} +0.5V

NOTE:
Stress above those listed above may cause permanent damage to the device. This is a stress rating only and functional operation at these or any other conditions above those listed in the operational sections of this specification is not implied.

Exposure to absolute maximum rating conditions for extended periods may affect device reliability. Although the 82380 contains protective circuitry to reset damage from static electric discharges, always take precautions against high static voltages or electric fields.

13.6 D.C. Specifications

T_{CASE} = 0°C to 85°C; V_{CC} = 5V ±5%; V_{SS} = 0V.

Table 13-1.

Symbol	Parameter	Min	Max	Unit	Notes
V_{IL}	Input Low Voltage	−0.3	0.8	V	(Note 1)
V_{IH}	Input High Voltage	2.0	V_{CC} + 0.3	V	
V_{ILC}	CLK2 Input Low Voltage	−0.3	0.8		(Note 1)
V_{IHC}	CLK2 Input High Voltage	V_{CC} − 0.8	V_{CC} + 0.3	V	
V_{OL}	Output Low Voltage I_{OL} = 4 mA: A2–A31, D0–D31 I_{OL} = 5 mA: All Others		 0.45 0.45	 V V	
V_{OH}	Output High Voltage I_{OH} = −1 mA: A2–A31, D0–D31 I_{OH} = −0.9 mA: All Others	 2.4 2.4		 V V	
I_{LI}	Input Leakage Current for all ins except: IRQ11#–IRQ23#, TOUT2/IRQ3#, EOP#, DREQ4		±15	µA	0V<V_{IN}<V_{CC}
I_{LI1}	Input Leakage Current for pins: IRQ11#–IRQ23#, TOUT2#/IRQ3#, EOP#, DREQ4	10	−300	µA	0V<V_{IN}<V_{CC} (Note 3)
I_{LO}	Output Leakage Current		±15	µA	0.45<V_{OUT}<V_{CC}
I_{CC}	Supply Current		300 325	mA mA	CLK2 = 32 MHz = 40 MHz (Note 4)
(CAP)	Capacitance (Input/IO)		12	pF	f_c = 1 MHz (Note 2)
CCLK	CLK2 Capacitance		20	pF	f_c = 1 MHz (Note 2)

NOTES:
1. Minimum value is not 100% tested.
2. Sampled only.
3. These pins have internal pullups on them.
4. I_{CC} is specified with inputs driven to CMOS levels. I_{CC} may be higher if driven to TTL levels.

13.6 D.C. Specifications (Continued)

T_{CASE} = 0°C to 85°C; V_{CC} = 5V ±5%; V_{SS} = 0V.

Table 13-2. 82380-25 D.C. Specifications

Symbol	Parameter	Min	Max	Unit	Notes
V_{IL}	Input Low Voltage	−0.3	0.8	V	(Note 1)
V_{IH}	Input High Voltage	2.0	V_{CC} + 0.3	V	
V_{ILC}	CLK2 Input Low Voltage	−0.3	0.8	V	(Note 1)
V_{IHC}	CLK2 Input High Voltage	V_{CC} − 0.8	V_{CC} + 0.3	V	
V_{OL}	Output Low Voltage I_{OL} = 4 mA: A_2–A_{31}, D_0–D_{31} I_{OL} = 5 mA: All Others		 0.45 0.45	 V V	
V_{OH}	Output High Voltage I_{OH} = −1 mA: A_2–A_{31}, D_0–D_{31} I_{OH} = −0.9 mA: All Others	 2.4 2.4		 V V	
I_{LI}	Input Leakage Current All Inputs except: IRQ11#–IRQ23#, EOP#, TOUT2/IRQ3#, DREQ4		±15	μA	
I_{LI1}	Input Leakage Current Inputs: IRQ11#–IRQ23#, EOP#, TOUT2/IRQ3#, DREQ4	10	−300	μA	0 < V_{IN} < V_{CC} (Note 3)
I_{LO}	Output Leakage Current		±15	μA	0 < V_{IN} < V_{CC}
I_{CC}	Supply Current (CLK2 = 50 MHz)		375	mA	(Note 4)
C_I	Input Capacitance		12	pF	(Note 2)
C_{CLK}	CLK2 Input Capacitance		20	pF	(Note 2)

NOTES:
1. Minimum value is not 100% tested.
2. f_C = 1 MHz; Sampled only.
3. These pins have weak internal pullups. They should not be left floating.
4. I_{CC} is specified with inputs driven to CMOS levels, and outputs driving CMOS loads. I_{CC} may be higher if inputs are driven to TTL levels, or if outputs are driving TTL loads.

4

13.7 A.C. Specifications

The A.C. specifications given in the following tables consist of output delays and input setup requirements. The A.C. diagram's purpose is to illustrate the clock edges from which the timing parameters are measured. The reader should not infer any other timing relationships from them. For specific information on timing relationships between signals, refer to the appropriate functional section.

A.C. spec measurement is defined in Figure 13.1. Inputs must be driven to the levels shown when A.C. specifications are measured. 82380 output delays are specified with minimum and maximum limits, which are measured as shown. The minimum 82380 output delay times are hold times for external circuitry. 82380 input setup and hold times are specified as minimums and define the smallest acceptable sampling window. Within the sampling window, a synchronous input signal must be stable for correct 82380 operation.

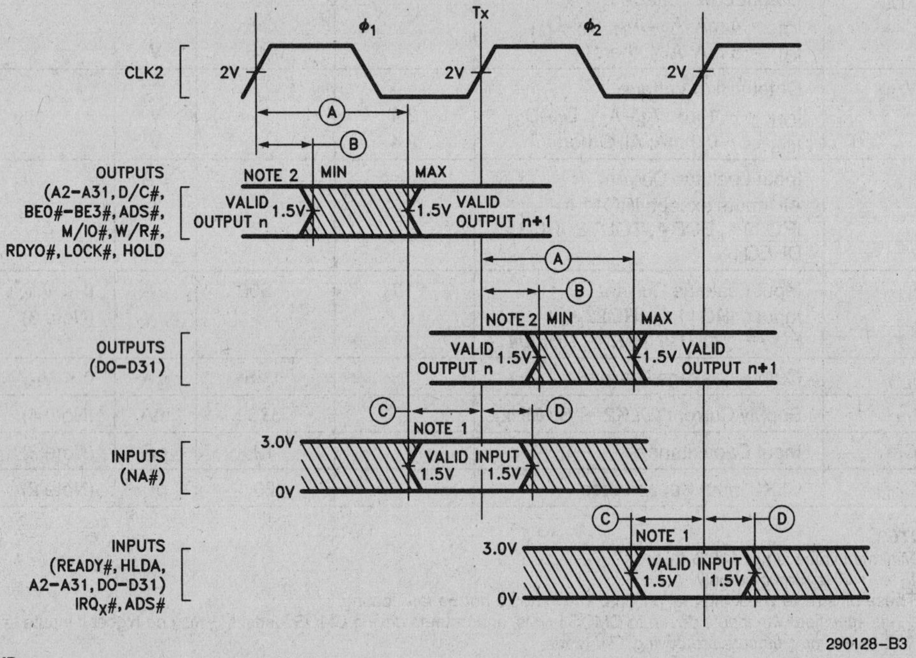

LEGEND:
- Ⓐ—maximum output delay spec
- Ⓑ—minimum output delay spec
- Ⓒ—minimum input setup spec
- Ⓓ—minimum input hold spec

NOTES:
1. Input waveforms have tr ≤ 2.0 ns from 0.8V to 2.0V.
2. Under rated loading (120 pF) 82380 output tr, tf is typically ≤ 4.0 ns from 0.8V to 2.0V.

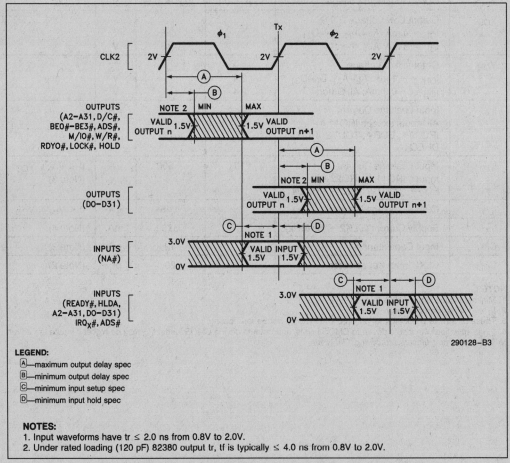

Figure 13-1. Drive Levels and Measurement Points for A.C. Specification

A.C. SPECIFICATION TABLES

Functional Operating Range: V_{CC} = 5V ±5%; T_{CASE} = 0°C to +85°C

Table 13-3. 82380 A.C. Characteristics

Symbol	Parameter	82380-16		82380-20		Notes
		Min	Max	Min	Max	
	Operating Frequency	4 MHz	16 MHz	4 MHz	20 MHz	Half CLK2 Frequency
t1	CLK2 Period	31 ns	125 ns	25 ns	125 ns	
t2a	CLK2 High Time	9		8		at 2.0V
t2b	CLK2 High Time	5		5		at (V_{CC}−0.8)V
t3a	CLK2 Low Time	9		8		at 2.0V
t3b	CLK2 Low Time	7		6		at 0.8V
t4	CLK2 Fall Time		8		8	(V_{CC}−0.8)V to 0.8V
t5	CLK2 Rise Time		8		8	0.8V to (V_{CC}−0.8)V
	A (2–31), BE (0–3) #, EDACK (0–2)					
t6	Valid Delay	4	36	4	30	CL = 120 pF
t7	Float Delay	4	40	4	32	(Note 1)
	A (2–31), BE (0–3) #					
t8	Setup Time	6		6		
t9	Hold Time	4		4		
	W/R#, M/IO#, D/C#,					
t10	Valid Delay	6	33	6	28	CL = 75 pF
t11	Float Delay	4	35	4	30	(Note 1)
t12	Setup Time	6		6		
t13	Hold Time	4		4		
t14	ADS# Valid Delay	6	33	6	28	CL = 75 pF
t15	Float Delay	4	35	4	30	
t16	Setup Time	21		15		
t17	Hold Time	4		4		
	Slave Mode— D(0–31) Read					
t18	Valid Delay	3	46	4	46	CL = 120 pF
t19	Float Delay	6	35	6	29	(Note 1)
	Slave Mode— D(0–31) Write					
t20	Setup Time	31		29		
t21	Hold Time	26		26		

4

A.C. SPECIFICATION TABLES (Continued)

Functional Operating Range: V_{CC} = 5V ±5%; T_{CASE} = 0°C to +85°C.

Table 13-3. 82380 A.C. Characteristics (Continued)

Symbol	Parameter	82380-16		82380-20		Notes
		Min	Max	Min	Max	
	Master Mode— D(0–31) Write					
t22	Valid Delay	4	48	4	38	CL = 120 pF
t23	Float Delay	4	35	4	27	(Note 1)
	Master Mode— D(0–31) Read					
t24	Setup Time	11		11		
t25	Hold Time	6		6		
t26	READY# Setup Time	21		12		
t27	Hold Time	4		4		
t28	WSC (0–1) Setup	6		6		
t29	Hold	21		21		
t31	RESET Setup Time	13		12		
t30	Hold Time	4		4		
t32	READYO# Valid Delay	4	31	4	23	CL = 25 pF
t33	CPU Reset From CLK2	2	18	2	16	CL = 50 pF
t34	HOLD Valid Delay	5	33	5	30	CL = 100 pF
t35	HLDA Setup Time	21		17		
t36	Hold Time	6		6		
t37a	EOP# Setup Time	21		17		Synch. EOP
t38a	EOP# Hold Time	4		4		
t37b	EOP# Setup Time	11		11		Asynch. EOP
t38b	EOP# Hold Time	11		11		
t39	EOP# Valid Delay	5	38	5	30	CL = 100 pF ('1'->'0')
t40	EOP# Float Delay	5	40	5	32	
t41a	DREQ Setup Time	21		19		Synchronous DREQ
t42a	Hold Time	4		4		
t41b	DREQ Setup Time	11		11		Asynchronous DREQ
t42b	Hold Time	11		11		
t43	INT Valid Delay		500		500	From IRQ Input CL = 75 pF
t44	NA# Setup Time	11		10		
t45	Hold Time	15		15		

A.C. SPECIFICATION TABLES (Continued)

Functional Operating Range: V_{CC} = 5V ±5%; T_{CASE} = 0°C to +85°C.

Table 13-3. 82380 A.C. Characteristics (Continued)

Symbol	Parameter	82380-16		82380-20		Notes
		Min	Max	Min	Max	
t46	CLKIN Frequency	0 MHz	10 MHz	0 MHz	10 MHz	
t47	CLKIN High Time	30		30		At 1.5V
t48	CLKIN Low Time	50		50		At 1.5V
t49	CLKIN Rise Time		10		10	0.8V to 3.7V
t50	CLKIN Fall Time		10		10	3.7V to 0.8V
t51	TOUT1/REF# Valid	4	36	4	30	From CLK2, CL = 25 pF
t52	TOUT1/REF# Valid	3	93	3	93	From CLKIN, CL = 120 pF
t53	TOUT2# Valid Delay	3	93	3	93	From CLKIN, CL = 120 pF (Falling Edge Only)
t54	TOUT2# Float Delay	3	40	3	40	From CLKIN (Note 1)
t55	TOUT3# Valid Delay	3	93	3	93	From CLKIN, CL = 120 pF

NOTE:
1. Float condition occurs when the maximum output current becomes less than ILO in magnitude. Float delay is not tested. For testing purposes, the float condition occurs when the dynamic output driven voltage changes with current loads.

4

Functional Operating Range: V_{CC} = 5V ±5%; T_{CASE} = 0°C to +85°C.
A.C. timings are tested at 1.5V thresholds; except as noted.

Table 13-4. 82380-25 A.C. Characteristics

Symbol	Parameter	82380-25		Unit	Notes
		Min	Max		
	Operating Frequency 1/(t1a × 2)	4	25	MHz	
t1	CLK2 Period	20	125	ns	
t2a	CLK2 High Time	7		ns	at 2.0V
t2b	CLK2 High Time	4		ns	at 3.7V
t3a	CLK2 Low Time	7		ns	at 2.0V
t3b	CLK2 Low Time	4		ns	at 0.8V
t4	CLK2 Fall Time		7	ns	3.7V to 0.8V
t5	CLK2 Rise Time		7	ns	0.8V to 3.7V
t6	A2–A31, BE0#–BE3# EDACK0–EDACK3 Valid Delay	4	20	ns	50 pF Load
t7	A2–A31, BE0#–BE3# EDACK0–EDACK3 Float Delay	4	27	ns	50 pF Load
t8	A2–A31, BE0#–BE3# Setup Time	6		ns	
t9	A2–A31, BE0#–BE3# Hold Time	4		ns	
t10	W/R#, M/IO#, D/C# Valid Delay	4	20	ns	50 pF Load
t11	W/R#, M/IO#, D/C# Float Delay	4	29	ns	50 pF Load

A.C. SPECIFICATION TABLES (Continued)

Functional Operating Range: V_{CC} = 5V ±5%; T_{CASE} = 0°C to +85°C.

A.C. timings are tested at 1.5V thresholds; except as noted.

Table 13-4. 82380-25 A.C. Characteristics (Continued)

Symbol	Parameter	82380-25		Unit	Notes
		Min	Max		
t12	W/R#, M/IO#, D/C# Setup Time	6		ns	
t13	W/R#, M/IO#, D/C# Hold Time	4		ns	
t14	ADS# Valid Delay	4	19	ns	50 pF Load
t15	ADS# Float Delay	4	29	ns	50 pF Load
t16	ADS# Setup Time	12		ns	
t17	ADS# Hold Time	4		ns	
t18	Slave Mode D0–D31 Read Valid	4	31	ns	50 pF Load
t19	Slave Mode D0–D31 Read Float	6	21	ns	50 pF Load
t20	Slave Mode D0–D31 Write Setup	20		ns	
t21	Slave Mode D0–D31 Write Hold	20		ns	
t22	Master Mode D0–D31 Write Valid	8	27	ns	50 pF Load
t23	Master Mode D0–D31 Write Float	4	19	ns	50 pF Load
t24	Master Mode D0–D31 Read Setup	7		ns	
t25	Master Mode D0–D31 Read Hold	4		ns	
t26	READY# Setup Time	9		ns	
t27	READY# Hold Time	4		ns	
t28	WSC0–WSC1 Setup Time	6		ns	
t29	WSC0–WSC1 Hold Time	15		ns	
t30	RESET Hold Time	4		ns	
t31	RESET Setup Time	9		ns	
t32	READYO# Valid Delay	3	21	ns	25 pF Load
t33	CPURST Valid Delay	2	14	ns	50 pF Load
t34	HOLD Valid Delay	4	22	ns	50 pF Load
t35	HLDA Setup Time	17		ns	
t36	HLDA Hold Time	4		ns	
t37a	EOP# Setup (Synchronous)	13		ns	
t38a	EOP# Hold (Synchronous)	4		ns	
t37b	EOP# Setup (Asynchronous)	10		ns	
t38b	EOP# Hold (Asynchronous)	10		ns	
t39	EOP# Valid Delay	4	21	ns	50 pF Load
t40	EOP# Float Delay	4	21	ns	50 pF Load
t41a	DREQ Setup (Synchronous)	17		ns	
t42a	DREQ Hold (Synchronous)	4		ns	
t41b	DREQ Setup (Asynchronous)	10		ns	
t42b	DREQ Hold (Asynchronous)	10		ns	
t43	INT Valid Delay from IRQn		500	ns	50 pF Load

A.C. SPECIFICATION TABLES (Continued)

Functional Operating Range: V_{CC} = 5V ±5%; T_{CASE} = 0°C to +85°C.
A.C. timings are tested at 1.5V thresholds; except as noted.

Table 13-4. 82380-25 A.C. Characteristics (Continued)

Symbol	Parameter	82380-25		Unit	Notes
		Min	Max		
t44	NA# Setup Time	7		ns	
t45	NA# Hold Time	8		ns	
t46	CLKIN Frequency	0	10	MHz	
t47	CLKIN High Time	30		ns	2.0V
t48	CLKIN Low Time	50		ns	0.8V
t49	CLKIN Rise Time		10	ns	0.8V to 3.7V
t50	CLKIN Fall Time		10	ns	3.7V to 0.8V
	TOUT1/REF# Valid Delay				
t51	from CLK2 (Refresh)	4	20	ns	50 pF Load
t52	from CLKIN (Timer)	3	90	ns	50 pF Load
t53	TOUT2# Valid Delay (Falling Edge Only)	3	90	ns	50 pF Load
t54	TOUT2# Float Delay	3	37	ns	50 pF Load
t55	TOUT3# Valid Delay	3	90	ns	50 pF Load

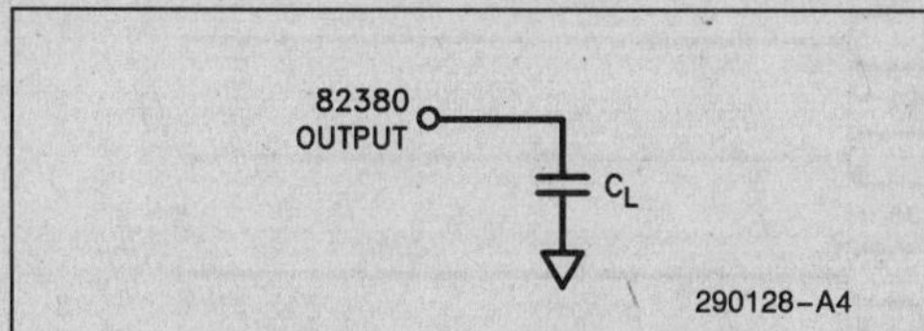

Figure 13-2. A.C. Test Load

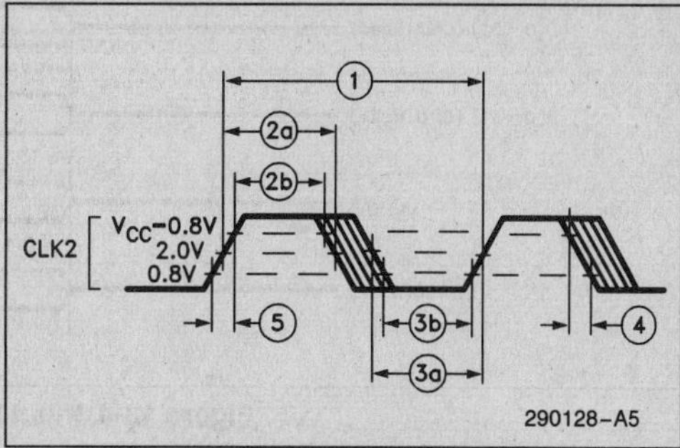

Figure 13-3. CLK2 Timing

4

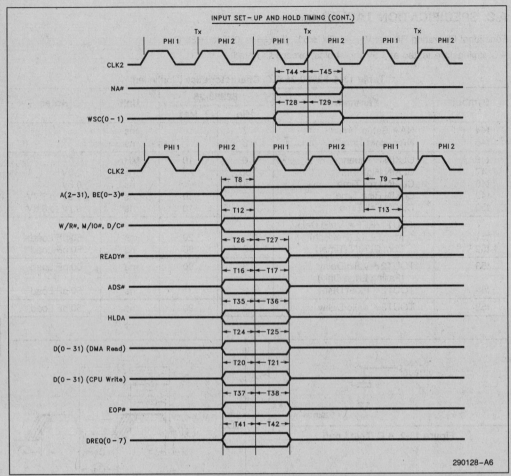

Figure 13-4. Input Setup and Hold Timing

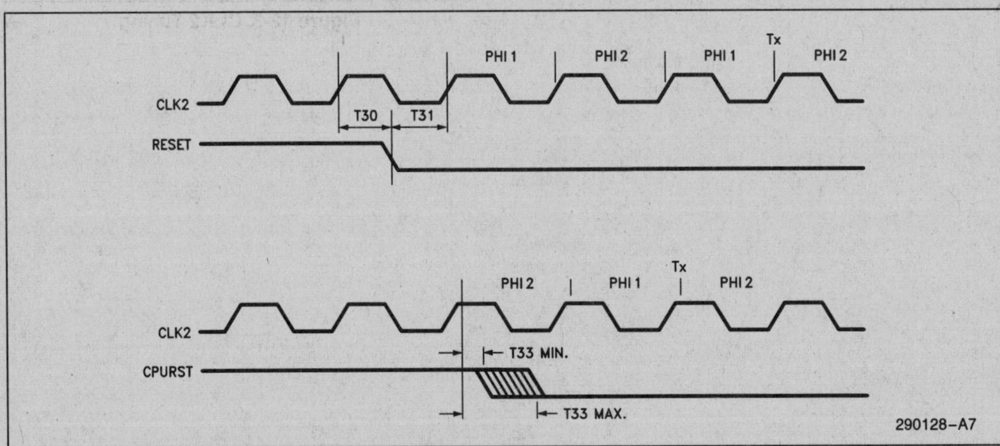

Figure 13-5. Reset Timing

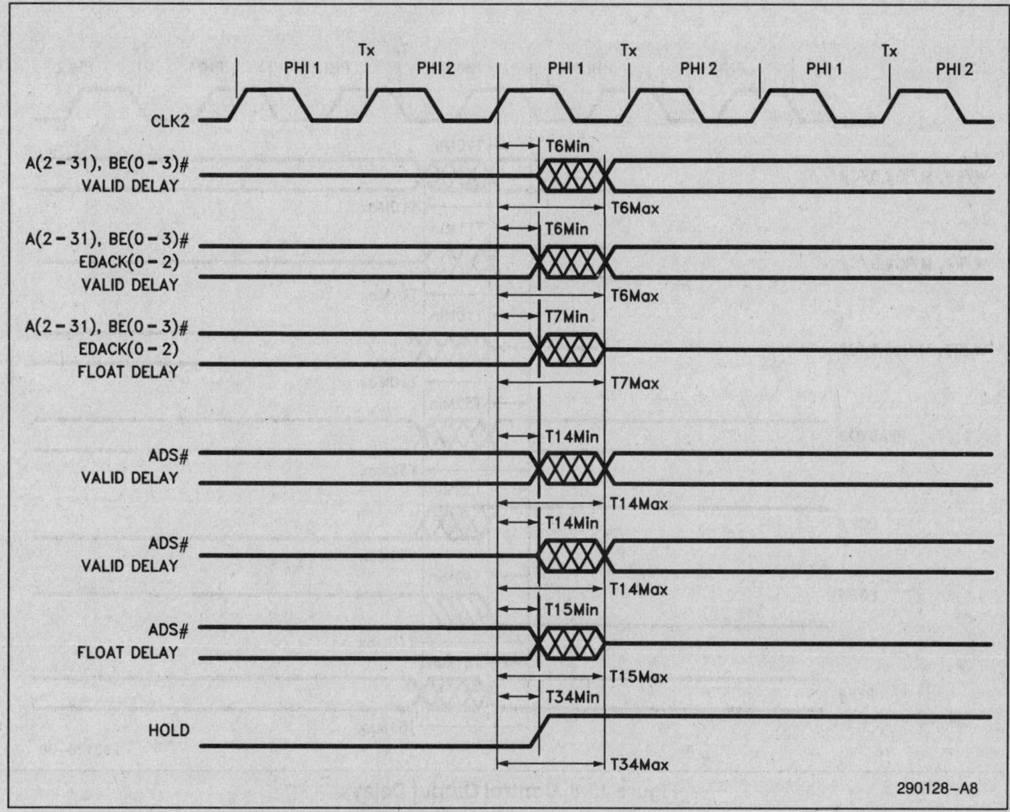

Tx Tx Tx
PHI 1 PHI 2 PHI 1 PHI 2 PHI 1 PHI 2
CLK2
A(2–31), BE(0–3)# VALID DELAY
T6Min
T6Max
A(2–31), BE(0–3)# EDACK(0–2) VALID DELAY
T6Min
T6Max
A(2–31), BE(0–3)# EDACK(0–2) FLOAT DELAY
T7Min
T7Max
ADS# VALID DELAY
T14Min
T14Max
ADS# VALID DELAY
T14Min
T14Max
ADS# FLOAT DELAY
T15Min
T15Max
HOLD
T34Min
T34Max
290128–A8

Figure 13-6. Address Output Delays

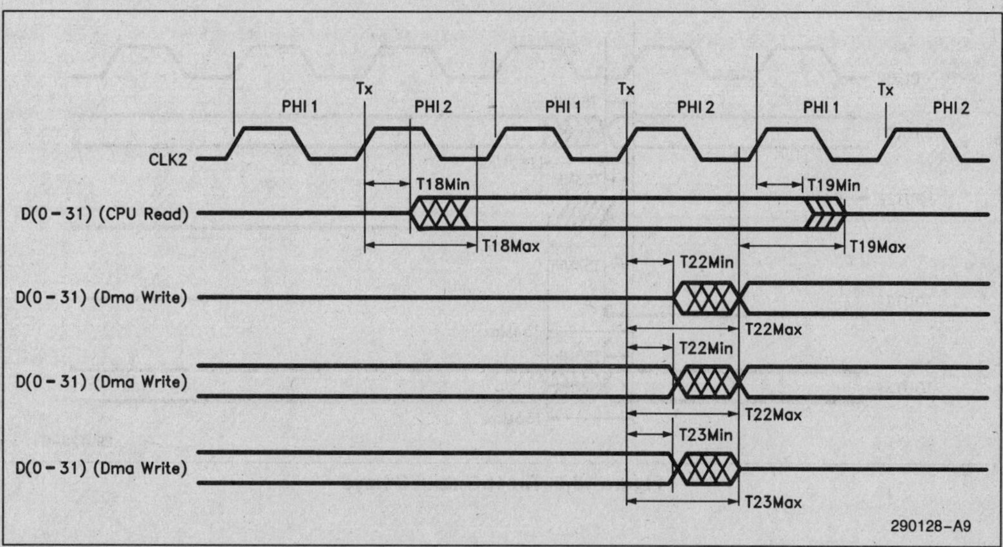

Figure 13-7. Data Bus Output Delays

4

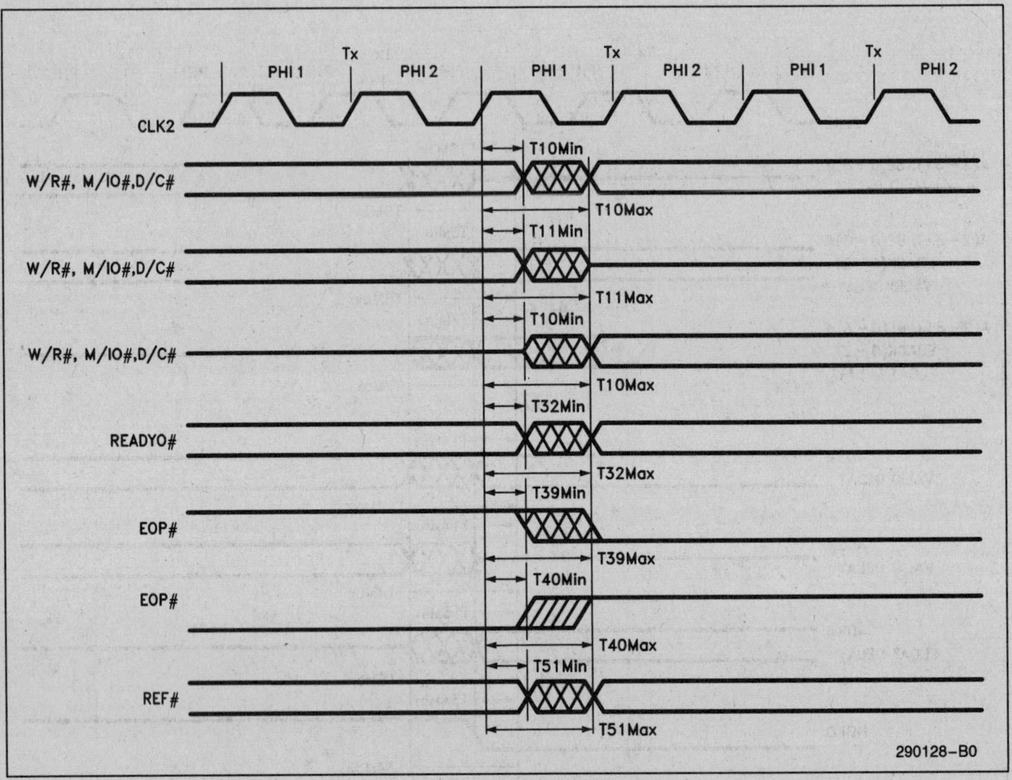

Tx Tx Tx
PHI 1 PHI 2 PHI 1 PHI 2 PHI 1 PHI 2
CLK2
W/R#, M/IO#,D/C#
T10Min
T10Max
W/R#, M/IO#,D/C#
T11Min
T11Max
W/R#, M/IO#,D/C#
T10Min
T10Max
READYO#
T32Min
T32Max
EOP#
T39Min
T39Max
EOP#
T40Min
T40Max
REF#
T51Min
T51Max
290128–B0

Figure 13-8. Control Output Delays

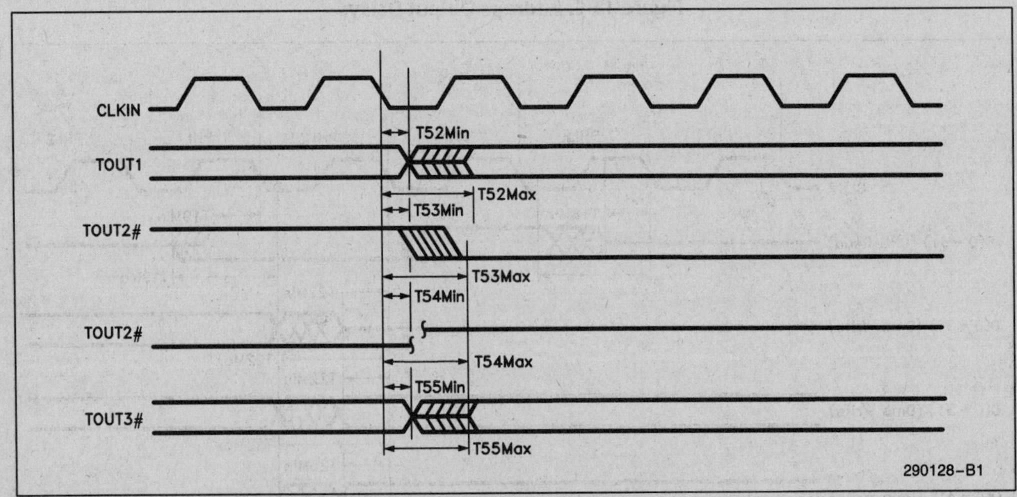

Figure 13-9. Timer Output Delays

APPENDIX A
Ports Listed by Address

Port Address (HEX)	Description
00	Read/Write DMA Channel 0 Target Address, A0–A15
01	Read/Write DMA Channel 0 Byte Count, B0–B15
02	Read/Write DMA Channel 1 Target Address, A0–A15
03	Read/Write DMA Channel 1 Byte Count, B0–B15
04	Read/Write DMA Channel 2 Target Address, A0–A15
05	Read/Write DMA Channel 2 Byte Count, B0–B15
06	Read/Write DMA Channel 3 Target Address, A0–A15
07	Read/Write DMA Channel 3 Byte Count, B0–B15
08	Read/Write DMA Channel 0–3 Status/Command I Register
09	Read/Write DMA Channel 0–3 Software Request Register
0A	Write DMA Channel 0–3 Set-Reset Mask Register
0B	Write DMA Channel 0–3 Mode Register I
0C	Write Clear Byte-Pointer FF
0D	Write DMA Master-Clear
0E	Write DMA Channel 0–3 Clear Mask Register
0F	Read/Write DMA Channel 0–3 Mask Register
10	Read/Write DMA Channel 0 Target Address, A24–A31
11	Read/Write DMA Channel 0 Byte Count, B16–B23
12	Read/Write DMA Channel 1 Target Address, A24–A31
13	Read/Write DMA Channel 1 Byte Count, B16–B23
14	Read/Write DMA Channel 2 Target Address, A24–A31
15	Read/Write DMA Channel 2 Byte Count, B16–B23
16	Read/Write DMA Channel 3 Target Address, A24–A31
17	Read/Write DMA Channel 3 Byte Count, B16–B23
18	Write DMA Channel 0–3 Bus Size Register
19	Read/Write DMA Channel 0–3 Chaining Register
1A	Write DMA Channel 0–3 Command Register II
1B	Write DMA Channel 0–3 Mode Register II
1C	Read/Write Refresh Control Register
1E	Reset Software Request Interrupt
20	Write Bank B ICW1, OCW2, or OCW3 Read Bank B Poll, Interrupt Request or In-Service Status Register
21	Write Bank B ICW2, ICW3, ICW4 or OCW1 Read Bank B Interrupt Mask Register
22	Read Bank B ICW2
28	Read/Write IRQ8 Vector Register
29	Read/Write IRQ9 Vector Register
2A	Reserved
2B	Read/Write IRQ11 Vector Register
2C	Read/Write IRQ12 Vector Register
2D	Read/Write IRQ13 Vector Register
2E	Read/Write IRQ14 Vector Register
2F	Read/Write IRQ15 Vector Register

4

APPENDIX A—Ports Listed by Address (Continued)

Port Address (HEX)	Description
30	Write Bank A ICW1, OCW2 or OCW3 Read Bank A Poll, Interrupt Request or In-Service Status Register
31	Write Bank A ICW2, ICW3, ICW4 or OCW1 Read Bank A Interrupt Mask Register
32	Read Bank A ICW2
38	Read/Write IRQ0 Vector Register
39	Read/Write IRQ1 Vector Register
3A	Read/Write IRQ1.5 Vector Register
3B	Read/Write IRQ3 Vector Register
3C	Read/Write IRQ4 Vector Register
3D	Reserved
3E	Reserved
3F	Read/Write IRQ7 Vector Register
40	Read/Write Counter 0 Register
41	Read/Write Counter 1 Register
42	Read/Write Counter 2 Register
43	Write Control Word Register I—Counter 0, 1, 2
44	Read/Write Counter 3 Register
45	Reserved
46	Reserved
47	Write Word Register II—Counter 3
61	Write Internal Control Port
64	Write CPU Reset Register (Data-1111XXX0H)
72	Read/Write Wait State Register 0
73	Read/Write Wait State Register 1
74	Read/Write Wait State Register 2
75	Read/Write Refresh Wait State Register
76	Reserved
77	Reserved
7D	Reserved
7E	Reserved
7F	Read/Write Relocation Register
80	Read/Write Internal Diagnostic Port 0
81	Read/Write DMA Channel 2 Target Address, A16–A23
82	Read/Write DMA Channel 3 Target Address, A16–A23
83	Read/Write DMA Channel 1 Target Address, A16–A23
87	Read/Write DMA Channel 0 Target Address, A16–A23
88	Read/Write Internal Diagnostic Port 1
89	Read/Write DMA Channel 6 Target Address, A16–A23
8A	Read/Write DMA Channel 7 Target Address, A16–A23
8B	Read/Write DMA Channel 5 Target Address, A16–A23
8F	Read/Write DMA Channel 4 Target Address, A16–A23

APPENDIX A—Ports Listed by Address (Continued)

Port Address (HEX)	Description
90	Read/Write DMA Channel 0 Requester Address, A0–A15
91	Read/Write DMA Channel 0 Requester Address, A16–A31
92	Read/Write DMA Channel 1 Requester Address, A0–A15
93	Read/Write DMA Channel 1 Requester Address, A16–A31
94	Read/Write DMA Channel 2 Requester Address, A0–A15
95	Read/Write DMA Channel 2 Requester Address, A16–A31
96	Read/Write DMA Channel 3 Requester Address, A0–A15
97	Read/Write DMA Channel 3 Requester Address, A16–A31
98	Read/Write DMA Channel 4 Requester Address, A0–A15
99	Read/Write DMA Channel 4 Requester Address, A16–A31
9A	Read/Write DMA Channel 5 Requester Address, A0–A15
9B	Read/Write DMA Channel 5 Requester Address, A16–A31
9C	Read/Write DMA Channel 6 Requester Address, A0–A15
9D	Read/Write DMA Channel 6 Requester Address, A16–A31
9E	Read/Write DMA Channel 7 Requester Address, A0–A15
9F	Read/Write DMA Channel 7 Requester Address, A16–A31
A0	Write Bank C ICW1, OCW2 or OCW3
	Read Bank C Poll, Interrupt Request or In-Service Status Register
A1	Write Bank C ICW2, ICW3, ICW4 or OCW1
	Read Bank C Interrupt Mask Register
A2	Read Bank C ICW2
A8	Read/Write IRQ16 Vector Register
A9	Read/Write IRQ17 Vector Register
AA	Read/Write IRQ18 Vector Register
AB	Read/Write IRQ19 Vector Register
AC	Read/Write IRQ20 Vector Register
AD	Read/Write IRQ21 Vector Register
AE	Read/Write IRQ22 Vector Register
AF	Read/Write IRQ23 Vector Register
C0	Read/Write DMA Channel 4 Target Address, A0–A15
C1	Read/Write DMA Channel 4 Byte Count, B0–B15
C2	Read/Write DMA Channel 5 Target Address, A0–A15
C3	Read/Write DMA Channel 5 Byte Count, B0–B15
C4	Read/Write DMA Channel 6 Target Address, A0–A15
C5	Read/Write DMA Channel 6 Byte Count, B0–B15
C6	Read/Write DMA Channel 7 Target Address, A0–A15
C7	Read/Write DMA Channel 7 Byte Count, B0–B15
C8	Read DMA Channel 4–7 Status/Command I Register
C9	Read/Write DMA Channel 4–7 Software Request Register
CA	Write DMA Channel 4–7 Set—Reset Mask Register
CB	Write DMA Channel 4–7 Mode Register I
CC	Reserved
CD	Reserved
CE	Write DMA Channel 4–7 Clear Mask Register
CF	Read/Write DMA Channel 4–7 Mask Register

APPENDIX A—Ports Listed by Address (Continued)

Port Address (HEX)	Description
D0	Read/Write DMA Channel 4 Target Address, A24–A31
D1	Read/Write DMA Channel 4 Byte Count, B16–B23
D2	Read/Write DMA Channel 5 Target Address, A24–A31
D3	Read/Write DMA Channel 5 Byte Count, B16–B23
D4	Read/Write DMA Channel 6 Target Address, A24–A31
D5	Read/Write DMA Channel 6 Byte Count, B16–B23
D6	Read/Write DMA Channel 7 Target Address, A24–A31
D7	Read/Write DMA Channel 7 Byte Count, B16–B23
D8	Write DMA Channel 4–7 Bus Size Register
D9	Read/Write DMA Channel 4–7 Chaining Register
DA	Write DMA Channel 4–7 Command Register II
DB	Write DMA Channel 4–7 Mode Register II

APPENDIX B
Ports Listed by Function

Port Address (HEX)	Description
	DMA CONTROLLER
0D	Write DMA Master-Clear
0C	Write DMA Clear Byte-Pointer FF
08	Read/Write DMA Channel 0–3 Status/Command I Register
C8	Read/Write DMA Channel 4–7 Status/Command I Register
1A	Write DMA Channel 0–3 Command Register II
DA	Write DMA Channel 4–7 Command Register II
0B	Write DMA Channel 0–3 Mode Register I
CB	Write DMA Channel 4–7 Mode Register I
1B	Write DMA Channel 0–3 Mode Register II
DB	Write DMA Channel 4–7 Mode Register II
09	Read/Write DMA Channel 0–3 Software Request Register
C9	Read/Write DMA Channel 4–7 Software Request Register
1E	Reset Software Request Interrupt
0E	Write DMA Channel 0–3 Clear Mask Register
CE	Write DMA Channel 4–7 Clear Mask Register
0F	Read/Write DMA Channel 0–3 Mask Register
CF	Read/Write DMA Channel 4–7 Mask Register
0A	Write DMA Channel 0–3 Set-Reset Mask Register
CA	Write DMA Channel 4–7 Set-Reset Mask Register
18	Write DMA Channel 0–3 Bus Size Register
D8	Write DMA Channel 4–7 Bus Size Register
19	Read/Write DMA Channel 0–3 Chaining Register
D9	Read/Write DMA Channel 4–7 Chaining Register
00	Read/Write DMA Channel 0 Target Address, A0–A15
87	Read/Write DMA Channel 0 Target Address, A16–A23
10	Read/Write DMA Channel 0 Target Address, A24–A31
01	Read/Write DMA Channel 0 Byte Count, B0–B15
11	Read/Write DMA Channel 0 Byte Count, B16–B23
90	Read/Write DMA Channel 0 Requester Address, A0–A15
91	Read/Write DMA Channel 0 Requester Address, A16–A31
02	Read/Write DMA Channel 1 Target Address, A0–A15
83	Read/Write DMA Channel 1 Target Address, A16–A23
12	Read/Write DMA Channel 1 Target Address, A24–A31
03	Read/Write DMA Channel 1 Byte Count, B0–B15
13	Read/Write DMA Channel 1 Byte Count, B16–B23
92	Read/Write DMA Channel 1 Requester Address, A0–A15
93	Read/Write DMA Channel 1 Requester Address, A16–A31

APPENDIX B—Ports Listed by Function (Continued)

Port Address (HEX)	Description
	DMA CONTROLLER
04	Read/Write DMA Channel 2 Target Address, A0–A15
81	Read/Write DMA Channel 2 Target Address, A16–A23
14	Read/Write DMA Channel 2 Target Address, A24–A31
05	Read/Write DMA Channel 2 Byte Count, B0–B15
15	Read/Write DMA Channel 2 Byte Count, B16–B23
94	Read/Write DMA Channel 2 Requester Address, A0–A15
95	Read/Write DMA Channel 2 Requester Address, A16–A31
06	Read/Write DMA Channel 3 Target Address, A0–A15
82	Read/Write DMA Channel 3 Target Address, A16–A23
16	Read/Write DMA Channel 3 Target Address, A24–A31
07	Read/Write DMA Channel 3 Byte Count, B0–B15
17	Read/Write DMA Channel 3 Byte Count, B16–B23
96	Read/Write DMA Channel 3 Requester Address, A0–A15
97	Read/Write DMA Channel 3 Requester Address, A16–A31
C0	Read/Write DMA Channel 4 Target Address, A0–A15
8F	Read/Write DMA Channel 4 Target Address, A16–A23
D0	Read/Write DMA Channel 4 Target Address, A24–A31
C1	Read/Write DMA Channel 4 Byte Count, B0–B15
D1	Read/Write DMA Channel 4 Byte Count, B16–B23
98	Read/Write DMA Channel 4 Requester Address, A0–A15
99	Read/Write DMA Channel 4 Requester Address, A16–A31
C2	Read/Write DMA Channel 5 Target Address, A0–A15
8B	Read/Write DMA Channel 5 Target Address, A16–A23
D2	Read/Write DMA Channel 5 Target Address, A24–A31
C3	Read/Write DMA Channel 5 Byte Count, B0–B15
D3	Read/Write DMA Channel 5 Byte Count, B16–B23
9A	Read/Write DMA Channel 5 Requester Address, A0–A15
9B	Read/Write DMA Channel 5 Requester Address, A16–A31
C4	Read/Write DMA Channel 6 Target Address, A0–A15
89	Read/Write DMA Channel 6 Target Address, A16–A23
D4	Read/Write DMA Channel 6 Target Address, A24–A31
C5	Read/Write DMA Channel 6 Byte Count, B0–B15
D5	Read/Write DMA Channel 6 Byte Count, B16–B23
9C	Read/Write DMA Channel 6 Requester Address, A0–A15
9D	Read/Write DMA Channel 6 Requester Address, A16–A31
C6	Read/Write DMA Channel 7 Target Address, A0–A15
8A	Read/Write DMA Channel 7 Target Address, A16–A23
D6	Read/Write DMA Channel 7 Target Address, A24–A31
C7	Read/Write DMA Channel 7 Byte Count, B0–B15
D7	Read/Write DMA Channel 7 Byte Count, B16–B23
9E	Read/Write DMA Channel 7 Requester Address, A0–A15
9F	Read/Write DMA Channel 7 Requester Address, A16–A31

APPENDIX B—Ports Listed by Function (Continued)

Port Address (HEX)	Description
	INTERRUPT CONTROLLER
20	Write Bank B ICW1, OCW2, or OCW3 Read Bank B Poll, Interrupt Request or In-Service Status Register
21	Write Bank B ICW2, ICW3, ICW4 or OCW1 Read Bank B Interrupt Mask Register
22	Read Bank B ICW2
28	Read/Write IRQ8 Vector Register
29	Read/Write IRQ9 Vector Register
2A	Reserved
2B	Read/Write IRQ11 Vector Register
2C	Read/Write IRQ12 Vector Register
2D	Read/Write IRQ13 Vector Register
2E	Read/Write IRQ14 Vector Register
2F	Read/Write IRQ15 Vector Register
A0	Write Bank C ICW1, OCW2 or OCW3 Read Bank C Poll, Interrupt Request or In-Service Status Register
A1	Write Bank C ICW2, ICW3, ICW4 or OCW1 Read Bank C Interrupt Mask Register
A2	Read Bank C ICW2
A8	Read/Write IRQ16 Vector Register
A9	Read/Write IRQ17 Vector Register
AA	Read/Write IRQ18 Vector Register
AB	Read/Write IRQ19 Vector Register
AC	Read/Write IRQ20 Vector Register
AD	Read/Write IRQ21 Vector Register
AE	Read/Write IRQ22 Vector Register
AF	Read/Write IRQ23 Vector Register
30	Write Bank A ICW1, OCW2 or OCW3 Read Bank A Poll, Interrupt Request oor In-Service Status Register
31	Write Bank A ICW2, ICW3, ICW4 or OCW1 Read Bank A Interrupt Mask Register
32	Read Bank A ICW2
38	Read/Write IRQ0 Vector Register
39	Read/Write IRQ1 Vector Register
3A	Read/Write IRQ1.5 Vector Register
3B	Read/Write IRQ3 Vector Register
3C	Read/Write IRQ4 Vector Register
3D	Reserved
3E	Reserved
3F	Read/Write IRQ7 Vector Register

APPENDIX B—Ports Listed by Function (Continued)

Port Address (HEX)	Description
	PROGRAMMABLE INTERVAL TIMER
40	Read/Write Counter 0 Register
41	Read/Write Counter 1 Register
42	Read/Write Counter 2 Register
43	Write Control Word Register I—Counter 0, 1, 2
44	Read/Write Counter 3 Register
47	Write Word Register II—Counter 3
	CPU RESET
64	Write CPU Reset Register (Data-1111XXX0H)
	WAIT STATE GENERATOR
72	Read/Write Wait State Register 0
73	Read/Write Wait State Register 1
74	Read/Write Wait State Register 2
75	Read/Write Refresh Wait State Register
	DRAM REFRESH CONTROLLER
1C	Read/Write Refresh Control Register
	INTERNAL CONTROL AND DIAGNOSTIC PORTS
61	Write Internal Control Port
80	Read/Write Internal Diagnostic Port 0
88	Read/Write Internal Diagnostic Port 1
	RELOCATION REGISTER
7F	Read/Write Relocation Register
	INTEL RESERVED PORTS
2A	Reserved
3D	Reserved
3E	Reserved
45	Reserved
46	Reserved
76	Reserved
77	Reserved
7D	Reserved
7E	Reserved
CC	Reserved
CD	Reserved

APPENDIX C
Pin Descriptions

The 82380 provides all of the signals necessary to interface it to an 80386 processor. It has separate 32-bit address and data buses. It also has a set of control signals to support operation as a bus master or a bus slave. Several special function signals exist on the 82380 for interfacing the system support peripherals to their respective system counterparts. Following are the definitions of the individual pins of the 82380. These brief descriptions are provided as a reference. Each signal is further defined within the sections which describe the associated 82380 function.

A2-A31 I/O ADDRESS BUS

This is the 32-bit address bus. The addresses are doubleword memory and I/O addresses. These are three-state signals which are active only during Master mode. The address lines should be connected directly to the 80386's local bus.

BE0# I/O BYTE-ENABLE 0

BE0# active indicates that data bits D0–D7 are being accessed or are valid. It is connected directly to the 80386's BE0#. The byte enable signals are active outputs when the 82380 is in the Master mode.

BE1# I/O BYTE-ENABLE 1

BE1# active indicates that data bits D8–D15 are being accessed or are valid. It is connected directly to the 80386's BE1#. The byte enable signals are active only when the 82380 is in the Master mode.

BE2# I/O BYTE-ENABLE 2

BE2# active indicates that data bits D15–D23 are being accessed or are valid. It is connected directly to the 80386's BE2#. The byte enable signals are active only when the 82380 is in the Master mode.

BE3# I/O BYTE-ENABLE 3

BE3# active indicates that data bits D24–D31 are being accessed or are valid. The byte enable signals are active only when the 82380 is in the Master mode. This pin should be connected directly to the 80386's BE3#. This pin is used for factory testing and must be low during reset. The 80386 drives BE3# low during reset.

D0–D31 I/O DATA BUS

This is the 32-bit data bus. These pins are active outputs during interrupt acknowledges, during Slave accesses, and when the 82380 is in the Master mode.

CLK2 I PROCESSOR CLOCK

This pin must be connected to CLK2. The 82380 monitors the phase of this clock in order to remain synchronized with the 80386. This clock drives all of the internal synchronous circuitry.

D/C# I/O DATA/CONTROL

D/C# is used to distinguish between 80386 control cycles and DMA or 80386 data access cycles. It is active as an output only in the Master mode.

W/R# I/O WRITE/READ

W/R# is used to distinguish between write and read cycles. It is active as an output only in the Master mode.

M/IO# I/O MEMORY/IO

M/IO# is used to distinguish between memory and IO accesses. It is active as an output only in the Master mode.

ADS# I/O ADDRESS STATUS

This signal indicates presence of a valid address on the address bus. It is active as output only in the Master mode. ADS# is active during the first T-state where addresses and control signals are valid.

NA# I NEXT ADDRESS

Asserted by a peripheral or memory to begin a pipelined address cycle. This pin is monitored only while the 82380 is in the Master mode. In the Slave mode, pipelining is determined by the current and past status of the ADS# and READY# signals.

HOLD O HOLD REQUEST

This is an active-high signal to the 80386 to request control of the system bus. When control is granted, the 80386 activates the hold acknowledge signal (HLDA).

HLDA I HOLD ACKNOWLEDGE

This input signal tells the DMA controller that the 80386 has relinquished control of the system bus to the DMA controller.

DREQ (0–3, 5–7) I DMA REQUEST

The DMA Request inputs monitor requests from peripherals requiring DMA service. Each of the eight DMA channels has one DREQ input. These active-high inputs are internally synchronized and prioritized. Upon reset, channel 0 has the highest priority and channel 7 the lowest.

DREQ4/IRQ9# I DMA/INTERRUPT REQUEST

This is the DMA request input for channel 4. It is also connected to the interrupt controller via interrupt request 9. This internal connection is available for DMA channel 4 only. The interrupt input is active low and can be programmed as either edge of level triggered. Either function can be masked by the appropriate mask register. Priorities of the DMA channel and the interrupt request are not related but follow the rules of the individual controllers.

Note that this pin has a weak internal pull-up. This causes the interrupt request to be inactive, but the DMA request will be active if there is no external connection made. Most applications will require that either one or the other of these functions be used, but not both. For this reason, it is advised that DMA channel 4 be used for transfers where a software request is more appropriate (such as memory-to-memory transfers). In such an application, DREQ4 can be masked by software, freeing IRQ9# for other purposes.

EOP# I/O END OF PROCESS

As an output, this signal indicates that the current Requester access is the last access of the currently operating DMA channel. It is activated when Terminal Count is reached. As an input, it signals the DMA channel to terminate the current buffer and proceed to the next buffer, if one is available. This signal may be programmed as an asynchronous or synchronous input.

EOP# must be connected to a pull-up resistor. This will prevent erroneous external requests for termination of a DMA process.

EDACK (0–2) O ENCODED DMA ACKNOWLEDGE

These signals contain the encoded acknowledgement of a request for DMA service by a peripheral. The binary code formed by the three signals indicates which channel is active. Channel 4 does not have a DMA acknowledge. The inactive state is indicated by the code 100. During a Requester access, EDACK presents the code for the active DMA channel. During a Target access, EDACK presents the inactive code 100.

IRQ (11–23)# I INTERRUPT REQUEST

These are active low interrupt request inputs. The inputs can be programmed to be edge or level sensitive. Interrupt priorities are programmable as either fixed or rotating. These inputs have weak internal pull-up resistors. Unused interrupt request inputs should be tied inactive externally.

INT O INTERRUPT OUT

INT signals the 80386 that an interrupt request is pending.

CLKIN I TIMER CLOCK INPUT

This is the clock input signal to all of the 82380's programmable timers. It is independent of the system clock input (CLK2).

TOUT1/REF# O TIMER 1 OUTPUT/REFRESH

This pin is software programmable as either the direct output of Timer 1, or as the indicator of a refresh cycle in progress. As REF#, this signal is active during the memory read cycle which occurs during refresh.

TOUT2#/IRQ3# I/O TIMER 2 OUTPUT/INTERRUPT REQUEST3

This is the inverted output of Timer 2. It is also connected directly to interrupt request 3. External hardware can use IRQ3# if Timer 2 is programmed as OUT=0 (TOUT2#=1)

TOUT3# O TIMER 3 OUTPUT

This is the inverted output of Timer 3.

READY# I READY INPUT

This active-low input indicates to the 82380 that the current bus cycle is complete. READY is sampled by the 82380 both while it is in the Master mode, and while it is in the Slave mode.

WSC (0–1) I WAIT STATE CONTROL

WSC0 AND WSC1 are inputs used by the Wait-State Generator to determine the number of wait states required by the currently accessed memory or I/O. The binary code on these ins, combined with the M/IO# signal, selects an internal register in which a wait-state count is stored. The combination WSC = 11 disables the wait-state generator.

READYO# O READY OUTPUT

This is the synchronized output of the wait-state generator. It is also valid during 80386 accesses to the 82380 in the Slave Mode when the 82380 requires wait states. READYO# should feed directly the 80386's READY# input.

RESET I RESET

This synchronous input serves to initialize the state of the 82380 and provides basis for the CPURST output. RESET must be held active for at least 15 CLK2 cycles in order to guarantee the state of the 82380. After Reset, the 82380 is in the Slave mode with all outputs except timers and interrupts in their inactive states. The state of the timers and interrupt controller must be initialized through software. This input must be active for the entire time required by the 80386 to guarantee proper reset.

CPURST O CPU RESET

CPURST provides a synchronized reset signal for the CPU. It is activated in the event of a software reset command, an 80386 shut-down detect, or a hardware reset via the RESET pin. The 82380 holds CPURST active for 62 clocks in response to either a software reset command or a shut-down detection. Otherwise CPURST reflects the RESET input.

V_{CC} +5V input power
V_{SS} Ground

Table C-1. Wait-State Select Inputs

Port Address	Wait-State Registers		Select Inputs	
	D7 D4	D3 D0	WSC1	WSC0
72H	Memory 0	I/O 0	0	0
73H	Memory 1	I/O 1	0	1
74H	Memory 2	I/O 2	1	1
	DISABLED		1	1
M/IO#	1	0		

APPENDIX D
82380 System Notes

82380 TIMER UNIT SYSTEM NOTES

The 82380 DMA controller with Integrated System Peripherals is functionally inconsistent with the data sheet. This document explains the behavior of the 82380 Timer Unit and outlines subsequent limitations of the timer unit. This document also provides recommended workarounds.

1.0 WRITE CYCLES TO THE 82380 TIMER UNIT

This errata applies only to SLAVE WRITE cycles to the 82380 timer unit. During these cycles, the data being written into the 82380 timer unit may be corrupted if CLKIN is not inhibited during a certain "window" of the write cycle.

1.1 Description

Please refer to Figure 1.

During write cycles to the 82380 timer unit, the 82380 translates the 386DX interface signals such as ADS#, W/R#, M/IO#, and D/C# into several internal signals that control the operation of the internal sub-blocks (e.g., Timer Unit).

The 82380 timer unit is controlled by such internal signals. These internal signals are generated and sampled with respect to two separate clock signals: CLK2 (the system clock) and CLKIN (the 82380 timer unit clock).

Since the CLKIN and CLK2 clock signals are used internally to generate control signals for the interface to the timer unit, some timing parameters must be met in order for the interface logic to function properly.

Those timing parameters are met by inhibiting the CLKIN signal for a specific window during Write Cycles to the 82380 Timer Unit.

The CLKIN signal must be inhibited using external logic, as the GATE function of the 82380 timer unit is not guaranteed to totally inhibit CLKIN.

1.2 Consequences

This CLKIN inhibit circuitry guarantees proper write cycles to the 82380 timer unit.

Without this solution, write cycles to the 82380 timer unit could place corrupted data into the timer unit registers. This, in turn, could yield inaccurate results and improper timer operation.

The proposed solution would involve a hardware modification for existing systems.

1.3 Solution

A timing waveform (Figure 2) shows the specific window during which CLKIN must be inhibited. Please note that CLKIN must only be inhibited during the window shown in Figure 2. This window is defined by two AC timing parameters:

t_a = 9 ns

t_b = 28 ns

The proposed solution provides a certain amount of system "guardband" to make sure that this window is avoided.

PAL equations for a suggested workaround are also included. Please refer to the comments in the PAL codes for stated assumptions of this particular workaround. A state diagram (Figure 3) is provided to help clarify how this PAL is designed.

Figure 4 shows how this PAL would fit into a system workaround. In order to show the effect of this workaround on the CLKIN signal, Figure 5 shows how CLKIN is inhibited. Note that you must still meet the CLKIN AC timing parameters (e.g., t_{47} (min), t_{48} (min)) in order for the timer unit to function properly.

Please note that this workaround has not been tested. It is provided as a suggested solution. Actual solutions will vary from system to system.

1.4 Long Term Plans

Intel has no plans to fix this behavior in the 82380 timer unit.

```
module Timer_82380_Fix
flag '-r2','-q2','-fl', '-t4', '-w1,3,6,5,4,16,7,12,17,18,15,14'
title '82380 Timer Unit CLKIN
      INHIBIT signal PAL Solution '
Timer_Unit_Fix device 'P16R6';

"This PAL inhibits the CLKIN signal (that comes from an oscillator)
"during Slave Writes to the 82380 Timer unit.
"
"ASSUMPTION:    This PAL assumes that an external system address
"               decoder provides a signal to indicate that an 82380
"               Timer Unit access is taking place. This input
"               signal is called TMR in this PAL. This PAL also
"               assumes that this TMR signal occurs during a
"               specific T-State. Please see Figure 3 of this
"               document to see when this signal is expected to
"               be active by this PAL.
"
"
"NOTE:          This PAL does not support pipelined 82380 SLAVE
"               cycles.
"
"(c) Intel Corporation 1989. This PAL is provided as a proposed
"method of solving a certain 82380 Timer Unit problem. This PAL
"has not been tested or validated. Please validate this solution
"for your system and application.
"
```

4

```
"Input Pins"

CLK2            pin      1; "System Clock
RESET           pin      2; "Microprocessor RESET signal
TMR             pin      3; "Input from Address Decoder, indicating
                            "an access to the timer unit of the
                            "82380.
!RDY            pin      4; "End of Cycle indicator
!ADS            pin      5; "Address and control strobe
CLK             pin      6; "PHI2 clock
W_R             pin      7; "Write/Read Signal"
nc1             pin      8; "No Connect 0"
nc3             pin      9; "No Connect 1"
GNDa            pin     10; "Tied to ground, documentation only
GNDb            pin     11; "Output enable, documentation only
CLKIN_IN        pin     12; "Input-CLKIN directly from oscillator

"Output Pins"

Q_0             pin     18; "Internal signal only, fed back to
                            "PAL logic"
CLKIN_OUT       pin     17; "CLKIN signal fed to 82380 Timer Unit
INHIBIT         pin     16; "CLKIN Inhibit signal
S0              pin     15; "Unused State Indicator Pin
S1              pin     14; "Unused State Indicator Pin

"Declarations"

Valid_ADS = ADS & CLK      ; "ADS# sampled in PHI1 of 386DX T-State

Valid_RDY = RDY & CLK      ; "RDY# sampled in PHI1 of 386DX T-State

Timer_Acc = TMR & CLK      ; "Timer Unit Access, as provided by
                             "external Address Decoder "

State_Diagram [INHIBIT, S1, S0]

state 000:     if RESET then 000
               else if Valid_ADS & W_R then 001
               else 000;

state 001:     if RESET then 000
               else if Timer_Acc then 010
               else if !Timer_Acc then 000
               else 001;

state 010:     if RESET then 000
               else if CLK then 110
               else 010;

state 110:     if RESET then 000
               else if CLK then 111
               else 110;
```

```
state 111:    if RESET then 000
              else if CLK then 011
              else 111;

state 011:    if RESET then 000
              else if Valid_RDY then 000
              else 011;

state 100:    if RESET then 000
              else 000;

state 101:    if RESET then 000
              else 000;

EQUATIONS

Q_0 := CLKIN_IN   ; "Latched incoming clock. This signal is used
                    "internally to feed into the MUX-ing logic"

CLKIN_OUT := (INHIBIT & CLKIN_OUT & !RESET)
            +( !INHIBIT & Q_0 & !RESET);

                          "Equation for CLKIN_OUT. This
                          "feeds directly to the 82380 Timer Unit."

END


Page 1

ABEL(tm) 3.10 - Document Generator 30-June 89 03:17
PM
82380 Timer Unit CLKIN
    INHIBIT signal PAL Solution
Equations for Module Timer_82380_Fix

Device Timer_Unit_Fix

- Reduced Equations:

    !INHIBIT := ( !CLK & !INHIBIT # CLK & S0 # RESET # !S1);

    !S1 := (RESET
            # INHIBIT & !S1
            # CLK & !INHIBIT & !~RDY & S0 & S1
            # !CLK & !S1
            # !S1 & !TMR
            # !S0 & !S1);

    !S0 := (RESET
            # INHIBIT & !S1
            # CLK & !INHIBIT & !~RDY & S1
            # !CLK & !S0
            # !INHIBIT & !S0 & S1
            # S0 & !S1
            # !S1 & !W_R
            # ~ADS & !S1);
```

```
    !Q_0 := (!CLKIN_IN);

    !CLKIN_OUT := (RESET # !CLKIN_OUT & INHIBIT # !INHIBIT & !Q_0);

Page 2

ABEL(tm) 3.10 - Document Generator 30-June 89 03:17
PM
82380 Timer Unit CLKIN
      INHIBIT signal PAL Solution
Chip diagram for Module Timer_82380_Fix

Device Timer_Unit_Fix
```

P16R6

Signal	Pin	Pin	Signal
CLK2	1	20	
RESET	2	19	
TMR	3	18	Q_0
$\overline{RDY}$	4	17	CLKIN_OUT
$\overline{ADS}$	5	16	INHIBIT
CLK	6	15	S0
W_R	7	14	S1
nc1	8	13	
nc3	9	12	CLKIN_IN
GNDa	10	11	GNDb

290128-B7

```
end of module Timer_82380_Fix
```

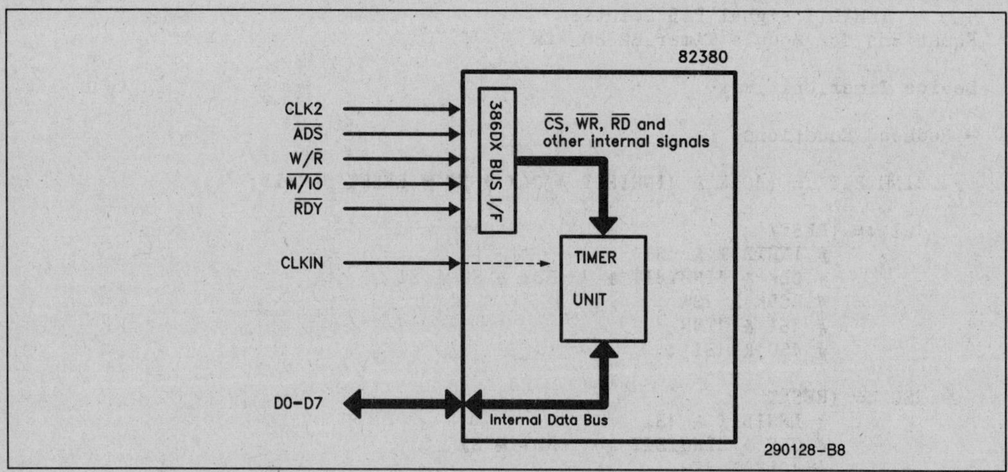

Figure 1. Translation of 386DX Signals to Internal 82380 Timer Unit Signals

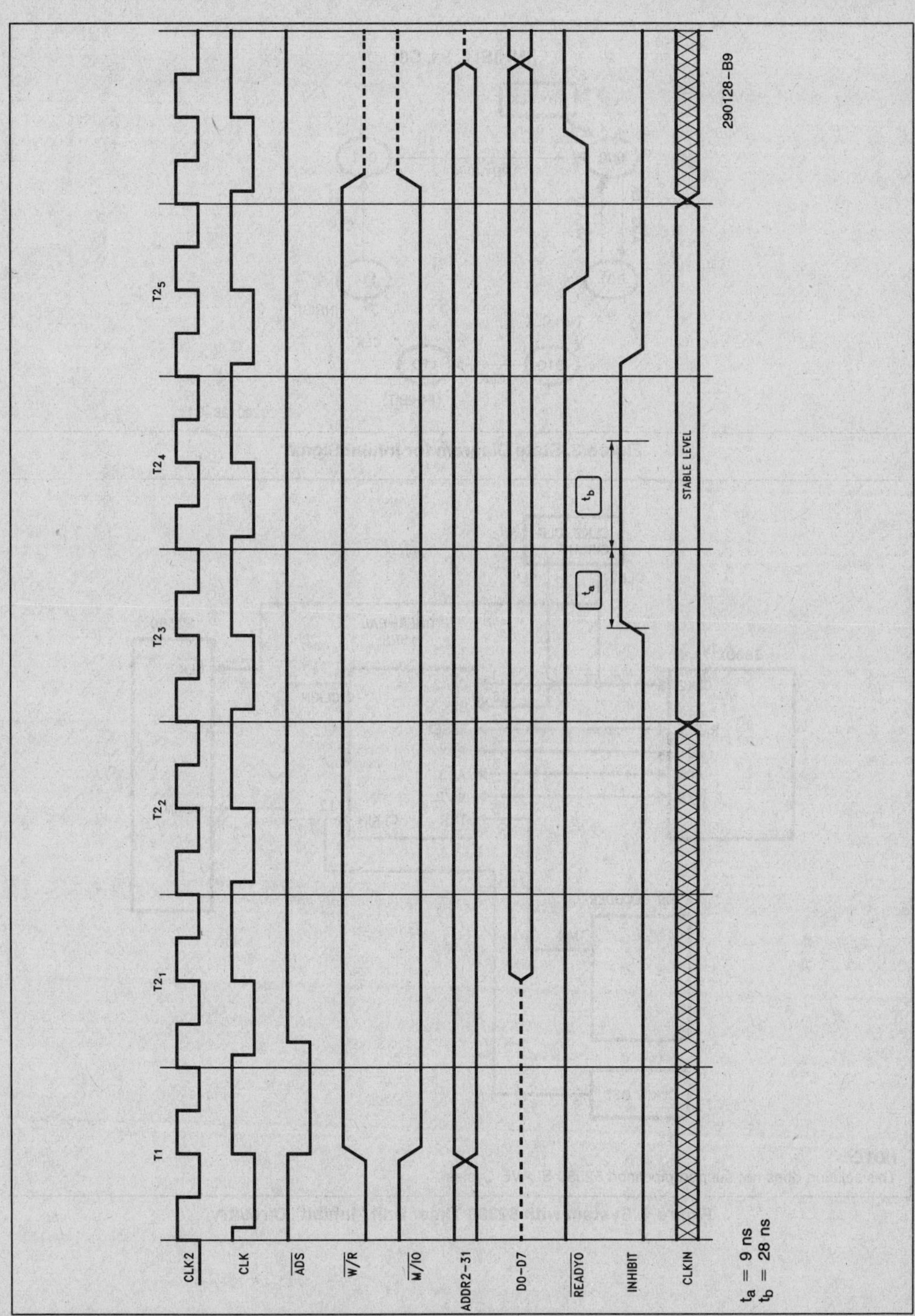

Figure 2. 82380 Timer Unit Write Cycle

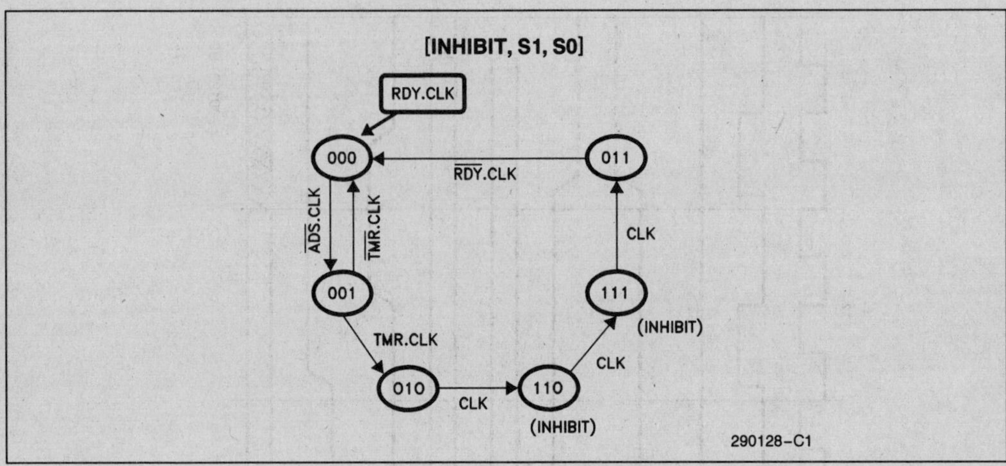

Figure 3. State Diagram for Inhibit Signal

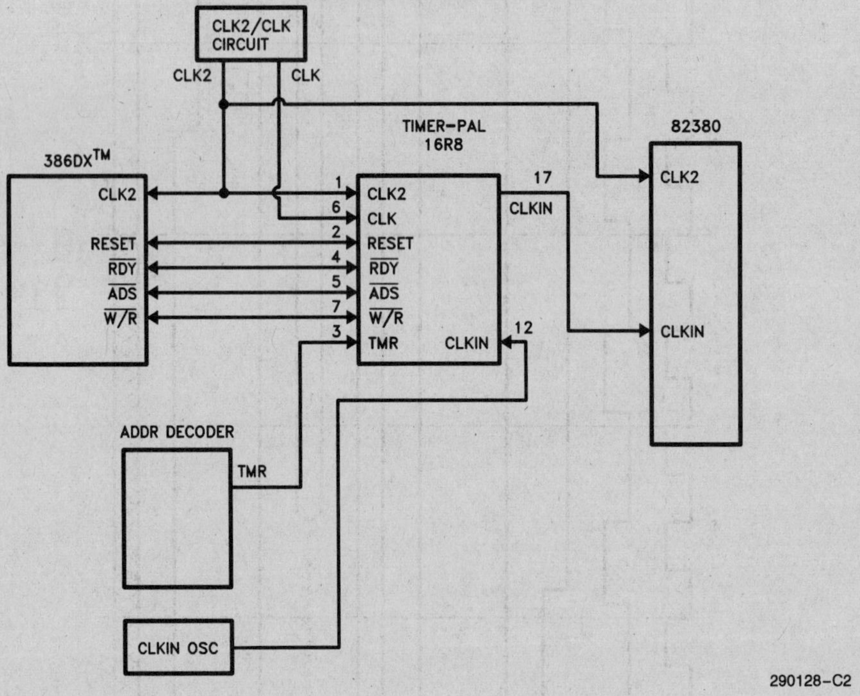

290128-C2

NOTE:
This solution does not support pipelined 82380 SLAVE Cycles.

Figure 4. System with 82380 Timer Unit "Inhibit" Circuitry

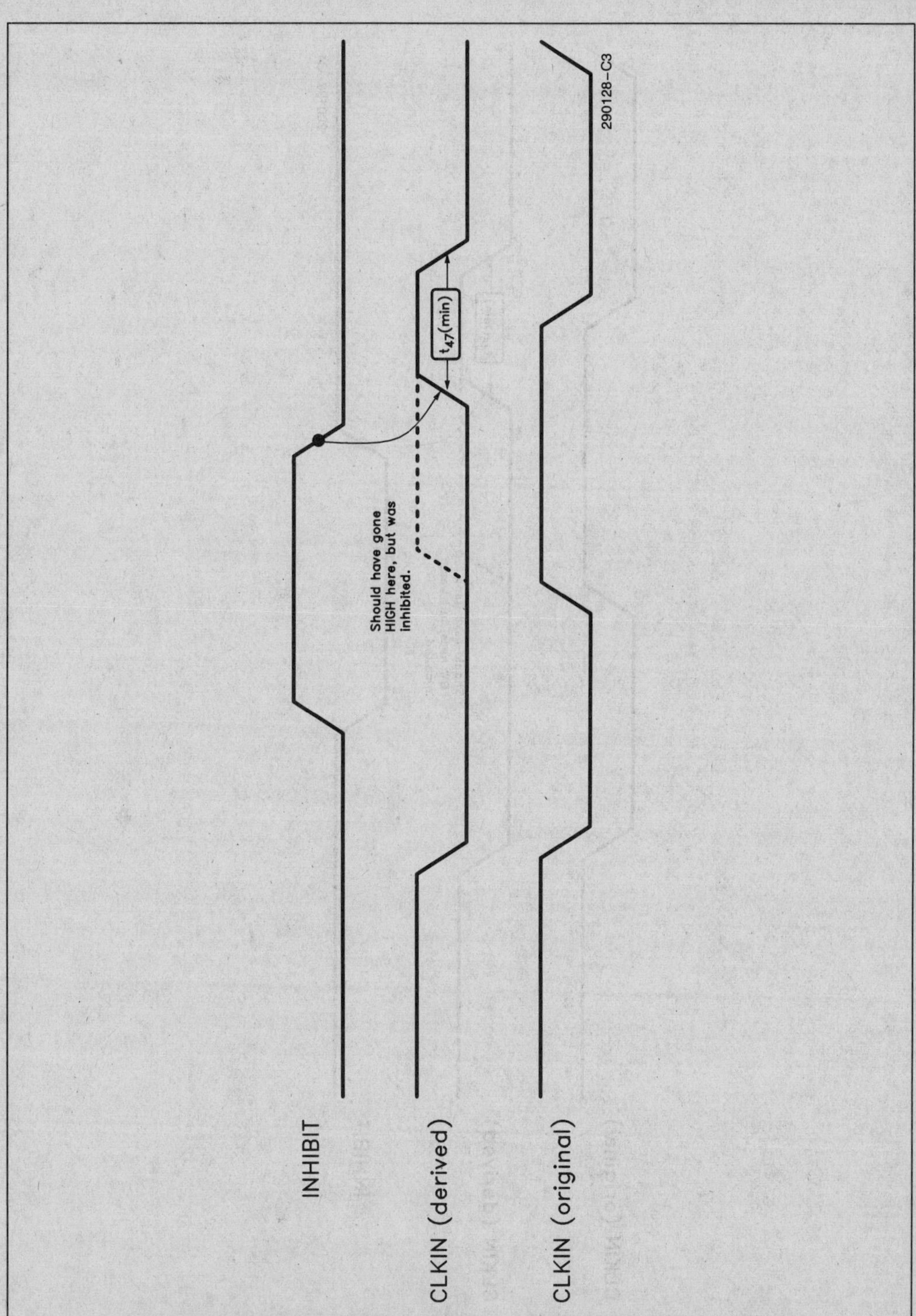

Figure 5(a). Inhibited CLKIN in an 82380 Timer Unit and CLKIN Minimum HIGH Time

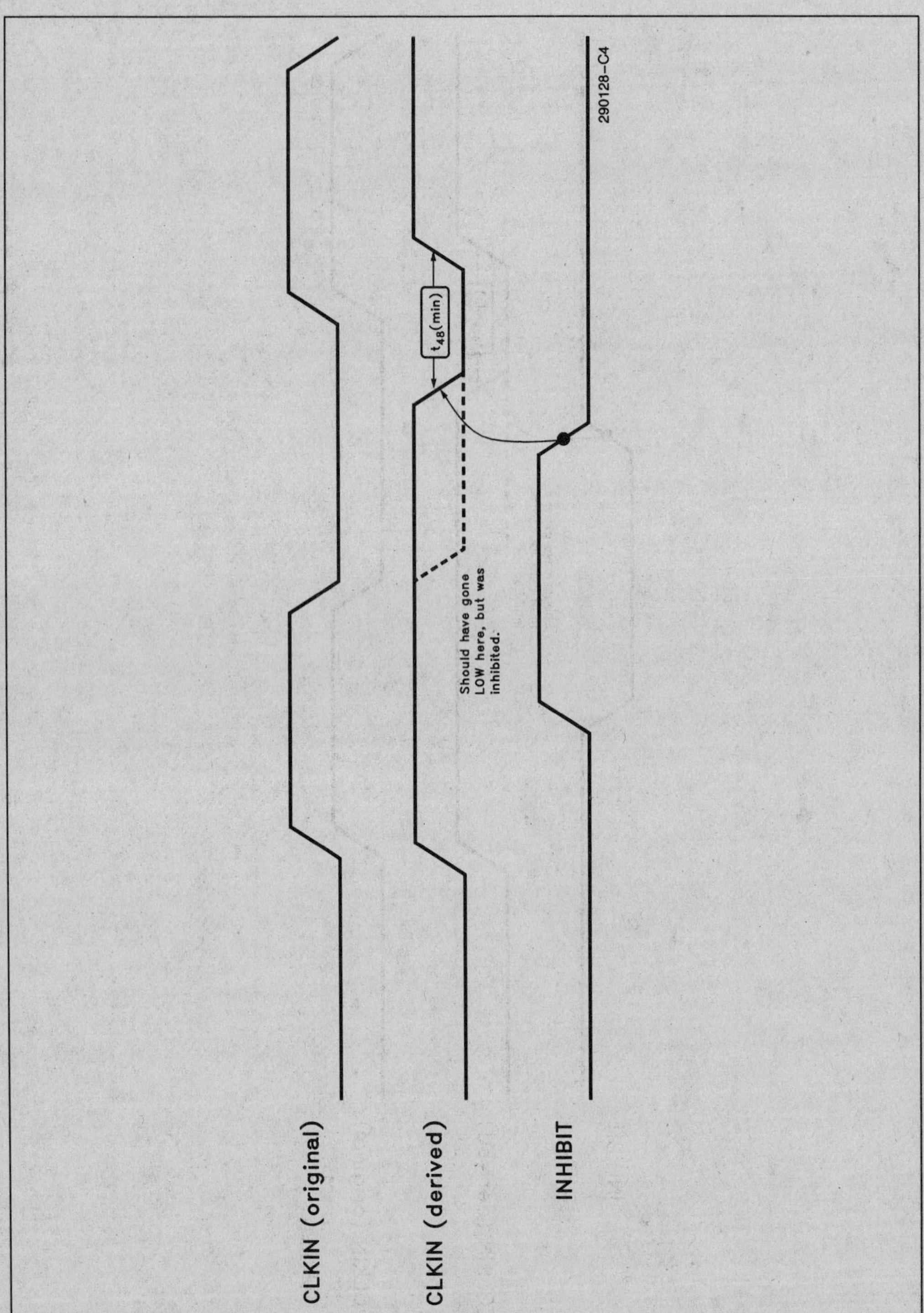

Figure 5(b). Inhibited CLKIN in an 82380 Timer Unit and CLKIN Minimum LOW Time

82380 DATA SHEET REVISION HISTORY

Changes in this revision:

Figure 4-1: Added details about IRQ3# and IRQ2#/IRQ1.5#.

Section 5.2.1: Added note referring reader to Appendix D (System Notes).

Table 13-2: Changed V_{IHC} MIN to $V_{CC} - 0.8V$.

Figure 13-1: Changed signal names to reflect accurate drive levels and measurement points for those signals.

Appendix D: Added this appendix to explain the restrictions on the CLKIN signal of the 82380 Timer Unit.

82370
INTEGRATED SYSTEM PERIPHERAL

- **High Performance 32-Bit DMA Controller for 16-Bit Bus**
  - **16 MBytes/Sec Maximum Data Transfer Rate at 16 MHz**
  - **8 Independently Programmable Channels**
- **20-Source Interrupt Controller**
  - **Individually Programmable Interrupt Vectors**
  - **15 External, 5 Internal Interrupts**
  - **82C59A Superset**
- **Four 16-Bit Programmable Interval Timers**
  - **82C54 Compatible**
- **Software Compatible to 82380**
- **Programmable Wait State Generator**
  - **0 to 15 Wait States Pipelined**
  - **1 to 16 Wait States Non-Pipelined**
- **DRAM Refresh Controller**
- **80376 Shutdown Detect and Reset Control**
  - **Software/Hardware Reset**
- **High Speed CHMOS III Technology**
- **100-Pin Plastic Quad Flat-Pack Package and 132-Pin Pin Grid Array Package**

  (See Packaging Handbook Order #240800-001, Package Type NG or Package Type A)
- **Optimized for Use with the 80376 Microprocessor**
  - **Resides on Local Bus for Maximum Bus Bandwidth**
  - **16 MHz Clock**

The 82370 is a multi-function support peripheral that integrates system functions necessary in an 80376 environment. It has eight channels of high performance 32-bit DMA (32-bit internal, 16-bit external) with the most efficient transfer rates possible on the 80376 bus. System support peripherals integrated into the 82370 provide Interrupt Control, Timers, Wait State generation, DRAM Refresh Control, and System Reset logic.

The 82370's DMA Controller can transfer data between devices of different data path widths using a single channel. Each DMA channel operates independently in any of several modes. Each channel has a temporary data storage register for handling non-aligned data without the need for external alignment logic.

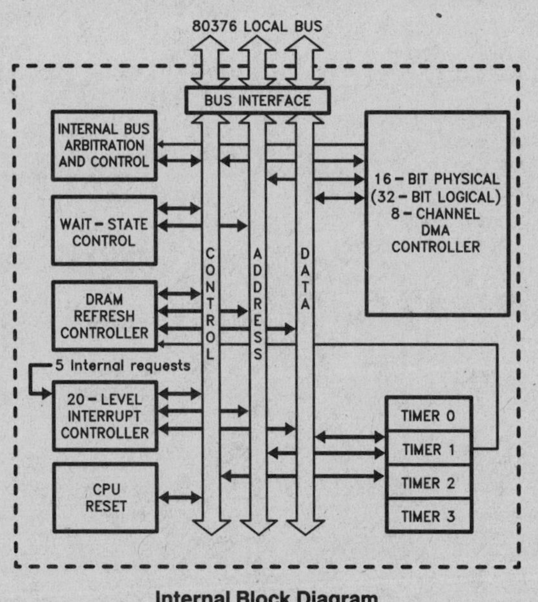

Internal Block Diagram

September 1991
Order Number: 290164-005

Table of Contents

CONTENTS

PAGE

4

CONTENTS

PAGE

CONTENTS

PAGE

CONTENTS

PAGE

CONTENTS

Pin Descriptions

The 82370 provides all of the signals necessary to interface an 80376 host processor. It has a separate 24-bit address and 16-bit data bus. It also has a set of control signals to support operation as a bus master or a bus slave. Several special function signals exist on the 82370 for interfacing the system support peripherals to their respective system counterparts. Following are the definitions of the individual pins of the 82370. These brief descriptions are provided as a reference. Each signal is further defined within the sections which describe the associated 82370 function.

Symbol	Type	Name and Function
A_1-A_{23}	I/O	**ADDRESS BUS:** Outputs physical memory or port I/O addresses. See **Address Bus** (2.2.3) for additional information.
BHE# BLE#	I/O	**BYTE ENABLES:** Indicate which data bytes of the data bus take part in a bus cycle. See **Byte Enable** (2.2.4) for additional information.
D_0-D_{15}	I/O	**DATA BUS:** This is the 16-bit data bus. These pins are active outputs during interrupt acknowledges, during Slave accesses, and when the 82370 is in the Master Mode.
CLK2	I	**PROCESSOR CLOCK:** This pin must be connected to the processor's clock, CLK2. The 82370 monitors the phase of this clock in order to remain synchronized with the CPU. This clock drives all of the internal synchronous circuitry.
D/C#	I/O	**DATA/CONTROL:** D/C# is used to distinguish between CPU control cycles and DMA or CPU data access cycles. It is active as an output only in the Master Mode.
W/R#	I/O	**WRITE/READ:** W/R# is used to distinguish between write and read cycles. It is active as an output only in the Master Mode.
M/IO#	I/O	**MEMORY/IO:** M/IO# is used to distinguish between memory and IO accesses. It is active as an output only in the Master Mode.
ADS#	I/O	**ADDRESS STATUS:** This signal indicates presence of a valid address on the address bus. It is active as output only in the Master Mode. ADS# is active during the first T-state where addresses and control signals are valid.
NA#	I	**NEXT ADDRESS:** Asserted by a peripheral or memory to begin a pipelined address cycle. This pin is monitored only while the 82370 is in the Master Mode. In the Slave Mode, pipelining is determined by the current and past status of the ADS# and READY# signals.
HOLD	O	**HOLD REQUEST:** This is an active-high signal to the Bus Master to request control of the system bus. When control is granted, the Bus Master activates the hold acknowledge signal (HLDA).
HLDA	I	**HOLD ACKNOWLEDGE:** This input signal tells the DMA controller that the Bus Master has relinquished control of the system bus to the DMA controller.

Pin Descriptions (Continued)

Symbol	Type	Name and Function
DREQ (0–3, 5–7)	I	**DMA REQUEST:** The DMA Request inputs monitor requests from peripherals requiring DMA service. Each of the eight DMA channels has one DREQ input. These active-high inputs are internally synchronized and prioritized. Upon request, channel 0 has the highest priority and channel 7 the lowest.
DREQ4/IRQ9#	I	**DMA/INTERRUPT REQUEST:** This is the DMA request input for channel 4. It is also connected to the interrupt controller via interrupt request 9. This internal connection is available for DMA channel 4 only. The interrupt input is active low and can be programmed as either edge or level triggered. Either function can be masked by the appropriate mask register. Priorities of the DMA channel and the interrupt request are not related but follow the rules of the individual controllers. Note that this pin has a weak internal pull-up. This causes the interrupt request to be inactive, but the DMA request will be active if there is no external connection made. Most applications will require that either one or the other of these functions be used, but not both. For this reason, it is advised that DMA channel 4 be used for transfers where a software request is more appropriate (such as memory-to-memory transfers). In such an application, DREQ4 can be masked by software, freeing IRQ9# for other purposes.
EOP#	I/O	**END OF PROCESS:** As an output, this signal indicates that the current Requester access is the last access of the currently operating DMA channel. It is activated when Terminal Count is reached. As an input, it signals the DMA channel to terminate the current buffer and proceed to the next buffer, if one is available. This signal may be programmed as an asynchronous or synchronous input. EOP# must be connected to a pull-up resistor. This will prevent erroneous external requests for termination of a DMA process.
EDACK (0–2)	O	**ENCODED DMA ACKNOWLEDGE:** These signals contain the encoded acknowledgment of a request for DMA service by a peripheral. The binary code formed by the three signals indicates which channel is active. Channel 4 does not have a DMA acknowledge. The inactive state is indicated by the code 100. During a Requester access, EDACK presents the code for the active DMA channel. During a Target access, EDACK presents the inactive code 100.
IRQ (11–23)#	I	**INTERRUPT REQUEST:** These are active low interrupt request inputs. The inputs can be programmed to be edge or level sensitive. Interrupt priorities are programmable as either fixed or rotating. These inputs have weak internal pull-up resistors. Unused interrupt request inputs should be tied inactive externally.
INT	O	**INTERRUPT OUT:** INT signals that an interrupt request is pending.
CLKIN	I	**TIMER CLOCK INPUT:** This is the clock input signal to all of the 82370's programmable timers. It is independent of the system clock input (CLK2).
TOUT1/REF#	O	**TIMER 1 OUTPUT/REFRESH:** This pin is software programmable as either the direct output of Timer 1, or as the indicator of a refresh cycle in progress. As REF#, this signal is active during the memory read cycle which occurs during refresh.

4

Pin Descriptions (Continued)

Symbol	Type	Name and Function
TOUT2#/IRQ3#	I/O	**TIMER 2 OUTPUT/INTERRUPT REQUEST:** This is the inverted output of Timer 2. It is also connected directly to interrupt request 3. External hardware can use IRQ3# if Timer 2 is programmed as OUT = 0 (TOUT2# = 1).
TOUT3#	O	**TIMER 3 OUTPUT:** This is the inverted output of Timer 3.
READY#	I	**READY INPUT:** This active-low input indicates to the 82370 that the current bus cycle is complete. READY is sampled by the 82370 both while it is in the Master Mode, and while it is in the Slave Mode.
WSC (0–1)	I	**WAIT STATE CONTROL:** WSC0 and WSC1 are inputs used by the Wait-State Generator to determine the number of wait states required by the currently accessed memory or I/O. The binary code on these pins, combined with the M/IO# signal, selects an internal register in which a wait-state count is stored. The combination WSC = 11 disables the wait-state generator.
READYO#	O	**READY OUTPUT:** This is the synchronized output of the wait-state generator. It is also valid during CPU accesses to the 82370 in the Slave Mode when the 82370 requires wait states. READYO# should feed directly the processor's READY# input.
RESET	I	**RESET:** This synchronous input serves to initialize the state of the 82370 and provides basis for the CPURST output. RESET must be held active for at least 15 CLK2 cycles in order to guarantee the state of the 82370. After Reset, the 82370 is in the Slave Mode with all outputs except timers and interrupts in their inactive states. The state of the timers and interrupt controller must be initialized through software. This input must be active for the entire time required by the host processor to guarantee proper reset.
CHPSEL#	O	**CHIP SELECT:** This pin is driven active whenever the 82370 is addressed in a slave bus read or write cycle. It is also active during interrupt acknowledge cycles when the 82370 is driving the Data Bus. It can be used to control the local bus transceivers to prevent contention with the system bus.
CPURST	O	**CPU RESET:** CPURST provides a synchronized reset signal for the CPU. It is activated in the event of a software reset command, a processor shut-down detect, or a hardware reset via the RESET pin. The 82370 holds CPURST active for 62 clocks in response to either a software reset command or a shut-down detection. Otherwise CPURST reflects the RESET input.
V_{CC}		**POWER:** +5V input power.
V_{SS}		Ground Reference.

Table 1. Wait-State Select Inputs

Port Address	Wait-State Registers				Select Inputs	
	D7	D4	D3	D0	WSC1	WSC0
72H	MEMORY 0		I/O 0		0	0
73H	MEMORY 1		I/O 1		0	1
74H	MEMORY 2		I/O 2		1	0
	DISABLED				1	1
M/IO#	1		0			

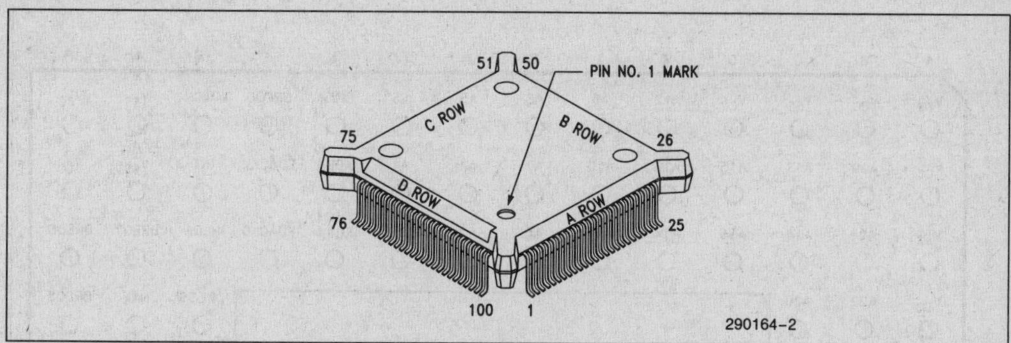

100 Pin Quad Flat-Pack Pin Out (Top View)

A Row		B Row		C Row		D Row	
Pin	Label	Pin	Label	Pin	Label	Pin	Label
1	CPURST	26	V_{CC}	51	A_{11}	76	DREQ5
2	INT	27	D_{11}	52	A_{10}	77	DREQ4/IRQ9#
3	V_{CC}	28	D_4	53	A_9	78	DREQ3
4	V_{SS}	29	D_{12}	54	A_8	79	DREQ2
5	TOUT2#/IRQ3#	30	D_5	55	A_7	80	DREQ1
6	TOUT3#	31	D_{13}	56	A_6	81	DREQ0
7	D/C#	32	D_6	57	A_5	82	IRQ23#
8	V_{CC}	33	V_{SS}	58	V_{CC}	83	IRQ22#
9	W/R#	34	D_{14}	59	A_4	84	IRQ21#
10	M/IO#	35	D_7	60	A_3	85	IRQ20#
11	HOLD	36	D_{15}	61	A_2	86	IRQ19#
12	TOUT1/REF#	37	A_{23}	62	A_1	87	IRQ18#
13	CLK2	38	A_{22}	63	V_{SS}	88	IRQ17#
14	V_{SS}	39	A_{21}	64	BLE#	89	IRQ16#
15	READYO#	40	A_{20}	65	BHE#	90	IRQ15#
16	EOP#	41	A_{19}	66	V_{SS}	91	IRQ14#
17	CHPSEL#	42	A_{18}	67	ADS#	92	IRQ13#
18	V_{CC}	43	V_{CC}	68	V_{CC}	93	IRQ12#
19	D_0	44	A_{17}	69	EDACK2	94	IRQ11#
20	D_8	45	A_{16}	70	EDACK1	95	CLKIN
21	D_1	46	A_{15}	71	EDACK0	96	WSC0
22	D_9	47	A_{14}	72	HLDA	97	WSC1
23	D_2	48	V_{SS}	73	DREQ7	98	RESET
24	D_{10}	49	A_{13}	74	DREQ6	99	READY#
25	D_3	50	A_{12}	75	NA#	100	V_{SS}

4

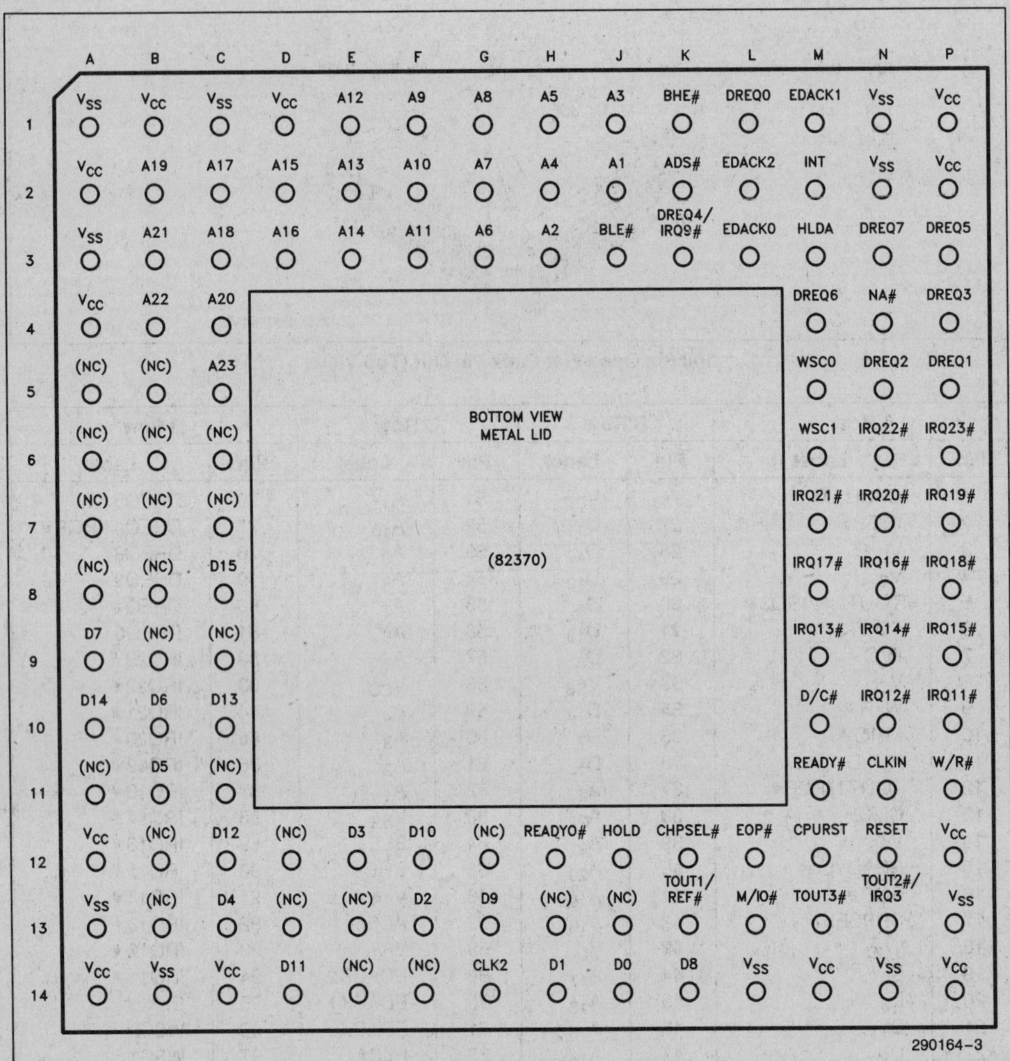

82370 PGA Pinout

Pin	Label	Pin	Label	Pin	Label	Pin	Label
G14	CLK2	D14	D_{11}	L1	DREQ0	A2	V_{CC}
N12	RESET	F12	D_{10}	P6	IRQ23#	P2	V_{CC}
M12	CPURST	G13	D_9	N6	IRQ22#	A4	V_{CC}
C5	A_{23}	K14	D_8	M7	IRQ21#	A12	V_{CC}
B4	A_{22}	A9	D_7	N7	IRQ20#	P12	V_{CC}
B3	A_{21}	B10	D_6	P7	IRQ19#	A14	V_{CC}
C4	A_{20}	B11	D_5	P8	IRQ18#	C14	V_{CC}
B2	A_{19}	C13	D_4	M8	IRQ17#	M14	V_{CC}
C3	A_{18}	E12	D_3	N8	IRQ16#	P14	V_{CC}
C2	A_{17}	F13	D_2	P9	IRQ15#	A5	NC
D3	A_{16}	H14	D_1	N9	IRQ14#	B5	NC
D2	A_{15}	J14	D_0	M9	IRQ13#	A6	NC
E3	A_{14}	P11	W/R#	N10	IRQ12#	B6	NC
E2	A_{13}	L13	M/IO#	P10	IRQ11#	C6	NC
E1	A_{12}	K2	ADS#	M5	WSC0	A7	NC
F3	A_{11}	M10	D/C#	M6	WSC1	B7	NC
F2	A_{10}	N4	NA#	M13	TOUT3#	C7	NC
F1	A_9	M11	READY#	N13	TOUT2#/IRQ3#	A8	NC
G1	A_8	H12	READYO#	K13	TOUT1/REF#	B8	NC
G2	A_7	J12	HOLD	N11	CLKIN	B9	NC
G3	A_6	M3	HLDA	A1	V_{SS}	C9	NC
H1	A_5	M2	INT	C1	V_{SS}	A11	NC
H2	A_4	L12	EOP#	N1	V_{SS}	B12	NC
J1	A_3	L2	EDACK2	N2	V_{SS}	C11	NC
H3	A_2	M1	EDACK1	A3	V_{SS}	D12	NC
J2	A_1	L3	EDACK0	A13	V_{SS}	G12	NC
J3	BLE#	N3	DREQ7	P13	V_{SS}	B13	NC
K1	BHE#	M4	DREQ6	B14	V_{SS}	D13	NC
K12	CHPSEL#	P3	DREQ5	L14	V_{SS}	E13	NC
C8	D_{15}	K3	DREQ4/IRQ9#	N14	V_{SS}	H13	NC
A10	D_{14}	P4	DREQ3	B1	V_{CC}	J13	NC
C10	D_{13}	N5	DREQ2	D1	V_{CC}	E14	NC
C12	D_{12}	P5	DREQ1	P1	V_{CC}	F14	NC

1.0 FUNCTIONAL OVERVIEW

The 82370 contains several independent functional modules. The following is a brief discussion of the components and features of the 82370. Each module has a corresponding detailed section later in this data sheet. Those sections should be referred to for design and programming information.

1.1 82370 Architecture

The 82370 is comprised of several computer system functions that are normally found in separate LSI and VLSI components. These include: a high-performance, eight-channel, 32-bit Direct Memory Access Controller; a 20-level Programmable Interrupt Controller which is a superset of the 82C59A; four 16-bit Programmable Interval Timers which are functionally equivalent to the 82C54 timers; a DRAM Refresh Controller; a Programmable Wait State Generator; and system reset logic. The interface to the 82370 is optimized for high-performance operation with the 80376 microprocessor.

The 82370 operates directly on the 80376 bus. In the Slave Mode, it monitors the state of the processor at all times and acts or idles according to the commands of the host. It monitors the address pipeline status and generates the programmed number of wait states for the device being accessed. The 82370 also has logic to the reset of the 80376 via hardware or software reset requests and processor shutdown status.

After a system reset, the 82370 is in the Slave Mode. It appears to the system as an I/O device. It becomes a bus master when it is performing DMA transfers.

To maintain compatibility with existing software, the registers within the 82370 are accessed as bytes. If the internal logic of the 82370 requires a delay before another access by the processor, wait states are automatically inserted into the access cycle. This allows the programmer to write initialization routines, etc. without regard to hardware recovery times.

Figure 1-1 shows the basic architectural components of the 82370. The following sections briefly discuss the architecture and function of each of the distinct sections of the 82370.

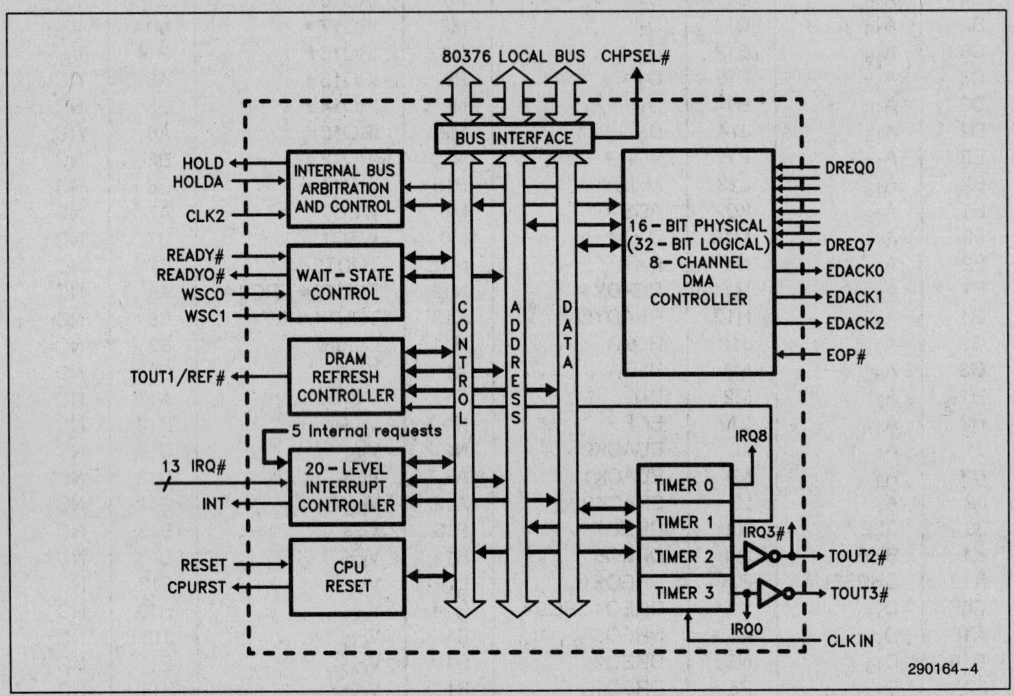

Figure 1-1. Architecture of the 82370

1.1.1 DMA CONTROLLER

The 82370 contains a high-performance, 8-channel DMA Controller. It provides a 32-bit internal data path. Through its 16-bit external physical data bus, it is capable of transferring data in any combination of bytes, words and double-words. The addresses of both source and destination can be independently incremented, decremented or held constant, and cover the entire 16-bit physical address space of the 80376. It can disassemble and assemble non-aligned data via a 32-bit internal temporary data storage register. Data transferred between devices of different data path widths can also be assembled and disassembled using the internal temporary data storage register. The DMA Controller can also transfer aligned data between I/O and memory on the fly, allowing data transfer rates up to 16 megabytes per second for an 82370 operating at 16 MHz. Figure 1-2 illustrates the functional components of the DMA Controller.

There are twenty-four general status and command registers in the 82370 DMA Controller. Through these registers any of the channels may be programmed into any of the possible modes. The operating modes of any one channel are independent of the operation of the other channels.

Each channel has three programmable registers which determine the location and amount of data to be transferred:

Byte Count Register—Number of bytes to transfer. (24-bits)

Requester Register — Byte Address of memory or peripheral which is requesting DMA service. (24-bits)

Target Register — Byte Address of peripheral or memory which will be accessed. (24-bits)

There are also port addresses which, when accessed, cause the 82370 to perform specific functions. The actual data written doesn't matter, the act of writing to the specific address causes the command to be executed. The commands which operate in this mode are: Master Clear, Clear Terminal Count Interrupt Request, Clear Mask Register, and Clear Byte Pointer Flip-Flop.

DMA transfers can be done between all combinations of memory and I/O; memory-to-memory, memory-to-I/O, I/O-to-memory, and I/O-to-I/O. DMA service can be requested through software and/or hardware. Hardware DMA acknowledge signals are available for all channels (except channel 4) through an encoded 3-bit DMA acknowledge bus (EDACK0–2).

4

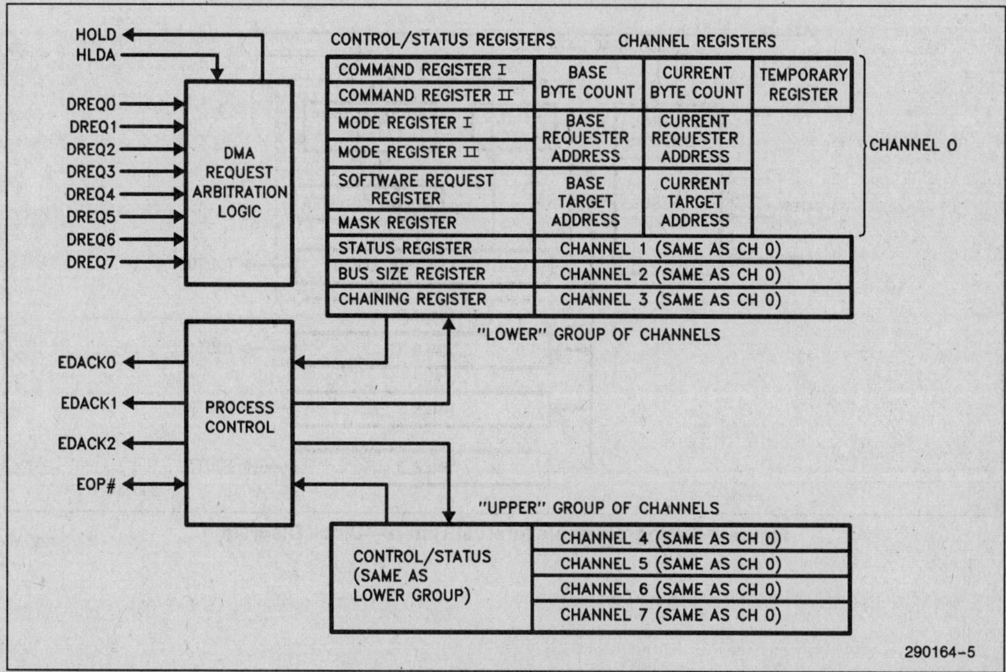

Figure 1-2. 82370 DMA Controller

The 82370 DMA Controller transfers blocks of data (buffers) in three modes: Single Buffer, Buffer Auto-Initialize, and Buffer Chaining. In the Single Buffer Process, the 82370 DMA Controller is programmed to transfer one particular block of data. Successive transfers then require reprogramming of the DMA channel. Single Buffer transfers are useful in systems where it is known at the time the transfer begins what quantity of data is to be transferred, and there is a contiguous block of data area available.

The Buffer Auto-Initialize Process allows the same data area to be used for successive DMA transfers without having to reprogram the channel.

The Buffer Chaining Process allows a program to specify a list of buffer transfers to be executed. The 82370 DMA Controller, through interrupt routines, is reprogrammed from the list. The channel is reprogrammed for a new buffer before the current buffer transfer is complete. This pipelining of the channel programming process allows the system to allocate non-contiguous blocks of data storage space, and transfer all of the data with one DMA process. The buffers that make up the chain do not have to be in contiguous locations.

Channel priority can be fixed or rotating. Fixed priority allows the programmer to define the priority of DMA channels based on hardware or other fixed parameters. Rotating priority is used to provide peripherals access to the bus on a shared basis.

With fixed priority, the programmer can set any channel to have the current lowest priority. This allows the user to reset or manually rotate the priority schedule without reprogramming the command registers.

1.1.2 PROGRAMMABLE INTERVAL TIMERS

Four 16-bit programmable interval timers reside within the 82370. These timers are identical in function to the timers in the 82C54 Programmable Interval Timer. All four of the timers share a common clock input which can be independent of the system clock. The timers are capable of operating in six different modes. In all of the modes, the current count can be latched and read by the 80376 at any time, making these very versatile event timers. Figure 1-3 shows the functional components of the Programmable Interval Timers.

The outputs of the timers are directed to key system functions, making system design simpler. Timer 0 is routed directly to an interrupt input and is not available externally. This timer would typically be used to generate time-keeping interrupts.

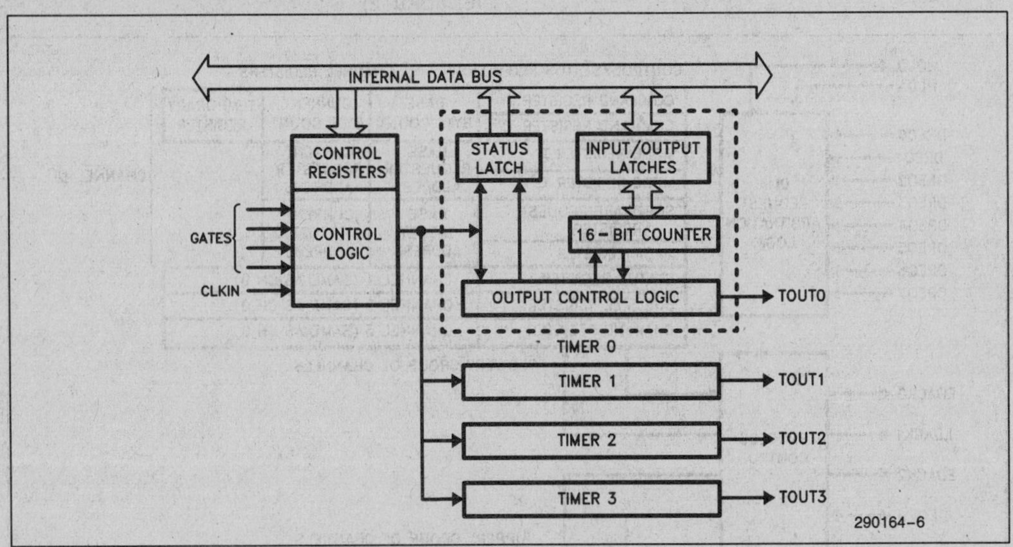

Figure 1-3. Programmable Interval Timers—Block Diagram

Timers 1 and 2 have outputs which are available for general timer/counter purposes as well as special functions. Timer 1 is routed to the refresh control logic to provide refresh timing. Timer 2 is connected to an interrupt request input to provide other timer functions. Timer 3 is a general purpose timer/counter whose output is available to external hardware. It is also connected internally to the interrupt request which defaults to the highest priority (IRQ0).

1.1.3 INTERRUPT CONTROLLER

The 82370 has the equivalent of three enhanced 82C59A Programmable Interrupt Controllers. These controllers can all be operated in the Master Mode, but the priority is always as if they were cascaded. There are 15 interrupt request inputs provided for the user, all of which can be inputs from external slave interrupt controllers. Cascading 82C59As to these request inputs allows a possible total of 120 external interrupt requests. Figure 1-4 is a block diagram of the 82370 Interrupt Controller.

Each of the interrupt request inputs can be individually programmed with its own interrupt vector, allowing more flexibility in interrupt vector mapping than was available with the 82C59A. An interrupt is provided to alert the system that an attempt is being made to program the vectors in the method of the 82C59A. This provides compatibility of existing software that used the 82C59A or 8259A with new designs using the 82370.

In the event of an unrequested or otherwise erroneous interrupt acknowledge cycle, the 82370 Interrupt Controller issues a default vector. This vector, programmed by the system software, will alert the system of unsolicited interrupts of the 80376.

The functions of the 82370 Interrupt Controller are identical to the 82C59A, except in regards to programming the interrupt vectors as mentioned above. Interrupt request inputs are programmable as either edge or level triggered and are software maskable. Priority can be either fixed or rotating and interrupt requests can be nested.

Enhancements are added to the 82370 for cascading external interrupt controllers. Master to Slave handshaking takes place on the data bus, instead of dedicated cascade lines.

4

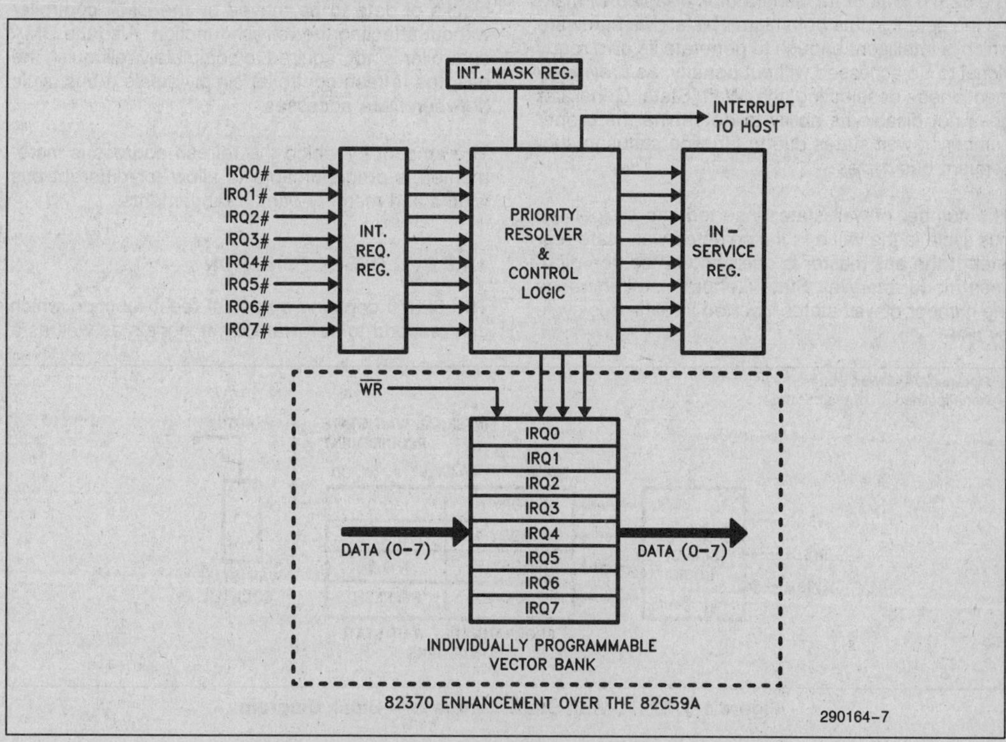

Figure 1-4. 82370 Interrupt Controller—Block Diagram

1.1.4 WAIT STATE GENERATOR

The Wait State Generator is a programmable READY generation circuit for the 80376 bus. A peripheral requiring wait states can request the Wait State Generator to hold the processor's READY input inactive for a predetermined number of bus states. Six different wait state counts can be programmed into the Wait State Generator by software; three for memory accesses and three for I/O accesses. A block diagram of the 82370 Wait State Generator is shown in Figure 1-5.

The peripheral being accessed selects the required wait state count by placing a code on a 2-bit wait state select bus. This code along with the M/IO# signal from the bus master is used to select one of six internal 4-bit wait state registers which has been programmed with the desired number of wait states. From zero to fifteen wait states can be programmed into the wait state registers. The Wait State generator tracks the state of the processor or current bus master at all times, regardless of which device is the current bus master and regardless of whether or not the wait state generator is currently active.

The 82370 Wait State Generator is disabled by making the select inputs both high. This allows hardware which is intelligent enough to generate its own ready signal to be accessed without penalty. As previously mentioned, deselecting the Wait State Generator does not disable its ability to determine the proper number of wait states due to pipeline status in subsequent bus cycles.

The number of wait states inserted into a pipelined bus cycle is the value in the selected wait state register. If the bus master is operating in the non-pipelined mode, the Wait State Generator will increase the number of wait states inserted into the bus cycle by one.

On reset, the Wait State Generator's registers are loaded with the value FFH, giving the maximum number of wait states for any access in which the wait state select inputs are active.

1.1.5 DRAM REFRESH CONTROLLER

The 82370 DRAM Refresh Controller consists of a 24-bit refresh address counter and bus arbitration logic. The output of Timer 1 is used to periodically request a refresh cycle. When the controller receives the request, it requests access to the system bus through the HOLD signal. When bus control is acknowledged by the processor or current bus master, the refresh controller executes a memory read operation at the address currently in the Refresh Address Register. At the same time, it activates a refresh signal (REF#) that the memory uses to force a refresh instead of a normal read. Control of the bus is transferred to the processor at the completion of this cycle. Typically a refresh cycle will take six clock cycles to execute on an 80376 bus.

The 82370 DRAM Refresh Controller has the highest priority when requesting bus access and will interrupt any active DMA process. This allows large blocks of data to be moved by the DMA controller without affecting the refresh function. Also the DMA controller is not required to completely relinquish the bus, the refresh controller simply steals a bus cycle between DMA accesses.

The amount by which the refresh address is incremented is programmable to allow for different bus widths and memory bank arrangements.

1.1.6 CPU RESET FUNCTION

The 82370 contains a special reset function which can respond to hardware reset signals as well as a

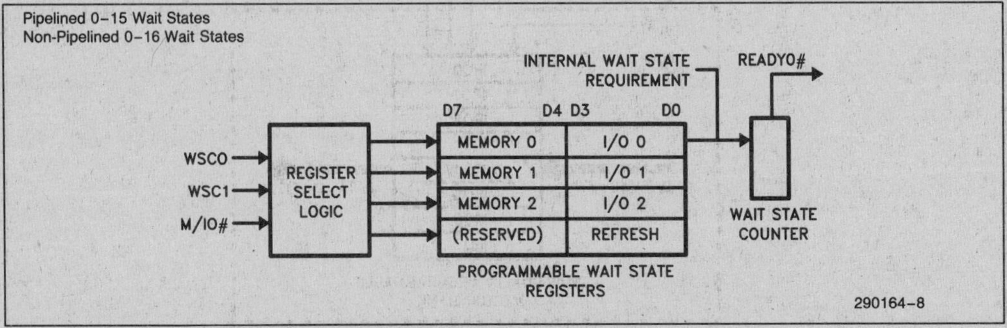

Figure 1-5. 82370 Wait State Generator—Block Diagram

software reset command. The circuit will hold the 80376's RESET line active while an external hardware reset signal is present at its RESET input. It can also reset the 80376 processor as the result of a software command. The software reset command causes the 82370 to hold the processor's RESET line active for a minimum of 62 clock cycles. The 80376 requires that its RESET line be held active for a minimum of 80 clock cycles to re-initialize. For a more detailed explanation and solution, see Appendix D (System Notes).

The 82370 can be programmed to sense the shutdown detect code on the status lines from the 80376. If the Shutdown Detect function is enabled, the 82370 will automatically reset the processor. A diagnostic register is available which can be used to determine the cause of reset.

1.1.7 REGISTER MAP RELOCATION

After a hardware reset, the internal registers of the 82370 are located in I/O space beginning at port address 0000H. The map of the 82370's registers is relocatable via a software command. The default mapping places the 82370 between I/O addresses 0000H and 00DBH. The relocation register allows this map to be moved to any even 256-byte boundary in the processor's 16-bit I/O address space or any even 64 kbyte boundary in the 24-bit memory address space.

1.2 Host Interface

The 82370 is designed to operate efficiently on the local bus of an 80376 microprocessor. The control signals of the 82370 are identical in function to those of the 80376. As a slave, the 82370 operates with all of the features available on the 80376 bus. When the 82370 is in the Master Mode, it looks identical to an 80376 to the connected devices.

The 82370 monitors the bus at all times, and determines whether the current bus cycle is a pipelined or non-pipelined access. All of the status signals of the processor are monitored.

The control, status, and data registers within the 82370 are located at fixed addresses relative to each other, but the group can be relocated to either memory or I/O space and to different locations within those spaces.

As a Slave device, the 82370 monitors the control/status lines of the CPU. The 82370 will generate all of the wait states it needs whenever it is accessed. This allows the programmer the freedom of accessing 82370 registers without having to insert NOPs in the program to wait for slower 82370 internal registers.

The 82370 can determine if a current bus cycle is a pipelined or a non-pipelined cycle. It does this by monitoring the ADS#, NA# and READY# signals and thereby keeping track of the current state of the 80376.

As a bus master, the 82370 looks like an 80376 to the rest of the system. This enables the designer greater flexibility in systems which include the 82370. The designer does not have to alter the interfaces of any peripherals designed to operate with the 80376 to accommodate the 82370. The 82370 will access any peripherals on the bus in the same manner as the 80376, including recognizing pipelined bus cycles.

The 82370 is accessed as an 8-bit peripheral. The 80376 places the data of all 8-bit accesses either on D(0–7) or D(8–15). The 82370 will only accept data on these lines when in the Slave Mode. When in the Master Mode, the 82370 is a full 16-bit machine, sending and receiving data in the same manner as the 80376.

2.0 80376 HOST INTERFACE

The 82370 contains a set of interface signals to operate efficiently with the 80376 host processor. These signals were designed so that minimal hardware is needed to connect the 82370 to the 80376. Figure 2-1 depicts a typical system configuration with the 80376 processor. As shown in the diagram, the 82370 is designed to interface directly with the 80376 bus.

Since the 82370 resides on the opposite side of the data bus transceivers with respect to the rest of the system peripherals, it is important to note that the transceivers should be controlled so that contention between the data bus transceivers and the 82370 will not occur. In order to ease the implementation of this, the 82370 activates the CHPSEL# signal which indicates that the 82370 has been addressed and may output data. This signal should be included in the direction and enable control logic of the transceiver. When any of the 82370 internal registers are read, the data bus transceivers should be disabled so that only the 82370 will drive the local bus.

This section describes the basic bus functions of the 82370 to show how this device interacts with the 80376 processor. Other signals which are not directly related to the host interface will be discussed in their associated functional block description.

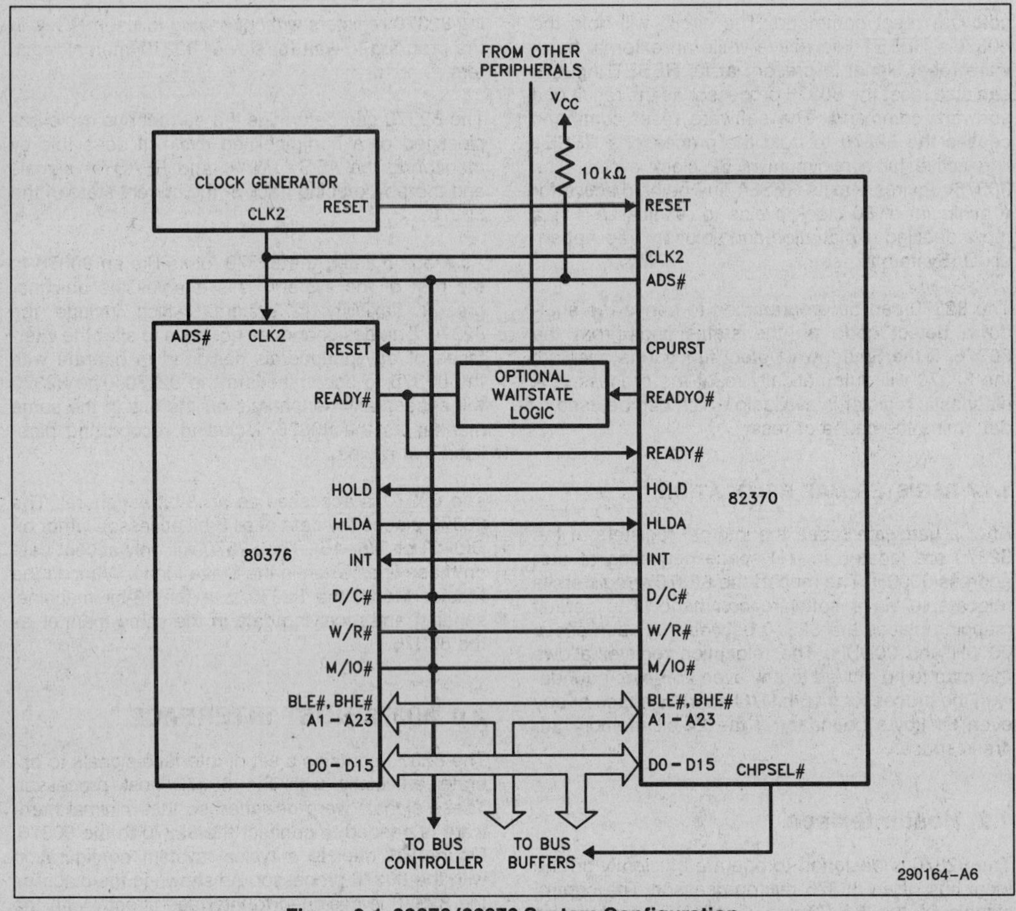

Figure 2-1. 80376/82370 System Configuration

2.1 Master and Slave Modes

At any time, the 82370 acts as either a Slave device or a Master device in the system. Upon reset, the 82370 will be in the Slave Mode. In this mode, the 80376 processor can read/write into the 82370 internal registers. Initialization information may be programmed into the 82370 during Slave Mode.

When DMA service (including DRAM Refresh Cycles generated by the 82370) is requested, the 82370 will request and subsequently get control of the 80376 local bus. This is done through the HOLD and HLDA (Hold Acknowledge) signals. When the 80376 processor responds by asserting the HLDA signal, the 82370 will switch into Master Mode and perform DMA transfers. In this mode, the 82370 is the bus master of the system. It can read/write data from/to memory and peripheral devices. The 82370 will return to the Slave Mode upon completion of DMA transfers, or when HLDA is negated.

2.2 80376 Interface Signals

As mentioned in the Architecture section, the Bus Interface module of the 82370 (see Figure 1-1) contains signals that are directly connected to the 80376 host processor. This module has separate

16-bit Data and 24-bit Address busses. Also, it has additional control signals to support different bus operations on the system. By residing on the 80376 local bus, the 82370 shares the same address, data and control lines with the processor. The following subsections discuss the signals which interface to the 80376 host processor.

2.2.1 CLOCK (CLK2)

The CLK2 input provides fundamental timing for the 82370. It is divided by two internally to generate the 82370 internal clock. Therefore, CLK2 should be driven with twice the 80376's frequency. In order to maintain synchronization with the 80376 host processor, the 82370 and the 80376 should share a common clock source.

The internal clock consists of two phases: PHI1 and PHI2. Each CLK2 period is a phase of the internal clock. PHI2 is usually used to sample input and set up internal signals and PHI1 is for latching internal data. Figure 2-2 illustrates the relationship of CLK2 and the 82370 internal clock signals. The CPURST signal generated by the 82370 guarantees that the 80376 will wake up in phase with PHI1.

2.2.2 DATA BUS (D_0-D_{15})

This 16-bit three-state bidirectional bus provides a general purpose data path between the 82370 and the system. These pins are tied directly to the corresponding Data Bus pins of the 80376 local bus. The Data Bus is also used for interrupt vectors generated by the 82370 in the Interrupt Acknowledge cycle.

During Slave I/O operations, the 82370 expects a single byte to be written or read. When the 80376 host processor writes into the 82370, either D_0-D_7 or D_8-D_{15} will be latched into the 82370, depending upon whether Byte Enable bit BLE# is 0 or 1 (see Table 2-1). When the 80376 host processor reads from the 82370, the single byte data will be duplicated twice on the Data Bus; i.e. on D_0-D_7 and D_8-D_{15}.

During Master Mode, the 82370 can transfer 16-, and 8-bit data between memory (or I/O devices) and I/O devices (or memory) via the Data Bus.

2.2.3 ADDRESS BUS ($A_{23}-A_1$)

These three-state bidirectional signals are connected directly to the 80376 Address Bus. In the Slave Mode, they are used as input signals so that the processor can address the 82370 internal ports/registers. In the Master Mode, they are used as output signals by the 82370 to address memory and peripheral devices. The Address Bus is capable of addressing 16 Mbytes of physical memory space (000000H to FFFFFFH), and 64 Kbytes of I/O addresses.

2.2.4 BYTE ENABLE (BHE#, BLE#)

The Byte Enable pins BHE# and BLE# select the specific byte(s) in the word addressed by A_1-A_{23}. During Master Mode operation, it is used as an output by the 82370 to address memory and I/O locations. The definition of BHE# and BLE# is further illustrated in Table 2-1.

NOTE:
The 82370 will activate BHE# when output in Master Mode. For a more detailed explanation and its solutions, see Appendix D (System Notes).

4

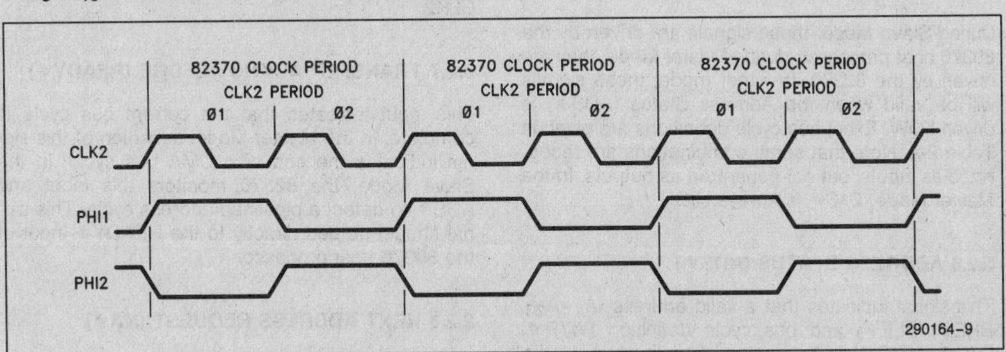

Figure 2-2. CLK2 and 82370 Internal Clock

As an output (Master Mode):

Table 2-1. Byte Enable Signals

BHE#	BLE#	Byte to be Accessed Relative to $A_{23}-A_1$	Logical Byte Presented on Data Bus During WRITE Only* $D_{15}-D_8$	D_7-D_0
0	0	0, 1	B	A
0	1	1	A	A
1	0	0	U	A
1	1	(Not Used)		

U = Undefined
A = Logical D_0-D_7
B = Logical D_8-D_{15}

***NOTE:**
Actual number of bytes accessed depends upon the programmed data path width.

Table 2-2. Bus Cycle Definition

M/IO#	D/C#	W/R#	As INPUTS	As OUTPUTS
0	0	0	Interrupt Acknowledge	NOT GENERATED
0	0	1	UNDEFINED	NOT GENERATED
0	1	0	I/O Read	I/O Read
0	1	1	I/O Write	I/O Write
1	0	0	UNDEFINED	NOT GENERATED
1	0	1	HALT if $A_1 = 1$ SHUTDOWN if $A_1 = 0$	NOT GENERATED
1	1	0	Memory Read	Memory Read
1	1	1	Memory Write	Memory Write

2.2.5 BUS CYCLE DEFINITION SIGNALS (D/C#, W/R#, M/IO#)

These three-state bidirectional signals define the type of bus cycle being performed. W/R# distinguishes between write and read cycles. D/C# distinguishes between processor data and control cycles. M/IO# distinguishes between memory and I/O cycles.

During Slave Mode, these signals are driven by the 80376 host processor; during Master Mode, they are driven by the 82370. In either mode, these signals will be valid when the Address Status (ADS#) is driven LOW. Exact bus cycle definitions are given in Table 2-2. Note that some combinations are recognized as inputs, but not generated as outputs. In the Master Mode, D/C# is always HIGH.

2.2.6 ADDRESS STATUS (ADS#)

This signal indicates that a valid address (A_1–A_{23}, BHE#, BLE#) and bus cycle definition (W/R#, D/C#, M/IO#) is being driven on the bus. In the Master Mode, it is driven by the 82370 as an output. In the Slave Mode, this signal is monitored as an input by the 82370. By the current and past status of ADS# and the READY# input, the 82370 is able to determine, during Slave Mode, if the next bus cycle is a pipelined address cycle. ADS# is asserted during T1 and T2P bus states (see Bus State Definition).

NOTE:
ADS# must be qualified with the rising edge of CLK2.

2.2.7 TRANSFER ACKNOWLEDGE (READY#)

This input indicates that the current bus cycle is complete. In the Master Mode, assertion of this signal indicates the end of a DMA bus cycle. In the Slave Mode, the 82370 monitors this input and ADS# to detect a pipelined address cycle. This signal should be tied directly to the READY# input of the 80376 host processor.

2.2.8 NEXT ADDRESS REQUEST (NA#)

This input is used to indicate to the 82370 in the Master Mode that the system is requesting address pipelining. When driven LOW by either memory or peripheral devices during Master Mode, it indicates that the system is prepared to accept a new address and bus cycle definition signals from the 82370 before the end of the current bus cycle. If this input is active when sampled by the 82370, the next address is driven onto the bus, provided a bus request is already pending internally.

This input pin is monitored only in the Master Mode. In the Slave Mode, the 82370 uses the ADS# and READY# signals to determine address pipelining cycles, and NA# will be ignored.

2.2.9 RESET (RESET, CPURST)

RESET

This synchronous input suspends any operation in progress and places the 82370 in a known initial state. Upon reset, the 82370 will be in the Slave Mode waiting to be initialized by the 80376 host processor. The 82370 is reset by asserting RESET for 15 or more CLK2 periods. When RESET is asserted, all other input pins are ignored, and all other bus pins are driven to an idle bus state as shown in Table 2-3. The 82370 will determine the phase of its internal clock following RESET going inactive.

RESET is level-sensitive and must be synchronous to the CLK2 signal. The RESET setup and hold time requirements are shown in Figure 2-3.

Table 2-3. Output Signals Following RESET

Signal	Level
A_1–A_{23}, D_0–D_{15}, BHE#, BLE#	Float
D/C#, W/R#, M/IO#, ADS#	Float
READYO#	'1'
EOP#	'1' (Weak Pull-UP)
EDACK2–EDACK0	'100'
HOLD	'0'
INT	UNDEFINED*
TOUT1/REF#, TOUT2#/IRQ3#, TOUT3#	UNDEFINED*
CPURST	'0'
CHPSEL#	'1'

***NOTE:**
The Interrupt Controller and Programmable Interval Timer are initialized by software commands.

CPURST

This output signal is used to reset the 80376 host processor. It will go active (HIGH) whenever one of the following events occurs: a) 82370's RESET input is active; b) a software RESET command is issued to the 82370; or c) when the 82370 detects a processor Shutdown cycle and when this detection feature is enabled (see CPU Reset and Shutdown Detect). When activated, CPURST will be held active for 62 clocks. The timing of CPURST is such that the 80376 processor will be in synchronization with the 82370. This timing is shown in Figure 2-4.

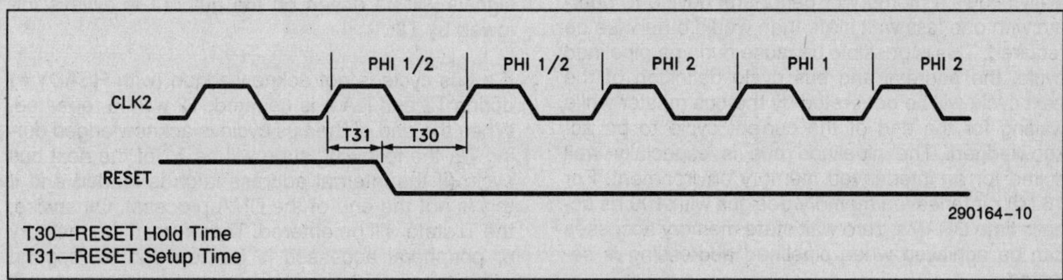

Figure 2-3. RESET Timing

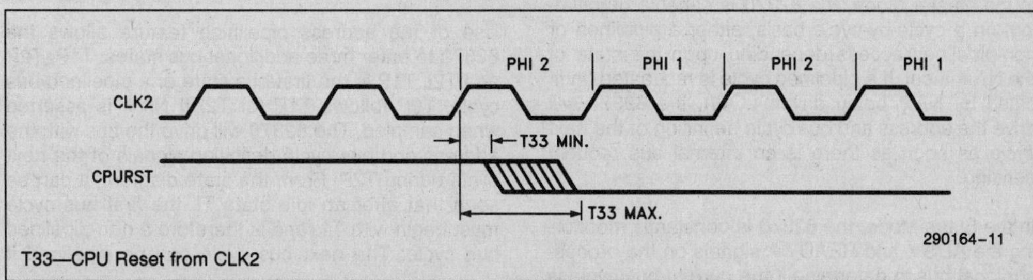

Figure 2-4. CPURST Timing

2.2.10 INTERRUPT OUT (INT)

This output pin is used to signal the 80376 host processor that one or more interrupt requests (either internal or external) are pending. The processor is expected to respond with an Interrupt Acknowledge cycle. This signal should be connected directly to the Maskable Interrupt Request (INTR) input of the 80376 host processor.

2.3 82370 Bus Timing

The 82370 internally divides the CLK2 signal by two to generate its internal clock. Figure 2-2 showed the relationship of CLK2 and the internal clock which consists of two phases: PHI1 and PHI2. Each CLK2 period is a phase of the internal clock.

In the 82370, whether it is in the Master or Slave Mode, the shortest time unit of bus activity is a bus state. A bus state, which is also referred as a 'T-state', is defined as one 82370 PHI2 clock period (i.e. two CLK2 periods). Recall in Table 2-2 various types of bus cycles in the 82370 are defined by the M/IO#, D/C# and W/R# signals. Each of these bus cycles is composed of two or more bus states. The length of a bus cycle depends on when the READY# input is asserted (i.e. driven LOW).

2.3.1 ADDRESS PIPELINING

The 82370 supports Address Pipelining as an option in both the Master and Slave Mode. This feature typically allows a memory or peripheral device to operate with one less wait state than would otherwise be required. This is possible because during a pipelined cycle, the address and bus cycle definition of the next cycle will be generated by the bus master while waiting for the end of the current cycle to be acknowledged. The pipelined bus is especially well suited for an interleaved memory environment. For 16 MHz interleaved memory designs with 100 ns access time DRAMs, zero wait state memory accesses can be achieved when pipelined addressing is selected.

In the Master Mode, the 82370 is capable of initiating, on a cycle-by-cycle basis, either a pipelined or non-pipelined access depending upon the state of the NA# input. If a pipelined cycle is requested (indicated by NA# being driven LOW), the 82370 will drive the address and bus cycle definition of the next cycle as soon as there is an internal bus request pending.

In the Slave Mode, the 82370 is constantly monitoring the ADS# and READY# signals on the processor local bus to determine if the current bus cycle is a pipelined cycle. If a pipelined cycle is detected, the 82370 will request one less wait state from the processor if the Wait State Generator feature is selected. On the other hand, during an 82370 internal register access in a pipelined cycle, it will make use of the advance address and bus cycle information. In all cases, Address Pipelining will result in a savings of one wait state.

2.3.2 MASTER MODE BUS TIMING

When the 82370 is in the Master Mode, it will be in one of six bus states. Figure 2-5 shows the complete bus state diagram of the Master Mode, including pipelined address states. As seen in the figure, the 82370 state diagram is very similar to that of the 80376. The major difference is that in the 82370, there is no Hold state. Also, in the 82370, the conditions for some state transitions depend upon whether it is the end of a DMA process.

NOTE:
The term 'end of a DMA process' is loosely defined here. It depends on the DMA modes of operation as well as the state of the EOP# and DREQ inputs. This is expained in detail in section 3—DMA Controller.

The 82370 will enter the idle state, Ti, upon RESET and whenever the internal address is not available at the end of a DMA cycle or at the end of a DMA process. When address pipelining is not used (NA# is not asserted), a new bus cycle always begins with state T1. During T1, address and bus cycle definition signals will be driven on the bus. T1 is always followed by T2.

If a bus cycle is not acknowledged (with READY#) during T2 and NA# is negated, T2 will be repeated. When the end of the bus cycle is acknowledged during T2, the following state will be T1 of the next bus cycle (if the internal address latch is loaded and if this is not the end of the DMA process). Otherwise, the Ti state will be entered. Therefore, if the memory or peripheral accessed is fast enough to respond within the first T2, the fastest non-pipelined cycle will take one T1 and one T2 state.

Use of the address pipelining feature allows the 82370 to enter three additional bus states: T1P, T2P and T2i. T1P is the first bus state of a pipelined bus cycle. T2P follows T1P (or T2) if NA# is asserted when sampled. The 82370 will drive the bus with the address and bus cycle definition signals of the next cycle during T2P. From the state diagram, it can be seen that after an idle state Ti, the first bus cycle must begin with T1, and is therefore a non-pipelined bus cycle. The next bus cycle can be pipelined if

NA# is asserted and the previous bus cycle ended in a T2P state. Once the 82370 is in a pipelined cycle and provided that NA# is asserted in subsequent cycles, the 82370 will be switching between T1P and T2P states. If the end of the current bus cycle is not acknowledged by the READY# input, the 82370 will extend the cycle by adding T2P states. The fastest pipelined cycle will consist of one T1P and one T2P state.

The 82370 will enter state T2i when NA# is asserted and when one of the following two conditions occurs. The first condition is when the 82370 is in state T2. T2i will be entered if READY# is not asserted and there is no next address available. This situation is similar to a wait state. The 82370 will stay in T2i for as long as this condition exists. The second condition which will cause the 82370 to enter T2i is when the 82370 is in state T1P. Before going to state T2P, the 82370 needs to wait in state T2i until the next address is available. Also, in both cases, if the DMA process is complete, the 82370 will enter the T2i state in order to finish the current DMA cycle.

Figure 2-6 is a timing diagram showing non-pipelined bus accesses in the Master Mode. Figure 2-7 shows the timing of pipelined accesses in the Master Mode.

2.3.3 SLAVE MODE BUS TIMING

Figure 2-8 shows the Slave Mode bus timing in both pipelined and non-pipelined cycles when the 82370 is being accessed. Recall that during Slave Mode, the 82370 will constantly monitor the ADS# and READY# signals to determine if the next cycle is pipelined. In Figure 2-8, the first cycle is non-pipelined and the second cycle is pipelined. In the pipelined cycle, the 82370 will start decoding the address and bus cycle signals one bus state earlier than in a non-pipelined cycle.

The READY# input signal is sampled by the 80376 host processor to determine the completion of a bus cycle. This occurs during the end of every T2, T2i and T2P state. Normally, the output of the 82370 Wait State Generator, READYO#, is directly connected to the READY# input of the 80376 host processor and the 82370. In such case, READYO# and READY# will be identical (see Wait State Generator).

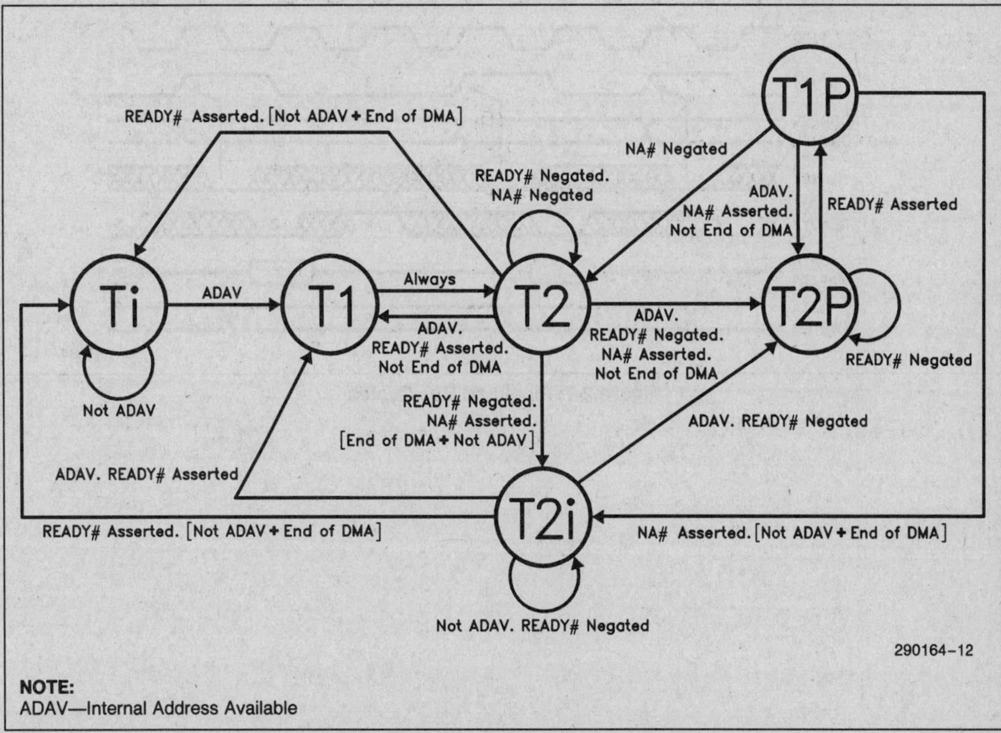

NOTE:
ADAV—Internal Address Available

Figure 2-5. Master Mode State Diagram

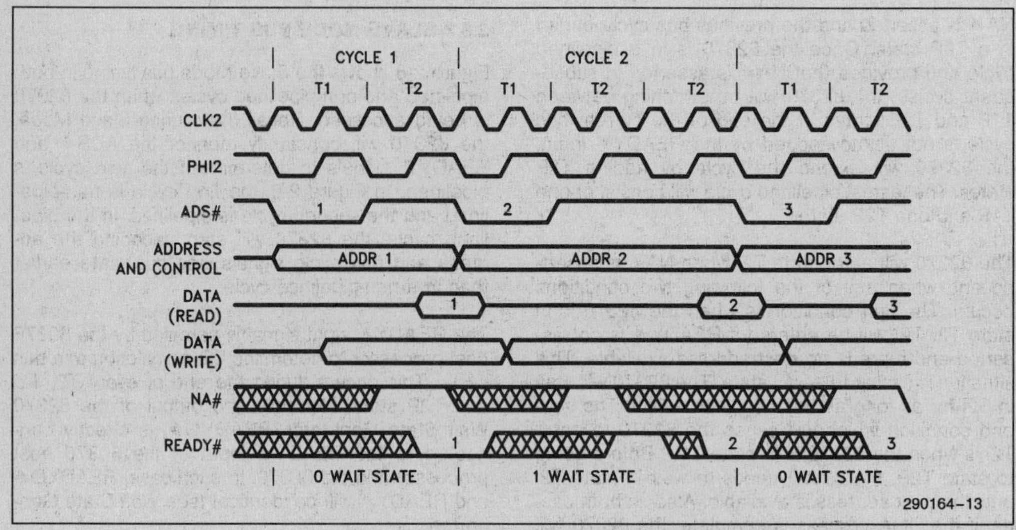

Figure 2-6. Non-Pipelined Bus Cycles

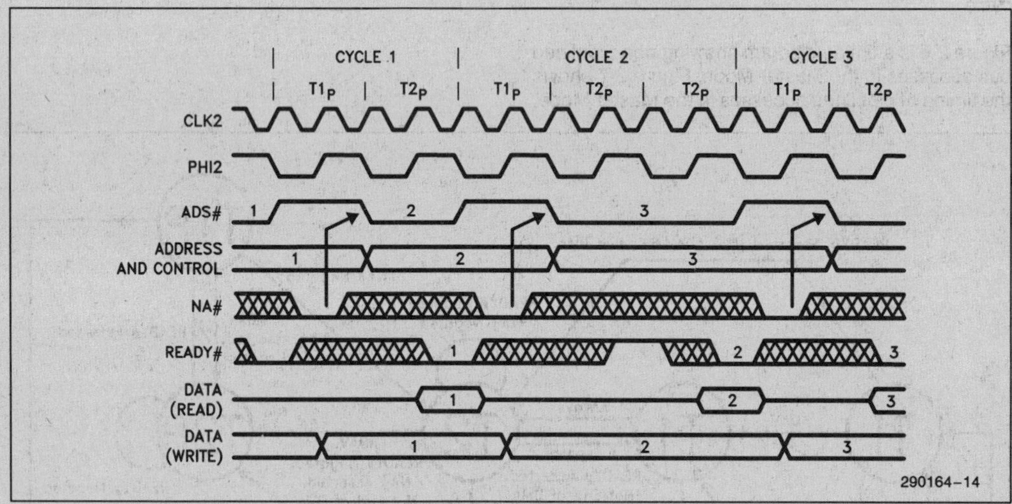

Figure 2-7. Pipelined Bus Cycles

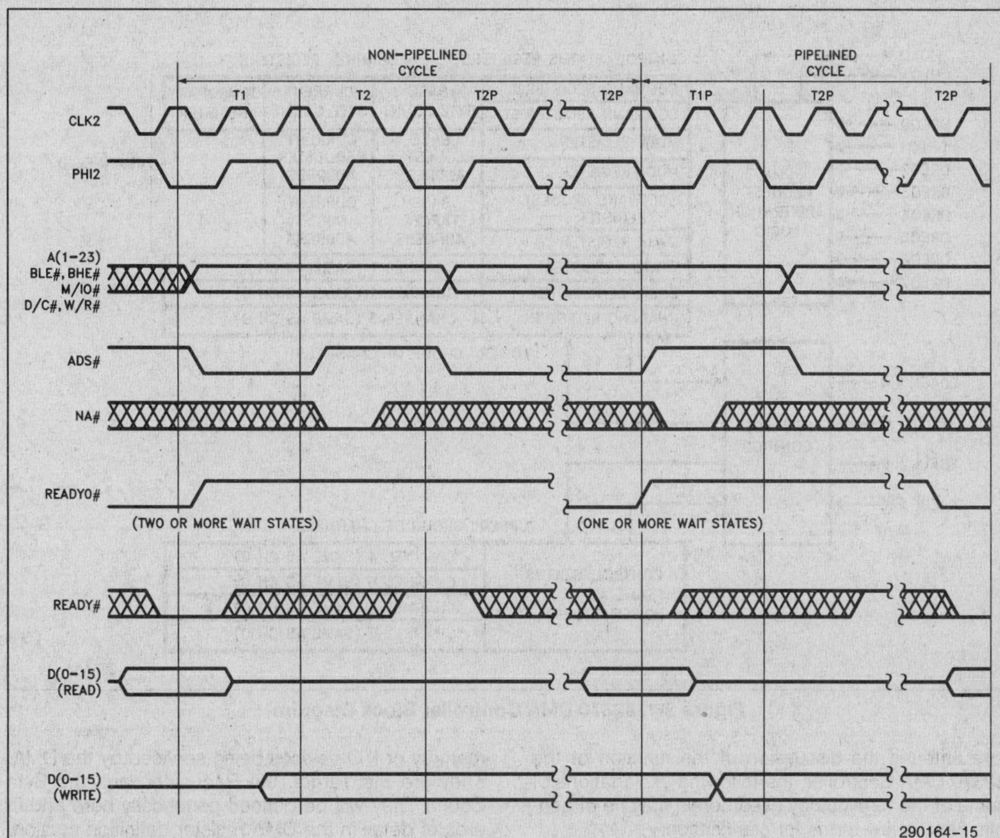

NOTE:
NA# is shown here only for timing reference. It is not sampled by the 82370 during Slave Mode.
When the 82370 registers are accessed, it will take one or more wait states in pipelined and two or more wait states in non-pipelined cycle to complete the internal access.

Figure 2-8. Slave Read/Write Timing

3.0 DMA CONTROLLER

The 82370 DMA Controller is capable of transferring data between any combination of memory and/or I/O, with any combination of data path widths. The 82370 DMA Controller can be programmed to accommodate 8- or 16-bit devices. With its 16-bit external data path, it can transfer data in units of byte or a word. Bus bandwidth is optimized through the use of an internal temporary register which can disassemble or assemble data to or from either an aligned or non-aligned destination or source. Figure 3-1 is a block diagram of the 82370 DMA Controller.

The 82370 has eight channels of DMA. Each channel operates independently of the others. Within the operation of the individual channels, there are many different modes of data transfer available. Many of the operating modes can be intermixed to provide a very versatile DMA controller.

3.1 Functional Description

In describing the operation of the 82370's DMA Controller, close attention to terminology is required. Be-

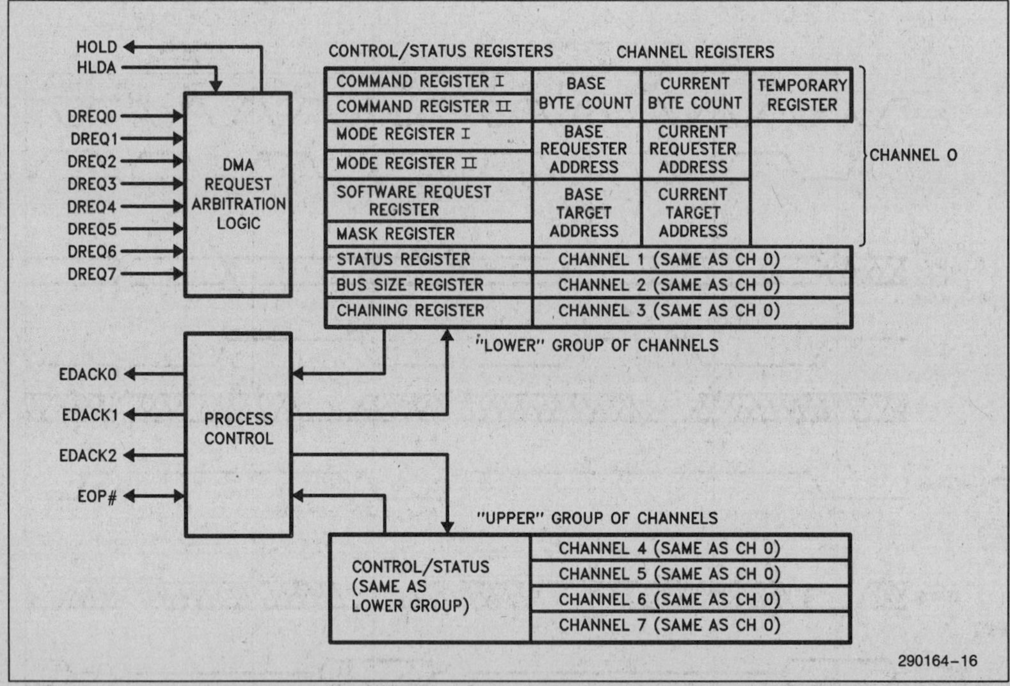

Figure 3-1. 82370 DMA Controller Block Diagram

fore entering the discussion of the function of the 82370 DMA Controller, the following explanations of some of the terminology used herein may be of benefit. First, a few terms for clarification:

DMA PROCESS—A DMA process is the execution of a programmed DMA task from beginning to end. Each DMA process requires intitial programming by the host 80376 microprocessor.

BUFFER—A contiguous block of data.

BUFFER TRANSFER—The action required by the DMA to transfer an entire buffer.

DATA TRANSFER—The DMA action in which a group of bytes or words are moved between devices by the DMA Controller. A data transfer operation may involve movement of one or many bytes.

BUS CYCLE—Access by the DMA to a single byte or word.

Each DMA channel consists of three major components. These components are identified by the contents of programmable registers which define the memory or I/O devices being serviced by the DMA. They are the Target, the Requester, and the Byte Count. They will be defined generically here and in greater detail in the DMA register definition section.

The Requester is the device which requires service by the 82370 DMA Controller, and makes the request for service. All of the control signals which the DMA monitors or generates for specific channels are logically related to the Requester. Only the Requester is considered capable of initiating or terminating a DMA process.

The Target is the device with which the Requester wishes to communicate. As far as the DMA process is concerned, the Target is a slave which is incapable of control over the process.

The direction of data transfer can be either from Requester to Target or from Target to Requester; i.e. each can be either a source or a destination.

The Requester and Target may each be either I/O or memory. Each has an address associated with it that can be incremented, decremented, or held constant. The addresses are stored in the Requester

Address Registers and Target Address Registers, respectively. These registers have two parts: one which contains the current address being used in the DMA process (Current Address Register), and one which holds the programmed base address (Base Address Register). The contents of the Base Registers are never changed by the 82370 DMA Controller. The Current Registers are incremented or decremented according to the progress of the DMA process.

The Byte Count is the component of the DMA process which dictates the amount of data which must be transferred. Current and Base Byte Count Registers are provided. The Current Byte Count Register is decremented once for each byte transferred by the DMA process. When the register is decremented past zero, the Byte Count is considered 'expired' and the process is terminated or restarted, depending on the mode of operation of the channel. The point at which the Byte Count expires is called 'Terminal Count' and several status signals are dependent on this event.

Each channel of the 82370 DMA Controller also contains a 32-bit Temporary Register for use in assembling and disassembling non-aligned data. The operation of this register is transparent to the user, although the contents of it may affect the timing of some DMA handshake sequences. Since there is data storage available for each channel, the DMA Controller can be interrupted without loss of data.

To avoid unexpected results, care should be taken in programming the byte count correctly when assembing and disassembling non-aligned data. For example:

Words to Bytes:
Transferring two words to bytes, but setting the byte count to three, will result in three bytes transferred and the final byte flushed.

Bytes to Words:
Transferring six bytes to three words, but setting the byte count to five, will result in the sixth byte transferred being undefined.

The 82370 DMA Controller is a slave on the bus until a request for DMA service is received via either a software request command or a hardware request signal. The host processor may access any of the control/status or channel registers at any time the 82370 is a bus slave. Figure 3-2 shows the flow of operations that the DMA Controller performs.

At the time a DMA service request is received, the DMA Controller issues a bus hold request to the host processor. The 82370 becomes the bus master when the host relinquishes the bus by asserting a hold acknowledge signal. The channel to be serviced will be the one with the highest priority at the time the DMA Controller becomes the bus master. The DMA Controller will remain in control of the bus until the hold acknowledge signal is removed, or until the current DMA transfer is complete.

While the 82370 DMA Controller has control of the bus, it will perform the required data transfer(s). The type of transfer, source and destination addresses, and amount of data to transfer are programmed in the control registers of the DMA channel which received the request for service.

At completion of the DMA process, the 82370 will remove the bus hold request. At this time the 82370 becomes a slave again, and the host returns to being a master. If there are other DMA channels with requests pending, the controller will again assert the hold request signal and restart the bus arbitration and switching process.

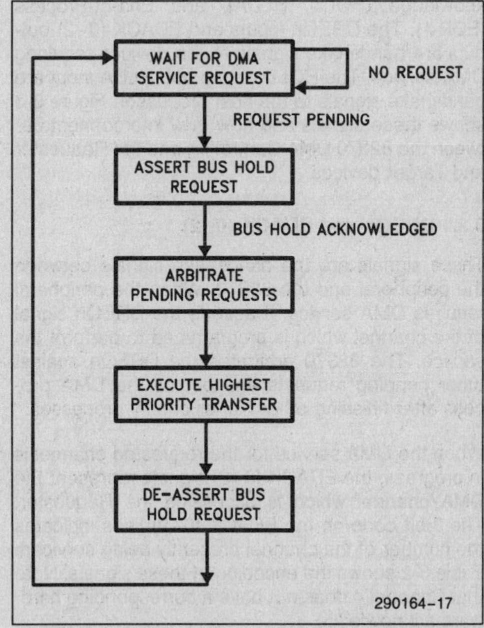

Figure 3-2. Flow of DMA Controller Operation

3.2 Interface Signals

There are fourteen control signals dedicated to the DMA process. They include eight DMA Channel Requests (DREQn), three Encoded DMA Acknowledge signals (EDACKn), Processor Hold and Hold Ac-

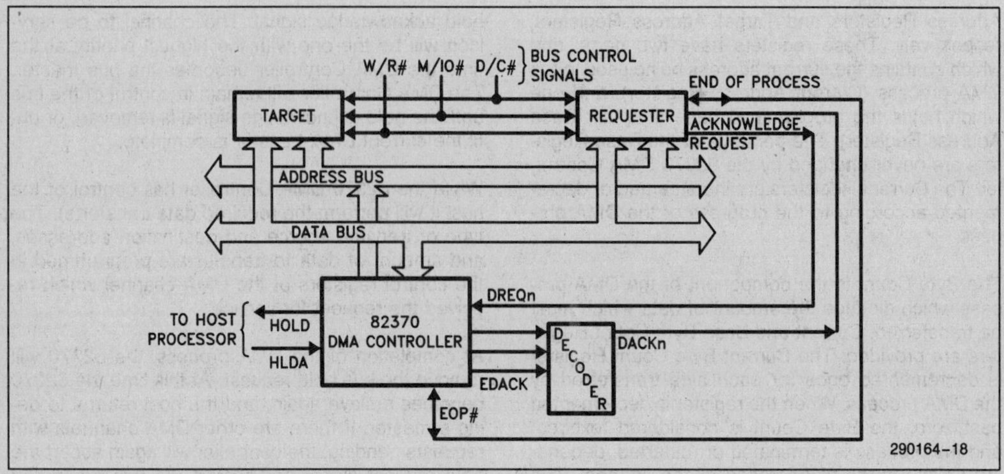

Figure 3-3. Requester, Target and DMA Controller Interconnection

knowledge (HOLD, HLDA), and End-of-Process (EOP#). The DREQn inputs and EDACK (0–2) outputs are handshake signals to the devices requiring DMA service. The HOLD output and HLDA input are handshake signals to the host processor. Figure 3-3 shows these signals and how they interconnect between the 82370 DMA Controller, and the Requester and Target devices.

3.2.1 DREQn and EDACK (0–2)

These signals are the handshake signals between the peripheral and the 82370. When the peripheral requires DMA service, it asserts the DREQn signal of the channel which is programmed to perform the service. The 82370 arbitrates the DREQn against other pending requests and begins the DMA process after finishing other higher priority processes.

When the DMA service for the requested channel is in progress, the EDACK (0–2) signals represent the DMA channel which is accessing the Requester. The 3-bit code on the EDACK (0–2) lines indicates the number of the channel presently being serviced. Table 3-2 shows the encoding of these signals. Note that Channel 4 does not have a corresponding hardware acknowledge.

The DMA acknowledge (EDACK) signals indicate the active channel only during DMA accesses to the Requester. During accesses to the Target, EDACK (0–2) has the idle code (100). EDACK (0–2) can thus be used to select a Requester device during a transfer.

DREQn can be programmed as either an Asynchronous or Synchronous input. See section 3.4.1 for details on synchronous versus asynchronous operation of these pins.

Table 3-2. EDACK Encoding During a DMA Transfer

EDACK2	EDACK1	EDACK0	Active Channel
0	0	0	0
0	0	1	1
0	1	0	2
0	1	1	3
1	0	0	Target Access
1	0	1	5
1	1	0	6
1	1	1	7

The EDACKn signals are always active. They either indicate 'no acknowledge' or they indicate a bus access to the requester. The acknowledge code is either 100, for an idle DMA or during a DMA access to the Target, or 'n' during a Requester access, where n is the binary value representing the channel. A simple 3-line to 8-line decoder can be used to provide discrete acknowledge signals for the peripherals.

3.2.2 HOLD AND HLDA

The Hold Request (HOLD) and Hold Acknowledge (HLDA) signals are the handshake signals between the DMA Controller and the host processor. HOLD is an output from the 82370 and HLDA is an input. HOLD is asserted by the DMA Controller when there is a pending DMA request, thus requesting the processor to give up control of the bus so the DMA process can take place. The 80376 responds by asserting HLDA when it is ready to relinquish control of the bus.

The 82370 will begin operations on the bus one clock cycle after the HLDA signal goes active. For this reason, other devices on the bus should be in the slave mode when HLDA is active.

HOLD and HLDA should not be used to gate or select peripherals requesting DMA service. This is because of the use of DMA-like operations by the DRAM Refresh Controller. The Refresh Controller is arbitrated with the DMA Controller for control of the bus, and refresh cycles have the highest priority. A refresh cycle will take place between DMA cycles without relinquishing bus control. See section 3.4.3 for a more detailed discussion of the interaction between the DMA Controller and the DRAM Refresh Controller.

3.2.3 EOP#

EOP# is a bi-directional signal used to indicate the end of a DMA process. The 82370 activates this as an output during the T2 states of the last Requester bus cycle for which a channel is programmed to execute. The Requester should respond by either withdrawing its DMA request, or interrupting the host processor to indicate that the channel needs to be programmed with a new buffer. As an input, this signal is used to tell the DMA Controller that the peripheral being serviced does not require any more data to be transferred. This indicates that the current buffer is to be terminated.

EOP# can be programmed as either an Asynchronous or a Synchronous input. See section 3.4.1 for details on synchronous versus asynchronous operation of this pin.

3.3 Modes of Operation

The 82370 DMA Controller has many independent operating functions. When designing peripheral interfaces for the 82370 DMA Controller, all of the functions or modes must be considered. All of the channels are independent of each other (except in priority of operation) and can operate in any of the modes. Many of the operating modes, though independently programmable, affect the operation of other modes. Because of the large number of combinations possible, each programmable mode is discussed here with its affects on the operation of other modes. The entire list of possible combinations will not be presented.

Table 3-1 shows the categories of DMA features available in the 82370. Each of the five major categories is independent of the others. The sub-categories are the available modes within the major function or mode category. The following sections explain each mode or function and its relation to other features.

Table 3-1. DMA Operating Modes

I. TARGET/REQUESTER DEFINITION
- a. Data Transfer Direction
- b. Device Type

II. BUFFER PROCESSES
- a. Single Buffer Process
- b. Buffer Auto-Initialize Process
- c. Buffer Chaining Process

III. DATA TRANSFER/HANDSHAKE MODES
- a. Single Transfer Mode
- b. Demand Transfer Mode
- c. Block Transfer Mode
- d. Cascade Mode

IV. PRIORITY ARBITRATION
- a. Fixed
- b. Rotating
- c. Programmable Fixed

V. BUS OPERATION
- a. Fly-By (Single-Cycle)/Two-Cycle
- b. Data Path Width
- c. Read, Write, or Verify Cycles

3.3.1 TARGET/REQUESTER DEFINITION

All DMA transfers involve three devices: the DMA Controller, the Requester, and the Target. Since the devices to be accessed by the DMA Controller vary widely, the operating characteristics of the DMA Controller must be tailored to the Requester and Target devices.

The Requester can be defined as either the source or the destination of the data to be transferred. This is done by specifying a Write or a Read transfer, respectively. In a Read transfer, the Target is the data source and the Requester is the destination for the data. In a Write transfer, the Requester is the source and the Target is the destination.

The Requester and Target addresses can each be independently programmed to be incremented, decremented, or held constant. As an example, the 82370 is capable of reversing a string of data by having the Requester address increment and the Target address decrement in a memory-to-memory transfer.

3.3.2 BUFFER TRANSFER PROCESSES

The 82370 DMA Controller allows three programmable Buffer Transfer Processes. These processes define the logical way in which a buffer of data is accessed by the DMA.

The three Buffer Transfer Processes include the Single Buffer Process, the Buffer Auto-Initialize Process, and the Buffer Chaining Process. These processes require special programming considerations. See the DMA Programming section for more details on setting up the Buffer Transfer Processes.

Single Buffer Process

The Single Buffer Process allows the DMA channel to transfer only one buffer of data. When the buffer has been completely transferred (Current Byte Count decremented past zero or EOP# input active), the DMA process ends and the channel becomes idle. In order for that channel to be used again, it must be reprogrammed.

The Single Buffer Process is usually used when the amount of data to be transferred is known exactly, and it is also known that there is not likely to be any data to follow before the operating system can reprogram the channel.

Buffer Auto-Initialize Process

The Buffer Auto-Initialize Process allows multiple groups of data to be transferred to or from a single buffer. This process does not require reprogramming. The Current Registers are automatically reprogrammed from the Base Registers when the current process is terminated, either by an expired Byte Count or by an external EOP# signal. The data transferred will always be between the same Target and Requester.

The auto-initialization/process-execution cycle is repeated until the channel is either disabled or re-programmed.

Buffer Chaining Process

The Buffer Chaining Process is useful for transferring large quantities of data into non-contiguous buffer areas. In this process, a single channel is used to process data from several buffers, while having to program the channel only once. Each new buffer is programmed in a pipelined operation that provides the new buffer information while the old buffer is being processed. The chain is created by loading new buffer information while the 82370 DMA Controller is processing the Current Buffer. When the Current Buffer expires, the 82370 DMA Controller automatically restarts the channel using the new buffer information.

Loading the new buffer information is done by an interrupt routine which is requested by the 82370. Interrupt Request 1 (IRQ1) is tied internally to the 82370 DMA Controller for this purpose. IRQ1 is generated by the 82370 when the new buffer information is loaded into the channel's Current Registers, leaving the Base Registers 'empty'. The interrupt service routine loads new buffer information into the Base Registers. The host processor is required to load the information for another buffer before the current Byte Count expires. The process repeats until the host programs the channel back to single buffer operation, or until the channel runs out of buffers.

The channel runs out of buffers when the Current Buffer expires and the Base Registers have not yet been loaded with new buffer information. When this occurs, the channel must be reprogrammed.

If an external EOP# is encountered while executing a Buffer Chaining Process, the current buffer is considered expired and the new buffer information is loaded into the Current Registers. If the Base Registers are 'empty', the chain is terminated.

The channel uses the Base Target Address Register as an indicator of whether or not the Base Registers are full. When the most significant byte of the Base Target Register is loaded, the channel considers all of the Base Registers loaded, and removes the interrupt request. This requires that the other Base Registers (Base Requester Address, Base Byte Count) must be loaded before the Base Target Address Register. The reason for implementing the reloading process this way is that, for most applications, the Byte Count and the Requester will not change from one buffer to the next, and therefore do not need to be reprogrammed. The details of programming the channel for the Buffer Chaining Process can be found in the section on DMA programming.

3.3.3 DATA TRANSFER MODES

Three Data Transfer modes are available in the 82370 DMA Controller. They are the Single Transfer, Block Transfer, and Demand Transfer Modes. These transfer modes can be used in conjunction with any one of three Buffer Transfer modes: Single Buffer, Auto-Initialized Buffer and Buffer Chaining. Any Data Transfer Mode can be used under any of the Buffer Transfer Modes. These modes are independently available for all DMA channels.

Different devices being serviced by the DMA Controller require different handshaking sequences for data transfers to take place. Three handshaking modes are available on the 82370, giving the designer the opportunity to use the DMA Controller as efficiently as possible. The speed at which data can be presented or read by a device can affect the way a DMA Controller uses the host's bus, thereby affecting not only data throughput during the DMA process, but also affecting the host's performance by limiting its access to the bus.

Single Transfer Mode

In the Single Transfer Mode, one data transfer to or from the Requester is performed by the DMA Controller at a time. The DREQn input is arbitrated and the HOLD/HLDA sequence is executed for each transfer. Transfers continue in this manner until the Byte Count expires, or until EOP# is sampled active. If the DREQn input is held active continuously, the entire DREQ-HOLD-HLDA-DACK sequence is repeated over and over until the programmed number of bytes has been transferred. Bus control is released to the host between each transfer. Figure 3-4 shows the logical flow of events which make up a buffer transfer using the Single Transfer Mode. Refer to section 3.4 for an explanation of the bus control arbitration procedure.

The Single Transfer Mode is used for devices which require complete handshake cycles with each data access. Data is transferred to or from the Requester only when the Requester is ready to perform the transfer. Each transfer requires the entire DREQ-HOLD-HLDA-DACK handshake cycle. Figure 3-5 shows the timing of the Single Transfer Mode cycle.

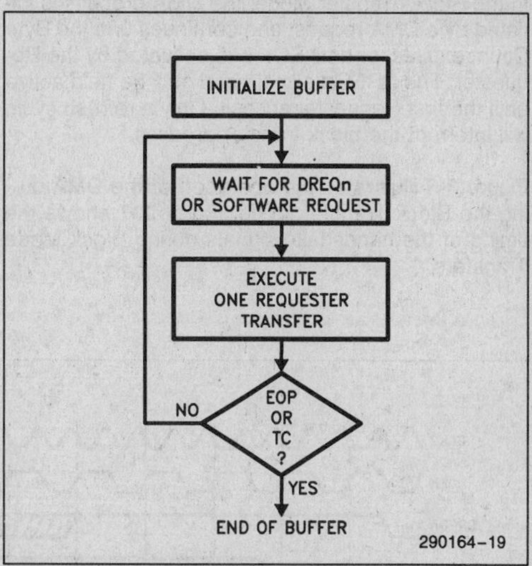

Figure 3-4. Buffer Transfer in Single Transfer Mode

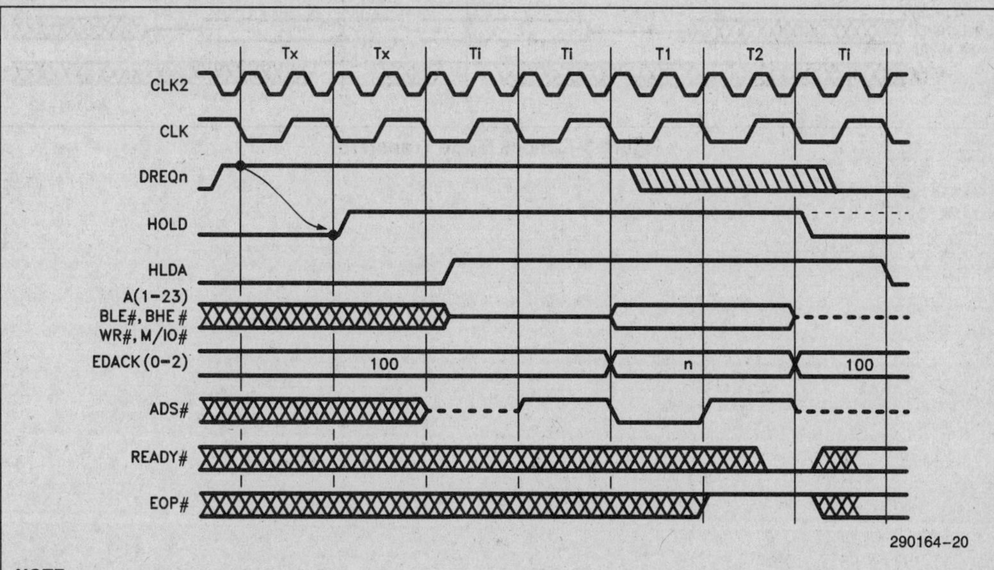

NOTE:
The Single Transfer Mode is more efficient (15%–20%) in the case where the source is the Target. Because of the internal pipeline of the 82370 DMA Controller, two idle states are added at the end of a transfer in the case where the source is the Requester.

Figure 3-5. DMA Single Transfer Mode

Block Transfer Mode

In the Block Transfer Mode, the DMA process is initiated by a DMA request and continues unti the Byte Count expires, or until EOP# is activated by the Requester. The DREQn signal need only be held active until the first Requester access. Only a refresh cycle will interrupt the block transfer process.

Figure 3-6 illustrates the operation of the DMA during the Block Transfer Mode. Figure 3-7 shows the timing of the handshake signals during Block Mode Transfers.

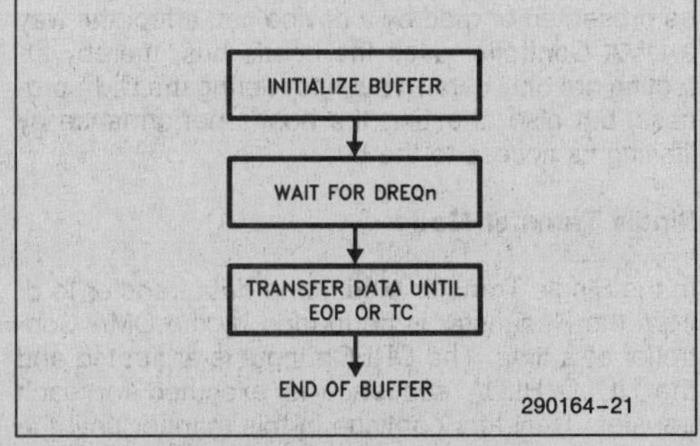

Figure 3-6. Buffer Transfer in Block Transfer Mode

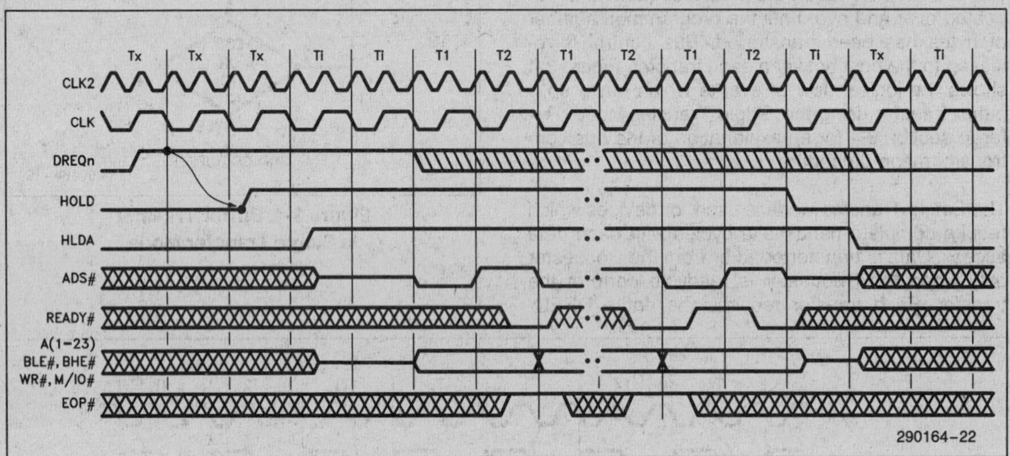

Figure 3-7. Block Mode Transfers

Demand Transfer Mode

The Demand Transfer Mode provides the most flexible handshaking procedures during the DMA process. A Demand Transfer is initiated by a DMA request. The process continues until the Byte Count expires, or an external EOP# is encountered. If the device being serviced (Requester) desires, it can interrupt the DMA process by de-activating the DREQn line. Action is taken on the condition of DREQn during Requester accesses only. The access during which DREQn is sampled inactive is the last Requester access which will be performed during the current transfer. Figure 3-8 shows the flow of events during the transfer of a buffer in the Demand Mode.

When the DREQn line goes inactive, the DMA Controller will complete the current transfer, including any necessary accesses to the Target, and relinquish control of the bus to the host. The current process information is saved (byte count, Requester and Target addresses, and Temporary Register).

The Requester can restart the transfer process by reasserting DREQn. The 82370 will arbitrate the request with other pending requests and begin the process where it left off. Figure 3-9 shows the timing of handshake signals during Demand Transfer Mode operation.

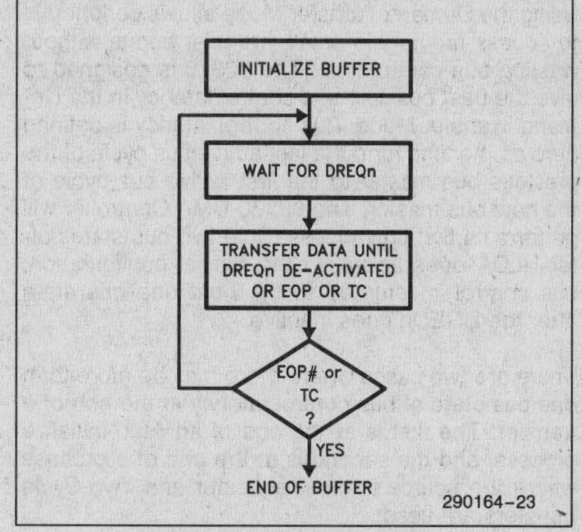

Figure 3-8. Buffer Transfer in Demand Transfer Mode

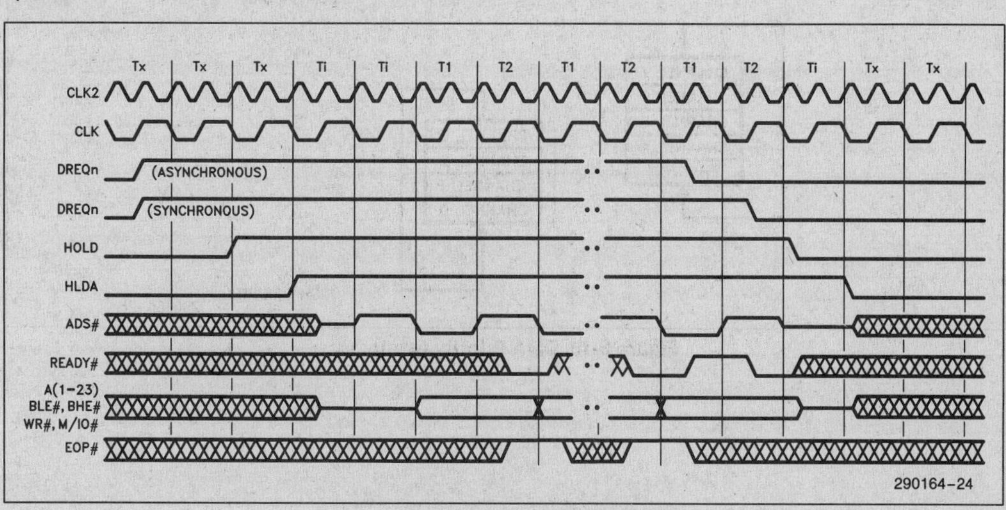

Figure 3-9. Demand Mode Transfers

4

Using the Demand Transfer Mode allows peripherals to access memory in small, irregular bursts without wasting bus control time. The 82370 is designed to give the best possible bus control latency in the Demand Transfer Mode. Bus control latency is defined here as the time form the last active bus cycle of the previous bus master to the first active bus cycle of the new bus master. The 82370 DMA Controller will perform its first bus access cycle two bus states after HLDA goes active. In the typical configuration, bus control is returned to the host one bus state after the DREQn goes inactive.

There are two cases where there may be more than one bus state of bus control latency at the end of a transfer. The first is at the end of an Auto-Initialize process, and the second is at the end of a process where the source is the Requester and Two-Cycle transfers are used.

When a Buffer Auto-Initialize Porcess is complete, the 82370 requires seven bus states to reload the Current Registers from the Base Registers of the Auto-Initialized channel. The reloading is done while the 82370 is still the bus master so that it is prepared to service the channel immediately after relinquishing the bus, if necessary.

In the case where the Requester is the source, and Two-Cycle transfers are being used, there are two extra idle states at the end of the transfer process. This occurs due to the housekeeping in the DMA's internal pipeline. These two idle states are present only after the very last Requester access, before the DMA Controller de-activates the HOLD signal.

3.3.4 CHANNEL PRIORITY ARBITRATION

DMA channel priority can be programmed into one of two arbitration methods: Fixed or Rotating. The four lower DMA channels and the four upper DMA channels operate as if they were two separate DMA controllers operating in cascade. The lower group of four channels (0–3) is always prioritized between channels 7 and 4 of the upper group of channels (4–7). Figure 3-10 shows a pictorial representation of the priority grouping.

The priority can thus be set up as rotating for one group of channels and fixed for the other, or any other combination. While in Fixed Priority, the programmer can also specify which channel has the lowest priority.

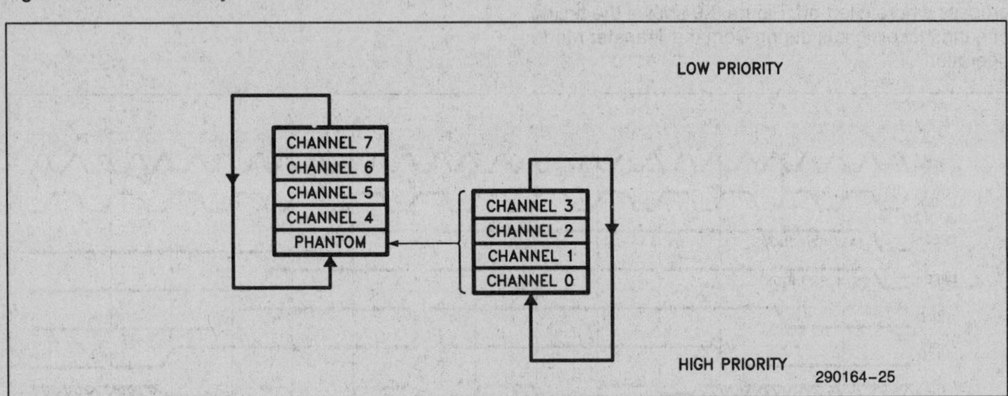

Figure 3-10. DMA Priority Grouping

The 82370 DMA Controller defaults to Fixed Priority. Channel 0 has the highest priority, then 1, 2, 3, 4, 5, 6, 7. Channel 7 has the lowest priority. Any time the DMA Controller arbitrates DMA requests, the requesting channel with the highest priority will be serviced next.

Fixed Priority can be entered into at any time by a software command. The priority levels in effect after the mode switch are determined by the current setting of the Programmable Priority.

Programmable Priority is available for fixing the priority of the DMA channels within a group to levels other than the default. Through a software command, the channel to have the lowest priority in a group can be specified. Each of the two groups of four channels can have the priority fixed in this way. The other channels in the group will follow the natural Fixed Priority sequence. This mode affects only the priority levels while operating with Fixed Priority.

For example, if channel 2 is programmed to have the lowest priority in its group, channel 3 has the highest priority. In descending order, the other channels would have the following priority: (3,0,1,2),4,5,6,7 (channel 2 lowest, channel 3 highest). If the upper group were programmed to have channel 5 as the lowest priority channel, the priority would be (again, highest to lowest): 6,7, (3,0,1,2), 4,5. Figure 3-11 shows this example pictorially. The lower group is always prioritized as a fifth channel of the upper group (between channels 4 and 7).

The DMA Controller will only accept Programmable Priority commands while the addressed group is operating in Fixed Priority. Switching from Fixed to Rotating Priority preserves the current priority levels. Switching from Rotating to Fixed Priority returns the priority levels to those which were last programmed by use of Programmable Priority.

Rotating Priority allows the devices using DMA to share the system bus more evenly. An individual channel does not retain highest priority after being serviced, priority is passed to the next highest priority channel in the group. The channel which was most recently serviced inherits the lowest priority. This rotation occurs each time a channel is serviced. Figure 3-12 shows the sequence of events as priority is passed between channels. Note that the lower group rotates within the upper group, and that servicing a channel within the lower group causes rotation within the group as well as rotation of the upper group.

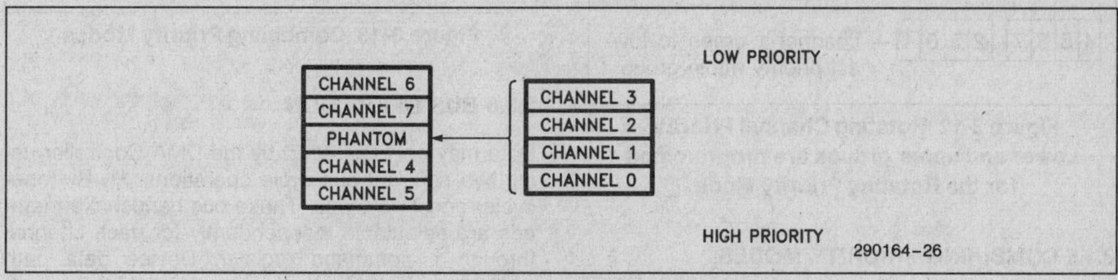

Figure 3-11. Example of Programmed Priority

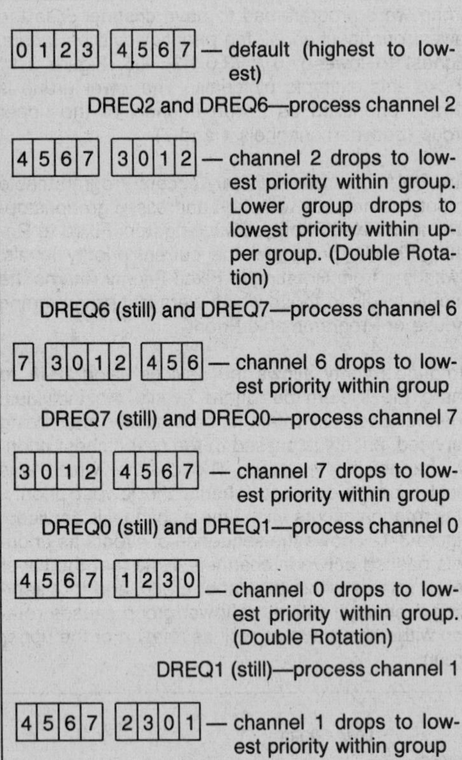

Figure 3-12. Rotating Channel Priority. Lower and upper groups are programmed for the Rotating Priority Mode.

3.3.5 COMBINING PRIORITY MODES

Since the DMA Controller operates as two four-channel controllers in cascade, the overall priority scheme of all eight channels can take on a variety of forms. There are four possible combinations of priority modes between the two groups of channels: Fixed Priority only (default), Fixed Priority upper group/Rotating Priority lower group, Rotating Priority upper group/Fixed Priority lower group, and Rotating Priority only. Figure 3-13 illustrates the operation of the two combined priority methods.

Case 1—
0–3 Fixed Priority, 4–7 Rotating Priority

	High ... Low
Default priority	0 1 2 3 4 5 6 7
After servicing channel 2	4 5 6 7 0 1 2 3
After servicing channel 6	7 0 1 2 3 4 5 6
After servicing channel 1	4 5 6 7 0 1 2 3

Case 2—
0–3 Rotating Priority, 4–7 Fixed Priority

	High ... Low
Default priority	0 1 2 3 4 5 6 7
After servicing channel 2	3 0 1 2 4 5 6 7
After servicing channel 6	3 0 1 2 4 5 6 7
After servicing channel 1	2 3 0 1 4 5 6 7

Figure 3-13. Combining Priority Modes

3.3.6 BUS OPERATION

Data may be transferred by the DMA Controller using two different bus cycle operations: Fly-By (one-cycle) and Two-Cycle. These bus handshake methods are selectable independently for each channel through a command register. Device data path widths are independently programmable for both Target and Requester. Also selectable through software is the direction of data transfer. All of these parameters affect the operation of the 82370 on a bus-cycle by bus-cycle basis.

3.3.6.1 Fly-By Transfers

The Fly-By Transfer Mode is the fastest and most efficient way to use the 82370 DMA Controller to transfer data. In this method of transfer, the data is written to the destination device at the same time it is read from the source. Only one bus cycle is used to accomplish the transfer.

In the Fly-By Mode, the DMA acknowledge signal is used to select the Requester. The DMA Controller simultaneously places the address of the Target on the address bus. The state of M/IO# and W/R# during the Fly-By transfer cycle indicate the type of Target and whether the Target is being written to or read from. The Target's Bus Size is used as an incrementer for the Byte Count. The Requester address registers are ignored during Fly-By transfers.

Note that memory-to-memory transfers cannot be done using the Fly-By Mode. Only one memory of I/O address is generated by the DMA Controller at a time during Fly-By transfers. Only one of the devices being accessed can be selected by an address. Also, the Fly-By method of data transfer limits the hardware to accesses of devices with the same data bus width. The Temporary Registers are not affected in the Fly-By Mode.

Fly-By transfers also require that the data paths of the Target and Requester be directly connected. This requires that successive Fly-By access be to word boundaries, or that the Requester be capable of switching its connections to the data bus.

3.3.6.2. Two-Cycle Transfers

Two-Cycle transfers can also be performed by the 82370 DMA Controller. These transfers require at least two bus cycles to execute. The data being transferred is read into the DMA Controller's Temporary Register during the first bus cycle(s). The second bus cycle is used to write the data from the Temporary Register to the destination.

If the addresses of the data being transferred are not word aligned, the 82370 will recognize the situation and read and write the data in groups of bytes, placing them always at the proper destination. This process of collecting the desired bytes and putting them together is called "byte assembly". The reverse process (reading from aligned locations and writing to non-aligned locations) is called "byte disassembly".

The assembly/disassembly process takes place transparent to the software, but can only be done while using the Two-Cycle transfer method. The 82370 will always perform the assembly/disassembly process as necessary for the current data transfer. Any data path widths for either the Requester or Target can be used in the Two-Cycle Mode. This is very convenient for interfacing existing 8- and 16-bit peripherals to the 80376's 16-bit bus.

The 82370 DMA Controller always reads and write data within the word boundaries; i.e. if a word to be read is crossing a word boundary, the DMA Controller will perform two read operations, each reading one byte, to read the 16-bit word into the Temporary Register. Also, the 82370 DMA Controller always attempts to fill the Temporary Register from the source before writing any data to the destination. If the process is terminated before the Temporary Register is filled (TC or EOP#), the 82370 will write the partial data to the destination. If a process is temporarily suspended (such as when DREQn is deactivated during a demand transfer), the contents of a partially filled Temporary Register will be stored within the 82370 until the process is restarted.

For example, if the source is specified as an 8-bit device and the destination as a 32-bit device, there will be four reads as necessary from the 8-bit source to fill the Temporary Register. Then the 82370 will write the 32-bit contents to the destination in two cycles of 16-bit each. This cycle will repeat until the process is terminated or suspended.

With Two-Cycle transfers, the devices that the 82370 accesses can reside at any address within I/O or memory space. The device must be able to decode the byte-enables (BLE#, BHE#). Also, if the device cannot accept data in byte quantities, the programmer must take care not to allow the DMA Controller to access the device on any address other than the device boundary.

3.3.6.3 Data Path Width and Data Transfer Rate Considerations

The number of bus cycles used to transfer a single "word" of data is affected by whether the Two-Cycle or the Fly-By (Single-Cycle) transfer method is used.

The number of bus cycles used to transfer data directly affects the data transfer rate. Inefficient use of bus cycles will decrease the effective data transfer rate that can be obtained. Generally, the data transfer rate is halved by using Two-Cycle transfers instead of Fly-By transfers.

The choice of data path widths of both Target and Requester affects the data transfer rate also. During each bus cycle, the largest pieces of data possible should be transferred.

The data path width of the devices to be accessed must be programmed into the DMA controller. The 82370 defaults after reset to 8-bit-to-8-bit data transfers, but the Target and Requester can have different data path widths, independent of each other and independent of the other channels. Since this is a software programmable function, more discussion of the uses of this feature are found in the section on programming.

3.3.6.4 Read, Write and Verify Cycles

Three different bus cycles types may be used in a data transfer. They are the Read, Write and Verify cycles. These cycle types dictate the way in which the 82370 operates on the data to be transferred.

A Read Cycle transfers data from the Target to the Requester. A Write Cycle transfers data from the Requester to the target. In a Fly-By transfer, the address and bus status signals indicate the access (read of write) to the Target; the access to the Requester is assumed to be the opposite.

The Verify Cycle is used to perform a data read only. No write access is indicated or assumed in a Verify Cycle. The Verify Cycle is useful for validating block fill operations. An external comparator must be provided to do any comparisons on the data read.

3.4 Bus Arbitration and Handshaking

Figure 3-14 shows the flow of events in the DMA request arbitration process. The arbitration sequence starts when the Requester asserts a DREQn (or DMA service is requested by software). Figure 3-15 shows the timing of the sequence of events following a DMA request. This sequence is executed for each channel that is activated. The DREQn signal can be replaced by a software DMA channel request with no change in the sequence.

After the Requester asserts the service request, the 82370 will request control of the bus via the HOLD signal. The 82370 will always assert the HOLD signal one bus state after the service request is asserted. The 80376 responds by asserting the HLDA signal, thus releasing control of the bus to the 82370 DMA Controller.

Priority of pending DMA service requests is arbitrated during the first state after HLDA is asserted by the 80376. The next state will be the beginning of the first transfer access of the highest priority process.

When the 82370 DMA Controller is finished with its current bus activity, it returns control of the bus to the host processor. This is done by driving the HOLD signal inactive. The 82370 does not drive any address or data bus signals after HOLD goes low. It enters the Slave Mode until another DMA process is requested. The processor acknowledges that it has regained control of the bus by forcing the HLDA signal inactive. Note that the 82370's DMA Controller will not re-request control of the bus until the entire HOLD/HLDA handshake sequence is complete.

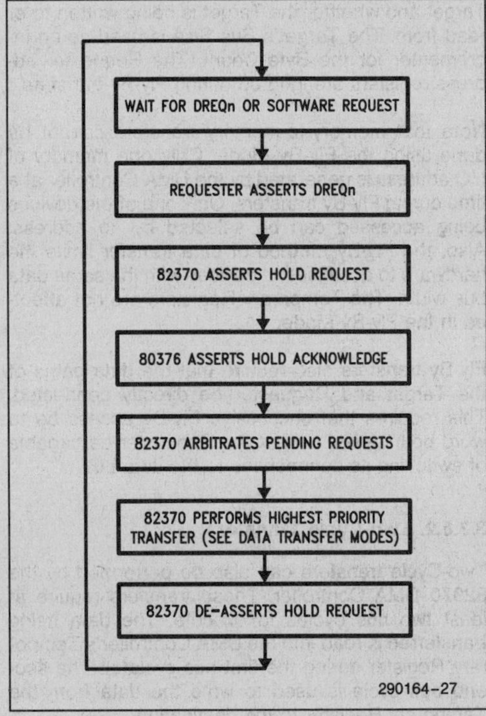

Figure 3-14. Bus Arbitration and DMA Sequence

The 82370 DMA Controller will terminate a current DMA process for one of three reasons: expired byte count, end-of-process command (EOP# activated) from a peripheral, or deactivated DMA request signal. In each case, the controller will de-assert HOLD immediately after completing the data transfer in progress. These three methods of process termination are illustrated in Figures 3-16, 3-19 and 3-18, respectively.

An expired byte count indicates that the current process is complete as programmed and the channel has no further transfers to process. The channel must be restarted according to the currently programmed Buffer Transfer Mode, or reprogrammed completely, including a new Buffer Transfer Mode.

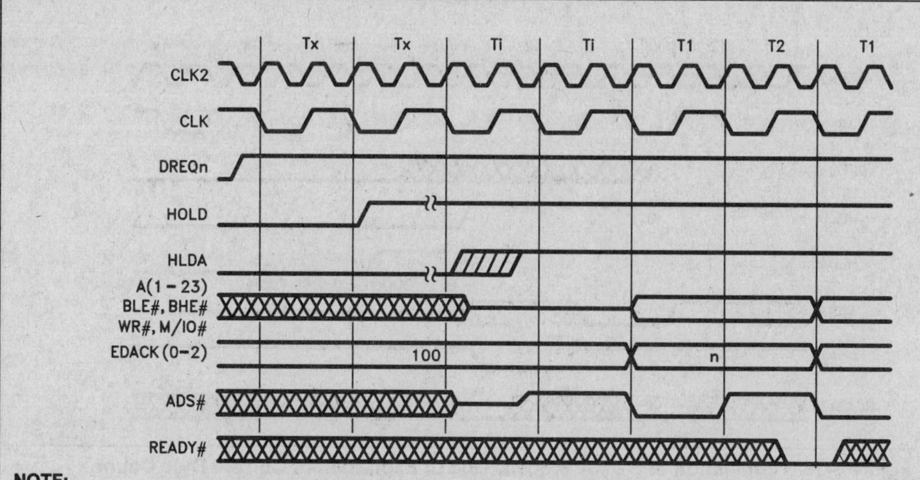

NOTE:
Channel priority resolution takes place during the bus state before HOLDA is asserted, allowing the DMA Controller to respond to HLDA without extra idle bus states.

Figure 3-15. Beginning of a DMA process

If the peripheral activates the EOP# signal, it is indicating that it will not accept or deliver any more data for the current buffer. The 82370 DMA Controller considers this as a completion of the channel's current process and interprets the condition the same way as if the byte count expired.

The action taken by the 82370 DMA Controller in response to a de-activated DREQn signal depends on the Data Transfer Mode of the channel. In the Demand Mode, data transfers will take place as long as the DREQn is active and the byte count has not expired. In the Block Mode, the controller will complete the entire block transfer without relinquishing the bus, even if DREQn goes inactive before the transfer is complete. In the Single Mode, the controller will execute single data transfers, relinquishing the bus between each transfer, as long as DREQn is active.

Normal termination of a DMA process due to expiration of the byte count (Terminal Count—TC) is shown if Figure 3-16. The condition of DREQn is ignored until after the process is terminated. If the channel is programmed to auto-initialize, HOLD will be held active for an additional seven clock cycles while the auto-initialization takes place.

Table 3-3 shows the DMA channel activity due to EOP# or Byte Count expiring (Terminal Count).

Table 3-3. DMA Channel Activity Due to Terminal Count or External EOP#

Buffer Process	Single or Chaining-Base Empty		Auto-Initialize		Chaining-Base Loaded	
EVENT						
Terminal Count	True	X	True	X	True	X
EOP#	X	0	X	0	X	0
RESULTS						
Current Registers			Load	Load	Load	Load
Channel Mask	Set	Set				
EOP# Output	0	X	0	X	1	X
Terminal Count Status	Set	Set	Set	Set		
Software Request	CLR	CLR	CLR	CLR		

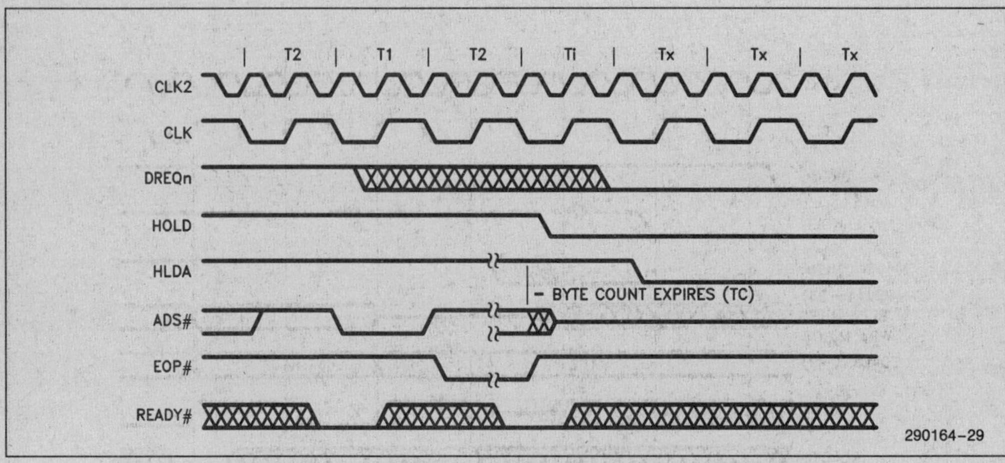

Figure 3-16. Termination of a DMA Process Due to Expiration of Current Byte Count

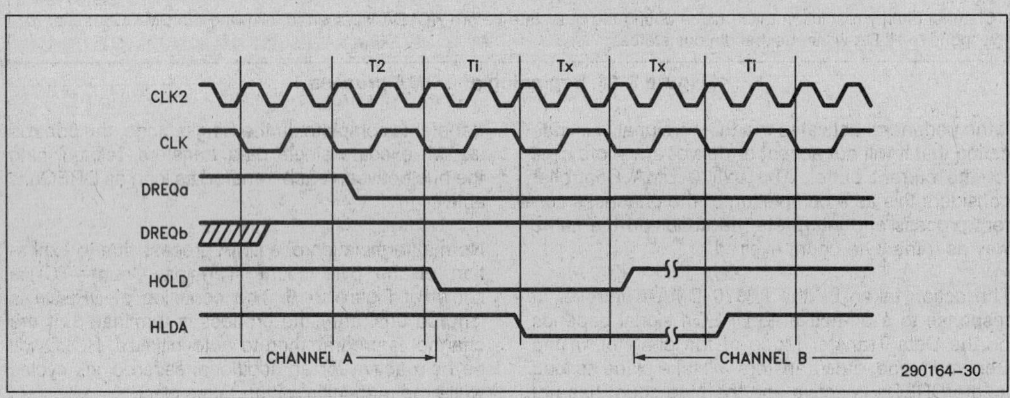

Figure 3-17. Switching between Active DMA Channels

The 82370 always relinquishes control of the bus between channel services. This allows the hardware designer the flexibility to externally arbitrate bus hold requests, if desired. If another DMA request is pending when a higher priority channel service is completed, the 82370 will relinquish the bus until the hold acknowledge is inactive. One bus state after the HLDA signal goes inactive, the 82370 will assert HOLD again. This is illustrated in Figure 3-17.

3.4.1 SYNCHRONOUS AND ASYNCHRONOUS SAMPLING OF DREQn AND EOP#

As an indicator that a DMA service is to be started, DREQn is always sampled asynchronous. It is sampled at the beginning of a bus state and acted upon at the end of the state. Figure 3-15 illustrates the start of a DMA process due to a DREQn input.

The DREQn and EOP# inputs can be programmed to be sampled either synchronously or asynchronously to signal the end of a transfer.

The synchronous mode affords the Requester one bus state of extra time to react to an access. This means the Requester can terminate a process on the current access, without losing any data. The asynchronous mode requires that the input signal be presented prior to the beginning of the last state of the Requester access.

The timing relationships of the DREQn and EOP# signals to the termination of a DMA transfer are shown in Figures 3-18 and 3-19. Figure 3-18 shows the termination of a DMA transfer due to inactive DREQn. Figure 3-19 shows the termination of a DMA process due to an active EOP# input.

In the Synchronous Mode, DREQn and EOP# are sampled at the end of the last state of every Requester data transfer cycle. If EOP# is active or DREQn is inactive at this time, the 82370 recognizes this access to the Requester as the last transfer. At this point, the 82370 completes the transfer in progress, if necessary, and returns bus control to the host.

In the asynchronous mode, the inputs are sampled at the beginning of every state of a Requester access. The 82370 waits until the end of the state to act on the input.

DREQn and EOP# are sampled at the latest possible time when the 82370 can determine if another transfer is required. In the Synchronous Mode, DREQn and EOP# are sampled on the trailing edge of the last bus state before another data access cycle begins. The Asynchronous Mode requires that the signals be valid one clock cycle earlier.

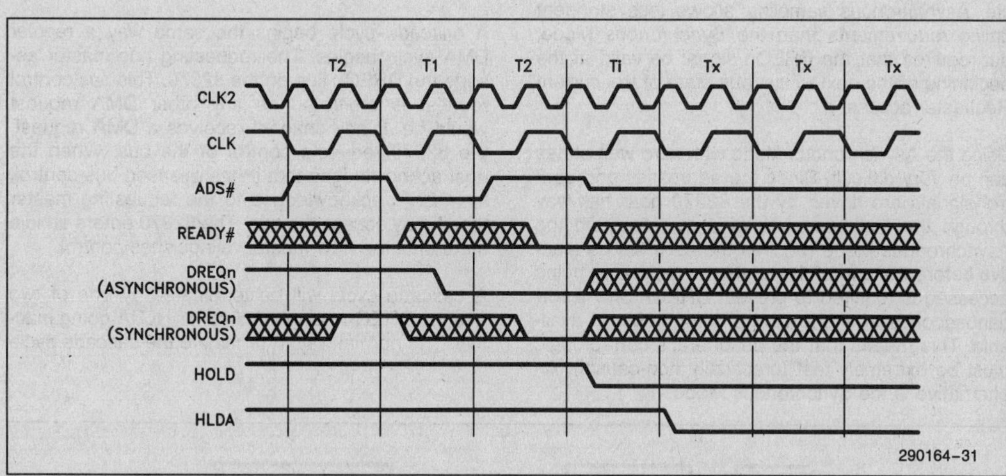

Figure 3-18. Termination of a DMA Process due to De-Asserting DREQn

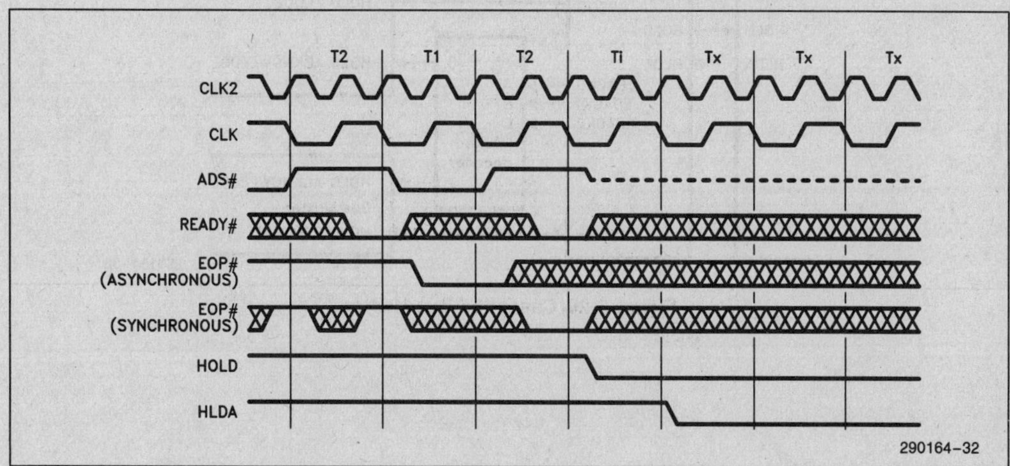

Figure 3-19. Termination of a DMA Process due to an External EOP#

While in the Pipeline Mode, if the NA# signal is sampled active during a transfer, the end of the state where NA# was sampled active is when the 82370 decides whether to commit to another transfer. The device must de-assert DREQn or assert EOP# before NA# is asserted, otherwise the 82370 will commit to another, possibly undesired, transfer.

Synchronous DREQn and EOP# sampling allows the peripheral to prevent the next transfer from occurring by de-activating DREQn or asserting EOP# during the current Requester access, before the 82370 DMA Controller commits itself to another transfer. The DMA Controller will not perform the next transfer if it has not already begun the bus cycle. Asynchronous sampling allows less stringent timing requirements than the Synchronous Mode, but requires that the DREQn signal be valid at the beginning of the next to last bus state of the current Requester access.

Using the Asynchronous Mode with zero wait states can be very difficult. Since the addresses and control signals are driven by the 82370 near half-way through the first bus state of a transfer, and the Asynchronous Mode requires that DREQn be inactive before the end of the state, the peripheral being accessed is required to present DREQn only a few nanoseconds after the control information is available. This means that the peripheral's control logic must be extremely fast (practically non-causal). An alternative is the Synchronous Mode.

3.4.2 ARBITRATION OF CASCADED MASTER REQUESTS

The Cascade Mode allows another DMA-type device to share the bus by arbitrating its bus accesses with the 82370's. Seven of the eight DMA channels (0–3 and 5–7) can be connected to a cascaded device. The cascaded device requests bus control through the DREQn line of the channel which is programmed to operate in Cascade Mode. Bus hold acknowledge is signalled to the cascaded device through the EDACK lines. When the EDACK lines are active with the code for the requested cascade channel, the bus is available to the cascaded master device.

A cascade cycle begins the same way a regular DMA cycle begins. The requesting bus master asserts the DREQn line on the 82370. This bus control request is arbitrated as any other DMA request would be. If any channel receives a DMA request, the 82370 requests control of the bus. When the host acknowledges that it has released bus control, the 82370 acknowledges to the requesting master that it may access the bus. The 82370 enters an idle state until the new master relinquishes control.

A cascade cycle will be terminated by one of two events: DREQn going inactive, or HLDA going inactive. The normal way to terminate the cascade cycle

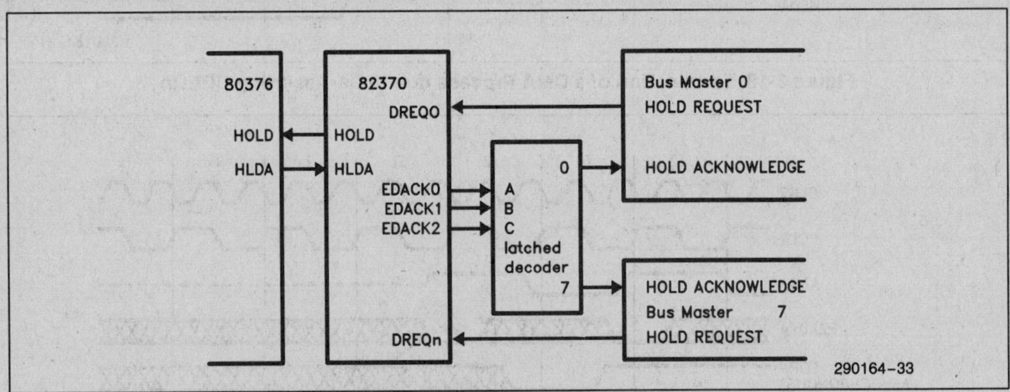

Figure 3-20. Cascaded Bus Master

is for the cascaded master to drop the DREQn signal. Figure 3-21 shows the two cascade cycle termination sequences.

The Refresh Controller may interrupt the cascaded master to perform a refresh cycle. If this occurs, the 82370 DMA Controller will de-assert the EDACK signal (hold acknowledge to cascaded master) and wait for the cascaded master to remove its hold request. When the 82370 regains bus control, it will perform the refresh cycle in its normal fashion. After the refresh cycle has been completed, and if the cascaded device has re-asserted its request, the 82370 will return control to the cascaded master which was interrupted.

The 82370 assumes that it is the only device monitoring the HLDA signal. If the system designer wishes to place other devices on the bus as bus masters, the HLDA from the processor must be intercepted before presenting it to the 82370. Using the Cascade capabililty of the 82370 DMA Controller offers a much better solution.

3.4.3 ARBITRATION OF REFRESH REQUESTS

The arbitration of refresh requests by the DRAM Refresh Controller is slightly different from normal DMA channel request arbitration. The 82370 DRAM Refresh Controller always has the highest priority of any DMA process. It also can interrupt a process in progress. Two types of processes in progress may be encountered: normal DMA, and bus master cascade.

In the event of a refresh request during a normal DMA process, the DMA Controller will complete the data transfer in progress and then execute the refresh cycle before continuing with the current DMA process. The priority of the interrupted process is not lost. If the data transfer cycle interrupted by the Refresh Controller is the last of a DMA process, the refresh cycle will always be executed before control of the bus is transferred back to the host.

When the Refresh Controller request occurs during a cascade cycle, the Refresh Controller must be assured that the cascaded master device has relinquished control of the bus before it can execute the refresh cycle. To do this, the DMA Controller drops the EDACK signal to the cascaded master and waits for the corresponding DREQn input to go inactive. By dropping the DREQn signal, the cascaded master relinquishes the bus. The Refresh Controller then performs the refresh cycle. Control of the bus is returned to the cascaded master if DREQn returns to an active state before the end of the refresh cycle, otherwise control is passed to the processor and the cascaded master loses its priority.

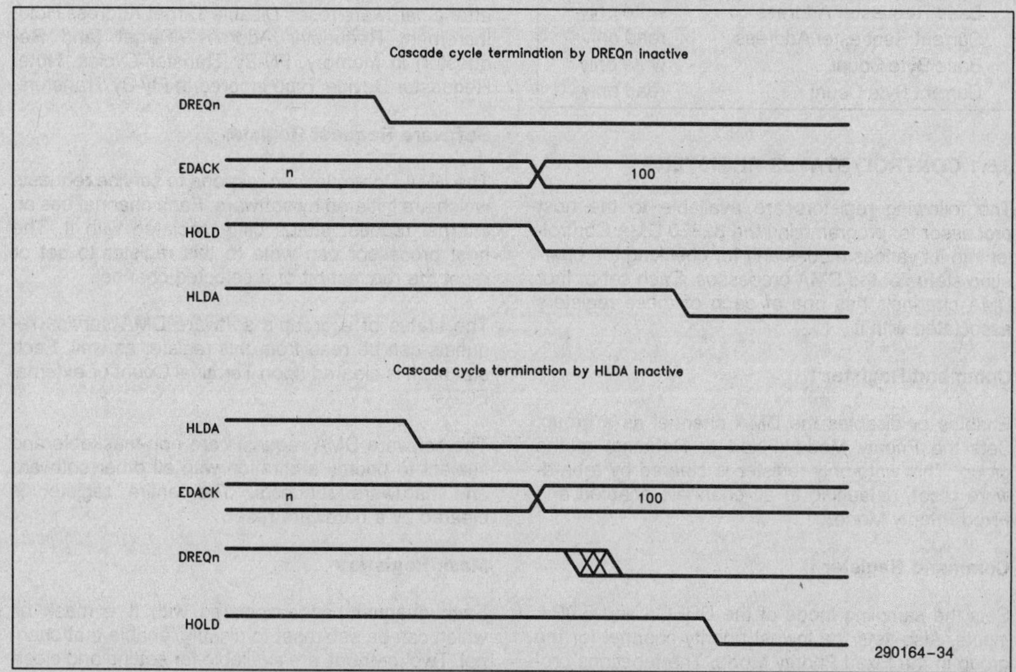

Figure 3-21. Cascade Cycle Termination

3.5 DMA Controller Register Overview

The 82370 DMA Controller contains 44 registers which are accessable to the host processor. Twenty-four of these registers contain the device addresses and data counts for the individual DMA channels (three per channel). The remaining registers are control and status registers for initiating and monitoring the operation of the 82370 DMA Controller. Table 3-4 lists the DMA Controller's registers and their accessability.

Table 3-4. DMA Controller Registers

Register Name	Access
Control/Status Registers—one each per group	
Command Register I	write only
Command Register II	write only
Mode Register I	write only
Mode Register II	write only
Software Request Register	read/write
Mask Set-Reset Register	write only
Mask Read-Write Register	read/write
Status Register	read only
Bus Size Register	write only
Chaining Register	read/write
Channel Registers—one each per channel	
Base Target Address	write only
Current Target Address	read only
Base Requester Address	write only
Current Requester Address	read only
Base Byte Count	write only
Current Byte Count	read only

3.5.1 CONTROL/STATUS REGISTERS

The following registers are available to the host processor for programming the 82370 DMA Controller into its various modes and for checking the operating status of the DMA processes. Each set of four DMA channels has one of each of these registers associated with it.

Command Register I

Enables or disables the DMA channel as a group. Sets the Priority Mode (Fixed or Rotating) of the group. This write-only register is cleared by a hardware reset, defaulting to all channels enabled and Fixed Priority Mode.

Command Register II

Sets the sampling mode of the DREQn and EOP# inputs. Also sets the lowest priority channel for the group in the Fixed Priority Mode. The functions programmed through Command Register II default after a hardware reset to: asynchronous DREQn and EOP#, and channels 3 and 7 lowest priority.

Mode Registers I

Mode Register I is identical in function to the Mode register of the 8237A. It programs the following functions for an individually selected channel:

Type of Transfer—read, write, verify
Auto-Initialize—enable or disable
Target Address Count—increment or decrement
Data Transfer Mode—demand, single, block, cascade

Mode Register I functions default to the following after reset: verify transfer, Auto-Initialize disabled, Increment Target address, Demand Mode.

Mode Register II

Programs the following functions for an individually selected channel:

Target Address Hold—enable or disable
Requester Address Count—increment or decrement
Requester Address Hold—enable or disable
Target Device Type—I/O or Memory
Requester Device Type—I/O or Memory
Transfer Cycles—Two-Cycle or Fly-By

Mode Register II functions are defined as follows after a hardware reset: Disable Target Address Hold, Increment Requester Address, Target (and Requester) in memory, Fly-By Transfer Cycles. Note: Requester Device Type ignored in Fly-By Transfers.

Software Request Register

The DMA Controller can respond to service requests which are initiated by software. Each channel has an internal request status bit associated with it. The host processor can write to this register to set or reset the request bit of a selected channel.

The status of a group's software DMA service requests can be read from this register as well. Each status bit is cleared upon Terminal Count or external EOP#.

The software DMA requests are non-maskable and subject to priority arbitration with all other software and hardware requests. The entire register is cleared by a hardware reset.

Mask Registers

Each channel has associated with it a mask bit which can be set/reset to disable/enable that channel. Two methods are available for setting and clearing the mask bits. The Mask Set/Reset Register is a write-only register which allows the host to select an individual channel and either set or reset the mask bit for that channel only. The Mask Read/Write Register is available for reading the mask bit status and for writing mask bits in groups of four.

The mask bits of a group may be cleared in one step by executing the Clear Mask Command. See the DMA Programming section for details. A hardware reset sets all of the channel mask bits, disabling all channels.

Status Register

The Status register is a read-only register which contains the Terminal Count (TC) and Service Request status for a group. Four bits indicate the TC status and four bits indicate the hardware request status for the four channels in the group. The TC bits are set when the Byte Count expires, or when and external EOP# is asserted. These bits are cleared by reading from the Status Register. The Service Request bit for a channel indicates when there is a hardware DMA request (DREQn) asserted for that channel. When the request has been removed, the bit is cleared.

Bus Size Register

This write-only register is used to define the bus size of the Target and Requester of a selected channel. The bus sizes programmed will be used to dictate the sizes of the data paths accessed when the DMA channel is active. The values programmed into this register affect the operation of the Temporary Register. When 32-bit bus width is programmed, the 82370 DMA Controller will access the device twice through its 16-bit external Data Bus to perform a 32-bit data transfer. Any byte-assembly required to make the transfers using the specified data path widths will be done in the Temporary Register. The Bus Size register of the Target is used as an increment/decrement value for the Byte Counter and Target Address when in the Fly-By Mode. Upon reset, all channels default to 8-bit Targets and 8-bit Requesters.

Chaining Register

As a command or write register, the Chaining register is used to enable or disable the Chaining Mode for a selected channel. Chaining can either be disabled or enabled for an individual channel, independently of the Chaining Mode status of other channels. After a hardware reset, all channels default to Chaining disabled.

When read by the host, the Chaining Register provides the status of the Chaining Interrupt of each of the channels. These interrupt status bits are cleared when the new buffer information has been loaded.

3.5.2 CHANNEL REGISTERS

Each channel has three individually programmable registers necessary for the DMA process; they are the Base Byte Count, Base Target Address, and Base Requester Address registers. The 24-bit Base Byte Count register contains the number of bytes to be transferred by the channel. The 24-bit Base Target Address Register contains the beginning address (memory or I/O) of the Target device. The 24-bit Base Requester Address register contains the base address (memory or I/O) of the device which is to request DMA service.

Three more registers for each DMA channel exist within the DMA Controller which are directly related to the registers mentioned above. These registers contain the current status of the DMA process. They are the Current Byte Count register, the Current Target Address, and the Current Requester Address. It is these registers which are manipulated (incremented, decremented, or held constant) by the 82370 DMA Controller during the DMA process. The Current registers are loaded from the Base registers at the beginning of a DMA process.

The Base registers are loaded when the host processor writes to the respective channel register addresses. Depending on the mode in which the channel is operating, the Current registers are typically loaded in the same operation. Reading from the channel register addresses yields the contents of the corresponding Current register.

To maintain compatibility with software which accesses an 8237A, a Byte Pointer Flip-Flop is used to control access to the upper and lower bytes of some words of the Channel Registers. These words are accessed as byte pairs at single port addresses. The Byte Pointer Flip-Flop acts as a one-bit pointer which is toggled each time a qualifying Channel Register byte is accessed.

It always points to the next logical byte to be accessed of a pair of bytes.

The Channel registers are arranged as pairs of words, each pair with its own port address. Addressing the port with the Byte Pointer Flip-Flop reset accesses the least significant byte of the pair. The most significant byte is accessed when the Byte Pointer is set.

For compatibility with existing 8237A designs, there is one exception to the above statements about the Byte Pointer Flip-Flop. The third byte (bits 16-23) of the Target Address is accessed through its own port address. The Byte Pointer Flip-Flop is not affected by any accesses to this byte.

4

The upper eight bits of the Byte Count Register are cleared when the least significant byte of the register is loaded. This provides compatibility with software which accesses an 8237A. The 8237A has 16-bit Byte Count Registers.

NOTE:
The 82370 is a subset of the Intel 82380 32-bit DMA Controller with Integrated System Peripherals.

Although the 82370 has 24 address bits externally, the programming model is actually a full 32 bits wide. For this reason, there are some "hidden" DMA registers in the 82370 register set. These hidden registers correspond to what would be A24–A31 in a 32-bit system.

Think of the 82370 addresses as though they were 32 bits wide, with only the lower 24 bits available externally.

This should be of concern in two areas:

1. Understanding the Byte Pointer Flip Flop
2. Removing the IRQ1 Chaining Interrupt

The byte pointer flip flop will behave as though the hidden upper address bits were accessible.

The IRQ1 Chaining Interrupt will be removed only when the hidden upper address bits are programmed. You will note that since the hidden upper address bits are not available externally, the **value** you program into the registers is not important. The **act** of programming the hidden register is critical in removing the IRQ1 Chaining interrupt for a DMA channel.

The port assignments for these hidden upper address bits come directly from the port assignments of the Intel 82380. For your convenience, those port definitions have been included in this data sheet in section 3.7.

3.5.3 TEMPORARY REGISTERS

Each channel has a 32-bit Temporary Register used for temporary data storage during two-cycle DMA transfers. It is this register in which any necessary byte assembly and disassembly of non-aligned data is performed. Figure 3-22 shows how a block of data will be moved between memory locations with different boundaries. Note that the order of the data does not change.

If the destination is the Requester and an early process termination has been indicated by the EOP# signal or DREQn inactive in the Demand Mode, the Temporary Register is not affected. If data remains in the Temporary Register due to differences in data path widths of the Target and Requester, it will not be transferred or otherwise lost, but will be stored for later transfer.

Source address	Source	Destination address	Destination
20H	A	50H	
21H	B	51H	
22H	C	52H	
23H	D	53H	A
24H	E	54H	B
25H	F	55H	C
26H	G	56H	D
27H		57H	E
		58H	F
		59H	G
		5AH	

Target = source = 00000020H
Requester = destination = 00000053H
Byte Count = 000007H

Figure 3-22. Transfer of data between memory locations with different boundaries. This will be the result, independent of data path width.

If the destination is the Target and the EOP# signal is sensed active during the Requester access of a transfer, the DMA Controller will complete the transfer by sending to the Target whatever information is in the Temporary Register at the time of process termination. This implies that the Target could be accessed with partial data in two accesses. For this reason it is advisable to have an I/O device designated as a Requester, unless it is capable of handling partial data transfers.

3.6 DMA Controller Programming

Programming a DMA Channel to perform a needed DMA function is in general a four step process. First the global attributes of the DMA Controller are programmed via the two Command Registers. These global attributes include: priority levels, channel group enables, priority mode, and DREQn/EOP# input sampling.

The second step involves setting the operating modes of the particular channel. The Mode Registers are used to define the type of transfer and the handshaking modes. The Bus Size Register and Chaining Register may also need to be programmed in this step.

The third step in setting up the channel is to load the Base Registers in accordance with the needs of the operating modes chosen in step two. The Current Registers are automatically loaded from the Base Registers, if required by the Buffer Transfer Mode in effect. The information loaded and the order in which it is loaded depends on the operating mode. A channel used for cascading, for example, needs no buffer information and this step can be skipped entirely.

The last step is to enable the newly programmed channel using one of the Mask Registers. The channel is then available to perform the desired data transfer. The status of the channel can be observed at any time through the Status Register, Mask Register, Chaining Register, and Software Request register.

Once the channel is programmed and enabled, the DMA process may be initiated in one of two ways, either by a hardware DMA request (DREQn) or a software request (Software Request Register).

Once programmed to a particular Process/Mode configuration, the channel will operate in that configuration until programmed otherwise. For this reason, restarting a channel after the current buffer expires does not require complete reprogramming of the channel. Only those parameters which have changed need to be reprogrammed. The Byte Count Register is always changed and must be reprogrammed. A Target or Requester Address Register which is incremented or decremented should be reprogrammed also.

3.6.1 BUFFER PROCESSES

The Buffer Process is determined by the Auto-Initialize bit of Mode Register I and the Chaining Register. If Auto-Initialize is enabled, Chaining should not be used.

3.6.1.1 Single Buffer Process

The Single Buffer Process is programmed by disabling Chaining via the Chaining Register and programming Mode Register I for non-Auto-Initialize.

3.6.1.2 Buffer Auto-Initialize Process

Setting the Auto-Initialize bit in Mode Register I is all that is necessary to place the channel in this mode. Buffer Auto-Initialize must not be enabled simultaneous to enabling the Buffer Chaining Mode as this will have unpredictable results.

Once the Base Registers are loaded, the channel is ready to be enabled. The channel will reload its Current Registers from the Base Registers each time the Current Buffer expires, either by an expired Byte Count or an external EOP#.

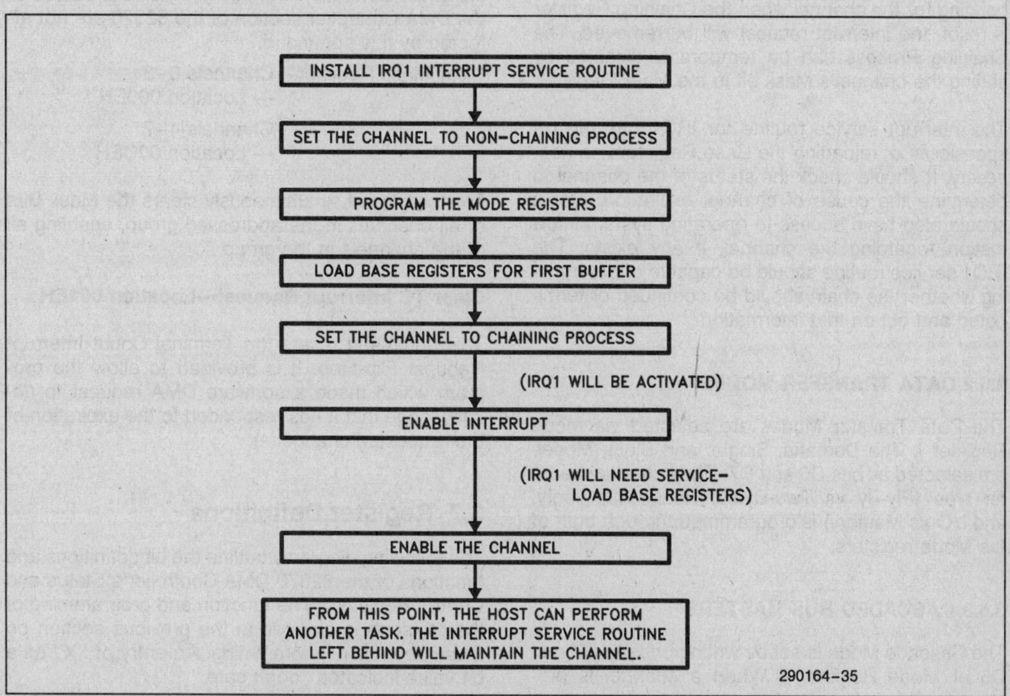

Figure 3-23. Flow of Events in the Buffer Chaining Process

4

3.6.1.3 Buffer Chaining Process

The Buffer Chaining Process is entered into from the Single Buffer Process. The Mode Registers should be programmed first, with all of the Transfer Modes defined as if the channel were to operate in the Single Buffer Process. The channel's Base Registers are then loaded. When the channel has been set up in this way, and the chaining interrupt service routine is in place, the Chaining Process can be entered by programming the Chaining Register. Figure 3-23 illustrates the Buffer Chaining Process.

An interrupt (IRQ1) will be generated immediately after the Chaining Process is entered, as the channel then perceives the Base Registers as empty and in need of reloading. It is important to have the interrupt service routine in place at the time the Chaining Process is entered into. The interrupt request is removed when the most significant byte of the Base Target Address is loaded.

The interrupt will occur again when the first buffer expires and the Current Registers are loaded from the Base Registers. The cycle continues until the Chaining Process is disabled, or the host fails to respond to IRQ1 before the Current Buffer expires.

Exiting the Chaining Process can be done by resetting the Chaining Mode Register. If an interrupt is pending for the channel when the Chaining Register is reset, the interrupt request will be removed. The Chaining Process can be temporarily disabled by setting the channel's Mask bit in the Mask Register.

The interrupt service routine for IRQ1 has the responsibility of reloading the Base Registers as necessary. It should check the status of the channel to determine the cause of channel expiration, etc. It should also have access to operating system information regarding the channel, if any exists. The IRQ1 service routine should be capable of determining whether the chain should be continued or terminated and act on that information.

3.6.2 DATA TRANSFER MODES

The Data Transfer Modes are selected via Mode Register I. The Demand, Single, and Block Modes are selected by bits D6 and D7. The individual transfer type (Fly-By vs Two-Cycle, Read-Write-Verify, and I/O vs Memory) is programmed through both of the Mode registers.

3.6.3 CASCADED BUS MASTERS

The Cascade Mode is set by writing ones to D7 and D6 of Mode Register I. When a channel is programmed to operate in the Cascade Mode, all of the other modes associated with Mode Registers I and II are ignored. The priority and DREQn/EOP# definitions of the Command Registers will have the same effect on the channel's operation as any other mode.

3.6.4 SOFTWARE COMMANDS

There are five port addresses which, when written to, command certain operations to be performed by the 82370 DMA Controller. The data written to these locations is not of consequence, writing to the location is all that is necessary to command the 82370 to perform the indicated function. Following are descriptions of the command functions.

Clear Byte Pointer Flip-Flop—Location 000CH

Resets the Byte Pointer Flip-Flop. This command should be performed at the beginning of any access to the channel registers in order to be assured of beginning at a predictable place in the register programming sequence.

Master Clear—Location 000DH

All DMA functions are set to their default states. This command is the equivalent of a hardware reset to the DMA Controller. Functions other than those in the DMA Controller section of the 82370 are not affected by this command.

Clear Mask Register—Channels 0–3
— Location 000EH

Channels 4–7
— Location 00CEH

This command simultaneously clears the Mask Bits of all channels in the addressed group, enabling all of the channels in the group.

Clear TC Interrupt Request—Location 001EH

This command resets the Terminal Count Interrupt Request Flip-Flop. It is provided to allow the program which made a software DMA request to acknowledge that it has responded to the expiration of the requested channel(s).

3.7 Register Definitions

The following diagrams outline the bit definitions and functions of the 82370 DMA Controller's Status and Control Registers. The function and programming of the registers is covered in the previous section on DMA Controller Programming. An entry of "X" as a bit value indicates "don't care."

Channel Registers (read Current, write Base)

Channel	Register Name	Address (hex)	Byte Pointer	Bits Accessed
Channel 0	Target Address	00	0	0–7
			1	8–15
		87	x	16–23
		10	0	24–31(*)
	Byte Count	01	0	0–7
			1	8–15
		11	0	16–23
	Requester Address	90	0	0–7
			1	8–15
		91	0	16–23
			1	24–31(*)
Channel 1	Target Address	02	0	0–7
			1	8–15
		83	x	16–23
		12	0	24–31(*)
	Byte Count	03	0	0–7
			1	8–15
		13	0	16–23
	Requester Address	92	0	0–7
			1	8–15
		93	0	16–23
			1	24–31(*)
Channel 2	Target Address	04	0	0–7
			1	8–15
		81	x	16–23
		14	0	24–31(*)
	Byte Count	05	0	0–7
			1	8–15
		15	0	16–23
	Requester Address	94	0	0–7
			1	8–15
		95	0	16–23
			1	24–31(*)
Channel 3	Target Address	06	0	0–7
			1	8–15
		82	x	16–23
		16	0	24–31(*)
	Byte Count	07	0	0–7
			1	8–15
		17	0	16–23
	Requester Address	96	0	0–7
			1	8–15
		97	0	16–23
			1	24–31(*)

4

Channel Registers (read Current, write Base) (Continued)

Channel	Register Name	Address (hex)	Byte Pointer	Bits Accessed
Channel 4	Target Address	C0	0	0–7
			1	8–15
		8F	x	16–23
		D0	0	24–31(*)
	Byte Count	C1	0	0–7
			1	8–15
		D1	0	16–23
	Requester Address	98	0	0–7
			1	8–15
		99	0	16–23
			1	24–31(*)
Channel 5	Target Address	C2	0	0–7
			1	8–15
		8B	x	16–23
		D2	0	24–31(*)
	Byte Count	C3	0	0–7
			1	8–15
		D3	0	16–23
	Requester Address	9A	0	0–7
			1	8–15
		9B	0	16–23
			1	24–31(*)
Channel 6	Target Address	C4	0	0–7
			1	8–15
		89	x	16–23
		D4	0	24–31(*)
	Byte Count	C5	0	0–7
			1	8–15
		D5	0	16–23
	Requester Address	9C	0	0–7
			1	8–15
		9D	0	16–23
			1	24–31(*)
Channel 7	Target Address	C6	0	0–7
			1	8–15
		8A	x	16–23
		D6	0	24–31(*)
	Byte Count	C7	0	0–7
			1	8–15
		D7	0	16–23
	Requester Address	9E	0	0–7
			1	8–15
		9F	0	16–23
			1	24–31(*)

NOTE:
(*)These bits are not available externally. You need to be aware of their existence for chaining and Byte Pointer Flip-Flop operations. Please see section 3.5.2 for further details.

Command Register I (write only)

Port Addresses— Channels 0-3—0008H
Channels 4-7—00C8H

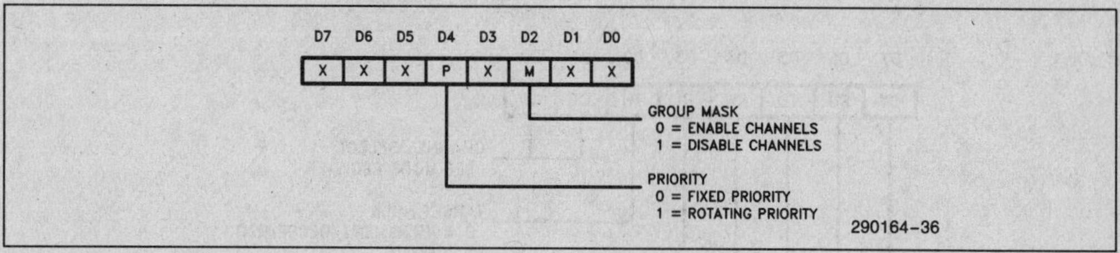

Command Register II (write only)

Port Addresses— Channels 0-3—001AH
Channels 4-7—00DAH

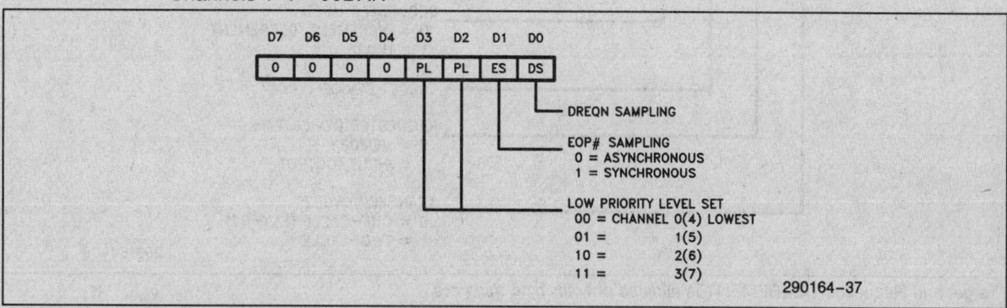

Mode Register I (write only)

Port Addresses— Channels 0-3—000BH
Channels 4-7—00CBH

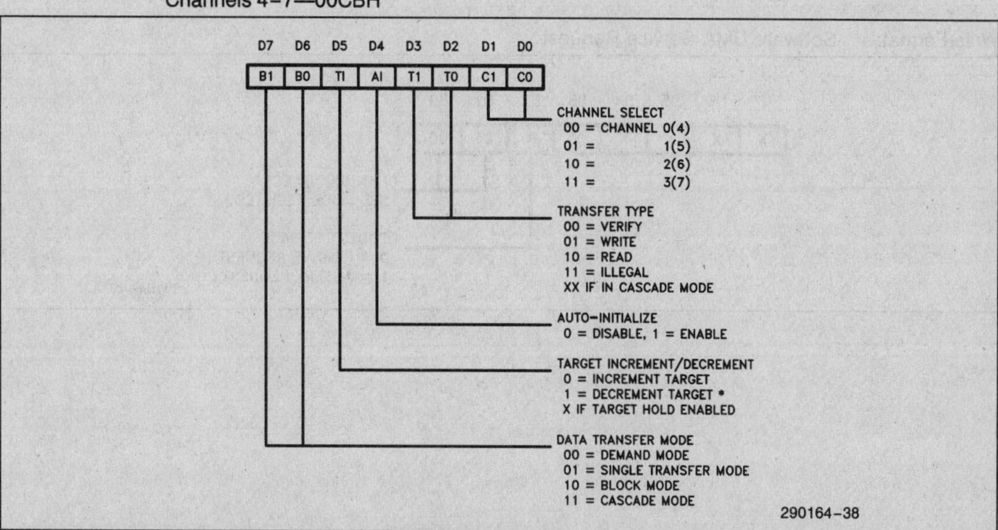

*Target and Requester DECREMENT is allowed only for byte transfers.

Mode Register II (write only)

Port Addresses— Channels 0-3—001BH
Channels 4-7—00DBH

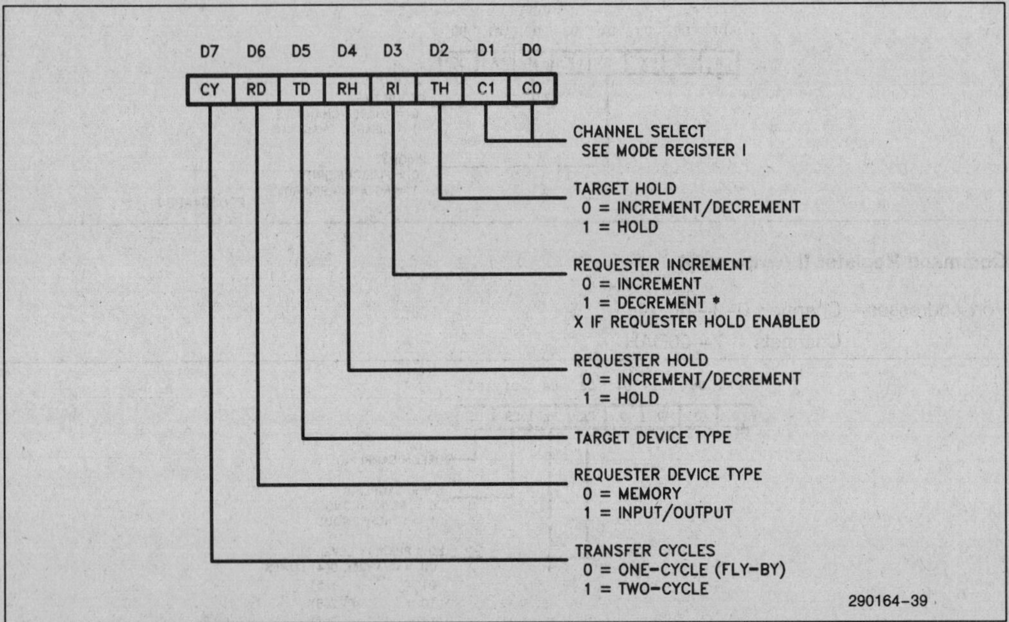

*Target and Requester DECREMENT is allowed only for byte transfers.

Software Request Register (read/write)

Port Addresses— Channels 0-3—0009H
Channels 4-7—00C9H

Write Format: Software DMA Service Request

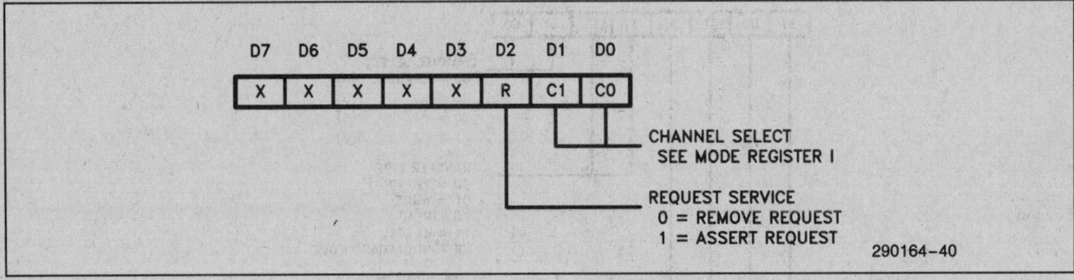

Read Format: Software Requests Pending

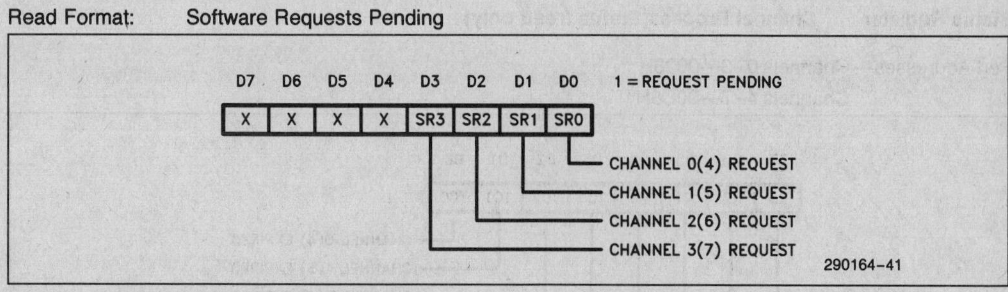

290164-41

Mask Set/Reset Register Individual Channel Mask (write only)

Port Addresses— Channels 0–3—000AH
Channels 4–7—00CAH

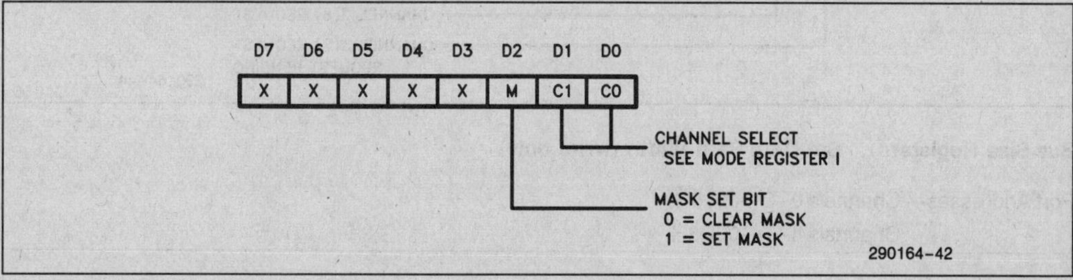

290164-42

Mask Read/Write Register Group Channel Mask (read/write)

Port Addresses— Channels 0–3—000FH
Channels 4–7—00CFH

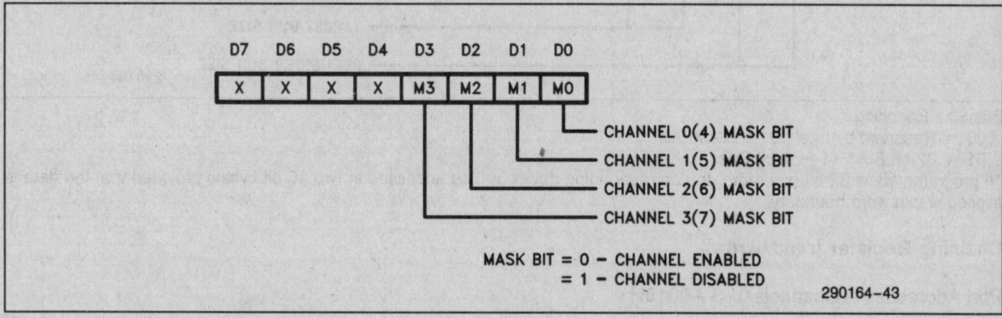

290164-43

Status Register **Channel Process Status (read only)**

Port Addresses— Channels 0-3—0008H
Channels 4-7—00C8H

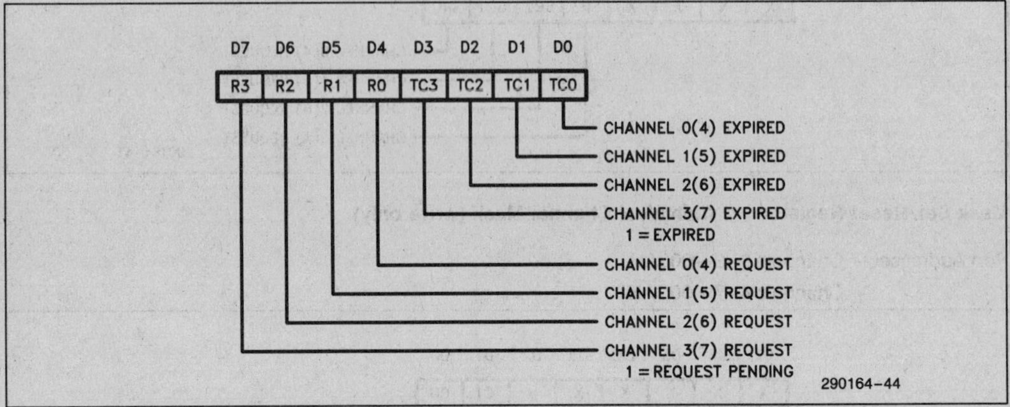

Bus Size Register **Set Data Path Width (write only)**

Port Addresses— Channels 0-3—0018H
Channels 4-7—00D8H

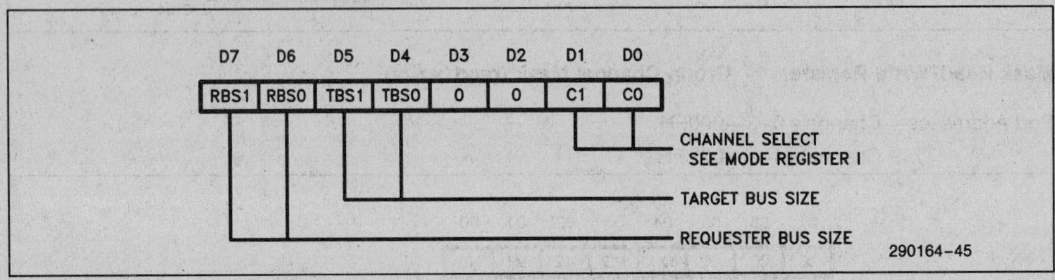

Bus Size Encoding:
00 = Reserved by Intel 10 = 16-bit Bus
01 = 32-bit Bus* 11 = 8-bit Bus
*If programmed as 32-bit bus width, the corresponding device will be accessed in two 16-bit cycles provided that the data is aligned within word boundary.

Chaining Register (read/write)

Port Addresses— Channels 0-3—0019H
Channels 4-7—00D9H

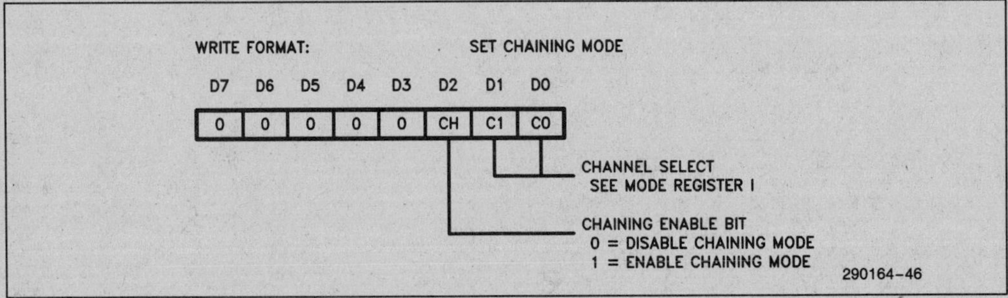

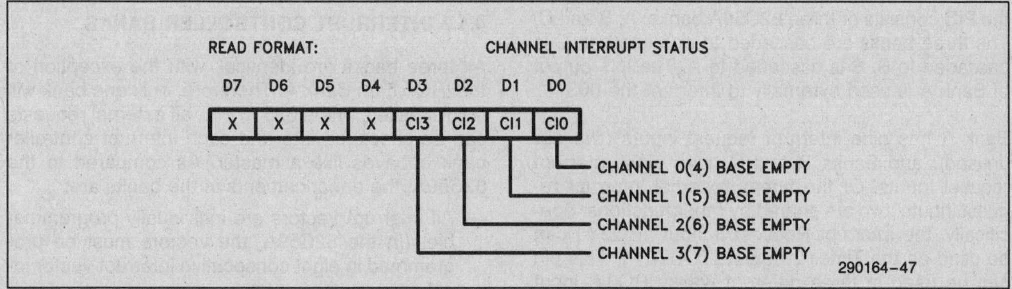

3.8 8237A Compatibility

The register arrangement of the 82370 DMA Controller is a superset of the 8237A DMA Controller. Functionally the 82370 DMA Controller is very different from the 8237A. Most of the functions of the 8237A are performed also by the 82370. The following discussion points out the differences between the 8237A and the 82370.

The 8237A is limited to transfers between I/O and memory only (except in one special case, where two channels can be used to perform memory-to-memory transfers). The 82370 DMA Controller can transfer between any combination of memory and I/O. Several other features of the 8237A are enhanced or expanded in the 82370 and other features are added.

The 8237A is an 8-bit only DMA device. For programming compatibility, all of the 8-bit registers are preserved in the 82370. The 82370 is programmed via 8-bit registers. The address registers in the 82370 are 24-bit registers in order to support the 80376's 24-bit bus. The Byte Count Registers are 24-bit registers, allowing support of larger data blocks than possible with the 8237A.

All of the 8237A's operating modes are supported by the 82370 (except the cumbersome two-channel memory-to-memory transfer). The 82370 performs memory-to-memory transfers using only one channel. The 82370 has the added features of buffer pipelining (Buffer Chaining Process) and programmable priority levels.

The 82370 also adds the feature of address registers for both destination and source. These addresses may be incremented, decremented, or held constant, as required by the application of the individual channel. This allows any combination of destination and source device.

Each DMA channel has associated with it a Target and a Requester. In the 8237A, the Target is the device which can be accessed by the address register, the Requester is the device which is accessed by the DMA Acknowledge signals and must be an I/O device.

4.0 PROGRAMMABLE INTERRUPT CONTROLLER (PIC)

4.1 Functional Description

The 82370 Programmable Interrupt Controller (PIC) consists of three enhanced 82C59A Interrupt Controllers. These three controllers together provide 15 external and 5 internal interrupt request inputs. Each external request input can be cascaded with an additional 82C59A slave controller. This scheme allows the 82370 to support a maximum of 120 (15 x 8) external interrupt request inputs.

Following one or more interrupt requests, the 82370 PIC issues an interrupt signal to the 80376. When the 80376 host processor responds with an interrupt acknowledge signal, the PIC will arbitrate between the pending interrupt requests and place the interrupt vector associated with the highest priority pending request on the data bus.

The major enhancement in the 82370 PIC over the 82C59A is that each of the interrupt request inputs can be individually programmed with its own interrupt vector, allowing more flexibility in interrupt vector mapping.

4.1.1 INTERNAL BLOCK DIAGRAM

The block diagram of the 82370 Programmable Interrupt Controller is shown in Figure 4-1. Internally,

4

the PIC consists of three 82C59A banks: A, B and C. The three banks are cascaded to one another: C is cascaded to B, B is cascaded to A. The INT output of Bank A is used externally to interrupt the 80376.

Bank A has nine interrupt request inputs (two are unused), and Banks B and C have eight interrupt request inputs. Of the fifteen external interrupt request inputs, two are shared by other functions. Specifically, the Interrupt Request 3 input (IRQ3#) can be used as the Timer 2 output (TOUT2#). This pin can be used in three different ways: IRQ3# input only, TOUT2# output only, or using TOUT2# to generate an IRQ3# interrupt request. Also, the Interrupt Request 9 input (IRQ9#) can be used as DMA Request 4 input (DREQ 4). Typically, only IRQ9# or DREQ4 can be used at a time.

4.1.2 INTERRUPT CONTROLLER BANKS

All three banks are identical, with the exception of the IRQ1.5 on Bank A. Therefore, only one bank will be discussed. In the 82370 PIC, all external requests can be cascaded into and each interrupt controller bank behaves like a master. As compared to the 82C59A, the enhancements in the banks are:

- All interrupt vectors are individually programmable. (In the 82C59A, the vectors must be programmed in eight consecutive interrupt vector locations.)
- The cascade address is provided on the Data Bus (D0-D7). (In the 82C59A, three dedicated control signals (CAS0, CAS1, CAS2) are used for master/slave cascading.)

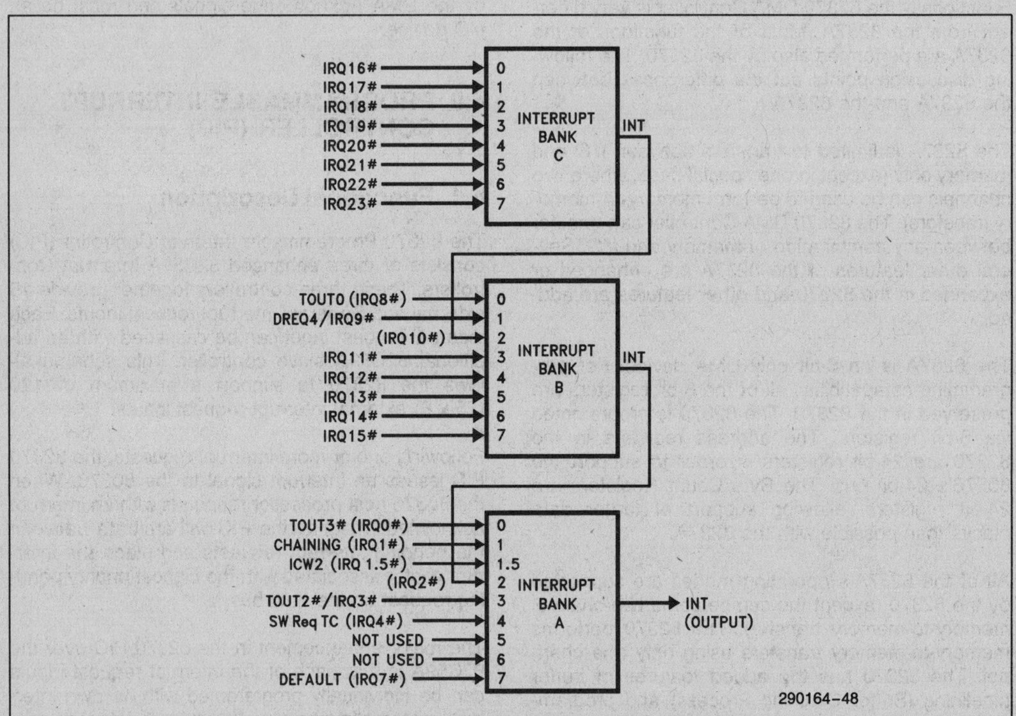

Figure 4-1. Interrupt Controller Block Diagram

The block diagram of a bank is shown in Figure 4-2. As can be seen from this figure, the bank consists of six major blocks: the Interrupt Request Register (IRR), the In-Service Register (ISR), the Interrupt Mask Register (IMR), the Priority Resolver (PR), the Vector Registers (VR), and the Control Logic. The functional description of each block is included below.

INTERRUPT REQUEST (IRR) AND IN-SERVICE REGISTER (ISR)

The interrupts at the Interrupt Request (IRQ) input lines are handled by two registers in cascade, the Interrupt Request Register (IRR) and the In-Service Register (ISR). The IRR is used to store all interrupt levels which are requesting service; and the ISR is used to store all interrupt levels which are being serviced.

PRIORITY RESOLVER (PR)

This logic block determines the priorities of the bits set in the IRR. The highest priority is selected and strobed into the corresponding bit of the ISR during an Interrupt Acknowledge cycle.

INTERRUPT MASK REGISTER (IMR)

The IMR stores the bits which mask the interrupt lines to be masked (disabled). The IMR operates on the IRR. Masking of a higher priority input will not affect the interrupt request lines of lower priority.

VECTOR REGISTERS (VR)

This block contains a set of Vector Registers, one for each interrupt request line, to store the pre-programmed interrupt vector number. The corresponding vector number will be driven onto the Data Bus of the 82370 during the Interrupt Acknowledge cycle.

CONTROL LOGIC

The Control Logic coordinates the overall operations of the other internal blocks within the same bank. This logic will drive the Interrupt Output signal (INT) HIGH when one or more unmasked interrupt inputs are active (LOW). The INT output signal goes directly to the 80376 (in bank A) or to another bank to which this bank is cascaded (see Figure 4-1). Also,

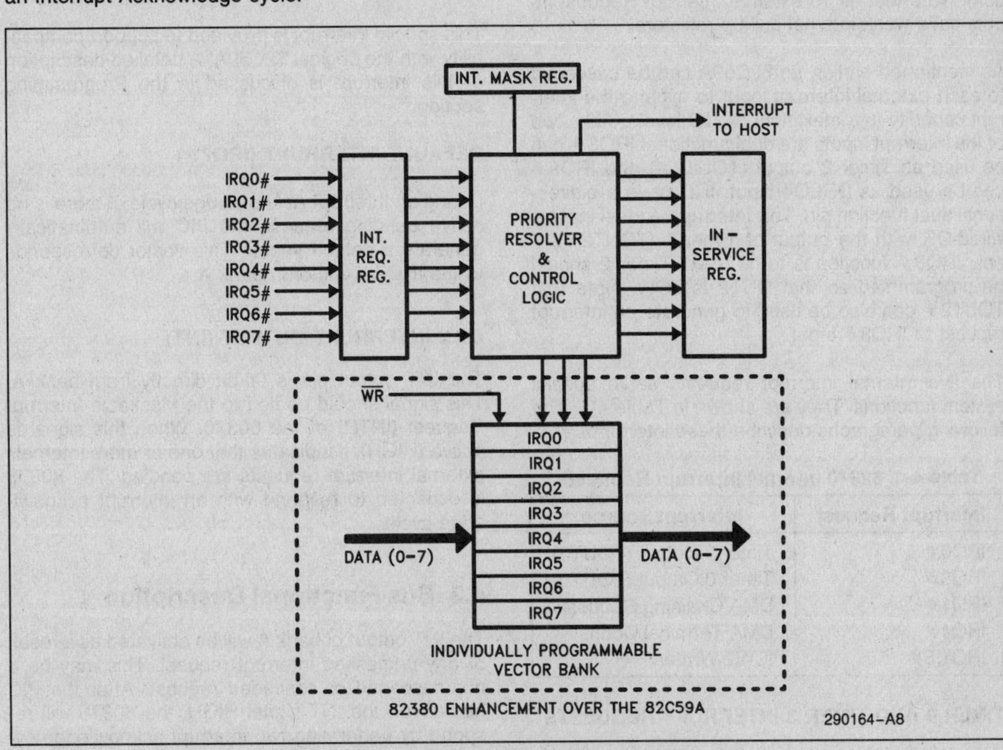

Figure 4-2. Interrupt Bank Block Diagram

this logic will recognize an Interrupt Acknowledge cycle (via M/IO#, D/C# and W/R# signals). During this bus cycle, the Control Logic will enable the corresponding Vector Register to drive the interrupt vector onto the Data Bus.

In bank A, the Control Logic is also responsible for handling the special ICW2 interrupt request input (IRQ1.5).

4.2 Interface Signals

4.2.1 INTERRUPT INPUTS

There are 15 external Interrupt Request inputs and 5 internal Interrupt Requests. The external request inputs are: IRQ3#, IRQ9#, IRQ11# to IRQ23#. They are shown in bold arrows in Figure 4-1. All IRQ inputs are active LOW and they can be programmed (via a control bit in the Initialization Command Word 1 (ICW1)) to be either edge-triggered or level-triggered. In order to be recognized as a valid interrupt request, the interrupt input must be active (LOW) until the first INTA cycle (see Bus Functional Description). Note that all 15 external Interrupt Request inputs have weak internal pull-up resistors.

As mentioned earlier, an 82C59A can be cascaded to each external interrupt input to expand the interrupt capacity to a maximum of 120 levels. Also, two of the interrupt inputs are dual functions: IRQ3# can be used as Timer 2 output (TOUT2#) and IRQ9# can be used as DREQ4 input. IRQ3# is a bidirectional dual function pin. This interrupt request input is wired-OR with the output of Timer 2 (TOUT2#). If only IRQ3# function is to be used, Timer 2 should be programmed so that OUT2 is LOW. Note that TOUT2# can also be used to generate an interrupt request to IRQ3# input.

The five internal interrupt requests serve special system functions. They are shown in Table 4-1. The following paragraphs describe these interrupts.

Table 4-1. 82370 Internal Interrupt Requests

Interrupt Request	Interrupt Source
IRQ0#	Timer 3 Output (TOUT3)
IRQ8#	Timer 0 Output (TOUT0)
IRQ1#	DMA Chaining Request
IRQ4#	DMA Terminal Count
IRQ1.5#	ICW2 Written

TIMER 0 AND TIMER 3 INTERRUPT REQUESTS

IRQ8# and IRQ0# interrupt requests are initiated by the output of Timers 0 and 3, respectively. Each of these requests is generated by an edge-detector flip-flop.

The flip-flops are activated by the following conditions:

Set — Rising edge of timer output (TOUT);

Clear — Interrupt acknowledge for this request; OR Request is masked (disabled); OR Hardware Reset.

CHAINING AND TERMINAL COUNT INTERRUPTS

These interrupt requests are generated by the 82370 DMA Controller. The chaining request (IRQ1#) indicates that the DMA Base Register is not loaded. The Terminal Count request (IRQ4#) indicates that a software DMA request was cleared.

ICW2 INTERRUPT REQUEST

Whenever an Initialization Control Word 2 (ICW2) is written to a Bank, a special ICW2 interrupt request is generated. The interrupt will be cleared when the newly programmed ICW2 Register is read. This interrupt request is in Bank A at level 1.5. This interrupt request is internally ORed with the Cascaded Request from Bank B and is always assigned a higher priority than the Cascaded Request.

This special interrupt is provided to support compatibility with the original 82C59A. A detailed description of this interrupt is discussed in the Programming section.

DEFAULT INTERRUPT (IRQ7#)

During an Interrupt Acknowledge cycle, if there is no active pending request, the PIC will automatically generate a default vector. This vector corresponds to the IRQ7# vector in bank A.

4.2.2 INTERRUPT OUTPUT (INT)

The INT output pin is taken directly from bank A. This signal should be tied to the Maskable Interrupt Request (INTR) of the 80376. When this signal is active (HIGH), it indicates that one or more internal/external interrupt requests are pending. The 80376 is expected to respond with an interrupt acknowledge cycle.

4.3 Bus Functional Description

The INT output of bank A will be activated as a result of any unmasked interrupt request. This may be a non-cascaded or cascaded request. After the PIC has driven the INT signal HIGH, the 80376 will respond by performing two interrupt acknowledge cycles. The timing diagram in Figure 4-3 shows a typical interrupt acknowledge process between the 82370 and the 80376 CPU.

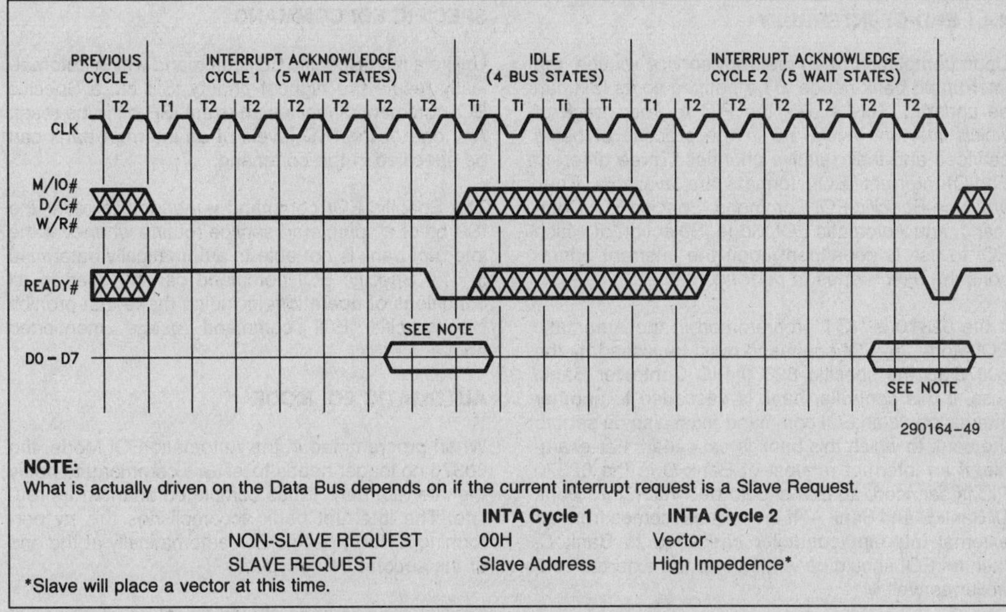

NOTE:
What is actually driven on the Data Bus depends on if the current interrupt request is a Slave Request.

	INTA Cycle 1	INTA Cycle 2
NON-SLAVE REQUEST	00H	Vector
SLAVE REQUEST	Slave Address	High Impedence*

*Slave will place a vector at this time.

Figure 4-3. Interrupt Acknowledge Cycle

After activating the INT signal, the 82370 monitors the status lines (M/IO#, D/C#, W/R#) and waits for the 80376 to initiate the first interrupt acknowledge cycle. In the 80376 environment, two successive interrupt acknowledge cycles (INTA) marked by M/IO# = LOW, D/C# = LOW, and W/R# = LOW are performed. During the first INTA cycle, the PIC will determine the highest priority request. Assuming this interrupt input has no external Slave Controller cascaded to it, the 82370 will drive the Data Bus with 00H in the first INTA cycle. During the second INTA cycle, the 82370 PIC will drive the Data Bus with the corresponding pre-programmed interrupt vector.

If the PIC determines (from the ICW3) that this interrupt input has an external Slave Controller cascaded to it, it will drive the Data Bus with the specific Slave Cascade Address (instead of 00H) during the first INTA cycle. This Slave Cascade Address is the preprogrammed content in the corresponding Vector Register. This means that no Slave Address should be chosen to be 00H. Note that the Slave Address and Interrupt Vector are different interpretations of the same thing. They are both the contents of the programmable Vector Register. During the second INTA cycle, the Data Bus will be floated so that the external Slave Controller can drive its interrupt vector on the bus. Since the Slave Interrupt Controller resides on the system bus, bus transceiver enable and direction control logic must take this into consideration.

In order to have a successful interrupt service, the interrupt request input must be held valid (LOW) until the beginning of the first interrupt acknowledge cycle. If there is no pending interrupt request when the first INTA cycle is generated, the PIC will generate a default vector, which is the IRQ7 vector (Bank A, level 7).

According to the Bus Cycle definition of the 80376, there will be four Bus Idle States between the two interrupt acknowledge cycles. These idle bus cycles will be initiated by the 80376. Also, during each interrupt acknowledge cycle, the internal Wait State Generator of the 82370 will automatically generate the required number of wait states for internal delays.

4.4 Modes of Operation

A variety of modes and commands are available for controlling the 82370 PIC. All of them are programmable; that is, they may be changed dynamically under software control. In fact, each bank can be programmed individually to operate in different modes. With these modes and commands, many possible configurations are conceivable, giving the user enough versatility for almost any interrupt controlled application.

This section is not intended to show how the 82370 PIC can be programmed. Rather, it describes the operation in different modes.

4.4.1 END-OF-INTERRUPT

Upon completion of an interrupt service routine, the interrupted bank needs to be notified so its ISR can be updated. This allows the PIC to keep track of which interrupt levels are in the process of being serviced and their relative priorities. Three different End-Of-Interrupt (EOI) formats are available. They are: Non-Specific EOI Command, Specific EOI Command, and Automatic EOI Mode. Selection of which EOI to use is dependent upon the interrupt operations the user wishes to perform.

If the 82370 is NOT programmed in the Automatic EOI Mode, an EOI command must be issued by the 80376 to the specific 82370 PIC Controller Bank. Also, if this controller bank is cascaded to another internal bank, an EOI command must also be sent to the bank to which this bank is cascaded. For example, if an interrupt request of Bank C in the 82370 PIC is serviced, an EOI should be written into Bank C, Bank B and Bank A. If the request comes from an external interrupt controller cascaded to Bank C, then an EOI should be written into the external controller as well.

NON-SPECIFIC EOI COMMAND

A Non-Specific EOI command sent from the 80376 lets the 82370 PIC bank know when a service routine has been completed, without specification of its exact interrupt level. The respective interrupt bank automatically determines the interrupt level and resets the correct bit in the ISR.

To take advantage of the Non-Specific EOI, the interrupt bank must be in a mode of operation in which it can predetermine its in-service routine levels. For this reason, the Non-Specific EOI command should only be used when the most recent level acknowledged and serviced is always the highest priority level (i.e. in the Fully Nested Mode structure to be described below). When the interrupt bank receives a Non-Specific EOI command, it simply resets the highest priority ISR bit to indicate that the highest priority routine in service is finished.

Special consideration should be taken when deciding to use the Non-Specific EOI command. Here are two operating conditions in which it is best NOT used since the Fully Nested Mode structure will be destroyed:

— Using the Set Priority command within an interrupt service routine.

— Using a Special Mask Mode.

These conditions are covered in more detail in their own sections, but are listed here for reference.

SPECIFIC EOI COMMAND

Unlike a Non-Specific EOI command which automatically resets the highest priority ISR bit, a Specific EOI command specifies an exact ISR bit to be reset. Any one of the IRQ levels of an interrupt bank can be specified in the command.

The Specific EOI command is needed to reset the ISR bit of a completed service routine whenever the interrupt bank is not able to automatically determine it. The Specific EOI command can be used in all conditions of operation, including those that prohibit Non-Specific EOI command usage mentioned above.

AUTOMATIC EOI MODE

When programmed in the Automatic EOI Mode, the 80376 no longer needs to issue a command to notify the interrupt bank it has completed an interrupt routine. The interrupt bank accomplishes this by performing a Non-Specific EOI automatically at the end of the second INTA cycle.

Special consideration should be taken when deciding to use the Automatic EOI Mode because it may disturb the Fully Nested Mode structure. In the Automatic EOI Mode, the ISR bit of a routine in service is reset right after it is acknowledged, thus leaving no designation in the ISR that a service routine is being executed. If any interrupt request within the same bank occurs during this time and interrupts are enabled, it will get serviced regardless of its priority. Therefore, when using this mode, the 80376 should keep its interrupt request input disabled during execution of a service routine. By doing this, higher priority interrupt levels will be serviced only after the completion of a routine in service. This guideline restores the Fully Nested Mode structure. However, in this scheme, a routine in service cannot be interrupted since the host's interrupt request input is disabled.

4.4.2 INTERRUPT PRIORITIES

The 82370 PIC provides various methods for arranging the interrupt priorities of the interrupt request inputs to suit different applications. The following subsections explain these methods in detail.

4.4.2.1 Fully Nested Mode

The Fully Nested Mode of operation is a general purpose priority mode. This mode supports a multi-level interrupt structure in which all of the Interrupt Request (IRQ) inputs within one bank are arranged from highest to lowest.

Unless otherwise programmed, the Fully Nested Mode is entered by default upon initialization. At this time, IRQ0# is assigned the highest priority (priority=0) and IRQ7# the lowest (priority=7). This default priority can be changed, as will be explained later in the Rotating Priority Mode.

When an interrupt is acknowledged, the highest priority request is determined from the Interrupt Request Register (IRR) and its vector is placed on the bus. In addition, the corresponding bit in the In-Service Register (ISR) is set to designate the routine in service. This ISR bit will remain set until the 80376 issues an End Of Interrupt (EOI) command immediately before returning from the service routine; or alternately, if the Automatic End Of Interrupt (AEOI) bit is set, the ISR bit will be reset at the end of the second INTA cycle.

While the ISR bit is set, all further interrupts of the same or lower priority are inhibited. Higher level interrupts can still generate an interrupt, which will be acknowledged only if the 80376 internal interrupt enable flip-flop has been reenabled (through software inside the current service routine).

4.4.2.2 Automatic Rotation–Equal Priority Devices

Automatic rotation of priorities serves in applications where the interrupting devices are of equal priority within an interrupt bank. In this kind of environment, once a device is serviced, all other equal priority peripherals should be given a chance to be serviced before the original device is serviced again. This is accomplished by automatically assigning a device the lowest priority after being serviced. Thus, in the worst case, the device would have to wait until all other peripherals connected to the same bank are serviced before it is serviced again.

There are two methods of accomplishing automatic rotation. One is used in conjunction with the Non-Specific EOI command and the other is used with the Automatic EOI mode. These two methods are discussed below.

ROTATE ON NON-SPECIFIC EOI COMMAND

When the Rotate On Non-Specific EOI command is issued, the highest ISR bit is reset as in a normal Non-Specific EOI command. However, after it is reset, the corresponding Interrupt Request (IRQ) level is assigned the lowest priority. Other IRQ priorities rotate to conform to the Fully Nested Mode based on the newly assigned low priority.

Figure 4-4 shows how the Rotate On Non-Specific EOI command affects the interrupt priorities. Assume the IRQ priorities were assigned with IRQ0 the highest and IRQ7 the lowest. IRQ6 and IRQ4 are

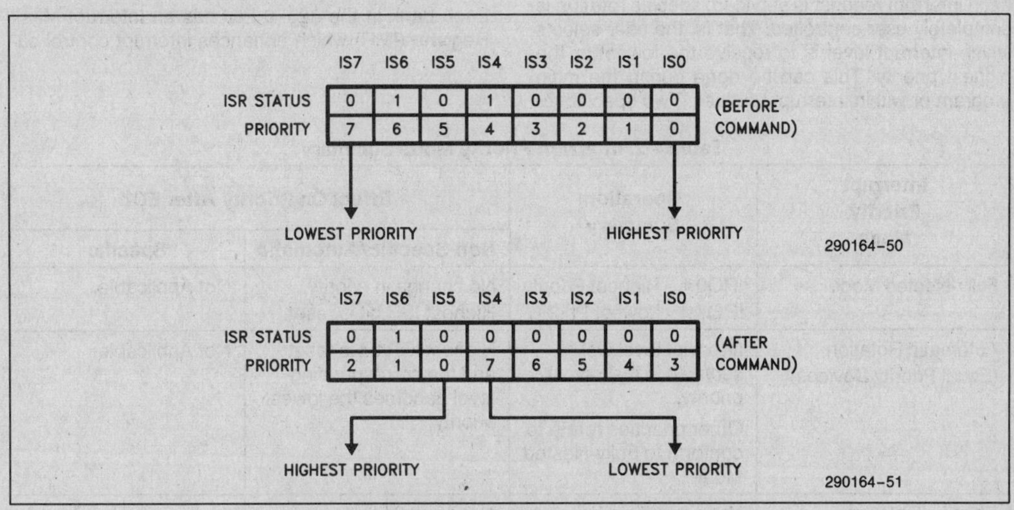

Figure 4-4. Rotate On Non-Specific EOI Command

already in service but neither is completed. Being the higher priority routine, IRQ4 is necessarily the routine being executed. During the IRQ4 routine, a rotate on Non-Specific EOI command is executed. When this happens, Bit 4 in the ISR is reset. IRQ4 then becomes the lowest priority and IRQ5 becomes the highest.

ROTATE ON AUTOMATIC EOI MODE

The Rotate On Automatic EOI Mode works much like the Rotate On Non-Specific EOI Command. The main difference is that priority rotation is done automatically after the second INTA cycle of an interrupt request. To enter or exit this mode, a Rotate-On-Automatic-EOI Set Command and Rotate-On-Automatic-EOI Clear Command is provided. After this mode is entered, no other commands are needed as in the normal Automatic EOI Mode. However, it must be noted again that when using any form of the Automatic EOI Mode, special consideration should be taken. The guideline presented in the Automatic EOI Mode also applies here.

4.4.2.3 Specific Rotation–Specific Priority

Specific rotation gives the user versatile capabilities in interrupt controlled operations. It serves in those applications in which a specific device's interrupt priority must be altered. As opposed to Automatic Rotation which will automatically set priorities after each interrupt request is serviced, specific rotation is completely user controlled. That is, the user selects which interrupt level is to receive the lowest or the highest priority. This can be done during the main program or within interrupt routines. Two specific rotation commands are available to the user: Set Priority Command and Rotate On Specific EOI Command.

SET PRIORITY COMMAND

The Set Priority Command allows the programmer to assign an IRQ level the lowest priority. All other interrupt levels will conform to the Fully Nested Mode based on the newly assigned low priority.

ROTATE ON SPECIFIC EOI COMMAND

The Rotate On Specific EOI Command is literally a combination of the Set Priority Command and the Specific EOI Command. Like the Set Priority Command, a specified IRQ level is assigned lowest priority. Like the Specific EOI Command, a specified level will be reset in the ISR. Thus, this command accomplishes both tasks in one single command.

4.4.2.4 Interrupt Priority Mode Summary

In order to simplify understanding the many modes of interrupt priority, Table 4-2 is provided to bring out their summary of operations.

4.4.3 INTERRUPT MASKING

VIA INTERRUPT MASK REGISTER

Each bank in the 82370 PIC has an Interrupt Mask Register (IMR) which enhances interrupt control ca-

Table 4-2. Interrupt Priority Mode Summary

Interrupt Priority Mode	Operation Summary	Effect On Priority After EOI	
		Non-Specific/Automatic	Specific
Fully-Nested Mode	IRQ0# - Highest Priority IRQ7# - Lowest Priority	No change in priority. Highest ISR bit is reset.	Not Applicable.
Automatic Rotation (Equal Priority Devices)	Interrupt level just serviced is the lowest priority. Other priorities rotate to conform to Fully-Nested Mode.	Highest ISR bit is reset and the corresponding level becomes the lowest priority.	Not Applicable.
Specific Rotation (Specific Priority Devices)	User specifies the lowest priority level. Other priorities rotate to conform to Fully-Nested Mode.	Not Applicable.	As described under "Operation Summary".

pabilities. This IMR allows individual IRQ masking. When an IRQ is masked, its interrupt request is disabled until it is unmasked. Each bit in the 8-bit IMR disables one interrupt channel if it is set (HIGH). Bit 0 masks IRQ0, Bit 1 masks IRQ1 and so forth. Masking an IRQ channel will only disable the corresponding channel and does not affect the others' operations.

The IMR acts only on the output of the IRR. That is, if an interrupt occurs while its IMR bit is set, this request is not "forgotten". Even with an IRQ input masked, it is still possible to set the IRR. Therefore, when the IMR bit is reset, an interrupt request to the 80376 will then be generated, providing that the IRQ request remains active. If the IRQ request is removed before the IMR is reset, the Default Interrupt Vector (Bank A, level 7) will be generated during the interrupt acknowledge cycle.

SPECIAL MASK MODE

In the Fully Nested Mode, all IRQ levels of lower priority than the routine in service are inhibited. However, in some applications, it may be desirable to let a lower priority interrupt request to interrupt the routine in service. One method to achieve this is by using the Special Mask Mode. Working in conjunction with the IMR, the Special Mask Mode enables interrupts from all levels except the level in service. This is usually done inside an interrupt service routine by masking the level that is in service and then issuing the Special Mask Mode Command. Once the Special Mask Mode is enabled, it remains in effect until it is disabled.

4.4.4 EDGE OR LEVEL INTERRUPT TRIGGERING

Each bank in the 82370 PIC can be programmed independently for either edge or level sensing for the interrupt request signals. Recall that all IRQ inputs are active LOW. Therefore, in the edge triggered mode, an active edge is defined as an input transition from an inactive (HIGH) to active (LOW) state. The interrupt input may remain active without generating another interrupt. During level triggered mode, an interrupt request will be recognized by an active (LOW) input, and there is no need for edge detection. However, the interrupt request must be removed before the EOI Command is issued, or the 80376 must be disabled to prevent a second false interrupt from occurring.

In either modes, the interrupt request input must be active (LOW) during the first INTA cycle in order to be recognized. Otherwise, the Default Interrupt Vector will be generated at level 7 of Bank A.

4.4.5 INTERRUPT CASCADING

As mentioned previously, the 82370 allows for external Slave interrupt controllers to be cascaded to any of its external interrupt request pins. The 82370 PIC indicates that an external Slave Controller is to be serviced by putting the contents of the Vector Register associated with the particular request on the 80376 Data Bus during the first INTA cycle (instead of 00H during a non-slave service). The external logic should latch the vector on the Data Bus using the INTA status signals and use it to select the external Slave Controller to be serviced (see Figure 4-5). The selected Slave will then respond to the second INTA cycle and place its vector on the Data Bus. This method requires that if external Slave Controllers are used in the system, no vector should be programmed to 00H.

Since the external Slave Cascade Address is provided on the Data Bus during INTA cycle 1, an external latch is required to capture this address for the Slave Controller. A simple scheme is depicted in Figure 4-5 below.

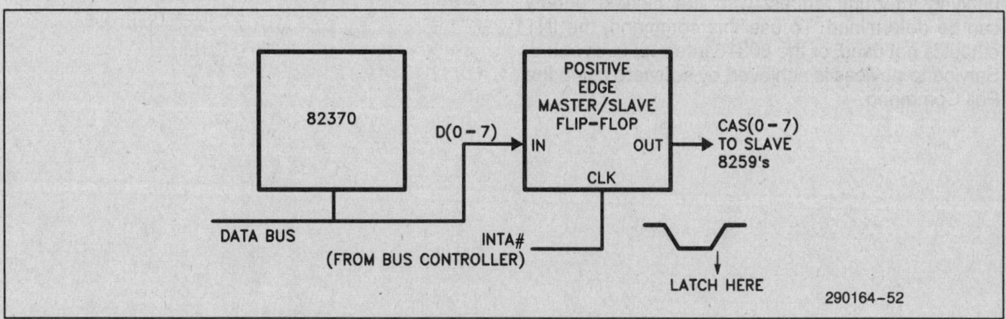

Figure 4-5. Slave Cascade Address Capturing

4.4.5.1 Special Fully Nested Mode

This mode will be used where cascading is employed and the priority is to be conserved within each Slave Controller. The Special Fully Nested Mode is similar to the "regular" Fully Nested Mode with the following exceptions:

— When an interrupt request from a Slave Controller is in service, this Slave Controller is not locked out from the Master's priority logic. Further interrupt requests from the higher priority logic within the Slave Controller will be recognized by the 82370 PIC and will initiate interrupts to the 80376. In comparing to the "regular" Fully Nested Mode, the Slave Controller is masked out when its request is in service and no higher requests from the same Slave Controller can be serviced.

— Before exiting the interrupt service routine, the software has to check whether the interrupt serviced was the only request from the Slave Controller. This is done by sending a Non-Specific EOI Command to the Slave Controller and then reading its In Service Register. If there are no requests in the Slave Controller, a Non-Specific EOI can be sent to the corresponding 82370 PIC bank also. Otherwise, no EOI should be sent.

4.4.6 READING INTERRUPT STATUS

The 82370 PIC provides several ways to read different status of each interrupt bank for more flexible interrupt control operations. These include polling the highest priority pending interrupt request and reading the contents of different interrupt status registers.

4.4.6.1 Poll Command

The 82370 PIC supports status polling operations with the Poll Command. In a Poll Command, the pending interrupt request with the highest priority can be determined. To use this command, the INT output is not used, or the 80376 interrupt is disabled. Service to devices is achieved by software using the Poll Command.

This mode is useful if there is a routine command common to several levels so that the INTA sequence is not needed. Another application is to use the Poll Command to expand the number of priority levels.

Notice that the ICW2 mechanism is not supported for the Poll Command. However, if the Poll Command is used, the programmable Vector Registers are of no concern since no INTA cycle will be generated.

4.4.6.2 Reading Interrupt Registers

The contents of each interrupt register (IRR, ISR, and IMR) can be read to update the user's program on the present status of the 82370 PIC. This can be a versatile tool in the decision making process of a service routine, giving the user more control over interrupt operations.

The reading of the IRR and ISR contents can be performed via the Operation Control Word 3 by using a Read Status Register Command and the content of IMR can be read via a simple read operation of the register itself.

4.5 Register Set Overview

Each bank of the 82370 PIC consists of a set of 8-bit registers to control its operations. The address map of all the registers is shown in Table 4-3 below. Since all three register sets are identical in functions, only one set will be described.

Functionally, each register set can be divided into five groups. They are: the four Initialization Command Words (ICW's), the three Operation Control Words (OCW's), the Poll/Interrupt Request/In-Service Register, the Interrupt Mask Register, and the Vector Registers. A description of each group follows.

Table 4-3. Interrupt Controller Register Address Map

Port Address	Access	Register Description
20H	Write	Bank B ICW1, OCW2, or OCW3
	Read	Bank B Poll, Request or In-Service Status Register
21H	Write	Bank B ICW2, ICW3, ICW4, OCW1
	Read	Bank B Mask Register
22H	Read	Bank B ICW2
28H	Read/Write	IRQ8 Vector Register
29H	Read/Write	IRQ9 Vector Register
2AH	Read/Write	Reserved
2BH	Read/Write	IRQ11 Vector Register
2CH	Read/Write	IRQ12 Vector Register
2DH	Read/Write	IRQ13 Vector Register
2EH	Read/Write	IRQ14 Vector Register
2FH	Read/Write	IRQ15 Vector Register
A0H	Write	Bank C ICW1, OCW2, or OCW3
	Read	Bank C Poll, Request or In-Service Status Register
A1H	Write	Bank C ICW2, ICW3, ICW4, OCW1
	Read	Bank C Mask Register
A2H	Read	Bank C ICW2
A8H	Read/Write	IRQ16 Vector Register
A9H	Read/Write	IRQ17 Vector Register
AAH	Read/Write	IRQ18 Vector Register
ABH	Read/Write	IRQ19 Vector Register
ACH	Read/Write	IRQ20 Vector Register
ADH	Read/Write	IRQ21 Vector Register
AEH	Read/Write	IRQ22 Vector Register
AFH	Read/Write	IRQ23 Vector Register
30H	Write	Bank A ICW1, OCW2, or OCW3
	Read	Bank A Poll, Request or In-Service Status Register
31H	Write	Bank A ICW2, ICW3, ICW4, OCW1
	Read	Bank A Mask Register
32H	Read	Bank ICW2
38H	Read/Write	IRQ0 Vector Register
39H	Read/Write	IRQ1 Vector Register
3AH	Read/Write	IRQ1.5 Vector Register
3BH	Read/Write	IRQ3 Vector Register
3CH	Read/Write	IRQ4 Vector Register
3DH	Read/Write	Reserved
3EH	Read/Write	Reserved
3FH	Read/Write	IRQ7 Vector Register

4

4.5.1 INITIALIZATION COMMAND WORDS (ICW)

Before normal operation can begin, the 82370 PIC must be brought to a known state. There are four 8-bit Initialization Command Words in each interrupt bank to setup the necessary conditions and modes for proper operation. Except for the second command word (ICW2) which is a read/write register, the other three are write-only registers. Without going into detail of the bit definitions of the command words, the following subsections give a brief description of what functions each command word controls.

ICW1

The ICW1 has three major functions. They are:

- To select between the two IRQ input triggering modes (edge- or level-triggered);
- To designate whether or not the interrupt bank is to be used alone or in the cascade mode. If the cascade mode is desired, the interrupt bank will accept ICW3 for further cascade mode programming. Otherwise, no ICW3 will be accepted;
- To determine whether or not ICW4 will be issued; that is, if any of the ICW4 operations are to be used.

ICW2

ICW2 is provided for compatibility with the 82C59A only. Its contents do not affect the operation of the interrupt bank in any way. Whenever the ICW2 of any of the three banks is written into, an interrupt is generated from bank A at level 1.5. The interrupt request will be cleared after the ICW2 register has been read by the 80376. The user is expected to program the corresponding vector register or to use it as an indicator that an attempt was made to alter the contents. Note that each ICW2 register has different addresses for read and write operations.

ICW3

The interrupt bank will only accept an ICW3 if programmed in the external cascade mode (as indicated in ICW1). ICW3 is used for specific programming within the cascade mode. The bits in ICW3 indicate which interrupt request inputs have a Slave cascaded to them. This will subsequently affect the interrupt vector generation during the interrupt acknowledge cycles as described previously.

ICW4

The ICW4 is accepted only if it was selected in ICW1. This command word register serves two functions:

- To select either the Automatic EOI mode or software EOI mode;
- To select if the Special Nested mode is to be used in conjunction with the cascade mode.

4.5.2 OPERATION CONTROL WORDS (OCW)

Once initialized by the ICW's, the interrupt banks will be operating in the Fully Nested Mode by default and they are ready to accept interrupt requests. However, the operations of each interrupt bank can be further controlled or modified by the use of OCW's. Three OCW's are available for programming various modes and commands. Note that all OCW's are 8-bit write-only registers.

The modes and operations controlled by the OCW's are:

- Fully Nested Mode;
- Rotating Priority Mode;
- Special Mask Mode;
- Poll Mode;
- EOI Commands;
- Read Status Commands.

OCW1

OCW1 is used solely for masking operations. It provides a direct link to the Internal Mask Register (IMR). The 80376 can write to this OCW register to enable or disable the interrupt inputs. Reading the pre-programmed mask can be done via the Interrupt Mask Register which will be discussed shortly.

OCW2

OCW2 is used to select End-Of-Interrupt, Automatic Priority Rotation, and Specific Priority Rotation operations. Associated commands and modes of these operations are selected using the different combinations of bits in OCW2.

Specifically, the OCW2 is used to:

- Designate an interrupt level (0–7) to be used to reset a specific ISR bit or to set a specific priority. This function can be enabled or disabled;
- Select which software EOI command (if any) is to be executed (i.e. Non-Specific or Specific EOI);
- Enable one of the priority rotation operations (i.e. Rotate On Non-Specific EOI, Rotate On Automatic EOI, or Rotate On Specific EOI).

OCW3

There are three main categories of operation that OCW3 controls. They are summarized as follows:

— To select and execute the Read Status Register Commands, either reading the Interrupt Request Register (IRR) or the In-Service Register (ISR);

— To issue the Poll Command. The Poll Command will override a Read Register Command if both functions are enabled simultaneously;

— To set or reset the Special Mask Mode.

4.5.3 POLL/INTERRUPT REQUEST/IN-SERVICE STATUS REGISTER

As the name implies, this 8-bit read-only register has multiple functions. Depending on the command issued in the OCW3, the content of this register reflects the result of the command executed. For a Poll Command, the register read contains the binary code of the highest priority level requesting service (if any). For a Read IRR Command, the register content will show the current pending interrupt request(s). Finally, for a Read ISR Command, this register will specify all interrupt levels which are being serviced.

4.5.4 INTERRUPT MASK REGISTER (IMR)

This is a read-only 8-bit register which, when read, will specify all interrupt levels within the same bank that are masked.

4.5.5 VECTOR REGISTERS (VR)

Each interrupt request input has an 8-bit read/write programmable vector register associated with it. The registers should be programmed to contain the interrupt vector for the corresponding request. The contents of the Vector Register will be placed on the Data Bus during the INTA cycles as described previously.

4.6 Programming

Programming the 82370 PIC is accomplished by using two types of command words: ICW's and OCW's. All modes and commands explained in the previous sections are programmable using the ICW's and OCW's. The ICW's are issued from the 80376 in a sequential format and are used to setup the banks in the 82370 PIC in an initial state of operation. The OCW's are issued as needed to vary and control the 82370 PIC's operations.

Both ICW's and OCW's are sent by the 80376 to the interrupt banks via the Data Bus. Each bank distinguishes between the different ICW's and OCW's by the I/O address map, the sequence they are issued (ICW's only), and by some dedicated bits among the ICW's and OCW's.

An example of programming the 82370 interrupt controllers is given in Appendix C (Programming the 82370 Interrupt Controllers).

All three interrupt banks are programmed in a similar way. Therefore, only a single bank will be described in the following sections.

4.6.1 INITIALIZATION (ICW)

Before normal operation can begin, each bank must be initialized by programming a sequence of two to four bytes written into the ICW's.

Figure 4-6 shows the initialization flow for an interrupt bank. Both ICW1 and ICW2 must be issued for any form of operation. However, ICW3 and ICW4 are used only if designated in ICW1. Once initialized, if any programming changes within the ICW's are to be made, the entire ICW sequence must be reprogrammed, not just an individual ICW.

Note that although the ICW2's in the 82370 PIC do not effect the Bank's operation, they still must be programmed in order to preserve the compatibility with the 82C59A. The contents programmed are not relevant to the overall operations of the interrupt banks. Also, whenever one of the three ICW2's is programmed, an interrupt level 1.5 in Bank A will be generated. This interrupt request will be cleared upon reading of the ICW2 registers. Since the three ICW2's share the same interrupt level and the system may not know the origin of the interrupt, all three ICW2's must be read.

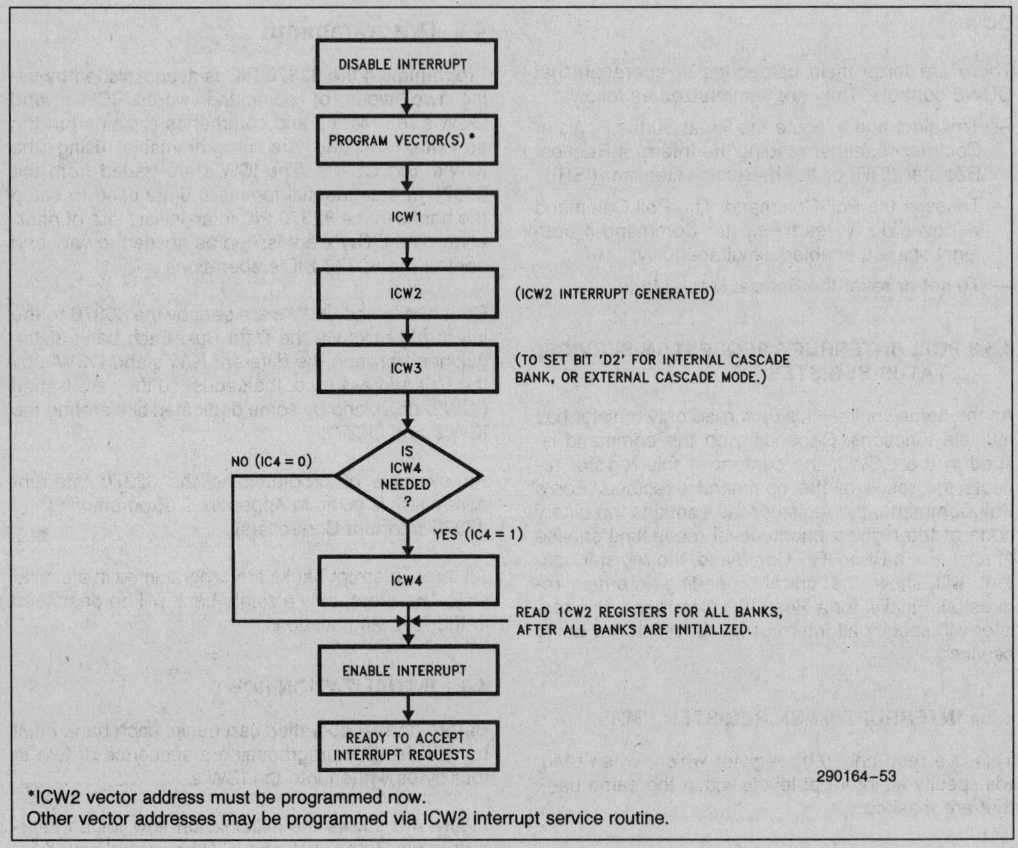

*ICW2 vector address must be programmed now.
Other vector addresses may be programmed via ICW2 interrupt service routine.

Figure 4-6. Initialization Sequence

Certain internal setup conditions occur automatically within the interrupt bank after the first ICW (ICW1) has been issued. These are:

— The edge sensitive circuit is reset, which means that following initialization, an interrupt request input must make a HIGH-to-LOW transition to generate an interrupt;

— The Interrupt Mask Register (IMR) is cleared; that is, all interrupt inputs are enabled;

— IRQ7 input of each bank is assigned priority 7 (lowest);

— Special Mask Mode is cleared and Status Read is set to IRR;

— If no ICW4 is needed, then no Automatic-EOI is selected.

4.6.2 VECTOR REGISTERS (VR)

Each interrupt request input has a separate Vector Register. These Vector Registers are used to store the pre-programmed vector number corresponding to their interrupt sources. In order to guarantee proper interrupt handling, all Vector Registers must be programmed with the predefined vector numbers. Since an interrupt request will be generated whenever an ICW2 is written during the initialization sequence, it is important that the Vector Register of IRQ1.5 in Bank A should be initialized and the interrupt service routine of this vector is set up before the ICW's are written.

4.6.3 OPERATION CONTROL WORDS (OCW)

After the ICW's are programmed, the operations of each interrupt controller bank can be changed by writing into the OCW's as explained before. There is no special programming sequence required for the OCW's. Any OCW may be written at any time in order to change the mode of or to perform certain operations on the interrupt banks.

4.6.3.1 Read Status and Poll Commands (OCW3)

Since the reading of IRR and ISR status as well as the result of a Poll Command are available on the same read-only Status Register, a special Read Status/Poll Command must be issued before the Poll/Interrupt Request/In-Service Status Register is read. This command can be specified by writing the required control word into OCW3. As mentioned earlier, if both the Poll Command and the Status Read Command are enabled simultaneously, the Poll Command will override the Status Read. That is, after the command execution, the Status Register will contain the result of the Poll Command.

Note that for reading IRR and ISR, there is no need to issue a Read Status Command to the OCW3 every time the IRR or ISR is to be read. Once a Read Status Command is received by the interrupt bank, it "remembers" which register is selected. However, this is not true when the Poll Command is used.

In the Poll Command, after the OCW3 is written, the 82370 PIC treats the next read to the Status Register as an interrupt acknowledge. This will set the appropriate IS bit if there is a request and read the priority level. Interrupt Request input status remains unchanged from the Poll Command to the Status Read.

In addition to the above read commands, the Interrupt Mask Register (IMR) can also be read. When read, this register reflects the contents of the preprogrammed OCW1 which contains information on which interrupt request(s) is(are) currently disabled.

4.7 Register Bit Definition

INITIALIZATION COMMAND WORD 1 (ICW1)

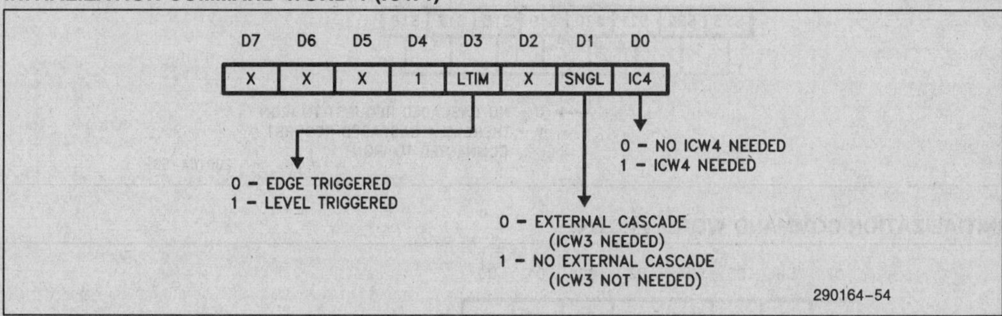

INITIALIZATION COMMAND WORD 2 (ICW2)

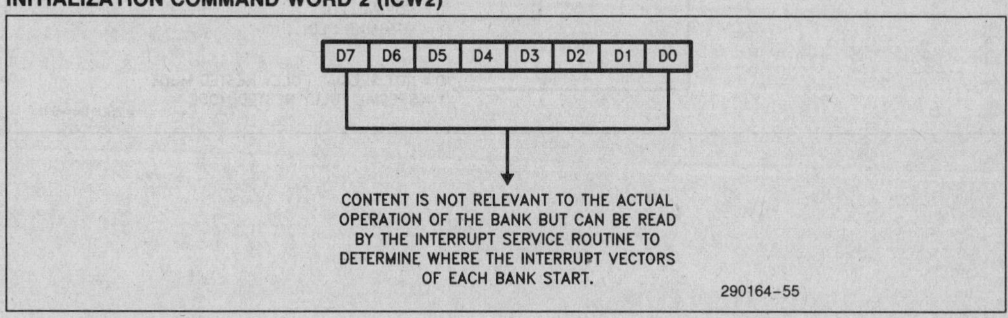

INITIALIZATION COMMAND WORD 3 (ICW3)

ICW3 for Bank A:

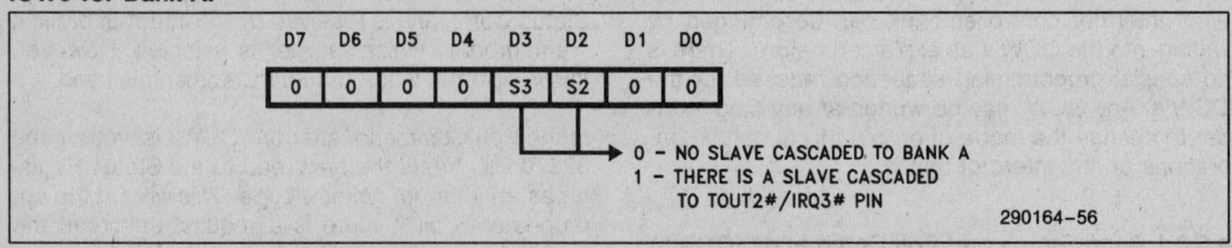

290164-56

ICW3 for Bank B:

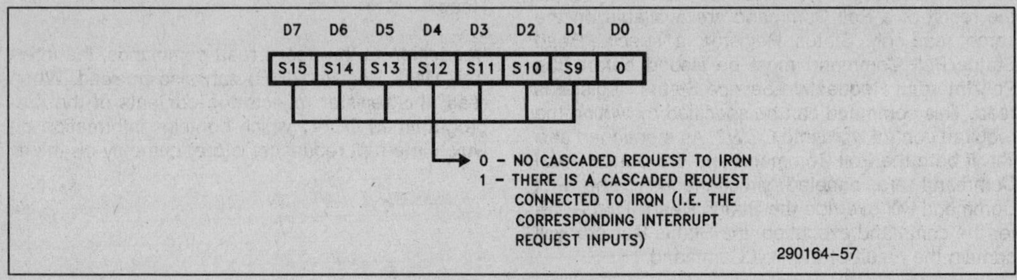

290164-57

ICW3 for Bank C:

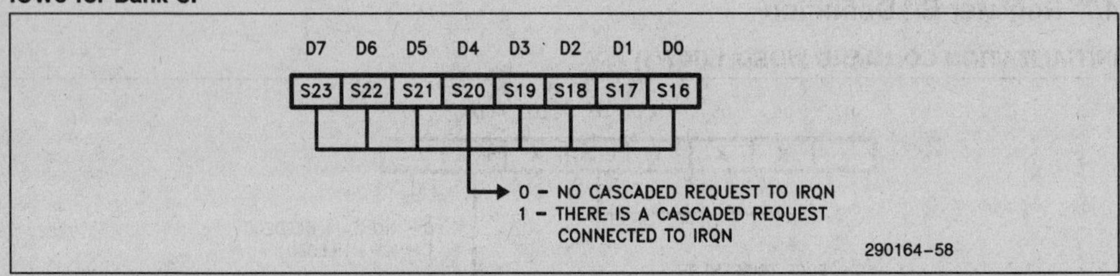

290164-58

INITIALIZATION COMMAND WORD 4 (ICW4)

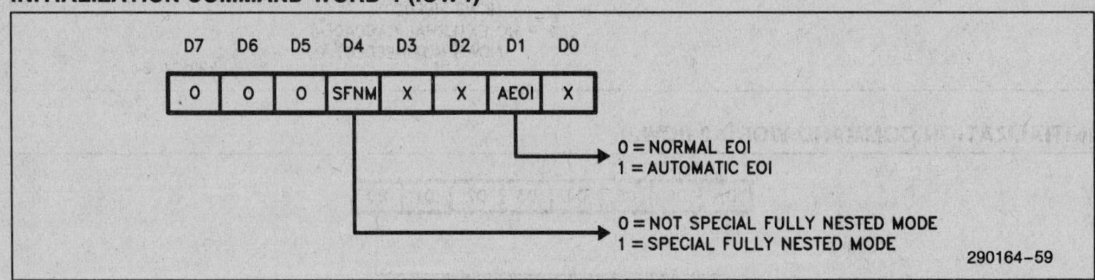

290164-59

OPERATION CONTROL WORD 1 (OCW1)

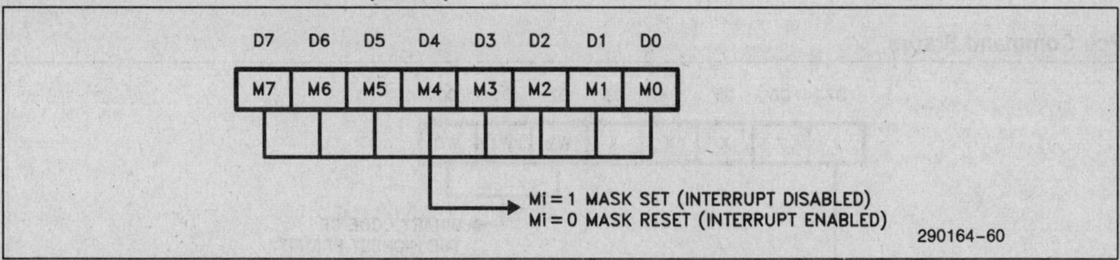

OPERATION CONTROL WORD 2 (OCW2)

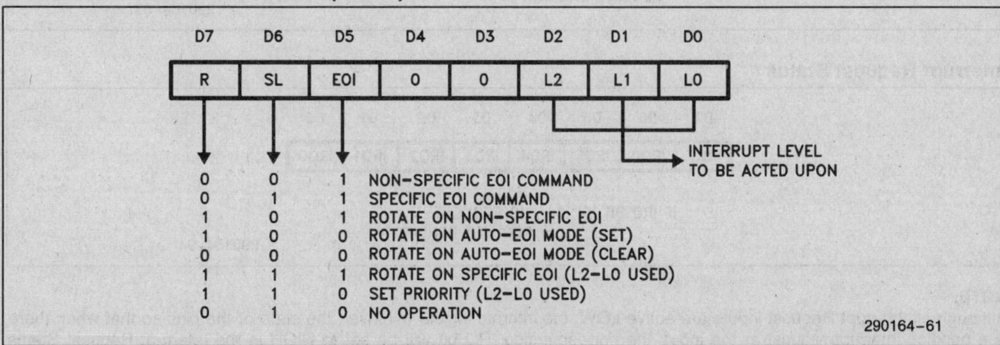

OPERATION CONTROL WORD 3 (OCW3)

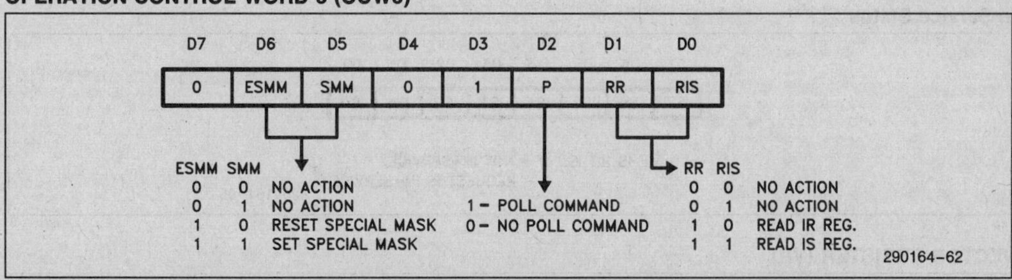

ESMM — Enable Special Mask Mode. When this bit is set to 1, it enables the SMM bit to set or reset the Special Mask Mode. When this bit is set to 0, SMM bit becomes don't care.

SMM — Special Mask Mode. If ESMM = 1 and SMM = 1, the interrupt controller bank will enter Special Mask Mode. If ESMM = 1 and SMM = 0, the bank will revert to normal mask mode. When ESMM = 0, SMM has no effect.

POLL/INTERRUPT REQUEST/IN-SERVICE STATUS REGISTER

Poll Command Status

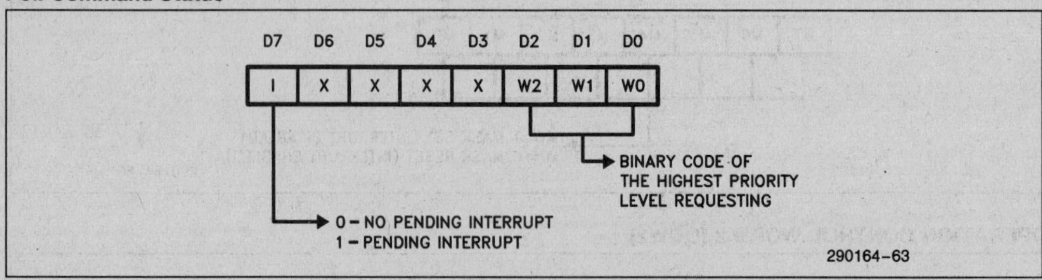

290164–63

Interrupt Request Status

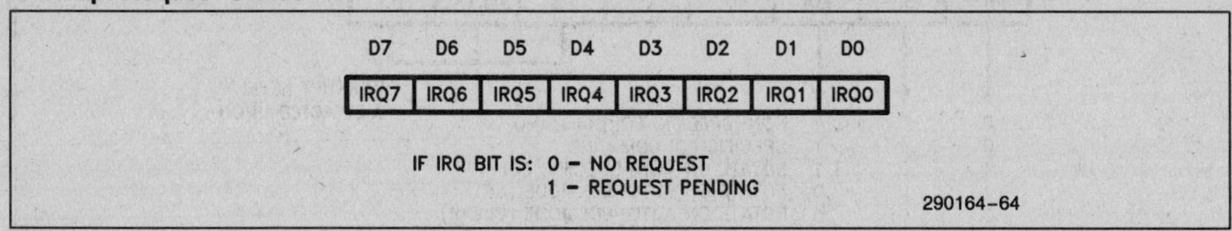

290164–64

NOTE:
Although all Interrupt Request inputs are active LOW, the internal logical will invert the state of the pins so that when there is a pending interrupt request at the input, the corresponding IRQ bit will be set to HIGH in the Interrupt Request Status register.

In-Service Status

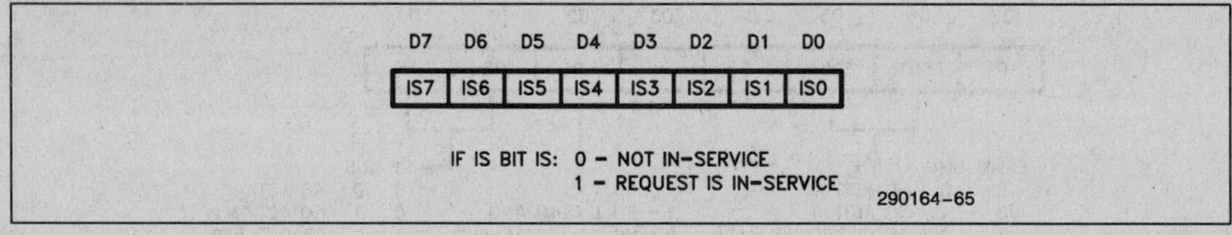

290164–65

VECTOR REGISTER (VR)

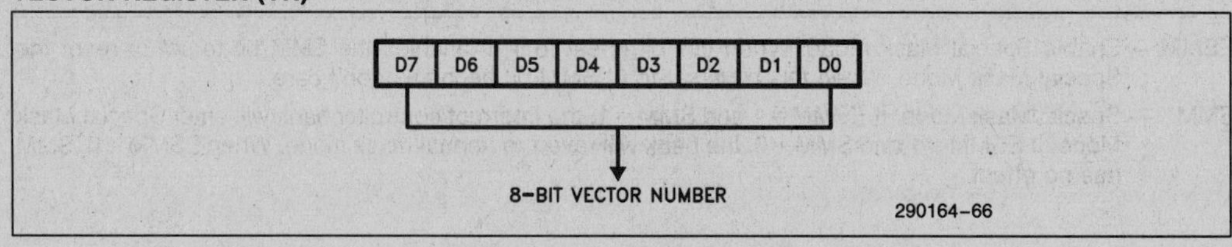

290164–66

Table 4-4. Register Operational Summary

Operational Description	Command Words	Bits
Fully Nested Mode	OCW-Default	
Non-specific EOI Command	OCW2	EOI
Specific EOI Command	OCW2	SL, EOI, L0–L2
Automatic EOI Mode	ICW1, ICW4	IC4, AEOI
Rotate On Non-Specific EOI Command	OCW2	EOI
Rotate On Automatic EOI Mode	OCW2	R, SL, EOI
Set Priority Command	OCW2	L0–L2
Rotate On Specific EOI Command	OCW2	R, SL, EOI
Interrupt Mask Register	OCW1	M0–M7
Special Mask Mode	OCW3	ESMM, SMM
Level Triggered Mode	ICW1	LTIM
Edge Triggered Mode	ICW1	LTIM
Read Register Command, IRR	OCW3	RR, RIS
Read Register Command, ISR	OCW3	RR, RIS
Read IMR	IMR	M0–M7
Poll Command	OCW3	P
Special Fully Nested Mode	ICW1, ICW4	IC4, SFNM

4.8 Register Operational Summary

For ease of reference, Table 4-4 gives a summary of the different operating modes and commands with their corresponding registers.

5.0 PROGRAMMABLE INTERVAL TIMER

5.1 Functional Description

The 82370 contains four independently Programmable Interval Timers: Timer 0–3. All four timers are functionally compatible to the Intel 82C54. The first three timers (Timer 0–2) have specific functions. The fourth timer, Timer 3, is a general purpose timer. Table 5-1 depicts the functions of each timer. A brief description of each timer's function follows.

Table 5-1. Programmable Interval Timer Functions

Timer	Output	Function
0	IRQ8	Event Based IRQ8 Generator
1	TOUT1/REF#	Gen. Purpose/DRAM Refresh Req.
2	TOUT2/IRQ3#	Gen. Purpose/Speaker Out/IRQ3#
3	TOUT3#	Gen. Purpose/IRQ0 Generator

TIMER 0—Event Based Interrupt Request 8 Generator

Timer 0 is intended to be used as an Event Counter. The output of this timer will generate an Interrupt Request 8 (IRQ8) upon a rising edge of the timer output (TOUT0). Normally, this timer is used to implement a time-of-day clock or system tick. The Timer 0 output is not available as an external signal.

TIMER 1—General Purpose/DRAM Refresh Request

The output of Timer 1, TOUT1, can be used as a general purpose timer or as a DRAM Refresh Request signal. The rising edge of this output creates a DRAM refresh request to the 82370 DRAM Refresh Controller. Upon reset, the Refresh Request function is disabled, and the output pin is the Timer 1 output.

TIMER 2—General Purpose/Speaker Out/IRQ3#

The Timer 2 output, TOUT2#, could be used to support tone generation to an external speaker. This pin is a bidirectional signal. When used as an input, a logic LOW asserted at this pin will generate an Interrupt Request 3 (IRQ3#) (see Programmable Interrupt Controller).

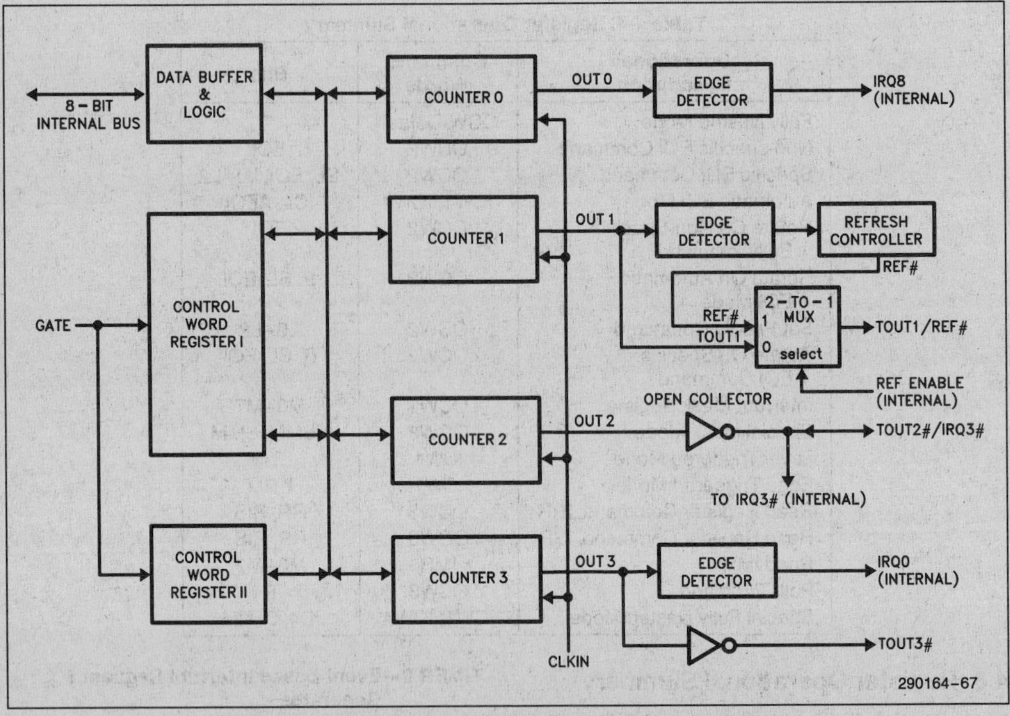

Figure 5-1. Block Diagram of Programmable Interval Timer

TIMER 3—General Purpose/Interrupt Request 0 Generator

The output of Timer 3 is fed to an edge detector and generates an Interrupt Request 0 (IRQ0) in the 82370. The inverted output of this timer (TOUT3#) is also available as an external signal for general purpose use.

5.1.1 INTERNAL ARCHITECTURE

The functional block diagram of the Programmable Interval Timer section is shown in Figure 5-1. Following is a description of each block.

DATA BUFFER & READ/WRITE LOGIC

This part of the Programmable Interval Timer is used to interface the four timers to the 82370 internal bus. The Data Buffer is for transferring commands and data between the 8-bit internal bus and the timers.

The Read/Write Logic accepts inputs from the internal bus and generates signals to control other functional blocks within the timer section.

CONTROL WORD REGISTERS I & II

The Control Word Registers are write-only registers. They are used to control the operating modes of the timers. Control Word Register I controls Timers 0, 1 and 2, and Control Word Register II controls Timer 3. Detailed description of the Control Word Registers will be included in the Register Set Overview section.

COUNTER 0, COUNTER 1, COUNTER 2, COUNTER 3

Counters 0, 1, 2, and 3 are the major parts of Timers 0, 1, 2, and 3, respectively. These four functional blocks are identical in operation, so only a single counter will be described. The internal block diagram of one counter is shown in Figure 5-2.

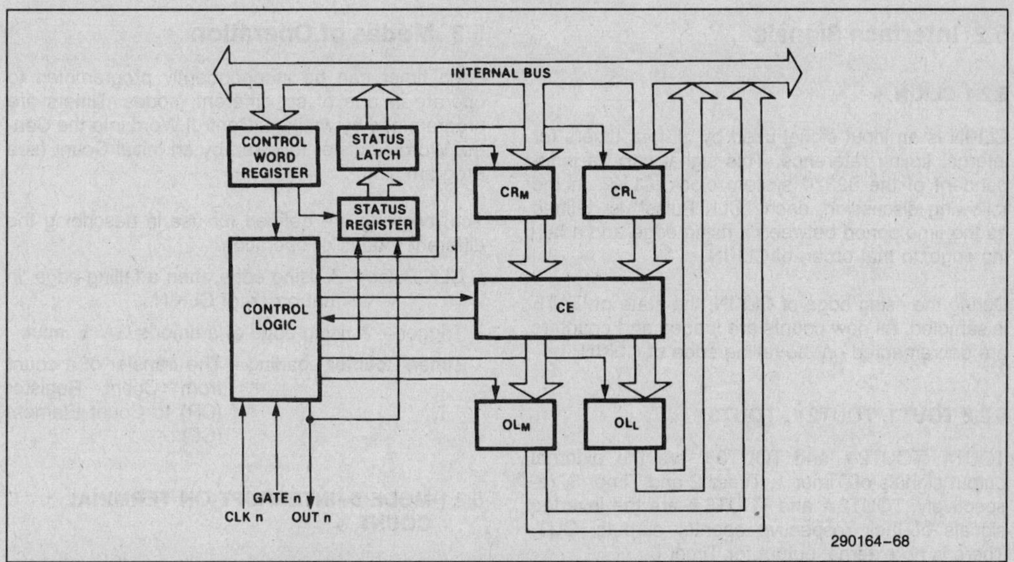

Figure 5-2. Internal Block Diagram of a Counter

The four counters share a common clock input (CLKIN), but otherwise are fully independent. Each counter is programmable to operate in a different mode.

Although the Control Word Register is shown in the figure, it is not part of the counter itself. Its programmed contents are used to control the operations of the counters.

The Status Register, when latched, contains the current contents of the Control Word Register and status of the output and Null Count Flag (see Read Back Command).

The Counting Element (CE) is the actual counter. It is a 16-bit presettable synchronous down counter.

The Output Latches (OL) contain two 8-bit latches (OLM and OLL). Normally, these latches "follow" the content of the CE. OLM contains the most significant byte of the counter and OLL contains the least significant byte. If the Counter Latch Command is sent to the counter, OL will latch the present count until read by the 80376 and then return to follow the CE. One latch at a time is enabled by the timer's Control Logic to drive the internal bus. This is how the 16-bit Counter communicates over the 8-bit internal bus. Note that CE cannot be read. Whenever the count is read, it is one of the OL's that is being read.

When a new count is written into the counter, the value will be stored in the Count Registers (CR), and transferred to CE. The transferring of the contents from CR's to CE is defined as "loading" of the counter. The Count Register contains two 8-bit registers: CRM (which contains the most significant byte) and CRL (which contains the least significant byte). Similar to the OL's, the Control Logic allows one register at a time to be loaded from the 8-bit internal bus. However, both bytes are transferred from the CR's to the CE simultaneously. Both CR's are cleared when the Counter is programmed. This way, if the Counter has been programmed for one byte count (either the most significant or the least significant byte only), the other byte will be zero. Note that CE cannot be written into directly. Whenever a count is written, it is the CR that is being written.

As shown in the diagram, the Control Logic consists of three signals: CLKIN, GATE, and OUT. CLKIN and GATE will be discussed in detail in the section that follows. OUT is the internal output of the counter. The external outputs of some timers (TOUT) are the inverted version of OUT (see TOUT1, TOUT2#, TOUT3#). The state of OUT depends on the mode of operation of the timer.

5.2 Interface Signals

5.2.1 CLKIN

CLKIN is an input signal used by all four timers for internal timing reference. This signal can be independent of the 82370 system clock, CLK2. In the following discussion, each "CLK Pulse" is defined as the time period between a rising edge and a falling edge, in that order, of CLKIN.

During the rising edge of CLKIN, the state of GATE is sampled. All new counts are loaded and counters are decremented on the falling edge of CLKIN.

5.2.2 TOUT1, TOUT2#, TOUT3#

TOUT1, TOUT2# and TOUT3# are the external output signals of Timer 1, Timer 2 and Timer 3, respectively. TOUT2# and TOUT3# are the inverted signals of their respective counter outputs, OUT. There is no external output for Timer 0.

If Timer 2 is to be used as a tone generator of a speaker, external buffering must be used to provide sufficient drive capability.

The Outputs of Timer 2 and 3 are dual function pins. The output pin of Timer 2 (TOUT2#/IRQ3#), which is a bidirectional open-collector signal, can also be used as interrupt request input. When the interrupt function is enabled (through the Programmable Interrupt Controller), a LOW on this input will generate an Interrupt Request 3# to the 82370 Programmable Interrupt Controller. This pin has a weak internal pull-up resistor. To use the IRQ3# function, Timer 2 should be programmed so that OUT2 is LOW. Additionally, OUT3 of Timer 3 is connected to an edge detector which will generate an Interrupt Request 0 (IRQ0) to the 82370 after the rising edge of OUT3 (see Figure 5-1).

5.2.3 GATE

GATE is not an externally controllable signal. Rather, it can be software controlled with the Internal Control Port. The state of GATE is always sampled on the rising edge of CLKIN. Depending on the mode of operation, GATE is used to enable/disable counting or trigger the start of an operation.

For Timer 0 and 1, GATE is always enabled (HIGH). For Timer 2 and 3, GATE is connected to Bit 0 and 6, respectively, of an Internal Control Port (at address 61H) of the 82370. After a hardware reset, the state of GATE of Timer 2 and 3 is disabled (LOW).

5.3 Modes of Operation

Each timer can be independently programmed to operate in one of six different modes. Timers are programmed by writing a Control Word into the Control Word Register followed by an Initial Count (see Programming).

The following are defined for use in describing the different modes of operation.

CLK Pulse— A rising edge, then a falling edge, in that order, of CLKIN.

Trigger— A rising edge of a timer's GATE input.

Timer/Counter Loading— The transfer of a count from Count Register (CR) to Count Element (CE).

5.3.1 MODE 0–INTERRUPT ON TERMINAL COUNT

Mode 0 is typically used for event counting. After the Control Word is written, OUT is initially LOW, and will remain LOW until the counter reaches zero. OUT then goes HIGH and remains HIGH until a new count or a new Mode 0 Control Word is written into the counter.

In this mode, GATE=HIGH enables counting; GATE = LOW disables counting. However, GATE has no effect on OUT.

After the Control Word and initial count are written to a timer, the initial count will be loaded on the next CLK pulse. This CLK pulse does not decrement the count, so for an initial count of N, OUT does not go HIGH until N+1 CLK pulses after the initial count is written.

If a new count is written to the timer, it will be loaded on the next CLK pulse and counting will continue from the new count. If a two-byte count is written, the following happens:

1. Writing the first byte disables counting, OUT is set LOW immediately (i.e. no CLK pulse required).

2. Writing the second byte allows the new count to be loaded on the next CLK pulse.

This allows the counting sequence to be synchronized by software. Again, OUT does not go HIGH until N+1 CLK pulses after the new count of N is written.

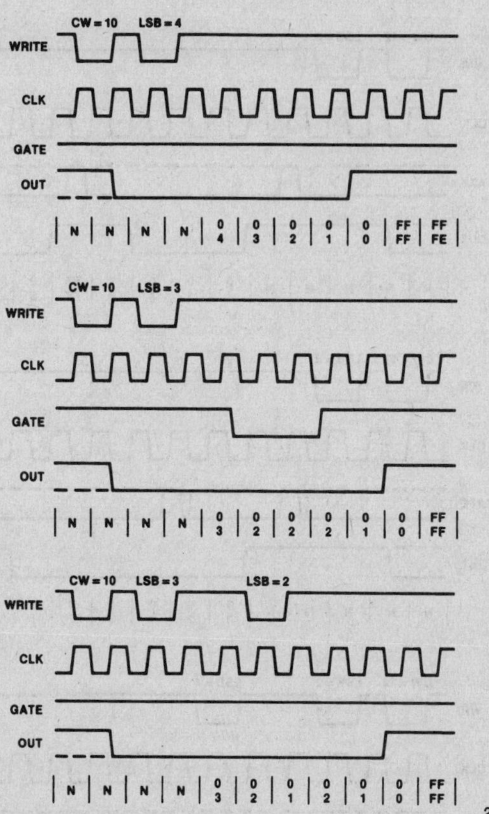

NOTES:

The following conventions apply to all mode timing diagrams.

1. Counters are programmed for binary (not BCD) counting and for reading/writing least significant byte (LSB) only.
2. The counter is always selected (CS# always low).
3. CW stands for "Control Word"; CW = 10 means a control word of 10, Hex is written to the counter.
4. LSB stands for "Least significant byte" of count.
5. Numbers below diagrams are count values.

The lower number is the least significant byte.

The upper number is the most significant byte. Since the counter is programmed to read/write LSB only, the most significant byte cannot be read.

N stands for an undefined count.

Vertical lines show transitions between count values.

Figure 5-3. Mode 0

If an initial count is written while GATE is LOW, the counter will be loaded on the next CLK pulse. When GATE goes HIGH, OUT will go HIGH N CLK pulses later; no CLK pulse is needed to load the counter as this has already been done.

5.3.2 MODE 1–GATE RETRIGGERABLE ONE-SHOT

In this mode, OUT will be initially HIGH. OUT will go LOW on the CLK pulse following a trigger to start the one-shot operation. The OUT signal will then remain LOW until the timer reaches zero. At this point, OUT will stay HIGH until the next trigger comes in. Since the state of GATE signals of Timer 0 and 1 are internally set to HIGH.

After writing the Control Word and initial count, the timer is considered "armed". A trigger results in loading the timer and setting OUT LOW on the next CLK pulse. Therefore, an initial count of N will result in a one-shot pulse width of N CLK cycles. Note

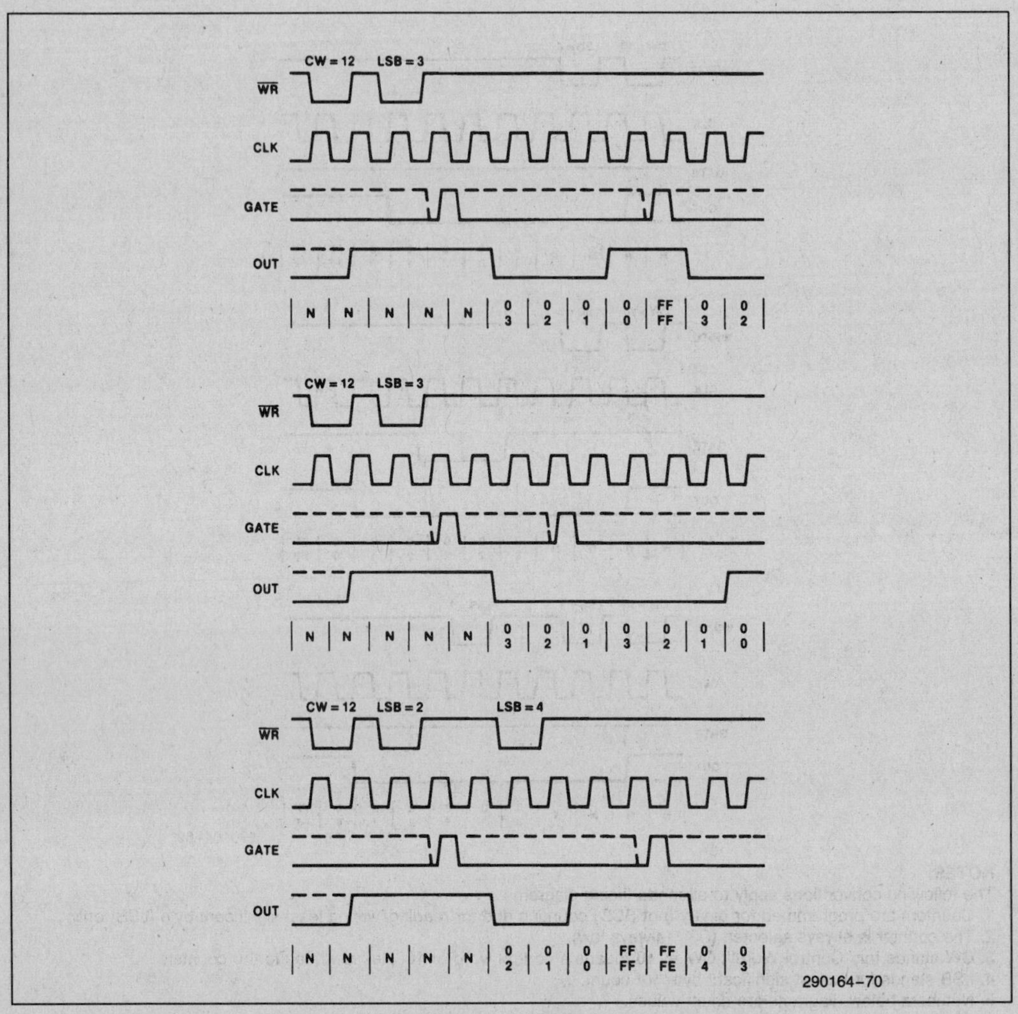

Figure 5-4. Mode 1

that this one-shot operation is retriggerable; i.e. OUT will remain LOW for N CLK pulses after every trigger. The one-shot operation can be repeated without re-writing the same count into the timer.

If a new count is written to the timer during a one-shot operation, the current one-shot pulse width will not be affected until the timer is retriggered. This is because loading of the new count to CE will occur only when the one-shot is triggered.

5.3.3 MODE 2-RATE GENERATOR

This mode is a divide-by-N counter. It is typically used to generate a Real Time Clock interrupt. OUT will initially be HIGH. When the initial count has decremented to 1, OUT goes LOW for one CLK pulse, then OUT goes HIGH again. Then the timer reloads the initial count and the process is repeated. In other words, this mode is periodic since the same sequence is repeated itself indefinitely. For an initial count of N, the sequence repeats every N CLK cycles.

Similar to Mode 0, GATE = HIGH enables counting, where GATE = LOW disables counting. If GATE goes LOW during an output pulse (LOW), OUT is set HIGH immediately. A trigger (rising edge on GATE) will reload the timer with the initial count on the next CLK pulse. Then, OUT will go LOW (for one CLK pulse) N CLK pulses after the new trigger. Thus, GATE can be used to synchronize the timer.

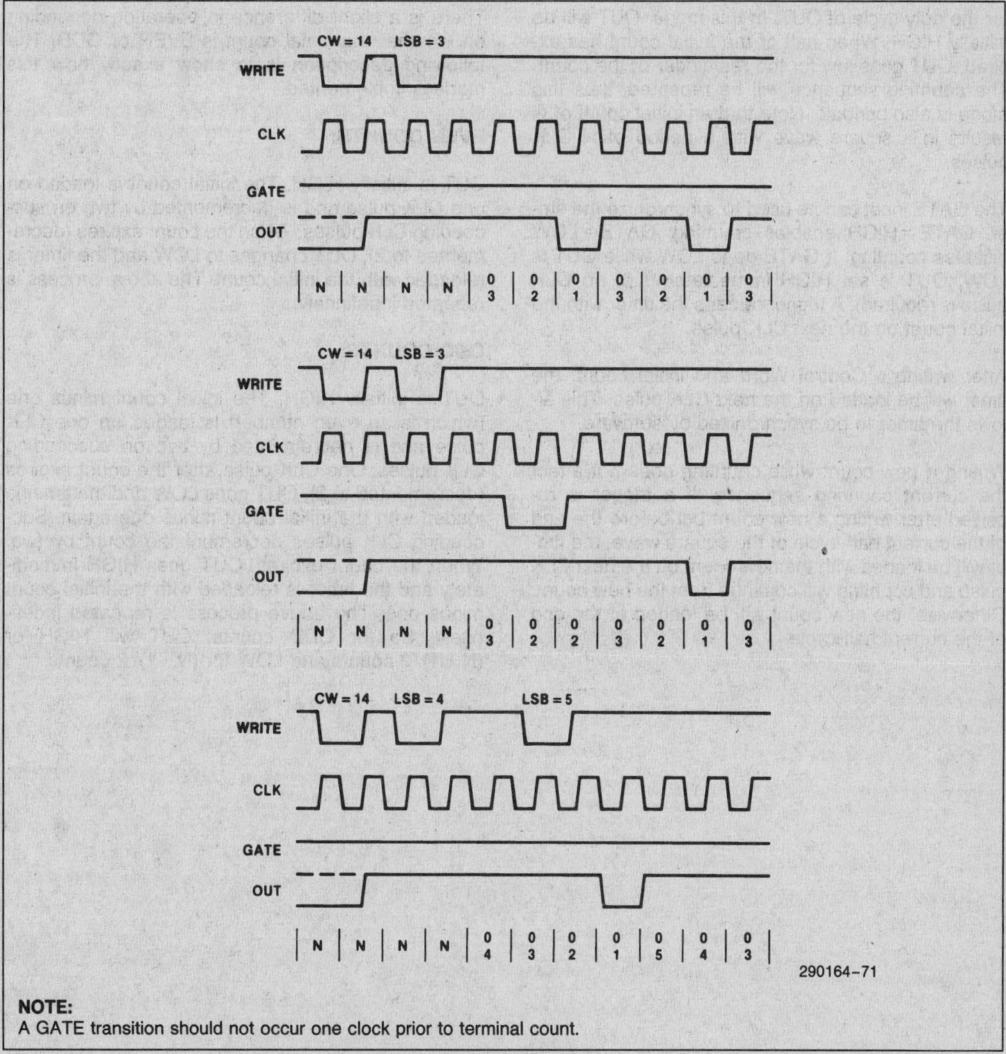

NOTE:
A GATE transition should not occur one clock prior to terminal count.

Figure 5-5. Mode 2

After writing a Control Word and initial count, the timer will be loaded on the next CLK pulse. OUT goes LOW (for one CLK pulse) N CLK pulses after the initial count is written. This is another way the timer may be synchronized by software.

Writing a new count while counting does not affect the current counting sequence because the new count will not be loaded until the end of the current counting cycle. If a trigger is received after writing a new count but before the end of the current period, the timer will be loaded with the new count on the next CLK pulse after the trigger, and counting will continue with the new count.

5.3.4 MODE 3—SQUARE WAVE GENERATOR

Mode 3 is typically used for Baud Rate generation. Functionally, this mode is similar to Mode 2 except for the duty cycle of OUT. In this mode, OUT will be initially HIGH. When half of the initial count has expired, OUT goes low for the remainder of the count. The counting sequence will be repeated, thus this mode is also periodic. Note that an initial count of N results in a square wave with a period of N CLK pulses.

The GATE input can be used to synchronize the timer. GATE = HIGH enables counting; GATE = LOW disables counting. If GATE goes LOW while OUT is LOW, OUT is set HIGH immediately (i.e. no CLK pulse is required). A trigger reloads the timer with the initial count on the next CLK pulse.

After writing a Control Word and initial count, the timer will be loaded on the next CLK pulse. This allows the timer to be synchronized by software.

Writing a new count while counting does not affect the current counting sequence. If a trigger is received after writing a new count but before the end of the current half-cycle of the square wave, the timer will be loaded with the new count on the next CLK pulse and counting will continue from the new count. Otherwise, the new count will be loaded at the end of the current half-cycle.

There is a slight difference in operation depending on whether the initial count is EVEN or ODD. The following description is to show exactly how this mode is implemented.

EVEN COUNTS:

OUT is initially HIGH. The initial count is loaded on one CLK pulse and is decremented by two on succeeding CLK pulses. When the count expires (decremented to 2), OUT changes to LOW and the timer is reloaded with the initial count. The above process is repeated indefinitely.

ODD COUNTS:

OUT is initially HIGH. The initial count minus one (which is an even number) is loaded on one CLK pulse and is decremented by two on succeeding CLK pulses. One CLK pulse after the count expires (decremented to 2), OUT goes LOW and the timer is loaded with the initial count minus one again. Succeeding CLK pulses decrement the count by two. When the count expires, OUT goes HIGH immediately and the timer is reloaded with the initial count minus one. The above process is repeated indefinitely. So for ODD counts, OUT will HIGH or $(N+1)/2$ counts and LOW for $(N-1)/2$ counts.

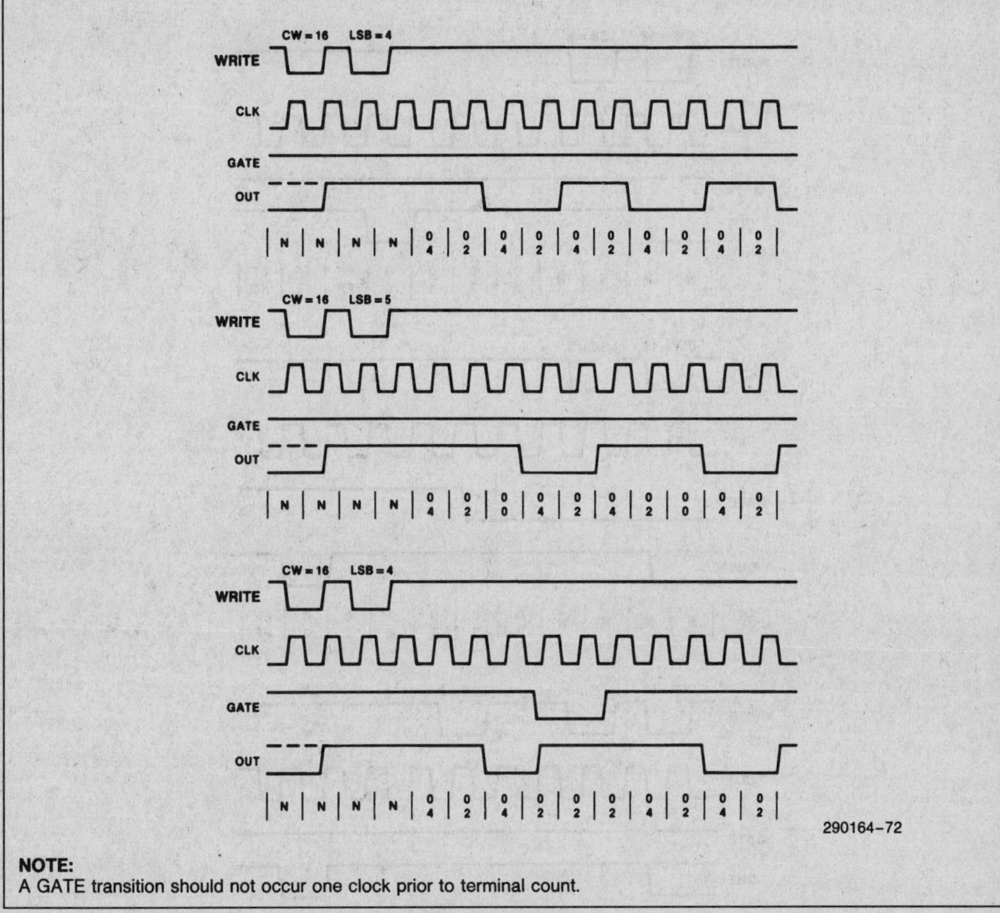

NOTE:
A GATE transition should not occur one clock prior to terminal count.

Figure 5-6. Mode 3

5.3.5 MODE 4–INITIAL COUNT TRIGGERED STROBE

This mode allows a strobe pulse to be generated by writing an initial count to the timer. Initially, OUT will be HIGH. When a new initial count is written into the timer, the counting sequence will begin. When the initial count expires (decremented to 1), OUT will go LOW for one CLK pulse and then go HIGH again.

Again, GATE = HIGH enables counting while GATE = LOW disables counting. GATE has no effect on OUT.

After writing the Control Word and initial count, the timer will be loaded on the next CLK pulse. This CLK pulse does not decrement the count, so for an initial count of N, OUT does not strobe LOW until N+1 CLK pulses after initial count is written.

If a new count is written during counting, it will be loaded in the next CLK pulse and counting will continue from the new count.

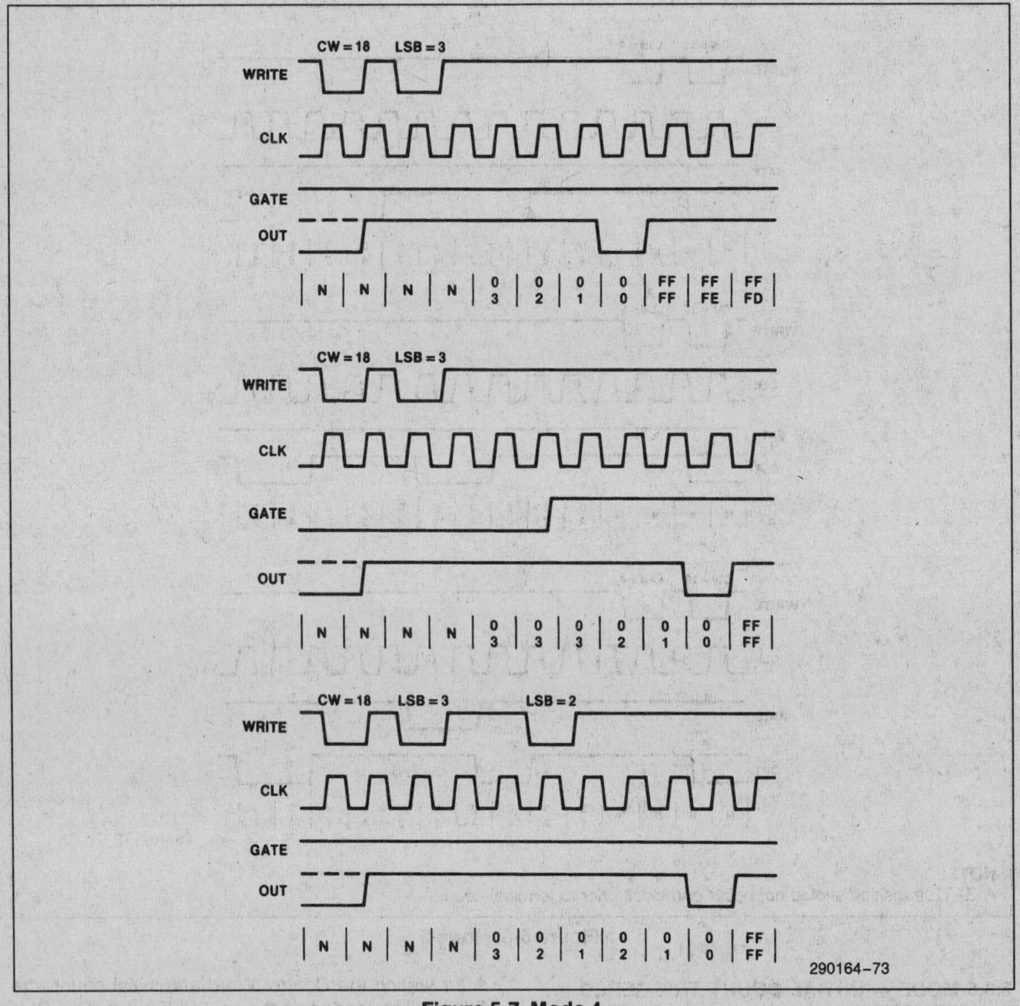

Figure 5-7. Mode 4

If a two-byte count is written, the following will occur:

1. Writing the first byte has no effect on counting.

2. Writing the second byte allows the new count to be loaded on the next CLK pulse.

OUT will strobe LOW N+1 CLK pulses after the new count of N is written. Therefore, when the strobe pulse will occur after a trigger depends on the value of the initial count loaded.

5.3.6 MODE 5—GATE RETRIGGERABLE STROBE

Mode 5 is very similar to Mode 4 except the count sequence is triggered by the gate signal instead of by writing an initial count. Initially, OUT will be HIGH. Counting is triggered by a rising edge of GATE. When the initial count has expired (decremented to 1), OUT will go LOW for one CLK pulse and then go HIGH again.

After loading the Control Word and initial count, the Count Element will not be loaded until the CLK pulse after a trigger. This CLK pulse does not decrement the count. Therefore, for an initial count of N, OUT does not strobe LOW until N+1 CLK pulses after a trigger.

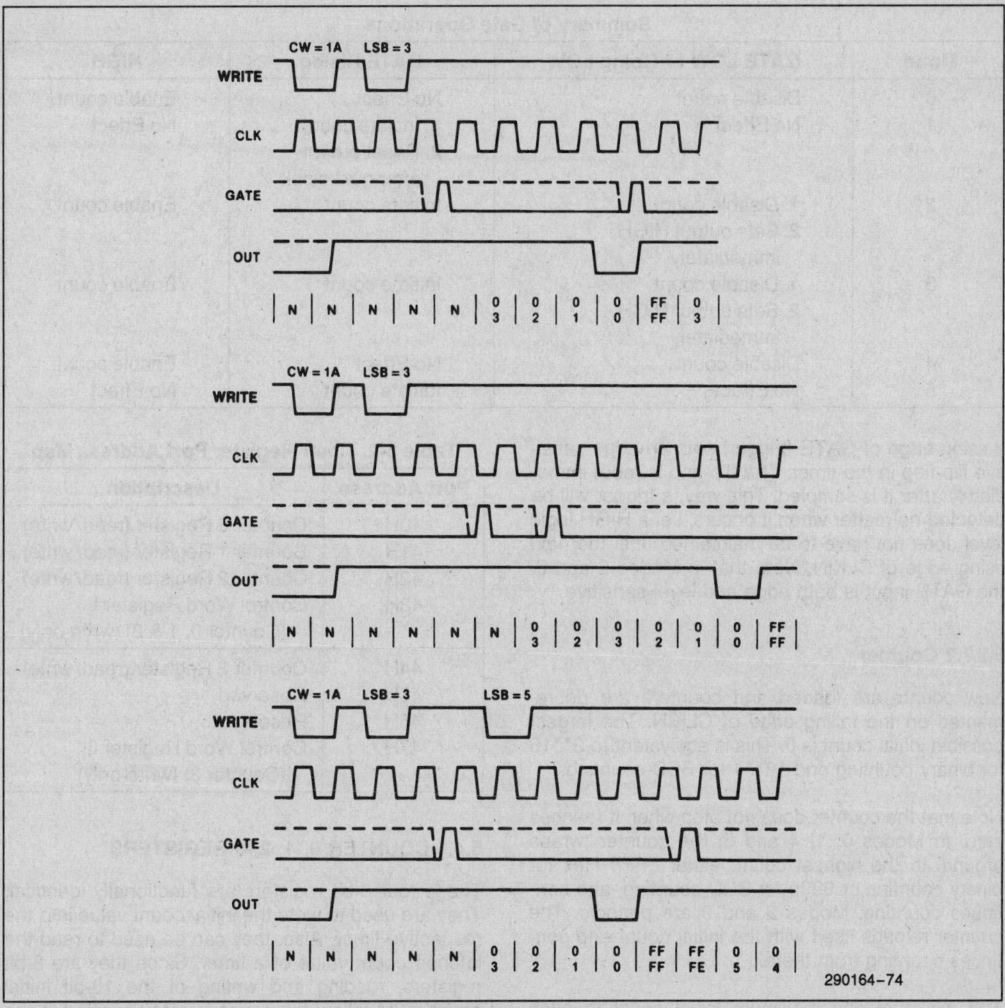

Figure 5-8. Mode 5

The counting sequence is retriggerable. Every trigger will result in the timer being loaded with the initial count on the next CLK pulse.

If the new count is written during counting, the current counting sequence will not be affected. If a trigger occurs after the new count is written but before the current count expires, the timer will be loaded with the new count on the next CLK pulse and a new count sequence will start from there.

5.3.7 OPERATION COMMON TO ALL MODES

5.3.7.1 GATE

The GATE input is always sampled on the rising edge of CLKIN. In Modes 0, 2, 3 and 4, the GATE input is level sensitive. The logic level is sampled on the rising edge of CLKIN. In Modes 1, 2, 3 and 5, the GATE input is rising edge sensitive. In these modes,

4

Summary of Gate Operations

Mode	GATE LOW or Going LOW	GATE Rising	HIGH
0	Disable count	No Effect	Enable count
1	No Effect	1. Initiate count 2. Reset output after next clock	No Effect
2	1. Disable count 2. Sets output HIGH immediately	Initiate count	Enable count
3	1. Disable count 2. Sets output HIGH immediately	Initiate count	Enable count
4	Disable count	No Effect	Enable count
5	No Effect	Initiate count	No Effect

a rising edge of GATE (trigger) sets an edge sensitive flip-flop in the timer. The flip-flop is reset immediately after it is sampled. This way, a trigger will be detected no matter when it occurs; i.e. a HIGH logic level does not have to be maintained until the next rising edge of CLKIN. Note that in Modes 2 and 3, the GATE input is both edge and level sensitive.

5.3.7.2 Counter

New counts are loaded and counters are decremented on the falling edge of CLKIN. The largest possible initial count is 0. This is equivalent to 2**16 for binary counting and 10**4 for BCD counting.

Note that the counter does not stop when it reaches zero. In Modes 0, 1, 4 and 5, the counter 'wraps around' to the highest count: either FFFF Hex for binary counting or 9999 for BCD counting, and continues counting. Modes 2 and 3 are periodic. The counter reloads itself with the initial count and continues counting from there.

The minimum and maximum initial count in each counter depends on the mode of operation. They are summarized below.

Mode	Min	Max
0	1	0
1	1	0
2	2	0
3	2	0
4	1	0
5	1	0

5.4 Register Set Overview

The Programmable Interval Timer module of the 82370 contains a set of six registers. The port address map of these registers is shown in Table 5-2.

Table 5-2. Timer Register Port Address Map

Port Address	Description
40H	Counter 0 Register (read/write)
41H	Counter 1 Register (read/write)
42H	Counter 2 Register (read/write)
43H	Control Word Register I (Counter 0, 1 & 2) (write-only)
44H	Counter 3 Register (read/write)
45H	Reserved
46H	Reserved
47H	Control Word Register II (Counter 3) (write-only)

5.4.1 COUNTER 0, 1, 2, 3 REGISTERS

These four 8-bit registers are functionally identical. They are used to write the initial count value into the respective timer. Also, they can be used to read the latched count value of a timer. Since they are 8-bit registers, reading and writing of the 16-bit initial count must follow the count format specified in the Control Word Registers; i.e. least significant byte only, most significant byte only, or least significant byte then most significant byte (see Programming).

5.4.2 CONTROL WORD REGISTER I & II

There are two Control Word Registers associated with the Timer section. One of the two registers (Control Word Register I) is used to control the operations of Counters 0, 1 and 2 and the other (Control Word Register II) is for Counter 3. The major functions of both Control Word Registers are listed below:

— Select the timer to be programmed.
— Define which mode the selected timer is to operate in.
— Define the count sequence; i.e. if the selected timer is to count as a Binary Counter or a Binary Coded Decimal (BCD) Counter.
— Select the byte access sequence during timer read/write operations; i.e. least significant byte only, most significant only, or least significant byte first, then most significant byte.

Also, the Control Word Registers can be programmed to perform a Counter Latch Command or a Read Back Command which will be described later.

5.5 Programming

5.5.1 INITIALIZATION

Upon power-up or reset, the state of all timers is undefined. The mode, count value, and output of all timers are random. From this point on, how each timer operates is determined solely by how it is programmed. Each timer must be programmed before it can be used. Since the outputs of some timers can generate interrupt signals to the 82370, all timers should be initialized to a known state.

Counters are programmed by writing a Control Word into their respective Control Word Registers. Then, an Initial Count can be written into the corresponding Count Register. In general, the programming procedure is very flexible. Only two conventions need to be remembered:

1. For each timer, the Control Word must be written before the initial count is written.

2. The 16-bit initial count must follow the count format specified in the Control Word (least significant byte only, most significant byte only, or least significant byte first, followed by most significant byte).

Since the two Control Word Registers and the four Counter Registers have separate addresses, and each timer can be individually selected by the appropriate Control Word Register, no special instruction sequence is required. Any programming sequence that follows the conventions above is acceptable.

A new initial count may be written to a timer at any time without affecting the timer's programmed mode in any way. Count sequence will be affected as described in the Modes of Operation section. Note that the new count must follow the programmed count format.

If a timer is previously programmed to read/write two-byte counts, the following precaution applies. A program must not transfer control between writing the first and second byte to another routine which also writes into the same timer. Otherwise, the read/write will result in incorrect count.

Whenever a Control Word is written to a timer, all control logic for that timer(s) is immediately reset (i.e. no CLK pulse is required). Also, the corresponding output in, TOUT#, goes to a known initial state.

5.5.2 READ OPERATION

Three methods are available to read the current count as well as the status of each timer. They are: Read Counter Registers, Counter Latch Command and Read Back Command. Below is a description of these methods.

READ COUNTER REGISTERS

The current count of a timer can be read by performing a read operation on the corresponding Counter Register. The only restriction of this read operation is that the CLKIN of the timers must be inhibited by using external logic. Otherwise, the count may be in the process of changing when it is read, giving an undefined result. Note that since all four timers are sharing the same CLKIN signal, inhibiting CLKIN to read a timer will unavoidably disable the other timers also. This may prove to be impractical. Therefore, it is suggested that either the Counter Latch Command or the Read Back Command can be used to read the current count of a timer.

Another alternative is to temporarily disable a timer before reading its Counter Register by using the GATE input. Depending on the mode of operation, GATE=LOW will disable the counting operation. However, this option is available on Timer 2 and 3 only, since the GATE signals of the other two timers are internally enabled all the time.

COUNTER LATCH COMMAND

A Counter Latch Command will be executed whenever a special Control Word is written into a Control Word Register. Two bits written into the Control Word Register distinguish this command from a 'regular' Control Word (see Register Bit Definition). Also, two other bits in the Control Word will select which counter is to be latched.

Upon execution of this command, the selected counter's Output Latch (OL) latches the count at the time the Counter Latch Command is received. This

4

count is held in the latch until it is read by the 80376, or until the timer is reprogrammed. The count is then unlatched automatically and the OL returns to "following" the Counting Element (CE). This allows reading the contents of the counters "on the fly" without affecting counting in progress. Multiple Counter Latch Commands may be used to latch more than one counter. Each latched count is held until it is read. Counter Latch Commands do not affect the programmed mode of the timer in any way.

If a counter is latched, and at some time later, it is latched again before the prior latched count is read, the second Counter Latch Command is ignored. The count read will then be the count at the time the first command was issued.

In any event, the latched count must be read according to the programmed format. Specifically, if the timer is programmed for two-byte counts, two bytes must be read. However, the two bytes do not have to be read right after the other. Read/write or programming operations of other timers may be performed between them.

Another feature of this Counter Latch Command is that read and write operations of the same timer may be interleaved. For example, if the timer is programmed for two-byte counts, the following sequence is valid.

1. Read least significant byte.
2. Write new least significant byte.
3. Read most significant byte.
4. Write new most significant byte.

If a timer is programmed to read/write two-byte counts, the following precaution applies. A program must not transfer control between reading the first and second byte to another routine which also reads from that same timer. Otherwise, an incorrect count will be read.

READ BACK COMMAND

The Read Back Command is another special Command Word operation which allows the user to read the current count value and/or the status of the selected timer(s). Like the Counter Latch Command, two bits in the Command Word identify this as a Read Back Command (see Register Bit Definition).

The Read Back Command may be used to latch multiple counter Output Latches (OL's) by selecting more than one timer within a Command Word. This single command is functionally equivalent to several Counter Latch Commands, one for each counter to be latched. Each counter's latched count will be held until it is read by the 80376 or until the timer is reprogrammed. The counter is automatically unlatched when read, but other counters remain latched until they are read. If multiple Read Back commands are issued to the same timer without reading the count, all but the first are ignored; i.e. the count read will correspond to the very first Read Back Command issued.

As mentioned previously, the Read Back Command may also be used to latch status information of the selected timer(s). When this function is enabled, the status of a timer can be read from the Counter Register after the Read Back Command is issued. The status information of a timer includes the following:

1. Mode of timer:

   This allows the user to check the mode of operation of the timer last programmed.

2. State of TOUT pin of the timer:

   This allows the user to monitor the counter's output pin via software, possibly eliminating some hardware from a system.

3. Null Count/Count available:

   The Null Count Bit in the status byte indicates if the last count written to the Count Register (CR) has been loaded into the Counting Element (CE). The exact time this happens depends on the mode of the timer and is described in the Programming section. Until the count is loaded into the Counting Element (CE), it cannot be read from the timer. If the count is latched or read before this occurs, the count value will not reflect the new count just written.

If multiple status latch operations of the timer(s) are performed without reading the status, all but the first command are ignored; i.e. the status read in will correspond to the first Read Back Command issued.

Both the current count and status of the selected timer(s) may be latched simultaneously by enabling both functions in a single Read Back Command. This is functionally the same as issuing two separate Read Back Commands at once. Once again, if multiple read commands are issued to latch both the count and status of a timer, all but the first command will be ignored.

If both count and status of a timer are latched, the first read operation of that timer will return the latched status, regardless of which was latched first. The next one or two (if two count bytes are to be read) read operations return the latched count. Note that subsequent read operations on the Counter Register will return the unlatched count (like the first read method discussed).

5.6 Register Bit Definitions

COUNTER 0, 1, 2, 3 REGISTER (READ/WRITE)

Port Address	Description
40H	Counter 0 Register (read/write)
41H	Counter 1 Register (read/write)
42H	Counter 2 Register (read/write)
44H	Counter 3 Register (read/write)
45H	Reserved
46H	Reserved

Note that these 8-bit registers are for writing and reading of one byte of the 16-bit count value, either the most significant or the least significant byte.

CONTROL WORD REGISTER I & II (WRITE-ONLY)

Port Address	Description
43H	Control Word Register I (Counter 0, 1, 2 (write-only)
47H	Control Word Register II (Counter 3) (write-only)

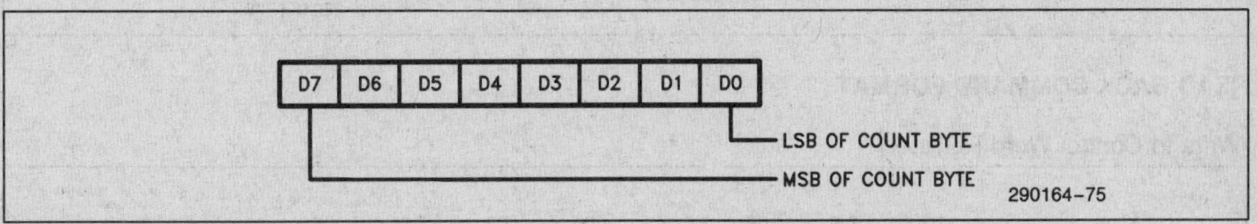

290164-75

Control Word Register I

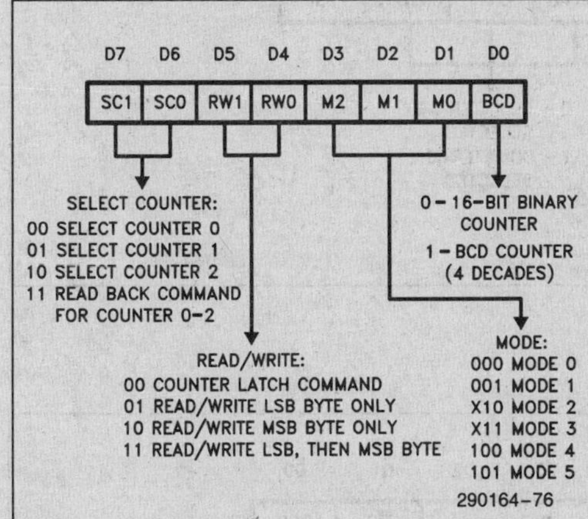

290164-76

Control Word Register II

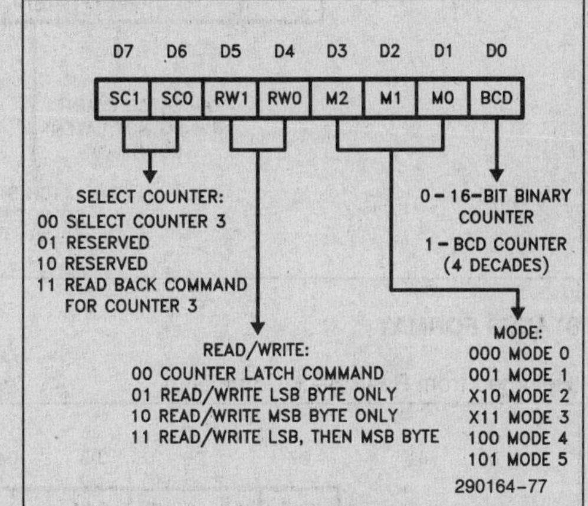

290164-77

COUNTER LATCH COMMAND FORMAT

(Write to Control Word Register)

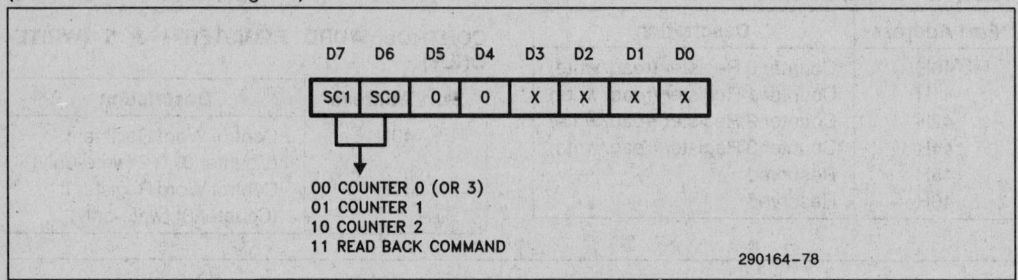

290164-78

READ BACK COMMAND FORMAT

(Write to Control Word Register)

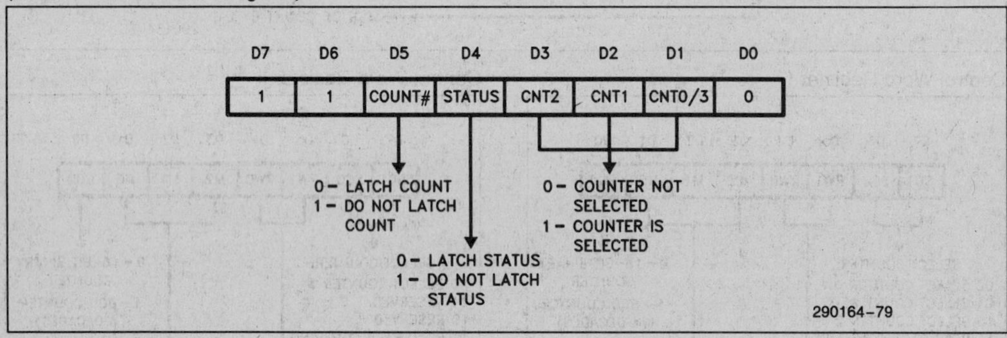

290164-79

STATUS FORMAT

(Returned from Read Back Command)

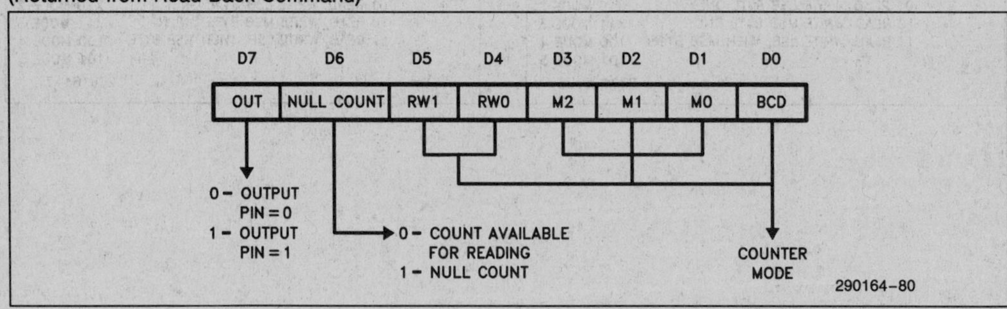

290164-80

6.0 WAIT STATE GENERATOR

6.1 Functional Description

The 82370 contains a programmable Wait State Generator which can generate a pre-programmed number of wait states during both CPU and DMA initiated bus cycles. This Wait State Generator is capable of generating 1 to 16 wait states in non-pipelined mode, and 0 to 15 wait states in pipelined mode. Depending on the bus cycle type and the two Wait State Control inputs (WSC 0–1), a pre-programmed number of wait states in the selected Wait State Register will be generated.

The Wait State Generator can also be disabled to allow the use of devices capable of generating their own READY# signals. Figure 6-1 is a block diagram of the Wait State Generator.

6.2 Interface Signals

The following describes the interface signals which affect the operation of the Wait State Generator. The READY#, WSC0 and WSC1 signals are inputs. READYO# is the ready output signal to the host processor.

6.2.1 READY#

READY# is an active LOW input signal which indicates to the 82370 the completion of a bus cycle. In the Master mode (e.g. 82370 initiated DMA transfer), this signal is monitored to determine whether a peripheral or memory needs wait states inserted in the current bus cycle. In the Slave mode, it is used (together with the ADS# signal) to trace CPU bus cycles to determine if the current cycle is pipelined.

6.2.2 READYO#

READYO# (Ready Out#) is an active LOW output signal and is the output of the Wait State Generator. The number of wait states generated depends on the WSC(0–1) inputs. Note that special cases are handled for access to the 82370 internal registers and for the Refresh cycles. For 82370 internal register access, READYO# will be delayed to take into the command recovery time of the register. One or more wait states will be generated in a pipelined cycle. During refresh, the number of wait states will be determined by the preprogrammed value in the Refresh Wait State Register.

In the simplest configuration, READYO# can be connected to the READY# input of the 82370 and the 80376 CPU. This is, however, not always the case. If external circuitry is to control the READY# inputs as well, additional logic will be required (see Application Issues).

6.2.3 WSC(0–1)

These two Wait State Control inputs, together with the M/IO# input, select one of the three pre-programmed 8-bit Wait State Registers which determines the number of wait states to be generated. The most significant half of the three Wait State Registers corresponds to memory accesses, the least significant half to I/O accesses. The combination WSC(0–1) = 11 disables the Wait State Generator.

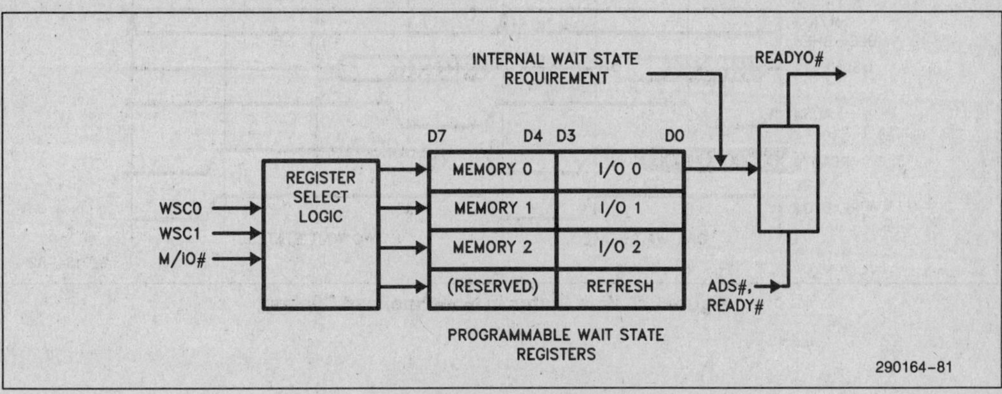

Figure 6-1. Wait State Generator Block Diagram

6.3 Bus Function

6.3.1 WAIT STATES IN NON-PIPELINED CYCLE

The timing diagram of two typical non-pipelined cycles with 82370 generated wait states is shown in Figure 6-2. In this diagram, it is assumed that the internal registers of the 82370 are not addressed. During the first T2 state of each bus cycle, the Wait State Control and the M/IO# inputs are sampled to determine which Wait State Register (if any) is selected. If the WSC inputs are active (i.e. not both are driven HIGH), the pre-programmed number of wait states corresponding to the selected Wait State Register will be requested. This is done by driving the READYO# output HIGH during the end of each T2 state.

The WSC (0–1) inputs need only be valid during the very first T2 state of each non-pipelined cycle. As a general rule, the WSC inputs are sampled on the rising edge of the next clock (82384 CLK) after the last state when ADS# (Address Status) is asserted.

The number of wait states generated depends on the type of bus cycle, and the number of wait states requested. The various combinations are discussed below.

1. Access the 82370 internal registers: 2 to 5 wait states, depending upon the specific register addressed. Some back-to-back sequences to the Interrupt Controller will require 7 wait states.

2. Interrupt Acknowledge to the 82370: 5 wait states.

3. Refresh: As programmed in the Refresh Wait State Register (see Register Set Overview). Note that if WCS (0–1) = 11, READYO# will stay inactive.

4. Other bus cycles: Depending on WCS (0–1) and M/IO# inputs, these inputs select a Wait State Register in which the number of wait states will be equal to the pre-programmed wait state count in the register plus 1. The Wait State Register selection is defined as follows (Table 6-1).

Table 6-1. Wait State Register Selection

M/IO#	WSC(0–1)	Register Selected
0	00	WAIT REG 0 (I/O half)
0	01	WAIT REG 1 (I/O half)
0	10	WAIT REG 2 (I/O half)
1	00	WAIT REG 0 (MEM half)
1	01	WAIT REG 1 (MEM half)
1	10	WAIT REG 2 (MEM half)
X	11	Wait State Gen. Disabled

The Wait State Control signals, WSC (0–1), can be generated with the address decode and the Read/Write control signals as shown in Figure 6-3.

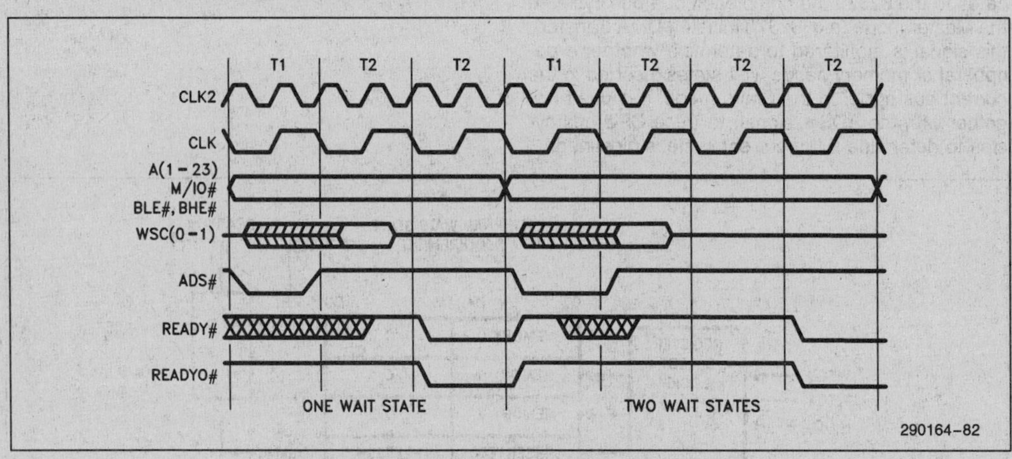

Figure 6-2. Wait States in Non-Pipelined Cycles

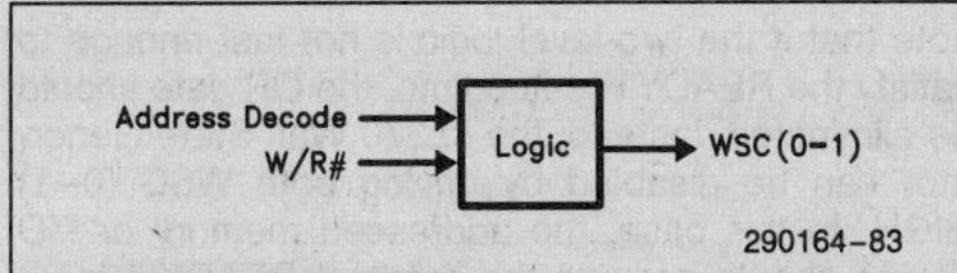

Figure 6-3. WSC (0–1) Generation

Note that during HALT and SHUTDOWN, the number of wait states will depend on the WSC (0–1) inputs, which will select the memory half of one of the Wait State Registers (see CPU Reset and Shutdown Detect).

6.3.2 WAIT STATES IN PIPELINED CYCLES

The timing diagram of two typical pipelined cycles with 82370 generated wait states is shown in Figure 6-4. Again, in this diagram, it is assumed that the 82370 internal registers are not addressed. As defined in the timing of the 80376 processor, the Address (A1–23), Byte Enable (BHE#, BLE#), and other control signals (M/IO#, ADS#) are asserted one T-state earlier than in a non-pipelined cycle; i.e. they are asserted at T2P. Similar to the non-pipelined case, the Wait State Control (WSC) inputs are sampled in the middle of the state after the last state the ADS# signal is asserted. Therefore, the WSC inputs should be asserted during the T1P state of each pipelined cycle (which is one T-state earlier than in the non-pipelined cycle).

The number of wait states generated in a pipelined cycle is selected in a similar manner as in the non-pipelined case discussed in the previous section. The only difference here is that the actual number of wait states generated will be one less than that of the non-pipelined cycle. This is done automatically by the Wait State Generator.

6.3.3 EXTENDING AND EARLY TERMINATING BUS CYCLE

The 82370 allows external logic to either add wait states or cause early termination of a bus cycle by controlling the READY# input to the 82370 and the host processor. A possible configuration is shown in Figure 6-5.

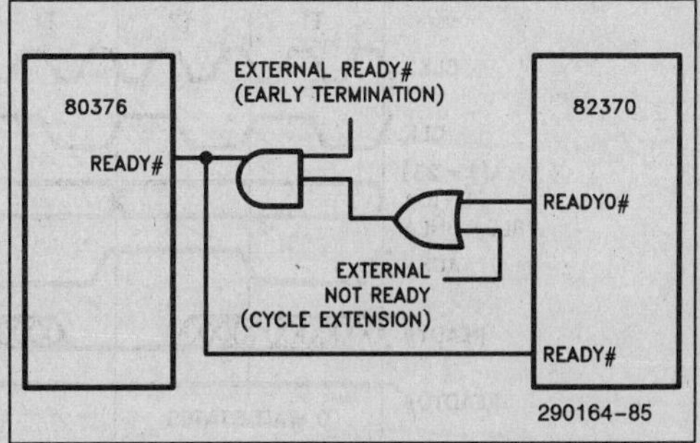

Figure 6-5. External 'READY' Control Logic

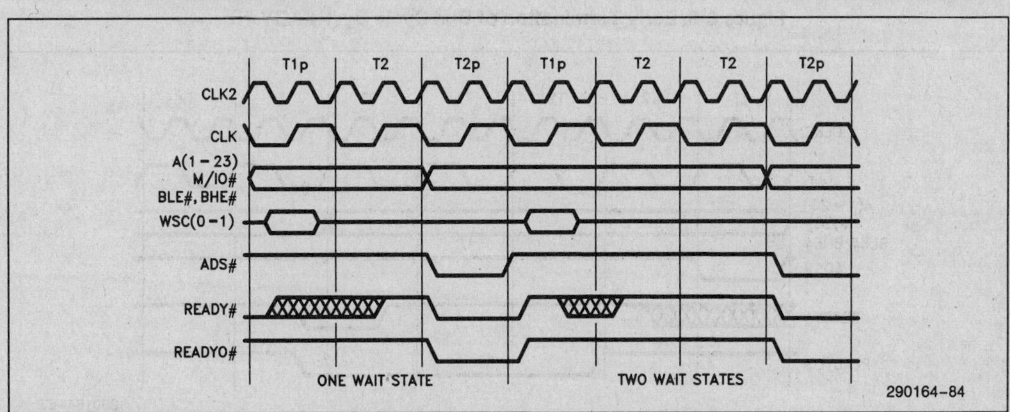

Figure 6-4. Wait States in Pipelined Cycles

The EXT. RDY# (External Ready) signal of Figure 6-5 allows external devices to cause early termination of a bus cycle. When this signal is asserted LOW, the output of the circuit will also go LOW (even though the READYO# of the 82370 may still be HIGH). This output is fed to the READY# input of the 80376 and the 82370 to indicate the completion of the current bus cycle.

Similarly, the EXT. NOT READY (External Not Ready) signal is used to delay the READY# input of the processor and the 82370. As long as this signal is driven HIGH, the output of the circuit will drive the READY# input HIGH. This will effectively extend the duration of a bus cycle. However, it is important to note that if the two-level logic is not fast enough to satisfy the READY# setup time, the OR gate should be eliminated. Instead, the 82370 Wait State Generator can be disabled by driving both WSC (0–1) HIGH. In this case, the addressed memory or I/O device should activate the external READY# input whenever it is ready to terminate the current bus cycle.

Figures 6-6 and 6-7 show the timing relationships of the ready signals for the early termination and extension of the bus cycles. Section 6-7, Application Issues, contains a detailed timing analysis of the external circuit.

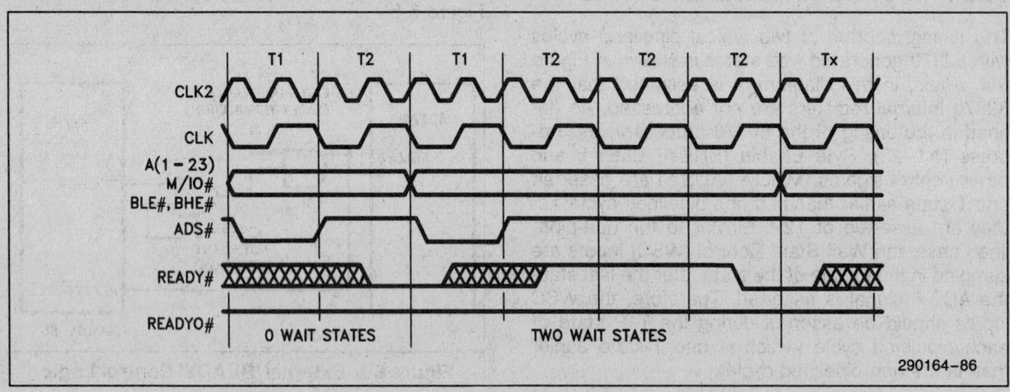

Figure 6-6. Early Termination of Bus Cycle By 'READY#'

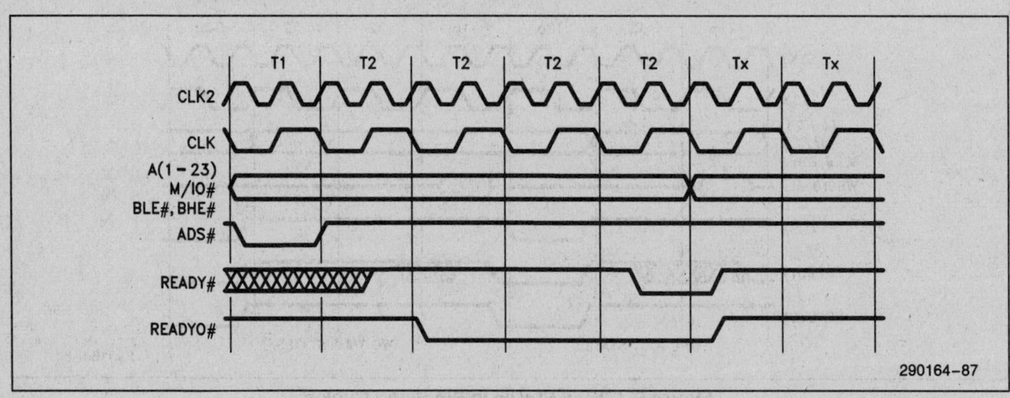

Figure 6-7. Extending Bus Cycle by 'READY#'

Due to the following implications, it should be noted that early termination of bus cycles in which 82370 internal registers are accessed is not recommended.

1. Erroneous data may be read from or written into the addressed register.

2. The 82370 must be allowed to recover either before HLDA (Hold Acknowledge) is asserted or before another bus cycle into an 82370 internal register is initiated.

The recovery time, in clock periods, equals the remaining wait states that were avoided plus 4.

6.4 Register Set Overview

Altogether, there are four 8-bit internal registers associated with the Wait State Genertor. The port address map of these registers is shown below in Table 6-2. A detailed description of each follows.

Table 6-2. Register Address Map

Port Address	Description
72H	Wait State Reg 0 (read/write)
73H	Wait State Reg 1 (read/write)
74H	Wait State Reg 2 (read/write)
75H	Ref. Wait State Reg (read/write)

WAIT STATE REGISTER 0, 1, 2

These three 8-bit read/write registers are functionally identical. They are used to store the pre-programmed wait state count. One half of each register contains the wait state count for I/O accesses while the other half contains the count for memory accesses. The total number of wait states generated will depend on the type of bus cycle. For a non-pipelined cycle, the actual number of wait states requested is equal to the wait state count plus 1. For a pipelined cycle, the number of wait states will be equal to the wait state count in the selected register. Therefore, the Wait State Generator is capable of generating 1 to 16 wait states in non-pipelined mode, and 0 to 15 wait states in pipelined mode.

Note that the minimum wait state count in each register is 0. This is equivalent to 0 wait states for a pipelined cycle and 1 wait state for a non-pipelined cycle.

REFRESH WAIT STATE REGISTER

Similar to the Wait State Registers discussed above, this 4-bit register is used to store the number of wait states to be generated during a DRAM refresh cycle.

Note that the Refresh Wait State Register is not selected by the WSC inputs. It will automatically be chosen whenever a DRAM refresh cycle occurs. If the Wait State Generator is disabled during the refresh cycle (WSC (0–1) = 11), READYO# will stay inactive and the Refresh Wait State Register is ignored.

6.5 Programming

Using the Wait State Generator is relatively straightforward. No special programming sequence is required. In order to ensure the expected number of wait states will be generated when a register is selected, the registers to be used must be programmed after power-up by writing the appropriate wait state count into each register. Note that upon hardware reset, all Wait State Registers are initialized with the value FFH, giving the maximum number of wait states possible. Also, each register can be read to check the wait state count previously stored in the register.

6.6 Register Bit Definition

WAIT STATE REGISTER 0, 1, 2

Port Address	Description
72H	Wait State Register 0 (read/write)
73H	Wait State Register 1 (read/write)
74H	Wait State Register 2 (read/write)

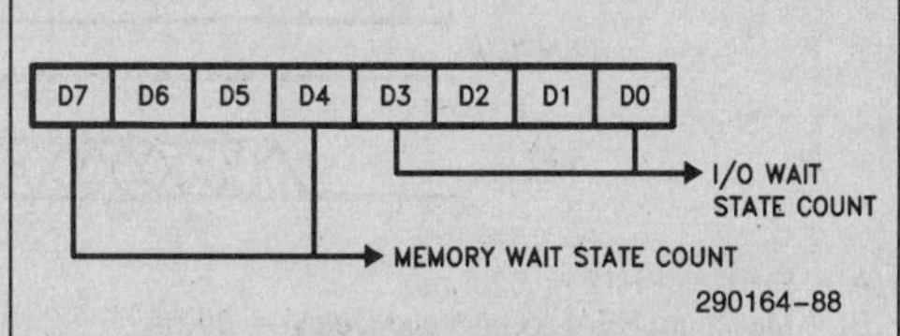

REFRESH WAIT STATE REGISTER

Port Address: 75H (Read/Write)

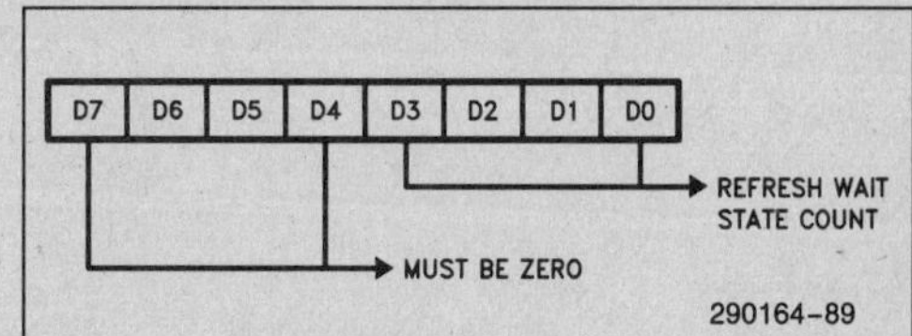

4

6.7 Application Issues

6.7.1 EXTERNAL 'READY' CONTROL LOGIC

As mentioned in section 6.3.3, wait state cycles generated by the 82370 can be terminated early or extended longer by means of additional external logic (see Figure 6-5). In order to ensure that the READY# input timing requirement of the 80376 and the 82370 is satisfied, special care must be taken when designing this external control logic. This section addresses the design requirements.

A simplified block diagram of the external logic along with the READY# timing diagram is shown in Figure 6-8. The purpose is to determine the maximum delay time allowed in the external control logic in order to satisfy the READY# setup time.

First, it will be assumed that the 80376 is running at 16 MHz (i.e. CLK2 is 32 MHz). Therefore, one bus state (two CLK2 periods) will be equivalent to 62.5 ns. According to the AC specifications of the 82370, the maximum delay time for valid READYO# signal is 31 ns after the rising edge of CLK2 in the beginning of T2 (for non-pipelined cycle) or T2P (for pipelined cycle). Also, the minimum READY# setup time of the 80376 and the 82370 should be 19 ns before the rising edge of CLK2 at the beginning of the next bus state. This limits the total delay time for the external READY# control logic to be 12.5 ns (62.5−31−19) in order to meet the READY# setup timing requirement.

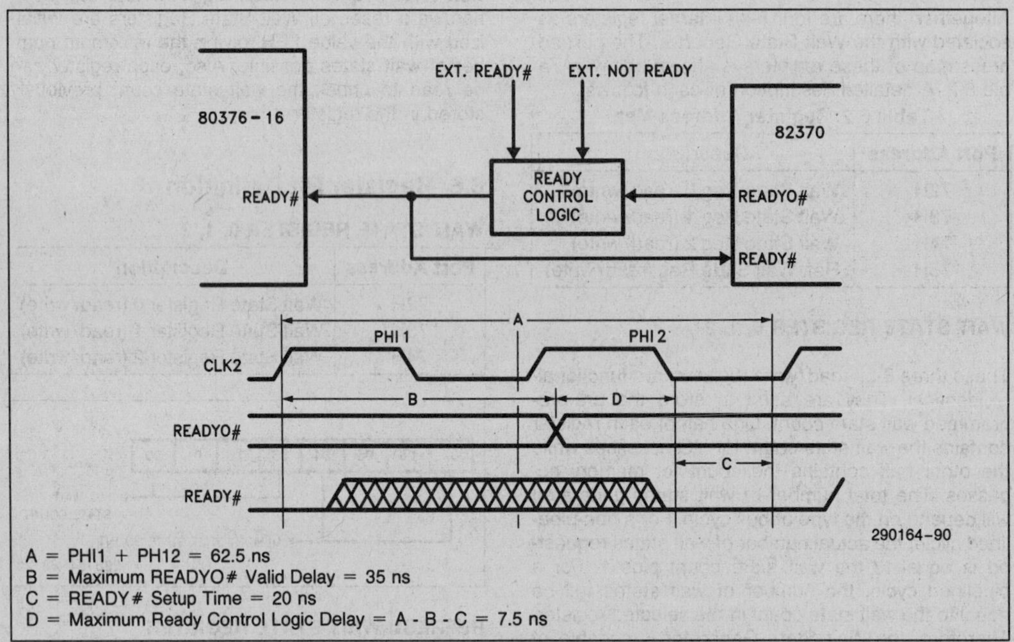

Figure 6-8. 'READY' Timing Consideration

7.0 DRAM REFRESH CONTROLLER

7.1 Functional Description

The 82370 DRAM Refresh Controller consists of a 24-bit Refresh Address Counter and Refresh Request logic for DRAM refresh operations (see Figure 7-1). TIMER 1 can be used as a trigger signal to the DRAM Refresh Request logic. The Refresh Bus Size can be programmed to be 8- or 16-bit wide. Depending on the Refresh Bus Size, the Refresh Address Counter will be incremented with the appropriate value after every refresh cycle. The internal logic of the 82370 will give the Refresh operation the highest priority in the bus control arbitration process. Bus control is not released and re-requested if the 82370 is already a bus master.

7.2 Interface Signals

7.2.1 TOUT1/REF#

The dual function output pin of TIMER 1 (TOUT1/REF#) can be programmed to generate DRAM Refresh signal. If this feature is enabled, the rising edge of TIMER 1 output (TOUT1#) will trigger the DRAM Refresh Request logic. After some delay for gaining access of the bus, the 82370 DRAM Controller will generate a DRAM Refresh signal by driving REF# output LOW. This signal is cleared after the refresh cycle has taken place, or by a hardware reset.

If the DRAM Refresh feature is disabled, the TOUT1/REF# output pin is simply the TIMER 1 output. Detailed information of how TIMER 1 operates is discussed in section 6—Programmable Interval Timer, and will not be repeated here.

7.3 Bus Function

7.3.1 ARBITRATION

In order to ensure data integrity of the DRAMs, the 82370 gives the DRAM Refresh signal the highest priority in the arbitration logic. It allows DRAM Refresh to interrupt DMA in progress in order to perform the DRAM Refresh cycle. The DMA service will be resumed after the refresh is done.

In case of a DRAM Refresh during a DMA process, the cascaded device will be requested to get off the bus. This is done by de-asserting the EDACK signal. Once DREQn goes inactive, the 82370 will perform the refresh operation. Note that the DMA controller does not completely relinquish the system bus during refresh. The Refresh Generator simply "steals" a bus cycle between DMA accesses.

Figure 7-2 shows the timing diagram of a Refresh Cycle. Upon expiration of TIMER 1, the 82370 will try to take control of the system bus by asserting HOLD. As soon as the 82370 see HLDA go active, the DRAM Refresh Cycle will be carried out by activating the REF# signal as well as the address and control signals on the system bus (Note that REF# will not be active until two CLK periods HLDA is asserted). The address bus will contain the 24-bit ad-

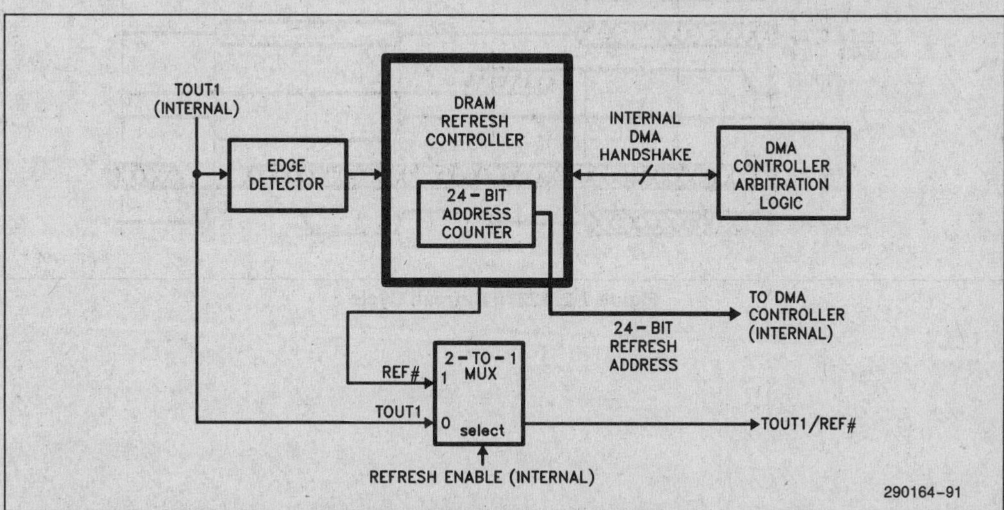

Figure 7-1. DRAM Refresh Controller

dress currently in the Refresh Address Counter. The control signals are driven the same way as in a Memory Read cycle. This "read" operation is complete when the READY# signal is driven LOW. Then, the 82370 will relinquish the bus by de-asserting HOLD. Typically, a Refresh Cycle without wait states will take five bus states to execute. If "n" wait states are added, the Refresh Cycle will last for five plus "n" bus states.

How often the Refresh Generator will initiate a refresh cycle depends on the frequency of CLKIN as will as TIMER 1's programmed mode of operation. For this specific application, TIMER 1 should be programmed to operate in Mode 2 to generate a constant clock rate. See section 6—Programmable Interval Timer for more information on programming the timer. One DRAM Refresh Cycle will be generated each time TIMER 1 expires (when TOUT1 changes from LOW to HIGH).

The Wait State Generator can be used to insert wait states during a refresh cycle. The 82370 will automatically insert the desired number of wait states as programmed in the Refresh Wait State Register (see Wait State Generator).

7.4 Modes of Operation

7.4.1 WORD SIZE AND REFRESH ADDRESS COUNTER

The 82370 supports 8- and 16-bit refresh cycle. The bus width during a refresh cycle is programmable (see Programming). The bus size can be programmed via the Refresh Control Register (see Register Overview). If the DRAM bus size is 8- or 16-bits, the Refresh Address Counter will be incremented by 1 or 2, respectively.

The Refresh Address Counter is cleared by a hardware reset.

7.5 Register Set Overview

The Refresh Generator has two internal registers to control its operation. They are the Refresh Control Register and the Refresh Wait State Register. Their port address map is shown in Table 7-1 below.

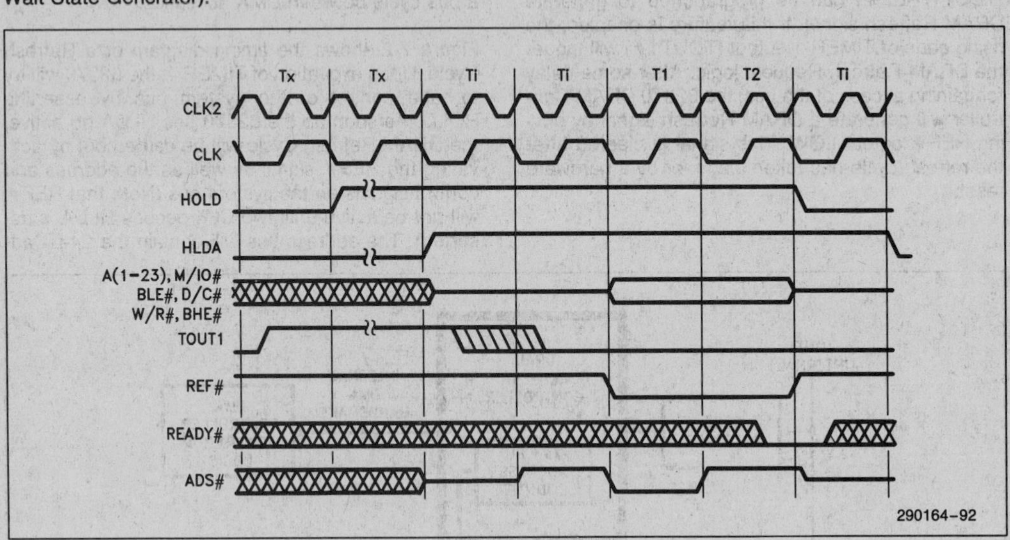

Figure 7-2. 82370 Refresh Cycle

Table 7-1. Register Address Map

Port Address	Description
1CH	Refresh Control Reg. (read/write)
75H	Ref. Wait State Reg. (read/write)

The Refresh Wait State Register is not part of the Refresh Generator. It is only used to program the number of wait states to be inserted during a refresh cycle. This register is discussed in detailed in section 7 (Wait State Generator) and will not be repeated here.

REFRESH CONTROL REGISTER

This 2-bit register serves two functions. First, it is used to enable/disable the DRAM Refresh function output. If disabled, the output of TIMER 1 is simply used as a general purpose timer. The second function of this register is to program the DRAM bus size for the refresh operation. The programmed bus size also determines how the Refresh Address Counter will be incremented after each refresh operation.

7.6 Programming

Upon hardware reset, the DRAM Refresh function is disabled (the Refresh Control Register is cleared). The following programming steps are needed before the Refresh Generator can be used. Since the rate of refresh cycles depends on how TIMER 1 is programmed, this timer must be initialized with the desired mode of operation as well as the correct refresh interval (see Programming Interval Timer). Whether or not wait states are to be generated during a refresh cycle, the Refresh Wait State Register must also be programmed with the appropriate value. Then, the DRAM Refresh feature must be enabled and the DRAM bus width should be defined. These can be done in one step by writing the appropriate control word into the Refresh Control Register (see Register Bit Definition). After these steps are done, the refresh operation will automatically be invoked by the Refresh Generator upon expiration of Timer 1.

In addition to the above programming steps, it should be noted that after reset, although the TOUT1/REF# becomes the Time 1 output, the state of this pin in undefined. This is because the Timer module has not been initialized yet. Therefore, if this output is used as a DRAM Refresh signal, this pin should be disqualified by external logic until the Refresh function is enabled. One simple solution is to logically AND this output with HLDA, since HLDA should not be active after reset.

7.7 Register Bit Definition

REFRESH CONTROL REGISTER

Port Address: 1CH (Read/Write)

8.0 RELOCATION REGISTER, ADDRESS DECODE, AND CHIP-SELECT (CHPSEL#)

8.1 Relocation Register

All the integrated peripheral devices in the 82370 are controlled by a set of internal registers. These registers span a total of 256 consecutive address locations (although not all the 256 locations are used). The 82370 provides a Relocation Register which allows the user to map this set of internal registers into either the memory or I/O address space. The function of the Relocation Register is to define the base address of the internal register set of the 82370 as well as if the registers are to be memory- or I/O-mapped. The format of the Relocation Register is depicted in Figure 8-1.

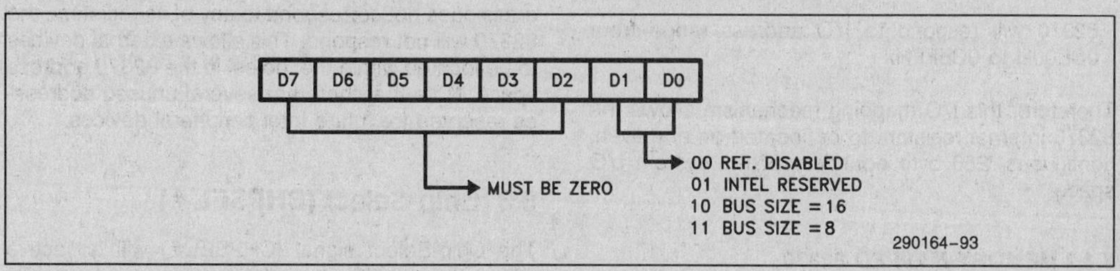

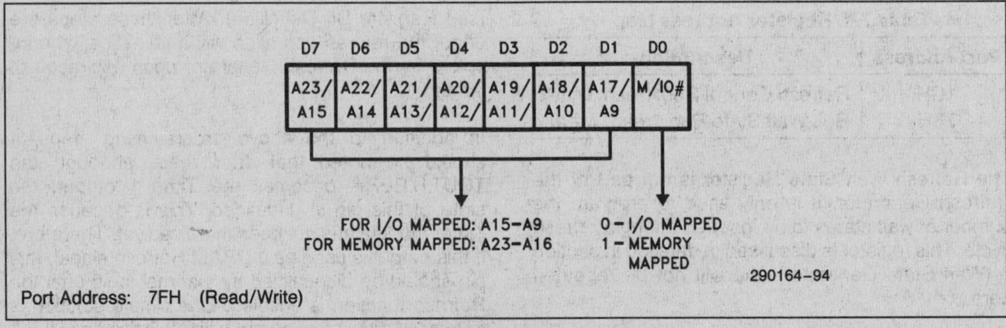

Figure 8-1. Relocation Register

Note that the Relocation Register is part of the internal register set of the 82370. It has a port address of 7FH. Therefore, any time the content of the Relocation Register is changed, the physical location of this register will also be moved. Upon reset of the 82370, the content of the Relocation Register will be cleared. This implies that the 82370 will respond to its I/O addresses in the range of 0000H to 00FFH.

8.1.1 I/O-MAPPED 82370

As shown in the figure, Bit 0 of the Relocation Register determines whether the 82370 registers are to be memory-mapped or I/O mapped. When Bit 0 is set to '0', the 82370 will respond to I/O Addresses. Address signals BHE#, BLE#, A1–A7 will be used to select one of the internal registers to be accessed. Bit 1 to Bit 7 of the Relocation Register will correspond to A9 to A15 of the Address bus, respectively. Together with A8 implied to be '0', A15 to A8 will be fully decoded by the 82370. The following shows how the 82370 is mapped into the I/O address space.

Example

Relocation Register = 11001110 (0CEH)

82370 will respond to I/O address range from 0CE00H to 0CEFFH.

Therefore, this I/O mapping mechanism allows the 82370 internal registers to be located on any even, contiguous, 256 byte boundary of the system I/O space.

8.1.2 MEMORY-MAPPED 82370

When Bit 0 of the Relocation Register is set to '1', the 82370 will respond to memory addresses. Again, Address signals BHE#, BLE#, A1–A7 will be used to select one of the internal registers to be accessed. Bit 1 to Bit 7 of the Relocation Register will correspond to A17–A23, respectively. A16 is assumed to be '0', and A8–A15 are ignored. Consider the following example.

Example

Relocation Register = 10100111 (0A7H)

The 82370 will respond to memory addresses in the range of A6XX00H to A60XXFFH (where 'X' is don't care).

This scheme implies that the internal registers can be located in any even, contiguous, 2**16 byte page of the memory space.

8.2 Address Decoding

As mentioned previously, the 82370 internal registers do not occupy the entire contiguous 256 address locations. Some of the locations are 'unoccupied'. The 82370 always decodes the lower 8 address signals (BHE#, BLE#, A1–A7) to determine if any one of its registers is being accessed. If the address does not correspond to any of its registers, the 82370 will not respond. This allows external devices to be located within the 'holes' in the 82370 address space. Note that there are several unused addresses reserved for future Intel peripheral devices.

8.3 Chip-Select (CHPSEL#)

The Chip-Select signal (CHPSEL#) will go active when the 82370 is addressed in a Slave bus

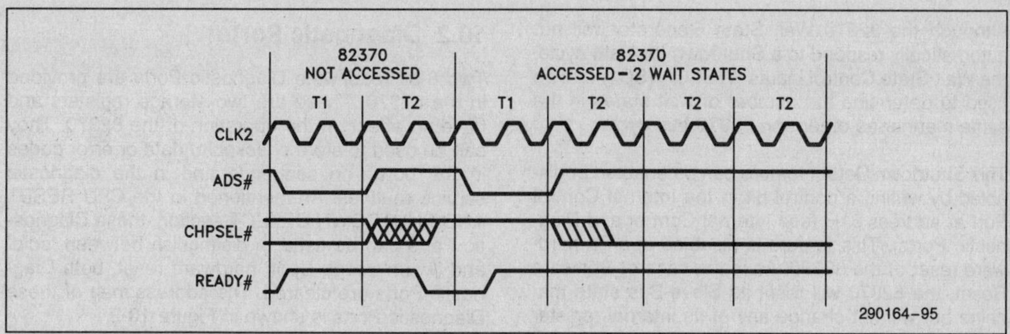

Figure 8-2. CHPSEL# Timing

cycle (either read or write), or in an interrupt acknowledge cycle in which the 82370 will drive the Data Bus. For a given bus cycle, CHPSEL# becomes active and valid in the first T2 (in a non-pipelined cycle) or in T1P (in a pipelined cycle). It will stay valid until the cycle is terminated by READY# driven active. As CHPSEL# becomes valid well before the 82370 drives the Data Bus, it can be used to control the transceivers that connect the local CPU bus to the system bus. The timing diagram of CHPSEL# is shown in Figure 8-2.

9.0 CPU RESET AND SHUTDOWN DETECT

The 82370 will activate the CPURST signal to reset the host processor when one of the following conditions occurs:

— 82370 RESET is active;

— 82370 detects a 80376 Shutdown cycle (this feature can be disabled);

— CPURST software command is issued to 80376.

Whenever the CPURST signal is activated, the 82370 will reset its own internal Slave-Bus state machine.

9.1 Hardware Reset

Following a hardware reset, the 82370 will assert its CPURST output to reset the host processor. This output will stay active for as long as the RESET input is active. During a hardware reset, the 82370 internal registers will be initialized as defined in the corresponding functional descriptions.

9.2 Software Reset

CPURST can be generated by writing the following bit pattern into 82370 register location 64H.

```
D7  . . .  D0
1 1 1 1 X X X 0
```

The Write operation into this port is considered as an 82370 access and the internal Wait State Generator will automatically determine the required number of wait states. The CPURST will be active following the completion of the Write cycle to this port. This signal will last for 80 CLK2 periods. The 82370 should not be accessed until the CPURST is deactivated.

This internal port is Write-Only and the 82370 will not respond to a Read operation to this location. Also, during a software reset command, the 82370 will reset its Slave-Bus state machine. However, its internal registers remain unchanged. This allows the operating system to distinguish a 'warm' reset by reading any 82370 internal register previously programmed for a non-default value. The Diagnostic registers can be used for this purpose (see Internal Control and Diagnostic Ports).

9.3 Shutdown Detect

The 82370 is constantly monitoring the Bus Cycle Definition signals (M/IO#, D/C#, W/R#) and is able to detect when the 80376 is in a Shutdown bus cycle. Upon detection of a processor shutdown, the 82370 will activate the CPURST output for 62 CLK2 periods to reset the host processor. This signal is generated after the Shutdown cycle is terminated by the READY# signal.

4

Although the 82370 Wait State Generator will not automatically respond to a Shutdown (or Halt) cycle, the Wait State Control inputs (WSC0, WSC1) can be used to determine the number of wait states in the same manner as other non-82370 bus cycles.

This Shutdown Detect feature can be enabled or disabled by writing a control bit in the Internal Control Port at address 61H (see Internal Control and Diagnostic Ports). This feature is disabled upon a hardware reset of the 82370. As in the case of Software Reset, the 82370 will reset its Slave-Bus state machine but will not change any of its internal register contents.

10.0 INTERNAL CONTROL AND DIAGNOSTIC PORTS

10.1 Internal Control Port

The format of the Internal Control Port of the 82370 is shown in Figure 10-1. This Control Port is used to enable/disable the Processor Shutdown Detect mechanism as well as controlling the Gate inputs of the Timer 2 and 3. Note that this is a Write-Only port. Therefore, the 82370 will not respond to a read operation to this port. Upon hardware reset, this port will be cleared; i.e., the Shutdown Detect feature and the Gate inputs of Timer 2 and 3 are disabled.

Port Address: 61H (Write only)

10.2 Diagnostic Ports

Two 8-bit read/write Diagnostic Ports are provided in the 82370. These are two storage registers and have no effect on the operation of the 82370. They can be used to store checkpoint data or error codes in the power-on sequence and in the diagnostic service routines. As mentioned in the CPU RESET AND SHUTDOWN DETECT section, these Diagnostic Ports can be used to distinguish between 'cold' and 'warm' reset. Upon hardware reset, both Diagnostic Ports are cleared. The address map of these Diagnostic Ports is shown in Figure 10-2.

Port		Address
Diagnostic Port 1	(Read/Write)	80H
Diagnostic Port 2	(Read/Write)	88H

Figure 10-2. Address Map of Diagnostic Ports

11.0 INTEL RESERVED I/O PORTS

There are nineteen I/O ports in the 82370 address space which are reserved for Intel future peripheral device use only. Their address locations are: 10H, 12H, 14H, 16H, 2AH, 3DH, 3EH, 45H, 46H, 76H, 77H, 7DH, 7EH, CCH, CDH, D0H, D2H, D4H, and D6H. These addresses should not be used in the system since the 82370 will respond to read/write operations to these locations and bus contention may occur if any peripheral is assigned to the same address location.

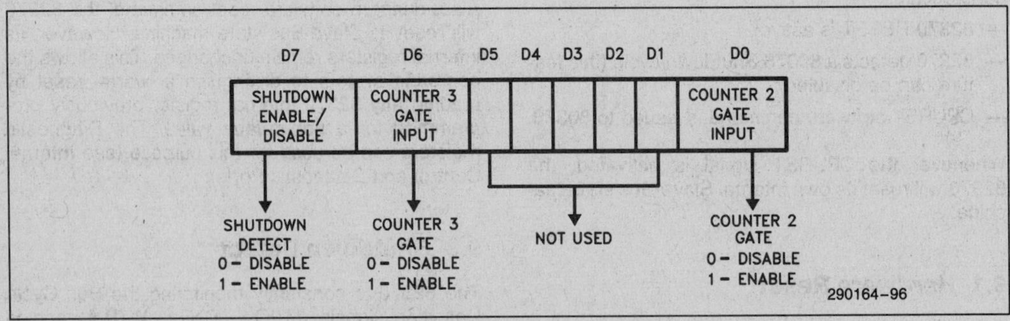

Figure 10-1. Internal Control Port

12.0 PACKAGE THERMAL SPECIFICATIONS

The intel 82370 Integrated System Peripheral is specified for operation when case temperature is within the range of 0°C to 96°C for the ceramic 132-pin PGA package, and 94°C for the 100-pin plastic package. The case temperature may be measured in any environment, to determine whether the 82370 is within specified operating range. The case temperature should be measured at the center of the top surface opposite the pins.

The ambient temperature is guaranteed as long as T_c is not violated. The ambient temperature can be calculated from the θ_{jc} and θ_{ja} from the following equations:

$$T_J = T_c + P^*\theta_{jc}$$

$$T_A = T_j - P^*\theta_{ja}$$

$$T_C = T_a + P^*[\theta_{ja} - \theta_{jc}]$$

Values for θ_{ja} and θ_{jc} are given in Table 12.1 for the 100-lead fine pitch. θ_{ja} is given at various airflows. Table 12.2 shows the maximum T_a allowable (without exceeding T_c) at various airflows. Note that T_a can be improved further by attaching "fins" or a "heat sink" to the package. P is calculated using the maximum ***hot*** I_{cc}.

Table 12.1 82370 Package Thermal Characteristics Thermal Resistances (°C/Watt) θ_{jc} and θ_{ja}

Package	θ_{jc}	θ_{ja} Versus Airflow-ft³/min (m³/sec)					
		0 (0)	200 (1.01)	400 (2.03)	600 (3.04)	800 (4.06)	1000 (5.07)
100L Fine Pitch	7	33	27	24	21	18	17
132L PGA	2	21	17	14	12	11	10

Table 12.2 82370 Maximum Allowable Ambient Temperature at Various Airflows

Package	θ_{jc}	T_a(c) Versus Airflow-ft³/min (m³/sec)					
		0 (0)	200 (1.01)	400 (2.03)	600 (3.04)	800 (4.06)	1000 (5.07)
100L Fine Pitch	7	63	74	79	85	91	92
132L PGA	2	74	83	88	93	97	99

100L PQFP Pkg:
$T_c = T_a + P^*(\theta_{ja} - \theta_{jc})$
$T_c = 63 + 1.21(33 - 7)$
$T_c = 63 + 1.21(26)$
$T_c = 63 + 31.46$
$T_c = 94\ °C$

132L PGA Pkg:
$T_c = T_a + P^*(\theta_{ja} - \theta_{jc})$
$T_c = 74 + 1.21(21 - 2)$
$T_c = 74 + 1.21(19)$
$T_c = 74 + 22.99$
$T_c = 96\ °C$

13.0 ELECTRICAL SPECIFICATIONS

82370 D.C. Specifications Functional Operating Range:
V_{CC} = 5.0V ±10%; T_{CASE} = 0°C to 96°C for 132-pin PGA, 0°C to 94°C for 100-pin plastic

Symbol	Parameter Description	Min	Max	Units	Notes
V_{IL}	Input Low Voltage	−0.3	0.8	V	(Note 1)
V_{IH}	Input High Voltage	2.0	V_{CC} + 0.3	V	
V_{ILC}	CLK2 Input Low Voltage	−0.3	0.8	V	(Note 1)
V_{IHC}	CLK2 Input High Voltage	V_{CC} − 0.8	V_{CC} + 0.3	V	
V_{OL}	Output Low Voltage I_{OL} = 4 mA: A_{1-23}, D_{0-15}, BHE#, BLE# I_{OL} = 5 mA: All Others		 0.45 0.45	 V V	
V_{OH}	Output High Voltage				
I_{OH} = −1 mA	A_{23}–A_1, D_{15}–D_0, BHE#, BLE#	2.4		V	(Note 5)
I_{OH} = −0.2 mA	A_{23}–A_1, D_{15}–D_0, BHE#, BLE#	V_{CC} − 0.5		V	(Note 5)
I_{OH} = −0.9 mA	All Others	2.4		V	(Note 5)
I_{OH} = −0.18 mA	All Others	V_{CC} − 0.5		V	(Note 5)
I_{LI}	Input Leakage Current All Inputs Except: IRQ11#–IRQ23# EOP#, TOUT2/IRQ3# DREQ4/IRQ9#		±15	μA	
I_{LI1}	Input Leakage Current Inputs: IRQ11#–IRQ23# EOP#, TOUT2/IRQ3 DREQ4/IRQ9	10	−300	μA	0 < V_{IN} < V_{CC} (Note 3)
I_{LO}	Output Leakage Current		±15	μA	0 < V_{IN} < V_{CC}
I_{CC}	Supply Current (CLK2 = 32 MHz)		220	mA	(Note 4)
C_I	Input Capacitance		12	pF	(Note 2)
C_{CLK}	CLK2 Input Capacitance		20	pF	(Note 2)

NOTES:
1. Minimum value is not 100% tested.
2. f_C = 1 MHz; sampled only.
3. These pins have weak internal pullups. They sould not be left floating.
4. I_{CC} is specified with inputs driven to CMOS levels, and outputs driving CMOS loads. I_{CC} may be higher if inputs are driven to TTL levels, or if outputs are driving TTL loads.
5. Tested at the minimum operating frequency of the part.

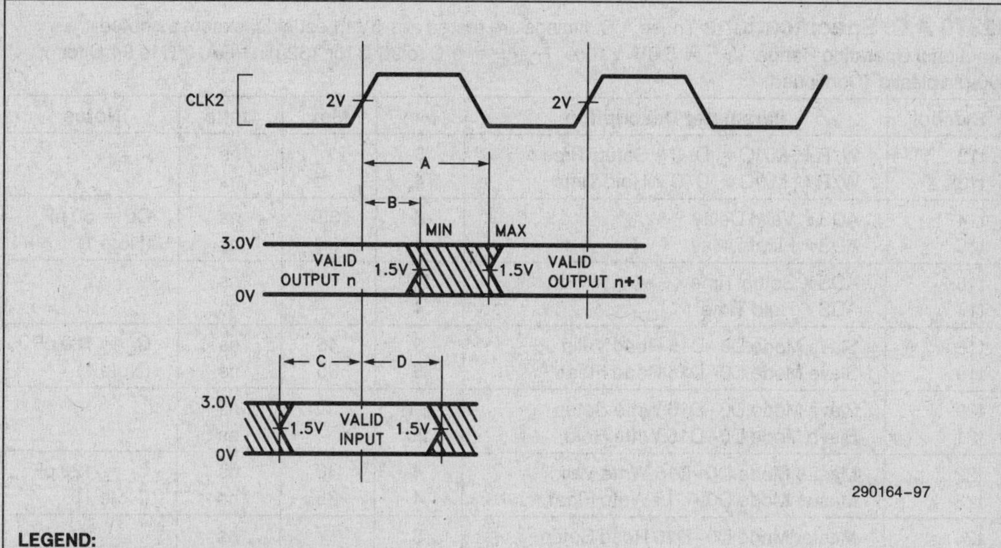

LEGEND:
A—Maximum output delay specification
B—Minimum output delay specification
C—Minimum input setup specification
D—Minimum input hold specification

Figure 13-1. Drive Levels and Measurement Points for A.C. Specification

4

82370 A.C. Specifications These A.C. timings are tested at 1.5V thresholds, except as noted. Functional Operating Range: V_{CC} = 5.0V ±10%; T_{CASE} = 0°C to 96°C for 132-pin PGA, 0°C to 94°C for 100-pin plastic

Symbol	Parameter Description	Min	Max	Units	Notes
	Operating Frequency 1/(t1a × 2)	4	16	MHz	
t1	CLK2 Period	31	125	ns	
t2a	CLK2 High Time	9		ns	At 2.0V
t2b	CLK2 High Time	5		ns	At V_{CC} − 0.8V
t3a	CLK2 Low Time	9		ns	At 2.0V
t3b	CLK2 Low Time	7		ns	At 0.8V
t4	CLK2 Fall Time		7	ns	V_{CC} − 0.8V to 0.8V
t5	CLK2 Rise Time		7	ns	0.8V to V_{CC} − 0.8V
t6	A1–A23, BHE#, BLE# EDACK0–EDACK2 Valid Delay	4	36	ns	C_L = 120 pF
t7	A1–A23, BHE#, BLE# EDACK0–EDACK3 Float Delay	4	40	ns	(Note 1)
t8	A1–A23, BHE#, BLE# Setup Time	6		ns	
t9	A1–A23, BHE#, BLE# Hold Time	4		ns	
t10	W/R#, M/IO#, D/C# Valid Delay	4	33	ns	C_L = 75 pF
t11	W/R#, M/IO#, D/C# Float Delay	4	35	ns	(Note 1)

82370 A.C. Specifications These A.C. timings are tested at 1.5V thresholds, except as noted.
Functional Operating Range: V_{CC} = 5.0V ±10%; T_{CASE} = 0°C to 96°C for 132-pin PGA, 0°C to 94°C for 100-pin plastic (Continued)

Symbol	Parameter Description	Min	Max	Units	Notes
t12 t13	W/R#, M/IO#, D/C# Setup Time W/R#, M/IO#, D/C# Hold Time	6 4		ns ns	
t14 t15	ADS# Valid Delay ADS# Float Delay	6 4	33 35	ns ns	CL = 50 pF (Note 1)
t16 t17	ADS# Setup Time ADS# Hold Time	21 4		ns ns	
t18 t19	Slave Mode D0–D15 Read Valid Slave Mode D0–D15 Read Float	3 6	46 35	ns ns	C_L = 120 pF (Note 1)
t20 t21	Slave Mode D0–D15 Write Setup Slave Mode D0–D15 Write Hold	31 26		ns ns	
t22 t23	Master Mode D0–D15 Write Valid Master Mode D0–D15 Write Float	4 4	40 35	ns ns	C_L = 120 pF (Note 1)
t24 t25	Master Mode D0–D15 Read Setup Master Mode D0–D15 Read Hold	8 6		ns ns	
t26 t27	READY# Setup Time READY# Hold Time	19 4		ns ns	
t28 t29	WSC0–WSC1 Setup Time WSC0–WSC1 Hold Time	6 21		ns ns	
t30 t31	RESET Setup Time RESET Hold Time	13 4		ns ns	
t32	READYO# Valid Delay	4	31	ns	C_L = 25 pF
t33	CPURST Valid Delay (Falling Edge Only)	2	18	ns	C_L = 50 pF
t34	HOLD Valid Delay	5	33	ns	C_L = 100 pF
t35 t36	HLDA Setup Time HLDA Hold Time	21 6		ns ns	
t37a t38a	EOP# Setup (Synchronous) EOP# Hold (Synchronous)	21 6		ns ns	
t37b t38b	EOP# Setup (Asynchronous) EOP# Hold (Asynchronous)	11 11		ns ns	
t39 t40	EOP# Valid Delay (Falling Edge Only) EOP# Float Delay	5 5	38 40	ns ns	C_L = 100 pF (Note 1)
t41a t42a	DREQ Setup (Synchronous) DREQ Hold (Synchronous)	21 4		ns ns	
t41b t42b	DREQ Setup (Asynchronous) DREQ Hold (Asynchronous)	11 11		ns ns	
t43	INT Valid Delay from IRQn		500	ns	
t44 t45	NA# Setup Time NA# Hold Time	5 15		ns ns	

82370 A.C. Specifications

These A.C. timings are tested at 1.5V thresholds, except as noted. Functional Operating Range: V_{CC} = 5.0V ±10%; T_{CASE} = 0°C to 96°C for 132-pin PGA, 0°C to 94°C for 100-pin plastic (Continued)

Symbol	Parameter Description	Min	Max	Units	Notes
t46	CLKIN Frequency	DC	10	MHz	
t47	CLKIN High Time	30		ns	2.0V
t48	CLKIN Low Time	50		ns	0.8V
t49	CLKIN Rise Time		10	ns	0.8V to 3.7V
t50	CLKIN Fall Time		10	ns	3.7V to 0.8V
	TOUT1#/REF# Valid Delay				
t51	from CLK2 (Refresh)	4	36	ns	C_L = 120 pF
t52	from CLKIN (Timer)	3	93	ns	C_L = 120 pF
t53	TOUT2# Valid Delay (from CLKIN, Falling Edge Only)	3	93	ns	C_L = 120 pf
t54	TOUT2# Float Delay	3	36	ns	(Note 1)
t55	TOUT3# Valid Delay (from CLKIN)	3	93	ns	C_L = 120 pF
t56	CHPSEL# Valid Delay	1	35	ns	C_L = 25 pF

NOTE:
1. Float condition occurs when the maximum output current becomes less than I_{LO} in magnitude. Float delay is not tested. For testing purposes, the float condition occurs when the dynamic output driven voltage changes with current loads.

4

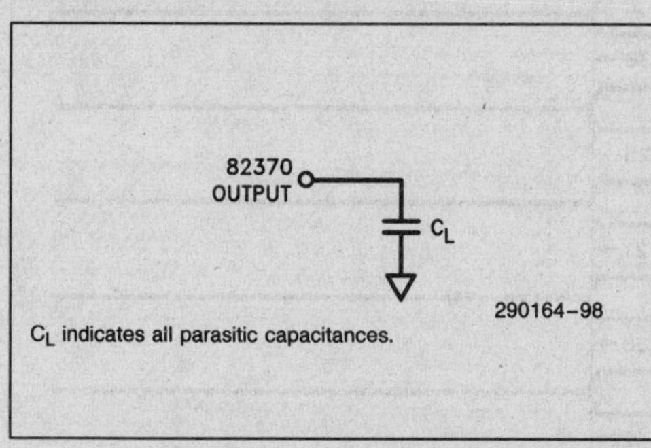

Figure 13-2. A.C. Test Load

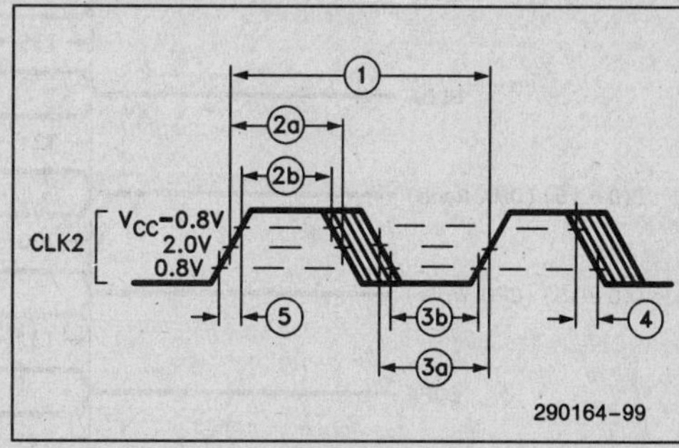

Figure 13-3

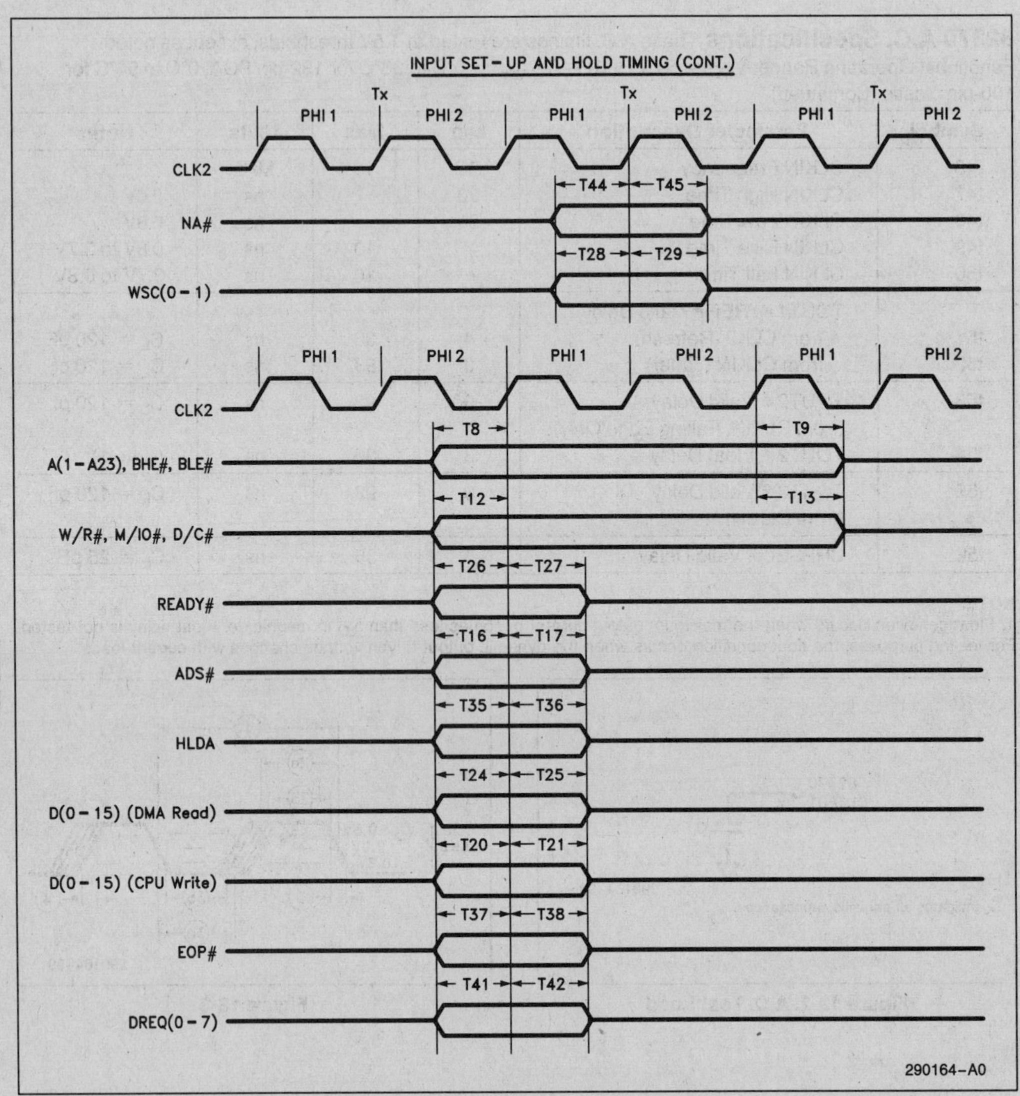

Figure 13-4. Input Setup and Hold Timing

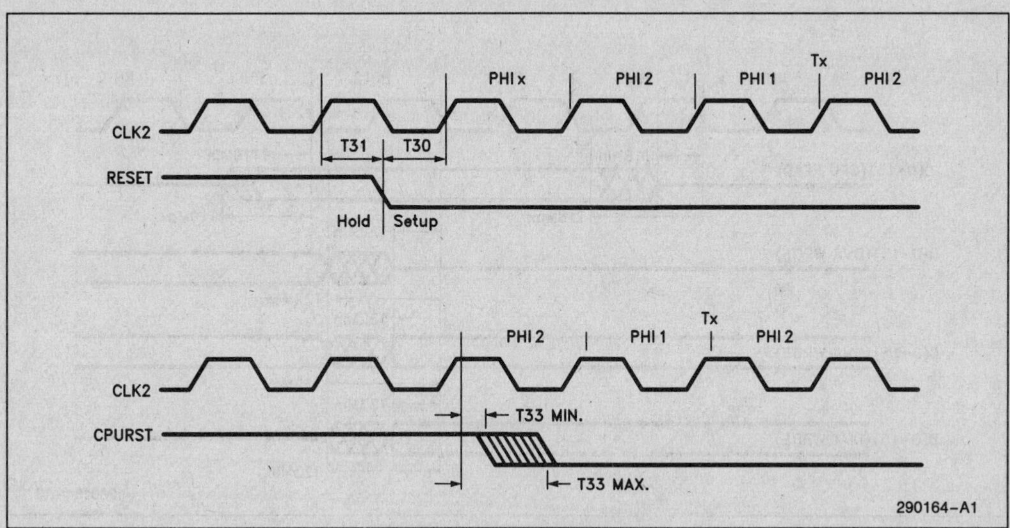

Figure 13-5. Reset Timing

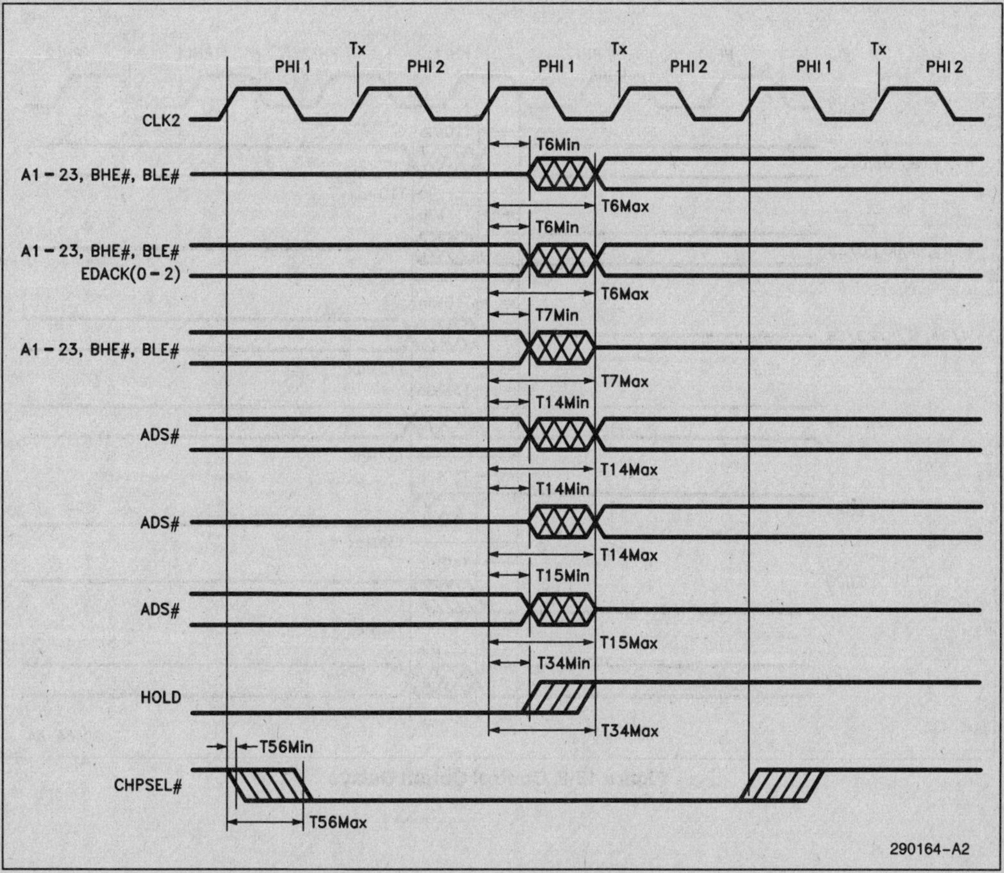

Figure 13-6. Address Output Delays

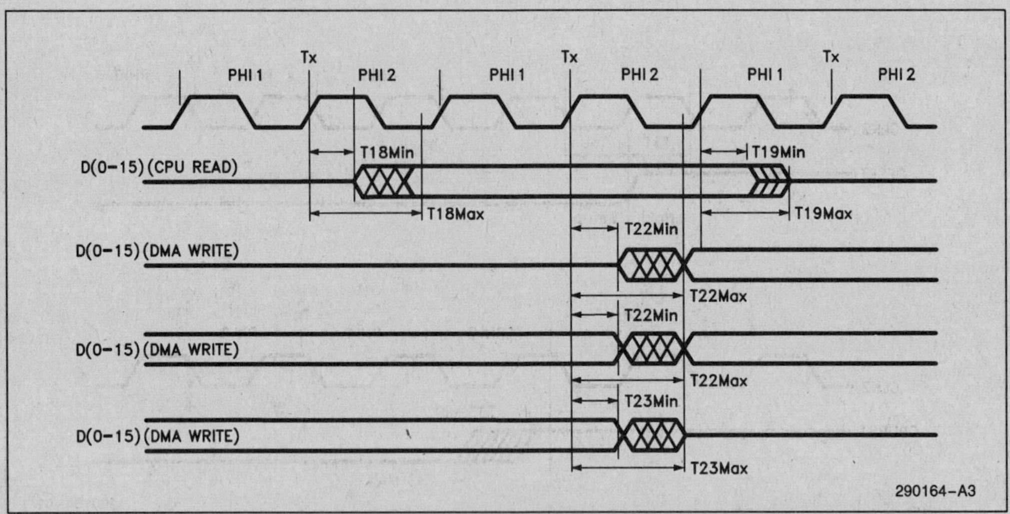

Figure 13-7. Data Bus Output Delays

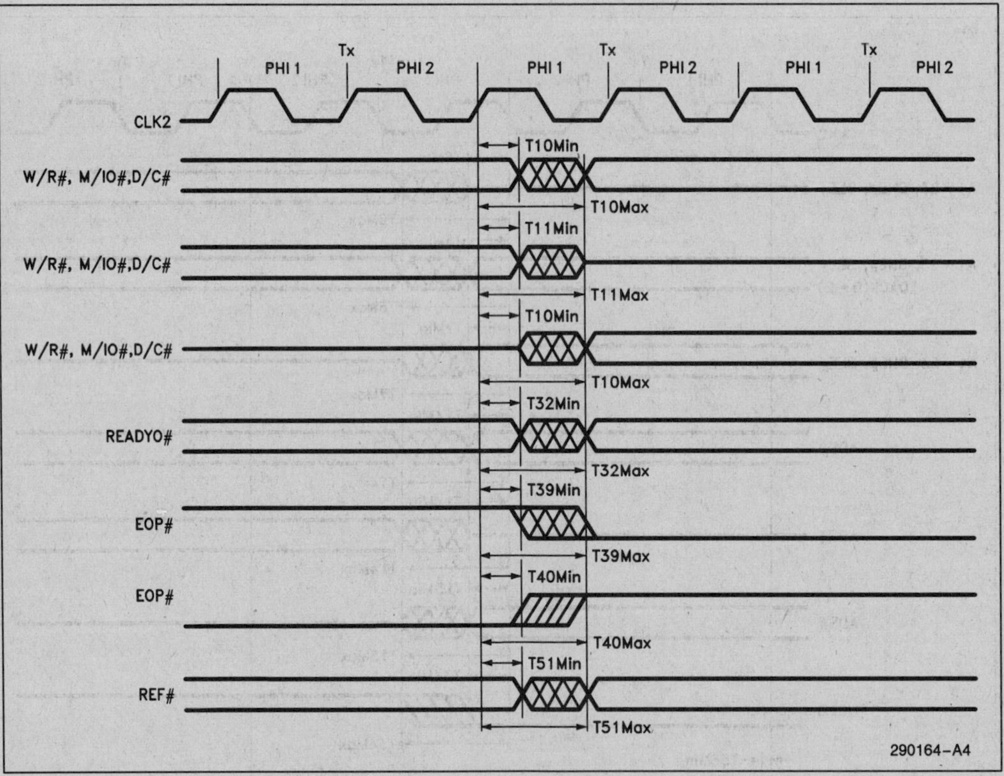

Figure 13-8. Control Output Delays

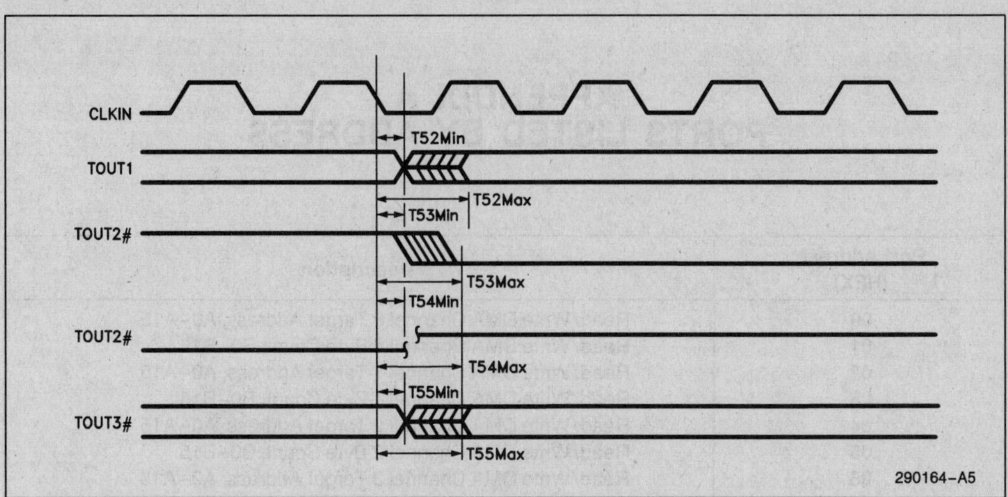

Figure 13-9. Timer Output Delays

4

APPENDIX A
PORTS LISTED BY ADDRESS

Port Address (HEX)	Description
00	Read/Write DMA Channel 0 Target Address, A0–A15
01	Read/Write DMA Channel 0 Byte Count, B0–B15
02	Read/Write DMA Channel 1 Target Address, A0–A15
03	Read/Write DMA Channel 1 Byte Count, B0–B15
04	Read/Write DMA Channel 2 Target Address, A0–A15
05	Read/Write DMA Channel 2 Byte Count, B0–B15
06	Read/Write DMA Channel 3 Target Address, A0–A15
07	Read/Write DMA Channel 3 Byte Count, B0–B15
08	Read/Write DMA Channel 0–3 Status/Command I Register
09	Read/Write DMA Channel 0–3 Software Request Register
0A	Write DMA Channel 0–3 Set-Reset Mask Register
0B	Write DMA Channel 0–3 Mode Register I
0C	Write Clear Byte-Pointer FF
0D	Write DMA Master-Clear
0E	Write DMA Channel 0–3 Clear Mask Register
0F	Read/Write DMA Channel 0–3 Mask Register
10	Intel Reserved
11	Read/Write DMA Channel 0 Byte Count, B16–B23
12	Intel Reserved
13	Read/Write DMA Channel 1 Byte Count, B16–B23
14	Intel Reserved
15	Read/Write DMA Channel 2 Byte Count, B16–B23
16	Intel Reserved
17	Read/Write DMA Channel 3 Byte Count, B16–B23
18	Write DMA Channel 0–3 Bus Size Register
19	Read/Write DMA Channel 0–3 Chaining Register
1A	Write DMA Channel 0–3 Command Register II
1B	Write DMA Channel 0–3 Mode Register II
1C	Read/Write Refresh Control Register
1E	Reset Software Request Interrupt
20	Write Bank B ICW1, OCW2 or OCW3 Read Bank B Poll, Interrupt Request or In-Service Status Register
21	Write Bank B ICW2, ICW3, ICW4 or OCW1 Read Bank B Interrupt Mask Register
22	Read Bank B ICW2
28	Read/Write IRQ8 Vector Register
29	Read/Write IRQ9 Vector Register
2A	Reserved

Port Address (HEX)	Description
2B	Read/Write IRQ11 Vector Register
2C	Read/Write IRQ12 Vector Register
2D	Read/Write IRQ13 Vector Register
2E	Read/Write IRQ14 Vector Register
2F	Read/Write IRQ15 Vector Register
30	Write Bank A ICW1, OCW2 or OCW3 Read Bank A Poll, Interrupt Request or In-Service Status Register
31	Write Bank A ICW2, ICW3, ICW4 or OCW1 Read Bank A Interrupt Mask Register
32	Read Bank A ICW2
38	Read/Write IRQ0 Vector Register
39	Read/Write IRQ1 Vector Register
3A	Read/Write IRQ1.5 Vector Register
3B	Read/Write IRQ3 Vector Register
3C	Read/Write IRQ4 Vector Register
3D	Reserved
3E	Reserved
3F	Read/Write IRQ7 Vector Register
40	Read/Write Counter 0 Register
41	Read/Write Counter 1 Register
42	Read/Write Counter 2 Register
43	Write Control Word Register I—Counter 0, 1, 2
44	Read/Write Counter 3 Register
45	Reserved
46	Reserved
47	Write Word Register II—Counter 3
61	Write Internal Control Port
64	Write CPU Reset Register (Data—1111XXX0H)
72	Read/Write Wait State Register 0
73	Read/Write Wait State Register 1
74	Read/Write Wait State Register 2
75	Read/Write Refresh Wait State Register
76	Reserved
77	Reserved
7D	Reserved
7E	Reserved
7F	Read/Write Relocation Register
80	Read/Write Internal Diagnostic Port 0
81	Read/Write DMA Channel 2 Target Address, A16–A23
82	Read/Write DMA Channel 3 Target Address, A16–A23
83	Read/Write DMA Channel 1 Target Address, A16–A23
87	Read/Write DMA Channel 0 Target Address, A16–A23
88	Read/Write Internal Diagnostic Port 1
89	Read/Write DMA Channel 6 Target Address, A16–A23
8A	Read/Write DMA Channel 7 Target Address, A16–A23
8B	Read/Write DMA Channel 5 Target Address, A16–A23
8F	Read/Write DMA Channel 4 Target Address, A16–A23

Port Address (HEX)	Description
90	Read/Write DMA Channel 0 Requester Address, A0–A15
91	Read/Write DMA Channel 0 Requester Address, A16–A23
92	Read/Write DMA Channel 1 Requester Address, A0–A15
93	Read/Write DMA Channel 1 Requester Address, A16–A23
94	Read/Write DMA Channel 2 Requester Address, A0–A15
95	Read/Write DMA Channel 2 Requester Address, A16–A23
96	Read/Write DMA Channel 3 Requester Address, A0–A15
97	Read/Write DMA Channel 3 Requester Address, A16–A23
98	Read/Write DMA Channel 4 Requester Address, A0–A15
99	Read/Write DMA Channel 4 Requester Address, A16–A23
9A	Read/Write DMA Channel 5 Requester Address, A0–A15
9B	Read/Write DMA Channel 5 Requester Address, A16–A23
9C	Read/Write DMA Channel 6 Requester Address, A0–A15
9D	Read/Write DMA Channel 6 Requester Address, A16–A23
9E	Read/Write DMA Channel 7 Requester Address, A0–A15
9F	Read/Write DMA Channel 7 Requester Address, A16–A23
A0	Write Bank C ICW1, OCW2 or OCW3 Read Bank C Poll, Interrupt Request or In-Service Status Register
A1	Write Bank C ICW2, ICW3, ICW4 or OCW1 Read Bank C Interrupt Mask Register
A2	Read Bank C ICW2
A8	Read/Write IRQ16 Vector Register
A9	Read/Write IRQ17 Vector Register
AA	Read/Write IRQ18 Vector Register
AB	Read/Write IRQ19 Vector Register
AC	Read/Write IRQ20 Vector Register
AD	Read/Write IRQ21 Vector Register
AE	Read/Write IRQ22 Vector Register
AF	Read/Write IRQ23 Vector Register
C0	Read/Write DMA Channel 4 Target Address, A0–A15
C1	Read/Write DMA Channel 4 Byte Count, B0–B15
C2	Read/Write DMA Channel 5 Target Address, A0–A15
C3	Read/Write DMA Channel 5 Byte Count, B0–B15
C4	Read/Write DMA Channel 6 Target Address, A0–A15
C5	Read/Write DMA Channel 6 Byte Count, B0–B15
C6	Read/Write DMA Channel 7 Target Address, A0–A15
C7	Read/Write DMA Channel 7 Byte Count, B0–B15
C8	Read DMA Channel 4–7 Status/Command I Register
C9	Read/Write DMA Channel 4–7 Software Request Register
CA	Write DMA Channel 4–7 Set-Reset Mask Register
CB	Write DMA Channel 4–7 Mode Register I
CC	Reserved
CD	Reserved
CE	Write DMA Channel 4–7 Clear Mask Register
CF	Read/Write DMA Channel 4–7 Mask Register
D0	Intel Reserved
D1	Read/Write DMA Channel 4 Byte Count, B16–B23
D2	Intel Reserved
D3	Read/Write DMA Channel 5 Byte Count, B16–B23

Port Address (HEX)	Description
D4	Intel Reserved
D5	Read/Write DMA Channel 6 Byte Count, B16–B23
D6	Intel Reserved
D7	Read/Write DMA Channel 7 Byte Count, B16–B23
D8	Write DMA Channel 4–7 Bus Size Register
D9	Read/Write DMA Channel 4–7 Chaining Register
DA	Write DMA Channel 4–7 Command Register II
DB	Write DMA Channel 4–7 Mode Register II

APPENDIX B
PORTS LISTED BY FUNCTION

Port Address (HEX)	Description
DMA CONTROLLER	
0D	Write DMA Master-Clear
0C	Write DMA Clear Byte-Pointer FF
08	Read/Write DMA Channel 0–3 Status/Command I Register
C8	Read/Write DMA Channel 4–7 Status/Command I Register
1A	Write DMA Channel 0–3 Command Register II
DA	Write DMA Channel 4–7 Command Register II
0B	Write DMA Channel 0–3 Mode Register I
CB	Write DMA Channel 4–7 Mode Register I
1B	Write DMA Channel 0–3 Mode Register II
DB	Write DMA Channel 4–7 Mode Register II
09	Read/Write DMA Channel 0–3 Software Request Register
C9	Read/Write DMA Channel 4–7 Software Request Register
1E	Reset Software Request Interrupt
0E	Write DMA Channel 0–3 Clear Mask Register
CE	Write DMA Channel 4–7 Clear Mask Register
0F	Read/Write DMA Channel 0–3 Mask Register
CF	Read/Write DMA Channel 4–7 Mask Register
0A	Write DMA Channel 0–3 Set-Reset Mask Register
CA	Write DMA Channel 4–7 Set-Reset Mask Register
18	Write DMA Channel 0–3 Bus Size Register
D8	Write DMA Channel 4–7 Bus Size Register
19	Read/Write DMA Channel 0–3 Chaining Register
D9	Read/Write DMA Channel 4–7 Chaining Register
00	Read/Write DMA Channel 0 Target Address, A0–A15
87	Read/Write DMA Channel 0 Target Address, A16–A23
01	Read/Write DMA Channel 0 Byte Count, B0–B15
11	Read/Write DMA Channel 0 Byte Count, B16–B23
90	Read/Write DMA Channel 0 Requester Address, A0–A15
91	Read/Write DMA Channel 0 Requester Address, A16–A23

Port Address (HEX)	Description
DMA CONTROLLER (Continued)	
02	Read/Write DMA Channel 1 Target Address, A0–A15
83	Read/Write DMA Channel 1 Target Address, A16–A23
03	Read/Write DMA Channel 1 Byte Count, B0–B15
13	Read/Write DMA Channel 1 Byte Count, B16–B23
92	Read/Write DMA Channel 1 Requester Address, A0–A15
93	Read/Write DMA Channel 1 Requester Address, A16–A23
04	Read/Write DMA Channel 2 Target Address, A0–A15
81	Read/Write DMA Channel 2 Target Address, A16–A23
05	Read/Write DMA Channel 2 Byte Count, B0–B15
15	Read/Write DMA Channel 2 Byte Count, B16–B23
94	Read/Write DMA Channel 2 Requester Address, A0–A15
95	Read/Write DMA Channel 2 Requester Address, A16–A23
06	Read/Write DMA Channel 3 Target Address, A0–A15
82	Read/Write DMA Channel 3 Target Address, A16–A23
07	Read/Write DMA Channel 3 Byte Count, B0–B15
17	Read/Write DMA Channel 3 Byte Count, B16–B23
96	Read/Write DMA Channel 3 Requester Address, A0–A15
97	Read/Write DMA Channel 3 Requester Address, A16–A23
C0	Read/Write DMA Channel 4 Target Address, A0–A15
8F	Read/Write DMA Channel 4 Target Address, A16–A23
C1	Read/Write DMA Channel 4 Byte Count, B0–B15
D1	Read/Write DMA Channel 4 Byte Count, B16–B23
98	Read/Write DMA Channel 4 Requester Address, A0–A15
99	Read/Write DMA Channel 4 Requester Address, A16–A23
C2	Read/Write DMA Channel 5 Target Address, A0–A15
8B	Read/Write DMA Channel 5 Target Address, A16–A23
C3	Read/Write DMA Channel 5 Byte Count, B0–B15
D3	Read/Write DMA Channel 5 Byte Count, B16–B23
9A	Read/Write DMA Channel 5 Requester Address, A0–A15
9B	Read/Write DMA Channel 5 Requester Address, A16–A23
C4	Read/Write DMA Channel 6 Target Address, A0–A15
89	Read/Write DMA Channel 6 Target Address, A16–A23
C5	Read/Write DMA Channel 6 Byte Count, B0–B15
D5	Read/Write DMA Channel 6 Byte Count, B16–B23
9C	Read/Write DMA Channel 6 Requester Address, A0–A15
9D	Read/Write DMA Channel 6 Requester Address, A16–A23
C6	Read/Write DMA Channel 7 Target Address, A0–A15
8A	Read/Write DMA Channel 7 Target Address, A16–A23
C7	Read/Write DMA Channel 7 Byte Count, B0–B15
D7	Read/Write DMA Channel 7 Byte Count, B16–B23
9E	Read/Write DMA Channel 7 Requester Address, A0–A15
9F	Read/Write DMA Channel 7 Requester Address, A16–A23

4

Port Address (HEX)	Description
INTERRUPT CONTROLLER	
20	Write Bank B ICW1, OCW2 or OCW3 Read Bank B Poll, Interrupt Request or In-Service Status Register
21	Write Bank B ICW2, ICW3, ICW4 or OCW1 Read Bank B Interrupt Mask Register
22	Read Bank B ICW2
28	Read/Write IRQ8 Vector Register
29	Read/Write IRQ9 Vector Register
2A	Reserved
2B	Read/Write IRQ11 Vector Register
2C	Read/Write IRQ12 Vector Register
2D	Read/Write IRQ13 Vector Register
2E	Read/Write IRQ14 Vector Register
2F	Read/Write IRQ15 Vector Register
A0	Write Bank C ICW1, OCW2 or OCW3 Read Bank C Poll, Interrupt Request or In-Service Status Register
A1	Write Bank C ICW2, ICW3, ICW4 or OCW1 Read Bank C Interrupt Mask Register
A2	Read Bank C ICW2
A8	Read/Write IRQ16 Vector Register
A9	Read/Write IRQ17 Vector Register
AA	Read/Write IRQ18 Vector Register
AB	Read/Write IRQ19 Vector Register
AC	Read/Write IRQ20 Vector Register
AD	Read/Write IRQ21 Vector Register
AE	Read/Write IRQ22 Vector Register
AF	Read/Write IRQ23 Vector Register
30	Write Bank A ICW1, OCW2 or OCW3 Read Bank A Poll, Interrupt Request or In-Service Status Register
31	Write Bank A ICW2, ICW3, ICW4 or OCW1 Read Bank A Interrupt Mask Register
32	Read Bank A ICW2
38	Read/Write IRQ0 Vector Register
39	Read/Write IRQ1 Vector Register
3A	Read/Write IRQ1.5 Vector Register
3B	Read/Write IRQ3 Vector Register
3C	Read/Write IRQ4 Vector Register
3D	Reserved
3E	Reserved
3F	Read/Write IRQ7 Vector Register

Port Address (HEX)	Description
PROGRAMMABLE INTERVAL TIMER	
40	Read/Write Counter 0 Register
41	Read/Write Counter 1 Register
42	Read/Write Counter 2 Register
43	Write Control Word Register I—Counter 0, 1, 2
44	Read/Write Counter 3 Register
47	Write Word Register II—Counter 3
CPU RESET	
64	Write CPU Reset Register (Data—1111XXX0H)
WAIT STATE GENERATOR	
72	Read/Write Wait State Register 0
73	Read/Write Wait State Register 1
74	Read/Write Wait State Register 2
75	Read/Write Refresh Wait State Register
DRAM REFRESH CONTROLLER	
1C	Read/Write Refresh Control Register
INTERNAL CONTROL AND DIAGNOSTIC PORTS	
61	Write Internal Control Port
80	Read/Write Internal Diagnostic Port 0
88	Read/Write Internal Diagnostic Port 1
RELOCATION REGISTER	
7F	Read/Write Relocation Register
INTEL RESERVED PORTS	
10	Reserved
12	Reserved
14	Reserved
16	Reserved
2A	Reserved
3D	Reserved
3E	Reserved
45	Reserved
46	Reserved
76	Reserved
77	Reserved
7D	Reserved
7E	Reserved
CC	Reserved
CD	Reserved
D0	Reserved
D2	Reserved
D4	Reserved
D6	Reserved

APPENDIX C
SYSTEM NOTES

1. BHE# IN MASTER MODE.

In Master Mode, BHE# will be activated during DMA to/from 8-bit devices residing at even locations when the remaining byte count is greater than 1.

For example, if an 8-bit device is located at 00000000 Hex and the number of bytes to be transferred is > 1, the first address/BHE# combination will be 00000000/0. In some systems this will cause the bus controller to perform two 8-bit accesses, the first to 0000000 Hex and the second to 00000001 Hex. However, the 82370's DMA will only read/write one byte. This may or may not cause a problem in the system depending on what is located at 00000001 Hex.

Solution:

There are two solutions if BH# active is unacceptable. Of the two, number 2 is the cleanest and most recommended.

1. If there is an 8-bit device that uses DMA located at an even address, do not use that address + 1. The limitation of this solution is that the user must have complete control over what addresses will be used in the end system.

2. Do not allow the Bus Controller to split cycles for the DMA.

82370 TIMER UNIT NOTES

The 82370 DMA Controller with Integrated System Peripherals is functionally inconsistent with the data sheet. This document explains the behavior of the 82370 Timer Unit and outlines subsequent limitations of the timer unit. This document also provides recommended workarounds.

1.0 WRITE CYCLES TO THE 82370 TIMER UNIT:

This errata applies only to SLAVE WRITE cycles to the 82370 timer unit. During these cycles, the data being written into the 82370 timer unit may be corrupted if asynchronous CLKIN is not inhibited during a certain "window" of the write cycle.

1.1 Description

Please refer to Figure C-2.

During write cycles to the 82370 timer unit, the 82370 translates the 80376 interface signals such as #ADS, #W/R, #M/IO, and #D/C into several internal signals that control the operation of the internal sub-blocks (e.g. Timer Unit).

The 82370 timer uint is controlled by such internal signals. These internal signals are generated and sampled with respect to two separate clock signals: CLK2 (the system clock) and CLKIN (the 82370 timer unit clock).

Since the CLKIN and CLK2 clock signals are used internally to generate control signals for the interface to the timer unit, some timing parameters must be met in order for the interface logic to function properly.

Those timing parameters are met by inhibiting the CLKIN signal for a specific window during Write Cycles to the 82370 Timer Unit.

The CLKIN signal must be inhibited using external logic, as the GATE function of the 82370 timer unit is not guaranteed to totally inhibit CLKIN.

1.2 Consequences

This CLKIN inhibits circuitry guarantees proper write cycles to the 82370 timer unit.

Without this solution, write cycles to the 82370 timer unit could place corrupted data into the timer unit registers. This, in turn, could yield inaccurate results and improper timer operation.

The proposed solution would involve a hardware modification for existing systems.

4

1.3 Solution

A timing waveform (Figure C-3) shows the specific window during which CLKIN must be inhibited. Please note that CLKIN must only be inhibited during the window shown in Figure C-3. This window is defined by two AC timing parameters:

$t_a = 9$ ns

$t_b = 28$ ns

The proposed solution provides a certain amount of system "guardband" to make sure that this window is avoided.

PAL equations for a suggested workaround are also included. Please refer to the comments in the PAL codes for stated assumptions of this particular workaround. A state diagram (Figure C-4) is provided to help clarify how this PAL is designed.

Figure C-5 shows how this PAL would fit into a system workaround. In order to show the effect of this work-around on the CLKIN signal, Figure C-6 shows how CLKIN is inhibited. Note that you must still meet the CLKIN AC timing parameters (e.g. t_{47} (min), t_{48} (min)) in order for the timer unit to function properly.

Please note that this workaround has not been tested. It is provided as a suggested solution. Actual solutions will vary from system to system.

1.4 Long Term Plans

Intel has no plans to fix this behavior in the 82370 timer unit.

```
module Timer_82370_Fix
flag '-r2', '-q2', '-fl', '-t4', '-wl,3,6,5,4,16,7,12,17,18,15,14'
title '82370 Timer Unit CLKIN
      INHIBIT signal PAL Solution '
Timer_Unit_Fix device 'P16R6';


"This PAL inhibits the CLKIN signal (that comes from an oscillator)
"during Slave Writes to the 82370 Timer unit.
"
"ASSUMPTION:   This PAL assumes that an external system address
"              decoder provides a signal to indicate that an 82370
"              Timer Unit access is taking place. This input
"              signal is called TMR in this PAL. This PAL also
"              assumes that this TMR signal occurs during a
"              specific T-State. Please see Figure 2 of this
"              document to see when this signal is expected to
"              be active by this PAL.
"
"
"NOTE:         This PAL does not support pipelined 82370 SLAVE
"              cycles.
"
"(c) Intel Corporation 1989. This PAL is provided as a proposed
"method of solving a certain 82370 Timer Unit problem. This PAL
"has not been tested or validated. Please validate this solution
"for your system and application.
"
"Input Pins"


CLK2          pin       1; "System Clock
RESET         pin       2; "Microprocessor RESET signal
TMR           pin       3; "Input from Address Decoder, indicating
                           "an access to the timer unit of the
                           "82370.
!RDY          pin       4; "End of Cycle indicator
!ADS          pin       5; "Address and control strobe
CLK           pin       6; "PHI2 clock
W_R           pin       7; "Write/Read Signal"
nc1           pin       8; "No Connect 0"
nc3           pin       9; "No Connect 1"
GNDa          pin      10; "Tied to ground, documentation only
GNDb          pin      11; "Output enable, documentation only
CLKIN_IN      pin      12; "Input-CLKIN directly from oscillator

"Output Pins"
Q_0           pin      18; "Internal signal only, fed back to
                           "PAL logic"
CLKIN_OUT     pin      17; "CLKIN signal fed to 82370 Timer Unit
INHIBIT       pin      16; "CLKIN Inhibit signal
S0            pin      15; "Unused State Indicator Pin
S1            pin      14; "Unused State Indicator Pin

"Declarations"
```

```
Valid_ADS = ADS & CLK     ; "#ADS sampled in PHI1 of 80376 T-State
Valid_RDY = RDY & CLK     ; "#RDY sampled in PHI1 of 80376 T-State
Timer_Acc = TMR & CLK     ; "Timer Unit Access, as provided by
                            "external Address Decoder"

State_Diagram [INHIBIT, S1, S0]

state 000:         if RESET then 000
                   else if Valid_ADS & W_R then 001
                   else 000;

state 001:         if RESET then 000
                   else if Timer_Acc then 010
                   else if !Timer_Acc then 000
                   else 001;

state 010:         if RESET then 000
                   else if CLK then 110
                   else 010;

state 110:         if RESET then 000
                   else if CLK then 111
                   else 110;

state 111:         if RESET then 000
                   else if CLK then 011
                   else 111;

state 011:         if RESET then 000
                   else if Valid_RDY then 000
                   else 011;

state 100:         if RESET then 000
                   else 000;

state 101:         if RESET then 000
                   else 000;

EQUATIONS
Q_0 := CLKIN_IN; "Latched incoming clock. This signal is used
                 "internally to feed into the MUX-ing logic"

CLKIN_OUT := (INHIBIT & CLKIN_OUT & !RESET)
           +(!INHIBIT & Q_0 & !RESET);

                         "Equation for CLKIN_OUT. This
                         "feeds directly to the 82370 Timer Unit."

END
```

4

82370 Timer Unit CLKIN
INHIBIT signal PAL Solution
Equations for Module Timer_82370_Fix

Device Timer_Unit_Fix

—Reduced Equations:

```
!INHIBIT := (!CLK & !INHIBIT # CLK & S0 # RESET # !S1);

!S1 := (RESET
  # INHIBIT & !S1
  # CLK & !INHIBIT & !~RDY & S0 & S1
  # !CLK & !S1
  # !S1 & !TMR
  # !S0 & !S1);


!S0 := (RESET
  # INHIBIT & !S1
  # CLK & !INHIBIT & !~RDY & S1
  #!INHIBIT & !S0 & S1
  # !CLK & !S0
  # !INHIBIT & !S0 & S1
  # S0 & !S1
  # !S1 & !W_R
  # ~ADS & !S1);


!Q_0 := (!CLKIN_IN);

!CLKIN_OUT := (RESET # !CLKIN_OUT & INHIBIT # !INHIBIT & !Q_0);
```

82370 Timer Unit CLKIN
INHIBIT signal PAL Solution
Chip diagram for Module Timer__82370__Fix

Device Timer__Unit__Fix

P16R6

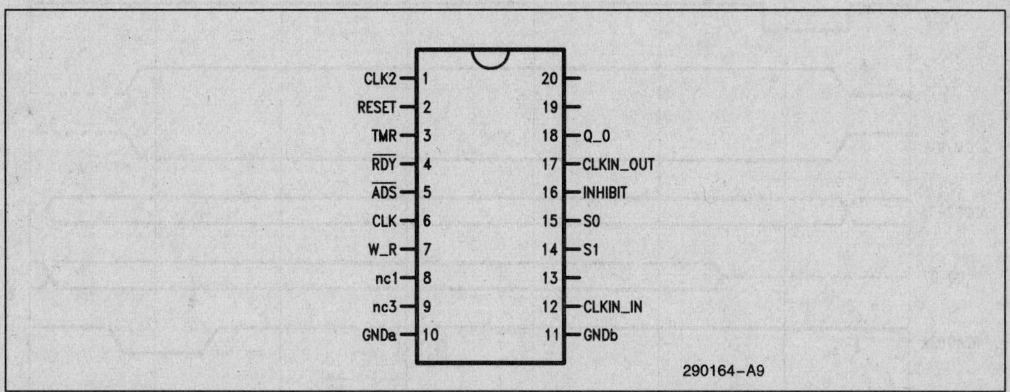

end of module Timer__82370__Fix

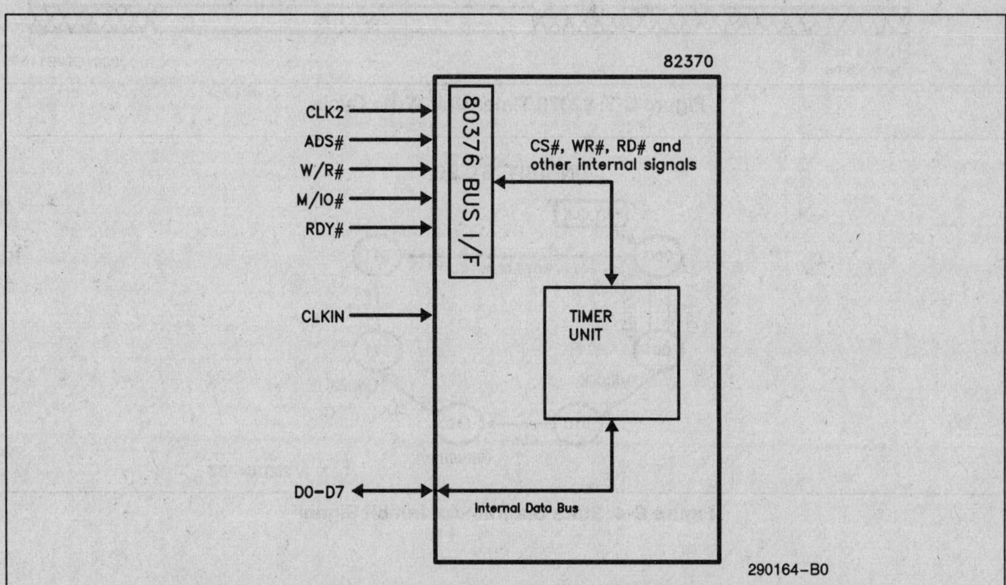

Figure C-2. Translation of 80376 Signals to Internal 82370 Timer Unit Signals

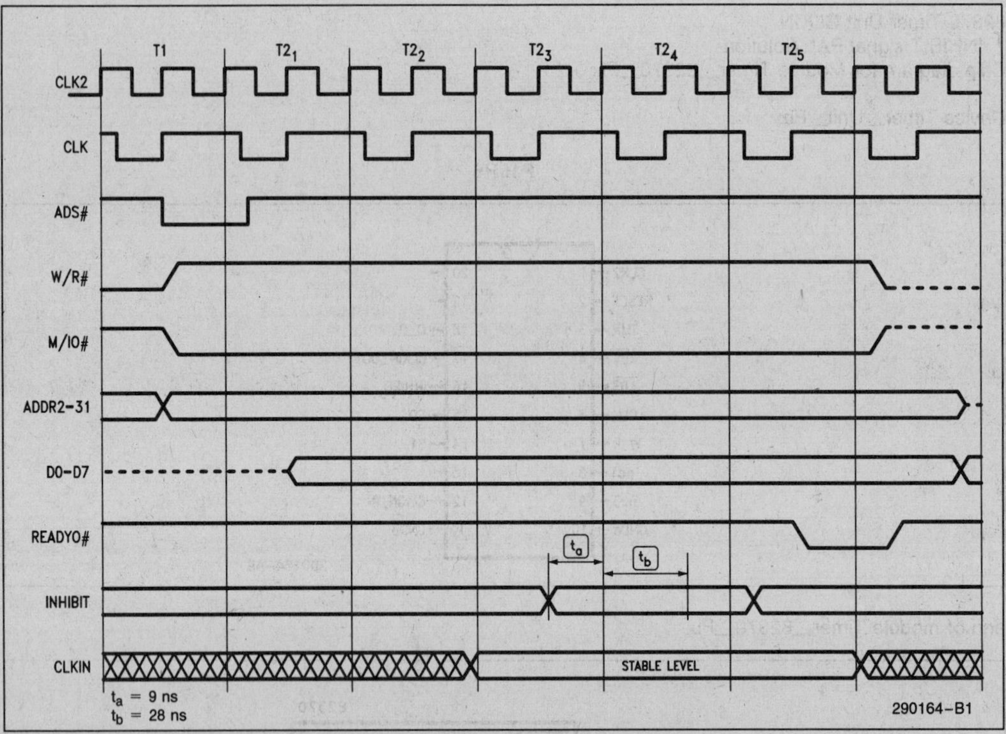

T1
$T2_1$
$T2_2$
$T2_3$
$T2_4$
$T2_5$
CLK2
CLK
ADS#
W/R#
M/IO#
ADDR2-31
D0-D7
READYO#
INHIBIT
CLKIN
t_a
t_b
STABLE LEVEL
t_a = 9 ns
t_b = 28 ns
290164-B1

Figure C-3. 82370 Timer Unit Write Cycle

[INHIBIT, S1, S0]
RDY.CLK
000
RDY#.CLK
011
ADS#.CLK
TMR.CLK
CLK
001
111
TMR.CLK
(INHIBIT)
CLK
010
110
CLK
(INHIBIT)
290164-B2

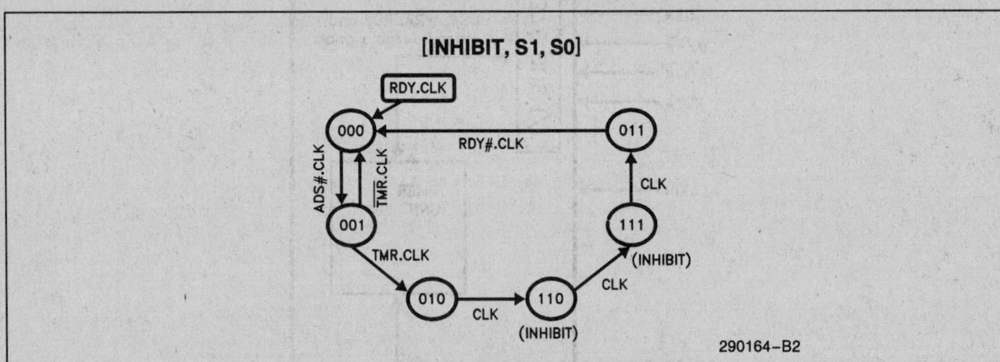

Figure C-4. State Diagram for Inhibit Signal

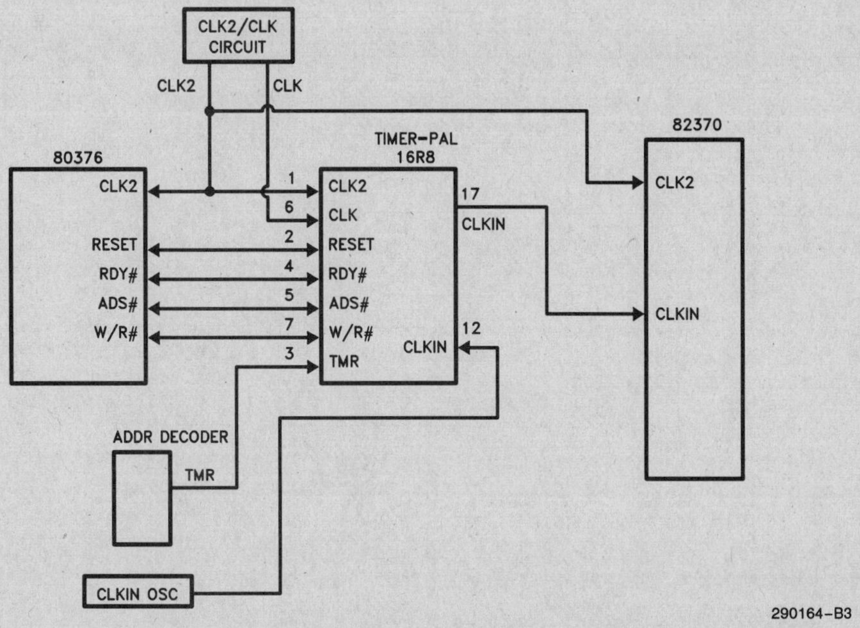

290164–B3

NOTE:
This solution does not support pipelined 82370 SLAVE Cycles.

Figure C-5. System with 82370 Timer Unit "INHIBIT" Circuitry

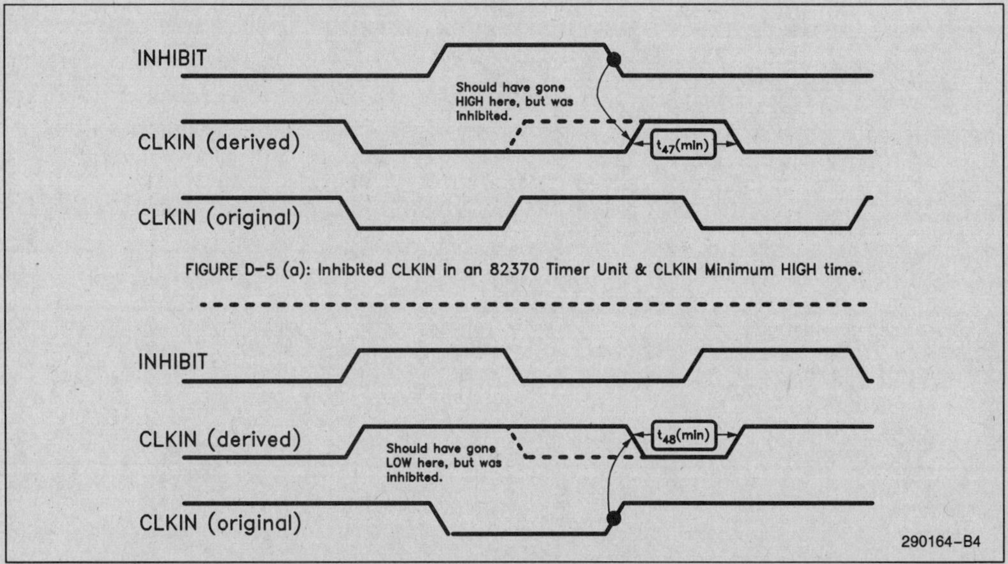

Figure C-6. Inhibited CLKIN in an 82370 Timer Unit and CLKIN Minimum LOW Time

80286 Microprocessor

5

80C286
HIGH PERFORMANCE CHMOS MICROPROCESSOR WITH MEMORY MANAGEMENT AND PROTECTION

- **High Speed CHMOS III Technology**
- **Pin for Pin, Clock for Clock, and Functionally Compatible with the HMOS 80286**
  (See 80286 Data Sheet, Order #210253)
- **Stop Clock Capability**
  — Uses Less Power (see I_{CCS} Specification)
- **12.5 MHz Clock Rate**
- **Available in a Variety of Packages:**
  — 68 Pin PLCC (Plastic Leaded Chip Carrier)
  — 68 Pin PGA (Pin Grid Array)
  (See Packaging Spec., Order #231369)

INTRODUCTION

The 80C286 is an advanced 16 bit CHMOS III microprocessor designed for multi-user and multi-tasking applications that require low power and high performance. The 80C286 is fully compatible with its predecessor the HMOS 80286 and object-code compatible with the 8086 and 80386 family of products. In addition, the 80C286 has a power down mode which uses less power, making it ideal for mobile applications. The 80C286 has built-in memory protection that maintains a four level protection mechanism for task isolation, a hardware task switching facility and memory management capabilities that map 2^{30} bytes (one gigabyte) of virtual address space per task (per user) into 2^{24} bytes (16 megabytes) of physical memory.

The 80C286 is upward compatible with 8086 and 8088 software. Using 8086 real address mode, the 80C286 is object code compatible with existing 8086, 8088 software. In protected virtual address mode, the 80C286 is source code compatible with 8086, 8088 software which may require upgrading to use virtual addresses supported by the 80C286's integrated memory management and protection mechanism. Both modes operate at full 80C286 performance and execute a superset of the 8086 and 8088 instructions.

The 80C286 provides special operations to support the efficient implementation and execution of operating systems. For example, one instruction can end execution of one task, save its state, switch to a new task, load its state, and start execution of the new task. The 80C286 also supports virtual memory systems by providing a segment-not-present exception and restartable instructions.

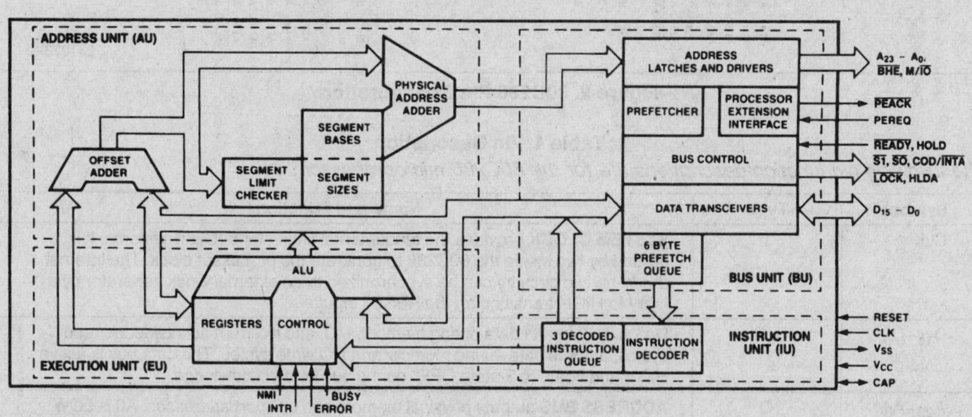

Figure 1. 80C286 Internal Block Diagram

October 1990
Order Number: 231923-003

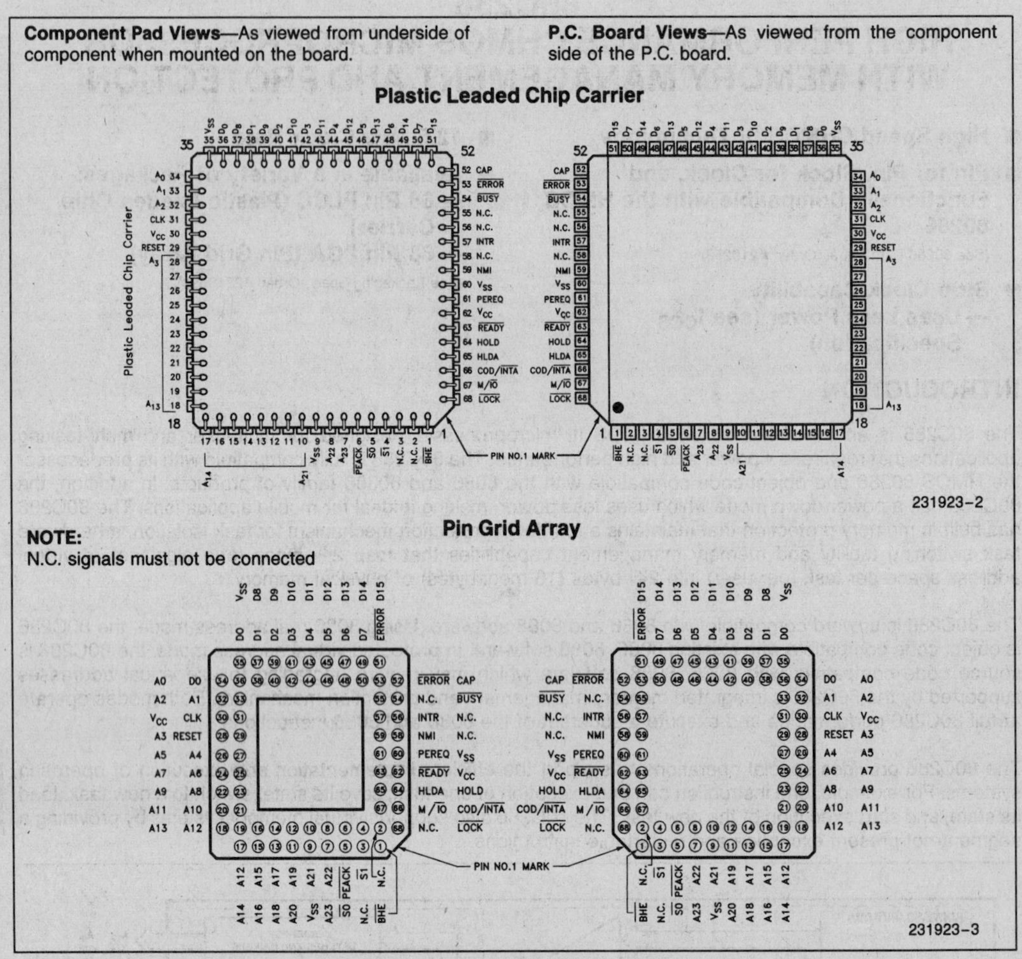

Component Pad Views—As viewed from underside of component when mounted on the board.
P.C. Board Views—As viewed from the component side of the P.C. board.
Plastic Leaded Chip Carrier
Plastic Leaded Chip Carrier
PIN NO.1 MARK
231923-2
NOTE:
N.C. signals must not be connected
Pin Grid Array
PIN NO.1 MARK
231923-3

Figure 2. 80C286 Pin Configuration

Table 1. Pin Description

The following pin function descriptions are for the 80C286 microprocessor:

Symbol	Type	Name and Function
CLK	I	**SYSTEM CLOCK** provides the fundamental timing for 80C286 systems. It is divided by two inside the 80C286 to generate the processor clock. The internal divide-by-two circuitry can be synchronized to an external clock generator by a LOW to HIGH transition on the RESET input.
$D_{15}-D_0$	I/O	**DATA BUS** inputs data during memory, I/O, and interrupt acknowledge read cycles; outputs data during memory and I/O write cycles. The data bus is active HIGH and floats to 3-state OFF* during bus hold acknowledge.
$A_{23}-A_0$	O	**ADDRESS BUS** outputs physical memory and I/O port addresses. A0 is LOW when data is to be transferred on pins D_{7-0}. $A_{23}-A_{16}$ are LOW during I/O transfers. The address bus is active HIGH and floats to 3-state OFF* during bus hold acknowledge.
$\overline{BHE}$	O	**BUS HIGH ENABLE** indicates transfer or data on the upper byte of the data bus. D_{15-8}. Eight-bit oriented devices assigned to the upper byte of the data bus would normally use $\overline{BHE}$ to condition chip select functions. $\overline{BHE}$ is active LOW and floats to 3-state OFF* during bus hold acknowledge.

*See bus hold circuitry section.

Table I. Pin Description (Continued)

Symbol	Type	Name and Function
$\overline{BHE}$ (Continued)		**$\overline{BHE}$ and A0 Encodings**

$\overline{BHE}$ Value	A0 Value	Function
0	0	Word transfer
0	1	Transfer on upper half of data bus ($D_{15}-D_8$)
1	0	Byte transfer on lower half of data bus (D_7-D_0)
1	1	Will never occur

Symbol	Type	Name and Function
$\overline{S1}$, $\overline{S0}$	O	**BUS CYCLE STATUS** indicates initiation of a bus cycle and, along with M/$\overline{IO}$ and COD/$\overline{INTA}$, defines the type of bus cycle. The bus is in a T_s state whenever one or both are LOW, $\overline{S1}$ and $\overline{S0}$ are active LOW and float to 3-state OFF* during bus hold acknowledge.

80C286 Bus Cycle Status Definition

COD/$\overline{INTA}$	M/$\overline{IO}$	$\overline{S1}$	$\overline{S0}$	Bus Cycle Initiated
0 (LOW)	0	0	0	Interrupt acknowledge
0	0	0	1	Will not occur
0	0	1	0	Will not occur
0	0	1	1	None; not a status cycle
0	1	0	0	IF A1 = 1 then halt; else shutdown
0	1	0	1	Memory data read
0	1	1	0	Memory data write
0	1	1	1	None; not a status cycle
1 (HIGH)	0	0	0	Will not occur
1	0	0	1	I/O read
1	0	1	0	I/O write
1	0	1	1	None; not a status cycle
1	1	0	0	Will not occur
1	1	0	1	Memory instruction read
1	1	1	0	Will not occur
1	1	1	1	None; not a status cycle

Symbol	Type	Name and Function
M/$\overline{IO}$	O	**MEMORY I/O SELECT** distinguishes memory access from I/O access. If HIGH during T_s, a memory cycle or a halt/shutdown cycle is in progress. If LOW, an I/O cycle or an interrupt acknowledge cycle is in progress. M/$\overline{IO}$ floats to 3-state OFF* during bus hold acknowledge.
COD/$\overline{INTA}$	O	**CODE/INTERRUPT ACKNOWLEDGE** distinguishes instruction fetch cycles from memory data read cycles. Also distinguishes interrupt acknowledge cycles from I/O cycles. COD/$\overline{INTA}$ floats to 3-state OFF* during bus hold acknowledge. Its timing is the same as M/$\overline{IO}$.
$\overline{LOCK}$	O	**BUS LOCK** indicates that other system bus masters are not to gain control of the system bus for the current and the following bus cycle. The $\overline{LOCK}$ signal may be activated explicitly by the "LOCK" instruction prefix or automatically by 80C286 hardware during memory XCHG instructions, interrupt acknowledge, or descriptor table access. $\overline{LOCK}$ is active LOW and floats to 3-state OFF* during bus hold acknowledge.
$\overline{READY}$	I	**BUS READY** terminates a bus cycle. Bus cycles are extended without limit until terminated by $\overline{READY}$ LOW. $\overline{READY}$ is an active LOW synchronous input requiring setup and hold times relative to the system clock be met for correct operation. $\overline{READY}$ is ignored during bus hold acknowledge.
HOLD HLDA	I O	**BUS HOLD REQUEST AND HOLD ACKNOWLEDGE** control ownership of the 80C286 local bus. The HOLD input allows another local bus master to request control of the local bus. When control is granted, the 80C286 will float its bus drivers to 3-state OFF* and then activate HLDA, thus entering the bus hold acknowledge condition. The local bus will remain granted to the requesting master until HOLD becomes inactive which results in the 80C286 deactivating HLDA and regaining control of the local bus. This terminates the bus hold acknowledge condition. HOLD may be asynchronous to the system clock. These signals are active HIGH.
INTR	I	**INTERRUPT REQUEST** requests the 80C286 to suspend its current program execution and service a pending external request. Interrupt requests are masked whenever the interrupt enable bit in the flag word is cleared. When the 80C286 responds to an interrupt request, it performs two interrupt acknowledge bus cycles to read an 8-bit interrupt vector that identifies the source of the interrupt. To assure program interruption, INTR must remain active until the first interrupt acknowledge cycle is completed. INTR is sampled at the beginning of each processor cycle and must be active HIGH at least two processor cycles before the current instruction ends in order to interrupt before the next instruction. INTR is level sensitive, active HIGH, and may be asynchronous to the system clock.

*See bus hold circuitry section.

Table 1. Pin Description (Continued)

<table>
<tr><th>Symbol</th><th>Type</th><th colspan="2">Name and Function</th></tr>
<tr><td>NMI</td><td>I</td><td colspan="2">NON-MASKABLE INTERRUPT REQUEST interrupts the 80C286 with an internally supplied vector value of 2. No interrupt acknowledge cycles are performed. The interrupt enable bit in the 80C286 flag word does not affect this input. The NMI input is active HIGH, may be asynchronous to the system clock, and is edge triggered after internal synchronization. For proper recognition, the input must have been previously LOW for at least four system clock cycles and remain HIGH for at least four system clock cycles.</td></tr>
<tr><td>PEREQ
$\overline{PEACK}$</td><td>I
O</td><td colspan="2">PROCESSOR EXTENSION OPERAND REQUEST AND ACKNOWLEDGE extend the memory management and protection capabilities of the 80C286 to processor extensions. The PEREQ input requests the 80C286 to perform a data operand transfer for a processor extension. The $\overline{PEACK}$ output signals the processor extension when the requested operand is being transferred. PEREQ is active HIGH and floats to 3-state OFF* during bus hold acknowledge. $\overline{PEACK}$ may be asynchronous to the system clock. $\overline{PEACK}$ is active LOW.</td></tr>
<tr><td>$\overline{BUSY}$
$\overline{ERROR}$</td><td>I
I</td><td colspan="2">PROCESSOR EXTENSION BUSY AND ERROR indicate the operating condition of a processor extension to the 80C286. An active $\overline{BUSY}$ input stops 80C286 program execution on WAIT and some ESC instructions until $\overline{BUSY}$ becomes inactive (HIGH). The 80C286 may be interrupted while waiting for $\overline{BUSY}$ to become inactive. An active $\overline{ERROR}$ input causes the 80C286 to perform a processor extension interrupt when executing WAIT or some ESC instructions. These inputs are active LOW and may be asynchronous to the system clock. These inputs have internal pull-up resistors.</td></tr>
<tr><td rowspan="5">RESET</td><td rowspan="5">I</td><td colspan="2">SYSTEM RESET clears the internal logic of the 80C286 and is active HIGH. The 80C286 may be reinitialized at any time with a LOW to HIGH transition on RESET which remains active for more than 16 system clock cycles. During RESET active, the output pins of the 80C286 enter the state shown below:</td></tr>
<tr><th colspan="2">80C286 Pin State During Reset</th></tr>
<tr><th>Pin Value</th><th>Pin Names</th></tr>
<tr><td>1 (HIGH)
0 (LOW)
3-state OFF*</td><td>$\overline{S0}$, $\overline{S1}$, $\overline{PEACK}$, A23–A0, $\overline{BHE}$, $\overline{LOCK}$
M/$\overline{IO}$, COD/$\overline{INTA}$, HLDA (Note 1)
D_{15}–D_0</td></tr>
<tr><td colspan="2">Operation of the 80C286 begins after a HIGH to LOW transition on RESET. The HIGH to LOW transition of RESET must be synchronous to the system clock. Approximately 38 CLK cycles from the trailing edge of RESET are required by the 80C286 for internal initialization before the first bus cycle, to fetch code from the power-on execution address, occurs.
A LOW to HIGH transition of RESET synchronous to the system clock will end a processor cycle at the second HIGH to LOW transition of the system clock. The LOW to HIGH transition of RESET may be asynchronous to the system clock; however, in this case it cannot be predetermined which phase of the processor clock will occur during the next system clock period. Synchronous LOW to HIGH transitions of RESET are required only for systems where the processor clock must be phase synchronous to another clock.</td></tr>
<tr><td>V_{SS}</td><td>I</td><td colspan="2">SYSTEM GROUND: 0 Volts.</td></tr>
<tr><td>V_{CC}</td><td>I</td><td colspan="2">SYSTEM POWER: +5 Volt Power Supply.</td></tr>
<tr><td>CAP</td><td>I</td><td colspan="2">SUBSTRATE FILTER CAPACITOR: a 0.047 μF ± 20% 12V capacitor can be connected between this pin and ground for compatibility with the HMOS 80286. For systems using only an 80C286, this pin can be left floating.</td></tr>
</table>

*See bus hold circuitry section.

NOTE:
1. HLDA is only Low if HOLD is inactive (Low).

FUNCTIONAL DESCRIPTION

Introduction

The 80C286 is an advanced, high-performance microprocessor with specially optimized capabilities for multiple user and multi-tasking systems. Depending on the application, a 12 MHz 80C286's performance is up to ten times faster than the standard 5 MHz 8086's, while providing complete upward software compatibility with Intel's 8086, 88, and 186 family of CPU's.

The 80C286 operates in two modes: 8086 real address mode and protected virtual address mode. Both modes execute a superset of the 8086 and 88 instruction set.

In 8086 real address mode programs use real addresses with up to one megabyte of address space. Programs use virtual addresses in protected virtual address mode, also called protected mode. In protected mode, the 80C286 CPU automatically maps 1 gigabyte of virtual addresses per task into a 16 megabyte real address space. This mode also provides memory protection to isolate the operating system and ensure privacy of each tasks' programs and data. Both modes provide the same base instruction set, registers, and addressing modes.

The following Functional Description describes first, the base 80C286 architecture common to both modes, second, 8086 real address mode, and third, protected mode.

80C286 BASE ARCHITECTURE

The 8086, 88, 186, and 286 CPU family all contain the same basic set of registers, instructions, and addressing modes. The 80C286 processor is upward compatible with the 8086, 8088, and 80186 CPU's and fully compatible with the HMOS 80286.

Register Set

The 80C286 base architecture has fifteen registers as shown in Figure 3. These registers are grouped into the following four categories:

General Registers: Eight 16-bit general purpose registers used to contain arithmetic and logical operands. Four of these (AX, BX, CX, and DX) can be used either in their entirety as 16-bit words or split into pairs of separate 8-bit registers.

Segment Registers: Four 16-bit special purpose registers select, at any given time, the segments of memory that are immediately addressable for code, stack, and data. (For usage, refer to Memory Organization.)

Base and Index Registers: Four of the general purpose registers may also be used to determine offset addresses of operands in memory. These registers may contain base addresses or indexes to particular locations within a segment. The addressing mode determines the specific registers used for operand address calculations.

Status and Control Registers: The 3 16-bit special purpose registers in figure 3A record or control certain aspects of the 80C286 processor state including the Instruction Pointer, which contains the offset address of the next sequential instruction to be executed.

5

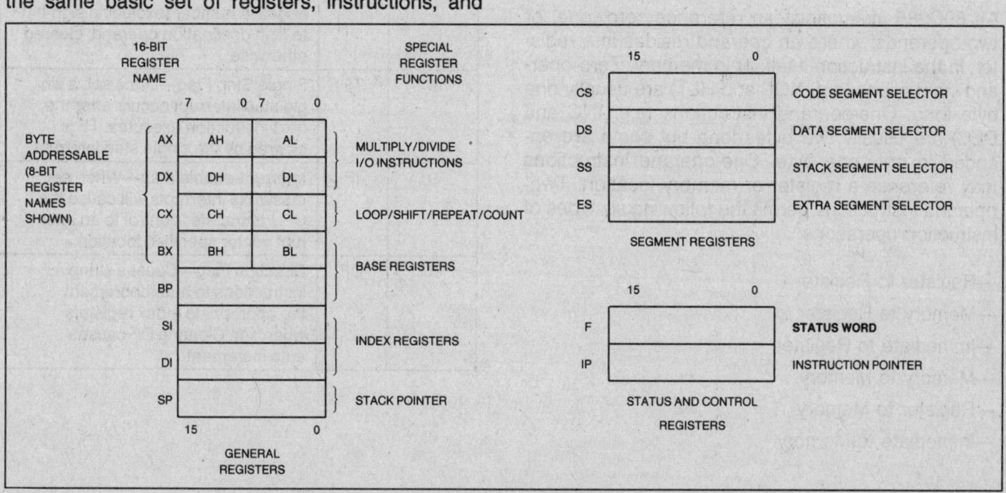

Figure 3. Register Set

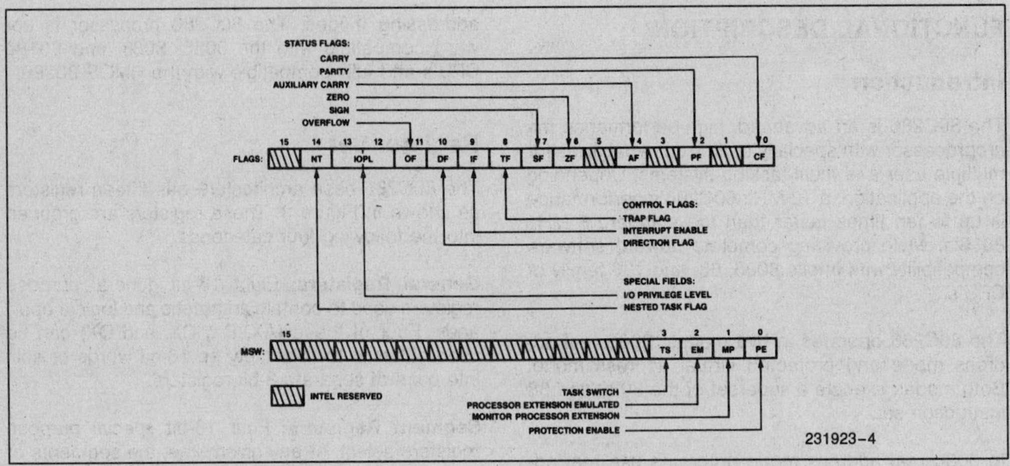

Figure 3a. Status and Control Register Bit Functions

Flags Word Description

The Flags word (Flags) records specific characteristics of the result of logical and arithmetic instructions (bits 0, 2, 4, 6, 7, and 11) and controls the operation of the 80C286 within a given operating mode (bits 8 and 9). Flags is a 16-bit register. The function of the flag bits is given in Table 2.

Table 2. Flags Word Bit Functions

Bit Position	Name	Function
0	CF	Carry Flag—Set on high-order bit carry or borrow; cleared otherwise
2	PF	Parity Flag—Set if low-order 8 bits of result contain an even number of 1-bits; cleared otherwise
4	AF	Set on carry from or borrow to the low order four bits of AL; cleared otherwise
6	ZF	Zero Flag—Set if result is zero; cleared otherwise
7	SF	Sign Flag—Set equal to high-order bit of result (0 if positive, 1 if negative)
11	OF	Overflow Flag—Set if result is a too-large positive number or a too-small negative number (excluding sign-bit) to fit in destination operand; cleared otherwise
8	TF	Single Step Flag—Once set, a single step interrupt occurs after the next instruction executes. TF is cleared by the single step interrupt.
9	IF	Interrupt-enable Flag—When set, maskable interrupts will cause the CPU to transfer control to an interrupt vector specified location.
10	DF	Direction Flag—Causes string instructions to auto decrement the appropriate index registers when set. Clearing DF causes auto increment.

Instruction Set

The instruction set is divided into seven categories: data transfer, arithmetic, shift/rotate/logical, string manipulation, control transfer, high level instructions, and processor control. These categories are summarized in Figure 4.

An 80C286 instruction can reference zero, one, or two operands; where an operand resides in a register, in the instruction itself, or in memory. Zero-operand instructions (e.g. NOP and HLT) are usually one byte long. One-operand instructions (e.g. INC and DEC) are usually two bytes long but some are encoded in only one byte. One-operand instructions may reference a register or memory location. Two-operand instructions permit the following six types of instruction operations:

—Register to Register

—Memory to Register

—Immediate to Register

—Memory to Memory

—Register to Memory

—Immediate to Memory

Two-operand instructions (e.g. MOV and ADD) are usually three to six bytes long. Memory to memory operations are provided by a special class of string instructions requiring one to three bytes. For detailed instruction formats and encodings refer to the instruction set summary at the end of this document.

For detailed operation and usage of each instruction, see Appendix B of the 80286/80287 Programmer's Reference Manual (Order No. 210498).

GENERAL PURPOSE	
MOV	Move byte or word
PUSH	Push word onto stack
POP	Pop word off stack
PUSHA	Push all registers on stack
POPA	Pop all registers from stack
XCHG	Exchange byte or word
XLAT	Translate byte
INPUT/OUTPUT	
IN	Input byte or word
OUT	Output byte or word
ADDRESS OBJECT	
LEA	Load effective address
LDS	Load pointer using DS
LES	Load pointer using ES
FLAG TRANSFER	
LAHF	Load AH register from flags
SAHF	Store AH register in flags
PUSHF	Push flags onto stack
POPF	Pop flags off stack

Figure 4a. Data Transfer Instructions

MOVS	Move byte or word string
INS	Input bytes or word string
OUTS	Output bytes or word string
CMPS	Compare byte or word string
SCAS	Scan byte or word string
LODS	Load byte or word string
STOS	Store byte or word string
REP	Repeat
REPE/REPZ	Repeat while equal/zero
REPNE/REPNZ	Repeat while not equal/not zero

Figure 4c. String Instructions

ADDITION	
ADD	Add byte or word
ADC	Add byte or word with carry
INC	Increment byte or word by 1
AAA	ASCII adjust for addition
DAA	Decimal adjust for addition
SUBTRACTION	
SUB	Subtract byte or word
SBB	Subtract byte or word with borrow
DEC	Decrement byte or word by 1
NEG	Negate byte or word
CMP	Compare byte or word
AAS	ASCII adjust for subtraction
DAS	Decimal adjust for subtraction
MULTIPLICATION	
MUL	Multiple byte or word unsigned
IMUL	Integer multiply byte or word
AAM	ASCII adjust for multiply
DIVISION	
DIV	Divide byte or word unsigned
IDIV	Integer divide byte or word
AAD	ASCII adjust for division
CBW	Convert byte to word
CWD	Convert word to doubleword

Figure 4b. Arithmetic Instructions

5

LOGICALS	
NOT	"Not" byte or word
AND	"And" byte or word
OR	"Inclusive or" byte or word
XOR	"Exclusive or" byte or word
TEST	"Test" byte or word
SHIFTS	
SHL/SAL	Shift logical/arithmetic left byte or word
SHR	Shift logical right byte or word
SAR	Shift arithmetic right byte or word
ROTATES	
ROL	Rotate left byte or word
ROR	Rotate right byte or word
RCL	Rotate through carry left byte or word
RCR	Rotate through carry right byte or word

Figure 4d. Shift/Rotate Logical Instructions

CONDITIONAL TRANSFERS	
JA/JNBE	Jump if above/not below nor equal
JAE/JNB	Jump if above or equal/not below
JB/JNAE	Jump if below/not above nor equal
JBE/JNA	Jump if below or equal/not above
JC	Jump if carry
JE/JZ	Jump if equal/zero
JG/JNLE	Jump if greater/not less nor equal
JGE/JNL	Jump if greater or equal/not less
JL/JNGE	Jump if less/not greater nor equal
JLE/JNG	Jump if less or equal/not greater
JNC	Jump if not carry
JNE/JNZ	Jump if not equal/not zero
JNO	Jump if not overflow
JNP/JPO	Jump if not parity/parity odd
JNS	Jump if not sign
JO	Jump if overflow
JP/JPE	Jump if parity/parity even
JS	Jump if sign

UNCONDITIONAL TRANSFERS	
CALL	Call procedure
RET	Return from procedure
JMP	Jump
ITERATION CONTROLS	
LOOP	Loop
LOOPE/LOOPZ	Loop if equal/zero
LOOPNE/LOOPNZ	Loop if not equal/not zero
JCXZ	Jump if register CX = 0
INTERRUPTS	
INT	Interrupt
INTO	Interrupt if overflow
IRET	Interrupt return

Figure 4e. Program Transfer Instructions

FLAG OPERATIONS	
STC	Set carry flag
CLC	Clear carry flag
CMC	Complement carry flag
STD	Set direction flag
CLD	Clear direction flag
STI	Set interrupt enable flag
CLI	Clear interrupt enable flag
EXTERNAL SYNCHRONIZATION	
HLT	Halt until interrupt or reset
WAIT	Wait for $\overline{BUSY}$ not active
ESC	Escape to extension processor
LOCK	Lock bus during next instruction
NO OPERATION	
NOP	No operation
EXECUTION ENVIRONMENT CONTROL	
LMSW	Load machine status word
SMSW	Store machine status word

Figure 4f. Processor Control Instructions

ENTER	Format stack for procedure entry
LEAVE	Restore stack for procedure exit
BOUND	Detects values outside prescribed range

Figure 4g. High Level Instructions

Memory Organization

Memory is organized as sets of variable length segments. Each segment is a linear contiguous sequence of up to 64K (2^{16}) 8-bit bytes. Memory is addressed using a two component address (a pointer) that consists of a 16-bit segment selector, and a 16-bit offset. The segment selector indicates the desired segment in memory. The offset component indicates the desired byte address within the segment.

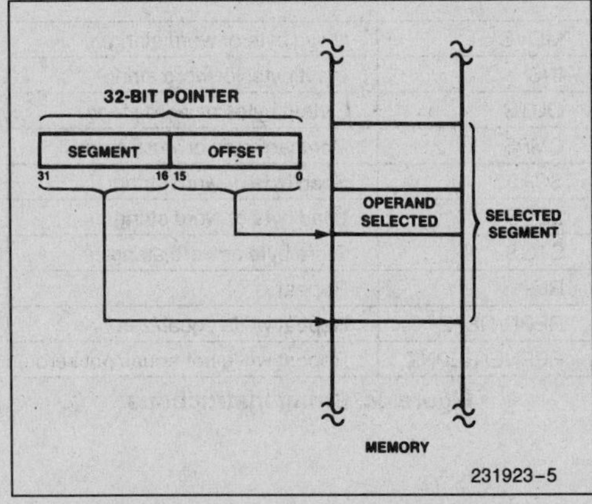

Figure 5. Two Component Address

Table 3. Segment Register Selection Rules

Memory Reference Needed	Segment Register Used	Implicit Segment Selection Rule
Instructions	Code (CS)	Automatic with instruction prefetch
Stack	Stack (SS)	All stack pushes and pops. Any memory reference which uses BP as a base register.
Local Data	Data (DS)	All data references except when relative to stack or string destination
External (Global) Data	Extra (ES)	Alternate data segment and destination of string operation

All instructions that address operands in memory must specify the segment and the offset. For speed and compact instruction encoding, segment selectors are usually stored in the high speed segment registers. An instruction need specify only the desired segment register and an offset in order to address a memory operand.

Most instructions need not explicitly specify which segment register is used. The correct segment register is automatically chosen according to the rules of Table 3. These rules follow the way programs are written (see Figure 6) as independent modules that require areas for code and data, a stack, and access to external data areas.

Special segment override instruction prefixes allow the implicit segment register selection rules to be overridden for special cases. The stack, data, and extra segments may coincide for simple programs. To access operands not residing in one of the four immediately available segments, a full 32-bit pointer or a new segment selector must be loaded.

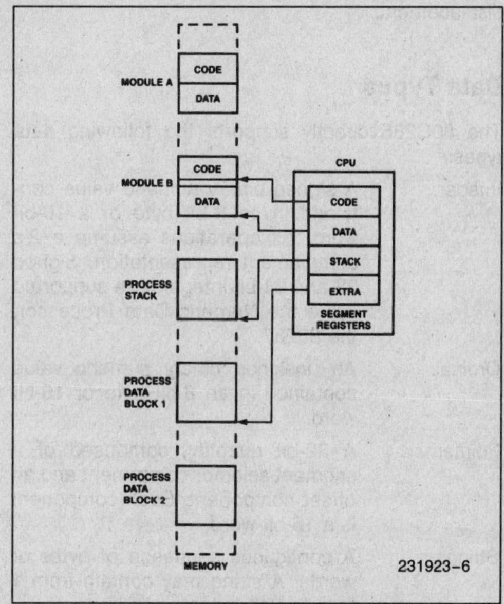

Figure 6. Segmented Memory Helps Structure Software

Addressing Modes

The 80C286 provides a total of eight addressing modes for instructions to specify operands. Two addressing modes are provided for instructions that operate on register or immediate operands:

Register Operand Mode: The operand is located in one of the 8 or 16-bit general registers.

Immediate Operand Mode: The operand is included in the instruction.

Six modes are provided to specify the location of an operand in a memory segment. A memory operand address consists of two 16-bit components: segment selector and offset. The segment selector is supplied by a segment register either implicitly chosen by the addressing mode or explicitly chosen by a segment override prefix. The offset is calculated by summing any combination of the following three address elements:

the **displacement** (an 8 or 16-bit immediate value contained in the instruction)

the **base** (contents of either the BX or BP base registers)

the **index** (contents of either the SI or DI index registers)

Any carry out from the 16-bit addition is ignored. Eight-bit displacements are sign extended to 16-bit values.

Combinations of these three address elements define the six memory addressing modes, described below.

Direct Mode: The operand's offset is contained in the instruction as an 8 or 16-bit displacement element.

Register Indirect Mode: The operand's offset is in one of the registers SI, DI, BX, or BP.

Based Mode: The operand's offset is the sum of an 8 or 16-bit displacement and the contents of a base register (BX or BP).

5

Indexed Mode: The operand's offset is the sum of an 8 or 16-bit displacement and the contents of an index register (SI or DI).

Based Indexed Mode: The operand's offset is the sum of the contents of a base register and an index register.

Based Indexed Mode with Displacement: The operand's offset is the sum of a base register's contents, an index register's contents, and an 8 or 16-bit displacement.

Data Types

The 80C286 directly supports the following data types:

- Integer: A signed binary numeric value contained in an 8-bit byte or a 16-bit word. All operations assume a 2's complement representation. Signed 32 and 64-bit integers are supported using the Numeric Data Processor, the 80287.
- Ordinal: An unsigned binary numeric value contained in an 8-bit byte or 16-bit word.
- Pointer: A 32-bit quantity, composed of a segment selector component and an offset component. Each component is a 16-bit word.
- String: A contiguous sequence of bytes or words. A string may contain from 1 byte to 64K bytes.
- ASCII: A byte representation of alphanumeric and control characters using the ASCII standard of character representation.
- BCD: A byte (unpacked) representation of the decimal digits 0–9.
- Packed BCD: A byte (packed) representation of two decimal digits 0–9 storing one digit in each nibble of the byte.
- Floating Point: A signed 32, 64, or 80-bit real number representation. (Floating point operands are supported using the 80287 Numeric Processor).

Figure 7 graphically represents the data types supported by the 80C286.

I/O Space

The I/O space consists of 64K 8-bit or 32K 16-bit ports. I/O instructions address the I/O space with either an 8-bit port address, specified in the instruction, or a 16-bit port address in the DX register. 8-bit port addresses are zero extended such that A_{15}–A_8 are LOW. I/O port addresses 00F8(H) through 00FF(H) are reserved.

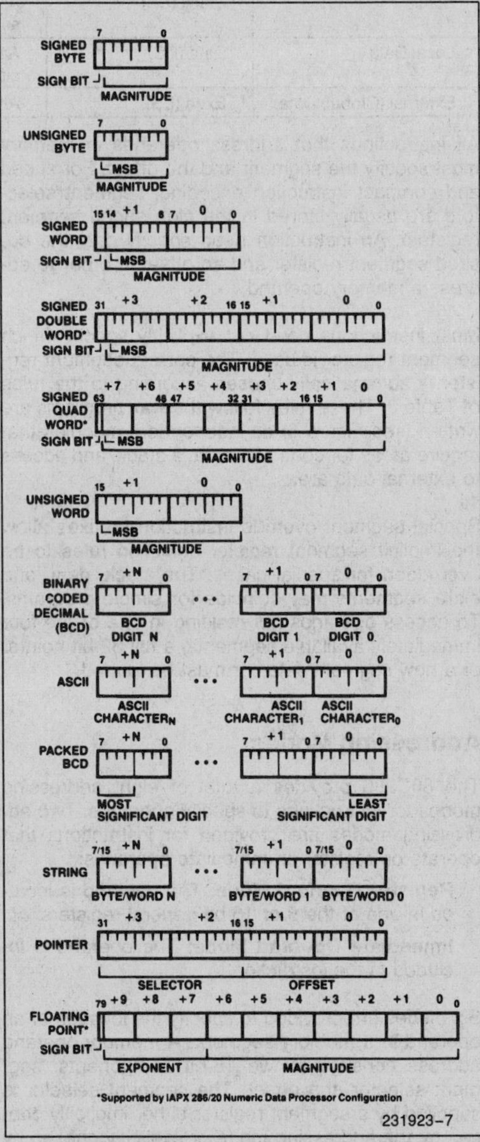

Figure 7. 80C286 Supported Data Types

Table 4. Interrupt Vector Assignments

Function	Interrupt Number	Related Instructions	Does Return Address Point to Instruction Causing Exception?
Divide error exception	0	DIV, IDIV	Yes
Single step interrupt	1	All	
NMI interrupt	2	INT 2 or NMI pin	
Breakpoint interrupt	3	INT 3	
INTO detected overflow exception	4	INTO	No
BOUND range exceeded exception	5	BOUND	Yes
Invalid opcode exception	6	Any undefined opcode	Yes
Processor extension not available exception	7	ESC or WAIT	Yes
Intel reserved–do not use	8-15		
Processor extension error interrupt	16	ESC or WAIT	
Intel reserved–do not use	17-31		
User defined	32-255		

Interrupts

An interrupt transfers execution to a new program location. The old program address (CS:IP) and machine state (Flags) are saved on the stack to allow resumption of the interrupted program. Interrupts fall into three classes: hardware initiated, INT instructions, and instruction exceptions. Hardware initiated interrupts occur in response to an external input and are classified as non-maskable or maskable. Programs may cause an interrupt with an INT instruction. Instruction exceptions occur when an unusual condition, which prevents further instruction processing, is detected while attempting to execute an instruction. The return address from an exception will always point at the instruction causing the exception and include any leading instruction prefixes.

A table containing up to 256 pointers defines the proper interrupt service routine for each interrupt. Interrupts 0–31, some of which are used for instruction exceptions, are reserved. For each interrupt, an 8-bit vector must be supplied to the 80C286 which identifies the appropriate table entry. Exceptions supply the interrupt vector internally. INT instructions contain or imply the vector and allow access to all 256 interrupts. Maskable hardware initiated interrupts supply the 8-bit vector to the CPU during an interrupt acknowledge bus sequence. Non-maskable hardware interrupts use a predefined internally supplied vector.

MASKABLE INTERRUPT (INTR)

The 80C286 provides a maskable hardware interrupt request pin, INTR. Software enables this input by setting the interrupt flag bit (IF) in the flag word. All 224 user-defined interrupt sources can share this input, yet they can retain separate interrupt handlers. An 8-bit vector read by the CPU during the interrupt acknowledge sequence (discussed in System Interface section) identifies the source of the interrupt.

Further maskable interrupts are disabled while servicing an interrupt by resetting the IF but as part of the response to an interrupt or exception. The saved flag word will reflect the enable status of the processor prior to the interrupt. Until the flag word is restored to the flag register, the interrupt flag will be zero unless specifically set. The interrupt return instruction includes restoring the flag word, thereby restoring the original status of IF.

NON-MASKABLE INTERRUPT REQUEST (NMI)

A non-maskable interrupt input (NMI) is also provided. NMI has higher priority than INTR. A typical use of NMI would be to activate a power failure routine. The activation of this input causes an interrupt with an internally supplied vector value of 2. No external interrupt acknowledge sequence is performed.

While executing the NMI servicing procedure, the 80C286 will service neither further NMI requests, INTR requests, nor the processor extension segment overrun interrupt until an interrupt return (IRET) instruction is executed or the CPU is reset. If NMI occurs while currently servicing an NMI, its presence will be saved for servicing after executing the first IRET instruction. IF is cleared at the beginning of an NMI interrupt to inhibit INTR interrupts.

SINGLE STEP INTERRUPT

The 80C286 has an internal interrupt that allows programs to execute one instruction at a time. It is called the single step interrupt and is controlled by the single step flag bit (TF) in the flag word. Once this bit is set, an internal single step interrupt will occur after the next instruction has been executed. The interrupt clears the TF bit and uses an internally supplied vector of 1. The IRET instruction is used to set the TF bit and transfer control to the next instruction to be single stepped.

Interrupt Priorities

When simultaneous interrupt requests occur, they are processed in a fixed order as shown in Table 5. Interrupt processing involves saving the flags, return address, and setting CS:IP to point at the first instruction of the interrupt handler. If other interrupts remain enabled they are processed before the first instruction of the current interrupt handler is executed. The last interrupt processed is therefore the first one serviced.

Table 5. Interrupt Processing Order

Order	Interrupt
1	Instruction exception
2	Single step
3	NMI
4	Processor extension segment overrun
5	INTR
6	INT instruction

Initialization and Processor Reset

Processor initialization or start up is accomplished by driving the RESET input pin HIGH. RESET forces the 80C286 to terminate all execution and local bus activity. No instruction or bus activity will occur as long as RESET is active. After RESET becomes inactive and an internal processing interval elapses, the 80C286 begins execution in real address mode with the instruction at physical location FFFFF0(H). RESET also sets some registers to predefined values as shown in Table 6.

Table 6. 80C286 Initial Register State after RESET

Register	Value
Flag word	0002(H)
Machine Status Word	FFF0(H)
Instruction pointer	FFF0(H)
Code segment	F000(H)
Data segment	0000(H)
Extra segment	0000(H)
Stack segment	0000(H)

HOLD must not be active during the time from the leading edge of RESET to 34 CLKs after the trailing edge of RESET.

Machine Status Word Description

The machine status word (MSW) records when a task switch takes place and controls the operating mode of the 80C286. It is a 16-bit register of which the lower four bits are used. One bit places the CPU into protected mode, while the other three bits, as shown in Table 7, control the processor extension interface. After RESET, this register contains FFF0(H) which places the 80C286 in 8086 real address mode.

Table 7. MSW Bit Functions

Bit Position	Name	Function
0	PE	Protected mode enable places the 80C286 into protected mode and cannot be cleared except by RESET.
1	MP	Monitor processor extension allows WAIT instructions to cause a processor extension not present exception (number 7).
2	EM	Emulate processor extension causes a processor extension not present exception (number 7) on ESC instructions to allow emulating a processor extension.
3	TS	Task switched indicates the next instruction using a processor extension will cause exception 7, allowing software to test whether the current processor extension context belongs to the current task.

The LMSW and SMSW instructions can load and store the MSW in real address mode. The recommended use of TS, EM, and MP is shown in Table 8.

Table 8. Recommended MSW Encodings For Processor Extension Control

TS	MP	EM	Recommended Use	Instructions Causing Exception 7
0	0	0	Initial encoding after RESET. 80C286 operation is identical to 8086, 88.	None
0	0	1	No processor extension is available. Software will emulate its function.	ESC
1	0	1	No processor extension is available. Software will emulate its function. The current processor extension context may belong to another task.	ESC
0	1	0	A processor extension exists.	None
1	1	0	A processor extension exists. The current processor extension context may belong to another task. The Exception 7 on WAIT allows software to test for an error pending from a previous processor extension operation.	ESC or WAIT

Halt

The HLT instruction stops program execution and prevents the CPU from using the local bus until restarted. Either NMI, INTR with IF = 1, or RESET will force the 80C286 out of halt. If interrupted, the saved CS:IP will point to the next instruction after the HLT.

8086 REAL ADDRESS MODE

The 80C286 executes a fully upward-compatible superset of the 8086 instruction set in real address mode. In real address mode the 80C286 is object code compatible with 8086 and 8088 software. The real address mode architecture (registers and addressing modes) is exactly as described in the 80C286 Base Architecture section of this Functional Description.

Memory Size

Physical memory is a contiguous array of up to 1,048,576 bytes (one megabyte) addressed by pins A_0 through A_{19} and $\overline{BHE}$. A_{20} through A_{23} should be ignored.

Memory Addressing

In real address mode physical memory is a contiguous array of up to 1,048,576 bytes (one megabyte) addressed by pins A_0 through A_{19} and $\overline{BHE}$. Address bits A_{20}–A_{23} may not always be zero in real mode. A_{20}–A_{23} should not be used by the system while the 80C286 is operating in Real Mode.

The selector portion of a pointer is interpreted as the upper 16 bits of a 20-bit segment address. The lower four bits of the 20-bit segment address are always zero. Segment addresses, therefore, begin on multiples of 16 bytes. See Figure 8 for a graphic representation of address information.

All segments in real address mode are 64K bytes in size and may be read, written, or executed. An exception or interrupt can occur if data operands or instructions attempt to wrap around the end of a segment (e.g. a word with its low order byte at offset FFFF(H) and its high order byte at offset 0000(H). If, in real address mode, the information contained in a segment does not use the full 64K bytes, the unused end of the segment may be overlayed by another segment to reduce physical memory requirements.

Reserved Memory Locations

The 80C286 reserves two fixed areas of memory in real address mode (see Figure 9); system initialization area and interrupt table area. Locations from addresses FFFF0(H) through FFFFF(H) are reserved for system initialization. Initial execution begins at location FFFF0(H). Locations 00000(H) through 003FF(H) are reserved for interrupt vectors.

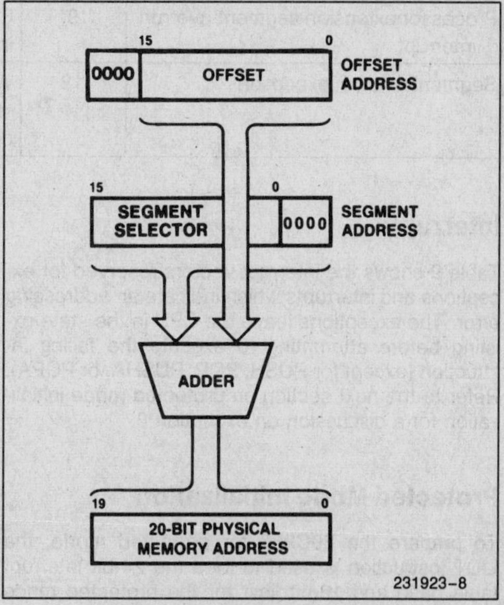

Figure 8. 8086 Real Address Mode Address Calculation

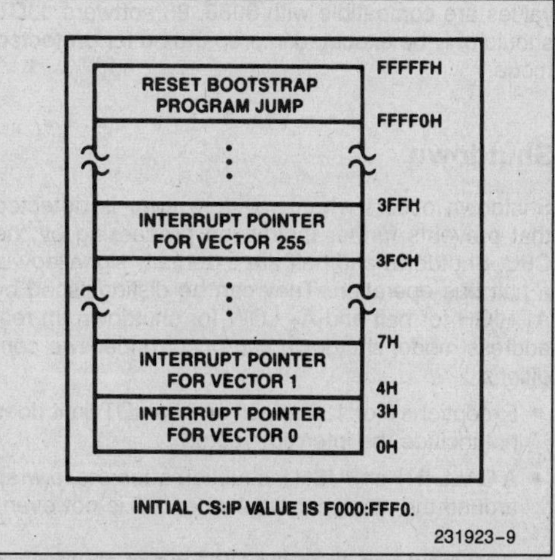

Figure 9. 8086 Real Address Mode Initially Reserved Memory Locations

5

Table 9. Real Address Mode Addressing Interrupts

Function	Interrupt Number	Related Instructions	Return Address Before Instruction?
Interrupt table limit too small exception	8	INT vector is not within table limit	Yes
Processor extension segment overrun interrupt	9	ESC with memory operand extending beyond offset FFFF(H)	No
Segment overrun exception	13	Word memory reference with offset = FFFF(H) or an attempt to execute past the end of a segment	Yes

Interrupts

Table 9 shows the interrupt vectors reserved for exceptions and interrupts which indicate an addressing error. The exceptions leave the CPU in the state existing before attempting to execute the failing instruction (except for PUSH, POP, PUSHA, or POPA). Refer to the next section on protected mode initialization for a discussion on exception 8.

Protected Mode Initialization

To prepare the 80C286 for protected mode, the LIDT instruction is used to load the 24-bit interrupt table base and 16-bit limit for the protected mode interrupt table. This instruction can also set a base and limit for the interrupt vector table in real address mode. After reset, the interrupt table base is initialized to 000000(H) and its size set to 03FF(H). These values are compatible with 8086, 88 software. LIDT should only be executed in preparation for protected mode.

Shutdown

Shutdown occurs when a severe error is detected that prevents further instruction processing by the CPU. Shutdown and halt are externally signalled via a halt bus operation. They can be distinguished by A_1 HIGH for halt and A_1 LOW for shutdown. In real address mode, shutdown can occur under two conditions:

- Exceptions 8 or 13 happen and the IDT limit does not include the interrupt vector.
- A CALL INT or PUSH instruction attempts to wrap around the stack segment when SP is not even.

An NMI input can bring the CPU out of shutdown if the IDT limit is at least 000F(H) and SP is greater than 0005(H), otherwise shutdown can only be exited via the RESET input.

PROTECTED VIRTUAL ADDRESS MODE

The 80C286 executes a fully upward-compatible superset of the 8086 instruction set in protected virtual address mode (protected mode). Protected mode also provides memory management and protection mechanisms and associated instructions.

The 80C286 enters protected virtual address mode from real address mode by setting the PE (Protection Enable) bit of the machine status word with the Load Machine Status Word (LMSW) instruction. Protected mode offers extended physical and virtual memory address space, memory protection mechanisms, and new operations to support operating systems and virtual memory.

All registers, instructions, and addressing modes described in the 80C286 Base Architecture section of this Functional Description remain the same. Programs for the 8086, 88, 186, and real address mode 80C286 can be run in protected mode; however, embedded constants for segment selectors are different.

Memory Size

The protected mode 80C286 provides a 1 gigabyte virtual address space per task mapped into a 16 megabyte physical address space defined by the address pin A_{23}–A_0 and $\overline{BHE}$. The virtual address space may be larger than the physical address space since any use of an address that does not map to a physical memory location will cause a restartable exception.

Memory Addressing

As in real address mode, protected mode uses 32-bit pointers, consisting of 16-bit selector and offset components. The selector, however, specifies an index into a memory resident table rather than the upper 16-bits of a real memory address. The 24-bit base address of the desired segment is obtained from the tables in memory. The 16-bit offset is added to the segment base address to form the physical address as shown in Figure 10. The tables are automatically referenced by the CPU whenever a segment register is loaded with a selector. All 80C286 instructions which load a segment register will reference the memory based tables without additional software. The memory based tables contain 8 byte values called descriptors.

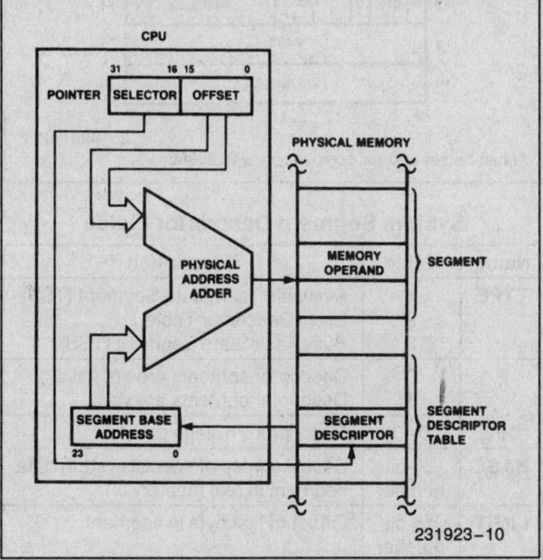

Figure 10. Protected Mode Memory Addressing

DESCRIPTORS

Descriptors define the use of memory. Special types of descriptors also define new functions for transfer of control and task switching. The 80C286 has segment descriptors for code, stack and data segments, and system control descriptors for special system data segments and control transfer operations. Descriptor accesses are performed as locked bus operations to assure descriptor integrity in multi-processor systems.

CODE AND DATA SEGMENT DESCRIPTORS (S = 1)

Besides segment base addresses, code and data descriptors contain other segment attributes including segment size (1 to 64K bytes), access rights (read only, read/write, execute only, and execute/read), and presence in memory (for virtual memory systems) (See Figure 11). Any segment usage violating a segment attribute indicated by the segment descriptor will prevent the memory cycle and cause an exception or interrupt.

Code or Data Segment Descriptor

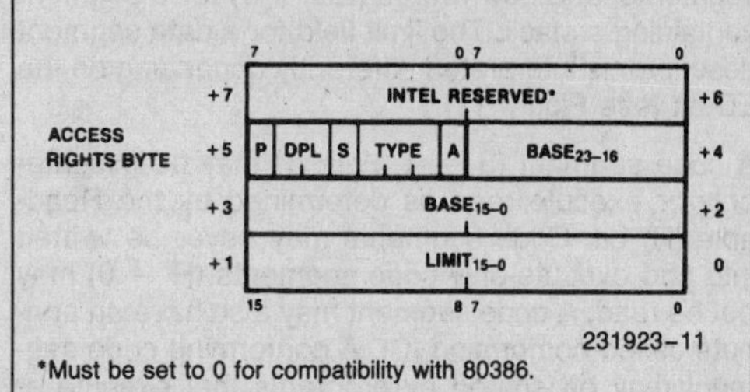

Access Rights Byte Definition

	Bit Position	Name		Function	
	7	Present (P)	P = 1 P = 0	Segment is mapped into physical memory. No mapping to physical memory exits, base and limit are not used.	
	6–5	Descriptor Privilege Level (DPL)		Segment privilege attribute used in privilege tests.	
	4	Segment Descriptor (S)	S = 1 S = 0	Code or Data (includes stacks) segment descriptor System Segment Descriptor or Gate Descriptor	
Type Field Definition	3 2 1	Executable (E) Expansion Direction (ED) Writeable (W)	E = 0 ED = 0 ED = 1 W = 0 W = 1	Data segment descriptor type is: Expand up segment, offsets must be ≤ limit. Expand down segment, offsets must be > limit. Data segment may not be written into. Data segment may be written into.	If Data Segment (S = 1, E = 0)
	3 2 1	Executable (E) Conforming (C) Readable (R)	E = 1 C = 1 R = 0 R = 1	Code Segment Descriptor type is: Code segment may only be executed when CPL ≥ DPL and CPL remains unchanged. Code segment may not be read Code segment may be read.	If Code Segment (S = 1, E = 1)
	0	Accessed (A)	A = 0 A = 1	Segment has not been accessed. Segment selector has been loaded into segment register or used by selector test instructions.	

Figure 11. Code and Data Segment Descriptor Formats

Code and data (including stack data) are stored in two types of segments: code segments and data segments. Both types are identified and defined by segment descriptors (S = 1). Code segments are identified by the executable (E) bit set to 1 in the descriptor access rights byte. The access rights byte of both code and data segment descriptor types have three fields in common: present (P) bit, Descriptor Privilege Level (DPL), and accessed (A) bit. If P = 0, any attempted use of this segment will cause a not-present exception. DPL specifies the privilege level of the segment descriptor. DPL controls when the descriptor may be used by a task (refer to privilege discussion below). The A bit shows whether the segment has been previously accessed for usage profiling, a necessity for virtual memory systems. The CPU will always set this bit when accessing the descriptor.

Data segments (S = 1, E = 0) may be either read-only or read-write as controlled by the W bit of the access rights byte. Read-only (W = 0) data segments may not be written into. Data segments may grow in two directions, as determined by the Expansion Direction (ED) bit: upwards (ED = 0) for data segments, and downwards (ED = 1) for a segment containing a stack. The limit field for a data segment descriptor is interpreted differently depending on the ED bit (see Figure 11).

A code segment (S = 1, E = 1) may be execute-only or execute/read as determined by the Readable (R) bit. Code segments may never be written into and execute-only code segments (R = 0) may not be read. A code segment may also have an attribute called conforming (C). A conforming code segment may be shared by programs that execute at different privilege levels. The DPL of a conforming code segment defines the range of privilege levels at which the segment may be executed (refer to privilege discussion below). The limit field identifies the last byte of a code segment.

SYSTEM SEGMENT DESCRIPTORS (S = 0, TYPE = 1–3)

In addition to code and data segment descriptors, the protected mode 80C286 defines System Segment Descriptors. These descriptors define special system data segments which contain a table of descriptors (Local Descriptor Table Descriptor) or segments which contain the execution state of a task (Task State Segment Descriptor).

Figure 12 gives the formats for the special system data segment descriptors. The descriptors contain a 24-bit base address of the segment and a 16-bit limit. The access byte defines the type of descriptor, its state and privilege level. The descriptor contents are valid and the segment is in physical memory if P = 1. If P = 0, the segment is not valid. The DPL field is only used in Task State Segment descriptors and indicates the privilege level at which the descriptor may be used (see Privilege). Since the Local Descriptor Table descriptor may only be used by a special privileged instruction, the DPL field is not used. Bit 4 of the access byte is 0 to indicate that it is a system control descriptor. The type field specifies the descriptor type as indicated in Figure 12.

System Segment Descriptor

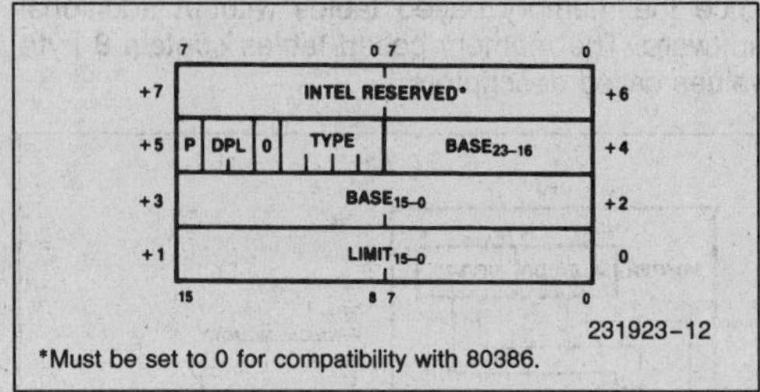

*Must be set to 0 for compatibility with 80386.

System Segment Descriptor Fields

Name	Value	Description
TYPE	1 2 3	Available Task State Segment (TSS) Local Descriptor Table Busy Task State Segment (TSS)
P	0 1	Descriptor contents are not valid Descriptor contents are valid
DPL	0–3	Descriptor Privilege Level
BASE	24-bit number	Base Address of special system data segment in real memory
LIMIT	16-bit number	Offset of last byte in segment

Figure 12. System Segment Descriptor Format

GATE DESCRIPTORS (S = 0, TYPE = 4–7)

Gates are used to control access to entry points within the target code segment. The gate descriptors are call gates, task gates, interrupt gates and trap gates. Gates provide a level of indirection between the source and destination of the control transfer. This indirection allows the CPU to automatically perform protection checks and control entry point of the destination. Call gates are used to change privilege levels (see Privilege), task gates are used to perform a task switch, and interrupt and trap gates are used to specify interrupt service routines. The interrupt gate disables interrupts (resets IF) while the trap gate does not.

Gate Descriptor

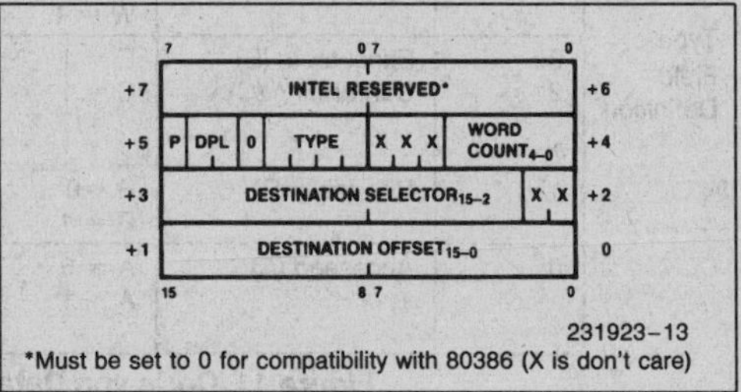

*Must be set to 0 for compatibility with 80386 (X is don't care)

Gate Descriptor Fields

Name	Value	Description
TYPE	4 5 6 7	–Call Gate –Task Gate –Interrupt Gate –Trap Gate
P	0 1	–Descriptor Contents are not valid –Descriptor Contents are valid
DPL	0–3	Descriptor Privilege Level
WORD COUNT	0–31	Number of words to copy from callers stack to called procedures stack. Only used with call gate.
DESTINATION SELECTOR	16-bit selector	Selector to the target code segment (Call, Interrupt or Trap Gate) Selector to the target task state segment (Task Gate)
DESTINATION OFFSET	16-bit offset	Entry point within the target code segment

Figure 13. Gate Descriptor Format

Figure 13 shows the format of the gate descriptors. The descriptor contains a destination pointer that points to the descriptor of the target segment and the entry point offset. The destination selector in an interrupt gate, trap gate, and call gate must refer to a code segment descriptor. These gate descriptors contain the entry point to prevent a program from constructing and using an illegal entry point. Task gates may only refer to a task state segment. Since task gates invoke a task switch, the destination offset is not used in the task gate.

Exception 13 is generated when the gate is used if a destination selector does not refer to the correct descriptor type. The word count field is used in the call gate descriptor to indicate the number of parameters (0–31 words) to be automatically copied from the caller's stack to the stack of the called routine when a control transfer changes privilege levels. The word count field is not used by any other gate descriptor.

The access byte format is the same for all gate descriptors. P = 1 indicates that the gate contents are valid. P = 0 indicates the contents are not valid and causes exception 11 if referenced. DPL is the descriptor privilege level and specifies when this descriptor may be used by a task (refer to privilege discussion below). Bit 4 must equal 0 to indicate a system control descriptor. The type field specifies the descriptor type as indicated in Figure 13.

SEGMENT DESCRIPTOR CACHE REGISTERS

A segment descriptor cache register is assigned to each of the four segment registers (CS, SS, DS, ES). Segment descriptors are automatically loaded (cached) into a segment descriptor cache register (Figure 14) whenever the associated segment register is loaded with a selector. Only segment descriptors may be loaded into segment descriptor cache registers. Once loaded, all references to that segment of memory use the cached descriptor information instead of reaccessing the descriptor. The descriptor cache registers are not visible to programs. No instructions exist to store their contents. They only change when a segment register is loaded.

SELECTOR FIELDS

A protected mode selector has three fields: descriptor entry index, local or global descriptor table indicator (TI), and selector privilege (RPL) as shown in Figure 15. These fields select one of two memory based tables of descriptors, select the appropriate table entry and allow highspeed testing of the selector's privilege attribute (refer to privilege discussion below).

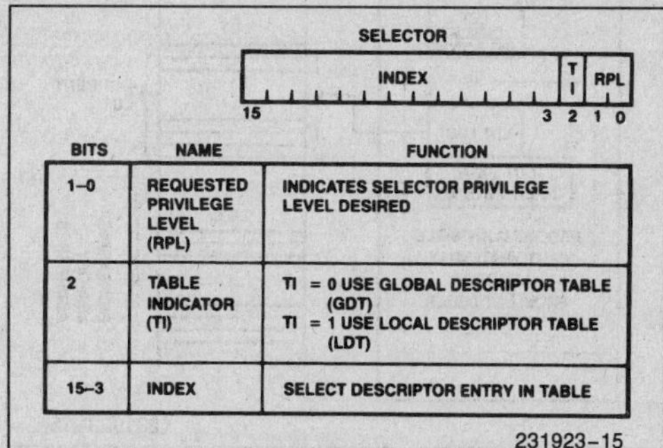

Figure 15. Selector Fields

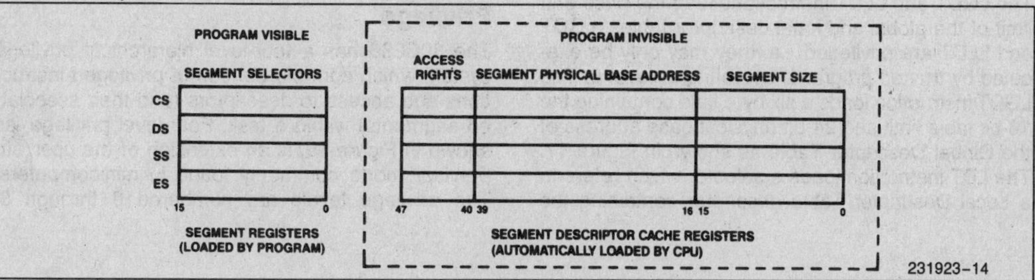

Figure 14. Descriptor Cache Registers

LOCAL AND GLOBAL DESCRIPTOR TABLES

Two tables of descriptors, called descriptor tables, contain all descriptors accessible by a task at any given time. A descriptor table is a linear array of up to 8192 descriptors. The upper 13 bits of the selector value are an index into a descriptor table. Each table has a 24-bit base register to locate the descriptor table in physical memory and a 16-bit limit register that confine descriptor access to the defined limits of the table as shown in Figure 16. A restartable exception (13) will occur if an attempt is made to reference a descriptor outside the table limits.

One table, called the Global Descriptor table (GDT), contains descriptors available to all tasks. The other table, called the Local Descriptor Table (LDT), contains descriptors that can be private to a task. Each task may have its own private LDT. The GDT may contain all descriptor types except interrupt and trap descriptors. The LDT may contain only segment, task gate, and call gate descriptors. A segment cannot be accessed by a task if its segment descriptor does not exist in either descriptor table at the time of access.

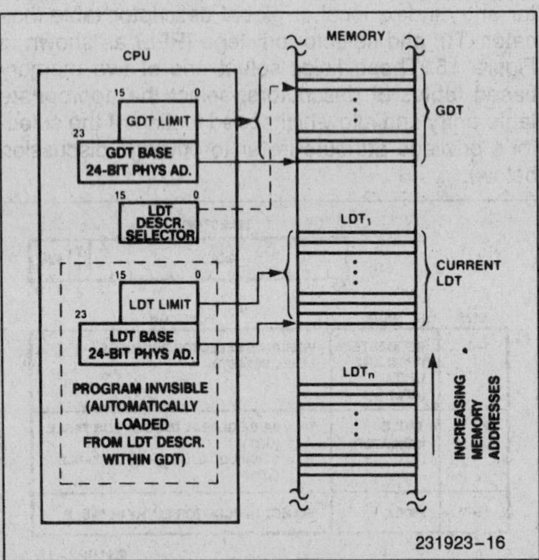

Figure 16. Local and Global Descriptor Table Definition

The LGDT and LLDT instructions load the base and limit of the global and local descriptor tables. LGDT and LLDT are privileged, i.e. they may only be executed by trusted programs operating at level 0. The LGDT instruction loads a six byte field containing the 16-bit table limit and 24-bit physical base address of the Global Descriptor Table as shown in Figure 17. The LDT instruction loads a selector which refers to a Local Descriptor Table descriptor containing the base address and limit for an LDT, as shown in Figure 12.

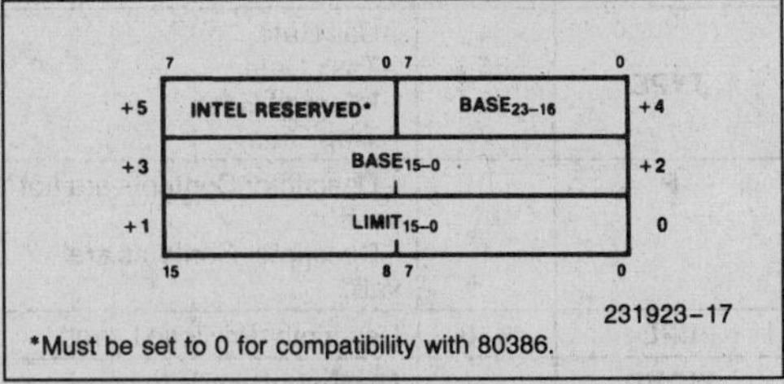

Figure 17. Global Descriptor Table and Interrupt Descriptor Table Data Type

INTERRUPT DESCRIPTOR TABLE

The protected mode 80C286 has a third descriptor table, called the Interrupt Descriptor Table (IDT) (see Figure 18), used to define up to 256 interrupts. It may contain only task gates, interrupt gates and trap gates. The IDT (Interrupt Descriptor Table) has a 24-bit physical base and 16-bit limit register in the CPU. The privileged LIDT instruction loads these registers with a six byte value of identical form to that of the LGDT instruction (see Figure 17 and Protected Mode Initialization).

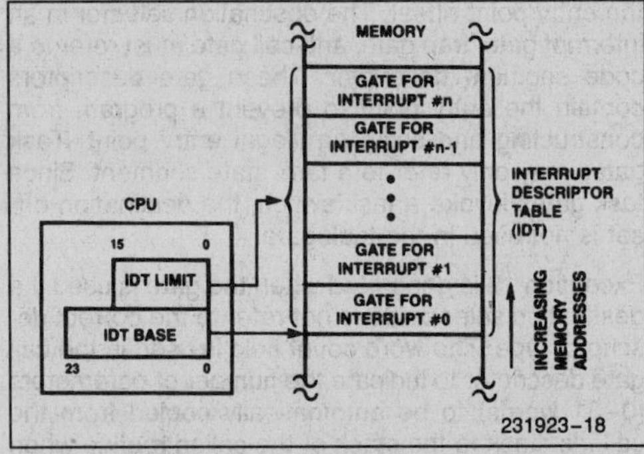

Figure 18. Interrupt Descriptor Table Definition

References to IDT entries are made via INT instructions, external interrupt vectors, or exceptions. The IDT must be at least 256 bytes in size to allocate space for all reserved interrupts.

Privilege

The 80C286 has a four-level hierarchical privilege system which controls the use of privileged instructions and access to descriptors (and their associated segments) within a task. Four-level privilege, as shown in Figure 19, is an extension of the user/supervisor mode commonly found in minicomputers. The privilege levels are numbered 0 through 3.

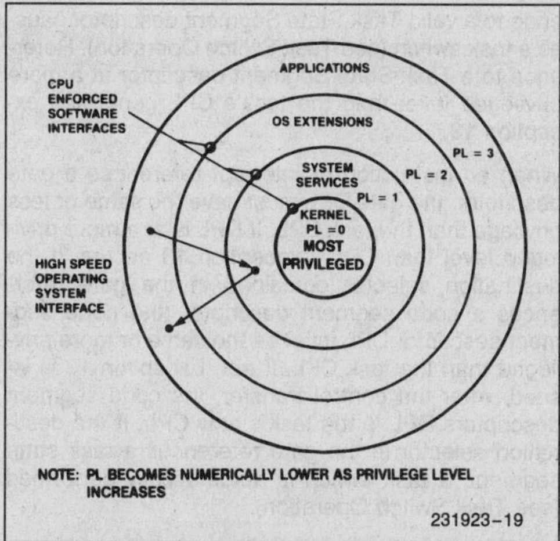

Level 0 is the most privileged level. Privilege levels provide protection within a task. (Tasks are isolated by providing private LDT's for each task.) Operating system routines, interrupt handlers, and other system software can be included and protected within the virtual address space of each task using the four levels of privilege. Each task in the system has a separate stack for each of its privilege levels.

Tasks, descriptors, and selectors have a privilege level attribute that determines whether the descriptor may be used. Task privilege effects the use of instructions and descriptors. Descriptor and selector privilege only effect access to the descriptor.

TASK PRIVILEGE

A task always executes at one of the four privilege levels. The task privilege level at any specific instant is called the Current Privilege Level (CPL) and is defined by the lower two bits of the CS register. CPL cannot change during execution in a single code segment. A task's CPL may only be changed by control transfers through gate descriptors to a new code segment (See Control Transfer). Tasks begin executing at the CPL value specified by the code segment selector within TSS when the task is initiated via a task switch operation (See Figure 20). A task executing at Level 0 can access all data segments defined in the GDT and the task's LDT and is considered the most trusted level. A task executing a Level 3 has the most restricted access to data and is considered the least trusted level.

DESCRIPTOR PRIVILEGE

Descriptor privilege is specified by the Descriptor Privilege Level (DPL) field of the descriptor access byte. DPL specifies the least trusted task privilege level (CPL) at which a task may access the descriptor. Descriptors with DPL = 0 are the most protected. Only tasks executing at privilege level 0 (CPL = 0) may access them. Descriptors with DPL = 3 are the least protected (i.e. have the least restricted access) since tasks can access them when CPL = 0, 1, 2, or 3. This rule applies to all descriptors, except LDT descriptors.

SELECTOR PRIVILEGE

Selector privilege is specified by the Requested Privilege Level (RPL) field in the least significant two bits of a selector. Selector RPL may establish a less trusted privilege level than the current privilege level for the use of a selector. This level is called the task's effective privilege level (EPL). RPL can only reduce the scope of a task's access to data with this selector. A task's effective privilege is the numeric maximum of RPL and CPL. A selector with RPL = 0 imposes no additional restriction on its use while a selector with RPL = 3 can only refer to segments at privilege Level 3 regardless of the task's CPL. RPL is generally used to verify that pointer parameters passed to a more trusted procedure are not allowed to use data at a more privileged level than the caller (refer to pointer testing instructions).

Descriptor Access and Privilege Validation

Determining the ability of a task to access a segment involves the type of segment to be accessed, the instruction used, the type of descriptor used and CPL, RPL, and DPL. The two basic types of segment accesses are control transfer (selectors loaded into CS) and data (selectors loaded into DS, ES or SS).

DATA SEGMENT ACCESS

Instructions that load selectors into DS and ES must refer to a data segment descriptor or readable code segment descriptor. The CPL of the task and the RPL of the selector must be the same as or more privileged (numerically equal to or lower than) than the descriptor DPL. In general, a task can only access data segments at the same or less privileged levels than the CPL or RPL (whichever is numerically higher) to prevent a program from accessing data it cannot be trusted to use.

An exception to the rule is a readable conforming code segment. This type of code segment can be read from any privilege level.

If the privilege checks fail (e.g. DPL is numerically less than the maximum of CPL and RPL) or an incorrect type of descriptor is referenced (e.g. gate descriptor or execute only code segment) exception 13 occurs. If the segment is not present, exception 11 is generated.

Instructions that load selectors into SS must refer to data segment descriptors for writable data segments. The descriptor privilege (DPL) and RPL must equal CPL. All other descriptor types or a privilege level violation will cause exception 13. A not present fault causes exception 12.

CONTROL TRANSFER

Four types of control transfer can occur when a selector is loaded into CS by a control transfer operation (see Table 10). Each transfer type can only occur if the operation which loaded the selector references the correct descriptor type. Any violation of these descriptor usage rules (e.g. JMP through a call gate or RET to a Task State Segment) will cause exception 13.

The ability to reference a descriptor for control transfer is also subject to rules of privilege. A CALL or JUMP instruction may only reference a code segment descriptor with DPL equal to the task CPL or a conforming segment with DPL of equal or greater privilege than CPL. The RPL of the selector used to reference the code descriptor must have as much privilege as CPL.

RET and IRET instructions may only reference code segment descriptors with descriptor privilege equal to or less privileged than the task CPL. The selector loaded into CS is the return address from the stack. After the return, the selector RPL is the task's new CPL. If CPL changes, the old stack pointer is popped after the return address.

When a JMP or CALL references a Task State Segment descriptor, the descriptor DPL must be the same or less privileged than the task's CPL. Reference to a valid Task State Segment descriptor causes a task switch (see Task Switch Operation). Reference to a Task State Segment descriptor at a more privileged level than the task's CPL generates exception 13.

When an instruction or interrupt references a gate descriptor, the gate DPL must have the same or less privilege than the task CPL. If DPL is at a more privileged level than CPL, exeception 13 occurs. If the destination selector contained in the gate references a code segment descriptor, the code segment descriptor DPL must be the same or more privileged than the task CPL. If not, Exception 13 is issued. After the control transfer, the code segment descriptors DPL is the task's new CPL. If the destination selector in the gate references a task state segment, a task switch is automatically performed (see Task Switch Operation).

The privilege rules on control transfer require:

- JMP or CALL direct to a code segment (code segment descriptor) can only be to a conforming segment with DPL of equal or greater privilege than CPL or a non-conforming segment at the same privilege level.
- interrupts within the task or calls that may change privilege levels, can only transfer control through a gate at the same or a less privileged level than CPL to a code segment at the same or more privileged level than CPL.
- return instructions that don't switch tasks can only return control to a code segment at the same or less privileged level.
- task switch can be performed by a call, jump or interrupt which references either a task gate or task state segment at the same or less privileged level.

Table 10. Descriptor Types Used for Control Transfer

Control Transfer Types	Operation Types	Descriptor Referenced	Descriptor Table
Intersegment within the same privilege level	JMP, CALL, RET, IRET*	Code Segment	GDT/LDT
Intersegment to the same or higher privilege level Interrupt within task may change CPL.	CALL	Call Gate	GDT/LDT
	Interrupt Instruction, Exception, External Interrupt	Trap or Interrupt Gate	IDT
Intersegment to a lower privilege level (changes task CPL)	RET, IRET*	Code Segment	GDT/LDT
Task Switch	CALL, JMP	Task State Segment	GDT
	CALL, JMP	Task Gate	GDT/LDT
	IRET** Interrupt Instruction, Exception, External Interrupt	Task Gate	IDT

*NT (Nested Task bit of flag word) = 0
**NT (Nested Task bit of flag word) = 1

PRIVILEGE LEVEL CHANGES

Any control transfer that changes CPL within the task, causes a change of stacks as part of the operation. Initial values of SS:SP for privilege levels 0, 1, and 2 are kept in the task state segment (refer to Task Switch Operation). During a JMP or CALL control transfer, the new stack pointer is loaded into the SS and SP registers and the previous stack pointer is pushed onto the new stack.

When returning to the original privilege level, its stack is restored as part of the RET or IRET instruction operation. For subroutine calls that pass parameters on the stack and cross privilege levels, a fixed number of words, as specified in the gate, are copied from the previous stack to the current stack. The inter-segment RET instruction with a stack adjustment value will correctly restore the previous stack pointer upon return.

Protection

The 80C286 includes mechanisms to protect critical instructions that affect the CPU execution state (e.g. HLT) and code or data segments from improper usage. These protection mechanisms are grouped into three forms:

Restricted *usage* of segments (e.g. no write allowed to read-only data segments). The only segments available for use are defined by descriptors in the Local Descriptor Table (LDT) and Global Descriptor Table (GDT).

Restricted *access* to segments via the rules of privilege and descriptor usage.

Privileged instructions or operations that may only be executed at certain privilege levels as determined by the CPL and I/O Privilege Level (IOPL). The IOPL is defined by bits 14 and 13 of the flag word.

These checks are performed for all instructions and can be split into three categories: segment load checks (Table 11), operand reference checks (Table 12), and privileged instruction checks (Table 13). Any violation of the rules shown will result in an exception. A not-present exception related to the stack segment causes exception 12.

The IRET and POPF instructions do not perform some of their defined functions if CPL is not of sufficient privilege (numerically small enough). Precisely these are:

- The IF bit is not changed if CPL > IOPL.
- The IOPL field of the flag word is not changed if CPL > 0.

No exceptions or other indication are given when these conditions occur.

Table 11. Segment Register Load Checks

Error Description	Exception Number
Descriptor table limit exceeded	13
Segment descriptor not-present	11 or 12
Privilege rules violated	13
Invalid descriptor/segment type segment register load: —Read only data segment load to SS —Special Control descriptor load to DS, ES, SS —Execute only segment load to DS, ES, SS —Data segment load to CS —Read/Execute code segment load to SS	13

Table 12. Operand Reference Checks

Error Description	Exception Number
Write into code segment	13
Read from execute-only code segment	13
Write to read-only data segment	13
Segment limit exceeded[1]	12 or 13

NOTE:
Carry out in offset calculations is ignored.

Table 13. Privileged Instruction Checks

Error Description	Exception Number
CPL ≠ 0 when executing the following instructions: LIDT, LLDT, LGDT, LTR, LMSW, CTS, HLT	13
CPL > IOPL when executing the following instructions: INS, IN, OUTS, OUT, STI, CLI, LOCK	13

EXCEPTIONS

The 80C286 detects several types of exceptions and interrupts, in protected mode (see Table 14). Most are restartable after the exceptional condition is removed. Interrupt handlers for most exceptions can read an error code, pushed on the stack after the return address, that identifies the selector involved (0 if none). The return address normally points to the failing instruction, including all leading prefixes. For a processor extension segment overrun exception, the return address will not point at the ESC instruction that caused the exception; however, the processor extension registers may contain the address of the failing instruction.

5

Table 14. Protected Mode Exceptions

Interrupt Vector	Function	Return Address At Falling Instruction?	Always Restart-able?	Error Code on Stack?
8	Double exception detected	Yes	No[2]	Yes
9	Processor extension segment overrun	No	No[2]	No
10	Invalid task state segment	Yes	Yes	Yes
11	Segment not present	Yes	Yes	Yes
12	Stack segment overrun or stack segment not present	Yes	Yes[1]	Yes
13	General protection	Yes	No[2]	Yes

NOTE:
1. When a PUSHA or POPA instruction attempts to wrap around the stack segment, the machine state after the exception will not be restartable because stack segment wrap around is not permitted. This condition is identified by the value of the saved SP being either 0000(H), 0001(H), FFFE(H), or FFFF(H).
2. These exceptions indicate a violation to privilege rules or usage rules has occurred. Restart is generally not attempted under those conditions.

These exceptions indicate a violation to privilege rules or usage rules has occurred. Restart is generally not attempted under those conditions.

All these checks are performed for all instructions and can be split into three categories: segment load checks (Table 11), operand reference checks (Table 12), and privileged instruction checks (Table 13). Any violation of the rules shown will result in an exception. A not-present exception causes exception 11 or 12 and is restartable.

Special Operations

TASK SWITCH OPERATION

The 80C286 provides a built-in task switch operation which saves the entire 80C286 execution state (registers, address space, and a link to the previous task), loads a new execution state, and commences execution in the new task. Like gates, the task switch operation is invoked by executing an inter-segment JMP or CALL instruction which refers to a Task State Segment (TSS) or task gate descriptor in the GDT or LDT. An INT n instruction, exception, or external interrupt may also invoke the task switch operation by selecting a task gate descriptor in the associated IDT descriptor entry.

The TSS descriptor points at a segment (see Figure 20) containing the entire 80C286 execution state while a task gate descriptor contains a TSS selector. The limit field of the descriptor must be >002B(H).

Each task must have a TSS associated with it. The current TSS is identified by a special register in the 80C286 called the Task Register (TR). This register contains a selector referring to the task state segment descriptor that defines the current TSS. A hidden base and limit register associated with TR are loaded whenever TR is loaded with a new selector.

The IRET instruction is used to return control to the task that called the current task or was interrupted. Bit 14 in the flag register is called the Nested Task (NT) bit. It controls the function of the IRET instruction. If NT = 0, the IRET instruction performs the regular current task by popping values off the stack; when NT = 1, IRET performs a task switch operation back to the previous task.

When a CALL, JMP, or INT instruction initiates a task switch, the old (except for case of JMP) and new TSS will be marked busy and the back link field of the new TSS set to the old TSS selector. The NT bit of the new task is set by CALL or INT initiated task switches. An interrupt that does not cause a task switch will clear NT. NT may also be set or cleared by POPF or IRET instructions.

The task state segment is marked busy by changing the descriptor type field from Type 1 to Type 3. Use of a selector that references a busy task state segment causes Exception 13.

PROCESSOR EXTENSION CONTEXT SWITCHING

The context of a processor extension (such as the 80287 numerics processor) is not changed by the task switch operation. A processor extension context need only be changed when a different task attempts to use the processor extension (which still contains the context of a previous task). The 80C286 detects the first use of a processor extension after a task switch by causing the processor extension not present exception (7). The interrupt handler may then decide whether a context change is necessary.

Whenever the 80C286 switches tasks, it sets the Task Switched (TS) bit of the MSW. TS indicates that a processor extension context may belong to a different task than the current one. The processor extension not present exception (7) will occur when attempting to execute an ESC or WAIT instruction if TS=1 and a processor extension is present (MP=1 in MSW).

POINTER TESTING INSTRUCTIONS

The 80C286 provides several instructions to speed pointer testing and consistency checks for maintaining system integrity (see Table 15). These instructions use the memory management hardware to verify that a selector value refers to an appropriate segment without risking an exception. A condition flag (ZF) indicates whether use of the selector or segment will cause an exception.

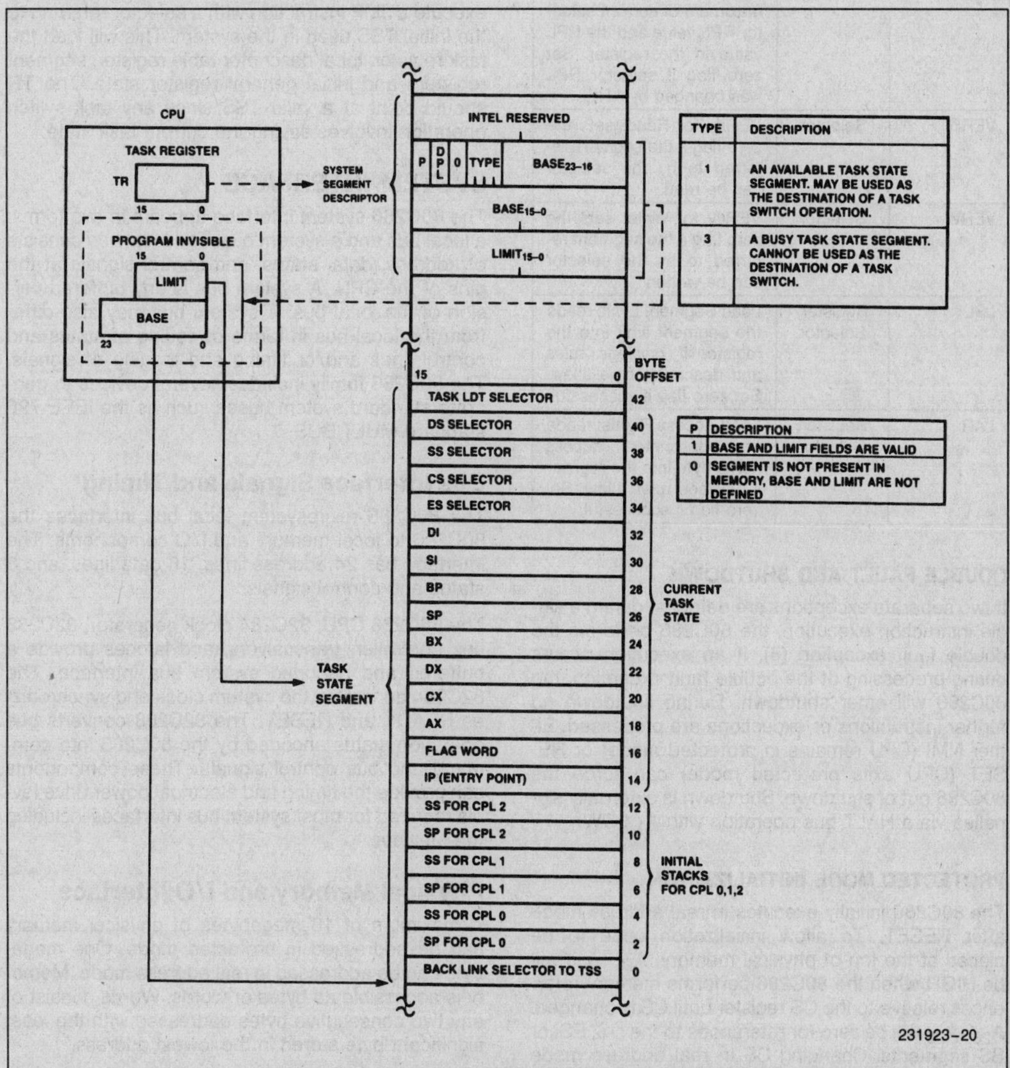

Figure 20. Task State Segment and TSS Registers

5

Table 15. 80C286 Pointer Test Instructions

Instruction	Operands	Function
ARPL	Selector, Register	Adjust Requested Privilege Level: adjusts the RPL of the selector to the numeric maximum of current selector RPL value and the RPL value in the register. Set zero flag if selector RPL was changed by ARPL.
VERR	Selector	VERify for Read: sets the zero flag if the segment referred to by the selector can be read.
VERW	Selector	VERify for Write: sets the zero flag if the segment referred to by the selector can be written.
LSL	Register, Selector	Load Segment Limit: reads the segment limit into the register if privilege rules and descriptor type allow. Set zero flag if successful.
LAR	Register, Selector	Load Access Rights: reads the descriptor access rights byte into the register if privilege rules allow. Set zero flag if successful.

DOUBLE FAULT AND SHUTDOWN

If two separate exceptions are detected during a single instruction execution, the 80C286 performs the double fault exception (8). If an execution occurs during processing of the double fault exception, the 80C286 will enter shutdown. During shutdown no further instructions or exceptions are processed. Either NMI (CPU remains in protected mode) or RESET (CPU exits protected mode) can force the 80C286 out of shutdown. Shutdown is externally signalled via a HALT bus operation with A_1 LOW.

PROTECTED MODE INITIALIZATION

The 80C286 initially executes in real address mode after RESET. To allow initialization code to be placed at the top of physical memory, $A_{23}-A_{20}$ will be HIGH when the 80C286 performs memory references relative to the CS register until CS is changed. $A_{23}-A_{20}$ will be zero for references to the DS, ES, or SS segments. Changing CS in real address mode will force $A_{23}-A_{20}$ LOW whenever CS is used again. The initial CS:IP value of F000:FFF0 provides 64K bytes of code space for initialization code without changing CS.

Protected mode operation requires several registers to be initialized. The GDT and IDT base registers must refer to a valid GDT and IDT. After executing the LMSW instruction to set PE, the 80C286 must immediately execute an intra-segment JMP instruction to clear the instruction queue of instructions decoded in real address mode.

To force the 80C286 CPU registers to match the initial protected mode state assumed by software, execute a JMP instruction with a selector referring to the initial TSS used in the system. This will load the task register, local descriptor table register, segment registers and initial general register state. The TR should point at a valid TSS since any task switch operation involves saving the current task state.

SYSTEM INTERFACE

The 80C286 system interface appears in two forms: a local bus and a system bus. The local bus consists of address, data, status, and control signals at the pins of the CPU. A system bus is any buffered version of the local bus. A system bus may also differ from the local bus in terms of coding of status and control lines and/or timing and loading of signals. The 80C286 family includes several devices to generate standard system buses such as the IEEE 796 standard MULTIBUS.

Bus Interface Signals and Timing

The 80C286 microsystem local bus interfaces the 80C286 to local memory and I/O components. The interface has 24 address lines, 16 data lines, and 8 status and control signals.

The 80C286 CPU, 82C284 clock generator, 82C288 bus controller, transceivers, and latches provide a buffered and decoded system bus interface. The 82C284 generates the system clock and synchronizes $\overline{\text{READY}}$ and RESET. The 82C288 converts bus operation status encoded by the 80C286 into command and bus control signals. These components can provide the timing and electrical power drive levels required for most system bus interfaces including the Multibus.

Physical Memory and I/O Interface

A maximum of 16 megabytes of physical memory can be addressed in protected mode. One megabyte can be addressed in real address mode. Memory is accessible as bytes or words. Words consist of any two consecutive bytes addressed with the least significant byte stored in the lowest address.

Byte transfers occur on either half of the 16-bit local data bus. Even bytes are accessed over D_7-D_0 while odd bytes are transferred over $D_{15}-D_8$. Even-addressed words are transferred over $D_{15}-D_0$ in one bus cycle, while odd-addressed word require *two* bus operations. The first transfers data on $D_{15}-D_8$, and the second transfers data on D_7-D_0. Both byte data transfers occur automatically, transparent to software.

Two bus signals, A_0 and $\overline{BHE}$, control transfers over the lower and upper halves of the data bus. Even address byte transfers are indicated by A_0 LOW and $\overline{BHE}$ HIGH. Odd address byte transfers are indicated by A_0 HIGH and $\overline{BHE}$ LOW. Both A_0 and $\overline{BHE}$ are LOW for even address word transfers.

The I/O address space contains 64K addresses in both modes. The I/O space is accessible as either bytes or words, as is memory. Byte wide peripheral devices may be attached to either the upper or lower byte of the data bus. Byte-wide I/O devices attached to the upper data byte (D_{15}–D_8) are accessed with odd I/O addresses. Devices on the lower data byte are accessed with even I/O addresses. An interrupt controller such as Intel's 82C59A-2 must be connected to the lower data byte (D_7–D_0) for proper return of the interrupt vector.

Bus Operation

The 80C286 uses a double frequency system clock (CLK input) to control bus timing. All signals on the local bus are measured relative to the system CLK input. The CPU divides the system clock by 2 to produce the internal processor clock, which determines bus state. Each processor clock is composed of two system clock cycles named phase 1 and phase 2. The 82C284 clock generator output (PCLK) identifies the next phase of the processor clock. (See Figure 21.)

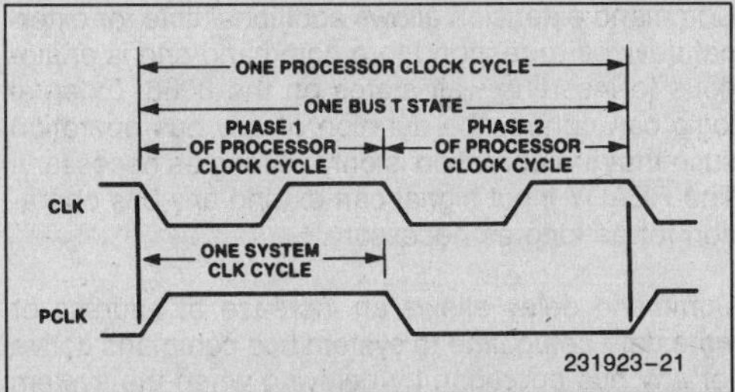

Figure 21. System and Processor Clock Relationships

Six types of bus operations are supported; memory read, memory write, I/O read, I/O write, interrupt acknowledge, and halt/shutdown. Data can be transferred at a maximum rate of one word per two processor clock cycles.

The 80C286 bus has three basic states: idle (T_i), send status (T_S), and perform command (T_c). The 80C286 CPU also has a fourth local bus state called hold (T_h). T_h indicates that the 80C286 has surrendered control of the local bus to another bus master in response to a HOLD request.

Each bus state is one processor clock long. Figure 22 shows the four 80C286 local bus states and allowed transitions.

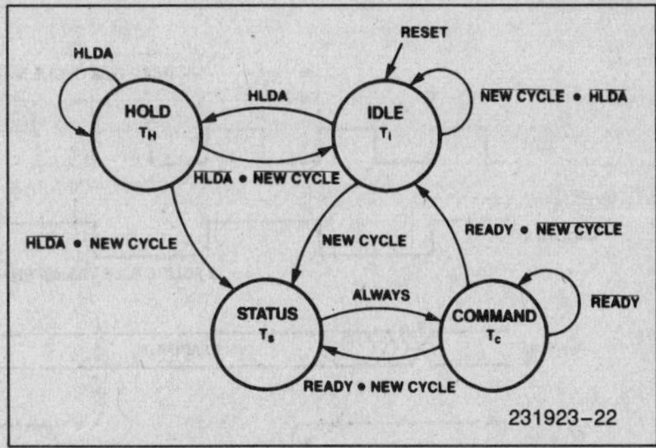

Figure 22. 80C286 Bus States

Bus States

The idle (T_i) state indicates that no data transfers are in progress or requested. The first active state T_S is signaled by status line $\overline{S1}$ or $\overline{S0}$ going LOW and identifying phase 1 of the processor clock. During T_S, the command encoding, the address, and data (for a write operation) are available on the 80C286 output pins. The 82C288 bus controller decodes the status signals and generates Multibus compatible read/write command and local transceiver control signals.

After T_S, the perform command (T_C) state is entered. Memory or I/O devices respond to the bus operation during T_C, either transferring read data to the CPU or accepting write data. T_C states may be repeated as often as necessary to assure sufficient time for the memory or I/O device to respond. The $\overline{READY}$ signal determines whether T_C is repeated. A repeated T_C state is called a wait state.

During hold (T_h), the 80C286 will float* all address, data, and status output pins enabling another bus master to use the local bus. The 80C286 HOLD input signal is used to place the 80C286 into the T_h state. The 80C286 HLDA output signal indicates that the CPU has entered T_h.

Pipelined Addressing

The 80C286 uses a local bus interface with pipelined timing to allow as much time as possible for data access. Pipelined timing allows a new bus operation to be initiated every two processor cycles, while allowing each individual bus operation to last for three processor cycles.

The timing of the address outputs is pipelined such that the address of the next bus operation becomes available during the current bus operation. Or in other words, the first clock of the next bus operation is overlapped with the last clock of the current bus operation. Therefore, address decode and routing logic can operate in advance of the next bus operation.

***NOTE:** See section on bus hold circuitry.

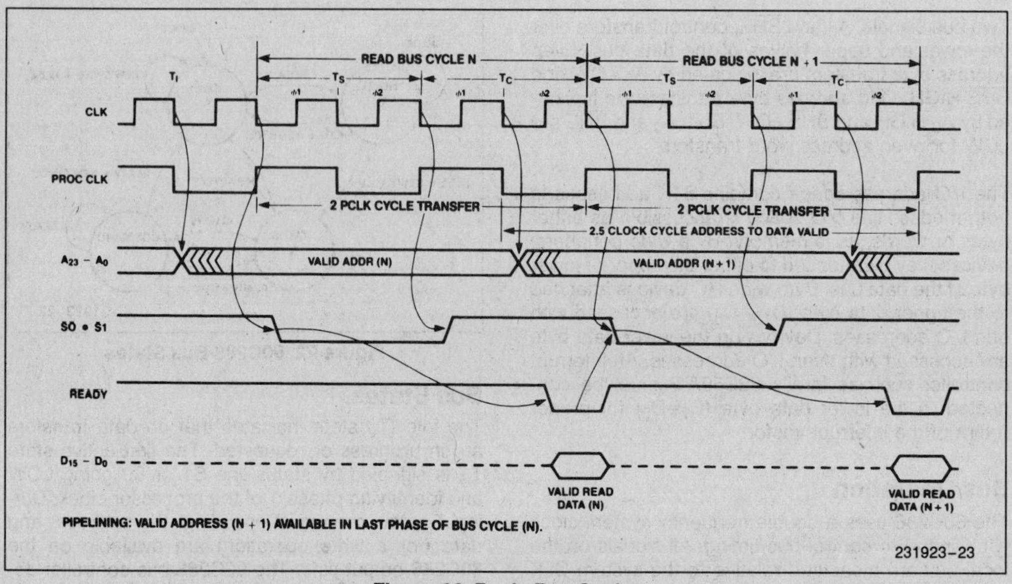

Figure 23. Basic Bus Cycle

External address latches may hold the address stable for the entire bus operation, and provide additional AC and DC buffering.

The 80C286 does not maintain the address of the current bus operation during all T_C states. Instead, the address for the next bus operation may be emitted during phase 2 of any T_C. The address remains valid during phase 1 of the first T_C to guarantee hold time, relative to ALE, for the address latch inputs.

Bus Control Signals

The 82C288 bus controller provides control signals; address latch enable (ALE), Read/Write commands, data transmit/receive (DT/$\overline{R}$), and data enable (DEN) that control the address latches, data transceivers, write enable, and output enable for memory and I/O systems.

The Address Latch Enable (ALE) output determines when the address may be latched. ALE provides at least one system CLK period of address hold time from the end of the previous bus operation until the address for the next bus operation appears at the latch outputs. This address hold time is required to support MULTIBUS and common memory systems.

The data bus transceivers are controlled by 82C288 outputs Data Enable (DEN) and Data Transmit/Receive (DT/$\overline{R}$). DEN enables the data transceivers; while DT/$\overline{R}$ controls tranceiver direction. DEN and DT/$\overline{R}$ are timed to prevent bus contention between the bus master, data bus transceivers, and system data bus transceivers.

Command Timing Controls

Two system timing customization options, command extension and command delay, are provided on the 80C286 local bus.

Command extension allows additional time for external devices to respond to a command and is analogous to inserting wait states on the 8086. External logic can control the duration of any bus operation such that the operation is only as long as necessary. The $\overline{\text{READY}}$ input signal can extend any bus operation for as long as necessary.

Command delay allows an increase of address or write data setup time to system bus command active for any bus operation by delaying when the system bus command becomes active. Command delay is controlled by the 82C288 CMDLY input. After T_S, the bus controller samples CMDLY at each failing edge of CLK. If CMDLY is HIGH, the 82C288 will not activate the command signal. When CMDLY is LOW, the 82C288 will activate the command signal. After the command becomes active, the CMDLY input is not sampled.

When a command is delayed, the available response time from command active to return read data or accept write data is less. To customize system bus timing, an address decoder can determine which bus operations require delaying the command. The CMDLY input does not affect the timing of ALE, DEN, or DT/$\overline{R}$.

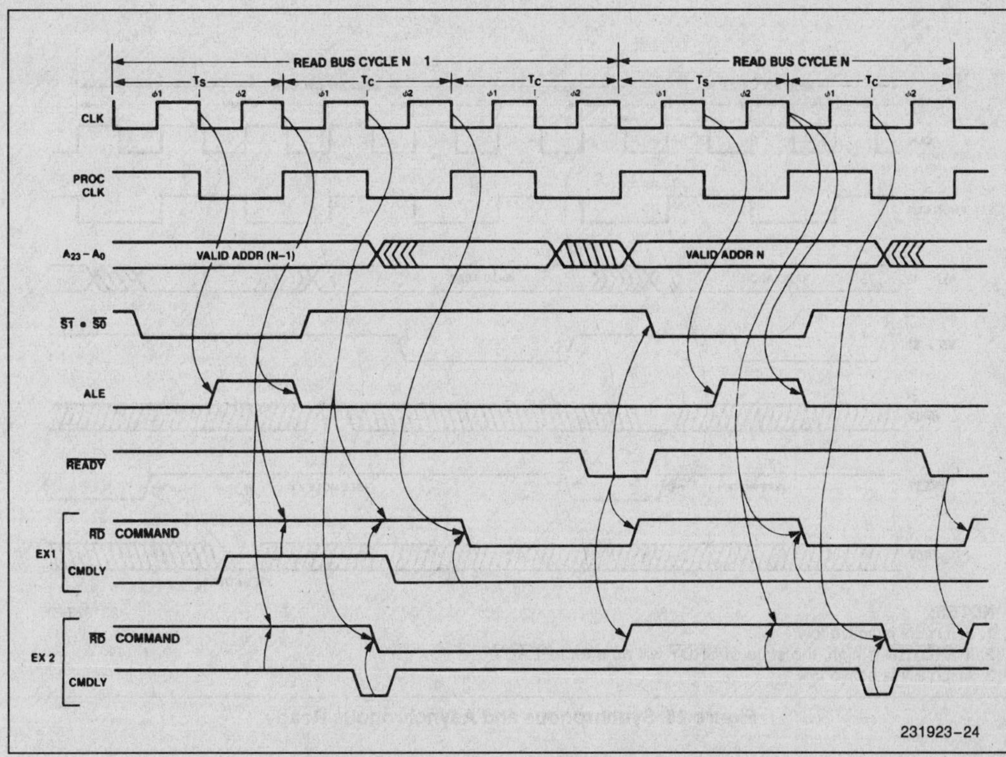

Figure 24. CMDLY Controls the Leading Edge of Command Signal

Figure 24 illustrates four uses of CMDLY. Example 1 shows delaying the read command two system CLKs for cycle N-1 and no delay for cycle N, and example 2 shows delaying the read command one system CLK for cycle N-1 and one system CLK delay for cycle N.

Bus Cycle Termination

At maximum transfer rates, the 80C286 bus alternates between the status and command states. The bus status signals become inactive after T_S so that they may correctly signal the start of the next bus operation after the completion of the current cycle. No external indication of T_C exists on the 80C286 local bus. The bus master and bus controller enter T_C directly after T_S and continue executing T_C cycles until terminated by READY.

READY Operation

The current bus master and 82C288 bus controller terminate each bus operation simultaneously to achieve maximum bus operation bandwidth. Both are informed in advance by READY active (open-collector output from 82C284) which identifies the last T_C cycle of the current bus operation. The bus master and bus controller must see the same sense of the READY signal, thereby requiring READY be synchronous to the system clock.

Synchronous Ready

The 82C284 clock generator provides READY synchronization from both synchronous and asynchronous sources (see Figure 25). The synchronous ready input (SRDY) of the clock generator is sampled with the falling edge of CLK at the end of phase 1 of each T_C. The state of SRDY is then broadcast to the bus master and bus controller via the READY output line.

Asynchronous Ready

Many systems have devices or subsystems that are asynchronous to the system clock. As a result, their ready outputs cannot be guaranteed to meet the 82C284 SRDY setup and hold time requirements. But the 82C284 asynchronous ready input (ARDY) is designed to accept such signals. The ARDY input is sampled at the beginning of each T_C cycle by 82C284 synchronization logic. This provides one system CLK cycle time to resolve its value before broadcasting it to the bus master and bus controller.

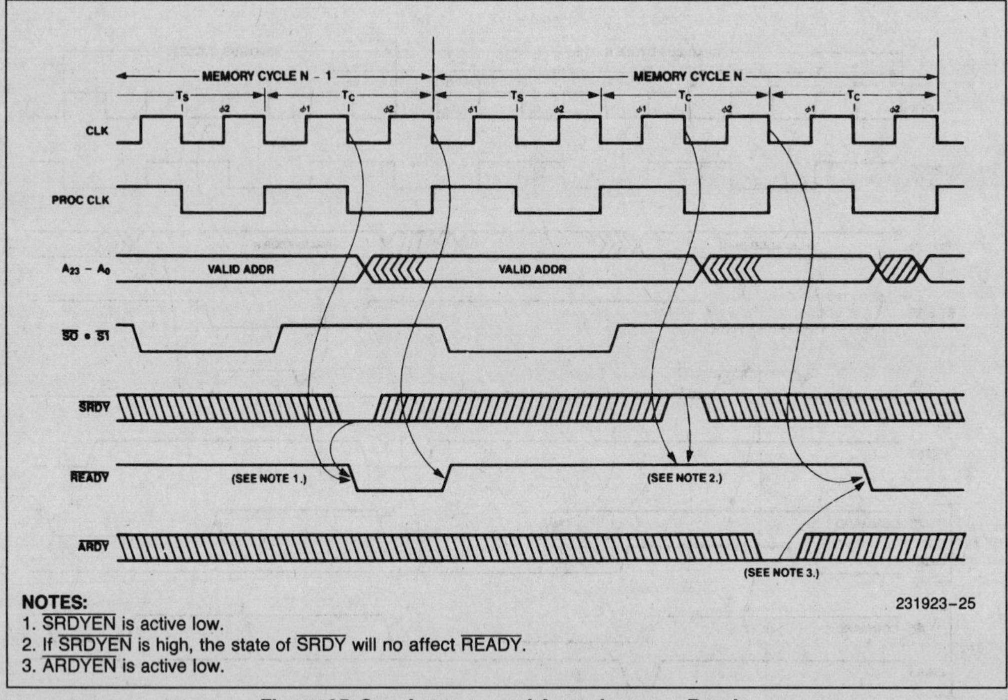

NOTES:
1. $\overline{\text{SRDYEN}}$ is active low.
2. If $\overline{\text{SRDYEN}}$ is high, the state of $\overline{\text{SRDY}}$ will no affect $\overline{\text{READY}}$.
3. $\overline{\text{ARDYEN}}$ is active low.

Figure 25. Synchronous and Asynchronous Ready

$\overline{\text{ARDY}}$ or $\overline{\text{ARDYEN}}$ must be HIGH at the end of T_S. $\overline{\text{ARDY}}$ cannot be used to terminate bus cycle with no wait states.

Each ready input of the 82C284 has an enable pin ($\overline{\text{SRDYEN}}$ and $\overline{\text{ARDYEN}}$) to select whether the current bus operation will be terminated by the synchronous or asynchronous ready. Either of the ready inputs may terminate a bus operation. These enable inputs are active low and have the same timing as their respective ready inputs. Address decode logic usually selects whether the current bus operation should be terminated by $\overline{\text{ARDY}}$ or $\overline{\text{SRDY}}$.

Data Bus Control

Figures 26, 27, and 28 show how the DT/$\overline{\text{R}}$, DEN, data bus, and address signals operate for different combinations of read, write, and idle bus operations. DT/$\overline{\text{R}}$ goes active (LOW) for a read operation. DT/$\overline{\text{R}}$ remains HIGH before, during, and between write operations.

The data bus is driven with write data during the second phase of T_S. The delay in write data timing allows the read data drivers, from a previous read cycle, sufficient time to enter 3-state OFF* before the 80C286 CPU begins driving the local data bus for write operations. Write data will always remain valid for one system clock past the last T_C to provide sufficient hold time for Multibus or other similar memory or I/O systems. During write-read or write-idle sequences the data bus enters 3-state OFF* during the second phase of the processor cycle after the last T_C. In a write-write sequence the data bus does not enter 3-state OFF* between T_C and T_S.

Bus Usage

The 80C286 local bus may be used for several functions: instruction data transfers, data transfers by other bus masters, instruction fetching, processor extension data transfers, interrupt acknowledge, and halt/shutdown. This section describes local bus activities which have special signals or requirements.

***NOTE:** See section on bus hold circuitry.

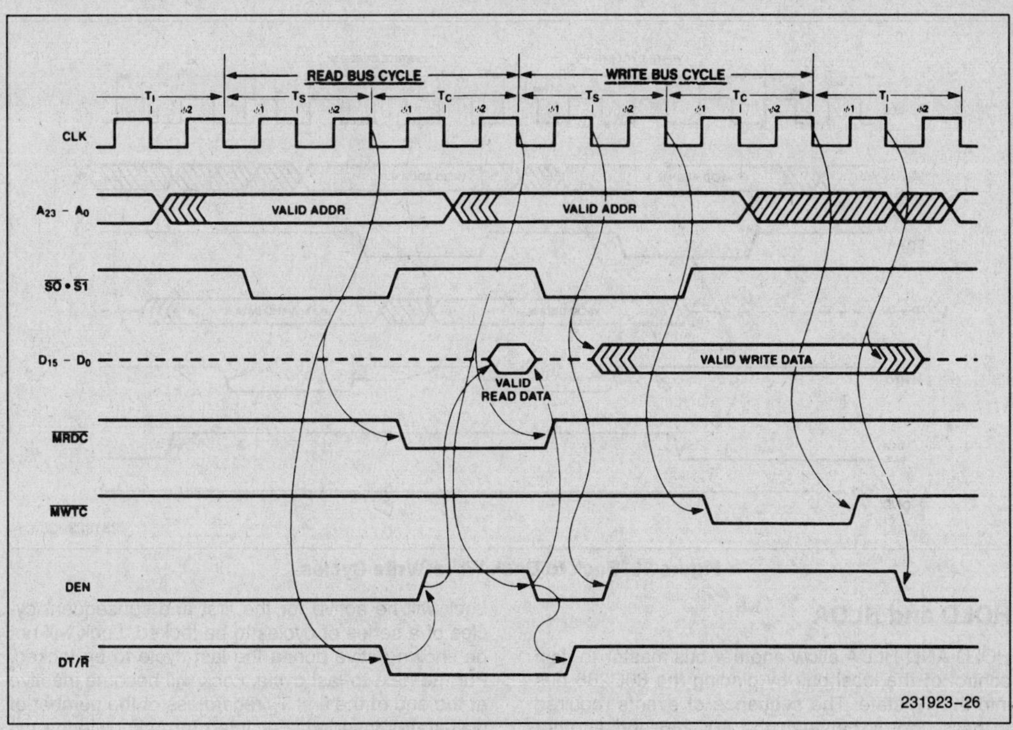

Figure 26. Back to Back Read-Write Cycles

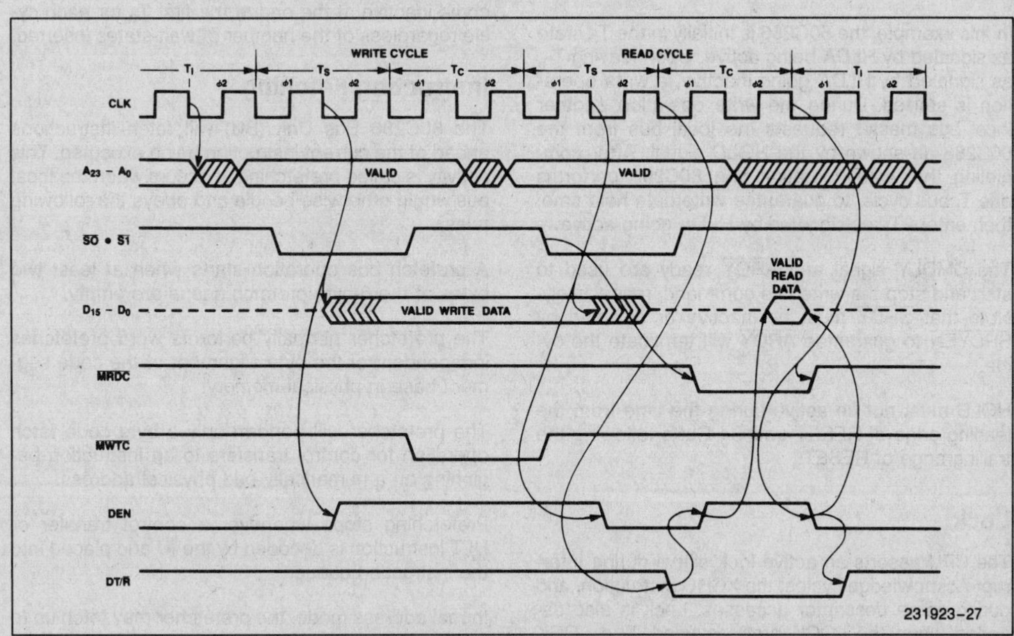

Figure 27. Back to Back Write-Read Cycles

5

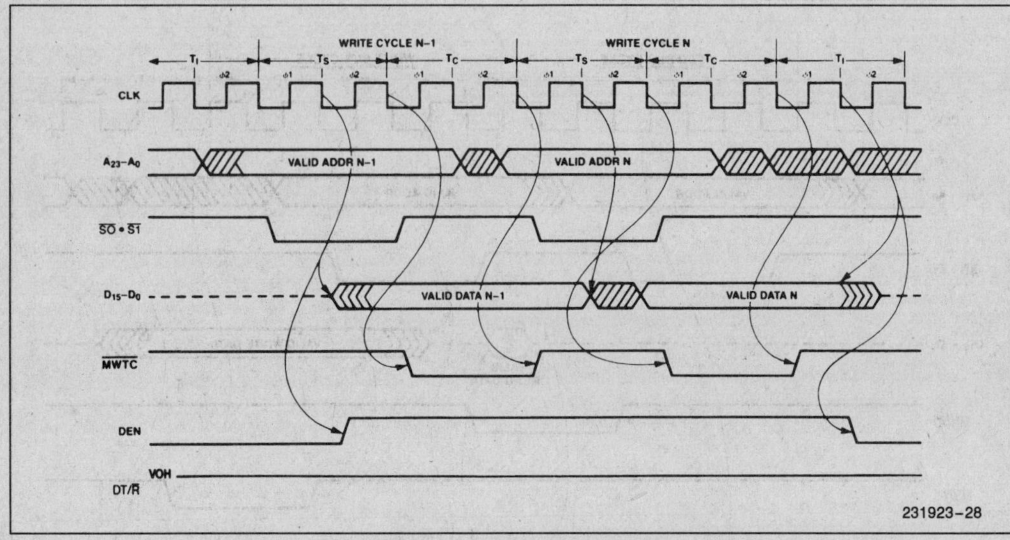

Figure 28. Back to Back Write-Write Cycles

HOLD and HLDA

HOLD AND HLDA allow another bus master to gain control of the local bus by placing the 80C286 bus into the T_h state. The sequence of events required to pass control between the 80C286 and another local bus master are shown in Figure 29.

In this example, the 80C286 is initially in the T_h state as signaled by HLDA being active. Upon leaving T_h, as signaled by HLDA going inactive, a write operation is started. During the write operation another local bus master requests the local bus from the 80C286 as shown by the HOLD signal. After completing the write operation, the 80C286 performs one T_i bus cycle, to guarantee write data hold time, then enters T_h as signaled by HLDA going active.

The CMDLY signal and $\overline{\text{ARDY}}$ ready are used to start and stop the write bus command, respectively. Note that $\overline{\text{SRDY}}$ must be inactive or disabled by $\overline{\text{SRDYEN}}$ to guarantee $\overline{\text{ARDY}}$ will terminate the cycle.

HOLD must not be active during the time from the leading edge of RESET until 34 CLKs following the trailing edge of RESET.

Lock

The CPU asserts an active lock signal during Interrupt-Acknowledge cycles, the XCHG instruction, and during some descriptor accesses. Lock is also asserted when the LOCK prefix is used. The LOCK prefix may be used with the following ASM-286 assembly instructions; MOVS, INS, and OUTS. For bus cycles other than Interrupt-Acknowledge cycles, Lock will be active for the first and subsequent cycles of a series of cycles to be locked. Lock will not be shown active during the last cycle to be locked. For the next-to-last cycle, Lock will become inactive at the end of the first T_c regardless of the number of wait-states inserted. For Interrupt-Acknowledge cycles, Lock will be active for each cycle, and will become inactive at the end of the first T_c for each cycle regardless of the number of wait-states inserted.

Instruction Fetching

The 80C286 Bus Unit (BU) will fetch instructions ahead of the current instruction being executed. This activity is called prefetching. It occurs when the local bus would otherwise be idle and obeys the following rules:

A prefetch bus operation starts when at least two bytes of the 6-byte prefetch queue are empty.

The prefetcher normally performs word prefetches independent of the byte alignment of the code segment base in physical memory.

The prefetcher will perform only a byte code fetch operation for control transfers to an instruction beginning on a numerically odd physical address.

Prefetching stops whenever a control transfer or HLT instruction is decoded by the IU and placed into the instruction queue.

In real address mode, the prefetcher may fetch up to 6 bytes beyond the last control transfer or HLT instruction in a code segment.

In protected mode, the prefetcher will never cause a segment overrun exception. The prefetcher stops at the last physical memory word of the code segment. Exception 13 will occur if the program attempts to execute beyond the last full instruction in the code segment.

If the last byte of a code segment appears on an even physical memory address, the prefetcher will read the next physical byte of memory (perform a word code fetch). The value of this byte is ignored and any attempt to execute it causes exception 13.

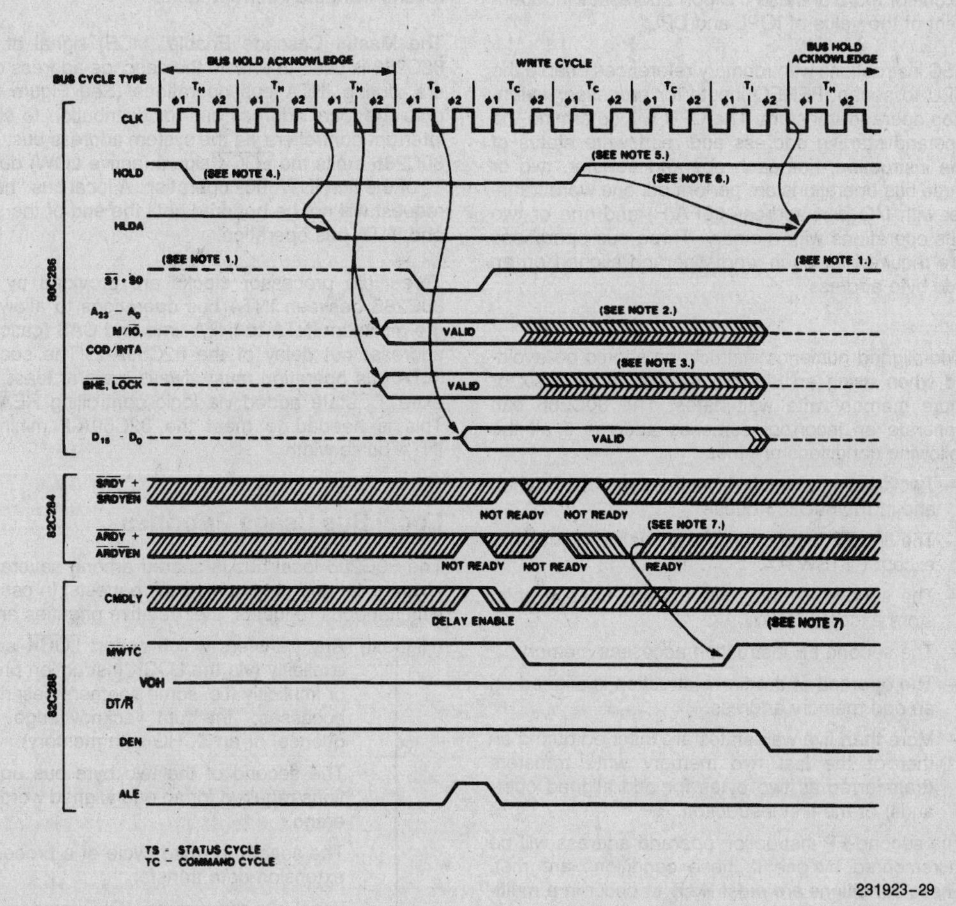

NOTES:

1. Status lines are not driven by 80C286, yet remain high due to internal pullup resistors during HOLD state. See section on bus hold circuitry.
2. Address, M/$\overline{IO}$ and COD/$\overline{INTA}$ may start floating during any T_C depending on when internal 80C286 bus arbiter decides to release bus to external HOLD. The float starts in $\phi 2$ of T_C. See section on bus hold circuitry.
3. $\overline{BHE}$ and $\overline{LOCK}$ may start floating after the end of any T_C depending on when internal 80C286 bus arbiter decides to release bus to external HOLD. The float starts in $\phi 1$ of T_C. See section on bus hold circuitry.
4. The minimum HOLD to HLDA time is shown. Maximum is one T_H longer.
5. The earliest HOLD time is shown. It will always allow a subsequent memory cycle if pending is shown.
6. The minimum HOLD to HLDA time is shown. Maximum is a function of the instruction, type of bus cycle and other machine state (i.e., Interrupts, Waits, Lock, etc.).
7. Asynchronous ready allows termination of the cycle. Synchronous ready does not signal ready in this example. Synchronous ready state is ignored after ready is signaled via the asynchronous input.

Figure 29. MULTIBUS® Write Terminated by Asynchronous Ready with Bus Hold

Processor Extension Transfers

The processor extension interface uses I/O port addresses 00F8(H), 00FA(H), and 00FC(H) which are part of the I/O port address range reserved by Intel. An ESC instruction with Machine Status Word bits EM = 0 and TS = 0 will perform I/O bus operations to one or more of these I/O port addresses independent of the value of IOPL and CPL.

ESC instructions with memory references enable the CPU to accept PEREQ inputs for processor extension operand transfers. The CPU will determine the operand starting address and read/write status of the instruction. For each operand transfer, two or three bus operations are performed, one word transfer with I/O port address 00FA(H) and one or two bus operations with memory. Three bus operations are required for each word operand aligned on an odd byte address.

NOTE:

Odd-aligned numerics instructions should be avoided when using an 80C286 system running six or more memory-write wait-states. The 80C286 can generate an incorrect numerics address if all the following conditions are met:

- Two floating point (FP) instructions are fetched and in the 80C286 queue.
- The first FP instruction is any floating point store except FSTSW AX.
- The second FP instruction is any floating point store except FSTSW AX.
- The second FP instruction accesses memory.
- The operand of the first instruction is aligned on an odd memory address.
- More than five wait-states are inserted during either of the last two memory write transfers (transferred as two bytes for odd aligned operands) of the first instruction.

The second FP instruction operand address will be incremented by one if these conditions are met. These conditions are most likely to occur in a multi-master system. For a hardware solution, contact your local Intel representative.

Ten or more command delays should not be used when accessing the numerics coprocessor. Excessive command delays can cause the 80C286 and 80287 to lose synchronization.

Interrupt Acknowledge Sequence

Figure 30 illustrates an interrupt acknowledge sequence performed by the 80C286 in response to an INTR input. An interrupt acknowledge sequence consists of two INTA bus operations. The first allows a master 82C59A-2 Programmable Interrupt Controller (PIC) to determine which if any of its slaves should return the interrupt vector. An eight bit vector is read on D0–D7 of the 80C286 during the second INTA bus operation to select an interrupt handler routine from the interrupt table.

The Master Cascade Enable (MCE) signal of the 82C288 is used to enable the cascade address drivers, during INTA bus operations (See Figure 30), onto the local address bus for distribution to slave interrupt controllers via the system address bus. The 80C286 emits the $\overline{LOCK}$ signal (active LOW) during T_S of the first INTA bus operation. A local bus "hold" request will not be honored until the end of the second INTA bus operation.

Three idle processor clocks are provided by the 80C286 between INTA bus operations to allow for the minimum INTA to INTA time and CAS (cascade address) out delay of the 82C59A-2. The second INTA bus operation must always have at least one extra T_C state added via logic controlling $\overline{READY}$. This is needed to meet the 82C59A-2 minimum INTA pulse width.

Local Bus Usage Priorities

The 80C286 local bus is shared among several internal units and external HOLD requests. In case of simultaneous requests, their relative priorities are:

(Highest) Any transfers which assert $\overline{LOCK}$ either explicitly (via the LOCK instruction prefix) or implicitly (i.e. some segment descriptor accesses, interrupt acknowledge sequence, or an XCHG with memory).

The second of the two byte bus operations required for an odd aligned word operand.

The second or third cycle of a processor extension data transfer.

Local bus request via HOLD input.

Processor extension data operand transfer via PEREQ input.

Data transfer performed by EU as part of an instruction.

(Lowest) An instruction prefetch request from BU. The EU will inhibit prefetching two processor clocks in advance of any data transfers to minimize waiting by EU for a prefetch to finish.

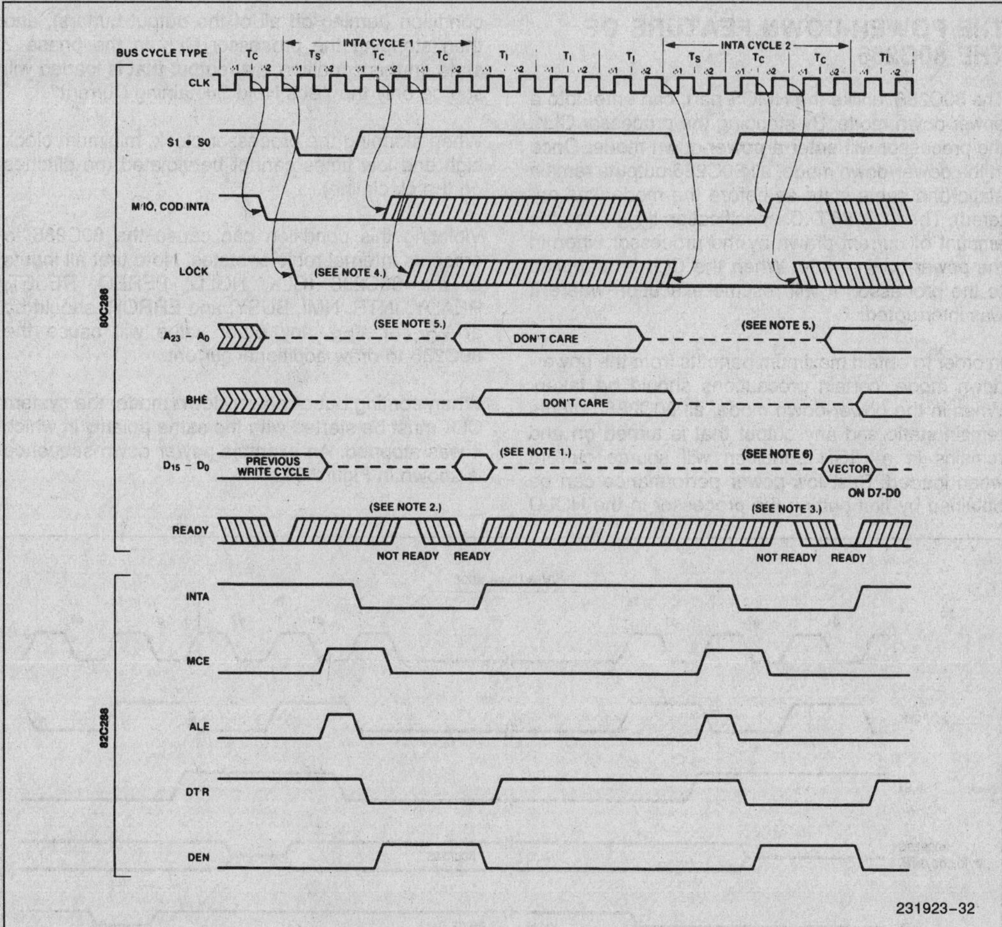

NOTES:

1. Data is ignored, upper data bus, D_8–D_{15}, should not change state during this time.
2. First INTA cycle should have at least one wait state inserted to meet 8259A minimum INTA pulse width.
3. Second INTA cycle should have at least one wait state inserted to meet 8259A minimum INTA pulse width.
4. $\overline{LOCK}$ is active for the first INTA cycle to prevent a bus arbiter from releasing the bus between INTA cycles in a multi-master system. $\overline{LOCK}$ is also active for the second INTA cycle.
5. A_{23}–A_0 exits 3-state OFF during $\phi 2$ of the second T_C in the INTA cycle. See section on bus hold circuitry.
6. Upper data bus should not change state during this time.

Figure 30. Interrupt Acknowledge Sequence

Halt or Shutdown Cycles

The 80C286 externally indicates halt or shutdown conditions as a bus operation. These conditions occur due to a HLT instruction or multiple protection exceptions while attempting to execute one instruction. A halt or shutdown bus operation is signalled when $\overline{S1}$, $\overline{S0}$ and COD/$\overline{INTA}$ are LOW and M/$\overline{IO}$ is HIGH. A_1 HIGH indicates halt, and A_1 LOW indicates shutdown. The 82C288 bus controller does not issue ALE, nor is $\overline{READY}$ required to terminate a halt or shutdown bus operation.

During halt or shutdown, the 80C286 may service PEREQ or HOLD requests. A processor extension segment overrun exception during shutdown will inhibit further service of PEREQ. Either NMI or RESET will force the 80C286 out of either halt or shutdown. An INTR, if interrupts are enabled, or a processor extension segment overrun exception will also force the 80C286 out of halt.

THE POWER-DOWN FEATURE OF THE 80C286

The 80C286, unlike the HMOS part, can enter into a power-down mode. By stopping the processor CLK, the processor will enter a power-down mode. Once in the power-down mode, all 80C286 outputs remain static (the same state as before the mode was entered). The 80C286 D.C. specification I_{CCS} rates the amount of current drawn by the processor when in the power-down mode. When the CLK is reapplied to the processor, it will resume execution where it was interrupted.

In order to obtain maximum benefits from the power-down mode, certain precautions should be taken. When in the power-down mode, all 80C286 outputs remain static and any output that is turned on and remains in a HIGH condition will source current when loaded. Best low-power performance can be obtained by first putting the processor in the HOLD condition (turning off all of the output buffers), and then stopping the processor CLK in the phase 2 state. In this condition, any output that is loaded will source only the "Bus Hold Sustaining Current".

When stopping the processor clock, minimum clock high and low times cannot be violated (no glitches on the clock line).

Violating this condition can cause the 80C286 to erase its internal register states. Note that all inputs to the 80C286 (CLK, HOLD, PEREQ, RESET, READY, INTR, NMI, BUSY, and ERROR) should be at V_{CC} or V_{SS}; any other value will cause the 80C286 to draw additional current.

When coming out of power-down mode, the system CLK must be started with the same polarity in which it was stopped. An example power down sequence is shown in Figure 31.

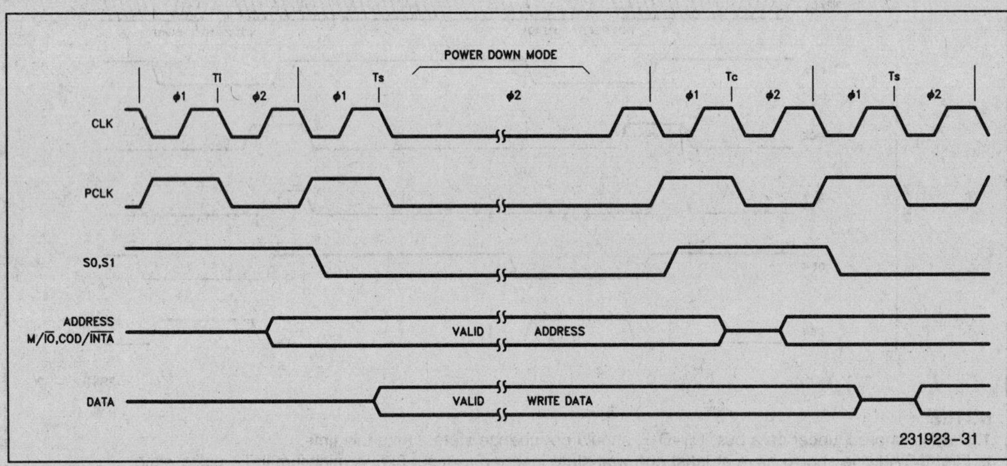

Figure 31. Example Power-Down Sequence

BUS HOLD CIRCUITRY

To avoid high current conditions caused by floating inputs to peripheral CMOS devices and eliminate the need for pull-up/down resistors, "bus-hold" circuitry has been used on all tri-state 80C286 outputs. See Table A for a list of these pins and Figures Ba and Bb for a complete description of which pins have bus hold circuitry. These circuits will maintain the last valid logic state if no driving source is present (i.e., an unconnected pin or a driving source which goes to a high impedance state). To overdrive the "bus hold" circuits, an external driver must be capable of supplying the maximum "Bus Hold Overdrive" sink or source current at valid input voltage levels. Since this "bus hold" circuitry is active and not a "resistive" type element, the associated power supply current is negligible and power dissipation is significantly reduced when compared to the use of passive pull-up resistors.

Bus Hold Circuitry on the 80C286

Signal	Pin Location	Polarity Pulled to when tri-stated
$\overline{S1}$, $\overline{S0}$, $\overline{PEACK}$, $\overline{LOCK}$	4–6, 68	Hi, See Figure Bb
Data Bus (D_0–D_{15})	36–51	Hi/Lo, See Figure Ba
COD/$\overline{INTA}$, M/$\overline{IO}$	66–67	Hi/Lo, See Figure Ba

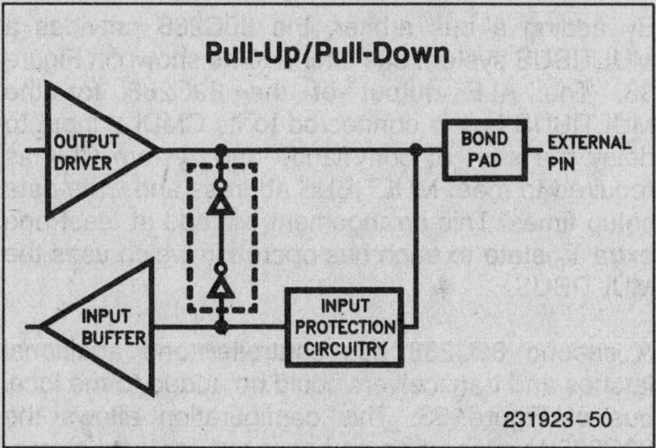

Figure Ba. Bus Hold Circuitry Pins 36–51, 66–67

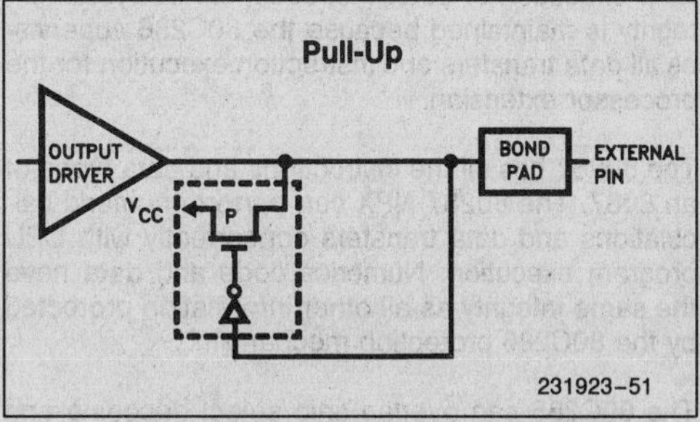

Figure Bb. Bus Hold Circuitry Pins 4–6, 68

5

SYSTEM CONFIGURATIONS

The versatile bus structure of the 80C286 microsystem, with a full complement of support chips, allows flexible configuration of a wide range of systems. The basic configuration, shown in Figure 32, is similar to an 8086 maximum mode system. It includes the CPU plus an 82C59A-2 interrupt controller, 82C284 clock generator, and the 82C288 Bus Controller.

As indicated by the dashed lines in Figure 32, the ability to add processor extensions is an integral feature of 80C286 microsystems. The processor extension interface allows external hardware to perform special functions and transfer data concurrent with CPU execution of other instructions. Full system integrity is maintained because the 80C286 supervises all data transfers and instruction execution for the processor extension.

The 80287 has all the instructions and data types of an 8087. The 80287 NPX can perform numeric calculations and data transfers concurrently with CPU program execution. Numerics code and data have the same integrity as all other information protected by the 80C286 protection mechanism.

The 80C286 can overlap chip select decoding and address propagation during the data transfer for the previous bus operation. This information is latched by ALE during the middle of a T_S cycle. The latched chip select and address information remains stable during the bus operation while the next cycle's address is being decoded and propagated into the system. Decode logic can be implemented with a high speed PROM or PAL.

The optional decode logic shown in Figure 32 takes advantage of the overlap between address and data of the 80C286 bus cycle to generate advanced memory and IO-select signals. This minimizes system performance degradation caused by address propagation and decode delays. In addition to selecting memory and I/O, the advanced selects may be used with configurations supporting local and system buses to enable the appropriate bus interface for each bus cycle. The COD/$\overline{\text{INTA}}$ and M/$\overline{\text{IO}}$ signals are applied to the decode logic to distinguish between interrupt, I/O, code and data bus cycles.

By adding a bus arbiter, the 80C286 provides a MULTIBUS system bus interface as shown in Figure 33. The ALE output of the 82C288 for the MULTIBUS bus is connected to its CMDLY input to delay the start of commands one system CLK as required to meet MULTIBUS address and write data setup times. This arrangement will add at least one extra T_C state to each bus operation which uses the MULTIBUS.

A second 82C288 bus controller and additional latches and transceivers could be added to the local bus of Figure 33. This configuration allows the 80C286 to support an on-board bus for local memory and peripherals, and the MULTIBUS for system bus interfacing.

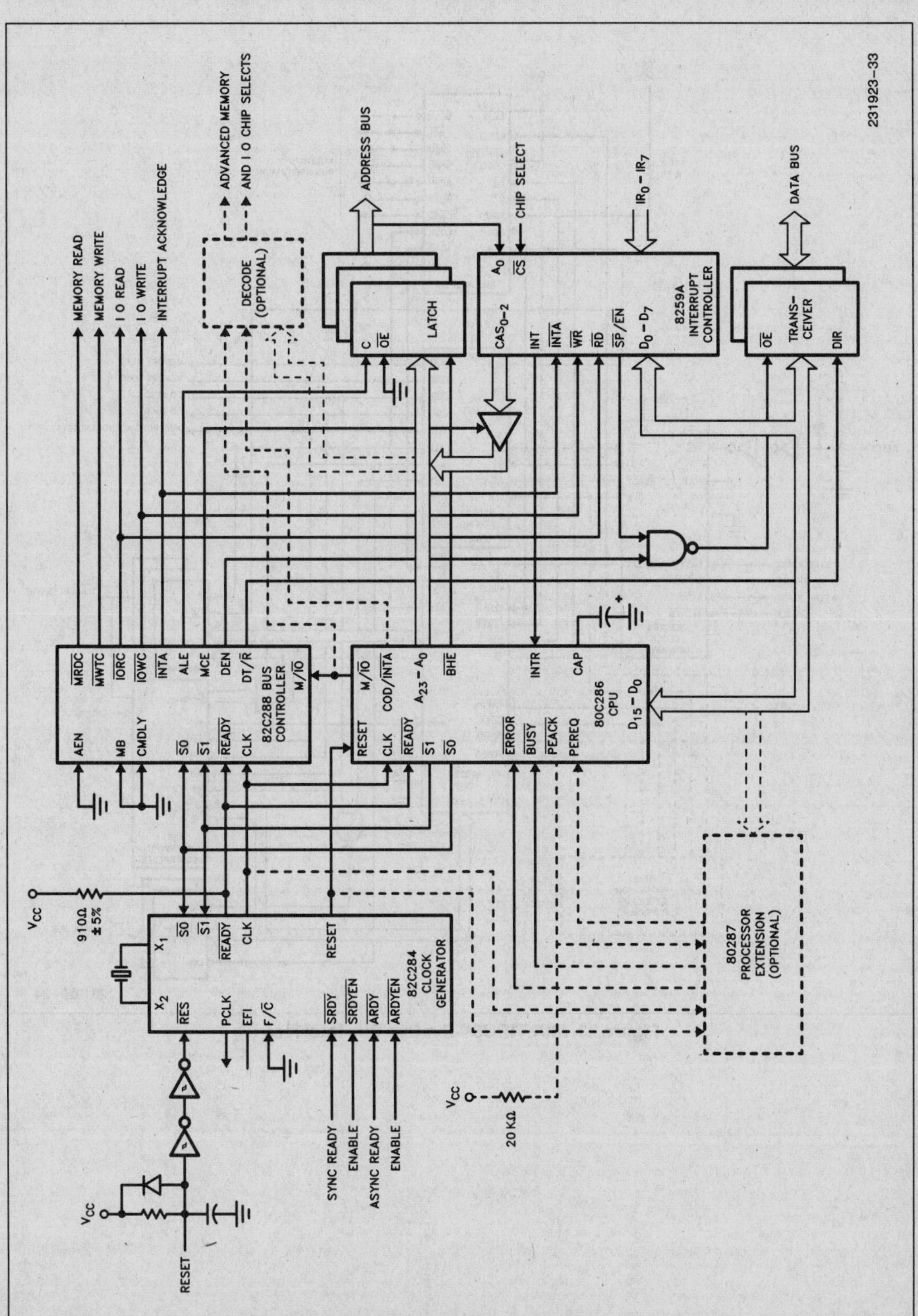

Figure 32. Basic 80C286 System Configuration

5

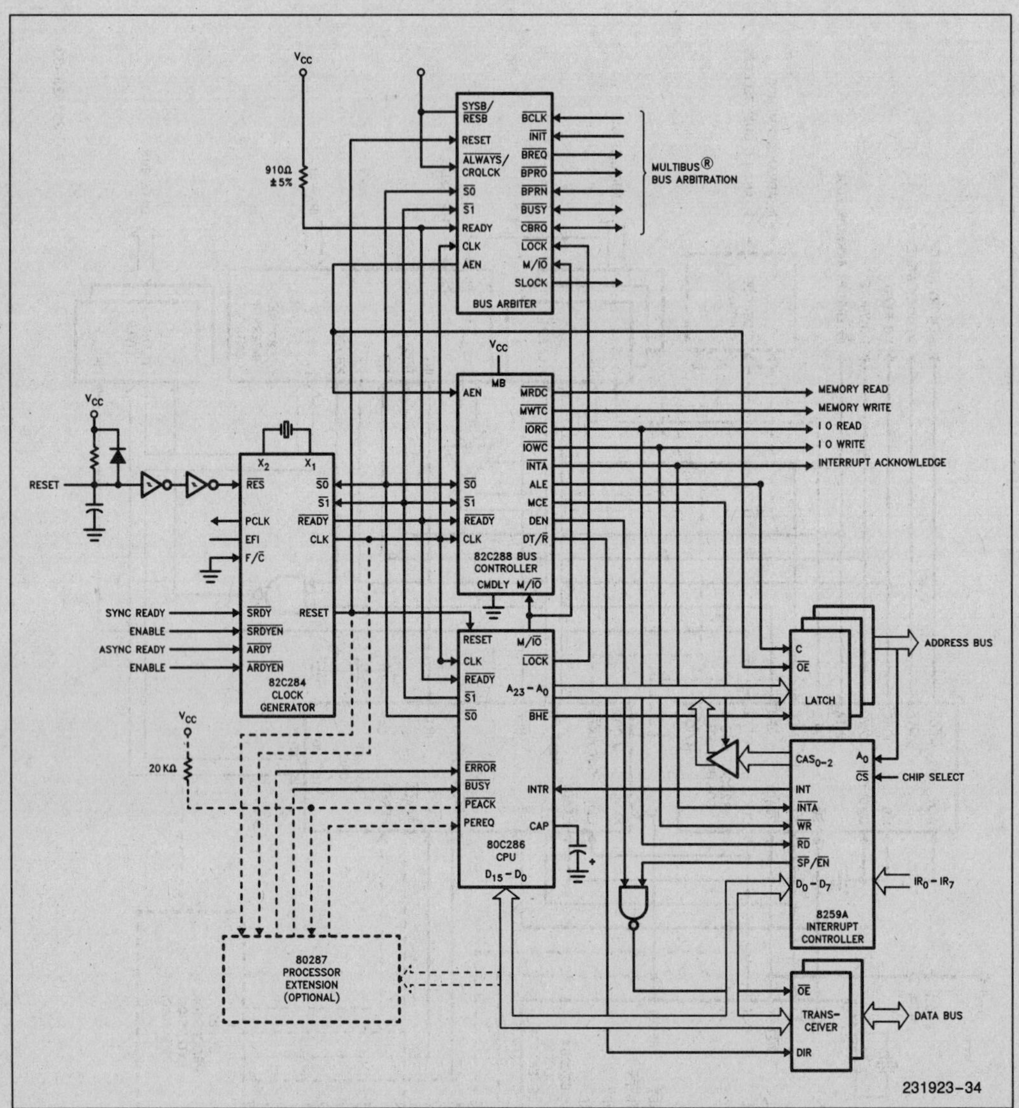

Figure 33. MULTIBUS® System Bus Interface

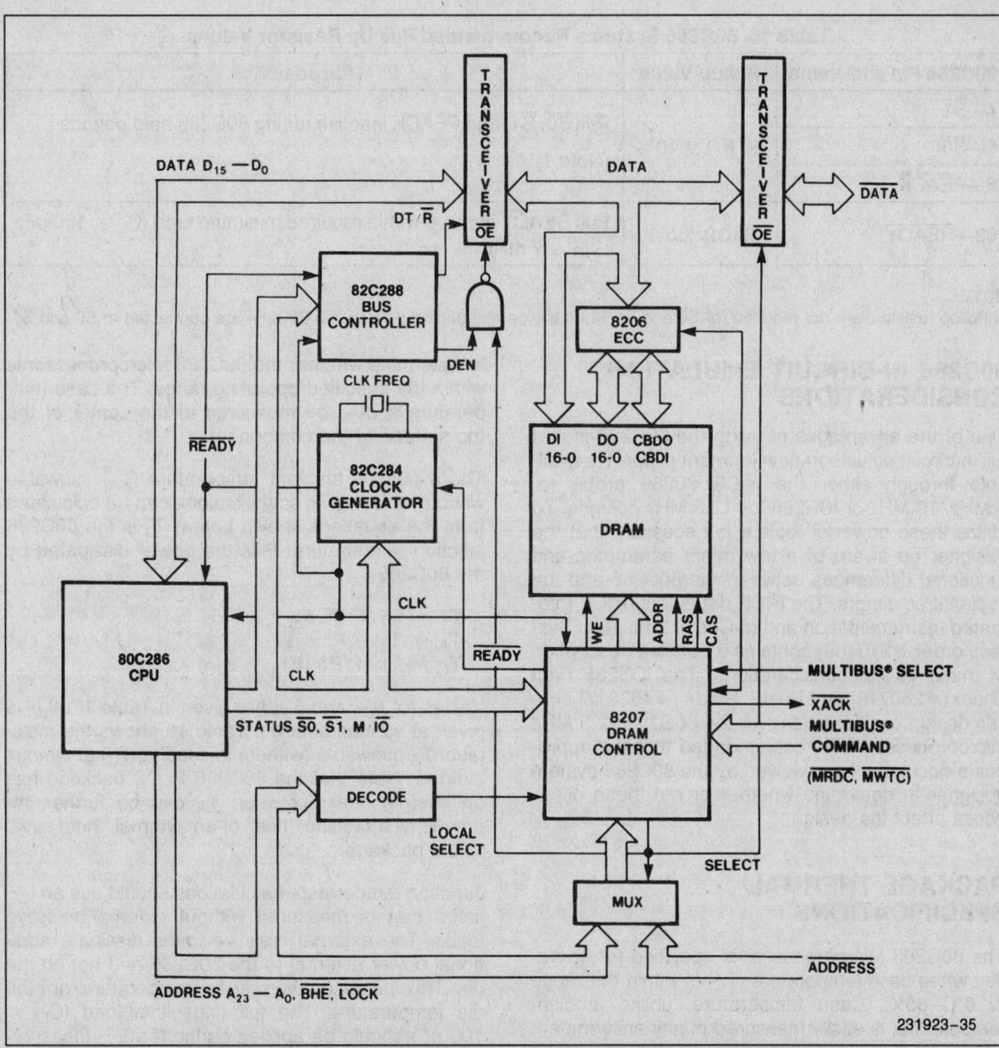

Figure 34. 80C286 System Configuration with Dual-Ported Memory

Figure 34 shows the addition of dual ported dynamic memory between the MULTIBUS system bus and the 80C286 local bus. The dual port interface is provided by the 8207 Dual Port DRAM Controller. The 8207 runs synchronously with the CPU to maximize throughput for local memory references. It also arbitrates between requests from the local and system buses and performs functions such as refresh, initialization of RAM, and read/modify/write cycles. The 8207 combined with the 8206 Error Checking and Correction memory controller provide for single bit error correction. The dual-ported memory can be combined with a standard MULTIBUS system bus interface to maximize performance and protection in multiprocessor system configurations.

5

Table 16. 80C286 Systems Recommended Pull Up Resistor Values

80C286 Pin and Name	Pullup Value	Purpose
4—$\overline{S1}$	20 KΩ ±10%	Pull $\overline{S0}$, $\overline{S1}$, and $\overline{PEACK}$ inactive during 80C286 hold periods (Note 1)
5—$\overline{S0}$		
6—$\overline{PEACK}$		
63—$\overline{READY}$	910Ω ±5%	Pull $\overline{READY}$ inactive within required minimum time (C_L = 150 pF, $I_R \leq 7$ mA)

NOTE:
1. Pullup resistors are not required for $\overline{S0}$ and $\overline{S1}$ when the corresponding pins on the 82C284 are connected to $\overline{S0}$ and $\overline{S1}$.

80C286 IN-CIRCUIT EMULATION CONSIDERATIONS

One of the advantages of using the 80C286 is that full in-circuit emulation development support is available through either the I²ICE 80286 probe for 8 MHz/10 MHz or ICE286 for 12.5 MHz designs. To utilize these powerful tools it is necessary that the designer be aware of a few minor parametric and functional differences between the 80C286 and the in-circuit emulators. The I²ICE datasheet (I²ICE Integrated Instrumentation and In-Circuit Emulation System, order #210469) contains a detailed description of these design considerations. The ICE286 Fact Sheet (#280718) and User's Guide (#452317) contain design considerations for the 80C286 12.5 MHz microprocessor. It is recommended that the appropriate document be reviewed by the 80C286 system designer to determine whether or not these differences affect the design.

PACKAGE THERMAL SPECIFICATIONS

The 80C286 Microprocessor is specified for operation when case temperature (T_C) is within the range of 0°C–85°C. Case temperature, unlike ambient temperature, is easily measured in any environment to determine whether the 80C286 Microprocessor is within the specified operating range. The case temperature should be measured at the center of the top surface of the component.

The maximum ambient temperature (T_A) allowable without violating T_C specifications can be calculated from the equations shown below. T_J is the 80C286 junction temperature. P is the power dissipated by the 80C286.

$$T_J = T_C + P^* \theta_{JC}$$
$$T_A = T_J - P^* \theta_{JA}$$
$$T_C = T_A + P^* [\theta_{JA} - \theta_{JC}]$$

Values for θ_{JA} and θ_{JC} are given in Table 17. θ_{JA} is given at various airflows. Table 18 shows the maximum T_A allowable (without exceeding T_C) at various airflows. Note that the 80C286 PLCC package has an internal heat spreader. T_A can be further improved by attaching "fins" or an external "heat sink" to the package.

Junction temperature calculations should use an I_{CC} value that is measured without external resistive loads. The external resistive loads dissipate additional power external to the 80C286 and not on the die. This increases the resistor temperature, not the die temperature. The full capacitive load (C_L = 100 pF) should be applied during the I_{CC} measurement.

Table 17. Thermal Resistances (°C/Watt) θ_{JC} and θ_{JA}

Package	θ_{JC}	θ_{JA} versus Airflow ft/min (m/sec)					
		0 (0)	200 (1.01)	400 (2.03)	600 (3.04)	800 (4.06)	1000 (5.07)
68-Lead PGA	5.5	29	22	16	15	14	13
68-Lead PLCC w/Internal Heat Speader	8	29	23	21	18	16	15

Table 18. Maximum T_A at Various Airflows

Package	T_A(°C) versus Airflow ft/min (m/sec)					
	0 (0)	200 (1.01)	400 (2.03)	600 (3.04)	800 (4.06)	1000 (5.07)
68-Lead PGA	68	73	78	78	79	80
68 Lead-PLCC w/Internal Heat Speader	70	74	76	78	79	80

NOTE:
The numbers in Table 18 were calculated using a V_{CC} of 5.0V, and an I_{CC} of 150 mA, which is representative of the worst case I_{CC} at T_C = 85°C with the outputs unloaded.

ABSOLUTE MAXIMUM RATINGS*

Ambient Temperature under Bias ....0°C to +70°C

Storage Temperature .... −65°C to +150°C

Voltage on Any Pin with Respect to Ground.............. −1.0V to +7V

Power Dissipation......................... 1.1W

NOTICE: This is a production data sheet. The specifications are subject to change without notice.

**WARNING: Stressing the device beyond the "Absolute Maximum Ratings" may cause permanent damage. These are stress ratings only. Operation beyond the "Operating Conditions" is not recommended and extended exposure beyond the "Operating Conditions" may affect device reliability.*

D.C. CHARACTERISTICS (V_{CC} = 5V ±10%, T_{CASE} = 0°C to +85°C)

Symbol	Parameter	Min	Max	Typ	Unit	Test Conditions
I_{CC}	Supply Current		200	125	mA	C_L = 100 pF (Note 1)
I_{CCS}	Supply Current (Static)		5	0.5	mA	(Note 2)
C_{CLK}	CLK Input Capacitance		20		pF	FREQ = 1 MHz (Note 3)
C_{IN}	Other Input Capacitance		10		pF	FREQ = 1 MHz (Note 3)
C_O	Input/Output Capacitance		20		pF	FREQ = 1 MHz (Note 3)

NOTES:
1. Tested at maximum frequency with no resistive loads on the outputs.
2. Tested while clock stopped in phase 2 and inputs at V_{CC} or V_{SS} with the outputs unloaded.
3. These are not tested but are guaranteed by design characterization.

D.C. CHARACTERISTICS (V_{CC} = 5V ±10%, T_{CASE} = 0°C to +85°C)

Symbol	Parameter	Min	Max	Unit	Test Conditions
V_{IL}	Input LOW Voltage	−0.5	0.8	V	FREQ = 2 MHz
V_{IH}	Input HIGH Voltage	2.0	V_{CC} + 0.5	V	FREQ = 2 MHz
V_{ILC}	CLK Input LOW Voltage	−0.5	0.8	V	FREQ = 2 MHz
V_{IHC}	CLK Input HIGH Voltage	3.8	V_{CC} + 0.5	V	FREQ = 2 MHz
V_{OL}	Output LOW Voltage		0.45	V	I_{OL} = 2.0 mA, FREQ = 2 MHz
V_{OH}	Output HIGH Voltage	3.0 V_{CC} − 0.5		V V	I_{OH} = −2.0 mA, FREQ = 2 MHz I_{OH} = −100 μA, FREQ = 2 MHz
I_{LI}	Input Leakage Current		±10	μA	V_{IN} = GND or V_{CC} (Note 1)
I_{LO}	Output Leakage Current		±10	μA	V_O = GND or V_{CC} (Note 1)
I_{IL}	Input Sustaining Current on BUSY# and ERROR# Pins	−30	−500	μA	V_{IN} = 0V (Note 1)
I_{BHL}	Input Sustaining Current (Bus Hold LOW)	38	150	μA	V_{IN} = 1.0V (Notes 1, 2)
I_{BHH}	Input Sustaining Current (Bus Hold HIGH)	−50	−350	μA	V_{IN} = 3.0V (Notes 1, 3)
I_{BHLO}	Bus Hold LOW Overdrive	200		μA	(Notes 1, 4)
I_{BHHO}	Bus Hold HIGH Overdrive	−400		μA	(Notes 1, 5)

NOTES:
1. Tested with the clock stopped.
2. I_{BHL} should be measured after lowering V_{IN} to GND and then raising to 1.0V on the following pins: 36–51, 66, 67.
3. I_{BHH} should be measured after raising V_{IN} to V_{CC} and then lowering to 3.0V on the following pins: 4–6, 36–51, 66–68.
4. An external driver must source at least I_{BHLO} to switch this node from LOW to HIGH.
5. An external driver must sink at least I_{BHHO} to switch this node from HIGH to LOW.

5

A.C. CHARACTERISTICS (V_{CC} = 5V ±10%, T_{CASE} = 0°C to +85°C)

A.C. timings are referenced to 1.5V points of signals as illustrated in datasheet waveforms, unless otherwise noted.

Symbol	Parameter	12.5 MHz		Unit	Test Conditions
		Min	Max		
1	System Clock (CLK) Period	40	DC	ns	(Note 1)
2	System Clock (CLK) LOW Time	11		ns	at 1.0V
3	System Clock (CLK) HIGH Time	13		ns	at 3.6V
17	System Clock (CLK) Rise Time		8	ns	1.0V to 3.6V (Note 2)
18	System Clock (CLK) Fall Time		8	ns	3.6V to 1.0V (Note 2)
4	Asynchronous Inputs Setup Time	16		ns	(Note 3)
5	Asynchronous Inputs Hold Time	16		ns	(Note 3)
6	RESET Setup Time	19		ns	
7	RESET Hold Time	6		ns	
8	Read Data Setup Time	6		ns	
9	Read Data Hold Time	7		ns	
10	$\overline{\text{READY}}$ Setup Time	23		ns	
11	$\overline{\text{READY}}$ Hold Time	21		ns	
12a1	Status Active Delay	5	16	ns	(Notes 4, 5, 7)
12a2	$\overline{\text{PEACK}}$ Active Delay	5	18	ns	(Notes 4, 5, 7)
12b	Status/$\overline{\text{PEACK}}$ Inactive Delay	5	20	ns	(Notes 4, 5, 7)
13	Address Valid Delay	4	29	ns	(Notes 4, 5, 7)
14	Write Data Valid Delay	3	27	ns	(Notes 4, 5, 7)
15	Address/Status/Data Float Delay	2	32	ns	(Notes 2, 4, 6)
16	HLDA Valid Delay	3	24	ns	(Notes 4, 5, 7)
19	Address Valid To Status Valid Setup Time	23		ns	(Notes 2, 4, 5)

NOTES:

1. Functionality at frequencies less than 2 MHz is not tested, but is guaranteed by design characterization.
2. These are not tested but are guaranteed by design characterization.
3. Asynchronous inputs are INTR, NMI, HOLD, PEREQ, $\overline{\text{ERROR}}$, and $\overline{\text{BUSY}}$. This specification is given only for testing purposes, to assure recognition at a specific CLK edge.
4. Delay from 1.0V on the CLK, to 1.5V or float on the output as appropriate for valid or floating condition.
5. Output load: C_L = 100 pF.
6. Float condition occurs when output current is less than I_{LO} in magnitude.
7. Minimum output delay timings are not tested, but are guaranteed by design characterization.

A.C. CHARACTERISTICS (Continued)

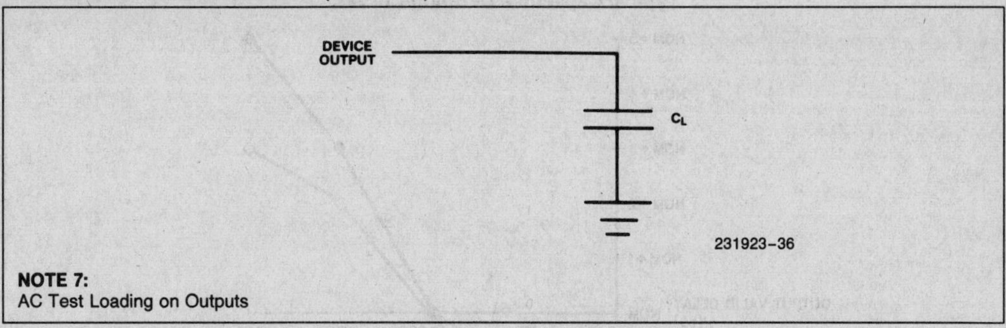

NOTE 7:
AC Test Loading on Outputs

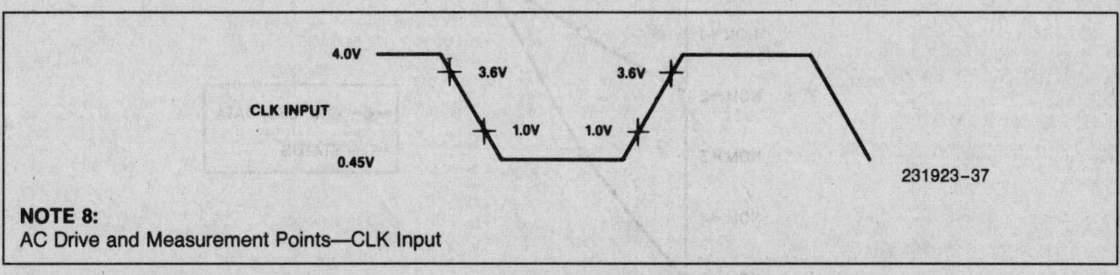

NOTE 8:
AC Drive and Measurement Points—CLK Input

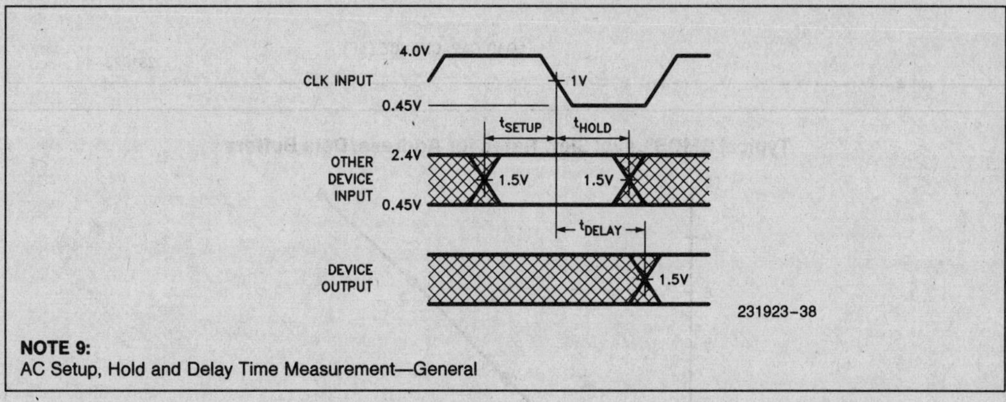

NOTE 9:
AC Setup, Hold and Delay Time Measurement—General

5

Typical Capacitive Derating Curves

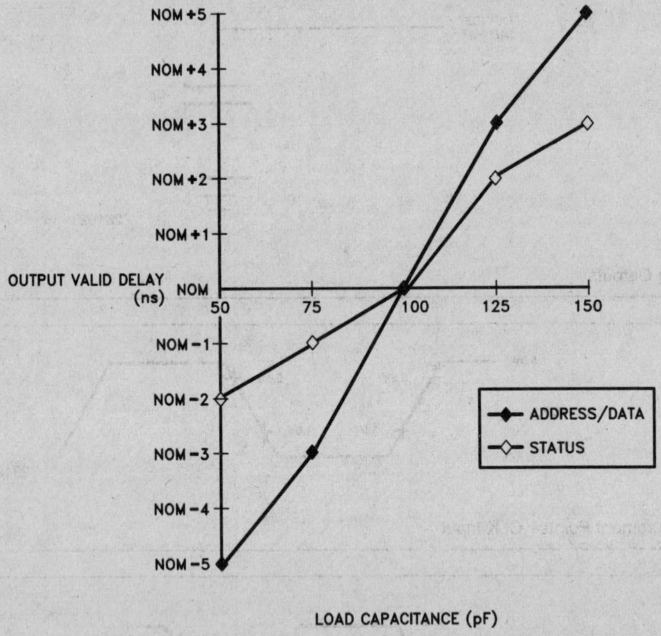

231923-46

Typical CMOS Level Slew Rates for Address/Data Buffers

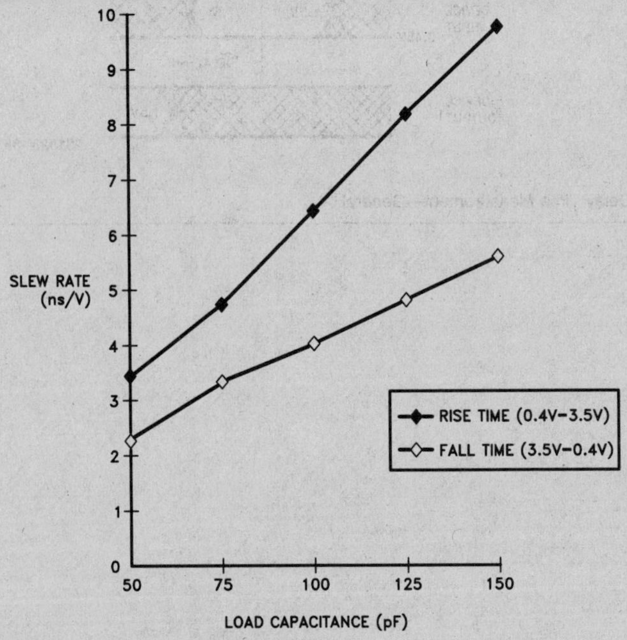

231923-47

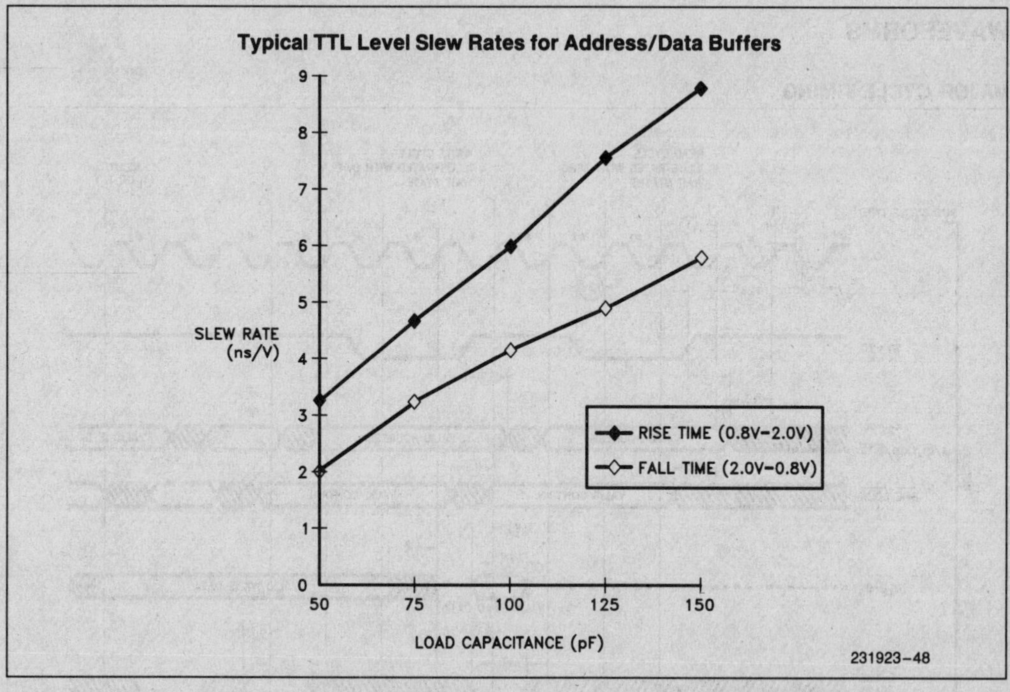

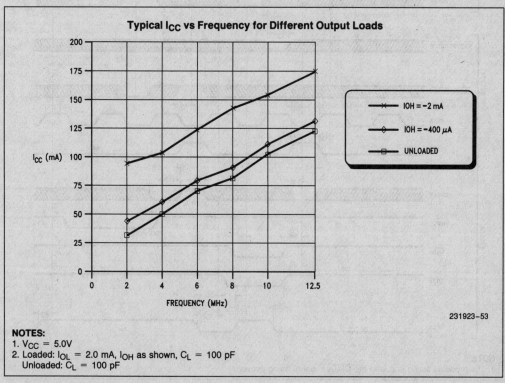

Typical I_{CC} vs Frequency for Different Output Loads

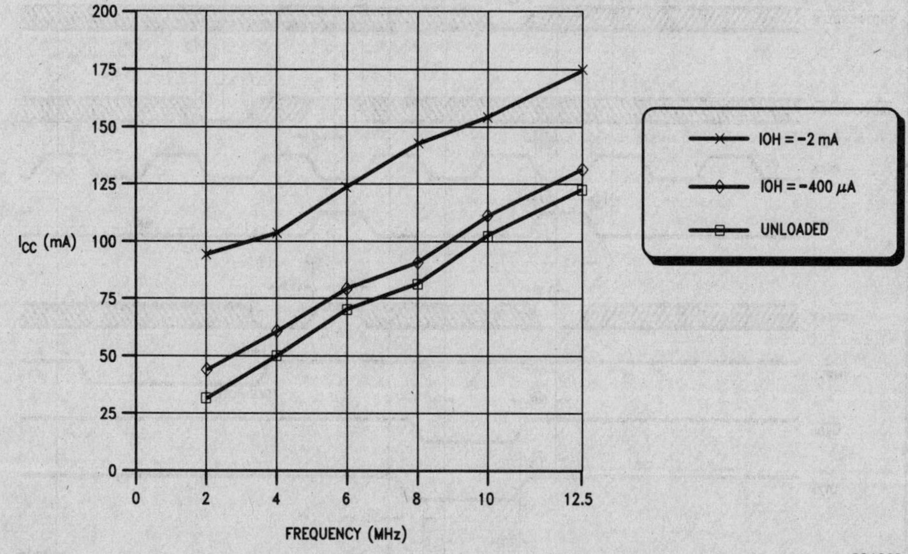

I_{CC} (mA)

200
175
150
125
100
75
50
25
0

0 2 4 6 8 10 12.5

FREQUENCY (MHz)

IOH = −2 mA

IOH = −400 μA

UNLOADED

231923–53

NOTES:

1. V_{CC} = 5.0V
2. Loaded: I_{OL} = 2.0 mA, I_{OH} as shown, C_L = 100 pF
   Unloaded: C_L = 100 pF

WAVEFORMS

MAJOR CYCLE TIMING

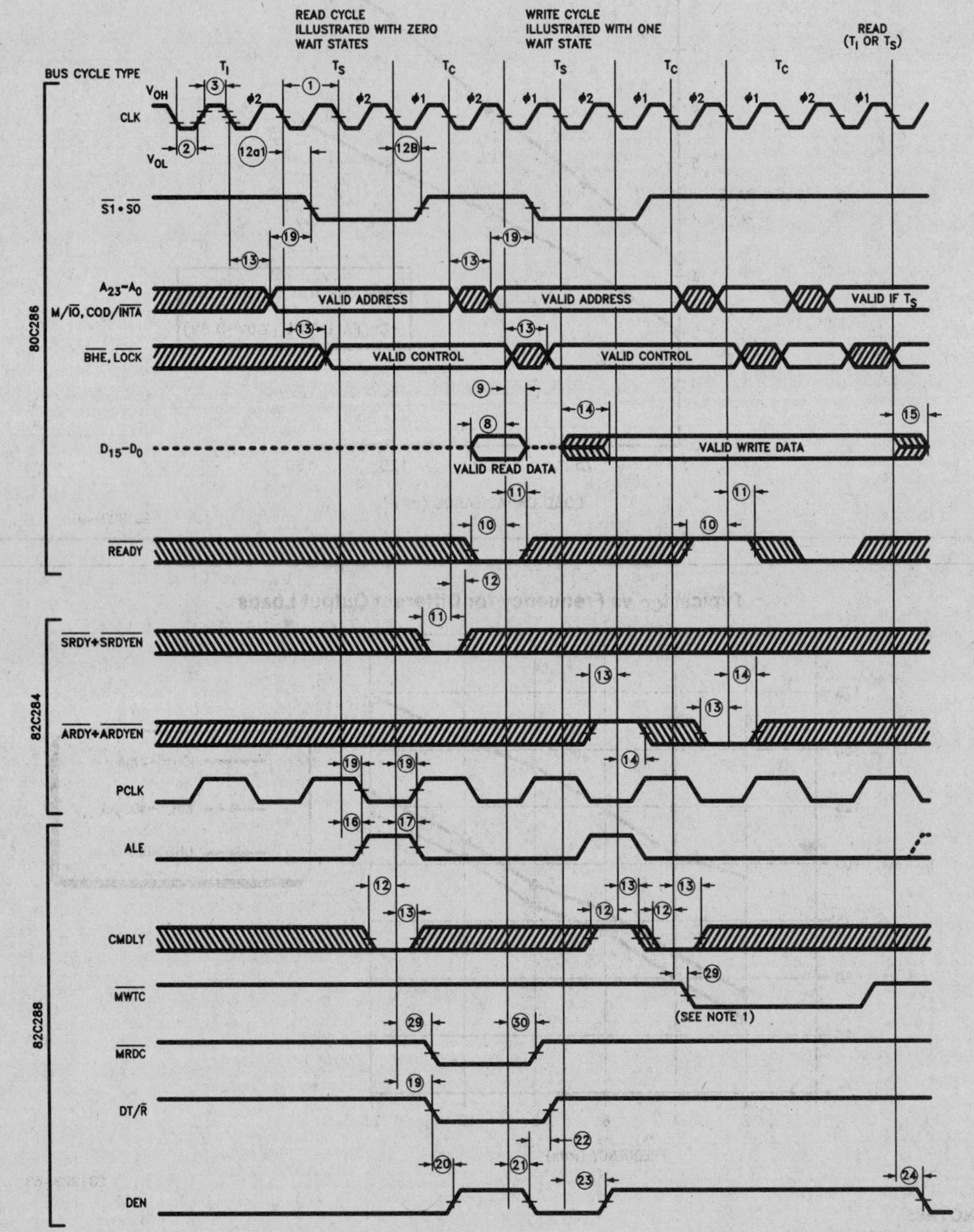

231923–52

NOTE:
1. The modified timing is due to the $\overline{\text{CMDLY}}$ signal being active.

WAVEFORMS (Continued)

80C286 ASYNCHRONOUS INPUT SIGNAL TIMING

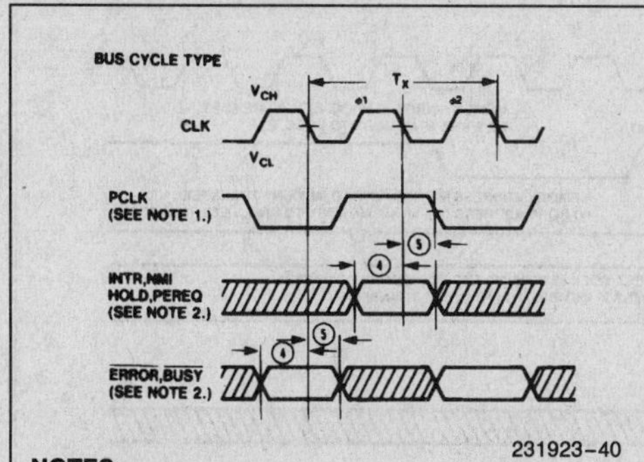

NOTES:

1. PCLK indicates which processor cycle phase will occur on the next CLK. PCLK may not indicate the correct phase until the first bus cycle is performed.
2. These inputs are asynchronous. The setup and hold times shown assure recognition for testing purposes.

80C286 RESET INPUT TIMING AND SUBSEQUENT PROCESSOR CYCLE PHASE

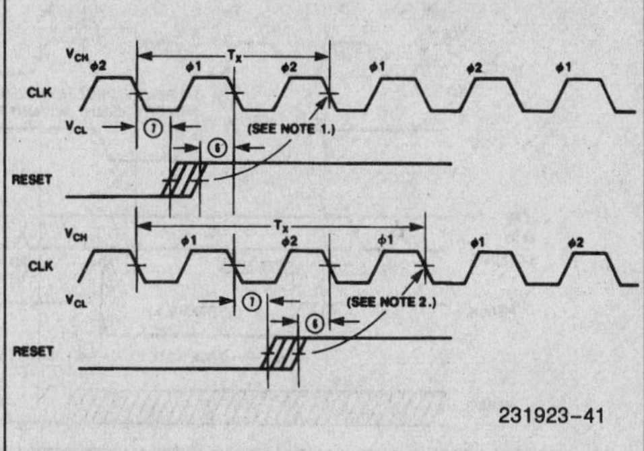

NOTES:

1. When RESET meets the setup time shown, the next CLK will start $\phi 2$ of a processor cycle.
2. When RESET meets the setup time shown, the next CLK will repeat $\phi 1$ of a processor cycle.

EXITING AND ENTERING HOLD

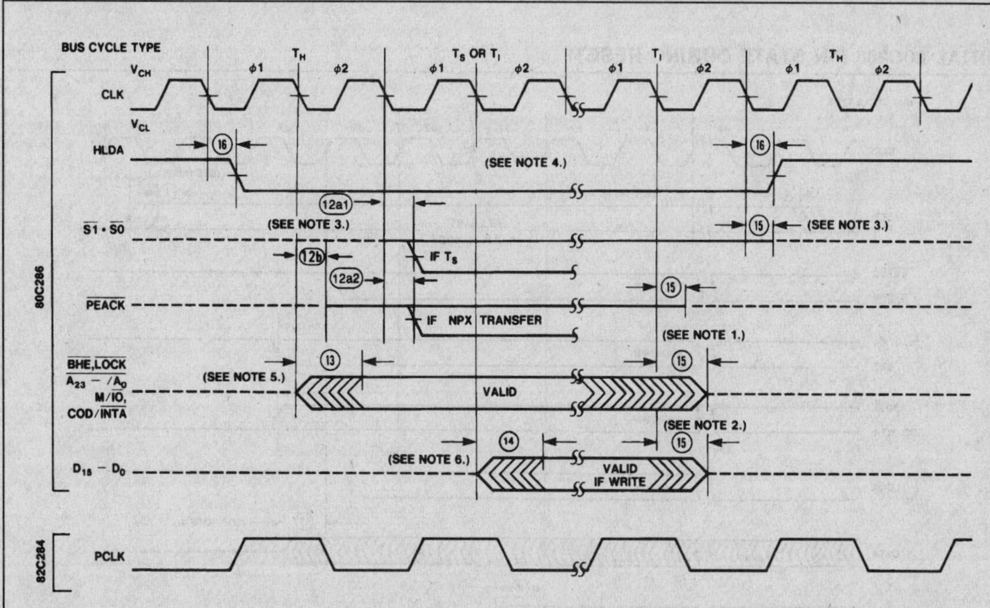

NOTES:

1. These signals may not be driven by the 80C286 during the time shown. The worst case in terms of latest float time is shown.
2. The data bus will be driven as shown if the last cycle before T_I in the diagram was a write T_C.
3. The 80C286 floats its status pins during T_H. External 20 KΩ resistors keep these signals high (see Table 16).
4. For HOLD request set up to HLDA, refer to Figure 29.
5. $\overline{BHE}$ and $\overline{LOCK}$ are driven at this time but will not become valid until T_S.
6. The data bus will remain in 3-state OFF if a read cycle is performed.

WAVEFORMS (Continued)

80C286 PEREQ/$\overline{\text{PEACK}}$ TIMING FOR ONE TRANSFER ONLY

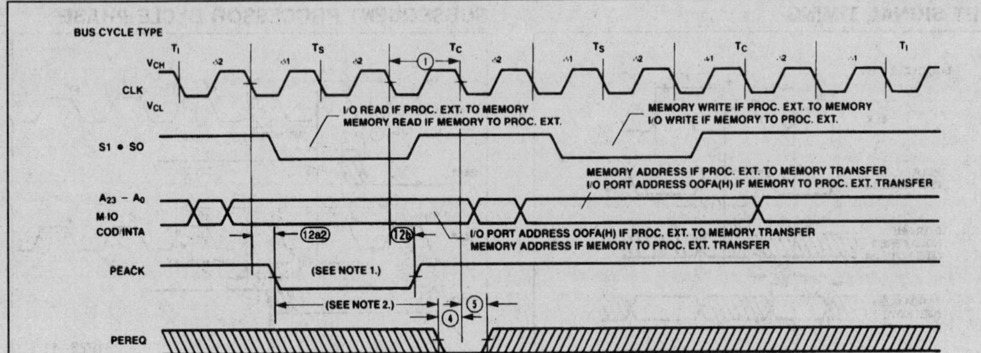

NOTES:

231923–43

1. $\overline{\text{PEACK}}$ always goes active during the first bus operation of a processor extension data operand transfer sequence. The first bus operation will be either a memory read at operand address or I/O read at port address OOFA(H).
2. To prevent a second processor extension data operand transfer, the worst case maximum time (Shown above) is: $3\times① - 12a2_{max.} - ④_{min.}$ The actual, configuration dependent, maximum time is: $3\times① - 12a2_{max.} - ④_{min.} + A\times2\times①$.

A is the number of extra T_C states added to either the first or second bus operation of the processor extension data operand transfer sequence.

INITIAL 80C286 PIN STATE DURING RESET

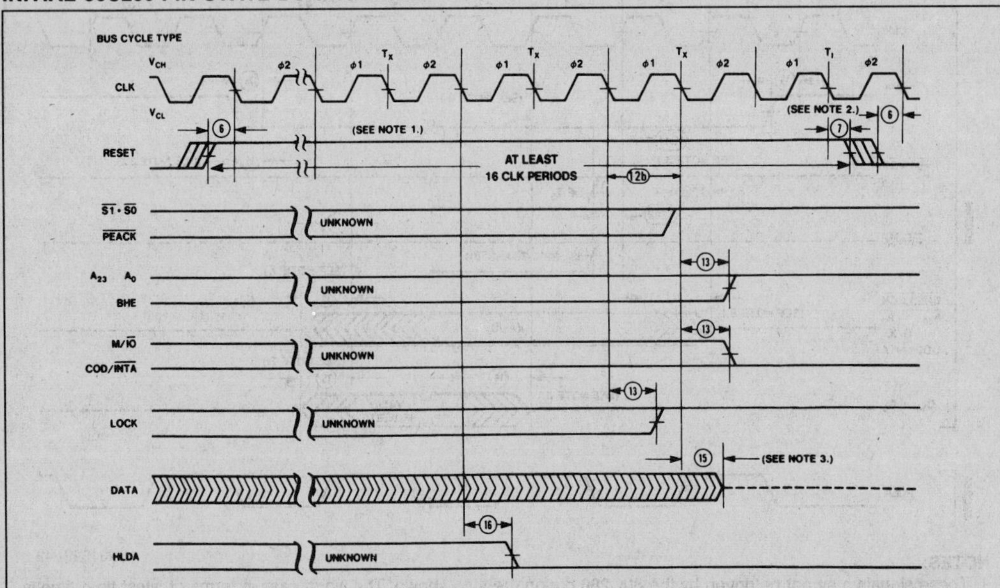

NOTES:

231923–44

1. Setup time for RESET ↑ may be violated with the consideration that $\phi1$ of the processor clock may begin one system CLK period later.
2. Setup and hold times for RESET ↓ must be met for proper operation, but RESET ↓ may occur during $\phi1$ or $\phi2$. If RESET ↓ occurs in $\phi1$, the reference clock edge can be $\phi2$ of the previous bus cycle.
3. The data bus is only guaranteed to be in 3-state OFF at the time shown.

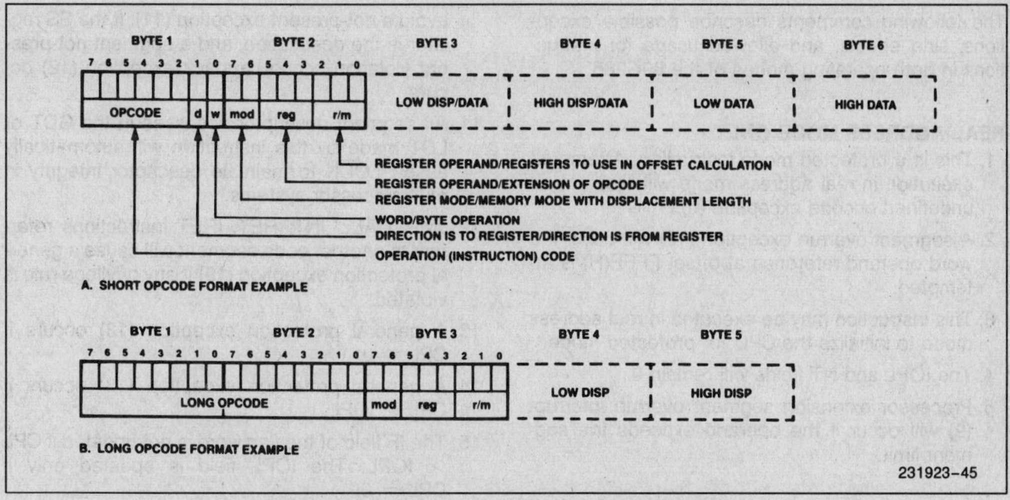

Figure 35. 80C286 Instruction Format Examples

80C286 INSTRUCTION SET SUMMARY

Instruction Timing Notes

The instruction clock counts listed below establish the maximum execution rate of the 80C286. With no delays in bus cycles, the actual clock count of an 80C286 program will average 5% more than the calculated clock count, due to instruction sequences which execute faster than they can be fetched from memory.

To calculate elapsed times for instruction sequences, multiply the sum of all instruction clock counts, as listed in the table below, by the processor clock period. A 12 MHz processor clock has a clock period of 83 nanoseconds and requires an 80C286 system clock (CLK input) of 24 MHz.

Instruction Clock Count Assumptions

1. The instruction has been prefetched, decoded, and is ready for execution. Control transfer instruction clock counts include all time required to fetch, decode, and prepare the next instruction for execution.
2. Bus cycles do not require wait states.
3. There are no processor extension data transfer or local bus HOLD requests.
4. No exceptions occur during instruction execution.

Instruction Set Summary Notes

Addressing displacements selected by the MOD field are not shown. If necessary they appear after the instruction fields shown.

Above/below refers to unsigned value

Greater refers to positive signed value

Less refers to less positive (more negative) signed values

if d = 1 then to register; if d = 0 then from register

if w = 1 then word instruction; if w = 0 then byte instruction

if s = 0 then 16-bit immediate data form the operand

if s = 1 then an immediate data byte is sign-extended to form the 16-bit operand

x don't care

z used for string primitives for comparison with ZF FLAG

If two clock counts are given, the smaller refers to a register operand and the larger refers to a memory operand

* = add one clock if offset calculation requires summing 3 elements

n = number of times repeated

m = number of bytes of code in next instruction

Level (L)—Lexical nesting level of the procedure

The following comments describe possible exceptions, side effects, and allowed usage for instructions in both operating modes of the 80C286.

REAL ADDRESS MODE ONLY

1. This is a protected mode instruction. Attempted execution in real address mode will result in an undefined opcode exception (6).
2. A segment overrun exception (13) will occur if a word operand reference at offset FFFF(H) is attempted.
3. This instruction may be executed in real address mode to initialize the CPU for protected mode.
4. The IOPL and NT fields will remain 0.
5. Processor extension segment overrun interrupt (9) will occur if the operand exceeds the segment limit.

EITHER MODE

6. An exception may occur, depending on the value of the operand.
7. $\overline{\text{LOCK}}$ is automatically asserted regardless of the presence or absence of the LOCK instruction prefix.
8. $\overline{\text{LOCK}}$ does not remain active between all operand transfers.

PROTECTED VIRTUAL ADDRESS MODE ONLY

9. A general protection exception (13) will occur if the memory operand cannot be used due to either a segment limit or access rights violation. If a stack segment limit is violated, a stack segment overrun exception (12) occurs.
10. For segment load operations, the CPL, RPL, and DPL must agree with privilege rules to avoid an exception. The segment must be present to avoid a not-present exception (11). If the SS register is the destination, and a segment not-present violation occurs, a stack exception (12) occurs.
11. All segment descriptor accesses in the GDT or LDT made by this instruction will automatically assert $\overline{\text{LOCK}}$ to maintain descriptor integrity in multiprocessor systems.
12. JMP, CALL, INT, RET, IRET instructions referring to another code segment will cause a general protection exception (13) if any privilege rule is violated.
13. A general protection exception (13) occurs if $CPL \neq 0$.
14. A general protection exception (13) occurs if $CPL > IOPL$.
15. The IF field of the flag word is not updated if $CPL > IOPL$. The IOPL field is updated only if $CPL = 0$.
16. Any violation of privilege rules as applied to the selector operand do not cause a protection exception; rather, the instruction does not return a result and the zero flag is cleared.
17. If the starting address of the memory operand violates a segment limit, or an invalid access is attempted, a general protection exception (13) will occur before the ESC instruction is executed. A stack segment overrun exception (12) will occur if the stack limit is violated by the operand's starting address. If a segment limit is violated during an attempted data transfer then a processor extension segment overrun exception (9) occurs.
18. The destination of an INT, JMP, CALL, RET or IRET instruction must be in the defined limit of a code segment or a general protection exception (13) will occur.

80C286 INSTRUCTION SET SUMMARY

FUNCTION	FORMAT	CLOCK COUNT Real Address Mode	CLOCK COUNT Protected Virtual Address Mode	COMMENTS Real Address Mode	COMMENTS Protected Virtual Address Mode
DATA TRANSFER					
MOV = Move:					
Register to Register/Memory	1000100w | mod reg r/m	2,3*	2,3*	2	9
Register/memory to register	1000101w | mod reg r/m	2,5*	2,5*	2	9
Immediate to register/memory	1100011w | mod 000 r/m | data | data if w = 1	2,3*	2,3*	2	9
Immediate to register	1011w reg | data | data if w = 1	2	2		
Memory to accumulator	1010000w | addr-low | addr-high	5	5	2	9
Accumulator to memory	1010001w | addr-low | addr-high	3	3	2	9
Register/memory to segment register	10001110 | mod 0 reg r/m	2,5*	17,19*	2	9,10,11
Segment register to register/memory	10001100 | mod 0 reg r/m	2,3*	2,3*	2	9
PUSH = Push:					
Memory	11111111 | mod 110 r/m	5*	5*	2	9
Register	01010 reg	3	3	2	9
Segment register	000 reg 110	3	3	2	9
Immediate	011010s0 | data | data if s = 0	3	3	2	9
PUSHA = Push All	01100000	17	17	2	9
POP = Pop:					
Memory	10001111 | mod 000 r/m	5*	5*	2	9
Register	01011 reg	5	5	2	9
Segment register	000 reg 111 (reg≠01)	5	20	2	9,10,11
POPA = Pop All	01100001	19	19	2	9
XCHG = Exhcange:					
Register/memory with register	1000011w | mod reg r/m	3,5*	3,5*	2,7	7,9
Register with accumulator	10010 reg	3	3		
IN = Input from:					
Fixed port	1110010w | port	5	5		14
Variable port	1110110w	5	5		14
OUT = Output to:					
Fixed port	1110011w | port	3	3		14
Variable port	1110111w	3	3		14
XLAT = Translate byte to AL	11010111	5	5		9
LEA = Load EA to register	10001101 | mod reg r/m	3*	3*		
LDS = Load pointer to DS	11000101 | mod reg r/m (mod≠11)	7*	21*	2	9,10,11
LES = Load pointer to ES	11000100 | mod reg r/m (mod≠1)	7*	21*	2	9,10,11

Shaded areas indicate instructions not available in 8086, 88 microsystems.

80C286 INSTRUCTION SET SUMMARY (Continued)

FUNCTION	FORMAT				CLOCK COUNT		COMMENTS	
					Real Address Mode	Protected Virtual Address Mode	Real Address Mode	Protected Virtual Address Mode
DATA TRANSFER (Continued)								
LAHF Load AH with flags	10011111				2	2		
SAHF = Store AH into flags	10011110				2	2		
PUSHF = Push flags	10011100				3	3	2	9
POPF = Pop flags	10011101				5	5	2,4	9,15
ARITHMETIC								
ADD = Add:								
Reg/memory with register to either	000000dw	mod reg r/m			2,7*	2,7*	2	9
Immediate to register/memory	100000sw	mod 000 r/m	data	data if s w = 01	3,7*	3,7*	2	9
Immediate to accumulator	0000010w	data	data if w = 1		3	3		
ADC = Add with carry:								
Reg/memory with register to either	000100dw	mod reg r/m			2,7*	2,7*	2	9
Immediate to register/memory	100000sw	mod 010 r/m	data	data if s w = 01	3,7*	3,7*	2	9
Immediate to accumulator	0001010w	data	data if w = 1		3	3		
INC = Increment:								
Register/memory	1111111w	mod 000 r/m			2,7*	2,7*	2	9
Register	01000reg				2	2		
SUB = Subtract:								
Reg/memory and register to either	001010dw	mod reg r/m			2,7*	2,7*	2	9
Immediate from register/memory	100000sw	mod 101 r/m	data	data if s w = 01	3,7*	3,7*	2	9
Immediate from accumulator	0010110w	data	data if w = 1		3	3		
SBB = Subtract with borrow:								
Reg/memory and register to either	000110dw	mod reg r/m			2,7*	2,7*	2	9
Immediate from register/memory	100000sw	mod 011 r/m	data	data if s w = 01	3,7*	3,7*	2	9
Immediate from accumulator	0001110w	data	data if w = 1		3	3		
DEC = Decrement								
Register/memory	1111111w	mod 001 r/m			2,7*	2,7*	2	9
Register	01001 reg				2	2		
CMP = Compare								
Register/memory with register	0011101w	mod reg r/m			2,6*	2,6*	2	9
Register with register/memory	0011100w	mod reg r/m			2,7*	2,7*	2	9
Immediate with register/memory	100000sw	mod 111 r/m	data	data if s w = 01	3,6*	3,6*	2	9
Immediate with accumulator	0011110w	data	data if w = 1		3	3		
NEG = Change sign	1111011w	mod 011 r/m			2	7*	2	9
AAA = ASCII adjust for add	00110111				3	3		
DAA = Decimal adjust for add	00100111				3	3		

80C286 INSTRUCTION SET SUMMARY (Continued)

FUNCTION	FORMAT					Clock Count: Real Address Mode	Clock Count: Protected Virtual Address Mode	Comments: Real Address Mode	Comments: Protected Virtual Address Mode
ARITHMETIC (Continued)									
AAS = ASCII adjust for subtract	00111111					3	3		
DAS = Decimal adjust for subtract	00101111					3	3		
MUL = Multiply (unsigned):	1111011w	mod 100 r/m							
Register-Byte						13	13		
Register-Word						21	21		
Memory-Byte						16*	16*	2	9
Memory-Word						24*	24*	2	9
IMUL = Integer multiply (signed):	1111011w	mod 101 r/m							
Register-Byte						13	13		
Register-Word						21	21		
Memory-Byte						16*	16*	2	9
Memory-Word						24*	24*	2	9
IMUL = Integer immediate multiply (signed)	011010s1	mod reg r/m	data	data if s = 0		21,24*	21,24*	2	9
DIV = Divide (unsigned)	1111011w	mod 110 r/m							
Register-Byte						14	14	6	6
Register-Word						22	22	6	6
Memory-Byte						17*	17*	2,6	6,9
Memory-Word						25*	25*	2,6	6,9
IDIV = Integer divide (signed)	1111011w	mod 111 r/m							
Register-Byte						17	17	6	6
Register-Word						25	25	6	6
Memory-Byte						20*	20*	2,6	6,9
Memory-Word						28*	28*	2,6	6,9
AAM = ASCII adjust for multiply	11010100	00001010				16	16		
AAD = ASCII adjust for divide	11010101	00001010				14	14		
CBW = Convert byte to word	10011000					2	2		
CWD = Convert word to double word	10011001					2	2		
LOGIC									
Shift/Rotate Instructions:									
Register/Memory by 1	1101000w	mod TTT r/m				2,7*	2,7*	2	9
Register/Memory by CL	1101001w	mod TTT r/m				5+n,8+n*	5+n,8+n*	2	9
Register/Memory by Count	1100000w	mod TTT r/m	count			5+n,8+n*	5+n,8+n*	2	9

TTT	Instruction
000	ROL
001	ROR
010	RCL
011	RCR
100	SHL/SAL
101	SHR
111	SAR

Shaded areas indicate instructions not available in 8086, 88 microsystems.

5

80C286 INSTRUCTION SET SUMMARY (Continued)

FUNCTION	FORMAT				CLOCK COUNT		COMMENTS	
					Real Address Mode	Protected Virtual Address Mode	Real Address Mode	Protected Virtual Address Mode
ARITHMETIC (Continued)								
AND = **And:**								
Reg/memory and register to either	001000dw	mod reg r/m			2,7*	2,7*	2	9
Immediate to register/memory	1000000w	mod 100 r/m	data	data if w = 1	3,7*	3,7*	2	9
Immediate to accumulator	0010010w	data	data if w = 1		3	3		
TEST = **And function to flags, no result:**								
Register/memory and register	1000010w	mod reg r/m			2,6*	2,6*	2	9
Immediate data and register/memory	1111011w	mod 000 r/m	data	data if w = 1	3,6*	3,6*	2	9
Immediate data and accumulator	1010100w	data	data if w = 1		3	3		
OR = **Or:**								
Reg/memory and register to either	000010dw	mod reg r/m			2,7*	2,7*	2	9
Immediate to register/memory	1000000w	mod 001 r/m	data	data if w = 1	3,7*	3,7*	2	9
Immediate to accumulator	0000110w	data	data if w = 1		3	3		
XOR = **Exclusive or:**								
Reg/memory and register to either	001100dw	mod reg r/m			2,7*	2,7*	2	9
Immediate to register/memory	1000000w	mod 110 r/m	data	data if w = 1	3,7*	3,7*	2	9
Immediate to accumulator	0011010w	data	data if w = 1		3	3		
NOT = Invert register/memory	1111011w	mod 010 r/m			2,7*	2,7*	2	9
STRING MANIPULATION:								
MOVS = Move byte/word	1010010w				5	5	2	9
CMPS = Compare byte/word	1010011w				8	8	2	9
SCAS = Scan byte/word	1010111w				7	7	2	9
LODS = Load byte/wd to AL/AX	1010110w				5	5	2	9
STOS = Stor byte/wd from AL/A	1010101w				3	3	2	9
INS = Input byte/wd from DX port	0110110w				5	5	2	9,14
OUTS = Output byte/wd to DX port	0110111w				5	5	2	9,14
Repeated by count in CX								
MOVS = Move string	11110011	1010010w			5+4n	5+4n	2	9
CMPS = Compare string	1111001z	1010011w			5+9n	5+9n	2,8	8,9
SCAS = Scan string	1111001z	1010111w			5+8n	5+8n	2,8	8,9
LODS = Load string	11110011	1010110w			5+4n	5+4n	2,8	8,9
STOS = Store string	11110011	1010101w			4+3n	4+3n	2,8	8,9
INS = Input string	11110011	0110110w			5+4n	5+4n	2	9,14
OUTS = Output string	11110011	0110111w			5+4n	5+4n	2	9,14

Shaded areas indicate instructions not available in 8086, 88 microsystems.

80C286 INSTRUCTION SET SUMMARY (Continued)

FUNCTION	FORMAT				CLOCK COUNT		COMMENTS	
					Real Address Mode	Protected Virtual Address Mode	Real Address Mode	Protected Virtual Address Mode
CONTROL TRANSFER								
CALL = Call:								
Direct within segment	11101000	disp-low	disp-high		7+m	7+m	2	18
Register/memory indirect within segment	11111111	mod 010 r/m			7+m, 11+m*	7+m, 11+m*	2,8	8,9,18
Direct intersegment	10011010	segment offset			13+m	26+m	2	11,12,18
Protected Mode Only (Direct intersegment):		segment selector						
Via call gate to same privilege level						41+m		8,11,12,18
Via call gate to different privilege level, no parameters						82+m		8,11,12,18
Via call gate to different privilege level, x parameters						86 +4x+m		8,11,12,18
Via TSS						177+m		8,11,12,18
Via task gate						182+m		8,11,12,18
Indirect intersegment	11111111	mod 011 r/m		(mod≠11)	16+m	29+m*	2	8,9,11,12,18
Protected Mode Only (Indirect intersegment):								
Via call gate to same privilege level						44+m*		8,9,11,12,18
Via call gate to different privilege level, no parameters						83 +m*		8,9,11,12,18
Via call gate to different privilege level, x parameters						90+4x +m*		8,9,11,12,18
Via TSS						180+m*		8,9,11,12,18
Via task gate						185+m*		8,9,11,12,18
JMP = Unconditional jump:								
Short/long	11101011	disp-low			7+m	7+m		18
Direct within segment	11101001	disp-low	disp-high		7+m	7+ m		18
Register/memory indirect within segment	11111111	mod 100 r/m			7 +m, 11+m*	7+m, 11+m*	2	9,18
Direct intersegment	11101010	segment offset			11+m	23+m		11,12,18
Protected Mode Only (Direct intersegment):		segment selector						
Via call gate to same privilege level						38+m		8,11,12,18
Via TSS						175+m		8,11,12,18
Via task gate						180+m		8,11,12,18
Indirect intersegment	11111111	mod 101 r/m		(mod≠11)	15+m*	26+m*	2	8,9,11,12,18
Protected Mode Only (Indirect intersegment):								
Via call gate to same privilege level						41+m*		8,9,11,12,18
Via TSS						178+m*		8,9,11,12,18
Via task gate						183+m*		8,9,11,12,18
RET = Return from CALL:								
Within segment	11000011				11+m	11+m	2	8,9,18
Within seg adding immed to SP	11000010	data-low	data-high		11+m	11+m	2	8,9,18
Intersegment	11001011				15+m	25+m	2	8,9,11,12,18
Intersegment adding immediate to SP	11001010	data-low	data-high		15+m		2	8,9,11,12,18
Protected Mode Only (RET):								
To different privilege level						55+m		9,11,12,18

5

80C286 INSTRUCTION SET SUMMARY (Continued)

FUNCTION	FORMAT	CLOCK COUNT Real Address Mode	CLOCK COUNT Protected Virtual Address Mode	COMMENTS Real Address Mode	COMMENTS Protected Virtual Address Mode
CONTROL TRANSFER (Continued)					
JE/JZ = Jump on equal zero	01110100 disp	7+m or 3	7+m or 3		18
JL/JNGE = Jump on less/not greater or equal	01111100 disp	7+m or 3	7+m or 3		18
JLE/JNG = Jump on less or equal/not greater	01111110 disp	7+m or 3	7+m or 3		18
JB/JNAE = Jump on below/not above or equal	01110010 disp	7+m or 3	7+m or 3		18
JBE/JNA = Jump on below or equal/not above	01110110 disp	7+m or 3	7+m or 3		18
JP/JPE = Jump on parity/parity even	01111010 disp	7+m or 3	7+m or 3		18
JO = Jump on overflow	01110000 disp	7+m or 3	7+m or 3		18
JS = Jump on sign	01111000 disp	7+m or 3	7+m or 3		18
JNE/JNZ = Jump on not equal/not zero	01110101 disp	7+m or 3	7+m or 3		18
JNL/JGE = Jump on not less/greater or equal	01111101 disp	7+m or 3	7+m or 3		18
JNLE/JG = Jump on not less or equal/greater	01111111 disp	7+m or 3	7+m or 3		18
JNB/JAE = Jump on not below/above or equal	01110011 disp	7+m or 3	7+m or 3		18
JNBE/JA = Jump on not below or equal/above	01110111 disp	7+m or 3	7+m or 3		18
JNP/JPO = Jump on not par/par odd	01111011 disp	7+m or 3	7+m or 3		18
JNO = Jump on not overflow	01110001 disp	7+m or 3	7+m or 3		18
JNS = Jump on not sign	01111001 disp	7+m or 3	7+m or 3		18
LOOP = Loop CX times	11100010 disp	8+m or 4	8+m or 4		18
LOOPZ/LOOPE = Loop while zero/equal	11100001 disp	8+m or 4	8+m or 4		18
LOOPNZ/LOOPNE = Loop while not zero/equal	11100000 disp	8+m or 4	8+m or 4		18
JCXZ = Jump on CX zero	11100011 disp	8+m or 4	8+m or 4		18
ENTER = Enter Procedure	11001000 data-low data-high L			2,8	8,9
L=0		11	11	2,8	8,9
L=1		15	15	2,8	8,9
L > 1		16+4(L − 1)	16+4(L − 1)	2,8	8,9
LEAVE = Leave Procedure	11001001	5	5		
INT = Interrupt:					
Type specified	11001101 type	23+m		2,7,8	
Type 3	11001100	23+m		2,7,8	
INTO = Interrupt on overflow	11001110	24+m or 3 (3 if no interrupt)	(3 if no interrupt)	2,6,8	

Shaded areas indicate instructions not available in 8086, 88 microsystems.

80C286 INSTRUCTION SET SUMMARY (Continued)

FUNCTION	FORMAT	Clock Count: Real Address Mode	Clock Count: Protected Virtual Address Mode	Comments: Real Address Mode	Comments: Protected Virtual Address Mode
CONTROL TRANSFER (Continued)					
Protected Mode Only:					
Via interrupt or trap gate to same privilege level			40+ m		7,8,11,12,18
Via interrupt or trap gate to fit different privilege level			78+ m		7,8,11,12,18
Via Task Gate			167+m		7,8,11,12,18
IRET = Interrupt return	11001111	17+m	31+ m	2,4	8,9,11,12,15,18
Protected Mode Only:					
To different privilege level			55+m		8,9,11,12,15,18
To different task (NT = 1)			169+m		8,9,11,12,18
BOUND = Detect value out of range	01100010 | mod reg r/m	13*	13* (Use INT clock count if exception 5)	2,6	6,8,9,11,12,18
PROCESSOR CONTROL					
CLC = Clear carry	11111000	2	2		
CMC = Complement carry	11110101	2	2		
STC = Set carry	11111001	2	2		
CLD = Clear direction	11111100	2	2		
STD = Set direction	11111101	2	2		
CLI = Clear interrupt	11111010	3	3		14
STI = Set interrupt	11111011	2	2		14
HLT = Halt	11110100	2	2		13
WAIT = Wait	10011011	3	3		
LOCK = Bus lock prefix	11110000	0	0		14
CTS = Clear task switched flag	00001111 | 00000110	2	2	3	13
ESC = Processor Extension Escape	11011TTT | mod LLL r/m (TTT LLL are opcode to processor extension)	9–20*	9–20*	5,8	8,17
SEG = Segment Override Prefix	001 reg 110	0	0		
PROTECTION CONTROL					
LGDT = Load global descriptor table register	00001111 | 00000001 | mod 010 r/m	11*	11*	2,3	9,13
SGDT = Store global descriptor table register	00001111 | 00000001 | mod 000 r/m	11*	11*	2,3	9
LIDT = Load interrupt descriptor table register	00001111 | 00000001 | mod 011 r/m	12*	12*	2,3	9,13
SIDT = Store interrupt descriptor table register	00001111 | 00000001 | mod 001 r/m	12*	12*	2,3	9
LLDT = Load local descriptor table register from register memory	00001111 | 00000000 | mod 010 r/m		17,19*	1	9,11,13
SLDT = Store local descriptor table register to register/memory	00001111 | 00000000 | mod 000 r/m		2,3*	1	9

Shaded areas indicate instructions not available in 8086, 88 microsystems.

80C286 INSTRUCTION SET SUMMARY (Continued)

FUNCTION	FORMAT			CLOCK COUNT		COMMENTS	
				Real Address Mode	Protected Virtual Address Mode	Real Address Mode	Protected Virtual Address Mode
PROTECTION CONTROL (Continued)							
LTR = Local task register from register/memory	00001111	00000000	mod 0 1 1 r/m		17,19*	1	9,11,13
STR = Store task register to register memory	00001111	00000000	mod 0 0 1 r/m		2,3*	1	9
LMSW = Load machine status word from register/memory	00001111	00000001	mod 1 1 0 r/m	3,6*	3,6*	2,3	9,13
SMSW = Store machine status word	00001111	00000001	mod 1 0 0 r/m	2,3*	2,3*	2,3	9
LAR = Load access rights from register/memory	00001111	00000010	mod reg r/m		14,16*	1	9,11,16
LSL = Load segment limit from register/memory	00001111	00000011	mod reg r/m		14,16*	1	9,11,16
ARPL = Adjust requested privilege level: from register/memory		01100011	mod reg r/m		10*,11*	2	8,9
VERR = Verify read access: register/memory	00001111	00000000	mod 1 0 0 r/m		14,16*	1	9,11,16
VERR = Verify write access:	00001111	00000000	mod 1 0 1 r/m		14,16*	1	9,11,16

Shaded areas indicate instructions not available in 8086, 88 microsystems.

Footnotes

The Effective Address (EA) of the memory operand is computed according to the mod and r/m fields:

if mod = 11 then r/m is treated as a REG field
if mod = 00 then DISP = 0*, disp-low and disp-high are absent
if mod = 01 then DISP = disp-low sign-extended to 16 bits, disp-high is absent
if mod = 10 then DISP = disp-high: disp-low

if r/m = 000 then EA = (BX) + (SI) + DISP
if r/m = 001 then EA = (BX) + (DI) + DISP
if r/m = 010 then EA = (BP) + (SI) + DISP
if r/m = 011 then EA = (BP) + (DI) + DISP
if r/m = 100 then EA = (SI) + DISP
if r/m = 101 then EA = (DI) + DISP
if r/m = 110 then EA = (BP) + DISP*
if r/m = 111 then EA = (BX) + DISP

DISP follows 2nd byte of instruction (before data if required)

*except if mod = 00 and r/m = 110 then EQ = disp-high: disp-low.

SEGMENT OVERRIDE PREFIX

0	0	1	reg	1	1	0

reg is assigned according to the following:

reg	Segment Register
00	ES
01	CS
10	SS
11	DC

REG is assigned according to the following table:

16-Bit (w = 1)		8-Bit (w = 0)	
000	AX	000	AL
001	CX	001	CL
010	DX	010	DL
011	BX	011	BL
100	SP	100	AH
101	BP	101	CH
110	SI	110	DH
111	DI	111	BH

The physical addresses of all operands addressed by the BP register are computed using the SS segment register. The physical addresses of the destination operands of the string primitive operations (those addressed by the DI register) are computed using the ES segment, which may not be overridden.

DATA SHEET REVISION REVIEW

The following list represents key differences between this and the −002 data sheet. Please review this summary carefully.

1. The test conditions in the A.C. Characteristics table has been changed.
2. The "Typical I_{CC} vs Frequency for Different Output Loads" graph has been modified.
3. The maximum ambient temperature (T_A) vs. various airflows has been updated.
4. Deleted the 82C284 and 82C288 A.C. Characteristics tables.
5. "PRELIMINARY" status was removed from the datasheet.

80286
High Performance Microprocessor with Memory Management and Protection
(80286-12, 80286-10, 80286-8)

- **High Performance HMOS III Technology**
- **Large Address Space:**
  - **— 16 Megabytes Physical**
  - **— 1 Gigabyte Virtual per Task**
- **Integrated Memory Management, Four-Level Memory Protection and Support for Virtual Memory and Operating Systems**
- **High Bandwidth Bus Interface (12.5 Megabyte/Sec)**
- **Industry Standard O.S. Support:**
  - **— MS-DOS*, UNIX**, XENIX*, iRMX®**
- **Optional Processor Extension:**
  - **— 80287 High Performance 80-bit Numeric Data Processor**
- **Two 8086 Upward Compatible Operating Modes:**
  - **— 8086 Real Address Mode**
  - **— Protected Virtual Address Mode**
- **Complete System Development Support:**
  - **— Assembler, PL/M, Pascal, FORTRAN, and In-Circuit-Emulator (ICE™-286)**
- **Available in:**
  - **— 68-Pin PLCC (Plastic Leaded Chip Carrier)**
  - **— 68-Pin LCC (Leadless Chip Carrier)**
  - **— 68-Pin PGA (Pin Grid Array)**

(See Packaging Spec., Order #231369)

The 80286 is an advanced, high-performance microprocessor with specially optimized capabilities for multiple user and multi-tasking systems. The 80286 has built-in memory protection that supports operating system and task isolation as well as program and data privacy within tasks. A 12.5 MHz 80286 provides six times or more throughput than the standard 5 MHz 8086. The 80286 includes memory management capabilities that map 2^{30} (one gigabyte) of virtual address space per task into 2^{24} bytes (16 megabytes) of physical memory.

The 80286 is upward compatible with 8086 and 88 software. Using 8086 real address mode, the 80286 is object code compatible with existing 8086, 88 software. In protected virtual address mode, the 80286 is source code compatible with 8086, 88 software and may require upgrading to use virtual addresses supported by the 80286's integrated memory management and protection mechanism. Both modes operate at full 80286 performance and execute a superset of the 8086 and 88 instructions.

The 80286 provides special operations to support the efficient implementation and execution of operating systems. For example, one instruction can end execution of one task, save its state, switch to a new task, load its state, and start execution of the new task. The 80286 also supports virtual memory systems by providing a segment-not-present exception and restartable instructions.

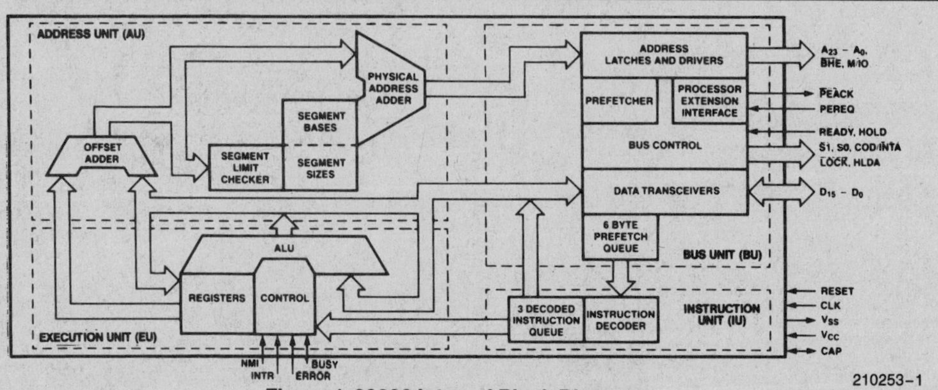

Figure 1. 80286 Internal Block Diagram

September 1991
Order Number: 210253-016

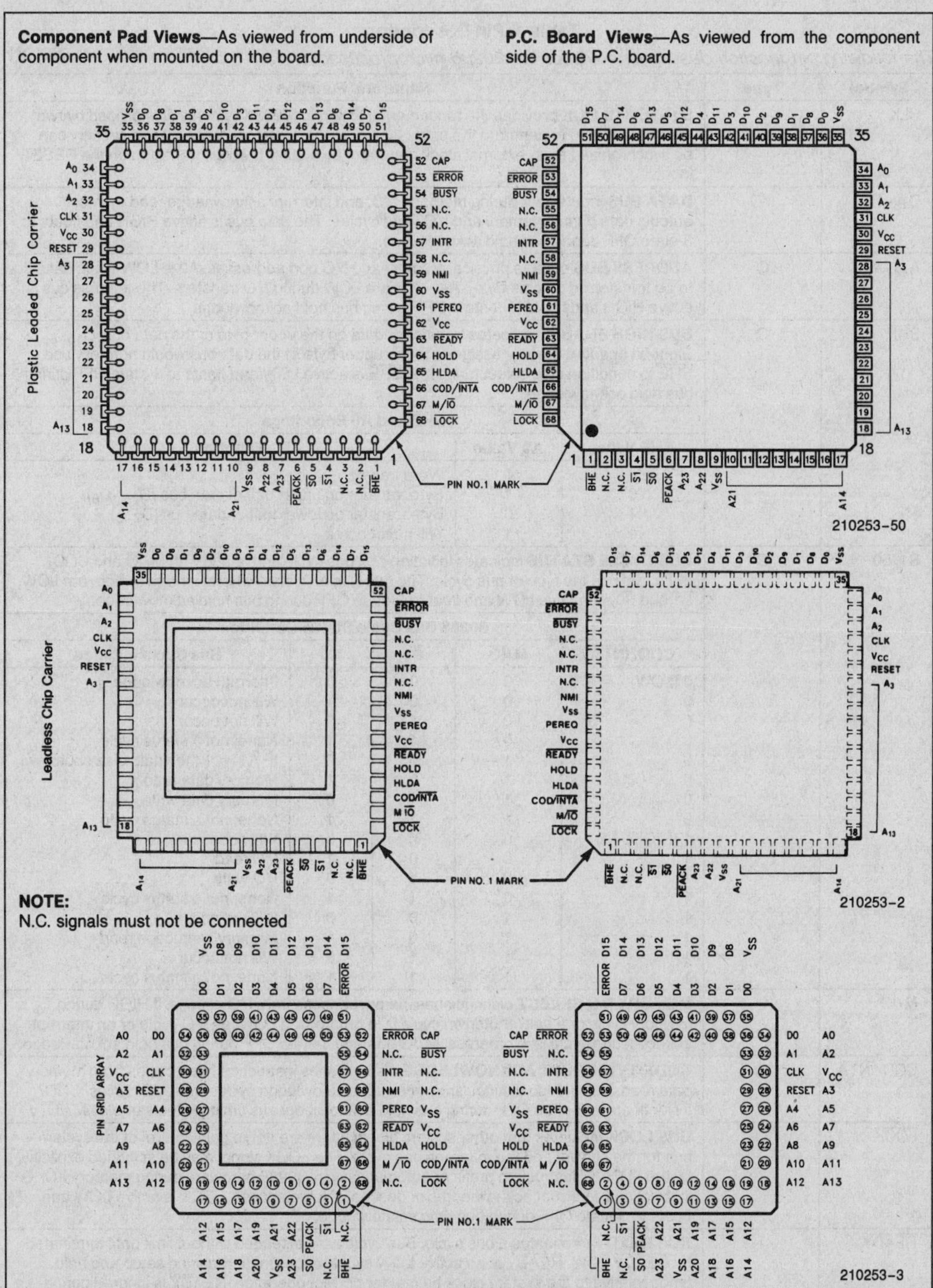

Figure 2. 80286 Pin Configuration

Table 1. Pin Description

The following pin function descriptions are for the 80286 microprocessor:

Symbol	Type	Name and Function
CLK	I	**SYSTEM CLOCK** provides the fundamental timing for 80286 systems. It is divided by two inside the 80286 to generate the processor clock. The internal divide-by-two circuitry can be synchronized to an external clock generator by a LOW to HIGH transition on the RESET input.
$D_{15}-D_0$	I/O	**DATA BUS** inputs data during memory, I/O, and interrupt acknowledge read cycles; outputs data during memory and I/O write cycles. The data bus is active HIGH and floats to 3-state OFF during bus hold acknowledge.
$A_{23}-A_0$	O	**ADDRESS BUS** outputs physical memory and I/O port addresses. A0 is LOW when data is to be transferred on pins D_{7-0}. $A_{23}-A_{16}$ are LOW during I/O transfers. The address bus is active HIGH and floats to 3-state OFF during bus hold acknowledge.
$\overline{\text{BHE}}$	O	**BUS HIGH ENABLE** indicates transfer or data on the upper byte of the data bus. D_{15-8}. Eight-bit oriented devices assigned to the upper byte of the data bus would normally use $\overline{\text{BHE}}$ to condition chip select functions. $\overline{\text{BHE}}$ is active LOW and floats to 3-state OFF during bus hold acknowledge.

$\overline{\text{BHE}}$ and A0 Encodings

$\overline{\text{BHE}}$ Value	A0 Value	Function
0	0	Word transfer
0	1	Byte transfer on upper half of data bus ($D_{15}-D_8$)
1	0	Byte transfer on lower half of data bus (D_{7-0})
1	1	Will never occur

Symbol	Type	Name and Function
$\overline{\text{S1}}$, $\overline{\text{S0}}$	O	**BUS CYCLE STATUS** indicates initiation of a bus cycle and, along with M/$\overline{\text{IO}}$ and COD/$\overline{\text{INTA}}$, defines the type of bus cycle. The bus is in a T_s state whenever one or both are LOW, $\overline{\text{S1}}$ and $\overline{\text{S0}}$ are active LOW and float to 3-state OFF during bus hold acknowledge.

80286 Bus Cycle Status Definition

COD/$\overline{\text{INTA}}$	M/$\overline{\text{IO}}$	$\overline{\text{S1}}$	$\overline{\text{S0}}$	Bus Cycle Initiated
0 (LOW)	0	0	0	Interrupt acknowledge
0	0	0	1	Will not occur
0	0	1	0	Will not occur
0	0	1	1	None; not a status cycle
0	1	0	0	IF A1 = 1 then halt; else shutdown
0	1	0	1	Memory data read
0	1	1	0	Memory data write
0	1	1	1	None; not a status cycle
1 (HIGH)	0	0	0	Will not occur
1	0	0	1	I/O read
1	0	1	0	I/O write
1	0	1	1	None; not a status cycle
1	1	0	0	Will not occur
1	1	0	1	Memory instruction read
1	1	1	0	Will not occur
1	1	1	1	None; not a status cycle

Symbol	Type	Name and Function
M/$\overline{\text{IO}}$	O	**MEMORY I/O SELECT** distinguishes memory access from I/O access. If HIGH during T_s, a memory cycle or a halt/shutdown cycle is in progress. If LOW, an I/O cycle or an interrupt acknowledge cycle is in progress. M/$\overline{\text{IO}}$ floats to 3-state OFF during bus hold acknowledge.
COD/$\overline{\text{INTA}}$	O	**CODE/INTERRUPT ACKNOWLEDGE** distinguishes instruction fetch cycles from memory data read cycles. Also distinguishes interrupt acknowledge cycles from I/O cycles. COD/$\overline{\text{INTA}}$ floats to 3-state OFF during bus hold acknowledge. Its timing is the same as M/$\overline{\text{IO}}$.
$\overline{\text{LOCK}}$	O	**BUS LOCK** indicates that other system bus masters are not to gain control of the system bus for the current and the following bus cycle. The $\overline{\text{LOCK}}$ signal may be activated explicitly by the "LOCK" instruction prefix or automatically by 80286 hardware during memory XCHG instructions, interrupt acknowledge, or descriptor table access. $\overline{\text{LOCK}}$ is active LOW and floats to 3-state OFF during bus hold acknowledge.
$\overline{\text{READY}}$	I	**BUS READY** terminates a bus cycle. Bus cycles are extended without limit until terminated by $\overline{\text{READY}}$ LOW. $\overline{\text{READY}}$ is an active LOW synchronous input requiring setup and hold times relative to the system clock be met for correct operation. $\overline{\text{READY}}$ is ignored during bus hold acknowledge.

Table 1. Pin Description (Continued)

Symbol	Type	Name and Function
HOLD HLDA	I O	**BUS HOLD REQUEST AND HOLD ACKNOWLEDGE** control ownership of the 80286 local bus. The HOLD input allows another local bus master to request control of the local bus. When control is granted, the 80286 will float its bus drivers to 3-state OFF and then activate HLDA, thus entering the bus hold acknowledge condition. The local bus will remain granted to the requesting master until HOLD becomes inactive which results in the 80286 deactivating HLDA and regaining control of the local bus. This terminates the bus hold acknowledge condition. HOLD may be asynchronous to the system clock. These signals are active HIGH.
INTR	I	**INTERRUPT REQUEST** requests the 80286 to suspend its current program execution and service a pending external request. Interrupt requests are masked whenever the interrupt enable bit in the flag word is cleared. When the 80286 responds to an interrupt request, it performs two interrupt acknowledge bus cycles to read an 8-bit interrupt vector that identifies the source of the interrupt. To assure program interruption, INTR must remain active until the first interrupt acknowledge cycle is completed. INTR is sampled at the beginning of each processor cycle and must be active HIGH at least two processor cycles before the current instruction ends in order to interrupt before the next instruction. INTR is level sensitive, active HIGH, and may be asynchronous to the system clock.
NMI	I	**NON-MASKABLE INTERRUPT REQUEST** interrupts the 80286 with an internally supplied vector value of 2. No interrupt acknowledge cycles are performed. The interrupt enable bit in the 80286 flag word does not affect this input. The NMI input is active HIGH, may be asynchronous to the system clock, and is edge triggered after internal synchronization. For proper recognition, the input must have been previously LOW for at least four system clock cycles and remain HIGH for at least four system clock cycles.
PEREQ $\overline{\text{PEACK}}$	I O	**PROCESSOR EXTENSION OPERAND REQUEST AND ACKNOWLEDGE** extend the memory management and protection capabilities of the 80286 to processor extensions. The PEREQ input requests the 80286 to perform a data operand transfer for a processor extension. The $\overline{\text{PEACK}}$ output signals the processor extension when the requested operand is being transferred. PEREQ is active HIGH and floats to 3-state OFF during bus hold acknowledge. $\overline{\text{PEACK}}$ may be asynchronous to the system clock. $\overline{\text{PEACK}}$ is active LOW.
$\overline{\text{BUSY}}$ $\overline{\text{ERROR}}$	I I	**PROCESSOR EXTENSION BUSY AND ERROR** indicate the operating condition of a processor extension to the 80286. An active $\overline{\text{BUSY}}$ input stops 80286 program execution on WAIT and some ESC instructions until $\overline{\text{BUSY}}$ becomes inactive (HIGH). The 80286 may be interrupted while waiting for $\overline{\text{BUSY}}$ to become inactive. An active $\overline{\text{ERROR}}$ input causes the 80286 to perform a processor extension interrupt when executing WAIT or some ESC instructions. These inputs are active LOW and may be asynchronous to the system clock. These inputs have internal pull-up resistors.

Table 1. Pin Description (Continued)

<table>
<tr><th>Symbol</th><th>Type</th><th colspan="2">Name and Function</th></tr>
<tr><td rowspan="5">RESET</td><td rowspan="5">I</td><td colspan="2">SYSTEM RESET clears the internal logic of the 80286 and is active HIGH. The 80286 may be reinitialized at any time with a LOW to HIGH transition on RESET which remains active for more than 16 system clock cycles. During RESET active, the output pins of the 80286 enter the state shown below:</td></tr>
<tr><td colspan="2">80286 Pin State During Reset</td></tr>
<tr><td>Pin Value</td><td>Pin Names</td></tr>
<tr><td>1 (HIGH)
0 (LOW)
3-state OFF</td><td>$\overline{S0}$, $\overline{S1}$, $\overline{PEACK}$, A23–A0, $\overline{BHE}$, $\overline{LOCK}$
M/$\overline{IO}$, COD/$\overline{INTA}$, HLDA (Note 1)
D_{15}–D_0</td></tr>
<tr><td colspan="2">Operation of the 80286 begins after a HIGH to LOW transition on RESET. The HIGH to LOW transition of RESET must be synchronous to the system clock. Approximately 38 CLK cycles from the trailing edge of RESET are required by the 80286 for internal initialization before the first bus cycle, to fetch code from the power-on execution address, occurs.
A LOW to HIGH transition of RESET synchronous to the system clock will end a processor cycle at the second HIGH to LOW transition of the system clock. The LOW to HIGH transition of RESET may be asynchronous to the system clock; however, in this case it cannot be predetermined which phase of the processor clock will occur during the next system clock period. Synchronous LOW to HIGH transitions of RESET are required only for systems where the processor clock must be phase synchronous to another clock.</td></tr>
<tr><td>V_{SS}</td><td>I</td><td colspan="2">SYSTEM GROUND: 0 Volts.</td></tr>
<tr><td>V_{CC}</td><td>I</td><td colspan="2">SYSTEM POWER: +5 Volt Power Supply.</td></tr>
<tr><td>CAP</td><td>I</td><td colspan="2">SUBSTRATE FILTER CAPACITOR: a 0.047 μF $\pm$ 20% 12V capacitor must be connected between this pin and ground. This capacitor filters the output of the internal substrate bias generator. A maximum DC leakage current of 1 μA is allowed through the capacitor.
For correct operation of the 80286, the substrate bias generator must charge this capacitor to its operating voltage. The capacitor chargeup time is 5 milliseconds (max.) after V_{CC} and CLK reach their specified AC and DC parameters. RESET may be applied to prevent spurious activity by the CPU during this time. After this time, the 80286 processor clock can be synchronized to another clock by pulsing RESET LOW synchronous to the system clock.</td></tr>
</table>

NOTE:
1. HLDA is only Low if HOLD is inactive (Low).

FUNCTIONAL DESCRIPTION

Introduction

The 80286 is an advanced, high-performance microprocessor with specially optimized capabilities for multiple user and multi-tasking systems. Depending on the application, a 12.5 MHz 80286's performance is up to six times faster than the standard 5 MHz 8086's, while providing complete upward software compatibility with Intel's 8086, 88, and 186 family of CPU's.

The 80286 operates in two modes: 8086 real address mode and protected virtual address mode. Both modes execute a superset of the 8086 and 88 instruction set.

In 8086 real address mode programs use real addresses with up to one megabyte of address space. Programs use virtual addresses in protected virtual address mode, also called protected mode. In protected mode, the 80286 CPU automatically maps 1 gigabyte of virtual addresses per task into a 16 megabyte real address space. This mode also provides memory protection to isolate the operating system and ensure privacy of each tasks' programs and data. Both modes provide the same base instruction set, registers, and addressing modes.

The following Functional Description describes first, the base 80286 architecture common to both modes, second, 8086 real address mode, and third, protected mode.

80286 BASE ARCHITECTURE

The 8086, 88, 186, and 286 CPU family all contain the same basic set of registers, instructions, and addressing modes. The 80286 processor is upward compatible with the 8086, 8088, and 80186 CPU's.

Register Set

The 80286 base architecture has fifteen registers as shown in Figure 3. These registers are grouped into the following four categories:

General Registers: Eight 16-bit general purpose registers used to contain arithmetic and logical operands. Four of these (AX, BX, CX, and DX) can be used either in their entirety as 16-bit words or split into pairs of separate 8-bit registers.

Segment Registers: Four 16-bit special purpose registers select, at any given time, the segments of memory that are immediately addressable for code, stack, and data. (For usage, refer to Memory Organization.)

Base and Index Registers: Four of the general purpose registers may also be used to determine offset addresses of operands in memory. These registers may contain base addresses or indexes to particular locations within a segment. The addressing mode determines the specific registers used for operand address calculations.

Status and Control Registers: The 3 16-bit special purpose registers in figure 3A record or control certain aspects of the 80286 processor state including the Instruction Pointer, which contains the offset address of the next sequential instruction to be executed.

5

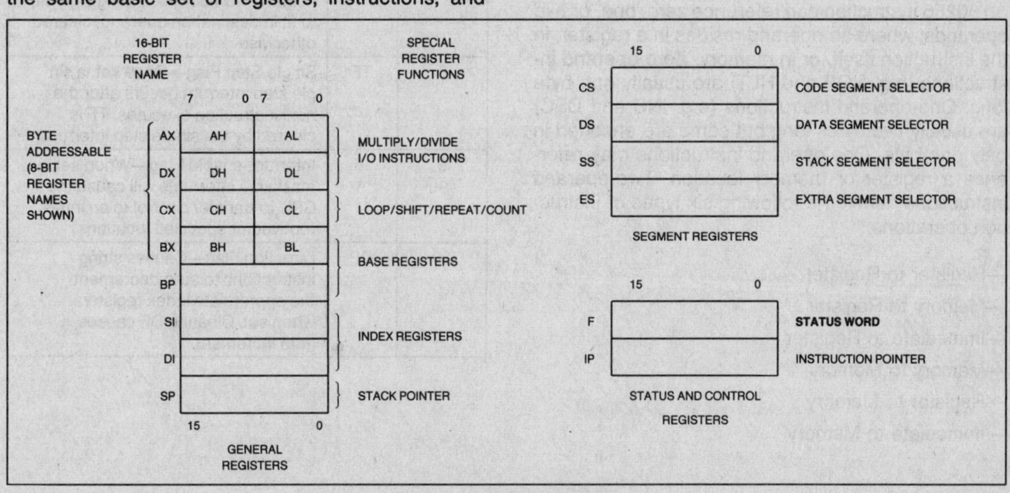

Figure 3. Register Set

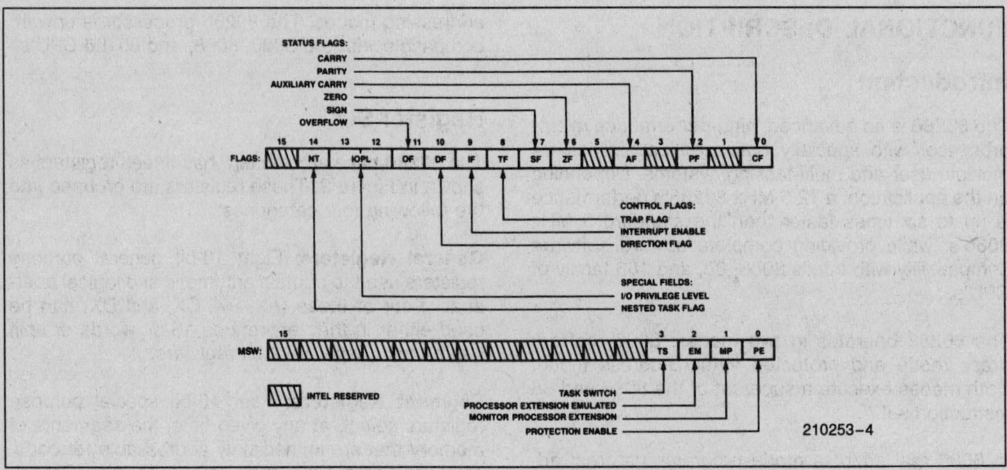

Figure 3a. Status and Control Register Bit Functions

Flags Word Description

The Flags word (Flags) records specific characteristics of the result of logical and arithmetic instructions (bits 0, 2, 4, 6, 7, and 11) and controls the operation of the 80286 within a given operating mode (bits 8 and 9). Flags is a 16-bit register. The function of the flag bits is given in Table 2.

Table 2. Flags Word Bit Functions

Bit Position	Name	Function
0	CF	Carry Flag—Set on high-order bit carry or borrow; cleared otherwise
2	PF	Parity Flag—Set if low-order 8 bits of result contain an even number of 1-bits; cleared otherwise
4	AF	Set on carry from or borrow to the low order four bits of AL; cleared otherwise
6	ZF	Zero Flag—Set if result is zero; cleared otherwise
7	SF	Sign Flag—Set equal to high-order bit of result (0 if positive, 1 if negative)
11	OF	Overflow Flag—Set if result is a too-large positive number or a too-small negative number (excluding sign-bit) to fit in destination operand; cleared otherwise
8	TF	Single Step Flag—Once set, a single step interrupt occurs after the next instruction executes. TF is cleared by the single step interrupt.
9	IF	Interrupt-enable Flag—When set, maskable interrupts will cause the CPU to transfer control to an interrupt vector specified location.
10	DF	Direction Flag—Causes string instructions to auto decrement the appropriate index registers when set. Clearing DF causes auto increment.

Instruction Set

The instruction set is divided into seven categories: data transfer, arithmetic, shift/rotate/logical, string manipulation, control transfer, high level instructions, and processor control. These categories are summarized in Figure 4.

An 80286 instruction can reference zero, one, or two operands; where an operand resides in a register, in the instruction itself, or in memory. Zero-operand instructions (e.g. NOP and HLT) are usually one byte long. One-operand instructions (e.g. INC and DEC) are usually two bytes long but some are encoded in only one byte. One-operand instructions may reference a register or memory location. Two-operand instructions permit the following six types of instruction operations:

—Register to Register
—Memory to Register
—Immediate to Register
—Memory to Memory
—Register to Memory
—Immediate to Memory

Two-operand instructions (e.g. MOV and ADD) are usually three to six bytes long. Memory to memory operations are provided by a special class of string instructions requiring one to three bytes. For detailed instruction formats and encodings refer to the instruction set summary at the end of this document.

For detailed operation and usage of each instruction, see Appendix of 80286 Programmer's Reference Manual (Order No. 210498)

GENERAL PURPOSE	
MOV	Move byte or word
PUSH	Push word onto stack
POP	Pop word off stack
PUSHA	Push all registers on stack
POPA	Pop all registers from stack
XCHG	Exchange byte or word
XLAT	Translate byte
INPUT/OUTPUT	
IN	Input byte or word
OUT	Output byte or word
ADDRESS OBJECT	
LEA	Load effective address
LDS	Load pointer using DS
LES	Load pointer using ES
FLAG TRANSFER	
LAHF	Load AH register from flags
SAHF	Store AH register in flags
PUSHF	Push flags onto stack
POPF	Pop flags off stack

Figure 4a. Data Transfer Instructions

ADDITION	
ADD	Add byte or word
ADC	Add byte or word with carry
INC	Increment byte or word by 1
AAA	ASCII adjust for addition
DAA	Decimal adjust for addition
SUBTRACTION	
SUB	Subtract byte or word
SBB	Subtract byte or word with borrow
DEC	Decrement byte or word by 1
NEG	Negate byte or word
CMP	Compare byte or word
AAS	ASCII adjust for subtraction
DAS	Decimal adjust for subtraction
MULTIPLICATION	
MUL	Multiple byte or word unsigned
IMUL	Integer multiply byte or word
AAM	ASCII adjust for multiply
DIVISION	
DIV	Divide byte or word unsigned
IDIV	Integer divide byte or word
AAD	ASCII adjust for division
CBW	Convert byte to word
CWD	Convert word to doubleword

Figure 4b. Arithmetic Instructions

MOVS	Move byte or word string
INS	Input bytes or word string
OUTS	Output bytes or word string
CMPS	Compare byte or word string
SCAS	Scan byte or word string
LODS	Load byte or word string
STOS	Store byte or word string
REP	Repeat
REPE/REPZ	Repeat while equal/zero
REPNE/REPNZ	Repeat while not equal/not zero

Figure 4c. String Instructions

LOGICALS	
NOT	"Not" byte or word
AND	"And" byte or word
OR	"Inclusive or" byte or word
XOR	"Exclusive or" byte or word
TEST	"Test" byte or word
SHIFTS	
SHL/SAL	Shift logical/arithmetic left byte or word
SHR	Shift logical right byte or word
SAR	Shift arithmetic right byte or word
ROTATES	
ROL	Rotate left byte or word
ROR	Rotate right byte or word
RCL	Rotate through carry left byte or word
RCR	Rotate through carry right byte or word

Figure 4d. Shift/Rotate Logical Instructions

5

CONDITIONAL TRANSFERS		UNCONDITIONAL TRANSFERS	
JA/JNBE	Jump if above/not below nor equal	CALL	Call procedure
JAE/JNB	Jump if above or equal/not below	RET	Return from procedure
JB/JNAE	Jump if below/not above nor equal	JMP	Jump
JBE/JNA	Jump if below or equal/not above		
JC	Jump if carry	ITERATION CONTROLS	
JE/JZ	Jump if equal/zero	LOOP	Loop
JG/JNLE	Jump if greater/not less nor equal		
JGE/JNL	Jump if greater or equal/not less	LOOPE/LOOPZ	Loop if equal/zero
JL/JNGE	Jump if less/not greater nor equal	LOOPNE/LOOPNZ	Loop if not equal/not zero
JLE/JNG	Jump if less or equal/not greater	JCXZ	Jump if register CX = 0
JNC	Jump if not carry		
JNE/JNZ	Jump if not equal/not zero	INTERRUPTS	
JNO	Jump if not overflow	INT	Interrupt
JNP/JPO	Jump if not parity/parity odd		
JNS	Jump if not sign	INTO	Interrupt if overflow
JO	Jump if overflow	IRET	Interrupt return
JP/JPE	Jump if parity/parity even		
JS	Jump if sign		

Figure 4e. Program Transfer Instructions

FLAG OPERATIONS	
STC	Set carry flag
CLC	Clear carry flag
CMC	Complement carry flag
STD	Set direction flag
CLD	Clear direction flag
STI	Set interrupt enable flag
CLI	Clear interrupt enable flag
EXTERNAL SYNCHRONIZATION	
HLT	Halt until interrupt or reset
WAIT	Wait for $\overline{\text{BUSY}}$ not active
ESC	Escape to extension processor
LOCK	Lock bus during next instruction
NO OPERATION	
NOP	No operation
EXECUTION ENVIRONMENT CONTROL	
LMSW	Load machine status word
SMSW	Store machine status word

Figure 4f. Processor Control Instructions

ENTER	Format stack for procedure entry
LEAVE	Restore stack for procedure exit
BOUND	Detects values outside prescribed range

Figure 4g. High Level Instructions

Memory Organization

Memory is organized as sets of variable length segments. Each segment is a linear contiguous sequence of up to 64K (2^{16}) 8-bit bytes. Memory is addressed using a two component address (a pointer) that consists of a 16-bit segment selector, and a 16-bit offset. The segment selector indicates the desired segment in memory. The offset component indicates the desired byte address within the segment.

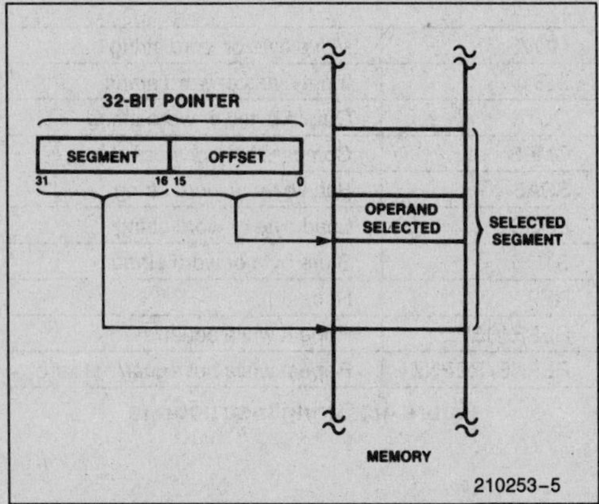

Figure 5. Two Component Address

Table 3. Segment Register Selection Rules

Memory Reference Needed	Segment Register Used	Implicit Segment Selection Rule
Instructions	Code (CS)	Automatic with instruction prefetch
Stack	Stack (SS)	All stack pushes and pops. Any memory reference which uses BP as a base register.
Local Data	Data (DS)	All data references except when relative to stack or string destination
External (Global) Data	Extra (ES)	Alternate data segment and destination of string operation

All instructions that address operands in memory must specify the segment and the offset. For speed and compact instruction encoding, segment selectors are usually stored in the high speed segment registers. An instruction need specify only the desired segment register and an offset in order to address a memory operand.

Most instructions need not explicitly specify which segment register is used. The correct segment register is automatically chosen according to the rules of Table 3. These rules follow the way programs are written (see Figure 6) as independent modules that require areas for code and data, a stack, and access to external data areas.

Special segment override instruction prefixes allow the implicit segment register selection rules to be overridden for special cases. The stack, data, and extra segments may coincide for simple programs. To access operands not residing in one of the four immediately available segments, a full 32-bit pointer or a new segment selector must be loaded.

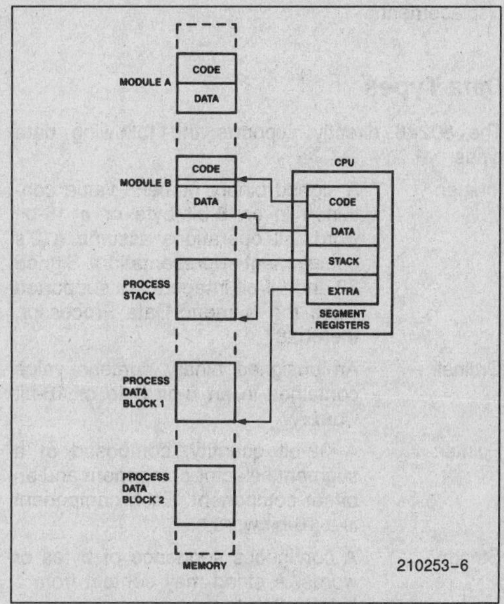

Figure 6. Segmented Memory Helps Structure Software

Addressing Modes

The 80286 provides a total of eight addressing modes for instructions to specify operands. Two addressing modes are provided for instructions that operate on register or immediate operands:

Register Operand Mode: The operand is located in one of the 8 or 16-bit general registers.

Immediate Operand Mode: The operand is included in the instruction.

Six modes are provided to specify the location of an operand in a memory segment. A memory operand address consists of two 16-bit components: segment selector and offset. The segment selector is supplied by a segment register either implicitly chosen by the addressing mode or explicitly chosen by a segment override prefix. The offset is calculated by summing any combination of the following three address elements:

the **displacement** (an 8 or 16-bit immediate value contained in the instruction)

the **base** (contents of either the BX or BP base registers)

the **index** (contents of either the SI or DI index registers)

Any carry out from the 16-bit addition is ignored. Eight-bit displacements are sign extended to 16-bit values.

Combinations of these three address elements define the six memory addressing modes, described below.

Direct Mode: The operand's offset is contained in the instruction as an 8 or 16-bit displacement element.

Register Indirect Mode: The operand's offset is in one of the registers SI, DI, BX, or BP.

Based Mode: The operand's offset is the sum of an 8 or 16-bit displacement and the contents of a base register (BX or BP).

5

Indexed Mode: The operand's offset is the sum of an 8 or 16-bit displacement and the contents of an index register (SI or DI).

Based Indexed Mode: The operand's offset is the sum of the contents of a base register and an index register.

Based Indexed Mode with Displacement: The operand's offset is the sum of a base register's contents, an index register's contents, and an 8 or 16-bit displacement.

Data Types

The 80286 directly supports the following data types:

- **Integer:** A signed binary numeric value contained in an 8-bit byte or a 16-bit word. All operations assume a 2's complement representation. Signed 32 and 64-bit integers are supported using the Numeric Data Processor, the 80287.
- **Ordinal:** An unsigned binary numeric value contained in an 8-bit byte or 16-bit word.
- **Pointer:** A 32-bit quantity, composed of a segment selector component and an offset component. Each component is a 16-bit word.
- **String:** A contiguous sequence of bytes or words. A string may contain from 1 byte to 64K bytes.
- **ASCII:** A byte representation of alphanumeric and control characters using the ASCII standard of character representation.
- **BCD:** A byte (unpacked) representation of the decimal digits 0–9.
- **Packed BCD:** A byte (packed) representation of two decimal digits 0–9 storing one digit in each nibble of the byte.
- **Floating Point:** A signed 32, 64, or 80-bit real number representation. (Floating point operands are supported using the 80287 Numeric Processor).

Figure 7 graphically represents the data types supported by the 80286.

I/O Space

The I/O space consists of 64K 8-bit or 32K 16-bit ports. I/O instructions address the I/O space with either an 8-bit port address, specified in the instruction, or a 16-bit port address in the DX register. 8-bit port addresses are zero extended such that $A_{15}-A_8$ are LOW. I/O port addresses 00F8(H) through 00FF(H) are reserved.

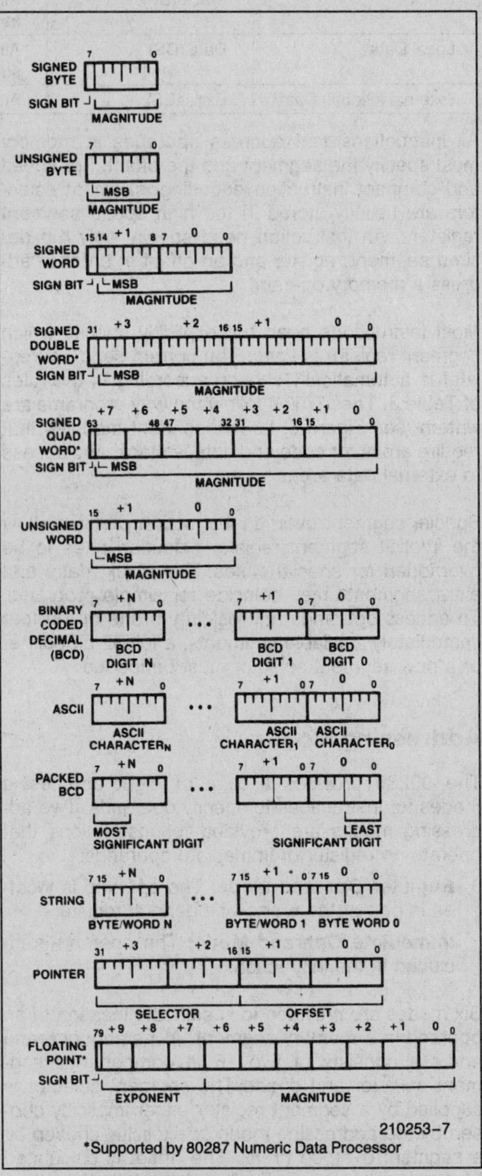

Figure 7. 80286 Supported Data Types

Table 4. Interrupt Vector Assignments

Function	Interrupt Number	Related Instructions	Does Return Address Point to Instruction Causing Exception?
Divide error exception	0	DIV, IDIV	Yes
Single step interrupt	1	All	
NMI interrupt	2	INT 2 or NMI pin	
Breakpoint interrupt	3	INT 3	
INTO detected overflow exception	4	INTO	No
BOUND range exceeded exception	5	BOUND	Yes
Invalid opcode exception	6	Any undefined opcode	Yes
Processor extension not available exception	7	ESC or WAIT	Yes
Intel reserved-do not use	8-15		
Processor extension error interrupt	16	ESC or WAIT	
Intel reserved-do not use	17-31		
User defined	32-255		

Interrupts

An interrupt transfers execution to a new program location. The old program address (CS:IP) and machine state (Flags) are saved on the stack to allow resumption of the interrupted program. Interrupts fall into three classes: hardware initiated, INT instructions, and instruction exceptions. Hardware initiated interrupts occur in response to an external input and are classified as non-maskable or maskable. Programs may cause an interrupt with an INT instruction. Instruction exceptions occur when an unusual condition, which prevents further instruction processing, is detected while attempting to execute an instruction. The return address from an exception will always point at the instruction causing the exception and include any leading instruction prefixes.

A table containing up to 256 pointers defines the proper interrupt service routine for each interrupt. Interrupts 0–31, some of which are used for instruction exceptions, are reserved. For each interrupt, an 8-bit vector must be supplied to the 80286 which identifies the appropriate table entry. Exceptions supply the interrupt vector internally. INT instructions contain or imply the vector and allow access to all 256 interrupts. Maskable hardware initiated interrupts supply the 8-bit vector to the CPU during an interrupt acknowledge bus sequence. Non-maskable hardware interrupts use a predefined internally supplied vector.

MASKABLE INTERRUPT (INTR)

The 80286 provides a maskable hardware interrupt request pin, INTR. Software enables this input by setting the interrupt flag bit (IF) in the flag word. All 224 user-defined interrupt sources can share this input, yet they can retain separate interrupt handlers. An 8-bit vector read by the CPU during the interrupt acknowledge sequence (discussed in System Interface section) identifies the source of the interrupt.

Further maskable interrupts are disabled while servicing an interrupt by resetting the IF bit as part of the response to an interrupt or exception. The saved flag word will reflect the enable status of the processor prior to the interrupt. Until the flag word is restored to the flag register, the interrupt flag will be zero unless specifically set. The interrupt return instruction includes restoring the flag word, thereby restoring the original status of IF.

NON-MASKABLE INTERRUPT REQUEST (NMI)

A non-maskable interrupt input (NMI) is also provided. NMI has higher priority than INTR. A typical use of NMI would be to activate a power failure routine. The activation of this input causes an interrupt with an internally supplied vector value of 2. No external interrupt acknowledge sequence is performed.

While executing the NMI servicing procedure, the 80286 will service neither further NMI requests, INTR requests, nor the processor extension segment overrun interrupt until an interrupt return (IRET) instruction is executed or the CPU is reset. If NMI occurs while currently servicing an NMI, its presence will be saved for servicing after executing the first IRET instruction. IF is cleared at the beginning of an NMI interrupt to inhibit INTR interrupts.

5

SINGLE STEP INTERRUPT

The 80286 has an internal interrupt that allows programs to execute one instruction at a time. It is called the single step interrupt and is controlled by the single step flag bit (TF) in the flag word. Once this bit is set, an internal single step interrupt will occur after the next instruction has been executed. The interrupt clears the TF bit and uses an internally supplied vector of 1. The IRET instruction is used to set the TF bit and transfer control to the next instruction to be single stepped.

Interrupt Priorities

When simultaneous interrupt requests occur, they are processed in a fixed order as shown in Table 5. Interrupt processing involves saving the flags, return address, and setting CS:IP to point at the first instruction of the interrupt handler. If other interrupts remain enabled they are processed before the first instruction of the current interrupt handler is executed. The last interrupt processed is therefore the first one serviced.

Table 5. Interrupt Processing Order

Order	Interrupt
1	Instruction exception
2	Single step
3	NMI
4	Processor extension segment overrun
5	INTR
6	INT instruction

Initialization and Processor Reset

Processor initialization or start up is accomplished by driving the RESET input pin HIGH. RESET forces the 80286 to terminate all execution and local bus activity. No instruction or bus activity will occur as long as RESET is active. After RESET becomes inactive and an internal processing interval elapses, the 80286 begins execution in real address mode with the instruction at physical location FFFFF0(H). RESET also sets some registers to predefined values as shown in Table 6.

Table 6. 80286 Initial Register State after RESET

Register	Value
Flag word	0002(H)
Machine Status Word	FFF0(H)
Instruction pointer	FFF0(H)
Code segment	F000(H)
Data segment	0000(H)
Extra segment	0000(H)
Stack segment	0000(H)

HOLD must not be active during the time from the leading edge of RESET to 34 CLKs after the trailing edge of RESET.

Machine Status Word Description

The machine status word (MSW) records when a task switch takes place and controls the operating mode of the 80286. It is a 16-bit register of which the lower four bits are used. One bit places the CPU into protected mode, while the other three bits, as shown in Table 7, control the processor extension interface. After RESET, this register contains FFF0(H) which places the 80286 in 8086 real address mode.

Table 7. MSW Bit Functions

Bit Position	Name	Function
0	PE	Protected mode enable places the 80286 into protected mode and cannot be cleared except by RESET.
1	MP	Monitor processor extension allows WAIT instructions to cause a processor extension not present exception (number 7).
2	EM	Emulate processor extension causes a processor extension not present exception (number 7) on ESC instructions to allow emulating a processor extension.
3	TS	Task switched indicates the next instruction using a processor extension will cause exception 7, allowing software to test whether the current processor extension context belongs to the current task.

The LMSW and SMSW instructions can load and store the MSW in real address mode. The recommended use of TS, EM, and MP is shown in Table 8.

Table 8. Recommended MSW Encodings For Processor Extension Control

TS	MP	EM	Recommended Use	Instructions Causing Exception 7
0	0	0	Initial encoding after RESET. 80286 operation is identical to 8086, 88.	None
0	0	1	No processor extension is available. Software will emulate its function.	ESC
1	0	1	No processor extension is available. Software will emulate its function. The current processor extension context may belong to another task.	ESC
0	1	0	A processor extension exists.	None
1	1	0	A processor extension exists. The current processor extension context may belong to another task. The Exception 7 on WAIT allows software to test for an error pending from a previous processor extension operation.	ESC or WAIT

Halt

The HLT instruction stops program execution and prevents the CPU from using the local bus until restarted. Either NMI, INTR with IF = 1, or RESET will force the 80286 out of halt. If interrupted, the saved CS:IP will point to the next instruction after the HLT.

8086 REAL ADDRESS MODE

The 80286 executes a fully upward-compatible superset of the 8086 instruction set in real address mode. In real address mode the 80286 is object code compatible with 8086 and 8088 software. The real address mode architecture (registers and addressing modes) is exactly as described in the 80286 Base Architecture section of this Functional Description.

Memory Size

Physical memory is a contiguous array of up to 1,048,576 bytes (one megabyte) addressed by pins A_0 through A_{19} and $\overline{BHE}$. A_{20} through A_{23} should be ignored.

Memory Addressing

In real address mode physical memory is a contiguous array of up to 1,048,576 bytes (one megabyte) addressed by pins A_0 through A_{19} and $\overline{BHE}$. Address bits A_{20}–A_{23} may not always be zero in real mode. A_{20}–A_{23} should not be used by the system while the 80286 is operating in Real Mode.

The selector portion of a pointer is interpreted as the upper 16 bits of a 20-bit segment address. The lower four bits of the 20-bit segment address are always zero. Segment addresses, therefore, begin on multiples of 16 bytes. See Figure 8 for a graphic representation of address information.

All segments in real address mode are 64K bytes in size and may be read, written, or executed. An exception or interrupt can occur if data operands or instructions attempt to wrap around the end of a segment (e.g. a word with its low order byte at offset FFFF(H) and its high order byte at offset 0000(H). If, in real address mode, the information contained in a segment does not use the full 64K bytes, the unused end of the segment may be overlayed by another segment to reduce physical memory requirements.

Reserved Memory Locations

The 80286 reserves two fixed areas of memory in real address mode (see Figure 9); system initialization area and interrupt table area. Locations from addresses FFFF0(H) through FFFFF(H) are reserved for system initialization. Initial execution begins at location FFFF0(H). Locations 00000(H) through 003FF(H) are reserved for interrupt vectors.

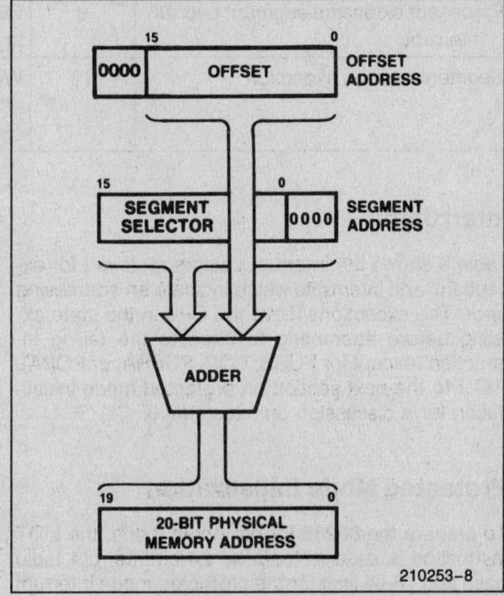

Figure 8. 8086 Real Address Mode Address Calculation

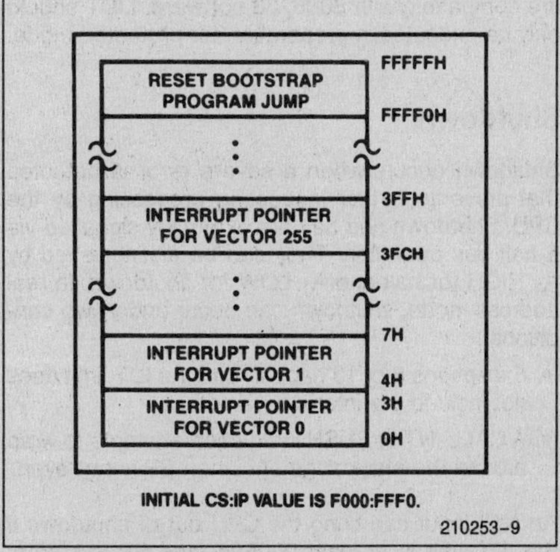

Figure 9. 8086 Real Address Mode Initially Reserved Memory Locations

5

Table 9. Real Address Mode Addressing Interrupts

Function	Interrupt Number	Related Instructions	Return Address Before Instruction?
Interrupt table limit too small exception	8	INT vector is not within table limit	Yes
Processor extension segment overrun interrupt	9	ESC with memory operand extending beyond offset FFFF(H)	No
Segment overrun exception	13	Word memory reference with offset = FFFF(H) or an attempt to execute past the end of a segment	Yes

Interrupts

Table 9 shows the interrupt vectors reserved for exceptions and interrupts which indicate an addressing error. The exceptions leave the CPU in the state existing before attempting to execute the failing instruction (except for PUSH, POP, PUSHA, or POPA). Refer to the next section on protected mode initialization for a discussion on exception 8.

Protected Mode Initialization

To prepare the 80286 for protected mode, the LIDT instruction is used to load the 24-bit interrupt table base and 16-bit limit for the protected mode interrupt table. This instruction can also set a base and limit for the interrupt vector table in real address mode. After reset, the interrupt table base is initialized to 000000(H) and its size set to 03FF(H). These values are compatible with 8086, 88 software. LIDT should only be executed in preparation for protected mode.

Shutdown

Shutdown occurs when a severe error is detected that prevents further instruction processing by the CPU. Shutdown and halt are externally signalled via a halt bus operation. They can be distinguished by A_1 HIGH for halt and A_1 LOW for shutdown. In real address mode, shutdown can occur under two conditions:

- Exceptions 8 or 13 happen and the IDT limit does not include the interrupt vector.
- A CALL INT or PUSH instruction attempts to wrap around the stack segment when SP is not even.

An NMI input can bring the CPU out of shutdown if the IDT limit is at least 000F(H) and SP is greater than 0005(H), otherwise shutdown can only be exited via the RESET input.

PROTECTED VIRTUAL ADDRESS MODE

The 80286 executes a fully upward-compatible superset of the 8086 instruction set in protected virtual address mode (protected mode). Protected mode also provides memory management and protection mechanisms and associated instructions.

The 80286 enters protected virtual address mode from real address mode by setting the PE (Protection Enable) bit of the machine status word with the Load Machine Status Word (LMSW) instruction. Protected mode offers extended physical and virtual memory address space, memory protection mechanisms, and new operations to support operating systems and virtual memory.

All registers, instructions, and addressing modes described in the 80286 Base Architecture section of this Functional Description remain the same. Programs for the 8086, 88, 186, and real address mode 80286 can be run in protected mode; however, embedded constants for segment selectors are different.

Memory Size

The protected mode 80286 provides a 1 gigabyte virtual address space per task mapped into a 16 megabyte physical address space defined by the address pin A_{23}–A_0 and $\overline{BHE}$. The virtual address space may be larger than the physical address space since any use of an address that does not map to a physical memory location will cause a restartable exception.

Memory Addressing

As in real address mode, protected mode uses 32-bit pointers, consisting of 16-bit selector and offset components. The selector, however, specifies an index into a memory resident table rather than the upper 16-bits of a real memory address. The 24-bit base address of the desired segment is obtained from the tables in memory. The 16-bit offset is added to the segment base address to form the physical address as shown in Figure 10. The tables are automatically referenced by the CPU whenever a segment register is loaded with a selector. All 80286 instructions which load a segment register will reference the memory based tables without additional software. The memory based tables contain 8 byte values called descriptors.

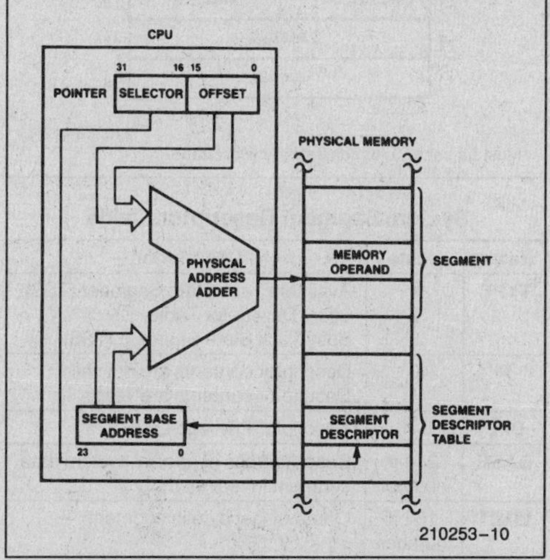

Figure 10. Protected Mode Memory Addressing

DESCRIPTORS

Descriptors define the use of memory. Special types of descriptors also define new functions for transfer of control and task switching. The 80286 has segment descriptors for code, stack and data segments, and system control descriptors for special system data segments and control transfer operations. Descriptor accesses are performed as locked bus operations to assure descriptor integrity in multi-processor systems.

CODE AND DATA SEGMENT DESCRIPTORS (S = 1)

Besides segment base addresses, code and data descriptors contain other segment attributes including segment size (1 to 64K bytes), access rights (read only, read/write, execute only, and execute/read), and presence in memory (for virtual memory systems) (See Figure 11). Any segment usage violating a segment attribute indicated by the segment descriptor will prevent the memory cycle and cause an exception or interrupt.

Code or Data Segment Descriptor

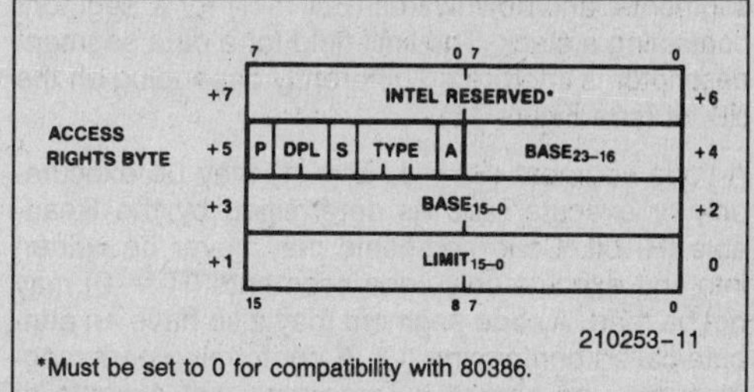

*Must be set to 0 for compatibility with 80386.

Access Rights Byte Definition

	Bit Position	Name		Function	
	7	Present (P)	P = 1 P = 0	Segment is mapped into physical memory. No mapping to physical memory exits, base and limit are not used.	
	6–5	Descriptor Privilege Level (DPL)		Segment privilege attribute used in privilege tests.	
	4	Segment Descriptor (S)	S = 1 S = 0	Code or Data (includes stacks) segment descriptor System Segment Descriptor or Gate Descriptor	
Type Field Definition	3 2 1	Executable (E) Expansion Direction (ED) Writeable (W)	E = 0 ED = 0 ED = 1 W = 0 W = 1	Data segment descriptor type is: Expand up segment, offsets must be ≤ limit. Expand down segment, offsets must be > limit. Data segment may not be written into. Data segment may be written into.	If Data Segment (S = 1, E = 0)
	3 2 1	Executable (E) Conforming (C) Readable (R)	E = 1 C = 1 R = 0 R = 1	Code Segment Descriptor type is: Code segment may only be executed when CPL ≥ DPL and CPL remains unchanged. Code segment may not be read Code segment may be read.	If Code Segment (S = 1, E = 1)
	0	Accessed (A)	A = 0 A = 1	Segment has not been accessed. Segment selector has been loaded into segment register or used by selector test instructions.	

Figure 11. Code and Data Segment Descriptor Formats

Code and data (including stack data) are stored in two types of segments: code segments and data segments. Both types are identified and defined by segment descriptors (S = 1). Code segments are identified by the executable (E) bit set to 1 in the descriptor access rights byte. The access rights byte of both code and data segment descriptor types have three fields in common: present (P) bit, Descriptor Privilege Level (DPL), and accessed (A) bit. If P = 0, any attempted use of this segment will cause a not-present exception. DPL specifies the privilege level of the segment descriptor. DPL controls when the descriptor may be used by a task (refer to privilege discussion below). The A bit shows whether the segment has been previously accessed for usage profiling, a necessity for virtual memory systems. The CPU will always set this bit when accessing the descriptor.

Data segments (S = 1, E = 0) may be either read-only or read-write as controlled by the W bit of the access rights byte. Read-only (W = 0) data segments may not be written into. Data segments may grow in two directions, as determined by the Expansion Direction (ED) bit: upwards (ED = 0) for data segments, and downwards (ED = 1) for a segment containing a stack. The limit field for a data segment descriptor is interpreted differently depending on the ED bit (see Figure 11).

A code segment (S = 1, E = 1) may be execute-only or execute/read as determined by the Readable (R) bit. Code segments may never be written into and execute-only code segments (R = 0) may not be read. A code segment may also have an attribute called conforming (C). A conforming code segment may be shared by programs that execute at different privilege levels. The DPL of a conforming code segment defines the range of privilege levels at which the segment may be executed (refer to privilege discussion below). The limit field identifies the last byte of a code segment.

SYSTEM SEGMENT DESCRIPTORS (S = 0, TYPE = 1–3)

In addition to code and data segment descriptors, the protected mode 80286 defines System Segment Descriptors. These descriptors define special system data segments which contain a table of descriptors (Local Descriptor Table Descriptor) or segments which contain the execution state of a task (Task State Segment Descriptor).

Figure 12 gives the formats for the special system data segment descriptors. The descriptors contain a 24-bit base address of the segment and a 16-bit limit. The access byte defines the type of descriptor, its state and privilege level. The descriptor contents are valid and the segment is in physical memory if P = 1. If P = 0, the segment is not valid. The DPL field is only used in Task State Segment descriptors and indicates the privilege level at which the descriptor may be used (see Privilege). Since the Local Descriptor Table descriptor may only be used by a special privileged instruction, the DPL field is not used. Bit 4 of the access byte is 0 to indicate that it is a system control descriptor. The type field specifies the descriptor type as indicated in Figure 12.

System Segment Descriptor

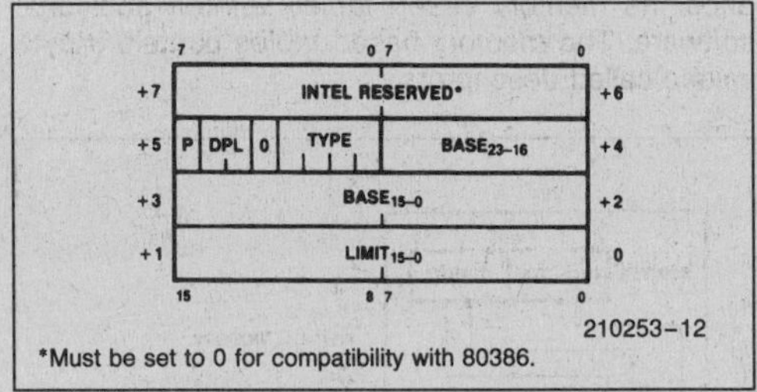

*Must be set to 0 for compatibility with 80386.

System Segment Descriptor Fields

Name	Value	Description
TYPE	1 2 3	Available Task State Segment (TSS) Local Descriptor Table Busy Task State Segment (TSS)
P	0 1	Descriptor contents are not valid Descriptor contents are valid
DPL	0–3	Descriptor Privilege Level
BASE	24-bit number	Base Address of special system data segment in real memory
LIMIT	16-bit number	Offset of last byte in segment

Figure 12. System Segment Descriptor Format

GATE DESCRIPTORS (S = 0, TYPE = 4–7)

Gates are used to control access to entry points within the target code segment. The gate descriptors are call gates, task gates, interrupt gates and trap gates. Gates provide a level of indirection between the source and destination of the control transfer. This indirection allows the CPU to automatically perform protection checks and control entry point of the destination. Call gates are used to change privilege levels (see Privilege), task gates are used to perform a task switch, and interrupt and trap gates are used to specify interrupt service routines. The interrupt gate disables interrupts (resets IF) while the trap gate does not.

Gate Descriptor

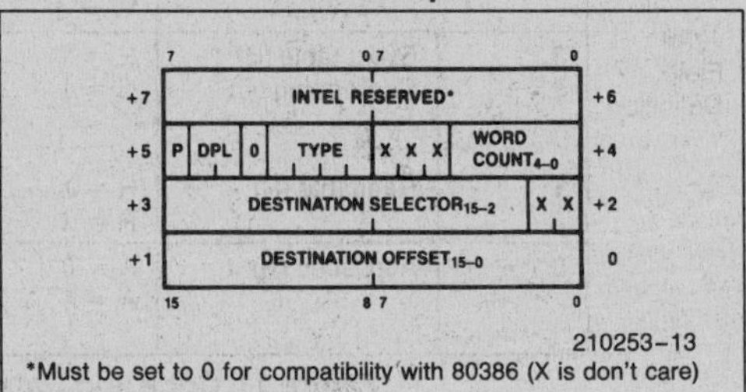

*Must be set to 0 for compatibility with 80386 (X is don't care)

Gate Descriptor Fields

Name	Value	Description
TYPE	4 5 6 7	–Call Gate –Task Gate –Interrupt Gate –Trap Gate
P	0 1	–Descriptor Contents are not valid –Descriptor Contents are valid
DPL	0–3	Descriptor Privilege Level
WORD COUNT	0–31	Number of words to copy from callers stack to called procedures stack. Only used with call gate.
DESTINATION SELECTOR	16-bit selector	Selector to the target code segment (Call, Interrupt or Trap Gate) Selector to the target task state segment (Task Gate)
DESTINATION OFFSET	16-bit offset	Entry point within the target code segment

Figure 13. Gate Descriptor Format

Figure 13 shows the format of the gate descriptors. The descriptor contains a destination pointer that points to the descriptor of the target segment and the entry point offset. The destination selector in an interrupt gate, trap gate, and call gate must refer to a code segment descriptor. These gate descriptors contain the entry point to prevent a program from constructing and using an illegal entry point. Task gates may only refer to a task state segment. Since task gates invoke a task switch, the destination offset is not used in the task gate.

Exception 13 is generated when the gate is used if a destination selector does not refer to the correct descriptor type. The word count field is used in the call gate descriptor to indicate the number of parameters (0–31 words) to be automatically copied from the caller's stack to the stack of the called routine when a control transfer changes privilege levels. The word count field is not used by any other gate descriptor.

The access byte format is the same for all gate descriptors. P = 1 indicates that the gate contents are valid. P = 0 indicates the contents are not valid and causes exception 11 if referenced. DPL is the descriptor privilege level and specifies when this descriptor may be used by a task (refer to privilege discussion below). Bit 4 must equal 0 to indicate a system control descriptor. The type field specifies the descriptor type as indicated in Figure 13.

SEGMENT DESCRIPTOR CACHE REGISTERS

A segment descriptor cache register is assigned to each of the four segment registers (CS, SS, DS, ES). Segment descriptors are automatically loaded (cached) into a segment descriptor cache register (Figure 14) whenever the associated segment register is loaded with a selector. Only segment descriptors may be loaded into segment descriptor cache registers. Once loaded, all references to that segment of memory use the cached descriptor information instead of reaccessing the descriptor. The descriptor cache registers are not visible to programs. No instructions exist to store their contents. They only change when a segment register is loaded.

SELECTOR FIELDS

A protected mode selector has three fields: descriptor entry index, local or global descriptor table indicator (TI), and selector privilege (RPL) as shown in Figure 15. These fields select one of two memory based tables of descriptors, select the appropriate table entry and allow highspeed testing of the selector's privilege attribute (refer to privilege discussion below).

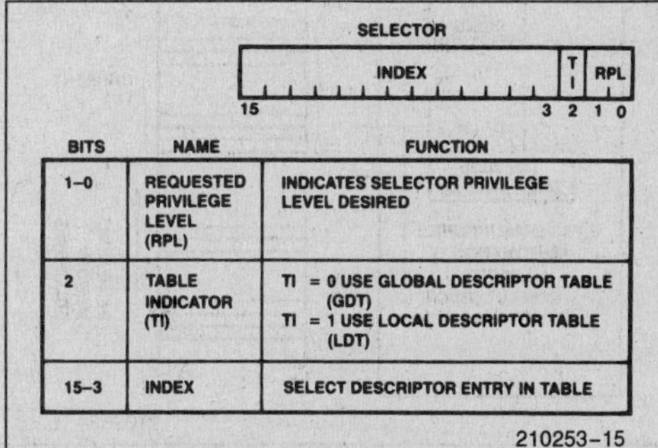

Figure 15. Selector Fields

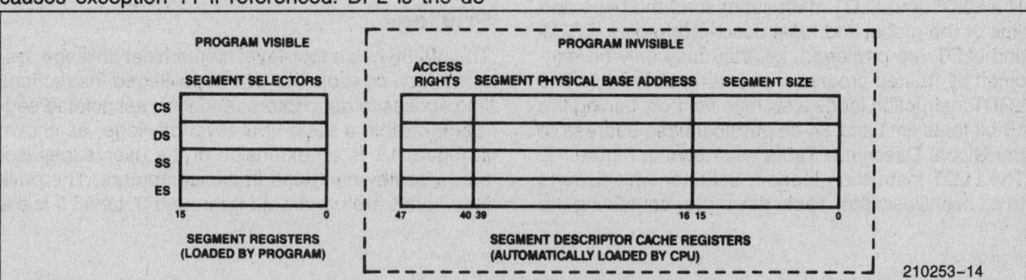

Figure 14. Descriptor Cache Registers

LOCAL AND GLOBAL DESCRIPTOR TABLES

Two tables of descriptors, called descriptor tables, contain all descriptors accessible by a task at any given time. A descriptor table is a linear array of up to 8192 descriptors. The upper 13 bits of the selector value are an index into a descriptor table. Each table has a 24-bit base register to locate the descriptor table in physical memory and a 16-bit limit register that confine descriptor access to the defined limits of the table as shown in Figure 16. A restartable exception (13) will occur if an attempt is made to reference a descriptor outside the table limits.

One table, called the Global Descriptor table (GDT), contains descriptors available to all tasks. The other table, called the Local Descriptor Table (LDT), contains descriptors that can be private to a task. Each task may have its own private LDT. The GDT may contain all descriptor types except interrupt and trap descriptors. The LDT may contain only segment, task gate, and call gate descriptors. A segment cannot be accessed by a task if its segment descriptor does not exist in either descriptor table at the time of access.

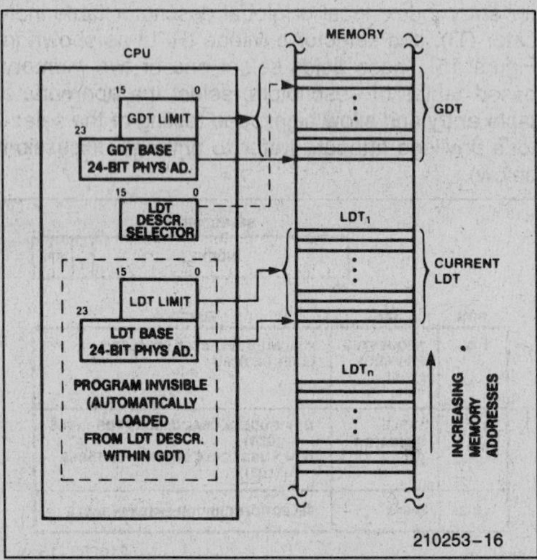

Figure 16. Local and Global Descriptor Table Definition

The LGDT and LLDT instructions load the base and limit of the global and local descriptor tables. LGDT and LLDT are privileged, i.e. they may only be executed by trusted programs operating at level 0. The LGDT instruction loads a six byte field containing the 16-bit table limit and 24-bit physical base address of the Global Descriptor Table as shown in Figure 17. The LLDT instruction loads a selector which refers to a Local Descriptor Table descriptor containing the base address and limit for an LDT, as shown in Figure 12.

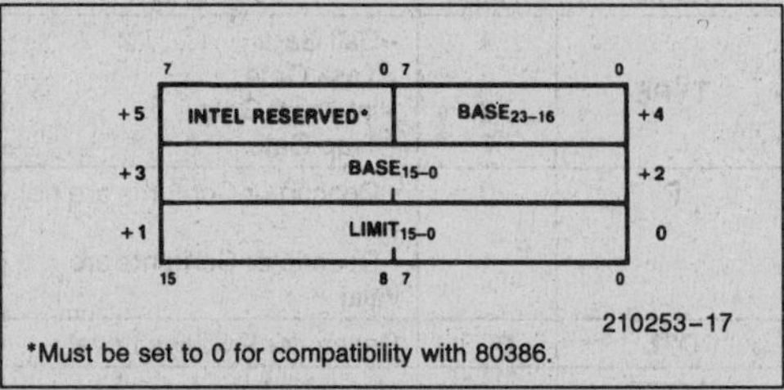

Figure 17. Global Descriptor Table and Interrupt Descriptor Table Data Type

INTERRUPT DESCRIPTOR TABLE

The protected mode 80286 has a third descriptor table, called the Interrupt Descriptor Table (IDT) (see Figure 18), used to define up to 256 interrupts. It may contain only task gates, interrupt gates and trap gates. The IDT (Interrupt Descriptor Table) has a 24-bit physical base and 16-bit limit register in the CPU. The privileged LIDT instruction loads these registers with a six byte value of identical form to that of the LGDT instruction (see Figure 17 and Protected Mode Initialization).

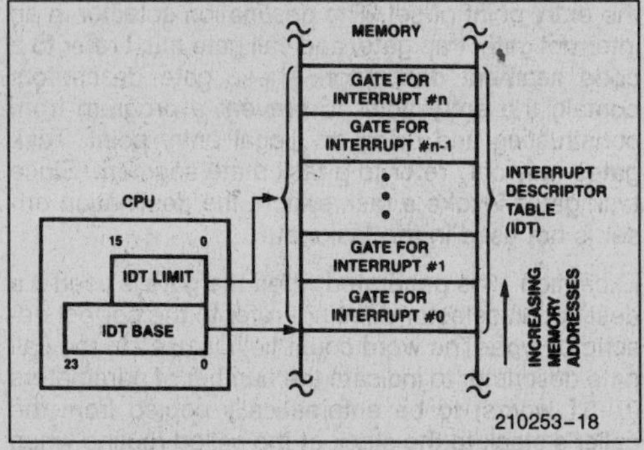

Figure 18. Interrupt Descriptor Table Definition

References to IDT entries are made via INT instructions, external interrupt vectors, or exceptions. The IDT must be at least 256 bytes in size to allocate space for all reserved interrupts.

Privilege

The 80286 has a four-level hierarchical privilege system which controls the use of privileged instructions and access to descriptors (and their associated segments) within a task. Four-level privilege, as shown in Figure 19, is an extension of the user/supervisor mode commonly found in minicomputers. The privilege levels are numbered 0 through 3. Level 0 is the

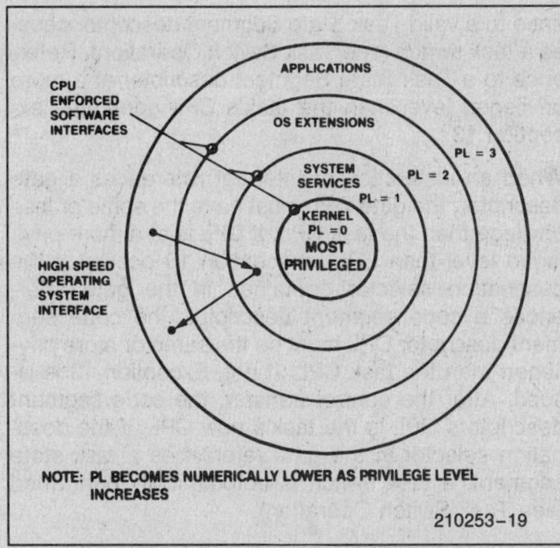

Figure 19. Four-Level Privilege

most privileged level. Privilege levels provide protection within a task. (Tasks are isolated by providing private LDT's for each task.) Operating system routines, interrupt handlers, and other system software can be included and protected within the virtual address space of each task using the four levels of privilege. Each task in the system has a separate stack for each of its privilege levels.

Tasks, descriptors, and selectors have a privilege level attribute that determines whether the descriptor may be used. Task privilege effects the use of instructions and descriptors. Descriptor and selector privilege only effect access to the descriptor.

TASK PRIVILEGE

A task always executes at one of the four privilege levels. The task privilege level at any specific instant is called the Current Privilege Level (CPL) and is defined by the lower two bits of the CS register. CPL cannot change during execution in a single code segment. A task's CPL may only be changed by control transfers through gate descriptors to a new code segment (See Control Transfer). Tasks begin executing at the CPL value specified by the code segment selector within TSS when the task is initiated via a task switch operation (See Figure 20). A task executing at Level 0 can access all data segments defined in the GDT and the task's LDT and is considered the most trusted level. A task executing a Level 3 has the most restricted access to data and is considered the least trusted level.

DESCRIPTOR PRIVILEGE

Descriptor privilege is specified by the Descriptor Privilege Level (DPL) field of the descriptor access byte. DPL specifies the least trusted task privilege level (CPL) at which a task may access the descriptor. Descriptors with DPL = 0 are the most protected. Only tasks executing at privilege level 0 (CPL = 0) may access them. Descriptors with DPL = 3 are the least protected (i.e. have the least restricted access) since tasks can access them when CPL = 0, 1, 2, or 3. This rule applies to all descriptors, except LDT descriptors.

SELECTOR PRIVILEGE

Selector privilege is specified by the Requested Privilege Level (RPL) field in the least significant two bits of a selector. Selector RPL may establish a less trusted privilege level than the current privilege level for the use of a selector. This level is called the task's effective privilege level (EPL). RPL can only reduce the scope of a task's access to data with this selector. A task's effective privilege is the numeric maximum of RPL and CPL. A selector with RPL = 0 imposes no additional restriction on its use while a selector with RPL = 3 can only refer to segments at privilege Level 3 regardless of the task's CPL. RPL is generally used to verify that pointer parameters passed to a more trusted procedure are not allowed to use data at a more privileged level than the caller (refer to pointer testing instructions).

Descriptor Access and Privilege Validation

Determining the ability of a task to access a segment involves the type of segment to be accessed, the instruction used, the type of descriptor used and CPL, RPL, and DPL. The two basic types of segment accesses are control transfer (selectors loaded into CS) and data (selectors loaded into DS, ES or SS).

DATA SEGMENT ACCESS

Instructions that load selectors into DS and ES must refer to a data segment descriptor or readable code segment descriptor. The CPL of the task and the RPL of the selector must be the same as or more privileged (numerically equal to or lower than) than the descriptor DPL. In general, a task can only access data segments at the same or less privileged levels than the CPL or RPL (whichever is numerically higher) to prevent a program from accessing data it cannot be trusted to use.

An exception to the rule is a readable conforming code segment. This type of code segment can be read from any privilege level.

If the privilege checks fail (e.g. DPL is numerically less than the maximum of CPL and RPL) or an incorrect type of descriptor is referenced (e.g. gate de-

5

scriptor or execute only code segment) exception 13 occurs. If the segment is not present, exception 11 is generated.

Instructions that load selectors into SS must refer to data segment descriptors for writable data segments. The descriptor privilege (DPL) and RPL must equal CPL. All other descriptor types or a privilege level violation will cause exception 13. A not present fault causes exception 12.

CONTROL TRANSFER

Four types of control transfer can occur when a selector is loaded into CS by a control transfer operation (see Table 10). Each transfer type can only occur if the operation which loaded the selector references the correct descriptor type. Any violation of these descriptor usage rules (e.g. JMP through a call gate or RET to a Task State Segment) will cause exception 13.

The ability to reference a descriptor for control transfer is also subject to rules of privilege. A CALL or JUMP instruction may only reference a code segment descriptor with DPL equal to the task CPL or a conforming segment with DPL of equal or greater privilege than CPL. The RPL of the selector used to reference the code descriptor must have as much privilege as CPL.

RET and IRET instructions may only reference code segment descriptors with descriptor privilege equal to or less privileged than the task CPL. The selector loaded into CS is the return address from the stack. After the return, the selector RPL is the task's new CPL. If CPL changes, the old stack pointer is popped after the return address.

When a JMP or CALL references a Task State Segment descriptor, the descriptor DPL must be the same or less privileged than the task's CPL. Reference to a valid Task State Segment descriptor causes a task switch (see Task Switch Operation). Reference to a Task State Segment descriptor at a more privileged level than the task's CPL generates exception 13.

When an instruction or interrupt references a gate descriptor, the gate DPL must have the same or less privilege than the task CPL. If DPL is at a more privileged level than CPL, exeception 13 occurs. If the destination selector contained in the gate references a code segment descriptor, the code segment descriptor DPL must be the same or more privileged than the task CPL. If not, Exception 13 is issued. After the control transfer, the code segment descriptors DPL is the task's new CPL. If the destination selector in the gate references a task state segment, a task switch is automatically performed (see Task Switch Operation).

The privilege rules on control transfer require:

— JMP or CALL direct to a code segment (code segment descriptor) can only be to a conforming segment with DPL of equal or greater privilege than CPL or a non-conforming segment at the same privilege level.

— interrupts within the task or calls that may change privilege levels, can only transfer control through a gate at the same or a less privileged level than CPL to a code segment at the same or more privileged level than CPL.

— return instructions that don't switch tasks can only return control to a code segment at the same or less privileged level.

— task switch can be performed by a call, jump or interrupt which references either a task gate or task state segment at the same or less privileged level.

Table 10. Descriptor Types Used for Control Transfer

Control Transfer Types	Operation Types	Descriptor Referenced	Descriptor Table
Intersegment within the same privilege level	JMP, CALL, RET, IRET*	Code Segment	GDT/LDT
Intersegment to the same or higher privilege level Interrupt within task may change CPL.	CALL	Call Gate	GDT/LDT
	Interrupt Instruction, Exception, External Interrupt	Trap or Interrupt Gate	IDT
Intersegment to a lower privilege level (changes task CPL)	RET, IRET*	Code Segment	GDT/LDT
	CALL, JMP	Task State Segment	GDT
Task Switch	CALL, JMP	Task Gate	GDT/LDT
	IRET** Interrupt Instruction, Exception, External Interrupt	Task Gate	IDT

*NT (Nested Task bit of flag word) = 0
**NT (Nested Task bit of flag word) = 1

PRIVILEGE LEVEL CHANGES

Any control transfer that changes CPL within the task, causes a change of stacks as part of the operation. Initial values of SS:SP for privilege levels 0, 1, and 2 are kept in the task state segment (refer to Task Switch Operation). During a JMP or CALL control transfer, the new stack pointer is loaded into the SS and SP registers and the previous stack pointer is pushed onto the new stack.

When returning to the original privilege level, its stack is restored as part of the RET or IRET instruction operation. For subroutine calls that pass parameters on the stack and cross privilege levels, a fixed number of words, as specified in the gate, are copied from the previous stack to the current stack. The inter-segment RET instruction with a stack adjustment value will correctly restore the previous stack pointer upon return.

Protection

The 80286 includes mechanisms to protect critical instructions that affect the CPU execution state (e.g. HLT) and code or data segments from improper usage. These protection mechanisms are grouped into three forms:

Restricted *usage* of segments (e.g. no write allowed to read-only data segments). The only segments available for use are defined by descriptors in the Local Descriptor Table (LDT) and Global Descriptor Table (GDT).

Restricted *access* to segments via the rules of privilege and descriptor usage.

Privileged instructions or operations that may only be executed at certain privilege levels as determined by the CPL and I/O Privilege Level (IOPL). The IOPL is defined by bits 14 and 13 of the flag word.

These checks are performed for all instructions and can be split into three categories: segment load checks (Table 11), operand reference checks (Table 12), and privileged instruction checks (Table 13). Any violation of the rules shown will result in an exception. A not-present exception related to the stack segment causes exception 12.

The IRET and POPF instructions do not perform some of their defined functions if CPL is not of sufficient privilege (numerically small enough). Precisely these are:

- The IF bit is not changed if CPL > IOPL.
- The IOPL field of the flag word is not changed if CPL > 0.

No exceptions or other indication are given when these conditions occur.

Table 11
Segment Register Load Checks

Error Description	Exception Number
Descriptor table limit exceeded	13
Segment descriptor not-present	11 or 12
Privilege rules violated	13
Invalid descriptor/segment type segment register load: —Read only data segment load to SS —Special Control descriptor load to DS, ES, SS —Execute only segment load to DS, ES, SS —Data segment load to CS —Read/Execute code segment load to SS	13

Table 12. Operand Reference Checks

Error Description	Exception Number
Write into code segment	13
Read from execute-only code segment	13
Write to read-only data segment	13
Segment limit exceeded[1]	12 or 13

NOTE:
Carry out in offset calculations is ignored.

Table 13. Privileged Instruction Checks

Error Description	Exception Number
CPL ≠ 0 when executing the following instructions: LIDT, LLDT, LGDT, LTR, LMSW, CTS, HLT	13
CPL > IOPL when executing the following instructions: INS, IN, OUTS, OUT, STI, CLI, LOCK	13

EXCEPTIONS

The 80286 detects several types of exceptions and interrupts, in protected mode (see Table 14). Most are restartable after the exceptional condition is removed. Interrupt handlers for most exceptions can read an error code, pushed on the stack after the return address, that identifies the selector involved (0 if none). The return address normally points to the failing instruction, including all leading prefixes. For a processor extension segment overrun exception, the return address will not point at the ESC instruction that caused the exception; however, the processor extension registers may contain the address of the failing instruction.

5

Table 14. Protected Mode Exceptions

Interrupt Vector	Function	Return Address At Failing Instruction?	Always Restart-able?	Error Code on Stack?
8	Double exception detected	Yes	No[2]	Yes
9	Processor extension segment overrun	No	No[2]	No
10	Invalid task state segment	Yes	Yes	Yes
11	Segment not present	Yes	Yes	Yes
12	Stack segment overrun or stack segment not present	Yes	Yes[1]	Yes
13	General protection	Yes	No[2]	Yes

NOTE:
1. When a PUSHA or POPA instruction attempts to wrap around the stack segment, the machine state after the exception will not be restartable because stack segment wrap around is not permitted. This condition is identified by the value of the saved SP being either 0000(H), 0001(H), FFFE(H), or FFFF(H).
2. These exceptions indicate a violation to privilege rules or usage rules has occurred. Restart is generally not attempted under those conditions.

These exceptions indicate a violation to privilege rules or usage rules has occurred. Restart is generally not attempted under those conditions.

All these checks are performed for all instructions and can be split into three categories: segment load checks (Table 11), operand reference checks (Table 12), and privileged instruction checks (Table 13). Any violation of the rules shown will result in an exception. A not-present exception causes exception 11 or 12 and is restartable.

Special Operations

TASK SWITCH OPERATION

The 80286 provides a built-in task switch operation which saves the entire 80286 execution state (registers, address space, and a link to the previous task), loads a new execution state, and commences execution in the new task. Like gates, the task switch operation is invoked by executing an inter-segment JMP or CALL instruction which refers to a Task State Segment (TSS) or task gate descriptor in the GDT or LDT. An INT n instruction, exception, or external interrupt may also invoke the task switch operation by selecting a task gate descriptor in the associated IDT descriptor entry.

The TSS descriptor points at a segment (see Figure 20) containing the entire 80286 execution state while a task gate descriptor contains a TSS selector. The limit field of the descriptor must be >002B(H).

Each task must have a TSS associated with it. The current TSS is identified by a special register in the 80286 called the Task Register (TR). This register contains a selector referring to the task state segment descriptor that defines the current TSS. A hidden base and limit register associated with TR are loaded whenever TR is loaded with a new selector.

The IRET instruction is used to return control to the task that called the current task or was interrupted. Bit 14 in the flag register is called the Nested Task (NT) bit. It controls the function of the IRET instruction. If NT = 0, the IRET instruction performs the regular current task by popping values off the stack; when NT = 1, IRET performs a task switch operation back to the previous task.

When a CALL, JMP, or INT instruction initiates a task switch, the old (except for case of JMP) and new TSS will be marked busy and the back link field of the new TSS set to the old TSS selector. The NT bit of the new task is set by CALL or INT initiated task switches. An interrupt that does not cause a task switch will clear NT. NT may also be set or cleared by POPF or IRET instructions.

The task state segment is marked busy by changing the descriptor type field from Type 1 to Type 3. Use of a selector that references a busy task state segment causes Exception 13.

PROCESSOR EXTENSION CONTEXT SWITCHING

The context of a processor extension (such as the 80287 numerics processor) is not changed by the task switch operation. A processor extension context need only be changed when a different task attempts to use the processor extension (which still contains the context of a previous task). The 80286 detects the first use of a processor extension after a task switch by causing the processor extension not present exception (7). The interrupt handler may then decide whether a context change is necessary.

Whenever the 80286 switches tasks, it sets the Task Switched (TS) bit of the MSW. TS indicates that a processor extension context may belong to a different task than the current one. The processor extension not present exception (7) will occur when attempting to execute an ESC or WAIT instruction if TS=1 and a processor extension is present (MP=1 in MSW).

POINTER TESTING INSTRUCTIONS

The 80286 provides several instructions to speed pointer testing and consistency checks for maintaining system integrity (see Table 15). These instructions use the memory management hardware to verify that a selector value refers to an appropriate segment without risking an exception. A condition flag (ZF) indicates whether use of the selector or segment will cause an exception.

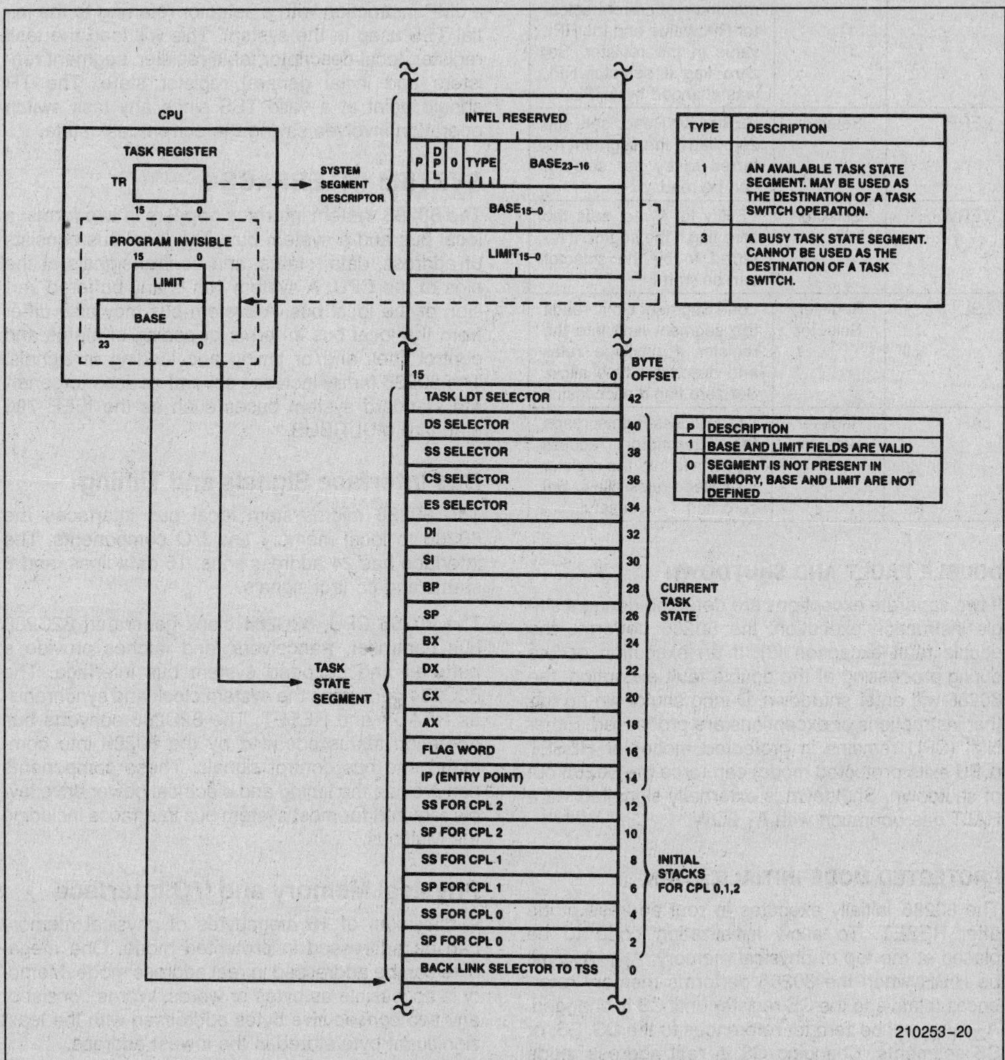

Figure 20. Task State Segment and TSS Registers

Table 15. 80286 Pointer Test Instructions

Instruction	Operands	Function
ARPL	Selector, Register	Adjust Requested Privilege Level: adjusts the RPL of the selector to the numeric maximum of current selector RPL value and the RPL value in the register. Set zero flag if selector RPL was changed by ARPL.
VERR	Selector	VERify for Read: sets the zero flag if the segment referred to by the selector can be read.
VERW	Selector	VERify for Write: sets the zero flag if the segment referred to by the selector can be written.
LSL	Register, Selector	Load Segment Limit: reads the segment limit into the register if privilege rules and descriptor type allow. Set zero flag if successful.
LAR	Register, Selector	Load Access Rights: reads the descriptor access rights byte into the register if privilege rules allow. Set zero flag if successful.

DOUBLE FAULT AND SHUTDOWN

If two separate exceptions are detected during a single instruction execution, the 80286 performs the double fault exception (8). If an execution occurs during processing of the double fault exception, the 80286 will enter shutdown. During shutdown no further instructions or exceptions are processed. Either NMI (CPU remains in protected mode) or RESET (CPU exits protected mode) can force the 80286 out of shutdown. Shutdown is externally signalled via a HALT bus operation with A_1 LOW.

PROTECTED MODE INITIALIZATION

The 80286 initially executes in real address mode after RESET. To allow initialization code to be placed at the top of physical memory, A_{23}–A_{20} will be HIGH when the 80286 performs memory references relative to the CS register until CS is changed. A_{23}–A_{20} will be zero for references to the DS, ES, or SS segments. Changing CS in real address mode will force A_{23}–A_{20} LOW whenever CS is used again. The initial CS:IP value of F000:FFF0 provides 64K bytes of code space for initialization code without changing CS.

Protected mode operation requires several registers to be initialized. The GDT and IDT base registers must refer to a valid GDT and IDT. After executing the LMSW instruction to set PE, the 80286 must immediately execute an intra-segment JMP instruction to clear the instruction queue of instructions decoded in real address mode.

To force the 80286 CPU registers to match the initial protected mode state assumed by software, execute a JMP instruction with a selector referring to the initial TSS used in the system. This will load the task register, local descriptor table register, segment registers and initial general register state. The TR should point at a valid TSS since any task switch operation involves saving the current task state.

SYSTEM INTERFACE

The 80286 system interface appears in two forms: a local bus and a system bus. The local bus consists of address, data, status, and control signals at the pins of the CPU. A system bus is any buffered version of the local bus. A system bus may also differ from the local bus in terms of coding of status and control lines and/or timing and loading of signals. The 80286 family includes several devices to generate standard system buses such as the IEEE 796 standard MULTIBUS.

Bus Interface Signals and Timing

The 80286 microsystem local bus interfaces the 80286 to local memory and I/O components. The interface has 24 address lines, 16 data lines, and 8 status and control signals.

The 80286 CPU, 82C284 clock generator, 82C288 bus controller, tranceivers, and latches provide a buffered and decoded system bus interface. The 82C284 generates the system clock and synchronizes $\overline{\text{READY}}$ and RESET. The 82C288 converts bus operation status encoded by the 80286 into command and bus control signals. These components can provide the timing and electrical power drive levels required for most system bus interfaces including the Multibus.

Physical Memory and I/O Interface

A maximum of 16 megabytes of physical memory can be addressed in protected mode. One megabyte can be addressed in real address mode. Memory is accessible as bytes or words. Words consist of any two consecutive bytes addressed with the least significant byte stored in the lowest address.

Byte transfers occur on either half of the 16-bit local data bus. Even bytes are accessed over D_{7-0} while odd bytes are transferred over D_{15-8}. Even-addressed words are transferred over D_{15-0} in one bus cycle, while odd-addressed word require *two* bus operations. The first transfers data on D_{15-8}, and the second transfers data on D_{7-0}. Both byte data transfers occur automatically, transparent to software.

Two bus signals, A_0 and $\overline{BHE}$, control transfers over the lower and upper halves of the data bus. Even address byte transfers are indicated by A_0 LOW and $\overline{BHE}$ HIGH. Odd address byte transfers are indicated by A_0 HIGH and $\overline{BHE}$ LOW. Both A_0 and $\overline{BHE}$ are LOW for even address word transfers.

The I/O address space contains 64K addresses in both modes. The I/O space is accessible as either bytes or words, as is memory. Byte wide peripheral devices may be attached to either the upper or lower byte of the data bus. Byte-wide I/O devices attached to the upper data byte (D_{15-8}) are accessed with odd I/O addresses. Devices on the lower data byte are accessed with even I/O addresses. An interrupt controller such as Intel's 8259A must be connected to the lower data byte (D_{7-0}) for proper return of the interrupt vector.

Bus Operation

The 80286 uses a double frequency system clock (CLK input) to control bus timing. All signals on the local bus are measured relative to the system CLK input. The CPU divides the system clock by 2 to produce the internal processor clock, which determines bus state. Each processor clock is composed of two system clock cycles named phase 1 and phase 2. The 82C284 clock generator output (PCLK) identifies the next phase of the processor clock. (See Figure 21.)

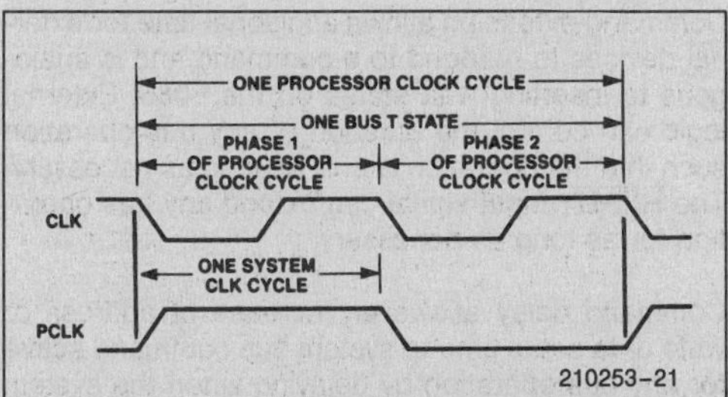

Figure 21. System and Processor Clock Relationships

Six types of bus operations are supported; memory read, memory write, I/O read, I/O write, interrupt acknowledge, and halt/shutdown. Data can be transferred at a maximum rate of one word per two processor clock cycles.

The 80286 bus has three basic states: idle (T_i), send status (T_S), and perform command (T_C). The 80286 CPU also has a fourth local bus state called hold (T_h). T_h indicates that the 80286 has surrendered control of the local bus to another bus master in response to a HOLD request.

Each bus state is one processor clock long. Figure 22 shows the four 80286 local bus states and allowed transitions.

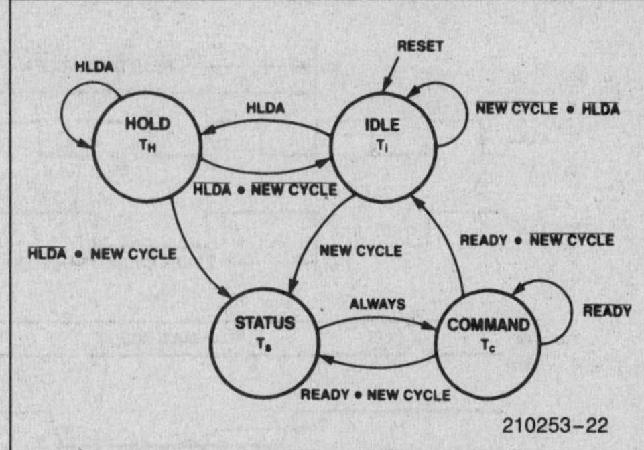

Figure 22. 80286 Bus States

Bus States

The idle (T_i) state indicates that no data transfers are in progress or requested. The first active state T_S is signaled by status line $\overline{S1}$ or $\overline{S0}$ going LOW and identifying phase 1 of the processor clock. During T_S, the command encoding, the address, and data (for a write operation) are available on the 80286 output pins. The 82C288 bus controller decodes the status signals and generates Multibus compatible read/write command and local transceiver control signals.

After T_S, the perform command (T_C) state is entered. Memory or I/O devices respond to the bus operation during T_C, either transferring read data to the CPU or accepting write data. T_C states may be repeated as often as necessary to assure sufficient time for the memory or I/O device to respond. The $\overline{READY}$ signal determines whether T_C is repeated. A repeated T_C state is called a wait state.

During hold (T_h), the 80286 will float all address, data, and status output pins enabling another bus master to use the local bus. The 80286 HOLD input signal is used to place the 80286 into the T_h state. The 80286 HLDA output signal indicates that the CPU has entered T_h.

Pipelined Addressing

The 80286 uses a local bus interface with pipelined timing to allow as much time as possible for data access. Pipelined timing allows a new bus operation to be initiated every two processor cycles, while allowing each individual bus operation to last for three processor cycles.

The timing of the address outputs is pipelined such that the address of the next bus operation becomes available during the current bus operation. Or in other words, the first clock of the next bus operation is overlapped with the last clock of the current bus operation. Therefore, address decode and routing logic can operate in advance of the next bus operation.

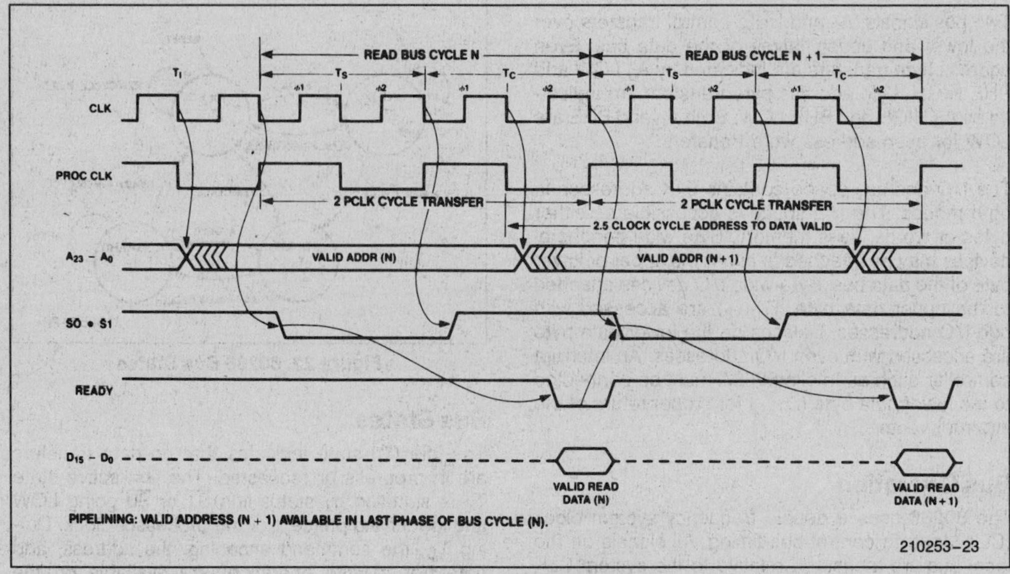

Figure 23. Basic Bus Cycle

External address latches may hold the address stable for the entire bus operation, and provide additional AC and DC buffering.

The 80286 does not maintain the address of the current bus operation during all T_C states. Instead, the address for the next bus operation may be emitted during phase 2 of any T_C. The address remains valid during phase 1 of the first T_C to guarantee hold time, relative to ALE, for the address latch inputs.

Bus Control Signals

The 82C288 bus controller provides control signals; address latch enable (ALE), Read/Write commands, data transmit/receive (DT/$\overline{R}$), and data enable (DEN) that control the address latches, data transceivers, write enable, and output enable for memory and I/O systems.

The Address Latch Enable (ALE) output determines when the address may be latched. ALE provides at least one system CLK period of address hold time from the end of the previous bus operation until the address for the next bus operation appears at the latch outputs. This address hold time is required to support MULTIBUS and common memory systems.

The data bus transceivers are controlled by 82C288 outputs Data Enable (DEN) and Data Transmit/Receive (DT/$\overline{R}$). DEN enables the data transceivers; while DT/$\overline{R}$ controls tranceiver direction. DEN and DT/$\overline{R}$ are timed to prevent bus contention between the bus master, data bus transceivers, and system data bus transceivers.

Command Timing Controls

Two system timing customization options, command extension and command delay, are provided on the 80286 local bus.

Command extension allows additional time for external devices to respond to a command and is analogous to inserting wait states on the 8086. External logic can control the duration of any bus operation such that the operation is only as long as necessary. The $\overline{\text{READY}}$ input signal can extend any bus operation for as long as necessary.

Command delay allows an increase of address or write data setup time to system bus command active for any bus operation by delaying when the system bus command becomes active. Command delay is controlled by the 82C288 CMDLY input. After T_S, the bus controller samples CMDLY at each failing edge of CLK. If CMDLY is HIGH, the 82C288 will not activate the command signal. When CMDLY is LOW, the 82C288 will activate the command signal. After the command becomes active, the CMDLY input is not sampled.

When a command is delayed, the available response time from command active to return read data or accept write data is less. To customize system bus timing, an address decoder can determine which bus operations require delaying the command. The CMDLY input does not affect the timing of ALE, DEN, or DT/$\overline{R}$.

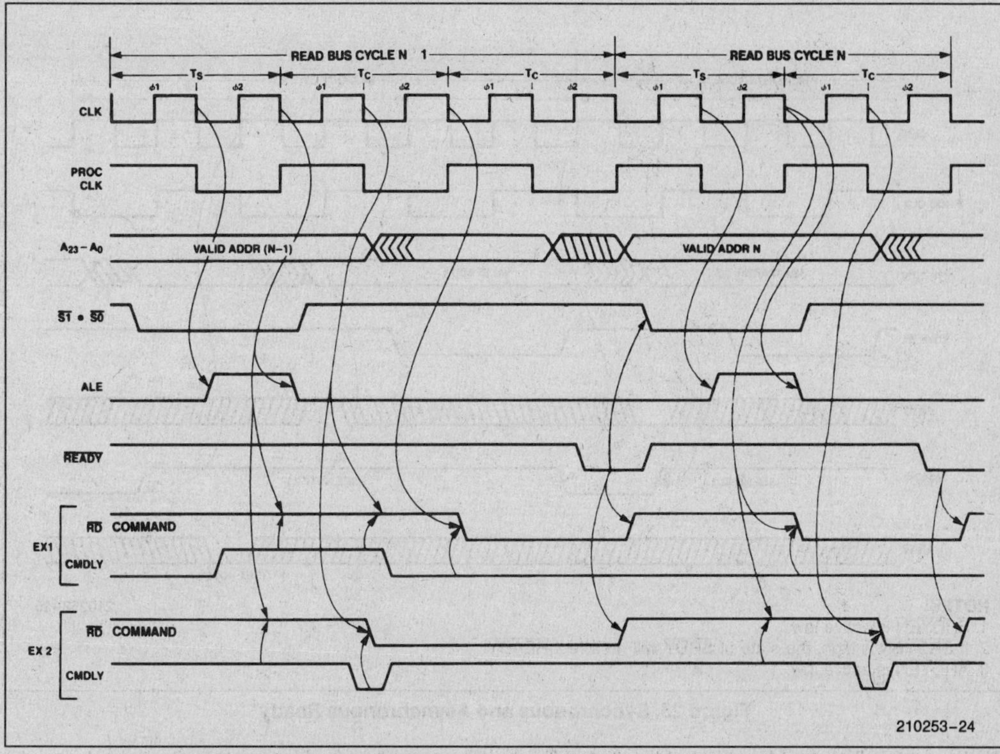

Figure 24. CMDLY Controls the Leading Edge of Command Signal

Figure 24 illustrates four uses of CMDLY. Example 1 shows delaying the read command two system CLKs for cycle N-1 and no delay for cycle N, and example 2 shows delaying the read command one system CLK for cycle N-1 and one system CLK delay for cycle N.

Bus Cycle Termination

At maximum transfer rates, the 80286 bus alternates between the status and command states. The bus status signals become inactive after T_S so that they may correctly signal the start of the next bus operation after the completion of the current cycle. No external indication of T_C exists on the 80286 local bus. The bus master and bus controller enter T_C directly after T_S and continue executing T_C cycles until terminated by $\overline{READY}$.

$\overline{READY}$ Operation

The current bus master and 82C288 bus controller terminate each bus operation simultaneously to achieve maximum bus operation bandwidth. Both are informed in advance by $\overline{READY}$ active (open-collector output from 82C284) which identifies the last T_C cycle of the current bus operation. The bus master and bus controller must see the same sense of the $\overline{READY}$ signal, thereby requiring $\overline{READY}$ be synchronous to the system clock.

Synchronous Ready

The 82C284 clock generator provides $\overline{READY}$ synchronization from both synchronous and asynchronous sources (see Figure 25). The synchronous ready input ($\overline{SRDY}$) of the clock generator is sampled with the falling edge of CLK at the end of phase 1 of each T_C. The state of $\overline{SRDY}$ is then broadcast to the bus master and bus controller via the $\overline{READY}$ output line.

Asynchronous Ready

Many systems have devices or subsystems that are asynchronous to the system clock. As a result, their ready outputs cannot be guaranteed to meet the 82C284 $\overline{SRDY}$ setup and hold time requirements. But the 82C284 asynchronous ready input ($\overline{ARDY}$) is designed to accept such signals. The $\overline{ARDY}$ input is sampled at the beginning of each T_C cycle by 82C284 synchronization logic. This provides one system CLK cycle time to resolve its value before broadcasting it to the bus master and bus controller.

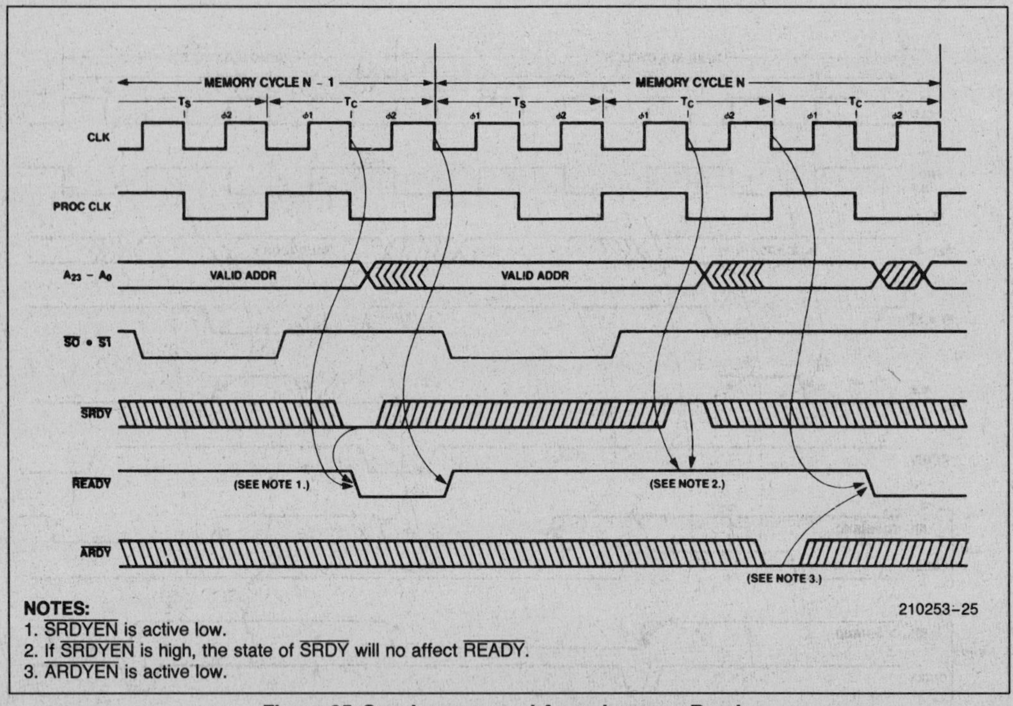

Figure 25. Synchronous and Asynchronous Ready

$\overline{ARDY}$ or $\overline{ARDYEN}$ must be HIGH at the end of T_S. $\overline{ARDY}$ cannot be used to terminate bus cycle with no wait states.

Each ready input of the 82C284 has an enable pin ($\overline{SRDYEN}$ and $\overline{ARDYEN}$) to select whether the current bus operation will be terminated by the synchronous or asynchronous ready. Either of the ready inputs may terminate a bus operation. These enable inputs are active low and have the same timing as their respective ready inputs. Address decode logic usually selects whether the current bus operation should be terminated by $\overline{ARDY}$ or $\overline{SRDY}$.

Data Bus Control

Figures 26, 27, and 28 show how the DT/$\overline{R}$, DEN, data bus, and address signals operate for different combinations of read, write, and idle bus operations. DT/$\overline{R}$ goes active (LOW) for a read operation. DT/$\overline{R}$ remains HIGH before, during, and between write operations.

The data bus is driven with write data during the second phase of T_S. The delay in write data timing allows the read data drivers, from a previous read cycle, sufficient time to enter 3-state OFF before the 80286 CPU begins driving the local data bus for write operations. Write data will always remain valid for one system clock past the last T_c to provide sufficient hold time for Multibus or other similar memory or I/O systems. During write-read or write-idle sequences the data bus enters 3-state OFF during the second phase of the processor cycle after the last T_C. In a write-write sequence the data bus does not enter 3-state OFF between T_C and T_S.

Bus Usage

The 80286 local bus may be used for several functions: instruction data transfers, data transfers by other bus masters, instruction fetching, processor extension data transfers, interrupt acknowledge, and halt/shutdown. This section describes local bus activities which have special signals or requirements.

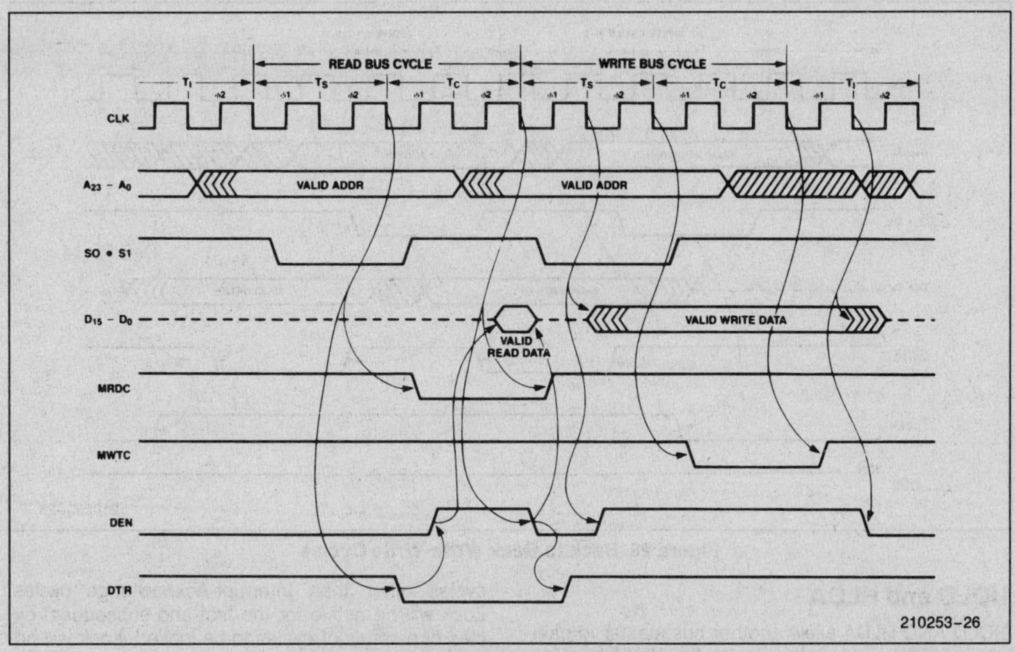

Figure 26. Back to Back Read-Write Cycles

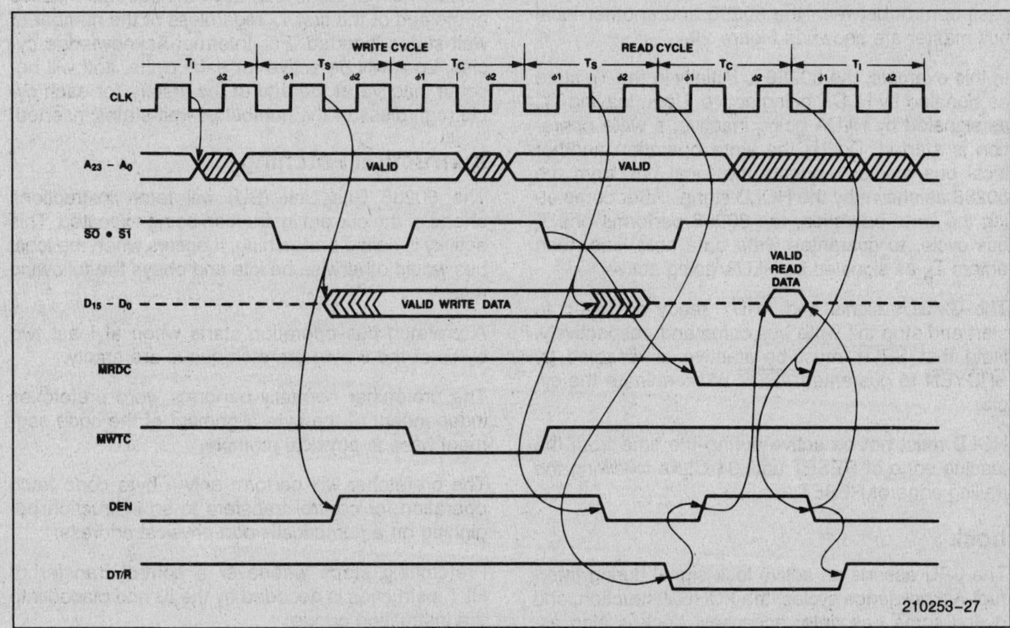

Figure 27. Back to Back Write-Read Cycles

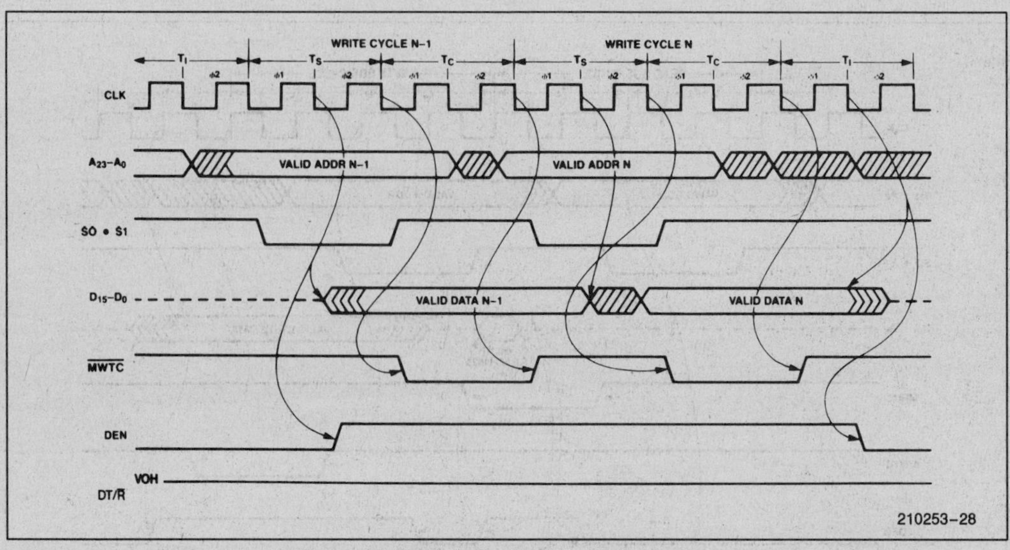

Figure 28. Back to Back Write-Write Cycles

HOLD and HLDA

HOLD AND HLDA allow another bus master to gain control of the local bus by placing the 80286 bus into the T_h state. The sequence of events required to pass control between the 80286 and another local bus master are shown in Figure 29.

In this example, the 80286 is initially in the T_h state as signaled by HLDA being active. Upon leaving T_h, as signaled by HLDA going inactive, a write operation is started. During the write operation another local bus master requests the local bus from the 80286 as shown by the HOLD signal. After completing the write operation, the 80286 performs one T_i bus cycle, to guarantee write data hold time, then enters T_h as signaled by HLDA going active.

The CMDLY signal and $\overline{ARDY}$ ready are used to start and stop the write bus command, respectively. Note that $\overline{SRDY}$ must be inactive or disabled by $\overline{SRDYEN}$ to guarantee $\overline{ARDY}$ will terminate the cycle.

HOLD must not be active during the time from the leading edge of RESET until 34 CLKs following the trailing edge of RESET.

Lock

The CPU asserts an active lock signal during Interrupt-Acknowledge cycles, the XCHG instruction, and during some descriptor accesses. Lock is also asserted when the LOCK prefix is used. The LOCK prefix may be used with the following ASM-286 assembly instructions; MOVS, INS, and OUTS. For bus cycles other than Interrupt-Acknowledge cycles, Lock will be active for the first and subsequent cycles of a series of cycles to be locked. Lock will not be shown active during the last cycle to be locked. For the next-to-last cycle, Lock will become inactive at the end of the first T_c regardless of the number of wait-states inserted. For Interrupt-Acknowledge cycles, Lock will be active for each cycle, and will become inactive at the end of the first T_c for each cycle regardless of the number of wait-states inserted.

Instruction Fetching

The 80286 Bus Unit (BU) will fetch instructions ahead of the current instruction being executed. This activity is called prefetching. It occurs when the local bus would otherwise be idle and obeys the following rules:

A prefetch bus operation starts when at least two bytes of the 6-byte prefetch queue are empty.

The prefetcher normally performs word prefetches independent of the byte alignment of the code segment base in physical memory.

The prefetcher will perform only a byte code fetch operation for control transfers to an instruction beginning on a numerically odd physical address.

Prefetching stops whenever a control transfer or HLT instruction is decoded by the IU and placed into the instruction queue.

In real address mode, the prefetcher may fetch up to 6 bytes beyond the last control transfer or HLT instruction in a code segment.

In protected mode, the prefetcher will never cause a segment overrun exception. The prefetcher stops at the last physical memory word of the code segment. Exception 13 will occur if the program attempts to execute beyond the last full instruction in the code segment.

If the last byte of a code segment appears on an even physical memory address, the prefetcher will read the next physical byte of memory (perform a word code fetch). The value of this byte is ignored and any attempt to execute it causes exception 13.

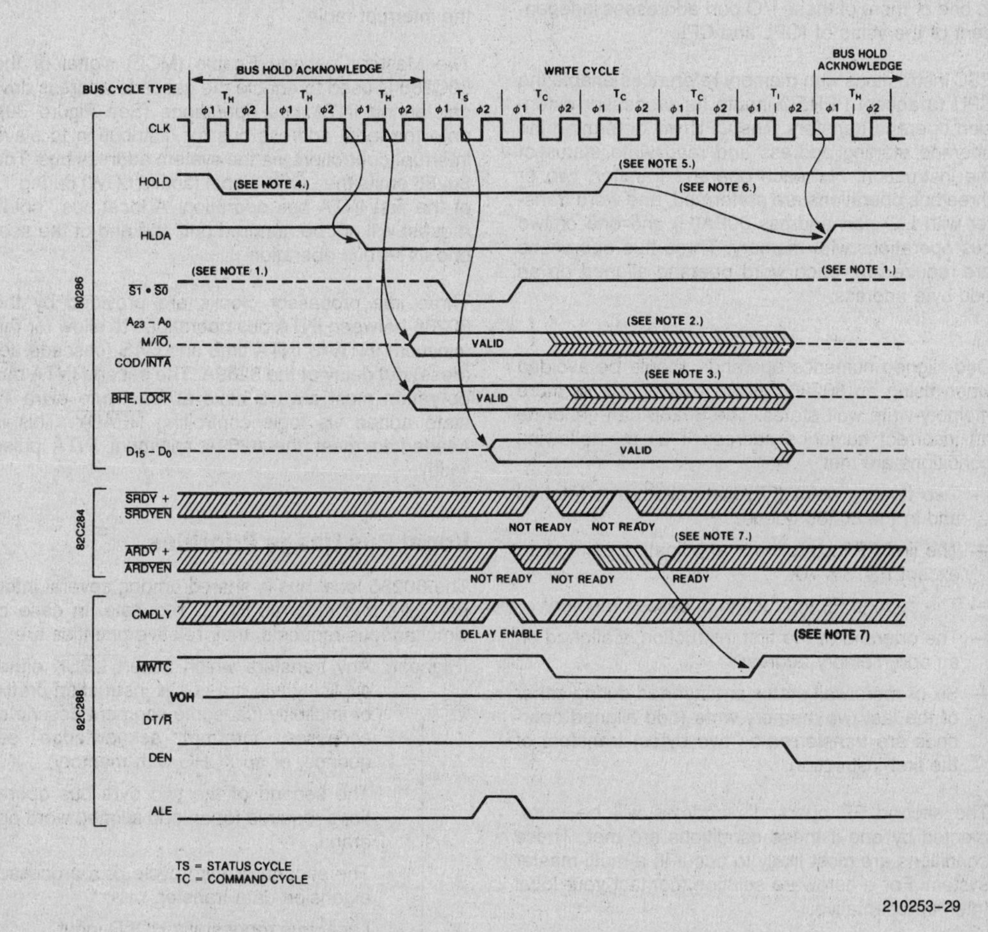

NOTES:

1. Status lines are not driven by 80286, yet remain high due to pullup resistors in 82C284 during HOLD state.
2. Address, M/IO and COD/INTA may start floating during any T_C depending on when internal 80286 bus arbiter decides to release bus to external HOLD. The float starts in $\phi 2$ of T_C.
3. BHE and LOCK may start floating after the end of any T_C depending on when internal 80286 bus arbiter decides to release bus to external HOLD. The float starts in $\phi 1$ of T_C.
4. The minimum HOLD to HLDA time is shown. Maximum is one T_H longer.
5. The earliest HOLD time is shown. It will always allow a subsequent memory cycle if pending is shown.
6. The minimum HOLD to HLDA time is shown. Maximum is a function of the instruction, type of bus cycle and other machine state (i.e., Interrupts, Waits, Lock, etc.).
7. Asynchronous ready allows termination of the cycle. Synchronous ready does not signal ready in this example. Synchronous ready state is ignored after ready is signaled via the asynchronous input.

Figure 29. MULTIBUS® Write Terminated by Asynchronous Ready with Bus Hold

Processor Extension Transfers

The processor extension interface uses I/O port addresses 00F8(H), 00FA(H), and 00FC(H) which are part of the I/O port address range reserved by Intel. An ESC instruction with Machine Status Word bits EM = 0 and TS = 0 will perform I/O bus operations to one or more of these I/O port addresses independent of the value of IOPL and CPL.

ESC instructions with memory references enable the CPU to accept PEREQ inputs for processor extension operand transfers. The CPU will determine the operand starting address and read/write status of the instruction. For each operand transfer, two or three bus operations are performed, one word transfer with I/O port address 00FA(H) and one or two bus operations with memory. Three bus operations are required for each word operand aligned on an odd byte address.

NOTE:

Odd-aligned numerics operands should be avoided when using an 80286 system running six or more memory-write wait states. The 80286 can generate an incorrect numerics address if all the following conditions are met:

- Two floating point (FP) instructions are fetched and in the 80286 queue.
- The first FP instruction is any floating point store except FSTSW AX.
- The second FP instruction accesses memory.
- The operand of the first instruction is aligned on an odd memory address.
- Six or more wait states are inserted during either of the last two memory write (odd aligned operands are transferred as two bytes) transfers of the first instruction.

The second FP operand's address will be incremented by one if these conditions are met. These conditions are most likely to occur in a multi-master system. For a hardware solution, contact your local Intel representative.

Commands to the numerics coprocessor should not be delayed by nine or more T-states. Excessive (nine or more) command-delays can cause the 80286 and 80287 to lose synchronization.

Interrupt Acknowledge Sequence

Figure 30 illustrates an interrupt acknowledge sequence performed by the 80286 in response to an INTR input. An interrupt acknowledge sequence consists of two INTA bus operations. The first allows a master 8259A Programmable Interrupt Controller (PIC) to determine which if any of its slaves should return the interrupt vector. An eight bit vector is read on D0–D7 of the 80286 during the second INTA bus operation to select an interrupt handler routine from the interrupt table.

The Master Cascade Enable (MCE) signal of the 82C288 is used to enable the cascade address drivers, during INTA bus operations (See Figure 30), onto the local address bus for distribution to slave interrupt controllers via the system address bus. The 80286 emits the $\overline{\text{LOCK}}$ signal (active LOW) during T_S of the first INTA bus operation. A local bus "hold" request will not be honored until the end of the second INTA bus operation.

Three idle processor clocks are provided by the 80286 between INTA bus operations to allow for the minimum INTA to INTA time and CAS (cascade address) out delay of the 8259A. The second INTA bus operation must always have at least one extra T_C state added via logic controlling $\overline{\text{READY}}$. This is needed to meet the 8259A minimum INTA pulse width.

Local Bus Usage Priorities

The 80286 local bus is shared among several internal units and external HOLD requests. In case of simultaneous requests, their relative priorities are:

(Highest) Any transfers which assert $\overline{\text{LOCK}}$ either explicitly (via the LOCK instruction prefix) or implicitly (i.e. some segment descriptor accesses, interrupt acknowledge sequence, or an XCHG with memory).

The second of the two byte bus operations required for an odd aligned word operand.

The second or third cycle of a processor extension data transfer.

Local bus request via HOLD input.

Processor extension data operand transfer via PEREQ input.

Data transfer performed by EU as part of an instruction.

(Lowest) An instruction prefetch request from BU. The EU will inhibit prefetching two processor clocks in advance of any data transfers to minimize waiting by EU for a prefetch to finish.

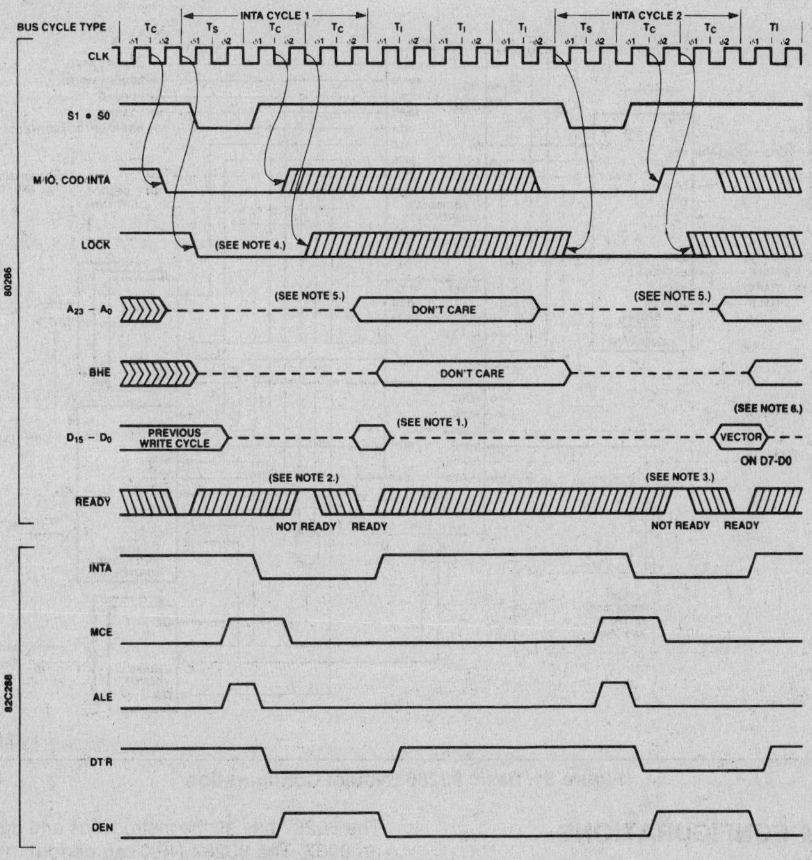

210253-31

NOTES:
1. Data is ignored, upper data bus, D_8–D_{15}, should not change state during this time.
2. First INTA cycle should have at least one wait state inserted to meet 8259A minimum INTA pulse width.
3. Second INTA cycle should have at least one wait state inserted to meet 8259A minimum INTA pulse width.
4. $\overline{\text{LOCK}}$ is active for the first INTA cycle to prevent the bus arbiter from releasing the bus between INTA cycles in a multi-master system. $\overline{\text{LOCK}}$ is also active for the second INTA cycle.
5. A_{23}–A_0 exits 3-state OFF during $\phi 2$ of the second T_C in the INTA cycle.
6. Upper data bus should not change state during this time.

Figure 30. Interrupt Acknowledge Sequence

Halt or Shutdown Cycles

The 80286 externally indicates halt or shutdown conditions as a bus operation. These conditions occur due to a HLT instruction or multiple protection exceptions while attempting to execute one instruction. A halt or shutdown bus operation is signalled when $\overline{\text{S1}}$, $\overline{\text{S0}}$ and COD/$\overline{\text{INTA}}$ are LOW and M/$\overline{\text{IO}}$ is HIGH. A_1 HIGH indicates halt, and A_1 LOW indicates shutdown. The 82C288 bus controller does not issue ALE, nor is $\overline{\text{READY}}$ required to terminate a halt or shutdown bus operation.

During halt or shutdown, the 80286 may service PEREQ or HOLD requests. A processor extension segment overrun exception during shutdown will inhibit further service of PEREQ. Either NMI or RESET will force the 80286 out of either halt or shutdown. An INTR, if interrupts are enabled, or a processor extension segment overrun exception will also force the 80286 out of halt.

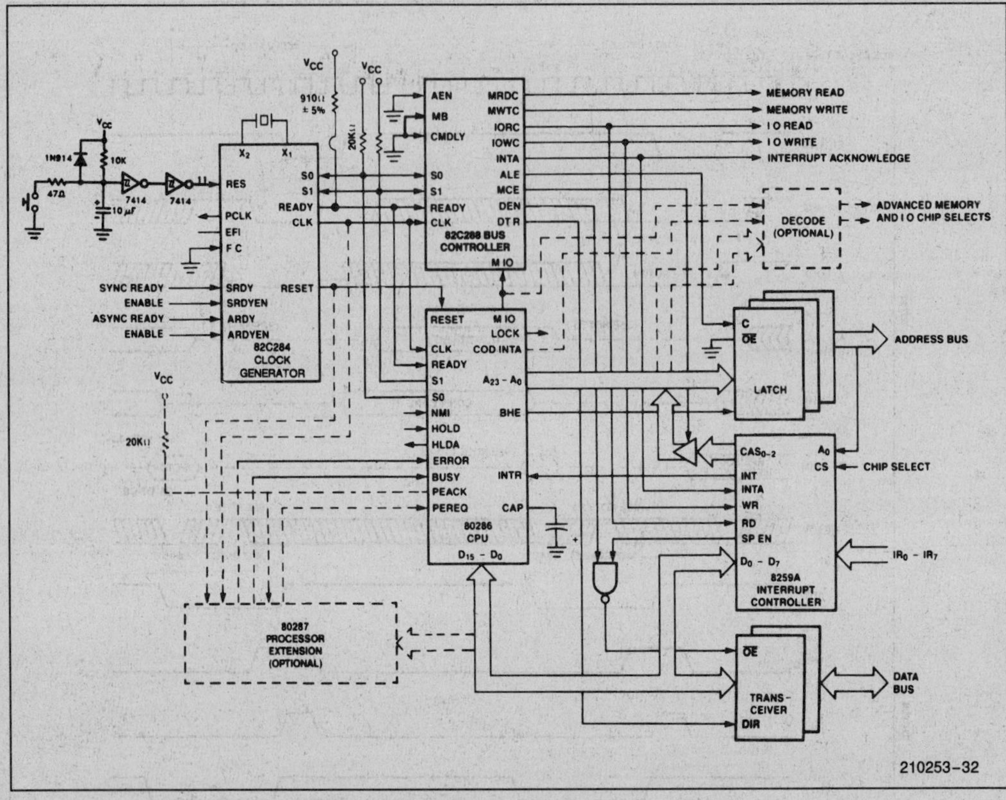

Figure 31. Basic 80286 System Configuration

SYSTEM CONFIGURATIONS

The versatile bus structure of the 80286 microsystem, with a full complement of support chips, allows flexible configuration of a wide range of systems. The basic configuration, shown in Figure 31, is similar to an 8086 maximum mode system. It includes the CPU plus an 8259A interrupt controller, 82C284 clock generator, and the 82C288 Bus Controller.

As indicated by the dashed lines in Figure 31, the ability to add processor extensions is an integral feature of 80286 microsystems. The processor extension interface allows external hardware to perform special functions and transfer data concurrent with CPU execution of other instructions. Full system integrity is maintained because the 80286 supervises all data transfers and instruction execution for the processor extension.

The 80287 has all the instructions and data types of an 8087. The 80287 NPX can perform numeric calculations and data transfers concurrently with CPU program execution. Numerics code and data have the same integrity as all other information protected by the 80286 protection mechanism.

The 80286 can overlap chip select decoding and address propagation during the data transfer for the previous bus operation. This information is latched by ALE during the middle of a T_S cycle. The latched chip select and address information remains stable during the bus operation while the next cycle's address is being decoded and propagated into the system. Decode logic can be implemented with a high speed bipolar PROM.

The optional decode logic shown in Figure 31 takes advantage of the overlap between address and data of the 80286 bus cycle to generate advanced memory and IO-select signals. This minimizes system

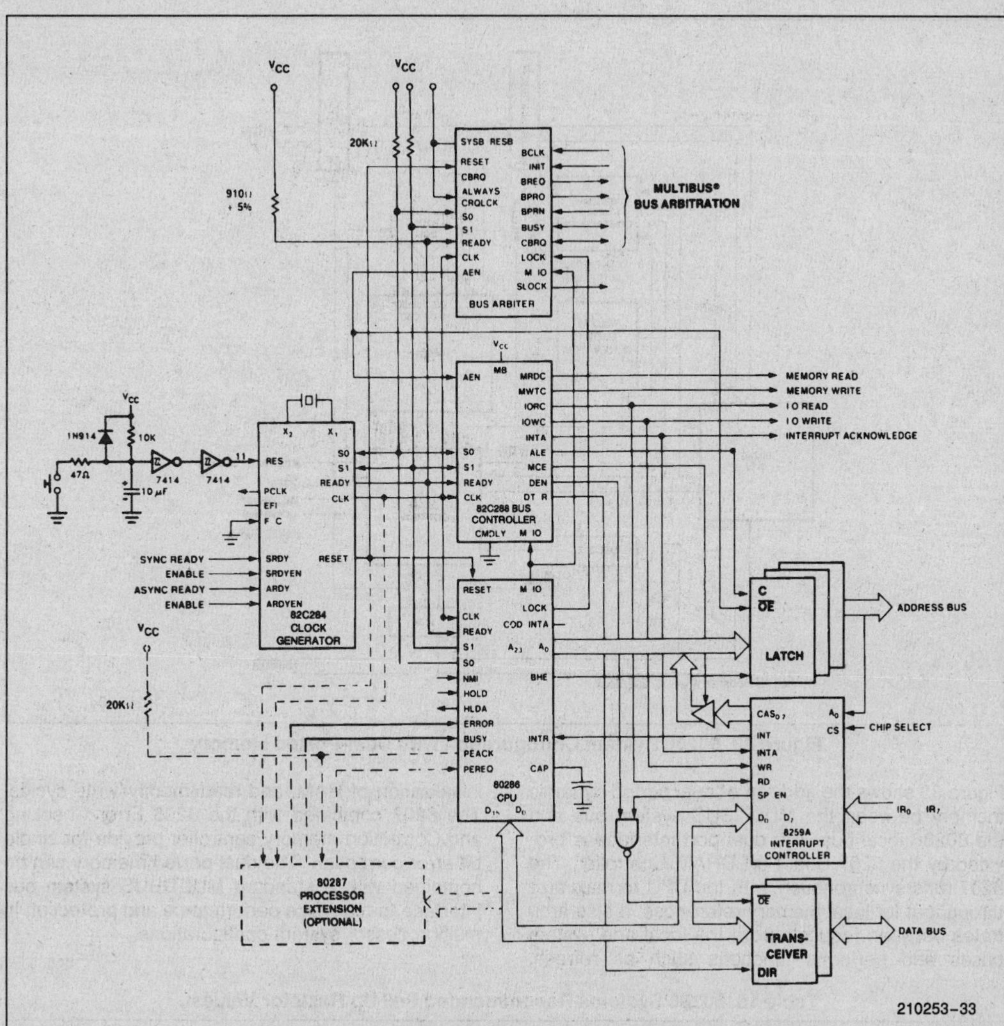

Figure 32. MULTIBUS® System Bus Interface

performance degradation caused by address propagation and decode delays. In addition to selecting memory and I/O, the advanced selects may be used with configurations supporting local and system buses to enable the appropriate bus interface for each bus cycle. The COD/$\overline{\text{INTA}}$ and M/$\overline{\text{IO}}$ signals are applied to the decode logic to distinguish between interrupt, I/O, code and data bus cycles.

By adding the 82289 bus arbiter chip, the 80286 provides a MULTIBUS system bus interface as shown in Figure 32. The ALE output of the 82C288 for the MULTIBUS bus is connected to its CMDLY input to delay the start of commands one system CLK as required to meet MULTIBUS address and write data setup times. This arrangement will add at least one extra T_C state to each bus operation which uses the MULTIBUS.

A second 82C288 bus controller and additional latches and transceivers could be added to the local bus of Figure 32. This configuration allows the 80286 to support an on-board bus for local memory and peripherals, and the MULTIBUS for system bus interfacing.

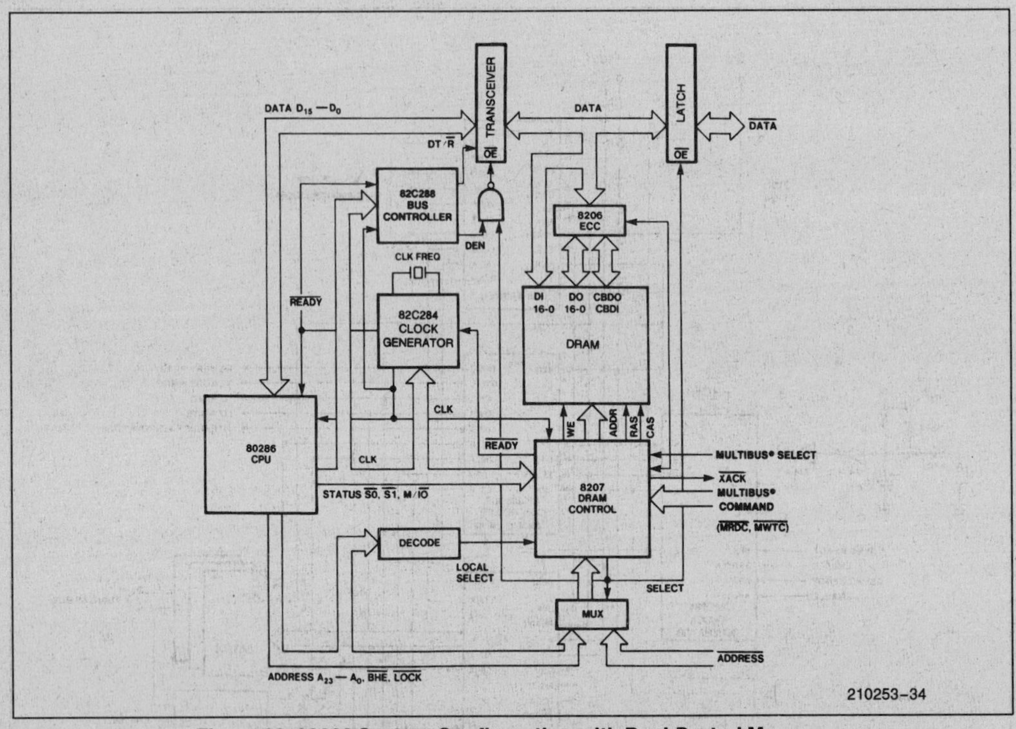

Figure 33. 80286 System Configuration with Dual-Ported Memory

Figure 33 shows the addition of dual ported dynamic memory between the MULTIBUS system bus and the 80286 local bus. The dual port interface is provided by the 8207 Dual Port DRAM Controller. The 8207 runs synchronously with the CPU to maximize throughput for local memory references. It also arbitrates between requests from the local and system buses and performs functions such as refresh, initialization of RAM, and read/modify/write cycles. The 8207 combined with the 8206 Error Checking and Correction memory controller provide for single bit error correction. The dual-ported memory can be combined with a standard MULTIBUS system bus interface to maximize performance and protection in multiprocessor system configurations.

Table 16. 80286 Systems Recommended Pull Up Resistor Values

80286 Pin and Name	Pullup Value	Purpose
4—$\overline{S1}$	20 KΩ ±10%	Pull $\overline{S0}$, $\overline{S1}$, and $\overline{PEACK}$ inactive during 80286 hold periods(1)
5—$\overline{S0}$		
6—$\overline{PEACK}$		
63—$\overline{READY}$	910Ω ±5%	Pull $\overline{READY}$ inactive within required minimum time (C_L = 150 pF, $I_R \le 7$ mA)

NOTE:
1. Pull-up resistors are not required on $\overline{S0}$ and $\overline{S1}$ when the corresponding pins of the 82C284 are connected to $\overline{S0}$ and $\overline{S1}$.

I²ICE™-286 System Design Considerations

One of the advantages of using the 80286 is that full in-circuit emulation debugging support is provided through the I²ICE system 80286 probe. To utilize this powerful tool it is necessary that the system designer be aware of a few minor parametric and functional differences between the 80286 and I²ICE system 80286 probe. The I²ICE data sheet (I²ICE Integrated Instrumentation and In-Circuit Emulation System, order #210469) contains a detailed description of these design considerations. It is recommended that this document be reviewed by the 80286 system designer to determine whether or not these differences affect his design.

PACKAGE THERMAL SPECIFICATIONS

The 80286 Microprocessor is specified for operation when case temperature (T_C) is within the range 0°C–85°C. Case temperature, unlike ambient temperature, is easily measured in any environment to determine whether the 80286 Microprocessor is within the specified operating range. The case temperature should be measured at the center of the top surface of the component.

The maximum ambient temperature (T_A) allowable without violating T_C specifications can be calculated from the equations shown below. T_J is the 80286 junction temperature. P is the power dissipated by the 80286.

$T_J = T_C + P * \theta_{JC}$

$T_A = T_J - P * \theta_{JA}$

$T_C = T_A + P * [\theta_{JA} - \theta_{JC}]$

Values for θ_{JA} and θ_{JC} are given in Table 17. θ_{JA} is given at various airflows. Table 18 shows the maximum T_A allowable (without exceeding T_C) at various airflows. Note that the 80286 PLCC package has an internal heat spreader. T_A can be further improved by attaching "fins" or an external "heat sink" to the package.

Junction temperature calculations should use an I_{CC} value that is measured without external resistive loads. The external resistive loads dissipate additional power external to the 80286 and not on the die. This increases the resistor temperature, not the die temperature. The full capacitive load (C_L = 100 pF) should be applied during the I_{CC} measurement.

Table 17. Thermal Resistances (°C/Watt) θ_{JC} and θ_{JA}

Package	θ_{JC}	θ_{JA} versus Airflow — ft/min (m/sec)					
		0 (0)	200 (1.01)	400 (2.03)	600 (3.04)	800 (4.06)	1000 (5.07)
68-Lead LCC	8	28	22	16	13	12	11
68-Lead PGA	5.5	28	22	16	15	14	13
68-Lead PLCC w/ Internal Heat Spreader	8	28	23	21	18	16	15

Table 18. Maximum T_A at Various Airflows

Package	T_A (°C) versus Airflow — ft/min (m/sec)					
	0 (0)	200 (1.01)	400 (2.03)	600 (3.04)	800 (4.06)	1000 (5.07)
68-Lead LCC	40	54	67	74	76	78
68-Lead PGA	34	48	61	64	66	68
68-Lead PLCC w/Internal Heat Spreader	40	51	56	63	67	69

NOTE:
The numbers in Table 18 were calculated using a V_{CC} of 5.0V, and an I_{CC} of 450 mA, which is representative of the worst case I_{CC} at T_C = 85°C with the outputs unloaded.

5

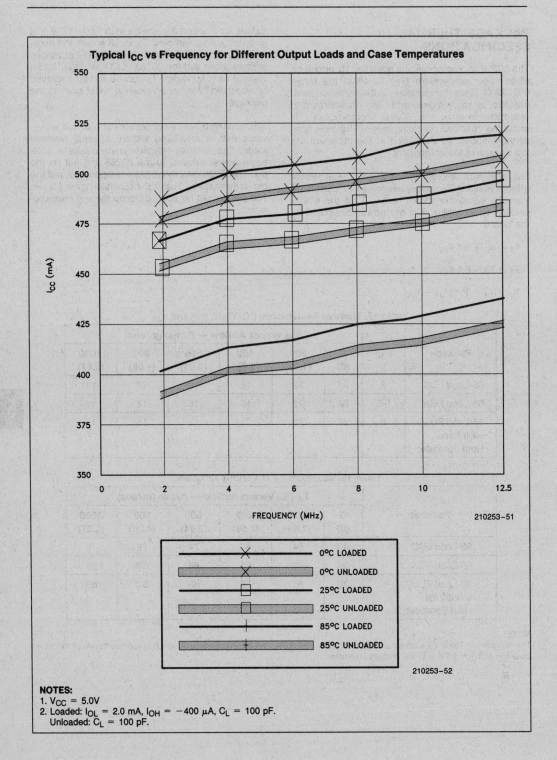

Typical I_{CC} vs Frequency for Different Output Loads and Case Temperatures

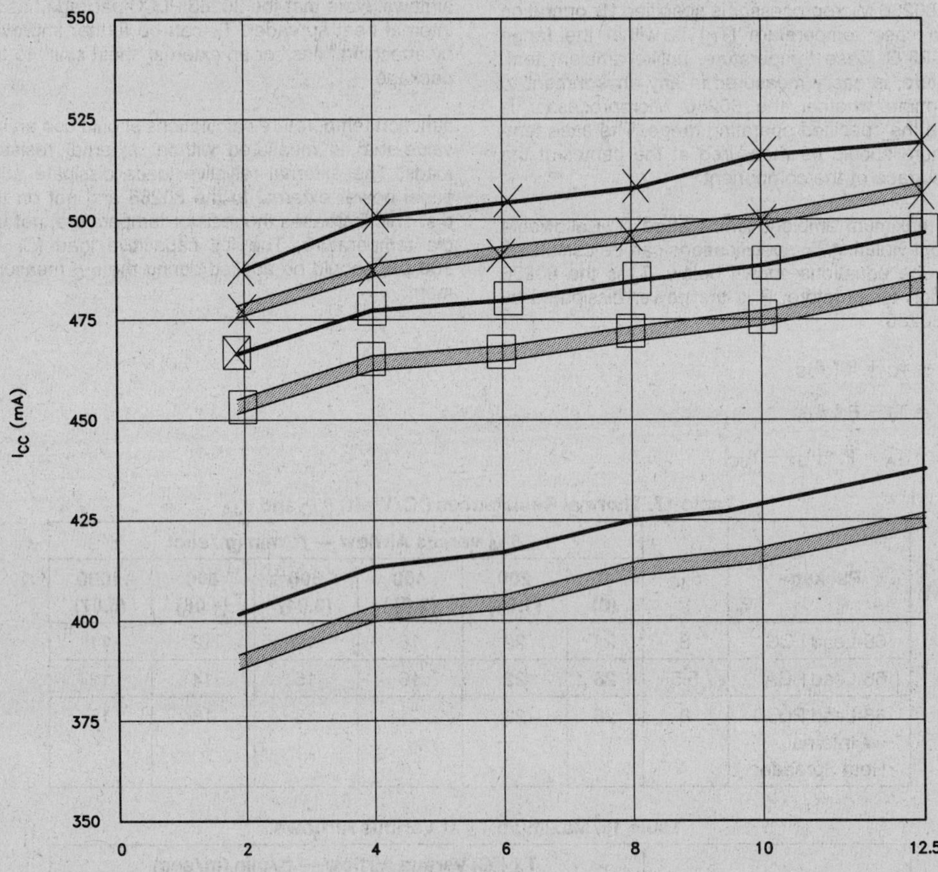

210253–51

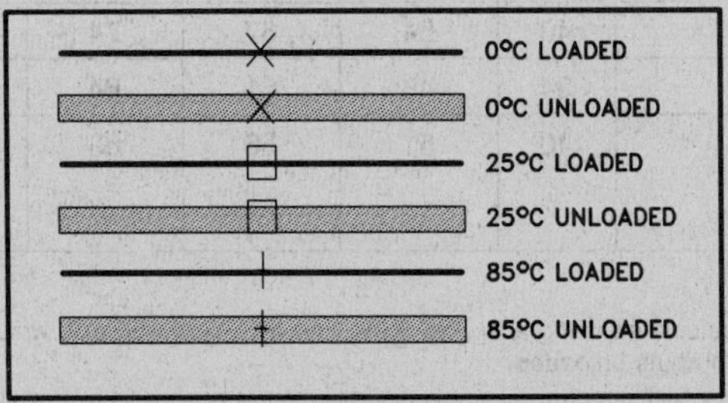

210253–52

NOTES:
1. V_{CC} = 5.0V
2. Loaded: I_{OL} = 2.0 mA, I_{OH} = −400 μA, C_L = 100 pF.
   Unloaded: C_L = 100 pF.

ABSOLUTE MAXIMUM RATINGS*

Ambient Temperature Under Bias ....0°C to +70°C
Storage Temperature .... −65°C to +150°C
Voltage on Any Pin with Respect to Ground.............. −1.0V to +7V
Power Dissipation..........................3.3W

NOTICE: This is a production data sheet. The specifications are subject to change without notice.

**WARNING: Stressing the device beyond the "Absolute Maximum Ratings" may cause permanent damage. These are stress ratings only. Operation beyond the "Operating Conditions" is not recommended and extended exposure beyond the "Operating Conditions" may affect device reliability.*

D.C. CHARACTERISTICS (V_{CC} = 5V ±5%, T_{CASE} = 0°C to +85°C)*

Symbol	Parameter	Min	Max	Unit	Test Condition
I_{CC}	Supply Current (0°C Turn On)		600	mA	(Note 1)
C_{CLK}	CLK Input Capacitance		20	pF	(Note 2)
C_{IN}	Other Input Capacitance		10	pF	(Note 2)
C_O	Input/Output Capacitance		20	pF	(Note 2)

NOTES:
1. C_L = 100 pF. Tested at maximum frequency without resistive loads on the outputs.
2. These are not tested. They are guaranteed by design characterization.

D.C. CHARACTERISTICS

(V_{CC} = 5V ±5%, T_{CASE} = 0°C to +85°C)* Tested at the minimum operating frequency of the part.

Symbol	Parameter	Min	Max	Unit	Test Condition
V_{IL}	Input LOW Voltage	−0.5	0.8	V	
V_{IH}	Input HIGH Voltage	2.0	V_{CC} +0.5	V	
V_{ILC}	CLK Input LOW Voltage	−0.5	0.6	V	
V_{IHC}	CLK Input HIGH Voltage	3.8	V_{CC} +0.5	V	
V_{OL}	Output LOW Voltge		0.45	V	I_{OL} = 2.0 mA
V_{OH}	Output HIGH Voltage	2.4		V	I_{OH} = −400 μA
I_{LI}	Input Leakage Current		±10	μA	0V ≤ V_{IN} ≤ V_{CC}
I_{IL}	Input Sustaining Current on $\overline{BUSY}$ and $\overline{ERROR}$ Pins	−30	−500	μA	V_{IN} = 0V
I_{LO}	Output Leakage Current		±10	μA	0V ≤ V_{OUT} ≤ V_{CC}

NOTE:
*T_A is guaranteed from 0°C to +55°C as long as T_{CASE} is not exceeded.

5

A.C. CHARACTERISTICS (V_{CC} = 5V ±5%, T_{CASE} = 0°C to +85°C)*

AC timings are referenced to 0.8V and 2.0V points of signals as illustrated in datasheet waveforms, unless otherwise noted.

Symbol	Parameter	8 MHz		10 MHz		12.5 MHz		Unit	Test Condition
		-8 Min	-8 Max	-10 Min	-10 Max	-12 Min	-12 Max		
1	System Clock (CLK) Period	62	250	50	250	40	250	ns	
2	System Clock (CLK) LOW Time	15		12		11		ns	at 1.0V
3	System Clock (CLK) HIGH Time	25		16		13		ns	at 3.6V
17	System Clock (CLK) Rise Time		10		8	—	8	ns	1.0V to 3.6V, (Note 7)
18	System Clock (CLK) Fall Time		10		8	—	8	ns	3.6V to 1.0V, (Note 7)
4	Asynch. Inputs Setup Time	20		20		15		ns	(Note 1)
5	Asynch. Inputs Hold Time	20		20		15		ns	(Note 1)
6	RESET Setup Time	28		23		18		ns	
7	RESET Hold Time	5		5		5		ns	
8	Read Data Setup Time	10		8		5		ns	
9	Read Data Hold Time	8		8		6		ns	
10	$\overline{\text{READY}}$ Setup Time	38		26		22		ns	
11	$\overline{\text{READY}}$ Hold Time	25		25		20		ns	
12	Status/$\overline{\text{PEACK}}$ Valid Delay	1	40	—	—	—	—	ns	(Notes 2, 3, 8)
12a1	Status Active Delay	—	—	1	22	3	18	ns	(Notes 2, 3, 8)
12a2	$\overline{\text{PEACK}}$ Active Delay	—	—	1	22	3	20	ns	(Notes 2, 3, 8)
12b	Status/$\overline{\text{PEACK}}$ Inactive Delay	—	—	1	30	3	22	ns	(Notes 2, 3, 8)
13	Address Valid Delay	1	60	1	35	1	32	ns	(Notes 2, 3, 8)
14	Write Data Valid Delay	0	50	0	30	0	30	ns	(Notes 2, 3, 8)
15	Address/Status/Data Float Delay	0	50	0	47	0	32	ns	(Notes 2, 4, 7)
16	HLDA Valid Delay	0	50	0	47	0	27	ns	(Notes 2, 3, 8)
19	Address Valid To Status Valid Setup Time	38		27		22		ns	(Notes 3, 5, 6, 7)

*T_A is guaranteed from 0°C to +55°C as long as T_{CASE} is not exceeded.

NOTES:

1. Asynchronous inputs are INTR, NMI, HOLD, PEREQ, $\overline{\text{ERROR}}$, and $\overline{\text{BUSY}}$. This specification is given only for testing purposes, to assure recognition at a specific CLK edge.
2. Delay from 1.0V on the CLK, to 0.8V or 2.0V or float on the output as appropriate for valid or floating condition.
3. Output load: C_L = 100 pF.
4. Float condition occurs when output current is less than I_{LO} in magnitude.
5. Delay measured from address either reaching 0.8V or 2.0V (valid) to status going active reaching 2.0V or status going inactive reaching 0.8V.
6. For load capacitance of 10 pF or more on STATUS/$\overline{\text{PEACK}}$ lines, subtract typically 7 ns.
7. These are not tested. They are guaranteed by design characterization.
8. Minimum output delay timings are not tested, but are guaranteed by design characterization.

A.C. CHARACTERISTICS (Continued)

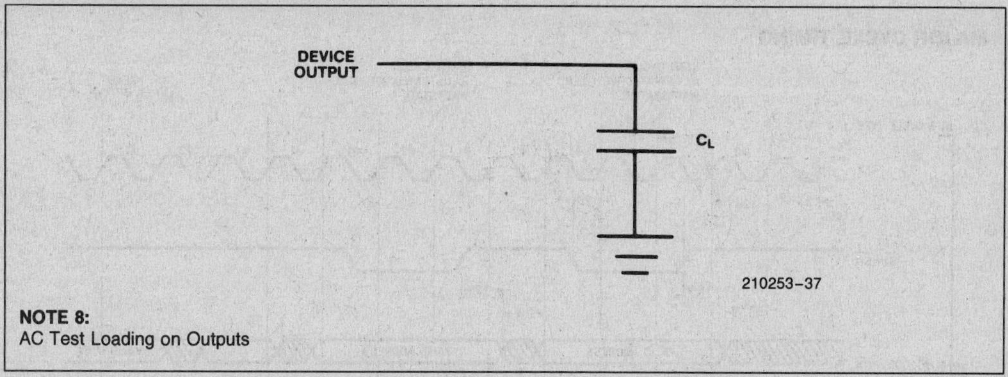

NOTE 8:
AC Test Loading on Outputs

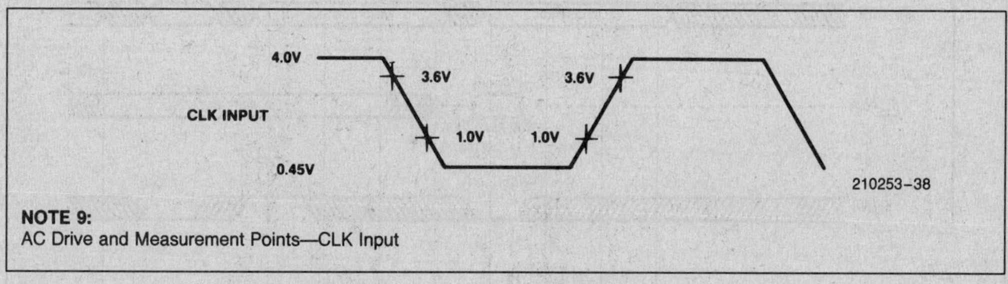

NOTE 9:
AC Drive and Measurement Points—CLK Input

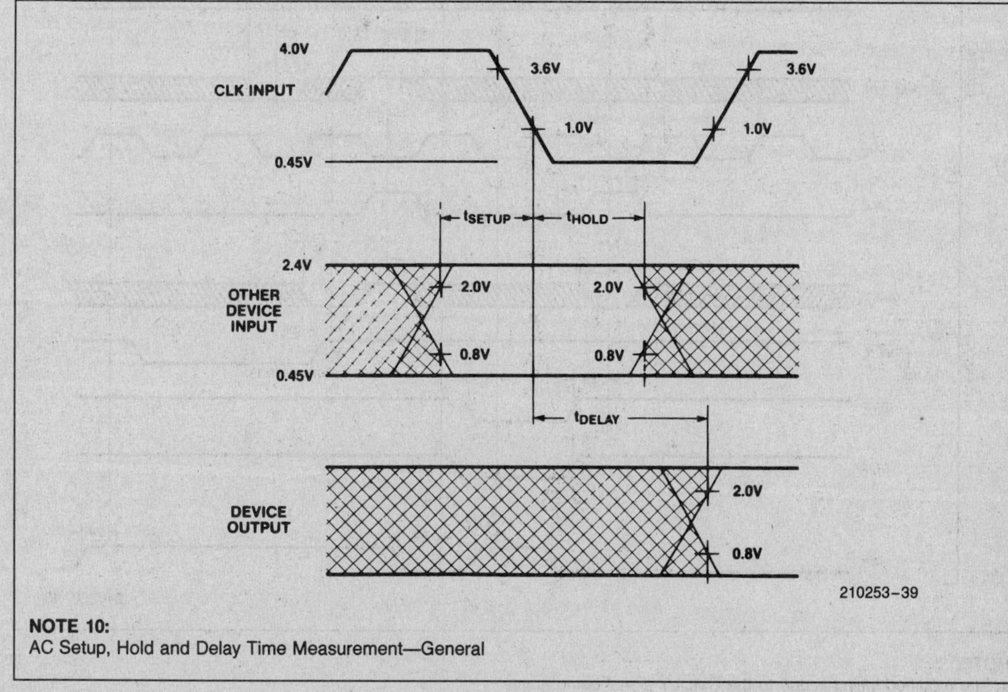

NOTE 10:
AC Setup, Hold and Delay Time Measurement—General

WAVEFORMS

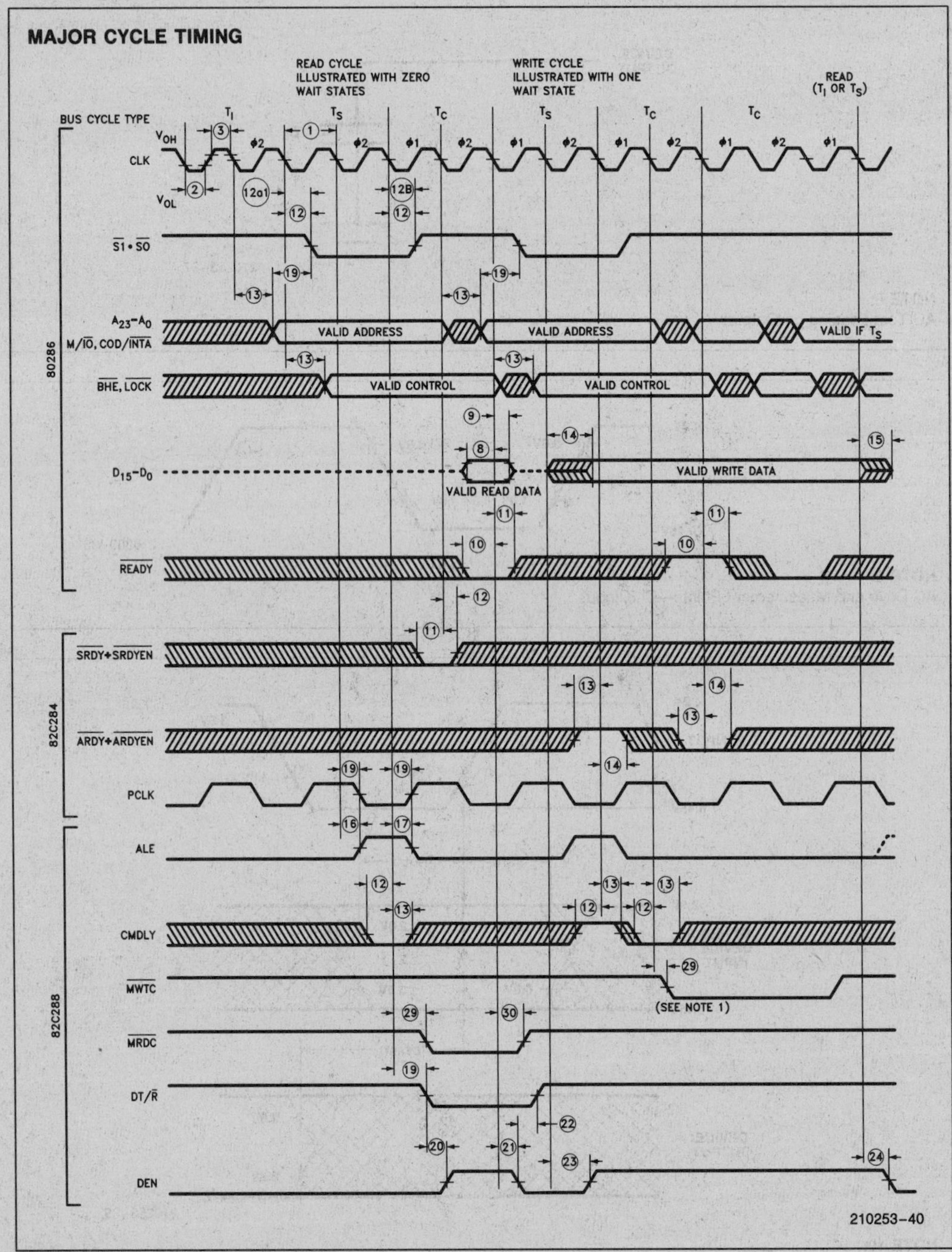

NOTE:
1. The modified timing is due to the $\overline{CMDLY}$ signal being active.

WAVEFORMS (Continued)

80286 ASYNCHRONOUS INPUT SIGNAL TIMING

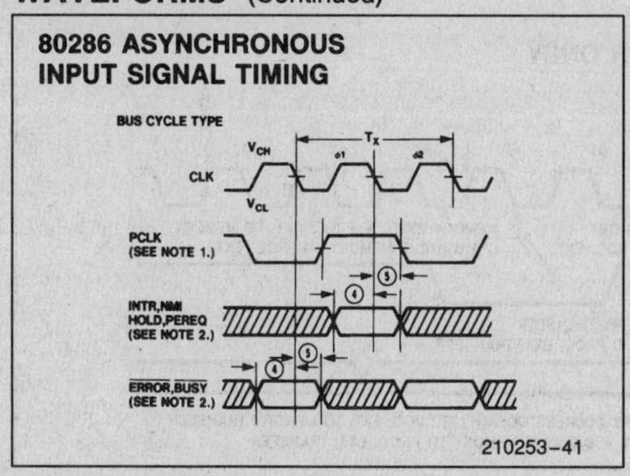

NOTES:

1. PCLK indicates which processor cycle phase will occur on the next CLK. PCLK may not indicate the correct phase until the first bus cycle is performed.
2. These inputs are asynchronous. The setup and hold times shown assure recognition for testing purposes.

80286 RESET INPUT TIMING AND SUBSEQUENT PROCESSOR CYCLE PHASE

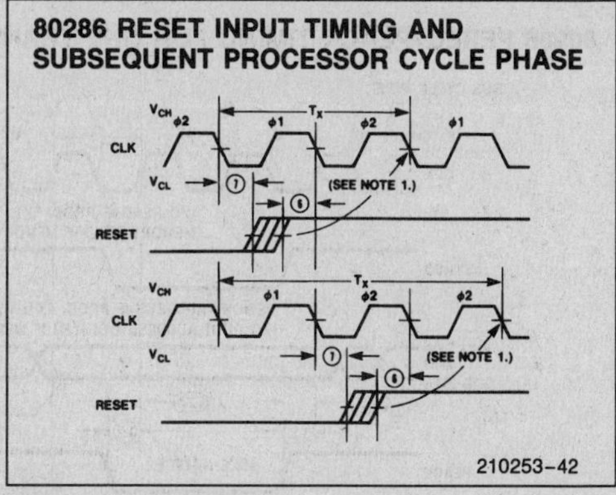

NOTE:

When RESET meets the setup time shown, the next CLK will start or repeat $\phi 2$ of a processor cycle.

EXITING AND ENTERING HOLD

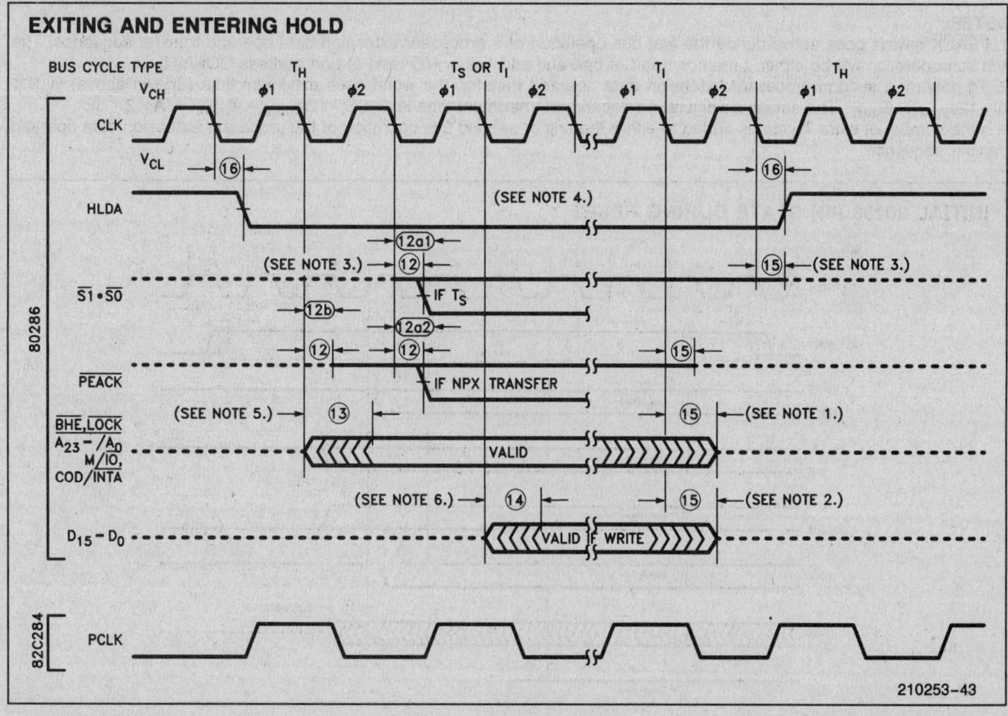

NOTES:

1. These signals may not be driven by the 80286 during the time shown. The worst case in terms of latest float time is shown.
2. The data bus will be driven as shown if the last cycle before T_I in the diagram was a write T_C.
3. The 80286 floats its status pins during T_H. External 20 KΩ resistors keep these signals high (see Table 16).
4. For HOLD request set up to HLDA, refer to Figure 29.
5. BHE and LOCK are driven at this time but will not become valid until T_S.
6. The data bus will remain in 3-state OFF if a read cycle is performed.

WAVEFORMS (Continued)

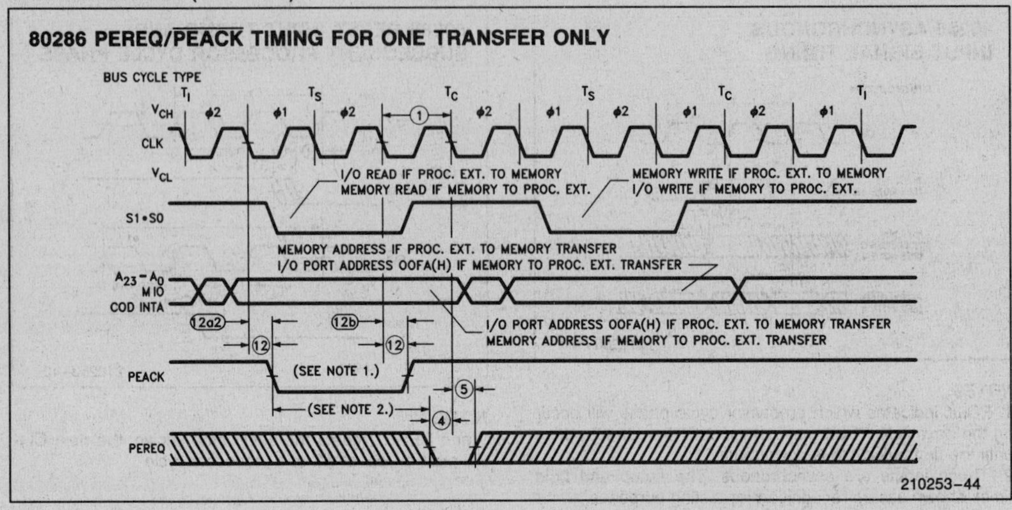

NOTES:
1. $\overline{PEACK}$ always goes active during the first bus operation of a processor extension data operand transfer sequence. The first bus operation will be either a memory read at operand address or I/O read at port address OOFA(H).
2. To prevent a second processor extension data operand transfer, the worst case maximum time (Shown above) is: $3 \times ① - 12a_{2max.} - ④_{min.}$. The actual, configuration dependent, maximum time is: $3 \times ① - 12a_{2max.} - ④_{min.} + A \times 2 \times ①$.
A is the number of extra T_C states added to either the first or second bus operation of the processor extension data operand transfer sequence.

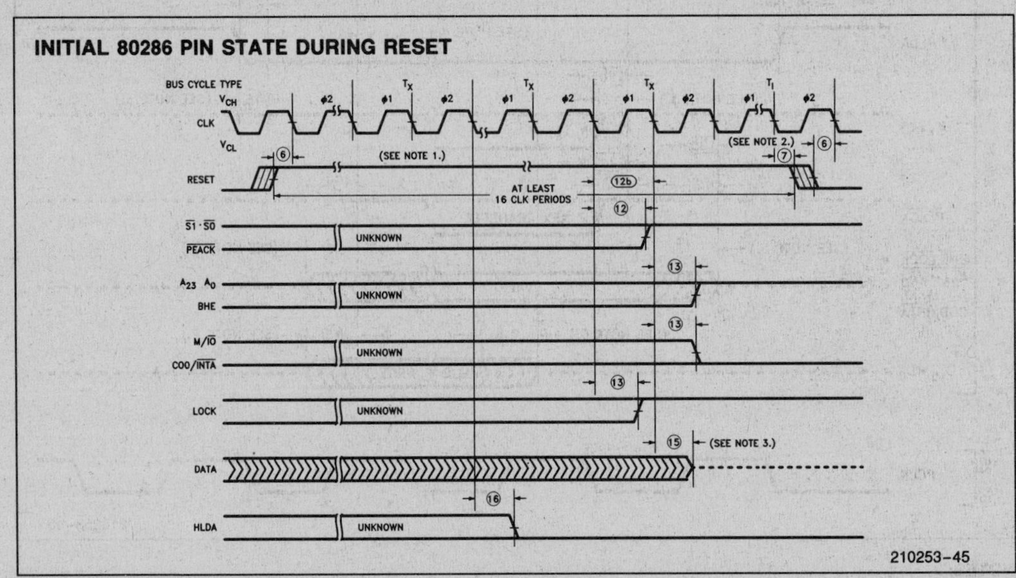

NOTES:
1. Setup time for RESET ↑ may be violated with the consideration that $\phi 1$ of the processor clock may begin one system CLK period later.
2. Setup and hold times for RESET ↓ must be met for proper operation, but RESET ↓ may occur during $\phi 1$ or $\phi 2$. If RESET ↓ occurs in ϕ, the reference clock edge can be ϕ_2 of the previous bus cycle.
3. The data bus is only guaranteed to be in 3-state OFF at the time shown.

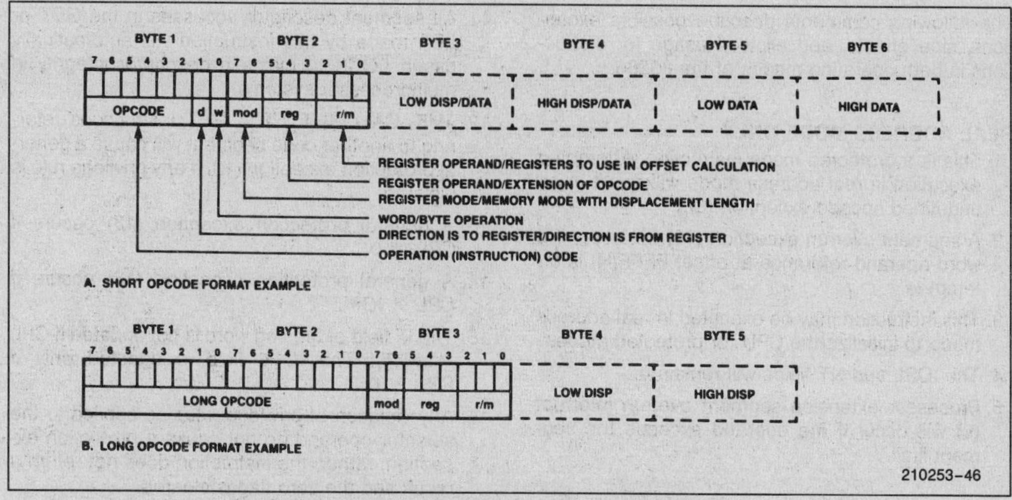

Figure 35. 80286 Instruction Format Examples

80286 INSTRUCTION SET SUMMARY

Instruction Timing Notes

The instruction clock counts listed below establish the maximum execution rate of the 80286. With no delays in bus cycles, the actual clock count of an 80286 program will average 5% more than the calculated clock count, due to instruction sequences which execute faster than they can be fetched from memory.

To calculate elapsed times for instruction sequences, multiply the sum of all instruction clock counts, as listed in the table below, by the processor clock period. An 8 MHz processor clock has a clock period of 125 nanoseconds and requires an 80286 system clock (CLK input) of 16 MHz.

Instruction Clock Count Assumptions

1. The instruction has been prefetched, decoded, and is ready for execution. Control transfer instruction clock counts include all time required to fetch, decode, and prepare the next instruction for execution.
2. Bus cycles do not require wait states.
3. There are no processor extension data transfer or local bus HOLD requests.
4. No exceptions occur during instruction execution.

Instruction Set Summary Notes

Addressing displacements selected by the MOD field are not shown. If necessary they appear after the instruction fields shown.

Above/below refers to unsigned value

Greater refers to positive signed value

Less refers to less positive (more negative) signed values

if d = 1 then to register; if d = 0 then from register

if w = 1 then word instruction; if w = 0 then byte instruction

if s = 0 then 16-bit immediate data form the operand

if s = 1 then an immediate data byte is sign-extended to form the 16-bit operand

x don't care

z used for string primitives for comparison with ZF FLAG

If two clock counts are given, the smaller refers to a register operand and the larger refers to a memory operand

* = add one clock if offset calculation requires summing 3 elements

n = number of times repeated

m = number of bytes of code in next instruction

Level (L)—Lexical nesting level of the procedure

5

The following comments describe possible exceptions, side effects, and allowed usage for instructions in both operating modes of the 80286.

REAL ADDRESS MODE ONLY

1. This is a protected mode instruction. Attempted execution in real address mode will result in an undefined opcode exception (6).
2. A segment overrun exception (13) will occur if a word operand reference at offset FFFF(H) is attempted.
3. This instruction may be executed in real address mode to initialize the CPU for protected mode.
4. The IOPL and NT fields will remain 0.
5. Processor extension segment overrun interrupt (9) will occur if the operand exceeds the segment limit.

EITHER MODE

6. An exception may occur, depending on the value of the operand.
7. $\overline{\text{LOCK}}$ is automatically asserted regardless of the presence or absence of the LOCK instruction prefix.
8. $\overline{\text{LOCK}}$ does not remain active between all operand transfers.

PROTECTED VIRTUAL ADDRESS MODE ONLY

9. A general protection exception (13) will occur if the memory operand cannot be used due to either a segment limit or access rights violation. If a stack segment limit is violated, a stack segment overrun exception (12) occurs.
10. For segment load operations, the CPL, RPL, and DPL must agree with privilege rules to avoid an exception. The segment must be present to avoid a not-present exception (11). If the SS register is the destination, and a segment not-present violation occurs, a stack exception (12) occurs.
11. All segment descriptor accesses in the GDT or LDT made by this instruction will automatically assert $\overline{\text{LOCK}}$ to maintain descriptor integrity in multiprocessor systems.
12. JMP, CALL, INT, RET, IRET instructions referring to another code segment will cause a general protection exception (13) if any privilege rule is violated.
13. A general protection exception (13) occurs if $CPL \neq 0$.
14. A general protection exception (13) occurs if $CPL > IOPL$.
15. The IF field of the flag word is not updated if $CPL > IOPL$. The IOPL field is updated only if $CPL = 0$.
16. Any violation of privilege rules as applied to the selector operand do not cause a protection exception; rather, the instruction does not return a result and the zero flag is cleared.
17. If the starting address of the memory operand violates a segment limit, or an invalid access is attempted, a general protection exception (13) will occur before the ESC instruction is executed. A stack segment overrun exception (12) will occur if the stack limit is violated by the operand's starting address. If a segment limit is violated during an attempted data transfer then a processor extension segment overrun exception (9) occurs.
18. The destination of an INT, JMP, CALL, RET or IRET instruction must be in the defined limit of a code segment or a general protection exception (13) will occur.

80286 INSTRUCTION SET SUMMARY

FUNCTION	FORMAT				Clock Count: Real Address Mode	Clock Count: Protected Virtual Address Mode	Comments: Real Address Mode	Comments: Protected Virtual Address Mode
DATA TRANSFER								
MOV = **Move:**								
Register to Register/Memory	1000100w	mod reg r/m			2,3*	2,3*	2	9
Register/memory to register	1000101w	mod reg r/m			2,5*	2,5*	2	9
Immediate to register/memory	1100011w	mod 000 r/m	data	data if w = 1	2,3*	2,3*	2	9
Immediate to register	1011w reg	data	data if w = 1		2	2		
Memory to accumulator	1010000w	addr-low	addr-high		5	5	2	9
Accumulator to memory	1010001w	addr-low	addr-high		3	3	2	9
Register/memory to segment register	10001110	mod 0 reg r/m			2,5*	17,19*	2	9,10,11
Segment register to register/memory	10001100	mod 0 reg r/m			2,3*	2,3*	2	9
PUSH = **Push:**								
Memory	11111111	mod 110 r/m			5*	5*	2	9
Register	01010 reg				3	3	2	9
Segment register	000 reg 110				3	3	2	9
Immediate	011010s0	data	data if s = 0		3	3	2	9
PUSHA = Push All	01100000				17	17	2	9
POP = Pop:								
Memory	10001111	mod 000 r/m			5*	5*	2	9
Register	01011 reg				5	5	2	9
Segment register	000 reg 111	(reg≠01)			5	20	2	9,10,11
POPA = Pop All	01100001				19	19	2	9
XCHG = **Exhcange:**								
Register/memory with register	1000011w	mod reg r/m			3,5*	3,5*	2,7	7,9
Register with accumulator	10010 reg				3	3		
IN = **Input from:**								
Fixed port	1110010w	port			5	5		14
Variable port	1110110w				5	5		14
OUT = **Output to:**								
Fixed port	1110011w	port			3	3		14
Variable port	1110111w				3	3		14
XLAT = Translate byte to AL	11010111				5	5		9
LEA = Load EA to register	10001101	mod reg r/m			3*	3*		
LDS = Load pointer to DS	11000101	mod reg r/m	(mod≠11)		7*	21*	2	9,10,11
LES = Load pointer to ES	11000100	mod reg r/m	(mod≠1)		7*	21*	2	9,10,11

Shaded areas indicate instructions not available in 8086, 88 microsystems.

5

80286 INSTRUCTION SET SUMMARY (Continued)

FUNCTION	FORMAT	CLOCK COUNT: Real Address Mode	CLOCK COUNT: Protected Virtual Address Mode	COMMENTS: Real Address Mode	COMMENTS: Protected Virtual Address Mode
DATA TRANSFER (Continued)					
LAHF Load AH with flags	10011111	2	2		
SAHF = Store AH into flags	10011110	2	2		
PUSHF = Push flags	10011100	3	3	2	9
POPF = Pop flags	10011101	5	5	2,4	9,15
ARITHMETIC					
ADD = **Add:**					
Reg/memory with register to either	000000dw | mod reg r/m	2,7*	2,7*	2	9
Immediate to register/memory	100000sw | mod 000 r/m | data | data if s w = 01	3,7*	3,7*	2	9
Immediate to accumulator	0000010w | data | data if w = 1	3	3		
ADC = **Add with carry:**					
Reg/memory with register to either	000100dw | mod reg r/m	2,7*	2,7*	2	9
Immediate to register/memory	100000sw | mod 010 r/m | data | data if s w = 01	3,7*	3,7*	2	9
Immediate to accumulator	0001010w | data | data if w = 1	3	3		
INC = **Increment:**					
Register/memory	1111111w | mod 000 r/m	2,7*	2,7*	2	9
Register	01000 reg	2	2		
SUB = **Subtract:**					
Reg/memory and register to either	001010dw | mod reg r/m	2,7*	2,7*	2	9
Immediate from register/memory	100000sw | mod 101 r/m | data | data if s w = 01	3,7*	3,7*	2	9
Immediate from accumulator	0010110w | data | data if w = 1	3	3		
SBB = **Subtract with borrow:**					
Reg/memory and register to either	000110dw | mod reg r/m	2,7*	2,7*	2	9
Immediate from register/memory	100000sw | mod 011 r/m | data | data if s w = 01	3,7*	3,7*	2	9
Immediate from accumulator	0001110w | data | data if w = 1	3	3		
DEC = **Decrement**					
Register/memory	1111111w | mod 001 r/m	2,7*	2,7*	2	9
Register	01001 reg	2	2		
CMP = **Compare**					
Register/memory with register	0011101w | mod reg r/m	2,6*	2,6*	2	9
Register with register/memory	0011100w | mod reg r/m	2,7*	2,7*	2	9
Immediate with register/memory	100000sw | mod 111 r/m | data | data if s w = 01	3,6*	3,6*	2	9
Immediate with accumulator	0011110w | data | data if w = 1	3	3		
NEG = Change sign	1111011w | mod 011 r/m	2	7*	2	9
AAA = ASCII adjust for add	00110111	3	3		
DAA = Decimal adjust for add	00100111	3	3		

80286 INSTRUCTION SET SUMMARY (Continued)

FUNCTION	FORMAT					CLOCK COUNT Real Address Mode	CLOCK COUNT Protected Virtual Address Mode	COMMENTS Real Address Mode	COMMENTS Protected Virtual Address Mode
ARITHMETIC (Continued)									
AAS = ASCII adjust for subtract	00111111					3	3		
DAS = Decimal adjust for subtract	00101111					3	3		
MUL = Multiply (unsigned):	1111011w	mod 100 r/m							
Register-Byte						13	13		
Register-Word						21	21		
Memory-Byte						16*	16*	2	9
Memory-Word						24*	24*	2	9
IMUL = Integer multiply (signed):	1111011w	mod 101 r/m							
Register-Byte						13	13		
Register-Word						21	21		
Memory-Byte						16*	16*	2	9
Memory-Word						24*	24*	2	9
IMUL = Integer immediate multiply (signed)	011010s1	mod reg r/m	data	data if s = 0		21,24*	21,24*	2	9
DIV = Divide (unsigned)	1111011w	mod 110 r/m							
Register-Byte						14	14	6	6
Register-Word						22	22	6	6
Memory-Byte						17*	17*	2,6	6,9
Memory-Word						25*	25*	2,6	6,9
IDIV = Integer divide (signed)	1111011w	mod 111 r/m							
Register-Byte						17	17	6	6
Register-Word						25	25	6	6
Memory-Byte						20*	20*	2,6	6,9
Memory-Word						28*	28*	2,6	6,9
AAM = ASCII adjust for multiply	11010100	00001010				16	16		
AAD = ASCII adjust for divide	11010101	00001010				14	14		
CBW = Convert byte to word	10011000					2	2		
CWD = Convert word to double word	10011001					2	2		
LOGIC									
Shift/Rotate Instructions:									
Register/Memory by 1	1101000w	mod TTT r/m				2,7*	2,7*	2	9
Register/Memory by CL	1101001w	mod TTT r/m				5+n,8+n*	5+n,8+n*	2	9
Register/Memory by Count	1100000w	mod TTT r/m	count			5+n,8+n*	5+n,8+n*	2	9

TTT	Instruction
000	ROL
001	ROR
010	RCL
011	RCR
100	SHL/SAL
101	SHR
111	SAR

Shaded areas indicate instructions not available in 8086, 88 microsystems.

5

80286 INSTRUCTION SET SUMMARY (Continued)

FUNCTION	FORMAT				Clock Count: Real Address Mode	Clock Count: Protected Virtual Address Mode	Comments: Real Address Mode	Comments: Protected Virtual Address Mode
ARITHMETIC (Continued)								
AND = **And:**								
Reg/memory and register to either	0 0 1 0 0 0 d w	mod reg r/m			2,7*	2,7*	2	9
Immediate to register/memory	1 0 0 0 0 0 0 w	mod 1 0 0 r/m	data	data if w = 1	3,7*	3,7*	2	9
Immediate to accumulator	0 0 1 0 0 1 0 w	data	data if w = 1		3	3		
TEST = **And function to flags, no result:**								
Register/memory and register	1 0 0 0 0 1 0 w	mod reg r/m			2,6*	2,6*	2	9
Immediate data and register/memory	1 1 1 1 0 1 1 w	mod 0 0 0 r/m	data	data if w = 1	3,6*	3,6*	2	9
Immediate data and accumulator	1 0 1 0 1 0 0 w	data	data if w = 1		3	3		
OR = **Or:**								
Reg/memory and register to either	0 0 0 0 1 0 d w	mod reg r/m			2,7*	2,7*	2	9
Immediate to register/memory	1 0 0 0 0 0 0 w	mod 0 0 1 r/m	data	data if w = 1	3,7*	3,7*	2	9
Immediate to accumulator	0 0 0 0 1 1 0 w	data	data if w = 1		3	3		
XOR = **Exclusive or:**								
Reg/memory and register to either	0 0 1 1 0 0 d w	mod reg r/m			2,7*	2,7*	2	9
Immediate to register/memory	1 0 0 0 0 0 0 w	mod 1 1 0 r/m	data	data if w = 1	3,7*	3,7*	2	9
Immediate to accumulator	0 0 1 1 0 1 0 w	data	data if w = 1		3	3		
NOT = Invert register/memory	1 1 1 1 0 1 1 w	mod 0 1 0 r/m			2,7*	2,7*	2	9
STRING MANIPULATION:								
MOVS = Move byte/word	1 0 1 0 0 1 0 w				5	5	2	9
CMPS = Compare byte/word	1 0 1 0 0 1 1 w				8	8	2	9
SCAS = Scan byte/word	1 0 1 0 1 1 1 w				7	7	2	9
LODS = Load byte/wd to AL/AX	1 0 1 0 1 1 0 w				5	5	2	9
STOS = Stor byte/wd from AL/A	1 0 1 0 1 0 1 w				3	3	2	9
INS = Input byte/wd from DX port	0 1 1 0 1 1 0 w				5	5	2	9,14
OUTS = Output byte/wd to DX port	0 1 1 0 1 1 1 w				5	5	2	9,14
Repeated by count in CX								
MOV$_5$ = Move string	1 1 1 1 0 0 1 1	1 0 1 0 0 1 0 w			5+4n	5+4n	2	9
CMPS = Compare string	1 1 1 1 0 0 1 z	1 0 1 0 0 1 1 w			5+9n	5+9n	2,8	8,9
SCAS = Scan string	1 1 1 1 0 0 1 z	1 0 1 0 1 1 1 w			5+8n	5+8n	2,8	8,9
LODS = Load string	1 1 1 1 0 0 1 1	1 0 1 0 1 1 0 w			5+4n	5+4n	2,8	8,9
STOS = Store string	1 1 1 1 0 0 1 1	1 0 1 0 1 0 1 w			4+3n	4+3n	2,8	8,9
INS = Input string	1 1 1 1 0 0 1 1	0 1 1 0 1 1 0 w			5+4n	5+4n	2	9,14
OUTS = Output string	1 1 1 1 0 0 1 1	0 1 1 0 1 1 1 w			5+4n	5+4n	2	9,14

Shaded areas indicate instructions not available in 8086, 88 microsystems.

80286 INSTRUCTION SET SUMMARY (Continued)

FUNCTION	FORMAT				Clock Count: Real Address Mode	Clock Count: Protected Virtual Address Mode	Comments: Real Address Mode	Comments: Protected Virtual Address Mode
CONTROL TRANSFER								
CALL = Call:								
Direct within segment	11101000	disp-low	disp-high		7+m	7+m	2	18
Register/memory indirect within segment	11111111	mod 010 r/m			7+m, 11+m*	7+m, 11+m*	2,8	8,9,18
Direct intersegment	10011010	segment offset			13+m	26+m	2	11,12,18
Protected Mode Only (Direct intersegment):		segment selector						
Via call gate to same privilege level						41+m		8,11,12,18
Via call gate to different privilege level, no parameters						82+m		8,11,12,18
Via call gate to different privilege level, x parameters						86 +4x+m		8,11,12,18
Via TSS						177+m		8,11,12,18
Via task gate						182+m		8,11,12,18
Indirect intersegment	11111111	mod 011 r/m		(mod≠11)	16+m	29+m*	2	8,9,11,12,18
Protected Mode Only (Indirect intersegment):								
Via call gate to same privilege level						44+m*		8,9,11,12,18
Via call gate to different privilege level, no parameters						83 +m*		8,9,11,12,18
Via call gate to different privilege level, x parameters						90+4x +m*		8,9,11,12,18
Via TSS						180+m*		8,9,11,12,18
Via task gate						185+m*		8,9,11,12,18
JMP = Unconditional jump:								
Short/long	11101011	disp-low			7+m	7+m		18
Direct within segment	11101001	disp-low	disp-high		7+m	7+ m		18
Register/memory indirect within segment	11111111	mod 100 r/m			7 +m, 11+m*	7+m, 11+m*	2	9,18
Direct intersegment	11101010	segment offset			11+m	23+m		11,12,18
Protected Mode Only (Direct intersegment):		segment selector						
Via call gate to same privilege level						38+m		8,11,12,18
Via TSS						175+m		8,11,12,18
Via task gate						180+m		8,11,12,18
Indirect intersegment	11111111	mod 101 r/m		(mod≠11)	15+m*	26+m*	2	8,9,11,12,18
Protected Mode Only (Indirect intersegment):								
Via call gate to same privilege level						41+m*		8,9,11,12,18
Via TSS						178+m*		8,9,11,12,18
Via task gate						183+m*		8,9,11,12,18
RET = Return from CALL:								
Within segment	11000011				11+m	11+m	2	8,9,18
Within seg adding immed to SP	11000010	data-low	data-high		11+m	11+m	2	8,9,18
Intersegment	11001011				15+m	25+m	2	8,9,11,12,18
Intersegment adding immediate to SP	11001010	data-low	data-high		15+m		2	8,9,11,12,18
Protected Mode Only (RET):								
To different privilege level						55+m		9,11,12,18

5

80286 INSTRUCTION SET SUMMARY (Continued)

FUNCTION	FORMAT	CLOCK COUNT		COMMENTS	
		Real Address Mode	Protected Virtual Address Mode	Real Address Mode	Protected Virtual Address Mode
CONTROL TRANSFER (Continued)					
JE/JZ = Jump on equal zero	01110100 disp	7+m or 3	7+m or 3		18
JL/JNGE = Jump on less/not greater or equal	01111100 disp	7+m or 3	7+m or 3		18
JLE/JNG = Jump on less or equal/not greater	01111110 disp	7+m or 3	7+m or 3		18
JB/JNAE = Jump on below/not above or equal	01110010 disp	7+m or 3	7+m or 3		18
JBE/JNA = Jump on below or equal/not above	01110110 disp	7+m or 3	7+m or 3		18
JP/JPE = Jump on parity/parity even	01111010 disp	7+m or 3	7+m or 3		18
JO = Jump on overflow	01110000 disp	7+m or 3	7+m or 3		18
JS = Jump on sign	01111000 disp	7+m or 3	7+m or 3		18
JNE/JNZ = Jump on not equal/not zero	01110101 disp	7+m or 3	7+m or 3		18
JNL/JGE = Jump on not less/greater or equal	01111101 disp	7+m or 3	7+m or 3		18
JNLE/JG = Jump on not less or equal/greater	01111111 disp	7+m or 3	7+m or 3		18
JNB/JAE = Jump on not below/above or equal	01110011 disp	7+m or 3	7+m or 3		18
JNBE/JA = Jump on not below or equal/above	01110111 disp	7+m or 3	7+m or 3		18
JNP/JPO = Jump on not par/par odd	01111011 disp	7+m or 3	7+m or 3		18
JNO = Jump on not overflow	01110001 disp	7+m or 3	7+m or 3		18
JNS = Jump on not sign	01111001 disp	7+m or 3	7+m or 3		18
LOOP = Loop CX times	11100010 disp	8+m or 4	8+m or 4		18
LOOPZ/LOOPE = Loop while zero/equal	11100001 disp	8+m or 4	8+m or 4		18
LOOPNZ/LOOPNE = Loop while not zero/equal	11100000 disp	8+m or 4	8+m or 4		18
JCXZ = Jump on CX zero	11100011 disp	8+m or 4	8+m or 4		18
ENTER = Enter Procedure	11001000 data-low data-high L			2,8	8,9
L=0		11	11	2,8	8,9
L=1		15	15	2,8	8,9
L > 1		16+4(L − 1)	16+4(L − 1)	2,8	8,9
LEAVE = Leave Procedure	11001001	5	5		
INT = Interrupt:					
Type specified	11001101 type	23+m		2,7,8	
Type 3	11001100	23+m		2,7,8	
INTO = Interrupt on overflow	11001110	24+m or 3 (3 if no interrupt)	(3 if no interrupt)	2,6,8	

Shaded areas indicate instructions not available in 8086, 88 microsystems.

80286 INSTRUCTION SET SUMMARY (Continued)

FUNCTION	FORMAT	CLOCK COUNT Real Address Mode	CLOCK COUNT Protected Virtual Address Mode	COMMENTS Real Address Mode	COMMENTS Protected Virtual Address Mode
CONTROL TRANSFER (Continued)					
Protected Mode Only:					
Via interrupt or trap gate to same privilege level			40+ m		7,8,11,12,18
Via interrupt or trap gate to fit different privilege level			78+ m		7,8,11,12,18
Via Task Gate			167+m		7,8,11,12,18
IRET = Interrupt return	11001111	17+m	31+ m	2,4	8,9,11,12,15,18
Protected Mode Only:					
To different privilege level			55+m		8,9,11,12,15,18
To different task (NT = 1)			169+m		8,9,11,12,18
BOUND = Detect value out of range	01100010 | mod reg r/m	13*	13* (Use INT clock count if exception 5)	2,6	6,8,9,11,12,18
PROCESSOR CONTROL					
CLC = Clear carry	11111000	2	2		
CMC = Complement carry	11110101	2	2		
STC = Set carry	11111001	2	2		
CLD = Clear direction	11111100	2	2		
STD = Set direction	11111101	2	2		
CLI = Clear interrupt	11111010	3	3		14
STI = Set interrupt	11111011	2	2		14
HLT = Halt	11110100	2	2		13
WAIT = Wait	10011011	3	3		
LOCK = Bus lock prefix	11110000	0	0		14
CTS = Clear task switched flag	00001111 | 00000110	2	2	3	13
ESC = Processor Extension Escape	11011TTT | mod LLL r/m (TTT LLL are opcode to processor extension)	9–20*	9–20*	5,8	8,17
SEG = Segment Override Prefix	001 reg 110	0	0		
PROTECTION CONTROL					
LGDT = Load global descriptor table register	00001111 | 00000001 | mod 010 r/m	11*	11*	2,3	9,13
SGDT = Store global descriptor table register	00001111 | 00000001 | mod 000 r/m	11*	11*	2,3	9
LIDT = Load interrupt descriptor table register	00001111 | 00000001 | mod 011 r/m	12*	12*	2,3	9,13
SIDT = Store interrupt descriptor table register	00001111 | 00000001 | mod 001 r/m	12*	12*	2,3	9
LLDT = Load local descriptor table register from register memory	00001111 | 00000000 | mod 010 r/m		17,19*	1	9,11,13
SLDT = Store local descriptor table register to register/memory	00001111 | 00000000 | mod 000 r/m		2,3*	1	9

Shaded areas indicate instructions not available in 8086, 88 microsystems.

5

80286 INSTRUCTION SET SUMMARY (Continued)

FUNCTION	FORMAT			CLOCK COUNT		COMMENTS	
				Real Address Mode	Protected Virtual Address Mode	Real Address Mode	Protected Virtual Address Mode
PROTECTION CONTROL (Continued)							
LTR = Local task register from register/memory	00001111	00000000	mod 0 1 1 r/m		17,19*	1	9,11,13
STR = Store task register to register memory	00001111	00000000	mod 0 0 1 r/m		2,3*	1	9
LMSW = Load machine status word from register/memory	00001111	00000001	mod 1 1 0 r/m	3,6*	3,6*	2,3	9,13
SMSW = Store machine status word	00001111	00000001	mod 1 0 0 r/m	2,3*	2,3*	2,3	9
LAR = Load access rights from register/memory	00001111	00000010	mod reg r/m		14,16*	1	9,11,16
LSL = Load segment limit from register/memory	00001111	00000011	mod reg r/m		14,16*	1	9,11,16
ARPL = Adjust requested privilege level: from register/memory		01100011	mod reg r/m		10*,11*	2	8,9
VERR = Verify read access: register/memory	00001111	00000000	mod 1 0 0 r/m		14,16*	1	9,11,16
VERR = Verify write access:	00001111	00000000	mod 1 0 1 r/m		14,16*	1	9,11,16

Shaded areas indicate instructions not available in 8086, 88 microsystems.

Footnotes

The Effective Address (EA) of the memory operand is computed according to the mod and r/m fields:

if mod = 11 then r/m is treated as a REG field
if mod = 00 then DISP = 0*, disp-low and disp-high are absent
if mod = 01 then DISP = disp-low sign-extended to 16 bits, disp-high is absent
if mod = 10 then DISP = disp-high: disp-low

if r/m = 000 then EA = (BX) + (SI) + DISP
if r/m = 001 then EA = (BX) + (DI) + DISP
if r/m = 010 then EA = (BP) + (SI) + DISP
if r/m = 011 then EA = (BP) + (DI) + DISP
if r/m = 100 then EA = (SI) + DISP
if r/m = 101 then EA = (DI) + DISP
if r/m = 110 then EA = (BP) + DISP*
if r/m = 111 then EA = (BX) + DISP

DISP follows 2nd byte of instruction (before data if required)

*except if mod = 00 and r/m = 110 then EQ = disp-high: disp-low.

SEGMENT OVERRIDE PREFIX

0 0 1 reg 1 1 0

reg is assigned according to the following:

reg	Segment Register
00	ES
01	CS
10	SS
11	DC

REG is assigned according to the following table:

16-Bit (w = 1)		8-Bit (w = 0)	
000	AX	000	AL
001	CX	001	CL
010	DX	010	DL
011	BX	011	BL
100	SP	100	AH
101	BP	101	CH
110	SI	110	DH
111	DI	111	BH

The physical addresses of all operands addressed by the BP register are computed using the SS segment register. The physical addresses of the destination operands of the string primitive operations (those addressed by the DI register) are computed using the ES segment, which may not be overridden.

DATA SHEET REVISION REVIEW

The following list represents key differences between this and the -015 data sheet. Please review this summary carefully.

1. Removed Input CLK, RESET Leakage Current (I_{LCR}) specs.
2. Updated output leakage current (I_{LO}) specs.

The following list represents key differences between this and the -014 data sheet. Please review this summary carefully.

1. Removed the Range of Clock Rates bullet.
2. The maximum ambient temperature (T_A) vs Various Airflows Table has been updated.
3. Removed the maximum values of System Clock (CLK) LOW period (t_2) of 8 MHz, 10 MHz, and 12.5 MHz parts in the A.C. Characteristics table.
4. Removed the maximum values of System Clock (CLK) HIGH period (t_3) of 8 MHz, 10 MHz, and 12.5 MHz parts in the A.C. Characteristics table.
5. Deleted the 82C284 and 82C288 A.C. Characteristics tables.

5

Intel287™ XL/XLT MATH COPROCESSOR

- **Interfaces with 80286 and 80C286 CPUs**
- **Operates in Any Socket Designed for Intel 80287 or Intel287™ XL MCP up to 12.5 MHz Clock Speeds**
- **Implements ANSI/IEEE Standard 754-1985 for Binary Floating-Point Arithmetic**
- **50% Higher Performance than Intel 80287**
- **Low Power CHMOS III Technology**
- **Upward Object Code Compatible from Intel 80287 and 8087**
- **Expands Data Types to Include 32-, 64-, 80-Bit Floating Point, or Integers, and 18 Digit BCD Operands**
- **Extends CPU Instruction Set to Include Tigonometric, Logarithmic, Exponential, and Arithmetic Instruction**
- **Implements Intel387™ Transcendental Operations for SINE, COSINE, TANGENT ARCTANGENT and LOGARITHM**
- **Eight 80-Bit Numeric Registers; for Stack use or Individual Access**
- **Available in 40-pin DIP as Intel287™ XL MCP and 44-pin PLCC as Intel287™ XLT MCP**

(See Packaging Outlined and Dimensions, order #231369)

The Intel287 XL Math CoProcessor is an extension of the Intel 80286 microprocessor architecture. When combined with an 80286 microprocessor, the Intel287 XL MCP dramatically increases the processing speed of computer application software which utilize floating point mathematical operations. This makes an ideal addition to a computer workstation platform for applications such as financial modeling and spreadsheets, CAD/CAM, or business graphics.

The Intel287 XL Math CoProcessor adds over seventy mnemonics to the Intel 80286 microprocessor instruction set. The Intel287 XL MCP is compatible with the Intel 80287 and 8087 Math CoProcessors. The Intel287 XL MCP increases performance by over 50% in typical floating-point tests, such as a Whetstone test, compared to the Intel 80287. The Intel287 XL MCP supports integer, floating point and BCD data formats and fully conforms to the ANSI/IEEE 754-1985 Floating Point Standard.

There are two versions of Intel287 XL MCP: the Intel287 XL MCP in a 40-pin DIP package and the Intel287 XLT MCP in a 44-pin PLCC package for small footprint applications such as portable personal computers. Each supports a clock speed up to 12.5 MHz which enables operation in any Math CoProcessor socket designed for the Intel 80287-6/8/10 or Intel 80C287A-12. Both versions are manufactured with low-power, CHMOS III technology.

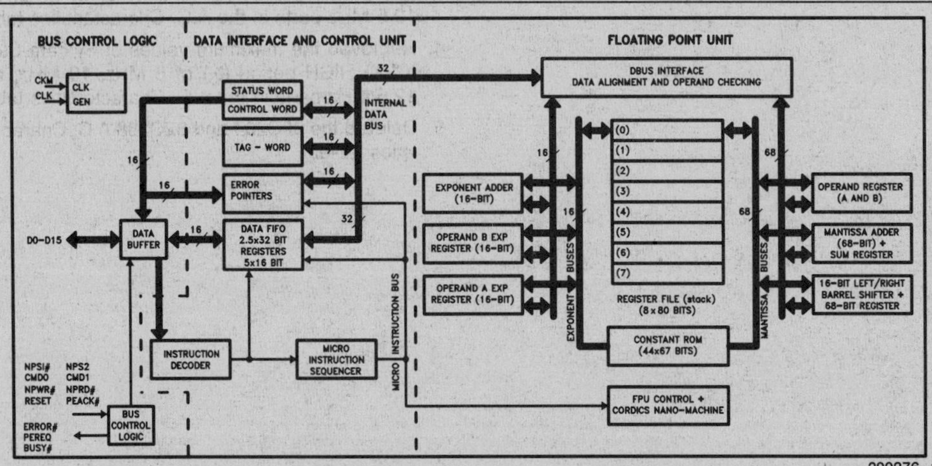

Figure 0.1. Intel287™ XL MCP Block Diagram

October 1991
Order Number: 290376-002

Intel287™ XL/XLT Math CoProcessor

CONTENTS

CONTENTS

CONTENTS PAGE

FIGURES

CONTENTS PAGE

TABLES

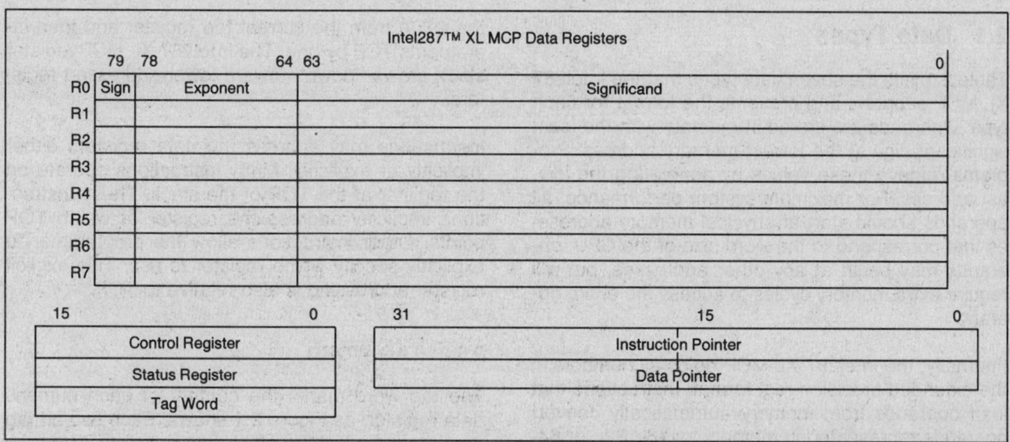

Figure 1.1. Intel287™ XL MCP Register Set

1.0 FUNCTIONAL DESCRIPTION

The Intel287 XL Math CoProcessor provides arithmetic instructions for a variety of numeric data types. It also executes numerous built-in transcendental functions (e.g. tangent, sine, cosine, and log functions). The Intel287 XL MCP effectively extends the register and instruction set of its CPU for existing data types and adds several new data types as well. Figure 1.1 shows the additional registers visible to programs in a system that includes the Intel287 XL MCP. Essentially, the Intel287 XL MCP can be treated as an additional resource or an extension to the CPU. The CPU together with an Intel287 XL Math CoProcessor can be used as a single unified system.

The Intel287 XL MCP has two operating modes. After reset, the Intel287 XL MCP is in the real-address mode. It can be placed into protected mode by executing the FSETPM instruction. It can be switched back to real-address mode by executing the FRSTPM instruction (note that this feature is useful only with CPU's that can also switch back to real-address mode). These instructions control the format of the administrative instructions FLDENV, FSTENV, FRSTOR, and FSAVE. Regardless of operating mode, all references to memory for numerics data or status information are performed by the CPU, and therefore obey the memory-management and protection rules of the CPU.

In real-address mode, a system that includes the Intel287 XL MCP is completely upward compatible with software for the 8086/8087 and for 80286/80287 or 80C287A real-address mode.

In protected mode, a system that includes the Intel287 XL MCP is completely upward compatible with software for 80286/80287 or 80C287A protected mode systems. The only differences of operation that may appear when 8086/8087 programs are ported to a protected-mode Intel287 XL MCP system are in the format of operands for the administrative instructions FLDENV, FSTENV, FRSTOR, and FSAVE. These instructions are normally used only by exception handlers and operating systems, not by applications programs.

2.0 PROGRAMMING INTERFACE

The Intel287 XL MCP adds to the CPU additional data types, registers, instructions, and interrupts specifically designed to facilitate high-speed numerics processing. To use the Intel287 XL MCP requires no special programming tools, because all new instructions and data types are directly supported by the assembler and compilers for high-level languages. All 8086/8088 development tools that support the 8087 can also be used to develop software for the 80286/Intel287 XL MCP in real-address mode. All 80286 development tools that support the 80287/80C287A can also be used to develop software for the 80286/Intel287 XL MCP and 80C286/Intel287 XL MCP. The Intel287 XL MCP supports all 80387 instructions, producing the same binary results.

All communication between the CPU and the Intel287 XL MCP is transparent to applications software. The CPU automatically controls the Intel287 XL MCP whenever a floating point instruction is executed. All physical memory and virtual memory of the CPU are available for storage of the instructions and operands of programs that use the Intel287 XL MCP. All memory addressing modes are available for addressing numerics operands.

Section 6 at the end of this data sheet lists the instructions that the Intel287 XL MCP adds to the 80286 instruction set.

2.1 Data Types

Table 2.1 lists the seven data types that the Intel287 XL MCP supports and presents the format for each type. Operands are stored in memory with the least significant digit at the lowest memory address. Programs retrieve these values by generating the lowest address. For maximum system performance, all operands should start at physical-memory addresses that correspond to the word size of the CPU; operands may begin at any other addresses, but will require extra memory cycles to access the entire operand.

Internally, the Intel287 XL MCP holds all numbers in the extended-precision real format. Instructions that load operands from memory automatically convert operands represented in memory as 16-, 32-, or 64-bit integers, 32- or 64-bit floating-point numbers, or 18-digit packed BCD numbers into extended-precision real format. Instructions that store operands in memory perform the inverse type conversion.

2.2 Numeric Operands

A typical MCP (Math CoProcessor) instruction accepts one or two operands and produces one (or sometimes two) results. In two-operand instructions, one operand is the contents of an MCP register, while the other may be a memory location. The operands of some instructions are predefined; for example, FSQRT always takes the square root of the number in the top stack element.

2.3 Register Set

Figure 1.1 shows the Intel287 XL MCP register set. When an Intel287 XL MCP is present in a system, programmers may use these registers in addition to the registers normally available on the CPU.

2.3.1 DATA REGISTERS

Intel287 XL MCP computations use the Intel287 XL MCP's data registers. These eight 80-bit registers provide the equivalent capacity of 20 32-bit registers. Each of the eight data registers in the Intel287 XL MCP is 80 bits wide and is divided into "fields" corresponding to the MCP's extended-precision real data type.

The Intel287 XL MCP register set can be accessed either as a stack, with instructions operating on the top one or two stack elements, or as individually addressable registers. The TOP field in the status word identifies the current top-of-stack register. A "push" operation decrements TOP by one and loads a value into the new top register. A "pop" operation stores the value from the current top register and then increments TOP by one. The Intel287 XL MCP register stack grows "down" toward lower-addressed registers.

Instructions may address the data registers either implicitly or explicitly. Many instructions operate on the register at the TOP of the stack. These instructions implicitly address the register at which TOP points. Other instructions allow the programmer to explicitly specify which register to use. This explicit register addressing is also relative to TOP.

2.3.2 TAG WORD

The tag word marks the content of each numeric data register, as Figure 2.1 shows. Each two-bit tag represents one of the eight data registers. The principal function of the tag word is to optimize the MCP's performance and stack handling by making it possible to distinguish between empty and nonempty register locations. It also enables exception handlers to identify special values (e.g. NaNs or denormals) in the contents of a stack location without the need to perform complex decoding of the actual data.

2.3.3 STATUS WORD

The 16-bit status word (in the status register) shown in Figure 2.2 reflects the overall state of the Intel287 XL MCP. It may be read and inspected by programs.

Bit 15, the B-bit (busy bit) is included for 8087 compatibility only. It always has the same value as the ES bit (bit 7 of the status word); it does **not** indicate the status of the BUSY# output of Intel287 XL MCP.

Bits 13–11 (TOP) point to the Intel287 XL MCP register that is the current top-of-stack.

The four numeric condition code bits (C_3–C_0) are similar to the flags in a CPU; instructions that perform arithmetic operations update these bits to reflect the outcome. The effects of these instructions on the condition code are summarized in Tables 2.2 through 2.5.

Bit 7 is the error summary (ES) status bit. This bit is set if any unmasked exception bit is set; it is clear otherwise. If this bit is set, the ERROR# signal is asserted.

Bit 6 is the stack flag (SF). This bit is used to distinguish invalid operations due to stack overflow or underflow from other kinds of invalid operations. When SF is set, bit 9 (C_1) distinguishes between stack overflow ($C_1 = 1$) and underflow ($C_1 = 0$).

Table 2.1. Intel287™ XL MCP Data Type Representation in Memory

Data Formats	Range	Precision	Most Significant Byte — HIGHEST ADDRESSED BYTE 7 0 | 7 0 | 7 0 | 7 0 | 7 0 | 7 0 | 7 0 | 7 0 | 7 0 | 7 0
Word Integer	$\pm 10^4$	16 Bits	15 … 0 (TWO S COMPLEMENT)
Short Integer	$\pm 10^9$	32 Bits	31 … 0 (TWO S COMPLEMENT)
Long Integer	$\pm 10^{18}$	64 Bits	63 … 0 (TWO S COMPLEMENT)
Packed BCD	$\pm 10^{18}$	18 Digits	S (79) | X (72) | MAGNITUDE: d_{17} d_{16} d_{15} d_{14} d_{13} d_{12} d_{11} d_{10} d_9 d_8 d_7 d_6 d_5 d_4 d_3 d_2 d_1 d_0 (0)
Single Precision	$\pm 10^{\pm 38}$	24 Bits	S (31) | BIASED EXPONENT (23) | SIGNIFICAND (0); I ▲
Double Precision	$\pm 10^{\pm 308}$	53 Bits	S (63) | BIASED EXPONENT (52) | SIGNIFICAND (0); I ▲
Extended Precision	$\pm 10^{\pm 4932}$	64 Bits	S (79) | BIASED EXPONENT (64) | I (63) ▲ | SIGNIFICAND (0)

290376–2

NOTES:

1. S = Sign bit (0 = positive, 1 = negative)
2. d_n = Decimal digit (two per byte)
3. X = Bits have no significance: Intel287 XL MCP ignores when loading, zeroes when storing
4. ▲ = Position of implicit binary point
5. I = Integer bit of significand; stored in temporary real, implicit in single and double precision
6. Exponent Bias (normalized values):
   Single: 127 (7FH)
   Double: 1023 (3FFH)
   Extended Real: 16383 (3FFFH)
7. Packed BCD: $(-1)^S (D_{17} \ldots D_0)$
8. Real: $(-1)^S (2^{E-BIAS}) (F_0 F_1 \ldots)$

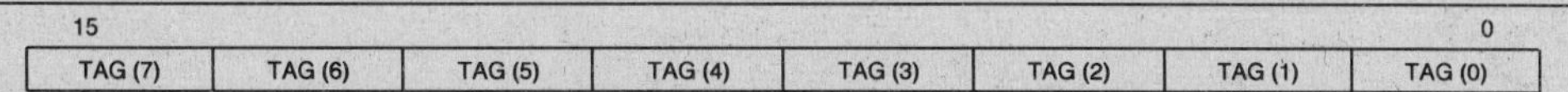

NOTE:
The index i of tag(i) is not top-relative. A program typically uses the "top" field of Status Word to determine which tag(i) field refers to logical top of stack.

TAG VALUES:
- 00 = Valid
- 01 = Zero
- 10 = QNaN, SNaN, Infinity, Denormal and Unsupported Formats
- 11 = Empty

Figure 2.1. Intel287™ XL MCP Tag Word

Figure 2.2 shows the six exception flags in bits 5–0 of the status word. Bits 5–0 are set to indicate that the Intel287 XL MCP has detected an exception while executing an instruction. A later section entitled "Exception Handling" explains how they are set and used.

Note that when a new value is loaded into the status word by the FLDENV or FRSTOR instruction, the value of ES (bit 7) and its reflection in the B-bit (bit 15) are not derived from the values loaded from memory but rather are dependent upon the values of the exception flags (bits 5–0) in the status word and their corresponding masks in the control word. If ES is set in such a case, the ERROR# output of the Intel287 XL MCP is activated immediately.

BUSY
TOP OF STACK POINTER
CONDITION CODE

15							7							0
B	C3	TOP	C2	C1	C0	ES	SF	PE	UE	OE	ZE	DE	IE

ERROR SUMMARY STATUS
STACK FLAG
EXCEPTION FLAGS
PRECISION
UNDERFLOW
OVERFLOW
ZERO DIVIDE
DENORMALIZED OPERAND
INVALID OPERATION

290376–3

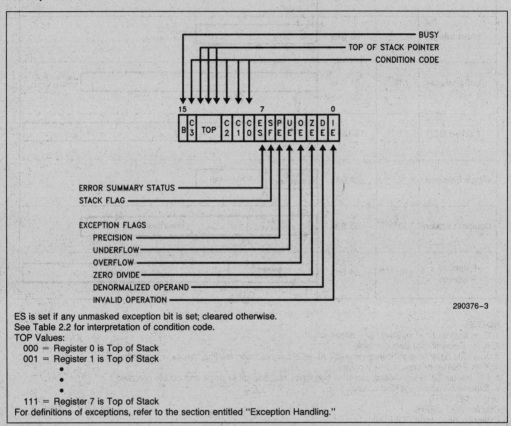

ES is set if any unmasked exception bit is set; cleared otherwise.
See Table 2.2 for interpretation of condition code.
TOP Values:
000 = Register 0 is Top of Stack
001 = Register 1 is Top of Stack
•
•
•
111 = Register 7 is Top of Stack
For definitions of exceptions, refer to the section entitled "Exception Handling."

Figure 2.2. Status Word

Table 2.2. Condition Code Interpretation

Instruction	C0 (S)	C3 (Z)	C1 (A)	C2 (C)
FPREM, FPREM1 (See Table 2.3)	Three Least Significant Bits of Quotient Q2	Q0	Q1 or O/U#	Reduction 0 = Complete 1 = Incomplete
FCOM, FCOMP, FCOMPP, FTST, FUCOM, FUCOMP, FUCOMPP, FICOM, FICOMP	Result of Comparison (See Table 2.4)		Zero or O/U#	Operand is Not Comparable (Table 2.4)
FXAM	Operand Class (See Table 2.5)		Sign or O/U#	Operand Class (Table 2.5)
FCHS, FABS, FXCH, FINCTOP, FDECTOP, Constant Loads, FXTRACT, FLD, FILD, FBLD, FSTP (Ext Real)	UNDEFINED		Zero or O/U#	UNDEFINED
FIST, FBSTP, FRNDINT, FST FSTP, FADD, FMUL, FDIV, FDIVR, FSUB, FSUBR, FSCALE, FSQRT, FPATAN, F2XM1, FYL2X, FYL2XP1	UNDEFINED		Roundup or O/U#	UNDEFINED
FPTAN, FSIN, FCOS, FSINCOS	UNDEFINED		Roundup or O/U# Undefined if C2 = 1	Reduction 0 = Complete 1 = Incomplete
FLDENV, FRSTOR	Each Bit Loaded from Memory			
FLDCW, FSTENV, FSTCW, FSTSW, FCLEX, FINIT, FSAVE	UNDEFINED			

O/U# When both IE and SF bits of status word are set, indicating a stack exception, this bit distinguishes between stack overflow (C1 = 1) and underflow (C1 = 0).

Reduction If FPREM or FPREM1 produces a remainder that is less than the modulus, reduction is complete. When reduction is incomplete the value at the top of the stack is a partial remainder, which can be used as input to further reduction. For FPTAN, FSIN, FCOS, and FSINCOS, the reduction bit is set if the operand at the top of the stack is too large. In this case the original operand remains at the top of the stack.

Roundup When the PE bit of the status word is set, this bit indicates whether one was added to the least significant bit of the result during the last rounding.

UNDEFINED Do not rely on finding any specific value in these bits.

Table 2.3. Condition Code Interpretation after FPREM and FPREM1 Instructions

Condition Code					Interpretation after FPREM and FPREM1
C2	C3	C1	C0		
1	X	X	X		**Incomplete Reduction:** Further iteration required for complete reduction.
	Q1	Q0	Q2	Q MOD 8	**Complete Reduction:** C0, C3, C1 contain three least significant bits of quotient.
0	0	0	0	0	
0	0	1	0	1	
0	1	0	0	2	
0	1	1	0	3	
0	0	0	1	4	
0	0	1	1	5	
0	1	0	1	6	
0	1	1	1	7	

Table 2.4. Condition Code Resulting from Comparison

Order	C3	C2	C0
TOP > Operand	0	0	0
TOP < Operand	0	0	1
TOP = Operand	1	0	0
Unordered	1	1	1

Table 2.5. Condition Code Defining Operand Class

C3	C2	C1	C0	Value at TOP
0	0	0	0	+ Unsupported
0	0	0	1	+ NaN
0	0	1	0	− Unsupported
0	0	1	1	− Nan
0	1	0	0	+ Normal
0	1	0	1	+ Infinity
0	1	1	0	− Normal
0	1	1	1	− Infinity
1	0	0	0	+ 0
1	0	0	1	+ Empty
1	0	1	0	− 0
1	0	1	1	− Empty
1	1	0	0	+ Denormal
1	1	1	0	− Denormal

2.3.4 CONTROL WORD

The MCP provides several processing options that are selected by loading a control word from memory into the control register. Figure 2.3 shows the format and encoding of fields in the control word.

The low-order byte of this control word configures exception masking. Bits 5–0 of the control word contain individual masks for each of the six exceptions that the Intel287 XL MCP recognizes.

The high-order byte of the control word configures the Intel287 XL MCP operating mode, including precision, rounding, and infinity control.

- The "infinity control bit" (bit 12) is not meaningful to the Intel287 XL MCP, and programs must ignore its value. To maintain compatibility with the 8087 and 80287, this bit can be programmed; however, regardless of its value, the Intel287 XL MCP always treats infinity in the affine sense ($-\infty < +\infty$). This bit is initialized to zero both after a hardware reset and after the FINIT instruction.
- The rounding control (RC) bits (bits 11–10) provide for directed rounding and true chop, as well as the unbiased round to nearest even mode specified in the IEEE standard. Rounding control affects only those instructions that perform rounding at the end of the operation (and thus can generate a precision exception); namely, FST, FSTP, FIST, all arithmetic instructions (except FPREM, FPREM1, FXTRACT, FABS, and FCHS), and all transcendental instructions.
- The precision control (PC) bits (bits 9–8) can be used to set the Intel287 XL MCP internal operating precision of the significand at less than the default of 64 bits (extended precision). This can be useful in providing compatibility with early generation arithmetic processors of smaller precision. PC affects only the instructions ADD, SUB, DIV, MUL, and SQRT. For all other instructions, either the precision is determined by the opcode or extended precision is used.

2.3.5 INSTRUCTION AND DATA POINTERS

Because the MCP operates in parallel with the CPU, any exceptions detected by the MCP may be reported after the CPU has executed the ESC instruction which caused it. To allow identification of the failing numeric instruction, the Intel287 XL MCP contains registers that aid in diagnosis. These registers supply the opcode of the failing numeric instruction, the address of the instruction, and the address of its numeric memory operand (if appropriate).

The instruction and data pointers are provided for user-written exception handlers. Whenever the Intel287 XL MCP executes a new ESC instruction, it saves the address of the instruction (including any prefixes that may be present), the address of the operand (if present), and the opcode. CPUs with 32-bit internal architectures contain 32-bit versions of these registers and do not use the contents of the MCP registers. This difference is not apparent to programmers, however.

The instruction and data pointers appear in one of four formats depending on the operating mode of the system (protected mode or real-address mode) and (for CPUs with 32-bit internal architectures) depending on the operand-size attribute in effect (32-bit operand or 16-bit operand). (See Figures 2.4, 2.5, 2.6, and 2.7.) The ESC instructions FLDENV, FSTENV, FSAVE, and FRSTOR are used to transfer these values between the registers and memory. Note that the value of the data pointer is *undefined* if the prior ESC instruction did not have a memory operand.

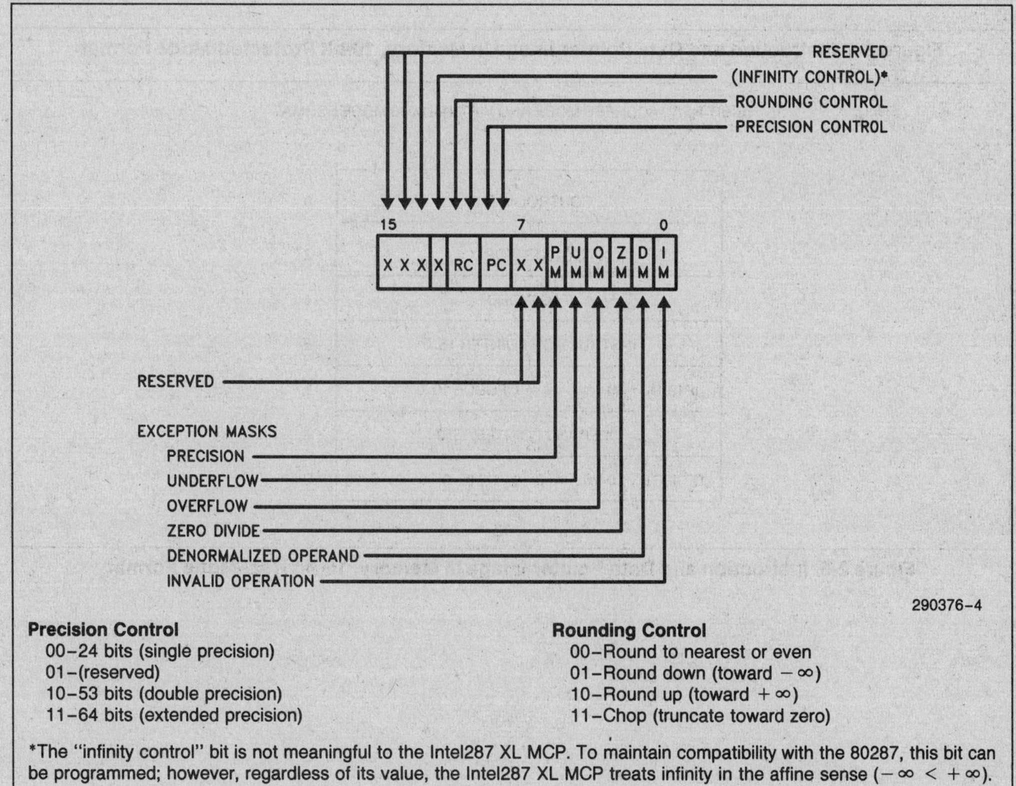

Precision Control
- 00–24 bits (single precision)
- 01–(reserved)
- 10–53 bits (double precision)
- 11–64 bits (extended precision)

Rounding Control
- 00–Round to nearest or even
- 01–Round down (toward $-\infty$)
- 10–Round up (toward $+\infty$)
- 11–Chop (truncate toward zero)

*The "infinity control" bit is not meaningful to the Intel287 XL MCP. To maintain compatibility with the 80287, this bit can be programmed; however, regardless of its value, the Intel287 XL MCP treats infinity in the affine sense ($-\infty < +\infty$).

Figure 2.3. Control Word

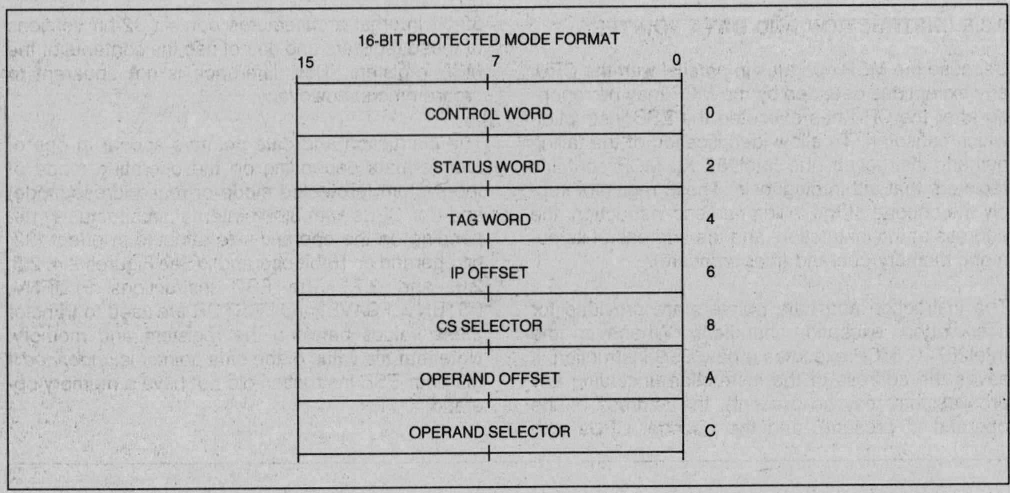

Figure 2-4. Instruction and Data Pointer Image in Memory, 16-bit Protected-Mode Format

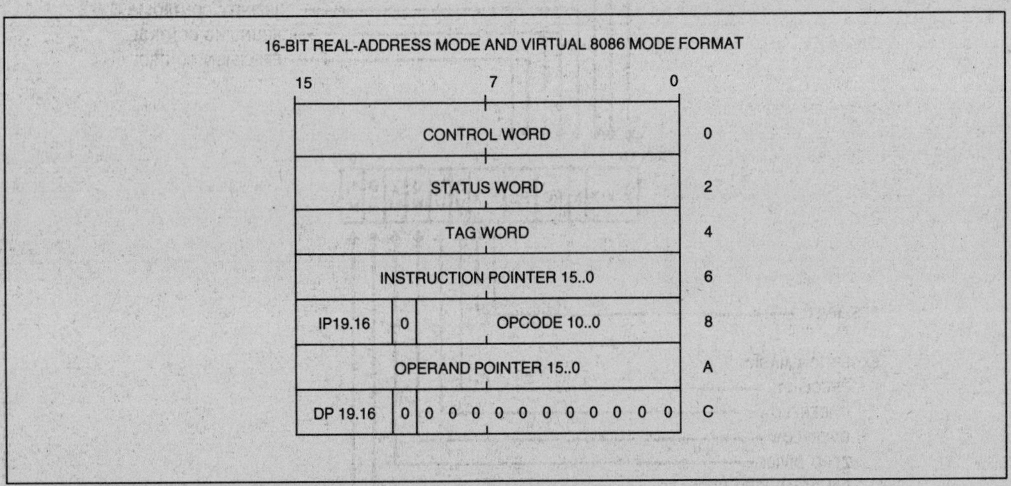

Figure 2-5. Instruction and Data Pointer Image in Memory, 16-bit Real-Mode Format

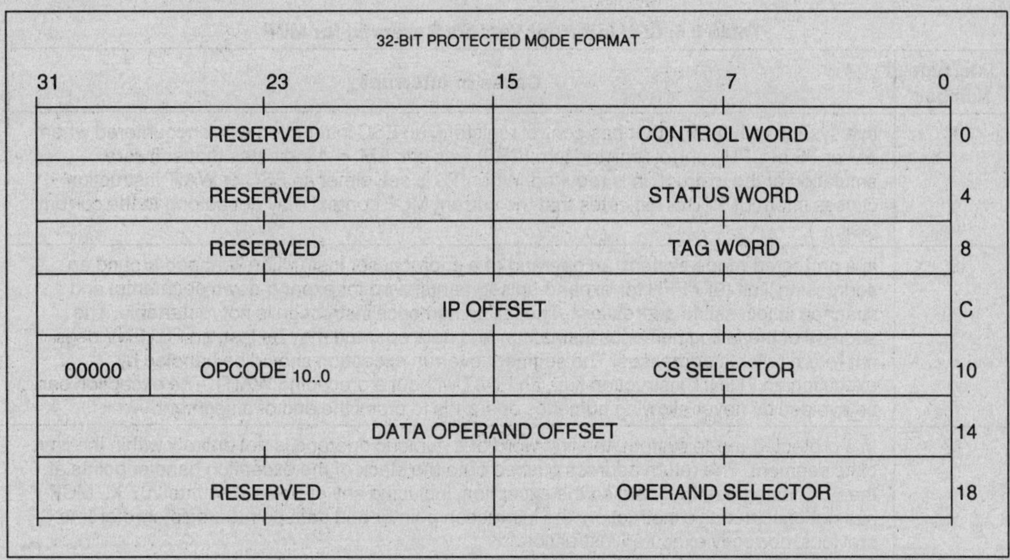

Figure 2-6.Instruction and Data Pointer Image in Memory, 32-bit Protected-Mode Format

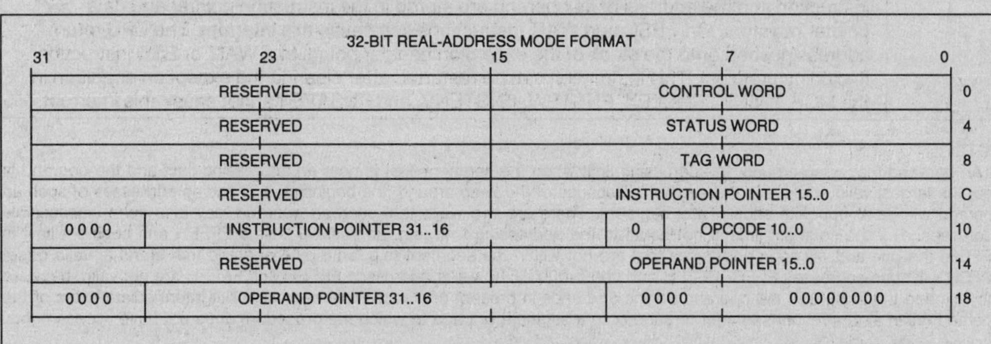

Figure 2-7. Instruction and Data Pointer Image in Memory, 32-bit Real-Mode Format

Table 2.6. CPU Interrupt Vectors Reserved for MCP

Interrupt Number	Cause of Interrupt
7	In a system with a CPU that has control registers, an ESC instruction was encountered when EM or TS of CPU control register zero (CR0) was set. EM = 1 indicates that software emulation of the instruction is required. When TS is set, either an ESC or WAIT instruction causes interrupt 7. This indicates that the current MCP context may not belong to the current task.
9	In a protected-mode system, an operand of a coprocessor instruction wrapped around an addressing limit (0FFFFH for expand-up segments, zero for expand-down segments) and spanned inaccessible addresses[1]. The failing numerics instruction is not restartable. The address of the failing numerics instruction and data operand may be lost; an FSTENV does not return reliable addresses. The segment overrun exception should be handled by executing an FNINIT instruction (i.e., an FINIT without a preceding WAIT). The exception can be avoided by never allowing numerics operands to cross the end of a segment.
13	In a protected-mode system, the first word of a numeric operand is not entirely within the limit of its segment. The return address pushed onto the stack of the exception handler points at the ESC instruction that caused the exception, including any prefixes. The Intel287 XL MCP has not executed this instruction; the instruction pointer and data pointer register refer to a previous, correctly executed instruction.
16	The previous numerics instruction caused an unmasked exception. The address of the faulty instruction and the address of its operand are stored in the instruction pointer and data pointer registers. Only ESC and WAIT instructions can cause this interrupt. The CPU return address pushed onto the stack of the exception handler points to a WAIT or ESC instruction (including prefixes). This instruction can be restarted after clearing the exception condition in the MCP. FNINIT, FNCLEX, FNSTSW, FNSTENV, and FNSAVE cannot cause this interrupt.

NOTE:
1. An operand may wrap around an addressing limit when the segment limit is near an addressing limit and the operand is near the largest valid address in the segment. Because of the wrap-around, the beginning and ending addresses of such an operand will be at opposite ends of the segment. There are two ways that such an operand may also span inaccessible addresses: 1) if the segment limit is not equal to the addressing limit (e.g. addressing limit is FFFFH and segment limit is FFFDH) the operand will span addresses that are not within the segment (e.g. an 8-byte operand that starts at valid offset FFFCH will span addresses FFFC–FFFFH and 0000–0003H; however addresses FFFEH and FFFFH are not valid, because they exceed the limit); 2) if the operand begins and ends in present and accessible segments but intermediate bytes of the operand fall in a not-present segment or page or in a segment or page to which the procedure does not have access rights.

2.4 Interrupt Description

CPU interrupts are used to report exceptional conditions while executing numeric programs in either real or protected mode. Table 2.6 shows these interrupts and their functions.

2.5 Exception Handling

The Intel287 XL MCP detects six different exception conditions that can occur during instruction execution. Table 2.7 lists the exception conditions in order of precedence, showing for each the cause and the

Table 2.7. Exceptions

Exception	Cause	Default Action (If Exception is Masked)
Invalid Operation	Operation on a signalling NaN, unsupported format, indeterminate form (0*∞, 0/0, (+∞) + (−∞), etc.), or stack overflow/underflow (SF is also set).	Result is a quiet NaN, integer indefinite, or BCD indefinite.
Denormalized Operand	At least one of the operands is denormalized, i.e., it has the smallest exponent but a nonzero significand.	The operand is normalized, and normal processing continues.
Zero Divisor	The divisor is zero while the dividend is a noninfinite, nonzero number.	Result is ∞.
Overflow	The result is too large in magnitude to fit in the specified format.	Result is largest finite value or ∞.
Underflow	The true result is nonzero but too small to be represented in the specified format, and, if underflow exception is masked, denormalization causes loss of accuracy.	Result is denormalized or zero.
Inexact Result (Precision)	The true result is not exactly representable in the specified format (e.g. ⅓); the result is rounded according to the rounding mode.	Normal processing continues.

default action taken by the Intel287 XL MCP if the exception is masked by its corresponding mask bit in the control word.

Any exception that is not masked by the control word sets the corresponding exception flag of the status word, sets the ES bit of the status word, and asserts the ERROR# signal. When the CPU attempts to execute another ESC instruction or WAIT, exception 16 occurs. The exception condition must be resolved via an interrupt service routine. The return address pushed onto the CPU stack upon entry to the service routine does not necessarily point to the failing instruction nor to the following instruction. The Intel287 XL MCP saves the address of the floating-point instruction that caused the exception and the address of any memory operand required by that instruction.

2.6 Initialization

After FNINIT or RESET, the control word contains the value 037FH (all exceptions masked, precision control 64 bits, rounding to nearest) the same values as in an 80287 after RESET. For compatibility with the 8087 and 80287, the bit that used to indicate infinity control (bit 12) is set to zero; however, regardless of its setting, infinity is treated in the affine sense. After FNINIT or RESET, the status word is initialized as follows:

- All exceptions are set to zero.
- Stack TOP is zero, so that after the first push the stack top will be register seven (111B).
- The condition code C_3–C_0 is **undefined.**
- The B-bit is zero.

The tag word contains FFFFH (all stack locations are empty).

80286/Intel287 XL MCP initialization software should execute an FNINIT instruction (i.e an FINIT without a preceding WAIT) after RESET. The FNINIT is not strictly required for either 80287, 80C287A or Intel287 XL MCP software, but Intel recommends its use to help ensure upward compatibility with other processors.

2.7 8087 and 80287 Compatibility

This section summarizes the differences between the Intel287 XL MCP and the 80287. Any migration from the 8087 directly to the Intel287 XL MCP must also take into account the differences between the 8087 and the 80287 as listed in the 80286 and 80287 Programmer's Reference Manual. There are no compatibility differences between the Intel287 XL MCP and 80C287A except the pinout configuration.

Many changes have been designed into the Intel287 XL MCP to directly support the IEEE standard in hardware. These changes result in increased performance by eliminating the need for software that supports the standard.

2.7.1 GENERAL DIFFERENCES

The Intel287 XL MCP supports only affine closure for infinity arithmetic, not projective closure.

Operands for FSCALE and FPATAN are no longer restricted in range (except for $\pm\infty$); F2XM1 and FPTAN accept a wider range of operands.

Rounding control is in effect for FLD *constant*.

Software cannot change entries of the tag word to values (other than empty) that differ from actual register contents.

After reset, FINIT, and incomplete FPREM, the Intel287 XL MCP resets to zero the condition code bits C_3-C_0 of the status word.

In conformance with the IEEE standard, the Intel287 XL MCP does not support the special data formats pseudozero, pseudo-NaN, pseudoinfinity, and unnormal.

The denormal exception has a different purpose on the Intel287 XL MCP. A system that uses the denormal-exception handler solely to normalize the denormal operands, would better mask the denormal exception on the Intel287 XL MCP. The Intel287 XL MCP automatically normalizes denormal operands when the denormal exception is masked.

2.7.2 EXCEPTIONS

A number of differences exist due to changes in the IEEE standard and to functional improvements to the architecture of the Intel287 XL MCP:

1. When the overflow or underflow exception is masked, the Intel287 XL MCP differs from the 80287 in rounding when overflow or underflow occurs. The Intel287 XL MCP produces results that are consistent with the rounding mode.
2. When the underflow exception is masked, the Intel287 XL MCP sets its underflow flag only if there is also a loss of accuracy during denormalization.
3. Fewer invalid-operation exceptions due to denormal operands, because the instructions FSQRT, FDIV, FPREM, and conversions to BCD or to integer normalize denormal operands before proceeding.
4. The FSQRT, FBSTP, and FPREM instructions may cause underflow, because they support denormal operands.
5. The denormal exception can occur during the transcendental instructions and the FXTRACT instruction.
6. The denormal exception no longer takes precedence over all other exceptions.
7. When the denormal exception is masked, the Intel287 XL MCP automatically normalizes denormal operands. The 8087/80287 performs unnormal arithmetic, which might produce an unnormal result.
8. When the operand is zero, the FXTRACT instruction reports a zero-divide exception and leaves $-\infty$ in ST(1).
9. The status word has a new bit (SF) that signals when invalid-operation exceptions are due to stack underflow or overflow.
10. FLD *extended precision* no longer reports denormal exceptions, because the instruction is not numeric.
11. FLD *single/double precision* when the operand is denormal converts the number to extended precision and signals the denormalized operand exception. When loading a signalling NaN, FLD *single/double precision* signals an invalid-operand exception.
12. The Intel287 XL MCP only generates quiet NaNs (as on the 80287); however, the Intel287 XL MCP distinguishes between quiet NaNs and signaling NaNs. Signaling NaNs trigger exceptions when they are used as operands; quiet NaNs do not (except for FCOM, FIST, and FBSTP which also raise IE for quiet NaNs).
13. When stack overflow occurs during FPTAN and overflow is masked, both ST(0) and ST(1) contain quiet NaNs. The 8087/80287 leaves the original operand in ST(1) intact.
14. When the scaling factor is $\pm\infty$, the FSCALE (ST(0), ST(1)) instruction behaves as follows (ST(0) and ST(1) contain the scaled and scaling operands respectively):
    - FSCALE(0,∞) generates the invalid operation exception.
    - FSCALE(finite, $-\infty$) generates zero with the same sign as the scaled operand.
    - FSCALE(finite, $+\infty$) generates $-\infty$ with the same sign as the scaled operand.

    The 8087/80287 returns zero in the first case and raises the invalid-operation exception in the other cases.

15. The Intel287 XL MCP returns signed infinity/zero as the unmasked response to massive overflow/underflow. The 8087 and 80287 support a limited range for the scaling factor; within this range either massive overflow/underflow do not occur or undefined results are produced.

3.0 HARDWARE INTERFACE

In the following description of hardware interface, the # symbol at the end of a signal name indicates that the active or asserted state occurs when the signal is at a low voltage. When no # is present after the signal name, the signal is asserted when at the high voltage level.

3.1 Signal Description

In the following signal descriptions, the Intel287 XL MCP pins are grouped by function as follows:

1. Execution control—CLK, CKM, RESET
2. MCP handshake—PEREQ, PEACK#, BUSY#, ERROR#
3. Bus interface pins—D_{15}–D_0, NPWR#, NPRD#
4. Chip/Port Select—NPS1#, NPS2, CMD0, CMD1
5. Power supplies—V_{CC}, V_{SS}

Table 3.1 lists every pin by its identifier, gives a brief description of its function, and lists some of its characteristics. Figure 3.1 shows the locations of pins on the Ceramic package, while Figure 3.2 shows the locations of pins on the PLCC package. Table 3.2 helps to locate pin identifiers in Figures 3.1 and 3.2.

Table 3.1. Pin Summary

Pin Name	Function	Active State	Input/ Output
CLK	CLocK		I
CKM	ClocKing Mode		I
RESET	System reset	High	I
PEREQ	Processor Extension REQuest	High	O
PEACK#	Processor Extension ACKnowledge	Low	I
BUSY#	Busy status	Low	O
ERROR#	Error status	Low	O
D15–D0	Data pins	High	I/O
NPRD#	Numeric Processor ReaD	Low	I
NPWR#	Numeric Processor WRite	Low	I
NPS1#	MCP select #1	Low	I
NPS2	MCP select #2	High	I
CMD0	CoMmanD 0	High	I
CMD1	CoMmanD 1	High	I
V_{CC}	System power		I
V_{SS}	System ground		I

5

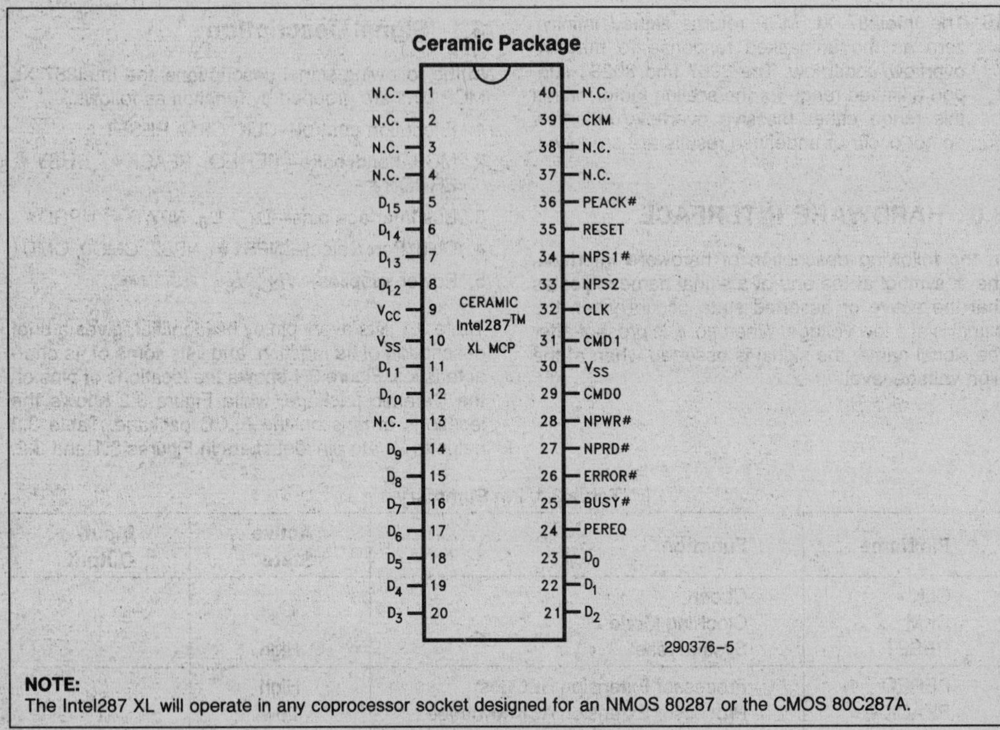

NOTE:
The Intel287 XL will operate in any coprocessor socket designed for an NMOS 80287 or the CMOS 80C287A.

Figure 3.1. DIP Pin Configuration

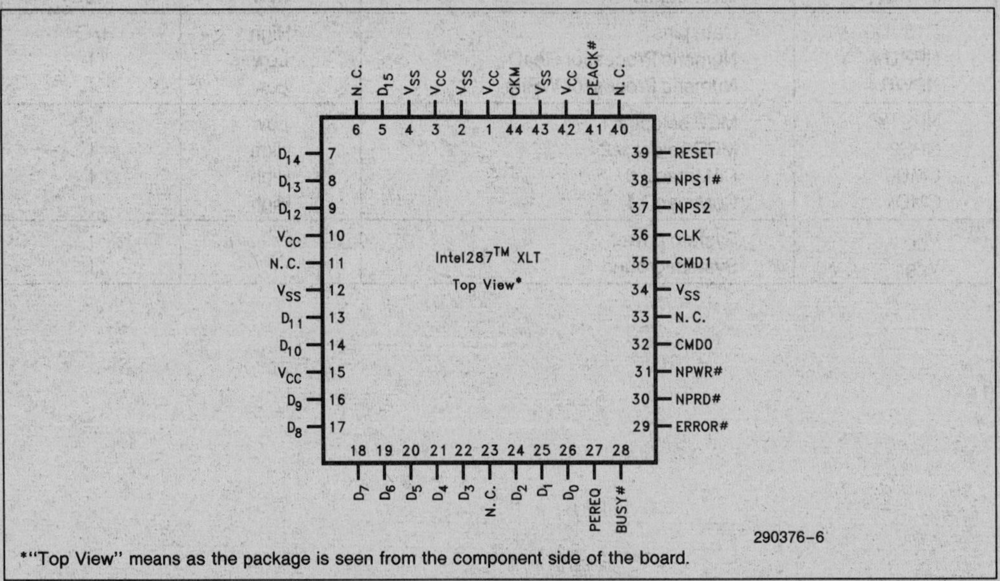

*"Top View" means as the package is seen from the component side of the board.

Figure 3.2. PLCC Pin Configuration

Table 3.2. PLCC Pin Cross-Reference

Pin Name	Ceramic Package	PLCC Package
BUSY#	25	28
CKM	39	44
CLK	32	36
CMD0	29	32
CMD1	31	35
D_0	23	26
D_1	22	25
D_2	21	24
D_3	20	22
D_4	19	21
D_5	18	20
D_6	17	19
D_7	16	18
D_8	15	17
D_9	14	16
D_{10}	12	14
D_{11}	11	13
D_{12}	8	9
D_{13}	7	8
D_{14}	6	7
D_{15}	5	5
ERROR#	26	29
No Connect	2	6,11,23,33,40
NPRD#	27	30
NPS1#	34	38
NPS2	33	37
NPWR#	28	31
PEACK#	36	41
PEREQ	24	27
RESET	35	39
V_{CC}	9	1,3,10,15,42
V_{SS}	10,30	2,4,12,34,43

3.1.1 CLOCK (CLK)

This input provides the basic timing for internal operation. This pin does not require MOS-level input; it will operate at either TTL or MOS levels up to the maximum allowed frequency. A minimum frequency must be provided to keep the internal logic properly functioning. Depending on the signal on CKM, the signal on CLK can be divided by two to produce the internal clock signal.

3.1.2 CLOCKING MODE (CKM)

This pin is a strapping option. When it is strapped to V_{CC} (HIGH), the CLK input is used directly; when strapped to V_{SS} (LOW), the CLK input is divided by two to produce the internal clock signal. During the RESET sequence, this input must be stable at least four internal clock cycles (i.e. CLK clocks when CKM is HIGH; 2 × CLK clocks when CKM is LOW) before RESET goes LOW.

3.1.3 SYSTEM RESET (RESET)

A LOW to HIGH transition on this pin causes the Intel287 XL MCP to terminate its present activity and to enter a dormant state. RESET must remain active (HIGH) for at least four CLK periods (i.e., the RESET signal presented to the Intel287 XL MCP must be at least four Intel287 XL MCP clocks long, regardless of the frequency of the CPU). Note that the Intel287 XL MCP is active internally for 25 clock cycles after the termination of the RESET signal (the HIGH to LOW transition of RESET); therefore, the first instruction should not be written to the Intel287 XL MCP until 25 clocks after the falling edge of RESET. Table 3.3 shows the status of the output pins during the reset sequence. After a reset, all output pins return to their inactive states.

Table 3.3. Output Pin Status during Reset

Output Pin Name	Value During Reset
BUSY#	HIGH
ERROR#	HIGH
PEREQ	LOW
D_{15}–D_0	Tristate OFF

3.1.4 PROCESSOR EXTENSION REQUEST (PEREQ)

When active, this pin signals to the CPU that the Intel287 XL MCP is ready for data transfer to/from its data FIFO. With 80286 and 80C286 CPUs, PEREQ can be deactivated after assertion of PEACK#. These CPUs rely on the MCP to deassert PEREQ when all operands have been transfered. When there are more than five data transfers, PEREQ is deactiviated after the first three transfers and subsequently after every four transfers. This signal always goes inactive before BUSY# goes inactive.

3.1.5 BUSY STATUS (BUSY#)

When active, this pin signals to the CPU that the Intel287 XL MCP is currently executing an instruction. It should be connected to the CPU's BUSY# pin. During the RESET sequence this pin is HIGH.

3.1.6 ERROR STATUS (ERROR#)

This pin reflects the ES bit of the status register. When active, it indicates that an unmasked exception has occurred. This signal can be changed to inactive state only by the following instructions (without a preceding WAIT): FNINIT, FNCLEX, FNSTENV, FNSAVE, FLDCW, FLDENV, and FRSTOR. This pin should be connected to the ERROR# pin of the CPU. ERROR# can change state only when BUSY# is active.

3.1.7 PROCESSOR EXTENSION ACKNOWLEDGE (PEACK#)

During execution of escape instructions, an 80286 or 80C286 CPU asserts PEACK# to acknowledge that the request signal (PEREQ) has been recognized and that data transfer is in progress. The 80286/80C286 also drives this signal HIGH during RESET.

This input may be asynchronous with respect to the Intel287 XL MCP clock except during a RESET sequence, when it must satisfy setup and hold requirements relative to RESET.

3.1.8 DATA PINS (D_{15}–D_0)

These bidirectional pins are used to transfer data and opcodes between the CPU and Intel287 XL MCP. They are normally connected directly to the corresponding CPU data pins. Other buffers/drivers driving the local data bus must be disabled when the CPU reads from the MCP. HIGH state indicates a value of one. D_0 is the least significant data bit.

3.1.9 NUMERIC PROCESSOR WRITE (NPWR#)

A signal on this pin enables transfers of data from the CPU to the MCP. This input is valid only when NPS1# and NPS2 are both active.

3.1.10 NUMERIC PROCESSOR READ (NPRD#)

A signal on this pin enables transfers of data from the MCP to the CPU. This input is valid only when NPS1# and NPS2 are both active.

3.1.11 NUMERIC PROCESSOR SELECTS (NPS1# and NPS2)

Concurrent assertion of these signals indicates that the CPU is performing an escape instruction and enables the Intel287 XL MCP to execute that instruction. No data transfer involving the Intel287 XL MCP occurs unless the device is selected by these lines.

3.1.12 COMMAND SELECTS (CMD0 AND CMD1)

These pins along with the select pins allow the CPU to direct the operation of the Intel287 XL MCP.

3.1.13 SYSTEM POWER (V_{CC})

System power provides the +5V ± 10% DC supply input. All V_{CC} pins should be tied together on the circuit board and local decoupling capacitors should be used between V_{CC} and V_{SS}.

3.1.14 SYSTEM GROUND (V_{SS})

All V_{SS} pins should be tied together on the circuit board and local decoupling capacitors should be used between V_{CC} and V_{SS}.

3.2 Processor Architecture

As shown by the block diagram on the front page, the Intel287 XL MCP is internally divided into three sections: the bus control logic (BCL), the data interface and control unit, and the floating point unit (FPU). The FPU (with the support of the control unit which contains the sequencer and other support units) executes all numerics instructions. The data interface and control unit is responsible for the data flow to and from the FPU and the control registers, for receiving the instructions, decoding them, and sequencing the microinstructions, and for handling some of the administrative instructions. The BCL is responsible for CPU bus tracking and interface.

3.2.1 BUS CONTROL LOGIC

The BCL communicates solely with the CPU using I/O bus cycles. The BCL appears to the CPU as a special peripheral device. It is special in two respects: the CPU initiates I/O automatically when it encounters ESC instructions, and the CPU uses reserved I/O addresses to communicate with the BCL. The BCL does not communicate directly with memory. The CPU performs all memory access, transferring input operands from memory to the Intel287 XL MCP and transferring outputs from the Intel287 XL MCP to memory. A dedicated communication protocol makes possible high-speed transfer of opcodes and operands between the CPU and Intel287 XL MCP.

3.2.2 DATA INTERFACE AND CONTROL UNIT

The data interface and control unit latches the data and, subject to BCL control, directs the data to the FIFO or the instruction decoder. The instruction de-

Table 3.4. Bus Cycles Definition

NPS1#	NPS2	CMD0	CMD1	NPRD#	NPWR#	Bus Cycle Type
x	0	x	x	x	x	Intel287 XL MCP not selected
1	x	x	x	x	x	Intel287 XL MCP not selected
0	1	0	0	1	0	Opcode write to Intel287 XL MCP
0	1	0	0	0	1	CW or SW read from Intel287 XL MCP
0	1	1	0	0	1	Read data from Intel287 XL MCP
0	1	1	0	1	0	Write data to Intel287 XL MCP
0	1	0	1	1	0	Write exception pointers
0	1	0	1	0	1	Reserved
0	1	1	1	0	1	Reserved
0	1	1	1	1	0	Reserved

coder decodes the ESC instructions sent to it by the CPU and generates controls that direct the data flow in the FIFO. It also triggers the microinstruction sequencer that controls execution of each instruction. If the ESC instruction is FINIT, FCLEX, FSTSW, FSTSW AX, FSTCW, FSETPM, or FRSTPM, the control executes it independent ly of the FPU and the sequencer. The data interface and control unit is the one that generates the BUSY#, PEREQ, and ERROR# signals that synchronize Intel287 XL activities with the CPU.

3.2.3 FLOATING-POINT UNIT

The FPU executes all instructions that involve the register stack, including arithmetic, logical, transcendental, constant, and data transfer instructions. The data path in the FPU is 84 bits wide (68 significant bits, 15 exponent bits, and a sign bit) which allows internal operand transfers to be performed at very high speeds.

3.3 Bus Cycles

The pins NPS1#, NPS2, CMD0, CMD1, NPRD#, and NPWR# identify bus cycles for the MCP. Table 3.4 defines the types of Intel287 XL MCP bus cycles.

3.3.1 Intel287™ XL MCP ADDRESSING

The NPS1#, NPS2, CMD0, and CMD1 signals allow the MCP to identify which bus cycles are intended for the MCP. The MCP responds to I/O cycles when the I/O address is 00F8H, 00FAH, 00FCH. The correspondence between I/O addresses and control signals is defined by Table 3.5. To guarantee correct operation of the MCP, programs must not perform any I/O operations to these reserved port addresses.

Table 3.5. I/O Address Decoding

I/O Address (Hexadecimal)	Intel287 XL MCP Select and Command Inputs			
	NPS2	NPS1#	CMD1	CMD0
00F8	1	0	0	0
00FA	1	0	0	1
00FC	1	0	1	0

3.3.2 CPU/MCP SYNCHRONIZATION

The pins BUSY#, PEREQ, and ERROR# are used for various aspects of synchronization between the CPU and the MCP.

BUSY# is used to synchronize instruction transfer from the CPU to the Intel287 XL MCP. When the Intel287 XL MCP recognizes an ESC instruction, it asserts BUSY#. For most ESC instructions, the CPU waits for the Intel287 XL MCP to deassert BUSY# before sending the new opcode.

The MCP uses the PEREQ pin of the CPU to signal that the MCP is ready for data transfer to or from its data FIFO. The MCP does not directly access memory; rather, the CPU provides memory access services for the MCP. Thus, memory access on behalf of the MCP always obeys the rules applicable to the mode of the CPU, whether the CPU be in real-address mode or protected mode.

Once the CPU initiates an Intel287 XL MCP instruction that has operands, the CPU waits for PEREQ signals that indicate when the Intel287 XL MCP is ready for operand transfer. Once all operands have been transferred (or if the instruction has no operands) the CPU continues program execution while the Intel287 XL MCP executes the ESC instruction.

In 8086/8087 systems, WAIT instructions may be required to achieve synchronization of both commands and operands. In Intel287 XL MCP systems, however, WAIT instructions are required only for operand synchronization; namely, after MCP stores to memory (except FSTSW and FSTCW) or load from memory. (In 80286/Intel287 XL MCP systems, WAIT is required before FLDENV and FRSTOR; with other CPU's, WAIT is not required in these cases.) Used this way, WAIT ensures that the value has already been written or read by the MCP before the CPU reads or changes the value.

Once it has started to execute a numerics instruction and has transferred the operands from the CPU, the Intel287 XL MCP can process the instruction in parallel with and independent of the host CPU. When the MCP detects an exception, it asserts the ERROR# signal, which causes a CPU interrupt.

3.4 Bus Operation

With respect to bus interface, the Intel287 XL MCP is fully asynchronous with the CPU, even when it operates from the same clock source as the CPU. The CPU initiates a bus cycle for the MCP by activating both NPS1# and NPS2, the MCP select signals. During the CLK period in which NPS1# and NPS2 are activated, the Intel287 XL MCP also examines the NPRD# and NPWR# input signals to determine whether the cycle is a read or a write cycle and examines the CMD0 and CMD1 inputs to determine whether an opcode, operand, or control/status register transfer is to occur. The Intel287 XL MCP activates its BUSY# output some time after the leading edge of the NPRD# or NPWR# signal. Input and output data are referenced to the trailing edges of the NPRD# and NPWR# signals.

The Intel287 XL MCP activates the PEREQ signal when it is ready for data transfer. In 80286/80C286 systems, the CPU activates PEACK# when no more data transfers are required, which causes the Intel287 XL MCP to deactivate PEREQ, halting the data transfer.

3.5 80286/Intel287™ XL MCP, 80C286/Intel287™ XL MCP Interface and Socket Compatibilty

The ceramic Intel287 XL MCP device can fit into existing 80287 sockets since the pin configuration is identical.

The CERDIP 80C287A utilizes a different pin configuration with extra power and ground pins. However, the Intel287 XL MCP operates in 80C287A sockets also. The extra power and ground pins are not connected inside the Intel287 XL MCP and not used. Refer to 80C287A data sheet (Order #240347).

Note that when the clock selection is CKM = 0, the Intel287 XL MCP divides the clock input by two, not by three as on the 80287. In this case, the Intel287 XL MCP will operate faster.

The interface between the Intel287 XL MCP and the 80286/80C286 CPU (illustrated in Figure 3.3) has these characteristics:

- The Intel287 XL MCP resides on the local data bus of the CPU.
- The CPU and Intel287 XL MCP share the same RESET signals. They may also share the same clock input; however, for greatest performance, an external oscillator may be needed.
- The corresponding BUSY#, ERROR#, PEREQ, and PEACK# pins are connected together.
- NPS2 is tied HIGH permanently, while NPS1#, CMD1, and CMD0 come from the latched address pins. The 80286 generates I/O addresses 00F8H, 00FAH, and 00FCH during MCP bus cycles. Address 00FEH is reserved.
- The Intel287 XL MCP NPRD# and NPWR# inputs are connected to I/O read and write signals from local bus control logic.

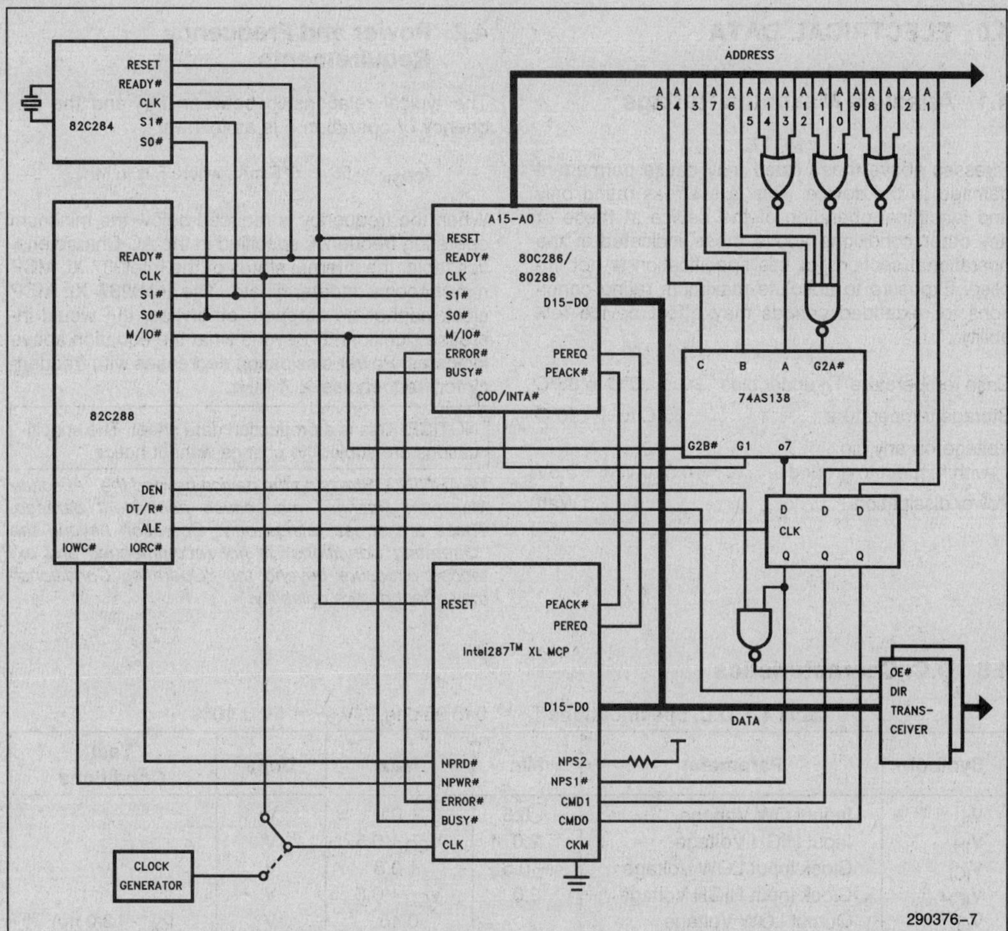

Figure 3.3. 80286/Intel287™ XL System Configuration

4.0 ELECTRICAL DATA

4.1 Absolute Maximum Ratings

NOTE

Stresses above those listed may cause permanent damage to the device. This is a stress rating only and functional operation of the device at these or any other conditions above those indicated in the operational sections of this specification is not implied. Exposure to absolute maximum rating conditions for extended periods may affect device reliability.

Case temperature T_C under bias ....0°C to 85°C

Storage temperature .... −65°C to +150°C

Voltage on any pin
with respect to ground .... −0.5 to V_{CC}+0.5V

Power dissipation .... 1.5 Watt

4.2 Power and Frequency Requirements

The typical relationship between I_{CC} and the frequency of operation F is as follows:

I_{CCtyp} = 55 + 5*F mA , where F is in MHz.

When the frequency is reduced below the minimum operating frequency specified in the AC Characteristics table, the internal states of the Intel287 XL MCP may become indeterminate. The Intel287 XL MCP clock cannot be stopped; otherwise, I_{CC} would increase significantly beyond what the equation above indicates. Power dissipation decreases with frequency for frequencies ≥ 4 MHz.

NOTICE: This is a production data sheet. The specifications are subject to change without notice.

**WARNING: Stressing the device beyond the "Absolute Maximum Ratings" may cause permanent damage. These are stress ratings only. Operation beyond the "Operating Conditions" is not recommended and extended exposure beyond the "Operating Conditions" may affect device reliability.*

4.3 D.C. Characteristics

Table 4.1. D.C. Specifications T_C = 0 to 85 deg C, V_{CC} = 5V ±10%

Symbol	Parameter	Min	Max	Units	Test Conditions
V_{IL}	Input LOW Voltage	−0.5	+0.8	V	
V_{IH}	Input HIGH Voltage	2.0	V_{CC}+0.5	V	
V_{ICL}	Clock Input LOW Voltage	−0.5	+0.8	V	
V_{ICH}	Clock Input HIGH Voltage	2.0	V_{CC}+0.5	V	
V_{OL}	Output LOW Voltage		0.45	V	I_{OL} = 3.0 mA
V_{OH}	Output HIGH Voltage	2.4		V	I_{OH} = −0.4 mA
I_{CC}	Power Supply Current		135	mA	Note 1
I_{LI}	Input Leakage Current		±10	μA	Note 2
I_{LO}	I/O Leakage Current		±10	μA	Note 3
C_{IN}	Input Capacitance		10	pF	Note 4
C_O	I/O or Output Capacitance		12	pF	Note 4
C_{CLK}	Clock Capacitance		20	pF	Note 4

NOTES:
1. 12.5 MHz operation, output load = 100 pF
2. 0V ≤ V_{IN} ≤ V_{CC}
3. 0.45V ≤ V_{OUT} ≤ V_{CC} −0.45
4. F_C = 1MHz

4.4 A.C. Characteristics

Table 4.2. Timing Requirements T_C = 0 to 85 deg C, V_{CC} = 5V ±10%
All timings are measured at 1.5V unless otherwise specified

Symbol	Parameter	12.5 MHz		Test Conditions
		Min (ns)	Max (ns)	
Tdvwh (t6)	Data setup to NPWR#	43		
Twhdx (t7)	Data hold from NPWR#	14		
Trlrh (t8)	NPRD# active time	59		
Twlwh (t9)	NPWR# active time	59		
Tavwl (t10)	Command valid to NPWR#	0		
Tavrl (t11)	Command valid to NPRD#	0		
Tmhrl (t12)	Min delay from PEREQ active to NPRD# active	40		
Tklkh (t33)	PEACK# active time	55		
Tkhkl (t34)	PEACK# inactive time	60		
Tkhch (t35)	PEACK# inactive to NPRD#, NPWR# inactive	30		
Tklcl (t36)	PEACK# active setup to NPRD#, NPWR# active	30		
Tchkl (t37)	NPRD#, NPWR# inactive to PEACK# active	−30		
Twhax (t18)	Command hold from NPWR#	12		
Trhax (t19)	Command hold from NPRD#	12		
Tivcl (t20)	NPRD#, NPWR#, RESET to CLK setup time	46		Note 1
Tclih (t21)	NPRD#, NPWR#, RESET from CLK hold time	26		Note 1
Tpaksu (t38)	PEACK# setup to RESET falling edge	80		
Tpakhd (t39)	PEACK# hold from RESET falling edge	80		
Trscl (t24)	RESET to CLK setup	21		Note 1
Tclrs (t25)	RESET from CLK hold	14		Note 1
Tcmdi (t26)	Command inactive time			
	Write to write	69		
	Read to read	69		
	Read to write	69		
	Write to read	69		

NOTE:
1. This is an asynchronous input. This specification is given for testing purposes only, to assure recognition at a specific CLK edge (not tested).

5

Table 4.3. Timing Responses

Symbol	Parameter	12.5 MHz Min (ns)	12.5 MHz Max (ns)	Test Conditions
Trhqz (t27) Trlqv (t28)	NPRD# inactive to data float* NPRD# active to data valid		18 50	Note 2 Note 3
Tilbh (t29)	ERROR# active to BUSY# inactive	104		Note 4
Twlbv (t30)	NPWR# active to BUSY# active		80	Note 4
Tklml (t31)	NPRD#, NPWR# or PEACK# active to PEREQ inactive		80	Note 5
Trhqh (t32)	Data hold from NPRD# inactive	2		Note 3

NOTES:
* The data float delay is not tested.
2. The float condition occurs when the measured output current is less than I_{OL} on $D_{15}-D_0$.
3. $D_{15}-D_0$ loading: C_L = 100pf.
4. BUSY# loading: C_L = 100pf.
5. On last data transfer of numeric instruction.

Table 4.4. Clock Timings

Symbol		Parameter		12.5 MHz Min (ns)	12.5 MHz Max (ns)	Test Conditions
Tclcl	(t1a)	CLK period	CKM = 1	80	250	
	(t1b)		CKM = 0	40	125	
Tclch	(t2a)	CLK low time	CKM = 1	35		
	(t2b)		CKM = 0	9		Note 6, 10
Tchcl	(t3a)	CLK high time	CKM = 1	35		V_{CC} = ±10%
			CKM = 1	28		V_{CC} = ±5%, Note 11
	(t3b)		CKM = 0	13		Note 7, 10
Tch1ch2	(t4)				10	Note 8
Tch2ch1	(t5)				10	Note 9

NOTES:
6. At 0.8V.
7. At 2.0V.
8. CKM = 1: 3.5V to 1.0V
9. CKM = 1: 1.0V to 3.5V
10. Proper operation can also be achieved by meeting the CPU specification
11. Provides compatibility for sockets designed for Intel 80287-6/8/10 MHz Math CoProcessors.

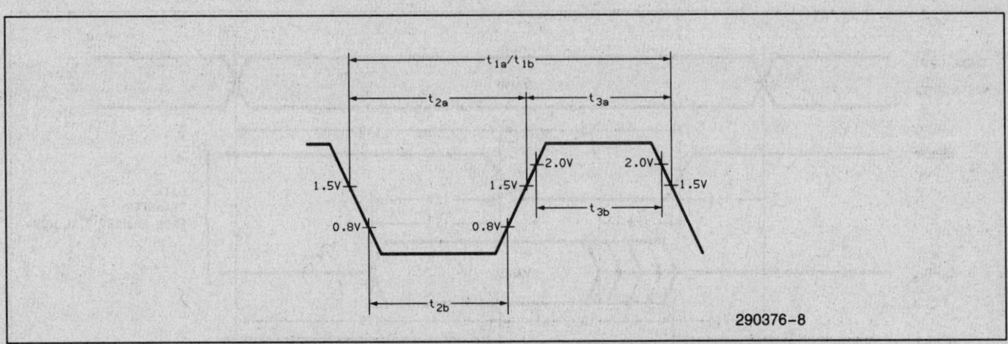

Figure 4.1. AC Drive and Measurement Points—CLK Input

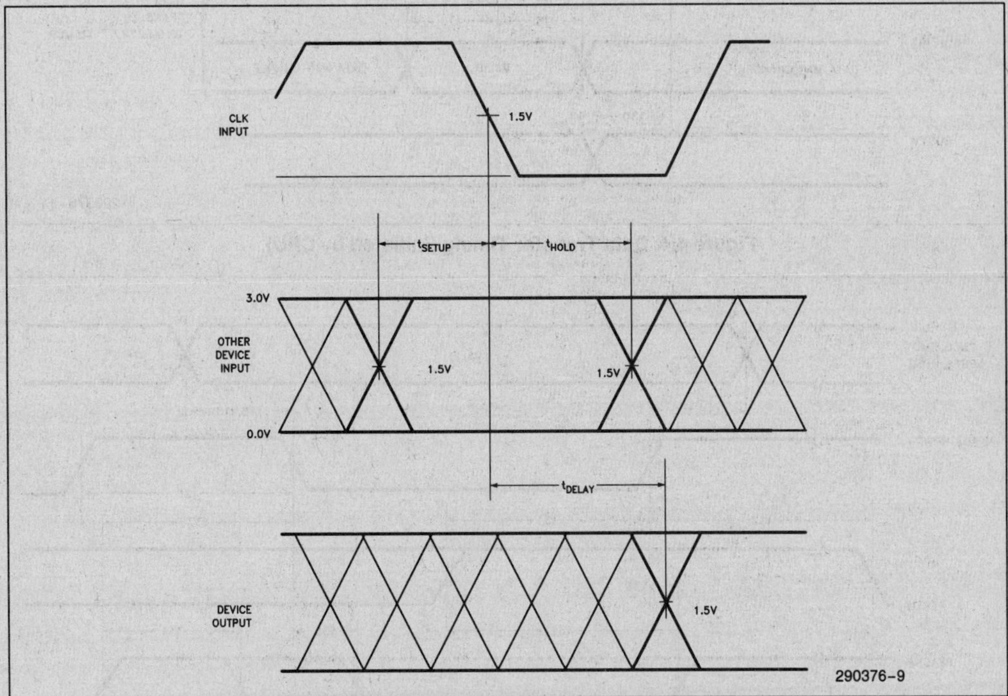

Figure 4.2. AC Setup, Hold, and Delay Time Measurements—General

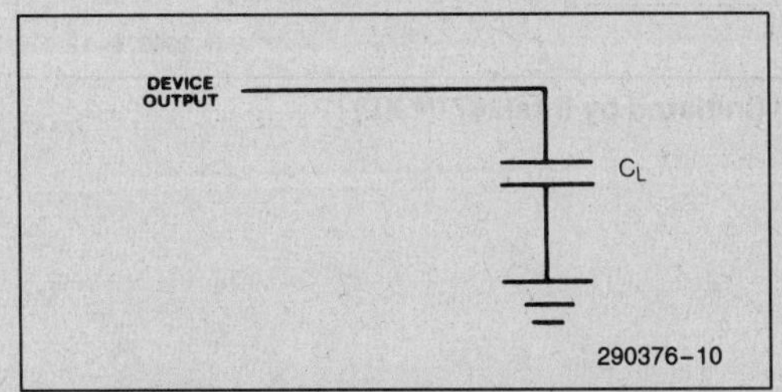

Figure 4.3. AC Test Loading on Outputs

RESET, NPWR#, NPRD# inputs are asynchronous to CLK. Timing requirements in Figures 4.7 through 4.10 are given for testing purposes only, to assure recognition at a specific CLK edge.

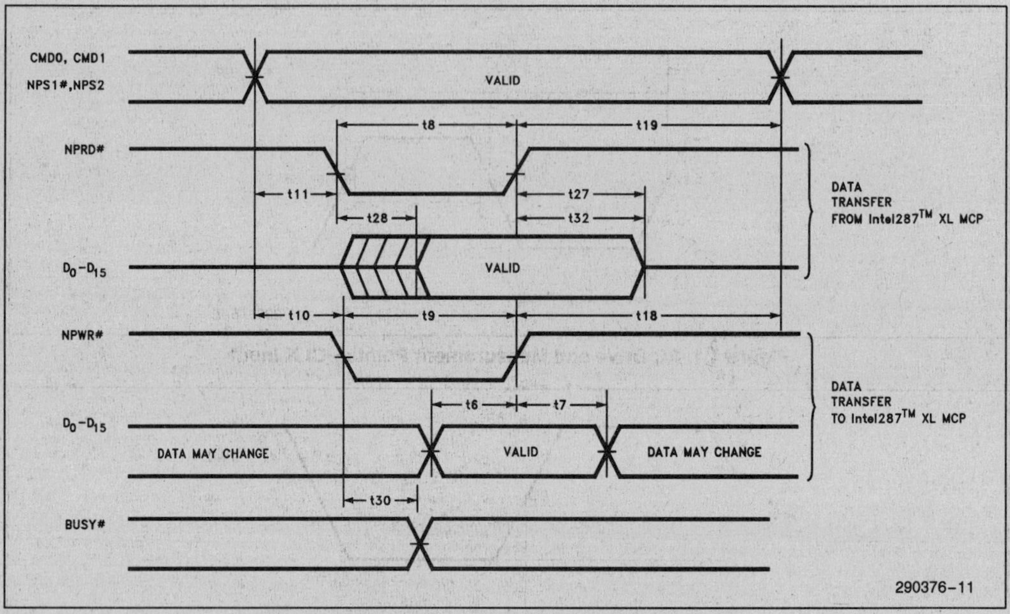

Figure 4.4. Data Transfer Timing (Initiated by CPU)

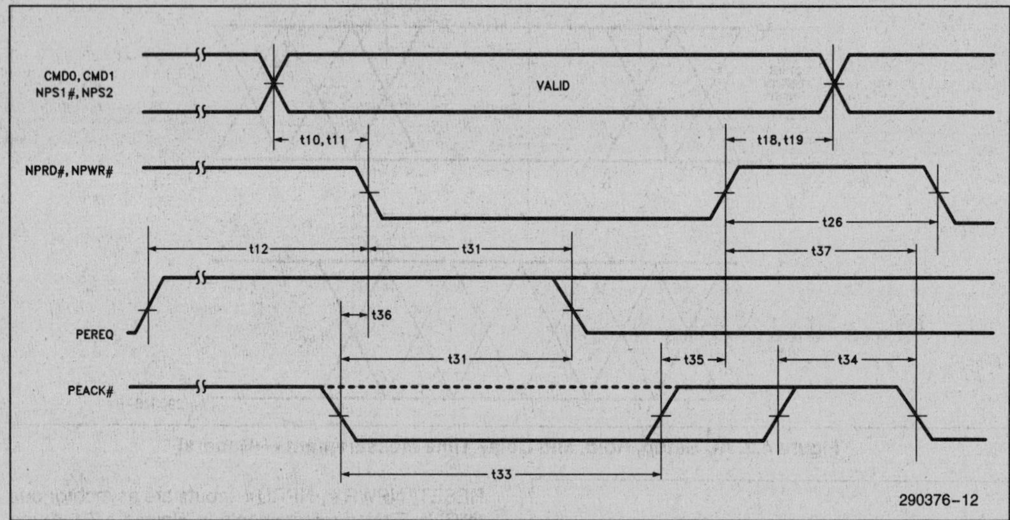

Figure 4.5. Data Channel Timing (Initiated by Intel287™ XL)

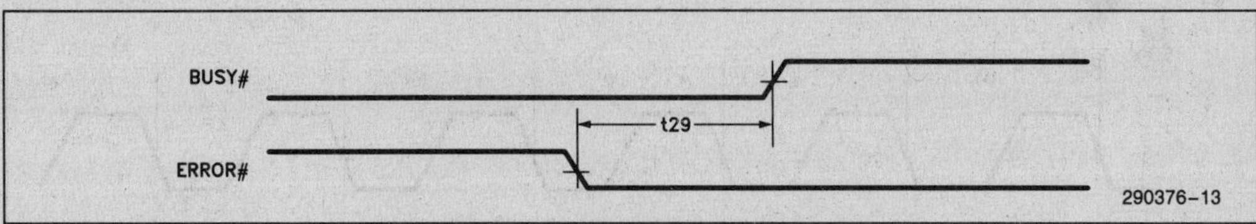

Figure 4.6. ERROR# Output Timing

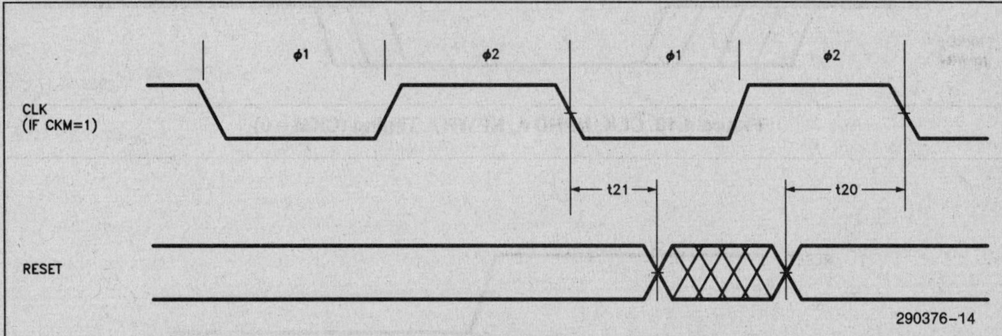

Figure 4.7. CLK, RESET Timing (CKM = 1)

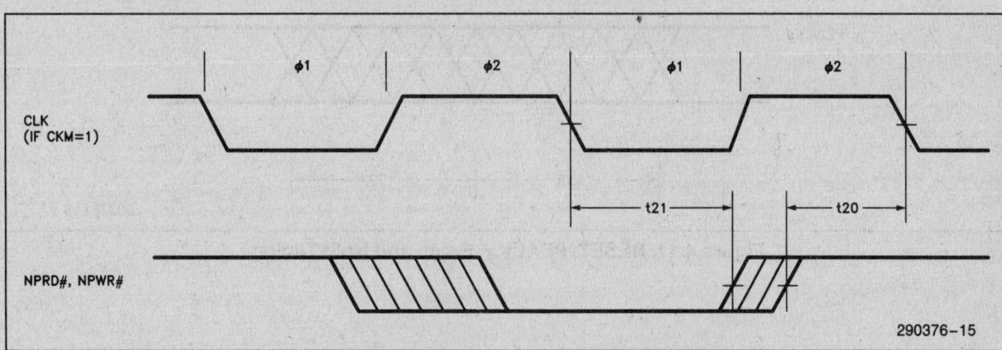

Figure 4.8. CLK, NPRD#, NPWR# Timing (CKM = 1)

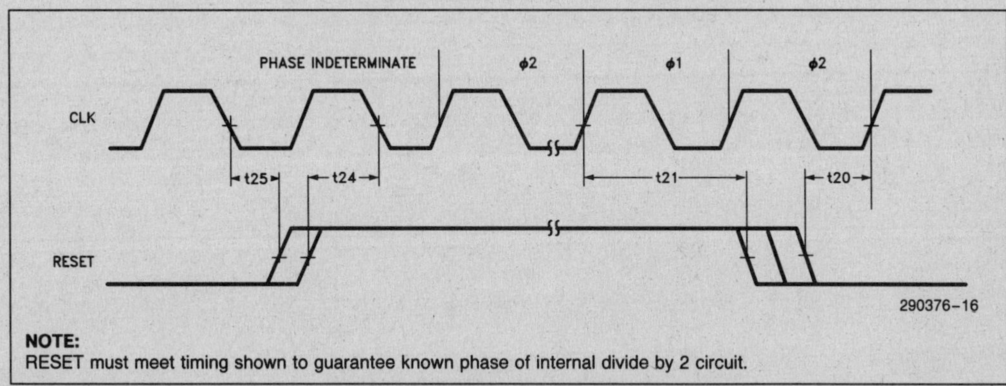

NOTE:
RESET must meet timing shown to guarantee known phase of internal divide by 2 circuit.

Figure 4.9. CLK, RESET Timing (CKM = 0)

5

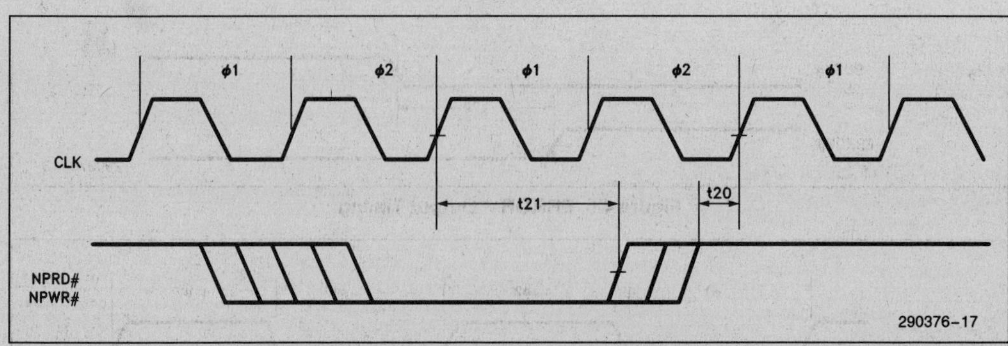

Figure 4.10. CLK, NPRD#, NPWR# Timing (CKM = 0)

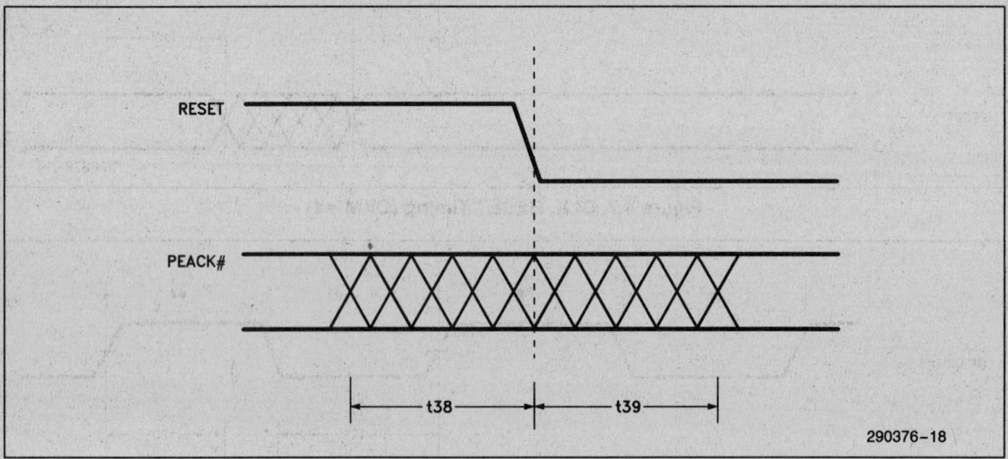

Figure 4.11. RESET, PEACK# Setup and Hold Timing

5.0 Intel287™ XL MCP EXTENSIONS TO THE CPU'S INSTRUCTION SET

Instructions for the Intel287 XL MCP assume one of the five forms shown in Table 5-1. In all cases, instructions are at least two bytes long and begin with the bit pattern 11011B, which identifies the ESCAPE class of instruction. Instructions that refer to memory operands specify addresses using the CPU's addressing modes.

MOD (Mode field) and R/M (Register/Memory specifier) have the same interpretation as the corresponding fields of CPU instructions (refer to Programmer's Reference Manual for the CPU). The DISP (displacement) is optionally present in instructions that have MOD and R/M fields. Its presence depends on the values of MOD and R/M, as for instructions of the CPU.

The instruction summaries that follow assume that the instruction has been prefetched, decoded, and is ready for execution; that bus cycles do not require wait states; that there are no local bus HOLD requests delaying processor access to the bus; and that no exceptions are detected during instruction execution. Timings are given in internal Intel287 XL MCP clocks and include the time for opcode and data transfer between the CPU and the MCP. If the instruction has MOD and R/M fields that call for both base and index registers, add one clock.

Table 5.1. Instruction Formats

	Instruction									Optional Field
	First Byte				Second Byte					
1	11011	OPA		1	MOD		1	OPB	R/M	DISP
2	11011	MF		OPA	MOD		OPB*		R/M	DISP
3	11011	d	P	OPA	1	1	OPB*		ST(i)	
4	11011	0	0	1	1	1	1	OP		
5	11011	0	1	1	1	1	1	OP		
	15–11	10	9	8	7	6	5	4 3	2 1 0	

OP = Instruction opcode, possibly split into two fields OPA and OPB

MF = Memory Format
00–32-bit real
01–32-bit integer
10–64-bit real
11–16-bit integer

d = Destination
0–Destination is ST(0)
1–Destination is ST(i)

R XOR d = 0-Destination (Op) Source
R XOR d = 1-Source (Op) Destination

*In FSUB and FDIV, the low-order bit of the OPB is the R (reversed) bit

P = Pop
0–Do not pop stack
1–Pop stack after operation

ESC = 11011

ST(i) = Register stack element i
000 = Stack top
001 = Second stack element
•
•
•
111 = Eighth stack element

Intel287™ XL MCP Extension to the CPU's Instruction Set

Instruction	Encoding			Clock Count Range			
	Byte 0	Byte 1	Optional Bytes 2–3	32-Bit Real	32-Bit Integer	64-Bit Real	16-Bit Integer
DATA TRANSFER							
FLD = Load[a]							
Integer/real memory to ST(0)	ESC MF 1	MOD 000 R/M	SIB/DISP	36	61–68	45	61–65
Long integer memory to ST(0)	ESC 111	MOD 101 R/M	SIB/DISP		76–87		
Extended real memory to ST(0)	ESC 011	MOD 101 R/M	SIB/DISP		48		
BCD memory to ST(0)	ESC 111	MOD 100 R/M	SIB/DISP		270–279		
ST(i) to ST(0)	ESC 001	11000 ST(i)			21		
FST = Store							
ST(0) to integer/real memory	ESC MF 1	MOD 010 R/M	SIB/DISP	51	86–100	56	88–101
ST(0) to ST(i)	ESC 101	11010 ST(i)			18		
FSTP = Store and Pop							
ST(0) to integer/real memory	ESC MF 1	MOD 011 R/M	SIB/DISP	51	86–100	56	88–101
ST(0) to long integer memory	ESC 111	MOD 111 R/M	SIB/DISP		91–108		
ST(0) to extended real	ESC 011	MOD 111 R/M	SIB/DISP		61		
ST(0) to BCD memory	ESC 111	MOD 110 R/M	SIB/DISP		520–542		
ST(0) to ST(i)	ESC 101	11001 ST (i)			19		
FXCH = Exchange							
ST(i) and ST(0)	ESC 001	11001 ST(i)			25		
COMPARISON							
FCOM = Compare							
Integer/real memory to ST(0)	ESC MF 0	MOD 010 R/M	SIB/DISP	42	72–79	51	71–75
ST(i) to ST(0)	ESC 000	11010 ST(i)			31		
FCOMP = Compare and pop							
Integer/real memory to ST	ESC MF 0	MOD 011 R/M	SIB/DISP	42	72–79	51	71–77
ST(i) to ST(0)	ESC 000	11011 ST(i)			33		
FCOMPP = Compare and pop twice							
ST(1) to ST(0)	ESC 110	1101 1001			33		
FTST = Test ST(0)	ESC 001	1110 0100			35		
FUCOM = Unordered compare	ESC 101	11100 ST(i)			31		
FUCOMP = Unordered compare and pop	ESC 101	11101 ST(i)			33		
FUCOMPP = Unordered compare and pop twice	ESC 010	1110 1001			33		
FXAM = Examine ST(0)	ESC 001	11100101			37–45		
CONSTANTS							
FLDZ = Load +0.0 into ST(0)	ESC 001	1110 1110			27		
FLD1 = Load +1.0 into ST(0)	ESC 001	1110 1000			31		
FLDPI = Load pi into ST(0)	ESC 001	1110 1011			47		
FLDL2T = Load $\log_2(10)$ into ST(0)	ESC 001	1110 1001			47		

Shaded areas indicate instructions not available in 8087/80287, but available on 80C287A and Intel287 XL MCP.

NOTE:
a. When loading single- or double-precision zero from memory, add 5 clocks.

Intel287™ XL MCP Extension to the CPU's Instruction Set (Continued)

Instruction	Encoding			Clock Count Range			
	Byte 0	Byte 1	Optional Bytes 2–3	32-Bit Real	32-Bit Integer	64-Bit Real	16-Bit Integer
CONSTANTS (Continued)							
FLDL2E = Load $\log_2(e)$ into ST(0)	ESC 001	1110 1010		47			
FLDLG2 = Load $\log_{10}(2)$ into ST(0)	ESC 001	1110 1100		48			
FLDLN2 = Load $\log_e(2)$ into ST(0)	ESC 001	1110 1101		48			
ARITHMETIC							
FADD = Add							
Integer/real memory with ST(0)	ESC MF 0	MOD 000 R/M	SIB/DISP	40–48	73–78	49–79	71–85
ST(i) and ST(0)	ESC d P 0	11000 ST(i)		30–38[b]			
FSUB = Subtract							
Integer/real memory with ST(0)	ESC MF 0	MOD 10 R R/M	SIB/DISP	40–48	73–98	49–77	71–83[c]
ST(i) and ST(0)	ESC d P 0	1110 R R/M		33–41[d]			
FMUL = Multiply							
Integer/real memory with ST(0)	ESC MF 0	MOD 001 R/M	SIB/DISP	43–51	77–88	52–77	76–87
ST(i) and ST(0)	ESC d P 0	1100 1 R/M		25–53[e]			
FDIV = Divide							
Integer/real memory with ST(0)	ESC MF 0	MOD 11 R R/M	SIB/DISP	105	136–143[f]	114	136–140[g]
ST(i) and ST(0)	ESC d P 0	1111 R R/M		95[h]			
FSQRT[i] = Square root	ESC 001	1111 1010		129–136			
FSCALE = Scale ST(0) by ST(1)	ESC 001	1111 1101		74–93			
FPREM = Partial remainder of ST(0) ÷ ST(1)	ESC 001	1111 1000		81–162			
FPREM1 = Partial remainder (IEEE)	ESC 001	1111 0101		102–192			
FRNDINT = Round ST(0) to integer	ESC 001	1111 1100		73–87			
FXTRACT = Extract components of ST(0)	ESC 001	1111 0100		75–83			
FABS = Absolute value of ST(0)	ESC 001	1110 0001		29			
FCHS = Change sign of ST(0)	ESC 001	1110 0000		31–37			

Shaded areas indicate instructions not available in 8087/80287, but available on Intel287 XL MCP and 80C287A.

NOTES:
b. Add 3 clocks to the range when d = 1.
c. Add 1 clock to **each** range when R = 1.
d. Add 3 clocks to the range when d = 0.
e. Typical = 48 (When d = 0, 42–50, typical = 45).
f. Add 1 clock to the range when R = 1.
g. 135–141 when R = 1.
h. Add 3 clocks to the range when d = 1.
i. $-0 \leq ST(0) \leq +\infty$.

5

Intel287™ XL MCP Extension to the CPU's Instruction Set (Continued)

Instruction	Encoding			Clock Count Range
	Byte 0	Byte 1	Optional Bytes 2–3	
TRANSCENDENTAL				
FCOS = Cosine of ST(0)	ESC 001	1111 1111		130–779[j]
FPTAN[k] = Partial tangent of ST(0)	ESC 001	1111 0010		198–504[j]
FPATAN = Partial arctangent	ESC 001	1111 0011		321–494
FSIN = Sine of ST(0)	ESC 001	1111 1110		129–778[j]
FSINCOS = Sine and cosine of ST(0)	ESC 001	1111 1011		201–816[j]
F2XM1[l] = $2^{ST(0)} - 1$	ESC 001	1111 0000		215–483
FYL2X[m] = $ST(1) * \log_2(ST(0))$	ESC 001	1111 0001		127–545
FYL2XP1[n] = $ST(1) * \log_2(ST(0) + 1.0)$	ESC 001	1111 1001		264–554
PROCESSOR CONTROL				
FINIT = Initialize MCP	ESC 011	1110 0011		25
FSETPM = Set protected mode	ESC 011	1110 0100		12
FRSTPM = Reset protected mode	ESC 011	1111 0100		12
FSTSW AX = Store status word	ESC 111	1110 0000		18
FLDCW = Load control word	ESC 001	MOD 101 R/M	SIB/DISP	33
FSTCW = Store control word	ESC 101	MOD 111 R/M	SIB/DISP	18
FSTSW = Store status word	ESC 101	MOD 111 R/M	SIB/DISP	18
FCLEX = Clear exceptions	ESC 011	1110 0010		8
FSTENV = Store environment	ESC 001	MOD 110 R/M	SIB/DISP	192–193
FLDENV = Load environment	ESC 001	MOD 100 R/M	SIB/DISP	85
FSAVE = Save state	ESC 101	MOD 110 R/M	SIB/DISP	521–522
FRSTOR = Restore state	ESC 101	MOD 100 R/M	SIB/DISP	396
FINCSTP = Increment stack pointer	ESC 001	1111 0111		28
FDECSTP = Decrement stack pointer	ESC 001	1111 0110		29
FFREE = Free ST(i)	ESC 101	1100 0 ST(i)		25
FNOP = No operations	ESC 001	1101 0000		19

Shaded areas indicate instructions not available in 8087/80287, but available on Intel287 XL MCP and 80C287A.

NOTES:

j. These timings hold for operands in the range $|x| < \pi/4$. For operands not in this range, up to 78 additional clocks may be needed to reduce the operand.

k. $0 \le |ST(0)| < 2^{63}$.

l. $-1.0 \le ST(0) \le 1.0$.

m. $0 \le ST(0) < \infty, -\infty < ST(1) < +\infty$.

n. $0 \le |ST(0)| < (2 - SQRT(2))/2, -\infty < ST(1) < +\infty$.

82C288
BUS CONTROLLER FOR 80286 PROCESSORS
(82C288-12, 82C288-10, 82C288-8)

- **Provides Commands and Controls for Local and System Bus**
- **Wide Flexibility in System Configurations**
- **High Speed CHMOS III Technology**
- **Fully Compatible with the HMOS 82288**
- **Fully Static Device**
- **Available in 20 Pin PLCC (Plastic Leaded Chip Carrier) and 20 Pin Cerdip Packages**
  (See Packaging Spec, Order #231369)

The Intel 82C288 Bus Controller is a 20-pin CHMOS III component for use in 80286 microsystems. The 82C288 is fully compatible with its predecessor the HMOS 82288. The bus controller is fully static and supports a low power mode. The bus controller provides command and control outputs with flexible timing options. Separate command outputs are used for memory and I/O devices. The data bus is controlled with separate data enable and direction control signals.

Two modes of operation are possible via a strapping option: MULTIBUS® I compatible bus cycles, and high speed bus cycles.

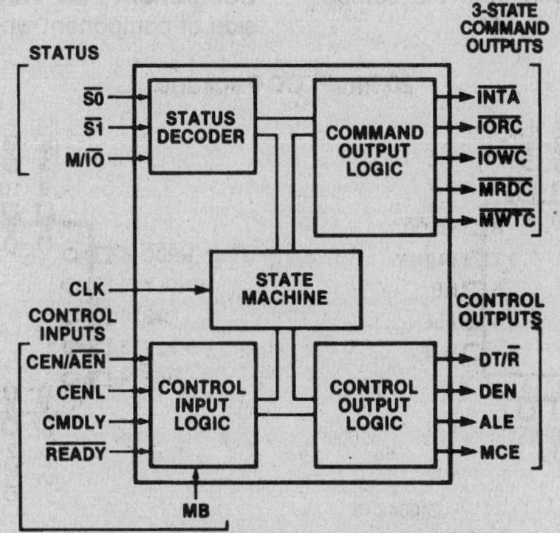

Figure 1. 82C288 Block Diagram

5

September 1989
Order Number: 240042-003

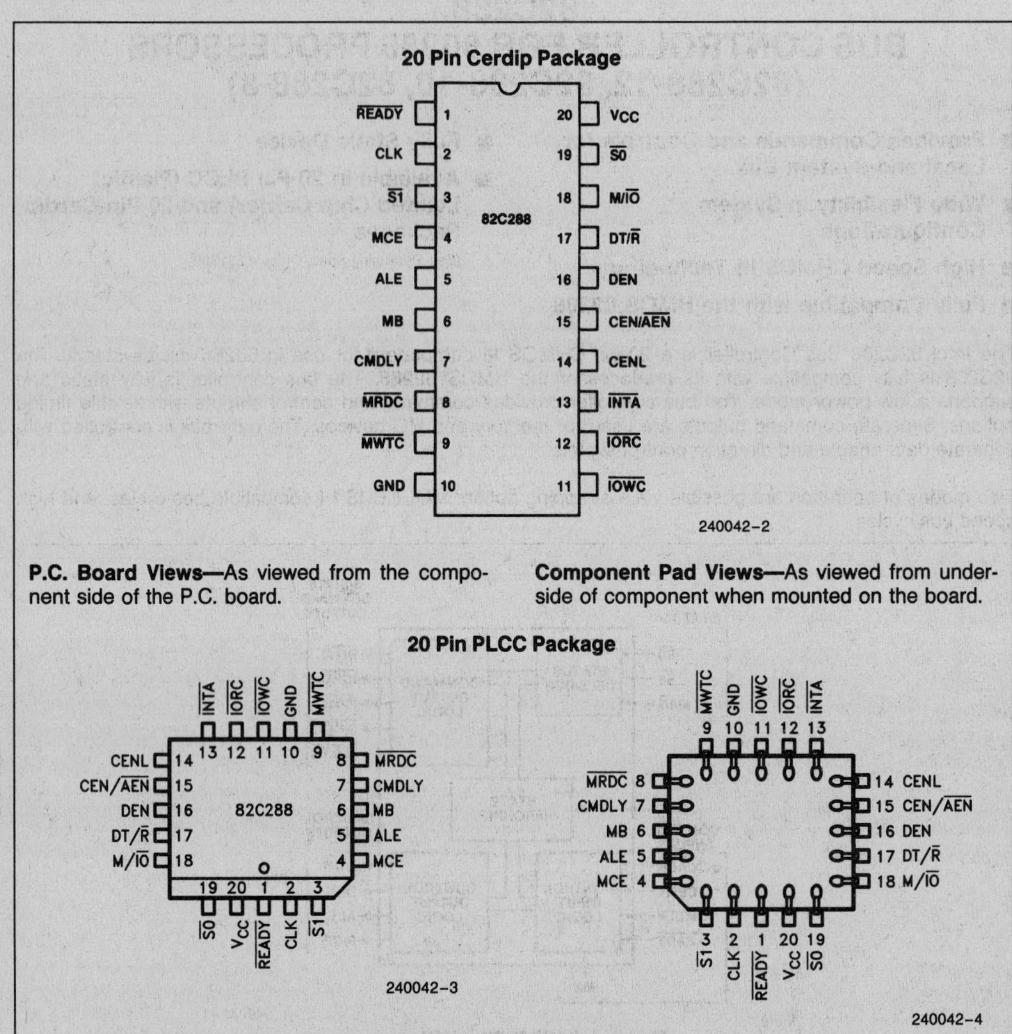

Figure 2. 82C288 Pin Configuration

Table 1. Pin Description

The following pin function descriptions are for the 82C288 bus controller.

<table>
<tr><th>Symbol</th><th>Type</th><th colspan="4">Name and Function</th></tr>
<tr><td>CLK</td><td>I</td><td colspan="4">SYSTEM CLOCK provides the basic timing control for the 82C288 in an 80286 microsystem. Its frequency is twice the internal processor clock frequency. The falling edge of this input signal establishes when inputs are sampled and command and control outputs change.</td></tr>
<tr><td rowspan="12">$\overline{S0}$, $\overline{S1}$</td><td rowspan="12">I</td><td colspan="4">BUS CYCLE STATUS starts a bus cycle and, along with M/$\overline{IO}$, defines the type of bus cycle. These inputs are active LOW. A bus cycle is started when either $\overline{S1}$ or $\overline{S0}$ is sampled LOW at the falling edge of CLK. Setup and hold times must be met for proper operation.</td></tr>
<tr><td colspan="4">80286 Bus Cycle Status Definition</td></tr>
<tr><td>M/$\overline{IO}$</td><td>$\overline{S1}$</td><td>$\overline{S0}$</td><td>Type of Bus Cycle</td></tr>
<tr><td>0</td><td>0</td><td>0</td><td>Interrupt Acknowledge</td></tr>
<tr><td>0</td><td>0</td><td>1</td><td>I/O Read</td></tr>
<tr><td>0</td><td>1</td><td>0</td><td>I/O Write</td></tr>
<tr><td>0</td><td>1</td><td>1</td><td>None; Idle</td></tr>
<tr><td>1</td><td>0</td><td>0</td><td>Halt or Shutdown</td></tr>
<tr><td>1</td><td>0</td><td>1</td><td>Memory Read</td></tr>
<tr><td>1</td><td>1</td><td>0</td><td>Memory Write</td></tr>
<tr><td>1</td><td>1</td><td>1</td><td>None; Idle</td></tr>
<tr><td colspan="4"></td></tr>
<tr><td>M/$\overline{IO}$</td><td>I</td><td colspan="4">MEMORY OR I/O SELECT determines whether the current bus cycle is in the memory space or I/O space. When LOW, the current bus cycle is in the I/O space. Setup and hold times must be met for proper operation.</td></tr>
<tr><td>MB</td><td>I</td><td colspan="4">MULTIBUS MODE SELECT determines timing of the command and control outputs. When HIGH, the bus controller operates with MULTIBUS I compatible timings. When LOW, the bus controller optimizes the command and control output timing for short bus cycles. The function of the CEN/$\overline{AEN}$ input pin is selected by this signal. This input is typically a strapping option and not dynamically changed.</td></tr>
<tr><td>CENL</td><td>I</td><td colspan="4">COMMAND ENABLE LATCHED is a bus controller select signal which enables the bus controller to respond to the current bus cycle being initiated. CENL is an active HIGH input latched internally at the end of each T_S cycle. CENL is used to select the appropriate bus controller for each bus cycle in a system where the CPU has more than one bus it can use. This input may be connected to V_{CC} to select this 82C288 for all transfers. No control inputs affect CENL. Setup and hold times must be met for proper operation.</td></tr>
<tr><td>CMDLY</td><td>I</td><td colspan="4">COMMAND DELAY allows delaying the start of a command. CMDLY is an active HIGH input. If sampled HIGH, the command output is not activated and CMDLY is again sampled at the next CLK cycle. When sampled LOW the selected command is enabled. If $\overline{READY}$ is detected LOW before the command output is activated, the 82C288 will terminate the bus cycle, even if no command was issued. Setup and hold times must be satisfied for proper operation. This input may be connected to GND if no delays are required before starting a command. This input has no effect on 82C288 control outputs.</td></tr>
<tr><td>$\overline{READY}$</td><td>I</td><td colspan="4">READY indicates the end of the current bus cycle. $\overline{READY}$ is an active LOW input. MULTIBUS I mode requires at least one wait state to allow the command outputs to become active. $\overline{READY}$ must be LOW during reset, to force the 82C288 into the idle state. Setup and hold times must be met for proper operation. The 82C284 drives $\overline{READY}$ LOW during RESET.</td></tr>
</table>

Table 1. Pin Description (Continued)

Symbol	Type	Name and Function
CEN/$\overline{\text{AEN}}$	I	**COMMAND ENABLE/ADDRESS ENABLE** controls the command and DEN outputs of the bus controller. CEN/$\overline{\text{AEN}}$ inputs may be asynchronous to CLK. Setup and hold times are given to assure a guaranteed response to synchronous inputs. This input may be connected to V_{CC} or GND. When MB is HIGH this pin has the $\overline{\text{AEN}}$ function. $\overline{\text{AEN}}$ is an active LOW input which indicates that the CPU has been granted use of a shared bus and the bus contoller command outputs may exit 3-state OFF and become inactive (HIGH). $\overline{\text{AEN}}$ HIGH indicates that the CPU does not have control of the shared bus and forces the command outputs into 3-state OFF and DEN inactive (LOW). When MB is LOW this pin has the CEN function. CEN is an unlatched active HIGH input which allows the bus controller to activate its command and DEN outputs. With MB LOW, CEN LOW forces the command and DEN outputs inactive but does not tristate them.
ALE	O	**ADDRESS LATCH ENABLE** controls the address latches used to hold an address stable during a bus cycle. This control output is active HIGH. ALE will not be issued for the halt bus cycle and is not affected by any of the control inputs.
MCE	O	**MASTER CASCADE ENABLE** signals that a cascade address from a master 8259A interrupt controller may be placed onto the CPU address bus for latching by the address latches under ALE control. The CPU's address bus may then be used to broadcast the cascade address to slave interrupt controllers so only one of them will respond to the interrupt acknowledge cycle. This control output is active HIGH. MCE is only active during interrupt acknowledge cycles and is not affected by any control input. Using MCE to enable cascade address drivers requires latches which save the cascade address on the falling edge of ALE.
DEN	O	**DATA ENABLE** controls when data transceivers connected to the local data bus should be enabled. DEN is an active HIGH control output. DEN is delayed for write cycles in the MULTIBUS I mode.
DT/$\overline{\text{R}}$	O	**DATA TRANSMIT/RECEIVE** establishes the direction of data flow to or from the local data bus. When HIGH, this control output indicates that a write bus cycle is being performed. A LOW indicates a read bus cycle. DEN is always inactive when DT/$\overline{\text{R}}$ changes states. This output is HIGH when no bus cycle is active. DT/$\overline{\text{R}}$ is not affected by any of the control inputs.
$\overline{\text{IOWC}}$	O	**I/O WRITE COMMAND** instructs an I/O device to read the data on the data bus. This command output is active LOW. The MB and CMDLY inputs control when this output becomes active. $\overline{\text{READY}}$ controls when it becomes inactive.
$\overline{\text{IORC}}$	O	**I/O READ COMMAND** instructs an I/O device to place data onto the data bus. This command output is active LOW. The MB and CMDLY inputs control when this output becomes active. $\overline{\text{READY}}$ controls when it becomes inactive.
$\overline{\text{MWTC}}$	O	**MEMORY WRITE COMMAND** instructs a memory device to read the data on the data bus. This command output is active LOW. The MB and CMDLY inputs control when this output becomes active. $\overline{\text{READY}}$ controls when it becomes inactive.
$\overline{\text{MRDC}}$	O	**MEMORY READ COMMAND** instructs the memory device to place data onto the data bus. This command output is active LOW. The MB and CMDLY inputs control when this output becomes active. $\overline{\text{READY}}$ controls when it becomes inactive.

Table 1. Pin Description (Continued)

Symbol	Type	Name and Function
$\overline{\text{INTA}}$	O	**INTERRUPT ACKNOWLEDGE** tells an interrupting device that its interrupt request is being acknowledged. This command output is active LOW. The MB and CMDLY inputs control when this output becomes active. $\overline{\text{READY}}$ controls when it becomes inactive.
V_{CC}		**System Power:** +5V Power Supply
GND		**System Ground:** 0V

Table 2. Command and Control Outputs for Each Type of Bus Cycle

Type of Bus Cycle	M/$\overline{\text{IO}}$	$\overline{\text{S1}}$	$\overline{\text{S0}}$	Command Activated	DT/$\overline{\text{R}}$ State	ALE, DEN Issued?	MCE Issued?
Interrupt Acknowledge	0	0	0	$\overline{\text{INTA}}$	LOW	YES	YES
I/O Read	0	0	1	$\overline{\text{IORC}}$	LOW	YES	NO
I/O Write	0	1	0	$\overline{\text{IOWC}}$	HIGH	YES	NO
None; Idle	0	1	1	None	HIGH	NO	NO
Halt/Shutdown	1	0	0	None	HIGH	NO	NO
Memory Read	1	0	1	$\overline{\text{MRDC}}$	LOW	YES	NO
Memory Write	1	1	0	$\overline{\text{MWTC}}$	HIGH	YES	NO
None; Idle	1	1	1	None	HIGH	NO	NO

Operating Modes

Two types of buses are supported by the 82C288: MULTIBUS I and non-MULTIBUS I. When the MB input is strapped HIGH, MULTIBUS I timing is used. In MULTIBUS I mode, the 82C288 delays command and data activation to meet IEEE-796 requirements on address to command active and write data to command active setup timing. MULTIBUS I mode requires at least one wait state in the bus cycle since the command outputs are delayed. The non-MULTIBUS I mode does not delay any outputs and does not require wait states. The MB input affects the timing of the command and DEN outputs.

Command and Control Outputs

The type of bus cycle performed by the local bus master is encoded in the M/$\overline{\text{IO}}$, $\overline{\text{S1}}$, and $\overline{\text{S0}}$ inputs. Different command and control outputs are activated depending on the type of bus cycle. Table 2 indicates the cycle decode done by the 82C288 and the effect on command, DT/$\overline{\text{R}}$, ALE, DEN, and MCE outputs.

Bus cycles come in three forms: read, write, and halt. Read bus cycles include memory read, I/O read, and interrupt acknowledge. The timing of the associated read command outputs ($\overline{\text{MRDC}}$, $\overline{\text{IORC}}$, and $\overline{\text{INTA}}$), control outputs (ALE, DEN, DT/$\overline{\text{R}}$) and control inputs (CEN/$\overline{\text{AEN}}$, CENL, CMDLY, MB, and $\overline{\text{READY}}$) are identical for all read bus cycles. Read cycles differ only in which command output is activated. The MCE control output is only asserted during interrupt acknowledge cycles.

Write bus cycles activate different control and command outputs with different timing than read bus cycles. Memory write and I/O write are write bus cycles whose timing for command outputs ($\overline{\text{MWTC}}$ and $\overline{\text{IOWC}}$), control outputs (ALE, DEN, DT/$\overline{\text{R}}$) and control inputs (CEN/$\overline{\text{AEN}}$, CENL, CMDLY, MB, and $\overline{\text{READY}}$) are identical. They differ only in which command output is activated.

Halt bus cycles are different because no command or control output is activated. All control inputs are ignored until the next bus cycle is started via $\overline{\text{S1}}$ and $\overline{\text{S0}}$.

Static Operation

All 82C288 circuitry is of static design. Internal registers and logic are static and require no refresh as with dynamic circuit design. This eliminates the minimum operating frequency restriction placed on the HMOS 82288. The CHMOS III 82C288 can operate from DC to the appropriate upper frequency limit.

5

The clock may be stopped in either state (HIGH/LOW) and held there indefinitely.

Power dissipation is directly related to operating frequency. As the system frequency is reduced, so is the operating power. When the clock is stopped to the 82C288, power dissipation is at a minimum. This is useful for low-power and portable applications.

FUNCTIONAL DESCRIPTION

Introduction

The 82C288 bus controller is used in 80286 systems to provide address latch control, data transceiver control, and standard level-type command outputs. The command outputs are timed and have sufficient drive capabilities for large TTL buses and meet all IEEE-796 requirements for MULTIBUS I. A special MULTIBUS I mode is provided to satisfy all address/data setup and hold time requirements. Command timing may be tailored to special needs via a CMDLY input to determine the start of a command and $\overline{\text{READY}}$ to determine the end of a command.

Connection to multiple buses are supported with a latched enable input (CENL). An address decoder can determine which, if any, bus controller should be enabled for the bus cycle. This input is latched to allow an address decoder to take full advantage of the pipelined timing on the 80286 local bus.

Buses shared by several bus controllers are supported. An $\overline{\text{AEN}}$ input prevents the bus controller from driving the shared bus command and data signals except when enabled by an external MULTIBUS I type bus arbiter.

Separate DEN and DT/$\overline{\text{R}}$ outputs control the data transceivers for all buses. Bus contention is eliminated by disabling DEN before changing DT/$\overline{\text{R}}$. The DEN timing allows sufficient time for tristate bus drivers to enter 3-state OFF before enabling other drivers onto the same bus.

The term CPU refers to any 80286 processor or 80286 support component which may become an 80286 local bus master and thereby drive the 82C288 status inputs.

Processor Cycle Definition

Any CPU which drives the local bus uses an internal clock which is one half the frequency of the system clock (CLK) (see Figure 3). Knowledge of the phase of the local bus master internal clock is required for proper operation of the 80286 local bus. The local bus master informs the bus controller of its internal clock phase when it asserts the status signals. Status signals are always asserted beginning in Phase 1 of the local bus master's internal clock.

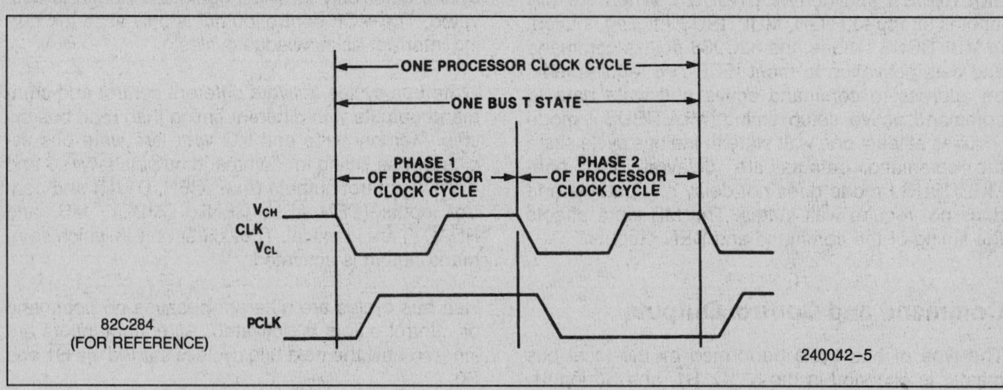

Figure 3. CLK Relationship to the Processor Clock and Bus T-States

Bus State Definition

The 82C288 bus controller has three bus states (see Figure 4): Idle (T_I) Status (T_S) and Command (T_C). Each bus state is two CLK cycles long. Bus state phases correspond to the internal CPU processor clock phases.

The T_I bus state occurs when no bus cycle is currently active on the 80286 local bus. This state may be repeated indefinitely. When control of the local bus is being passed between masters, the bus remains in the T_I state.

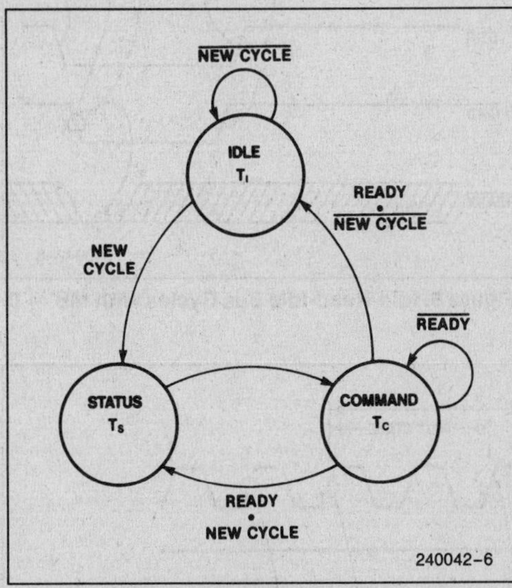

Figure 4. 82C288 Bus States

Bus Cycle Definition

The $\overline{S1}$ and $\overline{S0}$ inputs signal the start of a bus cycle. When either input becomes LOW, a bus cycle is started. The T_S bus state is defined to be the two CLK cycles during which either $\overline{S1}$ or $\overline{S0}$ are active (see Figure 5). These inputs are sampled by the 82C288 at every falling edge of CLK. When either $\overline{S1}$ or $\overline{S0}$ are sampled LOW, the next CLK cycle is considered the second phase of the internal CPU clock cycle.

The local bus enters the T_C bus state after the T_S state. The shortest bus cycle may have one T_S state and one T_C state. Longer bus cycles are formed by repeating T_C state. A repeated T_C bus state is called a wait state.

The $\overline{READY}$ input determines whether the current T_C bus state is to be repeated. The $\overline{READY}$ input has the same timing and effect for all bus cycles. $\overline{READY}$ is sampled at the end of each T_C bus state to see if it is active. If sampled HIGH, the T_C bus state is repeated. This is called inserting a wait state. The control and command outputs do not change during wait states.

When $\overline{READY}$ is sampled LOW, the current bus cycle is terminated. Note that the bus controller may enter the T_S bus state directly from T_C if the status lines are sampled active at the next falling edge of CLK.

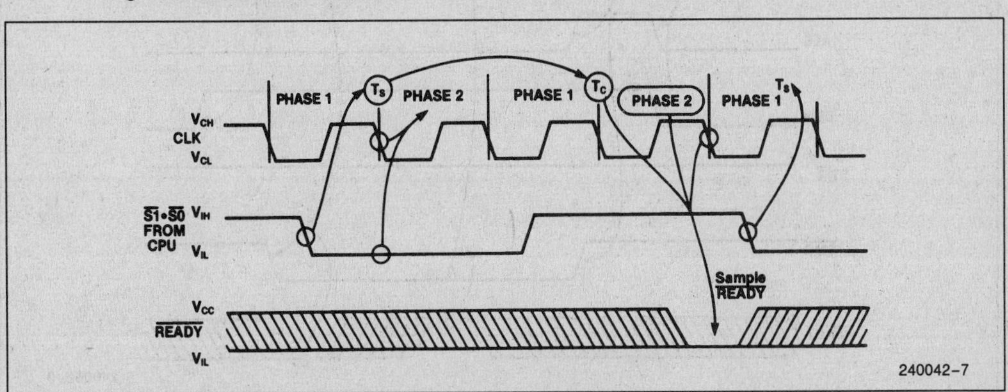

Figure 5. Bus Cycle Definition

Figures 6 through 10 show the basic command and control output timing for read and write bus cycles. Halt bus cycles are not shown since they activate no outputs. The basic idle-read-idle and idle-write-idle bus cycles are shown. The signal label CMD represents the appropriate command output for the bus cycle. For Figures 6 through 10, the CMDLY input is connected to GND and CENL to V_{CC}. The effects of CENL and CMDLY are described later in the section on control inputs.

Figures 6, 7 and 8 show non-MULTIBUS I cycles. MB is connected to GND while CEN is connected to V_{CC}. Figure 6 shows a read cycle with no wait states while Figure 7 shows a write cycle with one wait state. The $\overline{READY}$ input is shown to illustrate how wait states are added.

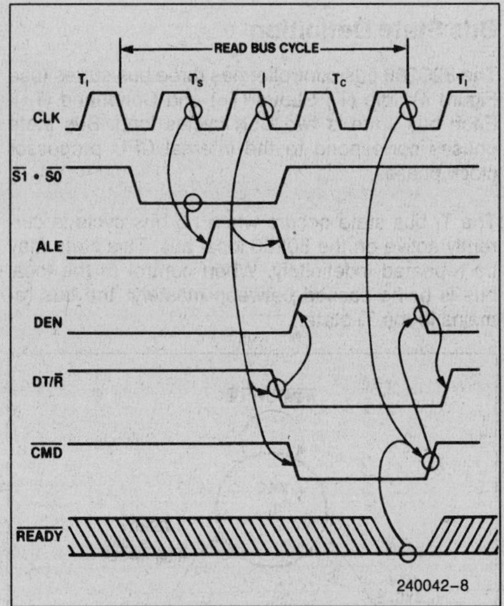

Figure 6. Idle-Read-Idle Bus Cycles with MB = 0

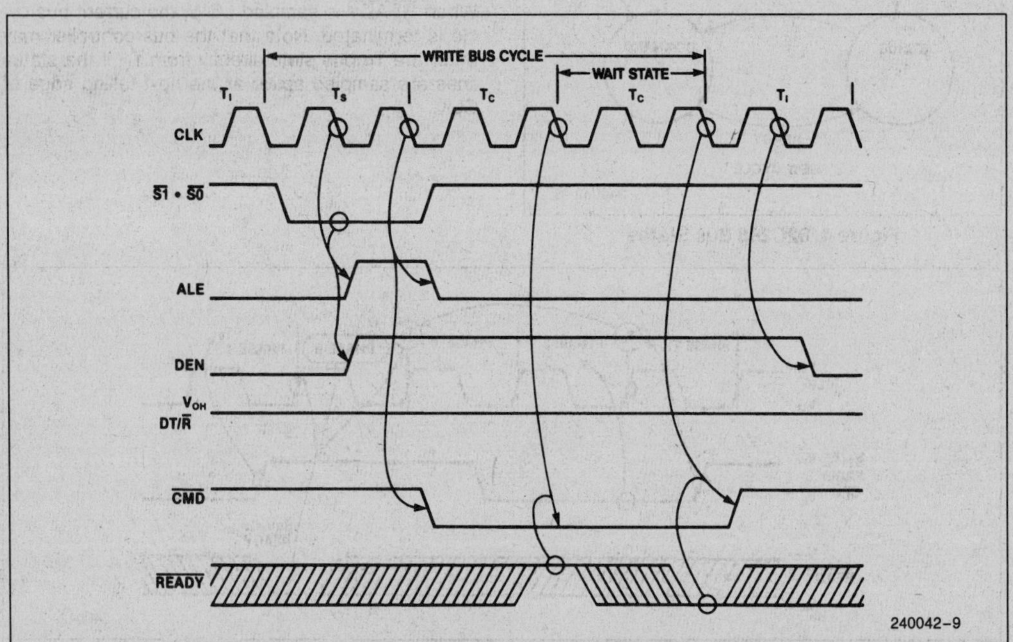

Figure 7. Idle-Write-Idle Bus Cycles with MB = 0

Bus cycles can occur back to back with no T_I bus states between T_C and T_S. Back to back cycles do not affect the timing of the command and control outputs. Command and control outputs always reach the states shown for the same clock edge (within T_S, T_C or following bus state) of a bus cycle.

A special case in control timing occurs for back to back write cycles with MB = 0. In this case, DT/$\overline{R}$ and DEN remain HIGH between the bus cycles (see Figure 8). The command and ALE output timing does not change.

Figures 9 and 10 show a MULTIBUS I cycle with MB = 1. $\overline{AEN}$ and CMDLY are connected to GND. The effects of CMDLY and $\overline{AEN}$ are described later in the section on control inputs. Figure 9 shows a read cycle with one wait state and Figure 10 shows a write cycle with two wait states. The second wait state of the write cycle is shown only for example purposes and is not required. The $\overline{READY}$ input is shown to illustrate how wait states are added.

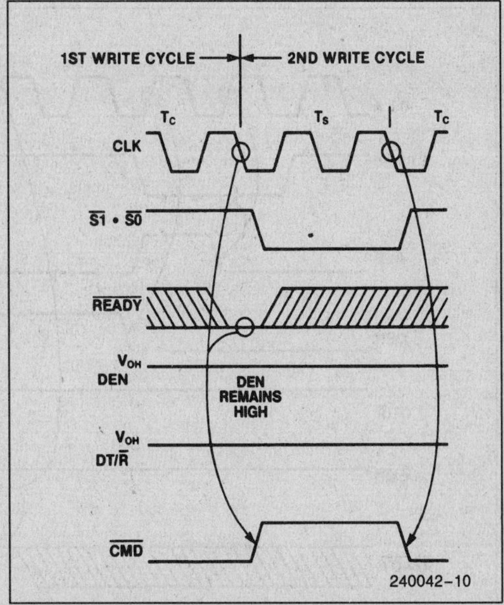

Figure 8. Write-Write Bus Cycles with MB = 0

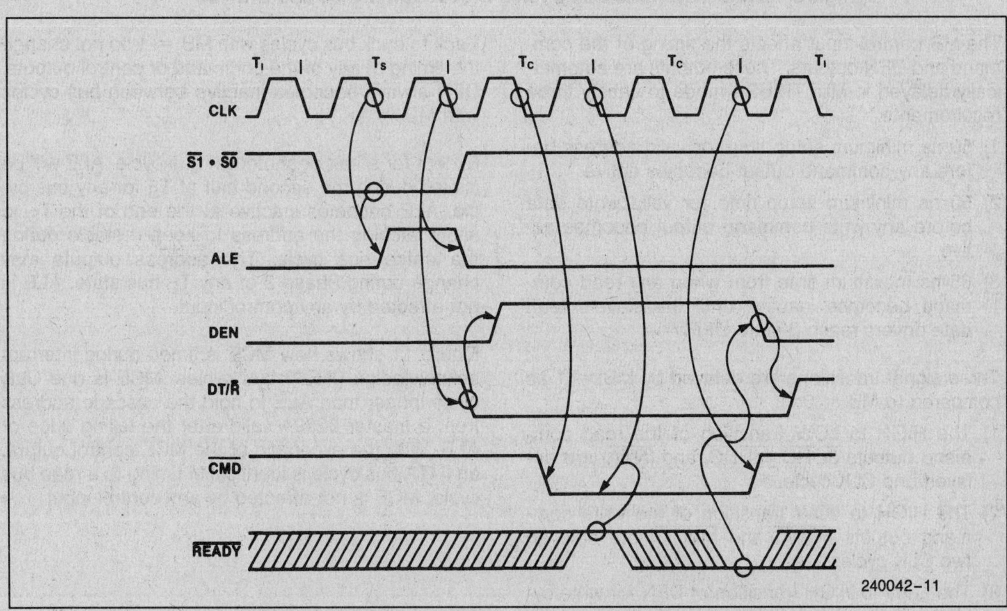

Figure 9. Idle-Read-Idle Bus Cycles with 1 Wait State and with MB = 1

5

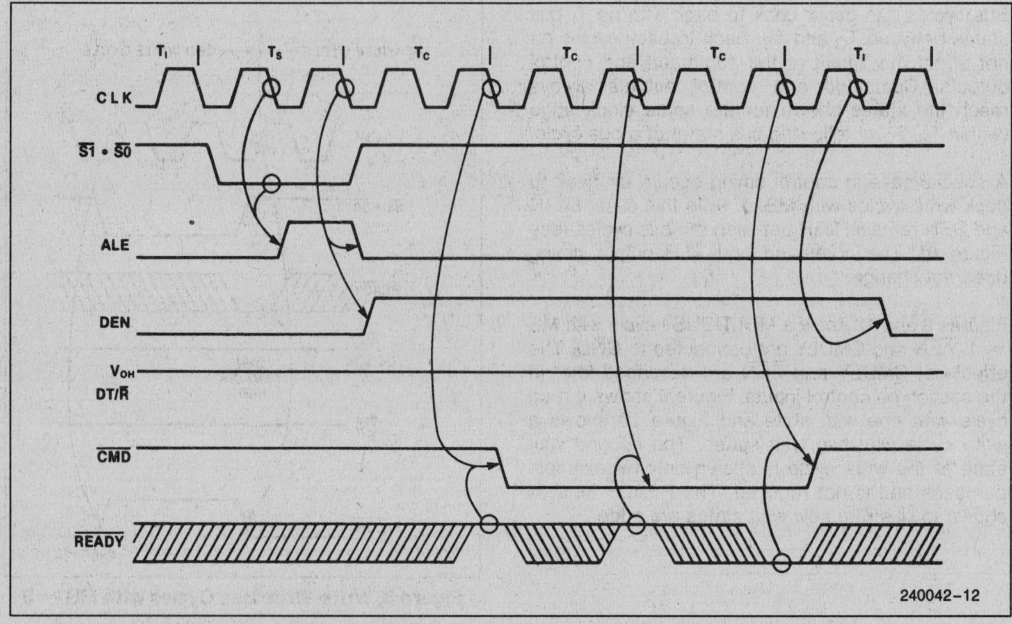

Figure 10. Idle-Write-Idle Bus Cycles with 2 Wait States and with MB = 1

The MB control input affects the timing of the command and DEN outputs. These outputs are automatically delayed in MULTIBUS I mode to satisfy three requirements:

1) 50 ns minimum setup time for valid address before any command output becomes active.
2) 50 ns minimum setup time for valid write data before any write command output becomes active.
3) 65 ns maximum time from when any read command becomes inactive until the slave's read data drivers reach 3-state OFF.

Three signal transitions are delayed by MB = 1 as compared to MB = 0:

1) The HIGH to LOW transition of the read command outputs ($\overline{IORC}$, $\overline{MRDC}$, and $\overline{INTA}$) are delayed one CLK cycle.
2) The HIGH to LOW transition of the write command outputs ($\overline{IOWC}$ and $\overline{MWTC}$) are delayed two CLK cycles.
3) The LOW to HIGH transition of DEN for write cycles is delayed one CLK cycle.

Back to back bus cycles with MB = 1 do not change the timing of any of the command or control outputs. DEN always becomes inactive between bus cycles with MB = 1.

Except for a halt or shutdown bus cycle, ALE will be issued during the second half of T_S for any bus cycle. ALE becomes inactive at the end of the T_S to allow latching the address to keep it stable during the entire bus cycle. The address outputs may change during Phase 2 of any T_C bus state. ALE is not affected by any control input.

Figure 11 shows how MCE is timed during interrupt acknowledlge (INTA) bus cycles. MCE is one CLK cycle longer than ALE to hold the cascade address from a master 8259A valid after the falling edge of ALE. With the exception of the MCE control output, an INTA bus cycle is identical in timing to a read bus cycle. MCE is not affected by any control input.

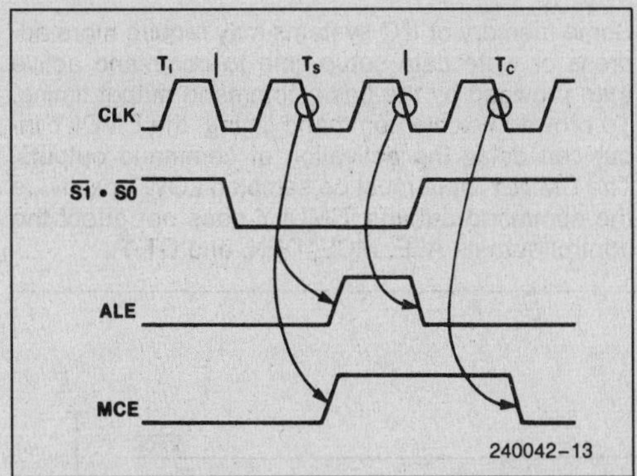

Figure 11. MCE Operation for an INTA Bus Cycle

Control Inputs

The control intputs can alter the basic timing of command outputs, allow interfacing to multiple buses, and share a bus between different masters. For many 80286 systems, each CPU will have more than one bus which may be used to perform a bus cycle. Normally, a CPU will only have one bus controller active for each bus cycle. Some buses may be shared by more than one CPU (i.e. MULTIBUS) requiring only one of them use the bus at a time.

Systems with multiple and shared buses use two control input signals of the 82C288 bus controller, CENL and $\overline{AEN}$ (see Figure 12). CENL enables the bus controller to control the current bus cycle. The $\overline{AEN}$ input prevents a bus controller from driving its command outputs. $\overline{AEN}$ HIGH means that another bus controller may be driving the shared bus.

In Figure 12, two buses are shown: a local bus and a MULTIBUS I. Only one bus is used for each CPU bus cycle. The CENL inputs of the bus controller select which bus controller is to perform the bus cycle. An address decoder determines which bus to use for each bus cycle. The 82C288 connected to the shared MULTIBUS I must be selected by CENL and be given access to the MULTIBUS I by $\overline{AEN}$ before it will begin a MULTIBUS I operation.

CENL must be sampled HIGH at the end of the T_S bus state (see waveforms) to enable the bus controller to activate its command and control outputs. If sampled LOW the commands and DEN will not go active and DT/$\overline{R}$ will remain HIGH. The bus controller will ignore the CMDLY, CEN, and $\overline{READY}$ inputs until another bus cycle is started via $\overline{S1}$ and $\overline{S0}$. Since an address decoder is commonly used to identify which bus is required for each bus cycle, CENL is latched to avoid the need for latching its input.

The CENL input can affect the DEN control output. When MB = 0, DEN normally becomes active during Phase 2 of T_S in write bus cycles. This transition occurs before CENL is sampled. If CENL is sampled LOW, the DEN output will be forced LOW during T_C as shown in the timing waveforms.

When MB = 1, CEN/$\overline{AEN}$ becomes $\overline{AEN}$. $\overline{AEN}$ controls when the bus controller command outputs enter and exit 3-state OFF. $\overline{AEN}$ is intended to be driven by a MULTIBUS I type bus arbiter, which assures only one bus controller is driving the shared bus at any time. When $\overline{AEN}$ makes a LOW to HIGH transition, the command outputs immediately enter 3-state OFF and DEN is forced inactive. An inactive DEN should force the local data transceivers connected to the shared data bus into 3-state OFF (see Figure 12). The LOW to HIGH transition of $\overline{AEN}$ should only occur during T_I or T_S bus states.

The HIGH to LOW transition of $\overline{AEN}$ signals that the bus controller may now drive the shared bus command signals. Since a bus cycle may be active or be in the process of starting, $\overline{AEN}$ can become active during any T-state. $\overline{AEN}$ LOW immediately allows DEN to go to the appropriate state. Three CLK edges later, the command outputs will go active (see timing waveforms). The MULTIBUS I requires this delay for the address and data to be valid on the bus before the command becomes active.

When MB = 0, CEN/$\overline{AEN}$ becomes CEN. CEN is an asynchronous input which immediately affects the command and DEN outputs. When CEN makes a HIGH to LOW transition, the commands and DEN are immediately forced inactive. When CEN makes a LOW to HIGH transition, the commands and DEN outputs immediately go to the appropriate state (see timing waveforms). $\overline{\text{READY}}$ must still become active to terminate a bus cycle if CEN remains LOW for a selected bus controller (CENL was latched HIGH).

Some memory or I/O systems may require more address or write data setup time to command active than provided by the basic command output timing. To provide flexible command timing, the CMDLY input can delay the activation of command outputs. The CMDLY input must be sampled LOW to activate the command outputs. CMDLY does not affect the control outputs ALE, MCE, DEN, and DT/$\overline{\text{R}}$.

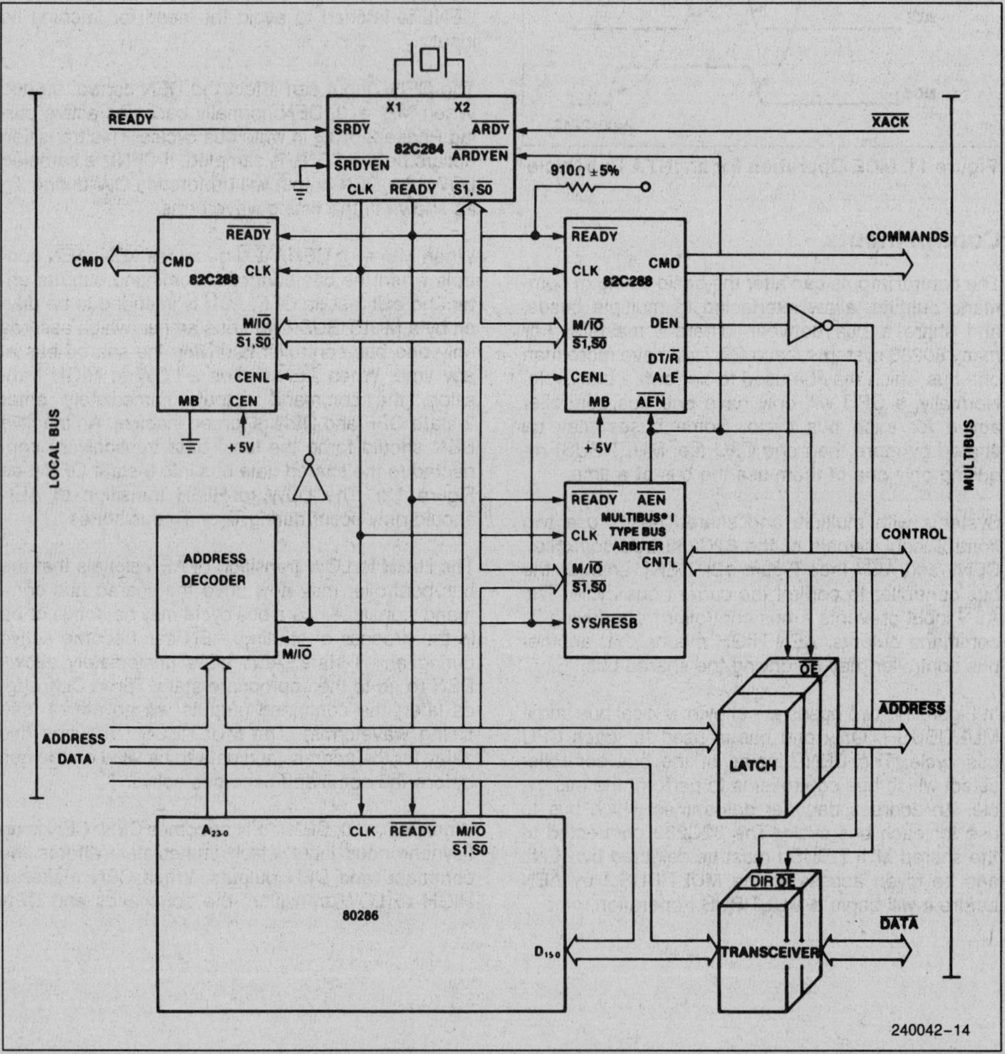

240042–14

Figure 12. System Use of $\overline{\text{AEN}}$ and CENL

CMDLY is first sampled on the falling edge of the CLK ending T_S. If sampled HIGH, the command output is not activated, and CMDLY is again sampled on the next falling edge of CLK. Once sampled LOW, the proper command output becomes active immediately if MB = 0. If MB = 1, the proper command goes active no earlier than shown in Figures 9 and 10.

$\overline{READY}$ can terminate a bus cycle before CMDLY allows a command to be issued. In this case no commands are issued an the bus controller will deactivate DEN and DT/$\overline{R}$ in the same manner as if a command had been issued.

Waveforms Discussion

The waveforms show the timing relationships of inputs and outputs and do not show all possible transitions of all signals in all modes. Instead, all signal timing relationships are shown via the general cases. Special cases are shown when needed. The waveforms provide some functional descriptions of the 82C288; however, most functional descriptions are provided in Figures 5 through 11.

To find the timing specification for a signal transition in a particular mode, first look for a special case in the waveforms. If no special case applies, then use a timing specification for the same or related function in another mode.

5

ABSOLUTE MAXIMUM RATINGS*

Ambient Temperature Under Bias 0°C to +70°C
Storage Temperature −65°C to +150°C
Voltage on Any Pin with Respect to GND −0.5V to +7V
Power Dissipation 1 Watt

NOTICE: This is a production data sheet. The specifications are subject to change without notice.

**WARNING: Stressing the device beyond the "Absolute Maximum Ratings" may cause permanent damage. These are stress ratings only. Operation beyond the "Operating Conditions" is not recommended and extended exposure beyond the "Operating Conditions" may affect device reliability.*

D.C. CHARACTERISTICS V_{CC} = 5V ±5%, T_{CASE} = 0°C to 85°C*

Symbol	Parameter	Min	Max	Units	Test Conditions
V_{IL}	Input LOW Voltage	−0.5	0.8	V	
V_{IH}	Input HIGH Voltage	2.0	V_{CC} + 0.5	V	
V_{ILC}	CLK Input LOW Voltage	−0.5	0.6	V	
V_{IHC}	CLK Input HIGH Voltage	3.8	V_{CC} + 0.5	V	
V_{OL}	Output LOW Voltage Command Outputs Control Outputs		 0.45 0.45	 V V	 I_{OL} = 32 mA (Note 1) I_{OL} = 16 mA (Note 2)
V_{OH}	Output HIGH Voltage Command Outputs Control Outputs 	 2.4 V_{CC} − 0.5 2.4 V_{CC} − 0.5		 V V V V	 I_{OH} = −5 mA (Note 1) I_{OH} = −1 mA (Note 1) I_{OH} = −1 mA (Note 2) I_{OH} = −0.2 mA (Note 2)
I_{IL}	Input Leakage Current		±10	μA	0V ≤ V_{IN} ≤ V_{CC}
I_{LO}	Output Leakage Current		±10	μA	0.45V ≤ V_{OUT} ≤ V_{CC}
I_{CC}	Power Supply Current		75	mA	
I_{CC_S}	Power Supply Current (Static)		3	mA	(Note 3)
C_{CLK}	CLK Input Capacitance		12	pF	F_C = 1 MHz
C_I	Input Capacitance		10	pF	F_C = 1 MHz
C_O	Input/Output Capacitance		20	pF	F_C = 1 MHz

*T_A is guaranteed from 0°C to +70°C as long as T_{CASE} is not exceeded.

NOTES:
1. Command Outputs are $\overline{INTA}$, $\overline{IORC}$, $\overline{IOWC}$, $\overline{MRDC}$ and $\overline{MWRC}$.
2. Control Outputs are DT/$\overline{R}$, DEN, ALE and MCE.
3. Tested while outputs are unloaded, and inputs at V_{CC} or V_{SS}.

A.C. CHARACTERISTICS

V_{CC} = 5V, ±5%, T_{CASE} = 0°C to +85°C.* AC timings are referenced to 0.8V and 2.0V points of signals as illustrated in data sheet waveforms, unless otherwise noted.

Symbol	Parameter	8 MHz		10 MHz		12.5 MHz		Unit	Test Condition
		-8 Min	-8 Max	-10 Min	-10 Max	-12 Min	-12 Max		
1	CLK Period	62	250	50	250	40	250	ns	
2	CLK HIGH Time	20		16		13		ns	at 3.6V
3	CLK LOW Time	15		12		11		ns	at 1.0V
4	CLK Rise Time		10		8		8	ns	1.0V to 3.6V
5	CLK Fall Time		10		8		8	ns	3.6V to 1.0V
6	M/$\overline{IO}$ and Status Setup Time	22		18		15		ns	
7	M/$\overline{IO}$ and Status Hold Time	1		1		1		ns	
8	CENL Setup Time	20		15		15		ns	
9	CENL Hold Time	1		1		1		ns	
10	$\overline{READY}$ Setup Time	38		26		18		ns	
11	$\overline{READY}$ Hold Time	25		25		20		ns	
12	CMDLY Setup Time	20		15		15		ns	
13	CMDLY Hold Time	1		1		1		ns	
14	$\overline{AEN}$ Setup Time	20		15		15		ns	(Note 3)
15	$\overline{AEN}$ Hold Time	0		0		0		ns	(Note 3)
16	ALE, MCE Active Delay from CLK	3	20	3	16	3	16	ns	(Note 4)
17	ALE, MCE Inactive Delay from CLK		25		19		19	ns	(Note 4)
18	DEN (Write) Inactive from CENL		35		23		23	ns	(Note 4)
19	DT/$\overline{R}$ LOW from CLK		25		23		23	ns	(Note 4)
20	DEN (Read) Active$\overline{R}$ from DT/	5	35	5	21	5	21	ns	(Note 4)
21	DEN (Read) Inactive Dly from CLK	3	35	3	21	3	19	ns	(Note 4)
22	DT/$\overline{R}$ HIGH from DEN Inactive	5	35	5	20	5	18	ns	(Note 4)
23	DEN (Write) Active Delay from CLK		30		23		23	ns	(Note 4)
24	DEN (Write) Inactive Dly from CLK	3	30	3	19	3	19	ns	(Note 4)

*T_A is guaranteed from 0°C to +70°C as long as T_{CASE} is not exceeded.

A.C. CHARACTERISTICS

V_{CC} = 5V, ±5%, T_{CASE} = 0°C to +85°C.* AC timings are referenced to 0.8V and 2.0V points of signals as illustrated in data sheet waveforms, unless otherwise noted. (Continued)

Symbol	Parameter	8 MHz		10 MHz		12.5 MHz		Unit	Test Condition
		-8 Min	-8 Max	-10 Min	-10 Max	-12 Min	-12 Max		
25	DEN Inactive from CEN		30		25		25	ns	(Note 4)
26	DEN Active from CEN		30		24		24	ns	(Note 4)
27	DT/$\overline{R}$ HIGH from CLK (when CEN = LOW)		35		25		25	ns	(Note 4)
28	DEN Active from $\overline{AEN}$		30		26		26	ns	(Note 4)
29	$\overline{CMD}$ Active Delay from CLK	3	25	3	21	3	21	ns	(Note 5)
30	$\overline{CMD}$ Inactive Delay from CLK	5	20	5	20	5	20	ns	(Note 5)
31	$\overline{CMD}$ Active from CEN		25		25		25	ns	(Note 5)
32	$\overline{CMD}$ Inactive from CEN		25		25		25	ns	(Note 5)
33	$\overline{CMD}$ Inactive Enable from $\overline{AEN}$		40		40		40	ns	(Note 5)
34	$\overline{CMD}$ Float Delay from $\overline{AEN}$		40		40		40	ns	(Note 6)
35	MB Setup Time	20		20		20		ns	
36	MB Hold Time	0		0		0		ns	
37	Command Inactive Enable from MB ↓		40		40		40	ns	(Note 5)
38	Command Float Time from MB ↑		40		40		40	ns	(Note 6)
39	DEN Inactive from MB ↑		30		26		26	ns	(Note 4)
40	DEN Active from MB ↓		30		30		30	ns	(Note 4)

*T_A is guaranteed from 0°C to +70°C as long as T_{CASE} is not exceeded.

NOTES:
3. $\overline{AEN}$ is an asynchronous input. This specification is for testing purposes only, to assure recognition at a specific CLK edge.
4. Control output load: Cl = 150 pF.
5. Command output load: Cl = 300 pF.
6. Float condition occurs when output current is less than I_{LO} in magnitude.

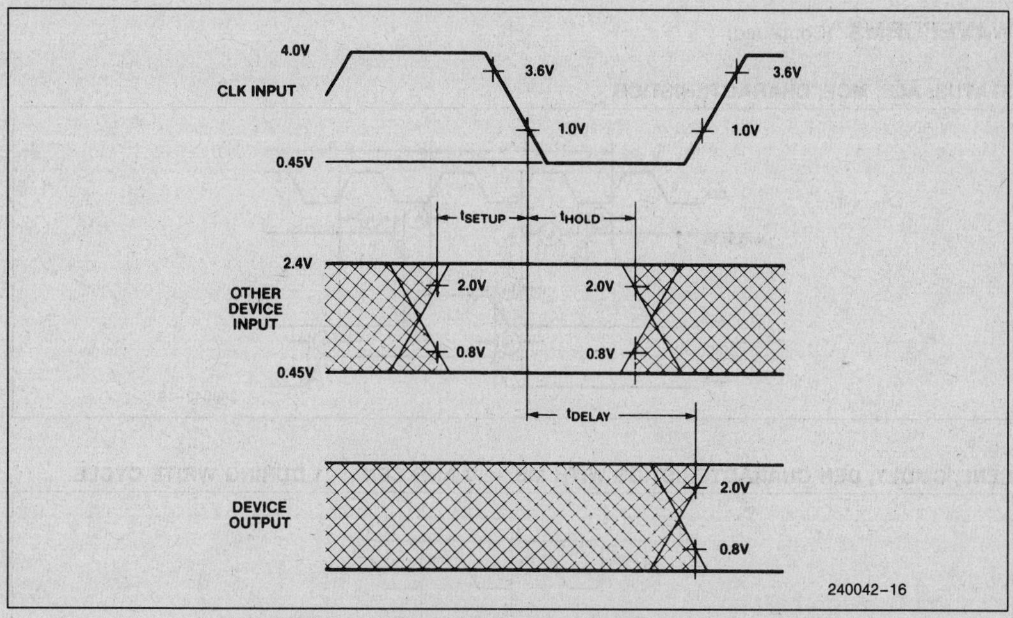

Note 7: AC Setup, Hold and Delay Time Measurement—General

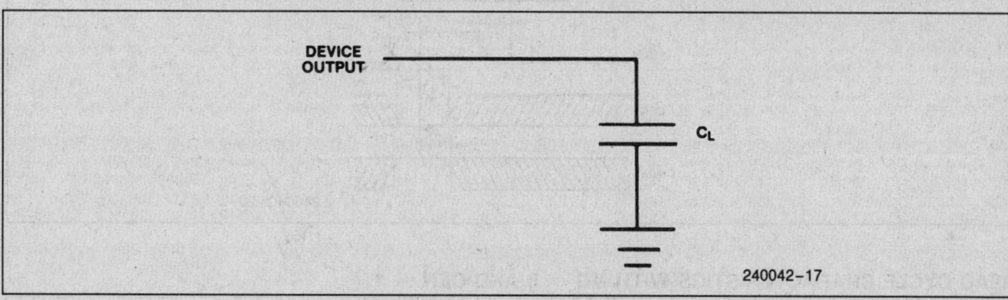

Note 8: AC Test Loading on Outputs

WAVEFORMS

CLK CHARACTERISTICS

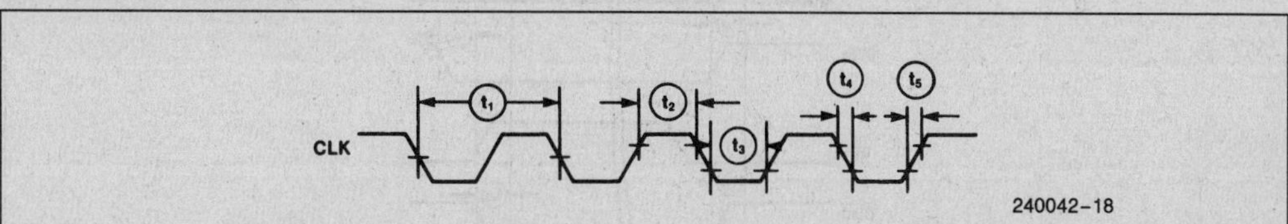

WAVEFORMS (Continued)

STATUS, ALE, MCE, CHARACTERISTICS

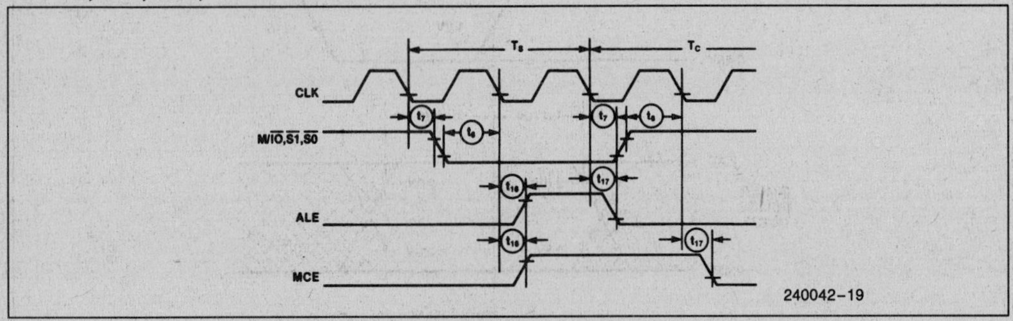

240042-19

CENL, CMDLY, DEN CHARACTERISTICS WITH MB = 0 AND CEN = 1 DURING WRITE CYCLE

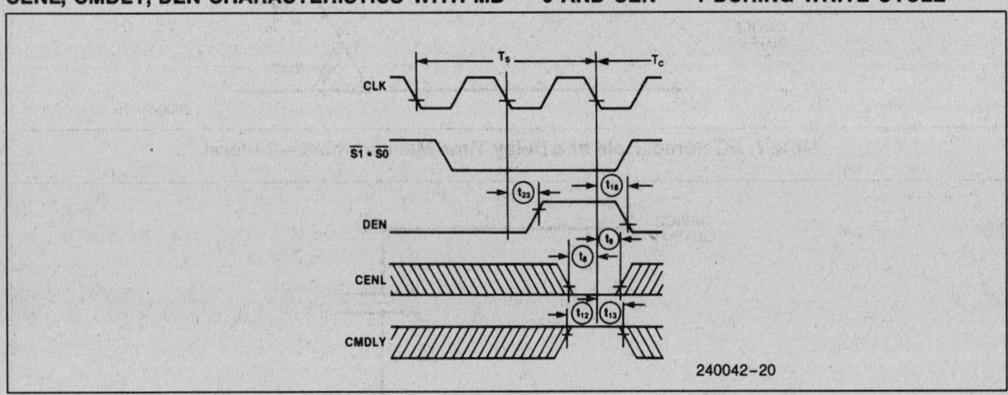

240042-20

READ CYCLE CHARACTERISTICS WITH MB = 0 AND CEN = 1

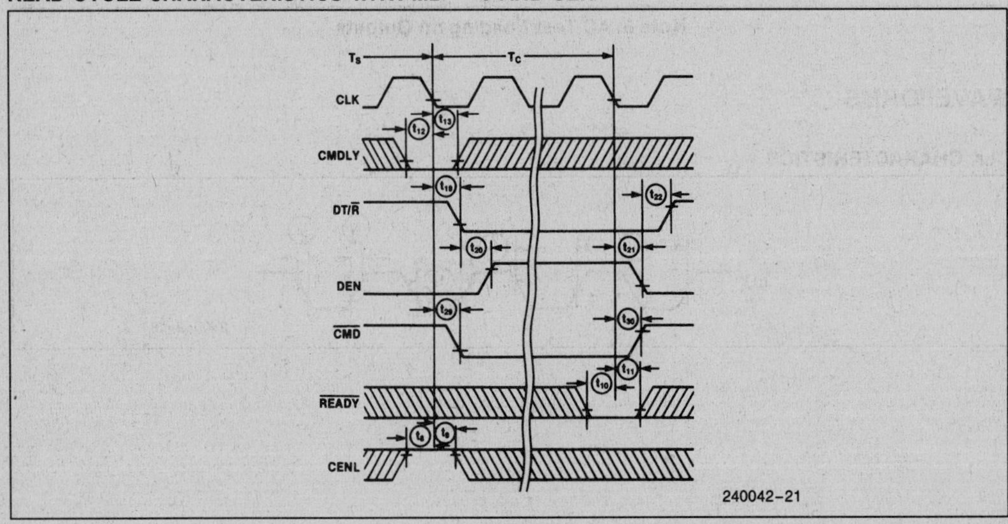

240042-21

WAVEFORMS (Continued)

WRITE CYCLE CHARACTERISTIC WITH MB = 0 AND CEN = 1

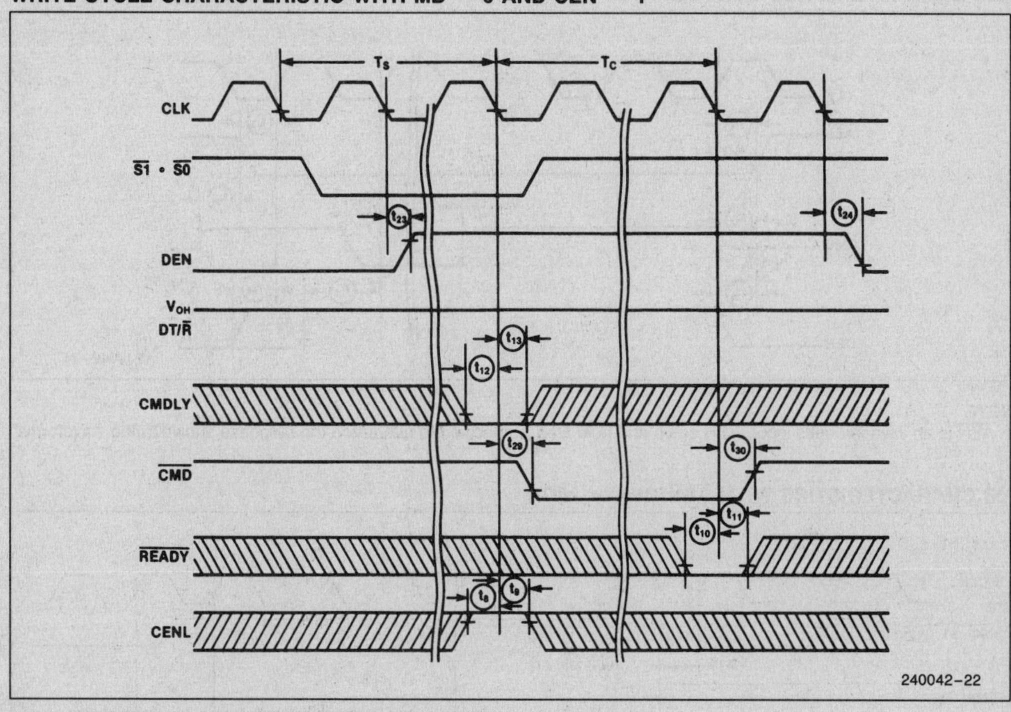

CEN CHARACTERISTICS WITH MB = 0

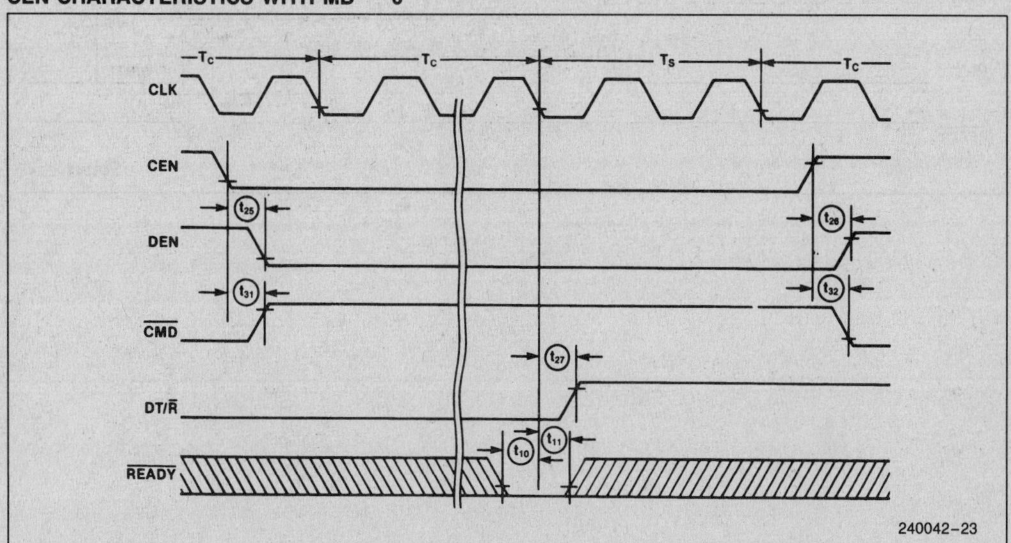

WAVEFORMS (Continued)

$\overline{AEN}$ CHARACTERISTICS WITH MB = 1

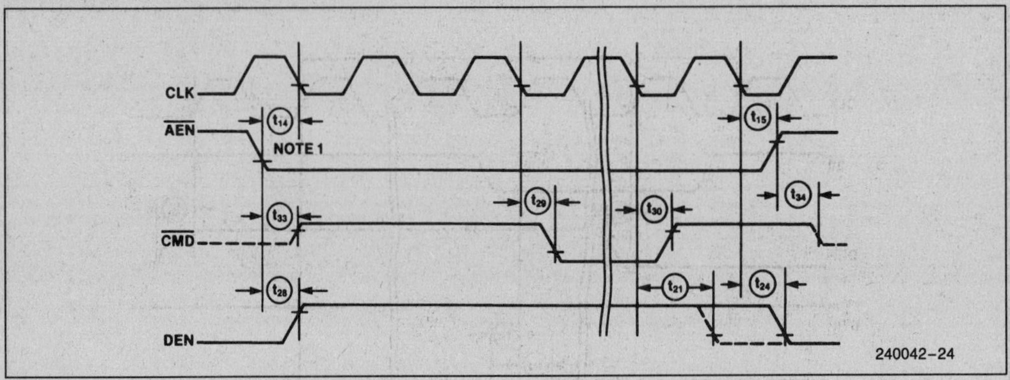

NOTE:
1. $\overline{AEN}$ is an asynchronous input. $\overline{AEN}$ setup and hold time is specified to guarantee the response shown in the waveforms.

MB CHARACTERISTICS WITH $\overline{AEN}$/CEN = HIGH

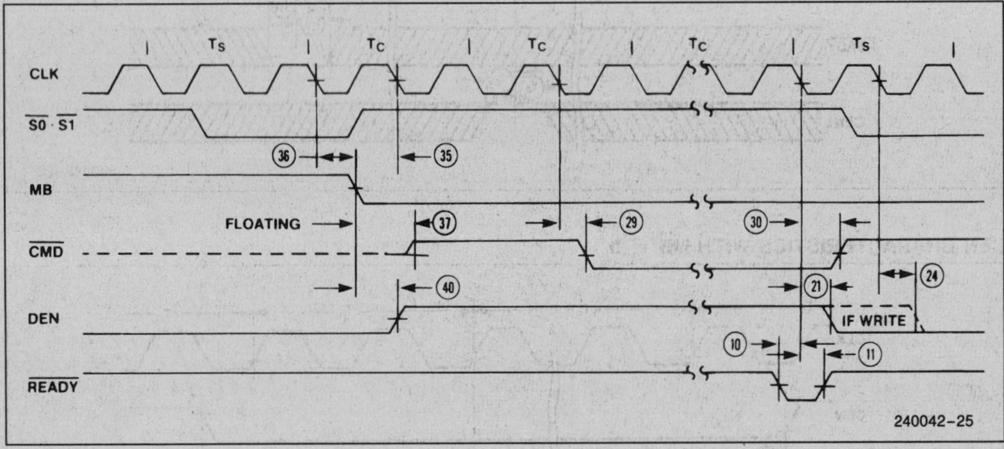

WAVEFORMS (Continued)

MB CHARACTERISTICS WITH $\overline{AEN}$/CEN = HIGH (Continued)

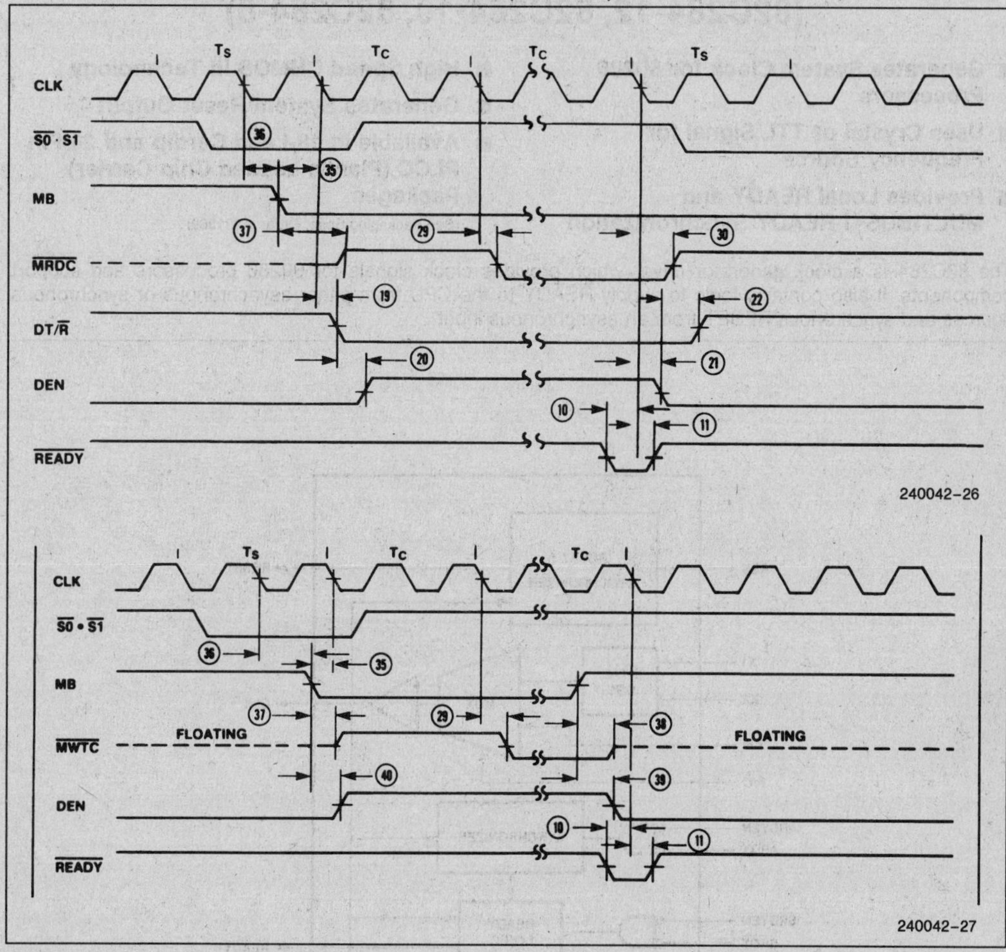

NOTES:
1. MB is an asynchronous input. MB setup and hold times specified to guarantee the response shown in the waveforms.
2. If the setup time, t35, is met two clock cycles will occur before $\overline{CMD}$ becomes active after the falling edge of MB.

DATA SHEET REVISION REVIEW

The following list represents key differences between this and the -002 data sheet. Please review this summary carefully.

1. The I_{CCS} specification was changed from 1 mA to 3 mA maximum.
2. The "PRELIMINARY" markings have been removed from the data sheet.

82C284
CLOCK GENERATOR AND READY INTERFACE FOR 80286 PROCESSORS
(82C284-12, 82C284-10, 82C284-8)

- Generates System Clock for 80286 Processors
- Uses Crystal or TTL Signal for Frequency Source
- Provides Local READY and MULTIBUS®I READY Synchronization
- High Speed CHMOS III Technology
- Generates System Reset Output
- Available in 18-Lead Cerdip and 20-Pin PLCC (Plastic Leaded Chip Carrier) Packages
  (See Packaging Spec, Order #231369)

The 82C284 is a clock generator/driver which provides clock signals for 80286 processors and support components. It also contains logic to supply $\overline{\text{READY}}$ to the CPU from either asynchronous or synchronous sources and synchronous RESET from an asynchronous input.

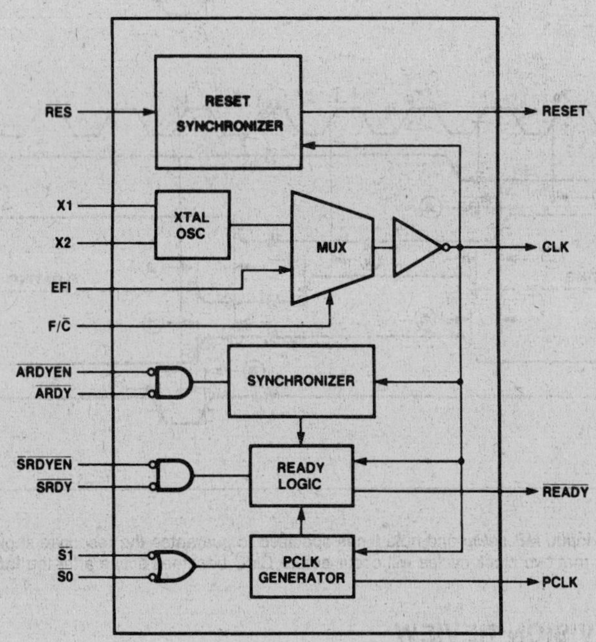

Figure 1. 82C284 Block Diagram

October 1990
Order Number: 210453-011

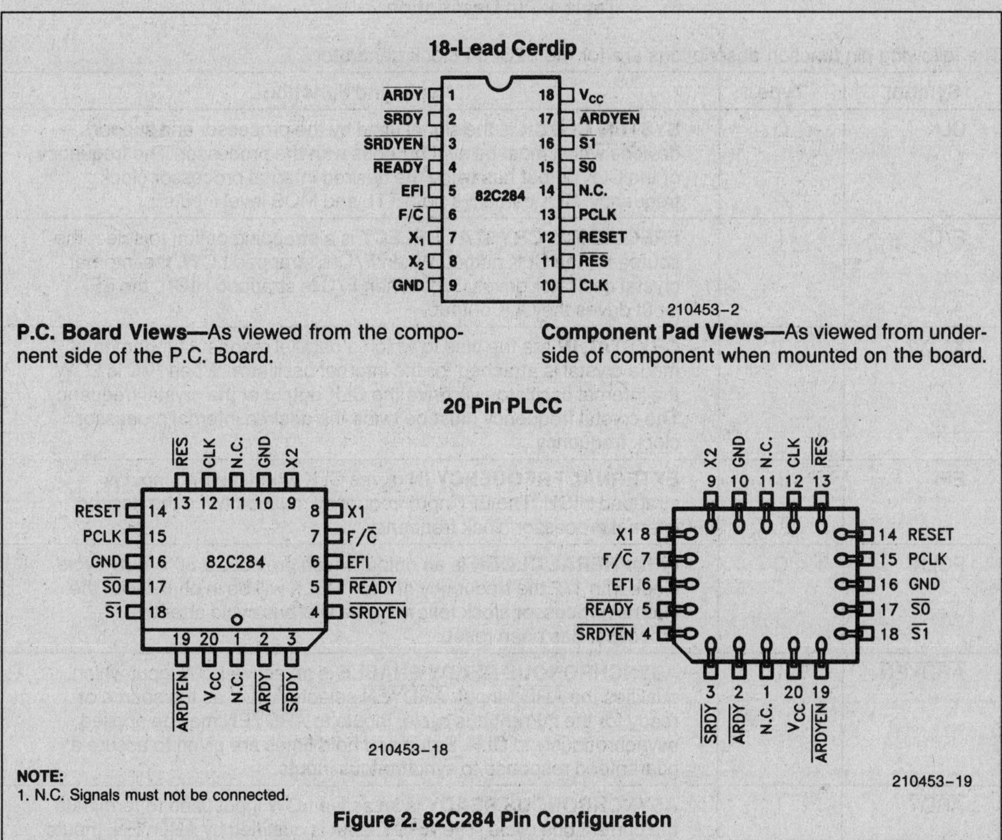

NOTE:
1. N.C. Signals must not be connected.

Figure 2. 82C284 Pin Configuration

5

Table 1. Pin Description

The following pin function descriptions are for the 82C284 clock generator.

Symbol	Type	Name and Function
CLK	O	**SYSTEM CLOCK** is the signal used by the processor and support devices which must be synchronous with the processor. The frequency of the CLK output has twice the desired internal processor clock frequency. CLK can drive both TTL and MOS level inputs.
F/$\overline{C}$	I	**FREQUENCY/CRYSTAL SELECT** is a strapping option to select the source for the CLK output. When F/$\overline{C}$ is strapped LOW, the internal crystal oscillator drives CLK. When F/$\overline{C}$ is strapped HIGH, the EFI input drives the CLK output.
X1, X2	I	**CRYSTAL IN** are the pins to which a parallel resonant fundamental mode crystal is attached for the internal oscillator. When F/$\overline{C}$ is LOW, the internal oscillator will drive the CLK output at the crystal frequency. The crystal frequency must be twice the desired internal processor clock frequency.
EFI	I	**EXTERNAL FREQUENCY IN** drives CLK when the F/$\overline{C}$ input is strapped HIGH. The EFI input frequency must be twice the desired internal processor clock frequency.
PCLK	O	**PERIPHERAL CLOCK** is an output which provides a 50% duty cycle clock with 1/2 the frequency of CLK. PCLK will be in phase with the internal processor clock following the first bus cycle after the processor has been reset.
$\overline{ARDYEN}$	I	**ASYNCHRONOUS READY ENABLE** is an active LOW input which qualifies the $\overline{ARDY}$ input. $\overline{ARDYEN}$ selects $\overline{ARDY}$ as the source of ready for the current bus cycle. Inputs to $\overline{ARDYEN}$ may be applied asynchronously to CLK. Setup and hold times are given to assure a guaranteed response to synchronous inputs.
$\overline{ARDY}$	I	**ASYNCHRONOUS READY** is an active LOW input used to terminate the current bus cycle. The $\overline{ARDY}$ input is qualified by $\overline{ARDYEN}$. Inputs to $\overline{ARDY}$ may be applied asynchronously to CLK. Setup and hold times are given to assure a guaranteed response to synchronous outputs.
$\overline{SRDYEN}$	I	**SYNCHRONOUS READY ENABLE** is an active LOW input which qualifies $\overline{SRDY}$. $\overline{SRDYEN}$ selects $\overline{SRDY}$ as the source for $\overline{READY}$ to the CPU for the current bus cycle. Setup and hold times must be satisfied for proper operation.
$\overline{SRDY}$	I	**SYNCHRONOUS READY** is an active LOW input used to terminate the current bus cycle. The $\overline{SRDY}$ input is qualified by the $\overline{SRDYEN}$ input. Setup and hold times must be satisfied for proper operation.
$\overline{READY}$	O	**READY** is an active LOW output which signals the current bus cycle is to be completed. The $\overline{SRDY}$, $\overline{SRDYEN}$, $\overline{ARDY}$, $\overline{ARDYEN}$, $\overline{S1}$, $\overline{S0}$ and RES inputs control $\overline{READY}$ as explained later in the $\overline{READY}$ generator section. $\overline{READY}$ is an open drain output requiring an external pull-up resistor.

Table 1. Pin Description (Continued)

The following pin function descriptions are for the 82C284 clock generator.

Symbol	Type	Name and Function
$\overline{S0}$, $\overline{S1}$	I	**STATUS** input prepare the 82C284 for a subsequent bus cycle. $\overline{S0}$ and $\overline{S1}$ synchronize PCLK to the internal processor clock and control $\overline{READY}$. These inputs have internal pull-up resistors to keep them HIGH if nothing is driving them. Setup and hold times must be satisfied for proper operation.
RESET	O	**RESET** is an active HIGH output which is derived from the $\overline{RES}$ input. RESET is used to force the system into an initial state. When RESET is active, $\overline{READY}$ will be active (LOW).
$\overline{RES}$	I	**RESET IN** is an active LOW input which generates the system reset signal, RESET. Signals to $\overline{RES}$ may be applied asynchronously to CLK. Setup and hold times are given to assure a guaranteed response to synchronous inputs.
V_{CC}		**SYSTEM POWER:** +5V Power Supply
GND		**SYSTEM GROUND:** 0V

FUNCTIONAL DESCRIPTION

Introduction

The 82C284 generates the clock, ready, and reset signals required for 80286 processors and support components. The 82C284 contains a crystal controlled oscillator, clock generator, peripheral clock generator, Multibus ready synchronization logic and system reset generation logic.

Clock Generator

The CLK output provides the basic timing control for an 80286 system. CLK has output characteristics sufficient to drive MOS devices. CLK is generated by either an internal crystal oscillator or an external source as selected by the F/$\overline{C}$ strapping option. When F/$\overline{C}$ is LOW, the crystal oscillator drives the CLK output. When F/$\overline{C}$ is HIGH, the EFI input drives the CLK output.

The 82C284 provides a second clock output, PCLK, for peripheral devices. PCLK is CLK divided by two. PCLK has a duty cycle of 50% and MOS output drive characteristics. PCLK is normally synchronized to the internal processor clock.

After reset, the PCLK signal may be out of phase with the internal processor clock. The $\overline{S1}$ and $\overline{S0}$ signals of the first bus cycle are used to synchronize PCLK to the internal processor clock. The phase of the PCLK output changes by extending its HIGH time beyond one system clock (see waveforms). PCLK is forced HIGH whenever either $\overline{S0}$ or $\overline{S1}$ were active (LOW) for the two previous CLK cycles. PCLK continues to oscillate when both $\overline{S0}$ and $\overline{S1}$ are HIGH.

Since the phase of the internal processor clock will not change except during reset, the phase of PCLK will not change except during the first bus cycle after reset.

Oscillator

The oscillator circuit of the 82C284 is a linear Pierce oscillator which requires an external parallel resonant, fundamental mode, crystal. The output of the oscillator is internally buffered. The crystal frequency chosen should be twice the required internal processor clock frequency. The crystal should have a typical load capacitance of 32 pF.

X1 and X2 are the oscillator crystal connections. For stable operation of the oscillator, two loading capacitors are recommended, as shown in Table 2. The sum of the board capacitance and loading capacitance should equal the values shown. It is advisable to limit stray board capacitances (not including the effect of the loading capacitors or crystal capacitance) to less than 10 pF between the X1 and X2 pins. Decouple V_{CC} and GND as close to the 82C284 as possible.

5

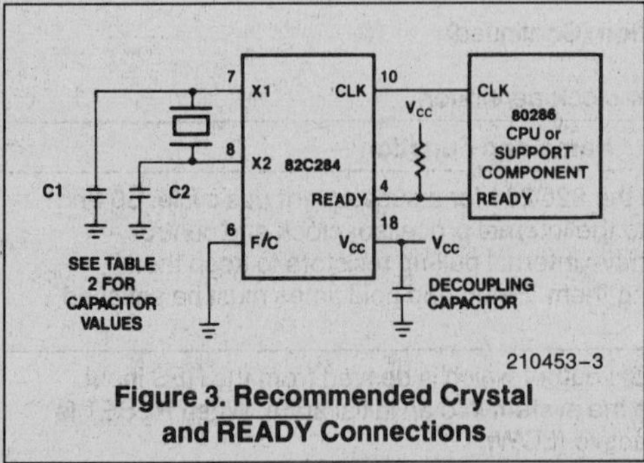

Figure 3. Recommended Crystal and $\overline{\text{READY}}$ Connections

CLK Termination

Due to the CLK output having a very fast rise and fall time, it is recommended to properly terminate the CLK line at frequencies above 10 MHz to avoid signal reflections and ringing. Termination is accomplished by inserting a small resistor (typically 10Ω–74Ω) in series with the output, as shown in Figure 4. This is known as series termination. The resistor value plus the circuit output impedance should be made equal to the impedance of the transmission line.

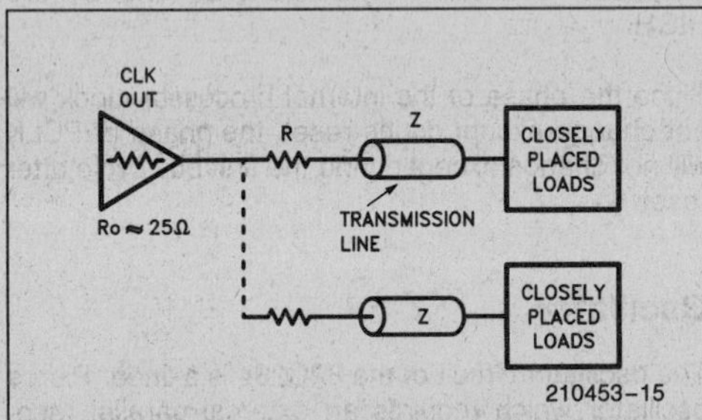

Figure 4. Series Termination

Reset Operation

The reset logic provides the RESET output to force the system into a known, initial state. When the $\overline{\text{RES}}$ input is active (LOW), the RESET output becomes active (HIGH). $\overline{\text{RES}}$ is synchronized internally at the falling edge of CLK before generating the RESET output (see waveforms). Synchronization of the $\overline{\text{RES}}$ input introduces a one or two CLK delay before affecting the RESET output.

At power up, a system does not have a stable V_{CC} and CLK. To prevent spurious activity, $\overline{\text{RES}}$ should be asserted until V_{CC} and CLK stabilize at their operating values. 80286 processors and support components also require their RESET inputs be HIGH a minimum of 16 CLK cycles. A network such as shown in Figure 5 will keep $\overline{\text{RES}}$ LOW long enough to satisfy both needs.

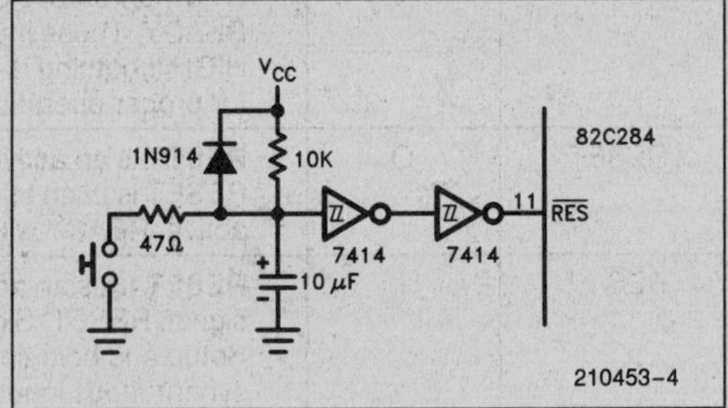

Figure 5. Typical $\overline{\text{RES}}$ Timing Circuit

Ready Operation

The 82C284 accepts two ready sources for the system ready signal which terminates the current bus cycle. Either a synchronous ($\overline{\text{SRDY}}$) or asynchronous ready ($\overline{\text{ARDY}}$) source may be used. Each ready input has an enable ($\overline{\text{SRDYEN}}$ and $\overline{\text{ARDYEN}}$) for selecting the type of ready source required to terminate the current bus cycle. An address decoder would normally select one of the enable inputs.

$\overline{\text{READY}}$ is enabled (LOW), if either $\overline{\text{SRDY}}$ + $\overline{\text{SRDYEN}}$ = 0 or $\overline{\text{ARDY}}$ + $\overline{\text{ARDYEN}}$ = 0 when sampled by the 82C284 $\overline{\text{READY}}$ generation logic. $\overline{\text{READY}}$ will remain active for at least two CLK cycles.

The $\overline{\text{READY}}$ output has an open-drain driver allowing other ready circuits to be wire or'ed with it, as shown in Figure 3. The $\overline{\text{READY}}$ signal of an 80286 system requires an external pull-up resistor. To force the $\overline{\text{READY}}$ signal inactive (HIGH) at the start of a bus cycle, the $\overline{\text{READY}}$ output floats when either $\overline{\text{S1}}$ or $\overline{\text{S0}}$ are sampled LOW at the falling edge of CLK. Two system clock periods are allowed for the pull-up resistor to pull the $\overline{\text{READY}}$ signal to V_{IH}. When RESET is active, $\overline{\text{READY}}$ is forced active one CLK later (see waveforms).

Figure 6 illustrates the operation of $\overline{\text{SRDY}}$ and $\overline{\text{SRDYEN}}$. These inputs are sampled on the falling edge of CLK when $\overline{\text{S1}}$ and $\overline{\text{S0}}$ are inactive and PCLK is HIGH. $\overline{\text{READY}}$ is forced active when both $\overline{\text{SRDY}}$ and $\overline{\text{SRDYEN}}$ are sampled as LOW.

Figure 7 shows the operation of $\overline{\text{ARDY}}$ and $\overline{\text{ARDYEN}}$. These inputs are sampled by an internal synchronizer at each falling edge of CLK. The output of the synchronizer is then sampled when PCLK is HIGH. If the synchronizer resolved both the $\overline{\text{ARDY}}$ and $\overline{\text{ARDYEN}}$ as active, the $\overline{\text{SRDY}}$ and $\overline{\text{SRDYEN}}$ inputs are ignored. Either $\overline{\text{ARDY}}$ or $\overline{\text{ARDYEN}}$ must be HIGH at the end of T_S (see Figure 7).

$\overline{\text{READY}}$ remains active until either $\overline{\text{S1}}$ or $\overline{\text{S0}}$ are sampled LOW, or the ready inputs are sampled as inactive.

Table 2. 82C284 Crystal Loading Capacitance Values

Crystal Frequency	C1 Capacitance (Pin 7)	C2 Capacitance (Pin 8)
1 to 8 MHz	60 pF	40 pF
8 to 20 MHz	25 pF	15 pF
Above 20 MHz	15 pF	15 pF

NOTE:
Capacitance values must include stray board capacitance.

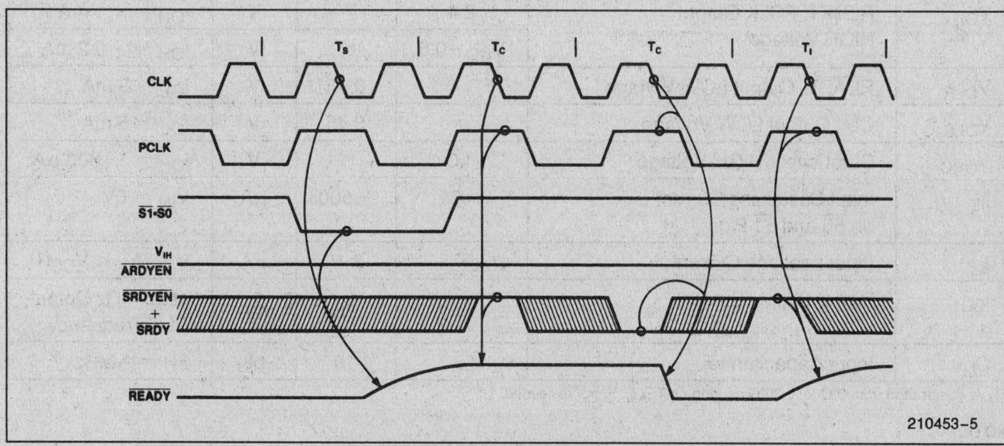

Figure 6. Synchronous Ready Operation

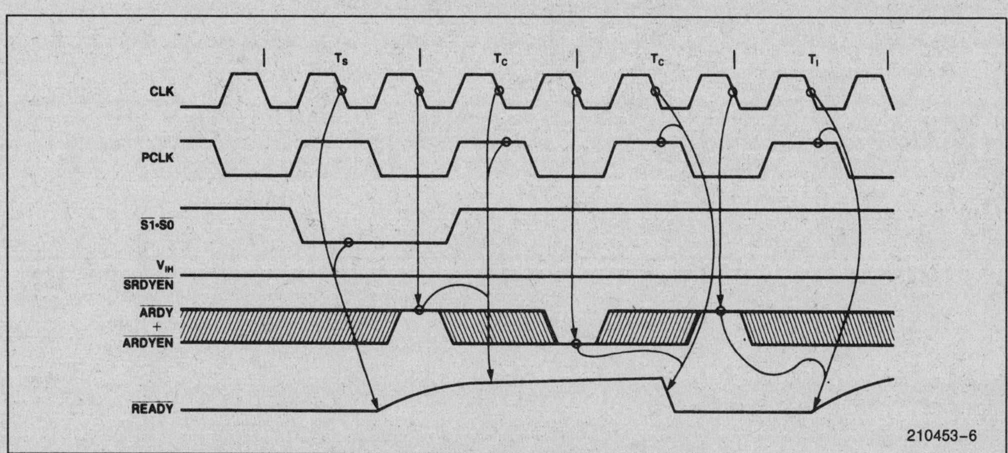

Figure 7. Asynchronous Ready Operation

ABSOLUTE MAXIMUM RATINGS*

Temperature Under Bias .... 0°C to +70°C
Storage Temperature .... −65°C to +150°C
All Output and Supply Voltages ..... −0.5V to +7V
All Input Voltages .... −1.0V to +5.5V
Power Dissipation .... 1 Watt

NOTICE: This is a production data sheet. The specifications are subject to change without notice.

**WARNING: Stressing the device beyond the "Absolute Maximum Ratings" may cause permanent damage. These are stress ratings only. Operation beyond the "Operating Conditions" is not recommended and extended exposure beyond the "Operating Conditions" may affect device reliability.*

D.C. CHARACTERISTICS T_{CASE} = 0°C to +85°C,* V_{CC} = 5V ±5%

Symbol	Parameter	Min	Max	Unit	Test Condition
V_{IL}	Input LOW Voltage		0.8	V	
V_{IH}	Input HIGH Voltage	2.0		V	
V_{IHR}	$\overline{RES}$ and EFI Input HIGH Voltage	2.6		V	
V_{OL}	RESET, PCLK Output LOW Voltage		0.45	V	I_{OL} = 5 mA
V_{OH}	RESET, PCLK Output HIGH Voltage	2.4		V	I_{OH} = −1 mA
		V_{CC}−0.5		V	I_{OH} = −0.2 mA
V_{OLR}	$\overline{READY}$, Output LOW Voltage		0.45	V	I_{OL} = 9 mA
V_{OLC}	CLK Output LOW Voltage		0.45	V	I_{OL} = 5 mA
V_{OHC}	CLK Output HIGH Voltage	4.0		V	I_{OH} = − 800 μA
I_{IL}	Input Sustaining Current on $\overline{S0}$ and $\overline{S1}$ Pins	−60	−500	μA	V_{IN} = 0V
I_{LI}	Input Leakage Current		±10	μA	$0 \leq V_{IN} \leq V_{CC}$(1)
I_{CC}	Power Supply Current		75	mA	at 25 MHz Output CLK Frequency
C_I	Input Capacitance		10	pF	F_C = 1 MHz

*T_A is guaranteed from 0°C to +70°C as long as T_{CASE} is not exceeded.

NOTE:
1. Status lines S0 and S1 excluded because they have internal pull-up resistors.

A.C. CHARACTERISTICS V_{CC} = 5V ±5%, T_{CASE} = 0°C to +85°C.*

Timings are referenced to 0.8V and 2.0V points of signals as illustrated in the datasheet waveforms, unless otherwise noted.

82C284 A.C. Timing Parameters

Symbol	Parameter	8 MHz		10 MHz		12.5 MHz		Units	Test Conditions
		Min	Max	Min	Max	Min	Max		
1	EFI to CLK Delay		25		25		25	ns	At 1.5V (1)
2	EFI LOW Time	28		22.5		13		ns	At 1.5V (1, 7)
3	EFI HIGH Time	28		22.5		22		ns	At 1.5V (1, 7)
4	CLK Period	62	500	50	500	40	500	ns	
5	CLK LOW Time	15		12		11		ns	At 1.0V (1, 2, 7, 8, 9, 10)
6	CLK HIGH Time	25		16		13		ns	At 3.6V (1, 2, 7, 8, 9, 10)
7	CLK Rise Time		10		8		8	ns	1.0V to 3.6V (1, 2, 10, 11)
8	CLK Fall Time		10		8		8	ns	3.6V to 1.0V (1, 9, 10, 11)
9	Status Setup Time	22		—		—		ns	(Note 1)
9a	Status Setup Time for Status Going Active	—		20		22		ns	(Note 1)
9b	Status Setup Time for Status Going Inactive	—		20		18		ns	(Note 1)
10	Status Hold Time	1		1		3		ns	(Note 1)
11	$\overline{SRDY}$ or $\overline{SRDYEN}$ Setup Time	20		17.5		17		ns	(Note 1)
12	$\overline{SRDY}$ or $\overline{SRDYEN}$ Hold Time	0		2		2		ns	(Notes 1, 11)
13	$\overline{ARDY}$ or $\overline{ARDYEN}$ Setup Time	0		0		0		ns	(Notes 1, 3)
14	$\overline{ARDY}$ or $\overline{ARDYEN}$ Hold Time	30		30		25		ns	(Notes 1, 3)
15	$\overline{RES}$ Setup Time	20		20		18		ns	(Notes 1, 3)
16	$\overline{RES}$ Hold Time	10		10		8		ns	(Notes 1, 3)
17	$\overline{READY}$ Inactive Delay	5		5		5		ns	At 0.8V (4)
18	$\overline{READY}$ Active Delay	0	24	0	24	0	18	ns	At 0.8V (4)
19	PCLK Delay	0	45	0	35	0	23	ns	(Note 5)
20	RESET Delay	5	34	5	27	3	22	ns	(Note 5)
21	PCLK LOW Time	t4−20		t4−20		t4−20		ns	(Notes 5, 6)
22	PCLK HIGH Time	t4−20		t4−20		t4−20		ns	(Notes 5, 6)

*T_A is guaranteed from 0°C to 70°C as long as T_{CASE} is not exceeded.

NOTES:

1. CLK loading: C_L = 100 pF. The 82C284's X1 and X2 inputs are designed primarily for parallel-resonant crystals. Serial-resonant crystals may also be used, however, they may oscillate up to 0.01% faster than their nominal frequencies when used with the 82C284. For either type of crystal, capacitive loading should be as specified by Table 2.
2. With the internal crystal oscillator using recommended crystal and capacitive loading; or with the EFI input meeting specifications t2 and t3. The recommended crystal loading for CLK frequencies of 8 MHz–20 MHz are 25 pF from pin X_1 to ground, and 15 pF from pin X_2 to ground; for CLK frequencies above 20 MHz 15 pF from pin X_1 to ground, and 15 pF from pin X_2 to ground. These recommended values are ±5 pF and include all stray capacitance. Decouple V_{CC} and GND as close to the 82C284 as possible.
3. This is an asynchronous input. This specification is given for testing purposes only, to assure recognition at specific CLK edge.

5

NOTES:

4. Pull-up Resistor values for READY Pin:

CPU Frequency	8 MHz	10 MHz	12.5 MHz
Resistor	910Ω	700Ω	600Ω
CL	150 pF	150 pF	150 pF
I_{OL}	7 mA	7 mA	9 mA

5. PCLK and RESET loading: C_L = 75 pF.
6. t4 refers to any allowable CLK period.
7. When driving the 82C284 with EFI, provide minimum EFI HIGH and LOW times as follows:

CLK Output Frequency	16 MHz	20 MHz	25 MHz
Min. Required EFI HIGH Time	28 ns	22.5 ns	22 ns
Min. Required EFI LOW Time	28 ns	22.5 ns	13 ns

8. When using a crystal (with recommended capacitive loading per Table 2) appropriate for the speed of the 80286, CLK output HIGH and LOW times guaranteed to meet the 80286 requirements.

Reset Drive EFI Drive and Measurement Points

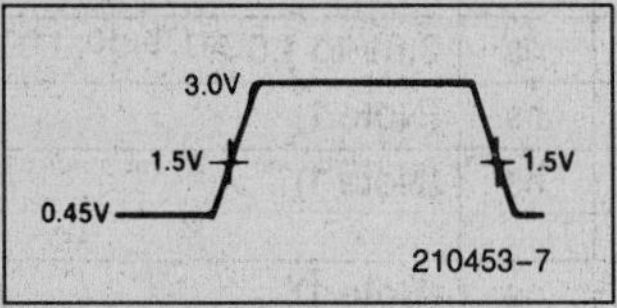

Note 9

CLK Output Measurement Points

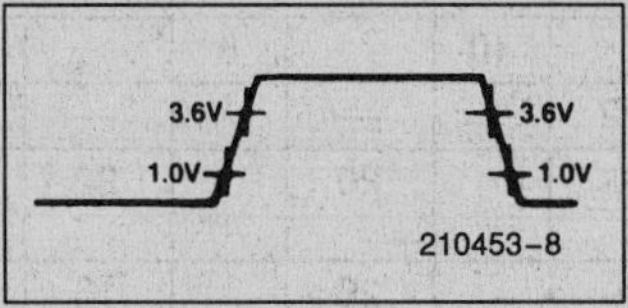

Note 10

F/C̄ Drive Points

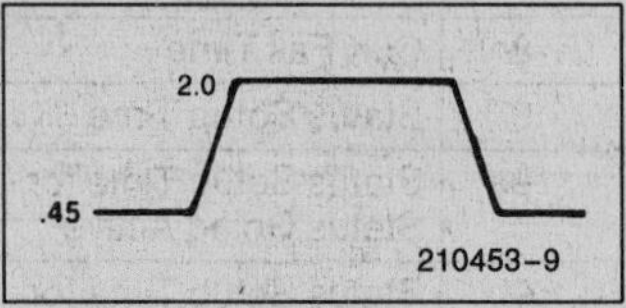

Note 11

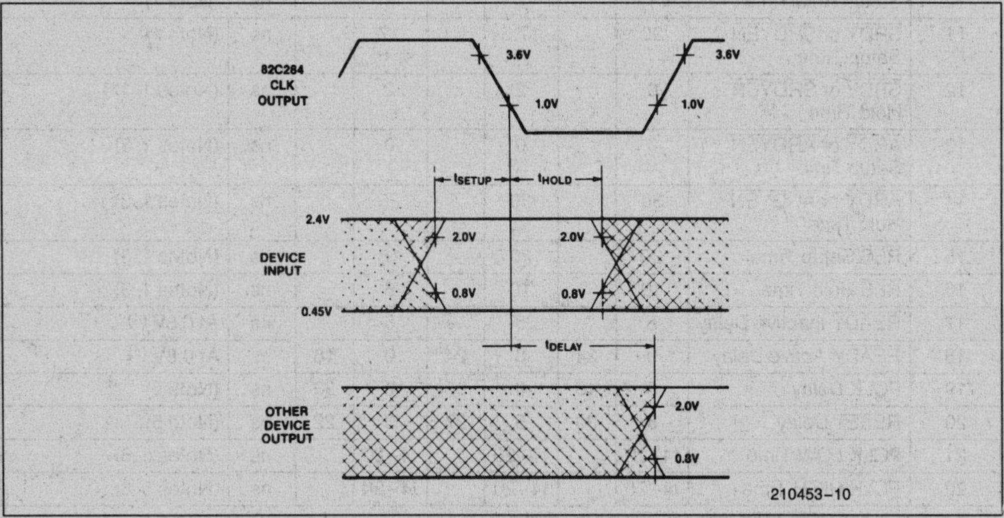

Note 12. AC Setup, Hold and Delay Time Measurement—General

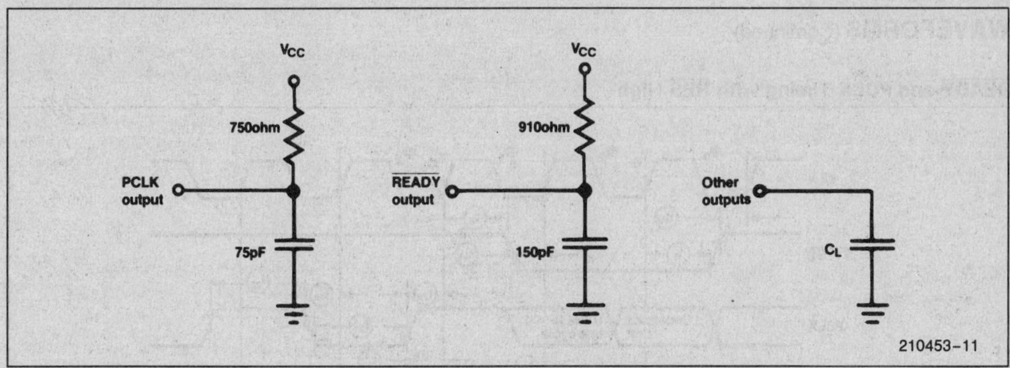

Note 13. AC Test Loading on Outputs

WAVEFORMS

CLK as a Function of EFI

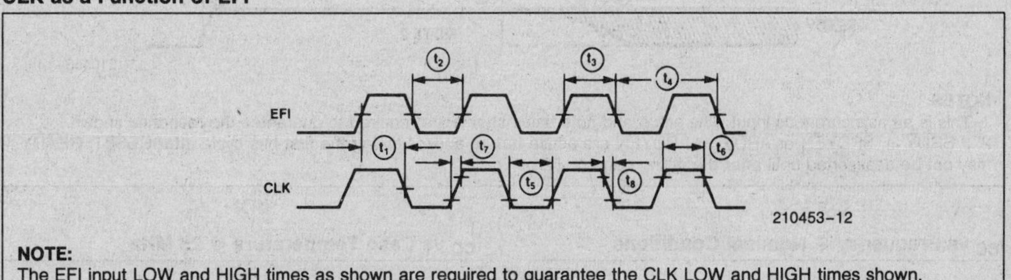

NOTE:
The EFI input LOW and HIGH times as shown are required to guarantee the CLK LOW and HIGH times shown.

5

$\overline{\text{RESET}}$ and $\overline{\text{READY}}$ Timing as a Function of $\overline{\text{RES}}$ with $\overline{\text{S1}}$, $\overline{\text{S0}}$, $\overline{\text{ARDY}}$ + $\overline{\text{ARDYEN}}$, and $\overline{\text{SRDY}}$ + $\overline{\text{SRDYEN}}$ High

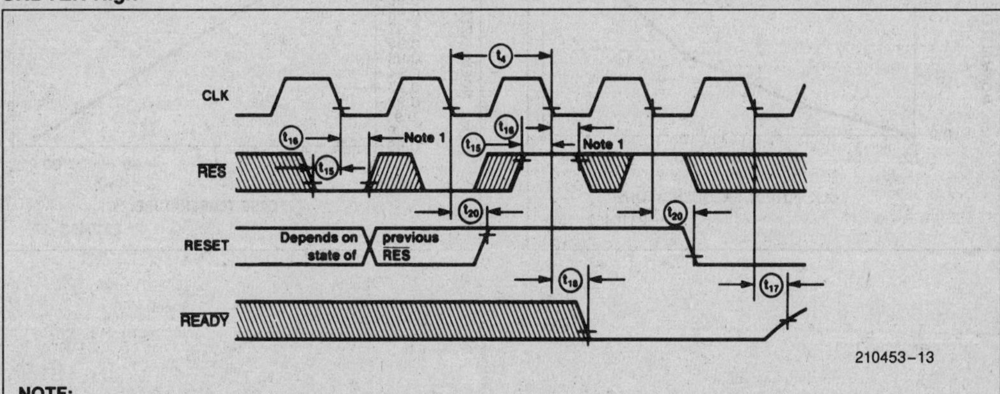

NOTE:
1. This is an asynchronous input. The setup and hold times shown are required to guarantee the response shown.

WAVEFORMS (Continued)

READY and PCLK Timing with RES High

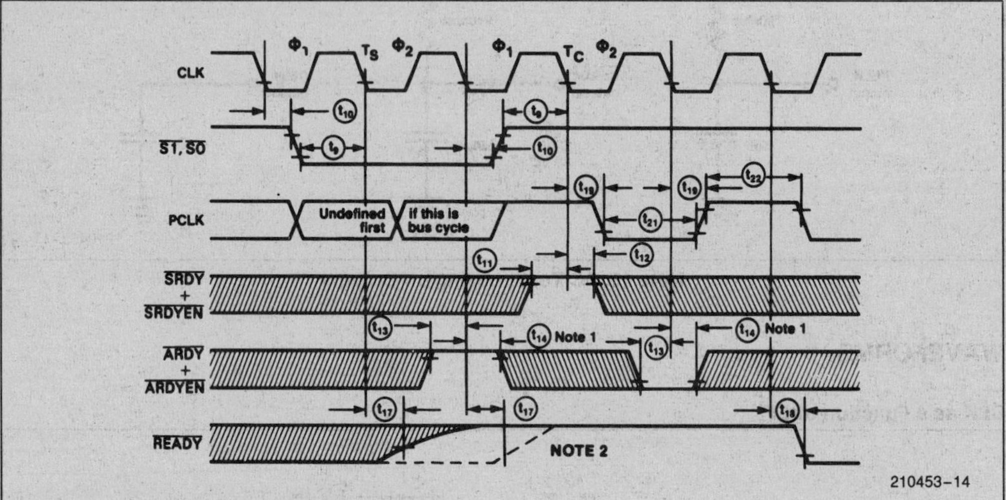

210453-14

NOTES:

1. This is an asynchronous input. The setup and hold times shown are required to guarantee the response shown.
2. If SRDY + SRDYEN or ARDY + ARDYEN are active before and/or during the first bus cycle after RESET, READY may not be deasserted until after the falling edge of $\phi 2$ of T_S.

I_{CC} vs Frequency @ Nominal Conditions

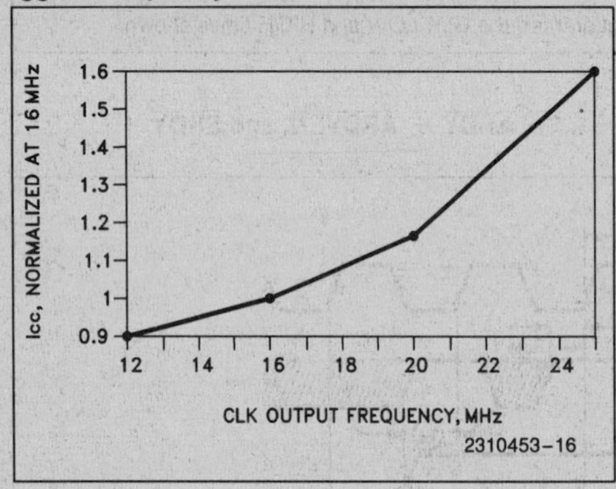

2310453-16

I_{CC} vs Case Temperature @ 25 MHz

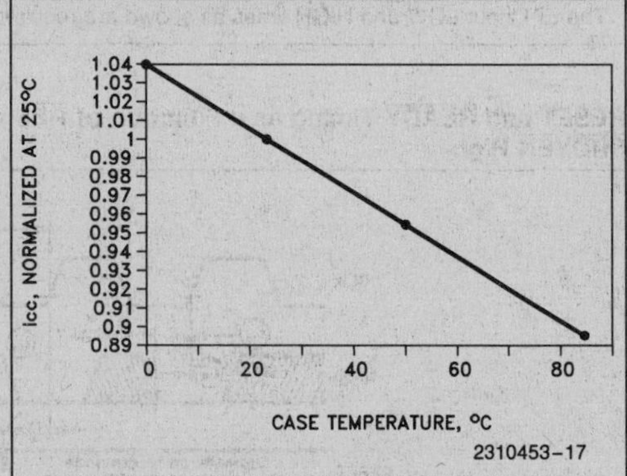

2310453-17

DATA SHEET REVISION REVIEW

The following list represents key differences between this and the -010 data sheet. Please review this summary carefully.

1. The DC Characteristics Input Sustaining Current on $\overline{S}_0$ and $\overline{S}_1$ pins (I_{IL}) has been changed from $-30\ \mu A$ to $-60\ \mu A$.
2. The AC Timing parameter $\overline{SRDY}$ or $\overline{SRDYEN}$ setup time (t_{11}) has been changed to 17.5 ns for the 10 MHz and 17 ns for the 12.5 MHz parts.

8086 Microprocessor

6

8086
16-BIT HMOS MICROPROCESSOR
8086/8086-2/8086-1

- **Direct Addressing Capability 1 MByte of Memory**
- **Architecture Designed for Powerful Assembly Language and Efficient High Level Languages**
- **14 Word, by 16-Bit Register Set with Symmetrical Operations**
- **24 Operand Addressing Modes**
- **Bit, Byte, Word, and Block Operations**
- **8 and 16-Bit Signed and Unsigned Arithmetic in Binary or Decimal Including Multiply and Divide**
- **Range of Clock Rates:**
  5 MHz for 8086,
  8 MHz for 8086-2,
  10 MHz for 8086-1
- **MULTIBUS® System Compatible Interface**
- **Available in EXPRESS**
  — Standard Temperature Range
  — Extended Temperature Range
- **Available in 40-Lead Cerdip and Plastic Package**
  (See Packaging Spec. Order #231369)

The Intel 8086 high performance 16-bit CPU is available in three clock rates: 5, 8 and 10 MHz. The CPU is implemented in N-Channel, depletion load, silicon gate technology (HMOS-III), and packaged in a 40-pin CERDIP or plastic package. The 8086 operates in both single processor and multiple processor configurations to achieve high performance levels.

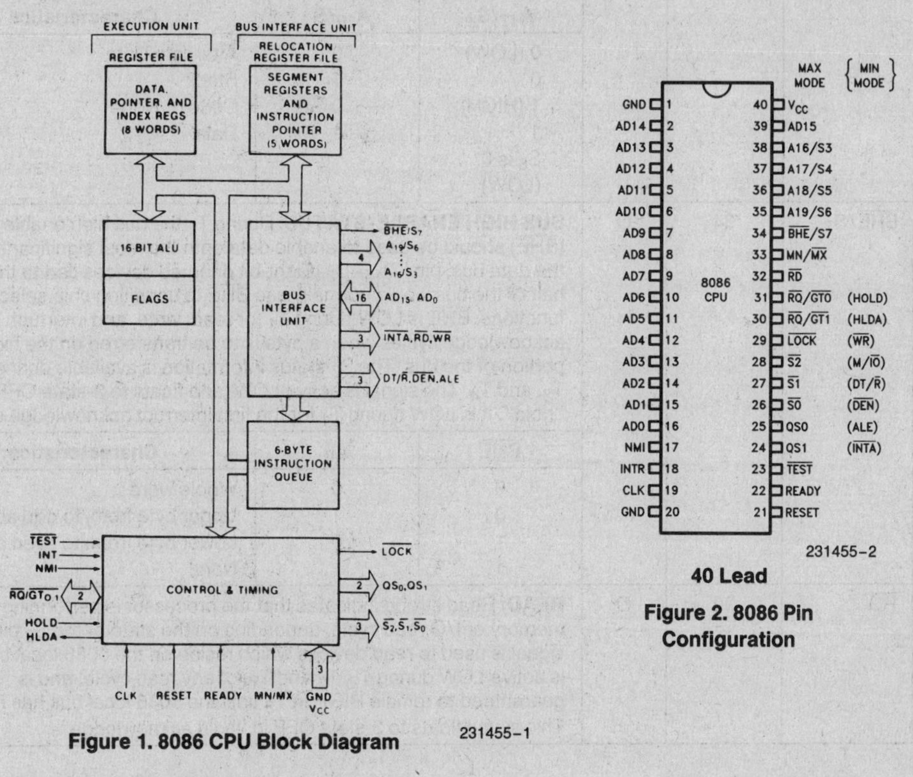

Figure 1. 8086 CPU Block Diagram

40 Lead

Figure 2. 8086 Pin Configuration

6

September 1990
Order Number: 231455-005

Table 1. Pin Description

The following pin function descriptions are for 8086 systems in either minimum or maximum mode. The "Local Bus" in these descriptions is the direct multiplexed bus interface connection to the 8086 (without regard to additional bus buffers).

<table>
<tr><th>Symbol</th><th>Pin No.</th><th>Type</th><th>Name and Function</th></tr>
<tr><td>$AD_{15}–AD_0$</td><td>2–16, 39</td><td>I/O</td><td>ADDRESS DATA BUS: These lines constitute the time multiplexed memory/IO address (T_1), and data (T_2, T_3, T_W, T_4) bus. A_0 is analogous to $\overline{BHE}$ for the lower byte of the data bus, pins $D_7–D_0$. It is LOW during T_1 when a byte is to be transferred on the lower portion of the bus in memory or I/O operations. Eight-bit oriented devices tied to the lower half would normally use A_0 to condition chip select functions. (See $\overline{BHE}$.) These lines are active HIGH and float to 3-state OFF during interrupt acknowledge and local bus "hold acknowledge".</td></tr>
<tr><td>A_{19}/S_6,
A_{18}/S_5,
A_{17}/S_4,
A_{16}/S_3</td><td>35–38</td><td>O</td><td>ADDRESS/STATUS: During T_1 these are the four most significant address lines for memory operations. During I/O operations these lines are LOW. During memory and I/O operations, status information is available on these lines during T_2, T_3, T_W, T_4. The status of the interrupt enable FLAG bit (S_5) is updated at the beginning of each CLK cycle. A_{17}/S_4 and A_{16}/S_3 are encoded as shown.
This information indicates which relocation register is presently being used for data accessing.
These lines float to 3-state OFF during local bus "hold acknowledge."
<table>
<tr><th>A_{17}/S_4</th><th>A_{16}/S_3</th><th>Characteristics</th></tr>
<tr><td>0 (LOW)</td><td>0</td><td>Alternate Data</td></tr>
<tr><td>0</td><td>1</td><td>Stack</td></tr>
<tr><td>1 (HIGH)</td><td>0</td><td>Code or None</td></tr>
<tr><td>1</td><td>1</td><td>Data</td></tr>
<tr><td>S_6 is 0 (LOW)</td><td></td><td></td></tr>
</table></td></tr>
<tr><td>$\overline{BHE}/S_7$</td><td>34</td><td>O</td><td>BUS HIGH ENABLE/STATUS: During T_1 the bus high enable signal ($\overline{BHE}$) should be used to enable data onto the most significant half of the data bus, pins $D_{15}–D_8$. Eight-bit oriented devices tied to the upper half of the bus would normally use $\overline{BHE}$ to condition chip select functions. $\overline{BHE}$ is LOW during T_1 for read, write, and interrupt acknowledge cycles when a byte is to be transferred on the high portion of the bus. The S_7 status information is available during T_2, T_3, and T_4. The signal is active LOW, and floats to 3-state OFF in "hold". It is LOW during T_1 for the first interrupt acknowledge cycle.
<table>
<tr><th>$\overline{BHE}$</th><th>A_0</th><th>Characteristics</th></tr>
<tr><td>0</td><td>0</td><td>Whole word</td></tr>
<tr><td>0</td><td>1</td><td>Upper byte from/to odd address</td></tr>
<tr><td>1</td><td>0</td><td>Lower byte from/to even address</td></tr>
<tr><td>1</td><td>1</td><td>None</td></tr>
</table></td></tr>
<tr><td>$\overline{RD}$</td><td>32</td><td>O</td><td>READ: Read strobe indicates that the processor is performing a memory or I/O read cycle, depending on the state of the S_2 pin. This signal is used to read devices which reside on the 8086 local bus. $\overline{RD}$ is active LOW during T_2, T_3 and T_W of any read cycle, and is guaranteed to remain HIGH in T_2 until the 8086 local bus has floated. This signal floats to 3-state OFF in "hold acknowledge".</td></tr>
</table>

Table 1. Pin Description (Continued)

Symbol	Pin No.	Type	Name and Function
READY	22	I	**READY:** is the acknowledgement from the addressed memory or I/O device that it will complete the data transfer. The READY signal from memory/IO is synchronized by the 8284A Clock Generator to form READY. This signal is active HIGH. The 8086 READY input is not synchronized. Correct operation is not guaranteed if the setup and hold times are not met.
INTR	18	I	**INTERRUPT REQUEST:** is a level triggered input which is sampled during the last clock cycle of each instruction to determine if the processor should enter into an interrupt acknowledge operation. A subroutine is vectored to via an interrupt vector lookup table located in system memory. It can be internally masked by software resetting the interrupt enable bit. INTR is internally synchronized. This signal is active HIGH.
$\overline{\text{TEST}}$	23	I	**$\overline{\text{TEST}}$:** input is examined by the "Wait" instruction. If the $\overline{\text{TEST}}$ input is LOW execution continues, otherwise the processor waits in an "Idle" state. This input is synchronized internally during each clock cycle on the leading edge of CLK.
NMI	17	I	**NON-MASKABLE INTERRUPT:** an edge triggered input which causes a type 2 interrupt. A subroutine is vectored to via an interrupt vector lookup table located in system memory. NMI is not maskable internally by software. A transition from LOW to HIGH initiates the interrupt at the end of the current instruction. This input is internally synchronized.
RESET	21	I	**RESET:** causes the processor to immediately terminate its present activity. The signal must be active HIGH for at least four clock cycles. It restarts execution, as described in the Instruction Set description, when RESET returns LOW. RESET is internally synchronized.
CLK	19	I	**CLOCK:** provides the basic timing for the processor and bus controller. It is asymmetric with a 33% duty cycle to provide optimized internal timing.
V_{CC}	40		**V_{CC}:** +5V power supply pin.
GND	1, 20		**GROUND**
MN/$\overline{\text{MX}}$	33	I	**MINIMUM/MAXIMUM:** indicates what mode the processor is to operate in. The two modes are discussed in the following sections.

The following pin function descriptions are for the 8086/8288 system in maximum mode (i.e., MN/$\overline{MX}$ = V_{SS}). Only the pin functions which are unique to maximum mode are described; all other pin functions are as described above.

Symbol	Pin No.	Type	Name and Function
$\overline{S_2}$, $\overline{S_1}$, $\overline{S_0}$	26–28	O	**STATUS:** active during T_4, T_1, and T_2 and is returned to the passive state (1, 1, 1) during T_3 or during T_W when READY is HIGH. This status is used by the 8288 Bus Controller to generate all memory and I/O access control signals. Any change by $\overline{S_2}$, $\overline{S_1}$, or $\overline{S_0}$ during T_4 is used to indicate the beginning of a bus cycle, and the return to the passive state in T_3 or T_W is used to indicate the end of a bus cycle.

6

Table 1. Pin Description (Continued)

<table>
<tr><th>Symbol</th><th>Pin No.</th><th>Type</th><th colspan="4">Name and Function</th></tr>
<tr><td rowspan="10">$\overline{S_2}$, $\overline{S_1}$, $\overline{S_0}$ (Continued)</td><td rowspan="10">26–28</td><td rowspan="10">O</td><td colspan="4">These signals float to 3-state OFF in "hold acknowledge". These status lines are encoded as shown.</td></tr>
<tr><td>$\overline{S_2}$</td><td>$\overline{S_1}$</td><td>$\overline{S_0}$</td><td>Characteristics</td></tr>
<tr><td>0 (LOW)</td><td>0</td><td>0</td><td>Interrupt Acknowledge</td></tr>
<tr><td>0</td><td>0</td><td>1</td><td>Read I/O Port</td></tr>
<tr><td>0</td><td>1</td><td>0</td><td>Write I/O Port</td></tr>
<tr><td>0</td><td>1</td><td>1</td><td>Halt</td></tr>
<tr><td>1 (HIGH)</td><td>0</td><td>0</td><td>Code Access</td></tr>
<tr><td>1</td><td>0</td><td>1</td><td>Read Memory</td></tr>
<tr><td>1</td><td>1</td><td>0</td><td>Write Memory</td></tr>
<tr><td>1</td><td>1</td><td>1</td><td>Passive</td></tr>
<tr><td>$\overline{RQ}/\overline{GT}_0$,
$\overline{RQ}/\overline{GT}_1$</td><td>30, 31</td><td>I/O</td><td colspan="4">REQUEST/GRANT: pins are used by other local bus masters to force the processor to release the local bus at the end of the processor's current bus cycle. Each pin is bidirectional with $\overline{RQ}/\overline{GT}_0$ having higher priority than $\overline{RQ}/\overline{GT}_1$. $\overline{RQ}/\overline{GT}$ pins have internal pull-up resistors and may be left unconnected. The request/grant sequence is as follows (see Page 2-24):
1. A pulse of 1 CLK wide from another local bus master indicates a local bus request ("hold") to the 8086 (pulse 1).
2. During a T_4 or T_1 clock cycle, a pulse 1 CLK wide from the 8086 to the requesting master (pulse 2), indicates that the 8086 has allowed the local bus to float and that it will enter the "hold acknowledge" state at the next CLK. The CPU's bus interface unit is disconnected logically from the local bus during "hold acknowledge".
3. A pulse 1 CLK wide from the requesting master indicates to the 8086 (pulse 3) that the "hold" request is about to end and that the 8086 can reclaim the local bus at the next CLK.
Each master-master exchange of the local bus is a sequence of 3 pulses. There must be one dead CLK cycle after each bus exchange. Pulses are active LOW.
If the request is made while the CPU is performing a memory cycle, it will release the local bus during T_4 of the cycle when all the following conditions are met:
1. Request occurs on or before T_2.
2. Current cycle is not the low byte of a word (on an odd address).
3. Current cycle is not the first acknowledge of an interrupt acknowledge sequence.
4. A locked instruction is not currently executing.
If the local bus is idle when the request is made the two possible events will follow:
1. Local bus will be released during the next clock.
2. A memory cycle will start within 3 clocks. Now the four rules for a currently active memory cycle apply with condition number 1 already satisfied.</td></tr>
<tr><td>$\overline{LOCK}$</td><td>29</td><td>O</td><td colspan="4">$\overline{LOCK}$: output indicates that other system bus masters are not to gain control of the system bus while $\overline{LOCK}$ is active LOW. The $\overline{LOCK}$ signal is activated by the "LOCK" prefix instruction and remains active until the completion of the next instruction. This signal is active LOW, and floats to 3-state OFF in "hold acknowledge".</td></tr>
</table>

Table 1. Pin Description (Continued)

Symbol	Pin No.	Type	Name and Function
QS_1, QS_0	24, 25	O	**QUEUE STATUS:** The queue status is valid during the CLK cycle after which the queue operation is performed. QS_1 and QS_0 provide status to allow external tracking of the internal 8086 instruction queue.

QS_1	QS_0	Characteristics
0 (LOW)	0	No Operation
0	1	First Byte of Op Code from Queue
1 (HIGH)	0	Empty the Queue
1	1	Subsequent Byte from Queue

The following pin function descriptions are for the 8086 in minimum mode (i.e., MN/$\overline{MX}$ = V_{CC}). Only the pin functions which are unique to minimum mode are described; all other pin functions are as described above.

Symbol	Pin No.	Type	Name and Function
M/$\overline{IO}$	28	O	**STATUS LINE:** logically equivalent to S_2 in the maximum mode. It is used to distinguish a memory access from an I/O access. M/$\overline{IO}$ becomes valid in the T_4 preceding a bus cycle and remains valid until the final T_4 of the cycle (M = HIGH, IO = LOW). M/$\overline{IO}$ floats to 3-state OFF in local bus "hold acknowledge".
$\overline{WR}$	29	O	**WRITE:** indicates that the processor is performing a write memory or write I/O cycle, depending on the state of the M/$\overline{IO}$ signal. $\overline{WR}$ is active for T_2, T_3 and T_W of any write cycle. It is active LOW, and floats to 3-state OFF in local bus "hold acknowledge".
$\overline{INTA}$	24	O	**$\overline{INTA}$:** is used as a read strobe for interrupt acknowledge cycles. It is active LOW during T_2, T_3 and T_W of each interrupt acknowledge cycle.
ALE	25	O	**ADDRESS LATCH ENABLE:** provided by the processor to latch the address into the 8282/8283 address latch. It is a HIGH pulse active during T_1 of any bus cycle. Note that ALE is never floated.
DT/$\overline{R}$	27	O	**DATA TRANSMIT/RECEIVE:** needed in minimum system that desires to use an 8286/8287 data bus transceiver. It is used to control the direction of data flow through the transceiver. Logically DT/$\overline{R}$ is equivalent to $\overline{S_1}$ in the maximum mode, and its timing is the same as for M/$\overline{IO}$. (T = HIGH, R = LOW.) This signal floats to 3-state OFF in local bus "hold acknowledge".
$\overline{DEN}$	26	O	**DATA ENABLE:** provided as an output enable for the 8286/8287 in a minimum system which uses the transceiver. $\overline{DEN}$ is active LOW during each memory and I/O access and for INTA cycles. For a read or $\overline{INTA}$ cycle it is active from the middle of T_2 until the middle of T_4, while for a write cycle it is active from the beginning of T_2 until the middle of T_4. $\overline{DEN}$ floats to 3-state OFF in local bus "hold acknowledge".
HOLD, HLDA	31, 30	I/O	**HOLD:** indicates that another master is requesting a local bus "hold." To be acknowledged, HOLD must be active HIGH. The processor receiving the "hold" request will issue HLDA (HIGH) as an acknowledgement in the middle of a T_4 or T_i clock cycle. Simultaneous with the issuance of HLDA the processor will float the local bus and control lines. After HOLD is detected as being LOW, the processor will LOWer the HLDA, and when the processor needs to run another cycle, it will again drive the local bus and control lines. Hold acknowledge (HLDA) and HOLD have internal pull-up resistors. The same rules as for $\overline{RQ}/\overline{GT}$ apply regarding when the local bus will be released. HOLD is not an asynchronous input. External synchronization should be provided if the system cannot otherwise guarantee the setup time.

FUNCTIONAL DESCRIPTION

General Operation

The internal functions of the 8086 processor are partitioned logically into two processing units. The first is the Bus Interface Unit (BIU) and the second is the Execution Unit (EU) as shown in the block diagram of Figure 1.

These units can interact directly but for the most part perform as separate asynchronous operational processors. The bus interface unit provides the functions related to instruction fetching and queuing, operand fetch and store, and address relocation. This unit also provides the basic bus control. The overlap of instruction pre-fetching provided by this unit serves to increase processor performance through improved bus bandwidth utilization. Up to 6 bytes of the instruction stream can be queued while waiting for decoding and execution.

The instruction stream queuing mechanism allows the BIU to keep the memory utilized very efficiently. Whenever there is space for at least 2 bytes in the queue, the BIU will attempt a word fetch memory cycle. This greatly reduces "dead time" on the memory bus. The queue acts as a First-In-First-Out (FIFO) buffer, from which the EU extracts instruction bytes as required. If the queue is empty (following a branch instruction, for example), the first byte into the queue immediately becomes available to the EU.

The execution unit receives pre-fetched instructions from the BIU queue and provides un-relocated operand addresses to the BIU. Memory operands are passed through the BIU for processing by the EU, which passes results to the BIU for storage. See the Instruction Set description for further register set and architectural descriptions.

MEMORY ORGANIZATION

The processor provides a 20-bit address to memory which locates the byte being referenced. The memory is organized as a linear array of up to 1 million bytes, addressed as 00000(H) to FFFFF(H). The memory is logically divided into code, data, extra data, and stack segments of up to 64K bytes each, with each segment falling on 16-byte boundaries. (See Figure 3a.)

All memory references are made relative to base addresses contained in high speed segment registers. The segment types were chosen based on the addressing needs of programs. The segment register to be selected is automatically chosen according to the rules of the following table. All information in one segment type share the same logical attributes (e.g. code or data). By structuring memory into relocatable areas of similar characteristics and by automatically selecting segment registers, programs are shorter, faster, and more structured.

Word (16-bit) operands can be located on even or odd address boundaries and are thus not constrained to even boundaries as is the case in many 16-bit computers. For address and data operands, the least significant byte of the word is stored in the lower valued address location and the most significant byte in the next higher address location. The BIU automatically performs the proper number of memory accesses, one if the word operand is on an even byte boundary and two if it is on an odd byte boundary. Except for the performance penalty, this double access is transparent to the software. This performance penalty does not occur for instruction fetches, only word operands.

Physically, the memory is organized as a high bank ($D_{15}-D_8$) and a low bank (D_7-D_0) of 512K 8-bit bytes addressed in parallel by the processor's address lines $A_{19}-A_1$. Byte data with even addresses is transferred on the D_7-D_0 bus lines while odd addressed byte data (A_0 HIGH) is transferred on the $D_{15}-D_8$ bus lines. The processor provides two enable signals, $\overline{BHE}$ and A_0, to selectively allow reading from or writing into either an odd byte location, even byte location, or both. The instruction stream is fetched from memory as words and is addressed internally by the processor to the byte level as necessary.

Memory Reference Need	Segment Register Used	Segment Selection Rule
Instructions	CODE (CS)	Automatic with all instruction prefetch.
Stack	STACK (SS)	All stack pushes and pops. Memory references relative to BP base register except data references.
Local Data	DATA (DS)	Data references when: relative to stack, destination of string operation, or explicitly overridden.
External (Global) Data	EXTRA (ES)	Destination of string operations: explicitly selected using a segment override.

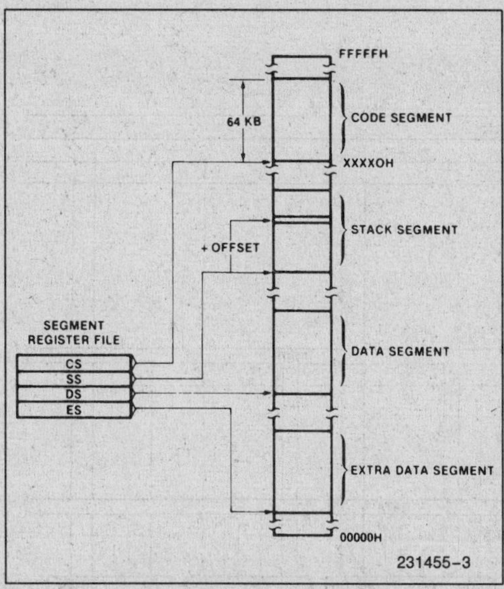

Figure 3a. Memory Organization

In referencing word data the BIU requires one or two memory cycles depending on whether or not the starting byte of the word is on an even or odd address, respectively. Consequently, in referencing word operands performance can be optimized by locating data on even address boundaries. This is an especially useful technique for using the stack, since odd address references to the stack may adversely affect the context switching time for interrupt processing or task multiplexing.

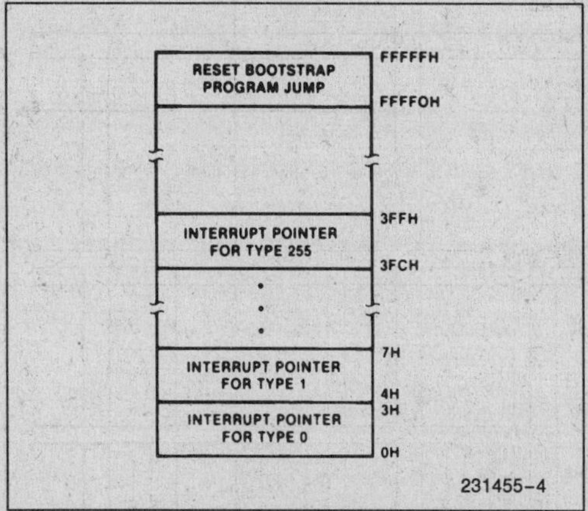

Figure 3b. Reserved Memory Locations

Certain locations in memory are reserved for specific CPU operations (see Figure 3b). Locations from address FFFF0H through FFFFFH are reserved for operations including a jump to the initial program loading routine. Following RESET, the CPU will always begin execution at location FFFF0H where the jump must be. Locations 00000H through 003FFH are reserved for interrupt operations. Each of the 256 possible interrupt types has its service routine pointed to by a 4-byte pointer element consisting of a 16-bit segment address and a 16-bit offset address. The pointer elements are assumed to have been stored at the respective places in reserved memory prior to occurrence of interrupts.

MINIMUM AND MAXIMUM MODES

The requirements for supporting minimum and maximum 8086 systems are sufficiently different that they cannot be done efficiently with 40 uniquely defined pins. Consequently, the 8086 is equipped with a strap pin (MN/$\overline{MX}$) which defines the system configuration. The definition of a certain subset of the pins changes dependent on the condition of the strap pin. When MN/$\overline{MX}$ pin is strapped to GND, the 8086 treats pins 24 through 31 in maximum mode. An 8288 bus controller interprets status information coded into $\overline{S_0}$, $\overline{S_2}$, $\overline{S_2}$ to generate bus timing and control signals compatible with the MULTIBUS® architecture. When the MN/$\overline{MX}$ pin is strapped to V_{CC}, the 8086 generates bus control signals itself on pins 24 through 31, as shown in parentheses in Figure 2. Examples of minimum mode and maximum mode systems are shown in Figure 4.

BUS OPERATION

The 8086 has a combined address and data bus commonly referred to as a time multiplexed bus. This technique provides the most efficient use of pins on the processor while permitting the use of a standard 40-lead package. This "local bus" can be buffered directly and used throughout the system with address latching provided on memory and I/O modules. In addition, the bus can also be demultiplexed at the processor with a single set of address latches if a standard non-multiplexed bus is desired for the system.

Each processor bus cycle consists of at least four CLK cycles. These are referred to as T_1, T_2, T_3 and T_4 (see Figure 5). The address is emitted from the processor during T_1 and data transfer occurs on the bus during T_3 and T_4. T_2 is used primarily for changing the direction of the bus during read operations. In the event that a "NOT READY" indication is given by the addressed device, "Wait" states (T_W) are inserted between T_3 and T_4. Each inserted "Wait" state is of the same duration as a CLK cycle. Periods

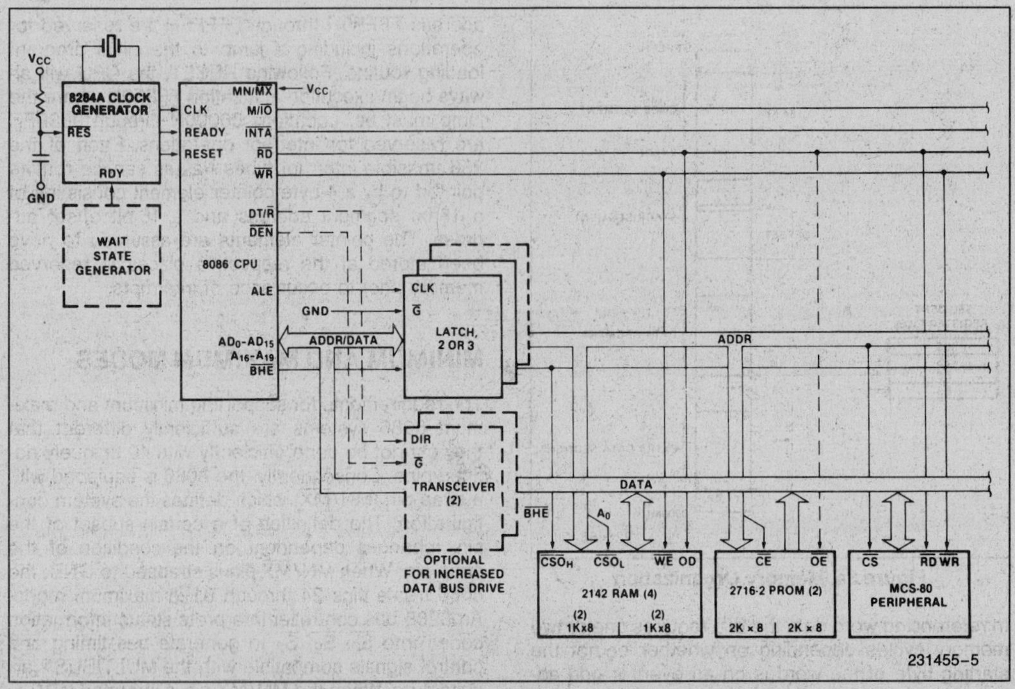

Figure 4a. Minimum Mode 8086 Typical Configuration

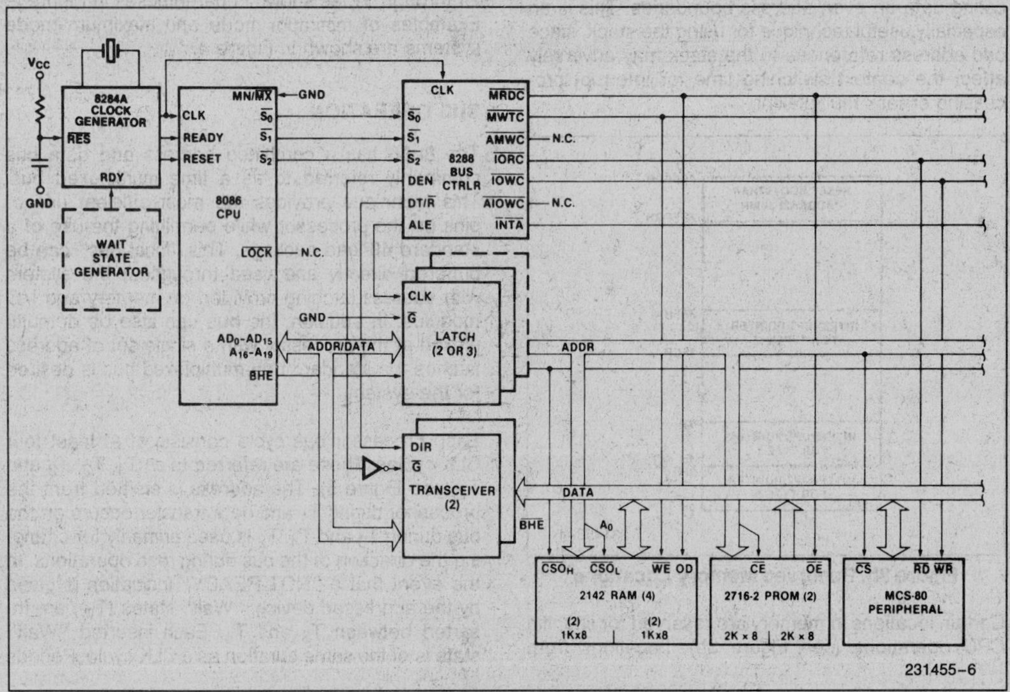

Figure 4b. Maximum Mode 8086 Typical Configuration

can occur between 8086 bus cycles. These are referred to as "Idle" states (T_i) or inactive CLK cycles. The processor uses these cycles for internal housekeeping.

During T_1 of any bus cycle the ALE (Address Latch Enable) signal is emitted (by either the processor or the 8288 bus controller, depending on the MN/$\overline{MX}$ strap). At the trailing edge of this pulse, a valid address and certain status information for the cycle may be latched.

Status bits $\overline{S_0}$, $\overline{S_1}$, and $\overline{S_2}$ are used, in maximum mode, by the bus controller to identify the type of bus transaction according to the following table:

$\overline{S_2}$	$\overline{S_1}$	$\overline{S_0}$	Characteristics
0 (LOW)	0	0	Interrupt Acknowledge
0	0	1	Read I/O
0	1	0	Write I/O
0	1	1	Halt
1 (HIGH)	0	0	Instruction Fetch
1	0	1	Read Data from Memory
1	1	0	Write Data to Memory
1	1	1	Passive (no bus cycle)

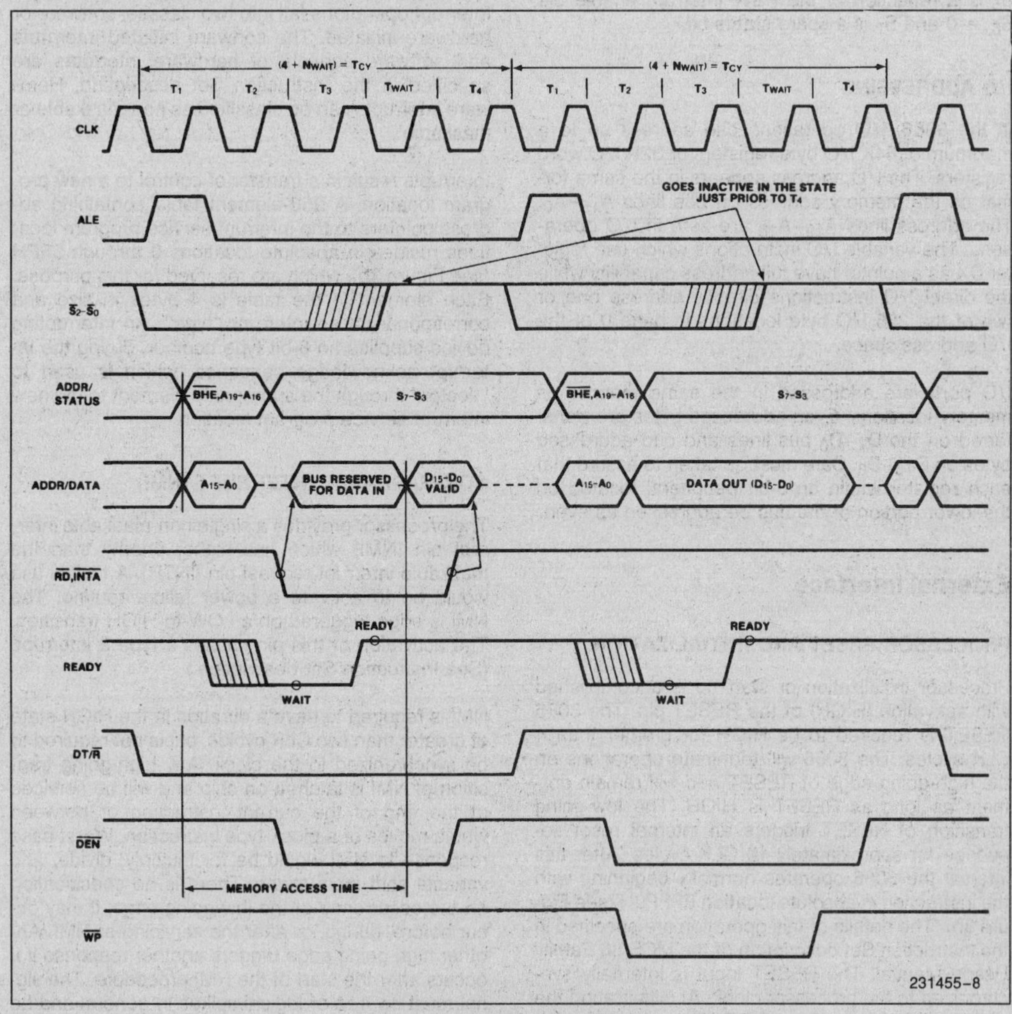

Figure 5. Basic System Timing

Status bits S_3 through S_7 are multiplexed with high-order address bits and the $\overline{BHE}$ signal, and are therefore valid during T_2 through T_4. S_3 and S_4 indicate which segment register (see Instruction Set description) was used for this bus cycle in forming the address, according to the following table:

S_4	S_3	Characteristics
0 (LOW)	0	Alternate Data (extra segment)
0	1	Stack
1 (HIGH)	0	Code or None
1	1	Data

S_5 is a reflection of the PSW interrupt enable bit. $S_6 = 0$ and S_7 is a spare status bit.

I/O ADDRESSING

In the 8086, I/O operations can address up to a maximum of 64K I/O byte registers or 32K I/O word registers. The I/O address appears in the same format as the memory address on bus lines $A_{15}-A_0$. The address lines $A_{19}-A_{16}$ are zero in I/O operations. The variable I/O instructions which use register DX as a pointer have full address capability while the direct I/O instructions directly address one or two of the 256 I/O byte locations in page 0 of the I/O address space.

I/O ports are addressed in the same manner as memory locations. Even addressed bytes are transferred on the D_7-D_0 bus lines and odd addressed bytes on $D_{15}-D_8$. Care must be taken to assure that each register within an 8-bit peripheral located on the lower portion of the bus be addressed as even.

External Interface

PROCESSOR RESET AND INITIALIZATION

Processor initialization or start up is accomplished with activation (HIGH) of the RESET pin. The 8086 RESET is required to be HIGH for greater than 4 CLK cycles. The 8086 will terminate operations on the high-going edge of RESET and will remain dormant as long as RESET is HIGH. The low-going transition of RESET triggers an internal reset sequence for approximately 10 CLK cycles. After this interval the 8086 operates normally beginning with the instruction in absolute location FFFF0H (see Figure 3b). The details of this operation are specified in the Instruction Set description of the MCS-86 Family User's Manual. The RESET input is internally synchronized to the processor clock. At initialization the HIGH-to-LOW transition of RESET must occur no sooner than 50 μs after power-up, to allow complete initialization of the 8086.

NMI asserted prior to the 2nd clock after the end of RESET will not be honored. If NMI is asserted after that point and during the internal reset sequence, the processor may execute one instruction before responding to the interrupt. A hold request active immediately after RESET will be honored before the first instruction fetch.

All 3-state outputs float to 3-state OFF during RESET. Status is active in the idle state for the first clock after RESET becomes active and then floats to 3-state OFF. ALE and HLDA are driven low.

INTERRUPT OPERATIONS

Interrupt operations fall into two classes; software or hardware initiated. The software initiated interrupts and software aspects of hardware interrupts are specified in the Instruction Set description. Hardware interrupts can be classified as non-maskable or maskable.

Interrupts result in a transfer of control to a new program location. A 256-element table containing address pointers to the interrupt service program locations resides in absolute locations 0 through 3FFH (see Figure 3b), which are reserved for this purpose. Each element in the table is 4 bytes in size and corresponds to an interrupt "type". An interrupting device supplies an 8-bit type number, during the interrupt acknowledge sequence, which is used to "vector" through the appropriate element to the new interrupt service program location.

NON-MASKABLE INTERRUPT (NMI)

The processor provides a single non-maskable interrupt pin (NMI) which has higher priority than the maskable interrupt request pin (INTR). A typical use would be to activate a power failure routine. The NMI is edge-triggered on a LOW-to-HIGH transition. The activation of this pin causes a type 2 interrupt. (See Instruction Set description.)

NMI is required to have a duration in the HIGH state of greater than two CLK cycles, but is not required to be synchronized to the clock. Any high-going transition of NMI is latched on-chip and will be serviced at the end of the current instruction or between whole moves of a block-type instruction. Worst case response to NMI would be for multiply, divide, and variable shift instructions. There is no specification on the occurrence of the low-going edge; it may occur before, during, or after the servicing of NMI. Another high-going edge triggers another response if it occurs after the start of the NMI procedure. The signal must be free of logical spikes in general and be free of bounces on the low-going edge to avoid triggering extraneous responses.

MASKABLE INTERRUPT (INTR)

The 8086 provides a single interrupt request input (INTR) which can be masked internally by software with the resetting of the interrupt enable FLAG status bit. The interrupt request signal is level triggered. It is internally synchronized during each clock cycle on the high-going edge of CLK. To be responded to, INTR must be present (HIGH) during the clock period preceding the end of the current instruction or the end of a whole move for a block-type instruction. During the interrupt response sequence further interrupts are disabled. The enable bit is reset as part of the response to any interrupt (INTR, NMI, software interrupt or single-step), although the FLAGS register which is automatically pushed onto the stack reflects the state of the processor prior to the interrupt. Until the old FLAGS register is restored the enable bit will be zero unless specifically set by an instruction.

During the response sequence (Figure 6) the processor executes two successive (back-to-back) interrupt acknowledge cycles. The 8086 emits the LOCK signal from T_2 of the first bus cycle until T_2 of the second. A local bus "hold" request will not be honored until the end of the second bus cycle. In the second bus cycle a byte is fetched from the external interrupt system (e.g., 8259A PIC) which identifies the source (type) of the interrupt. This byte is multiplied by four and used as a pointer into the interrupt vector lookup table. An INTR signal left HIGH will be continually responded to within the limitations of the enable bit and sample period. The INTERRUPT RETURN instruction includes a FLAGS pop which returns the status of the original interrupt enable bit when it restores the FLAGS.

HALT

When a software "HALT" instruction is executed the processor indicates that it is entering the "HALT" state in one of two ways depending upon which mode is strapped. In minimum mode, the processor issues one ALE with no qualifying bus control signals. In maximum mode, the processor issues appropriate HALT status on $\overline{S_2}$, $\overline{S_1}$, and $\overline{S_0}$; and the 8288 bus controller issues one ALE. The 8086 will not leave the "HALT" state when a local bus "hold" is entered while in "HALT". In this case, the processor reissues the HALT indicator. An interrupt request or RESET will force the 8086 out of the "HALT" state.

READ/MODIFY/WRITE (SEMAPHORE) OPERATIONS VIA LOCK

The $\overline{LOCK}$ status information is provided by the processor when directly consecutive bus cycles are required during the execution of an instruction. This provides the processor with the capability of performing read/modify/write operations on memory (via the Exchange Register With Memory instruction, for example) without the possibility of another system bus master receiving intervening memory cycles. This is useful in multi-processor system configurations to accomplish "test and set lock" operations. The $\overline{LOCK}$ signal is activated (forced LOW) in the clock cycle following the one in which the software "LOCK" prefix instruction is decoded by the EU. It is deactivated at the end of the last bus cycle of the instruction following the "LOCK" prefix instruction. While $\overline{LOCK}$ is active a request on a RQ/GT pin will be recorded and then honored at the end of the LOCK.

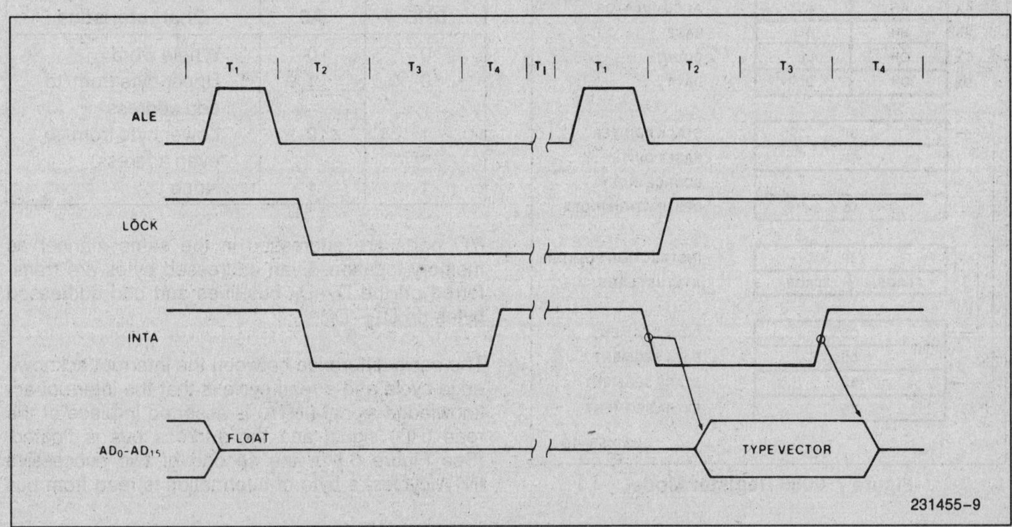

Figure 6. Interrupt Acknowledge Sequence

EXTERNAL SYNCHRONIZATION VIA TEST

As an alternative to the interrupts and general I/O capabilities, the 8086 provides a single software-testable input known as the $\overline{TEST}$ signal. At any time the program may execute a WAIT instruction. If at that time the $\overline{TEST}$ signal is inactive (HIGH), program execution becomes suspended while the processor waits for $\overline{TEST}$ to become active. It must remain active for at least 5 CLK cycles. The WAIT instruction is re-executed repeatedly until that time. This activity does not consume bus cycles. The processor remains in an idle state while waiting. All 8086 drivers go to 3-state OFF if bus "Hold" is entered. If interrupts are enabled, they may occur while the processor is waiting. When this occurs the processor fetches the WAIT instruction one extra time, processes the interrupt, and then re-fetches and re-executes the WAIT instruction upon returning from the interrupt.

Basic System Timing

Typical system configurations for the processor operating in minimum mode and in maximum mode are shown in Figures 4a and 4b, respectively. In minimum mode, the MN/$\overline{MX}$ pin is strapped to V_{CC} and the processor emits bus control signals in a manner similar to the 8085. In maximum mode, the MN/$\overline{MX}$ pin is strapped to V_{SS} and the processor emits coded status information which the 8288 bus controller uses to generate MULTIBUS compatible bus control signals. Figure 5 illustrates the signal timing relationships.

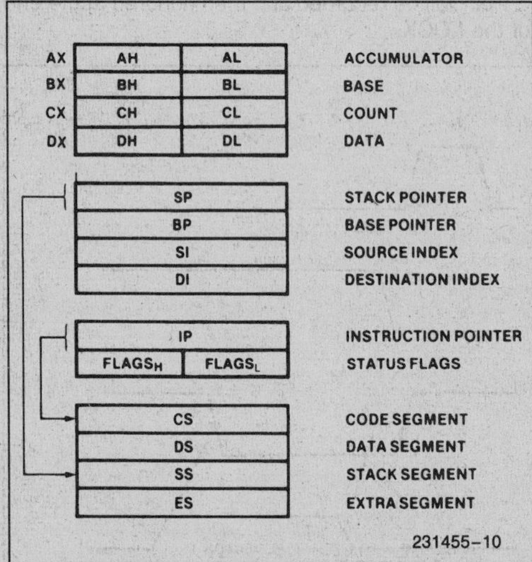

Figure 7. 8086 Register Model

SYSTEM TIMING—MINIMUM SYSTEM

The read cycle begins in T_1 with the assertion of the Address Latch Enable (ALE) signal. The trailing (low-going) edge of this signal is used to latch the address information, which is valid on the local bus at this time, into the address latch. The $\overline{BHE}$ and A_0 signals address the low, high, or both bytes. From T_1 to T_4 the M/$\overline{IO}$ signal indicates a memory or I/O operation. At T_2 the address is removed from the local bus and the bus goes to a high impedance state. The read control signal is also asserted at T_2. The read ($\overline{RD}$) signal causes the addressed device to enable its data bus drivers to the local bus. Some time later valid data will be available on the bus and the addressed device will drive the READY line HIGH. When the processor returns the read signal to a HIGH level, the addressed device will again 3-state its bus drivers. If a transceiver is required to buffer the 8086 local bus, signals DT/$\overline{R}$ and $\overline{DEN}$ are provided by the 8086.

A write cycle also begins with the assertion of ALE and the emission of the address. The M/$\overline{IO}$ signal is again asserted to indicate a memory or I/O write operation. In the T_2 immediately following the address emission the processor emits the data to be written into the addressed location. This data remains valid until the middle of T_4. During T_2, T_3, and T_W the processor asserts the write control signal. The write ($\overline{WR}$) signal becomes active at the beginning of T_2 as opposed to the read which is delayed somewhat into T_2 to provide time for the bus to float.

The $\overline{BHE}$ and A_0 signals are used to select the proper byte(s) of the memory/IO word to be read or written according to the following table:

$\overline{BHE}$	A0	Characteristics
0	0	Whole word
0	1	Upper byte from/to odd address
1	0	Lower byte from/to even address
1	1	None

I/O ports are addressed in the same manner as memory location. Even addressed bytes are transferred on the D_7–D_0 bus lines and odd addressed bytes on D_{15}–D_8.

The basic difference between the interrupt acknowledge cycle and a read cycle is that the interrupt acknowledge signal ($\overline{INTA}$) is asserted in place of the read ($\overline{RD}$) signal and the address bus is floated. (See Figure 6.) In the second of two successive INTA cycles, a byte of information is read from bus lines D_7-D_0 as supplied by the inerrupt system logic (i.e., 8259A Priority Interrupt Controller). This byte identifies the source (type) of the interrupt. It is multiplied by four and used as a pointer into an interrupt vector lookup table, as described earlier.

BUS TIMING—MEDIUM SIZE SYSTEMS

For medium size systems the MN/$\overline{MX}$ pin is connected to V_{SS} and the 8288 Bus Controller is added to the system as well as a latch for latching the system address, and a transceiver to allow for bus loading greater than the 8086 is capable of handling. Signals ALE, DEN, and DT/$\overline{R}$ are generated by the 8288 instead of the processor in this configuration although their timing remains relatively the same. The 8086 status outputs ($\overline{S_2}$, $\overline{S_1}$, and $\overline{S_0}$) provide type-of-cycle information and become 8288 inputs. This bus cycle information specifies read (code, data, or I/O), write (data or I/O), interrupt acknowledge, or software halt. The 8288 thus issues control signals specifying memory read or write, I/O read or write, or interrupt acknowledge. The 8288 provides two types of write strobes, normal and advanced, to be applied as required. The normal write strobes have data valid at the leading edge of write. The advanced write strobes have the same timing as read strobes, and hence data isn't valid at the leading edge of write. The transceiver receives the usual DIR and $\overline{G}$ inputs from the 8288's DT/$\overline{R}$ and DEN.

The pointer into the interrupt vector table, which is passed during the second INTA cycle, can derive from an 8259A located on either the local bus or the system bus. If the master 8259A Priority Interrupt Controller is positioned on the local bus, a TTL gate is required to disable the transceiver when reading from the master 8259A during the interrupt acknowledge sequence and software "poll".

6

ABSOLUTE MAXIMUM RATINGS*

Ambient Temperature Under Bias ......0°C to 70°C

Storage Temperature ....−65°C to +150°C

Voltage on Any Pin with
Respect to Ground..............−1.0V to +7V

Power Dissipation.........................2.5W

NOTICE: This is a production data sheet. The specifications are subject to change without notice.

**WARNING: Stressing the device beyond the "Absolute Maximum Ratings" may cause permanent damage. These are stress ratings only. Operation beyond the "Operating Conditions" is not recommended and extended exposure beyond the "Operating Conditions" may affect device reliability.*

D.C. CHARACTERISTICS

(8086: T_A = 0°C to 70°C, V_{CC} = 5V ±10%)
(8086-1: T_A = 0°C to 70°C, V_{CC} = 5V ±5%)
(8086-2: T_A = 0°C to 70°C, V_{CC} = 5V ±5%)

Symbol	Parameter	Min	Max	Units	Test Conditions
V_{IL}	Input Low Voltage	−0.5	+0.8	V	(Note 1)
V_{IH}	Input High Voltage	2.0	V_{CC} + 0.5	V	(Notes 1, 2)
V_{OL}	Output Low Voltage		0.45	V	I_{OL} = 2.5 mA
V_{OH}	Output High Voltage	2.4		V	I_{OH} = − 400 μA
I_{CC}	Power Supply Current: 8086 8086-1 8086-2		340 360 350	mA	T_A = 25°C
I_{LI}	Input Leakage Current		±10	μA	0V ≤ V_{IN} ≤ V_{CC} (Note 3)
I_{LO}	Output Leakage Current		±10	μA	0.45V ≤ V_{OUT} ≤ V_{CC}
V_{CL}	Clock Input Low Voltage	−0.5	+0.6	V	
V_{CH}	Clock Input High Voltage	3.9	V_{CC} + 1.0	V	
C_{IN}	Capacitance of Input Buffer (All input except AD_0–AD_{15}, $\overline{RQ}/\overline{GT}$)		15	pF	fc = 1 MHz
C_{IO}	Capacitance of I/O Buffer (AD_0–AD_{15}, $\overline{RQ}/\overline{GT}$)		15	pF	fc = 1 MHz

NOTES:
1. V_{IL} tested with MN/$\overline{MX}$ Pin = 0V. V_{IH} tested with MN/$\overline{MX}$ Pin = 5V. MN/$\overline{MX}$ Pin is a Strap Pin.
2. Not applicable to $\overline{RQ}/\overline{GT0}$ and $\overline{RQ}/\overline{GT1}$ (Pins 30 and 31).
3. HOLD and HLDA I_{LI} min = 30 μA, max = 500 μA.

A.C. CHARACTERISTICS

(8086: T_A = 0°C to 70°C, V_{CC} = 5V ± 10%)
(8086-1: T_A = 0°C to 70°C, V_{CC} = 5V ± 5%)
(8086-2: T_A = 0°C to 70°C, V_{CC} = 5V ± 5%)

MINIMUM COMPLEXITY SYSTEM TIMING REQUIREMENTS

Symbol	Parameter	8086		8086-1		8086-2		Units	Test Conditions
		Min	Max	Min	Max	Min	Max		
TCLCL	CLK Cycle Period	200	500	100	500	125	500	ns	
TCLCH	CLK Low Time	118		53		68		ns	
TCHCL	CLK High Time	69		39		44		ns	
TCH1CH2	CLK Rise Time		10		10		10	ns	From 1.0V to 3.5V
TCL2CL1	CLK Fall Time		10		10		10	ns	From 3.5V to 1.0V
TDVCL	Data in Setup Time	30		5		20		ns	
TCLDX	Data in Hold Time	10		10		10		ns	
TR1VCL	RDY Setup Time into 8284A (See Notes 1, 2)	35		35		35		ns	
TCLR1X	RDY Hold Time into 8284A (See Notes 1, 2)	0		0		0		ns	
TRYHCH	READY Setup Time into 8086	118		53		68		ns	
TCHRYX	READY Hold Time into 8086	30		20		20		ns	
TRYLCL	READY Inactive to CLK (See Note 3)	−8		−10		−8		ns	
THVCH	HOLD Setup Time	35		20		20		ns	
TINVCH	INTR, NMI, $\overline{\text{TEST}}$ Setup Time (See Note 2)	30		15		15		ns	
TILIH	Input Rise Time (Except CLK)		20		20		20	ns	From 0.8V to 2.0V
TIHIL	Input Fall Time (Except CLK)		12		12		12	ns	From 2.0V to 0.8V

A.C. CHARACTERISTICS (Continued)

TIMING RESPONSES

Symbol	Parameter	8086		8086-1		8086-2		Units	Test Conditions
		Min	Max	Min	Max	Min	Max		
TCLAV	Address Valid Delay	10	110	10	50	10	60	ns	*C_L = 20–100 pF for all 8086 Outputs (In addition to 8086 selfload)
TCLAX	Address Hold Time	10		10		10		ns	
TCLAZ	Address Float Delay	TCLAX	80	10	40	TCLAX	50	ns	
TLHLL	ALE Width	TCLCH-20		TCLCH-10		TCLCH-10		ns	
TCLLH	ALE Active Delay		80		40		50	ns	
TCHLL	ALE Inactive Delay		85		45		55	ns	
TLLAX	Address Hold Time	TCHCL-10		TCHCL-10		TCHCL-10		ns	
TCLDV	Data Valid Delay	10	110	10	50	10	60	ns	
TCHDX	Data Hold Time	10		10		10		ns	
TWHDX	Data Hold Time After WR	TCLCH-30		TCLCH-25		TCLCH-30		ns	
TCVCTV	Control Active Delay 1	10	110	10	50	10	70	ns	
TCHCTV	Control Active Delay 2	10	110	10	45	10	60	ns	
TCVCTX	Control Inactive Delay	10	110	10	50	10	70	ns	
TAZRL	Address Float to READ Active	0		0		0		ns	
TCLRL	$\overline{RD}$ Active Delay	10	165	10	70	10	100	ns	
TCLRH	$\overline{RD}$ Inactive Delay	10	150	10	60	10	80	ns	
TRHAV	$\overline{RD}$ Inactive to Next Address Active	TCLCL-45		TCLCL-35		TCLCL-40		ns	
TCLHAV	HLDA Valid Delay	10	160	10	60	10	100	ns	
TRLRH	$\overline{RD}$ Width	2TCLCL-75		2TCLCL-40		2TCLCL-50		ns	
TWLWH	$\overline{WR}$ Width	2TCLCL-60		2TCLCL-35		2TCLCL-40		ns	
TAVAL	Address Valid to ALE Low	TCLCH-60		TCLCH-35		TCLCH-40		ns	
TOLOH	Output Rise Time		20		20		20	ns	From 0.8V to 2.0V
TOHOL	Output Fall Time		12		12		12	ns	From 2.0V to 0.8V

NOTES:
1. Signal at 8284A shown for reference only.
2. Setup requirement for asynchronous signal only to guarantee recognition at next CLK.
3. Applies only to T2 state. (8 ns into T3).

A.C. TESTING INPUT, OUTPUT WAVEFORM

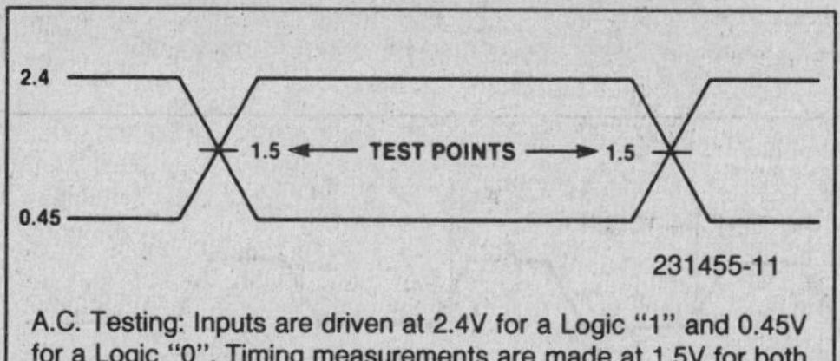

231455-11

A.C. Testing: Inputs are driven at 2.4V for a Logic "1" and 0.45V for a Logic "0". Timing measurements are made at 1.5V for both a Logic "1" and "0".

A.C. TESTING LOAD CIRCUIT

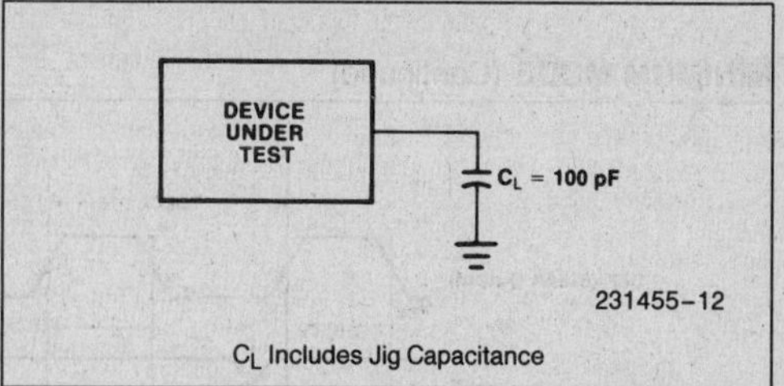

231455-12

C_L Includes Jig Capacitance

WAVEFORMS

MINIMUM MODE

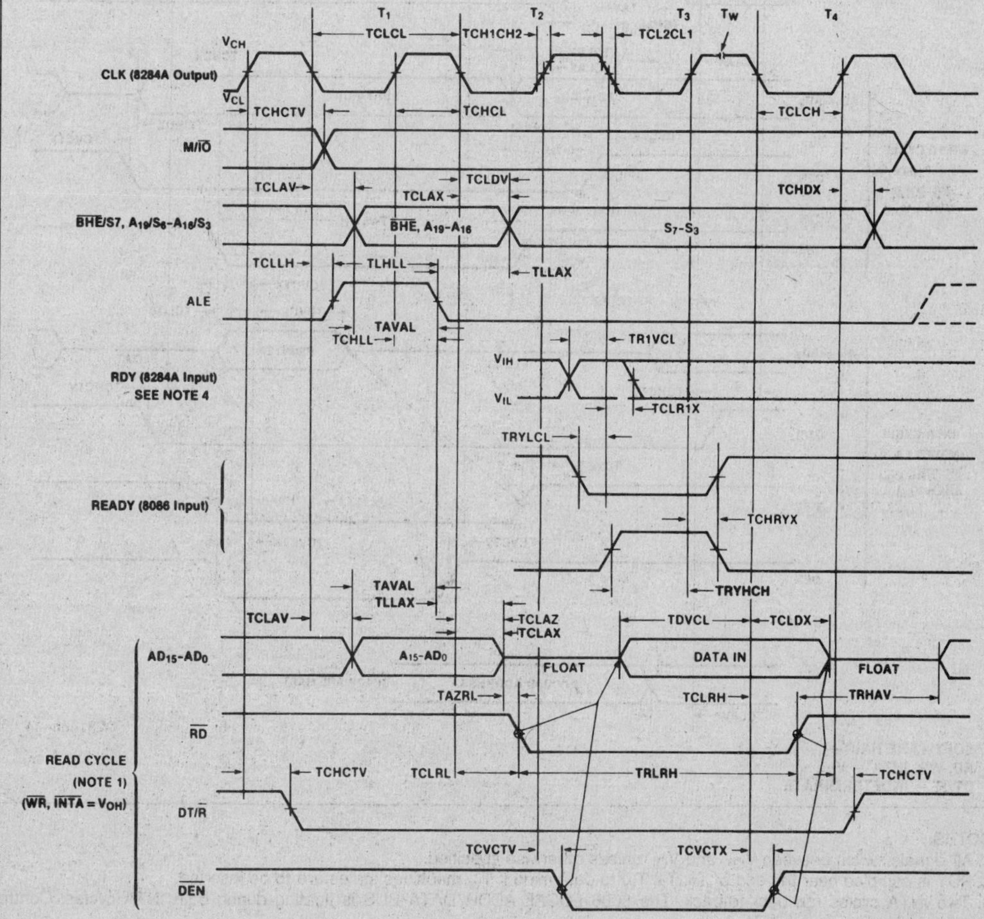

CLK (8284A Output), M/$\overline{IO}$, $\overline{BHE}$/S7, $A_{19}/S_6-A_{16}/S_3$, ALE, RDY (8284A Input) SEE NOTE 4, READY (8086 Input), READ CYCLE (NOTE 1) ($\overline{WR}$, $\overline{INTA}$ = V_{OH}): $AD_{15}-AD_0$, $\overline{RD}$, DT/$\overline{R}$, $\overline{DEN}$

231455-13

WAVEFORMS (Continued)

MINIMUM MODE (Continued)

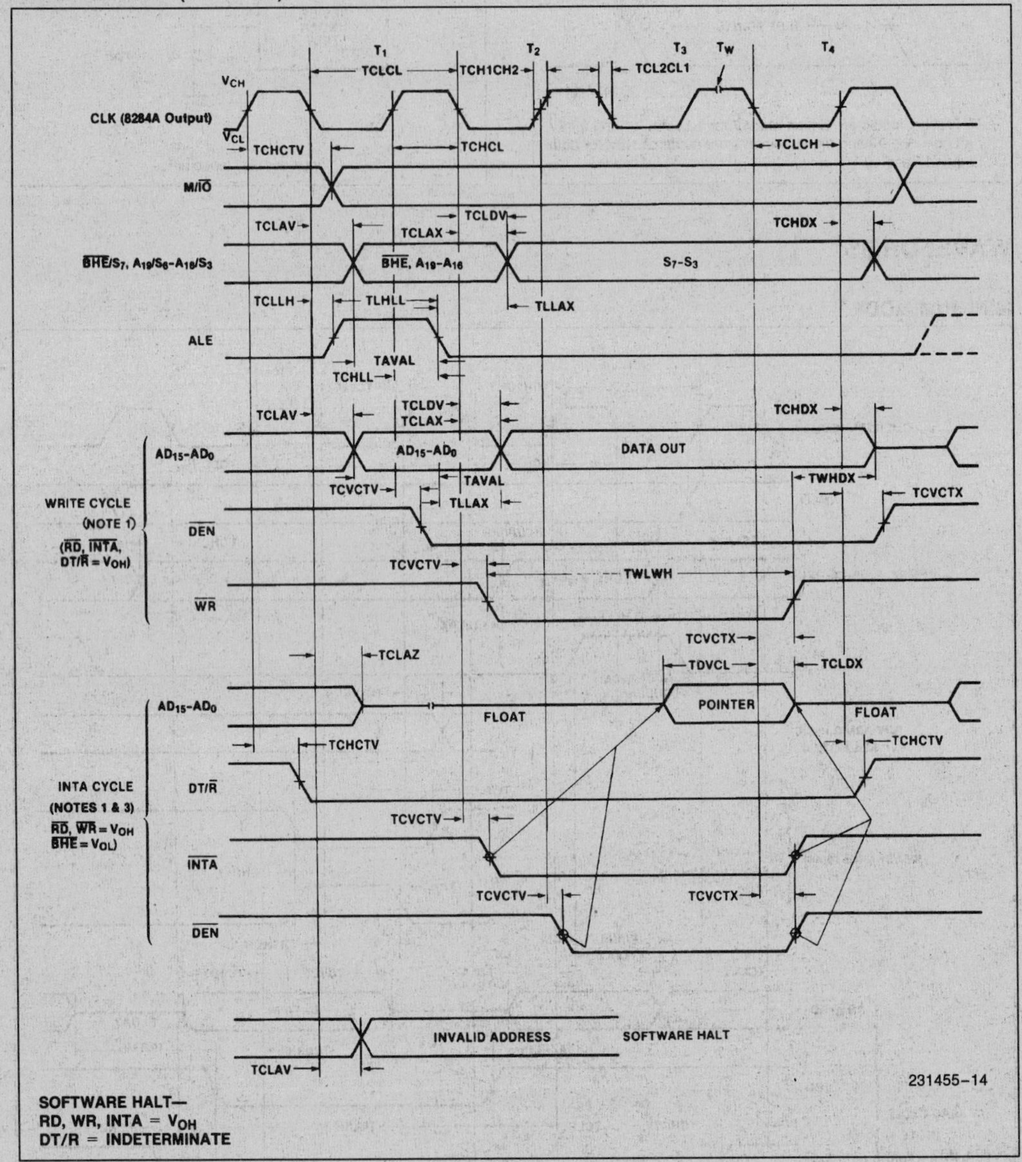

NOTES:
1. All signals switch between V_{OH} and V_{OL} unless otherwise specified.
2. RDY is sampled near the end of T_2, T_3, T_W to determine if T_W machines states are to be inserted.
3. Two INTA cycles run back-to-back. The 8086 LOCAL ADDR/DATA BUS is floating during both INTA cycles. Control signals shown for second INTA cycle.
4. Signals at 8284A are shown for reference only.
5. All timing measurements are made at 1.5V unless otherwise noted.

A.C. CHARACTERISTICS

MAX MODE SYSTEM (USING 8288 BUS CONTROLLER) TIMING REQUIREMENTS

Symbol	Parameter	8086		8086-1		8086-2		Units	Test Conditions
		Min	Max	Min	Max	Min	Max		
TCLCL	CLK Cycle Period	200	500	100	500	125	500	ns	
TCLCH	CLK Low Time	118		53		68		ns	
TCHCL	CLK High Time	69		39		44		ns	
TCH1CH2	CLK Rise Time		10		10		10	ns	From 1.0V to 3.5V
TCL2CL1	CLK Fall Time		10		10		10	ns	From 3.5V to 1.0V
TDVCL	Data in Setup Time	30		5		20		ns	
TCLDX	Data in Hold Time	10		10		10		ns	
TR1VCL	RDY Setup Time into 8284A (Notes 1, 2)	35		35		35		ns	
TCLR1X	RDY Hold Time into 8284A (Notes 1, 2)	0		0		0		ns	
TRYHCH	READY Setup Time into 8086	118		53		68		ns	
TCHRYX	READY Hold Time into 8086	30		20		20		ns	
TRYLCL	READY Inactive to CLK (Note 4)	−8		−10		−8		ns	
TINVCH	Setup Time for Recognition (INTR, NMI, $\overline{TEST}$) (Note 2)	30		15		15		ns	
TGVCH	$\overline{RQ}/\overline{GT}$ Setup Time (Note 5)	30		15		15		ns	
TCHGX	$\overline{RQ}$ Hold Time into 8086	40		20		30		ns	
TILIH	Input Rise Time (Except CLK)		20		20		20	ns	From 0.8V to 2.0V
TIHIL	Input Fall Time (Except CLK)		12		12		12	ns	From 2.0V to 0.8V

A.C. CHARACTERISTICS (Continued)

TIMING RESPONSES

Symbol	Parameter	8086		8086-1		8086-2		Units	Test Conditions
		Min	Max	Min	Max	Min	Max		
TCLML	Command Active Delay (See Note 1)	10	35	10	35	10	35	ns	C_L = 20–100 pF for all 8086 Outputs (In addition to 8086 self-load)
TCLMH	Command Inactive Delay (See Note 1)	10	35	10	35	10	35	ns	
TRYHSH	READY Active to Status Passive (See Note 3)		110		45		65	ns	
TCHSV	Status Active Delay	10	110	10	45	10	60	ns	
TCLSH	Status Inactive Delay	10	130	10	55	10	70	ns	
TCLAV	Address Valid Delay	10	110	10	50	10	60	ns	
TCLAX	Address Hold Time	10		10		10		ns	
TCLAZ	Address Float Delay	TCLAX	80	10	40	TCLAX	50	ns	
TSVLH	Status Valid to ALE High (See Note 1)		15		15		15	ns	
TSVMCH	Status Valid to MCE High (See Note 1)		15		15		15	ns	
TCLLH	CLK Low to ALE Valid (See Note 1)		15		15		15	ns	
TCLMCH	CLK Low to MCE High (See Note 1)		15		15		15	ns	
TCHLL	ALE Inactive Delay (See Note 1)		15		15		15	ns	
TCLMCL	MCE Inactive Delay (See Note 1)		15		15		15	ns	
TCLDV	Data Valid Delay	10	110	10	50	10	60	ns	
TCHDX	Data Hold Time	10		10		10		ns	
TCVNV	Control Active Delay (See Note 1)	5	45	5	45	5	45	ns	
TCVNX	Control Inactive Delay (See Note 1)	10	45	10	45	10	45	ns	
TAZRL	Address Float to READ Active	0		0		0		ns	
TCLRL	RD Active Delay	10	165	10	70	10	100	ns	
TCLRH	RD Inactive Delay	10	150	10	60	10	80	ns	

A.C. CHARACTERISTICS (Continued)

TIMING RESPONSES (Continued)

Symbol	Parameter	8086		8086-1		8086-2		Units	Test Conditions
		Min	Max	Min	Max	Min	Max		
TRHAV	RD Inactive to Next Address Active	TCLCL-45		TCLCL-35		TCLCL-40		ns	C_L = 20–100 pF for all 8086 Outputs (In addition to 8086 self-load)
TCHDTL	Direction Control Active Delay (Note 1)		50		50		50	ns	
TCHDTH	Direction Control Inactive Delay (Note 1)		30		30		30	ns	
TCLGL	GT Active Delay	0	85	0	38	0	50	ns	
TCLGH	GT Inactive Delay	0	85	0	45	0	50	ns	
TRLRH	RD Width	2TCLCL-75		2TCLCL-40		2TCLCL-50		ns	
TOLOH	Output Rise Time		20		20		20	ns	From 0.8V to 2.0V
TOHOL	Output Fall Time		12		12		12	ns	From 2.0V to 0.8V

NOTES:
1. Signal at 8284A or 8288 shown for reference only.
2. Setup requirement for asynchronous signal only to guarantee recognition at next CLK.
3. Applies only to T3 and wait states.
4. Applies only to T2 state (8 ns into T3).

WAVEFORMS

MAXIMUM MODE

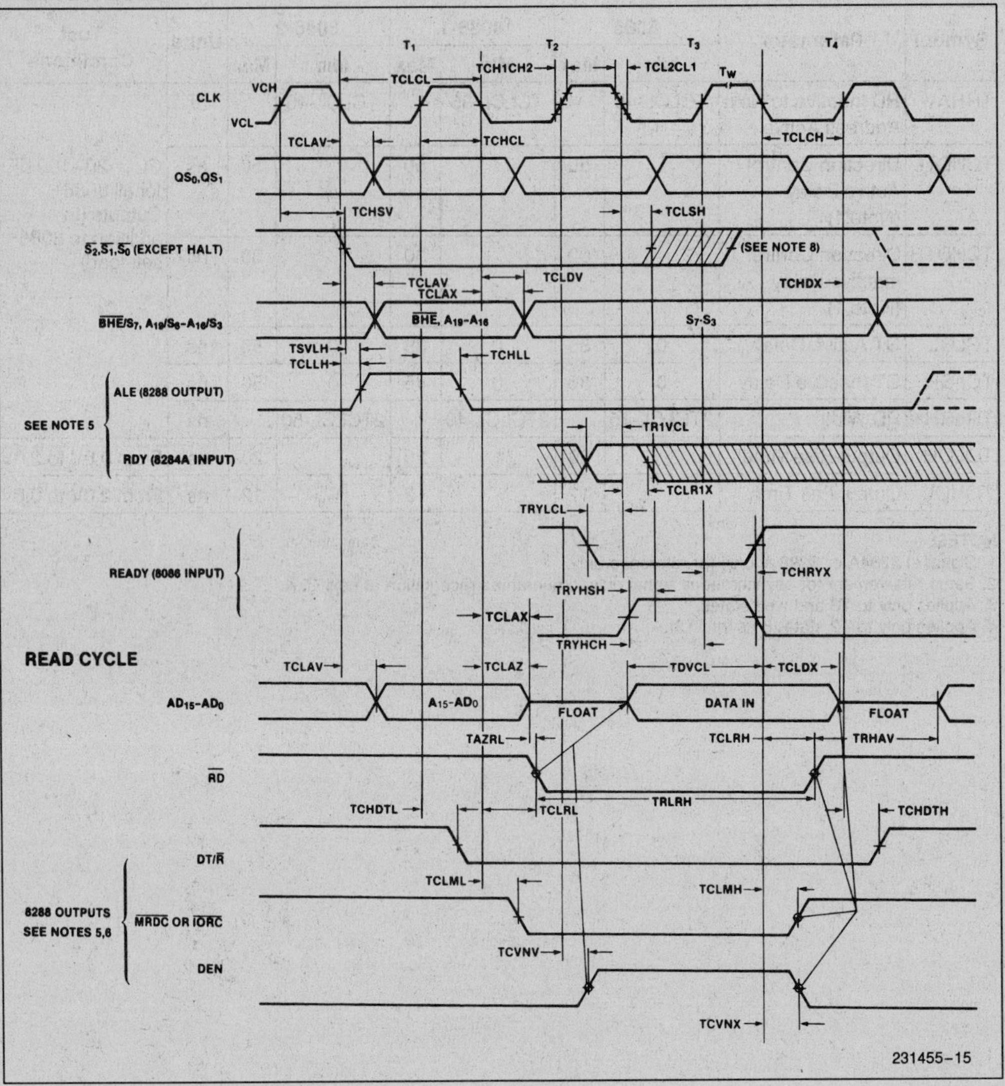

T1 T2 T3 Tw T4

TCLCL TCH1CH2 TCL2CL1

CLK VCH VCL

TCLAV TCHCL TCLCH

QS_0, QS_1

TCHSV TCLSH

$\overline{S_2}, \overline{S_1}, \overline{S_0}$ (EXCEPT HALT)

(SEE NOTE 8)

TCLAV TCLAX TCLDV TCHDX

$\overline{BHE}/S_7$, A_{19}/S_6–A_{16}/S_3

$\overline{BHE}$, A_{19}–A_{16}

S_7-S_3

TSVLH TCLLH TCHLL

SEE NOTE 5

ALE (8288 OUTPUT)

RDY (8284A INPUT)

TR1VCL TCLR1X

TRYLCL

READY (8086 INPUT)

TCHRYX TRYHSH TCLAX TRYHCH

READ CYCLE

TCLAV TCLAZ TDVCL TCLDX

AD_{15}–AD_0

A_{15}–AD_0 FLOAT DATA IN FLOAT

TAZRL TCLRH TRHAV

$\overline{RD}$

TCHDTL TCLRL TRLRH TCHDTH

DT/$\overline{R}$

TCLML TCLMH

8288 OUTPUTS
SEE NOTES 5,6

$\overline{MRDC}$ OR $\overline{IORC}$

TCVNV

DEN

TCVNX

231455–15

WAVEFORMS (Continued)

MAXIMUM MODE (Continued)

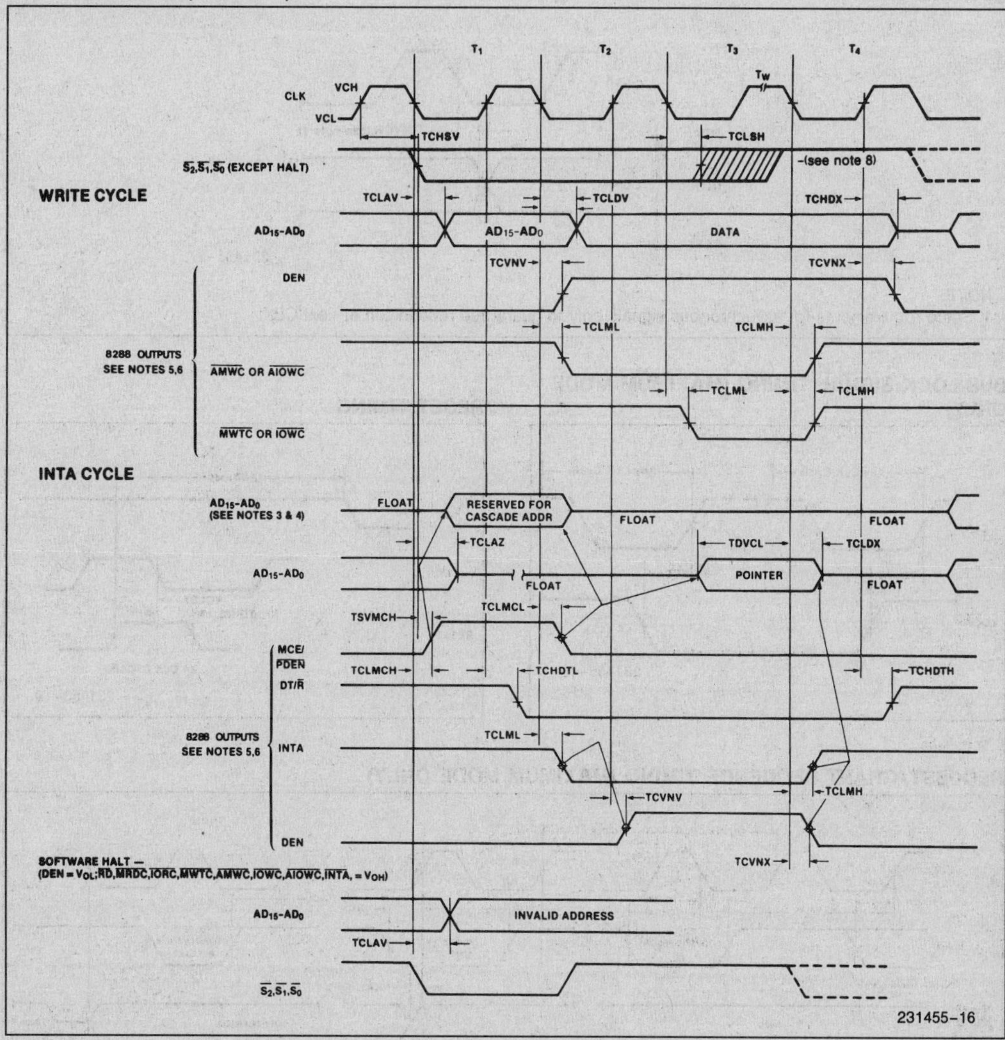

NOTES:
1. All signals switch between V_{OH} and V_{OL} unless otherwise specified.
2. RDY is sampled near the end of T_2, T_3, T_W to determine if T_W machines states are to be inserted.
3. Cascade address is valid between first and second INTA cycle.
4. Two INTA cycles run back-to-back. The 8086 LOCAL ADDR/DATA BUS is floating during both INTA cycles. Control for pointer address is shown for second INTA cycle.
5. Signals at 8284A or 8288 are shown for reference only.
6. The issuance of the 8288 command and control signals ($\overline{MRDC}$, $\overline{MWTC}$, $\overline{AMWC}$, $\overline{IORC}$, $\overline{IOWC}$, $\overline{AIOWC}$, $\overline{INTA}$ and DEN) lags the active high 8288 CEN.
7. All timing measurements are made at 1.5V unless otherwise noted.
8. Status inactive in state just prior to T_4.

WAVEFORMS (Continued)

ASYNCHRONOUS SIGNAL RECOGNITION

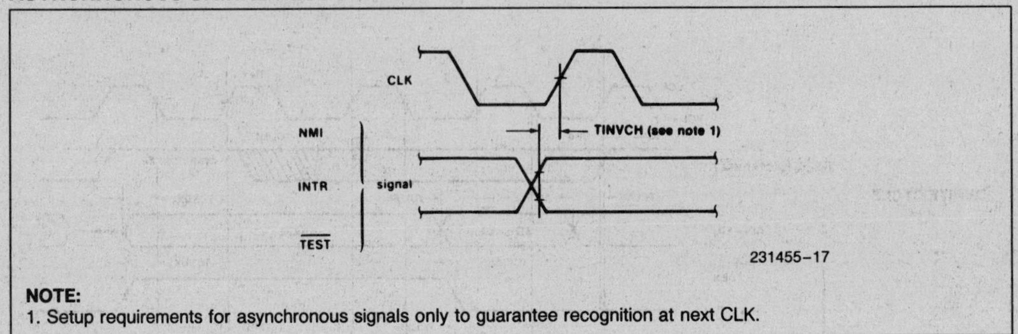

NOTE:
1. Setup requirements for asynchronous signals only to guarantee recognition at next CLK.

BUS LOCK SIGNAL TIMING (MAXIMUM MODE ONLY)

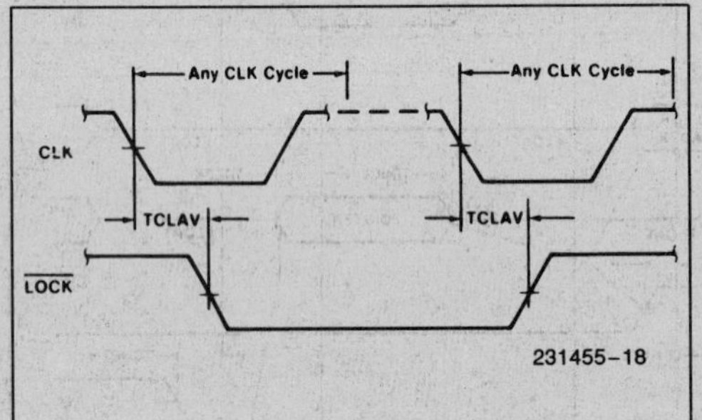

RESET TIMING

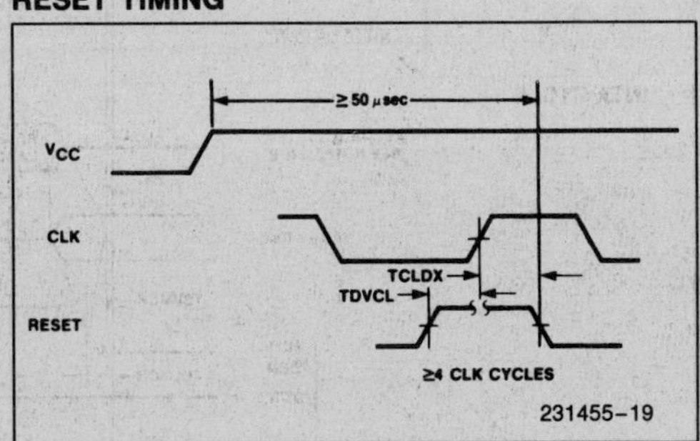

REQUEST/GRANT SEQUENCE TIMING (MAXIMUM MODE ONLY)

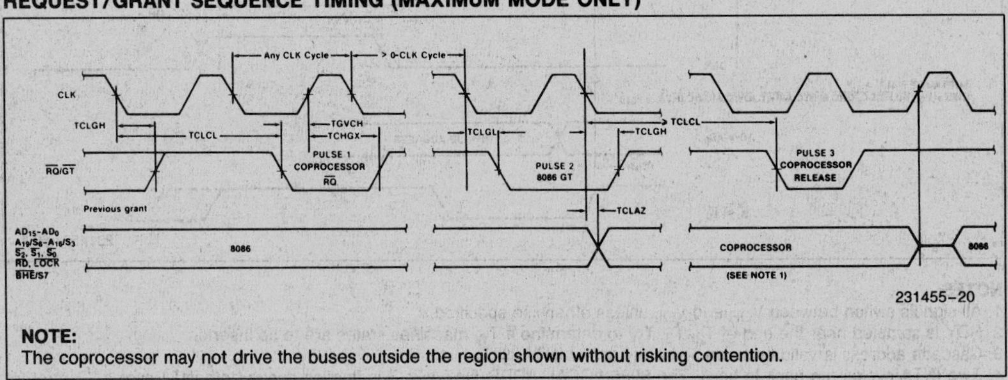

NOTE:
The coprocessor may not drive the buses outside the region shown without risking contention.

WAVEFORMS (Continued)

HOLD/HOLD ACKNOWLEDGE TIMING (MINIMUM MODE ONLY)

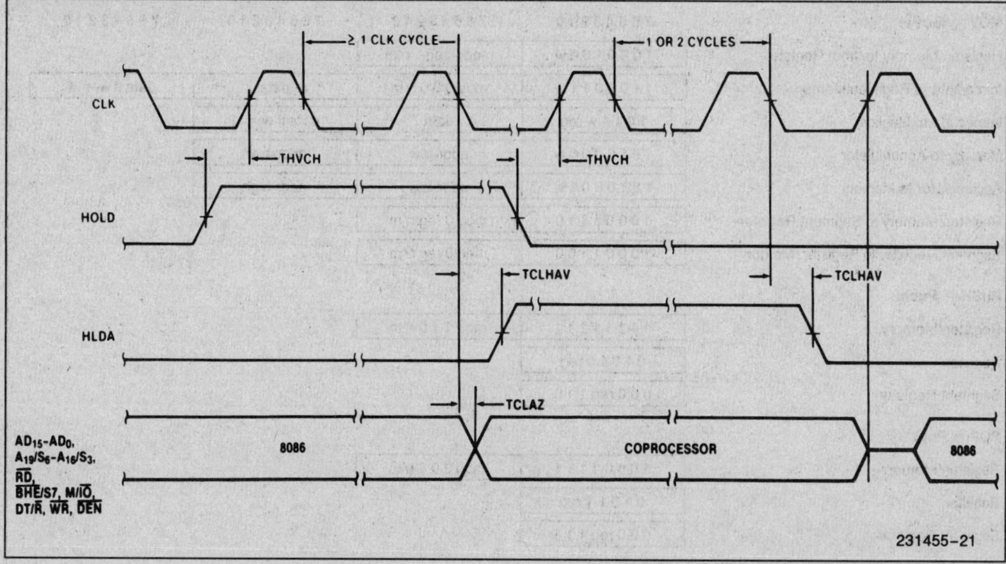

Table 2. Instruction Set Summary

Mnemonic and Description	Instruction Code			
DATA TRANSFER				
MOV = **Move:**	7 6 5 4 3 2 1 0	7 6 5 4 3 2 1 0	7 6 5 4 3 2 1 0	7 6 5 4 3 2 1 0
Register/Memory to/from Register	1 0 0 0 1 0 d w	mod reg r/m		
Immediate to Register/Memory	1 1 0 0 0 1 1 w	mod 0 0 0 r/m	data	data if w = 1
Immediate to Register	1 0 1 1 w reg	data	data if w = 1	
Memory to Accumulator	1 0 1 0 0 0 0 w	addr-low	addr-high	
Accumulator to Memory	1 0 1 0 0 0 1 w	addr-low	addr-high	
Register/Memory to Segment Register	1 0 0 0 1 1 1 0	mod 0 reg r/m		
Segment Register to Register/Memory	1 0 0 0 1 1 0 0	mod 0 reg r/m		
PUSH = **Push:**				
Register/Memory	1 1 1 1 1 1 1 1	mod 1 1 0 r/m		
Register	0 1 0 1 0 reg			
Segment Register	0 0 0 reg 1 1 0			
POP = **Pop:**				
Register/Memory	1 0 0 0 1 1 1 1	mod 0 0 0 r/m		
Register	0 1 0 1 1 reg			
Segment Register	0 0 0 reg 1 1 1			
XCHG = **Exchange:**				
Register/Memory with Register	1 0 0 0 0 1 1 w	mod reg r/m		
Register with Accumulator	1 0 0 1 0 reg			
IN = **Input from:**				
Fixed Port	1 1 1 0 0 1 0 w	port		
Variable Port	1 1 1 0 1 1 0 w			
OUT = **Output to:**				
Fixed Port	1 1 1 0 0 1 1 w	port		
Variable Port	1 1 1 0 1 1 1 w			
XLAT = Translate Byte to AL	1 1 0 1 0 1 1 1			
LEA = Load EA to Register	1 0 0 0 1 1 0 1	mod reg r/m		
LDS = Load Pointer to DS	1 1 0 0 0 1 0 1	mod reg r/m		
LES = Load Pointer to ES	1 1 0 0 0 1 0 0	mod reg r/m		
LAHF = Load AH with Flags	1 0 0 1 1 1 1 1			
SAHF = Store AH into Flags	1 0 0 1 1 1 1 0			
PUSHF = Push Flags	1 0 0 1 1 1 0 0			
POPF = Pop Flags	1 0 0 1 1 1 0 1			

Table 2. Instruction Set Summary (Continued)

Mnemonic and Description	Instruction Code			
ARITHMETIC	76543210	76543210	76543210	76543210
ADD = Add:				
Reg./Memory with Register to Either	0 0 0 0 0 0 d w	mod reg r/m		
Immediate to Register/Memory	1 0 0 0 0 0 s w	mod 0 0 0 r/m	data	data if s: w = 01
Immediate to Accumulator	0 0 0 0 0 1 0 w	data	data if w = 1	
ADC = Add with Carry:				
Reg./Memory with Register to Either	0 0 0 1 0 0 d w	mod reg r/m		
Immediate to Register/Memory	1 0 0 0 0 0 s w	mod 0 1 0 r/m	data	data if s: w = 01
Immediate to Accumulator	0 0 0 1 0 1 0 w	data	data if w = 1	
INC = Increment:				
Register/Memory	1 1 1 1 1 1 1 w	mod 0 0 0 r/m		
Register	0 1 0 0 0 reg			
AAA = ASCII Adjust for Add	0 0 1 1 0 1 1 1			
BAA = Decimal Adjust for Add	0 0 1 0 0 1 1 1			
SUB = Subtract:				
Reg./Memory and Register to Either	0 0 1 0 1 0 d w	mod reg r/m		
Immediate from Register/Memory	1 0 0 0 0 0 s w	mod 1 0 1 r/m	data	data if s w = 01
Immediate from Accumulator	0 0 1 0 1 1 0 w	data	data if w = 1	
SSB = Subtract with Borrow				
Reg./Memory and Register to Either	0 0 0 1 1 0 d w	mod reg r/m		
Immediate from Register/Memory	1 0 0 0 0 0 s w	mod 0 1 1 r/m	data	data if s w = 01
Immediate from Accumulator	0 0 0 1 1 1 w	data	data if w = 1	
DEC = Decrement:				
Register/memory	1 1 1 1 1 1 1 w	mod 0 0 1 r/m		
Register	0 1 0 0 1 reg			
NEG = Change sign	1 1 1 1 0 1 1 w	mod 0 1 1 r/m		
CMP = Compare:				
Register/Memory and Register	0 0 1 1 1 0 d w	mod reg r/m		
Immediate with Register/Memory	1 0 0 0 0 0 s w	mod 1 1 1 r/m	data	data if s w = 01
Immediate with Accumulator	0 0 1 1 1 1 0 w	data	data if w = 1	
AAS = ASCII Adjust for Subtract	0 0 1 1 1 1 1 1			
DAS = Decimal Adjust for Subtract	0 0 1 0 1 1 1 1			
MUL = Multiply (Unsigned)	1 1 1 1 0 1 1 w	mod 1 0 0 r/m		
IMUL = Integer Multiply (Signed)	1 1 1 1 0 1 1 w	mod 1 0 1 r/m		
AAM = ASCII Adjust for Multiply	1 1 0 1 0 1 0 0	0 0 0 0 1 0 1 0		
DIV = Divide (Unsigned)	1 1 1 1 0 1 1 w	mod 1 1 0 r/m		
IDIV = Integer Divide (Signed)	1 1 1 1 0 1 1 w	mod 1 1 1 r/m		
AAD = ASCII Adjust for Divide	1 1 0 1 0 1 0 1	0 0 0 0 1 0 1 0		
CBW = Convert Byte to Word	1 0 0 1 1 0 0 0			
CWD = Convert Word to Double Word	1 0 0 1 1 0 0 1			

6

Table 2. Instruction Set Summary (Continued)

Mnemonic and Description	Instruction Code			
LOGIC	76543210	76543210	76543210	76543210
NOT = Invert	1111011w	mod 010 r/m		
SHL/SAL = Shift Logical/Arithmetic Left	110100vw	mod 100 r/m		
SHR = Shift Logical Right	110100vw	mod 101 r/m		
SAR = Shift Arithmetic Right	110100vw	mod 111 r/m		
ROL = Rotate Left	110100vw	mod 000 r/m		
ROR = Rotate Right	110100vw	mod 001 r/m		
RCL = Rotate Through Carry Flag Left	110100vw	mod 010 r/m		
RCR = Rotate Through Carry Right	110100vw	mod 011 r/m		
AND = **And:**				
Reg./Memory and Register to Either	001000dw	mod reg r/m		
Immediate to Register/Memory	1000000w	mod 100 r/m	data	data if w = 1
Immediate to Accumulator	0010010w	data	data if w = 1	
TEST = **And Function to Flags, No Result:**				
Register/Memory and Register	1000010w	mod reg r/m		
Immediate Data and Register/Memory	1111011w	mod 000 r/m	data	data if w = 1
Immediate Data and Accumulator	1010100w	data	data if w = 1	
OR = **Or:**				
Reg./Memory and Register to Either	000010dw	mod reg r/m		
Immediate to Register/Memory	1000000w	mod 001 r/m	data	data if w = 1
Immediate to Accumulator	0000110w	data	data if w = 1	
XOR = **Exclusive or:**				
Reg./Memory and Register to Either	001100dw	mod reg r/m		
Immediate to Register/Memory	1000000w	mod 110 r/m	data	data if w = 1
Immediate to Accumulator	0011010w	data	data if w = 1	
STRING MANIPULATION				
REP = Repeat	1111001z			
MOVS = Move Byte/Word	1010010w			
CMPS = Compare Byte/Word	1010011w			
SCAS = Scan Byte/Word	1010111w			
LODS = Load Byte/Wd to AL/AX	1010110w			
STOS = Stor Byte/Wd from AL/A	1010101w			
CONTROL TRANSFER				
CALL = **Call:**				
Direct within Segment	11101000	disp-low	disp-high	
Indirect within Segment	11111111	mod 010 r/m		
Direct Intersegment	10011010	offset-low	offset-high	
		seg-low	seg-high	
Indirect Intersegment	11111111	mod 011 r/m		

Table 2. Instruction Set Summary (Continued)

Mnemonic and Description	Instruction Code		
JMP = Unconditional Jump:	7 6 5 4 3 2 1 0	7 6 5 4 3 2 1 0	7 6 5 4 3 2 1 0
Direct within Segment	1 1 1 0 1 0 0 1	disp-low	disp-high
Direct within Segment-Short	1 1 1 0 1 0 1 1	disp	
Indirect within Segment	1 1 1 1 1 1 1 1	mod 1 0 0 r/m	
Direct Intersegment	1 1 1 0 1 0 1 0	offset-low	offset-high
		seg-low	seg-high
Indirect Intersegment	1 1 1 1 1 1 1 1	mod 1 0 1 r/m	
RET = Return from CALL:			
Within Segment	1 1 0 0 0 0 1 1		
Within Seg Adding Immed to SP	1 1 0 0 0 0 1 0	data-low	data-high
Intersegment	1 1 0 0 1 0 1 1		
Intersegment Adding Immediate to SP	1 1 0 0 1 0 1 0	data-low	data-high
JE/JZ = Jump on Equal/Zero	0 1 1 1 0 1 0 0	disp	
JL/JNGE = Jump on Less/Not Greater or Equal	0 1 1 1 1 1 0 0	disp	
JLE/JNG = Jump on Less or Equal/ Not Greater	0 1 1 1 1 1 1 0	disp	
JB/JNAE = Jump on Below/Not Above or Equal	0 1 1 1 0 0 1 0	disp	
JBE/JNA = Jump on Below or Equal/ Not Above	0 1 1 1 0 1 1 0	disp	
JP/JPE = Jump on Parity/Parity Even	0 1 1 1 1 0 1 0	disp	
JO = Jump on Overflow	0 1 1 1 0 0 0 0	disp	
JS = Jump on Sign	0 1 1 1 1 0 0 0	disp	
JNE/JNZ = Jump on Not Equal/Not Zero	0 1 1 1 0 1 0 1	disp	
JNL/JGE = Jump on Not Less/Greater or Equal	0 1 1 1 1 1 0 1	disp	
JNLE/JG = Jump on Not Less or Equal/ Greater	0 1 1 1 1 1 1 1	disp	
JNB/JAE = Jump on Not Below/Above or Equal	0 1 1 1 0 0 1 1	disp	
JNBE/JA = Jump on Not Below or Equal/Above	0 1 1 1 0 1 1 1	disp	
JNP/JPO = Jump on Not Par/Par Odd	0 1 1 1 1 0 1 1	disp	
JNO = Jump on Not Overflow	0 1 1 1 0 0 0 1	disp	
JNS = Jump on Not Sign	0 1 1 1 1 0 0 1	disp	
LOOP = Loop CX Times	1 1 1 0 0 0 1 0	disp	
LOOPZ/LOOPE = Loop While Zero/Equal	1 1 1 0 0 0 0 1	disp	
LOOPNZ/LOOPNE = Loop While Not Zero/Equal	1 1 1 0 0 0 0 0	disp	
JCXZ = Jump on CX Zero	1 1 1 0 0 0 1 1	disp	
INT = Interrupt			
Type Specified	1 1 0 0 1 1 0 1	type	
Type 3	1 1 0 0 1 1 0 0		
INTO = Interrupt on Overflow	1 1 0 0 1 1 1 0		
IRET = Interrupt Return	1 1 0 0 1 1 1 1		

6

Table 2. Instruction Set Summary (Continued)

Mnemonic and Description	Instruction Code	
	76543210	76543210
PROCESSOR CONTROL		
CLC = Clear Carry	11111000	
CMC = Complement Carry	11110101	
STC = Set Carry	11111001	
CLD = Clear Direction	11111100	
STD = Set Direction	11111101	
CLI = Clear Interrupt	11111010	
STI = Set Interrupt	11111011	
HLT = Halt	11110100	
WAIT = Wait	10011011	
ESC = Escape (to External Device)	11011xxx	mod x x x r/m
LOCK = Bus Lock Prefix	11110000	

NOTES:
AL = 8-bit accumulator
AX = 16-bit accumulator
CX = Count register
DS = Data segment
ES = Extra segment
Above/below refers to unsigned value
Greater = more positive;
Less = less positive (more negative) signed values
if d = 1 then "to" reg; if d = 0 then "from" reg
if w = 1 then word instruction; if w = 0 then byte instruction
if mod = 11 then r/m is treated as a REG field
if mod = 00 then DISP = 0*, disp-low and disp-high are absent
if mod = 01 then DISP = disp-low sign-extended to 16 bits, disp-high is absent
if mod = 10 then DISP = disp-high; disp-low
if r/m = 000 then EA = (BX) + (SI) + DISP
if r/m = 001 then EA = (BX) + (DI) + DISP
if r/m = 010 then EA = (BP) + (SI) + DISP
if r/m = 011 then EA = (BP) + (DI) + DISP
if r/m = 100 then EA = (SI) + DISP
if r/m = 101 then EA = (DI) + DISP
if r/m = 110 then EA = (BP) + DISP*
if r/m = 111 then EA = (BX) + DISP
DISP follows 2nd byte of instruction (before data if required)
*except if mod = 00 and r/m = 110 then EA = disp-high; disp-low.

if s w = 01 then 16 bits of immediate data form the operand
if s w = 11 then an immediate data byte is sign extended to form the 16-bit operand
if v = 0 then "count" = 1; if v = 1 then "count" in (CL)
x = don't care
z is used for string primitives for comparison with ZF FLAG

SEGMENT OVERRIDE PREFIX

0 0 1 reg 1 1 0

REG is assigned according to the following table:

16-Bit (w = 1)	8-Bit (w = 0)	Segment
000 AX	000 AL	00 ES
001 CX	001 CL	01 CS
010 DX	010 DL	10 SS
011 BX	011 BL	11 DS
100 SP	100 AH	
101 BP	101 CH	
110 SI	110 DH	
111 DI	111 BH	

Instructions which reference the flag register file as a 16-bit object use the symbol FLAGS to represent the file:
FLAGS = X:X:X:X:(OF):(DF):(IF):(TF):(SF):(ZF):X:(AF):X:(PF):X:(CF)

DATA SHEET REVISION REVIEW

The following list represents key differences between this and the -004 data sheet. Please review this summary carefully.

1. The Intel® 8086 implementation technology (HMOS) has been changed to (HMOS-III).
2. Delete all "changes from 1985 Handbook Specification" sentences.

80C86A
16-BIT CHMOS MICROPROCESSOR

- Pin-for-Pin and Functionally Compatible to Industry Standard HMOS 8086
- Fully Static Design with Frequency Range from D.C. to:
  — 8 MHz for 80C86A-2
- Low Power Operation
  — Operating I_{CC} = 10 mA/MHz
  — Standby I_{CCS} = 500 μA max
- Bus-Hold Circuitry Eliminates Pull-Up Resistors
- Direct Addressing Capability of 1 MByte of Memory
- Architecture Designed for Powerful Assembly Language and Efficient High Level Languages
- 24 Operand Addressing Modes
- Byte, Word and Block Operations
- 8 and 16-Bit Signed and Unsigned Arithmetic
  — Binary or Decimal
  — Multiply and Divide
- Available in 40-Lead Plastic DIP

The Intel 80C86A is a high performance, CHMOS version of the industry standard HMOS 8086 16-bit CPU. The 80C86A available in 8 MHz clock rates, offers two modes of operation: MINimum for small systems and MAXimum for larger applications such as multiprocessing. It is available in 40-pin DIP package.

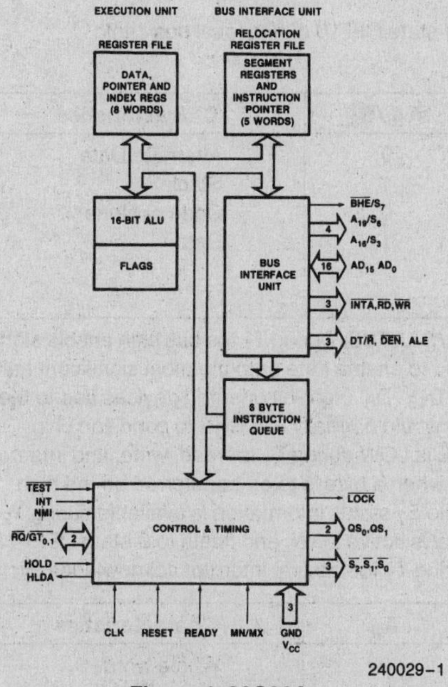

240029–1

Figure 1. 80C86A CPU Block Diagram

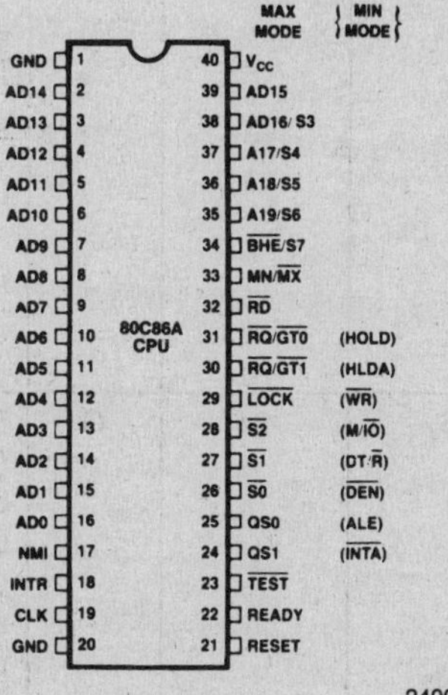

240029–2

Figure 2. 80C86A 40-Lead DIP Configuration

Table 1. Pin Description

The following pin function descriptions are for 80C86AA systems in either minimum or maximum mode. The "Local Bus" in these descriptions is the direct multiplexed bus interface connection to the 80C86A (without regard to additional bus buffers).

<table>
<tr><th>Symbol</th><th>Pin No.</th><th>Type</th><th>Name and Function</th></tr>
<tr><td>AD_{15}–AD_0</td><td>2–16, 39</td><td>I/O</td><td>ADDRESS DATA BUS: These lines constitute the time multiplexed memory/IO address (T_1) and data (T_2, T_3, T_W, T_4) bus. A_0 is analogous to $\overline{BHE}$ for the lower byte of the data bus, pins D_7–D_0. It is LOW during T_1 when a byte is to be transferred on the lower portion of the bus in memory or I/O operations. Eight-bit oriented devices tied to the lower half would normally use A_0 to condition chip select functions. (See $\overline{BHE}$.) These lines are active HIGH and float to 3-state OFF(1) during interrupt acknowledge and local bus "hold acknowledge."</td></tr>
<tr><td>A_{19}/S_6,
A_{18}/S_5,
A_{17}/S_4,
A_{16}/S_3</td><td>35–38</td><td>O</td><td>ADDRESS/STATUS: During T_1 these are the four most significant address lines for memory operations. During I/O operations these lines are LOW. During memory and I/O operations, status information is available on these lines during T_2, T_3, T_W, and T_4. The status of the interrupt enable FLAG bit (S_5) is updated at the beginning of each CLK cycle. A_{17}/S_4 and A_{16}/S_3 are encoded as shown.

This information indicates which relocation register is presently being used for data accessing.

These lines float to 3-state OFF(1) during local bus "hold acknowledge."

<table>
<tr><th>A_{17}/S_4</th><th>A_{16}/S_3</th><th>Characteristics</th></tr>
<tr><td>0 (LOW)</td><td>0</td><td>Alternate Data</td></tr>
<tr><td>0</td><td>1</td><td>Stack</td></tr>
<tr><td>1 (HIGH)</td><td>0</td><td>Code or None</td></tr>
<tr><td>1</td><td>1</td><td>Data</td></tr>
<tr><td>S_6 is 0 (LOW)</td><td></td><td></td></tr>
</table></td></tr>
<tr><td>$\overline{BHE}/S_7$</td><td>34</td><td>O</td><td>BUS HIGH ENABLE/STATUS: During T_1 the bus high enable signal ($\overline{BHE}$) should be used to enable data onto the most significant half of the data bus, pins D_{15}–D_8. Eight-bit oriented devices tied to the upper half of the bus would normally use $\overline{BHE}$ to condition chip select functions. $\overline{BHE}$ is LOW during T_1 for read, write, and interrupt acknowledge cycles when a byte is to be transferred on the high portion of the bus. The S_7 status information is available during T_2, T_3, and T_4. The signal is active LOW, and floats to 3-state OFF(1) in "hold." It is LOW during T_1 for the first interrupt acknowledge cycle.

<table>
<tr><th>$\overline{BHE}$</th><th>A_0</th><th>Characteristics</th></tr>
<tr><td>0</td><td>0</td><td>Whole word</td></tr>
<tr><td>0</td><td>1</td><td>Upper byte from/ to odd address</td></tr>
<tr><td>1</td><td>0</td><td>Lower byte from/ to even address</td></tr>
<tr><td>1</td><td>1</td><td>None</td></tr>
</table></td></tr>
</table>

Table 1. Pin Description (Continued)

Symbol	Pin No.	Type	Name and Function
$\overline{RD}$	32	O	**READ:** Read strobe indicates that the processor is performing a memory of I/O read cycle, depending on the state of the S_2 pin. This signal is used to read devices which reside on the 80C86A local bus. $\overline{RD}$ is active LOW during T_2, T_3 and T_W of any read cycle, and is guaranteed to remain HIGH in T_2 until the 80C86A local bus has floated. This floats to 3-state OFF in "hold acknowledge."
READY	22	I	**READY:** is the acknowledgement from the addressed memory or I/O device that it will complete the data transfer. The READY signal from memory/IO is synchronized by the 82C84A Clock Generator to form READY. This signal is active HIGH. The 80C86A READY input is not synchronized. Correct operation is not guaranteed if the setup and hold times are not met.
INTR	18	I	**INTERRUPT REQUEST:** is a level triggered input which is sampled during the last clock cycle of each instruction to determine if the processor should enter into an interrupt acknowledge operation. A subroutine is vectored to via an interrupt vector lookup table located in system memory. It can be internally masked by software resetting the interrupt enable bit. INTR is internally synchronized. This signal is active HIGH.
$\overline{TEST}$	23	I	**$\overline{TEST}$:** input is examined by the "Wait" instruction. If the $\overline{TEST}$ input is LOW execution continues, otherwise the processor waits in an "Idle" state. This input is synchronized internally during each clock cycle on the leading edge of CLK.
NMI	17	I	**NON-MASKABLE INTERRUPT:** an edge triggered input which causes a type 2 interrupt. A subroutine is vectored to via an interrupt vector lookup table located in system memory. NMI is not maskable internally by software. A transition from a LOW to HIGH initiates the interrupt at the end of the current instruction. This input is internally synchronized.
RESET	21	I	**RESET:** causes the processor to immediately terminate its present activity. The signal must be active HIGH for at least four clock cycles. It restarts execution, as described in the Instruction Set description, when RESET returns LOW. RESET is internally synchronized.
CLK	19	I	**CLOCK:** provides the basic timing for the processor and bus controller. It is asymmetric with a 33% duty cycle to provide optimized internal timing.
V_{CC}	40		**V_{CC}:** +5V power supply pin.
GND	1, 20		**GROUND:** Both must be connected.
MN/$\overline{MX}$	33	I	**MINIMUM/MAXIMUM:** indicates what mode the processor is to operate in. The two modes are discussed in the following sections.

6

Table 1. Pin Description (Continued)

The following pin function descriptions are for the 80C86A/82C88 system in maximum mode (i.e., $MN/\overline{MX} = V_{SS}$). Only the pin functions which are unique to maximum mode are described; all other pin functions are as described above.

<table>
<tr><th>Symbol</th><th>Pin No.</th><th>Type</th><th>Name and Function</th></tr>
<tr><td>$\overline{S_2}$, $\overline{S_1}$, $\overline{S_0}$</td><td>26–28</td><td>O</td><td>**STATUS:** active during T_4, T_1, and T_2 and is returned to the passive state (1,1,1) during T_3 or during T_W when READY is HIGH. This status is used by the 82C88 Bus Controller to generate all memory and I/O access control signals. Any change by $\overline{S_2}$, $\overline{S_1}$, $\overline{S_0}$ during T_4 is used to indicate the beginning of a bus cycle, and the return to the passive state in T_3 or T_W is used to indicate the end of a bus cycle.

These signals float to 3-state OFF(1) in "hold acknowledge." These status lines are encoded as shown.

<table>
<tr><th>$\overline{S_2}$</th><th>$\overline{S_1}$</th><th>$\overline{S_0}$</th><th>Characteristics</th></tr>
<tr><td>0 (LOW)</td><td>0</td><td>0</td><td>Interrupt Acknowledge</td></tr>
<tr><td>0</td><td>0</td><td>1</td><td>Read I/O Port</td></tr>
<tr><td>0</td><td>1</td><td>0</td><td>Write I/O Port</td></tr>
<tr><td>0</td><td>1</td><td>1</td><td>Halt</td></tr>
<tr><td>1 (HIGH)</td><td>0</td><td>0</td><td>Code Access</td></tr>
<tr><td>1</td><td>0</td><td>1</td><td>Read Memory</td></tr>
<tr><td>1</td><td>1</td><td>0</td><td>Write Memory</td></tr>
<tr><td>1</td><td>1</td><td>1</td><td>Passive</td></tr>
</table>
</td></tr>
<tr><td>$\overline{RQ}/\overline{GT}_0$,
$\overline{RQ}/\overline{GT}_1$</td><td>30, 31</td><td>I/O</td><td>**REQUEST/GRANT:** pins are used by other local bus masters to force the processor to release the local bus at the end of the processor's current bus cycle. Each pin is bidirectional with $\overline{RQ}/\overline{GT}_0$ having higher priority than $\overline{RQ}/\overline{GT}_1$. $\overline{RQ}/\overline{GT}$ has an internal pull-up resistor so may be left unconnected. The request/grant sequence is as follows (see timing diagram):

1. A pulse of 1 CLK wide from another local bus master indicates a local bus request ("hold") to the 80C86A (pulse 1).
2. During a T_4 or T_1 clock cycle, a pulse 1 CLK wide from the 80C86A to the requesting master (pulse 2), indicates that the 80C86A has allowed the local bus to float and that it will enter the "hold acknowledge" state at the next CLK. The CPU's bus interface unit is disconnected logically from the local bus during "hold acknowledge."
3. A pulse 1 CLK wide from the requesting master indicates to the 80C86A (pulse 3) that the "hold" request is about to end and that 80C86A can reclaim the local bus at the next CLK.

Each master-master exchange of the local bus is a sequence of 3 pulses. There must be one dead CLK cycle after each bus exchange. Pulses are active LOW.

If the request is made while the CPU is performing a memory cycle, it will release the local bus during T_4 of the cycle when all the following conditions are met:

1. Request occurs on or before T_2.
2. Current cycle is not the low byte of a word (on an odd address).
3. Current cycle is not the first acknowledge of an interrupt acknowledge sequence.
4. A locked instruction is not currently executing.</td></tr>
</table>

Table 1. Pin Description (Continued)

<table>
<tr><th>Symbol</th><th>Pin No.</th><th>Type</th><th>Name and Function</th></tr>
<tr><td></td><td></td><td></td><td>If the local bus is idle when the request is made the two possible events will follow:
1. Local bus will be released during the next clock.
2. A memory cycle will start within 3 clocks. Now the four rules for a currently active memory cycle apply with condition number 1 already satisfied.</td></tr>
<tr><td>$\overline{LOCK}$</td><td>29</td><td>O</td><td>$\overline{LOCK}$: output indicates that other system bus masters are not to gain control of the system bus while $\overline{LOCK}$ is active LOW. The $\overline{LOCK}$ signal is activated by the "LOCK" prefix instruction and remains active until the completion of the next instruction. This signal is active LOW, and floats to 3-state OFF(1) in "hold acknowledge."</td></tr>
<tr><td>QS_1, QS_0</td><td>24, 25</td><td>O</td><td>QUEUE STATUS: The queue status is valid during the CLK cycle after which the queue operation is performed.
QS_1 and QS_0 provide status to allow external tracking of the internal 80C86A instruction queue.
<table>
<tr><th>QS_1</th><th>QS_0</th><th>Characteristics</th></tr>
<tr><td>0 (LOW)</td><td>0</td><td>No Operation</td></tr>
<tr><td>0</td><td>1</td><td>First Byte of Op Code from Queue</td></tr>
<tr><td>1 (HIGH)</td><td>0</td><td>Empty the Queue</td></tr>
<tr><td>1</td><td>1</td><td>Subsequent Byte from Queue</td></tr>
</table></td></tr>
</table>

The following pin function descriptions are for the 80C86A in minimum mode (i.e., MN/$\overline{MX}$ = V_{CC}). Only the pin functions which are unique to minimum mode are described; all other pin functions are described above.

M/$\overline{IO}$	28	O	**STATUS LINE:** logically equivalent to S_2 in the maximum mode. It is used to distinguish a memory access from an I/O access. M/$\overline{IO}$ becomes valid in the T_4 preceding a bus cycle and remains valid until the final T_4 of the cycle (M = HIGH, IO = LOW). M/$\overline{IO}$ floats to 3-state OFF(1) in local bus "hold acknowledge."
$\overline{WR}$	29	O	**WRITE:** indicates that the processor is performing a write memory or write I/O cycle, depending on the state of the M/$\overline{IO}$ signal. $\overline{WR}$ is active for T_2, T_3 and T_W of any write cycle. It is active LOW, and floats to 3-state OFF(1) in local bus "hold acknowledge."
$\overline{INTA}$	24	O	$\overline{INTA}$ is used as a read strobe for interrupt acknowledge cycles. It is active LOW during T_2, T_3 and T_W of each interrupt acknowledge cycle.
ALE	25	O	**ADDRESS LATCH ENABLE:** provided by the processor to latch the address into an address latch. It is a HIGH pulse active during T_1 of any bus cycle. Note that ALE is never floated.
DT/$\overline{R}$	27	O	**DATA TRANSMIT/RECEIVE:** needed in minimum system that desires to use a data bus transceiver. It is used to control the direction of data flow through the transceiver. Logically DT/$\overline{R}$ is equivalent to $\overline{S_1}$ in the maximum mode, and its timing is the same as for M/$\overline{IO}$. (T = HIGH, R = LOW.) This signal floats to 3-state OFF(1) in local bus "hold acknowledge."

Table 1. Pin Description (Continued)

Symbol	Pin No.	Type	Name and Function
$\overline{DEN}$	26	O	**DATA ENABLE:** provided as an output enable for the transceiver in a minimum system which uses the transceiver. $\overline{DEN}$ is active LOW during each memory and I/O access and for INTA cycles. For a read or $\overline{INTA}$ cycle it is active from the middle of T_2 until the middle of T_4, while for a write cycle it is active from the beginning of T_2 until the middle of T_4. $\overline{DEN}$ floats to 3-state OFF(1) in local bus "hold acknowledge."
HOLD, HLDA	31, 30	I/O	**HOLD:** indicates that another master is requesting a local bus "hold." To be acknowledged, HOLD must be active HIGH. The processor receiving the "hold" request will issue HLDA (HIGH) as an acknowledgement in the middle of a T_4 or T_i clock cycle. Simultaneous with the issuance of HLDA the processor will float the local bus and control lines. After HOLD is detected as being LOW, the processor will LOWer the HLDA, and when the processor needs to run another cycle, it will again drive the local bus and control lines. The same rules as for $\overline{RQ}/\overline{GT}$ apply regarding when the local bus will be released. HOLD is not an asynchronous input. External synchronization should be provided if the system cannot otherwise guarantee the setup time.

NOTE:
1. See the section on Bus Hold Circuitry.

FUNCTIONAL DESCRIPTION

STATIC OPERATION

All 80C86A circuitry is of static design. Internal registers, counters and latches are static and require no refresh as with dynamic circuit design. This eliminates the minimum operating frequency restriction placed on other microprocessors. The CMOS 80C86A can operate from DC to the appropriate upper frequency limit. The processor clock may be stopped in either state (high/low) and held there indefinitely. This type of operation is especially useful for system debug or power critical applications.

The 80C86A can be single stepped using only the CPU clock. This state can be maintained as long as is necessary. Single step clock operation allows simple interface circuitry to provide critical information for bringing up your system.

Static design also allows very low frequency operation. In a power critical situation, this can provide extremely low power operation since 80C86A power dissipation is directly related to operating frequency. As the system frequency is reduced, so is the operating power until, ultimately, at a DC input frequency, the 80C86A power requirement is the standby current.

INTERNAL ARCHITECTURE

The internal functions of the 80C86A processor are partitioned logically into two processing units. The first is the Bus Interface Unit (BIU) and the second is the Execution Unit (EU) as shown in the block diagram of Figure 1.

These units can interact directly but for the most part perform as separate asynchronous operational processors. The bus interface unit provides the functions related to instruction fetching and queuing, operand fetch and store, and address relocation. This unit also provides the basic bus control. The overlap of instruction pre-fetching provided by this unit serves to increase processor performance through improved bus bandwidth utilization. Up to 6 bytes of the instruction stream can be queued while waiting for decoding and execution.

The instruction stream queuing mechanism allows the BIU to keep the memory utilized very efficiently. Whenever there is space for at least 2 bytes in the queue, the BIU will attempt a word fetch memory cycle. This greatly reduces "dead time" on the memory bus. The queue acts as a First-In-First Out (FIFO) buffer, from which the EU extracts instruction bytes as required. If the queue is empty (following a branch instruction, for example), the first byte into the queue immediately becomes available to the EU.

Memory Reference Need	Segment Register Used	Segment Selection Rule
Instructions	CODE (CS)	Automatic with all instruction prefetch.
Stack	STACK (SS)	All stack pushes and pops. Memory references relative to BP base register except data references.
Local Data	DATA (DS)	Data references when: relative to stack, destination of string operation, or explicitly overridden.
External (Global) Data	EXTRA (ES)	Destination of string operations: Explicitly selected using a segment override.

The execution units receives pre-fetched instructions from the BIU queue and provides un-relocated operand addresses to the BIU. Memory operands are passed through the BIU for processing by the EU, which passes results to the BIU for storage. See the Instruction Set description for further register set and architectural descriptions.

MEMORY ORGANIZATION

The processor provides a 20-bit address to memory which locates the byte being referenced. The memory is organized as a linear array of up to 1 million bytes, addressed as 00000(H) to FFFFF(H). The memory is logically divided into code, data, extra data, and stack segments of up to 64k bytes each, with each segment falling on 16-byte boundaries. (See Figure 3a.)

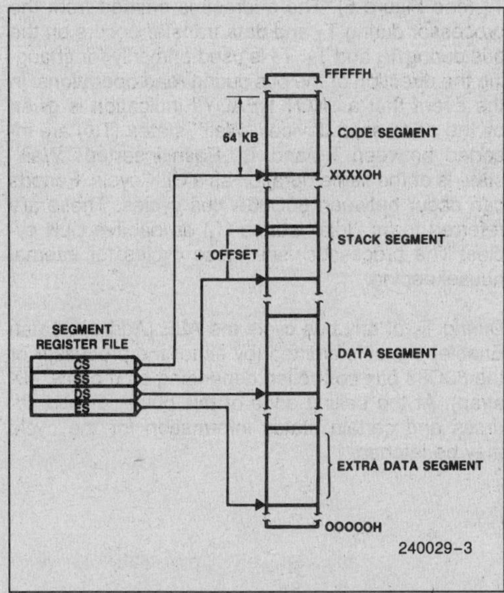

Figure 3a. Memory Organization

All memory references are made relative to base addresses contained in high speed segment registers. The segment types were chosen based on the addressing needs of programs. The segment register to be selected is automatically chosen according to the rules of the following table. All information in one segment type share the same logical attributes (e.g. code or data). By structuring memory into relocatable areas of similar characteristics and by automatically selecting segment registers, programs are shorter, faster, and more structured.

Word (16-bit) operands can be located on even or odd address boundaries and are thus not constrained to even boundaries as is the case in many 16-bit computers. For address and data operands, the least significant byte of the word is stored in the lower valued address location and the most significant byte in the next higher address location. The BIU automatically performs the proper number of memory accesses, one if the word operand is on an even byte boundary and two if it is on an odd byte boundary. Except for the performance penalty, this double access is transparent to the software. This performance penalty does not occur for instruction fetches, only word operands.

Physically, the memory is organized as a high bank (D_{15}–D_8) and a low bank (D_7–D_0) of 512k 8-bit bytes addressed in parallel by the processor's address lines.

A_{19}–A_1. Byte data with even addresses is transferred on the D_7-D_0 bus lines while odd addressed byte data (A_0 HIGH) is transferred on the D_{15}–D_8 bus lines. The processor provides two enable signals, $\overline{BHE}$ and A_0, to selectively allow reading from or writing into either an odd byte location, even byte location, or both. The instruction stream is fetched from memory as words and is addressed internally by the processor to the byte level as necessary.

In referencing word data the BIU requires one or two memory cycles depending on whether or not the starting byte of the word is on an even or odd address, respectively. Consequently, in referencing word operands performance can be optimized by locating data on even address boundaries. This is an especially useful technique for using the stack, since odd address references to the stack may adversely affect the context switching time for interrupt processing or task multiplexing.

Certain locations in memory are reserved for specific CPU operations (see Figure 3b.) Locations from address FFFF0H through FFFFFH are reserved for operations including a jump to the initial program loading routine. Following RESET, the CPU will always begin execution at location FFFF0H where the jump must be. Locations 00000H through 003FFH are reserved for interrupt operations. Each of the 256 possible interrupt types has its service routine pointed to by a 4-byte pointer element consisting of a 16-bit segment address and a 16-bit offset address. The pointer elements are assumed to have been stored at the respective places in reserved memory prior to occurrence of interrupts.

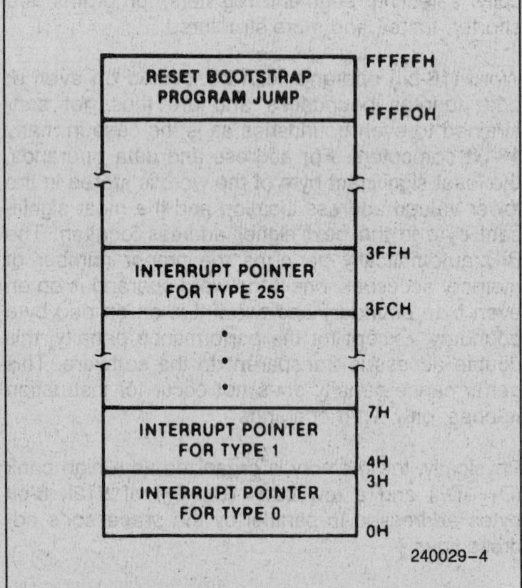

Figure 3b. Reserved Memory Locations

MINIMUM AND MAXIMUM MODES

The requirements for supporting minimum and maximum 80C86A systems are sufficiently different that they cannot be done efficiently with 40 uniquely defined pins. Consequently, the 80C86A is equipped with a strap pin (MN/$\overline{MX}$) which defines the system configuration. The definition of a certain subset of the pins changes dependent on the condition of the strap pin. When MN/$\overline{MX}$ pin is strapped to GND, the 80C86A treats pins 24 through 31 in maximum mode. An 82C88 bus controller interprets status information coded into $\overline{S}_0$, $\overline{S}_1$, $\overline{S}_2$ to generate bus timing and control signals compatible with the MULTIBUS® architecture. When the MN/$\overline{MX}$ pin is strapped to V_{CC}, the 80C86A generates bus control signals itself on pins 24 through 31, as shown in parentheses in Figure 2. Examples of minimum mode and maximum mode systems are shown in Figure 4.

BUS OPERATION

The 80C86A has a combined address and data bus commonly referred to as a time multiplexed bus. This technique provides the most efficient use of pins on the processor. This "local bus" can be buffered directly and used throughout the system with address latching provided on memory and I/O modules. In addition, the bus can also be demultiplexed at the processor with a single set of address latches if a standard non-multiplexed bus is desired for the system.

Each processor bus cycle consists of at least four CLK cycles. These are referred to as T_1, T_2, T_3 and T_4 (see Figure 5). The address is emitted from the processor during T_1 and data transfer occurs on the bus during T_3 and T_4. T_2 is used primarily for changing the direction of the bus during read operations. In the event that a "NOT READY" indication is given by the addressed device, "Wait" states (T_W) are inserted between T_3 and T_4. Each inserted "Wait" state is of the same duration as a CLK cycle. Periods can occur between 80C86A bus cycles. These are referred to as "Idle" states (T_i) or inactive CLK cycles. The processor uses these cycles for internal housekeeping.

During T_1 of any bus cycle the ALE (Address Latch Enable) signal is emitted (by either the processor or the 82C88 bus controller, depending on the MN/$\overline{MX}$ strap). At the trailing edge of this pulse, a valid address and certain status information for the cycle may be latched.

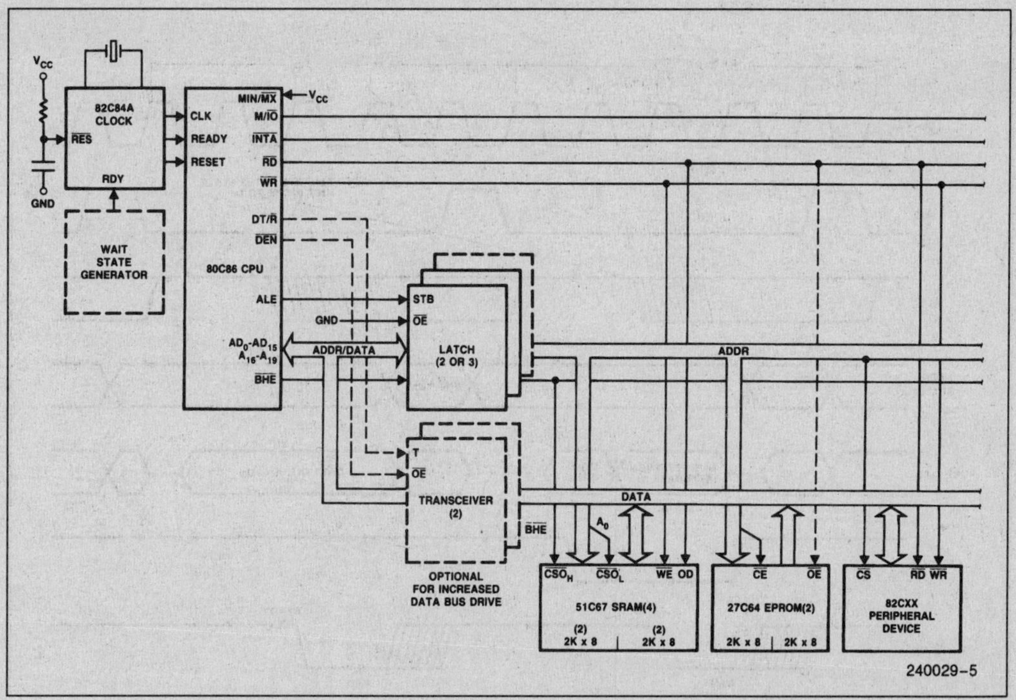

Figure 4a. Minimum Mode iAPX 80C86A Typical Configuration

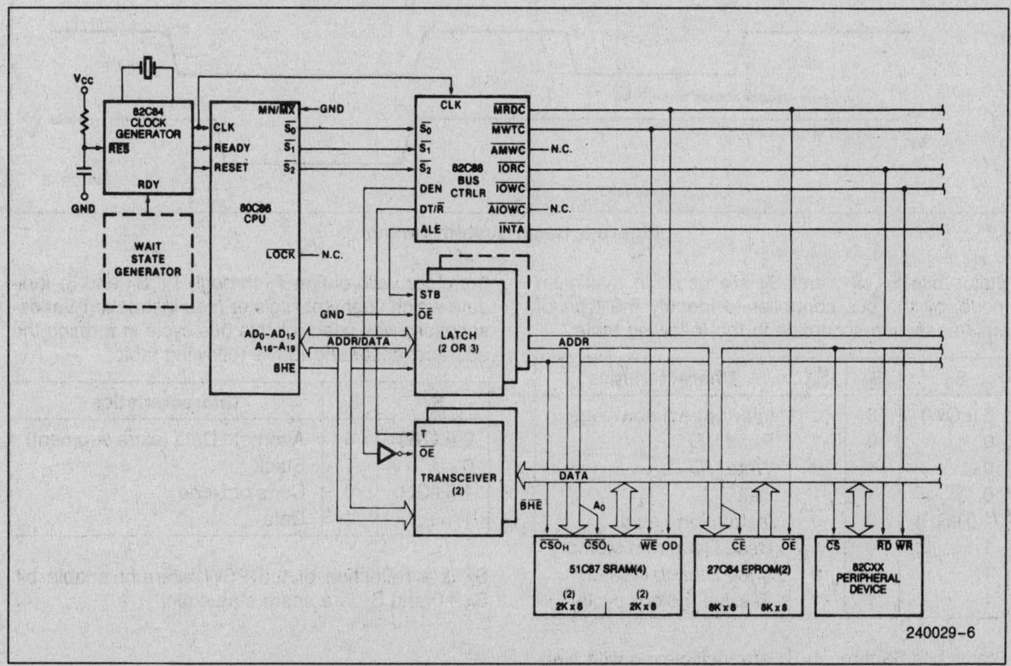

Figure 4b. Maximum Mode 80C86A Typical Configuration

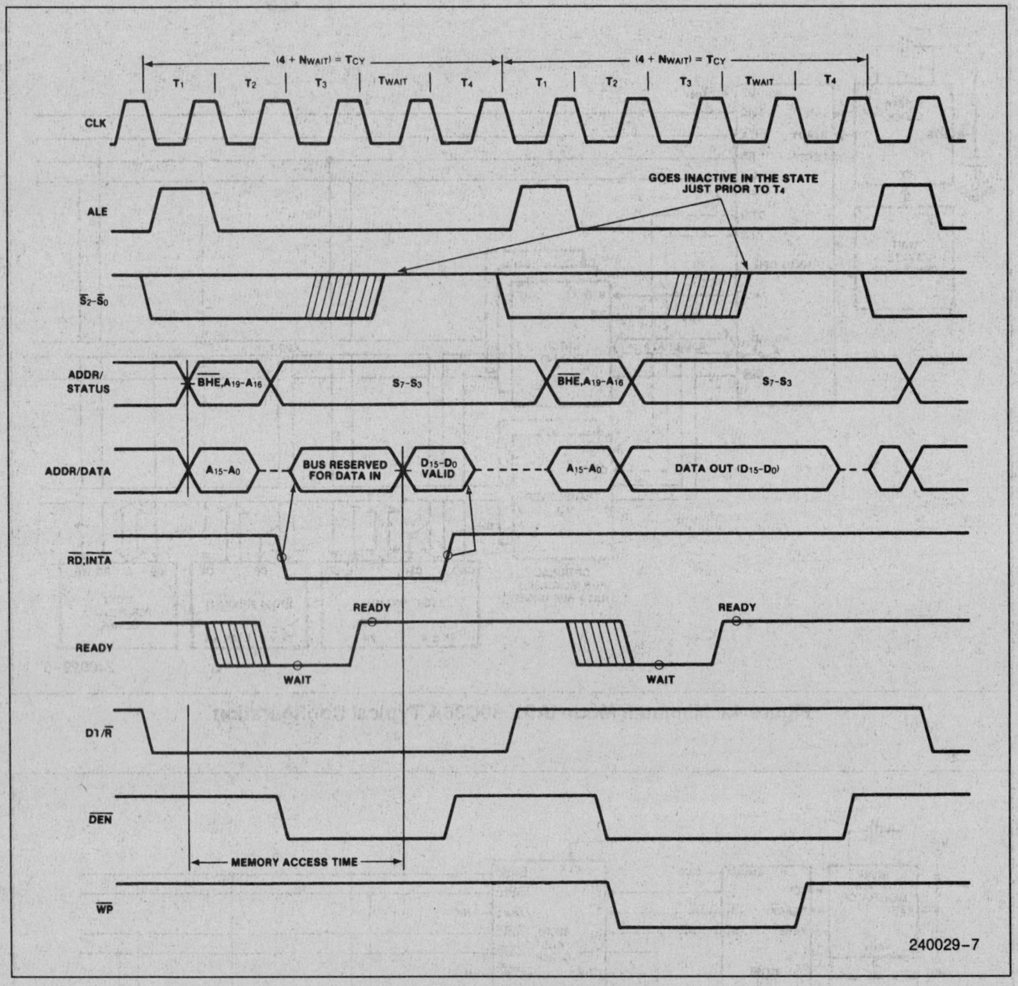

Figure 5. Basic System Timing

Status bits $\overline{S}_0$, $\overline{S}_1$, and $\overline{S}_2$ are used, in maximum mode, by the bus controller to identify the type of bus transaction according to the following table:

$\overline{S}_2$	$\overline{S}_1$	$\overline{S}_0$	Characteristics
0 (LOW)	0	0	Interrupt Acknowledge
0	0	1	Read I/O
0	1	0	Write I/O
0	1	1	Halt
1 (HIGH)	0	0	Instruction Fetch
1	0	1	Read Data from Memory
1	1	0	Write Data to Memory
1	1	1	Passive (no bus cycle)

Status bits S_3 through S_7 are multiplexed with high-order address bits and the $\overline{BHE}$ signal, and are therefore valid during T_2 through T_4. S_3 and S_4 indicate which segment register (see Instruction Set description) was used for this bus cycle in forming the address, according to the following table:

S_4	S_3	Characteristics
0 (LOW)	0	Alternate Data (extra segment)
0	1	Stack
1 (HIGH)	0	Code or None
1	1	Data

S_5 is a reflection of the PSW interrupt enable bit. $S_6 = 0$ and S_7 is a spare status pin.

I/O ADDRESSING

In the 80C86A, I/O operations can address up to a maximum of 64k I/O byte registers or 32k I/O word registers. The I/O address appears in the same format as the memory address on bus lines $A_{15}-A_0$. The address lines $A_{19}-A_{16}$ are zero in I/O operations. The variable I/O instructions which use register DX as a pointer have full address capability while the direct I/O instructions directly address one or two of the 256 I/O byte locations in page 0 of the I/O address space.

I/O ports are addressed in the same manner as memory locations. Even addressed bytes are transferred on the D_7-D_0 bus lines and odd addressed bytes on $D_{15}-D_8$. Care must be taken to assure that each register within an 8-bit peripheral located on the lower portion of the bus be addressed as even.

EXTERNAL INTERFACE

PROCESSOR RESET AND INITIALIZATION

Processor initialization or start up is accomplished with activation (HIGH) of the RESET pin. The 80C86A RESET is required to be HIGH for four or more CLK cycles. The 80C86A will terminate operations on the high-going edge of RESET and will remain dormant as long as RESET is HIGH. The low-going transition of RESET triggers an internal reset sequence for approximately 7 CLK cycles. After this interval the 80C86A operates normally beginning with the instruction in absolute location FFFF0H (see Figure 3b). The details of this operation are specified in the Instruction Set description of the MCS®-86 Family User's Manual. The RESET input is internally synchronized to the processor clock. At initialization the HIGH-to-LOW transition of RESET must occur no sooner than 50 μs after power-up, to allow complete initialization of the 80C86A.

NMI asserted prior to the 2nd clock after the end of RESET will not be honored. If NMI is asserted after that point and during the internal reset sequence, the processor may execute one instruction before responding to the interrupt. A hold request active immediately after RESET will be honored before the first instruction fetch.

All 3-state outputs float to 3-state OFF[1] during RESET. Status is active in the idle state for the first clock after RESET becomes active and then floats to 3-state OFF[1]. ALE and HLDA are driven low.

NOTE:
1. See the section on Bus Hold Circuitry.

BUS HOLD CIRCUITRY

To avoid high current conditions caused by floating inputs to CMOS devices and eliminate the need for pull-up/down resistors, "bus-hold" circuitry has been used on the 80C86A pins 2-16, 26-32, and 34-39 (Figures 6a, 6b). These circuits will maintain the last valid logic state if no driving source is present (i.e. an unconnected pin or a driving source which goes to a high impedance state). To overdrive the "bus hold" circuits, an external driver must be capable of supplying 350 μA minimum sink or source current at valid input voltage levels. Since this "bus hold" circuitry is active and not a "resistive" type element, the associated power supply current is negligible and power dissipation is significantly reduced when compared to the use of passive pull-up resistors.

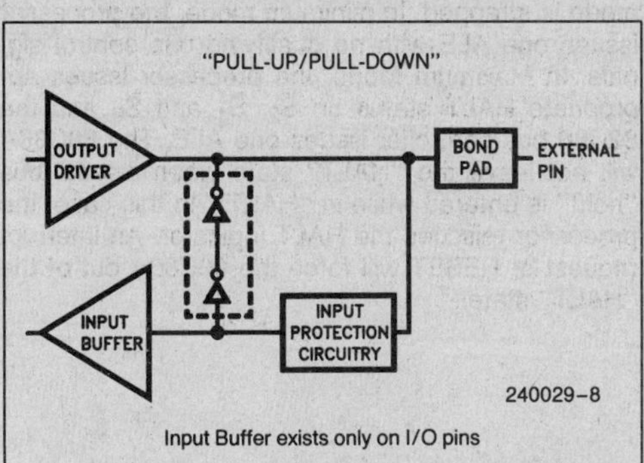

Figure 6a. Bus hold circuitry pin 2-16, 34-39.

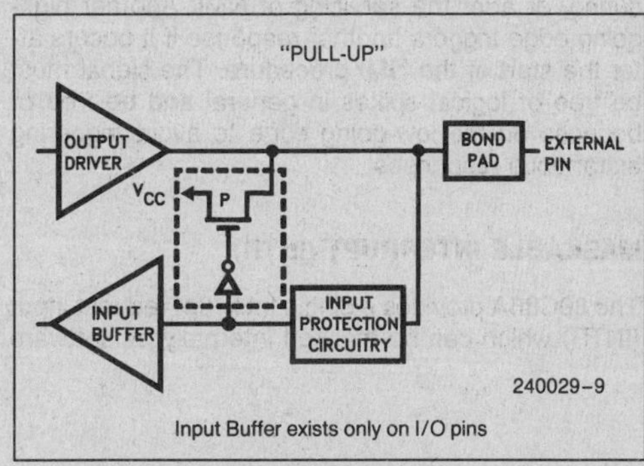

Figure 6b. Bus hold circuitry pin 26-32.

6

INTERRUPT OPERATIONS

Interrupt operations fall into two classes; software or hardware initiated. The software initiated interrupts and software aspects of hardware interrupts are specified in the Instruction Set description. Hardware interrupts can be classified as non-maskable or maskable.

Interrupts result in a transfer of control to a new program location. A 256-element table containing address pointers to the interrupt service program locations resides in absolute locations 0 through 3FFH (see Figure 3b), which are reserved for this purpose. Each element in the table is 4 bytes in size and corresponds to an interrupt "type". An interrupting device supplies an 8-bit type number, during the interrupt acknowledge sequence, which is used to "vector" through the appropriate element to the new interrupt service program location.

NON-MASKABLE INTERRUPT (NMI)

The processor provides a single non-maskable interrupt pin (NMI) which has higher priority than the maskable interrupt request pin (INTR). A typical use would be to activate a power failure routine. The NMI is edge-triggered on a LOW-to-HIGH transition. The activation of this pin causes a type 2 interrupt. (See Instruction Set description.) NMI is required to have a duration in the HIGH state of greater than two CLK cycles, but is not required to be synchronized to the clock. Any high-going transition of NMI is latched on-chip and will be serviced at the end of the current instruction or between whole moves of a block-type instruction. Worst case response to NMI would be for multiply, divide and variable shift instructions. There is no specification on the occurrence of the low-going edge; it may occur before, during, or after the servicing of NMI. Another high-going edge triggers another response if it occurs after the start of the NMI procedure. The signal must be free of logical spikes in general and be free of bounces on the low-going edge to avoid triggering extraneous responses.

MASKABLE INTERRUPT (INTR)

The 80C86A provides a single interrupt request input (INTR) which can be masked internally by software with the resetting of the interrupt enable FLAG status bit. The interrupt request signal is level triggered. It is internally synchronized during each clock cycle on the high-going edge of CLK. To be responded to, INTR must be present (HIGH) during the clock period preceding the end of the current instruction or the end of a whole move for a block-type instruction. During the interrupt response sequence further interrupts are disabled. The enable bit is reset as part of the response to any interrupt (INTR, NMI, software interrupt or single-step), although the FLAGS register which is automatically pushed onto the stack reflects the state of the processor prior to the interrupt. Until the old FLAGS register is restored the enable bit will be zero unless specifically set by an instruction.

During the response sequence (Figure 7) the processor executes two successive (back-to-back) interrupt acknowledge cycles. The 80C86A emits the LOCK signal from T_2 of the first bus cycle until T_2 of the second. A local bus "hold" request will not be honored until the end of the second bus cycle. In the second bus cycle a byte is fetched from the external interrupt system (e.g., 82C59 PIC) which identifies the source (type) of the interrupt. This byte is multiplied by four and used as a pointer into the interrupt vector lookup table. An INTR signal left HIGH will be continually responded to within the limitations of the enable bit and sample period. The INTERRUPT RETURN instruction includes a FLAGS pop which returns the status of the original interrupt enable bit when it restores the FLAGS.

HALT

When a software "HALT" instruction is executed the processor indicates that it is entering the "HALT" state in one of two ways depending upon which mode is strapped. In minimum mode, the processor issues one ALE with no qualifying bus control signals. In Maximum Mode, the processor issues appropriate HALT status on $\overline{S}_2$, $\overline{S}_1$ and $\overline{S}_0$ and the 82C88 bus controller issues one ALE. The 80C86A will not leave the "HALT" state when a local bus "hold" is entered while in "HALT". In this case, the processor reissues the HALT indicator. An interrupt request or RESET will force the 80C86A out of the "HALT" state.

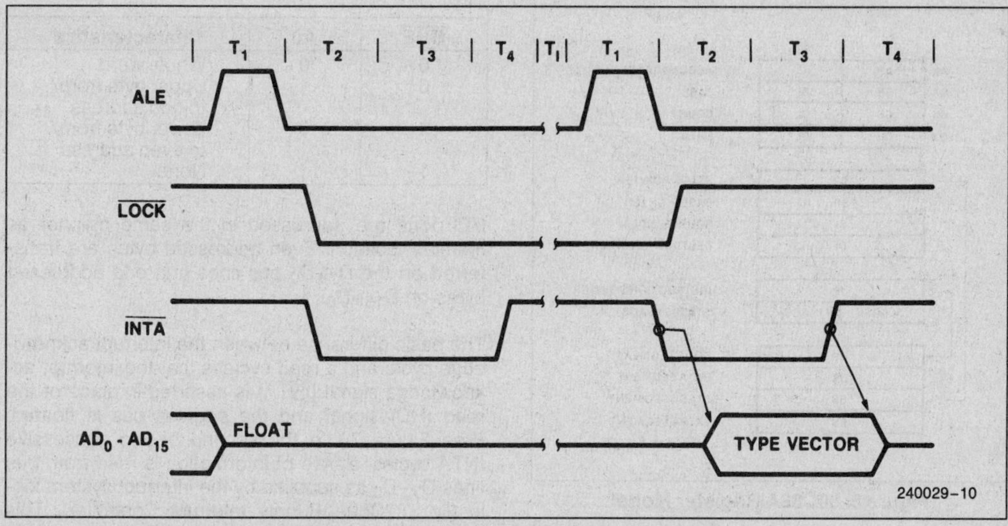

Figure 7. Interrupt Acknowledge Sequence

READ/MODIFY/WRITE (SEMAPHORE) OPERATIONS VIA LOCK

The $\overline{LOCK}$ status information is provided by the processor when directly consecutive bus cycles are required during the execution of an instruction. This provides the processor with the capability of performing read/modify/write operations on memory (via the Exchange Register With Memory instruction, for example) without the possibility of another system bus master receiving intervening memory cycles. This is useful in mutliprocessor system configurations to accomplish "test and set lock" operations. The $\overline{LOCK}$ signal is activated (forced LOW) in the clock cycle following the one in which the software "LOCK" prefix instruction is decoded by the EU. It is deactivated at the end of the last bus cycle of the instruction following the "LOCK" prefix instruction. While $\overline{LOCK}$ is active a request on a RQ/GT pin will be recorded and then honored at the end of the LOCK.

EXTERNAL SYNCHRONIZATION VIA TEST

As an alternative to the interrupts and general I/O capabilities, the 80C86A provides a single software-testable input known as the $\overline{TEST}$ signal. At any time the program may execute a WAIT instruction. If at that time the $\overline{TEST}$ signal is inactive (HIGH), program execution becomes suspended while the processor waits for $\overline{TEST}$ to become active. It must remain active for at least 5 CLK cycles. The WAIT instruction is re-executed repeatedly until that time. This activity does not consume bus cycles. The processor remains in an idle state while waiting. All 80C86A drivers go to 3-state OFF if bus "Hold" is entered. If interrupts are enabled, they may occur while the processor is waiting. When this occurs the processor fetches the WAIT instruction one extra time, processes the interrupt, and then re-fetches and re-executes the WAIT instruction upon returning from the interrupt.

BASIC SYSTEM TIMING

Typical system configurations for the processor operating in minimum mode and in maximum mode are shown in Figures 4a and 4b, respectively. In minimum mode, the MN/$\overline{MX}$ pin is strapped to V_{CC} and the processor emits bus control signals in a manner similar to the 8085. In maximum mode, the MN/$\overline{MX}$ pin is strapped to V_{SS} and the processor emits coded status information which the 82C88 bus controller uses to generate MULTIBUS compatible bus control signals. Figure 5 illustrates the signal timing relationships.

6

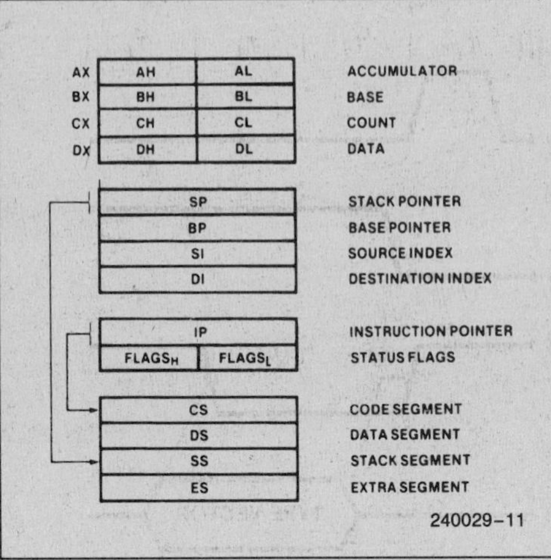

Figure 8. 80C86A Register Model

SYSTEM TIMING—MINIMUM SYSTEM

The read cycle begins in T_1 with the assertion of the Address Latch Enable (ALE) signal. The trailing (low-going) edge of this signal is used to latch the address information, which is valid on the local bus at this time, into a latch. The $\overline{BHE}$ and A_0 signals address the low, high, or both bytes. From T_1 to T_4 the M/$\overline{IO}$ signal indicates a memory or I/O operation. At T_2 the address is removed from the local bus and the bus goes to a high impedance state. The read control signal is also asserted at T_2. The read ($\overline{RD}$) signal causes the addressed device to enable its data bus drivers to the local bus. Some time later valid data will be available on the bus and the addressed device will drive the READY line HIGH. When the processor returns the read signal to a HIGH level, the addressed device will again 3-state its bus drivers. If a transceiver is required to buffer the 80C86A local bus, signals DT/$\overline{R}$ and $\overline{DEN}$ are provided by the 80C86A.

A write cycle also begins with the assertion of ALE and the emission of the address. The M/$\overline{IO}$ signal is again asserted to indicate a memory or I/O write operation. In the T_2 immediately following the address emission the processor emits the data to be written into the addressed location. This data remains valid until the middle of T_4. During T_2, T_3, and T_W the processor asserts the write control signal. The write ($\overline{WR}$) signal becomes active at the beginning of T_2 as opposed to the read which is delayed somewhat into T_2 to provide time for the bus to float.

The $\overline{BHE}$ and A_0 signals are used to select the proper byte(s) of the memory/IO word to be read or written according to the following table:

$\overline{BHE}$	A0	Characteristics
0	0	Whole word
0	1	Upper byte from/ to odd address
1	0	Lower byte from/ to even address
1	1	None

I/O ports are addressed in the same manner as memory location. Even addressed bytes are transferred on the D_7-D_0 bus lines and odd addressed bytes on $D_{15}-D_8$.

The basic difference between the interrupt acknowledge cycle and a read cycle is that the interrupt acknowledge signal ($\overline{INTA}$) is asserted in place of the read ($\overline{RD}$) signal and the address bus is floated. (See Figure 7.) In the second of two successive INTA cycles, a byte of information is read from bus lines D_7-D_0 as supplied by the interrupt system logic (i.e., 82C59A Priority Interrupt Controller). This byte identifies the source (type) of the interrupt. It is multiplied by four and used as a pointer into an interrupt vector lookup table, as described earlier.

BUS TIMING—MEDIUM SIZE SYSTEMS

For medium size systems the MN/$\overline{MX}$ pin is connected to V_{SS} and the 82C88 Bus Controller is added to the system as well as a latch for latching the system address, and a transceiver to allow for bus loading greater than the 80C86A is capable of handling. Signals ALE, DEN, and DT/$\overline{R}$ are generated by the 82C88 instead of the processor in this configuration although their timing remains relatively the same. The 80C86A status outputs ($\overline{S}_2$, $\overline{S}_1$, and $\overline{S}_0$) provide type-of-cycle information and become 82C88 inputs. This bus cycle information specifies read (code, data, or I/O), write (data or I/O), interrupt acknowledge, or software halt. The 82C88 thus issues control signals specifying memory read or write, I/O read or write, or interrupt acknowledge. The 82C88 provides two types of write strobes, normal and advanced, to be applied as required. The normal write strobes have data valid at the leading edge of write. The advanced write strobes have the same timing as read strobes, and hence data isn't valid at the leading edge of write. The transceiver receives the usual T and OE inputs from the 82C88 DT/$\overline{R}$ and DEN.

The pointer into the interrupt vector table, which is passed during the second INTA cycle, can derive from an 82C59A located on either the local bus or the system bus. If the master 82C59A Priority Interrupt Controller is positioned on the local bus, a TTL gate is required to disable the transceiver when reading from the master 82C59A during the interrupt acknowledge sequence and software "poll".

ABSOLUTE MAXIMUM RATINGS*

Supply Voltage
(With respect to ground) . . . . −0.5 to 7.0V
Input Voltage Applied
(w.r.t. ground) . . . . −0.5 to V_{CC} + 0.5V
Output Voltage Applied
(w.r.t. ground) . . . . −0.5 to V_{CC} + 0.5V
Power Dissipation 1.0W
Storage Temperature . . . . −65°C to 150°C
Ambient Temperature Under Bias . . . . . . 0°C to 70°C

NOTICE: This is a production data sheet. The specifications are subject to change without notice.

**WARNING: Stressing the device beyond the "Absolute Maximum Ratings" may cause permanent damage. These are stress ratings only. Operation beyond the "Operating Conditions" is not recommended and extended exposure beyond the "Operating Conditions" may affect device reliability.*

D.C. CHARACTERISTICS

(T_A = 0°C to 70°C, V_{CC} = 5V ±5%)

Symbol	Parameter	80C86A-2		Units	Test Conditions
		Min	Max		
V_{IL}	Input Low Voltage	−0.5	+0.8	V	
V_{IH}	Input High Voltage (All inputs except clock)	2.0		V	
V_{CH}	Clock Input High Voltage	V_{CC}−0.8		V	
V_{OL}	Output Low Voltage		0.45	V	I_{OL} = 2.5 mA
V_{OH}	Output High Voltage	3.0 V_{CC}−0.4		V	I_{OH} = −2.5 mA I_{OH} = −100 μA
I_{CC}	Power Supply Current		10 mA/MHz		V_{IL} = GND, V_{IH} = V_{CC}
I_{CCS}	Standby Supply Current		500	μA	V_{IN} = V_{CC} or GND Outputs Unloaded CLK = GND or V_{CC}
I_{LI}	Input Leakage Current		±1.0	μA	0V ≤ V_{IN} ≤ V_{CC}
I_{BHL}	Input Leakage Current (Bus Hold Low)	50	400	μA	V_{IN} = 0.8V (Note 4)
I_{BHH}	Input Leakage Current (Bus Hold High)	−50	−400	μA	V_{IN} = 3.0V (Note 5)
I_{BHLO}	Bus Hold Low Overdrive		600	μA	(Note 2)
I_{BHHO}	Bus Hold High Overdrive		−600	μA	(Note 3)
I_{LO}	Output Leakage Current		±10	μA	V_{OUT} = GND or V_{CC}
C_{IN}	Capacitance of Input Buffer (All inputs except AD_0–AD_{15}, $\overline{RQ}/\overline{GT}$)		5	pF	(Note 1)
C_{IO}	Capacitance of I/O Buffer (AD_0–AD_{15}, $\overline{RQ}/\overline{GT}$)		20	pF	(Note 1)
C_{OUT}	Output Capacitance		15	pF	(Note 1)

NOTES:
1. Characterization conditions are a) Frequency = 1 MHz; b) Unmeasured pins at GND; c) V_{IN} at +5.0V or GND.
2. An external driver must source at least I_{BHLO} to switch this node from LOW to HIGH.
3. An external driver must sink at least I_{BHHO} to switch this node from HIGH to LOW.
4. Test Condition is to lower V_{IN} to GND and then raise V_{IN} to 0.8V on pins 2-16 & 34-39.
5. Test Condition is to raise V_{IN} to V_{CC} and then lower V_{IN} to 3.0V on pins 2-16, 26-32 & 34-39.

A.C. CHARACTERISTICS

(T_A = 0°C to 70°C, V_{CC} = 5V ±5%)

MINIMUM COMPLEXITY SYSTEM TIMING REQUIREMENTS

Symbol	Parameter	80C86A-2		Units	Test Conditions
		Min	Max		
TCLCL	CLK Cycle Period	125	D.C.	ns	
TCLCH	CLK Low Time	68		ns	
TCHCL	CLK High Time	44		ns	
TCH1CH2	CLK Rise Time		10	ns	From 1.0V to 3.5V
TCL2CL1	CLK Fall Time		10	ns	From 3.5V to 1.0V
TDVCL	Data in Setup Time	20		ns	
TCLDX	Data in Hold Time	10		ns	
TR1VCL	RDY Setup Time into 82C84A (Notes 1, 2)	35		ns	
TCLR1X	RDY Hold Time into 82C84A (Notes 1, 2)	0		ns	
TRYHCH	READY Setup Time into 80C86A	68		ns	
TCHRYX	READY Hold Time into 80C86A	20		ns	
TRYLCL	READY Inactive to CLK (Note 3)	−8		ns	
THVCH	HOLD Setup Time	20		ns	
TINVCH	INTR, NMI, $\overline{\text{TEST}}$ Setup Time (Note 2)	15		ns	
TILIH	Input Rise Time (Except CLK)		15	ns	From 0.8V to 2.0V
TIHIL	Input Fall Time (Except CLK)		15	ns	From 2.0V to 0.8V

A.C. CHARACTERISTICS (Continued)

(T_A = 0°C to 70°C, V_{CC} = 5V ±5%)

Timing Responses

Symbol	Parameter	80C86A-2		Units	Test Conditions
		Min	Max		
TCLAV	Address Valid Delay	10	60	ns	
TCLAX	Address Hold Time	10		ns	
TCLAZ	Address Float Delay	TCLAX	50	ns	
TLHLL	ALE Width	TCLCH−10		ns	
TCLLH	ALE Active Delay		50	ns	
TCHLL	ALE Inactive Delay		55	ns	
TLLAX	Address Hold Time to ALE Inactive	TCHCL−10		ns	
TCLDV	Data Valid Delay	10	60	ns	
TCHDX	Data Hold Time	10		ns	
TWHDX	Data Hold Time After WR	TCLCH−30		ns	
TCVCTV	Control Active Delay 1	10	70	ns	
TCHCTV	Control Active Delay 2	10	60	ns	
TCVCTX	Control Inactive Delay	10	70	ns	
TAZRL	Address Float to READ Active	0		ns	
TCLRL	$\overline{RD}$ Active Delay	10	100	ns	
TCLRH	$\overline{RD}$ Inactive Delay	10	80	ns	
TRHAV	$\overline{RD}$ Inactive to Next Address Active	TCLCL−40		ns	
TCLHAV	HLDA Valid Delay	10	100	ns	
TRLRH	$\overline{RD}$ Width	2TCLCL−50		ns	
TWLWH	$\overline{WR}$ Width	2TCLCL−40		ns	
TAVAL	Address Valid to ALE Low	TCLCH−40		ns	
TOLOH	Output Rise Time		15	ns	From 0.8V to 2.0V
TOHOL	Output Fall Time		15	ns	From 2.0V to 0.8V

NOTES:
1. Signal at 82C84A shown for reference only. See 82C84A data sheet for the most recent specifications.
2. Setup requirement for asynchronous signal only to guarantee recognition at next CLK.
3. Applies only to T2 state. (8 ns into T3).

A.C. TESTING INPUT, OUTPUT WAVEFORM

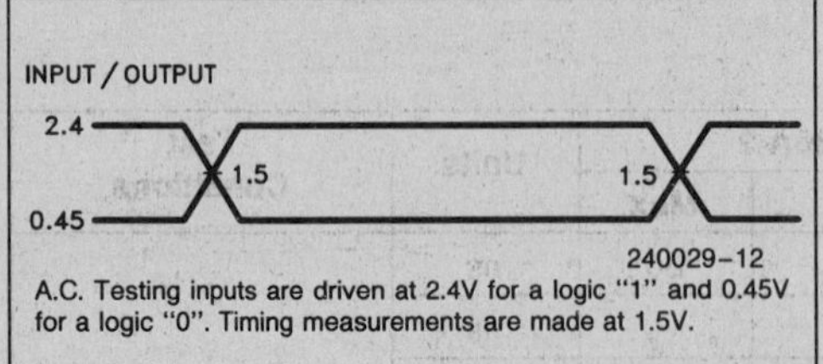

240029-12

A.C. Testing inputs are driven at 2.4V for a logic "1" and 0.45V for a logic "0". Timing measurements are made at 1.5V.

A.C. TESTING LOAD CIRCUIT

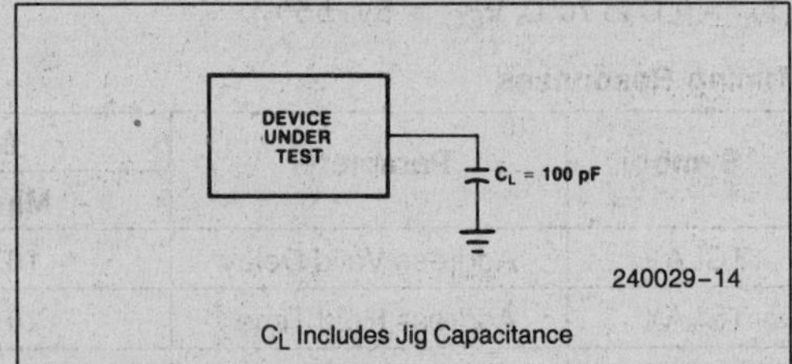

240029-14

C_L Includes Jig Capacitance

WAVEFORMS

MINIMUM MODE

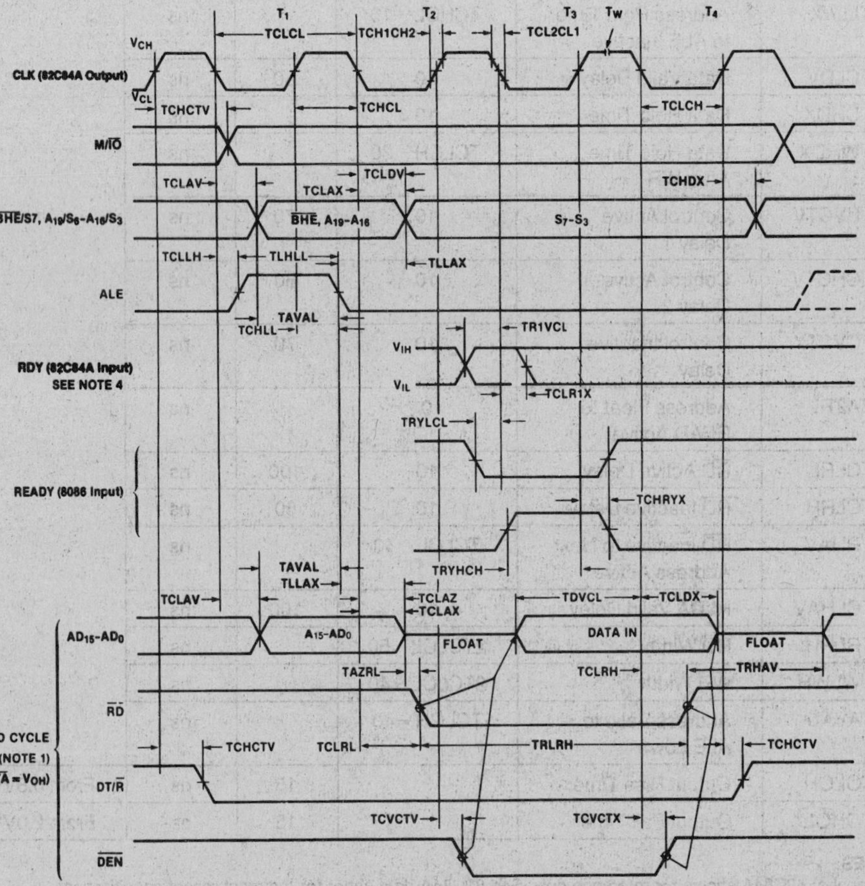

240029-13

WAVEFORMS (Continued)

MINIMUM MODE (Continued)

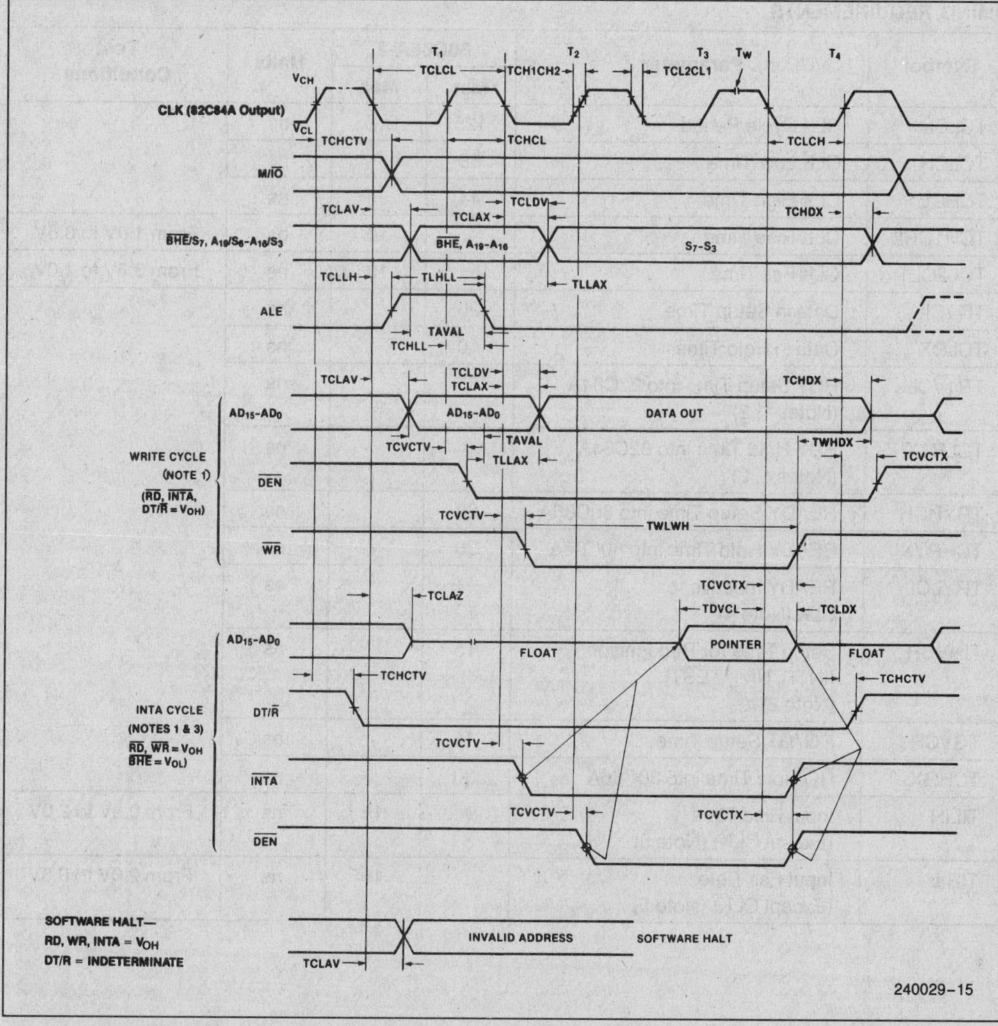

NOTES:

1. All output timing measurements are made at 1.5V unless otherwise noted.
2. RDY is sampled near the end of T_2, T_3, T_W to determine if T_W machines states are to be inserted.
3. Two INTA cycles run back-to-back. The 80C86A local ADDR/DATA BUS is floating during both INTA cycles. Control signals shown for second INTA cycle.
4. Signals at 82C84A are shown for reference only.

6

A.C. CHARACTERISTICS

MAX MODE SYSTEM (USING 82C88 BUS CONTROLLER) TIMING REQUIREMENTS

Symbol	Parameter	80C86A-2		Units	Test Conditions
		Min	Max		
TCLCL	CLK Cycle Period	125	D.C.	ns	
TCLCH	CLK Low Time	68		ns	
TCHCL	CLK High Time	44		ns	
TCH1CH2	CLK Rise Time		10	ns	From 1.0V to 3.5V
TCL2CL1	CLK Fall Time		10	ns	From 3.5V to 1.0V
TDVCL	Data in Setup Time	20		ns	
TCLDX	Data in Hold Time	10		ns	
TR1VCL	RDY Setup Time into 82C84A (Notes 1, 2)	35		ns	
TCLR1X	RDY Hold Time into 82C84A (Notes 1, 2)	0		ns	
TRYHCH	READY Setup Time into 80C86A	68		ns	
TCHRYX	READY Hold Time into 80C86A	20		ns	
TRYLCL	READY Inactive to CLK (Note 4)	−8		ns	
TINVCH	Setup Time for Recognition (INTR, NMI, $\overline{TEST}$) (Note 2)	15		ns	
TGVCH	$\overline{RQ}/\overline{GT}$ Setup Time	15		ns	
TCHGX	$\overline{RQ}$ Hold Time into 80C86A	30		ns	
TILIH	Input Rise Time (Except CLK) (Note 5)		15	ns	From 0.8V to 2.0V
TIHIL	Input Fall Time (Except CLK) (Note 5)		15	ns	From 2.0V to 0.8V

A.C. CHARACTERISTICS (Continued)

TIMING RESPONSES

Symbol	Parameter	80C86A-2		Units	Test Conditions
		Min	Max		
TCLML	Command Active Delay (Note 1)	5	35	ns	
TCLMH	Command Inactive Delay (Note 1)	5	35	ns	
TRYHSH	READY Active to Status Passive (Note 3)		65	ns	
TCHSV	Status Active Delay	10	60	ns	
TCLSH	Status Inactive Delay	10	70	ns	
TCLAV	Address Valid Delay	10	60	ns	
TCLAX	Address Hold Time	10		ns	
TCLAZ	Address Float Delay	TCLAX	50	ns	
TSVLH	Status Valid to ALE High (Note 1)		20	ns	
TSVMCH	Status Valid to MCE High (Note 1)		30	ns	
TCLLH	CLK Low to ALE Valid (Note 1)		20	ns	
TCLMCH	CLK Low to MCE High (Note 1)		25	ns	
TCHLL	ALE Inactive Delay (Note 1)	4	18	ns	
TCLDV	Data Valid Delay	10	60	ns	
TCHDX	Data Hold Time	10		ns	
TCVNV	Control Active Delay (Note 1)	5	45	ns	
TCVNX	Control Inactive Delay (Note 1)	10	45	ns	
TAZRL	Address Float to Read Active	0		ns	
TCLRL	RD Active Delay	10	100	ns	
TCLRH	RD Inactive Delay	10	80	ns	
TRHAV	RD Inactive to Next Address Active	TCLCL−40		ns	
TCHDTL	Direction Control Active Delay (Note 1)		50	ns	
TCHDTH	Direction Control Inactive Delay (Note 1)		30	ns	
TCLGL	GT Active Delay	0	50	ns	
TCLGH	GT Inactive Delay	0	50	ns	
TRLRH	RD Width	2TCLCL−50		ns	
TOLOH	Output Rise Time		15	ns	From 0.8V to 2.0V
TOHOL	Output Fall Time		15	ns	From 2.0V to 0.8V

NOTES:
1. Signal at 82C84A or 82C88 shown for reference only. See 82C84A and 82C88 for the most recent specifications.
2. Setup requirement for asynchronous signal only to guarantee recognition at next CLK.
3. Applies only to T3 and wait states.
4. Applies only to T2 state (8 ns into T3).
5. These parameters are characterized and not 100% tested.

A.C. TESTING INPUT, OUTPUT WAVEFORM

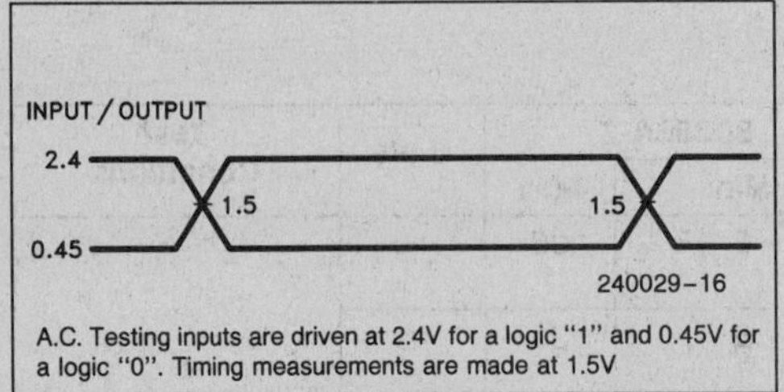

A.C. Testing inputs are driven at 2.4V for a logic "1" and 0.45V for a logic "0". Timing measurements are made at 1.5V

A.C. TESTING LOAD CIRCUIT

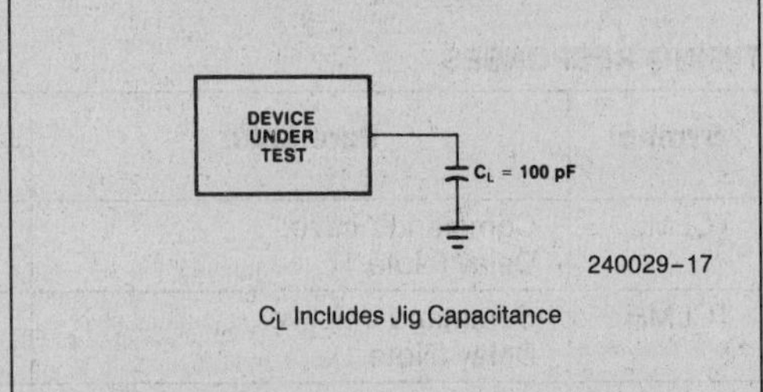

C_L Includes Jig Capacitance

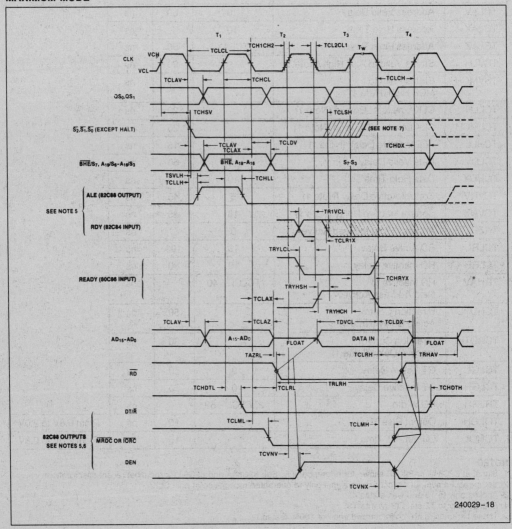

WAVEFORMS

MAXIMUM MODE

CLK, VCH, VCL, T_1, T_2, T_3, T_W, T_4, TCLCL, TCH1CH2, TCL2CL1, TCLAV, TCHCL, TCLCH, QS_0,QS_1, TCHSV, TCLSH, $\overline{S_2},\overline{S_1},\overline{S_0}$ (EXCEPT HALT), (SEE NOTE 7), TCLAV, TCLAX, TCLDV, TCHDX, $\overline{BHE}/S_7$, A_{19}/S_6–A_{16}/S_3, $\overline{BHE}$, A_{19}–A_{16}, S_7–S_3, TSVLH, TCLLH, TCHLL, SEE NOTE 5, ALE (82C88 OUTPUT), RDY (82C84 INPUT), TR1VCL, TCLR1X, TRYLCL, READY (80C86 INPUT), TCHRYX, TRYHSH, TCLAX, TRYHCH, TCLAV, TCLAZ, TDVCL, TCLDX, AD_{15}–AD_0, A_{15}–AD_0, FLOAT, DATA IN, FLOAT, TAZRL, TCLRH, TRHAV, $\overline{RD}$, TRLRH, TCHDTL, TCLRL, TCHDTH, DT/$\overline{R}$, TCLML, TCLMH, 82C88 OUTPUTS SEE NOTES 5,6, $\overline{MRDC}$ OR $\overline{IORC}$, TCVNV, DEN, TCVNX

240029–18

WAVEFORMS (Continued)

MAXIMUM MODE (Continued)

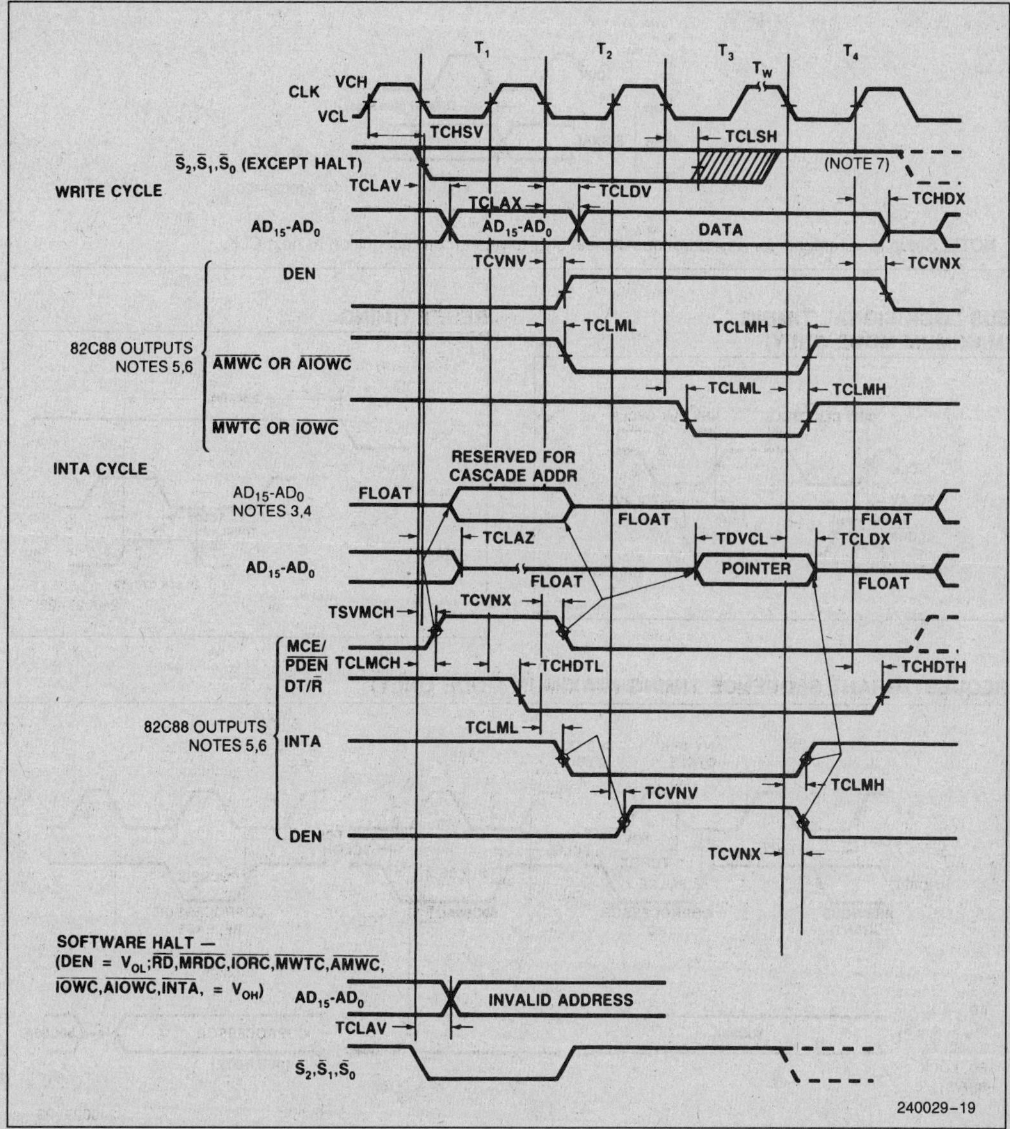

NOTES:

1. All timing measurements are made at 1.5V unless otherwise noted.
2. RDY is sampled near the end of T_2, T_3, T_W to determine if T_W machines states are to be inserted.
3. Cascade address is valid between first and second INTA cycle.
4. Two INTA cycles run back-to-back. The 80C86A local ADDR/DATA BUS is floating during both INTA cycles. Control for pointer address is shown for second INTA cycle.
5. Signals at 82C84A or 82C88 are shown for reference only.
6. The issuance of the 82C88 command and control signals ($\overline{MRDC}$, $\overline{MWTC}$, $\overline{AMWC}$, $\overline{IORC}$, $\overline{IOWC}$, $\overline{AIOWC}$, $\overline{INTA}$ and DEN) lags the active high 82C88 CEN.
7. Status inactive in state just prior to T_4.

WAVEFORMS (Continued)

ASYNCHRONOUS SIGNAL RECOGNITION

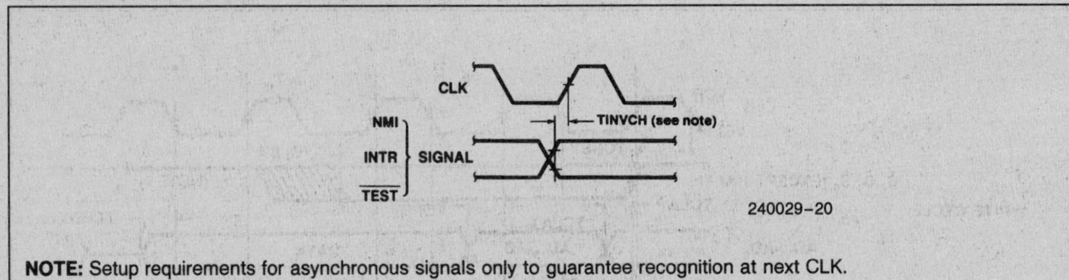

NOTE: Setup requirements for asynchronous signals only to guarantee recognition at next CLK.

BUS LOCK SIGNAL TIMING (MAXIMUM MODE ONLY)

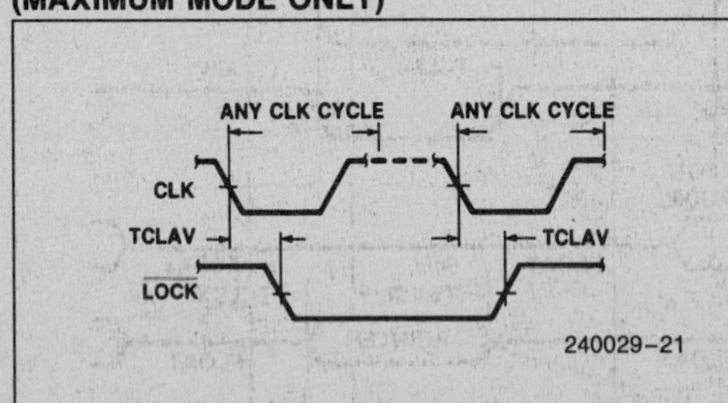

RESET TIMING

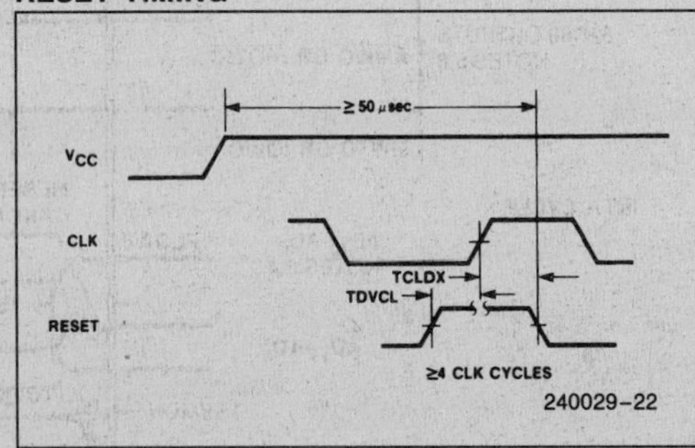

REQUEST/GRANT SEQUENCE TIMING (MAXIMUM MODE ONLY)

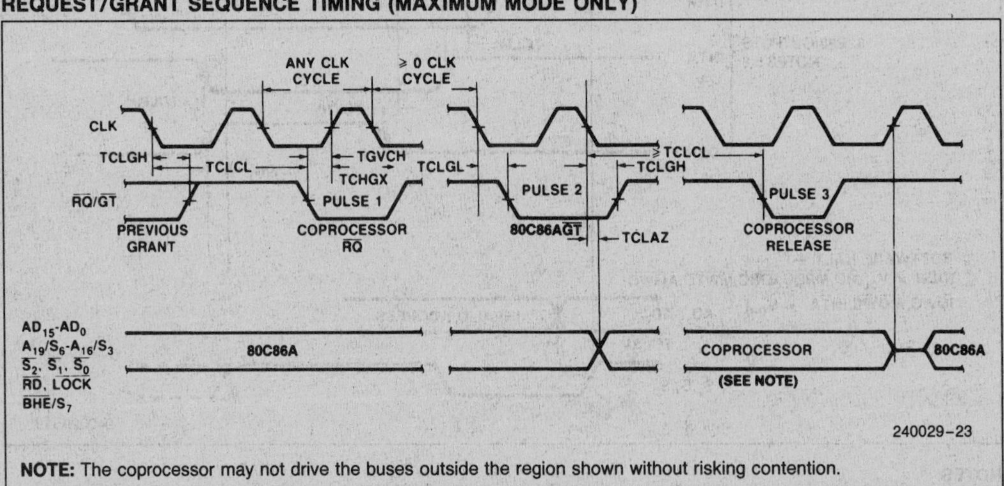

NOTE: The coprocessor may not drive the buses outside the region shown without risking contention.

WAVEFORMS (Continued)

HOLD/HOLD ACKNOWLEDGE TIMING (MINIMUM MODE ONLY)

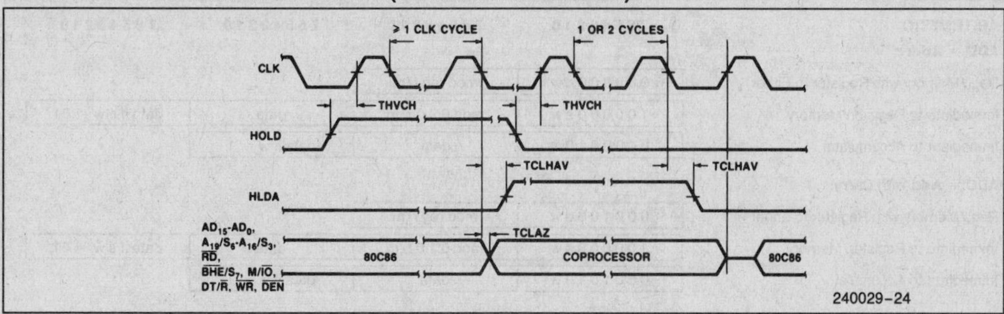

Table 2. Instruction Set Summary

Mnemonic and Description	Instruction Code			
DATA TRANSFER				
MOV = Move:	76543210	76543210	76543210	76543210
Register/Memory to/from Register**	100010dw	mod reg r/m		
Immediate to Register/Memory	1100011w	mod 000 r/m	data	data if w = 1
Immediate to Register	1011 w reg	data	data if w = 1	
Memory to Accumulator	1010000w	addr-low	addr-high	
Accumulator to Memory	1010001w	addr-low	addr-high	
Register/Memory to Segment Register**	10001110	mod 0 reg r/m		
Segment Register to Register/Memory	10001100	mod 0 reg r/m		
PUSH = Push:				
Register/Memory	11111111	mod 110 r/m		
Register	01010 reg			
Segment Register	000 reg 110			
POP = Pop:				
Register/Memory	10001111	mod 000 r/m		
Register	01011 reg			
Segment Register	000 reg 111			
XCHG = Exchange:				
Register/Memory with Register	1000011w	mod reg r/m		
Register with Accumulator	10010 reg			
IN = Input from:				
Fixed Port	1110010w	port		
Variable Port	1110110w			
OUT = Output to:				
Fixed Port	1110011w	port		
Variable Port	1110111w			
XLAT = Translate Byte to AL	11010111			
LEA = Load EA to Register	10001101	mod reg r/m		
LDS = Load Pointer to DS	11000101	mod reg r/m		
LES = Load Pointer to ES	11000100	mod reg r/m		
LAHF = Load AH with Flags	10011111			
SAHF = Store AH into Flags	10011110			
PUSHF = Push Flags	10011100			
POPF = Pop Flags	10011101			

6

Table 2. Instruction Set Summary (Continued)

Mnemonic and Description	Instruction Code			
ARITHMETIC	76543210	76543210	76543210	76543210
ADD = Add:				
Reg./Memory with Register to Either	0 0 0 0 0 0 d w	mod reg r/m		
Immediate to Register/Memory	1 0 0 0 0 0 s w	mod 0 0 0 r/m	data	data if s w = 01
Immediate to Accumulator	0 0 0 0 0 1 0 w	data	data if w = 1	
ADC = Add with Carry:				
Reg./Memory with Register to Either	0 0 0 1 0 0 d w	mod reg r/m		
Immediate to Register/Memory	1 0 0 0 0 0 s w	mod 0 1 0 r/m	data	data if s w = 01
Immediate to Accumulator	0 0 0 1 0 1 0 w	data	data if w = 1	
INC = Increment:				
Register/Memory	1 1 1 1 1 1 1 w	mod 0 0 0 r/m		
Register	0 1 0 0 0 reg			
AAA = ASCII Adjust for Add	0 0 1 1 0 1 1 1			
DAA = Decimal Adjust for Add	0 0 1 0 0 1 1 1			
SUB = Subtract:				
Reg./Memory and Register to Either	0 0 1 0 1 0 d w	mod reg r/m		
Immediate from Register/Memory	1 0 0 0 0 0 s w	mod 1 0 1 r/m	data	data if s w = 01
Immediate from Accumulator	0 0 1 0 1 1 0 w	data	data if w = 1	
SBB = Subtract with Borrow				
Reg./Memory and Register to Either	0 0 0 1 1 0 d w	mod reg r/m		
Immediate from Register/Memory	1 0 0 0 0 0 s w	mod 0 1 1 r/m	data	data if s w = 01
Immediate from Accumulator	0 0 0 1 1 1 0 w	data	data if w = 1	
DEC = Decrement:				
Register/Memory	1 1 1 1 1 1 1 w	mod 0 0 1 r/m		
Register	0 1 0 0 1 reg			
NEG = Change Sign	1 1 1 1 0 1 1 w	mod 0 1 1 r/m		
CMP = Compare:				
Register/Memory and Register	0 0 1 1 1 0 d w	mod reg r/m		
Immediate with Register/Memory	1 0 0 0 0 0 s w	mod 1 1 1 r/m	data	data if s w = 01
Immediate with Accumulator	0 0 1 1 1 1 0 w	data	data if w = 1	
AAS = ASCII Adjust for Subtract	0 0 1 1 1 1 1 1			
DAS = Decimal Adjust for Subtract	0 0 1 0 1 1 1 1			
MUL = Multiply (Unsigned)	1 1 1 1 0 1 1 w	mod 1 0 0 r/m		
IMUL = Integer Multiply (Signed)	1 1 1 1 0 1 1 w	mod 1 0 1 r/m		
AAM = ASCII Adjust for Multiply	1 1 0 1 0 1 0 0	0 0 0 0 1 0 1 0		
DIV = Divide (Unsigned)	1 1 1 1 0 1 1 w	mod 1 1 0 r/m		
IDIV = Integer Divide (Signed)	1 1 1 1 0 1 1 w	mod 1 1 1 r/m		
AAD = ASCII Adjust for Divide	1 1 0 1 0 1 0 1	0 0 0 0 1 0 1 0		
CBW = Convert Byte to Word	1 0 0 1 1 0 0 0			
CWD = Convert Word to Double Word	1 0 0 1 1 0 0 1			

Table 2. Instruction Set Summary (Continued)

Mnemonic and Description	Instruction Code			
LOGIC	76543210	76543210	76543210	76543210
NOT = Invert	1111011w	mod 010 r/m		
SHL/SAL = Shift Logical/Arithmetic Left	110100vw	mod 100 r/m		
SHR = Shift Logical Right	110100vw	mod 101 r/m		
SAR = Shift Arithmetic Right	110100vw	mod 111 r/m		
ROL = Rotate Left	110100vw	mod 000 r/m		
ROR = Rotate Right	110100vw	mod 001 r/m		
RCL = Rotate Through Carry Flag Left	110100vw	mod 010 r/m		
RCR = Rotate Through Carry Right	110100vw	mod 011 r/m		
AND = And:				
Reg./Memory and Register to Either	001000dw	mod reg r/m		
Immediate to Register/Memory	1000000w	mod 100 r/m	data	data if w = 1
Immediate to Accumulator	0010010w	data	data if w = 1	
TEST = And Function to Flags, No Result:				
Register/Memory and Register	1000010w	mod reg r/m		
Immediate Data and Register/Memory	1111011w	mod 000 r/m	data	data if w = 1
Immediate Data and Accumulator	1010100w	data	data if w = 1	
OR = Or:				
Reg./Memory and Register to Either	000010dw	mod reg r/m		
Immediate to Register/Memory	1000000w	mod 001 r/m	data	data if w = 1
Immediate to Accumulator	0000110w	data	data if w = 1	
XOR = Exclusive OR:				
Reg./Memory and Register to Either	001100dw	mod reg r/m		
Immediate to Register/Memory	1000000w	mod 110 r/m	data	data if w = 1
Immediate to Accumulator	0011010w	data	data if w = 1	
STRING MANIPULATION				
REP = Repeat	1111001z			
MOVS = Move Byte/Word	1010010w			
CMPS = Compare Byte/Word	1010011w			
SCAS = Scan Byte/Word	1010111w			
LODS = Load Byte/Wd to AL/AX	1010110w			
STOS = Stor Byte/Wd from AL/A	1010101w			
CONTROL TRANSFER				
CALL = Call:				
Direct Within Segment	11101000	disp-low	disp-high	
Indirect Within Segment	11111111	mod 010 r/m		
Direct Intersegment	10011010	offset-low	offset-high	
		seg-low	seg-high	
Indirect Intersegment	11111111	mod 011 r/m		

6

Table 2. Instruction Set Summary (Continued)

Mnemonic and Description	Instruction Code		
CONTROL TRANSFER (Continued)			
JMP = Unconditional Jump:	7 6 5 4 3 2 1 0	7 6 5 4 3 2 1 0	7 6 5 4 3 2 1 0
Direct Within Segment	1 1 1 0 1 0 0 1	disp-low	disp-high
Direct Within Segment-Short	1 1 1 0 1 0 1 1	disp	
Indirect Within Segment	1 1 1 1 1 1 1 1	mod 1 0 0 r/m	
Direct Intersegment	1 1 1 0 1 0 1 0	offset-low	offset-high
		seg-low	seg-high
Indirect Intersegment	1 1 1 1 1 1 1 1	mod 1 0 1 r/m	
RET = Return from CALL:			
Within Segment	1 1 0 0 0 0 1 1		
Within Seg. Adding Immed to SP	1 1 0 0 0 0 1 0	data-low	data-high
Intersegment	1 1 0 0 1 0 1 1		
Intersegment Adding Immediate to SP	1 1 0 0 1 0 1 0	data-low	data-high
JE/JZ = Jump on Equal/Zero	0 1 1 1 0 1 0 0	disp	
JL/JNGE = Jump on Less/Not Greater or Equal	0 1 1 1 1 1 0 0	disp	
JLE/JNG = Jump on Less or Equal/ Not Greater	0 1 1 1 1 1 1 0	disp	
JB/JNAE = Jump on Below/Not Above or Equal	0 1 1 1 0 0 1 0	disp	
JBE/JNA = Jump on Below or Equal/ Not Above	0 1 1 1 0 1 1 0	disp	
JP/JPE = Jump on Parity/Parity Even	0 1 1 1 1 0 1 0	disp	
JO = Jump on Overflow	0 1 1 1 0 0 0 0	disp	
JS = Jump on Sign	0 1 1 1 1 0 0 0	disp	
JNE/JNZ = Jump on Not Equal/Not Zero	0 1 1 1 0 1 0 1	disp	
JNL/JGE = Jump on Not Less/Greater or Equal	0 1 1 1 1 1 0 1	disp	
JNLE/JG = Jump on Not Less or Equal/ Greater	0 1 1 1 1 1 1 1	disp	
JNB/JAE = Jump on Not Below/Above or Equal	0 1 1 1 0 0 1 1	disp	
JNBE/JA = Jump on Not Below or Equal/Above	0 1 1 1 0 1 1 1	disp	
JNP/JPO = Jump on Not Par/Par Odd	0 1 1 1 1 0 1 1	disp	
JNO = Jump on Not Overflow	0 1 1 1 0 0 0 1	disp	
JNS = Jump on Not Sign	0 1 1 1 1 0 0 1	disp	
LOOP = Loop CX Times	1 1 1 0 0 0 1 0	disp	
LOOPZ/LOOPE = Loop While Zero/Equal	1 1 1 0 0 0 0 1	disp	
LOOPNZ/LOOPNE = Loop While Not Zero/Equal	1 1 1 0 0 0 0 0	disp	
JCXZ = Jump on CX Zero	1 1 1 0 0 0 1 1	disp	
INT = Interrupt			
Type Specified	1 1 0 0 1 1 0 1	type	
Type 3	1 1 0 0 1 1 0 0		
INTO = Interrupt on Overflow	1 1 0 0 1 1 1 0		
IRET = Interrupt Return	1 1 0 0 1 1 1 1		

Table 2. Instruction Set Summary (Continued)

Mnemonic and Description	Instruction Code	
PROCESSOR CONTROL	7 6 5 4 3 2 1 0	7 6 5 4 3 2 1 0
CLC = Clear Carry	1 1 1 1 1 0 0 0	
CMC = Complement Carry	1 1 1 1 0 1 0 1	
STC = Set Carry	1 1 1 1 1 0 0 1	
CLD = Clear Direction	1 1 1 1 1 1 0 0	
STD = Set Direction	1 1 1 1 1 1 0 1	
CLI = Clear Interrupt	1 1 1 1 1 0 1 0	
STI = Set Interrupt	1 1 1 1 1 0 1 1	
HLT = Halt	1 1 1 1 0 1 0 0	
WAIT = Wait	1 0 0 1 1 0 1 1	
ESC = Escape (to External Device)	1 1 0 1 1 x x x	mod x x x r/m
LOCK = Bus Lock Prefix	1 1 1 1 0 0 0 0	

NOTES:
AL = 8-bit accumulator
AX = 16-bit accumulator
CX = Count register
DS = Data segment
ES = Extra segment
Above/below refers to unsigned value.
Greater = more positive:
Less = less positive (more negative) signed values
if d = 1 then "to" reg; if d = 0 then "from" reg
if w = 1 then word instruction; if w = 0 then byte instruction
if mod = 11 then r/m is treated as a REG field
if mod = 00 then DISP = 0*, disp-low and disp-high are absent
if mod = 01 then DISP = disp-low sign-extended to 16 bits, disp-high is absent
if mod = 10 then DISP = disp-high: disp-low
if r/m = 000 then EA = (BX) + (SI) + DISP
if r/m = 001 then EA = (BX) + (DI) + DISP
if r/m = 010 then EA = (BP) + (SI) + DISP
if r/m = 011 then EA = (BP) + (DI) + DISP
if r/m = 100 then EA = (SI) + DISP
if r/m = 101 then EA = (DI) + DISP
if r/m = 110 then EA = (BP) + DISP*
if r/m = 111 then EA = (BX) + DISP
DISP follows 2nd byte of instruction (before data if required)
*except if mod = 00 and r/m = 110 then EA = disp-high: disp-low.
**MOV CS, REG/MEMORY not allowed.

if s w = 01 then 16 bits of immediate data form the operand
if s w = 11 then an immediate data byte is sign extended to form the 16-bit operand
if v = 0 then "count" = 1; if v = 1 then "count" in (CL) register
x = don't care
z is used for string primitives for comparison with ZF FLAG

SEGMENT OVERRIDE PREFIX

0 0 1 reg 1 1 0

REG is assigned according to the following table:

16-Bit (w = 1)	8-Bit (w = 0)	Segment
000 AX	000 AL	00 ES
001 CX	001 CL	01 CS
010 DX	010 DL	10 SS
011 BX	011 BL	11 DS
100 SP	100 AH	
101 BP	101 CH	
110 SI	110 DH	
111 DI	111 BH	

Instructions which reference the flag register file as a 16-bit object use the symbol FLAGS to represent the file:
FLAGS =
X:X:X:X:(OF):(DF):(IF):(TF):(SF):(ZF):X:(AF):X:(PF):X:(CF)

6

DATA SHEET REVISION REVIEW

The following list represents key differences between this and the -001 data sheet. Please review this summary carefully.

1. In the Pin Description Table (Table 1), the description of the HLDA signal being issued has been corrected. HLDA will be issued in the middle of either the T_4 or T_i state.

8088
8-BIT HMOS MICROPROCESSOR
8088/8088-2

- 8-Bit Data Bus Interface
- 16-Bit Internal Architecture
- Direct Addressing Capability to 1 Mbyte of Memory
- Direct Software Compatibility with 8086 CPU
- 14-Word by 16-Bit Register Set with Symmetrical Operations
- 24 Operand Addressing Modes
- Byte, Word, and Block Operations
- 8-Bit and 16-Bit Signed and Unsigned Arithmetic in Binary or Decimal, Including Multiply and Divide
- Two Clock Rates:
  - 5 MHz for 8088
  - 8 MHz for 8088-2
- Available in EXPRESS
  - Standard Temperature Range
  - Extended Temperature Range

The Intel® 8088 is a high performance microprocessor implemented in N-channel, depletion load, silicon gate technology (HMOS-II), and packaged in a 40-pin CERDIP package. The processor has attributes of both 8- and 16-bit microprocessors. It is directly compatible with 8086 software and 8080/8085 hardware and peripherals.

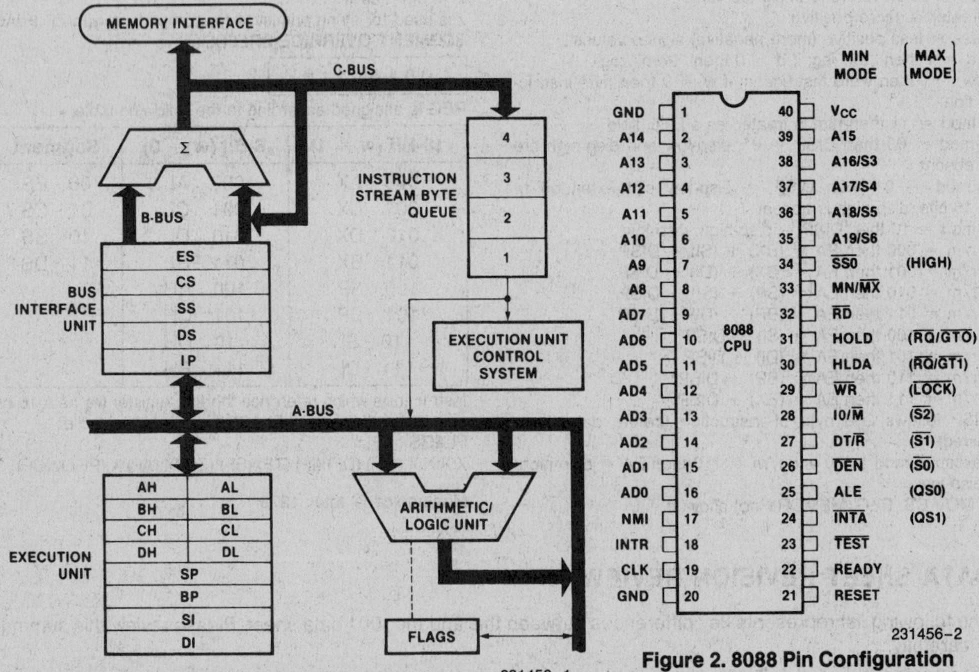

Figure 1. 8088 CPU Functional Block Diagram

Figure 2. 8088 Pin Configuration

August 1990
Order Number: 231456-006

Table 1. Pin Description

The following pin function descriptions are for 8088 systems in either minimum or maximum mode. The "local bus" in these descriptions is the direct multiplexed bus interface connection to the 8088 (without regard to additional bus buffers).

<table>
<tr><th>Symbol</th><th>Pin No.</th><th>Type</th><th>Name and Function</th></tr>
<tr><td>AD7–AD0</td><td>9–16</td><td>I/O</td><td>ADDRESS DATA BUS: These lines constitute the time multiplexed memory/IO address (T1) and data (T2, T3, Tw, T4) bus. These lines are active HIGH and float to 3-state OFF during interrupt acknowledge and local bus "hold acknowledge".</td></tr>
<tr><td>A15–A8</td><td>2–8, 39</td><td>O</td><td>ADDRESS BUS: These lines provide address bits 8 through 15 for the entire bus cycle (T1–T4). These lines do not have to be latched by ALE to remain valid. A15–A8 are active HIGH and float to 3-state OFF during interrupt acknowledge and local bus "hold acknowledge".</td></tr>
<tr><td>A19/S6, A18/S5, A17/S4, A16/S3</td><td>35–38</td><td>O</td><td>ADDRESS/STATUS: During T1, these are the four most significant address lines for memory operations. During I/O operations, these lines are LOW. During memory and I/O operations, status information is available on these lines during T2, T3, Tw, and T4. S6 is always low. The status of the interrupt enable flag bit (S5) is updated at the beginning of each clock cycle. S4 and S3 are encoded as shown.
This information indicates which segment register is presently being used for data accessing.
These lines float to 3-state OFF during local bus "hold acknowledge".
<table>
<tr><th>S4</th><th>S3</th><th>Characteristics</th></tr>
<tr><td>0 (LOW)</td><td>0</td><td>Alternate Data</td></tr>
<tr><td>0</td><td>1</td><td>Stack</td></tr>
<tr><td>1 (HIGH)</td><td>0</td><td>Code or None</td></tr>
<tr><td>1</td><td>1</td><td>Data</td></tr>
<tr><td>S6 is 0 (LOW)</td><td></td><td></td></tr>
</table></td></tr>
<tr><td>$\overline{RD}$</td><td>32</td><td>O</td><td>READ: Read strobe indicates that the processor is performing a memory or I/O read cycle, depending on the state of the IO/$\overline{M}$ pin or S2. This signal is used to read devices which reside on the 8088 local bus. $\overline{RD}$ is active LOW during T2, T3 and Tw of any read cycle, and is guaranteed to remain HIGH in T2 until the 8088 local bus has floated.
This signal floats to 3-state OFF in "hold acknowledge".</td></tr>
<tr><td>READY</td><td>22</td><td>I</td><td>READY: is the acknowledgement from the addressed memory or I/O device that it will complete the data transfer. The RDY signal from memory or I/O is synchronized by the 8284 clock generator to form READY. This signal is active HIGH. The 8088 READY input is not synchronized. Correct operation is not guaranteed if the set up and hold times are not met.</td></tr>
<tr><td>INTR</td><td>18</td><td>I</td><td>INTERRUPT REQUEST: is a level triggered input which is sampled during the last clock cycle of each instruction to determine if the processor should enter into an interrupt acknowledge operation. A subroutine is vectored to via an interrupt vector lookup table located in system memory. It can be internally masked by software resetting the interrupt enable bit. INTR is internally synchronized. This signal is active HIGH.</td></tr>
<tr><td>$\overline{TEST}$</td><td>23</td><td>I</td><td>$\overline{TEST}$: input is examined by the "wait for test" instruction. If the $\overline{TEST}$ input is LOW, execution continues, otherwise the processor waits in an "idle" state. This input is synchronized internally during each clock cycle on the leading edge of CLK.</td></tr>
</table>

Table 1. Pin Description (Continued)

Symbol	Pin No.	Type	Name and Function
NMI	17	I	**NON-MASKABLE INTERRUPT:** is an edge triggered input which causes a type 2 interrupt. A subroutine is vectored to via an interrupt vector lookup table located in system memory. NMI is not maskable internally by software. A transition from a LOW to HIGH initiates the interrupt at the end of the current instruction. This input is internally synchronized.
RESET	21	I	**RESET:** causes the processor to immediately terminate its present activity. The signal must be active HIGH for at least four clock cycles. It restarts execution, as described in the instruction set description, when RESET returns LOW. RESET is internally synchronized.
CLK	19	I	**CLOCK:** provides the basic timing for the processor and bus controller. It is asymmetric with a 33% duty cycle to provide optimized internal timing.
V_{CC}	40		**V_{CC}:** is the +5V ±10% power supply pin.
GND	1, 20		**GND:** are the ground pins.
MN/$\overline{MX}$	33	I	**MINIMUM/MAXIMUM:** indicates what mode the processor is to operate in. The two modes are discussed in the following sections.

The following pin function descriptions are for the 8088 minimum mode (i.e., MN/$\overline{MX}$ = V_{CC}). Only the pin functions which are unique to minimum mode are described; all other pin functions are as described above.

Symbol	Pin No.	Type	Name and Function
IO/$\overline{M}$	28	O	**STATUS LINE:** is an inverted maximum mode $\overline{S2}$. It is used to distinguish a memory access from an I/O access. IO/$\overline{M}$ becomes valid in the T4 preceding a bus cycle and remains valid until the final T4 of the cycle (I/O = HIGH, M = LOW). IO/$\overline{M}$ floats to 3-state OFF in local bus "hold acknowledge".
$\overline{WR}$	29	O	**WRITE:** strobe indicates that the processor is performing a write memory or write I/O cycle, depending on the state of the IO/$\overline{M}$ signal. WR is active for T2, T3, and Tw of any write cycle. It is active LOW, and floats to 3-state OFF in local bus "hold acknowledge".
$\overline{INTA}$	24	O	**INTA:** is used as a read strobe for interrupt acknowledge cycles. It is active LOW during T2, T3, and Tw of each interrupt acknowledge cycle.
ALE	25	O	**ADDRESS LATCH ENABLE:** is provided by the processor to latch the address into an address latch. It is a HIGH pulse active during clock low of T1 of any bus cycle. Note that ALE is never floated.
DT/$\overline{R}$	27	O	**DATA TRANSMIT/RECEIVE:** is needed in a minimum system that desires to use a data bus transceiver. It is used to control the direction of data flow through the transceiver. Logically, DT/$\overline{R}$ is equivalent to $\overline{S1}$ in the maximum mode, and its timing is the same as for IO/$\overline{M}$ (T = HIGH, R = LOW). This signal floats to 3-state OFF in local "hold acknowledge".
$\overline{DEN}$	26	O	**DATA ENABLE:** is provided as an output enable for the data bus transceiver in a minimum system which uses the transceiver. $\overline{DEN}$ is active LOW during each memory and I/O access, and for $\overline{INTA}$ cycles. For a read or $\overline{INTA}$ cycle, it is active from the middle of T2 until the middle of T4, while for a write cycle, it is active from the beginning of T2 until the middle of T4. $\overline{DEN}$ floats to 3-state OFF during local bus "hold acknowledge".

Table 1. Pin Description (Continued)

Symbol	Pin No.	Type	Name and Function
HOLD, HLDA	31, 30	I, O	**HOLD:** indicates that another master is requesting a local bus "hold". To be acknowledged, HOLD must be active HIGH. The processor receiving the "hold" request will issue HLDA (HIGH) as an acknowledgement, in the middle of a T4 or Ti clock cycle. Simultaneous with the issuance of HLDA the processor will float the local bus and control lines. After HOLD is detected as being LOW, the processor lowers HLDA, and when the processor needs to run another cycle, it will again drive the local bus and control lines. HOLD and HLDA have internal pull-up resistors. Hold is not an asynchronous input. External synchronization should be provided if the system cannot otherwise guarantee the set up time.
$\overline{SSO}$	34	O	**STATUS LINE:** is logically equivalent to $\overline{SO}$ in the maximum mode. The combination of $\overline{SSO}$, IO/$\overline{M}$ and DT/$\overline{R}$ allows the system to completely decode the current bus cycle status.

IO/$\overline{M}$	DT/$\overline{R}$	$\overline{SSO}$	Characteristics
1(HIGH)	0	0	Interrupt Acknowledge
1	0	1	Read I/O Port
1	1	0	Write I/O Port
1	1	1	Halt
0(LOW)	0	0	Code Access
0	0	1	Read Memory
0	1	0	Write Memory
0	1	1	Passive

The following pin function descriptions are for the 8088/8288 system in maximum mode (i.e., MN/$\overline{MX}$ = GND). Only the pin functions which are unique to maximum mode are described; all other pin functions are as described above.

Symbol	Pin No.	Type	Name and Function
$\overline{S2}$, $\overline{S1}$, $\overline{S0}$	26–28	O	**STATUS:** is active during clock high of T4, T1, and T2, and is returned to the passive state (1,1,1) during T3 or during Tw when READY is HIGH. This status is used by the 8288 bus controller to generate all memory and I/O access control signals. Any change by $\overline{S2}$, $\overline{S1}$, or $\overline{S0}$ during T4 is used to indicate the beginning of a bus cycle, and the return to the passive state in T3 and Tw is used to indicate the end of a bus cycle. These signals float to 3-state OFF during "hold acknowledge". During the first clock cycle after RESET becomes active, these signals are active HIGH. After this first clock, they float to 3-state OFF.

$\overline{S2}$	$\overline{S1}$	$\overline{S0}$	Characteristics
0(LOW)	0	0	Interrupt Acknowledge
0	0	1	Read I/O Port
0	1	0	Write I/O Port
0	1	1	Halt
1(HIGH)	0	0	Code Access
1	0	1	Read Memory
1	1	0	Write Memory
1	1	1	Passive

Table 1. Pin Description (Continued)

<table>
<tr><th>Symbol</th><th>Pin No.</th><th>Type</th><th>Name and Function</th></tr>
<tr><td>$\overline{RQ}/\overline{GT0}$,
$\overline{RQ}/\overline{GT1}$</td><td>30, 31</td><td>I/O</td><td>REQUEST/GRANT: pins are used by other local bus masters to force the processor to release the local bus at the end of the processor's current bus cycle. Each pin is bidirectional with $\overline{RQ}/\overline{GT0}$ having higher priority than $\overline{RQ}/\overline{GT1}$. $\overline{RQ}/\overline{GT}$ has an internal pull-up resistor, so may be left unconnected. The request/grant sequence is as follows (See Figure 8):
1. A pulse of one CLK wide from another local bus master indicates a local bus request ("hold") to the 8088 (pulse 1).
2. During a T4 or TI clock cycle, a pulse one clock wide from the 8088 to the requesting master (pulse 2), indicates that the 8088 has allowed the local bus to float and that it will enter the "hold acknowledge" state at the next CLK. The CPU's bus interface unit is disconnected logically from the local bus during "hold acknowledge". The same rules as for HOLD/HOLDA apply as for when the bus is released.
3. A pulse one CLK wide from the requesting master indicates to the 8088 (pulse 3) that the "hold" request is about to end and that the 8088 can reclaim the local bus at the next CLK. The CPU then enters T4.
Each master-master exchange of the local bus is a sequence of three pulses. There must be one idle CLK cycle after each bus exchange. Pulses are active LOW.
If the request is made while the CPU is performing a memory cycle, it will release the local bus during T4 of the cycle when all the following conditions are met:
1. Request occurs on or before T2.
2. Current cycle is not the low bit of a word.
3. Current cycle is not the first acknowledge of an interrupt acknowledge sequence.
4. A locked instruction is not currently executing.
If the local bus is idle when the request is made the two possible events will follow:
1. Local bus will be released during the next clock.
2. A memory cycle will start within 3 clocks. Now the four rules for a currently active memory cycle apply with condition number 1 already satisfied.</td></tr>
<tr><td>$\overline{LOCK}$</td><td>29</td><td>O</td><td>$\overline{LOCK}$: indicates that other system bus masters are not to gain control of the system bus while $\overline{LOCK}$ is active (LOW). The $\overline{LOCK}$ signal is activated by the "LOCK" prefix instruction and remains active until the completion of the next instruction. This signal is active LOW, and floats to 3-state off in "hold acknowledge".</td></tr>
<tr><td>QS1, QS0</td><td>24, 25</td><td>O</td><td>QUEUE STATUS: provide status to allow external tracking of the internal 8088 instruction queue.
The queue status is valid during the CLK cycle after which the queue operation is performed.
<table>
<tr><th>QS1</th><th>QS0</th><th>Characteristics</th></tr>
<tr><td>0(LOW)</td><td>0</td><td>No Operation</td></tr>
<tr><td>0</td><td>1</td><td>First Byte of Opcode from Queue</td></tr>
<tr><td>1(HIGH)</td><td>0</td><td>Empty the Queue</td></tr>
<tr><td>1</td><td>1</td><td>Subsequent Byte from Queue</td></tr>
</table></td></tr>
<tr><td>—</td><td>34</td><td>O</td><td>Pin 34 is always high in the maximum mode.</td></tr>
</table>

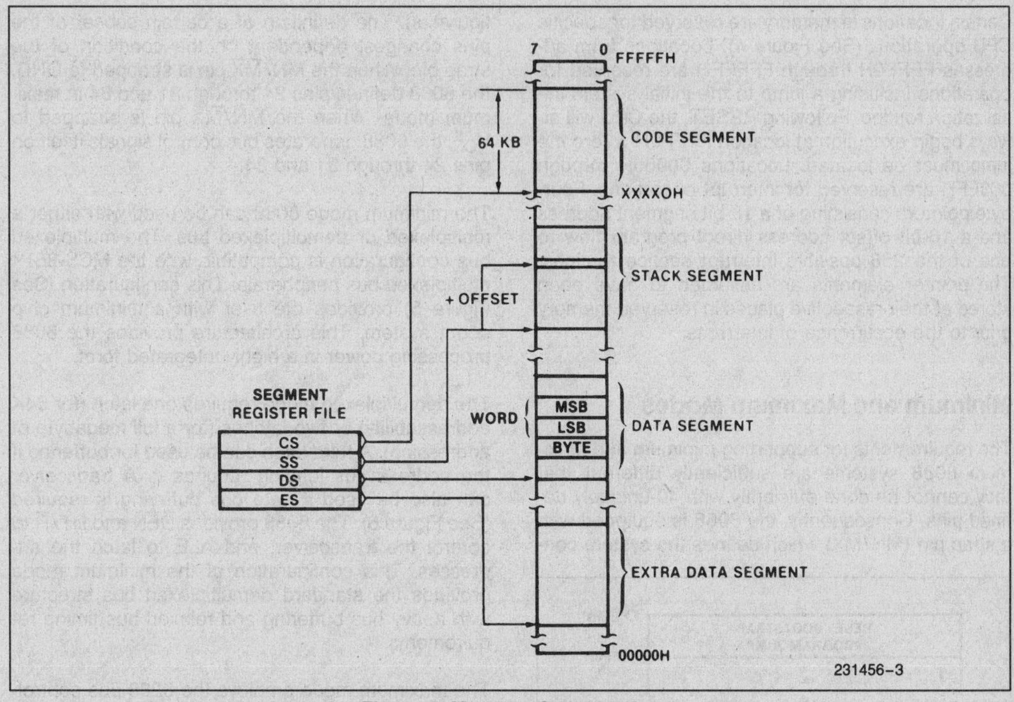

Figure 3. Memory Organization

FUNCTIONAL DESCRIPTION

Memory Organization

The processor provides a 20-bit address to memory which locates the byte being referenced. The memory is organized as a linear array of up to 1 million bytes, addressed as 00000(H) to FFFFF(H). The memory is logically divided into code, data, extra data, and stack segments of up to 64K bytes each, with each segment falling on 16-byte boundaries (See Figure 3).

All memory references are made relative to base addresses contained in high speed segment registers. The segment types were chosen based on the addressing needs of programs. The segment register to be selected is automatically chosen according to the rules of the following table. All information in one segment type share the same logical attributes (e.g. code or data). By structuring memory into relocatable areas of similar characteristics and by automatically selecting segment registers, programs are shorter, faster, and more structured.

Word (16-bit) operands can be located on even or odd address boundaries. For address and data operands, the least significant byte of the word is stored in the lower valued address location and the most significant byte in the next higher address location. The BIU will automatically execute two fetch or write cycles for 16-bit operands.

Memory Reference Used	Segment Register Used	Segment Selection Rule
Instructions	CODE (CS)	Automatic with all instruction prefetch.
Stack	STACK (SS)	All stack pushes and pops. Memory references relative to BP base register except data references.
Local Data	DATA (DS)	Data references when: relative to stack, destination of string operation, or explicity overridden.
External (Global) Data	EXTRA (ES)	Destination of string operations: Explicitly selected using a segment override.

6

Certain locations in memory are reserved for specific CPU operations (See Figure 4). Locations from addresses FFFF0H through FFFFFH are reserved for operations including a jump to the initial system initialization routine. Following RESET, the CPU will always begin execution at location FFFF0H where the jump must be located. Locations 00000H through 003FFH are reserved for interrupt operations. Four-byte pointers consisting of a 16-bit segment address and a 16-bit offset address direct program flow to one of the 256 possible interrupt service routines. The pointer elements are assumed to have been stored at their respective places in reserved memory prior to the occurrence of interrupts.

Minimum and Maximum Modes

The requirements for supporting minimum and maximum 8088 systems are sufficiently different that they cannot be done efficiently with 40 uniquely defined pins. Consequently, the 8088 is equipped with a strap pin (MN/$\overline{MX}$) which defines the system configuration. The definition of a certain subset of the pins changes, dependent on the condition of the strap pin. When the MN/$\overline{MX}$ pin is strapped to GND, the 8088 defines pins 24 through 31 and 34 in maximum mode. When the MN/$\overline{MX}$ pin is strapped to V_{CC}, the 8088 generates bus control signals itself on pins 24 through 31 and 34.

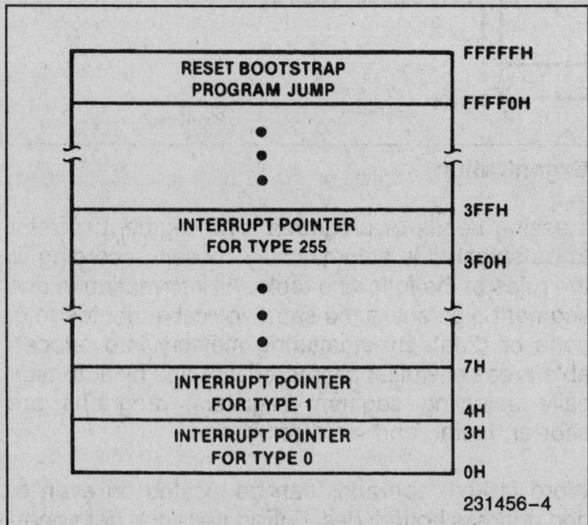

Figure 4. Reserved Memory Locations

The minimum mode 8088 can be used with either a multiplexed or demultiplexed bus. The multiplexed bus configuration is compatible with the MCS-85™ multiplexed bus peripherals. This configuration (See Figure 5) provides the user with a minimum chip count system. This architecture provides the 8088 processing power in a highly integrated form.

The demultiplexed mode requires one latch (for 64K addressability) or two latches (for a full megabyte of addressing). A third latch can be used for buffering if the address bus loading requires it. A transceiver can also be used if data bus buffering is required (See Figure 6). The 8088 provides $\overline{DEN}$ and DT/$\overline{R}$ to control the transceiver, and ALE to latch the addresses. This configuration of the minimum mode provides the standard demultiplexed bus structure with heavy bus buffering and relaxed bus timing requirements.

The maximum mode employs the 8288 bus controller (See Figure 7). The 8288 decodes status lines $\overline{S0}$, $\overline{S1}$, and $\overline{S2}$, and provides the system with all bus control signals. Moving the bus control to the 8288 provides better source and sink current capability to the control lines, and frees the 8088 pins for extended large system features. Hardware lock, queue status, and two request/grant interfaces are provided by the 8088 in maximum mode. These features allow co-processors in local bus and remote bus configurations.

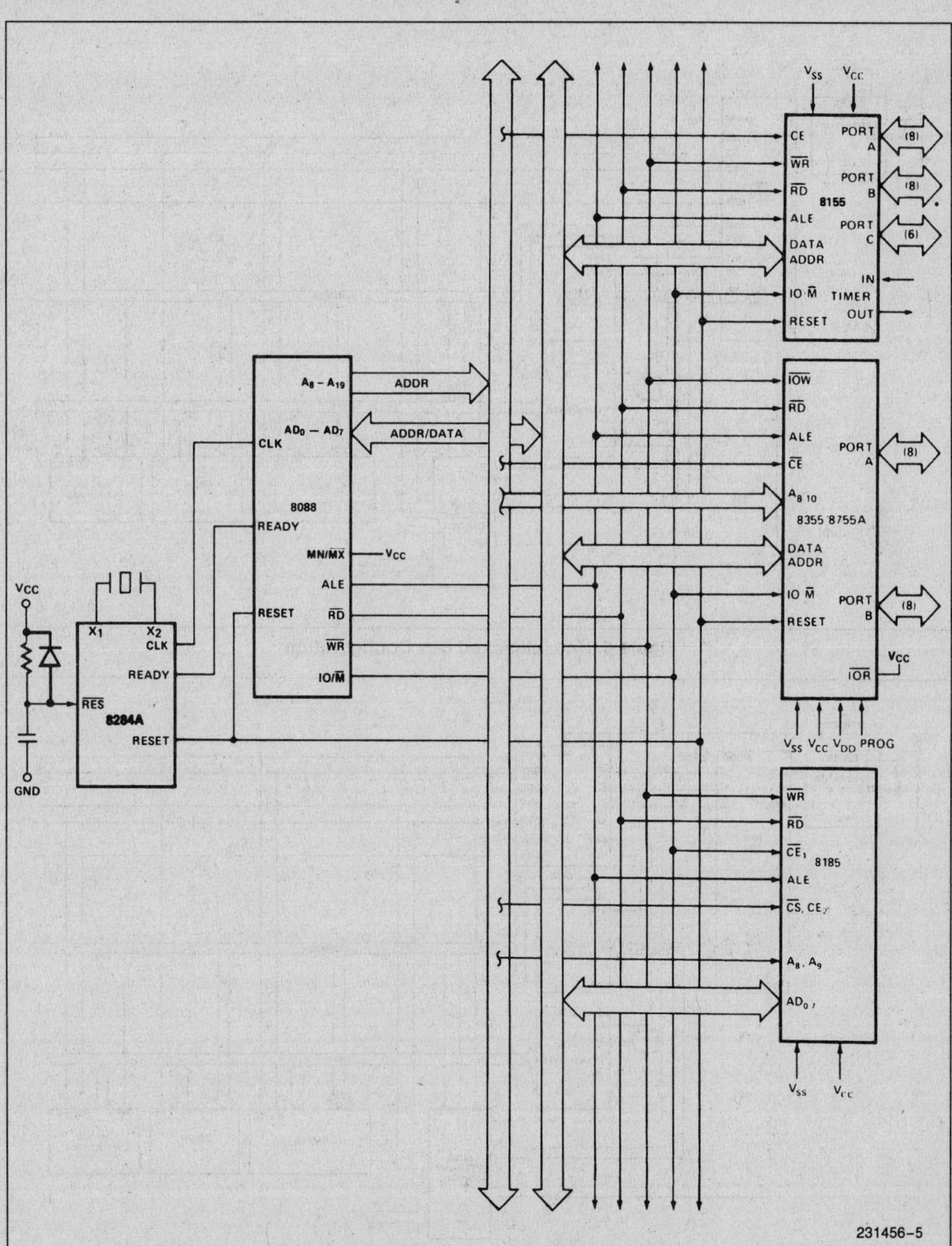

Figure 5. Multiplexed Bus Configuration

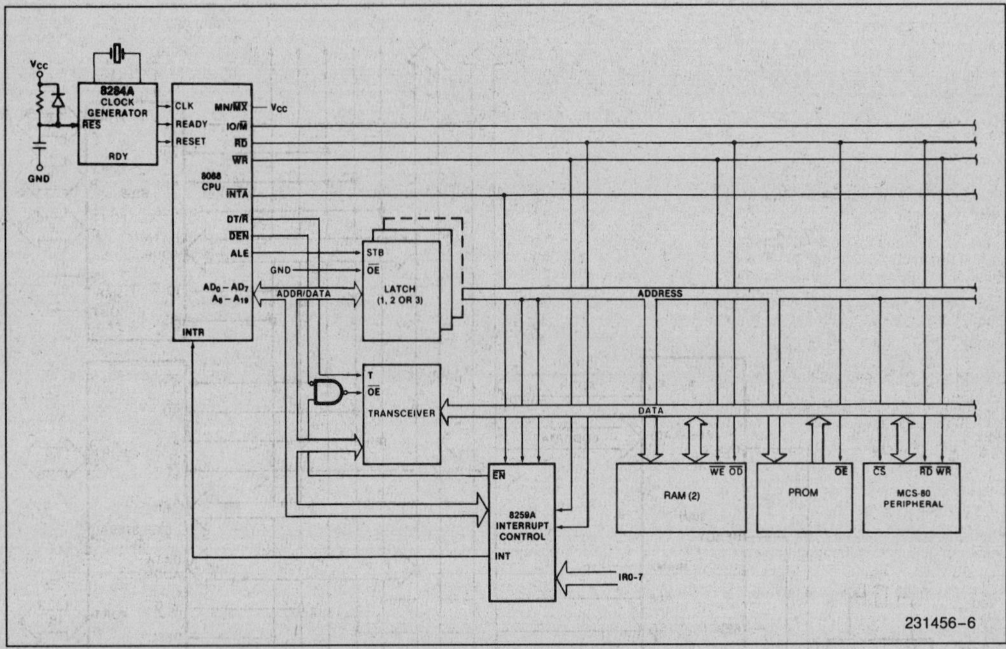

Figure 6. Demultiplexed Bus Configuration

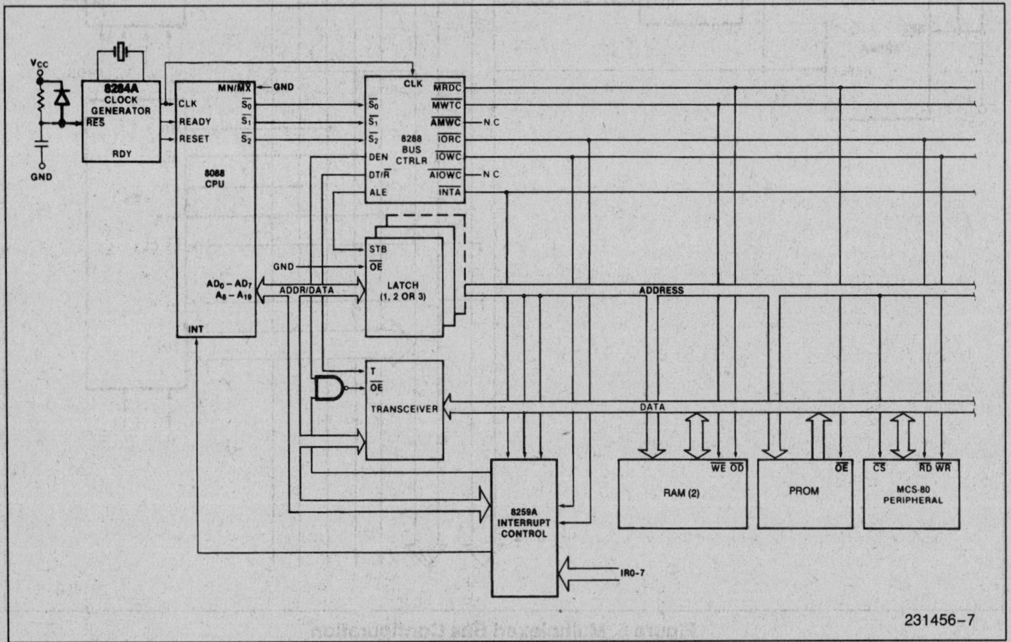

Figure 7. Fully Buffered System Using Bus Controller

Bus Operation

The 8088 address/data bus is broken into three parts—the lower eight address/data bits (AD0–AD7), the middle eight address bits (A8–A15), and the upper four address bits (A16–A19). The address/data bits and the highest four address bits are time multiplexed. This technique provides the most efficient use of pins on the processor, permitting the use of a standard 40 lead package. The middle eight address bits are not multiplexed, i.e. they remain valid throughout each bus cycle. In addition, the bus can be demultiplexed at the processor with a single address latch if a standard, non-multiplexed bus is desired for the system.

Each processor bus cycle consists of at least four CLK cycles. These are referred to as T1, T2, T3, and T4 (See Figure 8). The address is emitted from the processor during T1 and data transfer occurs on the bus during T3 and T4. T2 is used primarily for chang-

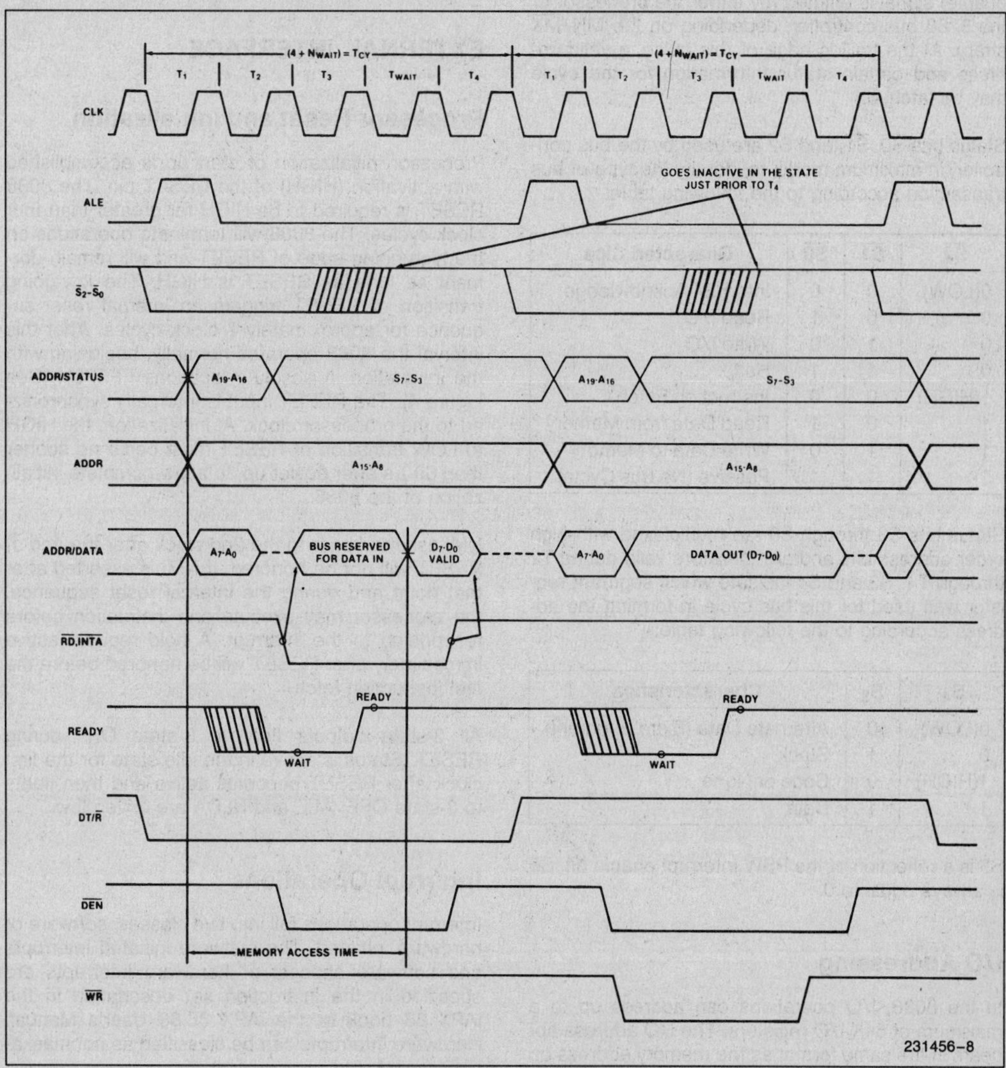

Figure 8. Basic System Timing

ing the direction of the bus during read operations. In the event that a "NOT READY" indication is given by the addressed device, "wait" states (Tw) are inserted between T3 and T4. Each inserted "wait" state is of the same duration as a CLK cycle. Periods can occur between 8088 driven bus cycles. These are referred to as "idle" states (Ti), or inactive CLK cycles. The processor uses these cycles for internal housekeeping.

During T1 of any bus cycle, the ALE (address latch enable) signal is emitted (by either the processor or the 8288 bus controller, depending on the MN/$\overline{MX}$ strap). At the trailing edge of this pulse, a valid address and certain status information for the cycle may be latched.

Status bits $\overline{S0}$, $\overline{S1}$, and $\overline{S2}$ are used by the bus controller, in maximum mode, to identify the type of bus transaction according to the following table:

$\overline{S2}$	$\overline{S1}$	$\overline{S0}$	Characteristics
0(LOW)	0	0	Interrupt Acknowledge
0	0	1	Read I/O
0	1	0	Write I/O
0	1	1	Halt
1(HIGH)	0	0	Instruction Fetch
1	0	1	Read Data from Memory
1	1	0	Write Data to Memory
1	1	1	Passive (No Bus Cycle)

Status bits S3 through S6 are multiplexed with high order address bits and are therefore valid during T2 through T4. S3 and S4 indicate which segment register was used for this bus cycle in forming the address according to the following table:

S_4	S_3	Characteristics
0(LOW)	0	Alternate Data (Extra Segment)
0	1	Stack
1(HIGH)	0	Code or None
1	1	Data

S5 is a reflection of the PSW interrupt enable bit. S6 is always equal to 0.

I/O Addressing

In the 8088, I/O operations can address up to a maximum of 64K I/O registers. The I/O address appears in the same format as the memory address on bus lines A15–A0. The address lines A19–A16 are zero in I/O operations. The variable I/O instructions, which use register DX as a pointer, have full address capability, while the direct I/O instructions directly address one or two of the 256 I/O byte locations in page 0 of the I/O address space. I/O ports are addressed in the same manner as memory locations.

Designers familiar with the 8085 or upgrading an 8085 design should note that the 8085 addresses I/O with an 8-bit address on both halves of the 16-bit address bus. The 8088 uses a full 16-bit address on its lower 16 address lines.

EXTERNAL INTERFACE

Processor Reset and Initialization

Processor initialization or start up is accomplished with activation (HIGH) of the RESET pin. The 8088 RESET is required to be HIGH for greater than four clock cycles. The 8088 will terminate operations on the high-going edge of RESET and will remain dormant as long as RESET is HIGH. The low-going transition of RESET triggers an internal reset sequence for approximately 7 clock cycles. After this interval the 8088 operates normally, beginning with the instruction in absolute locations FFFF0H (See Figure 4). The RESET input is internally synchronized to the processor clock. At initialization, the HIGH to LOW transition of RESET must occur no sooner than 50 μs after power up, to allow complete initialization of the 8088.

NMI asserted prior to the 2nd clock after the end of RESET will not be honored. If NMI is asserted after that point and during the internal reset sequence, the processor may execute one instruction before responding to the interrupt. A hold request active immediately after RESET will be honored before the first instruction fetch.

All 3-state outputs float to 3-state OFF during RESET. Status is active in the idle state for the first clock after RESET becomes active and then floats to 3-state OFF. ALE and HLDA are driven low.

Interrupt Operations

Interrupt operations fall into two classes: software or hardware initiated. The software initiated interrupts and software aspects of hardware interrupts are specified in the instruction set description in the iAPX 88 book or the iAPX 86,88 User's Manual. Hardware interrupts can be classified as nonmaskable or maskable.

Interrupts result in a transfer of control to a new program location. A 256 element table containing address pointers to the interrupt service program locations resides in absolute locations 0 through 3FFH (See Figure 4), which are reserved for this purpose. Each element in the table is 4 bytes in size and corresponds to an interrupt "type." An interrupting device supplies an 8-bit type number, during the interrupt acknowledge sequence, which is used to vector through the appropriate element to the new interrupt service program location.

Non-Maskable Interrupt (NMI)

The processor provides a single non-maskable interrupt (NMI) pin which has higher priority than the maskable interrupt request (INTR) pin. A typical use would be to activate a power failure routine. The NMI is edge-triggered on a LOW to HIGH transition. The activation of this pin causes a type 2 interrupt.

NMI is required to have a duration in the HIGH state of greater than two clock cycles, but is not required to be synchronized to the clock. Any higher going transition of NMI is latched on-chip and will be serviced at the end of the current instruction or between whole moves (2 bytes in the case of word moves) of a block type instruction. Worst case response to NMI would be for multiply, divide, and variable shift instructions. There is no specification on the occurrence of the low-going edge; it may occur before, during, or after the servicing of NMI. Another high-going edge triggers another response if it occurs after the start of the NMI procedure. The signal must be free of logical spikes in general and be free of bounces on the low-going edge to avoid triggering extraneous responses.

Maskable Interrupt (INTR)

The 8088 provides a single interrupt request input (INTR) which can be masked internally by software with the resetting of the interrupt enable (IF) flag bit. The interrupt request signal is level triggered. It is internally synchronized during each clock cycle on the high-going edge of CLK. To be responded to, INTR must be present (HIGH) during the clock period preceding the end of the current instruction or the end of a whole move for a block type instruction. During interrupt response sequence, further interrupts are disabled. The enable bit is reset as part of the response to any interrupt (INTR, NMI, software interrupt, or single step), although the FLAGS register which is automatically pushed onto the stack reflects the state of the processor prior to the interrupt. Until the old FLAGS register is restored, the enable bit will be zero unless specifically set by an instruction.

During the response sequence (See Figure 9), the processor executes two successive (back to back) interrupt acknowledge cycles. The 8088 emits the LOCK signal (maximum mode only) from T2 of the first bus cycle until T2 of the second. A local bus "hold" request will not be honored until the end of the second bus cycle. In the second bus cycle, a byte is fetched from the external interrupt system (e.g., 8259A PIC) which identifies the source (type) of the interrupt. This byte is multiplied by four and used as a pointer into the interrupt vector lookup table. An INTR signal left HIGH will be continually responded to within the limitations of the enable bit and sample period. The interrupt return instruction includes a flags pop which returns the status of the original interrupt enable bit when it restores the flags.

HALT

When a software HALT instruction is executed, the processor indicates that it is entering the HALT state in one of two ways, depending upon which mode is strapped. In minimum mode, the processor issues ALE, delayed by one clock cycle, to allow the system to latch the halt status. Halt status is available on $IO/\overline{M}$, $DT/\overline{R}$, and $\overline{SSO}$. In maximum mode, the processor issues appropriate HALT status on $\overline{S2}$, $\overline{S1}$, and $\overline{S0}$, and the 8288 bus controller issues one ALE. The 8088 will not leave the HALT state when a local bus hold is entered while in HALT. In this case, the processor reissues the HALT indicator at the end of the local bus hold. An interrupt request or RESET will force the 8088 out of the HALT state. 6

Read/Modify/Write (Semaphore) Operations via LOCK

The LOCK status information is provided by the processor when consecutive bus cycles are required during the execution of an instruction. This allows the processor to perform read/modify/write operations on memory (via the "exchange register with memory" instruction), without another system bus master receiving intervening memory cycles. This is useful in multiprocessor system configurations to accomplish "test and set lock" operations. The $\overline{LOCK}$ signal is activated (LOW) in the clock cycle following decoding of the LOCK prefix instruction. It is deactivated at the end of the last bus cycle of the instruction following the LOCK prefix. While $\overline{LOCK}$ is active, a request on a $\overline{RQ}/\overline{GT}$ pin will be recorded, and then honored at the end of the LOCK.

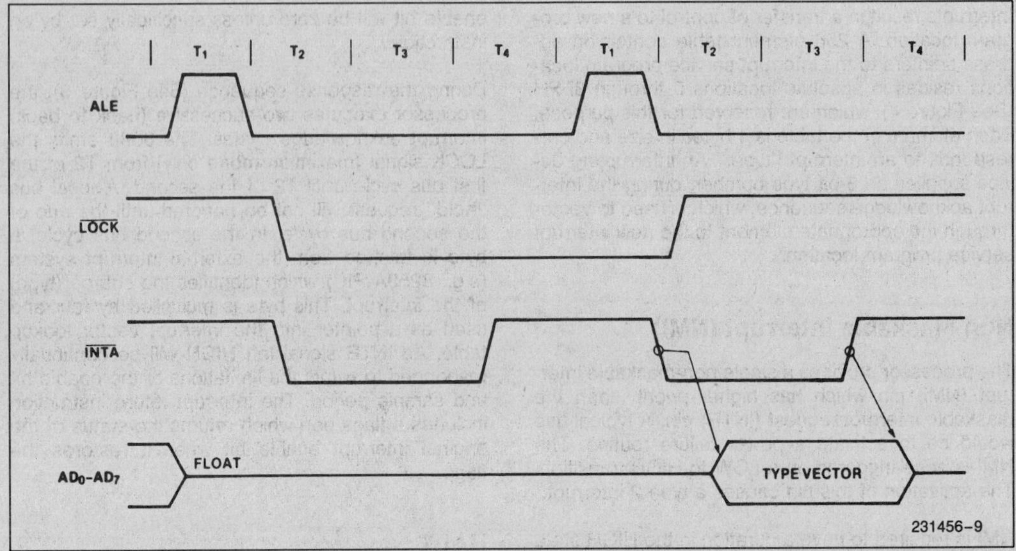

Figure 9. Interrupt Acknowledge Sequence

External Synchronization via TEST

As an alternative to interrupts, the 8088 provides a single software-testable input pin (TEST). This input is utilized by executing a WAIT instruction. The single WAIT instruction is repeatedly executed until the TEST input goes active (LOW). The execution of WAIT does not consume bus cycles once the queue is full.

If a local bus request occurs during WAIT execution, the 8088 3-states all output drivers. If interrupts are enabled, the 8088 will recognize interrupts and process them. The WAIT instruction is then refetched, and reexecuted.

Basic System Timing

In minimum mode, the MN/MX pin is strapped to V_{CC} and the processor emits bus control signals compatible with the 8085 bus structure. In maximum mode, the MN/MX pin is strapped to GND and the processor emits coded status information which the 8288 bus controller uses to generate MULTIBUS compatible bus control signals.

System Timing—Minimum System

(See Figure 8)

The read cycle begins in T1 with the assertion of the address latch enable (ALE) signal. The trailing (low going) edge of this signal is used to latch the address information, which is valid on the address/data bus (AD0–AD7) at this time, into the 8282/8283 latch. Address lines A8 through A15 do not need to be latched because they remain valid throughout the bus cycle. From T1 to T4 the IO/M signal indicates a memory or I/O operation. At T2 the address is removed from the address/data bus and the bus goes to a high impedance state. The read control signal is also asserted at T2. The read (RD) signal causes the addressed device to enable its data bus drivers to the local bus. Some time later, valid data will be available on the bus and the addressed device will drive the READY line HIGH. When the processor returns the read signal to a HIGH level, the addressed device will again 3-state its bus drivers. If a transceiver is required to buffer the 8088 local bus, signals DT/R and DEN are provided by the 8088.

A write cycle also begins with the assertion of ALE and the emission of the address. The IO/M signal is again asserted to indicate a memory or I/O write operation. In T2, immediately following the address emission, the processor emits the data to be written into the addressed location. This data remains valid until at least the middle of T4. During T2, T3, and Tw, the processor asserts the write control signal. The write (WR) signal becomes active at the beginning of T2, as opposed to the read, which is delayed somewhat into T2 to provide time for the bus to float.

The basic difference between the interrupt acknowledge cycle and a read cycle is that the interrupt acknowledge ($\overline{INTA}$) signal is asserted in place of the read ($\overline{RD}$) signal and the address bus is floated. (See Figure 9) In the second of two successive $\overline{INTA}$ cycles, a byte of information is read from the data bus, as supplied by the interrupt system logic (i.e. 8259A priority interrupt controller). This byte identifies the source (type) of the interrupt. It is multiplied by four and used as a pointer into the interrupt vector lookup table, as described earlier.

Bus Timing—Medium Complexity Systems

(See Figure 10)

For medium complexity systems, the MN/$\overline{MX}$ pin is connected to GND and the 8288 bus controller is added to the system, as well as a latch for latching the system address, and a transceiver to allow for bus loading greater than the 8088 is capable of handling. Signals ALE, $\overline{DEN}$, and DT/$\overline{R}$ are generated by the 8288 instead of the processor in this configuration, although their timing remains relatively the same. The 8088 status outputs ($\overline{S2}$, $\overline{S1}$, and $\overline{S0}$) provide type of cycle information and become 8288 inputs. This bus cycle information specifies read (code, data, or I/O), write (data or I/O), interrupt acknowledge, or software halt. The 8288 thus issues control signals specifying memory read or write, I/O read or write, or interrupt acknowledge. The 8288 provides two types of write strobes, normal and advanced, to be applied as required. The normal write strobes have data valid at the leading edge of write. The advanced write strobes have the same timing as read strobes, and hence, data is not valid at the leading edge of write. The transceiver receives the usual T and $\overline{OE}$ inputs from the 8288's DT/$\overline{R}$ and $\overline{DEN}$ outputs.

The pointer into the interrupt vector table, which is passed during the second $\overline{INTA}$ cycle, can derive from an 8259A located on either the local bus or the system bus. If the master 8289A priority interrupt controller is positioned on the local bus, a TTL gate is required to disable the transceiver when reading from the master 8259A during the interrupt acknowledge sequence and software "poll".

The 8088 Compared to the 8086

The 8088 CPU is an 8-bit processor designed around the 8086 internal structure. Most internal functions of the 8088 are identical to the equivalent 8086 functions. The 8088 handles the external bus the same way the 8086 does with the distinction of handling only 8 bits at a time. Sixteen-bit operands are fetched or written in two consecutive bus cycles. Both processors will appear identical to the software engineer, with the exception of execution time. The internal register structure is identical and all instructions have the same end result. The differences between the 8088 and 8086 are outlined below. The engineer who is unfamiliar with the 8086 is referred to the iAPX 86, 88 User's Manual, Chapters 2 and 4, for function description and instruction set information. Internally, there are three differences between the 8088 and the 8086. All changes are related to the 8-bit bus interface.

- The queue length is 4 bytes in the 8088, whereas the 8086 queue contains 6 bytes, or three words. The queue was shortened to prevent overuse of the bus by the BIU when prefetching instructions. This was required because of the additional time necessary to fetch instructions 8 bits at a time.
- To further optimize the queue, the prefetching algorithm was changed. The 8088 BIU will fetch a new instruction to load into the queue each time there is a 1 byte hole (space available) in the queue. The 8086 waits until a 2-byte space is available.
- The internal execution time of the instruction set is affected by the 8-bit interface. All 16-bit fetches and writes from/to memory take an additional four clock cycles. The CPU is also limited by the speed of instruction fetches. This latter problem only occurs when a series of simple operations occur. When the more sophisticated instructions of the 8088 are being used, the queue has time to fill and the execution proceeds as fast as the execution unit will allow.

The 8088 and 8086 are completely software compatible by virtue of their identical execution units. Software that is system dependent may not be completely transferable, but software that is not system dependent will operate equally as well on an 8088 and an 8086.

The hardware interface of the 8088 contains the major differences between the two CPUs. The pin assignments are nearly identical, however, with the following functional changes:

- A8–A15—These pins are only address outputs on the 8088. These address lines are latched internally and remain valid throughout a bus cycle in a manner similar to the 8085 upper address lines.
- $\overline{BHE}$ has no meaning on the 8088 and has been eliminated.

- $\overline{SSO}$ provides the $\overline{SO}$ status information in the minimum mode. This output occurs on pin 34 in minimum mode only. DT/$\overline{R}$, IO/$\overline{M}$, and $\overline{SSO}$ provide the complete bus status in minimum mode.
- IO/$\overline{M}$ has been inverted to be compatible with the MCS-85 bus structure.
- ALE is delayed by one clock cycle in the minimum mode when entering HALT, to allow the status to be latched with ALE.

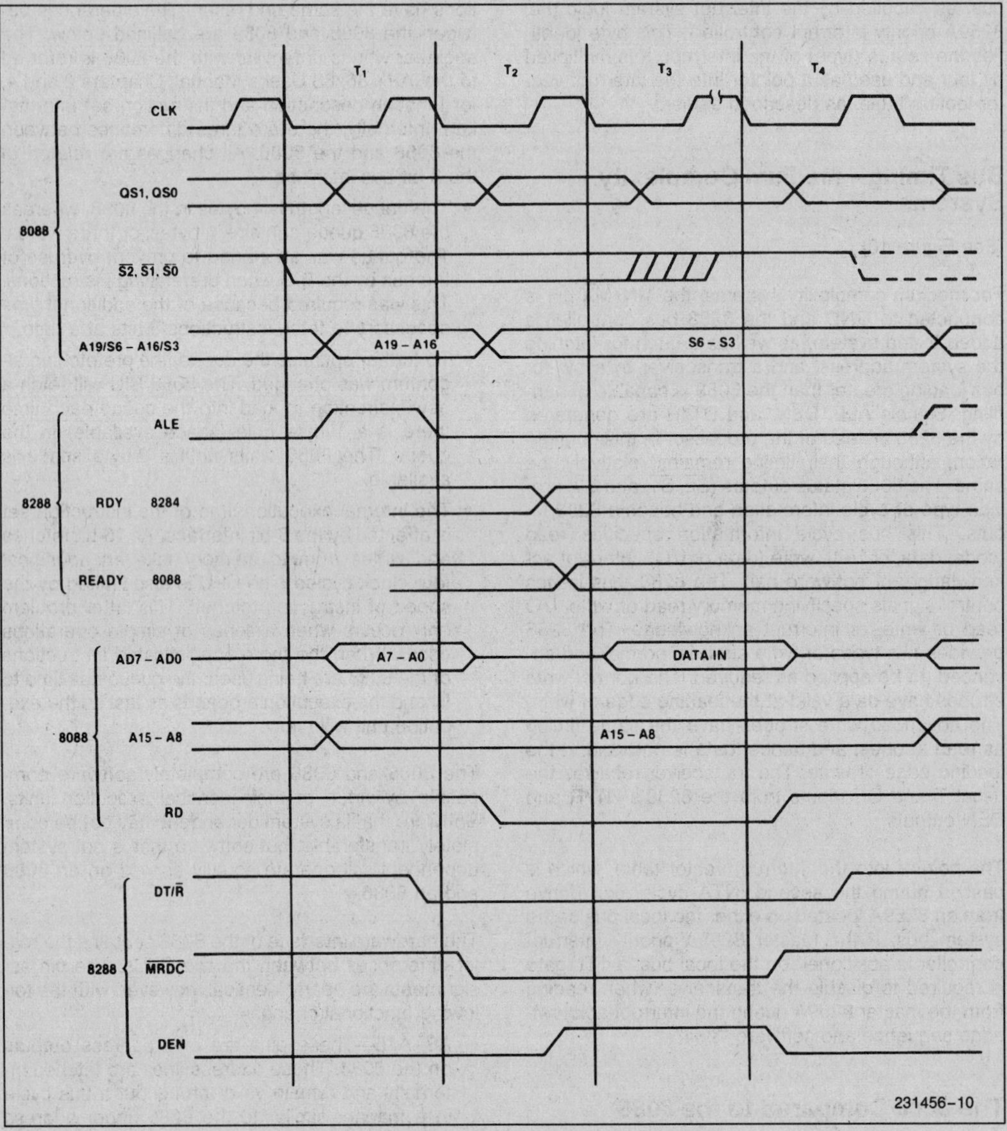

231456-10

Figure 10. Medium Complexity System Timing

ABSOLUTE MAXIMUM RATINGS*

Ambient Temperature Under Bias ....0°C to +70°C
Case Temperature (Plastic) ....0°C to +95°C
Case Temperature (CERDIP) ....0°C to +75°C
Storage Temperature ....−65°C to +150°C
Voltage on Any Pin with
Respect to Ground ....−1.0 to +7V
Power Dissipation ....2.5 Watt

NOTICE: This is a production data sheet. The specifications are subject to change without notice.

**WARNING: Stressing the device beyond the "Absolute Maximum Ratings" may cause permanent damage. These are stress ratings only. Operation beyond the "Operating Conditions" is not recommended and extended exposure beyond the "Operating Conditions" may affect device reliability.*

D.C. CHARACTERISTICS

(T_A = 0°C to 70°C, T_{CASE} (Plastic) = 0°C to 95°C, T_{CASE} (CERDIP) = 0°C to 75°C,
T_A = 0°C to 55°C and T_{CASE} = 0°C to 75°C for P8088-2 only
T_A is guaranteed as long as T_{CASE} is not exceeded)
(V_{CC} = 5V ±10% for 8088, V_{CC} = 5V ±5% for 8088-2 and Extended Temperature EXPRESS)

Symbol	Parameter	Min	Max	Units	Test Conditions
V_{IL}	Input Low Voltage	−0.5	+0.8	V	(Note 1)
V_{IH}	Input High Voltage	2.0	V_{CC} + 0.5	V	(Notes 1, 2)
V_{OL}	Output Low Voltage		0.45	V	I_{OL} = 2.0 mA
V_{OH}	Output High Voltage	2.4		V	I_{OH} = −400 μA
I_{CC}	Power Supply Current: 8088 8088-2 P8088		340 350 250	mA	T_A = 25°C
I_{LI}	Input Leakage Current		±10	μA	0V ≤ V_{IN} ≤ V_{CC} (Note 3)
I_{LO}	Output and I/O Leakage Current		±10	μA	0.45V ≤ V_{OUT} ≤ V_{CC}
V_{CL}	Clock Input Low Voltage	−0.5	+0.6	V	
V_{CH}	Clock Input High Voltage	3.9	V_{CC} + 1.0	V	
C_{IN}	Capacitance If Input Buffer (All Input Except AD_0–AD_7, RQ/GT)		15	pF	fc = 1 MHz
C_{IO}	Capacitance of I/O Buffer AD_0–AD_7, RQ/GT)		15	pF	fc = 1 MHz

NOTES:
1. V_{IL} tested with MN/$\overline{MX}$ Pin = 0V
V_{IH} tested with MN/$\overline{MX}$ Pin = 5V
MN/$\overline{MX}$ Pin is a strap Pin
2. Not applicable to $\overline{RQ}/\overline{GT0}$ and $\overline{RQ}/\overline{GT1}$ Pins (Pins 30 and 31)
3. HOLD and HLDA I_{LI} Min = 30 μA, Max = 500 μA

6

A.C. CHARACTERISTICS

(T_A = 0°C to 70°C, T_{CASE} (Plastic) = 0°C to 95°C, T_{CASE} (CERDIP) = 0°C to 75°C,
T_A = 0°C to 55°C and T_{CASE} = 0°C to 80°C for P8088-2 only
T_A is guaranteed as long as T_{CASE} is not exceeded)

(V_{CC} = 5V ±10% for 8088, V_{CC} = 5V ±5% for 8088-2 and Extended Temperature EXPRESS)

MINIMUM COMPLEXITY SYSTEM TIMING REQUIREMENTS

Symbol	Parameter	8088		8088-2		Units	Test Conditions
		Min	Max	Min	Max		
TCLCL	CLK Cycle Period	200	500	125	500	ns	
TCLCH	CLK Low Time	118		68		ns	
TCHCL	CLK High Time	69		44		ns	
TCH1CH2	CLK Rise Time		10		10	ns	From 1.0V to 3.5V
TCL2CL2	CLK Fall Time		10		10	ns	From 3.5V to 1.0V
TDVCL	Data in Setup Time	30		20		ns	
TCLDX	Data in Hold Time	10		10		ns	
TR1VCL	RDY Setup Time into 8284 (Notes 1, 2)	35		35		ns	
TCLR1X	RDY Hold Time into 8284 (Notes 1, 2)	0		0		ns	
TRYHCH	READY Setup Time into 8088	118		68		ns	
TCHRYX	READY Hold Time into 8088	30		20		ns	
TRYLCL	READY Inactive to CLK (Note 3)	−8		−8		ns	
THVCH	HOLD Setup Time	35		20		ns	
TINVCH	INTR, NMI, $\overline{\text{TEST}}$ Setup Time (Note 2)	30		15		ns	
TILIH	Input Rise Time (Except CLK)		20		20	ns	From 0.8V to 2.0V
TIHIL	Input Fall Time (Except CLK)		12		12	ns	From 2.0V to 0.8V

A.C. CHARACTERISTICS (Continued)

TIMING RESPONSES

Symbol	Parameter	8088		8088-2		Units	Test Conditions
		Min	Max	Min	Max		
TCLAV	Address Valid Delay	10	110	10	60	ns	
TCLAX	Address Hold Time	10		10		ns	
TCLAZ	Address Float Delay	TCLAX	80	TCLAX	50	ns	
TLHLL	ALE Width	TCLCH − 20		TCLCH − 10		ns	
TCLLH	ALE Active Delay		80		50	ns	
TCHLL	ALE Inactive Delay		85		55	ns	
TLLAX	Address Hold Time to ALE Inactive	TCHCL − 10		TCHCL − 10		ns	
TCLDV	Data Valid Delay	10	110	10	60	ns	
TCHDX	Data Hold Time	10		10		ns	
TWHDX	Data Hold Time after $\overline{WR}$	TCLCH − 30		TCLCH − 30		ns	
TCVCTV	Control Active Delay 1	10	110	10	70	ns	
TCHCTV	Control Active Delay 2	10	110	10	60	ns	
TCVCTX	Control Inactive Delay	10	110	10	70	ns	
TAZRL	Address Float to READ Active	0		0		ns	
TCLRL	$\overline{RD}$ Active Delay	10	165	10	100	ns	
TCLRH	$\overline{RD}$ Inactive Delay	10	150	10	80	ns	
TRHAV	$\overline{RD}$ Inactive to Next Address Active	TCLCL − 45		TCLCL − 40		ns	
TCLHAV	HLDA Valid Delay	10	160	10	100	ns	
TRLRH	$\overline{RD}$ Width	2TCLCL − 75		2TCLCL − 50		ns	
TWLWH	$\overline{WR}$ Width	2TCLCL − 60		2TCLCL − 40		ns	
TAVAL	Address Valid to ALE Low	TCLCH − 60		TCLCH − 40		ns	
TOLOH	Output Rise Time		20		20	ns	From 0.8V to 2.0V
TOHOL	Output Fall Time		12		12	ns	From 2.0V to 0.8V

NOTES:
1. Signal at 8284A shown for reference only. See 8284A data sheet for the most recent specifications.
2. Set up requirement for asynchronous signal only to guarantee recognition at next CLK.
3. Applies only to T2 state (8 ns into T3 state).

6

A.C. TESTING INPUT, OUTPUT WAVEFORM

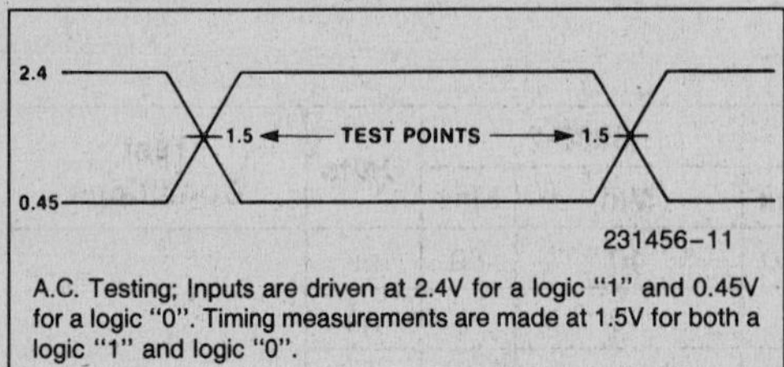

A.C. Testing; Inputs are driven at 2.4V for a logic "1" and 0.45V for a logic "0". Timing measurements are made at 1.5V for both a logic "1" and logic "0".

A.C. TESTING LOAD CIRCUIT

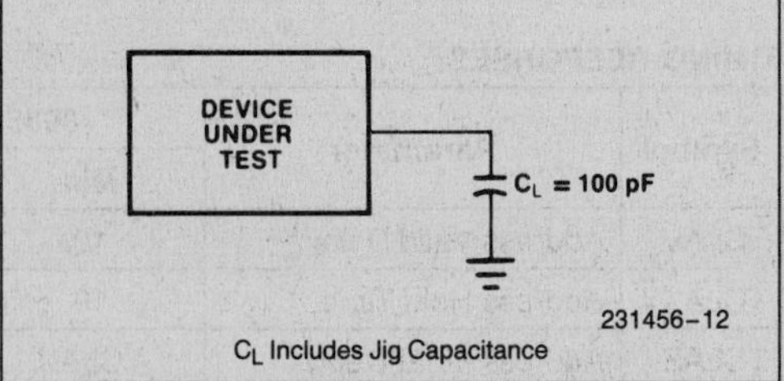

C_L Includes Jig Capacitance

WAVEFORMS

BUS TIMING—MINIMUM MODE SYSTEM

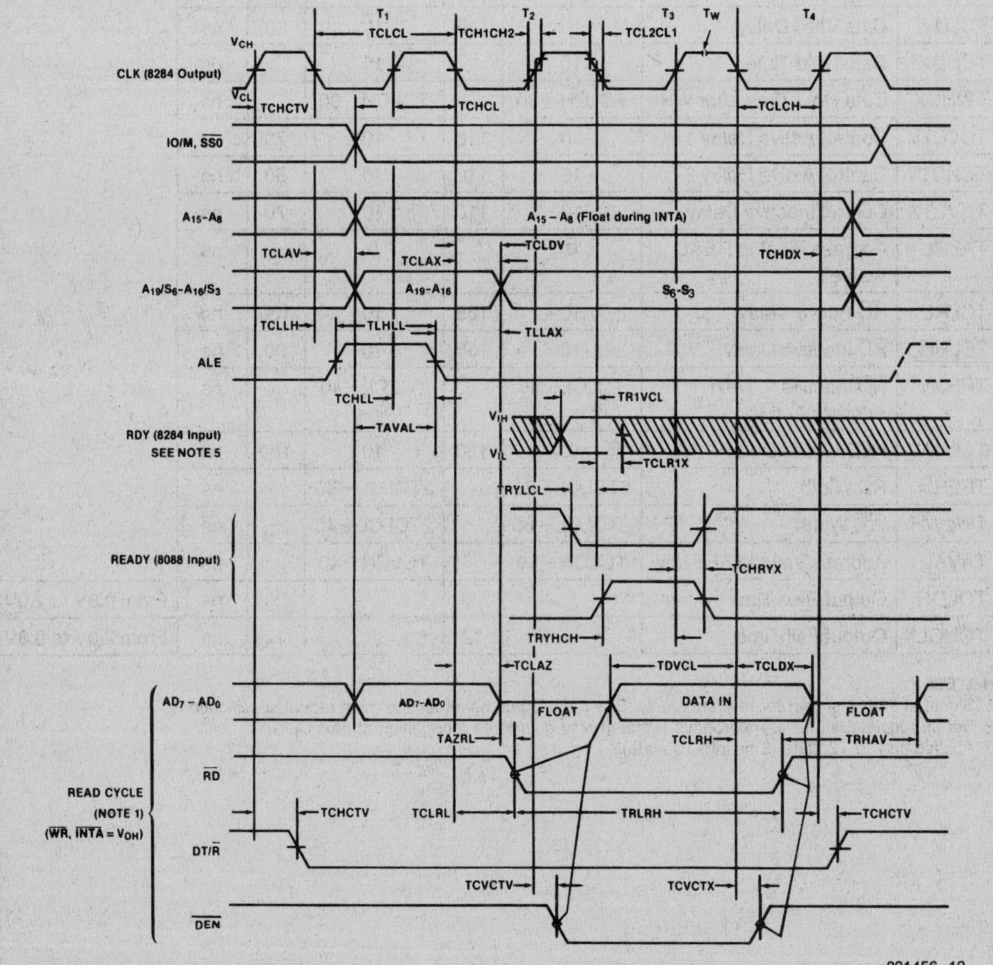

231456-13

WAVEFORMS (Continued)

BUS TIMING—MINIMUM MODE SYSTEM (Continued)

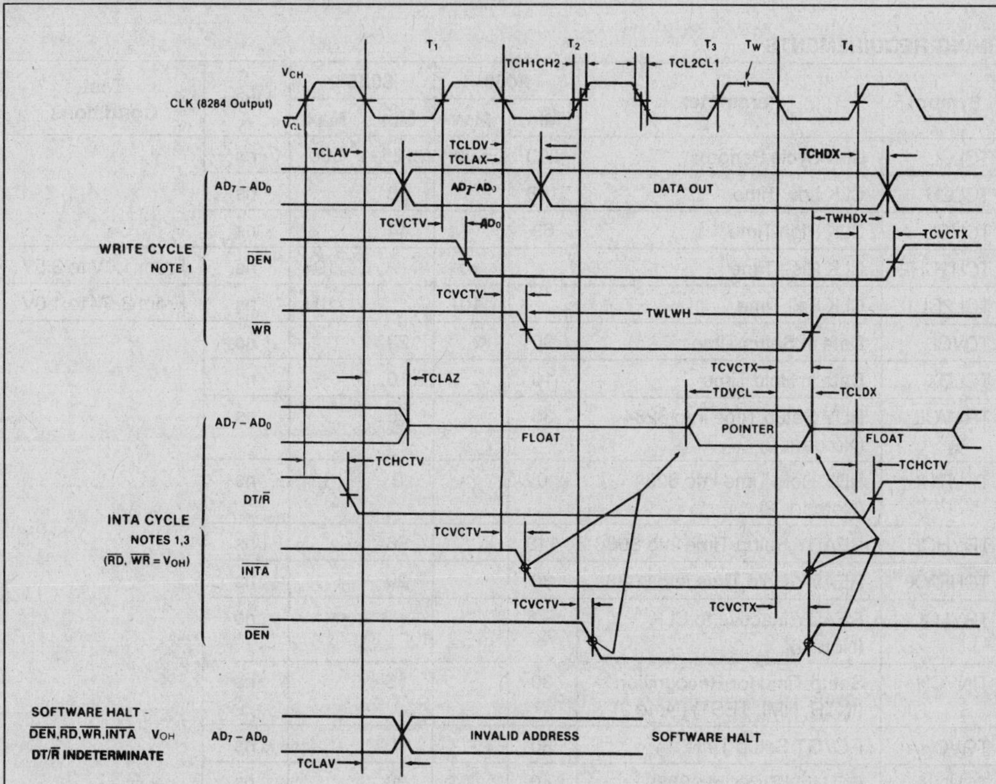

NOTES:

1. All signals switch between V_{OH} and V_{OL} unless otherwise specified.
2. RDY is sampled near the end of T_2, T_3, T_w to determine if T_w machines states are to be inserted.
3. Two INTA cycles run back-to-back. The 8088 local ADDR/DATA bus is floating during both INTA cycles. Control signals are shown for the second INTA cycle.
4. Signals at 8284 are shown for reference only.
5. All timing measurements are made at 1.5V unless otherwise noted.

6

A.C. CHARACTERISTICS

MAX MODE SYSTEM (USING 8288 BUS CONTROLLER)

TIMING REQUIREMENTS

Symbol	Parameter	8088		8088-2		Units	Test Conditions
		Min	Max	Min	Max		
TCLCL	CLK Cycle Period	200	500	125	500	ns	
TCLCH	CLK Low Time	118		68		ns	
TCHCL	CLK High Time	69		44		ns	
TCH1CH2	CLK Rise Time		10		10	ns	From 1.0V to 3.5V
TCL2CL1	CLK Fall Time		10		10	ns	From 3.5V to 1.0V
TDVCL	Data in Setup Time	30		20		ns	
TCLDX	Data in Hold Time	10		10		ns	
TR1VCL	RDY Setup Time into 8284 (Notes 1, 2)	35		35		ns	
TCLR1X	RDY Hold Time into 8284 (Notes 1, 2)	0		0		ns	
TRYHCH	READY Setup Time into 8088	118		68		ns	
TCHRYX	READY Hold Time into 8088	30		20		ns	
TRYLCL	READY Inactive to CLK (Note 4)	−8		−8		ns	
TINVCH	Setup Time for Recognition (INTR, NMI, TEST) (Note 2)	30		15		ns	
TGVCH	RQ/GT Setup Time	30		15		ns	
TCHGX	RQ Hold Time into 8088	40		30		ns	
TILIH	Input Rise Time (Except CLK)		20		20	ns	From 0.8V to 2.0V
TIHIL	Input Fall Time (Except CLK)		12		12	ns	From 2.0V to 0.8V

A.C. CHARACTERISTICS (Continued)

TIMING RESPONSES

Symbol	Parameter	8088 Min	8088 Max	8088-2 Min	8088-2 Max	Units	Test Conditions
TCLML	Command Active Delay (Note 1)	10	35	10	35	ns	C_L = 20–100 pF for All 8088 Outputs in Addition to Internal Loads
TCLMH	Command Inactive Delay (Note 1)	10	35	10	35	ns	
TRYHSH	READY Active to Status Passive (Note 3)		110		65	ns	
TCHSV	Status Active Delay	10	110	10	60	ns	
TCLSH	Status Inactive Delay	10	130	10	70	ns	
TCLAV	Address Valid Delay	10	110	10	60	ns	
TCLAX	Address Hold Time	10		10		ns	
TCLAZ	Address Float Delay	TCLAX	80	TCLAX	50	ns	
TSVLH	Status Valid to ALE High (Note 1)		15		15	ns	
TSVMCH	Status Valid to MCE High (Note 1)		15		15	ns	
TCLLH	CLK Low to ALE Valid (Note 1)		15		15	ns	
TCLMCH	CLK Low to MCE (Note 1)		15		15	ns	
TCHLL	ALE Inactive Delay (Note 1)		15		15	ns	
TCLMCL	MCE Inactive Delay (Note 1)		15		15	ns	
TCLDV	Data Valid Delay	10	110	10	60	ns	
TCHDX	Data Hold Time	10		10		ns	
TCVNV	Control Active Delay (Note 1)	5	45	5	45	ns	
TCVNX	Control Inactive Delay (Note 1)	10	45	10	45	ns	
TAZRL	Address Float to Read Active	0		0		ns	
TCLRL	$\overline{RD}$ Active Delay	10	165	10	100	ns	
TCLRH	$\overline{RD}$ Inactive Delay	10	150	10	80	ns	
TRHAV	$\overline{RD}$ Inactive to Next Address Active	TCLCL−45		TCLCL−40		ns	
TCHDTL	Direction Control Active Delay (Note 1)		50		50	ns	
TCHDTH	Direction Control Inactive Delay (Note 1)		30		30	ns	
TCLGL	GT Active Delay		85		50	ns	
TCLGH	GT Inactive Delay		85		50	ns	
TRLRH	$\overline{RD}$ Width	2TCLCL−75		2TCLCL−50		ns	
TOLOH	Output Rise Time		20		20	ns	From 0.8V to 2.0V
TOHOL	Output Fall Time		12		12	ns	From 2.0V to 0.8V

NOTES:
1. Signal at 8284 or 8288 shown for reference only.
2. Setup requirement for asynchronous signal only to guarantee recognition at next CLK.
3. Applies only to T3 and wait states.
4. Applies only to T2 state (8 ns into T3 state).

6

A.C. TESTING INPUT, OUTPUT WAVEFORM

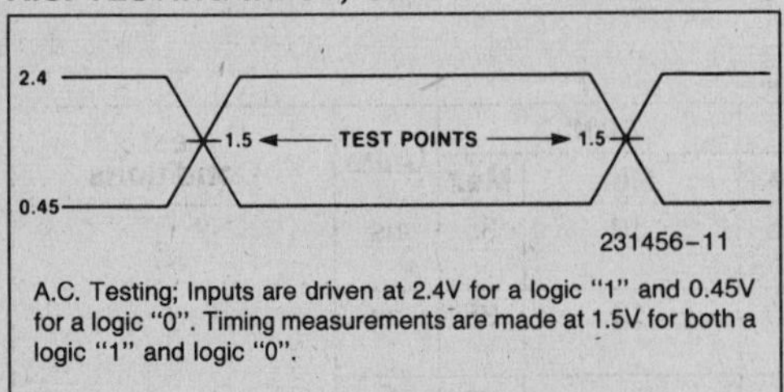

231456-11

A.C. Testing; Inputs are driven at 2.4V for a logic "1" and 0.45V for a logic "0". Timing measurements are made at 1.5V for both a logic "1" and logic "0".

A.C. TESTING LOAD CIRCUIT

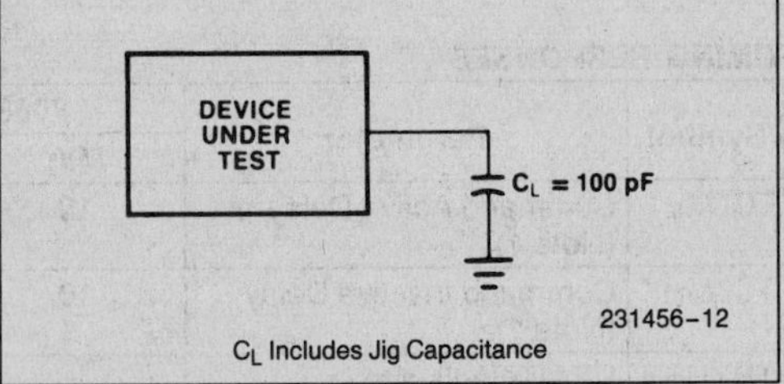

231456-12

C_L Includes Jig Capacitance

WAVEFORMS (Continued)

BUS TIMING—MAXIMUM MODE SYSTEM

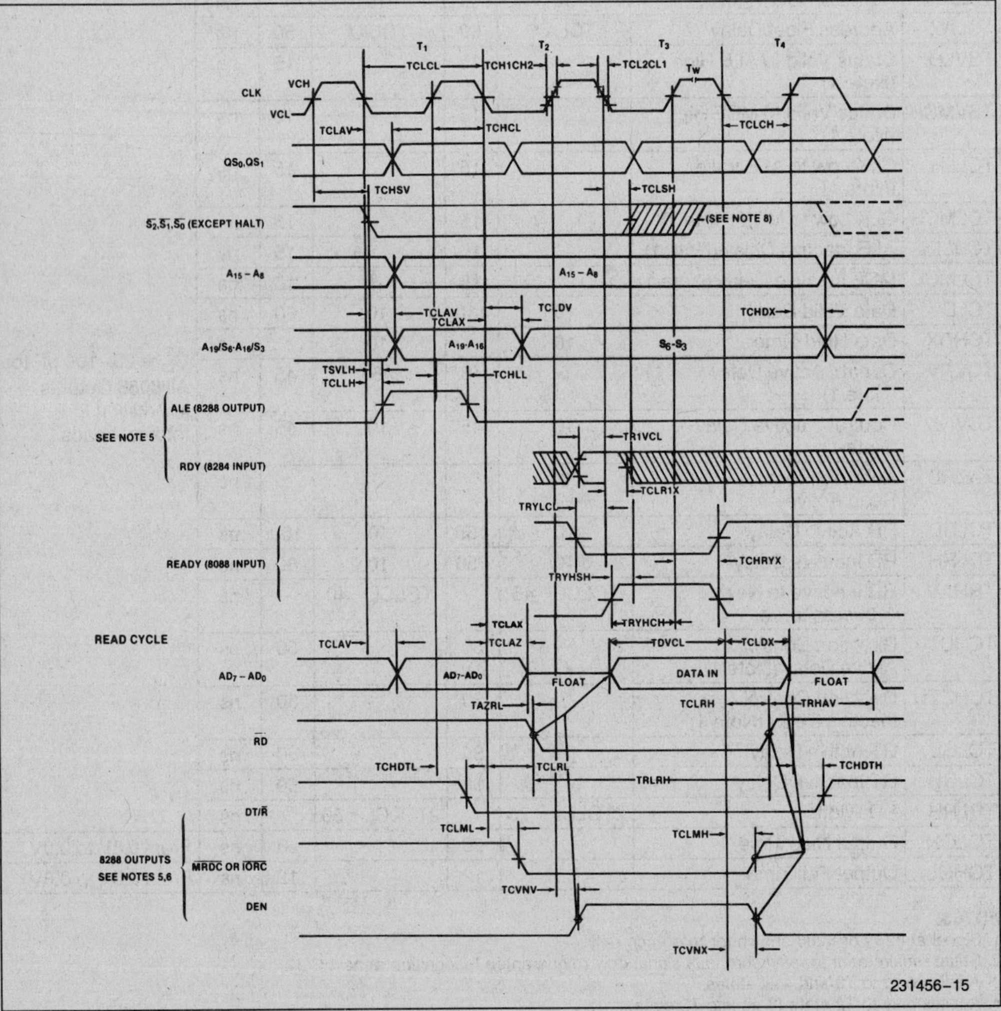

231456-15

WAVEFORMS (Continued)

BUS TIMING—MAXIMUM MODE SYSTEM (USING 8288)

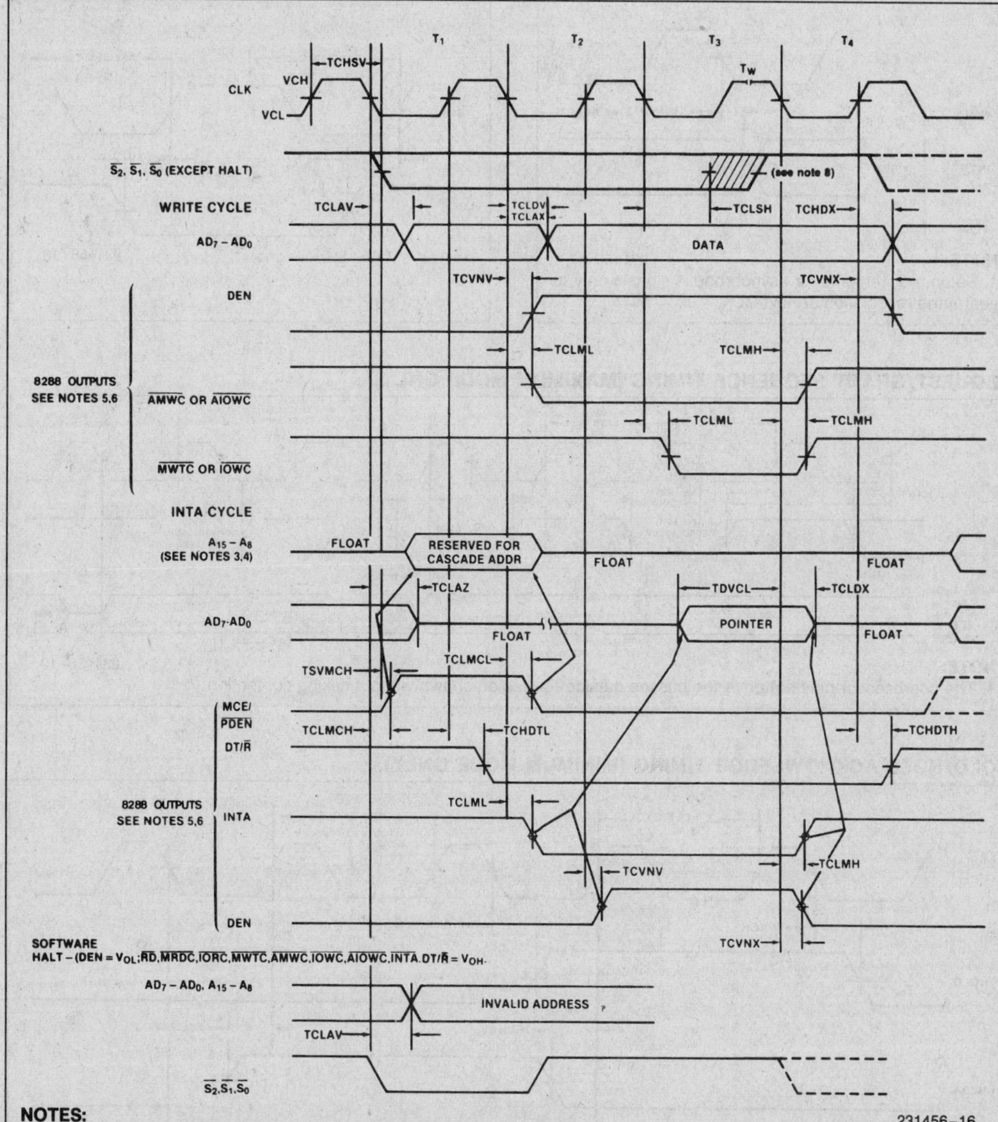

NOTES:

1. All signals switch between V_{OH} and V_{OL} unless otherwise specified.
2. RDY is sampled near the end of T_2, T_3, T_W to determine if T_W machines states are to be inserted.
3. Cascade address is valid between first and second INTA cycles.
4. Two INTA cycles run back-to-back. The 8088 local ADDR/DATA bus is floating during both INTA cycles. Control for pointer address is shown for second INTA cycle.
5. Signals at 8284 or 8288 are shown for reference only.
6. The issuance of the 8288 command and control signals ($\overline{MRDC}$, $\overline{MWTC}$, $\overline{AMWC}$, $\overline{IORC}$, $\overline{IOWC}$, $\overline{AIOWC}$, $\overline{INTA}$ and DEN) lags the active high 8288 CEN.
7. All timing measurements are made at 1.5V unless otherwise noted.
8. Status inactive in state just prior to T_4.

WAVEFORMS (Continued)

ASYNCHRONOUS SIGNAL RECOGNITION

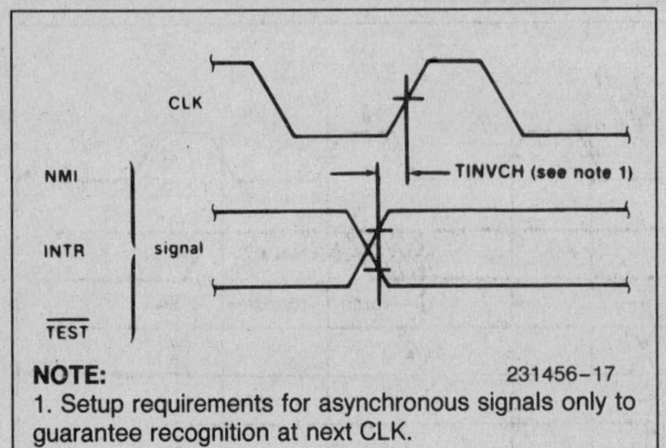

NOTE:
1. Setup requirements for asynchronous signals only to guarantee recognition at next CLK.

BUS LOCK SIGNAL TIMING (MAXIMUM MODE ONLY)

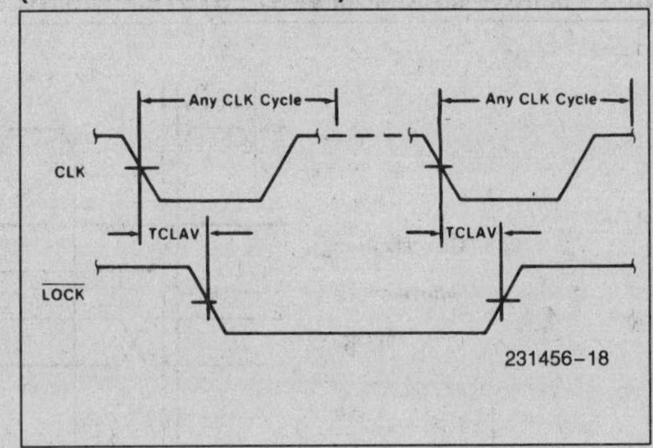

REQUEST/GRANT SEQUENCE TIMING (MAXIMUM MODE ONLY)

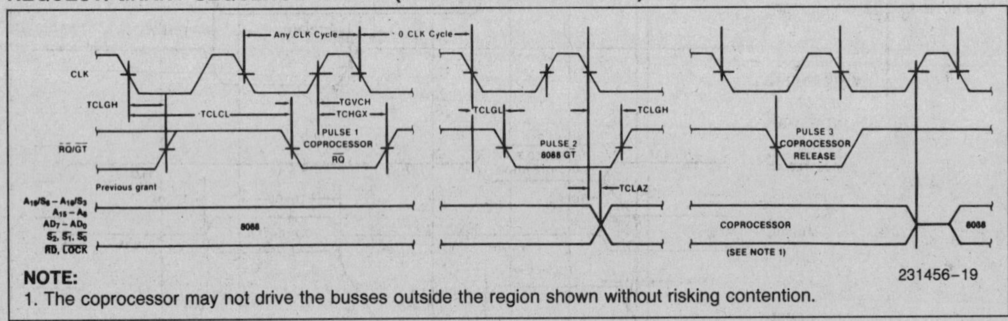

NOTE:
1. The coprocessor may not drive the busses outside the region shown without risking contention.

HOLD/HOLD ACKNOWLEDGE TIMING (MINIMUM MODE ONLY)

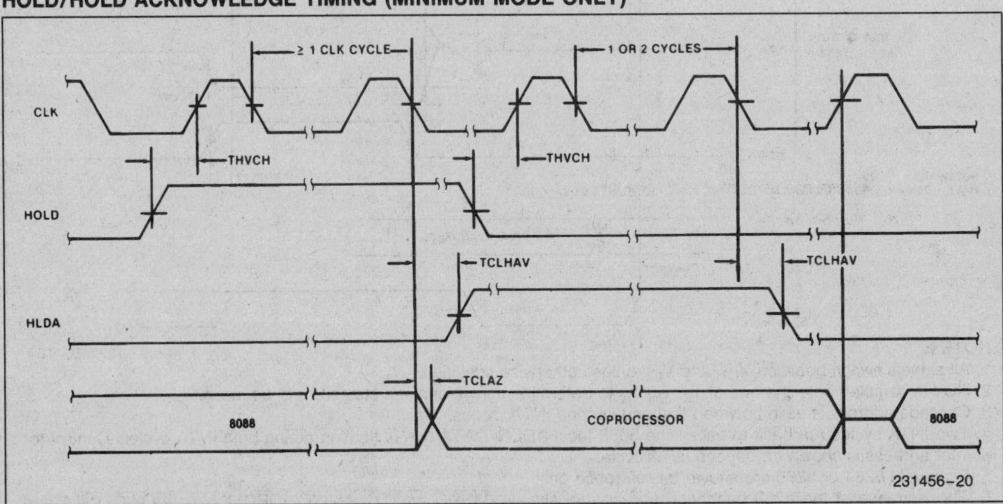

8086/8088 Instruction Set Summary

Mnemonic and Description	Instruction Code			
DATA TRANSFER				
MOV = **Move:**	7 6 5 4 3 2 1 0	7 6 5 4 3 2 1 0	7 6 5 4 3 2 1 0	7 6 5 4 3 2 1 0
Register/Memory to/from Register	1 0 0 0 1 0 d w	mod reg r/m		
Immediate to Register/Memory	1 1 0 0 0 1 1 w	mod 0 0 0 r/m	data	data if w = 1
Immediate to Register	1 0 1 1 w reg	data	data if w = 1	
Memory to Accumulator	1 0 1 0 0 0 0 w	addr-low	addr-high	
Accumulator to Memory	1 0 1 0 0 0 1 w	addr-low	addr-high	
Register/Memory to Segment Register	1 0 0 0 1 1 1 0	mod 0 reg r/m		
Segment Register to Register/Memory	1 0 0 0 1 1 0 0	mod 0 reg r/m		
PUSH = **Push:**				
Register/Memory	1 1 1 1 1 1 1 1	mod 1 1 0 r/m		
Register	0 1 0 1 0 reg			
Segment Register	0 0 0 reg 1 1 0			
POP = **Pop:**				
Register/Memory	1 0 0 0 1 1 1 1	mod 0 0 0 r/m		
Register	0 1 0 1 1 reg			
Segment Register	0 0 0 reg 1 1 1			
XCHG = **Exchange:**				
Register/Memory with Register	1 0 0 0 0 1 1 w	mod reg r/m		
Register with Accumulator	1 0 0 1 0 reg			
IN = **Input from:**				
Fixed Port	1 1 1 0 0 1 0 w	port		
Variable Port	1 1 1 0 1 1 0 w			
OUT = **Output to:**				
Fixed Port	1 1 1 0 0 1 1 w	port		
Variable Port	1 1 1 0 1 1 1 w			
XLAT = Translate Byte to AL	1 1 0 1 0 1 1 1			
LEA = Load EA to Register	1 0 0 0 1 1 0 1	mod reg r/m		
LDS = Load Pointer to DS	1 1 0 0 0 1 0 1	mod reg r/m		
LES = Load Pointer to ES	1 1 0 0 0 1 0 0	mod reg r/m		
LAHF = Load AH with Flags	1 0 0 1 1 1 1 1			
SAHF = Store AH into Flags	1 0 0 1 1 1 1 0			
PUSHF = Push Flags	1 0 0 1 1 1 0 0			
POPF = Pop Flags	1 0 0 1 1 1 0 1			

8086/8088 Instruction Set Summary (Continued)

Mnemonic and Description	Instruction Code			
ARITHMETIC	76543210	76543210	76543210	76543210
ADD = Add:				
Reg./Memory with Register to Either	0 0 0 0 0 0 d w	mod reg r/m		
Immediate to Register/Memory	1 0 0 0 0 0 s w	mod 0 0 0 r/m	data	data if s:w = 01
Immediate to Accumulator	0 0 0 0 0 1 0 w	data	data if w = 1	
ADC = Add with Carry:				
Reg./Memory with Register to Either	0 0 0 1 0 0 d w	mod reg r/m		
Immediate to Register/Memory	1 0 0 0 0 0 s w	mod 0 1 0 r/m	data	data if s:w = 01
Immediate to Accumulator	0 0 0 1 0 1 0 w	data	data if w = 1	
INC = Increment:				
Register/Memory	1 1 1 1 1 1 1 w	mod 0 0 0 r/m		
Register	0 1 0 0 0 reg			
AAA = ASCII Adjust for Add	0 0 1 1 0 1 1 1			
BAA = Decimal Adjust for Add	0 0 1 0 0 1 1 1			
SUB = Subtract:				
Reg./Memory and Register to Either	0 0 1 0 1 0 d w	mod reg r/m		
Immediate from Register/Memory	1 0 0 0 0 0 s w	mod 1 0 1 r/m	data	data if s:w = 01
Immediate from Accumulator	0 0 1 0 1 1 0 w	data	data if w = 1	
SSB = Subtract with Borrow				
Reg./Memory and Register to Either	0 0 0 1 1 0 d w	mod reg r/m		
Immediate from Register/Memory	1 0 0 0 0 0 s w	mod 0 1 1 r/m	data	data if s:w = 01
Immediate from Accumulator	0 0 0 1 1 1 w	data	data if w = 1	
DEC = Decrement:				
Register/memory	1 1 1 1 1 1 1 w	mod 0 0 1 r/m		
Register	0 1 0 0 1 reg			
NEG = Change sign	1 1 1 1 0 1 1 w	mod 0 1 1 r/m		
CMP = Compare:				
Register/Memory and Register	0 0 1 1 1 0 d w	mod reg r/m		
Immediate with Register/Memory	1 0 0 0 0 0 s w	mod 1 1 1 r/m	data	data if s:w = 01
Immediate with Accumulator	0 0 1 1 1 1 0 w	data	data if w = 1	
AAS = ASCII Adjust for Subtract	0 0 1 1 1 1 1 1			
DAS = Decimal Adjust for Subtract	0 0 1 0 1 1 1 1			
MUL = Multiply (Unsigned)	1 1 1 1 0 1 1 w	mod 1 0 0 r/m		
IMUL = Integer Multiply (Signed)	1 1 1 1 0 1 1 w	mod 1 0 1 r/m		
AAM = ASCII Adjust for Multiply	1 1 0 1 0 1 0 0	0 0 0 0 1 0 1 0		
DIV = Divide (Unsigned)	1 1 1 1 0 1 1 w	mod 1 1 0 r/m		
IDIV = Integer Divide (Signed)	1 1 1 1 0 1 1 w	mod 1 1 1 r/m		
AAD = ASCII Adjust for Divide	1 1 0 1 0 1 0 1	0 0 0 0 1 0 1 0		
CBW = Convert Byte to Word	1 0 0 1 1 0 0 0			
CWD = Convert Word to Double Word	1 0 0 1 1 0 0 1			

8086/8088 Instruction Set Summary (Continued)

Mnemonic and Description	Instruction Code			
LOGIC	7 6 5 4 3 2 1 0	7 6 5 4 3 2 1 0	7 6 5 4 3 2 1 0	7 6 5 4 3 2 1 0
NOT = Invert	1 1 1 1 0 1 1 w	mod 0 1 0 r/m		
SHL/SAL = Shift Logical/Arithmetic Left	1 1 0 1 0 0 v w	mod 1 0 0 r/m		
SHR = Shift Logical Right	1 1 0 1 0 0 v w	mod 1 0 1 r/m		
SAR = Shift Arithmetic Right	1 1 0 1 0 0 v w	mod 1 1 1 r/m		
ROL = Rotate Left	1 1 0 1 0 0 v w	mod 0 0 0 r/m		
ROR = Rotate Right	1 1 0 1 0 0 v w	mod 0 0 1 r/m		
RCL = Rotate Through Carry Flag Left	1 1 0 1 0 0 v w	mod 0 1 0 r/m		
RCR = Rotate Through Carry Right	1 1 0 1 0 0 v w	mod 0 1 1 r/m		
AND = And:				
Reg./Memory and Register to Either	0 0 1 0 0 0 d w	mod reg r/m		
Immediate to Register/Memory	1 0 0 0 0 0 0 w	mod 1 0 0 r/m	data	data if w = 1
Immediate to Accumulator	0 0 1 0 0 1 0 w	data	data if w = 1	
TEST = And Function to Flags. No Result:				
Register/Memory and Register	1 0 0 0 0 1 0 w	mod reg r/m		
Immediate Data and Register/Memory	1 1 1 1 0 1 1 w	mod 0 0 0 r/m	data	data if w = 1
Immediate Data and Accumulator	1 0 1 0 1 0 0 w	data	data if w = 1	
OR = Or:				
Reg./Memory and Register to Either	0 0 0 0 1 0 d w	mod reg r/m		
Immediate to Register/Memory	1 0 0 0 0 0 0 w	mod 0 0 1 r/m	data	data if w = 1
Immediate to Accumulator	0 0 0 0 1 1 0 w	data	data if w = 1	
XOR = Exclusive or:				
Reg./Memory and Register to Either	0 0 1 1 0 0 d w	mod reg r/m		
Immediate to Register/Memory	1 0 0 0 0 0 0 w	mod 1 1 0 r/m	data	data if w = 1
Immediate to Accumulator	0 0 1 1 0 1 0 w	data	data if w = 1	
STRING MANIPULATION				
REP = Repeat	1 1 1 1 0 0 1 z			
MOVS = Move Byte/Word	1 0 1 0 0 1 0 w			
CMPS = Compare Byte/Word	1 0 1 0 0 1 1 w			
SCAS = Scan Byte/Word	1 0 1 0 1 1 1 w			
LODS = Load Byte/Wd to AL/AX	1 0 1 0 1 1 0 w			
STOS = Stor Byte/Wd from AL/A	1 0 1 0 1 0 1 w			
CONTROL TRANSFER				
CALL = Call:				
Direct Within Segment	1 1 1 0 1 0 0 0	disp-low	disp-high	
Indirect Within Segment	1 1 1 1 1 1 1 1	mod 0 1 0 r/m		
Direct Intersegment	1 0 0 1 1 0 1 0	offset-low	offset-high	
		seg-low	seg-high	
Indirect Intersegment	1 1 1 1 1 1 1 1	mod 0 1 1 r/m		

6

8086/8088 Instruction Set Summary (Continued)

Mnemonic and Description	Instruction Code		
JMP = Unconditional Jump:	76543210	76543210	76543210
Direct Within Segment	11101001	disp-low	disp-high
Direct Within Segment-Short	11101011	disp	
Indirect Within Segment	11111111	mod 1 0 0 r/m	
Direct Intersegment	11101010	offset-low	offset-high
		seg-low	seg-high
Indirect Intersegment	11111111	mod 1 0 1 r/m	
RET = Return from CALL:			
Within Segment	11000011		
Within Seg Adding Immed to SP	11000010	data-low	data-high
Intersegment	11001011		
Intersegment Adding Immediate to SP	11001010	data-low	data-high
JE/JZ = Jump on Equal/Zero	01110100	disp	
JL/JNGE = Jump on Less/Not Greater or Equal	01111100	disp	
JLE/JNG = Jump on Less or Equal/ Not Greater	01111110	disp	
JB/JNAE = Jump on Below/Not Above or Equal	01110010	disp	
JBE/JNA = Jump on Below or Equal/ Not Above	01110110	disp	
JP/JPE = Jump on Parity/Parity Even	01111010	disp	
JO = Jump on Overflow	01110000	disp	
JS = Jump on Sign	01111000	disp	
JNE/JNZ = Jump on Not Equal/Not Zero	01110101	disp	
JNL/JGE = Jump on Not Less/Greater or Equal	01111101	disp	
JNLE/JG = Jump on Not Less or Equal/ Greater	01111111	disp	
JNB/JAE = Jump on Not Below/Above or Equal	01110011	disp	
JNBE/JA = Jump on Not Below or Equal/Above	01110111	disp	
JNP/JPO = Jump on Not Par/Par Odd	01111011	disp	
JNO = Jump on Not Overflow	01110001	disp	
JNS = Jump on Not Sign	01111001	disp	
LOOP = Loop CX Times	11100010	disp	
LOOPZ/LOOPE = Loop While Zero/Equal	11100001	disp	
LOOPNZ/LOOPNE = Loop While Not Zero/Equal	11100000	disp	
JCXZ = Jump on CX Zero	11100011	disp	
INT = Interrupt			
Type Specified	11001101	type	
Type 3	11001100		
INTO = Interrupt on Overflow	11001110		
IRET = Interrupt Return	11001111		

8086/8088 Instruction Set Summary (Continued)

Mnemonic and Description	Instruction Code	
	76543210	76543210
PROCESSOR CONTROL		
CLC = Clear Carry	11111000	
CMC = Complement Carry	11110101	
STC = Set Carry	11111001	
CLD = Clear Direction	11111100	
STD = Set Direction	11111101	
CLI = Clear Interrupt	11111010	
STI = Set Interrupt	11111011	
HLT = Halt	11110100	
WAIT = Wait	10011011	
ESC = Escape (to External Device)	11011xxx	mod xxx r/m
LOCK = Bus Lock Prefix	11110000	

NOTES:

AL = 8-bit accumulator
AX = 16-bit accumulator
CX = Count register
DS = Data segment
ES = Extra segment
Above/below refers to unsigned value
Greater = more positive:
Less = less positive (more negative) signed values
if d = 1 then "to" reg; if d = 0 then "from" reg
if w = 1 then word instruction; if w = 0 then byte instruction
if mod = 11 then r/m is treated as a REG field
if mod = 00 then DISP = 0*, disp-low and disp-high are absent
if mod = 01 then DISP = disp-low sign-extended to 16 bits, disp-high is absent
if mod = 10 then DISP = disp-high; disp-low
if r/m = 000 then EA = (BX) + (SI) + DISP
if r/m = 001 then EA = (BX) + (DI) + DISP
if r/m = 010 then EA = (BP) + (SI) + DISP
if r/m = 011 then EA = (BP) + (DI) + DISP
if r/m = 100 then EA = (SI) + DISP
if r/m = 101 then EA = (DI) + DISP
if r/m = 110 then EA = (BP) + DISP*
if r/m = 111 then EA = (BX) + DISP
DISP follows 2nd byte of instruction (before data if required)
*except if mod = 00 and r/m = then EA = disp-high: disp-low.
if s:w = 01 then 16 bits of immediate data form the operand
if s:w = 11 then an immediate data byte is sign extended to form the 16-bit operand
if v = 0 then "count" = 1; if v = 1 then "count" in (CL) register
x = don't care
z is used for string primitives for comparison with ZF FLAG
SEGMENT OVERRIDE PREFIX

0 0 1 reg 1 1 0

REG is assigned according to the following table:

16-Bit (w = 1)	8-Bit (w = 0)	Segment
000 AX	000 AL	00 ES
001 CX	001 CL	01 CS
010 DX	010 DL	10 SS
011 BX	011 BL	11 DS
100 SP	100 AH	
101 BP	101 CH	
110 SI	110 DH	
111 DI	111 BH	

Instructions which reference the flag register file as a 16-bit object use the symbol FLAGS to represent the file:
FLAGS =
X:X:X:X:(OF):(DF):(IF):(TF):(SF):(ZF):X:(AF):X:(PF):X:(CF)

DATA SHEET REVISION REVIEW

The following list represents key differences between this and the -005 data sheet. Please review this summary carefully.

1. The Intel® 8088 implementation technology (HMOS) has been changed to (HMOS-II).

6

8087
MATH COPROCESSOR

- **Adds Arithmetic, Trigonometric, Exponential, and Logarithmic Instructions to the Standard 8086/8088 and 80186/80188 Instruction Set for All Data Types**
- **CPU/8087 Supports 7 Data Types: 16-, 32-, 64-Bit Integers, 32-, 64-, 80-Bit Floating Point, and 18-Digit BCD Operands**
- **Compatible with IEEE Floating Point Standard 754**
- **Available in 5 MHz (8087), 8 MHz (8087-2) and 10 MHz (8087-1): 8 MHz 80186/80188 System Operation Supported with the 8087-1**
- **Adds 8 x 80-Bit Individually Addressable Register Stack to the 8086/8088 and 80186/80188 Architecture**
- **7 Built-In Exception Handling Functions**
- **MULTIBUS® System Compatible Interface**

The Intel 8087 Math CoProcessor is an extension to the Intel 8086/8088 microprocessor architecture. When combined with the 8086/8088 microprocessor, the 8087 dramatically increases the processing speed of computer applications which utilize mathematical operations such as CAM, numeric controllers, CAD or graphics.

The 8087 Math CoProcessor adds 68 mnemonics to the 8086 microprocessor instruction set. Specific 8087 math operations include logarithmic, arithmetic, exponential, and trigonometric functions. The 8087 supports integer, floating point and BCD data formats, and fully conforms to the ANSI/IEEE floating point standard.

The 8087 is fabricated with HMOS III technology and packaged in a 40-pin cerdip package.

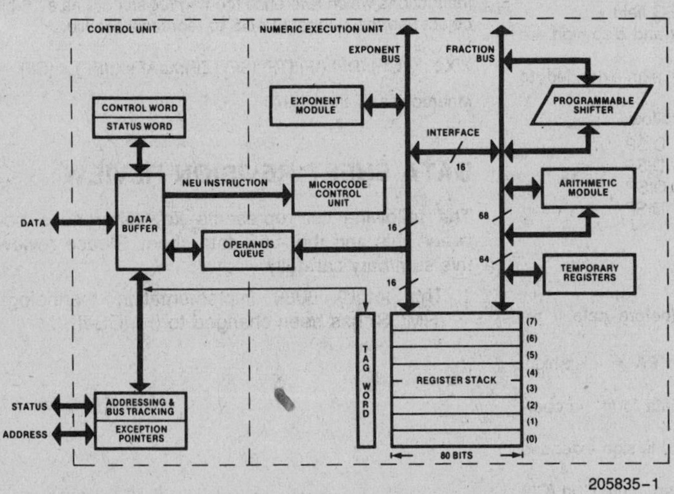

Figure 1. 8087 Block Diagram

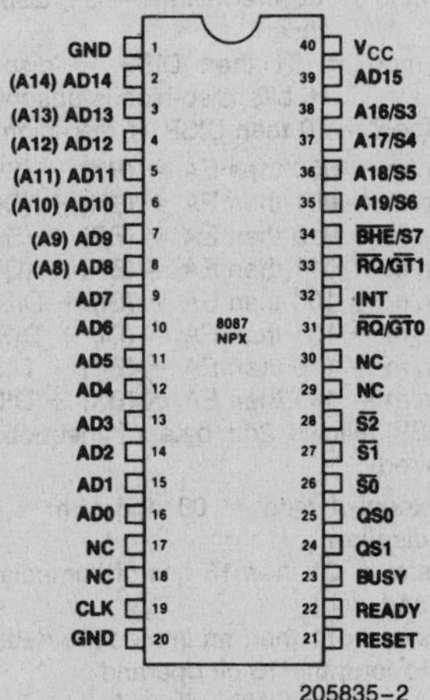

Figure 2. 8087 Pin Configuration

October 1989
Order Number: 205835-007

Table 1. 8087 Pin Description

Symbol	Type	Name and Function
AD15–AD0	I/O	**ADDRESS DATA:** These lines constitute the time multiplexed memory address (T_1) and data (T_2, T_3, T_W, T_4) bus. A0 is analogous to the $\overline{BHE}$ for the lower byte of the data bus, pins D7–D0. It is LOW during T_1 when a byte is to be transferred on the lower portion of the bus in memory operations. Eight-bit oriented devices tied to the lower half of the bus would normally use A0 to condition chip select functions. These lines are active HIGH. They are input/output lines for 8087-driven bus cycles and are inputs which the 8087 monitors when the CPU is in control of the bus. A15–A8 do not require an address latch in an 8088/8087 or 80188/8087. The 8087 will supply an address for the T_1–T_4 period.
A19/S6, A18/S5, A17/S4, A16/S3	I/O	**ADDRESS MEMORY:** During T_1 these are the four most significant address lines for memory operations. During memory operations, status information is available on these lines during T_2, T_3, T_W, and T_4. For 8087-controlled bus cycles, S6, S4, and S3 are reserved and currently one (HIGH), while S5 is always LOW. These lines are inputs which the 8087 monitors when the CPU is in control of the bus.
BHE/S7	I/O	**BUS HIGH ENABLE:** During T_1 the bus high enable signed ($\overline{BHE}$) should be used to enable data onto the most significant half of the data bus, pins D15–D8. Eight-bit-oriented devices tied to the upper half of the bus would normally use $\overline{BHE}$ to condition chip select functions. $\overline{BHE}$ is LOW during T_1 for read and write cycles when a byte is to be transferred on the high portion of the bus. The S7 status information is available during T_2, T_3, T_W, and T_4. The signal is active LOW. S7 is an input which the 8087 monitors during the CPU-controlled bus cycles.
$\overline{S2}$, $\overline{S1}$, $\overline{S0}$	I/O	**STATUS:** For 8087-driven, these status lines are encoded as follows: **$\overline{S2}$ $\overline{S1}$ $\overline{S0}$** 0 (LOW) X X Unused 1 (HIGH) 0 0 Unused 1 0 1 Read Memory 1 1 0 Write Memory 1 1 1 Passive Status is driven active during T_4, remains valid during T_1 and T_2, and is returned to the passive state (1, 1, 1) during T_3 or during T_W when READY is HIGH. This status is used by the 8288 Bus Controller (or the 82188 Integrated Bus Controller with an 80186/80188 CPU) to generate all memory access control signals. Any change in $\overline{S2}$, $\overline{S1}$, or $\overline{S0}$ during T_4 is used to indicate the beginning of a bus cycle, and the return to the passive state in T_3 or T_W is used to indicate the end of a bus cycle. These signals are monitored by the 8087 when the CPU is in control of the bus.
$\overline{RQ}/\overline{GT0}$	I/O	**REQUEST/GRANT:** This request/grant pin is used by the 8087 to gain control of the local bus from the CPU for operand transfers or on behalf of another bus master. It must be connected to one of the two processor request/grant pins. The request/grant sequence on this pin is as follows: 1. A pulse one clock wide is passed to the CPU to indicate a local bus request by either the 8087 or the master connected to the 8087 $\overline{RQ}/\overline{GT1}$ pin. 2. The 8087 waits for the grant pulse and when it is received will either initiate bus transfer activity in the clock cycle following the grant or pass the grant out on the $\overline{RQ}/\overline{GT1}$ pin in this clock if the initial request was for another bus master. 3. The 8087 will generate a release pulse to the CPU one clock cycle after the completion of the last 8087 bus cycle or on receipt of the release pulse from the bus master on $\overline{RQ}/\overline{GT1}$. For 80186/80188 systems the same sequence applies except $\overline{RQ}/\overline{GT}$ signals are converted to appropriate HOLD, HLDA signals by the 82188 Integrated Bus Controller. This is to conform with 80186/80188's HOLD, HLDA bus exchange protocol. Refer to the 82188 data sheet for further information.

Table 1. 8087 Pin Description (Continued)

Symbol	Type	Name and Function
$\overline{RQ}/\overline{GT}1$	I/O	**REQUEST/GRANT:** This request/grant pin is used by another local bus master to force the 8087 to request the local bus. If the 8087 is not in control of the bus when the request is made the request/grant sequence is passed through the 8087 on the $\overline{RQ}/\overline{GT}0$ pin one cycle later. Subsequent grant and release pulses are also passed through the 8087 with a two and one clock delay, respectively, for resynchronization. $\overline{RQ}/\overline{GT}1$ has an internal pullup resistor, and so may be left unconnected. If the 8087 has control of the bus the request/grant sequence is as follows: 1. A pulse 1 CLK wide from another local bus master indicates a local bus request to the 8087 (pulse 1). 2. During the 8087's next T_4 or T_1 a pulse 1 CLK wide from the 8087 to the requesting master (pulse 2) indicates that the 8087 has allowed the local bus to float and that it will enter the "RQ/GT acknowledge" state at the next CLK. The 8087's control unit is disconnected logically from the local bus during "RQ/GT acknowledge." 3. A pulse 1 CLK wide from the requesting master indicates to the 8087 (pulse 3) that the "RQ/GT" request is about to end and that the 8087 can reclaim the local bus at the next CLK. Each master-master exchange of the local bus is a sequence of 3 pulses. There must be one dead CLK cycle after each bus exchange. Pulses are active LOW. For 80186/80188 system, the $\overline{RQ}/\overline{GT}1$ line may be connected to the 82188 Integrated Bus Controller. In this case, a third processor with a HOLD, HLDA bus exchange system may acquire the bus from the 8087. For this configuration, $\overline{RQ}/\overline{GT}1$ will only be used if the 8087 is the bus master. Refer to 82188 data sheet for further information.
QS1, QS0	I	**QS1, QS0:** QS1 and QS0 provide the 8087 with status to allow tracking of the CPU instruction queue. **QS1 QS0** 0 (LOW) 0 No Operation 0 1 First Byte of Op Code from Queue 1 (HIGH) 0 Empty the Queue 1 1 Subsequent Byte from Queue
INT	O	**INTERRUPT:** This line is used to indicate that an unmasked exception has occurred during numeric instruction execution when 8087 interrupts are enabled. This signal is typically routed to an 8259A for 8086/8088 systems and to INT0 for 80186/80188 systems. INT is active HIGH.
BUSY	O	**BUSY:** This signal indicates that the 8087 NEU is executing a numeric instruction. It is connected to the CPU's $\overline{TEST}$ pin to provide synchronization. In the case of an unmasked exception BUSY remains active until the exception is cleared. BUSY is active HIGH.
READY	I	**READY:** READY is the acknowledgement from the addressed memory device that it will complete the data transfer. The RDY signal from memory is synchronized by the 8284A Clock Generator to form READY for 8086 systems. For 80186/80188 systems, RDY is synchronized by the 82188 Integrated Bus Controller to form READY. This signal is active HIGH.
RESET	I	**RESET:** RESET causes the processor to immediately terminate its present activity. The signal must be active HIGH for at least four clock cycles. RESET is internally synchronized.
CLK	I	**CLOCK:** The clock provides the basic timing for the processor and bus controller. It is asymmetric with a 33% duty cycle to provide optimized internal timing.
V_{CC}		**POWER:** V_{CC} is the +5V power supply pin.
GND		**GROUND:** GND are the ground pins.

NOTE:
For the pin descriptions of the 8086, 8088, 80186 and 80188 CPUs, reference the respective data sheets (8086, 8088, 80186, 80188).

APPLICATION AREAS

The 8087 provides functions meant specifically for high performance numeric processing requirements. Trigonometric, logarithmic, and exponential functions are built into the coprocessor hardware. These functions are essential in scientific, engineering, navigational, or military applications.

The 8087 also has capabilities meant for business or commercial computing. An 8087 can process Binary Coded Decimal (BCD) numbers up to 18 digits without roundoff errors. It can also perform arithmetic on integers as large as 64 bits $\pm 10^{18}$).

PROGRAMMING LANGUAGE SUPPORT

Programs for the 8087 can be written in Intel's high-level languages for 8086/8088 and 80186/80188 Systems; ASM-86 (the 8086, 8088 assembly language), PL/M-86, FORTRAN-86, and PASCAL-86.

RELATED INFORMATION

For 8086, 8088, 80186 or 80188 details, refer to the respective data sheets. For 80186 or 80188 systems, also refer to the 82188 Integrated Bus Controller data sheet.

FUNCTIONAL DESCRIPTION

The 8087 Math CoProcessor's architecture is designed for high performance numeric computing in conjunction with general purpose processing.

The 8087 is a numeric processor extension that provides arithmetic and logical instruction support for a variety of numeric data types. It also executes numerous built-in transcendental functions (e.g., tangent and log functions). The 8087 executes instructions as a coprocessor to a maximum mode CPU. It effectively extends the register and instruction set of the system and adds several new data types as well. Figure 3 presents the registers of the CPU+8087. Table 2 shows the range of data types supported by the 8087. The 8087 is treated as an extension to the CPU, providing register, data types, control, and instruction capabilities at the hardware level. At the programmer's level the CPU and the 8087 are viewed as a single unified processor.

System Configuration

As a coprocessor to an 8086 or 8088, the 8087 is wired in parallel with the CPU as shown in Figure 4. Figure 5 shows the 80186/80188 system configuration. The CPU's status (S0–S2) and queue status lines (QS0–QS1) enable the 8087 to monitor and decode instructions in synchronization with the CPU and without any CPU overhead. For 80186/80188 systems, the queue status signals of the 80186/80188 are synchronized to 8087 requirements by the 8288 Integrated Bus Controller. Once started, the 8087 can process in parallel with, and independent of, the host CPU. For resynchronization, the 8087's BUSY signal informs the CPU that the 8087 is executing an instruction and the CPU WAIT instruction tests this signal to insure that the 8087 is ready to execute subsequent instructions. The 8087 can interrupt the CPU when it detects an error or exception. The 8087's interrupt request line is typically routed to the CPU through an 8259A Programmable Interrupt Controller for 8086, 8088 systems and INT0 for 80186/80188.

6

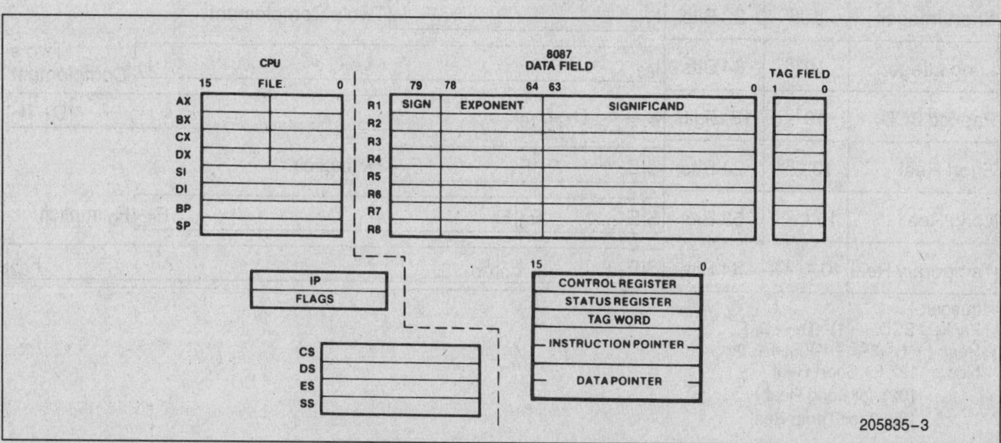

Figure 3. CPU+8087 Architecture

The 8087 uses one of the request/grant lines of the 8086/8088 architecture (typically $\overline{RQ}/\overline{GT}0$) to obtain control of the local bus for data transfers. The other request/grant line is available for general system use (for instance by an I/O processor in LOCAL mode). A bus master can also be connected to the 8087's $\overline{RQ}/\overline{GT}1$ line. In this configuration the 8087 will pass the request/grant handshake signals between the CPU and the attached master when the 8087 is not in control of the bus and will relinquish the bus to the master directly when the 8087 is in control. In this way two additional masters can be configured in an 8086/8088 system; one will share the 8086/8088 bus with the 8087 on a first-come first-served basis, and the second will be guaranteed to be higher in priority than the 8087.

For 80186/80188 systems, $\overline{RQ}/\overline{GT}0$ and $\overline{RQ}/\overline{GT}1$ are connected to the corresponding inputs of the 82188 Integrated Bus Controller. Because the 80186/80188 has a HOLD, HLDA bus exchange protocol, an interface is needed which will translate $\overline{RQ}/\overline{GT}$ signals to corresponding HOLD, HLDA signals and vice versa. One of the functions of the 82188 IBC is to provide this translation. $\overline{RQ}/\overline{GT}0$ is translated to HOLD, HLDA signals which are then directly connected to the 80186/80188. The $\overline{RQ}/\overline{GT}1$ line is also translated into HOLD, HLDA signals (referred to as SYSHOLD, SYSHLDA signals) by the 82188 IBC. This allows a third processor (using a HOLD, HLDA bus exchange protocol) to gain control of the bus.

Unlike an 8086/8087 system, $\overline{RQ}/\overline{GT}$ is only used when the 8087 has bus control. If the third processor requests the bus when the current bus master is the 80186/80188, the 82188 IBC will directly pass the request onto the 80186/80188 without going through the 8087. The third processor has the highest bus priority in the system. If the 8087 requests the bus while the third processor has bus control, the grant pulse will not be issued until the third processor releases the bus (using SYSHOLD). In this configuration, the third processor has the highest priority, the 8087 has the next highest, and the 80186/80188 has the lowest bus priority.

Bus Operation

The 8087 bus structure, operation and timing are identical to all other processors in the 8086/8088 series (maximum mode configuration). The address is time multiplexed with the data on the first 16/8 lines of the address/data bus. A16 through A19 are time multiplexed with four status lines S3–S6. S3, S4 and S6 are always one (HIGH) for 8087-driven bus cycles while S5 is always zero (LOW). When the 8087 is monitoring CPU bus cycles (passive mode) S6 is also monitored by the 8087 to differentiate 8086/8088 activity from that of a local I/O processor or any other local bus master. (The 8086/8088 must be the only processor on the local bus to drive S6 LOW). S7 is multiplexed with and has the same value as $\overline{BHE}$ for all 8087 bus cycles.

Table 2. 8087 Data Types

Data Formats	Range	Precision	Most Significant Byte (7 0 | 7 0 | 7 0 | 7 0 | 7 0 | 7 0 | 7 0 | 7 0 | 7 0 | 7 0)
Word Integer	10^4	16 Bits	I_{15} … I_0 Two's Complement
Short Integer	10^9	32 Bits	I_{31} … I_0 Two's Complement
Long Integer	10^{18}	64 Bits	I_{63} … I_0 Two's Complement
Packed BCD	10^{18}	18 Digits	S — $D_{17} D_{16}$ … D_1 D_0
Short Real	$10^{\pm 38}$	24 Bits	S E_7 … E_0 F_1 … F_{23} F_0 Implicit
Long Real	$10^{\pm 308}$	53 Bits	S E_{10} … E_0 F_1 … F_{52} F_0 Implicit
Temporary Real	$10^{\pm 4932}$	64 Bits	S E_{14} … E_0 F_0 … F_{63}

Integer: I
Packed BCD: $(-1)^S(D_{17}...D_0)$
Real: $(-1)^S(2^{E-Bias})(F_0 \bullet F_1...)$
bias = 127 for Short Real
1023 for Long Real
16383 for Temp Real

The first three status lines, $\overline{S0}-\overline{S2}$, are used with an 8288 bus controller or 82188 Integrated Bus Controller to determine the type of bus cycle being run:

$\overline{S2}$	$\overline{S1}$	$\overline{S0}$	
0	X	X	Unused
1	0	0	Unused
1	0	1	Memory Data Read
1	1	0	Memory Data Write
1	1	1	Passive (no bus cycle)

Programming Interface

The 8087 includes the standard 8086, 8088 instruction set for general data manipulation and program control. It also includes 68 numeric instructions for extended precision integer, floating point, trigonometric, logarithmic, and exponential functions. Sample execution times for several 8087 functions are shown in Table 3. Overall performance is up to 100 times that of an 8086 processor for numeric instructions.

Any instruction executed by the 8087 is the combined result of the CPU and 8087 activity. The CPU and the 8087 have specialized functions and registers providing fast concurrent operation. The CPU controls overall program execution while the 8087 uses the coprocessor interface to recognize and perform numeric operations.

Table 2 lists the seven data types the 8087 supports and presents the format for each type. Internally, the 8087 holds all numbers in the temporary real format. Load and store instructions automatically convert operands represented in memory as 16-, 32-, or 64-bit integers, 32- or 64-bit floating point numbers or 18-digit packed BCD numbers into temporary real format and vice versa. The 8087 also provides the capability to control round off, underflow, and overflow errors in each calculation.

Computations in the 8087 use the processor's register stack. These eight 80-bit registers provide the equivalent capacity of 20 32-bit registers. The 8087 register set can be accessed as a stack, with instructions operating on the top one or two stack elements, or as a fixed register set, with instructions operating on explicitly designated registers.

Table 5 lists the 8087's instructions by class. All appear as ESCAPE instructions to the host. Assembly language programs are written in ASM-86, the 8086, 8088 assembly language.

Table 3. Execution Times for Selected 8086/8087 Numeric Instructions and Corresponding 8086 Emulation

Floating Point Instruction	Approximate Execution Time (μs)	
	8086/8087 (8 MHz Clock)	8086 Emulation
Add/Subtract	10.6	1000
Multiply (Single Precision)	11.9	1000
Multiply (Extended Precision)	16.9	1312
Divide	24.4	2000
Compare	−5.6	812
Load (Double Precision)	−6.3	1062
Store (Double Precision)	13.1	750
Square Root	22.5	12250
Tangent	56.3	8125
Exponentiation	62.5	10687

NUMERIC PROCESSOR EXTENSION ARCHITECTURE

As shown in Figure 1, the 8087 is internally divided into two processing elements, the control unit (CU) and the numeric execution unit (NEU). The NEU executes all numeric instructions, while the CU receives and decodes instructions, reads and writes memory operands and executes 8087 control instructions. The two elements are able to operate independently of one another, allowing the CU to maintain synchronization with the CPU while the NEU is busy processing a numeric instruction.

Control Unit

The CU keeps the 8087 operating in synchronization with its host CPU. 8087 instructions are intermixed with CPU instructions in a single instruction stream. The CPU fetches all instructions from memory; by monitoring the status ($\overline{S0}-\overline{S2}$, S6) emitted by the CPU, the control unit determines when an instruction is being fetched. The CPU monitors the data bus in parallel with the CPU to obtain instructions that pertain to the 8087.

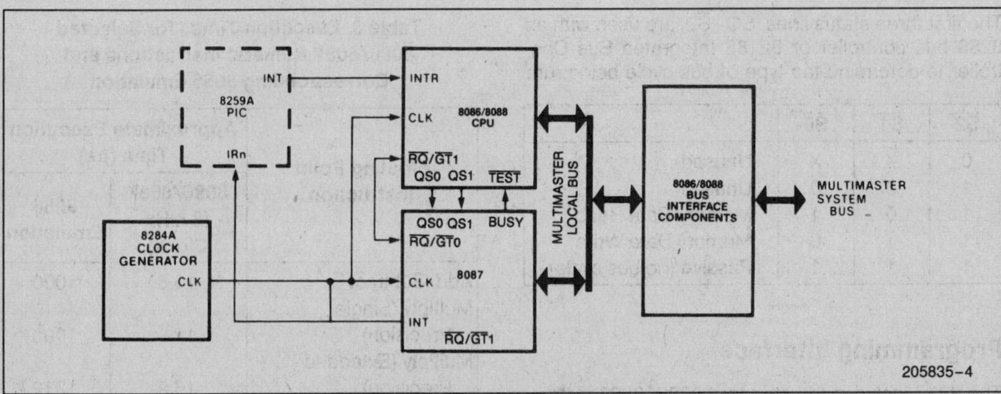

Figure 4. 8086/8087, 8088/8087 System Configuration

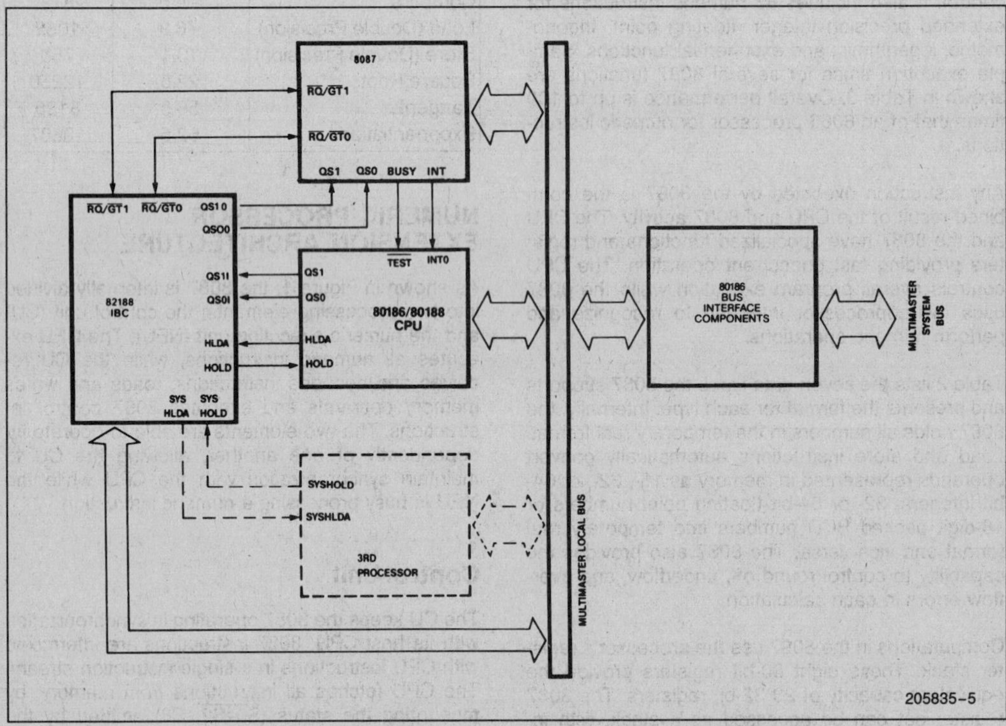

Figure 5. 80186/8087, 80188/8087 System Configuration

The CU maintains an instruction queue that is identical to the queue in the host CPU. The CU automatically determines if the CPU is an 8086/80186 or an 8088/80188 immediately after reset (by monitoring the $\overline{\text{BHE}}$/S7 line) and matches its queue length accordingly. By monitoring the CPU's queue status lines (QS0, QS1), the CU obtains and decodes instructions from the queue in synchronization with the CPU.

A numeric instruction appears as an ESCAPE instruction to the CPU. Both the CPU and 8087 decode and execute the ESCAPE instruction together. The 8087 only recognizes the numeric instructions shown in Table 5. The start of a numeric operation is accomplished when the CPU executes the ESCAPE instruction. The instruction may or may not identify a memory operand.

The CPU does, however, distinguish between ESC instructions that reference memory and those that do not. If the instruction refers to a memory operand, the CPU calculates the operand's address using any one of its available addressing modes, and then performs a "dummy read" of the word at that location. (Any location within the 1M byte address space is allowed.) This is a normal read cycle except that the CPU ignores the data it receives. If the ESC instruction does not contain a memory reference (e.g. an 8087 stack operation), the CPU simply proceeds to the next instruction.

An 8087 instruction can have one of three memory reference options: (1) not reference memory; (2) load an operand word from memory into the 8087; or (3) store an operand word from the 8087 into memory. If no memory reference is required, the 8087 simply executes its instruction. If a memory reference is required, the CU uses a "dummy read" cycle initiated by the CPU to capture and save the address that the CPU places on the bus. If the instruction is a load, the CU additionally captures the data word when it becomes available on the local data bus. If data required is longer than one word, the CU immediately obtains the bus from the CPU using the request/grant protocol and reads the rest of the information in consecutive bus cycles. In a store operation, the CU captures and saves the store address as in a load, and ignores the data word that follows in the "dummy read" cycle. When the 8087 is ready to perform the store, the CU obtains the bus from the CPU and writes the operand starting at the specified address.

Numeric Execution Unit

The NEU executes all instructions that involve the register stack; these include arithmetic, logical, transcendental, constant and data transfer instructions. The data path in the NEU is 84 bits wide (68 fractions bits, 15 exponent bits and a sign bit) which allows internal operand transfers to be performed at very high speeds.

When the NEU begins executing an instruction, it activates the 8087 BUSY signal. This signal can be used in conjunction with the CPU WAIT instruction to resynchronize both processors when the NEU has completed its current instruction.

Register Set

The CPU+8087 register set is shown in Figure 3. Each of the eight data registers in the 8087's register stack is 80 bits and is divided into "fields" corresponding to the 8087's temporary real data type.

At a given point in time the TOP field in the control word identifies the current top-of-stack register. A "push" operation decrements TOP by 1 and loads a value into the new top register. A "pop" operation stores the value from the current top register and then increments TOP by 1. Like CPU stacks in memory, the 8087 register stack grows "down" toward lower-addressed registers.

Instructions may address the data registers either implicitly or explicitly. Many instructions operate on the register at the top of the stack. These instructions implicitly address the register pointed to by the TOP. Other instructions allow the programmer to explicitly specify the register which is to be used. Explicit register addressing is "top-relative."

Status Word

The status word shown in Figure 6 reflects the overall state of the 8087; it may be stored in memory and then inspected by CPU code. The status word is a 16-bit register divided into fields as shown in Figure 6. The busy bit (bit 15) indicates whether the NEU is either executing an instruction or has an interrupt request pending (B=1), or is idle (B=0). Several instructions which store and manipulate the status word are executed exclusively by the CU, and these do not set the busy bit themselves.

6

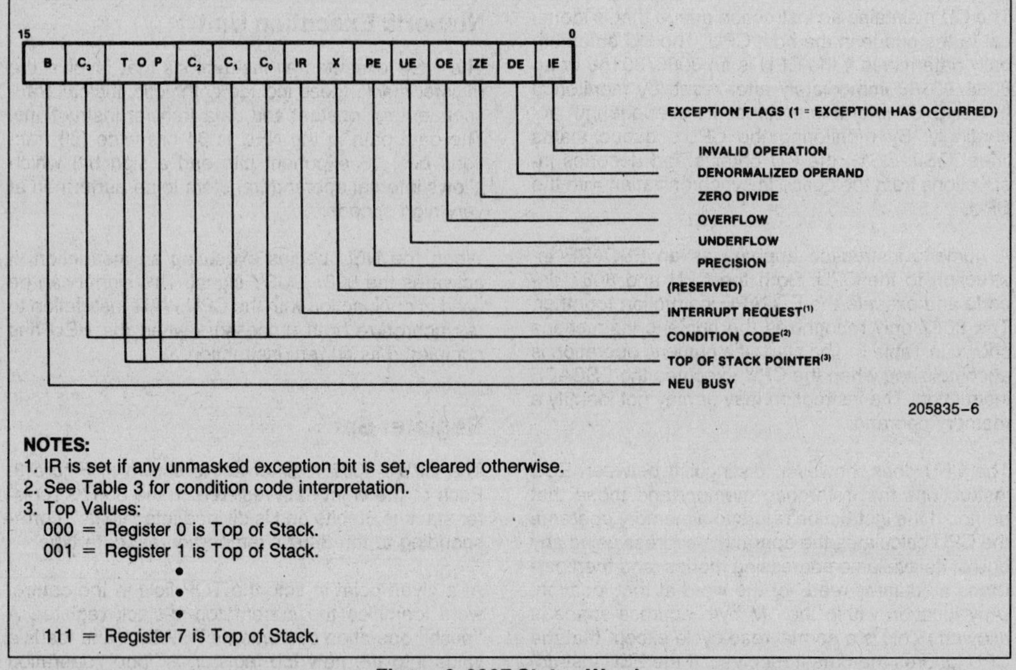

NOTES:
1. IR is set if any unmasked exception bit is set, cleared otherwise.
2. See Table 3 for condition code interpretation.
3. Top Values:
   000 = Register 0 is Top of Stack.
   001 = Register 1 is Top of Stack.
   •
   •
   •
   111 = Register 7 is Top of Stack.

Figure 6. 8087 Status Word

The four numeric condition code bits (C_0–C_3) are similar to flags in a CPU: various instructions update these bits to reflect the outcome of the 8087 operations. The effect of these instructions on the condition code bits is summarized in Table 4.

Bits 14–12 of the status word point to the 8087 register that is the current top-of-stack (TOP) as described above.

Bit 7 is the interrupt request bit. This bit is set if any unmasked exception bit is set and cleared otherwise.

Bits 5–0 are set to indicate that the NEU has detected an exception while executing an instruction.

Tag Word

The tag word marks the content of each register as shown in Figure 7. The principal function of the tag word is to optimize the 8087's performance. The tag word can be used, however, to interpret the contents of 8087 registers.

Instruction and Data Pointers

The instruction and data pointers (see Figure 8) are provided for user-written error handlers. Whenever the 8087 executes a math instruction, the CU saves the instruction address, the operand address (if present) and the instruction opcode. 8087 instructions can store this data into memory.

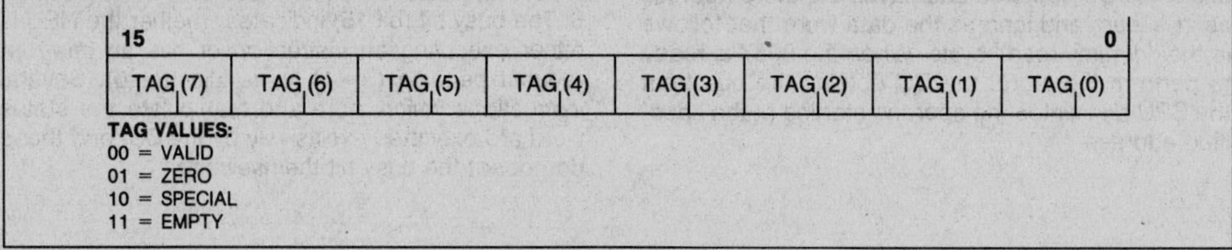

Figure 7. 8087 Tag Word

Table 4a. Condition Code Interpretation

Instruction Type	C_3	C_2	C_1	C_0	Interpretation
Compare, Test	0	0	X	0	ST > Source or 0 (FTST)
	0	0	X	1	ST < Source or 0 (FTST)
	1	0	X	0	ST = Source or 0 (FTST)
	1	1	X	1	ST is not comparable
Remainder	Q_1	0	Q_0	Q_2	Complete reduction with three low bits of quotient (See Table 4b)
	U	1	U	U	Incomplete Reduction
Examine	0	0	0	0	Valid, positive unnormalized
	0	0	0	1	Invalid, positive, exponent = 0
	0	0	1	0	Valid, negative, unnormalized
	0	0	1	1	Invalid, negative, exponent = 0
	0	1	0	0	Valid, positive, normalized
	0	1	0	1	Infinity, positive
	0	1	1	0	Valid, negative, normalized
	0	1	1	1	Infinity, negative
	1	0	0	0	Zero, positive
	1	0	0	1	Empty
	1	0	1	0	Zero, negative
	1	0	1	1	Empty
	1	1	0	0	Invalid, positive, exponent = 0
	1	1	0	1	Empty
	1	1	1	0	Invalid, negative, exponent = 0
	1	1	1	1	Empty

NOTES:
1. ST = Top of stack
2. X = value is not affected by instruction
3. U = value is undefined following instruction
4. Q_n = Quotient bit n

Table 4b. Condition Code Interpretation after FPREM Instruction As a Function of Divided Value

Dividend Range	Q_2	Q_1	Q_0
Dividend < 2 * Modulus	C_3[1]	C_1[1]	Q_0
Dividend < 4 * Modulus	C_3[1]	Q_1	Q_0
Dividend ≥ 4 * Modulus	Q_2	Q_1	Q_0

NOTE:
1. Previous value of indicated bit, not affected by FPREM instruction execution.

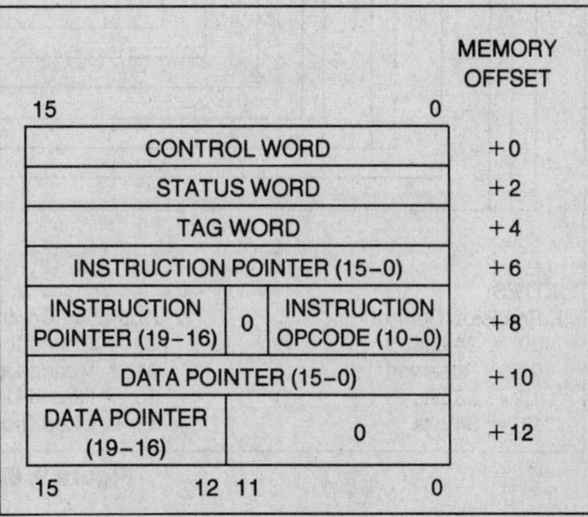

Figure 8. 8087 Instruction and Data Pointer Image in Memory

Control Word

The 8087 provides several processing options which are selected by loading a word from memory into the control word. Figure 9 shows the format and encoding of the fields in the control word.

The low order byte of this control word configures 8087 interrupts and exception masking. Bits 5–0 of the control word contain individual masks for each of the six exceptions that the 8087 recognizes and bit 7 contains a general mask bit for all 8087 interrupts. The high order byte of the control word configures the 8087 operating mode including precision, rounding, and infinity controls. The precision control bits (bits 9–8) can be used to set the 8087 internal operating precision at less than the default of temporary real precision. This can be useful in providing compatibility with earlier generation arithmetic processors of smaller precision than the 8087. The rounding control bits (bits 11–10) provide for directed rounding and true chop as well as the unbiased round to nearest mode specified in the proposed IEEE standard. Control over closure of the number space at infinity is also provided (either affine closure, $\pm\infty$, or projective closure, ∞, is treated as unsigned, may be specified).

Exception Handling

The 8087 detects six different exception conditions that can occur during instruction execution. Any or all exceptions will cause an interrupt if unmasked and interrupts are enabled.

If interrupts are disabled the 8087 will simply continue execution regardless of whether the host clears the exception. If a specific exception class is masked and that exception occurs, however, the 8087 will post the exception in the status register and perform an on-chip default exception handling procedure, thereby allowing processing to continue. The exceptions that the 8087 detects are the following:

1. INVALID OPERATION: Stack overflow, stack underflow, indeterminate form (0/0, $\infty - \infty$, etc.) or the use of a Non-Number (NAN) as an operand. An exponent value is reserved and any bit pattern with this value in the exponent field is termed a Non-Number and causes this exception. If this exception is masked, the 8087's default response is to generate a specific NAN called INDEFINITE, or to propagate already existing NANs as the calculation result.

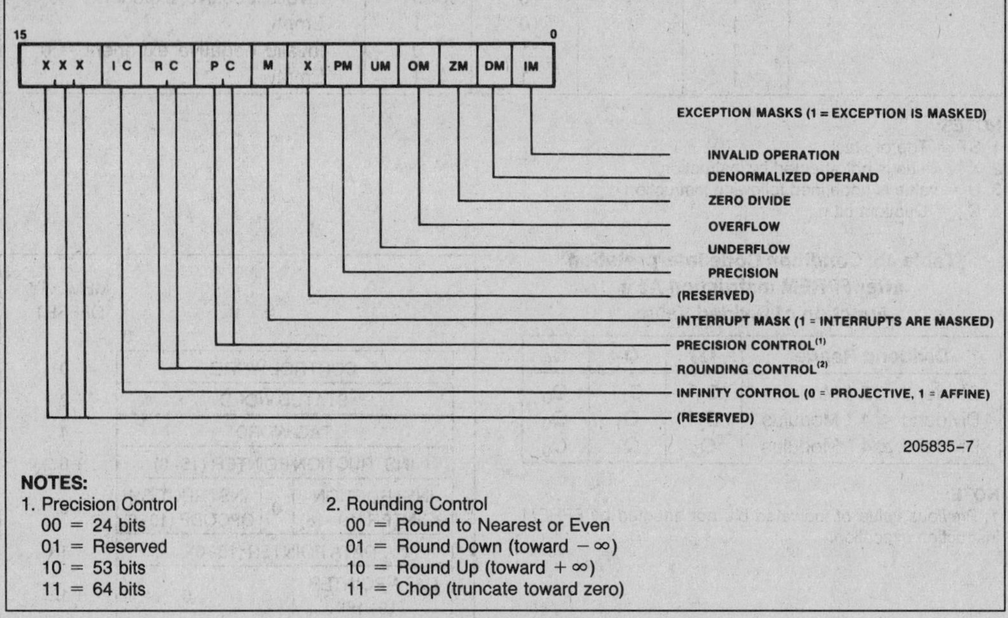

Figure 9. 8087 Control Word

2. OVERFLOW: The result is too large in magnitude to fit the specified format. The 8087 will generate an encoding for infinity if this exception is masked.
3. ZERO DIVISOR: The divisor is zero while the dividend is a non-infinite, non-zero number. Again, the 8087 will generate an encoding for infinity if this exception is masked.
4. UNDERFLOW: The result is non-zero but too small in magnitude to fit in the specified format. If this exception is masked the 8087 will denormalize (shift right) the fraction until the exponent is in range. This process is called gradual underflow.
5. DENORMALIZED OPERAND: At least one of the operands or the result is denormalized; it has the smallest exponent but a non-zero significand. Normal processing continues if this exception is masked off.
6. INEXACT RESULT: If the true result is not exactly representable in the specified format, the result is rounded according to the rounding mode, and this flag is set. If this exception is masked, processing will simply continue.

ABSOLUTE MAXIMUM RATINGS*

Ambient Temperature Under Bias ...... 0°C to 70°C

Storage Temperature .... −65°C to +150°C

Voltage on Any Pin with Respect to Ground .... −1.0V to +7V

Power Dissipation .... 3.0 Watt

NOTICE: This is a production data sheet. The specifications are subject to change without notice.

**WARNING: Stressing the device beyond the "Absolute Maximum Ratings" may cause permanent damage. These are stress ratings only. Operation beyond the "Operating Conditions" is not recommended and extended exposure beyond the "Operating Conditions" may affect device reliability.*

D.C. CHARACTERISTICS T_A = 0°C to 70°C, V_{CC} = 5V ±5%

Symbol	Parameter	Min	Max	Units	Test Conditions
V_{IL}	Input Low Voltage	−0.5	0.8	V	
V_{IH}	Input High Voltage	2.0	V_{CC} + 0.5	V	
V_{OL}	Output Low Voltage (Note 8)		0.45	V	I_{OL} = 2.5 mA
V_{OH}	Output High Voltage	2.4		V	I_{OH} = −400 μA
I_{CC}	Power Supply Current		475	mA	T_A = 25°C
I_{LI}	Input Leakage Current		±10	μA	0V ≤ V_{IN} ≤ V_{CC}
I_{LO}	Output Leakage Current		±10	μA	T_A = 25°C
V_{CL}	Clock Input Low Voltage	−0.5	0.6	V	
V_{CH}	Clock Input High Voltage	3.9	V_{CC} + 1.0	V	
C_{IN}	Capacitance of Inputs		10	pF	fc = 1 MHz
C_{IO}	Capacitance of I/O Buffer (AD0–15, A_{16}–A_{19}, BHE, S2–S0, RQ/GT) and CLK		15	pF	fc = 1 MHz
C_{OUT}	Capacitance of Outputs BUSY INT		10	pF	fc = 1 MHz

A.C. CHARACTERISTICS T_A = 0°C to 70°C, V_{CC} = 5V ±5%

TIMING REQUIREMENTS

Symbol	Parameter	8087		8087-2		8087-1 (See Note 7)		Units	Test Conditions
		Min	Max	Min	Max	Min	Max		
TCLCL	CLK Cycle Period	200	500	125	500	100	500	ns	
TCLCH	CLK Low Time	118		68		53		ns	
TCHCL	CLK High Time	69		44		39		ns	
TCH1CH2	CLK Rise Time		10		10		15	ns	From 1.0V to 3.5V
TCL2CL2	CLK Fall Time		10		10		15	ns	From 3.5V to 1.0V
TDVCL	Data In Setup Time	30		20		15		ns	
TCLDX	Data In Hold Time	10		10		10		ns	
TRYHCH	READY Setup Time	118		68		53		ns	
TCHRYX	READY Hold Time	30		20		5		ns	
TRYLCL	READY Inactive to CLK (Note 6)	−8		−8		−10		ns	
TGVCH	RQ/GT Setup Time (Note 8)	30		15		15		ns	
TCHGX	RQ/GT Hold Time	40		30		20		ns	
TQVCL	QS0−1 Setup Time (Note 8)	30		30		30		ns	
TCLQX	QS0−1 Hold Time	10		10		5		ns	
TSACH	Status Active Setup Time	30		30		30		ns	
TSNCL	Status Inactive Setup Time	30		30		30		ns	
TILIH	Input Rise Time (Except CLK)		20		20		20	ns	From 0.8V to 2.0V
TIHIL	Input Fall Time (Except CLK)		12		12		15	ns	From 2.0V to 0.8V

TIMING RESPONSES

Symbol	Parameter	8087		8087-2		8087-1 (See Note 7)		Units	Test Conditions
		Min	Max	Min	Max	Min	Max		
TCLML	Command Active Delay (Notes 1, 2)	10/0	35/70	10/0	35/70	10/0	35/70	ns	C_L = 20–100 pF for all 8087 Outputs (in addition to 8087 self-load)
TCLMH	Command Inactive Delay (Notes 1, 2)	10/0	35/55	10/0	35/55	10/0	35/70	ns	
TRYHSH	Ready Active to Status Passive (Note 5)		110		65		45	ns	
TCHSV	Status Active Delay	10	110	10	60	10	45	ns	
TCLSH	Status Inactive Delay	10	130	10	70	10	55	ns	
TCLAV	Address Valid Delay	10	110	10	60	10	55	ns	
TCLAX	Address Hold Time	10		10		10		ns	

A.C. CHARACTERISTICS T_A = 0°C to 70°C, V_{CC} = 5V ±5% (Continued)

TIMING RESPONSES (Continued)

Symbol	Parameter	8087		8087-2		8087-1 (See Note 7)		Units	Test Conditions
		Min	Max	Min	Max	Min	Max		
TCLAZ	Address Float Delay	TCLAX	80	TCLAX	50	TCLAX	45	ns	C_L = 20–100 pF for all 8087 Outputs (in addition to 8087 self-load)
TSVLH	Status Valid to ALE High (Notes 1, 2)		15/30		15/30		15/30	ns	
TCLLH	CLK Low to ALE Valid (Notes 1, 2)		15/30		15/30		15/30	ns	
TCHLL	ALE Inactive Delay (Notes 1, 2)		15/30		15/30		15/30	ns	
TCLDV	Data Valid Delay	10	110	10	60	10	50	ns	
TCHDX	Status Hold Time	10		10		10	45	ns	
TCLDOX	Data Hold Time	10		10		10		ns	
TCVNV	Control Active Delay (Notes 1, 3)	5	45	5	45	5	45	ns	
TCVNX	Control Inactive Delay (Notes 1, 3)	10	45	10	45	10	45	ns	
TCHBV	BUSY and INT Valid Delay	10	150	10	85	10	65	ns	
TCHDTL	Direction Control Active Delay (Notes 1, 3)		50		50		50	ns	
TCHDTH	Direction Control Inactive Delay (Notes 1, 3)		30		30		30	ns	
TSVDTV	STATUS to DT/$\overline{R}$ Delay (Notes 1, 4)	0	30	0	30	0	30	ns	
TCLDTV	DT/$\overline{R}$ Active Delay (Notes 1, 4)	0	55	0	55	0	55	ns	
TCHDNV	$\overline{DEN}$ Active Delay (Notes 1, 4)	0	55	0	55	0	55	ns	
TCHDNX	$\overline{DEN}$ Inactive Delay (Notes 1, 4)	5	55	5	55	5	55	ns	
TCLGL	RQ/GT Active Delay (Note 8)	0	85	0	50	0	38	ns	C_L = 40 pF (in addition to 8087 self-load)
TCLGH	RQ/GT Inactive Delay	0	85	0	50	0	45	ns	
TOLOH	Output Rise Time		20		20		15	ns	From 0.8V to 2.0V
TOHOL	Output Fall Time		12		12		12	ns	From 2.0V to 0.8V

NOTES:
1. Signal at 8284A, 8288, or 82188 shown for reference only.
2. 8288 timing/82188 timing.
3. 8288 timing.
4. 82188 timing.
5. Applies only to T_3 and wait states.
6. Applies only to T_2 state (8 ns into T_3).
7. IMPORTANT SYSTEM CONSIDERATION: Some 8087-1 timing parameters are constrained relative to the corresponding 8086-1 specifications. Therefore, 8086-1 systems incorporating the 8087-1 should be designed with the 8087-1 specifications.
8. Changes since last revision.

A.C. TESTING INPUT, OUTPUT WAVEFORM

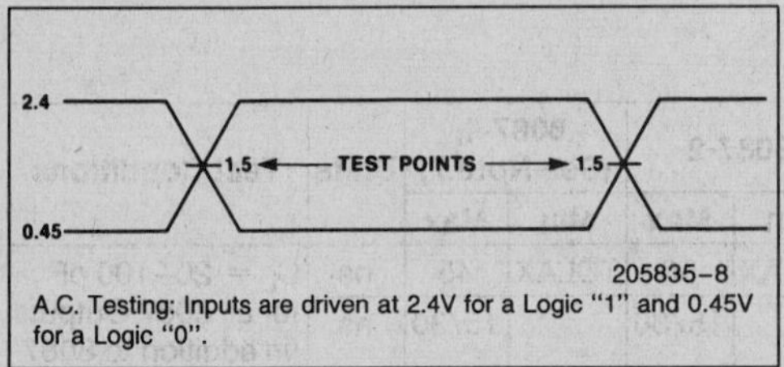

205835–8

A.C. Testing: Inputs are driven at 2.4V for a Logic "1" and 0.45V for a Logic "0".

A.C. TESTING LOAD CIRCUIT

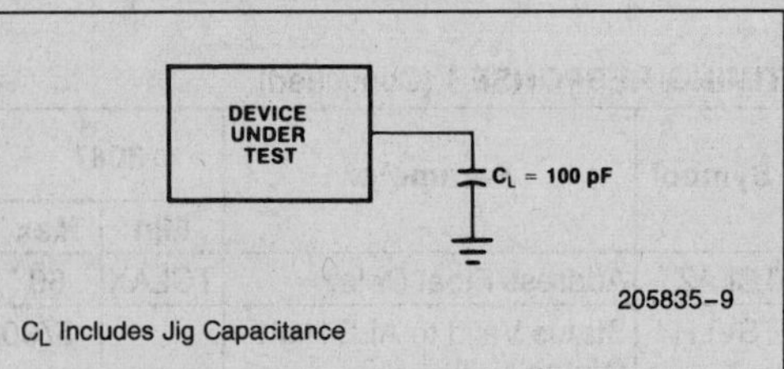

205835–9

C_L Includes Jig Capacitance

WAVEFORMS

MASTER MODE (with 8288 references)

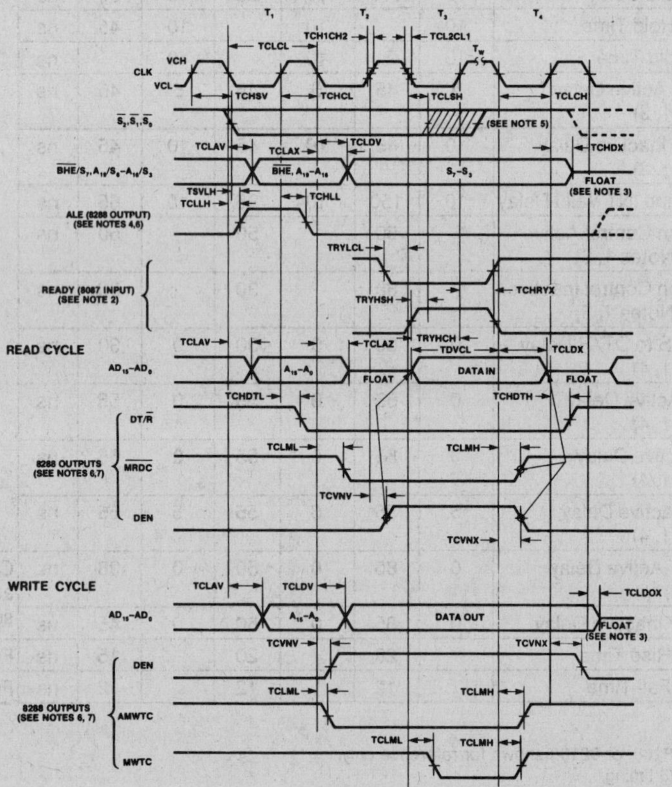

205835–10

NOTES:

1. All signals switch between V_{OL} and V_{OH} unless otherwise specified.
2. READY is sampled near the end of T_2, T_3 and T_W to determine if T_W machine states are to be inserted.
3. The local bus floats only if the 8087 is returning control to the 8086/8088.
4. ALE rises at later of (TSVLH, TCLLH).
5. Status inactive in state just prior to T_4.
6. Signals at 8284A or 8288 are shown for reference only.
7. The issuance of 8288 command and control signals ($\overline{MRDC}$, ($\overline{MWTC}$, $\overline{AMWC}$, and DEN) lags the active high 8288 CEN.
8. All timing measurements are made at 1.5V unless otherwise noted.

WAVEFORMS (Continued)

MASTER MODE (with 82188 references)

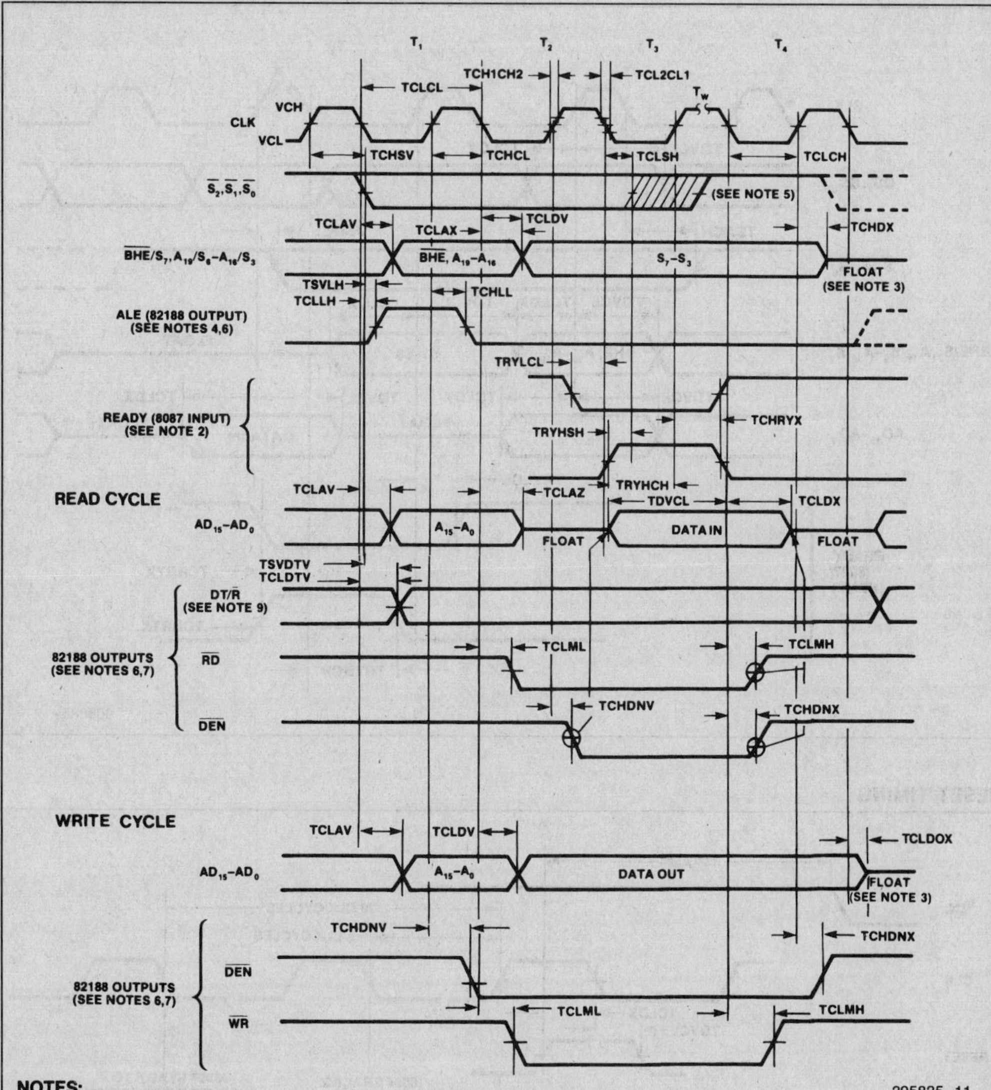

NOTES:

1. All signals switch between V_{OL} and V_{OH} unless otherwise specified.
2. READY is sampled near the end of T_2, T_3 and T_W to determine if T_W machine states are to be inserted.
3. The local bus floats only if the 8087 is returning control to the 80186/80188.
4. ALE rises at later of (TSVLH, TCLLH).
5. Status inactive in state just prior to T_4.
6. Signals at 8284A or 82188 are shown for reference only.
7. The issuance of 8288 command and control signals ($\overline{MRDC}$, ($\overline{MWTC}$, $\overline{AMWC}$, and DEN) lags the active high 8288 CEN.
8. All timing measurements are made at 1.5V unless otherwise noted.
9. DT/$\overline{R}$ becomes valid at the later of (TSVDTV, TCLDTV).

WAVEFORMS (Continued)

PASSIVE MODE

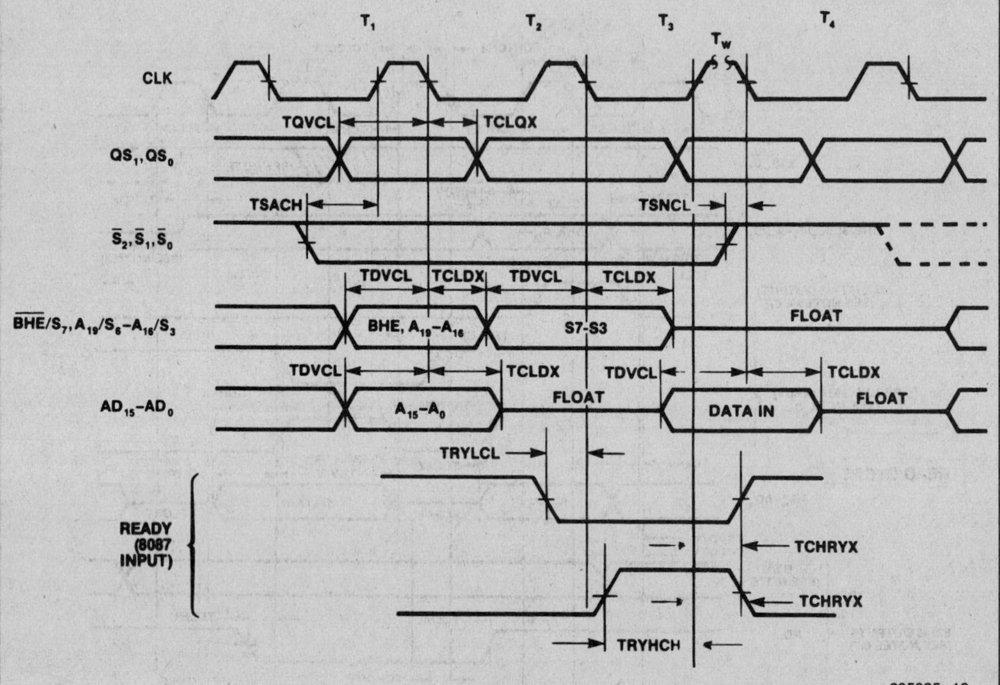

T1 T2 T3 TW T4
CLK
TQVCL TCLQX
QS_1, QS_0
TSACH TSNCL
$\overline{S}_2, \overline{S}_1, \overline{S}_0$
TDVCL TCLDX TDVCL TCLDX
$\overline{BHE}/S_7, A_{19}/S_6-A_{16}/S_3$
BHE, $A_{19}-A_{16}$
S7-S3
FLOAT
TDVCL TCLDX TDVCL TCLDX
$AD_{15}-AD_0$
$A_{15}-A_0$
FLOAT
DATA IN
FLOAT
TRYLCL
READY (8087 INPUT)
TCHRYX
TCHRYX
TRYHCH

205835-12

RESET TIMING

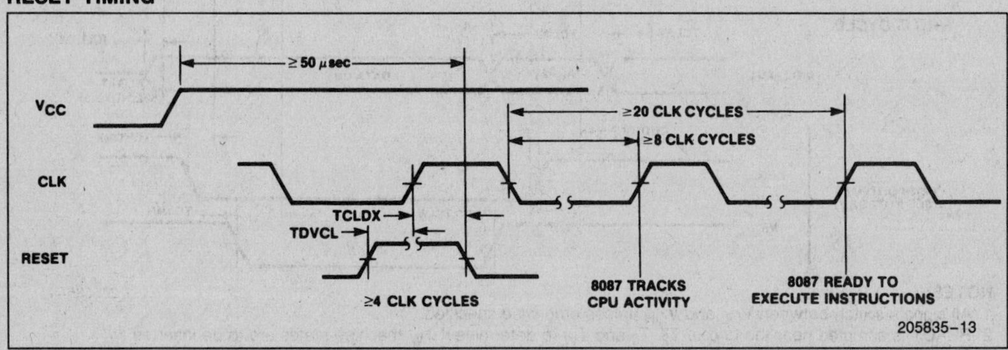

WAVEFORMS (Continued)

REQUEST/GRANT$_0$ TIMING

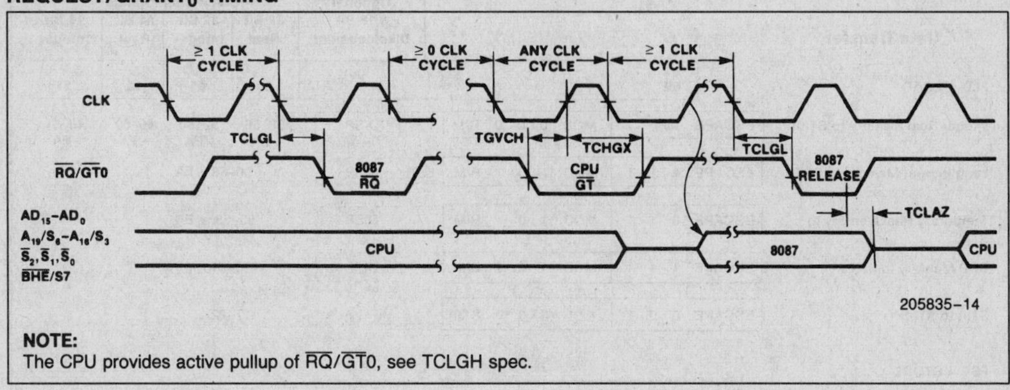

NOTE:
The CPU provides active pullup of $\overline{RQ}/\overline{GT}0$, see TCLGH spec.

REQUEST/GRANT$_1$ TIMING

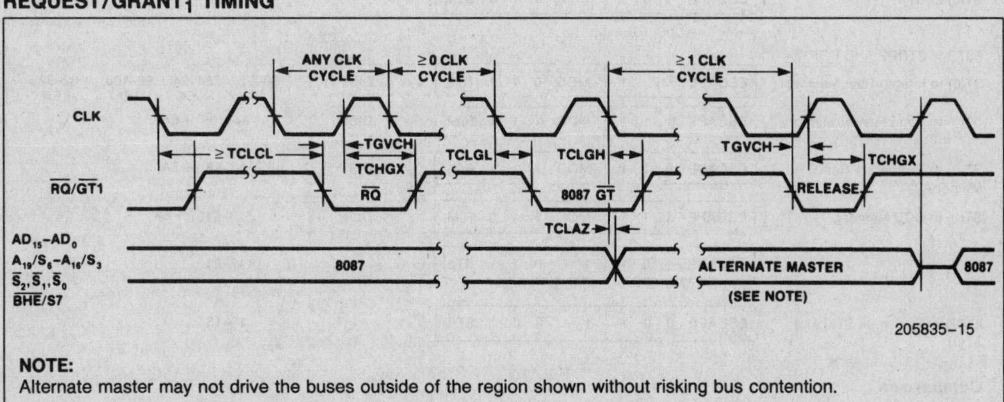

NOTE:
Alternate master may not drive the buses outside of the region shown without risking bus contention.

BUSY AND INTERRUPT TIMING

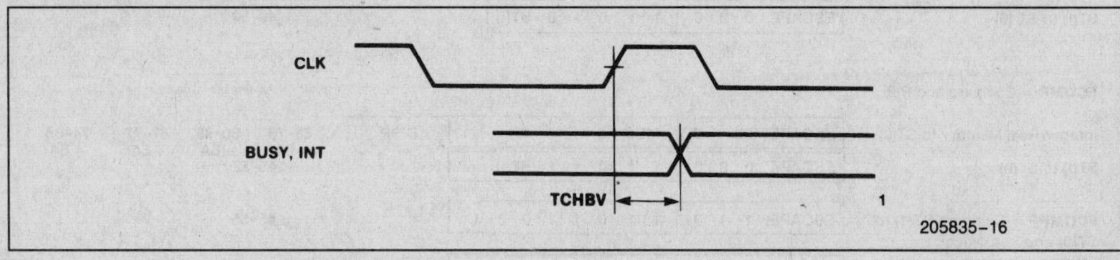

6

Table 5. 8087 Extensions to the 86/186 Instructions Sets

Data Transfer	Instruction Format		Optional 8,16 Bit Displacement	Clock Count Range 32 Bit Real	32 Bit Integer	64 Bit Real	16 Bit Integer
FLD = LOAD	MF =			00	01	10	11
Integer/Real Memory to ST(0)	ESCAPE MF 1	MOD 0 0 0 R/M	DISP	38–56 + EA	52–60 + EA	40–60 + EA	46–54 + EA
Long Integer Memory to ST(0)	ESCAPE 1 1 1	MOD 1 0 1 R/M	DISP	60–68 + EA			
Temporary Real Memory to ST(0)	ESCAPE 0 1 1	MOD 1 0 1 R/M	DISP	53–65 + EA			
BCD Memory to ST(0)	ESCAPE 1 1 1	MOD 1 0 0 R/M	DISP	290–310 + EA			
ST(i) to ST(0)	ESCAPE 0 0 1	1 1 0 0 0 ST(i)		17–22			
FST = STORE							
ST(0) to Integer/Real Memory	ESCAPE MF 1	MOD 0 1 0 R/M	DISP	84–90 + EA	82–92 + EA	96–104 + EA	80–90 + EA
ST(0) to ST(i)	ESCAPE 1 0 1	1 1 0 1 0 ST(i)		15–22			
FSTP = STORE AND POP							
ST(0) to Integer/Real Memory	ESCAPE MF 1	MOD 0 1 1 R/M	DISP	86–92 + EA	84–94 + EA	98–106 + EA	82–92 + EA
ST(0) to Long Integer Memory	ESCAPE 1 1 1	MOD 1 1 1 R/M	DISP	94–105 + EA			
ST(0) to Temporary Real Memory	ESCAPE 0 1 1	MOD 1 1 1 R/M	DISP	52–58 + EA			
ST(0) to BCD Memory	ESCAPE 1 1 1	MOD 1 1 0 R/M	DISP	520–540 + EA			
ST(0) to ST(i)	ESCAPE 1 0 1	1 1 0 1 1 ST(i)		17–24			
FXCH = Exchange ST(i) and ST(0)	ESCAPE 0 0 1	1 1 0 0 1 ST(i)		10–15			
Comparison							
FCOM = Compare							
Integer/Real Memory to ST(0)	ESCAPE MF 0	MOD 0 1 0 R/M	DISP	60–70 + EA	78–91 + EA	65–75 + EA	72–86 + EA
ST(i) to ST (0)	ESCAPE 0 0 0	1 1 0 1 0 ST(i)		40–50			
FCOMP = Compare and Pop							
Integer/Real Memory to ST(0)	ESCAPE MF 0	MOD 0 1 1 R/M	DISP	63–73 + EA	80–93 + EA	67–77 + EA	74–88 + EA
ST(i) to ST(0)	ESCAPE 0 0 0	1 1 0 1 1 ST(i)		45–52			
FCOMPP = Compare ST(1) to ST(0) and Pop Twice	ESCAPE 1 1 0	1 1 0 1 1 0 0 1		45–55			
FTST = Test ST(0)	ESCAPE 0 0 1	1 1 1 0 0 1 0 0		38–48			
FXAM = Examine ST(0)	ESCAPE 0 0 1	1 1 1 0 0 1 0 1		12–23			

205835–17

Table 5. 8087 Extensions to the 86/186 Instructions Sets (Continued)

Constants			Optional 8,16 Bit Displacement	Clock Count Range 32 Bit Real	32 Bit Integer	64 Bit Real	16 Bit Integer
	MF	=		00	01	10	11
FLDZ = LOAD + 0.0 into ST(0)	ESCAPE 0 0 1	1 1 1 0 1 1 1 0		11–17			
FLD1 = LOAD + 1.0 into ST(0)	ESCAPE 0 0 1	1 1 1 0 1 0 0 0		15–21			
FLDPI = LOAD π into ST(0)	ESCAPE 0 0 1	1 1 1 0 1 0 1 1		16–22			
FLDL2T = LOAD $\log_2 10$ into ST(0)	ESCAPE 0 0 1	1 1 1 0 1 0 0 1		16–22			
FLDL2E = LOAD $\log_2 e$ into ST(0)	ESCAPE 0 0 1	1 1 1 0 1 0 1 0		15–21			
FLDLG2 = LOAD $\log_{10} 2$ into ST(0)	ESCAPE 0 0 1	1 1 1 0 1 1 0 0		18–24			
FLDLN2 = LOAD $\log_e 2$ into ST(0)	ESCAPE 0 0 1	1 1 1 0 1 1 0 1		17–23			
Arithmetic							
FADD = Addition							
Integer/Real Memory with ST(0)	ESCAPE MF 0	MOD 0 0 0 R/M	DISP	90–120 + EA	108–143 + EA	95–125 + EA	102–137 + EA
ST(i) and ST(0)	ESCAPE d P 0	1 1 0 0 0 ST(i)		70–100 (Note 1)			
FSUB = Subtraction							
Integer/Real Memory with ST(0)	ESCAPE MF 0	MOD 1 0 R R/M	DISP	90–120 + EA	108–143 + EA	95–125 + EA	102–137 + EA
ST(i) and ST(0)	ESCAPE d P 0	1 1 1 0 R R/M		70–100 (Note 1)			
FMUL = Multiplication							
Integer/Real Memory with ST(0)	ESCAPE MF 0	MOD 0 0 1 R/M	DISP	110–125 + EA	130–144 + EA	112–168 + EA	124–138 + EA
ST(i) and ST(0)	ESCAPE d P 0	1 1 0 0 1 R/M		90–145 (Note 1)			
FDIV = Division							
Integer/Real Memory with ST(0)	ESCAPE MF 0	MOD 1 1 R R/M	DISP	215–225 + EA	230–243 + EA	220–230 + EA	224–238 + EA
ST(i) and ST(0)	ESCAPE d P 0	1 1 1 1 R R/M		193–203 (Note 1)			
FSQRT = Square Root of ST(0)	ESCAPE 0 0 1	1 1 1 1 1 0 1 0		180–186			
FSCALE = Scale ST(0) by ST(1)	ESCAPE 0 0 1	1 1 1 1 1 1 0 1		32–38			
FPREM = Partial Remainder of ST(0) ÷ST(1)	ESCAPE 0 0 1	1 1 1 1 1 0 0 0		15–190			
FRNDINT = Round ST(0) to Integer	ESCAPE 0 0 1	1 1 1 1 1 1 0 0		16–50			

205835–18

NOTE:
1. If P = 1 then add 5 clocks.

6

Table 5. 8087 Extensions to the 86/186 Instructions Sets (Continued)

Instruction			Optional 8,16 Bit Displacement	Clock Count Range
FXTRACT = Extract Components of St(0)	ESCAPE 0 0 1	1 1 1 1 0 1 0 0		27–55
FABS = Absolute Value of ST(0)	ESCAPE 0 0 1	1 1 1 0 0 0 0 1		10–17
FCHS = Change Sign of ST(0)	ESCAPE 0 0 1	1 1 1 0 0 0 0 0		10–17
Transcendental				
FPTAN = Partial Tangent of ST(0)	ESCAPE 0 0 1	1 1 1 1 0 0 1 0		30–540
FPATAN = Partial Arctangent of ST(0) ÷ST(1)	ESCAPE 0 0 1	1 1 1 1 0 0 1 1		250–800
F2XM1 = $2^{ST(0)}-1$	ESCAPE 0 0 1	1 1 1 1 0 0 0 0		310–630
FYL2X = ST(1) • Log_2 |ST(0)|	ESCAPE 0 0 1	1 1 1 1 0 0 0 1		900–1100
FYL2XP1 = ST(1) • Log_2 [ST(0) +1]	ESCAPE 0 0 1	1 1 1 1 1 0 0 1		700–1000
Processor Control				
FINIT = Initialized 8087	ESCAPE 0 1 1	1 1 1 0 0 0 1 1		2–8
FENI = Enable Interrupts	ESCAPE 0 1 1	1 1 1 0 0 0 0 0		2–8
FDISI = Disable Interrupts	ESCAPE 0 1 1	1 1 1 0 0 0 0 1		2–8
FLDCW = Load Control Word	ESCAPE 0 0 1	MOD 1 0 1 R/M	DISP	7–14 + EA
FSTCW = Store Control Word	ESCAPE 0 0 1	MOD 1 1 1 R/M	DISP	12–18 + EA
FSTSW = Store Status Word	ESCAPE 1 0 1	MOD 1 1 1 R/M	DISP	12–18 + EA
FCLEX = Clear Exceptions	ESCAPE 0 1 1	1 1 1 0 0 0 1 0		2–8
FSTENV = Store Environment	ESCAPE 0 0 1	MOD 1 1 0 R/M	DISP	40–50 + EA
FLDENV = Load Environment	ESCAPE 0 0 1	MOD 1 0 0 R/M	DISP	35–45 + EA
FSAVE = Save State	ESCAPE 1 0 1	MOD 1 1 0 R/M	DISP	197 – 207 + EA
FRSTOR = Restore State	ESCAPE 1 0 1	MOD 1 0 0 R/M	DISP	197 – 207 + EA
FINCSTP = Increment Stack Pointer	ESCAPE 0 0 1	1 1 1 1 0 1 1 1		6–12
FDECSTP = Decrement Stack Pointer	ESCAPE 0 0 1	1 1 1 1 0 1 1 0		6–12

205835–19

Table 5. 8087 Extensions to the 86/186 Instructions Sets (Continued)

Instruction	Encoding		Clock Count Range
FFREE = Free ST(i)	ESCAPE 1 0 1	1 1 0 0 0 ST(i)	9–16
FNOP = No Operation	ESCAPE 0 0 1	1 1 0 1 0 0 0 0	10–16
FWAIT = CPU Wait for 8087	1 0 0 1 1 0 1 1		3 + 5n*

205835–20

*n = number of times CPU examines TEST line before 8087 lowers BUSY.

NOTES:

1. if mod = 00 then DISP = 0*, disp-low and disp-high are absent
   if mod = 01 then DISP = disp-low sign-extended to 16-bits, disp-high is absent
   if mod = 10 then DISP = disp-high; disp-low
   if mod = 11 then r/m is treated as an ST(i) field
2. if r/m = 000 then EA = (BX) + (SI) + DISP
   if r/m = 001 then EA = (BX) + (DI) + DISP
   if r/m = 010 then EA = (BP) + (SI) + DISP
   if r/m = 011 then EA = (BP) + (DI) + DISP
   if r/m = 100 then EA = (SI) + DISP
   if r/m = 101 then EA = (DI) + DISP
   if r/m = 110 then EA = (BP) + DISP
   if r/m = 111 then EA = (BX) + DISP
   *except if mod = 000 and r/m = 110 then EA = disp-high; disp-low.
3. MF = Memory Format
   00–32-bit Real
   01–32-bit Integer
   10–64-bit Real
   11–16-bit Integer
4. ST(0) = Current stack top
   ST(i) = i^{th} register below stack top
5. d = Destination
   0—Destination is ST(0)
   1—Destination is ST(i)
6. P = Pop
   0—No pop
   1—Pop ST(0)
7. R = Reverse: When d = 1 reverse the sense of R
   0—Destination (op) Source
   1—Source (op) Destination
8. For **FSQRT:** $-0 \le ST(0) \le +\infty$
   For **FSCALE:** $-2^{15} \le ST(1) < +2^{15}$ and ST(1) integer
   For **F2XM1:** $0 \le ST(0) \le 2^{-1}$
   For **FYL2X:** $0 < ST(0) < \infty$
   $-\infty < ST(1) < +\infty$
   For **FYL2XP1:** $0 \le |ST(0)| < (2 - \sqrt{2})/2$
   $-\infty < ST(1) < \infty$
   For **FPTAN:** $0 \le ST(0) \le \pi/4$
   For **FPATAN:** $0 \le ST(0) < ST(1) < +\infty$

6

i860™ Supercomputing Microprocessor

7

7

intel®

PRELIMINARY

i860™ XP MICROPROCESSOR

- Parallel Architecture that Supports Up to Three Operations per Clock
  - One Integer or Control Instruction
  - Up to Two Floating-Point Results
- High Performance Design
  - 40/50 MHz Clock Rate
  - 100 Peak Single Precision MFLOPS
  - 75 Peak Double Precision MFLOPS
  - 64-Bit External Data Bus
  - 64-Bit Internal Code Bus
  - 128-Bit Internal Data Bus
- High Integration on One Chip
  - 32-Bit Integer and Control Unit
  - 32/64-Bit Pipelined Floating-Point
  - 64-Bit 3-D Graphics Unit
  - Paging Unit with 64 Four-Kbyte and 16 Four-Mbyte Pages
  - 16 Kbyte Code Cache
  - 16 Kbyte Data Cache
- Fast, Multiprocessor-Oriented Bus
  - Burst Cycles Move 400 Mbyte/Sec
  - Hardware Cache Snooping
  - MESI Cache Consistency Protocol
  - Supports Second-Level Cache
  - Supports DRAM
- Compatible with Industry Standards
  - ANSI/IEEE Standard 754-1985 for Binary Floating-Point Arithmetic
  - Intel 386™/Intel 486™/i860™ Data Formats and Page Table Entries
  - Binary Compatible with i860™ XR Applications Instruction Set
  - Detached Concurrency Control Unit (CCU) Supports Parallel Architecture Extensions (PAX)
  - JEDEC 262-pin Ceramic Pin Grid Array Package
  - IEEE Standard 1149.1/D6 Boundary-Scan Architecture
- Easy to Use
  - On-Chip Debug Register
  - UNIX*/860
  - APX Attached Processor Executive
  - Assembler, Linker, Simulator, Debugger, C and FORTRAN Compilers, FORTRAN Vectorizer, Scalar and Vector Math Libraries
  - Graphics Libraries

The Intel i860 XP Microprocessor (order code A80860XP) delivers supercomputing performance in a single VLSI component. The 32/64-bit architecture of the i860 XP microprocessor balances integer, floating point, and graphics performance for applications such as engineering workstations, scientific computing, 3-D graphics workstations, and multiuser systems. Its parallel architecture achieves high throughput with RISC design techniques, multiprocessor support, pipelined processing units, wide data paths, large on-chip caches, 2.5 million transistor design, and fast 0.8-micron silicon technology.

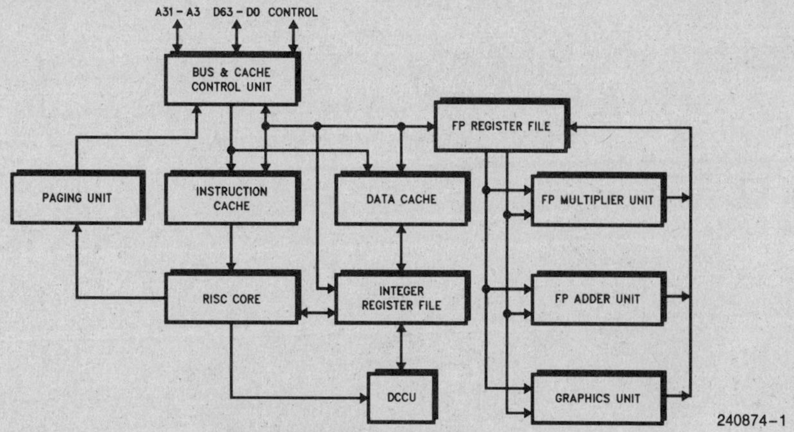

Figure 0.1. Block Diagram

*UNIX is a registered trademark of UNIX System Laboratories, Inc.
Intel, i860, Intel386 and Intel486 are trademarks of Intel Corporation.

For the complete data sheet on this device, refer to the Multimedia & Supercomputing Processors Handbook.

September 1991
Order Number: 240874-002

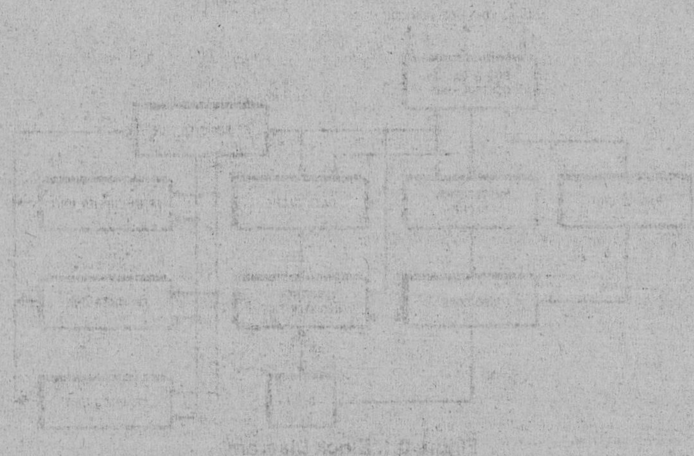

i860™ XR 64-BIT MICROPROCESSOR

- Parallel Architecture that Supports Up to Three Operations per Clock
  - One Integer or Control Instruction per Clock
  - Up to Two Floating-Point Results per Clock
- High Performance Design
  - 25/33.3/40 MHz Clock Rates
  - 80 Peak Single Precision MFLOPs
  - 60 Peak Double Precision MFLOPs
  - 64-Bit External Data Bus
  - 64-Bit Internal Instruction Cache Bus
  - 128-Bit Internal Data Cache Bus
- High Level of Integration on One Chip
  - 32-Bit Integer and Control Unit
  - 32/64-Bit Pipelined Floating-Point Adder and Multiplier Units
  - 64-Bit 3-D Graphics Unit
  - Paging Unit with Translation Lookaside Buffer
  - 4 Kbyte Instruction Cache
  - 8 Kbyte Data Cache
- Compatible with Industry Standards
  - ANSI/IEEE Standard 754-1985 for Binary Floating-Point Arithmetic
  - Intel386™/486™ Microprocessor Data Formats and Page Table Entries
  - JEDEC 168-pin Ceramic Pin Grid Array Package (see *Packaging Outlines and Dimensions*, order #231369)
- Easy to Use
  - On-Chip Debug Register
  - Assembler, Linker, Simulator, Debugger, C and FORTRAN Compilers, FORTRAN Vectorizer, Scalar and Vector Math Libraries for both OS/2* and UNIX* Environments

The Intel i860™ XR Microprocessor (order codes A80860XR-25, A80860XR-33 and A80860XR-40) delivers supercomputing performance in a single VLSI component. The 64-bit design of the i860 XR microprocessor balances integer, floating point, and graphics performance for applications such as engineering workstations, scientific computing, 3-D graphics workstations, and multiuser systems. Its parallel architecture achieves high throughput with RISC design techniques, pipelined processing units, wide data paths, large on-chip caches, million-transistor design, and fast one-micron CHMOS IV silicon technology.

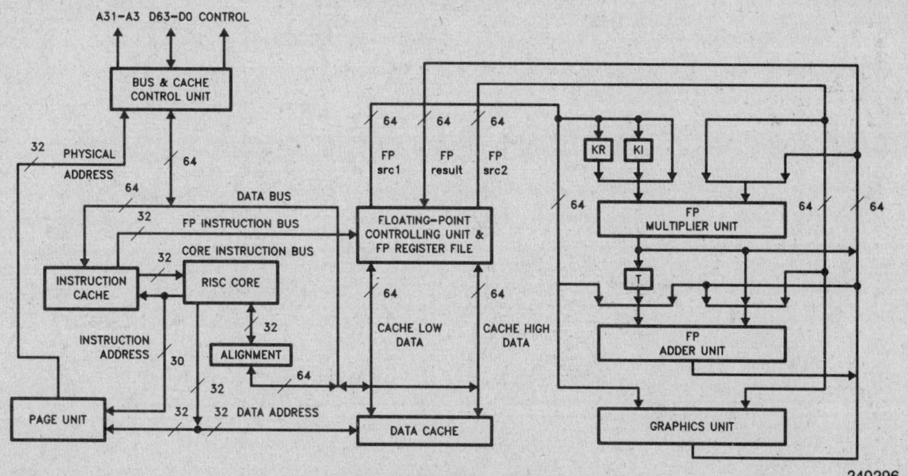

Figure 0.1. Block Diagram

Intel, int$_e$l, Intel386™, Intel486™, i860 XR, Multibus II and Parallel System Bus are trademarks of Intel Corporation.
*UNIX is a registered trademark of UNIX System Laboratories, Inc. OS/2 is a trademark of International Business Machines Corporation.

For the complete data sheet on this device, refer to the Multimedia & Supercomputing Processors Handbook.

August 1991
Order Number: 240296-005

82495XP CACHE CONTROLLER/ 82490XP CACHE RAM

- **Two-Way, Set Associative, Secondary Cache for i860™ XP Microprocessor**
- **50 MHz "No Glue" Interface with CPU**
- **Configurable**
  - **—Cache Size 256 or 512 Kbytes**
  - **—Line Width 32, 64 or 128 Bytes**
  - **—Memory Bus Width 64 or 128 Bits**
- **Dual-Ported Structure Permits Simultaneous Operations on CPU and Memory Buses**
- **Efficient MRU Way Prediction**
  - **—Zero Wait States on MRU Hit**
  - **—One Wait State on MRU Miss**
- **Dynamically Selectable Update Policies**
  - **—Write-Through**
  - **—Write-Once**
  - **—Write-Back**
- **MESI Cache Consistency Protocol**
- **Hardware Cache Snooping**
- **Maintains Consistency with Primary Cache via Inclusion Principle**
- **Flexible User-Implemented Memory Interface Enables Wide Range of Product Differentiation**
  - **—Clocked or Strobed**
  - **—Synchronous or Asynchronous**
  - **—Pipelining**
  - **—Memory Bus Protocol**
- **82495XP Cache Controller Available in 208-Lead Ceramic Pin Grid Array Package**
- **82490XP Cache RAM Available in 84-Lead Plastic Quad Flatpack Package**
  (See *Packaging Handbook*, Order #240800)

The Intel 82495XP cache controller and 82490XP cache RAM, when coupled with a user-implemented memory bus controller, provide a second-level cache subsystem that eliminates the memory latency and bandwidth bottleneck for a wide range of multiprocessor systems based on the i860 XP microprocessor. The CPU interface is optimized to serve the i860 XP microprocessor with zero wait states at up to 50 MHz. A secondary cache built from the 82495XP and 82490XP isolates the CPU from the memory subsystem; the memory can run slower and follow a different protocol than the i860 XP microprocessor.

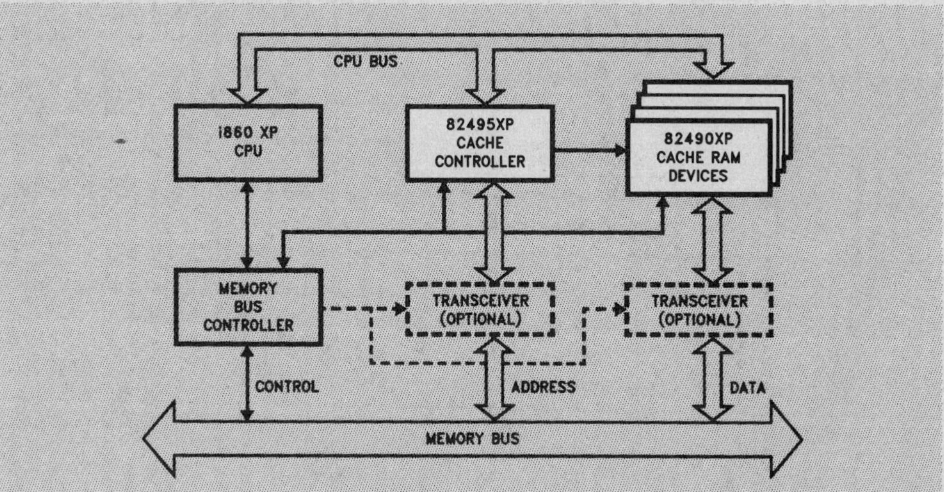

240956-60

Figure 0-1. Secondary Cache Configuration

For the complete data sheet on this device, refer to the Multimedia & Supercomputing Processors Handbook.

June 1991
Order Number: 240956-001

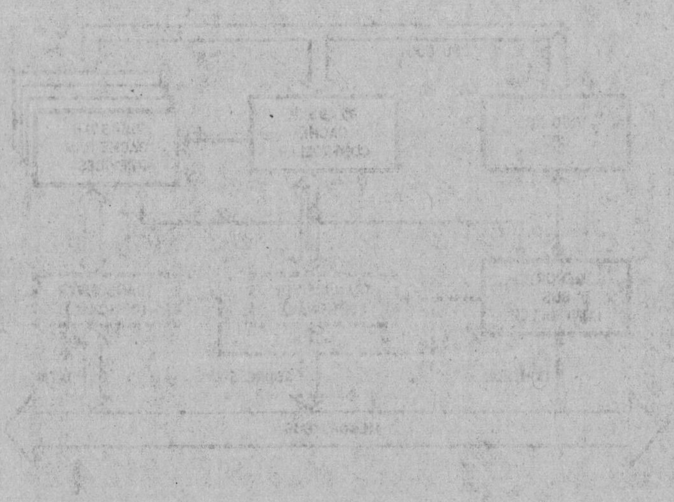

APPLICATION NOTE

PRELIMINARY

AP-452

September 1991

Designing a Memory Bus Controller for the 82495/82490 Cache

MARK ATKINS

ISIC SILAS

CHRIS KARLE

For the complete data sheet on this device, refer to the Multimedia & Supercomputing Processors Handbook.

Order Number: 240957-001

7

APPLICATION NOTE

AP-434

November 1989

Using i860™ Microprocessor Graphics Instructions for 3-D Rendering

For the complete data sheet on this device, refer to the Multimedia & Supercomputing Processors Handbook.

Order Number: 240856-001

APPLICATION NOTE

PRELIMINARY
AP-435

March 1990

FAST Fourier Transforms on the i860™ Microprocessor

MARK ATKINS
APPLICATIONS ENGINEER

For the complete data sheet on this device, refer to the Multimedia & Supercomputing Processors Handbook.

Order Number: 240658-001

7

i750® Video Processor 8

intel®

82750PB PIXEL PROCESSOR

- 25 MHz Clock with Single Cycle Execution
- Zero Branch Delay
- Wide Instruction Word Processor
- 512 x 48-Bit Instruction RAM
- 512 x 16-Bit Data RAM
- Two Internal 16-Bit Buses
- ALU with Dual-Add-With-Saturation Mode
- Variable Length Sequence Decoder
- Pixel Interpolator
- High Performance Memory Interface
  - 32-Bit Memory Data Bus
  - 50 MBytes per Second Maximum
  - 25 MBytes per Second with Standard VRAMs or DRAMs
- 16 General-Purpose Registers
- 4 Gbyte Linear Address Space
- 132-Pin PQFP
- Compatible with the 82750PA

Intel's 82750PB is a 25 MHz wide instruction processor that generates and manipulates pixels. When paired with its companion chip, the 82750DB, and used to implement a DVI Technology video subsystem, the 82750PB provides real time (30 images/sec) pixel processing, real time video compression, interactive motion video playback and real time video effects.

Real time pixel manipulations, including 30 images/sec video compression, are supported by the 25 MHz instruction rate. On-chip instruction RAM provides programmability for execution of a wide range of algorithms that support motion video decompression, text, and 2D and 3D graphics. Inner loops are optimized with the integration of sixteen 16-bit quad ported registers, on-chip DRAM, and two loop counters that provide zero delay two-way branching "free" in any instruction. Two, 16-bit internal buses enable two parallel register transfers on each 82750PB instruction, contributing to the real time performance of the video processing. Another feature that adds to the processing power of the 82750PB is the 16-bit ALU, which includes an 8-bit dual-add-with-saturate operation critical for pixel arithmetic. Other specialized features for pixel processing include a 2D pixel interpolator for image processing functions and a variable length sequence decoder for decoding compressed data.

The 82750PB is implemented using Intel's low-power CHMOS IV Technology and is packaged in a 132-lead space-saving, plastic quad flat pack (PQFP) package.

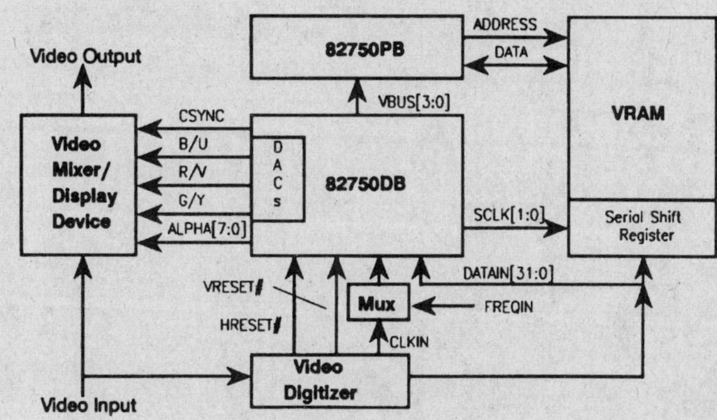

82750PB Subsystem Diagram

8

For the complete data sheet on this device, refer to the Multimedia & Supercomputing Processors Handbook.

February 1991
Order Number: 240854-003

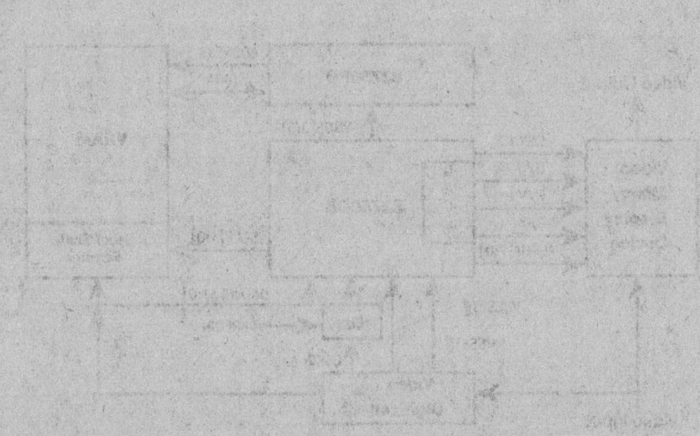

82750DB DISPLAY PROCESSOR

- Programmable Video Timing
  - 28 MHz Operating Frequency
  - Pixel/Line Address Range to 4096
  - Fully Programmable Sync, Equalization, and Serration Components
  - Fully Programmable Blanking and Active Display Start and Stop Times
  - Genlocking Capability
- Flexible Display Characteristics
  - 8-, Pseudo 16-, 16-, and 32-Bit/Pixel Modes
  - Selectable Pixel Widths of 1.0, 1.5, 2.0, 2.5, through 14 Periods of the Input Frequency
  - Support Popular Display Resolutions: VGA, NTSC, PAL, and SECAM
  - On-Chip Triple DAC for Analog RGB/YUV Output
  - Mix Graphics and Video Images on a Pixel by Pixel Basis
  - Real Time Expansion of the Reduced Sample Density Video Color Components (U, V) to Full Resolution
  - Three Independently Addressable Color Palettes
  - Programmable 2X Horizontal Interpolation of Y Channel
  - 16 x 16 x 2-Bit Cursor Map with Independently Programmable 2X Expansion Factors in X and Y Dimensions
  - YUV to RGB Color Space Conversion
  - 2X Vertical Replication of Y, U, and V Data for Displaying Full Motion Video on VGA Monitor
  - Register and Function Compatible with the 82750DA

Intel's 82750DB is a custom designed VLSI chip used for processing and displaying video graphic information. It is register and function compatible with the 82750DA.

Reset inputs allow the 82750DB to be genlocked to an external sync source. By programming internal control registers, this sync can be modified to accommodate a wide variety of scanning frequencies. A large selection of bits/pixel, pixels/line, and pixel widths are programmable, allowing a wide latitude in trading-off image quality vs update rate and VRAM requirements.

The 82750DB can operate in a digitizing mode, wherein it generates timing and control signals to the 82750PB and VRAM, but does not output display information. Besides digitizer support signals and video synchronization, the 82750DB outputs digital and analog RGB or YUV information and an 8-bit digital word of alpha data. This alpha channel data may be used to obtain a fractional mix of 82750DB outputs with another video source.

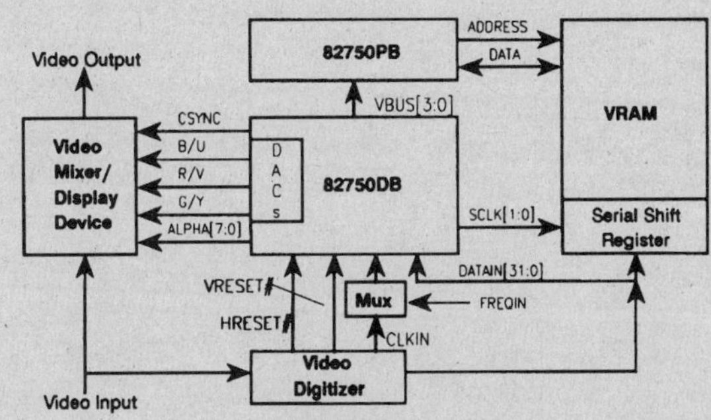

82750DB Subsystem Diagram

For the complete data sheet on this device, refer to the Multimedia & Supercomputing Processors Handbook.

February 1991
Order Number: 240855-003

Development Tools for the 80386, 80286, 80188, 80186 and 8086 Microprocessors

9

intel®

INTEL386™ AND INTEL486™ FAMILY DEVELOPMENT SUPPORT

280808-1

COMPREHENSIVE DEVELOPMENT SUPPORT FOR THE INTEL386™ AND INTEL486™ FAMILIES OF MICROPROCESSORS

The perfect complement to the Intel386™ and i486™ microprocessor family is a comprehensive development solution. Intel provides a complete, synergistic hardware and software development toolset, that delivers full access to the power of the Intel386 and i486 microprocessor family architectures.

Intel development tools are easy to use, yet powerful, with an up-date user interface and productivity boosting features such as symbolic debugging. Each tool is designed to help move your application from the lab to the market.

If what interests you is getting the best product to market in as little time as possible, Intel is the choice.

9

August 1991
Order Number: 280808-006

80C86/80C186/80C286 SOFTWARE DEVELOPMENT TOOLS

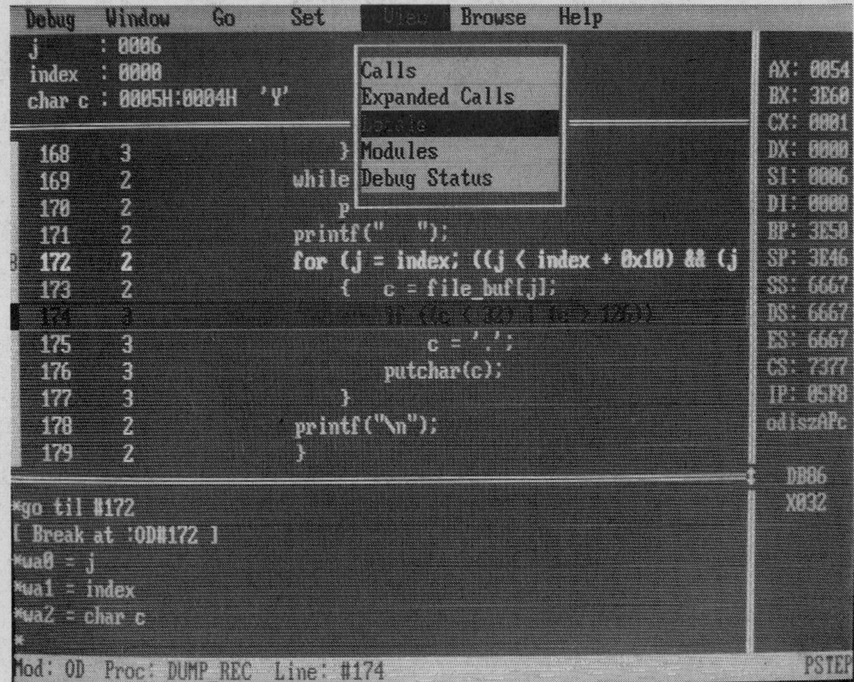

280809–1

Intel supports application development for the 80C86/80C186/80C286 family of microprocessors* with a complete set of development languages and utilities. Intel software tools generate fast and efficient code and are designed to give maximum control over the processor. Most importantly they can decrease the design time of an embedded system and accelerate your product's time-to-market.

FEATURES

- Macro assembler for high-performance code
- ANSI C compiler with numerous processor-specific extensions.
- PL/M compiler for high-level language programs with support for many low-level hardware functions
- FORTRAN for ANSI-compatible, numeric intensive applications
- Pascal to develop modular, portable applications that are easy to maintain
- Linker to link Intel-generated compiler and assembler modules together
- Locator to generate files with absolute addresses for execution from ROM-based systems
- Windowed, interactive source level debugger that works with all Intel languages
- AEDIT Source Code and text editor
- Library manager for creating and maintaining object module libraries
- Complete 8087/80C187/80C287 numeric libraries, including software emulator support
- Object-to-hex conversion utility for EPROM support

*80C86/8088, 80186/80188, 80C186/80C188, 80C186EB/80C188EB, 80C186XL/80C188XL, 80C186EA/80C188EA, 80C186EC/80C188EC, Real Mode 80286, and real mode Intel386™ microprocessors.

October 1991
Order Number: 280809-004

ASM-86, ASM-286 MACRO ASSEMBLER

ASM-86 and ASM-286 are used to translate symbolic assembly language source into relocatable object code where utmost speed, small code size and hardware control are critical.

HIGHLIGHTS AND BENEFITS

- Macro facility saves development and maintenance time, since common code sequences need only be developed once.
- Simplified instruction set makes program development easier.
- Saves development time by performing extensive checks on consistent usage of variables and labels. Inconsistencies are detected when the program is assembled, before linking or debugging is started.

iC-86, iC-286 COMPILER

Intel's iC-86 and iC-286 bring the full power of the C programming language to embedded applications based on the 80C86/80C186 family of microprocessors. iC-86 can also be used to develop real mode programs to be executed on the 80C286 or the Intel386™ microprocessors.

HIGHLIGHTS AND BENEFITS

- Generates compact efficient code — easily loaded into ROM-based systems.
- Highly optimized with four levels of optimization, including a jump optimizer and improved register manipulation via register history.
- Produces ROMable code — can be loaded directly into embedded target systems. Libraries completely ROMable, retargetable, and reentrant.
- Supports small, compact, medium, and large memory segmentation models. Allows memory modules to be mixed using "near" and "far" pointers.
- Extensive debug information, including type information and symbols, increases programming productivity.
- Built-in functions for automatic machine code generation improve compile-time and run-time performance. Eliminates need for in-line assembly code or making calls to assembly functions. Allows registers, I/O ports, interrupts and the numerics chips to be controlled directly in C and not in assembly code.
- ANSI C-conforming. Fully linkable with other Intel 80C86/80C186/80C286 languages such as ASM and PL/M. Allows programmers to choose optimal language(s) for application.

PL/M-86, PL/M-286 COMPILER

PL/M-86 and PL/M-286 are high-level programming languages designed to support the software requirements of advanced 16-bit microprocessors. The PL/M languages provide both the productivity advantages of a high-level language and access to the low-level hardware features found in the assembly language.

HIGHLIGHTS AND BENEFITS

- Modular and structured programming support. Final applications easier to understand, maintain, and support.
- Includes extensive list of built-in functions, e.g., TYPE CONVERSION functions, STRING manipulations, and functions for interrogating hardware flags.
- Define interrupt handling procedures using the INTERRUPT attribute. Compiler generates code to save and restore all registers for interrupt procedures.
- Compile-time options to increase flexibility of PL/M compiler. Options include four optimization levels, conditional compilation, inclusion of common PL/M source files from disk, symbol cross-referencing, and optional assembly language code in list file.
- Supports seven data types. Allows compiler to perform signed, unsigned, and floating-point arithmetic.
- Object modules compatible with all other object modules generated by Intel 80C86/80C186/80C286 languages.

FORTRAN-86, FORTRAN-286 COMPILER

FORTRAN-86 and FORTRAN-286 meet the ANSI FORTRAN 77 Language Subset Specification and include nearly all of the features of the full standard. This compatibility assures portability of existing FORTRAN programs and shortens the development process, since programmers are immediately productive without retraining.

HIGHLIGHTS AND BENEFITS

- Extensive support for numeric processing tasks and applications.
- Support for single, double, double extended precision, complex and double-complex floating point data types.
- Supports REALMATH IEEE floating point standard
- Full support for all other data types: integer, logical, and character
- Optional hardware (8087/80C287 numeric data processors) or software (simulator) floating-point support at link time.

PASCAL-86, PASCAL-286 COMPILER

Pascal-86 and Pascal-286 conform to the ISO Pascal standard, facilitating application portability, training, and maintenance. A well-defined and documented run-time operating system interface allows the user to execute applications under user-designed operating systems as an alternative to the development system environment.

HIGHLIGHTS AND BENEFITS

- Additional microcomputer support features such as interrupt handling, direct port I/O, and separate compilation.
- Modules are compatible and linkable with modules written in other Intel 80C86/80C186/80C286 languages.

LINK-86, BIND-286 TOOLS

Link-86 and Bind-286 combine multiple object modules into a single program and resolve references between independently compiled modules. Both tools can increase productivity by enabling the user to use modular programming, making applications easier to design, test, and maintain.

HIGHLIGHTS AND BENEFITS

- Incremental linking allows new modules to be easily added to existing software.
- Final linked module can be either a bound load-time- locatable module or a relocatable module.
- .EXE option allows modules to be generated that can be executed directly in a DOS system.
- Standard modules can be reused in different applications, decreasing software development time.

LOC-86, BUILD-286 TOOLS

The LOC-86 and Build-286 tools convert relocatable 80C86/80C186/80C286 object modules into absolute object modules. Both will allow you to assign addresses; Build-286 also enables you to create protected mode data structures, e.g., tasks that will execute in protected mode.

HIGHLIGHTS AND BENEFITS

- Default address assignment algorithm automatically assigns absolute addresses to object modules prior to loading code into target system. Frees user from concern regarding the final arrangement of the object code in memory.
- User has ability to override the control and specify absolute addresses for various Segments, Classes, and Groups in memory.
- User can reserve various parts of memory.
- Simplifies set up of bootstrap loader and initialization code for ROM-based systems. Very important and beneficial for embedded application development.
- Optional print file containing diagnostic information helpful in debugging may be generated.

LIB-86, LIB-286 TOOLS

Both Lib-86 and Lib-286 create and maintain libraries of software object modules. Standard modules can be placed in a library and linked to your application using the LINK-86/BIND-286 tools.

OH-86 OBJECT-TO-HEXADECIMAL CONVERTER

The OH-86 utiltity converts Intel 80C86/186/286 object modules into standard hexadecimal format, allowing the code to be loaded directly into PROM using industry standard PROM programmers.

NUMERICS SUPPORT LIBRARIES

The 8027/80C187/80C287 numerics libraries fully support the 8087, 80C187, and 80C287 math coprocessors, with or without the math coprocessor in the final system; numeric functions may be processed by the math coprocessor or by the corresponding software emulator.

Numerics Software Emulator

- For applications without a math coprocessor
- Executes instructions as though coprocessor present; functionality identical to math coprocessor.
- Ideal for prototyping and debugging floating point application code independent of hardware; supports portable code.

Numerics Support Library

- For applications with a math coprocessor
- Provide Intel ASM, C, PL/M, and FORTRAN users with enhanced numeric data processing capability; easy to do floating point math.

HIGHLIGHTS AND BENEFITS

- 4 functionally distinct libraries support floating point operations.
  - Common elementary function library: algebraic, logarithmic, exponential, trignometric and hyperbolic operations on real and complex numbers. Real-to-integer conversions
  - Initialization library: Set up the numerics processing environment (math coprocessor or software emulator).
  - Decimal conversion library: Converts floating point numbers from one binary storage format to another, from ASCII decimal strings to binary floating point format, or vise- versa.
  - Error handling library: Simplifies coding numerics exception handlers.
- All support library modules in OMF-86 format; can be linked with object output of any Intel language.
- All library routines reentrant and ROMable.
- Meets industry standard (ANSI/IEEE standard for binary floating point arithmetic, 754-1985)

DB-86 SOURCE LEVEL DEBUGGER

DB-86 is a DOS-hosted, high-level source code debugger for programs written in C, PL/M, FORTRAN, and Pascal. Its powerful, source-oriented interface allows users to focus their efforts on finding bugs, not learning how to use the debug environment.

HIGHLIGHTS AND FEATURES

- Drop-down menus and on-line help decrease learning time for beginning users.
- Watch windows, conditional breakpoints, trace points and fixed and temporary breakpoints can be set and modified as needed.
- Browse Source and Call Stack, review processor registers, observe watch window variables — all accessed via a pull down menu or single keystroke.
- Uses extensive debug information available in Intel languages to display program variables in their respective type formats.
- Provides support for overlayed programs and the math coprocessors.

AEDIT SOURCE CODE AND TEXT EDITOR

Aedit is a full-screen text editing system designed specifically for software engineers and technical writers. The output file is the pure ASCII text (or HEX code) you input — no special characters or proprietary formats. Its numerous features and advanced capabilities make it an excellent tool to support the 80C86/80C186/80C286 development environment.

HIGHLIGHTS AND BENEFITS

- Complete range of editing support—from document processing to HEX code entry and modification
- Supports system escape for quick execution of PC-DOS System level commands
- Full macro support for complex or repetitive editing tasks
- Supports multiple operating systems including DOS and iRMX
- Dual file support with optional split-screen windowing
- No limit to file size or line length
- Quick response with an easy to use menu driven interface
- Configurable and extensible for complete control of the editing process.

WORLDWIDE SERVICE, SUPPORT, AND TRAINING

To augment its development tools, Intel offers a full array of seminars, classes, and workshops, field application engineering expertise, hotline technical support and on-site service.

Intel also offers a Software Support package which includes technical software information, telephone support, automatic distribution of software and documentation updates, access to the "Tooltalk" electronic bulletin board. "iComments" publication, remote diagnostic software, and a development tools troubleshooting guide.

Intel's Hardware Support package includes technical hardware information, telephone support, warranty on parts, labor, material, and on-site hardware support.

SUMMARY

Intel provides a complete software development toolset that delivers full access to the 80C86/80C186/80C286 microprocessors. The development tools are easy to use, yet powerful, with productivity boosting features such as source-level symbolic debugging and an up-to-date user interface. Each tool is designed to help you move quickly your application from the lab to the market.

ORDERING INFORMATION

80C86/80C186

D86ASM86KIT	ASM-86	Assember for PC XT or AT system (or compatible) running DOS 3.0 or higher
R86ASM86SU	ASM-86	Assembler for Intel 80C86/3XX systems iRMX 86 operating system
R286ASM86EU	ASM-86	Assembler for Intel 80C286/3XX systems running iRMX II™ operating system

Note: ASM-86 includes Macro Assembler, Link-86, Loc-86, Lib-86, Cross-Reference utility, OH-86, Numerics Support, and DB-86 Source Level Debugger. (DB-86 available in DOS version only.)

D86C86NL	iC-86	Software Package for IBM PC XT/AT running PC DOS 3.0 or higher
R86C86SU	iC-86	Software Package for Intel System 80C86/3XX running iRMX 86 operating system
D86PLM86NL	PL/M-86	Software Package for IBM PC XT/AT running PC DOS 3.0 or higher
R86PLM86SU	PL/M-86	Software Package for Intel System 80C86/3XX running iRMX 86 operating system
D86PAS86NL	PASCAL-86	Software Package for IBM PC XT/AT running PC DOS 3.0 or higher
R86PAS86SU	PASCAL-86	Software Package for Intel System 80C86/3XX running iRMX 86
D86EDNL	AEDIT	AEDIT Source Code Editor for IBM PC XT/AT running PC DOS 3.0 or higher
D86FOR86NL	FORTRAN-86	Software Package for PC XT/AT (or compatible) running PC DOS 3.0 or higher
R86FOR86SU	FORTRAN-86	Software Package for Intel System 80C86/3XX running iRMX 86 operating system
R286PLM86EU	PL/M-86	Software package for Intel System 80C286/3XX running iRMX II operating system.

9

ORDERING INFORMATION

80C286

R286ASM286EU	ASM-286	Software package for Intel System 80C286/3XX running iRMX II operating system.
R286C286EU	iC-286	Software package for Intel System 80C286/3XX running iRMX II operating system
R286EDI286EU	AEDIT	AEDIT Source Code Editor for Intel System 80C286/3XX running iRMX II operating system
R286FOR286EU	FORTRAN-286	Software package for Intel System 80C286/3XX running iRMX II operating system
R286PAS286EU	Pascal-286	Software package for Intel System 80C286/3XX running iRMX II operating system
R286PLM286EU	PL/M-286	Software package for Intel System 80C286/3XX running iRMX II operating system
D86ASM286NL	ASM-286	Software package for IBM PC XT/AT running PC DOS 3.0 or higher.
D86C286NL	iC-286	Software package for IBM PC XT/AT running PC DOS 3.0 or higher.
D86FOR286NL	FORTRAN-286	Software package for IBM PC XT/AT running PC DOS 3.0 or higher.
D86PAS286NL	Pascal-286	Software package for IBM PC XT/AT running PC DOS 3.0 or higher.
D86PLM286NL	PL/M-286	Software package for IBM PC XT/AT running PC DOS 3.0 or higher.

intel®

DB86A ARTIC SOFTWARE DEBUGGER

280914-1

Multitasking Source Level Debugger

The DB86A ARTIC debugger from Intel is a powerful source-level debugger designed to support the development of multitasking applications targeted to run on the full family of IBM* ARTIC cards. The DB86A ARTIC debugger is hosted on an IBM PC/AT*, PS/2* or compatible computer running DOS or OS/2* (DOS compatibility box only). Using an RS232 link to an IBM ARTIC card, the debugger contains control and monitoring capabilities for on-target software debugging. The DB86A debugger delivers an optimum debugging environment for application code generated by IBM C/2*, IBM MASM/2*, Microsoft C*, and Microsoft MASM*.

The DB86A debugger features a contemporary windowed human interface, symbolic source level debug, tasking controls, extensive breakpoint modes, and flexible stepping capabilities. This multitasking debug environment boosts productivitiy by allowing you to focus efforts on finding bugs more quickly, and reducing time-to-market.

DB86A Debugger Features

- Menu-driven Windowed Human Interface
- Source Level Debug with various Source Window and Watch Window Operations
- Multitasking Debug Support
- High-level and Assembly Language Symbolic Debugging
- Extensive Breakpoint and Stepping Capabilities
- Powerful Procedural Command Language
- On-line Help Facility
- Built-in Assembler and Disassembler
- Memory and Register Manipulations
- Intel Service and Support

9

August 1991
Order Number: 280914-002

FEATURES

Windowed Human Interface

The DB86A Artic Debugger offers a windowed user interface that is easy for both experienced and new users.

Pull-down menus provide a set of commonly used debug operations, shortening learning curves. Many debugging functions can be executed with a single key stroke. Custom debug commands and the command line interface offer experienced users increased efficiency. Multiple windows simultaneously display source code, watch variables, and registers. Source breakpoints support the point-and-shoot technique of debugging, or breakpoints can be easily set through the source window. When the debugger completes a breakpoint or stepping operation, the various windows are updated. The watch window can track up to six program variables. The on-line help facility provides command syntax and explanation as well as error descriptions.

Event Monitor Capability

DB86A provides many ways to monitor events. There are four conditional breakpoints, ten source breakpoints, ten temporary breakpoints, and ten passpoints. Each type of breakpoint meets different debugging needs. The stepping commands not only allow execution of one machine-level instruction or one high-level language statement at a time, they also permit stepping over or stepping through a procedure until it returns.

Procedural Command Language

The command language of the DB86A debugger provides control constructs, procedures, and debug variables allowing the user to extend and customize the functionality of the debugger. Control constructs (e.g. If...else, do...while) facilitate the grouping of a sequence of debugger commands and control the execution of the sequence. For debug sequences that are repeated frequently, the user can define debug procedures containing a sequence of debugger commands, control constructs, and debug variables. DB86A debugger comes with a set of predefined debug procedures that display various ARTIC system data structures such as interface blocks, task tables, and task control block tables.

Multitasking Debug Support

The DB86A debugger delivers control and monitor capabilities to simplify multitasking debug. You can download multiple tasks to the target system, and easily select any task for viewing and debugging.

Corresponding windows are automatically updated when a task hits a breakpoint. Tasks can be suspended and resumed. Breakpoints can be set for all, or for specific tasks. Qualifiers are provided with the debugger commands to facilitate multitasking debug.

Symbolic Debug Capabilities

The debugger makes full use of the symbolic and typing information passed by the code translators. Source code symbolics are enabled in debugging operations and displays. The debugger supports easy browsing through modules in each task. The Callstack feature creates a snapshot of the active call chain, and call stack browsing lets you navigate through the source code of the procedure call chain. Task memory and registers can be displayed and modified easily. An on-line assembler is provided for in-target code patching.

Worldwide Service, Support, and Training

To augment its development tools, Intel offers a full array of seminars, classes, workshops, field application engineering expertise, hotline technical support, and on-site service.

Intel also offers a Software Support contract which includes technical software information, telephone support, automatic distributions of software and documentation updates, *iCOMMENTS* magazine, remote diagnostic software, and a development tools troubleshooting guide.

Intel Development Tools also offers a 30-day, money-back guarantee to customers who are not satisfied after purchasing any Intel development tool.

SPECIFICATIONS

Host System Requirements

IBM PC/AT or IBM PS/2 or fully compatible computers with the following minimum configurations:

- Minimum of 900Kbytes free hard disk space for DB86A
- 640Kbytes of RAM recommended; DB86A uses a minimum of 360Kbytes of RAM
- A serial port (COM1 or COM2)
- DOS V3.3 or later, OS/2 V1.2 (DOS Compatibility Box Only)
- One floppy drive capable of reading 5.25″ diskettes or 3.5″ diskettes

Target System Requirements

- One ARTIC RS232 serial port
- 8 Kbytes free RAM on the target ARTIC Board for DB86A debug support task
- Target system containing one of the following ARTIC cards:
  IBM Realtime Interface Coprocessor
  IBM Realtime Interface Coprocessor Multiport
  IBM Realtime Interface Coprocessor Multiport Model 2
  IBM X.25 Interface Coprocessor/2
  IBM Realtime Interface Coprocessor Multiport/2
  IBM Realtime Interface Coprocessor Portmaster/A

INTEL386™ FAMILY IN-CIRCUIT EMULATORS

280850–1

ACCURATE AND SOPHISTICATED EMULATION FOR THE INTEL386™ FAMILY OF MICROPROCESSORS

Intel386™ In-circuit Emulators are the cornerstone of the optimum development solution for the Intel386 Family of microprocessors. The ICE™-386 family of development tools delivers complete access and control over the Intel386.

Intel386 emulators feature realtime emulation to 33 MHz, source-level symbolic debugging, and a powerful windowed human interface. Intel product quality and world class technical support and service insure that your design requirements are met on time. And your investment in development tools is protected via interchangeable probes for the Intel386 DX, Intel386 SX, and Intel376™ microprocessors. Support for the Intel386 SL and Intel486™ is provided via an ICE upgrade package.

Maximize your productivity with Intel development tools. Reduced time to market and increased market acceptance for your microprocessor-based product are the benefits when Intel is the choice.

August 1991
Order Number: 280850-005

FEATURES

INTEL ICE™ FAMILY IN-CIRCUIT EMULATOR FEATURES

- ICE™-386 DX and ICE-386 SX emulators feature a powerful source-level, windowed human interface
- Unparalleled support of all of the Intel386 operating modes opens the door to the full potential of the Intel386 architecture
- Non-intrusive, 100% accurate emulation and execution history to processor speeds of 33 MHz
- Relocatable Expansion Memory (REM) Board options provide 2 MByte of mappable memory
- Versatile event recognition makes short work of uncovering complex bugs
- Dynamic trace display of bus and execution information during emulation
- Support for PGA and PQFP component packages
- Integrated software development environment provides complete access to the power of the Intel386 family
- Available on DOS and on Hewlett-Packard HP9000 UNIX*

FEATURES

100% ACCURATE EMULATION

Intel386 Family In-Circuit Emulators utilize technology that accesses internal processor states that are otherwise invisible. Intel386 microprocessors fetch and execute instructions in parallel; fetched instructions are not necessarily executed in any order. Because of this, an emulator without access to the core of the component is prone to error in determining what actually occurs inside the microprocessor. With Intel's technology, an Intel386 In-Circuit Emulator displays real-time execution history with one hundred percent accuracy.

OPENING THE DOOR TO PROTECTED MODE

The Intel386 family of In-circuit Emulators opens the door to the full potential of the architecture with unparalleled support of protected mode. Not only does the emulator display and modify task state segments and global, local, and interrupt descriptor tables (with symbolic access to all descriptor components), but emulator functions are sensitive to the operating mode of the processor, greatly improving ease of use. For instance, while debugging protected mode code, it is easy to change any field in any descriptor, including privelege, level, segment limit, segment access rights, etc.

The Intel386 family of In-circuit Emulators supports all aspects of protected mode addressing, including paged virtual memory. Processor tables are used to automatically translate virtual addresses to linear and physical addresses. Physical addresses can be translated to symbolic references to indicate the module, procedure, or data segment accessed. And when debugging a memory management system, components of the page table and directory can be displayed and modified.

FLEXIBLE AND VERSATILE EVENT RECOGNITION

Flexibility and versatility in event recognition makes short work of uncovering the most complex bugs. Bus event recognition circuitry may be used to trigger on specific or masked data input, output, read, written, or fetched at a physical address or range of addresses. Or on-chip debug registers may be used to trigger on virtual, linear, or symbolic addresses being executed, accessed, or written.

Versatility shows in other triggering options such as the ability to break upon a task switch, an external signal from another emulator or a logic analyzer, multiple occurrences of an event, a full trace buffer, halt or shutdown cycles, or interrupt acknowledge. And up to four sequential event triggers can be combined with a high-level construct to make it easier locating those hard to find real-time bugs.

The Intel386 family of In-circuit Emulators captures all bus activity and, as an option, execution information, into a trace buffer of 4 K frames. Information is captured in logic analyzer style, including the address and data busses, as well as a variety of important control signals. With PRE, POST, and CENTER collection modes it is possible to focus the trace buffer contents around a specified trigger event. ICE-386 DX also allows the user to selectively remove wait-states from trace.

ACCESSING THE POWER

The DOS hosted Intel386 DX and Intel386 SX emulators feature a windowed, menu-driven, human interface which provides easy access to the power of these emulators. This interface features pull-down menus, pop-up windows and templates for common actions such as configuring the emulator and setting breakpoints

A source code window allows display of program code as high-level source and/or assembly code, and most importantly, allows "point and shoot" breakpoints. This powerful feature, combined with the ability to view any section of program code in the source window, means that setting a breakpoint anywhere in the program is as simple as moving the cursor to a line of code and hitting a function key.

Multiple windows may be opened for simultaneous viewing of not only source code, but also memory, trace buffer contents, variables, and registers. All of these features are accessible from pull-down menus or function keys, making it easy for novice or infrequent users to get the most of every debug session.

Customized procedures with variables and literal definitions can be created to assist in debugging or for manufacturing test or field service applications.

FEATURES

SPEEDING DEVELOPMENT WITH SYMBOLICS

Intel386 processor data structures, such as registers, descriptor tables, and page tables, can be examined and modified using symbolic names. And with the symbolic debugging information that is a feature of Intel languages, memory locations can be accessed using symbolic references to the source program (such as a procedure and variable names, line numbers, or program labels) rather than via cumbersome virtual, linear, or physical addresses. The type information of variables (such as byte, word, record, or array) can also be displayed.

ADDITIONAL FEATURES

The Intel386 In-circuit Emulator can be combined with a variety of devices. I/O lines synchronize emulation starts and triggers with external tools such as a logic analyzer or another emulator. An optional Time Tag Board synchronizes multiple Intel386 emulators and records timestamp information in the trace buffer with 20 nanosecond resolution. An Optional Clips Pod allows 8 user defined data lines to be captured and displayed in the trace. The bus isolation board buffers the emulation processor from faults in an untested target. And with the Stand-Alone Self-Test board the emulator can be used to debug software before the target system is functional, as well as execute confidence tests.

RELOCATABLE EXPANSION MEMORY BOARDS

In addition to the 128 KBytes of mappable memory that is supplied with ICE-386 in-circuit emulators, the optional REM386DX and REM386SX376 Relocatable Expansion Memory boards provide an additional 2 MBytes of mappable memory. The memory is 2 wait-states up to 16 MHz, and 5 wait-states beyond 16 MHz. To reduce physical intrusion into the target system, these boards are shaped like, and connect to, the ICE processor module.

COMPONENT INTERCONNECT

Component interconnect between the ICE and the processor on your system is accomplished using either direct probe connection to the target system, or by using an optional hinge cable adapter. Hinge cable adapters allow the ICE to access components in hard-to-reach cases and in the case of the 80386 SX, to provide support for surface mounted devices via ONCE™ mode. ONCE mode is a mechanism of tri-stating the component pins, thus allowing a system with a surface mounted CPU to be emulated without removing the component. The dimensions and clearance requirements of the adapter are shown in the 386SXONCE Adapter Dimension figure on the following pages.

THE INVESTMENT PICTURE

As designs move from one Intel386 Family processor to another, the reinvestment cost is limited to probes that adapt the emulator base to the specific processor. Beside cost savings, migration from one processor to another is accomplished with minimum disruption in the engineering environment, as the same command language applies to the entire emulator family.

Upgrades are also available to support the Intel386 SL microprocessor and the Intel486™ family of microprocessors.

9

FEATURES

SOFTWARE COMPLETES THE SYSTEM

Intel wraps a comprehensive software development system around the emulator to deliver the most complete development environment available from a single vendor. Like the emulator, Intel's software development system supports every aspect of the Intel386 architecture.

Overlooked at times is the fact that a significant part of developing a system is making sure the code works. Intel languages and software debugger integrate seamlessly with the Intel386 emulator and provide the symbolics so important for efficient debugging. By using Intel software tools with the Intel386 emulator the full power of Intel development solution can be utilized.

The software development system offers a broad choice of languages with object code compatibility so performance can be maximized by using different languages for specialized, performance critical modules. Architectural extensions in the high-level languages allows hardware features such as interrupts, input/output, or flags to be controlled directly, avoiding the tediousness of coding assembly language routines.

Intel's software portfolio includes a unique, sophisticated, and very powerful system builder, which simplifies the generation of protected mode systems from simple flat model systems to the most complex paged multiple privelege level, multi-tasking systems. To further reduce the effort necessary to integrate software into the final target configuration, Intel tools produce ROM-able code directly from the development system.

WORLDWIDE SERVICE, SUPPORT, AND TRAINING

To augment its development tools, Intel offers a full array of seminars, classes, workshops, field application engineering expertise, hotline technical support, and on-site service.

Intel also offers a Software Support contract which includes technical software information, automatic distributions of software and documentation updates, *iCOMMENTS* publication, remote diagnostic software, and a development tools troubleshooting guide.

Intel's 90-day Hardware Support package includes technical hardware information, telephone support, warranty on parts, labor, material, and on-site hardware support.

Intel Development Tools also offers a 30-day, money-back guarantee to customers who are not satisfied after purchasing any Intel development tool.

ICE™-386 FAMILY SPECIFICATIONS AND REQUIREMENTS

Unless otherwise noted, the following specifications apply to ICE-386 DX 33, ICE-386 DX 25, ICE-386 SX 20, and ICE-376 20.

HOST SYSTEM REQUIREMENTS

The user supplied host system can be either an IBM* PC/AT* or Personal System/2* Model 60. Host system requirements to run the emulator include the following:

- DOS version 3.3 or 4.01 (All ICE Products) or Hewlett Packard HP9000 UNIX (386 DX Only)
- 640 KBytes of RAM in conventional memory
- 1 MByte of expanded memory (e.g., an Above™ board managed by a driver such as EMM.SYS, or an expanded memory manager such as QEMM* or 386MAX™ which conforms to the Lotus*/Intel®/Microsoft* Expanded Memory Specification, version 4.0 or later)
- A 20 MB hard disk
- A serial port or the National Instruments GPIB-PCII*, GPIB-PCIIA*, or MC-GPIB* board
- A math coprocessor if either the optional time tag board is used or if a math coprocessor resides on the target system

ICE™-386 FAMILY SPECIFICATIONS AND REQUIREMENTS

ELECTRICAL CHARACTERISTICS

100–120V or 220–240V selectable
50–60 Hz
2 amps (AC max) @ 120V
1 amp (AC max) @ 240V

ENVIRONMENTAL CHARACTERISTICS

Operating temperature:	+10°C to +40°C (50°F to 104°F)
Operating Humidity:	Maximum of 85% relative humidity, non-condensing

TESTED HOT SYSTEMS INCLUDE:

- IBM PC/AT (286) with MS-DOS 3.3 and an Intel Above Board with 1.5 MBytes of memory
- IBM PC/AT with Intel Inboard™ 386 with MS-DOS 3.3 and 3 MBytes of memory with a QEMM* or 386Max* memory manager
- Compaq* DESKPRO 386* with COMDOS 3.31 and 3 MBytes of memory with QEMM or 386MAX memory manager
- Intel Sys 301 with MS-DOS 3.3 and 2 MBytes of memory with a QEMM, EMM, or 386Max memory manager
- IBM PS/2 Model 80 with PC-DOS 4.01 and 2 MBytes of memory with QEMM or 386Max memory manager

Note: Future versions of ICE-386 Family emulators will use DOS extenders. Host systems will need at least a 386 SX or 386 DX based host with 4 MBytes of RAM.

THE EMULATOR'S PHYSICAL CHARACTERISTICS

Unit	Width		Height		Length	
	inches	cm	inches	cm	inches	cm
Base Unit	13.4	34.0	4.6	11.7	11.0	27.9
Processor Module	3.8	9.7	0.7	1.8	4.4	11.2
Optional Isolation Board	3.8	9.7	0.5	1.3	4.4	11.2
Power Supply	7.7	19.6	4.1	10.4	11.0	27.9
User Cable	1.9	4.8			17.3	43.9
100-Pin Target-Adapter Cable	2.3	5.3	0.5	1.3	5.1	13.0
88-Pin Target-Adapter Cable	2.3	5.3	0.5	1.3	5.8	14.7
Serial Cable					144	366
Optional Clips Pod	3.3	8.4	0.8	2.0	6.0	15.2

The Processor Module and Bus Isolation Board Dimensions

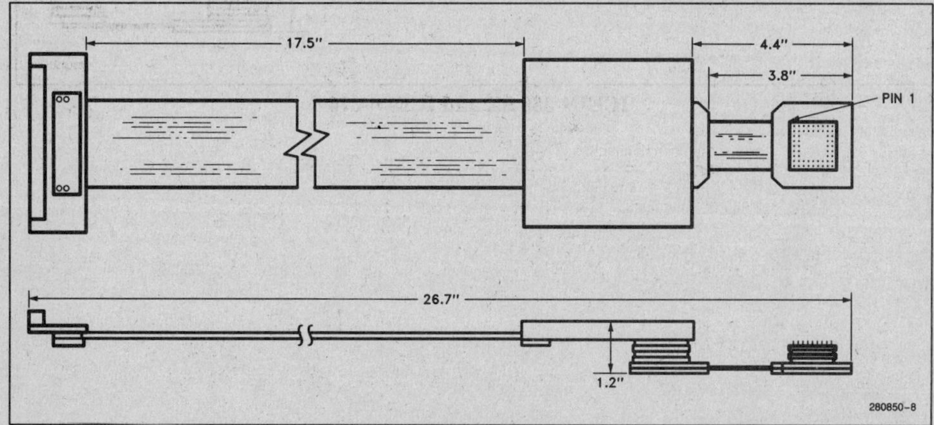

ICE™-386 DX

9

ICE™-386 FAMILY SPECIFICATIONS AND REQUIREMENTS

***The Processor Module and Bus Isolation Board Dimensions** (Continued)*

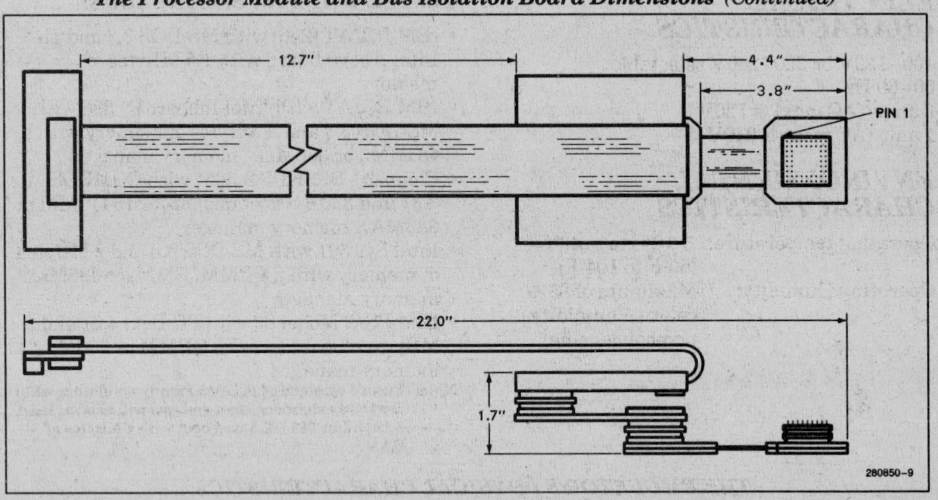

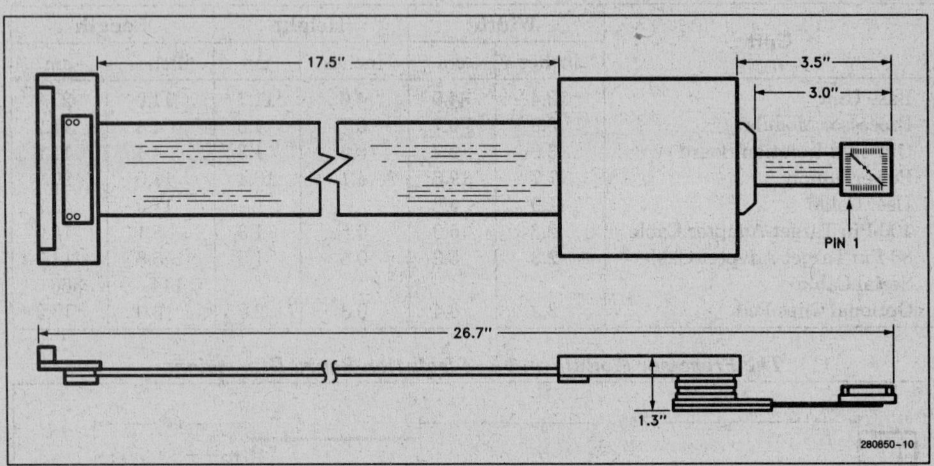

ICE™-386 SX and ICE™-376

ICE™-386 FAMILY SPECIFICATIONS AND REQUIREMENTS

***The Processor Module and Bus Isolation Board Dimensions** (Continued)*

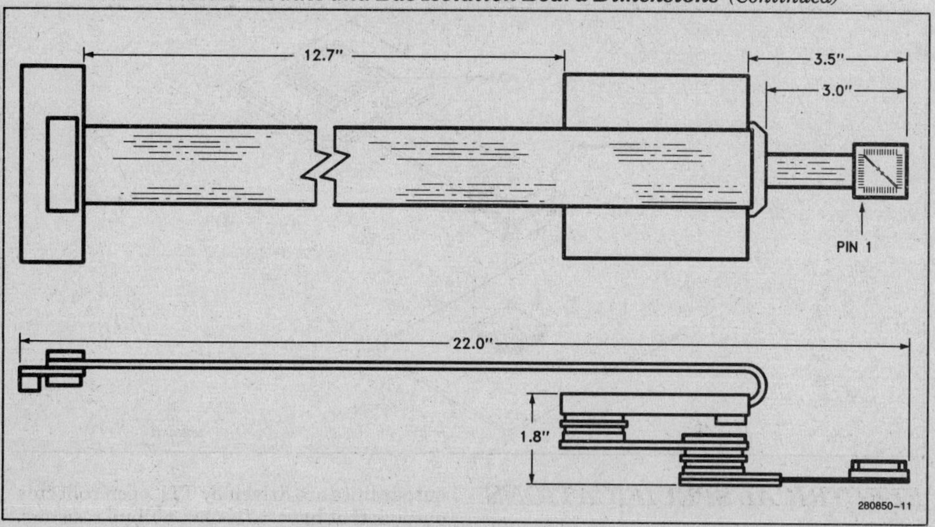

ICE-386 SX and ICE-376 Dimensions

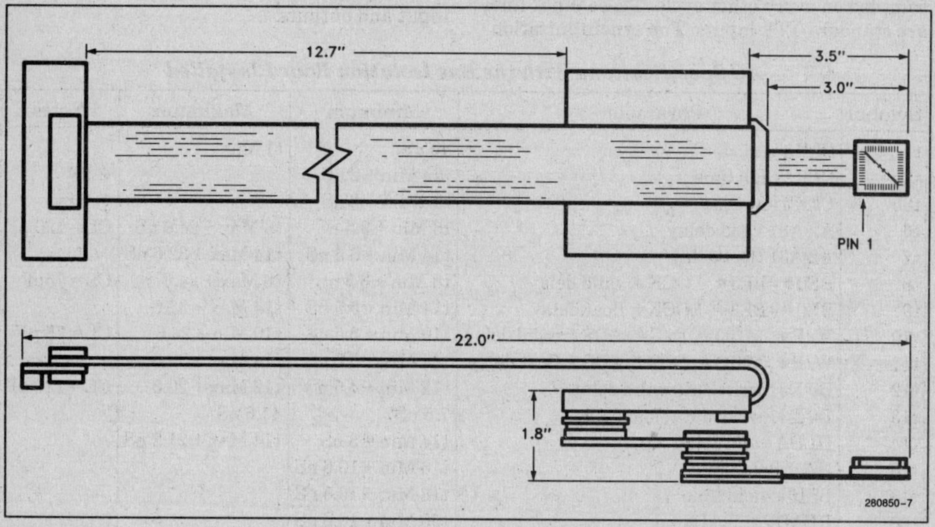

ICE™-386 FAMILY SPECIFICATIONS AND REQUIREMENTS

386SXONCE Hinge Cable Adapter Dimensions

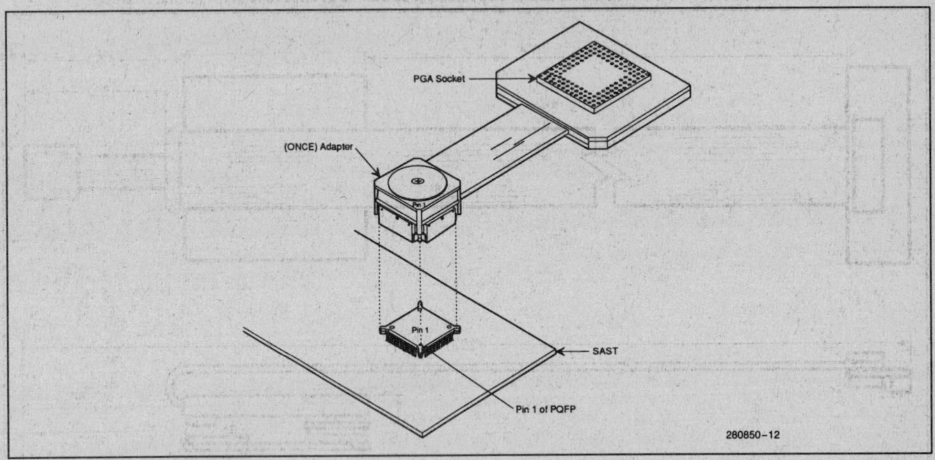

ELECTRICAL SPECIFICATIONS

The synchronization input lines must be valid for at least four CLK2 cycles as they are only sampled on every other cycle. These input lines are standard TTL inputs. The synchronization output lines are driven by TTL open collector outputs that have 4.7K-ohm pull-up resistors. The synchronization input and output signals on the optional clips pod are standard TTL input and outputs.

AC Specifications With the Bus Isolation Board Installed

Symbol	Parameter	Minimum	Maximum	Notes
t1	CLK2 period	40 nS	t1 Max	
t2a	CLK2 high time	t2a Min + 2 nS		@ 2V
t3b	CLK2 low time	t3b Min + 2 nS		@ 0.8v
t6	A2-A31 valid delay	t6 Min + 3.5 nS	t6 Max + 24.6 nS	CL = 120 pF
t7	A2-A31 float delay	t14 Min + 5.5 nS	t14 Max + 32.6 nS	
t8	BE0#-BE3#, LOCK# valid delay	t8 Min + 3.5 nS	t8 Max + 24.6	CL = 75pF
t9	BE0#-BE3#, LOCK# float delay	t14 Min + 5.5 nS	t14 Max + 32.6	
t10	W/R#, M/IO#, D/C#, ADS# valid delay	t10 Min + 3.5 nS	t10 Min + 24.6	CL = 75 pF
t11	W/R#, M/IO#, D/C#, ADS# float delay	t14 Min + 5.5 nS	t14 Max + 32.6	
t12	D0-D31 write data valid delay	t12 Min + 4.5 nS	t12 Max + 20.6	CL = 120 pF
t13	D0-D31 write data float delay	7.5 nS	41.6 nS	
t14	HLDA valid delay	t14 Min = 3 nS	t14 Max + 21.2 nS	
t16	NA# hold time	t16 Min + 10.6 nS		
t18	BS16# hold time	t18 Min + 10.6 nS		
t20	READY# hold time	t20 Min + 10.6 nS		
t21	D0-D31 read setup time	t21 Min + 8.5 nS		
t22	D0-D31 read hold time	t22 Min + 7.6 nS		
t24	HOLD hold time	t24 Min + 10.6 nS		
t25	RESET setup time	t25 Min + 2.1 nS		
t26	RESET hold time	t26 Min + 2.1 nS		
t28	NMI, INTR hold time	t28 Min + 10.6 nS		
t30	PEREQ, ERROR#, BUSY# hold time	t30 Min + 10.6 nS		

SPECIFICATIONS

ICE™-386 DX 25/33 Emulator DC Specifications Emulator Capacitance Specifications

Symbol	Description	386 DX Typical	386 DX w/ Hinge Cable	386 SX and 376 w/ Hinge Cable
C_{IN}	Input Capacitance			
	CLK2	35 pF	45 pF	55 pF
	READY#, NMI, BS16#	25 pF	35 pF	35 pF
	HOLD, BUSY#,	10 pF	20 pF	20 pF
	PEREQ, NA#, INTR, ERROR#, RESET	20 pF	30 pF	30 pF
C_{OUT}	Output or I/O Capacitance			
	D0–D31	40 pF	50 pF	50 pF
	A2–A31	30 pF	40 pF	40 pF
	BE0#–BE3#			30 pF
	D/C#	35 pF	45 pF	30 pF
	W/R#	40 pF	50 pF	55 pF
	ADS#, M/IO#	25 pF	35 pF	35 pF
	LOCK#, HLDA	25 pF	25 pF	55 pF

ICE™-386 DX 25/33 Emulator DC Specifications without the Bus Isolation Board Installed

Item	Description	Max	Notes
PM-I_{CC}	Processor Module Supply Current Component	I_{CC} + 1.5A	
I_{IH}	Input High Leakage Current	0.020 μA	1
	A2–A31, BE0#–BE3#, D0–D31, HLDA, NMI, BS16#	0.010 μA	1
	ADS#, M/IO#, LOCK#, READY#	0.010 μA	1
	W/R#, D/C#	0.030 μA	1
	CLK2	0.015 μA	1
	RESET	0.005 μA	2
I_{IL}	Input Low Leakage Current		
	A2–A31, BE0#–BE3#, D0–D31	0.600 μA	1
	HLDA, NMI, BS16#	0.010 μA	1
	ADS#, M/IO#, LOCK#, READY#	0.010 μA	1
	W/R#	0.110 μA	1
	D/C#	0.610 μA	1
	CLK2	0.015 μA	1
	RESET	0.005 μA	2

Note 1: Not tested. These specifications include the 80386 component and all additional emulator loading.
Note 2: The target-adapter cable adds a propagation delay of 0.5 ns.

SPECIFICATIONS

ICE™-386 SX or ICE™-386 20 MHz Emulator DC Specifications without the Bus Isolation Board Installed

Item	Description	Max	Notes
PM-I_{CC}	Processor Module Supply Current	3386SX-I_{CC} + 940 mA	
I_{IH}	Input High Leakage Current		
	A23–A1, BLE#, BHE#, D/C#, HLDA	20 μA	1
	D15–D0	60 μA	1
	ADS#, M/IO#, LOCK#, READY#, ERROR#	10 μA	1
	W/R#	30 μA	1
	CLK2	40 μA	1
	RESET	60 μA	2
I_{IL}	Input Low Leakage Current		
	A23–A1, BLE#, BHE#, D/C#	600 μA	1
	D15–D0	60 μA	1
	ADS#, M/IO#, LOCK#, READY#, ERROR#	10 μA	1
	W/R#	510 μA	1
	CLK2	620 μA	1
	RESET	600 μA	2
	HDLA	20 μA	1

Note 1: This specification is the DC input loading of the emulator circuitry only and does not include any component leakage current.
Note 2: This specification replaces the component specification for this signal.

ICE™-386 DX 25/33 Emulator DC Specifications with the Bus Isolation Board Installed

Item	Description	Min	Max
BIB-I_{CC}	Bus Isolation Board Supply Current		PM-I_{CC} + 475 mA
V_{OL}	Output Low Voltage (I_{OL} = 48 mA)		
	A2–A31, BE0#–BE3#, D/C#		0.5V
	ADS#		0.5V
	D0–D31, M/IO#, LOCK#, W/R#, HLDA (I_{OL} = 24 mA)		0.44V
V_{OH}	Output High Voltage (I_{OH} = 3 mA)		
	A2–A31, BE0#–BE3#, D/C#	2.4V	
	ADS#	2.4V	
	D0–D31, M/IO#, LOCK#, W/R#, HLDA (I_{OL} = 24 mA)	3.8V	
I_{IH}	Input High Current		
	CLK2, RESET		1.0 μA
	READY#		25 μA
I_{IL}	Input Low Current		
	CLK2, RESET		1.0 μA
	READY#		250 μA
I_{IO}	Output Leakage Current		
	A2–A31, BE0#–BE3#, D/C#, ADS#		±20 μA
	D0–D31, M/IO#, LOCK#, W/R#		±20 μA

SPECIFICATIONS

ICE™-386 SX or ICE™-376 20 MHz Emulator DC Specifications

Item	Description	Min	Max
BIB-I_{CC}	Bus Isolation Board Supply Current		PM-I_{CC} + 350 mA
V_{OL}	Output Low Voltage (I_{OL} = 48 mA) A23–A1, BLE#, BHE#, D/C, ADS# D15–D0, M/IO#, LOCK#, W/R# HLDA (I_{OL} = 24 mA)		 0.5V 0.5V 0.44V
V_{OH}	Output High Voltage (I_{OH} = 3 mA) A23–A1, BLE#, BHE#, D/C, ADS# D15–D0, M/IO#, LOCK#, W/R# HLDA (I_{OL} = 24 mA)	 2.4V 2.4V 3.8V	
I_{IH}	Input High Current CLK2, RESET READY#		 1.0 μA 25 μA
I_{IL}	Input Low Current CLK2, RESET READY#		 1.0 μA 250 μA
I_{IO}	Output Leakage Current A23–A1, BLE#, BHE#, D/C, ADS# D15–D0, M/IO#, LOCK#, W/R#		 ±20 μA ±20 μA

PROCESSOR MODULE INTERFACE CONSIDERATIONS

With the processor module directly attached to the target system without using the bus isolation board, the target system must meet the following requirements.

- The user bus controller must only drive the data bus during a valid read cycle of the emulator processor or while the emulator processor is in a hold state (the emulator processor uses the data bus to communicate with the emulator hardware).
- Before driving the address bus, the user system must gain control by asserting HOLD and receiving HLDA.
- The user reset signal is disabled during the interrogation mode. It is enabled in emulation, but is delayed by 2 or 4 CLK2 cycles.
- The user system must be able to drive one additional TTL load on all signals that go to the emulation processor.

When the target system does not satisfy the first two restrictions, the bus isolation board is used to isolate the emulation processor from the target system. With the isolation board installed, the processor CLK2 is restricted to running at 25 MHz.

The processor module drives its DC power from the target system through the Intel386 component family socket. It requires 1500 mA, including the 386 DX component current or 1400 mA, including the 386 SX or 376 component current. The isolation board requires an additional 475 mA for the 386 DX component and 350 mA for the 386 SX or 376 components.

386-DX PROCESSOR INTERCONNECT

The processor must be socketed. The printed circuit board design should locate the processor socket at the physical ends of the printed circuit board traces that connect the processor to the other logic of the target system. This reduces transmission line noise. Additionally, if the target system is enclosed in a box, pin one of the processor socket should be oriented to make connecting the processor module or target-adapter cable (TAC) easier.

ORDERING INFORMATION

The emulator uses the 386 microprocessor's pins C7, E13, and F13. The 386 High Performance 32-Bit Microprocessor With Integrated Memory Management data sheet specifies these pins as "N/C" (no connect). If the target system uses any of these pins, you must do one of the following:

- Use the bus isolation board
- Use the hinge cable adapter
- Build an adapter to disconnect pins C7, E13, and F13 (i.e., a socket with these pins removed).

386-SX PROCESSOR INTERCONNECT

The processor can be either socketed or surface-mount. Some examples of sockets which have been used include Textool 2-0100-07243-000 or AMP 821949-4 sockets. The standard ICE-386SX provides support for socketed components. To support surface-mount components, the optional 386SXONCE hinge cable adapter should be ordered. This adapter fits over a surface-mount 386SX and tri-states its pins using ONCE™ mode.

The printed circuit board design should locate the processor socket at the physical ends of the printed circuit board traces that connect the processor to the other logic of the target system. This reduces transmission line noise. Additionally, if the target system is enclosed in a box, pin one of the processor socket should be oriented to make connecting the processor module or hinge cable adapter easier.

376 PROCESSOR INTERCONNECT

The processor must be socketed. Some examples of sockets which have been used include Textool 2-0100-07243-000 or AMP821949-4 sockets.

The printed circuit board design should locate the processor socket at the physical ends of the printed circuit board traces that connect the processor to the other logic of the target system. This reduces transmission line noise. Additionally, if the target system is enclosed in a box, pin one of the processor socket should be oriented to make connecting the processor module or hinge cable adapter easier.

IN CIRCUIT EMULATOR CONVERSION KITS ORDER CODES

All In-Circuit Emulator codes include: control unit, power supply, processor module. Stand-Alone Self Test board, bus Isolation Board, either DOS or HP9000 host software and a serial interface cable.

pICE37620DZ	ICE-376 In-Circuit Emulator for the 80376 component to 20 MHz.
pICE386SX20D	ICE-386SX In-Circuit Emulator for the 80386 SX component to 20 MHz.
pICE386DX25DZ	ICE-386DX In-Circuit Emulator for the 80386 DX component to 25 MHz.
ICE386DX33D	ICE-386DX In-Circuit Emulator for the 80386 DX component to 33 MHz.
ICD48633D	In-Circuit Debugger for the 80486 microprocessor to 33 MHz.
pICE48633DZ	ICE-486 In-Circuit Emulator for the 80486 component to 33 MHz.

ORDERING INFORMATION

ICE CONVERSION KITS

KBASECONC	Converts ICE-486 to ICE-376, ICE-386SX, or ICE-386DX.
KBASECONV	Converts ICE-376, ICE-386SX or ICE-386DX to ICE-486.
TOICE37620D	Converts ICE-386SX or ICE-386DX to ICE-376 20 MHz.
TOICE386SX20D	Converts ICE-376 or ICE-386DX to ICE-386SX 20 MHz.
TOICE386DX25D	Converts ICE-376 or ICE-386SX to ICE-386DX 25 MHz.
TOICE48633D	Converts ICE-376, ICE-386SX or ICE-386DX to ICE-486 33 MHz.

IN-CIRCUIT EMULATOR OPTION ORDER CODES

p88GAADAPT	Adaptor for ICE376 emulator to support 88 pin PGA component packaging.
386SXONCE	"ONCE™" (On-Circuit Emulation) hinge cable adapter for ICE™-386 SX to support 100 pin PQFP component packaging in surface-mount. The standard ICE product includes a hinge cable adapter for socketed components.
REM386DX	2 Mbyte relocatable explansion memory option for ICE-386DX.
REM386SX376	2 Mbyte relocatable expansion memory option for ICE-386SX or ICE-376.
REM486A	2 Mbyte relocatable expansion memory option for ICD-486 (included with ICE-486).
pICE3XXCPO	Clips Pod Option for ICE376, ICE386SX 16 or 20 MHz, ICE386 25 MHz, and ICE386DX 33 MHz emulators.
pICE3XXTTB	Time Tag Board Option for ICE376, ICE386SX 16 or 20 MHz, ICE386 25 MHz, and ICE386DX 33 MHz emulators.
DT0AB	2 MB Above Board.

ICE™-186/188 FAMILY IN-CIRCUIT EMULATORS

280897-1

PRODUCT OVERVIEW

The Intel ICE™-186/188 family of in-circuit emulators delivers outstanding 16 MHz real-time emulation for the 80C186/80C188 family of microprocessors: 80C186EB, 80C188EB, 80C186XL, 80C188XL, 80C186EA, 80C188EA, 80C186EC, 80C188EC. The emulator is a versatile and efficient tool for developing, debugging, and testing products designed with Intel microprocessors. Intel provides a complete development environment, including language tools (assembler, C, PL/M, FORTRAN, PASCAL, and DB-86) to meet your embedded design needs and accelerate your time to market.

FEATURES

- Reliable full speed emulation up to 16 MHz
- Source level debug with effective source window and watch window operations
- Windowed Human Interface with mouse support
- 128K, 512K or 1 Mbytes of zero wait-state mapped memory
- 3K Frames dynamic trace buffer can be displayed without stopping emulation
- Powerful Go command with two-level breakpoints, event counters and single stepping capability
- High-Level language symbolic debug
- 80C187 Numeric Coprocessor support
- Emulation support for all commercial component packages
- High speed RS-232C and GPIB communication link
- Stand Alone Self Test unit for software development and self test
- Complete Intel service and support

October 1991
Order Number: 280897-004

ICE™-186/188 FAMILY IN-CIRCUIT EMULATORS

PRODUCT HIGHLIGHTS

- Superior Intel component bondout and advanced cable technology ensures accurate and reliable high speed emulation
- Supports debugging target systems with 80C187 numeric coprocessor
- Windowed Human Interface enables user to open multiple windows simultaneously, providing source code, watch variables, memory, registers, and trace information
- Powerful Go command permits precise emulation control through versatile event recognition, conditional constructs, and internal actions (e.g., full trace buffer, event counters)
- Breakpoints easily defined on execution and bus addresses and memory and I/O cycles
- Address and data specification based on single value, range, or "don't cares"
- Flexible single-step command for executing one machine-level or high-level instruction at a time
- 3K trace buffer collects both execution and data bus activity in real time. Display either instructions, cycles, or both
- Stand Alone Self Test (SAST) unit in conjunction with emulator map memory facilitates early software debugging and emulator confidence testing
- 128K, 512K and 1 MB zero wait-state memory modules can be used in place of target memory for code debugging
- Supports all Intel software products, including C, assembler, PL/M, FORTRAN, and PASCAL. Also accepts Microsoft and Borland object code when used in conjunction with Paradigm and SSI products
- Programmable fastbreak for monitoring target system
- DRAM contents preserved even when emulator halted
- RS-232C serial link provides transfer rate up to 57.6 Kbyte per second. GPIB driver (in conjunction with a user-supplied National Instruments (IEEE-488) GPIB communication board) provides parallel transfers at rates up to 300 Kbytes per second
- Logic analyzer support included via a 60-pin connector to emulator
- All component packages supported, either directly on the probe or through adapters
- World-wide service, support, and training available

BENEFITS

- Supports low power application needs. Probe draws low power current, supports true CMOS voltage input/output
- Minimal power consumption difference (90 mA) between using the emulator or actual component
- Windowed Interface increases productivity for both expert and casual users. Pull-down menus and on-line help simplifies debugging and decreases learning curve
- Source code window automatically updated when emulator halts, highlighting next instruction to be executed
- Breakpoints may be set directly in the source code window and facilitate precise emulation control
- Emulator can track up to ten user-defined program variables using the Watch Window. Emulator responsible for variable tracking, not the user
- "C"-based macro commands facilitate customized or repeated debug sessions. Extremely useful for automated manufacturing testing and debug
- Trace Buffer provides valuable reference for tracking down problems. User able to view trace buffer or modify trace conditions without stopping emulation
- Software developers may debug application code before target hardware is available using the Stand Alone Self Test (SAST) Unit with emulator map memory, as long as time and hardware interrupt support is not required
- Early debugging of ROM memory simplified using emulator map memory. Memory addressable in 32 Kbyte increments. Supports debugging ROM-based applications over entire 1 MB addressing range
- Mappable I/O ports, addressable in 4 Kbyte increments, enable user to debug suspect I/O behavior. PC resources allow data "input" from keyboard and data "output" to the screen
- Source code window displays source code in original high-level language used to produce the object code. Simplifies and accelerates debug process because it refers to source code window rather than hard copy listing
- Investigate privileged processor information during emulation using the fastbreak feature (e.g., PCB, registers, target memory). Emulator will halt while information is displayed to screen or written to a file (maximum time emulator halted is 5625 cycles, depending on operation)

ICE™-186/188 FAMILY IN-CIRCUIT EMULATORS

- DRAM refresh signals continue even when emulator halted and ensures DRAM memory not lost or corrupted. Also permits emulation in cost-sensitive applications that do not include DRAM controllers
- Continuous timer function while emulator halted allows emulator to respond to on-chip and external interrupts in real-time. Useful for critical applications where continuous interrupt-service is a requirement
- Detailed timing of specific events possible using a logic analyzer connected to the emulator. An external sync signal can trigger the logic analyzer, enabling complex event triggering
- Software support contract available, providing technical software information, telephone support, automatic software and manual updates, "iComments" publication and a development tools trouble-shooting guide
- 90-day hardware support package. Includes technical hardware information, telephone support, warranty on parts, labor, material, and on-site hardware support
- Intel Development Tools offer a 30-day, money-back guarantee to customers who are dissatisfied with their Intel development tool

SERVICE, SUPPORT AND TRAINING

- Intel offers full array of seminars, classes, workshops, field application engineering expertise, hotline technical support, and on-site service

PHYSICAL DESCRIPTION AND CHARACTERISTICS

The ICE-186EB/188EB Emulator consists of the following components:

Table 1. Emulator's Physical Characteristics

Unit	Width in.	Width cm	Height in.	Height cm	Length in.	Length cm
Emulator Control Unit	10.4	26.4	1.7	4.3	20.7	52.6
Power Supply	7.7	19.6	4.1	10.4	11.0	27.9
User Probe	4.0	10.0	0.75	1.8	6.75	17.5
User Probe Adapter Cable					2.5	6.2
Stand Alone Self Test	4.30	10.9	0.60	1.5	6.7	17.0
Serial Cable					144.0	366.0

SUMMARY

The ICE-186/188 family of In-Circuit Emulators provide a versatile and efficient tool for developing, debugging and testing products designed with the 80C186/80C188 family of microprocessors. The emulator includes numerous productivity boosting features to enable you to move your products to market as quickly as possible. Intel, the inventor of the 80C186/80C188 family of microprocessors, offers the most complete line of development tools from a single vendor to meet all of your development needs for your embedded design.

ICE™-186/188 FAMILY IN-CIRCUIT EMULATORS

SPECIFICATIONS

Personal Computer Requirements

The ICE-186EB/188EB emulator is hosted on an IBM PC AT platform or IBM PS/2. The emulator has been tested and evaluated on an IBM PC AT. The PC AT must meet the following minimum requirements:

- 640 Kbytes of Memory
- An additional 1 Mbytes of expanded memory. Above Board managed by emm.sys driver recommended. Other memory managers conforming to the Lotus/Intel/Microsoft Expanded Memory Specification Version 3.2 or later are available.
- One 20 Mbytes Hard Disk
- PC DOS 3.2 or 3.3
- A serial Port (COM1 or COM2) supporting minimally at 9600 Baud Data Transfers, or a National Instruments GPIB-PCIIA board.
- Math coprocessor (if Target Ssytem intends to use an 80C187, host PC must have one)

ICE-18XEB ORDERING INFORMATION

ICE17XEBP	ICE-18XEB 16 MHz system supports 80C186EB/80C188EB, includes control unit, PLCC probe, power supply, SAST, emulator s/w, Software Carousel and SAST adapter
UP18XEBP	16 MHz 80C186EB/80C188EB PLCC user probe

The above order codes MUST order a memory option

MEM128	128 Kbytes map memory
MEM512	512 Kbytes map memory
MEM1MB	1 Mbytes map memory

ICE-18XLEA Ordering Information

Call 800-874-6835 (U.S.) for latest information

ICE-18XEC Ordering Information

Call 800-874-6835 (U.S.) for latest information

NORTH AMERICAN SALES OFFICES

ALABAMA

Intel Corp.
5015 Bradford Dr., #2
Huntsville 35805
Tel: (205) 830-4010
FAX: (205) 837-2640

ARIZONA

†Intel Corp.
410 North 44th Street
Suite 500
Phoenix 85008
Tel: (602) 231-0386
FAX: (602) 244-0446

CALIFORNIA

†Intel Corp.
21515 Vanowen Street
Suite 116
Canoga Park 91303
Tel: (818) 704-8500
FAX: (818) 340-1144

Intel Corp.
1 Sierra Gate Plaza
Suite 280C
Roseville 95678
Tel: (916) 782-8086
FAX: (916) 782-8153

†Intel Corp.
9665 Chesapeake Dr.
Suite 325
San Diego 92123
Tel: (619) 292-8086
FAX: (619) 292-0628

*†Intel Corp.
400 N. Tustin Avenue
Suite 450
Santa Ana 92705
Tel: (714) 835-9642
TWX: 910-595-1114
FAX: (714) 541-9157

*†Intel Corp.
San Tomas 4
2700 San Tomas Expressway
2nd Floor
Santa Clara 95051
Tel: (408) 986-8086
TWX: 910-338-0255
FAX: (408) 727-2620

COLORADO

Intel Corp.
4445 Northpark Drive
Suite 100
Colorado Springs 80907
Tel: (719) 594-6622
FAX: (303) 594-0720

*†Intel Corp.
600 S. Cherry St.
Suite 700
Denver 80222
Tel: (303) 321-8086
TWX: 910-931-2289
FAX: (303) 322-8670

CONNECTICUT

†Intel Corp.
301 Lee Farm Corporate Park
83 Wooster Heights Rd.
Danbury 06810
Tel: (203) 748-3130
FAX: (203) 794-0339

FLORIDA

†Intel Corp.
800 Fairway Drive
Suite 160
Deerfield Beach 33441
Tel: (305) 421-0506
FAX: (305) 421-2444

†Intel Corp.
5850 T.G. Lee Blvd.
Suite 340
Orlando 32822
Tel: (407) 240-8000
FAX: (407) 240-8097

GEORGIA

†Intel Corp.
20 Technology Parkway
Suite 150
Norcross 30092
Tel: (404) 449-0541
FAX: (404) 605-9762

ILLINOIS

*†Intel Corp.
Woodfield Corp. Center III
300 N. Martingale Road
Suite 400
Schaumburg 60173
Tel: (708) 605-8031
FAX: (708) 706-9762

INDIANA

†Intel Corp.
8910 Purdue Road
Suite 350
Indianapolis 46268
Tel: (317) 875-0623
FAX: (317) 875-8938

MARYLAND

*†Intel Corp.
10010 Junction Dr.
Suite 200
Annapolis Junction 20701
Tel: (301) 206-2860
FAX: (301) 206-3677
(301) 206-3678

MASSACHUSETTS

*†Intel Corp.
Westford Corp. Center
3 Carlisle Road
2nd Floor
Westford 01886
Tel: (508) 692-0960
TWX: 710-343-6333
FAX: (508) 692-7867

MICHIGAN

†Intel Corp.
7071 Orchard Lake Road
Suite 100
West Bloomfield 48322
Tel: (313) 851-8096
FAX: (313) 851-8770

MINNESOTA

†Intel Corp.
3500 W. 80th St.
Suite 360
Bloomington 55431
Tel: (612) 835-6722
TWX: 910-576-2867
FAX: (612) 831-6497

NEW JERSEY

*†Intel Corp.
Lincroft Office Center
125 Half Mile Road
Red Bank 07701
Tel: (908) 747-2233
FAX: (908) 747-0983

NEW YORK

*Intel Corp.
850 Crosskeys Office Park
Fairport 14450
Tel: (716) 425-2750
TWX: 510-253-7391
FAX: (716) 223-2561

*†Intel Corp.
2950 Express Dr., South
Suite 130
Islandia 11722
Tel: (516) 231-3300
TWX: 510-227-6236
FAX: (516) 348-7939

†Intel Corp.
300 Westage Business Center
Suite 230
Fishkill 12524
Tel: (914) 897-3860
FAX: (914) 897-3125

OHIO

*†Intel Corp.
3401 Park Center Drive
Suite 220
Dayton 45414
Tel: (513) 890-5350
TWX: 810-450-2528
FAX: (513) 890-8658

*†Intel Corp.
25700 Science Park Dr.
Suite 100
Beachwood 44122
Tel: (216) 464-2736
TWX: 810-427-9298
FAX: (804) 282-0673

OKLAHOMA

Intel Corp.
6801 N. Broadway
Suite 115
Oklahoma City 73162
Tel: (405) 848-8086
FAX: (405) 840-9819

OREGON

†Intel Corp.
15254 N.W. Greenbrier Pkwy.
Building B
Beaverton 97006
Tel: (503) 645-8051
TWX: 910-467-8741
FAX: (503) 645-8181

PENNSYLVANIA

*†Intel Corp.
925 Harvest Drive
Suite 200
Blue Bell 19422
Tel: (215) 641-1000
FAX: (215) 641-0785

*†Intel Corp.
400 Penn Center Blvd.
Suite 610
Pittsburgh 15235
Tel: (412) 823-4970
FAX: (412) 829-7578

PUERTO RICO

†Intel Corp.
South Industrial Park
P.O. Box 910
Las Piedras 00671
Tel: (809) 733-8616

TEXAS

†Intel Corp.
8911 N. Capital of Texas Hwy.
Suite 4230
Austin 78759
Tel: (512) 794-8086
FAX: (512) 338-9335

*†Intel Corp.
12000 Ford Road
Suite 400
Dallas 75234
Tel: (214) 241-8087
FAX: (214) 484-1180

*†Intel Corp.
7322 S.W. Freeway
Suite 1490
Houston 77074
Tel: (713) 988-8086
TWX: 910-881-2490
FAX: (713) 988-3660

UTAH

†Intel Corp.
428 East 6400 South
Suite 104
Murray 84107
Tel: (801) 263-8051
FAX: (801) 268-1457

WASHINGTON

†Intel Corp.
155 108th Avenue N.E.
Suite 386
Bellevue 98004
Tel: (206) 453-8086
TWX: 910-443-3002
FAX: (206) 451-9556

Intel Corp.
408 N. Mullan Road
Suite 102
Spokane 99206
Tel: (509) 928-8086
FAX: (509) 928-9467

WISCONSIN

Intel Corp.
330 S. Executive Dr.
Suite 102
Brookfield 53005
Tel: (414) 784-8087
FAX: (414) 796-2115

CANADA

BRITISH COLUMBIA

Intel Semiconductor of Canada, Ltd.
4585 Canada Way
Suite 202
Burnaby V5G 4L6
Tel: (604) 298-0387
FAX: (604) 298-8234

ONTARIO

†Intel Semiconductor of Canada, Ltd.
2650 Queensview Drive
Suite 250
Ottawa K2B 8H6
Tel: (613) 829-9714
FAX: (613) 820-5936

†Intel Semiconductor of Canada, Ltd.
190 Attwell Drive
Suite 500
Rexdale M9W 6H8
Tel: (416) 675-2105
FAX: (416) 675-2438

QUEBEC

†Intel Semiconductor of Canada, Ltd.
1 Rue Holiday
Suite 115
Tour East
Pt. Claire H9R 5N3
Tel: (514) 694-9130
FAX: 514-694-0064

†Sales and Service Office
*Field Application Location

NORTH AMERICAN DISTRIBUTORS

ALABAMA

Arrow Electronics, Inc.
1015 Henderson Road
Huntsville 35806
Tel: (205) 837-6955
FAX: (205) 721-1581

Hamilton/Avnet Electronics
4960 Corporate Drive, #135
Huntsville 35805
Tel: (205) 837-7210
FAX: (205) 721-0356

MTI Systems Sales
4950 Corporate Drive
Suite 120
Huntsville 35805
Tel: (205) 830-9526
FAX: (205) 830-9557

Pioneer/Technologies Group, Inc.
4835 University Square, #5
Huntsville 35805
Tel: (205) 837-9300
FAX: (205) 837-9358

ARIZONA

†Arrow Electronics, Inc.
4134 E. Wood Street
Phoenix 85040
Tel: (602) 437-0750
FAX: (602) 252-9109

Avnet Computer
30 South McKemy Avenue
Chandler 85226
Tel: (602) 961-6460
FAX: (602) 961-4787

Hamilton/Avnet Electronics
30 South McKemy Avenue
Chandler 85226
Tel: (602) 961-6403
FAX: (602) 961-1331

Wyle Distribution Group
4141 E. Raymond
Phoenix 85040
Tel: (602) 437-2088
FAX: (602) 437-2124

CALIFORNIA

Arrow Commercial System Group
1502 Crocker Avenue
Hayward 94544
Tel: (415) 489-5371
FAX: (415) 489-9393

Arrow Commercial System Group
14242 Chambers Road
Tustin 92680
Tel: (714) 544-0200
FAX: (714) 731-8438

†Arrow Electronics, Inc.
19748 Dearborn Street
Chatsworth 91311
Tel: (818) 701-7500
FAX: (818) 772-8930

†Arrow Electronics, Inc.
9511 Ridgehaven Court
San Diego 92123
Tel: (619) 565-4800
FAX: (619) 279-8062

†Arrow Electronics, Inc.
1180 Murphy Avenue
San Jose 95131
Tel: (408) 441-9700
FAX: (408) 453-4810

†Arrow Electronics, Inc.
2961 Dow Avenue
Tustin 92680
Tel: (714) 838-5422
FAX: (714) 838-4151

Avnet Computer
3170 Pullman Street
Costa Mesa 92626
Tel: (714) 641-4121
FAX: (714) 641-4170

Avnet Computer
1361B West 190th Street
Gardena 90248
Tel: (800) 345-3870
FAX: (213) 327-5389

Avnet Computer
755 Sunrise Blvd., #150
Roseville 95661
Tel: (916) 781-2521
FAX: (916) 781-3819

Avnet Computer
1175 Bordeaux Drive, #A
Sunnyvale 94089
Tel: (408) 743-3304
FAX: (408) 743-3348

Avnet Computer
21150 Califa Street
Woodland Hills 91376
Tel: (808) 345-3870
FAX: (818) 594-8333

†Hamilton/Avnet Electronics
3170 Pullman Street
Costa Mesa 92626
Tel: (714) 641-4100
FAX: (714) 754-6033

†Hamilton/Avnet Electronics
1175 Bordeaux Drive, #A
Sunnyvale 94089
Tel: (408) 743-3300
FAX: (408) 745-6679

†Hamilton/Avnet Electronics
4545 Viewridge Avenue
San Diego 92123
Tel: (619) 571-1900
FAX: (619) 571-8761

†Hamilton/Avnet Electronics
21150 Califa St.
Woodland Hills 91367
Tel: (818) 594-0403
FAX: (818) 594-8234

†Hamilton/Avnet Electronics
1361B West 190th Street
Gardena 90248
Tel: (213) 516-8600
FAX: (213) 217-6822

†Hamilton/Avnet Electronics
755 Sunrise Avenue, #150
Roseville 95661
Tel: (916) 925-2216
FAX: (916) 925-3478

Pioneer/Technologies Group, Inc.
134 Rio Robles
San Jose 95134
Tel: (408) 954-9100
FAX: 408-954-9113

†Wyle Distribution Group
124 Maryland Street
El Segundo 90245
Tel: (213) 322-8100
FAX: (213) 416-1151

Wyle Distribution Group
7431 Chapman Ave.
Garden Grove 92641
Tel: (714) 891-1717
FAX: (714) 891-1621

†Wyle Distribution Group
2951 Sunrise Blvd., Suite 175
Rancho Cordova 95742
Tel: (916) 638-5282
FAX: (916) 638-1491

†Wyle Distribution Group
9525 Chesapeake Drive
San Diego 92123
Tel: (619) 565-9171
FAX: (619) 365-0512

†Wyle Distribution Group
3000 Bowers Avenue
Santa Clara 95051
Tel: (408) 727-2500
FAX: (408) 727-5896

†Wyle Distribution Group
17872 Cowan Avenue
Irvine 92714
Tel: (714) 863-9953
FAX: (714) 263-0473

†Wyle Distribution Group
26010 Mureau Road, #150
Calabasas 91302
Tel: (818) 880-9000
FAX: (818) 880-5510

COLORADO

Arrow Electronics, Inc.
3254 C Frazer Street
Aurora 80011
Tel: (303) 373-5616
FAX: (303) 373-5760

†Hamilton/Avnet Electronics
9605 Maroon Circle, #200
Englewood 80112
Tel: (303) 799-7800
FAX: (303) 799-7801

†Wyle Distribution Group
451 E. 124th Avenue
Thornton 80241
Tel: (303) 457-9953
FAX: (303) 457-4831

CONNECTICUT

†Arrow Electronics, Inc.
12 Beaumont Road
Wallingford 06492
Tel: (203) 265-7741
FAX: (203) 265-7988

Avnet Computer
55 Federal Road, #103
Danbury 06810
Tel: (203) 797-2880
FAX: (203) 791-9050

†Hamilton/Avnet Electronics
55 Federal Road, #103
Danbury 06810
Tel: (203) 743-6077
FAX: (203) 791-9050

†Pioneer/Standard Electronics
112 Main Street
Norwalk 06851
Tel: (203) 853-1515
FAX: (203) 838-9901

FLORIDA

†Arrow Electronics, Inc.
400 Fairway Drive, #102
Deerfield Beach 33441
Tel: (305) 429-8200
FAX: (305) 428-3991

†Arrow Electronics, Inc.
37 Skyline Drive, #3101
Lake Mary 32746
Tel: (407) 333-9300
FAX: (407) 333-9320

Avnet Computer
3343 W. Commercial Blvd.
Bldg. C/D, Suite 107
Ft. Lauderdale 33309
Tel: (305) 979-9067
FAX: (305) 730-0368

Avnet Computer
3247 Tech Drive North
St. Petersburg 33716
Tel: (813) 573-5524
FAX: (813) 572-4324

†Hamilton/Avnet Electronics
5371 N.W. 33rd Avenue
Ft. Lauderdale 33309
Tel: (305) 484-5016
FAX: (305) 484-8369

†Hamilton/Avnet Electronics
3247 Tech Drive North
St. Petersburg 33716
Tel: (813) 573-3930
FAX: (813) 572-4329

†Hamilton/Avnet Electronics
7079 University Boulevard
Winter Park 32791
Tel: (407) 657-3300
FAX: (407) 678-1878

†Pioneer/Technologies Group, Inc.
337 Northlake Blvd., Suite 1000
Alta Monte Springs 32701
Tel: (407) 834-9090
FAX: (407) 834-0865

Pioneer/Technologies Group, Inc.
674 S. Military Trail
Deerfield Beach 33442
Tel: (305) 428-8877
FAX: (305) 481-2950

GEORGIA

Arrow Commercial System Group
3400 C. Corporate Way
Duluth 30136
Tel: (404) 623-8825
FAX: (404) 623-8802

†Arrow Electronics, Inc.
4250 E. Rivergreen Pkwy., #E
Duluth 30136
Tel: (404) 497-1300
FAX: (404) 476-1493

Avnet Computer
3425 Corporate Way, #G
Duluth 30136
Tel: (404) 623-5452
FAX: (404) 476-0125

Hamilton/Avnet Electronics
3425 Corporate Way, #G
Duluth 30136
Tel: (404) 446-0611
FAX: (404) 446-1011

Pioneer/Technologies Group, Inc.
4250 C. Rivergreen Parkway
Duluth 30136
Tel: (404) 623-1003
FAX: (404) 623-0665

ILLINOIS

†Arrow Electronics, Inc.
1140 W. Thorndale Rd.
Itasca 60143
Tel: (708) 250-0500

Avnet Computer
1124 Thorndale Avenue
Bensenville 60106
Tel: (708) 860-8573
FAX: (708) 773-7976

†Hamilton/Avnet Electronics
1130 Thorndale Avenue
Bensenville 60106
Tel: (708) 860-7700
FAX: (708) 860-8530

MTI Systems
1140 W. Thorndale Avenue
Itasca 60143
Tel: (708) 250-8222
FAX: (708) 250-8275

†Pioneer/Standard Electronics
2171 Executive Dr., Suite 200
Addison 60101
Tel: (708) 495-9680
FAX: (708) 495-9831

INDIANA

†Arrow Electronics, Inc.
7108 Lakeview Parkway West Dr.
Indianapolis 46268
Tel: (317) 299-2071
FAX: (317) 299-2379

Avnet Computer
485 Gradle Drive
Carmel 46032
Tel: (317) 575-8029
FAX: (317) 844-4964

Hamilton/Avnet Electronics
485 Gradle Drive
Carmel 46032
Tel: (317) 844-9333
FAX: (317) 844-5921

†Pioneer/Standard Electronics
9350 Priority Way West Dr.
Indianapolis 46250
Tel: (317) 573-0880
FAX: (317) 573-0979

†Certified VAD

NORTH AMERICAN DISTRIBUTORS (Contd.)

IOWA

Hamilton/Avnet Electronics
2335A Blairsferry Rd., N.E.
Cedar Rapids 52402
Tel: (319) 362-4757
FAX: (319) 393-7050

KANSAS

Arrow Electronics, Inc.
8208 Melrose Dr., Suite 210
Lenexa 66214
Tel: (913) 541-9542
FAX: (913) 541-0328

Avnet Computer
15313 W. 95th Street
Lenexa 61219
Tel: (913) 541-7989
FAX: (913) 541-7904

†Hamilton/Avnet Electronics
15313 W. 95th
Overland Park 66215
Tel: (913) 888-1055
FAX: (913) 541-7951

KENTUCKY

Hamilton/Avnet Electronics
805 A. Newtown Circle
Lexington 40511
Tel: (606) 259-1475
FAX: (606) 252-3238

MARYLAND

Arrow Commercial Systems Group
200 Perry Parkway
Gaithersburg 20877
Tel: (301) 670-1600
FAX: (301) 670-0188

†Arrow Electronics, Inc.
8300 Guilford Road, #H
Columbia 21046
Tel: (301) 995-6002
FAX: (301) 995-6201

Avnet Computer
7172 Columbia Gateway Dr., #G
Columbia 21045
Tel: (301) 995-0020
FAX: (301) 995-3515

†Hamilton/Avnet Electronics
7172 Columbia Gateway Dr., #F
Columbia 21045
Tel: (301) 995-3554
FAX: (301) 995-3515

†North Atlantic Industries
Systems Division
7125 Riverwood Dr.
Columbia 21046
Tel: (301) 290-3999

†Pioneer/Technologies Group, Inc.
15810 Gaither Road
Gaithersburg 20877
Tel: (301) 921-0660
FAX: (301) 670-6746

MASSACHUSETTS

Arrow Electronics, Inc.
25 Upton Dr.
Wilmington 01887
Tel: (508) 658-0900
FAX: (508) 694-1754

Avnet Computer
10 D Centennial Drive
Peabody 01960
Tel: (508) 532-9886
FAX: (508) 532-9660

†Hamilton/Avnet Electronics
10D Centennial Drive
Peabody 01960
Tel: (508) 531-7430
FAX: (508) 532-9802

†Pioneer/Standard Electronics
44 Hartwell Avenue
Lexington 02173
Tel: (617) 861-9200
FAX: (617) 863-1547

Wyle Distribution Group
15 Third Avenue
Burlington 01803
Tel: (617) 272-7300
FAX: (617) 272-6809

MICHIGAN

†Arrow Electronics, Inc.
19880 Haggerty Road
Livonia 48152
Tel: (313) 665-4100
FAX: (313) 462-2686

Avnet Computer
2876 28th Street, S.W., #5
Grandville 49418
Tel: (616) 531-9607
FAX: (616) 531-0059

Avnet Computer
41650 Garden Road
Novi 48375
Tel: (313) 347-1820
FAX: (313) 347-4067

Hamilton/Avnet Electronics
2876 28th Street, S.W., #5
Grandville 49418
Tel: (616) 243-8805
FAX: (616) 531-0059

Hamilton/Avnet Electronics
41650 Garden Brook Rd., #100
Novi 48375
Tel: (313) 347-4270
FAX: (313) 347-4021

†Pioneer/Standard Electronics
4505 Broadmoor S.E.
Grand Rapids 49512
Tel: (616) 698-1800
FAX: (616) 698-1831

†Pioneer/Standard Electronics
13485 Stamford
Livonia 48150
Tel: (313) 525-1800
FAX: (313) 427-3720

MINNESOTA

†Arrow Electronics, Inc.
10120A West 76th Street
Eden Prairie 55344
Tel: (612) 829-5588
FAX: (612) 942-7803

Avnet Computer
10000 West 76th Street
Eden Prairie 55344
Tel: (612) 829-0025
FAX: (612) 944-2781

†Hamilton/Avnet Electronics
12400 Whitewater Drive
Minnetonka 55343
Tel: (612) 932-0600
FAX: (612) 932-0613

†Pioneer/Standard Electronics
7625 Golden Triange Dr., #G
Eden Prairie 55344
Tel: (612) 944-3355
FAX: (612) 944-3794

MISSOURI

†Arrow Electronics, Inc.
2380 Schuetz Road
St. Louis 63141
Tel: (314) 567-6888
FAX: (314) 567-1164

Avnet Computer
739 Goddard Avenue
Chesterfield 63005
Tel: (314) 537-2725
FAX: (314) 537-4248

†Hamilton/Avnet Electronics
741 Goddard
Chesterfield 63005
Tel: (314) 537-1600
FAX: (314) 537-4248

NEW HAMPSHIRE

Avnet Computer
2 Executive Park Drive
Bedford 03102
Tel: (603) 624-6630
FAX: (603) 624-2402

NEW JERSEY

†Arrow Electronics, Inc.
4 East Stow Road
Unit 11
Marlton 08053
Tel: (609) 596-8000
FAX: (609) 596-9632

†Arrow Electronics, Inc.
6 Century Drive
Parsipanny 07054
Tel: (201) 538-0900
FAX: (201) 538-4962

Avnet Computer
1-B Keystone Ave., Bldg. 36
Cherry Hill 08003
Tel: (609) 424-8961
FAX: (609) 751-2502

Avnet Computer
10 Industrial Road
Fairfield 07006
Tel: (201) 882-2879
FAX: (201) 808-9251

†Hamilton/Avnet Electronics
1 Keystone Ave., Bldg. 36
Cherry Hill 08003
Tel: (609) 424-0110
FAX: (609) 751-2552

†Hamilton/Avnet Electronics
10 Industrial
Fairfield 07006
Tel: (201) 575-3390
FAX: (201) 575-5839

†MTI Systems Sales
6 Century Drive
Parsippany 07054
Tel: (201) 539-6496
FAX: (201) 539-6430

†Pioneer/Standard Electronics
14-A Madison Rd.
Fairfield 07006
Tel: (201) 575-3510
FAX: (201) 575-3454

NEW MEXICO

Alliance Electronics Inc.
10510 Research Avenue
Albuquerque 87123
Tel: (505) 292-3360
FAX: (505) 275-6392

Avnet Computer
7801 Academy Road
Bldg. 1, Suite 204
Albuquerque 87109
Tel: (505) 828-9725
FAX: (505) 828-0360

†Hamilton/Avnet Electronics
7801 Academy Rd. N.E.
Bldg. 1, Suite 204
Albuquerque 87108
Tel: (505) 765-1500
FAX: (505) 243-1395

NEW YORK

†Arrow Electronics, Inc.
3375 Brighton Henrietta Townline Rd.
Rochester 14623
Tel: (716) 427-0300
FAX: (716) 427-0735

Arrow Electronics, Inc.
20 Oser Avenue
Hauppauge 11788
Tel: (516) 231-1000
FAX: (516) 231-1072

Avnet Computer
933 Motor Parkway
Hauppauge 11788
Tel: (516) 231-9040
FAX: (516) 434-7426

Avnet Computer
2060 Townline
Rochester 14623
Tel: (716) 272-9306
FAX: (716) 272-9685

†Hamilton/Avnet Electronics
933 Motor Parkway
Hauppauge 11788
Tel: (516) 231-9800
FAX: (516) 434-7426

†Hamilton/Avnet Electronics
2060 Townline Rd.
Rochester 14623
Tel: (716) 292-0730
FAX: (716) 292-0810

Hamilton/Avnet Electronics
103 Twin Oaks Drive
Syracuse 13120
Tel: (315) 437-2641
FAX: (315) 432-0740

MTI Systems
50 Horseblock Road
Brookhaven 11719
Tel: (516) 924-9400
FAX: (516) 924-1103

MTI Systems
1 Penn Plaza
250 W. 34th Street
New York 10119
Tel: (212) 643-1280
FAX: (212) 643-1288

Pioneer/Standard Electronics
68 Corporate Drive
Binghamton 13904
Tel: (607) 722-9300
FAX: (607) 722-9562

†Pioneer/Standard Electronics
60 Crossway Park West
Woodbury, Long Island 11797
Tel: (516) 921-8700
FAX: (516) 921-2143

†Pioneer/Standard Electronics
840 Fairport Park
Fairport 14450
Tel: (716) 381-7070
FAX: (716) 381-5955

NORTH CAROLINA

†Arrow Electronics, Inc.
5240 Greensdairy Road
Raleigh 27604
Tel: (919) 876-3132
FAX: (919) 878-9517

Avnet Computer
2725 Millbrook Rd., #123
Raleigh 27604
Tel: (919) 790-1735
FAX: (919) 872-4972

Hamilton/Avnet Electronics
5250-77 Center Dr. #350
Charlotte 28217
Tel: (704) 527-2485
FAX: (704) 527-8058

†Hamilton/Avnet Electronics
3510 Spring Forest Drive
Raleigh 27604
Tel: (919) 878-0819

Pioneer/Technologies Group, Inc.
9401 L-Southern Pine Blvd.
Charlotte 28210
Tel: (704) 527-8188
FAX: (704) 522-8564

Pioneer Technologies Group, Inc.
2810 Meridian Parkway, #148
Durham 27713
Tel: (919) 544-5400
FAX: (919) 544-5885

OHIO

Arrow Commercial System Group
284 Cramer Creek Court
Dublin 43017
Tel: (614) 889-9347
FAX: (614) 889-9680

†Arrow Electronics, Inc.
6573 Cochran Road, #E
Solon 44139
Tel: (216) 248-3990
FAX: (216) 248-1106

Arrow Electronics, Inc.
8200 Washington Village Dr.
Centerville 45458
Tel: (513) 435-5563
FAX: (513) 435-2049

†Certified VAD

NORTH AMERICAN DISTRIBUTORS (Contd.)

OHIO (Contd.)

Avnet Computer
7764 Washington Village Dr.
Dayton 45459
Tel: (513) 439-6756
FAX: (513) 439-6719

Avnet Computer
30325 Bainbridge Rd., Bldg. A
Solon 44139
Tel: (216) 349-2505
FAX: (216) 349-1894

†Hamilton/Avnet Electronics
7760 Washington Village Dr.
Dayton 45459
Tel: (513) 439-6733
FAX: (513) 439-6711

†Hamilton/Avnet Electronics
30325 Bainbridge
Solon 44139
Tel: (800) 543-2984
FAX: (216) 349-1894

Hamilton/Avnet Electronics
2600 Corp Exchange Drive, #180
Columbus 43231
Tel: (614) 882-7004
FAX: (614) 882-8650

MTI Systems Sales
23404 Commerce Park Road
Beachwood 44122
Tel: (216) 464-6688
FAX: (216) 464-3564

†Pioneer/Standard Electronics
4433 Interpoint Boulevard
Dayton 45424
Tel: (513) 236-9900
FAX: (513) 236-8133

†Pioneer/Standard Electronics
4800 E. 131st Street
Cleveland 44105
Tel: (216) 587-3600
FAX: (216) 663-1004

OKLAHOMA

Arrow Electronics, Inc.
12111 East 51st Street, #101
Tulsa 74146
Tel: (918) 252-7537
FAX: (918) 254-0917

†Hamilton/Avnet Electronics
12121 E. 51st St., Suite 102A
Tulsa 74146
Tel: (918) 664-0444
FAX: (918) 250-8763

OREGON

†Almac Electronics Corp.
1885 N.W. 169th Place
Beaverton 97006
Tel: (503) 629-8090
FAX: 503-645-0611

Avnet Computer
9409 Southwest Nimbus Ave.
Beaverton 97005
Tel: (503) 627-0900
FAX: (503) 526-6242

†Hamilton/Avnet Electronics
9409 S.W. Nimbus Ave.
Beaverton 97005
Tel: (503) 627-0201
FAX: (503) 641-4012

Wyle
9640 Sunshine Court
Bldg. G, Suite 200
Beaverton 97005
Tel: (503) 643-7900
FAX: (503) 646-5466

PENNSYLVANIA

Avnet Computer
213 Executive Drive, #320
Mars 16046
Tel: (412) 772-1888
FAX: (412) 772-1890

Hamilton/Avnet Electronics
213 Executive, #320
Mars 16045
Tel: (412) 281-4152
FAX: (412) 772-1890

Pioneer/Technologies Group, Inc.
259 Kappa Drive
Pittsburgh 15238
Tel: (412) 782-2300
FAX: (412) 963-8255

†Pioneer/Technologies Group, Inc.
500 Enterprise Road
Keith Valley Business Center
Horsham 19044
Tel: (215) 674-4000
FAX: (215) 674-3107

TENNESSEE

Arrow Commercial System Group
3635 Knight Road, #7
Memphis 38118
Tel: (901) 367-0540
FAX: (901) 367-2081

TEXAS

Arrow Electronics, Inc.
3220 Commander Drive
Carrollton 75006
Tel: (214) 380-6464
FAX: (214) 248-7208

Avnet Computer
4004 Beltline, Suite 200
Dallas 75244
Tel: (214) 308-8181
FAX: (214) 308-8129

Avnet Computer
1235 North Loop West, #525
Houston 77008
Tel: (713) 867-7500
FAX: (713) 861-6851

†Hamilton/Avnet Electronics
1826-F Kramer Lane
Austin 78758
Tel: (800) 772-5668
FAX: (512) 832-4315

†Hamilton/Avnet Electronics
4004 Beltline, #200
Dallas 75244
Tel: (214) 308-8111
FAX: (214) 308-8109

†Hamilton/Avnet Electronics
1235 N. Loop West, #521
Houston 77008
Tel: (713) 240-7733
FAX: (713) 861-6541

†Pioneer/Standard Electronics
1826-D Kramer Lane
Austin 78758
Tel: (512) 835-4000
FAX: (512) 835-9829

†Pioneer/Standard Electronics
13765 Beta Road
Dallas 75244
Tel: (214) 386-7300
FAX: (214) 490-6419

†Pioneer/Standard Electronics
10530 Rockley Road, #100
Houston 77099
Tel: (713) 495-4700
FAX: (713) 495-5642

†Wyle Distribution Group
1810 Greenville Avenue
Richardson 75081
Tel: (214) 235-9953
FAX: (214) 644-5064

Wyle Distribution Group
4030 West Braker Lane, #330
Austin 78758
Tel: (512) 345-8853
FAX: (512) 345-9330

Wyle Distribution Group
11001 South Wilcrest, #100
Houston 77099
Tel: (713) 879-9953
FAX: (713) 879-6540

UTAH

Arrow Electronics, Inc.
1946 W. Parkway Blvd.
Salt Lake City 84119
Tel: (801) 973-6913

Avnet Computer
1100 E. 6600 South, #150
Salt Lake City 84121
Tel: (801) 266-1115
FAX: (801) 266-0362

Avnet Computer
17761 Northeast 78th Place
Redmond 98052
Tel: (206) 867-0160
FAX: (206) 867-0161

†Hamilton/Avnet Electronics
1100 East 6600 South, #120
Salt Lake City 84121
Tel: (801) 972-2800
FAX: (801) 263-0104

†Wyle Distribution Group
1325 West 2200 South, #E
West Valley 84119
Tel: (801) 974-9953
FAX: (801) 972-2524

WASHINGTON

†Almac Electronics Corp.
14360 S.E. Eastgate Way
Bellevue 98007
Tel: (206) 643-9992
FAX: (206) 643-9709

†Hamilton/Avnet Electronics
17761 N.E. 78th Place, #C
Redmond 98052
Tel: (206) 241-8555
FAX: (206) 241-5472

Wyle Distribution Group
15385 N.E. 90th Street
Redmond 98052
Tel: (206) 881-1150
FAX: (206) 881-1567

WISCONSIN

Arrow Electronics, Inc.
200 N. Patrick Blvd., Ste. 100
Brookfield 53005
Tel: (414) 792-0150
FAX: (414) 792-0156

Avnet Computer
20875 Crossroads Circle, #400
Waukesha 53186
Tel: (414) 784-8205
FAX: (414) 784-6006

†Hamilton/Avnet Electronics
28875 Crossroads Circle, #400
Waukesha 53186
Tel: (414) 784-4510
FAX: (414) 784-9509

Pioneer/Standard Electronics
120 Bishops Way #163
Brookfield 53005
Tel: (414) 784-3480

ALASKA

Avnet Computer
1400 West Benson Blvd.
Suite 400
Anchorage 99503
Tel: (907) 274-9899
FAX: (907) 277-2639

CANADA

ALBERTA

Avnet Computer
2816 21st Street Northeast
Calgary T2E 6Z2
Tel: (403) 291-3284
FAX: (403) 250-1591

Zentronics
6815 8th Street N.E., #100
Calgary T2E 7H
Tel: (403) 295-8838
FAX: (403) 295-8714

BRITISH COLUMBIA

†Hamilton/Avnet Electronics
8610 Commerce Court
Burnaby V5A 4N6
Tel: (604) 420-4101
FAX: (604) 420-5376

Zentronics
11400 Bridgeport Rd., #108
Richmond V6X 1T2
Tel: (604) 273-5575
FAX: (604) 273-2413

ONTARIO

Arrow Electronics, Inc.
36 Antares Dr., Unit 100
Nepean K2E 7W5
Tel: (613) 226-6903
FAX: (613) 723-2018

†Arrow Electronics, Inc.
1093 Meyerside, Unit 2
Mississauga L5T 1M4
Tel: (416) 670-7769
FAX: (416) 670-7781

Avnet Computer
Canada System Engineering Group
3688 Nashua Dr., Unit 6
Mississuaga L4V 1M5
Tel: (416) 672-8638
FAX: (416) 677-5091

Avnet Computer
6845 Rexwood Road
Units 7–9
Mississuaga L4V 1M4
Tel: (416) 672-8638
FAX: (416) 672-8650

Avnet Computer
190 Colonade Road
Nepean K2E 7J5
Tel: (613) 727-7529
FAX: (613) 226-1184

†Hamilton/Avnet Electronics
6845 Rexwood Rd., Units 3–5
Mississauga L4T 1R2
Tel: (416) 677-7432
FAX: (416) 677-0940

†Hamilton/Avnet Electronics
190 Colonade Road
Nepean K2E 7J5
Tel: (613) 226-1700
FAX: (613) 226-1184

†Zentronics
1355 Meyerside Drive
Mississauga L5T 1C9
Tel: (416) 564-9600
FAX: (416) 564-3127

†Zentronics
155 Colonade Rd., South
Unit 17
Nepean K2E 7K1
Tel: (613) 226-8840
FAX: (613) 226-6352

QUEBEC

Arrow Electronics Inc.
1100 St. Regis Blvd.
Dorval H9P 2T5
Tel: (514) 421-7411
FAX: (514) 421-7430

Arrow Electronics, Inc.
500 Boul. St-Jean-Baptiste Ave.
Quebec H2E 5R9
Tel: (418) 871-7500
FAX: (418) 871-6816

Avnet Computer
2795 Rue Halpern
St. Laurent H4S 1P8
Tel: (514) 335-2483
FAX: (514) 335-2481

†Hamilton/Avnet Electronics
2795 Halpern
St. Laurent H4S 1P8
Tel: (514) 335-1000
FAX: (514) 335-2481

†Zentronics
520 McCaffrey
St. Laurent H4T 1N3
Tel: (514) 737-9700
FAX: (514) 737-5212

†Certified VAD

EUROPEAN SALES OFFICES

FINLAND

Intel Finland OY
Ruosilantie 2
00390 Helsinki
Tel. (358) 0 544 644
FAX: (358) 0 544 030

FRANCE

Intel Corporation S.A.R.L.
1, Rue Edison-BP 303
78054 St. Quentin-en-Yvelines
Cedex
Tel: (33) (1) 30 57 70 00
FAX: (33) (1) 30 64 60 32

GERMANY

Intel GmbH
Dornacher Strasse 1
8016 Feldkirchen bei Muenchen
Tel: (49) 089/90992-0
FAX: (49) 089/9043948

ISRAEL

Intel Semiconductor Ltd.
Atidim Industrial Park-Neve Sharet
P.O. Box 43202
Tel-Aviv 61430
Tel: (972) 03 498080
FAX: (972) 03 491870

ITALY

Intel Corporation Italia S.p.A.
Milanofiori Palazzo E
20094 Assago
Milano
Tel: (39) (02) 89200950
FAX: (39) (2) 3498464

NETHERLANDS

Intel Semiconductor B.V.
Postbus 84130
3009 CC Rotterdam
Tel: (31) 10 407 11 11
FAX: (31) 10 455 4688

SPAIN

Intel Iberia S.A.
Zubaran, 28
28010 Madrid
Tel: (34) 308 25 52
FAX: (34) 410 7570

SWEDEN

Intel Sweden A.B.
Dalvagen 24
171 36 Solna
Tel: (46) 8 734 01 00
FAX: (46) 8 278085

UNITED KINGDOM

Intel Corporation (U.K.) Ltd.
Pipers Way
Swindon, Wiltshire SN3 1RJ
Tel: (44) (0793) 696000
FAX: (44) (0793) 641440

EUROPEAN DISTRIBUTORS/REPRESENTATIVES

AUSTRIA

Bacher Electronics GmbH
Rotenmuehlgasse 26
A-1120 Wien
Tel: 43 222 81356460
FAX: 43 222 834276

BELGIUM

Inelco Belgium S.A.
Oorlogskruisenlaan 94
B-1120 Bruxelles
Tel: 32 2 244 2811
FAX: 32 2 216 4301

FRANCE

Almex
48, Rue de l'Aubepine
B.P. 102
92164 Antony Cedex
Tel: 33 1 4096 5400
FAX: 33 1 4666 6028

Lex Electronics
Silic 585
60 Rue des Gemeaux
94663 Rungis Cedex
Tel: 33 1 4978 4978
FAX: 33 1 4978 0596

Metrologie
Tour d'Asnieres
4, Avenue Laurent Cely
92606 Asnieres Cedex
Tel: 33 1 4790 6240
FAX: 33 1 4790 5947

Tekelec-Airtronic
Cite Des Bruyeres
Rue Carle Vernet
BP 2
92310 Sevres
Tel: 33 1 4623 2425
FAX: 33 1 4507 2191

GERMANY

E2000 Vertriebs-AG
Stahlgruberring 12
8000 Muenchen 82
Tel: 49 89 420010
FAX: 49 89 42001209

Jermyn GmbH
Im Dachsstueck 9
6250 Limburg
Tel: 49 6431 5080
FAX: 49 6431 508289

Metrologie GmbH
Steinerstrasse 15
8000 Muenchen 70
Tel: 49 89 724470
FAX: 49 89 72447111

Proelectron Vertriebs GmbH
Max-Planck-Strasse 1-3
6072 Dreieich
Tel: 49 6103 304343
FAX: 49 6103 304425

Rein Electronik GmbH
Loetscher Weg 66
4054 Nettetal 1
Tel: 49 2153 7330
FAX: 49 2153 733513

GREECE

Pouliadis Associates Corp.
5 Koumbari Street
Kolonaki Square
10674 Athens
Tel: 30 1 360 3741
FAX: 30 1 360 7501

IRELAND

Micro Marketing
Tany Hall
Eglinton Terrace
Dundrum
Dublin
Tel: 0001 989 400
FAX: 0001 989 8282

ISRAEL

Eastronics Ltd.
Rozanis 11
P.O.B. 39300
Tel Baruch
Tel-Aviv 61392
Tel: 972 3 475151
FAX: 972 3 475125

ITALY

Celdis Spa
Via F.11i Gracchi 36
20092 Cinisello Balsamo
Milano
Tel: 39 2 66012003
FAX: 39 2 6182433

Intesi Div. Della Deutsche
Divisione ITT
Industries GmbH
P.I. 06550110156
Milanofiori Palazzo E5
20094 Assago (Milano)
Tel: 39 2 824701
FAX: 39 2 8242631

Lasi Elettronica S.p.A.
P.I. 00839000155
Viale Fulvio Testi, N.280
20126 Milano
Tel: 39 2 66101370
FAX: 39 2 66101385

Telcom s.r.l. – Divisione MDS
Via Trombetta
Zona Marconi
Strada Cassanese
Segrate – Milano
Tel: 39 2 2138010
FAX: 39 2 216061

NETHERLANDS

Koning en Hartman B.V.
Energieweg 1
2627 AP Delft
Tel: 31 15 609 906
FAX: 31 15 619 194

PORTUGAL

ATD Electronica LDA
Rua Dr. Faria de
Vasconcelos, 3a
1900 Lisboa
Tel: 351 1 8472200
FAX: 351 1 8472197

SPAIN

ATD Electronica
Plaza Ciudad de Viena, 6
28040 Madrid
Tel: 34 1 534 4000/09
FAX: 34 1 534 7663

Metrologia Iberica
Ctra De Fuencarral N.80
28100 Alcobendas
Madrid
Tel: 34 1 6538611
FAX: 34 1 6517549

SCANDINAVIA

OY Fintronic AB
Heikkilantie 2a
SF-00210 Helsinki
Tel: 358 0 6926022
FAX: 358 0 6821251

ITT Multikomponent A/S
Naverland 29
DK-2600 Glostrup
Denmark
Tel: 010 45 42 451822
FAX: 010 45 42 457624

Nordisk Elektronik A/S
Postboks 122
Smedsvingen 4
N-1364 Hvalstad
Norway
Tel: 47 2 846210
FAX: 47 2 846545

Nordisk Electronik AB
Box 36
Torshamnsgatan 39
S-16493 Kista
Sweden
Tel: 46 8 7034630
FAX: 46 8 7039845

SWITZERLAND

Industrade A.G.
Hertistrasse 31
CH-8304 Wallisellen
Tel: 41 1 8328111
FAX: 41 1 8307550

TURKEY

EMPA
80050 Sishane
Refik Saydam Cad No. 89/5
Istanbul
Tel: 90 1 143 6212
FAX: 90 1 143 6547

UNITED KINGDOM

Access Elect Comp Ltd.
Jubilee House
Jubilee Road
Letchworth
Hertfordshire
SG6 1QH
Tel: 0462 480888
FAX: 0462 682467

Bytech Components Ltd.
12a Cedarwood
Chineham Business Park
Crockford Lane
Basingstoke
Hants RG12 1RW
Tel: 0256 707107
FAX: 0256 707162

Bytech Systems
Unit 3
The Western Centre
Western Road
Bracknell
Berks RG12 1RW
Tel: 0344 55333
FAX: 0344 867270

Metrologie
Rapid House
Oxford Road
High Wycombe
Bucks
Herts HP11 2EE
Tel: 0494 474147
FAX: 0494 452144

Jermyn
Vestry Estate
Otford Road
Sevenoaks
Kent TN14 5EU
Tel: 0732 450144
FAX: 0732 451251

MMD
3 Bennet Court
Bennet Road
Reading
Berkshire RG2 0QX
Tel: 0734 313232
FAX: 0734 313255

Rapid Silicon
3 Bennet Court
Bennet Road
Reading
Berks RG2 0QX
Tel: 0734 752266
FAX: 0734 312728

Metro Systems
Rapid House
Oxford Road
High Wycombe
Bucks HP11 2EE
Tel: 0494 474171
FAX: 0494 21860

YUGOSLAVIA

H.R. Microelectronics Corp.
2005 de la Cruz Blvd.
Suite 220
Santa Clara, CA 95050
U.S.A.
Tel: (408) 988-0286
FAX: (408) 988-0306

INTERNATIONAL SALES OFFICES

AUSTRALIA

Intel Australia Pty. Ltd.
Unit 13
Allambie Grove Business Park
25 Frenchs Forest Road East
Frenchs Forest, NSW, 2086
Sydney
Tel: 61-2-975-3300
FAX: 61-2-975-3375

Intel Australia Pty. Ltd.
711 High Street
1st Floor
East Kw. Vic., 3102
Melbourne
Tel: 61-3-810-2141
FAX: 61-3-819 7200

BRAZIL

Intel Semicondutores do Brazil LTDA
Avenida Paulista, 1159-CJS 404/405
01311 - Sao Paulo - S.P.
Tel: 55-11-287-5899
TLX: 11-37-557-ISDB
FAX: 55-11-287-5119

CHINA/HONG KONG

Intel PRC Corporation
15/F, Office 1, Citic Bldg.
Jian Guo Men Wai Street
Beijing, PRC
Tel: (1) 500-4850
TLX: 22947 INTEL CN
FAX: (1) 500-2953

Intel Semiconductor Ltd.*
10/F East Tower
Bond Center
Queensway, Central
Hong Kong
Tel: (852) 844-4555
FAX: (852) 868-1989

INDIA

Intel Asia Electronics, Inc.
4/2, Samrah Plaza
St. Mark's Road
Bangalore 560001
Tel: 91-812-215773
TLX: 953-845-2646 INTEL IN
FAX: 091-812-215067

JAPAN

Intel Japan K.K.
5-6 Tokodai, Tsukuba-shi
Ibaraki, 300-26
Tel: 0298-47-8511
FAX: 0298-47-8450

Intel Japan K.K.*
Hachioji ON Bldg.
4-7-14 Myojin-machi
Hachioji-shi, Tokyo 192
Tel: 0426-48-8770
FAX: 0426-48-8775

Intel Japan K.K.*
Bldg. Kumagaya
2-69 Hon-cho
Kumagaya-shi, Saitama 360
Tel: 0485-24-6871
FAX: 0485-24-7518

Intel Japan K.K.*
Kawa-asa Bldg.
2-11-5 Shin-Yokohama
Kohoku-ku, Yokohama-shi
Kanagawa, 222
Tel: 045-474-7661
FAX: 045-471-4394

Intel Japan K.K.*
Ryokuchi-Eki Bldg.
2-4-1 Terauchi
Toyonaka-shi, Osaka 560
Tel: 06-863-1091
FAX: 06-863-1084

Intel Japan K.K.
Shinmaru Bldg.
1-5-1 Marunouchi
Chiyoda-ku, Tokyo 100
Tel: 03-3201-3621
FAX: 03-3201-6850

Intel Japan K.K.
Green Bldg.
1-16-20 Nishiki
Naka-ku, Nagoya-shi
Aichi 460
Tel: 052-204-1261
FAX: 052-204-1285

KOREA

Intel Korea, Ltd.
16th Floor, Life Bldg.
61 Yoido-dong, Youngdeungpo-Ku
Seoul 150-010
Tel: (2) 784-8186
FAX: (2) 784-8096

SINGAPORE

Intel Singapore Technology, Ltd.
101 Thomson Road #08-03/06
United Square
Singapore 1130
Tel: (65) 250-7811
FAX: (65) 250-9256

TAIWAN

Intel Technology Far East Ltd.
Taiwan Branch Office
8th Floor, No. 205
Bank Tower Bldg.
Tung Hua N. Road
Taipei
Tel: 886-2-5144202
FAX: 886-2-717-2455

INTERNATIONAL DISTRIBUTORS/REPRESENTATIVES

ARGENTINA

Dafsys S.R.L.
Chacabuco, 90-6 Piso
1069-Buenos Aires
Tel: 54-1-34-7726
FAX: 54-1-34-1871

AUSTRALIA

Email Electronics
15-17 Hume Street
Huntingdale, 3166
Tel: 011-61-3-544-8244
TLX: AA 30895
FAX: 011-61-3-543-8179

NSD-Australia
205 Middleborough Rd.
Box Hill, Victoria 3128
Tel: 03 8900970
FAX: 03 8990819

BRAZIL

Microlinear
Largo do Arouche, 24
01219 Sao Paulo, SP
Tel: 5511-220-2215
FAX: 5511-220-5750

CHILE

Sisteco
Vecinal 40 – Las Condes
Santiago
Tel: 562-234-1644
FAX: 562-233-9895

CHINA/HONG KONG

Novel Precision Machinery Co., Ltd.
Room 728 Trade Square
681 Cheung Sha Wan Road
Kowloon, Hong Kong
Tel: (852) 360-8999
TWX: 32032 NVTNL HX
FAX: (852) 725-3695

GUATEMALA

Abinitio
11 Calle 2 – Zona 9
Guatemala City
Tel: 5022-32-4104
FAX: 5022-32-4123

INDIA

Micronic Devices
Arun Complex
No. 65 D.V.G. Road
Basavanagudi
Bangalore 560 004
Tel: 011-91-812-600-631
011-91-812-611-365
TLX: 9538458332 MDBG

Micronic Devices
No. 516 5th Floor
Swastik Chambers
Sion, Trombay Road
Chembur
Bombay 400 071
TLX: 9531 171447 MDEV

Micronic Devices
25/8, 1st Floor
Bada Bazaar Marg
Old Rajinder Nagar
New Delhi 110 060
Tel: 011-91-11-5723509
011-91-11-589771
TLX: 031-63253 MDND IN

Micronic Devices
6-3-348/12A Dwarakapuri Colony
Hyderabad 500 482
Tel: 011-91-842-226748

S&S Corporation
1587 Kooser Road
San Jose, CA 95118
Tel: (408) 978-6216
TLX: 820281
FAX: (408) 978-8635

JAMAICA

MC Systems
10-12 Grenada Crescent
Kingston 5
Tel: (809) 929-2638
(809) 926-0188
FAX: (809) 926-0104

JAPAN

Asahi Electronics Co. Ltd.
KMM Bldg. 2-14-1 Asano
Kokurakita-ku
Kitakyushu-shi 802
Tel: 093-511-6471
FAX: 093-551-7861

CTC Components Systems Co., Ltd.
4-8-1 Dobashi, Miyamae-ku
Kawasaki-shi, Kanagawa 213
Tel: 044-852-5121
FAX: 044-877-4268

Dia Semicon Systems, Inc.
Flower Hill Shinmachi Higashi-kan
1-23 Shinmachi, Setagaya-ku
Tokyo 154
Tel: 03-3439-1600
FAX: 03-3439-1601

Okaya Koki
2-4-18 Sakae
Naka-ku, Nagoya-shi 460
Tel: 052-204-8315
FAX: 052-204-8380

Ryoyo Electro Corp.
Konwa Bldg.
1-12-22 Tsukiji
Chuo-ku, Tokyo 104
Tel: 03-3546-5011
FAX: 03-3546-5044

KOREA

J-Tek Corporation
Dong Sung Bldg. 9/F
158-24, Samsung-Dong, Kangnam-Ku
Seoul 135-090
Tel: (822) 557-8039
FAX: (822) 557-8304

Samsung Electronics
Samsung Main Bldg.
150 Taepyung-Ro-2KA, Chung-Ku
Seoul 100-102
C.P.O. Box 8780
Tel: (822) 751-3680
TWX: KORSST K 27970
FAX: (822) 753-9065

MEXICO

PSI S.A. de C.V.
Fco. Villa esq. Ajusco s/n
Cuernavaca, MOR 62130
Tel: 52-73-13-9412
52-73-17-5340
FAX: 52-73-17-5333

NEW ZEALAND

Email Electronics
36 Olive Road
Penrose, Auckland
Tel: 011-64-9-591-155
FAX: 011-64-9-592-681

SAUDI ARABIA

AAE Systems, Inc.
642 N. Pastoria Ave.
Sunnyvale, CA 94086
U.S.A.
Tel: (408) 732-1710
FAX: (408) 732-3095
TLX: 494-3405 AAE SYS

SINGAPORE

Electronic Resources Pte, Ltd.
17 Harvey Road
#03-01 Singapore 1336
Tel: (65) 283-0888
TWX: RS 56541 ERS
FAX: (65) 289-5327

SOUTH AFRICA

Electronic Building Elements
178 Erasmus St. (off Watermeyet St.)
Meyerspark, Pretoria, 0184
Tel: 011-2712-803-7680
FAX: 011-2712-803-8294

TAIWAN

Micro Electronics Corporation
12th Floor, Section 3
285 Nanking East Road
Taipei, R.O.C.
Tel: (886) 2-7198419
FAX: (886) 2-7197916

Acer Sertek Inc.
15th Floor, Section 2
Chien Kuo North Rd.
Taipei 18479 R.O.C.
Tel: 886-2-501-0055
TWX: 23756 SERTEK
FAX: (886) 2-5012521

URUGUAY

Interfase
Zabala 1378
11000 Montevideo
Tel: 5982-96-0490
5982-96-1143
FAX: 5982-96-2965

VENEZUELA

Unixel C.A.
4 Transversal de Monte Cristo
Edf. AXXA, Piso 1, of. 1&2
Centro Empresarial Boleita
Caracas
Tel: 582-238-6082
FAX: 582-238-1816

*Field Application Location

NORTH AMERICAN SERVICE OFFICES

ALASKA

Intel Corp.
c/o TransAlaska Network
1515 Lore Rd.
Anchorage 99507
Tel: (907) 522-1776

Intel Corp.
c/o TransAlaska Data Systems
c/o GCI Operations
520 Fifth Ave., Suite 407
Fairbanks 99701
Tel: (907) 452-6264

ARIZONA

*Intel Corp.
410 North 44th Street
Suite 500
Phoenix 85008
Tel: (602) 231-0386
FAX: (602) 244-0446

*Intel Corp.
500 E. Fry Blvd., Suite M-15
Sierra Vista 85635
Tel: (602) 459-5010

ARKANSAS

Intel Corp.
c/o Federal Express
1500 West Park Drive
Little Rock 72204

CALIFORNIA

*Intel Corp.
21515 Vanowen St., Ste. 116
Canoga Park 91303
Tel: (818) 704-8500

*Intel Corp.
300 N. Continental Blvd.
Suite 100
El Segundo 90245
Tel: (213) 640-6040

*Intel Corp.
1900 Prairie City Rd.
Folsom 95630-9597
Tel: (916) 351-6143

*Intel Corp.
9665 Chesapeake Dr., Suite 325
San Diego 92123
Tel: (619) 292-8086

**Intel Corp.
400 N. Tustin Avenue
Suite 450
Santa Ana 92705
Tel: (714) 835-9642

**Intel Corp.
2700 San Tomas Exp., 1st Floor
Santa Clara 95051
Tel: (408) 970-1747

COLORADO

*Intel Corp.
600 S. Cherry St., Suite 700
Denver 80222
Tel: (303) 321-8086

CONNECTICUT

*Intel Corp.
301 Lee Farm Corporate Park
83 Wooster Heights Rd.
Danbury 06811
Tel: (203) 748-3130

FLORIDA

**Intel Corp.
800 Fairway Dr., Suite 160
Deerfield Beach 33441
Tel: (305) 421-0506
FAX: (305) 421-2444

*Intel Corp.
5850 T.G. Lee Blvd., Ste. 340
Orlando 32822
Tel: (407) 240-8000

GEORGIA

*Intel Corp.
20 Technology Park, Suite 150
Norcross 30092
Tel: (404) 449-0541

5523 Theresa Street
Columbus 31907

HAWAII

**Intel Corp.
Honolulu 96820
Tel: (808) 847-6738

ILLINOIS

**†Intel Corp.
Woodfield Corp. Center III
300 N. Martingale Rd., Ste. 400
Schaumburg 60173
Tel: (708) 605-8031

INDIANA

*Intel Corp.
8910 Purdue Rd., Ste. 350
Indianapolis 46268
Tel: (317) 875-0623

KANSAS

*Intel Corp.
10985 Cody, Suite 140
Overland Park 66210
Tel: (913) 345-2727

KENTUCKY

Intel Corp.
133 Walton Ave., Office 1A
Lexington 40508
Tel: (606) 255-2957

Intel Corp.
896 Hillcrest Road, Apt. A
Radcliff 40160 (Louisville)

LOUISIANA

Hammond 70401
(serviced from Jackson, MS)

MARYLAND

**Intel Corp.
10010 Junction Dr., Suite 200
Annapolis Junction 20701
Tel: (301) 206-2860

MASSACHUSETTS

**Intel Corp.
Westford Corp. Center
3 Carlisle Rd., 2nd Floor
Westford 01886
Tel: (508) 692-0960

MICHIGAN

*Intel Corp.
7071 Orchard Lake Rd., Ste. 100
West Bloomfield 48322
Tel: (313) 851-8905

MINNESOTA

*Intel Corp.
3500 W. 80th St., Suite 360
Bloomington 55431
Tel: (612) 835-6722

MISSISSIPPI

Intel Corp.
c/o Compu-Care
2001 Airport Road, Suite 205F
Jackson 39208
Tel: (601) 932-6275

MISSOURI

*Intel Corp.
3300 Rider Trail South
Suite 170
Earth City 63045
Tel: (314) 291-1990

Intel Corp.
Route 2, Box 221
Smithville 64089
Tel: (913) 345-2727

NEW JERSEY

**Intel Corp.
300 Sylvan Avenue
Englewood Cliffs 07632
Tel: (201) 567-0821

*Intel Corp.
Lincroft Office Center
125 Half Mile Road
Red Bank 07701
Tel: (908) 747-2233

NEW MEXICO

Intel Corp.
Rio Rancho 1
4100 Sara Road
Rio Rancho 87124-1025
(near Albuquerque)
Tel: (505) 893-7000

NEW YORK

*Intel Corp.
2950 Expressway Dr. South
Suite 130
Islandia 11722
Tel: (516) 231-3300

Intel Corp.
300 Westage Business Center
Suite 230
Fishkill 12524
Tel: (914) 897-3860

Intel Corp.
5858 East Molloy Road
Syracuse 13211
Tel: (315) 454-0576

NORTH CAROLINA

*Intel Corp.
5800 Executive Center Drive
Suite 105
Charlotte 28212
Tel: (704) 568-8966

**Intel Corp.
5540 Centerview Dr., Suite 215
Raleigh 27606
Tel: (919) 851-9537

OHIO

**Intel Corp.
3401 Park Center Dr., Ste. 220
Dayton 45414
Tel: (513) 890-5350

*Intel Corp.
25700 Science Park Dr., Ste. 100
Beachwood 44122
Tel: (216) 464-2736

OREGON

**Intel Corp.
15254 N.W. Greenbrier Pkwy.
Building B
Beaverton 97006
Tel: (503) 645-8051

PENNSYLVANIA

*†Intel Corp.
925 Harvest Drive
Suite 200
Blue Bell 19422
Tel: (215) 641-1000
1-800-468-3548
FAX: (215) 641-0785

**†Intel Corp.
400 Penn Center Blvd., Ste. 610
Pittsburgh 15235
Tel: (412) 823-4970

*Intel Corp.
1513 Cedar Cliff Dr.
Camp Hill 17011
Tel: (717) 761-0860

PUERTO RICO

Intel Corp.
South Industrial Park
P.O. Box 910
Las Piedras 00671
Tel: (809) 733-8616

TEXAS

**Intel Corp.
Westech 360, Suite 4230
8911 N. Capitol of Texas Hwy.
Austin 78752-1239
Tel : (512) 794-8086

**†Intel Corp.
12000 Ford Rd., Suite 401
Dallas 75234
Tel: (214) 241-8087

**Intel Corp.
7322 SW Freeway, Suite 1490
Houston 77074
Tel: (713) 988-8086

UTAH

Intel Corp.
428 East 6400 South
Suite 104
Murray 84107
Tel: (801) 263-8051
FAX: (801) 268-1457

VIRGINIA

*Intel Corp.
9030 Stony Point Pkwy.
Suite 360
Richmond 23235
Tel: (804) 330-9393

WASHINGTON

**Intel Corp.
155 108th Avenue N.E., Ste. 386
Bellevue 98004
Tel: (206) 453-8086

CANADA

ONTARIO

**Intel Semiconductor of
Canada, Ltd.
2650 Queensview Dr., Ste. 250
Ottawa K2B 8H6
Tel: (613) 829-9714

**Intel Semiconductor of
Canada, Ltd.
190 Attwell Dr., Ste. 102
Rexdale (Toronto) M9W 6H8
Tel: (416) 675-2105

QUEBEC

**Intel Semiconductor of
Canada, Ltd.
1 Rue Holiday
Suite 115
Tour East
Pt. Claire H9R 5N3
Tel: (514) 694-9130
FAX: 514-694-0064

CUSTOMER TRAINING CENTERS

ARIZONA

2402 W. Beardsley Road
Phoenix 85027
Tel: (602) 869-4288
1-800-468-3548

SYSTEMS ENGINEERING OFFICES

MINNESOTA

3500 W. 80th Street
Suite 360
Bloomington 55431
Tel: (612) 835-6722

NEW YORK

2950 Expressway Dr., South
Islandia 11722
Tel: (506) 231-3300

*Carry-in locations
**Carry-in/mail-in locations